INDEX OF ECONOMIC ARTICLES
In Journals and Collective Volumes

Index of
Economic Articles

IN JOURNALS AND COLLECTIVE VOLUMES

Volume XXIII · 1981

Part One—Subject Index

Prepared under the auspices of

THE JOURNAL OF ECONOMIC LITERATURE

of the

AMERICAN ECONOMIC ASSOCIATION

JOHN PENCAVEL

Managing Editor

MOSES ABRAMOVITZ

Associate Editor

DRUCILLA EKWURZEL

Associate Editor

ASATOSHI MAESHIRO

Editorial Consultant

LINDA C. SCOTT

Assistant Editor

Distributed by

RICHARD D. IRWIN, INC.

1818 RIDGE ROAD
HOMEWOOD, ILLINOIS 60430
1987

Student Classifiers: Jang-Bong Choi; A'Amer Farooqi; Tat P. Fong; Nayyer Hussain; Edgar L. Zamalloa, and Lorena M. Zamalloa.

Library of Congress Catalog Card Number: 61–8020
International Standard Book Number: 0–917290–12–7
International Standard Serial Number: 0536–647X
Printed in the United States of America

TABLE OF CONTENTS

INTRODUCTORY DISCUSSION

This volume of the *Index* lists, both by subject category and by author, articles in major economic journals and in collective volumes published during the year 1981. The articles listed include all articles published in English or with English summaries in the journals and books listed below (p. x). Part one includes the Subject Index of Articles in Journals and Collective Volumes, and Part Two consists of an alphabetical Author Index of all the articles indexed in Part One.

Relationship to JEL

This *Index* is prepared largely as an adjunct to the bibliographic activities of the *Journal of Economic Literature (JEL)*. Economies of joint production are pursued throughout the production process. Journals included are those indexed in the *JEL* quarterly; collective volumes are selected from the annotated 1981 books; the classification system is a more detailed version of the *JEL* system.

Journals Included

The 266 journals listed represent, in general, those journals that we believe will be most helpful to research workers and teachers of economics. These journals are listed below on p. x.

Generally, articles, notes, communications, comments, replies, rejoinders, as well as papers and formal discussions in proceedings and review articles in the included journals have been indexed. There are some exceptions; only articles in English or with English summaries are included—this practice results in a slightly reduced coverage compared with the *JEL* quarterly. Articles lacking author identification are omitted, as are articles without economic content. Identical articles appearing in two different journals in 1981 are listed from both sources. The journal issues included usually fall within a single volume. When a volume of a journal overlaps two calendar years, for example, Fall 1980 to Summer 1981, we include the issues from the two volumes relating to 1981 as best we can determine.

Collective Volumes

The collective volumes consist of the following:

1. *Festschriften*
2. Conference publications with individual papers
3. Collected essays, original, by one or more authors
4. Collected essays, reprinted, by one or more authors
5. Proceedings volumes with individual papers not included among the journal listings
6. Books of readings

All original articles in English are indexed with the exception of unsigned articles or articles without economic content. Reprinted articles are included on the basis that a researcher would be interested in knowing about another source of the article. The original publication dates are shown in italics on the citations of reprinted articles. Excerpts are not included. The same article appearing for the first time in different collective volumes in the same year is cited from both publications.

In the article citation, reference to the book in which the article appears is by author or editor of the volume. If the same person or persons wrote or edited more than one book included in the 1981 *Index*, it is indicated by a I or II appearing in both the source given in the article citation and the bibliographic reference in the book listing. If the same person wrote one book and edited another in 1981, the specification of "ed" in the reference indicates which book is being cited.

The collective volumes are listed alphabetically by author or editor beginning on p. xvi and include a full bibliographic reference. If there is more than one edition, the publisher cited is the one on the copy the *JEL* received, usually the American publisher.

Arrangement

The *Index* consists of two parts:
1. A Subject Index in which the articles are arranged by subject.
2. An Author Index.

Subject Index

In Part One, all articles are listed alphabetically by first author under each 4-digit subject category. Joint authors are listed up to three; beyond that, only the first author is listed, followed by *et al.*

There is one exception to the alphabetical author arrangement. In the 0322 category, a subdivision of **History of Thought** entitled **Individuals,** the arrangement is first alphabetical by the individual discussed in the article and then alphabetical by the article's author.

Articles with empirical content or discussing a particular geographic area carry a geographic descriptor (see discussion below).

Author Index

In the alphabetical Author Index in Part Two citations appear under each author (up to three) of an article. Wherever possible the full first name and middle initial or middle name(s) are used. Wherever it could be definitely ascertained, articles by the same person are grouped together with only one listing of the name. Authors' first names and initials are listed differently in various journals and books; for example, an individual may be identified as John L. Smith, J. L. Smith, or John Smith. Thus, despite our best efforts, we were left in doubt in several instances. Joint authors are listed up to three; beyond that, only the first author is listed, followed by *et al.* Under each author, articles are listed alphabetically. Names carrying prefixes are alphabetized according to the first *capitalized* letter, with occasional exceptions following national practices. Thus, van Arkadie would appear under A and D'Alabro under D.

Geographic Descriptors

Geographic descriptors appear in brackets at the end of any article entry in the Subject Index where the article cites data from or refers to a particular country or area. Research workers interested in these countries thus are made aware of the empirical content in the article. The descriptors used are countries or broader areas, such as southeast Asia (S.E. Asia); articles referring to cities or regions within a country are classified under the country. In general, the country name is written out in full with some adaptations and abbreviations, *e.g.,* U.S. is used for United States, U.K. for United Kingdom, and U.S.S.R. for Union of Soviet Socialist Republics. Abbreviations include: W. for West, E. for East, S. for South, N. for North. A shortened name such as W. Germany is used rather than the correct, but longer, Federal Republic of Germany. When broader regions are used as descriptors, the article may or may not refer to the full unit. For example, OECD has been used at times when most, but not all, of the OECD member countries are referred to.

Index volumes prior to 1979 sometimes did not include geographic descriptors on articles listed under subject categories 1210, 1211, 1220, 1221, 1230, 1240, and 1241, involving general or comparative economic country studies. In the 1979 *Index* and later volumes, these articles carry geographic descriptors in order to facilitate online identification in the ECONOMIC LITERATURE INDEX on DIALOG. Because the descriptor fields are limited to five, very general descriptors, such as LDCs (developing countries) and MDCs (developed countries), are often used on articles.

The fact that an article carries a geographic descriptor does not necessarily preclude its being primarily theoretical in nature. Any theoretical article drawing on empirical data to demonstrate its findings will carry a geographic descriptor.

Classification System

The classification system is an expansion of the 3-digit classification system used in the *Journal of Economic Literature* to a 4-digit system with slightly over 300 subcategories. The classification system, itself, is shown beginning on p. xxxiv (Part One). In most cases the classification heading is self-explanatory; however, in some cases notes have been added to clarify the coverage or indicate alternative subject classifications. The basic approach in classification is from the point of view of the researcher rather than the teacher; course content does not necessarily coincide with subfields of our classification system. In all cases where there are two or more 4-digit classifications under a 3-digit category, there is a zero classification; in most instances this is labeled "General." The zero or general category has been used both as an inclusive and a residual category; thus, when the subject matter of an article covers all or most of the subcategories, that article appears in the zero or general category. For example, an article discussing *all* aspects of international trade theory appears in the general category. There are also some articles that do not fall in any of the individual subcategories, and these, too, are classified in the general or zero category.

The criterion used in the classifying process is whether persons interested in this topic would wish to have the article drawn to their attention. With the advent of the online ECONOMIC LITERATURE INDEX on DIALOG, the interpretation of "interest" has broadened slightly to include cross-classifications that indicate the subject matter, particularly in such categories as industry studies or occupational designations. Over half of the articles are classified in more than one subcategory. From time to time, we find it desirable to add subject classifications as particular topics become prominent or to change subject headings to make them more descriptive of the contents of the category. In 1981 the subject classification, **2150 Experimental Economic Methods,** has been added. Also, a number of subject classification headings have been reworded to make the headings more descriptive of the subject matter.

Topical Guide to the Classification System

At the end of Part One there is an alphabetical listing of standard economic terms and concepts. References are to the appropriate 4-digit classification numbers, not to page numbers.

LIST OF JOURNALS INDEXED 1981

Accounting Review, Vol. 56.

Acta Oeconomica, Vol. 26; Vol. 27.

L'Actualité Economique, Vol. 57.

Agricultural Economics Research, Vol. 33.

American Economic Review, Vol. 71.
Includes American Economic Association **Papers and Proceedings** of the annual meeting in 71(2).

American Economist, Vol. 25.

American Historical Review, Vol. 86.

American Journal of Agricultural Economics, Vol. 63.
Title changed from **Journal of Farm Economics** in 1968.

American Journal of Economics and Sociology, Vol. 40.

American Political Science Review, Vol. 75.

American Real Estate and Urban Economics Association Journal, Vol. 9.

Annales de l'INSEE, Issue nos. 41–44.

Annales de Sciences Économiques Appliquées, Vol. 37.

Annals of the American Academy of Political and Social Science, Vols. 453–454, 456.

Annals of Public and Co-operative Economy, Vol. 52.

Antitrust Bulletin, Vol. 26.

Applied Economics, Vol. 13.

Artha-Vikas, Vol. 17.

ACES Bulletin (Association for Comparative Economic Studies Bulletin), Vol. 23.

Atlantic Economic Journal, Vol. 9.

Aussenwirtschaft, Vol. 36.

Australian Bulletin of Labor, Vol. 7, Issue nos. 3–5; Vol. 8, Issue no. 1.

Australian Economic History Review, Vol. 21.
Title changed from **Business Archives and History** in 1967; prior to 1962 entitled **Bulletin of the Business Archives Council of Australia.**

Australian Economic Papers, Vol. 20.

Australian Economic Review, Issue nos. 53–56.

Australian Journal of Agricultural Economics, Vol. 25.

Australian Journal of Management, Vol. 6.

Banca Nazionale del Lavoro—Quarterly Review, Issue nos. 136–139.

Bancaria, Vol. 37.

Bangladesh Development Studies, Vol. 9.
Title changed from **Bangladesh Economic Review** in 1974.

Bell Journal of Economics, Vol. 12.

British Journal of Industrial Relations, Vol. 19.

British Review of Economic Issues, Vol. 2, Issue no. 8; Vol. 3, Issue no. 9.

Brookings Papers on Economic Activity, Issue nos. 1–2, 1981.

Bulletin of Economic Research, Vol. 33.
Title changed from **Yorkshire Bulletin of Economic and Social Research** in 1971.

Bulletin of Indonesian Economic Studies, Vol. 17.

Bulletin for International Fiscal Documentation, Vol. 35.

Business Economics, Vol. 16.

Business History Review, Vol. 55.
Title changed from **Bulletin of the Business Historical Society** in 1954.

Cahiers Économiques de Bruxelles, Issue nos. 89–92.

California Management Review, Vol. 23, Issue nos. 3–4; Vol. 24, Issue nos. 1–2.

Cambridge Economic Policy Review, Vol. 7, Issue no. 2.

Cambridge Journal of Economics, Vol. 5.

Canadian Journal of Agricultural Economics, Vol. 29.

Canadian Journal of Economics, Vol. 14.

Canadian Public Policy, Vol. 7, Supplement.

Carnegie–Rochester Conference Series on Public Policy, Vol. 14; Vol. 15.
Formerly listed as a supplement to the Journal of Monetary Economics.

Cato Journal, Vol. 1.

Cepal Review, Issue nos. 13–15.

Challenge, Vol. 24, Issue nos. 2–5.

Chinese Economic Studies, Vol. 14; Issue nos. 2–4; Vol. 15, Issue no. 1.

Conflict Management and Peace Science, Vol. 5, Issue no. 2; Vol. 6, Issue no. 1.
Title changed from Journal of Peace Science in 1979–80.

Consommation, Vol. 28.

Cuadernos de Economia, Vol. 18.

Czechoslovak Economic Digest, Issue nos. 1–3, 5–8, 1981.

Demography, Vol. 18.

Eastern Economic Journal, Vol. 7.

Eastern European Economics, Vol. 19, Issue no. 4; Vol. 20, Issue nos. 1–2.

Econometrica, Vol. 49.

Economia, Vol. 5.

Economia Internazionale, Vol. 34.

Economic Affairs, Vol. 26.

Economic Analysis and Workers' Management, Vol. 15.

Economic Computation and Economic Cybernetics Studies and Research, Vol. 15.
Title changed from Studii şi Cercetări Economicè in 1974. Changed from issue numbers to volume numbers in 1978.

Economic Development and Cultural Change, Vol. 29, Issue nos. 2–4; Vol. 30, Issue no. 1.

Economic Forum, Vol. 12.
Title changed from Intermountain Economic Review in 1979.

Economic Geography, Vol. 57.

Economic History Review, Vol. 34.

Economic Inquiry, Vol. 19.
Title changed from Western Economic Journal in 1974.

Economic Journal, Vol. 91.

Economic Notes, Vol. 10.

Economic Record, Vol. 57.

Economic and Social Review, Vol. 12, Issue nos. 2–4; Vol. 13, Issue no. 1.

Economic Studies Quarterly, Vol. 32.

Economica, Vol. 48.
Title changed from Economica, N.S. in 1974.

Económica, Vol. 27.

Economics of Planning, Vol. 17.

Économie Appliqué, Vol. 34.

Economies et Sociétés, Vol. 15, Issue nos. 6–12.

Economisch en Sociaal Tijdschrift, Vol. 35, Issue nos. 3–5.

De Economist, Vol. 129.

Ekonomiska Samfundets Tidskrift, Vol. 34.

Empirica, Issue nos. 1–2, 1981.

Empirical Economics, Vol. 6.

Energy Economics, Vol. 3.

Energy Journal, Vol. 2, Issue nos. 2–4.

Engineering Economist, Vol. 26, Issue no. 2.

European Economic Review, Vol. 15; Vol. 16.

European Review of Agricultural Economics, Vol. 8.

Explorations in Economic History, Vol. 18.
Title changed from Explorations in Entrepreneurial History in 1969–70.

Federal Reserve Bank of Minneapolis Quarterly Review, Vol. 5.

Federal Reserve Bank of New York Quarterly Review, Vol. 6.

Federal Reserve Bank of San Francisco Economic Review, Winter, Spring, Summer, Fall, 1981.

Federal Reserve Bank of St. Louis Review, Vol. 63.

Federal Reserve Bulletin, Vol. 67.

Journal of Finance, Vol. 36.

Journal of Financial Economics, Vol. 9.

Journal of Financial and Quantitative Analysis, Vol. 16.

Journal of Futures Markets, Vol. 1.

Journal of Human Resources, Vol. 16.

Journal of Industrial Economics, Vol. 29, Issue nos. 3–4; Vol. 30, Issue nos. 1–2.

Journal of International Business Studies, Vol. 12.

Journal of International Economics, Vol. 11.

Journal of Labor Research, Vol. 2.

Journal of Law and Economics, Vol. 24.

Journal of Macroeconomics, Vol. 3.

Journal of Mathematical Economics, Vol. 8.

Journal of Monetary Economics, Vol. 7; Vol. 8.

Journal of Money, Credit and Banking, Vol. 13.

Journal of Policy Analysis and Management, Vol. 1, Issue no. 1.

Journal of Political Economy, Vol. 89.

Journal of Portfolio Management, Vol. 7, Issue nos. 2–4; Vol. 8, Issue no. 1.

Journal of Post Keynesian Economics, Vol. 3, Issue nos. 2–4; Vol. 4, Issue no. 1.

Journal of Public Economics, Vol. 15; Vol. 16.

Journal of Regional Science, Vol. 21.

Journal of Risk and Insurance, Vol. 48.

Journal of the Royal Statistical Society, Series A, Vol. 144.

Journal of Transport Economics and Policy, Vol. 15.

Journal of Urban Economics, Vol. 9; Vol. 10.

Journal of World Trade Law, Vol. 15.

Kansantaloudellinen Aikakauskirja, Vol. 77, Issue nos. 2–4.

Kobe Economic and Business Review, Vol. 27, 1981.

Konjunkturpolitik, Vol. 27.

Kredit und Kapital, Vol. 14.

Kyklos, Vol. 34.

Kyoto University Economic Review, Vol. 51.

Labor History, Vol. 22.

Land Economics, Vol. 57.

Law and Contemporary Problems, Vol. 44.

Liiketaloudellinen Aikakauskirja, Vol. 30.

Lloyds Bank Review, Issue nos. 139–42, 1981.

Malayan Economic Review, Vol. 26.

Management Accounting, Vol. 62, Issue nos. 7–12; Vol. 63, Issue nos. 1–6.

Managerial and Decision Economics, Vol. 2.

Manchester School of Economics and Social Studies, Vol. 49.
    Title changed from **The Manchester School** in 1939; prior to 1932 entitled **The Manchester School of Economics, Commerce and Administration.**

Matekon, Vol. 17, Issue nos. 3–4; Vol. 18, Issue nos. 1–2.
    Title changed from **Mathematical Studies in Economics and Statistics in the USSR and Eastern Europe** in 1969.

Metroeconomica, Vol. 33.

METU—Studies in Development, Vol. 8, Special Issue.

Michigan Academician, Vol. 13, Issue nos. 3–4.

Michigan Law Review, Vol. 79, Issue nos. 3, 7–8; Vol. 80, Issue nos. 1–2.

Mondo Aperto, Vol. 35.

Monthly Labor Review, Vol. 104.

National Institute Economic Review, Issue nos. 95–98, 1981.

National Tax Journal, Vol. 34.

National Westminster Bank Quarterly Review, Issue nos. 1–4, 1981.

Nationaløkonomisk Tidsskrift, Vol. 119.

Natural Resources Journal, Vol. 21.

Nebraska Journal of Economics and Business, Vol. 20.

New England Economic Review, Issue nos. 1–6, 1981.

Osaka Economic Papers, Vol. 30, Issue no. 4; Vol. 31, Issue nos. 1–3.

Oxford Bulletin of Economics and Statistics, Vol. 43.
   Title changed from **Bulletin Oxford University Institute of Economics and Statistics** in 1973. Prior to 1972 entitled **Bulletin of the Institute of Economics and Statistics.**

Oxford Economic Papers, N. S., Vol. 33, Supplement.

Pakistan Development Review, Vol. 20.

Pakistan Economic and Social Review, Vol. 19.

Philippine Economic Journal, Vol. 20.

Philippine Review of Economics and Business, Vol. 18.

Policy Analysis, Vol. 7.

Policy Review, Issue nos. 15–17, 1981.

Political Science Quarterly, Vol. 96.

Population and Development Review, Vol. 7.

Population Studies, Vol. 35.

Problems of Economics, Vol. 23, Issue nos. 9–12; Vol. 24, Issue nos. 1–8.

Public Budgeting and Finance, Vol. 1.

Public Choice, Vol. 36; Vol. 37.

Public Finance, Vol. 36.

Public Finance Quarterly, Vol. 9.

Public Policy, Vol. 29.

Quarterly Journal of Economics, Vol. 96.

Quarterly Review of Economics and Business, Vol. 21.

Quarterly Review of the Rural Economy, Vol. 3.
   Title change from **Quarterly Review of Agricultural Economics** in 1979.

Regional Science Perspectives, Vol. 11.

Regional Science and Urban Economics, Vol. 11.

Regional Studies, Vol. 15.

Review of Black Political Economy, Vol. 11, Issue nos. 2–3.

Review of Business and Economic Research, Vol. 16, Issue nos. 2–3; Vol. 17, Issue no. 1.
   Title changed from **Mississippi Valley Journal of Business and Economics** in 1975.

Review of the Economic Conditions in Italy, Issue nos. 1–3, 1981.

Review of Economic Studies, Vol. 48.

Review of Economics and Statistics, Vol. 63.
   Title changed from **The Review of Economic Statistics** in 1948.

Review of Income and Wealth, Vol. 27.

Review of Marketing and Agricultural Economics, Vol. 49.

Review of Public Data Use, Vol. 9.

Review of Radical Political Economics, Vol. 12, Issue no. 4; Vol. 13, Issue nos. 1–3.

Review of Regional Studies, Vol. 11, Issue nos. 2–3.

Review of Social Economy, Vol. 39.

Revue d'Economie Industrielle, Issue nos. 15–18, 1981.

Revue Économique, Vol. 32.

Rivista Internazionale di Scienze Economiche e Commerciali, Vol. 28.

Rivista di Politica Economica, Vol. 71, Supplement—Selected Papers.

Scandinavian Economic History Review, Vol. 29.

Scandinavian Journal of Economics, Vol. 83.
   Title changed from **Swedish Journal of Economics** in 1976; prior to 1965 entitled **Ekonomisk Tidskrift.**

Schweizerische Zeitschrift für Volkswirtschaft und Statistik, Vol. 117.

Science and Society, Vol. 45.

Scottish Journal of Political Economy, Vol. 28.

Sloan Management Review, Vol. 22, Issue nos. 2–4; Vol. 23, Issue no. 1.

Social and Economic Studies, Vol. 30, Issue nos. 1, 3–4.

Social Research, Vol. 48.

Social Science Quarterly, Vol. 62.

Social Security Bulletin, Vol. 44.

South African Journal of Economics, Vol. 49.

Southern Economic Journal, Vol. 47, Issue nos. 3–4; Vol. 48, Issue nos. 1–2.

Southern Journal of Agricultural Economics, Vol. 13.

Statistica, Vol. 41.

Survey of Current Business, Vol. 61.

Tijdschrift Voor Economie en Management, Vol. 26.
Title changed from Tijdschrift voor Economie in 1975.

Urban Studies, Vol. 18.

Water Resources Research, Vol. 17.

Weltwirtschaftliches Archiv, Vol. 117.

Wirtschaft und Recht, Vol. 33, Issue nos. 3–4.

World Development, Vol. 9.

Yale Law Journal, Vol. 90, Issue nos. 3–4, 6–8; Vol. 91, Issue nos. 1–2.

Zeitschrift für die gesamte Staatswissenschaft, Vol. 137.

Zeitschrift für Nationalökonomie, Vol. 41.

Zeitschrift fur Wirtschafts-und Socialwissenschaften, Vol. 101.

LIST OF COLLECTIVE VOLUMES INDEXED 1981

AARON, HENRY J., ed. *The Value-added Tax: Lessons from Europe.* Studies of Government Finance: Second Series. Washington, D.C.: Brookings Institution, 1981.

AARON, HENRY J. AND PECHMAN, JOSEPH A., eds. *How Taxes Affect Economic Behavior.* Studies of Government Finance: Second Series. Washington, D.C.: Brookings Institution, 1981.

ADEDEJI, ADEBAYO, ed. *Indigenization of African Economies.* New York: Holmes and Meier, Africana, 1981.

ALTENSTETTER, CHRISTA, ed. *Innovation in Health Policy and Service Delivery: A Cross-national Perspective.* Science Center Berlin, vol. 34. Research on Service Delivery series, vol. 3. Cambridge, Mass.: Oelgeschlager, Gunn and Hain; Königstein, West Germany: Anton Hain, 1981.

ALTMAN, EDWARD I., ed. *Financial Handbook.* Fifth edition. New York; Chichester, England; Brisbane and Toronto: Wiley, Ronald Press, [1925...1968] 1981.

AMJAD, RASHID, ed. *The Development of Labour Intensive Industry in ASEAN Countries.* Bangkok: International Labour Office, Asian Employment Programme, Asian Regional Team for Employment Promotion (ARTEP), 1981.

AMMAN, FERNANDO AND WILSON, RICHARD, eds. *Energy Demand and Efficient Use.* Ettore Majorana International Science Series: Physical Sciences, vol. 9. New York and London: Plenum Press, 1981.

ARONSON, J. RICHARD AND SCHWARTZ, ELI, eds. *Management Policies in Local Government Finance.* Fourth Edition. Municipal management series. Washington, D.C.: International City Management Association for the Institute for Training in Municipal Administration, [1937...1975] 1981.

ARROW, KENNETH J. AND INTRILIGATOR, MICHAEL D., eds. *Handbook of Mathematical Economics.* Volume 1. Handbooks in Economics series, Book 1. Amsterdam; New York and Oxford: North-Holland, 1981.

ATLANTIC INSTITUTE FOR INTERNATIONAL AFFAIRS AND AMERICAN NUCLEAR SOCIETY. *Nuclear Nonproliferation and Safeguards: A Conference Report.* Atlantic Papers, no. 42. Paris: Atlantic Institute for International Affairs; LaGrange Park, Ill.: American Nuclear Society; distributed in the U.S. by Allanheld, Osmun, Totowa, N.J., 1981.

AUSTIN, JAMES E. AND ZEITLIN, MARIAN F., eds. *Nutrition Intervention in Developing Countries: an Overview* Cambridge, Mass.: Oelgeschlager, Gunn and Hain, 1981.

BAER, WERNER AND GILLIS, MALCOLM, eds. *Export Diversification and the New Protectionism: The Experiences of Latin America.* Champaign: University of Illinois, Bureau of Economic and Business Research; Cambridge, Mass.: National Bureau of Economic Research, 1981.

BAGCHI, AMIYA KUMAR AND BANERJEE, NIRMALA, eds. *Change and Choice in Indian Industry.* Calcutta: Bagchi for Centre for Studies in Social Sciences, Calcutta, 1981.

BAHL, ROY, ed. *Urban Government Finance: Emerging Trends.* Urban Affairs Annual Reviews, vol. 20. Beverly Hills, Calif., and London: Sage, 1981.

BAILEY, ANNE M. AND LLOBERA, JOSEP R., eds. *The Asiatic Mode of Production: Science and Politics.* Boston and London: Routledge and Kegan Paul, 1981.

BAIROCH, PAUL AND LÉVY-LEBOYER, MAURICE, eds. *Disparities in Economic Development since the Industrial Revolution.* New York: St. Martin's Press, 1981.

BALAAM, DAVID N. AND CAREY, MICHAEL J., eds. *Food Politics: The Regional Conflict.* Totowa, N.J.: Littlefield, Adams; Allanheld, Osmun, 1981.

BALASSA, BELA. *The Newly Industrializing Countries in the World Economy.* Pergamon Policy Studies on International Development. New York; Oxford; Toronto and Sydney: Pergamon Press, 1981.

BALDERSTON, JUDITH B., ET AL., eds. *Malnourished Children of the Rural Poor: The Web of Food, Health, Education, Fertility, and Agricultural Production.* Forewords by BENSON, CHARLES S. AND MARGEN, SHELDON. Boston, Mass.: Auburn House, 1981.

BALDWIN, ROBERT E. AND RICHARDSON, J. DAVID, eds. *International Trade and Finance: Readings.* Second edition. Boston and Toronto: Little, Brown, [1974] 1981.

BALLABON, MAURICE B., ed. *Economic Perspectives: An Annual Survey of Economics*. Volume 2. Chur, Switzerland; London and New York: Harwood Academic, 1981.

BARRO, ROBERT J. *Money, Expectations, and Business Cycles: Essays on Macroeconomics*. Economic Theory, Econometrics, and Mathematical Economics series. New York; London; Toronto and Sydney: Harcourt Brace Jovanovich, Academic Press, 1981.

BATEMAN, FRED, ed. *Business in the New South: A Historical Perspective: Papers Presented at the First Annual Sewanee Economics Symposium April 3–5, 1980*. Sewanee, Tenn.: University Press, University of the South, 1981.

BAUER, P. T. *Equality, the Third World and Economic Delusion*. Cambridge, Mass.: Harvard University Press, 1981.

BAYRAKTAR, B. A., ET AL., eds. *Energy Policy Planning*. NATO Conference Series, no. 2, System Science, vol. 9. New York and London: Plenum Press in cooperation with NATO Scientific Affairs Division, 1981.

BERGER, SUZANNE, ed. *Organizing Interests in Western Europe: Pluralism, Corporatism, and the Transformation of Politics*. Cambridge Studies in Modern Political Economies series. Cambridge; New York and Sydney: Cambridge University Press, 1981.

[BERGSON, ABRAM.] *Economic Welfare and the Economics of Soviet Socialism: Essays in Honor of Abram Bergson*. Edited by STEVEN ROSEFIELDE. New York; Cambridge and Sydney: Cambridge University Press, 1981.

BERGSTEN, C. FRED, ed. *The World Economy in the 1980s: Selected Papers of C. Fred Bergsten, 1980*. Lexington, Mass., and Toronto: Heath, Lexington Books, 1981.

BERNDT, ERNST R. AND FIELD, BARRY C., eds. *Modeling and Measuring Natural Resource Substitution*. Cambridge, Mass., and London: MIT Press, 1981.

BERREMAN, GERALD D., ed. *Social Inequality: Comparative and Developmental Approaches*. Assisted by KATHLEEN M. ZARETSKY. Studies in Anthropology series. Burg Wartenstein Symposium, No. 80. New York; London; Toronto and Sydney: Harcourt Brace Jovanovich, Academic Press, 1981.

BESSEL, RICHARD AND FEUCHTWANGER, EDGAR J., eds. *Social Change and Political Development in Weimar Germany*. London: Croom Helm; Totowa, N. J.: Barnes and Noble Books, 1981.

BHAGWATI, JAGDISH N., ed. *International Trade: Selected Readings*. Cambridge, Mass., and London: MIT Press, 1981.

BHALLA, A. S., ed. *Technology and Employment in Industry: A Case Study Approach*. Foreword by AMARTYA SEN. Second, revised and enlarged edition. A WEP Study. Geneva: International Labour Office, [1975] 1981.

BIENEN, HENRY AND DIEJOMAOH, V. P., eds. *The Political Economy of Income Distribution in Nigeria*. Political Economy of Income Distribution in Developing Countries series, no. 2. New York and London: Holmes and Meier, 1981.

BLAIR, ROGER D. AND LANZILLOTTI, ROBERT F., eds. *The Conglomerate Corporation: An Antitrust Law and Economics Symposium*. Cambridge, Mass.: Oelgeschlager, Gunn and Hain, 1981.

BLOCK, WALTER AND OLSEN, EDGAR, eds. *Rent Control: Myths and Realities: International Evidence of the Effects of Rent Control in Six Countries*. Fraser Institute Housing and Land Economics series, no. 7. Vancouver: Fraser Institute; distributed outside Canada by Enslow, Hillside, N.J., 1981.

BLUM, ALBERT A., ed. *International Handbook of Industrial Relations: Contemporary Developments and Research*. Westport, Conn.: Greenwood Press, 1981.

BÖHNING, W. R., ed. *Black Migration to South Africa: A Selection of Policy-Oriented Research*. Geneva: International Labour Office, 1981.

BORNSTEIN, MORRIS, ed. *The Soviet Economy: Continuity and Change*. Boulder, Colo.: Westview Press, 1981.

BORNSTEIN, MORRIS; GITELMAN, ZVI AND ZIMMERMAN, WILLIAM, eds. *East–West Relations and the Future of Eastern Europe: Politics and Economics*. London; Boston and Sydney: Allen and Unwin, 1981.

BOWER, BLAIR T., ET AL., eds. *Incentives in Water Quality Management: France and the Ruhr*

CENTER FOR STRATEGIC AND INTERNATIONAL STUDIES, ed. *The Export Performance of the United States: Political, Strategic, and Economic Implications.* New York: Praeger, 1981. (II)

CHATTERJI, MANAS, ed. *Energy and Environment in the Developing Countries.* Chichester, England; New York; Toronto and Brisbane: Wiley, 1981.

CHIKÁN, ATTILA, ed. *The Economics and Management of Inventories.* Volume 2. *Part A: Inventories in the National Economy.* Studies in Production and Engineering Economics, no. 2A. Amsterdam; Oxford and New York: Elsevier Scientific; distributed in U.S. and Canada by Elsevier North-Holland, N.Y., 1981. (I)

CHIKÁN, ATTILA, ed. *The Economics and Management of Inventories.* Volume 2. *Part B. Inventory Management, Mathematical Models of Inventories.* Studies in Production and Engineering Economics, no. 2B. Amsterdam; Oxford and New York: Elsevier Scientific; distributed in U.S. and Canada by Elsevier North-Holland, N.Y., 1981. (II)

CLARK, TERRY NICHOLS, ed. *Urban Policy Analysis: Directions for Future Research.* Urban Affairs Annual Reviews, vol. 21. Beverly Hills, Calif., and London: Sage, 1981.

CLARKSON, KENNETH W. AND MURIS, TIMOTHY J., eds. *The Federal Trade Commission since 1970: Economic Regulation and Bureaucratic Behavior.* Cambridge; New York and Sydney: Cambridge University Press, 1981.

CLAUDON, MICHAEL P. AND CORNWALL, RICHARD R., eds. *An Incomes Policy for the United States: New Approaches.* Boston; The Hague and London: Martinus Nijhoff, 1981.

CLEVELAND, HARLAN, ed. *The Management of Sustainable Growth.* Pergamon Policy Studies on Business and Economics. New York; Oxford; Sydney and Toronto: Pergamon Press in cooperation with the Woodlands Conference, 1981.

CLINE, WILLIAM R. AND WEINTRAUB, SIDNEY, eds. *Economic Stabilization in Developing Countries.* Washington, D.C.: Brookings Institution, 1981.

CLINE, WILLIAM R., ET AL. *World Inflation and the Developing Countries.* Washington, D.C.: Brookings Institution, 1981.

COATS, A. W., ed. *Economists in Government: An International Comparative Study.* Durham, N.C.: Duke University Press, 1981.

COLVIN, LUCIE GALLISTEL, ET AL. *The Uprooted of the Western Sahel: Migrants' Quest for Cash in the Senegambia.* New York: Praeger, 1981.

COOMER, JAMES C., ed. *Quest for a Sustainable Society.* Pergamon Policy Studies on Business and Economics series. New York; Oxford; Sydney and Paris: Pergamon Press in cooperation with The Woodlands Conference, 1981.

COPELAND, MORRIS A. *Essays in Socioeconomic Evolution.* New York: Vantage Press, 1981.

COURAKIS, ANTHONY S., ed. *Inflation, Depression and Economic Policy in the West.* Totowa, N.J.: Barnes and Noble Books, 1981.

COURBIS, RAYMOND, ed. *International Trade and Multicountry Models.* Collection "Modèles et Macroéconomie Appliquée" Série "Travaux du G.A.M.A.," no. 3. Paris: Economica, 1981.

COWING, THOMAS G. AND STEVENSON, RODNEY E., eds. *Productivity Measurement in Regulated Industries.* Economic Theory, Econometrics, and Mathematical Economics series. New York; London; Toronto and Sydney: Harcourt Brace Jovanovich, Academic Press, 1981.

CRANDALL, ROBERT W. AND LAVE, LESTER B., eds. *The Scientific Basis of Health and Safety Regulation.* Studies in the Regulation of Economic Activity series. Washington, D.C.: Brookings Institution, 1981.

CRECINE, JOHN P., ed. *Research in Public Policy Analysis and Management.* Volume 1. *Basic Theory, Methods and Perspectives.* Greenwich, Conn.: JAI Press, 1981.

CREEDY, JOHN, ed. *The Economics of Unemployment in Britain.* London; Boston; Toronto and Sydney: Butterworths, 1981.

CRICK, BERNARD, ed. *Unemployment.* Reprinted from *The Political Quarterly.* New York and London: Methuen, 1981.

CURRIE, D.; NOBAY, R. AND PEEL, D., eds. *Macroeconomic Analysis: Essays in Macroeconomics and Econometrics.* London: Croom Helm; distributed by Biblio Distribution Center, Totowa, N.J., 1981.

FEDERAL RESERVE BANK OF BOSTON. *The Decline in Productivity Growth: Proceedings of a Conference Held at Edgartown, Massachusetts, June 1980.* Conference Series, no. 22. Boston: Author, 1981. (I)

FEDERAL RESERVE BANK OF BOSTON. *The Future of the Thrift Industry: Proceedings of a Conference Held at Harwichport, Massachusetts, October, 1981.* Conference Series, no. 24. Boston: Author, 1981. (II)

FEDERAL RESERVE BANK OF BOSTON AND NATIONAL SCIENCE FOUNDATION. *The Regulation of Financial Institutions: Proceedings of a Conference Held at Melvin Village, New Hampshire, October 1979.* Conference Series, no. 21. Boston: Authors, 1981.

FEDERAL RESERVE SYSTEM. *Public Policy and Capital Formation.* Washington, D.C.: Board of Governors of the Federal Reserve System, 1981.

FELDSTEIN, MARTIN, ed. *Hospital Costs and Health Insurance.* Cambridge, Mass., and London: Harvard University Press, 1981.

FELLNER, WILLIAM, ed. *Essays in Contemporary Economic Problems: Demand, Productivity, and Population.* 1981–1982 edition. Washington and London: American Enterprise Institute for Public Policy Research, 1981.

FERGUSON, ALLEN R., ed. *Attacking Regulatory Problems: An Agenda for Research in the 1980s.* Cambridge, Mass.: Harper and Row, Ballinger, 1981.

FERGUSON, ALLEN R. AND LeVEEN, E. PHILLIP, eds. *The Benefits of Health and Safety Regulations.* Cambridge, Mass.: Harper and Row, Ballinger, 1981.

FERGUSON, THOMAS AND ROGERS, JOEL, eds. *The Hidden Election: Politics and Economics in the 1980 Presidential Campaign.* A Nation Book. New York: Pantheon Books; Toronto: Random House, 1981.

FINGER, WILLIAM R., ed. *The Tobacco Industry in Transition: Policies for the 1980s.* Lexington, Mass., and Toronto: Heath, Lexington Books, 1981.

[FISHER, WILLIAM BAYNE.] *Change and Development in the Middle East: Essays in Honour of W. B. Fisher.* Edited by JOHN I. CLARKE AND HOWARD BOWEN-JONES. London and New York: Methuen, 1981.

FLOUD, RODERICK AND MCCLOSKEY, DONALD, eds. *The Economic History of Britain since 1700. Volume 1. 1700–1860.* New York; Cambridge and Sydney: Cambridge University Press, 1981.

FLOUD, RODERICK AND MCCLOSKEY, DONALD, eds. *The Economic History of Britain since 1700. Volume 2. 1860 to the 1970s.* New York; Cambridge and Sydney: Cambridge University Press, 1981.

FOSTER, JOHN, ET AL. *Energy for Development: An International Challenge: Prepared for the North–South Roundtable of the Society for International Development.* Foreword by MAURICE F. STRONG. New York: Praeger for the North–South Roundtable (SID) and the Overseas Development Council, 1981.

FREEMAN, CHRISTOPHER, ET AL. *Technical Innovation and National Economic Performance: Papers from a Workshop Held at the Institute of Production, Aalborg University Centre, December 8th, 1980.* IKE Seminar, Industrial Development Research Series, no. 12. Working papers. Aalborg, Denmark: Aalborg University Centre, Institute of Production; distributed by Aalborg University Press, 1981.

FROMM, GARY, ed. *Studies in Public Regulation.* Regulation of Economic Activity Series, no. 4. Cambridge, Mass., and London: MIT Press, 1981.

VAN DER GAAG, JACQUES AND PERLMAN, MARK, eds. *Health, Economics, and Health Economics: Proceedings of the World Congress on Health Economics, Leiden, the Netherlands, September 1980.* Contributions to Economic Analysis series, no. 137. Amsterdam; New York and Oxford: North-Holland, 1981.

GALATIN, MALCOLM AND LEITER, ROBERT D., eds. *Economics of Information.* Social Dimensions of Economics series. Boston; The Hague and London: Martinus Nijhoff, 1981.

GALE, WILLIAM A., ed. *Inflation: Causes, Consequents, and Control.* Cambridge, Mass.: Oelgeschlager, Gunn and Hain, 1981.

GASKIN, MAXWELL, ed. *The Political Economy of Tolerable Survival*. London: Croom Helm; distributed by Biblio Distribution Centre, Totowa, N.J., 1981.

GATTI, JAMES F., ed. *The Limits of Government Regulation*. Foreword by MALCOLM F. SEVERANCE. New York; London; Toronto and Sydney: Harcourt Brace Jovanovich, Academic Press, 1981.

GIERSCH, HERBERT, ed. *Macroeconomic Policies for Growth and Stability: A European Perspective: Symposium 1979*. Institut für Weltwirtschaft an der Universität Kiel, Symposien- und Konferenzbände series. Tübingen, West Germany: Mohr (Paul Siebeck), 1981. (I)

GIERSCH, HERBERT, ed. *Towards an Explanation of Economic Growth: Symposium 1980*. Institut für Weltwirtschaft an de Universität Kiel, Symposien- und Konferenzbände series. Tübingen, West Germany: Mohr (Paul Siebeck), 1981. (II)

GLEASON, HERBERT P., ed. *Getting Better: A Report on Health Care from the Salzburg Seminar*. Cambridge, Mass.: Oelgeschlager, Gunn and Hain, 1981.

GMÜR, CHARLES J., ed. *Trade Financing*. London: Euromoney, 1981.

GOODMAN, LOUIS J.; HAWKINS, JOHN N. AND LOVE, RALPH N., eds. *Small Hydroelectric Projects for Rural Development Planning and Management*. Pergamon Policy Studies on International Development. New York; Oxford; Toronto and Sydney: Pergamon Press in cooperation with the East–West Center, Hawaii, 1981.

GOODWIN, CRAUFURD D., ed. *Energy Policy in Perspective: Today's Problems, Yesterday's Solutions*. Washington, D.C.: Brookings Institution, 1981.

GRASSMAN, SVEN AND LUNDBERG, ERIK, eds. *The World Economic Order: Past and Prospects*. New York: St. Martin's Press, 1981.

[GRETHER, EWALD T.] *Regulation of Marketing and the Public Interest: Essays in Honor of Ewald T. Grether*. Edited by FREDERICK E. BALDERSTON, JAMES M. CARMAN, AND FRANCESCO M. NICOSIA. Pergamon Policy Studies on Business. New York; Oxford; Sydney and Paris: Pergamon Press, 1981.

GRIFFITHS, BRIAN AND WOOD, GEOFFREY E., eds. *Monetary Targets*. New York: St. Martin's Press, 1981.

GRÜNBAUM, ISI. *Essays in Political Economy*. Copenhagen: Akademisk, 1981.

[VON HABERLER, GOTTFRIED.] *ORDO: Jahrbuch für die Ordnung von Wirtschaft und Gesellschaft*. Volume 32. Edited by WALTER EUCKEN AND FRANZ BÖHM. Stuttgart and New York: Gustav Fischer, 1981.

HAIMES, YACOV Y., ed. *Risk/Benefit Analysis in Water Resources Planning and Management*. New York and London: Plenum Press, 1981.

HAKIM, SIMON AND RENGERT, GEORGE F., eds. *Crime Spillover*. Sage Research Progress Series in Criminology, vol. 23. Beverly Hills and London: Sage in cooperation with the American Society of Criminology, 1981.

HALEY, K. BRIAN, ed. *Applied Operations Research in Fishing*. NATO Conference Series II: Systems Science, vol. 10. New York and London: Plenum Press in cooperation with NATO Scientific Affairs Division, 1981.

HAMILTON, F. E. IAN AND LINGE, G. J. R., eds. *International Industrial Systems*. Spatial Analysis, Industry and the Industrial Environment: Progress in Research and Applications, vol. 2. Chichester, England; New York; Brisbane and Toronto: Wiley, 1981.

HANCOCK, KEITH, ed. *Incomes Policy in Australia*. Sydney: Harcourt Brace Jovanovich (Australia), 1981.

HARE, PAUL G.; RADICE, HUGO K. AND SWAIN, NIGEL, eds. *Hungary: A Decade of Economic Reform*. London; Boston and Sydney: Allen and Unwin, 1981.

HARRIS, STUART AND MAYNARD, GEOFFREY. *Economic Theory and Public Policy*. Centre for Applied Economic Research Paper, no. 12. Kensington, Australia: University of New South Wales, 1981.

HART, DONN V., ed. *Philippine Studies: Political Science, Economics and Linguistics*. Contributions by KIT G. MACHADO, RICHARD HOOLEY, AND LAWRENCE A. REID. Center for Southeast Asian Studies Occasional Paper, no. 8. DeKalb: Northern Illinois University, Center for Southeast Asian Studies; distributed by Cellar Book Shop, Detroit, 1981.

HAWKINS, ROBERT G. AND PRASAD, A. J., eds. *Research in International Business and Finance.* Volume 2. *Technology Transfer and Economic Development.* A Research Annual. Greenwich, Conn., and London: JAI Press, 1981.

HAWLEY, AMOS H. AND MAZIE, SARA MILLS, eds. *Nonmetropolitan America in Transition.* Institute for Research in Social Science Monograph series. Chapel Hill: University of North Carolina Press in association with the Institute for Research in Social Science, 1981.

HEERTJE, ARNOLD, ed. *Schumpeter's Vision: "Capitalism, Socialism and Democracy" after 40 Years.* New York: Praeger, 1981.

HEGGESTAD, ARNOLD A., ed. *Regulation of Consumer Financial Services.* Cambridge, Mass.: Abt Books, 1981.

HELLEINER, GERALD K. *International Economic Disorder: Essays in North–South Relations.* Toronto and Buffalo: University of Toronto Press, 1981.

HELLER, FRANCIS H., ed. *Economics and the Truman Administration.* Lawrence, Kansas: Regents Press, 1981.

HELMS, ROBERT B., ed. *Drugs and Health: Economic Issues and Policy Objectives.* AEI Symposia series, no. 81B. Washington, D.C. and London: American Enterprise Institute for Public Policy Research, 1981.

HENDERSON, J. VERNON, ed. *Research in Urban Economics: A Research Annual.* Volume 1. Greenwich, Conn.: JAI Press, 1981.

HERSHBERG, THEODORE, ed. *Philadelphia: Work, Space, Family, and Group Experience in the Nineteenth Century: Essays toward an Interdisciplinary History of the City.* New York and Oxford: Oxford University Press, 1981.

HESSEN, ROBERT, ed. *Does Big Business Rule America? Critical Commentaries on Charles E. Lindblom's "Politics and Markets."* Washington, D.C.: Ethics and Public Policy Center, 1981.

HEWETT, ROBERT B., ed. *Political Change and the Economic Future of East Asia. Papers Presented at Seminars Sponsored by the Pacific Forum.* Honolulu: Pacific Forum; distributed by University Press of Hawaii, 1981.

HEYER, JUDITH; ROBERTS, PEPE AND WILLIAMS, GAVIN, eds. *Rural Development in Tropical Africa.* Preface by KEITH GRIFFIN. New York: St. Martin's Press, 1981.

HIBBS, DOUGLAS A., JR. AND FASSBENDER, HEINO, eds. *Contemporary Political Economy: Studies on the Interdependence of Politics and Economics.* Assisted by R. DOUGLAS RIVERS. Contributions to Economic Analysis, no. 135. Amsterdam; New York and Oxford: North-Holland, 1981.

HICKS, JOHN. *Collected Essays on Economic Theory.* Volume 1. *Wealth and Welfare.* Cambridge, Mass.: Harvard University Press, 1981.

HILL, MARTHA S.; HILL, DANIEL H. AND MORGAN, JAMES N., eds. *Five Thousand American Families—Patterns of Economic Progress.* Volume IX. *Analyses of the First Twelve Years of the Panel Study of Income Dynamics.* With contributions by SUE A. AUGUSTYNIAK ET AL. Ann Arbor: University of Michigan, Institute for Social Research, Survey Research Center, 1981.

HINSHAW, RANDALL, ed. *Global Monetary Anarchy: Perspectives on Restoring Stability.* Beverly Hills and London: Sage in cooperation with Claremont Graduate School, 1981.

HIRSCHMAN, ALBERT O. *Essays in Trespassing: Economics to Politics and Beyond.* Cambridge; New York and Sydney: Cambridge University Press, 1981.

HOFFMAN, W. MICHAEL AND WYLY, THOMAS J., eds. *The Work Ethic in Business: Proceedings of the Third National Conference on Business Ethics.* Sponsored by THE CENTER FOR BUSINESS ETHICS, BENTLEY COLLEGE. Cambridge, Mass.: Oelgeschlager, Gunn and Hain in conjunction with The Ethics Resource Center, Washington, D.C., 1981.

HOGAN, JOHN D. AND CRAIG, ANNA M., eds. *Dimensions of Productivity Research: Proceedings of the Conference on Productivity Research, the American Productivity Center, Houston, Texas, April 21–24, 1980.* Volume 1. Houston: American Productivity Center, 1981.

HOGAN, JOHN D. AND CRAIG, ANNA M., eds. *Dimensions of Productivity Research: Proceedings of the Conference on Productivity Research, the American Productivity Center, Houston, Texas, April 21–24, 1980.* Volume 2. Houston: American Productivity Center, 1981.

HOLLIST, W. LADD AND ROSENAU, JAMES N., eds. *World System Structure: Continuity and Change.* Sage Focus Editions series, no. 37. Beverly Hills and London: Sage, 1981.

HONG, WONTACK AND KRAUSE, LAWRENCE B., eds. *Trade and Growth of the Advanced Developing Countries in the Pacific Basin: Papers and Proceedings of the Eleventh Pacific Trade and Development Conference.* Seoul: Korea Development Institute; distributed by the University Press of Hawaii, Honolulu, 1981.

HOOD, CHRISTOPHER AND WRIGHT, MAURICE, eds. *Big Government in Hard Times.* Oxford: Martin Robertson; distributed by Biblio Distribution Centre, Totowa, N.J., 1981.

HULTEN, CHARLES R., ed. *Depreciation, Inflation, and the Taxation of Income from Capital.* Assisted by JANICE MCCALLUM. URI no. 33800. Washington, D.C.: Urban Institute Press, 1981.

HUTCHISON, T. W. *The Politics and Philosophy of Economics: Marxians, Keynesians and Austrians.* New York and London: New York University Press; distributed by Columbia University Press, New York, 1981.

INDUSTRIAL INSTITUTE FOR ECONOMIC AND SOCIAL RESEARCH. *IUI 40 years, 1939–1979: The Firms in the Market Economy.* IUI Research Program 1979–1980. Stockholm: Author, 1981.

INSTITUTE FOR CONTEMPORARY STUDIES. *The Fairmont Papers: Black Alternatives Conference, San Francisco, December 1980.* San Francisco: Author, 1981.

INSTITUTE OF INTERNATIONAL PUBLIC LAW AND INTERNATIONAL RELATIONS OF THESSALONIKI. *The Law of the European Communities and Greece.* Thesaurus Acroasium series, vol. 8. Thessaloniki: Author, 1981.

JANSSEN, J. M. L.; PAU, L. F. AND STRASZAK, A. J., eds. *Dynamic Modelling and Control of National Economies: Proceedings of the 3rd IFAC/IFORS Conference, Warsaw, Poland, 16–19 June 1980.* Oxford; New York; Toronto and Sydney: Pergamon Press for the International Federation of Automatic Control, 1981.

JOHNSON, D. GALE, ed. *Food and Agricultural Policy for the 1980s.* AEI Symposia series, no. 81G. Washington, D.C., and London: American Enterprise Institute for Public Policy Research, 1981.

JOHNSON, GLENN AND MAUNDER, ALLEN, eds. *Rural Change: The Challenge for Agricultural Economists: Proceedings, Seventeenth International Conference of Agricultural Economists Held at Banff, Canada, 3rd–12th September 1979.* Totowa, N.J.: Allenheld, Osmun; Oxford: International Association of Agricultural Economists, Institute of Agricultural Economists, 1981.

JOHNSTON, DENIS F., ed. *Measurement of Subjective Phenomena.* Special Demographic Analyses series, CDS-80-3. Washington: U.S. Department of Commerce, Bureau of the Census; distributed by U.S.G.P.O., 1981.

JORDAN, K. FORBIS AND CAMBRON-MCCABE, NELDA H., eds. *Perspectives in State School Support Programs.* Second Annual Yearbook of the American Education Finance Association. Cambridge, Mass.: Harper and Row, Ballinger, 1981.

JUSTER, F. THOMAS AND LAND, KENNETH C., eds. *Social Accounting Systems: Essays on the State of the Art.* Studies in Population series. New York; London; Toronto and Tokyo: Harcourt Brace Jovanovich, Academic Press, 1981.

JÜTTNER, D. JOHANNES, ed. *Interest Rates: Papers and Proceedings of a Symposium.* Melbourne: Longman Cheshire, 1981.

KALDOR, NICHOLAS. *Essays on Value and Distribution.* Second edition. Collected Economic Essays, vol. 1. New York: Holmes and Meier, [1960] 1981.

KAMRANY, NAKE M. *Energy Independence for the United States: Alternative Policy Proposals.* Contributions by WALTER BAER ET AL. Santa Monica, Calif.: Fundamental Books for Newport Foundation for Study of Major Economic Issues, 1981.

KARNA, MAHENDRA NARAIN, ed. *Studies in Bihar's Economy and Society.* B.N. College, Patna Series, no. 1. New Delhi: Concept; distributed in U.S. by Humanities Press, Atlantic Highlands, N.J., 1981.

KAUFMAN, GEORGE G. AND ROSEN, KENNETH T., eds. *The Property Tax Revolt: The Case of Proposition 13.* Cambridge, Mass.: Harper and Row, Ballinger, 1981.

KHAN, ALI AND SIRAGELDIN, ISMAIL, eds. *Research in Human Capital and Development*. Volume 2. *Equity, Human Capital, and Development*. A Research Annual. Greenwich, Conn., and London: JAI Press, 1981.

KILLICK, TONY, ed. *Papers on the Kenyan Economy: Performance, Problems and Policies*. Studies in the Economics of Africa series. Exeter, N.H.; London; Nairobi and Ibadan: Heinemann Educational Books, 1981.

KINDLEBERGER, CHARLES P. *International Money: A Collection of Essays*. London; Boston and Sydney: Allen and Unwin, 1981.

KLAASSEN, L. H.; MOLLE, W. T. M. AND PAELINCK, J. H. P., eds. *The Dynamics of Urban Development: Proceedings of an International Conference Held on the Occasion of the 50th Anniversary of the Netherlands Economic Institute, in Rotterdam, September 4, 1979*. New York: St. Martin's Press, 1981.

KMENTA, J. AND RAMSEY, J. B., eds. *Large-scale Macro-econometric Models: Theory and Practice*. Contributions to Economic Analysis series, no. 141. Amsterdam; New York and Oxford: North-Holland, 1981.

KORNAI, JÁNOS AND MARTOS, BÉLA, eds. *Non-price Control*. Translated from the Hungarian by GY. HAJDÚ. Translation revised by P. G. HARE. Contributions to Economic Analysis, vol. 133. Budapest: Akadémiai Kiadó; Amsterdam; New York and Oxford: North-Holland, 1981.

KOROPECKYJ, I. S. AND SCHROEDER, GERTRUDE E., eds. *Economics of Soviet Regions*. New York: Praeger, 1981.

KRIEDTE, PETER; MEDICK, HANS AND SCHLUMBOHM, JÜRGEN. *Industrialization before Industrialization: Rural Industry in the Genesis of Capitalism*. English Edition. With contributions from HERBERT KISCH AND FRANKLIN F. MENDELS. Translated by BEATE SCHLEMPP. Studies in Modern Capitalism series. Cambridge; New York and Sydney: Cambridge University Press; Paris: Editions de la Maison des Science de l'Homme, [1977] 1981.

KRUEGER, ANNE O., ET AL., eds. *Trade and Employment in Developing Countries*. Volume 1. *Individual Studies*. Chicago and London: University of Chicago Press for the National Bureau of Economic Research, 1981.

KUMAR, KRISHNA AND MCLEOD, MAXWELL G., eds. *Multinationals from Developing Countries*. Lexington, Mass., and Toronto: Heath, Lexington Books, 1981.

LADMAN, JERRY R.; BALDWIN, DEBORAH J. AND BERGMAN, ELIHU, eds. *U.S.–Mexican Energy Relationships: Realities and Prospects*. Lexington, Mass., and Toronto: Heath, Lexington Books, 1981.

LALL, SANJAYA. *Developing Countries in the International Economy: Selected Papers*. London: Macmillan Press; distributed in the U.S. by Humanities Press, Atlantic Highlands, N.J., 1981.

LASZLO, ERVIN AND KURTZMAN, JOEL, eds. *Political and Institutional Issues of the New International Economic Order*. Pergamon Policy Studies on the New International Economic Order series. UNITAR–CEESTEM NIEO Library. New York; Oxford; Toronto and Sydney: Pergamon Press for UNITAR and the Center for Economic and Social Studies of the Third World (CEESTEM), 1981.

LAWSON, MERLIN P. AND BAKER, MAURICE E., eds. *The Great Plains: Perspectives and Prospects*. Lincoln: Center for Great Plains Studies in association with the Old West Regional Commission; distributed by University of Nebraska Press, Lincoln, 1981.

LEIGH, LEONARD H., ed. *Economic Crime in Europe*. New York: St. Martin's Press, 1981.

LEIJONHUFVUD, AXEL. *Information and Coordination: Essays in Macroeconomic Theory*. New York and Oxford: Oxford University Press, 1981.

LEIPZIGER, DANNY M., ed. *Basic Needs and Development*. Foreword by PAUL P. STREETEN. Cambridge, Mass.: Oelgeschlager, Gunn and Hain, 1981.

LEVITAN, SAR A. AND MANGUM, GARTH L., eds. *The T in CETA: Local and National Perspectives*. Kalamazoo, Mich.: Upjohn Institute for Employment Research, 1981.

LEVY, HAIM, ed. *Research in Finance. A Research Annual*. Volume 3. Greenwich, Conn.: JAI Press, 1981.

[LIPIŃSKI, EDWARD.] *Studies in Economic Theory and Practice: Essays in Honor of Edward Lipinski*.

Edited by N. Assorodobraj-Kula et al. Amsterdam; New York and Oxford: North-Holland, 1981.

Livingstone, Ian, ed. *Development Economics and Policy: Readings*. London; Boston and Sydney: Allen and Unwin, 1981.

Lozoya, Jorge A. and Bhattacharya, A. K., eds. *Asia and the New International Economic Order*. Pergamon Policy Studies on the New International Economic Order series. UNITAR–CEESTEM NIEO Library. New York; Oxford; Toronto and Sydney: Pergamon Press for UNITAR and the Center for Economic and Social Studies of the Third World (CEESTEM), 1981.

Lozoya, Jorge A. and Birgin, Haydee, eds. *Social and Cultural Issues of the New International Economic Order*. Pergamon Policy Studies on the New International Economic Order series. UNITAR–CEESTEM NIEO Library. New York; Oxford; Toronto and Sydney: Pergamon Press for UNITAR and the Center for Economic and Social Studies of the Third World (CEESTEM), 1981.

Lozoya, Jorge and Green, Rosario, eds. *International Trade Industrialization and the New International Economic Order*. Pergamon Policy Studies on the New International Economic Order series. UNITAR–CEESTEM NIEO Library. New York; Oxford; Toronto and Sydney: Pergamon Press for UNITAR and the Center for Economic and Social Studies of the Third World (CEESTEM), 1981.

Lucas, Robert E., Jr. *Studies in Business-cycle Theory*. Cambridge, Mass., and London: MIT Press, 1981.

Lucas, Robert E. and Sargent, Thomas J., eds. *Rational Expectations and Econometric Practice*. Minneapolis: University of Minnesota Press, 1981.

Lynch, Thomas D., ed. *Contemporary Public Budgeting*. New Brunswick, N.J., and London: Transaction Books: Washington, D.C.: *The Bureaucrat* , 1981.

Maisel, Sherman J., ed. *Risk and Capital Adequacy in Commercial Banks*. NBER Monograph series. Chicago and London: University of Chicago Press for the National Bureau of Economic Research, 1981.

Mann, Dean E., ed. *Environmental Policy Formation: The Impact of Values, Ideology, and Standards*. Policy Studies Organization series. Lexington, Mass., and Toronto: Heath, Lexington Books, 1981.

Manski, Charles F. and McFadden, Daniel, eds. *Structural Analysis of Discrete Data with Econometric Applications*. Cambridge, Mass., and London: MIT Press, 1981.

Marer, Paul and Tabaczynski, Eugeniusz, eds. *Polish–U.S. Industrial Cooperation in the 1980s: Findings of a Joint Research Project*. Indiana University, International Development Institute, Studies in East European and Soviet Planning, Development and Trade, no. 30. Bloomington: Indiana University Press, 1981.

Martin, George T., Jr., and Zald, Mayer N., eds. *Social Welfare in Society*. New York: Columbia University Press, 1981.

Martin, Lee R., ed. *A Survey of Agricultural Economics Literature*. Volume 3. *Economics of Welfare, Rural Development, and Natural Resources in Agriculture, 1940s to 1970s*. Minneapolis: University of Minnesota Press for American Agricultural Economics Association, 1981.

Martin, R. L., ed. *Regional Wage Inflation and Unemployment*. London: Pion; distributed in the U.S. by Methuen, N.Y., 1981.

Mauri, Arnaldo, ed. *Europe's Role in World Development: Conference of the European Association of Development Institutes, Milano, 19–22 September 1978*. Series of Monographs on Development, no. 1. Milan: Finafrica—Cassa di Risparmio delle Provincie Lombarde (CARIPLO), 1981.

McBride, Robert H., ed. *Mexico and the United States*. The American Assembly, Columbia University, series. Englewood Cliffs, N.J.: Prentice-Hall, Spectrum, 1981.

McCalla, Alex F. and Josling, Timothy E., eds. *Imperfect Markets in Agricultural Trade*. Totowa, N.J.: Allanheld, Osmun, 1981.

McCloskey, Donald N. *Enterprise and Trade in Victorian Britain: Essays in Historical Economics*. London; Boston and Sydney: Allen and Unwin, 1981.

MCCRAW, THOMAS K., ed. *Regulation in Perspective: Historical Essays.* Cambridge, Mass., and London: Harvard University, Graduate School of Business Administration, Division of Research; distributed by Harvard University Press, 1981.

MCGUIRE, THOMAS G. AND WEISBROD, BURTON A., eds. *Economics and Mental Health.* Series EN, no. 1. DHHS Publication No. (ADM) 81-1114. Rockville, Md.: National Institute of Mental Health; distributed by U.S.G.P.O., Washington, D.C., 1981.

MCNAMARA, ROBERT S. *The McNamara Years at the World Bank: Major Policy Addresses of Robert S. McNamara, 1968–1981.* Forewords by HELMUT SCHMIDT AND LÉOPOLD SENGHOR. Baltimore and London: Johns Hopkins University Press for the World Bank, 1981.

MERCER, ROGER, ed. *Farming Practice in British Prehistory.* Edinburgh: Edinburgh University Press; distributed by Columbia University Press, 1981.

MERGEN, FRANÇOIS, ed. *Tropical Forests Utilization and Conservation: Ecological, Sociopolitical and Economic Problems and Potentials: Proceedings of an International Symposium Held at Yale University, School of Forestry and Environmental Studies, New Haven, Connecticut, April 15 and 16, 1980.* New Haven, Conn.: Yale University, School of Forestry and Environmental Studies, 1981.

MEYER, LAURENCE H., ed. *The Supply-Side Effects of Economic Policy* Economic Policy Conference series. Boston; The Hague and London: Kluwer-Nijhoff; distributed in North America by Kluwer Boston, Hingham, Mass., 1981.

MILEIKOVSKY, A. G., ET AL. *Present-Day Non-Marxist Political Economy: A Critical Analysis.* Translation of the revised Russian text by GALINA SDOBNIKOVA. Moscow: Progress; distributed by Imported Publications, Chicago, [1975] 1981.

VON MISES, LUDWIG. *Epistemological Problems of Economics.* Reprint Edition. Translated by GEORGE REISMAN. The Institute for Humane Studies Series in Economic Theory. New York and London: New York University Press; distributed by Columbia University Press, New York, [1933] 1981.

MISHAN, E. J. *Economic Efficiency and Social Welfare: Selected Essays on Fundamental Aspects of the Economic Theory of Social Welfare.* London; Boston and Sydney: Allen and Unwin, 1981.

MITCHELL, SIMON, ed. *The Logic of Poverty: The Case of the Brazilian Northeast.* Routledge Direct Editions. London and Boston: Routledge and Kegan Paul, 1981.

MOLT, WALTER; HARTMANN, HANS ALBRECHT AND STRINGER, PETER, eds. *Advances in Economic Psychology: Third European Colloquium on Economic Psychology, 1978.* Heidelberg: Meyn, 1981.

MOMMSEN, W. J., ed. *The Emergence of the Welfare State in Britain and Germany, 1850–1950.* In collaboration with WOLFGANG MOCK. London: Croom Helm for the German Historical Institute, 1981.

MORK, KNUT ANTON, ed. *Energy Prices, Inflation and Economic Activity.* Cambridge, Mass.: Harper and Row, Ballinger, 1981.

MORSE, JOEL N., ed. *Organizations: Multiple Agents with Multiple Criteria: Proceedings of the Fourth International Conference on Multiple Criteria Decision-making, University of Delaware, Newark, August 10–15, 1980.* Lecture Notes in Economics and Mathematical Systems series, vol. 190. New York and Berlin: Springer, 1981.

MUÑOZ, HERALDO, ed. *From Dependency to Development: Strategies to Overcome Underdevelopment and Inequality.* Westview Special Studies in Social, Political and Economic Development. Boulder, Colo.: Westview Press, 1981.

MURRAY, ROBIN, ed. *Multinationals beyond the Market: Intra-firm Trade and the Control of Transfer Pricing.* New York: Wiley, Halsted Press, 1981.

NATIONAL SCIENCE FOUNDATION. *International Economic Policy Research: Papers and Proceedings of a Colloquium Held in Washington, D.C., October 3, 4, 1980.* Washington, D.C.: Author, 1981.

[NELSON, JAMES R.] *Economic Regulation: Essays in Honor of James R. Nelson.* Edited by KENNETH D. BOYER AND WILLIAM G. SHEPHERD. MSU Public Utility Papers series. East Lansing: Michigan

State University, Graduate School of Business Administration, Division of Research, Institute of Public Utilities, 1981.

NEMETZ, PETER N., ed. *Energy Crisis: Policy Response.* Montreal: Institute for Research on Public Policy in collaboration with *The Journal of Business Administration* , 1981.

NEPAL, MINISTRY OF FOOD AND AGRICULTURE. *Nepal's Experience in Hill Agricultural Development.* Kathmandu: Author, 1981.

DE NEUFVILLE, JUDITH I., ed. *The Land Use Policy Debate in the United States.* Environment, Development, and Public Policy series; Environmental Policy and Planning series. New York and London: Plenum Press, 1981.

NEVILE, J. W., ed. *Economics, Economists and Policy Formulation.* Centre for Applied Economic Research paper, no. 13. Kensington, Australia: University of New South Wales, 1981.

NEWTON, KENNETH, ed. *Urban Political Economy.* New York: St. Martin's Press, 1981.

NICOL, DAVIDSON; ECHEVERRIA, LUIS AND PECCEI, AURELIO, eds. *Regionalism and the New International Economic Order: Studies Presented to the UNITAR–CEESTEM–Club of Rome Conference at the United Nations.* Foreword by KURT WALDHEIM. Pergamon Policy Studies on the New International Economic Order series. Studies in Regional Cooperation. New York; Oxford; Toronto and Sydney: Pergamon Press, 1981.

NIJKAMP, PETER AND SPRONK, JAAP, eds. *Multiple Criteria Analysis: Operational Methods.* Aldershot, England: Gower, 1981.

NOVAK, MICHAEL, ed. *Liberation South, Liberation North.* With ROGER W. FONTAINE ET AL. AEI Studies in Philosophy, Religion, and Public Policy, no. 338. Washington and London: American Enterprise Institute for Public Policy Research, 1981.

NOVAK, MICHAEL AND COOPER, JOHN W., eds. *The Corporation: A Theological Inquiry.* AEI Symposia series, no. 81C. Washington and London: American Enterprise Institute for Public Policy Research, 1981.

NOVOSTI PRESS AGENCY. *Soviet Economy Today: With Guidelines for the Economic and Social Development of the USSR for 1981–1985 and for the Period Ending in 1990.* Contributions in Economics and Economic History, no. 41. Westport, Conn.: Greenwood Press, 1981.

NYSTROM, PAUL C. AND STARBUCK, WILLIAM H., eds. *Handbook of Organizational Design.* Volume 1. *Adapting Organizations to Their Environments.* Oxford and New York: Oxford University Press, 1981.

NYSTROM, PAUL C. AND STARBUCK, WILLIAM H., eds. *Handbook of Organizational Design.* Volume 2. *Remodeling Organizations and Their Environments.* Oxford and New York: Oxford University Press, 1981.

OKOCHI, AKIO AND SHIMOKAWA, KOICHI, eds. *Development of Mass Marketing: The Automobile and Retailing Industries: Proceedings of the Fuji Conference.* The International Conference on Business History, Second Series, no. 7. Tokyo: University of Tokyo Press; distributed by Columbia University Press, New York, 1981.

OLSON, MANCUR, ed. *A New Approach to the Economics of Health Care.* AEI Symposia series, no. 81E. Washington and London: American Enterprise Institute for Public Policy Research, 1981.

ONTARIO ECONOMIC COUNCIL. *Policies for Stagflation: Focus on Supply.* Volume 1. Special Research Report. Toronto: Author, 1981.

ONTARIO ECONOMIC COUNCIL. *Policies for Stagflation: Focus on Supply.* Volume 2. Special Research Report. Toronto: Author, 1981.

OPEC, PUBLIC INFORMATION DEPARTMENT. *OPEC and Future Energy Markets: The Proceedings of the OPEC Seminar Held in Vienna, Austria, in October 1979.* New York: St. Martin's Press, 1981.

OTTERBECK, LARS, ed. *The Management of Headquarters–Subsidiary Relationships in Multinational Corporations.* New York: St. Martin's Press, 1981.

PARNES, HERBERT S., ed. *Work and Retirement: A Longitudinal Study of Men.* Cambridge, Mass., and London: MIT Press, 1981.

PATINKIN, DON. *Essays on and in the Chicago Tradition.* Durham, N.C.: Duke University Press, 1981.

PAUL, JEFFREY, ed. *Reading Nozick: Essays on "Anarchy, State, and Utopia."* Philosophy and Society series. Totowa, N.J.: Rowman and Littlefield, 1981.

PEACH, CERI; ROBINSON, VAUGHAN AND SMITH, SUSAN, eds. *Ethnic Segregation in Cities.* Athens: University of Georgia Press, 1981.

PEACOCK, ALAN AND FORTE, FRANCESCO, eds. *The Political Economy of Taxation.* New York: St. Martin's Press, 1981.

PEARSON, M. N. *Coastal Western India: Studies from the Portuguese Records.* XCHR Studies series, no. 2. New Delhi: Concept; distributed by Humanities Press, Atlantic Highlands, N.J., 1981.

PEARSON, SCOTT R.; STRYKER, J. DIRCK AND HUMPHREYS, CHARLES P., ET AL. *Rice in West Africa: Policy and Economics.* Stanford: Stanford University Press, 1981.

PECHMAN, JOSEPH A., ed. *Setting National Priorities: The 1982 Budget.* Washington, D.C.: Brookings Institution, 1981.

[PEN, JAN.] *Inkomensverdeling en Openbare Financiën: Opstellen voor Jan Pen.* Edited by P. J. EIJGELSHOVEN AND L. J. VAN GEMERDEN. Het Wetenschappelijke Boek, no. 61. Utrecht, Netherlands and Antwerp, Belgium: Het Spectrum, 1981.

PESKIN, HENRY M.; PORTNEY, PAUL R. AND KNEESE, ALLEN V., eds. *Environmental Regulation and the U.S. Economy.* Reprint from *Natural Resources Journal*, July, 1981. Baltimore and London: Johns Hopkins University Press for Resources for the Future, 1981.

PHELPS BROWN, HENRY AND HOPKINS, SHEILA V. *A Perspective of Wages and Prices.* London and New York: Methuen, 1981.

PINDER, JOHN, ed. *Fifty Years of Political and Economic Planning: Looking Forward 1931–1981.* London and Exeter, N.H.: Heinemann, 1981.

PIOUS, RICHARD M., ed. *The Power to Govern: Assessing Reform in the United States.* Proceedings of the Academy of Political Science, vol. 34, no. 2. New York: Academy of Political Science, 1981.

PITT, JOSEPH C., ed. *Philosophy in Economics: Papers Deriving from and Related to a Workshop on Testability and Explanation in Economics Held at Virginia Polytechnic Institute and State University, 1979.* Series in Philosophy of Science, vol. 16. Dordrecht, Holland; Boston and London: Riedel; distributed in U.S. and Canada by Kluwer Boston, Hingham, Mass., 1981.

POSTON, DUDLEY L., JR. AND WELLER, ROBERT H., eds. *The Population of the South: Structure and Change in Social Demographic Context.* Austin: University of Texas Press, 1981.

POWERS, TERRY A., ed. *Estimating Accounting Prices for Project Appraisal: Case Studies in the Little–Mirrlees/Squire–van der Tak Method.* Washington, D.C.: Inter-American Development Bank, 1981.

PURCELL, SUSAN KAUFMAN, ed. *Mexico–United States Relations: Proceedings of the Academy of Political Science.* Volume 34, no. 1. New York: Academy of Political Science, 1981.

REES, JOHN; HEWINGS, GEOFFREY J. D. AND STAFFORD, HOWARD A., eds. *Industrial Location and Regional Systems: Spatial Organization in the Economic Sector.* South Hadley, Mass.: Bergin; London: Croom Helm, 1981.

REPETTO, ROBERT, ET AL. *Economic Development, Population Policy, and Demographic Transition in the Republic of Korea.* Studies in the Modernization of the Republic of Korea: 1945–1975. East Asian Monographs, no. 93. Cambridge, Mass.: Harvard University, Council on East Asian Studies; distributed by Harvard University Press, 1981.

REUBENS, EDWIN P., ed. *The Challenge of the New International Economic Order.* Westview Special Studies in Social, Political, and Economic Development. Boulder, Colo.: Westview Press, 1981.

RICHARDSON, BRADLEY M. AND UEDA, TAIZO, eds. *Business and Society in Japan: Fundamentals for Businessmen.* Columbus: Ohio State University, East Asian Studies Program; New York: Praeger, 1981.

ROBINSON, JOAN. *What Are the Questions? And Other Essays.* Further Contributions to Modern Economics series. Armonk, N.Y.: Sharpe, 1981.

RODGERS, GERRY AND STANDING, GUY, eds. *Child Work, Poverty and Underdevelopment.* WEP Study. Geneva: International Labour Office, 1981.

RODWIN, LLOYD. _Cities and City Planning._ With HUGH EVANS, ET AL. Environment, Development, and Public Policy series. New York and London: Plenum Press, 1981.

ROSEN, SHERWIN, ed. _Studies in Labor Markets._ Universities–National Bureau Committee for Economic Research Conference Report series, no. 31. Chicago and London: University of Chicago Press, 1981.

ROSKAMP, KARL W. AND FORTE, FRANCESCO, eds. _Reforms of Tax Systems: Proceedings of the 35th Congress of the International Institute of Public Finance, Taormina, 1979._ Detroit: Wayne State University Press, 1981.

THE ROYAL INSTITUTE OF INTERNATIONAL AFFAIRS. _The Chatham House Annual Review._ Volume 1. _International Economic and Monetary Issues._ Foreword by ISIAH FRANK. Pergamon Policy Studies on International Politics series. New York; Oxford; Toronto and Sydney: Pergamon Press for author, 1981.

RUBINSON, RICHARD, ed. _Dynamics of World Development._ Political Economy of the World-System Annuals, vol 4. Beverly Hills and London: Sage, 1981.

RUSSELL, CLIFFORD S. AND NICHOLSON, NORMAN K., eds. _Public Choice and Rural Development: The Proceedings of a Conference Sponsored by the U.S. Agency for International Development and Held in Washington, D.C. in September 1979, under the Auspices of Resources for the Future, Inc._ Research Paper R-21. Washington, D.C.: Resources for the Future; distributed by Johns Hopkins University Press, Baltimore, 1981.

SAGAFI-NEJAD, TAGI; MOXON, RICHARD W. AND PERLMUTTER, HOWARD V., EDS. _Controlling International Technology Transfer: Issues, Perspectives, and Policy Implications._ Technology Transfer Trilogy series. Pergamon Policy Studies on International Development series. New York; Oxford; Sydney and Paris: Pergamon Press, 1981

SAMETZ, ARNOLD W., ed. _Securities Activities of Commercial Banks._ Lexington, Mass., and Toronto: Heath, Lexington Books, 1981.

SAMUEL, RAPHAEL, ed. _People's History and Socialist Theory._ History Workshop Series. London and Boston: Routledge and Kegan Paul, 1981.

SARMA, J. S. _Growth and Equity: Policies and Implementation in Indian Agriculture._ With commentaries by ESTER BOSERUP, S. HIRASHIMA, AND OLAF F. LARSON. Research Report, no. 28. Washington, D.C.: International Food Policy Institute, 1981.

SAUNDERS, CHRISTOPHER T., ed. _East–West–South: Economic Interactions between Three Worlds._ East–West European Economic Interaction Workshop Papers, vol. 6. New York: St. Martin's Press, 1981. (I)

SAUNDERS, CHRISTOPHER T., ed. _The Political Economy of New and Old Industrial Countries._ Butterworths Studies in International Political Economy series. London; Boston; Durban, South Africa and Toronto: Butterworths, 1981. (II)

SCHACHTER, OSCAR AND HELLAWELL, ROBERT, eds. _Competition in International Business: Law and Policy on Restrictive Practices._ New York: Columbia University Press, 1981.

SCHAIBLE, SIEGFRIED AND ZIEMBA, WILLIAM T., eds. _Generalized Concavity in Optimization and Economics._ New York; London; Toronto and Sydney: Harcourt Brace Jovanovich, Academic Press, 1981.

SCHANZE, ERICH, ET AL. _Mining Ventures in Developing Countries._ Part 2. _Analysis of Project Agreements._ Translated by GARY M. FRIEDMAN. Studies in Transnational Law of Natural Resources, vol. 2. Deventer, The Netherlands: Kluwer; Frankfurt am Main: Metzner for the Institut fur Auslandisches und Internationales Wirtschaftsrecht, Frankfurt am Main, 1981.

SCHEFFLER, RICHARD M., ed. _Advances in Health Economics and Health Services Research._ A Research Annual, vol. 2. Greenwich, Conn., and London: JAI Press, 1981.

SCHMITT-RINK, GERHARD, ed. _Ghana's Foreign Trade 1968–1978: Trends and Structures._ Contributions to Quantitative Economics series, vol. 2. Bochum, West Germany: Brockmeyer, 1981.

SCHWARTZ, GAIL GARFIELD, ed. _Advanced Industrialization and the Inner Cities._ The Urban Roundtable Series. Lexington, Mass., and Toronto: Heath, Lexington Books, 1981.

SCIENCE COUNCIL OF CANADA, INDUSTRIAL POLICIES COMMITTEE. _The Adoption of Foreign Technology by Canadian Industry: Proceedings of a Workshop._ Ottawa: Author, 1981.

SEDJO, ROGER A., ed. *Issues in U.S. International Forest Products Trade: Proceedings of a Workshop Held in Washington, D.C. on March 6 and 7, 1980.* Research Paper R-23. Washington, D.C.: Resources for the Future; distributed by Johns Hopkins University Press, Baltimore, 1981.

SELDON, ARTHUR, ed. *The Emerging Consensus...? Essays on the Interplay between Ideas, Interests and Circumstances in the First 25 Years of the IEA.* London: Institute of Economic Affairs; distributed by Trans-atlantic Arts, Central Islip, N.Y., 1981.

SETHURAMAN, S. V., ed. *The Urban Informal Sector in Developing Countries: Employment, Poverty and Environment.* WEP Study. Geneva: International Labour Office, 1981.

SHACKLETON, J. R. AND LOCKSLEY, GARETH, eds. *Twelve Contemporary Economists.* New York: Wiley, Halsted Press; London: Macmillan Press, 1981.

SHADOW OPEN MARKET COMMITTEE. *Policy Statement and Position Papers: September 13–14, 1981.* PPS 81-8. Rochester, N.Y.: University of Rochester, Graduate School of Management, Center for Research in Government Policy and Business, 1981. (I)

SHADOW OPEN MARKET COMMITTEE. *Policy Statement and Position Papers, March 15–16, 1981.* PPS 81-4. Rochester, N.Y.: University of Rochester, Graduate School of Management, Center for Research in Government Policy and Business, 1981. (II)

SHERBINY, NAIEM A., ed. *Manpower Planning in the Oil Countries.* Research in Human Capital and Development: A Research Annual. Supplement no. 1. Greenwich, Conn.: JAI Press, 1981.

SHOWLER, BRIAN AND SINFIELD, ADRIAN, eds. *The Workless State: Studies in Unemployment.* Oxford: Robertson; distributed by Biblio Distribution Centre, Totowa, N.J., 1981.

SICHEL, WERNER AND GIES, THOMAS G., eds. *Applications of Economic Principles in Public Utility Industries.* Michigan Business Studies, New Series: vol. 2, no. 3. Ann Arbor: University of Michigan, Graduate School of Business Administration, Division of Research, 1981.

SIMON, JULIAN L. AND LINDERT, PETER H., eds. *Research in Population Economics.* Research Annual, vol. 3. Greenwich, Conn.: JAI Press, 1981.

SIRKIN, GERALD, ed. *Lexeconics: The Interaction of Law and Economics.* Social Dimensions of Economics, vol. 2. Boston; The Hague and London: Martinus Nijhoff, 1981.

SKIDMORE, FELICITY, ed. *Social Security Financing.* Cambridge, Mass., and London: MIT Press, 1981.

SMITH, ERIC OWEN, ed. *Trade Unions in the Developed Economies.* New York: St. Martin's Press, 1981.

SOLO, ROBERT A. AND ANDERSON, CHARLES W., eds. *Value Judgement and Income Distribution.* Foreword by JANOS HORVATH. Praeger Studies in Grants Economics series. New York: Praeger, 1981.

SOLOMON, RICHARD H., ed. *The China Factor: Sino–American Relations and the Global Scene.* The American Assembly, Columbia University, and Council on Foreign Relations, Inc. series. Englewood Cliffs, N.J.: Prentice-Hall, Spectrum Books, 1981.

STAVE, BRUCE M., ed. *Modern Industrial Cities: History, Policy, and Survival.* Sage Focus Editions, no. 44. Beverly Hills, Calif., and London: Sage, 1981.

STERNLIEB, GEORGE AND HUGHES, JAMES W., eds. *Shopping Centers: U.S.A.* Piscataway, N.J.: Rutgers University, Center for Urban Policy Research, 1981.

STERNLIEB, GEORGE AND LISTOKIN, DAVID, eds. *New Tools for Economic Development: The Enterprise Zone, Development Bank, and RFC.* Piscataway, N.J.: Rutgers University, Center for Urban Policy Research, 1981.

STEVENS, CHRISTOPHER, ed. *EEC and the Third World: A Survey 1.* New York: Holmes and Meier, 1981.

STIEBER, JACK; MCKERSIE, ROBERT B. AND MILLS, D. QUINN, eds. *U.S. Industrial Relations, 1950–1980: A Critical Assessment.* Industrial Relations Research Association Series. Madison: University of Wisconsin, Industrial Relations Research Association, 1981.

[STONE, SIR RICHARD.] *Essays in the Theory and Measurement of Consumer Behaviour: In Honour of Sir Richard Stone.* Edited by ANGUS DEATON. Cambridge; New York and Sydney: Cambridge University Press, 1981.

STOPHER, PETER R.; MEYBURG, ARNIM H. AND BRÖG, WERNER, eds. *New Horizons in Travel-Behavior Research.* Lexington, Mass., and Toronto: Heath, Lexington Books, 1981.

STREETEN, PAUL. *Development Perspectives.* New York: St. Martin's Press, 1981.

STREETEN, PAUL AND JOLLY, RICHARD, eds. *Recent Issues in World Development: A Collection of Survey Articles.* Oxford; New York; Toronto and Sydney: Pergamon Press, 1981.

STRØM, STEINAR, ed. *Measurement in Public Choice.* London: Macmillan Press; distributed in the U.S. by Humanities Press, Atlantic Highlands, N.J., 1981.

STRUYK, RAYMOND J. AND BENDICK, MARC, JR., eds. *Housing Vouchers for the Poor: Lessons from a National Experiment.* Washington, D.C.: Urban Institute Press, 1981.

STUNKEL, KENNETH R., ed. *National Energy Profiles.* New York: Praeger, 1981.

TARLOCK, A. DAN, ed. *Regulation, Federalism, and Interstate Commerce.* Principal paper by EDMUND W. KITCH. Cambridge, Mass.: Oelgeschlager, Gunn and Hain, 1981.

TEMPEST, PAUL, ed. *International Energy Options: An Agenda for the 1980s: Selected Papers from Leading Contributors to the 1980 Annual Conference of the International Association of Energy Economists in Cambridge, U.K.* Cambridge, Mass.: Oelgeschlager, Gunn and Hain; London: Graham and Trotman, 1981.

TEPASKE, JOHN J., ed. *Research Guide to Andean History: Bolivia, Chile, Equador, and Peru.* Contributing editors are JUDITH R. BAKEWELL ET AL. Durham, N.C.: Duke University Press, 1981.

TRISKA, JAN F. AND GATI, CHARLES, eds. *Blue-collar Workers in Eastern Europe.* London; Boston and Sydney: Allen and Unwin, 1981.

TUCCILLO, JOHN A. AND VILLANI, KEVIN E., eds. *House Prices and Inflation.* URI 33300. Washington, D.C.: Urban Institute Press, 1981.

TWITCHETT, CAROL COSGROVE, ed. *Harmonisation in the EEC.* New York: St. Martin's Press, 1981.

UNITED NATIONS INDUSTRIAL DEVELOPMENT ORGANIZATION. *Appropriate Industrial Technology for Basic Industries.* Monographs on Appropriate Industrial Technology, no. 13. New York: United Nations, 1981.

U.S. CONGRESS, JOINT ECONOMIC COMMITTEE. *The Economy of 1981: A Bipartisan Look: Proceedings of a Congressional Economic Conference on Wednesday, December 10, 1980, Cosponsored by the Joint Economic Committee, Lyndon Baines Johnson School of Public Affairs, Lyndon Baines Johnson Library, Harvard Competitiveness Group.* 97th Congress, 1st Session, Joint Committee Print. Washington: U.S.G.P.O., 1981. (I)

U.S. CONGRESS, JOINT ECONOMIC COMMITTEE. *Expectations and the Economy: A Volume of Essays.* 97th Congress, 1st Session. Joint Committee Print. Washington: U.S.G.P.O., 1981. (II)

U.S. CONGRESS, JOINT ECONOMIC COMMITTEE. *The Political Economy of the Western Hemisphere: Selected Issues for U.S. Policy: Selected Essays Prepared for the Use of the Subcommittee on International Trade, Finance, and Security Economics.* 97th Congress, 1st Session, Joint Committee Print. Washington, D.C.: U.S.G.P.O., 1981. (III)

U.S. DEPARTMENT OF ENERGY, ECONOMIC REGULATORY ADMINISTRATION, DIVISION OF REGULATORY ASSISTANCE. *Electric Rate Demonstration Conference: Papers and Proceedings, April 1–3, 1980, Denver, Colorado.* Washington, D.C.: Onyx Corporation for author, 1981.

USELDING, PAUL, ed. *Research in Economic History: A Research Annual.* Volume 6. Greenwich, Conn.: JAI Press, 1981.

[VALAVANIS, STEFAN.] *Proceedings of the Econometric Society European Meeting, 1979: Selected Econometric Papers in Memory of Stefan Valavanis.* Edited by E. G. CHARATSIS. Contributions to Economic Analysis, no. 138. Amsterdam; New York and Oxford: North-Holland, 1981.

VALDÉS, ALBERTO. *Food Security for Developing Countries.* A Westview Special Study. Boulder, Colo.: Westview Press, 1981.

VERHEIRSTRAETEN, ALBERT, ed. *Competition and Regulation in Financial Markets.* New York: St. Martin's Press, 1981.

VERNON, RAYMOND AND AHARONI, YAIR, eds. *State-Owned Enterprise in the Western Economies.* New York: St. Martin's Press, 1981.

WACHTER, MICHAEL L. AND WACHTER, SUSAN M., eds. *Toward a New U.S. Industrial Policy?* Philadelphia: University of Pennsylvania Press, 1981.

WALTON, GARY M. AND SHEPHERD, JAMES F., eds. *Market Institutions and Economic Progress in the New South, 1865–1900: Essays Stimulated by "One Kind of Freedom: The Economic Consequences of Emancipation."* New York; London; Toronto and Sydney: Harcourt Brace Jovanovich, Academic Press, 1981.

WALZER, NORMAN AND CHICOINE, DAVID L., eds. *Financing State and Local Governments in the 1980s: Issues and Trends.* Cambridge, Mass.: Oelgeschlager, Gunn and Hain, 1981.

WEICHER, JOHN C.; VILLANI, KEVIN E. AND ROISTACHER, ELIZABETH A., eds. *Rental Housing: Is There a Crisis?* Washington, D.C.: Urban Institute Press, 1981.

[WEILER, EMANUEL T.] *Essays in Contemporary Fields of Economics: In Honor of Emanuel T. Weiler (1914–1979).* Edited by GEORGE HORWICH AND JAMES P. QUIRK. West Lafayette, Ind.: Purdue University Press, 1981.

WEINSTEIN, STANLEY AND WALKER, MICHAEL A., eds. *Annual Accounting Review.* Volume 3. Chur, Switzerland; London and New York: Harwood Academic, 1981.

WERTHEIMER, BARBARA MAYER, ed. *Labor Education for Women Workers.* Philadelphia: Temple University Press, 1981.

WEISS, LEONARD W. AND KLASS, MICHAEL W., eds. *Case Studies in Regulation: Revolution and Reform.* Boston and Toronto: Little, Brown, 1981.

WILLIAMS, PETER, ed. *The Overseas Student Question: Studies for a Policy.* London: Heinemann for the Overseas Students Trust, 1981.

WILLIAMSON, JOHN, ed. *Exchange Rate Rules: The Theory, Performance and Prospects of the Crawling Peg.* New York: St. Martin's Press, 1981.

WIND, YORAM; MAHAJAN, VIJAY AND CARDOZO, RICHARD N., eds. *New-Product Forecasting: Models and Applications.* Lexington, Mass., and Toronto: Heath, Lexington Books, 1981.

WOLD, HERMAN, ed. *The Fix-Point Approach to Interdependent Systems.* Contributions to Economic Analysis series, no. 132. Amsterdam; New York and Oxford: North-Holland, 1981.

WOOD, W. D. AND KUMAR, PRADEEP, eds. *The Current Industrial Relations Scene in Canada, 1981.* Kingston, Ont.: Queen's University, Industrial Relations Centre, 1981.

WRIGHT, KEVIN N., ed. *Crime and Criminal Justice in a Declining Economy.* Cambridge, Mass.: Oelgeschlager, Gunn and Hain, 1981.

ZAREMBKA, PAUL, ed. *Research in Political Economy: A Research Annual.* Volume 4. Greenwich, Conn.: JAI Press, 1981.

ZERBE, RICHARD O., JR., ed. *Research in Law and Economics.* Volume 3. Greenwich, Conn.: JAI Press, 1981.

CLASSIFICATION SYSTEM

Editor's note: Notes on the *Classification System* further clarify the subject matter covered under specific categories or point out specific topics included. They also may contain cross references to other categories. In addition, the *Topical Guide* at the end of this volume provides an index to classification numbers appropriate for specific topics. Please note that "General" categories may include *both* detailed articles covering all subcategories and very general articles falling into no subcategory.

050 **Economic Systems** 99
For studies of particular countries, as distinct from discussions of a system, see category 120.

Includes articles discussing or critiquing capitalist systems. Also includes articles on the cooperative as a system in predominantly market economies. Articles on mixed enterprise systems and nontheoretical articles on entrepreneurship also appear here (for theoretical articles on entrepreneurship and profits, see 0224).

Articles discussing socialist or communist systems generally or in a specific country are included here. For theory, see the 027 category and for planning, see the 113 category. Studies of particular communist or socialist countries or of particular sectors in the countries will be found in either the country division (124 subcategories) or the appropriate subject category for the article. For example, an article dealing with agriculture in the Soviet Union would be classified in one of the 710 subcategories.

100 **Economic Growth; Development; Planning; Fluctuations**

For development theory see 1120; for empirical studies of an individual country, see category 120, or for primarily historical studies, 040.

Does not include theory and analyses of productivity, which appear in 2260.

Subject Index of Articles
in Current Periodicals and Collective Volumes

Abbreviated titles for journals are the same as those used in the *Journal of Economic Literature*. Full titles of journals may be found on pages x–xv.

Books have been identified by author or editor (noted *ed.*). In rare cases where two books by the same author appear, volumes are distinguished by I or II after the name. In some cases there appear two books by the same person, once as author, once as editor. These may be distinguished by *ed.* noted for the edited volume. Full titles and bibliographic references for books may be found on pages xvi–xxxiii.

Geographic Descriptors when appropriate appear in brackets at the end of the article citation.

E000 General Economics; Theory; History; Systems

010 GENERAL ECONOMICS

011 General Economics

0110 General

Ames, Edward. On Forgetting Economics with Em Weiler. In *[Weiler, E. T.]*, 1981, pp. 355–60.

Bailey, Richard. The Second Post-war Decade: 1954–64. In *Pinder, J., ed.*, 1981, pp. 117–35. [G: U.K.]

Bergson, Abram. Where Are the Young Specialists on the Soviet Economy and What Are They Doing? Comment. *J. Compar. Econ.*, March 1981, *5*(1), pp. 119. [G: U.S.]

Berresford, Susan Vail. How Foundations View Funding Proposals on Working Women. In *Wertheimer, B. M., ed.*, 1981, pp. 233–40. [G: U.S.]

Boulding, Kenneth E. Agricultural Economics in an Evolutionary Perspective. *Amer. J. Agr. Econ.*, December 1981, *63*(5), pp. 788–95.

Buchanan, James McGill and Tullock, Gordon. An American Perspective: From 'Markets Work' to Public Choice. In *Seldon, A., ed.*, 1981, pp. 79–97. [G: U.S.]

Button, Kenneth J. The Economic Analysis of Economic Literature: A Survey. *Amer. Econ.*, Fall 1981, *25*(2), pp. 36–43.

Carter, Charles. PSI and the Future. In *Pinder, J., ed.*, 1981, pp. 171–77. [G: U.K.]

Clark, Colin. The IEA and the Fabians: Comparison and Contrast. In *Seldon, A., ed.*, 1981, pp. 189–204.

Copeland, Morris A. The Evolutionary Process. In *Copeland, M. A.*, 1981, pp. 1–7.

Croham [Lord]. The IEA as Seen from the Civil Service. In *Seldon, A., ed.*, 1981, pp. 205–15.

Culyer, A. J. The IEA's Unorthodoxy. In *Seldon, A., ed.*, 1981, pp. 99–119.

Davidson, Paul and Weintraub, Sidney. Jacob and Paul Samuelson, Post-Keynesian. *J. Post Keynesian Econ.*, Summer 1981, *3*(4), pp. 602–04.

Eliasson—Gunnar. The Firms in the Market Economy—40 Years of Research at IUI. In *Industrial Inst. for Econ. and Soc. Research*, 1981, pp. 13–32. [G: Sweden]

Feldstein, Martin S. 'Twas a Night in the Sixties. *J. Polit. Econ.*, December 1981, *89*(6), pp. 1266–69.

Feliciano, Gloria D. Principal Sources of Information in Singapore, Malaysia, the Philippines and Indonesia: A Critical Survey. *Int. Soc. Sci. J.*, 1981, *33*(1), pp. 176–86. [G: Singapore; Malaysia; Philippines; Indonesia]

Fienup, Darrell F. and Riley, Harold M. Training Agricultural Economists to Serve the Needs of a Changing World. In *Johnson, G. and Maunder, A., eds.*, 1981, pp. 632–42. [G: U.S.; LDCs]

Finger, Joseph Michael. Policy Research. *J. Polit. Econ.*, December 1981, *89*(6), pp. 1270–71.

Fischer, Charles C. A Comment on "The Method Is the Ideology." *J. Econ. Issues*, March 1981, *15*(1), pp. 193–96.

Foster, J. Fagg. Policy Implications of Increasing Growth Rates in the More Developed Economies. *J. Econ. Issues*, December 1981, *15*(4), pp. 959–62.

Foster, J. Fagg. Syllabus for Problems of Modern Society: The Theory of Institutional Adjustment. *J. Econ. Issues*, December 1981, *15*(4), pp. 929–35.

Foster, J. Fagg. Syllabus for Problems of Modern Society: The Theory of Institutional Adjustment. *J. Econ. Issues*, December 1981, *15*(4), pp. 929–35.

Foster, J. Fagg. The American Economy. *J. Econ. Issues*, December 1981, *15*(4), pp. 981–84.

Goodman, Raymond. The First Post-war Decade. In *Pinder, J., ed.*, 1981, pp. 97–116. [G: U.K.]

Green, Richard D. and Hassan, Zuhair A. Choices and Consequences: Comment. *Amer. J. Agr. Econ.*, February 1981, *63*(1), pp. 174–75.

Greffe, Xavier. L'économie non officielle. (The Unofficial Economy. With English summary.) *Consommation*, July–September 1981, *28*(3), pp. 95–118.

Havlicek, Joseph, Jr. Funding for Agricultural Economics: Discussion. *Amer. J. Agr. Econ.*, December 1981, *63*(5), pp. 806–07.

Hicks, John R. The Mainspring of Economic Growth. *Amer. Econ. Rev.*, Special Issue December 1981, *71*(6), pp. 23–29.

Hirschman, Albert O. Exit, Voice, and the State. In *Hirschman, A. O.*, 1981, *1978*, pp. 246–65.

Hirschman, Albert O. Exit, Voice, and Loyalty: Further Reflections and a Survey of Recent Contributions. In *Hirschman, A. O.*, 1981, *1974*, pp. 213–35.

Holmes, A. S. The Good Fight. *Econ. Rec.*, March 1981, *57*(156), pp. 1–11. [G: Australia]

Horowitz, Irving Louis. Social Science and the Reagan Administration. *J. Policy Anal. Manage.*, Fall 1981, *1*(1), pp. 125–29. [G: U.S.]

Hughes, Jonathan. A Note on Early Cliometrica. In *[Weiler, E. T.]*, 1981, pp. 361–64.

Hutchison, Terence W. The Market Economy and the Franchise, or 1867 and All That. In *Hutchison, T. W.*, 1981, pp. 22–45.

Hutton, Graham. 'Why Did It Happen . . . Just Then?' In *Seldon, A., ed.*, 1981, pp. 1–18. [G: U.K.]

Isserlis, A. R. Plus ça Change ... In *Pinder, J., ed.*, 1981, pp. 162–70.

Kamien, Morton I. "It's Just like New York!" In *[Weiler, E. T.]*, 1981, pp. 265–68.

King, Richard A. Choices and Consequences: Reply. *Amer. J. Agr. Econ.*, February 1981, *63*(1), pp. 176–77.

Leijonhufvud, Axel. Life among the Econ. In *Leijonhufvud, A.*, 1981, *1973*, pp. 347–59.

Machan, Tibor R. The Non-Rational Domain and the Limits of Economic Analysis: Comment. *Southern Econ. J.*, April 1981, *47*(4), pp. 1123–27.

Makler, Harry; Sales, Arnaud and Smelser, Neil. Economy and Society. *Int. Soc. Sci. J.*, 1981, *33*(2), pp. 330–50.

McCain, Roger A. Tradition and Innovation: Some Economics of the Creative Arts, Science, Scholarship, and Technical Development. In *Galatin, M. and Leiter, R. D., eds.*, 1981, pp. 173–204.

McKenzie, Richard B. The Non-Rational Domain and the Limits of Economic Analysis: Reply. *Southern Econ. J.*, April 1981, *47*(4), pp. 1128–31.

Miller, Ronald E. Publication Lags in the *Journal of Regional Science*: A Note from the Editor. *J. Reg. Sci.*, February 1981, *21*(1), pp. 127–28.

von Mises, Ludwig. Conception and Understanding. In *von Mises, L.*, 1981, pp. 130–45.

von Mises, Ludwig. The Psychological Basis of the Opposition to Economic Theory. In *von Mises, L.*, 1981, pp. 183–203.

von Mises, Ludwig. The Task and Scope of the Science of Human Action. In *von Mises, L.*, 1981, pp. 1–67.

Mokhov, N. The Economics, Planning, and Organization of Culture. *Prob. Econ.*, July 1981, *24*(3), pp. 36–54. [G: U.S.S.R.]

Myrdal, Gunnar. What Is Political Economy? In *Solo, R. A. and Anderson, C. W., eds.*, 1981, pp. 41–53.

Negoiţă, C. V. Human Systems Cybernetics. *Econ. Computat. Cybern. Stud. Res.*, 1981, *15*(2), pp. 57–63.

O'Brien, Denis Patrick. The Emphasis on Market Economics. In *Seldon, A., ed.*, 1981, pp. 51–77.

Parry, Robert T. Presidential Address: NABE in the Eighties. *Bus. Econ.*, January 1981, *16*(1), pp. 10–13. [G: U.S.]

Pinder, John. 1964–1980: From PEP to PSI. In *Pinder, J., ed.*, 1981, pp. 136–61. [G: U.K.]

Reubens, Edwin P. Tradition and Innovation: Some Economics of the Creative Arts, Science, Scholarship, and Technical Development: Comments. In *Galatin, M. and Leiter, R. D., eds.*, 1981, pp. 205–08.

Roberts, Stephen A. and Brittain, J. Michael. Demand and Supply Patterns for Documents and Data in the United Kingdom. *Int. Soc. Sci. J.*, 1981, *33*(1), pp. 50–74. [G: U.K.]

Robinson, Joan. The Disintegration of Economics. In *Robinson, J.*, 1981, *1979*, pp. 96–104.

Rózsa, György. European Co-operation in Social Science Information and Documentation: A Process of Maturation. *Int. Soc. Sci. J.*, 1981, *33*(3), pp. 559–65.

Samuels, Warren J. The Current State of Economics. *Econ. Forum*, Winter 1981–82, *12*(2), pp. 1–8.

Schuh, G. Edward. Economics and International Relations: A Conceptual Framework. *Amer. J. Agr. Econ.*, December 1981, *63*(5), pp. 767–78.

Shackleton, J. R. and Locksley, Gareth. Twelve Contemporary Economists: Introduction. In *Shackleton, J. R. and Locksley, G., eds.*, 1981, pp. 1–11.

Sharp, Eric. The IEA as Seen from Industry. In *Seldon, A., ed.*, 1981, pp. 217–26. [G: U.K.]

Sherman, Howard J. Marx and Determinism. *J. Econ. Issues*, March 1981, *15*(1), pp. 61–71.

Sims, Christopher A. What Kind of Science is Economics? A Review Article on *Causality* in Economics by John R. Hicks. *J. Polit. Econ.*, June 1981, *89*(3), pp. 578–83.

Sinclair, Sol. The Function of the CAES Workshop: Past Performance and Suggestions for the Future. *Can. J. Agr. Econ.*, November 1981, *29*(3), pp. 257–64. [G: Canada]

Smith, Vernon L. Experimental Economics at Purdue. In *[Weiler, E. T.]*, 1981, pp. 369–73.

Soltow, Martha Jane. Twenty Year Cumulative Index to Labor History: Vol. 1, No. 1 (Spring, 1960)—Vol. 20, No. 4 (Fall, 1979). *Labor Hist.*, Winter 1981, *22*(1), pp. 57–135.

Stanton, Bernard F. and Farrell, Kenneth R. Funding for Agricultural Economics: Needs and Strategies for the 1980s. *Amer. J. Agr. Econ.*, December 1981, *63*(5), pp. 796–805.

Stephens, R. J. Social Economics: A Budding Scientific Research Programme? *Int. J. Soc. Econ.*, 1981, *8*(3), pp. 3–25.

Stolz, Peter. Experimente in der Ökonomie und Wirtschaftshistorische Erfahrung. (With English summary.) *Kyklos*, 1981, *34*(1), pp. 72–94.

Streeten, Paul P. Programmes and Prognoses [Introduction to Gunnar Myrdal]. In *Streeten, P.*, 1981, *1958*, pp. 3–34.

Swanson, Dorothy. Annual Bibliography on American Labor History, 1980: Periodicals, Dissertations, and Research in Progress. *Labor Hist.*, Fall 1981, *22*(4), pp. 545–72. [G: U.S.]

Tool, Marc R. Observations on the Fischer Comment [The Method Is the Ideology]. *J. Econ. Issues*, March 1981, *15*(1), pp. 197–99.

Toussaint, W. D. Funding for Agricultural Economics: Discussion. *Amer. J. Agr. Econ.*, December 1981, *63*(5), pp. 808–09.

Vinogradov, V. A., et al. Towards an International Information System. *Int. Soc. Sci. J.*, 1981, *33*(1), pp. 10–49.

Walton, John. *Social Science Quarterly:* Two Histories of Tradition and Renovation. *Soc. Sci. Quart.*, March 1981, *62*(1), pp. 1–6.

Watts, Michael W. The Non-Rational Domain and the Limits of Economic Analysis: Comment. *Southern Econ. J.*, April 1981, *47*(4), pp. 1120–22.

Weisskopf, Walter. Reply to Professor Fischer [The Method Is the Ideology]. *J. Econ. Issues*, March 1981, *15*(1), pp. 196–97.

White, Rudolph A.; Billings, C. David and Brown, Robert D., Jr. Assessing the Role of Business Schools in the Market for New Economics Ph.D.'s. *J. Econ. Educ.*, Summer 1981, *12*(2), pp. 34–44. [G: U.S.]

Wolff, Klaus. "Textile History": The First Ten Years: Review Article. *J. Econ. Hist.*, June 1981, *41*(2), pp. 411–14.

Wood, John B. How It All Began—Personal Recollections. In *Seldon, A., ed.*, 1981, pp. 247–64.

Woudenberg, Henry W. and McKee, David L. Musical Chairs and Revolving Doors: The Transmigration of Economists North American Style. *Eastern Econ. J.*, January 1981, *7*(1), pp. 35–38. [G: Canada; U.S.]

0112 Role of Economics; Role of Economists

Ambirajan, S. India: The Aftermath of Empire. In *Coats, A. W., ed.*, 1981, pp. 98–132. [G: India]

Ambirajan, Srinivasa. India: The Aftermath of Empire. *Hist. Polit. Econ.*, Fall 1981, *13*(3), pp. 436–70. [G: India]

Barber, William J. The United States: Economists in a Pluralistic Polity. *Hist. Polit. Econ.*, Fall 1981, *13*(3), pp. 513–47. [G: U.S.]

Barber, William J. The United States: Economists in a Pluralistic Polity. In *Coats, A. W., ed.*, 1981, pp. 175–209. [G: U.S.]

Bergh, Trond. Norway: The Powerful Servants. *Hist. Polit. Econ.*, Fall 1981, *13*(3), pp. 471–512. [G: Norway]

Bergh, Trond. Norway: The Powerful Servants. In *Coats, A. W., ed.*, 1981, pp. 133–74. [G: Norway]

Bjarnason, Harold F. Accomplishments of and Opportunities for Agricultural Economists in Parastatal Organizations. In *Johnson, G. and Maunder, A., eds.*, 1981, pp. 520–27.

Blankart, Charles B. Towards an Economic Theory of Advice and Its Application to the Deregulation Issue. *Kyklos*, 1981, *34*(1), pp. 95–105.

Boute, S., et al. Les économistes belges: tour d'ivoire ou tour de Babel. (With English summary.) *Cah. Écon. Bruxelles*, 4th Trimestre 1981, (92), pp. 539–56. [G: Belgium]

Britton, Denis K. Fifty Years of Agricultural Economics—and What Next? In *Johnson, G. and Maunder, A., eds.*, 1981, pp. 3–11.

Cairncross, Alec [Sir]. Academics and Policy Makers. In *[Cairncross, A.]*, 1981, pp. 5–22.

Coats, A. W. Britain: The Rise of the Specialists. *Hist. Polit. Econ.*, Fall 1981, *13*(3), pp. 365–404. [G: U.K.]

Coats, A. W. Britain: The Rise of the Specialists. In *Coats, A. W., ed.*, 1981, pp. 27–66. [G: U.K.]

Coats, A. W. Economists in Government: Conclusions. *Hist. Polit. Econ.*, Fall 1981, *13*(3), pp. 681–94.

Coats, A. W. Economists in Government: Introduction. *Hist. Polit. Econ.*, Fall 1981, *13*(3), pp. 341–64.

Coats, A. W. Economists in Government: Conclusions. In *Coats, A. W., ed.*, 1981, pp. 343–56.

Coats, A. W. Economists in Government: Introduction. In *Coats, A. W., ed.*, 1981, pp. 3–26.

Cromarty, William A. Challenges for Agricultural Economists Working for Multi-national Firms. In *Johnson, G. and Maunder, A., eds.*, 1981, pp. 509–17.

Culyer, A. J. Health, Economics, and Health Economics. In *van der Gaag, J. and Perlman, M., eds.*, 1981, pp. 3–11.

Fekete, Ferenc. Accomplishments of and Challenges for Agricultural Economists Working at the National Level of Centrally Managed Economies. In *Johnson, G. and Maunder, A., eds.*, 1981, pp. 285–94.

Ferraresi, Franco and Ferrari, Giuseppe. Italy: Economists in a Weak Political System. *Hist. Polit. Econ.*, Fall 1981, *13*(3), pp. 629–55. [G: Italy]

Ferraresi, Franco and Ferrari, Giuseppe. Italy: Economists in a Weak Political System. In *Coats, A. W., ed.*, 1981, pp. 291–317. [G: Italy]

Gross, Bertram R. The Employment Act of 1946. In *Heller, F. H., ed.*, 1981, pp. 101–04. [G: U.S.]

Haddad, Paulo Roberto. Brazil: Economists in a Bureaucratic-Authoritarian System. In *Coats, A. W., ed.*, 1981, pp. 318–42. [G: Brazil]

Haddad, Paulo Roberto. Brazil: Economists in a Bureaucratic-Authoritarian System. *Hist. Polit. Econ.*, Fall 1981, *13*(3), pp. 656–80. [G: Brazil]

Hardin, Lowell S. Emerging Roles of Agricultural Economists Working in International Research Institutions such as IRRI and CIMMYT. In *Johnson, G. and Maunder, A., eds.*, 1981, pp. 479–90. [G: Selected LDCs]

Hawkins, R. G. and FitzGerald, V. W. The Potential Contribution of Econometric Modelling. In *Nevile, J. W., ed.*, 1981, pp. 11–30. [G: Australia]

Hewson, John R. The Role of the Advisor. In *Nevile, J. W., ed.*, 1981, pp. 46–65.

Hutchison, Terence W. On the Aims and Methods of Economic Theorizing. In *Hutchison, T. W.*, 1981, pp. 266–307.

Hutchison, Terence W. The Limitations of General Theories in Macro Economics. In *Hutchison, T. W.*, 1981, pp. 233–65.

Johnson, Harry G. Networks of Economists: Their Role in International Monetary Reforms. In *Evan, W. M., ed.*, 1981, pp. 79–90.

Kemenes, Egon. Hungary: Economists in a Socialist Planning System. In *Coats, A. W., ed.*, 1981, pp. 242–61. [G: Hungary]

Kemenes, Egon. Hungary: Economists in a Socialist Planning System. *Hist. Polit. Econ.*, Fall 1981, *13*(3), pp. 580–99. **[G: Hungary]**

Keyserling, Leon H. The Employment Act of 1946. In *Heller, F. H., ed.*, 1981, pp. 104–07. **[G: U.S.]**

Keyserling, Leon H. The View from The Council of Economic Advisers. In *Heller, F. H., ed.*, 1981, pp. 79–95. **[G: U.S.]**

Kleiman, Ephraim. Israel: Economists in a New State. In *Coats, A. W., ed.*, 1981, pp. 210–41. **[G: Israel]**

Kleiman, Ephraim. Israel: Economists in a New State. *Hist. Polit. Econ.*, Fall 1981, *13*(3), pp. 548–79. **[G: Israel]**

Komiya, Ryutaro and Yamamoto, Kozo. Japan: The Officer in Charge of Economic Affairs. In *Coats, A. W., ed.*, 1981, pp. 262–90. **[G: Japan]**

Komiya, Ryutaro and Yamamoto, Kozo. Japan: The Officer in Charge of Economic Affairs. *Hist. Polit. Econ.*, Fall 1981, *13*(3), pp. 600–628. **[G: Japan]**

Leijonhufvud, Axel. Inflation and the Economists: Critique. In *Leijonhufvud, A.*, 1981, *1977*, pp. 271–89.

Lucas, Robert E., Jr. Rules, Discretion, and the Role of the Economic Advisor. In *Lucas, R. E., Jr.*, 1981, *1980*, pp. 248–61.

Mishan, Ezra J. The Nature of Economic Expertise Reconsidered. In *Mishan, E. J.*, 1981, pp. 175–86.

Moneta, Carlos. The Impact of Research on Policymaking. In *Laszlo, E. and Kurtzman, J., eds.*, 1981, pp. 133–72.

Nazarenko, Victor J. Accomplishments and Challenges for the Future for Agricultural Economists Working in COMECON. In *Johnson, G. and Maunder, A., eds.*, 1981, pp. 407–13. **[G: CMEA]**

Nazarenko, Victor J. The Part Played by Agricultural Economists in State Trading Bodies. In *Johnson, G. and Maunder, A., eds.*, 1981, pp. 546–47.

Nevile, J. W. Economics, Economists and Policy Formulation. In *Nevile, J. W., ed.*, 1981, pp. 1–10.

Niehans, Jürg. Economics: History, Doctrine, Science, Art. *Kyklos*, 1981, *34*(2), pp. 165–77.

O'Neil, R. F. The Artist's Perception of the Typical Businessman: Selfish, Greedy, Conniving and Thoroughly Amoral. *Int. J. Soc. Econ.*, 1981, *8*(4), pp. 31–39.

Ojala, Eric M. Accomplishments and Opportunities of Agricultural Economists Working in International Agencies. In *Johnson, G. and Maunder, A., eds.*, 1981, pp. 391–403.

Petit, Michel. Agriculture and Regional Development in Europe—The Role of Agricultural Economists. *Europ. Rev. Agr. Econ.*, 1981, *8*(2–3), pp. 137–53. **[G: Europe]**

Petridis, A. Australia: Economists in a Federal System. In *Coats, A. W., ed.*, 1981, pp. 67–97. **[G: Australia]**

Petridis, Anatasios. Australia: Economists in a Federal System. *Hist. Polit. Econ.*, Fall 1981, *13*(3), pp. 405–35. **[G: Australia]**

Ritson, Christopher. Accomplishments and Opportunities for Agricultural Economists on the Theoretical Front. In *Johnson, G. and Maunder, A., eds.*, 1981, pp. 605–17.

Rodwin, Lloyd. Training City Planners in Third World Countries. In *Rodwin, L.*, 1981, pp. 210–26.

Salant, Walter S. The Employment Act of 1946. In *Heller, F. H., ed.*, 1981, pp. 107–09. **[G: U.S.]**

Schuh, G. Edward. Challenges for Agricultural Economists Working in State Trading Agencies. In *Johnson, G. and Maunder, A., eds.*, 1981, pp. 544–46.

Sebestyén, Joseph. Accomplishments, Opportunities and Needs of Agricultural Economists vis-à-vis Quantitative Techniques. In *Johnson, G. and Maunder, A., eds.*, 1981, pp. 620–28.

Shah, C. H. Accomplishments, Present Status and Future Opportunities for Agricultural Economists in the Planning Processes in Less Developed Economies. In *Johnson, G. and Maunder, A., eds.*, 1981, pp. 247–57.

Sundquist, James L. The Employment Act of 1946. In *Heller, F. H., ed.*, 1981, pp. 98–100. **[G: U.S.]**

Thimm, Heinz-Ulrich. The Challenges for Western European Teachers of Agricultural Economics in Educating for Agrarian Change in their Own and Developing Countries. In *Johnson, G. and Maunder, A., eds.*, 1981, pp. 589–601.

Triffin, Robert. An Economist's Career: What? Why? How? *Banca Naz. Lavoro Quart. Rev.*, September 1981, (138), pp. 240–59.

Wright, John. Academics and Policy Makers: Comments. In *[Cairncross, A.]*, 1981, pp. 22–25.

0113 Relation of Economics to Other Disciplines

Anderson, Charles W. Value Judgement, the Policy Sciences, and the Aims of Political Education. In *Solo, R. A. and Anderson, C. W., eds.*, 1981, pp. 385–410.

Augé, Marc. Economic Anthropology and History: The Work of Karl Polanyi: Discussion. In *Dalton, G., ed.*, 1981, *1974*, pp. 62–63.

Barry, Brian. Social Science and Distributive Justice. In *Solo, R. A. and Anderson, C. W., eds.*, 1981, pp. 107–37.

Beit-Hallahmi, Benjamin. Ideology in Psychology: How Psychologists Explain Inequality. In *Solo, R. A. and Anderson, C. W., eds.*, 1981, pp. 70–106.

Blumberg, Georges. Psychology of Economic Development. In *Molt, W.; Hartmann, H. A. and Stringer, P., eds.*, 1981, pp. 295–304.

Breault, K. Modern Psychophysical Measurement of Marginal Utility: A Return to Introspective Cardinality? *Soc. Sci. Quart.*, December 1981, *62*(4), pp. 672–84.

Buchanan, James McGill and Faith, Roger L. Entrepreneurship and the Internalization of Externalities. *J. Law Econ.*, April 1981, *24*(1), pp. 95–111.

Chanier, Paul. L'assignation des rôles et les limites de la notion d'équilibre général. (With English summary.) *Écon. Appl.*, 1981, *34*(1), pp. 89–115.

Cook, Earl. The Tragedy of Turfdom [Environmental Disruption: Implications for the Social Sciences]. *Soc. Sci. Quart.*, March 1981, *62*(1), pp. 23–29.

Darity, William A., Jr. *Research in Economic Anthropology, Volume One:* A Review Article. *J. Econ. Issues,* March 1981, *15*(1), pp. 129–35.

Ederer, Rupert J. Solidarity: From Dogma to Economic System: Juan Donoso Cortes and Heinrich Pesch, S.J. *Int. J. Soc. Econ.,* 1981, *8*(4), pp. 40–49.

Ehrlich, Paul R. An Economist in Wonderland [Environmental Disruption: Implications for the Social Sciences]. *Soc. Sci. Quart.,* March 1981, *62*(1), pp. 44–49.

Ehrlich, Paul R. Environmental Disruption: Implications for the Social Sciences. *Soc. Sci. Quart.,* March 1981, *62*(1), pp. 7–22.

Godelier, Maurice. Economic Anthropology and History: The Work of Karl Polanyi: Discussion. In *Dalton, G., ed.,* 1981, *1974,* pp. 64–69.

Hartmann, Hans A. Causes and Cures of Traffic Behavior: Facts—Myths—Research—Planning. In *Molt, W.; Hartmann, H. A. and Stringer, P., eds.,* 1981, pp. 319–55.   [G: W. Germany]

Henry, Louis H. The Economic Benefits of the Arts: A Neuropsychological Comment. *J. Cult. Econ.,* June 1981, *5*(1), pp. 52–60.

Himes, James R. The Impact in Peru of the Vicos Project. In *Dalton, G., ed.,* 1981, pp. 141–213.   [G: Peru]

Johansen, Leif. Interaction in Economic Theory. *Écon. Appl.,* 1981, *34*(2–3), pp. 229–67.

Keto, David B. The Corporation and the Constitution: Economic Due Process and Corporate Speech. *Yale Law J.,* July 1981, *90*(8), pp. 1833–60.   [G: U.S.]

Köhler, Ulrich. Integrated Community Development: Vicos in Peru. In *Dalton, G., ed.,* 1981, pp. 111–40.   [G: Peru]

von Mises, Ludwig. Sociology and History. In *von Mises, L.,* 1981, pp. 68–129.

Moles, Abraham A. Micropsychology and Economic Motivation. In *Molt, W.; Hartmann, H. A. and Stringer, P., eds.,* 1981, pp. 105–17.   [G: France]

Molt, Walter. The Function of Needs for Planning in the Public Sector. In *Molt, W.; Hartmann, H. A. and Stringer, P., eds.,* 1981, pp. 273–79.

Molt, Walter. Traffic as an Economic and Psychological Problem. In *Molt, W.; Hartmann, H. A. and Stringer, P., eds.,* 1981, pp. 315–18.

Norman, Kent L. Assessing the Importance of Environmental and Societal Factors: A Way to Separate Relative Importance and Subjective Value. In *Molt, W.; Hartmann, H. A. and Stringer, P., eds.,* 1981, pp. 37–61.

Pejovich, Svetozar. Law as a Capital Good. In *Sirkin, G., ed.,* 1981, pp. 257–67.

Prezeau, Carl. L'équilibre social et l'équilibre général reconsidérés. (With English summary.) *Écon. Appl.,* 1981, *34*(1), pp. 29–60.

Pryor, Frederic L. A Survey of the Economic Systems of Wild Chimpanzees and Baboons. *J. Econ. Issues,* March 1981, *15*(1), pp. 33–59.

Rashid, Salim. Political Economy and Geology in the Early Nineteenth Century: Similarities and Contrasts. *Hist. Polit. Econ.,* Winter 1981, *13*(4), pp. 726–44.

Reynaud, P.-L. Introduction of Economic Psychology—A French Perspective. In *Molt, W.; Hart-*

mann, H. A. and Stringer, P., eds., 1981, pp. 21–25.

Reynaud, P.-L. Principles of Consumer Behavior. In *Molt, W.; Hartmann, H. A. and Stringer, P., eds.,* 1981, pp. 97–104.

von Rosenstiel, Lutz. Regarding Psychology of Reproductive Behavior—An Introduction. In *Molt, W.; Hartmann, H. A. and Stringer, P., eds.,* 1981, pp. 191–96.

Rüttinger, Bruno. Consumer Behavior. In *Molt, W.; Hartmann, H. A. and Stringer, P., eds.,* 1981, pp. 83–87.

Schelling, Thomas C. Analytic Methods and the Ethics of Policy. In *Caplan, A. L. and Callahan, D., eds.,* 1981, pp. 175–215.

Shackleton, J. R. Gary S. Becker: The Economist as Empire-builder. In *Shackleton, J. R. and Locksley, G., eds.,* 1981, pp. 12–32.

Silberer, Günter. Basic Concepts and Principles as a Framework for the Explanation of Consumer Behavior. In *Molt, W.; Hartmann, H. A. and Stringer, P., eds.,* 1981, pp. 89–95.

Silver, Morris. Law as a Capital Good: Comments. In *Sirkin, G., ed.,* 1981, pp. 268–71.

Simon, Julian L. Environmental disruption or Environmental Improvement? [Environmental Disruption: Implications for the Social Sciences]. *Soc. Sci. Quart.,* March 1981, *62*(1), pp. 30–43.

Sirkin, Gerald. Lexeconics: The Interaction of Law and Economics: Introduction. In *Sirkin, G., ed.,* 1981, pp. 9–13.

Stephens, R. J. Social Economics: A Budding Scientific Research Programme? *Int. J. Soc. Econ.,* 1981, *8*(3), pp. 3–25.

Streeten, Paul P. The Meaning and Purpose of Interdisciplinary Studies. In *Streeten, P.,* 1981, *1976,* pp. 52–61.

Sykes, Alan O. An Efficiency Analysis of Vicarious Liability under the Law of Agency. *Yale Law J.,* November 1981, *91*(1), pp. 168–206.   [G: U.S.]

Umaña, Alvaro F. Energy, Economics, and the Environment: Introduction. In *Daly, H. E. and Umana, A. F., eds.,* 1981, pp. 1–19.

Umaña, Alvaro F. Toward a Biophysical Foundation for Economics. In *Daly, H. E. and Umana, A. F., eds.,* 1981, pp. 21–41.

Valensi, Lucette. Economic Anthropology and History: The Work of Karl Polanyi. In *Dalton, G., ed.,* 1981, *1974,* pp. 3–12.

van Veldhoven, Gery M. Economic Psychology: A New Discipline? In *Molt, W.; Hartmann, H. A. and Stringer, P., eds.,* 1981, pp. 1–19.

Wärneryd, Karl-Erik. The Individual and the Economy. In *Molt, W.; Hartmann, H. A. and Stringer, P., eds.,* 1981, pp. 27–36.

Williams, Edward E. and Findlay, M. Chapman, III. A Reconsideration of the Rationality Postulate: 'Right Hemisphere Thinking' in Economics. *Amer. J. Econ. Soc.,* January 1981, *40*(1), pp. 17–36.

0114 Relation of Economics to Social Values

Anderson, Charles W. Value Judgement, the Policy Sciences, and the Aims of Political Education. In *Solo, R. A. and Anderson, C. W., eds.,* 1981, pp. 385–410.

Bauer, P. T. The Grail of Equality. In *Bauer, P. T.*, 1981, pp. 8–25.

Béteille, André. The Idea of Natural Inequality. In *Berreman, G. D., ed.*, 1981, pp. 59–80.

Boute, S., et al. Les économistes belges: tour d'ivoire ou tour de Babel. (With English summary.) *Cah. Écon. Bruxelles*, 4th Trimestre 1981, (92), pp. 539–56. **[G: Belgium]**

Bush, Paul D. The Normative Implications of Institutional Analysis. *Econ. Forum*, Winter 1981–82, *12*(2), pp. 9–29.

Chianese, Robert L. New Metaphors, Myths, and Values for a Steady-State Future. In *Coomer, J. C., ed.*, 1981, pp. 89–102.

Corbett, Timothy, et al. The Joint Responsibility of Business and Government. *Rivista Int. Sci. Econ. Com.*, January–February 1981, *28*(1–2), pp. 121–28.

Danner, Peter L. Exchange Value in the Value Hierarchy. *Int. J. Soc. Econ.*, 1981, *8*(4), pp. 70–84.

Debroy, B. Laodong and Primordial Ignorance. *Indian Econ. Rev.*, Oct.-Dec. 1981, *16*(4), pp. 297–307.

Ehrlich, Paul R. Diversity and the Steady State. In *Coomer, J. C., ed.*, 1981, pp. 13–31.

Evans, James W. Ethics and the Capitalist-Liberal Organisation: Implications for a Social Economy in the United States. *Int. J. Soc. Econ.*, 1981, *8*(4), pp. 85–99.

Firey, Walter. Variations on a Theme by Graftstein. *Soc. Sci. Quart.*, June 1981, *62*(2), pp. 213–17.

Grafstein, Robert. Sociologists, Economists and Legitimacy. *Soc. Sci. Quart.*, June 1981, *62*(2), pp. 218–20.

Haines, Walter W. The Economic Consequences of Altruism. *Int. J. Soc. Econ.*, 1981, *8*(4), pp. 50–69.

Hey, John D. Goodwill—Investment in the Intangible. In *Currie, D.; Peel, D. and Peters, W., eds.*, 1981, pp. 196–229.

Hirschman, Albert O. Morality and the Social Sciences: A Durable Tension. In *Hirschman, A. O.*, 1981, pp. 294–306.

Hirshleifer, Jack. It Pays to Do Good, but Not to do More Good than It Pays: A Note on the Survival of Altruism: Comment. *J. Econ. Behav. Organ.*, December 1981, *2*(4), pp. 387.

Inglehart, Ronald. Post-Materialism in an Environment of Insecurity. *Amer. Polit. Sci. Rev.*, December 1981, *75*(4), pp. 880–900. **[G: U.S.; EEC]**

Katsenelinboigen, Aron. Exchange and Values. In *Solo, R. A. and Anderson, C. W., eds.*, 1981, pp. 165–84.

McDaniel, Bruce A. Solar Energy and Social Economy. *Rev. Soc. Econ.*, October 1981, *39*(2), pp. 181–95. **[G: U.S.]**

McDaniel, Bruce A. The Integration of Economics and Society. *J. Econ. Issues*, June 1981, *15*(2), pp. 543–55.

Miller, William Lee. The Paradox of Plenty: Economic Growth and Moral Shrinkage. In *Cleveland, H., ed.*, 1981, pp. 79–114.

Mishan, Ezra J. Whatever Happened to Progress? In *Mishan, E. J.*, 1981, pp. 266–76.

Novak, Michael. A Theology of the Corporation. In *Novak, M. and Cooper, J. W., eds.*, 1981, pp. 203–24.

O'Brien, John Conway. The Economist's Quandary: Ethical Values. *Int. J. Soc. Econ.*, 1981, *8*(3), pp. 26–46.

O'Brien, John Conway. The Role of Economics and Ethics in Civilisation and Progress. *Int. J. Soc. Econ.*, 1981, *8*(4), pp. 1–20.

Papps, Ivy. Goodwill—Investment in the Intangible: Comment. In *Currie, D.; Peel, D. and Peters, W., eds.*, 1981, pp. 230–32.

Sadowski, Zdzislaw. The Principle of Rationality and the Social Effectiveness of Economic Activity. In *[Lipiński, E.]*, 1981, pp. 235–51.

Samuels, Warren J. The Historical Treatment of the Problem of Value Judgements: An Interpretation. In *Solo, R. A. and Anderson, C. W., eds.*, 1981, pp. 57–69.

Schelling, Thomas C. Analytic Methods and the Ethics of Policy. In *Caplan, A. L. and Callahan, D., eds.*, 1981, pp. 175–215.

Schweitzer, Arthur. Social Values in Economics. *Rev. Soc. Econ.*, December 1981, *39*(3), pp. 257–78.

Smith, Timothy. Churches and Corporate Responsibility. In *Novak, M. and Cooper, J. W., eds.*, 1981, pp. 60–73. **[G: U.S.]**

Solo, Robert A. Values and Judgements in the Discourse of the Sciences. In *Solo, R. A. and Anderson, C. W., eds.*, 1981, pp. 9–40.

Steve, Sergio. I fondamenti attuali della politica sociale. (The Present Foundations of Social Policy. With English summary.) *Giorn. Econ.*, July–August 1981, *40*(7–8), pp. 411–22.

Streeten, Paul P. Human Rights and Basic Needs. In *Streeten, P.*, 1981, pp. 366–73.

Streeten, Paul P. It *Is* a Moral Issue. In *Streeten, P.*, 1981, *1976*, pp. 232–36.

Taubman, Paul. On Heritability. *Economica*, November 1981, *48*(192), pp. 417–20.

Tinbergen, Jan. Misunderstandings Concerning Income Distribution Policies. *De Economist*, 1981, *129*(1), pp. 8–20.

Tropman, John E. Societal Values and Social Policy: Implications for Social Work. In *Martin, G. T., Jr., and Zald, M. N., eds.*, 1981, *1976*, pp. 87–104. **[G: U.S.]**

Wintrobe, Ronald. It Pays to Do Good, but Not to Do More Good than It Pays: A Note on the Survival of Altruism. *J. Econ. Behav. Organ.*, September 1981, *2*(3), pp. 201–13.

Wintrobe, Ronald. It Pays to Do Good, but Not to Do More Good than It Pays: A Note on the Survival of Altruism: Reply. *J. Econ. Behav. Organ.*, December 1981, *2*(4), pp. 389–90.

0115 Methods Used by Economists

Arrow, Kenneth J. and Intriligator, Michael D. Handbook of Mathematical Economics: Historical Introduction. In *Arrow, K. J. and Intriligator, M. D., eds.*, 1981, pp. 1–14.

Elfring, Tom. Assessing Eclecticism, a Reaction to Professor Pen's Article [On Eclecticism, or We are (almost) all Neo-Classical Neo-Keynesians Now]. *De Economist*, 1981, *129*(4), pp. 558–66.

Georgescu-Roegen, Nicholas. Methods in Economic Science: A Rejoinder. *J. Econ. Issues*, March 1981, *15*(1), pp. 188–93.

Green, Jerry R. and Heller, Walter P. Mathematical Analysis and Convexity with Applications to Economics. **In** *Arrow, K. J. and Intriligator, M. D., eds.*, 1981, pp. 15–52.

Hull, Terence M. Perspectives and Data Requirements for the Study of Children's Work. **In** *Rodgers, G. and Standing, G., eds.*, 1981, pp. 47–79.

Intriligator, Michael D. Mathematical Programming with Applications to Economics. **In** *Arrow, K. J. and Intriligator, M. D., eds.*, 1981, pp. 53–91.

Los, Jerzy. Is Mathematical Economics a New Science? **In** *[Lipiński, E.],* 1981, pp. 107–15.

Morice, Alain. The Exploitation of Children in the "Informal Sector": Proposals for Research. **In** *Rodgers, G. and Standing, G., eds.*, 1981, pp. 131–58.

Pen, Jan. Assessing Eclecticism, a Reaction to Professor Pen's Article: Reply [On Eclecticism, or We are (almost) all Neo-Classical Neo-Keynesians Now]. *De Economist*, 1981, *129*(4), pp. 566–67.

Pen, Jan. On Eclecticism, or We Are (Almost) All Neo-Classical Neo-Keynesians Now. *De Economist*, 1981, *129*(1), pp. 127–50.

du Plessis, J. C. Fiskale en Monetêre Beleid: Antwoord [Die Huidige Fiskale en Monetêre Beleid in Suid-Afrika]. *S. Afr. J. Econ.*, September 1981, *49*(3), pp. 269–78. **[G: S. Africa]**

Plott, Charles R. Experimental Methods in Political Economy: A Tool for Regulatory Research. **In** *Ferguson, A. R., ed.*, 1981, pp. 117–43.

Rashid, Salim. Methods in Economic Science: Comment. *J. Econ. Issues*, March 1981, *15*(1), pp. 183–88.

Termini, Valeria. Logical, Mechanical and Historical Time in Economics. *Econ. Notes*, 1981, *10*(3), pp. 58–104.

Truu, M. L. Fiscal and Monetary Policy: Rejoinder [Die Huidige Fiskale en Monetêre Beleid in Suid-Afrika]. *S. Afr. J. Econ.*, September 1981, *49*(3), pp. 279. **[G: S. Africa]**

Truu, M. L. The Minister and Quantification in Economics [Die Huidige Fiskale en Monetêre Belied in Suid-Affrika]. *S. Afr. J. Econ.*, March 1981, *49*(1), pp. 59–61. **[G: S. Africa]**

Varian, Hal R. Dynamical Systems with Applications to Economics. **In** *Arrow, K. J. and Intriligator, M. D., eds.*, 1981, pp. 93–110.

012 Teaching of Economics

0120 Teaching of Economics

Bergson, Abram. Where Are the Young Specialists on the Soviet Economy and What Are They Doing? Comment. *J. Compar. Econ.*, March 1981, *5*(1), pp. 119. **[G: U.S.]**

Blissett, Marlan; Schmandt, Jurgen and Warner, David. The Policy Research Project at the LBJ School of Public Affairs. *Policy Anal.*, Winter 1981, *7*(1), pp. 103–24. **[G: U.S.]**

Bornemann, Alfred H. Fifty Years of Ideology: A Selective Survey of Academic Economics in the United States, 1930 to 1980. *J. Econ. Stud.*, 1981, *8*(1), pp. 16–36. **[G: U.S.]**

Chizmar, John F. and Soper, John C. Specification and Development of New Pre-College Tests: *BET* and *TEL*. *Amer. Econ. Rev.*, May 1981, *71*(2), pp. 195–99. **[G: U.S.]**

Clark, J. R. and Barron, Deborah Durfee. Major Findings of the National Survey of Economic Education. *J. Econ. Educ.*, Summer 1981, *12*(2), pp. 45–51. **[G: U.S.]**

Fienup, Darrell F. and Riley, Harold M. Training Agricultural Economists to Serve the Needs of a Changing World. **In** *Johnson, G. and Maunder, A., eds.*, 1981, pp. 632–42. **[G: U.S.; LDCs]**

Gallagher, Daniel J. and Thompson, G. Rodney. A Readability Analysis of Selected Introductory Economics Textbooks. *J. Econ. Educ.*, Summer 1981, *12*(2), pp. 60–63.

Gay, David E. R. Towards a Theory of Entitlements in Comparative Economics. *Rivista Int. Sci. Econ. Com.*, March 1981, *28*(3), pp. 216–25.

Gillen, William J. A Survey of Advanced Undergraduate and Graduate Courses in Microeconomic Theory. *Amer. Econ.*, Fall 1981, *25*(2), pp. 68–72. **[G: U.S.]**

Hogan, Timothy D. Faculty Research Activity and the Quality of Graduate Training. *J. Human Res.*, Summer 1981, *16*(3), pp. 400–415. **[G: U.S.]**

Hughes, Joseph P. Methodological Confusion in Introductory Economics. *Amer. Econ.*, Fall 1981, *25*(2), pp. 7–11.

Leinhardt, Samuel. Data Analysis and Statistics Education in Public Policy Programs. **In** *Crecine, J. P., ed.*, 1981, pp. 53–61.

Luker, William and Proctor, Wanda. The Effect of an Introductory Course in Microeconomics on the Political Orientation of Students. *J. Econ. Educ.*, Summer 1981, *12*(2), pp. 54–57. **[G: U.S.]**

Nelson, C. Louise. The Response to Scarcity in Introductory Economics. *Amer. Econ.*, Fall 1981, *25*(2), pp. 3–6.

Page, A. N. An Experimental Buchanan-Type Economics Course. *J. Econ. Educ.*, Summer 1981, *12*(2), pp. 57–60.

Petit, Michel. Teaching Marxist Economics to Agricultural Economics Students in non-Marxist Countries. **In** *Johnson, G. and Maunder, A., eds.*, 1981, pp. 645–56.

Prince, Raymond; Kipps, Paul H. and Wilhelm, Howard M. Scholastic Effort: An Empirical Test of Student Choice Models. *J. Econ. Educ.*, Summer 1981, *12*(2), pp. 15–25. **[G: U.S.]**

Saunders, Phillip; Fels, Rendigs and Welsh, Arthur L. The Revised Test of Understanding College Economics. *Amer. Econ. Rev.*, May 1981, *71*(2), pp. 190–94. **[G: U.S.]**

Senesh, Lawrence. Closing the Gap between Frontier Thinking and the Curriculum in Economics. **In** *[Weiler, E. T.],* 1981, pp. 311–51. **[G: U.S.]**

Simon, Julian L. Unnecessary, Confusing, and Inadequate: The Marginal Analysis as a Tool for Decision Making. *Amer. Econ.*, Spring 1981, *25*(1), pp. 28–35.

Soper, John C. and Brenneke, Judith Staley. The Test of Economic Literacy as an Evaluation of the DEEP System. *J. Econ. Educ.*, Summer

1981, *12*(2), pp. 1–14. [G: U.S.]

Sterrett, Jack and Barr, Saul Z. A Comparative Study of Junior and Senior College Economics Programs in the Southeast. *J. Econ. Educ.*, Summer 1981, *12*(2), pp. 52–53. [G: U.S.]

Stone, Lewis. Selected Outlines in Microeconomic Theory. *Amer. Econ.*, Fall 1981, *25*(2), pp. 73–83.

Thimm, Heinz-Ulrich. The Challenges for Western European Teachers of Agricultural Economics in Educating for Agrarian Change in their Own and Developing Countries. In *Johnson, G. and Maunder, A., eds.*, 1981, pp. 589–601.

Uecker, Wilfred C. Behavioral Accounting Research as a Source for Experimental Teaching Aids: An Example. *Accounting Rev.*, April 1981, *56*(2), pp. 366–82.

Weidenaar, Dennis J. The Development of Economics Education through the Principles of Economics Course in the United States: Its Goals, Content, and Methodology. In *[Weiler, E. T.]*, 1981, pp. 277–89.

Wyzan, Michael L. The Emphasis on Comparative Economic Systems in Introductory Economics. *Amer. Econ.*, Fall 1981, *25*(2), pp. 12–18.

Yates, Judith N. Diversity as a Means of Individualizing Instruction. *J. Econ. Educ.*, Summer 1981, *12*(2), pp. 26–33.

020 GENERAL ECONOMIC THEORY

0200 General Economic Theory

Arrow, Kenneth J. and Intriligator, Michael D. Handbook of Mathematical Economics: Historical Introduction. In *Arrow, K. J. and Intriligator, M. D., eds.*, 1981, pp. 1–14.

Basu, Kaushik. Causality and Economic Theory. *Indian Econ. Rev.*, January–June 1981, *16*(1 and 2), pp. 41–53.

Bauer, P. T. Reflections on the State of Economics. In *Bauer, P. T.*, 1981, pp. 255–66.

Boland, Lawrence A. On the Futility of Criticizing the Neoclassical Maximization Hypothesis. *Amer. Econ. Rev.*, December 1981, *71*(5), pp. 1031–36.

Bornemann, Alfred H. Fifty Years of Ideology: A Selective Survey of Academic Economics in the United States, 1930 to 1980. *J. Econ. Stud.*, 1981, *8*(1), pp. 16–36. [G: U.S.]

Brown, William S. Market Adjustment and Catastrophe Theory. *J. Post Keynesian Econ.*, Summer 1981, *3*(4), pp. 510–18.

Dasgupta, A. K. Perfect Competition and Economic Theory. *Indian Econ. Rev.*, July-Sept. 1981, *16*(3), pp. 155–67.

Day, Richard H. Unstable Economic Systems. *Econ. Notes*, 1981, *10*(3), pp. 3–17.

Dow, Sheila C. Weintraub and Wiles: The Methodological Basis of Policy Conflict. *J. Post Keynesian Econ.*, Spring 1981, *3*(3), pp. 325–39.

Dugger, William M. A Note on Institutionalism, Straw Men, and Equality [Clarence Ayres's Critique of Orthodox Economic Theory]. *J. Econ. Issues*, September 1981, *15*(3), pp. 785–91.

Elfring, Tom. Assessing Eclecticism, a Reaction to Professor Pen's Article [On Eclecticism, or We

are (almost) all Neo-Classical Neo-Keynesians Now]. *De Economist*, 1981, *129*(4), pp. 558–66.

Elliott, John E. The Neoclassical–Keynesian Synthesis and Its Critics: Contending Perspectives in Political Economy. *Econ. Forum*, Winter 1981–82, *12*(2), pp. 31–53.

Feiwel, George R. Modern Neoclassical Economics. *Economia (Portugal)*, October 1981, *5*(3), pp. 407–29.

Forgang, William G. The Long Run and Social Economics: A Note to William Dugger [The Long Run and Its Significance to Social Economy]. *Rev. Soc. Econ.*, April 1981, *39*(1), pp. 85–86.

Foster, J. Fagg. John Dewey and Economic Value. *J. Econ. Issues*, December 1981, *15*(4), pp. 871–97.

Foster, J. Fagg. The Relation between the Theory of Value and Economic Analysis. *J. Econ. Issues*, December 1981, *15*(4), pp. 899–905.

Futia, Carl A. Rational Expectations in Stationary Linear Models. *Econometrica*, January 1981, *49*(1), pp. 171–92.

Gill, Flora. Some Methodological Implications of the Marginal Revolution. *Australian Econ. Pap.*, June 1981, *20*(36), pp. 72–82.

Green, Edward J. On the Role of Fundamental Theory in Positive Economics. In *Pitt, J. C., ed.*, 1981, pp. 5–15.

Green, Jerry R. and Heller, Walter P. Mathematical Analysis and Convexity with Applications to Economics. In *Arrow, K. J. and Intriligator, M. D., eds.*, 1981, pp. 15–52.

Gunnarsson, Jan. Marknaden. (The Market Process in Economic Theory—Some Critical Comments. With English summary.) *Nationaløkon. Tidsskr.*, 1981, *119*(2), pp. 258–75.

Halevi, Joseph. Some Notes on Classical Political Economy and the Rise to Dominance of Supply and Demand Theories. *Australian Econ. Pap.*, June 1981, *20*(36), pp. 96–103.

Hurwicz, Leonid. Perspectives on Economics. In *[Weiler, E. T.]*, 1981, pp. 290–310.

Hutchison, Terence W. On the Aims and Methods of Economic Theorizing. In *Hutchison, T. W.*, 1981, pp. 266–307.

Jesse, Richard R., Jr. and Radcliffe, Robert C. On Speculation and Price Stability under Uncertainty. *Rev. Econ. Statist.*, February 1981, *63*(1), pp. 129–32.

Johansen, Leif. Interaction in Economic Theory. *Écon. Appl.*, 1981, *34*(2–3), pp. 229–67.

Kaldor, Nicholas. Essays on Value and Distribution: General Introduction to Collected Economic Essays. In *Kaldor, N.*, 1981, pp. vii–xxxi.

Kaldor, Nicholas. The Determinateness of Static Equilibrium. In *Kaldor, N.*, 1981, *1934*, pp. 13–33.

Katz, Eliakim. A Note on a Comparative Statics Theorem for Choice under Risk. *J. Econ. Theory*, October 1981, *25*(2), pp. 318–19.

Kendry, Adrian. Paul Samuelson and the Scientific Awakening of Economics. In *Shackleton, J. R. and Locksley, G., eds.*, 1981, pp. 219–39.

Kirman, Alan P. Measure Theory with Applications to Economics. In *Arrow, K. J. and Intriligator, M. D., eds.*, 1981, pp. 159–209.

Kornai, János. Control by Norms. In *Kornai, J. and Martos, B., eds.,* 1981, 1976, pp. 113–27.

Kornai, János and Martos, Béla. Non-price Control: Introduction: Theoretical Background of the Research. In *Kornai, J. and Martos, B., eds.,* 1981, pp. 17–56.

Leijonhufvud, Axel. Schools, "Revolutions," and Research Programmes in Economic Theory. In *Leijonhufvud, A.,* 1981, 1976, pp. 291–345.

Los, Jerzy. Is Mathematical Economics a New Science? In *[Lipiński, E.],* 1981, pp. 107–15.

Machan, Tibor R. The Non-Rational Domain and the Limits of Economic Analysis: Comment. *Southern Econ. J.,* April 1981, 47(4), pp. 1123–27.

Mănescu, Manea. Cybernetic Scenario: Accumulation-Consumption Correlation. *Econ. Computat. Cybern. Stud. Res.,* 1981, 15(2), pp. 7–19.

Martos, Béla. Equivalence of Control Systems. Partitioned Systems. In *Kornai, J. and Martos, B., eds.,* 1981, pp. 187–200.

Martos, Béla. Non-price Control: Report on a Research Trend. In *Janssen, J. M. L.; Pau, L. F. and Straszak, A. J., eds.,* 1981, pp. 1–10.

McKenzie, Richard B. The Non-Rational Domain and the Limits of Economic Analysis: Reply. *Southern Econ. J.,* April 1981, 47(4), pp. 1128–31.

Mirowski, Philip. Is There a Mathematical Neoinstitutional Economics? *J. Econ. Issues,* September 1981, 15(3), pp. 593–613.

von Mises, Ludwig. The Controversy Over the Theory of Value. In *von Mises, L.,* 1981, pp. 204–16.

von Mises, Ludwig. The Psychological Basis of the Opposition to Economic Theory. In *von Mises, L.,* 1981, pp. 183–203.

Mishan, Ezra J. The Folklore of the Market: An Inquiry into the Economic Doctrines of the Chicago School. In *Mishan, E. J.,* 1981, 1975, pp. 219–55.

Morgan, Brian. Sir John Hicks's Contributions to Economic Theory. In *Shackleton, J. R. and Locksley, G., eds.,* 1981, pp. 108–40.

Patinkin, Don. Involuntary Unemployment and the Keynesian Supply Function: Mathematical Appendix. In *Patinkin, D.,* 1981, pp. 175–79.

Patinkin, Don. Reflections on the Neoclassical Dichotomy. In *Patinkin, D.,* 1981, 1972, pp. 149–54.

Patinkin, Don. The Indeterminacy of Absolute Prices in Classical Economic Theory. In *Patinkin, D.,* 1981, 1949, pp. 125–48.

Pen, Jan. Assessing Eclecticism, a Reaction to Professor Pen's Article: Reply [On Eclecticism, or We are (almost) all Neo-Classical Neo-Keynesians Now]. *De Economist,* 1981, 129(4), pp. 566–67.

Pen, Jan. On Eclecticism, or We Are (Almost) All Neo-Classical Neo-Keynesians Now. *De Economist,* 1981, 129(1), pp. 127–50.

Peston, Maurice. Lionel Robbins: Methodology, Policy and Modern Theory. In *Shackleton, J. R. and Locksley, G., eds.,* 1981, pp. 183–98.

Ranson, Baldwin. A Comment on Donald A. Walker's Article [Clarence Ayres's Critique of Orthodox Economic Theory]. *J. Econ. Issues,*

September 1981, 15(3), pp. 783–85.

Reiter, Stanley. A Dynamic Process of Exchange. In *[Weiler, E. T.],* 1981, pp. 3–23.

Robbins, Lionel. Economics and Political Economy. *Amer. Econ. Rev.,* May 1981, 71(2), pp. 1–10.

Robinson, Joan. Survey: 1950s. In *Robinson, J.,* 1981, pp. 105–11.

Robinson, Joan. Survey: 1960s. In *Robinson, J.,* 1981, pp. 112–22.

Robinson, Joan. The Disintegration of Economics. In *Robinson, J.,* 1981, 1979, pp. 96–104.

Robinson, Joan. Time in Economic Theory. In *Robinson, J.,* 1981, 1980, pp. 86–95.

Robinson, Joan. What Are the Questions? In *Robinson, J.,* 1981, 1977, pp. 1–32.

Roncaglia, Alessandro. Piero Sraffa's Contribution to Political Economy. In *Shackleton, J. R. and Locksley, G., eds.,* 1981, pp. 240–56.

Rugina, Anghel N. What Is the Alternative for the West? Neither Capitalism nor Socialism but "Social Liberalism." *Int. J. Soc. Econ.,* 1981, 8(2), pp. 3–46.

Samuels, Warren J. The Current State of Economics. *Econ. Forum,* Winter 1981–82, 12(2), pp. 1–8.

Seldon, James R. The Relevance of Subjective Costs: Comment [Does It Matter That Costs Are Subjective?]. *Southern Econ. J.,* July 1981, 48(1), pp. 216–21.

Senesh, Lawrence. Closing the Gap between Frontier Thinking and the Curriculum in Economics. In *[Weiler, E. T.],* 1981, pp. 311–51. [G: U.S.]

Skouras, Thanos. The Economics of Joan Robinson. In *Shackleton, J. R. and Locksley, G., eds.,* 1981, pp. 199–218.

Solo, Robert A. Values and Judgements in the Discourse of the Sciences. In *Solo, R. A. and Anderson, C. W., eds.,* 1981, pp. 9–40.

Stamatis, Georgios and Dimakis, Aristophanes. Zur Linearität der Relation zwischen dem Nominallohnsatz und der Profitrate bei post factum gezahlten Löhnen. (On the Linearity of the w-r-Relation under Post Factum Paid Wages. With English summary.) *Jahr. Nationalökon. Statist.,* March 1981, 196(2), pp. 147–69.

Tabellini, Guido. Equazioni e disequazioni differenziali nei modelli di economia dinamica: elementi di confronto. (Differential Equations and Differential Inequalities in Dynamic Economic Models: Elements for a Comparison. With English summary.) *Giorn. Econ.,* July–August 1981, 40(7–8), pp. 423–45.

Torr, C. S. W. The Role of the Entrepreneur (Review Note). *S. Afr. J. Econ.,* September 1981, 49(3), pp. 283–88.

Vaughn, Karen I. The Relevance of Subjective Costs: Reply [Does It Matter That Costs Are Subjective?]. *Southern Econ. J.,* July 1981, 48(1), pp. 222–26.

Vikor, Desider. Toward Qualitative Economic Analysis. *Int. J. Soc. Econ.,* 1981, 8(7), pp. 42–49.

Watts, Michael W. The Non-Rational Domain and the Limits of Economic Analysis: Comment. *Southern Econ. J.,* April 1981, 47(4), pp. 1120–22.

Zang, Israel. Concavifiability of C^2-Functions: A Unified Exposition. In *Schaible, S. and Ziemba, W. T., eds.*, 1981, pp. 131–52.

Zinam, Oleg. Paradigm Matters: Toward Reconstruction of the Neo-classical Economics. *Rivista Int. Sci. Econ. Com.*, January–February 1981, 28(1–2), pp. 61–89.

021 General Equilibrium and Disequilibrium Theory

0210 General

Äbel, István. The Labor Saving Principle with an Application to the Leontief-Type Economies. *Int. Econ. Rev.*, June 1981, 22(2), pp. 377–83.

Åberg, Morgan and Persson, Håkan. A Note on a Closed Input-Output Model with Finite Life-Times and Gestation Lags. *J. Econ. Theory*, June 1981, 24(3), pp. 446–52.

Aivazian, Varouj A. and Callen, Jeffrey L. The Coase Theorem and the Empty Core. *J. Law Econ.*, April 1981, 24(1), pp. 175–81.

Allen, Beth E. Generic Existence of Completely Revealing Equilibria for Economies with Uncertainty when Prices Convey Information. *Econometrica*, September 1981, 49(5), pp. 1173–99.

Allen, Beth E. Utility Perturbations and the Equilibrium Price Set. *J. Math. Econ.*, October 1981, 8(3), pp. 277–307.

Anderson, Robert M. Core Theory with Strongly Convex Preferences. *Econometrica*, November 1981, 49(6), pp. 1457–68.

Atsumi, Hiroshi. Taxes and Subsidies in the Input–Output Model. *Quart. J. Econ.*, February 1981, 96(1), pp. 27–45.

Aubin, Jean-Pierre. A Dynamical, Pure Exchange Economy with Feedback Pricing. *J. Econ. Behav. Organ.*, June 1981, 2(2), pp. 95–127.

Aubin, Jean-Pierre. Locally Lipschitz Cooperative Games. *J. Math. Econ.*, October 1981, 8(3), pp. 241–62.

Balasko, Yves and Shell, Karl. The Overlapping-Generations Model. II: The Case of Pure Exchange with Money. *J. Econ. Theory*, February 1981, 24(1), pp. 112–42.

Balasko, Yves and Shell, Karl. The Overlapping-Generations Model. III: The Case of Log-Linear Utility Functions. *J. Econ. Theory*, February 1981, 24(1), pp. 143–52.

Bewley, Truman F. A Critique of Tiebout's Theory of Local Public Expenditures. *Econometrica*, May 1981, 49(3), pp. 713–40.

Bewley, Truman F. Stationary Equilibrium. *J. Econ. Theory*, April 1981, 24(2), pp. 265–95.

Bocage, Ducarmel. The Human Agent and General Equilibrium Analysis from Cournot to Perroux. *Amer. Econ.*, Spring 1981, 25(1), pp. 36–42.

Bródy, András. An Economy Controlled by Stocks and Profits. In *Kornai, J. and Martos, B., eds.*, 1981, 1973, pp. 149–61.

Cave, Martin. Wassily Leontief: Input–Output and Economic Planning. In *Shackleton, J. R. and Locksley, G., eds.*, 1981, pp. 160–82.

Champsaur, Paul and Laroque, Guy. Fair Allocations in Large Economies. *J. Econ. Theory*, Octo-

ber 1981, 25(2), pp. 269–82.

Champsaur, Paul and Laroque, Guy. Le plan face aux comportements stratégiques des unités décentralisées. (Planning, Public Goods, and Strategic Behavior by Decentralized Units. With English summary.) *Ann. INSEE*, April–June 1981, (42), pp. 3–30.

Chanier, Paul. L'assignation des rôles et les limites de la notion d'équilibre général. (With English summary.) *Écon. Appl.*, 1981, 34(1), pp. 89–115.

Cheng, Hsueh-Cheng. On Dual Regularity and Value Convergence Theorems. *J. Math. Econ.*, March 1981, 8(1), pp. 37–57.

Cheng, Hsueh-Cheng. What Is the Normal Rate of Convergence of the Core? (Part I). *Econometrica*, January 1981, 49(1), pp. 73–83.

Chichilnisky, Graciela. Existence and Characterization of Optimal Growth Paths Including Models with Non-Convexities in Utilities and Technologies. *Rev. Econ. Stud.*, January 1981, 48(1), pp. 51–61.

Clark, Stephen A. A Combinatorial Analysis of the Overlapping Generations Model. *Rev. Econ. Stud.*, January 1981, 48(1), pp. 139–45.

Coase, R. H. The Coase Theorem and the Empty Core: A Comment. *J. Law Econ.*, April 1981, 24(1), pp. 183–87.

Coughlin, Peter J. Necessary and Sufficient Conditions for d-Relative Majority Voting Equilibria [Consistent Majority Rules over Compact Sets of Alternatives]. *Econometrica*, September 1981, 49(5), pp. 1223–24.

Crouzeix, Jean-Pierre. A Duality Framework in Quasiconvex Programming. In *Schaible, S. and Ziemba, W. T., eds.*, 1981, pp. 207–25.

Dancs, István; Hunyadi, László and Sivák, József. Discrete-Time Control with Time Lags. In *Kornai, J. and Martos, B., eds.*, 1981, pp. 131–47.

Diewert, W. Erwin. The Measurement of Deadweight Loss Revisited. *Econometrica*, September 1981, 49(5), pp. 1225–44.

Eckalbar, John C. Stable Quantities in Fixed Price Disequilibrium. *J. Econ. Theory*, October 1981, 25(2), pp. 302–13.

Filimon, Radu. Aggregation of Heterogeneous Goods in Models of the von Neumann Variety. *Z. Nationalökon.*, 1981, 41(3–4), pp. 253–64.

Fisher, Franklin M. Stability, Disequilibrium Awareness, and the Perception of New Opportunities. *Econometrica*, March 1981, 49(2), pp. 279–317.

Fleischmann, Bernd. Reduction to Dated Quantities of Labour. A Footnote on Mr. Sraffa. *Metroecon.*, Feb.-Oct. 1981, 33(1–2–3), pp. 233–37.

Friedman, James W. A Note on the Turnpike Properties of Time Dependent Supergames [Non-Cooperative Equilibria in Time Dependent Supergames]. *Econometrica*, June 1981, 49(4), pp. 1087–88.

Fujimoto, Takao. An Elementary Proof of Okishio's Theorem for Models with Fixed Capital and Heterogeneous Labour. *Metroecon.*, Feb.-Oct. 1981, 33(1–2–3), pp. 21–27.

Gale, Douglas. Improving Coalitions in a Monetary Economy. *Rev. Econ. Stud.*, July 1981, 48(3), pp. 365–84.

Gale, Douglas. Large Economies with Trading Uncertainty: A Correction. *Rev. Econ. Stud.*, April 1981, *48*(2), pp. 363–64.

Glycopantis, Dionysius. The Cusp Catastrophe in an Exchange Model. *Econ. Stud. Quart.*, August 1981, *32*(2), pp. 188–91.

Grossman, Sanford J. An Introduction to the Theory of Rational Expectations under Asymmetric Information. *Rev. Econ. Stud.*, October 1981, *48*(4), pp. 541–59.

Harris, Milton and Townsend, Robert M. Resource Allocation under Asymmetric Information. *Econometrica*, January 1981, *49*(1), pp. 33–64.

Hausman, Daniel M. Are General Equilibrium Theories Explanatory? In *Pitt, J. C., ed.*, 1981, pp. 17–32.

von Hayek, F. A. Economics and Knowledge. In *Buchanan, J. M. and Thirlby, G. F., eds.*, *1937*, pp. 43–68.

Hirota, Masayoshi. On the Stability of Competitive Equilibrium and the Patterns of Initial Holdings: An Example. *Int. Econ. Rev.*, June 1981, *22*(2), pp. 461–67.

Ichiishi, Tatsuro. A Social Coalitional Equilibrium Existence Lemma. *Econometrica*, March 1981, *49*(2), pp. 369–77.

Ichiishi, Tatsuro. Super-modularity: Applications to Convex Games and to the Greedy Algorithm for LP. *J. Econ. Theory*, October 1981, *25*(2), pp. 283–86.

Ingene, Charles A. and Yu, Eden S. H. Wage Distortion and Resource Allocation under Uncertainty. *Southern Econ. J.*, October 1981, *48*(2), pp. 283–95.

Iritani, Jun. On Uniqueness of General Equilibrium. *Rev. Econ. Stud.*, January 1981, *48*(1), pp. 167–71.

Jones, Ronald W. The Structure of Simple General Equilibrium Models. In *Bhagwati, J. N., ed.*, 1981, *1965*, pp. 30–49.

Kapitány, Zsuzsa. Uncertainty in Decision-Making: A Simulation Experiment. In *Kornai, J. and Martos, B., eds.*, 1981, pp. 247–66.

Keenan, Donald. Further Remarks on the Global Newton Method [A Convergent Process of Price Adjustment and Global Newton Methods]. *J. Math. Econ.*, July 1981, *8*(2), pp. 159–65.

Keiding, Hans. Existence of Budget Constrained Pareto Efficient Allocations. *J. Econ. Theory*, June 1981, *24*(3), pp. 393–97.

Khan, M. Ali and Yamazaki, Akira. On the Cores of Economies with Indivisible Commodities and a Continuum of Traders. *J. Econ. Theory*, April 1981, *24*(2), pp. 218–25.

van de Klundert, Theo. Optimal Capital Accumulation in Generalized Leontief Models. *De Economist*, 1981, *129*(1), pp. 21–40.

Kogelschatz, Hartmut. Equilibrium Preserving Aggregation in von Neumann Models. *Z. Nationalökon.*, 1981, *41*(3–4), pp. 265–78.

Kondor, George A. On the Asymptotic Local Stability of Autonomous Economic Systems with Non-negativity Conditions. *J. Econ. Theory*, December 1981, *25*(3), pp. 466–70.

Kornai, János and Martos, Béla. Vegetative Control: The First Step. In *Kornai, J. and Martos, B., eds.*, 1981, pp. 57–80.

Kornai, János and Simonovits, András. Control by Order Signals. In *Kornai, J. and Martos, B., eds.*, 1981, pp. 267–79.

Kornai, János and Simonovits, András. Stock-Signal Model Regulated from a Normal Path. In *Kornai, J. and Martos, B., eds.*, 1981, pp. 223–45.

Kreps, David M. Arbitrage and Equilibrium in Economies with Infinitely Many Commodities. *J. Math. Econ.*, March 1981, *8*(1), pp. 15–35.

Laise, Domenico and Tucci, Michele. Considerazioni su sistemi di equilibrio economico generale di tipo walrasiano. (On Walrasian General Equilibrium Models. With English summary.) *Giorn. Econ.*, January–February 1981, *40*(1–2), pp. 81–100.

Lane, John and Mitra, Tapan. On Nash Equilibrium Programs of Capital Accumulation under Altruistic Preferences. *Int. Econ. Rev.*, June 1981, *22*(2), pp. 309–31.

Laroque, Guy. A Comment on "Stable Spillovers among Substitutes." *Rev. Econ. Stud.*, April 1981, *48*(2), pp. 355–61.

Laroque, Guy. On the Local Uniqueness of the Fixed Price Equilibria. *Rev. Econ. Stud.*, January 1981, *48*(1), pp. 113–29.

Lorenzen, Gunter. Zur Charakterisierung der industriellen Verflechtung und der Endnachfragestruktur einer Volkswirtschaft. (On Economic Interrelatedness and the Structure of Final Demand. With English summary.) *Jahr. Nationalökon. Statist.*, November 1981, *196*(6), pp. 503–10.

Makarov, V. L. Some Results on General Assumptions about the Existence of Economic Equilibrium. *J. Math. Econ.*, March 1981, *8*(1), pp. 87–99.

Martos, Béla. Partially Coordinated Controls. In *Kornai, J. and Martos, B., eds.*, 1981, pp. 201–20.

Martos, Béla. Vegetative Control with Price Communication. In *Kornai, J. and Martos, B., eds.*, 1981, pp. 163–86.

McCabe, Peter J. On Two Market Equilibrium Theorems. *J. Math. Econ.*, July 1981, *8*(2), pp. 167–71.

McKenzie, Lionel W. The Classical Theorem on Existence of Competitive Equilibrium. *Econometrica*, June 1981, *49*(4), pp. 819–41.

Mehta, Ghanshyam. A New Extension Procedure for the Arrow-Hahn Theorem. *Int. Econ. Rev.*, February 1981, *22*(1), pp. 113–18.

Mori, Pier Angelo. Economie concorrenziali, banditore e disoccupazione. (Competitive Economies, Auctioneer and Unemployment. With English summary.) *Giorn. Econ.*, March–April 1981, *40*(3–4), pp. 231–38.

Nishimura, Kazuo. Kuhn's Intensity Hypothesis Revisited. *Rev. Econ. Stud.*, April 1981, *48*(2), pp. 351–54.

Nishimura, Kazuo. The Exclusion of Boundary Equilibria [Two Remarks on the Number of Equilibria of an Economy]. *Int. Econ. Rev.*, June 1981, *22*(2), pp. 475.

Nishimura, Kazuo and Friedman, James W. Existence of Nash Equilibrium in *n* Person Games without Quasi-Concavity. *Int. Econ. Rev.*, October 1981, *22*(3), pp. 637–48.

Nti, Kofi O. and Shubik, Martin. Noncooperative Oligopoly with Entry. *J. Econ. Theory*, April 1981, *24*(2), pp. 187–204.

Okuno, Masahiro and Zilcha, Itzhak. A Proof of the Existence of Competitive Equilibrium in a Generation-Overlapping Exchange Economy with Money. *Int. Econ. Rev.*, February 1981, *22*(1), pp. 239–52.

Ostroy, Joseph M. Differentiability as Convergence to Perfectly Competitive Equilibrium. *J. Math. Econ.*, March 1981, *8*(1), pp. 59–73.

Palomba, Giuseppe. Economie et géométrie de Walras et Pareto à nos jours. (With English summary.) *Écon. Appl.*, 1981, *34*(2–3), pp. 319–47.

Perroux, François. Structure et échange dit "International." L'équilibre général reconsidéré. (Structure and the So-called "International" Exchange: The General Equilibrium Revisited. With English summary.) *Rivista Int. Sci. Econ. Com.*, December 1981, *28*(12), pp. 1116–37.

Postelwaite, Andrew and Schmeidler, David. Approximate Walrasian Equilibria and Nearby Economies. *Int. Econ. Rev.*, February 1981, *22*(1), pp. 105–11.

Prezeau, Carl. L'équilibre social et l'équilibre général reconsidérés. (With English summary.) *Écon. Appl.*, 1981, *34*(1), pp. 29–60.

Radner, Roy. Monitoring Cooperative Agreements in a Repeated Principal–Agent Relationship. *Econometrica*, September 1981, *49*(5), pp. 1127–48.

Rogers, C. Classical and Neoclassical Theories of General Equilibrium (Review Note). *S. Afr. J. Econ.*, June 1981, *49*(2), pp. 172–76.

Sato, Fumitaka. On the Informational Size of Message Spaces for Resource Allocation Processes in Economies with Public Goods. *J. Econ. Theory*, February 1981, *24*(1), pp. 48–69.

Scarf, Herbert E. Comment on: "On the Stability of Competitive Equilibrium and the Patterns of Initial Holdings: An Example." *Int. Econ. Rev.*, June 1981, *22*(2), pp. 469–70.

Shefrin, Hersh M. Games with Self-Generating Distributions. *Rev. Econ. Stud.*, July 1981, *48*(3), pp. 511–19.

Shefrin, Hersh M. Transaction Costs, Uncertainty and Generally Inactive Futures Markets. *Rev. Econ. Stud.*, January 1981, *48*(1), pp. 131–37.

Shubik, Martin. A Price–Quantity Buy–Sell Market with and without Contingent Bids. In *[Lipiński, E.]*, 1981, pp. 117–24.

Shubik, Martin. Game Theory Models and Methods in Political Economy. In *Arrow, K. J. and Intriligator, M. D., eds.*, 1981, pp. 285–330.

Simonovits, András. Constrained Control and Destabilization. In *Kornai, J. and Martos, B., eds.*, 1981, pp. 281–320.

Smale, Steve. Global Analysis and Economics. In *Arrow, K. J. and Intriligator, M. D., eds.*, 1981, pp. 331–70.

Sobel, Joel. Proportional Distribution Schemes. *J. Math. Econ.*, July 1981, *8*(2), pp. 147–57.

Starr, Ross M. Approximation of Points of the Convex Hull of a Sum of Sets by Points of the Sum: An Elementary Approach. *J. Econ. Theory*, October 1981, *25*(2), pp. 314–17.

Svensson, Lars E. O. Effective Demand in a Sequence of Markets. *Scand. J. Econ.*, 1981, *83*(1), pp. 1–21.

Svensson, Lars E. O. Efficiency and Speculation in a Model with Price-Contingent Contracts. *Econometrica*, January 1981, *49*(1), pp. 131–51.

Varian, Hal R. Dynamical Systems with Applications to Economics. In *Arrow, K. J. and Intriligator, M. D., eds.*, 1981, pp. 93–110.

Weber, S. Some Results on the Weak Core of a Non-Side-Payment Game with Infinitely Many Players. *J. Math. Econ.*, March 1981, *8*(1), pp. 101–11.

Weiss, Ernst-August, Jr. Finitely Additive Exchange Economies. *J. Math. Econ.*, October 1981, *8*(3), pp. 221–40.

Weller, Paul A. Limit Theorems on the Core of a Many Good Economy with Individual Risks. *Int. Econ. Rev.*, October 1981, *22*(3), pp. 625–35.

Wilson, Charles A. Equilibrium in Dynamic Models with an Infinity of Agents. *J. Econ. Theory*, February 1981, *24*(1), pp. 95–111.

Wooders, Myrna. Equilibria, the Core and Jurisdiction Structures in Economies with a Local Public Good: A Correction. *J. Econ. Theory*, August 1981, *25*(1), pp. 144–51.

Yamazaki, Akira. Diversified Consumption Characteristics and Conditionally Dispersed Endowment Distribution: Regularizing Effect and Existence of Equilibria. *Econometrica*, May 1981, *49*(3), pp. 639–54.

Yun, Kwan Koo. A Note on Nishimura's Uniqueness Theorem of General Equilibrium [Two Remarks on the Number of Equilibria of an Economy]. *Int. Econ. Rev.*, June 1981, *22*(2), pp. 471–73.

022 Microeconomic Theory

0220 General

Ames, Edward. The Place of an Individual in an Economy. In *[Weiler, E. T.]*, 1981, pp. 24–40.

Arndt, Helmut. Das Dilemma der Wirtschaftstheorie. (The "Dilemma" of Economic Theory. With English summary.) *Z. Wirtschaft. Sozialwissen.*, 1981, *101*(5), pp. 459–77.

Aubin, Jean-Pierre. A Dynamical, Pure Exchange Economy with Feedback Pricing. *J. Econ. Behav. Organ.*, June 1981, *2*(2), pp. 95–127.

Brazelton, W. Robert. Post Keynesian Economics: An Institutional Compatibility? *J. Econ. Issues*, June 1981, *15*(2), pp. 531–42.

Buchanan, James M. L.S.E. Cost Theory in Retrospect. In *Buchanan, J. M. and Thirlby, G. F., eds.*, 1981, pp. 1–16.

De Vany, Arthur S. and Frey, N. G. Stochastic Equilibrium and Capacity Utilization. *Amer. Econ. Rev.*, May 1981, *71*(2), pp. 53–57.

DeAngelo, Harry. Competition and Unanimity. *Amer. Econ. Rev.*, March 1981, *71*(1), pp. 18–27.

Diamond, Peter A. and Maskin, Eric S. An Equilibrium Analysis of Search and Breach of Contract II. A Non-Steady State Example. *J. Econ. Theory*,

October 1981, 25(2), pp. 165–95.

Diewert, W. E. Generalized Concavity and Economics. In *Schaible, S. and Ziemba, W. T., eds.,* 1981, pp. 511–41.

Diewert, W. E.; Avriel, M. and Zang, Israel. Nine Kinds of Quasiconcavity and Concavity. *J. Econ. Theory,* December 1981, 25(3), pp. 397–420.

Epstein, Larry G. Generalized Duality and Integrability. *Econometrica,* May 1981, 49(3), pp. 655–78.

Green, Jerry R. Value of Information with Sequential Futures Markets. *Econometrica,* March 1981, 49(2), pp. 335–58.

Gregory, R. G. The Role of Microeconomic Theory in Policy Formulation: Comment. In *Harris, S. and Maynard, G.,* 1981, pp. 48–56.
[G: Australia]

Harris, Stuart. The Role of Microeconomic Theory in Policy Formulation. In *Harris, S. and Maynard, G.,* 1981, pp. 27–47.

von Hayek, F. A. Economics and Knowledge. In *Buchanan, J. M. and Thirlby, G. F., eds.,* 1981, 1937, pp. 43–68.

Hey, John D. Goodwill—Investment in the Intangible. In *Currie, D.; Peel, D. and Peters, W., eds.,* 1981, pp. 196–229.

Hjorth-Andersen, Christian. Price and Quality of Industrial Products: Some Results of an Empirical Investigation. *Scand. J. Econ.,* 1981, 83(3), pp. 372–89.
[G: Denmark]

Intriligator, Michael D. Mathematical Programming with Applications to Economics. In *Arrow, K. J. and Intriligator, M. D., eds.,* 1981, pp. 53–91.

Junker, Louis J. Instrumentalism, the Principle of Continuity and the Life Process. *Amer. J. Econ. Soc.,* October 1981, 40(4), pp. 381–400.

Klein, Benjamin and Leffler, Keith B. The Role of Market Forces in Assuring Contractual Performance. *J. Polit. Econ.,* August 1981, 89(4), pp. 615–41.

Kreps, David M. Arbitrage and Equilibrium in Economies with Infinitely Many Commodities. *J. Math. Econ.,* March 1981, 8(1), pp. 15–35.

Lancaster, Kelvin J. Information and Product Differentiation. In *Galatin, M. and Leiter, R. D., eds.,* 1981, pp. 17–36.

Lee, Frederic S. The Oxford Challenge to Marshallian Supply and Demand: The History of the Oxford Economists' Research Group. *Oxford Econ. Pap.,* November 1981, 33(3), pp. 339–51.

Lowe, Adolph. Is Economic Value Still a Problem? *Soc. Res.,* Winter 1981, 48(4), pp. 786–815.

Magill, Michael J. P. Infinite Horizon Programs. *Econometrica,* May 1981, 49(3), pp. 679–711.

McCain, Roger A. Information and Product Differentiation: Comments. In *Galatin, M. and Leiter, R. D., eds.,* 1981, pp. 37–41.

McFadden, Daniel. Econometric Models of Probabilistic Choice. In *Manski, C. F. and McFadden, D., eds.,* 1981, pp. 198–272.

von Mises, Ludwig. On the Development of the Subjective Theory of Value. In *von Mises, L.,* 1981, pp. 146–66.

von Mises, Ludwig. Remarks on the Fundamental Problem of the Subjective Theory of Value. In *von Mises, L.,* 1981, pp. 167–82.

Morrison, Clarence C. and Pfouts, Ralph W. A Postscript [Harold Hotelling and Marginal Cost Pricing]. *Atlantic Econ. J.,* December 1981, 9(4), pp. 41–42.

Morrison, Clarence C. and Pfouts, Ralph W. Hotelling's Proof of the Marginal Cost Pricing Theorem [Harold Hotelling and Marginal Cost Pricing]. *Atlantic Econ. J.,* December 1981, 9(4), pp. 34–37.

Muth, John F. Rational Expectations and the Theory of Price Movements. In *Lucas, R. E. and Sargent, T. J., eds.,* 1981, 1961, pp. 3–22.

Nishimura, Kiyohiko Giichi. On Uniqueness of a Steady State and Convergence of Optimal Paths in Multisector Models of Optimal Growth with a Discount Rate. *J. Econ. Theory,* April 1981, 24(2), pp. 157–67.

Papps, Ivy. Goodwill—Investment in the Intangible: Comment. In *Currie, D.; Peel, D. and Peters, W., eds.,* 1981, pp. 230–32.

Phelps, Edmund S. Okun's Micro-Macro System: A Review Article. *J. Econ. Lit.,* September 1981, 19(3), pp. 1065–73.

Polemarchakis, Heraklis M. Constrained Excess Demand Functions. *J. Econ. Theory,* December 1981, 25(3), pp. 323–37.

Riddell, W. Craig. Bargaining under Uncertainty. *Amer. Econ. Rev.,* September 1981, 71(4), pp. 579–90.

Robbins, Lionel. Remarks upon Certain Aspects of the Theory of Costs. In *Buchanan, J. M. and Thirlby, G. F., eds.,* 1981, 1934, pp. 19–41.

Rosen, Sherwin. The Economics of Superstars. *Amer. Econ. Rev.,* December 1981, 71(5), pp. 845–58.

Rosenberg, Alexander. A Skeptical History of Microeconomic Theory. In *Pitt, J. C., ed.,* 1981, pp. 47–61.

Rosenfield, Donald B. and Shapiro, Roy D. Optimal Adaptive Price Search. *J. Econ. Theory,* August 1981, 25(1), pp. 1–20.

Sandler, Todd and Tschirhart, John. On the Number and Membership Size of Consumer Managed Firms [The Economics of Consumer-Managed Firms]. *Southern Econ. J.,* April 1981, 47(4), pp. 1086–91.

Sato, Fumitaka. On the Informational Size of Message Spaces for Resource Allocation Processes in Economies with Public Goods. *J. Econ. Theory,* February 1981, 24(1), pp. 48–69.

Satterthwaite, Mark A. and Sonnenschein, Hugo. Strategy-Proof Allocation Mechanisms at Differentiable Points. *Rev. Econ. Stud.,* October 1981, 48(4), pp. 587–97.

Silberberg, Eugene. Harold Hotelling and Marginal Cost Pricing: Reply [Harold Hotelling and Marginal Cost Pricing]. *Atlantic Econ. J.,* December 1981, 9(4), pp. 38–40.

Spence, A. Michael. The Learning Curve and Competition. *Bell J. Econ. (See Rand J. Econ. after 4/85),* Spring 1981, 12(1), pp. 49–70.

Stein, Jerome L. Speculative Price: Economic Welfare and the Idiot of Chance. *Rev. Econ. Statist.,* May 1981, 63(2), pp. 223–32.
[G: U.S.]

Tomer, John F. Worker Motivation: A Neglected Element in Micro-Micro Theory. *J. Econ. Issues*, June 1981, *15*(2), pp. 351–62.

Weber, Robert James. Attainable Sets of Markets: An Overview. In *Schaible, S. and Ziemba, W. T., eds.*, 1981, pp. 613–25.

von Weizsäcker, Carl Christian. Rechte und Verhältnisse in der Modernen Wirtschaftslehre. (Rights and Relations in Modern Economic Theory. With English summary.) *Kyklos*, 1981, *34*(3), pp. 345–76.

0222 Theory of the Household (consumer demand)

Adler, Thomas J. Disaggregate Models for Decisions Other than Travel-Mode Choices. In *Stopher, P. R.; Meyburg, A. H. and Brög, W., eds.*, 1981, pp. 695–99.

Ahn, C. Y.; Singh, Inderjit and Squire, Lyn. A Model of an Agricultural Household in a Multi-Crop Economy: The Case of Korea. In *Johnson, G. and Maunder, A., eds.*, 1981, pp. 697– 708. [G: S. Korea]

Alcaly, Roger E. Consumer Information and Advertising: Comments. In *Galatin, M. and Leiter, R. D., eds.*, 1981, pp. 78–82. [G: U.S.]

Allen, R. G. D. A Reconsideration of the Theory of Value: Part II. A Mathematical Theory of Individual Demand Functions. In *Hicks, J.*, 1981, *1934*, pp. 30–55.

Anderson, Robert J., Jr. A Note on Option Value and the Expected Value of Consumer's Surplus. *J. Environ. Econ. Manage.*, June 1981, *8*(2), pp. 187–91.

Appelbaum, Elie and Katz, Eliakim. Market Constraints as a Rationale for the Friedman-Savage Utility Function. *J. Polit. Econ.*, August 1981, *89*(4), pp. 819–25.

Atkinson, A. B. and Stern, N. H. On Labour Supply and Commodity Demands. In *[Stone, R.]*, 1981, pp. 265–96. [G: U.K.]

Barnett, William A. and Kopecky, Kenneth J. Estimation of Implicit Utility Models. *Europ. Econ. Rev.*, March 1981, *15*(3), pp. 247–59.

Battalio, Raymond C.; Green, Leonard and Kagel, John H. Income–Leisure Tradeoffs of Animal Workers. *Amer. Econ. Rev.*, September 1981, *71*(4), pp. 621–32.

Battalio, Raymond C., et al. Commodity-Choice behavior with Pigeons as Subjects. *J. Polit. Econ.*, February 1981, *89*(1), pp. 67–91.

Becker, Gary S. Altruism in the Family and Selfishness in the Market Place. *Economica*, February 1981, *48*(189), pp. 1–15.

Becker, Gary S. An Equilibrium Theory of the Distribution of Income and Intergenerational Mobility. In *Currie, D.; Peel, D. and Peters, W., eds.*, 1981, *1979*, pp. 1–33.

Bell, Carolyn Shaw. Demand, Supply, and Labor Market Analysis. *J. Econ. Issues*, June 1981, *15*(2), pp. 423–34. [G: U.S.]

Benhabib, Jess and Day, Richard H. Rational Choice and Erratic Behaviour. *Rev. Econ. Stud.*, July 1981, *48*(3), pp. 459–71.

Bernardo, John J. A Programming Approach to Measure Attributes Utilities. *J. Econ. Bus.*, Spring/ Summer 1981, *33*(3), pp. 239–45.

Bewley, Truman F. Stationary Equilibrium. *J. Econ. Theory*, April 1981, *24*(2), pp. 265–95.

Binswanger, Hans P. Attitudes toward Risk: Theoretical Implications of an Experiment in Rural India. *Econ. J.*, December 1981, *91*(364), pp. 867– 90. [G: India]

Bolnick, Bruce R. Government as a Super Becker-Altruist: A Reply. *Public Choice*, 1981, *37*(3), pp. 603–06.

Bourguignon, François. Participation, emploi et travail domestiques des femmes mariées: Un modèle micro-économique appliqué aux pays en développement. (Participation, Domestic Employment and Domestic Work by Married Women: A Micro-Economic Model Applied to Developing Countries. With English summary.) *Consommation*, April–June 1981, *28*(2), pp. 75–98. [G: France]

Brandstätter, Hermann. Time Sampling of Subjective Well-being. In *Molt, W.; Hartmann, H. A. and Stringer, P., eds.*, 1981, pp. 63–76. [G: W. Germany]

Brandt, Richard B. Utilitarianism and Welfare Legislation. In *Brown, P. G.; Johnson, C. and Vernier, P., eds.*, 1981, pp. 7–24.

Braverman, Avishay and Dixit, Avinash. Consumer Search and Market Equilibria: A Note. *Rev. Econ. Stud.*, October 1981, *48*(4), pp. 657–58.

Breault, K. Modern Psychophysical Measurement of Marginal Utility: A Return to Introspective Cardinality? *Soc. Sci. Quart.*, December 1981, *62*(4), pp. 672–84.

Bresson, Yoland. Capital-temps et répartition des revenus. De la remise en cause des fondements théoriques de la microéconomie à une nouvelle loi macroéconomique de répartition des revenus. (With English summary.) *Écon. Appl.*, 1981, *34*(2–3), pp. 517–48.

Brown, Donald J. and Lewis, Lucinda M. Myopic Economic Agents. *Econometrica*, March 1981, *49*(2), pp. 359–68.

Burdett, Kenneth and Malueg, David A. The Theory of Search for Several Goods. *J. Econ. Theory*, June 1981, *24*(3), pp. 362–76.

Carey, Malachy. On Mutually Exclusive and Collectively Exhaustive Properties of Demand Functions. *Economica*, November 1981, *48*(192), pp. 407–15.

Charles, Susan and Westaway, Anthony J. Ignorance and Merit Wants. *Finanzarchiv*, 1981, *39*(1), pp. 74–78.

Chichilnisky, Graciela. Existence of Optimal Savings Policies with Imperfect Information and Non-Convexities. *J. Math. Econ.*, March 1981, *8*(1), pp. 1–14.

Cornes, Richard and Albon, Robert. Evaluation of Welfare Change in Quantity-Constrained Regimes. *Econ. Rec.*, June 1981, *57*(157), pp. 186– 90.

Cory, Dennis C., et al. Simplified Measurement of Consumer Welfare Change. *Amer. J. Agr. Econ.*, November 1981, *63*(4), pp. 715–17.

Daganzo, Carlos F. Calibration and Prediction with Random-Utility Models: Some Recent Advances and Unresolved Questions. In *Stopher, P. R.;*

Meyburg, A. H. and Brög, W., eds., 1981, pp. 35–53.

Dahlby, B. G. Measuring the Effect on a Consumer of Stabilizing the Price of a Commodity. *Can. J. Econ.*, August 1981, *14*(3), pp. 440–49.

Daly, Andrew J. Some Issues in the Application of Disaggregate Choice Models. In *Stopher, P. R.; Meyburg, A. H. and Brög, W., eds.*, 1981, pp. 55–72.

Daly, Vince and Hadjimatheou, George. Stochastic Implications of the Life Cycle-Permanent Income Hypothesis: Evidence for the U.K. Economy: Comment. *J. Polit. Econ.*, June 1981, *89*(3), pp. 596–99. **[G: U.K.]**

Danner, Peter L. Exchange Value in the Value Hierarchy. *Int. J. Soc. Econ.*, 1981, *8*(4), pp. 70–84.

Davies, James B. Uncertain Lifetime, Consumption, and Dissaving in Retirement. *J. Polit. Econ.*, June 1981, *89*(3), pp. 561–77.

Deaton, Angus. Theoretical and Empirical Approaches to Consumer Demand under Rationing. In *[Stone, R.]*, 1981, pp. 55–72. **[G: U.K.]**

Deaton, Angus and Muellbauer, John. Functional Forms for Labor Supply and Commodity Demands with and without Quantity Restrictions. *Econometrica*, November 1981, *49*(6), pp. 1521–32.

DeLorme, Charles D., Jr. and Mounts, William S., Jr. Small Saver Discrimination, Anticipated Inflation and Economic Welfare. *Amer. Econ.*, Spring 1981, *25*(1), pp. 53–56.

Dionne, Georges. Le risque moral et la sélection adverse: une revue critique de la littérature. (Moral Hazard and Adverse Selection: A Survey. With English summary.) *L'Actual. Econ.*, April–June 1981, *57*(2), pp. 193–224.

Doti, James L. and Sharir, Shmuel. Households' Grocery Shopping Behavior in the Short-Run: Theory and Evidence. *Econ. Inquiry*, April 1981, *19*(2), pp. 196–208. **[G: U.S.]**

Dybvig, Philip and Polemarchakis, Heraklis M. Recovering Cardinal Utility. *Rev. Econ. Stud.*, January 1981, *48*(1), pp. 159–66.

Edlefsen, Lee E. The Comparative Statics of Hedonic Price Functions and Other Nonlinear Constraints. *Econometrica*, November 1981, *49*(6), pp. 1501–20.

Ermisch, John F. An Economic Theory of Household Formation: Theory and Evidence from the General Household Survey. *Scot. J. Polit. Econ.*, February 1981, *28*(1), pp. 1–19. **[G: U.K.]**

Färe, Rolf and Primont, Daniel. Separability vs Strict Separability: A Further Result [Separability vs Functional Structure: A Characterization of their Differences]. *J. Econ. Theory*, December 1981, *25*(3), pp. 455–60.

Firey, Walter. Variations on a Theme by Graftstein. *Soc. Sci. Quart.*, June 1981, *62*(2), pp. 213–17.

Fischer, Gregory W. and Nagin, Daniel. Random versus Fixed Coefficient Quantal Choice Models. In *Manski, C. F. and McFadden, D., eds.*, 1981, pp. 273–304.

Fountain, John. Consumer Surplus When Preferences are Intransitive: Analysis and Interpretation. *Econometrica*, March 1981, *49*(2), pp. 379–94.

Fuchs-Seliger, Susanne. Aggregation with a Fixed Distribution of Income. *Z. Nationalökon.*, 1981, *41*(1–2), pp. 69–78.

George, Donald A. R. Equilibrium and Catastrophes in Economics. *Scot. J. Polit. Econ.*, February 1981, *28*(1), pp. 43–61.

Gorman, W. M. Some Engel Curves. In *[Stone, R.]*, 1981, pp. 7–29.

Gould, Joseph R. On the Interpretation of Inferior Goods and Factors. *Economica*, November 1981, *48*(192), pp. 397–405.

Grafstein, Robert. Sociologists, Economists and Legitmacy. *Soc. Sci. Quart.*, June 1981, *62*(2), pp. 218–20.

Graham, John W. An Explanation for the Correlation of Stocks of Nonhuman Capital with Investment in Human Capital. *Amer. Econ. Rev.*, March 1981, *71*(1), pp. 248–55.

Grunert, Klaus G. Consumer Information Programs and the Concept of "Perceived Risk." In *Molt, W.; Hartmann, H. A. and Stringer, P., eds.*, 1981, pp. 161–74.

Haines, Walter W. The Economic Consequences of Altruism. *Int. J. Soc. Econ.*, 1981, *8*(4), pp. 50–69.

Hall, Robert E. Stochastic Implications of the Life Cycle–Permanent Income Hypothesis: Theory and Evidence. In *Lucas, R. E. and Sargent, T. J., eds.*, 1981, *1978*, pp. 501–17. **[G: U.S.]**

Hanson, Susan and Burnett, K. Patricia. Understanding Complex Travel Behavior: Measurement Issues. In *Stopher, P. R.; Meyburg, A. H. and Brög, W., eds.*, 1981, pp. 207–30.

Haque, W. Direct and Indirect Weak Separability. *J. Econ. Theory*, October 1981, *25*(2), pp. 237–54.

Hausman, Jerry A. Exact Consumer's Surplus and Deadweight Loss. *Amer. Econ. Rev.*, September 1981, *71*(4), pp. 662–76.

Held, Martin. Needs and System Requirements: A Review of Some Relevant Topics. In *Molt, W.; Hartmann, H. A. and Stringer, P., eds.*, 1981, pp. 305–13.

Held, Martin. Some Thoughts about the Individual's Choice among Alternative Travel Modes and Its Determinants. In *Stopher, P. R.; Meyburg, A. H. and Brög, W., eds.*, 1981, pp. 155–69.

Helpman, Elhanan. Optimal Spending and Money Holdings in the Presence of Liquidity Constraints. *Econometrica*, November 1981, *49*(6), pp. 1559–70.

Hey, John D. and McKenna, Chris J. Consumer Search with Uncertain Product Quality. *J. Polit. Econ.*, February 1981, *89*(1), pp. 54–66.

Hicks, John R. A Reconsideration of the Theory of Value: Part I. In *Hicks, J.*, 1981, *1934*, pp. 5–29.

Hicks, John R. The Four Consumer's Surpluses. In *Hicks, J.*, 1981, *1943*, pp. 114–32.

Hicks, John R. The Rehabilitation of Consumers' Surplus. In *Hicks, J.*, 1981, *1941*, pp. 100–113.

Hicks, John R. Valuation of the Social Income II— The Utility Approach [The Measurement of Real Income]. In *Hicks, J.*, 1981, pp. 142–88.

Higa, Teruyuki. An Analysis of Structural Changes in the Food Stamp Program. *Amer. Econ.*, Fall

1981, 25(2), pp. 24–29.   [G: U.S.]

Hirschman, Albert O. An Alternative Explanation of Contemporary Harriedness. In *Hirschman, A. O.*, 1981, *1973*, pp. 290–93.

Hirshleifer, Jack. It Pays to Do Good, but Not to do More Good than It Pays: A Note on the Survival of Altruism: Comment. *J. Econ. Behav. Organ.*, December 1981, 2(4), pp. 387.

Holthausen, Duncan M. A Risk–Return Model with Risk and Return Measured as Deviations from a Target Return. *Amer. Econ. Rev.*, March 1981, 71(1), pp. 182–88.

Ippolito, Pauline M. Information and the Life Cycle Consumption of Hazardous Goods. *Econ. Inquiry*, October 1981, 19(4), pp. 529–58.

Johansen, Leif. Suggestions towards Freeing Systems of Demand Functions from a Strait-jacket. In *[Stone, R.]*, 1981, pp. 31–54.

Jolibert, Alain J. P. L'économie du consommateur: les nouvelles approches théoriques et commerciales sont-elles conciliables? (Consumer Economy: Are the New Theoretical and Commercial Approaches Reconcilable? With English summary.) *Écon. Soc.*, October–November–December 1981, 15(10–12), pp. 1457–80.

Kagel, John H., et al. Demand Curves for Animal Consumers. *Quart. J. Econ.*, February 1981, 96(1), pp. 1–15.

Kannai, Yakar. Concave Utility Functions—Existence, Constructions and Cardinality. In *Schaible, S. and Ziemba, W. T., eds.*, 1981, pp. 543–611.

Kau, James B. and Keenan, Donald. On the Theory of Interest Rates, Consumer Durables, and the Demand for Housing. *J. Urban Econ.*, September 1981, 10(2), pp. 183–200.

Kawai, Masahiro. The Behaviour of an Open-Economy Firm under Flexible Exchange Rates. *Economica*, February 1981, 48(189), pp. 45–60.

Keating, Barry P. United Way Contributions: Anomalous Philanthropy. *Quart. Rev. Econ. Bus.*, Spring 1981, 21(1), pp. 114–19.   [G: U.S.]

Kennan, John. The Existence of Expected Utility Maximizing Decisions When Utility Is Unbounded. *Econometrica*, January 1981, 49(1), pp. 215–18.

Kihlstrom, Richard E. and Mirman, Leonard J. Constant, Increasing and Decreasing Risk Aversion with Many Commodities. *Rev. Econ. Stud.*, April 1981, 48(2), pp. 271–80.

Kihlstrom, Richard E.; Romer, David and Williams, Steve. Risk Aversion with Random Initial Wealth. *Econometrica*, June 1981, 49(4), pp. 911–20.

Kinsey, Jean. Determinants of Credit Card Accounts: An Application of Tobit Analysis. *J. Cons. Res.*, September 1981, 8(2), pp. 172–82.

[G: U.S.]

Kleinhückelskoten, Hans-Dieter and Spaetling, Dieter. Aspekte der Inferiorität und Superiorität als ökonomische Phänomene—Ein Beitrag zur Neuorientierung der mikroökonomischen Theorie. (Aspects of Inferiority and Superiority as Economic Phenomena—A Contribution to the Re-orientation of Macroeconomic Theory. With English summary.) *Jahr. Nationalökon. Statist.*, November 1981, 196(6), pp. 511–26.

Kolm, Serge-Christophe. Efficacité et altruisme: les sophismes de Mandeville, Smith et Pareto. (Efficiency and Altruism: The Mandeville, Smith and Pareto Fallacies. With English summary.) *Revue Écon.*, January 1981, 32(1), pp. 5–31.

Kourilsky, Marilyn and Murray, Trudy. The Use of Economic Reasoning to Increase Satisfaction with Family Decision Making. *J. Cons. Res.*, September 1981, 8(2), pp. 183–88.

Krelle, Wilhelm and Pallaschke, Diethard. A General Demand System or: Utility Maximization and the Representative Household or Cost Minimization and the Representative Firm as Approximations. *Z. Nationalökon.*, 1981, 41(3–4), pp. 223–52.

Landsburg, Steven E. Taste Change in the United Kingdom, 1900–1955. *J. Polit. Econ.*, February 1981, 89(1), pp. 92–104.   [G: U.K.]

Ledyard, John O. The Paradox of Voting and Candidate Competition: A General Equilibrium Analysis. In *[Weiler, E. T.]*, 1981, pp. 54–80.

Leibenstein, Harvey. Economic Decision Theory and Human Fertility Behavior: A Speculative Essay. *Population Devel. Rev.*, September 1981, 7(3), pp. 381–400.

Lemennicier, Bertrand and Lévy-Garboua, Louis. L'arbitrage autarcie-marché: Une explication du travail féminin. (The Autarky/Market Trade-off: An Explanation of Female Labor. With English summary.) *Consommation*, April–June 1981, 28(2), pp. 41–74.   [G: France]

von Loesch, Heinrich. Economistic Theories of Fertility Motivation and Rich and Poor Populations; a Critical Evaluation and Proposals for Socio-Psychology Approaches. In *Molt, W.; Hartmann, H. A. and Stringer, P., eds.*, 1981, pp. 233–42.

Loury, Glenn C. Intergenerational Transfers and the Distribution of Earnings. *Econometrica*, June 1981, 49(4), pp. 843–67.

Lucas, Robert E., Jr. Equilibrium Search and Unemployment. In *Lucas, R. E., Jr.*, 1981, *1974*, pp. 156–78.

Manheim, L. Marvin and Sobel, Kenneth L. Modeling Individual Choice in Nontransportation Contexts. In *Stopher, P. R.; Meyburg, A. H. and Brög, W., eds.*, 1981, pp. 706–13.

Mark, John; Brown, Frank and Pierson, B. J. Consumer Demand Theory, Goods and Characteristics: Breathing Empirical Content into the Lancastrian Approach. *Managerial Dec. Econ.*, March 1981, 2(1), pp. 32–39.   [G: U.K.]

McElroy, Marjorie B. and Horney, Mary Jean. Nash-Bargained Household Decisions: Toward a Generalization of the Theory of Demand. *Int. Econ. Rev.*, June 1981, 22(2), pp. 333–49.

McEwin, R. Ian. Liability Rules, Insurance and the Coase Theorem. *Australian J. Manage.*, December 1981, 6(2), pp. 103–17.

Mehta, Ghanshyam. A New Extension Procedure for the Arrow-Hahn Theorem. *Int. Econ. Rev.*, February 1981, 22(1), pp. 113–18.

Meidinger, Claude. La théorie économique de la famille: Une critique méthodologique. (The Economic Theory of Family Decisions. With English summary.) *Consommation*, July–September 1981, 28(3), pp. 75–93.

Menz, Fredric C. and Mullen, John K. The Economics of Congestion: A Comment. *Public Finance Quart.*, January 1981, *9*(1), pp. 107–16.

Milne, Frank. Induced Preferences and the Theory of the Consumer. *J. Econ. Theory*, April 1981, *24*(2), pp. 205–17.

Mishan, Ezra J. The Plain Truth about Consumer Surplus. In *Mishan, E. J.*, 1981, *1977*, pp. 61–72.

Miyao, Takahiro and Shapiro, Perry. Discrete Choice and Variable Returns to Scale. *Int. Econ. Rev.*, June 1981, *22*(2), pp. 257–73.

Moles, Abraham A. Micropsychology and Economic Motivation. In *Molt, W.; Hartmann, H. A. and Stringer, P., eds.*, 1981, pp. 105–17.
[G: France]

Muellbauer, John. Linear Aggregation in Neoclassical Labour Supply. *Rev. Econ. Stud.*, January 1981, *48*(1), pp. 21–36.

Muellbauer, John. Testing Neoclassical Models of the Demand for Consumer Durables. In *[Stone, R.]*, 1981, pp. 213–35. [G: U.K.]

Murphy, F. P. A Note on Weak Separability. *Rev. Econ. Stud.*, October 1981, *48*(4), pp. 671–72.

Nelson, Phillip J. Consumer Information and Advertising. In *Galatin, M. and Leiter, R. D., eds.*, 1981, pp. 42–77. [G: U.S.]

Norman, Kent L. Assessing the Importance of Environmental and Societal Factors: A Way to Separate Relative Importance and Subjective Value. In *Molt, W.; Hartmann, H. A. and Stringer, P., eds.*, 1981, pp. 37–61.

Ölander, Folke. The Effects of Income Level upon the Efficiency of Buying, or Do the Poor Pay More? In *Molt, W.; Hartmann, H. A. and Stringer, P., eds.*, 1981, pp. 149–59.

Olson, Mancur and Bailey, Martin J. Positive Time Preference. *J. Polit. Econ.*, February 1981, *89*(1), pp. 1–25.

Patinkin, Don. Demand Curves and Consumer's Surplus. In *Patinkin, D.*, 1981, *1963*, pp. 181–208.

Patinkin, Don and Liviatan, Nissan. On the Economic Theory of Price Indexes. In *Patinkin, D.*, 1981, *1961*, pp. 209–39.

Pethig, Rüdiger. Möglichkeiten der Allokation gemeinschaftlich nutzbarer Güter mit nutzungsabhängiger Qualität. (Possibilities of Allocating Jointly Usable Goods with Use-Dependent Quality. With English summary.) *Z. ges. Staatswiss.*, June 1981, *137*(2), pp. 187–211.

Pudney, Stephen E. An Empirical Method of Approximating the Separable Structure of Consumer Preferences. *Rev. Econ. Stud.*, October 1981, *48*(4), pp. 561–77. [G: U.K.]

Pudney, Stephen E. Instrumental Variable Estimation of a Characteristics Model of Demand. *Rev. Econ. Stud.*, July 1981, *48*(3), pp. 417–33.

Rader, Trout. Utility over Time: The Homothetic Case. *J. Econ. Theory*, October 1981, *25*(2), pp. 219–36.

Rashid, Salim. Preferences under Certainty and Uncertainty: A Note [A Homiletic Exposition of the Expected Utility Hypothesis]. *Economica*, February 1981, *48*(189), pp. 93–94.

Reynaud, P.-L. Principles of Consumer Behavior. In *Molt, W.; Hartmann, H. A. and Stringer, P., eds.*, 1981, pp. 97–104.

Rigaux-Bricmont, B.; Sayegh, E. and Vlahopoulos, P. Pour un modèle du rôle de l'information et du risque perçu dans la prise de decision de consommation. (Building a Model of Consumer Decision-Making Emphasizing the Use of Information for Perceived Risk Reduction. With English summary.) *Ann. Sci. Écon. Appl.*, 1981, *37*(2), pp. 25–55.

Rüttinger, Bruno. Consumer Behavior. In *Molt, W.; Hartmann, H. A. and Stringer, P., eds.*, 1981, pp. 83–87.

Sandmo, Agnar. The Rate of Return and Personal Savings [The Rate of Return, Taxation and Personal Savings]. *Econ. J.*, June 1981, *91*(362), pp. 536–40.

Schnabl, Hermann. Das Preislimit-Konzept als alternativer Nachfrageansatz. (The Price Limit Approach to Demand Analysis. With English summary.) *Jahr. Nationalökon. Statist.*, January 1981, *196*(1), pp. 63–74.

Seaman, Bruce A. An Assessment of Recent Applications of Economic Theory to the Arts. *J. Cult. Econ.*, June 1981, *5*(1), pp. 36–51.

Shah, Anup R. Imperfections in the Capital Markets and Consumer Behavior. *Southern Econ. J.*, April 1981, *47*(4), pp. 1032–45.

Shapouri, S.; Folwell, R. J. and Baritelle, J. L. Statistical Estimation of Firm-Level Demand Functions: A Case Study in an Oligopolistic Industry. *Agr. Econ. Res.*, April 1981, *33*(2), pp. 18–25.

Siegers, J. J. and Zandanel, R. A Simultaneous Analysis of the Labour Force Participation of Married Women and the Presence of Young Children in the Family. *De Economist*, 1981, *129*(3), pp. 382–93. [G: Netherlands]

Silberer, Günter. Basic Concepts and Principles as a Framework for the Explanation of Consumer Behavior. In *Molt, W.; Hartmann, H. A. and Stringer, P., eds.*, 1981, pp. 89–95.

Sobel, Joel. Distortion of Utilities and the Bargaining Problem. *Econometrica*, May 1981, *49*(3), pp. 597–619.

Spinnewyn, Frans. Rational Habit Formation. *Europ. Econ. Rev.*, January 1981, *15*(1), pp. 91–109.

Strasnick, Steven. Neo-utilitarian Ethics and the Ordinal Representation Assumption. In *Pitt, J. C., ed.*, 1981, pp. 63–92.

Svensson, Lars E. O. Effective Demand in a Sequence of Markets. *Scand. J. Econ.*, 1981, *83*(1), pp. 1–21.

Terrebonne, R. Peter. Government as a Super Becker-Altruist: A Comment. *Public Choice*, 1981, *37*(3), pp. 595–601.

Tesfatsion, Leigh. Dynamic Investment, Risk Aversion, and Foresight Sensitivity. *J. Econ. Dynam. Control*, February 1981, *3*(1), pp. 65–96.

Tezel, Ahmet. Optimal Insurance Coverage. *Amer. Econ.*, Spring 1981, *25*(1), pp. 70–71.

Thaler, Richard H. and Shefrin, Hersh M. An Economic Theory of Self-Control. *J. Polit. Econ.*, April 1981, *89*(2), pp. 392–406.

Thayer, Mark A. Contingent Valuation Techniques for Assessing Environmental Impacts: Further

Evidence. *J. Environ. Econ. Manage.*, March 1981, *8*(1), pp. 27–44. [G: U.S.]

Theeuwes, J. Family Labour Force Participation: Multinomial Logit Estimates. *Appl. Econ.*, December 1981, *13*(4), pp. 481–98. [G: U.S.]

Theil, Henri and Laitinen, Kenneth. The Independence Transformation: A Review and Some Further Explorations. In [*Stone, R.*], 1981, pp. 73–112. [G: U.S.]

Timmer, C. Peter. Is There "Curvature" in the Slutsky Matrix? *Rev. Econ. Statist.*, August 1981, *63*(3), pp. 395–402. [G: U.S.]

Trognon, Alain. Composition des ménages et système linéaire de dépenses. (Household Composition and Linear System of Expenditures. With English summary.) *Ann. INSEE*, January–March 1981, (41), pp. 3–40. [G: France]

Turchi, Boone A. A Comprehensive Micro Theory of Fertility. In *Molt, W.; Hartmann, H. A. and Stringer, P., eds.*, 1981, pp. 197–210.

Val'tukh, K. K. and Ryzhenkov, A. V. An Analysis of Personal Consumption Structure in Austria Using a Theoretical Utility Function. *Empirical Econ.*, 1981, *6*(1), pp. 11–65. [G: Austria]

Vartia, Yrjö O. and Weymark, John A. Four Revealed Preference Tables. *Scand. J. Econ.*, 1981, *83*(3), pp. 408–18.

Vickerman, Roger W. Travel-Choice Models and the Limit of Their Applicability in Other Choice Situations. In *Stopher, P. R.; Meyburg, A. H. and Brög, W., eds.*, 1981, pp. 700–706.

Waid, C. Carter and Schoemaker, Paul J. H. On the Fidelity of Multiattribute Preference Representations: Some Analytical Considerations. In *Morse, J. N., ed.*, 1981, pp. 447–64.

Wärneryd, Karl-Erik. The Individual and the Economy. In *Molt, W.; Hartmann, H. A. and Stringer, P., eds.*, 1981, pp. 27–36.

Wickham, Elizabeth D. Relative Price Linearity and JRC Equilibrium. *Econ. Inquiry*, October 1981, *19*(4), pp. 672–86.

Willassen, Yngve. Expected Utility, Chebichev Bounds, Mean-Variance Analysis. *Scand. J. Econ.*, 1981, *83*(3), pp. 419–28.

Wintrobe, Ronald. It Pays to Do Good, but Not to Do More Good than It Pays: A Note on the Survival of Altruism: Reply. *J. Econ. Behav. Organ.*, December 1981, *2*(4), pp. 389–90.

Wintrobe, Ronald. It Pays to Do Good, but Not to Do More Good than It Pays: A Note on the Survival of Altruism. *J. Econ. Behav. Organ.*, September 1981, *2*(3), pp. 201–13.

Wolfson, R. J. New Consumer Theory and the Relations between Goods. In *Pitt, J. C., ed.*, 1981, pp. 33–46.

0223 Theory of Production

Abel, Andrew B. A Dynamic Model of Investment and Capacity Utilization. *Quart. J. Econ.*, August 1981, *96*(3), pp. 379–403.

Abel, Andrew B. Dynamic Adjustment in a Putty-Putty Model: Implications for Testing the Putty-Clay Hypothesis. *Int. Econ. Rev.*, February 1981, *22*(1), pp. 19–36.

Abel, Andrew B. Taxes, Inflation, and the Durability

of Capital. *J. Polit. Econ.*, June 1981, *89*(3), pp. 548–60.

Ábel, István. The Labor Saving Principle with an Application to the Leontief-Type Economies. *Int. Econ. Rev.*, June 1981, *22*(2), pp. 377–83.

Abraham-Frois, Gilbert and Berrebi, Edmond. La demade, face cachée de la production jointe. (Demand Analysis, the Hidden Side of Joint Production. With English summary.) *Revue Écon.*, November 1981, *32*(6), pp. 1154–65.

Albach, Horst. The Nature of the Firm—A Production-Theoretical Viewpoint. *Z. ges. Staatswiss.*, December 1981, *137*(4), pp. 717–22.

Allard, Marie; Bronsard, Camille and McDougall, Gilles. Note sur la théorie néo-keynésienne du producteur. (A Note on the Neo-Classical Theory of the Producer. With English summary.) *L'Actual. Econ.*, April–June 1981, *57*(2), pp. 131–47.

Allen, Robert C. and Diewert, W. Erwin. Direct versus Implicit Superlative Index Number Formulae. *Rev. Econ. Statist.*, August 1981, *63*(3), pp. 430–35.

Anderson, Richard G. On the Specification of Conditional Factor Demand Functions in Recent Studies of U.S. Manufacturing. In *Berndt, E. R. and Field, B. C., eds.*, 1981, pp. 119–44. [G: U.S.]

Artus, Patrick and Peyroux, Claude. Fonctions de production avec facteur énergie: estimations pour les grands pays de l'OCDE. (Production Functions with the Energy Factor: Estimates for the Large OECD Countries. With English summary.) *Ann. INSEE*, October–December 1981, (44), pp. 3–39. [G: OECD]

Atkinson, Sherry S. An Analysis of Finished Goods Inventory Behavior: A Microtheoretic Approach. *Southern Econ. J.*, October 1981, *48*(2), pp. 312–26.

Auerbach, Alan J. A Note on the Efficient Design of Investment Incentives. *Econ. J.*, March 1981, *91*(361), pp. 217–23.

Auerbach, Alan J. Inflation and the Tax Treatment of Firm Behavior. *Amer. Econ. Rev.*, May 1981, *71*(2), pp. 419–23.

Baetge, Jörg and Fischer, Thomas. Substitution des Markt-Preis-Mechanismus durch Steuerungs- und Regelungsmechanismen im Unternehmen. (Managerial Control Strategies Instead of Price Mechanism. With English summary.) *Z. ges. Staatswiss.*, December 1981, *137*(4), pp. 723–32.

Baron, David P. Price Regulation, Product Quality, and Asymmetric Information. *Amer. Econ. Rev.*, March 1981, *71*(1), pp. 212–20.

Baumol, William J. and Willig, Robert D. Fixed Costs, Sunk Costs, Entry Barriers, and Sustainability of Monopoly. *Quart. J. Econ.*, August 1981, *96*(3), pp. 405–31.

Beckmann, Martin J. Binary Choice and the Demand for Durables. In [*Lipiński, E.*], 1981, pp. 87–92. [G: U.S.]

Ben-Zion, Uri and Fixler, Dennis J. Market Structure and Product Innovation. *Southern Econ. J.*, October 1981, *48*(2), pp. 437–48.

Benhabib, Jess and Nishimura, Kazuo. Stability of Equilibrium in Dynamic Models of Capital Theory. *Int. Econ. Rev.*, June 1981, *22*(2), pp. 275–93.

Benninga, Simon and Muller, Eitan. Majority Choice and the Objective Function of the Firm under Uncertainty: Reply. *Bell J. Econ. (See Rand J. Econ. after 4/85)*, Spring 1981, *12*(1), pp. 338–39.

Bergman, Lars and Mäler, Karl-Göran. Efficiency–flexibility Trade-off and the Cost of Unexpected Oil Price Increases. *Scand. J. Econ.*, 1981, *83*(2), pp. 253–68. [G: Sweden]

Bergström, Villy and Södersten, Jan. Inflation, Taxation and Capital Cost. In *Eliasson, G. and Södersten, J., eds.*, 1981, pp. 233–66.

Berndt, Ernst R. and Wood, David O. Engineering and Econometric Interpretations of Energy–Capital Complementarity: Reply and Further Results. *Amer. Econ. Rev.*, December 1981, *71*(5), pp. 1105–10. [G: U.S.]

Bhattacharya, Prodyot K., et al. Variable Wages and Prices and the Demand for Capital with Discrete and Continuous Adjustments. *Int. Econ. Rev.*, June 1981, *22*(2), pp. 295–307.

Blackorby, Charles and Russell, R. Robert. The Morishima Elasticity of Substitution; Symmetry, Constancy, Separability, and Its Relationship to the Hicks and Allen Elasticities. *Rev. Econ. Stud.*, January 1981, *48*(1), pp. 147–58.

Bonin, John P. The Theory of the Labor-Managed Firm from the Membership's Perspective with Implications for Marshallian Industry Supply. *J. Compar. Econ.*, December 1981, *5*(4), pp. 337–51.

Borins, Sandford F. The Effect of Pricing Policy on the Optimal Timing of Investments in Transport Facilities. *J. Transp. Econ. Policy*, May 1981, *15*(2), pp. 121–33.

Bössmann, Eva. Weshalb gibt es Unternehmungen? Der Erklärungsansatz von Ronald H. Coase. (The Nature of the Firm: Ronald H. Coase's Interpretation. With English summary.) *Z. ges. Staatswiss.*, December 1981, *137*(4), pp. 667–74.

Bourguignon, Francoise and Sethi, Suresh P. Dynamic Optimal Pricing and (Possibly) Advertising in the Face of Various Kinds of Potential Entrants. *J. Econ. Dynam. Control*, May 1981, *3*(2), pp. 119–40.

Brinkmann, Tomas and Kübler, Friedrich. Überlegungen zur ökonomischen Analyse von Unternehmensrecht. (Thoughts on the Economic Analysis of the Firm. With English summary.) *Z. ges. Staatswiss.*, December 1981, *137*(4), pp. 681–88.

Brown, Randall S. and Christensen, Laurits R. Estimating Elasticities of Substitution in a Model of Partial Static Equilibrium: An Application to U.S. Agriculture, 1947 to 1974. In *Berndt, E. R. and Field, B. C., eds.*, 1981, pp. 209–29. [G: U.S.]

Buchanan, James McGill and Tollison, Robert D. The Homogenization of Heterogeneous Inputs. *Amer. Econ. Rev.*, March 1981, *71*(1), pp. 28–38.

Camacho, Antonio and White, William D. A Note on Loss of Control and the Optimum Size of the Firm [Supervision, Loss of Control, and the Optimum Size of the Firm]. *J. Polit. Econ.*, April 1981, *89*(2), pp. 407–10.

Caramanis, Michael C. Elasticity and Substitution between Capital and Disaggregated Labor: A Cost Function Application with Greek Data at the Level of the Firm. *Greek Econ. Rev.*, August 1981, *3*(2), pp. 187–96. [G: Greece]

Carter, E. Eugene. Resource Allocation. In *Nystrom, P. C. and Starbuck, W. H., eds.*, Vol. 2, 1981, pp. 152–65.

Chambers, Robert G. The Monopsonistic Firm in an Uncertain World. *Atlantic Econ. J.*, July 1981, *9*(2), pp. 35–39.

Chavas, Jean-Paul and Pope, Rulon D. A Welfare Measure of Production Activities under Risk Aversion. *Southern Econ. J.*, July 1981, *48*(1), pp. 187–96.

Chillemi, Ottorino. Sul regime del capitale nell'impresa autogestita. (Property Rights and the Labour-managed Firm. With English summary.) *Rivista Int. Sci. Econ. Com.*, January–February 1981, *28*(1–2), pp. 151–69.

Coase, R. H. Business Organization and the Accountant. In *Buchanan, J. M. and Thirlby, G. F., eds.*, 1981, pp. 95–132.

Cocks, Douglas L. Company Total Factor Productivity: Refinements, Production Functions, and Certain Effects of Regulation. *Bus. Econ.*, May 1981, *16*(3), pp. 5–14.

Cosimano, Thomas F. The Incentive to Adopt Cost Reducing Innovation in the Presence of a Non-Linear Demand Curve. *Southern Econ. J.*, July 1981, *48*(1), pp. 97–102.

Davidson, Russell and Harris, Richard G. Non-Convexities in Continuous-Time Investment Theory. *Rev. Econ. Stud.*, April 1981, *48*(2), pp. 235–53.

Davis, Jeffrey S. A Comparison of Procedures for Estimating Returns to Research Using Production Functions. *Australian J. Agr. Econ.*, April 1981, *25*(1), pp. 60–72. [G: Australia]

Diewert, W. Erwin. On Measuring the Loss of Output Due to Nonneutral Business Taxation. In *Hulten, C. R., ed.*, 1981, pp. 57–80.

Diewert, W. Erwin. The Elasticity of Derived Net Supply and a Generalized Le Chatelier Principle. *Rev. Econ. Stud.*, January 1981, *48*(1), pp. 63–80.

Duesing, Erick C. Multiple Objective Linear Programming: An Economist's Perspective. In *Morse, J. N., ed.*, 1981, pp. 77–90.

Edwards, R. S. The Rationale of Cost Accounting. In *Buchanan, J. M. and Thirlby, G. F., eds.*, 1981, *1937*, pp. 71–92.

Eichhorn, Wolfgang. Concavity and Quasiconcavity in the Theory of Production. In *Schaible, S. and Ziemba, W. T., eds.*, 1981, pp. 627–36.

El-Hodiri, Mohamed and Takayama, Akira. Dynamic Behavior of the Firm with Adjustment Costs, under Regulatory Constraint. *J. Econ. Dynam. Control*, February 1981, *3*(1), pp. 29–41.

Epstein, Larry G. Duality Theory and Functional Forms for Dynamic Factor Demands. *Rev. Econ. Stud.*, January 1981, *48*(1), pp. 81–95.

Eswaran, Mukesh; Kanemoto, Yoshitsugu and Ryan, David. A Dual Approach to the Locational Decision of the Firm. *J. Reg. Sci.*, November 1981, *21*(4), pp. 469–90.

Färe, Rolf and Lovell, C. A. Knox. Measuring the Technical Efficiency of Production: Reply. *J.*

Econ. Theory, December 1981, *25*(3), pp. 453–54.

Färe, Rolf and Lyon, Vern. The Determinateness Test and Economic Price Indices. *Econometrica*, January 1981, *49*(1), pp. 209–13.

Field, Barry C. and Allen, P. Geoffrey. A General Measure for Output-Variable Input Demand Elasticities. *Amer. J. Agr. Econ.*, August 1981, *63*(3), pp. 575–77.

Filimon, Radu. Aggregation of Heterogeneous Goods in Models of the von Neumann Variety. *Z. Nationalökon.*, 1981, *41*(3–4), pp. 253–64.

Francken, Dick A.; van Raaij, W. Fred and Verhallen, Theo M. M. Satisfaction with Leisure Activities. In *Molt, W.; Hartmann, H. A. and Stringer, P., eds.*, 1981, pp. 119–33. [G: Netherlands]

Frantz, Roger S. On the Existence of X-Efficiency: A Reply. *J. Post Keynesian Econ.*, Fall 1981, *4*(1), pp. 149–51. [G: U.S.]

Friedman, Bernard and Pauly, Mark V. Cost Functions for a Service Firm with Variable Quality and Stochastic Demand: The Case of Hospitals. *Rev. Econ. Statist.*, November 1981, *63*(4), pp. 620–24. [G: U.S.]

Gilbert, Richard J. and Harris, Richard G. Investment Decisions with Economies of Scale and Learning. *Amer. Econ. Rev.*, May 1981, *71*(2), pp. 172–77.

Gold, Bela. Changing Perspectives on Size, Scale, and Returns: An Interpretive Survey. *J. Econ. Lit.*, March 1981, *19*(1), pp. 5–33.

Gould, Joseph R. On the Interpretation of Inferior Goods and Factors. *Economica*, November 1981, *48*(192), pp. 397–405.

Green, Richard D.; Pope, Rulon D. and Phipps, Tim T. Discriminating among Alternative Habit Formation Schemes in Single-Equation Demand Models. *Appl. Econ.*, September 1981, *13*(3), pp. 399–409. [G: U.S.]

Greenberg, Edward; Marshall, William J. and Yawitz, Jess B. The Technology of Risk and Return: Reply. *Amer. Econ. Rev.*, June 1981, *71*(3), pp. 491–92.

Griffin, James M. Engineering and Econometric Interpretations of Energy–Capital Complementarity: Comment. *Amer. Econ. Rev.*, December 1981, *71*(5), pp. 1100–1104. [G: U.S.]

Griffin, James M. Statistical Cost Analysis Re-Revisited: Reply. *Quart. J. Econ.*, February 1981, *96*(1), pp. 183–87.

Gronberg, Timothy J. and Meyer, Jack. Transport Inefficiency and the Choice of Spatial Pricing Mode. *J. Reg. Sci.*, November 1981, *21*(4), pp. 541–49.

Gui, Benedetto. Investment Decisions in a Worker-Managed Firm. *Econ. Anal. Worker's Manage.*, 1981, *15*(1), pp. 45–65.

Gunther, William. "Profit versus Quasi Rent in Predicting Short Run Firm Behavior:" A Comment. *Amer. Econ.*, Spring 1981, *25*(1), pp. 80–81.

Haber, Lawrence J. Factor Transferability: The Efficiency of Single Product and Multiproduct Firms. *Eastern Econ. J.*, April 1981, *7*(2), pp. 119–24.

Harmatuck, Donald J. A Motor Carrier Joint Cost Function: A Flexible Functional Form with Activity Prices. *J. Transp. Econ. Policy*, May 1981,

15(2), pp. 135–53. [G: U.S.]

Harris, Donald J. On the Timing of Wage Payments. *Cambridge J. Econ.*, December 1981, *5*(4), pp. 369–81.

Harris, Frederick H. deB. Value-Maximizing Price and Advertising with Stochastic Demand. *Southern Econ. J.*, October 1981, *48*(2), pp. 296–311.

Haruna, Shoji. Investment and Input Choices of a Monopolistic Firm under Demand Uncertainty: A Long Run Analysis. (In Japanese. With English summary.) *Econ. Stud. Quart.*, April 1981, *32*(1), pp. 45–55.

Henry, Claude. Criteres Simples Pour La Prise En Compte Du Risque. (With English summary.) *Econometrica*, January 1981, *49*(1), pp. 153–70.

Hey, John D. A Unified Theory of the Behaviour of Profit-Maximising, Labour-Managed and Joint-Stock Firms Operating under Uncertainty. *Econ. J.*, June 1981, *91*(362), pp. 364–74.

Hey, John D. Hedging and the Competitive Labor-Managed Firm under Price Uncertainty [Hedging and the Competitive Firm under Price Uncertainty]. *Amer. Econ. Rev.*, September 1981, *71*(4), pp. 753–57.

Hey, John D. and Suckling, John. Risk-Bearing in a Yugoslavian Labour-Managed Firm: Comment. *Oxford Econ. Pap.*, March 1981, *33*(1), pp. 170–73. [G: Yugoslavia]

Hicks, John R. Optimisation and Specialisation. In *Hicks, J.*, 1981, pp. 269–82.

Hiebert, L. Dean. Production Uncertainty and Factor Demands for the Competitive Firm: An Extension. *Southern Econ. J.*, July 1981, *48*(1), pp. 211–15.

Hildenbrand, Werner. Short-Run Production Functions Based on Microdata. *Econometrica*, September 1981, *49*(5), pp. 1095–1125.

Hughes, Joseph P. Giffen Inputs and the Theory of Multiple Production [Substitution and Expansion Effects in Production Theory: The Case of Joint Production]. *J. Econ. Theory*, October 1981, *25*(2), pp. 287–301.

Humphrey, David Burras. Scale Economies at Automated Clearinghouses. *J. Bank Res.*, Summer 1981, *12*(2), pp. 71–81. [G: U.S.]

Huppert, Rémi. Stratégies de développement des P.M.I. françaises. (Strategies and Growth of French Small Businesses. With English summary.) *Rev. Econ. Ind.*, 3rd Trimestre 1981, (17), pp. 26–41. [G: France]

Ilmakunnas, Pekka. Giffen Phenomena for Normal Inputs: The Multiproduct, Sales-Maximizing Firm. *Southern Econ. J.*, January 1981, *47*(3), pp. 598–605.

Ireland, Norman J. The Behaviour of the Labour Managed Firm and Disutility from Supplying Factor Services. *Econ. Anal. Worker's Manage.*, 1981, *15*(1), pp. 21–43.

Irvine, F. Owen, Jr. An Optimal Middleman Firm Price Adjustment Policy: The "Short-Run Inventory-Based Pricing Policy." *Econ. Inquiry*, April 1981, *19*(2), pp. 245–69.

Irvine, F. Owen, Jr. Retail Inventory Investment and the Cost of Capital. *Amer. Econ. Rev.*, September 1981, *71*(4), pp. 633–48. [G: U.S.]

James, Christopher. The Technology of Risk and Return: Comment. *Amer. Econ. Rev.*, June 1981, *71*(3), pp. 485–90.

Johnson, Marc A. and Pasour, E. C., Jr. An Opportunity Cost View of Fixed Asset Theory and the Overproduction Trap. *Amer. J. Agr. Econ.*, February 1981, *63*(1), pp. 1–7.

Kaldor, Nicholas. The Controversy on the Theory of Capital. In *Kaldor, N.*, 1981, *1937*, pp. 153–205.

Kaldor, Nicholas. The Equilibrium of the Firm. In *Kaldor, N.*, 1981, *1934*, pp. 34–50.

Kang, Heejoon and Brown, Gardner M. Partial and Full Elasticities of Substitution and the Energy–Capital Complementarity Controversy. In *Berndt, E. R. and Field, B. C., eds.*, 1981, pp. 81–89. [G: U.S.]

Kleinhückelskoten, Hans-Dieter and Spaetling, Dieter. Aspekte der Inferiorität und Superiorität als ökonomische Phänomene—Ein Beitrag zur Neuorientierung der mikroökonomischen Theorie. (Aspects of Inferiority and Superiority as Economic Phenomena—A Contribution to the Re-orientation of Macroeconomic Theory. With English summary.) *Jahr. Nationalökon. Statist.*, November 1981, *196*(6), pp. 511–26.

Kogelschatz, Hartmut. Equilibrium Preserving Aggregation in von Neumann Models. *Z. Nationalökon.*, 1981, *41*(3–4), pp. 265–78.

Kopp, Raymond J. Measuring the Technical Efficiency of Production: A Comment. *J. Econ. Theory*, December 1981, *25*(3), pp. 450–52.

Kopp, Raymond J. The Measurement of Productive Efficiency: A Reconsideration. *Quart. J. Econ.*, August 1981, *96*(3), pp. 477–503.

Kopp, Raymond J. and Smith, V. Kerry. Measuring the Prospects for Resource Substitution under Input and Technology Aggregations. In *Berndt, E. R. and Field, B. C., eds.*, 1981, pp. 145–73.

Landsberger, Michael and Subotnik, A. Some Anomalies in the Production Strategy of a Labour-managed Firm. *Economica*, May 1981, *48*(190), pp. 195–97.

Lazear, Edward P. Agency, Earnings Profiles, Productivity, and Hours Restrictions. *Amer. Econ. Rev.*, September 1981, *71*(4), pp. 606–20.

Lim, Chin. Risk Pooling and Intermediate Trading Agents. *Can. J. Econ.*, May 1981, *14*(2), pp. 261–75.

Lim, Chin. Theory of the Firm: Uncertainty and Choice of Experiments. *J. Econ. Theory*, June 1981, *24*(3), pp. 328–61.

Lippman, Steven A. and McCall, John J. Competitive Production and Increases in Risk. *Amer. Econ. Rev.*, March 1981, *71*(1), pp. 207–11.

Lloyd, P. J. A Knightian Model for the Analysis of Structural Adjustments by Firms. *Weltwirtsch. Arch.*, 1981, *117*(4), pp. 672–86.

Lucas, Robert E., Jr. Capacity, Overtime, and Empirical Production Functions. In *Lucas, R. E., Jr.*, 1981, *1970*, pp. 146–55.

Lucas, Robert E., Jr. Distributed Lags and Optimal Investment Policy. In *Lucas, R. E. and Sargent, T. J., eds.*, 1981, pp. 39–54.

Lucas, Robert E., Jr. Optimal Investment with Rational Expectations. In *Lucas, R. E. and Sargent, T. J., eds.*, 1981, pp. 55–66.

Lucas, Robert E., Jr. and Prescott, Edward C. Investment under Uncertainty. In *Lucas, R. E. and Sargent, T. J., eds.*, 1981, *1971*, pp. 67–90.

Lyon, Kenneth S. A Note on Long-Run and Short-Run Elasticities in the Theory of the Firm. *Southern Econ. J.*, October 1981, *48*(2), pp. 506–12.

Maccini, Louis J. On the Theory of the Firm Underlying Empirical Models of Aggregate Price Behavior. *Int. Econ. Rev.*, October 1981, *22*(3), pp. 609–24.

Maddala, G. S. and Roberts, R. Blaine. Statistical Cost Analysis Re-Revisited: Comment. *Quart. J. Econ.*, February 1981, *96*(1), pp. 177–81.

Maddigan, Ruth J. The Measurement of Vertical Integration. *Rev. Econ. Statist.*, August 1981, *63*(3), pp. 328–35.

Mai, Chao-cheng. Optimum Location and the Theory of the Firm under Demand Uncertainty. *Reg. Sci. Urban Econ.*, November 1981, *11*(4), pp. 549–57.

Malcomson, James M. Corporate Tax Policy and the Service Life of Capital Equipment. *Rev. Econ. Stud.*, April 1981, *48*(2), pp. 311–16.

Manne, Henry G. The Publicly Held Corporation as a Market Creation. *Z. ges. Staatswiss.*, December 1981, *137*(4), pp. 689–93.

Manning, R. A Nonsubstitution Theorem with Many Primary Factors. *J. Econ. Theory*, December 1981, *25*(3), pp. 442–49.

Marshall, William J.; Yawitz, Jess B. and Greenberg, Edward. Optimal Regulation under Uncertainty. *J. Finance*, September 1981, *36*(4), pp. 909–21.

Martin, Robert E. Stochastic Input Deliveries. *Econ. Inquiry*, October 1981, *19*(4), pp. 640–49.

Mauskopf, Eileen and Conrad, William E. Taxes, Inflation, and the Allocation of Capital. In *Federal Reserve System*, 1981, pp. 201–20. [G: U.S.]

McElroy, F. William. Scale and Cost Elasticity in the Multiproduct Case. *Atlantic Econ. J.*, July 1981, *9*(2), pp. 60–61.

McGaw, Richard L. The Supply of Effort in a Fishery. *Appl. Econ.*, June 1981, *13*(2), pp. 245–53. [G: Canada]

McNally, Mary. On X-Efficiency: Comment [On the Existence of X-Efficiency]. *J. Post Keynesian Econ.*, Fall 1981, *4*(1), pp. 145–48. [G: U.S.]

Metcalfe, J. S. and Steedman, Ian W. On Two Production Possibility Frontiers. *Metroecon.*, Feb.-Oct. 1981, *33*(1–2–3), pp. 1–19.

de Meza, David. "Perverse" Long-run and Short-run Factor Demand Curves. *Economica*, August 1981, *48*(191), pp. 299–303.

Miller, Jeffrey B. and Murrell, Peter. Limitations on the Use of Information-Revealing Incentive Schemes in Economic Organizations. *J. Compar. Econ.*, September 1981, *5*(3), pp. 251–71.

Milne, Frank. The Firm's Objective Function as a Collective Choice Problem. *Public Choice*, 1981, *37*(3), pp. 473–86.

von Mises, Ludwig. Inconvertible Capital. In *von Mises, L.*, 1981, pp. 217–31.

Mittelhammer, Ron C.; Matulich, Scott C. and Bushaw, D. On Implicit Forms of Multiproduct–Multifactor Production Functions. *Amer. J. Agr. Econ.*, February 1981, *63*(1), pp. 164–68.

Moore, George R. Taxes, Inflation, and Capital Formation. In *Federal Reserve System*, 1981, pp. 303–26.

Morrison, Catherine J. and Berndt, Ernst R. Short-Run Labor Productivity in a Dynamic Model. *J. Econometrics*, August 1981, *16*(3), pp. 339–65.

Ng, Yew-Kwang. Incomes Policies: Conditions for Voluntary Compliance. *Manchester Sch. Econ. Soc. Stud.*, June 1981, *49*(2), pp. 111–28.

Norman, George. Uniform Pricing as an Optimal Spatial Pricing Policy. *Economica*, February 1981, *48*(189), pp. 87–91.

Oswald, Andrew J. The Theory of Internal Wage and Employment Structure. *Bell J. Econ. (See Rand J. Econ. after 4/85)*, Spring 1981, *12*(1), pp. 263–71.

Panagariya, Arvind. Variable Returns to Scale in Production and Patterns of Specialization. *Amer. Econ. Rev.*, March 1981, *71*(1), pp. 221–30.

Panzar, John C. and Willig, Robert D. Economies of Scope. *Amer. Econ. Rev.*, May 1981, *71*(2), pp. 268–72.

Perry, Martin K. The Manager and the Competitive Firm's Supply. *Southern Econ. J.*, January 1981, *47*(3), pp. 630–39.

Petrović, Pavle. Income Distribution, Prices and Choice of Technique in the Labour-Managed Economy. *Econ. Anal. Worker's Manage.*, 1981, *15*(4), pp. 433–44.

Phlips, Louis and Thisse, Jacques-François. Pricing, Distribution and the Supply of Storage. *Europ. Econ. Rev.*, February 1981, *15*(2), pp. 225–43.

Pissarides, Christopher A. Uncertainty and the Demand for Labour by Dynamically-Monopsonistic Firms. *Greek Econ. Rev.*, December 1981, *3*(3), pp. 279–94.

Prakash, Shri. Cost Based Prices in Indian Economy, 1951–74. *Malayan Econ. Rev. (See Singapore Econ. Rev.)*, April 1981, *26*(1), pp. 1–14.
[G: India]

Pratt, Michael D. Firm Behavior under Regulatory Constraint: An Immanent Criticism [Depreciation, Tax Policy and Firm Behavior under Regulatory Constraint]. *Southern Econ. J.*, July 1981, *48*(1), pp. 235–38. [G: U.S.]

Ramachandran, Rama V. Scale Elasticity in a Static and Dynamic Economy. *Indian Econ. J.*, October–December 1981, *29*(2), pp. 65–77.

Ramachandran, Rama V.; Russell, William R. and Seo, Tae Kun. Response to Comments by John D. Hey and John Suckling [Risk Bearing in a Yugoslavian Labour-Managed Firm]. *Oxford Econ. Pap.*, March 1981, *33*(1), pp. 174–75.
[G: Yugoslavia]

Rao, P. Someshwar. Factor Prices and Labour Productivity in the Canadian Manufacturing Industries. *Empirical Econ.*, 1981, *6*(4), pp. 187–202.
[G: Canada]

Reich, Michael and Devine, James. The Microeconomics of Conflict and Hierarchy in Capitalist Production. *Rev. Radical Polit. Econ.*, Winter 1981, *12*(4), pp. 27–45.

Reinganum, Jennifer F. On the Diffusion of New Technology: A Game Theoretic Approach. *Rev. Econ. Stud.*, July 1981, *48*(3), pp. 395–405.

Reinwald, Thomas P. Profit versus Quasi Rent in Predicting Short Run Firm Behavior: A Note. *Amer. Econ.*, Spring 1981, *25*(1), pp. 78–79.

Rempala, Ryszarda. On the Multicommodity Arrow–Karlin Inventory Model. In *Chikán, A., ed. (II)*, 1981, pp. 491–99.

Richter, Knut. Solving a Capacity Constrained Deterministic Dynamic Inventory Problem. In *Chikán, A., ed. (II)*, 1981, pp. 501–09.

Robinson, Joan. Misunderstanding in the Theory of Production. In *Robinson, J.*, 1981, *1979*, pp. 135–40.

Sakai, Yasuhiro. Uncertainty and the Multiproduct Firm: A Duality Approach. *Econ. Stud. Quart.*, April 1981, *32*(1), pp. 66–76.

Salvadori, Neri. Falling Rate of Profit with a Constant Real Wage: An Example. *Cambridge J. Econ.*, March 1981, *5*(1), pp. 59–66.

Sandler, Todd and Tschirhart, John. On the Number and Membership Size of Consumer Managed Firms [The Economics of Consumer-Managed Firms]. *Southern Econ. J.*, April 1981, *47*(4), pp. 1086–91.

Sarantis, Nicholas C. On Optimal Dynamic Adjustment of Capital and Labour under Non-Stationary Expectations. *Greek Econ. Rev.*, April 1981, *3*(1), pp. 46–58.

Satterthwaite, Mark A. On the Scope of the Stockholder Unanimity Theorems. *Int. Econ. Rev.*, February 1981, *22*(1), pp. 119–33.

Scarf, Herbert E. Production Sets with Indivisibilities—Part II: The Case of Two Activities. *Econometrica*, March 1981, *49*(2), pp. 395–423.

Scarf, Herbert E. Production Sets with Indivisibilities—Part I: Generalities. *Econometrica*, January 1981, *49*(1), pp. 1–32.

Schanze, Erich. Der Beitrag von Coase zu Recht und Ökonomie des Unternehmens. (Coase's Contribution to Law and Economics of Business Organizations. With English summary.) *Z. ges. Staatswiss.*, December 1981, *137*(4), pp. 694–701.

Schim van der Loeff, Sybrand and Harkema, Rins. Estimation and Testing of Alternative Production Function Models. *J. Macroecon.*, Winter 1981, *3*(1), pp. 33–53. [G: Netherlands]

Schmitz, Andrew; Shalit, Haim and Turnovsky, Stephen J. Producer Welfare and the Preference for Price Stability. *Amer. J. Agr. Econ.*, February 1981, *63*(1), pp. 157–60.

Shapiro, Nina. Pricing and the Growth of the Firm. *J. Post Keynesian Econ.*, Fall 1981, *4*(1), pp. 85–100.

Shapiro, Nina. The Neoclassical Concept of Capital. *Australian Econ. Pap.*, June 1981, *20*(36), pp. 42–62.

Sheffrin, Steven M. Dynamics of Investment in a Perfect Foresight Model. *J. Econ. Bus.*, Winter 1981, *33*(2), pp. 160–65.

Shipley, David D. Pricing Objectives in British Manufacturing Industry. *J. Ind. Econ.*, June 1981, *29*(4), pp. 429–43. [G: U.K.]

Shrieves, Ronald E. Uncertainty, the Theory of Production, and Optimal Operating Leverage. *Southern Econ. J.*, January 1981, *47*(3), pp. 690–702.

Siebert, W. Stanley and Addison, John T. A Geometric Derivation of the Firm's Input Decision.

Australian Econ. Pap., June 1981, *20*(36), pp. 142–49.

Sonnenschein, Hugo. Price Dynamics and the Disappearance of Short-Run Profits: An Example. *J. Math. Econ.*, July 1981, *8*(2), pp. 201–04.

Stapleton, David C. Inferring Long-term Substitution Possibilities from Cross-Section and Time-Series Data. In *Berndt, E. R. and Field, B. C., eds.*, 1981, pp. 93–118.

Stewart, Marion B. Uncertain Demand and Product Quality in a Price-Regulated Market. *Can. J. Econ.*, August 1981, *14*(3), pp. 507–14.

Stoneman, Patrick. Intra-Firm Diffusion, Bayesian Learning and Profitability. *Econ. J.*, June 1981, *91*(362), pp. 375–88.

Swan, Peter L. Durability and Taxes: Market Structure and Quasi-Capital Market Distortion. *Econometrica*, March 1981, *49*(2), pp. 425–35.

Taub, Allan J. Futures Markets and the Cooperative Firm under Price Uncertainty. *Eastern Econ. J.*, July-Oct. 1981, *7*(3–4), pp. 157–61.

Thirlby, G. F. Economists' Cost Rules and Equilibrium Theory. In *Buchanan, J. M. and Thirlby, G. F., eds.*, 1981, *1960*, pp. 273–87.

Thirlby, G. F. The Economist's Description of Business Behaviour. In *Buchanan, J. M. and Thirlby, G. F., eds.*, 1981, *1952*, pp. 201–24.

Thirlby, G. F. The Ruler. In *Buchanan, J. M. and Thirlby, G. F., eds.*, 1981, *1946*, pp. 163–98.

Thirlby, G. F. The Subjective Theory of Value and Accounting 'Cost.' In *Buchanan, J. M. and Thirlby, G. F., eds.*, 1981, *1946*, pp. 135–61.

Tompkinson, Paul. The Price Equation and Excess Demand. *Oxford Bull. Econ. Statist.*, May 1981, *43*(2), pp. 173–83.

Varri, Paolo. Il valore dei residui negli schemi di produzione congiunta. (The Value of Residual Scraps in Joint Production Schemes. With English summary.) *Giorn. Econ.*, July–August 1981, *40*(7–8), pp. 447–64.

Wagstaff, Peter. The Stability of Two Decentralized Adjustment Schemes. *J. Econ. Dynam. Control*, May 1981, *3*(2), pp. 183–90.

Wahlroos, Björn. On the Economics of Multiplant Operation: Some Concepts and an Example. *J. Ind. Econ.*, March 1981, *29*(3), pp. 231–45. [G: N. America; U.K.; W. Europe; Japan; India]

Watkins, Thayer H. In Multi-Plant Industries the Efficiency-Relevant Marginal Cost Is the Minimum Average Cost of the Marginal Plant. *Southern Econ. J.*, July 1981, *48*(1), pp. 149–55.

Weymark, John A. On Sums of Production Set Frontiers. *Rev. Econ. Stud.*, January 1981, *48*(1), pp. 179–83.

Whitmore, Harland William, Jr. Plant Location and the Demand for Investment: A Theoretical Analysis. *J. Reg. Sci.*, February 1981, *21*(1), pp. 89–101.

Williamson, Oliver E. On the Nature of the Firm: Some Recent Developments. *Z. ges. Staatswiss.*, December 1981, *137*(4), pp. 675–80.

Wills, Hugh R. Estimating Input Demand Equations by Direct and Indirect Methods. *Rev. Econ. Stud.*, April 1981, *48*(2), pp. 255–70. [G: U.S.]

Winter, Ralph A. Majority Choice and the Objective

Function of the Firm under Uncertainty: Note. *Bell J. Econ. (See Rand J. Econ. after 4/85)*, Spring 1981, *12*(1), pp. 335–37.

Winter, Sidney G. Attention Allocation and Input Proportions. *J. Econ. Behav. Organ.*, March 1981, *2*(1), pp. 31–46.

Wiseman, Jack. Uncertainty, Costs, and Collectivist Economic Planning. In *Buchanan, J. M. and Thirlby, G. F., eds.*, 1981, *1953*, pp. 227–43.

Womer, Norman Keith. Some Propositions on Cost Functions. *Southern Econ. J.*, April 1981, *47*(4), pp. 1111–19.

You, Jong S. Money, Technology, and the Production Function: An Empirical Study. *Can. J. Econ.*, August 1981, *14*(3), pp. 515–24. [G: Canada]

Zind, Richard G. Modèle d'estimation de l'élasticité de substitution et du progrès technologique. (Estimation of the Elasticity of Substitution and Technological Change: A Model. With English summary.) *L'Actual. Econ.*, April–June 1981, *57*(2), pp. 148–59.

Zylberberg, André. Flexibilité, incertain et théorie de la demande de travail. (Flexibility, Incertitude, and Theory of the Demand for Labor. With English summary.) *Ann. INSEE*, April–June 1981, (42), pp. 31–52.

0224 Theory of Factor Distribution and Distributive Shares

Barr, Kenneth. On the Capitalist Enterprise. *Rev. Radical Polit. Econ.*, Winter 1981, *12*(4), pp. 60–70.

Bellante, Don and Long, James E. The Political Economy of the Rent-Seeking Society: The Case of Public Employees and Their Unions. *J. Lab. Res.*, Spring 1981, *2*(1), pp. 1–14. [G: U.S.]

Gintis, Herbert and Bowles, Samuel. Structure and Practice in the Labor Theory of Value. *Rev. Radical Polit. Econ.*, Winter 1981, *12*(4), pp. 1–26.

von Hayek, F. A. The Repercussions of Rent Restrictions. In *Block, W. and Olsen, E., eds.*, 1981, pp. 171–86.

Labus, Miroljub. Fiksni kapital, negativne radne vrednosti i izbor tehnike. (Fixed Capital, Negative Labour Values and Choice of Technique. With English summary.) *Econ. Anal. Worker's Manage.*, 1981, *15*(4), pp. 445–58.

Olson, Mancur and Bailey, Martin J. Positive Time Preference. *J. Polit. Econ.*, February 1981, *89*(1), pp. 1–25.

Petrović, Pavle. Income Distribution, Prices and Choice of Technique in the Labour-Managed Economy. *Econ. Anal. Worker's Manage.*, 1981, *15*(4), pp. 433–44.

Robinson, Joan. Debate: 1970s. In *Robinson, J.*, 1981, pp. 123–30.

Robinson, Joan. Piero Sraffa: *Production of Commodities by Means of Commodities.* In *Robinson, J.*, 1981, *1961*, pp. 144–50.

Robinson, Joan. Retrospect: 1980. In *Robinson, J.*, 1981, pp. 131–34.

Samuels, Warren J. The Historical Treatment of the Problem of Value Judgements: An Interpretation. In *Solo, R. A. and Anderson, C. W., eds.*, 1981,

pp. 57–69.

Shapiro, Nina. The Neoclassical Concept of Capital. *Australian Econ. Pap.*, June 1981, *20*(36), pp. 42–62.

Silver, M. S. and Golder, P. Negative Value Added and the Measurement of Production Changes. *J. Econ. Stud.*, 1981, *8*(1), pp. 3–15.

Sirkin, Gerald. Rent Seeking: Comments. In *Sirkin, G., ed.*, 1981, pp. 191–94.

Stallaerts, Robert. The Effect of Capital Intensity on Income in Yugoslav Industry. *Econ. Anal. Worker's Manage.*, 1981, *15*(4), pp. 501–15.
[G: Yugoslavia]

Tinbergen, Jan. Misunderstandings Concerning Income Distribution Policies. *De Economist*, 1981, *129*(1), pp. 8–20.

Tullock, Gordon. Rent Seeking. In *Sirkin, G., ed.*, 1981, pp. 165–90.

0225 Theory of Firm and Industry under Competitive Market Structure

Amit, Eilon. On Quality and Price Regulation under Competition and under Monopoly. *Southern Econ. J.*, April 1981, *47*(4), pp. 1056–62.

Clark, Larry R. A Note on Arrow's Suggested Environment for Theories of Price Adjustment. *Scot. J. Polit. Econ.*, November 1981, *28*(3), pp. 284–90.

Cooper, Charles. Aspects of Transfer Pricing in Machinery Markets. In *Murray, R., ed.*, 1981, pp. 133–44.

Dasgupta, A. K. Perfect Competition and Economic Theory. *Indian Econ. Rev.*, July-Sept. 1981, *16*(3), pp. 155–67.

Dennis, Ken G. Provable Theorems and Refutable Hypotheses: The Case of Competitive Theory. *J. Econ. Issues*, March 1981, *15*(1), pp. 95–112.

Diewert, W. Erwin. The Comparative Statics of Industry Long-Run Equilibrium. *Can. J. Econ.*, February 1981, *14*(1), pp. 78–92.

Fink, Gerhard. Price Distortions in the Austrian and in the Hungarian Economy. *Z. Nationalökon.*, 1981, *41*(1–2), pp. 111–32.
[G: Austria; Hungary]

Gronberg, Timothy J. and Meyer, Jack. Competitive Equilibria in Uniform Delivered Pricing Models. *Amer. Econ. Rev.*, September 1981, *71*(4), pp. 758–63.

Hiebert, L. Dean. Production Uncertainty and Factor Demands for the Competitive Firm: An Extension. *Southern Econ. J.*, July 1981, *48*(1), pp. 211–15.

Isaac, R. Mark and Plott, Charles R. The Opportunity for Conspiracy in Restraint of Trade: An Experimental Study. *J. Econ. Behav. Organ.*, March 1981, *2*(1), pp. 1–30.

Kamien, Morton I. and Schwartz, Nancy L. Technical Change Inclinations of a Resource Monopolist. In *[Weiler, E. T.]*, 1981, pp. 41–53.

Levhari, David and Pindyck, Robert S. The Pricing of Durable Exhaustible Resources. *Quart. J. Econ.*, August 1981, *96*(3), pp. 365–77.

Mestelman, Stuart. Corrective Production Subsidies in an Increasing Cost Industry: A Note on a Baumol–Oates Proposition. *Can. J. Econ.*, February

1981, *14*(1), pp. 124–30.

Murray, Robin. Transfer Pricing and Its Control: Alternative Approaches. In *Murray, R., ed.*, 1981, pp. 147–76.

Pakravan, Karim. Exhaustible Resource Models and Predictions of Crude Oil Prices—Some Preliminary Results. *Energy Econ.*, July 1981, *3*(3), pp. 169–77.
[G: OPEC]

Pindyck, Robert S. Models of Resource Markets and the Explanation of Resource Price Behaviour. *Energy Econ.*, July 1981, *3*(3), pp. 130–39.

Riley, John G. and Samuelson, William F. Optimal Auctions. *Amer. Econ. Rev.*, June 1981, *71*(3), pp. 381–92.

Saving, T. R. and De Vany, Arthur S. Uncertain Markets, Reliability and Peak-Load Pricing. *Southern Econ. J.*, April 1981, *47*(4), pp. 908–23.

Schlesinger, Harris. A Note on the Consistency of Non-Profit-Maximizing Behavior with Perfect Competition. *Southern Econ. J.*, October 1981, *48*(2), pp. 513–16.

Smith, James L. Non-Aggressive Bidding Behavior and the "Winner's Curse." *Econ. Inquiry*, July 1981, *19*(3), pp. 380–88.

Smith, Vernon L. An Empirical Study of Decentralized Institutions of Monopoly Restraint. In *[Weiler, E. T.]*, 1981, pp. 83–106.

Taub, Allan J. Futures Markets and the Cooperative Firm under Price Uncertainty. *Eastern Econ. J.*, July-Oct. 1981, *7*(3–4), pp. 157–61.

Zabel, Edward. Competitive Firm Behavior under Risk in Disequilibrium Trading. *Econ. Inquiry*, July 1981, *19*(3), pp. 389–409.

0226 Theory of Firm and Industry under Imperfectly Competitive Market Structure

Amit, Eilon. On Quality and Price Regulation under Competition and under Monopoly. *Southern Econ. J.*, April 1981, *47*(4), pp. 1056–62.

Artle, Roland A. Competitive Behavior: Comments. In *[Grether, E. T.]*, 1981, pp. 128–30.

Barro, Robert J. A Theory of Monopolistic Price Adjustment. In *Barro, R. J.*, 1981, *1972*, pp. 203–12.

Baseman, Kenneth C. Sustainability and the Entry Process. *Amer. Econ. Rev.*, May 1981, *71*(2), pp. 273–77.

Baumol, William J. and Willig, Robert D. Fixed Costs, Sunk Costs, Entry Barriers, and Sustainability of Monopoly. *Quart. J. Econ.*, August 1981, *96*(3), pp. 405–31.

Beck, Roger L. Competition for Patent Monopolies. In *Zerbe, R. O., Jr., ed.*, 1981, pp. 91–110.

Bourguignon, Francoise and Sethi, Suresh P. Dynamic Optimal Pricing and (Possibly) Advertising in the Face of Various Kinds of Potential Entrants. *J. Econ. Dynam. Control*, May 1981, *3*(2), pp. 119–40.

Brennan, Geoffrey and Walsh, Cliff. A Monopoly Model of Public Goods Provision: The Uniform Pricing Case. *Amer. Econ. Rev.*, March 1981, *71*(1), pp. 196–206.

Bresnahan, Timothy F. Duopoly Models with Consistent Conjectures. *Amer. Econ. Rev.*, December 1981, *71*(5), pp. 934–45.

Bressler, Barry. Search, Information, and Market Structure: Comments. In *Galatin, M. and Leiter, R. D., eds.,* 1981, pp. 98–103.

Brick, Ivan E. and Jagpal, Harsharanjeet S. Monopoly Price-Advertising Decision-Making under Uncertainty. *J. Ind. Econ.,* March 1981, *29*(3), pp. 279–85.

Burns, Michael E. and Walsh, Cliff. Market Provision of Price-excludable Public Goods: A General Analysis. *J. Polit. Econ.,* February 1981, *89*(1), pp. 166–91.

Chambers, Donald R. and Lovell, C. A. Knox. Some Neglected Stackelberg Duopoly Models. *Atlantic Econ. J.,* July 1981, *9*(2), pp. 25–29.

Chambers, Robert G. The Monopsonistic Firm in an Uncertain World. *Atlantic Econ. J.,* July 1981, *9*(2), pp. 35–39.

Clarke, R. Sraffa's 'Laws of Returns'—A Reappraisal. *Indian Econ. J.,* January–March 1981, *28*(3), pp. 35–50.

Cooper, Charles. Aspects of Transfer Pricing in Machinery Markets. In *Murray, R., ed.,* 1981, pp. 133–44.

Cowling, Keith. Oligopoly, Distribution and the Rate of Profit. *Europ. Econ. Rev.,* February 1981, *15*(2), pp. 195–224.

Daniel, Coldwell, III. The New Theory of Public Utilities: The Case of the Natural Monopoly. *Antitrust Bull.,* Spring 1981, *26*(1), pp. 133–43.
    [G: U.S.]

Das, Satya P. Long Run Behavior of a Monopolistically Competitive Firm. *Int. Econ. Rev.,* February 1981, *22*(1), pp. 159–65.

Dasgupta, Partha. Resource Pricing and Technological Innovations under Oligopoly: A Theoretical Exploration. *Scand. J. Econ.,* 1981, *83*(2), pp. 289–317.

Dasgupta, Partha and Stiglitz, Joseph E. Entry, Innovation, Exit: Towards a Dynamic Theory of Oligopolistic Industrial Structure. *Europ. Econ. Rev.,* February 1981, *15*(2), pp. 137–58.

Dessant, J. W. and Morgan, R. H. Limit Pricing and the Theory of the Firm. *Brit. Rev. Econ. Issues,* Spring 1981, *2*(8), pp. 98–106.

DiLorenzo, Thomas J. Corporate Management, Property Rights and the X–istence of X-inefficiency. *Southern Econ. J.,* July 1981, *48*(1), pp. 116–23.

Dirlam, Joel B. Marginal Cost Pricing Tests for Predation: Naive Welfare Economics and Public Policy. *Antitrust Bull.,* Winter 1981, *26*(4), pp. 769–814.   [G: U.S.]

Dnes, A. W. The Case of Monopoly and Pollution [Monopoly Power as a Means to Pollution Control]. *J. Ind. Econ.,* December 1981, *30*(2), pp. 213–16.

Donaldson, David and Eaton, B. Curtis. Patience, More Than Its Own Reward: A Note on Price Discrimination. *Can. J. Econ.,* February 1981, *14*(1), pp. 93–105.

Dorward, Neil. "Impacts of Distance on Microeconomic Theory": A Critique. *Manchester Sch. Econ. Soc. Stud.,* September 1981, *49*(3), pp. 245–58.

Eaton, B. Curtis and Lipsey, Richard G. Capital,

Commitment, and Entry Equilibrium. *Bell J. Econ. (See Rand J. Econ. after 4/85),* Autumn 1981, *12*(2), pp. 593–604.

Eckalbar, John C. Stable Quantities in Fixed Price Disequilibrium. *J. Econ. Theory,* October 1981, *25*(2), pp. 302–13.

Eden, Benjamin. Toward a Theory of Competitive Price Adjustment. *Rev. Econ. Stud.,* April 1981, *48*(2), pp. 199–216.

Edwards, Clark. Keynes' Monopolistic Theory of Employment, Interest, and Money. *Agr. Econ. Res.,* April 1981, *33*(2), pp. 7–17.

Ekelund, Robert B., Jr.; Higgins, Richard S. and Smithson, Charles W. Can Discrimination Increase Employment: A Neoclassical Perspective. *Southern Econ. J.,* January 1981, *47*(3), pp. 664–73.

Endres, Alfred. The Provision of Product Attributes: Monopolistic Equilibrium and Social Optimum. *Metroecon.,* Feb.-Oct. 1981, *33*(1–2–3), pp. 129–44.

Faith, Roger L. and Tollison, Robert D. The Allocative Equivalence of Contracting and Regulation. *Atlantic Econ. J.,* July 1981, *9*(2), pp. 57–59.

Fan, Yiu-Kwan. Behavioral Rules, Inventory Adjustments and the Stability of Macroequilibria. *J. Econ. Behav. Organ.,* September 1981, *2*(3), pp. 257–72.

Finsinger, Jörg and Vogelsang, Ingo. Alternative Institutional Frameworks for Price Incentive Mechanism. *Kyklos,* 1981, *34*(3), pp. 388–404.

Freixas, Xavier. Une analyse coût-avantage des mécanismes d'allocation: l'approche prix-quantités. (A Cost–Benefit Analysis of Allocation Mechanisms: The Prices versus Quantities Approach. With English summary.) *Revue Écon.,* November 1981, *32*(6), pp. 1074–86.

Friedman, James W. A Note on the Turnpike Properties of Time Dependent Supergames [Non-Cooperative Equilibria in Time Dependent Supergames]. *Econometrica,* June 1981, *49*(4), pp. 1087–88.

Friedman, James W. Limit Pricing and Entry. *J. Econ. Dynam. Control,* August 1981, *3*(3), pp. 319–23.

Galatin, Malcolm. Search, Information, and Market Structure. In *Galatin, M. and Leiter, R. D., eds.,* 1981, pp. 83–97.

Gehrig, Wilhelm. On the Complete Solution of the Linear Cournot Oligopoly Model. *Rev. Econ. Stud.,* October 1981, *48*(4), pp. 667–70.

Gilley, Otis W. and Karels, Gordon V. The Competitive Effect in Bonus Bidding: New Evidence. *Bell J. Econ. (See Rand J. Econ. after 4/85),* Autumn 1981, *12*(2), pp. 637–48.

Greenhut, Melvyn L. Mr. Dorward and Impacts of Distance on Microeconomic Theory. *Manchester Sch. Econ. Soc. Stud.,* September 1981, *49*(3), pp. 259–65.

Grossman, Sanford J. Nash Equilibrium and the Industrial Organization of Markets with Large Fixed Costs. *Econometrica,* September 1981, *49*(5), pp. 1149–72.

Grossman, Sanford J. The Informational Role of Warranties and Private Disclosure about Product Quality. *J. Law Econ.,* December 1981, *24*(3),

pp. 461–83.

Harris, Milton and Raviv, Artur. A Theory of Monopoly Pricing Schemes with Demand Uncertainty. *Amer. Econ. Rev.*, June 1981, *71*(3), pp. 347–65.

Harris, Richard G. Price and Entry Regulations with Large Fixed Costs. *Quart. J. Econ.*, November 1981, *96*(4), pp. 643–55.

Hoel, Michael. Resource Extraction by a Monopolist with Influence over the Rate of Return on Non-Resource Assets. *Int. Econ. Rev.*, February 1981, *22*(1), pp. 147–57.

Holahan, William L. and Schuler, Richard E. Competitive Entry in a Spatial Economy: Market Equilibrium and Welfare Implications. *J. Reg. Sci.*, August 1981, *21*(3), pp. 341–57.

Horowitz, Ira. Limit Pricing in a Cournot-Stackelberg Market. *Z. Nationalökon.*, 1981, *41*(1–2), pp. 133–39.

Hüpen, Rolf and Seitz, Tycho. Neues zu einem alten Problem—Preisdifferenzierung bei willkürlicher Marktteilung. (An Old Problem Reconsidered—Price Discrimination with Arbitrary Market Segmentation. With English summary.) *Jahr. Nationalökon. Statist.*, July 1981, *196*(4), pp. 333–40.

Isaac, R. Mark and Plott, Charles R. Price Controls and the Behavior of Auction Markets: An Experimental Examination. *Amer. Econ. Rev.*, June 1981, *71*(3), pp. 448–59.

Isaac, R. Mark and Plott, Charles R. The Opportunity for Conspiracy in Restraint of Trade: An Experimental Study. *J. Econ. Behav. Organ.*, March 1981, *2*(1), pp. 1–30.

Ishii, Yasunori. A Study on Quantity Setting Monopoly under Demand Uncertainty. *Econ. Stud. Quart.*, April 1981, *32*(1), pp. 56–65.

Jørgensen, Steffen. En note om Dorfman-Steiner teoremet. (A Note on the Dorfman-Steiner Theorem. With English summary.) *Nationaløkon. Tidsskr.*, 1981, *119*(3), pp. 409–10.

Jovanovic, Boyan. Entry with Private Information. *Bell J. Econ. (See Rand J. Econ. after 4/85)*, Autumn 1981, *12*(2), pp. 649–60.

Kaldor, Nicholas. Market Imperfection and Excess Capacity. In *Kaldor, N.*, 1981, *1935*, pp. 62–80.

Kaldor, Nicholas. Mrs. Robinson's 'Economics of Imperfect Competition.' In *Kaldor, N.*, 1981, *1934*, pp. 53–61.

Kaldor, Nicholas. Professor Chamberlin on Monopolistic and Imperfect Competition. In *Kaldor, N.*, 1981, *1938*, pp. 81–95.

Kaneko, Mamoru. A Bilateral Monopoly and the Nash Cooperative Solution. *J. Econ. Theory*, June 1981, *24*(3), pp. 311–27.

Kelly, William A., Jr. A Generalized Interpretation of the Herfindahl Index. *Southern Econ. J.*, July 1981, *48*(1), pp. 50–57.

Koenker, Roger W. and Perry, Martin K. Product Differentiation, Monopolistic Competition, and Public Policy. *Bell J. Econ. (See Rand J. Econ. after 4/85)*, Spring 1981, *12*(1), pp. 217–31.

Krugman, Paul R. Increasing Returns, Monopolistic Competition, and International Trade. In *Bhagwati, J. N., ed.*, 1981, *1979*, pp. 88–99.

Lee, Dwight R. Monopoly, Price Controls, and the Exploitation of Nonrenewable Resources. *J. Energy Devel.*, Autumn 1981, *7*(1), pp. 111–20.

Lefever, J. Timothy. Predatory Pricing Rules: A Comment on Williamson's Output Restriction Rule [Predatory Pricing: A Strategic and Welfare Analysis]. *Yale Law J.*, June 1981, *90*(7), pp. 1639–45. **[G: U.S.]**

Leland, Hayne E. The Informational Role of Warranties and Private Disclosure about Product Quality: Comment. *J. Law Econ.*, December 1981, *24*(3), pp. 485–89.

Leontief, Wassily W. Multiple-Plant Firms: Comment. In *Patinkin, D.*, 1981, *1947*, pp. 115.

Levhari, David and Pindyck, Robert S. The Pricing of Durable Exhaustible Resources. *Quart. J. Econ.*, August 1981, *96*(3), pp. 365–77.

Lim, Chin. Theory of the Firm: Uncertainty and Choice of Experiments. *J. Econ. Theory*, June 1981, *24*(3), pp. 328–61.

Littlechild, S. C. Misleading Calculations of the Social Costs of Monopoly Power. *Econ. J.*, June 1981, *91*(362), pp. 348–63. **[G: U.S.; U.K.]**

Loomes, Graham. Why Oligopoly Prices Don't Stick. *J. Econ. Stud.*, 1981, *8*(1), pp. 37–46.

Lovell, C. A. Knox and Wertz, Kenneth L. Price Discrimination in Related Markets. *Econ. Inquiry*, July 1981, *19*(3), pp. 488–94.

Mabawonku, A. F. Monopoly and Market Concentration in the Process of Economic Development: A Review of the Literature. *Indian Econ. J.*, October–December 1981, *29*(2), pp. 23–34.

Makepeace, Gerald H. Measuring the Effects of Monopolies in a Partial Monopoly Model. *Scot. J. Polit. Econ.*, November 1981, *28*(3), pp. 236–55.

Meisel, John B. Entry, Multiple-Brand Firms and Market Share Instability. *J. Ind. Econ.*, June 1981, *29*(4), pp. 375–84. **[G: U.S.]**

Ménard, Claude. D'un objet économique non identifié. (With English summary.) *Écon. Appl.*, 1981, *34*(1), pp. 141–59.

Moulin, Hervé. Deterrence and Cooperation: A Classification of Two-Person Games. *Europ. Econ. Rev.*, February 1981, *15*(2), pp. 179–93.

Mueller, Dennis C. and Cowling, Keith. The Social Costs of Monopoly Power Revisited. *Econ. J.*, September 1981, *91*(363), pp. 721–25. **[G: U.S.; U.K.]**

Murray, Robin. Transfer Pricing and Its Control: Alternative Approaches. In *Murray, R., ed.*, 1981, pp. 147–76.

Narver, John C. On the Unresponsiveness of Market Price. In *[Grether, E. T.]*, 1981, pp. 14–29.

Newbery, David M. G. Dominant Firm Models of Resource Depletion: Comment. In *Currie, D.; Peel, D. and Peters, W., eds.*, 1981, pp. 101–06.

Newbery, David M. G. Oil Prices, Cartels, and the Problem of Dynamic Inconsistency. *Econ. J.*, September 1981, *91*(363), pp. 617–46.

Nishimura, Kazuo and Friedman, James W. Existence of Nash Equilibrium in *n* Person Games without Quasi-Concavity. *Int. Econ. Rev.*, October 1981, *22*(3), pp. 637–48.

Norman, George. Spatial Competition and Spatial Price Discrimination. *Rev. Econ. Stud.*, January 1981, *48*(1), pp. 97–111.

Nti, Kofi O. and Shubik, Martin. Duopoly with Differentiated Products and Entry Barriers. *South-*

ern Econ. J., July 1981, *48*(1), pp. 129–86.

Nti, Kofi O. and Shubik, Martin. Noncooperative Oligopoly with Entry. *J. Econ. Theory,* April 1981, *24*(2), pp. 187–204.

Ohta, Hiroshi. The Price Effects of Spatial Competition. *Rev. Econ. Stud.,* April 1981, *48*(2), pp. 317–25.

Ong, Nai-Pew. Target Pricing, Competition, and Growth. *J. Post Keynesian Econ.,* Fall 1981, *4*(1), pp. 101–16.

Oren, Shmuel S. and Smith, Stephen A. Critical Mass and Tariff Structure in Electronic Communications Markets. *Bell J. Econ. (See Rand J. Econ. after 4/85),* Autumn 1981, *12*(2), pp. 467–87.

Pakravan, Karim. Exhaustible Resource Models and Predictions of Crude Oil Prices—Some Preliminary Results. *Energy Econ.,* July 1981, *3*(3), pp. 169–77. **[G: OPEC]**

Paroush, Jacob and Peles, Yoram C. A Combined Monopoly and Optimal Packaging. *Europ. Econ. Rev.,* March 1981, *15*(3), pp. 373–83.

Patinkin, Don. Multiple-Plant Firms, Cartels, and Imperfect Competition. **In** *Patinkin, D.,* 1981, *1947,* pp. 91–114.

Patinkin, Don. Multiple-Plant Firms, Cartels, and Imperfect Competition: Note on the Allocation of Output. **In** *Patinkin, D.,* 1981, *1947,* pp. 116–20.

Patinkin, Don. Multiple-Plant Firms, Cartels, and Imperfect Competition: Postscript. **In** *Patinkin, D.,* 1981, pp. 120–23.

Perroux, François. Commerce entre grandes firmes ou commerce entre nations? (With English summary.) *Écon. Appl.,* 1981, *34*(4), pp. 567–91.

Phillips, Almarin. Predation and Antitrust Rules: The Complications When Quality is Considered. **In** *[Grether, E. T.],* 1981, pp. 113–27.

Pindyck, Robert S. Models of Resource Markets and the Explanation of Resource Price Behaviour. *Energy Econ.,* July 1981, *3*(3), pp. 130–39.

Reinganum, Jennifer F. On the Diffusion of New Technology: A Game Theoretic Approach. *Rev. Econ. Stud.,* July 1981, *48*(3), pp. 395–405.

Rice, Edward M. and Ulen, Thomas S. Rent-Seeking and Welfare Loss. **In** *Zerbe, R. O., Jr., ed.,* 1981, pp. 53–65.

Riley, John G. and Samuelson, William F. Optimal Auctions. *Amer. Econ. Rev.,* June 1981, *71*(3), pp. 381–92.

Rosenthal, Robert W. Games of Perfect Information, Predatory Pricing and the Chain-Store Paradox. *J. Econ. Theory,* August 1981, *25*(1), pp. 92–100.

Rothschild, R. Cartel Problems: Note. *Amer. Econ. Rev.,* March 1981, *71*(1), pp. 179–81.

Saving, T. R. and De Vany, Arthur S. Uncertain Markets, Reliability and Peak-Load Pricing. *Southern Econ. J.,* April 1981, *47*(4), pp. 908–23.

Scherr, Frederick C. Focal Points and Pricing Behavior: Results in an Experimental Oligopoly. *J. Behav. Econ.,* Summer 1981, *10*(1), pp. 47–65. **[G: U.S.]**

Schmalensee, Richard. Economies of Scale and Barriers to Entry. *J. Polit. Econ.,* December 1981, *89*(6), pp. 1228–38.

Schmalensee, Richard. Monopolistic Two-Part Pricing Arrangements. *Bell J. Econ. (See Rand J. Econ. after 4/85),* Autumn 1981, *12*(2), pp. 445–66.

Schmalensee, Richard. Output and Welfare Implications of Monopolistic Third-Degree Price Discrimination. *Amer. Econ. Rev.,* March 1981, *71*(1), pp. 242–47.

Seton, Francis A. A Quasi-Competitive Price Basis for Intersystem Comparisons of Economic Structure and Performance. *J. Compar. Econ.,* December 1981, *5*(4), pp. 367–91. **[G: Kenya; U.S.S.R.; Japan; U.K.; U.S.]**

Shaked, Avner and Sutton, John. Heterogeneous Consumers and Product Differentiation in a Market for Professional Services. *Europ. Econ. Rev.,* February 1981, *15*(2), pp. 159–77.

Shaked, Avner and Sutton, John. The Self-Regulating Profession. *Rev. Econ. Stud.,* April 1981, *48*(2), pp. 217–34.

Shapouri, S.; Folwell, R. J. and Baritelle, J. L. Statistical Estimation of Firm-Level Demand Functions: A Case Study in an Oligopolistic Industry. *Agr. Econ. Res.,* April 1981, *33*(2), pp. 18–25.

Sharkey, William W. Existence of Sustainable Prices for Natural Monopoly Outputs. *Bell J. Econ. (See Rand J. Econ. after 4/85),* Spring 1981, *12*(1), pp. 144–54.

Shubik, Martin. A Price–Quantity Buy–Sell Market with and without Contingent Bids. **In** *[Lipiński, E.],* 1981, pp. 117–24.

Shubik, Martin. Game Theory Models and Methods in Political Economy. **In** *Arrow, K. J. and Intriligator, M. D., eds.,* 1981, pp. 285–330.

Siegfried, John J. and Wheeler, Edwin H. Cost Efficiency and Monopoly Power: A Survey. *Quart. Rev. Econ. Bus.,* Spring 1981, *21*(1), pp. 25–46.

Simon, Julian L. Unnecessary, Confusing, and Inadequate: The Marginal Analysis as a Tool for Decision Making. *Amer. Econ.,* Spring 1981, *25*(1), pp. 28–35.

Skinner, Andrew S. Of Factor and Commodity Markets: A Note on E. H. Chamberlin. *Oxford Econ. Pap.,* March 1981, *33*(1), pp. 122–34.

Smith, Richard L., II. Efficiency Gains from Strategic Investment. *J. Ind. Econ.,* September 1981, *30*(1), pp. 1–23. **[G: U.S.]**

Smith, W. James and Formby, John P. Output Changes under Third Degree Price Discrimination: A Reexamination. *Southern Econ. J.,* July 1981, *48*(1), pp. 164–71.

Spulber, Daniel F. Spatial Nonlinear Pricing. *Amer. Econ. Rev.,* December 1981, *71*(5), pp. 923–33.

Stiglitz, Joseph E. and Dasgupta, Partha. Market Structure and Resource Extraction under Uncertainty. *Scand. J. Econ.,* 1981, *83*(2), pp. 318–33.

Stokey, Nancy L. Rational Expectations and Durable Goods Pricing. *Bell J. Econ. (See Rand J. Econ. after 4/85),* Spring 1981, *12*(1), pp. 112–28.

Thépot, Jacques. Stratégies d'investissement des entreprises d'un duopole au cours d'un cycle économique. (Investment Strategy of Firms in a Price Setting Duopoly through a Business Cycle. With English summary.) *Écon. Soc.,* October–November–December 1981, *15*(10–12), pp. 1835–68.

Thomas, Christopher R. A Theory of the Vertically Integrated Input Monopolist with a Depletion Allowance. *Southern Econ. J.*, January 1981, *47*(3), pp. 799–804.

Ulph, Alistair M. and Folie, G. Michael. Dominant Firm Models of Resource Depletion. In *Currie, D.; Peel, D. and Peters, W.*, eds., 1981, pp. 77–100.

von Ungern-Sternberg, Thomas and von Weizsäcker, Carl Christian. Marktstruktur und Marktverhalten bei Qualitätsunsicherheit. (Structure and Conduct on Markets with Quality Uncertainty. With English summary.) *Z. Wirtschaft. Sozialwissen.*, 1981, *101*(6), pp. 609–26.

Vander Weide, James H. and Zalkind, Julie H. Deregulation and Oligopolistic Price–Quality Rivalry. *Amer. Econ. Rev.*, March 1981, *71*(1), pp. 144–54.

Varian, Hal R. A Model of Sales: Errata. *Amer. Econ. Rev.*, June 1981, *71*(3), pp. 517.

Vastrup, Claus. Monopoler og udtømmelige ressourcer. (The Extraction of Exhaustible Resources by a Monopoly. With English summary.) *Nationaløkon. Tidsskr.*, 1981, *119*(1), pp. 21–31.

Veendorp, E. C. H. Instability in Competition: Two Variations on a Hotelling Theme. *Atlantic Econ. J.*, July 1981, *9*(2), pp. 30–34.

Wahlroos, Björn. On the Economics of Multiplant Operation: Some Concepts and an Example. *J. Ind. Econ.*, March 1981, *29*(3), pp. 231–45.
[G: N. America; U.K.; W. Europe; Japan; India]

West, Douglas S. Testing for Market Preemption Using Sequential Location Data. *Bell J. Econ. (See Rand J. Econ. after 4/85)*, Spring 1981, *12*(1), pp. 129–43. [G: Canada]

Westfield, Fred M. Vertical Integration: Does Product Price Rise or Fall? *Amer. Econ. Rev.*, June 1981, *71*(3), pp. 334–46.

Williamson, Oliver E. Reply to Lefever [Predatory Pricing: A Strategic and Welfare Analysis]. *Yale Law J.*, June 1981, *90*(7), pp. 1646–49.
[G: U.S.]

Zabel, Edward. Competitive Price Adjustment without Market Clearing. *Econometrica*, September 1981, *49*(5), pp. 1201–21.

0227 Theory of Auction Markets

Gilley, Otis W. and Karels, Gordon V. The Competitive Effect in Bonus Bidding: New Evidence. *Bell J. Econ. (See Rand J. Econ. after 4/85)*, Autumn 1981, *12*(2), pp. 637–48.

Harris, Milton and Raviv, Artur. Allocation Mechanisms and the Design of Auctions. *Econometrica*, November 1981, *49*(6), pp. 1477–99.

Hoffman, Elizabeth and Plott, Charles R. The Effect of Intertemporal Speculation on the Outcomes in Seller Posted Offer Auction Markets. *Quart. J. Econ.*, May 1981, *96*(2), pp. 223–41.

Isaac, R. Mark and Plott, Charles R. Price Controls and the Behavior of Auction Markets: An Experimental Examination. *Amer. Econ. Rev.*, June 1981, *71*(3), pp. 448–59.

Milgrom, Paul R. Rational Expectations, Information Acquisition, and Competitive Bidding. *Econometrica*, June 1981, *49*(4), pp. 921–43.

Plott, Charles R. and Uhl, Jonathan T. Competitive

Equilibrium with Middlemen: An Empirical Study. *Southern Econ. J.*, April 1981, *47*(4), pp. 1063–71.

Riley, John G. and Samuelson, William F. Optimal Auctions. *Amer. Econ. Rev.*, June 1981, *71*(3), pp. 381–92.

Smith, James L. Non-Aggressive Bidding Behavior and the "Winner's Curse." *Econ. Inquiry*, July 1981, *19*(3), pp. 380–88.

Smith, Vernon L. An Empirical Study of Decentralized Institutions of Monopoly Restraint. In *[Weiler, E. T.]*, 1981, pp. 83–106.

Smith, Vernon L. and Williams, Arlington W. On Nonbinding Price Controls in a Competitive Market. *Amer. Econ. Rev.*, June 1981, *71*(3), pp. 467–74.

0228 Agent Theory

Dionne, Georges. Le risque moral et la sélection adverse: une revue critique de la littérature. (Moral Hazard and Adverse Selection: A Survey. With English summary.) *L'Actual. Econ.*, April–June 1981, *57*(2), pp. 193–224.

Harris, Milton and Townsend, Robert M. Resource Allocation under Asymmetric Information. *Econometrica*, January 1981, *49*(1), pp. 33–64.

Lazear, Edward P. Agency, Earnings Profiles, Productivity, and Hours Restrictions. *Amer. Econ. Rev.*, September 1981, *71*(4), pp. 606–20.

Mori, Pier Angelo. Economie concorrenziali, banditore e disoccupazione. (Competitive Economies, Auctioneer and Unemployment. With English summary.) *Giorn. Econ.*, March–April 1981, *40*(3–4), pp. 231–38.

Radner, Roy. Monitoring Cooperative Agreements in a Repeated Principal–Agent Relationship. *Econometrica*, September 1981, *49*(5), pp. 1127–48.

Sykes, Alan O. An Efficiency Analysis of Vicarious Liability under the Law of Agency. *Yale Law J.*, November 1981, *91*(1), pp. 168–206. [G: U.S.]

Hildenbrand, Werner. Short-Run Production Functions Based on Microdata. *Econometrica*, September 1981, *49*(5), pp. 1095–1125.

023 Macroeconomic Theory

0230 General

Ahmad, Syed. Metzler on Classical Interest Theory: Comment. *Amer. Econ. Rev.*, December 1981, *71*(5), pp. 1092–93.

Aiginger, Karl. Empirical Evidence on the Rational Expectations Hypothesis Using Reported Expectations. *Empirica*, 1981, (1), pp. 25–72.
[G: Scandinavia; Austria; U.S.; Japan; France]

Ambrosi, G. M. Keynes and the 45° Cross. *J. Post Keynesian Econ.*, Summer 1981, *3*(4), pp. 503–09.

Andersen, Torben M. Rationelle forventninger—nogle kritiske kommentarer. (The Rational Expectations Model—Some Critical Comments. With English summary.) *Nationaløkon. Tidsskr.*, 1981, *119*(2), pp. 240–57.

Ando, Albert. On a Theoretical and Empirical Basis

of Macroeconometric Models. In *Kmenta, J. and Ramsey, J. B., eds.*, 1981, pp. 329–67.

Arestis, P. and Karakitsos, Elias. The "Economics of Keynes" and Leijonhufvud. *Econ. Int.*, May–August–November 1981, *34*(2–3–4), pp. 222–41.

Attfield, C. L. F.; Demery, D. and Duck, Nigel W. Unanticipated Monetary Growth, Output and the Price Level: U.K., 1946–77. *Europ. Econ. Rev.*, June/July 1981, *16*(2/3), pp. 367–85. [G: U.K.]

Azariadis, Costas. A Reexamination of Natural Rate Theory. *Amer. Econ. Rev.*, December 1981, *71*(5), pp. 946–60.

Azariadis, Costas. Self-Fulfilling Prophecies. *J. Econ. Theory*, December 1981, *25*(3), pp. 380–96.

Backhouse, Roger E. Keynesian Unemployment and the One-Sector Neoclassical Growth Model. *Econ. J.*, March 1981, *91*(361), pp. 174–87.

Barnett, William A. The New Monetary Aggregates: A Comment. *J. Money, Credit, Banking*, November 1981, *13*(4), pp. 485–89. [G: U.S.]

Barro, Robert J. A Capital Market in an Equilibrium Business Cycle Model. In *Barro, R. J.*, 1981, *1980*, pp. 111–36.

Barro, Robert J. Intertemporal Substitution and the Business Cycle. *Carnegie-Rochester Conf. Ser. Public Policy*, Spring 1981, *14*, pp. 237–68.

Barro, Robert J. Money and the Price Level under the Gold Standard. In *Barro, R. J.*, 1981, *1979*, pp. 355–75.

Barro, Robert J. Unanticipated Money Growth and Economic Activity in the United States. In *Barro, R. J.*, 1981, pp. 137–69.

Barro, Robert J. and Grossman, Herschel I. A General Disequilibrium Model of Income and Employment. In *Barro, R. J.*, 1981, *1971*, pp. 173–84.

Barro, Robert J. and Grossman, Herschel I. Suppressed Inflation and the Supply Multiplier. In *Barro, R. J.*, 1981, *1974*, pp. 185–202.

Batchelor, R. A. Aggregate Expectations under the Stable Laws. *J. Econometrics*, June 1981, *16*(2), pp. 199–210.

Benavie, Arthur. Continuous versus Discrete-Time Comparative Macrostatics. *Atlantic Econ. J.*, July 1981, *9*(2), pp. 1–11.

Benhabib, Jess and Miyao, Takahiro. Some New Results on the Dynamics of the Generalized Tobin Model. *Int. Econ. Rev.*, October 1981, *22*(3), pp. 589–96.

Benhabib, Jess and Nishimura, Kazuo. Stability of Equilibrium in Dynamic Models of Capital Theory. *Int. Econ. Rev.*, June 1981, *22*(2), pp. 275–93.

Bhandari, Jagdeep S. A Stochastic Macroequilibrium Approach to a Floating Exchange Rate Economy with Interest-Bearing Assets. *Weltwirtsch. Arch.*, 1981, *117*(1), pp. 1–19.

Bhandari, Jagdeep S. The Simple Macroeconomics of an Oil-Dependent Economy. *Europ. Econ. Rev.*, June/July 1981, *16*(2/3), pp. 333–54.

Blad, Michael C. Exchange of Stability in a Disequilibrium Model. *J. Math. Econ.*, July 1981, *8*(2), pp. 121–45.

Blanchard, Olivier J. Output, the Stock Market, and

Interest Rates. *Amer. Econ. Rev.*, March 1981, *71*(1), pp. 132–43.

Blanchard, Olivier J. What Is Left of the Multiplier Accelerator? *Amer. Econ. Rev.*, May 1981, *71*(2), pp. 150–54.

Blanchard, Olivier J. and Wyplosz, Charles. An Empirical Structural Model of Aggregate Demand. *J. Monet. Econ.*, January 1981, *7*(1), pp. 1–28. [G: U.S.]

Blatt, John M. Classical Economics of Involuntary Unemployment. *J. Post Keynesian Econ.*, Summer 1981, *3*(4), pp. 552–59.

Blinder, Alan S. Inventories and the Structure of Macro Models. *Amer. Econ. Rev.*, May 1981, *71*(2), pp. 11–16. [G: U.S.]

Blinder, Alan S. Monetary Accommodation of Supply Shocks under Rational Expectations. *J. Money, Credit, Banking*, November 1981, *13*(4), pp. 425–38.

Blinder, Alan S. and Fischer, Stanley. Inventories, Rational Expectations, and the Business Cycle. *J. Monet. Econ.*, November 1981, *8*(3), pp. 277–304.

Boskin, Michael J. Some Issues in "Supply-Side" Economics. *Carnegie-Rochester Conf. Ser. Public Policy*, Spring 1981, *14*, pp. 201–20.

Brazelton, W. Robert. A Survey of Some Textbook Misinterpretations of Keynes. *J. Post Keynesian Econ.*, Winter 1980–81, *3*(2), pp. 256–70.

Brazelton, W. Robert. Post Keynesian Economics: An Institutional Compatibility? *J. Econ. Issues*, June 1981, *15*(2), pp. 531–42.

Brazelton, W. Robert. 45° Keynesianism, Imperfect Competition, and Macroeconomic Disequilibrium: A Comment. *Quart. Rev. Econ. Bus.*, Autumn 1981, *21*(3), pp. 98–100.

Brock, William A. and Turnovsky, Stephen J. The Analysis of Macroeconomic Policies in Perfect Foresight Equilibrium. *Int. Econ. Rev.*, February 1981, *22*(1), pp. 179–209.

Brown, Elba K. The Neoclassical and Post-Keynesian Research Programs: The Methodological Issues. *Rev. Soc. Econ.*, October 1981, *39*(2), pp. 111–32.

Brunner, Karl. The Case against Monetary Activism. *Lloyds Bank Rev.*, January 1981, (139), pp. 20–39.

Buiter, Willem H. The Role of Economic Policy after the New Classical Macroeconomics. In *Currie, D.; Nobay, R. and Peel, D., eds.*, 1981, pp. 233–79.

Buiter, Willem H. The Superiority of Contingent Rules over Fixed Rules in Models with Rational Expectations. *Econ. J.*, September 1981, *91*(363), pp. 647–70.

Buiter, Willem H. and Jewitt, Ian. Staggered Wage Setting with Real Wage Relativities: Variations on a Theme of Taylor. *Manchester Sch. Econ. Soc. Stud.*, September 1981, *49*(3), pp. 211–28.

Burmeister, Edwin; Flood, Robert P. and Turnovsky, Stephen J. Dynamic Macroeconomic Stability with or without Equilibrium in Money and Labour Markets. *Economica*, August 1981, *48*(191), pp. 251–65.

Butterfield, David W. and Kubursi, Atif A. Wage Indexation and the Unemployment-Inflation

Trade-Off. *J. Macroecon.*, Spring 1981, *3*(2), pp. 227–45.

Canarella, Giorgio and Garston, Neil. The Rational Expectation of Income: A Test with Italian Data. *Rivista Int. Sci. Econ. Com.*, June 1981, *28*(6), pp. 597–611. **[G: Italy]**

Cansier, Dieter. Vermögenseffekte der Staatsverschuldung—Multiplikatorwirkungen und Implikationen für den "konjunkturneutralen öffentlichen Haushalt". (Wealth Effects of Government Debt. With English summary.) *Kredit Kapital*, 1981, *14*(3), pp. 390–411.

Canto, Victor A. and Miles, Marc A. The Missing Equation: The Wedge Model Alternative. *J. Macroecon.*, Spring 1981, *3*(2), pp. 247–69.

Casarosa, Carlo. The Microfoundations of Keynes's Aggregate Supply and Expected Demand Analysis. *Econ. J.*, March 1981, *91*(361), pp. 188–94.

Casson, M. C. Unemployment and the New Macroeconomics. In *Creedy, J., ed.*, 1981, pp. 48–98.

Chappell, David. On the Revenue Maximizing Rate of Inflation: A Comment [Monetary Dynamics, Growth, and the Efficiency of Inflationary Finance]. *J. Money, Credit, Banking*, August 1981, *13*(3), pp. 391–92.

Chase, Richard. The Development of Contemporary Mainstream Macroeconomics: Vision, Ideology, and Theory Debate. *Nebr. J. Econ. Bus.*, Summer 1981, *20*(3), pp. 5–36.

Chase, Richard. Vision, Theory Debate and the Development of Mainstream Macroeconomics. *Rivista Int. Sci. Econ. Com.*, June 1981, *28*(6), pp. 558–96.

Chick, V. Reply to Professor Harrison [The Nature of the Keynesian Revolution: A Reassessment]. *Australian Econ. Pap.*, December 1981, *20*(37), pp. 405–08.

Chow, Gregory C. Estimation and Control of Rational Expectations Models. *Amer. Econ. Rev.*, May 1981, *71*(2), pp. 211–16.

Chow, Gregory C. Estimation and Optimal Control of Dynamic Game Models under Rational Expectations. In *Lucas, R. E. and Sargent, T. J., eds.*, 1981, pp. 681–89.

Colander, David C. and Guthrie, Robert S. Great Expectations: What the Dickens Do "Rational Expectations" Mean? *J. Post Keynesian Econ.*, Winter 1980–81, *3*(2), pp. 219–34.

Corden, W. M. Taxation, Real Wage Rigidity and Employment. *Econ. J.*, June 1981, *91*(362), pp. 309–30.

Costabile, Lilia. Keynesian Unemployment in Patinkin and in the "Rationing Models." *Econ. Notes*, 1981, *10*(2), pp. 64–80.

Costrell, Robert M. Stability of Zero Production under Life-Cycle Savings. *Rev. Econ. Stud.*, October 1981, *48*(4), pp. 661–65.

Cuddington, John T. Money, Income, and Causality in the United Kingdom: An Empirical Reexamination. *J. Money, Credit, Banking*, August 1981, *13*(3), pp. 342–51. **[G: U.K.; U.S.]**

Darity, William A., Jr. and Marrero, Wanda I. Distribution, Effective Demand, and the Orthodox Macromodel. *J. Macroecon.*, Fall 1981, *3*(4), pp. 455–87.

Davidson, Paul. A Critical Analysis of Monetarist–

Rational Expectation–Supply-Side (Incentive) Economics Approach to Accumulation during a Period of Inflationary Expectations. *Kredit Kapital*, 1981, *14*(4), pp. 496–504.

Davidson, Paul. Expectations and Economic Decisionmaking. In *U.S. Congress, Joint Economic Committee (II)*, 1981, pp. 10–25.

Deleau, Michel; Malgrange, Pierre and Muet, Pierre-Alain. Une maquette représentative des modèles macroéconomiques. (A Representative, Small-Scale Macroeconomic Model. With English summary.) *Ann. INSEE*, April–June 1981, (42), pp. 53–92. **[G: France]**

Dervis, Kemal. IS/LM in the Tropics: Diagrammatics of the New Structuralist Macro Critique: Comment. In *Cline, W. R. and Weintraub, S., eds.*, 1981, pp. 503–06. **[G: LDCs]**

Drazen, Allan. Disequilibrium Dynamics with Inventories and Anticipatory Price-Setting by Green and Laffont: Comment. *Europ. Econ. Rev.*, May 1981, *16*(1), pp. 223–27.

Eckstein, Otto and Warburg, Paul M. Economic Theory and Econometric Models. In *Kmenta, J. and Ramsey, J. B., eds.*, 1981, pp. 155–76. **[G: U.S.]**

Edwards, Clark. Keynes' Monopolistic Theory of Employment, Interest, and Money. *Agr. Econ. Res.*, April 1981, *33*(2), pp. 7–17.

Eichner, Alfred S. Expectations in Economics. In *U.S. Congress, Joint Economic Committee (II)*, 1981, pp. 113–18.

Eisner, Robert. Expectations in Economics. In *U.S. Congress, Joint Economic Committee (II)*, 1981, pp. 54–61.

Eltis, Walter. The Failure of the Keynesian Conventional Wisdom. In *Courakis, A. S., ed.*, 1981, pp. 92–110.

Fan, Yiu-Kwan. Behavioral Rules, Inventory Adjustments and the Stability of Macroequilibria. *J. Econ. Behav. Organ.*, September 1981, *2*(3), pp. 257–72.

Feiwel, George R. Keynesian Economics, Neoclassical Synthesis and Resurgence of Classical Macroeconomics. *Economia (Portugal)*, May 1981, *5*(2), pp. 209–57.

Feldstein, Martin S. The Distribution of the U.S. Capital Stock Between Residential and Industrial Uses. *Econ. Inquiry*, January 1981, *19*(1), pp. 26–37. **[G: U.S.]**

Fethke, Gary C. and Policano, Andrew J. Cooperative Responses by Public and Private Agents to Aggregate Demand and Supply Disturbances. *Economica*, May 1981, *48*(190), pp. 155–71.

Fischer, Stanley. Expectations in Macroeconomics. In *U.S. Congress, Joint Economic Committee (II)*, 1981, pp. 66–69.

Forman, Leonard and Eichner, Alfred S. A Post Keynesian Short-Period Model: Some Preliminary Econometric Results. *J. Post Keynesian Econ.*, Fall 1981, *4*(1), pp. 117–35.

Foster, J. Fagg. The Reality of the Present and the Challenge of the Future. *J. Econ. Issues*, December 1981, *15*(4), pp. 963–68.

Fourçans, André and Fratianni, Michele. Du côté ou à côté de l'offre de monnaie? Un commentaire sur Sterdyniak et Villa [Du côté de l'offre de monnaie]. (On the Supply of Money? A Comment on Sterdyniak and Villa. With English summary.) *Ann. INSEE*, January–March 1981, (41), pp. 79–94.   [G: France]

Fourgeaud, Claude; Lenclud, Bernard and Michel, Philippe. Two-Sector Model with Quantity Rationing. *J. Econ. Theory*, June 1981, 24(3), pp. 413–36.

Frenkel, Jacob A. Adjustment Lags versus Information Lags: A Test of Alternative Explanations of the Phillips Curve Phenomenon: A Comment. *J. Money, Credit, Banking*, November 1981, 13(4), pp. 490–93.

Gapinski, James H. Steady Growth, Policy Shocks, and Speed of Adjustment under Embodiment and Putty-Clay. *J. Macroecon.*, Spring 1981, 3(2), pp. 147–76.

Gesick, Esther. A Critical Evaluation of Supply Side Economics. *Econ. Forum*, Winter 1981–82, 12(2), pp. 103–11.

Gordon, Robert J. Output Fluctuations and Gradual Price Adjustment. *J. Econ. Lit.*, June 1981, 19(2), pp. 493–530.   [G: U.S.]

Green, Jerry R. and Laffont, Jean-Jacques. Disequilibrium Dynamics with Inventories and Anticipatory Price-Setting. *Europ. Econ. Rev.*, May 1981, 16(1), pp. 199–221.

Griffiths, Brian and Wood, Geoffrey E. Monetary Targets: Introduction. In *Griffiths, B. and Wood, G. E., eds.*, 1981, pp. 1–12.

Grossman, Herschel I. Incomplete Information, Risk Shifting, and Employment Fluctuations. *Rev. Econ. Stud.*, April 1981, 48(2), pp. 189–97.

Grossman, Sanford J. An Introduction to the Theory of Rational Expectations under Asymmetric Information. *Rev. Econ. Stud.*, October 1981, 48(4), pp. 541–59.

Grünbaum, Isi. Incongruous Expectations and the Concept of Monetary Equilibrium. In *Grünbaum, I.*, 1981, 1945, pp. 91–109.

Grünbaum, Isi. Relative Inertias and the Long-run Analysis. In *Grünbaum, I.*, 1981, pp. 65–90.

Hannah, S. P. Equilibrium, Disequilibrium and Unemployment Theory: A Simple Illustrative Model. *J. Econ. Stud.*, 1981, 8(3), pp. 22–39.

Hansen, Bent. Unemployment, Keynes, and the Stockholm School. *Hist. Polit. Econ.*, Summer 1981, 13(2), pp. 256–77.

Harberger, Arnold C. Comment on Papers by Boskin [Some Issues in "Supply-Side" Economics] and Piggott and Whalley [A Summary of Some Findings from a General Equilibrium Tax Model for the United Kingdom]. *Carnegie-Rochester Conf. Ser. Public Policy*, Spring 1981, 14, pp. 221–29.

Harck, Søren. The Supply Side in a Post-Keynesian Two-Sector Model. *Z. Nationalökon.*, 1981, 41(1–2), pp. 1–26.

Harrison, Glenn W. The Nature of the Keynesian Revolution—Comment. *Australian Econ. Pap.*, December 1981, 20(37), pp. 398–404.

Henin, Pierre Yves. Equilibres avec rationnement dans un modèle macroéconomique avec décision d'investissement endogène. (With English summary.) *Écon. Appl.*, 1981, 34(4), pp. 697–728.

Hicks, John R. IS–LM: An Explanation. *J. Post Keynesian Econ.*, Winter 1980–81, 3(2), pp. 139–54.

Holly, Sean. The Role of Economic Policy after the New Classical Macroeconomics: Comment. In *Currie, D.; Nobay, R. and Peel, D., eds.*, 1981, pp. 280–85.

Holmes, James M. and Rhoda, Kenneth L. A Nonparametric Analysis of "Keynesian" and "Monetarist" Models. *Rev. Bus. Econ. Res.*, Spring 1981, 16(3), pp. 26–37.   [G: U.S.]

Horwich, George and Hu, Sheng-Cheng. The Stability of Macro Models. In *[Weiler, E. T.]*, 1981, pp. 242–73.

Hsiao, Cheng. Autoregressive Modelling and Money–Income Causality Detection. *J. Monet. Econ.*, January 1981, 7(1), pp. 85–106.   [G: U.S.]

Hutchison, Terence W. Keynes versus the Keynesians. In *Hutchison, T. W.*, 1981, pp. 108–54.

Hutchison, Terence W. The Limitations of General Theories in Macro Economics. In *Hutchison, T. W.*, 1981, pp. 233–65.

Ip, Pui Chi. A General Equilibrium Analysis in the Phillips Space. *J. Macroecon.*, Summer 1981, 3(3), pp. 355–67.

Jaeger, Klaus. Economic Policy Effectiveness in Hicksian Analysis: A Note. *Kredit Kapital*, 1981, 14(2), pp. 177–79.

Jameson, Kenneth P. and Philips, Joseph. Supply-Side Economics: A Skeptical View. *Econ. Forum*, Summer 1981, 12(1), pp. 81–88.

Jarsulic, Marc. Unemployment in a Flexible Price Competitive Model. *J. Post Keynesian Econ.*, Fall 1981, 4(1), pp. 32–43.

Jespersen, Jesper. Clower og Leijonhufvuds bidrag til det mikroøkonomiske fundament for makroteori. (The Contributions of Clower and Leijonhufvud to the Microeconomic Foundation of Macroeconomics. With English summary.) *Nationaløkon. Tidsskr.*, 1981, 119(2), pp. 220–38.

Joyce, Joseph P. Money and Production in the Developing Economies: An Analytical Survey of the Issues. *J. Econ. Devel.*, December 1981, 6(2), pp. 41–70.   [G: LDCs]

Kaldor, Nicholas and Trevithick, James. A Keynesian Perspective on Money. *Lloyds Bank Rev.*, January 1981, (139), pp. 1–19.

Kaliski, S. F. Inflation, Stagflation and Macroeconomics: Does Received Macro-Theory Explain Our Economic Circumstances? *Can. Public Policy*, Supplement, April 1981, 7, pp. 189–203.   [G: Canada]

Katona, George. Expectations in Economics. In *U.S. Congress, Joint Economic Committee (II)*, 1981, pp. 26–34.   [G: U.S.]

Klein, Lawrence R. Expectations and the Economy: Statement. In *U.S. Congress, Joint Economic Committee (II)*, 1981, pp. 62–65.

Kohn, Meir. A Loanable Funds Theory of Unemployment and Monetary Disequilibrium. *Amer. Econ. Rev.*, December 1981, 71(5), pp. 859–79.

Kohn, Meir. In Defense of the Finance Constraint. *Econ. Inquiry*, April 1981, 19(2), pp. 177–95.

Kohn, Meir. Metzler on Classical Interest Theory: Comment. *Amer. Econ. Rev.*, December 1981, 71(5), pp. 1094–95.

Kregel, J. A. On Distinguishing between Alternative Methods of Approach to the Demand for Output as a Whole. *Australian Econ. Pap.*, June 1981, *20*(36), pp. 63–71.

Kuipers, Simon K. Keynesian and Neo-Classical Growth Models: A Sequential Analytical Approach. *De Economist*, 1981, *129*(1), pp. 58–104.

Lahiri, Kajal and Lee, Y. H. An Empirical Study on the Econometric Implications of Rational Expectations Hypothesis. *Empirical Econ.*, 1981, *6*(2), pp. 111–27.

Laidler, David. Monetarism: An Interpretation and an Assessment. *Econ. J.*, March 1981, *91*(361), pp. 1–28.

Lawson, Tony. Keynesian Model Building and the Rational Expectations Critique. *Cambridge J. Econ.*, December 1981, *5*(4), pp. 311–26.

Leijonhufvud, Axel. Effective Demand Failures. In *Leijonhufvud, A.*, 1981, *1973*, pp. 103–29.

Leijonhufvud, Axel. Expectations: Policymaker's Predicament. In *U.S. Congress, Joint Economic Committee (II)*, 1981, pp. 40–47.

Leijonhufvud, Axel. Keynes and the Classics: Second Lecture. In *Leijonhufvud, A.*, 1981, *1969*, pp. 55–78.

Leijonhufvud, Axel. Keynes and the Classics: First Lecture. In *Leijonhufvud, A.*, 1981, *1969*, pp. 39–54.

Leijonhufvud, Axel. Keynes and the Effectiveness of Monetary Policy. In *Leijonhufvud, A.*, 1981, *1968*, pp. 17–37.

Leijonhufvud, Axel. Keynes and the Keynesians: A Suggested Interpretation. In *Leijonhufvud, A.*, 1981, *1967*, pp. 3–15.

Leijonhufvud, Axel. The Wicksell Connection: Variations on a Theme. In *Leijonhufvud, A.*, 1981, pp. 131–202.

Leijonhufvud, Axel and Clower, Robert W. Say's Principle, What It Means and Doesn't Mean. In *Leijonhufvud, A.*, 1981, *1973*, pp. 79–101.

Lephardt, George P. Taxes and Aggregate Supply: A Case of a Misplaced Blade. *J. Macroecon.*, Winter 1981, *3*(1), pp. 117–24.

Lewis, Geoffrey W. The Phillips Curve and Bayesian Learning. *J. Econ. Theory*, April 1981, *24*(2), pp. 240–64.

Lipsey, Richard G. Supply-side Economics: A Survey. In *Ontario Economic Council, Vol. 1*, 1981, pp. 5–30.

Lipsey, Richard G. The Understanding and Control of Inflation: Is There a Crisis in Macro-Economics? *Can. J. Econ.*, November 1981, *14*(4), pp. 545–76.

Lorie, Henri R. Asset Prices and Temporary Equilibrium with Rationing. *Scand. J. Econ.*, 1981, *83*(3), pp. 457–62.

Lucas, Robert E., Jr. Econometric Policy Evaluation: A Critique. In *Lucas, R. E., Jr.*, 1981, *1976*, pp. 104–30.

Lucas, Robert E., Jr. Expectations and the Neutrality of Money. In *Lucas, R. E., Jr.*, 1981, *1972*, pp. 66–89.

Lucas, Robert E., Jr. Methods and Problems in Business Cycle Theory. In *Lucas, R. E., Jr.*, 1981, *1980*, pp. 271–96.

Lucas, Robert E., Jr. Studies in Business-Cycle Theory: Introduction. In *Lucas, R. E., Jr.*, 1981, pp. 1–18.

Lucas, Robert E., Jr. Tobin and Monetarism: A Review Article. *J. Econ. Lit.*, June 1981, *19*(2), pp. 558–67.

Lucas, Robert E., Jr. Understanding Business Cycles. In *Lucas, R. E., Jr.*, 1981, *1977*, pp. 215–39.

Lucas, Robert E., Jr. and Sargent, Thomas J. After Keynesian Macroeconomics. In *Lucas, R. E. and Sargent, T. J.*, eds., 1981, *1979*, pp. 295–319.

Lucas, Robert E., Jr. and Sargent, Thomas J. Rational Expectations and Econometric Practice: Introduction. In *Lucas, R. E. and Sargent, T. J.*, eds., 1981, pp. xi–xl.

Malinvaud, Edmond. Econometrics Faced with the Needs of Macroeconomic Policy. *Econometrica*, November 1981, *49*(6), pp. 1363–75.

Matthews, R. C. O. Comment on the Papers by Professors Laidler [Monetarism: An Interpretation and an Assessment] and Tobin [The Monetarist Counter Revolution Today—An Appraisal]. *Econ. J.*, March 1981, *91*(361), pp. 43–48.

Mayes, David G. The Controversy over Rational Expectations. *Nat. Inst. Econ. Rev.*, May 1981, (96), pp. 53–61. [G: U.K.]

McCallum, Bennett T. Price Level Determinacy with an Interest Rate Policy Rule and Rational Expectations. *J. Monet. Econ.*, November 1981, *8*(3), pp. 319–29.

McCallum, Bennett T. Price-Level Stickiness and the Feasibility of Monetary Stabilization Policy with Rational Expectations. In *Lucas, R. E. and Sargent, T. J.*, eds., 1981, *1977*, pp. 277–84.

McCallum, Bennett T. The Role of Expectations in Economics: An Essay. In *U.S. Congress, Joint Economic Committee (II)*, 1981, pp. 48–53.

McCallum, John C. P. Modigliani on Flexible Wages and Prices: Comment. *J. Post Keynesian Econ.*, Winter 1980–81, *3*(2), pp. 281–84. [G: Canada]

McElhattan, Rose. The Response of Real Output and Inflation to Monetary Policy. *Fed. Res. Bank San Francisco Econ. Rev.*, Summer 1981, pp. 45–70.

McElroy, F. William. Classical Misconceptions and Keynesian Innovations. *Rivista Int. Sci. Econ. Com.*, October–November 1981, *28*(10–11), pp. 1053–69.

McGee, Robert T. A Graphical Exposition of a More Complete Keynesian System. *J. Macroecon.*, Fall 1981, *3*(4), pp. 559–70.

Meade, James E. Comment on the Papers by Professors Laidler [Monetarism: An Interpretation and an Assessment] and Tobin [The Monetarist Counter Revolution Today—An Appraisal]. *Econ. J.*, March 1981, *91*(361), pp. 49–55.

Meltzer, Allan H. Keynes's *General Theory*: A Different Perspective. *J. Econ. Lit.*, March 1981, *19*(1), pp. 34–64.

Minford, Patrick. Dynamic Predictive Tests of a Rational Expectations Model of the U.K. *Brit. Rev. Econ. Issues*, Autumn 1981, *3*(9), pp. 39–50. [G: U.K.]

Minoguchi, Takeo. The Process of Writing the General Theory as 'A Monetary Theory of Production.' *Hitotsubashi J. Econ.*, February 1981,

21(2), pp. 33–43.

Minsky, Hyman P. James Tobin's *Asset Accumulation and Economic Activity*: A Review Article. *Eastern Econ. J.*, July–Oct. 1981, *7*(3–4), pp. 199–209.

Minsky, Hyman P. The United States' Economy in the 1980s: The Financial Past and Present as a Guide to the Future. *Giorn. Econ.*, May–June 1981, *40*(5–6), pp. 301–17.   [G: U.S.]

Mitchell, Douglas W. Deficit and Inflation in a Post Keynesian Model. *J. Post Keynesian Econ.*, Summer 1981, *3*(4), pp. 560–67.

Mitchell, Douglas W. Stability of the Government Budget Constraint with a Constant Exogenous Monetary Growth Rate. *Quart. Rev. Econ. Bus.*, Autumn 1981, *21*(3), pp. 15–22.

Montesano, Aldo. Propagazione di uno shock esogeno sulle produzioni che richiedono tempo. (The Propogation of an Exogenous Shock over Time-Consuming Productions. With English summary.) *Rivista Int. Sci. Econ. Com.*, December 1981, *28*(12), pp. 1105–15.

Mortensen, Dale T. A Comment on Barro's Intertemporal Substitution and the Business Cycle. *Carnegie-Rochester Conf. Ser. Public Policy*, Spring 1981, *14*, pp. 269–71.

Muth, John F. Rational Expectations and the Theory of Price Movements. **In** *Lucas, R. E. and Sargent, T. J., eds.*, 1981, *1961*, pp. 3–22.

Nelson, Charles R. Adjustment Lags versus Information Lags: A Test of Alternative Explanations of the Phillips Curve Phenomenon. *J. Money, Credit, Banking*, February 1981, *13*(1), pp. 1–11.

Nelson, Charles R. Adjustment Lags versus Information Lags: A Test of Alternative Explanations of the Phillips Curve Phenomenon: A Reply. *J. Money, Credit, Banking*, November 1981, *13*(4), pp. 494–96.

Norman, N. R. The Impact Macrofix: An Exposition. *Australian Econ. Pap.*, June 1981, *20*(36), pp. 183–85.

Obstfeld, Maurice. Capital Mobility and Devaluation in an Optimizing Model with Rational Expectations. *Amer. Econ. Rev.*, May 1981, *71*(2), pp. 217–21.

Ohlin, Bertil. Stockholm and Cambridge: Four Papers on the Monetary and Employment Theory of the 1930s. *Hist. Polit. Econ.*, Summer 1981, *13*(2), pp. 189–255.

Osadchaya, I. M. The Present Stage of the "Antimarginalist Revolution" and Keynesianism. **In** *Mileikovsky, A. G., et al.*, 1981, pp. 74–117.

Oswald, Rudolph A. The Role of Expectations in Economics. **In** *U.S. Congress, Joint Economic Committee (II)*, 1981, pp. 94–101.

Parguez, Alain. Ordre social, monnaie et régulation. (With English summary.) *Écon. Appl.*, 1981, *34*(2–3), pp. 383–448.

Patel, Meena. A Note on Transfer Pricing by Transnational Corporations. *Indian Econ. Rev.*, January–June 1981, *16*(1 and 2), pp. 139–52.

Patinkin, Don. Keynes and Chicago. **In** *Patinkin, D.*, 1981, *1979*, pp. 289–308.

Patinkin, Don. The Chicago Tradition, the Quantity Theory, and Friedman: Postscript. **In** *Patinkin,*

D., 1981, pp. 264–74.

Patinkin, Don. The Chicago Tradition, the Quantity Theory, and Friedman. **In** *Patinkin, D.*, 1981, *1969*, pp. 241–64.

Peel, David A. and Chappell, David. Rational Expectations and Wage and Price Inflexibility: A Note. *Scand. J. Econ.*, 1981, *83*(1), pp. 115–20.

Penner, Rudolph G. Discussion of the Papers by Piggott and Whalley [A Summary of Some Findings from a General Equilibrium Tax Model for the United Kingdom] and Boskin [Some Issues in "Supply-Side" Economics]. *Carnegie-Rochester Conf. Ser. Public Policy*, Spring 1981, *14*, pp. 231–35.

Pesek, Boris P. Reply [A Note on the Theory of Permanent Income]. *J. Post Keynesian Econ.*, Fall 1981, *4*(1), pp. 157–58.

Peston, Maurice H. An Aspect of the Crowding Out Problem. *Oxford Econ. Pap.*, March 1981, *33*(1), pp. 19–27.

Peterson, R. D. 45° Keynesianism, Imperfect Competition, and Macroeconomic Disequilibrium: Reply. *Quart. Rev. Econ. Bus.*, Autumn 1981, *21*(3), pp. 100–102.

Pettersen, Øystein. Monetary Policy Rules and Variances in Difference Equation Models Containing Autocorrelated Disturbance Terms: Comment [On the Implications of Monetary Rules in a Stochastic Framework]. *Weltwirtsch. Arch.*, 1981, *117*(3), pp. 574–77.

Phelps, Edmund S. Okun's Micro-Macro System: A Review Article. *J. Econ. Lit.*, September 1981, *19*(3), pp. 1065–73.

Picard, Pierre. Croissance et inflation dans un modèle de déséquilibres. (Growth and Inflation in a Disequilibrium Model. With English summary.) *Revue Écon.*, November 1981, *32*(6), pp. 1013–44.

Pitchford, J. D. Taxation, Real Wage Rigidity and Employment: The Flexible Price Case. *Econ. J.*, September 1981, *91*(363), pp. 716–20.

Pizzutto, Giorgio. Flussi finanziari e teoria monetaria. (Financial Flows and Monetary Theory. With English summary.) *Rivista Int. Sci. Econ. Com.*, December 1981, *28*(12), pp. 1168–80.

Portes, Richard. Disequilibrium Dynamics with Inventories and Anticipatory Price-Setting by Green and Laffont: Comment. *Europ. Econ. Rev.*, May 1981, *16*(1), pp. 229–32.

Poschl, Josef and Locksley, Gareth. Michal Kalecki: A Comprehensive Challenge to Orthodoxy. **In** *Shackleton, J. R. and Locksley, G., eds.*, 1981, pp. 141–59.

Prescott, Edward C. Economic Theory, Model Size and Model Purpose: Remarks. **In** *Kmenta, J. and Ramsey, J. B., eds.*, 1981, pp. 273–77.

Rabin, Alan. Comment on Don Roper: What Is the "Demand for Money"? *Econ. Forum*, Summer 1981, *12*(1), pp. 115–16.

Raymon, Neil. Stability in the Barro–Grossman Model. *Scand. J. Econ.*, 1981, *83*(4), pp. 563–69.

Redhead, Keith J. On Keynesian Economics and the Economics of Keynes: A Suggested Interpretation [Keynes and the Keynesians: A Suggested Interpretation]. *Bull. Econ. Res.*, May 1981, *33*(1),

pp. 48–55.

Riese, Hajo. Wirtschaftspolitik unter dem Regime der Stagnation: Bemerkungen zu einem Symposium des Deutschen Instituts für Wirtschaftsforschung. (Economic Policy and Stagnation. With English summary.) *Konjunkturpolitik*, 1981, 27(4), pp. 227–46.

Robinson, Joan. Marxism and Modern Economics. In *Robinson, J.*, 1981, pp. 192–202.

Robinson, Joan and Bhaduri, Amit. Accumulation and Exploitation: An Analysis in the Tradition of Marx, Sraffa and Kalecki. In *Robinson, J.*, 1981, 1980, pp. 64–77.

Roper, Don E. What Is the "Demand for Money"? A Reply. *Econ. Forum*, Summer 1981, 12(1), pp. 117–20.

Rutledge, John. The Role of Expectations in Economics. In *U.S. Congress, Joint Economic Committee (II)*, 1981, pp. 121–29.

Salmon, Richard A. and Lotspeich, Richard. Supply-Side Economics: Personal Income Tax and the Aggregate Supply of Labor. *Econ. Forum*, Summer 1981, 12(1), pp. 89–93.

Sarantis, Nicholas C. Employment, Labor Supply and Real Wages in Market Disequilibrium. *J. Macroecon.*, Summer 1981, 3(3), pp. 335–54. [G: U.S.]

Sargent, Thomas J. A Classical Macroeconomic Model for the United States. In *Lucas, R. E. and Sargent, T. J., eds.*, 1981, 1976, pp. 521–51. [G: U.S.]

Sargent, Thomas J. Rational Expectations, the Real Rate of Interest, and the Natural Rate of Unemployment. In *Lucas, R. E. and Sargent, T. J., eds.*, 1981, 1973, pp. 159–98. [G: U.S.]

Sargent, Thomas J. and Wallace, Neil. "Rational" Expectations, the Optimal Monetary Instrument, and the Optimal Money Supply Rule. In *Lucas, R. E. and Sargent, T. J., eds.*, 1981, 1975, pp. 215–28.

Sargent, Thomas J. and Wallace, Neil. Rational Expectations and the Theory of Economic Policy. In *Lucas, R. E. and Sargent, T. J., eds.*, 1981, 1976, pp. 199–213.

Sauernheimer, Karlhans. Beschäftigungseffekte in makroökonomischen Modellen offener Volkswirtschaften mit flexiblen Wechselkursen. (Macroeconomic Policy under Flexible Exchange Rates and Flexible Wages. With English summary.) Z. *Wirtschaft. Sozialwissen.*, 1981, 101(1), pp. 61–81.

Schinasi, Garry J. A Nonlinear Dynamic Model of Short Run Fluctuations. *Rev. Econ. Stud.*, October 1981, 48(4), pp. 649–56.

Seoka, Yoshihiko. The Effectiveness of Monetary Policy in the Keynesian Model with Rational Expectations: A Comment on Mr. Yoshikawa. *Econ. Stud. Quart.*, August 1981, 32(2), pp. 181–87.

Shapiro, Edward. "Supply-Side" Economics: A Diagrammatic Exposition. *Nebr. J. Econ. Bus.*, Spring 1981, 20(2), pp. 37–46.

Simos, Evangelos O. and Triantis, John. The Theory of Permanent Income: Comment [A Note on the Theory of Permanent Income]. *J. Post Keynesian Econ.*, Fall 1981, 4(1), pp. 152–56.

Sims, Christopher A. Money, Income, and Causal-

ity. In *Lucas, R. E. and Sargent, T. J., eds.*, 1981, 1972, pp. 387–403. [G: U.S.]

Siven, Claes-Henric. The General Supply–Demand Multiplier. *Scand. J. Econ.*, 1981, 83(1), pp. 22–37.

Smyth, David J. and Holmes, James M. The Employment Ratio and the Potential Labor Surplus in Phillips-Type Relationships: A Note. *J. Post Keynesian Econ.*, Fall 1981, 4(1), pp. 75–80.

Startz, Richard. Unemployment and Real Interest Rates: Econometric Testing of Inflation Neutrality. *Amer. Econ. Rev.*, December 1981, 71(5), pp. 969–77.

Steedman, Ian W. and Metcalfe, J. S. On Duality and Basic Commodities in an Open Economy. *Australian Econ. Pap.*, June 1981, 20(36), pp. 133–41.

Stein, Jerome L. Monetarist, Keynesian, and New Classical Economics. *Amer. Econ. Rev.*, May 1981, 71(2), pp. 139–44. [G: U.S.]

Tatom, John A. We Are All Supply-Siders Now! *Fed. Res. Bank St. Louis Rev.*, May 1981, 63(5), pp. 18–30. [G: U.S.]

Tavlas, George S. Keynesian and Monetarist Theories of the Monetary Transmission Process: Doctrinal Aspects. *J. Monet. Econ.*, May 1981, 7(3), pp. 317–37.

Taylor, John B. Estimation and Control of a Macroeconomic Model with Rational Expectations. In *Lucas, R. E. and Sargent, T. J., eds.*, 1981, 1979, pp. 659–80. [G: U.S.]

Taylor, Lance. IS/LM in the Tropics: Diagrammatics of the New Structuralist Macro Critique. In *Cline, W. R. and Weintraub, S., eds.*, 1981, pp. 465–503. [G: LDCs]

Teigen, Ronald L. The Evolution of Monetarism. Z. *ges. Staatswiss.*, March 1981, 137(1), pp. 1–16.

Termini, Valeria. Logical, Mechanical and Historical Time in Economics. *Econ. Notes*, 1981, 10(3), pp. 58–104.

Thurow, Lester C. Psychic Income: A Market Failure. *J. Post Keynesian Econ.*, Winter 1980–81, 3(2), pp. 183–93.

Tobin, James. Comment on the Paper by Professor Laidler [Monetarism: An Interpretation and an Assessment]. *Econ. J.*, March 1981, 91(361), pp. 56–57.

Tobin, James. On a Theoretical and Empirical Basis of Macroeconometric Models: Comment. In *Kmenta, J. and Ramsey, J. B., eds.*, 1981, pp. 391–92.

Tobin, James. The Monetarist Counter-Revolution Today—An Appraisal. *Econ. J.*, March 1981, 91(361), pp. 29–42.

Tool, Marc R. The Compulsive Shift to Institutional Analysis. *J. Econ. Issues*, September 1981, 15(3), pp. 569–92.

Torr, C. S. W. Microfoundations for Keynes's Point of Effective Demand. *S. Afr. J. Econ.*, December 1981, 49(4), pp. 334–48.

Tuchscherer, Thomas. The Unnatural "Natural" Rate of Unemployment. *J. Post Keynesian Econ.*, Fall 1981, 4(1), pp. 25–31.

Turner, Thomas H. and Whiteman, Charles H. Econometric Policy Evaluation under Rational

Expectations. *Fed. Res. Bank Minn. Rev.*, Spring-Summer 1981, *5*(2), pp. 6–15.

Usoskin, V. M. The "Stability" Problem: Monetarism vs. Keynesianism. In *Mileikovsky, A. G., et al.*, 1981, pp. 118–65.

Van Cott, T. Norman. Inflation as a Tax on Money: Integration into IS–LM Analysis. *Public Finance Quart.*, January 1981, *9*(1), pp. 61–74.

Visco, Ignazio. On the Derivation of Reduced Forms of Rational Expectations Models. *Europ. Econ. Rev.*, June/July 1981, *16*(2/3), pp. 355–65.

Visholm, Torben. Keynesmodellen—ufuldkommen koordination over tiden. (Time and Adjustment in Keynesian Theory. With English summary.) *Nationaløkon. Tidsskr.*, 1981, *119*(2), pp. 229–39.

Wagner, Helmut. Wirtschaftspolitik im Lichte rationaler Erwartungen. (Economic Policy and Rational Expectations. With English summary.) *Konjunkturpolitik*, 1981, *27*(1), pp. 1–11.

Waldo, Douglas G. Sticky Nominal Wages and the Optimal Employment Rule. *J. Monet. Econ.*, May 1981, *7*(3), pp. 339–53.

Wallace, Myles S. Government Provided Information and Economic Stability. *Econ. Forum*, Winter 1981–82, *12*(2), pp. 69–76.

Wallis, Kenneth F. Econometric Implications of the Rational Expectations Hypothesis. In *Lucas, R. E. and Sargent, T. J., eds.*, 1981, *1980*, pp. 329–54.

Watkins, John P. Religious Parable: A Comment [Supply-Side Economics: A Religious Parable]. *Econ. Forum*, Winter 1981–82, *12*(2), pp. 117–22.

Weintraub, Sidney. Monetarism's Muddles. *Kredit Kapital*, 1981, *14*(4), pp. 463–95.
[G: W. Germany; U.S.]

Wells, Paul. Modigliani on Flexible Wages and Prices: Reply. *J. Post Keynesian Econ.*, Winter 1980–81, *3*(2), pp. 284–86.

Weniger, Anna and Robison, Hank. Supply-Side Economics: A Religious Parable. *Econ. Forum*, Summer 1981, *12*(1), pp. 75–80.

Wood, John H. Metzler on Classical Interest Theory: Reply. *Amer. Econ. Rev.*, December 1981, *71*(5), pp. 1096–97.

Zannoni, Diane C. and McKenna, Edward J. A Test of the Monetarist "Puzzle." *J. Post Keynesian Econ.*, Summer 1981, *3*(4), pp. 479–90.

0232 Theory of Aggregate Demand: Consumption

Alogoskoufis, George S. and Nissim, John. Consumption–Income Dynamics under Rational Expectations: Theory and Evidence. *Greek Econ. Rev.*, August 1981, *3*(2), pp. 128–47.
[G: Greece]

Ballentine, J. Gregory. The Cost of the Intersectoral and Intertemporal Price Distortions of a Corporation Income Tax. *Southern Econ. J.*, July 1981, *48*(1), pp. 87–96.

Bulkley, George. Personal Savings and Anticipated Inflation. *Econ. J.*, March 1981, *91*(361), pp. 124–35.

Cebula, Richard J. The Positively Sloped IS Curve and Joint Balance: An Analysis in Light of Recent New Evidence on the Interest Sensitivity of Commodity Demand. *Rivista Int. Sci. Econ. Com.*, April 1981, *28*(4), pp. 366–77.

Chrystal, K. Alec. The 'New Cambridge' Aggregate Expenditure Function: The Emperor's Old Clothes? *J. Monet. Econ.*, May 1981, *7*(3), pp. 395–402.
[G: U.K.]

Daly, Vince and Hadjimatheou, George. Stochastic Implications of the Life Cycle-Permanent Income Hypothesis: Evidence for the U.K. Economy: Comment. *J. Polit. Econ.*, June 1981, *89*(3), pp. 596–99.
[G: U.K.]

Davidson, James E. H. and Hendry, David F. Interpreting Econometric Evidence: The Behaviour of Consumers' Expenditure in the UK. *Europ. Econ. Rev.*, May 1981, *16*(1), pp. 177–92.
[G: U.K.]

Davies, James B. Uncertain Lifetime, Consumption, and Dissaving in Retirement. *J. Polit. Econ.*, June 1981, *89*(3), pp. 561–77.

Federenko, N. P. and Rimashevskaya, N. M. The Analysis of Consumption and Demand in the USSR. In *[Stone, R.]*, 1981, pp. 113–28.

Fischer, Stanley. Is There a Real-Balance Effect in Equilibrium? *J. Monet. Econ.*, July 1981, *8*(1), pp. 25–39.

Flavin, Marjorie A. The Adjustment of Consumption to Changing Expectations about Future Income. *J. Polit. Econ.*, October 1981, *89*(5), pp. 974–1009.
[G: U.S.]

Fralick, James S. Tax Incentives and Private Saving: Some Policy Options. In *Federal Reserve System*, 1981, pp. 143–59.

Fry, Maxwell J. The Permanent Income Hypothesis in Underdeveloped Countries: Mea Culpa. *J. Devel. Econ.*, April 1981, *8*(2), pp. 263–68.
[G: Asia; LDCs]

Fuchs-Seliger, Susanne. Aggregation with a Fixed Distribution of Income. *Z. Nationalökon.*, 1981, *41*(1–2), pp. 69–78.

Green, Francis G. The Effect of Occupational Pension Schemes on Saving in the United Kingdom: A Test of the Life Cycle Hypothesis. *Econ. J.*, March 1981, *91*(361), pp. 136–44.
[G: U.K.]

Gylfason, Thorvaldur. Interest Rates, Inflation, and the Aggregate Consumption Function. *Rev. Econ. Statist.*, May 1981, *63*(2), pp. 233–45.

Hall, Robert E. Interpreting Econometric Evidence by Davidson and Hendry: Comment. *Europ. Econ. Rev.*, May 1981, *16*(1), pp. 193–94.

Hall, Robert E. Stochastic Implications of the Life Cycle–Permanent Income Hypothesis: Theory and Evidence. In *Lucas, R. E. and Sargent, T. J., eds.*, 1981, *1978*, pp. 501–17.
[G: U.S.]

Hendry, David F. and von Ungern-Sternberg, Thomas. Liquidity and Inflation Effects on Consumers' Expenditure. In *[Stone, R.]*, 1981, pp. 237–60.
[G: U.K.]

Hymans, Saul H. Saving, Investment, and Social Security. *Nat. Tax J.*, March 1981, *34*(1), pp. 1–8.
[G: U.S.]

Jorgenson, Dale W.; Lau, L. J. and Stoker, T. M. Aggregate Consumer Behaviour and Individual Welfare. In *Currie, D.; Nobay, R. and Peel, D., eds.*, 1981, pp. 35–61.
[G: U.S.]

Kohli, Ulrich R. Permanent Income in the Consumption and the Demand for Money Functions. *J.*

Monet. Econ., March 1981, 7(2), pp. 227–38.
[G: Canada]

Krohn, Lawrence D. The Generational Optimum Economy: Extracting Monopoly Gains from Posterity through Taxation of Capital. *Amer. Econ. Rev.*, June 1981, 71(3), pp. 411–20.

Laitner, John P. The Steady States of a Stochastic Decentralized Growth Model. *J. Econ. Theory*, June 1981, 24(3), pp. 377–92.

Laumas, G. S. Discount Rate and Wealth. *J. Polit. Econ.*, February 1981, 89(1), pp. 196–98.
[G: U.S.]

Laumas, Prem S. and Mohabbat, Khan A. A Note on the Two Concepts of Permanent Income. *Eastern Econ. J.*, July-Oct. 1981, 7(3–4), pp. 187–91.
[G: U.S.]

Leijonhufvud, Axel. Effective Demand Failures. In *Leijonhufvud, A.*, 1981, *1973*, pp. 103–29.

Marchal, Jean and Poulon, Frédéric. Multiplicateur et probabilité. (Multiplier and Probability. With English summary.) *L'Actual. Econ.*, January–March 1981, 57(1), pp. 70–86.

Milanović, Branko. Godišnje potrošne funkcije za Jugoslaviju 1952–78. (Yearly Consumption Functions for Yugoslavia, 1952–1978. With English summary.) *Econ. Anal. Worker's Manage.*, 1981, 15(3), pp. 291–334.
[G: Yugoslavia]

Montesano, Aldo. The Notion of Money Illusion. *Rivista Polit. Econ.*, Supplement December 1981, 71, pp. 139–47.

Muellbauer, John. Testing Neoclassical Models of the Demand for Consumer Durables. In *[Stone, R.]*, 1981, pp. 213–35.
[G: U.K.]

Ouliaris, Sam. Household Saving and the Rate of Interest. *Econ. Rec.*, September 1981, 57(158), pp. 205–14.
[G: Australia]

Ram, Rati. Applicability of the Permanent Income Hypothesis to Underdeveloped Economies: A Comment [The Permanent Income Hypothesis in Underdeveloped Economies: Additional Evidence]. *J. Devel. Econ.*, April 1981, 8(2), pp. 259–62.
[G: Asia; LDCs]

Ramm, Wolfhard. Tax Design and Individual Saving. In *Federal Reserve System*, 1981, pp. 115–32.

Skott, Peter. On the 'Kaldorian' Saving Function. *Kyklos*, 1981, 34(4), pp. 563–81.

Steedman, Ian W. Time Preference, the Rate of Interest and Abstinence from Accumulation. *Australian Econ. Pap.*, December 1981, 20(37), pp. 219–34.

Steindel, Charles. The Determinants of Private Saving. In *Federal Reserve System*, 1981, pp. 101–14.
[G: U.S.]

Summers, Lawrence H. Capital Taxation and Accumulation in a Life Cycle Growth Model. *Amer. Econ. Rev.*, September 1981, 71(4), pp. 533–44.

Svensson, Lars E. O. Effective Demand in a Sequence of Markets. *Scand. J. Econ.*, 1981, 83(1), pp. 1–21.

Thomas, R. Leighton. Wealth and Aggregate Consumption. *Manchester Sch. Econ. Soc. Stud.*, June 1981, 49(2), pp. 129–52.

Thomas, T. Aggregate Demand in the United Kingdom 1918–45. In *Floud, R. and McCloskey, D., eds., Vol. 2*, 1981, pp. 332–46.
[G: U.K.]

von Ungern-Sternberg, Thomas. Inflation and Savings: International Evidence on Inflation-Induced Income Losses. *Econ. J.*, December 1981, 91(364), pp. 961–76.
[G: W. Germany; U.K.]

Wallace, Neil. A Modigliani-Miller Theorem for Open-Market Operations. *Amer. Econ. Rev.*, June 1981, 71(3), pp. 267–74.

Westphal, Uwe. Interpreting Econometric Evidence by Davidson and Hendry: Comment. *Europ. Econ. Rev.*, May 1981, 16(1), pp. 195–97.

Woglom, Geoffrey R. H. A Reexamination of the Role of Stocks in the Consumption Function and the Transmission Mechanism: A Note. *J. Money, Credit, Banking*, May 1981, 13(2), pp. 215–20.

Wolff, Edward N. The Accumulation of Household Wealth over the Life-Cycle: A Microdata Analysis. *Rev. Income Wealth*, March 1981, 27(1), pp. 75–96.
[G: U.S.]

0233 Theory of Aggregate Demand: Investment

Abel, Andrew B. Dynamic Adjustment in a Putty-Putty Model: Implications for Testing the Putty-Clay Hypothesis. *Int. Econ. Rev.*, February 1981, 22(1), pp. 19–36.

Abel, Andrew B. Taxes, Inflation, and the Durability of Capital. *J. Polit. Econ.*, June 1981, 89(3), pp. 548–60.

Anckar, Dag. On Information Inventories and Political Responsiveness. In *Chikán, A., ed. (1)*, 1981, pp. 29–37.
[G: Finland]

Anderson, G. J. A New Approach to the Empirical Investigation of Investment Expenditures. *Econ. J.*, March 1981, 91(361), pp. 88–103.
[G: U.K.]

Anderson, G. J. An Econometric Model of Manufacturing Investment in the U.K.: A Comment. *Econ. J.*, March 1981, 91(361), pp. 122–23.

Andersson, Åke E. Structural Change and Technological Development. *Reg. Sci. Urban Econ.*, August 1981, 11(3), pp. 351–61.

Artus, Patrick, et al. Economic Policy and Private Investment since the Oil Crisis: A Comparative Study of France and Germany. *Europ. Econ. Rev.*, May 1981, 16(1), pp. 7–51.
[G: France; W. Germany]

Auerbach, Alan J. A Note on the Efficient Design of Investment Incentives. *Econ. J.*, March 1981, 91(361), pp. 217–23.

Bauer, P. T. The Investment Fetish. In *Bauer, P. T.*, 1981, pp. 239–54.

Beach, E. F. A Generalization of the Accelerator. In *Chikán, A., ed. (1)*, 1981, pp. 39–48.

Bean, Charles R. A New Approach to the Empirical Investigation of Investment Expenditures: A Comment. *Econ. J.*, March 1981, 91(361), pp. 104–05.

Bean, Charles R. An Econometric Model of Manufacturing Investment in the UK. *Econ. J.*, March 1981, 91(361), pp. 106–21.
[G: U.K.]

Blinder, Alan S. Inventories and the Structure of Macro Models. *Amer. Econ. Rev.*, May 1981, 71(2), pp. 11–16.
[G: U.S.]

Bradford, David F. Issues in the Design of Savings and Investment Incentives. In *Hulten, C. R., ed.*, 1981, pp. 13–47.

Chikán, Attila. Market Disequilibrium and the Volume of Stocks. In *Chikán, A., ed. (I)*, 1981, pp. 73–85. **[G: Selected Countries]**

Chrystal, K. Alec. The 'New Cambridge' Aggregate Expenditure Function: The Emperor's Old Clothes? *J. Monet. Econ.*, May 1981, *7*(3), pp. 395–402. **[G: U.K.]**

Dernburg, Thomas. Issues in the Design of Savings and Investment Incentives: Discussion. In *Hulten, C. R., ed.*, 1981, pp. 48–52.

Di Matteo, Massimo. Capital Theory and Investment Theory: Some Reflections on a Book by C. J. Bliss. *Econ. Notes*, 1981, *10*(3), pp. 138–45.

Eaton, Jonathan. Fiscal Policy, Inflation and the Accumulation of Risky Capital. *Rev. Econ. Stud.*, July 1981, *48*(3), pp. 435–45.

Enzler, Jared J.; Conrad, William E. and Johnson, Lewis. Public Policy and Capital Formation: Introduction. In *Federal Reserve System*, 1981, pp. 1–44. **[G: U.S.; OECD]**

Enzler, Jared J.; Conrad, William E. and Johnson, Lewis. Public Policy and Capital Formation. *Fed. Res. Bull.*, October 1981, *67*(10), pp. 749–61. **[G: U.S.]**

Fiorito, Riccardo. Inventory Investment and Demand for Factors in Disequilibrium. In *Chikán, A., ed. (I)*, 1981, pp. 139–56. **[G: Italy]**

Fralick, James S. Tax Policy and the Demand for Real Capital. In *Federal Reserve System*, 1981, pp. 177–90.

Galloni, Nino. Towards a Post-Keynesian Equilibrium. *Econ. Notes*, 1981, *10*(2), pp. 116–19.

Hendershott, Patric H. Estimates of Investment Functions and Some Implications for Productivity Growth. In *Meyer, L. H., ed.*, 1981, pp. 149–63.

Irvine, F. Owen, Jr. The Dependence of Aggregate Inventory Investment on Inventory Carrying Costs. A Critique of Recent Research. In *Chikán, A., ed. (I)*, 1981, pp. 199–208.

Jorgenson, Dale W. Economic Policy and Private Investment since the Oil Crisis by Artus, et al.: Comment. *Europ. Econ. Rev.*, May 1981, *16*(1), pp. 53–56.

Jorgenson, Dale W. Issues in the Design of Savings and Investment Incentives: Discussion. In *Hulten, C. R., ed.*, 1981, pp. 52–56.

Jüttner, D. Johannes. A Note on Tobin's Supply Price of Capital. *Australian Econ. Pap.*, December 1981, *20*(37), pp. 409–13.

Ketterer, Karl-Heinz and Vollmer, Rainer. Tobin's q und private Investitionsausgaben. Einige analytische Aspekte und empirische Ergebnisse. (Tobin's q and Private Investment Expenditures—Some Analytical and Empirical Issues. With English summary.) *Z. Wirtschaft. Sozialwissen.*, 1981, *101*(2), pp. 153–80. **[G: W. Germany]**

Kotlikoff, Laurence J. and Summers, Lawrence H. The Role of Intergenerational Transfers in Aggregate Capital Accumulation. *J. Polit. Econ.*, August 1981, *89*(4), pp. 706–32. **[G: U.S.]**

Lapidus, André. Investissements et salaires nominaux dans la détermination de l'emploi et de la répartition. (Investment and Money Wages in the Determination of Employment and Distribution. With English summary.) *Revue Écon.*, January 1981, *32*(1), pp. 63–85.

Lovell, Michael C. Aggregation in a Multi-sector Model of the Inventory Cycle. In *Chikán, A., ed. (I)*, 1981, pp. 229–40.

Lucas, Robert E., Jr. Optimal Investment with Rational Expectations. In *Lucas, R. E. and Sargent, T. J., eds.*, 1981, pp. 55–66.

Lucas, Robert E., Jr. and Prescott, Edward C. Investment under Uncertainty. In *Lucas, R. E. and Sargent, T. J., eds.*, 1981, *1971*, pp. 67–90.

Maccini, Louis J. Return-to-Normal Expectations and Investment Demand Functions. *J. Macroecon.*, Summer 1981, *3*(3), pp. 317–34.

Manzetti, Fabio A. On the Stability Implications of Inventory Cycles: An Econometric Analysis of Some Italian Sectors. In *Chikán, A., ed. (I)*, 1981, pp. 241–53. **[G: Italy]**

Nickell, Stephen J. Economic Policy and Private Investment since the Oil Crisis by Artus, et al.: Comment. *Europ. Econ. Rev.*, May 1981, *16*(1), pp. 57–59.

Oulton, Nicholas. Aggregate Investment and Tobin's Q: The Evidence from Britain. *Oxford Econ. Pap.*, July 1981, *33*(2), pp. 177–202. **[G: U.K.]**

Sakovich, V. A. Modelling of Processes of Intercoordinated Planning of Economic Ties and Material Inventories. In *Chikán, A., ed. (I)*, 1981, pp. 301–06.

Sargent, Thomas J. Interpreting Economic Time Series. *J. Polit. Econ.*, April 1981, *89*(2), pp. 213–48.

Skowronek, Czeslaw. Inventory Intensity of Industrial Production and the Possibilities of its Reduction. In *Chikán, A., ed. (I)*, 1981, pp. 307–18.

Steindl, Josef. Some Comments on the Three Versions of Kalecki's Theory of the Trade Cycle. In *[Lipiński, E.]*, 1981, pp. 125–33.

Stojanović, Dragiša. The Model of Inventories Based on the Matrix of Growth. In *Chikán, A., ed. (I)*, 1981, pp. 319–31.

Sumner, Michael T. Investment Grants. In *Currie, D.; Nobay, R. and Peel, D., eds.*, 1981, pp. 286–320. **[G: U.K.]**

Tatom, John A. Investment and the New Energy Regime. In *Federal Reserve System*, 1981, pp. 221–30. **[G: U.S.]**

0234 Theory of Aggregate Supply

Apostolakis, Bobby. A Transcendental Logarithmic Cost Function: An Empirical Case. *Metroecon.*, Feb.-Oct. 1981, *33*(1–2–3), pp. 193–204. **[G: Italy]**

Artus, Patrick and Peyroux, Claude. Fonctions de production avec facteur énergie: estimations pour les grands pays de l'OCDE. (Production Functions with the Energy Factor: Estimates for the Large OECD Countries. With English summary.) *Ann. INSEE*, October–December 1981, (44), pp. 3–39. **[G: OECD]**

Baffi, Paolo. Allocazione delle risorse e politica economica nelle economie contemporanee. (Allocation of Resources and Economic Policy in Contemporary Economies. With English summary.) *Bancaria*, August 1981, *37*(8), pp. 771–73. **[G: Italy]**

Bagi, Faqir S. and Bagi, S. K. Aggregate Production Function and Marginal Productivity Theory of

Distribution. *Indian Econ. J.*, April–June 1981, 28(4), pp. 55–59.

Benavie, Arthur. Stabilization Policies Which Reverse Stagflation in a Short Run Macromodel. *Southern Econ. J.*, July 1981, 48(1), pp. 17–25.

Blinder, Alan S. Thoughts on the Laffer Curve. In *Meyer, L. H., ed.*, 1981, pp. 81–92. [G: U.S.]

Brown, C. V. Macroeconomic Implications I: Income Taxation and Employment—An Integration of Neo-classical and Keynesian Approaches. In *Brown, C. V., ed.*, 1981, pp. 213–22.

Canto, Victor A.; Joines, Douglas H. and Laffer, Arthur B. Tax Rates, Factor Employment, and Market Production. In *Meyer, L. H., ed.*, 1981, pp. 3–32. [G: U.S.]

Chakraborty, Debesh. A Note on the Neoclassical Theory of Investment. *Indian Econ. J.*, January–March 1981, 28(3), pp. 63–69.

Conrad, William E. and Cohen, Darrel S. Inflation, Taxes, and the Capital Stock: A Long-run Analysis. In *Federal Reserve System*, 1981, pp. 267–74.

Faber, Malte. Modern Austrian Capital Theory and Orosel's Standard Neoclassical Analysis: A Reply. *Z. Nationalökon.*, 1981, 41(1–2), pp. 157–76.

Fiorito, Riccardo. Inventory Investment and Demand for Factors in Disequilibrium. In *Chikán, A., ed. (I)*, 1981, pp. 139–56. [G: Italy]

Funke, Michael and Stamatis, Georgios. Towards an Unequivocal Definition of Labor Values in Joint Production as Examined by Ochoa [Steedman after Marx: A Marxian Analysis of Fixed Capital and Joint Production]. *Econ. Forum*, Winter 1981–82, 12(2), pp. 85–91.

Gahlen, Bernhard. How Useful are Post-Keynesian and Neo-Classical Models in Explaining Growth? In *Giersch, H., ed. (II)*, 1981, pp. 1–20.

Glaister, K. W. Macroeconomic Implications II: Labour Supply and Fiscal Policy in a Disequilibrium Model. In *Brown, C. V., ed.*, 1981, pp. 223–54.

Grünbaum, Isi. Keynes in the Light of Marx. In *Grünbaum, I.*, 1981, 1979, pp. 191–216.

Grünbaum, Isi. On Wage Increases as a means to check Oversaving-Unemployment. In *Grünbaum, I.*, 1981, 1939, pp. 11–56.

Hanson, James A. La relación de corto plazo entre crecimiento e inflación en Latinoamérica: Un enfoque de expectativas cuasi racionales o consistentes. (With English summary.) *Cuadernos Econ.*, April 1981, 18(53), pp. 15–41. [G: Brazil; Chile; Colombia; Mexico; Peru]

Hicks, John R. Measurement of Capital—In Practice. In *Hicks, J.*, 1981, 1969, pp. 204–17.

Hicks, John R. Measurement of Capital—In Theory. In *Hicks, J.*, 1981, 1961, pp. 189–203.

Hoel, Michael. Employment Effects of an Increased Oil Price in an Economy with Short-run Labor Immobility. *Scand. J. Econ.*, 1981, 83(2), pp. 269–76.

Johnson, Lewis. Capital Formation in the Long Run. In *Federal Reserve System*, 1981, pp. 91–98.

Johnson, Lewis. Life-cycle Saving, Social Security, and the Long-run Capital Stock. In *Federal Reserve System*, 1981, pp. 275–79.

Kohli, Ulrich R. Nonjointness and Factor Intensity in U.S. Production. *Int. Econ. Rev.*, February 1981, 22(1), pp. 3–18. [G: U.S.]

Kohli, Ulrich R. Valeur adoutée et progrès technique en Suisse, 1948–1976. (Value Added and Technological Change in Switzerland, 1948–1976. With English summary.) *Schweiz. Z. Volkswirtsch. Statist.*, March 1981, 117(1), pp. 11–24. [G: Switzerland]

Leijonhufvud, Axel and Clower, Robert W. Say's Principle, What It Means and Doesn't Mean. In *Leijonhufvud, A.*, 1981, 1973, pp. 79–101.

Lucas, Robert E., Jr. Capacity, Overtime, and Empirical Production Functions. In *Lucas, R. E., Jr.*, 1981, 1970, pp. 146–55.

Lucas, Robert E., Jr. Econometric Testing of the Natural Rate Hypothesis. In *Lucas, R. E., Jr.*, 1981, 1972, pp. 90–103.

Lucas, Robert E., Jr. Equilibrium Search and Unemployment. In *Lucas, R. E., Jr.*, 1981, 1974, pp. 156–78.

Lucas, Robert E., Jr. Real Wages, Employment, and Inflation. In *Lucas, R. E., Jr.*, 1981, 1969, pp. 19–58. [G: U.S.]

Maddison, Angus. How Useful are Post-Keynesian and Neo-Classical Models in Explaining Growth? Comments. In *Giersch, H., ed. (II)*, 1981, pp. 21–25.

Marty, Alvin L. The Aggregate Supply Function Once Again [A Study of Keynes' Theory of Effective Demand]. *Econ. Inquiry*, April 1981, 19(2), pp. 350–51.

McMullen, B. Starr. The Laffer Curve: Fact or Convenient Fantasy. *Econ. Forum*, Winter 1981–82, 12(2), pp. 113–15. [G: U.S.]

Metcalfe, J. S. and Steedman, Ian W. On Two Production Possibility Frontiers. *Metroecon.*, Feb.-Oct. 1981, 33(1–2–3), pp. 1–19.

Mohabbat, Khan A. The Stability of the Production Function and the Marginal Productivity of Inputs: An Empirical Study. *J. Macroecon.*, Spring 1981, 3(2), pp. 283–92. [G: U.S.]

Moore, George R. Taxes, Inflation, and Capital Formation. In *Federal Reserve System*, 1981, pp. 303–26.

Ochoa, Edward M. Labor Values and Joint Production: Reply and Further Thoughts [Steedman after Marx: A Marxian Analysis of Fixed Capital and Joint Production]. *Econ. Forum*, Winter 1981–82, 12(2), pp. 93–102.

Okuguchi, Koji. Joint Production and Specific Factor: A Dynamic Analysis. *Econ. Stud. Quart.*, December 1981, 32(3), pp. 267–71.

Orosel, Gerhard O. Faber's Capital Theory: A Rejoinder. *Z. Nationalökon.*, 1981, 41(1–2), pp. 177–81.

Orosel, Gerhard O. Faber's Modern Austrian Capital Theory: A Critical Survey. *Z. Nationalökon.*, 1981, 41(1–2), pp. 141–55.

Patinkin, Don. Involuntary Unemployment and the Keynesian Supply Function. In *Patinkin, D.*, 1981, 1949, pp. 155–75.

Prachowny, Martin F. J. Aggregate Supply Management in a Small Open Economy. *J. Macroecon.*, Summer 1981, 3(3), pp. 409–21.

Robinson, Joan. Misunderstanding in the Theory of Production. In *Robinson, J.*, 1981, 1979, pp. 135–40.

Robinson, Joan. Piero Sraffa: *Production of Commodities by Means of Commodities*. In *Robinson, J.*,

1981, *1961*, pp. 144–50.

Salvadori, Neri. Falling Rate of Profit with a Constant Real Wage: An Example. *Cambridge J. Econ.*, March 1981, *5*(1), pp. 59–66.

Schim van der Loeff, Sybrand and Harkema, Rins. Estimation and Testing of Alternative Production Function Models. *J. Macroecon.*, Winter 1981, *3*(1), pp. 33–53. **[G: Netherlands]**

Simos, Evangelos O. Real Money Balances as a Productive Input: Further Evidence. *J. Monet. Econ.*, March 1981, *7*(2), pp. 207–25. **[G: U.S.]**

Sinai, Allen and Stokes, Houston H. Money and the Production Function—A Reply to Boyes and Kavanaugh [Money and the Production Function: A Test for Specification Errors]. *Rev. Econ. Statist.*, May 1981, *63*(2), pp. 313–18.

Streissler, Erich. How Useful are Post-Keynesian and Neo-Classical Models in Explaining Growth? Comments. In *Giersch, H., ed. (II)*, 1981, pp. 26–35.

Weymark, John A. On Sums of Production Set Frontiers. *Rev. Econ. Stud.*, January 1981, *48*(1), pp. 179–83.

0235 Theory of Aggregate Distribution

Alberro, José and Persky, Joseph. The Dynamics of Fixed Capital Revaluation and Scrapping. *Rev. Radical Polit. Econ.*, Summer 1981, *13*(2), pp. 32–37.

Amsden, Alice H. An International Comparison of the Rate of Surplus Value in Manufacturing Industry. *Cambridge J. Econ.*, September 1981, *5*(3), pp. 229–49.

Asimakopulos, Athanasios. Themes in a Post Keynesian Theory of Income Distribution. *J. Post Keynesian Econ.*, Winter 1980–81, *3*(2), pp. 158–69.

Baranzini, Mauro. Taux d'intérêt, distribution du revenu, théorie des cycles vitaux et choix du portefeuille. (With English summary.) *Kyklos*, 1981, *34*(4), pp. 593–610.

Bombach, Gottfried. Ein Modell und sein Echo. (With English summary.) *Kyklos*, 1981, *34*(4), pp. 517–39. **[G: W. Germany; Switzerland]**

Bourguignon, François. Pareto Superiority of Unegalitarian Equilibria in Stiglitz' Model of Wealth Distribution with Convex Saving Function. *Econometrica*, November 1981, *49*(6), pp. 1469–75.

Bronfenbrenner, Martin and Conerly, W. B. On Pasinetti's Distribution Paradox. In *[Pen, J.]*, 1981, pp. 25–30.

Brown, W. W. and Santoni, Gary J. Unreal Estimates of the Real Rate of Interest. *Fed. Res. Bank St. Louis Rev.*, January 1981, *63*(1), pp. 18–26. **[G: U.S.]**

Cogoy, Mario. The Fundamental Theorem of Value Analysis. *Metroecon.*, Feb.-Oct. 1981, *33*(1–2–3), pp. 29–40.

Darity, William A., Jr. The Simple Analytics of Neo-Ricardian Growth and Distribution. *Amer. Econ. Rev.*, December 1981, *71*(5), pp. 978–93.

Del Punta, Veniero. A Singular Reasoning about Incentives in Favour of Southern Italy. *Rivista Polit. Econ.*, Supplement December 1981, *71*, pp. 39–60. **[G: Italy]**

Delaunay, J.-C. L'évolution du taux de la plus-value en France (1951–1980). (The Rate of Surplus-Value in France (1951–1980). With English summary.) *L'Actual. Econ.*, April–June 1981, *57*(2), pp. 160–92. **[G: France]**

Di Matteo, Massimo. Capital Theory and Investment Theory: Some Reflections on a Book by C. J. Bliss. *Econ. Notes*, 1981, *10*(3), pp. 138–45.

Dixon, Robert J. A Model of Distribution. *J. Post Keynesian Econ.*, Spring 1981, *3*(3), pp. 383–402.

Dixon, Robert J. The Wage Share and Capital Accumulation. *J. Post Keynesian Econ.*, Fall 1981, *4*(1), pp. 3–9.

Eygelshoven, P. J. and Kuipers, Simon K. A Note on Pasinetti's "Ricardian System" [A Mathematical Formulation of the Ricardian System]. *Rev. Econ. Stud.*, January 1981, *48*(1), pp. 185–86.

Fazi, Elido and Salvadori, Neri. The Existence of a Two-Class Economy in the Kaldor Model of Growth and Distribution. *Kyklos*, 1981, *34*(4), pp. 582–92.

Folkers, Cay. Grundsatzfragen und Konzepte der dynamischen Inzidenzanalyse. (Basic Problems and Concepts of Dynamic Incidence. With English summary.) *Z. Wirtschaft. Sozialwissen.*, 1981, *101*(2), pp. 127–51.

Fujimori, Yoriaki. Theory of Value and Joint-Production. *Econ. Stud. Quart.*, August 1981, *32*(2), pp. 146–55.

Fujimoto, Takao. An Elementary Proof of Okishio's Theorem for Models with Fixed Capital and Heterogeneous Labour. *Metroecon.*, Feb.-Oct. 1981, *33*(1–2–3), pp. 21–27.

Funke, Michael and Stamatis, Georgios. Towards an Unequivocal Definition of Labor Values in Joint Production as Examined by Ochoa [Steedman after Marx: A Marxian Analysis of Fixed Capital and Joint Production]. *Econ. Forum*, Winter 1981–82, *12*(2), pp. 85–91.

Grahl, John. Capital Theory and Overaccumulation. *Brit. Rev. Econ. Issues*, Spring 1981, *2*(8), pp. 76–88.

Grünbaum, Isi. Keynes in the Light of Marx. In *Grünbaum, I.*, 1981, *1979*, pp. 191–216.

Grünbaum, Isi. Marginal Productivity in the Profit-multiplier Growth Model. In *Grünbaum, I.*, 1981, *1963*, pp. 159–90.

Harris, Donald J. Profits, Productivity, and Thrift: The Neoclassical Theory of Capital and Distribution Revisited. *J. Post Keynesian Econ.*, Spring 1981, *3*(3), pp. 359–82.

Hicks, John R. Measurement of Capital—In Theory. In *Hicks, J.*, 1981, *1961*, pp. 189–203.

Hicks, John R. The Mainspring of Economic Growth. *Amer. Econ. Rev.*, Special Issue December 1981, *71*(6), pp. 23–29.

Hodgson, Geoff M. Money and the Sraffa System. *Australian Econ. Pap.*, June 1981, *20*(36), pp. 83–95.

Kaldor, Nicholas. Alternative Theories of Distribution. In *Kaldor, N.*, 1981, *1955*, pp. 209–36.

Kaldor, Nicholas. The Controversy on the Theory of Capital. In *Kaldor, N.*, 1981, *1937*, pp. 153–205.

Krause, Ulrich. Heterogeneous Labour and the Fundamental Marxian Theorem. *Rev. Econ. Stud.*,

January 1981, *48*(1), pp. 173–78.

Krause, Ulrich. Marxian Inequalities in a von Neumann Setting. *Z. Nationalökon.*, 1981, *41*(1–2), pp. 59–67.

Kurz, Heinz D. Smithian Themes in Piero Sraffa's Theory. *J. Post Keynesian Econ.*, Winter 1980–81, *3*(2), pp. 271–80.

Lapidus, André. Investissements et salaires nominaux dans la détermination de l'emploi et de la répartition. (Investment and Money Wages in the Determination of Employment and Distribution. With English summary.) *Revue Écon.*, January 1981, *32*(1), pp. 63–85.

von Mises, Ludwig. Inconvertible Capital. In *von Mises, L.*, 1981, pp. 217–31.

Munley, Frank. Wages, Salaries, and the Profit Share: A Reassessment of the Evidence. *Cambridge J. Econ.*, June 1981, *5*(2), pp. 159–73. [G: U.S.]

Obrinsky, Mark. The Profit Prophets. *J. Post Keynesian Econ.*, Summer 1981, *3*(4), pp. 491–502.

Ochoa, Edward M. Labor Values and Joint Production: Reply and Further Thoughts [Steedman after Marx: A Marxian Analysis of Fixed Capital and Joint Production]. *Econ. Forum*, Winter 1981–82, *12*(2), pp. 93–102.

Olson, Mancur and Bailey, Martin J. Positive Time Preference. *J. Polit. Econ.*, February 1981, *89*(1), pp. 1–25.

Pasinetti, Luigi L. On the Ricardian Theory of Value: A Note [A Mathematical Formulation of Ricardian System]. *Rev. Econ. Stud.*, October 1981, *48*(4), pp. 673–75.

Pasinetti, Luigi L. The Rate of Interest and the Distribution of Income in a Pure Labor Economy. *J. Post Keynesian Econ.*, Winter 1980–81, *3*(2), pp. 170–82.

Perelman, Michael. Capital, Constant Capital and the Social Division of Labor. *Rev. Radical Polit. Econ.*, Fall 1981, *13*(3), pp. 43–53.

Reca, Lucio G. and Verstraeten, Juan. La tasa social de retorno al capital en la Argentina (1935–1973). Un intento de estimación. (The Social Rate of Return to Capital in Argentina, 1935–1973. With English summary.) *Económica*, January–August 1981, *27*(1–2), pp. 57–92. [G: Argentina]

Riese, Hajo. Theorie der Produktion und Einkommensverteilung. (With English summary.) *Kyklos*, 1981, *34*(4), pp. 540–62.

Robinson, Joan. Debate: 1970s. In *Robinson, J.*, 1981, pp. 123–30.

Robinson, Joan. Retrospect: 1980. In *Robinson, J.*, 1981, pp. 131–34.

Sardoni, Claudio. Multi-Sectoral Models of Balanced Growth and the Marxian Schemes of Expanded Reproduction. *Australian Econ. Pap.*, December 1981, *20*(37), pp. 383–97.

Shah, Anup R. and Desai, Meghnad. Growth Cycles with Induced Technical Change. *Econ. J.*, December 1981, *91*(364), pp. 1006–10.

Skott, Peter. Technological Advance with Depletion of Innovation Possibilities: A Comment and Some Extensions. *Econ. J.*, December 1981, *91*(364), pp. 977–87.

Steedman, Ian W. Time Preference, the Rate of Interest and Abstinence from Accumulation. *Aus-* *tralian Econ. Pap.*, December 1981, *20*(37), pp. 219–34.

Sylos Labini, Paolo. On the Concept of the Optimum Rate of Profit. In *[Lipiński, E.]*, 1981, pp. 141–54.

Weintraub, Sidney. An Eclectic Theory of Income Shares. *J. Post Keynesian Econ.*, Fall 1981, *4*(1), pp. 10–24.

Weisskopf, Thomas E. Wages, Salaries and the Profit Share: A Rejoinder [Marxian Crisis Theory and the Rate of Profit in the Postwar US Economy]. *Cambridge J. Econ.*, June 1981, *5*(2), pp. 175–82. [G: U.S.]

Woodfield, Alan and McDonald, John. Income Distribution in the Pasinetti Model: An Extension. *Australian Econ. Pap.*, June 1981, *20*(36), pp. 104–14.

024 Welfare Theory

0240 General

Aranson, Peter H. and Ordeshook, Peter C. Regulation, Redistribution, and Public Choice. *Public Choice*, 1981, *37*(1), pp. 69–100.

Arrow, Kenneth J. Optimal and Voluntary Income Distribution. In *[Bergson, A.]*, 1981, pp. 267–88.

Barnett, A. H. Soliciting Accurate Evaluations of Public Goods. *Public Finance Quart.*, April 1981, *9*(2), pp. 221–34.

Bates, Robert H. Public Choice Processes. In *Russell, C. S. and Nicholson, N. K., eds.*, 1981, pp. 81–117.

Becker, Gary S. Altruism in the Family and Selfishness in the Market Place. *Economica*, February 1981, *48*(189), pp. 1–15.

Bergstrom, Ted C. When Does Majority Rule Supply Public Goods Efficiently? In *Strøm, S., ed.*, 1981, *1979*, pp. 75–85.

Blackorby, Charles; Donaldson, David and Auersperg, Maria. A New Procedure for the Measurement of Inequality within and among Population Subgroups. *Can. J. Econ.*, November 1981, *14*(4), pp. 665–85. [G: Canada]

Bohm, Peter. Estimating Willingness to Pay: Why and How? In *Strøm, S., ed.*, 1981, *1979*, pp. 1–12.

Bordes, Georges. Individualisme, ordinalisme et bien-être social. (Individualism, Ordinalism, and Social Welfare. With English summary.) *Ann. INSEE*, January–March 1981, (41), pp. 41–66.

Buchanan, James M. L.S.E. Cost Theory in Retrospect. In *Buchanan, J. M. and Thirlby, G. F., eds.*, 1981, pp. 1–16.

Burns, Michael E. and Walsh, Cliff. Market Provision of Price-excludable Public Goods: A General Analysis. *J. Polit. Econ.*, February 1981, *89*(1), pp. 166–91.

Butlin, J. A. Environmental Quality and Resource Use under Laissez-faire. In *Butlin, J. A., ed.*, 1981, pp. 3–8.

Canterbery, E. Ray. Income Redistribution and Rawlsian Justice. *J. Econ. Bus.*, Spring/Summer 1981, *33*(3), pp. 188–201.

Cartwright, Philip. Welfare Economics and the Log

Export Policy Issue: Discussion. In *Sedjo, R. A.*, *ed.*, 1981, pp. 209–15.   [G: U.S.]

Cebula, Richard J. A Note on the Determinants of AFDC Policies [State Tax Structure and the Supply of AFDC Assistance]. *Public Choice*, 1981, 37(2), pp. 327–30.   [G: U.S.]

Champsaur, Paul and Laroque, Guy. Le plan face aux comportements stratégiques des unités décentralisées. (Planning, Public Goods, and Strategic Behavior by Decentralized Units. With English summary.) *Ann. INSEE*, April–June 1981, (42), pp. 3–30.

Charles, Susan and Westaway, Anthony J. Ignorance and Merit Wants. *Finanzarchiv*, 1981, 39(1), pp. 74–78.

Collard, David. Market Failure and Government Failure. In *Seldon, A., ed.*, 1981, pp. 121–46.

Conybeare, John A. C. The Private and Social Utility of Extortion. *Amer. Econ. Rev.*, December 1981, 71(5), pp. 1028–30.

Cory, Dennis C., et al. Use of Paasche and Laspeyres Variations to Estimate Consumer Welfare Change. *Agr. Econ. Res.*, April 1981, 33(2), pp. 1–6.

Cowell, Frank A. and Kuga, Kiyoshi. Additivity and the Entropy Concept: An Axiomatic Approach to Inequality Measurement. *J. Econ. Theory*, August 1981, 25(1), pp. 131–43.

Cowell, Frank A. and Kuga, Kiyoshi. Inequality Measurement: An Axiomatic Approach. *Europ. Econ. Rev.*, March 1981, 15(3), pp. 287–305.

Darcy, Robert L. Value Issues in Program Evaluation. *J. Econ. Issues*, June 1981, 15(2), pp. 449–61.

Dworkin, Gerald. Paternalism and Welfare Policy. In *Brown, P. G.; Johnson, C. and Vernier, P.*, *eds.*, 1981, pp. 43–55.

Eichhorn, Wolfgang and Gehrig, Wilhelm. Generalized Convexity and the Measurement of Inequality. In *Schaible, S. and Ziemba, W. T., eds.*, 1981, pp. 637–42.

Encarnación, José, Jr. Group Choice with Lexicographic Preferences. *Phillipine Rev. Econ. Bus.*, Sept. & Dec. 1981, 18(3/4), pp. 104–15.

Endres, Alfred. The Provision of Product Attributes: Monopolistic Equilibrium and Social Optimum. *Metroecon.*, Feb.-Oct. 1981, 33(1–2–3), pp. 129–44.

Faulhaber, Gerald R. and Levinson, Stephen B. Subsidy-Free Prices and Anonymous Equity [Cross-Subsidization: Pricing in Public Enterprises]. *Amer. Econ. Rev.*, December 1981, 71(5), pp. 1083–91.

Fesmire, James M. and Truscott, Michael H. The Net Demand for Public Goods. *Eastern Econ. J.*, July-Oct. 1981, 7(3–4), pp. 151–56.

Fogarty, T. M. Prisoner's Dilemma and Other Public Goods Games. *Conflict Manage. Peace Sci.*, Spring 1981, 5(2), pp. 111–20.

Fountain, John. Consumer Surplus When Preferences are Intransitive: Analysis and Interpretation. *Econometrica*, March 1981, 49(2), pp. 379–94.

Fujigaki, Yoshifumi and Sato, Kimitoshi. Incentives in the Generalized MDP Procedure for the Provision of Public Goods. *Rev. Econ. Stud.*, July 1981,

48(3), pp. 473–85.

Gaertner, Wulf. Rawlsianism, Utilitarianism, and Profiles of Extended Orderings. *Z. ges. Staatswiss.*, March 1981, 137(1), pp. 78–96.

Gierer, Alfred. Socioeconomic Inequalities: Effects of Self-Enhancement, Depletion and Redistribution. *Jahr. Nationalökon. Statist.*, July 1981, 196(4), pp. 309–31.

Goldberg, Victor P. Pigou on Complex Contracts and Welfare Economics. In *Zerbe, R. O., Jr.*, *ed.*, 1981, pp. 39–51.

Grout, Paul. On Minimax Regret and Welfare Economics: Addendum and Correction. *J. Public Econ.*, December 1981, 16(3), pp. 395–96.

Grout, Paul. Social Welfare and Exhaustible Resources. In *Butlin, J. A., ed.*, 1981, pp. 88–109.

Hansmann, Henry B. Consumer Perceptions of Nonprofit Enterprise: Reply [The Role of Nonprofit Enterprise]. *Yale Law J.*, June 1981, 90(7), pp. 1633–38.

Harstad, Ronald M. and Marrese, Michael. Implementation of Mechanism by Processes: Public Good Allocation Experiments. *J. Econ. Behav. Organ.*, June 1981, 2(2), pp. 129–51.

Hausman, Jerry A. Exact Consumer's Surplus and Deadweight Loss. *Amer. Econ. Rev.*, September 1981, 71(4), pp. 662–76.

Hicks, John R. A Manifesto. In *Hicks, J.*, 1981, pp. 135–41.

Hicks, John R. The Foundations of Welfare Economics. In *Hicks, J.*, 1981, 1939, pp. 59–77.

Hicks, John R. The Four Consumer's Surpluses. In *Hicks, J.*, 1981, 1943, pp. 114–32.

Hicks, John R. The Rehabilitation of Consumers' Surplus. In *Hicks, J.*, 1981, 1941, pp. 100–113.

Hicks, John R. The Scope and Status of Welfare Economics. In *Hicks, J.*, 1981, 1975, pp. 218–39.

Hicks, John R. Valuation of the Social Income II—The Utility Approach [The Measurement of Real Income]. In *Hicks, J.*, 1981, pp. 142–88.

Hicks, John R. Valuation of Social Income I. In *Hicks, J.*, 1981, 1940, pp. 78–99.

Hildebrandt, Gregory G. and Tregarthen, Timothy D. Observing Preferences for Educational Quality: The Weak Complementarity Approach. In *Strum, S., ed.*, 1981, 1979, pp. 47–56. [G: U.S.]

Howe, Roger E. and Roemer, John E. Rawlsian Justice as the Core of a Game. *Amer. Econ. Rev.*, December 1981, 71(5), pp. 880–95.

Inada, Ken-ichi. On "The Marginal Substitution Rate of Distribution." (In Japanese. With English summary.) *Econ. Stud. Quart.*, April 1981, 32(1), pp. 1–11.

Irvine, I. J. The Use of Cross-Section Microdata in Life Cycle Models: An Application to Inequality Theory in Nonstationary Economies. *Quart. J. Econ.*, May 1981, 96(2), pp. 301–16. [G: U.S.]

Jackson, Raymond. A Rejoinder [Optimal Studies for Public Transit]. *J. Transp. Econ. Policy*, January 1981, 15(1), pp. 72–75.

James, Jeffrey and Stewart, Frances. New Products: A Discussion of the Welfare Effects of the Introduction of New Products in Developing Countries. *Oxford Econ. Pap.*, March 1981, 33(1), pp. 81–107.   [G: LDCs]

Johansen, Leif. Incentives in Public Decision Making: Review and Comments. *J. Public Econ.*, August 1981, *16*(1), pp. 123–28.

Johnson, Conrad. Equity: Its Scope and Its Relation to Other Objectives. In *Brown, P. G.; Johnson, C. and Vernier, P.*, eds., 1981, pp. 125–45.

Judge, Ken. Pricing and Public Choice in Social Welfare. In *Seldon, A.*, ed., 1981, pp. 147–69.

Juster, F. Thomas; Courant, Paul N. and Dow, Greg K. A Theoretical Framework for the Measurement of Well-Being. *Rev. Income Wealth*, March 1981, *27*(1), pp. 1–31.

Kakwani, Nanak. Note on a New Measure of Poverty. *Econometrica*, March 1981, *49*(2), pp. 525–26.

Kakwani, Nanak. Welfare Measures: An International Comparison. *J. Devel. Econ.*, February 1981, *8*(1), pp. 21–45.

Kaldor, Nicholas. Welfare Propositions in Economics. In *Kaldor, N.*, 1981, *1939*, pp. 143–46.

Kalt, Joseph P. Public Goods and the Theory of Government. *Cato J.*, Fall 1981, *1*(2), pp. 565–84.

Kaneko, Mamoru. The Nash Social Welfare Function for a Measure Space of Individuals. *J. Math. Econ.*, July 1981, *8*(2), pp. 173–200.

Kolm, Serge-Christophe. Efficacité et altruisme: les sophismes de Mandeville, Smith et Pareto. (Efficiency and Altruism: The Mandeville, Smith and Pareto Fallacies. With English summary.) *Revue Écon.*, January 1981, *32*(1), pp. 5–31.

Krutilla, John V. Reflections of an Applied Welfare Economist. *J. Environ. Econ. Manage.*, March 1981, *8*(1), pp. 1–10.

Laffont, Jean-Jacques. Théorie des incitations: un exemple introductif. (With English summary.) *Écon. Appl.*, 1981, *34*(1), pp. 117–40.

Laffont, Jean-Jacques and Maskin, Eric S. On the Difficulty of Attaining Distributional Goals with Imperfect Information about Consumers. In *Strøm, S.*, ed., 1981, *1979*, pp. 86–96.

Lall, Sanjaya. Welfare Economics and Development Problems. In *Lall, S.*, 1981, *1976*, pp. 24–50.

Littlechild, S. C. Misleading Calculations of the Social Costs of Monopoly Power. *Econ. J.*, June 1981, *91*(362), pp. 348–63.   [G: U.S.; U.K.]

MacRae, Duncan, Jr. Valuative Problems of Public Policy Analysis. In *Crecine, J. P.*, ed., 1981, pp. 175–94.

Marwell, Gerald and Ames, Ruth E. Economists Free Ride, Does Anyone Else?: Experiments on the Provision of Public Goods, IV. *J. Public Econ.*, June 1981, *15*(3), pp. 295–310.

McClennen, E. F. Constitutional Choice: Rawls vs. Harsanyi. In *Pitt, J. C.*, ed., 1981, pp. 93–109.

McGuckin, J. Thomas and Young, Robert A. On the Economics of Desalination of Brackish Household Water Supplies. *J. Environ. Econ. Manage.*, March 1981, *8*(1), pp. 79–91.   [G: U.S.]

McKee, Michael and West, Edwin G. The Theory of Second Best: A Solution in Search of a Problem. *Econ. Inquiry*, July 1981, *19*(3), pp. 436–48.

McKenzie, Richard B. The Construction of the Demand for Public Goods and the Theory of Income Redistribution. *Public Choice*, 1981, *36*(2), pp. 337–44.

Menz, Fredric C. and Mullen, John K. The Economics of Congestion: A Comment. *Public Finance Quart.*, January 1981, *9*(1), pp. 107–16.

Mishan, Ezra J. Economic Criteria for Intergenerational Comparisons. In *Mishan, E. J.*, 1981, *1977*, pp. 46–58.

Mishan, Ezra J. Pareto Optimality and the Law. In *Mishan, E. J.*, 1981, *1967*, pp. 105–24.

Mishan, Ezra J. Rent as a Measure of Welfare Change. In *Mishan, E. J.*, 1981, *1959*, pp. 73–78.

Mishan, Ezra J. Second Thoughts on Second Best. In *Mishan, E. J.*, 1981, *1962*, pp. 14–21.

Mishan, Ezra J. The Plain Truth about Consumer Surplus. In *Mishan, E. J.*, 1981, *1977*, pp. 61–72.

Mishan, Ezra J. The Recent Debate on Welfare Criteria. In *Mishan, E. J.*, 1981, *1965*, pp. 22–32.

Mishan, Ezra J. The Value of Trying to Value Life [Trying to Value a Life]. *J. Public Econ.*, February 1981, *15*(1), pp. 133–37.

Mishan, Ezra J. Welfare Criteria: Resolution of a Paradox. In *Mishan, E. J.*, 1981, *1973*, pp. 33–44.

Moore, Thomas Gale. Comments on Aranson & Ordershook's Regulation, Redistribution, and Public Choice. *Public Choice*, 1981, *37*(1), pp. 101–05.

Mueller, Dennis C. and Cowling, Keith. The Social Costs of Monopoly Power Revisited. *Econ. J.*, September 1981, *91*(363), pp. 721–25. [G: U.S.; U.K.]

Myerson, Roger B. Utilitarianism, Egalitarianism, and the Timing Effect in Social Choice Problems. *Econometrica*, June 1981, *49*(4), pp. 883–97.

Nagarajan, Karatholuvu V. Rawls, Nozick, Justice and Welfare: An Economic Interpretation. *Indian Econ. J.*, April–June 1981, *28*(4), pp. 36–47.

Nakatani, Iwao. A "Sample" Tâtonnement Process for Public Goods. *Osaka Econ. Pap.*, December 1981, *31*(2–3), pp. 115–20.

Ng, Yew-Kwang. Welfarism: A Defence against Sen's Attack [Personal Utilities and Public Judgements: Or What's Wrong with Welfare Economics]. *Econ. J.*, June 1981, *91*(362), pp. 527–30.

Nicholson, Norman K. Applications of Public Choice Theory to Rural Development—A Statement of the Problem. In *Russell, C. S. and Nicholson, N. K.*, eds., 1981, pp. 17–41.

Nielsen, Kai. A Rationale for Egalitarianism. *Soc. Res.*, Summer 1981, *48*(2), pp. 260–76.

O'Hare, Michael. Information Management and Public Choice. In *Crecine, J. P.*, ed., 1981, pp. 223–56.

Pasour, E. C., Jr. Pareto Optimality as a Guide to Income Redistribution. *Public Choice*, 1981, *36*(1), pp. 75–87.

Patinkin, Don. Demand Curves and Consumer's Surplus. In *Patinkin, D.*, 1981, *1963*, pp. 181–208.

Permut, Steven E. Consumer Perceptions of Nonprofit Enterprise: A Comment on Hansmann [The Role of Nonprofit Enterprise]. *Yale Law J.*, June 1981, *90*(7), pp. 1623–32.

Petersen, Jørn Henrik. Decentralisering i den offentlige sektor. (Collective Decision-Making and Decentralization. With English summary.) *Na-*

tionaløkon. Tidsskr., 1981, *119*(3), pp. 378–91.

Plotnick, Robert. A Measure of Horizontal Inequity. *Rev. Econ. Statist.*, May 1981, *63*(2), pp. 283–88. [G: U.S.]

Pollak, Robert A. The Social Cost of Living Index. *J. Public Econ.*, June 1981, *15*(3), pp. 311–36.

Rader, Trout. Utility over Time: The Homothetic Case. *J. Econ. Theory*, October 1981, *25*(2), pp. 219–36.

Reynolds, Larry. Foundations of an Institutional Theory of Regulation. *J. Econ. Issues*, September 1981, *15*(3), pp. 641–56. [G: U.S.]

Robbins, Lionel. Remarks upon Certain Aspects of the Theory of Costs. In *Buchanan, J. M. and Thirlby, G. F.*, eds., 1981, *1934*, pp. 19–41.

Rodriguez, Alvaro. Rawls' Maximin Criterion and Time Consistency: A Generalization. *Rev. Econ. Stud.*, October 1981, *48*(4), pp. 599–605.

Russell, Clifford S. Public Choice and Rural Development: Introduction. In *Russell, C. S. and Nicholson, N. K.*, eds., 1981, pp. 1–15.

Samuelson, Paul A. Bergsonian Welfare Economics. In *[Bergson, A.]*, 1981, pp. 223–66.

Saposnik, Rubin. Rank-Dominance in Income Distributions. *Public Choice*, 1981, *36*(1), pp. 147–51.

Sato, Fumitaka. On the Informational Size of Message Spaces for Resource Allocation Processes in Economies with Public Goods. *J. Econ. Theory*, February 1981, *24*(1), pp. 48–69.

Schneider, Friedrich and Pommerehne, Werner W. Free Riding and Collective Action: An Experiment in Public Microeconomics. *Quart. J. Econ.*, November 1981, *96*(4), pp. 689–704.

Schulze, William D.; Brookshire, David S. and Sandler, Todd. The Social Rate of Discount for Nuclear Waste Storage: Economics or Ethics? *Natural Res. J.*, October 1981, *21*(4), pp. 811–32.

Sen, Amartya. A Reply to 'Welfarism: A Defence against Sen's Attack' [Personal Utilities and Public Judgements: Or What's Wrong with Welfare Economics]. *Econ. J.*, June 1981, *91*(362), pp. 531–35.

Sen, Amartya. Ingredients of Famine Analysis: Availability and Entitlements. *Quart. J. Econ.*, 1981, *96*(3), pp. 433–64. [G: India; Bangladesh]

Shilony, Yuval. A Methodological Note on Welfare Calculus [Optimal Subsidies for Public Transit]. *J. Transp. Econ. Policy*, January 1981, *15*(1), pp. 69–72.

Siebert, Horst. Ökonomische Theorie natürlicher Ressourcen. Ein Uberblick. (The Economic Theory of Natural Resources: A Survey. With English summary.) *Z. Wirtschaft. Sozialwissen.*, 1981, *101*(3), pp. 267–98.

Small, Kenneth A. and Rosen, Harvey S. Applied Welfare Economics with Discrete Choice Models. *Econometrica*, January 1981, *49*(1), pp. 105–30.

Smith, Vernon L. An Experimental Comparison of Three Public Good Decision Mechanisms. In *Strm, S.*, ed., 1981, *1979*, pp. 57–74. [G: U.S.]

Steve, Sergio. I fondamenti attuali della politica sociale. (The Present Foundations of Social Policy. With English summary.) *Giorn. Econ.*, July–August 1981, *40*(7–8), pp. 411–22.

Thomson, William. A Class of Solutions to Bargaining Problems [Independence of Irrelevant Alternatives and Solutions to Nash's Bargaining Problem]. *J. Econ. Theory*, December 1981, *25*(3), pp. 431–41.

Tideman, T. Nicolaus and Tullock, Gordon. Coalitions under Demand Revealing [A New and Superior Process of Making Social Choices]. *Public Choice*, 1981, *36*(2), pp. 323–28.

Tirole, Jean. Taux d'actualisation et optimum second. (The Social Rate of Discount and the Theory of the Second Best. With English summary.) *Revue Écon.*, September 1981, *32*(5), pp. 829–69.

Walsh, Cliff. A Reconsideration of Some Aspects of the Private Production of Public Goods. *Rev. Soc. Econ.*, April 1981, *39*(1), pp. 19–35.

Welch, Robert L. Incentives and Risk Aversion in the Provision of a Public Input. *J. Public Econ.*, February 1981, *15*(1), pp. 87–103.

Wiseman, A. Clark and Sedjo, Roger. Welfare Economics and the Log Export Policy Issue. In *Sedjo, R. A.*, ed., 1981, pp. 187–208. [G: U.S.]

Wooders, Myrna. Equilibria, the Core and Jurisdiction Structures in Economies with a Local Public Good: A Correction. *J. Econ. Theory*, August 1981, *25*(1), pp. 144–51.

Worland, Stephen T. Exploitative Capitalism: The Natural-Law Perspective. *Soc. Res.*, Summer 1981, *48*(2), pp. 277–305.

Yaari, Menahem E. Rawls, Edgeworth, Shapley, Nash: Theories of Distributive Justice Re-examined. *J. Econ. Theory*, February 1981, *24*(1), pp. 1–39.

0242 Allocative Efficiency Including Theory of Cost/Benefit

Aivazian, Varouj A. and Callen, Jeffrey L. The Coase Theorem and the Empty Core. *J. Law Econ.*, April 1981, *24*(1), pp. 175–81.

Alam, M. Shahid. Rentiers or Rent-Seekers? Some Clarifications. *Indian Econ. J.*, April–June 1981, *28*(4), pp. 48–54.

Arrow, Kenneth J. Pareto Efficiency with Costly Tranfers. In *[Lipiński, E.]*, 1981, pp. 73–86.

Balasko, Yves and Shell, Karl. The Overlapping-Generations Model. II: The Case of Pure Exchange with Money. *J. Econ. Theory*, February 1981, *24*(1), pp. 112–42.

Balasko, Yves and Shell, Karl. The Overlapping-Generations Model. III: The Case of Log-Linear Utility Functions. *J. Econ. Theory*, 1981, *24*(1), pp. 143–52.

Baldwin, G. B. A Layman's Guide to Little–Mirrlees. In *Livingstone, I.*, ed., 1981, *1972*, pp. 223–28.

Baumol, William J. Application of the Theory of Superfairness. In *Currie, D.; Peel, D. and Peters, W.*, eds., 1981, pp. 34–50.

Becker, Robert A. The Duality of a Dynamic Model of Equilibrium and an Optimal Growth Model: The Heterogeneous Capital Goods Case. *Quart. J. Econ.*, May 1981, *96*(2), pp. 271–300.

Bewley, Truman F. Stationary Equilibrium. *J. Econ. Theory*, April 1981, *24*(2), pp. 265–95.

Boulding, Kenneth E. Allocation and Distribution: The Quarrelsome Twins. In *Solo, R. A. and An-*

derson, C. W., eds., 1981, pp. 141–64.

Bourguignon, François. Pareto Superiority of Unegalitarian Equilibria in Stiglitz' Model of Wealth Distribution with Convex Saving Function. *Econometrica*, November 1981, *49*(6), pp. 1469–75.

Brookshire, David S. and Crocker, Thomas D. The Advantages of Contingent Valuation Methods for Benefit-Cost Analysis. *Public Choice*, 1981, *36*(2), pp. 235–52.

Brown, H. James. Market Failure: Efficiency or Equity? In *de Neufville, J. I., ed.*, 1981, pp. 143–47.

Browning, Edgar K. A Theory of Paternalistic In-Kind Transfers. *Econ. Inquiry*, October 1981, *19*(4), pp. 579–97.

Cesario, Frank J. Benefit-Cost Analysis under Pricing Constraints. *Appl. Econ.*, June 1981, *13*(2), pp. 215–24.

Champsaur, Paul and Laroque, Guy. Fair Allocations in Large Economies. *J. Econ. Theory*, October 1981, *25*(2), pp. 269–82.

Clark, Stephen A. A Combinatorial Analysis of the Overlapping Generations Model. *Rev. Econ. Stud.*, January 1981, *48*(1), pp. 139–45.

Coase, R. H. The Coase Theorem and the Empty Core: A Comment. *J. Law Econ.*, April 1981, *24*(1), pp. 183–87.

Cohon, Jared L.; ReVelle, Charles S. and Palmer, Richard N. Multiobjective Generating Techniques for Risk/Benefit Analysis. In *Haimes, Y. Y., ed.*, 1981, pp. 123–34. [G: U.S.]

Cooper, Charles. Professor Pearce on 'The Limits of Cost-Benefit Analysis as a Guide to Environmental Policy': A Comment. *Kyklos*, 1981, *34*(2), pp. 274–78.

Cornes, Richard and Albon, Robert. Evaluation of Welfare Change in Quantity-Constrained Regimes. *Econ. Rec.*, June 1981, *57*(157), pp. 186–90.

Dnes, A. W. The Case of Monopoly and Pollution [Monopoly Power as a Means to Pollution Control]. *J. Ind. Econ.*, December 1981, *30*(2), pp. 213–16.

Drummond, M. F. Welfare Economics and Cost Benefit Analysis in Health Care. *Scot. J. Polit. Econ.*, June 1981, *28*(2), pp. 125–45.

Faith, Roger L. and Thompson, Earl A. A Paradox in the Theory of Second Best. *Econ. Inquiry*, April 1981, *19*(2), pp. 235–44.

Feldstein, Martin S. The Welfare Loss of Excess Health Insurance. In *Feldstein, M., ed.*, 1973, pp. 175–204. [G: U.S.]

Foster, Edward. The Treatment of Rents in Cost–Benefit Analysis. *Amer. Econ. Rev.*, March 1981, *71*(1), pp. 171–78.

Freixas, Xavier. Une analyse coût-avantage des mécanismes d'allocation: l'approche prix-quantités. (A Cost–Benefit Analysis of Allocation Mechanisms: The Prices versus Quantities Approach. With English summary.) *Revue Écon.*, November 1981, *32*(6), pp. 1074–86.

Gaertner, Wulf and Krüger, Lorenz. Self-Supporting Preferences and Individual Rights: The Possibility of Paretian Libertarianism. *Economica*, February 1981, *48*(189), pp. 17–28.

Gardner, Roy. Wealth and Power in a Collegial Pol-

ity. *J. Econ. Theory*, December 1981, *25*(3), pp. 353–66.

Gärtner, Manfred. Legislative Profits and the Rate of Change of Money Wages: A Reply. *Public Choice*, 1981, *37*(3), pp. 589–93. [G: W. Germany]

Goodrich, Chris. Legislative Profits and the Rate of Change of Money Wages: A Comment. *Public Choice*, 1981, *37*(3), pp. 585–88. [G: W. Germany]

Graham, Daniel A. Cost-Benefit Analysis under Uncertainty. *Amer. Econ. Rev.*, September 1981, *71*(4), pp. 715–25.

Guesnerie, Roger and Oddou, Claude. Second Best Taxation as a Game. *J. Econ. Theory*, August 1981, *25*(1), pp. 67–91.

Hammond, Peter J. *Ex-ante* and *Ex-post* Welfare Optimality under Uncertainty. *Economica*, August 1981, *48*(191), pp. 235–50.

Hanke, Steve H. On the Feasibility of Benefit-Cost Analysis. *Public Policy*, Spring 1981, *29*(2), pp. 147–57.

Hansen, Ronald W. Pharmaceutical Innovation, Product Imitation, and Public Policy: Comment. In *Helms, R. B., ed.*, 1981, pp. 293–99.

Harris, Milton and Townsend, Robert M. Resource Allocation under Asymmetric Information. *Econometrica*, January 1981, *49*(1), pp. 33–64.

Heiner, Ronald A. Length and Cycle Equalization. *J. Econ. Theory*, August 1981, *25*(1), pp. 101–30.

Hoffman, Elizabeth and Plott, Charles R. The Effect of Intertemporal Speculation on the Outcomes in Seller Posted Offer Auction Markets. *Quart. J. Econ.*, May 1981, *96*(2), pp. 223–41.

Howard, Ronald A. The Risks of Benefit-Cost-Risk Analysis. In *Haimes, Y. Y., ed.*, 1981, pp. 135–47. [G: U.S.]

Hurwicz, Leonid. On Incentive Problems in the Design of Non-Wasteful Resource Allocation Systems. In *[Lipiński, E.]*, 1981, pp. 93–106.

Jewitt, Ian. Preference Structure and Piecemeal Second Best Policy. *J. Public Econ.*, October 1981, *16*(2), pp. 215–31.

Joshi, V. The Rationale and Relevance of the Little–Mirrlees Criterion. In *Livingstone, I., ed.*, 1972, pp. 229–44.

Keiding, Hans. Existence of Budget Constrained Pareto Efficient Allocations. *J. Econ. Theory*, June 1981, *24*(3), pp. 393–97.

Keyes, Lucile S. A Non-Paretian Approach to Market Regulation. *J. Post Keynesian Econ.*, Spring 1981, *3*(3), pp. 440–51.

Krohn, Lawrence D. The Generational Optimum Economy: Extracting Monopoly Gains from Posterity through Taxation of Capital. *Amer. Econ. Rev.*, June 1981, *71*(3), pp. 411–20.

Lane, John and Mitra, Tapan. On Nash Equilibrium Programs of Capital Accumulation under Altruistic Preferences. *Int. Econ. Rev.*, June 1981, *22*(2), pp. 309–31.

Lewis, Tracy R. Markets and Environmental Management with a Storable Pollutant. *J. Environ. Econ. Manage.*, March 1981, *8*(1), pp. 11–18.

Magill, Michael J. P. Infinite Horizon Programs. *Econometrica*, May 1981, *49*(3), pp. 679–711.

Matthews, R. C. O. Morality, Competition and Efficiency. *Manchester Sch. Econ. Soc. Stud.*, December 1981, *49*(4), pp. 289–309.

McDonald, John F. The Use of Weighted Discount Rates in Cost-Benefit Analysis: A Further Analysis. *Water Resources Res.*, June 1981, *17*(3), pp. 478–80.

Mishan, Ezra J. A Reappraisal of the Principles of Resource Allocation. In *Mishan, E. J.*, 1981, *1957*, pp. 3–13.

Mishan, Ezra J. Distributive Implications of Economic Controls. In *Ferguson, A. R. and LeVeen, E. P., eds.*, 1981, pp. 155–75.

Mishan, Ezra J. Do Economic Evaluations of Allocative Changes Have Any Validity in the West Today? In *Mishan, E. J.*, 1981, pp. 256–65.

Mishan, Ezra J. Evaluation of Life and Limb: A Theoretical Approach. In *Mishan, E. J.*, 1981, *1971*, pp. 89–99.

Mishan, Ezra J. Flexibility and Consistency in Project Evaluation. In *Mishan, E. J.*, 1981, *1974*, pp. 155–64.

Mishan, Ezra J. The Difficulty in Evaluating Long-lived Projects. In *Mishan, E. J.*, 1981, pp. 196–205.

Mishan, Ezra J. The Nature of Economic Expertise Reconsidered. In *Mishan, E. J.*, 1981, pp. 175–86.

Mishan, Ezra J. The Use of Compensating and Equivalent Variations in Cost–Benefit Analysis. In *Mishan, E. J.*, 1981, *1976*, pp. 165–73.

Mishan, Ezra J. The Use of DPV in Public Investment Criteria: A Critique. In *Mishan, E. J.*, 1981, pp. 188–95.

Mishan, Ezra J. What Is Wrong with Roskill? In *Mishan, E. J.*, 1981, *1970*, pp. 209–18. [G: U.K.]

Mitra, Tapan. Efficiency, Weak Value Maximality and Weak Value Optimality in a Multisector Model. *Rev. Econ. Stud.*, October 1981, *48*(4), pp. 643–47.

Mori, Toru. On the Existence of Satisfactory Dynamic Revelation Processes for Public Good Provision. *Scand. J. Econ.*, 1981, *83*(3), pp. 429–43.

Morrison, Clarence C. Second Best and Monopoly: A Cautionary Tale. *Public Choice*, 1981, *37*(2), pp. 275–85.

Moulin, Hervé. Implementing Just and Efficient Decision-Making. *J. Public Econ.*, October 1981, *16*(2), pp. 193–213.

Murrell, Peter. The Microeconomic Efficiency Argument for Socialism Revisited: Comment. *J. Econ. Issues*, March 1981, *15*(1), pp. 211–19.

Nakao, Takeo. The Effects of Demonopolization on the Aggregate Stock of Capital and the Welfare of a Society. *Southern Econ. J.*, October 1981, *48*(2), pp. 358–64.

Noam, Eli M. A Cost–Benefit Model of Criminal Courts. In *Zerbe, R. O., Jr., ed.*, 1981, pp. 173–83. [G: U.S.]

Okuguchi, Koji. Innovation and Intergenerational Equity in a Model with Many Exhaustible and Renewable Resources. *Econ. Stud. Quart.*, December 1981, *32*(3), pp. 272–75.

Palomba, Giuseppe. Economie et géométrie de Walras et Pareto à nos jours. (With English summary.) *Écon. Appl.*, 1981, *34*(2–3), pp. 319–47.

Rivera-Batiz, Francisco L. The Price System vs. Rationing: An Extension [Is the Price System or Rationing More Effective in Getting a Commodity to Those Who Need It Most?]. *Bell J. Econ. (See Rand J. Econ. after 4/85)*, Spring 1981, *12*(1), pp. 245–48.

Sage, Andrew P. and White, Elbert B. On the Value Dependent Role of the Identification Processing and Evaluation of Information in Risk/Benefit Analysis. In *Haimes, Y. Y., ed.*, 1981, pp. 245–62.

Sagoff, Mark. Economic Theory and Environmental Law. *Mich. Law Rev.*, June 1981, *79*(7), pp. 1393–1419.

Scapparone, Paolo. Una nota sulle economie di baratto. (A Note on Barter Economies. With English summary.) *Giorn. Econ.*, March–April 1981, *40*(3–4), pp. 217–29.

Sentis, Philippe. L'encadrement de l'équilibre économique par l'équilibre social. (With English summary.) *Écon. Appl.*, 1981, *34*(2–3), pp. 269–78.

Sherman, Roger. Pricing Inefficiency under Profit Regulation. *Southern Econ. J.*, October 1981, *48*(2), pp. 475–89.

Sinn, Hans-Werner and Schmoltzi, Ulrich. Eigentumsrechte, Kompensationsregeln und Marktmacht—Anmerkungen zum "Coase Theorem." (Property Rights, Compensation Rules and Market Power—Comments on the "Coase Theorem." With English summary.) *Jahr. Nationalökon. Statist.*, March 1981, *196*(2), pp. 97–117.

Smith, Vernon L. An Empirical Study of Decentralized Institutions of Monopoly Restraint. In *[Weiler, E. T.]*, 1981, pp. 83–106.

Sobel, Joel. Proportional Distribution Schemes. *J. Math. Econ.*, July 1981, *8*(2), pp. 147–57.

Stein, Jerome L. Speculative Price: Economic Welfare and the Idiot of Chance. *Rev. Econ. Statist.*, May 1981, *63*(2), pp. 223–32. [G: U.S.]

Stiglitz, Joseph E. Potential Competition May Reduce Welfare. *Amer. Econ. Rev.*, May 1981, *71*(2), pp. 184–89.

Suzumura, Kotaro. On Pareto-Efficiency and the No-Envy Concept of Equity. *J. Econ. Theory*, December 1981, *25*(3), pp. 267–79.

Svensson, Lars E. O. Efficiency and Speculation in a Model with Price-Contingent Contracts. *Econometrica*, January 1981, *49*(1), pp. 131–51.

Thurow, Lester C. Psychic Income: A Market Failure. *J. Post Keynesian Econ.*, Winter 1980–81, *3*(2), pp. 183–93.

Tomita, Yasunobu. Interdependent Utilities and Pareto Optimality. (In Japanese. With English summary.) *Osaka Econ. Pap.*, December 1981, *31*(2–3), pp. 199–208.

Tullock, Gordon. Lobbying and Welfare: A Comment. *J. Public Econ.*, December 1981, *16*(3), pp. 391–94.

Walker, Mark. A Simple Incentive Compatible Scheme for Attaining Lindahl Allocations. *Econometrica*, January 1981, *49*(1), pp. 65–71.

Warr, Peter G. and Wright, Brian D. The Isolation Paradox and the Discount Rate for Benefit–Cost Analysis. *Quart. J. Econ.*, February 1981, *96*(1),

pp. 129–45.

Weymark, John A. On Sums of Production Set Frontiers. *Rev. Econ. Stud.*, January 1981, *48*(1), pp. 179–83.

Wihlborg, Clas G. and Wijkman, Per Magnus. Outer Space Resources in Efficient and Equitable Use: New Frontiers for Old Principles. *J. Law Econ.*, April 1981, *24*(1), pp. 23–43.

Wilde, Louis L. On the Use of Laboratory Experiments in Economics. In *Pitt, J. C., ed.*, 1981, pp. 137–48.

Wiseman, Jack. The Theory of Public Utility Price— An Empty Box. In *Buchanan, J. M. and Thirlby, G. F., eds.*, 1981, *1957*, pp. 245–71.

Wolf, Charles, Jr. A Non-Paretian Approach to Market Regulation: Comment. *J. Post Keynesian Econ.*, Spring 1981, *3*(3), pp. 457–58.

Wu, S. Y. Pharmaceutical Innovation, Product Imitation, and Public Policy. In *Helms, R. B., ed.*, 1981, pp. 272–89.

Yunker, James A. The Microeconomic Efficiency of Market Socialism: Reply [The Microeconomic Efficiency Argument for Socialism Revisited]. *J. Econ. Issues*, March 1981, *15*(1), pp. 220–27.

0243 Redistribution Analyses

Allen, Jodie T. The Concept of Vertical Equity and Its Application to Social Program Design. In *Brown, P. G.; Johnson, C. and Vernier, P., eds.*, 1981, pp. 87–107.   [G: U.S.]

Anderson, Terry L. and Hill, P. J. Economic Growth in a Transfer Society: The United States Experience. *J. Econ. Hist.*, March 1981, *41*(1), pp. 113–19.   [G: U.S.]

Arrow, Kenneth J. Optimal and Voluntary Income Distribution. In *[Bergson, A.]*, 1981, pp. 267–88.

Atkinson, A. B. The Measurement of Economic Mobility. In *[Pen, J.]*, 1981, pp. 9–24.

Barry, Brian. Social Science and Distributive Justice. In *Solo, R. A. and Anderson, C. W., eds.*, 1981, pp. 107–37.

Bauer, P. T. The Grail of Equality. In *Bauer, P. T.*, 1981, pp. 8–25.

Baumol, William J. and Fischer, Dietrich. The Output Distribution Frontier: Reply. *Amer. Econ. Rev.*, September 1981, *71*(4), pp. 800.

Bennett, John. A Variable-Production Generalisation of Lerner's Theorem. *J. Public Econ.*, December 1981, *16*(3), pp. 371–76.

Bennett, John. The Probable Gain from Egalitarian Redistribution. *Oxford Econ. Pap.*, March 1981, *33*(1), pp. 165–69.

Berthélemy, Jean-Claude. La théorie des transferts: une approche en termes de déséquilibres. (The Transfer Theory: A Disequilibrium Approach. With English summary.) *Revue Écon.*, January 1981, *32*(1), pp. 32–62.

Bolnick, Bruce R. Government as a Super Becker-Altruist: A Reply. *Public Choice*, 1981, *37*(3), pp. 603–06.

Boulding, Kenneth E. Allocation and Distribution: The Quarrelsome Twins. In *Solo, R. A. and Anderson, C. W., eds.*, 1981, pp. 141–64.

Brandt, Richard B. Utilitarianism and Welfare Legislation. In *Brown, P. G.; Johnson, C. and Vernier, P., eds.*, 1981, pp. 7–24.

Brennan, Geoffrey and Friedman, David D. A Libertarian Perspective on Welfare. In *Brown, P. G.; Johnson, C. and Vernier, P., eds.*, 1981, pp. 25–42.

Brody, Baruch. Work Requirements and Welfare Rights. In *Brown, P. G.; Johnson, C. and Vernier, P., eds.*, 1981, pp. 247–57.

Buiter, Willem H. Time Preference and International Lending and Borrowing in an Overlapping-Generations Model. *J. Polit. Econ.*, August 1981, *89*(4), pp. 769–97.

Canterbery, E. Ray. Income Redistribution and Rawlsian Justice. *J. Econ. Bus.*, Spring/Summer 1981, *33*(3), pp. 188–201.

Cebula, Richard J.; Carlos, Christopher and Koch, James V. The 'Crowding Out' Effect of Federal Government Outlay Decisions: An Empirical Note [The 'Crowding Out' Effect of Government Transfers on Private Charitable Contributions]. *Public Choice*, 1981, *36*(2), pp. 329–36.
          [G: U.S.]

Chowdhury, Omar Haider. Estimating Distributional Weights for Bangladesh. *Bangladesh Devel. Stud.*, Summer 1981, *9*(2), pp. 103–11.
          [G: Bangladesh]

Christiansen, Vidar. Optimization and Quantitative Assessment of Child Allowances. In *Strøm, S., ed.*, 1981, *1979*, pp. 103–22.   [G: Norway]

Creedy, John. Education versus Cash Redistribution: A Comment. *J. Public Econ.*, April 1981, *15*(2), pp. 269–72.

Daniels, Norman. Conflicting Objectives and the Priorities Problem. In *Brown, P. G.; Johnson, C. and Vernier, P., eds.*, 1981, pp. 147–64.

Debroy, B. Laodong and Primordial Ignorance. *Indian Econ. Rev.*, Oct.-Dec. 1981, *16*(4), pp. 297–307.

Fei, John C. H. Equity Oriented Fiscal Programs. *Econometrica*, June 1981, *49*(4), pp. 869–81.

Fioravanti-Molinié, Antoinette. Reciprocity and the INCA State: From Karl Polanyi to John V. Murra: Discussion. In *Dalton, G., ed.*, 1981, *1974*, pp. 54–58.

Gevers, Louis; Glejser, Herbert and Rouyer, Jean. Professed Inequality Aversion and Its Error Component. In *Strøm, S., ed.*, 1981, *1979*, pp. 97–102.   [G: Belgium]

Guesnerie, Roger. La gratuité, outil de politique économique? (Could Giving out Freely a Private Good be a Tool of Economic Policy? With English summary.) *Can. J. Econ.*, May 1981, *14*(2), pp. 232–60.

Haines, Walter W. The Economic Consequences of Altruism. *Int. J. Soc. Econ.*, 1981, *8*(4), pp. 50–69.

Hamm, Walter. An den Grenzen des Wohlfahrtsstaats. (The Welfare State at its Limits. With English Summary.) In *[von Haberler, G.]*, 1981, pp. 117–39.   [G: W. Germany]

Hammer, Jeffrey S. Optimal Growth and Income Redistribution. *Metroecon.*, Feb.-Oct. 1981, *33*(1–2–3), pp. 145–57.

Hirshleifer, Jack. It Pays to Do Good, but Not to do More Good than It Pays: A Note on the Survival of Altruism: Comment. *J. Econ. Behav. Organ.*, December 1981, *2*(4), pp. 387.

Holcombe, Randall G. and Meiners, Roger E. Corrective Taxes and Auctions of Rights in the Control of Externalities: A Reply. *Public Finance Quart.*, October 1981, *9*(4), pp. 479–84.

Hylland, Aanund and Zeckhauser, Richard. Distributional Objectives Should Affect Taxes but Not Program Choice or Design. In *Strøm, S., ed.*, 1981, *1979*, pp. 123–43.

Intriligator, Michael D. Probabilistic Mechanisms of Social Choice and Income Redistribution. In *Solo, R. A. and Anderson, C. W., eds.*, 1981, pp. 185–98.

Jakobsson, Ulf and Normann, Göran. Welfare Effects of Changes in Income Tax Progression in Sweden. In *Eliasson, G.; Holmlund, B. and Stafford, F. P., eds.*, 1981, pp. 313–38.
[G: Sweden]

Johnson, Lewis. Life-cycle Saving, Social Security, and the Long-run Capital Stock. In *Federal Reserve System*, 1981, pp. 275–79.

Judge, Ken. Pricing and Public Choice in Social Welfare. In *Seldon, A., ed.*, 1981, pp. 147–69.

Keating, Barry P. United Way Contributions: Anomalous Philanthropy. *Quart. Rev. Econ. Bus.*, Spring 1981, *21*(1), pp. 114–19.   [G: U.S.]

Keenan, Donald and Rubin, Paul H. The Output Distribution Frontier: Comment. *Amer. Econ. Rev.*, September 1981, *71*(4), pp. 796–99.

Kirzner, Israel M. Entrepreneurship, Entitlement, and Economic Justice. In *Paul, J., ed.*, 1981, *1978*, pp. 383–411.

Klevorick, Alvin K. Income-Distribution Concerns in Regulatory Policymaking: Comment. In *Fromm, G., ed.*, 1981, pp. 108–11.   [G: U.S.]

Kornai, János. Ethical Issues in Income Distribution: National and International: Comments. In *Grassman, S. and Lundberg, E., eds.*, 1981, pp. 495–97.

Layard, Richard. Reply to John Creedy's Comment [Education versus Cash Redistribution: The Lifetime Context]. *J. Public Econ.*, April 1981, *15*(2), pp. 273.

Loury, Glenn C. Intergenerational Transfers and the Distribution of Earnings. *Econometrica*, June 1981, *49*(4), pp. 843–67.

Lyons, David. The New Indian Claims and Original Rights to Land. In *Paul, J., ed.*, 1981, *1977*, pp. 355–79.

McKee, Arnold F. What Is "Distributive" Justice? *Rev. Soc. Econ.*, April 1981, *39*(1), pp. 1–17.

McKenzie, Richard B. Taxation and Income Redistribution: An Unsympathetic Critique of Practice and Theory. *Cato J.*, Fall 1981, *1*(2), pp. 339–71.   [G: U.S.]

Melden, A. I. Are There Welfare Rights? In *Brown, P. G.; Johnson, C. and Vernier, P., eds.*, 1981, pp. 259–78.

Menchik, Paul L. Some Issues in the Measurement of Income Inequality. In *Solo, R. A. and Anderson, C. W., eds.*, 1981, pp. 227–49.

Mishan, Ezra J. Economic Criteria for Intergenerational Comparisons. In *Mishan, E. J.*, 1981, *1977*, pp. 46–58.

Mishan, Ezra J. What Is Producer's Surplus? In

Mishan, E. J., 1981, *1968*, pp. 79–86.

Moon, Marilyn. Measuring Economic Status: Recent Contributions and Future Directions. In *Ballabon, M. B., ed.*, 1981, pp. 131–53.

Morrison, Clarence C. The Lerner Equal Distribution Theorem: A Possible Extension. *Atlantic Econ. J.*, March 1981, *9*(1), pp. 1–6.

Murra, John V. Reciprocity and the Inca State: From Karl Polanyi to John V. Murra: Discussion. In *Dalton, G., ed.*, 1981, *1974*, pp. 51–54.
[G: Peru]

O'Neill, Onora. Nozick's Entitlements. In *Paul, J., ed.*, 1981, *1976*, pp. 305–22.

Oates, Wallace E. Corrective Taxes and Auctions of Rights in the Control of Externalities: Some Further Thoughts. *Public Finance Quart.*, October 1981, *9*(4), pp. 471–78.

Olsen, Edgar O. The Simple Analytics of the Externality Argument for Redistribution. In *Ballabon, M. B., ed.*, 1981, pp. 155–73.

Ordover, Janusz A. Redistributing Incomes: Ex Ante or Ex Post. *Econ. Inquiry*, April 1981, *19*(2), pp. 333–49.

Pasour, E. C., Jr. Pareto Optimality as a Guide to Income Redistribution. *Public Choice*, 1981, *36*(1), pp. 75–87.

Paul, Jeffrey. Reading Nozick: Essays on *Anarchy, State, and Utopia*: Introduction. In *Paul, J., ed.*, 1981, pp. 1–23.

Pfaff, Martin. Redistribution, Social Security and Growth: Comments. In *Giersch, H., ed. (II)*, 1981, pp. 426–45.   [G: W. Germany; LDCs]

Phillips, John and Stevens, Dana. A Just, Non-Binary Choice Rule. *Amer. Econ.*, Fall 1981, *25*(2), pp. 44–48.

Pinstrup-Andersen, Per. Economic Theory Needed in Studying the Economics of Getting Poorer While Redistributing. In *Johnson, G. and Maunder, A., eds.*, 1981, pp. 369–78.

Plotnick, Robert. A Measure of Horizontal Inequity. *Rev. Econ. Statist.*, May 1981, *63*(2), pp. 283–88.   [G: U.S.]

Rae, Douglas W. and Fessler, Carol. The Varieties of Equality. In *Solo, R. A. and Anderson, C. W., eds.*, 1981, pp. 201–26.

Ricketts, Martin. Tax Theory and Tax Policy. In *Peacock, A. and Forte, F., eds.*, 1981, pp. 29–46.

Rothbard, Murray N. The Myth of Neutral Taxation. *Cato J.*, Fall 1981, *1*(2), pp. 519–64.

Samuels, Warren J. The Historical Treatment of the Problem of Value Judgements: An Interpretation. In *Solo, R. A. and Anderson, C. W., eds.*, 1981, pp. 57–69.

Scanlon, Thomas. Nozick on Rights, Liberty, and Property. In *Paul, J., ed.*, 1981, *1976*, pp. 107–29.

Schmalensee, Richard. Income-Distribution Concerns in Regulatory Policymaking: Comment. In *Fromm, G., ed.*, 1981, pp. 112–17.   [G: U.S.]

Sellier, François. Les transformations sociales du système économique capitaliste. (With English summary.) *Écon. Appl.*, 1981, *34*(2–3), pp. 279–318.

Sen, Amartya K. Ethical Issues in Income Distribution: National and International. In *Grassman, S. and Lundberg, E., eds.*, 1981, pp. 464–94.

Shubik, Martin. Society. Land, Love, or Money: A Strategic Model of How to Glue the Generations Together. *J. Econ. Behav. Organ.*, December 1981, *2*(4), pp. 359–85.

Solo, Robert A. A Progressive Expenditure Tax Reconsidered. In *Solo, R. A. and Anderson, C. W., eds.*, 1981, pp. 379–81.

Steiner, Hillel. Justice and Entitlement. In *Paul, J., ed.*, 1981, *1977*, pp. 380–82.

Streeten, Paul P. Taxation and Enterprise. In *Streeten, P.*, 1981, *1958*, pp. 407–17.

Streeten, Paul P. Values, Facts and the Compensation Principle. In *Streeten, P.*, 1981, *1963*, pp. 35–51.

Terrebonne, R. Peter. Government as a Super Becker-Altruist: A Comment. *Public Choice*, 1981, *37*(3), pp. 595–601.

Thomson, Judith Jarvis. Some Ruminations on Rights. In *Paul, J., ed.*, 1981, *1977*, pp. 130–47.

Thurow, Lester C. Equity, Efficiency, Social Justice, and Redistribution. *Nebr. J. Econ. Bus.*, Spring 1981, *20*(2), pp. 5–24. [G: U.S.]

Thurow, Lester C. The Illusion of Economic Necessity. In *Solo, R. A. and Anderson, C. W., eds.*, 1981, pp. 250–75. [G: U.S.]

Tinbergen, Jan. Misunderstandings Concerning Income Distribution Policies. *De Economist*, 1981, *129*(1), pp. 8–20.

Tomes, Nigel. The Family, Inheritance, and the Intergenerational Transmission of Inequality. *J. Polit. Econ.*, October 1981, *89*(5), pp. 928–58. [G: U.S.]

Tullock, Gordon. The Rhetoric and Reality of Redistribution. *Southern Econ. J.*, April 1981, *47*(4), pp. 895–907.

Ulen, Thomas S. Discussion [Economic Growth in a Transfer Society: The United States Experience]. *J. Econ. Hist.*, March 1981, *41*(1), pp. 120–21. [G: U.S.]

Vaubel, Roland. Redistribution, Social Security and Growth. In *Giersch, H., ed. (II)*, 1981, pp. 387–425.

Walton, A. L. Intergenerational Equity and Resource Use. *Amer. J. Econ. Soc.*, July 1981, *40*(3), pp. 239–48.

Willig, Robert D. and Bailey, Elizabeth E. Income-Distribution Concerns in Regulatory Policymaking. In *Fromm, G., ed.*, 1981, pp. 79–107. [G: U.S.]

Wintrobe, Ronald. It Pays to Do Good, but Not to Do More Good than It Pays: A Note on the Survival of Altruism. *J. Econ. Behav. Organ.*, September 1981, *2*(3), pp. 201–13.

Wintrobe, Ronald. It Pays to Do Good, but Not to Do More Good than It Pays: A Note on the Survival of Altruism: Reply. *J. Econ. Behav. Organ.*, December 1981, *2*(4), pp. 389–90.

Witte, John F. Tax Philosophy and Income Equality. In *Solo, R. A. and Anderson, C. W., eds.*, 1981, pp. 340–78.

0244 Externalities

Anderson, Terry L. and Hill, Peter J. Establishing Property Rights in Energy: Efficient vs. Inefficient Processes. *Cato J.*, Spring 1981, *1*(1), pp. 87–105. [G: U.S.; U.K.]

Archibald, G. C. and Davidson, Russell. On the Intertemporal Incidence of Externalities. *Economica*, August 1981, *48*(191), pp. 267–77.

Beavis, Brian and Walker, Martin. Long-Run Efficiency and Property Rights Sharing for Pollution Control: A Comment. *Public Choice*, 1981, *37*(3), pp. 607–08.

Bentley, J. Marvin and Oberhofer, Tom. Property Rights and Economic Development. *Rev. Soc. Econ.*, April 1981, *39*(1), pp. 51–65. [G: W. Africa]

Braden, John B. and Bromley, Daniel W. The Economics of Cooperation over Collective Bads. *J. Environ. Econ. Manage.*, June 1981, *8*(2), pp. 134–50.

Buchanan, James McGill and Faith, Roger L. Entrepreneurship and the Internalization of Externalities. *J. Law Econ.*, April 1981, *24*(1), pp. 95–111.

Cross, Melvin L. and Ekelund, Robert B., Jr. A. T. Hadley: The American Invention of the Economics of Property Rights and Public Goods. *Rev. Soc. Econ.*, April 1981, *39*(1), pp. 37–50.

Gay, David E. R. Towards a Theory of Entitlements in Comparative Economics. *Rivista Int. Sci. Econ. Com.*, March 1981, *28*(3), pp. 216–25.

Glazer, Amihai. Congestion Tolls and Consumer Welfare. *Public Finance*, 1981, *36*(1), pp. 77–83.

Griffin, Ronald C. Property Rights and Welfare Economics: Miller et al. v. Schoene Revisited: Comment. *Land Econ.*, November 1981, *57*(4), pp. 645–51. [G: U.S.]

Hageman, Ronda K. Nuclear Waste Disposal: Potential Property Value Impacts. *Natural Res. J.*, October 1981, *21*(4), pp. 789–810.

Holcombe, Randall G. and Stecher, Edwin L. Intra-Industry Adjustment and the Correction of an Externality. *Atlantic Econ. J.*, September 1981, *9*(3), pp. 79–84.

Ito, Yozo and Kaneko, Mamoru. Ratio Equilibrium in an Economy with Externalities. *Z. Nationalökon.*, 1981, *41*(3–4), pp. 279–94.

Keto, David B. The Corporation and the Constitution: Economic Due Process and Corporate Speech. *Yale Law J.*, July 1981, *90*(8), pp. 1833–60. [G: U.S.]

Martinet, Alain. Externalités et comportements stratégiques à la recherche de nouvelles équilibrations. (With English summary.) *Écon. Appl.*, 1981, *34*(1), pp. 61–88.

McEwin, R. Ian. Liability Rules, Insurance and the Coase Theorem. *Australian J. Manage.*, December 1981, *6*(2), pp. 103–17.

Mercuro, Nicholas and Ryan, Timothy. Property Rights and Welfare Economics: Miller et al. v. Schoene Revisited: Reply. *Land Econ.*, November 1981, *57*(4), pp. 657–59. [G: U.S.]

Mills, David E. Ownership Arrangements and Congestion-Prone Facilities. *Amer. Econ. Rev.*, June 1981, *71*(3), pp. 493–502.

Mishan, Ezra J. Interpretation of the Benefits of Private Transport. In *Mishan, E. J.*, 1981, *1967*, pp. 100–104.

Mishan, Ezra J. The Postwar Literature on Externalities: An Interpretative Essay. In *Mishan, E. J.*, 1981, *1971*, pp. 132–52.

Mishan, Ezra J. What Is the Optimal Level of Pollution? In *Mishan, E. J.*, 1981, *1974*, pp. 125–31.

Mumy, Gene E. Long-Run Efficiency and Property Rights Sharing for Pollution Control: A Reply. *Public Choice*, 1981, 37(3), pp. 609.

Olsen, Edgar O. The Simple Analytics of the Externality Argument for Redistribution. In *Ballabon, M. B.*, ed., 1981, pp. 155–73.

Pethig, Rüdiger. Möglichkeiten der Allokation gemeinschaftlich nutzbarer Güter mit nutzungsabhängiger Qualität. (Possibilities of Allocating Jointly Usable Goods with Use-Dependent Quality. With English summary.) *Z. ges. Staatswiss.*, June 1981, *137*(2), pp. 187–211.

Runge, Carlisle Ford. Common Property Externalities: Isolation, Assurance, and Resource Depletion in a Traditional Grazing Context. *Amer. J. Agr. Econ.*, November 1981, *63*(4), pp. 595–606.

Ryan, Cheyney C. Yours, Mine, and Ours: Property Rights and Individual Liberty. In *Paul, J.*, ed., 1981, *1977*, pp. 323–43.

Sinn, Hans-Werner and Schmoltzi, Ulrich. Eigentumsrechte, Kompensationsregeln und Marktmacht—Anmerkungen zum "Coase Theorem." (Property Rights, Compensation Rules and Market Power—Comments on the "Coase Theorem." With English summary.) *Jahr. Nationalökon. Statist.*, March 1981, *196*(2), pp. 97–117.

Swaney, James A. Externality and Community. *J. Econ. Issues*, September 1981, *15*(3), pp. 615–27.

Umbeck, John. Might Makes Rights: A Theory of the Formation and Initial Distribution of Property Rights. *Econ. Inquiry*, January 1981, *19*(1), pp. 38–59.   [G: U.S.]

Wagstaff, Peter. The Stability of Two Decentralized Adjustment Schemes. *J. Econ. Dynam. Control*, May 1981, *3*(2), pp. 183–90.

von Weizsäcker, Carl Christian. Rechte und Verhältnisse in der Modernen Wirtschaftslehre. (Rights and Relations in Modern Economic Theory. With English summary.) *Kyklos*, 1981, *34*(3), pp. 345–76.

Wetzel, James N. Congestion and Economic Valuation: A Reconsideration: Comment [Estimating the Benefits of Recreation under Conditions of Congestion]. *J. Environ. Econ. Manage.*, June 1981, *8*(2), pp. 192–95.

Whitney, Gerald. Property Rights and Welfare Economics: Miller et al. v. Schoene Revisited: Comment. *Land Econ.*, November 1981, *57*(4), pp. 652–56.   [G: U.S.]

Wihlborg, Clas G. and Wijkman, Per Magnus. Outer Space Resources in Efficient and Equitable Use: New Frontiers for Old Principles. *J. Law Econ.*, April 1981, *24*(1), pp. 23–43.

025 Social Choice

0250 Social Choice

Abrams, Burton A. Political Power and the Market for Governors. *Public Choice*, 1981, 37(3), pp. 521–29.

Adams, James D. Daylight Savings: An Endogenous Law. *Public Choice*, 1981, 36(2), pp. 345–49.

Alt, James E. and Chrystal, K. Alec. Politico-economic Models of British Fiscal Policy. In *Hibbs, D. A., Jr. and Fassbender, H.*, eds., 1981, pp. 185–207.   [G: U.K.]

Alt, James E. and Chrystal, K. Alec. Public Sector Behaviour: The Status of the Political Business Cycle. In *Currie, D.; Nobay, R. and Peel, D.*, eds., 1981, pp. 353–76.   [G: U.K.]

Aranson, Peter H. and Ordeshook, Peter C. Regulation, Redistribution, and Public Choice. *Public Choice*, 1981, 37(1), pp. 69–100.

Arnold, R. Douglas. Legislators, Bureaucrats, and Locational Decisions. *Public Choice*, 1981, 37(1), pp. 107–32.

Austen-Smith, David. Party Policy and Campaign Costs in a Multi-Constituency Model of Electoral Competition. *Public Choice*, 1981, 37(3), pp. 389–402.

Austen-Smith, David. Voluntary Pressure Groups. *Economica*, May 1981, *48*(190), pp. 143–53.

Axelrod, Robert. The Emergence of Cooperation among Egoists. *Amer. Polit. Sci. Rev.*, June 1981, *75*(2), pp. 306–18.

Barnett, Richard R. Frequent Voter Recontracting: On Constitutional Choice and Minority Group Power. *Public Finance Quart.*, July 1981, *9*(3), pp. 309–19.

Bates, Robert H. Public Choice Processes. In *Russell, C. S. and Nicholson, N. K.*, eds., 1981, pp. 81–117.

Batteau, Pierre; Blin, Jean-Marie and Monjardet, Bernard. Stability of Aggregation Procedures, Ultrafilters, and Simple Games. *Econometrica*, March 1981, *49*(2), pp. 527–34.

Bauer, P. T. The Grail of Equality. In *Bauer, P. T.*, 1981, pp. 8–25.

Behn, Robert D. Policy Analysis and Policy Politics. *Policy Anal.*, Spring 1981, *7*(2), pp. 199–226.

Bell, Colin E. A Random Voting Graph Almost Surely Has a Hamiltonian Cycle When the Number of Alternatives Is Large. *Econometrica*, November 1981, *49*(6), pp. 1597–1603.

Benson, Bruce L. Why Are Congressional Committees Dominated by "High-Demand" Legislators?—A Comment on Niskanen's View of Bureaucrats and Politicians [Bureaucrats and Politicians]. *Southern Econ. J.*, July 1981, *48*(1), pp. 68–77.   [G: U.S.]

Bental, Benjamin and Ben-Zion, Uri. A Simple Model of Political Contributions. *Public Finance Quart.*, April 1981, *9*(2), pp. 143–57.   [G: U.S.]

Berger, Suzanne. Organizing Interests in Western Europe: Introduction. In *Berger, S.*, ed., 1981, pp. 1–23.

Berger, Suzanne. Regime and Interest Representation: The French Traditional Middle Classes. In *Berger, S.*, ed., 1981, pp. 83–101.   [G: France]

Berglas, Eitan. The Market Provision of Club Goods Once Again. *J. Public Econ.*, June 1981, *15*(3), pp. 377–93.

Bergsten, Gordon S. Toward a New Normative (Economic) Theory of Politics. *Rev. Soc. Econ.*, April 1981, *39*(1), pp. 67–79.

Bergstrom, Ted C. When Does Majority Rule Supply Public Goods Efficiently? In *Strøm, S.*, ed., 1981, *1979*, pp. 75–85.

Béteille, André. The Idea of Natural Inequality. **In** *Berreman, G. D., ed.*, 1981, pp. 59–80.

Bigman, David. Decisive Sets, Majority Voting and the Existence of a Group Preference Function. *De Economist*, 1981, *129*(2), pp. 241–52.

Blair, Douglas H. On the Ubiquity of Strategic Voting Opportunities. *Int. Econ. Rev.*, October 1981, *22*(3), pp. 649–55.

Blake, Judith and Del Pinal, Jorge H. Negativism, Equivocation, and Wobbly Assent: Public "Support" for the Prochoice Platform on Abortion. *Demography*, August 1981, *18*(3), pp. 309–20.

Bolnick, Bruce R. Government as a Super Becker-Altruist: A Reply. *Public Choice*, 1981, *37*(3), pp. 603–06.

Bonus, Holger. The Political Party as a Firm. *Z. ges. Staatswiss.*, December 1981, *137*(4), pp. 710–16.

Bordes, Georges. Individualisme, ordinalisme et bien-être social. (Individualism, Ordinalism, and Social Welfare. With English summary.) *Ann. INSEE*, January–March 1981, (41), pp. 41–66.

Boyd, William L. Comments on E. G. West and R. J. Staaf [Extra-Governmental Powers in Public Schooling: The Unions and the Courts]. *Public Choice*, 1981, *36*(3), pp. 639–40.

Brennan, Geoffrey. Why So Much Stability? Appendix. *Public Choice*, 1981, *37*(2), pp. 203–04.

Brennan, Geoffrey and Buchanan, James McGill. Revenue Implications of Money Creation under Leviathan. *Amer. Econ. Rev.*, May 1981, *71*(2), pp. 347–51.

Breton, Albert. Representative Governments and the Formation of National and International Policies. *Revue Écon.*, March 1981, *32*(2), pp. 356–73.

Bronner, Fred and de Hoog, Robert. Choice Models and Voting Behaviour: The Case of the Dutch Electorate. *Public Choice*, 1981, *37*(3), pp. 531–46. **[G: Netherlands]**

Buchanan, Allen. Deriving Welfare Rights from Libertarian Rights. **In** *Brown, P. G.; Johnson, C. and Vernier, P., eds.*, 1981, pp. 233–46.

Burton, John; Hawkins, M. J. and Hughes, G. L. Is Liberal Democracy Especially Prone to Inflation? An Analytical Treatment. **In** *Hibbs, D. A., Jr. and Fassbender, H., eds.*, 1981, pp. 248–68.

Calvert, Randall L. and Isaac, R. Mark. The Inherent Disadvantage of the Presidential Party in Midterm Congressional Elections. *Public Choice*, 1981, *36*(1), pp. 141–46. **[G: U.S.]**

Chamberlain, Gary and Rothschild, Michael. A Note on the Probability of Casting a Decisive Vote. *J. Econ. Theory*, August 1981, *25*(1), pp. 152–62.

Champernowne, D. G. Income Distribution and Egalitarian Policy. The Outlook in 1980. **In** *[Pen, J.]*, 1981, pp. 31–50. **[G: U.K.]**

Chappell, Henry W., Jr. Campaign Contributions and Voting on the Cargo Preference Bill: A Comparison of Simultaneous Models. *Public Choice*, 1981, *36*(2), pp. 301–12. **[G: U.S.]**

Chappell, Henry W., Jr. Conflict of Interest and Congressional Voting: A Note. *Public Choice*, 1981, *37*(2), pp. 331–35. **[G: U.S.]**

Chisholm, Michael; Devereux, Bernard and Versey, Roy. The Myth of Non-partisan Cartography: The Tale Continued. *Urban Stud.*, June 1981, *18*(2), pp. 213–18. **[G: U.K.]**

Chrystal, K. Alec and Alt, James E. Some Problems in Formulating and Testing a Politico-Economic Model of the United Kingdom. *Econ. J.*, September 1981, *91*(363), pp. 730–36. **[G: U.K.]**

Chubb, Judith. The Social Bases of an Urban Political Machine: The Case of Palermo. *Polit. Sci. Quart.*, Spring 1981, *96*(1), pp. 107–25. **[G: Italy]**

Collard, David. Market Failure and Government Failure. **In** *Seldon, A., ed.*, 1981, pp. 121–46.

Collins, William P. Political Participation under the Unit Rule: A Research Note. *Public Choice*, 1981, *36*(1), pp. 165–69. **[G: U.S.]**

Cornell, Bradford and Roll, Richard. Strategies for Pairwise Competitions in Markets and Organizations. *Bell J. Econ. (See Rand J. Econ. after 4/ 85)*, Spring 1981, *12*(1), pp. 201–13.

Coughlin, Peter J. Necessary and Sufficient Conditions for d-Relative Majority Voting Equilibria [Consistent Majority Rules over Compact Sets of Alternatives]. *Econometrica*, September 1981, *49*(5), pp. 1223–24.

Coughlin, Peter J. and Nitzan, Shmuel. Directional and Local Electoral Equilibria with Probabilistic Voting. *J. Econ. Theory*, April 1981, *24*(2), pp. 226–39.

Coughlin, Peter J. and Nitzan, Shmuel. Electoral Outcomes with Probabilistic Voting and Nash Social Welfare Maxima. *J. Public Econ.*, February 1981, *15*(1), pp. 113–21.

Cowart, Susan Cooper. Representation of High Demand Constituencies on Review Committees: A Research Note. *Public Choice*, 1981, *37*(2), pp. 337–42. **[G: U.S.]**

Cowell, Frank A. and Kuga, Kiyoshi. Inequality Measurement: An Axiomatic Approach. *Europ. Econ. Rev.*, March 1981, *15*(3), pp. 287–305.

Cuzán, Alfred G. Political Profit: Taxing and Spending in Democracies and Dictatorships. *Amer. J. Econ. Soc.*, October 1981, *40*(4), pp. 329–40.

Daly, George. Politics as a Filter. *Public Choice*, 1981, *36*(1), pp. 171–77.

DeAngelo, Harry. Competition and Unanimity. *Amer. Econ. Rev.*, March 1981, *71*(1), pp. 18–27.

Deb, Rajat. k-Monotone Social Decision Functions and the Veto. *Econometrica*, June 1981, *49*(4), pp. 899–909.

DeLorme, Charles D., Jr.; Hill, R. Carter and Wood, Norman J. The Determinants of Voting by the National Labor Relations Board on Unfair Labor Practice Cases: 1955–1975. *Public Choice*, 1981, *37*(2), pp. 207–18. **[G: U.S.]**

DiLorenzo, Thomas J. An Empirical Assessment of the Factor-Supplier Pressure Group Hypothesis. *Public Choice*, 1981, *37*(3), pp. 559–78. **[G: U.S.]**

Dinkel, Reiner. Political Business Cycles in Germany and the United States: Some Theoretical and Empirical Considerations. **In** *Hibbs, D. A., Jr. and Fassbender, H., eds.*, 1981, pp. 209–230. **[G: U.S.; W. Germany]**

Dobell, W. M. A Limited Corrective to Plurality Voting. *Can. Public Policy*, Winter 1981, *7*(1), pp. 75–81. [G: Canada]

Dobra, John and Tullock, Gordon. An Approach to Empirical Measures of Voting Paradoxes. *Public Choice*, 1981, *36*(1), pp. 193–94.

Dorff, Robert H. and Steiner, Jürg. Political Decision Making in Face-to-Face Groups: Theory, Methods, and an Empirical Application in Switzerland. *Amer. Polit. Sci. Rev.*, June 1981, *75*(2), pp. 368–80. [G: Switzerland]

Downing, Paul B. and Stafford, Elizabeth Ann. Citations as an Indicator of Classic Works and Major Contributors in Social Choice. *Public Choice*, 1981, *37*(2), pp. 219–30.

Dutter, Lee E. Voter Preferences, Simple Electoral Games, and Equilibria in Two-Candidate Contests. *Public Choice*, 1981, *37*(3), pp. 403–23.

Ehrenberg, Ronald G. Comments on E. G. West and R. J. Staaf [Extra-Governmental Powers in Public Schooling: The Unions and the Courts]. *Public Choice*, 1981, *36*(3), pp. 641–45.

Eisel, Leo M. Uncertainty: The Water Resources Decisionmaking Dilemma. In *Haimes, Y. Y., ed.*, 1981, pp. 5–11.

Ekelund, Robert B., Jr. and Saba, Richard P. A Note on Politics and Franchise Bidding. *Public Choice*, 1981, *37*(2), pp. 343–48.

Elden, J. Maxwell. Political Efficacy at Work: The Connection between More Autonomous Forms of Workplace Organization and a More Participatory Politics. *Amer. Polit. Sci. Rev.*, March 1981, *75*(1), pp. 43–58. [G: U.S.]

Encarnación, José, Jr. Group Choice with Lexicographic Preferences. *Phillipine Rev. Econ. Bus.*, Sept. & Dec. 1981, *18*(3/4), pp. 104–15.

Epple, Dennis and Schipper, Katherine. Municipal Pension Funding: A Theory and Some Evidence. *Public Choice*, 1981, *37*(1), pp. 141–78.

Epple, Dennis and Zelenitz, Allan. The Roles of Jurisdictional Competition and of Collective Choice Institutions in the Market for Local Public Goods. *Amer. Econ. Rev.*, May 1981, *71*(2), pp. 87–92.

Faith, Roger L. and Buchanan, James McGill. Towards a Theory of Yes-No Voting. *Public Choice*, 1981, *37*(2), pp. 231–45.

Faith, Roger L. and Thompson, Earl A. A Paradox in the Theory of Second Best. *Econ. Inquiry*, April 1981, *19*(2), pp. 235–44.

Fassbender, Heino. From Conventional IS–LM to Political-Economic Models. In *Hibbs, D. A., Jr. and Fassbender, H., eds.*, 1981, pp. 153–67.

Feldman, Gerald D. German Interest Group Alliances in War and Inflation, 1914–23. In *Berger, S., ed.*, 1981, pp. 159–84. [G: Germany]

Feller, Irwin. Public-Sector Innovation as "Conspicuous Production." *Policy Anal.*, Winter 1981, *7*(1), pp. 1–20. [G: U.S.]

Fiorina, Morris. Short- and Long-term Effects of Economic Conditions on Individual Voting Decisions. In *Hibbs, D. A., Jr. and Fassbender, H., eds.*, 1981, pp. 73–100. [G: U.S.]

Fiorina, Morris P. Universalism, Reciprocity, and Distributive Policymaking in Majority Rule Institutions. In *Crecine, J. P., ed.*, 1981, pp. 197–221.

Fishburn, Peter C. Majority Committees. *J. Econ. Theory*, October 1981, *25*(2), pp. 255–68.

Fishburn, Peter C. and Brams, Steven J. Approval Voting, Condorcet's Principle, and Runoff Elections. *Public Choice*, 1981, *36*(1), pp. 89–114.

Fishburn, Peter C. and Brams, Steven J. Efficacy, Power and Equity under Approval Voting. *Public Choice*, 1981, *37*(3), pp. 425–34.

Flowers, Marilyn R. Agenda Control and Budget Size: An Extension of the Romer-Rosenthal Model [Political Resource Allocation, Controlled Agendas and the Status Quo]. *Public Choice*, 1981, *37*(3), pp. 579–84.

Flowers, Marilyn R. Majority Voting on Tax Shares: A Simple Life-Cycle Model. *Public Finance Quart.*, January 1981, *9*(1), pp. 47–59.

Frasca, Ralph R. Instability in Voluntary Contributions Based upon Jointness in Supply. *Public Choice*, 1981, *37*(3), pp. 435–45.

Frey, Bruno S. Elemente einer zukünftigen Theorie der Wirtschaftspolitik. (With English summary.) *Z. Wirtschaft. Sozialwissen.*, 1981, *101*(4), pp. 361–77.

Frey, Bruno S. Politometrics of Government Behavior in a Democracy. In *Strøm, S., ed.*, 1981, *1979*, pp. 167–81. [G: W. Germany; Sweden; U.K.; U.S.]

Frey, Bruno S. and Schneider, Friedrich. A Politico-Economic Model of the U.K.: New Estimates and Predictions. *Econ. J.*, September 1981, *91*(363), pp. 737–40. [G: U.K.]

Frey, Bruno S. and Schneider, Friedrich. Recent Research on Empirical Politico-economic Models. In *Hibbs, D. A., Jr. and Fassbender, H., eds.*, 1981, pp. 11–27. [G: Selected countries]

Frey, Bruno S. and Weck, Hannelore. Hat Arbeitslosigkeit den Aufstieg des Nationalsozialismus bewirkt? (Did Unemployment Lead to the Rise of National Socialism? With English summary.) *Jahr. Nationalökon. Statist.*, January 1981, *196*(1), pp. 1–31. [G: Germany]

Fukuchi, Takao and Seki, Koh. An Econometric Analysis of Voting Behavior. (In Japanese. With English summary.) *Econ. Stud. Quart.*, April 1981, *32*(1), pp. 29–44. [G: Japan]

Gaertner, Wulf. Rawlsianism, Utilitarianism, and Profiles of Extended Orderings. *Z. ges. Staatswiss.*, March 1981, *137*(1), pp. 78–96.

Gaertner, Wulf and Krüger, Lorenz. Self-Supporting Preferences and Individual Rights: The Possibility of Paretian Libertarianism. *Economica*, February 1981, *48*(189), pp. 17–28.

Gardner, Roy. The Borda Game: A Correction. *Public Choice*, 1981, *37*(2), pp. 375–76.

Gardner, Roy. Wealth and Power in a Collegial Polity. *J. Econ. Theory*, December 1981, *25*(3), pp. 353–66.

Gärtner, Manfred. Legislative Profits and the Rate of Change of Money Wages: A Reply. *Public Choice*, 1981, *37*(3), pp. 589–93. [G: W. Germany]

Gazon, Jules. La transmission de l'opinion, une approche structurale du pouvoir au sein des structures fortement connexes. (With English summary.) *Écon. Appl.*, 1981, *34*(4), pp. 749–84.

Gehrlein, William V. Single-Stage Election Procedures for Large Electorates. *J. Math. Econ.*, October 1981, *8*(3), pp. 263–75.

Gessaman, Paul H. Rugged Individualism: Recurring Myth or Reemerging Giant? In *Lawson, M. P. and Baker, M. E., eds.*, 1981, pp. 267–75. [G: U.S.]

Gevers, Louis; Glejser, Herbert and Rouyer, Jean. Professed Inequality Aversion and Its Error Component. In *Strøm, S., ed.*, 1981, *1979*, pp. 97–102. [G: Belgium]

Gist, John R. and Hill, R. Carter. The Economics of Choice in the Allocation of Federal Grants: An Empirical Test. *Public Choice*, 1981, *36*(1), pp. 63–73. [G: U.S.]

Goodrich, Chris. Legislative Profits and the Rate of Change of Money Wages: A Comment. *Public Choice*, 1981, *37*(3), pp. 585–88. [G: W. Germany]

Goodsell, Charles, et al. Bureaucracy Expresses Itself: How State Documents Address the Public. *Soc. Sci. Quart.*, September 1981, *62*(3), pp. 576–91. [G: U.S.]

Gordon, Milton M. Models of Pluralism: The New American Dilemma. *Ann. Amer. Acad. Polit. Soc. Sci.*, March 1981, *454*, pp. 178–88. [G: U.S.]

Grafstein, Robert. The Problem of Choosing Your Alternatives: A Revision of the Public Choice Theory of Constitutions. *Soc. Sci. Quart.*, June 1981, *62*(2), pp. 199–212. [G: U.S.]

Gramlich, Edward M.; Rubinfeld, Daniel L. and Swift, Deborah A. Why Voters Turn out for Tax Limitation Votes. *Nat. Tax J.*, March 1981, *34*(1), pp. 115–24. [G: U.S.]

Gupta, Dipak K. and Venieris, Yiannis P. Introducing New Dimensions in Macro Models: The Sociopolitical and Institutional Environments. *Econ. Develop. Cult. Change*, October 1981, *30*(1), pp. 31–58. [G: U.K.]

Hall, Warren A. Risk Assessment: The Role of Government in a Multiple Objective Framework. In *Haimes, Y. Y., ed.*, 1981, pp. 181–89.

Hansen, Pierre and Thisse, Jacques-François. Outcomes of Voting and Planning: Condorcet, Weber and Rawls Locations. *J. Public Econ.*, August 1981, *16*(1), pp. 1–15.

Heiner, Ronald A. Length and Cycle Equalization. *J. Econ. Theory*, August 1981, *25*(1), pp. 101–30.

Heiner, Ronald A. The Collective Decision Problem, and the Theory of Preference. *Econ. Inquiry*, April 1981, *19*(2), pp. 297–332.

Hernes, Gudmund and Selvik, Arne. Local Corporatism. In *Berger, S., ed.*, 1981, pp. 103–19. [G: Norway]

Heuss, Ernst. Wie man Sozialwissenschaften nicht betreiben soll. (Social Sciences Going Astray. With English Summary.) In *[von Haberler, G.]*, 1981, pp. 109–15.

Hibbs, Douglas A., Jr. and Vasilatos, Nicholas. Macroeconomic Performance and Mass Political Support in the United States and Great Britain. In *Hibbs, D. A., Jr. and Fassbender, H., eds.*, 1981, pp. 31–47. [G: U.K.; U.S.]

Hicks, Alexander; Friedland, Roger and Johnson, Edwin. Class Power and State Policy. In *Martin, G. T., Jr., and Zald, M. N., eds.*, 1981, *1978*, pp. 131–46. [G: U.S.]

Hicks, John R. The Rationale of Majority Rule. In *Hicks, J.*, 1981, pp. 283–99.

Hill, Kim Quaile. Taxpayer Support for the Presidential Election Campaign Fund. *Soc. Sci. Quart.*, December 1981, *62*(4), pp. 767–71. [G: U.S.]

Hinich, Melvin J. Voting as an Act of Contribution. *Public Choice*, 1981, *36*(1), pp. 135–40.

Hirschman, Albert O. Exit, Voice, and the State. In *Hirschman, A. O.*, 1981, *1978*, pp. 246–65.

Hirschman, Albert O. Exit, Voice, and Loyalty: Further Reflections and a Survey of Recent Contributions. In *Hirschman, A. O.*, 1981, *1974*, pp. 213–35.

Holmes, A. S. The Good Fight. *Econ. Rec.*, March 1981, *57*(156), pp. 1–11. [G: Australia]

Howe, Roger E. and Roemer, John E. Rawlsian Justice as the Core of a Game. *Amer. Econ. Rev.*, December 1981, *71*(5), pp. 880–95.

Hunt, Lester H. Some Advantages of Social Control: An Individualist Defense. *Public Choice*, 1981, *36*(1), pp. 3–16.

Inada, Ken-ichi. On "The Marginal Substitution Rate of Distribution." (In Japanese. With English summary.) *Econ. Stud. Quart.*, April 1981, *32*(1), pp. 1–11.

Ingram, Robert W. and Copeland, Ronald M. Municipal Accounting Information and Voting Behavior. *Accounting Rev.*, October 1981, *56*(4), pp. 830–43. [G: U.S.]

Inman, Robert P. "Municipal Pension Funding: A Theory and Some Evidence" by Dennis Epple and Katherine Schipper: A Comment. *Public Choice*, 1981, *37*(1), pp. 179–87.

Inoue, K., et al. A Trial towards Group Decisions in Structuring Environmental Science. In *Morse, J. N., ed.*, 1981, pp. 157–70.

Intriligator, Michael D. Probabilistic Mechanisms of Social Choice and Income Redistribution. In *Solo, R. A. and Anderson, C. W., eds.*, 1981, pp. 185–98.

Johansen, Leif. Incentives in Public Decision Making: Review and Comments. *J. Public Econ.*, August 1981, *16*(1), pp. 123–28.

Johnson, Conrad. Equity: Its Scope and Its Relation to Other Objectives. In *Brown, P. G.; Johnson, C. and Vernier, P., eds.*, 1981, pp. 125–45.

Johnston, R. J. Regional Variations in British Voting Trends—1966–1979: Tests of an Ecological Model. *Reg. Stud.*, 1981, *15*(1), pp. 23–32. [G: U.K.]

Johnston, R. J. and Rossiter, D. J. Shape and the Definition of Parliamentary Constituencies. *Urban Stud.*, June 1981, *18*(2), pp. 219–23. [G: U.K.]

Jonung, Lars and Wadensjö, Eskil. The Effect of Unemployment, Inflation and Real Income Growth on Government Popularity in Sweden. In *Strøm, S., ed.*, 1981, *1979*, pp. 202–12. [G: Sweden]

Judge, Ken. Pricing and Public Choice in Social Welfare. In *Seldon, A., ed.*, 1981, pp. 147–69.

Kafoglis, Milton Z. and Cebula, Richard J. The Buchanan–Tullock Model: Some Extensions. *Public Choice*, 1981, *36*(1), pp. 179–86.

Kaneko, Mamoru. The Nash Social Welfare Function for a Measure Space of Individuals. *J. Math. Econ.*, July 1981, *8*(2), pp. 173–200.

Kau, James B. and Rubin, Paul H. The Impact of Labor Unions on the Passage of Economic Legislation. *J. Lab. Res.*, Spring 1981, *2*(1), pp. 133–45. **[G: U.S.]**

Keating, Barry P. Standards: Implicit, Explicit and Mandatory. *Econ. Inquiry*, July 1981, *19*(3), pp. 449–58. **[G: U.S.]**

Kemp, Kathleen. Symbolic and Strict Regulation in the American States. *Soc. Sci. Quart.*, September 1981, *62*(3), pp. 516–26. **[G: U.S.]**

Kernell, Samuel and Hibbs, Douglas A., Jr. A Critical Threshold Model of Presidential Popularity. In *Hibbs, D. A., Jr. and Fassbender, H., eds.*, 1981, pp. 49–71. **[G: U.S.]**

Kiefer, David. The Dynamic Behavior of Public Budgets: An Empirical Study of Australian Local Governments. *Rev. Econ. Statist.*, August 1981, *63*(3), pp. 422–29. **[G: Australia]**

Kiewiet, D. Roderick. Policy-Oriented Voting in Response to Economic Issues. *Amer. Polit. Sci. Rev.*, June 1981, *75*(2), pp. 448–59. **[G: U.S.]**

Kim, Ki Hang and Roush, Fred W. Effective Nondictatorial Domains. *J. Econ. Theory*, February 1981, *24*(1), pp. 40–47.

Klevorick, Alvin K. Income-Distribution Concerns in Regulatory Policymaking: Comment. In *Fromm, G., ed.*, 1981, pp. 108–11. **[G: U.S.]**

Kuklinski, James H. and West, Darrell M. Economic Expectations and Voting Behavior in United States House and Senate Elections. *Amer. Polit. Sci. Rev.*, June 1981, *75*(2), pp. 436–47. **[G: U.S.]**

Lafay, Jean-Dominique. The Impact of Economic Variables on Political Behavior in France. In *Hibbs, D. A., Jr. and Fassbender, H., eds.*, 1981, pp. 137–49. **[G: France]**

Laffont, Jean-Jacques and Maskin, Eric S. On the Difficulty of Attaining Distributional Goals with Imperfect Information about Consumers. In *Strnm, S., ed.*, 1981, *1979*, pp. 86–96.

Lambro, Donald. Congressional Oversights. *Policy Rev.*, Spring 1981, (16), pp. 115–28.

Lawrence, David G. Comment on Sullivan, Piereson, and Marcus [The Sources of Political Tolerance: A Multivariate Analysis]. *Amer. Polit. Sci. Rev.*, December 1981, *75*(4), pp. 1013–14.

Lecaillon, Jacques. Cycle électoral et répartition du revenu national. (Political Business Cycle and Distribution of National Income. With English summary.) *Revue Écon.*, March 1981, *32*(2), pp. 213–36.

Lecaillon, Jacques. Popularité des gouvernants et politique économique. (The Popularity of Government and Economic Policy. With English summary.) *Consommation*, July–September 1981, *28*(3), pp. 17–49. **[G: France]**

Ledyard, John O. The Paradox of Voting and Candidate Competition: A General Equilibrium Analysis. In *[Weiler, E. T.]*, 1981, pp. 54–80.

Lekachman, Robert. Economic Justice in Hard Times. In *Caplan, A. L. and Callahan, D., eds.*, 1981, pp. 91–115.

Lentz, Bernard F. Political and Economic Determinants of County Government Pay. *Public Choice*, 1981, *36*(2), pp. 253–71. **[G: U.S.]**

Locksley, Gareth. Individuals, Contracts and Constitutions: The Political Economy of James M. Buchanan. In *Shackleton, J. R. and Locksley, G., eds.*, 1981, pp. 33–52.

Locksley, Gareth. The Minister's Memos: The Re-Election Issue. *Public Choice*, 1981, *36*(1), pp. 33–41.

Machina, Mark J. and Parks, Robert P. On Path Independent Randomized Choice: Comment. *Econometrica*, September 1981, *49*(5), pp. 1345–47.

MacIntyre, I. and Pattanaik, Prasanta K. Strategic Voting under Minimally Binary Group Decision Functions. *J. Econ. Theory*, December 1981, *25*(3), pp. 338–52.

Mack, Eric. Nozick on Unproductivity: The Unintended Consequences. In *Paul, J., ed.*, 1981, pp. 169–90.

Mackay, Robert J. and Weaver, Carolyn L. Agenda Control by Budget Maximizers in a Multi-Bureau Setting. *Public Choice*, 1981, *37*(3), pp. 447–72.

Macnaughton, Bruce D. and Winn, Conrad J. Economic Policy and Electoral Self Interest: The Allocations of the Department of Regional Economic Expansion. *Can. Public Policy*, Spring 1981, *7*(2), pp. 318–27. **[G: Canada]**

MacRae, Duncan. On the Political Business Cycle. In *Hibbs, D. A., Jr. and Fassbender, H., eds.*, 1981, pp. 169–84. **[G: U.S.]**

MacRae, Duncan, Jr. Valuative Problems of Public Policy Analysis. In *Crecine, J. P., ed.*, 1981, pp. 175–94.

Madsen, Henrik Jess. Partisanship and Macroeconomic Outcomes: A Reconsideration. In *Hibbs, D. A., Jr. and Fassbender, H., eds.*, 1981, pp. 269–82. **[G: Norway; OECD]**

Maier, Charles S. "Fictitious Bonds...of Wealth and Law": On the Theory and Practice of Interest Representation. In *Berger, S., ed.*, 1981, pp. 27–61. **[G: W. Europe]**

Maloney, Kevin J. and Smirlock, Michael L. Business Cycles and the Political Process. *Southern Econ. J.*, October 1981, *48*(2), pp. 377–92.

Marcus, George E., et al. Reply [The Sources of Political Tolerance: A Multivariate Analysis]. *Amer. Polit. Sci. Rev.*, December 1981, *75*(4), pp. 1014.

Martinez-Vazquez, Jorge. Selfishness versus Public 'Regardingness' in Voting Behavior. *J. Public Econ.*, June 1981, *15*(3), pp. 349–61. **[G: U.S.]**

McClennen, E. F. Constitutional Choice: Rawls vs. Harsanyi. In *Pitt, J. C., ed.*, 1981, pp. 93–109.

McGuire, Thomas G. Budget-Maximizing Governmental Agencies: An Empirical Test. *Public Choice*, 1981, *36*(2), pp. 313–22. **[G: U.S.]**

Mehta, Ghanshyam. Recent Developments in Keynesian Economics. *Indian Econ. J.*, April–June 1981, *28*(4), pp. 1–17.

Meltzer, Allan H. and Richard, Scott F. A Rational Theory of the Size of Government. *J. Polit. Econ.*, October 1981, *89*(5), pp. 914–27.

Merkies, Arnold H. Q. M. and Nijam, T. E. Preference Functions of Dutch Political Parties. *Écon. Appl.*, 1981, *34*(4), pp. 784–818. **[G: Netherlands]**

Merrill, Samuel, III. Strategic Decisions under One-Stage Multi-Candidate Voting Systems. *Public*

Choice, 1981, 36(1), pp. 115–34.   [G: U.S.]

Messerlin, Patrick A. The Political Economy of Protectionism: The Bureaucratic Case. Weltwirtsch. Arch., 1981, 117(3), pp. 469–96.

Mestmäcker, Ernst-Joachim. Vom Bürgerkrieg als Utopie. (A Utopianism Resulting in Civil War. With English Summary.) In [von Haberler, G.], 1981, pp. 103–07.

Michaels, Robert and Kalish, Lionel. The Incentives of Regulators: Evidence from Banking. Public Choice, 1981, 36(1), pp. 187–92.   [G: U.S.]

Milne, Frank. The Firm's Objective Function as a Collective Choice Problem. Public Choice, 1981, 37(3), pp. 473–86.

Mirrlees, J. A. Property and Commodity taxes and Under-Provision in the Public Sector: Comment. In Currie, D.; Peel, D. and Peters, W., eds., 1981, pp. 136–38.

Moore, Thomas Gale. Comments on Aranson & Ordershook's Regulation, Redistribution, and Public Choice. Public Choice, 1981, 37(1), pp. 101–05.

Moulin, Hervé. Implementing Just and Efficient Decision-Making. J. Public Econ., October 1981, 16(2), pp. 193–213.

Moulin, Hervé. Prudence versus Sophistication in Voting Strategy. J. Econ. Theory, June 1981, 24(3), pp. 398–412.

Moulin, Hervé. The Proportional Veto Principle. Rev. Econ. Stud., July 1981, 48(3), pp. 407–16.

Myerson, Roger B. Utilitarianism, Egalitarianism, and the Timing Effect in Social Choice Problems. Econometrica, June 1981, 49(4), pp. 883–97.

Nagel, Stuart S. Optimally Allocating Campaign Expenditures. Public Choice, 1981, 36(1), pp. 159–64.   [G: U.S.]

Nelson, William B.; Stone, Gerald W., Jr. and Swint, J. Michael. An Economic Analysis of Public Sector Collective Bargaining and Strike Activity. J. Lab. Res., Spring 1981, 2(1), pp. 77–98.   [G: U.S.]

Ng, Yew-Kwang. All "NG" up on Clubs? A "Bran-New Flawer" of Brennan–Flowers. Public Finance Quart., January 1981, 9(1), pp. 75–78.

Ng, Yew-Kwang. Bentham or Nash? On the Acceptable Form of Social Welfare Functions. Econ. Rec., September 1981, 57(158), pp. 238–50.

Ng, Yew-Kwang. Welfarism: A Defence against Sen's Attack [Personal Utilities and Public Judgements: Or What's Wrong with Welfare Economics]. Econ. J., June 1981, 91(362), pp. 527–30.

Nitzan, Shmuel and Rubinstein, Ariel. A Further Characterization of Borda Ranking Method. Public Choice, 1981, 36(1), pp. 153–58.

Noll, Roger G. and Joskow, Paul L. Regulation in Theory and Practice: An Overview. In Fromm, G., ed., 1981, pp. 1–65.   [G: U.S.]

Offe, Claus. The Attribution of Public Status to Interest Groups: Observations on the West German Case. In Berger, S., ed., 1981, pp. 123–58.   [G: W. Germany]

Olsen, Johan P. Integrated Organizational Participation in Government. In Nystrom, P. C. and Starbuck, W. H., eds., Vol. 2, 1981, pp. 492–516.

Oppenheimer, Joe. Does the Route to Development Pass through Public Choice? In Russell, C. S.

and Nicholson, N. K., eds., 1981, pp. 271–99.   [G: LDCs]

Oppenheimer, Joe A. Legislators, Bureaucrats and Locational Decisions and Beyond: Some Comments. Public Choice, 1981, 37(1), pp. 133–40.

Oren, Ishai. The Structure of Exactly Strongly Consistent Social Choice Functions. J. Math. Econ., October 1981, 8(3), pp. 207–20.

Ott, Mack. Bureaucratic Incentives, Social Efficiency, and the Conflict in Federal Land Policy. Cato J., Fall 1981, 1(2), pp. 585–607. [G: U.S.]

Packel, Edward W. Social Decision Functions and Strongly Decisive Sets. Rev. Econ. Stud., April 1981, 48(2), pp. 343–49.

Paldam, Martin. An Essay on the Rationality of Economic Policy: The Test-Case of the Electional Cycle. Public Choice, 1981, 37(2), pp. 287–305.

Paul, Jeffrey. Reading Nozick: Essays on Anarchy, State, and Utopia: Introduction. In Paul, J., ed., 1981, pp. 1–23.

Peel, David A. Some Empirical Evidence on the Influence of Political Parties on the Behaviour of the Unemployment Rate. Empirical Econ., 1981, 6(1), pp. 67–73.   [G: U.K.]

Peirce, William S. Bureaucratic Politics and the Labor Market. Public Choice, 1981, 37(2), pp. 307–20.

Peretz, Paul. The Effect of Economic Change on Political Parties in West Germany. In Hibbs, D. A., Jr. and Fassbender, H., eds., 1981, pp. 101–20.   [G: W. Germany]

Pizzorno, Alessandro. Interests and Parties in Pluralism. In Berger, S., ed., 1981, pp. 247–84.

Polsby, Nelson W. Contemporary Transformations of American Politics: Thoughts on the Research Agendas of Political Scientists. Polit. Sci. Quart., Winter 1981–82, 96(4), pp. 551–70.   [G: U.S.]

Pommerehne, Werner W.; Schneider, Friedrich and Lafay, Jean-Dominique. Les interactions entre économie et politique: synthèses des analyses theoriques et empiriques. (Interactions between the Economy and the Polity: A Synthesis of Theoretical and Empirical Studies. With English summary.) Revue Écon., January 1981, 32(1), pp. 110–62.

Putterman, Louis. On Optimality in Collective Institutional Choice. J. Compar. Econ., December 1981, 5(4), pp. 392–403.

Rattinger, Hans. Unemployment and the 1976 Election in Germany: Some Findings at the Aggregate and the Individual Level of Analysis. In Hibbs, D. A., Jr. and Fassbender, H., eds., 1981, pp. 121–35.

Rob, Rafael. A Condition Guaranteeing the Optimality of Public Choice. Econometrica, November 1981, 49(6), pp. 1605–13.

Rose-Ackerman, Susan. Does Federalism Matter? Political Choice in a Federal Republic. J. Polit. Econ., February 1981, 89(1), pp. 152–65.

Russell, Clifford S. Public Choice and Rural Development: Introduction. In Russell, C. S. and Nicholson, N. K., eds., 1981, pp. 1–15.

Saposnik, Rubin. Rank-Dominance in Income Distributions. Public Choice, 1981, 36(1), pp. 147–51.

Satterthwaite, Mark A. and Sonnenschein, Hugo. Strategy-Proof Allocation Mechanisms at Differentiable Points. *Rev. Econ. Stud.*, October 1981, *48*(4), pp. 587–97.

Şaylan, Gencay. Planlama ve Bürokrasi. (Planning and Bureaucracy. With English summary.) *METU*, Special Issue, 1981, pp. 183–205.
[G: Turkey]

Scanlon, Thomas. Nozick on Rights, Liberty, and Property. In *Paul, J., ed.*, 1981, *1976*, pp. 107–29.

Schmalensee, Richard. Income-Distribution Concerns in Regulatory Policymaking: Comment. In *Fromm, G., ed.*, 1981, pp. 112–17. [G: U.S.]

Schmitter, Philippe C. Interest Intermediation and Regime Governability in Contemporary Western Europe and North America. In *Berger, S., ed.*, 1981, pp. 285–327. [G: W. Europe; N. America]

Schneider, Friedrich; Pommerehne, Werner W. and Frey, Bruno S. Politico-economic Interdependence in a Direct Democracy: The Case of Switzerland. In *Hibbs, D. A., Jr. and Fassbender, H., eds.*, 1981, pp. 231–48. [G: Switzerland]

Schott, Kerry. Public Sector Behaviour: The Status of the Political Business Cycle: Comment. In *Currie, D.; Nobay, R. and Peel, D., eds.*, 1981, pp. 377–82. [G: U.K.]

Schulze, William D.; Brookshire, David S. and Sandler, Todd. The Social Rate of Discount for Nuclear Waste Storage: Economics or Ethics? *Natural Res. J.*, October 1981, *21*(4), pp. 811–32.

Schumaker, Paul D. Citizen Preferences and Policy Responsiveness. In *Clark, T. N., ed.*, 1981, pp. 227–43.

Schwartz, Thomas. The Universal-Instability Theorem. *Public Choice*, 1981, *37*(3), pp. 487–501.

Sen, Amartya. A Reply to 'Welfarism: A Defence against Sen's Attack' [Personal Utilities and Public Judgements: Or What's Wrong with Welfare Economics]. *Econ. J.*, June 1981, *91*(362), pp. 531–35.

Shariff, Zahid. Contemporary Challenges to Public Administration. *Soc. Sci. Quart.*, September 1981, *62*(3), pp. 555–68.

Shepsle, Kenneth A. and Weingast, Barry R. Structure-Induced Equilibrium and Legislative Choice. *Public Choice*, 1981, *37*(3), pp. 503–19.

Simon, William E. Government Regulation and a Free Society. In *Gatti, J. F., ed.*, 1981, pp. 11–24.

Sirkin, Gerald. Rent Seeking: Comments. In *Sirkin, G., ed.*, 1981, pp. 191–94.

Sisk, David E. A Theory of Government Enterprise: University Ph.D. Production. *Public Choice*, 1981, *37*(2), pp. 357–63. [G: U.S.]

Sjoquist, David L. A Median Voter Analysis of Variations in the Use of Property Taxes among Local Governments. *Public Choice*, 1981, *36*(2), pp. 273–85. [G: U.S.]

Strasnick, Steven. Neo-utilitarian Ethics and the Ordinal Representation Assumption. In *Pitt, J. C., ed.*, 1981, pp. 63–92.

Sullivan, John L., et al. The Sources of Political Tolerance: A Multivariate Analysis. *Amer. Polit. Sci. Rev.*, March 1981, *75*(1), pp. 92–106. [G: U.S.]

Suzumura, Kotaro. On the Possibility of "Fair" Col-

lective Choice Rule. *Int. Econ. Rev.*, June 1981, *22*(2), pp. 351–64.

Suzumura, Kotaro. On Pareto-Efficiency and the No-Envy Concept of Equity. *J. Econ. Theory*, December 1981, *25*(3), pp. 267–79.

Swaney, James A. Externality and Community. *J. Econ. Issues*, September 1981, *15*(3), pp. 615–27.

Tanino, T.; Nakayama, H. and Sawaragi, Y. On Methodology for Group Decision Support. In *Morse, J. N., ed.*, 1981, pp. 409–23.

Tate, C. Neal. Personal Attribute Models of the Voting Behavior of U.S. Supreme Court Justices: Liberalism in Civil Liberties and Economics Decisions, 1946–1978. *Amer. Polit. Sci. Rev.*, June 1981, *75*(2), pp. 355–67. [G: U.S.]

Terrebonne, R. Peter. Government as a Super Becker-Altruist: A Comment. *Public Choice*, 1981, *37*(3), pp. 595–601.

Thompson, Earl A. and Faith, Roger L. A Pure Theory of Strategic Behavior and Social Institutions. *Amer. Econ. Rev.*, June 1981, *71*(3), pp. 366–80.

Thompson, Fred. Utility-Maximizing Behavior in Organized Anarchies: An Empirical Investigation of the Breneman Thesis. *Public Choice*, 1981, *36*(1), pp. 17–32. [G: U.S.]

Thomson, William. Nash's Bargaining Solution and Utilitarian Choice Rules. *Econometrica*, March 1981, *49*(2), pp. 535–38.

Tideman, T. Nicolaus and Tullock, Gordon. Coalitions under Demand Revealing [A New and Superior Process of Making Social Choices]. *Public Choice*, 1981, *36*(2), pp. 323–28.

Toma, Eugenia Froedge. Bureaucratic Structures and Educational Spending. *Southern Econ. J.*, January 1981, *47*(3), pp. 640–54. [G: U.S.]

Topham, Neville. Property and Commodity Taxes and Under-Provision in the Public Sector. In *Currie, D.; Peel, D. and Peters, W., eds.*, 1981, pp. 107–35.

Townley, Peter G. C. Public Choice and the Social Insurance Paradox: A Note. *Can. J. Econ.*, November 1981, *14*(4), pp. 712–17.

Tullock, Gordon. Lobbying and Welfare: A Comment. *J. Public Econ.*, December 1981, *16*(3), pp. 391–94.

Tullock, Gordon. Rent Seeking. In *Sirkin, G., ed.*, 1981, pp. 165–90.

Tullock, Gordon. Why So Much Stability? *Public Choice*, 1981, *37*(2), pp. 189–202.

Umbeck, John. Might Makes Rights: A Theory of the Formation and Initial Distribution of Property Rights. *Econ. Inquiry*, January 1981, *19*(1), pp. 38–59. [G: U.S.]

Upton, Graham J. G. and Särlvik, B. A Loyalty-Distance Model for Voting Change. *J. Roy. Statist. Soc.*, Part 2, 1981, *144*, pp. 247–59. [G: Sweden]

Warner, Stanley L. Balanced Information: The Pickering Airport Experiment. *Rev. Econ. Statist.*, May 1981, *63*(2), pp. 256–62. [G: Canada]

Weber, James W. Of Legislative Bills and Markov Chains: An Inquiry into the Technologies of the Legislative Policy Process. *Mich. Academician*, Spring 1981, *13*(4), pp. 435–49.

Weingast, Barry R. Regulation, Reregulation, and Deregulation: The Political Foundations of Agency Clientele Relationships. *Law Contemp. Probl.*, Winter 1981, *44*(1), pp. 147–77.
[G: U.S.]

Weingast, Barry R. and Hall, Kent S. Congress, Regulation, and the Courts: Economic Perspectives on Political Choice. In *Ferguson, A. R., ed.*, 1981, pp. 55–93.
[G: U.S.]

Weingast, Barry R.; Shepsle, Kenneth A. and Johnsen, Christopher. The Political Economy of Benefits and Costs: A Neoclassical Approach to Distributive Politics. *J. Polit. Econ.*, August 1981, *89*(4), pp. 642–64.

Welch, Robert L. Incentives and Risk Aversion in the Provision of a Public Input. *J. Public Econ.*, February 1981, *15*(1), pp. 87–103.

Welch, W. P. Money and Votes: A Simultaneous Equation Model. *Public Choice*, 1981, *36*(2), pp. 209–34.
[G: U.S.]

West, Edwin G. and McKee, Michael. The Public Choice of Price Control and Rationing of Oil. *Southern Econ. J.*, July 1981, *48*(1), pp. 204–10.

West, Edwin G. and Staaf, Robert J. Extra-Governmental Powers in Public Schooling: The Unions and the Courts: Rejoinder. *Public Choice*, 1981, *36*(3), pp. 647–50.

West, Edwin G. and Staaf, Robert J. Extra-Governmental Powers in Public Schooling: The Unions and the Courts. *Public Choice*, 1981, *36*(3), pp. 619–37.

Willig, Robert D. Social Welfare Dominance. *Amer. Econ. Rev.*, May 1981, *71*(2), pp. 200–204.

Willig, Robert D. and Bailey, Elizabeth E. Income-Distribution Concerns in Regulatory Policymaking. In *Fromm, G., ed.*, 1981, pp. 79–107.
[G: U.S.]

Yaari, Menahem E. Rawls, Edgeworth, Shapley, Nash: Theories of Distributive Justice Re-examined. *J. Econ. Theory*, February 1981, *24*(1), pp. 1–39.

Yinger, John. Capitalization and the Median Voter. *Amer. Econ. Rev.*, May 1981, *71*(2), pp. 99–103.

Ziemer, Rod F.; White, Fred C. and Clifton, Ivery D. An Analysis of Factors Affecting Differential Assessment Legislation. *Public Choice*, 1981, *36*(1), pp. 43–52.
[G: U.S.]

026 Economics of Uncertainty and Information; Game Theory and Bargaining Theory

0260 Economics of Uncertainty and Information; Game Theory and Bargaining Theory

Allen, Beth E. Generic Existence of Completely Revealing Equilibria for Economies with Uncertainty when Prices Convey Information. *Econometrica*, September 1981, *49*(5), pp. 1173–99.

Jesse, Richard R., Jr. and Radcliffe, Robert C. On Speculation and Price Stability under Uncertainty. *Rev. Econ. Statist.*, February 1981, *63*(1), pp. 129–32.

Laitner, John P. The Steady States of a Stochastic Decentralized Growth Model. *J. Econ. Theory*, June 1981, *24*(3), pp. 377–92.

Rashid, Salim. Preferences under Certainty and Uncertainty: A Note [A Homiletic Exposition of the Expected Utility Hypothesis]. *Economica*, February 1981, *48*(189), pp. 93–94.

Yefimov, Vladimir M. Gaming-Simulation of the Functioning of Economic Systems. *J. Econ. Behav. Organ.*, June 1981, *2*(2), pp. 187–200.

0261 Theory of Uncertainty and Information

Albin, Peter S. "Strategic Mind Set" and the Assessment of Information in Serious Games. In *Galatin, M. and Leiter, R. D., eds.*, 1981, pp. 209–55.

Albrecht, James W. A Procedure for Testing the Signalling Hypothesis. *J. Public Econ.*, February 1981, *15*(1), pp. 123–32.
[G: Sweden; U.S.]

Appelbaum, Elie and Katz, Eliakim. Market Constraints as a Rationale for the Friedman-Savage Utility Function. *J. Polit. Econ.*, August 1981, *89*(4), pp. 819–25.

Balcer, Yves. Equilibrium Distributions of Sales and Advertising Prices over Space. *J. Econ. Theory*, October 1981, *25*(2), pp. 196–218.

Bell, D. E. Explaining Utility Theory Paradoxes by Decision Regret. In *Morse, J. N., ed.*, 1981, pp. 28–39.

Berczi, Andrew. Information as a Factor of Production. *Bus. Econ.*, January 1981, *16*(1), pp. 14–20.

Binswanger, Hans P. Attitudes toward Risk: Theoretical Implications of an Experiment in Rural India. *Econ. J.*, December 1981, *91*(364), pp. 867–90.
[G: India]

Bodily, Samuel E. Stability, Equality, Balance, and Multivariate Risk. In *Morse, J. N., ed.*, 1981, pp. 40–55.

Bradford, David F. and Kelejian, Harry H. The Value of Information in a Storage Model with Open- and Closed-Loop Controls: A Numerical Example. *J. Econ. Dynam. Control*, August 1981, *3*(3), pp. 307–17.

Bressler, Barry. Search, Information, and Market Structure: Comments. In *Galatin, M. and Leiter, R. D., eds.*, 1981, pp. 98–103.

Burdett, Kenneth and Malueg, David A. The Theory of Search for Several Goods. *J. Econ. Theory*, June 1981, *24*(3), pp. 362–76.

Burdett, Kenneth and Mortensen, Dale T. Testing for Ability in a Competitive Labor Market. *J. Econ. Theory*, August 1981, *25*(1), pp. 42–66.

Chan, Yuk-shee. A Note on Risk and the Value of Information. *J. Econ. Theory*, December 1981, *25*(3), pp. 461–65.

Charles, Susan and Westaway, Anthony J. Ignorance and Merit Wants. *Finanzarchiv*, 1981, *39*(1), pp. 74–78.

Chowdhury, Tawfiq-e-Elahi. Fertility Behaviour under Uncertainty—A Mathematical Model. *Bangladesh Devel. Stud.*, Summer 1981, *9*(2), pp. 97–101.

Christensen, John. Communication in Agencies. *Bell J. Econ. (See Rand J. Econ. after 4/85)*, Autumn 1981, *12*(2), pp. 661–74.

Dacey, Raymond. Some Implications of 'Theory Absorption' for Economic Theory and the Economics of Information. In *Pitt, J. C., ed.*, 1981, pp. 111–36.

Dahlby, B. G. Adverse Selection and Pareto Improvements through Compulsory Insurance. *Public Choice*, 1981, 37(3), pp. 547–58.

Danthine, Jean-Pierre and Donaldson, John B. Certainty Planning in an Uncertain World: A Reconsideration. *Rev. Econ. Stud.*, July 1981, 48(3), pp. 507–10.

Diamond, Peter A. and Maskin, Eric S. An Equilibrium Analysis of Search and Breach of Contract II. A Non-Steady State Example. *J. Econ. Theory*, October 1981, 25(2), pp. 165–95.

Dionne, Georges. Le risque moral et la sélection adverse: une revue critique de la littérature. (Moral Hazard and Adverse Selection: A Survey. With English summary.) *L'Actual. Econ.*, April–June 1981, 57(2), pp. 193–224.

Eden, Benjamin. Toward a Theory of Competitive Price Adjustment. *Rev. Econ. Stud.*, April 1981, 48(2), pp. 199–216.

Eden, Benjamin and Pakes, Ariél. On Measuring the Variance-Age Profile of Lifetime Earnings. *Rev. Econ. Stud.*, July 1981, 48(3), pp. 385–94.

Etgar, Michael and Malhotra, Naresh K. Determinants of Price Dependency: Personal and Perceptual Factors. *J. Cons. Res.*, September 1981, 8(2), pp. 217–22.

Finley, D. R. and Liao, Woody M. A General Decision Model for Cost–Volume–Profit Analysis under Uncertainty: A Comment. *Accounting Rev.*, April 1981, 56(2), pp. 400–403.

Fraser, Clive D. The Value of Non-Marginal Changes in Physical Risk: Comment. In *Currie, D.; Peel, D. and Peters, W., eds.*, 1981, pp. 269–75.

Friedman, David D. Why There are No Risk Preferrers. *J. Polit. Econ.*, June 1981, 89(3), pp. 600.

Galatin, Malcolm. Search, Information, and Market Structure. In *Galatin, M. and Leiter, R. D., eds.*, 1981, pp. 83–97.

Green, Jerry R. Value of Information with Sequential Futures Markets. *Econometrica*, March 1981, 49(2), pp. 335–58.

Greenberg, Edward; Marshall, William J. and Yawitz, Jess B. The Technology of Risk and Return: Reply. *Amer. Econ. Rev.*, June 1981, 71(3), pp. 491–92.

Grossman, Herschel I. Incomplete Information, Risk Shifting, and Employment Fluctuations. *Rev. Econ. Stud.*, April 1981, 48(2), pp. 189–97.

Grossman, Sanford J. The Informational Role of Warranties and Private Disclosure about Product Quality. *J. Law Econ.*, December 1981, 24(3), pp. 461–83.

Grunert, Klaus G. Consumer Information Programs and the Concept of "Perceived Risk." In *Molt, W.; Hartmann, H. A. and Stringer, P., eds.*, 1981, pp. 161–74.

Haimes, Yacov Y. Risk-benefit Analysis in a Multiobjective Framework. In *Haimes, Y. Y., ed.*, 1981, pp. 89–122.

Hammond, Peter J. *Ex-ante* and *Ex-post* Welfare Optimality under Uncertainty. *Economica*, August 1981, 48(191), pp. 235–50.

Harris, Milton and Townsend, Robert M. Resource Allocation under Asymmetric Information. *Econometrica*, January 1981, 49(1), pp. 33–64.

Heinkel, Robert. Uncertain Product Quality: The Market for Lemons with an Imperfect Testing Technology. *Bell J. Econ. (See Rand J. Econ. after 4/85)*, Autumn 1981, 12(2), pp. 625–36.

Helleiner, G. K. The International Economics of the Information Industry and the Developing Countries. In *Murray, R., ed.*, 1981, pp. 207–20.

Henry, Claude. Criteres Simples Pour La Prise En Compte Du Risque. (With English summary.) *Econometrica*, January 1981, 49(1), pp. 153–70.

Hey, John D. Are Optimal Search Rules Reasonable? And Vice Versa? (And Does It Matter Anyway?) *J. Econ. Behav. Organ.*, March 1981, 2(1), pp. 47–70.

Hey, John D. Hedging and the Competitive Labor-Managed Firm under Price Uncertainty [Hedging and the Competitive Firm under Price Uncertainty]. *Amer. Econ. Rev.*, September 1981, 71(4), pp. 753–57.

Hey, John D. and McKenna, Chris J. Consumer Search with Uncertain Product Quality. *J. Polit. Econ.*, February 1981, 89(1), pp. 54–66.

Hiebert, L. Dean. Production Uncertainty and Factor Demands for the Competitive Firm: An Extension. *Southern Econ. J.*, July 1981, 48(1), pp. 211–15.

Hilton, Ronald W. and Swieringa, Robert J. Perception of Initial Uncertainty as a Determinant of Information Value. *J. Acc. Res.*, Spring 1981, 19(1), pp. 109–19.

Hilton, Ronald W.; Swieringa, Robert J. and Hoskin, Robert E. Perception of Accuracy as a Determinant of Information Value. *J. Acc. Res.*, Spring 1981, 19(1), pp. 86–108.

Holthausen, Duncan M. A Risk–Return Model with Risk and Return Measured as Deviations from a Target Return. *Amer. Econ. Rev.*, March 1981, 71(1), pp. 182–88.

James, Christopher. The Technology of Risk and Return: Comment. *Amer. Econ. Rev.*, June 1981, 71(3), pp. 485–90.

Jones-Lee, M. The Value of Non-Marginal Changes in Physical Risk. In *Currie, D.; Peel, D. and Peters, W., eds.*, 1981, pp. 232–68.

Katz, Eliakim. A Note on a Comparative Statics Theorem for Choice under Risk. *J. Econ. Theory*, October 1981, 25(2), pp. 318–19.

Kihlstrom, Richard E.; Romer, David and Williams, Steve. Risk Aversion with Random Initial Wealth. *Econometrica*, June 1981, 49(4), pp. 911–20.

Kotz, Rolf and Spremann, Klaus. Risk-Aversion and Mixing. *Z. Nationalökon.*, 1981, 41(3–4), pp. 307–28.

Laffont, Jean-Jacques and Maskin, Eric S. On the Difficulty of Attaining Distributional Goals with Imperfect Information about Consumers. In *Strm, S., ed.*, 1981, 1979, pp. 86–96.

Lancaster, Kelvin J. Information and Product Differentiation. In *Galatin, M. and Leiter, R. D., eds.*, 1981, pp. 17–36.

Lau, Amy Hing-Ling and Lau, Hon-Shiang. A Comment on Shih's General Decision Model for CVP

Analysis. *Accounting Rev.*, October 1981, *56*(4), pp. 980–83.

Leland, Hayne E. The Informational Role of Warranties and Private Disclosure about Product Quality: Comment. *J. Law Econ.*, December 1981, *24*(3), pp. 485–89.

Lim, Chin. Risk Pooling and Intermediate Trading Agents. *Can. J. Econ.*, May 1981, *14*(2), pp. 261–75.

Lim, Chin. Theory of the Firm: Uncertainty and Choice of Experiments. *J. Econ. Theory*, June 1981, *24*(3), pp. 328–61.

Lippman, Steven A. and McCall, John J. The Economics of Uncertainty: Selected Topics and Probabilistic Methods. In *Arrow, K. J. and Intriligator, M. D., eds.*, 1981, pp. 211–84.

Lorigny, Jacques. Théorie de l'information appliquée aux systèmes sociaux. (Theory of Information Applied to Social Systems. With English summary.) *Ann. INSEE*, July–September 1981, (43), pp. 47–97.

Mack, Eric. Nozick on Unproductivity: The Unintended Consequences. In *Paul, J., ed.*, 1981, pp. 169–90.

Marty, Alvin L. Adaptations to Information Impactedness: A Survey: Comments. In *Galatin, M. and Leiter, R. D., eds.*, 1981, pp. 119–22.

McCain, Roger A. Information and Product Differentiation: Comments. In *Galatin, M. and Leiter, R. D., eds.*, 1981, pp. 37–41.

Milgrom, Paul R. An Axiomatic Characterization of Common Knowledge. *Econometrica*, January 1981, *49*(1), pp. 219–22.

Milgrom, Paul R. Good News and Bad News: Representation Theorems and Applications. *Bell J. Econ. (See Rand J. Econ. after 4/85)*, Autumn 1981, *12*(2), pp. 380–91.

Milgrom, Paul R. Rational Expectations, Information Acquisition, and Competitive Bidding. *Econometrica*, June 1981, *49*(4), pp. 921–43.

Miller, Jeffrey B. and Murrell, Peter. Limitations on the Use of Information-Revealing Incentive Schemes in Economic Organizations. *J. Compar. Econ.*, September 1981, *5*(3), pp. 251–71.

Morse, Joel N. Compound Lotteries: Call Option Spreads in Black–Scholes Markets. In *Morse, J. N., ed.*, 1981, pp. 239–47.

Mumy, Gene E. A Superior Solution to Captain MacWhirr's Problem: An Illustration of Information Problems and Entitlement Structures. *J. Polit. Econ.*, October 1981, *89*(5), pp. 1039–43.

Niculescu-Mizil, E. Information Processing for Managing Economic Units. *Econ. Computat. Cybern. Stud. Res.*, 1981, *15*(1), pp. 13–22.

North, Ronald M. Risk Analyses Applicable to Water Resources Program and Project Planning and Evaluation. In *Haimes, Y. Y., ed.*, 1981, pp. 163–74. [G: U.S.]

O'Hare, Michael. Information Management and Public Choice. In *Crecine, J. P., ed.*, 1981, pp. 223–56.

Ohlson, James A. and Buckman, A. G. Toward a Theory of Financial Accounting: Welfare and Public Information. *J. Acc. Res.*, Autumn 1981, *19*(2), pp. 399–433.

Pissarides, Christopher A. Uncertainty and the De-mand for Labour by Dynamically-Monopsonistic Firms. *Greek Econ. Rev.*, December 1981, *3*(3), pp. 279–94.

Pohjola, Matti T. Uncertainty and the Vigour of Policy: Some Implications of Quadratic Preferences. *J. Econ. Dynam. Control*, August 1981, *3*(3), pp. 299–305.

Posner, Richard A. The Economics of Privacy. *Amer. Econ. Rev.*, May 1981, *71*(2), pp. 405–09. [G: U.S.]

Rigaux-Bricmont, B.; Sayegh, E. and Vlahopoulos, P. Pour un modèle du rôle de l'information et du risque perçu dans la prise de decision de consommation. (Building a Model of Consumer Decision-Making Emphasizing the Use of Information for Perceived Risk Reduction. With English summary.) *Ann. Sci. Écon. Appl.*, 1981, *37*(2), pp. 25–55.

Roberts, Kevin and Weitzman, Martin L. Funding Criteria for Research, Development, and Exploration Projects. *Econometrica*, September 1981, *49*(5), pp. 1261–88.

Rosenfield, Donald B. and Shapiro, Roy D. Optimal Adaptive Price Search. *J. Econ. Theory*, August 1981, *25*(1), pp. 1–20.

Rosenthal, Robert W. Games of Perfect Information, Predatory Pricing and the Chain-Store Paradox. *J. Econ. Theory*, August 1981, *25*(1), pp. 92–100.

Ross, Stephen A. Some Stronger Measures of Risk Aversion in the Small and the Large with Applications. *Econometrica*, May 1981, *49*(3), pp. 621–38.

Rowe, William D. Methodology and Myth. In *Haimes, Y. Y., ed.*, 1981, pp. 59–88.

Sage, Andrew P. and White, Elbert B. On the Value Dependent Role of the Identification Processing and Evaluation of Information in Risk/Benefit Analysis. In *Haimes, Y. Y., ed.*, 1981, pp. 245–62.

Schotter, Andrew and Braunstein, Yale M. Economic Search: An Experimental Study. *Econ. Inquiry*, January 1981, *19*(1), pp. 1–25.

Shih, Wei. A Comment on Shih's General Decision Model for CVP Analysis—A Reply. *Accounting Rev.*, October 1981, *56*(4), pp. 984–85.

Shih, Wei. A General Decision Model for Cost–Volume–Profit Analysis under Uncertainty: A Reply. *Accounting Rev.*, April 1981, *56*(2), pp. 404–08.

Silver, Morris. Adaptations to Information Impactedness: A Survey. In *Galatin, M. and Leiter, R. D., eds.*, 1981, pp. 104–18.

Szaniawski, Klemens. The Concept of Unreliable Information. In *[Lipiński, E.]*, 1981, pp. 135–39.

Theiler, G. and Tövissi, L. Useful Versions of Entropy with Weights. *Econ. Computat. Cybern. Stud. Res.*, 1981, *15*(3), pp. 19–29.

von Ungern-Sternberg, Thomas and von Weizsäcker, Carl Christian. Marktstruktur und Marktverhalten bei Qualitätsunsicherheit. (Structure and Conduct on Markets with Quality Uncertainty. With English summary.) *Z. Wirtschaft. Sozialwissen.*, 1981, *101*(6), pp. 609–26.

Wilde, Louis L. Information Costs, Duration of Search, and Turnover: Theory and Applications. *J. Polit. Econ.*, December 1981, *89*(6), pp. 1122–41.

0262 Game Theory and Bargaining Theory

Aubin, Jean-Pierre. Locally Lipschitz Cooperative Games. *J. Math. Econ.*, October 1981, *8*(3), pp. 241–62.

Brams, Steven J. and Wittman, Donald. Nonmyopic Equilibria in 2 x 2 Games. *Conflict Manage. Peace Sci.*, Fall 1981, *6*(1), pp. 39–62.

Chow, Gregory C. Estimation and Optimal Control of Dynamic Game Models under Rational Expectations. In *Lucas, R. E. and Sargent, T. J., eds.*, 1981, pp. 681–89.

Denzer, D. Eine Methode zur Auswertung von Gefechtssimulationen. (With English summary.) In *Fandel, G., et al., eds.*, 1981, pp. 45–48.

Diskin, Abraham and Felsenthal, Dan S. An Experimental Examination of Samson's Dilemma. *Conflict Manage. Peace Sci.*, Spring 1981, *5*(2), pp. 121–37.

Fandel, Günter. Decision Concepts for Organizations. In *Morse, J. N., ed.*, 1981, pp. 91–109.

Fogarty, T. M. Prisoner's Dilemma and Other Public Goods Games. *Conflict Manage. Peace Sci.*, Spring 1981, *5*(2), pp. 111–20.

Friedman, James W. A Note on the Turnpike Properties of Time Dependent Supergames [Non-Cooperative Equilibria in Time Dependent Supergames]. *Econometrica*, June 1981, *49*(4), pp. 1087–88.

Galatin, Malcolm. "Strategic Mind Set" and the Assessment of Information in Serious Games: Comments. In *Galatin, M. and Leiter, R. D., eds.*, 1981, pp. 256–57.

Jansen, M. J. M. and Tijs, S. H. Arbitration Games. A Survey. In *Fandel, G., et al., eds.*, 1981, pp. 116–26.

Johansen, Leif. Interaction in Economic Theory. *Écon. Appl.*, 1981, *34*(2–3), pp. 229–67.

Landa, Janet and Grofman, Bernard. Games of Breach and the Role of Contract Law in Protecting the Expectation Interest. In *Zerbe, R. O., Jr., ed.*, 1981, pp. 67–90.

Moulin, Hervé. Deterrence and Cooperation: A Classification of Two-Person Games. *Europ. Econ. Rev.*, February 1981, *15*(2), pp. 179–93.

Moulin, Hervé and d'Alcantara, G. Application of Game Theory to the Multicountry Models: Methodology and an Example with Comet. In *Courbis, R., ed.*, 1981, pp. 327–36.

Radner, Roy. Monitoring Cooperative Agreements in a Repeated Principal–Agent Relationship. *Econometrica*, September 1981, *49*(5), pp. 1127–48.

Ratick, Samuel J.; Cohon, Jared L. and ReVelle, Charles S. Multiobjective Programming Solutions to N-Person Bargaining Games. In *Morse, J. N., ed.*, 1981, pp. 296–319.

Riddell, W. Craig. Bargaining under Uncertainty. *Amer. Econ. Rev.*, September 1981, *71*(4), pp. 579–90.

Roth, Alvin E.; Malouf, Michael W. K. and Murnighan, J. Keith. Sociological versus Strategic Factors in Bargaining. *J. Econ. Behav. Organ.*, June 1981, *2*(2), pp. 153–77.

Rustem, Berc and Zarrop, Martin B. A Newton-Type Algorithm for a Class of N-Player Dynamic Games Using Nonlinear Econometric Models. In *Janssen, J. M. L.; Pau, L. F. and Straszak, A. J., eds.*, 1981, pp. 349–54.

Shefrin, Hersh M. Games with Self-Generating Distributions. *Rev. Econ. Stud.*, July 1981, *48*(3), pp. 511–19.

Shubik, Martin. Game Theory Models and Methods in Political Economy. In *Arrow, K. J. and Intriligator, M. D., eds.*, 1981, pp. 285–330.

Sobel, Joel. Distortion of Utilities and the Bargaining Problem. *Econometrica*, May 1981, *49*(3), pp. 597–619.

Szidarovszky, Ferenc. On the Generalization of Nash's Cooperative Solution Concept. *Acta Oecon.*, 1981, *26*(3–4), pp. 361–67.

Thomson, William. A Class of Solutions to Bargaining Problems [Independence of Irrelevant Alternatives and Solutions to Nash's Bargaining Problem]. *J. Econ. Theory*, December 1981, *25*(3), pp. 431–41.

Tolwinski, B. and Sosnowski, J. Planning Model with Decentralized Structure of Decision Making. In *Janssen, J. M. L.; Pau, L. F. and Straszak, A. J., eds.*, 1981, pp. 367–74.

Weber, Robert James. Attainable Sets of Markets: An Overview. In *Schaible, S. and Ziemba, W. T., eds.*, 1981, pp. 613–25.

Weber, S. Some Results on the Weak Core of a Non-Side-Payment Game with Infinitely Many Players. *J. Math. Econ.*, March 1981, *8*(1), pp. 101–11.

Zagare, Frank C. Nonmyopic Equilibria and the Middle East Crisis of 1967. *Conflict Manage. Peace Sci.*, Spring 1981, *5*(2), pp. 139–62.

[G: Israel]

027 Economics of Centrally Planned Economies

0270 Economics of Centrally Planned Economies

Antal, László. Historical Development of the Hungarian System of Economic Control and Management. *Acta Oecon.*, 1981, *27*(3–4), pp. 251–66.

[G: Hungary]

Antsyshkin, S. V. and Polianskaia, T. M. On Possible Ways of Using Optimal Branch Plans to Improve the Price System—The Case of Power Station Coals. *Matekon*, Fall 1981, *18*(1), pp. 15–34.

[G: U.S.S.R.]

Avrămiţă, G. M. An Optimal Proceeding for Solving Large-Scale Problems: Vertical Decomposition. *Econ. Computat. Cybern. Stud. Res.*, 1981, *15*(3), pp. 81–96.

Bródy, András. An Economy Controlled by Stocks and Profits. In *Kornai, J. and Martos, B., eds.*, 1981, *1973*, pp. 149–61.

Cave, Martin. Soviet Planning Models: Introduction. *Matekon*, Summer 1981, *17*(4), pp. 3–10.

[G: U.S.S.R.]

Dancs, István; Hunyadi, László and Sivák, József. Discrete-Time Control with Time Lags. In *Kornai, J. and Martos, B., eds.*, 1981, pp. 131–47.

Granberg, A. Modelling the Processes of Coordinating National Economic and Regional Planning Decisions. In *Janssen, J. M. L.; Pau, L. F. and*

027 Economics of Centrally Planned Economies

Straszak, A. J., eds., 1981, pp. 187–93.

Guran, M., et al. Multilevel Approach to Real Time Management and Control Systems. *Econ. Computat. Cybern. Stud. Res.,* 1981, 15(1), pp. 22–33.

Hoós, János. Characteristics of the New Growth Path of the Economy in Hungary. *Acta Oecon.,* 1981, 27(3–4), pp. 207–19.   [G: Hungary]

Kornai, János and Martos, Béla. Vegetative Control: The First Step. In *Kornai, J. and Martos, B., eds.,* 1981, pp. 57–80.

Maiminas, E. Z. Theoretical Problems of Modeling the Socioeconomic System. *Matekon,* Spring 1981, 17(3), pp. 9–34.   [G: U.S.S.R.]

Mănescu, Manea. Cybernetic Scenario: Accumulation-Consumption Correlation. *Econ. Computat. Cybern. Stud. Res.,* 1981, 15(2), pp. 7–19.

Mănescu, Manea. The System of Scientific Research and Technological Development: Cybernetic—Economic Models of the system. *Econ. Computat. Cybern. Stud. Res.,* 1981, 15(1), pp. 7–12.

Martos, Béla. Vegetative Control with Price Communication. In *Kornai, J. and Martos, B., eds.,* 1981, pp. 163–86.

Mikhailov, A. G. and Tokarev, V. V. The Principle of a Guaranteed Result in Problems of Economic Control. In *Janssen, J. M. L.; Pau, L. F. and Straszak, A. J., eds.,* 1981, pp. 383–86.

Miloslavskii, N. On Uniform Principles in Determining the Economic Effectiveness of New Technology and Capital Investments. *Prob. Econ.,* July 1981, 24(3), pp. 55–72.   [G: U.S.S.R.]

Nistorescu, G. Problems of Value in the Context of Production Cybernetization. *Econ. Computat. Cybern. Stud. Res.,* 1981, 15(2), pp. 65–73.

Özler, Güntaç. A Note on Novozhilov's Optimal Plan Prices [A Suggested Planning Procedure with Scarcity in a Centrally Planned Economy]. *METU,* 1981, 8(1 & 2), pp. 571–75.

Pertot, Nada. Integracijski procesi v našem gospodarstvu: Modeli in metode za ugotavljanje smiselnosti in učinkovitosti takih povezovanj. (Integration Models in Yugoslav Economy: Models and Methods to Prove the Rationale and Efficiency of Merging. With English summary.) *Econ. Anal. Worker's Manage.,* 1981, 15(3), pp. 365–81.   [G: Yugoslavia]

Petrakov, N. Ia. The Operating Mechanism of a Socialist Economy and the Problem of the Economy's Optimality Criterion. *Matekon,* Spring 1981, 17(3), pp. 35–54.   [G: U.S.S.R.]

Raichur, Satish. Economic 'Laws,' the Law of Value, and Chinese Socialism. *Australian Econ. Pap.,* December 1981, 20(37), pp. 205–18. [G: China]

Sadowski, Zdzislaw. The Principle of Rationality and the Social Effectiveness of Economic Activity. In *[Lipiński, E.],* 1981, pp. 235–51.

Schweitzer, Iván. Some Interrelations between Enterprise Organization and the Economic Mechanism in Hungary. *Acta Oecon.,* 1981, 27(3–4), pp. 289–300.   [G: Hungary]

Simonovits, András. Maximal Convergence Speed of Decentralized Control. *J. Econ. Dynam. Control,* February 1981, 3(1), pp. 51–64.

Sirotkovic, Jakov. Influence of the Self-Management System on the Development of the Yugoslav

Economy. *Eastern Europ. Econ.,* Winter 1981–82, 20(2), pp. 46–62.   [G: Yugoslavia]

Stojanović, Dragiša. Special Models Based on the Matrix of Growth. *Econ. Computat. Cybern. Stud. Res.,* 1981, 15(3), pp. 97–106.

Stroe, R. Production Cybernetization—A Basic Component of the New Higher Stage of Development of the Romanian Socialist Society. *Econ. Computat. Cybern. Stud. Res.,* 1981, 15(1), pp. 43–52.   [G: Romania]

Thomas, Ewart A. C. Effort and Optimality in the New Soviet Incentive Model. *Econ. Planning,* 1981, 17(1), pp. 23–36.

Vatel', I. A. and Moiseev, N. N. On Modeling Economic Mechanisms. *Matekon,* Spring 1981, 17(3), pp. 78–101.

Zelić, Nikola. Income Distribution and the Allocation of Resources in the Yugoslav Economy. *Econ. Anal. Worker's Manage.,* 1981, 15(3), pp. 277–89.   [G: Yugoslavia]

0271 Microeconomic Theory

Äbel, István. The Labor Saving Principle with an Application to the Leontief-Type Economies. *Int. Econ. Rev.,* June 1981, 22(2), pp. 377–83.

Anatskov, Vasil. Problems of Management of Production Stocks at Agricultural Organizations in the Bulgarian People's Republic. In *Chikán, A., ed. (II),* 1981, pp. 11–21.   [G: Bulgaria]

Belkin, M. I., et al. Modeling the Impact of the Economic Mechanism on the Indicators of Enterprise Activity. *Matekon,* Winter 1981–82, 18(2), pp. 32–52.   [G: U.S.S.R.]

Bod, Péter. Strategic Decisions on the Development of the Aluminum Industry. *Matekon,* Winter 1981–82, 18(2), pp. 3–18.   [G: Hungary]

Bonin, John P. The Theory of the Labor-Managed Firm from the Membership's Perspective with Implications for Marshallian Industry Supply. *J. Compar. Econ.,* December 1981, 5(4), pp. 337–51.

Borozdin, Iu. Trends toward Change in Socially Necessary Expenditures of Labor and Prices. *Prob. Econ.,* December 1981, 24(8), pp. 64–80.   [G: U.S.S.R.]

Bulgaru, M. The Micro-Economic Equilibrium and the Enterprise Management Problems. *Econ. Computat. Cybern. Stud. Res.,* 1981, 15(3), pp. 5–18.

Bunich, P. G. Wages as an Economic Incentive. *Prob. Econ.,* May 1981, 24(1), pp. 3–18.   [G: U.S.S.R.]

Chillemi, Ottorino. Sul regime del capitale nell'impresa autogestita. (Property Rights and the Labour-managed Firm. With English summary.) *Rivista Int. Sci. Econ. Com.,* January–February 1981, 28(1–2), pp. 151–69.

Ciobanu, G. and Stoica, M. Production Scheduling in Fuzzy Conditions. *Econ. Computat. Cybern. Stud. Res.,* 1981, 15(3), pp. 67–79.

Farkas, Katalin. The Changing Role of Inventories in the Enterprise. An Example for the Adaptation of the Management. In *Chikán, A., ed. (II),* 1981, pp. 85–98.   [G: Hungary]

Fink, Gerhard. Price Distortions in the Austrian and

in the Hungarian Economy. *Z. Nationalökon.*, 1981, *41*(1–2), pp. 111–32. **[G: Austria; Hungary]**

Granick, David. Soviet Use of Fixed Prices: Hypothesis of a Job-Right Constraint. In *[Bergson, A.]*, 1981, pp. 85–103.

Gui, Benedetto. Investment Decisions in a Worker-Managed Firm. *Econ. Anal. Worker's Manage.*, 1981, *15*(1), pp. 45–65.

Gürmann, Klaus. Complex Stock Planning by the Improvement of Plan Indicators. In *Chikán, A., ed. (I)*, 1981, pp. 167–78. **[G: E. Germany]**

Hey, John D. A Unified Theory of the Behaviour of Profit-Maximising, Labour-Managed and Joint-Stock Firms Operating under Uncertainty. *Econ. J.*, June 1981, *91*(362), pp. 364–74.

Hey, John D. and Suckling, John. Risk-Bearing in a Yugoslavian Labour-Managed Firm: Comment. *Oxford Econ. Pap.*, March 1981, *33*(1), pp. 170–73. **[G: Yugoslavia]**

Iakovlev, A. Methods of Determining Economic Effectiveness and of Pricing New Machinery and Equipment. *Prob. Econ.*, July 1981, *24*(3), pp. 73–85. **[G: U.S.S.R.]**

Ireland, Norman J. The Behaviour of the Labour Managed Firm and Disutility from Supplying Factor Services. *Econ. Anal. Worker's Manage.*, 1981, *15*(1), pp. 21–43.

Ireland, Norman J. and Law, Peter J. Efficiency, Incentives, and Individual Labor Supply in the Labor-Managed Firm. *J. Compar. Econ.*, March 1981, *5*(1), pp. 1–23.

Kheifets, L. Material Rewards for the Work Force and the Improvement of the Economic Mechanism. *Prob. Econ.*, June 1981, *24*(2), pp. 32–45. **[G: U.S.S.R.]**

Klinger, Harry; Przyborowski, Claus-Jürgen and Wilhelm, Klaus. Centralization of Material Stocks Justified by Economic Reasons. Decision Aids and Results in Their Application. In *Chikán, A., ed. (II)*, 1981, pp. 121–34.

Landsberger, Michael and Subotnik, A. Some Anomalies in the Production Strategy of a Labour-managed Firm. *Economica*, May 1981, *48*(190), pp. 195–97.

Miller, Jeffrey B. and Murrell, Peter. Limitations on the Use of Information-Revealing Incentive Schemes in Economic Organizations. *J. Compar. Econ.*, September 1981, *5*(3), pp. 251–71.

Murrell, Peter. The Microeconomic Efficiency Argument for Socialism Revisited: Comment. *J. Econ. Issues*, March 1981, *15*(1), pp. 211–19.

Negoiţă, C. V. On the Fundamental Research in Modelling Decision-Making Processes. *Econ. Computat. Cybern. Stud. Res.*, 1981, *15*(1), pp. 35–42.

Niculescu-Mizil, E. Informatics on Industrial Platforms. *Econ. Computat. Cybern. Stud. Res.*, 1981, *15*(2), pp. 25–30.

Niculescu-Mizil, E. Information Processing for Managing Economic Units. *Econ. Computat. Cybern. Stud. Res.*, 1981, *15*(1), pp. 13–22.

Ostojić, Slobodan. Interna alokacija rada i razlike u ličnim dohocima izmedu OOUR-a U SOUR-ima. (Inter-boal Personal Income Differences and the Internal Allocation of Labour in Large Yugoslav

Enterprises [COALs]. With English summary.) *Econ. Anal. Worker's Manage.*, 1981, *15*(4), pp. 481–500. **[G: Yugoslavia]**

Petrović, Pavle. Income Distribution, Prices and Choice of Technique in the Labour-Managed Economy. *Econ. Anal. Worker's Manage.*, 1981, *15*(4), pp. 433–44.

Rácz, Lászlo. On the New Price System. *Eastern Europ. Econ.*, Fall 1981, *20*(1), pp. 49–69. **[G: Hungary]**

Ramachandran, Rama V.; Russell, William R. and Seo, Tae Kun. Response to Comments by John D. Hey and John Suckling [Risk Bearing in a Yugoslavian Labour-Managed Firm]. *Oxford Econ. Pap.*, March 1981, *33*(1), pp. 174–75. **[G: Yugoslavia]**

Roca, Santiago. An Approach towards Differentiating Self-Managed from Non-Selfmanaged Enterprises. *Econ. Anal. Worker's Manage.*, 1981, *15*(1), pp. 1–19.

Snowberger, Vinson. Firm Response to Planner Initiative in Centrally Planned Economy. *Econ. Planning*, 1981, *17*(2–3), pp. 113–25.

Song, Yangyan. A Discussion on the Starting Point and Main Basis for the Reform of Economic Structure. *Chinese Econ. Stud.*, Summer 1981, *14*(4), pp. 30–37. **[G: China]**

Spechler, Martin. The Welfare Economics of Product Quality Under Socialism. In *[Bergson, A.]*, 1981, pp. 311–31.

Stallaerts, Robert. The Effect of Capital Intensity on Income in Yugoslav Industry. *Econ. Anal. Worker's Manage.*, 1981, *15*(4), pp. 501–15. **[G: Yugoslavia]**

Stolbov, A. Prices on Agricultural Products and the Stimulation of Production. *Prob. Econ.*, June 1981, *24*(2), pp. 66–77. **[G: U.S.S.R.]**

Stroe, R. Dimension and Homogeneity of the Microeconomic Cybernetic Systems. *Econ. Computat. Cybern. Stud. Res.*, 1981, *15*(2), pp. 51–56.

Tam, Mo-Yin S. Reward Structures in a Planned Economy: The Problem of Incentives and Efficient Allocation of Resources. *Quart. J. Econ.*, February 1981, *96*(1), pp. 111–28.

Tsurkov, V. I. Aggregation in a Branch Planning Problem. *Matekon*, Winter 1981–82, *18*(2), pp. 75–90.

Varga, György. Management—In a Fast Changing Environment. *Acta Oecon.*, 1981, *27*(3–4), pp. 301–26. **[G: Hungary]**

Wiseman, Jack. Uncertainty, Costs, and Collectivist Economic Planning. In *Buchanan, J. M. and Thirlby, G. F., eds.*, 1981, *1953*, pp. 227–43.

Yunker, James A. The Microeconomic Efficiency of Market Socialism: Reply [The Microeconomic Efficiency Argument for Socialism Revisited]. *J. Econ. Issues*, March 1981, *15*(1), pp. 220–27.

Zhang, Zhuoyuan. Le recenti riforme nella struttura dell'economia cinese. (Recent Reforms in the Structure of Chinese Economy. With English summary.) *Rivista Int. Sci. Econ. Com.*, September 1981, *28*(9), pp. 799–810. **[G: China]**

Zhou, Shulian; Wu, Jinglian and Wang, Haibo. The Profit Category and Socialist Business Management. *Chinese Econ. Stud.*, Winter–Spring 1980-81, *14*(2–3), pp. 3–138. **[G: China]**

027 Economics of Centrally Planned Economies

0272 Macroeconomic Theory

Äbel, István and Riecke, Werner. A Model of Aggregate Inventory Behaviour in the Hungarian Economy. In *Chikán, A., ed. (I),* 1981, pp. 13–28.
[G: Hungary]

Augusztinovics, Mária. Changes in the Macro-Structure of the Hungarian Economy (1950–2000). *Acta Oecon.,* 1981, 27(3–4), pp. 267–88.
[G: Hungary]

Baranov, E. F.; Danilov-Danil'ian, V. I. and Zavel-'skii, M. G. On a System of Models for Optimal Long-Term Planning. *Matekon,* Summer 1981, 17(4), pp. 11–38.

Bertinelli, Roberto. Alcune considerazioni sulla moneta nella R.P.C. (A Few Thoughts on Money in the P.R.C. With English summary.) *Rivista Int. Sci. Econ. Com.,* September 1981, 28(9), pp. 852–63.
[G: China]

Boratav, Korkut. The Market, Self-Management and Socialism. *Econ. Anal. Worker's Manage.,* 1981, 15(2), pp. 197–206.

Cheng, Hang-Sheng. Money and Credit in China. *Fed. Res. Bank San Francisco Econ. Rev.,* Fall 1981, pp. 19–36.
[G: China]

Csikós-Nagy, Béla. Some Aspects of Stock Economy (A Case Study of Hungary). In *Chikán, A., ed. (I),* 1981, pp. 87–97.
[G: Hungary]

Dadaian, V. S. and Raiatskas, R. L. Integrated Sets of Macroeconomic Models. *Matekon,* Summer 1981, 17(4), pp. 94–111.

Dirksen, Erik. The Control of Inflation? Errors in the Interpretation of CPE Data. *Economica,* August 1981, 48(191), pp. 305–08.
[G: Cent. Planned Econ.]

Fábri, Ervin. Paradoxes of Macroeconomic Inventory Developments. In *Chikán, A., ed. (I),* 1981, pp. 109–23.
[G: Hungary]

Fényes, Tamás and Sári, József. On the Difference Equation System of the Composition of the Amount of Money. *Acta Oecon.,* 1981, 26(3–4), pp. 335–59.

Gardner, Roy and Strauss, Jonathan. Repressed Inflation in the Soviet Union: A Temporary Equilibrium Approach. *Europ. Econ. Rev.,* June/July 1981, 16(2/3), pp. 387–404.
[G: U.S.S.R.]

Gligorov, Kiro. The Social and Economic Basis of Socialist Self-Management in Yugoslavia. *Eastern Europ. Econ.,* Winter 1981–82, 20(2), pp. 3–22.

Halevi, Joseph. The Composition of Investment under Conditions of Non Uniform Changes. *Banca Naz. Lavoro Quart. Rev.,* June 1981, (137), pp. 213–32.

Iakovets, Iu. Prices and the Improvement of Planning and the Economic Mechanism. *Prob. Econ.,* April 1981, 23(12), pp. 49–66.
[G: U.S.S.R.]

Inyutina, Klara V. The Role of Inventories in the Improvement of Economic Efficiency. In *Chikán, A., ed. (I),* 1981, pp. 189–98.
[G: U.S.S.R.]

Kapitány, Zsuzsa. Dynamic Stochastic Systems Controlled by Stock and Order Signals. In *Chikán, A., ed. (I),* 1981, pp. 209–21.

Khachaturov, Tigran. The Effectiveness of Socialist Social Production. *Prob. Econ.,* April 1981, 23(12), pp. 3–27.
[G: U.S.S.R.]

Kovács, János and Virág, Ildikó. Periodic versus

Continuous Growth. *Acta Oecon.,* 1981, 27(1–2), pp. 41–55.

Kubrin, Edward J. Some Characteristics of Stocks. In *Chikán, A., ed. (I),* 1981, pp. 223–28.

Luo, Jingfen. The Administrative System of the Economy Should be Separated from the Administrative System of State Power. *Chinese Econ. Stud.,* Summer 1981, 14(4), pp. 17–29.
[G: China]

Mikovsky, Vasil. Approach to Data Processing in Rating Inventory in Supply Enterprises. In *Chikán, A., ed. (II),* 1981, pp. 183–94.

Nagy, Márta. Some Special Features of the Connection between Material Flows and Stocks in the Hungarian Economy. In *Chikán, A., ed. (I),* 1981, pp. 269–80.
[G: Hungary]

Portes, Richard. Macroeconomic Equilibrium and Disequilibrium in Centrally Planned Economies. *Econ. Inquiry,* October 1981, 19(4), pp. 559–78.

Pugachev, V. F. A Multistage Set of Models for Optimal Production Planning. *Matekon,* Summer 1981, 17(4), pp. 39–57.

Pugachev, V. F. On Improving the Multistage System for Optimizing Long-Term Economic Plans. *Matekon,* Summer 1981, 17(4), pp. 58–71.

Sadowski, Zdzislaw; Kotowicz, Joanna and Cwalina, Kazimierz. An Experimental Model of General Growth Proportions in the National Economy: The MODO Model. *Econ. Planning,* 1981, 17(2–3), pp. 64–73.

Tallós, György. Objectives, Means and Methods in Inventory Control and in the Financing of Circulating Funds. In *Chikán, A., ed. (I),* 1981, pp. 333–40.
[G: Hungary]

Tsakmakov, Stoino Ivanov. Effects of Progressive Forms of Supply on Stocks of Means of Production. In *Chikán, A., ed. (I),* 1981, pp. 341–48.
[G: Bulgaria]

030 HISTORY OF THOUGHT; METHODOLOGY

031 History of Economic Thought

0310 General

Bauer, P. T. Economic History as Theory. In *Bauer, P. T.,* 1981, pp. 221–38.

Béteille, André. The Idea of Natural Inequality. In *Berreman, G. D., ed.,* 1981, pp. 59–80.

Bornemann, Alfred H. Fifty Years of Ideology: A Selective Survey of Academic Economics in the United States, 1930 to 1980. *J. Econ. Stud.,* 1981, 8(1), pp. 16–36.
[G: U.S.]

Danner, Peter L. Exchange Value in the Value Hierarchy. *Int. J. Soc. Econ.,* 1981, 8(4), pp. 70–84.

Das Gupta, A. K. How One May View the Development of Economic Theory. *Indian Econ. J.,* January–March 1981, 28(3), pp. 1–15.

Fischer, Charles C. A Comment on "The Method Is the Ideology." *J. Econ. Issues,* March 1981, 15(1), pp. 193–96.

Foster, J. Fagg. Economics. *J. Econ. Issues,* December 1981, 15(4), pp. 857–69.

Hutchison, Terence W. Walter Eucken and the German Social-Market Economy. In *Hutchison, T. W.,* 1981, pp. 155–75.
[G: W. Germany]

von Mises, Ludwig. The Task and Scope of the Science of Human Action. **In** *von Mises, L.*, 1981, pp. 1–67.

Niehans, Jürg. Economics: History, Doctrine, Science, Art. *Kyklos*, 1981, *34*(2), pp. 165–77.

Pourvoyeur, Robert. Pre-Ricardiaanse theorieën over de buitenlandse handel. (Pre-Ricardian Foreign Trade Theories. With English summary.) *Econ. Soc. Tijdschr.*, October 1981, *35*(5), pp. 575–84.

Rashid, Salim. Political Economy and Geology in the Early Nineteenth Century: Similarities and Contrasts. *Hist. Polit. Econ.*, Winter 1981, *13*(4), pp. 726–44.

Robbins, Lionel. Economics and Political Economy. *Amer. Econ. Rev.*, May 1981, *71*(2), pp. 1–10.

Tool, Marc R. Observations on the Fischer Comment [The Method Is the Ideology]. *J. Econ. Issues*, March 1981, *15*(1), pp. 197–99.

Ureña, Enrique M. A Note on "Marx and Darwin." *Hist. Polit. Econ.*, Winter 1981, *13*(4), pp. 772–73.

Weisskopf, Walter. Reply to Professor Fischer [The Method Is the Ideology]. *J. Econ. Issues*, March 1981, *15*(1), pp. 196–97.

Williams, Edward E. and Findlay, M. Chapman, III. A Reconsideration of the Rationality Postulate: 'Right Hemisphere Thinking' in Economics. *Amer. J. Econ. Soc.*, January 1981, *40*(1), pp. 17–36.

0311 Ancient, Medieval

Lowry, S. Todd. The Roots of Hedonism: An Ancient Analysis of Quantity and Time. *Hist. Polit. Econ.*, Winter 1981, *13*(4), pp. 812–23.

0312 Pre-Classical Except Mercantilist

Grampp, William D. The Classical Economics of the Pre-Classical Economists. *Eastern Econ. J.*, April 1981, *7*(2), pp. 125–31.

Leijonhufvud, Axel. Effective Demand Failures. **In** *Leijonhufvud, A.*, 1981, *1973*, pp. 103–29.

O'Neill, Onora. Nozick's Entitlements. **In** *Paul, J., ed.*, 1981, *1976*, pp. 305–22.

0313 Mercantilist

Patinkin, Don. Mercantilism and the Readmission of the Jews to England. **In** *Patinkin, D.*, 1981, *1946*, pp. 75–89. **[G: U.K.]**

Schaeffer, Robert K. The Entelechies of Mercantilism. *Scand. Econ. Hist. Rev.*, 1981, *29*(2), pp. 81–96.

0314 Classical

Arena, Richard. Note sur les apports de Sismondi à la théorie classique. (On the contribution of Sismondi's Economic Analysis to the Classical Economic Theory. With English summary.) *L'Actual. Econ.*, October–December 1981, *57*(4), pp. 565–88.

Bloomfield, Arthur I. British Thought on the Influence of Foreign Trade and Investment on Growth, 1800–1880. *Hist. Polit. Econ.*, Spring 1981, *13*(1), pp. 95–120. **[G: U.K.]**

Bradley, Ian. Intellectual Influences in Britain: Past and Present. **In** *Seldon, A., ed.*, 1981, pp. 171–88. **[G: U.K.]**

Caminati, Mauro. The Theory of Interest in the Classical Economists. *Metroecon.*, Feb.-Oct. 1981, *33*(1–2–3), pp. 79–104.

Claeys, Gregory and Kerr, Prue. Mechanical Political Economy: Review Article. *Cambridge J. Econ.*, September 1981, *5*(3), pp. 251–72.

Halevi, Joseph. Some Notes on Classical Political Economy and the Rise to Dominance of Supply and Demand Theories. *Australian Econ. Pap.*, June 1981, *20*(36), pp. 96–103.

Hollander, Samuel. Marxian Economics as 'General Equilibrium' Theory. *Hist. Polit. Econ.*, Spring 1981, *13*(1), pp. 121–55.

Howard, M. C. Ricardo's Analysis of Profit: An Evaluation in Terms of Piero Sraffa's Production of Commodities by Means of Commodities. *Metroecon.*, Feb.-Oct. 1981, *33*(1–2–3), pp. 105–28.

Hutchison, Terence W. The Changing Intellectual Climate In Economics. **In** *Seldon, A., ed.*, 1981, pp. 19–49. **[G: U.K.]**

Hutchison, Terence W. The Market Economy and the Franchise, or 1867 and All That. **In** *Hutchison, T. W.*, 1981, pp. 22–45.

Laidler, David. Adam Smith as a Monetary Economist. *Can. J. Econ.*, May 1981, *14*(2), pp. 185–200.

Leijonhufvud, Axel and Clower, Robert W. Say's Principle, What It Means and Doesn't Mean. **In** *Leijonhufvud, A.*, 1981, *1973*, pp. 79–101.

Matteucci, Andrea. Sraffa's "Two Ricardos": About the Interconnection between the Ricardian Theories of Value and Distribution. *Rivista Polit. Econ.*, Supplement December 1981, *71*, pp. 109–37.

O'Brien, D. P. Ricardian Economics and the Economics of David Ricardo. *Oxford Econ. Pap.*, November 1981, *33*(3), pp. 352–86.

Patinkin, Don. Involuntary Unemployment and the Keynesian Supply Function: Mathematical Appendix. **In** *Patinkin, D.*, 1981, pp. 175–79.

Patinkin, Don. Reflections on the Neoclassical Dichotomy. **In** *Patinkin, D.*, 1981, *1972*, pp. 149–54.

Patinkin, Don. The Indeterminacy of Absolute Prices in Classical Economic Theory. **In** *Patinkin, D.*, 1981, *1949*, pp. 125–48.

Ricciardi, Joseph. Class Struggle, the Classical Economists, and the Factory Acts: Towards a 'Reformulation.' **In** *Zarembka, P., ed.*, 1981, pp. 81–100. **[G: U.K.]**

Ryan, Cheyney C. The Fiends of Commerce: Romantic and Marxist Criticisms of Classical Political Economy. *Hist. Polit. Econ.*, Spring 1981, *13*(1), pp. 80–94.

Skinner, Andrew S. Sir James Steuart: Author of a System. *Scot. J. Polit. Econ.*, February 1981, *28*(1), pp. 20–42.

Sylos Labini, Paolo. On the Concept of the Optimum Rate of Profit. **In** *[Lipiński, E.]*, 1981, pp. 141–54.

Vint, John. A Two Sector Model of the Wages Fund: Mill's Recantation Revisited. *Brit. Rev. Econ. Is-*

sues, Autumn 1981, 3(9), pp. 71–88.
Wiltgen, Richard J. Marx and Engels on Malthus and Population: A Reconstruction and Reconsideration. *Quart. Rev. Econ. Bus.*, Winter 1981, 21(4), pp. 107–26.

0315 Austrian, Marshallian, Neoclassical

Bradley, Ian. Intellectual Influences in Britain: Past and Present. In *Seldon, A., ed.*, 1981, pp. 171–88. [G: U.K.]
Faber, Malte. Modern Austrian Capital Theory and Orosel's Standard Neoclassical Analysis: A Reply. *Z. Nationalökon.*, 1981, 41(1–2), pp. 157–76.
Gill, Flora. Some Methodological Implications of the Marginal Revolution. *Australian Econ. Pap.*, June 1981, 20(36), pp. 72–82.
Hutchison, Terence W. Austrians on Philosophy and Method (since Menger). In *Hutchison, T. W.*, 1981, pp. 203–32.
Hutchison, Terence W. The Changing Intellectual Climate In Economics. In *Seldon, A., ed.*, 1981, pp. 19–49. [G: U.K.]
Hutchison, Terence W. The Market Economy and the Franchise, or 1867 and All That. In *Hutchison, T. W.*, 1981, pp. 22–45.
Lee, Frederic S. The Oxford Challenge to Marshallian Supply and Demand: The History of the Oxford Economists' Research Group. *Oxford Econ. Pap.*, November 1981, 33(3), pp. 339–51.
Orosel, Gerhard O. Faber's Capital Theory: A Rejoinder. *Z. Nationalökon.*, 1981, 41(1–2), pp. 177–81.
Orosel, Gerhard O. Faber's Modern Austrian Capital Theory: A Critical Survey. *Z. Nationalökon.*, 1981, 41(1–2), pp. 141–55.
Osadchaya, I. M. Evolution of Economic Growth Theory. In *Mileikovsky, A. G., et al.*, 1981, pp. 51–73.
Osadchaya, I. M. The Present Stage of the "Antimarginalist Revolution" and Keynesianism. In *Mileikovsky, A. G., et al.*, 1981, pp. 74–117.
Patinkin, Don. More on the Chicago Monetary Tradition. In *Patinkin, D.*, 1981, 1973, pp. 277–84.
Patinkin, Don. More on the Chicago Monetary Tradition: Postscript. In *Patinkin, D.*, 1981, pp. 284–87.
Patinkin, Don. The Chicago Tradition, the Quantity Theory, and Friedman: Postscript. In *Patinkin, D.*, 1981, pp. 264–74.
Patinkin, Don. The Chicago Tradition, the Quantity Theory, and Friedman. In *Patinkin, D.*, 1981, 1969, pp. 241–64.
Rosenberg, Alexander. A Skeptical History of Microeconomic Theory. In *Pitt, J. C., ed.*, 1981, pp. 47–61.
Steedman, Ian W. Time Preference, the Rate of Interest and Abstinence from Accumulation. *Australian Econ. Pap.*, December 1981, 20(37), pp. 219–34.

0316 General Equilibrium until 1945

Rogers, C. Classical and Neoclassical Theories of General Equilibrium (Review Note). *S. Afr. J. Econ.*, June 1981, 49(2), pp. 172–76.

0317 Socialist and Marxian until 1945

Bailey, Anne M. and Llobera, Josep R. The Asiatic Mode of Production: Science and Politics: General Introduction. In *Bailey, A. M. and Llobera, J. R., eds.*, 1981, pp. 1–10.
Bailey, Anne M. and Llobera, Josep R. The AMP: Sources and Formation of the Concept. In *Bailey, A. M. and Llobera, J. R., eds.*, 1981, pp. 11–45.
Bailey, Anne M. and Llobera, Josep R. The Contemporary Debate on the AMP: Editors' Introduction. In *Bailey, A. M. and Llobera, J. R., eds.*, 1981, pp. 237–41.
Bailey, Anne M. and Llobera, Josep R. The Fate of the AMP from Plekhanov to Stalin: Editors' Introduction. In *Bailey, A. M. and Llobera, J. R., eds.*, 1981, pp. 49–52.
Banu, Ioan. The 'Tributary' Social Formation. In *Bailey, A. M. and Llobera, J. R., eds.*, 1981, 1967, pp. 278–80.
Chase-Dunn, Christopher. Interstate System and Capitalist World-Economy. In *Hollist, W. L. and Rosenau, J. N., eds.*, 1981, pp. 30–53.
Clark, Colin. The IEA and the Fabians: Comparison and Contrast. In *Seldon, A., ed.*, 1981, pp. 189–204.
DiMaio, Alfred J., Jr. Evolution of Soviet Population Thought: From Marxism-Leninism to the *Literaturnaya Gazeta* Debate. In *Desfosses, H., ed.*, 1981, pp. 157–78. [G: U.S.S.R.]
England, Richard and Greene, Michael. A Comment on John Roemer's Theory of Differentially Exploited Labor. *Rev. Radical Polit. Econ.*, Winter 1981, 12(4), pp. 71–74.
Funke, Michael and Stamatis, Georgios. Towards an Unequivocal Definition of Labor Values in Joint Production as Examined by Ochoa [Steedman after Marx: A Marxian Analysis of Fixed Capital and Joint Production]. *Econ. Forum*, Winter 1981–82, 12(2), pp. 85–91.
Godelier, Maurice. The Asiatic Mode of Production. In *Bailey, A. M. and Llobera, J. R., eds.*, 1981, 1978, pp. 264–77.
Heinsohn, Gunnar and Steiger, Otto. Money, Productivity and Uncertainty in Capitalism and Socialism. *Metroecon.*, Feb.-Oct. 1981, 33(1–2–3), pp. 41–77.
Ignatieff, Michael. Marxism and Classical Political Economy. In *Samuel, R., ed.*, 1981, pp. 344–52.
King, J. E. Perish Commerce! Free Trade and Underconsumption in Early British Radical Economics. *Australian Econ. Pap.*, December 1981, 20(37), pp. 235–57. [G: U.K.]
Kingston-Mann, Esther. Marxism and Russian Rural Development: Problems of Evidence, Experience, and Culture. *Amer. Hist. Rev.*, October 1981, 86(4), pp. 731–52. [G: U.S.S.R.]
Krader, Lawrence. Principles and Critique of the Asiatic Mode of Production. In *Bailey, A. M. and Llobera, J. R., eds.*, 1981, 1975, pp. 325–34.
Lewin, Gunter. Wittfogel on the Asiatic Mode of Production. In *Bailey, A. M. and Llobera, J. R., eds.*, 1981, 1967, pp. 158–63.
Lipset, Seymour Martin. Industrial Proletariat in Comparative Perspective. In *Triska, J. F. and*

Gati, C., eds., 1981, pp. 1–28.   [G: OECD; U.S.S.R.]

MacLean, Brian. Kōzō Uno's Principles of Political Economy: Review Article. *Sci. Soc.*, Summer 1981, *45*(2), pp. 212–27.

Mad'iar, L. I. The Legitimacy of the AMP. In *Bailey, A. M. and Llobera, J. R., eds.*, 1981, *1930*, pp. 76–94.

Mileikovsky, A. G. Radical Political Economy and the "New Left." In *Mileikovsky, A. G., et al.*, 1981, pp. 533–46.

Ochoa, Edward M. Labor Values and Joint Production: Reply and Further Thoughts [Steedman after Marx: A Marxian Analysis of Fixed Capital and Joint Production]. *Econ. Forum*, Winter 1981–82, *12*(2), pp. 93–102.

Plekhanov, G. The Fate of the AMP from Plekhanov to Stalin: Our Differences. In *Bailey, A. M. and Llobera, J. R., eds.*, 1981, *1881*, pp. 53–57.

Robinson, Joan. Marxism and Modern Economics. In *Robinson, J.*, 1981, pp. 192–202.

Robinson, Joan. Marxism: Religion and Science. In *Robinson, J.*, 1981, *1962*, pp. 155–64.

Robinson, Joan. The Labour Theory of Value. In *Robinson, J.*, 1981, *1977*, pp. 183–91.

Roemer, John E. Reply to England and Greene [Differentially Exploited Labor: A Marxian Theory of Discrimination]. *Rev. Radical Polit. Econ.*, Winter 1981, *12*(4), pp. 75.

Ryan, Cheyney C. The Fiends of Commerce: Romantic and Marxist Criticisms of Classical Political Economy. *Hist. Polit. Econ.*, Spring 1981, *13*(1), pp. 80–94.

Sherman, Howard J. Marx and Determinism. *J. Econ. Issues*, March 1981, *15*(1), pp. 61–71.

Shuklian, Steven. Marx, Means-Ends, and Instrumentalism: A Critique of Tool. *J. Econ. Issues*, September 1981, *15*(3), pp. 775–79.

Tökei, Ferenc. The Asiatic Mode of Production. In *Bailey, A. M. and Llobera, J. R., eds.*, 1981, *1966*, pp. 249–63.

Tool, Marc R. Response to Shuklian [Marx, Means-Ends, and Instrumentalism: A Critique of Tool]. *J. Econ. Issues*, September 1981, *15*(3), pp. 779–83.

Welskopf, Elisabeth C. Problems of Periodisation in Ancient History. In *Bailey, A. M. and Llobera, J. R., eds.*, 1981, *1957*, pp. 242–48.

0318 Historical and Institutional

Barbash, Jack. Theories of the Labor Movement in an Institutional Setting. *J. Econ. Issues*, June 1981, *15*(2), pp. 299–309.

Brazelton, W. Robert. Post Keynesian Economics: An Institutional Compatibility? *J. Econ. Issues*, June 1981, *15*(2), pp. 531–42.

Brinkman, Richard L. Culture in Neoinstitutional Economics: An Integration of Myrdal and Galbraith into the Veblen-Ayres Matrix. *Amer. J. Econ. Soc.*, October 1981, *40*(4), pp. 401–13.

Bush, Paul D. 'Radical Individualism' vs. Institutionalism, I: The Division of Institutionalists into 'Humanists' and 'Behaviorists.' *Amer. J. Econ. Soc.*, April 1981, *40*(2), pp. 139–47.

Bush, Paul D. 'Radical Individualism' vs. Institution-

alism, II: Philosophical Dualisms as Apologetic Constructs Based on Obsolete Psychological Preconceptions. *Amer. J. Econ. Soc.*, July 1981, *40*(3), pp. 287–98.

Foster, J. Fagg. Current Structure and Future Prospects of Institutional Economics. *J. Econ. Issues*, December 1981, *15*(4), pp. 943–47.

Foster, J. Fagg. John Dewey and Economic Value. *J. Econ. Issues*, December 1981, *15*(4), pp. 871–97.

Foster, J. Fagg. The Fundamental Principles of Economics. *J. Econ. Issues*, December 1981, *15*(4), pp. 937–42.

Foster, J. Fagg. The Institutionalist Theory of Government Ownership. *J. Econ. Issues*, December 1981, *15*(4), pp. 915–22.

Foster, J. Fagg. The Relation between the Theory of Value and Economic Analysis. *J. Econ. Issues*, December 1981, *15*(4), pp. 899–905.

Foster, J. Fagg. The Theory of Institutional Adjustment. *J. Econ. Issues*, December 1981, *15*(4), pp. 923–28.

Gruchy, Allan G. Organized Labor and Institutional Economics. *J. Econ. Issues*, June 1981, *15*(2), pp. 311–24.   [G: U.S.]

Junker, Louis J. Instrumentalism, the Principle of Continuity and the Life Process. *Amer. J. Econ. Soc.*, October 1981, *40*(4), pp. 381–400.

Kozlova, K. B. Institutionalism. In *Mileikovsky, A. G., et al.*, 1981, pp. 333–69.

Lissner, Will. Adolph Lowe's Methodological Alternative for Economic Research and Policy: "Political Economics" as an Experimental Method for Achieving Growth, Stability and Continuity. *Amer. J. Econ. Soc.*, July 1981, *40*(3), pp. 277–86.

Loescher, Samuel M. Public Interest Movements and Private Interest Systems: A Healthy Schizophrenia. *J. Econ. Issues*, June 1981, *15*(2), pp. 557–68.

Mirowski, Philip. Is There a Mathematical Neoinstitutional Economics? *J. Econ. Issues*, September 1981, *15*(3), pp. 593–613.

Ramstad, Yngve. Institutional Economics: How Prevalent in the Labor Literature? *J. Econ. Issues*, June 1981, *15*(2), pp. 339–50.   [G: U.S.]

Ranson, Baldwin. AFEE or AFIT: Which Represents Institutional Economics? *J. Econ. Issues*, June 1981, *15*(2), pp. 521–29.

Rutherford, Malcolm H. Clarence Ayres and the Instrumental Theory of Value. *J. Econ. Issues*, September 1981, *15*(3), pp. 657–73.

Rutherford, Malcolm H. Veblen on Owners, Managers, and the Control of Industry: A Rejoinder. *Hist. Polit. Econ.*, Spring 1981, *13*(1), pp. 156–58.

Seckler, David W. Individualism and Institutionalism Revisited: A Response to Professor Bush. *Amer. J. Econ. Soc.*, October 1981, *40*(4), pp. 415–26.

Sherman, Howard J. Marx and Determinism. *J. Econ. Issues*, March 1981, *15*(1), pp. 61–71.

Shuklian, Steven. Marx, Means-Ends, and Instrumentalism: A Critique of Tool. *J. Econ. Issues*, September 1981, *15*(3), pp. 775–79.

Tool, Marc R. Response to Shuklian [Marx, Means-

Ends, and Instrumentalism: A Critique of Tool].
J. Econ. Issues, September 1981, *15*(3), pp. 779–
83.

Tool, Marc R. The Compulsive Shift to Institutional
Analysis. *J. Econ. Issues*, September 1981, *15*(3),
pp. 569–92.

032 History of Economic Thought (continued)

0321 Other Schools Since 1800

Cate, Tom. Keynes on Monetary Theory and Policy:
Comment [Some Further Observations on the
Monetary Economics of Chicagoans and Non-Chi-
cagoans]. *Southern Econ. J.*, April 1981, *47*(4),
pp. 1132–36.

Feiwel, George R. Keynesian Economics, Neoclassical Synthesis and Resurgence of Classical Macroeconomics. *Economia (Portugal)*, May 1981, *5*(2),
pp. 209–57.

Foster, J. Fagg. Understandings and Misunderstandings of Keynesian Economics. *J. Econ. Issues*,
December 1981, *15*(4), pp. 949–57.

Hutchison, Terence W. The Philosophy and Politics
of the Cambridge School. In *Hutchison, T. W.*,
1981, pp. 46–107.

Hutton, Graham. 'Why Did It Happen . . . Just
Then?' In *Seldon, A., ed.*, 1981, pp. 1–18.
[G: U.K.]

Kuznetsov, V. I. and Kudryavtsev, A. K. Attempts
to Sociologise Bourgeois Political Economy: The
French School. In *Mileikovsky, A. G., et al.*,
1981, pp. 370–91.

von Mises, Ludwig. Remarks on the Fundamental
Problem of the Subjective Theory of Value. In
von Mises, L., 1981, pp. 167–82.

Patinkin, Don. Reminiscences of Chicago, 1941–47.
In *Patinkin, D.*, 1981, pp. 3–20.

Tavlas, George S. Keynes on Monetary Theory and
Policy: Reply [Some Further Observations on the
Monetary Economics of Chicagoans and Non-Chi-
cagoans]. *Southern Econ. J.*, April 1981, *47*(4),
pp. 1137–42.

0322 Individuals

Amin, Samir
Schiffer, Jonathan. The Changing Post-war Pattern of Development: The Accumulated Wisdom of Samir Amin. *World Devel.*, June 1981,
9(6), pp. 515–37.

Attwood, Thomas
Moss, David John. Banknotes versus Gold: The
Monetary Theory of Thomas Attwood in His
Early Writings, 1816–19. *Hist. Polit. Econ.*,
Spring 1981, *13*(1), pp. 19–38.

Ayres, Clarence E.
Dugger, William M. A Note on Institutionalism,
Straw Men, and Equality [Clarence Ayres's
Critique of Orthodox Economic Theory]. *J.
Econ. Issues*, September 1981, *15*(3), pp. 785–
91.

Hamilton, David. Ayres' Theory of Economic
Progress: An Evaluation of Its Place in Economic Literature. *Amer. J. Econ. Soc.*, Octo-

ber 1981, *40*(4), pp. 427–38.

Mayhew, Anne. Ayresian Technology, Technological Reasoning, and Doomsday. *J. Econ.
Issues*, June 1981, *15*(2), pp. 513–20.

Ranson, Baldwin. A Comment on Donald A.
Walker's Article [Clarence Ayres's Critique of
Orthodox Economic Theory]. *J. Econ. Issues*,
September 1981, *15*(3), pp. 783–85.

Rutherford, Malcolm H. Clarence Ayres and the
Instrumental Theory of Value. *J. Econ. Issues*,
September 1981, *15*(3), pp. 657–73.

Barfod, Børge
Jørgensen, Steffen. En note om Dorfman-Steiner
teoremet. (A Note on the Dorfman-Steiner
Theorem. With English summary.) *Nationaløk-
kon. Tidsskr.*, 1981, *119*(3), pp. 409–10.

Beard, Charles A.
Diggins, John Patrick. Power and Authority in
American History: The Case of Charles A.
Beard and His Critics. *Amer. Hist. Rev.*, Octo-
ber 1981, *86*(4), pp. 701–30. [G: U.S.]

Becker, Gary S.
Shackleton, J. R. Gary S. Becker: The Economist
as Empire-builder. In *Shackleton, J. R. and
Locksley, G., eds.*, 1981, pp. 12–32.

Bergson, Abram
Samuelson, Paul A. Bergsonian Welfare Economics. In *[Bergson, A.]*, 1981, pp. 223–66.

Braudel, Fernand
Kinser, Samuel. *Annaliste* Paradigm? The Geohistorical Structuralism of Fernand Braudel.
Amer. Hist. Rev., February 1981, *86*(1), pp.
63–105.

Buchanan, James M.
Locksley, Gareth. Individuals, Contracts and
Constitutions: The Political Economy of James
M. Buchanan. In *Shackleton, J. R. and Lock-
sley, G., eds.*, 1981, pp. 33–52.

Campbell, Angus
Converse, Philip E. On the Passing of Angus
Campbell. *Amer. J. Econ. Soc.*, October 1981,
40(4), pp. 341–42.

Cantillon, Richard
Gilardi, Jean-Claude. Profit, domination et équilibre dans "l'essai sur la nature du commerce
en général" de R. Cantillon. (With English
summary.) *Écon. Appl.*, 1981, *34*(1), pp. 161–
201.

Hébert, Robert F. Richard Cantillon's Early Contributions to Spatial Economics. *Economica*,
February 1981, *48*(189), pp. 71–77.

Tarascio, Vincent J. Cantillon's Theory of Population Size and Distribution. *Atlantic Econ. J.*,
July 1981, *9*(2), pp. 12–18.

Chamberlin, E. H.
Skinner, Andrew S. Of Factor and Commodity
Markets: A Note on E. H. Chamberlin. *Oxford
Econ. Pap.*, March 1981, *33*(1), pp. 122–34.

Clark, John Maurice
Benz, George A. The Theoretical Background of
John M. Clark and His Theory of Wages. *Rev.
Soc. Econ.*, December 1981, *39*(3), pp. 307–
21.

Gruchy, Allan G. Theory and Policy in John M.
Clark's Social Economics. *Rev. Soc. Econ.*,
December 1981, *39*(3), pp. 241–55.

Herschede, Fred and Wiltgen, Richard J. Japan's Alternative Road to Serfdom: J. M. Clark and the Japanese Experience. *Rev. Soc. Econ.*, December 1981, *39*(3), pp. 323–42.
[G: U.S.; Japan]

Hickerson, Steven. John Maurice Clark's View of Social Valuation and Accounting: Potential Applications of Policy Assessment Techniques. *Rev. Soc. Econ.*, December 1981, *39*(3), pp. 289–305.

Rohrlich, George F. John Maurice Clark's Unmet Challenge. *Rev. Soc. Econ.*, December 1981, *39*(3), pp. 343–48.

Schweitzer, Arthur. Social Values in Economics. *Rev. Soc. Econ.*, December 1981, *39*(3), pp. 257–78.

Stanfield, J. Ron. The Instructive Vision of John Maurice Clark. *Rev. Soc. Econ.*, December 1981, *39*(3), pp. 279–87.

Coase, Ronald H.

Baetge, Jörg and Fischer, Thomas. Substitution des Markt-Preis-Mechanismus durch Steuerungs- und Regelungsmechanismen im Unternehmen. (Managerial Control Strategies Instead of Price Mechanism. With English summary.) *Z. ges. Staatswiss.*, December 1981, *137*(4), pp. 723–32.

Bössmann, Eva. Weshalb gibt es Unternehmungen? Der Erklärungsansatz von Ronald H. Coase. (The Nature of the Firm: Ronald H. Coase's Interpretation. With English summary.) *Z. ges. Staatswiss.*, December 1981, *137*(4), pp. 667–74.

Brinkmann, Tomas and Kübler, Friedrich. Überlegungen zur ökonomischen Analyse von Unternehmensrecht. (Thoughts on the Economic Analysis of the Firm. With English summary.) *Z. ges. Staatswiss.*, December 1981, *137*(4), pp. 681–88.

Schanze, Erich. Der Beitrag von Coase zu Recht und Ökonomie des Unternehmens. (Coase's Contribution to Law and Economics of Business Organizations. With English summary.) *Z. ges. Staatswiss.*, December 1981, *137*(4), pp. 694–701.

Williamson, Oliver E. On the Nature of the Firm: Some Recent Developments. *Z. ges. Staatswiss.*, December 1981, *137*(4), pp. 675–80.

Edgeworth, Francis Y.

Samuels, Warren J. Edgeworth's *Mathematical Psychics*: A Centennial Notice. *Eastern Econ. J.*, July-Oct. 1981, *7*(3–4), pp. 193–98.

Engels, Friedrich

Hutchison, Terence W. Friedrich Engels and Marxian Political Economy. **In** *Hutchison, T. W.*, 1981, pp. 1–21.

Wiltgen, Richard J. Marx and Engels on Malthus and Population: A Reconstruction and Reconsideration. *Quart. Rev. Econ. Bus.*, Winter 1981, *21*(4), pp. 107–26.

Fanno, Marco

Palomba, Giuseppe. La disgregazione delle leggi economiche. (The Collapse of Economic Laws. With English summary.) *Rivista Int. Sci. Econ. Com.*, October–November 1981, *28*(10–11), pp. 1070–81.

Fisher, Irving

Steedman, Ian W. Time Preference, the Rate of Interest and Abstinence from Accumulation. *Australian Econ. Pap.*, December 1981, *20*(37), pp. 219–34.

Friedman, Milton

Burton, John. Positively Milton Friedman. **In** *Shackleton, J. R. and Locksley, G., eds.*, 1981, pp. 53–71.

Mason, Will E. Some Negative Thoughts on Friedman's Positive Economics. *J. Post Keynesian Econ.*, Winter 1980–81, *3*(2), pp. 235–55.

Prebisch, Raúl. Dialogue on Friedman and Hayek: From the Standpoint of the Periphery. *Cepal Rev.*, December 1981, (15), pp. 153–74.

Wood, John H. The Economics of Professor Friedman. **In** *[Weiler, E. T.]*, 1981, pp. 191–241.

Frisch, Ragnar

Andvig, Jens Christopher. Ragnar Frisch and Business Cycle Research during the Interwar Years. *Hist. Polit. Econ.*, Winter 1981, *13*(4), pp. 695–725.

Galbraith, John K.

Reisman, David. The Dissenting Economist: J. K. Galbraith. **In** *Shackleton, J. R. and Locksley, G., eds.*, 1981, pp. 72–86.

George, Henry

Kelly, John M. The New Barbarians: The Continuing Relevance of Henry George. *Amer. J. Econ. Soc.*, July 1981, *40*(3), pp. 299–308.

Petrella, Frank. Henry George, the Classical Model and Technological Change: The Ignored Alternative to the Single Tax in Progress and Poverty. *Amer. J. Econ. Soc.*, April 1981, *40*(2), pp. 190–206.

Gray, Simon

Masuda, Etsusuke and Newman, Peter. Gray and Giffen Goods. *Econ. J.*, December 1981, *91*(364), pp. 1011–14.

Hadley, Arthur Twining

Cross, Melvin L. and Ekelund, Robert B., Jr. A. T. Hadley: The American Invention of the Economics of Property Rights and Public Goods. *Rev. Soc. Econ.*, April 1981, *39*(1), pp. 37–50.

Harrod, Roy [Sir]

Phelps Brown, Henry. Sir Roy Harrod: A Note [Sir Roy Harrod: A Bibliographical Memoir]. *Econ. J.*, March 1981, *91*(361), pp. 231.

von Hayek, Friedrich A.

Barry, Norman P. Re-stating the Liberal Order: Hayek's Philosophical Economics. **In** *Shackleton, J. R. and Locksley, G., eds.*, 1981, pp. 87–107.

Gordon, Scott. The Political Economy of F. A. Hayek: Review Article. *Can. J. Econ.*, August 1981, *14*(3), pp. 470–87.

Prebisch, Raúl. Dialogue on Friedman and Hayek: From the Standpoint of the Periphery. *Cepal Rev.*, December 1981, (15), pp. 153–74.

Hegel, Georg Friedrich
Bruyn, Severyn T. Social Economy: A Note on Its Theoretical Foundations. *Rev. Soc. Econ.*, April 1981, *39*(1), pp. 81–84.
Hirschman, Albert O. On Hegel, Imperialism, and Structural Stagnation. **In** *Hirschman, A. O.*, 1981, *1976*, 167–76.
Hennipman, Pieter
Zijlstra, J. Hennipman and De Economist. *De Economist*, 1981, *129*(1), pp. 1–7.
Hicks, John R.
Basu, Kaushik. Causality and Economic Theory. *Indian Econ. Rev.*, January–June 1981, *16*(1 and 2), pp. 41–53.
Bauer, P. T. Economic History as Theory. **In** *Bauer, P. T.*, 1981, pp. 221–38.
Leijonhufvud, Axel. Monetary Theory in Hicksian Perspective. **In** *Leijonhufvud, A.*, 1981, *1968*, pp. 203–26.
Morgan, Brian. Sir John Hicks's Contributions to Economic Theory. **In** *Shackleton, J. R. and Locksley, G., eds.*, 1981, pp. 108–40.
Hobson, J. A.
Cain, P. J. Hobson's Developing Theory of Imperialism. *Econ. Hist. Rev., 2nd Ser.*, May 1981, *34*(2), pp. 313–16.
Clarke, P. F. Hobson, Free Trade, and Imperialism. *Econ. Hist. Rev., 2nd Ser.*, May 1981, *34*(2), pp. 308–12.
Hotelling, Harold
Devarajan, Shantayanan and Fisher, Anthony C. Hotelling's "Economics of Exhaustible Resources": Fifty Years Later. *J. Econ. Lit.*, March 1981, *19*(1), pp. 65–73.
Ischboldin, Boris
Ederer, Rupert J. Heinrich Pesch's Solidarism and Boris Ischboldin's Scientific Reformism. *Int. J. Soc. Econ.*, 1981, *8*(7), pp. 73–86.
Sharp, John A. Economic Synthesis: A Review of the Work of Boris Ischboldin. *Int. J. Soc. Econ.*, 1981, *8*(7), pp. 8–13.
Jaffé, William
Hollander, Samuel. William Jaffé, 1898–1980. *Can. J. Econ.*, February 1981, *14*(1), pp. 106–09.
Tarascio, Vincent J. William Jaffé, 1898–1980. *Hist. Polit. Econ.*, Summer 1981, *13*(2), pp. 301–12.
Walker, Donald A. William Jaffé, Historian of Economic Thought, 1898–1980. *Amer. Econ. Rev.*, December 1981, *71*(5), pp. 1012–19.
Kaldor, Nicholas
Baranzini, Mauro. Taux d'intérêt, distribution du revenu, théorie des cycles vitaux et choix du portefeuille. (With English summary.) *Kyklos*, 1981, *34*(4), pp. 593–610.
Bombach, Gottfried. Ein Modell und sein Echo. (With English summary.) *Kyklos*, 1981, *34*(4), pp. 517–39. [G: W. Germany; Switzerland]
Fazi, Elido and Salvadori, Neri. The Existence of a Two-Class Economy in the Kaldor Model of Growth and Distribution. *Kyklos*, 1981, *34*(4), pp. 582–92.
Riese, Hajo. Theorie der Produktion und Einkommensverteilung. (With English summary.) *Kyklos*, 1981, *34*(4), pp. 540–62.

Shea, Koon-lam. An Alternative Theory of Inflation. *Kyklos*, 1981, *34*(4), pp. 611–28.
Skott, Peter. On the 'Kaldorian' Saving Function. *Kyklos*, 1981, *34*(4), pp. 563–81.
Kalecki, Michal
Poschl, Josef and Locksley, Gareth. Michal Kalecki: A Comprehensive Challenge to Orthodoxy. **In** *Shackleton, J. R. and Locksley, G., eds.*, 1981, pp. 141–59.
Steindl, Josef. A Personal Portrait of Michal Kalecki. *J. Post Keynesian Econ.*, Summer 1981, *3*(4), pp. 590–96.
Keynes, John Maynard
Ambrosi, G. M. Keynes and the 45° Cross. *J. Post Keynesian Econ.*, Summer 1981, *3*(4), pp. 503–09.
Arestis, P. and Karakitsos, Elias. The "Economics of Keynes" and Leijonhufvud. *Econ. Int.*, May–August–November 1981, *34*(2–3–4), pp. 222–41.
Brazelton, W. Robert. A Survey of Some Textbook Misinterpretations of Keynes. *J. Post Keynesian Econ.*, Winter 1980–81, *3*(2), pp. 256–70.
Cate, Tom. Keynes on Monetary Theory and Policy: Comment [Some Further Observations on the Monetary Economics of Chicagoans and Non-Chicagoans]. *Southern Econ. J.*, April 1981, *47*(4), pp. 1132–36.
Chase, Richard. The Development of Contemporary Mainstream Macroeconomics: Vision, Ideology, and Theory Debate. *Nebr. J. Econ. Bus.*, Summer 1981, *20*(3), pp. 5–36.
Chase, Richard. Vision, Theory Debate and the Development of Mainstream Macroeconomics. *Rivista Int. Sci. Econ. Com.*, June 1981, *28*(6), pp. 558–96.
D'Adda, Carlo. La determinazione delle funzioni aggregate di offerta e di domanda: una nota di "ermeneutica" keynesiana. (The Determination of the Aggregate Supply and Demand Functions: A Note of Keynesian "Hermeneutics". With English summary.) *Giorn. Econ.*, January–February 1981, *40*(1–2), pp. 19–29.
Gold, Joseph. Keynes and the Articles of the Fund: Review Article. *Finance Develop.*, September 1981, *18*(3), pp. 38–42.
Hansen, Bent. Unemployment, Keynes, and the Stockholm School. *Hist. Polit. Econ.*, Summer 1981, *13*(2), pp. 256–77.
Harcourt, G. C. "Marshall, Sraffa and Keynes: Incompatible Bedfellows?" *Eastern Econ. J.*, January 1981, *7*(1), pp. 39–50.
Hutchison, Terence W. Keynes versus the Keynesians. **In** *Hutchison, T. W.*, 1981, pp. 108–54.
Kregel, J. A. On Distinguishing between Alternative Methods of Approach to the Demand for Output as a Whole. *Australian Econ. Pap.*, June 1981, *20*(36), pp. 63–71.
Leijonhufvud, Axel. Keynes and the Classics: Second Lecture. **In** *Leijonhufvud, A.*, 1981, *1969*, pp. 55–78.
Leijonhufvud, Axel. Keynes and the Classics: First Lecture. **In** *Leijonhufvud, A.*, 1981, *1969*, pp. 39–54.

Leijonhufvud, Axel. Keynes and the Effectiveness of Monetary Policy. In *Leijonhufvud, A., 1981, 1968,* pp. 17–37.

Leijonhufvud, Axel. Keynes and the Keynesians: A Suggested Interpretation. In *Leijonhufvud, A., 1981, 1967,* pp. 3–15.

Mehta, Ghanshyam. Recent Developments in Keynesian Economics. *Indian Econ. J.,* April–June 1981, *28*(4), pp. 1–17.

Meltzer, Allan H. Keynes's *General Theory:* A Different Perspective. *J. Econ. Lit.,* March 1981, *19*(1), pp. 34–64.

Minoguchi, Takeo. The Process of Writing the General Theory as 'A Monetary Theory of Production.' *Hitotsubashi J. Econ.,* February 1981, *21*(2), pp. 33–43.

Patinkin, Don. Keynes and Chicago. In *Patinkin, D., 1981, 1979,* pp. 289–308.

Redhead, Keith J. On Keynesian Economics and the Economics of Keynes: A Suggested Interpretation [Keynes and the Keynesians: A Suggested Interpretation]. *Bull. Econ. Res.,* May 1981, *33*(1), pp. 48–55.

Robinson, Joan. Keynes and Ricardo. In *Robinson, J., 1981, 1978,* pp. 78–85.

Rotheim, Roy J. Keynes' Monetary Theory of Value (1933). *J. Post Keynesian Econ.,* Summer 1981, *3*(4), pp. 568–85.

Tavlas, George S. Keynes on Monetary Theory and Policy: Reply [Some Further Observations on the Monetary Economics of Chicagoans and Non-Chicagoans]. *Southern Econ. J.,* April 1981, *47*(4), pp. 1137–42.

Torr, C. S. W. Microfoundations for Keynes's Point of Effective Demand. *S. Afr. J. Econ.,* December 1981, *49*(4), pp. 334–48.

Wells, Paul. Keynes' Demand for Finance. *J. Post Keynesian Econ.,* Summer 1981, *3*(4), pp. 586–89.

Klein, Lawrence R.

Ball, R. James. On Lawrence R. Klein's Contributions to Economics. *Scand. J. Econ.,* 1981, *83*(1), pp. 81–103.

Knight, Frank

Patinkin, Don. Frank Knight as Teacher. In *Patinkin, D., 1981, 1973,* pp. 23–51.

Patinkin, Don. In Search of the "Wheel of Wealth": On the Origins of Frank Knight's Circular-Flow Diagram. In *Patinkin, D., 1981, 1973,* pp. 53–65.

Patinkin, Don. In Search of the "Wheel of Wealth": On the Origins of Frank Knight's Circular-Flow Diagram: Postscript. In *Patinkin, D., 1981,* pp. 65–72.

Laspeyres, Ernst Louis Etienne

Rinne, Horst. Ernst Louis Etienne Laspeyres, 1834–1913. (With English summary.) *Jahr. Nationalökon. Statist.,* May 1981, *196*(3), pp. 194–216.

Leijonhufvud, Axel

Arestis, P. and Karakitsos, Elias. The "Economics of Keynes" and Leijonhufvud. *Econ. Int.,* May–August–November 1981, *34*(2–3–4), pp. 222–41.

Leontief, Wassily

Cave, Martin. Wassily Leontief: Input–Output

and Economic Planning. In *Shackleton, J. R. and Locksley, G., eds.,* 1981, pp. 160–82.

List, Friedrich

Henderson, W. O. Friedrich List and the Social Question. *J. Europ. Econ. Hist.,* Winter 1981, *10*(3), pp. 697–708.

Lowe, Adolph

Lissner, Will. Adolph Lowe's Methodological Alternative for Economic Research and Policy: "Political Economics" as an Experimental Method for Achieving Growth, Stability and Continuity. *Amer. J. Econ. Soc.,* July 1981, *40*(3), pp. 277–86.

Luxemburg, Rosa

Yannacopoulos, Nicos A. Rosa Luxemburg's Theory of Capitalist Catastrophe. *J. Post Keynesian Econ.,* Spring 1981, *3*(3), pp. 452–56.

Malthus, Thomas Robert

Grampp, William D. Ricardo and Malthus: Review Article. *J. Econ. Hist.,* June 1981, *41*(2), pp. 421–23.

Maitra, Priyatosh. Malthus Revisited—Population, Poverty and Pollution. *Int. J. Soc. Econ.,* 1981, *8*(3), pp. 47–61.

Pullen, John M. Malthus' Theological Ideas and Their Influence on His Principle of Population. *Hist. Polit. Econ.,* Spring 1981, *13*(1), pp. 39–54.

Pullen, John M. Notes from Malthus: The Inverarity Manuscript. *Hist. Polit. Econ.,* Winter 1981, *13*(4), pp. 794–811.

Rashid, Salim. Malthus' *Principles* and British Economic Thought, 1820–1835. *Hist. Polit. Econ.,* Spring 1981, *13*(1), pp. 55–79.

Shields, Michael P. On Malthus's Analytical Sophistication. *Econ. Forum,* Summer 1981, *12*(1), pp. 109–14.

Wiltgren, Richard J. Marx and Engels on Malthus and Population: A Reconstruction and Reconsideration. *Quart. Rev. Econ. Bus.,* Winter 1981, *21*(4), pp. 107–26.

de Mandeville, Bernard

Kolm, Serge-Christophe. Efficacité et altruisme: les sophismes de Mandeville, Smith et Pareto. (Efficiency and Altruism: The Mandeville, Smith and Pareto Fallacies. With English summary.) *Revue Écon.,* January 1981, *32*(1), pp. 5–31.

Marcuse, Herbert

Malinovich, Myriam Miedzian. Herbert Marcuse in 1978: An Interview. *Soc. Res.,* Summer 1981, *48*(2), pp. 362–94.

Marshall, Alfred

Harcourt, G. C. "Marshall, Sraffa and Keynes: Incompatible Bedfellows?" *Eastern Econ. J.,* January 1981, *7*(1), pp. 39–50.

Wearne, Bruce C. Talcott Parsons's Appraisal and Critique of Alfred Marshall. *Soc. Res.,* Winter 1981, *48*(4), pp. 816–51.

Marx, Karl

Barr, Kenneth. On the Capitalist Enterprise. *Rev. Radical Polit. Econ.,* Winter 1981, *12*(4), pp. 60–70.

Bowles, Samuel and Gintis, Herbert. Labour Heterogeneity and the Labour Theory of Value: A Reply [The Marxian Theory of Value and Heterogeneous Labour: A Critique and Reformulation]. *Cambridge J. Econ.*, September 1981, 5(3), pp. 285–88.

Bruyn, Severyn T. Social Economy: A Note on Its Theoretical Foundations. *Rev. Soc. Econ.*, April 1981, 39(1), pp. 81–84.

Catephores, George. On Heterogeneous Labour and the Labour Theory of Value [The Marxian Theory of Value and Heterogeneous Labour: A Critique and Reformulation]. *Cambridge J. Econ.*, September 1981, 5(3), pp. 273–80.

Gintis, Herbert and Bowles, Samuel. Structure and Practice in the Labor Theory of Value. *Rev. Radical Polit. Econ.*, Winter 1981, 12(4), pp. 1–26.

Hirata, Kiyoaki. Conceptual Evolution of "Capital in Process" in "Foundations of the Critique of Political Economy." *Kyoto Univ. Econ. Rev.*, April–October 1981, 51(1–2), pp. 1–35.

Hodgson, Geoff. On Exploitation and Labor-Value. *Sci. Soc.*, Summer 1981, 45(2), pp. 228–33.

Hollander, Samuel. Marxian Economics as 'General Equilibrium' Theory. *Hist. Polit. Econ.*, Spring 1981, 13(1), pp. 121–55.

Itoh, Makoto. On Marx's Theory of Accumulation: A Reply to Weeks [The Process of Accumulation and the 'Profit Squeeze' Hypothesis]. *Sci. Soc.*, Spring 1981, 45(1), pp. 71–84.

Krause, Ulrich. Heterogeneous Labour and the Fundamental Marxian Theorem. *Rev. Econ. Stud.*, January 1981, 48(1), pp. 173–78.

Krause, Ulrich. Marxian Inequalities in a von Neumann Setting. *Z. Nationalökon.*, 1981, 41(1–2), pp. 59–67.

Mattick, Paul, Jr. Some Aspects of the Value-Price Problem. *Écon. Soc.*, June–July 1981, 15(6–7), pp. 725–81.

McKenna, Edward J. A Comment on Bowles and Gintis' Marxian Theory of Value [The Marxian Theory of Value and Heterogeneous Labour: A Critique and Reformulation]. *Cambridge J. Econ.*, September 1981, 5(3), pp. 281–84.

Meiksins, Peter. Productive and Unproductive Labor and Marx's Theory of Class. *Rev. Radical Polit. Econ.*, Fall 1981, 13(3), pp. 32–42.

Minogue, K. R. Marxism: The Apologetics of Power. *Policy Rev.*, Winter 1981, (15), pp. 41–60.

O'Brien, John Conway. Karl Marx, the Social Theorist. *Int. J. Soc. Econ.*, 1981, 8(6), pp. 3–35.

O'Brien, John Conway. The Outraged Moralist? *Int. J. Soc. Econ.*, 1981, 8(6), pp. 36–66.

Perelman, Michael. Capital, Constant Capital and the Social Division of Labor. *Rev. Radical Polit. Econ.*, Fall 1981, 13(3), pp. 43–53.

Robinson, Joan. Marxism and Modern Economics. In *Robinson, J.*, 1981, pp. 192–202.

Robinson, Joan. Marxism: Religion and Science. In *Robinson, J.*, 1981, 1962, pp. 155–64.

Sardoni, Claudio. Multi-Sectoral Models of Balanced Growth and the Marxian Schemes of Expanded Reproduction. *Australian Econ. Pap.*, December 1981, 20(37), pp. 383–97.

Ureña, Enrique M. A Note on "Marx and Dar-

win." *Hist. Polit. Econ.*, Winter 1981, 13(4), pp. 772–73.

Wiltgen, Richard J. Marx and Engels on Malthus and Population: A Reconstruction and Reconsideration. *Quart. Rev. Econ. Bus.*, Winter 1981, 21(4), pp. 107–26.

Menger, Carl

Hutchison, Terence W. Carl Menger on Philosophy and Method. In *Hutchison, T. W.*, 1981, pp. 176–202.

Meyer, Fritz W.

Willgerodt, Hans. Fritz Walter Meyer. (With English Summary.) In *[von Haberler, G.]*, 1981, pp. 199–217.

Mill, John Stuart

Ekelund, Robert B., Jr. and Kordsmeier, William F. J. S. Mill, Unions, and the Wages Fund Recantation: A Reinterpretation—Comment. *Quart. J. Econ.*, August 1981, 96(3), pp. 531–41.

Vint, John. A Two Sector Model of the Wages Fund: Mill's Recantation Revisited. *Brit. Rev. Econ. Issues*, Autumn 1981, 3(9), pp. 71–88.

de Vivo, Giancarlo. John Stuart Mill on Value. *Cambridge J. Econ.*, March 1981, 5(1), pp. 67–69.

West, Edwin G. and Hafer, R. W. J. S. Mill, Unions, and the Wages Fund Recantation: A Reinterpretation—Reply. *Quart. J. Econ.*, August 1981, 96(3), pp. 543–49.

Mosca, Gaetano

Violante, Sante. L'economica e la politica come scienze. Itinerario ventennale di uno studioso: Gaetano Mosca, docente bocconiano. (Economics and Politics as Sciences: The Twenty-Year Itinerary of a Scholar: Gaetano Mosca, Professor at the Bocconi University of Milan. With English summary.) *Giorn. Econ.*, January–February 1981, 40(1–2), pp. 51–64.

Myrdal, Gunnar

Robinson, Joan. Gunnar Myrdal: *Against the Stream*. In *Robinson, J.*, 1981, 1979, pp. 151–54.

Streeten, Paul P. Gunnar Myrdal. In *Streeten, P.*, 1981, 1979, pp. 418–31.

Streeten, Paul P. Programmes and Prognoses [Introduction to Gunnar Myrdal]. In *Streeten, P.*, 1981, 1958, pp. 3–34.

Ohlin, Bertil

Ohlin, Bertil. Stockholm and Cambridge: Four Papers on the Monetary and Employment Theory of the 1930s. *Hist. Polit. Econ.*, Summer 1981, 13(2), pp. 189–255.

Samuelson, Paul A. Bertil Ohlin (1899–1979). *Scand. J. Econ.*, 1981, 83(3), pp. 355–71.

Samuelson, Paul A. Bertil Ohlin: 1899–1979. *J. Int. Econ.*, May 1981, 11(2), pp. 147–63.

Steiger, Otto. Bertil Ohlin, 1899–1979. *Hist. Polit. Econ.*, Summer 1981, 13(2), pp. 179–88.

Okun, Arthur M.

Phelps, Edmund S. Okun's Micro-Macro System: A Review Article. *J. Econ. Lit.*, September 1981, 19(3), pp. 1065–73.

Pareto, Vilfredo

Bourgain, Jean and Vaneecloo, Nicolas. Inégalité, paupérisme et loi de Pareto. (Inequality,

Pauperism and Pareto. With English summary.) *Revue Écon.*, September 1981, *32*(5), pp. 950–64.

Kolm, Serge-Christophe. Efficacité et altruisme: les sophismes de Mandeville, Smith et Pareto. (Efficiency and Altruism: The Mandeville, Smith and Pareto Fallacies. With English summary.) *Revue Écon.*, January 1981, *32*(1), pp. 5–31.

Patinkin, Don

Patinkin, Don. Reminiscences of Chicago, 1941–47. In *Patinkin, D.*, 1981, pp. 3–20.

Pesch, Heinrich

Ederer, Rupert J. Heinrich Pesch's Solidarism and Boris Ischboldin's Scientific Reformism. *Int. J. Soc. Econ.*, 1981, *8*(7), pp. 73–86.

Plekhanov, G.

Lenin, V. I. A Letter to the St. Petersburg Workers. In *Bailey, A. M. and Llobera, J. R.*, eds., 1981, *1906*, pp. 71–75.

Polanyi, Karl

Dalton, George. Economic Anthropology and History: The Work of Karl Polanyi: Comment. In *Dalton, G.*, ed., 1981, *1974*, pp. 69–93.

Godelier, Maurice. Economic Anthropology and History: The Work of Karl Polanyi: Discussion. In *Dalton, G.*, ed., 1981, *1974*, pp. 64–69.

Stanfield, J. Ron. The Social Economics of Karl Polanyi. *Int. J. Soc. Econ.*, 1981, *8*(5), pp. 3–20.

Valensi, Lucette. Economic Anthropology and History: The Work of Karl Polanyi. In *Dalton, G.*, ed., 1981, *1974*, pp. 3–12.

Redlich, Fritz

Arcand, Charles Gaston, Jr. Fritz Redlich, 1892–1978: The Man and the Scholar. *Amer. J. Econ. Soc.*, April 1981, *40*(2), pp. 217–21.

Ricardo, David

Claeys, Gregory and Kerr, Prue. Mechanical Political Economy: Review Article. *Cambridge J. Econ.*, September 1981, *5*(3), pp. 251–72.

Eygelshoven, P. J. and Kuipers, Simon K. A Note on Pasinetti's "Ricardian System" [A Mathematical Formulation of the Ricardian System]. *Rev. Econ. Stud.*, January 1981, *48*(1), pp. 185–86.

Grampp, William D. Ricardo and Malthus: Review Article. *J. Econ. Hist.*, June 1981, *41*(2), pp. 421–23.

Howard, M. C. Ricardo's Analysis of Profit: An Evaluation in Terms of Piero Sraffa's Production of Commodities by Means of Commodities. *Metroecon.*, Feb.-Oct. 1981, *33*(1–2–3), pp. 105–28.

Jonung, Lars. Ricardo on Machinery and the Present Unemployment: An Unpublished Manuscript by Knut Wicksell. *Econ. J.*, March 1981, *91*(361), pp. 195–205.

Matteucci, Andrea. Sraffa's "Two Ricardos": About the Interconnection between the Ricardian Theories of Value and Distribution. *Rivista Polit. Econ.*, Supplement December 1981, *71*, pp. 109–37.

O'Brien, D. P. Ricardian Economics and the Economics of David Ricardo. *Oxford Econ. Pap.*, November 1981, *33*(3), pp. 352–86.

Pasinetti, Luigi L. On the Ricardian Theory of Value: A Note [A Mathematical Formulation of Ricardian System]. *Rev. Econ. Stud.*, October 1981, *48*(4), pp. 673–75.

Robbins, Lionel

Peston, Maurice. Lionel Robbins: Methodology, Policy and Modern Theory. In *Shackleton, J. R. and Locksley, G.*, eds., 1981, pp. 183–98.

Targetti, Ferdinando. La base economica dei conflitti o la base conflittuale dell'economia. (The Economic Basis of Class Conflicts or the Conflictual Basis of Economy. With English summary.) *Giorn. Econ.*, March–April 1981, *40*(3–4), pp. 239–42.

Robinson, Joan

Skouras, Thanos. The Economics of Joan Robinson. In *Shackleton, J. R. and Locksley, G.*, eds., 1981, pp. 199–218.

Samuelson, Marion Crawford

Manger, Gary J. Summing up on the Australian Case for Protection: Comment. *Quart. J. Econ.*, February 1981, *96*(1), pp. 161–67. [G: Australia]

Samuelson, Paul A. Summing up on the Australian Case for Protection. *Quart. J. Econ.*, February 1981, *96*(1), pp. 147–60. [G: Australia]

Samuelson, Paul A.

Davidson, Paul and Weintraub, Sidney. Jacob and Paul Samuelson, Post-Keynesian. *J. Post Keynesian Econ.*, Summer 1981, *3*(4), pp. 602–04.

Feiwel, George R. Modern Neoclassical Economics. *Economia (Portugal)*, October 1981, *5*(3), pp. 407–29.

Kendry, Adrian. Paul Samuelson and the Scientific Awakening of Economics. In *Shackleton, J. R. and Locksley, G.*, eds., 1981, pp. 219–39.

Say, J. B.

Leijonhufvud, Axel and Clower, Robert W. Say's Principle, What It Means and Doesn't Mean. In *Leijonhufvud, A.*, 1981, *1973*, pp. 79–101.

Schumpeter, Joseph A.

Beach, E. F. A Modified Schumpeterian Process. *Indian Econ. J.*, January–March 1981, *28*(3), pp. 51–62.

Bottomore, Tom. The Decline of Capitalism, Sociologically Considered. In *Heertje, A.*, ed., 1981, pp. 22–44.

Cramer, Dale L. and Leathers, Charles G. Schumpeter's Corporatist Views: Links among His Social Theory, Quadragesimo Anno, and Moral Reform. *Hist. Polit. Econ.*, Winter 1981, *13*(4), pp. 745–71.

Fellner, William. March into Socialism, or Viable Postwar Stage of Capitalism? In *Heertje, A.*, ed., 1981, pp. 45–68.

Haberler, Gottfried. Schumpeter's *Capitalism, Socialism and Democracy* after Forty Years. In *Heertje, A.*, ed., 1981, pp. 69–94.

Heilbroner, Robert L. Was Schumpeter Right? In *Heertje, A.*, ed., 1981, pp. 95–106.

Heilbroner, Robert L. Was Schumpeter Right? *Soc. Res.*, Autumn 1981, *48*(3), pp. 456–71.

Lambers, Hendrik Wilm. The Vision. In *Heertje,*

A., ed., 1981, pp. 107–29.

Robinson, Joan. Joseph Schumpeter: *Capitalism, Socialism and Democracy.* In *Robinson, J.*, 1981, *1943*, pp. 141–43.

Samuelson, Paul A. Schumpeter's *Capitalism, Socialism and Democracy.* In *Heertje, A., ed.*, 1981, pp. 1–21.

Smithies, Arthur. Schumpeter's Predictions. In *Heertje, A., ed.*, 1981, pp. 130–49.

Wiles, Peter. A Sovietological View. In *Heertje, A., ed.*, 1981, pp. 150–69.

Zassenhaus, Herbert K. Capitalism, Socialism and Democracy: The 'Vision' and the 'Theories.' In *Heertje, A., ed.*, 1981, pp. 170–202.

Shackle, G. L. S.

Harcourt, G. C. Notes on an Economic Querist: G. L. S. Shackle. *J. Post Keynesian Econ.*, Fall 1981, *4*(1), pp. 136–44.

Simon, Herbert A.

Boland, Lawrence A. Satisficing in Methodology: A Reply. *J. Econ. Lit.*, March 1981, *19*(1), pp. 84–86.

Fels, Rendigs. Boland Ignores Simon: A Comment. *J. Econ. Lit.*, March 1981, *19*(1), pp. 83–84.

Lackman, Conway L. Herbert Simon: Microeconomist in Administrative Clothing? *Revista Int. Sci. Econ. Com.*, March 1981, *28*(3), pp. 201–15.

Simons, Henry

Kiesling, H. J. Henry Simons, Equality, and the Personal Income Tax. *Nat. Tax J.*, June 1981, *34*(2), pp. 257–59.

Patinkin, Don. Keynes and Chicago. In *Patinkin, D.*, 1981, *1979*, pp. 289–308.

Sismonde de Sismondi, Jean

Arena, Richard. Note sur les apports de Sismondi à la théorie classique. (On the contribution of Sismondi's Economic Analysis to the Classical Economic Theory. With English summary.) *L'Actual. Econ.*, October–December 1981, *57*(4), pp. 565–88.

Smith, Adam

Gee, J. M. A. The Origin of Rent in Adam Smith's *Wealth of Nations:* An Anti-Neoclassical View. *Hist. Polit. Econ.*, Spring 1981, *13*(1), pp. 1–18.

Jackson, John. A Note on Adam Smith's Second Regulator of Wealth. *Indian Econ. J.*, January–March 1981, *28*(3), pp. 105–06.

Kolm, Serge-Christophe. Efficacité et altruisme: les sophismes de Mandeville, Smith et Pareto. (Efficiency and Altruism: The Mandeville, Smith and Pareto Fallacies. With English summary.) *Revue Écon.*, January 1981, *32*(1), pp. 5–31.

Kurz, Heinz D. Smithian Themes in Piero Sraffa's Theory. *J. Post Keynesian Econ.*, Winter 1980–81, *3*(2), pp. 271–80.

Laidler, David. Adam Smith as a Monetary Economist. *Can. J. Econ.*, May 1981, *14*(2), pp. 185–200.

Merrill, Bruce. Adam Smith's Commercial Society as a Surrogate for Morals. *Econ. Forum*, Summer 1981, *12*(1), pp. 65–74.

Miller, William L. Adam Smith on Wage Differ-

entials against Agricultural Laborers. *Atlantic Econ. J.*, July 1981, *9*(2), pp. 19–24.

Ross, I. S. and Webster, A. M. Adam Smith: Two Letters. *Scot. J. Polit. Econ.*, June 1981, *28*(2), pp. 206–09.

Sraffa, Piero

Bidard, Christian. Travail et salaire chez Sraffa. (Labour and Wage in Sraffa's Work. With English summary.) *Revue Écon.*, May 1981, *32*(3), pp. 448–67.

Fleischmann, Bernd. Reduction to Dated Quantities of Labour. A Footnote on Mr. Sraffa. *Metroecon.*, Feb.-Oct. 1981, *33*(1–2–3), pp. 233–37.

Harcourt, G. C. "Marshall, Sraffa and Keynes: Incompatible Bedfellows?" *Eastern Econ. J.*, January 1981, *7*(1), pp. 39–50.

Kurz, Heinz D. Smithian Themes in Piero Sraffa's Theory. *J. Post Keynesian Econ.*, Winter 1980–81, *3*(2), pp. 271–80.

Robinson, Joan. Piero Sraffa: *Production of Commodities by Means of Commodities.* In *Robinson, J.*, 1981, *1961*, pp. 144–50.

Robinson, Joan and Bhaduri, Amit. Accumulation and Exploitation: An Analysis in the Tradition of Marx, Sraffa and Kalecki. In *Robinson, J.*, 1981, *1980*, pp. 64–77.

Roncaglia, Alessandro. Piero Sraffa's Contribution to Political Economy. In *Shackleton, J. R. and Locksley, G., eds.*, 1981, pp. 240–56.

von Stackelberg, Heinrich

Chambers, Donald R. and Lovell, C. A. Knox. Some Neglected Stackelberg Duopoly Models. *Atlantic Econ. J.*, July 1981, *9*(2), pp. 25–29.

Steuart, James [Sir]

Skinner, Andrew S. Sir James Steuart: Author of a System. *Scot. J. Polit. Econ.*, February 1981, *28*(1), pp. 20–42.

Tobin, James

Ketterer, Karl-Heinz. James Tobin—Nobel Laureat. *Kredit Kapital*, 1981, *14*(4), pp. 449–50.

Lucas, Robert E., Jr. Tobin and Monetarism: A Review Article. *J. Econ. Lit.*, June 1981, *19*(2), pp. 558–67.

Veblen, Thorstein

Bush, Paul D. 'Radical Individualism' vs. Institutionalism, II: Philosophical Dualisms as Apologetic Constructs Based on Obsolete Psychological Preconceptions. *Amer. J. Econ. Soc.*, July 1981, *40*(3), pp. 287–98.

Rutherford, Malcolm H. Veblen on Owners, Managers, and the Control of Industry: A Rejoinder. *Hist. Polit. Econ.*, Spring 1981, *13*(1), pp. 156–58.

Weed, Frank J. Interpreting 'Institutions' in Veblen's Evolutionary Theory. *Amer. J. Econ. Soc.*, January 1981, *40*(1), pp. 67–78.

Walras, Auguste

Cirillo, Renato. The Influence of Auguste Walras on Léon Walras. *Amer. J. Econ. Soc.*, July 1981, *40*(3), pp. 309–16.

Walras, Léon

Denizet, Jean. Equilibre économique et social chez Walras. (With English summary.) *Écon.*

Appl., 1981, *34*(1), pp. 5–28.

Jaffé, William. Another Look at Léon Walras's Theory of *Tâtonnement. Hist. Polit. Econ.*, Summer 1981, *13*(2), pp. 313–36.

Warburton, Clark

Cargill, Thomas F. A Tribute to Clark Warburton, 1896–1979: A Note. *J. Money, Credit, Banking*, February 1981, *13*(1), pp. 89–93.

Yeager, Leland B. Clark Warburton, 1896–1979. *Hist. Polit. Econ.*, Summer 1981, *13*(2), pp. 279–84.

Weiler, Emanuel T.

Ames, Edward. On Forgetting Economics with Em Weiler. In *[Weiler, E. T.]*, 1981, pp. 355–60.

Wicksell, Knut

Honohan, Patrick. A New Look at Wicksell's Inflationary Process. *Manchester Sch. Econ. Soc. Stud.*, December 1981, *49*(4), pp. 319–33.

Jonung, Lars. Ricardo on Machinery and the Present Unemployment: An Unpublished Manuscript by Knut Wicksell. *Econ. J.*, March 1981, *91*(361), pp. 195–205.

Wulff, Julius

Topp, Niels-Henrik. A Nineteenth-Century Multiplier and Its Fate: Julius Wulff and the Multiplier Theory in Denmark, 1896–1932. *Hist. Polit. Econ.*, Winter 1981, *13*(4), pp. 824–45.

Young, Allyn

Currie, Lauchlin. Allyn Young and the Development of Growth Theory. *J. Econ. Stud.*, 1981, *8*(1), pp. 52–60.

Young, John Humphrey

Reisman, Simon S. John Humphrey Young, 1922–80. *Can. J. Econ.*, February 1981, *14*(1), pp. 110–14.

Zappa, Gino

Onida, Pietro. Gino Zappa, Il Maestro. (Gino Zappa, the Master. With English summary.) *Bancaria*, April 1981, *37*(4), pp. 368–80.

Saraceno, Pasquale. Il reddito d'impresa: attualità del pensiero di Gino Zappa. (Business Profit: Topicality of Gino Zappa's Thinking. With English summary.) *Bancaria*, April 1981, *37*(4), pp. 381–85.

0329 Other Special Topics

Debroy, B. Laodong and Primordial Ignorance. *Indian Econ. Rev.*, Oct.-Dec. 1981, *16*(4), pp. 297–307.

Demaria, Giovanni. Those Dynamic Years, 1930–31–32. *Banca Naz. Lavoro Quart. Rev.*, March 1981, (136), pp. 3–34.

Ekelund, Robert B., Jr. and Hébert, Robert F. The Proto-History of Franchise Bidding. *Southern Econ. J.*, October 1981, *48*(2), pp. 464–74.

Hicks, John R. The Scope and Status of Welfare Economics. In *Hicks, J.*, 1981, *1975*, pp. 218–39.

Hughes, Jonathan. Professor Hobsbawm on the Evolution of Modern Capitalism. In *[Weiler, E. T.]*, 1981, pp. 168–87. [G: U.K.]

Jørgensen, Steffen. En note om Dorfman-Steiner teoremet. (A Note on the Dorfman-Steiner Theorem. With English summary.) *Nationaløkon. Tidsskr.*, 1981, *119*(3), pp. 409–10.

Leijonhufvud, Axel. Schools, "Revolutions," and Research Programmes in Economic Theory. In *Leijonhufvud, A.*, 1981, *1976*, pp. 291–345.

Leijonhufvud, Axel. The Wicksell Connection: Variations on a Theme. In *Leijonhufvud, A.*, 1981, pp. 131–202.

Lerner, Ralph. Commerce and Character: The Anglo-American as New-Model Man. In *Novak, M., ed.*, 1981, *1979*, pp. 24–49.

Montias, J. M. Reflections on Historical Materialism, Economic Theory, and the History of Art in the Context of Renaissance and 17th Century Painting. *J. Cult. Econ.*, December 1981, *5*(2), pp. 19–38.

Obrinsky, Mark. The Profit Prophets. *J. Post Keynesian Econ.*, Summer 1981, *3*(4), pp. 491–502.

Patinkin, Don. In Search of the "Wheel of Wealth": On the Origins of Frank Knight's Circular-Flow Diagram. In *Patinkin, D.*, 1981, *1973*, pp. 53–65.

Patinkin, Don. In Search of the "Wheel of Wealth": On the Origins of Frank Knight's Circular-Flow Diagram: Postscript. In *Patinkin, D.*, 1981, pp. 65–72.

Porta, Pier Luigi. L'economia politica in Italia. (Political Economy in Italy. With English summary.) *Rivista Int. Sci. Econ. Com.*, April 1981, *28*(4), pp. 391–93. [G: Italy]

Robinson, Joan. An Open Letter from a Keynesian to a Marxist. In *Robinson, J.*, 1981, *1979*, pp. 165–69.

Robinson, Joan. The Disintegration of Economics. In *Robinson, J.*, 1981, *1979*, pp. 96–104.

Robinson, Joan. The Labour Theory of Value. In *Robinson, J.*, 1981, *1977*, pp. 183–91.

Robinson, Joan. The Organic Composition of Capital. In *Robinson, J.*, 1981, *1978*, pp. 170–82.

Samuelson, Paul A. Bertil Ohlin (1899–1979). *Scand. J. Econ.*, 1981, *83*(3), pp. 355–71.

Sylos Labini, Paolo. On the Concept of the Optimum Rate of Profit. In *[Lipiński, E.]*, 1981, pp. 141–54.

036 Economic Methodology

0360 Economic Methodology

Barry, Norman P. Re-stating the Liberal Order: Hayek's Philosophical Economics. In *Shackleton, J. R. and Locksley, G., eds.*, 1981, pp. 87–107.

Bocage, Ducarmel. The Human Agent and General Equilibrium Analysis from Cournot to Perroux. *Amer. Econ.*, Spring 1981, *25*(1), pp. 36–42.

Boland, Lawrence A. Satisficing in Methodology: A Reply. *J. Econ. Lit.*, March 1981, *19*(1), pp. 84–86.

Brown, Elba K. The Neoclassical and Post-Keynesian Research Programs: The Methodological Issues. *Rev. Soc. Econ.*, October 1981, *39*(2), pp. 111–32.

Bush, Paul D. The Normative Implications of Institutional Analysis. *Econ. Forum*, Winter 1981–82, *12*(2), pp. 9–29.

Cumming, Robert D. Giving Back Words: Things, Money, Persons. *Soc. Res.*, Summer 1981, *48*(2), pp. 227–59.

Dalton, George. Economic Anthropology and History: The Work of Karl Polanyi: Comment. In *Dalton, G., ed.*, 1981, *1974*, pp. 69–93.

Dennis, Ken G. Provable Theorems and Refutable Hypotheses: The Case of Competitive Theory. *J. Econ. Issues*, March 1981, *15*(1), pp. 95–112.

Dow, Sheila C. Weintraub and Wiles: The Methodological Basis of Policy Conflict. *J. Post Keynesian Econ.*, Spring 1981, *3*(3), pp. 325–39.

Fels, Rendigs. Boland Ignores Simon: A Comment. *J. Econ. Lit.*, March 1981, *19*(1), pp. 83–84.

Fischer, Charles C. A Comment on "The Method Is the Ideology." *J. Econ. Issues*, March 1981, *15*(1), pp. 193–96.

Georgescu-Roegen, Nicholas. Methods in Economic Science: A Rejoinder. *J. Econ. Issues*, March 1981, *15*(1), pp. 188–93.

Gill, Flora. Some Methodological Implications of the Marginal Revolution. *Australian Econ. Pap.*, June 1981, *20*(36), pp. 72–82.

Good, I. J. Some Logic and History of Hypothesis Testing. In *Pitt, J. C., ed.*, 1981, pp. 149–74.

Green, Edward J. On the Role of Fundamental Theory in Positive Economics. In *Pitt, J. C., ed.*, 1981, pp. 5–15.

Hausman, Daniel M. Are General Equilibrium Theories Explanatory? In *Pitt, J. C., ed.*, 1981, pp. 17–32.

von Hayek, F. A. Economics and Knowledge. In *Buchanan, J. M. and Thirlby, G. F., eds.*, 1981, *1937*, pp. 43–68.

Hughes, Joseph P. Methodological Confusion in Introductory Economics. *Amer. Econ.*, Fall 1981, *25*(2), pp. 7–11.

Hutchison, Terence W. Austrians on Philosophy and Method (since Menger). In *Hutchison, T. W.*, 1981, pp. 203–32.

Hutchison, Terence W. Carl Menger on Philosophy and Method. In *Hutchison, T. W.*, 1981, pp. 176–202.

Hutchison, Terence W. On the Aims and Methods of Economic Theorizing. In *Hutchison, T. W.*, 1981, pp. 266–307.

Hutchison, Terence W. The Philosophy and Politics of the Cambridge School. In *Hutchison, T. W.*, 1981, pp. 46–107.

Junker, Louis J. Instrumentalism, the Principle of Continuity and the Life Process. *Amer. J. Econ. Soc.*, October 1981, *40*(4), pp. 381–400.

Leijonhufvud, Axel. Schools, "Revolutions," and Research Programmes in Economic Theory. In *Leijonhufvud, A.*, 1981, *1976*, pp. 291–345.

Locksley, Gareth. Individuals, Contracts and Constitutions: The Political Economy of James M. Buchanan. In *Shackleton, J. R. and Locksley, G., eds.*, 1981, pp. 33–52.

Machan, Tibor R. The Non-Rational Domain and the Limits of Economic Analysis: Comment. *Southern Econ. J.*, April 1981, *47*(4), pp. 1123–27.

Mason, Will E. Some Negative Thoughts on Friedman's Positive Economics. *J. Post Keynesian Econ.*, Winter 1980–81, *3*(2), pp. 235–55.

Mayo, Deborah. Testing Statistical Testing. In *Pitt, J. C., ed.*, 1981, pp. 175–203.

McKenzie, Richard B. The Necessary Normative Context of Positive Economics. *J. Econ. Issues*, September 1981, *15*(3), pp. 703–19.

McKenzie, Richard B. The Non-Rational Domain and the Limits of Economic Analysis: Reply. *Southern Econ. J.*, April 1981, *47*(4), pp. 1128–31.

von Mises, Ludwig. Conception and Understanding. In *von Mises, L.*, 1981, pp. 130–45.

von Mises, Ludwig. Sociology and History. In *von Mises, L.*, 1981, pp. 68–129.

von Mises, Ludwig. The Task and Scope of the Science of Human Action. In *von Mises, L.*, 1981, pp. 1–67.

Musgrave, Alan. 'Unreal Assumptions' in Economic Theory: The F-Twist Untwisted. *Kyklos*, 1981, *34*(3), pp. 377–87.

Niehans, Jürg. Economics: History, Doctrine, Science, Art. *Kyklos*, 1981, *34*(2), pp. 165–77.

O'Brien, John Conway. The Economist's Quandary: Ethical Values. *Int. J. Soc. Econ.*, 1981, *8*(3), pp. 26–46.

Peston, Maurice. Lionel Robbins: Methodology, Policy and Modern Theory. In *Shackleton, J. R. and Locksley, G., eds.*, 1981, pp. 183–98.

Prezeau, Carl. L'équilibre social et l'équilibre général reconsidérés. (With English summary.) *Écon. Appl.*, 1981, *34*(1), pp. 29–60.

Rashid, Salim. Methods in Economic Science: Comment. *J. Econ. Issues*, March 1981, *15*(1), pp. 183–88.

Rashid, Salim. Political Economy and Geology in the Early Nineteenth Century: Similarities and Contrasts. *Hist. Polit. Econ.*, Winter 1981, *13*(4), pp. 726–44.

Robbins, Lionel. Economics and Political Economy. *Amer. Econ. Rev.*, May 1981, *71*(2), pp. 1–10.

Robinson, Joan. Thinking about Thinking. In *Robinson, J.*, 1981, *1979*, pp. 54–63.

Rousseas, Stephen. Wiles' Wily *Weltanschauung* [Ideology, Methodology, and Neoclassical Economics]. *J. Post Keynesian Econ.*, Spring 1981, *3*(3), pp. 340–51.

Samuels, Warren J. A Necessary Normative Context of Positive Economics? *J. Econ. Issues*, September 1981, *15*(3), pp. 721–27.

Sharp, John A. Economic Synthesis: A Review of the Work of Boris Ischboldin. *Int. J. Soc. Econ.*, 1981, *8*(7), pp. 8–13.

Sims, Christopher A. What Kind of Science is Economics? A Review Article on *Causality* in Economics by John R. Hicks. *J. Polit. Econ.*, June 1981, *89*(3), pp. 578–83.

Solo, Robert A. Values and Judgements in the Discourse of the Sciences. In *Solo, R. A. and Anderson, C. W., eds.*, 1981, pp. 9–40.

Termini, Valeria. Logical, Mechanical and Historical Time in Economics. *Econ. Notes*, 1981, *10*(3), pp. 58–104.

Tietzel, Manfred. "Annahmen" in der Wirtschaftstheorie. (Assumptions in Economic Theory. With English summary.) *Z. Wirtschaft. Sozialwissen.*, 1981, *101*(3), pp. 237–65.

Tinbergen, Jan. Misunderstandings Concerning Income Distribution Policies. *De Economist*, 1981, *129*(1), pp. 8–20.

Tool, Marc R. Observations on the Fischer Comment [The Method Is the Ideology]. *J. Econ. Issues*, March 1981, *15*(1), pp. 197–99.

Watts, Michael W. The Non-Rational Domain and the Limits of Economic Analysis: Comment. *Southern Econ. J.*, April 1981, *47*(4), pp. 1120–22.

Weisskopf, Walter. Reply to Professor Fischer [The Method Is the Ideology]. *J. Econ. Issues*, March 1981, *15*(1), pp. 196–97.

Wickins, P. L. Reconciliation of Facts and Hypotheses: The Golden Mean of Economic Historiography. *S. Afr. J. Econ.*, September 1981, *49*(3), pp. 241–55.

Wiles, Peter. Rejoinder [Ideology, Methodology, and Neoclassical Economics]. *J. Post Keynesian Econ.*, Spring 1981, *3*(3), pp. 352–58.

Williams, Edward E. and Findlay, M. Chapman, III. A Reconsideration of the Rationality Postulate: 'Right Hemisphere Thinking' in Economics. *Amer. J. Econ. Soc.*, January 1981, *40*(1), pp. 17–36.

Zellner, Arnold. Philosophy and Objectives of Econometrics. In *Currie, D.; Nobay, R. and Peel, D., eds.*, 1981, pp. 24–34.

040 ECONOMIC HISTORY

041 Economic History: General

0410 General

Busch, Lawrence and Sachs, Carolyn. The Agricultural Sciences and the Modern World System. In *Busch, L., ed.*, 1981, pp. 131–56.
[G: Selected Countries]

Cain, P. J. Hobson's Developing Theory of Imperialism. *Econ. Hist. Rev.*, 2nd Ser., May 1981, *34*(2), pp. 313–16.

Clarke, P. F. Hobson, Free Trade, and Imperialism. *Econ. Hist. Rev.*, 2nd Ser., May 1981, *34*(2), pp. 308–12.

Duby, Georges. Economic Anthropology and History: The Work of Karl Polanyi: Discussion. In *Dalton, G., ed.*, 1981, *1974*, pp. 58–60.

Freudenberger, Herman. Continuity in Administration: The Historical Uses of Business Records. In *Bateman, F., ed.*, 1981, pp. 129–36.
[G: U.S.]

Godelier, Maurice. Economic Anthropology and History: The Work of Karl Polanyi: Discussion. In *Dalton, G., ed.*, 1981, *1974*, pp. 64–69.

Hedlin, Edie. Maintaining Historical Records: The Current Situation. In *Bateman, F., ed.*, 1981, pp. 137–43. [G: U.S.]

Hershberg, Theodore. The New Urban History: Toward an Interdisciplinary History of the City. In *Hershberg, T., ed.*, 1981, *1978*, pp. 3–35.

Lovett, Robert. Preserving the Record of Southern Business: Comment. In *Bateman, F., ed.*, 1981, pp. 157–58. [G: U.S.]

Medick, Hans. The Transition from Feudalism to Capitalism: Renewal of the Debate. In *Samuel, R., ed.*, 1981, pp. 120–30.

Meillassoux, Claude. Economic Anthropology and History: The Work of Karl Polanyi: Discussion. In *Dalton, G., ed.*, 1981, *1974*, pp. 60–62.

Mooney, Philip F. From the Corporate Perspective: The Value of the Archival Function in Contemporary Business. In *Bateman, F., ed.*, 1981, pp. 144–48. [G: U.S.]

Panic, Mica. Evolution of the Concept of International Economic Order: Comments. In *[Cairncross, A.]*, 1981, pp. 182–87.

Stolz, Peter. Experimente in der Ökonomie und Wirtschaftshistorische Erfahrung. (With English summary.) *Kyklos*, 1981, *34*(1), pp. 72–94.

Tumlir, Jan. Evolution of the Concept of International Economic Order. In *[Cairncross, A.]*, 1981, pp. 152–82.

Valensi, Lucette. Economic Anthropology and History: The Work of Karl Polanyi. In *Dalton, G., ed.*, 1981, *1974*, pp. 3–12.

Wanjohi, N. Gatheru. Historical Scholarship in the East African Context. *Int. Soc. Sci. J.*, 1981, *33*(4), pp. 667–74.

0411 Development of the Discipline

Bailey, Anne M. and Llobera, Josep R. The Asiatic Mode of Production: Science and Politics: General Introduction. In *Bailey, A. M. and Llobera, J. R., eds.*, 1981, pp. 1–10.

Bailey, Anne M. and Llobera, Josep R. The AMP: Sources and Formation of the Concept. In *Bailey, A. M. and Llobera, J. R., eds.*, 1981, pp. 11–45.

Banu, Ioan. The 'Tributary' Social Formation. In *Bailey, A. M. and Llobera, J. R., eds.*, 1981, *1967*, pp. 278–80.

Clubb, Jerome M. History as a Social Science. *Int. Soc. Sci. J.*, 1981, *33*(4), pp. 596–610.

Davin, Anna. Feminism and Labour History. In *Samuel, R., ed.*, 1981, pp. 176–81.

Godelier, Maurice. The Asiatic Mode of Production. In *Bailey, A. M. and Llobera, J. R., eds.*, 1981, *1978*, pp. 264–77.

Godes, M. The Reaffirmation of Unilinealism. In *Bailey, A. M. and Llobera, J. R., eds.*, 1981, *1931*, pp. 99–105.

Kinser, Samuel. *Annaliste* Paradigm? The Geohistorical Structuralism of Fernand Braudel. *Amer. Hist. Rev.*, February 1981, *86*(1), pp. 63–105.

Krader, Lawrence. Principles and Critique of the Asiatic Mode of Production. In *Bailey, A. M. and Llobera, J. R., eds.*, 1981, *1975*, pp. 325–34.

Mad'iar, L. I. The Legitimacy of the AMP. In *Bailey, A. M. and Llobera, J. R., eds.*, 1981, *1930*, pp. 76–94.

McCloskey, Donald N. Does the Past Have Useful Economics? In *McCloskey, D. N.*, 1981, *1976*, pp. 19–52.

McCloskey, Donald N. The Achievements of the Cliometric School. In *McCloskey, D. N.*, 1981, *1978*, pp. 3–18. [G: U.K.]

Mokyr, Joel. Industrialization in Two Languages. *Econ. Hist. Rev.*, 2nd Ser., February 1981, *34*(1), pp. 143–49. [G: Netherlands; Belgium]

Romano, Ruggiero. History Today. *Int. Soc. Sci. J.*, 1981, *33*(4), pp. 641–49.

041 Economic History: General

Tishkov, Valery. Modern Soviet Historiography. *Int. Soc. Sci. J.*, 1981, *33*(4), pp. 650–66.
[G: U.S.S.R.]

Tökei, Ferenc. The Asiatic Mode of Production. In *Bailey, A. M. and Llobera, J. R., eds.*, 1981, *1966*, pp. 249–63.

Wickins, P. L. Reconciliation of Facts and Hypotheses: The Golden Mean of Economic Historiography. *S. Afr. J. Econ.*, September 1981, *49*(3), pp. 241–55.

Wolff, Klaus. "Textile History": The First Ten Years: Review Article. *J. Econ. Hist.*, June 1981, *41*(2), pp. 411–14.

0412 Comparative Intercountry or Intertemporal Economic History

Aujac, Henri. Cultures and Growth. In *Saunders, C. T., ed. (II)*, 1981, pp. 47–70.
[G: Brazil; France; Ivory Coast; Japan]

Bairoch, Paul. The Main Trends in National Economic Disparities since the Industrial Revolution. In *Bairoch, P. and Lévy-Leboyer, M., eds.*, 1981, pp. 3–17.
[G: LDCs; MDCs]

Ellsworth, P. T. The Terms of Trade between Primary-Producing and Industrial Countries. In *Livingstone, I., ed.*, 1981, *1961*, pp. 129–36.
[G: Global]

Flora, P. Solution or Source of Crises? The Welfare State in Historical Perspective. In *Mommsen, W. J., ed.*, 1981, pp. 343–89.
[G: Europe]

Hoselitz, B. F. Small Industry in Underdeveloped Countries. In *Livingstone, I., ed.*, 1981, *1959*, pp. 203–11.
[G: LDCs; Japan; W. Europe]

Ingham, Barbara and Simmons, Colin. The Two World Wars and Economic Development: Editors' Introduction. *World Devel.*, August 1981, *9*(8), pp. 701–05.

Issawi, Charles. Egypt, Iran and Turkey, 1800–1970: Patterns of Growth and Development. In *Bairoch, P. and Lévy-Leboyer, M., eds.*, 1981, pp. 65–77.
[G: Egypt; Iran; Turkey]

Jones, F. Stuart. Growth and Fluctuations, 1870–1913 (Review Note). *S. Afr. J. Econ.*, December 1981, *49*(4), pp. 407–14.
[G: U.K.; France; W. Germany; U.S.]

Jonung, Lars. The Depression in Sweden and the United States: A Comparison of Causes and Policies. In *Brunner, K., ed.*, 1981, pp. 286–315.
[G: Sweden; U.S.]

Kindleberger, Charles P. Debt Situation of the Developing Countries in Historical Perspective (1800–1945) *Aussenwirtschaft*, December 1981, *36*(4), pp. 372–80.

Lewis, W. Arthur. The Rate of Growth of World Trade, 1830–1973. In *Grassman, S. and Lundberg, E., eds.*, 1981, pp. 11–74.
[G: Global]

Maitra, Priyatosh. Technology Transfer, Population Growth and the Development Gap since the Industrial Revolution. In *Bairoch, P. and Lévy-Leboyer, M., eds.*, 1981, pp. 78–85.
[G: LDCs; W. Europe]

McCloskey, Donald N. International Differences in Productivity? Coal and Steel in America and Britain before World War I. In *McCloskey, D. N.*, 1981, *1973*, pp. 73–93.
[G: U.K.; U.S.]

McGowan, Patrick J. Imperialism in World-System Perspective. In *Hollist, W. L. and Rosenau, J. N., eds.*, 1981, pp. 54–79.
[G: U.K.]

Rimlinger, G. V. Comments on Professor Peter Flora's Analytical Perspective of the Welfare State [Solution or Source of Crises? The Welfare State in Historical Perspective]. In *Mommsen, W. J., ed.*, 1981, pp. 390–94.
[G: Europe]

Svedberg, Peter. Colonial Enforcement of Foreign Direct Investment. *Manchester Sch. Econ. Soc. Stud.*, March 1981, *49*(1), pp. 21–38.

Yeats, Alexander J. The Rate of Growth of World Trade, 1830–1973: Comments. In *Grassman, S. and Lundberg, E., eds.*, 1981, pp. 75–81.
[G: Europe; U.S.; Japan]

042 Economic History: United States and Canada

0420 General

Anders, Gary C. The Reduction of a Self-Sufficient People to Poverty and Welfare Dependence: An Analysis of the Causes of Cherokee Indian Underdevelopment. *Amer. J. Econ. Soc.*, July 1981, *40*(3), pp. 225–37.
[G: U.S.]

Anderson, Terry L. and Hill, Peter J. Economic Growth in a Transfer Society: The United States Experience. *J. Econ. Hist.*, March 1981, *41*(1), pp. 113–19.
[G: U.S.]

Atack, Jeremy. Business in the New South: The Early Problems: Comment. In *Bateman, F., ed.*, 1981, pp. 151–53.
[G: U.S.]

Atack, Jeremy and Bateman, Fred. Egalitarianism, Inequality, and Age: The Rural North in 1860. *J. Econ. Hist.*, March 1981, *41*(1), pp. 85–93.
[G: U.S.]

Atack, Jeremy and Bateman, Fred. The "Egalitarian Ideal" and the Distribution of Wealth in the Northern Agricultural Community: A Backward Look. *Rev. Econ. Statist.*, February 1981, *63*(1), pp. 124–29.
[G: U.S.]

Baskerville, Peter. Americans in Britain's Backyard: The Railway Era in Upper Canada, 1850–1880. *Bus. Hist. Rev.*, Autumn 1981, *55*(3), pp. 314–36.
[G: Canada]

Bateman, Fred. Business in the New South: The Interaction between History and Economics. In *Bateman, F., ed.*, 1981, pp. 8–13.
[G: U.S.]

Berry, Brian J. L. Inner-City Futures: An American Dilemma Revisited. In *Stave, B. M., ed.*, 1981, *1980*, pp. 187–219.
[G: U.S.]

Blum, Albert A. United States. In *Blum, A. A., ed.*, 1981, pp. 621–45.
[G: U.S.]

Bordo, Michael David and Schwartz, Anna J. Money and Prices in the 19th Century: Was Thomas Tooke Right? *Exploration Econ. Hist.*, April 1981, *18*(2), pp. 97–127.
[G: U.S.; U.K.]

Boyer, M. Christine. National Land Use Policy: Instrument and Product of the Economic Cycle. In *de Neufville, J. I., ed.*, 1981, pp. 109–25.
[G: U.S.]

Brunner, Karl. Epilogue: Understanding the Great Depression. In *Brunner, K., ed.*, 1981, pp. 316–58.
[G: U.S.]

Burstein, Alan N. Immigrants and Residential Mobility: The Irish and Germans in Philadelphia, 1850–1880. In *Hershberg, T., ed.*, 1981, pp. 174–203. [G: U.S.]

Claggett, William. Turnout and Core Voters in the Nineteenth and Twentieth Centuries: A Reconsideration [Voter Turnout in the Midwest, 1840–1872]. *Soc. Sci. Quart.*, September 1981, *62*(3), pp. 443–49. [G: U.S.]

Dale, Christopher. Agricultural Research as State Intervention. In *Busch, L., ed.*, 1981, pp. 69–82. [G: U.S.]

DeCanio, Stephen J. Accumulation and Discrimination in the Postbellum South. In *Walton, G. M. and Shepherd, J. F., eds.*, 1981, *1980*, pp. 103–25. [G: U.S.]

Diggins, John Patrick. Power and Authority in American History: The Case of Charles A. Beard and His Critics. *Amer. Hist. Rev.*, October 1981, *86*(4), pp. 701–30. [G: U.S.]

Engerman, Stanley L. Agriculture as Business: The Southern Context. In *Bateman, F., ed.*, 1981, pp. 17–26. [G: U.S.]

Engerman, Stanley L. Notes on the Patterns of Economic Growth in the British North American Colonies in the Seventeenth, Eighteenth and Nineteenth Centuries. In *Bairoch, P. and Lévy-Leboyer, M., eds.*, 1981, pp. 46–57. [G: Caribbean; U.S.]

Field, Alexander James. The Problem with Neoclassical Institutional Economics: A Critique with Special Reference to the North/Thomas Model of Pre-1500 Europe. *Exploration Econ. Hist.*, April 1981, *18*(2), pp. 174–98. [G: Europe]

Furstenberg, Frank F., Jr.; Modell, John and Hershberg, Theodore. The Origins of the Female-Headed Black Family: The Impact of the Urban Experience. In *Hershberg, T., ed.*, 1981, *1975*, pp. 435–54. [G: U.S.]

Gilb, Corinne Lathrop. Public or Private Governments? In *Nystrom, P. C. and Starbuck, W. H., eds., Vol. 2*, 1981, pp. 464–91. [G: U.S.; W. Europe]

Goldfield, David R. The Urban South: A Regional Framework. *Amer. Hist. Rev.*, December 1981, *86*(5), pp. 1009–34. [G: U.S.]

Goldin, Claudia Dale. Credit Merchandising in the New South: The Role of Competition and Risk. In *Walton, G. M. and Shepherd, J. F., eds.*, 1981, pp. 3–23. [G: U.S.]

Goodstein, Marvin E. The Study of Southern Economic and Business History: Challenges and Opportunities. In *Bateman, F., ed.*, 1981, pp. 1–7. [G: U.S.]

Gordon, Robert J. and Wilcox, James A. Monetarist Interpretations of the Great Depression: A Rejoinder. In *Brunner, K., ed.*, 1981, pp. 165–73. [G: U.S.; W. Europe]

Gordon, Robert J. and Wilcox, James A. Monetarist Interpretations of the Great Depression: An Evaluation and Critique. In *Brunner, K., ed.*, 1981, pp. 49–107. [G: U.S.]

Grantham, Dewey W. The Contours of Southern Progressivism. *Amer. Hist. Rev.*, December 1981, *86*(5), pp. 1035–59. [G: U.S.]

Greenberg, Stephanie W. Industrial Location and

Ethnic Residential Patterns in an Industrializing City: Philadelphia, 1880. In *Hershberg, T., ed.*, 1981, pp. 204–32. [G: U.S.]

Guest, Avery M. Social Structure and U.S. Inter-State Fertility Differentials in 1900. *Demography*, November 1981, *18*(4), pp. 465–86. [G: U.S.]

Haines, Michael R. Poverty, Economic Stress, and the Family in a Late Nineteenth-Century American City: Whites in Philadelphia, 1880. In *Hershberg, T., ed.*, 1981, pp. 240–76. [G: U.S.]

Halsey, Harlan I. The Choice between High-Pressure and Low-Pressure Steam Power in America in the Early Nineteenth Century. *J. Econ. Hist.*, December 1981, *41*(4), pp. 723–44. [G: U.S.]

Handlin, Oscar. The Development of the Corporation. In *Novak, M. and Cooper, J. W., eds.*, 1981, pp. 1–10.

Hanner, John. Government Response to the Buffalo Hide Trade, 1871–1883. *J. Law Econ.*, October 1981, *24*(2), pp. 239–71. [G: U.S.]

Harper-Fender, Ann. Discouraging the Use of a Common Resource: The Crees of Saskatchewan. *J. Econ. Hist.*, March 1981, *41*(1), pp. 163–70. [G: Canada]

Harrison, William B. Annals of a Crusade: Wright Patman and the Federal Reserve System. *Amer. J. Econ. Soc.*, July 1981, *40*(3), pp. 317–20. [G: U.S.]

Harvey, Charles E. Religion and Industrial Relations: John D. Rockefeller, Jr., and the Interchurch World Movement of 1919–1920. In *Zarembka, P., ed.*, 1981, pp. 199–227.

Hershberg, Theodore. Free Blacks in Antebellum Philadelphia: A Study of Ex-Slaves, Freeborn, and Socioeconomic Decline. In *Hershberg, T., ed.*, 1981, *1971*, pp. 368–91. [G: U.S.]

Hershberg, Theodore and Williams, Henry. Mulattoes and Blacks: Intra-group Color Differences and Social Stratification in Nineteenth-Century Philadelphia. In *Hershberg, T., ed.*, 1981, pp. 392–434.

Hershberg, Theodore, et al. The "Journey-to-Work": An Empirical Investigation of Work, Residence and Transportation, Philadelphia, 1850 and 1880. In *Hershberg, T., ed.*, 1981, pp. 128–73. [G: U.S.]

Higgs, Robert. Discussion [Regulation, Property Rights, and Definition of "The Market": Law and the American Economy]. *J. Econ. Hist.*, March 1981, *41*(1), pp. 110–11. [G: U.S.]

Johnson, H. Thomas. Toward a New Understanding of Nineteenth-Century Cost Accounting. *Accounting Rev.*, July 1981, *56*(3), pp. 510–18. [G: U.K.; U.S.]

Katzman, Martin T. An Ecology of Family Decisions: Suburbanization, Schooling, and Fertility in Philadelphia, 1880–1920: Comment. In *Stave, B. M., ed.*, 1981, pp. 61–67. [G: U.S.]

Laurie, Bruce and Schmitz, Mark. Manufacture and Productivity: The Making of an Industrial Base, Philadelphia, 1850–1880. In *Hershberg, T., ed.*, 1981, pp. 43–92. [G: U.S.]

Leinenweber, Charles. The Class and Ethnic Bases of New York City Socialism, 1904–1915. *Labor Hist.*, Winter 1981, *22*(1), pp. 31–56. [G: U.S.]

Lewis, Frank D. Farm Settlement on the Canadian

Prairies, 1898 to 1911. *J. Econ. Hist.*, September 1981, *41*(3), pp. 517–35. [G: Canada]

Lindert, Peter H. Understanding 1929–33: Comments. In *Brunner, K., ed.*, 1981, pp. 125–33. [G: U.S.]

Lockeretz, William. The Dust Bowl: Its Relevance to Contemporary Environmental Problems. In *Lawson, M. P. and Baker, M. E., eds.*, 1981, pp. 11–31. [G: U.S.]

Lothian, James R. Monetarist Interpretations of the Great Depression: Comment. In *Brunner, K., ed.*, 1981, pp. 134–47. [G: U.S.]

Maggard, Sally. From Farmers to Miners: The Decline of Agriculture in Eastern Kentucky. In *Busch, L., ed.*, 1981, pp. 25–66. [G: U.S.]

Mandelbaum, Seymour J. The Economy of Cities: Comment. In *Stave, B. M., ed.*, 1981, pp. 251–57. [G: U.S.]

Mandle, Jay R. The Economic Underdevelopment of the United States South in the Post-Bellum Era. In *Bairoch, P. and Lévy-Leboyer, M., eds.*, 1981, pp. 86–97. [G: U.S.]

McCormick, Richard L. The Discovery That Business Corrupts Politics: A Reappraisal of the Origins of Progressivism. *Amer. Hist. Rev.*, April 1981, *86*(2), pp. 247–74. [G: U.S.]

McGuire, Robert A. Economic Causes of Late-Nineteenth Century Agrarian Unrest: New Evidence. *J. Econ. Hist.*, December 1981, *41*(4), pp. 835–52. [G: U.S.]

McPherson, W. W. and Langham, Max R. Commercial Agriculture in Historical Perspective. *Amer. J. Agr. Econ.*, December 1981, *63*(5), pp. 894–901. [G: U.S.]

Meltzer, Allan H. Monetarist Interpretations of the Great Depression: Comments. In *Brunner, K., ed.*, 1981, pp. 148–64. [G: U.S.]

Mins, Henry F. Science & Society: The Early Days. *Sci. Soc.*, Spring 1981, *45*(1), pp. 85–88. [G: U.S.]

Modell, John. An Ecology of Family Decisions: Suburbanization, Schooling, and Fertility in Philadelphia, 1880–1920. In *Stave, B. M., ed.*, 1981, *1980*, pp. 39–59. [G: U.S.]

Modell, John; Hershberg, Theodore and Furstenberg, Frank F., Jr. Social Change and Transitions to Adulthood in Historical Perspective. In *Hershberg, T., ed.*, 1981, *1975*, pp. 311–41. [G: U.S.]

Modell, John and Lees, Lynn H. The Irish Countryman Urbanized: A Comparative Perspective on the Famine Migration. In *Hershberg, T., ed.*, 1981, *1977*, pp. 351–67. [G: U.S.; U.K.]

Mohammadi, S. Buik. American Capitalism and Agricultural Development. In *Busch, L., ed.*, 1981, pp. 9–24. [G: U.S.]

Mokyr, Joel. Discussion [The Organization of Exchange in Early Christian Ireland] [Discouraging the Use of a Common Resource: The Crees of Saskatchewan]. *J. Econ. Hist.*, March 1981, *41*(1), pp. 177–78. [G: Canada; Ireland]

Pomfret, Richard. The Staple Theory as an Approach to Canadian and Australian Economic Development. *Australian Econ. Hist. Rev.*, September 1981, *21*(2), pp. 133–46. [G: Canada; Australia]

Pope, Clayne L. Discussion [Egalitarianism, Inequality, and Age: The Rural North in 1860]. *J. Econ. Hist.*, March 1981, *41*(1), pp. 94–95. [G: U.S.]

Randolph, S. Randi and Sachs, Carolyn. The Establishment of Applies Sciences: Medicine and Agriculture Compared. In *Busch, L., ed.*, 1981, pp. 83–111. [G: U.S.]

Ransom, Roger L. and Sutch, Richard. Credit Merchandising in the Post-emancipation South: Structure, Conduct, and Performance. In *Walton, G. M. and Shepherd, J. F., eds.*, 1981, *1980*, pp. 57–81. [G: U.S.]

Ransom, Roger L. and Sutch, Richard. Growth and Welfare in the American South in the Nineteenth Century. In *Walton, G. M. and Shepherd, J. F., eds.*, 1981, *1980*, pp. 127–53. [G: U.S.]

Reid, Joseph D., Jr. White Land, Black Labor, and Agricultural Stagnation: The Causes and Effects of Sharecropping in the Postbellum South. In *Walton, G. M. and Shepherd, J. F., eds.*, 1981, *1980*, pp. 33–55. [G: U.S.]

Scheiber, Harry N. Regulation, Property Rights, and Definition of "The Market": Law and the American Economy. *J. Econ. Hist.*, March 1981, *41*(1), pp. 103–09. [G: U.S.]

Schwartz, Anna J. Understanding 1929–1933. In *Brunner, K., ed.*, 1981, pp. 5–48. [G: U.S.]

Serow, William J. An Economic Approach to Population Change in the South. In *Poston, D. L., Jr. and Weller, R. H., eds.*, 1981, pp. 198–226. [G: U.S.]

Sexton, Robert L. The Effect of Alternative Regional Delineations on Historical Interpretation. *Econ. Forum*, Winter 1981–82, *12*(2), pp. 77–83. [G: U.S.]

Shortridge, Ray M. Nineteenth Century Turnout: A Rejoinder [Voter Turnout in the Midwest, 1840–1872]. *Soc. Sci. Quart.*, September 1981, *62*(3), pp. 450–52. [G: U.S.]

Sly, David F. The Population of the South: Migration. In *Poston, D. L., Jr. and Weller, R. H., eds.*, 1981, pp. 109–36. [G: U.S.]

Smiley, Gene. The Expansion of New York Securities Market at the Turn of the Century. *Bus. Hist. Rev.*, Spring 1981, *55*(1), pp. 75–85. [G: U.S.]

Soltow, Martha Jane. Twenty Year Cumulative Index to Labor History: Vol. 1, No. 1 (Spring, 1960)—Vol. 20, No. 4 (Fall, 1979). *Labor Hist.*, Winter 1981, *22*(1), pp. 57–135.

Temin, Peter. Freedom and Coercion: Notes on the Analysis of Debt Peonage in *One Kind of Freedom*. In *Walton, G. M. and Shepherd, J. F., eds.*, 1981, *1980*, pp. 25–32. [G: U.S.]

Temin, Peter. Notes on the Causes of the Great Depression. In *Brunner, K., ed.*, 1981, pp. 108–24. [G: U.S.]

Tolnay, Stewart E. Trends in Total and Marital Fertility for Black Americans, 1886–1899. *Demography*, November 1981, *18*(4), pp. 443–63. [G: U.S.]

Ulen, Thomas S. Discussion [Economic Growth in a Transfer Society: The United States Experience]. *J. Econ. Hist.*, March 1981, *41*(1), pp. 120–21. [G: U.S.]

Vinovskis, Maris A. Estimating the Wealth of Americans on the Eve of the Revolution: Review Article. *J. Econ. Hist.*, June 1981, *41*(2), pp. 415–20. [G: U.S.]

Walsh, Margaret. Another New Look? The Encyclopedia of American Economic History—A Review Article. *Bus. Hist. Rev.*, Autumn 1981, *55*(3), pp. 403–18. [G: U.S.]

Weiss, Thomas. Southern Business Never had it so Good!! A Look at Antebellum Industrialization. In *Bateman, F., ed.*, 1981, pp. 27–34. [G: U.S.]

Williams, Jeffrey C. Economics and Politics: Voting Behavior in Kansas during the Populist Decade. *Exploration Econ. Hist.*, July 1981, *18*(3), pp. 233–56. [G: U.S.]

Williamson, Jeffrey G. Inequality and Regional Development: The View from America. In *Bairoch, P. and Lévy-Leboyer, M., eds.*, 1981, pp. 373–91. [G: U.S.]

Woodman, Harold D. Agriculture and Business in the Postbellum South: The Transformation of a Slave Society. In *Bateman, F., ed.*, 1981, pp. 51–61. [G: U.S.]

Wright, Gavin. Freedom and the Southern Economy. In *Walton, G. M. and Shepherd, J. F., eds.*, 1981, *1980*, pp. 85–102. [G: U.S.]

0421 History of Product Prices and Markets

Aduddell, Robert M. and Cain, Louis P. The Consent Decree in the Meatpacking Industry, 1920–1956. *Bus. Hist. Rev.*, Autumn 1981, *55*(3), pp. 359–78. [G: U.S.]

Allen, Robert C. Accounting for Price Changes: American Steel Rails, 1879–1910. *J. Polit. Econ.*, June 1981, *89*(3), pp. 512–28. [G: U.S.]

Armentano, D. T. The Petroleum Industry: A Historical Study in Power. *Cato J.*, Spring 1981, *1*(1), pp. 53–85. [G: U.S.]

Badger, Anthony J. The Tobacco Program and the Farmer: Early Efforts to Control the Market—and Why they Failed. In *Finger, W. R., ed.*, 1981, pp. 3–12. [G: U.S.]

Barkin, Solomon. Management and Ownership in the New England Cotton Textile Industry. *J. Econ. Issues*, June 1981, *15*(2), pp. 463–75. [G: U.S.]

Carlos, Ann. The Causes and Origins of the North American Fur Trade Rivalry: 1804–1810. *J. Econ. Hist.*, December 1981, *41*(4), pp. 777–94. [G: Canada]

Church, Roy. The Marketing of Automobiles in Britain and the United States before 1939. In *Okochi, A. and Shimokawa, K., eds.*, 1981, pp. 59–87. [G: U.K.; U.S.]

Fridenson, Patrick. The Marketing of Automobiles in Britain and the United States before 1939: Comment. In *Okochi, A. and Shimokawa, K., eds.*, 1981, pp. 88–90. [G: U.K.; U.S.]

Guth, James L. Herbert Hoover, the U.S. Food Administration, and the Dairy Industry, 1917–1918. *Bus. Hist. Rev.*, Summer 1981, *55*(2), pp. 170–87. [G: U.S.]

Hekman, John S. and Strong, John S. The Evolution of New England Industry. *New Eng. Econ. Rev.*, March–April 1981, pp. 35–46. [G: U.S.]

Killick, J. R. The Transformation of Cotton Marketing in the Late Nineteenth Century: Alexander Sprunt and Son of Wilmington, N.C., 1884–1956. *Bus. Hist. Rev.*, Summer 1981, *55*(2), pp. 143–69. [G: U.S.]

Lebergott, Stanley. Through the Blockade: The Profitability and Extent of Cotton Smuggling, 1861–1865. *J. Econ. Hist.*, December 1981, *41*(4), pp. 867–88. [G: U.S.]

Livesay, Harold C. Nineteenth Century Precursors to Automobile Marketing in the United States. In *Okochi, A. and Shimokawa, K., eds.*, 1981, pp. 39–52. [G: U.S.]

Marr, William L. The Wheat Economy in Reverse: Ontario's Wheat Production, 1887–1917. *Can. J. Econ.*, February 1981, *14*(1), pp. 136–45. [G: Canada]

Nash, Gerald D. Energy Crises in Historical Perspective. *Natural Res. J.*, April 1981, *21*(2), pp. 341–54. [G: U.S.]

Petzel, Todd E. A New Look at Some Old Evidence: The Wheat Market Scandal of 1925. *Food Res. Inst. Stud.*, 1981, *18*(1), pp. 117–28. [G: U.S.]

Rothenberg, Winifred B. The Market and Massachusetts Farmers, 1750–1855. *J. Econ. Hist.*, June 1981, *41*(2), pp. 283–314. [G: U.S.]

Samson, Peter. The Department Store, Its Past and Its Future: A Review Article. *Bus. Hist. Rev.*, Spring 1981, *55*(1), pp. 26–34. [G: U.S.]

Taylor, Graham D. Management Relations in a Multinational Enterprise: The Case of Canadian Industries Limited, 1928–1948. *Bus. Hist. Rev.*, Autumn 1981, *55*(3), pp. 337–58. [G: Canada]

Toba, Kin'ichiro. Nineteenth Century Precursors to Automobile Marketing in the United States: Comment. In *Okochi, A. and Shimokawa, K., eds.*, 1981, pp. 53–55. [G: U.S.]

Tucker, Barbara M. The Merchant, the Manufacturer, and the Factory Manager: The Case of Samuel Slater. *Bus. Hist. Rev.*, Autumn 1981, *55*(3), pp. 297–313. [G: U.S.]

Ward, James A. Image and Reality: The Railway Corporate-State Metaphor. *Bus. Hist. Rev.*, Winter 1981, *55*(4), pp. 491–516. [G: U.S.]

Wright, Gavin. Cheap Labor and Southern Textiles, 1880–1930. *Quart. J. Econ.*, November 1981, *96*(4), pp. 605–29. [G: U.S.]

Yamada, Makiko. Nineteenth Century Precursors to Automobile Marketing in the United States: Comment. In *Okochi, A. and Shimokawa, K., eds.*, 1981, pp. 55–57. [G: U.S.]

Yuzawa, Takeshi. The Marketing of Automobiles in Britain and the United States before 1939: Comment. In *Okochi, A. and Shimokawa, K., eds.*, 1981, pp. 90–92. [G: U.K.; U.S.]

0422 History of Factor Prices and Markets

Adelman, William. Labor History through Field Trips. In *Wertheimer, B. M., ed.*, 1981, pp. 159–70. [G: U.S.]

Alston, Lee J. Tenure Choice in Southern Agriculture, 1930–1960. *Exploration Econ. Hist.*, July 1981, *18*(3), pp. 211–32. [G: U.S.]

Anderson, Terry L. From the Parts to the Whole: Modeling Chesapeake Population [The Growth of Population and Labor Force in the 17th-Century Chesapeake]. *Exploration Econ. Hist.*, October 1981, *18*(4), pp. 411–14.   [G: U.S.]

Benson, Susan Porter. The Cinderalla of Occupations: Managing the Work of Department Store Saleswomen, 1900–1940. *Bus. Hist. Rev.*, Spring 1981, *55*(1), pp. 1–25.   [G: U.S.]

Blewett, Mary H. Discussion [Mechanization and Work in the American Shoe Industry: Lynn, Massachusetts, 1852–1883]. *J. Econ. Hist.*, March 1981, *41*(1), pp. 64.   [G: U.S.]

Bonnell, Sheila. Real Wages and Employment in the Great Depression. *Econ. Rec.*, September 1981, *57*(158), pp. 277–81.   [G: U.K.; U.S.; Sweden; Germany]

Cain, Louis P. and Paterson, Donald G. Factor Biases and Technical Change in Manufacturing: The American System, 1850–1919. *J. Econ. Hist.*, June 1981, *41*(2), pp. 341–60.   [G: U.S.]

Carlson, Leonard A. Labor Supply, the Acquisition of Skills, and the Location of Southern Textile Mills, 1880–1900. *J. Econ. Hist.*, March 1981, *41*(1), pp. 65–71.   [G: U.S.]

Chiles, Frederic. General Strike: San Francisco, 1934—An Historical Compilation Film Storyboard. *Labor Hist.*, Summer 1981, *22*(3), pp. 430–65.   [G: U.S.]

Christensen, Paul P. Land Abundance and Cheap Horsepower in the Mechanization of the Antebellum United States Economy. *Exploration Econ. Hist.*, October 1981, *18*(4), pp. 309–29.   [G: U.S.]

Cohn, Raymond L. Antebellum Regional Incomes: Another Look. *Exploration Econ. Hist.*, October 1981, *18*(4), pp. 330–46.   [G: U.S.]

Conk, Margo A. Immigrant Workers in the City, 1870–1930: Agents of Growth or Threats to Democracy. *Soc. Sci. Quart.*, December 1981, *62*(4), pp. 704–20.   [G: U.S.]

Dubofsky, Melvyn. Film as History: History as Drama—Some Comments on "The Wobblies," a Play by Stewart Bird and Peter Robilotta, and "The Wobblies" a Film by Stewart Bird and Deborah Shaffer. *Labor Hist.*, Winter 1981, *22*(1), pp. 136–40.   [G: U.S.]

Erickson, Charlotte. Emigration from the British Isles to the U.S.A. in 1831. *Population Stud.*, July 1981, *35*(2), pp. 175–97.   [G: U.S.; U.K.]

Fenoltea, Stefano. The Slavery Debate: A Note from the Sidelines. *Exploration Econ. Hist.*, July 1981, *18*(3), pp. 304–08.   [G: U.S.]

Fones-Wolf, Elizabeth and Fones-Wolf, Kenneth. Knights versus the Trade Unionists: The Case of the Washington, D.C. Carpenters, 1881–1896. *Labor Hist.*, Spring 1981, *22*(2), pp. 192–212.   [G: U.S.]

Fujii, Edwin T. and Mak, James. The Effect of Acculturation and Assimilation on the Income of Immigrant Filipino Men in Hawaii. *Phillipine Rev. Econ. Bus.*, March & June 1981, *18*(1 & 2), pp. 75–85.   [G: U.S.]

Galenson, David W. The Market Evaluation of Human Capital: The Case of Indentured Servitude. *J. Polit. Econ.*, June 1981, *89*(3), pp. 446–67.   [G: U.S.]

Galenson, David W. White Servitude and the Growth of Black Slavery in Colonial America. *J.*

Econ. Hist., March 1981, *41*(1), pp. 39–47.   [G: U.S.]

Gildemeister, Glen A. The Founding of the American Federation of Labor. *Labor Hist.*, Spring 1981, *22*(2), pp. 262–68.   [G: U.S.]

Goldin, Claudia Dale. Family Strategies and the Family Economy in the Late Nineteenth Century: The Role of Secondary Workers. In *Hershberg, T., ed.*, 1981, pp. 277–310.   [G: U.S.]

Gomez, Joseph A. History, Documentary, and Audience Manipulation: A View of "The Wobblies." *Labor Hist.*, Winter 1981, *22*(1), pp. 141–45.   [G: U.S.]

Graziosi, Andrea. Common Laborers, Unskilled Workers: 1880-1915. *Labor Hist.*, Fall 1981, *22*(4), pp. 512–44.   [G: U.S.]

Harris, William H. Federal Intervention in Union Discrimination: FEPC and West Coast Shipyards during World War II. *Labor Hist.*, Summer 1981, *22*(3), pp. 325–47.   [G: U.S.]

Havira, Barbara S. Managing Industrial and Social Tensions in a Rural Setting: Women Silk Workers in Belding, Michigan, 1885–1932. *Mich. Academician*, Winter 1981, *13*(3), pp. 257–73.   [G: U.S.]

Hershberg, Theodore, et al. A Tale of Three Cities: Blacks, Immigrants, and Opportunity in Philadelphia, 1850–1880, 1930, 1970. In *Hershberg, T., ed.*, 1981, pp. 461–91.   [G: U.S.]

James, John A. Some Evidence on Relative Labor Scarcity in 19th-Century American Manufacturing. *Exploration Econ. Hist.*, October 1981, *18*(4), pp. 376–88.   [G: U.S.]

Kaufman, Stuart Bruce. Birth of a Federation: Mr. Gompers Endeavors 'Not to Build a Bubble.' *Mon. Lab. Rev.*, November 1981, *104*(11), pp. 23–36.   [G: U.S.]

Kornbluh, Joyce L. and Goldfarb, Lyn. Labor Education and Women Workers: An Historical Perspective. In *Wertheimer, B. M., ed.*, 1981, pp. 15–31.   [G: U.S.]

Laurie, Bruce; Alter, George and Hershberg, Theodore. Immigrants and Industry: The Philadelphia Experience, 1850–1880. In *Hershberg, T., ed.*, 1981, *1975*, pp. 93–119.   [G: U.S.]

Lazonick, William H. Production Relations, Labor Productivity, and Choice of Technique: British and U.S. Cotton Spinning. *J. Econ. Hist.*, September 1981, *41*(3), pp. 491–516.   [G: U.S.; U.K.]

Levenstein, Harvey. Leninists Undone by Leninism: Communism and Unionism in the United States and Mexico, 1935–1939. *Labor Hist.*, Spring 1981, *22*(2), pp. 237–61.   [G: U.S.; Mexico]

Lucas, Robert E., Jr. Unemployment in the Great Depression: Is There a Full Explanation? In *Lucas, R. E., Jr.*, 1981, *1972*, pp. 59–65. [G: U.S]

Maccoby, Michael and Terzi, Katherine A. What Happened to the Work Ethic? In *Hoffman, W. M. and Wyly, T. J., eds.*, 1981, pp. 19–58.   [G: U.S.]

Masson, Jack and Guimary, Donald. Asian Labor Contractors in the Alaskan Canned Salmon Industry: 1880–1937. *Labor Hist.*, Summer 1981, *22*(3), pp. 377–97.   [G: U.S.]

Menard, Russell R. The Growth of Population in

the Chesapeake Colonies: A Comment [The Growth of Population and Labor Force in the 17th-Century Chesapeake]. *Exploration Econ. Hist.*, October 1981, *18*(4), pp. 399–410. [G: U.S.]

Miller, Randall M. The Fabric of Control: Slavery in Antebellum Southern Textile Mills. *Bus. Hist. Rev.*, Winter 1981, *55*(4), pp. 471–90. [G: U.S.]

Moggridge, D. E. Financial Crises and Lenders of Last Resort: Policy in the Crises of 1920 and 1929. *J. Europ. Econ. Hist.*, Spring 1981, *10*(1), pp. 47–69.

Mulligan, William H., Jr. Mechanization and Work in the American Shoe Industry: Lynn, Massachusetts, 1852–1883. *J. Econ. Hist.*, March 1981, *41*(1), pp. 59–63. [G: U.S.]

Musoke, Moses S. Mechanizing Cotton Production in the American South: The Tractor, 1915–1960. *Exploration Econ. Hist.*, October 1981, *18*(4), pp. 347–75. [G: U.S.]

Oates, Mary J. Discussion [Labor Supply, the Acquisition of Skills, and the Location of Southern Textile Mills, 1880–1900]. *J. Econ. Hist.*, March 1981, *41*(1), pp. 72–73. [G: U.S.]

Oestreicher, Richard. Socialism and the Knights of Labor in Detroit, 1877–1886. *Labor Hist.*, Winter 1981, *22*(1), pp. 5–30. [G: U.S.]

Perrier, Hubert. The Socialists and the Working Class in New York: 1890–1896. *Labor Hist.*, Fall 1981, *22*(4), pp. 485–511. [G: U.S.]

Pessen, Edward. A Young Industrial Worker in Early World War II in New York City. *Labor Hist.*, Spring 1981, *22*(2), pp. 269–81. [G: U.S.]

Peterson, Joyce Shaw. Auto Workers and Their Work, 1900–1933. *Labor Hist.*, Spring 1981, *22*(2), pp. 213–36. [G: U.S.]

Pomfret, Richard. Capital Formation in Canada, 1870–1900. *Exploration Econ. Hist.*, January 1981, *18*(1), pp. 84–96. [G: Canada]

Poulin Simon, Lise. Une théorie économique du loisir industriel; le cas du Canada. (An Economic Theory of Industrial Leisure. With English summary.) *L'Actual. Econ.*, January–March 1981, *57*(1), pp. 33–53. [G: Canada]

Rosemont, Henry P. Benjamin Franklin and the Philadelphia Typographical Strikers of 1786. *Labor Hist.*, Summer 1981, *22*(3), pp. 398–429. [G: U.S.]

Rotella, Elyce J. The Transformation of the American Office: Changes in Employment and Technology. *J. Econ. Hist.*, March 1981, *41*(1), pp. 51–57. [G: U.S.]

Salinger, Sharon V. Colonial Labor in Transition: The Decline of Indentured Servitude in Late Eighteenth-Century Philadelphia. *Labor Hist.*, Spring 1981, *22*(2), pp. 165–91. [G: U.S.]

Schmitz, Mark. The Elasticity of Substitution in 19th-Century Manufacturing. *Exploration Econ. Hist.*, July 1981, *18*(3), pp. 290–303. [G: U.S.]

Schmitz, Mark and Schaefer, Donald. Paradox Lost: Westward Expansion and Slave Prices before the Civil War. *J. Econ. Hist.*, June 1981, *41*(2), pp. 402–07. [G: U.S.]

Sheflin, Neil; Troy, Leo and Koeller, C. Timothy. Structural Stability in Models of American Trade Union Growth. *Quart. J. Econ.*, February 1981,

96(1), pp. 77–88. [G: U.S.]

Smiley, Gene. Regional Variation in Bank Loan Rates in the Interwar Years. *J. Econ. Hist.*, December 1981, *41*(4), pp. 889–901. [G: U.S.]

Stauffer, Robert F. The Bank Failures of 1930–31: A Comment. *J. Money, Credit, Banking*, February 1981, *13*(1), pp. 109–13. [G: U.S.]

Swanson, Dorothy. Annual Bibliography on American Labor History, 1980: Periodicals, Dissertations, and Research in Progress. *Labor Hist.*, Fall 1981, *22*(4), pp. 545–72. [G: U.S.]

Thomson, Andrew W. J. Trade Unions in the Developed Economies: The United States of America. In *Smith, E. O., ed.*, 1981, pp. 155–77. [G: U.S.]

Tygiel, Jules. Tramping Artisans: The Case of the Carpenters in Industrial America. *Labor Hist.*, Summer 1981, *22*(3), pp. 348–76. [G: U.S.]

Wall, Paul L. Changes in the Black Community. *Amer. J. Agr. Econ.*, December 1981, *63*(5), pp. 902–04. [G: U.S.]

Walsh, Lorena S. Discussion [White Servitude and the Growth of Black Slavery in Colonial America]. *J. Econ. Hist.*, March 1981, *41*(1), pp. 48–49. [G: U.S.]

Wellenreuther, Hermann. Labor in the Era of the American Revolution: A Discussion of Recent Concepts and Theories. *Labor Hist.*, Fall 1981, *22*(4), pp. 573–600. [G: U.S.]

Wright, Gavin. Black and White Labor in the Old New South. In *Bateman, F., ed.*, 1981, pp. 35–50. [G: U.S.]

Wright, Gavin. Cheap Labor and Southern Textiles, 1880–1930. *Quart. J. Econ.*, November 1981, *96*(4), pp. 605–29. [G: U.S.]

0423 History of Public Economic Policy (all levels)

Aduddell, Robert M. and Cain, Louis P. Public Policy toward "The Greatest Trust in the World." *Bus. Hist. Rev.*, Summer 1981, *55*(2), pp. 217–42. [G: U.S.]

Benston, George J. The Ideological Origins of the Revolution in American Financial Policies: Comments. In *Brunner, K., ed.*, 1981, pp. 253–57.

Berk, Gerald P. Approaches to the History of Regulation. In *McCraw, T. K., ed.*, 1981, pp. 187–204.

Black, Charles L., Jr. Perspectives on the American Common Market [Regulation and the American Common Market]. In *Tarlock, A. D., ed.*, 1981, pp. 59–66. [G: U.S.]

Bordo, Michael David. The Classical Gold Standard: Some Lessons for Today. *Fed. Res. Bank St. Louis Rev.*, May 1981, *63*(5), pp. 2–17. [G: U.K.; U.S.]

Braeutigam, Ronald R. The Deregulation of Natural Gas. In *Weiss, L. W. and Klass, M. W., eds.*, 1981, pp. 142–86. [G: U.S.]

Bryant, John. Bank Collapse and Depression. *J. Money, Credit, Banking*, November 1981, *13*(4), pp. 454–64. [G: U.S.]

Buenker, John D. The Ratification of the Federal Income Tax Amendment. *Cato J.*, Spring 1981, *1*(1), pp. 183–223. [G: U.S.]

Cagan, Phillip. Some Macroeconomic Impacts of the

National Industrial Recovery Act, 1933–35: Comments. In *Brunner, K., ed.*, 1981, pp. 282–85.
[G: U.S.]

Carlson, Leonard A. Land Allotment and the Decline of American Indian Farming. *Exploration Econ. Hist.*, April 1981, *18*(2), pp. 128–54.
[G: U.S.]

Conley, John A. Revising Conceptions about the Origin of Prisons: The Importance of Economic Considerations. *Soc. Sci. Quart.*, June 1981, *62*(2), pp. 247–58.
[G: U.S.]

Cox, Charles C. Monopoly Explanations of the Great Depression and Public Policies toward Business. In *Brunner, K., ed.*, 1981, pp. 174–207.
[G: U.S.]

Ekirch, Arthur A., Jr. The Sixteenth Amendment: The Historical Background. *Cato J.*, Spring 1981, *1*(1), pp. 161–82.
[G: U.S.]

Fisher, Glenn W. The Changing Role of Property Taxation. In *Walzer, N. and Chicoine, D. L., eds.*, 1981, pp. 37–60.
[G: U.S.]

Fisher, Louis. Developing Fiscal Responsibility. In *Pious, R. M., ed.*, 1981, pp. 62–75.
[G: U.S.]

Green, George D. The Ideological Origins of the Revolution in American Financial Policies. In *Brunner, K., ed.*, 1981, pp. 220–52.

Harris, William H. Federal Intervention in Union Discrimination: FEPC and West Coast Shipyards during World War II. *Labor Hist.*, Summer 1981, *22*(3), pp. 325–47.
[G: U.S.]

Hawley, Ellis. Three Facets of Hooverian Associationalism: Lumber, Aviation, and Movies, 1921–1930. In *McCraw, T. K., ed.*, 1981, pp. 95–123.
[G: U.S.]

Hays, Samuel P. Political Choice in Regulatory Administration. In *McCraw, T. K., ed.*, 1981, pp. 124–54.
[G: U.S.]

Howe, Charles W. Guidelines for a Responsible Natural Resources Policy. In *[Weiler, E. T.]*, 1981, pp. 131–51.
[G: U.S.]

Jackson, Kenneth T. The Spatial Dimensions of Social Control: Race, Ethnicity, and Government Housing Policy in the United States, 1918–1968. In *Stave, B. M., ed.*, 1981, pp. 79–128.
[G: U.S.]

James, John A. The Optimal Tariff in the Antebellum United States. *Amer. Econ. Rev.*, September 1981, *71*(4), pp. 726–34.
[G: U.S.]

Keeler, Theodore E. The Revolution in Airline Regulation. In *Weiss, L. W. and Klass, M. W., eds.*, 1981, pp. 53–85.
[G: U.S.]

Keller, Morton. The Pluralist State: American Economic Regulation in Comparative Perspective, 1900–1930. In *McCraw, T. K., ed.*, 1981, pp. 56–94.
[G: U.S.]

Kitch, Edmund W. Regulation and the American Common Market. In *Tarlock, A. D., ed.*, 1981, pp. 9–55.
[G: U.S.]

Libecap, Gary D. Bureaucratic Opposition to the Assignment of Property Rights: Overgrazing on the Western Range. *J. Econ. Hist.*, March 1981, *41*(1), pp. 151–58.
[G: U.S.]

Marcuse, Peter A. Class Tension and the Mechanisms of Social Control: The Housing Experience: Comment. In *Stave, B. M., ed.*, 1981, pp. 175–81.
[G: Europe; U.S.]

Martin, George T., Jr. Historical Overview of Social Welfare. In *Martin, G. T., Jr., and Zald, M. N., eds.*, 1981, pp. 11–17.
[G: Europe; U.S.]

Mayer, Thomas. Monopoly Explanations of the Great Depression and Public Policies toward Business: Comments. In *Brunner, K., ed.*, 1981, pp. 211–19.

McCraw, Thomas K. Rethinking the Trust Question. In *McCraw, T. K., ed.*, 1981, pp. 1–55.
[G: U.S.]

McGraw, Thomas K. Discussion [The Response of the Giant Corporations to Wage and Price Controls in World War II] [Planning for Peace: The Surplus Property Act of 1944]. *J. Econ. Hist.*, March 1981, *41*(1), pp. 136–37.
[G: U.S.]

North, Douglass C. An Economist's Perspective on the American Common Market [Regulation and the American Common Market]. In *Tarlock, A. D., ed.*, 1981, pp. 77–81.
[G: U.S.]

Officer, Lawrence H. The Floating Dollar in the Greenback Period: A Test of Theories of Exchange-Rate Determination. *J. Econ. Hist.*, September 1981, *41*(3), pp. 629–50.
[G: U.S.]

Pierce, James L. The Ideological Origins of the Revolution in American Financial Policies: Comments. In *Brunner, K., ed.*, 1981, pp. 258–61.

Pincus, Jonathan J. Discussion [Government Policy and Economic Development in Germany and Japan: A Skeptical Reevaluation] [Bureaucratic Opposition to the Assignment of Property Rights: Overgrazing on the Western Range]. *J. Econ. Hist.*, March 1981, *41*(1), pp. 159–61.
[G: Germany; Japan; U.S.]

Poole, William. Monopoly Explanations of the Great Depression and Public Policies toward Business: Comments. In *Brunner, K., ed.*, 1981, pp. 208–10.

Rockoff, Hugh. Price and Wage Controls in Four Wartime Periods. *J. Econ. Hist.*, June 1981, *41*(2), pp. 381–401.
[G: U.S.]

Rockoff, Hugh. The Response of the Giant Corporations to Wage and Price Controls in World War II. *J. Econ. Hist.*, March 1981, *41*(1), pp. 123–28.
[G: U.S.]

Rosen, Christine M. Class Tension and the Mechanisms of Social Control: The Housing Experience: Comment. In *Stave, B. M., ed.*, 1981, pp. 165–75.

Schwartz, Gary T. Tort Law and the Economy in Nineteenth-Century America: A Reinterpretation. *Yale Law J.*, July 1981, *90*(8), pp. 1717–75.
[G: U.S.]

St. Clair, David J. The Motorization and Decline of Urban Public Transit, 1935–1950. *J. Econ. Hist.*, September 1981, *41*(3), pp. 579–600.
[G: U.S.]

Stoff, Michael B. The Anglo-American Oil Agreement and the Wartime Search for Foreign Oil Policy. *Bus. Hist. Rev.*, Spring 1981, *55*(1), pp. 59–74.
[G: U.S.]

Tedlow, Richard S. From Competitor to Consumer: The Changing Focus of Federal Regulation of Advertising, 1914–1938. *Bus. Hist. Rev.*, Spring 1981, *55*(1), pp. 35–58.
[G: U.S.]

Timberlake, Richard H., Jr. The Significance of Unaccounted Currencies. *J. Econ. Hist.*, December 1981, *41*(4), pp. 853–66.   **[G: U.S.]**

Vasey, Wayne. Recurring Themes in the Income Support Policy Debate— Obstacles to Change. **In** *Brown, P. G.; Johnson, C. and Vernier, P., eds.*, 1981, pp. 283–303.   **[G: U.S.]**

Vogel, David. The "New" Social Regulation in Historical and Comparative Perspective. **In** *McCraw, T. K., ed.*, 1981, pp. 155–85.   **[G: U.S.]**

Wallis, John Joseph and Benjamin, Daniel K. Public Relief and Private Employment in the Great Depression. *J. Econ. Hist.*, March 1981, *41*(1), pp. 97–102.   **[G: U.S.]**

Warburton, Clark. Monetary Disequilibrium Theory in the First Half of the Twentieth Century. *Hist. Polit. Econ.*, Summer 1981, *13*(2), pp. 285–99.   **[G: U.S.]**

Weidenbaum, Murray L. The New Regulation and the American Common Market [Regulation and the American Common Market]. **In** *Tarlock, A. D., ed.*, 1981, pp. 83–92.   **[G: U.S.]**

Weinstein, Michael M. Some Macroeconomic Impacts of the National Industrial Recovery Act, 1933–1935. **In** *Brunner, K., ed.*, 1981, pp. 262–81.   **[G: U.S.]**

White, Eugene Nelson. State-Sponsored Insurance of Bank Deposits in the United States, 1907–1929. *J. Econ. Hist.*, September 1981, *41*(3), pp. 537–57.   **[G: U.S.]**

043 Economic History: Ancient and Medieval (until 1453)

0430 General

Abulafia, David Samuel Harrard. Southern Italy and the Florentine Economy, 1265–1370. *Econ. Hist. Rev., 2nd Ser.*, August 1981, *34*(3), pp. 377–88.   **[G: Italy]**

Anderson, J. L. Climatic Change in European Economic History. **In** *Uselding, P., ed.*, 1981, pp. 1–34.   **[G: Europe]**

Copeland, Morris A. Bank Demand Deposit Currency before 1700 A.D. **In** *Copeland, M. A.*, 1981, pp. 163–74.

Copeland, Morris A. Bank Deposit Currency before A.D. 1700. **In** *Uselding, P., ed.*, 1981, pp. 245–54.

Copeland, Morris A. Concerning the Origin of a Money Economy. **In** *Copeland, M. A.*, 1981, *1974*, pp. 8–28.

Copeland, Morris A. Developments in Military Technology and Government Organization in the Ancient Near East. **In** *Copeland, M. A.*, 1981, pp. 64–129.   **[G: Middle East]**

Copeland, Morris A. Foreign Exchange in the Eastern Mediterranean in the Fourth Century B.C. **In** *Copeland, M. A.*, 1981, *1977*, pp. 130–46.   **[G: Greece]**

Copeland, Morris A. Health Care in Ancient Times. **In** *Copeland, M. A.*, 1981, pp. 147–62.   **[G: Greece; Egypt]**

Copeland, Morris A. The Economies of Two Great Nonpecuniary Civilizations. **In** *Copeland, M. A.*, 1981, pp. 29–63.   **[G: Egypt; S. America]**

Fenton, Alexander J. Early Manuring Techniques.

In *Mercer, R., ed.*, 1981, pp. 210–17.   **[G: U.K.]**

Fowler, Peter. Wildscape to Landscape: 'Enclosure' in Prehistoric Britain. **In** *Mercer, R., ed.*, 1981, pp. 9–54.   **[G: U.K.]**

Golte, Jürgen. The Economy of the Inca State and the Notion of the AMP. **In** *Bailey, A. M. and Llobera, J. R., eds.*, 1981, pp. 290–300.   **[G: Peru]**

Halliday, S. P.; Hill, P. J. and Stevenson, J. B. Early Agriculture in Scotland. **In** *Mercer, R., ed.*, 1981, pp. 55–65.   **[G: U.K.]**

Hillman, Gordon. Reconstructing Crop Husbandry Practices from Charred Remains of Crops. **In** *Mercer, R., ed.*, 1981, pp. 123–62.   **[G: U.K.]**

Jewell, Peter. A Summing-Up. **In** *Mercer, R., ed.*, 1981, pp. 223–30.   **[G: U.K.]**

Klep, Paul M. M. Regional Disparities in Brabantine Urbanisation before and after the Industrial Revolution (1374–1970): Some Aspects of Measurement and Explanation. **In** *Bairoch, P. and Lévy-Leboyer, M., eds.*, 1981, pp. 259–69.   **[G: Belgium]**

Le, Thanh Khoi. A Contribution to the Study of the AMP: The Case of Ancient Vietnam. **In** *Bailey, A. M. and Llobera, J. R., eds.*, 1981, *1973*, pp. 281–89.   **[G: Vietnam]**

Legge, A. J. Aspects of Cattle Husbandry. **In** *Mercer, R., ed.*, 1981, pp. 169–81.   **[G: U.K.]**

Mercer, Roger. Farming Practice in British Prehistory: Introduction. **In** *Mercer, R., ed.*, 1981, pp. ix–xxvi.   **[G: U.K.]**

Mercer, Roger. Farming Practice in British Prehistory: Appendix. **In** *Mercer, R., ed.*, 1981, pp. 231–37.

Orrman, Eljas. The Progress of Settlement in Finland during the late Middle Ages. *Scand. Econ. Hist. Rev.*, 1981, *29*(2), pp. 129–43.   **[G: Finland]**

Peragallo, Edward. Closing Procedures in the 15th Century Ledger of Jachomo Badoer, A Venetian Merchant. *Accounting Rev.*, July 1981, *56*(3), pp. 587–95.

Rees, Sian. Agricultural Tools: Function and Use. **In** *Mercer, R., ed.*, 1981, pp. 66–84.   **[G: U.K.]**

Reynolds, Peter. Deadstock and Livestock. **In** *Mercer, R., ed.*, 1981, pp. 97–122.   **[G: U.K.]**

Ryder, Michael J. Livestock Products: Skins and Fleeces. **In** *Mercer, R., ed.*, 1981, pp. 182–209.   **[G: U.K.]**

Schremmer, Eckart. Proto-Industrialisation: A Step towards Industrialisation? *J. Europ. Econ. Hist.*, Winter 1981, *10*(3), pp. 653–70.   **[G: Germany]**

Stuard, Susan Mosher. Dowry Increase and Increments in Wealth in Medieval Ragusa (Dubrovnik). *J. Econ. Hist.*, December 1981, *41*(4), pp. 795–811.   **[G: Yugoslavia]**

Topolski, Jerzy. Continuity and Discontinuity in the Development of the Feudal System in Eastern Europe (Xth to XVIIth Centuries). *J. Europ. Econ. Hist.*, Fall 1981, *10*(2), pp. 373–400.   **[G: E. Europe]**

Wittfogel, Karl. The Stages of Development in Chinese Economic and Social History. **In** *Bailey, A. M. and Llobera, J. R., eds.*, 1981, *1935*, pp. 113–40.   **[G: China]**

043 Economic History: Ancient and Medieval (until 1453)

0431 History of Product Prices and Markets

Childs, W. R. England's Iron Trade in the Fifteenth Century. *Econ. Hist. Rev.*, *2nd Ser.*, February 1981, *34*(1), pp. 25–47. [G: U.K.]

0432 History of Factor Prices and Markets

Jones, Ernest D. Some Reasons Behind Land Transfers Involving East Anglian Freemen in the Thirteenth Century. *Australian Econ. Hist. Rev.*, September 1981, *21*(2), pp. 147–62. [G: U.K.]

0433 History of Public Economic Policy (all levels)

Larson, Olaf F. Agricultural Policies for Growth and Equity: The Perspective of the American Experience. In *Sarma, J. S.*, 1981, pp. 70–76. [G: U.S.]

von Stromer, Wolfgang. Commercial Policy and Economic Conjuncture in Nuremberg at the Close of the Middle Ages: A Model of Economic Policy. *J. Europ. Econ. Hist.*, Spring 1981, *10*(1), pp. 119–29. [G: Germany]

044 Economic History: Europe

0440 General

Adams, Thomas M. From Old Regime to New: Business, Bureaucracy, and Social Change in Eighteenth-Century France—A Review Article. *Bus. Hist. Rev.*, Winter 1981, *55*(4), pp. 541–61. [G: France]

Alba, Victor. Spain. In *Blum, A. A., ed.*, 1981, pp. 515–37. [G: Spain]

Aldcroft, Derek H. McCloskey on Victorian Growth: A Comment. In *McCloskey, D. N.*, 1981, pp. 111–15. [G: U.K.]

Alford, B. W. E. New Industries for Old? British Industry between the Wars. In *Floud, R. and McCloskey, D., eds.*, Vol. 2, 1981, pp. 308–31. [G: U.K.]

Anderson, J. L. Climatic Change in European Economic History. In *Uselding, P., ed.*, 1981, pp. 1–34. [G: Europe]

Armstrong, John and Hannam, June. List of Publications on the Economic and Social History of Great Britain and Ireland. *Econ. Hist. Rev.*, *2nd Ser.*, November 1981, *34*(4), pp. 598–642. [G: U.K.]

Armstrong, W. A. The Trend of Mortality in Carlisle between the 1780s and the 1840s: A Demographic Contribution to the Standard of Living Debate. *Econ. Hist. Rev.*, *2nd Ser.*, February 1981, *34*(1), pp. 94–114. [G: U.K.]

Auffret, Marc; Hau, Michel and Lévy-Leboyer, Maurice. Regional Inequalities and Economic Development: French Agriculture in the Nineteenth and Twentieth Centuries. In *Bairoch, P. and Lévy-Leboyer, M., eds.*, 1981, pp. 273–89. [G: France]

Baker-Lampe, Anita B. Discussion [The Development of the Peasant Commune in Russia]. *J. Econ. Hist.*, March 1981, *41*(1), pp. 185–86. [G: U.S.S.R.]

Becker, Walter. Methodological Aspects in Describing the Bourgeois and Industrial Revolutions. In *Bairoch, P. and Lévy-Leboyer, M., eds.*, 1981, pp. 131–36. [G: Europe]

Bédarida, François and Sutcliffe, Anthony R. The Street in the Structure and Life of the City: Reflections on Nineteenth-Century London and Paris. In *Stave, B. M., ed.*, 1981, *1980*, pp. 21–38. [G: U.K.; France]

Bordo, Michael David. The U.K. Money Supply 1870–1914. In *Uselding, P., ed.*, 1981, pp. 107–25. [G: U.K.]

Bordo, Michael David and Schwartz, Anna J. Money and Prices in the 19th Century: Was Thomas Tooke Right? *Exploration Econ. Hist.*, April 1981, *18*(2), pp. 97–127. [G: U.S.; U.K.]

Bridbury, A. R. English Provincial Towns in the Later Middle Ages. *Econ. Hist. Rev.*, *2nd Ser.*, February 1981, *34*(1), pp. 1–24. [G: U.K.]

Briggs, Asa. Social History 1900–45. In *Floud, R. and McCloskey, D., eds.*, Vol. 2, 1981, pp. 347–69. [G: U.K.]

Buchheim, Christoph. Aspects of XIXth Century Anglo-German Trade Rivalry Reconsidered. *J. Europ. Econ. Hist.*, Fall 1981, *10*(2), pp. 273–89. [G: U.K.; W. Germany]

Cameron, Rondo. Economic Relations of France with Central and Eastern Europe, 1800–1914. *J. Europ. Econ. Hist.*, Winter 1981, *10*(3), pp. 537–52. [G: France]

Carter, Ian. The Scottish Peasantry. In *Samuel, R., ed.*, 1981, pp. 85–92. [G: U.K.]

Coquery-Vidrovitch, Catherine. Industry and Empire: The Beginnings of French Industrial Politics in the Colonies under the Vichy Regime. In *Bairoch, P. and Lévy-Leboyer, M., eds.*, 1981, pp. 29–33. [G: France; Selected LDCs]

Crafts, N. F. R. The Eighteenth Century: A Survey. In *Floud, R. and McCloskey, D., eds.*, Vol. 1, 1981, pp. 1–16. [G: U.K.]

Crafts, N. F. R. Victorian Britain Did Fail. In *McCloskey, D. N.*, 1981, *1978*, pp. 126–31. [G: U.K.]

Davis, Lance E. and Huttenback, Robert A. In Search of the Historical Imperialist. In *[Weiler, E. T.]*, 1981, pp. 152–67. [G: U.K.]

Del Treppo, Mario. Federigo Melis and the Renaissance Economy. *J. Europ. Econ. Hist.*, Winter 1981, *10*(3), pp. 709–42.

Drummond, I. Britain and the World Economy 1900–45. In *Floud, R. and McCloskey, D., eds.*, Vol. 2, 1981, pp. 286–307. [G: U.K.]

Feinstein, C. H. Capital Accumulation and the Industrial Revolution. In *Floud, R. and McCloskey, D., eds.*, Vol. 1, 1981, pp. 128–42. [G: U.K.]

Feldenkirchen, Wilfried. The Banks and the Steel Industry in the Ruhr: Developments in Relations from 1873 to 1914. In *Engels, W. and Pohl, H., eds.*, 1981, pp. 27–51. [G: W. Germany]

Feldman, Gerald D. German Interest Group Alliances in War and Inflation, 1914–23. In *Berger, S., ed.*, 1981, pp. 159–84. [G: Germany]

Floud, R. C. Britain 1860–1914: A Survey. In *Floud, R. and McCloskey, D., eds.*, Vol. 2, 1981, pp. 1–26. [G: U.K.]

Ford, A. G. The Trade Cycle in Britain 1860–1914. In *Floud, R. and McCloskey, D., eds.*, Vol. 2, 1981, pp. 27–49. [G: U.K.]

Fowler, Peter. Wildscape to Landscape: 'Enclosure' in Prehistoric Britain. In *Mercer, R., ed.,* 1981, pp. 9–54. **[G: U.K.]**

Freudenberger, Herman and Mensch, Gerhard. Regional Differences, Differential Development and Generative Regional Growth. In *Bairoch, P. and Lévy-Leboyer, M., eds.,* 1981, pp. 199–209. **[G: Czechoslovakia]**

Galenson, David W. Literacy and Age in Preindustrial England: Quantitative Evidence and Implications. *Econ. Develop. Cult. Change,* July 1981, 29(4), pp. 813–29. **[G: U.K.]**

Gatrell, Peter. The Impact of War on Russian and Soviet Development, 1850–1950. *World Devel.,* August 1981, 9(8), pp. 793–802. **[G: U.S.S.R.]**

Gelb, Michael. Roots of Soviet Industrial Management, 1917–1941. *Rev. Radical Polit. Econ.,* Spring 1981, 13(1), pp. 55–66. **[G: U.S.S.R.]**

Gerriets, Marilyn. The Organization of Exchange in Early Christian Ireland. *J. Econ. Hist.,* March 1981, 41(1), pp. 171–76. **[G: Ireland]**

Gilb, Corinne Lathrop. Public or Private Governments? In *Nystrom, P. C. and Starbuck, W. H., eds., Vol. 2,* 1981, pp. 464–91. **[G: U.S.; W. Europe]**

Gömmel, R. The Development of a Growth Pole in the Nineteenth Century Illustrated by the Example of Nuremberg. In *Bairoch, P. and Lévy-Leboyer, M., eds.,* 1981, pp. 210–15. **[G: Germany]**

Good, David F. Economic Integration and Regional Development in Austria-Hungary, 1867–1913. In *Bairoch, P. and Lévy-Leboyer, M., eds.,* 1981, pp. 137–50. **[G: Austria; Hungary]**

Gregory, Paul R. Economic Growth and Structural Change in Czarist Russia and the Soviet Union: A Long-term Comparison. In *[Bergson, A.],* 1981, pp. 25–52. **[G: U.S.S.R.; OECD]**

Harley, C. K. and McCloskey, D. N. Foreign Trade: Competition and the Expanding International Economy. In *Floud, R. and McCloskey, D., eds., Vol. 2,* 1981, pp. 50–69. **[G: U.K.]**

Hause, Steven C. and Kenney, Anne R. The Limits of Suffragist Behavior: Legalism and Militancy in France, 1876–1922. *Amer. Hist. Rev.,* October 1981, 86(4), pp. 781–806. **[G: France]**

Hawke, G. R. and Higgins, J. P. P. Transport and Social Overhead Capital. In *Floud, R. and McCloskey, D., eds., Vol. 1,* 1981, pp. 227–52. **[G: U.K.]**

Haywood, Richard Mowbray. The Development of Steamboats on the Volga River and Its Tributaries, 1817–1856. In *Uselding, P., ed.,* 1981, pp. 127–92. **[G: U.S.S.R.]**

Henderson, W. O. Friedrich List and the Social Question. *J. Europ. Econ. Hist.,* Winter 1981, 10(3), pp. 697–708.

Henning, Hansjoachim. The Social Integration of Entrepreneurs in Westphalia 1860–1914. In *Engels, W. and Pohl, H., eds.,* 1981, pp. 83–106. **[G: W. Germany]**

Hobza, Jaroslav. Sixty Years of Struggle for Social and Economic Development. *Czech. Econ. Digest.,* September 1981, (6), pp. 3–26. **[G: Czechoslovakia]**

Howson, S. Slump and Unemployment. In *Floud,*

R. and McCloskey, D., eds., Vol. 2, 1981, pp. 265–85. **[G: U.K.]**

Hughes, Jonathan. Professor Hobsbawm on the Evolution of Modern Capitalism. In *[Weiler, E. T.],* 1981, pp. 168–87. **[G: U.K.]**

Hutchison, Terence W. The Changing Intellectual Climate In Economics. In *Seldon, A., ed.,* 1981, pp. 19–49. **[G: U.K.]**

Ignatieff, Michael. Primitive Accumulation Revisited. In *Samuel, R., ed.,* 1981, pp. 130–35. **[G: U.K.]**

Islamoglu, Huri and Keyder, Caglar. The Ottoman Social Formation. In *Bailey, A. M. and Llobera, J. R., eds.,* 1981, 1977, pp. 301–24. **[G: Ottoman Empire]**

Johnson, H. Thomas. Toward a New Understanding of Nineteenth-Century Cost Accounting. *Accounting Rev.,* July 1981, 56(3), pp. 510–18. **[G: U.K.; U.S.]**

Kahk, J. and Koval'chenko, I. D. Regional Differences in the Position of Peasants in the European Part of Russia in the Nineteenth Century. In *Bairoch, P. and Lévy-Leboyer, M., eds.,* 1981, pp. 244–47. **[G: U.S.S.R.]**

Kaser, Michael C. From Versailles to Helsinki: Structural Change in the Economies of Eastern Europe. *Acta Oecon.,* 1981, 27(3–4), pp. 343–50. **[G: E. Europe]**

Kindleberger, Charles P. Historical Perspective on the Decline in U.S. Productivity. In *Hogan, J. D. and Craig, A. M., eds., Vol. 1,* 1981, pp. 715–24. **[G: U.K.; U.S.]**

Kirchner, Walther. Russian Tariffs and Foreign Industries before 1914: The German Entrepreneur's Perspective. *J. Econ. Hist.,* June 1981, 41(2), pp. 361–79. **[G: U.S.S.R.; Germany]**

Klep, Paul M. M. Regional Disparities in Brabantine Urbanisation before and after the Industrial Revolution (1374–1970): Some Aspects of Measurement and Explanation. In *Bairoch, P. and Lévy-Leboyer, M., eds.,* 1981, pp. 259–69. **[G: Belgium]**

Kocka, Jürgen. Capitalism and Bureaucracy in German Industrialization before 1914. *Econ. Hist. Rev., 2nd Ser.,* August 1981, 34(3), pp. 453–68. **[G: W. Germany]**

Kocka, Jürgen. The Entrepreneur, the Family and Capitalism: Some Examples from the Early Phase of Industrialisation in Germany. In *Engels, W. and Pohl, H., eds.,* 1981, pp. 53–82. **[G: W. Germany]**

Komlos, John. Economic Growth and Industrialization in Hungary, 1830–1913. *J. Europ. Econ. Hist.,* Spring 1981, 10(1), pp. 5–46. **[G: Hungary]**

Krantz, Olle and Nilsson, Carl-Axel. National Product Series in Historical Analysis: A Case Study of Sweden, 1861–1975. In *Bairoch, P. and Lévy-Leboyer, M., eds.,* 1981, pp. 411–19. **[G: Sweden]**

Kriedte, Peter. Proto-Industrialization between Industrialization and De-Industrialization. In *Kriedte, P.; Medick, H. and Schlumbohm, J.,* 1981, pp. 135–60. **[G: Europe]**

Kriedte, Peter. The Origins, the Agrarian Context, and the Conditions in the World Market. In

Kriedte, P.; Medick, H. and Schlumbohm, J.,
1981, pp. 12–37.   [G: Europe]

Lee, Clive Howard. Regional Growth and Structural
Change in Victorian Britain. *Econ. Hist. Rev.,*
2nd Ser., August 1981, *34*(3), pp. 438–52.
[G: U.K.]

Lee, Geoffrey A. The Francis Willughby Executorship Accounts, 1672–1682: An Early Double-
Entry System in England. *Accounting Rev.,* July
1981, *56*(3), pp. 539–53.   [G: U.K.]

Lee, R. D. and Schofield, R. S. British Population
in the Eighteenth Century. In *Floud, R. and*
McCloskey, D., eds., Vol. 1, 1981, pp. 17–35.
[G: U.K.]

Lesnodorski, Boguslaw. On Some Values of Enlightenment in Poland. In *[Lipiński, E.],* 1981, pp.
39–52.   [G: Poland]

Lincoln, Andrew. Through the Undergrowth: Capitalist Development and Social Formation in Nineteenth-Century France. In *Samuel, R., ed.,* 1981,
pp. 255–67.   [G: France]

Locke, Robert R. French Industrialization: The
Roehl Thesis Reconsidered [French Industrializa-
tion: A Reconsideration]. *Exploration Econ.*
Hist., October 1981, *18*(4), pp. 415–33.
[G: France]

Maier, Charles S. "Fictitious Bonds...of Wealth and
Law": On the Theory and Practice of Interest
Representation. In *Berger, S., ed.,* 1981, pp. 27–
61.   [G: W. Europe]

Maier, Charles S. The Two Postwar Eras and the
Conditions for Stability in Twentieth-Century
Western Europe. *Amer. Hist. Rev.,* April 1981,
86(2), pp. 327–52.   [G: W. Europe]

Major, J. Russell. Noble Income, Inflation, and the
Wars of Religion in France. *Amer. Hist. Rev.,*
February 1981, *86*(1), pp. 21–48.   [G: France]

Marcuse, Peter A. Class Tension and the Mechanisms of Social Control: The Housing Experience:
Comment. In *Stave, B. M., ed.,* 1981, pp. 175–
81.   [G: Europe; U.S.]

Mayer, Jean. Regional Development in Portugal
(1929–1977): An Assessment. In *Bairoch, P. and*
Lévy-Leboyer, M., eds., 1981, pp. 331–45.
[G: Portugal]

Mazoyer, Marcel L. Origins and Mechanisms of Reproduction of the Regional Discrepancies in Agricultural Development in Europe. *Europ. Rev.*
Agr. Econ., 1981, *8*(2–3), pp. 177–96.
[G: Europe]

McCloskey, Donald N. Did Victorian Britain Fail?
In *McCloskey, D. N.,* 1981, *1970,* pp. 94–110.
[G: U.K.]

McCloskey, Donald N. From Dependence to Autonomy: Judgments on Trade as an Engine of British
Growth. In *McCloskey, D. N.,* 1981, pp. 139–
54.   [G: U.K.]

McCloskey, Donald N. Magnanimous Albion: Free
Trade and British National Income, 1841–1881.
In *McCloskey, D. N.,* 1981, *1980,* pp. 155–72.
[G: U.K.]

McCloskey, Donald N. No It Did Not: A Reply to
Crafts. In *McCloskey, D. N.,* 1981, *1978,* pp. 131–
35.   [G: U.K.]

McCloskey, Donald N. The Industrial Revolution
1780–1860: A Survey. In *Floud, R. and McClos-*

key, D., eds., Vol. 1, 1981, pp. 103–27.
[G: U.K.]

McCloskey, Donald N. Victorian Growth: A Rejoinder to Derek Aldcroft. In *McCloskey, D. N.,*
1981, *1974,* pp. 115–19.   [G: U.K.]

McCloskey, Donald N. and Sandberg, Lars G. From
Damnation to Redemption: Judgments on the
Late Victorian Entrepreneur. In *McCloskey,*
D. N., 1981, *1971,* pp. 55–72.   [G: U.K.]

McCloskey, Donald N. and Zecher, J. Richard. How
the Gold Standard Worked, 1880–1913. In
McCloskey, D. N., 1981, *1976,* pp. 184–208.
[G: U.K.; U.S.; Sweden; Germany]

McCusker, John J. The Tonnage of Ships Engaged
in British Colonial Trade during the Eighteenth
Century. In *Uselding, P., ed.,* 1981, pp. 73–105.
[G: U.K.]

McGowan, Patrick J. Imperialism in World-System
Perspective. In *Hollist, W. L. and Rosenau,*
J. N., eds., 1981, pp. 54–79.   [G: U.K.]

Medick, Hans. The Proto-Industrial Family Economy. In *Kriedte, P.; Medick, H. and Schlum-*
bohm, J., 1981, pp. 38–73.   [G: Europe]

Medick, Hans. The Structures and Function of Population-Development under the Protoindustrial
System. In *Kriedte, P.; Medick, H. and Schlum-*
bohm, J., 1981, pp. 74–93.   [G: Europe]

Mendels, Franklin F. Agriculture and Peasant Industry in Eighteenth-Century Flanders. In *Kriedte,*
P.; Medick, H. and Schlumbohm, J., 1981, pp.
161–77.   [G: Belgium; France; Netherlands]

Meyers, Frederic. France. In *Blum, A. A., ed.,*
1981, pp. 169–208.   [G: France]

Modell, John and Lees, Lynn H. The Irish Countryman Urbanized: A Comparative Perspective on
the Famine Migration. In *Hershberg, T., ed.,*
1981, *1977,* pp. 351–67.   [G: U.S.; U.K.]

Mokyr, Joel. Discussion [The Organization of Exchange in Early Christian Ireland] [Discouraging
the Use of a Common Resource: The Crees of
Saskatchewan]. *J. Econ. Hist.,* March 1981, *41*(1),
pp. 177–78.   [G: Canada; Ireland]

Mokyr, Joel. Industrialization in Two Languages.
Econ. Hist. Rev., 2nd Ser., February 1981, *34*(1),
pp. 143–49.   [G: Netherlands; Belgium]

Moore, Gerry. Socio-Economic Aspects of Anti-Sem-
itism in Ireland, 1880–1905. *Econ. Soc. Rev.,*
April 1981, *12*(3), pp. 187–201.   [G: Ireland]

Morineau, Michel. History and Tithes. *J. Europ.*
Econ. Hist., Fall 1981, *10*(2), pp. 437–80.
[G: France; U.K.]

Mosk, Carl. The Evolution of Premodern Demo-
graphic Regimes: A Research Note. *Exploration*
Econ. Hist., April 1981, *18*(2), pp. 199–208.
[G: Sweden; Japan]

Nazarenko, Victor J. Origins and Mechanisms of Reproduction of the Regional Discrepancies in Agricultural Development in Europe: Comment.
Europ. Rev. Agr. Econ., 1981, *8*(2–3), pp. 197–
98.   [G: Europe]

Niethammer, Lutz. Some Elements of the Housing
Reform Debate in Nineteenth-Century Europe:
Or, On the Making of a New Paradigm of Social
Control. In *Stave, B. M., ed.,* 1981, pp. 129–
64.   [G: Europe]

Orridge, Andrew W. Who Supported the Land War?

An Aggregate-Data Analysis of Irish Agrarian Discontent, 1879–1882. *Econ. Soc. Rev.*, April 1981, *12*(3), pp. 203–33. [G: Ireland]

Parker, R. H. The Third International Congress of Accounting Historians. *J. Europ. Econ. Hist.*, Winter 1981, *10*(3), pp. 743–54.

Payne, Adrian F. T. Options, Premium Contracts, and the EOE. *De Economist*, 1981, *129*(2), pp. 224–40. [G: Netherlands]

Payne, Geoff; Ford, Graeme and Ulas, Marion. Occupational Change and Social Mobility in Scotland Since the First World War. In *Gaskin, M., ed.,* 1981, pp. 200–17. [G: U.K.]

Perkins, J. A. The Agricultural Revolution in Germany, 1850–1914. *J. Europ. Econ. Hist.*, Spring 1981, *10*(1), pp. 71–118. [G: Germany]

Phelps Brown, Henry. The Economic Consequences of Collective Bargaining. In *Phelps Brown, H. and Hopkins, S. V.,* 1981, *1966*, pp. 191–214. [G: OECD]

Phelps Brown, Henry and Handfield-Jones, S. J. The Climacteric of the 1890's: A Study in the Expanding Economy. In *Phelps Brown, H. and Hopkins, S. V.,* 1981, *1952*, pp. 131–72. [G: U.K.; OECD]

Phelps Brown, Henry and Ozga, S. A. Economic Growth and the Price Level. In *Phelps Brown, H. and Hopkins, S. V.,* 1981, *1955*, pp. 173–90. [G: U.K.]

Pollard, Sidney. Sheffield and Sweet Auburn—Amenities and Living Standards in the British Industrial Revolution: A Comment. *J. Econ. Hist.*, December 1981, *41*(4), pp. 902–04. [G: U.K.]

Porter, Andrew. Britain, the Cape Colony, and Natal, 1870–1914: Capital, Shipping, and the Imperial Connexion. *Econ. Hist. Rev., 2nd Ser.,* November 1981, *34*(4), pp. 554–77. [G: U.K.; S. Africa]

Pound, J. F. The Validity of the Freemen's Lists: Some Norwich Evidence. *Econ. Hist. Rev., 2nd Ser.,* February 1981, *34*(1), pp. 48–59. [G: U.K.]

Ránki, György. On the Economic Development of the Habsburg Monarchy. In *Bairoch, P. and Lévy-Leboyer, M., eds.,* 1981, pp. 165–74. [G: Austria; Hungary]

Ringrose, David R. Madrid and the Castilian Economy. *J. Europ. Econ. Hist.*, Fall 1981, *10*(2), pp. 481–90. [G: Spain]

Roehl, Richard. French Industrialization: A Reply [French Industrialization: A Reconsideration]. *Exploration Econ. Hist.*, October 1981, *18*(4), pp. 434–35. [G: France]

Roehl, Richard. Medieval Texts: A Review Article. *J. Econ. Hist.*, June 1981, *41*(2), pp. 408–10.

Rose, M. E. Social Change and the Industrial Revolution. In *Floud, R. and McCloskey, D., eds.,* Vol. 1, 1981, pp. 253–75. [G: U.K.]

Rosen, Christine M. Class Tension and the Mechanisms of Social Control: The Housing Experience: Comment. In *Stave, B. M., ed.,* 1981, pp. 165–75.

Rosen, Marvin. The Dictatorship of the Bougeoisie: England, 1688–1721. *Sci. Soc.*, Spring 1981, *45*(1), pp. 24–51. [G: U.K.]

Rosenberg, William G. The Democratization of Rus-

sia's Railroads in 1917. *Amer. Hist. Rev.*, December 1981, *86*(5), pp. 983–1008. [G: U.S.S.R.]

Rowley-Conwy, P. Slash and Burn in the Temperate European Neolithic. In *Mercer, R., ed.,* 1981, pp. 85–96. [G: U.K.]

Sakai, Akihiro. Popular Education and the Industrial Revolution: A Study on the Intellectual Origins of Industrialization in England. (In Japanese. With English summary.) *Osaka Econ. Pap.*, June 1981, *31*(1), pp. 73–97. [G: U.K.]

Sandberg, Lars G. The Entrepreneur and Technological Change. In *Floud, R. and McCloskey, D., eds.,* Vol. 2, 1981, pp. 99–120. [G: U.K.]

Sarnat, Marshall and Engelhardt, Annerose. The Pattern of Risk and Return in Germany, Selected Industries, 1928–1976. *Konjunkturpolitik*, 1981, *27*(2), pp. 105–25. [G: W. Germany]

Schlumbohm, Jürgen. Excursus: The Political and Institutional Framework of Proto-Industrialization. In *Kriedte, P.; Medick, H. and Schlumbohm, J.,* 1981, pp. 126–34. [G: Europe]

Schlumbohm, Jürgen. Relations of Production—Productive Forces—Crises in Proto-Industrialization. In *Kriedte, P.; Medick, H. and Schlumbohm, J.,* 1981, pp. 94–125. [G: Europe]

Schneider, Jürgen. Terms of Trade between France and Latin America, 1826–1856: Causes of Increasing Economic Disparities? In *Bairoch, P. and Lévy-Leboyer, M., eds.,* 1981, pp. 110–119. [G: France; Latin America]

Schremmer, Eckart. Proto-Industrialisation: A Step towards Industrialisation? *J. Europ. Econ. Hist.*, Winter 1981, *10*(3), pp. 653–70. [G: Germany]

Slack, Paul. The Disappearance of Plague: An Alternative View: Comment. *Econ. Hist. Rev., 2nd Ser.,* August 1981, *34*(3), pp. 469–76. [G: Europe]

Smith, Richard M. Fertility, Economy, and Household Formation in England over Three Centuries. *Population Devel. Rev.*, December 1981, *7*(4), pp. 595–622. [G: U.K.]

Snell, Keith David Malcolm. Agricultural Seasonal Unemployment, the Standard of Living, and Women's Work in the South and East, 1690–1860. *Econ. Hist. Rev., 2nd Ser.,* August 1981, *34*(3), pp. 407–37. [G: U.K.]

Soltow, Lee. The Distribution of Property Values in England and Wales in 1798. *Econ. Hist. Rev., 2nd Ser.,* February 1981, *34*(1), pp. 60–70. [G: U.K.]

Soltow, Lee. The Distribution of Wealth in Belgium in 1814–1815. *J. Europ. Econ. Hist.*, Fall 1981, *10*(2), pp. 401–13. [G: Belgium]

Soltow, Lee. Wealth Distribution in Finland in 1800. *Scand. Econ. Hist. Rev.*, 1981, *29*(1), pp. 21–32. [G: Finland; Norway]

Soubeyroux, Nicole. The Spread of Agricultural Growth over the Departments of France from the Mid-nineteenth to the Mid-twentieth Century. In *Bairoch, P. and Lévy-Leboyer, M., eds.,* 1981, pp. 290–301. [G: France]

Southern, David B. The Impact of the Inflation: Inflation, the Courts and Revaluation. In *Bessel, R. and Feuchtwanger, E. J., eds.,* 1981, pp. 55–76. [G: Germany]

Teichova, Alice. Structural Change and Industrialisation in Inter-war Central-East Europe. In *Bairoch, P. and Lévy-Leboyer, M., eds.*, 1981, pp. 175–86.   [G: E. Europe]

Thane, P. Social History 1860–1914. In *Floud, R. and McCloskey, D., eds., Vol. 2*, 1981, pp. 198–238.   [G: U.K.]

Thomas, T. Aggregate Demand in the United Kingdom 1918–45. In *Floud, R. and McCloskey, D., eds., Vol. 2*, 1981, pp. 332–46.   [G: U.K.]

Thompson, Francis Michael Longstreth. Social Control in Victorian Britain. *Econ. Hist. Rev., 2nd Ser.*, May 1981, *34*(2), pp. 189–208.   [G: U.K.]

Toumanoff, Peter. The Development of the Peasant Commune in Russia. *J. Econ. Hist.*, March 1981, *41*(1), pp. 179–84.   [G: U.S.S.R.]

Toutain, Jean-Claude. The Uneven Growth of Regional Incomes in France from 1840–1970. In *Bairoch, P. and Lévy-Leboyer, M., eds.*, 1981, pp. 302–15.   [G: France]

von Tunzelmann, G. N. Britain 1900–45: A Survey. In *Floud, R. and McCloskey, D., eds., Vol. 2*, 1981, pp. 239–64.   [G: U.K.]

de Vries, Jan. Regional Economic Inequality in the Netherlands since 1600. In *Bairoch, P. and Lévy-Leboyer, M., eds.*, 1981, pp. 189–98.   [G: Netherlands]

Wallerstein, Immanuel and Kasaba, Reşat. Incorporation into the World-Economy: Change in the Structure of the Ottoman Empire, 1750–1839. *METU*, 1981, *8*(1 & 2), pp. 537–70.   [G: Turkey]

Williamson, Jeffrey G. Some Myths Die Hard—Urban Disamenities One More Time: A Reply. *J. Econ. Hist.*, December 1981, *41*(4), pp. 905–07.   [G: U.K.]

Williamson, Jeffrey G. Urban Disamenities, Dark Satanic Mills, and the British Standard of Living Debate. *J. Econ. Hist.*, March 1981, *41*(1), pp. 75–83.   [G: U.K.]

Worsley, Peter. Village Economies. In *Samuel, R., ed.*, 1981, pp. 80–85.   [G: U.K.]

Wyczansky, Andrzey. The Adjustment of the Polish Economy to Economic Checks in the XVIIth Century. *J. Europ. Econ. Hist.*, Spring 1981, *10*(1), pp. 207–12.   [G: Poland]

0441 History of Product Prices and Markets

Aldcroft, Derek H. McCloskey on Victorian Growth: A Comment. In *McCloskey, D. N.*, 1981, pp. 111–15.   [G: U.K.]

Allen, Robert C. Entrepreneurship and Technical Progress in the Northeast Coast Pig Iron Industry: 1850–1913. In *Uselding, P., ed.*, 1981, pp. 35–71.   [G: U.K.]

Attman, Artur. The Russian Market in World Trade, 1500–1860. *Scand. Econ. Hist. Rev.*, 1981, *29*(3), pp. 177–202.   [G: U.S.S.R.]

Barro, Robert J. Inflation, the Payments Period, and the Demand for Money. In *Barro, R. J.*, 1981, *1970*, pp. 301–36.   [G: Selected Countries]

Blaich, Fritz. The Development of the Distribution Sector in the German Car Industry. In *Okochi, A. and Shimokawa, K., eds.*, 1981, pp. 93–117.   [G: Germany]

Boserup, Ester. Indian Agriculture from the Perspective of Western Europe. In *Sarma, J. S.*, 1981, pp. 55–58.   [G: India; W. Europe]

Britnell, Richard Hugh. The Proliferation of Markets in England, 1200–1349. *Econ. Hist. Rev., 2nd Ser.*, May 1981, *34*(2), pp. 209–21.   [G: U.K.]

Channon, Geoffrey. The Great Western Railway under the British Railways Act of 1921. *Bus. Hist. Rev.*, Summer 1981, *55*(2), pp. 188–216.   [G: U.K.]

Chorley, G. P. H. The Agricultural Revolution in Northern Europe, 1750–1880: Nitrogen, Legumes, and Crop Productivity. *Econ. Hist. Rev., 2nd Ser.*, February 1981, *34*(1), pp. 71–93.   [G: Belgium; France; Germany; Netherlands]

Church, Roy. French Automobile Marketing, 1890–1979: Comment. In *Okochi, A. and Shimokawa, K., eds.*, 1981, pp. 155–60.   [G: France]

Church, Roy. The Marketing of Automobiles in Britain and the United States before 1939. In *Okochi, A. and Shimokawa, K., eds.*, 1981, pp. 59–87.   [G: U.K.; U.S.]

Ciriacono, Salvatore. Silk Manufacturing in France and Italy in the XVIIth Century: Two Models Compared. *J. Europ. Econ. Hist.*, Spring 1981, *10*(1), pp. 167–99.   [G: France; Italy]

Cohen, Jon S. Managers and Machinery: An Analysis of the Rise of Factory Production. *Australian Econ. Pap.*, June 1981, *20*(36), pp. 24–41.   [G: U.K.]

Cole, W. A. Factors in Demand 1700–80. In *Floud, R. and McCloskey, D., eds., Vol. 1*, 1981, pp. 36–65.   [G: U.K.]

Crafts, N. F. R. Victorian Britain Did Fail. In *McCloskey, D. N.*, 1981, *1978*, pp. 126–31.   [G: U.K.]

Engwall, Lars. Newspaper Competition: A Case for Theories of Oligopoly: Review Article. *Scand. Econ. Hist. Rev.*, 1981, *29*(2), pp. 145–54.   [G: Sweden]

Foreman-Peck, James S. The Effect of Market Failure on the British Motor Industry before 1939. *Exploration Econ. Hist.*, July 1981, *18*(3), pp. 257–89.   [G: U.K.]

Fridenson, Patrick. French Automobile Marketing, 1890–1979. In *Okochi, A. and Shimokawa, K., eds.*, 1981, pp. 127–54.   [G: France]

Fridenson, Patrick. The Marketing of Automobiles in Britain and the United States before 1939: Comment. In *Okochi, A. and Shimokawa, K., eds.*, 1981, pp. 88–90.   [G: U.K.; U.S.]

Gessner, Dieter. The Dilemma of German Agriculture during the Weimar Republic. In *Bessel, R. and Feuchtwanger, E. J., eds.*, 1981, pp. 134–54.   [G: Germany]

Hara, Terushi. French Automobile Marketing, 1890–1979: Comment. In *Okochi, A. and Shimokawa, K., eds.*, 1981, pp. 160–62.   [G: France]

Heywood, Colin Michael. The Launching of an "Infant Industry"? The Cotton Industry of Troyes under Protectionism, 1793–1860. *J. Europ. Econ. Hist.*, Winter 1981, *10*(3), pp. 553–81.   [G: France]

Hodne, Fritz and Gjølberg, Ole. Market Integration during the Period of Industrialisation in Norway. In *Bairoch, P. and Lévy-Leboyer, M., eds.*, 1981, pp. 216–25.   [G: Norway]

Holland, Robert Featherstone. The Federation of British Industries and the International Economy, 1929–39. *Econ. Hist. Rev.*, *2nd Ser.*, May 1981, *34*(2), pp. 287–300. [G: U.K.]

Hueckel, G. Agriculture during Industrialisation. In *Floud, R. and McCloskey, D., eds., Vol. 1*, 1981, pp. 182–203. [G: U.K.]

Hughes, Thomas P. Transfer and Style: A Historical Account. In *Sagafi-nejad, T.; Moxon, R. W. and Perlmutter, H. V., eds.*, 1981, pp. 42–54. [G: U.S.; U.K.]

Inikori, J. E. Market Structure and the Profits of the British African Trade in the Late Eighteenth Century. *J. Econ. Hist.*, December 1981, *41*(4), pp. 745–76. [G: U.K.]

Jones, E. L. Agriculture, 1700–80. In *Floud, R. and McCloskey, D., eds., Vol. 1*, 1981, pp. 66–86. [G: U.K.]

Keckova, Antonina. Polish Salt-Mines as a State Enterprise (XIIIth-XVIIIth Centuries). *J. Europ. Econ. Hist.*, Winter 1981, *10*(3), pp. 619–31. [G: Poland]

Kelly, William J. Crisis Management in the Russian Oil Industry: The 1905 Revolution. *J. Europ. Econ. Hist.*, Fall 1981, *10*(2), pp. 291–342. [G: U.S.S.R.]

Kirk, Robert and Simmons, Colin. Engineering and the First World War: A Case Study of the Lancashire Cotton Spinning Machine Industry. *World Devel.*, August 1981, *9*(8), pp. 773–91. [G: U.K.]

Kisch, Herbert. The Textile Industries in Silesia and the Rhineland: A Comparative Study in Industrialization. In *Kriedte, P.; Medick, H. and Schlumbohm, J.*, 1981, pp. 178–200. [G: Germany; Poland]

McCloskey, Donald N. Britain's Loss from Foreign Industrialization: A Provisional Estimate. In *McCloskey, D. N.*, 1981, pp. 173–83. [G: U.K.]

McCloskey, Donald N. Did Victorian Britain Fail? In *McCloskey, D. N.*, 1981, *1970*, pp. 94–110. [G: U.K.]

McCloskey, Donald N. No It Did Not: A Reply to Crafts. In *McCloskey, D. N.*, 1981, *1978*, pp. 131–35. [G: U.K.]

McCloskey, Donald N. Victorian Growth: A Rejoinder to Derek Aldcroft. In *McCloskey, D. N.*, 1981, *1974*, pp. 115–19. [G: U.K.]

Mori, Giorgio. The Process of Industrialisation in General and the Process of Industrialisation in Italy: Some Suggestions, Problems and Questions. In *Bairoch, P. and Lévy-Leboyer, M., eds.*, 1981, pp. 151–64. [G: Italy]

Ó Gráda, Cormac. Agricultural Decline 1860–1914. In *Floud, R. and McCloskey, D., eds., Vol. 2*, 1981, pp. 175–97. [G: U.K.]

O'Malley, Eoin. The Decline of Irish Industry in the Nineteenth Century. *Econ. Soc. Rev.*, October 1981, *13*(1), pp. 21–42. [G: Ireland]

Phelps Brown, Henry and Hopkins, Sheila V. Builders' Wage-rates, Prices and Population: Some Further Evidence. In *Phelps Brown, H. and Hopkins, S. V.*, 1981, *1959*, pp. 78–98. [G: Europe]

Phelps Brown, Henry and Hopkins, Sheila V. Seven Centuries of the Prices of Consumables Compared with Builders' Wage-rates. In *Phelps Brown, H. and Hopkins, S. V.*, 1981, *1956*, pp. 13–59. [G: U.K.]

Phelps Brown, Henry and Hopkins, Sheila V. Wage-rates and Prices: Evicence for Population Pressure in the Sixteenth Century. In *Phelps Brown, H. and Hopkins, S. V.*, 1981, *1957*, pp. 60–77. [G: U.K.; France]

Ranis, Gustav. Transfer and Style: A Historical Account: Comment. In *Sagafi-nejad, T.; Moxon, R. W. and Perlmutter, H. V., eds.*, 1981, pp. 55–63. [G: Selected Countries: U.K.; U.S.]

Samura, Terutoshi. The Proto-Industrialization and the Development of Textile Industries in the North of France. (In Japanese. With English summary.) *Osaka Econ. Pap.*, December 1981, *31*(2–3), pp. 338–60. [G: France]

Sargent, Thomas J. The Demand for Money during Hyperinflations under Rational Expectations. In *Lucas, R. E. and Sargent, T. J., eds.*, 1981, *1977*, pp. 429–52. [G: Europe]

Sargent, Thomas J. and Wallace, Neil. Rational Expectations and the Dynamics of Hyperinflation. In *Lucas, R. E. and Sargent, T. J., eds.*, 1981, *1973*, pp. 405–28. [G: Europe]

Shimokawa, Koichi. The Development of the Distribution Sector in the German Car Industry: Comment. In *Okochi, A. and Shimokawa, K., eds.*, 1981, pp. 118–21. [G: Germany]

Supple, B. E. Income and Demand 1860–1914. In *Floud, R. and McCloskey, D., eds., Vol. 2*, 1981, pp. 121–43. [G: U.K.]

Thomas, R. P. and McCloskey, Donald N. Overseas Trade and Empire 1700–1860. In *Floud, R. and McCloskey, D., eds., Vol. 1*, 1981, pp. 87–102. [G: U.K.]

Todd, Douglas. Synthetic Rubber in the German War Economy: A Case of Economic Dependence. *J. Europ. Econ. Hist.*, Spring 1981, *10*(1), pp. 153–65. [G: Germany]

Walton, John K. The Demand for Working-Class Seaside Holidays in Victorian England. *Econ. Hist. Rev.*, *2nd Ser.*, May 1981, *34*(2), pp. 249–65. [G: U.K.]

Watanabe, Hisashi. The Development of the Distribution Sector in the German Car Industry: Comment. In *Okochi, A. and Shimokawa, K., eds.*, 1981, pp. 121–25. [G: Germany]

Yuzawa, Takeshi. The Marketing of Automobiles in Britain and the United States before 1939: Comment. In *Okochi, A. and Shimokawa, K., eds.*, 1981, pp. 90–92. [G: U.K.; U.S]

0442 History of Factor Prices and Markets

Awty, Brian G. The Continental Origins of Wealden Ironworkers, 1451–1544. *Econ. Hist. Rev.*, *2nd Ser.*, November 1981, *34*(4), pp. 524–39. [G: U.K.]

Baines, D. E. The Labour Supply and the Labour Market 1860–1914. In *Floud, R. and McCloskey, D., eds., Vol. 2*, 1981, pp. 144–74. [G: U.K.]

Bonnell, Sheila. Real Wages and Employment in the Great Depression. *Econ. Rec.*, September 1981, *57*(158), pp. 277–81. [G: U.K.; U.S.; Sweden; Germany]

Brüggemeier, Franz-Josef. Ruhr Miners and Their

Historians. In *Samuel, R., ed.*, 1981, pp. 326–32. [G: W. Germany]

Christiansen, Niels Finn and Rasmussen, Jens Rahbek. 'To Be or Not to Be': Socialist Historians in Denmark. In *Samuel, R., ed.*, 1981, pp. 278–83. [G: Denmark]

Daultrey, Stuart; Dickson, David and Ó Gráda, Cormac. Eighteenth-Century Irish Population: New Perspectives from Old Sources. *J. Econ. Hist.*, September 1981, *41*(3), pp. 601–28. [G: Ireland]

Daunton, Martin James. Down the Pit: Work in the Great Northern and South Wales Coalfields, 1870–1914. *Econ. Hist. Rev., 2nd Ser.*, November 1981, *34*(4), pp. 578–97. [G: U.K.]

Edelstein, M. Foreign Investment and Empire 1860–1914. In *Floud, R. and McCloskey, D., eds., Vol. 2*, 1981, pp. 70–98. [G: U.K.]

Erickson, Charlotte. Emigration from the British Isles to the U.S.A. in 1831. *Population Stud.*, July 1981, *35*(2), pp. 175–97. [G: U.S.; U.K.]

Firestone, Ya'akov. Land Equalization and Factor Scarcities: Holding Size and the Burden of Impositions in Imperial Central Russia and the Late Ottoman Levant. *J. Econ. Hist.*, December 1981, *41*(4), pp. 813–33. [G: Ottoman Empire; U.S.S.R.]

Goodman, Jordan. Financing Pre-Modern European Industry: An Example from Florence, 1580–1660. *J. Europ. Econ. Hist.*, Fall 1981, *10*(2), pp. 415–35. [G: Italy]

Grage, Elsa-Britta. Capital Supply in Gothenburg's Foreign Trade, 1765–1810. *Scand. Econ. Hist. Rev.*, 1981, *29*(2), pp. 97–128. [G: Sweden]

Hall, Catherine. Gender Divisions and Class Formation in the Birmingham Middle Class, 1780–1850. In *Samuel, R., ed.*, 1981, pp. 164–75. [G: U.K.]

Harrison, Royden. The Webbs as Historians of Trade Unionism. In *Samuel, R., ed.*, 1981, pp. 322–23. [G: U.K.]

Heywood, Colin Michael. The Role of the Peasantry in French Industrialization, 1815–80. *Econ. Hist. Rev., 2nd Ser.*, August 1981, *34*(3), pp. 359–76. [G: France]

Hodne, Fritz and Gjølberg, Ole. Market Integration during the Period of Industrialisation in Norway. In *Bairoch, P. and Lévy-Leboyer, M., eds.*, 1981, pp. 216–25. [G: Norway]

Hudson, Pat. The Role of Banks in the Finance of the West Yorkshire Wool Textile Industry, c. 1780–1850. *Bus. Hist. Rev.*, Autumn 1981, *55*(3), pp. 379–402. [G: U.K.]

Johnston, T. L. Trade Unions in the Developed Economies: Sweden. In *Smith, E. O., ed.*, 1981, pp. 97–122. [G: Sweden]

Jörberg, Lennart and Bengtsson, Tommy. Regional Wages in Sweden during the Nineteenth Century. In *Bairoch, P. and Lévy-Leboyer, M., eds.*, 1981, pp. 226–43. [G: Sweden]

Kiesewetter, Hubert. Regional Disparities in Wages: The Cotton Industry in Nineteenth-century Germany—Some Methodological Considerations. In *Bairoch, P. and Lévy-Leboyer, M., eds.*, 1981, pp. 248–58. [G: Germany]

King, J. E. Perish Commerce! Free Trade and Underconsumption in Early British Radical Economics. *Australian Econ. Pap.*, December 1981, *20*(37), pp. 235–57. [G: U.K.]

Knodel, J. and Wilson, C. The Secular Increase in Fecundity in German Village Populations: An Analysis of Reproductive Histories of Couples Married, 1750–1899. *Population Stud.*, March 1981, *35*(1), pp. 53–84. [G: Germany]

Kocka, Jürgen. Class Formation, Interest Articulation, and Public Policy: The Origins of the German White-Collar Class in the Late Nineteenth and Early Twentieth Centuries. In *Berger, S., ed.*, 1981, pp. 63–81. [G: Germany]

Koval'chenko, I. D. and Selunskaia, N. B. Labor Rental in the Manorial Economy of European Russia at the End of the 19th Century and the Beginning of the 20th. *Exploration Econ. Hist.*, January 1981, *18*(1), pp. 1–20. [G: U.S.S.R.]

Kussmaul, Ann Sturm. The Ambiguous Mobility of Farm Servants. *Econ. Hist. Rev., 2nd Ser.*, May 1981, *34*(2), pp. 222–35. [G: U.K.]

Lazonick, William H. Competition, Specialization, and Industrial Decline. *J. Econ. Hist.*, March 1981, *41*(1), pp. 31–38. [G: U.K.]

Lazonick, William H. Factor Costs and the Diffusion of Ring Spinning in Britain Prior to World War I. *Quart. J. Econ.*, February 1981, *96*(1), pp. 89–109. [G: U.K.]

Lazonick, William H. Production Relations, Labor Productivity, and Choice of Technique: British and U.S. Cotton Spinning. *J. Econ. Hist.*, September 1981, *41*(3), pp. 491–516. [G: U.S.; U.K.]

McLernon, Douglas S. Trade Union Organisation in the South of Ireland in the XIXth Century. *J. Europ. Econ. Hist.*, Spring 1981, *10*(1), pp. 145–52. [G: Ireland]

Millward, R. The Emergence of Wage Labor in Early Modern England. *Exploration Econ. Hist.*, January 1981, *18*(1), pp. 21–39. [G: U.K.]

Mirowski, Philip. The Rise (and Retreat) of a Market: English Joint Stock Shares in the Eighteenth Century. *J. Econ. Hist.*, September 1981, *41*(3), pp. 559–77. [G: U.K.]

Moggridge, D. E. Financial Crises and Lenders of Last Resort: Policy in the Crises of 1920 and 1929. *J. Europ. Econ. Hist.*, Spring 1981, *10*(1), pp. 47–69.

Newman, Allen R. A Test of the Okun–Richardson Model of Internal Migration. *Econ. Develop. Cult. Change*, January 1981, *29*(2), pp. 295–307. [G: Germany]

O'Brien, P. K. and Engerman, Stanley L. Changes in Income and Its Distribution during the Industrial Revolution. In *Floud, R. and McCloskey, D., eds., Vol. 1*, 1981, pp. 164–81. [G: U.K.]

Pescarolo, Sandra. From Gramsci to 'Workerism': Notes on Italian Working-Class History. In *Samuel, R., ed.*, 1981, pp. 273–78. [G: Italy]

Phelps Brown, Henry and Hart, P. E. The Share of Wages in National Income. In *Phelps Brown, H. and Hopkins, S. V.*, 1981, 1952, pp. 106–30. [G: U.K.; U.S.]

Phelps Brown, Henry and Hopkins, Sheila V. Builders' Wage-rates, Prices and Population: Some Further Evidence. In *Phelps Brown, H. and*

Hopkins, S. V., 1981, *1959*, pp. 78–98.
[G: Europe]

Phelps Brown, Henry and Hopkins, Sheila V. Seven Centuries of the Prices of Consumables Compared with Builders' Wage-rates. **In** *Phelps Brown, H. and Hopkins, S. V.*, 1981, *1956*, pp. 13–59. [G: U.K.]

Phelps Brown, Henry and Hopkins, Sheila V. Seven Centuries of Building Wages. **In** *Phelps Brown, H. and Hopkins, S. V.*, 1981, *1955*, pp. 1–12.
[G: U.K.]

Phelps Brown, Henry and Hopkins, Sheila V. Seven Centuries of Wages and Prices: Some Earlier Estimates. **In** *Phelps Brown, H. and Hopkins, S. V.*, 1981, *1961*, pp. 99–105. [G: U.K.]

Phelps Brown, Henry and Hopkins, Sheila V. Wage-rates and Prices: Evicence for Population Pressure in the Sixteenth Century. **In** *Phelps Brown, H. and Hopkins, S. V.*, 1981, *1957*, pp. 60–77.
[G: U.K.; France]

Rancière, Jacques. 'Le Socail': The Lost Tradition in French Labour History. **In** *Samuel, R., ed.*, 1981, pp. 267–72. [G: France]

Riley, James C. Mortality on Long-Distance Voyages in the Eighteenth Century. *J. Econ. Hist.*, September 1981, *41*(3), pp. 651–56.
[G: Netherlands]

Saito, Osamu. Labour Supply Behaviour of the Poor in the English Industrial Revolution. *J. Europ. Econ. Hist.*, Winter 1981, *10*(3), pp. 633–52.
[G: U.K.]

Seabrook, Jeremy. Unemployment Now and in the 1930s. **In** *Crick, B., ed.*, 1981, *1981*, pp. 7–15.
[G: U.K.]

Smith, Eric Owen. Trade Unions in the Developed Economies: The United Kingdom. **In** *Smith, E. O., ed.*, 1981, pp. 123–54. [G: U.K.]

Solow, Barbara Lewis. A New Look at the Irish Land Question. *Econ. Soc. Rev.*, July 1981, *12*(4), pp. 301–14. [G: Ireland]

Soltow, Lee. Age and Economic Achievement in an Irish Barony in 1821. *Exploration Econ. Hist.*, October 1981, *18*(4), pp. 389–98. [G: U.K.]

Supple, B. E. Income and Demand 1860–1914. **In** *Floud, R. and McCloskey, D., eds., Vol. 2*, 1981, pp. 121–43. [G: U.K.]

Svejnar, Jan. Relative Wage Effects of Unions, Dictatorship and Codetermination: Econometric Evidence from Germany. *Rev. Econ. Statist.*, May 1981, *63*(2), pp. 188–97. [G: W. Germany]

Tranter, N. L. The Labour Supply 1780–1860. **In** *Floud, R. and McCloskey, D., eds., Vol. 1*, 1981, pp. 204–26. [G: U.K.]

von Tunzelmann, G. N. Technical Progress during the Industrial Revolution. **In** *Floud, R. and McCloskey, D., eds., Vol. 1*, 1981, pp. 143–63.
[G: U.K.]

Walker, Jill. Markets, Industrial Processes and Class Struggle: The Evolution of the Labor Process in the U.K. Engineering Industry. *Rev. Radical Polit. Econ.*, Winter 1981, *12*(4), pp. 46–59.
[G: U.K.]

Walton, John K. The Demand for Working-Class Seaside Holidays in Victorian England. *Econ. Hist. Rev., 2nd Ser.*, May 1981, *34*(2), pp. 249–65. [G: U.K.]

0443 History of Public Economic Policy (all levels)

Amsler, Christine E.; Bartlett, Robin L. and Bolton, Craig J. Thoughts of Some British Economists on Early Limited Liability and Corporate Legislation. *Hist. Polit. Econ.*, Winter 1981, *13*(4), pp. 774–93. [G: U.K.]

Barbier, Jacques A. and Klein, Herbert S. Revolutionary Wars and Public Finances: The Madrid Treasury, 1784–1807. *J. Econ. Hist.*, June 1981, *41*(2), pp. 315–39. [G: Spain]

Bettelheim, Charles and Chavance, Bernard. Stalinism as the Ideology of State Capitalism. *Rev. Radical Polit. Econ.*, Spring 1981, *13*(1), pp. 40–54.
[G: U.S.S.R.]

Boltho, Andrea. Are the British So Different from Everyone Else? Comments. **In** *[Cairncross, A.]*, 1981, pp. 244–47. [G: U.K.; Italy]

Bordo, Michael David. The Classical Gold Standard: Some Lessons for Today. *Fed. Res. Bank St. Louis Rev.*, May 1981, *63*(5), pp. 2–17. [G: U.K.; U.S.]

Bridge, Carl. Britain and the Indian Currency Crisis, 1930–2: A Comment. *Econ. Hist. Rev., 2nd Ser.*, May 1981, *34*(2), pp. 301–04. [G: U.K.; India]

Buck, N. H. The Analysis of State Intervention in Nineteenth-Century Cities: The Case of Municipal Labour Policy in East London, 1886–1914. **In** *Dear, M. and Scott, A. J., eds.*, 1981, pp. 501–33. [G: U.K.]

Capie, Forrest H. Shaping the British Tariff Structure in the 1930s. *Exploration Econ. Hist.*, April 1981, *18*(2), pp. 155–73. [G: U.K.]

Capie, Forrest H. Tariffs, Elasticities and Prices in Britain in the 1930s: Comment. *Econ. Hist. Rev., 2nd Ser.*, February 1981, *34*(1), pp. 140–42.
[G: U.K.]

Carli, Guido. Are the British So Different from Everyone Else? **In** *[Cairncross, A.]*, 1981, pp. 232–44. [G: U.K.; Italy]

Davidson, R. and Lowe, R. Bureaucracy and Innovation in British Welfare Policy 1870-1945. **In** *Mommsen, W. J., ed.*, 1981, pp. 263–95.
[G: U.K.]

Dimsdale, N. H. British Monetary Policy and the Exchange Rate, 1920–1938. *Oxford Econ. Pap.*, Supplement July 1981, *33*, pp. 306–49.
[G: U.K.]

Faust, A. State and Unemployment in Germany 1890–1918 (Labour Exchanges, Job Creation and Unemployment Insurance). **In** *Mommsen, W. J., ed.*, 1981, pp. 150–63. [G: Germany]

Foreman-Peck, James S. The British Tariff and Industrial Protection in the 1930s: An Alternative Model: Comment. *Econ. Hist. Rev., 2nd Ser.*, February 1981, *34*(1), pp. 132–39. [G: U.K.]

Fraser, Derek. The English Poor Law and the Origins of the British Welfare State. **In** *Mommsen, W. J., ed.*, 1981, pp. 9–31. [G: U.K.]

Gash, Norman. The Power of Ideas over Policy. **In** *Seldon, A., ed.*, 1981, pp. 227–45. [G: U.K.]

Gessner, Dieter. The Dilemma of German Agriculture during the Weimar Republic. **In** *Bessel, R. and Feuchtwanger, E. J., eds.*, 1981, pp. 134–54. [G: Germany]

Giersch, Herbert and Lehment, Harmen. Monetary

Policy: Does Independence Make a Difference?—The German Experience. In *[von Haberler, G.]*, 1981, pp. 3–15. **[G: W. Germany]**

Grampp, William D. The Controversy over Usury in the Seventeenth Century. *J. Europ. Econ. Hist.*, Winter 1981, *10*(3), pp. 671–95. **[G: U.K.]**

Harris, José. Some Aspects of Social Policy in Britain During the Second World War. In *Mommsen, W. J., ed.*, 1981, pp. 247–62. **[G: U.K.]**

Harrison, Mark. Soviet Primary Accumulation Processes: Some Unresolved Problems. *Sci. Soc.*, Winter 1981–1982, *45*(4), pp. 387–408. **[G: U.S.S.R.]**

Hartwell, Ronald Max. Taxation in England during the Industrial Revolution. *Cato J.*, Spring 1981, *1*(1), pp. 129–53. **[G: U.K.]**

Hausman, William J. and Neufeld, John L. Excise Anatomized: The Political Economy of Walpole's 1733 Tax Scheme. *J. Europ. Econ. Hist.*, Spring 1981, *10*(1), pp. 131–43.

Hay, J. R. The British Business Community, Social Insurance and the German Example. In *Mommsen, W. J., ed.*, 1981, pp. 107–32. **[G: U.K.; Germany]**

Hennock, E. P. The Origins of British National Insurance and the German Precedent 1880–1914. In *Mommsen, W. J., ed.*, 1981, pp. 84–106. **[G: U.K.; Germany]**

Heywood, Colin Michael. The Launching of an "Infant Industry"? The Cotton Industry of Troyes under Protectionism, 1793–1860. *J. Europ. Econ. Hist.*, Winter 1981, *10*(3), pp. 553–81. **[G: France]**

Holland, Robert Featherstone. The Federation of British Industries and the International Economy, 1929–39. *Econ. Hist. Rev., 2nd Ser.*, May 1981, *34*(2), pp. 287–300. **[G: U.K.]**

Jago, Charles. Habsburg Absolutism and the Cortes of Castile. *Amer. Hist. Rev.*, April 1981, *86*(2), pp. 307–26. **[G: Spain]**

Jones, Stuart. The First Currency Revolution. *J. Europ. Econ. Hist.*, Winter 1981, *10*(3), pp. 583–618. **[G: U.K.]**

Kaji, Naoki. On the Introduction of the Poor Rate in England and Its Ideas. (In Japanese. With English summary.) *Osaka Econ. Pap.*, June 1981, *31*(1), pp. 42–54. **[G: U.K.]**

Kallenautio, Jorma. Finnish Prohibition as an Economic Policy Issue. *Scand. Econ. Hist. Rev.*, 1981, *29*(3), pp. 203–28. **[G: Finland]**

Kingston-Mann, Esther. Marxism and Russian Rural Development: Problems of Evidence, Experience, and Culture. *Amer. Hist. Rev.*, October 1981, *86*(4), pp. 731–52. **[G: U.S.S.R.]**

Kirchner, Walther. Russian Tariffs and Foreign Industries before 1914: The German Entrepreneur's Perspective. *J. Econ. Hist.*, June 1981, *41*(2), pp. 361–79. **[G: U.S.S.R.; Germany]**

Knight, Arthur [Sir]. Industrial Policy. In *[Cairncross, A.]*, 1981, pp. 114–37. **[G: U.K.]**

Lieberman, Sima. The Idological Foundations of Western European Planning. *J. Europ. Econ. Hist.*, Fall 1981, *10*(2), pp. 343–71. **[G: W. Europe]**

Likierman, Andrew. Industrial Policy; Comments. In *[Cairncross, A.]*, 1981, pp. 137–39. **[G: U.K.]**

Lindsay, Kenneth. PEP through the 1930s: Organisation, Structure, People. In *Pinder, J., ed.*, 1981, pp. 9–31. **[G: U.K.]**

Martin, George T., Jr. Historical Overview of Social Welfare. In *Martin, G. T., Jr., and Zald, M. N., eds.*, 1981, pp. 11–17. **[G: Europe; U.S.]**

McCloskey, Donald N. "Taxation in England during the Industrial Revolution": A Comment. *Cato J.*, Spring 1981, *1*(1), pp. 155–59. **[G: U.K.]**

Middleton, Roger. The Constant Employment Budget Balance and British Budgetary Policy, 1929–39. *Econ. Hist. Rev., 2nd Ser.*, May 1981, *34*(2), pp. 266–86. **[G: U.K.]**

Moss, David John. The Bank of England and the Country Banks: Birmingham, 1827–33. *Econ. Hist. Rev., 2nd Ser.*, November 1981, *34*(4), pp. 540–53. **[G: U.K.]**

Myrdal, Gunnar. A Parallel: The First Blum Government 1936—A Footnote to History. In *[Lipiński, E.]*, 1981, pp. 53–62. **[G: France]**

Nicholson, Max. PEP through the 1930s: Growth, Thinking, Performance. In *Pinder, J., ed.*, 1981, pp. 32–53. **[G: U.K.]**

Nicholson, Max. The Proposal for a National Plan. In *Pinder, J., ed.*, 1981, pp. 5–8. **[G: U.K.]**

Outhwaite, Richard Brian. Dearth and Government Intervention in English Grain Markets, 1590–1700. *Econ. Hist. Rev., 2nd Ser.*, August 1981, *34*(3), pp. 389–406. **[G: U.K.]**

Patinkin, Don. Mercantilism and the Readmission of the Jews to England. In *Patinkin, D.*, 1981, *1946*, pp. 75–89. **[G: U.K.]**

Pettengill, John S. Firearms and the Distribution of Income: A Neo-Classical Model. *Rev. Radical Polit. Econ.*, Summer 1981, *13*(2), pp. 1–10.

Pincus, Jonathan J. Discussion [Government Policy and Economic Development in Germany and Japan: A Skeptical Reevaluation] [Bureaucratic Opposition to the Assignment of Property Rights: Overgrazing on the Western Range]. *J. Econ. Hist.*, March 1981, *41*(1), pp. 159–61. **[G: Germany; Japan; U.S.]**

Pogge von Strandmann, Hartmut. Industrial Primacy in German Foreign Policy? Myths and Realities in German-Russian Relations at the End of the Weimar Republic. In *Bessel, R. and Feuchtwanger, E. J., eds.*, 1981, pp. 241–67. **[G: U.S.S.R.; Germany]**

Reulecke, J. English Social Policy around the Middle of the Nineteenth Century as Seen by German Social Reformers. In *Mommsen, W. J., ed.*, 1981, pp. 32–49. **[G: U.K.]**

Ricciardi, Joseph. Class Struggle, the Classical Economists, and the Factory Acts: Towards a 'Reformulation.' In *Zarembka, P., ed.*, 1981, pp. 81–100. **[G: U.K.]**

Risch, Bodo. Gewerkschaftseigene Arbeitslosenversicherung vor 1914. (Trade Union Unemployment Insurance before 1914. With English summary.) *Weltwirtsch. Arch.*, 1981, *117*(3), pp. 513–45. **[G: Germany]**

Rose, M. E. The Crisis of Poor Relief in England,

1860–1890. In *Mommsen, W. J., ed.*, 1981, pp. 50–70. [G: U.K.]

Roskill, Oliver. PEP through the 1930s: The Industries Group. In *Pinder, J., ed.*, 1981, pp. 54–80. [G: U.K.]

Rosted, Jørgen. Udviklingstendenser i den makroøkonomiske planlægning i Danmark. (The Development of Macroeconomic Planning in Denmark. With English summary.) *Nationaløkon. Tidsskr.*, 1981, *119*(2), pp. 276–94. [G: Denmark]

Samura, Terutoshi. French Monetary Policy and Its Effects in the Latter Half of the Seventeenth Century. (In Japanese. With English summary.) *Osaka Econ. Pap.*, March 1981, *30*(4), pp. 16–35. [G: France]

Skidelsky, R. Keynes and the Treasury View: The Case For and Against an Active Unemployment Policy 1920–1939. In *Mommsen, W. J., ed.*, 1981, pp. 167–87. [G: U.K.]

Tampke, J. Bismarck's Social Legislation: A Genuine Breakthrough? In *Mommsen, W. J., ed.*, 1981, pp. 71–83. [G: Germany]

Thomas, R. P. and McCloskey, Donald N. Overseas Trade and Empire 1700–1860. In *Floud, R. and McCloskey, D., eds., Vol. 1*, 1981, pp. 87–102. [G: U.K.]

Tipton, Frank B., Jr. Government Policy and Economic Development in Germany and Japan: A Skeptical Reevaluation. *J. Econ. Hist.*, March 1981, *41*(1), pp. 139–50. [G: Germany; Japan]

Tomlinson, B. R. Britain and the Indian Currency Crisis, 1930–2: A Reply. *Econ. Hist. Rev., 2nd Ser.*, May 1981, *34*(2), pp. 305–07. [G: U.K.; India]

Turner, Michael Edward. Cost, Finance, and Parliamentary Enclosure. *Econ. Hist. Rev., 2nd Ser.*, May 1981, *34*(2), pp. 236–48. [G: U.K.]

Ullmann, H.-P. German Industry and Bismarck's Social Security System. In *Mommsen, W. J., ed.*, 1981, pp. 133–49. [G: Germany]

Vamplew, Wray. Tithes and Agriculture: Some Comments on Commutation. *Econ. Hist. Rev., 2nd Ser.*, February 1981, *34*(1), pp. 115–19. [G: U.K.]

Verlinden, Charles. Economic Fluctuations and Government Policy in the Netherlands in the Late XVIth Century. *J. Europ. Econ. Hist.*, Spring 1981, *10*(1), pp. 201–06. [G: Netherlands]

Wallerstein, Immanuel and Kasaba, Reşat. Incorporation into the World-Economy: Change in the Structure of the Ottoman Empire, 1750–1839. *METU*, 1981, *8*(1 & 2), pp. 537–70. [G: Turkey]

Weisbrod, Bernd. The Crisis of German Unemployment Insurance in 1928/1929 and its Political Repercussions. In *Mommsen, W. J., ed.*, 1981, pp. 188–204. [G: Germany]

Wolffsohn, M. Creation of Employment as a Welfare Policy. The Final Phase of the Weimar Republic. In *Mommsen, W. J., ed.*, 1981, pp. 205–44.

Wright, J. F. Britain's Inter-War Experience. *Oxford Econ. Pap.*, Supplement July 1981, *33*, pp. 282–305. [G: U.K.]

Young, Michael. The Second World War. In *Pinder, J., ed.*, 1981, pp. 81–96. [G: U.K.]

045 Economic History: Asia

0450 General

Akimoto, Hiroya. Capital Formation and Economic Growth in Mid-19th Century Japan. *Exploration Econ. Hist.*, January 1981, *18*(1), pp. 40–59. [G: Japan]

Blumenthal, Tuvia. Factor Proportions and Choice of Technology: The Japanese Experience: Reply. *Econ. Develop. Cult. Change*, July 1981, *29*(4), pp. 845–48. [G: Japan]

Brown, Shannon R. Technology Transfer and Economic Systems: The Case of China in the Nineteenth Century. *ACES Bull. (See Comp. Econ. Stud. after 8/85)*, Spring 1981, *23*(1), pp. 79–88. [G: China]

Chandra, Nirmal K. The New International Economic Order and Industrialization in India. In *Lozoya, J. A. and Bhattacharya, A. K., eds.*, 1981, pp. 90–140. [G: India]

Clark, Brian D. Urban Planning in Iran. In *[Fisher, W. B.]*, 1981, pp. 280–88. [G: Iran]

Fei, John C. H. and Ranis, Gustav. Factor Proportions and Choice of Technology: The Japanese Experience: Comment. *Econ. Develop. Cult. Change*, July 1981, *29*(4), pp. 841–44. [G: Japan]

Harada, Toshimaru. On the Subordinate Social Rank Called "Kerai" in the Rural Communities of Early Modern Times in Ōmni Province. (In Japanese. With English summary.) *Osaka Econ. Pap.*, December 1981, *31*(2–3), pp. 261–73. [G: Japan]

Hiroyama, Kensuke. A Middle-Sized Osaka Money Exchanging Business at the End of the Edo Period—A Case Study of the Tomiko Family. (In Japanese. With English summary.) *Osaka Econ. Pap.*, June 1981, *31*(1), pp. 138–61. [G: Japan]

Islamoglu, Huri and Keyder, Caglar. The Ottoman Social Formation. In *Bailey, A. M. and Llobera, J. R., eds.*, 1981, 1977, pp. 301–24. [G: Ottoman Empire]

Kim, Dae Young and Sloboda, John E. Migration and Korean Development. In *Repetto, R., et al.*, 1981, pp. 36–138. [G: S. Korea]

Kumar, Dharma and Krishnamurty, J. Regional and International Economic Disparities since the Industrial Revolution: The Indian Evidence. In *Bairoch, P. and Lévy-Leboyer, M., eds.*, 1981, pp. 361–72. [G: India]

Kwon, Tai Hwan. The Historical Background to Korea's Demographic Transition. In *Repetto, R., et al.*, 1981, pp. 10–35. [G: S. Korea]

Liang, Ernest P. L. Market Accessibility and Agricultural Development in Prewar China. *Econ. Develop. Cult. Change*, October 1981, *30*(1), pp. 77–105. [G: China]

Mosk, Carl. The Evolution of Premodern Demographic Regimes: A Research Note. *Exploration Econ. Hist.*, April 1981, *18*(2), pp. 199–208. [G: Sweden; Japan]

Okyay, Vildan. Bati Anadolu Bölgesinde Ulaşim Sistemindeki Değişikliğin Merkezler Kademelenmesi Üzerindeki Etkileri (1844–1914). (With

English summary.) *METU*, 1981, *8*(3&4), pp. 649–82. [G: Turkey]

Pearson, M. N. Banyas and Brahmins: Their Role in the Portuguese Indian Economy. In *Pearson, M. N.*, 1981, pp. 93–115. [G: India]

Pearson, M. N. The Port City of Goa: Policy and Practice in the Sixteenth Century. In *Pearson, M. N.*, 1981, pp. 67–92. [G: India]

Robb, Peter Graham. British Rule and Indian "Improvement." *Econ. Hist. Rev., 2nd Ser.*, November 1981, *34*(4), pp. 507–23. [G: India]

Simmons, Colin. Imperial Dictate: The Effect of the Two World Wars on the Indian Coal Industry. *World Devel.*, August 1981, *9*(8), pp. 749–71. [G: India]

Stivers, William. International Politics and Iraqi Oil, 1918–1928: A Study in Anglo–American Diplomacy. *Bus. Hist. Rev.*, Winter 1981, *55*(4), pp. 517–40. [G: Iraq; U.S.; U.K.]

Uekawa, Yoshimi. A Study on the Reformation Movement of Dogyokumiai Junsoku (Trade Association Regulations) by the Association of Chambers of Commerce. (In Japanese. With English summary.) *Osaka Econ. Pap.*, June 1981, *31*(1), pp. 115–37. [G: Japan]

Wallerstein, Immanuel and Kasaba, Reşat. Incorporation into the World-Economy: Change in the Structure of the Ottoman Empire, 1750–1839. *METU*, 1981, *8*(1 & 2), pp. 537–70. [G: Turkey]

Wiegersma, Nancy. Women in the Transition to Capitalism: Nineteenth to Mid-twentieth Century Vietnam. In *Zarembka, P., ed.*, 1981, pp. 1–28. [G: Vietnam]

Wittfogel, Karl. The Theory of Oriental Society. In *Bailey, A. M. and Llobera, J. R., eds.*, 1981, *1968*, pp. 141–57.

0451 History of Product Prices and Markets

Blaich, Fritz. Japan's Automobile Marketing: Its Introduction, Consolidation, Development and Characteristics: Comment. In *Okochi, A. and Shimokawa, K., eds.*, 1981, pp. 188–90. [G: Japan]

Boserup, Ester. Indian Agriculture from the Perspective of Western Europe. In *Sarma, J. S.*, 1981, pp. 55–58. [G: India; W. Europe]

Brown, Shannon R. and Wright, Tim. Technology, Economics, and Politics in the Modernization of China's Coal-Mining Industry, 1850–1895. *Exploration Econ. Hist.*, January 1981, *18*(1), pp. 60–83. [G: China]

Chakepaichayon, Vichian. Joint-Stock Companies in the Early Meiji Era (1)—An Analysis on 81 Articles of Corporations. (In Japanese. With English summary.) *Osaka Econ. Pap.*, June 1981, *31*(1), pp. 98–114. [G: Japan]

Doeppers, Daniel F. Construction Cycles in Prewar Manila. *Philippine Econ. J.*, 1981, *20*(1), pp. 44–57. [G: Philippines]

Fieldhouse, D. K. Decolonisation and the Multinational Company: Unilever in India, 1917–65. In *Bairoch, P. and Lévy-Leboyer, M., eds.*, 1981, pp. 58–64. [G: India]

Hirashima, S. Some Issues in Indian Agriculture Viewed from the Japanese Experience. In *Sarma,*

J. S., 1981, pp. 59–69. [G: India; Japan]

Miyamoto, Matao. Relationships among Local Rice Markets in the Tokugawa Period, 1651–1850—Correlation Analysis on Regional Prices of Rice. (In Japanese. With English summary.) *Osaka Econ. Pap.*, December 1981, *31*(2–3), pp. 274–307. [G: Japan]

Sakudō, Yōtarō. The Characteristics and the Genealogy of the Entrepreneurs of the Kansai Area. (In Japanese. With English summary.) *Osaka Econ. Pap.*, December 1981, *31*(2–3), pp. 308–28. [G: Japan]

Udagawa, Masaru. Japan's Automobile Marketing: Its Introduction, Consolidation, Development and Characteristics. In *Okochi, A. and Shimokawa, K., eds.*, 1981, pp. 163–87. [G: Japan]

Uemura, Masahiro. Ako Salt Transport and Shipping Operations in Late Tokugawa and Meiji Period. (In Japanese. With English summary.) *Osaka Econ. Pap.*, March 1981, *30*(4), pp. 80–113. [G: Japan]

Wagle, Dileep M. Imperial Preference and the Indian Steel Industry, 1924–39. *Econ. Hist. Rev., 2nd Ser.*, February 1981, *34*(1), pp. 120–31. [G: India]

0452 History of Factor Prices and Markets

Allen, G. C. Trade Unions in the Developed Economies: Japan. In *Smith, E. O., ed.*, 1981, pp. 73–96. [G: Japan]

Minami, Ryoshin and Ono, Akira. Behavior of Income Shares in a Labor Surplus Economy: Japan's Experience. *Econ. Develop. Cult. Change*, January 1981, *29*(2), pp. 309–24. [G: Japan]

Nakamura, James I. Human Capital Accumulation in Premodern Rural Japan. *J. Econ. Hist.*, June 1981, *41*(2), pp. 263–81. [G: Japan]

Taniguchi, Shinkichi. The Patni System—A Modern Origin of the "Sub-Infeudation" of Bengal in the Nineteenth Century. *Hitotsubashi J. Econ.*, June 1981, *22*(1), pp. 32–60. [G: India]

0453 History of Public Economic Policy (all levels)

Andic, Fuat M. and Andic, Suphan. Fritz Neumark, Teacher and Reformer: A Turkish View. *Finanzarchiv*, 1981, *39*(1), pp. 11–19. [G: Turkey]

Günçe, Ergin. Türkiye'de Planlamanin "Dünü—Bugünü—Yarini." (Past, Present and Future of Planning in Turkey. With English summary.) *METU*, Special Issue, 1981, pp. 117–32. [G: Turkey]

Kim, Son-Ung. Population Policies in Korea. In *Repetto, R., et al.*, 1981, pp. 196–221. [G: S. Korea]

Küçük, Yalçin. Türkiye'de Planlama Kavraminin Gelişimi Üzerine. (On the Development of the Planning Concept in Turkey. With English summary.) *METU*, Special Issue, 1981, pp. 79–115. [G: Turkey]

Matsuda, Yoshiro. Formation of the Census System in Japan: 1871–1945—Development of the Statistical System in Japan Proper and Her Colonies. *Hitotsubashi J. Econ.*, February 1981, *21*(2), pp. 44–68. [G: Japan]

Pettengill, John S. Firearms and the Distribution

of Income: A Neo-Classical Model. *Rev. Radical Polit. Econ.*, Summer 1981, *13*(2), pp. 1–10.

Pincus, Jonathan J. Discussion [Government Policy and Economic Development in Germany and Japan: A Skeptical Reevaluation] [Bureaucratic Opposition to the Assignment of Property Rights: Overgrazing on the Western Range]. *J. Econ. Hist.*, March 1981, *41*(1), pp. 159–61.
[G: Germany; Japan; U.S.]

Tipton, Frank B., Jr. Government Policy and Economic Development in Germany and Japan: A Skeptical Reevaluation. *J. Econ. Hist.*, March 1981, *41*(1), pp. 139–50. [G: Germany; Japan]

Uekawa, Yoshimi. A Study on the Reformation Movement of Dogyokumiai junsoku (Trade Association Regulations)—The Case of Tokyo Chamber of Commerce in the mid Meiji Period. (In Japanese. With English summary.) *Osaka Econ. Pap.*, March 1981, *30*(4), pp. 114–33.
[G: Japan]

Wallerstein, Immanuel and Kasaba, Reşat. Incorporation into the World-Economy: Change in the Structure of the Ottoman Empire, 1750–1839. *METU*, 1981, *8*(1 & 2), pp. 537–70.
[G: Turkey]

046 Economic History: Africa

0460 General

Adedeji, Adebayo. General Background to Indigenization: The Economic Dependence of Africa. In *Adedeji, A., ed.*, 1981, pp. 15–28. [G: Africa]

Adedeji, Adebayo. Historical and Theoretical Background. In *Adedeji, A., ed.*, 1981, pp. 29–41.
[G: Africa]

Amin, Samir. Senegal. In *Adedeji, A., ed.*, 1981, pp. 309–27. [G: Senegal]

Austen, Ralph. Capitalism, Class, and African Colonial Agriculture: The Mating of Marxism and Empiricism: Review Article. *J. Econ. Hist.*, September 1981, *41*(3), pp. 657–63. [G: Africa]

Barry, Boubacar. Economic Anthropology of Precolonial Senegambia from the Fifteenth through the Nineteenth Centuries. In *Colvin, L. G., et al.*, 1981, pp. 27–57. [G: W. Africa]

Bauer, P. T. British Colonial Africa: Economic Retrospect and Aftermath. In *Bauer, P. T.*, 1981, pp. 163–84. [G: Africa]

Chrétien, Jean-Pierre. Exchanges and Hierarchies in the East African Interlacustrine Kingdoms. In *Dalton, G., ed.*, 1981, *1974*, pp. 19–30.
[G: E. Africa]

Chrétien, Jean-Pierre. Exchanges and Hierarchies in the East African Interlacustrine Kingdoms: Reply. In *Dalton, G., ed.*, 1981, pp. 64.
[G: E. Africa]

Colvin, Lucie Gallistel. Labor and Migration in Colonial Senegambia. In *Colvin, L. G., et al.*, 1981, pp. 58–80. [G: W. Africa]

Fako, Thabo. Development in Sub-Saharan Africa and the Decline of Folk Knowledge in Agriculture. In *Busch, L., ed.*, 1981, pp. 157–66.
[G: Africa]

Hanafi, Mohammed N. Egypt. In *Adedeji, A., ed.*, 1981, pp. 49–80. [G: Egypt]

Khalafalla, Elfatih ShaaelDin. Capital Accumulation and the Consolidation of a Bourgeois Dependent State in Sudan, 1898–1978. In *Zarembka, P., ed.*, 1981, pp. 29–80. [G: Sudan]

Lawless, Richard I. Social and Economic Change in North African Medinas: The Case of Tunis. In *[Fisher, W. B.]*, 1981, pp. 264–79.
[G: Tunisia]

Lonsdale, John. State and Peasantry in Colonial Africa. In *Samuel, R., ed.*, 1981, pp. 106–17.
[G: Africa]

Magubane, Bernard. Social Inequality: The South Africa Case. In *Berreman, G. D., ed.*, 1981, pp. 257–76. [G: S. Africa]

Porter, Andrew. Britain, the Cape Colony, and Natal, 1870–1914: Capital, Shipping, and the Imperial Connexion. *Econ. Hist. Rev.*, 2nd Ser., November 1981, *34*(4), pp. 554–77. [G: U.K.; S. Africa]

Randles, W. G. L. Reciprocity in Bantu Africa. In *Dalton, G., ed.*, 1981, *1974*, pp. 12–19.
[G: Africa]

Roberts, Pepe. 'Rural Development' and the Rural Economy in Niger, 1900–75. In *Heyer, J.; Roberts, P. and Williams, G., eds.*, 1981, pp. 193–221. [G: Niger]

Spencer, Ian R. G. The First World War and the Origins of the Dual Policy of Development in Kenya, 1914–1922. *World Devel.*, August 1981, *9*(8), pp. 735–48. [G: Kenya]

Triulzi, Alessandro. Decolonising African History. In *Samuel, R., ed.*, 1981, pp. 286–97.
[G: Africa]

Wanjohi, N. Gatheru. Historical Scholarship in the East African Context. *Int. Soc. Sci. J.*, 1981, *33*(4), pp. 667–74.

0461 History of Product Prices and Markets

Marais, G. Structural Changes in Manufacturing Industry, 1916 to 1975. *S. Afr. J. Econ.*, March 1981, *49*(1), pp. 26–45. [G: S. Africa]

0462 History of Factor Prices and Markets

Müller, A. L. Slavery and the Development of South Africa. *S. Afr. J. Econ.*, June 1981, *49*(2), pp. 153–65. [G: S. Africa]

Müller, A. L. The Economics of Slave Labour at the Cape of Good Hope. *S. Afr. J. Econ.*, March 1981, *49*(1), pp. 46–58. [G: S. Africa]

Rathbone, Richard. Slavery in Pre-Colonial Africa. In *Samuel, R., ed.*, 1981, pp. 309–12.
[G: Africa]

Stahl, C. W. Migrant Labour Supplies, Past, Present and Future; with Special Reference to the Gold-Mining Industry. In *Böhning, W. R., ed.*, 1981, pp. 7–44. [G: S. Africa]

0463 History of Public Economic Policy (all levels)

Forrest, Tom. Agricultural Policies in Nigeria 1900–78. In *Heyer, J.; Roberts, P. and Williams, G., eds.*, 1981, pp. 222–58. [G: Nigeria]

Wickins, P. L. The Natives Land Act of 1913: A Cautionary Essay on Simple Explanations of Complex Change. *S. Afr. J. Econ.*, June 1981, *49*(2), pp. 105–29. [G: S. Africa]

047 Economic History: Latin America and Caribbean

0470 General

Albert, Bill and Henderson, Paul. Latin America and the Great War: A Preliminary Survey of Developments in Chile, Peru, Argentina and Brazil. *World Devel.*, August 1981, *9*(8), pp. 717–34.
[G: Chile; Peru; Argentina; Brazil]

Buescu, Mircea. Regional Inequalities in Brazil during the Second Half of the Nineteenth Century. In *Bairoch, P. and Lévy-Leboyer, M.*, eds., 1981, pp. 349–58. [G: Brazil]

Carmagnani, Marcello. Archives and Their Usage: Economic History in Colonial Chile. In *TePaske, J. J.*, ed., 1981, pp. 67–72. [G: Chile]

Copeland, Morris A. The Economies of Two Great Nonpecuniary Civilizations. In *Copeland, M. A.*, 1981, pp. 29–63. [G: Egypt; S. America]

Edwards, S. F. Archival Resources for Chilean Economic History, 1800–1850. In *TePaske, J. J.*, ed., 1981, pp. 73–83. [G: Chile]

Engerman, Stanley L. Notes on the Patterns of Economic Growth in the British North American Colonies in the Seventeenth, Eighteenth and Nineteenth Centuries. In *Bairoch, P. and Lévy-Leboyer, M.*, eds., 1981, pp. 46–57.
[G: Caribbean; U.S.]

Fioravanti-Molinié, Antoinette. Reciprocity and the INCA State: From Karl Polanyi to John V. Murra: Discussion. In *Dalton, G.*, ed., 1981, *1974*, pp. 54–58.

Margarido, Alfredo. Reciprocity in a Peasant Movement in Southern Brasil. In *Dalton, G.*, ed., 1981, *1974*, pp. 30–38. [G: Brazil]

Morrissey, Marietta. A Political Class Theory of the Satellite State: Jamaica, 1830–1930. In *Zarembka, P.*, ed., 1981, pp. 173–98. [G: Jamaica]

Murra, John V. Reciprocity and the Inca State: From Karl Polanyi to John V. Murra: Discussion. In *Dalton, G.*, ed., 1981, *1974*, pp. 51–54.
[G: Peru]

O'Brien, Thomas F., Jr. Notarial and Judicial Archives as Sources for Nineteenth-Century Chilean Economic History. In *TePaske, J. J.*, ed., 1981, pp. 96–97. [G: Chile]

Ocampo, José-Antonio. Export Growth and Capitalist Development in Colombia in the Nineteenth Century. In *Bairoch, P. and Lévy-Leboyer, M.*, eds., 1981, pp. 98–109. [G: Colombia]

Oppenheimer, Robert. Chilean Economic Development, 1850–1900: A Primary Source Guide. In *TePaske, J. J.*, ed., 1981, pp. 88–95. [G: Chile]

Schneider, Jürgen. Terms of Trade between France and Latin America, 1826–1856: Causes of Increasing Economic Disparities? In *Bairoch, P. and Lévy-Leboyer, M.*, eds., 1981, pp. 110–119.
[G: France; Latin America]

Wachtel, N. Reciprocity and the Inca State: From Karl Polanyi to John V. Murra. In *Dalton, G.*, ed., 1981, *1974*, pp. 38–50. [G: Peru]

0471 History of Product Prices and Markets

Leveson, Sidney M. Comments [Possible Dimensions of Mexican Petroleum] [PEMEX in a Dependent Society]. In *Ladman, J. R.; Baldwin, D. J. and Bergman, E.*, eds., 1981, pp. 117–21.
[G: Mexico; U.S.]

Miller, Rory. Latin American Manufacturing and the First World War: An Exploratory Essay. *World Devel.*, August 1981, *9*(8), pp. 707–16.
[G: Latin America]

Sepúlveda, Isidro. PEMEX in a Dependent Society. In *Ladman, J. R.; Baldwin, D. J. and Bergman, E.*, eds., 1981, pp. 45–68. [G: Mexico]

Trouillot, Michel-Rolph. Peripheral Vibrations: The Case of Saint-Domingue's Coffee Revolution. In *Rubinson, R.*, ed., 1981, pp. 27–41. [G: Haiti]

0472 History of Factor Prices and Markets

Baseo, Sahadeo. The Role of the British Labour Movement in the Development of Labour Organisation in Trinidad 1919–1929. *Soc. Econ. Stud.*, September 1981, *30*(3), pp. 21–41.
[G: Trinidad and Tobago; U.K.]

Johansen, Hans Chr. Slave Demography of the Danish West Indian Islands. *Scand. Econ. Hist. Rev.*, 1981, *29*(1), pp. 1–20. [G: W. Indies]

Levenstein, Harvey. Leninists Undone by Leninism: Communism and Unionism in the United States and Mexico, 1935–1939. *Labor Hist.*, Spring 1981, *22*(2), pp. 237–61. [G: U.S.; Mexico]

Loveman, Brian. Sources for the Study of Chilean Labor History. In *TePaske, J. J.*, ed., 1981, pp. 118–27. [G: Chile]

0473 History of Public Economic Policy (all levels)

Cardoso, Eliana A. The Great Depression and Commodity-exporting LDCs: The Case of Brazil. *J. Polit. Econ.*, December 1981, *89*(6), pp. 1239–50. [G: Brazil]

Curzon, Gerard and Price, Victoria Curzon. Protección antigua y nueva: Una revisión histórica. (With English summary.) *Cuadernos Econ.*, August–December 1981, *18*(54–55), pp. 129–40.
[G: Chile]

Douglas, Hernán Cortés; Butelmann, Andrea and Videla, Pedro. Proteccionismo en Chile: Una visión retrospectiva. (With English summary.) *Cuadernos Econ.*, August–December 1981, *18*(54–55), pp. 141–94. [G: Chile]

048 Economic History: Oceania

0480 General

Mayne, A. J. C. Commuter Travel and Class Mobility in Sydney, 1858–88. *Australian Econ. Hist. Rev.*, March 1981, *21*(1), pp. 53–65.
[G: Australia]

Neale, R. S., et al. Life and Death in Hillgrove, 1870–1914. *Australian Econ. Hist. Rev.*, September 1981, *21*(2), pp. 91–113. [G: Australia]

Pomfret, Richard. The Staple Theory as an Approach to Canadian and Australian Economic Development. *Australian Econ. Hist. Rev.*, September

1981, *21*(2), pp. 133–46. [G: Canada; Australia]

Pope, David H. Contours of Australian Immigration, 1901–30. *Australian Econ. Hist. Rev.*, March 1981, *21*(1), pp. 29–52. [G: Australia]

0481 History of Product Prices and Markets

Purcell, W. R. The Development of Japan's Trading Company Network in Australia, 1890–1941. *Australian Econ. Hist. Rev.*, September 1981, *21*(2), pp. 114–32. [G: Australia]

0482 History of Factor Prices and Markets

Cupper, Les and Hearn, June M. Trade Unions in the Developed Economies: Australia. In *Smith, E. O., ed.*, 1981, pp. 13–42. [G: Australia]

McLean, Ian W. The Analysis of Agricultural Productivity: Alternative Views and Victorian Evidence. *Australian Econ. Hist. Rev.*, March 1981, *21*(1), pp. 6–28. [G: Australia]

Sinclair, W. A. Women at Work in Melbourne and Adelaide since 1871. *Econ. Rec.*, December 1981, *57*(159), pp. 344–53. [G: Australia]

0483 History of Public Economic Policy (all levels)

Manger, Gary J. The Australian Case for Protection Reconsidered. *Australian Econ. Pap.*, December 1981, *20*(37), pp. 193–204. [G: Australia]

Pope, David H. Modelling the Peopling of Australia: 1900–1930. *Australian Econ. Pap.*, December 1981, *20*(37), pp. 258–82. [G: Australia]

050 ECONOMIC SYSTEMS

0500 General

Alker, Hayward R., Jr. Dialectical Foundations of Global Disparities. In *Hollist, W. L. and Rosenau, J. N., eds.*, 1981, pp. 80–109.

Bailey, Anne M. and Llobera, Josep R. The Asiatic Mode of Production: Science and Politics: General Introduction. In *Bailey, A. M. and Llobera, J. R., eds.*, 1981, pp. 1–10.

Bailey, Anne M. and Llobera, Josep R. The AMP: Sources and Formation of the Concept. In *Bailey, A. M. and Llobera, J. R., eds.*, 1981, pp. 11–45.

Banu, Ioan. The 'Tributary' Social Formation. In *Bailey, A. M. and Llobera, J. R., eds.*, 1981, *1967*, pp. 278–80.

Bierfelder, Wilhelm. Exploration of Needs under Conditions of a Free Marketsystem and of a Planned Economy. In *Molt, W.; Hartmann, H. A. and Stringer, P., eds.*, 1981, pp. 281–84.

Coats, A. W. and Thompstone, S. Against 'Against Convergence.' *Cambridge J. Econ.*, December 1981, *5*(4), pp. 383–86.

Darity, William A., Jr. *Research in Economic Anthropology, Volume One:* A Review Article. *J. Econ. Issues*, March 1981, *15*(1), pp. 129–35.

Ellman, Michael. Reply to 'Against "Against Convergence".' *Cambridge J. Econ.*, December 1981, *5*(4), pp. 387–89.

Godelier, Maurice. The Asiatic Mode of Production. In *Bailey, A. M. and Llobera, J. R., eds.*, 1981,

1978, pp. 264–77.

Godes, M. The Reaffirmation of Unilinealism. In *Bailey, A. M. and Llobera, J. R., eds.*, 1981, *1931*, pp. 99–105.

Gregory, C. A. A Conceptual Analysis of a Non-Capitalist Gift Economy with Particular Reference to Papua New Guinea. *Cambridge J. Econ.*, June 1981, *5*(2), pp. 119–35.
[G: Papua New Guinea]

Hollist, W. Ladd. Anticipating World System Theory Synthesis. In *Hollist, W. L. and Rosenau, J. N., eds.*, 1981, pp. 289–300.

Krader, Lawrence. Principles and Critique of the Asiatic Mode of Production. In *Bailey, A. M. and Llobera, J. R., eds.*, 1981, *1975*, pp. 325–34.

Lewin, Gunter. Wittfogel on the Asiatic Mode of Production. In *Bailey, A. M. and Llobera, J. R., eds.*, 1981, *1967*, pp. 158–63.

Mad'iar, L. I. The Legitimacy of the AMP. In *Bailey, A. M. and Llobera, J. R., eds.*, 1981, *1930*, pp. 76–94.

Price, Barbara. Irrigation: Sociopolitical Dynamics and the Growth of Civilization. In *Bailey, A. M. and Llobera, J. R., eds.*, 1981, *1973*, pp. 216–32.

Tökei, Ferenc. The Asiatic Mode of Production. In *Bailey, A. M. and Llobera, J. R., eds.*, 1981, *1966*, pp. 249–63.

Welskopf, Elisabeth C. Problems of Periodisation in Ancient History. In *Bailey, A. M. and Llobera, J. R., eds.*, 1981, *1957*, pp. 242–48.

Wittfogel, Karl. The Theory of Oriental Society. In *Bailey, A. M. and Llobera, J. R., eds.*, 1981, *1968*, pp. 141–57.

Yefimov, Vladimir M. Gaming-Simulation of the Functioning of Economic Systems. *J. Econ. Behav. Organ.*, June 1981, *2*(2), pp. 187–200.

051 Capitalist Economic Systems

0510 Market Economies

Abramovitz, Moses. Welfare Quandaries and Productivity Concerns. *Amer. Econ. Rev.*, March 1981, *71*(1), pp. 1–17. [G: U.S.]

Agnew, J. A. Homeownership and the Capitalist Social Order. In *Dear, M. and Scott, A. J., eds.*, 1981, pp. 457–80. [G: U.K.; U.S.]

Aharoni, Yair. Toward an Age of Humility. *Calif. Manage. Rev.*, Winter 1981, *24*(2), pp. 49–59.
[G: U.S.]

Albach, Horst. On the Re-Discovery of the Entrepreneur in Economic Policy Discussion. In *Engels, W. and Pohl, H., eds.*, 1981, pp. 12–26.

Allen, Robert C. Entrepreneurship and Technical Progress in the Northeast Coast Pig Iron Industry: 1850–1913. In *Uselding, P., ed.*, 1981, pp. 35–71. [G: U.K.]

Amin, Samir. Some Thoughts of Self-reliant Development, Collective Self-reliance and the New International Economic Order. In *Grassman, S. and Lundberg, E., eds.*, 1981, pp. 534–52.

Austen-Smith, David. Society and Economy: A Review Article. *Scot. J. Polit. Econ.*, November 1981, *28*(3), pp. 291–96.

Barbash, Jack. Theories of the Labor Movement in

an Institutional Setting. *J. Econ. Issues*, June 1981, *15*(2), pp. 299–309.

Barry, Norman P. Re-stating the Liberal Order: Hayek's Philosophical Economics. In *Shackleton, J. R. and Locksley, G., eds.*, 1981, pp. 87–107.

Bauer, P. T. Class on the Brain. In *Bauer, P. T.*, 1981, pp. 26–39.   [G: U.K.]

Baumol, William J. and Willig, Robert D. Intertemporal Failures of the Invisible Hand: Theory and Implications for International Market Dominance. *Indian Econ. Rev.*, January–June 1981, *16*(1 and 2), pp. 1–12.

Becker, Walter. Methodological Aspects in Describing the Bourgeois and Industrial Revolutions. In *Bairoch, P. and Lévy-Leboyer, M., eds.*, 1981, pp. 131–36.   [G: Europe]

Bentley, J. Marvin and Oberhofer, Tom. Property Rights and Economic Development. *Rev. Soc. Econ.*, April 1981, *39*(1), pp. 51–65.
                    [G: W. Africa]

Berger, Suzanne. Regime and Interest Representation: The French Traditional Middle Classes. In *Berger, S., ed.*, 1981, pp. 83–101.   [G: France]

Bergesen, Albert. Long Economic Cycles and the Size of Industrial Enterprise. In *Rubinson, R., ed.*, 1981, pp. 179–89.   [G: MDCs]

Bitunov, Vladimir V. Economic Planning and Management. In *Novosti Press Agency*, 1981, pp. 63–76.   [G: U.S.S.R.]

Bottomore, Tom. The Decline of Capitalism, Sociologically Considered. In *Heertje, A., ed.*, 1981, pp. 22–44.

Bowles, Samuel. Technical Change and the Profit Rate: A Simple Proof of the Okishio Theorem: Note [Technical Change and the Rate of Profit]. *Cambridge J. Econ.*, June 1981, *5*(2), pp. 183–86.

Bradley, Keith and Gelb, Alan. Motivation and Control in the Mondragon Experiment. *Brit. J. Ind. Relat.*, July 1981, *19*(2), pp. 211–31. [G: Spain]

Brandis, Royall. An Alarmist View of Corporate Influence. In *Hessen, R., ed.*, 1981, pp. 17–22.

Bruyn, Severyn T. Social Economy: A Note on Its Theoretical Foundations. *Rev. Soc. Econ.*, April 1981, *39*(1), pp. 81–84.

Camilleri, Joseph. The Advanced Capitalist State and the Contemporary World Crisis. *Sci. Soc.*, Summer 1981, *45*(2), pp. 130–58.

Chary, Joseph. The Kibbutz: An Applied Socio-economic Experiment. *Int. J. Soc. Econ.*, 1981, *8*(7), pp. 56–59.   [G: Israel]

Chase-Dunn, Christopher. Interstate System and Capitalist World-Economy. In *Hollist, W. L. and Rosenau, J. N., eds.*, 1981, pp. 30–53.

Clark, Gordon L. and Dear, Michael. The State in Capitalism and the Capitalist State. In *Dear, M. and Scott, A. J., eds.*, 1981, pp. 45–61.

Corbett, Timothy, et al. The Joint Responsibility of Business and Government. *Rivista Int. Sci. Econ. Com.*, January–February 1981, *28*(1–2), pp. 121–28.

Cox, Kevin R. Capitalism and Conflict Around the Communal Living Space. In *Dear, M. and Scott, A. J., eds.*, 1981, pp. 432–55.

Cramer, Dale L. and Leathers, Charles G. Schumpeter's Corporatist Views: Links among His Social

Theory, Quadragesimo Anno, and Moral Reform. *Hist. Polit. Econ.*, Winter 1981, *13*(4), pp. 745–71.

Davis, Lance E. and Huttenback, Robert A. In Search of the Historical Imperialist. In *[Weiler, E. T.]*, 1981, pp. 152–67.   [G: U.K.]

Delaunay, J.-C. L'évolution du taux de la plus-value en France (1951–1980). (The Rate of Surplus-Value in France (1951–1980). With English summary.) *L'Actual. Econ.*, April–June 1981, *57*(2), pp. 160–92.   [G: France]

Deutsch, K. W. From the National Welfare State to the International Welfare System. In *Mommsen, W. J., ed.*, 1981, pp. 424–37.

Duvall, Raymond D. and Freeman, John R. The State and Dependent Capitalism. In *Hollist, W. L. and Rosenau, J. N., eds.*, 1981, pp. 223–42.

Eckberg, Douglas Lee. Intelligence as an Economic Concept: A Critique of Gonzalez's History. *Rev. Radical Polit. Econ.*, Fall 1981, *13*(3), pp. 54–57.

Edel, Matthew. Capitalism, Accumulation and the Explanation of Urban Phenomena. In *Dear, M. and Scott, A. J., eds.*, 1981, pp. 19–44.

Falkena, H. B. Public and Private Enterprise (Review Note). *S. Afr. J. Econ.*, September 1981, *49*(3), pp. 289–94.

Fellner, William. March into Socialism, or Viable Postwar Stage of Capitalism? In *Heertje, A., ed.*, 1981, pp. 45–68.

Ferreira da Costa, Fernando. Co-operative Democracy among Consumers and Workers. *Ann. Pub. Co-op. Econ.*, January–June 1981, *52*(1/2), pp. 101–15.

Flora, P. Solution or Source of Crises? The Welfare State in Historical Perspective. In *Mommsen, W. J., ed.*, 1981, pp. 343–89.   [G: Europe]

Gay, David E. R. Towards a Theory of Entitlements in Comparative Economics. *Rivista Int. Sci. Econ. Com.*, March 1981, *28*(3), pp. 216–25.

Gilb, Corinne Lathrop. Public or Private Governments? In *Nystrom, P. C. and Starbuck, W. H., eds., Vol. 2*, 1981, pp. 464–91.   [G: U.S.; W. Europe]

Gordon, David M. Capital–Labor Conflict and the Productivity Slowdown. *Amer. Econ. Rev.*, May 1981, *71*(2), pp. 30–35.   [G: U.S.]

Gordon, David M. The Best Defense is a Good Defense: Toward a Marxian Theory of Labor Union Structure and Behavior. In *Carter, M. J. and Leahy, W. H., eds.*, 1981, pp. 167–214.

Gordon, Theodore J. The Revival of Enterprise. In *Cleveland, H., ed.*, 1981, pp. 330–59. [G: U.S.]

Gramm, Warren S. Property Rights in Work: Capitalism, Industrialism, and Democracy. *J. Econ. Issues*, June 1981, *15*(2), pp. 363–75.

Greenberg, Edward S. Industrial Self-Management and Political Attitudes. *Amer. Polit. Sci. Rev.*, March 1981, *75*(1), pp. 29–42.   [G: U.S.]

Greenfield, Sidney M. and Strickon, Arnold. A New Paradigm for the Study of Entrepreneurship and Social Change. *Econ. Develop. Cult. Change*, April 1981, *29*(3), pp. 467–99.

Grossman, Gregory. The "Second Economy" of the U.S.S.R. In *Bornstein, M., ed.*, 1981, *1977*, pp. 71–93.   [G: U.S.S.R.]

Gruchy, Allan G. Organized Labor and Institutional Economics. *J. Econ. Issues*, June 1981, *15*(2), pp. 311–24.   [G: U.S.]

Haberler, Gottfried. Schumpeter's *Capitalism, Socialism and Democracy* after Forty Years. In *Heertje, A., ed.*, 1981, pp. 69–94.

Halpern, Paul J. Business, Government, the Public: Who Manipulates Whom? In *Hessen, R., ed.*, 1981, pp. 40–49.

Hannesson, Rögnvaldur. Stagflation: A Problem of the Aging Welfare State? A Comment on the Baumol-Oates "Cost-Disease" Model. *Scand. J. Econ.*, 1981, *83*(1), pp. 104–08.

Harvey, David. The Urban Process under Capitalism: A Framework for Analysis. In *Dear, M. and Scott, A. J., eds.*, 1981, pp. 91–121.

Heilbroner, Robert L. Was Schumpeter Right? In *Heertje, A., ed.*, 1981, pp. 95–106.

Heilbroner, Robert L. Was Schumpeter Right? *Soc. Res.*, Autumn 1981, *48*(3), pp. 456–71.

Henning, Hansjoachim. The Social Integration of Entrepreneurs in Westphalia 1860–1914. In *Engels, W. and Pohl, H., eds.*, 1981, pp. 83–106.   [G: W. Germany]

Hernes, Gudmund and Selvik, Arne. Local Corporatism. In *Berger, S., ed.*, 1981, pp. 103–19.   [G: Norway]

Herschede, Fred and Wiltgen, Richard J. Japan's Alternative Road to Serfdom: J. M. Clark and the Japanese Experience. *Rev. Soc. Econ.*, December 1981, *39*(3), pp. 323–42.   [G: U.S.; Japan]

Hessen, Robert. Does Big Business Rule America? Introduction. In *Hessen, R., ed.*, 1981, pp. 1–7.

Higgs, Robert. Discussion [Regulation, Property Rights, and Definition of "The Market": Law and the American Economy]. *J. Econ. Hist.*, March 1981, *41*(1), pp. 110–11.   [G: U.S.]

Himmelstrand, Ulf. Sweden: Paradise in Trouble. In *Denitch, B., ed.*, 1981, pp. 149–62.   [G: Sweden]

Hirsch, Joachim. The Apparatus of the State, the Reproduction of Capital and Urban Conflicts. In *Dear, M. and Scott, A. J., eds.*, 1981, pp. 593–607.

Hirschman, Albert O. A Generalized Linkage Approach to Development, with Special Reference to Staples. In *Hirschman, A. O.*, 1981, *1977*, pp. 59–97.

Hirschman, Albert O. The Turn to Authoritarianism in Latin America and the Search for its Economic Determinants. In *Hirschman, A. O.*, 1981, *1979*, pp. 98–135.   [G: Latin America]

Hodgson, Geoff. On Exploitation and Labor-Value. *Sci. Soc.*, Summer 1981, *45*(2), pp. 228–33.

Hopkins, Terence K. and Wallerstein, Immanuel. Structural Transformations of the World-Economy. In *Rubinson, R., ed.*, 1981, pp. 233–61.   [G: Global]

Howe, Geoffrey [Sir]. Liberating Free Enterprise: A New Experiment. In *Sternlieb, G. and Listokin, D., eds.*, 1981, pp. 13–24.   [G: U.K.]

Hughes, Jonathan. Professor Hobsbawm on the Evolution of Modern Capitalism. In *[Weiler, E. T.]*, 1981, pp. 168–87.   [G: U.K.]

Hutchison, Terence W. The Market Economy and the Franchise, or 1867 and All That. In *Hutchison, T. W.*, 1981, pp. 22–45.

Hutchison, Terence W. Walter Eucken and the German Social-Market Economy. In *Hutchison, T. W.*, 1981, pp. 155–75.   [G: W. Germany]

Ignatieff, Michael. Primitive Accumulation Revisited. In *Samuel, R., ed.*, 1981, pp. 130–35.   [G: U.K.]

Ishikawa, Akihiro. Experiments in Self-Management in Japan. *Econ. Anal. Worker's Manage.*, 1981, *15*(1), pp. 115–24.   [G: Japan]

Itoh, Makoto. On Marx's Theory of Accumulation: A Reply to Weeks [The Process of Accumulation and the 'Profit Squeeze' Hypothesis]. *Sci. Soc.*, Spring 1981, *45*(1), pp. 71–84.

Izraeli, Oded and Groll, Shalom. Implications of an Ideological Constraint: The Case of Hired Labor in the Kibbutz. *Econ. Develop. Cult. Change*, January 1981, *29*(2), pp. 341–51.   [G: Israel]

Johnson, Dale L. Intermediate Classes in a Bipolarizing Structure. In *Rubinson, R., ed.*, 1981, pp. 167–78.

Khalafalla, Elfatih ShaaelDin. Capital Accumulation and the Consolidation of a Bourgeois Dependent State in Sudan, 1898–1978. In *Zarembka, P., ed.*, 1981, pp. 29–80.   [G: Sudan]

Kirzner, Israel M. Entrepreneurship, Entitlement, and Economic Justice. In *Paul, J., ed.*, 1981, *1978*, pp. 383–411.

Kochevrin, Yu. B. The Economic Theory of Managerial Capitalism. In *Mileikovsky, A. G., et al.*, 1981, pp. 453–91.

Kocka, Jürgen. The Entrepreneur, the Family and Capitalism: Some Examples from the Early Phase of Industrialisation in Germany. In *Engels, W. and Pohl, H., eds.*, 1981, pp. 53–82.   [G: W. Germany]

Kriedte, Peter. Proto-Industrialization between Industrialization and De-Industrialization. In *Kriedte, P.; Medick, H. and Schlumbohm, J.*, 1981, pp. 135–60.   [G: Europe]

Kuipers, Simon K. Disequilibrium, Power and Economic Systems: A Review Article of Schouten's New Book "Power and Disorder, a Comparison of Economic Systems." *De Economist*, 1981, *129*(4), pp. 546–57.

Kuznetsov, V. I. and Kudryavtsev, A. K. Attempts to Sociologise Bourgeois Political Economy: The French School. In *Mileikovsky, A. G., et al.*, 1981, pp. 370–91.

Lambers, Hendrik Wilm. The Vision. In *Heertje, A., ed.*, 1981, pp. 107–29.

Lane, Robert E. Waiting for Lefty: The Capitalist Genesis of Socialist Man. In *Denitch, B., ed.*, 1981, pp. 36–60.

Lange, Peter. Unions, Parties, the State, and Liberal Corporatism. In *Denitch, B., ed.*, 1981, pp. 82–103.   [G: Italy]

Lansbury, Russell D. and Prideaux, Geoffrey J. Industrial Democracy: Toward an Analytical Framework. *J. Econ. Issues*, June 1981, *15*(2), pp. 325–38.

Lele, Uma. Co-operatives and the Poor: A Comparative Perspective. *World Devel.*, January 1981, *9*(1), pp. 55–72.

Lerner, Ralph. Commerce and Character: The Anglo-American as New-Model Man. In *Novak, M., ed.*, 1981, *1979*, pp. 24–49.

Lincoln, Andrew. Through the Undergrowth: Capitalist Development and Social Formation in Nineteenth-Century France. In *Samuel, R., ed.*, 1981, pp. 255–67. [G: France]

Lindbeck, Assar. Some Thoughts of Self-reliant Development, Collective Self-reliance and the New International Economic Order: Comments. In *Grassman, S. and Lundberg, E., eds.*, 1981, pp. 553–57.

Linz, Juan J. A Century of Politics and Interests in Spain. In *Berger, S., ed.*, 1981, pp. 365–415. [G: Spain]

Loescher, Samuel M. Public Interest Movements and Private Interest Systems: A Healthy Schizophrenia. *J. Econ. Issues*, June 1981, *15*(2), pp. 557–68.

Lonsdale, John. State and Peasantry in Colonial Africa. In *Samuel, R., ed.*, 1981, pp. 106–17. [G: Africa]

Lorenz, James. Expanding Choice and Opportunities for Entrepreneurship. In *Inst. for Contemp. Studies*, 1981, pp. 93–97. [G: U.S.]

Lowenthal, Richard. The Postwar Transformation of European Social Democracy. In *Denitch, B., ed.*, 1981, pp. 20–35. [G: Europe]

Magubane, Bernard. Social Inequality: The South Africa Case. In *Berreman, G. D., ed.*, 1981, pp. 257–76. [G: S. Africa]

Maier, Charles S. "Fictitious Bonds...of Wealth and Law": On the Theory and Practice of Interest Representation. In *Berger, S., ed.*, 1981, pp. 27–61. [G: W. Europe]

McCracken, Paul W. The Corporation and the Liberal Order. In *Novak, M. and Cooper, J. W., eds.*, 1981, pp. 34–46. [G: U.S.]

McDaniel, Bruce A. The Integration of Economics and Society. *J. Econ. Issues*, June 1981, *15*(2), pp. 543–55.

Medick, Hans. The Transition from Feudalism to Capitalism: Renewal of the Debate. In *Samuel, R., ed.*, 1981, pp. 120–30.

Mileikovsky, A. G. Structural Changes in the Economy of Capitalism and Theories of its Social Transformation. In *Mileikovsky, A. G., et al.*, 1981, pp. 392–452.

Mileikovsky, A. G. The General Crisis of Capitalism and Bourgeois Economic Doctrines of World Development. In *Mileikovsky, A. G., et al.*, 1981, pp. 547–75.

Mileikovsky, A. G. The Present Stage in the Crisis of Bourgeois Economics: Introduction. In *Mileikovsky, A. G., et al.*, 1981, pp. 13–49.

Mills, Catherine. Du sacrifice de l'équilibre social à l'aggravation des déséquilibres économiques. (With English summary.) *Écon. Appl.*, 1981, *34*(2–3), pp. 349–81. [G: France]

Mishan, Ezra J. The Folklore of the Market: An Inquiry into the Economic Doctrines of the Chicago School. In *Mishan, E. J.*, 1981, *1975*, pp. 219–55.

Morrissey, Marietta. A Political Class Theory of the Satellite State: Jamaica, 1830–1930. In *Zarembka, P., ed.*, 1981, pp. 173–98. [G: Jamaica]

Munley, Frank. Wages, Salaries, and the Profit Share: A Reassessment of the Evidence. *Cambridge J. Econ.*, June 1981, *5*(2), pp. 159–73. [G: U.S.]

Murchland, Bernard. The Socialist Critique of the Corporation. In *Novak, M. and Cooper, J. W., eds.*, 1981, pp. 156–71.

Myrdal, Hans-Göran. Collective Wage-Earner Funds in Sweden: A Road to Socialism and the End of Freedom of Association. *Int. Lab. Rev.*, May–June 1981, *120*(3), pp. 319–34. [G: Sweden]

Naschold, Frieder. The Future of the Welfare State. In *Mommsen, W. J., ed.*, 1981, pp. 394–407.

Neffa, Julio César. Improvement of Working Conditions and Environment: A Peruvian Experiment with New Forms of Work Organisation. *Int. Lab. Rev.*, July–August 1981, *120*(4), pp. 473–90. [G: Peru]

Nelson, Richard R. Assessing Private Enterprise: An Exegesis of Tangled Doctrine. *Bell J. Econ. (See Rand J. Econ. after 4/85)*, Spring 1981, *12*(1), pp. 93–111.

Noam, Eli M. The Valuation of Legal Rights. *Quart. J. Econ.*, August 1981, *96*(3), pp. 465–76. [G: Switzerland]

O'Brien, Denis Patrick. The Emphasis on Market Economics. In *Seldon, A., ed.*, 1981, pp. 51–77.

Obern, Catheryn C. and Jones, Steven D. Critical Factors Affecting Agricultural Production Cooperatives: A Review. *Ann. Pub. Co-op. Econ.*, September 1981, *52*(3), pp. 317–49.

Painton, Frederick. I guai dello stato assistenziale in Europa. (Woes of the Welfare State. With English summary.) *Mondo Aperto*, December 1981, *35*(6), pp. 345–57. [G: W. Europe]

Peterson, Richard A. Entrepreneurship and Organization. In *Nystrom, P. C. and Starbuck, W. H., eds.*, Vol. 1, 1981, pp. 65–83.

Poschl, Josef and Locksley, Gareth. Michal Kalecki: A Comprehensive Challenge to Orthodoxy. In *Shackleton, J. R. and Locksley, G., eds.*, 1981, pp. 141–59.

Posner, Richard A. The Economics of Privacy. *Amer. Econ. Rev.*, May 1981, *71*(2), pp. 405–09. [G: U.S.]

Pryor, Frederic L. The 'New Class': Analysis of the Concept, the Hypothesis and the Idea as a Research Tool. *Amer. J. Econ. Soc.*, October 1981, *40*(4), pp. 367–79.

Ramirez, Francisco O. and Thomas, George M. Structural Antecedents and Consequences of Statism. In *Rubinson, R., ed.*, 1981, pp. 139–64.

Ramos, Joseph. On the Prospects of Social Market Democracy—or Democratic Capitalism—in Latin America. In *Novak, M., ed.*, 1981, pp. 68–72. [G: Latin America]

Rauter, Anton. Co-operatives and the Democracy of Members. *Ann. Pub. Co-op. Econ.*, January–June 1981, *52*(1/2), pp. 117–25. [G: Austria]

Reiman, Jeffrey H. and Headlee, Sue. Crime and Crisis. In *Wright, K. N., ed.*, 1981, pp. 27–38. [G: U.S.]

Reisman, David. The Dissenting Economist: J. K. Galbraith. In *Shackleton, J. R. and Locksley, G.,* eds., 1981, pp. 72–86.

Rimlinger, G. V. Comments on Professor Peter Flora's Analytical Perspective of the Welfare State [Solution or Source of Crises? The Welfare State in Historical Perspective]. In *Mommsen, W. J., ed.*, 1981, pp. 390–94. **[G: Europe]**

Robinson, Joan. The Age of Growth. In *Robinson, J.*, 1981, *1979*, pp. 33–42.

Robinson, Joan and Bhaduri, Amit. Accumulation and Exploitation: An Analysis in the Tradition of Marx, Sraffa and Kalecki. In *Robinson, J.*, 1981, *1980*, pp. 64–77.

Rogerson, Christian M. Industrialization in the Shadows of Apartheid: A World-Systems Analysis. In *Hamilton, F. E. I. and Linge, G. J. R., eds.*, 1981, pp. 395–421. **[G: Southern Africa]**

Room, G. J. The End of the Welfare State? In *Mommsen, W. J., ed.*, 1981, pp. 408–23. **[G: U.K.]**

Rosser, J. Barkley, Jr. The Emergence of the Megacorpstate and the Acceleration of Global Inflation. *J. Post Keynesian Econ.*, Spring 1981, *3*(3), pp. 429–39.

Roweis, Shoukry T. Urban Planning in Early and Late Capitalist Societies: Outline of a Theoretical Perspective. In *Dear, M. and Scott, A. J., eds.*, 1981, pp. 159–77.

Rugina, Anghel N. What Is the Alternative for the West? Neither Capitalism nor Socialism but "Social Liberalism." *Int. J. Soc. Econ.*, 1981, *8*(2), pp. 3–46.

Sáinz, Juan Pablo Pérez. Capital, State and Fetishization. In *Zarembka, P., ed.*, 1981, pp. 129–45.

Saive, Marie-Anne. L'État et le développement coopératif. Quatre expériences. (The State and the Co-operative Movement: Four Experiments. With English summary.) *Ann. Pub. Co-op. Econ.*, September 1981, *52*(3), pp. 301–15. **[G: France; Canada; U.S.; U.K.]**

Saive, Marie-Anne. Note sur Mondragon et les aspects doctrinaux du projet coopératif. (Co-operative Doctrine and Rent in Mondragon: A Note. With English summary.) *Ann. Pub. Co-op. Econ.*, September 1981, *52*(3), pp. 369–79. **[G: Spain]**

Salvati, Michele. May 1968 and the Hot Autumn of 1969: The Responses of Two Ruling Classes. In *Berger, S., ed.*, 1981, pp. 329–63. **[G: France; Italy]**

Samuelson, Paul A. Schumpeter's *Capitalism, Socialism and Democracy.* In *Heertje, A., ed.*, 1981, pp. 1–21.

Sandberg, Lars G. The Entrepreneur and Technological Change. In *Floud, R. and McCloskey, D., eds., Vol. 2*, 1981, pp. 99–120. **[G: U.K.]**

Scheiber, Harry N. Regulation, Property Rights, and Definition of "The Market": Law and the American Economy. *J. Econ. Hist.*, March 1981, *41*(1), pp. 103–09. **[G: U.S.]**

Schlumbohm, Jürgen. Excursus: The Political and Institutional Framework of Proto-Industrialization. In *Kriedte, P.; Medick, H. and Schlumbohm, J.*, 1981, pp. 126–34. **[G: Europe]**

Schlumbohm, Jürgen. Relations of Production—Productive Forces—Crises in Proto-Industrialization. In *Kriedte, P.; Medick, H. and Schlumbohm, J.*, 1981, pp. 94–125. **[G: Europe]**

Shenayev, V. N. The Crisis of Neoliberalism and the Evolution of the "Social Market Economy" Theory. In *Mileikovsky, A. G., et al.*, 1981, pp. 253–82.

Simon, William E. Government Regulation and a Free Society. In *Gatti, J. F., ed.*, 1981, pp. 11–24.

Slater, David. Some Theoretical Considerations on the Peruvian State, 1968–1978. In *Zarembka, P., ed.*, 1981, pp. 147–72. **[G: Peru]**

Smithies, Arthur. Schumpeter's Predictions. In *Heertje, A., ed.*, 1981, pp. 130–49.

de Sola Pool, Ithiel. How Powerful is Business? In *Hessen, R., ed.*, 1981, pp. 23–34.

Stephens, John D. The Ideological Development of the Swedish Social Democrats. In *Denitch, B., ed.*, 1981, pp. 136–48. **[G: Sweden]**

Stockman, David. How the Market Outwits the Planners. In *Hessen, R., ed.*, 1981, pp. 57–74.

Szelenyi, Ivan. The Relative Autonomy of the State or State Mode of Production? In *Dear, M. and Scott, A. J., eds.*, 1981, pp. 565–91.

Taylor, Barbara. Socialist Feminism: Utopian or Scientific? In *Samuel, R., ed.*, 1981, pp. 158–63.

Theophanides, Stavros M. The Consumer Firm: The Popular Shipping Companies in Greece—A Case-Study of Consumer Participation in the Creation of Firms. *Econ. Anal. Worker's Manage.*, 1981, *15*(2), pp. 231–50. **[G: Greece]**

Thimm, Alfred L. How Far Should German Codetermination Go? *Challenge*, July/August 1981, *24*(3), pp. 13–22. **[G: W. Germany]**

Tíkal, Svatopluk. The Balance of Forces between the U.S.A. and the European Communities. *Czech. Econ. Digest.*, March 1981, (2), pp. 55–72. **[G: U.S.; EEC]**

Trouillot, Michel-Rolph. Peripheral Vibrations: The Case of Saint-Domingue's Coffee Revolution. In *Rubinson, R., ed.*, 1981, pp. 27–41. **[G: Haiti]**

Umbeck, John. Might Makes Rights: A Theory of the Formation and Initial Distribution of Property Rights. *Econ. Inquiry*, January 1981, *19*(1), pp. 38–59. **[G: U.S.]**

Vogt, Roy. Property Rights and Employee Decision Making in West Germany. *J. Econ. Issues*, June 1981, *15*(2), pp. 377–86. **[G: W. Germany]**

Wachtel, Howard M. The Future of Social Democracy. *Econ. Forum*, Winter 1981–82, *12*(2), pp. 55–68.

Wallerstein, Immanuel. Dependence in an Interdependent World: The Limited Possibilities of Transformation within the Capitalist World Economy. In *Muñoz, H., ed.*, 1981, *1974*, pp. 267–93.

Ward, Sally K. Dependency, National Economy, and Inequality. In *Rubinson, R., ed.*, 1981, pp. 211–29. **[G: U.S.]**

Weisskopf, Thomas E. Wages, Salaries and the Profit Share: A Rejoinder [Marxian Crisis Theory and the Rate of Profit in the Postwar US Economy]. *Cambridge J. Econ.*, June 1981, *5*(2), pp. 175–82. **[G: U.S.]**

Wiegersma, Nancy. Women in the Transition to Capitalism: Nineteenth to Mid-twentieth Century Vietnam. In *Zarembka, P., ed.*, 1981, pp. 1–28. **[G: Vietnam]**

Wiles, Peter. A Sovietological View. In *Heertje, A., ed.*, 1981, pp. 150–69.

Wilson, James Q. Democracy and the Corporation. In *Hessen, R., ed.*, 1981, pp. 35–39.

Woodworth, Warner. The Emergence of Economic Democracy in the United States. *Econ. Anal. Worker's Manage.*, 1981, 15(2), pp. 207–18. [G: U.S.]

Worland, Stephen T. Exploitative Capitalism: The Natural-Law Perspective. *Soc. Res.*, Summer 1981, 48(2), pp. 277–305.

Worsley, Peter. Social Class and Development. In *Berreman, G. D., ed.*, 1981, pp. 221–55.

Yannacopoulos, Nicos A. Rosa Luxemburg's Theory of Capitalist Catastrophe. *J. Post Keynesian Econ.*, Spring 1981, 3(3), pp. 452–56.

Young, Michael. How Large a Future for Co-operatives? Some Personal Reflections on the OECD Seminar of 12–14 September 1980. *Econ. Anal. Worker's Manage.*, 1981, 15(3), pp. 396–416.

Zaikina, V. I. Concept of "Democratisation of Capital." In *Mileikovsky, A. G., et al.*, 1981, pp. 514–32. [G: W. Germany]

Zassenhaus, Herbert K. Capitalism, Socialism and Democracy: The 'Vision' and the 'Theories.' In *Heertje, A., ed.*, 1981, pp. 170–202.

052 Socialist and Communist Economic Systems

0520 Socialist and Communist Economic Systems

Äbel, István and Riecke, Werner. A Model of Aggregate Inventory Behaviour in the Hungarian Economy. In *Chikán, A., ed. (I)*, 1981, pp. 13–28. [G: Hungary]

Altvater, Elmar. The Primacy of Politics in Post-Revolutionary Societies. *Rev. Radical Polit. Econ.*, Spring 1981, 13(1), pp. 1–10.

Antal, László. Historical Development of the Hungarian System of Economic Control and Management. *Acta Oecon.*, 1981, 27(3–4), pp. 251–66. [G: Hungary]

Bailey, Anne M. and Llobera, Josep R. The Fate of the AMP from Plekhanov to Stalin: Editors' Introduction. In *Bailey, A. M. and Llobera, J. R., eds.*, 1981, pp. 49–52.

Balassa, Bela. The Economic Reform in Hungary Ten Years After. In *Balassa, B.*, 1981, pp. 329–46. [G: Hungary]

Bazarova, G. The Financial and Credit Mechanism for Increasing Effectiveness. *Prob. Econ.*, April 1981, 23(12), pp. 28–48. [G: U.S.S.R.]

Behrendt, Willy. The Concept of Public Needs as Used in the Socialist States. In *Molt, W.; Hartmann, H. A. and Stringer, P., eds.*, 1981, pp. 285–94.

Berliner, Joseph S. The Prospects for Technological Progress. In *Bornstein, M., ed.*, 1981, 1976, pp. 293–311.

Bettelheim, Charles and Chavance, Bernard. Stalinism as the Ideology of State Capitalism. *Rev. Radical Polit. Econ.*, Spring 1981, 13(1), pp. 40–54. [G: U.S.S.R.]

Bielasiak, Jack. Workers and Mass Participation in 'Socialist Democracy.' In *Triska, J. F. and Gati, C., eds.*, 1981, pp. 88–107. [G: E. Europe]

Böttcher, Dieter Joachim. Some Problems of the Stability and Flexibility of the National Economic Reproduction Process with Special Regard to the Role of Material and Financial Reserves. In *Chikán, A., ed. (I)*, 1981, pp. 63–71.

Bunich, P. G. Wages as an Economic Incentive. *Prob. Econ.*, May 1981, 24(1), pp. 3–18. [G: U.S.S.R.]

Cain, P. J. Hobson's Developing Theory of Imperialism. *Econ. Hist. Rev.*, 2nd Ser., May 1981, 34(2), pp. 313–16.

Capian, Alain. La socialisation du salaire. (The Socialization of Wages. With English summary.) *Revue Écon.*, November 1981, 32(6), pp. 1087–1112.

Clarke, P. F. Hobson, Free Trade, and Imperialism. *Econ. Hist. Rev.*, 2nd Ser., May 1981, 34(2), pp. 308–12.

Comisso, Ellen Turkish. Can a Party of the Working Class Be a Working-Class Party? In *Triska, J. F. and Gati, C., eds.*, 1981, pp. 70–87. [G: Yugoslavia; Italy]

Connor, Walter D. Workers and Power. In *Triska, J. F. and Gati, C., eds.*, 1981, pp. 157–72. [G: E. Europe]

Denitch, Bogdan. Yugoslav Exceptionalism. In *Triska, J. F. and Gati, C., eds.*, 1981, pp. 253–67. [G: Yugoslavia]

Desai, Padma and Bhagwati, Jagdish N. Three Alternative Concepts of Foreign Exchange Difficulties in Centrally Planned Economies. In *Bhagwati, J. N., ed.*, 1981, 1979, pp. 349–59.

Dyker, David A. Decentralization and the Command-Principle—Some Lessons from Soviet Experience. *J. Compar. Econ.*, June 1981, 5(2), pp. 121–48. [G: U.S.S.R.]

Edelstein, Joel C. The Evolution of Cuban Development Strategy, 1959–1979. In *Muñoz, H., ed.*, 1981, pp. 225–66. [G: Cuba]

Ellman, Michael. Agricultural Productivity under Socialism. *World Devel.*, September/October 1981, 9(9/10), pp. 979–89. [G: China; U.S.S.R.]

Fábri, Ervin. Paradoxes of Macroeconomic Inventory Developments. In *Chikán, A., ed. (I)*, 1981, pp. 109–23. [G: Hungary]

Feiwel, George R. A Socialist Model of Economic Development: The Polish and Bulgarian Experiences. *World Devel.*, September/October 1981, 9(9/10), pp. 929–50. [G: Poland; Bulgaria]

Fekete, Ferenc. Accomplishments of and Challenges for Agricultural Economists Working at the National Level of Centrally Managed Economies. In *Johnson, G. and Maunder, A., eds.*, 1981, pp. 285–94.

Fellner, William. March into Socialism, or Viable Postwar Stage of Capitalism? In *Heertje, A., ed.*, 1981, pp. 45–68.

Fenichel, Allen and Khan, Azfar. The Burmese Way to 'Socialism.' *World Devel.*, September/October 1981, 9(9/10), pp. 813–24. [G: Burma]

Fényes, Tamás I. Potential Applicability of Certain Socialistic Farming Practices for Rural Development in Non-Socialist Less Developed Countries. In *Johnson, G. and Maunder, A., eds.*, 1981, pp. 659–69.

Flakierski, Henryk. Economic Reform and Income Distribution in Poland: The Negative Evidence.

Cambridge J. Econ., June 1981, 5(2), pp. 137–58. [G: Poland]

Gati, Charles. Workers' Assertiveness, Western Dilemmas. In *Triska, J. F. and Gati, C., eds.*, 1981, pp. 283–94. [G: E. Europe]

Gebethner, Stanislaw. Political and Institutional Changes in the Management of the Socialist Economy: the Polish Case. In *Bornstein, M.; Gitelman, Z. and Zimmerman, W., eds.*, 1981, pp. 252–82. [G: Poland]

Gelb, Michael. Roots of Soviet Industrial Management, 1917–1941. *Rev. Radical Polit. Econ.*, Spring 1981, 13(1), pp. 55–66. [G: U.S.S.R.]

Glushkov, N. The Economic Mechanism and Planned Pricing Practices. *Prob. Econ.*, January 1981, 23(9), pp. 77–102. [G: U.S.S.R.]

Gowdy, John M. Radical Economics and Resource Scarcity. *Rev. Soc. Econ.*, October 1981, 39(2), pp. 165–80.

Grossman, Gregory. The "Second Economy" of the U.S.S.R. In *Bornstein, M., ed.*, 1981, 1977, pp. 71–93. [G: U.S.S.R.]

Halliday, Jon. The North Korean Model: Gaps and Questions. *World Devel.*, September/October 1981, 9(9/10), pp. 889–905. [G: N. Korea]

Hare, Paul G. The Investment System in Hungary. In *Hare, P. G.; Radice, H. K. and Swain, N., eds.*, 1981, pp. 83–106. [G: Hungary]

Holzman, Franklyn D. The Second Economy in CMEA: A Terminological Note. *ACES Bull. (See Comp. Econ. Stud. after 8/85)*, Spring 1981, 23(1), pp. 111–14. [G: CMEA]

Horvat, Branko. Establishing Self-governing Socialism in a Less Developed Country. *World Devel.*, September/October 1981, 9(9/10), pp. 951–64. [G: LDCs]

Iakovets, Iu. Prices and the Improvement of Planning and the Economic Mechanism. *Prob. Econ.*, April 1981, 23(12), pp. 49–66. [G: U.S.S.R.]

Jameson, Kenneth P. Socialist Cuba and the Intermediate Regimes of Jamaica and Guyana. *World Devel.*, September/October 1981, 9(9/10), pp. 871–88. [G: Cuba; Jamaica; Guyana]

Jameson, Kenneth P. and Wilber, Charles K. Socialism and Development: Editors' Introduction. *World Devel.*, September/October 1981, 9(9/10), pp. 803–11. [G: U.S.S.R.; China]

Johnson, Paul M. Changing Social Structure and the Political Role of Manual Workers. In *Triska, J. F. and Gati, C., eds.*, 1981, pp. 29–42. [G: E. Europe]

Karabín, Štefan. For a More Effective Use of Manpower. *Czech. Econ. Digest.*, February 1981, (1), pp. 38–53. [G: Czechoslovakia]

Khachaturov, Tigran. Soviet Economy Today: Introduction. In *Novosti Press Agency*, 1981, pp. 3–16. [G: U.S.S.R.]

Knaack, Ruud. Economic Reform in China. *ACES Bull. (See Comp. Econ. Stud. after 8/85)*, Summer 1981, 23(2), pp. 1–29. [G: China]

Kofi, Tetteh A. Prospects and Problems of the Transition from Agrarianism to Socialism: The Case of Angola, Guinea-Bissau and Mozambique. *World Devel.*, September/October 1981, 9(9/10), pp. 851–70. [G: Angola; Guinea-Bissau; Mozambique]

Kojima, Kiyoshi. A New Capitalism for a New International Economic Order. *Hitotsubashi J. Econ.*, June 1981, 22(1), pp. 1–19.

Kolankiewicz, George. Poland, 1980: The Working Class under 'Anomic Socialism.' In *Triska, J. F. and Gati, C., eds.*, 1981, pp. 136–56. [G: Poland]

Komarov, V. and Ulanovskaia, V. The Service Sector and Increasing the Effectiveness of Production. *Prob. Econ.*, May 1981, 24(1), pp. 19–38. [G: U.S.S.R.]

Kónya, Lajos. Conditions of Setting Up Simple Forms of Cooperatives in the Hungarian Industry. *Acta Oecon.*, 1981, 27(1–2), pp. 77–92. [G: Hungary]

Kornai, János. Some Properties of the Eastern European Growth Pattern. *World Devel.*, September/October 1981, 9(9/10), pp. 965–70. [G: E. Europe]

Laluha, Ivan. Higher Quality of Living Conditions—An Essential Prerequisite of Development of the Socialist Way of Life. *Czech. Econ. Digest.*, December 1981, (8), pp. 39–54. [G: Czechoslovakia]

Maiminas, E. Z. Theoretical Problems of Modeling the Socioeconomic System. *Matekon*, Spring 1981, 17(3), pp. 9–34. [G: U.S.S.R.]

Mandel, Ernest. The Laws of Motion of the Soviet Economy. *Rev. Radical Polit. Econ.*, Spring 1981, 13(1), pp. 35–39. [G: U.S.S.R.]

Marrese, M. The Evolution of Wage Regulation in Hungary. In *Hare, P. G.; Radice, H. K. and Swain, N., eds.*, 1981, pp. 54–80. [G: Hungary]

McIntyre, Robert J. and Thornton, James R. Energy Systems and Comparative Systems: A Reply to Ryding [Urban Design and Energy Utilization: A Comparative Analysis of Soviet Practice]. *J. Compar. Econ.*, December 1981, 5(4), pp. 414–17. [G: U.S.S.R.]

Molyneux, Maxine. Women's Emancipation under Socialism: A Model for the Third World? *World Devel.*, September/October 1981, 9(9/10), pp. 1019–37. [G: LDCs; E. Europe; U.S.S.R.; China]

Montias, J. M. Observations on Strikes, Riots and Other Disturbances. In *Triska, J. F. and Gati, C., eds.*, 1981, pp. 173–86.

Montias, J. M. and Rose-Ackerman, Susan. Corruption in a Soviet-type Economy: Theoretical Considerations. In *[Bergson, A.]*, 1981, pp. 53–83.

Mujžel, Jan. The Working System of the Economy (Problems with Its Further Development in Poland). *Eastern Europ. Econ.*, Fall 1981, 20(1), pp. 20–48. [G: Poland]

Murrell, Peter. The Microeconomic Efficiency Argument for Socialism Revisited: Comment. *J. Econ. Issues*, March 1981, 15(1), pp. 211–19.

Nelson, Daniel. Romania: Participatory Dynamics in 'Developed Socialism.' In *Triska, J. F. and Gati, C., eds.*, 1981, pp. 236–52. [G: Romania]

Nuti, D. M. Socialism on Earth. *Cambridge J. Econ.*, December 1981, 5(4), pp. 391–403.

Petrakov, N. Ia. The Operating Mechanism of a Socialist Economy and the Problem of the Economy's Optimality Criterion. *Matekon*, Spring 1981, 17(3), pp. 35–54. [G: U.S.S.R.]

Plekhanov, G. The Fate of the AMP from Plekhanov to Stalin: Our Differences. In *Bailey, A. M. and*

Llobera, J. R., eds., 1981, *1881*, pp. 53–57.

Pollis, Adamantia. Human Rights, Third World Socialism and Cuba. *World Devel.*, September/October 1981, 9(9/10), pp. 1005–17.   [G: LDCs; Cuba]

Portes, Richard. Reply to E. Dirksen, "The Control of Inflation? Errors in the Interpretation of CPE Data." *Economica*, August 1981, 48(191), pp. 309–11.   [G: Cent. Planned Econ.]

Pravda, Alex. Political Attitudes and Activity. In *Triska, J. F. and Gati, C., eds.*, 1981, pp. 43–69.   [G: E. Europe]

Pryor, Frederic L. The 'New Class': Analysis of the Concept, the Hypothesis and the Idea as a Research Tool. *Amer. J. Econ. Soc.*, October 1981, 40(4), pp. 367–79.

Raichur, Satish. Economic 'Laws,' the Law of Value, and Chinese Socialism. *Australian Econ. Pap.*, December 1981, 20(37), pp. 205–18. [G: China]

Rosefielde, Steven. Knowledge and Socialism: Deciphering the Soviet Experience. In *[Bergson, A.]*, 1981, pp. 5–23.   [G: U.S.S.R.]

Ryding, Helene. Municipal Energy Supply and District Heating: A Comment on Robert J. McIntyre and James R. Thornton, "Urban Design and Energy Utilization: A Comparative Analysis of Soviet Practice." *J. Compar. Econ.*, December 1981, 5(4), pp. 404–13.   [G: U.S.S.R.]

Schweitzer, Iván. Some Interrelations between Enterprise Organization and the Economic Mechanism in Hungary. *Acta Oecon.*, 1981, 27(3–4), pp. 289–300.   [G: Hungary]

Shaozhi, Su. Some Questions in China's Socialist Economic Construction. *Econ. Notes*, 1981, 10(3), pp. 18–36.   [G: China]

Silver, Geoffrey and Tarpinian, Gregory. Marxism and Socialism: A Response to Paul Sweezy and Ernest Mandel. *Rev. Radical Polit. Econ.*, Spring 1981, 13(1), pp. 11–21.   [G: U.S.S.R.]

Skurski, Roger. Socialism and the Consumer in the U.S.S.R. *Rev. Radical Polit. Econ.*, Spring 1981, 13(1), pp. 22–30.   [G: U.S.S.R.]

Triska, Jan F. Workers' Assertiveness and Soviet Policy Choices. In *Triska, J. F. and Gati, C., eds.*, 1981, pp. 268–82.

Tyson, Laura D'Andrea. Aggregate Economic Difficulties and Workers' Welfare. In *Triska, J. F. and Gati, C., eds.*, 1981, pp. 108–35.   [G: Hungary; Poland]

Valenta, Jiri. Czechoslovakia: A 'Prolétariat Embourgeoisé'? In *Triska, J. F. and Gati, C., eds.*, 1981, pp. 209–23.   [G: Czechoslovakia]

Volgyes, Ivan. Hungary: The Lumpenproletarianization of the Working Class. In *Triska, J. F. and Gati, C., eds.*, 1981, pp. 224–35. [G: Hungary]

Weaver, James H. and Kronemer, Alexander. Tanzanian and African Socialism. *World Devel.*, September/October 1981, 9(9/10), pp. 839–49.   [G: Tanzania]

Wesolowski, Wlodzimierz and Krauze, Tadeusz. Socialist Society and the Meritocratic Principle of Remuneration. In *Berreman, G. D., ed.*, 1981, pp. 337–49.   [G: Poland]

de Weydenthal, Jan B. Poland: Workers and Politics. In *Triska, J. F. and Gati, C., eds.*, 1981, pp. 187–208.   [G: Poland]

Whyte, Martin King. Destratification and Restratification in China. In *Berreman, G. D., ed.*, 1981, pp. 309–36.   [G: China]

Wiedemann, Paul. Economic Reform in Bulgaria: Coping with "The kj Problem." *Eastern Europ. Econ.*, Fall 1981, 20(1), pp. 90–108.

Xue, Muqiao. Tentative Study on the Reform of the Economic System. *Chinese Econ. Stud.*, Winter–Spring 1980-81, 14(2–3), pp. 139–68.

[G: China]

Yunker, James A. The Microeconomic Efficiency of Market Socialism: Reply [The Microeconomic Efficiency Argument for Socialism Revisited]. *J. Econ. Issues*, March 1981, 15(1), pp. 220–27.

Zassenhaus, Herbert K. Capitalism, Socialism and Democracy: The 'Vision' and the 'Theories.' In *Heertje, A., ed.*, 1981, pp. 170–202.

Zhou, Shulian; Wu, Jinglian and Wang, Haibo. The Profit Category and Socialist Business Management. *Chinese Econ. Stud.*, Winter–Spring 1980-81, 14(2–3), pp. 3–138.   [G: China]

Zimbalist, Andrew. On the Role of Management in Socialist Development. *World Devel.*, September/October 1981, 9(9/10), pp. 971–77.

[G: Yugoslavia; U.S.S.R.; Cuba; Chile]

053 Comparative Economic Systems

0530 Comparative Economic Systems

Bardach, Eugene. Pluralism Reconsidered. In *Hessen, R., ed.*, 1981, pp. 11–16.

Boncher, William. A Comparative Engineering-Economic Analysis of the Evolution of the Soviet Mainline Freight Locomotive. *J. Compar. Econ.*, June 1981, 5(2), pp. 149–68.   [G: U.S.; U.S.S.R.]

Burakow, Nicholas. Romania and Greece—Socialism vs Capitalism. *World Devel.*, September/October 1981, 9(9/10), pp. 907–28.   [G: Romania; Greece]

Foster, J. Fagg. The United States, Russia, and Democracy. *J. Econ. Issues*, December 1981, 15(4), pp. 975–80.   [G: U.S.; U.S.S.R.]

Gottheil, Fred. Iraqi and Syrian Socialism: An Economic Appraisal. *World Devel.*, September/October 1981, 9(9/10), pp. 825–37.   [G: Iraq; Syria; Jordan; Morocco]

Heinsohn, Gunnar and Steiger, Otto. Money, Productivity and Uncertainty in Capitalism and Socialism. *Metroecon.*, Feb.-Oct. 1981, 33(1–2–3), pp. 41–77.

Lipset, Seymour Martin. Industrial Proletariat in Comparative Perspective. In *Triska, J. F. and Gati, C., eds.*, 1981, pp. 1–28.   [G: OECD; U.S.S.R.]

Murrell, Peter. An Evaluation of the Success of the Hungarian Economic Reform: An Analysis Using International-Trade Data. *J. Compar. Econ.*, December 1981, 5(4), pp. 352–66.
[G: Mediterranean Europe; Austria; U.K.; Hungary; E. Europe]

Pommerehne, Werner W.; Schneider, Friedrich and Lafay, Jean-Dominique. Les interactions entre économie et politique: synthèses des analyses theoriques et empiriques. (Interactions between the Economy and the Polity: A Synthesis of Theoretical and Empirical Studies. With English summary.) *Revue Écon.*, January 1981, *32*(1), pp. 110–62.

Scholing, Eberhard and Timmermann, Vincenz. Ost-West-Vergleich interindustrieller Verflechtungsstrukturen auf der Basis von Input-Output-Tabellen. (With English summary.) *Kyklos,* 1981, *34*(2), pp. 230–41.

Seton, Francis A. A Quasi-Competitive Price Basis for Intersystem Comparisons of Economic Structure and Performance. *J. Compar. Econ.*, December 1981, *5*(4), pp. 367–91. [G: Kenya; U.S.S.R.; Japan; U.K.; U.S.]

Spalter-Roth, Roberta M. and Zeitz, Eileen. Production and Reproduction of Everyday Life. In *Rubinson, R., ed.,* 1981, pp. 193–209. [G: Philippines]

100 Economic Growth; Development; Planning; Fluctuations

110 ECONOMIC GROWTH; DEVELOPMENT; AND PLANNING THEORY AND POLICY

111 Economic Growth Theory and Models

1110 Growth Theories

Baranzini, Mauro. Taux d'intérêt, distribution du revenu, théorie des cycles vitaux et choix du portefeuille. (With English summary.) *Kyklos,* 1981, *34*(4), pp. 593–610.

Burmeister, Edwin. On the Uniqueness of Dynamically Efficient Steady States. *Int. Econ. Rev.,* February 1981, *22*(1), pp. 211–19.

Chiang, Alpha C. Hicks-Neutral and Harrod-Neutral Technological Progress: The Solution of a Puzzle [Neutrality of Technological Progress: A Synthetic View and a Puzzle]. *Rivista Int. Sci. Econ. Com.,* April 1981, *28*(4), pp. 304–10.

Currie, Lauchlin. Allyn Young and the Development of Growth Theory. *J. Econ. Stud.,* 1981, *8*(1), pp. 52–60.

Davenport, Paul. Unemployment and Technology in a Model of Steady Growth. *Australian Econ. Pap.,* June 1981, *20*(36), pp. 115–32.

Fazi, Elido and Salvadori, Neri. The Existence of a Two-Class Economy in the Kaldor Model of Growth and Distribution. *Kyklos,* 1981, *34*(4), pp. 582–92.

Fischer, Wolfram. Driving Forces of Economic Growth: What Can We Learn from History? Comments. In *Giersch, H., ed. (II),* 1981, pp. 59–64.

Folkers, Cay. Grundsatzfragen und Konzepte der dynamischen Inzidenzanalyse. (Basic Problems and Concepts of Dynamic Incidence. With English summary.) *Z. Wirtschaft. Sozialwissen.,* 1981, *101*(2), pp. 127–51.

Gahlen, Bernhard. How Useful are Post-Keynesian and Neo-Classical Models in Explaining Growth? In *Giersch, H., ed. (II),* 1981, pp. 1–20.

Ganti, Subrahmanyam and Kolluri, Bharat R. The Limits to Growth Hypothesis: Some Empirical Evidence. *J. Econ. Devel.,* July 1981, *6*(1), pp. 101–10.

Gapinski, James H. Steady Growth, Policy Shocks, and Speed of Adjustment under Embodiment and Putty-Clay. *J. Macroecon.,* Spring 1981, *3*(2), pp. 147–76.

Gaude, J. Capital-Labour Substitution Possibilities: A Review of Empirical Evidence. In *Bhalla, A. S., ed.,* 1981, *1975,* pp. 41–64. [G: Selected LDCs]

Hammer, Jeffrey S. Optimal Growth and Income Redistribution. *Metroecon.,* Feb.-Oct. 1981, *33*(1–2–3), pp. 145–57.

Kuipers, Simon K. Keynesian and Neo-Classical Growth Models: A Sequential Analytical Approach. *De Economist,* 1981, *129*(1), pp. 58–104.

Kuznets, Simon. Driving Forces of Economic Growth: What Can We Learn from History? In *Giersch, H., ed. (II),* 1981, pp. 37–58.

Laitner, John P. The Stability of Steady States in Perfect Foresight Models. *Econometrica,* March 1981, *49*(2), pp. 319–33.

Laitner, John P. The Steady States of a Stochastic Decentralized Growth Model. *J. Econ. Theory,* June 1981, *24*(3), pp. 377–92.

Laski, Kazimierz. International Financing: Comment. In *Saunders, C. T., ed. (I),* 1981, pp. 162–64. [G: LDCs]

Leibenstein, Harvey. Economic Growth as an Endogenous Process—Human Resources and Motivation: Comments. In *Giersch, H., ed. (II),* 1981, pp. 88–91.

Little, Ian M. D. Driving Forces of Economic Growth: What Can We Learn from History? Comments. In *Giersch, H., ed. (II),* 1981, pp. 65–69.

Maddison, Angus. How Useful are Post-Keynesian and Neo-Classical Models in Explaining Growth? Comments. In *Giersch, H., ed. (II),* 1981, pp. 21–25.

McClelland, David C. Economic Growth as an Endogenous Process—Human Resources and Motivation: Comments. In *Giersch, H., ed. (II),* 1981, pp. 92–100.

Millendorfer, Johann. Economic Growth as an Endogenous Process—Human Resources and Motivation: Comments. In *Giersch, H., ed. (II),* 1981, pp. 101–10.

Mishan, Ezra J. Whatever Happened to Progress? In *Mishan, E. J.,* 1981, pp. 266–76.

Mitra, Tapan and Zilcha, Itzhak. On Optimal Economic Growth with Changing Technology and Tastes: Characterization and Stability Results. *Int. Econ. Rev.,* February 1981, *22*(1), pp. 221–38.

Nelson, Richard R. Research on Productivity Growth and Productivity Differences: Dead Ends and New Departures. *J. Econ. Lit.,* September 1981, *19*(3), pp. 1029–64.

Ognev, Alexandre P. The Role of Development Aid Facilities: Comment. In *Saunders, C. T., ed. (I),* 1981, pp. 165–66. [G: LDCs]

Osadchaya, I. M. Evolution of Economic Growth Theory. In *Mileikovsky, A. G., et al.,* 1981, pp. 51–73.

Osadchaya, I. M. The Present Stage of the "Antimarginalist Revolution" and Keynesianism. In *Milei-kovsky, A. G., et al.*, 1981, pp. 74–117.

Reinhardt, Paul G. Is the Neoclassical Growth Economy a Market Economy? *Z. Wirtschaft. Sozialwissen.*, 1981, *101*(4), pp. 441–43.

Rossi, Enzo. A Lemma on Relative Stability with an Application to an Economic Case Study. *J. Math. Econ.*, March 1981, *8*(1), pp. 75–85.

Seton, Francis. The Role of Development Aid Facilities. In *Saunders, C. T., ed. (I)*, 1981, pp. 127–59. [G: LDCs]

Simon, Julian L. and Steinmann, Gunter. Population Growth and Phelps' Technical Progress Model: Interpretation and Generalization. In *Simon, J. L. and Lindert, P. H., eds.*, 1981, pp. 239–54.

Soldaczuk, Józef. The Role of Development Aid Facilities: Comment. In *Saunders, C. T., ed. (I)*, 1981, pp. 167–71. [G: LDCs]

Steindl, Josef. Ideas and Concepts of Long Run Growth. *Banca Naz. Lavoro Quart. Rev.*, March 1981, (136), pp. 35–48.

Streeten, Paul P. From Growth to Basic Needs. In *Streeten, P.*, 1981, pp. 323–33.

Streissler, Erich. How Useful are Post-Keynesian and Neo-Classical Models in Explaining Growth? Comments. In *Giersch, H., ed. (II)*, 1981, pp. 26–35.

Vaizey [Lord]. Economic Growth as an Endogenous Process—Human Resources and Motivation. In *Giersch, H., ed. (II)*, 1981, pp. 71–87.

Yu, Eden S. H. On Factor Market Distortions and Economic Growth. *Southern Econ. J.*, July 1981, *48*(1), pp. 172–78.

1112 One and Two Sector Growth Models and Related Topics

Andersson, Åke E. Structural Change and Technological Development. *Reg. Sci. Urban Econ.*, August 1981, *11*(3), pp. 351–61.

Augusztinovics, Mária. The Rate of Economic Growth in Hungary, 1950–2000. *Acta Oecon.*, 1981, *26*(3–4), pp. 223–42. [G: Hungary]

Backhouse, Roger E. Keynesian Unemployment and the One-Sector Neoclassical Growth Model. *Econ. J.*, March 1981, *91*(361), pp. 174–87.

Becker, Robert A. The Duality of a Dynamic Model of Equilibrium and an Optimal Growth Model: The Heterogeneous Capital Goods Case. *Quart. J. Econ.*, May 1981, *96*(2), pp. 271–300.

Cigno, Alessandro. Growth with Exhaustible Resources and Endogenous Population. *Rev. Econ. Stud.*, April 1981, *48*(2), pp. 281–87.

Danthine, Jean-Pierre and Donaldson, John B. Certainty Planning in an Uncertain World: A Reconsideration. *Rev. Econ. Stud.*, July 1981, *48*(3), pp. 507–10.

Danthine, Jean-Pierre and Donaldson, John B. Stochastic Properties of Fast vs. Slow Growing Economies. *Econometrica*, June 1981, *49*(4), pp. 1007–33.

Dixon, Robert J. The Wage Share and Capital Accumulation. *J. Post Keynesian Econ.*, Fall 1981, *4*(1), pp. 3–9.

Findlay, Ronald and Rodriguez, Carlos Alfredo. A

Model of Economic Growth with Investment in Human Capital. In *Khan, A. and Sirageldin, I., eds.*, 1981, pp. 57–72.

Freixas, Xavier. Optimal Growth with Experimentation. *J. Econ. Theory*, April 1981, *24*(2), pp. 296–309.

Grünbaum, Isi. Experiments with a Profit-multiplier Growth Model. In *Grünbaum, I.*, 1981, pp. 111–57.

Grünbaum, Isi. Marginal Productivity in the Profit-multiplier Growth Model. In *Grünbaum, I.*, 1981, *1963*, pp. 159–90.

Hansen, Jørgen Drud. Om regionale uligheder i neoklassisk vækstteori. (The Regional Level of Income per Capita in a Neoclassical One-Sector Growth Model. With English summary.) *Nationaløkon. Tidsskr.*, 1981, *119*(3), pp. 392–408.

Hung, N. M. L'instabilité structurelle dans le modèle de croissance avec ressource non renouvelable. (Structural Instability in the Growth Model with Exhaustible Resources. With English summary.) *L'Actual. Econ.*, July–September 1981, *57*(3), pp. 387–406.

Kohli, Ulrich R. Nonjointness and Factor Intensity in U.S. Production. *Int. Econ. Rev.*, February 1981, *22*(1), pp. 3–18. [G: U.S.]

Kosobud, Richard F. and O'Neill, William D. On the Dependence of Population Growth on Income: New Results in a Ricardian-Malthus Model. *De Economist*, 1981, *129*(2), pp. 206–23.

Laibman, David. Two-Sector Growth with Endogenous Technical Change: A Marxian Simulation Model. *Quart. J. Econ.*, February 1981, *96*(1), pp. 47–75.

MacLean, L. C.; Field, C. A. and Sutherland, W. R. S. Optimal Growth and Uncertainty: The Borrowing Models. *J. Econ. Theory*, April 1981, *24*(2), pp. 168–86.

Murrell, Peter. Endogenous Technological Change and Optimal Growth. *Eastern Econ. J.*, April 1981, *7*(2), pp. 97–109.

Olson, Dennis O. Neoclassical Growth Models and Regional Growth in the U.S.: A Comment. *J. Reg. Sci.*, August 1981, *21*(3), pp. 425–30. [G: U.S.]

Pikoulakis, Emmanuel. Growth, Saving, the Balance of Payments and the Neo-Classical Growth Diagram. *Bull. Econ. Res.*, November 1981, *33*(2), pp. 104–14.

Pohjola, Matti T. Stable, Cyclic and Chaotic Growth: The Dynamics of a Discrete-Time Version of Goodwin's Growth Cycle Model. *Z. Nationalökon.*, 1981, *41*(1–2), pp. 27–38.

Sgro, Pasquale M. and Takayama, Akira. On the Long-Run Growth Effects of a Minimum Wage for a Two-Sector Economy. *Econ. Rec.*, June 1981, *57*(157), pp. 180–85.

Sinn, Hans-Werner. Capital Income Taxation, Depreciation Allowances and Economic Growth: A Perfect-Foresight General Equilibrium Model. *Z. Nationalökon.*, 1981, *41*(3–4), pp. 295–305.

Smith, Donald Mitchell. Neoclassical Growth Models and Regional Growth in the U.S.: A Reply. *J. Reg. Sci.*, August 1981, *21*(3), pp. 431–32. [G: U.S.]

Smith, M. Alasdair M. Capital Accumulation in the Open Two-Sector Economy. In *Bhagwati, J. N.*, ed., 1981, 1977, pp. 329–41.

Stewart, Frances. Capital Goods in Developing Countries. In *Livingstone, I., ed., 1981, 1976,* pp. 194–202.

Withagen, C. The Optimal Exploitation of Exhaustible Resources, A Survey. *De Economist,* 1981, *129*(4), pp. 504–31.

1113 Multisector Growth Models and Related Topics

Bolnick, Bruce R. Government as a Super Becker-Altruist: A Reply. *Public Choice,* 1981, *37*(3), pp. 603–06.

Chichilnisky, Graciela. Existence and Characterization of Optimal Growth Paths Including Models with Non-Convexities in Utilities and Technologies. *Rev. Econ. Stud.,* January 1981, *48*(1), pp. 51–61.

Crouzeix, Jean-Pierre. A Duality Framework in Quasiconvex Programming. In *Schaible, S. and Ziemba, W. T., eds., 1981,* pp. 207–25.

Kapitány, Zsuzsa. Uncertainty in Decision-Making: A Simulation Experiment. In *Kornai, J. and Martos, B., eds., 1981,* pp. 247–66.

Kornai, János and Simonovits, András. Control by Order Signals. In *Kornai, J. and Martos, B., eds., 1981,* pp. 267–79.

Kornai, János and Simonovits, András. Stock-Signal Model Regulated from a Normal Path. In *Kornai, J. and Martos, B., eds., 1981,* pp. 223–45.

Mitra, Tapan. Efficiency, Weak Value Maximality and Weak Value Optimality in a Multisector Model. *Rev. Econ. Stud.,* October 1981, *48*(4), pp. 643–47.

Mitra, Tapan. Some Results on the Optimal Depletion of Exhaustible Resources under Negative Discounting. *Rev. Econ. Stud.,* July 1981, *48*(3), pp. 521–32.

Nishimura, Kiyohiko Giichi. On Uniqueness of a Steady State and Convergence of Optimal Paths in Multisector Models of Optimal Growth with a Discount Rate. *J. Econ. Theory,* April 1981, *24*(2), pp. 157–67.

Okuguchi, Koji. Population Growth, Costly Innovation and Modified Hartwick's Rule [Costly Innovation and Natural Resources]. *Int. Econ. Rev.,* October 1981, *22*(3), pp. 657–61.

Sardoni, Claudio. Multi-Sectoral Models of Balanced Growth and the Marxian Schemes of Expanded Reproduction. *Australian Econ. Pap.,* December 1981, *20*(37), pp. 383–97.

Steenge, Albert E. The Verification of Efficient Growth: An Approach via Stojanović's Matrix of Growth. *J. Macroecon.,* Spring 1981, *3*(2), pp. 271–81.

Terrebonne, R. Peter. Government as a Super Becker-Altruist: A Comment. *Public Choice,* 1981, *37*(3), pp. 595–601.

1114 Monetary Growth Models

Barro, Robert J. and Fischer, Stanley. Recent Developments in Monetary Theory. In *Barro, R. J., 1981, 1976,* pp. 3–40.

Benhabib, Jess and Miyao, Takahiro. Some New Results on the Dynamics of the Generalized Tobin

Model. *Int. Econ. Rev.,* October 1981, *22*(3), pp. 589–96.

Chand, Sheetal K. Stocks, Flows, and Market Equilibrium in Neoclassical Monetary Growth Models. *J. Monet. Econ.,* July 1981, *8*(1), pp. 117–29.

Drazen, Allan. Inflation and Capital Accumulation under a Finite Horizon. *J. Monet. Econ.,* September 1981, *8*(2), pp. 247–60.

Pereira Leite, Sérgio. International Reserves in a Neo-Classical Growth Model. *Economia (Portugal),* May 1981, *5*(2), pp. 389–99.

de Santibañez, Fernando J. Dinero y actividad económica. (Money and Economic Activity. With English summary.) *Económica,* January–August 1981, *27*(1–2), pp. 93–116.

Søndergaard, Jørgen. Samspillet mellem indkomstskatter og inflation. (Long-run and Short-run Interaction of Inflation and Income Taxation. With English summary.) *Nationaløkon. Tidsskr.,* 1981, *119*(3), pp. 343–61.

112 Economic Development Models and Theories

1120 Economic Development Models and Theories

Adedeji, Adebayo. Prospects and Limitations of Indigenization. In *Adedeji, A., ed., 1981,* pp. 384–94. **[G: Africa]**

Ahluwalia, Montek S. Inequality, Poverty and Development. In *Livingstone, I., ed., 1981, 1976,* pp. 30–48.

Ahmed, Iqbal. Wage Determination in Bangladesh Agriculture. *Oxford Econ. Pap.,* July 1981, *33*(2), pp. 298–322. **[G: Bangladesh]**

Altimir, Oscar. Poverty in Latin America: A Review of Concepts and Data. *Cepal Rev.,* April 1981, (13), pp. 65–91. **[G: Latin America]**

Amin, Samir. Some Thoughts of Self-reliant Development, Collective Self-reliance and the New International Economic Order. In *Grassman, S. and Lundberg, E., eds., 1981,* pp. 534–52.

Amsden, Alice H. The Military in Development: Comment. In *Streeten, P. and Jolly, R, eds., 1981, 1977,* pp. 267–75.

Arndt, Heinz W. Economic Development: A Semantic History. *Econ. Develop. Cult. Change,* April 1981, *29*(3), pp. 457–66.

Aujac, Henri. Cultures and Growth. In *Saunders, C. T., ed. (II), 1981,* pp. 47–70. **[G: Brazil; France; Ivory Coast; Japan]**

Balassa, Bela. The Process of Industrial Development and Alternative Development Strategies. In *Balassa, B., 1981,* pp. 1–26. **[G: LDCs]**

Baldwin, G. B. A Layman's Guide to Little–Mirrlees. In *Livingstone, I., ed., 1981, 1972,* pp. 223–28.

Bale, Malcolm D. The Role of Export Cropping in Less Developed Countries: Discussion. *Amer. J. Agr. Econ.,* May 1981, *63*(2), pp. 396–98.

Balogh, T. and Streeten, Paul P. The Coefficient of Ignorance. In *Livingstone, I., ed., 1981, 1963,* pp. 25–29.

Bates, Robert H. Public Choice Processes. In *Russell, C. S. and Nicholson, N. K., eds., 1981,* pp. 81–117.

Bauer, P. T. Broadcasting the Liberal Death Wish.

In *Bauer, P. T.*, 1981, pp. 191–211. [G: Africa]

Bauer, P. T. Reflections on the State of Economics. In *Bauer, P. T.*, 1981, pp. 255–66.

Bauer, P. T. The Vicious Circle of Poverty. In *Livingstone, I., ed.*, 1981, *1965*, pp. 3–9.
[G: LDCs]

Bauer, P. T. Western Guilt and Third World Poverty. In *Bauer, P. T.*, 1981, pp. 66–85.

Beckford, G. L. The Economics of Agricultural Resource Use and Development in Plantation Economies. In *Livingstone, I., ed.*, 1981, *1969*, pp. 277–86.

Bentley, J. Marvin and Oberhofer, Tom. Property Rights and Economic Development. *Rev. Soc. Econ.*, April 1981, *39*(1), pp. 51–65.
[G: W. Africa]

Berry, A. and Sabot, R. H. Labour Market Performance in Developing Countries: A Survey. In *Streeten, P. and Jolly, R, eds.*, 1981, *1978*, pp. 149–92.

Bhaduri, Amit. Class Relations and the Pattern of Accumulation in an Agrarian Economy. *Cambridge J. Econ.*, March 1981, *5*(1), pp. 33–46.
[G: India]

Bhagwati, Jagdish N. Need for Reforms in Underdeveloped Countries: Comments. In *Grassman, S. and Lundberg, E., eds.*, 1981, pp. 526–33.

Blumberg, Georges. Psychology of Economic Development. In *Molt, W.; Hartmann, H. A. and Stringer, P., eds.*, 1981, pp. 295–304.

Blumenthal, Tuvia. Factor Proportions and Choice of Technology: The Japanese Experience: Reply. *Econ. Develop. Cult. Change*, July 1981, *29*(4), pp. 845–48. [G: Japan]

Brandão, Antonio. Alternative Agricultural Development Models Commonly Advocated in Latin America. In *Johnson, G. and Maunder, A., eds.*, 1981, pp. 346–55. [G: Latin America]

Bruneau, Thomas C. and Faucher, Philippe. Authoritarian Capitalism: Brazil's Contempory Economic and Political Development: Introduction. In *Bruneau, T. C. and Faucher, P., eds.*, 1981, pp. 1–9.

Bruton, Henry J. Labour Market Performance in Developing Countries: A Survey: Comment. In *Streeten, P. and Jolly, R, eds.*, 1981, *1978*, pp. 197–200. [G: LDCs]

Bruton, Henry J. The Import-Substitution Strategy of Economic Development: A Survey. In *Livingstone, I., ed.*, 1981, *1970*, pp. 167–76.

Bryson, Judy C. Women and Agriculture in sub-Saharan Africa: Implications for Development (An Exploratory Study) *J. Devel. Stud.*, April 1981, *17*(3), pp. 29–46. [G: sub-Saharan Africa]

Bueno, G. M. A New Order in Financial and Technological Relations with the Third World? *Tijdschrift Econ. Manage.*, 1981, *26*(1), pp. 95–116.

Campbell, David C. and Tobal, Carlos. The Efficiency Price of Labor in Developed and Developing Nations. *J. Econ. Issues*, June 1981, *15*(2), pp. 435–47.

Campos, Roberto de Oliveira and Valentino, Raphael. Theories of Diffusion and Dependency. In *Saunders, C. T., ed. (II)*, 1981, pp. 71–80.
[G: LDCs; MDCs]

Caporaso, James A. Industrialization in the Periphery: The Evolving Global Division of Labor. In *Hollist, W. L. and Rosenau, J. N., eds.*, 1981, pp. 140–71. [G: LDCs]

Caporaso, James A. and Zare, Behrouz. An Interpretation and Evaluation of Dependency Theory. In *Muñoz, H., ed.*, 1981, pp. 43–56.

Cardoso, Eliana A. Celso Furtado Revisited: The Postwar Years. *Econ. Develop. Cult. Change*, October 1981, *30*(1), pp. 117–28. [G: Brazil]

Cardoso, Eliana A. Food Supply and Inflation. *J. Devel. Econ.*, June 1981, *8*(3), pp. 269–84.
[G: Latin America]

Cardoso, Eliana A. The Great Depression and Commodity-exporting LDCs: The Case of Brazil. *J. Polit. Econ.*, December 1981, *89*(6), pp. 1239–50. [G: Brazil]

Cardoso, Fernando Henrique. Towards Another Development. In *Muñoz, H., ed.*, 1981, *1977*, pp. 295–313.

Cassen, Robert, et al. World Development Report 1981—Principal Themes. *Finance Develop.*, September 1981, *18*(3), pp. 6–10. [G: LDCs]

Cassen, Robert H. Population and Development: A Survey. In *Streeten, P. and Jolly, R, eds.*, 1981, *1976*, pp. 1–46.

Chichilnisky, Graciela. Terms of Trade and Domestic Distribution: Export-Led Growth with Abundant Labour. *J. Devel. Econ.*, April 1981, *8*(2), pp. 163–92.

Civelek, Mehmet A. Education and Economic Growth Revisited: The Evidence from the Turkish Development Experience. *Rivista Int. Sci. Econ. Com.*, March 1981, *28*(3), pp. 257–69.
[G: Turkey]

Cline, William R. and Weintraub, Sidney. Economic Stabilization in Developing Countries: Introduction and Overview. In *Cline, W. R. and Weintraub, S., eds.*, 1981, pp. 1–42. [G: LDCs]

Coles, Flournoy A., Jr. Rethinking Economic Development. *Rev. Black Polit. Econ.*, Winter 1981, *11*(2), pp. 277–81.

da Conceição Tavares, María and Teixeira, Aloisia. Transnational Enterprises and the Internationalization of Capital in Brazilian Industry. *Cepal Rev.*, August 1981, (14), pp. 85–105.
[G: Brazil]

Couriel, Alberto. Comment [The Latin American Periphery in the Global System of Capitalism]. *Cepal Rev.*, April 1981, (13), pp. 161–64.

Crockett, Andrew D. Stabilization Policies in Developing Countries: Some Policy Considerations. *Int. Monet. Fund Staff Pap.*, March 1981, *28*(1), pp. 55–79. [G: LDCs]

Crosswell, Michael J. Basic Human Needs: A Development Planning Approach. In *Leipziger, D. M., ed.*, 1981, pp. 1–28.

Datta-Chaudhuri, Mrinal. Labour-Intensive Industrialisation, Organisation of Trade and the Role of the State. *Indian Econ. Rev.*, July-Sept. 1981, *16*(3), pp. 199–212.

Dervis, Kemal. IS/LM in the Tropics: Diagrammatics of the New Structuralist Macro Critique: Comment. In *Cline, W. R. and Weintraub, S., eds.*, 1981, pp. 503–06. [G: LDCs]

Dervis, Kemal; de Melo, Jaime and Robinson, Sher-

man. A General Equilibrium Analysis of Foreign Exchange Shortages in a Developing Economy. *Econ. J.*, December 1981, *91*(364), pp. 891–906. [G: Turkey]

Donaldson, Loraine. Efficiency Ranges for Intermediate Technology: A General Equilibrium Approach. *Greek Econ. Rev.*, April 1981, *3*(1), pp. 59–70.

Dos Santos, T. The Structure of Dependence. In *Livingstone, I., ed., 1981, 1970*, pp. 143–47. [G: Latin America]

Edelman, David J. A Macroeconomic Policy Simulation of the Energy Crisis and the Development of Low-Income Countries. In *Chatterji, M., ed., 1981*, pp. 167–92. [G: LDCs]

Edwards, E. O. Investment in Education in Developing Nations: Policy Responses When Private and Social Signals Conflict. In *Livingstone, I., ed., 1981, 1975*, pp. 85–88. [G: U.S.]

Ehrlich, Eva. Comparison of Development Levels: Inequalities in the Physical Structures of National Economies. In *Bairoch, P. and Lévy-Leboyer, M., eds., 1981*, pp. 395–410. [G: LDCs; MDCs]

Ekundare, Richard O. Constraints to Economic Development in Africa: Some Determinants of Economic Disparities. In *Bairoch, P. and Lévy-Leboyer, M., eds., 1981*, pp. 34–45. [G: Nigeria; Sub-Saharan Africa]

El Serafy, Salah. Absorptive Capacity, the Demand for Revenue, and the Supply of Petroleum. *J. Energy Devel.*, Autumn 1981, *7*(1), pp. 73–88. [G: OPEC]

Eliou, Marie. Alternative Development Strategies. In *Mauri, A., ed., 1981*, pp. 81–90. [G: LDCs]

Ellis, Gene. Development Planning and Appropriate Technology: A Dilemma and a Proposal. *World Devel.*, March 1981, *9*(3), pp. 251–62.

Eralp, Atilâ. Türkiye'de Izlenen Ithal Ikameci Kalkinma Stratejisi ve Yabanci Sermaye. (Import Substitution Strategy and Foreign Capital in Turkey. With English summary.) *METU*, Special Issue, 1981, pp. 613–33. [G: Turkey]

Evans, D. Unequal Exchange and Economic Policies: Some Implications of the Neo-Ricardian Critique of the Theory of Comparative Advantage. In *Livingstone, I., ed., 1981*, pp. 117–28.

Fajnzylber, Fernando. Some Reflections on South-East Asian Export Industrialization. *Cepal Rev.*, December 1981, (15), pp. 111–32. [G: S. Korea; Taiwan; Hong Kong; Singapore]

Farooq, Ghazi M. Population, Human Resources and Development Planning: Towards an Integrated Approach. *Int. Lab. Rev.*, May–June 1981, *120*(3), pp. 335–49.

Farrag, Nureddin. Basic Issues of Energy and Development: I. *J. Energy Devel.*, Autumn 1981, *7*(1), pp. 27–33. [G: LDCs; MDCs]

Feder, Gershon. Growth and External Borrowing in Trade Gap Economies of Less Developed Countries. *Aussenwirtschaft*, December 1981, *36*(4), pp. 381–95. [G: LDCs]

Fei, John C. H. and Ranis, Gustav. Factor Proportions and Choice of Technology: The Japanese Experience: Comment. *Econ. Develop. Cult. Change*, July 1981, *29*(4), pp. 841–44. [G: Japan]

Findlay, Ronald. Export-Led Industrial Growth Reconsidered: Comment. In *Hong, W. and Krause, L. B., eds., 1981*, pp. 30–33. [G: LDCs]

Friedmann, John. The Active Community: Toward a Political–Territorial Framework for Rural Development in Asia. *Econ. Develop. Cult. Change*, January 1981, *29*(2), pp. 235–61. [G: Asia]

Fry, Maxwell J. Inflation and Economic Growth in Pacific Basin Developing Economies. *Fed. Res. Bank San Francisco Econ. Rev.*, Fall 1981, pp. 8–18. [G: LDCs]

Galtung, Johan. The Politics of Self-reliance. In *Muñoz, H., ed., 1981*, pp. 173–96.

Garavello, Oscar. processi di sviluppo e dipendenza dai flussi esterni di capitale. (Growth: The L.D.C. Dependency on Foreign Capital Inflows. With English summary.) *Rivista Int. Sci. Econ. Com.*, October–November 1981, *28*(10–11), pp. 959–76. [G: LDCs]

Gierer, Alfred. Socioeconomic Inequalities: Effects of Self-Enhancement, Depletion and Redistribution. *Jahr. Nationalökon. Statist.*, July 1981, *196*(4), pp. 309–31.

Goetz, Arturo L. Beyond the Slogan of South-South Co-operation: Comment. *World Devel.*, June 1981, *9*(6), pp. 583–85.

Gorman, Lyn. The Funding of Development Research. *World Devel.*, May 1981, *9*(5), pp. 465–83. [G: OECD]

Greenfield, Sidney M. and Strickon, Arnold. A New Paradigm for the Study of Entrepreneurship and Social Change. *Econ. Develop. Cult. Change*, April 1981, *29*(3), pp. 467–99.

Griffin, Keith. Economic Development in a Changing World. *World Devel.*, March 1981, *9*(3), pp. 221–26.

Gülalp, Haldun. Gelişme Stratejileri Tartişmasi: Bir Eleştiriye Yanit. (The Debate on Development Strategies: Reply to a Critique. With English summary.) *METU*, 1981, *8*(3&4), pp. 755–70. [G: Turkey]

Gupta, Suraj B. The Productivity of Workers' Consumption and the Choice of Techniques. *Indian Econ. Rev.*, Oct.-Dec. 1981, *16*(4), pp. 279–96.

Hablützel, Rudolf. Issues in Economic Diversification for the Oil-Rich Countries. *Finance Develop.*, June 1981, *18*(2), pp. 10–13. [G: Arab OPEC]

Hager, Wolfgang. The Strains on the International System. In *Saunders, C. T., ed. (II), 1981*, pp. 287–309. [G: LDCs; MDCs]

Harris, John R. and Todaro, Michael P. Migration, Unemployment and Development: A Two-Sector Analysis. In *Livingstone, I., ed., 1981, 1970*, pp. 89–96.

Hazledine, Tim and Moreland, R. Scott. Population and Economic Growth: A Rejoinder. *Rev. Econ. Statist.*, February 1981, *63*(1), pp. 153–55.

Heady, Christopher John. Shadow Wages and Induced Migration. *Oxford Econ. Pap.*, March 1981, *33*(1), pp. 108–21.

Helleiner, Gerald K. Aid and Dependence: Issues for Recipients. In *Helleiner, G. K., 1981*, pp. 219–38.

Herrera, Amilcar O. The Generation of Technologies in Rural Areas. *World Devel.*, January 1981, *9*(1), pp. 21–35. [G: LDCs]

Hershlag, Zvi Y. Pitfalls of Development Strategy and Planning. *METU*, Special Issue, 1981, pp. 19–54. [G: LDCs]

Heyer, Judith; Roberts, Pepe and Williams, Gavin. Rural Development. In *Heyer, J.; Roberts, P. and Williams, G., eds.*, 1981, pp. 1–15.

Hillman, Jimmye S. The Role of Export Cropping in Less Developed Countries. *Amer. J. Agr. Econ.*, May 1981, 63(2), pp. 375–83. [G: LDCs]

Hirschman, Albert O. A Generalized Linkage Approach to Development, with Special Reference to Staples. In *Hirschman, A. O.*, 1981, 1977, pp. 59–97.

Hirschman, Albert O. Beyond Asymmetry: Critical Notes on Myself as a Young Man and on Some Other Old Friends. In *Hirschman, A. O.*, 1981, 1978, pp. 27–33.

Hirschman, Albert O. On Hegel, Imperialism, and Structural Stagnation. In *Hirschman, A. O.*, 1981, 1976, pp. 167–76.

Hirschman, Albert O. The Changing Tolerance for Income Inequality in the Course of Economic Development. In *Hirschman, A. O.*, 1981, 1973, pp. 39–58.

Hirschman, Albert O. The Rise and Decline of Development Economics. In *Hirschman, A. O.*, 1981, pp. 1–24.

Hirschman, Albert O. The Turn to Authoritarianism in Latin America and the Search for its Economic Determinants. In *Hirschman, A. O.*, 1981, 1979, pp. 98–135. [G: Latin America]

Hirschman, Charles. The Uses of Demography in Development Planning. *Econ. Develop. Cult. Change*, April 1981, 29(3), pp. 561–75.

Hopkins, Terence K. and Wallerstein, Immanuel. Structural Transformations of the World-Economy. In *Rubinson, R., ed.*, 1981, pp. 233–61. [G: Global]

Horvat, Branko. Establishing Self-governing Socialism in a Less Developed Country. *World Devel.*, September/October 1981, 9(9/10), pp. 951–64. [G: LDCs]

Hoselitz, B. F. Small Industry in Underdeveloped Countries. In *Livingstone, I., ed.*, 1981, 1959, pp. 203–11. [G: LDCs; Japan; W. Europe]

Hughes, Helen. The New Industrial Countries in the World Economy: Pessimism and a Way Out. In *Saunders, C. T., ed. (II)*, 1981, pp. 97–131. [G: LDCs; MDCs]

Hunter, Holland; Bresnahan, Timothy F. and Rutan, Everett J., III. Modeling Structural Change Using Early Soviet Data. *J. Devel. Econ.*, August 1981, 9(1), pp. 65–87. [G: U.S.S.R.]

Iglesias, Enrique V. Development and Equity: The Challenge of the 1980s. *Cepal Rev.*, December 1981, (15), pp. 7–46. [G: Latin America]

Immink, Maarten D. C. and Viteri, Fernando E. Energy Intake and Productivity of Guatemalan Sugarcane Cutters: An Empirical Test of the Efficiency Wage Hypothesis—Part II. *J. Devel. Econ.*, October 1981, 9(2), pp. 273–87. [G: Guatemala]

Immink, Maarten D. C. and Viteri, Fernando E. Energy Intake and Productivity of Guatemalan Sugarcane Cutters: An Empirical Test of the Efficiency Wage Hypothesis—Part I. *J. Devel. Econ.*, October 1981, 9(2), pp. 251–71. [G: Guatemala]

James, Jeffrey. Growth, Technology and the Environment in Less Developed Countries: A Survey. In *Streeten, P. and Jolly, R, eds.*, 1981, 1978, pp. 115–43. [G: LDCs]

James, Jeffrey and Stewart, Frances. New Products: A Discussion of the Welfare Effects of the Introduction of New Products in Developing Countries. *Oxford Econ. Pap.*, March 1981, 33(1), pp. 81–107. [G: LDCs]

Jha, Raghbendra and Lächler, Ulrich. Optimum Taxation and Public Production in a Dynamic Harris-Todaro World. *J. Devel. Econ.*, December 1981, 9(3), pp. 357–73.

Jorgensen, D. W. Testing Alternative Theories of the Development of a Dual Economy. In *Livingstone, I., ed.*, 1981, 1967, pp. 67–74. [G: Japan; LDCs]

Joshi, V. The Rationale and Relevance of the Little–Mirrlees Criterion. In *Livingstone, I., ed.*, 1981, 1972, pp. 229–44.

Kadhim, Mihssen. A Note on "Downstream" Industrialization and the Security of Oil Supplies. *J. Energy Devel.*, Autumn 1981, 7(1), pp. 99–109. [G: OAPEC; U.S.]

Kaldor, Mary. The Military in Development: Reply. In *Streeten, P. and Jolly, R, eds.*, 1981, 1977, pp. 277.

Kaldor, Mary. The Military in Development. In *Streeten, P. and Jolly, R, eds.*, 1981, 1976, pp. 241–64.

Kao, C. H. C.; Anschel, K. R. and Eicher, C. K. Disguised Unemployment in Agriculture: A Survey. In *Livingstone, I., ed.*, 1981, 1964, pp. 59–66. [G: Greece; India; Italy; Thailand]

Khan, Mohsin S. and Knight, Malcolm D. Stabilization Programs in Developing Countries: A Formal Framework. *Int. Monet. Fund Staff Pap.*, March 1981, 28(1), pp. 1–53. [G: LDCs]

Kidron, Michael. The Military in Development: Comment. In *Streeten, P. and Jolly, R, eds.*, 1981, 1976, pp. 265–66.

Kim, Kwang Suk. Export-Led Industrial Growth Reconsidered: Comment. In *Hong, W. and Krause, L. B., eds.*, 1981, pp. 28–29. [G: LDCs]

Kirkpatrick, Colin H. and Nixson, F. I. The Origins of Inflation in Less Developed Countries: A Selective Review. In *Livingstone, I., ed.*, 1981, 1976, pp. 311–32. [G: LDCs]

Kisch, Herbert. The Textile Industries in Silesia and the Rhineland: A Comparative Study in Industrialization. In *Kriedte, P.; Medick, H. and Schlumbohm, J.*, 1981, pp. 178–200. [G: Germany; Poland]

Knight, Peter T. and Morán, Ricardo. Bringing the Poor into the Growth Process: The Case of Brazil. *Finance Develop.*, December 1981, 18(4), pp. 22–25. [G: Brazil]

Kreye, Otto. Dependency in the 1980s. In *Saunders, C. T., ed. (II)*, 1981, pp. 81–93. [G: LDCs]

Kriedte, Peter. Proto-Industrialization between Industrialization and De-Industrialization. In *Kriedte, P.; Medick, H. and Schlumbohm, J.*, 1981, pp. 135–60. [G: Europe]

Kriedte, Peter. The Origins, the Agrarian Context,

and the Conditions in the World Market. **In** *Kriedte, P.; Medick, H. and Schlumbohm, J.,* 1981, pp. 12–37. **[G: Europe]**

Krueger, Anne O. Export-Led Industrial Growth Reconsidered. **In** *Hong, W. and Krause, L. B., eds.,* 1981, pp. 3–27. **[G: LDCs]**

Krueger, Anne O. Interactions between Inflation and Trade Regime Objectives in Stabilization Programs. **In** *Cline, W. R. and Weintraub, S., eds.,* 1981, pp. 83–114. **[G: LDCs]**

Krueger, Anne O. Trade and Employment in Developing Countries: The Framework of the Country Studies. **In** *Krueger, A. O., et al., eds.,* 1981, pp. 1–28. **[G: LDCs]**

Krugman, Paul R. Trade, Accumulation, and Uneven Development. *J. Devel. Econ.,* April 1981, *8*(2), pp. 149–61.

Kulikowski, R. Modelling of Rural–Urban Development. **In** *Janssen, J. M. L.; Pau, L. F. and Straszak, A. J., eds.,* 1981, pp. 195–99.

Lall, Sanjaya. Dependence and Underdevelopment. **In** *Lall, S.,* 1981, *1975,* pp. 3–23.

Lall, Sanjaya. Developing Countries and Foreign Investment. **In** *Lall, S.,* 1981, *1974,* pp. 53–67.

Lall, Sanjaya. Technology and Developing Countries: A Review and an Agenda for Research. **In** *Lall, S.,* 1981, pp. 123–52. **[G: LDCs]**

Lall, Sanjaya. The Patent System and the Transfer of Technology to Less-Developed Countries. **In** *Lall, S.,* 1981, *1976,* pp. 153–70. **[G: LDCs]**

Lall, Sanjaya. Welfare Economics and Development Problems. **In** *Lall, S.,* 1981, *1976,* pp. 24–50.

Lambsdorff, Otto Graf. Basic Issues of Energy and Development: II. *J. Energy Devel.,* Autumn 1981, *7*(1), pp. 35–38.

Laszlo, Ervin; Moneta, Carlos and Kurtzman, Joel. The Place of Regional Approaches in Current Negotiations on International Development. **In** *Nicol, D.; Echeverria, L. and Peccei, A., eds.,* 1981, pp. 251–61.

Leipziger, Danny M. Policy Issues and the Basic Human Needs Approach. **In** *Leipziger, D. M., ed.,* 1981, pp. 107–36. **[G: LDCs]**

Leistner, G. M. E. Towards a Regional Development Strategy for Southern Africa. *S. Afr. J. Econ.,* December 1981, *49*(4), pp. 349–64. **[G: Africa]**

Lele, Uma and Mellor, John W. Technological Change, Distributive Bias and Labor Transfer in a Two-Sector Economy. *Oxford Econ. Pap.,* November 1981, *33*(3), pp. 426–41.

Leontief, Wassily W. Population Growth and Economic Development: Illustrative Projections. **In** *Reubens, E. P., ed.,* 1981, *1979,* pp. 39–60.

Levy, Victor. Total Factor Productivity, Non-Neutral Technical Change and Economic Growth: A Parametric Study of a Developing Economy. *J. Devel. Econ.,* February 1981, *8*(1), pp. 93–109. **[G: Iraq]**

Lewis, Maureen A. Sectoral Aspects of a Basic Human Needs Approach: The Linkages among Population, Nutrition, and Health. **In** *Leipziger, D. M., ed.,* 1981, pp. 29–105. **[G: LDCs]**

Lewis, W. Arthur. Development Strategy in a Limping World Economy. **In** *Johnson, G. and Maunder, A., eds.,* 1981, pp. 12–26. **[G: U.S.; LDCs]**

Lindbeck, Assar. Some Thoughts of Self-reliant Development, Collective Self-reliance and the New International Economic Order: Comments. **In** *Grassman, S. and Lundberg, E., eds.,* 1981, pp. 553–57.

Lipton, Michael. The Theory of the Optimising Peasant. **In** *Livingstone, I., ed.,* 1981, *1968,* pp. 263–71.

Love, J. Commodity Diversification: A Market Model. *J. Devel. Stud.,* October 1981, *18*(1), pp. 94–103. **[G: Latin America; Africa; Asia]**

Mabawonku, A. F. Monopoly and Market Concentration in the Process of Economic Development: A Review of the Literature. *Indian Econ. J.,* October–December 1981, *29*(2), pp. 23–34.

Makler, Harry; Sales, Arnaud and Smelser, Neil. Economy and Society. *Int. Soc. Sci. J.,* 1981, *33*(2), pp. 330–50.

Manser, W. A. P. and Webley, Simon. Technology Transfer to Developing Countries. **In** *The Royal Inst. of Internat. Affairs,* 1981, pp. 1–58. **[G: LDCs; MDCs]**

Marinho, Luiz Claudio. The Transnational Corporations and Latin America's Present Form of Economic Growth. *Cepal Rev.,* August 1981, (14), pp. 9–34. **[G: Latin America; Brazil; Mexico]**

Maurice, Nelson. Exploiting Crop-Credit Insurance for Development Purposes in Developing Nations. *Artha-Vikas,* January–December 1981, *17*(1–2), pp. 5–54. **[G: India]**

Maxwell, S. J. and Singer, H. W. Food Aid to Developing Countries: A Survey. **In** *Streeten, P. and Jolly, R, eds.,* 1981, pp. 219–40. **[G: LDCs]**

McKinnon, Ronald I. Foreign Exchange Constraints in Economic Development and Efficient Aid Allocation. **In** *Bhagwati, J. N., ed.,* 1981, *1964,* pp. 342–48.

McNamara, Robert S. Lo sviluppo del Terzo Mondo e il ruolo della Banca Mondiale negli anni Ottanta. (Third World Development and the Role of the World Bank in the '70s. With English summary.) *Bancaria,* January 1981, *37*(1), pp. 7–29. **[G: LDCs]**

McNamara, Robert S. To the Board of Governors, Copenhagen, Denmark, September 21, 1970. **In** *McNamara, R. S.,* 1981, *1970,* pp. 111–34. **[G: Selected LDCs]**

McNamara, Robert S. To the Board of Governors, Belgrade, Yugoslavia, October 2, 1979. **In** *McNamara, R. S.,* 1981, *1979,* pp. 565–610. **[G: OECD; LDCs]**

McNamara, Robert S. To the Board of Governors, Washington, D.C., September 29, 1969. **In** *McNamara, R. S.,* 1981, *1969,* pp. 69–94.

McNamara, Robert S. To the Board of Governors, Washington, D.C., September 1, 1975. **In** *McNamara, R. S.,* 1981, *1975,* pp. 297–334. **[G: OECD; LDCs]**

McNamara, Robert S. To the Board of Governors, Washington, D.C., September 27, 1971. **In** *McNamara, R. S.,* 1981, *1971,* pp. 137–67.

McNamara, Robert S. To the Columbia University Conference on International Economic Development, New York, New York, February 20, 1970. **In** *McNamara, R. S.,* 1981, *1970,* pp. 97–108.

McNamara, Robert S. To the United Nations Conference on the Human Environment, Stockholm,

Sweden, June 8, 1972. In *McNamara, R. S.*, 1981, *1972*, pp. 193–206.

McNamara, Robert S. To the University of Notre Dame, Notre Dame, Indiana, May 1, 1969. In *McNamara, R. S.*, 1981, *1969*, pp. 33–52.

Medick, Hans. The Proto-Industrial Family Economy. In *Kriedte, P.; Medick, H. and Schlumbohm, J.*, 1981, pp. 38–73.   [G: Europe]

Medick, Hans. The Structures and Function of Population-Development under the Protoindustrial System. In *Kriedte, P.; Medick, H. and Schlumbohm, J.*, 1981, pp. 74–93.   [G: Europe]

de Melo, Jaime and Robinson, Sherman. Trade Policy and Resource Allocation in the Presence of Product Differentiation. *Rev. Econ. Statist.*, May 1981, *63*(2), pp. 169–77.   [G: Turkey]

de Melo, Martha. Modeling the Effects of Alternative Approaches to Basic Human Needs: Case Study of Sri Lanka. In *Leipziger, D. M., ed.*, 1981, pp. 137–80.   [G: Sri Lanka]

Mendels, Franklin F. Agriculture and Peasant Industry in Eighteenth-Century Flanders. In *Kriedte, P.; Medick, H. and Schlumbohm, J.*, 1981, pp. 161–77.   [G: Belgium; France; Netherlands]

Michaely, Michael. Foreign Aid, Economic Structure, and Dependence. *J. Devel. Econ.*, December 1981, *9*(3), pp. 313–30.

Mundlak, Yair. Agricultural Growth—Formulation, Evaluation and Policy Consequences. In *Johnson, G. and Maunder, A., eds.*, 1981, pp. 672–84.

Muñoz, Heraldo. The Strategic Dependency of the Centers and the Economic Importance of the Latin American Periphery. In *Muñoz, H., ed.*, 1981, pp. 59–92.   [G: U.S.; Latin America]

Muñoz, Heraldo. The Various Roads to Development. In *Muñoz, H., ed.*, 1981, pp. 1–11.

Myrdal, Gunnar. Need for Reforms in Underdeveloped Countries. In *Grassman, S. and Lundberg, E., eds.*, 1981, pp. 501–25.

Nandi, Sukumar. A Note on Equilibrium Theory of International Trade and Underdevelopment. *Econ. Aff.*, April–June 1981, *26*(2), pp. 117–23.

Neary, J. Peter. On the Harris–Todaro Model with Intersectoral Capital Mobility. *Economica*, August 1981, *48*(191), pp. 219–34.   [G: LDCs]

Nelson, Nici. African Women in the Development Process: Introduction. *J. Devel. Stud.*, April 1981, *17*(3), pp. 1–9.   [G: sub-Saharan Africa]

Nixson, Frederick I. State Intervention, Economic Planning and Import-Substituting Industrialisation: The Experience of the Less Developed Countries. *METU*, Special Issue, 1981, pp. 55–78.   [G: LDCs]

Núñez del Prado, Arturo. The Transnational Corporations in a New Planning Process. *Cepal Rev.*, August 1981, (14), pp. 35–50.
   [G: Latin America]

Olgun, Hasan. Ithal Ikamesi Tartişmasi ve G. Özler. (The Crisis of Import Substitution: A Reply. With English summary.) *METU*, 1981, *8*(3&4), pp. 771–76.   [G: Turkey]

Olgun, Hasan. Türkiye'de Ithal Ikamesi Bunalimi ve Dişa Açilma: Ikinci Eleştiri. (The Crisis of Import Substitution: A Second Critique. With English summary.) *METU*, 1981, *8*(3&4), pp. 777–93.   [G: Turkey]

Oshima, Harry T. A. Lewis' Dualistic Theory and Its Relevance for Postwar Asian Growth. *Malayan Econ. Rev. (See Singapore Econ. Rev.)*, October 1981, *26*(2), pp. 1–26.   [G: Asia]

Özler, Güntaç. Gülalp-Oglun Tartişmasi Üzerine. (On Gülalp-Olgun Controversy. With English summary.) *METU*, 1981, *8*(3&4), pp. 747–53.
   [G: Turkey]

Pack, Howard. Fostering the Capital–Goods Sector in LDCs. *World Devel.*, March 1981, *9*(3), pp. 227–50.   [G: LDCs]

Palma, Gabriel. Dependency: A Formal Theory of Underdevelopment or a Methodology for the Analysis of Concrete Situations of Underdevelopment? In *Streeten, P. and Jolly, R, eds.*, 1981, pp. 383–426.   [G: Latin America]

Perlman, Mark. *Population and Economic Change in Developing Countries:* A Review Article. *J. Econ. Lit.*, March 1981, *19*(1), pp. 74–82.

Prebisch, Raúl. Dialogue on Friedman and Hayek: From the Standpoint of the Periphery. *Cepal Rev.*, December 1981, (15), pp. 153–74.

Prebisch, Raúl. The Latin American Periphery in the Global System of Capitalism. *Cepal Rev.*, April 1981, (13), pp. 143–50.
   [G: Latin America]

Quibria, M. G. Domestic Policies and Foreign Resource Requirements. *Quart. J. Econ.*, February 1981, *96*(1), pp. 17–26.

Quibria, M. G. Foreign Dependence, Domestic Policies, and Economic Development in a Poor Labour Surplus Economy. *Bangladesh Devel. Stud.*, Summer 1981, *9*(2), pp. 21–41.

Raj, K. N. Alternative Development Strategies. In *Mauri, A., ed.*, 1981, pp. 91–99.   [G: LDCs]

Ram, Rati. Population and Economic Growth: A Critical Note. *Rev. Econ. Statist.*, February 1981, *63*(1), pp. 149–53.

Ramirez, Francisco O. and Thomas, George M. Structural Antecedents and Consequences of Statism. In *Rubinson, R., ed.*, 1981, pp. 139–64.

Ramos, Joseph. Dependency and Development: An Attempt to Clarify the Issues. In *Novak, M., ed.*, 1981, pp. 61–67.

Resnick, Stephen and Wolff, Richard. Class Structures in Developing Societies. In *Hollist, W. L. and Rosenau, J. N., eds.*, 1981, pp. 243–60.

Rimmer, Douglas. "Basic Needs" and the Origins of the Development Ethos. *J. Devel. Areas*, January 1981, *15*(2), pp. 215–37.

Robinson, W. C. Population Control and Development Strategy. In *Livingstone, I., ed.*, 1981, *1972*, pp. 51–58.   [G: LDCs]

Rodríguez, Octavio. On Peripheral Capitalism and Its Transformation: Comment [The Latin American Periphery in the Global System of Capitalism]. *Cepal Rev.*, April 1981, (13), pp. 151–59.

Roemer, Michael. Dependence and Industrialization Strategies. *World Devel.*, May 1981, *9*(5), pp. 429–34.

Rosenberg, N. Capital Goods, Technology, and Economic Growth. In *Livingstone, I., ed.*, 1981, *1963*, pp. 188–93.   [G: LDCs]

Sachs, Ignacy. Ecodevelopment: A Paradigm for Strategic Planning? Comment on James [Growth, Technology and the Environment in Less Devel-

oped Countries: A Survey]. In *Streeten, P. and Jolly, R, eds.*, 1981, *1978*, pp. 145–47.
[G: LDCs]

Sakellariou, Dimitri M. A Simple Method for Finding Shadow Prices Using Leontief Matrices. *Rev. Econ. Statist.*, May 1981, *63*(2), pp. 309–10.

Santiago, Carlos E. Male–Female Labor Force Participation and Rapid Industrialization. *J. Econ. Devel.*, December 1981, *6*(2), pp. 7–40.
[G: Puerto Rico]

Saunders, Christopher T. Joint Strategies for World Development. In *Saunders, C. T., ed. (I)*, 1981, pp. 1–17.

Schiavo-Campo, Salvatore. Instability of Developmental Imports and Economic Growth: A Theoretical Framework. *Weltwirtsch. Arch.*, 1981, *117*(3), pp. 562–73.

Schiffer, Jonathan. The Changing Post-war Pattern of Development: The Accumulated Wisdom of Samir Amin. *World Devel.*, June 1981, *9*(6), pp. 515–37.

Schlumbohm, Jürgen. Excursus: The Political and Institutional Framework of Proto-Industrialization. In *Kriedte, P.; Medick, H. and Schlumbohm, J.*, 1981, pp. 126–34.
[G: Europe]

Schlumbohm, Jürgen. Relations of Production—Productive Forces—Crises in Proto-Industrialization. In *Kriedte, P.; Medick, H. and Schlumbohm, J.*, 1981, pp. 94–125.
[G: Europe]

Seers, Dudley. European Conscience and Social Science. In *Mauri, A., ed.*, 1981, pp. 9–19.
[G: Europe; LDCs]

Sen, Amartya K. Some Notes on the Choice of Capital-Intensity in Development Planning. In *Livingstone, I., ed.*, 1981, *1957*, pp. 215–22.
[G: LDCs]

Sethuraman, S. V. The Role of the Urban Informal Sector. In *Sethuraman, S. V., ed.*, 1981, pp. 1–47.

Sharma, Brij Mohan. Technology and Economic Growth. *Econ. Aff.*, July–September 1981, *26*(3), pp. 174–81.
[G: India]

Siggel, Eckhard. Immizerizing Technical Progress: The Effect of Product Innovations on Consumption and Welfare of the Poor in Less Developed Countries: Theoretical Analysis and Empirical Observations in Zaire. *J. Econ. Devel.*, July 1981, *6*(1), pp. 7–31.
[G: Zaire]

Simon, D. Informal Sector Research: Note and Comment. *S. Afr. J. Econ.*, September 1981, *49*(3), pp. 295–98.

Simoniya, N. A. The Unevenness of the Socio-economic Development and Prospects for the Economic Self-sufficiency of the Countries of the East. In *Bairoch, P. and Lévy-Leboyer, M., eds.*, 1981, pp. 120–27.
[G: LDCs]

Soza, Héctor. The Industrialization Debate in Latin America. *Cepal Rev.*, April 1981, (13), pp. 35–64.
[G: Latin America]

Stark, Oded. On the Optimal Choice of Capital Intensity in LDCs with Migration. *J. Devel. Econ.*, August 1981, *9*(1), pp. 31–41.
[G: LDCs]

Stavenhagen, Rodolfo. The Future of Latin America: Between Underdevelopment and Revolution. In *Muñoz, H., ed.*, 1981, pp. 207–23.
[G: Latin America]

Stecher, Bernd. The Role of Economic Policies. In *Saunders, C. T., ed. (II)*, 1981, pp. 27–46.
[G: Selected LDCs]

Stein, Leslie. The Growth and Implications of LDC Manufactured Exports to Advanced Countries. *Kyklos*, 1981, *34*(1), pp. 36–59.
[G: LDCs.]

Stewart, Frances. Capital Goods in Developing Countries. In *Livingstone, I., ed.*, 1981, *1976*, pp. 194–202.

Stewart, Frances and Streeten, Paul P. New Strategies for Development: Poverty, Income Distribution, and Growth. In *Streeten, P.*, 1981, *1976*, pp. 148–74.

Streeten, Paul P. Alternatives in Development. In *Streeten, P.*, 1981, pp. 140–47.

Streeten, Paul P. Basic Needs and Development: Foreword. In *Leipziger, D. M., ed.*, 1981, pp. xi–xxii.
[G: LDCs]

Streeten, Paul P. Development Ideas in Historical Perspective. In *Streeten, P.*, 1981, *1977*, pp. 100–132.
[G: LDCs]

Streeten, Paul P. From Growth to Basic Needs. In *Streeten, P.*, 1981, pp. 323–33.

Streeten, Paul P. Self-reliant Industrialization. In *Streeten, P.*, 1981, *1979*, pp. 193–212.

Streeten, Paul P. The Distinctive Features of a Basic-Needs Approach to Development. In *Streeten, P.*, 1981, pp. 334–65.

Streeten, Paul P. The Limits of Development Research. In *Streeten, P.*, 1981, *1974*, pp. 62–99.

Streeten, Paul P. The Meaning and Purpose of Interdisciplinary Studies. In *Streeten, P.*, 1981, *1976*, pp. 52–61.

Streeten, Paul P. The Multi-national Enterprise and the Theory of Development Policy. In *Streeten, P.*, 1981, *1973*, pp. 267–97.

Takagi, Yasuoki. Aid and Debt Problems in Less–Developed Countries. *Oxford Econ. Pap.*, July 1981, *33*(2), pp. 323–37.
[G: LDCs]

Tarp, Finn. Vaekst og indkomstforderling i udviklingslandene. (The Relationship between Growth and Income Distribution in Developing Countries. With English summary.) *Nationaløkon. Tidsskr.*, 1981, *119*(1), pp. 32–46.
[G: LDCs]

Taylor, Lance. IS/LM in the Tropics: Diagrammatics of the New Structuralist Macro Critique. In *Cline, W. R. and Weintraub, S., eds.*, 1981, pp. 465–503.
[G: LDCs]

Teitel, Simón. Productivity, Mechanization and Skills: A Test of the Hirschman Hypothesis for Latin American Industry. *World Devel.*, April 1981, *9*(4), pp. 355–71.
[G: Latin America]

Teitelbaum, Michael S. Population and Development: A Survey: Comment. In *Streeten, P. and Jolly, R, eds.*, 1981, *1976*, pp. 47–51.

Tekiner, Ahmet C. Social and Political Components of Economic Performance for the 1960s: A Note on Adelman and Morris' 'Society, Politics and Economic Development.' *J. Devel. Econ.*, April 1981, *8*(2), pp. 249–58.
[G: LDCs]

Thirlwall, A. P. The Valuation of Labour in Surplus Labour Economies: A Synoptic View. In *Livingstone, I., ed.*, 1981, *1971*, pp. 245–53.

Tinbergen, Jan. Manpower Planning in the Oil Countries: The Issues. In *Sherbiny, N. A., ed.*, 1981, pp. 3–20.

Todaro, Michael P. Labour Market Performance in Developing Countries: A Survey: Comment. In *Streeten, P. and Jolly, R, eds.*, 1981, *1978*, pp. 193–95. [G: LDCs]

Tokman, Víctor E. The Development Strategy and Employment in the 1980s. *Cepal Rev.*, December 1981, (15), pp. 133–41. [G: Latin America]

de la Torre, José. Foreign Investment and Economic Development: Conflict and Negotiation. *J. Int. Bus. Stud.*, Fall 1981, *12*(2), pp. 9–32. [G: LDCs]

Tsegaye, Asrat. The Specification of the Foreign Trade Multiplier for a Developing Country. *Oxford Bull. Econ. Statist.*, August 1981, *43*(3), pp. 287–300. [G: LDCs]

Tyler, William G. Growth and Export Expansion in Developing Countries: Some Empirical Evidence. *J. Devel. Econ.*, August 1981, *9*(1), pp. 121–30. [G: LDCs]

Valenzuela, J. Samuel and Valenzuela, Arturo. Modernization and Dependency: Alternative Perspectives in the Study of Latin American Underdevelopment. In *Muñoz, H., ed.*, 1981, pp. 15–41. [G: Latin America]

Van der Wees, Gerrit. Multinational Corporations, Transfer of Technology, and the Socialist Strategy of a Developing Nation: Perspectives from Tanzania. In *Hamilton, F. E. I. and Linge, G. J. R., eds.*, 1981, pp. 529–47. [G: Tanzania]

de Vries, Barend A. Public Policy and the Private Sector. *Finance Develop.*, September 1981, *18*(3), pp. 11–15. [G: LDCs]

Wallerstein, Immanuel. Dependence in an Interdependent World: The Limited Possibilities of Transformation within the Capitalist World Economy. In *Muñoz, H., ed.*, 1981, *1974*, pp. 267–93.

Weisskoff, Richard and Wolff, Edward N. The Structure of Income Inequality in Puerto Rico. *J. Devel. Econ.*, October 1981, *9*(2), pp. 205–28.

Wheaton, William C. and Shishido, Hisanobu. Urban Concentration, Agglomeration Economies, and the Level of Economic Development. *Econ. Develop. Cult. Change*, October 1981, *30*(1), pp. 17–30.

Willoughby, Christopher R. Infrastructure: Doing More with Less. *Finance Develop.*, December 1981, *18*(4), pp. 30–32.

Worsley, Peter. Social Class and Development. In *Berreman, G. D., ed.*, 1981, pp. 221–55.

Zevin, Leon. Concepts of Economic Development of the Developing Nations and Problems of Tripartite Cooperation. In *Saunders, C. T., ed. (I)*, 1981, pp. 295–302.

113 Economic Planning Theory and Policy

1130 Economic Planning Theory and Policy

Antsyshkin, S. V. and Polianskaia, T. M. On Possible Ways of Using Optimal Branch Plans to Improve the Price System—The Case of Power Station Coals. *Matekon*, Fall 1981, *18*(1), pp. 15–34. [G: U.S.S.R.]

Balassa, Bela. The Economic Reform in Hungary Ten Years After. In *Balassa, B.*, 1981, pp. 329–46. [G: Hungary]

Bazarova, G. The Financial and Credit Mechanism for Increasing Effectiveness. *Prob. Econ.*, April 1981, *23*(12), pp. 28–48. [G: U.S.S.R.]

Biţă, V. Objectives for the Informatic Systems. *Econ. Computat. Cybern. Stud. Res.*, 1981, *15*(2), pp. 41–49. [G: Romania]

Boev, Vasily. Food Production for New Industrial Development Regions of the USSR. *Int. Lab. Rev.*, May–June 1981, *120*(3), pp. 351–60. [G: U.S.S.R.]

Brada, Josef C.; Jackson, Marvin R. and King, Arthur E. The Optimal Rate of Industrialization in Developed and Developing Centrally-planned Economies: A General Equilibrium Approach. *World Devel.*, September/October 1981, *9*(9/10), pp. 991–1004. [G: Czechoslovakia; Romania]

Bulutay, Tuncer. Türkiye'nin 1950–1980 Dönemindeki Iktisadi Büyüesi Üzerine Düşünceler. (Reflections on the Economic Growth of Turkey in the Period 1950–1980. With English summary.) *METU*, Special Issue, 1981, pp. 493–539. [G: Turkey]

Bunich, P. G. Wages as an Economic Incentive. *Prob. Econ.*, May 1981, *24*(1), pp. 3–18. [G: U.S.S.R.]

Cai, Yanchu. Does the Key to the Overextension of the Basic Construction Front Lie in Uncompensated Allocation of Funds? *Chinese Econ. Stud.*, Fall 1981, *15*(1), pp. 31–37. [G: China]

Campbell, Robert W. The Foreign Trade System in Poland: Comment. In *Marer, P. and Tabaczynski, E., eds.*, 1981, pp. 92–96. [G: Poland]

Cave, Martin. Soviet Planning Models: Introduction. *Matekon*, Summer 1981, *17*(4), pp. 3–10. [G: U.S.S.R.]

Černý, Miroslav and Holeček, Josef. Traditionally, but with New Approaches. *Czech. Econ. Digest.*, August 1981, (5), pp. 49–62. [G: CMEA]

Chittle, Charles R. Foreign-Exchange Distribution in Yugoslavia's New Planning System: An Input–Output Approach. *J. Compar. Econ.*, March 1981, *5*(1), pp. 79–86. [G: Yugoslavia]

Czerwinski, Z., et al. System of Models for Medium-term Planning of National Economy. In *Janssen, J. M. L.; Pau, L. F. and Straszak, A. J., eds.*, 1981, pp. 79–84. [G: Poland]

Danilov-Danil'ian, V. I. Goal-Related Programs and Optimal Long-Term Planning. *Matekon*, Spring 1981, *17*(3), pp. 55–77.

Delp, Peter. District Planning in Kenya. In *Killick, T., ed.*, 1981, pp. 117–26. [G: Kenya]

Dong, Yusheng. Instituting an Intrafactory Economic Contract System Is a Good Device to Strengthen Business Management. *Chinese Econ. Stud.*, Fall 1981, *15*(1), pp. 38–46. [G: China]

Doran, Howard E. and Deen, Rozany R. The Use of Linear Difference Equations in Manpower Planning: A Criticism. *J. Devel. Econ.*, April 1981, *8*(2), pp. 193–204.

Dyker, David A. Decentralization and the Command-Principle—Some Lessons from Soviet Experience. *J. Compar. Econ.*, June 1981, *5*(2), pp. 121–48. [G: U.S.S.R.]

Dzarasov, S. Economic Initiative and the Organization of Centralized Planning. *Prob. Econ.*, December 1981, *24*(8), pp. 81–95.   [G: U.S.S.R.]

Edelstein, Joel C. The Evolution of Cuban Development Strategy, 1959–1979. In *Muñoz, H., ed.*, 1981, pp. 225–66.   [G: Cuba]

Ellis, Gene. Development Planning and Appropriate Technology: A Dilemma and a Proposal. *World Devel.*, March 1981, *9*(3), pp. 251–62.

Farooq, Ghazi M. Population, Human Resources and Development Planning: Towards an Integrated Approach. *Int. Lab. Rev.*, May–June 1981, *120*(3), pp. 335–49.

Giezgala, Jan. The Foreign Trade System in Poland: Reply. In *Marer, P. and Tabaczynski, E., eds.*, 1981, pp. 96–97.   [G: Poland]

Giezgala, Jan. The Foreign Trade System in Poland. In *Marer, P. and Tabaczynski, E., eds.*, 1981, pp. 87–91.   [G: Poland]

Glushkov, N. The Economic Mechanism and Planned Pricing Practices. *Prob. Econ.*, January 1981, *23*(9), pp. 77–102.   [G: U.S.S.R.]

Gómez, Guillermo L. and Tintner, Gerhard. The Application of Diffusion Processes in Problems of Developmental Economic Planning: A Case Study (Colombia). In *[Lipiński, E.]*, 1981, pp. 177–94.   [G: Colombia]

Goodman, Raymond. The First Post-war Decade. In *Pinder, J., ed.*, 1981, pp. 97–116.   [G: U.K.]

Granberg, A. Modelling the Processes of Coordinating National Economic and Regional Planning Decisions. In *Janssen, J. M. L.; Pau, L. F. and Straszak, A. J., eds.*, 1981, pp. 187–93.

Günçe, Ergin. Türkiye'de Planlamanin "Dünü—Bugünü—Yarini." (Past, Present and Future of Planning in Turkey. With English summary.) *METU*, Special Issue, 1981, pp. 117–32.   [G: Turkey]

Hare, Paul G. The Organization of Information Flows in Systems of Economic Planning. *Econ. Planning*, 1981, *17*(1), pp. 1–19.

Hare, Paul G.; Radice, H. K. and Swain, N. Hungary: A Decade of Economic Reform: Introduction. In *Hare, P. G.; Radice, H. K. and Swain, N., eds.*, 1981, pp. 3–22.   [G: Hungary]

Hershlag, Zvi Y. Pitfalls of Development Strategy and Planning. *METU*, Special Issue, 1981, pp. 19–54.   [G: LDCs]

Hirschman, Albert O. Policymaking and Policy Analysis in Latin America—a Return Journey. In *Hirschman, A. O.*, 1981, *1975*, pp. 142–66.   [G: Latin America]

Hoós, János. Characteristics of the New Growth Path of the Economy in Hungary. *Acta Oecon.*, 1981, *27*(3–4), pp. 207–19.   [G: Hungary]

Hughes Hallett, A. J. Data Analysis as a Sufficient Condition for Economic Planning: The Case of Sri Lanka's Development Plans. *Rev. Public Data Use (See J. Econ. Soc. Meas. after 4/85)*, December 1981, *9*(4), pp. 283–300.   [G: Sri Lanka]

Hunter, Holland. Soviet Economic Problems and Alternative Policy Responses. In *Bornstein, M., ed.*, 1981, *1979*, pp. 345–62.   [G: U.S.S.R.]

Hunter, Holland; Bresnahan, Timothy F. and Rutan, Everett J., III. Modeling Structural Change Using Early Soviet Data. *J. Devel. Econ.*, August 1981, *9*(1), pp. 65–87.   [G: U.S.S.R.]

Joshi, V. The Rationale and Relevance of the Little–

Mirrlees Criterion. In *Livingstone, I., ed.*, 1981, *1972*, pp. 229–44.

Killick, Tony. By Their Fruits Ye Shall Know Them: The Fourth Development Plan. In *Killick, T., ed.*, 1981, pp. 97–108.   [G: Kenya]

Killick, Tony and Kinyua, J. K. Development Plan Implementation in Kenya. In *Killick, T., ed.*, 1981, pp. 109–16.   [G: Kenya]

Korum, Uğur. Türk Planlamasinda Kisa Dönem Makroekonometrik Model Gereksinimi. (The Need for Short-Term Macroeconometric Models in Turkish Planning. With English summary.) *METU*, Special Issue, 1981, pp. 427–36.   [G: Turkey]

Kosta, Jiři. Decentral Planning and Workers' Participation in Decision-Making: The Polish and the Czechoslovak Experience. *Econ. Anal. Worker's Manage.*, 1981, *15*(3), pp. 383–96.   [G: Poland; Czechoslovakia]

Kruzsz, Karl. Material Consumption Norms. The Basis for Planning Demand and Stocks. In *Chikán, A., ed. (II)*, 1981, pp. 135–43.   [G: U.S.S.R.]

Küçük, Yalçin. Türkiye'de Planlama Kavraminin Gelişimi Üzerine. (On the Development of the Planning Concept in Turkey. With English summary.) *METU*, Special Issue, 1981, pp. 79–115.   [G: Turkey]

Lindsay, Kenneth. PEP through the 1930s: Organisation, Structure, People. In *Pinder, J., ed.*, 1981, pp. 9–31.   [G: U.K.]

Los, Marc. Some Reflexions on Epistemology, Design and Planning Theory. In *Dear, M. and Scott, A. J., eds.*, 1981, pp. 63–88.

Manjappa, H. D. Mathematical Models in Development Planning. *Econ. Aff.*, July–September 1981, *26*(3), pp. 211–16.

Manzoor, Nayyer. Economic Growth Model for Pakistan. *Pakistan Econ. Soc. Rev.*, Summer 1981, *19*(1), pp. 24–49.   [G: Pakistan]

Mokhov, N. The Economics, Planning, and Organization of Culture. *Prob. Econ.*, July 1981, *24*(3), pp. 36–54.   [G: U.S.S.R.]

Nicholson, Max. PEP through the 1930s: Growth, Thinking, Performance. In *Pinder, J., ed.*, 1981, pp. 32–53.   [G: U.K.]

Nicholson, Max. The Proposal for a National Plan. In *Pinder, J., ed.*, 1981, pp. 5–8.   [G: U.K.]

Niculescu-Mizil, E. The Place and Role of Cybernetics as a Science and Practice in the Socio-Economic Development of Socialist Romania. *Econ. Computat. Cybern. Stud. Res.*, 1981, *15*(4), pp. 47–61.   [G: Romania]

Pěnkava, Jaromír and Koláček, František. Development through Intensification. *Czech. Econ. Digest.*, December 1981, (8), pp. 19–38.   [G: U.S.S.R.]

Penson, John B., Jr. Synthesis of Optimal Macro Production Plans in Planned Economies: A Syrian Example. *J. Devel. Areas*, October 1981, *16*(1), pp. 31–45.   [G: Syria]

Pertot, Nada. Integracijski procesi v našem gospodarstvu: Modeli in metode za ugotavljanje smiselnosti in učinkovitosti takih povezovanj. (Integration Models in Yugoslav Economy: Models and Methods to Prove the Rationale and Efficiency of Merging. With English summary.)

Econ. Anal. Worker's Manage., 1981, *15*(3), pp. 365–81. [G: Yugoslavia]

Petrakov, N. Ia. The Operating Mechanism of a Socialist Economy and the Problem of the Economy's Optimality Criterion. *Matekon*, Spring 1981, *17*(3), pp. 35–54. [G: U.S.S.R.]

Portes, Richard. Macroeconomic Equilibrium and Disequilibrium in Centrally Planned Economies. *Econ. Inquiry*, October 1981, *19*(4), pp. 559–78.

Powell, Raymond P. Plan Execution and the Workability of Soviet Planning. In *Bornstein, M., ed.*, 1981, *1977*, pp. 39–59. [G: U.S.S.R.]

Ren, Tao. Why Did the Four Hundred Pilot Experiment Enterprises in Sichuan Achieve Swift Results? *Chinese Econ. Stud.*, Fall 1981, *15*(1), pp. 72–86. [G: China]

Richet, X. Is There an 'Hungarian' Model of Planning? In *Hare, P. G.; Radice, H. K. and Swain, N., eds.*, 1981, pp. 23–37. [G: Hungary]

Rosenstein-Rodan, P. M. Planning for Full Employment. In *[Lipiński, E.]*, 1981, pp. 223–34.

Roskill, Oliver. PEP through the 1930s: The Industries Group. In *Pinder, J., ed.*, 1981, pp. 54–80. [G: U.K.]

Schreiner, Per. Makroøkonomisk planlegging i Norge. (Macroeconomic Planning in Norway. With English summary.) *Nationaløkon. Tidsskr.*, 1981, *119*(2), pp. 295–308. [G: Norway]

Sezer, A. Deha. Türkiye'de Planlamanin Hukuki Cerçevesine Ilişkin Sorunlar ve Seçenekler Üzerine Bazi Gözlemler. (Some Observations on Issues and Alternatives Pertaining to the Legal Framework of Planning in Turkey. With English summary.) *METU*, Special Issue, 1981, pp. 163–82. [G: Turkey]

Stojanovic, Radmila. Planning Economic Development in Yugoslavia. *Eastern Europ. Econ.*, Winter 1981–82, *20*(2), pp. 23–45.

Stroe, R. Production Cybernetization—A Basic Component of the New Higher Stage of Development of the Romanian Socialist Society. *Econ. Computat. Cybern. Stud. Res.*, 1981, *15*(1), pp. 43–52. [G: Romania]

Štrougal, Lubomír. With Responsibility and Initiative at the Start of the 7th Five-Year Plan. *Czech. Econ. Digest.*, May 1981, (3), pp. 22–38. [G: Czechoslovakia]

Tardos, Márton M. Options in Hungary's Foreign Trade. *Acta Oecon.*, 1981, *26*(1–2), pp. 29–49. [G: Hungary]

Türel, Oktar. Planlama ve Ulusararasi Örgütler: Turkiye'nin Dünya Bankasi ile Ilişkileri Örnek Olayi. (Planning and International Organizations: The Case of Turkey's Relations with the World Bank. With English summary.) *METU*, Special Issue, 1981, pp. 635–54. [G: Turkey]

Tüzün, Gürel. Bunalim, Ekonomi Politikalari, Planlama ve Devlet: Bir Yaklaşim Önerisi. (Crisis, Economic Policies, Planning and the State: A Suggested Approach. With English summary.) *METU*, Special Issue, 1981, pp. 3–17. [G: Turkey]

Uygur, Ercan. Etki, Yönlendirme ve Öngörüler Açisindan Planlar. (Impact, Orientation and Predictions of the Plans. With English summary.) *METU*, Special Issue, 1981, pp. 437–74. [G: Turkey]

Vatel', I. A. and Moiseev, N. N. On Modeling Economic Mechanisms. *Matekon*, Spring 1981, *17*(3), pp. 78–101.

Voronin, E. Utilize Labor Resources More Completely. *Prob. Econ.*, July 1981, *24*(3), pp. 20–35. [G: U.S.S.R.]

Wan, Jing. Exploit the Potential of Enterprises and Speed up the Circulation of Materiel. *Chinese Econ. Stud.*, Fall 1981, *15*(1), pp. 20–30. [G: China]

Yağci, Fahrettin. Macro Planning in Turkey: A Critical Evaluation. *METU*, Special Issue, 1981, pp. 407–25. [G: Turkey]

Ye, Yinsong. Review of Thirty Years of Management of Commercial Undertakings and Suggestions for Its Future Reform. *Chinese Econ. Stud.*, Summer 1981, *14*(4), pp. 3–16. [G: China]

Young, Michael. The Second World War. In *Pinder, J., ed.*, 1981, pp. 81–96. [G: U.K.]

1132 Economic Planning Theory

Amey, Lloyd R. and Bonaert, Axel P. The Theory of Fuzzy Subsets: A Review and Application to Planning and Control. *Rivista Int. Sci. Econ. Com.*, January–February 1981, *28*(1–2), pp. 1–32.

Anckar, Dag. On Information Inventories and Political Responsiveness. In *Chikán, A., ed. (I)*, 1981, pp. 29–37. [G: Finland]

Baranov, E. F.; Danilov-Danil'ian, V. I. and Zavel'skii, M. G. On a System of Models for Optimal Long-Term Planning. *Matekon*, Summer 1981, *17*(4), pp. 11–38.

Baumgartner, Thomas; Burns, Tom R. and DeVillé, Philippe. Autogestion and Planning: Dilemmas and Possibilities. *Econ. Anal. Worker's Manage.*, 1981, *15*(4), pp. 459–79.

Behrendt, Willy. The Concept of Public Needs as Used in the Socialist States. In *Molt, W.; Hartmann, H. A. and Stringer, P., eds.*, 1981, pp. 285–94.

Bitunov, Vladimir V. Economic Planning and Management. In *Novosti Press Agency*, 1981, pp. 63–76. [G: U.S.S.R.]

Böttcher, Dieter Joachim. Some Problems of the Stability and Flexibility of the National Economic Reproduction Process with Special Regard to the Role of Material and Financial Reserves. In *Chikán, A., ed. (I)*, 1981, pp. 63–71.

Csaki, Csaba. National Agricultural Sector Models for Centrally Planned Economies. In *Johnson, G. and Maunder, A., eds.*, 1981, pp. 312–23. [G: Hungary; CMEA]

Dadaian, V. S. and Raiatskas, R. L. Integrated Sets of Macroeconomic Models. *Matekon*, Summer 1981, *17*(4), pp. 94–111.

Davies, R. W. Economic Planning in the USSR. In *Bornstein, M., ed.*, 1981, pp. 7–38. [G: U.S.S.R.]

Easley, David and Spulber, Daniel F. Stochastic Equilibrium and Optimality with Rolling Plans. *Int. Econ. Rev.*, February 1981, *22*(1), pp. 79–103.

Fallenbuchl, Zbigniew M. Poland: Command Planning in Crisis. *Challenge*, July/August 1981, *24*(3), pp. 5–12. [G: Poland]

Freixas, Xavier. Comparaison de mécanismes d'allocation. (Comparing Allocation Mechanisms. With English summary.) *Revue Écon.*, September 1981, *32*(5), pp. 870–86.

Frisch, Ragnar. From Utopian Theory to Practical Applications: The Case of Econometrics. *Amer. Econ. Rev.*, Special Issue December 1981, *71*(6), pp. 1–16.

Granberg, A. G. A Modified Version of the Optimal Multisectoral Interregional Model. *Matekon*, Summer 1981, *17*(4), pp. 72–93.

Granick, David. Soviet Use of Fixed Prices: Hypothesis of a Job-Right Constraint. In *[Bergson, A.]*, 1981, pp. 85–103.

Hare, Paul G. Aggregate Planning by Means of Input-Output and Material-Balances Systems. *J. Compar. Econ.*, September 1981, *5*(3), pp. 272–91.

Holeček, Josef. Topical Questions Concerning Management of the Process of International Socialist Economic Integration. *Czech. Econ. Digest.*, December 1981, (8), pp. 69–82.   [G: CMEA]

Houdek, Karel. Electric Energy in the 6th and 7th Five-Year Plans. *Czech. Econ. Digest.*, February 1981, (1), pp. 71–78.   [G: Czechoslovakia]

Inyutina, Klara V. The Role of Inventories in the Improvement of Economic Efficiency. In *Chikán, A., ed. (I)*, 1981, pp. 189–98.   [G: U.S.S.R.]

Jech, Otto. Social Consumption of the Population and Its Expected Trends. *Czech. Econ. Digest.*, February 1981, (1), pp. 18–37.
    [G: Czechoslovakia]

Karabín, Štefan. For a More Effective Use of Manpower. *Czech. Econ. Digest.*, February 1981, (1), pp. 38–53.   [G: Czechoslovakia]

Karacal, Hasan. Sosyal Planlamanin Problemleri Üzerine. (On the Problems of Social Planning. With English summary.) *METU*, Special Issue, 1981, pp. 263–86.   [G: Turkey]

Kornai, János. Some Properties of the Eastern European Growth Pattern. *World Devel.*, September/October 1981, *9*(9/10), pp. 965–70.
    [G: E. Europe]

Krishnamurty, J. Indirect Employment Effects of Investment. In *Bhalla, A. S., ed.*, 1981, *1975*, pp. 65–87.   [G: LDCs]

Kubrin, Edward J. Some Characteristics of Stocks. In *Chikán, A., ed. (I)*, 1981, pp. 223–28.

Kydland, Finn E. and Prescott, Edward C. Rules Rather than Discretion: The Inconsistency of Optimal Plans. In *Lucas, R. E. and Sargent, T. J., eds.*, 1981, *1977*, pp. 619–37.

Leibkind, A. R.; Rudnik, B. L. and Chukhnov, A. I. Models for Forming Organizational Structures—A Survey. *Matekon*, Spring 1981, *17*(3), pp. 102–35.

Lieberman, Sima. The Idological Foundations of Western European Planning. *J. Europ. Econ. Hist.*, Fall 1981, *10*(2), pp. 343–71.
    [G: W. Europe]

Nijkamp, Peter and Rietveld, Piet. Multi-Objective Multi-Level Policy Models: An Application to Regional and Environmental Planning. *Europ. Econ. Rev.*, January 1981, *15*(1), pp. 63–89.
    [G: Netherlands]

Orsan, H. Suat and Tayanç, Tunç. Türkiye'de Makro Modellere Genel Bir Bakiş. (Macro Models

in Turkey: A General Outlook. With English summary.) *METU*, Special Issue, 1981, pp. 393–404.

Özler, Güntaç. A Note on Novozhilov's Optimal Plan Prices [A Suggested Planning Procedure with Scarcity in a Centrally Planned Economy]. *METU*, 1981, *8*(1 & 2), pp. 571–75.

Papazov, Christu. Organizational and Planning Problems of Material Stocks. In *Chikán, A., ed. (I)*, 1981, pp. 281–90.

Pugachev, V. F. A Multistage Set of Models for Optimal Production Planning. *Matekon*, Summer 1981, *17*(4), pp. 39–57.

Pugachev, V. F. On Improving the Multistage System for Optimizing Long-Term Economic Plans. *Matekon*, Summer 1981, *17*(4), pp. 58–71.

Říha, Ladislav. Plan-Based Management of Science and Research in Czechoslovakia. *Czech. Econ. Digest.*, February 1981, (1), pp. 54–70.
    [G: Czechoslovakia]

Sadowski, Zdzislaw; Kotowicz, Joanna and Cwalina, Kazimierz. An Experimental Model of General Growth Proportions in the National Economy: The MODO Model. *Econ. Planning*, 1981, *17*(2–3), pp. 64–73.

Simonovits, András. Maximal Convergence Speed of Decentralized Control. *J. Econ. Dynam. Control*, February 1981, *3*(1), pp. 51–64.

Šmíd, Ladislav and Součková, Natalja. International Cooperation in Rational Utilization of Material Resources. *Czech. Econ. Digest.*, February 1981, (1), pp. 3–17.   [G: CMEA]

Snowberger, Vinson. Firm Response to Planner Initiative in Centrally Planned Economy. *Econ. Planning*, 1981, *17*(2–3), pp. 113–25.

Tam, Mo-Yin S. Reward Structures in a Planned Economy: The Problem of Incentives and Efficient Allocation of Resources. *Quart. J. Econ.*, February 1981, *96*(1), pp. 111–28.

Thomas, Ewart A. C. Effort and Optimality in the New Soviet Incentive Model. *Econ. Planning*, 1981, *17*(1), pp. 23–36.

Wiseman, Jack. Uncertainty, Costs, and Collectivist Economic Planning. In *Buchanan, J. M. and Thirlby, G. F., eds.*, 1981, *1953*, pp. 227–43.

Wohltmann, Hans-Werner. Complete, Perfect, and Maximal Controllability of Discrete Economic Systems. *Z. Nationalökon.*, 1981, *41*(1–2), pp. 39–58.

Zahariev, Zahary. Optimization of Inventories as a Factor of Increasing Efficiency of Production. In *Chikán, A., ed. (I)*, 1981, pp. 349–59.
    [G: Bulgaria]

1136 Economic Planning Policy

Al-Ameen, Abdul Wahab. Investment Allocations and Plan Implementation: Iraq's Absorptive Capacity, 1951–1980. *J. Energy Devel.*, Spring 1981, *6*(2), pp. 263–80.   [G: Iraq]

Balassa, Bela. Development Strategy and the Six Year Plan in Taiwan. In *Balassa, B.*, 1981, pp. 381–406.   [G: Taiwan]

Balassa, Bela. Incentive Policies in Brazil. In *Balassa, B.*, 1981, pp. 231–54.   [G: Brazil]

Balassa, Bela. Incentives for Economic Growth in Taiwan. In *Balassa, B.*, 1981, pp. 407–22.
    [G: Taiwan]

Balassa, Bela. Inflation and Trade Liberalization in Korea. In *Balassa, B.*, 1981, pp. 365–79.
[G: South Korea]

Balassa, Bela. Planning and Policy Making in Greece. In *Balassa, B.*, 1981, pp. 281–96.
[G: Greece]

Balassa, Bela. The 15-Year Social and Economic Development Plan for Korea. In *Balassa, B.*, 1981, pp. 347–63.
[G: South Korea]

Bánkövi, G.; Veliczky, József and Ziermann, M. Dynamic Factor Models of the Hungarian National Economy. In *Janssen, J. M. L.; Pau, L. F. and Straszak, A. J., eds.*, 1981, pp. 117–21.
[G: Hungary]

Bauer, Tamás and Soós, Károly Attila. The Current Debate among Soviet Economists over Transformation of the System of Economic Control. *Eastern Europ. Econ.*, Fall 1981, 20(1), pp. 70–89.
[G: U.S.S.R.]

Berend, Iván T. Continuity and Changes of Industrialization in Hungary after the Turn of 1956/57. *Acta Oecon.*, 1981, 27(3–4), pp. 221–50.
[G: Hungary]

Berend, Iván T. Reflections on the Sixth Hungarian Five-Year Plan (1981–1985). *Acta Oecon.*, 1981, 26(1–2), pp. 17–27.
[G: Hungary]

Bergson, Abram. Can the Soviet Slowdown be Reversed? *Challenge*, November–December 1981, 24(5), pp. 33–42.
[G: U.S.S.R.]

Berliner, Joseph S. Technological Progress and the Evolution of Soviet Pricing Policy. In *[Bergson, A.]*, 1981, pp. 105–25.

Bluma, Aleš. Le processus de décision d'achat dans le système socialiste. (The Procedure behind the Decision to Purchase in the Socialist System. With English summary.) *Ann. Sci. Écon. Appl.*, 1981, 37(3), pp. 145–66.
[G: Czechoslovakia]

Brada, Josef C.; King, Arthur E. and Schlagenhauf, Don E. The Optimality of Socialist Development Strategies: An Empirical Inquiry. *J. Econ. Dynam. Control*, February 1981, 3(1), pp. 1–27.
[G: Czechoslovakia]

Brainard, Lawrence J. Foreign Economic Constraints on Soviet Economic Policy in the 1980s. In *Bornstein, M., ed.*, 1981, 1979, pp. 217–31.
[G: U.S.S.R.]

Chenery, Hollis B. Comments on "Challenges and Opportunities Posed by Asia's Superexporters: Implications for Manufactured Exports from Latin America" *Quart. Rev. Econ. Bus.*, Summer 1981, 21(2), pp. 227–30. [G: Latin America; E. Asia]

Civelek, Mehmet A. Education and Economic Growth Revisited: The Evidence from the Turkish Development Experience. *Rivista Int. Sci. Econ. Com.*, March 1981, 28(3), pp. 257–69.
[G: Turkey]

Csikós-Nagy, Béla. Some Aspects of Stock Economy (A Case Study of Hungary). In *Chikán, A., ed. (1)*, 1981, pp. 87–97. [G: Hungary]

Degefe, Befekadu. Ethiopia. In *Adedeji, A., ed.*, 1981, pp. 238–77. [G: Ethiopia]

Ekundare, Richard O. Constraints to Economic Development in Africa: Some Determinants of Economic Disparities. In *Bairoch, P. and Lévy-Leboyer, M., eds.*, 1981, pp. 34–45.
[G: Nigeria; Sub-Saharan Africa]

Ekzen, Aykut. Kamu Iktisadi Kuruluşlarinin Yeniden Düzenlenmesi Yaklaşimlari ve Dördüncü Beş Yillik Plan'in Politikalari. (Approaches to the Reorganization of the State Economic Enterprises and the Policies of the Fourth Plan. With English summary.) *METU*, Special Issue, 1981, pp. 227–60. [G: Turkey]

El-Shibly, M. and Thirlwall, A. P. Dual-Gap Analysis for the Sudan. *World Devel.*, February 1981, 9(2), pp. 193–200. [G: Sudan]

Fenichel, Allen and Khan, Azfar. The Burmese Way to 'Socialism.' *World Devel.*, September/October 1981, 9(9/10), pp. 813–24. [G: Burma]

Grindle, Merilee S. Anticipating Failure: The Implementation of Rural Development Programs. *Public Policy*, Winter 1981, 29(1), pp. 51–74.

Havasi, Ferenc. The Sixth Five-Year Plan of the Hungarian National Economy (1981–1985). *Acta Oecon.*, 1981, 26(1–2), pp. 1–16. [G: Hungary]

Hůla, Václav. Higher Performance of the Economy—Prerequisite of Certainties. *Czech. Econ. Digest.*, March 1981, (2), pp. 3–23.
[G: Czechoslovakia]

Hutchison, Terence W. Walter Eucken and the German Social-Market Economy. In *Hutchison, T. W.*, 1981, pp. 155–75. [G: W. Germany]

Ikram, Khalid. Meeting the Social Contract in Egypt. *Finance Develop.*, September 1981, 18(3), pp. 30–33. [G: Egypt]

Isenman, Paul. Basic Needs: The Case of Sri Lanka: Reply. *World Devel.*, February 1981, 9(2), pp. 217–18. [G: Sri Lanka]

Katsenelinboigen, Aron and Levine, Herbert S. Market and Plan, Plan and Market: The Soviet Case. In *Bornstein, M., ed.*, 1981, 1977, pp. 61–70. [G: U.S.S.R.]

Kedrova, K. Financial Provision for the Scientific and Technical Development of the Branch. *Prob. Econ.*, May 1981, 24(1), pp. 61–77.
[G: U.S.S.R.]

Khachaturov, Tigran. New Perspectives on the Economic and Social Development of the USSR. *Prob. Econ.*, December 1981, 24(8), pp. 3–23.
[G: U.S.S.R.]

Khaikhin, V. P. An Analysis of the State of Plan Discipline in Enterprises. *Matekon*, Winter 1981–82, 18(2), pp. 53–74. [G: U.S.S.R.]

Kheinman, S. A. Organizational–Structural Factors in Economic Growth [Part II]. *Prob. Econ.*, January 1981, 23(9), pp. 25–52. [G: U.S.S.R.]

Kheinman, S. A. Organizational–Structural Factors in Economic Growth [Part I]. *Prob. Econ.*, January 1981, 23(9), pp. 3–24. [G: U.S.S.R.]

Lér, Leopold. Another Step in the Development of the Czechoslovak Economy. *Czech. Econ. Digest.*, August 1981, (5), pp. 39–48.

Mička, Vladimír. The Need for Economy-Oriented Thinking and Acting. *Czech. Econ. Digest.*, August 1981, (5), pp. 25–38. [G: Czechoslovakia]

Moore, John H. Agency Costs, Technological Change, and Soviet Central Planning. *J. Law Econ.*, October 1981, 24(2), pp. 189–214.
[G: U.S.S.R.]

Mujžel, Jan. The Working System of the Economy (Problems with Its Further Development in Poland). *Eastern Europ. Econ.*, Fall 1981, 20(1), pp. 20–48. [G: Poland]

Özhan, H. Gazi. An Evaluation of the 1973 Soviet Industrial Reorganization. *METU*, 1981, *8*(3&4), pp. 715–46. [G: U.S.S.R.]

Panov, Vladimir P. The Supreme Goal of Social Production. In *Novosti Press Agency*, 1981, pp. 191–215. [G: U.S.S.R.]

Pfajfar, Lovro, et al. Upotreba ekonometrijskog modela u prognoziranju razvoja Jugoslavije za period 1981–1985. (The Application of an Econometric Model for Yugoslavia's 1981–1985 Medium-Term Plan. With English summary.) *Econ. Anal. Worker's Manage.*, 1981, *15*(2), pp. 143–61. [G: Yugoslavia]

Porokhovsky, Anatoly. A Comparative Study of Indicative Planning in Turkey and Planning in Socialist Countries. *METU*, Special Issue, 1981, pp. 133–43. [G: Turkey; U.S.S.R.]

Rabevazaha, C. Control of Development by the People: Regional Planning and Basic Needs in Madagascar. *Int. Lab. Rev.*, July–August 1981, *120*(4), pp. 439–52. [G: Madagascar]

Ranis, Gustav. Challenges and Opportunities Posed by Asia's Superexporters: Implications for Manufactured Exports from Latin America. *Quart. Rev. Econ. Bus.*, Summer 1981, *21*(2), pp. 204–26. [G: Latin America; E. Asia]

Richards, Peter J. Comment on Isenman, 'Basic Needs: The Case of Sri Lanka.' *World Devel.*, February 1981, *9*(2), pp. 215–16. [G: Sri Lanka]

del Rio, Abel Beltran. The Mexican Oil Syndrome: Early Symptoms, Preventive Efforts, and Prognosis. *Quart. Rev. Econ. Bus.*, Summer 1981, *21*(2), pp. 115–30. [G: Mexico; OPEC]

Rosted, Jørgen. Udviklingstendenser i den makroøkonomiske planlægning i Danmark. (The Development of Macroeconomic Planning in Denmark. With English summary.) *Nationaløkon. Tidsskr.*, 1981, *119*(2), pp. 276–94. [G: Denmark]

Şaylan, Gencay. Planlama ve Bürokrasi. (Planning and Bureaucracy. With English summary.) *METU*, Special Issue, 1981, pp. 183–205. [G: Turkey]

Szakolczai, György. Foreign Trade in the Hungarian Models. In *Courbis, R., ed.*, 1981, pp. 65–75. [G: Hungary]

Tan, Turgut. 20 yillik planlama deneyimi işiğinda— Türkiye'de Planlamanin idari ve Hukuki Sorunlari. (Administrative and Legal Problems of Planning in Turkey in the Light of Twenty Years of Experience. With English summary.) *METU*, Special Issue, 1981, pp. 147–61. [G: Turkey]

Türel, Oktar. 1970'li Yillarda Mühendislik Sanayilerindeki Kamu Yatirimlari: Gözlem ve Değerlendirmeler. (Public Investments in Engineering Industries in the '70's: Some Observations and Comments. With English summary.) *METU*, Special Issue, 1981, pp. 575–612. [G: Turkey]

Vĕrtelář, Václav. Drafting the Plan for 1982. *Czech. Econ. Digest.*, September 1981, (6), pp. 27–36. [G: Czechoslovakia]

Vojnic, Dragomir. Investment Policy. *Eastern Europ. Econ.*, Winter 1981–82, *20*(2), pp. 63–83. [G: Yugoslavia]

Wiedemann, Paul. Economic Reform in Bulgaria:

Coping with "The kj Problem." *Eastern Europ. Econ.*, Fall 1981, *20*(1), pp. 90–108.

Xue, Muqiao. Tentative Study on the Reform of the Economic System. *Chinese Econ. Stud.*, Winter–Spring 1980-81, *14*(2–3), pp. 139–68. [G: China]

114 Economics of War, Defense, and Disarmament

1140 Economics of War, Defense, and Disarmament

Albert, Bill and Henderson, Paul. Latin America and the Great War: A Preliminary Survey of Developments in Chile, Peru, Argentina and Brazil. *World Devel.*, August 1981, *9*(8), pp. 717–34. [G: Chile; Peru; Argentina; Brazil]

Amsden, Alice H. The Military in Development: Comment. In *Streeten, P. and Jolly, R, eds.*, 1981, *1977*, pp. 267–75.

Barro, Robert J. Output Effects of Government Purchases. *J. Polit. Econ.*, December 1981, *89*(6), pp. 1086–1121. [G: U.S.]

Borcherding, Thomas E. Comment: The Demand for Military Expenditures: An International Comparison. *Public Choice*, 1981, *37*(1), pp. 33–39.

Brito, Dagobert L. and Intriligator, Michael D. Strategic Arms Limitation Treaties and Innovations in Weapons Technology. *Public Choice*, 1981, *37*(1), pp. 41–59. [G: U.S.; U.S.S.R.]

Cain, Louis P. and Neumann, George R. Planning for Peace: The Surplus Property Act of 1944. *J. Econ. Hist.*, March 1981, *41*(1), pp. 129–35. [G: U.S.]

Capra, James R. The National Defense Budget and Its Economic Effects. *Fed. Res. Bank New York Quart. Rev.*, Summer 1981, *6*(2), pp. 21–31. [G: U.S.]

Cooper, Orah and Fogarty, Carol. Soviet Military and Economic Aid to the Less Developed Countries, 1954–78. In *Bornstein, M., ed.*, 1981, *1979*, pp. 253–66. [G: U.S.S.R.; LDCs]

Davis, Lance E. and Huttenback, Robert A. In Search of the Historical Imperialist. In *[Weiler, E. T.]*, 1981, pp. 152–67. [G: U.K.]

Denzer, D. Eine Methode zur Auswertung von Gefechtssimulationen. (With English summary.) In *Fandel, G., et al., eds.*, 1981, pp. 45–48.

Desai, Meghnad and Blake, David. Modelling the Ultimate Absurdity: A Comment on "A Quantitative Study of the Strategic Arms Race in the Missile Age." *Rev. Econ. Statist.*, November 1981, *63*(4), pp. 629–32. [G: U.S.; U.S.S.R.]

Dudley, Leonard and Montmarquette, Claude. The Demand for Military Expenditures: An International Comparison. *Public Choice*, 1981, *37*(1), pp. 5–31.

Dumas, Lloyd J. Taxes and Militarism. *Cato J.*, Spring 1981, *1*(1), pp. 277–92. [G: U.S.]

Feldman, Gerald D. German Interest Group Alliances in War and Inflation, 1914–23. In *Berger, S., ed.*, 1981, pp. 159–84. [G: Germany]

Franko, Lawrence G. and Stephenson, Sherry. French Export Behavior in Third World Markets. In *Center for Strategic and Internat. Studies, ed.*

(I), 1981, pp. 171–251.   [G: France; OECD; LDCs]

Gansler, Jacques S. Our Ailing Defense Industry. *Challenge,* November–December 1981, *24*(5), pp. 43–48.   [G: U.S.]

Goodwin, Crauford A. The Economic Problems Facing Truman. In *Heller, F. H., ed.,* 1981, pp. 2–12.   [G: U.S.]

Hartley, Keith. UK Defence: A Case Study of Spending Cuts. In *Hood, C. and Wright, M., eds.,* 1981, pp. 125–51.   [G: U.K.]

Hartley, Keith and McLean, Pat. U.K. Defence Expenditure. *Public Finance,* 1981, *36*(2), pp. 171–92.   [G: U.K.]

Hogan, William W. Energy and Security Policy. In *Wachter, M. L. and Wachter, S. M., eds.,* 1981, pp. 202–71.   [G: U.S.; Selected Countries]

Hossfeld, B. Verlustraten und numerische Stabilität in Lanchester-Modellen. (With English summary.) In *Fandel, G., et al., eds.,* 1981, pp. 56–63.

Huq, Muzammel. The Role of the Military in the NIEO. In *Lozoya, J. A. and Birgin, H., eds.,* 1981, pp. 193–206.   [G: Global]

Ingham, Barbara and Simmons, Colin. The Two World Wars and Economic Development: Editors' Introduction. *World Devel.,* August 1981, *9*(8), pp. 701–05.

Intriligator, Michael D. and Brito, Dagobert L. Nuclear Proliferation and the Probability of Nuclear War. *Public Choice,* 1981, *37*(2), pp. 247–60.

Kaldor, Mary. The Military in Development: Reply. In *Streeten, P. and Jolly, R, eds.,* 1981, *1977,* pp. 277.

Kaldor, Mary. The Military in Development. In *Streeten, P. and Jolly, R, eds.,* 1981, *1976,* pp. 241–64.

Kaufmann, William W. The Defense Budget. In *Pechman, J. A., ed.,* 1981, pp. 133–83.   [G: U.S.]

Kidron, Michael. The Military in Development: Comment. In *Streeten, P. and Jolly, R, eds.,* 1981, *1976,* pp. 265–66.

Kirk, Robert and Simmons, Colin. Engineering and the First World War: A Case Study of the Lancashire Cotton Spinning Machine Industry. *World Devel.,* August 1981, *9*(8), pp. 773–91.   [G: U.K.]

Mackay, Robert J. Strategic Arms Limitation Treaties and Innovations in Weapons Technology: A Comment. *Public Choice,* 1981, *37*(1), pp. 61–68.

McGraw, Thomas K. Discussion [The Response of the Giant Corporations to Wage and Price Controls in World War II] [Planning for Peace: The Surplus Property Act of 1944]. *J. Econ. Hist.,* March 1981, *41*(1), pp. 136–37.   [G: U.S.]

McGuire, Martin. A Quantitative Study of the Strategic Arms Race in the Missile Age: A Reply. *Rev. Econ. Statist.,* November 1981, *63*(4), pp. 632–33.   [G: U.S.; U.S.S.R.]

McNamara, Robert S. At the University of Chicago on Development and the Arms Race, Chicago, Illinois, May 22, 1979. In *McNamara, R. S.,* 1981, *1979,* pp. 553–61.

Miller, Rory. Latin American Manufacturing and the

First World War: An Exploratory Essay. *World Devel.,* August 1981, *9*(8), pp. 707–16.   [G: Latin America]

Moskos, Charles C. Making the All-Volunteer Force Work: A National Service Approach. *Foreign Aff.,* Fall 1981, *60*(1), pp. 17–34.   [G: U.S.]

Okuguchi, Koji. Stability of the Arms Race Models. *Z. Nationalökon.,* 1981, *41*(3–4), pp. 353–60.

Pettengill, John S. Firearms and the Distribution of Income: A Neo-Classical Model. *Rev. Radical Polit. Econ.,* Summer 1981, *13*(2), pp. 1–10.

Proost, Stef; Schokkaert, Erik and Van Elewijck, Paul. Enkele economische aspecten van de Belgische defensie-uitgaven. (Some Economic Aspects of the Belgian Military Spending. With English summary.) *Cah. Écon. Bruxelles,* 4th Trimestre 1981, (92), pp. 571–99.   [G: Belgium]

Short, John. Defence Spending in the U.K. Regions. *Reg. Stud.,* 1981, *15*(2), pp. 101–10.   [G: U.K.]

Simmons, Colin. Imperial Dictate: The Effect of the Two World Wars on the Indian Coal Industry. *World Devel.,* August 1981, *9*(8), pp. 749–71.   [G: India]

Spencer, Ian R. G. The First World War and the Origins of the Dual Policy of Development in Kenya, 1914–1922. *World Devel.,* August 1981, *9*(8), pp. 735–48.   [G: Kenya]

Stowe, David H. Economics and the Truman Administration: Comments. In *Heller, F. H., ed.,* 1981, pp. 129–31.   [G: U.S.]

Todd, D. Regional Variations in Naval Construction: The British Experience, 1895–1966. *Reg. Stud.,* 1981, *15*(2), pp. 123–42.   [G: U.K.]

Wassermann, Ursula. Apartheid and Economic Sanctions. *J. World Trade Law,* July–August 1981, *15*(4), pp. 367–69.   [G: S. Africa]

Young, Michael. The Second World War. In *Pinder, J., ed.,* 1981, pp. 81–96.   [G: U.K.]

Zagare, Frank C. Nonmyopic Equilibria and the Middle East Crisis of 1967. *Conflict Manage. Peace Sci.,* Spring 1981, *5*(2), pp. 139–62.   [G: Israel]

Zimmerman, William. Soviet–East European Relations in the 1980s and the Changing International System. In *Bornstein, M.; Gitelman, Z. and Zimmerman, W., eds.,* 1981, pp. 87–104.   [G: U.S.S.R.; E. Europe]

120 COUNTRY STUDIES

121 Economic Studies of Developing Countries

1210 General

Balassa, Bela. The Process of Industrial Development and Alternative Development Strategies. In *Balassa, B.,* 1981, pp. 1–26.   [G: LDCs]

Barraclough, Solon. Agricultural Finance and Rural Credit in Poor Countries: Comment. In *Streeten, P. and Jolly, R, eds.,* 1981, *1976,* pp. 215–17.   [G: LDCs]

Benjenk, Munir C. Compiti e propositi del Gruppo Banca Mondiale. (Role and Aims of the World Bank Group. With English summary.) *Bancaria,* February 1981, *37*(2), pp. 123–28.   [G: LDCs]

Black, Stanley W. The Impact of Changes in the

World Economy on Stabilization Policies in the 1970s. In *Cline, W. R. and Weintraub, S., eds.*, 1981, pp. 43–77. [G: LDCs]

Chenery, Hollis B. Comments on "Challenges and Opportunities Posed by Asia's Superexporters: Implications for Manufactured Exports from Latin America" *Quart. Rev. Econ. Bus.*, Summer 1981, 21(2), pp. 227–30. [G: Latin America; E. Asia]

Cline, William R. and Weintraub, Sidney. Economic Stabilization in Developing Countries: Introduction and Overview. In *Cline, W. R. and Weintraub, S., eds.*, 1981, pp. 1–42. [G: LDCs]

Dell, Sidney. The Impact of Changes in the World Economy on Stabilization Policies in the 1970s: Comment. In *Cline, W. R. and Weintraub, S., eds.*, 1981, pp. 77–81. [G: LDCs]

Dunning, John H. Multinational Enterprises and Trade Flows of Developing Countries. In *Dunning, J. H.*, 1981, pp. 304–20.

Feder, Gershon; Just, Richard E. and Ross, Knud. Projecting Debt Servicing Capacity of Developing Countries. *J. Finan. Quant. Anal.*, December 1981, 16(5), pp. 651–69.

Glezakos, C. Export Instability and Economic Growth: A Statistical Verification. In *Livingstone, I., ed.*, 1981, 1973, pp. 137–42. [G: LDCs; MDCs]

Hicks, Norman and Streeten, Paul. Reply [Indicators of Development: The Search for a Basic Needs Yardstick]. *World Devel.*, April 1981, 9(4), pp. 399.

Hicks, Norman and Streeten, Paul P. Indicators of Development: The Search for a Basic Needs Yardstick. In *Streeten, P. and Jolly, R, eds.*, 1981, 1979, pp. 53–66.

Hürni, Bettina. IFC: The New Five-Year Programme. *J. World Trade Law*, September–October 1981, 15(5), pp. 461–65.

Krueger, Anne O. Trade and Employment in Developing Countries: The Framework of the Country Studies. In *Krueger, A. O., et al., eds.*, 1981, pp. 1–28. [G: LDCs]

Lall, Sanjaya. Developing Countries and Foreign Investment. In *Lall, S.*, 1981, 1974, pp. 53–67.

Lipton, Michael. Agricultural Finance and Rural Credit in Poor Countries. In *Streeten, P. and Jolly, R, eds.*, 1981, 1976, pp. 201–11. [G: LDCs]

McGranahan, Donald; Richard, Claude and Pizarro, Eduardo. Development Statistics and Correlations: A Comment on Hicks and Streeten [Indicators of Development: The Search for a Basic Needs Yardstick]. *World Devel.*, April 1981, 9(4), pp. 389–97.

McNamara, Robert S. To the Board of Governors, Washington, D.C., September 26, 1977. In *McNamara, R. S.*, 1981, 1977, pp. 437–75. [G: OECD; LDCs]

McNamara, Robert S. To the Board of Governors, Belgrade, Yugoslavia, October 2, 1979. In *McNamara, R. S.*, 1981, 1979, pp. 565–610. [G: OECD; LDCs]

McNamara, Robert S. To the Board of Governors, Washington, D.C., September 30, 1980. In *McNamara, R. S.*, 1981, 1980, pp. 613–60. [G: LDCs; OECD]

McNamara, Robert S. To the Board of Governors, Washington, D.C., September 25, 1978. In *McNamara, R. S.*, 1981, 1978, pp. 479–518. [G: OECD; LDCs]

McNamara, Robert S. To the Board of Governors, Washington, D.C., September 30, 1974. In *McNamara, R. S.*, 1981, 1974, pp. 267–93. [G: OECD; LDCs]

McNamara, Robert S. To the United Nations Conference on Trade and Development, Santiago, Chile, April 14, 1972. In *McNamara, R. S.*, 1981, 1972, pp. 171–89. [G: OECD; LDCs]

Oshima, Harry T. A. Lewis' Dualistic Theory and Its Relevance for Postwar Asian Growth. *Malayan Econ. Rev. (See Singapore Econ. Rev.)*, October 1981, 26(2), pp. 1–26. [G: Asia]

Palma, Gabriel. Dependency: A Formal Theory of Underdevelopment or a Methodology for the Analysis of Concrete Situations of Underdevelopment? In *Streeten, P. and Jolly, R, eds.*, 1981, pp. 383–426. [G: Latin America]

Ranis, Gustav. Challenges and Opportunities Posed by Asia's Superexporters: Implications for Manufactured Exports from Latin America. *Quart. Rev. Econ. Bus.*, Summer 1981, 21(2), pp. 204–26. [G: Latin America; E. Asia]

Robson, Peter. Regional Economic Cooperation among Developing Countries: Some Further Considerations. In *Streeten, P. and Jolly, R, eds.*, 1981, pp. 331–37. [G: LDCs; ASEAN]

Schiffer, Jonathan. The Changing Post-war Pattern of Development: The Accumulated Wisdom of Samir Amin. *World Devel.*, June 1981, 9(6), pp. 515–37.

Seers, Dudley. Massive Transfers and Mutual Interests. *World Devel.*, June 1981, 9(6), pp. 557–62.

Sen, Amartya. Public Action and the Quality of Life in Developing Countries. *Oxford Bull. Econ. Statist.*, November 1981, 43(4), pp. 287–319.

Solomon, Robert. The Debt of Developing Countries: Another Look. *Brookings Pap. Econ. Act.*, 1981, (2), pp. 592–606. [G: LDCs]

Tsegaye, Asrat. The Specification of the Foreign Trade Multiplier for a Developing Country. *Oxford Bull. Econ. Statist.*, August 1981, 43(3), pp. 287–300. [G: LDCs]

Tyler, William G. Growth and Export Expansion in Developing Countries: Some Empirical Evidence. *J. Devel. Econ.*, August 1981, 9(1), pp. 121–30. [G: LDCs]

Vaitsos, Constantine V. Crisis in Regional Economic Cooperation (Integration) among Developing Countries: A Survey. In *Streeten, P. and Jolly, R, eds.*, 1981, 1978, pp. 279–329. [G: Latin America]

Wheaton, William C. and Shishido, Hisanobu. Urban Concentration, Agglomeration Economies, and the Level of Economic Development. *Econ. Develop. Cult. Change*, October 1981, 30(1), pp. 17–30.

Wionczek, Miguel S. Can the Broken Humpty-Dumpty Be Put Together Again and by Whom? Comments on the Vaitsos Survey [Crisis in Regional Economic Cooperation (Integration) among Developing Countries: A Survey]. In *Streeten,*

121 Economic Studies of Developing Countries

P. and Jolly, R, eds., 1981, *1978*, pp. 339–42. **[G: LDCs]**

Yudelman, Montague. Agricultural Finance and Rural Credit in Poor Countries: Comment. In *Streeten, P. and Jolly, R, eds.*, 1981, *1976*, pp. 213–14. **[G: LDCs]**

1211 Comparative Country Studies

Amsden, Alice H. The Military in Development: Comment. In *Streeten, P. and Jolly, R, eds.*, 1981, *1977*, pp. 267–75.

Balassa, Bela. The Newly-Industrializing Developing Countries after the Oil Crisis. *Weltwirtsch. Arch.*, 1981, *117*(1), pp. 142–94. **[G: LDCs]**

Balassa, Bela. The Newly-Industrializing Developing Countries after the Oil Crisis. In *Balassa, B.*, 1981, pp. 29–81. **[G: LDCs]**

Desai, Ashok V. Effects of the Rise in Oil Prices on South Asian Countries, 1972–78. *Int. Lab. Rev.*, March–April 1981, *120*(2), pp. 129–47. **[G: S. Asia]**

Fautz, Wolfgang. Il "miracolo economico" dell'est asiatico e le sue origini. (The "Economic Miracle" of South East Asia and Its Origin. With English summary.) *Mondo Aperto*, October 1981, *35*(5), pp. 289–97. **[G: S.E. Asia]**

Issawi, Charles. Egypt, Iran and Turkey, 1800–1970: Patterns of Growth and Development. In *Bairoch, P. and Lévy-Leboyer, M., eds.*, 1981, pp. 65–77. **[G: Egypt; Iran; Turkey]**

Kaldor, Mary. The Military in Development. In *Streeten, P. and Jolly, R, eds.*, 1981, *1976*, pp. 241–64.

Kaldor, Mary. The Military in Development: Reply. In *Streeten, P. and Jolly, R, eds.*, 1981, *1977*, pp. 277.

Kidron, Michael. The Military in Development: Comment. In *Streeten, P. and Jolly, R, eds.*, 1981, *1976*, pp. 265–66.

1213 European Countries

Aiyer, T. Sriram. The Economic Consequences of the April 25th Revolution: Comment. In *Braga de Macedo, J. and Serfaty, S., eds.*, 1981, pp. 89–94. **[G: Portugal]**

Bacon, Robert and Karayiannis-Bacon, Hariklia. The Growth of the Non-Market Sector and the Greek Economy: A Reply to Hadjimatheou and Skouras. *Greek Econ. Rev.*, April 1981, *3*(1), pp. 81–82. **[G: Greece]**

Balassa, Bela. Planning and Policy Making in Greece. In *Balassa, B.*, 1981, pp. 281–96. **[G: Greece]**

Balassa, Bela. Portugal in Face of the Common Market. In *Balassa, B.*, 1981, pp. 255–80. **[G: Portugal]**

Beleza, Luis Miguel. The Economic Consequences of the April 25th Revolution: Comment. In *Braga de Macedo, J. and Serfaty, S., eds.*, 1981, pp. 95–100. **[G: Portugal]**

Burakow, Nicholas. Romania and Greece—Socialism vs Capitalism. *World Devel.*, September/October 1981, *9*(9/10), pp. 907–28. **[G: Romania; Greece]**

Georgiou, George C. Alternative Trade Strategies and Employment in Cyprus. *J. Econ. Devel.*, December 1981, *6*(2), pp. 113–31. **[G: Cyprus]**

Gligorov, Kiro. The Social and Economic Basis of Socialist Self-Management in Yugoslavia. *Eastern Europ. Econ.*, Winter 1981–82, *20*(2), pp. 3–22.

Krugman, Paul R. and Braga de Macedo, Jorge. The Economic Consequences of the April 25th Revolution. In *Braga de Macedo, J. and Serfaty, S., eds.*, 1981, pp. 53–87. **[G: Portugal]**

Sapir, André. Economic Reform and Migration in Yugoslavia: An Econometric Model. *J. Devel. Econ.*, October 1981, *9*(2), pp. 149–81. **[G: Yugoslavia]**

Sirotkovic, Jakov. Influence of the Self-Management System on the Development of the Yugoslav Economy. *Eastern Europ. Econ.*, Winter 1981–82, *20*(2), pp. 46–62. **[G: Yugoslavia]**

Varga, Werner. Yugoslavia's Battle for Economic Stability. *Eastern Europ. Econ.*, Summer 1981, *19*(4), pp. 58–74. **[G: Yugoslavia]**

1214 Asian Countries

Ahmad, Masood. Incremental Capital-Output Ratios and Growth Rates in the Short-Run Evidence from Pakistan. *Pakistan Econ. Soc. Rev.*, Winter 1981, *19*(2), pp. 123–30. **[G: Selected MDCs; Selected LDCs; Pakistan]**

Akrasanee, Narongchai. Trade Strategy for Employment Growth in Thailand. In *Krueger, A. O., et al., eds.*, 1981, pp. 393–433. **[G: Thailand]**

Al-Ameen, Abdul Wahab. Investment Allocations and Plan Implementation: Iraq's Absorptive Capacity, 1951–1980. *J. Energy Devel.*, Spring 1981, *6*(2), pp. 263–80. **[G: Iraq]**

Arndt, Heinz W. Survey of Recent Developments. *Bull. Indonesian Econ. Stud.*, November 1981, *17*(3), pp. 1–24. **[G: Indonesia]**

Balassa, Bela. Development Strategy and the Six Year Plan in Taiwan. In *Balassa, B.*, 1981, pp. 381–406. **[G: Taiwan]**

Balassa, Bela. Incentives for Economic Growth in Taiwan. In *Balassa, B.*, 1981, pp. 407–22. **[G: Taiwan]**

Balassa, Bela. Policies for Stable Economic Growth in Turkey. In *Balassa, B.*, 1981, pp. 297–328. **[G: Turkey]**

Balassa, Bela. The 15-Year Social and Economic Development Plan for Korea. In *Balassa, B.*, 1981, pp. 347–63. **[G: South Korea]**

Balasubramanyan, V. N. Prospects for the NICs: India. In *Saunders, C. T., ed. (II)*, 1981, pp. 183–203. **[G: India]**

Bauer, P. T. The Lesson of Hong Kong. In *Bauer, P. T.*, 1981, pp. 185–90. **[G: Hong Kong]**

Bhaduri, Amit. Class Relations and the Pattern of Accumulation in an Agrarian Economy. *Cambridge J. Econ.*, March 1981, *5*(1), pp. 33–46. **[G: India]**

Bowen-Jones, Howard. Development in the Middle East. In *[Fisher, W. B.]*, 1981, pp. 3–23. **[G: Middle East]**

Bulmuş, Ismail. Türkiye'de Tarimsal Taban Fiyat Politikasi ve Etkileri. (Price Support Policies in Turkey and Their Impacts. With English sum-

mary.) *METU*, Special Issue, 1981, pp. 541–73.
[G: Turkey]

Bulutay, Tuncer. Türkiye'nin 1950–1980 Dönemindeki Iktisadi Büyüesi Üzerine Düşünceler. (Reflections on the Economic Growth of Turkey in the Period 1950–1980. With English summary.) *METU*, Special Issue, 1981, pp. 493–539.
[G: Turkey]

Burki, Shahid Javed. Pakistan's Development: An Overview. *World Devel.*, March 1981, 9(3), pp. 301–14. [G: Pakistan]

Chandavarkar, A. G. Some Aspects of Interest Rate Policies in Less Developed Economies: The Experience of Selected Asian Countries. In *Livingstone, I., ed.*, 1981, *1971*, pp. 333–50.
[G: Taiwan; S. Korea; Malaysia; Singapore]

Chandra, Nirmal K. The New International Economic Order and Industrialization in India. In *Lozoya, J. A. and Bhattacharya, A. K., eds.*, 1981, pp. 90–140. [G: India]

Chow, Steven C. and Papanek, Gustav F. Laissez-Faire, Growth and Equity—Hong Kong. *Econ. J.*, June 1981, 91(362), pp. 466–85.
[G: Hong Kong]

Christensen, Laurits R. and Cummings, Dianne. Real Product, Real Factor Input, and Productivity in the Republic of Korea, 1960–1973. *J. Devel. Econ.*, June 1981, 8(3), pp. 285–302.
[G: S. Korea]

Corden, W. Max. Export Growth and the Balance of Payments in Korea, 1960–78: Comment. In *Hong, W. and Krause, L. B., eds.*, 1981, pp. 253–56. [G: S. Korea]

Daroesman, Ruth. Survey of Recent Developments. *Bull. Indonesian Econ. Stud.*, July 1981, 17(2), pp. 1–41. [G: Indonesia]

Desai, Ashok V. Effects of the Rise in Oil Prices on South Asian Countries, 1972–78. *Int. Lab. Rev.*, March–April 1981, 120(2), pp. 129–47.
[G: S. Asia]

English, H. Edward. Export-Oriented Growth and Industrial Diversification in Hong Kong: Comment. In *Hong, W. and Krause, L. B., eds.*, 1981, pp. 124–28. [G: Hong Kong]

Fenichel, Allen and Khan, Azfar. The Burmese Way to 'Socialism.' *World Devel.*, September/October 1981, 9(9/10), pp. 813–24. [G: Burma]

Girgis, Maurice. Growth Patterns and Structural Changes in Output and Employment in the Arab World. In *Sherbiny, N. A., ed.*, 1981, pp. 21–54. [G: Arab Countries]

Glassburner, Bruce. The Indonesian Economy: A Review Essay. *Bull. Indonesian Econ. Stud.*, November 1981, 17(3), pp. 94–101.
[G: Indonesia]

Gottheil, Fred. Iraqi and Syrian Socialism: An Economic Appraisal. *World Devel.*, September/October 1981, 9(9/10), pp. 825–37. [G: Iraq; Syria; Jordan; Morocco]

Guisinger, Stephen E. Stabilization Policies in Pakistan: The 1970–77 Experience. In *Cline, W. R. and Weintraub, S., eds.*, 1981, pp. 375–99.
[G: Pakistan]

Guisinger, Stephen E. Trade Policies and Employment: The Case of Pakistan. In *Krueger, A. O., et al., eds.*, 1981, pp. 291–340. [G: Pakistan]

Healey, Derek. Survey of Recent Developments. *Bull. Indonesian Econ. Stud.*, March 1981, 17(1), pp. 1–35. [G: Indonesia]

Hong, Lee Fook. Singapore's 1981 Budget: Summary. *Bull. Int. Fiscal Doc.*, June 1981, 35(6), pp. 243–53. [G: Singapore]

Hooley, Richard. Philippine Economics: Development and Major Issues. In *Hart, D. V., ed.*, 1981, pp. 98–211. [G: Philippines]

Hughes Hallett, A. J. Data Analysis as a Sufficient Condition for Economic Planning: The Case of Sri Lanka's Development Plans. *Rev. Public Data Use (See J. Econ. Soc. Meas. after 4/85)*, December 1981, 9(4), pp. 283–300.
[G: Sri Lanka]

Isenman, Paul. Basic Needs: The Case of Sri Lanka: Reply. *World Devel.*, February 1981, 9(2), pp. 217–18. [G: Sri Lanka]

Kim, Key W. Prospects for the NICs: South Korea. In *Saunders, C. T., ed. (II)*, 1981, pp. 159–82.
[G: S. Korea]

Ladejinsky, W. Ironies of India's Green Revolution. In *Livingstone, I., ed.*, 1981, *1970*, pp. 293–96.
[G: India]

Laumas, Prem S. and Williams, Martin. Energy and Economic Development. *Weltwirtsch. Arch.*, 1981, 117(4), pp. 706–16. [G: India]

Lazaridis, A. S. and Basu, D. R. Stochastic Optimal Control by Pseudoinverse. An Application. In *Janssen, J. M. L.; Pau, L. F. and Straszak, A. J., eds.*, 1981, pp. 361–65. [G: India]

Levy, Victor. Total Factor Productivity, Non-Neutral Technical Change and Economic Growth: A Parametric Study of a Developing Economy. *J. Devel. Econ.*, February 1981, 8(1), pp. 93–109.
[G: Iraq]

Liang, Ernest P. L. Market Accessibility and Agricultural Development in Prewar China. *Econ. Develop. Cult. Change*, October 1981, 30(1), pp. 77–105. [G: China]

Liang, Kuo-Shu and Liang, Ching-ing Hou. Trade Strategy and the Exchange Rate Policies in Taiwan. In *Hong, W. and Krause, L. B., eds.*, 1981, pp. 150–78. [G: Taiwan]

Lim, Chong-Yah. The Economic Development of the Members of the Association of Southeast Asian Nations (ASEAN). In *Lozoya, J. A. and Bhattacharya, A. K., eds.*, 1981, pp. 174–88.
[G: S. E. Asia]

Lin, Tzong Biau and Ho, Yin Ping. Export-Oriented Growth and Industrial Diversification in Hong Kong. In *Hong, W. and Krause, L. B., eds.*, 1981, pp. 69–123. [G: Hong Kong]

Méng-Try, EA. Kampuchea: A Country Adrift. *Population Devel. Rev.*, June 1981, 7(2), pp. 209–28. [G: Kampuchea]

Mohammad, Sharif. Trade, Growth and Income Redistribution: A Case Study of India. *J. Devel. Econ.*, August 1981, 9(1), pp. 131–47.
[G: India]

Oshima, Harry T. Policy Implications for Southeast Asia in the Low Growth Decade of the 1980s. *Phillipine Rev. Econ. Bus.*, Sept. & Dec. 1981, 18(3/4), pp. 116–31. [G: Asian LDCs]

Pal, Dipti Prakas and Pal, Gunendra Prasad. Macro Measurers of Import Substitution. *Econ. Aff.*, October–December 1981, *26*(4), pp. 241–49.

[G: India]

Papanek, Gustav F. Stabilization Policies in Pakistan: The 1970–77 Experience: Comment. In *Cline, W. R. and Weintraub, S., eds.*, 1981, pp. 399–405.

[G: Pakistan]

Park, Yung Chul. Export Growth and the Balance of Payments in Korea, 1960–78. In *Hong, W. and Krause, L. B., eds.*, 1981, pp. 218–51.

[G: S. Korea]

Pitt, Mark M. Alternative Trade Strategies and Employment in Indonesia. In *Krueger, A. O., et al., eds.*, 1981, pp. 181–237. [G: Indonesia]

Porokhovsky, Anatoly. A Comparative Study of Indicative Planning in Turkey and Planning in Socialist Countries. *METU*, Special Issue, 1981, pp. 133–43. [G: Turkey; U.S.S.R.]

Power, J. H. Industrialisation in Pakistan: A Case of Frustrated Take-off? In *Livingstone, I., ed.*, 1981, *1963*, pp. 177–81. [G: Pakistan]

Richards, Peter J. Comment on Isenman, 'Basic Needs: The Case of Sri Lanka.' *World Devel.*, February 1981, *9*(2), pp. 215–16.

[G: Sri Lanka]

Safarian, A. E. The Financing of Trade and Development in the ADCs: The Experience of Singapore: Comment. In *Hong, W. and Krause, L. B., eds.*, 1981, pp. 145–47. [G: Singapore]

Sandeman, Hugh. L'amico ricco della Cina. (China's Rich Friend. With English summary.) *Mondo Aperto*, October 1981, *35*(5), pp. 267–87.

[G: Hong Kong]

Schlegel, Charles C. Development, Equity, and Level of Living in Peninsular Malaysia. *J. Devel. Areas*, January 1981, *15*(2), pp. 297–316.

[G: Malaysia]

Şenses, Fikret. Short-Term Stabilization Policies in a Developing Economy: The Turkish Experience in 1980 in Long-Term Perspective. *METU*, 1981, *8*(1 & 2), pp. 409–52. [G: Turkey]

Song, Jiwen. On the Question of Adjusting the Proportional Relationship between the Means of Production and the Means of Livelihood. *Chinese Econ. Stud.*, Fall 1981, *15*(1), pp. 62–71.

[G: China]

Tamaschke, H. U. and Duriyaprapan, C. Economic Development through Export Expansion: An Econometric Study of Thailand. *Philippine Econ. J.*, 1981, *20*(2), pp. 159–74. [G: Thailand]

Tüzün, Gürel. Bunalim, Ekonomi Politikalari, Planlama ve Devlet: Bir Yaklaşim Önerisi. (Crisis, Economic Policies, Planning and the State: A Suggested Approach. With English summary.) *METU*, Special Issue, 1981, pp. 3–17.

[G: Turkey]

Willner, Ann Ruth. Reptition in Change: Cyclical Movement and Indonesian "Development": Review Article. *Econ. Develop. Cult. Change*, January 1981, *29*(2), pp. 409–17. [G: Indonesia]

Wong, Kum Poh. The Financing of Trade and Development in the ADCs: The Experience of Singapore. In *Hong, W. and Krause, L. B., eds.*, 1981, pp. 129–44. [G: Singapore]

Zagoria, Donald S. The New Equilibrium in East Asia. In *Hewett, R. B., ed.*, 1981, pp. 1–18.

[G: East Asia]

1215 African Countries

Acharya, Shankar N. Development Perspectives and Priorities in Sub-Saharan Africa. *Finance Develop.*, March 1981, *18*(1), pp. 16–19. [G: Sub-Saharan Africa]

Acharya, Shankar N. Perspectives and Problems of Development in Sub-Saharan Africa. *World Devel.*, February 1981, *9*(2), pp. 109–47.

[G: Sub-Saharan Africa]

Adedeji, Adebayo. General Background to Indigenization: The Economic Dependence of Africa. In *Adedeji, A., ed.*, 1981, pp. 15–28. [G: Africa]

Adedeji, Adebayo. Historical and Theoretical Background. In *Adedeji, A., ed.*, 1981, pp. 29–41.

[G: Africa]

Baffoe, Frank. Southern Africa. In *Adedeji, A., ed.*, 1981, pp. 278–308. [G: S. Africa]

Bernard, Frank E. and Thom, Derrick J. Population Pressure and Human Carrying Capacity in Selected Locations of Machakos and Kitui Districts. *J. Devel. Areas*, April 1981, *15*(3), pp. 381–406.

[G: Kenya]

Frank, Lawrence. Khama and Jonathan: Leadership Strategies in Contemporary Southern Africa. *J. Devel. Areas*, January 1981, *15*(2), pp. 173–98.

[G: Southern Africa]

Girgis, Maurice. Growth Patterns and Structural Changes in Output and Employment in the Arab World. In *Sherbiny, N. A., ed.*, 1981, pp. 21–54. [G: Arab Countries]

Hanafi, Mohammed N. Egypt. In *Adedeji, A., ed.*, 1981, pp. 49–80. [G: Egypt]

Helleiner, Gerald K. Stabilization and Development of the Tanzanian Economy in the 1970s: Comment. In *Cline, W. R. and Weintraub, S., eds.*, 1981, pp. 369–74. [G: Tanzania]

Ikiara, G. K. Structural Changes in the Kenyan Economy. In *Killick, T., ed.*, 1981, pp. 20–32.

[G: Kenya]

Ikiara, G. K. and Killick, Tony. The Performance of the Economy since Independence. In *Killick, T., ed.*, 1981, pp. 5–19. [G: Kenya]

Ikram, Khalid. Meeting the Social Contract in Egypt. *Finance Develop.*, September 1981, *18*(3), pp. 30–33. [G: Egypt]

Kofi, Tetteh A. Prospects and Problems of the Transition from Agrarianism to Socialism: The Case of Angola, Guinea-Bissau and Mozambique. *World Devel.*, September/October 1981, *9*(9/10), pp. 851–70. [G: Angola; Guinea-Bissau; Mozambique]

Manu, J. E. A. Ghana's Economic Performance in the Seventies. In *Schmitt-Rink, G., ed.*, 1981, pp. 3–25. [G: Ghana]

Monson, Terry. Trade Strategies and Employment in the Ivory Coast. In *Krueger, A. O., et al., eds.*, 1981, pp. 239–90. [G: Ivory Coast]

Nabli, Mustapha K. Alternative Trade Policies and Employment in Tunisia. In *Krueger, A. O., et al., eds.*, 1981, pp. 435–98. [G: Tunisia]

Palmer, P. N. Industrialising the National States: The Bophuthatswana Example. *Finance Trade Rev.*, June 1981, *14*(3), pp. 118–34.

[G: S. Africa]

Rimmer, Douglas. Development in Nigeria: an

Overview. In *Bienen, H. and Diejomaoh, V. P.*, *eds.*, 1981, pp. 29–87.   [G: Nigeria]

Spencer, Ian R. G. The First World War and the Origins of the Dual Policy of Development in Kenya, 1914–1922. *World Devel.*, August 1981, *9*(8), pp. 735–48.   [G: Kenya]

Stewart, Frances. Kenya Strategies for Development. In *Killick, T., ed.*, 1981, *1976*, pp. 75–89.   [G: Kenya]

Weaver, James H. and Anderson, Arne. Stabilization and Development of the Tanzanian Economy in the 1970s. In *Cline, W. R. and Weintraub, S., eds.*, 1981, pp. 335–69.   [G: Tanzania]

Weaver, James H. and Kronemer, Alexander. Tanzanian and African Socialism. *World Devel.*, September/October 1981, *9*(9/10), pp. 839–49.   [G: Tanzania]

1216 Latin American and Caribbean Countries

Albert, Bill and Henderson, Paul. Latin America and the Great War: A Preliminary Survey of Developments in Chile, Peru, Argentina and Brazil. *World Devel.*, August 1981, *9*(8), pp. 717–34.
[G: Chile; Peru; Argentina; Brazil]

Aponte, Juan B. The Lash of Inflation on a Developing Economy: Puerto Rico, A Case Study. *Ann. Amer. Acad. Polit. Soc. Sci.*, July 1981, *456*, pp. 132–53.   [G: Puerto Rico]

Balassa, Bela. Incentive Policies in Brazil. In *Balassa, B.*, 1981, pp. 231–54.   [G: Brazil]

Balassa, Bela. Policy Responses to External Shocks in Selected Latin-American Countries. *Quart. Rev. Econ. Bus.*, Summer 1981, *21*(2), pp. 131–64.   [G: Brazil; Mexico; Uruguay]

Beltran del Rio, Abel. The Mexican Oil Syndrome: Early Symptoms, Preventive Efforts, and Prognosis. In *Baer, W. and Gillis, M., eds.*, 1981, pp. 115–30.   [G: Mexico; OPEC]

Bension, Alberto and Caumont, Jorge. Uruguay: Alternative Trade Strategies and Employment Implications. In *Krueger, A. O., et al., eds.*, 1981, pp. 499–529.   [G: Uruguay]

Black, Stanley W. Inflation and Growth: Exchange Rate Alternatives for Mexico: Comment. In *Williamson, J., ed.*, 1981, pp. 349–50. [G: Mexico]

Bourne, Compton. Government Foreign Borrowing and Economic Growth: The Jamaican Experience. *Soc. Econ. Stud.*, December 1981, *30*(4), pp. 52–74.   [G: Jamaica]

Brown, Adlith. Economic Policy and the IMF in Jamaica. *Soc. Econ. Stud.*, December 1981, *30*(4), pp. 1–51.   [G: Jamaica]

Campos, Roberto de Oliveira and Valentino, Raphael. Prospects for the NICs: Brazil. In *Saunders, C. T., ed. (II)*, 1981, pp. 204–14.
[G: Brazil]

Cardoso, Eliana A. Celso Furtado Revisited: The Postwar Years. *Econ. Develop. Cult. Change*, October 1981, *30*(1), pp. 117–28.   [G: Brazil]

Cardoso, Eliana A. The Great Depression and Commodity-exporting LDCs: The Case of Brazil. *J. Polit. Econ.*, December 1981, *89*(6), pp. 1239–50.   [G: Brazil]

Carvalho, José L. and Haddad, Cláudio, L. S. Foreign Trade Strategies and Employment in Brazil.

In *Krueger, A. O., et al., eds.*, 1981, pp. 29–81.
[G: Brazil]

Casimir, Jean. Main Challenges of Social Development in the Caribbean. *Cepal Rev.*, April 1981, (13), pp. 125–42.   [G: Caribbean]

Castagnino, Ernesto S. Estimating Accounting Prices for Project Appraisal: Paraguay. In *Powers, T. A., ed.*, 1981, pp. 147–223.   [G: Paraguay]

Cline, William R. Economic Stabilization in Peru, 1975–78. In *Cline, W. R. and Weintraub, S., eds.*, 1981, pp. 297–326.   [G: Peru]

Corbo, Vittorio and Meller, Patricio. Alternative Trade Strategies and Employment Implications: Chile. In *Krueger, A. O., et al., eds.*, 1981, pp. 83–134.   [G: Chile]

Devlin, Robert. Transnational Banks, External Debt and Peru: Results of a Recent Study. *Cepal Rev.*, August 1981, (14), pp. 153–84.   [G: Peru]

Donoso R., Gregorio. Estimating Accounting Prices for Project Appraisal: Ecuador. In *Powers, T. A., ed.*, 1981, pp. 323–67.   [G: Ecuador]

Edelstein, Joel C. The Evolution of Cuban Development Strategy, 1959–1979. In *Muñoz, H., ed.*, 1981, pp. 225–66.   [G: Cuba]

Faucher, Philippe. The Paradise T hat Never Was: The Breakdown of the Brazilian Authoritarian Order. In *Bruneau, T. C. and Faucher, P., eds.*, 1981, pp. 11–39.   [G: Brazil]

Fendt, Roberto, Jr. Inflation and Growth: Exchange Rate Alternatives for Mexico: Comment. In *Williamson, J., ed.*, 1981, pp. 347–48. [G: Mexico]

Girgis, Maurice. Foreign Trade and Development in Egypt [Review Article]. *Weltwirtsch. Arch.*, 1981, *117*(2), pp. 389–96.   [G: Egypt]

Gómez, Guillermo L. and Tintner, Gerhard. The Application of Diffusion Processes in Problems of Developmental Economic Planning: A Case Study (Colombia). In *[Lipiński, E.]*, 1981, pp. 177–94.   [G: Colombia]

Hirschman, Albert O. The Turn to Authoritarianism in Latin America and the Search for its Economic Determinants. In *Hirschman, A. O.*, 1981, *1979*, pp. 98–135.   [G: Latin America]

Hollist, W. Ladd. Brazilian Dependence: An Evolutionary, World-System Perspective. In *Hollist, W. L. and Rosenau, J. N., eds.*, 1981, pp. 202–20.   [G: Brazil]

Iglesias, Enrique V. Development and Equity: The Challenge of the 1980s. *Cepal Rev.*, December 1981, (15), pp. 7–46.   [G: Latin America]

Jameson, Kenneth P. Socialist Cuba and the Intermediate Regimes of Jamaica and Guyana. *World Devel.*, September/October 1981, *9*(9/10), pp. 871–88.   [G: Cuba; Jamaica; Guyana]

Knight, Peter T. Brazilian Socioeconomic Development: Issues for the Eighties. *World Devel.*, November/December 1981, *9*(11/12), pp. 1063–82.
[G: Brazil]

Lahera, Eugenio. The Transnational Corporations in the Chilean Economy. *Cepal Rev.*, August 1981, (14), pp. 107–25.   [G: Chile]

Lanfranco, Sam. Mexican Oil, Export-led Development and Agricultural Neglect. *J. Econ. Devel.*, July 1981, *6*(1), pp. 125–51.   [G: Mexico]

Londero, Elio H. Estimating Accounting Prices for Project Appraisal: El Salvador. In *Powers, T. A.*, *ed.*, 1981, pp. 225–321.   [G: El Salvador]

Long, Millard F. External Debt and the Trade Imperative in Latin America. *Quart. Rev. Econ. Bus.*, Summer 1981, *21*(2), pp. 280–301.
[G: Latin America]

Longo, Carlos A. Comment on "Policy Responses to External Shocks in Selected Latin-American Countries." *Quart. Rev. Econ. Bus.*, Summer 1981, *21*(2), pp. 165–67.   [G: Brazil; Mexico; Uruguay]

Mayio, Albert. The Future of the New Style Military Regimes of South America. In *U.S. Congress, Joint Economic Committee (III)*, 1981, pp. 66–99. [G: Argentina; Brazil; Peru; Uruguay; Chile]

McBain, Helen. The Political Economy of Capital Flows: The Case of Jamaica. *Soc. Econ. Stud.*, December 1981, *30*(4), pp. 75–110.
[G: Jamaica]

McDonough, Peter. Developmental Priorities among Brazilian Elites. *Econ. Develop. Cult. Change*, April 1981, *29*(3), pp. 535–59.
[G: Brazil]

Miller, Rory. Latin American Manufacturing and the First World War: An Exploratory Essay. *World Devel.*, August 1981, *9*(8), pp. 707–16.
[G: Latin America]

Morales Bayro, Luis. Estimating Accounting Prices for Project Appraisal: Barbados. In *Powers, T. A., ed.*, 1981, pp. 369–430.   [G: Barbados]

Mortimore, Michael D. The State and Transnational Banks: Lessons from the Bolivian Crisis of External Public Indebtedness. *Cepal Rev.*, August 1981, (14), pp. 127–51.   [G: Bolivia]

Ortiz, Guillermo and Solís, Leopoldo. Inflation and Growth: Exchange Rate Alternatives for Mexico. In *Williamson, J., ed.*, 1981, pp. 327–46.
[G: Mexico]

Ramos, Joseph. Latin America: The End of Democratic Reformism? In *Novak, M., ed.*, 1981, pp. 73–81.   [G: Latin America]

Randall, Laura R. Mexican Development and Its Effects upon United States Trade. In *McBride, R. H., ed.*, 1981, pp. 49–76. [G: Mexico; U.S.]

del Rio, Abel Beltran. The Mexican Oil Syndrome: Early Symptoms, Preventive Efforts, and Prognosis. *Quart. Rev. Econ. Bus.*, Summer 1981, *21*(2), pp. 115–30.   [G: Mexico; OPEC]

Selowsky, Marcelo. Income Distribution, Basic Needs and Trade-Offs with Growth: The Case of Semi-Industrialized Latin American Countries. *World Devel.*, January 1981, *9*(1), pp. 73–92.
[G: Latin America]

Soza, Héctor. The Industrialization Debate in Latin America. *Cepal Rev.*, April 1981, (13), pp. 35–64.   [G: Latin America]

St. Cyr, E. B. A. Wages, Prices and Balance of Payments: Trinidad and Tobago; 1956–1976. *Soc. Econ. Stud.*, December 1981, *30*(4), pp. 111–33.
[G: Trinidad and Tobago]

Trejo Reyes, Saúl. Case Study of Economic Stabilization: Mexico: Comment. In *Cline, W. R. and Weintraub, S., eds.*, 1981, pp. 292–95.
[G: Mexico]

Weintraub, Sidney. Case Study of Economic Stabilization: Mexico. In *Cline, W. R. and Weintraub, S., eds.*, 1981, pp. 271–92.   [G: Mexico]

Worrell, Delisle. External Influences and Domestic Policies: The Economies of Barbados and Jamaica. *Soc. Econ. Stud.*, December 1981, *30*(4), pp. 134–55.   [G: Barbados; Jamaica]

1217 Oceanic Countries

Gregory, C. A. A Conceptual Analysis of a Non-Capitalist Gift Economy with Particular Reference to Papua New Guinea. *Cambridge J. Econ.*, June 1981, *5*(2), pp. 119–35.
[G: Papua New Guinea]

Lam, Ngo Van. Government Responses to Export Instability in Papua New Guinea. *Malayan Econ. Rev. (See Singapore Econ. Rev.)*, October 1981, *26*(2), pp. 27–45.   [G: Papua New Guinea]

122 Economic Studies of Developed Countries

1220 General

Fabritius, Jan F. R. and Petersen, Christian Ettrup. OPEC Respending and the Economic Impact of an Increase in the Price of Oil. *Scand. J. Econ.*, 1981, *83*(2), pp. 220–36.   [G: OPEC]

Fieleke, Norman S. Rising Oil Prices and the Industrial Countries. *New Eng. Econ. Rev.*, January/February 1981, pp. 17–28.   [G: U.S.]

Gärtner, Manfred and Heri, Erwin W. Oil Imports and Inflation: A Comment [Oil Imports and Inflation: An Empirical International Analysis of the "Imported" Inflation Thesis]. *Kyklos*, 1981, *34*(3), pp. 461–67.   [G: EEC; Japan; U.S.; Australia]

Lafay, Gérard and Brender, Anton. Modèles et Prospective en Période de Crise: Le Cas Du Modèle Moise. (With English summary.) In *Courbis, R., ed.*, 1981, pp. 295–307.   [G: OECD]

1221 Comparative Country Studies

Baily, Martin Neil. Relative Productivity Levels, 1947–1963 by Christensen, et al.: Comment. *Europ. Econ. Rev.*, May 1981, *16*(1), pp. 95–97.

Boyer, Robert and Petit, Pascal. Employment and Productivity in the EEC. *Cambridge J. Econ.*, March 1981, *5*(1), pp. 47–58.   [G: EEC]

Christensen, Laurits R.; Cummings, Dianne and Jorgenson, Dale W. Relative Productivity Levels, 1947–1973: An International Comparison. *Europ. Econ. Rev.*, May 1981, *16*(1), pp. 61–94.

Formby, John P.; Seaks, Terry G. and Smith, W. James. A Comparison of Two New Measures of Tax Progressivity [Measurement of Tax Progressivity: An International Comparison]. [Measurement of Tax Progressivity]. *Econ. J.*, December 1981, *91*(364), pp. 1015–19.
[G: U.S.; U.K.; Australia; Canada]

Norton, W. E. and McDonald, Robin. Implications for Australia of Cross-Country Comparisons in Economic Performance. *Econ. Rec.*, December 1981, *57*(159), pp. 301–18.   [G: Australia]

Sautter, Christian. Relative Productivity Levels, 1947–1973 by Christensen, et al.: Comment. *Europ. Econ. Rev.*, May 1981, *16*(1), pp. 99–102.

Thoroe, Carsten S. Changes in the Regional Growth Pattern in the European Community. In *Giersch,*

H., ed. (II), 1981, pp. 283–311.
[G: W. Germany; France; Italy; U.K.]

Verner, Joel G. Legislative Systems and Public Policy: A Comparative Analysis of 78 Developing Countries. *J. Devel. Areas,* January 1981, *15*(2), pp. 275–96.

1223 European Countries

Ackley, Gardner. Macroeconomic Policies in Western European Countries: 1973–1977: Comment. In *Giersch, H, ed. (I),* 1981, pp. 137–42.
[G: W. Europe]

Bohman, Gösta. Demokrati och kapitalism under 80-talet. (Democracy and Capitalism in the '80. With English summary.) *Ekon. Samfundets Tidskr.,* 1981, *34*(1), pp. 55–68. **[G: Sweden]**

Boltho, Andrea. Italian and Japanese Postwar Growth: Some Similarities and Differences. *Rivista Int. Sci. Econ. Com.,* July–August 1981, *28*(7–8), pp. 626–43. **[G: Italy; Japan]**

Brada, Josef C.; King, Arthur E. and Schlagenhauf, Don E. The Optimality of Socialist Development Strategies: An Empirical Inquiry. *J. Econ. Dynam. Control,* February 1981, *3*(1), pp. 1–27.
[G: Czechoslovakia]

Brittan, Samuel. The Roots of the British Sickness. In *Currie, D.; Nobay, R. and Peel, D., eds.,* 1981, pp. 321–52. **[G: U.K.]**

Buiter, Willem H. and Miller, Marcus. The Thatcher Experiment: The First Two Years. *Brookings Pap. Econ. Act.,* 1981, (2), pp. 315–67. **[G: U.K.]**

Cairncross, Alec [Sir]. The Postwar Years 1945–77. In *Floud, R. and McCloskey, D., eds., Vol. 2,* 1981, pp. 370–416. **[G: U.K.]**

Contini, Bruno B. Labor Market Segmentation and the Development of the Parallel Economy—The Italian Experience. *Oxford Econ. Pap.,* November 1981, *33*(3), pp. 401–12. **[G: Italy]**

Cripps, Francis. Government Planning as a Means to Economic Recovery in the UK. *Cambridge J. Econ.,* March 1981, *5*(1), pp. 95–106.
[G: U.K.]

Drummond, I. Britain and the World Economy 1900–45. In *Floud, R. and McCloskey, D., eds., Vol. 2,* 1981, pp. 286–307. **[G: U.K.]**

Floud, R. C. Britain 1860–1914: A Survey. In *Floud, R. and McCloskey, D., eds., Vol. 2,* 1981, pp. 1–26. **[G: U.K.]**

Halttunen, Hannu, et al. Sveriges ekonomiska långtidsproblem. (Sweden's Long-term Economic Problems. With English summary.) *Ekon. Samfundets Tidskr.,* 1981, *34*(4), pp. 305–24.
[G: Sweden]

Henke, Josef. Economic Reconstruction in Europe: The Reintegration of Western Germany—Report on the Relevant Historical Material in the Bundesarchiv. *Z. ges. Staatswiss.,* September 1981, *137*(3), pp. 469–90. **[G: W. Germany]**

Ietto Gillies, Grazia. The De-Industrialisation of the UK: Some Issues and Hypotheses. *Brit. Rev. Econ. Issues,* Spring 1981, *2*(8), pp. 1–20.
[G: U.K.]

Izzo, Lucio and Spaventa, Luigi. Macroeconomic Policies in Western European Countries: 1973–

1977. In *Giersch, H, ed. (I),* 1981, pp. 73–136.
[G: W. Europe]

Jossa, Bruno and Vinci, Salvatore. The Italian Economy from 1963 to Today: An Interpretation. *Rev. Econ. Cond. Italy,* February 1981, (1), pp. 9–40. **[G: Italy]**

Kádár, Béla. Adjustment Problems, Patterns and Policies in Small Countries. *Acta Oecon.,* 1981, *27*(1–2), pp. 125–39. **[G: W. Europe]**

Kivikari, Urpo. Problems and Prospects of an Open Economy: Finland's Case. *Acta Oecon.,* 1981, *26*(1–2), pp. 157–74. **[G: Finland]**

Knapp, Manfred. Reconstruction and West-Integration: The Impact of the Marshall Plan on Germany. *Z. ges. Staatswiss.,* September 1981, *137*(3), pp. 415–33. **[G: W. Germany]**

Lesthaeghe, Ron J. Demographic Change, Social Security and Economic Growth: Inferences from the Belgian Example. *Schweiz. Z. Volkswirtsch. Statist.,* September 1981, *117*(3), pp. 225–55.
[G: Belgium]

Lienert, Ian. The Macroeconomic Effects of the 1979/80 Oil Price Rise on Four Nordic Economies. *Scand. J. Econ.,* 1981, *83*(2), pp. 201–19.
[G: Denmark; Finland; Sweden; Norway]

Marczewski, Jean. Théorie de la stagflation et expérience comparée de la France et de l'Allemagne 1971–1979. (With English summary.) *Écon. Appl.,* 1981, *34*(4), pp. 667–96. **[G: France; W. Germany]**

Marquand, David. Tolerable Survival and Politics. In *Gaskin, M., ed.,* 1981, pp. 34–51. **[G: U.K.]**

Möller, Hans. The Reconstruction of the International Economic Order after the Second World War and the Integration of the Federal Republic of Germany into the World Economy. *Z. ges. Staatswiss.,* September 1981, *137*(3), pp. 344–66.
[G: W. Germany]

Petzina, Dietmar. The Origin of the European Coal and Steel Community: Economic Forces and Political Interests. *Z. ges. Staatswiss.,* September 1981, *137*(3), pp. 450–68. **[G: W. Europe]**

Stammati, Gaetano. Italy and Japan Facing the New Oil and Monetary Crises. *Rivista Int. Sci. Econ. Com.,* July–August 1981, *28*(7–8), pp. 755–61.
[G: Japan; Italy]

Stuart, Charles E. Swedish Tax Rates, Labor Supply, and Tax Revenues. *J. Polit. Econ.,* October 1981, *89*(5), pp. 1020–38. **[G: Sweden]**

Travaglini, Guido. Accumulazione del capitale, occupazione ed inflazione nel Regno Unito dal 1960 al 1977: Analisi teorica a ricerca empirica. (Accumulation of Capital, Employment and Inflation in the United Kingdom, 1960–1977: Theoretical Analysis and Empirical Research. With English summary.) *Bancaria,* December 1981, *37*(12), pp. 1257–73. **[G: U.K.]**

Tumlir, Jan and La Haye, Laura. The Two Attempts at European Economic Reconstruction after 1945. *Z. ges. Staatswiss.,* September 1981, *137*(3), pp. 367–89. **[G: W. Europe]**

von Tunzelmann, G. N. Britain 1900–45: A Survey. In *Floud, R. and McCloskey, D., eds., Vol. 2,* 1981, pp. 239–64. **[G: U.K.]**

Wallich, Henry C. and Wilson, John F. Economic Orientations in Postwar Germany: Critical

Choices on the Road toward Currency Convertibility. *Z. ges. Staatswiss.*, September 1981, *137*(3), pp. 390–406. [G: W. Germany]

1224 Asian Countries

Ariki, Soichiro. Japan's Economy at the Crossroads: An Analysis of Conditions for Her Survival. *Rivista Int. Sci. Econ. Com.*, July–August 1981, *28*(7–8), pp. 644–62. [G: Japan]

Blumenthal, Tuvia. Factor Proportions and Choice of Technology: The Japanese Experience: Reply. *Econ. Develop. Cult. Change*, July 1981, *29*(4), pp. 845–48. [G: Japan]

Boltho, Andrea. Italian and Japanese Postwar Growth: Some Similarities and Differences. *Rivista Int. Sci. Econ. Com.*, July–August 1981, *28*(7–8), pp. 626–43. [G: Italy; Japan]

Fei, John C. H. and Ranis, Gustav. Factor Proportions and Choice of Technology: The Japanese Experience: Comment. *Econ. Develop. Cult. Change*, July 1981, *29*(4), pp. 841–44. [G: Japan]

Halliday, Jon. The Specificity of Japan's Re-integration into the World Capitalist Economy after 1945: Notes on Some Myths and Misconceptions. *Rivista Int. Sci. Econ. Com.*, July–August 1981, *28*(7–8), pp. 663–81. [G: Japan]

Imazato, Hiroki. Japanese Economy in the Eighties. *Rivista Int. Sci. Econ. Com.*, July–August 1981, *28*(7–8), pp. 682–88. [G: Japan]

Keidel, Albert. Japan's Economic Modernization. In *Richardson, B. M. and Ueda, T., eds.*, 1981, pp. 67–74. [G: Japan]

Keidel, Albert. Japan's Growth Record. In *Richardson, B. M. and Ueda, T., eds.*, 1981, pp. 75–82. [G: Japan]

Lombardo, Antonio. Japan's and Italy's Political Systems: Developmental and Comparative Perspectives. *Rivista Int. Sci. Econ. Com.*, July–August 1981, *28*(7–8), pp. 731–54. [G: Japan; Italy]

Mahler, Walter R. Japan's Adjustment to the Increased Cost of Energy. *Finance Develop.*, December 1981, *18*(4), pp. 26–29. [G: Japan]

Matsurra, Tamotsu. The Development of the Welfare State in Japan. *Giorn. Econ.*, January–February 1981, *40*(1–2), pp. 3–17. [G: Japan]

Sinai, Allen and Stokes, Houston H. Real Money Balances and Production: A Partial Explanation of Japanese Economic Development for 1952–1968. *Hitotsubashi J. Econ.*, February 1981, *21*(2), pp. 69–81. [G: Japan]

Stammati, Gaetano. Italy and Japan Facing the New Oil and Monetary Crises. *Rivista Int. Sci. Econ. Com.*, July–August 1981, *28*(7–8), pp. 755–61. [G: Japan; Italy]

1227 Oceanic Countries

Norton, W. E. and McDonald, Robin. Implications for Australia of Cross-Country Comparisons in Economic Performance. *Econ. Rec.*, December 1981, *57*(159), pp. 301–18. [G: Australia]

1228 North American Countries

Baumann, Harry; Irvine, Russell and Paquet, Bertrand. The Impact of Higher Energy Prices in

Canada: Comment. *Can. Public Policy*, Winter 1981, *7*(1), pp. 39–41. [G: Canada]

Drummond, Don and Grady, Patrick. The Impact of Higher Energy Prices in Canada: Comment. *Can. Public Policy*, Winter 1981, *7*(1), pp. 42–49. [G: Canada]

Empey, W. F. The Impact of Higher Energy Prices in Canada. *Can. Public Policy*, Winter 1981, *7*(1), pp. 28–35. [G: Canada]

Jump, Gregory V. On Interpreting Simulations with a Macroeconometric Model: Comment [The Impact of Higher Enery Prices in Canada]. *Can. Public Policy*, Winter 1981, *7*(1), pp. 35–38. [G: Canada]

Kumar, Pradeep. The Current Industrial Relations Scene in Canada 1981: Technical Notes. In *Wood, W. D. and Kumar, P., eds.*, 1981, pp. 465–76. [G: Canada]

Kumar, Pradeep. The Economy: Summary Outline. In *Wood, W. D. and Kumar, P., eds.*, 1981, pp. 1–25. [G: Canada]

Lester, John. The Impact of Higher Energy Prices in Canada: Comment. *Can. Public Policy*, Winter 1981, *7*(1), pp. 52–58. [G: Canada]

McCracken, M. C. and Jarvis, W. D. What Is the Impact of Higher Energy Prices? Comment [The Impact of Higher Energy Prices in Canada]. *Can. Public Policy*, Winter 1981, *7*(1), pp. 50–52. [G: Canada]

Muller, Patrice and White, W. R. The Impact of Higher Energy Prices in Canada: Comment. *Can. Public Policy*, Winter 1981, *7*(1), pp. 59–65. [G: Canada]

Nelson, Richard R. Regional Life-Cycles and U.S. Industrial Rejuvenation. In *Giersch, H., ed. (II)*, 1981, pp. 281. [G: U.S.]

Norton, R. D. Regional Life-Cycles and U.S. Industrial Rejuvenation. In *Giersch, H., ed. (II)*, 1981, pp. 253–80. [G: U.S.]

Tatom, John A. Capital Utilization and Okun's Law. *Rev. Econ. Statist.*, February 1981, *63*(1), pp. 155–58. [G: U.S.]

You, Jong Keun. Capital Utilization and Okun's Law: A Reply. *Rev. Econ. Statist.*, February 1981, *63*(1), pp. 158–60. [G: U.S.]

123 Comparative Economic Studies of Developing, Developed, and/or Centrally Planned Economies

1230 Comparative Economic Studies of Developing, Developed, and/or Centrally Planned Economies

Ahluwalia, Montek S. Inequality, Poverty and Development. In *Livingstone, I., ed.*, 1981, *1976*, pp. 30–48.

Ahmad, Masood. Incremental Capital-Output Ratios and Growth Rates in the Short-Run Evidence from Pakistan. *Pakistan Econ. Soc. Rev.*, Winter 1981, *19*(2), pp. 123–30. [G: Selected MDCs; Selected LDCs; Pakistan]

Baer, Werner and Samuelson, Larry. Toward a Service-oriented Growth Strategy. *World Devel.*, June 1981, *9*(6), pp. 499–514.

Bairoch, Paul. The Main Trends in National Economic Disparities since the Industrial Revolution. In *Bairoch, P. and Lévy-Leboyer, M., eds.*, 1981, pp. 3–17.   [G: LDCs; MDCs]

Balaam, David N. East and Southeast Asian Food Systems: Structural Constraints, Political Arenas, and Appropriate Food Strategies. In *Balaam, D. N. and Carey, M. J., eds.*, 1981, pp. 106–42.
[G: Asia]

Balassa, Bela. Policy Responses to External Shocks in Selected Latin American Countries. In *Balassa, B.*, 1981, pp. 83–108.

Balassa, Bela. The Changing International Division of Labor in Manufactured Goods. In *Balassa, B.*, 1981, pp. 169–91.

Berry, A. and Sabot, R. H. Labour Market Performance in Developing Countries: A Survey. In *Streeten, P. and Jolly, R, eds.*, 1981, *1978*, pp. 149–92.

Braga de Macedo, Jorge. Portugal and Europe: The Channels of Structural Interdependence. In *Braga de Macedo, J. and Serfaty, S., eds.*, 1981, pp. 153–202.   [G: W. Europe; Portugal]

Bruton, Henry J. Labour Market Performance in Developing Countries: A Survey: Comment. In *Streeten, P. and Jolly, R, eds.*, 1981, *1978*, pp. 197–200.   [G: LDCs]

Burakow, Nicholas. Romania and Greece—Socialism vs Capitalism. *World Devel.*, September/October 1981, *9*(9/10), pp. 907–28.   [G: Romania; Greece]

Caldwell, J. Alexander. The Economic and Financial Outlook for the Developing Countries of East Asia: Trends and Issues. In *Hewett, R. B., ed.*, 1981, pp. 127–52.   [G: East Asia]

Cameron, Norman E. Economic Growth in the USSR, Hungary, and East and West Germany. *J. Compar. Econ.*, March 1981, *5*(1), pp. 24–42.
[G: U.S.S.R.; Hungary; E. Germany; W. Germany]

Donges, Juergen B. Portugal and Europe: The Channels of Structural Interdependence: Comment. In *Braga de Macedo, J. and Serfaty, S., eds.*, 1981, pp. 209–14.   [G: W. Europe; Portugal]

Dunning, John H. Explaining the International Direct Investment Position of Countries: Towards a Dynamic or Developmental Approach. In *Dunning, J. H.*, 1981, *1981*, pp. 109–41.

Dunning, John H. Explaining the International Direct Investment Position of Countries: Towards a Dynamic or Developmental Approach. *Weltwirtsch. Arch.*, 1981, *117*(1), pp. 30–64.
[G: Selected Countries]

Ehrlich, Eva. Comparison of Development Levels: Inequalities in the Physical Structures of National Economies. In *Bairoch, P. and Lévy-Leboyer, M., eds.*, 1981, pp. 395–410. [G: LDCs; MDCs]

Glezakos, C. Export Instability and Economic Growth: A Statistical Verification. In *Livingstone, I., ed.*, 1981, *1973*, pp. 137–42.   [G: LDCs; MDCs]

Gordon, Lincoln. Changing Growth Patterns and World Order. In *Cleveland, H., ed.*, 1981, pp. 266–98.

Gregory, Paul R. Economic Growth and Structural Change in Czarist Russia and the Soviet Union: A Long-term Comparison. In *[Bergson, A.]*,

1981, pp. 25–52.   [G: U.S.S.R.; OECD]

Gyulavári, Antal. Stocks and Stockpiling in Hungary—An International Comparison. *Acta Oecon.*, 1981, *27*(1–2), pp. 57–76.   [G: Hungary; W. Germany; U.K.]

Hafer, R. W. and Heyne-Hafer, Gail. The Relationship between Inflation and Its Variability: International Evidence from the 1970s. *J. Macroecon.*, Fall 1981, *3*(4), pp. 571–77.

Hazledine, Tim and Moreland, R. Scott. Population and Economic Growth: A Rejoinder. *Rev. Econ. Statist.*, February 1981, *63*(1), pp. 153–55.

Kakwani, Nanak. Welfare Measures: An International Comparison. *J. Devel. Econ.*, February 1981, *8*(1), pp. 21–45.

Kislev, Yoav. International Farm Prices and the Social Cost of Cheap Food Policies: Comment. *Amer. J. Agr. Econ.*, May 1981, *63*(2), pp. 280.
[G: LDCs]

Koo, Anthony Y. C.; Quan, Nguyen and Rasche, Robert H. Identification of the Lorenz Curve by Lorenz Coefficient. *Weltwirtsch. Arch.*, 1981, *117*(1), pp. 125–35.   [G: Selected Countries]

Kuznets, Simon. A Note on Production Structure and Aggregate Growth. In *[Bergson, A.]*, 1981, pp. 289–303.   [G: Global]

Leontief, Wassily W. Population Growth and Economic Development: Illustrative Projections. In *Reubens, E. P., ed.*, 1981, *1979*, pp. 39–60.

Linge, G. J. R. and Hamilton, F. E. Ian. International Industrial Systems. In *Hamilton, F. E. I. and Linge, G. J. R., eds.*, 1981, pp. 1–117.
[G: OECD; CMEA; LDCs]

Lucas, Robert E., Jr. Some International Evidence on Output-Inflation Tradeoffs. In *Lucas, R. E., Jr.*, 1981, *1973*, pp. 131–45.
[G: Selected Countries]

McAleese, Dermot and Carey, Patrick. Employment Coefficients for Irish Trade with Extra-EEC Countries: Measurement and Implications. *Econ. Soc. Rev.*, January 1981, *12*(2), pp. 115–32.
[G: Ireland]

McCombie, J. S. L. Are International Growth Rates Constrained by the Balance of Payments? A Comment on Professor Thirlwall [The Balance of Payments Constraint as an Explanation of International Growth Rate Differences]. *Banca Naz. Lavoro Quart. Rev.*, December 1981, (139), pp. 455–58.

Meister, Jürgen. Taxes, Tax Systems and Economic Growth: Comments. In *Giersch, H., ed. (II)*, 1981, pp. 354–57.   [G: Selected Countries]

Murrell, Peter. An Evaluation of the Success of the Hungarian Economic Reform: An Analysis Using International-Trade Data. *J. Compar. Econ.*, December 1981, *5*(4), pp. 352–66.
[G: Mediterranean Europe; Austria; U.K.; Hungary; E. Europe]

Neumark, Fritz. Taxes, Tax Systems and Economic Growth: Comments. In *Giersch, H., ed. (II)*, 1981, pp. 348–53.   [G: Selected Countries]

Paldam, Martin. Is There an Electional Cycle? A Comparative Study of National Accounts. In *Strim, S., ed.*, 1981, *1979*, pp. 182–201.
[G: OECD]

Petersen, Hans-Georg. Taxes, Tax Systems and Economic Growth. In *Giersch, H., ed. (II)*, 1981, pp. 313–47. [G: Selected Countries]

Peterson, Peter G. Proceedings of the Seminar on International Economic Problems: Statement. In *U.S. Congress, Joint Economic Committee (I)*, 1981, pp. 233–91. [G: U.S.; OECD]

Porokhovsky, Anatoly. A Comparative Study of Indicative Planning in Turkey and Planning in Socialist Countries. *METU*, Special Issue, 1981, pp. 133–43. [G: Turkey; U.Ş.Ş.R.]

Ram, Rati. Inequalities in Income and Schooling: A Different Point of View. *De Economist*, 1981, 129(2), pp. 253–61.

Ram, Rati. Population and Economic Growth: A Critical Note. *Rev. Econ. Statist.*, February 1981, 63(1), pp. 149–53.

Rostow, Walt W. Energy and the Economy. In *U.S. Congress, Joint Economic Committee (I)*, 1981, 1980, pp. 348–434. [G: U.S.; Selected Countries]

Schmitt, Hans. Portugal and Europe: The Channels of Structural Interdependence: Comment. In *Braga de Macedo, J. and Serfaty, S., eds.*, 1981, pp. 203–07. [G: W. Europe; Portugal]

Theil, Henri. The Quality of Consumption in the U.S. and Abroad. *Sloan Manage. Rev.*, Fall 1981, 23(1), pp. 31–36. [G: U.S.]

Thirlwall, A. P. A Reply to Mr. McCombie [The Balance of Payments Constraint as an Explanation of International Growth Rate Differences]. *Banca Naz. Lavoro Quart. Rev.*, December 1981, (139), pp. 458–59.

Todaro, Michael P. Labour Market Performance in Developing Countries: A Survey: Comment. In *Streeten, P. and Jolly, R, eds.*, 1981, 1978, pp. 193–95. [G: LDCs]

124 Economic Studies of Centrally Planned Economies

1241 Comparative Country Studies

Feiwel, George R. Bulgarian Industrialization Strategy in Comparative Perspective. *Écon. Soc.*, August–September 1981, 15(8–9), pp. 1267–1316. [G: Bulgaria; CMEA]

1243 European Countries

Askanas, Benedykt. Poland. *Eastern Europ. Econ.*, Summer 1981, 19(4), pp. 34–40. [G: Poland]

Askanas, Benedykt and Levcik, Friedrich. The CMEA Countries: Overview. *Eastern Europ. Econ.*, Summer 1981, 19(4), pp. 4–17. [G: CMEA; Yugoslavia]

Augusztinovics, Mária. Changes in the Macro-Structure of the Hungarian Economy (1950–2000). *Acta Oecon.*, 1981, 27(3–4), pp. 267–88. [G: Hungary]

Brada, Josef C.; Jackson, Marvin R. and King, Arthur E. The Optimal Rate of Industrialization in Developed and Developing Centrally-planned Economies: A General Equilibrium Approach. *World Devel.*, September/October 1981, 9(9/10), pp. 991–1004. [G: Czechoslovakia; Romania]

Dietz, Raimund. The German Democratic Republic.

Eastern Europ. Econ., Summer 1981, 19(4), pp. 28–33. [G: E. Germany]

Fallenbuchl, Zbigniew M. Poland: Command Planning in Crisis. *Challenge*, July/August 1981, 24(3), pp. 5–12. [G: Poland]

Fáy, József and Nyers, Reszö. Specialization and Cooperation in the Hungarian Economy and the CMEA. *Acta Oecon.*, 1981, 27(1–2), pp. 1–18. [G: CMEA; Hungary]

Feiwel, George R. A Socialist Model of Economic Development: The Polish and Bulgarian Experiences. *World Devel.*, September/October 1981, 9(9/10), pp. 929–50. [G: Poland; Bulgaria]

Feiwel, George R. Bulgarian Industrialization Strategy in Comparative Perspective. *Écon. Soc.*, August–September 1981, 15(8–9), pp. 1267–1316. [G: Bulgaria; CMEA]

Fink, Gerhard. The USSR. *Eastern Europ. Econ.*, Summer 1981, 19(4), pp. 53–57. [G: U.S.S.R.]

Flakierski, Henryk. Economic Reform and Income Distribution in Poland: The Negative Evidence. *Cambridge J. Econ.*, June 1981, 5(2), pp. 137–58. [G: Poland]

Gatrell, Peter. The Impact of War on Russian and Soviet Development, 1850–1950. *World Devel.*, August 1981, 9(8), pp. 793–802. [G: U.S.S.R.]

Gregory, Paul R. Economic Growth and Structural Change in Czarist Russia and the Soviet Union: A Long-term Comparison. In *[Bergson, A.]*, 1981, pp. 25–52. [G: U.S.S.R.; OECD]

Grosser, Ilse and Wiedemann, Paul. Bulgaria. *Eastern Europ. Econ.*, Summer 1981, 19(4), pp. 18–22. [G: Bulgaria]

Hobza, Jaroslav. Sixty Years of Struggle for Social and Economic Development. *Czech. Econ. Digest.*, September 1981, (6), pp. 3–26. [G: Czechoslovakia]

Huber, Pau. Il blocco orientale e i problemi economici. (The Eastern European Countries and Their Economic Problems. With English summary.) *Mondo Aperto*, April 1981, 35(2), pp. 99–107. [G: CMEA]

Hunter, Holland; Bresnahan, Timothy F. and Rutan, Everett J., III. Modeling Structural Change Using Early Soviet Data. *J. Devel. Econ.*, August 1981, 9(1), pp. 65–87. [G: U.S.S.R.]

Jameson, Kenneth P. and Wilber, Charles K. Socialism and Development: Editors' Introduction. *World Devel.*, September/October 1981, 9(9/10), pp. 803–11. [G: U.S.S.R.; China]

Kalicki, Krzysztof. Economic Reforms in Poland. *Kansant. Aikak.*, 1981, 77(4), pp. 460–67. [G: Poland]

Karmarics, Gabriel. Hungary. *Eastern Europ. Econ.*, Summer 1981, 19(4), pp. 47–52. [G: Hungary]

Kaser, Michael C. From Versailles to Helsinki: Structural Change in the Economies of Eastern Europe. *Acta Oecon.*, 1981, 27(3–4), pp. 343–50. [G: E. Europe]

Katsenelinboigen, Aron and Levine, Herbert S. Market and Plan, Plan and Market: The Soviet Case. In *Bornstein, M., ed.*, 1981, 1977, pp. 61–70. [G: U.S.S.R.]

Khachaturov, Tigran. New Perspectives on the Economic and Social Development of the USSR.

Prob. Econ., December 1981, *24*(8), pp. 3–23.
[G: U.S.S.R.]

Kheinman, S. A. Organizational–Structural Factors in Economic Growth [Part II]. *Prob. Econ.*, January 1981, *23*(9), pp. 25–52. [G: U.S.S.R.]

Kheinman, S. A. Organizational–Structural Factors in Economic Growth [Part I]. *Prob. Econ.*, January 1981, *23*(9), pp. 3–24. [G: U.S.S.R.]

Krč, Rudolf. Slovakia in the Economy of the Czechoslovak Socialist Republic. *Czech. Econ. Digest.*, March 1981, (2), pp. 33–54.
[G: Czechoslovakia]

Lesnodorski, Boguslaw. On Some Values of Enlightenment in Poland. In *[Lipiński, E.]*, 1981, pp. 39–52. [G: Poland]

Levcik, Friedrich. Czechoslovakia. *Eastern Europ. Econ.*, Summer 1981, *19*(4), pp. 23–27.
[G: Czechoslovakia]

Mandel, Ernest. The Laws of Motion of the Soviet Economy. *Rev. Radical Polit. Econ.*, Spring 1981, *13*(1), pp. 35–39. [G: U.S.S.R.]

Meilakhs, Abram. Facts and Figures: Statistical Supplement. In *Novosti Press Agency*, 1981, pp. 263–76. [G: U.S.S.R.]

Murrell, Peter. An Evaluation of the Success of the Hungarian Economic Reform: An Analysis Using International-Trade Data. *J. Compar. Econ.*, December 1981, *5*(4), pp. 352–66.
[G: Mediterranean Europe; Austria; U.K.; Hungary; E. Europe]

Pravda, Alex. East–West Interdependence and the Social Compact in Eastern Europe. In *Bornstein, M.; Gitelman, Z. and Zimmerman, W., eds.*, 1981, pp. 162–87. [G: E. Europe]

Tardos, Márton M. Importing Western Technology into Hungary. In *Bornstein, M.; Gitelman, Z. and Zimmerman, W., eds.*, 1981, pp. 221–41.
[G: Hungary]

Tuitz, Gabriele. Romania. *Eastern Europ. Econ.*, Summer 1981, *19*(4), pp. 41–46. [G: Romania]

1244 Asian Countries

Cai, Yanchu. Does the Key to the Overextension of the Basic Construction Front Lie in Uncompensated Allocation of Funds? *Chinese Econ. Stud.*, Fall 1981, *15*(1), pp. 31–37. [G: China]

Halliday, Jon. The North Korean Model: Gaps and Questions. *World Devel.*, September/October 1981, *9*(9/10), pp. 889–905. [G: N. Korea]

Hidasi, Gábor. China's Economy in the Nineteen-Eighties (Problems and Prospects). *Acta Oecon.*, 1981, *27*(1–2), pp. 141–62. [G: China]

Knaack, Ruud. Economic Reform in China. *ACES Bull. (See Comp. Econ. Stud. after 8/85)*, Summer 1981, *23*(2), pp. 1–29. [G: China]

Lin, Paul T. K. The People's Republic of China and the New International Economic Order: The Strategy of Domestic Development. In *Lozoya, J. A. and Bhattacharya, A. K., eds.*, 1981, pp. 39–52. [G: China]

Paine, Suzanne. Spatial Aspects of Chinese Development: Issues, Outcomes and Policies, 1949–79. *J. Devel. Stud.*, January 1981, *17*(2), pp. 135–95. [G: China]

Perkins, Dwight H. The International Consequences

of China's Economic Development. In *Solomon, R. H., ed.*, 1981, pp. 114–36. [G: China]

Stefani, Giorgio. Finanza locale, investimenti e servizi urbani in Cina. (Local Finance, Investment and Urban Services in China. With English summary.) *Bancaria*, May 1981, *37*(5), pp. 454–69.
[G: China]

Ye, Yinsong. Review of Thirty Years of Management of Commercial Undertakings and Suggestions for Its Future Reform. *Chinese Econ. Stud.*, Summer 1981, *14*(4), pp. 3–16. [G: China]

Zhang, Xuansan. Réajustement de l'économie chinoise et perspectives des échanges économiques entre la Chine et les autres pays. (The Readjustment of Chinese Economy and Prospects for Trade between China and Foreign Countries. With English summary.) *Rivista Int. Sci. Econ. Com.*, September 1981, *28*(9), pp. 811–22.
[G: China]

1246 Latin American and Caribbean Countries

Brundenius, Claes. Growth with Equity: The Cuban Experience (1959–1980). *World Devel.*, November/December 1981, *9*(11/12), pp. 1083–96.
[G: Cuba]

Jameson, Kenneth P. Socialist Cuba and the Intermediate Regimes of Jamaica and Guyana. *World Devel.*, September/October 1981, *9*(9/10), pp. 871–88. [G: Cuba; Jamaica; Guyana]

Swanson, Russell. Cuba: Revolution Put to the Test. In *U.S. Congress, Joint Economic Committee (III)*, 1981, pp. 117–23. [G: Cuba]

130 ECONOMIC FLUCTUATIONS; FORECASTING; STABILIZATION; AND INFLATION

131 Economic Fluctuations

1310 Economic Fluctuations: General

Alt, James E. and Chrystal, K. Alec. Public Sector Behaviour: The Status of the Political Business Cycle. In *Currie, D.; Nobay, R. and Peel, D., eds.*, 1981, pp. 353–76. [G: U.K.]

Andvig, Jens Christopher. Ragnar Frisch and Business Cycle Research during the Interwar Years. *Hist. Polit. Econ.*, Winter 1981, *13*(4), pp. 695–725.

Assenmacher, Walter. Tarifpolitik, Kapitalstock und konjunkturelle Entwicklung. Ein Jahrgangsmodell. (Negotiated Wages, Capital Stock and the Business Cycle: A Vintage Approach. With English summary.) *Jahr. Nationalökon. Statist.*, March 1981, *196*(2), pp. 119–36.

Azariadis, Costas. Self-Fulfilling Prophecies. *J. Econ. Theory*, December 1981, *25*(3), pp. 380–96.

Barro, Robert J. A Capital Market in an Equilibrium Business Cycle Model. In *Barro, R. J.*, 1981, 1980, pp. 111–36.

Barro, Robert J. Intertemporal Substitution and the Business Cycle. *Carnegie-Rochester Conf. Ser. Public Policy*, Spring 1981, *14*, pp. 237–68.

Barro, Robert J. The Equilibrium Approach to Business Cycles. In *Barro, R. J.*, 1981, pp. 41–78.

Beach, E. F. A Generalization of the Accelerator. In *Chikán, A., ed. (1)*, 1981, pp. 39–48.

Bernanke, Ben S. Bankruptcy, Liquidity, and Recession. *Amer. Econ. Rev.*, May 1981, *71*(2), pp. 155–59.

Beveridge, Stephen and Nelson, Charles R. A New Approach to Decomposition of Economic Time Series into Permanent and Transitory Components with Particular Attention to Measurement of the 'Business Cycle.' *J. Monet. Econ.*, March 1981, *7*(2), pp. 151–74. [G: U.S.]

Blanchard, Olivier J. What Is Left of the Multiplier Accelerator? *Amer. Econ. Rev.*, May 1981, *71*(2), pp. 150–54.

Blinder, Alan S. Inventories and the Structure of Macro Models. *Amer. Econ. Rev.*, May 1981, *71*(2), pp. 11–16. [G: U.S.]

Blinder, Alan S. Retail Inventory Behavior and Business Fluctuations. *Brookings Pap. Econ. Act.*, 1981, (2), pp. 443–505. [G: U.S.]

Blinder, Alan S. and Fischer, Stanley. Inventories, Rational Expectations, and the Business Cycle. *J. Monet. Econ.*, November 1981, *8*(3), pp. 277–304.

Clemhout, Simone and Neftci, Salih N. Policy Evaluation of Housing Cyclicality: A Spectral Analysis. *Rev. Econ. Statist.*, August 1981, *63*(3), pp. 385–94. [G: U.S.]

Cline, William R. Cyclical Growth Links between Industrial and Developing Countries. In *Cline, W. R., et al.*, 1981, pp. 240–56. [G: LDCs; MDCs]

Cukierman, Alex. Interest Rates during the Cycle, Inventories and Monetary Policy—A Theoretical Analysis. *Carnegie-Rochester Conf. Ser. Public Policy*, Autumn 1981, *15*, pp. 87–144.

Edel, Matthew. Land Policy, Economic Cycles, and Social Conflict. In *de Neufville, J. I., ed.*, 1981, pp. 127–39.

van Ewijk, Casper. The Long Wave—A Real Phenomenon? *De Economist*, 1981, *129*(3), pp. 324–72. [G: U.K.; France; W. Germany; U.S.]

Fiorito, Riccardo. Inventory Investment and Demand for Factors in Disequilibrium. In *Chikán, A., ed. (1)*, 1981, pp. 139–56. [G: Italy]

Forman, Leonard. Expectations and the Economy: Statement. In *U.S. Congress, Joint Economic Committee (II)*, 1981, pp. 119–20.

Fusfeld, Daniel R. Response to Professor Gurley [The Next Great Depression II: The Impending Financial Collapse]. *J. Econ. Issues*, March 1981, *15*(1), pp. 181–83. [G: U.S.; Europe]

George, Donald A. R. Equilibrium and Catastrophes in Economics. *Scot. J. Polit. Econ.*, February 1981, *28*(1), pp. 43–61.

Giersch, Herbert. Aspects of Growth, Structural Changes, and Employment—A Schumpeterian Perspective. In *Giersch, H, ed. (1)*, 1981, pp. 181–206. [G: OECD]

Gordon, Robert J. Output Fluctuations and Gradual Price Adjustment. *J. Econ. Lit.*, June 1981, *19*(2), pp. 493–530. [G: U.S.]

Grünbaum, Isi. Relative Inertias and the Long-run Analysis. In *Grünbaum, I.*, 1981, pp. 65–90.

Kaufman, Bruce E. Bargaining Theory, Inflation, and Cyclical Strike Activity in Manufacturing. *Ind. Lab. Relat. Rev.*, April 1981, *34*(3), pp. 333–55. [G: U.S.]

Kindleberger, Charles P. Historical Perspective on the Decline in U.S. Productivity. In *Hogan, J. D. and Craig, A. M., eds., Vol. 1*, 1981, pp. 715–24. [G: U.K.; U.S.]

King, Robert G. Monetary Information and Monetary Neutrality. *J. Monet. Econ.*, March 1981, *7*(2), pp. 195–206.

Klein, Philip A. and Moore, Geoffrey H. Growth Cycles in France. *Revue Écon.*, May 1981, *32*(3), pp. 468–89. [G: France]

Kovács, János and Virág, Ildikó. Periodic versus Continuous Growth. *Acta Oecon.*, 1981, *27*(1–2), pp. 41–55.

Lecaillon, Jacques. Cycle électoral et répartition du revenu national. (Political Business Cycle and Distribution of National Income. With English summary.) *Revue Écon.*, March 1981, *32*(2), pp. 213–36.

Lovell, Michael C. Aggregation in a Multi-sector Model of the Inventory Cycle. In *Chikán, A., ed. (1)*, 1981, pp. 229–40.

Lucas, Robert E., Jr. An Equilibrium Model of the Business Cycle. In *Lucas, R. E., Jr.*, 1981, *1979*, pp. 179–214.

Lucas, Robert E., Jr. Methods and Problems in Business Cycle Theory. In *Lucas, R. E., Jr.*, 1981, *1980*, pp. 271–96.

Lucas, Robert E., Jr. Studies in Business-Cycle Theory: Introduction. In *Lucas, R. E., Jr.*, 1981, pp. 1–18.

Lucas, Robert E., Jr. Understanding Business Cycles. In *Lucas, R. E., Jr.*, 1981, *1977*, pp. 215–39.

Lucas, Robert E., Jr. and Sargent, Thomas J. After Keynesian Macroeconomics. In *Lucas, R. E. and Sargent, T. J., eds.*, 1981, *1979*, pp. 295–319.

Luukkainen, Pecca A. Debatten om den svenska industrins strukturproblem. (The Debate on the Structural Problem of Swedish Industry: A Survey. With English summary.) *Ekon. Samfundets Tidskr.*, 1981, *34*(2), pp. 147–62. [G: Sweden]

MacRae, Duncan. On the Political Business Cycle. In *Hibbs, D. A., Jr. and Fassbender, H., eds.*, 1981, pp. 169–84. [G: U.S.]

Manzetti, Fabio A. On the Stability Implications of Inventory Cycles: An Econometric Analysis of Some Italian Sectors. In *Chikán, A., ed. (1)*, 1981, pp. 241–53. [G: Italy]

McCulloch, J. Huston. Misintermediation and Macroeconomic Fluctuations. *J. Monet. Econ.*, July 1981, *8*(1), pp. 103–15.

Meyer, Peter B. "Survival" in Economic Downturns: Some Implications for the Criminal Justice System. In *Wright, K. N., ed.*, 1981, pp. 39–50. [G: U.S.]

Molnár, Ferenc. Consumers' Investment versus Capital Investment (A Contribution to the Theory of Contemporary Business Fluctuations). *Acta Oecon.*, 1981, *26*(1–2), pp. 133–55. [G: U.S.]

Mortensen, Dale T. A Comment on Barro's Intertemporal Substitution and the Business Cycle. *Carnegie-Rochester Conf. Ser. Public Policy*, Spring 1981, *14*, pp. 269–71.

Neumann, Manfred J. M. Der Beitrag der Geldpoli-

tik zur konjunkturellen Entwicklung in der Bundesrepublik Deutschland 1973–1980. (With English summary.) *Kyklos*, 1981, *34*(3), pp. 405–31.
[G: W. Germany]

Paldam, Martin. An Essay on the Rationality of Economic Policy: The Test-Case of the Electional Cycle. *Public Choice*, 1981, *37*(2), pp. 287–305.

Palomba, Giuseppe. La disgregazione delle leggi economiche. (The Collapse of Economic Laws. With English summary.) *Rivista Int. Sci. Econ. Com.*, October–November 1981, *28*(10–11), pp. 1070–81.

Schinasi, Garry J. A Nonlinear Dynamic Model of Short Run Fluctuations. *Rev. Econ. Stud.*, October 1981, *48*(4), pp. 649–56.

Schott, Kerry. Public Sector Behaviour: The Status of the Political Business Cycle: Comment. In *Currie, D.; Nobay, R. and Peel, D.*, eds., 1981, pp. 377–82.
[G: U.K.]

Siegel, Jeremy J. Interest Rates during the Cycle, Inventories and Monetary Policy—A Theoretical Analysis: A Comment. *Carnegie-Rochester Conf. Ser. Public Policy*, Autumn 1981, *15*, pp. 145–50.

Steindl, Josef. Some Comments on the Three Versions of Kalecki's Theory of the Trade Cycle. In *[Lipiński, E.]*, 1981, pp. 125–33.

Stenbäck, Pär. Regeringens ekonomisk-politiska utskott. Funktion och problematik. (The Government Commission on Economic Policy. With English summary.) *Ekon. Samfundets Tidskr.*, 1981, *34*(4), pp. 295–303.
[G: Finland]

Talamona, Mario. Economic Efficiency, Structural Change and Social Policies for the 1980s. *Giorn. Econ.*, May–June 1981, *40*(5–6), pp. 379–87.

von Weizsäcker, Carl Christian. Aspects of Growth, Structural Changes, and Employment—A Schumpeterian Perspective: Comment. In *Giersch, H*, ed. *(I)*, 1981, pp. 207–09.
[G: OECD]

1313 Economic Fluctuations: Studies

Abbott, George C. The Recycling of Surplus Oil Funds. *Econ. Int.*, May–August–November 1981, *34*(2–3–4), pp. 203–21.
[G: OPEC; OECD]

Bachár, Vladislav. Crisis Processes in Present-Day Capitalism. *Czech. Econ. Digest.*, May 1981, (3), pp. 54–74.
[G: OECD; MDCs]

Baqir, Ghalib M. The Long-Wave Cycles and Reindustrialisation. *Int. J. Soc. Econ.*, 1981, *8*(7), pp. 117–23.
[G: U.S.; France; U.K.]

Benston, George J. The Ideological Origins of the Revolution in American Financial Policies: Comments. In *Brunner, K.*, ed., 1981, pp. 253–57.

Bergesen, Albert. Long Economic Cycles and the Size of Industrial Enterprise. In *Rubinson, R.*, ed., 1981, pp. 179–89.
[G: MDCs]

Black, W. The Effects of the Recession on the Economy of Northern Ireland. *Irish Banking Rev.*, December 1981, pp. 16–23.
[G: U.K.]

Bonnell, Sheila. Real Wages and Employment in the Great Depression. *Econ. Rec.*, September 1981, *57*(158), pp. 277–81.
[G: U.K.; U.S.; Sweden; Germany]

Bossier, Francis and Hugé, Pierre. Une vérification empirique de l'existence de cycles longs à partir de données belges. (An Empirical Examination of the Long Cycles Existence from Belgian Data. With English summary.) *Cah. Écon. Bruxelles*, 2nd Trimestre 1981, (90), pp. 253–67.
[G: Belgium]

Boyer, M. Christine. National Land Use Policy: Instrument and Product of the Economic Cycle. In *de Neufville, J. I.*, ed., 1981, pp. 109–25.
[G: U.S.]

Brunner, Karl. Epilogue: Understanding the Great Depression. In *Brunner, K.*, ed., 1981, pp. 316–58.
[G: U.S.]

Camaiti, R. The Long Italian Economic Recession: 1981–1982. *Econ. Notes*, 1981, *10*(3), pp. 159–64.
[G: Italy]

Chikán, Attila. Market Disequilibrium and the Volume of Stocks. In *Chikán, A.*, ed. *(I)*, 1981, pp. 73–85.
[G: Selected Countries]

Corcione, Frank P. and Thornton, Robert J. The Economic Determinants of Strike Activity: An Industry Approach. *Rev. Bus. Econ. Res.*, Fall 1981, *17*(1), pp. 15–26.
[G: U.S.]

Cox, Charles C. Monopoly Explanations of the Great Depression and Public Policies toward Business. In *Brunner, K.*, ed., 1981, pp. 174–207.
[G: U.S.]

Csikós-Nagy, Béla. Some Aspects of Stock Economy (A Case Study of Hungary). In *Chikán, A.*, ed. *(I)*, 1981, pp. 87–97.
[G: Hungary]

Dinkel, Reiner. Political Business Cycles in Germany and the United States: Some Theoretical and Empirical Considerations. In *Hibbs, D. A., Jr. and Fassbender, H.*, eds., 1981, pp. 209–230.
[G: U.S.; W. Germany]

Doeppers, Daniel F. Construction Cycles in Prewar Manila. *Philippine Econ. J.*, 1981, *20*(1), pp. 44–57.
[G: Philippines]

Duke, John and Brand, Horst. Cyclical Behavior of Productivity in the Machine Tool Industry. *Mon. Lab. Rev.*, November 1981, *104*(11), pp. 27–34.
[G: U.S.]

Evans, Richard D. Residential Construction Volatility: A Seasonal and Cyclical Inventory Adjustment Analysis. *Amer. Real Estate Urban Econ. Assoc. J.*, Spring 1981, *9*(1), pp. 74–82.
[G: U.S.]

Fábri, Ervin. Paradoxes of Macroeconomic Inventory Developments. In *Chikán, A.*, ed. *(I)*, 1981, pp. 109–23.
[G: Hungary]

Favereau, Olivier and Mouillart, Michel. La stabilité du lien emploi-croissance et la loi d'Okun: Une application à l'économie française. (The Stability of the Relationship between Employment and Growth in Okun's Law: An Application to the French Economy. With English summary.) *Consommation*, January–March 1981, *28*(1), pp. 85–117.
[G: France]

Ferguson, Lorna Crowley. Fiscal Strain in American Cities: Some Limitations to Popular Explanations. In *Newton, K.*, ed., 1981, pp. 156–78.
[G: U.S.]

Fernández Diaz, Andrés. Inventories and Stabilization Policy. In *Chikán, A.*, ed. *(I)*, 1981, pp. 125–37.
[G: Spain]

Finegan, T. Aldrich. Discouraged Workers and Economic Fluctuations. *Ind. Lab. Relat. Rev.*, October 1981, *35*(1), pp. 88–102.   [G: U.S.]

Fischer, Wolfram. The World Economy in the 20th Century—Continuity and Change. In *Engels, W. and Pohl, H., eds.*, 1981, pp. 107–27.

Ford, A. G. The Trade Cycle in Britain 1860–1914. In *Floud, R. and McCloskey, D., eds., Vol. 2,* 1981, pp. 27–49.   [G: U.K.]

Ghysels, Eric and Vuchelen, Jozef. Het gebruik van de DULBEA-BNP cijfers in konjunktuuranalyses. (The Use of the DULBEA GNP-Figures in Business Cycle Analysis. With English summary.) *Cah. Écon. Bruxelles,* 1st Trimestre 1981, (89), pp. 53–73.   [G: Belgium]

Gordon, Robert J. and Wilcox, James A. Monetarist Interpretations of the Great Depression: A Rejoinder. In *Brunner, K., ed.,* 1981, pp. 165–73.   [G: U.S.; W. Europe]

Gordon, Robert J. and Wilcox, James A. Monetarist Interpretations of the Great Depression: An Evaluation and Critique. In *Brunner, K., ed.,* 1981, pp. 49–107.   [G: U.S.]

Green, George D. The Ideological Origins of the Revolution in American Financial Policies. In *Brunner, K., ed.,* 1981, pp. 220–52.

Honkapohja, Seppo and Kanniainen, Vesa. Corporate Taxation, Inventory Undervaluation and Neutrality. *Kansant. Aikak.,* 1981, *77*(4), pp. 435–45.   [G: Finland]

Howson, S. Slump and Unemployment. In *Floud, R. and McCloskey, D., eds., Vol. 2,* 1981, pp. 265–85.   [G: U.K.]

Jonung, Lars. The Depression in Sweden and the United States: A Comparison of Causes and Policies. In *Brunner, K., ed.,* 1981, pp. 286–315.   [G: Sweden; U.S.]

Kleiman, Ephraim and Pincus, Jonathan J. The Cyclical Effects of Incremental Export Subsidies. *Econ. Rec.,* June 1981, *57*(157), pp. 140–49.   [G: Australia]

Klein, Philip A. and Moore, Geoffrey H. Industrial Surveys in the UK: Part I—New Orders. *Appl. Econ.,* June 1981, *13*(2), pp. 167–79. [G: U.K.]

Klein, Philip A. and Moore, Geoffrey H. Industrial Surveys in the UK: Part II—Stocks, Profits and Business Confidence over the Business Cycle. *Appl. Econ.,* December 1981, *13*(4), pp. 465–80.   [G: U.K.]

Kozlowski, Paul J. Forecasting Cyclical Turning Points in Local Market Areas. *Bus. Econ.,* September 1981, *16*(4), pp. 43–49.   [G: U.S.]

Laffargue, Jean-Pierre. Interprétation économique des caractéristiques quasi-cycliques d'un modèle macroéconométrique évoluant en environnement aléatoire. (Economic Interpretation of the Quasi-cyclical Characteristics of a Macroeconometric Model in a Stochastic Environment. With English summary.) *Ann. INSEE,* July–September 1981, (43), pp. 3–34.

Lindert, Peter H. Understanding 1929–33: Comments. In *Brunner, K., ed.,* 1981, pp. 125–33.   [G: U.S.]

Lothian, James R. Monetarist Interpretations of the Great Depression: Comment. In *Brunner, K., ed.,* 1981, pp. 134–47.   [G: U.S.]

Magill, W. G.; Felmingham, B. S. and Wells, G. M. Cyclical Interdependencies between Nations in the Pacific Basin. *Econ. Int.,* February

1981, *34*(1), pp. 34–45.   [G: U.S.; Canada; Japan; Australia; New Zealand]

Maloney, Kevin J. and Smirlock, Michael L. Business Cycles and the Political Process. *Southern Econ. J.,* October 1981, *48*(2), pp. 377–92.

Mayer, Thomas. Monopoly Explanations of the Great Depression and Public Policies toward Business: Comments. In *Brunner, K., ed.,* 1981, pp. 211–19.

Meltzer, Allan H. Monetarist Interpretations of the Great Depression: Comments. In *Brunner, K., ed.,* 1981, pp. 148–64.   [G: U.S.]

Mickwitz, Gösta. Att förutsäga konjunkturer. (On Economic Forecasting. With English summary.) *Ekon. Samfundets Tidskr.,* 1981, *34*(1), pp. 19–21.   [G: Finland]

Otani, Ichiro. Real Wages, Business Cycles, and the Speed of Adjustment: A Reply [Real Wages and Business Cycles Revisited]. *Rev. Econ. Statist.,* May 1981, *63*(2), pp. 312–13. [G: W. Europe; Japan; U.K.; U.S.]

Paldam, Martin. Is There an Electional Cycle? A Comparative Study of National Accounts. In *Strøm, S., ed.,* 1981, *1979,* pp. 182–201.   [G: OECD]

Poole, William. Monopoly Explanations of the Great Depression and Public Policies toward Business: Comments. In *Brunner, K., ed.,* 1981, pp. 208–10.

Qualls, P. David. Cyclical Wage Flexibility, Inflation, and Industrial Structure: An Alternative View and Some Empirical Evidence. *J. Ind. Econ.,* June 1981, *29*(4), pp. 345–56. [G: U.S.]

Schwartz, Anna J. Understanding 1929–1933. In *Brunner, K., ed.,* 1981, pp. 5–48.   [G: U.S.]

Smyth, David J. Real Wages, Business Cycles and the Speed of Adjustment of Employment in Manufacturing Sectors of Industrialized Countries [Real Wages and Business Cycles Revisited]. *Rev. Econ. Statist.,* May 1981, *63*(2), pp. 311–12.   [G: W. Europe; Japan; U.K.; U.S.]

Sutton, C. J. Merger Cycles: An Exploratory Discussion. *Brit. Rev. Econ. Issues,* Spring 1981, *2*(8), pp. 89–97.   [G: U.K.]

Talley, Ronald J. Identifying a Cyclical Peak in Interest Rates. *Bus. Econ.,* January 1981, *16*(1), pp. 5–9.

Talvas, G. S. and Aschheim, J. The Chicago Monetary Growth-Rate Rule: Friedman on Simons Reconsidered. *Banca Naz. Lavoro Quart. Rev.,* March 1981, (136), pp. 75–89.   [G: U.S.]

Tatom, John A. Capital Utilization and Okun's Law. *Rev. Econ. Statist.,* February 1981, *63*(1), pp. 155–58.   [G: U.S.]

Temin, Peter. Notes on the Causes of the Great Depression. In *Brunner, K., ed.,* 1981, pp. 108–24.   [G: U.S.]

You, Jong Keun. Capital Utilization and Okun's Law: A Reply. *Rev. Econ. Statist.,* February 1981, *63*(1), pp. 158–60.   [G: U.S.]

132 Forecasting; Econometric Models

1320 General

Carli, Guido. Experience with Econometric Models in Italy: Aims and Results: Final Remarks. *Rev.*

Econ. Cond. Italy, June 1981, (2), pp. 371–75. [G: Italy]

Cazalet, Edward G. A Progress Report on the Development of Generalized Equilibrium Modeling. In *Bayraktar, B. A., et al., eds.*, 1981, pp. 321–34.

Courbis, R. Les Problèmes Internationaux a la Lumière des Modèles. (With English summary.) In *Courbis, R., ed.*, 1981, pp. 337–50.

D'Adda, Carlo and Stagni, Anna. The Bologna Econometric Model: Interpretative Framework and Simulation. *Rev. Econ. Cond. Italy*, June 1981, (2), pp. 267–80. [G: Italy]

Ginsburgh, V. and Waelbroeck, Jean. Some Calculations of the Impact of Tariffs on World Trade and Welfare with a General Equilibrium Model of World Economy. In *Courbis, R., ed.*, 1981, pp. 279–94. [G: Global]

Harris, Britton. Policy-Making, Programming, and Design. In *Crecine, J. P., ed.*, 1981, pp. 279–88.

Hawkins, R. G. and FitzGerald, V. W. The Potential Contribution of Econometric Modelling. In *Nevile, J. W., ed.*, 1981, pp. 11–30. [G: Australia]

Holmes, A. S. Macro, Micro and Modelling—What Else? In *Nevile, J. W., ed.*, 1981, pp. 34–42.

Jöhr, Walter Adolf. Das Bariloche-Modell. Ein lateinamerikanisches Weltmodell. (The Bariloche Model: A Latin American World Model. With English summary.) *Schweiz. Z. Volkswirtsch. Statist.*, June 1981, *117*(2), pp. 109–74.

Keen, Howard, Jr. Who Forecasts Best? Some Evidence from the Livingston Survey. *Bus. Econ.*, September 1981, *16*(4), pp. 24–29. [G: U.S.]

Keyfitz, Nathan. The Limits of Population Forecasting. *Population Devel. Rev.*, December 1981, *7*(4), pp. 579–93.

Khazzoom, J. Daniel. The Dilemma of Economic versus Statistical Models of Energy (and Some Results of Forecasting Monthly Peak Electricity Demand Using a Transfer Function Model) *Energy J.*, July 1981, *2*(3), pp. 134–37.

Klaassen, Leo H. and Pawlowski, Zbigniew. Long-Term Forecasting: Meditations of Two Pitfall Collectors. *De Economist*, 1981, *129*(4), pp. 455–75.

Klein, Lawrence R. Project Link: Policy Implications for the World Economy. In *Evan, W. M., ed.*, 1981, pp. 91–106.

Kost, William E. The Agricultural Component in Macroeconomic Models. *Agr. Econ. Res.*, July 1981, *33*(3), pp. 1–10. [G: LDCs; MDCs]

Manjappa, H. D. Mathematical Models in Development Planning. *Econ. Aff.*, July–September 1981, *26*(3), pp. 211–16.

Marbach, George M. R. Conditions and Problems of the Scientific Study of the Future. *Econ. Notes*, 1981, *10*(2), pp. 3–13.

Martelli, Antonio. Further Outlook for the Use of Econometric Models at the Confindustria Research Department. *Rev. Econ. Cond. Italy*, June 1981, (2), pp. 239–46. [G: Italy]

Martin, Robert Dee. The Illusion of Uncritical Evaluations of Econometrics. *Bus. Econ.*, September 1981, *16*(4), pp. 53–56.

McNees, Stephen K. The Optimists and the Pessimists: Can We Tell Whose Forecast Will Be Better? *New Eng. Econ. Rev.*, May/June 1981, pp. 5–14. [G: U.S.]

McNees, Stephen K. The Recent Record of Thirteen Forecasters. *New Eng. Econ. Rev.*, September–October 1981, pp. 5–21. [G: U.S.]

McNees, Stephen K. and Perna, Nicholas S. Forecasting Macroeconomic Variables: An Eclectic Approach. *New Eng. Econ. Rev.*, May/June 1981, pp. 15–30. [G: U.S.]

Meadows, Donella H. Global Modeling after Its First Decade. *Agr. Econ. Res.*, July 1981, *33*(3), pp. 25–26.

Mesarovic, Mihajlo D. and Hughes, Barry B. Global Modeling and Decision-Making. In *Evan, W. M., ed.*, 1981, pp. 107–20.

Mitchell, John. Use of Models in Decision Making: A Policy Maker's View. In *Bayraktar, B. A., et al., eds.*, 1981, pp. 35–45.

Naylor, Thomas H. Experience with Corporate Econometric Models: A Survey. *Bus. Econ.*, January 1981, *16*(1), pp. 79–83. [G: U.S.]

Sarcinelli, Mario. Policy-Making and Macro-economic Models: A Symbiosis? *Econ. Notes*, 1981, *10*(1), pp. 3–12.

Sartori, Franco. Simulation with the ISPE Model: Income Policies and Indexation Mechanisms. *Rev. Econ. Cond. Italy*, June 1981, (2), pp. 293–304. [G: Italy]

Sebenius, James K. The Computer as Mediator: Law of the Sea and Beyond. *J. Policy Anal. Manage.*, Fall 1981, *1*(1), pp. 77–95.

1322 General Forecasts and Models

Aagaard-Svendsen, Rolf. Estimation of Econometric Models by Kalman Filtering and Iterative Instrumental Variables. In *Janssen, J. M. L.; Pau, L. F. and Straszak, A. J., eds.*, 1981, pp. 291–96. [G: Denmark]

Aislabie, C. J. The Sectoral Impact on Employment of Some Economic Policies: An Australian Case Study. *Metroecon.*, Feb.-Oct. 1981, *33*(1–2–3), pp. 175–91. [G: Australia]

Attfield, C. L. F.; Demery, D. and Duck, Nigel W. A Quarterly Model of Unanticipated Monetary Growth, Output and the Price Level in the U.K., 1963–1978. *J. Monet. Econ.*, November 1981, *8*(3), pp. 331–50. [G: U.K.]

Attfield, C. L. F.; Demery, D. and Duck, Nigel W. Unanticipated Monetary Growth, Output and the Price Level: U.K., 1946–77. *Europ. Econ. Rev.*, June/July 1981, *16*(2/3), pp. 367–85. [G: U.K.]

Bánkövi, G.; Veliczky, József and Ziermann, M. Dynamic Factor Models of the Hungarian National Economy. In *Janssen, J. M. L.; Pau, L. F. and Straszak, A. J., eds.*, 1981, pp. 117–21. [G: Hungary]

Barten, Anton P. Comet in a Nutshell. In *Courbis, R., ed.*, 1981, pp. 211–19. [G: EEC]

Basu, D. R. A Multisectoral Stochastic Optimal Control Model for UK to Derive Future Energy Policies. In *Janssen, J. M. L.; Pau, L. F. and Straszak, A. J., eds.*, 1981, pp. 129–39. [G: U.K.]

Baumann, Harry; Irvine, Russell and Paquet, Bertrand. The Impact of Higher Energy Prices in Canada: Comment. *Can. Public Policy*, Winter 1981, *7*(1), pp. 39–41. [G: Canada]

Berde, E. Comparative Analysis of Dynamic Factor

Models of Current and Constant Prices. In *Janssen, J. M. L.; Pau, L. F. and Straszak, A. J., eds.*, 1981, pp. 285–90.

Blanchard, Olivier J. and Wyplosz, Charles. An Empirical Structural Model of Aggregate Demand. *J. Monet. Econ.*, January 1981, 7(1), pp. 1–28. [G: U.S.]

Bradley, J. and O'Raifeartaigh, C. Optimal Control and Policy Analysis with a Model of a Small Open Economy: The Case of Ireland. In *Janssen, J. M. L.; Pau, L. F. and Straszak, A. J., eds.*, 1981, pp. 85–90. [G: Ireland]

Bruno, Michael and Sachs, Jeffrey. Supply versus Demand Approaches to the Problem of Stagflation. In *Giersch, H, ed.* (1), 1981, pp. 15–60. [G: Selected OECD]

Burki, Shahid Javed. The Prospects for the Developing World: A Review of Recent Forecasts. *Finance Develop.*, March 1981, 18(1), pp. 20–24. [G: LDCs]

Chiesa, G. Monetary and Fiscal Policy in a Small Open Economy. In *Janssen, J. M. L.; Pau, L. F. sm and Straszak, A. J., eds.*, 1981, pp. 253–61. [G: Italy]

Cichocki, K. Optimization Techniques in Modelling of Economic Policy. In *Janssen, J. M. L.; Pau, L. F. and Straszak, A. J., eds.*, 1981, pp. 105–16. [G: Poland]

Cullison, William E. Monetarist Econometric Models and Tax Cuts: Comment [Monetarist Econometric Models and the Effects of Tax Cuts: Further Evidence]. *Econ. Inquiry*, January 1981, 19(1), pp. 173–75.

Daub, Mervin. The Accuracy of Canadian Short-Term Economic Forecasts Revisited. *Can. J. Econ.*, August 1981, 14(3), pp. 499–507. [G: Canada]

Davis, Robert R. and Genetski, Robert J. Federal Budget Outlook and Economic Prospects through 1982. In *Shadow Open Market Committee (I)*, 1981, pp. 51–61. [G: U.S.]

Del Monte, Carlo. Theory and Practice in the Construction of Mosyl DF/70. *Rev. Econ. Cond. Italy*, June 1981, (2), pp. 323–27. [G: Italy]

Dramais, A. Le Modèle Desmos. (With English summary.) In *Courbis, R., ed.*, 1981, pp. 221–34. [G: EEC]

Drummond, Don and Grady, Patrick. The Impact of Higher Energy Prices in Canada: Comment. *Can. Public Policy*, Winter 1981, 7(1), pp. 42–49. [G: Canada]

Eckstein, Otto. Shock Inflation, Core Inflation, and Energy Disturbances in the DRI Model. In *Mork, K. A., ed.*, 1981, pp. 63–98. [G: U.S.]

Eckstein, Otto and Warburg, Paul M. Economic Theory and Econometric Models. In *Kmenta, J. and Ramsey, J. B., eds.*, 1981, pp. 155–76. [G: U.S.]

Empey, W. F. The Impact of Higher Energy Prices in Canada. *Can. Public Policy*, Winter 1981, 7(1), pp. 28–35. [G: Canada]

Fazio, Antonio. The Banca d'Italia Model: Structure, Experiences and Problems. *Rev. Econ. Cond. Italy*, June 1981, (2), pp. 199–209. [G: Italy]

Feltenstein, Andrew. A General-Equilibrium Approach to the Analysis of Monetary and Fiscal Policies. *Int. Monet. Fund Staff Pap.*, December 1981, 28(4), pp. 653–81. [G: U.S.]

Forman, Leonard and Eichner, Alfred S. A Post Keynesian Short-Period Model: Some Preliminary Econometric Results. *J. Post Keynesian Econ.*, Fall 1981, 4(1), pp. 117–35.

Genetski, Robert J. The Impact of the Reagan Administration's Economic Proposals (Simulations with the Harris Monetarist–Supply Side Model). In *Shadow Open Market Committee (II)*, 1981, pp. 13–38. [G: U.S.]

Guillaume, Y. Marco II, un Modèle Structure-Conjoncture de L'Economie Mondiale. (With English summary.) In *Courbis, R., ed.*, 1981, pp. 137–47.

Gupta, Dipak K. and Venieris, Yiannis P. Introducing New Dimensions in Macro Models: The Sociopolitical and Institutional Environments. *Econ. Develop. Cult. Change*, October 1981, 30(1), pp. 31–58. [G: U.K.]

Hernandez, Ruby Daniel. Un modelo econométrico para la República Argentina: Valor Agregado Sectorial 1950–1979. (An Econometric Model for Argentina: Sectoral Value Added, 1950–1979. With English summary.) *Económica*, September–December 1981, 27(3), pp. 175–222. [G: Argentina]

Hieronymi, Otto. Prospect-Italy: Structure and Results of a Short-Term Forecasting Program. *Rev. Econ. Cond. Italy*, June 1981, (2), pp. 349–69. [G: Italy]

Howe, Howard, et al. Assessing International Interdependence with a Multi-Country Model. *J. Econometrics*, January 1981, 15(1), pp. 65–92. [G: Japan; W. Germany; U.S.]

Ioannidis, C. P. and Matthews, K. G. P. Rational Expectations and the St. Louis Model for the U.K. *Empirical Econ.*, 1981, 6(2), pp. 87–102. [G: U.K.]

Jump, Gregory V. On Interpreting Simulations with a Macroeconometric Model: Comment [The Impact of Higher Enery Prices in Canada]. *Can. Public Policy*, Winter 1981, 7(1), pp. 35–38. [G: Canada]

Kawaller, Ira G. and Koch, Timothy W. Housing as a Monetary Phenomenon: Forecasting Housing Starts Using the Monetary Aggregate Targets. *Bus. Econ.*, September 1981, 16(4), pp. 30–35. [G: U.S.]

Kelejian, Harry H. and Vavrichek, Bruce. An Evaluation of the Forecasting Performance of Macro Economic Models, with Special Emphasis on Model Size. In *Kmenta, J. and Ramsey, J. B., eds.*, 1981, pp. 93–122. [G: U.S.]

Kemme, David M. Econometric Models of East European Economies: A Survey of Models of Poland. *ACES Bull. (See Comp. Econ. Stud. after 8/85)*, Summer 1981, 23(2), pp. 51–69. [G: Poland]

Klein, Lawrence R. The Link Project. In *Courbis, R., ed.*, 1981, pp. 197–209. [G: OECD]

Kooyman, Jan. The Meteor Model. In *Courbis, R., ed.*, 1981, pp. 235–42. [G: OECD]

Korum, Uğur. Türk Planlamasinda Kisa Dönem Makroekonometrik Model Gereksinimi. (The Need for Short-Term Macroeconometric Models in Turkish Planning. With English summary.)

METU, Special Issue, 1981, pp. 427–36.
[G: Turkey]

Kumar, Pradeep. The Economy: Summary Outline. In *Wood, W. D. and Kumar, P., eds.*, 1981, pp. 1–25. [G: Canada]

Kutscher, Ronald E. New Economic Projections through 1900—An Overview. *Mon. Lab. Rev.*, August 1981, *104*(8), pp. 9–17. [G: U.S.]

Lafay, Gérard and Brender, Anton. Modèles et Prospective en Période de Crise: Le Cas Du Modèle Moise. (With English summary.) In *Courbis, R., ed.*, 1981, pp. 295–307. [G: OECD]

Leontief, Wassily W. Population Growth and Economic Development: Illustrative Projections. In *Reubens, E. P., ed.*, 1981, *1979*, pp. 39–60.

Lester, John. The Impact of Higher Energy Prices in Canada: Comment. *Can. Public Policy*, Winter 1981, 7(1), pp. 52–58. [G: Canada]

Lucas, Robert E., Jr. An Equilibrium Model of the Business Cycle. In *Lucas, R. E., Jr.*, 1981, *1979*, pp. 179–214.

Malinvaud, Edmond. Supply versus Demand Approaches to the Problem of Stagflation: Comment. In *Giersch, H, ed. (I)*, 1981, pp. 70–72. [G: Selected OECD]

McCracken, M. C. and Jarvis, W. D. What Is the Impact of Higher Energy Prices? Comment [The Impact of Higher Energy Prices in Canada]. *Can. Public Policy*, Winter 1981, 7(1), pp. 50–52. [G: Canada]

Meade, James E. Note on the Inflationary Implications of the Wage-Fixing Assumption of the Cambridge Economic Policy Group. *Oxford Econ. Pap.*, March 1981, *33*(1), pp. 28–41. [G: U.K.]

Meyer, Laurence H. and Varvares, Chris. A Comparison of the St. Louis Model and Two Variations: Predictive Performance and Policy Implications. *Fed. Res. Bank St. Louis Rev.*, December 1981, *63*(10), pp. 13–25. [G: U.S.]

Minford, Patrick. Comparison of NIESR and Liverpool Model Errors: A Note. *Nat. Inst. Econ. Rev.*, August 1981, (97), pp. 81. [G: U.K.]

Minford, Patrick. Dynamic Predictive Tests of a Rational Expectations Model of the U.K. *Brit. Rev. Econ. Issues*, Autumn 1981, 3(9), pp. 39–50. [G: U.K.]

Mork, Knut Anton and Hall, Robert E. Macroeconomic Analysis of Energy Price Shocks and Offsetting Policies: An Integrated Approach. In *Mork, K. A., ed.*, 1981, pp. 43–62. [G: U.S.]

Moulin, Hervé and d'Alcantara, G. Application of Game Theory to the Multicountry Models: Methodology and an Example with Comet. In *Courbis, R., ed.*, 1981, pp. 327–36.

Muller, Patrice and White, W. R. The Impact of Higher Energy Prices in Canada: Comment. *Can. Public Policy*, Winter 1981, 7(1), pp. 59–65. [G: Canada]

Norton, Roger D. and Rhee, Seung Yoon. A Macroeconomic Model of Inflation and Growth in South Korea. In *Cline, W. R. and Weintraub, S., eds.*, 1981, pp. 407–57. [G: S. Korea]

Nyhus, D. E. INFORUM-IIASA System of National Economic Models. In *Janssen, J. M. L.; Pau, L. F. and Straszak, A. J., eds.*, 1981, pp. 123–28. [G: U.S.]

Pawlowski, Z. A Demoeconometric Model of Poland and Its Simulations. In *Janssen, J. M. L.; Pau, L. F. and Straszak, A. J., eds.*, 1981, pp. 37–41. [G: Poland]

Pfajfar, Lovro, et al. Upotreba ekonometrijskog modela u prognoziranju razvoja Jugoslavije za period 1981–1985. (The Application of an Econometric Model for Yugoslavia's 1981–1985 Medium-Term Plan. With English summary.) *Econ. Anal. Worker's Manage.*, 1981, *15*(2), pp. 143–61. [G: Yugoslavia]

Plasmans, J. E. J. Interplay: A Linked Model for Economic Policy in the EEC. In *Janssen, J. M. L.; Pau, L. F. and Straszak, A. J., eds.*, 1981, pp. 43–56. [G: EEC]

Posta, G. and Veliczky, József. Forecasting and Simulation by Controlled Dynamic Factors of Open Economies. In *Janssen, J. M. L.; Pau, L. F. and Straszak, A. J., eds.*, 1981, pp. 279–84. [G: Hungary]

Rasche, Robert H. Comments on the Size of Macroeconomic Models. In *Kmenta, J. and Ramsey, J. B., eds.*, 1981, pp. 265–71.

Rashid, M. Ali. A Macro-Econometric Model of Bangladesh. *Bangladesh Devel. Stud.*, Monsoon 1981, 9(3), pp. 21–44. [G: Bangladesh]

Rasmussen, T. V. and Kaergård, N. A Growth Model of the Danish Economy. In *Janssen, J. M. L.; Pau, L. F. and Straszak, A. J., eds.*, 1981, pp. 99–104. [G: Denmark]

del Rio, Abel Beltran. The Mexican Oil Syndrome: Early Symptoms, Preventive Efforts, and Prognosis. *Quart. Rev. Econ. Bus.*, Summer 1981, *21*(2), pp. 115–30. [G: Mexico; OPEC]

Robinson, P. W. Medium Term Forecasting in the European Communities: The Use of the Comet Model. In *Courbis, R., ed.*, 1981, pp. 251–58.

Sadowski, Zdzislaw; Kotowicz, Joanna and Cwalina, Kazimierz. An Experimental Model of General Growth Proportions in the National Economy: The MODO Model. *Econ. Planning*, 1981, *17*(2–3), pp. 64–73.

Sadun, Arrigo. The Track Record of Chase Econometrics Italian Forecasting Model: The 1977–80 Experience. *Rev. Econ. Cond. Italy*, June 1981, (2), pp. 329–48. [G: Italy]

Sallin-Kornberg, Eugenia and Fontela, Emilio. Scenarios Building with the Explor-Multitrade 85 Model. In *Courbis, R., ed.*, 1981, pp. 309–25.

Samuelson, Lee W. OECD World Trade Model: Some Recent Extensions. In *Courbis, R., ed.*, 1981, pp. 149–62. [G: OECD]

Sandblom, C. L. and Banasik, J. L. Optimal and Suboptimal Controls of a Canadian Model. In *Janssen, J. M. L.; Pau, L. F. and Straszak, A. J., eds.*, 1981, pp. 71–78. [G: Canada]

Sapir, André. Economic Reform and Migration in Yugoslavia: An Econometric Model. *J. Devel. Econ.*, October 1981, 9(2), pp. 149–81. [G: Yugoslavia]

Sarkar, Hiren and Subbarao, S. V. A Short Term Macro Forecasting Model for India—Structure and Uses. *Indian Econ. Rev.*, January–June 1981, *16*(1 and 2), pp. 55–80. [G: India]

Saunders, Norman C. The U.S. Economy through 1990—An Update. *Mon. Lab. Rev.*, August 1981, *104*(8), pp. 18–27. [G: U.S.]

Savona, Paolo. The State of Econometric Modelling in Italy: Some Reflections on the Two CSC Models. *Rev. Econ. Cond. Italy*, June 1981, (2), pp. 211–37. [G: Italy]

Shapiro, Harold T. and Garman, David M. Perspectives on the Accuracy of Macro-econometric Forecasting Models. In *Kmenta, J. and Ramsey, J. B., eds.*, 1981, pp. 59–91. [G: U.S.]

Suzuki, K. and Takenaka, H. The Role of Investment for Energy Conservation: Future Japanese Economic Growth. *Energy Econ.*, October 1981, *3*(4), pp. 233–43. [G: Japan]

Taylor, John B. Estimation and Control of a Macroeconomic Model with Rational Expectations. In *Lucas, R. E. and Sargent, T. J., eds.*, 1981, *1979*, pp. 659–80. [G: U.S.]

Thurman, Stephan and Berner, Richard. Analysis of Oil Price Shocks in the MPS Model. In *Mork, K. A., ed.*, 1981, pp. 99–124. [G: U.S.]

Tobin, James. Supply versus Demand Approaches to the Problem of Stagflation: Comment. In *Giersch, H, ed. (I)*, 1981, pp. 61–69. [G: Selected OECD]

Uygur, Ercan. Etki, Yönlendirme ve Öngörüler Açisindan Planlar. (Impact, Orientation and Predictions of the Plans. With English summary.) *METU*, Special Issue, 1981, pp. 437–74. [G: Turkey]

Val'tukh, K. K. Optimization and Balance of National Economy Models. In *Janssen, J. M. L.; Pau, L. F. and Straszak, A. J., eds.*, 1981, pp. 21–30. [G: W. Germany]

Vishwakarma, K. P. An Application of the Generalized Inverse in Input–Output and Macroeconomic Analysis. In *Janssen, J. M. L.; Pau, L. F. and Straszak, A. J., eds.*, 1981, pp. 63–69. [G: Netherlands]

Westphal, Larry E. A Macroeconomic Model of Inflation and Growth in South Korea: Comment. In *Cline, W. R. and Weintraub, S., eds.*, 1981, pp. 457–62. [G: S. Korea]

Zandano, Gianni. A Two-Sector Model of the Italian Economy. *Rev. Econ. Cond. Italy*, June 1981, (2), pp. 247–66. [G: Italy]

Zwick, Burton. Economic Projections. In *Shadow Open Market Committee (I)*, 1981, pp. 63–70. [G: U.S.]

1323 Specific Forecasts and Models

Abed, George T. and Kubursi, Atif A. A Macroeconomic Simulation Model of High Level Manpower Requirements in Iraq. In *Sherbiny, N. A., ed.*, 1981, pp. 145–71. [G: Iraq]

Ábel, István and Riecke, Werner. A Model of Aggregate Inventory Behaviour in the Hungarian Economy. In *Chikán, A., ed. (I)*, 1981, pp. 13–28. [G: Hungary]

Alessandroni, A.; Leporelli, C. and Rey, G. M. Economic Industry Model Building: The Synthetic Fibres Case. In *Janssen, J. M. L.; Pau, L. F. and Straszak, A. J., eds.*, 1981, pp. 169–75. [G: Italy]

Anderson, G. J. A New Approach to the Empirical Investigation of Investment Expenditures. *Econ. J.*, March 1981, *91*(361), pp. 88–103. [G: U.K.]

Anderson, G. J. An Econometric Model of Manufacturing Investment in the U.K.: A Comment. *Econ. J.*, March 1981, *91*(361), pp. 122–23.

Ando, Albert. An Econometric Model Incorporating the Supply-Side Effects of Economic Policy: Discussion. In *Meyer, L. H., ed.*, 1981, pp. 103–11. [G: U.S.]

Arestis, P. Fiscal Actions and "Crowding-Out" in the United Kingdom. *Metroecon.*, Feb.-Oct. 1981, *33*(1–2–3), pp. 205–32. [G: U.K.]

Artus, Jacques R. and McGuirk, Anne Kenny. A New Version of the I.M.F. Multilateral Exchange Rate Model (MERM2). In *Courbis, R., ed.*, 1981, pp. 111–21.

Artus, Jacques R. and McGuirk, Anne Kenny. A Revised Version of the Multilateral Exchange Rate Model. *Int. Monet. Fund Staff Pap.*, June 1981, *28*(2), pp. 275–309.

Balas, Egon. The Strategic Petroleum Reserve: How Large Should It Be? In *Bayraktar, B. A., et al., eds.*, 1981, pp. 335–86.

Basile, Paul S. An Integrated Energy Modeling Approach: Experience at IIASA. In *Bayraktar, B. A., et al., eds.*, 1981, pp. 287–305.

Basile, Paul S. Balancing Energy Supply and Demand: A Fifty-Year Global Perspective. *Energy J.*, July 1981, *2*(3), pp. 1–15.

Bass, Frank M. A New-Product Growth Model for Consumer Durables. In *Wind, Y.; Mahajan, V. and Cardozo, R. N., eds.*, 1981, *1969*, pp. 457–74. [G: U.S.]

Bean, Charles R. A New Approach to the Empirical Investigation of Investment Expenditures: A Comment. *Econ. J.*, March 1981, *91*(361), pp. 104–05.

Bean, Charles R. An Econometric Model of Manufacturing Investment in the UK. *Econ. J.*, March 1981, *91*(361), pp. 106–21. [G: U.K.]

Behling, David J., Jr. Use of Energy Models for Business Decisions. In *Bayraktar, B. A., et al., eds.*, 1981, pp. 215–20.

Bergendahl, Per-Anders and Bergström, Clas. Long-term Oil Substitution—The IEA-MARKAL Model and Some Simulation Results for Sweden. *Scand. J. Econ.*, 1981, *83*(2), pp. 237–52. [G: Sweden]

Bessler, David A. and Brandt, Jon A. Forecasting Livestock Prices with Individual and Composite Methods. *Appl. Econ.*, December 1981, *13*(4), pp. 513–22. [G: U.S.]

Blattberg, Robert and Golanty, John. TRACKER: An Early Test-Market Forecasting and Diagnostic Model for New-Product Planning. In *Wind, Y.; Mahajan, V. and Cardozo, R. N., eds.*, 1981, *1978*, pp. 387–409.

Bopp, Anthony, et al. Air Quality Implications of a Nuclear Moratorium: An Alternative Analysis. *Energy J.*, July 1981, *2*(3), pp. 33–48. [G: U.S.]

Boyle, G. A Time Series Forecast of Pigs Received at Irish Bacon Factories. *Irish J. Agr. Econ. Rural Soc.*, 1981, *8*(2), pp. 179–89. [G: Ireland]

Brada, Josef C.; Jackson, Marvin R. and King, Arthur E. The Optimal Rate of Industrialization in

Developed and Developing Centrally-planned Economies: A General Equilibrium Approach. *World Devel.*, September/October 1981, *9*(9/10), pp. 991–1004. **[G: Czechoslovakia; Romania]**

Brandt, Jon A. and Bessler, David A. Composite Forecasting: An Application with U.S. Hog Prices. *Amer. J. Agr. Econ.*, February 1981, *63*(1), pp. 135–40. **[G: U.S.]**

Braun, Steven. An Econometric Model Incorporating the Supply-Side Effects of Economic Policy: Discussion. In *Meyer, L. H., ed.*, 1981, pp. 93–101. **[G: U.S.]**

Brown, Bryan W. and Maital, Shlomo. What Do Economists Know? An Empirical Study of Experts' Expectations. *Econometrica*, March 1981, *49*(2), pp. 491–504. **[G: U.S.]**

Caramanis, Michael C. Capital, Energy, and Labor Cross-Substitution Elasticities in a Developing Country: The Case of Greek Manufacturing. In *Bayraktar, B. A., et al., eds.*, 1981, pp. 307–16. **[G: Greece]**

Carhart, Steven C. Energy Demand Analysis and Modeling. In *Bayraktar, B. A., et al., eds.*, 1981, pp. 221–32.

Carman, Peter. The Trouble with Asset Allocation. *J. Portfol. Manage.*, Fall 1981, *8*(1), pp. 17–22. **[G: U.S.]**

Chan, M. W. Luke. An Econometric Model of the Canadian Agricultural Economy. *Can. J. Agr. Econ.*, November 1981, *29*(3), pp. 265–82.

Cherniavsky, E. A. Multiobjective Energy Analysis. In *Bayraktar, B. A., et al., eds.*, 1981, pp. 399–420.

Christensen, Laurits R. On the Formation of Price Expectations by König, et al.: Comment. *Europ. Econ. Rev.*, May 1981, *16*(1), pp. 139.

Conrad, K. Energy Policy Planning: Discussion of the Session on Demand Modeling. In *Bayraktar, B. A., et al., eds.*, 1981, pp. 233–43.

Cornelius, James C.; Ikerd, John E. and Nelson, A. Gene. A Preliminary Evaluation of Price Forecasting Performance by Agricultural Economists. *Amer. J. Agr. Econ.*, November 1981, *63*(4), pp. 712–14. **[G: U.S.]**

Craine, Roger and Havenner, Arthur. Choosing a Monetary Instrument: The Case of Supply-Side Shocks. *J. Econ. Dynam. Control*, August 1981, *3*(3), pp. 217–34. **[G: U.S.]**

Csaki, Csaba. National Agricultural Sector Models for Centrally Planned Economies. In *Johnson, G. and Maunder, A., eds.*, 1981, pp. 312–23. **[G: Hungary; CMEA]**

D'Hoop, H. and Laughton, M. A. Survey of Present Energy Models with Particular Reference to the European Community. In *Bayraktar, B. A., et al., eds.*, 1981, pp. 245–58.

Dewald, W. G. and Gavin, W. T. Money and Inflation in a Small Model of the German Economy. *Empirical Econ.*, 1981, *6*(3), pp. 173–85. **[G: W. Germany]**

Dodson, Joe A. Application and Utilization of Test-Market-Based New-Product Forecasting Models. In *Wind, Y.; Mahajan, V. and Cardozo, R. N., eds.*, 1981, pp. 411–21.

Dohner, Robert S. Energy Prices, Economic Activity, and Inflation: A Survey of Issues and Results.

In *Mork, K. A., ed.*, 1981, pp. 7–41. **[G: U.S.]**

Dufour, Jean-Marie. Variables binaires et tests prédictifs contre les changements structurels: une application à l'équation de St. Louis. (Predictive Tests for Structural Change and the St. Louis Equation. With English summary.) *L'Actual. Econ.*, July–September 1981, *57*(3), pp. 376–86. **[G: U.S.]**

Egberts, G. and Voss, A. Energy Models and Technology Assessment. In *Bayraktar, B. A., et al., eds.*, 1981, pp. 159–72.

Eklöf, J. A. On Optimal Macro-economic Control with Inaccurate Data. In *Janssen, J. M. L.; Pau, L. F. and Straszak, A. J., eds.*, 1981, pp. 57–62. **[G: Sweden]**

Eliasson, Gunnar and Lindberg, Thomas. Allocation and Growth Effects of Corporate Income Taxes. In *Eliasson, G. and Södersten, J., eds.*, 1981, pp. 381–435. **[G: Sweden]**

Evans, Michael K. An Econometric Model Incorporating the Supply-Side Effects of Economic Policy. In *Meyer, L. H., ed.*, 1981, pp. 33–80. **[G: U.S.]**

Foster, John. Comment on "Balancing Energy Supply and Demand." *Energy J.*, July 1981, *2*(3), pp. 29–32.

Gamaletsos, Theodore. A Dynamic Generalized Linear Expenditure System of the Demand for Consumer Goods in Greece. In *[Valavanis, S.]*, 1981, pp. 379–89. **[G: Greece]**

Gass, Saul I. Validation and Assessment Issues of Energy Models. In *Bayraktar, B. A., et al., eds.*, 1981, pp. 421–41.

Gellatly, Colin. Forecasting N.S.W. Beef Production: A Reply [Forecasting N.S.W. Beef Production: An Evaluation of Alternative Techniques]. *Rev. Marketing Agr. Econ.*, August 1981, *49*(2), pp. 127–30.

Giles, David E. A. and Goss, Barry A. Futures Prices as Forecasts of Commodity Spot Prices: Live Cattle and Wool. *Australian J. Agr. Econ.*, April 1981, *25*(1), pp. 1–13. **[G: Australia]**

Goldie, Raymond and Ambachtsheer, Keith P. The Battle of Insider Trading vs. Market Efficiency: Comment. *J. Portfol. Manage.*, Winter 1981, *7*(2), pp. 88. **[G: U.S.]**

Green, Paul E. and Carroll, J. Douglas. New Computer Tools for Product Strategy. In *Wind, Y.; Mahajan, V. and Cardozo, R. N., eds.*, 1981, pp. 109–54. **[G: U.S.]**

Häfele, Wolf. Energy in a Finite World—Expansio ad Absurdum? A Rebuttal. *Energy J.*, October 1981, *2*(4), pp. 35–42. **[G: LDCs]**

Henriksson, Roy D. and Merton, Robert C. On Market Timing and Investment Performance. II. Statistical Procedures for Evaluating Forecasting Skills. *J. Bus.*, October 1981, *54*(4), pp. 513–33. **[G: U.S.]**

Hopwood, William S. and McKeown, James C. An Evaluation of Univariate Time-Series Earnings Models and Their Generalization to a Single Input Transfer Function. *J. Acc. Res.*, Autumn 1981, *19*(2), pp. 313–22. **[G: U.S.]**

Horowitz, Joel L. Sources of Error and Uncertainty in Behavioral Travel-Demand Models. In *Stopher, P. R.; Meyburg, A. H. and Brög, W., eds.*,

1981, pp. 543–58.

Hudson, Edward A. Modeling Production and Pricing within an Interindustry Framework. In *Bayraktar, B. A., et al., eds.*, 1981, pp. 201–14.

Hutber, F. W. Energy Policy Planning: Comments on the Papers Presented in the Session on Supply Modeling. In *Bayraktar, B. A., et al., eds.*, 1981, pp. 183–86.

Jacobson, Robert. Forecasting Bank Portfolios. In *Maisel, S. J., ed.*, 1981, pp. 249–70. [G: U.S.]

Jöckel, Karl-Heinz and Pflaumer, Peter. Die Vorhersage des Goldpreises mit dem Box-Jenkins-Verfahren. (Forecasting Monthly Gold Prices with the Box-Jenkins Approach. With English summary.) *Jahr. Nationalökon. Statist.*, November 1981, *196*(6), pp. 481–501.

Johannes, James M. and Rasche, Robert H. Forecasting Multipliers for the "New–New" Monetary Aggregates. In *Shadow Open Market Committee (I)*, 1981, pp. 39–49. [G: U.S.]

Johannes, James M. and Rasche, Robert H. Updated Forecasts of Money Multipliers. In *Shadow Open Market Committee (II)*, 1981, pp. 53–65. [G: U.S.]

Just, Richard E. and Rausser, Gordon C. Commodity Price Forecasting with Large-Scale Econometric Models and the Futures Market. *Amer. J. Agr. Econ.*, May 1981, *63*(2), pp. 197–208. [G: U.S.]

Kaufman, Alvin and Bodilly, Susan J. Supplemental Sources of Natural Gas: An Economic Comparison. *Energy J.*, October 1981, *2*(4), pp. 63–83. [G: U.S.]

Kaufman, Herbert M. and Schlagenhauf, Don E. FNMA Auction Results as a Forecaster of Residential Mortgage Yields. *J. Money, Credit, Banking*, August 1981, *13*(3), pp. 352–64. [G: U.S.]

Keesing, Donald B. Exports and Policy in Latin-American Countries: Prospects for the World Economy and for Latin-American Exports, 1980–90. In *Baer, W. and Gillis, M., eds.*, 1981, pp. 18–43. [G: Latin America]

Klein, Lawrence R.; Fardoust, Shahrokh and Filatov, Victor. Purchasing Power Parity in Medium Term Simulation of the World Economy. *Scand. J. Econ.*, 1981, *83*(4), pp. 479–96.

König, Heinz; Nerlove, Marc and Oudiz, Gilles. On the Formation of Price Expectations: An Analysis of Business Test Data by Log-Linear Probability Models. *Europ. Econ. Rev.*, May 1981, *16*(1), pp. 103–38. [G: Germany; France]

Kreicher, Lawrence L. An International Evaluation of the Fisher Hypothesis Using Rational Expectations. *Southern Econ. J.*, July 1981, *48*(1), pp. 58–67. [G: U.K.; W. Germany; Italy; U.S.]

Kuh, Edwin and Neese, John. Parameter Sensitivity, Dynamic Behavior, and Model Reliability: An Initial Exploration with the MQEM Monetary Sector. In *[Valavanis, S.]*, 1981, pp. 121–68. [G: U.S.]

Langworthy, Mark; Pearson, Scott R. and Josling, Timothy. Macroeconomic Influences on Future Agricultural Prices in the European Community. *Europ. Rev. Agr. Econ.*, 1981, *8*(1), pp. 5–26. [G: EEC]

Lawrence, Kenneth D. and Lawton, William H. Applications of Diffusion Models: Some Empirical Results. In *Wind, Y.; Mahajan, V. and Cardozo, R. N., eds.*, 1981, pp. 529–41. [G: U.S.]

Lawrence, Kenneth D. and Reeves, Gary R. Consensus Time Series Forecasting. In *Morse, J. N., ed.*, 1981, pp. 199–204.

Leimer, Dean R. and Petri, Peter A. Cohort-Specific Effects of Social Security Policy. *Nat. Tax J.*, March 1981, *34*(1), pp. 9–28. [G: U.S.]

Levich, Richard M. Tests of Forecasting Models and Market Efficiency in the International Money Market. In *Baldwin, R. E. and Richardson, J. D., eds.*, 1981, 1978, pp. 362–68.

Lovins, Amory B. Expansio ad Absurdum. *Energy J.*, October 1981, *2*(4), pp. 25–34. [G: LDCs]

Mahajan, Vijay and Muller, Eitan. Innovation Diffusion and New-Product Growth Models in Marketing. In *Wind, Y.; Mahajan, V. and Cardozo, R. N., eds.*, 1981, 1979, pp. 425–56.

Martin, Larry J. and Garcia, Philip. The Price-Forecasting Performance of Futures Markets for Live Cattle and Hogs: A Disaggregated Analysis. *Amer. J. Agr. Econ.*, May 1981, *63*(2), pp. 209–15. [G: U.S.]

Marzouk, M. Shokri. An Econometric/Input–Output Approach for Projecting Sectoral Manpower Requirements: The Case of Kuwait. In *Sherbiny, N. A., ed.*, 1981, pp. 111–44. [G: Kuwait]

McGregor, Peter G. The Portfolio Selection Approach and Short-Run Econometric Models of Capital Flows and the Foreign Exchange Market: A Theoretical Analysis. *J. Econ. Stud.*, 1981, *8*(2), pp. 3–24.

Melvin, John G. Energy: The Future Has Come. In *Nemetz, P. N., ed.*, 1981, pp. 61–81. [G: Canada]

Mészáros, S. Econometric Forecasting by a Fertiliser Sectoral Model. In *Janssen, J. M. L.; Pau, L. F. and Straszak, A. J., eds.*, 1981, pp. 163–68.

Midgley, David F. A Simple Mathematical Theory of Innovative Behavior. In *Wind, Y.; Mahajan, V. and Cardozo, R. N., eds.*, 1981, 1976, pp. 475–98. [G: U.S.]

Mishkin, Frederic S. Are Market Forecasts Rational? *Amer. Econ. Rev.*, June 1981, *71*(3), pp. 295–306.

Mitropoulos, C. S.; Samouilidis, J. E. and Protonotarios, E. N. Using Kalman Filtering for Energy Forecasting. In *Janssen, J. M. L.; Pau, L. F. and Straszak, A. J., eds.*, 1981, pp. 317–24. [G: Greece]

Moses, Lincoln E. One Statistician's Observations Concerning Energy Modeling. In *Bayraktar, B. A., et al., eds.*, 1981, pp. 17–33.

Muellbauer, John. Testing Neoclassical Models of the Demand for Consumer Durables. In *[Stone, R.]*, 1981, pp. 213–35. [G: U.K.]

Mueller, R. K.; Eggert, D. J. and Swanson, H. S. Petroleum Decline Analysis Using Time Series. *Energy Econ.*, October 1981, *3*(4), pp. 256–67. [G: U.S.]

Murphy, Terence. Aspects of High-Level Manpower Forecasting and University Development in Papua New Guinea. *J. Devel. Areas*, April 1981, *15*(3), pp. 417–33. [G: New Guinea]

Mylander, W. Charles. Energy Policy Planning: Discussion of Papers Presented in Comprehensive/

Integrated Modeling Systems Session. In *Bayraktar, B. A., et al., eds.*, 1981, pp. 317–19.

Nachane, D. M., et al. Forecasting Freight and Passenger Traffic on Indian Railways: A Generalized Adaptive-Filtering Approach. *Indian Econ. J.*, October–December 1981, *29*(2), pp. 98–116.
[G: India]

Narasimhan, Chakravarthi and Sen, Subrata K. Test-Market Models for New-Product Introduction. In *Wind, Y.; Mahajan, V. and Cardozo, R. N., eds.*, 1981, pp. 293–321.

Ottenwaelter, Benoît and Vuong, Quang. Modèles conditionnels log-linéaires de probabilité et systèmes récursifs. (Conditional Log-Linear Models of Probability and Recursive Systems. With English summary.) *Ann. INSEE*, October–December 1981, (44), pp. 81–120.

Pagan, Adrian Rodney. Interest Rates Using the Survey Method and a Time Series Method: Comments. In *Jüttner, D. J., ed.*, 1981, pp. 339–41.
[G: Australia]

Personick, Valerie A. The Outlook for Industry Output and Employment through 1990. *Mon. Lab. Rev.*, August 1981, *104*(8), pp. 28–41. [G: U.S.]

Pesando, James E. On Forecasting Interest Rates: An Efficient Markets Perspective. *J. Monet. Econ.*, November 1981, *8*(3), pp. 305–18.
[G: Canada]

Plihon, D. Un Modéle Sectoriel de la Balance Commerciale Française. (With English summary.) In *Courbis, R., ed.*, 1981, pp. 47–63. [G: France]

Portney, Paul R. The Macroeconomic Impacts of Federal Environmental Regulation. In *Peskin, H. M.; Portney, P. R. and Kneese, A. V., eds.*, 1981, pp. 25–54. [G: U.S.]

Portney, Paul R. The Macroeconomic Impacts of Federal Environmental Regulation. *Natural Res. J.*, July 1981, *21*(3), pp. 459–88. [G: U.S.]

Rao, Vithala R. New-Product Sales Forecasting Using the Hendry System. In *Wind, Y.; Mahajan, V. and Cardozo, R. N., eds.*, 1981, pp. 499–527.

Revell, B. J. Box–Jenkins Forecasting Models: Comment [Forecasting NSW Beef Production: An Evaluation of Alternative Techniques] [Comparing the Box–Jenkins and Econometric Techniques for Forecasting Beef Prices]. *Rev. Marketing Agr. Econ.*, April 1981, *49*(1), pp. 61–64.

Ridker, Ronald G. and Watson, William D. Long-run Effects of Environmental Regulation. In *Peskin, H. M.; Portney, P. R. and Kneese, A. V., eds.*, 1981, pp. 131–53. [G: U.S.]

Ridker, Ronald G. and Watson, William D. Long–Run Effects of Environmental Regulation. *Natural Res. J.*, July 1981, *21*(3), pp. 565–87.
[G: U.S.]

Ripley, Duncan. The I.M.F. World Trade Model: A Progress Report. In *Courbis, R., ed.*, 1981, pp. 123–36.

Robinson, Patrick J. Comparison of Pre-test-market New-Product Forecasting Models. In *Wind, Y.; Mahajan, V. and Cardozo, R. N., eds.*, 1981, pp. 181–204.

Rodekohr, Mark. An Examination of Econometric Energy Modeling and Comparison with Alternative Methodologies. In *Bayraktar, B. A., et al., eds.*, 1981, pp. 387–97.

Saunders, Peter G. The Formation of Producers' Price Expectations in Australia. *Econ. Rec.*, December 1981, *57*(159), pp. 368–78.
[G: Australia]

Scott, Elton and Teycock, Stefan. Published Results on Speculative Markets: Some Evidence from the Stock Market. *Bus. Econ.*, January 1981, *16*(1), pp. 67–74. [G: U.S.]

Sherbiny, Naiem A. Sectoral Employment Projections with Minimum Data: The Case of Saudi Arabia. In *Sherbiny, N. A., ed.*, 1981, pp. 173–206. [G: Saudi Arabia]

Shihab-Eldin, Adnan and Al-Qudsi, Sulayman S. Energy Needs of the Less Developed Countries (LDCs). In *Amman, F. and Wilson, R., eds.*, 1981, pp. 349–93. [G: LDCs]

Signora, André. Les Leçons D'Une Expérience D'Application De Modèles Mondiaux au Niveau Sectoriel. (With English summary.) In *Courbis, R., ed.*, 1981, pp. 163–70.

Silk, Alvin J. and Urban, Glen L. Pre-test-market Evaluation of New Packaged Goods: A Model and Measurement Methodology. In *Wind, Y.; Mahajan, V. and Cardozo, R. N., eds.*, 1981, *1978*, pp. 205–48.

Smith, A. W. and Smith, Rhonda L. The Impact of Changing Economic Conditions on the Australian Agricultural Sector. In *Johnson, G. and Maunder, A., eds.*, 1981, pp. 326–37. [G: Australia]

Stitt, William C. Resource Modeling: Problems in the State of the Art. In *Bayraktar, B. A., et al., eds.*, 1981, pp. 127–58.

Sweeney, James L. Model Comparison for Energy Policy and Planning. In *Bayraktar, B. A., et al., eds.*, 1981, pp. 259–85. [G: U.S.]

Szumilak, J. and Wasik, B. Simulation Analysis of Goods Flows Stability in the Food Products Distribution System. In *Janssen, J. M. L.; Pau, L. F. and Straszak, A. J., eds.*, 1981, pp. 177–85.

Talley, Ronald J. Identifying a Cyclical Peak in Interest Rates. *Bus. Econ.*, January 1981, *16*(1), pp. 5–9.

Talvitie, Antti P. Inaccurate or Incomplete Data as a Source of Uncertainty in Econometric or Attitudinal Models of Travel Behavior. In *Stopher, P. R.; Meyburg, A. H. and Brög, W., eds.*, 1981, pp. 559–75. [G: U.S.]

Tauber, Edward M. Utilization of Concept Testing for New-Product Forecasting: Traditional versus Multiattribute Approaches. In *Wind, Y.; Mahajan, V. and Cardozo, R. N., eds.*, 1981, pp. 169–78.

Taylor, Robert R. Forecasting Interest Rates Using the Survey Method and a Time Series Model. In *Jüttner, D. J., ed.*, 1981, pp. 316–35.
[G: Australia]

Wagner, H. F. Energy in Europe: Demand, Forecast, Control and Supply. In *Amman, F. and Wilson, R., eds.*, 1981, pp. 23–97. [G: W. Europe]

Westcott, Paul C. Monthly Food Price Forecasts. *Agr. Econ. Res.*, July 1981, *33*(3), pp. 27–30.
[G: U.S.]

Wills, Hugh R. On the Formation of Price Expectations by König, et al.: Comment. *Europ. Econ. Rev.*, May 1981, *16*(1), pp. 141–44.

Wind, Yoram. A Framework for Classifying New-Product Forecasting Models. In *Wind, Y.; Mahajan, V. and Cardozo, R. N., eds., 1981, 1981,* pp. 3–42.

Wolf, Charles, Jr.; Relles, Daniel A. and Navarro, Jaime. Oil and Energy Demand in Developing Countries in 1990. *Energy J.,* October 1981, 2(4), pp. 1–24. [G: non OPEC LDCs]

Wolf, Thomas A. Modelling Energy in the Soviet Economy: Differences between SOVMOD and SOVSIM. *ACES Bull. (See Comp. Econ. Stud. after 8/85),* Fall–Winter 1981, 23(3–4), pp. 73–79. [G: U.S.S.R.]

1324 Forecasting and Econometric Models: Theory and Methodology

Ansley, Craig F. and Newbold, Paul. On the Bias in Estimates of Forecast Mean Squared Error. *J. Amer. Statist. Assoc.,* September 1981, 76(375), pp. 569–78.

Badach, A. Adaptive Models in Econometric Forecasting. In *Janssen, J. M. L.; Pau, L. F. and Straszak, A. J., eds., 1981,* pp. 271–77.

Bhansali, R. J. Effects of Not Knowing the Order of an Autoregressive Process on the Mean Squared Error of Prediction—I. *J. Amer. Statist. Assoc.,* September 1981, 76(375), pp. 588–97.

Bianchi, C. and de Bianchi, P. Ranuzzi. Some Problems Related to the Construction of Linkage Models. In *Courbis, R., ed., 1981,* pp. 185–96.

Bomberger, William A. and Frazer, William J., Jr. Interest Rates, Uncertainty and the Livingston Data. *J. Finance,* June 1981, 36(3), pp. 661–75. [G: U.S.]

Bourke, I. J. Forecasting Beef Prices: A Reply [Comparing the Box–Jenkins and Econometric Techniques for Forecasting Beef Prices]. *Rev. Marketing Agr. Econ.,* August 1981, 49(2), pp. 125–26.

Brooks, Simon. Systematic Econometric Comparisons: Exports of Manufactured Goods. *Nat. Inst. Econ. Rev.,* August 1981, (97), pp. 67–80. [G: U.K.]

Caines, P. E.; Keng, C. W. and Sethi, Suresh P. Causality Analysis and Multivariate Autoregressive Modelling with an Application to Supermarket Sales Analysis. *J. Econ. Dynam. Control,* August 1981, 3(3), pp. 267–98. [G: U.S.]

Casti, J. Systemism, System Theory and Social System Modeling. *Reg. Sci. Urban Econ.,* August 1981, 11(3), pp. 405–24.

Cattier, John and Gerard, Marcel. La dynamisation des coefficients économétriques: une application à des données sectorielles belges. (With English summary.) *Cah. Écon. Bruxelles,* 3rd Trimestre 1981, (91), pp. 447–74. [G: Belgium]

Courbis, R. La Construction de Modèles Multinationaux: Problèmes Méthodologiques. (With English summary.) In *Courbis, R., ed., 1981,* pp. 243–47.

Crivellini, Marco. Instruments and Objectives of Economic Analysis: Reflections on Experiences with Italian Econometric Models. *Rev. Econ. Cond. Italy,* June 1981, (2), pp. 281–92. [G: Italy]

Currie, David A. Some Long Run Features of Dynamic Time Series Models. *Econ. J.,* September 1981, 91(363), pp. 704–15.

Dadaian, V. S. and Raiatskas, R. L. Integrated Sets of Macroeconomic Models. *Matekon,* Summer 1981, 17(4), pp. 94–111.

Deheuvels, Paul. La prévision des séries économiques: Une technique subjective. (With English summary.) *Écon. Appl.,* 1981, 34(4), pp. 729–47.

Deleau, Michel; Malgrange, Pierre and Muet, Pierre-Alain. Une maquette représentative des modèles macroéconomiques. (A Representative, Small-Scale Macroeconomic Model. With English summary.) *Ann. INSEE,* April–June 1981, (42), pp. 53–92. [G: France]

Fair, Ray C. Comments [An Autoregressive Index Model for the U.S., 1948–1975] [The Methodology of Macroeconometric Model Comparisons]. In *Kmenta, J. and Ramsey, J. B., eds., 1981,* pp. 389–90.

Freedman, David. Some Pitfalls in Large Econometric Models: A Case Study. *J. Bus.,* July 1981, 54(3), pp. 479–500. [G: U.S.]

Froment, René. Matrices de Structure: Propriétés et Problèmes de Projection. (With English summary.) In *Courbis, R., ed., 1981,* pp. 171–82.

Fromm, Gary and Klein, Lawrence R. Scale of Macro-econometric Models and Accuracy of Forecasting. In *Kmenta, J. and Ramsey, J. B., eds., 1981,* pp. 369–88. [G: U.S.]

Geurts, Michael D. and Buchman, Thomas A. Accounting for 'Shocks' in Forecasts. *Manage. Account.,* April 1981, 62(10), pp. 21–26, 39.

Granger, C. W. J. The Comparison of Time Series and Econometric Forecasting Strategies. In *Kmenta, J. and Ramsey, J. B., eds., 1981,* pp. 123–28.

Greenberg, Harvey J. Implementation Aspects of Model Management: A Focus on Computer-Assisted Analysis. In *Bayraktar, B. A., et al., eds., 1981,* pp. 443–59.

Howe, Howard, et al. Assessing International Interdependence with a Multi-Country Model. *J. Econometrics,* January 1981, 15(1), pp. 65–92. [G: Japan; W. Germany; U.S.]

Hughes Hallett, A. J. Some Extensions and Comparisons in the Theory of Gauss–Seidel Iterative Techniques for Solving Large Equation Systems. In *[Valavanis, S.], 1981,* pp. 297–318.

Karlqvist, Anders. The Role of Modeling in Social Sciences: Some Concluding Remarks. *Reg. Sci. Urban Econ.,* August 1981, 11(3), pp. 425–30.

Kmenta, Jan and Ramsey, James B. Large-Scale Macro-econometric Models: Summary of the General Discussion. In *Kmenta, J. and Ramsey, J. B., eds., 1981,* pp. 449–62.

Kmenta, Jan and Ramsey, James B. Model Size, Quality of Forecast Accuracy, and Economic Theory. In *Kmenta, J. and Ramsey, J. B., eds., 1981,* pp. 3–16.

Lawson, Tony. Keynesian Model Building and the Rational Expectations Critique. *Cambridge J. Econ.,* December 1981, 5(4), pp. 311–26.

Maki, Wilbur R. Regional Economic Forecast System for Resource Development Planning. *Reg. Sci. Persp.,* 1981, 11(1), pp. 22–31.

Malgrange, Pierre. Note sur le calcul des valeurs propres d'un modèle macroéconométrique. (A Note on the Calculation of the Eigen Values of a Macroeconometric Model. With English summary.) *Ann. INSEE,* January–March 1981, (41), pp. 67–77.

Malinvaud, Edmond. Econometrics Faced with the Needs of Macroeconomic Policy. *Econometrica,* November 1981, *49*(6), pp. 1363–75.

Marois, Bernard and Behar, Michel. La prévision du risque politique liée aux investissements à l'étranger. (Forecasting the Political Risks of Foreign Investments. With English summary.) *Rev. Econ. Ind.,* 2nd Trimester 1981, (16), pp. 34–43.

McNees, Stephen K. The Methodology of Macroeconometric Model Comparisons. In *Kmenta, J. and Ramsey, J. B., eds.,* 1981, pp. 397–422.

Meadows, Dennis. A Critique of the IIASA Energy Models. *Energy J.,* July 1981, *2*(3), pp. 17–28.

Merkies, Arnold H. Q. M. and Nijam, T. E. Preference Functions of Dutch Political Parties. *Écon. Appl.,* 1981, *34*(4), pp. 784–818.
[G: Netherlands]

Modigliani, Franco. Scale of Macro-econometric Models and Accuracy of Forecasting: Comment. In *Kmenta, J. and Ramsey, J. B., eds.,* 1981, pp. 393–94.

Muth, John F. Optimal Properties of Exponentially Weighted Forecasts. In *Lucas, R. E. and Sargent, T. J., eds.,* 1981, *1960,* pp. 23–31.

Neumann, Manfred J. M. Der Beitrag der Geldpolitik zur konjunkturellen Entwicklung in der Bundesrepublik Deutschland 1973–1980. (With English summary.) *Kyklos,* 1981, *34*(3), pp. 405–31.
[G: W. Germany]

Ormerod, Paul. The Maintenance of Large Macro-Economic Models: A Case Study with the NIESR Model of the UK Economy. *Appl. Econ.,* December 1981, *13*(4), pp. 431–47. [G: U.K.]

Rey, Guido M. Statistical Difficulties in the Construction and Use of Italian Econometric Models. *Rev. Econ. Cond. Italy,* June 1981, (2), pp. 181–97. [G: Italy]

Sims, Christopher A. An Autoregressive Index Model for the U.S., 1948–1975. In *Kmenta, J. and Ramsey, J. B., eds.,* 1981, pp. 283–327.
[G: U.S.]

Smyth, David J. and Ash, J. C. K. The Underestimation of Forecasts and the Variability of Predictions and Outcomes. *Bull. Econ. Res.,* May 1981, *33*(1), pp. 37–44. [G: U.K.]

Suciu, Camelia Raţiu. On the Cause-Effect Relation in the Study of Goods Demand. *Econ. Computat. Cybern. Stud. Res.,* 1981, *15*(3), pp. 31–39.
[G: 9212]

Sweeney, James L. Model Comparison for Energy Policy and Planning. In *Bayraktar, B. A., et al., eds.,* 1981, pp. 259–85. [G: U.S.]

Sylos Labini, Paolo. Some Reflections on a Model Built with Rudimentary Means. *Rev. Econ. Cond. Italy,* June 1981, (2), pp. 305–08. [G: Italy]

Ugonotto, Elio. Modelling Culture Snags Met While Working on Mosyl. *Rev. Econ. Cond. Italy,* June 1981, (2), pp. 309–22. [G: Italy]

Visco, Ignazio. On the Derivation of Reduced Forms of Rational Expectations Models. *Europ. Econ. Rev.,* June/July 1981, *16*(2/3), pp. 355–65.

133 General Outlook and Stabilization Theories and Policies

1330 General Outlook

Alho, Kari. Pääoman tuotto Suomessa. (The Rate of Return in Finland. With English summary.) *Kansant. Aikak.,* 1981, *77*(2), pp. 151–61.
[G: Finland]

Anderson, William S. Proceedings of the Seminar on Productivity: Statement. In *U.S. Congress, Joint Economic Committee (I),* 1981, pp. 149–66.
[G: U.S.; Japan]

Ariki, Soichiro. Japan's Economy at the Crossroads: An Analysis of Conditions for Her Survival. *Rivista Int. Sci. Econ. Com.,* July–August 1981, *28*(7–8), pp. 644–62. [G: Japan]

Arndt, Heinz W. Survey of Recent Developments. *Bull. Indonesian Econ. Stud.,* November 1981, *17*(3), pp. 1–24. [G: Indonesia]

Ayres, Robert L. Mexico–United States Relations: The Future of the Relationship. In *Purcell, S. K., ed.,* 1981, pp. 195–208. [G: Mexico; U.S.]

Bachár, Vladislav. Crisis Processes in Present-Day Capitalism. *Czech. Econ. Digest.,* May 1981, (3), pp. 54–74. [G: OECD; MDCs]

Balassa, Bela. Policies for Stable Economic Growth in Turkey. In *Balassa, B.,* 1981, pp. 297–328.
[G: Turkey]

Bautista, Romeo M. Incomes and Prices: Assessment and Prospects. *Philippine Econ. J.,* 1981, *20*(2), pp. 151–58. [G: Philippines]

Bergsten, C. Fred. The International Economic Policy of the United States: An Assessment and Agenda for the Future. In *Bergsten, C. F., ed.,* 1981, pp. 3–21. [G: U.S.]

Bombach, Gottfried. The Contributions of the Economics of Growth to Economic Policies: Comment. In *Giersch, H., ed. (II),* 1981, pp. 467–75.

Bosworth, Barry P. The Economic Environment for Regulation in the 1980s. *Natural Res. J.,* July 1981, *21*(3), pp. 441–58. [G: U.S.]

Bosworth, Barry P. The Economic Environment for Regulation in the 1980s. In *Peskin, H. M.; Portney, P. R. and Kneese, A. V., eds.,* 1981, pp. 7–24. [G: U.S.]

Brown, Gary and Krislov, Joseph. The Determinants of Mediation Activity: A Two-Country Comparison. *J. Lab. Res.,* Spring 1981, *2*(1), pp. 157–62. [G: U.S.; U.K.]

Browning, E. S. East Asia in Search of a Second Economic Miracle. *Foreign Aff.,* Fall 1981, *60*(1), pp. 123–47. [G: E. Asia]

Buira Seira, Ariel. Recession, Inflation and the International Monetary System. *World Devel.,* November/December 1981, *9*(11/12), pp. 1115–28.
[G: MDCs; LDCs]

Burki, Shahid Javed. The Prospects for the Developing World: A Review of Recent Forecasts. *Finance Develop.,* March 1981, *18*(1), pp. 20–24.
[G: LDCs]

Caldwell, J. Alexander. The Economic and Financial Outlook for the Developing Countries of East Asia: Trends and Issues. In *Hewett, R. B., ed.*, 1981, pp. 127–52. **[G: East Asia]**

Camaiti, R. The Long Italian Economic Recession: 1981–1982. *Econ. Notes*, 1981, *10*(3), pp. 159–64. **[G: Italy]**

Colombo, Umberto. Energy in Europe in the 1980s. *Giorn. Econ.*, May–June 1981, *40*(5–6), pp. 319–51. **[G: EEC]**

Cornelius, Wayne A. Immigration, Mexican Development Policy, and the Future of U.S.–Mexican Relations. In *McBride, R. H., ed.*, 1981, pp. 104–27. **[G: Mexico; U.S.]**

Daroesman, Ruth. Survey of Recent Developments. *Bull. Indonesian Econ. Stud.*, July 1981, *17*(2), pp. 1–41. **[G: Indonesia]**

Dobozi, István. The Fifth Hungarian-US Economic Round-Table. *Acta Oecon.*, 1981, *26*(1–2), pp. 186–94. **[G: Hungary; U.S.]**

Dobozi, István and Inotai, András. Prospects of Economic Cooperation between CMEA Countries and Developing Countries. In *Saunders, C. T., ed. (I)*, 1981, pp. 48–65. **[G: CMEA; LDCs]**

Dobrska, Zofia. The Present World Economic Situation and Structural Changes in Developing Countries. In *[Lipiński, E.]*, 1981, pp. 165–76. **[G: LDCs]**

Downer, Joseph P. Proceedings of the Seminar on Energy: Statement. In *U.S. Congress, Joint Economic Committee (I)*, 1981, pp. 505–14. **[G: U.S.; Other Countries]**

Eckstein, Otto. Expectations and the Economy: Statement. In *U.S. Congress, Joint Economic Committee (II)*, 1981, pp. 7–9. **[G: U.S.]**

El-Shibly, M. and Thirlwall, A. P. Dual-Gap Analysis for the Sudan. *World Devel.*, February 1981, *9*(2), pp. 193–200. **[G: Sudan]**

Gasparini, Innocenzo. Economic Trends and Problems in the 1980s. *Giorn. Econ.*, May–June 1981, *40*(5–6), pp. 267–86. **[G: EEC; LDCs]**

Genetski, Robert J. The Impact of the Reagan Administration's Economic Proposals (Simulations with the Harris Monetarist–Supply Side Model). In *Shadow Open Market Committee (II)*, 1981, pp. 13–38. **[G: U.S.]**

Glassman, James E. and Sege, Ronald A. The Recent Inflation Experience. *Fed. Res. Bull.*, May 1981, *67*(5), pp. 389–97. **[G: U.S.]**

Haberler, Gottfried. The Economic Malaise of the 1980s: A Positive Program for a Benevolent and Enlightened Dictator. In *Fellner, W., ed.*, 1981, pp. 215–44.

Hager, Wolfgang. The Strains on the International System. In *Saunders, C. T., ed. (II)*, 1981, pp. 287–309. **[G: LDCs; MDCs]**

Hamrin, Robert. The Road to Qualitative Growth. In *Cleveland, H., ed.*, 1981, pp. 115–52. **[G: U.S.]**

Hartman, Robert W. The Budget Outlook. In *Pechman, J. A., ed.*, 1981, pp. 185–228. **[G: U.S.]**

Hästö, Stig H. Industrins konjunkturutsikter. (Industry's Economic Prospects. With English summary.) *Ekon. Samfundets Tidskr.*, 1981, *34*(1), pp. 23–27. **[G: Finland]**

Hatch, Orrin G. The Politics of Supply-Side Eco-

nomics. In *Meyer, L. H., ed.*, 1981, pp. 255–62. **[G: U.S.]**

Healey, Derek. Survey of Recent Developments. *Bull. Indonesian Econ. Stud.*, March 1981, *17*(1), pp. 1–35. **[G: Indonesia]**

Hidasi, Gábor. China's Economy in the Nineteen-Eighties (Problems and Prospects). *Acta Oecon.*, 1981, *27*(1–2), pp. 141–62. **[G: China]**

Hirschman, Albert O. Policymaking and Policy Analysis in Latin America—a Return Journey. In *Hirschman, A. O.*, 1981, *1975*, pp. 142–66. **[G: Latin America]**

Hughes, Helen. The New Industrial Countries in the World Economy: Pessimism and a Way Out. In *Saunders, C. T., ed. (II)*, 1981, pp. 97–131. **[G: LDCs; MDCs]**

Imazato, Hiroki. Japanese Economy in the Eighties. *Rivista Int. Sci. Econ. Com.*, July–August 1981, *28*(7–8), pp. 682–88. **[G: Japan]**

Jones, Reginald H. Toward a New Industrial Policy. In *Wachter, M. L. and Wachter, S. M., eds.*, 1981, pp. 9–16. **[G: U.S.]**

Jonung, Lars. The Depression in Sweden and the United States: A Comparison of Causes and Policies. In *Brunner, K., ed.*, 1981, pp. 286–315. **[G: Sweden; U.S.]**

Katano, Hikoji. Current Situations of World Economy and Global Adjustment of Industries. *Kobe Econ. Bus. Rev.*, 1981, (27), pp. 11–35. **[G: Global]**

Klein, Lawrence R. Project Link: Policy Implications for the World Economy. In *Evan, W. M., ed.*, 1981, pp. 91–106.

Kouri, Pentti J. K. and Braga de Macedo, Jorge. Perspectives on the Stagflation of the 1970's. In *Giersch, H, ed. (I)*, 1981, pp. 211–53. **[G: OECD]**

Leijonhufvud, Axel. Expectations: Policymaker's Predicament. In *U.S. Congress, Joint Economic Committee (II)*, 1981, pp. 40–47.

Loesch, Dieter. The Economic Present and the Future of West Germany. *Giorn. Econ.*, May–June 1981, *40*(5–6), pp. 287–99. **[G: W. Germany]**

Luben, Dušan. L'économie tchécoslovaque et ses perspectives. (Czechoslovakian Economy and Perspectives. With English summary.) *Ann. Sci. Écon. Appl.*, 1981, *37*(3), pp. 109–27. **[G: Czechoslovakia]**

Lundberg, Erik. The Contributions of the Economics of Growth to Economic Policies. In *Giersch, H., ed. (II)*, 1981, pp. 447–66.

de Macedo, Jorge Braga. International Investment, Migration and Finance: Issues and Policies: Comment. *Economia (Portugal)*, January 1981, *5*(1), pp. 111–15.

Mazzocchi, Giancarlo. Unemployment in Italy and Europe in the 1980s. *Giorn. Econ.*, May–June 1981, *40*(5–6), pp. 363–70. **[G: Italy; W. Europe]**

McNamara, Robert S. To the Board of Governors, Belgrade, Yugoslavia, October 2, 1979. In *McNamara, R. S.*, 1981, *1979*, pp. 565–610. **[G: OECD; LDCs]**

McNees, Stephen K. The Optimists and the Pessimists: Can We Tell Whose Forecast Will Be Better? *New Eng. Econ. Rev.*, May/June 1981, pp. 5–14. **[G: U.S.]**

Melchor, Alejandro, Jr. Resource Management: Some Problems and Issues in the 1980s. In *Hewett, R. B., ed.*, 1981, pp. 164–76.
[G: Pacific Basin]

Minsky, Hyman P. The United States' Economy in the 1980s: The Financial Past and Present as a Guide to the Future. *Giorn. Econ.*, May–June 1981, *40*(5–6), pp. 301–17. **[G: U.S.]**

Molitor, Bernhard. International Investment, Migration and Finance: Issues and Policies: Comment. *Economia (Portugal)*, January 1981, *5*(1), pp. 105–10.

Nelson, Richard R. The Contributions of the Economics of Growth to Economic Policies: Comments. In *Giersch, H., ed. (II)*, 1981, pp. 476.

Neumann, Manfred J. M. Under Compulsion for Adjustment: The Annual Report 1980/81 of the West German Council of Economic Experts. *Z. ges. Staatswiss.*, June 1981, *137*(2), pp. 309–17.
[G: W. Germany]

O'Sullivan, John. Is Mrs. Thatcher Curing the British Disease? In *Gatti, J. F., ed.*, 1981, pp. 59–85. **[G: U.K.]**

Odell, Peter R. International Energy Issues: The Next Ten Years. In *Tempest, P., ed.*, 1981, pp. 187–202.

Packer, Arnold and Steger, Wilbur. Energy/Employment Policy Analysis: International Impacts of Alternative Energy Technologies. In *Tempest, P., ed.*, 1981, pp. 99–117.

Paine, Suzanne. International Investment, Migration and Finance: Issues and Policies. *Economia (Portugal)*, January 1981, *5*(1), pp. 63–104.

Parra, Francisco Ramon. World Energy Balances: Looking to 2020: Commentary. In *OPEC, Public Information Dept.*, 1981, pp. 73–75.

Pechman, Joseph A. Setting National Priorities: The 1982 Budget: Introduction and Summary. In *Pechman, J. A., ed.*, 1981, pp. 1–16. **[G: U.S.]**

Pechman, Joseph A. and Bosworth, Barry P. The Federal Budget, Fiscal Years 1980–82. In *Pechman, J. A., ed.*, 1981, pp. 17–44. **[G: U.S.]**

Pekkala, Ahti. Talousarvio vuodelle 1982. (The Budget for 1982. With English summary.) *Kansant. Aikak.*, 1981, *77*(4), pp. 403–11.

Regan, Donald T. Peas, People, and the Economy. In *Wachter, M. L. and Wachter, S. M., eds.*, 1981, pp. 17–22. **[G: U.S.]**

Reichley, A. James. Setting National Priorities: The 1982 Budget: A Change in Direction. In *Pechman, J. A., ed.*, 1981, pp. 229–60. **[G: U.S.]**

Reuss, Henry S. Can American Industry Be Born Again? In *Wachter, M. L. and Wachter, S. M., eds.*, 1981, pp. 23–29. **[G: U.S.]**

Reuss, Henry S. Expectations and the Economy: Introduction. In *U.S. Congress, Joint Economic Committee (II)*, 1981, pp. 1–3. **[G: U.S.]**

Russell, Milton. The Energy Problem in the 1980s. *Giorn. Econ.*, May–June 1981, *40*(5–6), pp. 353–61.

Ruttley, E. World Energy Balances: Looking to 2020. In *OPEC, Public Information Dept.*, 1981, pp. 51–71. **[G: Global]**

Sansón, Carlos E. Latin America and the Caribbean:

A Medium-Term Outlook. *Finance Develop.*, September 1981, *18*(3), pp. 34–37.
[G: Latin America; Caribbean]

Saunders, Christopher T. The Political Economy of New and Old Industrial Countries: Introduction and Selective Summary. In *Saunders, C. T., ed. (II)*, 1981, pp. 1–24. **[G: Global]**

Sloan, Judith. The Australian Labour Market. *Australian Bull. Lab.*, December 1981, *8*(1), pp. 3–20. **[G: MDCs; Australia]**

Stanković, Dušan. Matrica pokazatelja poslovnog uspeha osnovne organizacije udruženog rada. (Matrix of Indicators of Business Results of the Firm. With English summary.) *Econ. Anal. Worker's Manage.*, 1981, *15*(4), pp. 539–54.
[G: Yugoslavia]

Strümpel, Burkhard. Needs and Economic Paradigms. In *Molt, W.; Hartmann, H. A. and Stringer, P., eds.*, 1981, pp. 269–72.

Talamona, Mario. Economic Efficiency, Structural Change and Social Policies for the 1980s. *Giorn. Econ.*, May–June 1981, *40*(5–6), pp. 379–87.

Thurow, Lester C. Employment and Public Expenditure in USA in the 1980s. *Giorn. Econ.*, May–June 1981, *40*(5–6), pp. 371–78. **[G: U.S.]**

Volcker, Paul A. Statement to Senate Committee on Appropriations, January 27, 1981. *Fed. Res. Bull.*, February 1981, *67*(2), pp. 135–37.
[G: U.S.]

Wasserman, Mark A. and Watt, Shirley N. The Economy in 1980. *Fed. Res. Bull.*, January 1981, *67*(1), pp. 1–12. **[G: U.S.]**

Weidenbaum, Murray L. The Uncertain Recovery in 1981, the Carter Legacy and the Reagan Opportunity. In *U.S. Congress, Joint Economic Committee (I)*, 1981, pp. 100–103. **[G: U.S.]**

Weintraub, Sidney. Inflationary "Expectations": Some Modern Economic Faddishness. In *U.S. Congress, Joint Economic Committee (II)*, 1981, pp. 4–6. **[G: U.S.]**

Yankelovich, Daniel and Kaagan, Larry. "Working Through" to Economic Realism. In *Wachter, M. L. and Wachter, S. M., eds.*, 1981, pp. 509–14. **[G: U.S.]**

Zwass, Adam. The Economic Situation in Poland in Light of the Eighth Party Congress. *Eastern Europ. Econ.*, Fall 1981, *20*(1), pp. 3–19.
[G: Poland]

1331 Stabilization Theories and Policies

Ackley, Gardner. Macroeconomic Policies in Western European Countries: 1973–1977: Comment. In *Giersch, H, ed. (I)*, 1981, pp. 137–42.
[G: W. Europe]

Akiba, Hiroya. Beggar Thy Neighbor, Better Thy Neighbor? Comment. *J. Post Keynesian Econ.*, Fall 1981, *4*(1), pp. 159–61.

Andreatta, Beniamino. Linee essenziali della politica finanziaria e monetaria. (Essential Guidelines of Financial and Monetary Policy. With English summary.) *Bancaria*, April 1981, *37*(4), pp. 348–67. **[G: Italy]**

Arestis, P. Fiscal Actions and "Crowding-Out" in the United Kingdom. *Metroecon.*, Feb.-Oct. 1981, *33*(1–2–3), pp. 205–32. **[G: U.K.]**

Baffi, Paolo. Allocazione delle risorse e politica economica nelle economie contemporanee. (Allocation of Resources and Economic Policy in Contemporary Economies. With English summary.) *Banca-ria*, August 1981, *37*(8), pp. 771–73.   [G: Italy]

Barber, William J. Economics and the Truman Administration: An Academic Perspective. In *Heller, F. H., ed.*, 1981, pp. 135–41.   [G: U.S.]

Barro, Robert J. Rational Expectations and the Role of Monetary Policy. In *Lucas, R. E. and Sargent, T. J., eds.*, 1981, *1976*, pp. 229–59.

Barro, Robert J. The Equilibrium Approach to Business Cycles. In *Barro, R. J.*, 1981, pp. 41–78.

Batchelor, Roy A. Choosing between Money Targets and Targets for Credit: Comments. In *Griffiths, B. and Wood, G. E., eds.*, 1981, pp. 81–85.   [G: U.S.; W. Germany; Italy; Japan]

Benavie, Arthur. Stabilization Policies Which Reverse Stagflation in a Short Run Macromodel. *Southern Econ. J.*, July 1981, *48*(1), pp. 17–25.

Bhalla, Surjit S. India's Closed Economy and World Inflation. In *Cline, W. R., et al.*, 1981, pp. 136–65.   [G: India]

Bird, Peter J. W. N. Reply [Beggar Thy Neighbor, Better Thy Neighbor?]. *J. Post Keynesian Econ.*, Fall 1981, *4*(1), pp. 162.

Black, Stanley W. The Impact of Changes in the World Economy on Stabilization Policies in the 1970s. In *Cline, W. R. and Weintraub, S., eds.*, 1981, pp. 43–77.   [G: LDCs]

Blackaby, F. Monetary Targets: Their Nature and Record in the Major Economies: Comments. In *Griffiths, B. and Wood, G. E., eds.*, 1981, pp. 54–61.   [G: OECD]

Blejer, Mario I. and Mathieson, Donald J. The Preannouncement of Exchange Rate Changes as a Stabilization Instrument. *Int. Monet. Fund Staff Pap.*, December 1981, *28*(4), pp. 760–92.

Boskin, Michael. Economic Growth: The Central Issue: Answers: Economic Reforms are Important. In *Inst. for Contemp. Studies*, 1981, pp. 53–55.   [G: U.S.]

Boskin, Michael J. Economic Growth: The Central Issue. In *Inst. for Contemp. Studies*, 1981, pp. 39–47.   [G: U.S.]

Bosworth, Barry P. The Economic Environment for Regulation in the 1980s. In *Peskin, H. M.; Portney, P. R. and Kneese, A. V., eds.*, 1981, pp. 7–24.   [G: U.S.]

Boyes, William J. and Schlagenhauf, Don E. Price Controls in an Open Economy. *J. Macroecon.*, Summer 1981, *3*(3), pp. 391–408.

Bradley, J. and O'Raifeartaigh, C. Optimal Control and Policy Analysis with a Model of a Small Open Economy: The Case of Ireland. In *Janssen, J. M. L.; Pau, L. F. and Straszak, A. J., eds.*, 1981, pp. 85–90.   [G: Ireland]

Bray, J. Design and Testing of Economic Policy in a Mixed Economy. In *Janssen, J. M. L.; Pau, L. F. and Straszak, A. J., eds.*, 1981, pp. 11–20.   [G: U.K.]

Brittain, Bruce. Choosing between Money Targets and Targets for Credit. In *Griffiths, B. and Wood, G. E., eds.*, 1981, pp. 62–80.   [G: U.S.; W. Germany; Italy; Japan]

Brough, A. T. and Curtin, T. R. C. Growth and

Stability: An Account of Fiscal and Monetary Policy. In *Killick, T., ed.*, 1981, pp. 37–51.   [G: Kenya]

Bruno, Michael and Sachs, Jeffrey. Supply versus Demand Approaches to the Problem of Stagflation. In *Giersch, H, ed. (1)*, 1981, pp. 15–60.   [G: Selected OECD]

Budd, Alan. Problems of Monetary Targeting in the UK: Comments. In *Griffiths, B. and Wood, G. E., eds.*, 1981, pp. 121–28.   [G: U.K.]

Budd, Alan. The Development of Demand Management: Comments. In *[Cairncross, A.]*, 1981, pp. 52–56.

Buiter, Willem H. The Role of Economic Policy after the New Classical Macroeconomics. In *Currie, D.; Nobay, R. and Peel, D., eds.*, 1981, pp. 233–79.

Buiter, Willem H. The Superiority of Contingent Rules over Fixed Rules in Models with Rational Expectations. *Econ. J.*, September 1981, *91*(363), pp. 647–70.

Buiter, Willem H. and Gersovitz, Mark. Issues in Controllability and the Theory of Economic Policy. *J. Public Econ.*, February 1981, *15*(1), pp. 33–43.

Buiter, Willem H. and Miller, Marcus. The Thatcher Experiment: The First Two Years. *Brookings Pap. Econ. Act.*, 1981, (2), pp. 315–67.   [G: U.K.]

Cady, Darrel. Economics and the Truman Administration: The Historical Record: A Bibliographic Essay. In *Heller, F. H., ed.*, 1981, pp. 143–70.   [G: U.S.]

Cagan, Phillip. Some Macroeconomic Impacts of the National Industrial Recovery Act, 1933–35: Comments. In *Brunner, K., ed.*, 1981, pp. 282–85.   [G: U.S.]

Cagan, Phillip. Two Pitfalls in the Conduct of Antiinflationary Monetary Policy. In *Fellner, W., ed.*, 1981, pp. 19–52.   [G: U.S.]

Cairncross, Alec. The Relationship between Fiscal and Monetary Policy. *Banca Naz. Lavoro Quart. Rev.*, December 1981, (139), pp. 375–93.

Calvo, Guillermo A. On the Time Consistency of Optimal Policy in a Monetary Economy. In *Lucas, R. E. and Sargent, T. J., eds.*, 1981, *1978*, pp. 639–58.

Canzoneri, Matthew B. Stability in Financial and Labor Markets: Is There a Tradeoff? *Southern Econ. J.*, January 1981, *47*(3), pp. 617–29.

Cargill, Thomas F. and Meyer, Robert A. Revealed Preferences in Macroeconomic Policy Decisions. *J. Macroecon.*, Spring 1981, *3*(2), pp. 205–26.   [G: U.S.]

Caspersen, Finn M. W. Proceedings of the Seminar on Inflation: Statement. In *U.S. Congress, Joint Economic Committee (1)*, 1981, pp. 43–48.   [G: U.S.]

Cavaco Silva, Aníbal. Enquadramento global do desenvolvimento económico português. (The Global Framework of the Portuguese Economic Development. With English summary.) *Economia (Portugal)*, May 1981, *5*(2), pp. 375–88.   [G: Portugal]

Chander, R.; Robless, C. L. and Teh, K. P. Malaysian Growth and Price Stabilization. In *Cline,*

W. R., et al., 1981, pp. 208–27. [G: Malaysia]

Chenery, Hollis B. Interactions between Inflation and Trade Regime Objectives in Stabilization Programs: Comment. In *Cline, W. R. and Weintraub, S., eds.*, 1981, pp. 114–16. [G: LDCs]

Chiesa, G. Monetary and Fiscal Policy in a Small Open Economy. In *Janssen, J. M. L.; Pau, L. F. and Straszak, A. J., eds.*, 1981, pp. 253–61. [G: Italy]

Chouraqui, Jean-Claude. Monetary Policy and Economic Activity in France. In *Courakis, A. S., ed.*, 1981, pp. 204–16. [G: France]

Chow, Gregory C. Estimation and Optimal Control of Dynamic Game Models under Rational Expectations. In *Lucas, R. E. and Sargent, T. J., eds.*, 1981, pp. 681–89.

Ciampi, Carlo Azeglio. Il ricupero della stabilità della moneta quale condizione di progresso. (Recovery of Stability of the Lira as a Condition for Progress. With English summary.) *Bancaria*, July 1981, 37(7), pp. 659–65. [G: Italy]

Cleveland, Harold van B. and Bhagavatula, Ramachandra. The Continuing World Economic Crisis. *Foreign Aff.*, 1981, 59(3), pp. 594–616. [G: MDCs]

Cline, William R. Cyclical Growth Links between Industrial and Developing Countries. In *Cline, W. R., et al.*, 1981, pp. 240–56. [G: LDCs; MDCs]

Cline, William R. Economic Stabilization in Peru, 1975–78. In *Cline, W. R. and Weintraub, S., eds.*, 1981, pp. 297–326. [G: Peru]

Cline, William R. World Inflation and the Developing Countries: Policy Response to External Fluctuations. In *Cline, W. R., et al.*, 1981, pp. 228–39. [G: LDCs]

Cline, William R. and Weintraub, Sidney. Economic Stabilization in Developing Countries: Introduction and Overview. In *Cline, W. R. and Weintraub, S., eds.*, 1981, pp. 1–42. [G: LDCs]

Corden, Max. Choosing between Money Targets and Targets for Credit: Comments. In *Griffiths, B. and Wood, G. E., eds.*, 1981, pp. 86–94.

Coutts, Ken, et al. The Economic Consequences of Mrs. Thatcher. *Cambridge J. Econ.*, March 1981, 5(1), pp. 81–93. [G: U.K.]

Craine, Roger and Havenner, Arthur. On Control with Instruments of Differing Frequency. *J. Econ. Dynam. Control*, May 1981, 3(2), pp. 177–81.

Crockett, Andrew D. Stabilization Policies in Developing Countries: Some Policy Considerations. *Int. Monet. Fund Staff Pap.*, March 1981, 28(1), pp. 55–79. [G: LDCs]

Crouch, Colin. The Political Economy of Inflation. In *Gaskin, M., ed.*, 1981, pp. 79–97.

Davidson, Paul. Expectations and Economic Decisionmaking. In *U.S. Congress, Joint Economic Committee (II)*, 1981, pp. 10–25.

Deacon, Alan. Unemployment and Politics in Britain since 1945. In *Showler, B. and Sinfield, A., eds.*, 1981, pp. 59–88. [G: U.K.]

Deissenberg, Christophe. Optimal Stabilization Policy with Control Lags and Imperfect State Observations. *Z. Nationalökon.*, 1981, 41(3–4), pp. 329–52.

Dell, Sidney. The Impact of Changes in the World Economy on Stabilization Policies in the 1970s: Comment. In *Cline, W. R. and Weintraub, S., eds.*, 1981, pp. 77–81. [G: LDCs]

Dervis, Kemal. IS/LM in the Tropics: Diagrammatics of the New Structuralist Macro Critique: Comment. In *Cline, W. R. and Weintraub, S., eds.*, 1981, pp. 503–06. [G: LDCs]

Díaz-Alejandro, Carlos F. Southern Cone Stabilization Plans. In *Cline, W. R. and Weintraub, S., eds.*, 1981, pp. 119–41. [G: Argentina; Chile; Uruguay]

Donovan, Robert J. Truman's Perspective. In *Heller, F. H., ed.*, 1981, pp. 13–21. [G: U.S.]

Drèze, Jacques H. and Modigliani, Franco. The Trade-off between Real Wages and Employment in an Open Economy (Belgium). *Europ. Econ. Rev.*, January 1981, 15(1), pp. 1–40. [G: Belgium]

den Dunnen, Emile. Dutch Economic and Monetary Problems in the 1970s. In *Courakis, A. S., ed.*, 1981, pp. 182–201. [G: Netherlands]

Eliasson, Gunnar. The Firms in the Market Economy—40 Years of Research at IUI. In *Industrial Inst. for Econ. and Soc. Research*, 1981, pp. 13–32. [G: Sweden]

Eltis, Walter. The Failure of the Keynesian Conventional Wisdom. In *Courakis, A. S., ed.*, 1981, pp. 92–110.

Epstein, Gerald. Domestic Stagflation and Monetary Policy: The Federal Reserve and the Hidden Election. In *Ferguson, T. and Rogers, J., eds.*, 1981, pp. 141–95. [G: U.S.]

Fellner, William. Why Policy Makers Need to Pay More Attention to the Crucial Role of Market Expectations. In *U.S. Congress, Joint Economic Committee (II)*, 1981, pp. 35–39.

Fethke, Gary C. and Policano, Andrew J. Cooperative Responses by Public and Private Agents to Aggregate Demand and Supply Disturbances. *Economica*, May 1981, 48(190), pp. 155–71.

Fethke, Gary C. and Policano, Andrew J. Long-Term Contracts and the Effectiveness of Demand and Supply Policies. *J. Money, Credit, Banking*, November 1981, 13(4), pp. 439–53.

Fischer, Stanley. Addendum: Response to Comments by Lucas [Towards an Understanding of the Costs of Inflation: II]. *Carnegie-Rochester Conf. Ser. Public Policy*, Autumn 1981, 15, pp. 53–55. [G: U.S.]

Fischer, Stanley. Long-term Contracts, Rational Expectations, and the Optimal Money Supply Rule. In *Lucas, R. E. and Sargent, T. J., eds.*, 1981, 1977, pp. 261–75.

Fischer, Stanley. Towards an Understanding of the Costs of Inflation: II. *Carnegie-Rochester Conf. Ser. Public Policy*, Autumn 1981, 15, pp. 5–41. [G: U.S.]

Fishlow, Albert. Comment [Employment, Income Distribution, and Programs to Remedy Balance-of-Payments Difficulties] [Stabilization Policies and Their Effects on Employment and Income Distribution: A Latin American Perspective]. In *Cline, W. R. and Weintraub, S., eds.*, 1981, pp. 229–32. [G: Malaysia; Latin America]

FitzRoy, Felix R. Work-Sharing and Insurance Policy: A Cure for Stagflation. *Kyklos*, 1981, *34*(3), pp. 432–47.

de Fontenay, Patrick. Portugal and the IMF: The Political Economy of Stabilization: Comment. In *Braga de Macedo, J. and Serfaty, S., eds.*, 1981, pp. 137–42. **[G: Portugal]**

Foot, M. D. K. W. Monetary Targets: Their Nature and Record in the Major Economies. In *Griffiths, B. and Wood, G. E., eds.*, 1981, pp. 13–46. **[G: OECD]**

Fowler, Henry H. Economics and the Truman Administration: Comments. In *Heller, F. H., ed.*, 1981, pp. 124–28. **[G: U.S.]**

Foxley, Alejandro. Stabilization Policies and Their Effects on Employment and Income Distribution: A Latin American Perspective. In *Cline, W. R. and Weintraub, S., eds.*, 1981, pp. 191–225. **[G: Argentina; Brazil; Chile; Uruguay]**

Freeman, George E. Some Thoughts about Supply Policies. In *Ontario Economic Council, Vol. 2*, 1981, pp. 1–7. **[G: Canada]**

Frenkel, Jacob A. and Mussa, Michael L. Monetary and Fiscal Policies in an Open Economy. *Amer. Econ. Rev.*, May 1981, *71*(2), pp. 253–58.

Friedman, Irving S. The Role of Private Banks in Stabilization Programs. In *Cline, W. R. and Weintraub, S., eds.*, 1981, pp. 235–65. **[G: LDCs]**

Frydman, Roman. Sluggish Price Adjustments and the Effectiveness of Monetary Policy under Rational Expectations: A Comment. *J. Money, Credit, Banking*, February 1981, *13*(1), pp. 94–102.

Giersch, Herbert. Aspects of Growth, Structural Changes, and Employment—A Schumpeterian Perspective. In *Giersch, H, ed. (I)*, 1981, pp. 181–206. **[G: OECD]**

Giersch, Herbert and Lehment, Harmen. Monetary Policy: Does Independence Make a Difference?— The German Experience. In *[von Haberler, G.]*, 1981, pp. 3–15. **[G: W. Germany]**

Goodhart, Charles A. E. Problems of Monetary Targeting in the UK: Comments. In *Griffiths, B. and Wood, G. E., eds.*, 1981, pp. 129–34. **[G: U.K.]**

Goodwin, Crauford A. The Economic Problems Facing Truman. In *Heller, F. H., ed.*, 1981, pp. 2–12. **[G: U.S.]**

Grant, John. Financial Measures as 'Supply-Side' Policies. In *Ontario Economic Council, Vol. 2*, 1981, pp. 63–66.

Griffiths, Brian and Wood, Geoffrey E. Monetary Targets: Introduction. In *Griffiths, B. and Wood, G. E., eds.*, 1981, pp. 1–12.

Guha, Sunil. Income Redistribution through Labour-Intensive Rural Public Works: Some Policy Issues. *Int. Lab. Rev.*, January–February 1981, *120*(1), pp. 67–82. **[G: LDCs]**

Guisinger, Stephen E. Stabilization Policies in Pakistan: The 1970–77 Experience. In *Cline, W. R. and Weintraub, S., eds.*, 1981, pp. 375–99. **[G: Pakistan]**

Gutierrez-Camara, José L. and Vaubel, Roland. Reducing the Cost of Reducing Inflation through Gradualism, Preannouncement or Indexation? The International Evidence. *Weltwirtsch. Arch.*, 1981, *117*(2), pp. 244–61.

Hadjimichalakis, Michael G. The Rose-Wicksell Model: Inside Money, Stability, and Stabilization Policies. *J. Macroecon.*, Summer 1981, *3*(3), pp. 369–90.

Harberger, Arnold C. Comment [Employment, Income Distribution, and Programs to Remedy Balance-of-Payments Difficulties] [Stabilization Policies and Their Effects on Employment and Income Distribution: A Latin American Perspective]. In *Cline, W. R. and Weintraub, S., eds.*, 1981, pp. 226–29. **[G: Malaysia; Latin America]**

Hartle, Douglas G., et al. Stagflation Consequences of the Canadian Tax/Transfer System. In *Ontario Economic Council, Vol. 1*, 1981, pp. 67–105. **[G: Canada; U.S.]**

Helleiner, Gerald K. Stabilization and Development of the Tanzanian Economy in the 1970s: Comment. In *Cline, W. R. and Weintraub, S., eds.*, 1981, pp. 369–74. **[G: Tanzania]**

Heller, H. Robert. The Role of Private Banks in Stabilization Programs: Comment. In *Cline, W. R. and Weintraub, S., eds.*, 1981, pp. 265–68. **[G: LDCs]**

Holly, Sean. The Role of Economic Policy after the New Classical Macroeconomics: Comment. In *Currie, D.; Nobay, R. and Peel, D., eds.*, 1981, pp. 280–85.

Hopkin, Bryan [Sir]. The Development of Demand Management. In *[Cairncross, A.]*, 1981, pp. 33–52. **[G: U.K.]**

Hutchison, Terence W. The Changing Intellectual Climate In Economics. In *Seldon, A., ed.*, 1981, pp. 19–49. **[G: U.K.]**

Izzo, Lucio and Spaventa, Luigi. Macroeconomic Policies in Western European Countries: 1973–1977. In *Giersch, H, ed. (I)*, 1981, pp. 73–136. **[G: W. Europe]**

Jeffers, Dean W. Proceedings of the Seminar on Inflation: Statement. In *U.S. Congress, Joint Economic Committee (I)*, 1981, pp. 56–59. **[G: U.S.]**

Juster, F. Thomas. The Role of Expectations in Economics. In *U.S. Congress, Joint Economic Committee (II)*, 1981, pp. 130–38. **[G: U.S.]**

Karakitsos, Elias and Rustem, Berc. Rules v Discretion: An Optimization Framework. *Brit. Rev. Econ. Issues*, Autumn 1981, *3*(9), pp. 51–70. **[G: W. Germany]**

Katona, George. Expectations in Economics. In *U.S. Congress, Joint Economic Committee (II)*, 1981, pp. 26–34. **[G: U.S.]**

Katznelson, Ira. A Radical Departure: Social Welfare and the Election. In *Ferguson, T. and Rogers, J., eds.*, 1981, pp. 313–40. **[G: U.S.]**

Kaufman, Henry. Reaganomics: Why Isn't Wall Street Convinced? *Challenge*, September/October 1981, *24*(4), pp. 43–48. **[G: U.S.]**

Khan, Mohsin S. and Knight, Malcolm D. Stabilization Programs in Developing Countries: A Formal Framework. *Int. Monet. Fund Staff Pap.*, March 1981, *28*(1), pp. 1–53. **[G: LDCs]**

Kim, Key W. Prospects for the NICs: South Korea. In *Saunders, C. T., ed. (II)*, 1981, pp. 159–82. **[G: S. Korea]**

Kouri, Pentti J. K. The Political Economy of Stabilization: Comment. In *Braga de Macedo, J. and Serfaty, S., eds.*, 1981, pp. 143–52.

[G: Portugal]

Krueger, Anne O. Interactions between Inflation and Trade Regime Objectives in Stabilization Programs. In *Cline, W. R. and Weintraub, S., eds.*, 1981, pp. 83–114. [G: LDCs]

Kydland, Finn E. and Prescott, Edward C. Rules Rather than Discretion: The Inconsistency of Optimal Plans. In *Lucas, R. E. and Sargent, T. J., eds.*, 1981, *1977*, pp. 619–37.

Laffer, Arthur B. and Canto, Victor A. The Measurement of Expectations in an Efficient Market. In *U.S. Congress, Joint Economic Committee (II)*, 1981, pp. 70–93. [G: U.S.]

Laidler, David. Inflation and Unemployment in an Open Economy: A Monetarist View. *Can. Public Policy*, Supplement, April 1981, *7*, pp. 179–88.

[G: Canada]

Laidler, David. Monetarism: An Interpretation and an Assessment. *Econ. J.*, March 1981, *91*(361), pp. 1–28.

Laidler, David. Monetary Targets and The Public Sector Borrowing Requirement: Comments. In *Griffiths, B. and Wood, G. E., eds.*, 1981, pp. 176–79. [G: U.K.]

Lam, Ngo Van. Government Responses to Export Instability in Papua New Guinea. *Malayan Econ. Rev. (See Singapore Econ. Rev.)*, October 1981, *26*(2), pp. 27–45. [G: Papua New Guinea]

Leibinger, Hans-Bodo and Rohwer, Bernd. Die Fiskalpolitik in den Jahren 1974 bis 1979: Ineffiziente Instrumente oder unzulängliche Anwendung? (Fiscal Policy from 1974 to 1979: Inefficient Instruments or Insufficient Application? With English summary.) *Konjunkturpolitik*, 1981, *27*(5), pp. 261–78. [G: W. Germany]

Leijonhufvud, Axel. Keynes and the Classics: First Lecture. In *Leijonhufvud, A.*, 1981, *1969*, pp. 39–54.

Leijonhufvud, Axel. Keynes and the Effectiveness of Monetary Policy. In *Leijonhufvud, A.*, 1981, *1968*, pp. 17–37.

Lipsey, Richard G. Targeting the Base—The Swiss Experience: Comments. In *Griffiths, B. and Wood, G. E., eds.*, 1981, pp. 226–28.

[G: Switzerland]

Lucas, Robert E., Jr. A Review: Paul McCracken et al., *Towards Full Employment and Price Stability*, A Report to the OECD by a Group of Independent Experts, OECD, June 1977. In *Lucas, R. E., Jr.*, 1981, *1976*, pp. 262–70. [G: OECD]

Lucas, Robert E., Jr. Discussion of: Stanley Fischer, "Towards an Understanding of the Costs of Inflation: II." *Carnegie-Rochester Conf. Ser. Public Policy*, Autumn 1981, *15*, pp. 43–52. [G: U.S.]

Lucas, Robert E., Jr. Econometric Policy Evaluation: A Critique. In *Lucas, R. E., Jr.*, 1981, *1976*, pp. 104–30.

Lucas, Robert E., Jr. Rules, Discretion, and the Role of the Economic Advisor. In *Lucas, R. E., Jr.*, 1981, *1980*, pp. 248–61.

Lucas, Robert E., Jr. Unemployment Policy. In *Lucas, R. E., Jr.*, 1981, *1978*, pp. 240–47.

Maldague, Robert. Les politiques "d'ajustement positif" dans la Communauté européenne. (Posi-

tive Adjustment Policies in the European Community. With English summary.) *Revue Écon.*, July 1981, *32*(4), pp. 625–35. [G: EEC]

Malinvaud, Edmond. Supply versus Demand Approaches to the Problem of Stagflation: Comment. In *Giersch, H, ed. (I)*, 1981, pp. 70–72.

[G: Selected OECD]

Martos, Béla. Non-price Control: Report on a Research Trend. In *Janssen, J. M. L.; Pau, L. F. and Straszak, A. J., eds.*, 1981, pp. 1–10.

Matsurra, Tamotsu. The Development of the Welfare State in Japan. *Giorn. Econ.*, January–February 1981, *40*(1–2), pp. 3–17. [G: Japan]

Matthews, R. C. O. Comment on the Papers by Professors Laidler [Monetarism: An Interpretation and an Assessment] and Tobin [The Monetarist Counter Revolution Today—An Appraisal]. *Econ. J.*, March 1981, *91*(361), pp. 43–48.

Maynard, Geoffrey. Macroeconomic Theory and United Kingdom Economic Policy. In *Harris, S. and Maynard, G.*, 1981, pp. 1–19. [G: U.K.]

McCallum, Bennett T. Monetarist Principles and the Money Stock Growth Rule. *Amer. Econ. Rev.*, May 1981, *71*(2), pp. 134–38.

McCallum, Bennett T. Price-Level Stickiness and the Feasibility of Monetary Stabilization Policy with Rational Expectations. In *Lucas, R. E. and Sargent, T. J., eds.*, 1981, *1977*, pp. 277–84.

McCallum, Bennett T. Sluggish Price Adjustments and the Effectiveness of Monetary Policy under Rational Expectations: A Reply. *J. Money, Credit, Banking*, February 1981, *13*(1), pp. 103–04.

McCallum, Bennett T. The Current State of the Policy-Ineffectiveness Debate. In *Lucas, R. E. and Sargent, T. J., eds.*, 1981, *1979*, pp. 285–92.

[G: U.S.]

McCrickard, Donald L. Macroeconomic Stability and the Initiation of Exchange-Rate Adjustments. *Southern Econ. J.*, January 1981, *47*(3), pp. 655–63.

McKinnon, Ronald I. Southern Cone Stabilization Plans: Comment. In *Cline, W. R. and Weintraub, S., eds.*, 1981, pp. 141–46. [G: Argentina; Chile; Uruguay]

Meade, James E. Changing Perceptions of Economic Policy: Concluding Remarks. In *[Cairncross, A.]*, 1981, pp. 259–66. [G: U.K.]

Middleton, P. E., et al. Monetary Targets and the Public Sector Borrowing Requirement. In *Griffiths, B. and Wood, G. E., eds.*, 1981, pp. 135–75. [G: U.K.]

Minford, Patrick. Monetary Targets: Their Nature and Record in the Major Economies: Comments. In *Griffiths, B. and Wood, G. E., eds.*, 1981, pp. 47–53. [G: OECD]

Mitchell, Austin. Political Aspects of Unemployment: The Alternative Policy. In *Crick, B., ed.*, 1981, *1981*, pp. 38–50. [G: U.K.]

Mork, Knut Anton and Hall, Robert E. Macroeconomic Analysis of Energy Price Shocks and Offsetting Policies: An Integrated Approach. In *Mork, K. A., ed.*, 1981, pp. 43–62. [G: U.S.]

Morse, David A. The Role of the Labor Department. In *Heller, F. H., ed.*, 1981, pp. 37–49.

[G: U.S.]

Nordhaus, William D. Policy Responses to the Productivity Slowdown. In *Federal Reserve Bank of Boston (1)*, 1981, pp. 147–72. [G: U.S.]

Obstfeld, Maurice. Macroeconomic Policy, Exchange-Rate Dynamics, and Optimal Asset Accumulation. *J. Polit. Econ.*, December 1981, *89*(6), pp. 1142–61.

Olson, Mancur. "Incentives-Based" Stabilization Policies and the Evolution of the Macroeconomic Problem. In *Claudon, M. P. and Cornwall, R. R., eds.*, 1981, pp. 37–77.

Oshima, Harry T. Policy Implications for Southeast Asia in the Low Growth Decade of the 1980s. *Phillipine Rev. Econ. Bus.*, Sept. & Dec. 1981, *18*(3/4), pp. 116–31. [G: Asian LDCs]

Papanek, Gustav F. Stabilization Policies in Pakistan: The 1970–77 Experience: Comment. In *Cline, W. R. and Weintraub, S., eds.*, 1981, pp. 399–405. [G: Pakistan]

Peel, David A. On Fiscal and Monetary Stabilization Policy under Rational Expectations. *Public Finance*, 1981, *36*(2), pp. 290–96.

Peston, Maurice H. The Integration of Monetary, Fiscal and Incomes Policy. *Lloyds Bank Rev.*, July 1981, (141), pp. 1–13.

Prachowny, Martin F. J. Sectoral Conflict over Stabilisation Policies in Small Open Economies. *Econ. J.*, September 1981, *91*(363), pp. 671–84.

Quiggin, John C. and Anderson, Jock R. Price Bands and Buffer Funds. *Econ. Rec.*, March 1981, *57*(156), pp. 67–73.

Riese, Hajo. Wirtschaftspolitik unter dem Regime der Stagnation: Bemerkungen zu einem Symposium des Deutschen Instituts für Wirtschaftsforschung. (Economic Policy and Stagnation. With English summary.) *Konjunkturpolitik*, 1981, *27*(4), pp. 227–46.

Robinson, Joan. The Age of Growth. In *Robinson, J.*, 1981, *1979*, pp. 33–42.

Rosner, Peter. Notes on "The Welfare Cost of Permanent Inflation and Optimal Short-Run Economic Policy" *Empirica*, 1981, (2), pp. 291–300.

Ruini, Carlo. Disinflation and Productive Investments in the Government's Programme. *Rev. Econ. Cond. Italy*, October 1981, (3), pp. 515–30. [G: Italy]

Saks, Daniel H. Wage Determination During Periods of High Inflation. In *Dennis, B. D., ed.*, 1981, pp. 128–34. [G: U.S.]

Salvati, Michele. May 1968 and the Hot Autumn of 1969: The Responses of Two Ruling Classes. In *Berger, S., ed.*, 1981, pp. 329–63. [G: France; Italy]

Sandblom, C. L. and Banasik, J. L. Optimal and Suboptimal Controls of a Canadian Model. In *Janssen, J. M. L.; Pau, L. F. and Straszak, A. J., eds.*, 1981, pp. 71–78. [G: Canada]

Sarcinelli, Mario. Policy-Making and Macro-economic Models: A Symbiosis? *Econ. Notes*, 1981, *10*(1), pp. 3–12.

Sargent, J. R. Problems of Monetary Targeting in the UK. In *Griffiths, B. and Wood, G. E., eds.*, 1981, pp. 95–120. [G: U.K.]

Sargent, Thomas J. The Observational Equivalence of Natural and Unnatural Rate Theories of Macroeconomics. In *Lucas, R. E. and Sargent, T. J., eds.*, 1981, *1976*, pp. 553–62.

Sargent, Thomas J. and Wallace, Neil. "Rational" Expectations, the Optimal Monetary Instrument, and the Optimal Money Supply Rule. In *Lucas, R. E. and Sargent, T. J., eds.*, 1981, *1975*, pp. 215–28.

Sargent, Thomas J. and Wallace, Neil. Rational Expectations and the Theory of Economic Policy. In *Lucas, R. E. and Sargent, T. J., eds.*, 1981, *1976*, pp. 199–213.

Sargent, Thomas J. and Wallace, Neil. Some Unpleasant Monetarist Arithmetic. *Fed. Res. Bank Minn. Rev.*, Fall 1981, *5*(3), pp. 1–17.

Saulnier, Raymond J. The President's Economic Report: A Critique. *J. Portfol. Manage.*, Summer 1981, *7*(4), pp. 17–18. [G: U.S.]

Schelbert, H.; Chassot, M. and Granziol, Markus. Stabilisierungspolitik in kleinen offenen Volkswirtschaften am Beispiel der Schweiz empirisch illustriert. (With English summary.) *Z. Wirtschaft. Sozialwissen.*, 1981, *101*(4), pp. 379–416. [G: Switzerland]

Schiltknecht, Kurt. Targeting the Base—The Swiss Experience. In *Griffiths, B. and Wood, G. E., eds.*, 1981, pp. 211–25. [G: Switzerland]

Schmitt, Hans O. Estabilização económica e crescimento em Portugal. (With English summary.) *Economia (Portugal)*, May 1981, *5*(2), pp. 325–73. [G: Portugal]

Schydlowsky, Daniel M. Economic Stabilization in Peru, 1975–78: Comment. In *Cline, W. R. and Weintraub, S., eds.*, 1981, pp. 326–32. [G: Peru]

Şenses, Fikret. Short-Term Stabilization Policies in a Developing Economy: The Turkish Experience in 1980 in Long-Term Perspective. *METU*, 1981, *8*(1 & 2), pp. 409–52. [G: Turkey]

Sheffrin, Steven M. Taxation and Automatic Stabilizers. *Public Finance*, 1981, *36*(1), pp. 99–107.

Showler, Brian. Political Economy and Unemployment. In *Showler, B. and Sinfield, A., eds.*, 1981, pp. 27–58. [G: U.K.]

Shoyama, T. K. Stagflation Consequences of the Canadian Tax/Transfer System: Comments. In *Ontario Economic Council, Vol. 1*, 1981, pp. 105–13. [G: Canada; U.S.]

Siebert, Horst. Strategische Ansatzpunkte der Rohstoffpolitik der Industrienationen nach der Theorie des intertemporalen Ressourcenangebots. (Strategies of Natural Resource Policy for the Industrial Nations According to the Theory of Intertemporal Allocation. With English summary.) *Konjunkturpolitik*, 1981, *27*(5), pp. 297–310. [G: W. Germany]

Sinai, Allen. New Approaches to Stabilization Policy and the Effects on U.S. Financial Markets. *Nat. Tax J.*, September 1981, *34*(3), pp. 341–72.

Siri, Gabriel and Domínguez, Luis Raúl. Central American Accommodation to External Disruptions. In *Cline, W. R., et al.*, 1981, pp. 166–207. [G: El Salvador; Guatemala]

Skidelsky, R. Keynes and the Treasury View: The Case For and Against an Active Unemployment Policy 1920–1939. In *Mommsen, W. J., ed.*, 1981, pp. 167–87. [G: U.K.]

Smith, James F. Proceedings of the Seminar on Inflation: Statement. In *U.S. Congress, Joint Eco-*

nomic Committee (I), 1981, pp. 72–91.
[G: U.S.]

Snyder, John W. The Treasury and Economic Policy. In *Heller, F. H., ed.*, 1981, pp. 23–36.
[G: U.S.]

Solow, Robert M. Policy Responses to the Productivity Slowdown: Discussion. In *Federal Reserve Bank of Boston (I)*, 1981, pp. 173–77. [G: U.S.]

Spence, A. Michael. Policies for Stagflation: Rapporteur's Remarks. In *Ontario Economic Council, Vol. 2*, 1981, pp. 55–62.

Sprinkel, Beryl W. Proceedings of the Seminar on Inflation: Statement. In *U.S. Congress, Joint Economic Committee (I)*, 1981, pp. 51–54.
[G: U.S.]

Stallings, Barbara. Portugal and the IMF: The Political Economy of Stabilization. In *Braga de Macedo, J. and Serfaty, S., eds.*, 1981, pp. 101–35.
[G: Portugal; U.K.; Italy]

Stammer, D. W. Macroeconomic Theory and United Kingdom Economic Policy: Comment. In *Harris, S. and Maynard, G.*, 1981, pp. 20–23.
[G: Australia]

Stein, Herbert. The Chief Executive as Chief Economist. In *Fellner, W., ed.*, 1981, pp. 53–78.
[G: U.S.]

Streit, Manfred E. Demand Management and Catallaxy—Reflections on a Poor Policy Record. In *[von Haberler, G.]*, 1981, pp. 17–34.

Supel, Thomas M. Macroeconomic Implications for Tax Indexing in the McCallum-Whitaker Framework. *J. Monet. Econ.*, July 1981, *8*(1), pp. 131–37.

Sushka, Marie Elizabeth. Discussion [Why Problems Do not Go Away: The Case of Inflation]. *J. Econ. Hist.*, March 1981, *41*(1), pp. 29–30.
[G: U.S.]

Tarshis, Lorie. Understanding and Treating Stagflation in Canada's Open Economy. In *Ontario Economic Council, Vol. 2*, 1981, pp. 67–91.
[G: Canada]

Taub, Leon W. The Role of Expectations in Economic Policy. In *U.S. Congress, Joint Economic Committee (II)*, 1981, pp. 139–43.

Taylor, John B. Estimation and Control of a Macroeconomic Model with Rational Expectations. In *Lucas, R. E. and Sargent, T. J., eds.*, 1981, *1979*, pp. 659–80. [G: U.S.]

Taylor, John B. Stabilization, Accommodation, and Monetary Rules. *Amer. Econ. Rev.*, May 1981, *71*(2), pp. 145–49.

Taylor, Lance. IS/LM in the Tropics: Diagrammatics of the New Structuralist Macro Critique. In *Cline, W. R. and Weintraub, S., eds.*, 1981, pp. 465–503. [G: LDCs]

Thurman, Stephan and Berner, Richard. Analysis of Oil Price Shocks in the MPS Model. In *Mork, K. A., ed.*, 1981, pp. 99–124. [G: U.S.]

Tobin, James. Supply versus Demand Approaches to the Problem of Stagflation: Comment. In *Giersch, H, ed. (I)*, 1981, pp. 61–69.
[G: Selected OECD]

Trejo Reyes, Saúl. Case Study of Economic Stabilization: Mexico: Comment. In *Cline, W. R. and Weintraub, S., eds.*, 1981, pp. 292–95.
[G: Mexico]

Trevithick, James. Monetary Targets and The Public Sector Borrowing Requirement: Comment. In *Griffiths, B. and Wood, G. E., eds.*, 1981, pp. 180–82. [G: U.K.]

Tuma, Elias H. Why Problems Do not Go Away: The Case of Inflation. *J. Econ. Hist.*, March 1981, *41*(1), pp. 21–28. [G: U.K.; U.S.]

Turner, Thomas H. and Whiteman, Charles H. Econometric Policy Evaluation under Rational Expectations. *Fed. Res. Bank Minn. Rev.*, Spring-Summer 1981, *5*(2), pp. 6–15.

Turnovsky, Stephen J. The Optimal Intertemporal Choice of Inflation and Unemployment: An Analysis of the Steady State and Transitional Dynamics. *J. Econ. Dynam. Control*, November 1981, *3*(4), pp. 357–84.

Wagner, Helmut. Wirtschaftspolitik im Lichte rationaler Erwartungen. (Economic Policy and Rational Expectations. With English summary.) *Konjunkturpolitik*, 1981, *27*(1), pp. 1–11.

Waldauer, Charles. Comment on "The Variable Rate Value Added Tax as an Anti-Inflation Fiscal Stabilizer." *Nat. Tax J.*, March 1981, *34*(1), pp. 131–32. [G: U.S.]

Wallich, Henry C. Statement to Temporary Subcommittee on Industrial Growth and Productivity, Senate Committee on the Budget, January 27, 1981. *Fed. Res. Bull.*, February 1981, *67*(2), pp. 137–40. [G: U.S.]

Weaver, James H. and Anderson, Arne. Stabilization and Development of the Tanzanian Economy in the 1970s. In *Cline, W. R. and Weintraub, S., eds.*, 1981, pp. 335–69. [G: Tanzania]

Weinstein, Michael M. Some Macroeconomic Impacts of the National Industrial Recovery Act, 1933–1935. In *Brunner, K., ed.*, 1981, pp. 262–81. [G: U.S.]

Weintraub, Sidney. Case Study of Economic Stabilization: Mexico. In *Cline, W. R. and Weintraub, S., eds.*, 1981, pp. 271–92. [G: Mexico]

von Weizsäcker, Carl Christian. Aspects of Growth, Structural Changes, and Employment—A Schumpeterian Perspective: Comment. In *Giersch, H, ed. (I)*, 1981, pp. 207–09.
[G: OECD]

White, Daniel L. The Variable Rate Value Added Tax as an Anti-Inflation Fiscal Stabilizer: A Response. *Nat. Tax J.*, March 1981, *34*(1), pp. 133.
[G: U.S.]

Whitehead, Donald and Bonnell, Sheila. What Ails the Lucky Country: The Debate about Diagnosis. In *Hancock, K., ed.*, 1981, pp. 89–140.
[G: Australia]

Willes, Mark H. Expectations and the Design of Government Economic Policy. In *U.S. Congress, Joint Economic Committee (II)*, 1981, pp. 102–12.

Willett, Thomas D. Macroeconomic Instability and Exchange-rate Volatility. In *[von Haberler, G.]*, 1981, pp. 35–50.

Wohltmann, Hans-Werner. Complete, Perfect, and Maximal Controllability of Discrete Economic Systems. *Z. Nationalökon.*, 1981, *41*(1–2), pp. 39–58.

Wood, Geoffrey E. Targeting the Base—The Swiss Experience: Comments. In *Griffiths, B. and*

Wood, G. E., eds., 1981, pp. 229–34.
[G: Switzerland]

Worrell, Delisle. External Influences and Domestic Policies: The Economies of Barbados and Jamaica. *Soc. Econ. Stud.*, December 1981, *30*(4), pp. 134–55. [G: Barbados; Jamaica]

Yeager, Leland B. Rules versus Authorities Revisited. *Atlantic Econ. J.*, September 1981, *9*(3), pp. 1–9.

Ysander, Bengt-Christer. Taxes and Market Stability. In *Eliasson, G. and Södersten, J., eds.*, 1981, pp. 191–231. [G: Sweden; U.S.]

Zayas, Edison R. Proceedings of the Seminar on Employment: Statement. In *U.S. Congress, Joint Economic Committee (I)*, 1981, pp. 119–24.
[G: U.S.]

1332 Wage and Price Controls

Addison, John T. Incomes Policy: The Recent European Experience. In *Fallick, J. L. and Elliott, R. F., eds.*, 1981, pp. 187–245.
[G: W. Europe]

Andersen, P. S. and Turner, P. Incomes Policy in Australia: The Overseas Experience. In *Hancock, K., ed.*, 1981, *1980*, pp. 51–88. [G: OECD]

Artis, Michael J. Incomes Policies: Some Rationales. In *Fallick, J. L. and Elliott, R. F., eds.*, 1981, pp. 6–22.

Auld, D. A. L., et al. The Impact of the Anti-Inflation Board on Negotiated Wage Settlements: A Reply. *Can. J. Econ.*, May 1981, *14*(2), pp. 328–31.
[G: Canada]

Ault, Richard W. The Presumed Advantages and Real Disadvantages of Rent Control. In *Block, W. and Olsen, E., eds.*, 1981, pp. 55–81.
[G: U.S.]

Bautista, Romeo M. Incomes and Prices: Assessment and Prospects. *Philippine Econ. J.*, 1981, *20*(2), pp. 151–58. [G: Philippines]

Bazdarich, Michael. Some Perspectives on Controlling U.S. Inflation. In *Gale, W. A., ed.*, 1981, pp. 167–91. [G: U.S.]

Bennett, Paul and Kuenstner, Deborah. Natural Gas Controls and Decontrol. *Fed. Res. Bank New York Quart. Rev.*, Winter 1981–82, *6*(4), pp. 50–60. [G: U.S.]

Bentley, Philip. The Industrial Relations Consequences of Incomes Policies. In *Hancock, K., ed.*, 1981, pp. 235–58. [G: Australia]

Bianchi, Patrizio. Price Control in Italy. *Ann. Pub. Co-op. Econ.*, December 1981, *52*(4), pp. 449–64. [G: Italy]

Blandy, Richard. The Political Economy of Incomes Policy. In *Hancock, K., ed.*, 1981, pp. 371–85.
[G: Australia; OECD]

Blinder, Alan S. and Newton, William J. The 1971–1974 Controls Program and the Price Level: An Econometric Post-Mortem. *J. Monet. Econ.*, July 1981, *8*(1), pp. 1–23. [G: U.S.]

Block, Walter. Rent Control: Postscript: A Reply to the Critics. In *Block, W. and Olsen, E., eds.*, 1981, pp. 285–319. [G: Canada]

Bodkin, Ronald G. The Challenge of Inflation and Unemployment in Canada during the 1980s: Would a Tax-Based Incomes Policy Help? *Can.*

Public Policy, Supplement, April 1981, 7, pp. 204–14. [G: Canada]

Boyes, William J. and Schlagenhauf, Don E. The Optimal Structure and Length of an Incomes Policy. *Quart. Rev. Econ. Bus.*, Winter 1981, *21*(4), pp. 45–63.

Chapman, D. R. and Junor, C. W. Profits, Variability of Profits and the Prices Justification Tribunal. *Econ. Rec.*, June 1981, *57*(157), pp. 128–39.
[G: Australia]

Chew, Soon-Beng. Incomes Policy and Wage Inflation in the UK: An Empirical Study. *Malayan Econ. Rev. (See Singapore Econ. Rev.)*, April 1981, *26*(1), pp. 52–73. [G: U.K.]

Chirinko, Robert S. A Further Comment on "Would Tax Shifting Undermine the Tax-Based Incomes Policy?" *J. Econ. Issues*, March 1981, *15*(1), pp. 177–81.

Christensen, Sandra. The Impact of the Anti-Inflation Board on Negotiated Wage Settlements: Comment. *Can. J. Econ.*, May 1981, *14*(2), pp. 327–28. [G: Canada]

Colander, David. Tax- and Market-Based Incomes Policies: The Interface of Theory and Practice. In *Claudon, M. P. and Cornwall, R. R., eds.*, 1981, pp. 79–97.

Colander, David C. New Approaches to Anti-Inflation Policy. *Public Finance*, 1981, *36*(1), pp. 39–54.

Crowley, R. W. Income Control Policies and Industrial Relations in Canada. *Can. Public Policy*, Autumn 1981, *7*(4), pp. 534–49. [G: Canada]

Dahlby, B. G. Measuring the Effect on a Consumer of Stabilizing the Price of a Commodity. *Can. J. Econ.*, August 1981, *14*(3), pp. 440–49.

Davidson, Lawrence S. and Houston, Douglas. A Reexamination of the Nixon Wage-Price Controls: An Application of Time Series Methods. *J. Econ. Bus.*, Spring/Summer 1981, *33*(3), pp. 246–53.
[G: U.S.]

Dienstfrey, Ted. The Politics of Rent Control in the United States: A Program at the Yellow Light. In *Block, W. and Olsen, E., eds.*, 1981, pp. 5–31. [G: U.S.]

Dorfman, Nancy S. Gasoline Distribution Policies in a Shortage: Welfare Impacts on Rich and Poor. *Public Policy*, Fall 1981, *29*(4), pp. 473–505.
[G: U.S.]

Duffy, Norman F. Australia. In *Blum, A. A., ed.*, 1981, pp. 3–36. [G: Australia]

Dugger, William M. Entrenched Corporate Power and Our Options for Dealing with It. *Rev. Soc. Econ.*, October 1981, *39*(2), pp. 133–44.
[G: U.S.]

Elliott, Robert F. and Fallick, J. L. Incomes Policies, Inflation and Relative Pay: An Overview. In *Fallick, J. L. and Elliott, R. F., eds.*, 1981, pp. 246–63.

Fallick, J. L. and Elliott, Robert F. Incomes Policies, Inflation and Relative Pay: Introduction. In *Fallick, J. L. and Elliott, R. F., eds.*, 1981, pp. 1–5.

Fallick, J. L. and Elliott, Robert F. Incomes Policy and the Public Sector. In *Fallick, J. L. and Elliott, R. F., eds.*, 1981, pp. 100–27. [G: U.K.]

Fels, Allan. Policies for Prices. In *Hancock, K., ed.*,

1981, pp. 319–48.   [G: Australia]

Friedman, Milton and Stigler, George J. Roofs or Ceilings? The Current Housing Problem. In *Block, W. and Olsen, E., eds.*, 1981, pp. 87–103.
                                     [G: U.S.]

Frye, Jon and Gordon, Robert J. Government Intervention in the Inflation Process: The Econometrics of "Self-Inflicted Wounds" *Amer. Econ. Rev.*, May 1981, *71*(2), pp. 288–94.   [G: U.S.]

Goodwin, William B. and Carlson, John A. Job-Advertising and Wage Control Spillovers. *J. Human Res.*, Winter 1981, *16*(1), pp. 80–93.   [G: U.S.]

Gribbin, J. D. The Operation of Price Control in the United Kingdom. *Ann. Pub. Co-op. Econ.*, December 1981, *52*(4), pp. 425–48.   [G: U.K.]

Hancock, Keith. The Roles of Incomes Policy: An Introductory Statement. In *Hancock, K., ed.*, 1981, pp. 1–22.

Henry, S. G. B. Incomes Policy and Aggregate Pay. In *Fallick, J. L. and Elliott, R. F., eds.*, 1981, pp. 23–44.   [G: U.K.]

Hochman, Harold M. The Over-Regulated City: A Perspective on Regulatory Procedures in the City of New York. *Public Finance Quart.*, April 1981, *9*(2), pp. 197–219.   [G: U.S.]

Ingham, M. Incomes Policy: A Short History. In *Fallick, J. L. and Elliott, R. F., eds.*, 1981, pp. 264–80.   [G: U.K.]

Isaac, R. Mark and Plott, Charles R. Price Controls and the Behavior of Auction Markets: An Experimental Examination. *Amer. Econ. Rev.*, June 1981, *71*(3), pp. 448–59.

Jenny, F. From Price Controls to Competition Policy in France: The Uneasy Alliance of Economical and Political Considerations. *Ann. Pub. Co-op. Econ.*, December 1981, *52*(4), pp. 477–90.
                                     [G: France]

de Jouvenel, Bertrand. Rent Control: No Vacancies. In *Block, W. and Olsen, E., eds.*, 1981, *1948*, pp. 189–97.   [G: France]

Kaish, Stanley. What Is 'Just and Reasonable' in Rent Control? Why Historic Cost Is More Rational Than Current Value. *Amer. J. Econ. Soc.*, April 1981, *40*(2), pp. 129–37.

Kalymon, Basil A. Apartment Shortages and Rent Control. In *Block, W. and Olsen, E., eds.*, 1981, pp. 233–45.   [G: Canada]

Kristof, Frank S. The Effects of Rent Control and Rent Stabilization in New York City. In *Block, W. and Olsen, E., eds.*, 1981, pp. 125–47.
                                     [G: U.S.]

Lee, Dwight R. Monopoly, Price Controls, and the Exploitation of Nonrenewable Resources. *J. Energy Devel.*, Autumn 1981, *7*(1), pp. 111–20.

Lerner, Abba P. and Colander, David. There is a Cure for Inflation. In *Claudon, M. P. and Cornwall, R. R., eds.*, 1981, pp. 101–08.   [G: U.S.]

Mayer, Thomas. Innovative Incomes Policies: A Skeptic's View. In *Claudon, M. P. and Cornwall, R. R., eds.*, 1981, pp. 197–214.   [G: U.S.]

Mayhew, Ken. Incomes Policy and the Private Sector. In *Fallick, J. L. and Elliott, R. F., eds.*, 1981, pp. 72–99.   [G: U.K.]

McGraw, Thomas K. Discussion [The Response of the Giant Corporations to Wage and Price Controls in World War II] [Planning for Peace: The

Surplus Property Act of 1944]. *J. Econ. Hist.*, March 1981, *41*(1), pp. 136–37.   [G: U.S.]

Mills, D. Quinn. U.S. Incomes Policies in the 1970's—Underlying Assumptions, Objectives, Results. *Amer. Econ. Rev.*, May 1981, *71*(2), pp. 283–87.   [G: U.S.]

Mitchell, Daniel J. B. Direct Intervention in Wage and Price Decisions. In *Ballabon, M. B., ed.*, 1981, pp. 27–69.   [G: U.S.; OECD]

Mortara, Alberto. Price Control: Foreword. *Ann. Pub. Co-op. Econ.*, December 1981, *52*(4), pp. 421–24.   [G: U.K.; Belgium; France; Italy; W. Germany]

Ng, Yew-Kwang. Incomes Policies: Conditions for Voluntary Compliance. *Manchester Sch. Econ. Soc. Stud.*, June 1981, *49*(2), pp. 111–28.

Noakes, B. M. Incomes Policies: An Employer Perspective. In *Hancock, K., ed.*, 1981, pp. 259–71.
                                     [G: Australia]

Nolan, P. I. Incomes Policies: A Trade Union Perspective. In *Hancock, K., ed.*, 1981, pp. 273–95.
                                     [G: Australia]

Nordhaus, William D. Tax-Based Incomes Policies: A Better Mousetrap? In *Claudon, M. P. and Cornwall, R. R., eds.*, 1981, pp. 135–51.
                                     [G: U.S.]

Norman, Neville R. Policies towards Prices—The Influence of Regulation. In *Hancock, K., ed.*, 1981, pp. 349–69.   [G: Australia]

Olsen, Edgar O. Questions and Some Answers about Rent Control: An Empirical Analysis of New York's Experience. In *Block, W. and Olsen, E., eds.*, 1981, pp. 107–21.   [G: U.S.]

Olsen, Edgar O. and Walker, M. A. Rent Control: Alternatives. In *Block, W. and Olsen, E., eds.*, 1981, pp. 267–82.   [G: U.S.]

Paish, F. W. The Economics of Rent Restriction. In *Block, W. and Olsen, E., eds.*, 1981, pp. 151–60.   [G: U.K.]

Pencavel, John H. The American Experience with Incomes Policies. In *Fallick, J. L. and Elliott, R. F., eds.*, 1981, pp. 155–86.   [G: U.S.]

Pennance, F. G. Recent British Experience: A Postscript from 1975. In *Block, W. and Olsen, E., eds.*, 1981, pp. 163–68.   [G: U.K.]

Peston, Maurice H. The Integration of Monetary, Fiscal and Incomes Policy. *Lloyds Bank Rev.*, July 1981, (141), pp. 1–13.

Quaden, Guy. Price Control Policy in Belgium. *Ann. Pub. Co-op. Econ.*, December 1981, *52*(4), pp. 465–76.   [G: Belgium]

Reid, Frank. Control and Decontrol of Wages in the United States: An Empirical Analysis. *Amer. Econ. Rev.*, March 1981, *71*(1), pp. 108–20.
                                     [G: U.S.]

Renshaw, Edward F. Time for an Incomes Policy. *Challenge*, November–December 1981, *24*(5), pp. 50–54.   [G: U.S.]

Rockoff, Hugh. Price and Wage Controls in Four Wartime Periods. *J. Econ. Hist.*, June 1981, *41*(2), pp. 381–401.   [G: U.S.]

Rockoff, Hugh. The Response of the Giant Corporations to Wage and Price Controls in World War II. *J. Econ. Hist.*, March 1981, *41*(1), pp. 123–28.   [G: U.S.]

Rosenberg, Samuel. Incomes Policy: The "TIP" of

the Iceberg. In *Claudon, M. P. and Cornwall, R. R., eds.*, 1981, pp. 175–95. [G: U.S.]

Rydenfelt, Sven. The Rise, Fall, and Revival of Swedish Rent Control. In *Block, W. and Olsen, E., eds.*, 1981, pp. 201–30. [G: Sweden]

Scherer, Peter. The Goals of Incomes Policy. In *Hancock, K., ed.*, 1981, pp. 23–50. [G: Australia; W. Europe]

Seidel, Hans. Incomes Policy in Austria. *Challenge*, September/October 1981, *24*(4), pp. 58–60. [G: Austria]

Seidman, Laurence S. Equity and Tradeoffs in a Tax-Based Incomes Policy. *Amer. Econ. Rev.*, May 1981, *71*(2), pp. 295–300. [G: U.S.]

Seidman, Laurence S. Insurance for Labor under a Tax-Based Incomes Policy. In *Claudon, M. P. and Cornwall, R. R., eds.*, 1981, pp. 109–33. [G: U.S.]

Sheahan, John. Incomes Policies in an Open Economy: Domestic and External Interactions. In *Claudon, M. P. and Cornwall, R. R., eds.*, 1981, pp. 155–74.

Sheehan, Peter. Wages Policy and the Economy in the Seventies and Beyond. In *Hancock, K., ed.*, 1981, pp. 141–70. [G: Australia]

Shulman, David. Real Estate Valuation under Rent Control: The Case of Santa Monica. *Amer. Real Estate Urban Econ. Assoc. J.*, Spring 1981, *9*(1), pp. 38–53. [G: U.S.]

Smith, Vernon L. and Williams, Arlington W. On Nonbinding Price Controls in a Competitive Market. *Amer. Econ. Rev.*, June 1981, *71*(3), pp. 467–74.

Snape, Richard H. Wages Policy and the Economy in the Seventies and Beyond. In *Hancock, K., ed.*, 1981, pp. 170–93. [G: Australia]

Steele, R. Incomes Policies and Low Pay. In *Fallick, J. L. and Elliott, R. F., eds.*, 1981, pp. 128–54. [G: U.K.]

Stollery, Kenneth R. Price Controls on Nonrenewable Resources When Capacity Is Constrained [Price Controls on Non-Renewable Resources: An Intertemporal Analysis]. *Southern Econ. J.*, October 1981, *48*(2), pp. 490–98.

Stowe, David H. Economics and the Truman Administration: Comments. In *Heller, F. H., ed.*, 1981, pp. 129–31. [G: U.S.]

Tanner, Lucretia Dewey and Converse, Mary. The 1978–80 Pay Guidelines: Meeting the Need for Flexibility. *Mon. Lab. Rev.*, July 1981, *104*(7), pp. 16–21. [G: U.S.]

Walker, M. A. A Short Course in Housing Economics. In *Block, W. and Olsen, E., eds.*, 1981, pp. 37–52.

Walker, M. A. Rent Control: Decontrol. In *Block, W. and Olsen, E., eds.*, 1981, pp. 249–61. [G: Canada]

Wallich, Henry C. Statement to Temporary Subcommittee on Industrial Growth and Productivity, Senate Committee on the Budget, January 27, 1981. *Fed. Res. Bull.*, February 1981, *67*(2), pp. 137–40. [G: U.S.]

Weintraub, Sidney. The Carter Economic Council's Thalidomide TIP. *J. Post Keynesian Econ.*, Spring 1981, *3*(3), pp. 459–62.

Weintraub, Sidney. Tips Against Inflation. In *Clau-

don, M. P. and Cornwall, R. R., eds.*, 1981, pp. 7–34. [G: U.S.]

Yerbury, D. The Government, the Arbitration Commission and Wages Policy: The Role of the 'Supporting Mechanisms' under the Whitlam Government. In *Hancock, K., ed.*, 1981, pp. 195–234. [G: Australia]

134 Inflation and Deflation

1340 General

Aho, Teemu and Virtanen, Ilkka. Adequacy of Depreciation Allowances under Inflation. *Liiketaloudellinen Aikak.*, 1981, *30*(4), pp. 351–79. [G: Finland]

Aho, Teemu and Virtanen, Ilkka. Analysis of Lease Financing under Inflation. *Liiketaloudellinen Aikak.*, 1981, *30*(3), pp. 239–77.

Aiginger, Karl. Accelerated Depreciation Matters After All: A Note on the Effects of the Existence and the Utilization of Accelerated Depreciation on Feldstein's Extra Tax on Fictitious Profits. *Empirica*, 1981, (2), pp. 263–75.

Antonioli Corigliano, Magda. Sugli effetti inflazionistici della finanza pubblica in Italia negli anni '70. (On the Inflationary Effects of Public Finance in Italy during the 1970s. With English summary.) *Giorn. Econ.*, March–April 1981, *40*(3–4), pp. 167–82. [G: Italy]

Aponte, Juan B. The Lash of Inflation on a Developing Economy: Puerto Rico, A Case Study. *Ann. Amer. Acad. Polit. Soc. Sci.*, July 1981, *456*, pp. 132–53. [G: Puerto Rico]

Ashley, Richard. Inflation and the Distribution of Price Changes across Markets: A Causal Analysis. *Econ. Inquiry*, October 1981, *19*(4), pp. 650–60. [G: U.S.]

Aubry, Jean-Pierre and Kierzkowski, Henryk. The Transmission of Foreign Price Inflation under Alternative Exchange Rate Regimes: Some Experiments with the RDX2 and MPS Models. In *Courbis, R., ed.*, 1981, pp. 259–77. [G: Canada; U.S.]

Babbel, David F. Inflation, Indexation, and Life Insurance Sales in Brazil. *J. Risk Ins.*, March 1981, *48*(1), pp. 111–35. [G: Brazil]

Baffi, Paolo. L'euroscudo in taluni rapporti finanziari. (The Role of the E.C.U. in Certain Financial Relations. With English summary.) *Bancaria*, March 1981, *37*(3), pp. 251–53. [G: EEC]

Balassa, Bela. Inflation and Trade Liberalization in Korea. In *Balassa, B.*, 1981, pp. 365–79. [G: South Korea]

Behrend, Hilde. Research into Public Accounting Attitudes and the Attitudes of the Public to Inflation. *Managerial Dec. Econ.*, March 1981, *2*(1), pp. 1–8. [G: U.K.]

Berg, Ivar. The Effects of Inflation on and in Higher Education. *Ann. Amer. Acad. Polit. Soc. Sci.*, July 1981, *456*, pp. 99–111.

Bergström, Villy and Södersten, Jan. Inflation, Taxation and Capital Cost. In *Eliasson, G. and Södersten, J., eds.*, 1981, pp. 233–66.

Bhalla, Surjit S. India's Closed Economy and World Inflation. In *Cline, W. R., et al.*, 1981, pp. 136–65. [G: India]

Bhalla, Surjit S. The Transmission of Inflation into Developing Economies. In *Cline, W. R., et al.,* 1981, pp. 52–101. [G: LDCs]

Björklund, Anders and Holmlund, Bertil. The Duration of Unemployment and Unexpected Inflation: An Empirical Analysis. *Amer. Econ. Rev.,* March 1981, *71*(1), pp. 121–31. [G: U.S.; Sweden]

Black, Thomas G. Usefulness of Constant Dollar Accounting Information. *Rev. Bus. Econ. Res.,* Spring 1981, *16*(3), pp. 58–68. [G: U.S.]

Blaich, Robert and Schuster, Walter. Did Fictitious Profits Contribute to the Decline in the Rate of Profit? *Empirica,* 1981, (2), pp. 241–54. [G: Austria]

Blejer, Mario I. Strike Activity and Wage Determination under Rapid Inflation: The Chilean Case. *Ind. Lab. Relat. Rev.,* April 1981, *34*(3), pp. 356–64. [G: Chile]

Blejer, Mario I. The Dispersion of Relative Commodity Prices under Very Rapid Inflation. *J. Devel. Econ.,* December 1981, *9*(3), pp. 347–56. [G: Argentina]

Blinder, Alan S. Monetarism Is Obsolete. *Challenge,* September/October 1981, *24*(4), pp. 35–41. [G: U.S.]

Bondonio, Piervincenzo. Personal Income Taxation, Wage Differentials, and Inflation with Special Reference to Italy. In *Peacock, A. and Forte, F., eds.,* 1981, pp. 49–62. [G: Italy]

Bosworth, Barry P. The Economic Environment for Regulation in the 1980s. *Natural Res. J.,* July 1981, *21*(3), pp. 441–58. [G: U.S.]

Botha, D. J. J. Die Minister en die Ekonomie [Die Huidige Fiskale en Monetêre Beleid in Suid-Afrika]. (With English summary.) *S. Afr. J. Econ.,* 1981, *49*(1), pp. 69–90. [G: S. Africa]

Bowring, Joseph. How Bad Were the Seventies? *Challenge,* July/August 1981, *24*(3), pp. 47–50. [G: U.S.]

van Breda, Michael F. Accounting Rates of Return under Inflation. *Sloan Manage. Rev.,* Summer 1981, *22*(4), pp. 15–28.

Bronfenbrenner, Martin. Some Neglected Microeconomics of Inflation Control. In *Claudon, M. P. and Cornwall, R. R., eds.,* 1981, pp. 233–49. [G: U.S.]

Brown, Ralph J. Inflation and the New Monetary Aggregates. *Bus. Econ.,* May 1981, *16*(3), pp. 30–33.

Bruni, Franco and Porta, Angelo. Allocazione delle risorse e inflazione: Il caso dei mercati finanziari. (Inflation and Resource Allocation: The Case of Financial Markets. With English summary.) *Econ. Int.,* May–August–November 1981, *34*(2–3–4), pp. 261–321. [G: Italy]

Cagan, Phillip. Two Pitfalls in the Conduct of Antiinflationary Monetary Policy. In *Fellner, W., ed.,* 1981, pp. 19–52. [G: U.S.]

Callahan, David W. Defining the Rate of Underlying Inflation. *Mon. Lab. Rev.,* September 1981, *104*(9), pp. 16–19. [G: U.S.]

Callahan, David W.; Clem, Andrew and Wetmore, John. Inflation Cross-Currents: Energy, Food, and Homeownership. *Mon. Lab. Rev.,* June 1981, *104*(6), pp. 14–21. [G: U.S.]

Calleo, David P. Inflation and American Power. *For-eign Aff.,* Spring 1981, *59*(4), pp. 781–812. [G: U.S.]

Caplovitz, David. Making Ends Meet: How Families Cope with Inflation and Recession. *Ann. Amer. Acad. Polit. Soc. Sci.,* July 1981, *456,* pp. 88–98. [G: U.S.]

Carlson, John A. Perceptions (or Misperceptions) of Inflation. In *Gale, W. A., ed.,* 1981, pp. 13–49. [G: U.S.]

Caspersen, Finn M. W. Proceedings of the Seminar on Inflation: Statement. In *U.S. Congress, Joint Economic Committee (I),* 1981, pp. 43–48. [G: U.S.]

Chaikin, Sol C. Proceedings of the Seminar on Employment: Statement. In *U.S. Congress, Joint Economic Committee (I),* 1981, pp. 106–09. [G: U.S.]

Chander, R.; Robless, C. L. and Teh, K. P. Malaysian Growth and Price Stabilization. In *Cline, W. R., et al.,* 1981, pp. 208–27. [G: Malaysia]

Chu, Ke-young and Feltenstein, Andrew. The Welfare Implications of Relative Price Distortions and Inflation: An Analysis of the Recent Argentine Experience. In *Khan, A. and Sirageldin, I., eds.,* 1981, pp. 181–223. [G: Argentina]

Cline, William R. Brazil's Aggressive Response to External Shocks. In *Cline, W. R., et al.,* 1981, pp. 102–35. [G: Brazil]

Cline, William R. Real Economic Effects of World Inflation and Recession. In *Cline, W. R., et al.,* 1981, pp. 10–51. [G: LDCs]

Cline, William R. World Inflation and the Developing Countries: Policy Response to External Fluctuations. In *Cline, W. R., et al.,* 1981, pp. 228–39. [G: LDCs]

Congdon, Tim. Is the Provision of a Sound Currency a Necessary Function of the State? *Nat. Westminster Bank Quart. Rev.,* August 1981, pp. 2–21.

Cornell, Bradford. Relative vs. Absolute Price Changes: An Empirical Study. *Econ. Inquiry,* July 1981, *19*(3), pp. 506–14. [G: U.S.]

Cristini, Giovanni. Il mercato dei titoli a reddito fisso negli anni '70. (The Fixed-Interest Securities Market in the 1970s. With English summary.) *Bancaria,* March 1981, *37*(3), pp. 260–69. [G: Italy]

Curtis, Lynn A. Inflation, Economic Policy, and the Inner City. *Ann. Amer. Acad. Polit. Soc. Sci.,* July 1981, *456,* pp. 46–59. [G: U.S.]

Dawson, Alistair. Sargan's Wage Equation: A Theoretical and Empirical Reconstruction. *Appl. Econ.,* September 1981, *13*(3), pp. 351–63. [G: U.S.]

Dockson, Robert R. and Vance, Jack O. Retirement in Peril: Inflation and the Executive Compensation Program. *Calif. Manage. Rev.,* Summer 1981, *23*(4), pp. 87–94. [G: U.S.]

Dohner, Robert S. Energy Prices, Economic Activity, and Inflation: A Survey of Issues and Results. In *Mork, K. A., ed.,* 1981, pp. 7–41. [G: U.S.]

Doud, Arthur A. and Summers, Anita A. Inflation and the Philadelphia Economy. *Ann. Amer. Acad. Polit. Soc. Sci.,* July 1981, *456,* pp. 13–31. [G: U.S.]

Draper, Anne. Proceedings of the Seminar on Inflation: Statement. In *U.S. Congress, Joint Eco-*

nomic Committee (1), 1981, pp. 54–56.
[G: U.S.]

Eichner, Alfred S. Reagan's Doubtful Game Plan. *Challenge*, May/June 1981, *24*(2), pp. 19–27.
[G: U.S.]

Elliott, Robert F. and Fallick, J. L. Incomes Policies, Inflation and Relative Pay: An Overview. In *Fallick, J. L. and Elliott, R. F., eds.*, 1981, pp. 246–63.

Epstein, Gerald. Domestic Stagflation and Monetary Policy: The Federal Reserve and the Hidden Election. In *Ferguson, T. and Rogers, J., eds.*, 1981, pp. 141–95.
[G: U.S.]

Fellner, William. On the Merits of Gradualism and on a Fall-back Position if It Should Nevertheless Fail: Introductory Remarks. In *Fellner, W., ed.*, 1981, pp. 3–18.
[G: U.S.]

Fieleke, Norman S. Rising Oil Prices and the Industrial Countries. *New Eng. Econ. Rev.*, January/February 1981, pp. 17–28.
[G: U.S.]

Fishburn, Geoffrey. Tax Evasion and Inflation. *Australian Econ. Pap.*, December 1981, *20*(37), pp. 325–32.

Foster, Edward. Who Loses from Inflation? *Ann. Amer. Acad. Polit. Soc. Sci.*, July 1981, *456*, pp. 32–45.

Freebairn, J. W. Assessing Some Effects of Inflation on the Agricultural Sector. *Australian J. Agr. Econ.*, August 1981, *25*(2), pp. 107–22.
[G: Australia]

Freund, William C. and Manchester, Paul B. Productivity and Inflation. In *Hogan, J. D. and Craig, A. M., eds.*, *Vol. 1*, 1981, pp. 53–75.
[G: U.S.]

Fuller, John W. Inflationary Effects on Transportation. *Ann. Amer. Acad. Polit. Soc. Sci.*, July 1981, *456*, pp. 112–22.
[G: U.S.]

Fuller, Russell J. and Petry, Glenn H. Inflation, Return on Equity, and Stock Prices. *J. Portfol. Manage.*, Summer 1981, *7*(4), pp. 19–25.
[G: U.S.]

Gaskin, Maxwell. The Political Economy of Tolerable Survival. In *Gaskin, M., ed.*, 1981, pp. 15–33.
[G: U.K.]

Glassman, James E. and Sege, Ronald A. The Recent Inflation Experience. *Fed. Res. Bull.*, May 1981, *67*(5), pp. 389–97.
[G: U.S.]

Gorham, Michael. The Effect of Inflation on the Rules of Futures Exchanges: A Case Study of the Chicago Mercantile Exchange. *J. Futures Markets*, Fall 1981, *1*(3), pp. 337–45.
[G: U.S.]

Greenwald, Eleanor. Why Doesn't Business Float Indexed Bonds? *Bus. Econ.*, May 1981, *16*(3), pp. 62.
[G: U.S.]

Guthrie, Robert S. The Relationship between Wholesale and Consumer Prices. *Southern Econ. J.*, April 1981, *47*(4), pp. 1046–55.
[G: U.S.]

Gutierrez-Camara, José L. and Vaubel, Roland. Reducing the Cost of Reducing Inflation through Gradualism, Preannouncement or Indexation? The International Evidence. *Weltwirtsch. Arch.*, 1981, *117*(2), pp. 244–61.

Gylfason, Thorvaldur. Interest Rates, Inflation, and the Aggregate Consumption Function. *Rev. Econ. Statist.*, May 1981, *63*(2), pp. 233–45.

Hadaway, Samuel C. and Hadaway, Beverly L. Inflation Protection from Multi-Asset Sector Investments: A Long-Run Examination of Correlation Relationships with Inflation Rates. *Rev. Bus. Econ. Res.*, Spring 1981, *16*(3), pp. 80–89.
[G: U.S.]

Hall, Robert E. Tax Treatment of Depreciation, Capital Gains, and Interest in an Inflationary Economy. In *Hulten, C. R., ed.*, 1981, pp. 149–66.

Haralz, Jonas H. Inflation Experience in Iceland. *J. Post Keynesian Econ.*, Spring 1981, *3*(3), pp. 312–24.
[G: Iceland]

Heller, H. Robert. International Reserves and World-Wide Inflation: Further Analysis. *Int. Monet. Fund Staff Pap.*, March 1981, *28*(1), pp. 230–33.

Hendry, David F. and von Ungern-Sternberg, Thomas. Liquidity and Inflation Effects on Consumers' Expenditure. In *[Stone, R.]*, 1981, pp. 237–60.
[G: U.K.]

Henry, S. G. B. Incomes Policy and Aggregate Pay. In *Fallick, J. L. and Elliott, R. F., eds.*, 1981, pp. 23–44.
[G: U.K.]

Herman, James. Inflationary Expectations and Capital Markets. *Rev. Bus. Econ. Res.*, Spring 1981, *16*(3), pp. 69–79.
[G: U.S.]

Hill, Stephen and Gough, Julian. Discounting Inflation—A Note. *Managerial Dec. Econ.*, June 1981, *2*(2), pp. 121–23.
[G: U.K.]

Hirschman, Albert O. The Social and Political Matrix of Inflation: Elaborations on the Latin American Experience. In *Hirschman, A. O.*, 1981, pp. 177–207.
[G: Latin America]

Janis, Jay. Dealing with Inflation: Ideology vs. Pragmatism. In *Federal Home Loan Bank of San Francisco.*, 1981, pp. 7–12.
[G: U.S.]

Jeffers, Dean W. Proceedings of the Seminar on Inflation: Statement. In *U.S. Congress, Joint Economic Committee (1)*, 1981, pp. 56–59.
[G: U.S.]

Jonung, Lars. Perceived and Expected Rates of Inflation in Sweden. *Amer. Econ. Rev.*, December 1981, *71*(5), pp. 961–68.
[G: Sweden]

Kaufman, Bruce E. Bargaining Theory, Inflation, and Cyclical Strike Activity in Manufacturing. *Ind. Lab. Relat. Rev.*, April 1981, *34*(3), pp. 333–55.
[G: U.S.]

Kaufman, George G. Inflation, Proposition 13 Fever, and Suggested Relief. In *Kaufman, G. G. and Rosen, K. T., eds.*, 1981, pp. 215–21.
[G: U.S.]

Kay, John A. Measuring Economic Performance in an Inflationary Environment. In *Courakis, A. S., ed.*, 1981, pp. 82–90.
[G: U.K.]

Kendrick, John W. Tax Treatment of Depreciation, Capital Gains, and Interest in an Inflationary Economy: Discussion. In *Hulten, C. R., ed.*, 1981, pp. 167–70.

Kiefer, David. The Interaction of Inflation and the U.S. Tax Subsidies of Housing. *Nat. Tax J.*, December 1981, *34*(4), pp. 433–46.
[G: U.S.]

Kincaid, G. Russell. Inflation and the External Debt of Developing Countries. *Finance Develop.*, December 1981, *18*(4), pp. 45–48.
[G: Non-Oil LDCs]

Kouri, Pentti J. K. and Braga de Macedo, Jorge. Perspectives on the Stagflation of the 1970's. In

Giersch, H, ed. (1), 1981, pp. 211–53.
[G: OECD]

Lage, Gerald M. and Greer, Charles R. Adjusting Salaries for the Effects of Inflation. *Rev. Bus. Econ. Res.*, Spring 1981, *16*(3), pp. 1–13.

Lamfalussy, Alexandre. Regole o discrezionalità? Saggio sulla politica monetaria in un contesto inflazionistico. (Rules or Discretionary Powers? Monetary Policy in an Inflationary Context. With English summary.) *Bancaria*, December 1981, *37*(12), pp. 1235–56. [G: Western MDCs]

Landskroner, Yoram. Index-Linked Bond and the Pricing of Capital Assets. *J. Econ. Bus.*, Winter 1981, *33*(2), pp. 143–46.

Leeds, Morton. Inflation and the Elderly: A Housing Perspective. *Ann. Amer. Acad. Polit. Soc. Sci.*, July 1981, *456*, pp. 60–69. [G: U.S.]

Leijonhufvud, Axel. Expectations: Policymaker's Predicament. In *U.S. Congress, Joint Economic Committee (II)*, 1981, pp. 40–47.

Lerner, Abba P. and Colander, David. There is a Cure for Inflation. In *Claudon, M. P. and Cornwall, R. R., eds.*, 1981, pp. 101–08. [G: U.S.]

Levi, Maurice D. and Makin, John H. Fisher, Phillips, Friedman and the Measured Impact of Inflation on Interest: A Reply. *J. Finance*, September 1981, *36*(4), pp. 963–69. [G: U.S.]

Lutz, Mark A. Stagflation as an Institutional Problem. *J. Econ. Issues*, September 1981, *15*(3), pp. 745–68. [G: MDCs]

Macón, Jorge. Argentina: Adjustment for Inflation in Argentine Income Tax Law. *Bull. Int. Fiscal Doc.*, July 1981, *35*(7), pp. 295–300.
[G: Argentina]

Mangiameli, Paul M.; Banks, Jerry and Schwarzbach, Henry. Static Inventory Models and Inflationary Cost Increases. *Eng. Econ.*, Winter 1981, *26*(2), pp. 91–112.

Marquand, David. Tolerable Survival and Politics. In *Gaskin, M., ed.*, 1981, pp. 34–51. [G: U.K.]

Massone, Pedro. Adjustment of Profits for Inflation: Part II. *Bull. Int. Fiscal Doc.*, February 1981, *35*(2), pp. 51–61. [G: Latin America]

Massone, Pedro. Adjustment of Profits for Inflation: Part I. *Bull. Int. Fiscal Doc.*, January 1981, *35*(1), pp. 3–15. [G: Latin America]

McElhattan, Rose. The Response of Real Output and Inflation to Monetary Policy. *Fed. Res. Bank San Francisco Econ. Rev.*, Summer 1981, pp. 45–70.

McFate, Patricia A. The Effects of Inflation on the Arts. *Ann. Amer. Acad. Polit. Soc. Sci.*, July 1981, *456*, pp. 70–87. [G: U.S.]

McHugh, Richard. Income Tax Indexation in the States: A Quantitative Appraisal of Partial Indexation. *Nat. Tax J.*, June 1981, *34*(2), pp. 193–206.
[G: U.S.]

McKee, Arnold F. Inflation: The Moral Behavioural Aspect. *Int. J. Soc. Econ.*, 1981, *8*(4), pp. 21–30.

Meloe, Tor. Oil and the Transfer Problem. *J. Energy Devel.*, Autumn 1981, *7*(1), pp. 17–25.
[G: Global]

Michel, Allen. The Inflation Audit. *Calif. Manage. Rev.*, Winter 1981, *24*(2), pp. 68–74.

Minford, Patrick. Locomotives, Convoys or What?— The International Adjustment Problem. In *Gas-*

kin, M., ed., 1981, pp. 125–39. [G: OECD]

Mishkin, Frederic S. Are Market Forecasts Rational? *Amer. Econ. Rev.*, June 1981, *71*(3), pp. 295–306.

Moore, Geoffrey H. Inflation and Statistics—Again. In *Fellner, W., ed.*, 1981, pp. 79–95. [G: U.S.]

Neudeck, Werner. Inflation and the Taxation of Capital Income: A Note. *Empirica*, 1981, (2), pp. 255–61. [G: Austria]

Neumann, Manfred J. M. Inflation und Staatsverschuldung. (Inflation and Debted Financing Deficits. With English summary.) *Z. Wirtschaft. Sozialwissen.*, 1981, *101*(2), pp. 113–26.

Norton, Roger D. and Rhee, Seung Yoon. A Macroeconomic Model of Inflation and Growth in South Korea. In *Cline, W. R. and Weintraub, S., eds.*, 1981, pp. 407–57. [G: S. Korea]

Olsen, Robert A. An Empirical Investigation of the Association between Common Stock Returns and Uncertain Inflation. *Rev. Bus. Econ. Res.*, Winter 1981, *16*(2), pp. 56–67.

Parkin, Michael. The Political Economy of Inflation in the United Kingdom. In *Brunner, K.; Parkin, M. and Weintraub, R. E.*, 1981, pp. 73–92.
[G: U.K.]

Paul, M. Thomas. The Demand for Money and the Variability of the Rate of Inflation (India—1951–52 to 1977–78) *Indian Econ. J.*, July–September 1981, *29*(1), pp. 65–74. [G: India]

Perry, L. J. Inflation in the USA, UK and Australia: Some Comparisons. *Econ. Rec.*, December 1981, *57*(159), pp. 319–31. [G: U.S.; U.K.; Australia]

du Plessis, J. C. Fiskale en Monetêre Beleid: Antwoord [Die Huidige Fiskale en Monetêre Beleid in Suid-Afrika]. *S. Afr. J. Econ.*, September 1981, *49*(3), pp. 269–78. [G: S. Africa]

Popov, Sofija. Međunarodna analiza efekata diferencijacija zarada na njihov opšti rast. (An International Analysis of the Effects of Differentiation of Earnings on Their General Growth. With English summary.) *Econ. Anal. Worker's Manage.*, 1981, *15*(2), pp. 163–76. [G: E. Europe; MDCs]

Rabin, Alan and Pratt, Leila J. A Note on Heller's Use of Regression Analysis [International Reserves and World-Wide Inflation]. *Int. Monet. Fund Staff Pap.*, March 1981, *28*(1), pp. 225–29.

Randall, Maury R. Inflation, Income, and Erosion of Household Wealth. *Bus. Econ.*, September 1981, *16*(4), pp. 20–23. [G: U.S.]

Randall, Maury R. and Greenfield, Robert L. Effects of Changes in Anticipated Inflation and Taxes on Stock Prices. *Nebr. J. Econ. Bus.*, Winter 1981, *20*(1), pp. 49–58. [G: U.S.]

Rosser, J. Barkley, Jr. The Emergence of the Megacorpstate and the Acceleration of Global Inflation. *J. Post Keynesian Econ.*, Spring 1981, *3*(3), pp. 429–39.

Sackey, James A. Inflation and Government Tax Revenue: The Case of Trinidad and Tobago with Comparative Reference to Barbados and Jamaica. *Soc. Econ. Stud.*, September 1981, *30*(3), pp. 76–103.
[G: Barbados; Jamaica; Trinidad and Tobago]

Samuel, Howard D. Proceedings of the Seminar on Inflation: Statement. In *U.S. Congress, Joint Economic Committee (I)*, 1981, pp. 49–51.
[G: U.S.]

Sarcinelli, Mario. Stagflazione e strutture finanziarie: il caso dell'Italia. (Stagflation and Financial Structures: The Case of Italy. With English summary.) *Bancaria*, November 1981, *37*(11), pp. 1105–31. [G: Italy]

Schwert, G. William. The Adjustment of Stock Prices to Information about Inflation. *J. Finance*, March 1981, *36*(1), pp. 15–29. [G: U.S.]

Siegel, Jeremy J. Inflation, Bank Profits, and Government Seigniorage. *Amer. Econ. Rev.*, May 1981, *71*(2), pp. 352–55.

Siri, Gabriel and Domínguez, Luis Raúl. Central American Accommodation to External Disruptions. In *Cline, W. R., et al.*, 1981, pp. 166–207. [G: El Salvador; Guatemala]

Smith, James F. Proceedings of the Seminar on Inflation: Statement. In *U.S. Congress, Joint Economic Committee (I)*, 1981, pp. 72–91. [G: U.S.]

Søndergaard, Jørgen. Samspillet mellem indkomstskatter og inflation. (Long-run and Short-run Interaction of Inflation and Income Taxation. With English summary.) *Nationaløkon. Tidsskr.*, 1981, *119*(3), pp. 343–61.

Southern, David B. The Impact of the Inflation: Inflation, the Courts and Revaluation. In *Bessel, R. and Feuchtwanger, E. J.*, eds., 1981, pp. 55–76. [G: Germany]

Spellman, Lewis J. Inflation and Housing Prices. *Amer. Real Estate Urban Econ. Assoc. J.*, Fall 1981, *9*(3), pp. 205–22. [G: U.S.]

Spence, A. Michael. Policies for Stagflation: Rapporteur's Remarks. In *Ontario Economic Council, Vol. 2*, 1981, pp. 55–62.

Sprinkel, Beryl W. Proceedings of the Seminar on Inflation: Statement. In *U.S. Congress, Joint Economic Committee (I)*, 1981, pp. 51–54. [G: U.S.]

Staats, Elmer B. Inflation: Cancer on the American Body Politic. *Ann. Amer. Acad. Polit. Soc. Sci.*, July 1981, *456*, pp. 123–31. [G: U.S.]

Stein, Herbert. The Chief Executive as Chief Economist. In *Fellner, W.*, ed., 1981, pp. 53–78. [G: U.S.]

Tait, Alan. Is the Introduction of a Value-Added Tax Inflationary? *Finance Develop.*, June 1981, *18*(2), pp. 38–42. [G: Selected Countries]

Tarshis, Lorie. Understanding and Treating Stagflation in Canada's Open Economy. In *Ontario Economic Council, Vol. 2*, 1981, pp. 67–91. [G: Canada]

Taylor, Herbert. Fisher, Phillips, Friedman and the Measured Impact of Inflation on Interest: A Comment. *J. Finance*, September 1981, *36*(4), pp. 955–62. [G: U.S.]

Thurow, Lester C. Stagflation, Productivity, and the Labor Market. In *Carter, M. J. and Leahy, W. H.*, eds., 1981, pp. 61–106. [G: U.S.]

Truu, M. L. Fiscal and Monetary Policy: Rejoinder [Die Huidige Fiskale en Monetêre Beleid in Suid-Afrika]. *S. Afr. J. Econ.*, September 1981, *49*(3), pp. 279. [G: S. Africa]

Truu, M. L. The Minister and Quantification in Economics [Die Huidige Fiskale en Monetêre Belied in Suid-Affrika]. *S. Afr. J. Econ.*, March 1981, *49*(1), pp. 59–61. [G: S. Africa]

Tuccillo, John A. and Villani, Kevin E. House Prices and Inflation: Introduction. In *Tuccillo, J. A. and Villani, K. E.*, eds., 1981, pp. 1–9.

Turner, John A. Inflation and the Accumulation of Assets in Private Pension Funds. *Econ. Inquiry*, July 1981, *19*(3), pp. 410–25.

Turnovsky, Stephen J. Secular Inflation and Dynamics of Exchange Rates under Perfect Myopic Foresight. *Scand. J. Econ.*, 1981, *83*(4), pp. 522–40.

Volcker, Paul A. Statement to House Committee on Ways and Means, March 3, 1981. *Fed. Res. Bull.*, March 1981, *67*(3), pp. 243–46. [G: U.S.]

Volcker, Paul A. Statement to Joint Economic Committee, February 5, 1981. *Fed. Res. Bull.*, February 1981, *67*(2), pp. 141–43. [G: U.S.]

Volcker, Paul A. Statement to Senate Committee on Appropriations, January 27, 1981. *Fed. Res. Bull.*, February 1981, *67*(2), pp. 135–37. [G: U.S.]

Wallich, Henry C. Statement to Temporary Subcommittee on Industrial Growth and Productivity, Senate Committee on the Budget, January 27, 1981. *Fed. Res. Bull.*, February 1981, *67*(2), pp. 137–40. [G: U.S.]

Weintraub, Robert E. Political Economy of Inflation. In *Brunner, K.; Parkin, M. and Weintraub, R. E.*, 1981, pp. 37–72. [G: U.S.]

Westphal, Larry E. A Macroeconomic Model of Inflation and Growth in South Korea: Comment. In *Cline, W. R. and Weintraub, S.*, eds., 1981, pp. 457–62. [G: S. Korea]

Wright, John Winthrop. Proceedings of the Seminar on International Economic Problems: Statement. In *U.S. Congress, Joint Economic Committee (I)*, 1981, pp. 295–312. [G: U.S.]

1342 Inflation Theories; Studies Illustrating Inflation Theories

Abbott, Walter F. Income Level and Inflation Strain in the United States: 1971–1975. *Amer. J. Econ. Soc.*, April 1981, *40*(2), pp. 97–106. [G: U.S.]

Abel, Andrew B. Taxes, Inflation, and the Durability of Capital. *J. Polit. Econ.*, June 1981, *89*(3), pp. 548–60.

Addison, John T.; Burton, John and Torrance, Thomas S. "On the Causation of Inflation": Some Further Clarifications. *Manchester Sch. Econ. Soc. Stud.*, December 1981, *49*(4), pp. 355–56.

Aghevli, Bijan B. Experiences of Asian Countries with Various Exchange Rate Policies. In *Williamson, J.*, ed., 1981, pp. 298–318. [G: Asia]

Alberro, José. The Lucas Hypothesis on the Phillips Curve: Further International Evidence. *J. Monet. Econ.*, March 1981, *7*(2), pp. 239–50.

Allen, Stuart D. and Crickard, Donald L. The Impact of Demand and Cost Factors on Inflation in Open Economies. *Southern Econ. J.*, April 1981, *47*(4), pp. 1092–1104. [G: OECD]

Alperovitz, Gar. The New Inflation. *Ann. Amer. Acad. Polit. Soc. Sci.*, July 1981, *456*, pp. 1–12. [G: U.S.]

Amihud, Yakov. Price-Level Uncertainty, Indexation and Employment. *Southern Econ. J.*, January 1981, *47*(3), pp. 776–87. [G: U.S.]

Arestis, P. and Hadjimatheou, George. Money,

Prices and Causality. *Brit. Rev. Econ. Issues*, Autumn 1981, *3*(9), pp. 19–38. [G: U.K.]

Artis, Michael J. Is there a Wage Equation? In *Courakis, A. S., ed.*, 1981, pp. 65–80. [G: U.K.]

Artus, Jacques R. and Young, John H. Fixed and Flexible Exchange Rates: A Renewal of the Debate. In *Baldwin, R. E. and Richardson, J. D., eds.*, 1981, 1979, pp. 327–51.

Asako, Kazumi. Heterogeneity of Labor, the Phillips Curve, and Stagflation. *Econ. Stud. Quart.*, August 1981, *32*(2), pp. 117–34.

Ashworth, J. S. Wages, Prices and Unemployment. In *Creedy, J., ed.*, 1981, pp. 186–234.

Auerbach, Alan J. Inflation and the Tax Treatment of Firm Behavior. *Amer. Econ. Rev.*, May 1981, *71*(2), pp. 419–23.

Auld, D. A. L., et al. The Impact of the Anti-Inflation Board on Negotiated Wage Settlements: A Reply. *Can. J. Econ.*, May 1981, *14*(2), pp. 328–31. [G: Canada]

Barro, Robert J. Inflation, the Payments Period, and the Demand for Money. In *Barro, R. J.*, 1981, 1970, pp. 301–36. [G: Selected Countries]

Barro, Robert J. Long-term Contracting, Sticky Prices, and Monetary Policy. In *Barro, R. J.*, 1981, 1977, pp. 213–24.

Barro, Robert J. The Equilibrium Approach to Business Cycles. In *Barro, R. J.*, 1981, pp. 41–78.

Barro, Robert J. Unanticipated Money, Output, and the Price Level in the United States. In *Lucas, R. E. and Sargent, T. J., eds.*, 1981, 1978, pp. 585–616. [G: U.S.]

Barro, Robert J. and Fischer, Stanley. Recent Developments in Monetary Theory. In *Barro, R. J.*, 1981, 1976, pp. 3–40.

Barro, Robert J. and Grossman, Herschel I. Suppressed Inflation and the Supply Multiplier. In *Barro, R. J.*, 1981, 1974, pp. 185–202.

Batten, Dallas S. Inflation: The Cost-Push Myth. *Fed. Res. Bank St. Louis Rev.*, June–July 1981, *63*(6), pp. 20–26. [G: U.S.]

Batten, Dallas S. Money Growth Stability and Inflation: An International Comparison. *Fed. Res. Bank St. Louis Rev.*, October 1981, *63*(8), pp. 7–12. [G: U.S.; W. Germany; U.K.; Switzerland]

Bazdarich, Michael. Some Perspectives on Controlling U.S. Inflation. In *Gale, W. A., ed.*, 1981, pp. 167–91. [G: U.S.]

Beigie, Carl E. Stagflation and Relative-wage Rates: Comments. In *Ontario Economic Council, Vol. 1*, 1981, pp. 50–56. [G: Canada]

Belongia, Mike. A Note on the Specification of Wage Rates in Cost-Push Models of Food Price Determination. *Southern J. Agr. Econ.*, December 1981, *13*(2), pp. 119–24. [G: U.S.]

Benavie, Arthur. Stabilization Policies Which Reverse Stagflation in a Short Run Macromodel. *Southern Econ. J.*, July 1981, *48*(1), pp. 17–25.

Blejer, Mario I. and Mathieson, Donald J. The Preannouncement of Exchange Rate Changes as a Stabilization Instrument. *Int. Monet. Fund Staff Pap.*, December 1981, *28*(4), pp. 760–92.

Blinder, Alan S. Monetary Accommodation of Supply Shocks under Rational Expectations. *J. Money, Credit, Banking*, November 1981, *13*(4),

pp. 425–38.

Bordo, Michael David and Schwartz, Anna J. Money and Prices in the 19th Century: Was Thomas Tooke Right? *Exploration Econ. Hist.*, April 1981, *18*(2), pp. 97–127. [G: U.S.; U.K.]

Bosworth, Barry P. Stagflation and Relative-wage Rates. In *Ontario Economic Council, Vol. 1*, 1981, pp. 31–49. [G: U.S.]

Boughton, James M. and Fackler, James S. The Nominal Rate of Interest, the Rate of Return on Money, and Inflationary Expectations. *J. Macroecon.*, Fall 1981, *3*(4), pp. 531–45.

Boyes, William J. and Schlagenhauf, Don E. Price Controls in an Open Economy. *J. Macroecon.*, Summer 1981, *3*(3), pp. 391–408.

Brissimis, Sophocles N. and Leventakis, John A. Estimating Autonomous and Induced Cost Inflation. *Empirical Econ.*, 1981, *6*(2), pp. 103–10. [G: Greece]

Brown, W. W. and Santoni, Gary J. Unreal Estimates of the Real Rate of Interest. *Fed. Res. Bank St. Louis Rev.*, January 1981, *63*(1), pp. 18–26. [G: U.S.]

Brunner, Karl. The Political Economy of Inflation: A Critique of the Sociological Approach and a Reinterpretation of Social Facts. In *Brunner, K.; Parkin, M. and Weintraub, R. E.*, 1981, pp. 7–36.

Bruno, Michael and Sachs, Jeffrey. Supply versus Demand Approaches to the Problem of Stagflation. In *Giersch, H, ed. (I)*, 1981, pp. 15–60. [G: Selected OECD]

Burton, John; Hawkins, M. J. and Hughes, G. L. Is Liberal Democracy Especially Prone to Inflation? An Analytical Treatment. In *Hibbs, D. A., Jr. and Fassbender, H., eds.*, 1981, pp. 248–68.

Butterfield, David W. and Kubursi, Atif A. Wage Indexation and the Unemployment-Inflation Trade-Off. *J. Macroecon.*, Spring 1981, *3*(2), pp. 227–45.

Cardoso, Eliana A. Food Supply and Inflation. *J. Devel. Econ.*, June 1981, *8*(3), pp. 269–84. [G: Latin America]

Cebula, Richard J., et al. On the Responsiveness of Money Wages to Anticipated Inflation and the Unemployment-Inflation Trade-Off: The Case of the United States. *Econ. Int.*, February 1981, *34*(1), pp. 1–12. [G: U.S.]

Chappell, David. On the Revenue Maximizing Rate of Inflation: A Comment [Monetary Dynamics, Growth, and the Efficiency of Inflationary Finance]. *J. Money, Credit, Banking*, August 1981, *13*(3), pp. 391–92.

Christensen, Sandra. The Impact of the Anti-Inflation Board on Negotiated Wage Settlements: Comment. *Can. J. Econ.*, May 1981, *14*(2), pp. 327–28. [G: Canada]

Cifarelli, Giulio. Some Econometric Implications of the Natural Rate of Unemployment with Rational Expectations Model. *Econ. Notes*, 1981, *10*(2), pp. 92–115.

Cobham, David. "On the Causation of Inflation": Some Comments. *Manchester Sch. Econ. Soc. Stud.*, December 1981, *49*(4), pp. 348–54.

Cohn, Richard A. and Lessard, Donald R. The Effect of Inflation on Stock Prices: International Evidence. *J. Finance*, May 1981, *36*(2), pp. 277–89.

Colander, David. Tax- and Market-Based Incomes Policies: The Interface of Theory and Practice. In *Claudon, M. P. and Cornwall, R. R., eds.*, 1981, pp. 79–97.

Colander, David C. New Approaches to Anti-Inflation Policy. *Public Finance*, 1981, *36*(1), pp. 39–54.

Conrad, William E. and Cohen, Darrel S. Inflation, Taxes, and the Capital Stock: A Long-run Analysis. In *Federal Reserve System*, 1981, pp. 267–74.

Cornwall, John. Do We Need Separate Theories of Inflation and Unemployment? *Can. Public Policy*, Supplement, April 1981, *7*, pp. 165–78.

Cornwall, John. Unemployment and Inflation: Institutionalist and Structuralist Views: A Review Article. *J. Econ. Issues*, March 1981, *15*(1), pp. 113–27.

Crouch, Colin. The Political Economy of Inflation. In *Gaskin, M., ed.*, 1981, pp. 79–97.

Cukierman, Alex. Interest Rates during the Cycle, Inventories and Monetary Policy—A Theoretical Analysis. *Carnegie-Rochester Conf. Ser. Public Policy*, Autumn 1981, *15*, pp. 87–144.

Daniel, Betty C. International Transmission of a Real Shock under Flexible Exchange Rates: A Comment. *J. Polit. Econ.*, August 1981, *89*(4), pp. 813–18.

Daniel, Betty C. The International Transmission of Economic Disturbances under Flexible Exchange Rates. *Int. Econ. Rev.*, October 1981, *22*(3), pp. 491–509.

Darby, Michael R. The International Economy as a Source of and Restraint on U.S. Inflation. In *Gale, W. A., ed.*, 1981, pp. 115–31. [G: U.S.]

Dean, James W. The Inflation Process: Where Conventional Theory Falters. *Amer. Econ. Rev.*, May 1981, *71*(2), pp. 362–67.

Desai, Meghnad. Inflation, Unemployment and Monetary Policy—The UK Experience. *Brit. Rev. Econ. Issues*, Autumn 1981, *3*(9), pp. 1–18. [G: U.K.]

Dewald, W. G. and Gavin, W. T. Money and Inflation in a Small Model of the German Economy. *Empirical Econ.*, 1981, *6*(3), pp. 173–85. [G: W. Germany]

Dirksen, Erik. The Control of Inflation? Errors in the Interpretation of CPE Data. *Economica*, August 1981, *48*(191), pp. 305–08. [G: Cent. Planned Econ.]

Drazen, Allan. Inflation and Capital Accumulation under a Finite Horizon. *J. Monet. Econ.*, September 1981, *8*(2), pp. 247–60.

Dror, David M. Flexible Indexation: A Proposal to Improve Wage Indexation Made in the Light of Israeli Experience. *Int. Lab. Rev.*, March–April 1981, *120*(2), pp. 183–200. [G: Israel]

den Dunnen, Emile. Dutch Economic and Monetary Problems in the 1970s. In *Courakis, A. S., ed.*, 1981, pp. 182–201. [G: Netherlands]

Dwyer, Gerald P., Jr. Are Expectations of Inflation Rational? Or Is Variation of the Expected Real Interest Rate Unpredictable? *J. Monet. Econ.*, July 1981, *8*(1), pp. 59–84. [G: U.S.]

Earley, James S. What Caused Worldwide Inflation:

Excess Liquidity, Excessive Credit, or Both? *Weltwirtsch. Arch.*, 1981, *117*(2), pp. 213–43.

Eckard, E. Woodrow, Jr. Concentration Changes and Inflation: Some Evidence [A Note on Inflation and Concentration]. *J. Polit. Econ.*, October 1981, *89*(5), pp. 1044–51. [G: U.S.]

Eckstein, Otto. Shock Inflation, Core Inflation, and Energy Disturbances in the DRI Model. In *Mork, K. A., ed.*, 1981, pp. 63–98. [G: U.S.]

Eidman, Vernon R. Microeconomic Impacts of Inflation on the Food and Agriculture Sector: Discussion. *Amer. J. Agr. Econ.*, December 1981, *63*(5), pp. 962–64. [G: U.S.]

Eltis, Walter. The Failure of the Keynesian Conventional Wisdom. In *Courakis, A. S., ed.*, 1981, pp. 92–110.

Entov, R. M. The Problem of Inflation. In *Mileikovsky, A. G., et al.*, 1981, pp. 166–252.

Erdös, Péter. The Acceleration of Inflation in the United States in the Seventies. *Acta Oecon.*, 1981, *27*(1–2), pp. 111–23. [G: U.S.]

Evans, Jean Lynne and Yarrow, George Keith. Some Implications of Alternative Expectations Hypotheses in the Monetary Analysis of Hyperinflations. *Oxford Econ. Pap.*, March 1981, *33*(1), pp. 61–80.

Evans, Paul. Why the Great Inflation Has Been a Catastrophe. In *Gale, W. A., ed.*, 1981, pp. 133–65. [G: U.S.]

Evans, William H. Expectations of Inflation and Nominal Interest Rates in Australia 1969(1)–1979(2): Comments. In *Jüttner, D. J., ed.*, 1981, pp. 279–81. [G: Australia]

Fama, Eugene F. Stock Returns, Real Activity, Inflation, and Money. *Amer. Econ. Rev.*, September 1981, *71*(4), pp. 545–65. [G: U.S.]

Fautz, Wolfgang. A Simple Dynamic Model of Autonomous Wage Policy, Price Expectations, and Monetary Accommodation. *Schweiz. Z. Volkswirtsch. Statist.*, March 1981, *117*(1), pp. 25–40.

Fazio, Antonio. Inflation and Wage Indexation in Italy. *Banca Naz. Lavoro Quart. Rev.*, June 1981, (137), pp. 147–70. [G: Italy]

Feige, Edgar L. and Singleton, Kenneth J. Multinational Inflation under Fixed Exchange Rates: Some Empirical Evidence from Latent Variable Models. *Rev. Econ. Statist.*, February 1981, *63*(1), pp. 11–19. [G: W. Europe]

Feldstein, Martin. Private Pensions and Inflation. *Amer. Econ. Rev.*, May 1981, *71*(2), pp. 424–28.

Feldstein, Martin S. Adjusting Depreciation in an Inflationary Economy: Indexing versus Acceleration. *Nat. Tax J.*, March 1981, *34*(1), pp. 29–43. [G: U.S.]

Feldstein, Martin S. Inflation and the American Economy. *Empirica*, 1981, (2), pp. 155–68. [G: U.S.]

Fellner, William. Why Policy Makers Need to Pay More Attention to the Crucial Role of Market Expectations. In *U.S. Congress, Joint Economic Committee (II)*, 1981, pp. 35–39.

Fields, T. Windsor and Noble, Nicholas R. Testing the Friedman-Phelps Natural Rate Hypothesis Using Survey Data: An Instrumental Variable Approach. *J. Monet. Econ.*, March 1981, *7*(2), pp. 251–59. [G: U.S.]

Figlewski, Stephen and Wachtel, Paul. The Formation of Inflationary Expectations. *Rev. Econ. Statist.*, February 1981, *63*(1), pp. 1–10. **[G: U.S.]**

Fischer, Stanley. Addendum: Response to Comments by Lucas [Towards an Understanding of the Costs of Inflation: II]. *Carnegie-Rochester Conf. Ser. Public Policy*, Autumn 1981, *15*, pp. 53–55. **[G: U.S.]**

Fischer, Stanley. Relative Shocks, Relative Price Variability, and Inflation. *Brookings Pap. Econ. Act.*, 1981, (2), pp. 381–431. **[G: U.S.]**

Fischer, Stanley. Towards an Understanding of the Costs of Inflation: II. *Carnegie-Rochester Conf. Ser. Public Policy*, Autumn 1981, *15*, pp. 5–41. **[G: U.S.]**

Fishe, Raymond P. H. and Lahiri, Kajal. On the Estimation of Inflationary Expectations from Qualitative Responses. *J. Econometrics*, May 1981, *16*(1), pp. 89–102. **[G: U.S.]**

FitzRoy, Felix R. Work-Sharing and Insurance Policy: A Cure for Stagflation. *Kyklos*, 1981, *34*(3), pp. 432–47.

Flannery, Mark J. and Johnson, Lewis. Indexing the U.S. Economy: Simulation Results with the MPS Model. *J. Econometrics*, January 1981, *15*(1), pp. 93–114. **[G: U.S.]**

Fortune, J. Neill. Voluntary (Dis) Saving and Expected Inflation. *Southern Econ. J.*, July 1981, *48*(1), pp. 134–43. **[G: U.S.]**

Franco, Giampiero and Mengarelli, Gianluigi. Debito pubblico, base monetaria e inflazione. (Public Debt, Monetary Base and Inflation. With English summary.) *Bancaria*, November 1981, *37*(11), pp. 1141–45. **[G: Italy]**

Fratianni, Michele and Spinelli, F. Sylos Labini on Spinelli and Fratianni on Inflation: A Reply [Money, Prices and Wages in Italy] [Wage Inflation in Italy: A Reappraisal]. *Banca Naz. Lavoro Quart. Rev.*, December 1981, (139), pp. 466–69.

Frenkel, Jacob A. Adjustment Lags versus Information Lags: A Test of Alternative Explanations of the Phillips Curve Phenomenon: A Comment. *J. Money, Credit, Banking*, November 1981, *13*(4), pp. 490–93.

Frisch, Helmut and Hof, Franz. A "Textbook"—Model of Inflation and Unemployment. *Kredit Kapital*, 1981, *14*(2), pp. 159–76.

Fry, Maxwell J. Government Revenue from Monopoly Supply of Currency and Deposits. *J. Monet. Econ.*, September 1981, *8*(2), pp. 261–70. **[G: Turkey]**

Fry, Maxwell J. Inflation and Economic Growth in Pacific Basin Developing Economies. *Fed. Res. Bank San Francisco Econ. Rev.*, Fall 1981, pp. 8–18. **[G: LDCs]**

Fry, Maxwell J. Monopoly Finance and Portugal's Government Deficit. *Economia (Portugal)*, May 1981, *5*(2), pp. 315–23. **[G: Portugal]**

Frye, Jon and Gordon, Robert J. Government Intervention in the Inflation Process: The Econometrics of "Self-Inflicted Wounds". *Amer. Econ. Rev.*, May 1981, *71*(2), pp. 288–94. **[G: U.S.]**

Gale, William A. Temporal Variability of United States Consumer Price Index. *J. Money, Credit, Banking*, August 1981, *13*(3), pp. 273–97. **[G: U.S.]**

Garbarino, Joseph W. Collective Bargaining under Adverse Conditions, or Hard Times in the Mill: Discussion. In *Dennis, B. D., ed.*, 1981, pp. 143–46.

Gardner, Roy and Strauss, Jonathan. Repressed Inflation in the Soviet Union: A Temporary Equilibrium Approach. *Europ. Econ. Rev.*, June/July 1981, *16*(2/3), pp. 387–404. **[G: U.S.S.R.]**

Gärtner, Manfred. A Politicoeconomic Model of Wage Inflation. *De Economist*, 1981, *129*(2), pp. 183–205. **[G: W. Germany]**

Gärtner, Manfred and Heri, Erwin W. Oil Imports and Inflation: A Comment [Oil Imports and Inflation: An Empirical International Analysis of the "Imported" Inflation Thesis]. *Kyklos*, 1981, *34*(3), pp. 461–67. **[G: EEC; Japan; U.S.; Australia]**

Gärtner, Manfred and Ursprung, Heinrich W. An Empirical Analysis of a Scandinavian Exchange Rate Model. *Scand. J. Econ.*, 1981, *83*(1), pp. 38–54. **[G: Switzerland]**

Gelber, Frank. The Inter-Industry Effect of Cumulative Wage Indexation—A Critical Comment. *Australian Econ. Pap.*, June 1981, *20*(36), pp. 186–88.

Giffin, Phillip E.; Macomber, James H. and Berry, Robert E. An Empirical Examination of Current Inflation and Deficit Spending. *J. Post Keynesian Econ.*, Fall 1981, *4*(1), pp. 63–67. **[G: U.S.]**

Gonedes, Nicholas J. Evidence on the "Tax Effects" of Inflation under Historical Cost Accounting Methods. *J. Bus.*, April 1981, *54*(2), pp. 227–70.

Gordon, Robert J. International Monetarism, Wage Push, and Monetary Accommodation. In *Courakis, A. S., ed.*, 1981, pp. 1–63. **[G: OECD]**

Gordon, Robert J. Output Fluctuations and Gradual Price Adjustment. *J. Econ. Lit.*, June 1981, *19*(2), pp. 493–530. **[G: U.S.]**

Gørtz, Erik. Overvaeltning af inflation i obligationsrenten i et vaekstperspektiv: Et simpelt estimationsresultat. (Inflation, Growth and the Interest Rate. With English summary.) *Nationaløkon. Tidsskr.*, 1981, *119*(1), pp. 95–104.

Gray, H. Peter. Oil-Push Inflation: A Broader Examination. *Banca Naz. Lavoro Quart. Rev.*, March 1981, (136), pp. 49–67.

Grünbaum, Isi. Inflationary Measures and Inflationary Systems. In *Grünbaum, I.*, 1981, *1940*, pp. 57–64.

Hafer, R. W. and Heyne-Hafer, Gail. The Relationship between Inflation and Its Variability: International Evidence from the 1970s. *J. Macroecon.*, Fall 1981, *3*(4), pp. 571–77.

Hamburger, Michael J. and Zwick, Burton. Deficits, Money and Inflation. *J. Monet. Econ.*, January 1981, *7*(1), pp. 141–50. **[G: U.S.]**

Hannesson, Rögnvaldur. Stagflation: A Problem of the Aging Welfare State? A Comment on the Baumol-Oates "Cost-Disease" Model. *Scand. J. Econ.*, 1981, *83*(1), pp. 104–08.

Hanson, James A. La relación de corto plazo entre crecimiento e inflación en Latinoamérica: Un enfoque de expectativas cuasi racionales o consistentes. (With English summary.) *Cuadernos Econ.*, April 1981, *18*(53), pp. 15–41. **[G: Brazil; Chile; Colombia; Mexico; Peru]**

Hartle, Douglas G., et al. Stagflation Consequences

of the Canadian Tax/Transfer System. In *Ontario Economic Council*, Vol. 1, 1981, pp. 67–105.
[G: Canada; U.S.]

Hein, Scott E. Deficits and Inflation. *Fed. Res. Bank St. Louis Rev.*, March 1981, 63(3), pp. 3–10.
[G: U.S.]

Helliwell, John F. The Stagflationary Effects of Higher Energy Prices in an Open Economy. *Can. Public Policy*, Supplement, April 1981, 7, pp. 155–64. [G: Canada]

Hendershott, Patric H. and Hu, Sheng-Cheng. Inflation and Extraordinary Returns on Owner-Occupied Housing: Some Implications for Capital Allocation and Productivity Growth. *J. Macroecon.*, Spring 1981, 3(2), pp. 177–203.
[G: U.S.]

Henry, C. Michael. U.S. Inflation and the Import Demand of Ghana and Nigeria, 1967–1976. *Rev. Black Polit. Econ.*, Winter 1981, 11(2), pp. 217–28. [G: Ghana; Nigeria]

Hercowitz, Zvi. Money and the Dispersion of Relative Prices. *J. Polit. Econ.*, April 1981, 89(2), pp. 328–56. [G: Germany]

Hoa, Tran Van. A Bivariate Model of Wages and Money for West Germany [Causality and Wage Price Inflation in West Germany, 1964–1979]. *Weltwirtsch. Arch.*, 1981, 117(4), pp. 752–55.
[G: W. Germany]

Hoa, Tran Van. Causality and Wage Price Inflation in West Germany, 1964–1979. *Weltwirtsch. Arch.*, 1981, 117(1), pp. 110–24.

Hodes, Daniel A. and Snyder, Christopher L. How Good Is Inflation Theory? A Call to Action. *Bus. Econ.*, September 1981, 16(4), pp. 15–19.

Honohan, Patrick. A New Look at Wicksell's Inflationary Process. *Manchester Sch. Econ. Soc. Stud.*, December 1981, 49(4), pp. 319–33.

Horne, Jocelyn. Rational Expectations and the Defris–Williams Inflationary Expectations Series. *Econ. Rec.*, September 1981, 57(158), pp. 261–68. [G: Australia]

Howell, Craig and Callahan, David W. Price Changes in 1980: Double-Digit Inflation Persists. *Mon. Lab. Rev.*, April 1981, 104(4), pp. 3–12.
[G: U.S.]

Hvidding, James M. Policy Implications of a Non-Linear Phillips Curve in a Stochastic Environment. *J. Macroecon.*, Winter 1981, 3(1), pp. 125–28.

Iglesias, C. H. and Iglesias, F. H. Is There a Stable Demand for Money? A Critical View of the "Independence Phenomenon." In *Janssen, J. M. L.; Pau, L. F. and Straszak, A. J., eds.*, 1981, pp. 263–69. [G: Spain; Germany]

Ip, Pui Chi. A General Equilibrium Analysis in the Phillips Space. *J. Macroecon.*, Summer 1981, 3(3), pp. 355–67.

Jenner, Stephen R. Inflation, Exchange Rates, and the Location of Automobile Manufacturing. *Bus. Econ.*, January 1981, 16(1), pp. 26–29.
[G: EEC; U.S.; Japan]

Jetzer, Martin. Causality and Wage Price Inflation in West Germany, 1964–1979: A Note [Causality and Wage Price Inflation in West Germany, 1964–1979]. *Weltwirtsch. Arch.*, 1981, 117(4), pp. 749–51. [G: W. Germany]

Kaldor, Nicholas and Trevithick, James. A Keynesian Perspective on Money. *Lloyds Bank Rev.*, January 1981, (139), pp. 1–19.

Kaliski, S. F. Inflation, Stagflation and Macroeconomics: Does Received Macro-Theory Explain Our Economic Circumstances? *Can. Public Policy*, Supplement, April 1981, 7, pp. 189–203.
[G: Canada]

Karatzas, George. Inflationary Forces in Fifty-Four Countries in the Past Decade: An Analysis. *Econ. Int.*, May–August–November 1981, 34(2–3–4), pp. 322–55. [G: Selected LDCs; Selected MDCs]

Kiewiet, D. Roderick. Policy-Oriented Voting in Response to Economic Issues. *Amer. Polit. Sci. Rev.*, June 1981, 75(2), pp. 448–59. [G: U.S.]

Kirby, Michael G. A Variable Expectations Coefficient Model of the Australian Phillips Curve. *Australian Econ. Pap.*, December 1981, 20(37), pp. 351–58. [G: Australia]

Kirkpatrick, Colin H. and Nixson, F. I. The Origins of Inflation in Less Developed Countries: A Selective Review. In *Livingstone, I., ed.*, 1981, 1976, pp. 311–32. [G: LDCs]

Kite, R. C. and Roop, J. M. Changing Agricultural Prices and Their Impact on Food Prices under Inflation. *Amer. J. Agr. Econ.*, December 1981, 63(5), pp. 956–61.

Kolluri, Bharat R. Gold as a Hedge against Inflation: An Empirical Investigation. *Quart. Rev. Econ. Bus.*, Winter 1981, 21(4), pp. 13–24. [G: U.S.]

Kopcke, Richard W. Inflation, Corporate Income Taxation, and the Demand for Capital Assets. *J. Polit. Econ.*, February 1981, 89(1), pp. 122–31.
[G: U.S.]

Kreicher, Lawrence L. An International Evaluation of the Fisher Hypothesis Using Rational Expectations. *Southern Econ. J.*, July 1981, 48(1), pp. 58–67. [G: U.K.; W. Germany; Italy; U.S.]

Kulkarni, Kishore G. and Dhekane, Sunil G. The Monetarist Model of Imported Inflation in Small Open Economy. *Econ. Aff.*, July–September 1981, 26(3), pp. 188–92.

Laffer, Arthur B. and Canto, Victor A. The Measurement of Expectations in an Efficient Market. In *U.S. Congress, Joint Economic Committee (II)*, 1981, pp. 70–93. [G: U.S.]

Lahiri, Kajal and Lee, Jung Soo. Inflationary Expectations and the Wage–Price Dynamics: An Econometric Analysis. In *[Valavanis, S.]*, 1981, pp. 421–36. [G: U.S.]

Laidler, David. Inflation and Unemployment in an Open Economy: A Monetarist View. *Can. Public Policy*, Supplement, April 1981, 7, pp. 179–88.
[G: Canada]

Lamm, Ray McFall, Jr. The Impact of the Voluntary Anti-Inflation Program on Retail Food Prices. *Agr. Econ. Res.*, January 1981, 33(1), pp. 28–33.
[G: U.S.]

Lawson, G. H. and Stark, A. W. Equity Values and Inflation: A Rejoinder. *Lloyds Bank Rev.*, October 1981, (142), pp. 39–43. [G: U.K.]

Lawson, G. H. and Stark, A. W. Equity Values and Inflation: Dividends and Debt Financing. *Lloyds Bank Rev.*, January 1981, (139), pp. 40–54.
[G: U.K.]

de Leeuw, Frank and McKelvey, Michael J. Price Expectations of Business Firms. *Brookings Pap. Econ. Act.*, 1981, (1), pp. 299–314.   [G: U.S.]

Leggett, Robert E. Measuring Inflation in the Soviet Machinebuilding Sector, 1960–1973. *J. Compar. Econ.*, June 1981, 5(2), pp. 169–84.
   [G: U.S.S.R.]

Leibenstein, Harvey. The Inflation Process: A Micro-Behavioral Analysis. *Amer. Econ. Rev.*, May 1981, 71(2), pp. 368–73.

Leijonhufvud, Axel. Costs and Consequences of Inflation. In *Leijonhufvud, A.*, 1981, 1977, pp. 227–69.

Leijonhufvud, Axel. Inflation and the Economists: Critique. In *Leijonhufvud, A.*, 1981, 1977, pp. 271–89.

Levy, Mickey D. Factors Affecting Monetary Policy in an Era of Inflation. *J. Monet. Econ.*, November 1981, 8(3), pp. 351–73.   [G: U.S.]

Levy, Victor. Oil Prices, Relative Prices, and Balance-of-Payments Adjustment: The Turkish Experience. *Europ. Econ. Rev.*, March 1981, 15(3), pp. 357–72.   [G: Turkey]

Lintner, John. Are Markets Efficient? Tests of Alternative Hypotheses: Discussion. *J. Finance*, May 1981, 36(2), pp. 307–11.

Lipsey, Richard G. Supply-side Economics: A Survey. In *Ontario Economic Council, Vol. 1*, 1981, pp. 5–30.

Lipsey, Richard G. The Understanding and Control of Inflation: Is There a Crisis in Macro-Economics? *Can. J. Econ.*, November 1981, 14(4), pp. 545–76.

Littmann, David L. A Leading Index of U.S. Inflation. *Bus. Econ.*, January 1981, 16(1), pp. 87–89.   [G: U.S.]

Logue, Dennis E. and Sweeney, Richard James. Inflation and Real Growth: Some Empirical Results: A Note. *J. Money, Credit, Banking*, November 1981, 13(4), pp. 497–501.

Long, John B., Jr. Are Markets Efficient? Tests of Alternative Hypotheses: Discussion. *J. Finance*, May 1981, 36(2), pp. 304–07.

Lucas, Robert E., Jr. A Review: Paul McCracken et al., *Towards Full Employment and Price Stability*, A Report to the OECD by a Group of Independent Experts, OECD, June 1977. In *Lucas, R. E., Jr.*, 1981, 1976, pp. 262–70. [G: OECD]

Lucas, Robert E., Jr. Discussion of: Stanley Fischer, "Towards an Understanding of the Costs of Inflation: II." *Carnegie-Rochester Conf. Ser. Public Policy*, Autumn 1981, 15, pp. 43–52.   [G: U.S.]

Lucas, Robert E., Jr. Econometric Policy Evaluation: A Critique. In *Lucas, R. E., Jr.*, 1981, 1976, pp. 104–30.

Lucas, Robert E., Jr. Econometric Testing of the Natural Rate Hypothesis. In *Lucas, R. E., Jr.*, 1981, 1972, pp. 90–103.

Lucas, Robert E., Jr. Real Wages, Employment, and Inflation. In *Lucas, R. E., Jr.*, 1981, 1969, pp. 19–58.   [G: U.S.]

Lucas, Robert E., Jr. Some International Evidence on Output-Inflation Tradeoffs. In *Lucas, R. E., Jr.*, 1981, 1973, pp. 131–45.
   [G: Selected Countries]

Maccini, Louis J. Adjustment Lags, Economically

Rational Expectations and Price Behavior. *Rev. Econ. Statist.*, May 1981, 63(2), pp. 213–22.
   [G: U.S.]

Maccini, Louis J. On the Theory of the Firm Underlying Empirical Models of Aggregate Price Behavior. *Int. Econ. Rev.*, October 1981, 22(3), pp. 609–24.

Maital, Shlomo and Maital, Sharone. Individual-Rational and Group-Rational Inflation Expectations: Theory and Cross-section Evidence. *J. Econ. Behav. Organ.*, June 1981, 2(2), pp. 179–86.
   [G: Israel]

Malinvaud, Edmond. Supply versus Demand Approaches to the Problem of Stagflation: Comment. In *Giersch, H, ed. (I)*, 1981, pp. 70–72.
   [G: Selected OECD]

Manser, W. A. P. The Monetary Year. *Nat. Westminster Bank Quart. Rev.*, May 1981, pp. 40–50.

Marczewski, Jean. La concurrence macroéconomique par les taux d'inflation et les taux de change. (With English summary.) *Écon. Appl.*, 1981, 34(4), pp. 619–37.   [G: U.S.]

Marczewski, Jean. Théorie de la stagflation et expérience comparée de la France et de l'Allemagne 1971–1979. (With English summary.) *Écon. Appl.*, 1981, 34(4), pp. 667–96.   [G: France; W. Germany]

Mayer, Thomas. Innovative Incomes Policies: A Skeptic's View. In *Claudon, M. P. and Cornwall, R. R., eds.*, 1981, pp. 197–214.   [G: U.S.]

McCallum, John C. P. Modigliani on Flexible Wages and Prices: Comment. *J. Post Keynesian Econ.*, Winter 1980–81, 3(2), pp. 281–84. [G: Canada]

Meade, James E. Fiscal Devices for the Control of Inflation. *Atlantic Econ. J.*, December 1981, 9(4), pp. 1–11.

Meade, James E. Note on the Inflationary Implications of the Wage-Fixing Assumption of the Cambridge Economic Policy Group. *Oxford Econ. Pap.*, March 1981, 33(1), pp. 28–41.   [G: U.K.]

Meissner, Werner and Fassing, Werner. Concentration and Inflation. *Konjunkturpolitik*, 1981, 27(4), pp. 247–59.   [G: W. Germany]

Mills, Terence C. Modelling the Formation of Australian Inflation Expectations. *Australian Econ. Pap.*, June 1981, 20(36), pp. 150–60.
   [G: Australia]

Mitchell, Douglas W. Deficit and Inflation in a Post Keynesian Model. *J. Post Keynesian Econ.*, Summer 1981, 3(4), pp. 560–67.

Mitchell, Douglas W. Determinants of Inflation Uncertainty. *Eastern Econ. J.*, April 1981, 7(2), pp. 111–17.   [G: U.S.]

Mixon, J. Wilson, Jr.; Pratt, Lelia J. and Wallace, Myles S. The Short-Run Transmission of U.S. Price Changes under Fixed and Flexible Exchange Rates: Evidence from the U.K. *Southern Econ. J.*, April 1981, 47(4), pp. 1072–79.
   [G: U.K.; U.S.]

Modigliani, Franco and Cohn, Richard A. Inflation and the Stock Market. *Rev. Econ. Cond. Italy*, October 1981, (3), pp. 415–31.   [G: U.S.]

Montesano, Aldo. Inflazione e finanziamento del deficit pubblico. (Inflation and Public-Debt Financing. With English summary.) *Bancaria*,

November 1981, 37(11), pp. 1146–52.

Moore, Basil J. Equity Values and Inflation: Reply. *Lloyds Bank Rev.*, October 1981, (142), pp. 44–45. **[G: U.K.]**

Moore, Basil J. Equity Values and Inflation: Reply. *Lloyds Bank Rev.*, January 1981, (139), pp. 55–57.

Morciano, Michele. Schemi per l'analisi della dinamica inflazionistica. (Schemes for the Analysis of Inflation. With English summary.) *Giorn. Econ.*, July–August 1981, 40(7–8), pp. 521–49. **[G: Italy]**

Müller, Norbert. Ökonomische Macht sozialer Gruppen und Inflation. (Economic Power of Social Groups and Inflation. With English summary.) *Kredit Kapital*, 1981, 14(1), pp. 74–93.

Mussa, Michael L. Sticky Individual Prices and the Dynamics of the General Price Level. *Carnegie-Rochester Conf. Ser. Public Policy*, Autumn 1981, 15, pp. 261–96.

Mussa, Michael L. Sticky Prices and Disequilibrium Adjustment in a Rational Model of the Inflationary Process. *Amer. Econ. Rev.*, December 1981, 71(5), pp. 1020–27.

Nagarajan, Karatholuvu V. Testing Theories of Inflation and Its Acceleration in the United States, 1960–1979. *Nebr. J. Econ. Bus.*, Autumn 1981, 20(4), pp. 63–69. **[G: U.S.]**

Nelson, Charles R. Adjustment Lags versus Information Lags: A Test of Alternative Explanations of the Phillips Curve Phenomenon. *J. Money, Credit, Banking*, February 1981, 13(1), pp. 1–11.

Nelson, Charles R. Adjustment Lags versus Information Lags: A Test of Alternative Explanations of the Phillips Curve Phenomenon: A Reply. *J. Money, Credit, Banking*, November 1981, 13(4), pp. 494–96.

Neri, Fabio. On the Inflationary Consequences of a Keynesian Model: Variations on a Theme of Meade. *Metroecon.*, Feb.-Oct. 1981, 33(1–2–3), pp. 159–73.

Nielsen, Niels Christian. Inflation and Taxation: Nominal and Real Rates of Return. *J. Monet. Econ.*, March 1981, 7(2), pp. 261–70.

Niemi, Beth T. and Lloyd, Cynthia B. Female Labor Supply in the Context of Inflation. *Amer. Econ. Rev.*, May 1981, 71(2), pp. 70–75. **[G: U.S.]**

Nordhaus, William D. Tax-Based Incomes Policies: A Better Mousetrap? In *Claudon, M. P. and Cornwall, R. R., eds.*, 1981, pp. 135–51. **[G: U.S.]**

Nosse, Tetsuya. The Effects of Tax Structure Change upon Income Redistribution under Inflationary Economic Growth. *Public Finance*, 1981, 36(2), pp. 145–61. **[G: Japan]**

O'Carroll, Francis X. The Differential Impacts of Inflation on Southern Plains Farms by Selected Farm Characteristics. *Amer. J. Agr. Econ.*, December 1981, 63(5), pp. 947–55. **[G: U.S.]**

Olson, Mancur. "Incentives-Based" Stabilization Policies and the Evolution of the Macroeconomic Problem. In *Claudon, M. P. and Cornwall, R. R., eds.*, 1981, pp. 37–77.

Ostrosky, Anthony L. Recflation: Recession and Inflation in the United States: A Comment. *Econ.*

Notes, 1981, 10(2), pp. 57–58. **[G: U.S.]**

Paelinck, J. H. P. Integrated Macro-Models of Price Formation. *Greek Econ. Rev.*, August 1981, 3(2), pp. 148–57.

Papademos, Lucas. Maximum Employment and Anti-Inflation Policy. *Greek Econ. Rev.*, August 1981, 3(2), pp. 93–127.

Park, Ung-suh K. Dynamic Sources of Inflation under Economic Development: The Case of Korea. *J. Econ. Devel.*, July 1981, 6(1), pp. 77–99. **[G: Korea]**

Paunio, Jouko and Suvanto, Antti. Wage Inflation, Expectations and Indexation. *J. Monet. Econ.*, September 1981, 8(2), pp. 165–82. **[G: Finland]**

Pautler, Paul A. Uncertainty in the Demand for Money during Hyperinflation. *Econ. Inquiry*, January 1981, 19(1), pp. 165–72. **[G: Germany; Hungary; Poland]**

Persico, Pasquale. Inflazione e prezzi relativi o degli effetti di scala sul livello assoluto dei prezzi in Italia. (Inflation, and Relative Prices, or on Scale Effects on the Absolute Level of Prices in Italy. With English summary.) *Giorn. Econ.*, January–February 1981, 40(1–2), pp. 65–79. **[G: Italy]**

Phipps, A. J. The Impact of Wage Indexation on Wage Inflation in Australia: 1975(2)–1980(2) *Australian Econ. Pap.*, December 1981, 20(37), pp. 333–50. **[G: Australia]**

Picard, Pierre. Croissance et inflation dans un modèle de déséquilibres. (Growth and Inflation in a Disequilibrium Model. With English summary.) *Revue Écon.*, November 1981, 32(6), pp. 1013–44.

Pitchford, J. D. A Consistent Model of the Expectations-Augmented Phillips Curve and Inflation. *J. Macroecon.*, Fall 1981, 3(4), pp. 489–99.

Plosser, Charles I. Comments on Mussa's Paper [Sticky Individual Prices and the Dynamics of the General Price Level]. *Carnegie-Rochester Conf. Ser. Public Policy*, Autumn 1981, 15, pp. 297–300.

Portes, Richard. Reply to E. Dirksen, "The Control of Inflation? Errors in the Interpretation of CPE Data." *Economica*, August 1981, 48(191), pp. 309–11. **[G: Cent. Planned Econ.]**

Prachowny, Martin F. J. Wage Indexation: Social Benefits and Private Incentives. *J. Lab. Res.*, Spring 1981, 2(1), pp. 15–24. **[G: Canada; U.S.]**

Praet, Peter. A Comparative Approach to the Measurement of Expected Inflation. *Cah. Écon. Bruxelles*, 2nd Trimestre 1981, (90), pp. 147–71. **[G: EEC; Canada; U.S.]**

Pyo, Hak K. and Yoo, Jang H. A Note on the Effects of Imported Inflation in a Small Open Economy. *J. Econ. Devel.*, July 1981, 6(1), pp. 111–23. **[G: S. Korea]**

Qadir, A. and Qadir, K. Inflation in a Growing Economy. *Pakistan Econ. Soc. Rev.*, Winter 1981, 19(2), pp. 149–56.

Reid, Frank and Smith, Douglas A. The Impact of Demographic Changes on Unemployment. *Can. Public Policy*, Spring 1981, 7(2), pp. 348–51.

Reinhardt, Paul G. and Abner, Brian D. Inflation-Induced Price Lags and Their Redistributive Effect. *Kredit Kapital*, 1981, 14(2), pp. 153–58.

Rhea, Nolan W. A Method for Predicting the Basic

Rate of Inflation. *Bus. Econ.*, January 1981, *16*(1), pp. 90–91. **[G: U.S.]**

Risch, Bodo. "Phillips-Loops" und endogener Konjunkturzyklus. (Phillips-Loops and Endogenous Cycles. With English summary.) *Z. ges. Staatswiss.*, March 1981, *137*(1), pp. 108–24.

Robinson, Joan. Stagflation. In *Robinson, J.*, 1981, *1979*, pp. 43–53.

Roos, Lawrence K. Lessons We Can Learn. *Fed. Res. Bank St. Louis Rev.*, October 1981, *63*(8), pp. 3–6. **[G: U.K.; Switzerland; W. Germany]**

Rosefielde, Steven. Are Soviet Industrial-Production Statistics Significantly Distorted by Hidden Inflation? *J. Compar. Econ.*, June 1981, *5*(2), pp. 185–99. **[G: U.S.S.R.]**

Rosenberg, Sam and Weisskopf, Thomas E. A Conflict Theory Approach to Inflation in the Postwar U.S. Economy. *Amer. Econ. Rev.*, May 1981, *71*(2), pp. 42–47. **[G: U.S.]**

Rosenberg, Samuel. Incomes Policy: The "TIP" of the Iceberg. In *Claudon, M. P. and Cornwall, R. R., eds.*, 1981, pp. 175–95. **[G: U.S.]**

Rosenberg, Y. and Zilberfarb, Ben-Zion. An Indicator of the Dominance of Cost or Demand Factors in Periods of Inflation. *Appl. Econ.*, December 1981, *13*(4), pp. 523–30. **[G: Israel]**

Rosner, Peter. Notes on "The Welfare Cost of Permanent Inflation and Optimal Short-Run Economic Policy" *Empirica*, 1981, (2), pp. 291–300.

Saks, Daniel H. Wage Determination During Periods of High Inflation. In *Dennis, B. D., ed.*, 1981, pp. 128–34. **[G: U.S.]**

Sargent, Thomas J. A Note on the "Accelerationist" Controversy. In *Lucas, R. E. and Sargent, T. J., eds.*, 1981, *1971*, pp. 33–38.

Sargent, Thomas J. Rational Expectations, the Real Rate of Interest, and the Natural Rate of Unemployment. In *Lucas, R. E. and Sargent, T. J., eds.*, 1981, *1973*, pp. 159–98. **[G: U.S.]**

Sargent, Thomas J. The Demand for Money during Hyperinflations under Rational Expectations. In *Lucas, R. E. and Sargent, T. J., eds.*, 1981, *1977*, pp. 429–52. **[G: Europe]**

Sargent, Thomas J. and Wallace, Neil. Rational Expectations and the Dynamics of Hyperinflation. In *Lucas, R. E. and Sargent, T. J., eds.*, 1981, *1973*, pp. 405–28. **[G: Europe]**

Sargent, Thomas J. and Wallace, Neil. Some Unpleasant Monetarist Arithmetic. *Fed. Res. Bank Minn. Rev.*, Fall 1981, *5*(3), pp. 1–17.

Saunders, Anthony and Tress, Richard B. Inflation and Stock Market Returns: Some Australian Evidence. *Econ. Rec.*, March 1981, *57*(156), pp. 58–66. **[G: Australia]**

Sawhill, Isabel V. Labor Market Policies and Inflation. In *Claudon, M. P. and Cornwall, R. R., eds.*, 1981, pp. 217–31. **[G: U.S.]**

Schaafsma, Joseph. Inflation and the Standard of Living of Pensioners: A Case Study. *Can. Public Policy*, Winter 1981, *7*(1), pp. 115–18. **[G: Canada]**

Schröder, Wolfgang. Theories of Inflation and Their Recent Empirical Evidence in the Federal Republic of Germany. *Z. Wirtschaft. Sozialwissen.*, 1981, *101*(1), pp. 25–44. **[G: W. Germany]**

Schultze, Charles L. Some Macro Foundations for

Micro Theory. *Brookings Pap. Econ. Act.*, 1981, (2), pp. 521–76. **[G: U.S.]**

Scott, Maurice FG. How Best to Deflate the Economy. *Oxford Econ. Pap.*, Supplement July 1981, *33*, pp. 47–69. **[G: U.K.]**

Shapiro, Edward. Wage Inflation, Manpower Training, and the Phillips Curve: A Graphic Integration. *Amer. Econ.*, Spring 1981, *25*(1), pp. 17–21.

Shea, Koon-lam. An Alternative Theory of Inflation. *Kyklos*, 1981, *34*(4), pp. 611–28.

Sheahan, John. Incomes Policies in an Open Economy: Domestic and External Interactions. In *Claudon, M. P. and Cornwall, R. R., eds.*, 1981, pp. 155–74.

Shostak, E. The Natural Rate Hypothesis: An Econometric Test for the South African Economy. *S. Afr. J. Econ.*, March 1981, *49*(1), pp. 1–9. **[G: S. Africa]**

Shoyama, T. K. Stagflation Consequences of the Canadian Tax/Transfer System: Comments. In *Ontario Economic Council, Vol. 1*, 1981, pp. 105–13. **[G: Canada; U.S.]**

Siegel, Jeremy J. Interest Rates during the Cycle, Inventories and Monetary Policy—A Theoretical Analysis: A Comment. *Carnegie-Rochester Conf. Ser. Public Policy*, Autumn 1981, *15*, pp. 145–50.

Silva, Ricardo. Inflación reprimida en Chile: El período 1970–1973. (With English summary.) *Cuadernos Econ.*, April 1981, *18*(53), pp. 97–106. **[G: Chile]**

Stockman, Alan C. Anticipated Inflation and the Capital Stock in a Cash-in-Advance Economy. *J. Monet. Econ.*, November 1981, *8*(3), pp. 387–93.

Summers, Lawrence H. Inflation, the Stock Market, and Owner-Occupied Housing. *Amer. Econ. Rev.*, May 1981, *71*(2), pp. 429–34. **[G: U.S.]**

Summers, Lawrence H. Optimal Inflation Policy. *J. Monet. Econ.*, March 1981, *7*(2), pp. 175–94. **[G: U.S.]**

Sushka, Marie Elizabeth. Discussion [Why Problems Do not Go Away: The Case of Inflation]. *J. Econ. Hist.*, March 1981, *41*(1), pp. 29–30. **[G: U.S.]**

Sutton, John. A Formal Model of the Long-run Phillips Curve Trade-off. *Economica*, November 1981, *48*(192), pp. 329–43.

Sylos Labini, Paolo. Spinelli and Fratianni on Inflation: A Comment [Money, Prices and Wages in Italy] [Wage Inflation in Italy: A Reappraisal]. *Banca Naz. Lavoro Quart. Rev.*, December 1981, (139), pp. 461–66.

Taylor, John B. On the Relation between the Variability of Inflation and the Average Inflation Rate. *Carnegie-Rochester Conf. Ser. Public Policy*, Autumn 1981, *15*, pp. 57–85. **[G: U.S.]**

Tobin, James. Supply versus Demand Approaches to the Problem of Stagflation: Comment. In *Giersch, H, ed. (1)*, 1981, pp. 61–69. **[G: Selected OECD]**

Tompkinson, Paul. The Price Equation and Excess Demand. *Oxford Bull. Econ. Statist.*, May 1981, *43*(2), pp. 173–83.

Tuma, Elias H. Why Problems Do not Go Away:

The Case of Inflation. *J. Econ. Hist.*, March 1981, *41*(1), pp. 21–28. [G: U.K.; U.S.]

Turnovsky, Stephen J. The Optimal Intertemporal Choice of Inflation and Unemployment: An Analysis of the Steady State and Transitional Dynamics. *J. Econ. Dynam. Control*, November 1981, *3*(4), pp. 357–84.

von Ungern-Sternberg, Thomas. Inflation and Savings: International Evidence on Inflation-Induced Income Losses. *Econ. J.*, December 1981, *91*(364), pp. 961–76. [G: W. Germany; U.K.]

Van Cott, T. Norman. Inflation as a Tax on Money: Integration into IS–LM Analysis. *Public Finance Quart.*, January 1981, *9*(1), pp. 61–74.

Vartia, Pentti. Wage and Price Changes in Indexed and Non-Indexed Wage Agreements. *Ekon. Samfundets Tidskr.*, 1981, *34*(3), pp. 223–48.

Vaughan, William J. Dollar Depreciation and Domestic Inflation: A Survey of Recent Applied Research. **In** *Ballabon, M. B., ed.*, 1981, pp. 1–26. [G: U.S.]

Volker, Paul A. Expectations of Inflation and Nominal Interest Rates in Australia 1968(1)–1979(2). **In** *Jüttner, D. J., ed.*, 1981, pp. 235–56. [G: Australia]

Waldauer, Charles. Comment on "The Variable Rate Value Added Tax as an Anti-Inflation Fiscal Stabilizer." *Nat. Tax J.*, March 1981, *34*(1), pp. 131–32. [G: U.S.]

Walden, Michael L. Microeconomic Impacts of Inflation on the Food and Agriculture Sector: Discussion. *Amer. J. Agr. Econ.*, December 1981, *63*(5), pp. 965–66. [G: U.S.]

Wallace, Myles S. A Backward Bending Supply of Labor Schedule and the Short Run Phillips Curve. *Southern Econ. J.*, October 1981, *48*(2), pp. 502–05.

Watson, Donald. The Inter-Industry Effect of Cumulative Wage Indexation—A Critical Comment. *Australian Econ. Pap.*, June 1981, *20*(36), pp. 189–90.

Weintraub, Sidney. Bedrock in the Money Wage—Money Supply Inflation Controversy. *Banca Naz. Lavoro Quart. Rev.*, December 1981, (139), pp. 439–46.

Weintraub, Sidney. Tips Against Inflation. **In** *Claudon, M. P. and Cornwall, R. R., eds.*, 1981, pp. 7–34. [G: U.S.]

Welcker, Johannes. Der Eurodollarmarkt: Tatsächliche und vermeintliche Probleme. (The Euro-Dollar Market—Actual and Alleged Problems. With English summary.) *Konjunkturpolitik*, 1981, *27*(5), pp. 279–96. [G: W. Germany]

Wells, Donald R. and Gootzeit, Michael J. Rational Expectations and the Positively-Sloped Phillips Curve. *Econ. Forum*, Summer 1981, *12*(1), pp. 121–29.

Wells, Paul. Modigliani on Flexible Wages and Prices: Reply. *J. Post Keynesian Econ.*, Winter 1980–81, *3*(2), pp. 284–86.

White, Daniel L. The Variable Rate Value Added Tax as an Anti-Inflation Fiscal Stabilizer: A Response. *Nat. Tax J.*, March 1981, *34*(1), pp. 133. [G: U.S.]

Whitman, Marina v. N. International Interdependence and the U.S. Economy. **In** *Baldwin,*

R. E. and Richardson, J. D., eds., 1981, *1977*, pp. 389–408. [G: U.S.]

Wibulswasdi, Chaiyawat. Experiences of Asian Countries with Various Exchange Rate Policies: Comment. **In** *Williamson, J., ed.*, 1981, pp. 319–21. [G: Asia]

Wirick, Ronald G. The Battle against Inflation: The Bank of Canada and Its Critics. *Can. Public Policy*, Supplement, April 1981, *7*, pp. 249–59. [G: Canada]

200 Quantitative Economic Methods and Data

210 ECONOMETRIC, STATISTICAL, AND MATHEMATICAL METHODS AND MODELS

211 Econometric and Statistical Methods and Models

2110 General

Agresti, Alan. Measures of Nominal-Ordinal Association. *J. Amer. Statist. Assoc.*, September 1981, *76*(375), pp. 524–29.

Ahn, Choong Yong; Singh, Inderjit and Squire, Lyn. A Model of an Agricultural Household in a Multi-Crop Economy: The Case of Korea. *Rev. Econ. Statist.*, November 1981, *63*(4), pp. 520–25. [G: Korea]

Akaike, Hirotugu. Likelihood of a Model and Information Criteria. *J. Econometrics*, May 1981, *16*(1), pp. 3–14.

Atkinson, A. C. Likelihood Ratios, Posterior Odds and Information Criteria. *J. Econometrics*, May 1981, *16*(1), pp. 15–20.

Avery, R. C. and Hakkert, R. Comment on 'The Random Variation in Rates Based on Total Enumeration of Events' by J. R. Udry, C. Teddlie, C. M. Suchindran. *Population Stud.*, November 1981, *35*(3), pp. 467–71.

Bailey, R. A. A Unified Approach to Design of Experiments. *J. Roy. Statist. Soc.*, Part 2, 1981, *144*, pp. 214–23.

Batchelor, R. A. Aggregate Expectations under the Stable Laws. *J. Econometrics*, June 1981, *16*(2), pp. 199–210.

Berndt, Ernst R. and Wood, David O. Engineering and Econometric Interpretations of Energy–Capital Complementarity: Reply and Further Results. *Amer. Econ. Rev.*, December 1981, *71*(5), pp. 1105–10. [G: U.S.]

Brockwell, P. J. and Brown, B. M. High-Efficiency Estimation for the Positive Stable Laws. *J. Amer. Statist. Assoc.*, September 1981, *76*(375), pp. 626–31.

Chandra, Mahesh; Singpurwalla, Nozer D. and Stephens, Michael A. Kolmogorov Statistics for Tests of Fit for the Extreme-Value and Weibull Distributions. *J. Amer. Statist. Assoc.*, September 1981, *76*(375), pp. 729–31.

Chow, Gregory C. A Comparison of the Information and Posterior Probability Criteria for Model Selection. *J. Econometrics*, May 1981, *16*(1), pp. 21–33.

Costantini, Domenico and Geymonat, Ludovico. Per una concezione oggettivista della probabilità. (For an Objectivist Notion of Probability. With English summary.) *Statistica*, October–December 1981, *41*(4), pp. 519–33.

Cox, D. R. Theory and General Principle in Statistics. *J. Roy. Statist. Soc.*, Part 3, 1981, *144*, pp. 289–97.

de Cristofaro, Rodolfo. Outlines for a Refoundation of Classical Statistics. *Statistica*, July–September 1981, *41*(3), pp. 375–94.

Durbin, J. Approximations for Densities of Sufficient Estimators. *J. Econometrics*, May 1981, *16*(1), pp. 165.

Fisher, Gordon R. and McAleer, Michael. Alternative Procedures and Associated Tests of Significance for Non-Nested Hypotheses. *J. Econometrics*, May 1981, *16*(1), pp. 103–19.

Gallant, A. Ronald. On the Bias in Flexible Functional Forms and an Essentially Unbiased Form: The Fourier Flexible Form. *J. Econometrics*, February 1981, *15*(2), pp. 211–45. [G: U.S.]

Geweke, John. The Approximate Slopes of Econometric Tests. *Econometrica*, November 1981, *49*(6), pp. 1427–42.

Gili, Adolfo. Valori medi e misure di variabilità nel pensiero di Paolo Fortunati. (Mean Values and Indices of Variability in Paolo Fortunati's Thought. With English summary.) *Statistica*, October–December 1981, *41*(4), pp. 511–18.

Godfrey, Lesley G. On the Invariance of the Lagrange Multiplier Test with Respect to Certain Changes in the Alternative Hypothesis. *Econometrica*, November 1981, *49*(6), pp. 1443–55.

Griffin, James M. Engineering and Econometric Interpretations of Energy–Capital Complementarity: Comment. *Amer. Econ. Rev.*, December 1981, *71*(5), pp. 1100–1104. [G: U.S.]

de Haan, Laurens. Estimation of the Minimum of a Function Using Order Statistics. *J. Amer. Statist. Assoc.*, June 1981, *76*(374), pp. 467–69.

Karlin, Samuel and Rinott, Yosef. Univariate and Multivariate Total Positivity, Generalized Convexity and Related Inequalities. In *Schaible, S. and Ziemba, W. T.*, eds., 1981, pp. 703–18.

Kronmal, Richard A. and Peterson, Arthur V., Jr. A Variant of the Acceptance-Rejection Method for Computer Generation of Random Variables. *J. Amer. Statist. Assoc.*, June 1981, *76*(374), pp. 446–51.

Kruskal, William. Statistics in Society: Problems Unsolved and Unformulated. *J. Amer. Statist. Assoc.*, September 1981, *76*(375), pp. 505–15.

Leamer, Edward E. Sets of Estimates of Location. *Econometrica*, January 1981, *49*(1), pp. 193–204.

Leinhardt, Samuel. Data Analysis and Statistics Education in Public Policy Programs. In *Crecine, J. P.*, ed., 1981, pp. 53–61.

Leitch, Robert A., et al. Implementation of Upper Multinomial Bound Using Clustering. *J. Amer. Statist. Assoc.*, September 1981, *76*(375), pp. 530–33.

Lippman, Steven A. and McCall, John J. The Economics of Uncertainty: Selected Topics and Probabilistic Methods. In *Arrow, K. J. and Intriligator, M. D.*, eds., 1981, pp. 211–84.

Lucas, Robert E., Jr. and Sargent, Thomas J. Rational Expectations and Econometric Practice: Introduction. In *Lucas, R. E. and Sargent, T. J.*, eds., 1981, pp. xi–xl.

Malinvaud, Edmond. Econometrics Faced with the Needs of Macroeconomic Policy. *Econometrica*, November 1981, *49*(6), pp. 1363–75.

Martin, Margaret E. Statistical Practice in Bureaucracies. *J. Amer. Statist. Assoc.*, March 1981, *76*(373), pp. 1–8. [G: U.S.]

Mayo, Deborah. Testing Statistical Testing. In *Pitt, J. C.*, ed., 1981, pp. 175–203.

McDonald, James B. and Ransom, Michael R. An Analysis of the Bounds for the Gini Coefficient. *J. Econometrics*, November 1981, *17*(2), pp. 177–88.

Merkies, Arnold H. Q. M. and Bikker, Jacob A. Aggregation of Lag Patterns with an Application in the Construction Industry. *Europ. Econ. Rev.*, March 1981, *15*(3), pp. 385–405.
[G: Netherlands]

Monari, Paola. La media geometrica in uno schema teorico generalizzato di variabilità. (The Geometric Mean in a Generalized Model for Variability. With English summary.) *Statistica*, January–March 1981, *41*(1), pp. 115–27.

Moors, J. J. A. Inadmissibility of Linearly Invariant Estimators in Truncated Parameter Spaces. *J. Amer. Statist. Assoc.*, December 1981, *76*(376), pp. 910–15.

Muliere, Pietro. Sull'invarianza del rapporto di concentrazione *R* di gini. (On the Invariance of Gini's Concentration Ratio R. With English summary.) *Statistica*, April–June 1981, *41*(2), pp. 333–44.

Pesaran, M. H. Pitfalls of Testing Non-Nested Hypotheses by the Lagrange Multiplier Method. *J. Econometrics*, December 1981, *17*(3), pp. 323–31.

Poirier, Dale J. and Klepper, Steven. Model Occurrence and Model Selection in Panel Data Sets. *J. Econometrics*, December 1981, *17*(3), pp. 333–50.

Rosa, Rodolfo. Metodo Monte Carlo e modelli probabilistici nello studio delle interazioni atomiche. (Monte Carlo Method and Probabilistic Models in Atomic Interactions Studies. With English summary.) *Statistica*, April–June 1981, *41*(2), pp. 211–35.

Scardovi, Italo. Fondamenti statistici delle scienze sociali: annotazioni storiografiche. (Statistical Foundations in Social Science: Historiographic Notes. With English summary.) *Statistica*, January–March 1981, *41*(1), pp. 149–78.

Sebestyén, Joseph. Accomplishments, Opportunities and Needs of Agricultural Economists vis-à-vis Quantitative Techniques. In *Johnson, G. and Maunder, A.*, eds., 1981, pp. 620–28.

Suchindran, C. M. A Reply to Avery and Hakkert [The Random Variation in Rates Based on Total Enumeration of Events]. *Population Stud.*, November 1981, *35*(3), pp. 473–75.

Taeuber, Conrad. Transfer of Methodology. *Rev. Public Data Use (See J. Econ. Soc. Meas. after 4/85)*, April 1981, *9*(1), pp. 39–45.

Zaman, Asad. Estimators without Moments: The Case of the Reciprocal of a Normal Mean. *J.*

Econometrics, February 1981, *15*(2), pp. 289–98.

Zellner, Arnold. Philosophy and Objectives of Econometrics. **In** *Currie, D.; Nobay, R. and Peel, D., eds.,* 1981, pp. 24–34.

2112 Inferential Problems in Simultaneous Equation Systems

Ågren, Anders. The GEID Specification: An Interpretation and Some of Its Consequences. **In** *Wold, H., ed.,* 1981, pp. 65–75.

Amemiya, Takeshi. Qualitative Response Models: A Survey. *J. Econ. Lit.,* December 1981, *19*(4), pp. 1483–1536.

Avery, Robert B. Estimating Credit Constraints by Switching Regressions. **In** *Manski, C. F. and McFadden, D., eds.,* 1981, pp. 435–72.
[G: U.S.]

Baillie, Richard T. Prediction from the Dynamic Simultaneous Equation Model with Vector Autoregressive Errors. *Econometrica,* September 1981, *49*(5), pp. 1331–37.

Baltagi, Badi H. Simultaneous Equations with Error Components. *J. Econometrics,* November 1981, *17*(2), pp. 189–200.

Barnett, William A. and Kopecky, Kenneth J. Estimation of Implicit Utility Models. *Europ. Econ. Rev.,* March 1981, *15*(3), pp. 247–59.

Bergström, Reinhold. Extensions of the GEID and IIV Estimators: The Case of Serially Correlated Residuals and Lagged Endogenous Variables. **In** *Wold, H., ed.,* 1981, pp. 197–223. [G: U.S.]

Bianchi, Carlo; Calzolari, Giorgio and Corsi, Paolo. Estimating Asymptotic Standard Errors and Inconsistencies of Impact Multipliers in Nonlinear Econometric Models. *J. Econometrics,* August 1981, *16*(3), pp. 277–94.

Binkley, James K. The Relationship between Elasticity and Least Squares Bias. *Rev. Econ. Statist.,* May 1981, *63*(2), pp. 307–09.

Bodin, Lennart. Algorithms for Reordering Interdependent Systems. **In** *Wold, H., ed.,* 1981, pp. 225–41.

Bodin, Lennart. Iterative Algorithms for Fix-Point Estimation, Their Design and Convergence Properties. **In** *Wold, H., ed.,* 1981, pp. 37–63.

Bowden, R. J. and Turkington, D. A. A Comparative Study of Instrumental Variables Estimators for Nonlinear Simultaneous Models. *J. Amer. Statist. Assoc.,* December 1981, *76*(376), pp. 988–95.

Breusch, T. S. and Godfrey, Lesley G. A Review of Recent Work on Testing for Auto-correlation in Dynamic Simultaneous Models. **In** *Currie, D.; Nobay, R. and Peel, D., eds.,* 1981, pp. 63–l05.

Brown, Bryan W. Sample Size Requirements in Full Information Maximum Likelihood Estimation. *Int. Econ. Rev.,* June 1981, *22*(2), pp. 443–59.

Chow, Gregory C. Estimation of Rational Expectations Models. **In** *Lucas, R. E. and Sargent, T. J., eds.,* 1981, *1980,* pp. 355–67.

Chow, Gregory C. Selection of Econometric Models by the Information Criterion. **In** *[Valavanis, S.],* 1981, pp. 199–214.

Edgerton, David. An Analysis of the Nonlinear Klein–Goldberger Model Using Fix-Point Esti-

mation and Other Methods. **In** *Wold, H., ed.,* 1981, pp. 243–82. [G: U.S.]

Fisher, Gordon R. Two Types of Residuals and the Classical Identifiability Test Statistic. **In** *[Valavanis, S.],* 1981, pp. 215–30.

Goldfeld, Stephen M. and Quandt, Richard E. Econometric Modelling with Non-Normal Disturbances. *J. Econometrics,* November 1981, *17*(2), pp. 141–55.

Goldfeld, Stephen M. and Quandt, Richard E. Single-Market Disequilibrium Models: Estimation and Testing. *Econ. Stud. Quart.,* April 1981, *32*(1), pp. 12–28.

Goldfeld, Stephen M. and Quandt, Richard E. Single-Market Disequilibrium Model: Estimating and Testing. *J. Econometrics,* May 1981, *16*(1), pp. 157.

Harvey, Andrew C. and Phillips, Garry D. A. Testing for Heteroscedasticity in Simultaneous Equation Models. *J. Econometrics,* April 1981, *15*(3), pp. 311–40.

Harvey, Andrew C. and Phillips, Garry D. A. Testing for Serial Correlation in Simultaneous Equation Models: Some Further Results. *J. Econometrics,* September 1981, *17*(1), pp. 99–105.

Heckman, James J. Statistical Models for Discrete Panel Data. **In** *Manski, C. F. and McFadden, D., eds.,* 1981, pp. 114–78.

Kunitomo, Naoto. Asymptotic Optimality of the Limited Information Maximum Likelihood Estimator in Large Econometric Models. *Econ. Stud. Quart.,* December 1981, *32*(3), pp. 247–66.

Kunitomo, Naoto; Morimune, Kimio and Tsukuda, Yoshihiko. Asymptotic Expansions of the Distributions of k-Class Estimators When the Disturbances Are Small. *Econ. Stud. Quart.,* August 1981, *32*(2), pp. 156–63.

Leamer, Edward E. Is It a Demand Curve, or Is It a Supply Curve? Partial Identification through Inequality Constraints. *Rev. Econ. Statist.,* August 1981, *63*(3), pp. 319–27. [G: U.S.]

Lee, Lung-Fei. Fully Recursive Probability Models and Multivariate Log-Linear Probability Models for the Analysis of Qualitative Data. *J. Econometrics,* May 1981, *16*(1), pp. 51–69. [G: U.S.]

Lee, Lung-Fei. Simultaneous Equations Models with Discrete and Censored Dependent Variables. **In** *Manski, C. F. and McFadden, D., eds.,* 1981, pp. 347–64.

Lerman, Steven R. and Manski, Charles F. On the Use of Simulated Frequencies to Approximate Choice Probabilities. **In** *Manski, C. F. and McFadden, D., eds.,* 1981, pp. 305–19.

Lyttkens, Ejnar. The Parametric Fix-Point (PFP) and the Algebraic Fix-Point (AFP) Methods. **In** *Wold, H., ed.,* 1981, pp. 77–107.

Maddala, G. S. Statistical Inference in Relation to the Size of the Model. **In** *Kmenta, J. and Ramsey, J. B., eds.,* 1981, pp. 191–218.

Maddala, G. S. Statistical Inference in Relation to the Size of the Model: Discussion. **In** *Kmenta, J. and Ramsey, J. B., eds.,* 1981, pp. 279–80.

Maddala, G. S. and Trost, Robert P. Alternative Formulations of the Nerlove-Press Models. *J. Econometrics,* May 1981, *16*(1), pp. 35–49.
[G: U.S.]

May, Sydney. Fix-Point Estimates of the Structure of a Model Using Different Y Proxy Starts. In *Wold, H., ed.*, 1981, pp. 303–18.

McCarthy, Michael D. A Note on the Moments of Partially Restricted Reduced Forms. *J. Econometrics*, December 1981, *17*(3), pp. 383–87.

McDonald, John and Darroch, John. Large Sample Estimation and Testing Procedures for Dynamic Equation Systems: Comment. *J. Econometrics*, September 1981, *17*(1), pp. 127–30.

Morimune, Kimio. Asymptotic Expansions of the Distribution of an Improved Limited Information Maximum Likelihood Estimator. *J. Amer. Statist. Assoc.*, June 1981, *76*(374), pp. 476–78.

Osborn, Denise R. A Review of Recent Work on Testing for Auto-correlation in Dynamic Simultaneous Models: Comment. In *Currie, D.; Nobay, R. and Peel, D., eds.*, 1981, pp. 106–10.

Otter, P. W. Identification and Estimation of Linear (Economic) Systems, Operating under Linear Closed-Loop Control. In *Janssen, J. M. L.; Pau, L. F. and Straszak, A. J., eds.*, 1981, pp. 305–16.

Paass, G. Assessing the Quality of Prediction Baykal: Bayesian Prediction by Kalman Filtering. In *Janssen, J. M. L.; Pau, L. F. and Straszak, A. J., eds.*, 1981, pp. 297–303.

Pesaran, M. H. Identification of Rational Expectations Models. *J. Econometrics*, August 1981, *16*(3), pp. 375–98.

Poirier, Dale J. A Switching Simultaneous Equations Model of Physician Behaviour in Ontario. In *Manski, C. F. and McFadden, D., eds.*, 1981, pp. 392–421. **[G: Canada]**

Poirier, Dale J. and Ruud, Paul A. On the Appropriateness of Endogenous Switching. *J. Econometrics*, June 1981, *16*(2), pp. 249–56.

Rhodes, George F., Jr. Exact Density Functions and Approximate Critical Regions for Likelihood Ratio Identifiability Test Statistics. *Econometrica*, June 1981, *49*(4), pp. 1035–55.

Rhodes, George F., Jr. and Westbrook, M. Daniel. A Study of Estimator Densities and Performance under Misspecification. *J. Econometrics*, August 1981, *16*(3), pp. 311–37.

Sargan, J. D. Identification in Models with Autoregressive Errors. *J. Econometrics*, May 1981, *16*(1), pp. 160–61.

Schmidt, Peter. Constraints on the Parameters in Simultaneous Tobit and Probit Models. In *Manski, C. F. and McFadden, D., eds.*, 1981, pp. 422–34.

Selén, Jan. A Search for Asymptotically Efficient Estimators: Especially Estimators of the GEID (FP) Type in the Case of Autoregressive Errors. In *Wold, H., ed.*, 1981, pp. 159–96. **[G: U.S.]**

Speakes, Jeffrey K. Inference in Some Disaggregated Models with Special Covariance Structure. *J. Econometrics*, June 1981, *16*(2), pp. 257–74.

Spencer, David E. and Berk, Kenneth N. A Limited Information Specification Test [Specification Tests in Econometrics]. *Econometrica*, June 1981, *49*(4), pp. 1079–85.

Swamy, P. A. V. B. and Mehta, J. S. On the Existence of Moments of Partially Restricted Reduced Form Estimators: A Comment. *J. Econometrics*, December 1981, *17*(3), pp. 389–92.

Vermeulen, P. J. Parameter and Structural Sensitivity of Econometric Models. In *Janssen, J. M. L.; Pau, L. F. and Straszak, A. J., eds.*, 1981, pp. 411–17. **[G: U.S.]**

Waldman, Donald M. An Economic Interpretation of Parameter Constraints in a Simultaneous-Equations Model with Limited Dependent Variables. *Int. Econ. Rev.*, Oct. 1981, *22*(3), pp. 731–39.

Wallis, Kenneth F. Econometric Implications of the Rational Expectations Hypothesis. In *Lucas, R. E. and Sargent, T. J., eds.*, 1981, *1980*, pp. 329–54.

Westlund, Anders. On Fix-Point Estimation in Interdependent Systems with Specification Errors. In *Wold, H., ed.*, 1981, pp. 283–302.

Wold, Herman. The Fix-Point Approach to Interdependent Systems: Review and Current Outlook. In *Wold, H., ed.*, 1981, pp. 1–36.

2113 Distributed Lags and Serially Correlated Disturbance Terms; Inferential Problems in Single Equation Models

Amato, Vittorio. Il coefficiente di correlazione multipla è una distanza di Mahalanobis. (The Multiple Correlation Coefficient as a Mahalanobis Distance. With English summary.) *Rivista Int. Sci. Econ. Com.*, June 1981, *28*(6), pp. 612–16.

Amemiya, Takeshi. Qualitative Response Models: A Survey. *J. Econ. Lit.*, December 1981, *19*(4), pp. 1483–1536.

Amemiya, Takeshi and Powell, James L. A Comparison of the Box-Cox Maximum Likelihood Estimator and the Non-Linear Two-Stage Least Squares Estimator. *J. Econometrics*, December 1981, *17*(3), pp. 351–81.

Anderson, T. W. and Hsiao, Cheng. Estimation of Dynamic Models with Error Components. *J. Amer. Statist. Assoc.*, September 1981, *76*(375), pp. 598–606.

Arabmazar, Abbas and Schmidt, Peter. Further Evidence on the Robustness of the Tobit Estimator to Heteroskedasticity. *J. Econometrics*, November 1981, *17*(2), pp. 253–58.

Baltagi, Badi H. Pooling: An Experimental Study of Alternative Testing and Estimation Procedures in a Two-Way Error Component Model. *J. Econometrics*, September 1981, *17*(1), pp. 21–49.

Bartels, Robert and Goodhew, John. The Robustness of the Durbin–Watson Test. *Rev. Econ. Statist.*, February 1981, *63*(1), pp. 136–39.

Belsley, David A. Assessing the Quality of Regression Estimates through a Test for Signal-to-Noise and Its Application to Detecting Harmful Collinearity. *J. Econometrics*, May 1981, *16*(1), pp. 167.

Ben-Akiva, Moshe and Watanatada, Thawat. Application of a Continuous Spatial Choice Logit Model. In *Manski, C. F. and McFadden, D., eds.*, 1981, pp. 320–43.

Bergström, Reinhold. Estimation of Real-World Models by Fix-Point and Other Methods. In *Wold, H., ed.*, 1981, pp. 109–57. **[G: U.S.]**

Betancourt, Roger R. and Kelejian, Harry H.

Lagged Endogenous Variables and the Cochrane-Orcutt Procedure. *Econometrica*, June 1981, 49(4), pp. 1073–78.

Bickel, Peter J. and Doksum, Kjell A. An Analysis of Transformations Revisited. *J. Amer. Statist. Assoc.*, June 1981, 76(374), pp. 296–311.

Binkley, James K. The Relationship between Elasticity and Least Squares Bias. *Rev. Econ. Statist.*, May 1981, 63(2), pp. 307–09.

Biørn, Erik. Estimating Economic Relations from Incomplete Cross-Section/Time-Series Data. *J. Econometrics*, June 1981, 16(2), pp. 221–36.

Bishop, Robert V. The Use and Misuse of Summary Statistics in Regression Analysis. *Agr. Econ. Res.*, January 1981, 33(1), pp. 13–18.

Breusch, T. S. and Godfrey, Lesley G. A Review of Recent Work on Testing for Auto-correlation in Dynamic Simultaneous Models. In *Currie, D.; Nobay, R. and Peel, D.*, *eds.*, 1981, pp. 63–105.

Buck, Andrew J. and Hakim, Simon. Appropriate Roles for Statistical Decision Theory and Hypothesis Testing in Model Selection: An Exposition. *Reg. Sci. Urban Econ.*, February 1981, 11(1), pp. 135–47. [G: U.S.]

Buck, Andrew J. and Hakim, Simon. Inequality Constraints, Multicollinearity and Models of Police Expenditure. *Southern Econ. J.*, October 1981, 48(2), pp. 449–63.

Buse, A. Pooling Time Series and Cross Section Data: A Minimum Chi-Squared Approach. *Manchester Sch. Econ. Soc. Stud.*, September 1981, 49(3), pp. 229–44.

Carter, R. A. L. Improved Stein-rule Estimator for Regression Problems: Comment. *J. Econometrics*, September 1981, 17(1), pp. 113–23.

Chamberlain, Gary. Models of Duration Dependence. *J. Econometrics*, May 1981, 16(1), pp. 164.

Chen, Chan-Fu. The EM Approach to the Multiple Indicators and Multiple Causes Model via the Estimation of the Latent Variable. *J. Amer. Statist. Assoc.*, September 1981, 76(375), pp. 704–08.

Cooley, Thomas F. and LeRoy, Stephen F. Identification and Estimation of Money Demand. *Amer. Econ. Rev.*, December 1981, 71(5), pp. 825–44. [G: U.S.]

Corradi, Corrado. On the Characterization of Smooth Distributed Lag Estimators: A Comment. *Statistica*, April–June 1981, 41(2), pp. 301–04.

Cosslett, Stephen R. Efficient Estimation of Discrete-Choice Models. In *Manski, C. F. and McFadden, D.*, *eds.*, 1981, pp. 51–111.

Cosslett, Stephen R. Maximum Likelihood Estimator for Choice-Based Samples. *Econometrica*, September 1981, 49(5), pp. 1289–1316.

Cotterman, Robert F. A Note on the Consistency of the GLS Estimator in Triangular Structural Systems. *Econometrica*, November 1981, 49(6), pp. 1589–91.

Davidson, James E. H. Problems with the Estimation of Moving Average Processes. *J. Econometrics*, August 1981, 16(3), pp. 295–310.

Davidson, Russell and MacKinnon, James G. Several Tests for Model Specification in the Presence of Alternative Hypotheses. *Econometrica*, May 1981, 49(3), pp. 781–93.

Deutsch, E. and Tintner, Gerhard. Aggregation und empirische Modelle: Untersuchungen anhand eines Produktionsmodells. (Aggregation and Empirical Models: Investigations by Means of a Production Model. With English summary.) *Jahr. Nationalökon. Statist.*, July 1981, 196(4), pp. 289–308.

Dhrymes, Phoebus J. On the Estimation of the Polynomial Lag Hypothesis. *Greek Econ. Rev.*, April 1981, 3(1), pp. 18–24.

Doran, Howard E. Omission of an Observation from a Regression Analysis: A Discussion on Efficiency Loss, with Applications. *J. Econometrics*, August 1981, 16(3), pp. 367–74.

Erickson, Gary M. Using Ridge Regression to Estimate Directly Lagged Effects in Marketing. *J. Amer. Statist. Assoc.*, December 1981, 76(376), pp. 766–73. [G: U.S.]

Estes, Edmund A.; Blakeslee, Leroy L. and Mittelhammer, Ron C. On Variances of Conditional Linear Least-Squares Search Parameter Estimates. *Amer. J. Agr. Econ.*, February 1981, 63(1), pp. 141–45.

Evans, G. B. A. and Savin, N. E. Testing for Unit Roots: 1. *Econometrica*, May 1981, 49(3), pp. 753–79.

Fischer, Gregory W. and Nagin, Daniel. Random versus Fixed Coefficient Quantal Choice Models. In *Manski, C. F. and McFadden, D.*, *eds.*, 1981, pp. 273–304.

Florens, J.-P.; Mouchart, M. and Richard, Jean-François. Specification and Inference in Linear Models. *J. Econometrics*, May 1981, 16(1), pp. 153.

Friedman, Jerome H. and Stuetzle, Werner. Projection Pursuit Regression. *J. Amer. Statist. Assoc.*, December 1981, 76(376), pp. 817–23.

Fuller, Wayne A. and Hasza, David P. Properties of Predictors for Autoregressive Time Series. *J. Amer. Statist. Assoc.*, March 1981, 76(373), pp. 155–61.

Gale, William A. How Well Can We Measure Price Changes? In *Gale, W. A.*, *ed.*, 1981, pp. 51–114. [G: U.S.]

Geweke, John F. and Meese, Richard. Estimating Regression Models of Finite but Unknown Order. *J. Econometrics*, May 1981, 16(1), pp. 162.

Geweke, John F. and Meese, Richard. Estimating Regression Models of Finite but Unknown Order. *Int. Econ. Rev.*, February 1981, 22(1), pp. 55–70.

Gibbons, Diane Galarneau. A Simulation Study of Some Ridge Estimators. *J. Amer. Statist. Assoc.*, March 1981, 76(373), pp. 131–39.

Giles, David E. A. and Low, Chan Kee. Choosing between Alternative Structural Equations Estimated by Instrumental Variables. *Rev. Econ. Statist.*, August 1981, 63(3), pp. 476–68.

Godfrey, Lesley G. and Wickens, Michael R. Testing Linear and Log-Linear Regressions for Functional Form. *Rev. Econ. Stud.*, July 1981, 48(3), pp. 487–96.

Goel, Prem K. and DeGroot, Morris H. Information about Hyperparameters in Hierarchical Models. *J. Amer. Statist. Assoc.*, March 1981, 76(373), pp. 140–47.

Goldberger, Arthur S. Linear Regression after Selection. *J. Econometrics*, April 1981, *15*(3), pp. 357–66.

Goldfeld, Stephen M. and Quandt, Richard E. Econometric Modelling with Non-Normal Disturbances. *J. Econometrics*, November 1981, *17*(2), pp. 141–55.

Goldfeld, Stephen M. and Quandt, Richard E. Single-Market Disequilibrium Model: Estimating and Testing. *J. Econometrics*, May 1981, *16*(1), pp. 157.

Gottschalk, Peter T. A Note on Estimating Treatment Effects [The Estimation of Labor Supply Models Using Experimental Data]. *Amer. Econ. Rev.*, September 1981, *71*(4), pp. 764–69. [G: U.S.]

Gourieroux, Christian; Holly, Alberto and Monfort, Alain. Kuhn-Tucker, Likelihood Ratio and Wald Tests for Nonlinear Models with Inequality Constraints on the Parameters. *J. Econometrics*, May 1981, *16*(1), pp. 166.

Gourieroux, Christian and Monfort, Alain. Asymptotic Properties of the Maximum Likelihood Estimator in Dichotomous Logit Models. *J. Econometrics*, September 1981, *17*(1), pp. 83–97.

Gourieroux, Christian and Monfort, Alain. On the Problem of Missing Data in Linear Models. *Rev. Econ. Stud.*, October 1981, *48*(4), pp. 579–86.

Greene, William H. On the Asymptotic Bias of the Ordinary Least Squares Estimator of the Tobit Model. *Econometrica*, March 1981, *49*(2), pp. 505–13.

Greene, William H. Sample Selection Bias as a Specification Error: Comment. *Econometrica*, May 1981, *49*(3), pp. 795–98.

Guilkey, David K. and Price, J. Michael. On Comparing Restricted Least Squares Estimators. *J. Econometrics*, April 1981, *15*(3), pp. 397–404.

Gupta, Yash P. and Maasoumi, Esfandiar. Specification Analysis in a Dynamic Model. In *[Valavanis, S.]*, 1981, pp. 89–103.

Hall, Anthony David and Pagan, Adrian Rodney. The LIML and Related Estimators of an Equation with Moving Average Disturbances. *Int. Econ. Rev.*, October 1981, *22*(3), pp. 719–30.

Harrison, M. J. A Comparison of the Bounds, Beta-approximate, and Exact Variants of Two Tests for Heteroscedasticity Based on Ordinary Least Squares Residuals. *Econ. Soc. Rev.*, July 1981, *12*(4), pp. 235–52.

Harvey, Andrew C. and McAvinchey, Ian D. On the Relative Efficiency of Various Estimators of Regression Models with Moving Average Disturbances. In *[Valavanis, S.]*, 1981, pp. 105–18.

Hatanaka, Michio. Confidence Judgment of the Extrapolation from a Dynamic Money Demand Function. (In Japanese. With English summary.) *Osaka Econ. Pap.*, December 1981, *31*(2–3), pp. 149–62.

Hausman, Jerry A. and Taylor, William E. Panel Data and Unobservable Individual Effects. *J. Econometrics*, May 1981, *16*(1), pp. 155.

Hausman, Jerry A. and Taylor, William E. Panel Data and Unobservable Individual Effects. *Econometrica*, November 1981, *49*(6), pp. 1377–98. [G: U.S.]

Hausman, Jerry A. and Wise, David A. Stratification

on Endogenous Variables and Estimation: The Gary Income Maintenance Experiment. In *Manski, C. F. and McFadden, D., eds.*, 1981, pp. 365–91. [G: U.S.]

Havenner, Arthur and Craine, Roger. Estimation Analogies in Control. *J. Amer. Statist. Assoc.*, December 1981, *76*(376), pp. 850–59.

Heckman, James J. Statistical Models for Discrete Panel Data. In *Manski, C. F. and McFadden, D., eds.*, 1981, pp. 114–78.

Heckman, James J. The Incidental Parameters Problem and the Problem of Initial Conditions in Estimating a Discrete Time-Discrete Data Stochastic Process. In *Manski, C. F. and McFadden, D., eds.*, 1981, pp. 179–95.

Hendry, David F. and Richard, Jean-François. Model Formulation to Simplify Selection When Specification Is Uncertain. *J. Econometrics*, May 1981, *16*(1), pp. 159.

Hill, R. Carter; Ziemer, Rod F. and White, Fred C. Mitigating the Effects of Multicollinearity Using Exact and Stochastic Restrictions: The Case of an Aggregate Agricultural Production Function in Thailand: Comment. *Amer. J. Agr. Econ.*, May 1981, *63*(2), pp. 298–300. [G: Thailand]

Hoffman, Dennis L. and Schmidt, Peter. Testing the Restrictions Implied by the Rational Expectations Hypothesis. *J. Econometrics*, February 1981, *15*(2), pp. 265–87.

Hulten, Charles R. and Wykoff, Frank C. The Estimation of Economic Depreciation Using Vintage Asset Prices: An Application of the Box-Cox Power Transformation. *J. Econometrics*, April 1981, *15*(3), pp. 367–96. [G: U.S.]

Jarque, Carlos M. Efficient Grouping of Observations in Regression Analysis. *Int. Econ. Rev.*, October 1981, *22*(3), pp. 709–18.

Kariya, Takeaki. Bounds for the Covariance Matrices of Zellner's Estimator in the SUR Model and the 2SAE in a Heteroscedastic Model. *J. Amer. Statist. Assoc.*, December 1981, *76*(376), pp. 975–79.

Keller, Wouter J. Public Sector Employment and the Distribution of Income. *J. Public Econ.*, April 1981, *15*(2), pp. 235–49. [G: Netherlands]

Kennedy, Peter E. Estimation with Correctly Interpreted Dummy Variables in Semilogarithmic Equations [The Interpretation of Dummy Variables in Semilogarithmic Equations]. *Amer. Econ. Rev.*, September 1981, *71*(4), pp. 801.

Kennedy, Peter E. The "Ballentine": A Graphical Aid for Econometrics [An Alternative Approach to Specification Errors]. *Australian Econ. Pap.*, December 1981, *20*(37), pp. 414–16.

King, Maxwell L. A Note on Szroeter's Bounds Test. *Oxford Bull. Econ. Statist.*, August 1981, *43*(3), pp. 315–21.

King, Maxwell L. The Alternative Durbin–Watson Test: An Assessment of Durbin and Watson's Choice of Test Statistic. *J. Econometrics*, September 1981, *17*(1), pp. 51–66.

King, Maxwell L. The Durbin-Watson Test for Serial Correlation: Bounds for Regressions with Trend and/or Seasonal Dummy Variables. *Econometrica*, November 1981, *49*(6), pp. 1571–81.

King, Maxwell L. The Durbin–Watson Bounds Test

and Regressions without an Intercept. *Australian Econ. Pap.*, June 1981, *20*(36), pp. 161–70.

Kirkpatrick, Grant. Further Results on the Time Series Analysis of Real Wages and Employment for U.S. Manufacturing, 1948–1977. *Weltwirtsch. Arch.*, 1981, *117*(2), pp. 326–51. **[G: U.S.]**

Kloek, T. OLS Estimation in a Model Where a Microvariable Is Explained by Aggregates and Contemporaneous Disturbances Are Equicorrelated. *Econometrica*, January 1981, *49*(1), pp. 205–07.

Kmenta, Jan. On the Problem of Missing Measurements in the Estimation of Economic Relationships. In *[Valavanis, S.]*, 1981, pp. 233–57.

Koenker, Roger W. A Note on Studentizing a Test for Heteroscedasticity. *J. Econometrics*, September 1981, *17*(1), pp. 107–12.

Kourouklis, S. and Paige, C. C. A Constrained Least Squares Approach to the General Gauss-Markov Linear Model. *J. Amer. Statist. Assoc.*, September 1981, *76*(375), pp. 620–25.

Krasker, William S. The Role of Bounded-Influence Estimation in Model Selection. *J. Econometrics*, May 1981, *16*(1), pp. 131–38. **[G: U.S.]**

Lahiri, Kajal and Egy, Daniel. Joint Estimation and Testing for Functional Form and Heteroskedasticity. *J. Econometrics*, February 1981, *15*(2), pp. 299–307.

Lawless, J. F. Mean Squared Error Properties of Generalized Ridge Estimators. *J. Amer. Statist. Assoc.*, June 1981, *76*(374), pp. 462–66.

Leamer, Edward E. Coordinate-Free Ridge Regression Bounds. *J. Amer. Statist. Assoc.*, December 1981, *76*(376), pp. 842–49.

Lee, Lung-Fei. Fully Recursive Probability Models and Multivariate Log-Linear Probability Models for the Analysis of Qualitative Data. *J. Econometrics*, May 1981, *16*(1), pp. 51–69. **[G: U.S.]**

Lerman, Steven R. and Manski, Charles F. On the Use of Simulated Frequencies to Approximate Choice Probabilities. In *Manski, C. F. and McFadden, D., eds.*, 1981, pp. 305–19.

Liu, Lon-Mu and Hanssens, Dominique M. A Bayesian Approach to Time-Varying Cross-Sectional Regression Models. *J. Econometrics*, April 1981, *15*(3), pp. 341–56.

Lütkepohl, Helmut. A Model for Non-Negative and Non-Positive Distributed Lag Functions. *J. Econometrics*, June 1981, *16*(2), pp. 211–19. **[G: U.S.]**

Maddala, G. S. and Trost, Robert P. Alternative Formulations of the Nerlove-Press Models. *J. Econometrics*, May 1981, *16*(1), pp. 35–49. **[G: U.S.]**

Manski, Charles F. and McFadden, Daniel. Alternative Estimators and Sample Designs for Discrete Choice Analysis. In *Manski, C. F. and McFadden, D., eds.*, 1981, pp. 2–50.

McFadden, Daniel. Econometric Models of Probabilistic Choice. In *Manski, C. F. and McFadden, D., eds.*, 1981, pp. 198–272.

Mittelhammer, Ron C. and Young, Douglas L. Mitigating the Effects of Multicollinearity Using Exact and Stochastic Restrictions: The Case of an Aggregate Agricultural Production Function in Thailand: Reply. *Amer. J. Agr. Econ.*, May 1981, *63*(2), pp. 301–04. **[G: Thailand]**

Mundlak, Yair. On the Concept of Non-Significant Functions and Its Implications for Regression Analysis. *J. Econometrics*, May 1981, *16*(1), pp. 139–49.

Mundlak, Yair and Yahav, Joseph A. Random Effects, Fixed Effects, Convolution, and Separation. *Econometrica*, November 1981, *49*(6), pp. 1399–1416.

Murray, David. The Inequality of Household Incomes in Australia. *Econ. Rec.*, March 1981, *57*(156), pp. 12–22. **[G: Australia]**

Nakamura, Alice and Nakamura, Masao. On the Relationships among Several Specification Error Tests Presented by Durbin, Wu, and Hausman. *Econometrica*, November 1981, *49*(6), pp. 1583–88.

Nelson, Forrest D. A Test for Misspecification in the Censored Normal Model. *Econometrica*, September 1981, *49*(5), pp. 1317–29.

Nickell, Stephen J. Biases in Dynamic Models with Fixed Effects. *Econometrica*, November 1981, *49*(6), pp. 1417–26.

Nowak, Eugen. Identifikation und Schätzung ökonometrischer Zeitreihenmodelle mit Fehlern in den Variablen. (Identification and Estimation of Econometric Time Series Models with Errors in the Variables. With English summary.) *Z. Wirtschaft. Sozialwissen.*, 1981, *101*(5), pp. 519–36.

Ohtani, Kazuhiro. On the Use of a Proxy Variable in Prediction: An MSE Comparison. *Rev. Econ. Statist.*, November 1981, *63*(4), pp. 627–28.

Oman, Samuel D. A Confidence Bound Approach to Choosing the Biasing Parameter in Ridge Regression. *J. Amer. Statist. Assoc.*, June 1981, *76*(374), pp. 452–61.

Osborn, Denise R. A Review of Recent Work on Testing for Auto-correlation in Dynamic Simultaneous Models: Comment. In *Currie, D.; Nobay, R. and Peel, D., eds.*, 1981, pp. 106–10.

Pagano, Marcello and Hartley, Michael J. On Fitting Distributed Lag Models Subject to Polynomial Restrictions. *J. Econometrics*, June 1981, *16*(2), pp. 171–98. **[G: U.S.]**

Palm, Franz and Zellner, Arnold. Large Sample Estimation and Testing Procedures for Dynamic Equation Systems: Rejoinder. *J. Econometrics*, September 1981, *17*(1), pp. 131–38.

Pesaran, M. H. Diagnostic Testing and Exact Maximum Likelihood Estimation of Dynamic Models. In *[Valavanis, S.]*, 1981, pp. 63–87.

Pesaran, M. H. Pitfalls of Testing Non-Nested Hypotheses by the Lagrange Multiplier Method. *J. Econometrics*, May 1981, *16*(1), pp. 158.

Pfeffermann, Dan and Nathan, Gad. Regression Analysis of Data from a Cluster Sample. *J. Amer. Statist. Assoc.*, September 1981, *76*(375), pp. 681–89.

Poirier, Dale J. and Ruud, Paul A. On the Appropriateness of Endogenous Switching. *J. Econometrics*, June 1981, *16*(2), pp. 249–56.

Pratt, John W. Concavity of the Log Likelihood. *J. Amer. Statist. Assoc.*, March 1981, *76*(373), pp. 103–06.

Quinn, Barry G. and Nicholls, Desmond F. The Stability of Random Coefficient Autoregressive Models. *Int. Econ. Rev.*, October 1981, *22*(3),

pp. 741–44.

Rao, Poduri S. R. S.; Kaplan, Jack and Cochran, William G. Estimators for the One-Way Random Effects Model with Unequal Error Variances. *J. Amer. Statist. Assoc.*, March 1981, *76*(373), pp. 89–97.

Royall, Richard M. and Cumberland, William G. The Finite-Population Linear Regression Estimator and Estimators of Its Variance—An Empirical Study. *J. Amer. Statist. Assoc.*, December 1981, *76*(376), pp. 924–30.

Sallas, William M. and Harville, David A. Best Linear Recursive Estimation for Mixed Linear Models. *J. Amer. Statist. Assoc.*, December 1981, *76*(376), pp. 860–69.

Sargan, J. D. and Tse, Y. K. Edgeworth Approximations to the Distribution of Various Test Statistics. **In** *[Valavanis, S.]*, 1981, pp. 281–95.

Sargent, Thomas J. A Note on Maximum Likelihood Estimation of the Rational Expectations Model of the Term Structure. **In** *Lucas, R. E. and Sargent, T. J.*, eds., 1981, *1979*, pp. 453–62. **[G: U.S.]**

Schmidt, Peter. Constraints on the Parameters in Simultaneous Tobit and Probit Models. **In** *Manski, C. F. and McFadden, D.*, eds., 1981, pp. 422–34.

Schmidt, Peter. Further Results on the Value of Sample Separation Information [Discrete Parameter Variation: Efficient Estimation of a Switching Regression Model]. *Econometrica*, September 1981, *49*(5), pp. 1339–43.

Shiller, Robert J. Alternative Tests of Rational Expectations Models: The Case of the Term Structure. *J. Econometrics*, May 1981, *16*(1), pp. 71–87. **[G: U.S.]**

Smith, Marvin M. A Note on Tests of Significance and Wage Discrimination. *Amer. Econ.*, Spring 1981, *25*(1), pp. 72–75.

Spencer, David E. and Berk, Kenneth N. A Limited Information Specification Test [Specification Tests in Econometrics]. *Econometrica*, June 1981, *49*(4), pp. 1079–85.

Stromback, C. T. Aggregation in Logarithmic Models: Some Experiments with UK Export Functions: A Comment. *Oxford Bull. Econ. Statist.*, November 1981, *43*(4), pp. 363–65. **[G: U.K.]**

Taylor, William E. On the Efficiency of the Cochrane–Orcutt Estimator. *J. Econometrics*, September 1981, *17*(1), pp. 67–82.

Thélot, Claude. Note sur la loi logistique et l'imitation. (A Note on the Logistic Law and Imitation. With English summary.) *Ann. INSEE*, April–June 1981, (42), pp. 111–26.

Thursby, Jerry G. A Test Strategy for Discriminating between Autocorrelation and Misspecification in Regression Analysis. *Rev. Econ. Statist.*, February 1981, *63*(1), pp. 117–23.

Tishler, Asher and Zang, Israel. A New Maximum Likelihood Algorithm for Piecewise Regression. *J. Amer. Statist. Assoc.*, December 1981, *76*(376), pp. 980–87.

Trost, Robert P. Interpretation of Error Covariances with Nonrandom Data: An Empirical Illustration of Returns to College Education. *Atlantic Econ. J.*, September 1981, *9*(3), pp. 85–90. **[G: U.S.]**

Tsurumi, Hiroki and Shiba, Tsunemasa. On Cooley and Prescott's Time Varying Parameter Model. *Econ. Stud. Quart.*, August 1981, *32*(2), pp. 176–80.

Ullah, A.; Vinod, H. D. and Kadiyala, R. K. A Family of Improved Shrinkage Factors for the Ordinary Ridge Estimator. *Econ. Stud. Quart.*, August 1981, *32*(2), pp. 164–75.

Ullah, A.; Vinod, H. D. and Kadiyala, R. K. A Family of Improved Shrinkage Factors for the Ordinary Ridge Estimator. **In** *[Valavanis, S.]*, 1981, pp. 259–77.

Vinod, H. D. Improved Stein-rule Estimator for Regression Problems: Reply. *J. Econometrics*, September 1981, *17*(1), pp. 125.

Viviani, Alessandro. Sulla possibilità di ridurre la distorsione delle stime dei parametri di una relazione non correttamente specificata mediante l'impiego d'informazioni "a priori." (On the Possibility to Reduce the Bias in Estimation of the Parameters of a Misspecified Relationship by Introducing "a priori" information. With English summary.) *Statistica*, January–March 1981, *41*(1), pp. 141–47.

Wansbeek, Tom and Kapteyn, Arie. Estimators of the Covariance Structure of a Model for Longitudinal Data. **In** *[Valavanis, S.]*, 1981, pp. 341–55.

Wegge, Leon L. Maximum Likelihood Estimators of Latent Multivariate Normal Processes when the Observations Are Intervals. **In** *[Valavanis, S.]*, 1981, pp. 357–78.

White, Halbert. Consequences and Detection of Misspecified Nonlinear Regression Models. *J. Amer. Statist. Assoc.*, June 1981, *76*(374), pp. 419–33.

Whittemore, Alice S. Sample Size for Logistic Regression with Small Response Probability. *J. Amer. Statist. Assoc.*, March 1981, *76*(373), pp. 27–32.

Winters, L. A. Aggregation in Logarithmic Models: Some Experiments with UK Exports: A Reply. *Oxford Bull. Econ. Statist.*, November 1981, *43*(4), pp. 367–69. **[G: U.K.]**

Yamamoto, Taku. A Note on the Effect of Misspecification and Temporal Aggregation in the GLS Model. *Econ. Stud. Quart.*, April 1981, *32*(1), pp. 77–82.

Ziemer, Rod F. and Hill, R. Carter. Principal Components and Stein-Like Estimation. *Can. J. Agr. Econ.*, July 1981, *29*(2), pp. 243–46.

2114 Multivariate Analysis, Statistical Information Theory, and Other Special Inferential Problems; Queuing Theory; Markov Chains

Arrow, Kenneth J.; Pesotchinsky, Leon and Sobel, Milton. On Partitioning a Sample with Binary-Type Questions in Lieu of Collecting Observations. *J. Amer. Statist. Assoc.*, June 1981, *76*(374), pp. 402–09.

Ashikaga, Takamaru and Chang, Potter C. Robustness of Fisher's Linear Discriminant Function under Two-Component Mixed Normal Models. *J. Amer. Statist. Assoc.*, September 1981, *76*(375), pp. 676–80.

211 Econometric and Statistical Methods and Models

Beckman, Richard J. and Johnson, Mark E. A Ranking Procedure for Partial Discriminant Analysis. *J. Amer. Statist. Assoc.*, September 1981, 76(375), pp. 671–75.

Dempster, A. P.; Rubin, D. B. and Tsutakawa, R. K. Estimation in Covariance Components Models. *J. Amer. Statist. Assoc.*, June 1981, 76(374), pp. 341–53.

Devlin, S. J.; Gnanadesikan, R. and Kettenring, J. R. Robust Estimation of Dispersion Matrices and Principal Components. *J. Amer. Statist. Assoc.*, June 1981, 76(374), pp. 354–62.

Flath, David and Leonard, E. W. A Comparison of Two Logit Models in the Analysis of Qualitative Marketing Data. In *Wind, Y.; Mahajan, V. and Cardozo, R. N., eds.*, 1981, 1979, pp. 155–67.

Flury, Bernhard and Riedwyl, Hans. Graphical Representation of Multivariate Data by Means of Asymmetrical Faces. *J. Amer. Statist. Assoc.*, December 1981, 76(376), pp. 757–65.

Füstös, László; Meszéna, György and Mosolygó-Simon, Nóra. Cluster Analysis. *Acta Oecon.*, 1981, 26(3–4), pp. 291–334.

Goodman, Leo A. Association Models and Canonical Correlation in the Analysis of Cross-Classifications Having Ordered Categories. *J. Amer. Statist. Assoc.*, June 1981, 76(374), pp. 320–34.

Grablowsky, Bernie J. and Talley, Wayne K. Probit and Discriminant Functions for Classifying Credit Applicants: A Comparison. *J. Econ. Bus.*, Spring/Summer 1981, 33(3), pp. 254–61. [G: U.S.]

Heckman, James J. The Incidental Parameters Problem and the Problem of Initial Conditions in Estimating a Discrete Time-Discrete Data Stochastic Process. In *Manski, C. F. and McFadden, D., eds.*, 1981, pp. 179–95.

Kelton, Christina M. L. Estimation of Time-Independent Markov Processes with Aggregate Data: A Comparison of Techniques. *Econometrica*, March 1981, 49(2), pp. 517–18.

Leredde, Henri and Outreville, J.-François. Un Exemple de l'utilisation des méthodes de l'analyse des données dans la démarche scientifique en économie. (The Use of Multivariate Analysis Procedures in Economic Methodology. With English summary.) *L'Actual. Econ.*, October–December 1981, 57(4), pp. 507–24.

Manski, Charles F. and McFadden, Daniel. Alternative Estimators and Sample Designs for Discrete Choice Analysis. In *Manski, C. F. and McFadden, D., eds.*, 1981, pp. 2–50.

Mazanec, J. Deterministische und probabilistische Klassifikation in der Konsumverhaltens-Forschung. Ein empirischer Anwendungsversuch der Quervalidierung cluster-analytischer Verfahren für qualitative Daten mit der Latent Class-Analyse. (With English summary.) In *Fandel, G., et al., eds.*, 1981, pp. 296–305.

Ronning, Gerd. Ökonometrische Analyse von aggregierten Tendenzdaten aus Panelerhebungen. (Econometric Analysis of Aggregated Tendency Data from Panel Surveys. With English summary.) *Z. Wirtschaft. Sozialwissen.*, 1981, 101(2), pp. 181–209.

Theiler, G. and Tövissi, L. Useful Versions of Entropy with Weights. *Econ. Computat. Cybern.*,

Stud. Res., 1981, 15(3), pp. 19–29.

Wegge, Leon L. Maximum Likelihood Estimators of Latent Multivariate Normal Processes when the Observations Are Intervals. In *[Valavanis, S.]*, 1981, pp. 357–78.

2115 Bayesian Statistics and Bayesian Econometrics

Colombo, A. G. and Costantini, Domenico. A Rational Reconstruction of the Beta Distribution. *Statistica*, January–March 1981, 41(1), pp. 3–10.

Crosby, Michael A. Bayesian Statistics in Auditing: A Comparison of Probability Elicitation Techniques. *Accounting Rev.*, April 1981, 56(2), pp. 355–65.

Deely, J. J. and Lindley, D. V. Bayes Empirical Bayes. *J. Amer. Statist. Assoc.*, December 1981, 76(376), pp. 833–41.

Dickey, David A. and Fuller, Wayne A. Likelihood Ratio Statistics for Autoregressive Time Series with a Unit Root. *Econometrica*, June 1981, 49(4), pp. 1057–72.

Good, I. J. Some Logic and History of Hypothesis Testing. In *Pitt, J. C., ed.*, 1981, pp. 149–74.

Kiefer, Nicholas M. Limited Information Analysis of a Small Underidentified Macroeconomic Model. *Int. Econ. Rev.*, June 1981, 22(2), pp. 429–42.

Liu, Lon-Mu and Hanssens, Dominique M. A Bayesian Approach to Time-Varying Cross-Sectional Regression Models. *J. Econometrics*, April 1981, 15(3), pp. 341–56.

Paass, G. Assessing the Quality of Prediction Baykal: Bayesian Prediction by Kalman Filtering. In *Janssen, J. M. L.; Pau, L. F. and Straszak, A. J., eds.*, 1981, pp. 297–303.

Trivedi, P. K. and Lee, B. M. S. Seasonal Variability in a Distributed Lag Model. *Rev. Econ. Stud.*, July 1981, 48(3), pp. 497–505.

Vedaldi, R. and Diana, G. Su alcuni piani di campionamento a tre decisioni terminali. (On Some Sampling Plans with Three Terminal Decisions. With English summary.) *Statistica*, January–March 1981, 41(1), pp. 23–37.

Weerahandi, S. and Zidek, J. V. Multi-Bayesian Statistical Decision Theory. *J. Roy. Statist. Soc.*, Part 1, 1981, 144, pp. 85–93.

Zellner, Arnold. Posterior Odds Ratios for Regression Hypotheses: General Considerations and Some Specific Results. *J. Econometrics*, May 1981, 16(1), pp. 151–52.

2116 Time Series and Spectral Analysis

Anderson, T. W. and Hsiao, Cheng. Estimation of Dynamic Models with Error Components. *J. Amer. Statist. Assoc.*, September 1981, 76(375), pp. 598–606.

Ansley, Craig F. and Newbold, Paul. On the Bias in Estimates of Forecast Mean Squared Error. *J. Amer. Statist. Assoc.*, September 1981, 76(375), pp. 569–78.

Beveridge, Stephen and Nelson, Charles R. A New Approach to Decomposition of Economic Time Series into Permanent and Transitory Components with Particular Attention to Measurement of the 'Business Cycle.' *J. Monet. Econ.*, March 1981, 7(2), pp. 151–74. [G: U.S.]

Bhansali, R. J. Effects of Not Knowing the Order of an Autoregressive Process on the Mean Squared Error of Prediction—I. *J. Amer. Statist. Assoc.*, September 1981, 76(375), pp. 588–97.

Bickel, Peter J.; Herzberg, Agnes M. and Schilling, M. F. Robustness of Design against Autocorrelation in Time II: Optimality, Theoretical and Numerical Results for the First-Order Autoregressive Process. *J. Amer. Statist. Assoc.*, December 1981, 76(376), pp. 870–77.

Caines, P. E.; Keng, C. W. and Sethi, Suresh P. Causality Analysis and Multivariate Autoregressive Modelling with an Application to Supermarket Sales Analysis. *J. Econ. Dynam. Control*, August 1981, 3(3), pp. 267–98. [G: U.S.]

Cholette, Pierre A. La prévision à l'aide des modèles ARMMI et d'information à priori. (Forecasting by Means of ARIMA Models and Prior Information. With English summary.) *L'Actual. Econ.*, October–December 1981, 57(4), pp. 553–64.

Colletaz, Gilbert and Marois, William. L'analyse des relations dynamiques entre variables: une application au taux du marché monetaire français. (The Analysis of the Dynamic Relationships between Variables: An Application to the French Money Market Rate. With English summary.) *Revue Écon.*, January 1981, 32(1), pp. 86–109.
[G: France]

Davidson, James. Small Sample Properties of Estimators of the Moving Average Process. In *[Valavanis, S.]*, 1981, pp. 27–62.

Davidson, James E. H. Problems with the Estimation of Moving Average Processes. *J. Econometrics*, August 1981, 16(3), pp. 295–310.

Deheuvels, Paul. La prévision des séries économiques: Une technique subjective. (With English summary.) *Écon. Appl.*, 1981, 34(4), pp. 729–47.

Deligönül, Z. Şeyda. Planlamada Bir Tepkinin Geçisim Fazi İçin Zaman Dizisi Profili. (Time Series Profile for the Transient Phase of a Response in Planning. With English summary.) *METU*, Special Issue, 1981, pp. 475–89.

Dunsmuir, W. and Robinson, P. M. Estimation of Time Series Models in the Presence of Missing Data. *J. Amer. Statist. Assoc.*, September 1981, 76(375), pp. 560–68.

Enächescu, D. M. Digital Methods in Estimating Spectral Densities. *Econ. Computat. Cybern. Stud. Res.*, 1981, 15(1), pp. 63–75.

Engle, Robert and Watson, Mark. A One-Factor Multivariate Time Series Model of Metropolitan Wage Rates. *J. Amer. Statist. Assoc.*, December 1981, 76(376), pp. 774–81. [G: U.S.]

Evans, G. B. A. and Savin, N. E. Testing for Unit Roots: 1. *Econometrica*, May 1981, 49(3), pp. 753–79.

Fair, Ray C. Comments [An Autoregressive Index Model for the U.S., 1948–1975] [The Methodology of Macroeconometric Model Comparisons]. In *Kmenta, J. and Ramsey, J. B., eds.*, 1981, pp. 389–90.

Fernández, Roque B. A Methodological Note on the Estimation of Time Series. *Rev. Econ. Statist.*, August 1981, 63(3), pp. 471–76.

Geweke, John F. A Comparison of Tests of the Independence of Two Covariance-Stationary Time Series. *J. Amer. Statist. Assoc.*, June 1981, 76(374), pp. 363–73.

Geweke, John F. and Singleton, Kenneth J. Latent Variable Models for Time Series: A Frequency Domain Approach with an Application to the Permanent Income Hypothesis. *J. Econometrics*, December 1981, 17(3), pp. 287–304. [G: U.S.]

Geweke, John F. and Singleton, Kenneth J. Maximum Likelihood "Confirmatory" Factor Analysis of Economic Time Series. *Int. Econ. Rev.*, February 1981, 22(1), pp. 37–54.

Gourieroux, Christian and Le Gallo, Françoise. Construction de moyennes mobiles par minimisation sous contraintes d'une forme quadratique des coefficients. (The Construction of Moving Averages by the Constrained Minimisation of a Quadratic Form of the Coefficients. With English summary.) *Ann. INSEE*, April–June 1981, (42), pp. 93–110.

Granger, C. W. J. Investigating Causal Relations by Econometric Models and Cross-Spectral Methods. In *Lucas, R. E. and Sargent, T. J., eds.*, 1981, 1969, pp. 371–86.

Granger, C. W. J. Some Properties of Time Series Data and Their Use in Econometric Model Specification. *J. Econometrics*, May 1981, 16(1), pp. 121–30.

Hansen, Lars Peter and Sargent, Thomas J. Formulating and Estimating Dynamic Linear Rational Expectations Models. In *Lucas, R. E. and Sargent, T. J., eds.*, 1981, 1980, pp. 91–125.

Hansen, Lars Peter and Sargent, Thomas J. Linear Rational Expectations Models for Dynamically Interrelated Variables. In *Lucas, R. E. and Sargent, T. J., eds.*, 1981, pp. 127–56.

Harvey, Andrew C. and McAvinchey, Ian D. On the Relative Efficiency of Various Estimators of Regression Models with Moving Average Disturbances. In *[Valavanis, S.]*, 1981, pp. 105–18.

Harvey, Andrew C. and Phillips, Garry D. A. Testing for Serial Correlation in Simultaneous Equation Models: Some Further Results. *J. Econometrics*, September 1981, 17(1), pp. 99–105.

Hausman, Jerry A. and Taylor, William E. Panel Data and Unobservable Individual Effects. *Econometrica*, November 1981, 49(6), pp. 1377–98. [G: U.S.]

Havenner, Arthur and Swamy, P. A. V. B. A Random Coefficient Approach to Seasonal Adjustment of Economic Time Series. *J. Econometrics*, February 1981, 15(2), pp. 177–209.

Hsiao, Cheng. Autoregressive Modelling and Money–Income Causality Detection. *J. Monet. Econ.*, January 1981, 7(1), pp. 85–106.
[G: U.S.]

Huot, Guy. L'effet des points aberrants dans la désaisonnalisation. (The Presence of Outliers in the Estimation of the Seasonal Factors. With English summary.) *L'Actual. Econ.*, July–September 1981, 57(3), pp. 407–22.

Kirkpatrick, Grant. Further Results on the Time Series Analysis of Real Wages and Employment for U.S. Manufacturing, 1948–1977. *Weltwirtsch.*

Arch., 1981, *117*(2), pp. 326–51. [G: U.S.]

Liu, Lon-Mu and Hanssens, Dominique M. A Bayesian Approach to Time-Varying Cross-Sectional Regression Models. *J. Econometrics*, April 1981, *15*(3), pp. 341–56.

Manegold, James G. Time-Series Properties of Earnings: A Comparison of Extrapolative and Component Models. *J. Acc. Res.*, Autumn 1981, *19*(2), pp. 360–73. [G: U.S.]

Maravall, Augustin. A Note on Identification of Multivariate Time-Series Models. *J. Econometrics*, June 1981, *16*(2), pp. 237–47.

McDonald, John and Darroch, John. Large Sample Estimation and Testing Procedures for Dynamic Equation Systems: Comment. *J. Econometrics*, September 1981, *17*(1), pp. 127–30.

Muth, John F. Optimal Properties of Exponentially Weighted Forecasts. In *Lucas, R. E. and Sargent, T. J., eds.*, 1981, *1960*, pp. 23–31.

Nelson, Charles R. and Kang, Heejoon. Spurious Periodicity in Inappropriately Detrended Time Series. *Econometrica*, May 1981, *49*(3), pp. 741–51.

Nickell, Stephen J. Biases in Dynamic Models with Fixed Effects. *Econometrica*, November 1981, *49*(6), pp. 1417–26.

Nowak, Eugen. Identifikation und Schätzung ökonometrischer Zeitreihenmodelle mit Fehlern in den Variablen. (Identification and Estimation of Econometric Time Series Models with Errors in the Variables. With English summary.) *Z. Wirtschaft. Sozialwissen.*, 1981, *101*(5), pp. 519–36.

Palm, Franz and Zellner, Arnold. Large Sample Estimation and Testing Procedures for Dynamic Equation Systems: Rejoinder. *J. Econometrics*, September 1981, *17*(1), pp. 131–38.

Pesaran, M. H. Diagnostic Testing and Exact Maximum Likelihood Estimation of Dynamic Models. In *[Valavanis, S.]*, 1981, pp. 63–87.

Piccolo, Domenico. Regioni Osservabili per modelli AR e MA. (Observable Regions for Autoregressive or Moving Average Models. With English summary.) *Statistica*, January–March 1981, *41*(1), pp. 11–22.

Pierce, David A. Sources of Error in Economic Time Series. *J. Econometrics*, December 1981, *17*(3), pp. 305–21. [G: U.S.]

Quinn, Barry G. and Nicholls, Desmond F. The Stability of Random Coefficient Autoregressive Models. *Int. Econ. Rev.*, October 1981, *22*(3), pp. 741–44.

Ryder, N. B. A Time Series of Instrumental Fertility Variables. *Demography*, November 1981, *18*(4), pp. 487–509. [G: U.S.]

Sargan, J. D. and Tse, Y. K. Edgeworth Approximations to the Distribution of Various Test Statistics. In *[Valavanis, S.]*, 1981, pp. 281–95.

Sargent, Thomas J. Interpreting Economic Time Series. *J. Polit. Econ.*, April 1981, *89*(2), pp. 213–48.

Schlicht, Ekkehart. A Seasonal Adjustment Principle and a Seasonal Adjustment Method Derived from This Principle. *J. Amer. Statist. Assoc.*, June 1981, *76*(374), pp. 374–78.

Sims, Christopher A. An Autoregressive Index Model for the U.S., 1948–1975. In *Kmenta, J. and Ramsey, J. B., eds.*, 1981, pp. 283–327. [G: U.S.]

Sims, Christopher A. Money, Income, and Causality. In *Lucas, R. E. and Sargent, T. J., eds.*, 1981, *1972*, pp. 387–403. [G: U.S.]

Taylor, William E. On the Efficiency of the Cochrane–Orcutt Estimator. *J. Econometrics*, September 1981, *17*(1), pp. 67–82.

Thisted, Ronald A. and Wecker, William E. Predicting a Multitude of Time Series. *J. Amer. Statist. Assoc.*, September 1981, *76*(375), pp. 516–23.

Thury, Gerhard. Discrimination between Alternative Arima Model Specifications. *Empirica*, 1981, (1), pp. 3–24.

Tiao, G. C. and Box, G. E. P. Modeling Multiple Time Series with Applications. *J. Amer. Statist. Assoc.*, December 1981, *76*(376), pp. 802–16. [G: U.K.]

Tjøstheim, Dag. Granger-Causality in Multiple Time Series. *J. Econometrics*, November 1981, *17*(2), pp. 157–76.

Trivedi, P. K. and Lee, B. M. S. Seasonal Variability in a Distributed Lag Model. *Rev. Econ. Stud.*, July 1981, *48*(3), pp. 497–505.

Vandaele, Walter. Robust Estimation of ARIMA Models. *J. Econometrics*, May 1981, *16*(1), pp. 163.

Wecker, William E. Asymmetric Time Series. *J. Amer. Statist. Assoc.*, March 1981, *76*(373), pp. 16–21. [G: U.S.]

Woodward, Wayne A. and Gray, H. L. On the Relationship between the S Array and the Box-Jenkins Method of ARMA Model Identification. *J. Amer. Statist. Assoc.*, September 1981, *76*(375), pp. 579–87.

2117 Survey Methods; Sampling Methods

Cosslett, Stephen R. Efficient Estimation of Discrete-Choice Models. In *Manski, C. F. and McFadden, D., eds.*, 1981, pp. 51–111.

Hausman, Jerry A. and Trimble, John L. Sample Design Considerations and Sample Selection for the Vermont Time-of-Day Electricity Use Survey. *Rev. Public Data Use (See J. Econ. Soc. Meas. after 4/85)*, July 1981, *9*(2), pp. 83–96.

Hidiroglou, Michael A. and Srinath, Kadaba P. Some Estimators of a Population Total from Simple Random Samples Containing Large Units. *J. Amer. Statist. Assoc.*, September 1981, *76*(375), pp. 690–95.

Hill, Martha S. Some Illustrative Design Effects: Proper Sampling Errors versus Simple Random Sample Assumptions. In *Hill, M. S.; Hill, D. H. and Morgan, J. N., eds.*, 1981, pp. 457–65. [G: U.S.]

Long, John F. Survey of Federally Produced National Level Demographic Projections. *Rev. Public Data Use (See J. Econ. Soc. Meas. after 4/85)*, December 1981, *9*(4), pp. 309–19. [G: U.S.]

Manski, Charles F. and McFadden, Daniel. Alternative Estimators and Sample Designs for Discrete Choice Analysis. In *Manski, C. F. and McFadden, D., eds.*, 1981, pp. 2–50.

Matsuda, Yoshiro. Formation of the Census System

in Japan: 1871–1945—Development of the Statistical System in Japan Proper and Her Colonies. *Hitotsubashi J. Econ.*, February 1981, *21*(2), pp. 44–68. [G: Japan]

Peck, Jon K. and Dresch, Stephen P. Financial Incentives, Survey Response, and Sample Representativeness: Does Money Matter? *Rev. Public Data Use (See J. Econ. Soc. Meas. after 4/85),* December 1981, *9*(4), pp. 245–66. [G: U.S.]

Pleeter, Saul and Trotta, Joseph. An Evaluation of the Bureau of Labor Statistics Methodology for Calculating Local Unemployment Rates: A Case Study of Cincinnati. *Rev. Public Data Use (See J. Econ. Soc. Meas. after 4/85),* July 1981, *9*(2), pp. 115–22. [G: U.S.]

Rao, J. N. K. and Scott, A. J. The Analysis of Categorical Data from Complex Sample Surveys: Chi-Squared Tests for Goodness of Fit and Independence in Two-Way Tables. *J. Amer. Statist. Assoc.*, June 1981, *76*(374), pp. 221–30.

Thayer, Mark A. Contingent Valuation Techniques for Assessing Environmental Impacts: Further Evidence. *J. Environ. Econ. Manage.*, March 1981, *8*(1), pp. 27–44. [G: U.S.]

Vaessen, M. Knowledge of Contraceptives: An Assessment of World Fertility Survey Data Collection Procedures. *Population Stud.*, November 1981, *35*(3), pp. 357–73. [G: Colombia; Sri Lanka; Thailand; LDCs]

Ycas, Martynas A. and Lininger, Charles A. The Income Survey Development Program: Design Features and Initial Findings. *Soc. Sec. Bull.*, November 1981, *44*(11), pp. 13–19. [G: U.S.]

2118 Theory of Index Numbers and Aggregation

Afriat, S. N. On the Constructability of Consistent Price Indices between Several Periods Simultaneously. In *[Stone, R.],* 1981, pp. 133–61.

Aghevli, B. B. and Mehran, F. Optimal Grouping of Income Distribution Data. *J. Amer. Statist. Assoc.*, March 1981, *76*(373), pp. 22–26.

Allen, Robert C. and Diewert, W. Erwin. Direct versus Implicit Superlative Index Number Formulae. *Rev. Econ. Statist.*, August 1981, *63*(3), pp. 430–35.

Balk, Bert M. Second Thoughts on Wald's Cost-of-Living Index and Frisch's Double Expenditure Method. *Econometrica*, November 1981, *49*(6), pp. 1553–58.

Cherif, M'hamed. Indices d'utilité pour la consommation d'énergie dans le secteur résidentiel. (With English summary.) *Cah. Écon. Bruxelles*, 4th Trimestre 1981, (92), pp. 557–70.

Clements, Kenneth W. and Izan, H. Y. A Note on Estimating Divisia Index Numbers. *Int. Econ. Rev.*, October 1981, *22*(3), pp. 745–47.

Cory, Dennis C., et al. Use of Paasche and Laspeyres Variations to Estimate Consumer Welfare Change. *Agr. Econ. Res.*, April 1981, *33*(2), pp. 1–6.

Das, Tarun and Parikh, Ashok. Decompositions of Atkinson's Measure of Inequality. *Australian Econ. Pap.*, June 1981, *20*(36), pp. 171–78.

Deutsch, E. and Tintner, Gerhard. Aggregation und empirische Modelle: Untersuchungen anhand

eines Produktionsmodells. (Aggregation and Empirical Models: Investigations by Means of a Production Model. With English summary.) *Jahr. Nationalökon. Statist.*, July 1981, *196*(4), pp. 289–308.

Diewert, W. E. The Economic Theory of Index Numbers: A Survey. In *[Stone, R.],* 1981, pp. 163–208.

Färe, Rolf and Lyon, Vern. The Determinateness Test and Economic Price Indices. *Econometrica*, January 1981, *49*(1), pp. 209–13.

Filimon, Radu. Aggregation of Heterogeneous Goods in Models of the von Neumann Variety. *Z. Nationalökon.*, 1981, *41*(3–4), pp. 253–64.

Forsyth, F. G. and Fowler, R. F. The Theory and Practice of Chain Price Index Numbers. *J. Roy. Statist. Soc.*, Part 2, 1981, *144*, pp. 224–46.

Guccione, Antonio. Perfect Aggregation and Disaggregation of Complementarity Problems: Comment. *Amer. J. Agr. Econ.*, November 1981, *63*(4), pp. 753–55.

Kogelschatz, Hartmut. Equilibrium Preserving Aggregation in von Neumann Models. *Z. Nationalökon.*, 1981, *41*(3–4), pp. 265–78.

Morgan, Barrie S. and Norbury, John. Some Further Observations on the Index of Residential Differentiation. *Demography*, May 1981, *18*(2), pp. 251–56. [G: U.S.]

Paris, Quirino. Perfect Aggregation and Disaggregation of Complementarity Problems: Reply. *Amer. J. Agr. Econ.*, November 1981, *63*(4), pp. 756–57.

Patinkin, Don and Liviatan, Nissan. On the Economic Theory of Price Indexes. In *Patinkin, D.,* 1981, *1961*, pp. 209–39.

Ringwald, Karl. Variablenfehler und Spezifikationsfehler in hierarchischen Modellen. (Errors in the Variables and Specification Errors in Hierarchical Models. With English summary.) *Jahr. Nationalökon. Statist.*, November 1981, *196*(6), pp. 527–40.

Sakoda, James M. A Generalized Index of Dissimilarity. *Demography*, May 1981, *18*(2), pp. 245–50.

Silver, M. S. and Golder, P. Negative Value Added and the Measurement of Production Changes. *J. Econ. Stud.*, 1981, *8*(1), pp. 3–15.

Stromback, C. T. Aggregation in Logarithmic Models: Some Experiments with UK Export Functions: A Comment. *Oxford Bull. Econ. Statist.*, November 1981, *43*(4), pp. 363–65. [G: U.K.]

Trivedi, P. K. Some Discrete Approximations to Divisia Integral Indices. *Int. Econ. Rev.*, February 1981, *22*(1), pp. 71–77.

Winters, L. A. Aggregation in Logarithmic Models: Some Experiments with UK Exports: A Reply. *Oxford Bull. Econ. Statist.*, November 1981, *43*(4), pp. 367–69. [G: U.K.]

2119 Experimental Design; Social Experiments

Acton, Jan Paul. Planning, Processing, and Analyzing Data for Residential Load Studies. In *U.S. Dept. of Energy*, 1981, pp. 137–51. [G: U.S.]

Bennis, Jerome. Developing and Maintaining a Load Research Data Base: Comment. In *U.S. Dept.*

of Energy, 1981, pp. 118–21. [G: U.S.]

Berry, Sandra H. Contacting and Interviewing Residential Electricity Customers. In *U.S. Dept. of Energy*, 1981, pp. 60–72.

Bishop, Lane. Considerations in Analysing and Generalizing from Time-of-Use Electricity Pricing Studies. In *U.S. Dept. of Energy*, 1981, pp. 158–65.

Clayton, C. Andrew. Drawing a Sample and Allocating Customers to Design Points. In *U.S. Dept. of Energy*, 1981, pp. 32–48.

Crano, William D. Variables Affecting Treatment Perception in an Electric Time-of-Use Rate Demonstration: Analytic and Interpretative Implications. In *U.S. Dept. of Energy*, 1981, pp. 287–304. [G: U.S.]

Famadas, Nelson. The Role of Survey Data in Load Research. In *U.S. Dept. of Energy*, 1981, pp. 49–52.

Goyco, Osvaldo C. Procedures for Collecting, Translating, and Editing Meter Data: Comment. In *U.S. Dept. of Energy*, 1981, pp. 81–92.

[G: U.S.]

Groves, Robert M. Definition of the Population and Formation and Use of Strata. In *U.S. Dept. of Energy*, 1981, pp. 23–31.

Hausman, Jerry A. and Wise, David A. Stratification on Endogenous Variables and Estimation: The Gary Income Maintenance Experiment. In *Manski, C. F. and McFadden, D., eds.*, 1981, pp. 365–91. [G: U.S.]

Heberlein, Thomas A. Electric Rate Demonstration Conference: Questionnaire Development. In *U.S. Dept. of Energy*, 1981, pp. 53–59.

Hendricks, Wallace E. Evaluation and Future Uses of the DOE Sponsored Demonstration Data. In *U.S. Dept. of Energy*, 1981, pp. 279–86.

[G: U.S.]

Hill, Daniel H. Electric Rate Demonstration Conference: Limitations on Analysis. In *U.S. Dept. of Energy*, 1981, pp. 152–57. [G: U.S.]

James, Richard E. Procedures for Collecting, Translating, and Editing Meter Data. In *U.S. Dept. of Energy*, 1981, pp. 73–80.

Levy, Roger. Developing and Maintaining a Load Research Data Base. In *U.S. Dept. of Energy*, 1981, pp. 93–117. [G: U.S.]

Lifson, Dale P. Practical Considerations in Modelling the Demand for Electricity. In *U.S. Dept. of Energy*, 1981, pp. 166–86. [G: U.S.]

Metcalf, Charles E. Sample Design for Rate Demonstrations and Load Research. In *U.S. Dept. of Energy*, 1981, pp. 15–22.

Struyk, Raymond J. Housing Vouchers for the Poor: Social Experimentation and Policy Research. In *Struyk, R. J. and Bendick, M., Jr., eds.*, 1981, pp. 295–310. [G: U.S.]

212 Construction, Analysis, and Use of Econometric Models

2120 Construction, Analysis, and Use of Econometric Models

Aagaard-Svendsen, Rolf. Estimation of Econometric Models by Kalman Filtering and Iterative Instrumental Variables. In *Janssen, J. M. L.; Pau, L. F. and Straszak, A. J., eds.*, 1981, pp. 291–96. [G: Denmark]

Akaike, Hirotugu. Likelihood of a Model and Information Criteria. *J. Econometrics*, May 1981, *16*(1), pp. 3–14.

Amey, Lloyd R. and Bonaert, Axel P. The Theory of Fuzzy Subsets: A Review and Application to Planning and Control. *Rivista Int. Sci. Econ. Com.*, January–February 1981, *28*(1–2), pp. 1–32.

Anderson, Richard G. On the Specification of Conditional Factor Demand Functions in Recent Studies of U.S. Manufacturing. In *Berndt, E. R. and Field, B. C., eds.*, 1981, pp. 119–44. [G: U.S.]

Ando, Albert. On a Theoretical and Empirical Basis of Macroeconometric Models. In *Kmenta, J. and Ramsey, J. B., eds.*, 1981, pp. 329–67.

Atkinson, A. C. Likelihood Ratios, Posterior Odds and Information Criteria. *J. Econometrics*, May 1981, *16*(1), pp. 15–20.

Augustyniak, Sue. Some Econometric Advantages of Panel Data. In *Hill, M. S.; Hill, D. H. and Morgan, J. N., eds.*, 1981, pp. 405–20.

Badach, A. Adaptive Models in Econometric Forecasting. In *Janssen, J. M. L.; Pau, L. F. and Straszak, A. J., eds.*, 1981, pp. 271–77.

Bergström, Reinhold. Estimation of Real-World Models by Fix-Point and Other Methods. In *Wold, H., ed.*, 1981, pp. 109–57. [G: U.S.]

Bergström, Reinhold. Extensions of the GEID and IIV Estimators: The Case of Serially Correlated Residuals and Lagged Endogenous Variables. In *Wold, H., ed.*, 1981, pp. 197–223. [G: U.S.]

Berndt, Ernst R.; Morrison, Catherine J. and Watkins, G. Campbell. Dynamic Models of Energy Demand: An Assessment and Comparison. In *Berndt, E. R. and Field, B. C., eds.*, 1981, pp. 259–89. [G: U.S.]

Bianchi, Carlo; Calzolari, Giorgio and Corsi, Paolo. Estimating Asymptotic Standard Errors and Inconsistencies of Impact Multipliers in Nonlinear Econometric Models. *J. Econometrics*, August 1981, *16*(3), pp. 277–94.

Bodin, Lennart. Algorithms for Reordering Interdependent Systems. In *Wold, H., ed.*, 1981, pp. 225–41.

Bodin, Lennart. Iterative Algorithms for Fix-Point Estimation, Their Design and Convergence Properties. In *Wold, H., ed.*, 1981, pp. 37–63.

Bradford, David F. and Kelejian, Harry H. The Value of Information in a Storage Model with Open- and Closed-Loop Controls: A Numerical Example. *J. Econ. Dynam. Control*, August 1981, *3*(3), pp. 307–17.

Brown, Randall S. and Christensen, Laurits R. Estimating Elasticities of Substitution in a Model of Partial Static Equilibrium: An Application to U.S. Agriculture, 1947 to 1974. In *Berndt, E. R. and Field, B. C., eds.*, 1981, pp. 209–29. [G: U.S.]

Brunner, Karl. The Problem with What They Do and Why They Do It: Comment. In *Kmenta, J. and Ramsey, J. B., eds.*, 1981, pp. 129–38.

Buiter, Willem H. The Superiority of Contingent Rules over Fixed Rules in Models with Rational Expectations. *Econ. J.*, September 1981, *91*(363),

pp. 647–70.

Buiter, Willem H. and Gersovitz, Mark. Issues in Controllability and the Theory of Economic Policy. *J. Public Econ.*, February 1981, *15*(1), pp. 33–43.

Caines, P. E.; Keng, C. W. and Sethi, Suresh P. Causality Analysis and Multivariate Autoregressive Modelling with an Application to Supermarket Sales Analysis. *J. Econ. Dynam. Control*, August 1981, *3*(3), pp. 267–98.   [G: U.S.]

Calzolari, Giorgio. A Note on the Variance of Ex-Post Forecasts in Econometric Models. *Econometrica*, November 1981, *49*(6), pp. 1593–95.

Cargill, Thomas F. and Meyer, Robert A. Revealed Preferences in Macroeconomic Policy Decisions. *J. Macroecon.*, Spring 1981, *3*(2), pp. 205–26.
[G: U.S.]

Chamberlain, Gary. Models of Duration Dependence. *J. Econometrics*, May 1981, *16*(1), pp. 164.

Chow, Gregory C. A Comparison of the Information and Posterior Probability Criteria for Model Selection. *J. Econometrics*, May 1981, *16*(1), pp. 21–33.

Chow, Gregory C. Estimation and Control of Rational Expectations Models. *Amer. Econ. Rev.*, May 1981, *71*(2), pp. 211–16.

Chow, Gregory C. Estimation of Rational Expectations Models. In *Lucas, R. E. and Sargent, T. J., eds.*, 1981, *1980*, pp. 355–67.

Chow, Gregory C. Evaluation of Econometric Models by Decomposition and Aggregation. In *Kmenta, J. and Ramsey, J. B., eds.*, 1981, pp. 423–44.

Chow, Gregory C. On the Control of Structural Models—Comment. *J. Econometrics*, January 1981, *15*(1), pp. 25–28.

Chow, Gregory C. Selection of Econometric Models by the Information Criterion. In *[Valavanis, S.]*, 1981, pp. 199–214.

Cichocki, K. Optimization Techniques in Modelling of Economic Policy. In *Janssen, J. M. L.; Pau, L. F. and Straszak, A. J., eds.*, 1981, pp. 105–16.   [G: Poland]

Cosslett, Stephen R. Efficient Estimation of Discrete-Choice Models. In *Manski, C. F. and McFadden, D., eds.*, 1981, pp. 51–111.

Craine, Roger and Havenner, Arthur. On Control with Instruments of Differing Frequency. *J. Econ. Dynam. Control*, May 1981, *3*(2), pp. 177–81.

Currie, David A. Some Long Run Features of Dynamic Time Series Models. *Econ. J.*, September 1981, *91*(363), pp. 704–15.

Danao, Rolando A. Nonnegative Approximate Solutions to an Econometric Model with Prescribed Goals. *Phillipine Rev. Econ. Bus.*, March & June 1981, *18*(1 & 2), pp. 45–53.

Deissenberg, Christophe. Optimal Stabilization Policy with Control Lags and Imperfect State Observations. *Z. Nationalökon.*, 1981, *41*(3–4), pp. 329–52.

Dickhoven, S. Implementierung von mikroanalytischen Modellen zur Unterstützung von staatlichen Transferentscheidungen. (With English summary.) In *Fandel, G., et al., eds.*, 1981, pp. 422–29.

Eckstein, Otto and Warburg, Paul M. Economic Theory and Econometric Models. In *Kmenta, J. and Ramsey, J. B., eds.*, 1981, pp. 155–76.
[G: U.S.]

Edgerton, David. An Analysis of the Nonlinear Klein–Goldberger Model Using Fix-Point Estimation and Other Methods. In *Wold, H., ed.*, 1981, pp. 243–82.   [G: U.S.]

Eklöf, J. A. On Optimal Macro-economic Control with Inaccurate Data. In *Janssen, J. M. L.; Pau, L. F. and Straszak, A. J., eds.*, 1981, pp. 57–62.   [G: Sweden]

Fair, Ray C. Comments [An Autoregressive Index Model for the U.S., 1948–1975] [The Methodology of Macroeconometric Model Comparisons]. In *Kmenta, J. and Ramsey, J. B., eds.*, 1981, pp. 389–90.

Fischer, Gregory W. and Nagin, Daniel. Random versus Fixed Coefficient Quantal Choice Models. In *Manski, C. F. and McFadden, D., eds.*, 1981, pp. 273–304.

Fisher, Gordon R. and McAleer, Michael. Alternative Procedures and Associated Tests of Significance for Non-Nested Hypotheses. *J. Econometrics*, May 1981, *16*(1), pp. 103–19.

Friedmann, Ralph. The Reliability of Policy Recommendations and Forecasts from Linear Econometric Models. *Int. Econ. Rev.*, June 1981, *22*(2), pp. 415–28.   [G: U.S.]

Frisch, Ragnar. From Utopian Theory to Practical Applications: The Case of Econometrics. *Amer. Econ. Rev.*, Special Issue December 1981, *71*(6), pp. 1–16.

Fromm, Gary and Klein, Lawrence R. Scale of Macro-econometric Models and Accuracy of Forecasting. In *Kmenta, J. and Ramsey, J. B., eds.*, 1981, pp. 369–88.   [G: U.S.]

Goldfeld, Stephen M. An Evaluation of the Forecasting Performance of Macro Economic Models, with Special Emphasis on Model Size: Discussion. In *Kmenta, J. and Ramsey, J. B., eds.*, 1981, pp. 139–43.

Goldfeld, Stephen M. and Quandt, Richard E. Single-Market Disequilibrium Models: Estimation and Testing. *Econ. Stud. Quart.*, April 1981, *32*(1), pp. 12–28.

Granger, C. W. J. Some Properties of Time Series Data and Their Use in Econometric Model Specification. *J. Econometrics*, May 1981, *16*(1), pp. 121–30.

Granger, C. W. J. The Comparison of Time Series and Econometric Forecasting Strategies. In *Kmenta, J. and Ramsey, J. B., eds.*, 1981, pp. 123–28.

Griliches, Zvi. Evaluation of Econometric Models by Decomposition and Aggregation: Discussion. In *Kmenta, J. and Ramsey, J. B., eds.*, 1981, pp. 445–46.

Hansen, Lars Peter and Sargent, Thomas J. Formulating and Estimating Dynamic Linear Rational Expectations Models. In *Lucas, R. E. and Sargent, T. J., eds.*, 1981, *1980*, pp. 91–125.

Hansen, Lars Peter and Sargent, Thomas J. Linear Rational Expectations Models for Dynamically Interrelated Variables. In *Lucas, R. E. and Sargent, T. J., eds.*, 1981, pp. 127–56.

Heckman, James J. Statistical Models for Discrete Panel Data. In *Manski, C. F. and McFadden, D., eds.*, 1981, pp. 114–78.

Heckman, James J. The Incidental Parameters Problem and the Problem of Initial Conditions in Estimating a Discrete Time-Discrete Data Stochastic Process. In *Manski, C. F. and McFadden, D., eds.*, 1981, pp. 179–95.

Hellwig, Z. H. Formal Designing of Stochastic Control Linear Systems. In *Janssen, J. M. L.; Pau, L. F. and Straszak, A. J., eds.*, 1981, pp. 375–78.

Hendry, David F. and Richard, Jean-François. Model Formulation to Simplify Selection When Specification Is Uncertain. *J. Econometrics*, May 1981, *16*(1), pp. 159.

Hoffman, Dennis L. and Schmidt, Peter. Testing the Restrictions Implied by the Rational Expectations Hypothesis. *J. Econometrics*, February 1981, *15*(2), pp. 265–87.

Howrey, E. Philip, et al. The Practice of Macroeconometric Model Building and Its Rationale. In *Kmenta, J. and Ramsey, J. B., eds.*, 1981, pp. 19–58.

Hsiao, Cheng. Autoregressive Modelling and Money–Income Causality Detection. *J. Monet. Econ.*, January 1981, *7*(1), pp. 85–106.
[G: U.S.]

Hughes Hallett, A. J. Some Extensions and Comparisons in the Theory of Gauss–Seidel Iterative Techniques for Solving Large Equation Systems. In *[Valavanis, S.]*, 1981, pp. 297–318.

Hughes Hallett, A. J. The Qualitative Design of Economic Policies and Planner-Model Interaction. In *Janssen, J. M. L.; Pau, L. F. and Straszak, A. J., eds.*, 1981, pp. 325–32.

Ito, Takatoshi and Ueda, Kazuo. Tests of the Equilibrium Hypothesis in Disequilibrium Econometrics: An International Comparison of Credit Rationing. *Int. Econ. Rev.*, October 1981, *22*(3), pp. 691–708.
[G: U.S.; Japan]

Johansen, Leif. Suggestions towards Freeing Systems of Demand Functions from a Strait-jacket. In *[Stone, R.]*, 1981, pp. 31–54.

Jorgenson, Dale W.; Lau, L. J. and Stoker, T. M. Aggregate Consumer Behaviour and Individual Welfare. In *Currie, D.; Nobay, R. and Peel, D., eds.*, 1981, pp. 35–61.
[G: U.S.]

Kelejian, Harry H. and Vavrichek, Bruce. An Evaluation of the Forecasting Performance of Macro Economic Models, with Special Emphasis on Model Size. In *Kmenta, J. and Ramsey, J. B., eds.*, 1981, pp. 93–122.
[G: U.S.]

Kiefer, Nicholas M. Limited Information Analysis of a Small Underidentified Macroeconomic Model. *Int. Econ. Rev.*, June 1981, *22*(2), pp. 429–42.

Kmenta, Jan and Ramsey, James B. Large-Scale Macro-econometric Models: Summary of the General Discussion. In *Kmenta, J. and Ramsey, J. B., eds.*, 1981, pp. 449–62.

Kmenta, Jan and Ramsey, James B. Model Size, Quality of Forecast Accuracy, and Economic Theory. In *Kmenta, J. and Ramsey, J. B., eds.*, 1981, pp. 3–16.

Kopp, Raymond J. and Smith, V. Kerry. Measuring the Prospects for Resource Substitution under Input and Technology Aggregations. In *Berndt, E. R. and Field, B. C., eds.*, 1981, pp. 145–73.

Kouris, George. Elasticities—Science or Fiction? *Energy Econ.*, April 1981, *3*(2), pp. 66–70.
[G: U.K.]

Krasker, William S. The Role of Bounded-Influence Estimation in Model Selection. *J. Econometrics*, May 1981, *16*(1), pp. 131–38.
[G: U.S.]

Kuh, Edwin and Neese, John. Parameter Sensitivity, Dynamic Behavior, and Model Reliability: An Initial Exploration with the MQEM Monetary Sector. In *[Valavanis, S.]*, 1981, pp. 121–68.
[G: U.S.]

Laffargue, Jean-Pierre. Interprétation économique des caractéristiques quasi-cycliques d'un modèle macroéconométrique évoluant en environnement aléatoire. (Economic Interpretation of the Quasi-cyclical Characteristics of a Macroeconometric Model in a Stochastic Environment. With English summary.) *Ann. INSEE*, July–September 1981, (43), pp. 3–34.

Lawson, Tony. Keynesian Model Building and the Rational Expectations Critique. *Cambridge J. Econ.*, December 1981, *5*(4), pp. 311–26.

Lee, Lung-Fei. Fully Recursive Probability Models and Multivariate Log-Linear Probability Models for the Analysis of Qualitative Data. *J. Econometrics*, May 1981, *16*(1), pp. 51–69.
[G: U.S.]

Lucas, Robert E., Jr. Econometric Policy Evaluation: A Critique. In *Lucas, R. E., Jr.*, 1981, *1976*, pp. 104–30.

Lucas, Robert E., Jr. and Sargent, Thomas J. After Keynesian Macroeconomics. In *Lucas, R. E. and Sargent, T. J., eds.*, 1981, *1979*, pp. 295–319.

Lucas, Robert E., Jr. and Sargent, Thomas J. Rational Expectations and Econometric Practice: Introduction. In *Lucas, R. E. and Sargent, T. J., eds.*, 1981, pp. xi–xl.

Maddala, G. S. Statistical Inference in Relation to the Size of the Model. In *Kmenta, J. and Ramsey, J. B., eds.*, 1981, pp. 191–218.

Maddala, G. S. Statistical Inference in Relation to the Size of the Model: Discussion. In *Kmenta, J. and Ramsey, J. B., eds.*, 1981, pp. 279–80.

Maddala, G. S. and Trost, Robert P. Alternative Formulations of the Nerlove-Press Models. *J. Econometrics*, May 1981, *16*(1), pp. 35–49.
[G: U.S.]

Malgrange, Pierre. Note sur le calcul des valeurs propres d'un modèle macroéconométrique. (A Note on the Calculation of the Eigen Values of a Macroeconometric Model. With English summary.) *Ann. INSEE*, January–March 1981, (41), pp. 67–77.

Malinvaud, Edmond. Econometrics Faced with the Needs of Macroeconomic Policy. *Econometrica*, November 1981, *49*(6), pp. 1363–75.

Manski, Charles F. and McFadden, Daniel. Alternative Estimators and Sample Designs for Discrete Choice Analysis. In *Manski, C. F. and McFadden, D., eds.*, 1981, pp. 2–50.

Matatko, John and Mayes, David G. A Multivariate Approach to Data Analysis. In *Currie, D.; Nobay, R. and Peel, D., eds.*, 1981, pp. 460–91.
[G: U.S.; U.K.]

McAleer, Michael, et al. Estimation of the Consumption Function: A Systems Approach to Employment Effects on the Purchase of Durables. In *[Valavanis, S.]*, 1981, pp. 169–97.
[G: Australia]

McFadden, Daniel. Econometric Models of Probabilistic Choice. In *Manski, C. F. and McFadden, D., eds.*, 1981, pp. 198–272.

McNees, Stephen K. The Methodology of Macroeconometric Model Comparisons. In *Kmenta, J. and Ramsey, J. B., eds.*, 1981, pp. 397–422.

Mikhailov, A. G. and Tokarev, V. V. The Principle of a Guaranteed Result in Problems of Economic Control. In *Janssen, J. M. L.; Pau, L. F. and Straszak, A. J., eds.*, 1981, pp. 383–86.

Mitropoulos, C. S.; Samouilidis, J. E. and Protonotarios, E. N. Using Kalman Filtering for Energy Forecasting. In *Janssen, J. M. L.; Pau, L. F. and Straszak, A. J., eds.*, 1981, pp. 317–24.
[G: Greece]

Modigliani, Franco. Scale of Macro-econometric Models and Accuracy of Forecasting: Comment. In *Kmenta, J. and Ramsey, J. B., eds.*, 1981, pp. 393–94.

Muth, John F. Estimation of Economic Relationships Containing Latent Expectations Variables. In *Lucas, R. E. and Sargent, T. J., eds.*, 1981, pp. 321–28.

Muth, John F. Rational Expectations and the Theory of Price Movements. In *Lucas, R. E. and Sargent, T. J., eds.*, 1981, *1961*, pp. 3–22.

Norman, Alfred L. On the Control of Structural Models. *J. Econometrics*, January 1981, *15*(1), pp. 13–24.
[G: U.S.]

Norman, Alfred L. On the Control of Structural Models—Reply. *J. Econometrics*, January 1981, *15*(1), pp. 29.

Otter, P. W. Identification and Estimation of Linear (Economic) Systems, Operating under Linear Closed-Loop Control. In *Janssen, J. M. L.; Pau, L. F. and Straszak, A. J., eds.*, 1981, pp. 305–16.

Paass, G. Assessing the Quality of Prediction Baykal: Bayesian Prediction by Kalman Filtering. In *Janssen, J. M. L.; Pau, L. F. and Straszak, A. J., eds.*, 1981, pp. 297–303.

Palash, Carl J. On the Accuracy and Efficiency of Polynomial Approximations in Optimal Macroeconomic Policy Determination. *J. Econometrics*, January 1981, *15*(1), pp. 49–62.

Perez, Howard. The Illusion of Econometrics. *Bus. Econ.*, January 1981, *16*(1), pp. 84–86.

Pesaran, M. H. Pitfalls of Testing Non-Nested Hypotheses by the Lagrange Multiplier Method. *J. Econometrics*, May 1981, *16*(1), pp. 158.

Pohjola, Matti T. Uncertainty and the Vigour of Policy: Some Implications of Quadratic Preferences. *J. Econ. Dynam. Control*, August 1981, *3*(3), pp. 299–305.

Poirier, Dale J. A Switching Simultaneous Equations Model of Physician Behaviour in Ontario. In *Manski, C. F. and McFadden, D., eds.*, 1981, pp. 392–421.
[G: Canada]

Poirier, Dale J. and Klepper, Steven. Model Occurrence and Model Selection in Panel Data Sets. *J. Econometrics*, December 1981, *17*(3), pp. 333–50.

Powell, Alan A. The Major Streams of Economy-Wide Modeling: Is Rapprochement Possible? In *Kmenta, J. and Ramsey, J. B., eds.*, 1981, pp. 219–64.
[G: Australia]

Pratt, John W. and Schlaifer, Robert. On the Nature and Discovery of Structure. *J. Econometrics*, May 1981, *16*(1), pp. 154.

Prescott, Edward C. Economic Theory, Model Size and Model Purpose: Remarks. In *Kmenta, J. and Ramsey, J. B., eds.*, 1981, pp. 273–77.

Rasche, Robert H. Comments on the Size of Macroeconomic Models. In *Kmenta, J. and Ramsey, J. B., eds.*, 1981, pp. 265–71.

Royer, D. Qualitative Hierarchies among Variables of a Macroeconomic Decision Model. In *Janssen, J. M. L.; Pau, L. F. and Straszak, A. J., eds.*, 1981, pp. 355–60.

Rupnik, V., et al. A Non-terminal Control Approach to Dynamic Economic Modelling in Non-compact Space. In *Janssen, J. M. L.; Pau, L. F. and Straszak, A. J., eds.*, 1981, pp. 333–37.

Sargent, Thomas J. Interpreting Economic Time Series. *J. Polit. Econ.*, April 1981, *89*(2), pp. 213–48.

Selén, Jan. A Search for Asymptotically Efficient Estimators: Especially Estimators of the GEID (FP) Type in the Case of Autoregressive Errors. In *Wold, H., ed.*, 1981, pp. 159–96.
[G: U.S.]

Shapiro, Harold T. and Garman, David M. Perspectives on the Accuracy of Macro-econometric Forecasting Models. In *Kmenta, J. and Ramsey, J. B., eds.*, 1981, pp. 59–91.
[G: U.S.]

Shiller, Robert J. Alternative Tests of Rational Expectations Models: The Case of the Term Structure. *J. Econometrics*, May 1981, *16*(1), pp. 71–87.
[G: U.S.]

Simmons, P. Consistent Estimation of a Large Generalised Strongly Separable Demand System. In *Currie, D.; Nobay, R. and Peel, D., eds.*, 1981, pp. 139–73.
[G: U.K.]

Sims, Christopher A. An Autoregressive Index Model for the U.S., 1948–1975. In *Kmenta, J. and Ramsey, J. B., eds.*, 1981, pp. 283–327.
[G: U.S.]

Spencer, J. E. Consistent Estimation of a Large Generalised Strongly Separable Demand System: Comment. In *Currie, D.; Nobay, R. and Peel, D., eds.*, 1981, pp. 174–77.
[G: U.K.]

Spivey, W. Allen. Model Size and the Evaluation of the Forecasting Performance of Macroeconomic Models: A Discussion. In *Kmenta, J. and Ramsey, J. B., eds.*, 1981, pp. 145–51.

Stapleton, David C. Inferring Long-term Substitution Possibilities from Cross-Section and Time-Series Data. In *Berndt, E. R. and Field, B. C., eds.*, 1981, pp. 93–118.

Taylor, John B. Economic Theory, Model Size, and Model Purpose. In *Kmenta, J. and Ramsey, J. B., eds.*, 1981, pp. 177–90.

Theil, Henri and Laitinen, Kenneth. The Independence Transformation: A Review and Some Further Explorations. In *[Stone, R.]*, 1981, pp. 73–112.
[G: U.S.]

Tinbergen, Jan. The Use of Models: Experience and Prospects. *Amer. Econ. Rev.*, Special Issue December 1981, *71*(6), pp. 17–22.

Tinsley, P. A. and von zur Muehlen, P. A Maximum Probability Approach to Short-Run Policy. *J. Econometrics*, January 1981, *15*(1), pp. 31–48. [G: U.S.]

Tobin, James. On a Theoretical and Empirical Basis of Macroeconometric Models: Comment. In *Kmenta, J. and Ramsey, J. B., eds.*, 1981, pp. 391–92.

Turner, Thomas H. and Whiteman, Charles H. Econometric Policy Evaluation under Rational Expectations. *Fed. Res. Bank Minn. Rev.*, Spring-Summer 1981, *5*(2), pp. 6–15.

Vermeulen, P. J. Parameter and Structural Sensitivity of Econometric Models. In *Janssen, J. M. L.; Pau, L. F. and Straszak, A. J., eds.*, 1981, pp. 411–17. [G: U.S.]

Visco, Ignazio. On the Derivation of Reduced Forms of Rational Expectations Models. *Europ. Econ. Rev.*, June/July 1981, *16*(2/3), pp. 355–65.

Wallis, Kenneth F. Econometric Implications of the Rational Expectations Hypothesis. In *Lucas, R. E. and Sargent, T. J., eds.*, 1981, *1980*, pp. 329–54.

Wansbeek, Tom and Kapteyn, Arie. Estimators of the Covariance Structure of a Model for Longitudinal Data. In *[Valavanis, S.]*, 1981, pp. 341–55.

Westlund, Anders. On Fix-Point Estimation in Interdependent Systems with Specification Errors. In *Wold, H., ed.*, 1981, pp. 283–302.

Yagolnitcer, M. A. Hybrid Models of Statistical Economics. In *Janssen, J. M. L.; Pau, L. F. and Straszak, A. J., eds.*, 1981, pp. 379–82.

213 Mathematical Methods and Models

2130 General

Amey, Lloyd R. and Bonaert, Axel P. The Theory of Fuzzy Subsets: A Review and Application to Planning and Control. *Rivista Int. Sci. Econ. Com.*, January–February 1981, *28*(1–2), pp. 1–32.

Arrow, Kenneth J. and Intriligator, Michael D. Handbook of Mathematical Economics: Historical Introduction. In *Arrow, K. J. and Intriligator, M. D., eds.*, 1981, pp. 1–14.

Bánkövi, György; Veliczky, József and Ziermann, Margit. New Ways and Means in Econometrics. *Acta Oecon.*, 1981, *26*(3–4), pp. 403–08. [G: Hungary]

Ciobanu, G. Characteristics of Feasible Solutions for Project Scheduling Problem. *Econ. Computat. Cybern. Stud. Res.*, 1981, *15*(1), pp. 53–62.

Constantinescu, P. Cybernetic Systems. *Econ. Computat. Cybern. Stud. Res.*, 1981, *15*(4), pp. 63–71.

Constantinescu, P. and Nicorovici, Al. Cybernetic Models for Two De Broglie's Formulas. *Econ. Computat. Cybern. Stud. Res.*, 1981, *15*(2), pp. 97–105.

Diewert, W. Erwin; Avriel, M. and Zang, Israel. Nine Kinds of Quasiconcavity and Concavity. *J. Econ. Theory*, December 1981, *25*(3), pp. 397–420.

Eichhorn, Wolfgang and Gehrig, Wilhelm. General-

ized Convexity and the Measurement of Inequality. In *Schaible, S. and Ziemba, W. T., eds.*, 1981, pp. 637–42.

Färe, Rolf and Primont, Daniel. Separability vs Strict Separability: A Further Result [Separability vs Functional Structure: A Characterization of their Differences]. *J. Econ. Theory*, December 1981, *25*(3), pp. 455–60.

Florescu, M. Industrial Process Cybernetization. *Econ. Computat. Cybern. Stud. Res.*, 1981, *15*(4), pp. 19–34. [G: Romania]

George, Donald A. R. Equilibrium and Catastrophes in Economics. *Scot. J. Polit. Econ.*, February 1981, *28*(1), pp. 43–61.

Glycopantis, Dionysius. The Cusp Catastrophe in an Exchange Model. *Econ. Stud. Quart.*, August 1981, *32*(2), pp. 188–91.

Green, Jerry R. and Heller, Walter P. Mathematical Analysis and Convexity with Applications to Economics. In *Arrow, K. J. and Intriligator, M. D., eds.*, 1981, pp. 15–52.

Kirman, Alan P. Measure Theory with Applications to Economics. In *Arrow, K. J. and Intriligator, M. D., eds.*, 1981, pp. 159–209.

Kornai, János. On the Difficulties and Deficiencies of Mathematical-Economic Research in Hungary. *Acta Oecon.*, 1981, *26*(1–2), pp. 175–85. [G: Hungary]

Lindberg, P. O. Power Convex Functions. In *Schaible, S. and Ziemba, W. T., eds.*, 1981, pp. 153–65.

Murphy, F. P. A Note on Weak Separability. *Rev. Econ. Stud.*, October 1981, *48*(4), pp. 671–72.

Niculescu-Mizil, E. The Place and Role of Cybernetics as a Science and Practice in the Socio-Economic Development of Socialist Romania. *Econ. Computat. Cybern. Stud. Res.*, 1981, *15*(4), pp. 47–61. [G: Romania]

Simonovits, András. Maximal Convergence Speed of Decentralized Control. *J. Econ. Dynam. Control*, February 1981, *3*(1), pp. 51–64.

Starr, Ross M. Approximation of Points of the Convex Hull of a Sum of Sets by Points of the Sum: An Elementary Approach. *J. Econ. Theory*, October 1981, *25*(2), pp. 314–17.

Stojanović, Dragiša. Special Models Based on the Matrix of Growth. *Econ. Computat. Cybern. Stud. Res.*, 1981, *15*(3), pp. 97–106.

Tabellini, Guido. Equazioni e disequazioni differenziali nei modelli di economia dinamica: elementi di confronto. (Differential Equations and Differential Inequalities in Dynamic Economic Models: Elements for a Comparison. With English summary.) *Giorn. Econ.*, July–August 1981, *40*(7–8), pp. 423–45.

2132 Optimization Techniques

Avriel, M., et al. Introduction to Concave and Generalized Concave Functions. In *Schaible, S. and Ziemba, W. T., eds.*, 1981, pp. 21–50.

Ben-Tal, A. and Ben-Israel, A. F-Convex Functions: Properties and Applications. In *Schaible, S. and Ziemba, W. T., eds.*, 1981, pp. 301–34.

Bereanu, B. Minimum Risk Criterion in Stochastic Optimization. *Econ. Computat. Cybern. Stud.*

Res., 1981, *15*(2), pp. 31–39.

Borwein, J. M. Convex Relations in Analysis and Optimization. In *Schaible, S. and Ziemba, W. T., eds.*, 1981, pp. 335–77.

Borwein, J. M. and Wolkowicz, H. Cone-Convex Programming: Stability and Affine Constraint Functions. In *Schaible, S. and Ziemba, W. T., eds.*, 1981, pp. 379–97.

Bródy, András. An Economy Controlled by Stocks and Profits. In *Kornai, J. and Martos, B., eds.*, 1981, *1973*, pp. 149–61.

Brumelle, Shelby L. and Puterman, Martin L. Newton's Method for W-Convex Operators. In *Schaible, S. and Ziemba, W. T., eds.*, 1981, pp. 399–414.

Cambini, Alberto. An Algorithm for a Special Class of Generalized Convex Programs. In *Schaible, S. and Ziemba, W. T., eds.*, 1981, pp. 491–508.

Craven, B. D. Duality for Generalized Convex Fractional Programs. In *Schaible, S. and Ziemba, W. T., eds.*, 1981, pp. 473–89.

Craven, B. D. Vector-Valued Optimization. In *Schaible, S. and Ziemba, W. T., eds.*, 1981, pp. 661–87.

Crouzeix, Jean-Pierre. A Duality Framework in Quasiconvex Programming. In *Schaible, S. and Ziemba, W. T., eds.*, 1981, pp. 207–25.

Crouzeix, Jean-Pierre. Continuity and Differentiability Properties of Quasiconvex Functions on I. In *Schaible, S. and Ziemba, W. T., eds.*, 1981, pp. 109–30.

Crouzeix, Jean-Pierre and Ferland, Jacques A. Criteria for Quasiconvexity and Pseudoconvexity and Their Relationships. In *Schaible, S. and Ziemba, W. T., eds.*, 1981, pp. 199–204.

Dancs, István; Hunyadi, László and Sivák, József. Discrete-Time Control with Time Lags. In *Kornai, J. and Martos, B., eds.*, 1981, pp. 131–47.

Di Guglielmo, F. Estimates of the Duality Gap for Discrete and Quasiconvex Optimization Problems. In *Schaible, S. and Ziemba, W. T., eds.*, 1981, pp. 281–98.

Diewert, W. E. Alternative Characterizations of Six Kinds of Quasiconcavity in the Nondifferentiable Case with Applications to Nonsmooth Programming. In *Schaible, S. and Ziemba, W. T., eds.*, 1981, pp. 51–93.

Diewert, W. E. Generalized Concavity and Economics. In *Schaible, S. and Ziemba, W. T., eds.*, 1981, pp. 511–41.

Ferland, Jacques A. Quasiconvexity and Pseudoconvexity of Functions on the Nonnegative Orthant. In *Schaible, S. and Ziemba, W. T., eds.*, 1981, pp. 169–81.

von Hohenbalken, Balder. The Simplicial Decomposition Approach in Optimization over Polytopes. In *Schaible, S. and Ziemba, W. T., eds.*, 1981, pp. 643–59.

Intriligator, Michael D. Mathematical Programming with Applications to Economics. In *Arrow, K. J. and Intriligator, M. D., eds.*, 1981, pp. 53–91.

Kallberg, J. G. and Ziemba, W. T. Generalized Concave Functions in Stochastic Programming and Portfolio Theory. In *Schaible, S. and Ziemba, W. T., eds.*, 1981, pp. 719–67.

Karlin, Samuel and Rinott, Yosef. Univariate and Multivariate Total Positivity, Generalized Convexity and Related Inequalities. In *Schaible, S. and Ziemba, W. T., eds.*, 1981, pp. 703–18.

Kendrick, David. Control Theory with Applications to Economics. In *Arrow, K. J. and Intriligator, M. D., eds.*, 1981, pp. 111–58.

Kornai, János and Martos, Béla. Vegetative Control: The First Step. In *Kornai, J. and Martos, B., eds.*, 1981, pp. 57–80.

Kornai, János and Simonovits, András. Control by Order Signals. In *Kornai, J. and Martos, B., eds.*, 1981, pp. 267–79.

Martin, D. H. Connectedness of Level Sets As a Generalization of Concavity. In *Schaible, S. and Ziemba, W. T., eds.*, 1981, pp. 95–107.

Martos, Béla. Concepts and Theorems from the Control Theory. In *Kornai, J. and Martos, B., eds.*, 1981, pp. 81–112.

Martos, Béla. Equivalence of Control Systems. Partitioned Systems. In *Kornai, J. and Martos, B., eds.*, 1981, pp. 187–200.

Martos, Béla. Partially Coordinated Controls. In *Kornai, J. and Martos, B., eds.*, 1981, pp. 201–20.

Martos, Béla. Vegetative Control with Price Communication. In *Kornai, J. and Martos, B., eds.*, 1981, pp. 163–86.

Michel, Philippe. Choice of Projects and Their Starting Dates: An Extension of Pontryagin's Maximum Principle to a Case Which Allows Choice among Different Possible Evolution Equations. *J. Econ. Dynam. Control*, February 1981, *3*(1), pp. 97–118.

Oettli, W. Optimality Conditions Involving Generalized Convex Mappings. In *Schaible, S. and Ziemba, W. T., eds.*, 1981, pp. 227–38.

Passy, Ury. Pseudo Duality and Non-Convex Programming. In *Schaible, S. and Ziemba, W. T., eds.*, 1981, pp. 239–61.

Robson, Arthur J. Sufficiency of the Pontryagin Conditions for Optimal Control When the Time Horizon Is Free. *J. Econ. Theory*, June 1981, *24*(3), pp. 437–45.

Schaible, Siegfried. A Survey of Fractional Programming. In *Schaible, S. and Ziemba, W. T., eds.*, 1981, pp. 417–40.

Schaible, Siegfried. Generalized Convexity of Quadratic Functions. In *Schaible, S. and Ziemba, W. T., eds.*, 1981, pp. 183–97.

Sethi, Suresh P. and Lehoczky, John P. A Comparison of the Ito and Stratonovich Formulations of Problems in Finance. *J. Econ. Dynam. Control*, November 1981, *3*(4), pp. 343–56.

Simonovits, András. Constrained Control and Destabilization. In *Kornai, J. and Martos, B., eds.*, 1981, pp. 281–320.

Varian, Hal R. Dynamical Systems with Applications to Economics. In *Arrow, K. J. and Intriligator, M. D., eds.*, 1981, pp. 93–110.

2133 Existence and Stability Conditions of Equilibrium

Conlisk, John. Bear's Theorem with Infinite Lags. *J. Econ. Dynam. Control*, February 1981, *3*(1), pp. 43–49.

Hartfiel, D. J. Bounds on the Solutions to $x' = SAx$ Where A Is S-Stable. *J. Econ. Theory*, June 1981, 24(3), pp. 453–57.

Ibaraki, Toshihide. Solving Mathematical Programming Problems with Fractional Objective Functions. In *Schaible, S. and Ziemba, W. T.*, eds., 1981, pp. 441–72.

Keenan, Donald. Further Remarks on the Global Newton Method [A Convergent Process of Price Adjustment and Global Newton Methods]. *J. Math. Econ.*, July 1981, 8(2), pp. 159–65.

Kimura, Yoshio. A Note on Sufficient Conditions for D-Stability. *J. Math. Econ.*, March 1981, 8(1), pp. 113–20.

Kondor, George A. On the Asymptotic Local Stability of Autonomous Economic Systems with Nonnegativity Conditions. *J. Econ. Theory*, December 1981, 25(3), pp. 466–70.

Makarov, V. L. Some Results on General Assumptions about the Existence of Economic Equilibrium. *J. Math. Econ.*, March 1981, 8(1), pp. 87–99.

Nishimura, Kazuo. Kuhn's Intensity Hypothesis Revisited. *Rev. Econ. Stud.*, April 1981, 48(2), pp. 351–54.

Rossi, Enzo. A Lemma on Relative Stability with an Application to an Economic Case Study. *J. Math. Econ.*, March 1981, 8(1), pp. 75–85.

Smale, Steve. Global Analysis and Economics. In *Arrow, K. J. and Intriligator, M. D.*, eds., 1981, pp. 331–70.

Varian, Hal R. Dynamical Systems with Applications to Economics. In *Arrow, K. J. and Intriligator, M. D.*, eds., 1981, pp. 93–110.

2134 Computational Techniques

Brumelle, Shelby L. and Puterman, Martin L. Newton's Method for W-Convex Operators. In *Schaible, S. and Ziemba, W. T.*, eds., 1981, pp. 399–414.

Gonçalves, Amilcar S. Explicit Solutions for Zero-One Linear Programming Problems. *Economia (Portugal)*, October 1981, 5(3), pp. 463–69.

Kendrick, David. Control Theory with Applications to Economics. In *Arrow, K. J. and Intriligator, M. D.*, eds., 1981, pp. 111–58.

Lazaridis, A. S. and Basu, D. R. Stochastic Optimal Control by Pseudoinverse. An Application. In *Janssen, J. M. L.; Pau, L. F. and Straszak, A. J.*, eds., 1981, pp. 361–65. [G: India]

Martić, Ljubomir. Limitations on the Procedure of Rounding. *Econ. Anal. Worker's Manage.*, 1981, 15(1), pp. 83–84.

Rustem, Berc and Zarrop, Martin B. A Newton-Type Algorithm for a Class of N-Player Dynamic Games Using Nonlinear Econometric Models. In *Janssen, J. M. L.; Pau, L. F. and Straszak, A. J.*, eds., 1981, pp. 349–54.

von Wülfingen, G. B. On Some Advantages of the Application of Newton's Method for the Solution of Nonlinear Economic Models. In *Janssen, J. M. L.; Pau, L. F. and Straszak, A. J.*, eds., 1981, pp. 339–47.

2135 Construction, Analysis, and Use of Mathematical Programming Models

Albegov, M. M., et al. Regional Agricultural Policy Design on the Basis of a Detailed Linear Economic and Agrotechnical Model. In *Janssen, J. M. L.; Pau, L. F. and Straszak, A. J.*, eds., 1981, pp. 221–29.

Avrămiţă, G. M. An Optimal Proceeding for Solving Large-Scale Problems: Vertical Decomposition. *Econ. Computat. Cybern. Stud. Res.*, 1981, 15(3), pp. 81–96.

Cambini, Alberto. An Algorithm for a Special Class of Generalized Convex Programs. In *Schaible, S. and Ziemba, W. T.*, eds., 1981, pp. 491–508.

Candler, Wilfred; Fortuny-Amat, Jose and McCarl, Bruce A. The Potential Role of Multilevel Programming in Agricultural Economics. *Amer. J. Agr. Econ.*, August 1981, 63(3), pp. 521–31.

Craven, B. D. Duality for Generalized Convex Fractional Programs. In *Schaible, S. and Ziemba, W. T.*, eds., 1981, pp. 473–89.

Day, Richard H. Unstable Economic Systems. *Econ. Notes*, 1981, 10(3), pp. 3–17.

Di Guglielmo, F. Estimates of the Duality Gap for Discrete and Quasiconvex Optimization Problems. In *Schaible, S. and Ziemba, W. T.*, eds., 1981, pp. 281–98.

Duesing, Erick C. Multiple Objective Linear Programming: An Economist's Perspective. In *Morse, J. N.*, ed., 1981, pp. 77–90.

Fernandes, Manuel C. C. Objectivos múltiplos em programaçao. (With English summary.) *Economia (Portugal)*, October 1981, 5(3), pp. 471–87.

Gal, T. Postefficient Sensitivity Analysis in Linear Vector-Maximum Problems. In *Nijkamp, P. and Spronk, J.*, eds., 1981, pp. 259–71.

Gol'shtein, E. G. and Tretiakov, N. V. On Modified Lagrange Functions for a Convex Programming Problem. *Matekon*, Winter 1981–82, 18(2), pp. 91–99.

Gonçalves, Amilcar S. A Unified Theory of Primal-Dual Techniques in Linear Programming. *Economia (Portugal)*, May 1981, 5(2), pp. 259–70.

Gonçalves, Amilcar S. Explicit Solutions for Zero-One Linear Programming Problems. *Economia (Portugal)*, October 1981, 5(3), pp. 463–69.

Hellwig, Z. H. Formal Designing of Stochastic Control Linear Systems. In *Janssen, J. M. L.; Pau, L. F. and Straszak, A. J.*, eds., 1981, pp. 375–78.

Hordijk, A. Linear Programming Methods for Solving Finite Markovian Decision Problems. In *Fandel, G., et al.*, eds., 1981, pp. 468–90.

Ibaraki, Toshihide. Solving Mathematical Programming Problems with Fractional Objective Functions. In *Schaible, S. and Ziemba, W. T.*, eds., 1981, pp. 441–72.

Ichiishi, Tatsuro. Super-modularity: Applications to Convex Games and to the Greedy Algorithm for LP. *J. Econ. Theory*, October 1981, 25(2), pp. 283–86.

Intriligator, Michael D. Mathematical Programming with Applications to Economics. In *Arrow, K. J. and Intriligator, M. D.*, eds., 1981, pp. 53–91.

Ionescu, V., et al. Optimizing the Dimensioning of

a Ramified Network of Pipe Lines with a Flow Variable in Time. *Econ. Computat. Cybern. Stud. Res.*, 1981, *15*(3), pp. 41–49.

Jeroslow, Robert. Some Influences of Generalized and Ordinary Convexity in Disjunctive and Integer Programming. In *Schaible, S. and Ziemba, W. T., eds.*, 1981, pp. 689–99.

Johnson, Donald and Boehlje, Michael. Minimizing Mean Absolute Deviations to Exactly Solve Expected Utility Problems. *Amer. J. Agr. Econ.*, November 1981, *63*(4), pp. 728–29.

Kallberg, J. G. and Ziemba, W. T. Generalized Concave Functions in Stochastic Programming and Portfolio Theory. In *Schaible, S. and Ziemba, W. T., eds.*, 1981, pp. 719–67.

Kennedy, John O. S. Applications of Dynamic Programming to Agriculture, Forestry and Fisheries: Review and Prognosis. *Rev. Marketing Agr. Econ.*, December 1981, *49*(3), pp. 141–73.

Lee, S. M. and Wynne, A. J. Separable Goal Programming. In *Nijkamp, P. and Spronk, J., eds.*, 1981, pp. 117–36.

Mond, B. and Weir, T. Generalized Concavity and Duality. In *Schaible, S. and Ziemba, W. T., eds.*, 1981, pp. 263–79.

Nijkamp, Peter and Rietveld, P. Hierarchical Multiobjective Models in a Spatial System. In *Nijkamp, P. and Spronk, J., eds.*, 1981, pp. 163–86.

Paris, Quirino. Multiple Optimal Solutions in Linear Programming Models. *Amer. J. Agr. Econ.*, November 1981, *63*(4), pp. 724–27.

Passy, Ury. Pseudo Duality and Non-Convex Programming. In *Schaible, S. and Ziemba, W. T., eds.*, 1981, pp. 239–61.

Patkar, Vivek; Saxena, P. C. and Parkash, Om. Dual Program for a Convex Fractional Function. *Econ. Computat. Cybern. Stud. Res.*, 1981, *15*(1), pp. 77–80.

Rowse, John. Solving the Generalized Transportation Problem. *Reg. Sci. Urban Econ.*, February 1981, *11*(1), pp. 57–68.

Rupnik, V., et al. A Non-terminal Control Approach to Dynamic Economic Modelling in Non-compact Space. In *Janssen, J. M. L.; Pau, L. F. and Straszak, A. J., eds.*, 1981, pp. 333–37.

Rupnik, Viljem. Eksistenca možne in optimalne rešitve zvezno-variabilnega dinamičnega linearnega programa v posplošeni obliki. (The Existence of Feasible and Optimal Solutions of a Continuously Variable Dynamic Linear Program in a Generalized Form. With English summary.) *Econ. Anal. Worker's Manage.*, 1981, *15*(4), pp. 527–37.

Samouilidis, J. E. A Planning Model for the Optimal Development of the Greek Energy Sector. In *Janssen, J. M. L.; Pau, L. F. and Straszak, A. J., eds.*, 1981, pp. 141–49.   [G: Greece]

Sazdanović, Stojadin. Optimizacija ekonomskih sistema po kriterijumu maksimalna produktivnost, ekonomičnost i rentabilnost modelima višekiterijumgkog programiranja. (Optimization of Economic Systems According to the Criterion of Maximal Productivity, Economy and Profitability Using Multi-Criteria Programmizing Models. With English summary.) *Econ. Anal. Worker's Manage.*, 1981, *15*(1), pp. 67–81.

Scarf, Herbert E. Production Sets with Indivisibilities—Part II: The Case of Two Activities. *Econometrica*, March 1981, *49*(2), pp. 395–423.

Scarf, Herbert E. Production Sets with Indivisibilities—Part I: Generalities. *Econometrica*, January 1981, *49*(1), pp. 1–32.

Schaible, Siegfried. A Survey of Fractional Programming. In *Schaible, S. and Ziemba, W. T., eds.*, 1981, pp. 417–40.

Schiefer, G. Agricultural Policy Planning with Programming Models: Problems of Centralized Planning in Decentralized Decision Situations. In *Janssen, J. M. L.; Pau, L. F. and Straszak, A. J., eds.*, 1981, pp. 157–62.   [G: LDCs]

Tsurkov, V. I. Aggregation in a Branch Planning Problem. *Matekon*, Winter 1981–82, *18*(2), pp. 75–90.

Werczberger, E. The Versatility Model in Decision Making under Uncertainty with Regard to Goals and Constraints. In *Nijkamp, P. and Spronk, J., eds.*, 1981, pp. 187–99.

Yagolnitcer, M. A. Hybrid Models of Statistical Economics. In *Janssen, J. M. L.; Pau, L. F. and Straszak, A. J., eds.*, 1981, pp. 379–82.

Young, Donovan and Sherali, Hanif D. Constructive Derivation in Dynamic Programing Modeling. *Water Resources Res.*, April 1981, *17*(2), pp. 293–94.

Zang, Israel. Concavifiability of C^2-Functions: A Unified Exposition. In *Schaible, S. and Ziemba, W. T., eds.*, 1981, pp. 131–52.

Zijm, W. H. M. Nonnegative Matrices, Generalized Eigenvectors and Dynamic Programming. In *Fandel, G., et al., eds.*, 1981, pp. 492–99.

214 Computer Programs

2140 Computer Programs

Diediw, A. and Nudds, D. Econometric Input–Output Tables Data Base. In *Janssen, J. M. L.; Pau, L. F. and Straszak, A. J., eds.*, 1981, pp. 387–98.

Drud, A. Combining an Optimal Control Program with the Time Series Processor System. In *Janssen, J. M. L.; Pau, L. F. and Straszak, A. J., eds.*, 1981, pp. 399–403.

Finley, D. R. and Liao, Woody M. A General Decision Model for Cost–Volume–Profit Analysis under Uncertainty: A Comment. *Accounting Rev.*, April 1981, *56*(2), pp. 400–403.

Greenberg, Harvey J. Implementation Aspects of Model Management: A Focus on Computer-Assisted Analysis. In *Bayraktar, B. A., et al., eds.*, 1981, pp. 443–59.

Lau, Amy Hing-Ling and Lau, Hon-Shiang. A Comment on Shih's General Decision Model for CVP Analysis. *Accounting Rev.*, October 1981, *56*(4), pp. 980–83.

Shih, Wei. A Comment on Shih's General Decision Model for CVP Analysis—A Reply. *Accounting Rev.*, October 1981, *56*(4), pp. 984–85.

Shih, Wei. A General Decision Model for Cost–Volume–Profit Analysis under Uncertainty: A Reply. *Accounting Rev.*, April 1981, *56*(2), pp. 404–08.

Tarabout, A.; Rechenmann, F. and Sefsaf, B. MODULECO: An Integrated, Modular Computer System for Economists. In *Janssen, J. M. L.; Pau, L. F. and Straszak, A. J., eds.,* 1981, pp. 405–10.

215 Experimental Economic Methods

2150 Experimental Economic Methods

Battalio, Raymond C.; Green, Leonard and Kagel, John H. Income–Leisure Tradeoffs of Animal Workers. *Amer. Econ. Rev.,* September 1981, *71*(4), pp. 621–32.

Battalio, Raymond C., et al. Commodity-Choice behavior with Pigeons as Subjects. *J. Polit. Econ.,* February 1981, *89*(1), pp. 67–91.

Harstad, Ronald M. and Marrese, Michael. Implementation of Mechanism by Processes: Public Good Allocation Experiments. *J. Econ. Behav. Organ.,* June 1981, *2*(2), pp. 129–51.

Kagel, John H., et al. Demand Curves for Animal Consumers. *Quart. J. Econ.,* February 1981, *96*(1), pp. 1–15.

Roth, Alvin E.; Malouf, Michael W. K. and Murnighan, J. Keith. Sociological versus Strategic Factors in Bargaining. *J. Econ. Behav. Organ.,* June 1981, *2*(2), pp. 153–77.

Thompson, Dennis. The Ethics of Social Experimentation: The Case of the DIME. *Public Policy,* Summer 1981, *29*(3), pp. 369–98. [G: U.S.]

Yefimov, Vladimir M. Gaming-Simulation of the Functioning of Economic Systems. *J. Econ. Behav. Organ.,* June 1981, *2*(2), pp. 187–200.

220 ECONOMIC AND SOCIAL STATISTICAL DATA AND ANALYSIS

2200 General

Aquino, Antonio. The Measurement of Intra-Industry Trade When Overall Trade Is Imbalanced. *Weltwirtsch. Arch.,* 1981, *117*(4), pp. 763–66.

Burtle, James L. The International Monetary System. In *Altman, E. I., ed.,* 1981, pp. 11.3–28.

Cherif, M'hamed. Note sur l'impact cumulé des mesures de conservation de l'énergie sur les principales grandeurs macro-économiques. (With English summary.) *Cah. Écon. Bruxelles,* 4th Trimestre 1981, (92), pp. 527–37.

Cohn, Richard M. Public Use Samples from the 1940 and 1950 Censuses. *Rev. Public Data Use (See J. Econ. Soc. Meas. after 4/85),* November 1981, *9*(3), pp. 241–43. [G: U.S.]

David, Martin and Robbin, Alice. The Great Rift: Gaps between Administrative Records and Knowledge Created through Secondary Analysis. *Rev. Public Data Use (See J. Econ. Soc. Meas. after 4/85),* November 1981, *9*(3), pp. 153–66. [G: U.S.]

Donoso R., Gregorio. Estimating Accounting Prices for Project Appraisal: Ecuador. In *Powers, T. A., ed.,* 1981, pp. 323–67. [G: Ecuador]

Eckaus, Richard S.; McCarthy, F. Desmond and Mohie-Eldin, Amr. A Social Accounting Matrix for Egypt, 1976. *J. Devel. Econ.,* October 1981, *9*(2), pp. 183–203. [G: Egypt]

Goldfield, Edwin D. Measurement of Subjective

Phenomena: Afterword. In *Johnston, D. F., ed.,* 1981, pp. 191–93.

Goldsmith, Raymond W. A Tentative Secular National Balance Sheet for Switzerland. *Schweiz. Z. Volkswirtsch. Statist.,* June 1981, *117*(2), pp. 175–87. [G: Switzerland]

Greene, J. E. and Robb, Reive. National Primary Socio-Economic Data Structures. IX: Barbados, Jamaica, Trinidad and Tobago. *Int. Soc. Sci. J.,* 1981, *33*(2), pp. 393–414. [G: Barbados; Jamaica; Trinidad; Tobago]

Hickerson, Steven. John Maurice Clark's View of Social Valuation and Accounting: Potential Applications of Policy Assessment Techniques. *Rev. Soc. Econ.,* December 1981, *39*(3), pp. 289–305.

Hughes Hallett, A. J. Data Analysis as a Sufficient Condition for Economic Planning: The Case of Sri Lanka's Development Plans. *Rev. Public Data Use (See J. Econ. Soc. Meas. after 4/85),* December 1981, *9*(4), pp. 283–300. [G: Sri Lanka]

Juster, F. Thomas; Courant, Paul N. and Dow, Greg K. A Theoretical Framework for the Measurement of Well-Being. *Rev. Income Wealth,* March 1981, *27*(1), pp. 1–31.

Matatko, John and Mayes, David G. A Multivariate Approach to Data Analysis. In *Currie, D.; Nobay, R. and Peel, D., eds.,* 1981, pp. 460–91. [G: U.S.; U.K.]

Meilakhs, Abram. Facts and Figures: Statistical Supplement. In *Novosti Press Agency,* 1981, pp. 263–76. [G: U.S.S.R.]

Morva, T.; Drechsler, L. and Hajnal, A. National Primary Socio-Economic Data Structures. VIII: Hungary. *Int. Soc. Sci. J.,* 1981, *33*(1), pp. 163–75. [G: Hungary]

Mullner, Ross. The American Hospital Association's Hospital Data Center: An Overview. *Rev. Public Data Use (See J. Econ. Soc. Meas. after 4/85),* November 1981, *9*(3), pp. 231–33. [G: U.S.]

Nicol, Kenneth J. Farm Sector Data: Presentation and Improvement. *Amer. J. Agr. Econ.,* May 1981, *63*(2), pp. 353–60. [G: U.S.]

Pierce, David A. Sources of Error in Economic Time Series. *J. Econometrics,* December 1981, *17*(3), pp. 305–21. [G: U.S.]

Rodefeld, Richard D. Farm Sector Data: Presentation and Improvement: Discussion. *Amer. J. Agr. Econ.,* May 1981, *63*(2), pp. 365–66. [G: U.S.]

Scott, Wolf. A Development Monitoring Service at the Local Level. *Int. Soc. Sci. J.,* 1981, *33*(1), pp. 82–90. [G: India]

Sicron, Moshe. National Primary Socio-Economic Data Structures. X: Israel. *Int. Soc. Sci. J.,* 1981, *33*(4), pp. 677–95. [G: Israel]

Smith, Tom W. Can We Have Confidence in Confidence? Revisited. In *Johnston, D. F., ed.,* 1981, pp. 119–89. [G: U.S.]

Stanković, Dušan. Matrica pokazatelja poslovnog uspeha osnovne organizacije udruženog rada. (Matrix of Indicators of Business Results of the Firm. With English summary.) *Econ. Anal. Worker's Manage.,* 1981, *15*(4), pp. 539–54. [G: Yugoslavia]

Stein, Linette S. The Conference Board Data Base. *Rev. Public Data Use (See J. Econ. Soc. Meas.*

after 4/85), July 1981, 9(2), pp. 151–52.
[G: U.S.]

Vavra, Janet K. The Inter-University Consortium for Political and Social Research: A Resource for the Social Scientist. *Rev. Public Data Use (See J. Econ. Soc. Meas. after 4/85),* November 1981, 9(3), pp. 237–39.

Wang, Zheng. Some Questions of Right and Wrong in Statistics Work Must Be Clarified. *Chinese Econ. Stud.,* Fall 1981, 15(1), pp. 47–61.
[G: China]

221 National Income Accounting

2210 National Income Accounting Theory and Procedures

Beck, Morris. On Measuring Public Sector Shares [Diverging Trends in the Shares of Nominal and Real Government Expenditure in GDP: Implications for Policy]. *Nat. Tax J.,* December 1981, 34(4), pp. 487–88. [G: MDCs; LDCs]

Black, Andrew P.; Horz, Kurt and Reich, Utz-Peter. Die Erfassung des Staatssektors in der Input–Output–Rechnung. (The Government Sector in Input–Output Accounting. With English summary.) *Ifo-Studien,* 1981, 27(1), pp. 1–33. [G: Sweden; U.K.; W. Germany]

Carson, Carol S. and Jaszi, George. The National Income and Products Accounts of the United States: An Overview. *Surv. Curr. Bus.,* February 1981, 61(2), pp. 22–34. [G: U.S.]

Dellacasa, Giorgio. Level of Living and National Product per Capita—Some Empirical Results. *Konjunkturpolitik,* 1981, 27(1), pp. 38–46.

Gutmann, Pierre. The Measurement of Terms of Trade Effects. *Rev. Income Wealth,* December 1981, 27(4), pp. 433–53. [G: Saudi Arabia; OECD]

Heller, Peter S. Diverging Trends in the Shares of Nominal and Real Government Expenditure in GDP: Implications for Policy. *Nat. Tax J.,* March 1981, 34(1), pp. 61–74. [G: MDCs; LDCs]

Hicks, John R. Valuation of the Social Income III—The Cost Approach. In *Hicks, J.,* 1981, pp. 243–68.

Hicks, John R. Valuation of the Social Income II—The Utility Approach [The Measurement of Real Income]. In *Hicks, J.,* 1981, pp. 142–88.

Hicks, John R. Valuation of Social Income I. In *Hicks, J.,* 1981, 1940, pp. 78–99.

Hicks, Norman and Streeten, Paul P. Reply [Indicators of Development: The Search for a Basic Needs Yardstick]. *World Devel.,* April 1981, 9(4), pp. 399.

Hicks, Norman and Streeten, Paul P. The Search for a Basic-Needs Yardstick. In *Streeten, P.,* 1981, pp. 374–97.

Holub, Hans Werner. Some Reflections on a Universal System of National Accounting. *Rev. Income Wealth,* September 1981, 27(3), pp. 333–38.

Holzman, Franklyn D. The Second Economy in CMEA: A Terminological Note. *ACES Bull. (See Comp. Econ. Stud. after 8/85),* Spring 1981, 23(1), pp. 111–14. [G: CMEA]

Kravis, Irving B. An Approximation of the Relative Real per Capita GDP of the People's Republic of China. *J. Compar. Econ.,* March 1981, 5(1), pp. 60–78. [G: China]

Kravis, Irving B.; Heston, Alan and Summers, Robert. New Insights into the Structure of the World Economy. *Rev. Income Wealth,* December 1981, 27(4), pp. 339–55. [G: Global]

Leipert, Christian. Kompensatorische Ausgaben, Symptombekämpfung und Kontraproduktivität im Staatssektor. (Compensating Expenditures, Curing of Symptoms and Negative Productivity in the Public Sector. With English summary.) *Ifo-Studien,* 1981, 27(1), pp. 35–51.

Martino, Antonio. Measuring Italy's Underground Economy. *Policy Rev.,* Spring 1981, (16), pp. 87–106. [G: Italy]

McGranahan, Donald; Richard, Claude and Pizarro, Eduardo. Development Statistics and Correlations: A Comment on Hicks and Streeten [Indicators of Development: The Search for a Basic Needs Yardstick]. *World Devel.,* April 1981, 9(4), pp. 389–97.

Mirus, Rolf and Smith, Roger S. Canada's Irregular Economy. *Can. Public Policy,* Summer 1981, 7(3), pp. 444–53. [G: Canada]

Nosse, Nobuko. Accounting Systems of Non-Market Oriented Activities. *Kobe Econ. Bus. Rev.,* 1981, (27), pp. 1–10.

Peskin, Henry M. National Income Accounts and the Environment. In *Peskin, H. M.; Portney, P. R. and Kneese, A. V., eds.,* 1981, pp. 77–103.
[G: U.S.]

Peskin, Henry M. National Income Accounts and the Environment. *Natural Res. J.,* July 1981, 21(3), pp. 511–37. [G: U.S.]

Peskin, Henry M.; Portney, Paul R. and Kneese, Allen V. Regulation and the Economy: Concluding Thoughts. *Natural Res. J.,* July 1981, 21(3), pp. 589–91. [G: U.S.]

Pommier, Philippe. Social Expenditure: Socialization of Expenditure? The French Experiment with Satellite Accounts. *Rev. Income Wealth,* December 1981, 27(4), pp. 373–86. [G: France]

Reich, Utz-Peter. Zur Berechnung der realen Staatsquote. (On the Calculation of the State's Share in Domestic Production. With English summary.) *Ifo-Studien,* 1981, 27(1), pp. 75–102.
[G: W. Germany]

Smith, Adrian. The Informal Economy. *Lloyds Bank Rev.,* July 1981, (141), pp. 45–61. [G: EEC]

Theret, Bruno. Un point de vue macroéconomique sur le traitement de la taxe sur la valeur ajoutée dans le système élargi de comptabilité nationale française. (A Macroeconomic View on the Treatment of the Value-Added Tax in the Extended French National Accounting System. With English summary.) *Public Finance,* 1981, 36(1), pp. 108–24. [G: France]

Treml, Vladimir G. Losses in Soviet National Income and Agriculture: A Puzzle. *ACES Bull. (See Comp. Econ. Stud. after 8/85),* Spring 1981, 23(1), pp. 103–09. [G: U.S.S.R.]

Tybout, Richard A. Social Accounting for Pollution. *Land Econ.,* November 1981, 57(4), pp. 507–25.
[G: U.S.]

Woodward, John T. Plant and Equipment Expenditures, Quarters of 1981 and First and Second Quarters of 1982. *Surv. Curr. Bus.*, December 1981, *61*(12), pp. 25–30.

2212 National Income Accounts

Abizadeh, Sohrab and Yousefi, Mahmood. Iran: Tax Structure Changes—A Time Series Analysis. *Bull. Int. Fiscal Doc.*, May 1981, *35*(5), pp. 202–06. [G: Iran]

Acharya, Shankar N. Perspectives and Problems of Development in Sub-Saharan Africa. *World Devel.*, February 1981, *9*(2), pp. 109–47.
[G: Sub-Saharan Africa]

Bach, Christopher L. U.S. International Transactions, Fourth Quarter and Year 1980. *Surv. Curr. Bus.*, March 1981, *61*(3), pp. 40–67. [G: U.S.]

Belli, R. David. U.S. Business Enterprises Acquired or Established by Foreign Direct Investors in 1980. *Surv. Curr. Bus.*, August 1981, *61*(8), pp. 58–71.

Bhalla, A. S. The Concept and Measurement of Labour Intensity. In *Bhalla, A. S., ed., 1981, 1975*, pp. 17–39. [G: Selected LDCs]

Bigsten, Arne. Regional Inequality in Kenya. In *Killick, T., ed., 1981*, pp. 180–88. [G: Kenya]

Bolyard, Joan E. International Travel and Passenger Fares, 1980. *Surv. Curr. Bus.*, May 1981, *61*(5), pp. 29–34. [G: U.S.]

Brophy, Theodore F. Toward a New U.S. Industrial Policy? Capital Formation: Comment. In *Wachter, M. L. and Wachter, S. M., eds., 1981*, pp. 152–55. [G: U.S.]

Carlson, Keith M. Recent Revisions of GNP. *Fed. Res. Bank St. Louis Rev.*, March 1981, *63*(3), pp. 27–32. [G: U.S.]

Caspersen, Finn M. W. Toward a New U.S. Industrial Policy? Capital Formation: Comment. In *Wachter, M. L. and Wachter, S. M., eds., 1981*, pp. 143–45. [G: U.S.]

Chittle, Charles R. Foreign-Exchange Distribution in Yugoslavia's New Planning System: An Input–Output Approach. *J. Compar. Econ.*, March 1981, *5*(1), pp. 79–86. [G: Yugoslavia]

Chung, William K. and Fouch, Gregory G. Foreign Direct Investment in the United States in 1980. *Surv. Curr. Bus.*, August 1981, *61*(8), pp. 40–51. [G: U.S.]

De Wulf, Luc. Statistical Analysis of Under- and Overinvoicing of Imports. *J. Devel. Econ.*, June 1981, *8*(3), pp. 303–23.

Denison, Edward F. International Transactions in Measures of the Nation's Production. *Surv. Curr. Bus.*, May 1981, *61*(5), pp. 17–28. [G: U.S.]

DiLullo, Anthony J. Service Transactions in the U.S. International Accounts, 1970–80. *Surv. Curr. Bus.*, November 1981, *61*(11), pp. 29–46.
[G: U.S.]

DiLullo, Anthony J. U.S. International Transactions, Third Quarter 1981. *Surv. Curr. Bus.*, December 1981, *61*(12), pp. 31–35, 56. [G: U.S.]

Eckstein, Otto and Tannenwald, Robert. Productivity and Capital Formation. In *Wachter, M. L. and Wachter, S. M., eds., 1981*, pp. 127–42.
[G: U.S.]

Eisner, Robert and Nebhut, David H. An Extended

Measure of Government Product: Preliminary Results for the United States, 1946–76. *Rev. Income Wealth*, March 1981, *27*(1), pp. 33–64.
[G: U.S.]

Enzler, Jared J.; Conrad, William E. and Johnson, Lewis. Public Policy and Capital Formation: Introduction. In *Federal Reserve System, 1981*, pp. 1–44. [G: U.S.; OECD]

Enzler, Jared J.; Conrad, William E. and Johnson, Lewis. Public Policy and Capital Formation. *Fed. Res. Bull.*, October 1981, *67*(10), pp. 749–61.
[G: U.S.]

Falkinger, Josef and Walther, Herbert. Eine kritische Bemerkung zur Frage der Lohnquotenbereinigung. (A Critical Remark on Correcting Wage Income Shares. With English summary.) *Jahr. Nationalökon. Statist.*, March 1981, *196*(2), pp. 137–46.

Fernández Diaz, Andrés. Inventories and Stabilization Policy. In *Chikán, A., ed. (I), 1981*, pp. 125–37. [G: Spain]

Friedlaender, Ann F. Saving: Comments. In *Aaron, H. J. and Pechman, J. A., eds., 1981*, pp. 390–96.

Friedman, Benjamin M. Financing Capital Formation in the 1980s: Issues for Public Policy. In *Wachter, M. L. and Wachter, S. M., eds., 1981*, pp. 95–126. [G: U.S.]

von Furstenberg, George M. Domestic Determinants of Net U.S. Foreign Investment. In *Hogan, J. D. and Craig, A. M., eds., Vol. 1, 1981*, pp. 115–63. [G: U.S.]

von Furstenberg, George M. Saving. In *Aaron, H. J. and Pechman, J. A., eds., 1981*, pp. 327–90. [G: U.S.]

Gaetani-d'Aragona, Gabriele. The Hidden Economy: Concealed Labor Markets in Italy. *Rivista Int. Sci. Econ. Com.*, March 1981, *28*(3), pp. 270–80. [G: Italy]

Ghysels, Eric and Vuchelen, Jozef. Het gebruik van de DULBEA-BNP cijfers in konjunktuuranalyses. (The Use of the DULBEA GNP-Figures in Business Cycle Analysis. With English summary.) *Cah. Écon. Bruxelles*, 1st Trimestre 1981, (89), pp. 53–73. [G: Belgium]

Gørtz, Erik. The Effect of Changes in Real Income and Relative Price on the Share of a Sector, with Special Reference to the Public Sector. *Scand. J. Econ.*, 1981, *83*(1), pp. 55–67.
[G: Denmark]

Gyulavári, Antal. Stocks and Stockpiling in Hungary—An International Comparison. *Acta Oecon.*, 1981, *27*(1–2), pp. 57–76. [G: Hungary; W. Germany; U.K.]

Hare, Paul G. The Investment System in Hungary. In *Hare, P. G.; Radice, H. K. and Swain, N., eds., 1981*, pp. 83–106. [G: Hungary]

Hinrichs, John C. and Eckman, Anthony D. Constant-Dollar Manufacturing Inventories. *Surv. Curr. Bus.*, November 1981, *61*(11), pp. 16–23.
[G: U.S.]

Hudson, Edward A. U.S. Energy Price Decontrol: Energy, Trade and Economic Effects. *Scand. J. Econ.*, 1981, *83*(2), pp. 180–200.

Hunt, Lacy H. Toward a New U.S. Industrial Policy? Capital Formation: Comment. In *Wachter,*

M. L. and Wachter, S. M., eds., 1981, pp. 145–49. [G: U.S.]

Johnson, Dana B. Capital Formation in the United States: The Postwar Perspective. In *Federal Reserve System*, 1981, pp. 47–58. [G: U.S.; OECD]

Kassirov, L. and Nikitina, M. On Determining the Share of Agriculture in the Social Product. *Prob. Econ.*, June 1981, 24(2), pp. 46–65. [G: U.S.S.R.]

Khan, M. H. and Zerby, J. A. The Socioeconomic Position of Pakistan in the Third World. *Pakistan Devel. Rev.*, Autumn 1981, 20(3), pp. 347–65. [G: Pakistan; LDCs]

Krantz, Olle and Nilsson, Carl-Axel. National Product Series in Historical Analysis: A Case Study of Sweden, 1861–1975. In *Bairoch, P. and Lévy-Leboyer, M., eds.*, 1981, pp. 411–19. [G: Sweden]

Krueger, Russell C. U.S. International Transactions, Second Quarter 1981. *Surv. Curr. Bus.*, September 1981, 61(9), pp. 42–45, 64. [G: U.S.]

de Leeuw, Frank and McKelvey, Michael J. The Realization of Plans Reported in the BEA Plant and Equipment Survey. *Surv. Curr. Bus.*, October 1981, 61(10), pp. 28–37. [G: U.S.]

Lienert, Ian. The Macroeconomic Effects of the 1979/80 Oil Price Rise on Four Nordic Economies. *Scand. J. Econ.*, 1981, 83(2), pp. 201–19. [G: Denmark; Finland; Sweden; Norway]

Lowe, Jeffrey H. Capital Expenditures by Majority-Owned Foreign Affiliates of U.S. Companies, 1981. *Surv. Curr. Bus.*, March 1981, 61(3), pp. 34–39. [G: U.S.]

Lowe, Jeffrey H. Capital Expenditures by Majority-Owned Foreign Affiliates of U.S. Companies, 1981 and 1982. *Surv. Curr. Bus.*, October 1981, 61(10), pp. 58–68. [G: U.S.]

Lubitz, Raymond. Capital Formation and Saving in Major Industrial Countries. In *Federal Reserve System*, 1981, pp. 59–73. [G: OECD]

Mǎnescu, Manea. Cybernetic Scenario: Accumulation-Consumption Correlation. *Econ. Computat. Cybern. Stud. Res.*, 1981, 15(2), pp. 7–19.

Marion, Gérald and Boury, Aly. La part salariale dans le revenu national: l'expérience contemporaine. (Wage Share in National Income: Recent Experience. With English summary.) *L'Actual. Econ.*, October–December 1981, 57(4), pp. 437–53. [G: Canada]

McKelvey, Michael J. Constant-Dollar Estimates of New Plant and Equipment Expenditures in the United States, 1947–80. *Surv. Curr. Bus.*, September 1981, 61(9), pp. 26–41.

Minami, Ryoshin and Ono, Akira. Behavior of Income Shares in a Labor Surplus Economy: Japan's Experience. *Econ. Develop. Cult. Change*, January 1981, 29(2), pp. 309–24. [G: Japan]

Oswald, Rudolph A. Toward a New U.S. Industrial Policy? Capital Formation: Comment. In *Wachter, M. L. and Wachter, S. M., eds.*, 1981, pp. 149–52. [G: U.S.]

Paldam, Martin. Is There an Electional Cycle? A Comparative Study of National Accounts. In *Strøm, S., ed.*, 1981, 1979, pp. 182–201. [G: OECD]

Park, Thae S. Relationship between Personal Income and Adjusted Gross Income, 1947–78. *Surv. Curr. Bus.*, November 1981, 61(11), pp. 24–28, 46. [G: U.S.]

Phelps Brown, Henry and Hart, P. E. The Share of Wages in National Income. In *Phelps Brown, H. and Hopkins, S. V.*, 1981, 1952, pp. 106–30. [G: U.K.; U.S.]

Powers, Terry A. An Overview of the LMST Accounting Price System. In *Powers, T. A., ed.*, 1981, pp. 1–59.

Powers, Terry A. Using Input–Output Analysis to Calculate Sectoral APRs. In *Powers, T. A., ed.*, 1981, pp. 61–122. [G: El Salvador; Paraguay; Barbados; Equador]

Rao, M. J. Manohar. Diminishing Returns—Fact or Fiction? *Indian Econ. J.*, January–March 1981, 28(3), pp. 107–14. [G: India]

Rutledge, Gary L. and O'Connor, Betsy D. Plant and Equipment Expenditures by Business for Pollution Abatement, 1973–80, and Planned 1981. *Surv. Curr. Bus.*, June 1981, 61(6), pp. 19–25, 30, 72. [G: U.S.]

Rutledge, Gary L. and Trevathan, Susan L. Pollution Abatement and Control Expenditures, 1972–79. *Surv. Curr. Bus.*, March 1981, 61(3), pp. 19–27. [G: U.S.]

Scholl, Russell B. The International Investment Position of the United States: Developments in 1980. *Surv. Curr. Bus.*, August 1981, 61(8), pp. 52–57.

Sirotkovic, Jakov. Influence of the Self-Management System on the Development of the Yugoslav Economy. *Eastern Europ. Econ.*, Winter 1981–82, 20(2), pp. 46–62. [G: Yugoslavia]

Tatom, John A. Energy Prices and Short-Run Economic Performance. *Fed. Res. Bank St. Louis Rev.*, January 1981, 63(1), pp. 3–17. [G: U.S.]

Vojnic, Dragomir. Investment Policy. *Eastern Europ. Econ.*, Winter 1981–82, 20(2), pp. 63–83. [G: Yugoslavia]

Weber, Warren E. Saving: Comments. In *Aaron, H. J. and Pechman, J. A., eds.*, 1981, pp. 396–402. [G: U.S.]

Whichard, Obie G. U.S. Direct Investment Abroad in 1980. *Surv. Curr. Bus.*, August 1981, 61(8), pp. 20–39. [G: U.S.]

Woodward, John T. Plant and Equipment Expenditures, the Four Quarters of 1981. *Surv. Curr. Bus.*, September 1981, 61(9), pp. 21–25, 41. [G: U.S.]

Woodward, John T. Plant and Equipment Expenditures, the Four Quarters of 1981. *Surv. Curr. Bus.*, June 1981, 61(6), pp. 26–30. [G: U.S.]

Woodward, John T. Plant and Equipment Expenditures, First and Second Quarters and Second Half of 1981. *Surv. Curr. Bus.*, March 1981, 61(3), pp. 28–33. [G: U.S.]

Woodward, John T. Plant and Equipment Expenditures: 1981. *Surv. Curr. Bus.*, January 1981, 61(1), pp. 24–25. [G: U.S.]

Zaitsev, A. The Personal Savings of the Working People under Developed Socialism. *Prob. Econ.*, February 1981, 23(10), pp. 64–77. [G: U.S.S.R.]

2213 Income Distribution

Aghevli, B. B. and Mehran, F. Optimal Grouping of Income Distribution Data. *J. Amer. Statist. Assoc.*, March 1981, 76(373), pp. 22–26.

Ahluwalia, Montek S. Inequality, Poverty and Development. In *Livingstone, I., ed.*, 1981, 1976, pp. 30–48.

Akpa, E. K. The Size Distribution of Income in Liberia. *Rev. Income Wealth*, December 1981, 27(4), pp. 387–400. [G: Liberia]

Altimir, Oscar. Poverty in Latin America: A Review of Concepts and Data. *Cepal Rev.*, April 1981, (13), pp. 65–91. [G: Latin America]

Amos, Orley M., Jr. Urban–Rural Regional Development Diffusion and Personal Income Inequality. *Rev. Reg. Stud.*, Winter 1981, 11(3), pp. 12–21. [G: U.S.]

Atack, Jeremy and Bateman, Fred. Egalitarianism, Inequality, and Age: The Rural North in 1860. *J. Econ. Hist.*, March 1981, 41(1), pp. 85–93. [G: U.S.]

Baldwin, Robert E. Trade, Growth and Income Distribution: The Korean Experience: Comment. In *Hong, W. and Krause, L. B., eds.*, 1981, pp. 287–89. [G: S. Korea]

Berry, Roger. Redistribution, Demand Structure and Factor Requirements: The Case of India. *World Devel.*, July 1981, 9(7), pp. 621–35. [G: India]

Bienen, Henry. The Political Economy of Income Distribution in Nigeria. In *Bienen, H. and Diejomaoh, V. P., eds.*, 1981, pp. 1–27. [G: Nigeria]

Bienen, Henry. The Politics of Income Distribution: Institutions, Class, and Ethnicity. In *Bienen, H. and Diejomaoh, V. P., eds.*, 1981, pp. 127–71. [G: Nigeria]

Blackorby, Charles; Donaldson, David and Auersperg, Maria. A New Procedure for the Measurement of Inequality within and among Population Subgroups. *Can. J. Econ.*, November 1981, 14(4), pp. 665–85. [G: Canada]

Blomquist, N. Sören. A Comparison of Distributions of Annual and Lifetime Income: Sweden around 1970. *Rev. Income Wealth*, September 1981, 27(3), pp. 243–64. [G: Sweden]

Bourgain, Jean and Vaneecloo, Nicolas. Inégalité, paupérisme et loi de Pareto. (Inequality, Pauperism and Pareto. With English summary.) *Revue Écon.*, September 1981, 32(5), pp. 950–64.

Bowring, Joseph. How Bad Were the Seventies? *Challenge*, July/August 1981, 24(3), pp. 47–50. [G: U.S.]

Bresson, Yoland. Capital-temps et répartition des revenus. De la remise en cause des fondements théoriques de la microéconomie à une nouvelle loi macroéconomique de répartition des revenus. (With English summary.) *Écon. Appl.*, 1981, 34(2–3), pp. 517–48.

Brown, C. V.; Levin, E. and Ulph, David T. Inflation, Taxation and Income Distribution. In *Brown, C. V., ed.*, 1981, 1977, pp. 255–68. [G: U.K.; Australia]

Burkhauser, Richard V. and Warlick, Jennifer L. Disentangling the Annuity from the Redistributive Aspects of Social Security in the United States. *Rev. Income Wealth*, December 1981, 27(4), pp. 401–21. [G: U.S.]

Champernowne, D. G. Income Distribution and Egalitarian Policy. The Outlook in 1980. In *[Pen, J.]*, 1981, pp. 31–50. [G: U.K.]

Chesnais, Jean-Claude. Génération et gain: une simulation de bilans financiers individuels par classe sociale. (Generation and Earnings: A Simulation of Individual Financial Balances per Social Group. With English summary.) *Consommation*, January–March 1981, 28(1), pp. 37–50. [G: France]

Chow, Steven C. and Papanek, Gustav F. Laissez-Faire, Growth and Equity—Hong Kong. *Econ. J.*, June 1981, 91(362), pp. 466–85. [G: Hong Kong]

Creedy, John. Education versus Cash Redistribution: A Comment. *J. Public Econ.*, April 1981, 15(2), pp. 269–72.

Crosswell, Michael J. Growth, Poverty Alleviation, and Foreign Assistance. In *Leipziger, D. M., ed.*, 1981, pp. 181–218. [G: LDCs]

Cutright, Phillips. Income Redistribution: A Cross-National Analysis. In *Martin, G. T., Jr., and Zald, M. N., eds.*, 1981, 1967, pp. 38–54. [G: LDCs; MDCs]

Dalrymple, Robert, et al. Quantitative Aspects of Tax Burdens—Methodology and Appraisal. In *Roskamp, K. W. and Forte, F., eds.*, 1981, pp. 309–30. [G: Netherlands; U.S.]

Das, Tarun and Parikh, Ashok. Decompositions of Atkinson's Measure of Inequality. *Australian Econ. Pap.*, June 1981, 20(36), pp. 171–78.

Diejomaoh, V. P. and Anusionwu, E. C. The Structure of Income Inequality in Nigeria: a Macro Analysis. In *Bienen, H. and Diejomaoh, V. P., eds.*, 1981, pp. 89–125. [G: Nigeria]

Dookeran, Winston. The Distribution of Income in Trinidad and Tobago, 1957–76. *Rev. Income Wealth*, June 1981, 27(2), pp. 195–206. [G: Trinidad; Tobago]

Estrin, Saul. Income Dispersion in a Self-managed Economy. *Economica*, May 1981, 48(190), pp. 181–94. [G: Yugoslavia]

Filgueira, Carlos. Consumption in the new Latin American Models. *Cepal Rev.*, December 1981, (15), pp. 71–110. [G: Latin America]

Flakierski, Henryk. Economic Reform and Income Distribution in Poland: The Negative Evidence. *Cambridge J. Econ.*, June 1981, 5(2), pp. 137–58. [G: Poland]

Formby, John P.; Seaks, Terry G. and Smith, W. James. A Comparison of Two New Measures of Tax Progressivity [Measurement of Tax Progressivity: An International Comparison]. [Measurement of Tax Progressivity]. *Econ. J.*, December 1981, 91(364), pp. 1015–19. [G: U.S.; U.K.; Australia; Canada]

Foxley, Alejandro. Stabilization Policies and Their Effects on Employment and Income Distribution: A Latin American Perspective. In *Cline, W. R. and Weintraub, S., eds.*, 1981, pp. 191–225. [G: Argentina; Brazil; Chile; Uruguay]

Garrison, Charles B. and Chang, Hui S. Subregional Income Differentials: A Study of the Tennessee Valley Region. *Rev. Reg. Stud.*, Winter 1981, 11(3), pp. 22–37. [G: U.S.]

Goldin, Claudia Dale. Credit Merchandising in the New South: The Role of Competition and Risk. In *Walton, G. M. and Shepherd, J. F., eds.*, 1981, pp. 3–23. [G: U.S.]

Gregory, Mary B., et al. Urban Poverty and Some Policy Options: An Analysis for India. *Urban Stud.*, June 1981, *18*(2), pp. 155–67. [G: India]

Grosse, Scott and Morgan, James N. Intertemporal Variability in Income and the Interpersonal Distribution of Economic Welfare. In *Hill, M. S.; Hill, D. H. and Morgan, J. N., eds.*, 1981, pp. 297–315. [G: U.S.]

Grüske, Karl-Dieter. An International Comparison of Quantitative Aspects of Tax Burdens and Specific Expenditure Benefits. In *Roskamp, K. W. and Forte, F., eds.*, 1981, pp. 331–39. [G: U.S.; W. Germany]

Grüske, Karl-Dieter. Umverteilung der Einkommen nach Generationen—Eine Analyse anhand Paglins verteilungstheoretischem Konzept. (Redistribution of Income According to Generations—An Analysis Based on Paglin's Distribution Concept. With English summary.) *Jahr. Nationalökon. Statist.*, May 1981, *196*(3), pp. 239–55. [G: W. Germany]

Harris, Richard J. Rewards of Migration for Income Change and Income Attainment, 1968–73. *Soc. Sci. Quart.*, June 1981, *62*(2), pp. 275–93. [G: U.S.]

Harrison, Alan. Earnings by Size: A Tale of Two Distributions. *Rev. Econ. Stud.*, October 1981, *48*(4), pp. 621–31. [G: U.K.]

Hazlewood, Arthur. Income Distribution and Poverty—An Unfashionable View. In *Killick, T., ed.*, 1981, *1978*, pp. 150–56. [G: Kenya]

Hong, Wontack. Trade, Growth and Income Distribution: The Korean Experience. In *Hong, W. and Krause, L. B., eds.*, 1981, pp. 258–83. [G: S. Korea]

House, William J. and Killick, Tony. Inequality and Poverty in the Rural Economy, and the Influence of Some Aspects of Policy. In *Killick, T., ed.*, 1981, pp. 157–79. [G: Kenya]

Hughes, Gordon A. and Islam, I. Inequality in Indonesia: A Decomposition Analysis. *Bull. Indonesian Econ. Stud.*, July 1981, *17*(2), pp. 42–71. [G: Indonesia]

Irvine, I. J. The Use of Cross-Section Microdata in Life Cycle Models: An Application to Inequality Theory in Nonstationary Economies. *Quart. J. Econ.*, May 1981, *96*(2), pp. 301–16. [G: U.S.]

Ishikawa, Tsuneo. Dual Labor Market Hypothesis and Long-Run Income Distribution. *J. Devel. Econ.*, August 1981, *9*(1), pp. 1–30. [G: U.S.]

Keidel, Albert. Income Distribution in Contemporary Japan. In *Richardson, B. M. and Ueda, T., eds.*, 1981, pp. 125–33. [G: Japan]

Knowles, James C. and Anker, Richard. An Analysis of Income Transfers in a Developing Country: The Case of Kenya. *J. Devel. Econ.*, April 1981, *8*(2), pp. 205–26. [G: Kenya]

Koo, Anthony Y. C.; Quan, Nguyen and Rasche, Robert H. Identification of the Lorenz Curve by Lorenz Coefficient. *Weltwirtsch. Arch.*, 1981, *117*(1), pp. 125–35. [G: Selected Countries]

Krug, Walter. Lineare und nicht-lineare Regressionen zur personellen Einkommensverteilung bei aggregierten Daten. (Linear and Non-linear Regressions Applied to Aggregated Data Concerning Personal Income Distribution. With English summary.) *Jahr. Nationalökon. Statist.*, September 1981, *196*(5), pp. 443–67. [G: W. Germany]

Kuznets, Simon. Size of Households and Income Disparities. In *Simon, J. L. and Lindert, P. H., eds.*, 1981, pp. 1–40. [G: Selected Countries]

Ladipo, O. O. and Adesimi, A. A. Income Distribution in the Rural Sector. In *Bienen, H. and Diejomaoh, V. P., eds.*, 1981, pp. 299–321. [G: Nigeria]

Lawrence, Edward C. and Elliehausen, Gregory E. The Impact of Federal Interest Rate Regulations on the Small Saver: Further Evidence. *J. Finance*, June 1981, *36*(3), pp. 677–84. [G: U.S.]

Layard, Richard. Reply to John Creedy's Comment [Education versus Cash Redistribution: The Lifetime Context]. *J. Public Econ.*, April 1981, *15*(2), pp. 273. [G: U.S.]

Lehrer, Evelyn and Nerlove, Marc. The Impact of Female Work on Family Income Distribution in the United States: Black-White Differentials. *Rev. Income Wealth*, December 1981, *27*(4), pp. 423–31. [G: U.S.]

Lorenzen, Gunter. Hierarchische Strukturen und die Verteilung der Lohn- und Gehaltseinkommen. (Hierarchical Structures of Earnings and the Distribution of Wage and Salary Incomes. With English summary.) *Z. ges. Staatswiss.*, March 1981, *137*(1), pp. 36–44.

MacMillan, J. A. and Winter, G. R. Income Improvement versus Efficiency in Canadian Rural Development Programmes. In *Johnson, G. and Maunder, A., eds.*, 1981, pp. 381–88. [G: Canada]

Matlon, Peter. The Structure of Production and Rural Incomes in Northern Nigeria: Results of Three Village Case Studies. In *Bienen, H. and Diejomaoh, V. P., eds.*, 1981, pp. 323–72. [G: Nigeria]

McDonald, James B. and Ransom, Michael R. An Analysis of the Bounds for the Gini Coefficient. *J. Econometrics*, November 1981, *17*(2), pp. 177–88.

McKenzie, Richard B. Taxation and Income Redistribution: An Unsympathetic Critique of Practice and Theory. *Cato J.*, Fall 1981, *1*(2), pp. 339–71. [G: U.S.]

Menchik, Paul L. Some Issues in the Measurement of Income Inequality. In *Solo, R. A. and Anderson, C. W., eds.*, 1981, pp. 227–49.

Mohammad, Sharif. Trade, Growth and Income Redistribution: A Case Study of India. *J. Devel. Econ.*, August 1981, *9*(1), pp. 131–47. [G: India]

Moreh, J. Income Inequality and the Social Welfare Function. *J. Econ. Stud.*, 1981, *8*(2), pp. 25–37. [G: U.K.]

Morley, Samuel A. The Effect of Changes in the Population on Several Measures of Income Distribution. *Amer. Econ. Rev.*, June 1981, *71*(3), pp.

285–94. [G: Brazil]

Morrison, Donald G. Inequalities of Social Rewards: Realities and Perceptions in Nigeria. In *Bienen, H. and Diejomaoh, V. P., eds.*, 1981, pp. 173–92. [G: Nigeria]

Muliere, Pietro. Sull'invarianza del rapporto di concentrazione R di gini. (On the Invariance of Gini's Concentration Ratio R. With English summary.) *Statistica*, April–June 1981, *41*(2), pp. 333–44.

Musgrove, Philip. The Oil Price Increases and the Alleviation of Poverty: Income Distribution in Caracas, Venezuela, in 1966 and 1975. *J. Devel. Econ.*, October 1981, *9*(2), pp. 229–50.

Nolan, Brian. Redistribution of Household Income in Ireland by Taxes and Benefits. *Econ. Soc. Rev.*, October 1981, *13*(1), pp. 59–88. [G: Ireland]

Nygård, Fredrik. Inkomstfördelningen i finländsk statistikproduktion. (The Income Distribution According to Finnish Official Statistics. With English summary.) *Ekon. Samfundets Tidskr.*, 1981, *34*(3), pp. 209–21. [G: Finland]

O'Brien, P. K. and Engerman, Stanley L. Changes in Income and Its Distribution during the Industrial Revolution. In *Floud, R. and McCloskey, D., eds., Vol. 1*, 1981, pp. 164–81. [G: U.K.]

Odufalu, Johnson O. The Distributive Impact of Public Expenditures in Nigeria. In *Bienen, H. and Diejomaoh, V. P., eds.*, 1981, pp. 455–83. [G: Nigeria]

Omorogiuwa, P. Ada. Personal Income Taxation and Income Distribution in Nigeria. In *Bienen, H. and Diejomaoh, V. P., eds.*, 1981, pp. 421–53. [G: Nigeria]

Orans, Martin. Hierarchy and Happiness in a Western Samoan Community. In *Berreman, G. D., ed.*, 1981, pp. 123–47. [G: W. Samoa]

Pfeffer, Jeffrey and Ross, Jerry. Unionization and Income Inequality. *Ind. Relat.*, Fall 1981, *20*(3), pp. 271–85. [G: U.S.]

Pope, Clayne L. Discussion [Egalitarianism, Inequality, and Age: The Rural North in 1860]. *J. Econ. Hist.*, March 1981, *41*(1), pp. 94–95. [G: U.S.]

Psacharopoulos, George. Education, Employment and Inequality in LDCs. *World Devel.*, January 1981, *9*(1), pp. 37–54. [G: LDCs]

Radner, Daniel B. An Example of the Use of Statistical Matching in the Estimation and Analysis of the Size Distribution of Income. *Rev. Income Wealth*, September 1981, *27*(3), pp. 211–42. [G: U.S.]

Ram, Rati. Inequalities in Income and Schooling: A Different Point of View. *De Economist*, 1981, *129*(2), pp. 253–61.

Reuss, Henry S. Inequality, Here We Come. *Challenge*, September/October 1981, *24*(4), pp. 49–52. [G: U.S.]

Rossi, José W. Income Distribution in Brazil: A Regional Approach. *J. Devel. Stud.*, January 1981, *17*(2), pp. 226–34. [G: Brazil]

Ruggles, Patricia and O'Higgins, Michael. The Distribution of Public Expenditure among Households in the United States. *Rev. Income Wealth*, June 1981, *27*(2), pp. 137–64. [G: U.S.; U.K.]

Russett, Bruce, et al. Health and Population Patterns

as Indicators of Income Inequality. *Econ. Develop. Cult. Change*, July 1981, *29*(4), pp. 759–79. [G: LDCs]

Sada, P. O. Urbanization and Income Distribution in Nigeria. In *Bienen, H. and Diejomaoh, V. P., eds.*, 1981, pp. 269–98. [G: Nigeria]

Seiver, Daniel A. Projecting the Income Distribution in a Regional Economy. *Growth Change*, October 1981, *12*(4), pp. 9–15. [G: U.S.]

Selowsky, Marcelo. Income Distribution, Basic Needs and Trade-Offs with Growth: The Case of Semi-Industrialized Latin American Countries. *World Devel.*, January 1981, *9*(1), pp. 73–92. [G: Latin America]

Sethuraman, S. V. Implications for Environment and Development Policies. In *Sethuraman, S. V., ed.*, 1981, pp. 171–208. [G: Selected LDCs]

Stano, Miron. State Variations in Income Inequality: A Multiple-Equation Approach. *Amer. Econ.*, Spring 1981, *25*(1), pp. 10–16. [G: U.S.]

Summers, Robert; Kravis, Irving B. and Heston, Alan. Inequality among Nations: 1950 and 1975. In *Bairoch, P. and Lévy-Leboyer, M., eds.*, 1981, pp. 18–25. [G: LDCs; MDCs]

Supple, B. E. Income and Demand 1860–1914. In *Floud, R. and McCloskey, D., eds., Vol. 2*, 1981, pp. 121–43. [G: U.K.]

Tachibanaki, Toshiaki. A Note on the Impact of Tax on Income Redistribution. *Rev. Income Wealth*, September 1981, *27*(3), pp. 327–32. [G: OECD]

Tarp, Finn. Vaekst og indkomstforderling i udviklingslandene. (The Relationship between Growth and Income Distribution in Developing Countries. With English summary.) *Nationaløkon. Tidsskr.*, 1981, *119*(1), pp. 32–46. [G: LDCs]

Thurow, Lester C. Equity, Efficiency, Social Justice, and Redistribution. *Nebr. J. Econ. Bus.*, Spring 1981, *20*(2), pp. 5–24. [G: U.S.]

Thurow, Lester C. Stagflation, Productivity, and the Labor Market. In *Carter, M. J. and Leahy, W. H., eds.*, 1981, pp. 61–106. [G: U.S.]

Thurow, Lester C. The Illusion of Economic Necessity. In *Solo, R. A. and Anderson, C. W., eds.*, 1981, pp. 250–75. [G: U.S.]

Tinbergen, Jan. Skill Scarcity, Monopoloid and Hierarchical Incomes in Some Western Countries. In *[Lipiński, E.]*, 1981, pp. 155–62. [G: U.S.; W. Germany; Netherlands]

Tomes, Nigel. The Family, Inheritance, and the Intergenerational Transmission of Inequality. *J. Polit. Econ.*, October 1981, *89*(5), pp. 928–58. [G: U.S.]

Toutain, Jean-Claude. The Uneven Growth of Regional Incomes in France from 1840–1970. In *Bairoch, P. and Lévy-Leboyer, M., eds.*, 1981, pp. 302–15. [G: France]

Ward, Sally K. Dependency, National Economy, and Inequality. In *Rubinson, R., ed.*, 1981, pp. 211–29. [G: U.S.]

Weisskoff, Richard and Wolff, Edward N. The Structure of Income Inequality in Puerto Rico. *J. Devel. Econ.*, October 1981, *9*(2), pp. 205–28.

Yasuba, Yasukichi. Trade, Growth and Income Distribution: The Korean Experience: Comment. In

Hong, W. and Krause, L. B., eds., 1981, pp. 284–86. [G: S. Korea]

Ycas, Martynas A. and Lininger, Charles A. The Income Survey Development Program: Design Features and Initial Findings. *Soc. Sec. Bull.*, November 1981, *44*(11), pp. 13–19. [G: U.S.]

Zelić, Nikola. Income Distribution and the Allocation of Resources in the Yugoslav Economy. *Econ. Anal. Worker's Manage.*, 1981, *15*(3), pp. 277–89. [G: Yugoslavia]

222 Input-Output

2220 Input-Output

Åberg, Morgan and Persson, Håkan. A Note on a Closed Input-Output Model with Finite Life-Times and Gestation Lags. *J. Econ. Theory*, June 1981, *24*(3), pp. 446–52.

Black, Andrew P.; Horz, Kurt and Reich, Utz-Peter. Die Erfassung des Staatssektors in der Input–Output–Rechnung. (The Government Sector in Input–Output Accounting. With English summary.) *Ifo-Studien*, 1981, *27*(1), pp. 1–33. [G: Sweden; U.K.; W. Germany]

Boyer, Marcel, et al. Mise à jour de la matrice des coefficients de capital pour l'économie québécoise. (Up-dating of the Capital Coefficient Matrix for the Quebec Economy. With English summary.) *L'Actual. Econ.*, January–March 1981, *57*(1), pp. 5–32. [G: Canada]

Burford, Roger L. and Katz, Joseph L. A Method for Estimation of Input-Output Type Output Multipliers When no I-O Model Exists. *J. Reg. Sci.*, May 1981, *21*(2), pp. 151–61. [G: U.S.]

Caravani, Paolo. Technology and Technical Change in a Dynamic Production Model. *Reg. Sci. Urban Econ.*, August 1981, *11*(3), pp. 335–49.

Castagnino, Ernesto S. Estimating Accounting Prices for Project Appraisal: Paraguay. In *Powers, T. A., ed.*, 1981, pp. 147–223. [G: Paraguay]

Cave, Martin. Wassily Leontief: Input–Output and Economic Planning. In *Shackleton, J. R. and Locksley, G., eds.*, 1981, pp. 160–82.

Cherif, M'hamed. Note sur l'impact cumulé des mesures de conservation de l'énergie sur les principales grandeurs macro-économiques. (With English summary.) *Cah. Écon. Bruxelles*, 4th Trimestre 1981, (92), pp. 527–37.

Chng, M. K. The Empirical Identification of a Capital-Goods Sector. *Oxford Bull. Econ. Statist.*, May 1981, *43*(2), pp. 207–23. [G: U.S.; Japan; U.S.S.R.]

Collins, Keith J. and Glade, Edward H., Jr. Regional and Functional Disaggregation of the Cotton Industry in a National Input–Output Model. *Southern J. Agr. Econ.*, July 1981, *13*(1), pp. 111–18. [G: U.S.]

Costanza, Robert. Embodied Energy, Energy Analysis, and Economics. In *Daly, H. E. and Umana, A. F., eds.*, 1981, pp. 119–45. [G: U.S.]

Czerwinski, Z., et al. System of Models for Medium-term Planning of National Economy. In *Janssen, J. M. L.; Pau, L. F. and Straszak, A. J., eds.*, 1981, pp. 79–84. [G: Poland]

Diediw, A. and Nudds, D. Econometric Input–Output Tables Data Base. In *Janssen, J. M. L.; Pau, L. F. and Straszak, A. J., eds.*, 1981, pp. 387–98.

Drabek, Zdenek. The Product Substitution and Technological Change in Czechoslovakia and Austria: The RAS Approach. *Greek Econ. Rev.*, December 1981, *3*(3), pp. 325–46. [G: Czechoslovakia; Austria]

Figueroa, Adolfo. Effects of Changes in Consumption and Trade Patterns on Agricultural Development in Latin America. *Quart. Rev. Econ. Bus.*, Summer 1981, *21*(2), pp. 83–97. [G: Latin America]

Ghosh, A. and Bugumbe, P. K. Computation of an Optimal Ordering for an Input–Output Matrix by an Application of Dynamic Programming. *Econ. Planning*, 1981, *17*(1), pp. 20–22.

Giannini, Carlo. Una nota sul cambiamento tecnologico nei sistemi input-output. (A Note on Technological Change in Input-Output Systems. With English summary.) *Giorn. Econ.*, January–February 1981, *40*(1–2), pp. 101–09.

Greenaway, David and Milner, Chris. Trade Imbalance Effects in the Measurement of Intra-Industry Trade. *Weltwirtsch. Arch.*, 1981, *117*(4), pp. 756–62. [G: U.K.]

Hanseman, Dennis J. and Gustafson, Elizabeth F. Stochastic Input–Output Analysis: A Comment [Input–Output as a Simple Econometric Model]. *Rev. Econ. Statist.*, August 1981, *63*(3), pp. 468–70.

Hare, Paul G. Aggregate Planning by Means of Input-Output and Material-Balances Systems. *J. Compar. Econ.*, September 1981, *5*(3), pp. 272–91.

Henry, Mark S., et al. A Cost-effective Approach to Primary Input-Output Data Collection. *Rev. Public Data Use (See J. Econ. Soc. Meas. after 4/85)*, December 1981, *9*(4), pp. 331–36.

Karunaratne, Neil Dias. An Input-Output Analysis of Australian Energy Planning Issues. *Energy Econ.*, July 1981, *3*(3), pp. 159–68. [G: Australia]

Kigyóssy-Schmidt, Éva. Sectoral Interrelations between Material and Non–Material Spheres of the National Economy in a Dynamic System (On the Basis of a Dynamic Input–Output Analysis with Several Years Lag Covering Also Non–Material Sectors.) *Acta Oecon.*, 1981, *26*(3–4), pp. 275–89. [G: E. Germany]

van de Klundert, Theo. Optimal Capital Accumulation in Generalized Leontief Models. *De Economist*, 1981, *129*(1), pp. 21–40.

Krishnamurty, J. Indirect Employment Effects of Investment. In *Bhalla, A. S., ed.*, 1981, *1975*, pp. 65–87. [G: LDCs]

Leipert, Christian. Kompensatorische Ausgaben, Symptombekämpfung und Kontraproduktivität im Staatssektor. (Compensating Expenditures, Curing of Symptoms and Negative Productivity in the Public Sector. With English summary.) *Ifo-Studien*, 1981, *27*(1), pp. 35–51.

Londero, Elio H. Estimating Accounting Prices for Project Appraisal: El Salvador. In *Powers, T. A.,* *ed.*, 1981, pp. 225–321. [G: El Salvador]

Lorenzen, Gunter. Zur Charakterisierung der industriellen Verflechtung und der Endnachfragestruktur einer Volkswirtschaft. (On Economic Interrelatedness and the Structure of Final Demand. With English summary.) *Jahr. Nationalökon. Statist.*, November 1981, *196*(6), pp. 503–10.

Marzi, Graziella. La misura della produttività in un modello con capitale fisso: i risultati disaggregati per l'economia italiana, 1970–1974. (Productivity Changes: A Disaggregated Analysis of the Italian Economy, 1970–1974. With English summary.) *Rivista Int. Sci. Econ. Com.*, April 1981, *28*(4), pp. 327–37. [G: Italy]

Meller, Patricio and Marfán, Manuel. Small and Large Industry: Employment Generation, Linkages, and Key Sectors. *Econ. Develop. Cult. Change*, January 1981, *29*(2), pp. 263–74.
[G: Chile]

Miglierina, Claudio and Folloni, Giuseppe. Significato economico di proiezioni spaziali di tavole input-output nazionali: alcune verifiche. (The Economic Meaning of the Spatial Projections of I/O National Tables: Some Tests. With English summary.) *Giorn. Econ.*, March–April 1981, *40*(3–4), pp. 199–215. [G: Italy]

Moore, Stuart A. Environmental Repercussions and the Economic Structure: Some Further Comments. *Rev. Econ. Statist.*, February 1981, *63*(1), pp. 139–42.

Morales Bayro, Luis. Estimating Accounting Prices for Project Appraisal: Barbados. In *Powers, T. A., ed.*, 1981, pp. 369–430. [G: Barbados]

Nyhus, D. E. INFORUM-IIASA System of National Economic Models. In *Janssen, J. M. L.; Pau, L. F. and Straszak, A. J., eds.*, 1981, pp. 123–28. [G: U.S.]

Park, Se-Hark; Mohtadi, Malek and Kubursi, Atif A. Errors in Regional Nonsurvey Input–Output Models: Analytical and Simulation Results. *J. Reg. Sci.*, August 1981, *21*(3), pp. 321–39.
[G: U.S.]

Powers, Terry A. Estimating Accounting Prices for Project Appraisal: Summary of Results. In *Powers, T. A., ed.*, 1981, pp. 123–45.
[G: Barbados; Paraguay; Ecuador; El Salvador]

Powers, Terry A. Using Input–Output Analysis to Calculate Sectoral APRs. In *Powers, T. A., ed.*, 1981, pp. 61–122. [G: El Salvador; Paraguay; Barbados; Equador]

Prakash, Shri. Cost Based Prices in Indian Economy, 1951–74. *Malayan Econ. Rev. (See Singapore Econ. Rev.)*, April 1981, *26*(1), pp. 1–14.
[G: India]

Richter, Josef and Zelle, Karl. Interregionale Lieferverflechtungen in Österreich 1976: Möglichkeiten der Schätzung einer multiregionalen Input-Output-Tabelle durch ein "information minimizing model." (With English summary.) *Empirica*, 1981, (1), pp. 73–110. [G: Austria]

Rocherieux, François. Sur la théorie des modèles inter-industriels: Quelques remarques appliquées à l'analyse de l'emploi et du commerce international. (On Input-Output Models Theory: Some Remarks Applied to Employment and Interna-

tional Trade Analysis. With English summary.) *Revue Écon.*, September 1981, *32*(5), pp. 887–922. [G: France]

Schluter, Gerald and Beeson, Patty. Components of Labor Productivity Growth in the Food System, 1958–67. *Rev. Econ. Statist.*, August 1981, *63*(3), pp. 378–84. [G: U.S.]

Scholing, Eberhard and Timmermann, Vincenz. Ost-West-Vergleich interindustrieller Verflechtungsstrukturen auf der Basis von Input-Output-Tabellen. (With English summary.) *Kyklos*, 1981, *34*(2), pp. 230–41.

Seton, Francis A. A Quasi-Competitive Price Basis for Intersystem Comparisons of Economic Structure and Performance. *J. Compar. Econ.*, December 1981, *5*(4), pp. 367–91. [G: Kenya; U.S.S.R.; Japan; U.K.; U.S.]

Steenge, Albert E. The Verification of Efficient Growth: An Approach via Stojanović's Matrix of Growth. *J. Macroecon.*, Spring 1981, *3*(2), pp. 271–81.

Stone, Richard. The Relationship of Demographic Accounts to National Income and Product Accounts. In *Juster, F. T. and Land, K. C., eds.*, 1981, pp. 307–76. [G: U.S.; U.K.]

Vishwakarma, K. P. An Application of the Generalized Inverse in Input–Output and Macroeconomic Analysis. In *Janssen, J. M. L.; Pau, L. F. and Straszak, A. J., eds.*, 1981, pp. 63–69.
[G: Netherlands]

Wessels, Hans. Auswirkungen des öffentlichen Verbrauchs auf die Struktur der Vorleistungen. (The Effects of the Public Sector's Consumption on the Structure of Intermediate Inputs. With English summary.) *Ifo-Studien*, 1981, *27*(1), pp. 53–74.
[G: W. Germany]

223 Financial Accounts

2230 Financial Accounts; Financial Statistics; Empirical Analyses of Capital Adequacy

Altman, Edward I. Bankruptcy and Reorganization. In *Altman, E. I., ed.*, 1981, pp. 35.3–47.
[G: U.S.]

Bench, Joseph. Money and Capital Markets: Institutional Framework and Federal Reserve Control. In *Altman, E. I., ed.*, 1981, pp. 1.3–33.
[G: U.S.]

Cramer, J. S. The Volume of Transactions and of Payments in the United Kingdom, 1968–1977. *Oxford Econ. Pap.*, July 1981, *33*(2), pp. 234–55. [G: U.K.]

Denison, Edward F. Capital Accumulation and Potential Growth: Discussion. In *Federal Reserve Bank of Boston (I)*, 1981, pp. 54–59. [G: U.S.]

Friedman, Benjamin M. Financing Capital Formation in the 1980s: Issues for Public Policy. In *Wachter, M. L. and Wachter, S. M., eds.*, 1981, pp. 95–126. [G: U.S.]

Kopcke, Richard W. Capital Accumulation and Potential Growth. In *Federal Reserve Bank of Boston (I)*, 1981, pp. 26–53. [G: U.S.]

Laidler, David. Monetary Targets and The Public Sector Borrowing Requirement: Comments. In *Griffiths, B. and Wood, G. E., eds.*, 1981, pp.

176–79. [G: U.K.]

Middleton, P. E., et al. Monetary Targets and the Public Sector Borrowing Requirement. In *Griffiths, B. and Wood, G. E., eds.*, 1981, pp. 135–75. [G: U.K.]

Moore, Peter G. The Wilson Committee Review of the Functioning of Financial Institutions—Some Statistical Aspects. *J. Roy. Statist. Soc.*, Part 1, 1981, *144*, pp. 32–46. [G: U.K.]

Munnell, Alicia H. Pensions and Capital Accumulation. In *Federal Reserve System*, 1981, pp. 133–42. [G: U.S.]

Ruggeri, Giovanni. Estimating the Enlarged Public Sector Borrowing Requirement: Comments and Prospects. *Rev. Econ. Cond. Italy*, February 1981, (1), pp. 121–44. [G: Italy]

Sharpley, Jennifer. Resource Transfers between the Agricultural and Non-agricultural Sectors: 1964–1977. In *Killick, T., ed.*, 1981, pp. 311–19. [G: Kenya]

Sinai, Allen. Economic Impacts of Accelerated Capital Cost Recovery. In *U.S. Congress, Joint Economic Committee (I)*, 1981, pp. 610–28. [G: U.S.]

Strichman, George A. The Economy of 1981: A Bipartisan Look: The Proceedings of a Congressional Economic Conference: Statement. In *U.S. Congress, Joint Economic Committee (I)*, 1981, pp. 590–609. [G: OECD]

Trevithick, James. Monetary Targets and The Public Sector Borrowing Requirement: Comment. In *Griffiths, B. and Wood, G. E., eds.*, 1981, pp. 180–82. [G: U.K.]

224 National Wealth and Balance Sheets

2240 National Wealth and Balance Sheets

Aaron, Henry J. The Economic Effects of the OASI Program: Comment. In *Skidmore, F., ed.*, 1981, pp. 81–84. [G: U.S.]

Atack, Jeremy and Bateman, Fred. The "Egalitarian Ideal" and the Distribution of Wealth in the Northern Agricultural Community: A Backward Look. *Rev. Econ. Statist.*, February 1981, *63*(1), pp. 124–29. [G: U.S.]

Barnard, A. and Butlin, N. G. Australian Public and Private Capital Formation, 1901–75. *Econ. Rec.*, December 1981, *57*(159), pp. 354–67. [G: Australia]

Benedetti, Alain; Consolo, Georges and Fouquet, Annie. L'experience française de compatabilite patrimoniale: sources, méthodes et résultats. (With English summary.) *Rev. Income Wealth*, September 1981, *27*(3), pp. 265–97. [G: France]

Blume, Marshall E.; Crockett, Jean A. and Friend, Irwin. Stimulation of Capital Formation: Ends and Means. In *Wachter, M. L. and Wachter, S. M., eds.*, 1981, pp. 41–94. [G: U.S.]

Bourguignon, François. Pareto Superiority of Unegalitarian Equilibria in Stiglitz' Model of Wealth Distribution with Convex Saving Function. *Econometrica*, November 1981, *49*(6), pp. 1469–75.

Break, George F. The Economic Effects of the OASI Program. In *Skidmore, F., ed.*, 1981, pp. 45–81. [G: U.S.]

Brophy, Theodore F. Toward a New U.S. Industrial Policy? Capital Formation: Comment. In *Wachter, M. L. and Wachter, S. M., eds.*, 1981, pp. 152–55. [G: U.S.]

Caspersen, Finn M. W. Toward a New U.S. Industrial Policy? Capital Formation: Comment. In *Wachter, M. L. and Wachter, S. M., eds.*, 1981, pp. 143–45. [G: U.S.]

Chowdhury, Nuimuddin. An Enquiry into the Nature and Determinants of Polarisation in Personal Wealth: A Case Study Using Handloom Industry Data. *Bangladesh Devel. Stud.*, Autumn 1981, *9*(4), pp. 51–76. [G: Bangladesh]

Christiano, Lawrence J. A Survey of Measures of Capacity Utilization. *Int. Monet. Fund Staff Pap.*, March 1981, *28*(1), pp. 144–98. [G: U.S.]

Corcoran, Patrick J. Inflation, Taxes, and the Composition of Business Investment. In *Federal Reserve System*, 1981, pp. 191–200. [G: U.S.]

Csikós-Nagy, Béla. Some Aspects of Stock Economy (A Case Study of Hungary). In *Chikán, A., ed. (I)*, 1981, pp. 87–97. [G: Hungary]

DeCanio, Stephen J. Accumulation and Discrimination in the Postbellum South. In *Walton, G. M. and Shepherd, J. F., eds.*, 1981, *1980*, pp. 103–25. [G: U.S.]

Dimitrov, Pavel. Analysis of Import Effects on Aggregate Inventories. In *Chikán, A., ed. (I)*, 1981, pp. 99–107. [G: Bulgaria]

Eckstein, Otto and Tannenwald, Robert. Productivity and Capital Formation. In *Wachter, M. L. and Wachter, S. M., eds.*, 1981, pp. 127–42. [G: U.S.]

Enzler, Jared J.; Conrad, William E. and Johnson, Lewis. Public Policy and Capital Formation: Introduction. In *Federal Reserve System*, 1981, pp. 1–44. [G: U.S.; OECD]

Feinstein, C. H. Capital Accumulation and the Industrial Revolution. In *Floud, R. and McCloskey, D., eds., Vol. 1*, 1981, pp. 128–42. [G: U.K.]

Feldstein, Martin S. The Distribution of the U.S. Capital Stock Between Residential and Industrial Uses. *Econ. Inquiry*, January 1981, *19*(1), pp. 26–37. [G: U.S.]

Fernández Diaz, Andrés. Inventories and Stabilization Policy. In *Chikán, A., ed. (I)*, 1981, pp. 125–37. [G: Spain]

Friedman, Benjamin M. Financing Capital Formation in the 1980s: Issues for Public Policy. In *Wachter, M. L. and Wachter, S. M., eds.*, 1981, pp. 95–126. [G: U.S.]

Gillula, James W. Selected Problems of Regional Development in the USSR: The Growth and Structure of Fixed Capital. In *Koropeckyj, I. S. and Schroeder, G. E., eds.*, 1981, pp. 157–93. [G: U.S.S.R.]

Gravelle, Jane G. The Social Cost of Nonneutral Taxation: Estimates for Nonresidential Capital. In *Hulten, C. R., ed.*, 1981, pp. 239–50. [G: U.S.]

Hibbert, Jack. National and Sector Balance Sheets in the United Kingdom. *Rev. Income Wealth*, December 1981, *27*(4), pp. 357–71. [G: U.K.]

Hicks, John R. Measurement of Capital—In Practice. In *Hicks, J.*, 1981, *1969*, pp. 204–17.

Hitchens, D. M. W. N. Life Insurance and Asset Holding in the United Kingdom: Comment. In *Currie, D.; Peel, D. and Peters, W., eds.,* 1981, pp. 165–68. [G: U.K.]

Hober, Rolf-Jürgen and Mierheim, Horst. Die Bedeutung des Versorgungsvermögens für die personelle Vermögensverteilung der privaten Haushalte in der Bundesrepublik Deutschland 1973: Eine vergleichende Untersuchung. (Significance of Pension-Property for Personal Distribution of Wealth of Private Households in the Federal Republic of Germany, 1973: A Comparative Investigation. With English summary.) *Jahr. Nationalökon. Statist.,* September 1981, *196*(5), pp. 385–419. [G: W. Germany]

Hulten, Charles R. and Wykoff, Frank C. The Measurement of Economic Depreciation. In *Hulten, C. R., ed.,* 1981, pp. 81–125. [G: U.S.; Japan]

Hunt, Lacy H. Toward a New U.S. Industrial Policy? Capital Formation: Comment. In *Wachter, M. L. and Wachter, S. M., eds.,* 1981, pp. 145–49. [G: U.S.]

Johnson, Dana B. Capital Formation in the United States: The Postwar Perspective. In *Federal Reserve System,* 1981, pp. 47–58. [G: U.S.; OECD]

Jorgenson, Dale W. and Sullivan, Martin A. Inflation and Corporate Capital Recovery. In *Hulten, C. R., ed.,* 1981, pp. 171–237. [G: U.S.]

Kotlikoff, Laurence J. and Summers, Lawrence H. The Role of Intergenerational Transfers in Aggregate Capital Accumulation. *J. Polit. Econ.,* August 1981, *89*(4), pp. 706–32. [G: U.S.]

de Leeuw, Frank. The Measurement of Economic Depreciation: Discussion. In *Hulten, C. R., ed.,* 1981, pp. 126–29. [G: U.S.; Japan]

Lubitz, Raymond. Capital Formation and Saving in Major Industrial Countries. In *Federal Reserve System,* 1981, pp. 59–73. [G: OECD]

Munnell, Alicia H. Pensions and Capital Accumulation. In *Federal Reserve System,* 1981, pp. 133–42. [G: U.S.]

Musgrave, John C. Fixed Capital Stock in the United States: Revised Estimates. *Surv. Curr. Bus.,* February 1981, *61*(2), pp. 57–68. [G: U.S.]

Oswald, Rudolph A. Toward a New U.S. Industrial Policy? Capital Formation: Comment. In *Wachter, M. L. and Wachter, S. M., eds.,* 1981, pp. 149–52. [G: U.S.]

Phelps Brown, Henry and Handfield-Jones, S. J. The Climacteric of the 1890's: A Study in the Expanding Economy. In *Phelps Brown, H. and Hopkins, S. V.,* 1981, *1952,* pp. 131–72. [G: U.K.; OECD]

Reischauer, Robert. The Economic Effects of the OASI Program: Comment. In *Skidmore, F., ed.,* 1981, pp. 84–88. [G: U.S.]

Shorrocks, A. F. Life Insurance and Asset Holding in the United Kingdom. In *Currie, D.; Peel, D. and Peters, W., eds.,* 1981, pp. 139–64. [G: U.K.]

Spånt, Roland. The Development of the Distribution of Wealth in Sweden. *Rev. Income Wealth,* March 1981, *27*(1), pp. 65–74. [G: Sweden]

Summers, Lawrence H. Tax Policy and Corporate Investment. In *Meyer, L. H., ed.,* 1981, pp. 115–48. [G: U.S.]

Tatom, John A. Investment and the New Energy Regime. In *Federal Reserve System,* 1981, pp. 221–30. [G: U.S.]

Taubman, Paul. The Measurement of Economic Depreciation: Discussion. In *Hulten, C. R., ed.,* 1981, pp. 129–32. [G: U.S.; Japan]

Thurow, Lester C. Stagflation, Productivity, and the Labor Market. In *Carter, M. J. and Leahy, W. H., eds.,* 1981, pp. 61–106. [G: U.S.]

Tomes, Nigel. The Family, Inheritance, and the Intergenerational Transmission of Inequality. *J. Polit. Econ.,* October 1981, *89*(5), pp. 928–58. [G: U.S.]

Ture, Norman B. Tax Policy and Corporate Investment: Discussion. In *Meyer, L. H., ed.,* 1981, pp. 165–70. [G: U.S.]

Wolff, Edward N. The Accumulation of Household Wealth over the Life-Cycle: A Microdata Analysis. *Rev. Income Wealth,* March 1981, *27*(1), pp. 75–96. [G: U.S.]

225 Social Indicators: Data and Analysis

2250 Social Indicators: Data and Analysis

Andorka, Rudolf and Falussy, Béla. The Way of Life of the Hungarian Society as Reflected by the Time Budget Survey of 1976–1977. *Acta Oecon.,* 1981, *26*(3–4), pp. 243–73. [G: Hungary]

Andrews, Frank M. Dissatisfaction with Satisfaction: Subjective Social Indicators and the Quality of Life: Comments. In *Johnston, D. F., ed.,* 1981, pp. 21–30. [G: U.S.]

Andrews, Frank M. Subjective Social Indicators, Objective Social Indicators, and Social Accounting Systems. In *Juster, F. T. and Land, K. C., eds.,* 1981, pp. 377–419.

Briggs, Asa. Social History 1900–45. In *Floud, R. and McCloskey, D., eds., Vol. 2,* 1981, pp. 347–69. [G: U.K.]

Brodsky, David A. and Rodrik, Dani. Indicators of Development and Data Availability: The Case of the PQLI. *World Devel.,* July 1981, *9*(7), pp. 695–99. [G: LDCs]

Campbell, Angus. Surveys of Subjective Phenomena: A Working Paper: Irregularities in Survey Data. In *Johnston, D. F., ed.,* 1981, pp. 79–84. [G: U.S.]

Castro, Alfonso Peter; Hakansson, N. Thomas and Brokensha, David. Indicators of Rural Inequality. *World Devel.,* May 1981, *9*(5), pp. 401–27.

Chandrasekar, Krishnamurti. Productivity and Social Indicators. *Ann. Amer. Acad. Polit. Soc. Sci.,* January 1981, *453,* pp. 153–68. [G: U.S.]

Dahmann, Donald C. Subjective Indicators of Neighborhood Quality. In *Johnston, D. F., ed.,* 1981, pp. 97–117. [G: U.S.]

Felson, Marcus. Social Accounts Based on Map, Clock, and Calendar. In *Juster, F. T. and Land, K. C., eds.,* 1981, pp. 219–39. [G: U.S.]

Fox, Karl A. and Ghosh, Syamal K. A Behavior Setting Approach to Social Accounts Combining Concepts and Data from Ecological Psychology, Economics, and Studies of Time Use. In *Juster, F. T. and Land, K. C., eds.,* 1981, pp. 131–217. [G: U.S.]

Goldfield, Edwin D. Measurement of Subjective

Phenomena: Afterword. In *Johnston, D. F., ed.*, 1981, pp. 191–93.

Hicks, Norman and Streeten, Paul P. Reply [Indicators of Development: The Search for a Basic Needs Yardstick]. *World Devel.*, April 1981, 9(4), pp. 399.

Hicks, Norman and Streeten, Paul P. Indicators of Development: The Search for a Basic Needs Yardstick. In *Streeten, P. and Jolly, R, eds.*, 1981, 1979, pp. 53–66.

Hicks, Norman and Streeten, Paul P. The Search for a Basic-Needs Yardstick. In *Streeten, P.*, 1981, pp. 374–97.

Horowitz, Harold. The UNESCO Framework for Cultural Statistics and a Cultural Data Bank for Europe. *J. Cult. Econ.*, December 1981, 5(2), pp. 1–17. [G: Europe]

House, James S. Social Indicators, Social Change, and Social Accounting: Toward More Integrated and Dynamic Models. In *Juster, F. T. and Land, K. C., eds.*, 1981, pp. 421–52.

Johnston, Denis F. and Carley, Michael J. Social Measurement and Social Indicators. *Ann. Amer. Acad. Polit. Soc. Sci.*, January 1981, 453, pp. 237–53.

Juster, F. Thomas; Courant, Paul N. and Dow, Greg K. The Theory and Measurement of Well-Being: A Suggested Framework for Accounting and Analysis. In *Juster, F. T. and Land, K. C., eds.*, 1981, pp. 23–94. [G: U.S.]

Khan, M. H. and Zerby, J. A. The Socioeconomic Position of Pakistan in the Third World. *Pakistan Devel. Rev.*, Autumn 1981, 20(3), pp. 347–65. [G: Pakistan; LDCs]

Land, Kenneth C. and Juster, F. Thomas. Social Accounting Systems: An Overview. In *Juster, F. T. and Land, K. C., eds.*, 1981, pp. 1–21.

Land, Kenneth C. and McMillen, Marilyn M. Demographic Accounts and the Study of Social Change, with Applications to the Post-World War II United States. In *Juster, F. T. and Land, K. C., eds.*, 1981, pp. 241–306. [G: U.S.]

Lunde, Anders Steen. Health in the United States. *Ann. Amer. Acad. Polit. Soc. Sci.*, January 1981, 453, pp. 28–69. [G: U.S.]

Mare, Robert D. Trends in Schooling: Demography, Performance, and Organization. *Ann. Amer. Acad. Polit. Soc. Sci.*, January 1981, 453, pp. 96–122. [G: U.S.]

McGranahan, Donald; Richard, Claude and Pizarro, Eduardo. Development Statistics and Correlations: A Comment on Hicks and Streeten [Indicators of Development: The Search for a Basic Needs Yardstick]. *World Devel.*, April 1981, 9(4), pp. 389–97.

Peterson, Richard A. Measuring Culture, Leisure, and Time Use. *Ann. Amer. Acad. Polit. Soc. Sci.*, January 1981, 453, pp. 169–79. [G: U.S.]

Pommier, Philippe. Social Expenditure: Socialization of Expenditure? The French Experiment with Satellite Accounts. *Rev. Income Wealth*, December 1981, 27(4), pp. 373–86. [G: France]

Power, Thomas M. Urban Size (Dis)amenities Revisited. *J. Urban Econ.*, January 1981, 9(1), pp. 85–89. [G: U.S.]

Ruggles, Richard. The Conceptual and Empirical Strengths and Limitations of Demographic and Time-Based Accounts. In *Juster, F. T. and Land, K. C., eds.*, 1981, pp. 453–76.

Sen, Amartya. Public Action and the Quality of Life in Developing Countries. *Oxford Bull. Econ. Statist.*, November 1981, 43(4), pp. 287–319.

Simon, Julian L. Environmental disruption or Environmental Improvement? [Environmental Disruption: Implications for the Social Sciences]. *Soc. Sci. Quart.*, March 1981, 62(1), pp. 30–43.

Stone, Richard. The Relationship of Demographic Accounts to National Income and Product Accounts. In *Juster, F. T. and Land, K. C., eds.*, 1981, pp. 307–76. [G: U.S.; U.K.]

Terleckyj, Nestor E. A Social Production Framework for Resource Accounting. In *Juster, F. T. and Land, K. C., eds.*, 1981, pp. 95–129. [G: U.S.]

Terleckyj, Nestor E. Contribution of Government to the Quality of Life. In *Hogan, J. D. and Craig, A. M., eds.*, Vol. 2, 1981, pp. 1085–93. [G: U.S.]

Thane, P. Social History 1860–1914. In *Floud, R. and McCloskey, D., eds.*, Vol. 2, 1981, pp. 198–238. [G: U.K.]

Turner, Charles F. Surveys of Subjective Phenomena: A Working Paper: Patterns of Disagreement: A Reply to Angus Campbell. In *Johnston, D. F., ed.*, 1981, pp. 85–95. [G: U.S.]

Turner, Charles F. Surveys of Subjective Phenomena: A Working Paper. In *Johnston, D. F., ed.*, 1981, pp. 37–78. [G: U.S.]

Verner, Joel G. Legislative Systems and Public Policy: A Comparative Analysis of 78 Developing Countries. *J. Devel. Areas*, January 1981, 15(2), pp. 275–96.

Wilcox, Allen R. Dissatisfaction with Satisfaction: Subjective Social Indicators and the Quality of Life: Response to Comments. In *Johnston, D. F., ed.*, 1981, pp. 31–35. [G: U.S.]

Wilcox, Allen R. Dissatisfaction with Satisfaction: Subjective Social Indicators and the Quality of Life. In *Johnston, D. F., ed.*, 1981, pp. 1–20. [G: U.S.]

Ziegler, Joseph A. and Britton, Charles R. A Comparative Analysis of Socioeconomic Variations in Measuring the Quality of Life. *Soc. Sci. Quart.*, June 1981, 62(2), pp. 303–12. [G: U.S.]

226 Productivity and Growth: Theory and Data

2260 Productivity and Growth: Theory and Data

Abramovitz, Moses. Welfare Quandaries and Productivity Concerns. *Amer. Econ. Rev.*, March 1981, 71(1), pp. 1–17. [G: U.S.]

Adams, Thomas M. From Old Regime to New: Business, Bureaucracy, and Social Change in Eighteenth-Century France—A Review Article. *Bus. Hist. Rev.*, Winter 1981, 55(4), pp. 541–61. [G: France]

Ahmad, Masood. Incremental Capital-Output Ratios and Growth Rates in the Short-Run Evidence from Pakistan. *Pakistan Econ. Soc. Rev.*, Winter 1981, 19(2), pp. 123–30. [G: Selected MDCs; Selected LDCs; Pakistan]

Alho, Kari. Pääoman tuotto Suomessa. (The Rate of Return in Finland. With English summary.) *Kan-*

sant. Aikak., 1981, 77(2), pp. 151–61.
[G: Finland]

Amendola, Adalgiso and Jossa, Bruno. Italian Economic Development: Comment on an Interpretation. *Rev. Econ. Cond. Italy*, October 1981, (3), pp. 481–512. [G: Italy]

Ando, Albert. An Econometric Model Incorporating the Supply-Side Effects of Economic Policy: Discussion. In *Meyer, L. H., ed.*, 1981, pp. 103–11. [G: U.S.]

Augusztinovics, Mária. Changes in the Macro-Structure of the Hungarian Economy (1950–2000). *Acta Oecon.*, 1981, 27(3–4), pp. 267–88.
[G: Hungary]

Augusztinovics, Mária. The Rate of Economic Growth in Hungary, 1950–2000. *Acta Oecon.*, 1981, 26(3–4), pp. 223–42. [G: Hungary]

Aujac, Henri. Cultures and Growth. In *Saunders, C. T., ed. (II)*, 1981, pp. 47–70. [G: Brazil; France; Ivory Coast; Japan]

Baer, Werner and Samuelson, Larry. Toward a Service-oriented Growth Strategy. *World Devel.*, June 1981, 9(6), pp. 499–514.

Baily, Martin Neil. Productivity and the Services of Capital and Labor. *Brookings Pap. Econ. Act.*, 1981, (1), pp. 1–50. [G: U.S.]

Baily, Martin Neil. Relative Productivity Levels, 1947–1963 by Christensen, et al.: Comment. *Europ. Econ. Rev.*, May 1981, 16(1), pp. 95–97.

Baily, Martin Neil. The Productivity Growth Slowdown and Capital Accumulation. *Amer. Econ. Rev.*, May 1981, 71(2), pp. 326–31. [G: U.S.]

Bairoch, Paul. The Main Trends in National Economic Disparities since the Industrial Revolution. In *Bairoch, P. and Lévy-Leboyer, M., eds.*, 1981, pp. 3–17. [G: LDCs; MDCs]

Baruch, Jordon. The Role of Government in Promoting Research and Development. In *Hogan, J. D. and Craig, A. M., eds., Vol. 1*, 1981, pp. 87–92. [G: U.S.]

Bauer, P. T. The Investment Fetish. In *Bauer, P. T.*, 1981, pp. 239–54.

Begg, Iain; Cripps, Francis and Ward, Terry. The European Community: Problems and Prospects. *Cambridge Econ. Pol. Rev.*, December 1981, 7(2), pp. 1–65. [G: EEC]

Benarey, Henry A. International Productivity: A European View. In *Hogan, J. D. and Craig, A. M., eds., Vol. 1*, 1981, pp. 639–44. [G: W. Europe]

Berndt, Ernst R. Energy Price Increases and the Productivity Slowdown in United States Manufacturing. In *Federal Reserve Bank of Boston (1)*, 1981, pp. 60–89. [G: U.S.]

Bernolak, Imre. The Whole and Its Parts: Micro and Macro Productivity Research. In *Hogan, J. D. and Craig, A. M., eds., Vol. 2*, 1981, pp. 755–64. [G: Canada]

Blume, Marshall E.; Crockett, Jean A. and Friend, Irwin. Stimulation of Capital Formation: Ends and Means. In *Wachter, M. L. and Wachter, S. M., eds.*, 1981, pp. 41–94. [G: U.S.]

Bolino, Paul. A Century of Human Capital Development by On-the-Job Training. *Int. J. Soc. Econ.*, 1981, 8(7), pp. 24–41. [G: U.S.]

Bombach, Gottfried. The Contributions of the Economics of Growth to Economic Policies: Comment. In *Giersch, H., ed. (II)*, 1981, pp. 467–75.

Bourne, Compton. Government Foreign Borrowing and Economic Growth: The Jamaican Experience. *Soc. Econ. Stud.*, December 1981, 30(4), pp. 52–74. [G: Jamaica]

Bowen, William. Productivity: A Journalist's Perspective. In *Hogan, J. D. and Craig, A. M., eds., Vol. 1*, 1981, pp. 725–36. [G: U.S.]

Boyer, Robert and Petit, Pascal. Employment and Productivity in the EEC. *Cambridge J. Econ.*, March 1981, 5(1), pp. 47–58. [G: EEC]

Boyer, Robert and Petit, Pascal. Progrès technique, croissance et emploi: Un modèle d'inspiration kaldorienne pour six industries européennes. (Technical Progress, Growth and Employment: A Kaldorian Model for Six European Industries. With English summary.) *Revue Écon.*, November 1981, 32(6), pp. 1113–53. [G: W. Europe; U.K.]

Braun, Steven. An Econometric Model Incorporating the Supply-Side Effects of Economic Policy: Discussion. In *Meyer, L. H., ed.*, 1981, pp. 93–101. [G: U.S.]

Brittan, Samuel. The Roots of the British Sickness. In *Currie, D.; Nobay, R. and Peel, D., eds.*, 1981, pp. 321–52. [G: U.K.]

Brockhoff, Klaus. Competition, Innovation, Productivity Growth, and Public Policy: Comments. In *Giersch, H., ed. (II)*, 1981, pp. 180–86.

Brown, Clarence J. Proceedings of the Seminar on Productivity: Statement. In *U.S. Congress, Joint Economic Committee (I)*, 1981, pp. 125–26.
[G: U.S.]

Bruch, Mathias. X-Efficiency Theory, Productivity and Growth: Comments. In *Giersch, H., ed. (II)*, 1981, pp. 217–19.

Cameron, Norman E. Economic Growth in the USSR, Hungary, and East and West Germany. *J. Compar. Econ.*, March 1981, 5(1), pp. 24–42.
[G: U.S.S.R.; Hungary; E. Germany; W. Germany]

Carlsson, Bo. The Content of Productivity Growth in Swedish Manufacturing. In *Industrial Inst. for Econ. and Soc. Research*, 1981, pp. 33–46.
[G: Sweden]

Chandrasekar, Krishnamurti. Productivity and Social Indicators. *Ann. Amer. Acad. Polit. Soc. Sci.*, January 1981, 453, pp. 153–68. [G: U.S.]

Chatterji, M. and Wickens, Michael R. Verdoorn's Law—The Externalities Hypothesis and Economic Growth in the U.K. In *Currie, D.; Nobay, R. and Peel, D., eds.*, 1981, pp. 405–29.
[G: U.K.]

Christensen, Laurits R. and Cummings, Dianne. Real Product, Real Factor Input, and Productivity in the Republic of Korea, 1960–1973. *J. Devel. Econ.*, June 1981, 8(3), pp. 285–302.
[G: S. Korea]

Christensen, Laurits R.; Cummings, Dianne and Jorgenson, Dale W. Relative Productivity Levels, 1947–1973: An International Comparison. *Europ. Econ. Rev.*, May 1981, 16(1), pp. 61–94.

Christensen, Paul P. Land Abundance and Cheap Horsepower in the Mechanization of the Antebellum United States Economy. *Exploration Econ. Hist.*, October 1981, 18(4), pp. 309–29.
[G: U.S.]

Christiansen, Gregory B. and Haveman, Robert H.

The Contribution of Environmental Regulations to the Slowdown in Productivity Growth. *J. Environ. Econ. Manage.*, December 1981, *8*(4), pp. 381–90. [G: U.S.]

Clauss, Franz Joachim. Einkommens-Produktivität und Quotienten-Mechanik. Die Produktivitäts-Statistik als Gegenstand der Konjunkturforschung. (Income Productivity and Quotient Mechanics: Productivity Statistics as an Object of Business Cycle Research. With English summary.) *Ifo-Studien*, 1981, *27*(4), pp. 291–337.

Cleveland, Harlan. We Changed our Minds in the 1970s. In *Cleveland, H., ed.*, 1981, pp. 3–15.

Cline, William R. Cyclical Growth Links between Industrial and Developing Countries. In *Cline, W. R., et al.*, 1981, pp. 240–56. [G: LDCs; MDCs]

Connally, John B. Productivity and National Policy. In *Hogan, J. D. and Craig, A. M., eds., Vol. 2*, 1981, pp. 1189–95. [G: U.S.]

Coomer, James C. The Nature of the Quest for a Sustainable Society. In *Coomer, J. C., ed.*, 1981, pp. 1–9.

Costanza, Robert. Embodied Energy, Energy Analysis, and Economics: Reply: An Embodied Energy Theory of Value. In *Daly, H. E. and Umana, A. F., eds.*, 1981, pp. 187–91.

Crandall, Robert W. Regulation and Productivity Growth. In *Federal Reserve Bank of Boston (1)*, 1981, pp. 93–111. [G: U.S.]

Daly, Herman E. Energy, Economics, and the Environment: Postscript: Unresolved Problems and Issues for Further Research. In *Daly, H. E. and Umana, A. F., eds.*, 1981, pp. 165–85.

Davenport, Paul. The Productivity Problem: Comment. In *Ontario Economic Council, Vol. 2*, 1981, pp. 35–43. [G: U.S.; Canada]

Denison, Edward F. Capital Accumulation and Potential Growth: Discussion. In *Federal Reserve Bank of Boston (1)*, 1981, pp. 54–59. [G: U.S.]

Denison, Edward F. Research Concerning the Effect of Regulation on Productivity. In *Hogan, J. D. and Craig, A. M., eds., Vol. 2*, 1981, pp. 1015–25. [G: U.S.]

Du Plooy, R. M. Productivity and the National Productivity Institute. *Finance Trade Rev.*, December 1981, *14*(4), pp. 148–64. [G: S. Africa]

Eads, George C. and McClain, David. The Role of Government Policy in Productivity. In *Hogan, J. D. and Craig, A. M., eds., Vol. 1*, 1981, pp. 41–51. [G: U.S.]

Easterlin, Richard A. Why Isn't the Whole World Developed? *J. Econ. Hist.*, March 1981, *41*(1), pp. 1–19.

Eccles, Mary E. Productivity Research Needs: The Congressional Viewpoint. In *Hogan, J. D. and Craig, A. M., eds., Vol. 2*, 1981, pp. 987–91. [G: U.S.]

Eckstein, Otto and Tannenwald, Robert. Productivity and Capital Formation. In *Wachter, M. L. and Wachter, S. M., eds.*, 1981, pp. 127–42. [G: U.S.]

Ehrlicher, Werner. Zukunftsprobleme unserer Wirtschaft. (Future Problems of Our Economy. With English summary.) *Kredit Kapital*, 1981, *14*(1), pp. 3–25.

Etzioni, Amitai. Productivity: The Human Factor. In *Hogan, J. D. and Craig, A. M., eds., Vol. 1*, 1981, pp. 27–38. [G: U.S.]

Evans, Michael K. An Econometric Model Incorporating the Supply-Side Effects of Economic Policy. In *Meyer, L. H., ed.*, 1981, pp. 33–80. [G: U.S.]

Fal'tsman, V. The Capacity Equivalent of Fixed Capital. *Prob. Econ.*, May 1981, *24*(1), pp. 39–60. [G: U.S.S.R.]

Feldstein, Martin S. Inflation and the American Economy. *Empirica*, 1981, (2), pp. 155–68. [G: U.S.]

Felli, Ernesto. Labour Productivity, Returns to Scale and Capital Accumulation in Italian Manufacturing Industry (1954–1978). *Rivista Polit. Econ.*, Supplement December 1981, *71*, pp. 61–107. [G: Italy]

Ferris, Tom. Comparisons of Productivity on Living Standards: Ireland and other EEC Countries. *Irish Banking Rev.*, March 1981, pp. 7–15. [G: Ireland; U.K.; Denmark; Benelux]

Fieleke, Norman S. Productivity and Labor Mobility in Japan, the United Kingdom, and the United States. *New Eng. Econ. Rev.*, November/December 1981, pp. 27–36. [G: Japan; U.K.; U.S.]

Fischer, Wolfram. Driving Forces of Economic Growth: What Can We Learn from History? Comments. In *Giersch, H., ed. (II)*, 1981, pp. 59–64.

Freund, William C. and Manchester, Paul B. Productivity and Inflation. In *Hogan, J. D. and Craig, A. M., eds., Vol. 1*, 1981, pp. 53–75. [G: U.S.]

Fromm, Gary. Research on Capital and Productivity. In *Hogan, J. D. and Craig, A. M., eds., Vol. 1*, 1981, pp. 109–14. [G: U.S.]

Fuchs, Victor R. Economic Growth and the Rise of Service Employment. In *Giersch, H., ed. (II)*, 1981, pp. 221–42. [G: U.S.; OECD]

Fulco, Lawrence J. Productivity Drops, Output and Hours Rise during the Fourth Quarter. *Mon. Lab. Rev.*, June 1981, *104*(6), pp. 40–43. [G: U.S.]

Ganti, Subrahmanyam and Kolluri, Bharat R. The Limits to Growth Hypothesis: Some Empirical Evidence. *J. Econ. Devel.*, July 1981, *6*(1), pp. 101–10.

Gatti, James F. Reindustrialization: A Cure Worse than the Disease? In *Gatti, J. F., ed.*, 1981, pp. 167–86. [G: U.S.; Japan]

Georgescu-Roegen, Nicholas. Energy, Matter, and Economic Valuation: Where Do We Stand? Reply. In *Daly, H. E. and Umana, A. F., eds.*, 1981, pp. 193–200.

Giersch, Herbert. Aspects of Growth, Structural Changes, and Employment—A Schumpeterian Perspective. In *Giersch, H, ed. (I)*, 1981, pp. 181–206. [G: OECD]

Golladay, Fredrick L. Productivity Problems in Developing Countries. In *Hogan, J. D. and Craig, A. M., eds., Vol. 1*, 1981, pp. 737–49. [G: LDCs]

Gollop, Frank M. Scale Effects and Technical Change as Sources of Productivity Growth. In *Hogan, J. D. and Craig, A. M., eds., Vol. 2*, 1981, pp. 805–38. [G: U.S.]

Gordon, David M. Capital–Labor Conflict and the

Productivity Slowdown. *Amer. Econ. Rev.*, May 1981, *71*(2), pp. 30–35. [G: U.S.]

Gordon, Lincoln. Changing Growth Patterns and World Order. **In** *Cleveland, H., ed.*, 1981, pp. 266–98.

Gordon, Robert J. Comment on Rasche and Tatom, "Energy Price Shocks, Aggregate Supply and Monetary Policy: The Theory and the International Evidence." *Carnegie-Rochester Conf. Ser. Public Policy*, Spring 1981, *14*, pp. 95–102.
[G: U.S.]

Gordon, Theodore J. The Revival of Enterprise. **In** *Cleveland, H., ed.*, 1981, pp. 330–59. [G: U.S.]

Graham, Edward M. A Comment on "The Dilemmas of Technology." *J. Econ. Issues*, March 1981, *15*(1), pp. 199–204. [G: U.S.S.R.; U.S.]

Granberg, A. G. Siberia in the National Economic Complex. *Prob. Econ.*, January 1981, *23*(9), pp. 53–76. [G: U.S.S.R.]

Grayson, C. Jackson, Jr. Proceedings of the Seminar on Productivity: Statement. **In** *U.S. Congress, Joint Economic Committee (I)*, 1981, pp. 127–44.
[G: U.S.; OECD]

Greenwood, Mary Ann. The Case for a Technologically Significant Capital Stock. *Bus. Econ.*, January 1981, *16*(1), pp. 94–96. [G: U.S.]

Gregory, Paul R. Energy Price Increases and the Productivity Slowdown in United States Manufacturing: Discussion. **In** *Federal Reserve Bank of Boston (I)*, 1981, pp. 90–92. [G: U.S.]

Gross, Bertram R. Economics and the Truman Administration: Comments. **In** *Heller, F. H., ed.*, 1981, pp. 131–34. [G: U.S.]

Hall, P. H. Patterns of Energy Use in Australian Manufacturing Industry. *Australian J. Manage.*, December 1981, *6*(2), pp. 43–58. [G: Australia]

Halttunen, Hannu, et al. Sveriges ekonomiska långtidsproblem. (Sweden's Long-term Economic Problems. With English summary.) *Ekon. Samfundets Tidskr.*, 1981, *34*(4), pp. 305–24.
[G: Sweden]

Hamrin, Robert. The Road to Qualitative Growth. **In** *Cleveland, H., ed.*, 1981, pp. 115–52.
[G: U.S.]

Harcourt, G. C. Notes on the Social Limits to Growth. *Econ. Forum*, Summer 1981, *12*(1), pp. 1–8.

Hardin, Garrett. Ending the Squanderarchy. **In** *Daly, H. E. and Umana, A. F., eds.*, 1981, pp. 147–64.

Haveman, Robert H. and Christainsen, Gregory B. Environmental Regulations and Productivity Growth. **In** *Peskin, H. M.; Portney, P. R. and Kneese, A. V., eds.*, 1981, pp. 55–75. [G: U.S.]

Haveman, Robert H. and Christainsen, Gregory B. Environmental Regulations and Productivity Growth. *Natural Res. J.*, July 1981, *21*(3), pp. 489–509. [G: U.S.]

Herman, Arthur S. Productivity Slows or Drops in 1979 in More Than Half of Industries Measured. *Mon. Lab. Rev.*, April 1981, *104*(4), pp. 58–61.
[G: U.S.]

Heywood, Colin Michael. The Role of the Peasantry in French Industrialization, 1815–80. *Econ. Hist. Rev.*, 2nd Ser., August 1981, *34*(3), pp. 359–76.
[G: France]

Hoffmann, Lutz. X-Efficiency Theory, Productivity and Growth: Comments. **In** *Giersch, H., ed. (II)*, 1981, pp. 213–16.

Hoós, János. Characteristics of the New Growth Path of the Economy in Hungary. *Acta Oecon.*, 1981, *27*(3–4), pp. 207–19. [G: Hungary]

Houthakker, Hendrik S. Regulation and Productivity Growth: Discussion. **In** *Federal Reserve Bank of Boston (I)*, 1981, pp. 112–14. [G: U.S.]

Hudson, Edward A. U.S. Energy Price Decontrol: Energy, Trade and Economic Effects. *Scand. J. Econ.*, 1981, *83*(2), pp. 180–200.

Hughes, Helen. The New Industrial Countries in the World Economy: Pessimism and a Way Out. **In** *Saunders, C. T., ed. (II)*, 1981, pp. 97–131.
[G: LDCs; MDCs]

Humphrey, Craig R. and Buttel, Frederick H. The Sociology of the Growth/No-Growth Debate. **In** *Mann, D. E., ed.*, 1981, pp. 125–35.

Ibielski, Dieter. Productivity Research in the Federal Republic of Germany. **In** *Hogan, J. D. and Craig, A. M., eds., Vol. 1*, 1981, pp. 685–98.
[G: W. Germany]

Johnson, Lewis. Capital Formation in the Long Run. **In** *Federal Reserve System*, 1981, pp. 91–98.

Jonas, Hans. Reflections on Technology, Progress, and Utopia. *Soc. Res.*, Autumn 1981, *48*(3), pp. 411–55.

Jones, F. Stuart. Growth and Fluctuations, 1870–1913 (Review Note). *S. Afr. J. Econ.*, December 1981, *49*(4), pp. 407–14. [G: U.K.; France; W. Germany; U.S.]

Jorgenson, Dale W. Energy Prices and Productivity Growth. **In** *Tempest, P., ed.*, 1981, pp. 75–92.
[G: U.S.]

Jorgenson, Dale W. Energy Prices and Productivity Growth. *Scand. J. Econ.*, 1981, *83*(2), pp. 165–79. [G: U.S.]

Jorgenson, Dale W. Proceedings of the Seminar on Productivity: Statement. **In** *U.S. Congress, Joint Economic Committee (I)*, 1981, pp. 166–84.
[G: U.S.]

Jorgenson, Dale W. U.S. Productivity Growth: Retrospect and Prospect. **In** *Hogan, J. D. and Craig, A. M., eds., Vol. 1*, 1981, pp. 5–25. [G: U.S.]

Kádár, Béla. Adjustment Problems, Patterns and Policies in Small Countries. *Acta Oecon.*, 1981, *27*(1–2), pp. 125–39. [G: W. Europe]

Kahn, Herman and Schneider, Ernest. Globaloney 2000. *Policy Rev.*, Spring 1981, (16), pp. 129–47.

Kaldor, Nicholas. Verdoorn's Law—The Externalities Hypothesis and Economic Growth in the U.K.: Comment. **In** *Currie, D.; Nobay, R. and Peel, D., eds.*, 1981, pp. 430–433. [G: U.K.]

Kallek, Shirley. Government Statistics for Productivity Research. **In** *Hogan, J. D. and Craig, A. M., eds., Vol. 2*, 1981, pp. 1071–84. [G: U.S.]

Katano, Hikoji. Current Situations of World Economy and Global Adjustment of Industries. *Kobe Econ. Bus. Rev.*, 1981, (27), pp. 11–35.
[G: Global]

Keidel, Albert. Japan's Economic Modernization. **In** *Richardson, B. M. and Ueda, T., eds.*, 1981, pp. 67–74. [G: Japan]

Keidel, Albert. Japan's Growth Record. **In** *Richard-*

son, B. M. and Ueda, T., eds., 1981, pp. 75–82. [G: Japan]

Keidel, Albert. The Postwar Economic Miracle. In Richardson, B. M. and Ueda, T., eds., 1981, pp. 82–89. [G: Japan]

Kendrick, John W. International Comparisons of Recent Productivity Trends. In Fellner, W., ed., 1981, pp. 125–70. [G: OECD]

Kendrick, John W. Survey of the Factors Contributing to the Decline in U.S. Productivity Growth. In Federal Reserve Bank of Boston (I), 1981, pp. 1–21. [G: U.S.]

Kendrick, John W. Why Productivity Growth Rates Change and Differ. In Giersch, H., ed. (II), 1981, pp. 111–40. [G: U.S.]

Khachaturov, Tigran. The Effectiveness of Socialist Social Production. Prob. Econ., April 1981, 23(12), pp. 3–27. [G: U.S.S.R.]

Kindleberger, Charles P. Historical Perspective on the Decline in U.S. Productivity. In Hogan, J. D. and Craig, A. M., eds., Vol. 1, 1981, pp. 715–24. [G: U.K.; U.S.]

Koch, Donald L. and Thomas, Ward. A Productivity Solution: Managing Human Performance. Bus. Econ., May 1981, 16(3), pp. 55–58. [G: U.S.]

Kopcke, Richard W. Capital Accumulation and Potential Growth. In Federal Reserve Bank of Boston (I), 1981, pp. 26–53. [G: U.S.]

Koropeckyj, I. S. Selected Problems of Regional Development in the USSR: Growth and Productivity. In Koropeckyj, I. S. and Schroeder, G. E., eds., 1981, pp. 92–117. [G: U.S.S.R.]

Kouri, Pentti J. K. and Braga de Macedo, Jorge. Perspectives on the Stagflation of the 1970's. In Giersch, H, ed. (I), 1981, pp. 211–53. [G: OECD]

Kuznets, Simon. A Note on Production Structure and Aggregate Growth. In [Bergson, A.], 1981, pp. 289–303. [G: Global]

Kuznets, Simon. Driving Forces of Economic Growth: What Can We Learn from History? In Giersch, H., ed. (II), 1981, pp. 37–58.

Kuznets, Simon. Economic Growth and the Rise of Service Employment: Comments. In Giersch, H., ed. (II), 1981, pp. 249–52. [G: U.S.; OECD]

Leibenstein, Harvey. Economic Growth as an Endogenous Process—Human Resources and Motivation: Comments. In Giersch, H., ed. (II), 1981, pp. 88–91.

Leibenstein, Harvey. X-Efficiency Theory, Productivity and Growth. In Giersch, H., ed. (II), 1981, pp. 187–212.

Levy, Victor. Total Factor Productivity, Non-Neutral Technical Change and Economic Growth: A Parametric Study of a Developing Economy. J. Devel. Econ., February 1981, 8(1), pp. 93–109. [G: Iraq]

Little, Ian M. D. Driving Forces of Economic Growth: What Can We Learn from History? Comments. In Giersch, H., ed. (II), 1981, pp. 65–69.

Lundberg, Erik. The Contributions of the Economics of Growth to Economic Policies. In Giersch, H., ed. (II), 1981, pp. 447–66.

Maddison, Angus. International Productivity Comparisons: National Differentials. In Hogan, J. D. and Craig, A. M., eds., Vol. 1, 1981, pp. 607–

37. [G: OECD]

Maitha, J. K. and Manundu, M. Production Techniques, Factor Proportions and Elasticities of Substitution. In Killick, T., ed., 1981, pp. 245–53. [G: Kenya]

Mansfield, Edwin. Why Productivity Growth Rates Change and Differ: Comments. In Giersch, H., ed. (II), 1981, pp. 141–48. [G: U.S.]

Marzi, Graziella. La misura della produttività in un modello con capitale fisso: i risultati disaggregati per l'economia italiana, 1970–1974. (Productivity Changes: A Disaggregated Analysis of the Italian Economy, 1970–1974. With English summary.) Rivista Int. Sci. Econ. Com., April 1981, 28(4), pp. 327–37. [G: Italy]

McClelland, David C. Economic Growth as an Endogenous Process—Human Resources and Motivation: Comments. In Giersch, H., ed. (II), 1981, pp. 92–100.

McCombie, J. S. L. Are International Growth Rates Constrained by the Balance of Payments? A Comment on Professor Thirlwall [The Balance of Payments Constraint as an Explanation of International Growth Rate Differences]. Banca Naz. Lavoro Quart. Rev., December 1981, (139), pp. 455–58.

McCombie, J. S. L. What Still Remains of Kaldor's Laws? Econ. J., March 1981, 91(361), pp. 206–16.

Meister, Jürgen. Taxes, Tax Systems and Economic Growth: Comments. In Giersch, H., ed. (II), 1981, pp. 354–57. [G: Selected Countries]

Mesarovic, Mihajlo D. and Hughes, Barry B. Global Modeling and Decision-Making. In Evan, W. M., ed., 1981, pp. 107–20.

Millendorfer, Johann. Economic Growth as an Endogenous Process—Human Resources and Motivation: Comments. In Giersch, H., ed. (II), 1981, pp. 101–10.

Miller, William Lee. The Paradox of Plenty: Economic Growth and Moral Shrinkage. In Cleveland, H., ed., 1981, pp. 79–114.

Minami, Ryoshin and Ono, Akira. Behavior of Income Shares in a Labor Surplus Economy: Japan's Experience. Econ. Develop. Cult. Change, January 1981, 29(2), pp. 309–24. [G: Japan]

Modelski, George. World Politics and Sustainable Growth: A Structural Model of the World System. In Coomer, J. C., ed., 1981, pp. 145–63.

Mohr, Michael F. Concepts in the Theory and Measurement of Productivity. In Hogan, J. D. and Craig, A. M., eds., Vol. 2, 1981, pp. 855–934. [G: U.S.]

Moore, John H. Agency Costs, Technological Change, and Soviet Central Planning. J. Law Econ., October 1981, 24(2), pp. 189–214. [G: U.S.S.R.]

Nagy, András. Growth and Trade: the Hungarian Case. In Bornstein, M.; Gitelman, Z. and Zimmerman, W., eds., 1981, pp. 192–220. [G: Hungary]

Nakamura, Toru. Productivity Losses through Capital Misallocation in the U.S., Japan, and West Germany. Quart. Rev. Econ. Bus., Autumn 1981, 21(3), pp. 65–76. [G: W. Germany; Japan; U.S.]

Nelson, Richard R. Competition, Innovation, Productivity Growth, and Public Policy. In Giersch, H., ed. (II), 1981, pp. 151–79.

Nelson, Richard R. Research on Productivity Growth and Productivity Differences: Dead Ends and New Departures. J. Econ. Lit., September 1981, 19(3), pp. 1029–64.

Nelson, Richard R. The Contributions of the Economics of Growth to Economic Policies: Comments. In Giersch, H., ed. (II), 1981, pp. 476.

Nelson, Richard R. Why Productivity Growth Rates Change and Differ: Comment. In Giersch, H., ed. (II), 1981, pp. 149–50.   [G: U.S.]

Nelson, Richard R. X-Efficiency Theory, Productivity and Growth: Comments. In Giersch, H., ed. (II), 1981, pp. 220.

Neumark, Fritz. Taxes, Tax Systems and Economic Growth: Comments. In Giersch, H., ed. (II), 1981, pp. 348–53.   [G: Selected Countries]

Nordhaus, William D. Policy Responses to the Productivity Slowdown. In Federal Reserve Bank of Boston (I), 1981, pp. 147–72.   [G: U.S.]

Norsworthy, J. R. Capital, Energy and Productivity Research. In Hogan, J. D. and Craig, A. M., eds., Vol. 1, 1981, pp. 171–81.   [G: U.S.]

Norsworthy, J. R. The Productivity Slowdown: A Labor Problem? Discussion. In Federal Reserve Bank of Boston (I), 1981, pp. 143–46. [G: U.S.]

O'Toole, James. Work in an Era of Slow Economic Growth. In Cleveland, H., ed., 1981, pp. 195–235.   [G: U.S.]

Osadchaya, I. M. Evolution of Economic Growth Theory. In Mileikovsky, A. G., et al., 1981, pp. 51–73.

Peacock, Alan. Economic Growth and the Rise of Service Employment: Comments. In Giersch, H., ed. (II), 1981, pp. 243–48.   [G: U.S.; OECD]

Perloff, Jeffrey M. and Wachter, Michael L. The Productivity Slowdown: A Labor Problem? In Federal Reserve Bank of Boston (I), 1981, pp. 115–42.   [G: U.S.]

Petersen, Hans-Georg. Taxes, Tax Systems and Economic Growth. In Giersch, H., ed. (II), 1981, pp. 313–47.   [G: Selected Countries]

Pfaff, Martin. Redistribution, Social Security and Growth: Comments. In Giersch, H., ed. (II), 1981, pp. 426–45.   [G: W. Germany; LDCs]

Phelps Brown, Henry and Handfield-Jones, S. J. The Climacteric of the 1890's: A Study in the Expanding Economy. In Phelps Brown, H. and Hopkins, S. V., 1981, 1952, pp. 131–72.
      [G: U.K.; OECD]

Phelps Brown, Henry and Ozga, S. A. Economic Growth and the Price Level. In Phelps Brown, H. and Hopkins, S. V., 1981, 1955, pp. 173–90.
      [G: U.K.]

Pincus, Jonathan J. Discussion [Government Policy and Economic Development in Germany and Japan: A Skeptical Reevaluation] [Bureaucratic Opposition to the Assignment of Property Rights: Overgrazing on the Western Range]. J. Econ. Hist., March 1981, 41(1), pp. 159–61.
      [G: Germany; Japan; U.S.]

Poliak, A. Ways to Lower the Materials-Output Ratio. Prob. Econ., December 1981, 24(8), pp. 44–63.   [G: U.S.S.R.]

Pomfret, Richard. The Staple Theory as an Approach to Canadian and Australian Economic Development. Australian Econ. Hist. Rev., September 1981, 21(2), pp. 133–46. [G: Canada; Australia]

Pratten, C. F. International Productivity Comparisons. In Hogan, J. D. and Craig, A. M., eds., Vol. 1, 1981, pp. 657–67.   [G: U.K.; Selected OECD]

Rao, M. J. Manohar. Diminishing Returns—Fact or Fiction? Indian Econ. J., January–March 1981, 28(3), pp. 107–14.   [G: India]

Rasche, Robert H. and Tatom, John A. Energy Price Shocks, Aggregate Supply and Monetary Policy: The Theory and the International Evidence. Carnegie-Rochester Conf. Ser. Public Policy, Spring 1981, 14, pp. 9–93.   [G: N. America; U.K.; Germany; France; Japan]

Rasche, Robert H. and Tatom, John A. Reply to Gordon [Energy Price Shocks, Aggregate Supply and Monetary Policy: The Theory and the International Evidence]. Carnegie-Rochester Conf. Ser. Public Policy, Spring 1981, 14, pp. 103–07.

Reisman, David. Social Limits to Tolerable Survival. In Gaskin, M., ed., 1981, pp. 52–75.

Resnikoff, Howard L. and Weiss, Edward C. Adapting Use of Information and Knowledge to Enhance Productivity: Productivity, Information and Energy. In Hogan, J. D. and Craig, A. M., eds., Vol. 1, 1981, pp. 507–49.   [G: U.S.]

Reubens, Edwin P. The Services and Productivity: Comment. Challenge, May/June 1981, 24(2), pp. 59–63.   [G: U.S.]

Roberts, Walter Orr and Slater, Lloyd E. The Interaction of Food, Climate, and Population. In Cleveland, H., ed., 1981, pp. 239–65.

Robinson, Joan. The Age of Growth. In Robinson, J., 1981, 1979, pp. 33–42.

Rostow, Walt W. Energy and the Economy. In U.S. Congress, Joint Economic Committee (I), 1981, 1980, pp. 348–434.   [G: U.S.; Selected Countries]

Rothschild, K. W. Futurology and the Economist. In [Lipiński, E.], 1981, pp. 63–70.

Sant, Roger W. Energy Productivity: Its Role in the Growth of the American Economy. In Hogan, J. D. and Craig, A. M., eds., Vol. 1, 1981, pp. 183–90.   [G: U.S.]

Sapsford, D. Productivity Growth in the UK: A Reconsideration. Appl. Econ., December 1981, 13(4), pp. 499–511.   [G: U.K.]

Sautter, Christian. Relative Productivity Levels, 1947–1973 by Christensen, et al.: Comment. Europ. Econ. Rev., May 1981, 16(1), pp. 99–102.

Schankerman, Mark A. The Effects of Double-Counting and Expensing on the Measured Returns to R&D. Rev. Econ. Statist., August 1981, 63(3), pp. 454–58.   [G: U.S.]

Scherer, F. M. Regulatory Dynamics and Economic Growth. In Wachter, M. L. and Wachter, S. M., eds., 1981, pp. 289–320.   [G: U.S.]

Schmitt, Hans O. Estabilização económica e crescimento em Portugal. (With English summary.) Economia (Portugal), May 1981, 5(2), pp. 325–73.   [G: Portugal]

Scott, Maurice FG. The Contribution of Investment

to Growth. *Scot. J. Polit. Econ.*, November 1981, 28(3), pp. 211–26. [G: U.K.]

Shepherd, Mark, Jr. America's Productivity Crisis: The Problem, Its Causes and Suggested Solutions. In *U.S. Congress, Joint Economic Committee (I)*, 1981, pp. 186–90. [G: U.S.]

Siebert, Horst. Ökonomische Theorie natürlicher Ressourcen. Ein Uberblick. (The Economic Theory of Natural Resources: A Survey. With English summary.) *Z. Wirtschaft. Sozialwissen.*, 1981, 101(3), pp. 267–98.

Siegel, Irving H. Need for Improvement in Government Productivity Information. In *Hogan, J. D. and Craig, A. M., eds., Vol. 2*, 1981, pp. 1057–69. [G: U.S.]

Simon, Julian L. and Steinmann, Gunter. Population Growth and Phelps' Technical Progress Model: Interpretation and Generalization. In *Simon, J. L. and Lindert, P. H., eds.*, 1981, pp. 239–54.

Simos, Evangelos O. Learning-by-Doing or Doing-by-Learning? Evidence on Factor Learning and Biased Factor Efficiency Growth in the United States. *Rev. Bus. Econ. Res.*, Spring 1981, 16(3), pp. 14–25. [G: U.S.]

Sinai, Allen and Stokes, Houston H. Real Money Balances and Production: A Partial Explanation of Japanese Economic Development for 1952–1968. *Hitotsubashi J. Econ.*, February 1981, 21(2), pp. 69–81. [G: Japan]

Sirotkovic, Jakov. Influence of the Self-Management System on the Development of the Yugoslav Economy. *Eastern Europ. Econ.*, Winter 1981–82, 20(2), pp. 46–62. [G: Yugoslavia]

Solo, Robert. The Dilemmas of Technology: A Reply. *J. Econ. Issues*, March 1981, 15(1), pp. 204–11. [G: U.S.S.R.; U.S.]

Solow, Robert M. Policy Responses to the Productivity Slowdown: Discussion. In *Federal Reserve Bank of Boston (I)*, 1981, pp. 173–77. [G: U.S.]

Stamper, M. T. Proceedings of the Seminar on Productivity: Statement. In *U.S. Congress, Joint Economic Committee (I)*, 1981, pp. 224–29. [G: U.S.]

Strong, Maurice F. Action for New Growth. In *Cleveland, H., ed.*, 1981, pp. 367–81.

Summers, Robert; Kravis, Irving B. and Heston, Alan. Inequality among Nations: 1950 and 1975. In *Bairoch, P. and Lévy-Leboyer, M., eds.*, 1981, pp. 18–25. [G: LDCs; MDCs]

Sveikauskas, Leo. Technological Inputs and Multifactor Productivity Growth. *Rev. Econ. Statist.*, May 1981, 63(2), pp. 275–82. [G: U.S.]

Takeuchi, Hirotaka. Productivity: Learning from the Japanese. *Calif. Manage. Rev.*, Summer 1981, 23(4), pp. 5–19. [G: Japan]

Tatom, John A. Energy Prices and Short-Run Economic Performance. *Fed. Res. Bank St. Louis Rev.*, January 1981, 63(1), pp. 3–17. [G: U.S.]

Tatom, John A. We Are All Supply-Siders Now! *Fed. Res. Bank St. Louis Rev.*, May 1981, 63(5), pp. 18–30. [G: U.S.]

Terleckyj, Nestor E. Contribution of Government to the Quality of Life. In *Hogan, J. D. and Craig, A. M., eds., Vol. 2*, 1981, pp. 1085–93. [G: U.S.]

Thirlwall, A. P. A Reply to Mr. McCombie [The Balance of Payments Constraint as an Explanation of International Growth Rate Differences]. *Banca Naz. Lavoro Quart. Rev.*, December 1981, (139), pp. 458–59.

Thoroe, Carsten S. Changes in the Regional Growth Pattern in the European Community. In *Giersch, H., ed. (II)*, 1981, pp. 283–311. [G: W. Germany; France; Italy; U.K.]

Thurow, Lester C. Survey of the Factors Contributing to the Decline in U.S. Productivity Growth: Discussion. In *Federal Reserve Bank of Boston (I)*, 1981, pp. 22–25. [G: U.S.]

Thurow, Lester C. The Productivity Problem. In *Ontario Economic Council, Vol. 2*, 1981, pp. 11–35. [G: U.S.]

Tipton, Frank B., Jr. Government Policy and Economic Development in Germany and Japan: A Skeptical Reevaluation. *J. Econ. Hist.*, March 1981, 41(1), pp. 139–50. [G: Germany; Japan]

Tomer, John F. Organizational Change, Organization Capital and Economic Growth. *Eastern Econ. J.*, January 1981, 7(1), pp. 1–14. [G: U.S.]

Usery, W. J., Jr. Proceedings of the Seminar on Productivity: Statement. In *U.S. Congress, Joint Economic Committee (I)*, 1981, pp. 144–47. [G: U.S.]

Vaizey [Lord]. Economic Growth as an Endogenous Process—Human Resources and Motivation. In *Giersch, H., ed. (II)*, 1981, pp. 71–87.

Vanderslice, Thomas A. Closing the Technology–Productivity Gap. In *Hogan, J. D. and Craig, A. M., eds., Vol. 2*, 1981, pp. 1231–38. [G: U.S.]

Vaubel, Roland. Redistribution, Social Security and Growth. In *Giersch, H., ed. (II)*, 1981, pp. 387–425.

Visser, Jan H. Productivity Research in the Republic of South Africa. In *Hogan, J. D. and Craig, A. M., eds., Vol. 1*, 1981, pp. 699–711. [G: S. Africa]

Vogel, Ezra F. Proceedings of the Seminar on International Economic Problems: Statement. In *U.S. Congress, Joint Economic Committee (I)*, 1981, pp. 292–95. [G: Japan; U.S.]

Walker, Charls E. Proceedings of the Seminar on Productivity: Statement. In *U.S. Congress, Joint Economic Committee (I)*, 1981, pp. 147–48. [G: U.S.]

Watts, Glenn E. Productivity and Employment: The Social Gains and Costs. In *Hogan, J. D. and Craig, A. M., eds., Vol. 1*, 1981, pp. 77–83. [G: U.S.]

Weidenbaum, Murray L. Proceedings of the Seminar on Inflation: Statement. In *U.S. Congress, Joint Economic Committee (I)*, 1981, pp. 92–100. [G: U.S.]

von Weizsäcker, Carl Christian. Aspects of Growth, Structural Changes, and Employment—A Schumpeterian Perspective: Comment. In *Giersch, H, ed. (I)*, 1981, pp. 207–09. [G: OECD]

Wenban-Smith, G. C. A Study of the Movements of Productivity in Individual Industries in the

United Kingdom, 1968–79. *Nat. Inst. Econ. Rev.*, August 1981, (97), pp. 57–66. [G: U.K.]

Yankelovich, Daniel and Lefkowitz, Bernard. The Public Debate about Growth. In *Cleveland, H., ed.*, 1981, pp. 16–78. [G: U.S.]

227 Prices

2270 Prices

Afriat, S. N. On the Constructability of Consistent Price Indices between Several Periods Simultaneously. In *[Stone, R.]*, 1981, pp. 133–61.

Ashley, Richard. Inflation and the Distribution of Price Changes across Markets: A Causal Analysis. *Econ. Inquiry*, October 1981, *19*(4), pp. 650–60. [G: U.S.]

Barro, Robert J. Unanticipated Money, Output, and the Price Level in the United States. In *Lucas, R. E. and Sargent, T. J., eds.*, 1981, *1978*, pp. 585–616. [G: U.S.]

Bertinelli, Roberto. Alcune considerazioni sulla moneta nella R.P.C. (A Few Thoughts on Money in the P.R.C. With English summary.) *Rivista Int. Sci. Econ. Com.*, September 1981, *28*(9), pp. 852–63. [G: China]

Bessler, David A. and Brandt, Jon A. Forecasting Livestock Prices with Individual and Composite Methods. *Appl. Econ.*, December 1981, *13*(4), pp. 513–22. [G: U.S.]

Bhalla, Surjit S. India's Closed Economy and World Inflation. In *Cline, W. R., et al.*, 1981, pp. 136–65. [G: India]

Blejer, Mario I. The Dispersion of Relative Commodity Prices under Very Rapid Inflation. *J. Devel. Econ.*, December 1981, *9*(3), pp. 347–56. [G: Argentina]

Bowring, Joseph. How Bad Were the Seventies? *Challenge*, July/August 1981, *24*(3), pp. 47–50. [G: U.S.]

Brandt, Jon A. and Bessler, David A. Composite Forecasting: An Application with U.S. Hog Prices. *Amer. J. Agr. Econ.*, February 1981, *63*(1), pp. 135–40. [G: U.S.]

Cagan, Phillip and Moore, Geoffrey H. Some Proposals to Improve the Consumer Price Index. *Mon. Lab. Rev.*, September 1981, *104*(9), pp. 20–25. [G: U.S.]

Callahan, David W. Defining the Rate of Underlying Inflation. *Mon. Lab. Rev.*, September 1981, *104*(9), pp. 16–19. [G: U.S.]

Carlson, John A. Perceptions (or Misperceptions) of Inflation. In *Gale, W. A., ed.*, 1981, pp. 13–49. [G: U.S.]

Christensen, Laurits R. On the Formation of Price Expectations by König, et al.: Comment. *Europ. Econ. Rev.*, May 1981, *16*(1), pp. 139.

Chu, Ke-young and Feltenstein, Andrew. The Welfare Implications of Relative Price Distortions and Inflation: An Analysis of the Recent Argentine Experience. In *Khan, A. and Sirageldin, I., eds.*, 1981, pp. 181–223. [G: Argentina]

Cline, William R. Imports and Consumer Prices: A Survey Analysis. In *Baldwin, R. E. and Richardson, J. D., eds.*, 1981, *1979*, pp. 110–17. [G: U.S.]

Cornelius, James C.; Ikerd, John E. and Nelson, A. Gene. A Preliminary Evaluation of Price Forecasting Performance by Agricultural Economists. *Amer. J. Agr. Econ.*, November 1981, *63*(4), pp. 712–14. [G: U.S.]

Cornell, Bradford. Relative vs. Absolute Price Changes: An Empirical Study. *Econ. Inquiry*, July 1981, *19*(3), pp. 506–14. [G: U.S.]

Dale, Charles, et al. Measuring Export Prices. *Rev. Public Data Use (See J. Econ. Soc. Meas. after 4/85)*, November 1981, *9*(3), pp. 199–209. [G: U.S.]

DeMilner, Lawrence. Discussion [Inflation and Housing Costs] [Expanding and Improving the CPI Rent Component] [Measuring the Cost of Shelter for Homeowners]. In *Tuccillo, J. A. and Villani, K. E., eds.*, 1981, pp. 131–33. [G: U.S.]

Diewert, W. E. The Economic Theory of Index Numbers: A Survey. In *[Stone, R.]*, 1981, pp. 163–208.

Dougherty, Ann and Van Order, Robert. Inflation and Housing Costs. In *Tuccillo, J. A. and Villani, K. E., eds.*, 1981, pp. 87–108. [G: U.S.]

Fischer, Stanley. Relative Shocks, Relative Price Variability, and Inflation. *Brookings Pap. Econ. Act.*, 1981, (2), pp. 381–431. [G: U.S.]

Forsyth, F. G. and Fowler, R. F. The Theory and Practice of Chain Price Index Numbers. *J. Roy. Statist. Soc.*, Part 2, 1981, *144*, pp. 224–46.

von Furstenberg, George M. Price Deflators for Special Drawing Rights over the Past Decade. *Rev. Public Data Use (See J. Econ. Soc. Meas. after 4/85)*, April 1981, *9*(1), pp. 1–20.

Gale, William A. How Well Can We Measure Price Changes? In *Gale, W. A., ed.*, 1981, pp. 51–114. [G: U.S.]

Gale, William A. Temporal Variability of United States Consumer Price Index. *J. Money, Credit, Banking*, August 1981, *13*(3), pp. 273–97. [G: U.S.]

Glazer, Amihai. Advertising, Information, and Prices—A Case Study. *Econ. Inquiry*, October 1981, *19*(4), pp. 661–71. [G: U.S.]

Grady, Stephen T. Estimation and Evaluation of State Price Indexes for the Period 1967–1978: An Empirical Note. *Rev. Reg. Stud.*, Winter 1981, *11*(3), pp. 51–62. [G: U.S.]

Guthrie, Robert S. The Relationship between Wholesale and Consumer Prices. *Southern Econ. J.*, April 1981, *47*(4), pp. 1046–55. [G: U.S.]

Halvorsen, Robert and Pollakowski, Henry O. Choice of Functional Form for Hedonic Price Equations. *J. Urban Econ.*, July 1981, *10*(1), pp. 37–49.

Hamilton, Bruce W. and Cooke, Timothy W. The Price of Housing, 1950–1975: Synopsis. In *Tuccillo, J. A. and Villani, K. E., eds.*, 1981, pp. 69–71. [G: U.S.]

Heins, A. James and Primeaux, Walter J., Jr. Regional Prices and the Conflict between Horizontal and Vertical Equity. *Public Finance Quart.*, April 1981, *9*(2), pp. 235–40. [G: U.S.]

Hekman, Christine R. The Effect of Trade Credit on Price and Price Level Comparisons. *Rev.*

Econ. Statist., November 1981, *63*(4), pp. 526–32.

Hercowitz, Zvi. Money and the Dispersion of Relative Prices. *J. Polit. Econ.*, April 1981, *89*(2), pp. 328–56. [G: Germany]

Hjorth-Andersen, Christian. Price and Quality of Industrial Products: Some Results of an Empirical Investigation. *Scand. J. Econ.*, 1981, *83*(3), pp. 372–89. [G: Denmark]

Horne, Jocelyn. Rational Expectations and the Defris–Williams Inflationary Expectations Series. *Econ. Rec.*, September 1981, *57*(158), pp. 261–68. [G: Australia]

Howell, Craig and Callahan, David W. Price Changes in 1980: Double-Digit Inflation Persists. *Mon. Lab. Rev.*, April 1981, *104*(4), pp. 3–12. [G: U.S.]

Iakovets, Iu. Prices and the Improvement of Planning and the Economic Mechanism. *Prob. Econ.*, April 1981, *23*(12), pp. 49–66. [G: U.S.S.R.]

Jarjour, Gabi. Long-Term Gas Pricing Strategy. *J. Energy Devel.*, Autumn 1981, *7*(1), pp. 89–98. [G: Global]

Jöckel, Karl-Heinz and Pflaumer, Peter. Die Vorhersage des Goldpreises mit dem Box-Jenkins-Verfahren. (Forecasting Monthly Gold Prices with the Box-Jenkins Approach. With English summary.) *Jahr. Nationalökon. Statist.*, November 1981, *196*(6), pp. 481–501.

Jonung, Lars. Perceived and Expected Rates of Inflation in Sweden. *Amer. Econ. Rev.*, December 1981, *71*(5), pp. 961–68. [G: Sweden]

Kite, R. C. and Roop, J. M. Changing Agricultural Prices and Their Impact on Food Prices under Inflation. *Amer. J. Agr. Econ.*, December 1981, *63*(5), pp. 956–61.

König, Heinz; Nerlove, Marc and Oudiz, Gilles. On the Formation of Price Expectations: An Analysis of Business Test Data by Log-Linear Probability Models. *Europ. Econ. Rev.*, May 1981, *16*(1), pp. 103–38. [G: Germany; France]

Kulshreshtha, Surendra N. and Bamford, John A. Feeder Cattle Price Determination in Saskatchewan. *Can. J. Agr. Econ.*, February 1981, *29*(1), pp. 49–62. [G: Canada]

Lamm, Ray McFall. Prices and Concentration in the Food Retailing Industry. *J. Ind. Econ.*, September 1981, *30*(1), pp. 67–78. [G: U.S.]

Lamm, Ray McFall, Jr. and Westcott, Paul C. The Effects of Changing Input Costs on Food Prices. *Amer. J. Agr. Econ.*, May 1981, *63*(2), pp. 187–96. [G: U.S.]

Langworthy, Mark; Pearson, Scott R. and Josling, Timothy. Macroeconomic Influences on Future Agricultural Prices in the European Community. *Europ. Rev. Agr. Econ.*, 1981, *8*(1), pp. 5–26. [G: EEC]

de Leeuw, Frank. Discussion [Inflation and Housing Costs] [Expanding and Improving the CPI Rent Component] [Measuring the Cost of Shelter for Homeowners]. In *Tuccillo, J. A. and Villani, K. E., eds.*, 1981, pp. 133–36. [G: U.S.]

de Leeuw, Frank and McKelvey, Michael J. Price Expectations of Business Firms. *Brookings Pap. Econ. Act.*, 1981, (1), pp. 299–314. [G: U.S.]

Leggett, Robert E. Measuring Inflation in the Soviet Machinebuilding Sector, 1960–1973. *J. Compar. Econ.*, June 1981, *5*(2), pp. 169–84. [G: U.S.S.R.]

Maccini, Louis J. Adjustment Lags, Economically Rational Expectations and Price Behavior. *Rev. Econ. Statist.*, May 1981, *63*(2), pp. 213–22. [G: U.S.]

Mussa, Michael L. Sticky Individual Prices and the Dynamics of the General Price Level. *Carnegie-Rochester Conf. Ser. Public Policy*, Autumn 1981, *15*, pp. 261–96.

Norwood, Janet L. Two Consumer Price Index Issues: Weighting and Homeownership. *Mon. Lab. Rev.*, March 1981, *104*(3), pp. 58–59. [G: U.S.]

Nziramasanga, Mudziviri T. and Obidegwu, Chukwuma. Primary Commodity Price Fluctuations and Developing Countries: An Econometric Model of Copper and Zambia. *J. Devel. Econ.*, August 1981, *9*(1), pp. 89–119. [G: Zambia]

Ozanne, Larry J. Expanding and Improving the CPI Rent Component. In *Tuccillo, J. A. and Villani, K. E., eds.*, 1981, pp. 109–21. [G: U.S.]

Paelinck, J. H. P. Integrated Macro-Models of Price Formation. *Greek Econ. Rev.*, August 1981, *3*(2), pp. 148–57.

Patinkin, Don and Liviatan, Nissan. On the Economic Theory of Price Indexes. In *Patinkin, D.*, 1981, *1961*, pp. 209–39.

Perry, L. J. Inflation in the USA, UK and Australia: Some Comparisons. *Econ. Rec.*, December 1981, *57*(159), pp. 319–31. [G: U.S.; U.K.; Australia]

Phelps Brown, Henry and Hopkins, Sheila V. Builders' Wage-rates, Prices and Population: Some Further Evidence. In *Phelps Brown, H. and Hopkins, S. V.*, 1981, *1959*, pp. 78–98. [G: Europe]

Phelps Brown, Henry and Hopkins, Sheila V. Seven Centuries of the Prices of Consumables Compared with Builders' Wage-rates. In *Phelps Brown, H. and Hopkins, S. V.*, 1981, *1956*, pp. 13–59. [G: U.K.]

Phelps Brown, Henry and Hopkins, Sheila V. Seven Centuries of Wages and Prices: Some Earlier Estimates. In *Phelps Brown, H. and Hopkins, S. V.*, 1981, *1961*, pp. 99–105. [G: U.K.]

Phelps Brown, Henry and Hopkins, Sheila V. Wage-rates and Prices: Evicence for Population Pressure in the Sixteenth Century. In *Phelps Brown, H. and Hopkins, S. V.*, 1981, *1957*, pp. 60–77. [G: U.K.; France]

Phelps Brown, Henry and Ozga, S. A. Economic Growth and the Price Level. In *Phelps Brown, H. and Hopkins, S. V.*, 1981, *1955*, pp. 173–90. [G: U.K.]

Piccolo, Domenico and Tunnicliffe Wilson, Granville. Time Series Models of Wholesale Retail Price Relationships in Italy. *Econ. Notes*, 1981, *10*(2), pp. 35–56. [G: Italy]

Plosser, Charles I. Comments on Mussa's Paper [Sticky Individual Prices and the Dynamics of the General Price Level]. *Carnegie-Rochester Conf. Ser. Public Policy*, Autumn 1981, *15*, pp. 297–300.

Praet, Peter. A Comparative Approach to the Measurement of Expected Inflation. *Cah. Écon. Bruxelles*, 2nd Trimestre 1981, (90), pp. 147–71. [G: EEC; Canada; U.S.]

Rosefielde, Steven. Are Soviet Industrial-Production Statistics Significantly Distorted by Hidden Inflation? *J. Compar. Econ.*, June 1981, *5*(2), pp. 185–99. [G: U.S.S.R.]

Runyon, Herbert. Indexes, Inflation and Public Policy. *Fed. Res. Bank San Francisco Econ. Rev.*, Spring 1981, pp. 44–56. [G: U.S.]

Saunders, Peter G. Price Determination in Australian Manufacturing Firms: A Cross-Section Study. *Australian Econ. Pap.*, December 1981, *20*(37), pp. 359–75. [G: Australia]

Saunders, Peter G. The Formation of Producers' Price Expectations in Australia. *Econ. Rec.*, December 1981, *57*(159), pp. 368–78. [G: Australia]

Shepherd, W. F. and Prasada Rao, D. S. A Comparison of Purchasing Power Parity between the Pound Sterling and the Australian Dollar in 1979. *Econ. Rec.*, September 1981, *57*(158), pp. 215–23. [G: U.K.; Australia]

Silver, M. S. and Golder, P. Negative Value Added and the Measurement of Production Changes. *J. Econ. Stud.*, 1981, *8*(1), pp. 3–15.

St. Cyr, E. B. A. Wages, Prices and Balance of Payments: Trinidad and Tobago; 1956–1976. *Soc. Econ. Stud.*, December 1981, *30*(4), pp. 111–33. [G: Trinidad and Tobago]

Sulvetta, Anthony J. The Price of Housing, 1950–1975: Synopsis: Discussion. In *Tuccillo, J. A. and Villani, K. E., eds.*, 1981, pp. 76–79. [G: U.S.]

Swan, Craig. The Price of Housing, 1950–1975: Synopsis: Discussion. In *Tuccillo, J. A. and Villani, K. E., eds.*, 1981, pp. 73–76. [G: U.S.]

Tompkinson, Paul. The Price Equation and Excess Demand. *Oxford Bull. Econ. Statist.*, May 1981, *43*(2), pp. 173–83.

Triplett, Jack E. Reconciling the CPI and the PCE Deflator. *Mon. Lab. Rev.*, September 1981, *104*(9), pp. 3–15. [G: U.S.]

Walden, Michael L. Microeconomic Impacts of Inflation on the Food and Agriculture Sector: Discussion. *Amer. J. Agr. Econ.*, December 1981, *63*(5), pp. 965–66. [G: U.S.]

Wecker, William E. Asymmetric Time Series. *J. Amer. Statist. Assoc.*, March 1981, *76*(373), pp. 16–21. [G: U.S.]

Westcott, Paul C. Monthly Food Price Forecasts. *Agr. Econ. Res.*, July 1981, *33*(3), pp. 27–30. [G: U.S.]

Wills, Hugh R. On the Formation of Price Expectations by König, et al.: Comment. *Europ. Econ. Rev.*, May 1981, *16*(1), pp. 141–44.

228 Regional Statistics

2280 Regional Statistics

Amos, Orley M., Jr. Urban–Rural Regional Development Diffusion and Personal Income Inequality. *Rev. Reg. Stud.*, Winter 1981, *11*(3), pp. 12–21. [G: U.S.]

Ashby, Lowell D. Economic Measurement and Regional Science. *Rev. Reg. Stud.*, Winter 1981, *11*(3), pp. 1–11.

Bretzfelder, Robert and Friedenberg, Howard. State Personal Income, Second Quarter 1981.

Surv. Curr. Bus., October 1981, *61*(10), pp. 26–27. [G: U.S.]

Bretzfelder, Robert and Friedenberg, Howard. Third-Quarter Acceleration in State Personal Income. *Surv. Curr. Bus.*, January 1981, *61*(1), pp. 27. [G: U.S.]

Dreifelds, Juris. Economic Development in Individual Regions in the USSR: Belorussia and Baltics. In *Koropeckyj, I. S. and Schroeder, G. E., eds.*, 1981, pp. 323–85. [G: U.S.S.R.]

Eason, Warren W. Selected Problems of Regional Development in the USSR: Population and Labor Force. In *Koropeckyj, I. S. and Schroeder, G. E., eds.*, 1981, pp. 11–91. [G: U.S.S.R.]

Espenshade, Thomas J.; Hobbs, Frank B. and Pol, Louis G. An Experiment in Estimating Postcensal Age Distributions of State Populations from Death Registration Data. *Rev. Public Data Use (See J. Econ. Soc. Meas. after 4/85)*, July 1981, *9*(2), pp. 97–114. [G: U.S.]

Garrison, Charles B. and Chang, Hui S. Subregional Income Differentials: A Study of the Tennessee Valley Region. *Rev. Reg. Stud.*, Winter 1981, *11*(3), pp. 22–37. [G: U.S.]

Gillula, James W. Selected Problems of Regional Development in the USSR: The Growth and Structure of Fixed Capital. In *Koropeckyj, I. S. and Schroeder, G. E., eds.*, 1981, pp. 157–93. [G: U.S.S.R.]

Gordijew, Ihor. Economic Development in Individual Regions in the USSR: Moldavia. In *Koropeckyj, I. S. and Schroeder, G. E., eds.*, 1981, pp. 305–22. [G: U.S.S.R.]

Gordijew, Ihor and Koropeckyj, I. S. Economic Development in Individual Regions in the USSR: Ukraine. In *Koropeckyj, I. S. and Schroeder, G. E., eds.*, 1981, pp. 267–304. [G: U.S.S.R.]

Hamilton, F. E. Ian. Economic Development in Individual Regions in the USSR: The European USSR. In *Koropeckyj, I. S. and Schroeder, G. E., eds.*, 1981, pp. 197–234. [G: U.S.S.R.]

Koropeckyj, I. S. Selected Problems of Regional Development in the USSR: Growth and Productivity. In *Koropeckyj, I. S. and Schroeder, G. E., eds.*, 1981, pp. 92–117. [G: U.S.S.R.]

Leser, C. E. V. Regional Differences in Industrial Structure: A Note. *Bull. Econ. Res.*, November 1981, *33*(2), pp. 72–73. [G: U.K.]

Lythe, Charlotte and Majmudar, Madhavi. Scottish Gross Domestic Product Statistics for 1961–71. *J. Roy. Statist. Soc.*, Part 3, 1981, *144*, pp. 352–59. [G: U.K.]

Matley, Ian M. Economic Development in Individual Regions in the USSR: Central Asia and Kazakhstan. In *Koropeckyj, I. S. and Schroeder, G. E., eds.*, 1981, pp. 417–53. [G: U.S.S.R.]

McCauley, James. A Critical Examination of the Dun & Bradstreet Data Files—A Rebuttal. *Rev. Public Data Use (See J. Econ. Soc. Meas. after 4/85)*, July 1981, *9*(2), pp. 145–48. [G: U.S.]

Schroeder, Gertrude E. Selected Problems of Regional Development in the USSR: Regional Living Standards. In *Koropeckyj, I. S. and Schroeder, G. E., eds.*, 1981, pp. 118–56. [G: U.S.S.R.]

Verway, David I. Reply to James McCauley [A Critical Examination of the Dun & Bradstreet Data Files]. *Rev. Public Data Use (See J. Econ. Soc. Meas. after 4/85)*, July 1981, *9*(2), pp. 149. [G: U.S.]

Whitehouse, F. Douglas and Kamerling, David S. Economic Development in Individual Regions in the USSR: The Asiatic RSFSR. In *Koropeckyj, I. S. and Schroeder, G. E., eds.*, 1981, pp. 235–66. [G: U.S.S.R.]

Zinam, Oleg. Economic Development in Individual Regions in the USSR: Transcaucasus. In *Koropeckyj, I. S. and Schroeder, G. E., eds.*, 1981, pp. 386–416. [G: U.S.S.R.]

229 Microdata and Database Analysis

2290 Microdata and Database Analysis

Imhof, Karen. Census and Property Survey Data Files Available. *Rev. Public Data Use (See J. Econ. Soc. Meas. after 4/85)*, December 1981, *9*(4), pp. 339. [G: U.S.]

Irvine, I. J. The Use of Cross-Section Microdata in Life Cycle Models: An Application to Inequality Theory in Nonstationary Economies. *Quart. J. Econ.*, May 1981, *96*(2), pp. 301–16. [G: U.S.]

Morgan, James N. Consistency of Reports of Hourly Earnings. In *Hill, M. S.; Hill, D. H. and Morgan, J. N., eds.*, 1981, pp. 427–39. [G: U.S.]

Peck, Jon K. and Dresch, Stephen P. Financial Incentives, Survey Response, and Sample Representativeness: Does Money Matter? *Rev. Public Data Use (See J. Econ. Soc. Meas. after 4/85)*, December 1981, *9*(4), pp. 245–66. [G: U.S.]

300 Domestic Monetary and Fiscal Theory and Institutions

310 DOMESTIC MONETARY AND FINANCIAL THEORY AND INSTITUTIONS

3100 General

Arak, Marcelle. Innovations in the Financial Markets. *Fed. Res. Bank New York Quart. Rev.*, Winter 1981–82, *6*(4), pp. 1–3. [G: U.S.]

Baffi, Paolo. Comment [Mobilité et mouvements de capitaux en Europe]. *Giorn. Econ.*, Sept.-Dec. 1981, *40*(9–12), pp. 621–33. [G: EEC]

Benston, George J. The Ideological Origins of the Revolution in American Financial Policies: Comments. In *Brunner, K., ed.*, 1981, pp. 253–57.

Bingham, Gavin, et al. Some Developments in Financial and Monetary Research in Finland. *Kansant. Aikak.*, 1981, *77*(3), pp. 342–56. [G: Finland]

Bourne, Compton. Issues of Public Financial Enterprise in Jamaica: The Case of the Jamaica Development Bank. *Soc. Econ. Stud.*, March 1981, *30*(1), pp. 197–208. [G: Jamaica]

Cheng, Hang-Sheng. Money and Credit in China. *Fed. Res. Bank San Francisco Econ. Rev.*, Fall 1981, pp. 19–36. [G: China]

Christelow, Dorothy B. Financial Innovation and Monetary Indicators in Japan. *Fed. Res. Bank*

New York Quart. Rev., Spring 1981, *6*(1), pp. 42–53. [G: Japan]

Courakis, Anthony S. Financial Structure and Policy in Greece: Retrospect and Prospect. *Greek Econ. Rev.*, December 1981, *3*(3), pp. 205–44. [G: Greece]

De Mattia, Renato. Problemi dell'equilibrio finanziario, ieri e oggi. (Past and Present Financial Equilibrium Problems. With English summary.) *Bancaria*, June 1981, *37*(6), pp. 572–77. [G: Italy]

Fusfeld, Daniel R. Response to Professor Gurley [The Next Great Depression II: The Impending Financial Collapse]. *J. Econ. Issues*, March 1981, *15*(1), pp. 181–83. [G: U.S.; Europe]

Green, George D. The Ideological Origins of the Revolution in American Financial Policies. In *Brunner, K., ed.*, 1981, pp. 220–52.

Lamfalussy, Alexandre. Introduzione al tema. (Introductory Paper and Verbal Statement. With English summary.) *Bancaria*, October 1981, *37*(10), pp. 988–1004. [G: U.S.; W. Europe; Japan]

Micossi, Stefano. Comment [Mobilité et mouvements de capitaux en Europe]. *Giorn. Econ.*, Sept.-Dec. 1981, *40*(9–12), pp. 641–43. [G: EEC]

Minsky, Hyman P. The United States' Economy in the 1980s: The Financial Past and Present as a Guide to the Future. *Giorn. Econ.*, May–June 1981, *40*(5–6), pp. 301–17. [G: U.S.]

Moore, Peter G. The Wilson Committee Review of the Functioning of Financial Institutions—Some Statistical Aspects. *J. Roy. Statist. Soc.*, Part 1, 1981, *144*, pp. 32–46. [G: U.K.]

Pierce, James L. The Ideological Origins of the Revolution in American Financial Policies: Comments. In *Brunner, K., ed.*, 1981, pp. 258–61.

Swoboda, Alexander K. Comment [Mobilité et mouvements de capitaux en Europe]. *Giorn. Econ.*, Sept.-Dec. 1981, *40*(9–12), pp. 635–40. [G: EEC]

311 Domestic Monetary and Financial Theory and Policy

3110 Monetary Theory and Policy

Artis, M. J. and Currie, David A. Monetary Targets and the Exchange Rate: A Case for Conditional Targets. *Oxford Econ. Pap.*, Supplement July 1981, *33*, pp. 176–200. [G: U.K.]

Atkinson, P. E.; Blundell-Wignall, A. and Chouraqui, J. C. Budget Financing and Monetary Targets with Special Reference to the Seven Major OECD Countries. *Greek Econ. Rev.*, December 1981, *3*(3), pp. 245–78. [G: U.S.; EEC; Canada; Japan]

Axilrod, Stephen H. and Lindsey, David E. Federal Reserve System Implementation of Monetary Policy: Analytical Foundations of the New Approach. *Amer. Econ. Rev.*, May 1981, *71*(2), pp. 246–52.

Baillie, Richard T. and McMahon, Patrick C. Multi-

variate Causality and the Relationship between the Free Liquid Reserves and Interest Rates. *Z. ges. Staatswiss.*, June 1981, *137*(2), pp. 284–88.
[G: W. Germany]

Barber, Clarence L. and McCallum, John C. P. The Failure of Monetarism in Theory and Policy. *Can. Public Policy*, Supplement, April 1981, 7, pp. 221–32. [G: Canada]

Barnett, William A.; Offenbacher, Edward and Spindt, Paul. New Concepts of Aggregated Money. *J. Finance*, May 1981, *36*(2), pp. 497–505. [G: U.S.]

Barry, Norman P. Austrian Economists on Money and Society. *Nat. Westminster Bank Quart. Rev.*, May 1981, pp. 20–31.

Batchelor, R. A. Aggregate Expectations under the Stable Laws. *J. Econometrics*, June 1981, *16*(2), pp. 199–210.

Batten, Dallas S. Money Growth Stability and Inflation: An International Comparison. *Fed. Res. Bank St. Louis Rev.*, October 1981, *63*(8), pp. 7–12. [G: U.S.; W. Germany; U.K.; Switzerland]

Bertinelli, Roberto. Alcune considerazioni sulla moneta nella R.P.C. (A Few Thoughts on Money in the P.R.C. With English summary.) *Rivista Int. Sci. Econ. Com.*, September 1981, *28*(9), pp. 852–63. [G: China]

Bomberger, William A. and Frazer, William J., Jr. Interest Rates, Uncertainty and the Livingston Data. *J. Finance*, June 1981, *36*(3), pp. 661–75. [G: U.S.]

Brennan, Geoffrey and Buchanan, James McGill. Revenue Implications of Money Creation under Leviathan. *Amer. Econ. Rev.*, May 1981, *71*(2), pp. 347–51.

Brimmer, Andrew F. and Sinai, Allen. Rational Expectations and the Conduct of Monetary Policy. *Amer. Econ. Rev.*, May 1981, *71*(2), pp. 259–67. [G: U.S.]

Brunner, Karl. The Case against Monetary Activism. *Lloyds Bank Rev.*, January 1981, (139), pp. 20–39.

Cagan, Phillip. Two Pitfalls in the Conduct of Anti-inflationary Monetary Policy. In *Fellner, W., ed.*, 1981, pp. 19–52. [G: U.S.]

Cairncross, Alec. The Relationship between Fiscal and Monetary Policy. *Banca Naz. Lavoro Quart. Rev.*, December 1981, (139), pp. 375–93.

Canzoneri, Matthew B. Stability in Financial and Labor Markets: Is There a Tradeoff? *Southern Econ. J.*, January 1981, *47*(3), pp. 617–29.

Cebula, Richard J. The Positively Sloped IS Curve and Joint Balance: An Analysis in Light of Recent New Evidence on the Interest Sensitivity of Commodity Demand. *Rivista Int. Sci. Econ. Com.*, April 1981, *28*(4), pp. 366–77.

Coats, Warren L., Jr. The Weekend Eurodollar Game. *J. Finance*, June 1981, *36*(3), pp. 649–59. [G: U.S.]

Cobham, David. Sterilisation and the Exchange Equalisation Account. *Scot. J. Polit. Econ.*, November 1981, *28*(3), pp. 278–83.

Copeland, Morris A. Bank Deposit Currency before A.D. 1700. In *Uselding, P., ed.*, 1981, pp. 245–54.

Courchene, Thomas J. The Attack on Monetarism: Muddled and Misdirected? *Can. Public Policy*, Supplement, April 1981, 7, pp. 239–48.
[G: Canada]

Davis, Richard G. Recent Evolution in U.S. Financial Markets—Implications for Monetary Policy. *Greek Econ. Rev.*, December 1981, *3*(3), pp. 295–309. [G: U.S.]

Dennis, Geoffrey E. J. A Modified Money Supply Multiplier for the UK in the 1970s. *J. Econ. Stud.*, 1981, *8*(2), pp. 38–45. [G: U.K.]

Dewald, W. G. and Gavin, W. T. Money and Inflation in a Small Model of the German Economy. *Empirical Econ.*, 1981, *6*(3), pp. 173–85.
[G: W. Germany]

Driscoll, M. J.; du Plessis, J. J. A. and Ford, J. L. Monetary Aggregates and Economic Activity in South Africa: Some Preliminary Findings. *S. Afr. J. Econ.*, September 1981, *49*(3), pp. 215–31.
[G: S. Africa]

Eltis, W. A. The Fundamental Problem. *Oxford Econ. Pap.*, Supplement July 1981, *33*, pp. 1–8.
[G: U.K.]

Evans, Paul. Why Have Interest Rates Been So Volatile? *Fed. Res. Bank San Francisco Econ. Rev.*, Summer 1981, pp. 7–20. [G: U.S.]

Fellner, William. Gold and the Uneasy Case for Responsibly Managed Fiat Money. In *Fellner, W., ed.*, 1981, pp. 97–121.

Feltenstein, Andrew. A General-Equilibrium Approach to the Analysis of Monetary and Fiscal Policies. *Int. Monet. Fund Staff Pap.*, December 1981, *28*(4), pp. 653–81. [G: U.S.]

Flannery, Mark J. and Johnson, Lewis. Indexing the U.S. Economy: Simulation Results with the MPS Model. *J. Econometrics*, January 1981, *15*(1), pp. 93–114. [G: U.S.]

Fourçans, André and Fratianni, Michele. Du côté ou à côté de l'offre de monnaie? Un commentaire sur Sterdyniak et Villa [Du côté de l'offre de monnaie]. (On the Supply of Money? A Comment on Sterdyniak and Villa. With English summary.) *Ann. INSEE*, January–March 1981, (41), pp. 79–94. [G: France]

Freeman, G. E. Has Monetarism Failed: A Central Banker Responds. *Can. Public Policy*, Supplement, April 1981, 7, pp. 260–64. [G: Canada]

Frey, Bruno S. and Schneider, Friedrich. Central Bank Behavior: A Positive Empirical Analysis. *J. Monet. Econ.*, May 1981, *7*(3), pp. 291–315.
[G: W. Germany]

Genberg, Hans. Effects of Central Bank Intervention in the Foreign Exchange Market. *Int. Monet. Fund Staff Pap.*, September 1981, *28*(3), pp. 451–76.

Gordon, Robert J. Comment on Rasche and Tatom, "Energy Price Shocks, Aggregate Supply and Monetary Policy: The Theory and the International Evidence." *Carnegie-Rochester Conf. Ser. Public Policy*, Spring 1981, *14*, pp. 95–102.
[G: U.S.]

Gutierrez-Camara, José L. and Vaubel, Roland. Reducing the Cost of Reducing Inflation through Gradualism, Preannouncement or Indexation? The International Evidence. *Weltwirtsch. Arch.*, 1981, *117*(2), pp. 244–61.

Hacche, Graham and Townend, John C. Exchange Rates and Monetary Policy: Modelling Sterling's Effective Exchange Rate, 1972–80. *Oxford Econ. Pap.*, Supplement July 1981, *33*, pp. 201–47. [G: U.K.]

Hafer, R. W. Much Ado about M2. *Fed. Res. Bank St. Louis Rev.*, October 1981, *63*(8), pp. 13–18. [G: U.S.]

Jones, Stuart. The First Currency Revolution. *J. Europ. Econ. Hist.*, Winter 1981, *10*(3), pp. 583–618. [G: U.K.]

Jonson, P. D. and Trevor, R. G. Monetary Rules: A Preliminary Analysis. *Econ. Rec.*, June 1981, *57*(157), pp. 150–67.

Kaldor, Nicholas. Fallacies of Monetarism. *Kredit Kapital*, 1981, *14*(4), pp. 451–62. [G: U.K.]

Kapur, Basant K. Monetary Policy in an Inside-Money, Open Economy: Comment. *Quart. J. Econ.*, May 1981, *96*(2), pp. 349–56.

Kelleher, R. The Role of Monetary Policy. *Irish Banking Rev.*, September 1981, pp. 15–20. [G: Ireland]

Kindleberger, Charles P. Quantity and Price, Especially in Financial Markets. In *Kindleberger, C. P.*, 1981, *1975*, pp. 256–68.

Laidler, David. Inflation and Unemployment in an Open Economy: A Monetarist View. *Can. Public Policy*, Supplement, April 1981, *7*, pp. 179–88. [G: Canada]

Laidler, David. Monetarism: An Interpretation and an Assessment. *Econ. J.*, March 1981, *91*(361), pp. 1–28.

Langohr, Herwig. Banks Borrowing from the Central Bank and Reserve Position Doctrine: Belgium, 1960–1973. *J. Monet. Econ.*, January 1981, *7*(1), pp. 107–24. [G: Belgium]

Laurent, Robert D. Reserve Requirements, Deposit Insurance and Monetary Control. *J. Money, Credit, Banking*, August 1981, *13*(3), pp. 314–24.

MacKinnon, S. The Money Transmission Mechanism. *Irish Banking Rev.*, March 1981, pp. 16–20. [G: Ireland]

Manser, W. A. P. The Monetary Year. *Nat. Westminster Bank Quart. Rev.*, May 1981, pp. 40–50.

Martino, Antonio. Measuring Italy's Underground Economy. *Policy Rev.*, Spring 1981, (16), pp. 87–106. [G: Italy]

Masera, Rainer Stefano. The Behaviour of the Euromarkets and the Problem of Monetary Control in Europe: Comment. *Giorn. Econ.*, Sept.-Dec. 1981, *40*(9–12), pp. 723–31. [G: EEC]

Mathieson, Donald J. Monetary Policy in an Inside-Money, Open Economy: Reply. *Quart. J. Econ.*, May 1981, *96*(2), pp. 357–61.

Matthews, R. C. O. Comment on the Papers by Professors Laidler [Monetarism: An Interpretation and an Assessment] and Tobin [The Monetarist Counter Revolution Today—An Appraisal]. *Econ. J.*, March 1981, *91*(361), pp. 43–48.

Mayer, Helmut W. The Behaviour of the Euro-markets and the Problem of Monetary Control in Europe. *Giorn. Econ.*, Sept.-Dec. 1981, *40*(9–12), pp. 681–721. [G: EEC]

Mayes, David G. The Controversy over Rational Ex-

pectations. *Nat. Inst. Econ. Rev.*, May 1981, (96), pp. 53–61. [G: U.K.]

McCallum, Bennett T. The Current State of the Policy-Ineffectiveness Debate. In *Lucas, R. E. and Sargent, T. J., eds.*, 1981, *1979*, pp. 285–92. [G: U.S.]

Meade, James E. Comment on the Papers by Professors Laidler [Monetarism: An Interpretation and an Assessment] and Tobin [The Monetarist Counter Revolution Today—An Appraisal]. *Econ. J.*, March 1981, *91*(361), pp. 49–55.

Miles, Marc A. Currency Substitution: Some Further Results and Conclusions. *Southern Econ. J.*, July 1981, *48*(1), pp. 78–86. [G: U.S.; W. Germany]

Miller, Marcus. Monetary Control in the UK. *Cambridge J. Econ.*, March 1981, *5*(1), pp. 71–79. [G: U.K.]

Minford, Patrick. The Exchange Rate and Monetary Policy. *Oxford Econ. Pap.*, Supplement July 1981, *33*, pp. 120–42. [G: U.K.]

Moore, Basil J. The Difficulty of Controlling the Money Stock. *J. Portfol. Manage.*, Summer 1981, *7*(4), pp. 7–14. [G: U.S.]

Owen, P. Dorian. Dynamic Models of Portfolio Behavior: A General Integrated Model Incorporating Sequencing Effects [Dynamic Models of Portfolio Behavior: More on Pitfalls in Financial Model Building]. *Amer. Econ. Rev.*, March 1981, *71*(1), pp. 231–38.

Peters, Douglas D. and Donner, Arthur W. Monetarism: A Costly Experiment. *Can. Public Policy*, Supplement, April 1981, *7*, pp. 233–38. [G: Canada]

Pierce, David A., et al. Uncertainty in the Monetary Aggregates: Sources, Measurement and Policy Effects. *J. Finance*, May 1981, *36*(2), pp. 507–15. [G: U.S.]

Rasche, Robert H. and Tatom, John A. Energy Price Shocks, Aggregate Supply and Monetary Policy: The Theory and the International Evidence. *Carnegie-Rochester Conf. Ser. Public Policy*, Spring 1981, *14*, pp. 9–93. [G: N. America; U.K.; Germany; France; Japan]

Rasche, Robert H. and Tatom, John A. Reply to Gordon [Energy Price Shocks, Aggregate Supply and Monetary Policy: The Theory and the International Evidence]. *Carnegie-Rochester Conf. Ser. Public Policy*, Spring 1981, *14*, pp. 103–07.

Santoni, Gary J. and Stone, Courtenay C. What Really Happened to Interest Rates?: A Longer-Run Analysis. *Fed. Res. Bank St. Louis Rev.*, November 1981, *63*(9), pp. 3–14. [G: U.S.]

Scott, Maurice FG. How Best to Deflate the Economy. *Oxford Econ. Pap.*, Supplement July 1981, *33*, pp. 47–69. [G: U.K.]

Siegel, Jeremy J. Inflation, Bank Profits, and Government Seigniorage. *Amer. Econ. Rev.*, May 1981, *71*(2), pp. 352–55.

Simpson, Thomas D. and Williams, John R. Recent Revisions in the Money Stock: Benchmark, Seasonal Adjustment, and Calculation of Shift-Adjusted M1-B. *Fed. Res. Bull.*, July 1981, *67*(7), pp. 539–42. [G: U.S.]

Sims, Christopher A. Current Monetary Policy Research at the Federal Reserve Board: Discussion.

J. Finance, May 1981, *36*(2), pp. 515–17.

Smith, James H., Jr. The Monetary Base and Interest Rates. *J. Portfol. Manage.*, Fall 1981, *8*(1), pp. 56–60. [G: U.S.]

Stauffer, Robert F. The Bank Failures of 1930–31: A Comment. *J. Money, Credit, Banking*, February 1981, *13*(1), pp. 109–13. [G: U.S.]

Teigen, Ronald L. The Evolution of Monetarism. *Z. ges. Staatswiss.*, March 1981, *137*(1), pp. 1–16.

Thompson, Earl A. Who Should Control the Money Supply? *Amer. Econ. Rev.*, May 1981, *71*(2), pp. 356–61.

Thygesen, Niels. Monetarismen—teoretiske principper og praktiske erfaringer. (Monetarism—Theoretical Propositions and Practical Experiences. With English summary.) *Nationaløkon. Tidsskr.*, 1981, *119*(2), pp. 139–66. [G: U.K.; U.S.; W. Germany]

Tobin, James. Comment on the Paper by Professor Laidler [Monetarism: An Interpretation and an Assessment]. *Econ. J.*, March 1981, *91*(361), pp. 56–57.

Tobin, James. The Monetarist Counter-Revolution Today—An Appraisal. *Econ. J.*, March 1981, *91*(361), pp. 29–42.

Tullio, Giuseppe. Demand Management and Exchange Rate Policy: The Italian Experience. *Int. Monet. Fund Staff Pap.*, March 1981, *28*(1), pp. 80–117. [G: Italy]

Wallich, Henry C. The Limits of Monetary Control. *Quart. Rev. Econ. Bus.*, Autumn 1981, *21*(3), pp. 6–14. [G: U.S.]

Warburton, Clark. Monetary Disequilibrium Theory in the First Half of the Twentieth Century. *Hist. Polit. Econ.*, Summer 1981, *13*(2), pp. 285–99. [G: U.S.]

Weber, Warren E. Prior Information and the Observational Equivalence Problem [The Observational Equivalence of Natural and Unnatural Rate Theories of Macroeconomics]. *J. Polit. Econ.*, April 1981, *89*(2), pp. 411–15.

Weintraub, Sidney. Monetarism's Muddles. *Kredit Kapital*, 1981, *14*(4), pp. 463–95. [G: W. Germany; U.S.]

Weise, Peter and Kraft, Manfred. Minsky's View of Fragility: A Game Theoretic Interpretation. *J. Post Keynesian Econ.*, Summer 1981, *3*(4), pp. 519–27.

Wenzel, H.-Dieter. Zur Effizienz und Stabilität geld- und bondfinanzierter Staatsausgabenpolitik in Makromodellen mit Government Budget Restraint. (Efficiency and Stability Aspects of Money- vs. Bond-Financed Government Expenditure Policies in Macro Models with Government Budget Restraint. With English summary.) *Z. ges. Staatswiss.*, March 1981, *137*(1), pp. 17–35.

Wilson, Thomas. The Monetarist Controversy and the British Experiment. *Atlantic Econ. J.*, December 1981, *9*(4), pp. 13–26. [G: U.K.]

Witte, Willard E. Expectations, Monetary Policy Rules, and Macroeconomic Stability: Analysis of an Open Economy with Flexible Exchange Rates. *J. Int. Econ.*, August 1981, *11*(3), pp. 379–94.

Worswick, G. D. N. The Money Supply and the Exchange Rate. *Oxford Econ. Pap.*, Supplement July 1981, *33*, pp. 9–22. [G: U.K.]

3112 Monetary Theory; Empirical Studies Illustrating Theory

Addison, John T.; Burton, John and Torrance, Thomas S. "On the Causation of Inflation": Some Further Clarifications. *Manchester Sch. Econ. Soc. Stud.*, December 1981, *49*(4), pp. 355–56.

Aghevli, Bijan B. Monetary Control and the Crawling Peg: Comment. In *Williamson, J., ed.*, 1981, pp. 53–54. [G: OECD; LDCs]

Ahmad, Syed. Metzler on Classical Interest Theory: Comment. *Amer. Econ. Rev.*, December 1981, *71*(5), pp. 1092–93.

Ajayi, S. Ibi. Money Supply and the Demand for Money: Comments and Extension. *Indian Econ. J.*, July–September 1981, *29*(1), pp. 82–88.

Akerlof, George A. Problems and Resolutions of Problems Concerning the Short Run Demand for Money. In *Currie, D.; Nobay, R. and Peel, D., eds.*, 1981, pp. 209–32.

Allen, Stuart D.; Hatfield, Beverly and Williams, David. A Cubic Estimate of the Term Structure of Interest Rates for a Money Demand Function. *J. Macroecon.*, Winter 1981, *3*(1), pp. 91–96. [G: U.S.]

Amihud, Yakov. A Possible Error in the Expectations Theory: A Rejoinder. *J. Money, Credit, Banking*, February 1981, *13*(1), pp. 107–08.

Arango, Sebastian and Nadiri, M. Ishaq. Demand for Money in Open Economies. *J. Monet. Econ.*, January 1981, *7*(1), pp. 69–83. [G: Canada; Germany; U.K.; U.S.]

Arestis, P. and Hadjimatheou, George. Money, Prices and Causality. *Brit. Rev. Econ. Issues*, Autumn 1981, *3*(9), pp. 19–38. [G: U.K.]

Artis, M. J. From Monetary to Exchange Rate Targets. *Banca Naz. Lavoro Quart. Rev.*, September 1981, (138), pp. 339–58.

Artus, Jacques R. Monetary Stabilization with and without Government Credibility. *Int. Monet. Fund Staff Pap.*, September 1981, *28*(3), pp. 495–533. [G: W. Germany]

Arzac, Enrique R.; Schwartz, Robert A. and Whitcomb, David K. The Leverage Structure of Interest Rates. *J. Money, Credit, Banking*, February 1981, *13*(1), pp. 72–88.

Attfield, C. L. F.; Demery, D. and Duck, Nigel W. A Quarterly Model of Unanticipated Monetary Growth, Output and the Price Level in the U.K., 1963–1978. *J. Monet. Econ.*, November 1981, *8*(3), pp. 331–50. [G: U.K.]

Attfield, C. L. F.; Demery, D. and Duck, Nigel W. Unanticipated Monetary Growth, Output and the Price Level: U.K., 1946–77. *Europ. Econ. Rev.*, June/July 1981, *16*(2/3), pp. 367–85. [G: U.K.]

Backhouse, Roger E. Credit Rationing in a General Equilibrium Model. *Economica*, May 1981, *48*(190), pp. 173–79.

Balasko, Yves and Shell, Karl. The Overlapping-Generations Model. III: The Case of Log-Linear Utility Functions. *J. Econ. Theory*, February 1981, *24*(1), pp. 143–52.

Balasko, Yves and Shell, Karl. The Overlapping-Generations Model. II: The Case of Pure Exchange with Money. *J. Econ. Theory*, February 1981, *24*(1), pp. 112–42.

Balbach, Anatol B. How Controllable Is Money Growth? *Fed. Res. Bank St. Louis Rev.*, April 1981, *63*(4), pp. 3–12. [G: U.S.]

Ballendux, Frans J. and Jonkhart, Marius J. L. A Possible Error in the Expectations Theory: A Comment. *J. Money, Credit, Banking*, February 1981, *13*(1), pp. 105–06.

Barro, Robert J. A Capital Market in an Equilibrium Business Cycle Model. **In** *Barro, R. J.*, 1981, *1980*, pp. 111–36.

Barro, Robert J. Inflation, the Payments Period, and the Demand for Money. **In** *Barro, R. J.*, 1981, *1970*, pp. 301–36. [G: Selected Countries]

Barro, Robert J. Long-term Contracting, Sticky Prices, and Monetary Policy. **In** *Barro, R. J.*, 1981, *1977*, pp. 213–24.

Barro, Robert J. Money and the Price Level under the Gold Standard. **In** *Barro, R. J.*, 1981, *1979*, pp. 355–75.

Barro, Robert J. Rational Expectations and the Role of Monetary Policy. **In** *Lucas, R. E. and Sargent, T. J.*, eds., 1981, *1976*, pp. 229–59.

Barro, Robert J. Rational Expectations and the Role of Monetary Policy. **In** *Barro, R. J.*, 1981, *1976*, pp. 79–110.

Barro, Robert J. The Equilibrium Approach to Business Cycles. **In** *Barro, R. J.*, 1981, pp. 41–78.

Barro, Robert J. Unanticipated Money Growth and Unemployment in the United States. **In** *Lucas, R. E. and Sargent, T. J.*, eds., 1981, *1977*, pp. 563–84. [G: U.S.]

Barro, Robert J. Unanticipated Money Growth and Economic Activity in the United States. **In** *Barro, R. J.*, 1981, pp. 137–69.

Barro, Robert J. Unanticipated Money, Output, and the Price Level in the United States. **In** *Lucas, R. E. and Sargent, T. J.*, eds., 1981, *1978*, pp. 585–616. [G: U.S.]

Barro, Robert J. and Fischer, Stanley. Recent Developments in Monetary Theory. **In** *Barro, R. J.*, 1981, *1976*, pp. 3–40.

Barro, Robert J. and Santomero, Anthony M. Household Money Holdings and the Demand Deposit Rate. **In** *Barro, R. J.*, 1981, *1972*, pp. 337–53. [G: U.S.]

Batchelor, Roy A. Choosing between Money Targets and Targets for Credit: Comments. **In** *Griffiths, B. and Wood, G. E.*, eds., 1981, pp. 81–85. [G: U.S.; W. Germany; Italy; Japan]

Bazdarich, Michael. Some Perspectives on Controlling U.S. Inflation. **In** *Gale, W. A.*, ed., 1981, pp. 167–91. [G: U.S.]

Beenstock, Michael; Budd, Alan and Warburton, Peter. Monetary Policy, Expectations and Real Exchange Rate Dynamics. *Oxford Econ. Pap.*, Supplement July 1981, *33*, pp. 85–119. [G: U.K.]

Beenstock, Michael and Longbottom, J. Andrew. The Term Structure of Interest Rates in a Small Open Economy. *J. Money, Credit, Banking*, February 1981, *13*(1), pp. 44–59. [G: U.K.]

Bellhouse, David R. and Panjer, Harry H. Stochastic Modelling of Interest Rates with Applications to Life Contingencies—Part II. *J. Risk Ins.*, December 1981, *48*(4), pp. 628–37. [G: U.S.]

Bench, Joseph. Money and Capital Markets: Institutional Framework and Federal Reserve Control.

In *Altman, E. I., ed.*, 1981, pp. 1.3–33. [G: U.S.]

Bernstein, Jeffrey I. and Fisher, Douglas. The Demand for Money and the Term Structure of Interest Rates: A Portfolio Approach. *Southern Econ. J.*, October 1981, *48*(2), pp. 400–411.

Bhandari, Jagdeep S. A Simple Transnational Model of Large Open Economies. *Southern Econ. J.*, April 1981, *47*(4), pp. 990–1006.

Blackaby, F. Monetary Targets: Their Nature and Record in the Major Economies: Comments. **In** *Griffiths, B. and Wood, G. E.*, eds., 1981, pp. 54–61. [G: OECD]

Blanchard, Olivier J. Output, the Stock Market, and Interest Rates. *Amer. Econ. Rev.*, March 1981, *71*(1), pp. 132–43.

Blinder, Alan S. Monetarism Is Obsolete. *Challenge*, September/October 1981, *24*(4), pp. 35–41. [G: U.S.]

Blinder, Alan S. Monetary Accommodation of Supply Shocks under Rational Expectations. *J. Money, Credit, Banking*, November 1981, *13*(4), pp. 425–38.

Bolnick, B. R. The Behaviour of the Proximate Determinants of Money in Kenya. **In** *Killick, T., ed.*, 1981, pp. 52–58. [G: Kenya]

Bordo, Michael David. The U.K. Money Supply 1870–1914. **In** *Uselding, P., ed.*, 1981, pp. 107–25. [G: U.K.]

Bordo, Michael David and Jonung, Lars. The Long Run Behavior of the Income Velocity of Money in Five Advanced Countries, 1870–1975: An Institutional Approach. *Econ. Inquiry*, January 1981, *19*(1), pp. 96–116. [G: Canada; U.S.; U.K.; Norway; Sweden]

Bordo, Michael David and Schwartz, Anna J. Money and Prices in the 19th Century: Was Thomas Tooke Right? *Exploration Econ. Hist.*, April 1981, *18*(2), pp. 97–127. [G: U.S.; U.K.]

Boughton, James M. Money and Its Substitutes. *J. Monet. Econ.*, November 1981, *8*(3), pp. 375–86. [G: U.S.]

Boughton, James M. Recent Instability of the Demand for Money: An International Perspective. *Southern Econ. J.*, January 1981, *47*(3), pp. 579–97. [G: N. America; U.K.; Japan; France; W. Germany]

Boughton, James M. and Fackler, James S. The Nominal Rate of Interest, the Rate of Return on Money, and Inflationary Expectations. *J. Macroecon.*, Fall 1981, *3*(4), pp. 531–45.

Bourne, Compton. The Stability and Predictive Efficiency of the Traditional Money Multiplier: Rejoinder [The Determination of Jamaica Money Stock: 1961–71]. *Soc. Econ. Stud.*, September 1981, *30*(3), pp. 144–48. [G: Jamaica]

Brannen, Pamela P. and Ulveling, Edwin F. The Implication of the Rational Expectations Hypothesis for Monetary Policy. *Indian Econ. J.*, July-September 1981, *29*(1), pp. 55–64.

Bray, J. Design and Testing of Economic Policy in a Mixed Economy. **In** *Janssen, J. M. L.; Pau, L. F. and Straszak, A. J.*, eds., 1981, pp. 11–20. [G: U.K.]

Bredahl, Maury E. Interrelationships between Monetary Instruments and Agricultural Commodity Trade: Discussion. *Amer. J. Agr. Econ.*, December 1981, 63(5), pp. 944–46.   [G: U.S.]

Brissimis, Sophocles N. and Leventakis, John A. Inflationary Expectations and the Demand for Money: The Greek Experience. *Kredit Kapital*, 1981, 14(4), pp. 561–73.   [G: Greece]

Brittain, Bruce. Choosing between Money Targets and Targets for Credit. In *Griffiths, B. and Wood, G. E., eds.*, 1981, pp. 62–80.   [G: U.S.; W. Germany; Italy; Japan]

Brittain, Bruce. International Currency Substitution and the Apparent Instability of Velocity in Some Western European Economies and in the United States. *J. Money, Credit, Banking*, May 1981, 13(2), pp. 135–55.   [G: U.S.; W. Germany; U.K.]

Bronfenbrenner, Martin. Price Change and Output Change: A Short-Run Three-Equation Analysis. *Kredit Kapital*, 1981, 14(4), pp. 505–20.   [G: U.S.]

Brown, W. W. and Santoni, Gary J. Unreal Estimates of the Real Rate of Interest. *Fed. Res. Bank St. Louis Rev.*, January 1981, 63(1), pp. 18–26.   [G: U.S.]

Brunner, Karl. Epilogue: Understanding the Great Depression. In *Brunner, K., ed.*, 1981, pp. 316–58.   [G: U.S.]

Brunner, Karl and Meltzer, Allan H. Time Deposits in the Brunner–Meltzer Model of Asset Markets. *J. Monet. Econ.*, January 1981, 7(1), pp. 129–39.

Budd, Alan. Problems of Monetary Targeting in the UK: Comments. In *Griffiths, B. and Wood, G. E., eds.*, 1981, pp. 121–28.   [G: U.K.]

Buiter, Willem H. and Miller, Marcus. Monetary Policy and International Competitiveness: The Problems of Adjustment. *Oxford Econ. Pap.*, Supplement July 1981, 33, pp. 143–75.

Butkiewicz, James L. The Impact of Debt Finance on Aggregate Demand. *J. Macroecon.*, Winter 1981, 3(1), pp. 77–90.   [G: U.S.]

den Butter, F. A. G. and Fase, M. M. G. The Demand for Money in EEC Countries. *J. Monet. Econ.*, September 1981, 8(2), pp. 201–30.   [G: EEC]

Calvo, Guillermo A. On the Time Consistency of Optimal Policy in a Monetary Economy. In *Lucas, R. E. and Sargent, T. J., eds.*, 1981, 1978, pp. 639–58.

Caminati, Mauro. The Theory of Interest in the Classical Economists. *Metroecon.*, Feb.-Oct. 1981, 33(1–2–3), pp. 79–104.

Canarella, Giorgio and Garston, Neil. Money, Expectations, and Interest Rates. *J. Macroecon.*, Fall 1981, 3(4), pp. 517–30.   [G: Italy]

Canarella, Giorgio and Garston, Neil. The Rational Expectation of Income: A Test with Italian Data. *Rivista Int. Sci. Econ. Com.*, June 1981, 28(6), pp. 597–611.   [G: Italy]

Carkovic, Maruja. Estabilidad de la demanda por dinero en Chile: Período 1947 a 1970. (With English summary.) *Cuadernos Econ.*, April 1981, 18(53), pp. 65–87.   [G: Chile]

Carr, Jack and Darby, Michael R. The Role of Money Supply Shocks in the Short-Run Demand for Money. *J. Monet. Econ.*, September 1981, 8(2), pp. 183–99.

Chambers, Robert G. Interrelationships between

Monetary Instruments and Agricultural Commodity Trade. *Amer. J. Agr. Econ.*, December 1981, 63(5), pp. 934–41.   [G: U.S.]

Chappell, David. On the Revenue Maximizing Rate of Inflation: A Comment [Monetary Dynamics, Growth, and the Efficiency of Inflationary Finance]. *J. Money, Credit, Banking*, August 1981, 13(3), pp. 391–92.

Chen, Chau-nan and Tsaur, Tien-wang. Monetary Approaches to Devaluation: Reply [IS, LM, BT and a Simplified Synthesis of the Elasticity, Absorption and Monetary Approaches to Devaluation]. *Southern Econ. J.*, April 1981, 47(4), pp. 1147–51.

Chen, Chau-nan; Tsaur, Tien-wang and Chou, Chein-fu. Gross Substitution, Gresham's Law, and Hayek's Free Currency System. *J. Macroecon.*, Fall 1981, 3(4), pp. 547–57.

Chick, Victoria. On the Structure of the Theory of Monetary Policy. In *Currie, D.; Nobay, R. and Peel, D., eds.*, 1981, pp. 178–208.

Clark, Gordon L. Regional Economic Systems, Spatial Interdependence and the Role of Money. In *Rees, J.; Hewings, G. J. D. and Stafford, H. A., eds.*, 1981, pp. 91–105.

Clark, Lawrence T. Time Lags: A Controversy in Monetary Policy: A Note. *Amer. Econ.*, Fall 1981, 25(2), pp. 63–67.

Cobham, David. "On the Causation of Inflation": Some Comments. *Manchester Sch. Econ. Soc. Stud.*, December 1981, 49(4), pp. 348–54.

Cobham, David. Definitions of Domestic Credit Expansion for the United Kingdom. *J. Econ. Stud.*, 1981, 8(3), pp. 65–78.   [G: U.K.]

Coghlan, Richard. Money Supply in an Open Economy. *Appl. Econ.*, June 1981, 13(2), pp. 181–91.   [G: U.K.]

Congdon, Tim. Is the Provision of a Sound Currency a Necessary Function of the State? *Nat. Westminster Bank Quart. Rev.*, August 1981, pp. 2–21.

Cooley, Thomas F. and LeRoy, Stephen F. Identification and Estimation of Money Demand. *Amer. Econ. Rev.*, December 1981, 71(5), pp. 825–44.   [G: U.S.]

Corbo, Vittorio. Inflation Expectations and the Specification of Demand for Money Equations: A Note. *J. Money, Credit, Banking*, August 1981, 13(3), pp. 381–87.   [G: Chile]

Corden, Max. Choosing between Money Targets and Targets for Credit: Comments. In *Griffiths, B. and Wood, G. E., eds.*, 1981, pp. 86–94.

Corden, W. M. The Exchange Rate, Monetary Policy and North Sea Oil: The Economic Theory of the Squeeze on Tradeables. *Oxford Econ. Pap.*, Supplement July 1981, 33, pp. 23–46.   [G: U.K.]

Courakis, Anthony S. Monetary Targets: Conceptual Antecedents and Recent Policies in the U.S., U.K. and West Germany. In *Courakis, A. S., ed.*, 1981, pp. 260–357.   [G: U.S.; U.K.; W. Germany]

Cox, John C.; Ingersoll, Jonathan E., Jr. and Ross, Stephen A. A Re-examination of Traditional Hypotheses about the Term Structure of Interest Rates. *J. Finance*, September 1981, 36(4), pp. 769–99.

Craine, Roger and Havenner, Arthur. Choosing a

Monetary Instrument: The Case of Supply-Side Shocks. *J. Econ. Dynam. Control*, August 1981, 3(3), pp. 217–34. [G: U.S.]

Cramer, J. S. The Volume of Transactions and of Payments in the United Kingdom, 1968–1977. *Oxford Econ. Pap.*, July 1981, 33(2), pp. 234–55. [G: U.K.]

Cramer, J. S. The Work Money Does: The Transaction Velocity of Circulation of Money in the Netherlands, 1950–1978. *Europ. Econ. Rev.*, March 1981, 15(3), pp. 307–26. [G: Netherlands]

Cuddington, John T. Money, Income, and Causality in the United Kingdom: An Empirical Reexamination. *J. Money, Credit, Banking*, August 1981, 13(3), pp. 342–51. [G: U.K.; U.S.]

Cukierman, Alex. Interest Rates during the Cycle, Inventories and Monetary Policy—A Theoretical Analysis. *Carnegie-Rochester Conf. Ser. Public Policy*, Autumn 1981, 15, pp. 87–144.

Cullison, William E. Monetarist Econometric Models and Tax Cuts: Comment [Monetarist Econometric Models and the Effects of Tax Cuts: Further Evidence]. *Econ. Inquiry*, January 1981, 19(1), pp. 173–75.

Cumby, Robert E. and Obstfeld, Maurice. A Note on Exchange-Rate Expectations and Nominal Interest Differentials: A Test of the Fisher Hypothesis. *J. Finance*, June 1981, 36(3), pp. 697–703.

Currie, David A. Some Long Run Features of Dynamic Time Series Models. *Econ. J.*, September 1981, 91(363), pp. 704–15.

Daniel, Betty C. Real Output Effects of Announced Monetary Policy in a Small Open Economy. *Weltwirtsch. Arch.*, 1981, 117(3), pp. 428–42.

Darby, Michael R. The International Economy as a Source of and Restraint on U.S. Inflation. In *Gale, W. A., ed.*, 1981, pp. 115–31. [G: U.S.]

Davidson, Paul. A Critical Analysis of Monetarist–Rational Expectation–Supply-Side (Incentive) Economics Approach to Accumulation during a Period of Inflationary Expectations. *Kredit Kapital*, 1981, 14(4), pp. 496–504.

Deadman, Derek and Ghatak, Subrata. On the Stability of the Demand for Money in India. *Indian Econ. J.*, July–September 1981, 29(1), pp. 41–54. [G: India]

Deiss, Joseph. Le processus d'ajustement au sein d'une union monétaire. (The Adjustment Process in a Monetary Union. With English summary.) *Rivista Int. Sci. Econ. Com.*, October–November 1981, 28(10–11), pp. 1015–26.

Desai, Meghnad. Inflation, Unemployment and Monetary Policy—The UK Experience. *Brit. Rev. Econ. Issues*, Autumn 1981, 3(9), pp. 1–18. [G: U.K.]

Desai, Meghnad. Testing Monetarism: An Econometric Analysis of Professor Stein's Model of Monetarism. *J. Econ. Dynam. Control*, May 1981, 3(2), pp. 141–56. [G: U.K.]

Dornbusch, Rudiger. Comment [From Monetary to Exchange Rate Targets]. *Banca Naz. Lavoro Quart. Rev.*, September 1981, (138), pp. 359–64.

Dornbusch, Rudiger. Monetary Policy under Exchange-Rate Flexibility. In *Baldwin, R. E. and Richardson, J. D., eds.*, 1981, 1978, pp. 408–24.

Drazen, Allan. Inflation and Capital Accumulation under a Finite Horizon. *J. Monet. Econ.*, September 1981, 8(2), pp. 247–60.

Driskill, Robert A. Exchange-Rate Dynamics: An Empirical Investigation. *J. Polit. Econ.*, April 1981, 89(2), pp. 357–71. [G: U.S.; Switzerland]

Dufour, Jean-Marie. Variables binaires et tests prédictifs contre les changements structurels: une application à l'équation de St. Louis. (Predictive Tests for Structural Change and the St. Louis Equation. With English summary.) *L'Actual. Econ.*, July–September 1981, 57(3), pp. 376–86. [G: U.S.]

den Dunnen, Emile. Dutch Economic and Monetary Problems in the 1970s. In *Courakis, A. S., ed.*, 1981, pp. 182–201. [G: Netherlands]

Dwyer, Gerald P., Jr. Are Expectations of Inflation Rational? Or Is Variation of the Expected Real Interest Rate Unpredictable? *J. Monet. Econ.*, July 1981, 8(1), pp. 59–84. [G: U.S.]

Eltis, Walter. The Failure of the Keynesian Conventional Wisdom. In *Courakis, A. S., ed.*, 1981, pp. 92–110.

Erös, Gyula. Some Problems of the International Monetary System. *Acta Oecon.*, 1981, 26(1–2), pp. 107–22. [G: W. Europe; Japan; U.S.]

Evans, Jean Lynne and Yarrow, George Keith. Some Implications of Alternative Expectations Hypotheses in the Monetary Analysis of Hyperinflations. *Oxford Econ. Pap.*, March 1981, 33(1), pp. 61–80.

Evans, William H. Expectations of Inflation and Nominal Interest Rates in Australia 1969(1)–1979(2): Comments. In *Jüttner, D. J., ed.*, 1981, pp. 279–81. [G: Australia]

Fama, Eugene F. Stock Returns, Real Activity, Inflation, and Money. *Amer. Econ. Rev.*, September 1981, 71(4), pp. 545–65. [G: U.S.]

Fautz, Wolfgang. A Simple Dynamic Model of Autonomous Wage Policy, Price Expectations, and Monetary Accommodation. *Schweiz. Z. Volkswirtsch. Statist.*, March 1981, 117(1), pp. 25–40.

Feige, Edgar L. and Johannes, James M. Testing the Causal Relationship between the Domestic Credit and Reserve Components of a Country's Monetary Base. *J. Macroecon.*, 3(1), pp. 55–76. [G: W. Europe]

Feige, Edgar L. and Singleton, Kenneth J. Multinational Inflation under Fixed Exchange Rates: Some Empirical Evidence from Latent Variable Models. *Rev. Econ. Statist.*, February 1981, 63(1), pp. 11–19. [G: W. Europe]

Fényes, Tamás and Sári, József. On the Difference Equation System of the Composition of the Amount of Money. *Acta Oecon.*, 1981, 26(3–4), pp. 335–59.

Ferris, J. Stephen. A Transactions Theory of Trade Credit Use. *Quart. J. Econ.*, May 1981, 96(2), pp. 243–70. [G: U.S.]

Fethke, Gary C. and Policano, Andrew J. Long-Term Contracts and the Effectiveness of Demand and Supply Policies. *J. Money, Credit, Banking*, November 1981, 13(4), pp. 439–53.

Findlay, M. Chapman, III and Williams, Edward E. Financial Theory and Political Reality under Fundamental Uncertainty. *J. Post Keynesian*

Econ., Summer 1981, *3*(4), pp. 528–44.

Fischer, Stanley. Addendum: Response to Comments by Lucas [Towards an Understanding of the Costs of Inflation: II]. *Carnegie-Rochester Conf. Ser. Public Policy*, Autumn 1981, *15*, pp. 53–55. [G: U.S.]

Fischer, Stanley. Is There a Real-Balance Effect in Equilibrium? *J. Monet. Econ.*, July 1981, *8*(1), pp. 25–39.

Fischer, Stanley. Long-term Contracts, Rational Expectations, and the Optimal Money Supply Rule. In *Lucas, R. E. and Sargent, T. J., eds.*, 1981, 1977, pp. 261–75.

Fischer, Stanley. Towards an Understanding of the Costs of Inflation: II. *Carnegie-Rochester Conf. Ser. Public Policy*, Autumn 1981, *15*, pp. 5–41. [G: U.S.]

Foot, M. D. K. W. Monetary Targets: Their Nature and Record in the Major Economies. In *Griffiths, B. and Wood, G. E., eds.*, 1981, pp. 13–46. [G: OECD]

Franco, Giampiero and Mengarelli, Gianluigi. Debito pubblico, base monetaria e inflazione. (Public Debt, Monetary Base and Inflation. With English summary.) *Bancaria*, November 1981, *37*(11), pp. 1141–45. [G: Italy]

Freeman, George E. A Central Banker's View of Targeting. In *Griffiths, B. and Wood, G. E., eds.*, 1981, pp. 191–201.

Frenkel, Jacob A. and Mussa, Michael L. Monetary and Fiscal Policies in an Open Economy. *Amer. Econ. Rev.*, May 1981, *71*(2), pp. 253–58.

Friedman, Benjamin M. and Froewiss, Kenneth C. More on Bank Behavior: Reply to Van Loo [Bank Behavior in the Brunner–Meltzer Model]. *J. Monet. Econ.*, January 1981, *7*(1), pp. 125–28.

Fry, Maxwell J. Government Revenue from Monopoly Supply of Currency and Deposits. *J. Monet. Econ.*, September 1981, *8*(2), pp. 261–70. [G: Turkey]

Fry, Maxwell J. Monopoly Finance and Portugal's Government Deficit. *Economia (Portugal)*, May 1981, *5*(2), pp. 315–23. [G: Portugal]

Gay, Phillip. Interest Rates in Futures Markets. In *Jüttner, D. J., ed.*, 1981, pp. 361–72. [G: Australia]

Geary, R. C. Monetarism in Ireland: A Simple Statistical Approach. *Econ. Soc. Rev.*, April 1981, *12*(3), pp. 163–68. [G: Ireland]

Gertler, Mark L. Long-Term Contracts, Imperfect Information, and Monetary Policy. *J. Econ. Dynam. Control*, August 1981, *3*(3), pp. 197–216.

Giffin, Phillip E.; Macomber, James H. and Berry, Robert E. An Empirical Examination of Current Inflation and Deficit Spending. *J. Post Keynesian Econ.*, Fall 1981, *4*(1), pp. 63–67. [G: U.S.]

Girton, Lance and Roper, Don E. Theory and Implications of Currency Substitution. *J. Money, Credit, Banking*, February 1981, *13*(1), pp. 12–30.

Goodfriend, Marvin S. and King, Robert G. A Note on the Neutrality of Temporary Monetary Disturbances. *J. Monet. Econ.*, May 1981, *7*(3), pp. 371–85.

Goodhart, Charles A. E. Problems of Monetary Management: The U.K. Experience. In *Courakis,*

A. S., ed., 1981, pp. 112–43. [G: U.K.]

Goodhart, Charles A. E. Problems of Monetary Targeting in the UK: Comments. In *Griffiths, B. and Wood, G. E., eds.*, 1981, pp. 129–34. [G: U.K.]

Gordon, Robert J. International Monetarism, Wage Push, and Monetary Accommodation. In *Courakis, A. S., ed.*, 1981, pp. 1–63. [G: OECD]

Gordon, Robert J. and Wilcox, James A. Monetarist Interpretations of the Great Depression: An Evaluation and Critique. In *Brunner, K., ed.*, 1981, pp. 49–107. [G: U.S.]

Gordon, Robert J. and Wilcox, James A. Monetarist Interpretations of the Great Depression: A Rejoinder. In *Brunner, K., ed.*, 1981, pp. 165–73. [G: U.S.; W. Europe]

Gørtz, Erik. Overvaeltning af inflation i obligationsrenten i et vaekstperspektiv: Et simpelt estimationsresultat. (Inflation, Growth and the Interest Rate. With English summary.) *Nationaløkon. Tidsskr.*, 1981, *119*(1), pp. 95–104.

Gramley, Lyle E. Statement to Subcommittee on Domestic Monetary Policy of the House Committee on Banking, Finance and Urban Affairs, October 27, 1981. *Fed. Res. Bull.*, November 1981, *67*(11), pp. 832–35. [G: U.S.]

Grassman, Sven. Financial Repression and the Liberalisation Problem within Less-developed Countries: Comments. In *Grassman, S. and Lundberg, E., eds.*, 1981, pp. 387–90. [G: LDCs; MDCs]

Gregory, Allan W. and McAleer, Michael. Simultaneity and the Demand for Money in Canada: Comments and Extensions. *Can. J. Econ.*, August 1981, *14*(3), pp. 488–96. [G: Canada]

Griffiths, Brian and Wood, Geoffrey E. Monetary Targets: Introduction. In *Griffiths, B. and Wood, G. E., eds.*, 1981, pp. 1–12.

Grossman, Jacob. The "Rationality" of Money Supply Expectations and the Short-Run Response of Interest Rates to Monetary Surprises. *J. Money, Credit, Banking*, November 1981, *13*(4), pp. 409–24. [G: U.S.]

Hadjimichalakis, Michael G. Expectations of the 'Myopic Perfect Foresight' Variety in Monetary Dynamics: Stability and Non-neutrality of Money. *J. Econ. Dynam. Control*, May 1981, *3*(2), pp. 157–76.

Hadjimichalakis, Michael G. The Rose-Wicksell Model: Inside Money, Stability, and Stabilization Policies. *J. Macroecon.*, Summer 1981, *3*(3), pp. 369–90.

Hakkio, Craig S. The Term Structure of the Forward Premium. *J. Monet. Econ.*, July 1981, *8*(1), pp. 41–58. [G: U.S.; Canada]

Hamburger, Michael J. A Central Banker's View of Targeting: Comments. In *Griffiths, B. and Wood, G. E., eds.*, 1981, pp. 203–10. [G: U.S.; Canada]

Hanson, James A. La relación de corto plazo entre crecimiento e inflación en Latinoamérica: Un enfoque de expectativas cuasi racionales o consistentes. (With English summary.) *Cuadernos Econ.*, April 1981, *18*(53), pp. 15–41. [G: Brazil; Chile; Colombia; Mexico; Peru]

Hatanaka, Michio. Confidence Judgment of the Extrapolation from a Dynamic Money Demand

Function. (In Japanese. With English summary.) *Osaka Econ. Pap.*, December 1981, *31*(2–3), pp. 149–62.

Hayashi, Toshihiko. The Yield on Government Bonds and the Structure of Expected Short Term Interest Rates. (In Japanese. With English summary.) *Osaka Econ. Pap.*, December 1981, *31*(2–3), pp. 132–48.　　　**[G: Japan]**

van Heerden, J. H. P. Income and Interest Rate Elasticities of the Demand-for-Money in South Africa, 1970–1979. *Indian Econ. J.*, July–September 1981, *29*(1), pp. 89–96.　**[G: S. Africa]**

Hein, Scott E. Deficits and Inflation. *Fed. Res. Bank St. Louis Rev.*, March 1981, *63*(3), pp. 3–10.
　　　　　　　　　　　　　　[G: U.S.]

Heins, A. James and Primeaux, Walter J., Jr. Regional Prices and the Conflict between Horizontal and Vertical Equity. *Public Finance Quart.*, April 1981, *9*(2), pp. 235–40.

Heller, H. Robert. International Reserves and World-Wide Inflation: Further Analysis. *Int. Monet. Fund Staff Pap.*, March 1981, *28*(1), pp. 230–33.

Helpman, Elhanan. Optimal Spending and Money Holdings in the Presence of Liquidity Constraints. *Econometrica*, November 1981, *49*(6), pp. 1559–70.

Hercowitz, Zvi. Money and the Dispersion of Relative Prices. *J. Polit. Econ.*, April 1981, *89*(2), pp. 328–56.　　　　　　　　**[G: Germany]**

Hernández-Iglesias, C. and Hernández-Iglesias, Feliciano. Causality and the Independence Phenomenon: The Case of the Demand for Money. *J. Econometrics*, February 1981, *15*(2), pp. 247–63.　　　　　　　　　　**[G: Spain]**

Hodgson, Geoff M. Money and the Sraffa System. *Australian Econ. Pap.*, June 1981, *20*(36), pp. 83–95.

Holmes, James M. and Rhoda, Kenneth L. A Nonparametric Analysis of "Keynesian" and "Monetarist" Models. *Rev. Bus. Econ. Res.*, Spring 1981, *16*(3), pp. 26–37.　　　**[G: U.S.]**

Howitt, Peter W. Activist Monetary Policy under Rational Expectations. *J. Polit. Econ.*, April 1981, *89*(2), pp. 249–69.

Hsiao, Cheng. Autoregressive Modelling and Money–Income Causality Detection. *J. Monet. Econ.*, January 1981, *7*(1), pp. 85–106.
　　　　　　　　　　　　　　[G: U.S.]

Hunt, Ben F. Rate Sensitivity of Financial Flows: Comment. In *Jüttner, D. J., ed.*, 1981, pp. 171–72.　　　　　　　　　**[G: Australia]**

Hunt, Ben F. and Volker, Paul A. A Simplified Portfolio Analysis of the Long-Run Demand for Money in Australia. *J. Monet. Econ.*, November 1981, *8*(3), pp. 395–404.　　**[G: Australia]**

Hwang, Hae-shin. Demand for Money: Tests of Functional Forms and Stability. *Appl. Econ.*, June 1981, *13*(2), pp. 235–44.　　**[G: U.S.]**

Iglesias, C. H. and Iglesias, F. H. Is There a Stable Demand for Money? A Critical View of the "Independence Phenomenon." In *Janssen, J. M. L.; Pau, L. F. and Straszak, A. J., eds.*, 1981, pp. 263–69.　　　　**[G: Spain; Germany]**

Ip, Pui C. International Interest-rate Linkages and Speculative Behaviour: Comments. In *Jüttner,*

D. J., ed., 1981, pp. 397.

Jaeger, Klaus. Economic Policy Effectiveness in Hicksian Analysis: A Note. *Kredit Kapital*, 1981, *14*(2), pp. 177–79.

Johannes, James M. Testing the Exogeneity Specification Underlying the Monetary Approach to the Balance of Payments. *Rev. Econ. Statist.*, February 1981, *63*(1), pp. 29–34.　　**[G: Australia; France; W. Germany; Norway; Sweden]**

Jonung, Lars. An Empirical Identification of the Swedish Money Stock. *Scand. J. Econ.*, 1981, *83*(1), pp. 68–78.　　　　　　**[G: Sweden]**

Joyce, Joseph P. Money and Production in the Developing Economies: An Analytical Survey of the Issues. *J. Econ. Devel.*, December 1981, *6*(2), pp. 41–70.　　　　　　　　　**[G: LDCs]**

Judd, John P. and Scadding, John L. Liability Management, Bank Loans and Deposit "Market" Disequilibrium. *Fed. Res. Bank San Francisco Econ. Rev.*, Summer 1981, pp. 21–44.

Jüttner, D. Johannes. Interest Rates, Capital Markets and Loanable Funds. In *Jüttner, D. J., ed.*, 1981, pp. 257–78.　　　**[G: Australia]**

Jüttner, D. Johannes and Tuckwell, Roger H. Some Comments on the Stability of the Demand for Money. *Kredit Kapital*, 1981, *14*(3), pp. 384–89.
　　　　　　　　　　　　　[G: Australia]

Kaldor, Nicholas and Trevithick, James. A Keynesian Perspective on Money. *Lloyds Bank Rev.*, January 1981, (139), pp. 1–19.

Karakitsos, Elias and Rustem, Berc. Rules v Discretion: An Optimization Framework. *Brit. Rev. Econ. Issues*, Autumn 1981, *3*(9), pp. 51–70.
　　　　　　　　　　　　[G: W. Germany]

Karakitsos, Elias; Rustem, Berc and Zarrop, Martin B. The Indicator System and U.K. Monetary Policy. *Bull. Econ. Res.*, November 1981, *33*(2), pp. 91–101.　　　　　　　　**[G: U.K.]**

Keating, G. R. and Sharpe, Ian G. Australian Interest Rates: A Cross Correlation Analysis. In *Jüttner, D. J., ed.*, 1981, pp. 181–203.
　　　　　　　　　　　　　[G: Australia]

Keinath, Karl. Die Bedeutung der Einkommenskreislaufgeschwindigkeit des Geldes für die Effizienz der Geldpolitik bei festen und flexiblen Wechselkursen. (The Significance of the Income-Velocity of Monetary for the Efficiency of Monetary Policy with Fixed and Flexible Exchange Rates. With English summary.) *Kredit Kapital*, 1981, *14*(2), pp. 180–85.

Keller, Robert R. and Revier, Charles F. The Hazards of a Monetarist Rule Extended. *Southern Econ. J.*, January 1981, *47*(3), pp. 824–30.

Kiernan, Eric. Australian Interest Rates: A Cross Correlation Analysis: Comment. In *Jüttner, D. J., ed.*, 1981, pp. 224–28.　**[G: Australia]**

Kiernan, Eric. Interest Rate Sensitivity of Financial Flows. In *Jüttner, D. J., ed.*, 1981, pp. 127–43.
　　　　　　　　　　　　　[G: Australia]

Kimball, Ralph C. Trends in the Use of Currency. *New Eng. Econ. Rev.*, September–October 1981, pp. 43–53.　　　　　　　**[G: U.S.]**

Kindleberger, Charles P. Money Illusion and Foreign Exchange. In *Kindleberger, C. P.*, 1981, 1973, pp. 87–99.

King, Robert G. Monetary Information and Monetary Neutrality. *J. Monet. Econ.*, March 1981, 7(2), pp. 195–206.

Kohli, Ulrich R. Permanent Income in the Consumption and the Demand for Money Functions. *J. Monet. Econ.*, March 1981, 7(2), pp. 227–38. [G: Canada]

Kohn, Meir. In Defense of the Finance Constraint. *Econ. Inquiry*, April 1981, 19(2), pp. 177–95.

Kohn, Meir. Metzler on Classical Interest Theory: Comment. *Amer. Econ. Rev.*, December 1981, 71(5), pp. 1094–95.

Kopecky, Kenneth J. Required Reserve Ratios and Monetary Control. *J. Econ. Bus.*, Spring/Summer 1981, 33(3), pp. 212–17.

Kreicher, Lawrence L. An International Evaluation of the Fisher Hypothesis Using Rational Expectations. *Southern Econ. J.*, July 1981, 48(1), pp. 58–67. [G: U.K.; W. Germany; Italy; U.S.]

Kuh, Edwin and Neese, John. Parameter Sensitivity, Dynamic Behavior, and Model Reliability: An Initial Exploration with the MQEM Monetary Sector. In *[Valavanis, S.]*, 1981, pp. 121–68. [G: U.S.]

Kulkarni, Kishore G. and Dhekane, Sunil G. The Monetarist Model of Imported Inflation in Small Open Economy. *Econ. Aff.*, July–September 1981, 26(3), pp. 188–92.

Laffer, Arthur B. and Canto, Victor A. The Measurement of Expectations in an Efficient Market. In *U.S. Congress, Joint Economic Committee (II)*, 1981, pp. 70–93. [G: U.S.]

Lahiri, Ashok Kumar. Liquidity Behaviour of Indian Business Firms. *Indian Econ. J.*, July–September 1981, 29(1), pp. 1–9. [G: India]

Laidler, David. Monetary Targets and The Public Sector Borrowing Requirement: Comments. In *Griffiths, B. and Wood, G. E.*, eds., 1981, pp. 176–79. [G: U.K.]

Laidler, David. Some Policy Implications of the Monetary Approach to Balance of Payments and Exchange Rate Analysis. *Oxford Econ. Pap.*, Supplement July 1981, 33, pp. 70–84.

Laumas, G. S. The Demand for Money by the Household Sector: Some Empirical Results. *Eastern Econ. J.*, January 1981, 7(1), pp. 27–33. [G: U.S.]

Leiderman, Leonardo. The Demand for Money under Rational Expectations of Inflation: FIML Estimates for Brazil. *Int. Econ. Rev.*, October 1981, 22(3), pp. 679–89. [G: Brazil]

Leijonhufvud, Axel. Costs and Consequences of Inflation. In *Leijonhufvud, A.*, 1981, 1977, pp. 227–69.

Leijonhufvud, Axel. Keynes and the Classics: Second Lecture. In *Leijonhufvud, A.*, 1981, 1969, pp. 55–78.

Leijonhufvud, Axel. Keynes and the Effectiveness of Monetary Policy. In *Leijonhufvud, A.*, 1981, 1968, pp. 17–37.

Leijonhufvud, Axel. Monetary Theory in Hicksian Perspective. In *Leijonhufvud, A.*, 1981, 1968, pp. 203–26.

Leijonhufvud, Axel. The Wicksell Connection: Variations on a Theme. In *Leijonhufvud, A.*, 1981, pp. 131–202.

Leonard, David C. and Kehr, James B. Stock Mar-

ket Returns and Monetary Aggregates: Recent Evidence on the Issue of Causality. *Rev. Bus. Econ. Res.*, Fall 1981, 17(1), pp. 40–50. [G: U.S.]

Levi, Maurice D. and Makin, John H. Fisher, Phillips, Friedman and the Measured Impact of Inflation on Interest: A Reply. *J. Finance*, September 1981, 36(4), pp. 963–69. [G: U.S.]

Levy, Mickey D. Factors Affecting Monetary Policy in an Era of Inflation. *J. Monet. Econ.*, November 1981, 8(3), pp. 351–73. [G: U.S.]

Lewis, Geoffrey W. The Phillips Curve and Bayesian Learning. *J. Econ. Theory*, April 1981, 24(2), pp. 240–64.

Lewis, Mervyn K. Interest Rate Sensitivity of Financial Flows: Comments: Interest Rates and Monetary Policy. In *Jüttner, D. J.*, ed., 1981, pp. 173–76. [G: Australia]

Lindert, Peter H. Understanding 1929–33: Comments. In *Brunner, K.*, ed., 1981, pp. 125–33. [G: U.S.]

Lipsey, Richard G. Targeting the Base—The Swiss Experience: Comments. In *Griffiths, B. and Wood, G. E.*, eds., 1981, pp. 226–28. [G: Switzerland]

Liviatan, Nissan. Monetary Expansion and Real Exchange Rate Dynamics. *J. Polit. Econ.*, December 1981, 89(6), pp. 1218–27.

Lothian, James R. Monetarist Interpretations of the Great Depression: Comment. In *Brunner, K.*, ed., 1981, pp. 134–47. [G: U.S.]

Lucas, Robert E., Jr. Discussion of: Stanley Fischer, "Towards an Understanding of the Costs of Inflation: II." *Carnegie-Rochester Conf. Ser. Public Policy*, Autumn 1981, 15, pp. 43–52. [G: U.S.]

Lucas, Robert E., Jr. Expectations and the Neutrality of Money. In *Lucas, R. E., Jr.*, 1981, 1972, pp. 66–89.

Lucas, Robert E., Jr. Tobin and Monetarism: A Review Article. *J. Econ. Lit.*, June 1981, 19(2), pp. 558–67.

Mai, Chao-cheng. Is the Optimum Quantity of Money Compatible with the Unique Price Level under Laissez-Faire? *J. Macroecon.*, Summer 1981, 3(3), pp. 435–40.

Malan, Pedro S. Monetary Control and the Crawling Peg: Comment. In *Williamson, J.*, ed., 1981, pp. 50–52. [G: OECD; LDCs]

Masera, Rainer Stefano. The Interaction between Money, the Exchange Rate and Prices: The Italian Experience in the 1970s. In *Courakis, A. S.*, ed., 1981, pp. 234–47. [G: Italy]

McCallum, Bennett T. Monetarist Principles and the Money Stock Growth Rule. *Amer. Econ. Rev.*, May 1981, 71(2), pp. 134–38.

McCallum, Bennett T. Price Level Determinacy with an Interest Rate Policy Rule and Rational Expectations. *J. Monet. Econ.*, November 1981, 8(3), pp. 319–29.

McCallum, Bennett T. Price-Level Stickiness and the Feasibility of Monetary Stabilization Policy with Rational Expectations. In *Lucas, R. E. and Sargent, T. J.*, eds., 1981, 1977, pp. 277–84.

McCallum, Bennett T. The Current State of the Policy-Ineffectiveness Debate. In *Lucas, R. E. and*

Sargent, T. J., eds., 1981, 1979, pp. 285–92. [G: U.S.]

McCloskey, Donald N. and Zecher, J. Richard. How the Gold Standard Worked, 1880–1913. In McCloskey, D. N., 1981, 1976, pp. 184–208. [G: U.K.; U.S.; Sweden; Germany]

McCulloch, J. Huston. Misintermediation and Macroeconomic Fluctuations. J. Monet. Econ., July 1981, 8(1), pp. 103–15.

McKinnon, Ronald I. Financial Repression and the Liberalisation Problem within Less-developed Countries. In Grassman, S. and Lundberg, E., eds., 1981, pp. 365–86. [G: LDCs; MDCs]

McKinnon, Ronald I. Monetary Control and the Crawling Peg. In Williamson, J., ed., 1981, pp. 38–49. [G: OECD; LDCs]

McLean, Wendel. The Stability and Predictive Efficiency of the Traditional Money Multiplier in the Jamaican Context: A Comment on Bourne's Analysis [The Determination of Jamaica Money Stock: 1961–71]. Soc. Econ. Stud., September 1981, 30(3), pp. 137–43. [G: Jamaica]

McMillin, W. Douglas. A Dynamic Analysis of the Impact of Fiscal Policy on the Money Supply: A Note. J. Money, Credit, Banking, May 1981, 13(2), pp. 221–26. [G: U.S.]

McMillin, W. Douglas and Beard, Thomas R. The Impact of Fiscal Policy on the Money Supply in the U.S.: Theory and Empirical Evidence. Rivista Int. Sci. Econ. Com., October–November 1981, 28(10–11), pp. 941–58. [G: U.S.]

Meltzer, Allan H. Monetarist Interpretations of the Great Depression: Comments. In Brunner, K., ed., 1981, pp. 148–64. [G: U.S.]

Middleton, P. E., et al. Monetary Targets and the Public Sector Borrowing Requirement. In Griffiths, B. and Wood, G. E., eds., 1981, pp. 135–75. [G: U.K.]

Minford, Patrick. Locomotives, Convoys or What?—The International Adjustment Problem. In Gaskin, M., ed., 1981, pp. 125–39. [G: OECD]

Minford, Patrick. Monetary Targets: Their Nature and Record in the Major Economies: Comments. In Griffiths, B. and Wood, G. E., eds., 1981, pp. 47–53. [G: OECD]

Minford, Patrick and Peel, David A. Is the Government's Economic Strategy on Course? Lloyds Bank Rev., April 1981, (140), pp. 1–19. [G: U.K.]

Minford, Patrick and Peel, David A. The Role of Monetary Stabilization Policy under Rational Expectations. Manchester Sch. Econ. Soc. Stud., March 1981, 49(1), pp. 39–50.

Minoguchi, Takeo. The Process of Writing the General Theory as 'A Monetary Theory of Production.' Hitotsubashi J. Econ., February 1981, 21(2), pp. 33–43.

Mishkin, Frederic S. Monetary Policy and Long-Term Interest Rates: An Efficient Markets Approach. J. Monet. Econ., January 1981, 7(1), pp. 29–55. [G: U.S.]

Mishkin, Frederic S. Reply to Singleton [The Real Interest Rate: An Empirical Investigation]. Carnegie-Rochester Conf. Ser. Public Policy, Autumn 1981, 15, pp. 213–18. [G: U.S.]

Mishkin, Frederic S. The Real Interest Rate: An Empirical Investigation. Carnegie-Rochester Conf. Ser. Public Policy, Autumn 1981, 15, pp. 151–200. [G: U.S.]

Mitchell, Douglas W. Stability of the Government Budget Constraint with a Constant Exogenous Monetary Growth Rate. Quart. Rev. Econ. Bus., Autumn 1981, 21(3), pp. 15–22.

Montes, Manuel F. Truncation Bias in Household Money Demand Tests. Phillipine Rev. Econ. Bus., March & June 1981, 18(1 & 2), pp. 1–21. [G: Philippines]

Montesano, Aldo. Inflazione e finanziamento del deficit pubblico. (Inflation and Public-Debt Financing. With English summary.) Bancaria, November 1981, 37(11), pp. 1146–52.

Montesano, Aldo. The Notion of Money Illusion. Rivista Polit. Econ., Supplement December 1981, 71, pp. 139–47.

Moosa, Suleman A. On the Empirical Existence of a Monetarist Steady State. Kredit Kapital, 1981, 14(3), pp. 350–83. [G: U.S.]

Mussa, Michael L. Public Policy Issues in International Finance. In National Science Foundation, 1981, pp. I76–104.

Niehans, Jürg. Static Deviations from Purchasing-Power Parity. J. Monet. Econ., January 1981, 7(1), pp. 57–68.

Ohlin, Bertil. Stockholm and Cambridge: Four Papers on the Monetary and Employment Theory of the 1930s. Hist. Polit. Econ., Summer 1981, 13(2), pp. 189–255.

Olivera, Julio H. G. Sobre la estabilidad del dinero pasivo. (On the Stability of Passive Money. With English summary.) Económica, January–August 1981, 27(1–2), pp. 51–55.

Osagie, E. Ghosa and Osayimwese, Iz. Conceptual, Measurement and Estimation Problems in the Demand for and Supply of Money. Indian Econ. J., July–September 1981, 29(1), pp. 75–81.

Pagan, Adrian Rodney. Interest Rates Using the Survey Method and a Time Series Method: Comments. In Jüttner, D. J., ed., 1981, pp. 339–41. [G: Australia]

Pagan, Adrian Rodney and Volker, Paul A. The Short-run Demand for Transactions Balances in Australia. Economica, November 1981, 48(192), pp. 381–95. [G: Australia]

Parguez, Alain. Ordre social, monnaie et régulation. (With English summary.) Écon. Appl., 1981, 34(2–3), pp. 383–448.

Pathak, D. S. Demand for Money in Developing Kenya—An Econometric Study (1969–78) Indian Econ. J., July–September 1981, 29(1), pp. 10–16. [G: Kenya]

Patinkin, Don. Involuntary Unemployment and the Keynesian Supply Function: Mathematical Appendix. In Patinkin, D., 1981, pp. 175–79.

Patinkin, Don. Keynes and Chicago. In Patinkin, D., 1981, 1979, pp. 289–308.

Patinkin, Don. More on the Chicago Monetary Tradition: Postscript. In Patinkin, D., 1981, pp. 284–87.

Patinkin, Don. More on the Chicago Monetary Tradition. In Patinkin, D., 1981, 1973, pp. 277–84.

Patinkin, Don. Reflections on the Neoclassical Dichotomy. In *Patinkin, D.*, 1981, *1972*, pp. 149–54.

Patinkin, Don. The Chicago Tradition, the Quantity Theory, and Friedman: Postscript. In *Patinkin, D.*, 1981, pp. 264–74.

Patinkin, Don. The Chicago Tradition, the Quantity Theory, and Friedman. In *Patinkin, D.*, 1981, *1969*, pp. 241–64.

Patinkin, Don. The Indeterminacy of Absolute Prices in Classical Economic Theory. In *Patinkin, D.*, 1981, *1949*, pp. 125–48.

Paul, M. Thomas. The Demand for Money and the Variability of the Rate of Inflation (India—1951–52 to 1977–78) *Indian Econ. J.*, July–September 1981, *29*(1), pp. 65–74. [G: India]

Pautler, Paul A. Uncertainty in the Demand for Money during Hyperinflation. *Econ. Inquiry*, January 1981, *19*(1), pp. 165–72. [G: Germany; Hungary; Poland]

Peel, David A. On Fiscal and Monetary Stabilization Policy under Rational Expectations. *Public Finance*, 1981, *36*(2), pp. 290–96.

Pettersen, Øystein. Monetary Policy Rules and Variances in Difference Equation Models Containing Autocorrelated Disturbance Terms: Comment [On the Implications of Monetary Rules in a Stochastic Framework]. *Weltwirtsch. Arch.*, 1981, *117*(3), pp. 574–77.

Pippenger, John. The Nature of the Theoretical Debate about Monetarism. *Kredit Kapital*, 1981, *14*(1), pp. 26–31.

Pizzutto, Giorgio. Flussi finanziari e teoria monetaria. (Financial Flows and Monetary Theory. With English summary.) *Rivista Int. Sci. Econ. Com.*, December 1981, *28*(12), pp. 1168–80.

Pope, Robin. Interest Rates, Capital Markets and Loanable Funds: Comments. In *Jüttner, D. J.*, ed., 1981, pp. 282–89. [G: Australia]

Praet, Peter. A Comparative Approach to the Measurement of Expected Inflation. *Cah. Écon. Bruxelles*, 2nd Trimestre 1981, (90), pp. 147–71. [G: EEC; Canada; U.S.]

Rabin, Alan. Comment on Don Roper: What Is the "Demand for Money"? *Econ. Forum*, Summer 1981, *12*(1), pp. 115–16.

Rabin, Alan and Pratt, Leila J. A Note on Heller's Use of Regression Analysis [International Reserves and World-Wide Inflation]. *Int. Monet. Fund Staff Pap.*, March 1981, *28*(1), pp. 225–29.

Ram, Rati. Business Demand for Money in India: A Suggestion for Inferential Caution. *Indian Econ. J.*, July–September 1981, *29*(1), pp. 37–40. [G: India]

Roos, Lawrence K. General Comments on Monetary Policy. In *Griffiths, B. and Wood, G. E., eds.*, 1981, pp. 183–90.

Roper, Don E. What Is the "Demand for Money"? A Reply. *Econ. Forum*, Summer 1981, *12*(1), pp. 117–20.

Saidi, Nasser. The Square-Root Law, Uncertainty and International Reserves under Alternative Regimes: Canadian Experience, 1950–1976. *J. Monet. Econ.*, May 1981, *7*(3), pp. 271–90. [G: Canada]

Sampath, R. K. and Hussain, Zakir. Demand for Money in India. *Indian Econ. J.*, July–September

1981, *29*(1), pp. 17–36. [G: India]

Santomero, Anthony M. and Seater, John J. Partial Adjustment in the Demand for Money: Theory and Empirics. *Amer. Econ. Rev.*, September 1981, *71*(4), pp. 566–78. [G: U.S.]

Santomero, Anthony M. and Siegel, Jeremy J. Bank Regulation and Macro-Economic Stability. *Amer. Econ. Rev.*, March 1981, *71*(1), pp. 39–53.

Sargent, J. R. Problems of Monetary Targeting in the UK. In *Griffiths, B. and Wood, G. E., eds.*, 1981, pp. 95–120. [G: U.K.]

Sargent, Thomas J. A Classical Macroeconomic Model for the United States. In *Lucas, R. E. and Sargent, T. J., eds.*, 1981, *1976*, pp. 521–51. [G: U.S.]

Sargent, Thomas J. A Note on Maximum Likelihood Estimation of the Rational Expectations Model of the Term Structure. In *Lucas, R. E. and Sargent, T. J., eds.*, 1981, *1979*, pp. 453–62. [G: U.S.]

Sargent, Thomas J. Rational Expectations, the Real Rate of Interest, and the Natural Rate of Unemployment. In *Lucas, R. E. and Sargent, T. J., eds.*, 1981, *1973*, pp. 159–98. [G: U.S.]

Sargent, Thomas J. The Demand for Money during Hyperinflations under Rational Expectations. In *Lucas, R. E. and Sargent, T. J., eds.*, 1981, *1977*, pp. 429–52. [G: Europe]

Sargent, Thomas J. The Observational Equivalence of Natural and Unnatural Rate Theories of Macroeconomics. In *Lucas, R. E. and Sargent, T. J., eds.*, 1981, *1976*, pp. 553–62.

Sargent, Thomas J. and Wallace, Neil. "Rational" Expectations, the Optimal Monetary Instrument, and the Optimal Money Supply Rule. In *Lucas, R. E. and Sargent, T. J., eds.*, 1981, *1975*, pp. 215–28.

Sargent, Thomas J. and Wallace, Neil. Rational Expectations and the Dynamics of Hyperinflation. In *Lucas, R. E. and Sargent, T. J., eds.*, 1981, *1973*, pp. 405–28. [G: Europe]

Sargent, Thomas J. and Wallace, Neil. Rational Expectations and the Theory of Economic Policy. In *Lucas, R. E. and Sargent, T. J., eds.*, 1981, *1976*, pp. 199–213.

Sargent, Thomas J. and Wallace, Neil. Some Unpleasant Monetarist Arithmetic. *Fed. Res. Bank Minn. Rev.*, Fall 1981, *5*(3), pp. 1–17.

Schaefer, Stephen M. Measuring a Tax-Specific Term Structure of Interest Rates in the Market for British Government Securities. *Econ. J.*, June 1981, *91*(362), pp. 415–38. [G: U.K.]

Schiltknecht, Kurt. Targeting the Base—The Swiss Experience. In *Griffiths, B. and Wood, G. E., eds.*, 1981, pp. 211–25. [G: Switzerland]

Schwartz, Anna J. Understanding 1929–1933. In *Brunner, K., ed.*, 1981, pp. 5–48. [G: U.S.]

Semudram, M. The Demand for Money in the Malaysian Economy: Empirical Estimates and an Analysis of Stability. *Malayan Econ. Rev. (See Singapore Econ. Rev.)*, October 1981, *26*(2), pp. 53–63. [G: Malaysia]

Seoka, Yoshihiko. The Effectiveness of Monetary Policy in the Keynesian Model with Rational Expectations: A Comment on Mr. Yoshikawa. *Econ. Stud. Quart.*, August 1981, *32*(2), pp. 181–87.

Shieh, Yeung-nan. Monetary Approaches to Devaluation: Comment [IS, LM, BT and a Simplified Synthesis of the Elasticity, Absorption and Monetary Approaches to Devaluation]. *Southern Econ. J.*, April 1981, 47(4), pp. 1143–46.

Shiller, Robert J. Alternative Tests of Rational Expectations Models: The Case of the Term Structure. *J. Econometrics*, May 1981, 16(1), pp. 71–87. [G: U.S.]

Siegel, Jeremy J. Interest Rates during the Cycle, Inventories and Monetary Policy—A Theoretical Analysis: A Comment. *Carnegie-Rochester Conf. Ser. Public Policy*, Autumn 1981, 15, pp. 145–50.

Silva, Ricardo. Inflación reprimida en Chile: El período 1970–1973. (With English summary.) *Cuadernos Econ.*, April 1981, 18(53), pp. 97–106. [G: Chile]

Simos, Evangelos O. Real Money Balances as a Productive Input: Further Evidence. *J. Monet. Econ.*, March 1981, 7(2), pp. 207–25. [G: U.S.]

Sims, Christopher A. Money, Income, and Causality. In *Lucas, R. E. and Sargent, T. J., eds.*, 1981, 1972, pp. 387–403. [G: U.S.]

Singleton, Kenneth J. Extracting Measures of Ex Ante Real Interest Rates from Ex Post Rates: A Comment [The Real Interest Rate: An Empirical Investigation]. *Carnegie-Rochester Conf. Ser. Public Policy*, Autumn 1981, 15, pp. 201–12. [G: U.S.]

Sprenkle, Case M. and Stanhouse, Bryan E. A Theoretical Framework for Evaluating the Impact of Universal Reserve Requirements. *J. Finance*, September 1981, 36(4), pp. 825–40. [G: U.S.]

Stadler, G. The Demand for Money in South Africa. *S. Afr. J. Econ.*, June 1981, 49(2), pp. 145–52. [G: S. Africa]

Startz, Richard. Implicit Interest on Demand Deposits: Reply. *J. Monet. Econ.*, May 1981, 7(3), pp. 403–04. [G: U.S.]

Stein, Jerome L. Monetarist, Keynesian, and New Classical Economics. *Amer. Econ. Rev.*, May 1981, 71(2), pp. 139–44. [G: U.S.]

Stiglitz, Joseph E. and Weiss, Andrew. Credit Rationing in Markets with Imperfect Information. *Amer. Econ. Rev.*, June 1981, 71(3), pp. 393–410.

Stockman, Alan C. Anticipated Inflation and the Capital Stock in a Cash-in-Advance Economy. *J. Monet. Econ.*, November 1981, 8(3), pp. 387–93.

Summers, Lawrence H. Optimal Inflation Policy. *J. Monet. Econ.*, March 1981, 7(2), pp. 175–94. [G: U.S.]

Talvas, G. S. and Aschheim, J. The Chicago Monetary Growth-Rate Rule: Friedman on Simons Reconsidered. *Banca Naz. Lavoro Quart. Rev.*, March 1981, (136), pp. 75–89. [G: U.S.]

Tavlas, George S. Keynesian and Monetarist Theories of the Monetary Transmission Process: Doctrinal Aspects. *J. Monet. Econ.*, May 1981, 7(3), pp. 317–37.

Taylor, Herbert. Fisher, Phillips, Friedman and the Measured Impact of Inflation on Interest: A Comment. *J. Finance*, September 1981, 36(4), pp. 955–62. [G: U.S.]

Taylor, John B. Estimation and Control of a Macroeconomic Model with Rational Expectations. In *Lucas, R. E. and Sargent, T. J., eds.*, 1981, 1979, pp. 659–80. [G: U.S.]

Taylor, John B. Stabilization, Accommodation, and Monetary Rules. *Amer. Econ. Rev.*, May 1981, 71(2), pp. 145–49. [G: U.S.]

Taylor, Robert R. Forecasting Interest Rates Using the Survey Method and a Time Series Model. In *Jüttner, D. J., ed.*, 1981, pp. 316–35. [G: Australia]

Temin, Peter. Notes on the Causes of the Great Depression. In *Brunner, K., ed.*, 1981, pp. 108–24. [G: U.S.]

Thornton, Daniel L. Bank Money as Net Wealth: A Comment. *Atlantic Econ. J.*, December 1981, 9(4), pp. 43–45.

Trevithick, James. Monetary Targets and The Public Sector Borrowing Requirement: Comment. In *Griffiths, B. and Wood, G. E., eds.*, 1981, pp. 180–82. [G: U.K.]

Turnbull, Stuart M. Measurement of the Real Rate of Interest and Related Problems in a World of Uncertainty. *J. Money, Credit, Banking*, May 1981, 13(2), pp. 177–91.

Turnovsky, Stephen J. Monetary Policy and Foreign Price Disturbances under Flexible Exchange Rates: A Stochastic Approach. *J. Money, Credit, Banking*, May 1981, 13(2), pp. 156–76.

Turnovsky, Stephen J. and Eaton, Jonathan. International Interest Rate Linkages and Speculative Behaviour. In *Jüttner, D. J., ed.*, 1981, pp. 385–96.

Usoskin, V. M. The "Stability" Problem: Monetarism vs. Keynesianism. In *Mileikovsky, A. G., et al.*, 1981, pp. 118–65.

Vickers, Douglas. Real Time and the Choice-Decision Point: A Comment on Findlay and Williams' "Financial Theory." *J. Post Keynesian Econ.*, Summer 1981, 3(4), pp. 545–51.

Volker, Paul A. Expectations of Inflation and Nominal Interest Rates in Australia 1968(1)–1979(2). In *Jüttner, D. J., ed.*, 1981, pp. 235–56. [G: Australia]

Vuchelen, Jozef. Monetary Policy and the Loan Rate in the Netherlands: Comment. In *Verheirstraeten, A., ed.*, 1981, pp. 191–94. [G: Netherlands]

Wagner, John R. Some Implications of a Stable Demand for Money Function. *Southern Econ. J.*, October 1981, 48(2), pp. 499–501.

Wallace, Neil. A Hybrid Fiat—Commodity Monetary System. *J. Econ. Theory*, December 1981, 25(3), pp. 421–30.

Wallace, Neil. A Modigliani-Miller Theorem for Open-Market Operations. *Amer. Econ. Rev.*, June 1981, 71(3), pp. 267–74.

Webb, David C. The Net Wealth Effect of Government Bonds When Credit Markets are Imperfect. *Econ. J.*, June 1981, 91(362), pp. 405–14.

Weber, Warren E. Output Variability under Monetary Policy and Exchange Rate Rules. *J. Polit. Econ.*, August 1981, 89(4), pp. 733–51.

Wells, Paul. Keynes' Demand for Finance. *J. Post Keynesian Econ.*, Summer 1981, 3(4), pp. 586–89.

Wenninger, John; Radecki, Lawrence and Hammond, Elizabeth. Recent Instability in the Demand for Money. *Fed. Res. Bank New York Quart. Rev.*, Summer 1981, *6*(2), pp. 1–9. [G: U.S.]

Wessels, Roberto E. Monetary Policy and the Loan Rate in the Netherlands. In *Verheirstraeten, A., ed.*, 1981, pp. 175–90. [G: Netherlands]

White, William H. The Case for and against "Disequilibrium" Money. *Int. Monet. Fund Staff Pap.*, September 1981, *28*(3), pp. 534–72.

Wilford, D. Sykes and Nattress, W. Dayle. Monetary and Financial Integration in North America. *Law Contemp. Probl.*, Summer 1981, *44*(3), pp. 55–79. [G: U.S.; Canada; Mexico]

Woglom, Geoffrey R. H. A Reexamination of the Role of Stocks in the Consumption Function and the Transmission Mechanism: A Note. *J. Money, Credit, Banking*, May 1981, *13*(2), pp. 215–20.

Wood, Geoffrey E. Targeting the Base—The Swiss Experience: Comments. In *Griffiths, B. and Wood, G. E., eds.*, 1981, pp. 229–34. [G: Switzerland]

Wood, John H. Financial Intermediaries and Monetary Control: An Example. *J. Monet. Econ.*, September 1981, *8*(2), pp. 145–63.

Wood, John H. Metzler on Classical Interest Theory: Reply. *Amer. Econ. Rev.*, December 1981, *71*(5), pp. 1096–97.

Wood, John H. The Economics of Professor Friedman. In *[Weiler, E. T.]*, 1981, pp. 191–241.

Yoshikawa, Hiroshi. Alternative Monetary Policies and Stability in a Stochastic Keynesian Model. *Int. Econ. Rev.*, October 1981, *22*(3), pp. 541–65.

You, Jong S. Money, Technology, and the Production Function: An Empirical Study. *Can. J. Econ.*, August 1981, *14*(3), pp. 515–24. [G: Canada]

Zannoni, Diane C. and McKenna, Edward J. A Test of the Monetarist "Puzzle." *J. Post Keynesian Econ.*, Summer 1981, *3*(4), pp. 479–90.

3116 Monetary Policy, Including All Central Banking Topics

Alcaly, Roger E. New Policies on Interstate Banking: Some Lessons from Reforms in the 1930s. In *[Nelson, J. R.]*, 1981, pp. 245–62. [G: U.S.]

Allison, Theodore E. Statement to Subcommittee on Government Information and Individual Rights of the House Committee on Government Operations, October 22, 1981. *Fed. Res. Bull.*, November 1981, *67*(11), pp. 828–32. [G: U.S.]

Andreatta, Beniamino. Linee essenziali della politica finanziaria e monetaria. (Essential Guidelines of Financial and Monetary Policy. With English summary.) *Bancaria*, April 1981, *37*(4), pp. 348–67. [G: Italy]

Artus, Patrick, et al. Economic Policy and Private Investment since the Oil Crisis: A Comparative Study of France and Germany. *Europ. Econ. Rev.*, May 1981, *16*(1), pp. 7–51. [G: France; W. Germany]

Axilrod, Stephen H. New Monetary Control Procedure: Findings and Evaluation from a Federal Reserve Study. *Fed. Res. Bull.*, April 1981, *67*(4), pp. 277–90. [G: U.S.]

Baade, Robert A. A Monetary (Asset) Approach to Exchange Rate Determination: The Evidence since 1973. *Kredit Kapital*, 1981, *14*(3), pp. 341–49. [G: Switzerland; EEC; Japan; Canada]

Baltensperger, Ernst. Geldpolitik und Wechselkursdynamik. (Monetary Policy and Exchange Rate Dynamics. With English summary.) *Kredit Kapital*, 1981, *14*(3), pp. 320–40.

Barnett, William A. The New Monetary Aggregates: A Comment. *J. Money, Credit, Banking*, November 1981, *13*(4), pp. 485–89. [G: U.S.]

Batchelor, Roy A. and Griffiths, Brian. Monetary Restraint through Credit Control in the United Kingdom—The Lessons of Recent Practice. In *Verheirstraeten, A., ed.*, 1981, pp. 195–217. [G: U.K.]

Batko, William. Proposals for Regulatory Reform in the Consumer Financial Services Sector. In *Heggestad, A. A., ed.*, 1981, pp. 92–123. [G: U.S.]

Beek, David C. Excess Reserves and Reserve Targeting. *Fed. Res. Bank New York Quart. Rev.*, Autumn 1981, *6*(3), pp. 15–22. [G: U.S.]

Bench, Joseph. Money and Capital Markets: Institutional Framework and Federal Reserve Control. In *Altman, E. I., ed.*, 1981, pp. 1.3–33. [G: U.S.]

Berkman, Neil G. Open Market Operations under the New Monetary Policy. *New Eng. Econ. Rev.*, March–April 1981, pp. 5–20. [G: U.S.]

Bhalla, Surjit S. The Transmission of Inflation into Developing Economies. In *Cline, W. R., et al.*, 1981, pp. 52–101. [G: LDCs]

Blackaby, F. Monetary Targets: Their Nature and Record in the Major Economies: Comments. In *Griffiths, B. and Wood, G. E., eds.*, 1981, pp. 54–61. [G: OECD]

Bockelmann, Horst. Problems of Monetary Policy in Germany. In *Courakis, A. S., ed.*, 1981, pp. 249–58. [G: W. Germany]

Boll, Frank. Monetary Restraint through Credit Control in the United Kingdom—The Lessons of Recent Practice: Comment. In *Verheirstraeten, A., ed.*, 1981, pp. 218–19. [G: U.K.]

Bolnick, B. R. The Behaviour of the Proximate Determinants of Money in Kenya. In *Killick, T., ed.*, 1981, pp. 52–58. [G: Kenya]

Borchert, Manfred. On the Efficiency of Monetary Policy in the EMS. *Z. Wirtschaft. Sozialwissen.*, 1981, *101*(4), pp. 417–28. [G: EEC]

Boyd, John H. and Kwast, Myron L. Bank Regulation and the Efficiency of Financial Intermediation. In *Federal Reserve System*, 1981, pp. 233–49. [G: U.S.]

Brough, A. T. and Curtin, T. R. C. Growth and Stability: An Account of Fiscal and Monetary Policy. In *Killick, T., ed.*, 1981, pp. 37–51. [G: Kenya]

Brown, Kathleen Hope. Effects of Changes in the Discount Rate on the Foreign Exchange Value of the Dollar: 1973 to 1978. *Quart. J. Econ.*, August 1981, *96*(3), pp. 551–58. [G: U.S.]

Brown, R. V. Selective Controls on the Lending of Financial Institutions. *Irish Banking Rev.*, September 1981, pp. 21–27.

Brown, Ralph J. Inflation and the New Monetary Aggregates. *Bus. Econ.*, May 1981, *16*(3), pp. 30–33.

Brunner, Karl. Policymaking, Accountability, and the Social Responsibility of the Fed. In *Shadow Open Market Committee (II)*, 1981, pp. 67–83. [G: U.S.]

Brunner, Karl. Transition to a New Regime. In *Shadow Open Market Committee (I)*, 1981, pp. 7–15. [G: U.S.]

Buiter, Willem H. and Miller, Marcus. The Thatcher Experiment: The First Two Years. *Brookings Pap. Econ. Act.*, 1981, (2), pp. 315–67. [G: U.K.]

Butkiewicz, James L. and Miller, Jeffrey B. Implications of the Merrill Decision for the Implementation of Monetary Policy. *Nebr. J. Econ. Bus.*, Summer 1981, *20*(3), pp. 47–53. [G: U.S.]

Cagan, Phillip. Financial Futures Markets: Is More Regulation Needed? *J. Futures Markets*, Summer 1981, *1*(2), pp. 169–89. [G: U.S.]

Carney, Owen. "The Regulation of Futures and Forward Trading by Depository Institutions: A Legal and Economic Analysis": Comment. *J. Futures Markets*, Summer 1981, *1*(2), pp. 219–23.

Chandavarkar, A. G. Some Aspects of Interest Rate Policies in Less Developed Economies: The Experience of Selected Asian Countries. In *Livingstone, I.*, ed., 1981, *1971*, pp. 333–50. [G: Taiwan; S. Korea; Malaysia; Singapore]

Chouraqui, Jean-Claude. Monetary Policy and Economic Activity in France. In *Courakis, A. S.*, ed., 1981, pp. 204–16. [G: France]

Chow, Gregory C. On the Control of Structural Models—Comment. *J. Econometrics*, January 1981, *15*(1), pp. 25–28.

Christelow, Dorothy B. Financial Innovation and Monetary Indicators in Japan. *Fed. Res. Bank New York Quart. Rev.*, Spring 1981, *6*(1), pp. 42–53. [G: Japan]

Ciampi, Carlo Azeglio. Funzioni della banca centrale nell'economia di oggi. (Role of the Central Bank in Today's Economy. With English summary.) *Bancaria*, December 1981, *37*(12), pp. 1219–25. [G: Italy]

Ciampi, Carlo Azeglio. Il ricupero della stabilità della moneta quale condizione di progresso. (Recovery of Stability of the Lira as a Condition for Progress. With English summary.) *Bancaria*, July 1981, *37*(7), pp. 659–65. [G: Italy]

Ciampi, Carlo Azeglio. Le condizioni per il ritorno a una moneta stabile. (Requirements for Restoration of Monetary Stability. With English summary.) *Bancaria*, March 1981, *37*(3), pp. 227–44. [G: Italy]

Coats, Warren L., Jr. Recent Monetary Policy Strategies in the United States. *Kredit Kapital*, 1981, *14*(4), pp. 521–49. [G: U.S.]

Courakis, Anthony S. Banking Policy and Commercial Bank Behaviour in Greece. In *Verheirstraeten, A.*, ed., 1981, pp. 220–63. [G: Greece]

Courakis, Anthony S. Financial Structure and Policy in Greece: Retrospect and Prospect. *Greek Econ. Rev.*, December 1981, *3*(3), pp. 205–44. [G: Greece]

Courakis, Anthony S. Monetary Targets: Conceptual Antecedents and Recent Policies in the U.S., U.K. and West Germany. In *Courakis, A. S.*, ed., 1981, pp. 260–357. [G: U.S.; U.K.; W. Germany]

Coutts, Ken, et al. The Economic Consequences of Mrs. Thatcher. *Cambridge J. Econ.*, March 1981, *5*(1), pp. 81–93. [G: U.K.]

Cross, Sam Y. Treasury and Federal Reserve Foreign Exchange Operations. *Fed. Res. Bank New York Quart. Rev.*, Winter 1981–82, *6*(4), pp. 67–69. [G: U.S.]

Cross, Sam Y. Treasury and Federal Reserve Foreign Exchange Operations. *Fed. Res. Bank New York Quart. Rev.*, Autumn 1981, *6*(3), pp. 45–64. [G: U.S.]

Dasmahapatra, Rajkrishna. Black Money and the Special Bearer Bonds. *Econ. Aff.*, July–September 1981, *26*(3), pp. 161–66. [G: India]

Davis, Kevin. Banks, Thrifts and Interest Rates: Comments: Intermediaries and Interest Rates. In *Jüttner, D. J.*, ed., 1981, pp. 106–13. [G: Australia]

Davis, Richard G. Recent Evolution in U.S. Financial Markets—Implications for Monetary Policy. *Greek Econ. Rev.*, December 1981, *3*(3), pp. 295–309. [G: U.S.]

Davis, Robert R. and Genetski, Robert J. Federal Budget Outlook and Economic Prospects through 1982. In *Shadow Open Market Committee (I)*, 1981, pp. 51–61. [G: U.S.]

Davis, Stuart. Deregulation and the Thrift Industry: Comments. In *Federal Home Loan Bank of San Francisco.*, 1981, pp. 61–70. [G: U.S.]

De Grauwe, Paul. Bank Intermediation under Flexible Deposit Rates and Controlled Credit Allocation: The Italian Experience: Comment. In *Verheirstraeten, A.*, ed., 1981, pp. 154–56. [G: Italy]

Degamo, Julia Thelma Y. The Rediscount Policy and Its Impact on the Lending Patterns of Commercial Banks and on the Economy. *Philippine Econ. J.*, 1981, *20*(3&4), pp. 311–36. [G: Philippines]

DeLorme, Charles D., Jr. and Mounts, William S., Jr. Small Saver Discrimination, Anticipated Inflation and Economic Welfare. *Amer. Econ.*, Spring 1981, *25*(1), pp. 53–56.

Dimsdale, N. H. British Monetary Policy and the Exchange Rate, 1920–1938. *Oxford Econ. Pap.*, Supplement July 1981, *33*, pp. 306–49. [G: U.K.]

Dotsey, Michael; Englander, Steven and Partlan, John C. Money Market Mutual Funds and Monetary Control. *Fed. Res. Bank New York Quart. Rev.*, Winter 1981–82, *6*(4), pp. 9–17. [G: U.S.]

Dunkelberg, William C. and De Magistris, Robin. Measuring the Impact of Credit Regulation on Consumers. In *Fed. Res. Bank of Boston and National Sci. Foundation*, 1981, pp. 44–62. [G: U.S.]

Durkin, Thomas A. Discussion [Effects of Creditor Remedies and Rate Restrictions] [Measuring the Impact of Credit Regulation on Consumers]. In *Fed. Res. Bank of Boston and National Sci. Foundation*, 1981, pp. 63–67. [G: U.S.]

Ebaugh, Dwight D. The Users and Providers of Consumer Financial Services: A Legal Framework.

In *Heggestad, A. A., ed.*, 1981, pp. 62–91.
[G: U.S.]

Edgar, Robert J. Banks and Interest Rates. In *Jüttner, D. J., ed.*, 1981, pp. 67–85. [G: Australia]

Edwards, Franklin R. The Regulation of Futures and Forward Trading by Depository Institutions: A Legal and Economic Analysis. *J. Futures Markets*, Summer 1981, *1*(2), pp. 201–18.

Epstein, Gerald. Domestic Stagflation and Monetary Policy: The Federal Reserve and the Hidden Election. In *Ferguson, T. and Rogers, J., eds.*, 1981, pp. 141–95. [G: U.S.]

Ettin, Edward C. The Implications for Federal Reserve Policy of Deregulation of the Thrift Industry: One View. In *Federal Home Loan Bank of San Francisco.*, 1981, pp. 73–79. [G: U.S.]

Fair, Ray C. Estimated Effects of the October 1979 Change in Monetary Policy on the 1980 Economy. *Amer. Econ. Rev.*, May 1981, *71*(2), pp. 160–65.
[G: U.S.]

Fausto, Domenicantonio. The Market for Government Securities in Italy, 1961–1971. *Econ. Notes*, 1981, *10*(2), pp. 14–34. [G: Italy]

Feldstein, Martin S. Inflation and the American Economy. *Empirica*, 1981, (2), pp. 155–68.
[G: U.S.]

Foot, M. D. K. W. Monetary Targets: Their Nature and Record in the Major Economies. In *Griffiths, B. and Wood, G. E., eds.*, 1981, pp. 13–46.
[G: OECD]

Froewiss, Kenneth C. "Financial Futures Markets: Is More Regulation Needed?": Comment. *J. Futures Markets*, Summer 1981, *1*(2), pp. 191–92.
[G: U.S.]

Fry, Maxwell J. Inflation and Economic Growth in Pacific Basin Developing Economies. *Fed. Res. Bank San Francisco Econ. Rev.*, Fall 1981, pp. 8–18. [G: LDCs]

Frydman, Roman. Sluggish Price Adjustments and the Effectiveness of Monetary Policy under Rational Expectations: A Comment. *J. Money, Credit, Banking*, February 1981, *13*(1), pp. 94–102.

Giersch, Herbert and Lehment, Harmen. Monetary Policy: Does Independence Make a Difference?— The German Experience. In *[von Haberler, G.]*, 1981, pp. 3–15. [G: W. Germany]

Gilbert, R. Alton and Trebing, Michael E. The FOMC in 1980: A Year of Reserve Targeting. *Fed. Res. Bank St. Louis Rev.*, August/September 1981, *63*(7), pp. 2–22. [G: U.S.]

Goodhart, Charles A. E. Problems of Monetary Management: The U.K. Experience. In *Courakis, A. S., ed.*, 1981, pp. 112–43. [G: U.K.]

Gramley, Lyle E. Statement to Senate Forum, July 27, 1981. *Fed. Res. Bull.*, August 1981, *67*(8), pp. 623–24. [G: U.S.]

Hafer, R. W. Selecting a Monetary Indicator: A Test of the New Monetary Aggregates. *Fed. Res. Bank St. Louis Rev.*, February 1981, *63*(2), pp. 12–18.
[G: U.S.]

Hafer, R. W. The Impact of Energy Prices and Money Growth on Five Industrial Countries. *Fed. Res. Bank St. Louis Rev.*, March 1981, *63*(3), pp. 19–26. [G: W. Germany; U.S.; U.K.; Japan; Canada]

Hahn, Oswald. Financing of Raw Material Reserves by Banks of Issue. In *Chikán, A., ed. (I)*, 1981, pp. 179–87. [G: W. Germany]

Hamburger, Michael J. and Zwick, Burton. Deficits, Money and Inflation. *J. Monet. Econ.*, January 1981, *7*(1), pp. 141–50. [G: U.S.]

Heggestad, Arnold A. Regulation of Consumer Financial Services: Introduction. In *Heggestad, A. A., ed.*, 1981, pp. 1–16. [G: U.S.]

Heinemann, H. Erich. At a Critical Juncture. In *Shadow Open Market Committee (II)*, 1981, pp. 39–47. [G: U.S.]

Heinemann, H. Erich. Risk and Federal Reserve Action and Monetary Growth. In *Shadow Open Market Committee (I)*, 1981, pp. 25–37.
[G: U.S.]

Hester, Donald D. Innovations and Monetary Control. *Brookings Pap. Econ. Act.*, 1981, (1), pp. 141–89. [G: U.S.]

Hetzel, Robert L. The Federal Reserve System and Control of the Money Supply in the 1970s. *J. Money, Credit, Banking*, February 1981, *13*(1), pp. 31–43.

Humes, Dorla. Foreign Reserves Management in Belize: An Assessment of the Liquidity Constraints in 1979. *Soc. Econ. Stud.*, December 1981, *30*(4), pp. 187–200. [G: Belize]

Humphrey, David Burras. Economies to Scale in Federal Reserve Check Processing Operations. *J. Econometrics*, January 1981, *15*(1), pp. 155–73. [G: U.S.]

Humphrey, David Burras and Savage, Donald T. Bank Use of Downstreamed Commercial Paper and the Impact of Reserve Requirements in Controlling Liability Usage. *J. Econ. Bus.*, Winter 1981, *33*(2), pp. 109–14. [G: U.S.]

Huszti, Ernö. Main Trends in the Development of Socialist Banking Systems and Organization (Relations between the Functions of Issuing [Central] and Credit Banks). *Acta Oecon.*, 1981, *26*(1–2), pp. 71–91. [G: E. Europe]

Issing, Otmar. Recent Developments in U.S. Monetary Policy. *Kredit Kapital*, 1981, *14*(4), pp. 550–60. [G: U.S.]

Johannes, James M. and Rasche, Robert H. Can the Reserves Approach to Monetary Control Really Work? *J. Money, Credit, Banking*, August 1981, *13*(3), pp. 298–313. [G: U.S.]

Johannes, James M. and Rasche, Robert H. Forecasting Multipliers for the "New–New" Monetary Aggregates. In *Shadow Open Market Committee (I)*, 1981, pp. 39–49. [G: U.S.]

Johannes, James M. and Rasche, Robert H. Updated Forecasts of Money Multipliers. In *Shadow Open Market Committee (II)*, 1981, pp. 53–65.
[G: U.S.]

Jorgenson, Dale W. Economic Policy and Private Investment since the Oil Crisis by Artus, et al.: Comment. *Europ. Econ. Rev.*, May 1981, *16*(1), pp. 53–56.

Kane, Edward J. Reregulation, Savings and Loan Diversification, and the Flow of Housing Finance. In *Federal Home Loan Bank of San Francisco.*, 1981, pp. 81–109. [G: U.S.]

Kapur, Basant K. Rejoinder to Mathieson's "Further Reply" [Traded Goods, Nontraded Goods, and the Balance of Payments]. *Int. Econ. Rev.*, June 1981, 22(2), pp. 485.

Kapur, Basant K. Traded Goods, Nontraded Goods, and the Balance of Payments: Further Comment. *Int. Econ. Rev.*, June 1981, 22(2), pp. 477–80.

Karakitsos, Elias; Zarrop, Martin B. and Rustem, Berc. Optimal Instruments for Monetary Control. In *Janssen, J. M. L.; Pau, L. F. and Straszak, A. J., eds.*, 1981, pp. 247–52. **[G: U.K.]**

Kaufman, Henry. Reaganomics: Why Isn't Wall Street Convinced? *Challenge*, September/October 1981, 24(4), pp. 43–48. **[G: U.S.]**

Keyserling, Leon H. International Implications of U.S. Economic Performance and National Policies. *Atlantic Econ. J.*, December 1981, 9(4), pp. 27–33. **[G: U.S.]**

Kim, Kyung Moo. An Econometric Examination of Central Bank Behavior. *J. Econ. Devel.*, July 1981, 6(1), pp. 153–71. **[G: U.S.]**

Kindleberger, Charles P. The Eurodollar and the Internationalization of United States Monetary Policy. In *Kindleberger, C. P.*, 1981, 1969, pp. 100–110.

Kitching, Beverly. New Powers to the Federal Reserve to Lend to Foreigners. *Rivista Int. Sci. Econ. Com.*, October–November 1981, 28(10–11), pp. 1082–85. **[G: U.S.]**

Kitching, Beverly. The Federal Reserve System Furnished the Money for World War II: Why Can't It Do the Same for Social Security? *Int. J. Soc. Econ.*, 1981, 8(7), pp. 70–72. **[G: U.S.]**

Klein, Michael A. Monetary-Control Implications of the Monetary Control Act. *Fed. Res. Bank San Francisco Econ. Rev.*, Winter 1981, pp. 6–21. **[G: U.S.]**

de Kock, Gerhard. New Developments in Monetary Policy in South Africa. *S. Afr. J. Econ.*, December 1981, 49(4), pp. 321–33. **[G: S. Africa]**

Kopcke, Richard W. and Woglom, Geoffrey R. H. Regulation Q and Savings Bank Solvency—The Connecticut Experience. In *Fed. Res. Bank of Boston and National Sci. Foundation*, 1981, pp. 68–95. **[G: U.S.]**

Kullberg, Rolf. Kan penningpolitiken styra vår ekonomi? (Can the Finnish Economy be Controlled by Monetary Policy? With English summary.) *Ekon. Samfundets Tidskr.*, 1981, 34(1), pp. 37–47. **[G: Finland]**

Lamfalussy, Alexandre. Regole o discrezionalità? Saggio sulla politica monetaria in un contesto inflazionistico. (Rules or Discretionary Powers? Monetary Policy in an Inflationary Context. With English summary.) *Bancaria*, December 1981, 37(12), pp. 1235–56. **[G: Western MDCs]**

Lawrence, Edward C. and Elliehausen, Gregory E. The Impact of Federal Interest Rate Regulations on the Small Saver: Further Evidence. *J. Finance*, June 1981, 36(3), pp. 677–84. **[G: U.S.]**

Lipsey, Richard G. Targeting the Base—The Swiss Experience: Comments. In *Griffiths, B. and Wood, G. E., eds.*, 1981, pp. 226–28. **[G: Switzerland]**

Lynge, Morgan J., Jr. Money Supply Announcements and Stock Prices. *J. Portfol. Manage.*, Fall 1981, 8(1), pp. 40–43. **[G: U.S.]**

Maes, Marcel. Deregulation of Deposit Rate Ceilings in the United States: Prospects and Consequences: Comment. In *Verheirstraeten, A., ed.*, 1981, pp. 52–54. **[G: Belgium]**

Magnifico, Giovanni. Governo della moneta, disavanzi pubblici e inflazione: il caso italiano. (Money Management, Public Deficits and Inflation: The Italian Case. With English summary.) *Bancaria*, September 1981, 37(9), pp. 908–17. **[G: Italy]**

Marois, William. Les interactions entre les mouvements de capitaux et la politique monétaire en systèmes de changes quasi fixes. (The Interactions between the Capital Movements and the Monetary Policy in a Quasi-Fixed Exchange Rates System. With English summary.) *Revue Écon.*, March 1981, 32(2), pp. 374–404.

Mathieson, Donald J. A Final Reply to Kapur [Traded Goods, Nontraded Goods and the Balance of Payments]. *Int. Econ. Rev.*, June 1981, 22(2), pp. 487.

Mathieson, Donald J. Traded Goods, Nontraded Goods, and the Balance of Payments: Further Reply. *Int. Econ. Rev.*, June 1981, 22(2), pp. 481–83.

Matthes, Heinrich. Il sistema creditizio della Germania Federale. (The West German Credit System. With English summary.) *Bancaria*, November 1981, 37(11), pp. 1099–1104. **[G: W. Germany]**

Mattson, Gustav. Penningpolitiska aspekt på konjunkturbilden. (Monetary Policy and the Business Cycle. With English summary.) *Ekon. Samfundets Tidskr.*, 1981, 34(1), pp. 33–34. **[G: Finland]**

McCallum, Bennett T. Price-Level Stickiness and the Feasibility of Monetary Stabilization Policy with Rational Expectations. In *Lucas, R. E. and Sargent, T. J., eds.*, 1981, 1977, pp. 277–84.

McCallum, Bennett T. Sluggish Price Adjustments and the Effectiveness of Monetary Policy under Rational Expectations: A Reply. *J. Money, Credit, Banking*, February 1981, 13(1), pp. 103–04.

McElhattan, Rose. The Response of Real Output and Inflation to Monetary Policy. *Fed. Res. Bank San Francisco Econ. Rev.*, Summer 1981, pp. 45–70.

McLean, Kenneth A. Legislative Background of the Depository Institutions Deregulation and Monetary Control Act of 1980. In *Federal Home Loan Bank of San Francisco.*, 1981, pp. 17–30. **[G: U.S.]**

Minford, Patrick. Monetary Targets: Their Nature and Record in the Major Economies: Comments. In *Griffiths, B. and Wood, G. E., eds.*, 1981, pp. 47–53. **[G: OECD]**

Minford, Patrick and Peel, David A. Is the Government's Economic Strategy on Course? *Lloyds Bank Rev.*, April 1981, (140), pp. 1–19. **[G: U.K.]**

Mingo, John J. The Economic Impact of Deposit Rate Ceilings. In *Heggestad, A. A., ed.*, 1981, pp. 124–43. **[G: U.S.]**

Minsky, Hyman P. Financial Markets and Economic Instability, 1965–1980. *Nebr. J. Econ. Bus.*, Autumn 1981, 20(4), pp. 5–16. **[G: U.S.]**

Mishan, Ezra J. The Iron Lady's Monetarism. *Chal-*

lenge, November–December 1981, *24*(5), pp. 57–58. **[G: U.K.]**

Mitchell, George W. and Hodgdon, Raymond F. Federal Reserve and the Payments System: Upgrading Electronic Capabilities for the 1980s. *Fed. Res. Bull.*, February 1981, *67*(2), pp. 109–16. **[G: U.S.]**

Monti, Mario and Padoa-Schioppa, Tommaso. Structural Changes and Cyclical Behaviour of the Italian Banking System. In *Courakis, A. S., ed.,* 1981, pp. 217–31. **[G: Italy]**

Monti, Mario and Porta, Angelo. Bank Intermediation under Flexible Deposit Rates and Controlled Credit Allocation: The Italian Experience. In *Verheirstraeten, A., ed.,* 1981, pp. 117–53. **[G: Italy]**

Moore, Basil J. Is the Money Stock Really a Control Variable? *Challenge,* July/August 1981, *24*(3), pp. 43–46. **[G: U.S.]**

Mushi, S. S. Tanzania. In *Adedeji, A., ed.,* 1981, pp. 204–37. **[G: Tanzania]**

Neumann, Manfred J. M. Der Beitrag der Geldpolitik zur konjunkturellen Entwicklung in der Bundesrepublik Deutschland 1973–1980. (With English summary.) *Kyklos,* 1981, *34*(3), pp. 405–31. **[G: W. Germany]**

Neumann, Manfred J. M. Inflation und Staatsverschuldung. (Inflation and Debted Financing Deficits. With English summary.) *Z. Wirtschaft. Sozialwissen.,* 1981, *101*(2), pp. 113–26.

Nickell, Stephen J. Economic Policy and Private Investment since the Oil Crisis by Artus, et al.: Comment. *Europ. Econ. Rev.,* May 1981, *16*(1), pp. 57–59.

Norman, Alfred L. On the Control of Structural Models. *J. Econometrics,* January 1981, *15*(1), pp. 13–24. **[G: U.S.]**

Norman, Alfred L. On the Control of Structural Models—Reply. *J. Econometrics,* January 1981, *15*(1), pp. 29.

O'Brien, James M. Estimating the Information Value of Immediate Disclosure of the FOMC Policy Directive. *J. Finance,* December 1981, *36*(5), pp. 1047–61. **[G: U.S.]**

Oteri, Carmelo. L'evoluzione degli schemi di controllo pubblico sui dati di bilancio delle aziende di credito. (The Evolution of Methods for Public Control of Commercial Banks' Financial Statements. With English summary.) *Bancaria,* July 1981, *37*(7), pp. 673–83. **[G: Italy]**

Palmerio, Giovanni. Tasso di cambio, ritmi di inflazione e movimenti di capitali. (Exchange Rate, Inflation Rates and Capital Movements. With English summary.) *Rivista Int. Sci. Econ. Com.,* October–November 1981, *28*(10–11), pp. 990–1000.

Pardee, Scott E. Treasury and Federal Reserve Foreign Exchange Operations. *Fed. Res. Bank New York Quart. Rev.,* Spring 1981, *6*(1), pp. 54–74. **[G: U.S.]**

Pardee, Scott E. Treasury and Federal Reserve Foreign Exchange Operations. *Fed. Res. Bank New York Quart. Rev.,* Summer 1981, *6*(2), pp. 76–78.

Perryman, M. Ray. Policy Intent, Policy Formulation and Policy Effectiveness: An Appraisal of Federal Reserve Actions. *Appl. Econ.,* September 1981, *13*(3), pp. 365–76. **[G: U.K.]**

Peston, Maurice H. The Integration of Monetary, Fiscal and Incomes Policy. *Lloyds Bank Rev.,* July 1981, (141), pp. 1–13.

Peterson, Richard L. Effects of Creditor Remedies and Rate Restrictions. In *Fed. Res. Bank of Boston and National Sci. Foundation,* 1981, pp. 24–43. **[G: U.S.]**

Pierce, David A. and Cleveland, William P. Seasonal Adjustment Methods for the Monetary Aggregates. *Fed. Res. Bull.,* December 1981, *67*(12), pp. 875–87. **[G: U.S.]**

Poloušek, Stanislav and Novotný, Zdeněk. The Influence of the Monetarist Concept of the State Monopoly Regulation in the United States. *Czech. Econ. Digest.,* November 1981, (7), pp. 60–76. **[G: U.S.]**

Poole, William. Banks, Thrifts and Interest Rates: Comments. In *Jüttner, D. J., ed.,* 1981, pp. 120–24. **[G: Australia]**

Raymond, Robert. Strutture finanziarie, stabilità economica e allocazione delle risorse: il caso della Francia. (Financial Structures, Economic Stability and the Allocation of Resources: The French Example. With English summary.) *Bancaria,* October 1981, *37*(10), pp. 1023–37. **[G: France]**

Reuber, G. L. Steps to Improve International Economic Policy Co-ordination. *Can. Public Policy,* Autumn 1981, *7*(4), pp. 596–603.

Revell, Jack R. S. Gli effetti dei trasferimenti di fondi a mezzo sistemi elettronici nella struttura di un sistema bancario. (The Effects of Electronic Fund Transfers on the Structure of Banking Systems. With English summary.) *Bancaria,* August 1981, *37*(8), pp. 774–83. **[G: W. Europe]**

Ribnikar, Ivan. The Yugoslav Monetary System. *ACES Bull. (See Comp. Econ. Stud. after 8/85),* Spring 1981, *23*(1), pp. 67–78. **[G: Yugoslavia]**

Rieke, Wolfgang. Comment [Are Monetary Policies and Performances Converging?]. *Banca Naz. Lavoro Quart. Rev.,* September 1981, (138), pp. 323–26. **[G: EEC]**

Riordan, Dale P. and Hartzog, Jerry. The Impact of the Deregulation Act on Policy Choices of the Federal Home Loan Bank Board. In *Federal Home Loan Bank of San Francisco.,* 1981, pp. 33–58. **[G: U.S.]**

Roos, Lawrence K. Lessons We Can Learn. *Fed. Res. Bank St. Louis Rev.,* October 1981, *63*(8), pp. 3–6. **[G: U.K.; Switzerland; W. Germany]**

Rowan, D. C. Implementing Monetarism: Some Reflections on the U.K. Experience. *Banca Naz. Lavoro Quart. Rev.,* June 1981, (137), pp. 119–45. **[G: U.K.]**

Rowen, Harvey A. The Probable Impacts of Expanded Securities and Other Financing Activities of Banks and Securities Firms in the 1980s: Impacts on the Securities Industry. In *Sametz, A. W., ed.,* 1981, pp. 164–66. **[G: U.S.]**

Royama, Shoichi. Deposit-Postal Saving Rate Setting and Monetary Policy: A Political Economy of Interest Rates Regulation. (In Japanese. With English summary.) *Osaka Econ. Pap.,* December 1981, *31*(2–3), pp. 121–31. **[G: Japan]**

Santoni, Gary J. and Stone, Courtenay C. Navigating through the Interest Rate Morass: Some Basic

Principles. *Fed. Res. Bank St. Louis Rev.*, March 1981, *63*(3), pp. 11–18. [G: U.S.]

Sarcinelli, Mario. The Role of the Central Bank in the Domestic Economy. *Rev. Econ. Cond. Italy*, October 1981, (3), pp. 433–54. [G: Italy]

Schiltknecht, Kurt. Targeting the Base—The Swiss Experience. **In** *Griffiths, B. and Wood, G. E., eds.*, 1981, pp. 211–25. [G: Switzerland]

Schultz, Frederich K. Statement to Domestic Monetary Policy Subcommittee of the House Committee on Banking, Finance and Urban Affairs, September 29, 1981. *Fed. Res. Bull.*, October 1981, *67*(10), pp. 774–75. [G: U.S.]

Schultz, Frederick H. Statement to House Committee on Small Business, April 7, 1981. *Fed. Res. Bull.*, April 1981, *67*(4), pp. 297–301. [G: U.S.]

Shadow Open Market Committee. Policy Statement, March 16, 1981. **In** *Shadow Open Market Committee (II)*, 1981, pp. 5–9. [G: U.S.]

Shadow Open Market Committee. Policy Statement, September 14, 1981. **In** *Shadow Open Market Committee (I)*, 1981, pp. 1–5. [G: U.S.]

Siegel, Jeremy J. Bank Reserves and Financial Stability. *J. Finance*, December 1981, *36*(5), pp. 1073–84. [G: U.S.]

Smith, Adrian. The Informal Economy. *Lloyds Bank Rev.*, July 1981, (141), pp. 45–61. [G: EEC]

Stevenson, Andrew. Italian Monetary Policy: Comparisons and Contrasts with the UK. *Lloyds Bank Rev.*, April 1981, (140), pp. 36–50. [G: Italy; U.K.]

Stone, Alan. State and Market: Economic Regulation and the Great Productivity Debate. **In** *Ferguson, T. and Rogers, J., eds.*, 1981, pp. 232–59. [G: U.S.]

Struble, Frederick M. "Financial Futures Markets: Is More Regulation Needed?": Comment. *J. Futures Markets*, Summer 1981, *1*(2), pp. 193–99. [G: U.S.]

Taggart, Robert A., Jr. Deregulation of Deposit Rate Ceilings in the United States: Prospects and Consequences. **In** *Verheirstraeten, A., ed.*, 1981, pp. 35–51. [G: U.S.]

Teeters, Nancy H. Statement to Subcommittee on Financial Institutions, Senate Committee on Banking, Housing, and Urban Affairs, July 21, 1981. *Fed. Res. Bull.*, August 1981, *67*(8), pp. 618–20. [G: U.S.]

Teeters, Nancy H. Statement to Subcommittee on Economic Stabilization, House Committee on Banking, Finance and Urban Affairs, April 30, 1981. *Fed. Res. Bull.*, May 1981, *67*(5), pp. 424–29. [G: U.S.]

Thygesen, Niels. Are Monetary Policies and Performances Converging? *Banca Naz. Lavoro Quart. Rev.*, September 1981, (138), pp. 297–322. [G: EEC]

Tiivloa, Mika. Vår penningpolitik. (Finland's Monetary Policy. With English summary.) *Ekon. Samfundets Tidskr.*, 1981, *34*(1), pp. 49–53. [G: Finland]

Tinsley, P. A. and von zur Muehlen, P. A Maximum Probability Approach to Short-Run Policy. *J. Econometrics*, January 1981, *15*(1), pp. 31–48. [G: U.S.]

Tinsley, P. A., et al. The Impact of Uncertainty on the Feasibility of Humphrey-Hawkins Objectives. *J. Finance*, May 1981, *36*(2), pp. 489–96. [G: U.S.]

Tucker, Donald P. Regulation Q and Savings Bank Solvency—The Connecticut Experience: Discussion. **In** *Fed. Res. Bank of Boston and National Sci. Foundation*, 1981, pp. 96–100. [G: U.S.]

Urich, Thomas and Wachtel, Paul. Market Response to the Weekly Money Supply Announcements in the 1970s. *J. Finance*, December 1981, *36*(5), pp. 1063–72. [G: U.S.]

Verga, Giovanni. La funzione di reazione della banca d'Italia: una stima per il periodo 1963–1980. (The Bank of Italy's Reaction Function: An Estimation for the Period 1963–80. With English summary.) *Giorn. Econ.*, March–April 1981, *40*(3–4), pp. 183–98. [G: Italy]

Vila, Gérard. Banking Policy and Commercial Bank Behaviour in Greece: Comment. **In** *Verheirstraeten, A., ed.*, 1981, pp. 264–66. [G: Greece]

Volcker, Paul A. Statement to House Committee on Banking, Finance and Urban Affairs, July 21, 1981. *Fed. Res. Bull.*, August 1981, *67*(8), pp. 613–18. [G: U.S.]

Volcker, Paul A. Statement to House Committee on the Budget, March 27, 1981. *Fed. Res. Bull.*, April 1981, *67*(4), pp. 293–96. [G: U.S.]

Volcker, Paul A. Statement to House Committee on Ways and Means, March 3, 1981. *Fed. Res. Bull.*, March 1981, *67*(3), pp. 243–46. [G: U.S.]

Volcker, Paul A. Statement to Joint Economic Committee, February 5, 1981. *Fed. Res. Bull.*, February 1981, *67*(2), pp. 141–43. [G: U.S.]

Volcker, Paul A. Statement to Joint Economic Committee, July 16, 1981. *Fed. Res. Bull.*, August 1981, *67*(8), pp. 610–13. [G: U.S.]

Volcker, Paul A. Statement to Senate Committee on Banking, Housing, and Urban Affairs, January 7, 1981. *Fed. Res. Bull.*, January 1981, *67*(1), pp. 17–21. [G: U.S.]

Volcker, Paul A. Statement to Senate Committee on Banking, Housing, and Urban Affairs, February 25, 1981. *Fed. Res. Bull.*, March 1981, *67*(3), pp. 237–41. [G: U.S.]

Volcker, Paul A. Statement to Senate Committee on Appropriations, January 27, 1981. *Fed. Res. Bull.*, February 1981, *67*(2), pp. 135–37. [G: U.S.]

Volcker, Paul A. Statement to Subcommittee on Financial Institutions Supervision, Regulation and Insurance of the House Committee on Banking, Finance and Urban Affairs, October 1, 1981. *Fed. Res. Bull.*, October 1981, *67*(10), pp. 775–78. [G: U.S.]

Vuchelen, Jozef. Monetary Policy and the Loan Rate in the Netherlands: Comment. **In** *Verheirstraeten, A., ed.*, 1981, pp. 191–94. [G: Netherlands]

Weinrobe, Maurice. Savings and Loan Demand for Liquid Assets: Theory, Evidence and Implications for Policy. *Amer. Real Estate Urban Econ. Assoc. J.*, Spring 1981, *9*(1), pp. 18–37. [G: U.S.]

Welcker, Johannes. Der Eurodollarmarkt: Tatsächliche und vermeintliche Probleme. (The Euro-Dollar Market—Actual and Alleged Problems. With English summary.) *Konjunkturpolitik*, 1981,

27(5), pp. 279–96.   [G: W. Germany]

Wessels, G. M. Depositokoersbeheer as Monetêre Beheermaatreël. (With English summary.) *S. Afr. J. Econ.*, June 1981, 49(2), pp. 130–44.
                                        [G: S. Africa]

Wessels, Roberto E. Monetary Policy and the Loan Rate in the Netherlands. In *Verheirstraeten, A., ed.*, 1981, pp. 175–90.   [G: Netherlands]

White, Betsy Buttrill. Monetary Policy without Regulation Q. *Fed. Res. Bank New York Quart. Rev.*, Winter 1981–82, 6(4), pp. 4–8.   [G: U.S.]

Wirick, Ronald G. The Battle against Inflation: The Bank of Canada and Its Critics. *Can. Public Policy*, Supplement, April 1981, 7, pp. 249–59.
                                        [G: Canada]

Wood, Geoffrey E. Targeting the Base—The Swiss Experience: Comments. In *Griffiths, B. and Wood, G. E., eds.*, 1981, pp. 229–34.
                                        [G: Switzerland]

Wright, John Winthrop. Proceedings of the Seminar on International Economic Problems: Statement. In *U.S. Congress, Joint Economic Committee (I)*, 1981, pp. 295–312.   [G: U.S.]

Zimmerman, Gary C. The Pricing of Federal Reserve Services under MCA. *Fed. Res. Bank San Francisco Econ. Rev.*, Winter 1981, pp. 22–40.
                                        [G: U.S.]

Zwick, Burton. Economic Projections. In *Shadow Open Market Committee (I)*, 1981, pp. 63–70.
                                        [G: U.S.]

312 Commercial Banking

3120 Commercial Banking

Aftalion, Florin. Government Intervention in the French Financial System. In *Verheirstraeten, A., ed.*, 1981, pp. 157–72.   [G: France]

Aharony, Joseph and Swary, Itzhak. Effects of the 1970 Bank Holding Company Act: Evidence from Capital Markets. *J. Finance*, September 1981, 36(4), pp. 841–53.   [G: U.S.]

Alcaly, Roger E. New Policies on Interstate Banking: Some Lessons from Reforms in the 1930s. In *[Nelson, J. R.]*, 1981, pp. 245–62.   [G: U.S.]

Alessandroni, Alessandro. L'intermediazione bancaria internazionale: evoluzione del passato e prospettive attuali. (International Banking Intermediation: Retrospect and Current Prospects. With English summary.) *Bancaria*, February 1981, 37(2), pp. 132–39.

Angermueller, Hans H. Current Regulatory Framework for Banks' Securities Activities as Viewed by Regulators: Comment. In *Sametz, A. W., ed.*, 1981, pp. 43–45.   [G: U.S.]

Arcuti, Luigi. Dalla regolamentazione alla liberalizzazione del movimento valutario. (From Control to Liberalization of Capital Movements. With English summary.) *Bancaria*, September 1981, 37(9), pp. 891–94.   [G: Italy]

Asay, Michael R.; Gonzalez, Gisela A. and Wolkowitz, Benjamin. Financial Futures, Bank Portfolio Risk, and Accounting. *J. Futures Markets*, Winter 1981, 1(4), pp. 607–18.

Bannock, Graham. The Clearing Banks and Small Firms. *Lloyds Bank Rev.*, October 1981, (142),

pp. 15–25.   [G: U.K.]

Batchelor, Roy A. and Griffiths, Brian. Monetary Restraint through Credit Control in the United Kingdom—The Lessons of Recent Practice. In *Verheirstraeten, A., ed.*, 1981, pp. 195–217.
                                        [G: U.K.]

Batko, William. Proposals for Regulatory Reform in the Consumer Financial Services Sector. In *Heggestad, A. A., ed.*, 1981, pp. 92–123. [G: U.S.]

Beason, Amos T. The Legal, Economic, and Social Case for Banks' Underwriting Municipal Revenue Bonds. In *Sametz, A. W., ed.*, 1981, pp. 123–27.   [G: U.S.]

Beedles, William L. and Buschmann, Nancy K. Describing Bank Equity Returns: The Year-by-Year Record. *J. Money, Credit, Banking*, May 1981, 13(2), pp. 241–47.   [G: U.S.]

Beek, David C. Excess Reserves and Reserve Targeting. *Fed. Res. Bank New York Quart. Rev.*, Autumn 1981, 6(3), pp. 15–22.   [G: U.S.]

Beim, David O. The Public-Policy Case for Private-Placement Services by Commercial Banks. In *Sametz, A. W., ed.*, 1981, pp. 109–13.
                                        [G: U.S.]

Bevan, Robert L. Current Regulatory Framework for Banks' Securities Activities as Viewed by Regulators: Comment. In *Sametz, A. W., ed.*, 1981, pp. 69–71.   [G: U.S.]

Bewley, R. A. The Portfolio Behaviour of the London Clearing Banks: 1963–1971. *Manchester Sch. Econ. Soc. Stud.*, September 1981, 49(3), pp. 191–210.   [G: U.K.]

Bianchi, Tancredi. Sulla lettura dei bilanci bancari. (The Reading of Financial Statements. With English summary.) *Bancaria*, April 1981, 37(4), pp. 386–97.   [G: Italy]

Biederman, Kenneth R. Non-mortgage Lending: Panel Presentation. In *Federal Home Loan Bank of San Francisco.*, 1981, pp. 343–52. [G: U.S.]

Bitros, George C. The Fungibility Factor in Credit and the Question of the Efficacy of Selective Controls. *Oxford Econ. Pap.*, November 1981, 33(3), pp. 459–77.   [G: Greece]

Black, Harold A. and Schweitzer, Robert L. An Analysis of Market Segmentation in Mortgage Lending between a Commercial Bank and a Mutual Savings Bank. *Amer. Real Estate Urban Econ. Assoc. J.*, Fall 1981, 9(3), pp. 234–40.
                                        [G: U.S.]

Boll, Frank. Monetary Restraint through Credit Control in the United Kingdom—The Lessons of Recent Practice: Comment. In *Verheirstraeten, A., ed.*, 1981, pp. 218–19.   [G: U.K.]

Bonds, W. Kenneth. Commingled-Agency Accounts for Bank Trust Departments—An Idea Whose Time Has Come. In *Sametz, A. W., ed.*, 1981, pp. 85–89.   [G: U.S.]

Boyd, John H. and Kwast, Myron L. Bank Regulation and the Efficiency of Financial Intermediation. In *Federal Reserve System*, 1981, pp. 233–49.   [G: U.S.]

Brunner, Karl and Meltzer, Allan H. Time Deposits in the Brunner–Meltzer Model of Asset Markets. *J. Monet. Econ.*, January 1981, 7(1), pp. 129–39.

Bryant, John. Bank Collapse and Depression. *J. Money, Credit, Banking*, November 1981, 13(4),

pp. 454–64. [G: U.S.]

Budd, Alan. Problems of Monetary Targeting in the UK: Comments. In *Griffiths, B. and Wood, G. E., eds.*, 1981, pp. 121–28. [G: U.K.]

Buser, Stephen A.; Chen, Andrew H. and Kane, Edward J. Federal Deposit Insurance, Regulatory Policy, and Optimal Bank Capital. *J. Finance*, March 1981, *36*(1), pp. 51–60. [G: U.S.]

Cagan, Phillip. Comment [The Legal, Economic, and Social Case for Banks' Underwriting Municipal Revenue Bonds] [The Public-Policy Case against Banks' Underwriting Revenue Bonds]. In *Sametz, A. W., ed.*, 1981, pp. 136–38. [G: U.S.]

Caldwell, J. Alexander and Villamil, J. Antonio. Factors Affecting Creditworthiness. In *Ensor, R., ed.*, 1981, pp. 19–25. [G: Iran; Nicaragua; Bolivia; Turkey; Zaire]

Canner, Glenn. The Community Reinvestment Act: A Second Progress Report. *Fed. Res. Bull.*, November 1981, *67*(11), pp. 813–23. [G: U.S.]

Carney, Owen. "The Regulation of Futures and Forward Trading by Depository Institutions: A Legal and Economic Analysis": Comment. *J. Futures Markets*, Summer 1981, *1*(2), pp. 219–23.

Castaldi, Giovanni and Clemente, Claudio. I controlli di vigilanza sugli enti creditizi—II. (Supervisory Controls of Banks in Italy—II. With English summary.) *Bancaria*, September 1981, *37*(9), pp. 918–30. [G: Italy]

Castaldi, Giovanni and Clemente, Claudio. I controlli di vigilanza sugli enti creditizi—I. (Supervisory Controls of Banks. With English summary.) *Bancaria*, August 1981, *37*(8), pp. 797–806. [G: Italy]

Ciampi, Carlo Azeglio. Discrzionalità nell'orientamento del sistema creditizio e tutela dell'imprenditorialità bancaria. (Discretionary Powers in Credit-System Guidelines and Protection of Bankers' Entrepreneurial Capabilities. With English summary.) *Bancaria*, April 1981, *37*(4), pp. 342–47. [G: Italy]

Cingano, Francesco. L'euroscudo nei rapporti bancari. (The E.C.U. in Banking Business. With English summary.) *Bancaria*, March 1981, *37*(3), pp. 254–56. [G: EEC]

Coats, Warren L., Jr. The Weekend Eurodollar Game. *J. Finance*, June 1981, *36*(3), pp. 649–59. [G: U.S.]

Cole, Roger T. Financial Performance of Small Banks, 1977–80. *Fed. Res. Bull.*, June 1981, *67*(6), pp. 480–85. [G: U.S.]

Cooke, Peter. Sviluppi nella cooperazione fra le autorità di vigilanza bancaria. (Developments in Cooperation among Banking Supervisory Authorities. With English summary.) *Bancaria*, June 1981, *37*(6), pp. 578–86. [G: EEC]

Cornyn, Anthony G. and Zearley, Thomas L. Financial Developments of Bank Holding Companies in 1980. *Fed. Res. Bull.*, June 1981, *67*(6), pp. 473–79. [G: U.S.]

Courakis, Anthony S. Banking Policy and Commercial Bank Behaviour in Greece. In *Verheirstraeten, A., ed.*, 1981, pp. 220–63. [G: Greece]

Craine, Roger N. and Pierce, James L. Multivariate Analysis of Interest Rate Risk. In *Maisel, S. J.,* ed., 1981, pp. 271–83. [G: U.S.]

Crawford, Donald J. Current Regulatory Framework for Banks' Securities Activities as Viewed by Regulators: Comment. In *Sametz, A. W., ed.*, 1981, pp. 46–47. [G: U.S.]

Crockett, John H. and Ungar, Meyer. Capital Investment in Commercial Banking Reconsidered. *Rev. Bus. Econ. Res.*, Winter 1981, *16*(2), pp. 76–88. [G: U.S.]

Cummings, F. Jay. The Tyler Decision and the Development of Texas Multibank Holding Companies. *Antitrust Bull.*, Spring 1981, *26*(1), pp. 183–93. [G: U.S.]

Curry, Timothy J. The Pre-Acquisition Characteristics of Banks Acquired by Multibank Holding Companies. *J. Bank Res.*, Summer 1981, *12*(2), pp. 82–89. [G: U.S.]

D'Andrea, Edoardo. L'autonomia delle aziende di credito nella concessione di fidi "eccedenti": un'nalaisi retrospettiva. (On the Autonomy of Banks in Lending beyond the Prescribed Limits: A Retrospective Analysis. With English summary.) *Bancaria*, August 1981, *37*(8), pp. 807–11. [G: Italy]

Dale, Richard S. Prudential Regulation of Multinational Banking: The Problem Outlined. *Nat. Westminster Bank Quart. Rev.*, February 1981, pp. 14–24.

David, Martin. The Transition in Smallholder Banking in Kenya: Evidence from Rural Branch Bank Loans. *J. Devel. Areas*, October 1981, *16*(1), pp. 71–85. [G: Kenya]

Davies, Alun G. The Commonwealth of the Bahamas as a Center of International Business Investment. *Bull. Int. Fiscal Doc.*, April 1981, *35*(4), pp. 165–69. [G: Bahamas]

Davies, David G. Property Rights and Economic Behavior in Private and Government Enterprises: The Case of Australia's Banking System. In *Zerbe, R. O., Jr., ed.*, 1981, pp. 111–42. [G: Australia]

Davis, Kevin. Banks, Thrifts and Interest Rates: Comments: Intermediaries and Interest Rates. In *Jüttner, D. J., ed.*, 1981, pp. 106–13. [G: Australia]

Davis, Robert R. Alternative Techniques for Country Risk Evaluation. *Bus. Econ.*, May 1981, *16*(3), pp. 34–41.

De Grauwe, Paul. Bank Intermediation under Flexible Deposit Rates and Controlled Credit Allocation: The Italian Experience: Comment. In *Verheirstraeten, A., ed.*, 1981, pp. 154–56. [G: Italy]

De Smet, Michel and Martin, Georges. Concentration and Economies of Scale in the Belgian Financial Sector: Comment. In *Verheirstraeten, A., ed.*, 1981, pp. 92–96. [G: Belgium]

Dean, James W. and Giddy, Ian H. Strangers and Neighbors: Cross-Border Banking in North America. *Banca Naz. Lavoro Quart. Rev.*, June 1981, (137), pp. 191–211.

Degamo, Julia Thelma Y. The Rediscount Policy and Its Impact on the Lending Patterns of Commercial Banks and on the Economy. *Philippine Econ. J.*, 1981, *20*(3&4), pp. 311–36. [G: Philippines]

Demattè, Claudio. International Financial Intermediation: Implications for Bankers and Regulators.

Banca Naz. Lavoro Quart. Rev., March 1981, (136), pp. 91–110.

Dini, Lamberto. L'attività creditizia: problemi e metodi di controllo. (The Provision of Credit: Aspects and Methods of Control. With English summary.) *Bancaria*, July 1981, *37*(7), pp. 666–72. [G: Italy]

Dod, David P. Bank Lending to Developing Countries: Recent Developments in Historical Perspective. *Fed. Res. Bull.*, September 1981, *67*(9), pp. 647–56. [G: LDCs]

Doyle, P.; Fenwick, I. and Savage, G. P. A Model for Evaluating Branch Location and Performance. *J. Bank Res.*, Summer 1981, *12*(2), pp. 90–95. [G: U.K.]

Dunham, Constance. Commercial Bank Costs and Correspondent Banking. *New Eng. Econ. Rev.*, September–October 1981, pp. 22–36. [G: U.S.]

Dunkelberg, William C. and De Magistris, Robin. Measuring the Impact of Credit Regulation on Consumers. In *Fed. Res. Bank of Boston and National Sci. Foundation*, 1981, pp. 44–62. [G: U.S.]

Durkin, Thomas A. Discussion [Effects of Creditor Remedies and Rate Restrictions] [Measuring the Impact of Credit Regulation on Consumers]. In *Fed. Res. Bank of Boston and National Sci. Foundation*, 1981, pp. 63–67. [G: U.S.]

Dwyer, Gerald P., Jr. The Effects of the Banking Acts of 1933 and 1935 on Capital Investment in Commercial Banking. *J. Money, Credit, Banking*, May 1981, *13*(2), pp. 192–204. [G: U.S.]

Edgar, Robert J. Banks and Interest Rates. In *Jüttner, D. J., ed.*, 1981, pp. 67–85. [G: Australia]

Edwards, Franklin R. Current Regulatory Framework for Banks' Securities Activities as Viewed by Regulators: Comment. In *Sametz, A. W., ed.*, 1981, pp. 74–76. [G: U.S.]

Edwards, Franklin R. Financial Institutions and Regulation in the 21st Century: After the Crash? In *Verheirstraeten, A., ed.*, 1981, pp. 1–13.

Edwards, Franklin R. The Regulation of Futures and Forward Trading by Depository Institutions: A Legal and Economic Analysis. *J. Futures Markets*, Summer 1981, *1*(2), pp. 201–18.

Eilenberger, Guido. Wachsende Geschäftsvolumina als Problem der Unternehmenspolitik von Banken. (Growing Business Volumes as a Problem of Bank Management Policy. With English summary.) *Kredit Kapital*, 1981, *14*(1), pp. 114–35. [G: W. Germany]

Engler, Rolf. Automation of Payments in the Federal Republic of Germany: Status and Future Prospects. *J. Bank Res.*, Winter 1981, *11*(4), pp. 233–41. [G: W. Germany]

Farrar, Donald E. and Girton, Lance. Institutional Investors and Concentration of Financial Power: Berle and Means Revisited. *J. Finance*, May 1981, *36*(2), pp. 369–81. [G: U.S.]

Feder, Gershon; Just, Richard E. and Ross, Knud. Projecting Debt Servicing Capacity of Developing Countries. *J. Finan. Quant. Anal.*, December 1981, *16*(5), pp. 651–69.

Feldenkirchen, Wilfried. The Banks and the Steel Industry in the Ruhr: Developments in Relations from 1873 to 1914. In *Engels, W. and Pohl, H.,*

eds., 1981, pp. 27–51. [G: W. Germany]

Fieleke, Norman S. Foreign-Currency Positioning by U.S. Firms: Some New Evidence. *Rev. Econ. Statist.*, February 1981, *63*(1), pp. 35–42. [G: U.S.]

Flannery, Mark J. Market Interest Rates and Commercial Bank Profitability: An Empirical Investigation. *J. Finance*, December 1981, *36*(5), pp. 1085–1101. [G: U.S.]

Forster, Edgar. Versicherung, Geld und Wirtschaftswachstum. (Insurance, Money and Economic Growth. With English summary.) *Konjunkturpolitik*, 1981, *27*(2), pp. 89–104.

Frey, Luigi. Verso nuove ricerche in tema di produttività, costi e prezzi nel settore bancario. (Further Research into Banking Productivity, Costs and Prices. With English summary.) *Bancaria*, August 1981, *37*(8), pp. 784–90. [G: W. Europe]

Friedman, Benjamin M. and Froewiss, Kenneth C. More on Bank Behavior: Reply to Van Loo [Bank Behavior in the Brunner–Meltzer Model]. *J. Monet. Econ.*, January 1981, *7*(1), pp. 125–28.

Friedman, Irving S. The Evolution of Country Risk Assessment. In *Ensor, R., ed.*, 1981, pp. 9–15.

Friedman, Stephen J. Rapidly Changing Financial Markets. In *Sametz, A. W., ed.*, 1981, pp. 31–34. [G: U.S.]

Gammaldi, Domenico and Lanciotti, Giulio. Misure alternative dell' "attività internazionale" del sistema bancario italiano 1975–1979. (Alternative Measures for the International Activity of the Italian Banking System, 1975–1979. With English summary.) *Bancaria*, February 1981, *37*(2), pp. 146–51. [G: Italy]

Garil, Barnard H. The Probable Impacts of Expanded Securities and Other Financing Activities of Banks and Securities Firms in the 1980s: Impacts on the Securities Industry. In *Sametz, A. W., ed.*, 1981, pp. 161–64. [G: U.S.]

Gheysens, Lieven. Profitability and Risk of the Belgian Financial Sector: A Stock Market Analysis and a Comparison with Accounting Data. In *Verheirstraeten, A., ed.*, 1981, pp. 97–113. [G: Belgium]

Giddy, Ian H. International Commercial Banking. In *Altman, E. I., ed.*, 1981, pp. 14.3–52.

Giddy, Ian H. Risk and Return in the Eurocurrency Interbank Market. *Greek Econ. Rev.*, August 1981, *3*(2), pp. 158–86. [G: Europe]

Gilbert, R. Alton. Will the Removal of Regulation Q Raise Mortgage Interest Rates? *Fed. Res. Bank St. Louis Rev.*, December 1981, *63*(10), pp. 3–12. [G: U.S.]

Gilliam, Kenneth P. and Hunter, William C. Some Normative Aspects of Bank Loan Commitment Pricing. *Econ. Notes*, 1981, *10*(3), pp. 105–13.

Giroux, Gary; Grossman, Steven and Kratchman, Stanley. What FAS No. 33 Does to Bank Financial Statements. *Manage. Account.*, January 1981, *62*(7), pp. 42–47. [G: U.S.]

Glassman, Cynthia A. The Impact of Banks' Statewide Economic Power on Their Political Power: An Empirical Analysis. *Atlantic Econ. J.*, July 1981, *9*(2), pp. 53–56. [G: U.S.]

Godano, Giuseppe. L'evoluzione della normativa sulle banche estere negli Stati Uniti. (Evolution of Regulations of Foreign Banks in the United States. With English summary.) *Bancaria*, July 1981, *37*(7), pp. 716–25. [G: U.S.]

Goldberg, Lawrence G. and Saunders, Anthony. The Growth of Organizational Forms of Foreign Banks in the U.S.: A Note. *J. Money, Credit, Banking*, August 1981, *13*(3), pp. 365–74. [G: U.S.]

Goldberg, Michael A. The Impact of Regulatory and Monetary Factors on Bank Loan Charges. *J. Finan. Quant. Anal.*, June 1981, *16*(2), pp. 227–46. [G: U.S.]

Golzio, Silvio. L'angusto sentiero delle banche italiane. (The Narrow Path of Italian Banks. With English summary.) *Bancaria*, April 1981, *37*(4), pp. 331–41. [G: Italy]

Goodhart, Charles A. E. Problems of Monetary Management: The U.K. Experience. In *Courakis, A. S., ed.*, 1981, pp. 112–43. [G: U.K.]

Goodhart, Charles A. E. Problems of Monetary Targeting in the UK: Comments. In *Griffiths, B. and Wood, G. E., eds.*, 1981, pp. 129–34. [G: U.K.]

Gradi, Florio. Il problema della liquidità nella gestione e nell'economia della banca. (The Liquidity Aspect in Banking Management. With English summary.) *Bancaria*, July 1981, *37*(7), pp. 684–97.

Graham, Stanley L. Limited Branching in Minnesota: Its Impact on Banking Consumers. *Fed. Res. Bank Minn. Rev.*, Winter 1981, *5*(1), pp. 1–6. [G: U.S.]

Gramley, Lyle E. Statement to Subcommittee on Monopolies and Commercial Law, House Committee on the Judiciary, July 8, 1981. *Fed. Res. Bull.*, July 1981, *67*(7), pp. 555–60. [G: U.S.]

Grassman, Sven. Financial Repression and the Liberalisation Problem within Less-developed Countries: Comments. In *Grassman, S. and Lundberg, E., eds.*, 1981, pp. 387–90. [G: LDCs; MDCs]

Green, Charles. La banca degli anni novanta. (The Bank in Its Nineties. With English summary.) *Mondo Aperto*, February 1981, *35*(1), pp. 11–23. [G: U.K.]

Hanselmann, Guido. Petrodollars and the Banks. In *Burghardt, A. M., ed.*, 1981, pp. 23–36. [G: LDCs; OECD; OPEC]

Hartman, Bart P. and Lee, Johng Y. Influence of Company Debt Burden on Reported Replacement Cost Values. *J. Bank Res.*, Spring 1981, *12*(1), pp. 56–59. [G: U.S.]

Haywood, Charles F. Provision of Consumer Financial Services. In *Heggestad, A. A., ed.*, 1981, pp. 17–61. [G: U.S.]

Haywood, Charles F. Regulation, Structure, and Technological Change in the Consumer Financial Services Industry. In *Heggestad, A. A., ed.*, 1981, pp. 163–67. [G: U.S.]

Haywood, Charles F. Regulation, Technological Change, and Productivity in Commercial Banking. In *Cowing, T. G. and Stevenson, R. E., eds.*, 1981, pp. 283–307. [G: U.S.]

Heggestad, Arnold A. Regulation of Consumer Financial Services: Introduction. In *Heggestad, A. A., ed.*, 1981, pp. 1–16. [G: U.S.]

Heimann, John G. The Probable Impacts of Expanded Securities and Other Financing Activities of Banks and Securities Firms in the 1980s: Impacts on the Regulatory Structure. In *Sametz, A. W., ed.*, 1981, pp. 145–47. [G: U.S.]

Heremans, Dirk. The Complementary Nature of Competition and Regulation in the Financial Sector: Comment. In *Verheirstraeten, A., ed.*, 1981, pp. 32–34.

Ho, Thomas S. Y. and Saunders, Anthony. The Determinants of Bank Interest Margins: Theory and Empirical Evidence. *J. Finan. Quant. Anal.*, November 1981, *16*(4), pp. 581–600. [G: U.S.]

Hogg, Gordon H. J. Payment Systems Developments in New Zealand. *J. Bank Res.*, Winter 1981, *11*(4), pp. 219–22. [G: New Zealand]

Houpt, James V. Performance and Characteristics of Edge Corporations. *Fed. Res. Bull.*, January 1981, *67*(1), pp. 13–14. [G: U.S.]

Humes, Dorla. Foreign Reserves Management in Belize: An Assessment of the Liquidity Constraints in 1979. *Soc. Econ. Stud.*, December 1981, *30*(4), pp. 187–200. [G: Belize]

Humphrey, David Burras. Economies to Scale in Federal Reserve Check Processing Operations. *J. Econometrics*, January 1981, *15*(1), pp. 155–73. [G: U.S.]

Humphrey, David Burras. Scale Economies at Automated Clearinghouses. *J. Bank Res.*, Summer 1981, *12*(2), pp. 71–81. [G: U.S.]

Humphrey, David Burras and Savage, Donald T. Bank Use of Downstreamed Commercial Paper and the Impact of Reserve Requirements in Controlling Liability Usage. *J. Econ. Bus.*, Winter 1981, *33*(2), pp. 109–14. [G: U.S.]

Hunt, Ben F. Rate Sensitivity of Financial Flows: Comment. In *Jüttner, D. J., ed.*, 1981, pp. 171–72. [G: Australia]

Huszti, Ernö. Main Trends in the Development of Socialist Banking Systems and Organization (Relations between the Functions of Issuing [Central] and Credit Banks). *Acta Oecon.*, 1981, *26*(1–2), pp. 71–91. [G: E. Europe]

Jacobs, Klaas Peter. The Probable Impacts of Expanded Securities and Other Financing Activities of Banks and Securities Firms in the 1980s: Impacts on International Banking and Finance. In *Sametz, A. W., ed.*, 1981, pp. 171–78. [G: U.S.; W. Europe]

Jacobson, Robert. Forecasting Bank Portfolios. In *Maisel, S. J., ed.*, 1981, pp. 249–70. [G: U.S.]

James, Christopher. Self-Selection and the Pricing of Bank Services: An Analysis of the Market for Loan Commitments and the Role of Compensating Balance Requirements. *J. Finan. Quant. Anal.*, December 1981, *16*(5), pp. 725–46.

Kalish, Lionel. Application of the "Probable Future Competition" Doctrine to the Commercial Banking and Savings and Loan Industries. *Atlantic Econ. J.*, July 1981, *9*(2), pp. 49–52. [G: U.S.]

Kalish, Lionel. The 'Protest' in the Bank Entry Process. *Public Choice*, 1981, *36*(2), pp. 287–99. [G: U.S.]

Kane, Edward J. Accelerating Inflation, Technological Innovation, and the Decreasing Effectiveness of Banking Regulation. *J. Finance*, May 1981,

36(2), pp. 355–67. [G: U.S.]

Kareken, John H. Commercial Banking as a Line of Commerce: An Appraisal. *Fed. Res. Bank Minn. Rev.*, Winter 1981, *5*(1), pp. 7–13. [G: U.S.]

Kareken, John H. Deregulating Commercial Banks: The Watchword Should Be Caution. *Fed. Res. Bank Minn. Rev.*, Spring-Summer 1981, *5*(2), pp. 1–5. [G: U.S.]

Karmel, Roberta S. Critique of Current Regulatory Approaches to the Separation of Commercial and Investment Banking. In *Sametz, A. W., ed.*, 1981, pp. 23–30. [G: U.S.]

Kaufman, George G. Comment [The Legal, Economic, and Social Case for Banks' Underwriting Municipal Revenue Bonds] [The Public-Policy Case against Banks' Underwriting Revenue Bonds]. In *Sametz, A. W., ed.*, 1981, pp. 138–42. [G: U.S.]

Kearney, Kevin J. The New Payment Technology. *J. Bank Res.*, Winter 1981, *11*(4), pp. 197–99.

Kiernan, Eric. Interest Rate Sensitivity of Financial Flows. In *Jüttner, D. J., ed.*, 1981, pp. 127–43. [G: Australia]

Klein, Hans E. The Impact of Planning on Growth and Profit. *J. Bank Res.*, Summer 1981, *12*(2), pp. 105–09. [G: U.S.]

Kleinheyer, Norbert. Bankenfreihandelszonen in den USA. (Free Banking Zones in the USA. With English summary.) *Kredit Kapital*, 1981, *14*(3), pp. 412–22. [G: U.S.]

Koch, Timothy W. Commercial Bank Size, Relative Profitability and the Demand for Tax-Exempt Securities. *J. Bank Res.*, Autumn 1981, *12*(3), pp. 136–44. [G: U.S.]

Kwast, Myron L. New Minority-Owned Commercial Banks: A Statistical Analysis. *J. Bank Res.*, Spring 1981, *12*(1), pp. 37–45. [G: U.S.]

Lanciotti, Giulio. Una postilla. (A Marginal Note. With English summary.) *Bancaria*, June 1981, *37*(6), pp. 587–88. [G: Italy]

Lane, David and Golen, Lawrence. Some Simulation-Based Estimates of Commercial Bank Deposit Insurance Premiums. In *Maisel, S. J., ed.*, 1981, pp. 341–65. [G: U.S.]

Langohr, Herwig. Banks Borrowing from the Central Bank and Reserve Position Doctrine: Belgium, 1960–1973. *J. Monet. Econ.*, January 1981, *7*(1), pp. 107–24. [G: Belgium]

Langohr, Herwig. Profitability and Risk of the Belgian Financial Sector: A Stock Market Analysis and a Comparison with Accounting Data: Comment. In *Verheirstraeten, A., ed.*, 1981, pp. 114–16. [G: Belgium]

Lawler, Thomas A. Reserve Requirements and the Structure of the CD Market: A Note. *J. Finance*, September 1981, *36*(4), pp. 935–40. [G: U.S.]

Lawrence, Edward C. and Elliehausen, Gregory E. The Impact of Federal Interest Rate Regulations on the Small Saver: Further Evidence. *J. Finance*, June 1981, *36*(3), pp. 677–84. [G: U.S.]

Lerner, Eugene M. The Determinants of Bank Interest Margins: Theory and Empirical Evidence: Discussion. *J. Finan. Quant. Anal.*, November 1981, *16*(4), pp. 601–02.

Levinson, Richard D. Interstate Taxation and Apportionment of Bank Income. *Nat. Tax J.*, December 1981, *34*(4), pp. 447–55. [G: U.S.]

Levitt, Arthur, Jr. The Probable Impacts of Expanded Securities and Other Financing Activities of Banks and Securities Firms in the 1980s: Impacts on the Exchanges. In *Sametz, A. W., ed.*, 1981, pp. 155–56. [G: U.S.]

Lewin, Wayne B. Productivity and the Banking Industry. In *Hogan, J. D. and Craig, A. M., eds.*, Vol. 2, 1981, pp. 1177–83. [G: U.S.]

Lewis, Mervyn K. Interest Rate Sensitivity of Financial Flows: Comments: Interest Rates and Monetary Policy. In *Jüttner, D. J., ed.*, 1981, pp. 173–76. [G: Australia]

Lomax, David F. The Current Account Levy. *Nat. Westminster Bank Quart. Rev.*, May 1981, pp. 2–10. [G: U.K.]

Loomis, Philip C. A Critique of Current Regulatory Procedures in the Municipal Securities Industry. In *Sametz, A. W., ed.*, 1981, pp. 65–69. [G: U.S.]

Luckett, Dudley G. The Future of Banking in the United States: An Application of Institutionalist Economic Theory. *Nebr. J. Econ. Bus.*, Spring 1981, *20*(2), pp. 25–36. [G: U.S.]

Lybecker, Martin E. Comment [Commingled-Agency Accounts for Bank Trust Departments—An Idea Whose Time Has Come] [Preserving Barriers against Banks' Engaging in the Personal-Investment Business]. In *Sametz, A. W., ed.*, 1981, pp. 100–107. [G: U.S.]

Macy, Jonathan R. A Conduct-Oriented Approach to the Glass-Steagall Act. *Yale Law J.*, November 1981, *91*(1), pp. 102–20. [G: U.S.]

Maes, Marcel. Deregulation of Deposit Rate Ceilings in the United States: Prospects and Consequences: Comment. In *Verheirstraeten, A., ed.*, 1981, pp. 52–54. [G: Belgium]

Maged, Mark J. The Probable Impacts of Expanded Securities and Other Financing Activities of Banks and Securities Firms in the 1980s: Impacts on International Banking and Finance. In *Sametz, A. W., ed.*, 1981, pp. 167–71. [G: U.S.; W. Europe]

Maisel, Sherman J. Risk and Capital Adequacy in Banks. In *Fed. Res. Bank of Boston and National Sci. Foundation*, 1981, pp. 203–24. [G: U.S.]

Maisel, Sherman J. Risk and Capital Adequacy in Commercial Banks: Introduction. In *Maisel, S. J., ed.*, 1981, pp. 1–16. [G: U.S.]

Maisel, Sherman J. The Theory and Measurement of Risk and Capital Adequacy. In *Maisel, S. J., ed.*, 1981, pp. 17–183. [G: U.S.]

Maisel, Sherman J. and Jacobson, Robert. Interest Rate Changes and Commercial Bank Revenues and Costs. In *Maisel, S. J., ed.*, 1981, pp. 203–22. [G: U.S.]

Mandell, Lewis; Lachman, Ran and Orgler, Yair. Interpreting the Image of Banking. *J. Bank Res.*, Summer 1981, *12*(2), pp. 96–104.

Marbacher, Josef. Characteristics and Problems of Modern Payment Systems. *J. Bank Res.*, Winter 1981, *11*(4), pp. 206–13.

Martell, Terrence F. and Fitts, Robert L. A Quadratic Discriminant Analysis of Bank Credit Card

User Characteristics. *J. Econ. Bus.*, Winter 1981, 33(2), pp. 153–59. [G: U.S.]

Mattson, Gustav. Penningpolitiska aspekt på konjunkturbilden. (Monetary Policy and the Business Cycle. With English summary.) *Ekon. Samfundets Tidskr.*, 1981, 34(1), pp. 33–34. [G: Finland]

McCabe, George M. and Blackwell, James M. The Hedging Strategy: A New Approach to Spread Management Banking and Commercial Lending. *J. Bank Res.*, Summer 1981, 12(2), pp. 114–18. [G: U.S.]

McCallum, John S. The Empirical Impact of Changes in Government on Bond Yields: The Canadian Provincial Experience. *J. Bank Res.*, Winter 1981, 11(4), pp. 245–47. [G: Canada]

McCulloch, J. Huston. Interest Rate Risk and Capital Adequacy for Traditional Banks and Financial Intermediaries. In *Maisel, S. J., ed.*, 1981, pp. 223–48. [G: U.S.]

McKinnon, Ronald I. Financial Repression and the Liberalisation Problem within Less-developed Countries. In *Grassman, S. and Lundberg, E., eds.*, 1981, pp. 365–86. [G: LDCs; MDCs]

McMahon, Christopher W. L'evoluzione del sistema di intermediazione finanziaria nel Regno Unito. (The Changing Pattern of Financial Intermediation in the United Kingdom during the Seventies. With English summary.) *Bancaria*, October 1981, 37(10), pp. 1014–22. [G: U.K.]

Mehle, Roger W. The Public-Policy Case against Banks' Underwriting Revenue Bonds. In *Sametz, A. W., ed.*, 1981, pp. 129–35. [G: U.S.]

Melton, William C. and Mahr, Jean M. Bankers' Acceptances. *Fed. Res. Bank New York Quart. Rev.*, Summer 1981, 6(2), pp. 39–55. [G: U.S.]

Melton, William C. and Roley, V. Vance. Imperfect Asset Elasticities and Financial Model Building. *J. Econometrics*, January 1981, 15(1), pp. 139–54.

Menell, Howard. Current Regulatory Framework for Banks' Securities Activities as Viewed by Regulators: Comment. In *Sametz, A. W., ed.*, 1981, pp. 76–81. [G: U.S.]

Merton, Robert C. Discussion [Risk and Capital Adequacy in Banks] [Capital Requirements for Entry into Property and Liability Underwriting: An empirical Examination]. In *Fed. Res. Bank of Boston and National Sci. Foundation*, 1981, pp. 256–63. [G: U.S.]

Michaels, Robert and Kalish, Lionel. The Incentives of Regulators: Evidence from Banking. *Public Choice*, 1981, 36(1), pp. 187–92. [G: U.S.]

Mingo, John J. A Comparison of European Housing Finance Systems: Discussion. In *Federal Reserve Bank of Boston (II)*, 1981, pp. 161–63.
[G: France; W. Germany; U.K.]

Mingo, John J. The Economic Impact of Deposit Rate Ceilings. In *Heggestad, A. A., ed.*, 1981, pp. 124–43. [G: U.S.]

Minsky, Hyman P. Financial Markets and Economic Instability, 1965–1980. *Nebr. J. Econ. Bus.*, Autumn 1981, 20(4), pp. 5–16. [G: U.S.]

Mitchell, George W. and Hodgdon, Raymond F. Federal Reserve and the Payments System: Upgrading Electronic Capabilities for the 1980s. *Fed.*

Res. Bull., February 1981, 67(2), pp. 109–16. [G: U.S.]

Monti, Mario and Padoa-Schioppa, Tommaso. Structural Changes and Cyclical Behaviour of the Italian Banking System. In *Courakis, A. S., ed.*, 1981, pp. 217–31. [G: Italy]

Monti, Mario and Porta, Angelo. Bank Intermediation under Flexible Deposit Rates and Controlled Credit Allocation: The Italian Experience. In *Verheirstraeten, A., ed.*, 1981, pp. 117–53.
[G: Italy]

Morrison, Jay B. and Pyle, David H. Interest Rate Risk and the Regulation of Financial Institutions. In *Maisel, S. J., ed.*, 1981, pp. 285–314.
[G: U.S.]

Mortimore, Michael D. The State and Transnational Banks: Lessons from the Bolivian Crisis of External Public Indebtedness. *Cepal Rev.*, August 1981, (14), pp. 127–51. [G: Bolivia]

Moss, David John. The Bank of England and the Country Banks: Birmingham, 1827–33. *Econ. Hist. Rev., 2nd Ser.*, November 1981, 34(4), pp. 540–53. [G: U.K.]

Mukhopadhyay, Arun. Institutional Finance: North-Eastern Region Chapter. *Econ. Aff.*, April–June 1981, 26(2), pp. 104–09. [G: India]

Murphy, Neil B. Commercial Banking. In *Altman, E. I., ed.*, 1981, pp. 6.3–32. [G: U.S.]

Nadauld, Stephen D. Calculating the Present Value of an Asset's Uncertain Future Cash Flows. In *Maisel, S. J., ed.*, 1981, pp. 315–39. [G: U.S.]

Nagy, Pancras. The Use of Quantified Country Risk in Decision Making in Banks. In *Ensor, R., ed.*, 1981, pp. 103–10. [G: Selected Countries]

Opper, Barbara Negri. Profitability of Insured Commercial Banks. *Fed. Res. Bull.*, September 1981, 67(9), pp. 657–69. [G: U.S.]

Opper, Franz F. Current Regulatory Framework for Banks' Securities Activities as Viewed by Regulators: Comment. In *Sametz, A. W., ed.*, 1981, pp. 47–51. [G: U.S.]

Osborne, D. K. and Wendel, Jeanne. A Note on Concentration and Checking Account Prices. *J. Finance*, March 1981, 36(1), pp. 181–86.
[G: U.S.]

Oteri, Carmelo. L'evoluzione degli schemi di controllo pubblico sui dati di bilancio delle aziende di credito. (The Evolution of Methods for Public Control of Commercial Banks' Financial Statements. With English summary.) *Bancaria*, July 1981, 37(7), pp. 673–83. [G: Italy]

Pacolet, Jozef and Verheirstraeten, Albert. Concentration and Economies of Scale in the Belgian Financial Sector. In *Verheirstraeten, A., ed.*, 1981, pp. 55–91. [G: Belgium]

Partee, J. Charles. Statement to Subcommittee on General Oversight and Renegotiation, House Committee on Banking, Finance and Urban Affairs, June 4, 1981. *Fed. Res. Bull.*, June 1981, 67(6), pp. 490–93. [G: U.S.]

Peterson, Richard L. An Investigation of Sex Discrimination in Commercial Banks' Direct Consumer Lending. *Bell J. Econ. (See Rand J. Econ. after 4/85)*, Autumn 1981, 12(2), pp. 547–61.
[G: U.S.]

Peterson, Richard L. and Ginsberg, Michael D.

Determinants of Commercial Bank Auto Loan Rates. *J. Bank Res.*, Spring 1981, *12*(1), pp. 46–55. [G: U.S.]

Phillips, Almarin. Comment [The Public-Policy Case for Private-Placement Services by Commercial Banks] [Banks' Unfair Advantages in Private-Placement Activity]. In *Sametz, A. W., ed.*, 1981, pp. 121–22. [G: U.S.]

Phillips, Almarin. Competition and Regulation in Financial Markets: Concluding Observations. In *Verheirstraeten, A., ed.*, 1981, pp. 267–74.

Phillips, Richard M. Preserving Barriers against Banks' Engaging in the Personal-Investment Business. In *Sametz, A. W., ed.*, 1981, pp. 91–95. [G: U.S.]

Podshivalenko, P. Strengthening the Role of Financial and Credit Levers in Increasing the Effectiveness of Capital Investments. *Prob. Econ.*, February 1981, *23*(10), pp. 78–95. [G: U.S.S.R.]

Pompili, Luigi. Le banche nel sistema valutario italiano. (Banks and the Italian Foreign Exchange Regulation. With English summary.) *Bancaria*, September 1981, *37*(9), pp. 895–907. [G: Italy]

Poole, William. Banks, Thrifts and Interest Rates: Comments. In *Jüttner, D. J., ed.*, 1981, pp. 120–24. [G: Australia]

Pozen, Robert C. A Broad Critique of the Current Regulatory Framework. In *Sametz, A. W., ed.*, 1981, pp. 55–58. [G: U.S.]

Priewasser, Erich. Implementation of OR/MS Models in German Banks. *J. Bank Res.*, Summer 1981, *12*(2), pp. 124–27. [G: W. Germany]

Ratti, Ronald A. Erratum: Bank Attitude toward Risk, Implicit Rates of Interest, and the Behavior of an Index of Risk Aversion for Commercial Banks. *Quart. J. Econ.*, May 1981, *96*(2), pp. 363. [G: U.S.]

Raymond, Robert. Strutture finanziarie, stabilità economica e allocazione delle risorse: il caso della Francia. (Financial Structures, Economic Stability and the Allocation of Resources: The French Example. With English summary.) *Bancaria*, October 1981, *37*(10), pp. 1023–37. [G: France]

Revell, Jack R. S. Gli effetti dei trasferimenti di fondi a mezzo sistemi elettronici nella struttura di un sistema bancario. (The Effects of Electronic Fund-Transfers on the Structure of Banking Systems. With English summary.) *Bancaria*, August 1981, *37*(8), pp. 774–83. [G: W. Europe]

Revell, Jack R. S. The Complementary Nature of Competition and Regulation in the Financial Sector. In *Verheirstraeten, A., ed.*, 1981, pp. 16–31.

Rhoades, Stephen A. Are the Big Banks Big Enough? *Antitrust Bull.*, Summer 1981, *26*(2), pp. 315–25. [G: U.S.]

Rhoades, Stephen A. Does Market Structure Matter in Commercial Banking? *Antitrust Bull.*, Spring 1981, *26*(1), pp. 155–81. [G: U.S.]

Rhoades, Stephen A. Federal Reserve Decisions on Bank Mergers and Acquisitions during the 1970s. *Fed. Res. Bull.*, August 1981, *67*(8), pp. 607. [G: U.S.]

Rhoades, Stephen A. and Rutz, Roger D. A Reexamination and Extension of the Relationship be-

tween Concentration and Firm Rank Stability [Concentration and Firm Stability in Commercial Banking]. *Rev. Econ. Statist.*, August 1981, *63*(3), pp. 446–51. [G: U.S.]

Rhoades, Stephen A. and Savage, Donald T. The Relative Performance of Bank Holding Companies and Branch Banking Systems. *J. Econ. Bus.*, Winter 1981, *33*(2), pp. 132–41. [G: U.S.]

Ribnikar, Ivan. The Yugoslav Monetary System. *ACES Bull. (See Comp. Econ. Stud. after 8/85)*, Spring 1981, *23*(1), pp. 67–78. [G: Yugoslavia]

Rondelli, Lucio. Alcuni aspetti dell'evoluzione delle aziende di credito italiane. (Aspects of the Evolution of Italian Commercial Banks. With English summary.) *Bancaria*, November 1981, *37*(11), pp. 1132–40. [G: Italy]

Rose, John T. and Rutz, Roger D. Organizational Form and Risk in Bank-Affiliated Mortgage Companies: A Note. *J. Money, Credit, Banking*, August 1981, *13*(3), pp. 375–80. [G: U.S.]

Rose, John T. and Savage, Donald T. Bank Holding Company De Novo Entry and Market Share Accumulation. *Antitrust Bull.*, Winter 1981, *26*(4), pp. 753–67. [G: U.S.]

Rose, Peter S. and Scott, William L. A Return-on-Equity Analysis of Eleven Largest U.S. Bank Failures. *Rev. Bus. Econ. Res.*, Winter 1981, *16*(2), pp. 1–11. [G: U.S.]

Rosen, Kenneth T. A Comparison of European Housing Finance Systems. In *Federal Reserve Bank of Boston (II)*, 1981, pp. 144–60. [G: U.K.; W. Germany; France]

Rosenberg, Barr and Perry, Philip R. The Fundamental Determinants of Risk in Banking. In *Maisel, S. J., ed.*, 1981, pp. 367–407. [G: U.S.]

Roussakis, Emmanuel N. Il processo di "internazionalizzazione" delle banche americane. (The Internationalization of U.S. Commercial Banks. With English summary.) *Bancaria*, July 1981, *37*(7), pp. 698–715. [G: U.S.; W. Europe; Japan; Canada]

Rowen, Harvey A. The Probable Impacts of Expanded Securities and Other Financing Activities of Banks and Securities Firms in the 1980s: Impacts on the Securities Industry. In *Sametz, A. W., ed.*, 1981, pp. 164–66. [G: U.S.]

Royama, Shoichi. Deposit-Postal Saving Rate Setting and Monetary Policy: A Political Economy of Interest Rates Regulation. (In Japanese. With English summary.) *Osaka Econ. Pap.*, December 1981, *31*(2–3), pp. 121–31. [G: Japan]

Ruding, H. O. Co-ordinating IMF and Commercial Bank Policies. In *Ensor, R., ed.*, 1981, pp. 149–52.

Rudolph, Bernd. Ein dynamisches Modell der Kreditbeziehungen zwischen einer Bank und ihren Kreditnehmern. (A Dynamic Model of Credit Relations between a Bank and Its Borrowers. With English summary.) *Kredit Kapital*, 1981, *14*(1), pp. 94–113.

Ruozi, Roberto. L'attività internazionale delle banche italiane. (Italian Banks' International Business. With English summary.) *Bancaria*, February 1981, *37*(2), pp. 140–45. [G: Italy]

Ruta, Guido. Risparmio e depositi nel sistema della legislazione bancaria. (Banking Legislation Relating to Savings and Deposits in Italy. With English summary.) *Bancaria*, May 1981, *37*(5), pp. 443–53. [G: Italy]

Ryan, John E. Statement to Subcommittee on General Oversight and Renegotiation, House Committee on Banking, Finance and Urban Affairs, July 21, 1981. *Fed. Res. Bull.*, August 1981, *67*(8), pp. 620–22. [G: U.S.]

Sacerdote, Peter M. Banks' Unfair Advantages in Private-Placement Activity. In *Sametz, A. W., ed.*, 1981, pp. 115–19. [G: U.S.]

Saito, Katrine Anderson and Villanueva, Delano P. Transaction Costs of Credit to the Small-Scale Sector in the Philippines. *Econ. Develop. Cult. Change*, April 1981, *29*(3), pp. 631–40.
[G: Philippines]

Sametz, A. W. Impact of Regulation on Economic Behavior: Discussion. *J. Finance*, May 1981, *36*(2), pp. 393–95.

Sametz, Arnold W. Background of the Controversy over Banks' Securities Activities—A Briefing. In *Sametz, A. W., ed.*, 1981, pp. 3–19. [G: U.S.]

Sametz, Arnold W. Comment [The Public-Policy Case for Private-Placement Services by Commercial Banks] [Banks' Unfair Advantages in Private-Placement Activity]. In *Sametz, A. W., ed.*, 1981, pp. 119–21. [G: U.S.]

Santomero, Anthony M. Comment [Commingled-Agency Accounts for Bank Trust Departments—An Idea Whose Time Has Come] [Preserving Barriers against Banks' Engaging in the Personal-Investment Business]. In *Sametz, A. W., ed.*, 1981, pp. 95–100. [G: U.S.]

Santomero, Anthony M. and Siegel, Jeremy J. Bank Regulation and Macro-Economic Stability. *Amer. Econ. Rev.*, March 1981, *71*(1), pp. 39–53.

Sargent, J. R. Problems of Monetary Targeting in the UK. In *Griffiths, B. and Wood, G. E., eds.*, 1981, pp. 95–120. [G: U.K.]

Scheiner, James H. Income Smoothing: An Analysis in the Banking Industry. *J. Bank Res.*, Summer 1981, *12*(2), pp. 119–23. [G: U.S.]

Schmidt, Hartmut. Wege zur Ermittlung und Beurteilung der Marktzinsrisiken von Banken. (Towards the Determination and Assessment of Market Interest Risks of Banks. With English summary.) *Kredit Kapital*, 1981, *14*(3), pp. 249–86. [G: W. Germany]

Schönwitz, Dietrich. Zunehmende Unternehmenskonzentration in der Bundesrepublik Deutschland: Zur bankbetrieblichen Bedeutung des dritten Hauptgutachtens der Monopolkommission. (Increasing Business Concentration in the Federal Republic of Germany: On the Significance of the Third Major Opinion of the Monopoly Commission for Banking. With English summary.) *Kredit Kapital*, 1981, *14*(2), pp. 222–35.
[G: W. Germany]

Schott, Francis H. The Probable Impacts of Expanded Securities and Other Financing Activities of Banks and Securities Firms in the 1980s: Impacts on Financing Nonfinancial Business. In *Sametz, A. W., ed.*, 1981, pp. 179–81.
[G: U.S.]

Schultz, Frederick H. Statement to Senate Committee on Banking, Housing, and Urban Affairs, April 28, 1981. *Fed. Res. Bull.*, May 1981, *67*(5), pp. 419–24. [G: U.S.]

Selby, Edward B., Jr. The Role of Director Deposits in New Bank Growth. *J. Bank Res.*, Spring 1981, *12*(1), pp. 60–61. [G: U.S.]

Sharpe, W. F. Bank Capital Adequacy, Deposit Insurance, and Security Values. In *Maisel, S. J., ed.*, 1981, *1978*, pp. 187–202.

Shay, Robert P. and Brandt, William K. Public Regulation of Financial Services: The Truth in Lending Act. In *Heggestad, A. A., ed.*, 1981, pp. 168–207. [G: U.S.]

Shay, Robert P.; Brandt, William K. and Sexton, Donald E., Jr. Public Regulation of Financial Services: The Equal Credit Opportunity Act. In *Heggestad, A. A., ed.*, 1981, pp. 208–39.
[G: U.S.]

Siaens, Alain. Government Intervention in the French Financial System: Comment. In *Verheirstraeten, A., ed.*, 1981, pp. 173–74.
[G: France]

Siebert, Muriel. The Probable Impacts of Expanded Securities and Other Financing Activities of Banks and Securities Firms in the 1980s: Impacts on the Regulatory Structure. In *Sametz, A. W., ed.*, 1981, pp. 147–51. [G: U.S.]

Siegel, Jeremy J. Bank Reserves and Financial Stability. *J. Finance*, December 1981, *36*(5), pp. 1073–84. [G: U.S.]

Siegel, Jeremy J. Inflation, Bank Profits, and Government Seigniorage. *Amer. Econ. Rev.*, May 1981, *71*(2), pp. 352–55.

Singh, Bhagwan Prasad. Commercial Banks in Rural India: Bihar's Relative Position. In *Karna, M. N., ed.*, 1981, pp. 57–85. [G: India]

Smiley, Gene. Regional Variation in Bank Loan Rates in the Interwar Years. *J. Econ. Hist.*, December 1981, *41*(4), pp. 889–901. [G: U.S.]

Smith, William M. The Probable Impacts of Expanded Securities and Other Financing Activities of Banks and Securities Firms in the 1980s: Impacts on the Exchanges. In *Sametz, A. W., ed.*, 1981, pp. 156–59. [G: U.S.]

Soleil, M. A New Payment Technique: The Memory Card. *J. Bank Res.*, Winter 1981, *11*(4), pp. 214–18. [G: France]

Spellman, Lewis J. Commercial Banks and the Profits of Savings and Loan Markets. *J. Bank Res.*, Spring 1981, *12*(1), pp. 32–36. [G: U.S.]

Spencer, Roger W. Rationale of Current Regulatory Approaches to Banks' Securities Activities. In *Sametz, A. W., ed.*, 1981, pp. 35–43. [G: U.S.]

Sprenkle, Case M. and Stanhouse, Bryan E. A Theoretical Framework for Evaluating the Impact of Universal Reserve Requirements. *J. Finance*, September 1981, *36*(4), pp. 825–40. [G: U.S.]

Starke, Wolfgang. Payment Methods of the Future. *J. Bank Res.*, Winter 1981, *11*(4), pp. 223–26.

Startz, Richard. Implicit Interest on Demand Deposits: Reply. *J. Monet. Econ.*, May 1981, *7*(3), pp. 403–04. [G: U.S.]

Stauffer, Robert F. The Bank Failures of 1930–31: A Comment. *J. Money, Credit, Banking*, February 1981, *13*(1), pp. 109–13. [G: U.S.]

Stiglitz, Joseph E. and Weiss, Andrew. Credit Rationing in Markets with Imperfect Information.

Amer. Econ. Rev., June 1981, *71*(3), pp. 393–410.

Taggart, Robert A., Jr. Deregulation of Deposit Rate Ceilings in the United States: Prospects and Consequences. In *Verheirstraeten, A., ed.*, 1981, pp. 35–51. [G: U.S.]

Teeters, Nancy H. Statement to Subcommittee on Consumer Affairs and Coinage of the House Committee on Banking, Finance, and Urban Affairs, October 21, 1981. *Fed. Res. Bull.*, November 1981, *67*(11), pp. 826–28. [G: U.S.]

Teeters, Nancy H. Statement to Subcommittee on Financial Institutions, Senate Committee on Banking, Housing, and Urban Affairs, July 21, 1981. *Fed. Res. Bull.*, August 1981, *67*(8), pp. 618–20. [G: U.S.]

Teriba, O. Financial Institutions, Financial Markets, and Income Distribution. In *Bienen, H. and Diejomaoh, V. P., eds.*, 1981, pp. 485–512. [G: Nigeria]

Tinic, S. M. Impact of Regulation on Economic Behavior: Discussion. *J. Finance*, May 1981, *36*(2), pp. 395–97.

Tinsley, P. A.; Garrett, Bonnie and Friar, Monica. An Exposé of Disguised Deposits. *J. Econometrics*, January 1981, *15*(1), pp. 117–37. [G: U.S.]

Trebing, Michael E. The New Bank-Thrift Competition: Will It Affect Bank Acquisition and Merger Analysis? *Fed. Res. Bank St. Louis Rev.*, February 1981, *63*(2), pp. 3–11. [G: U.S.]

Trepeta, Warren T. Changes in Bank Lending Practices, 1979–81. *Fed. Res. Bull.*, September 1981, *67*(9), pp. 671–86. [G: U.S.]

Trotman, K. T.; Yetton, Philip W. and Zimmer, I. Group Size and Performance: Prediction of Failure by Loan Officers [Correction]. *Australian J. Manage.*, December 1981, *6*(2), pp. 127–36. [G: Australia]

Trotman, K. T.; Yetton, Philip W. and Zimmer, I. Group Size and Performance: Prediction of Failure by Loan Officers. *Australian J. Manage.*, June 1981, *6*(1), pp. 137–43. [G: Australia]

Tunney, Joseph J. Bank Perspectives in Measuring Risk. In *Ensor, R., ed.*, 1981, pp. 83–85.

Verplaetse, Alfons. Financial Institutions and Regulation in the 21st Century: After the Crash?: Comment. In *Verheirstraeten, A., ed.*, 1981, pp. 14–15.

Vila, Gérard. Banking Policy and Commercial Bank Behaviour in Greece: Comment. In *Verheirstraeten, A., ed.*, 1981, pp. 264–66. [G: Greece]

Vogel, Robert C. Rural Financial Market Performance: Implications of Low Delinquency Rates. *Amer. J. Agr. Econ.*, February 1981, *63*(1), pp. 58–65. [G: Costa Rica]

Volcker, Paul A. Statement to Senate Committee on Banking, Housing, and Urban Affairs, October 29, 1981. *Fed. Res. Bull.*, November 1981, *67*(11), pp. 835–45. [G: U.S.]

Wallich, Henry C. Le banche americane durante gli anni Settanta ed oltre. (American Banks during the Seventies and Beyond. With English summary.) *Bancaria*, October 1981, *37*(10), pp. 1005–13. [G: U.S.]

Wallich, Henry C. Statement to Commerce, Consumer, and Monetary Affairs Subcommittee of the House Committee on Government Operations, September 23, 1981. *Fed. Res. Bull.*, October 1981, *67*(10), pp. 769–74. [G: U.S.; OPEC]

Wallich, Henry C. Statement to Subcommittee on International Finance and Monetary Policy, Senate Committee on Banking, Housing, and Urban Affairs, February 17, 1981. *Fed. Res. Bull.*, March 1981, *67*(3), pp. 233–35. [G: U.S.]

Wallich, Henry C. The Probable Impacts of Expanded Securities and Other Financing Activities of Banks and Securities Firms in the 1980s: Impacts on the Regulatory Structure. In *Sametz, A. W., ed.*, 1981, pp. 151–54. [G: U.S.]

Wessels, G. M. Depositokoersbeheer as Monetêre Beheermaatreël. (With English summary.) *S. Afr. J. Econ.*, June 1981, *49*(2), pp. 130–44. [G: S. Africa]

White, Betsy Buttrill. Monetary Policy without Regulation Q. *Fed. Res. Bank New York Quart. Rev.*, Winter 1981–82, *6*(4), pp. 4–8. [G: U.S.]

White, George C., Jr. Developments in United States Payment Systems. *J. Bank Res.*, Winter 1981, *11*(4), pp. 200–205. [G: U.S.]

White, Lawrence J. Current Regulatory Framework for Banks' Securities Activities as Viewed by Regulators: Comment. In *Sametz, A. W., ed.*, 1981, pp. 51–54. [G: U.S.]

Williamson, J. M. Pricing Money Transfer Services. *J. Bank Res.*, Winter 1981, *11*(4), pp. 227–32.

Wilson, Dick. Come operano le banche cinesi. (The Chinese Banking System. With English summary.) *Mondo Aperto*, June–August 1981, *35*(3–4), pp. 177–88. [G: China]

Withers, Glenn. Efficiency Gains from Banking Deregulation. *Australian Econ. Rev.*, 1st Quarter 1981, (53), pp. 35–40. [G: Australia]

Zimmerman, Gary C. The Pricing of Federal Reserve Services under MCA. *Fed. Res. Bank San Francisco Econ. Rev.*, Winter 1981, pp. 22–40. [G: U.S.]

313 Capital Markets

3130 General

Adler, Michael. Investor Recognition of Corporation International Diversification: Comment. *J. Finance*, March 1981, *36*(1), pp. 187–90.

Aftalion, Florin. Government Intervention in the French Financial System. In *Verheirstraeten, A., ed.*, 1981, pp. 157–72. [G: France]

Agmon, Tamir and Lessard, Donald R. Investor Recognition of Corporate International Diversification: Reply. *J. Finance*, March 1981, *36*(1), pp. 191–92.

Allen, Franklin. The Prevention of Default. *J. Finance*, May 1981, *36*(2), pp. 271–76.

Beaver, William H. Econometric Properties of Alternative Security Return Methods. *J. Acc. Res.*, Spring 1981, *19*(1), pp. 163–84.

Bidwell, Clinton M., III. SUE/PE Revista. *J. Portfol. Manage.*, Winter 1981, *7*(2), pp. 85–87.

Bowman, Robert G. The Theoretical Relationship between Systematic Risk and Financial (Accounting) Variables: Reply. *J. Finance*, June 1981, *36*(3), pp. 749–50.

Bruni, Franco and Porta, Angelo. Allocazione delle risorse e inflazione: Il caso dei mercati finanziari. (Inflation and Resource Allocation: The Case of Financial Markets. With English summary.) *Econ. Int.*, May–August–November 1981, *34*(2–3–4), pp. 261–321. [G: Italy]

Buss, James A. and Buss, William E. A Note on the Economic Impact from the Financed Capitalist Plan. In *Zerbe, R. O., Jr., ed.*, 1981, pp. 227–39.

Caks, John. The Pricing of Premium Bonds: Comment. *J. Finan. Quant. Anal.*, September 1981, *16*(3), pp. 397–401. [G: U.S.]

Carman, Peter. The Trouble with Asset Allocation. *J. Portfol. Manage.*, Fall 1981, *8*(1), pp. 17–22. [G: U.S.]

Chen, Son-Nan. Beta Nonstationarity, Portfolio Residual Risk and Diversification. *J. Finan. Quant. Anal.*, March 1981, *16*(1), pp. 95–111. [G: U.S.]

Chen, Son-Nan and Keown, Arthur J. An Examination of the Relationship between Pure Residual and Market Risk: A Note. *J. Finance*, December 1981, *36*(5), pp. 1203–09. [G: U.S.]

Cornell, Bradford and Roll, Richard. Strategies for Pairwise Competitions in Markets and Organizations. *Bell J. Econ. (See Rand J. Econ. after 4/85)*, Spring 1981, *12*(1), pp. 201–13.

Curley, Anthony J. GNMA Passthrough Securities: Discussion. *J. Finance*, May 1981, *36*(2), pp. 486–87.

Davis, Kevin. Banks, Thrifts and Interest Rates: Comments: Intermediaries and Interest Rates. In *Jüttner, D. J., ed.*, 1981, pp. 106–13. [G: Australia]

De Grauwe, Paul. Bank Intermediation under Flexible Deposit Rates and Controlled Credit Allocation: The Italian Experience: Comment. In *Verheirstraeten, A., ed.*, 1981, pp. 154–56. [G: Italy]

Dufey, Gunter. International Capital Markets: Structure and Response in an Era of Instability. *Sloan Manage. Rev.*, Spring 1981, *22*(3), pp. 35–45.

Dunn, Kenneth B. and McConnell, John J. A Comparison of Alternative Models for Pricing GNMA Mortgage-Backed Securities. *J. Finance*, May 1981, *36*(2), pp. 471–84. [G: U.S.]

Dunn, Kenneth B. and McConnell, John J. Valuation of GNMA Mortgage-Backed Securities. *J. Finance*, June 1981, *36*(3), pp. 599–616. [G: U.S.]

Edwards, Franklin R. Financial Institutions and Regulation in the 21st Century: After the Crash? In *Verheirstraeten, A., ed.*, 1981, pp. 1–13.

Elstone, Robert G. Interest Rates and Thrift Institutions. In *Jüttner, D. J., ed.*, 1981, pp. 86–105. [G: Australia]

Enzler, Jared J.; Conrad, William E. and Johnson, Lewis. Public Policy and Capital Formation. *Fed. Res. Bull.*, October 1981, *67*(10), pp. 749–61. [G: U.S.]

Feldstein, Martin S. and Seligman, Stephanie. Pension Funding, Share Prices, and National Savings. *J. Finance*, September 1981, *36*(4), pp. 801–24. [G: U.S.]

Frankle, Alan W. and Hawkins, Clark A. Characteristics of Temporal Price Behavior of Long-Term

Corporate Bonds. *Rev. Bus. Econ. Res.*, Winter 1981, *16*(2), pp. 43–55. [G: U.S.]

Fry, Maxwell J. Inflation and Economic Growth in Pacific Basin Developing Economies. *Fed. Res. Bank San Francisco Econ. Rev.*, Fall 1981, pp. 8–18. [G: LDCs]

Gibbons, Michael R. and Hess, Patrick. Day of the Week Effects and Asset Returns. *J. Bus.*, October 1981, *54*(4), pp. 579–96.

Goldberg, Michael A. and Vora, Ashok. The Inconsistency of the Relationship between Security and Market Returns. *J. Econ. Bus.*, Winter 1981, *33*(2), pp. 97–107. [G: U.S.]

Goldie, Raymond and Ambachtsheer, Keith P. The Battle of Insider Trading vs. Market Efficiency: Comment. *J. Portfol. Manage.*, Winter 1981, *7*(2), pp. 88. [G: U.S.]

Gupta, Sanjeev. A Note on the Efficiency of Black Markets in Foreign Currencies. *J. Finance*, June 1981, *36*(3), pp. 705–10. [G: India; S. Korea; Taiwan]

Healy, James P. and Piderit, John J. The Time Series Properties of the Spot Exchange Rate: A Multiple Input Transfer Function. *J. Econ. Devel.*, July 1981, *6*(1), pp. 47–76. [G: U.S.]

Heremans, Dirk. The Complementary Nature of Competition and Regulation in the Financial Sector: Comment. In *Verheirstraeten, A., ed.*, 1981, pp. 32–34.

Howenstine, E. Jay. Private Rental Housing Abroad: Dwindling Supply Stirs Concern. *Mon. Lab. Rev.*, September 1981, *104*(9), pp. 38–42. [G: W. Europe; N. America; Japan]

Jacque, Laurent L. Management of Foreign Exchange Risk: A Review Article. *J. Int. Bus. Stud.*, Spring/Summer 1981, *12*(1), pp. 81–101.

Kim, Kee S. The Theoretical Relationship between Systematic Risk and Financial (Accounting) Variables: Comment. *J. Finance*, June 1981, *36*(3), pp. 747–48.

Kindleberger, Charles P. Quantity and Price, Especially in Financial Markets. In *Kindleberger, C. P.*, 1981, *1975*, pp. 256–68.

Lamfalussy, Alexandre. Introduzione al tema. (Introductory Paper and Verbal Statement. With English summary.) *Bancaria*, October 1981, *37*(10), pp. 988–1004. [G: U.S.; W. Europe; Japan]

Latané, Henry A. The CAPM and the Investment Horizon: Comment. *J. Portfol. Manage.*, Fall 1981, *8*(1), pp. 64–65. [G: U.S.]

Lawson, G. H. and Stark, A. W. Equity Values and Inflation: Dividends and Debt Financing. *Lloyds Bank Rev.*, January 1981, (139), pp. 40–54. [G: U.K.]

Lawson, G. H. and Stark, A. W. Equity Values and Inflation: A Rejoinder. *Lloyds Bank Rev.*, October 1981, (142), pp. 39–43. [G: U.K.]

Levy, Haim. The CAPM and the Investment Horizon. *J. Portfol. Manage.*, Winter 1981, *7*(2), pp. 32–40. [G: U.S.]

Livingston, Miles. The Pricing of Premium Bonds: Reply. *J. Finan. Quant. Anal.*, September 1981, *16*(3), pp. 403–06. [G: U.S.]

Maes, Marcel. Deregulation of Deposit Rate Ceilings in the United States: Prospects and Consequences: Comment. In *Verheirstraeten, A., ed.*,

1981, pp. 52–54. [G: Belgium]

McMahon, Christopher W. L'evoluzione del sistema di intermediazione finanziaria nel Regno Unito. (The Changing Pattern of Financial Intermediation in the United Kingdom during the Seventies. With English summary.) *Bancaria*, October 1981, *37*(10), pp. 1014–22. [G: U.K.]

McWilliams, James D. and Wei, James. Some Like To-matoes and Some Like To-mätoes. *J. Portfol. Manage.*, Summer 1981, *7*(4), pp. 43–47. [G: U.S.]

Monti, Mario and Porta, Angelo. Bank Intermediation under Flexible Deposit Rates and Controlled Credit Allocation: The Italian Experience. In *Verheirstraeten, A., ed.*, 1981, pp. 117–53. [G: Italy]

Moore, Basil J. Equity Values and Inflation: Reply. *Lloyds Bank Rev.*, October 1981, (142), pp. 44–45. [G: U.K.]

Moore, Basil J. Equity Values and Inflation: Reply. *Lloyds Bank Rev.*, January 1981, (139), pp. 55–57.

Morrison, Jay B. and Pyle, David H. Interest Rate Risk and the Regulation of Financial Institutions. In *Maisel, S. J., ed.*, 1981, pp. 285–314. [G: U.S.]

Murthy, N. R. Vasudeva. Fiscal Policy and Government Savings in a Developing Economy: Some Empirical Evidence in the Indian Economy. *Bull. Int. Fiscal Doc.*, March 1981, *35*(3), pp. 120–25. [G: India]

Nakamura, Toru. Productivity Losses through Capital Misallocation in the U.S., Japan, and West Germany. *Quart. Rev. Econ. Bus.*, Autumn 1981, *21*(3), pp. 65–76. [G: W. Germany; Japan; U.S.]

Oppenheimer, Henry R. and Schlarbaum, Gary G. Investing with Ben Graham: An Ex Ante Test of the Efficient Markets Hypothesis. *J. Finan. Quant. Anal.*, September 1981, *16*(3), pp. 341–60. [G: U.S.]

Phillips, Almarin. Competition and Regulation in Financial Markets: Concluding Observations. In *Verheirstraeten, A., ed.*, 1981, pp. 267–74.

Poole, William. Banks, Thrifts and Interest Rates: Comments. In *Jüttner, D. J., ed.*, 1981, pp. 120–24. [G: Australia]

Raymond, Robert. Strutture finanziarie, stabilità economica e allocazione delle risorse: il caso della Francia. (Financial Structures, Economic Stability and the Allocation of Resources: The French Example. With English summary.) *Bancaria*, October 1981, *37*(10), pp. 1023–37. [G: France]

Revell, Jack R. S. The Complementary Nature of Competition and Regulation in the Financial Sector. In *Verheirstraeten, A., ed.*, 1981, pp. 16–31.

Sametz, Arnold W. The "New" Financial Environment. In *Altman, E. I., ed.*, 1981, pp. I3–I10. [G: U.S.]

Schipper, Katherine and Thompson, Rex. Common Stocks as Hedges against Shifts in the Consumption or Investment Opportunity Set. *J. Bus.*, April 1981, *54*(2), pp. 305–28. [G: U.S.]

Shah, Anup R. Imperfections in the Capital Markets and Consumer Behavior. *Southern Econ. J.*, April

1981, *47*(4), pp. 1032–45.

Sharpe, W. F. Decentralized Investment Management. *J. Finance*, May 1981, *36*(2), pp. 217–34.

Shiller, Robert J. Do Stock Prices Move Too Much to be Justified by Subsequent Changes in Dividends? *Amer. Econ. Rev.*, June 1981, *71*(3), pp. 421–36.

Siaens, Alain. Government Intervention in the French Financial System: Comment. In *Verheirstraeten, A., ed.*, 1981, pp. 173–74. [G: France]

Smith, James H., Jr. The Monetary Base and Interest Rates. *J. Portfol. Manage.*, Fall 1981, *8*(1), pp. 56–60. [G: U.S.]

Statman, Meir. Betas Compared: Merrill Lynch vs. Value Line. *J. Portfol. Manage.*, Winter 1981, *7*(2), pp. 41–44. [G: U.S.]

Summers, Lawrence H. Taxation and Corporate Investment: A *q*-Theory Approach. *Brookings Pap. Econ. Act.*, 1981, (1), pp. 67–127.

Taggart, Robert A., Jr. Deregulation of Deposit Rate Ceilings in the United States: Prospects and Consequences. In *Verheirstraeten, A., ed.*, 1981, pp. 35–51. [G: U.S.]

Tauber, Ronald S. Is Gold a Prudent Investment under ERISA? *J. Portfol. Manage.*, Fall 1981, *8*(1), pp. 28–31. [G: U.S.]

Tsung, Stephen. Interest Rates and Thrift Institutions: Comments. In *Jüttner, D. J., ed.*, 1981, pp. 114–19. [G: Australia]

Verplaetse, Alfons. Financial Institutions and Regulation in the 21st Century: After the Crash?: Comment. In *Verheirstraeten, A., ed.*, 1981, pp. 14–15.

Weiss, Stanley and McCarthy, Phillip A. Summary of Final Regulations on Treatment of Certain Interests in Corporations as Stock or Debt. *Bull. Int. Fiscal Doc.*, June 1981, *35*(6), pp. 272–76. [G: U.S.]

3131 Capital Markets: Theory, Including Portfolio Selection, and Empirical Studies Illustrating Theory

Anderson, Ronald. "Margins and Futures Contracts": Comment. *J. Futures Markets*, Summer 1981, *1*(2), pp. 259–64.

Anderson, Ronald W. and Danthine, Jean-Pierre. Cross Hedging. *J. Polit. Econ.*, December 1981, *89*(6), pp. 1182–96.

Apel, Emmanuel. Une méthode asymptotique pour tester la validité du modèle d'équilibre d'actifs financiers (MEDAF) avec pour exemple la bourse de Paris. (An Asymptotic Method to Test the Validity of the Capital Asset Pricing Model (CAPM) with the Paris Stock Exchange as an Example. With English summary.) *L'Actual. Econ.*, April–June 1981, *57*(2), pp. 225–43. [G: France]

Arzac, Enrique R.; Schwartz, Robert A. and Whitcomb, David K. A Theory and Test of Credit Rationing: Some Further Results. *Amer. Econ. Rev.*, September 1981, *71*(4), pp. 735–37.

Arzac, Enrique R.; Schwartz, Robert A. and Whitcomb, David K. The Leverage Structure of Interest Rates. *J. Money, Credit, Banking*, February 1981, *13*(1), pp. 72–88.

Ballentine, J. Gregory. Corporation Finance: Comments. In *Aaron, H. J. and Pechman, J. A., eds.*, 1981, pp. 192–96. [G: U.S.]

Barnea, Amir; Haugen, Robert A. and Senbet, Lemma W. An Equilibrium Analysis of Debt Financing under Costly Tax Arbitrage and Agency Problems. *J. Finance*, June 1981, *36*(3), pp. 569–81.

Barro, Robert J. A Capital Market in an Equilibrium Business Cycle Model. In *Barro, R. J.*, 1981, *1980*, pp. 111–36.

Bearman, Arlene Erlich and Kuhn, Betsey Epstein. A Test of Efficiency: Cash versus Futures Markets. *J. Portfol. Manage.*, Fall 1981, *8*(1), pp. 44–49. [G: U.S.]

Beaver, William H. Market Efficiency. *Accounting Rev.*, January 1981, *56*(1), pp. 23–37.

Ben-Horim, Moshe. Alternative Estimators of Rates of Return Distribution Parameters of Financial Assets. In *Levy, H., ed.*, 1981, pp. 157–77.

Bensoussan, Claude. Comportements comparés des marchés boursiers (1974–1979). (Stock Markets Behaviour (1974–1979). With English summary.) *L'Actual. Econ.*, April–June 1981, *57*(2), pp. 244–58. [G: W. Europe; N. America; Japan; U.K.; Australia]

Bewley, R. A. The Portfolio Behaviour of the London Clearing Banks: 1963–1971. *Manchester Sch. Econ. Soc. Stud.*, September 1981, *49*(3), pp. 191–210. [G: U.K.]

Bhattacharya, Sudipto. Notes on Multiperiod Valuation and the Pricing of Options. *J. Finance*, March 1981, *36*(1), pp. 163–80.

Bierwag, G. O., et al. The Art of Risk Management in Bond Portfolios. *J. Portfol. Manage.*, Spring 1981, *7*(3), pp. 27–36. [G: U.S.]

Biger, Nahum. An Analytical Examination of Real versus Nominal Rates of Return Matrices in Portfolio Management: A Comment. *J. Econ. Bus.*, Winter 1981, *33*(2), pp. 172–73.

Bildersee, John S. and Roberts, Gordon S. Beta Instability When Interest Rate Levels Change. *J. Finan. Quant. Anal.*, September 1981, *16*(3), pp. 375–80.

Blanchard, Olivier J. Output, the Stock Market, and Interest Rates. *Amer. Econ. Rev.*, March 1981, *71*(1), pp. 132–43.

Bookstaber, Richard M. and Clarke, Roger. Options Can Alter Portfolio Return Distributions. *J. Portfol. Manage.*, Spring 1981, *7*(3), pp. 63–70.

Boughton, James M. Money and Its Substitutes. *J. Monet. Econ.*, November 1981, *8*(3), pp. 375–86. [G: U.S.]

Bray, Margaret M. Futures Trading, Rational Expectations, and the Efficient Markets Hypothesis. *Econometrica*, May 1981, *49*(3), pp. 575–96.

Brennan, M. J. Empirical Tests of Multi-Factor Pricing Model: Discussion. *J. Finance*, May 1981, *36*(2), pp. 352–53.

Brennan, M. J. and Solanki, R. Optimal Portfolio Insurance. *J. Finan. Quant. Anal.*, September 1981, *16*(3), pp. 279–300.

Brinner, Roger E. and Brooks, Stephen H. Stock Prices. In *Aaron, H. J. and Pechman, J. A., eds.*, 1981, pp. 199–238. [G: U.S.]

Burghardt, Galen, Jr. and Kohn, Donald L. "Mar-

gins and Futures Contracts": Comment. *J. Futures Markets*, Summer 1981, *1*(2), pp. 255–57. [G: U.S.]

Callier, Philippe. One Way Arbitrage, Foreign Exchange and Securities Markets: A Note. *J. Finance*, December 1981, *36*(5), pp. 1177–86.

Camp, Robert C. and Eubank, Arthur A., Jr. The Beta Quotient: A New Measure of Portfolio Risk. *J. Portfol. Manage.*, Summer 1981, *7*(4), pp. 53–57.

Campbell, Tim S. and Kracaw, William A. Sorting Equilibria in Financial Markets: The Incentive Problem. *J. Finan. Quant. Anal.*, November 1981, *16*(4), pp. 477–92.

Canarella, Giorgio and Garston, Neil. Money, Expectations, and Interest Rates. *J. Macroecon.*, Fall 1981, *3*(4), pp. 517–30. [G: Italy]

Carpenter, Michael D. and Henderson, Glenn V., Jr. Estimation Procedures and Stability of the Market-Model Parameters. *Rev. Bus. Econ. Res.*, Fall 1981, *17*(1), pp. 51–63. [G: U.S.]

Carpenter, Michael D. and Upton, David E. Trading Volume and Beta Stability. *J. Portfol. Manage.*, Winter 1981, *7*(2), pp. 60–64.

Chen, Son-Nan and Keown, Arthur J. Risk Decomposition and Portfolio Diversification When Beta Is Nonstationary: A Note. *J. Finance*, September 1981, *36*(4), pp. 941–47. [G: U.S.]

Clements, Kenneth W. A Note on the Interpretation and Estimation of Parkin's Discount House Portfolio Model. *Rev. Econ. Stud.*, July 1981, *48*(3), pp. 533–35.

Cohen, Kalman J., et al. Transaction Costs, Order Placement Strategy, and Existence of the Bid–Ask Spread. *J. Polit. Econ.*, April 1981, *89*(2), pp. 287–305.

Cohn, Richard A. and Lessard, Donald R. The Effect of Inflation on Stock Prices: International Evidence. *J. Finance*, May 1981, *36*(2), pp. 277–89.

Conine, Thomas E., Jr. and Tamarkin, Maurry, J. On Diversification Given Asymmetry in Returns. *J. Finance*, December 1981, *36*(5), pp. 1143–55. [G: U.S.]

Conroy, Robert M. and Winkler, Robert L. Informational Differences between Limit and Market Orders for a Market Maker. *J. Finan. Quant. Anal.*, December 1981, *16*(5), pp. 703–24.

Cornell, Bradford. The Consumption Based Asset Pricing Model: A Note on Potential Tests and Applications. *J. Finan. Econ.*, March 1981, *9*(1), pp. 103–08.

Cox, John C.; Ingersoll, Jonathan E., Jr. and Ross, Stephen A. A Re-examination of Traditional Hypotheses about the Term Structure of Interest Rates. *J. Finance*, September 1981, *36*(4), pp. 769–99.

Cox, John C.; Ingersoll, Jonathan E., Jr. and Ross, Stephen A. The Relation between Forward Prices and Futures Prices. *J. Finan. Econ.*, December 1981, *9*(4), pp. 321–46.

Craine, Roger N. and Pierce, James L. Multivariate Analysis of Interest Rate Risk. In *Maisel, S. J., ed.*, 1981, pp. 271–83. [G: U.S.]

Dewbre, Joe H. Interrelationships between Spot and Futures Markets: Some Implications of Rational Expectations. *Amer. J. Agr. Econ.*, December

1981, *63*(5), pp. 926–33.

Diamond, Douglas W. and Verrecchia, Robert E. Information Aggregation in a Noisy Rational Expectations Economy. *J. Finan. Econ.*, Summer 1981, *9*(3), pp. 221–35.

Dietz, Peter O.; Fogler, H. Russell and Rivers, Anthony U. Duration, Nonlinearity, and Bond Portfolio Performance. *J. Portfol. Manage.*, Spring 1981, *7*(3), pp. 37–41. [G: U.S.]

Doherty, Neil A. and Tinic, S. M. Reinsurance under Conditions of Capital Market Equilibrium: A Note. *J. Finance*, September 1981, *36*(4), pp. 949–53.

Durez-Demal, Martine. The Inclusion of Real Estate in the Capital Asset Pricing Model Tests. *Tijdschrift Econ. Manage.*, 1981, *26*(4), pp. 499–513.

Epps, Thomas W. Necessary and Sufficient Conditions for the Mean-Variance Portfolio Model with Constant Risk Aversion. *J. Finan. Quant. Anal.*, June 1981, *16*(2), pp. 169–76.

Eun, Cheol S. Global Purchasing Power View of Exchange Risk. *J. Finan. Quant. Anal.*, December 1981, *16*(5), pp. 639–50.

Fama, Eugene F. Stock Returns, Real Activity, Inflation, and Money. *Amer. Econ. Rev.*, September 1981, *71*(4), pp. 545–65. [G: U.S.]

Farrell, James L., Jr. Security Analysis. In *Altman, E. I.*, ed., 1981, pp. 16.3–33.

Figlewski, Stephen. The Informational Effects of Restrictions on Short Sales: Some Empirical Evidence. *J. Finan. Quant. Anal.*, November 1981, *16*(4), pp. 463–76. [G: U.S.]

Findlay, M. Chapman, III and Williams, Edward E. Financial Theory and Political Reality under Fundamental Uncertainty. *J. Post Keynesian Econ.*, Summer 1981, *3*(4), pp. 528–44.

Fogler, H. Russell; John, Kose and Tipton, James. Three Factors, Interest Rate Differentials and Stock Groups. *J. Finance*, May 1981, *36*(2), pp. 323–35. [G: U.S.]

Frankfurter, George M. and Hill, Joanne M. A Normative Approach to Pension Fund Management. *J. Finan. Quant. Anal.*, November 1981, *16*(4), pp. 533–55.

Frenkel, Jacob A. Flexible Exchange Rates, Prices, and the Role of "News": Lessons from the 1970s. *J. Polit. Econ.*, August 1981, *89*(4), pp. 665–705. [G: U.S.]

Freund, William C. Corporation Finance: Comments. In *Aaron, H. J. and Pechman, J. A.*, eds., 1981, pp. 197–98. [G: U.S.]

Friedman, Daniel. Makin's MARP: A Comment [Portfolio Theory and the Problem of Foreign Exchange Risk]. *J. Finance*, June 1981, *36*(3), pp. 739–41.

Friend, Irwin. Empirical Tests of Multi-Factor Pricing Model: Discussion. *J. Finance*, May 1981, *36*(2), pp. 350–52.

Fuller, Russell J. and Kerr, Halbert S. Estimating the Divisional Cost of Capital: An Analysis of the Pure-Play Technique. *J. Finance*, December 1981, *36*(5), pp. 997–1009.

von Furstenberg, George M. Incentives for International Currency Diversification by U.S. Financial Investors. *Int. Monet. Fund Staff Pap.*, September 1981, *28*(3), pp. 477–94. [G: U.S.]

Garbade, Kenneth D. and Rentzler, Joel. Testing the Hypothesis of Beta Stationarity. *Int. Econ. Rev.*, October 1981, *22*(3), pp. 577–87.

Garman, Mark B. and Ohlson, James A. Valuation of Risky Assets in Arbitrage-Free Economies with Transactions Costs. *J. Finan. Econ.*, Summer 1981, *9*(3), pp. 271–80.

Gay, Phillip. Interest Rates in Futures Markets. In *Jüttner, D. J.*, ed., 1981, pp. 361–72. [G: Australia]

Goldberg, Michael A. An Explanation of Security β Regression Tendencies. *Southern Econ. J.*, January 1981, *47*(3), pp. 809–15.

Grauer, Robert R. A Comparison of Growth Optimal and Mean Variance Investment Policies. *J. Finan. Quant. Anal.*, March 1981, *16*(1), pp. 1–21.

Grauer, Robert R. Investment Policy Implications of the Capital Asset Pricing Model. *J. Finance*, March 1981, *36*(1), pp. 127–41. [G: U.S.]

Grosen, Anders and Møller, Peder Fredslund. Fast-forrentede fordringers rentefølsomhed og varighed. (Duration of Bonds and Interest Sensitivity of Fixed Income Portfolios. With English summary.) *Nationaløkon. Tidsskr.*, 1981, *119*(1), pp. 105–25.

Grossman, Sanford J. and Shiller, Robert J. The Determinants of the Variability of Stock Market Prices. *Amer. Econ. Rev.*, May 1981, *71*(2), pp. 222–27.

Groth, John C. and Martin, John D. Impact of Firm Size on Capital Market Efficiency. *J. Econ. Bus.*, Winter 1981, *33*(2), pp. 166–71. [G: U.S.]

Hagin, Robert L. Modern Portfolio Theory and Management. In *Altman, E. I.*, ed., 1981, pp. 17.3–27.

Hakkio, Craig S. The Term Structure of the Forward Premium. *J. Monet. Econ.*, July 1981, *8*(1), pp. 41–58. [G: U.S.; Canada]

Hamaui, Rony. La determinazione del tasso di cambio nel breve periodo: una rassegna della letteratura empirica. (Exchange Rate Determination in the Short Run: A Survey of Empirical Literature. With English summary.) *Giorn. Econ.*, July-August 1981, *40*(7–8), pp. 501–20.

Harris, Richard G. and Purvis, Douglas D. Diverse Information and Market Efficiency in a Monetary Model of the Exchange Rate. *Econ. J.*, December 1981, *91*(364), pp. 829–47.

Hawanini, Gabriel A. and Vora, Ashok. The Capital Asset Pricing Model and the Investment Horizon: Comment. *Rev. Econ. Statist.*, November 1981, *63*(4), pp. 633–36.

Heinkel, Robert. Sorting Equilibria in Financial Markets: The Incentive Problem: Discussion. *J. Finan. Quant. Anal.*, November 1981, *16*(4), pp. 493–94.

Hemmings, Dan B. Exchange Controls, Security Prices and Exchange Rates. *Bull. Econ. Res.*, November 1981, *33*(2), pp. 82–90. [G: U.K.]

Hendershott, Patric H. The Decline in Aggregate Share Values: Taxation, Valuation Errors, Risk and Profitability. *Amer. Econ. Rev.*, December 1981, *71*(5), pp. 909–22. [G: U.S.]

Hessel, Christopher A. Extensions to Portfolio Theory to Reflect Vast Wealth Differences among Investors. *J. Finan. Quant. Anal.*, March 1981,

16(1), pp. 53–70.

Hessel, Christopher A. and Huffman, Lucy. The Effect of Taxation on Immunization Rules and Duration Estimation. *J. Finance*, December 1981, *36*(5), pp. 1127–42.

Hill, Joanne M. Is Optimal Portfolio Management Worth the Candle? *J. Portfol. Manage.*, Summer 1981, *7*(4), pp. 59–69. **[G: U.S.]**

Hinich, Melvin J. and Roll, Richard. Measuring Nonstationarity in the Parameters of the Market Model. **In** *Levy, H., ed.*, 1981, pp. 1–51. **[G: U.S.]**

Ho, Thomas S. Y. and Stoll, Hans R. Optimal Dealer Pricing under Transactions and Return Uncertainty. *J. Finan. Econ.*, March 1981, *9*(1), pp. 47–73.

Hodrick, Robert J. International Asset Pricing with Time-Varying Risk Premia. *J. Int. Econ.*, November 1981, *11*(4), pp. 573–87.

Holloway, Clark. A Note on Testing an Aggressive Investment Strategy Using Value Line Ranks. *J. Finance*, June 1981, *36*(3), pp. 711–19. **[G: U.S.]**

Holthausen, Duncan M. A Risk–Return Model with Risk and Return Measured as Deviations from a Target Return. *Amer. Econ. Rev.*, March 1981, *71*(1), pp. 182–88.

Jabson, J. D. and Korkie, Bob M. Putting Markowitz Theory to Work. *J. Portfol. Manage.*, Summer 1981, *7*(4), pp. 70–74.

Jacquillat, Bernard. Les processus de diffusion et leur utilisation dans l'évaluation des actifs financiers conditionnels. (Diffusion Processes and Their Use in the Assessment of Financial Option Contracts. With English summary.) *Écon. Soc.*, October–November–December 1981, *15*(10–12), pp. 1483–1511.

Jarrow, Robert A. and Oldfield, George S., Jr. Forward Contracts and Futures Contracts. *J. Finan. Econ.*, December 1981, *9*(4), pp. 373–82.

Jennings, Robert H.; Starks, Laura T. and Fellingham, John C. An Equilibrium Model of Asset Trading with Sequential Information Arrival. *J. Finance*, March 1981, *36*(1), pp. 143–61.

Jesse, Richard R., Jr. and Radcliffe, Robert C. On Speculation and Price Stability under Uncertainty. *Rev. Econ. Statist.*, February 1981, *63*(1), pp. 129–32.

Jobson, J. D. and Korkie, Bob M. Performance Hypothesis Testing with the Sharpe and Treynor Measures. *J. Finance*, September 1981, *36*(4), pp. 889–908.

John, Kose. Efficient Funds in a Financial Market with Options: A New Irrelevance Proposition. *J. Finance*, June 1981, *36*(3), pp. 685–95.

Johnson, Dana J. and Deckro, Richard F. The Role of Economic Variables in Relating Changes in a Firm's Earnings to Changes in the Price of Its Common Stock. *Rev. Bus. Econ. Res.*, Fall 1981, *17*(1), pp. 27–39. **[G: U.S.]**

Johnson, James M. and Lanser, Howard P. Dividend Risk Measurement and Tests of the CAPM. *J. Portfol. Manage.*, Winter 1981, *7*(2), pp. 50–54.

Johnston, H. Neil; Russell, Don E. and Freeland, B. A. The Relationship between Dividend Yields,

Interest Rates and Stock Market Prices. **In** *Jüttner, D. J., ed.*, 1981, pp. 204–23. **[G: Australia]**

Jüttner, D. Johannes. A Note on Tobin's Supply Price of Capital. *Australian Econ. Pap.*, December 1981, *20*(37), pp. 409–13.

Jüttner, D. Johannes. Interest Rates, Capital Markets and Loanable Funds. **In** *Jüttner, D. J., ed.*, 1981, pp. 257–78. **[G: Australia]**

Kallberg, J. G. and Ziemba, W. T. Generalized Concave Functions in Stochastic Programming and Portfolio Theory. **In** *Schaible, S. and Ziemba, W. T., eds.*, 1981, pp. 719–67.

Katz, Eliakim. On Destabilizing Profitable Speculation. *Econ. Notes*, 1981, *10*(3), pp. 114–17.

Keenan, Michael. A Normative Approach to Pension Fund Management: Discussion. *J. Finan. Quant. Anal.*, November 1981, *16*(4), pp. 557–58.

Kihlstrom, Richard E. and Mirman, Leonard J. Constant, Increasing and Decreasing Risk Aversion with Many Commodities. *Rev. Econ. Stud.*, April 1981, *48*(2), pp. 271–80.

Kihlstrom, Richard E.; Romer, David and Williams, Steve. Risk Aversion with Random Initial Wealth. *Econometrica*, June 1981, *49*(4), pp. 911–20.

Kwan, Clarence C. Y. Efficient Market Tests of the Informational Content of Dividend Announcements: Critique and Extension. *J. Finan. Quant. Anal.*, June 1981, *16*(2), pp. 193–206. **[G: U.S.]**

Lakonishok, Josef. Performance of Mutual Funds versus Their Expenses. *J. Bank Res.*, Summer 1981, *12*(2), pp. 110–13. **[G: U.S.]**

Landskroner, Yoram. Index-Linked Bond and the Pricing of Capital Assets. *J. Econ. Bus.*, Winter 1981, *33*(2), pp. 143–46.

Landskroner, Yoram and Liviatan, Nissan. Risk Premia and the Sources of Inflation. *J. Money, Credit, Banking*, May 1981, *13*(2), pp. 205–14.

Lane, David and Golen, Lawrence. Some Simulation-Based Estimates of Commercial Bank Deposit Insurance Premiums. **In** *Maisel, S. J., ed.*, 1981, pp. 341–65. **[G: U.S.]**

Lee, C. Jevons. The Pricing of Corporate Debt: A Note. *J. Finance*, December 1981, *36*(5), pp. 1187–89.

Lee, Cheng Few; Lee, Jack C. and Zumwalt, J. Kenton. An Analytical Examination of Real versus Nominal Rates of Return Matrices in Portfolio Management: A Reply. *J. Econ. Bus.*, Winter 1981, *33*(2), pp. 173–74.

Lee, Wayne Y.; Rao, Ramesh K. S. and Auchmuty, J. F. G. Option Pricing in a Lognormal Securities Market with Discrete Trading. *J. Finan. Econ.*, March 1981, *9*(1), pp. 75–101.

Leibowitz, Martin L. and Weinberger, Alfred. The Uses of Contingent Immunization. *J. Portfol. Manage.*, Fall 1981, *8*(1), pp. 51–55. **[G: U.S.]**

LeRoy, Stephen F. and LaCivita, C. J. Risk Aversion and the Dispersion of Asset Prices. *J. Bus.*, October 1981, *54*(4), pp. 535–47.

LeRoy, Stephen F. and Porter, Richard D. The Present-Value Relation: Tests Based on Implied Variance Bounds. *Econometrica*, May 1981, *49*(3), pp. 555–74. **[G: U.S.]**

Levhari, David and Levy, Haim. The Capital Asset Pricing Model and the Investment Horizon: Reply. *Rev. Econ. Statist.*, November 1981, *63*(4),

pp. 637–38.

Levy, Haim. Optimal Portfolio of Foreign Currencies with Borrowing and Lending. *J. Money, Credit, Banking*, August 1981, *13*(3), pp. 325–41.
[G: U.S.]

Lintner, John. Are Markets Efficient? Tests of Alternative Hypotheses: Discussion. *J. Finance*, May 1981, *36*(2), pp. 307–11.

Long, John B., Jr. Are Markets Efficient? Tests of Alternative Hypotheses: Discussion. *J. Finance*, May 1981, *36*(2), pp. 304–07.

Makin, John H. Portfolio Theory and the Problem of Foreign Exchange Risk: Reply. *J. Finance*, June 1981, *36*(3), pp. 743–45.

Markowitz, Harry M. and Perold, André F. Portfolio Analysis with Factors and Scenarios. *J. Finance*, September 1981, *36*(4), pp. 871–77.

Mason, Scott P. and Bhattacharya, Sudipto. Risky Debt, Jump Processes, and Safety Covenants. *J. Finan. Econ.*, Summer 1981, *9*(3), pp. 281–307.

Mayshar, Joram. Transaction Costs and the Pricing of Assets. *J. Finance*, June 1981, *36*(3), pp. 583–97.

McGregor, Peter G. The Portfolio Selection Approach and Short-Run Econometric Models of Capital Flows and the Foreign Exchange Market: A Theoretical Analysis. *J. Econ. Stud.*, 1981, *8*(2), pp. 3–24.

Melton, William C. and Roley, V. Vance. Imperfect Asset Elasticities and Financial Model Building. *J. Econometrics*, January 1981, *15*(1), pp. 139–54.

Mennis, Edmund A.; Valentine, Jerome L. and Mennis, Daniel L. New Perspectives on Pension Fund Management. *J. Portfol. Manage.*, Spring 1981, *7*(3), pp. 46–50.

Merton, Robert C. On Market Timing and Investment Performance. I. An Equilibrium Theory of Value for Market Forecasts. *J. Bus.*, July 1981, *54*(3), pp. 363–406.

Michaud, Richard O. Risk Policy and Long-Term Investment. *J. Finan. Quant. Anal.*, June 1981, *16*(2), pp. 147–67.

Milgrom, Paul R. Good News and Bad News: Representation Theorems and Applications. *Bell J. Econ. (See Rand J. Econ. after 4/85)*, Autumn 1981, *12*(2), pp. 380–91.

Milgrom, Paul R. Rational Expectations, Information Acquisition, and Competitive Bidding. *Econometrica*, June 1981, *49*(4), pp. 921–43.

Mishkin, Frederic S. Are Market Forecasts Rational? *Amer. Econ. Rev.*, June 1981, *71*(3), pp. 295–306.

Nadauld, Stephen D. Calculating the Present Value of an Asset's Uncertain Future Cash Flows. In *Maisel, S. J., ed.*, 1981, pp. 315–39. [G: U.S.]

Oldfield, George S., Jr. and Rogalski, Richard J. Treasury Bill Factors and Common Stock Returns. *J. Finance*, May 1981, *36*(2), pp. 337–50.
[G: U.S.]

Olsen, Robert A. An Empirical Investigation of the Association between Common Stock Returns and Uncertain Inflation. *Rev. Bus. Econ. Res.*, Winter 1981, *16*(2), pp. 56–67.

Owen, P. Dorian. Dynamic Models of Portfolio Behavior: A General Integrated Model Incorporat-

ing Sequencing Effects [Dynamic Models of Portfolio Behavior: More on Pitfalls in Financial Model Building]. *Amer. Econ. Rev.*, March 1981, *71*(1), pp. 231–38.

Pagan, Adrian Rodney. Interest Rates Using the Survey Method and a Time Series Method: Comments. In *Jüttner, D. J., ed.*, 1981, pp. 339–41.
[G: Australia]

Pesando, James E. On Forecasting Interest Rates: An Efficient Markets Perspective. *J. Monet. Econ.*, November 1981, *8*(3), pp. 305–18.
[G: Canada]

Poole, William. Short-term Interest Rates and Futures Markets: Comments. In *Jüttner, D. J., ed.*, 1981, pp. 373–78. [G: Australia; U.S.]

Poole, William. The Relationship between Dividend Yields, Interest Rates and Stock Market Prices: Comment. In *Jüttner, D. J., ed.*, 1981, pp. 229–32. [G: Australia]

Pope, Robin. Interest Rates, Capital Markets and Loanable Funds: Comments. In *Jüttner, D. J., ed.*, 1981, pp. 282–89. [G: Australia]

Pulley, Lawrence B. A General Mean-Variance Approximation to Expected Utility for Short Holding Periods. *J. Finan. Quant. Anal.*, September 1981, *16*(3), pp. 361–73.

Pulliam, Kenneth P. How to Produce Value from Portfolio Measurement. *J. Portfol. Manage.*, Fall 1981, *8*(1), pp. 13–16. [G: U.S.]

Reinganum, Marc R. A New Empirical Perspective on the CAPM. *J. Finan. Quant. Anal.*, November 1981, *16*(4), pp. 439–62. [G: U.S.]

Reinganum, Marc R. Misspecification of Capital Asset Pricing: Empirical Anomalies Based on Earnings' Yields and Market Values. *J. Finan. Econ.*, March 1981, *9*(1), pp. 19–46.

Reinganum, Marc R. The Arbitrage Pricing Theory: Some Empirical Results. *J. Finance*, May 1981, *36*(2), pp. 313–21. [G: U.S.]

Richard, Scott F. and Sundaresan, M. A Continuous Time Equilibrium Model of Forward Prices and Futures Prices in a Multigood Economy. *J. Finan. Econ.*, December 1981, *9*(4), pp. 347–71.

Roll, Richard. Performance Evaluation and Benchmark Errors (II) *J. Portfol. Manage.*, Winter 1981, *7*(2), pp. 17–22. [G: U.S.]

Rosenberg, Barr. The Capital Asset Pricing Model and the Market Model. *J. Portfol. Manage.*, Winter 1981, *7*(2), pp. 5–16.

Ross, Stephen A. Some Stronger Measures of Risk Aversion in the Small and the Large with Applications. *Econometrica*, May 1981, *49*(3), pp. 621–38.

Rubinstein, Mark. A Discrete-Time Synthesis of Financial Theory. In *Levy, H., ed.*, 1981, pp. 53–102.

Rudd, Andrew. Social Responsibility and Portfolio Performance. *Calif. Manage. Rev.*, Summer 1981, *23*(4), pp. 55–61.

Rutledge, David J. S. Short-term Interest Rates and Futures Markets: Comments. In *Jüttner, D. J., ed.*, 1981, pp. 379–81. [G: U.S.; Australia]

Ryan, Peter J. and Lefoll, Jean. A Comment on Mean-Variance Portfolio Selection with Either a Singular or a Non-Singular Variance-Covariance Matrix. *J. Finan. Quant. Anal.*, September 1981,

16(3), pp. 389–95.

Satterthwaite, Mark A. On the Scope of the Stockholder Unanimity Theorems. *Int. Econ. Rev.*, February 1981, 22(1), pp. 119–33.

Schmalensee, Richard. Risk and Return on Long-Lived Tangible Assets. *J. Finan. Econ.*, June 1981, 9(2), pp. 185–205.

Schnabel, J. A. A Note on the Specification of Financial Asset Demand Functions. *Atlantic Econ. J.*, December 1981, 9(4), pp. 46–48.

Schrieves, Ronald E. and Wachowicz, John M., Jr. A Utility Theoretic Basis for "Generalized" Mean-Coefficient of Variation (MCV) Analysis. *J. Finan. Quant. Anal.*, December 1981, 16(5), pp. 671–83.

Schwert, G. William. Using Financial Data to Measure Effects of Regulation. *J. Law Econ.*, April 1981, 24(1), pp. 121–58. [G: U.S.]

Sercu, Piet. A Note on Real and Nominal Efficient Sets. *J. Finance*, June 1981, 36(3), pp. 721–37.

Sethi, Suresh P. and Lehoczky, John P. A Comparison of the Ito and Stratonovich Formulations of Problems in Finance. *J. Econ. Dynam. Control*, November 1981, 3(4), pp. 343–56.

Sheffrin, Steven M. Dynamics of Investment in a Perfect Foresight Model. *J. Econ. Bus.*, Winter 1981, 33(2), pp. 160–65.

Shefrin, Hersh M. Transaction Costs, Uncertainty and Generally Inactive Futures Markets. *Rev. Econ. Stud.*, January 1981, 48(1), pp. 131–37.

Shiller, Robert J. The Use of Volatility Measures in Assessing Market Efficiency. *J. Finance*, May 1981, 36(2), pp. 291–304.

Sinclair, N. A. An Empirical Examination of the Required Number of Leading and Lagged Variables for ACM Beta Estimation. *Australian J. Manage.*, December 1981, 6(2), pp. 119–26.

Smith, Gary N. Investment and q in a Stock Valuation Model. *Southern Econ. J.*, April 1981, 47(4), pp. 1007–20.

Smith, Gary N. The Systematic Specification of a Full Prior Covariance Matrix for Asset Demand Equations. *Quart. J. Econ.*, May 1981, 96(2), pp. 317–39.

Stiglitz, Joseph E. Ownership, Control, and Efficient Markets: Some Paradoxes in the Theory of Capital Markets. In *[Nelson, J. R.]*, 1981, pp. 311–40.

Stiglitz, Joseph E. Pareto Optimality and Competition. *J. Finance*, May 1981, 36(2), pp. 235–51.

Stock, Duane. A Canonical Correlation Analysis of the Moments of Bond Portfolio Return Distributions. *Rev. Bus. Econ. Res.*, Fall 1981, 17(1), pp. 64–71. [G: U.S.]

Stulz, René M. A Model of International Asset Pricing. *J. Finan. Econ.*, December 1981, 9(4), pp. 383–406.

Stulz, René M. On the Effects of Barriers to International Investment. *J. Finance*, September 1981, 36(4), pp. 923–34.

Sullivan, James D. Interrelationships between Spot and Futures Markets: Some Implications of Rational Expectations: Discussion. *Amer. J. Agr. Econ.*, December 1981, 63(5), pp. 942–43. [G: U.S.]

Summers, Lawrence H. Inflation, the Stock Market, and Owner-Occupied Housing. *Amer. Econ.*

Rev., May 1981, 71(2), pp. 429–34. [G: U.S.]

Tabatoni, Olivier. Modèle opérationnel d'évaluation de contrats conditionnels. (Operational Valuation Model of Conditional Contracts. With English summary.) *Écon. Soc.*, October–November–December 1981, 15(10–12), pp. 1513–52.

Taub, Allan J. Futures Markets and the Cooperative Firm under Price Uncertainty. *Eastern Econ. J.*, July-Oct. 1981, 7(3–4), pp. 157–61.

Taylor, Robert R. Forecasting Interest Rates Using the Survey Method and a Time Series Model. In *Jüttner, D. J., ed.*, 1981, pp. 316–35. [G: Australia]

Telser, Lester G. Margins and Futures Contracts. *J. Futures Markets*, Summer 1981, 1(2), pp. 225–53.

Telser, Lester G. Why There Are Organized Futures Markets. *J. Law Econ.*, April 1981, 24(1), pp. 1–22.

Tesfatsion, Leigh. Dynamic Investment, Risk Aversion, and Foresight Sensitivity. *J. Econ. Dynam. Control*, February 1981, 3(1), pp. 65–96.

Theobald, Michael. Beta Stationarity and Estimation Period: Some Analytical Results. *J. Finan. Quant. Anal.*, December 1981, 16(5), pp. 747–57.

Thompson, A. Frank, Jr. Immunization of Pension Funds and Sensitivity to Actuarial Assumptions: Comment. *J. Risk Ins.*, March 1981, 48(1), pp. 148–53.

Throop, Adrian W. Interest Rate Forecasts and Market Efficiency. *Fed. Res. Bank San Francisco Econ. Rev.*, Spring 1981, pp. 29–43. [G: U.S.]

Tole, Thomas M. How to Maximize Stationarity of Beta. *J. Portfol. Manage.*, Winter 1981, 7(2), pp. 45–49.

Umstead, David A. Volatility, Growth, and Investment Policy. *J. Portfol. Manage.*, Winter 1981, 7(2), pp. 55–59.

Vandell, Robert F. and Pontius, Marcia L. The Impact of Tax Status on Stock Selection. *J. Portfol. Manage.*, Summer 1981, 7(4), pp. 35–42.

Vickers, Douglas. Real Time and the Choice-Decision Point: A Comment on Findlay and Williams' "Financial Theory." *J. Post Keynesian Econ.*, Summer 1981, 3(4), pp. 545–51.

Wallace, Neil. A Modigliani-Miller Theorem for Open-Market Operations. *Amer. Econ. Rev.*, June 1981, 71(3), pp. 267–74.

Welcker, Johannes. Technische Analyse durch Computertest bestätigt—Random Walk Theorie widerlegt. (Technical Analysis Confirmed by Computer Test—Random Walk Theory Refuted. With English summary.) *Kredit Kapital*, 1981, 14(1), pp. 136–46.

Wenglowski, Gary M. Stock Prices: Comments. In *Aaron, H. J. and Pechman, J. A., eds.*, 1981, pp. 238–40. [G: U.S.]

Willassen, Yngve. Expected Utility, Chebichev Bounds, Mean-Variance Analysis. *Scand. J. Econ.*, 1981, 83(3), pp. 419–28.

Wolff, M. R. A Control-Theoretic Approach to the Portfolio Selection Problem Including Cash Balance. In *Fandel, G., et al., eds.*, 1981, pp. 594–600.

Yawitz, Jess B. and Marshall, William J. Measuring the Effect of Callability on Bond Yields. *J. Money,*

Credit, Banking, February 1981, *13*(1), pp. 60–71. [G: U.S.]

Zéghal, Daniel. L'effet de l'information non comptable sur la valeur informationnelle des états financiers dans le marché des capitaux. (The Effect of Non-Accounting Information on the Informational Value of Financial Statements. With English summary.) *Can. J. Econ.*, May 1981, *14*(2), pp. 298–312.

3132 Capital Markets: Empirical Studies, including Regulation

Agnew, Jonathan G. The Yankee Bond Market. **In** *Burghardt, A. M., ed.,* 1981, pp. 65–72. [G: U.S.]

Akhoury, Ravi. Bond Management Issues. **In** *Altman, E. I., ed.,* 1981, pp. 18.3–31. [G: U.S. New York]

Alderman, C. Wayne. The Effect of Changes in Accounting Techniques on Systematic Risk. *Rev. Bus. Econ. Res.,* Winter 1981, *16*(2), pp. 12–22. [G: U.S.]

Alexander, Michael O. Discussion of The SEC "Reversal" of FASB Statement No. 19: An Investigation of Information Effects. *J. Acc. Res.,* Supplement 1981, *19*, pp. 212–17. [G: U.S.]

Altman, Edward I. and Brenner, Menachem. Information Effects and Stock Market Response to Signs of Firm Deterioration. *J. Finan. Quant. Anal.,* March 1981, *16*(1), pp. 35–51. [G: U.S.]

Ambachtsheer, Keith P. International Investing: Structuring the Process. *J. Portfol. Manage.,* Fall 1981, *8*(1), pp. 23–27. [G: W. Europe; U.S.]

Anderson, Ronald. "Margins and Futures Contracts": Comment. *J. Futures Markets,* Summer 1981, *1*(2), pp. 259–64.

Angermueller, Hans H. Current Regulatory Framework for Banks' Securities Activities as Viewed by Regulators: Comment. **In** *Sametz, A. W., ed.,* 1981, pp. 43–45. [G: U.S.]

Arbit, Hal. The Nature of the Game. *J. Portfol. Manage.,* Fall 1981, *8*(1), pp. 5–9. [G: U.S.]

Argy, V. and Semudram, M. Test of a Simple Model of the Determination of the Effective Exchange Rate for the Mark (March 1973–December 1979). *Empirical Econ.,* 1981, *6*(3), pp. 163–71. [G: W. Germany]

Arrow, Kenneth J. Futures Markets: Some Theoretical Perspectives. *J. Futures Markets,* Summer 1981, *1*(2), pp. 107–15.

Asay, Michael R. Implied Margin Requirements on Options and Stocks. *J. Portfol. Manage.,* Spring 1981, *7*(3), pp. 55–59. [G: U.S.]

Asay, Michael R.; Gonzalez, Gisela A. and Wolkowitz, Benjamin. Financial Futures, Bank Portfolio Risk, and Accounting. *J. Futures Markets,* Winter 1981, *1*(4), pp. 607–18.

Banz, Rolf W. The Relationship between Return and Market Value of Common Stocks. *J. Finan. Econ.,* March 1981, *9*(1), pp. 3–18. [G: U.S.]

Barnhill, Theodore M. and Powell, James A. Silver Price Volatility: A Perspective on the July 1979–April 1980 Period. *J. Futures Markets,* Winter 1981, *1*(4), pp. 619–47. [G: U.S.]

Barry, Peter J. Capital Asset Pricing and Farm Real Estate: Reply. *Amer. J. Agr. Econ.,* August 1981, *63*(3), pp. 580–81. [G: U.S.]

Bart, John and Masse, Isidore J. Divergence of Opinion and Risk. *J. Finan. Quant. Anal.,* March 1981, *16*(1), pp. 23–34. [G: Canada]

Basu, S. Market Reactions to Accounting Policy Deliberations: The Inflation Accounting Case Revisited. *Accounting Rev.,* October 1981, *56*(4), pp. 942–54. [G: U.S.]

Beaver, William H. and Landsman, Wayne R. Note on the Behavior of Residual Security Returns for Winner and Loser Portfolios. *J. Acc. Econ.,* December 1981, *3*(3), pp. 233–41. [G: U.S.]

Beckers, Stan. A Note on Estimating the Parameters of the Diffusion-Jump Model of Stock Returns. *J. Finan. Quant. Anal.,* March 1981, *16*(1), pp. 127–40. [G: U.S.]

Bench, Joseph. Government Obligations: U.S. Treasury and Federal Agency Securities. **In** *Altman, E. I., ed.,* 1981, pp. 2.3–19. [G: U.S.]

Bench, Joseph. Money and Capital Markets: Institutional Framework and Federal Reserve Control. **In** *Altman, E. I., ed.,* 1981, pp. 1.3–33. [G: U.S.]

Benson, Earl D., et al. Systematic Variation in Yield Spreads for Tax-Exempt General Obligation Bonds. *J. Finan. Quant. Anal.,* December 1981, *16*(5), pp. 685–702. [G: U.S.]

Bevan, Robert L. Current Regulatory Framework for Banks' Securities Activities as Viewed by Regulators: Comment. **In** *Sametz, A. W., ed.,* 1981, pp. 69–71. [G: U.S.]

Biffignandi, Silvia and Stefani, Silvana. Stochastic Analysis on Share Prices in Italy. *Econ. Notes,* 1981, *10*(1), pp. 67–82. [G: Italy]

Bilson, John F. O. The "Speculative Efficiency" Hypothesis. *J. Bus.,* July 1981, *54*(3), pp. 435–51. [G: OECD]

Black, Deborah G.; Garbade, Kenneth D. and Silber, William L. The Impact of the GNMA Pass-through Program on FHA Mortgage Costs. *J. Finance,* May 1981, *36*(2), pp. 457–69. [G: U.S.]

Blackie, Henry and Antl, Boris. Currency Strategy in Multicurrency Portfolio Management. **In** *Ensor, R. and Muller, P., eds.,* 1981, pp. 227–40.

Blau, Leslie A. and Barber, James S. Proposed Amendment of Section 4d(2) of the Commodity Exchange Act: Concerning Investment of Customer Funds. *J. Futures Markets,* Winter 1981, *1*(4), pp. 657–58. [G: U.S.]

Boardman, Calvin M. and McEnally, Richard W. Factors Affecting Seasoned Corporate Bond Prices. *J. Finan. Quant. Anal.,* June 1981, *16*(2), pp. 207–26. [G: U.S.]

Bohan, James. Relative Strength: Further Positive Evidence. *J. Portfol. Manage.,* Fall 1981, *8*(1), pp. 36–39. [G: U.S.]

Bonaduce, Michele. La Deputazione, autorità locale di Borsa. (Deputazione di Borsa as a Local Stock Exchange Authority. With English summary.) *Bancaria,* March 1981, *37*(3), pp. 270–73. [G: Italy]

Bonds, W. Kenneth. Commingled-Agency Accounts for Bank Trust Departments—An Idea Whose Time Has Come. **In** *Sametz, A. W., ed.,* 1981, pp. 85–89. [G: U.S.]

Bookstaber, Richard M. Observed Option Mispricing and the Nonsimultaneity of Stock and Option Quotations. *J. Bus.*, January 1981, *54*(1), pp. 141–55. [G: U.S.]

Brewer, H. L. Investor Benefits from Corporate International Diversification. *J. Finan. Quant. Anal.*, March 1981, *16*(1), pp. 113–26. [G: U.S.]

Brown, R. L. and Rainbow, K. A. Exercising of Options in the Australian Options Market. *Australian J. Manage.*, June 1981, *6*(1), pp. 1–21. [G: Australia]

Burghardt, Galen, Jr. and Kohn, Donald L. "Margins and Futures Contracts": Comment. *J. Futures Markets*, Summer 1981, *1*(2), pp. 255–57. [G: U.S.]

Cagan, Phillip. Financial Futures Markets: Is More Regulation Needed? *J. Futures Markets*, Summer 1981, *1*(2), pp. 169–89. [G: U.S.]

Caird, Kathryn G. and Emanuel, David M. Some Time Series Properties of Accounting Income Numbers. *Australian J. Manage.*, December 1981, *6*(2), pp. 7–15. [G: New Zealand]

Callier, Philippe. Covered Arbitrage Margin and Transaction Costs. *Weltwirtsch. Arch.*, 1981, *117*(2), pp. 262–75.

Cantoni, Renato. Le Borse estere nel 1980. (Foreign Stock Markets in 1980. With English summary.) *Bancaria*, February 1981, *37*(2), pp. 152–61. [G: U.S.; Europe; Japan; Australia]

Cantoni, Renato. Le Borse italiane nel 1980. (The Italian Stock Market in 1980. With English summary.) *Bancaria*, January 1981, *37*(1), pp. 49–57. [G: Italy]

Cantoni, Renato. Le Borse Italiane nel 1981. (The Italian Stock Exchange in 1981. With English summary.) *Bancaria*, December 1981, *37*(12), pp. 1274–83. [G: Italy]

Carney, Owen. "The Regulation of Futures and Forward Trading by Depository Institutions: A Legal and Economic Analysis": Comment. *J. Futures Markets*, Summer 1981, *1*(2), pp. 219–23.

Carter, Colin. Capital Asset Pricing and Farm Real Estate: Comment. *Amer. J. Agr. Econ.*, August 1981, *63*(3), pp. 578–79. [G: U.S.]

Casella, Angelo. Il mercato monetario statunitense—I. (The United States Money Market—I. With English summary.) *Bancaria*, November 1981, *37*(11), pp. 1153–61. [G: U.S.]

Casella, Angelo. Il mercato monetario statunitense—II. (The United States Money Market—II. With English summary.) *Bancaria*, December 1981, *37*(12), pp. 1284–93. [G: U.S.]

Castagna, Anthony D. A Review of Bond Rating Systems and an Assessment of Their Likely Contribution to the Australian Capital Market. In *Jüttner, D. J., ed.*, 1981, pp. 293–315. [G: U.S.; Australia]

Chance, Don M. Leverage and the Valuation of Risk Assets: A Comment. *Quart. Rev. Econ. Bus.*, Spring 1981, *21*(1), pp. 125–27. [G: U.S.]

Chen, Son-Nan. Residual Variance Heteroscedasticity, Portfolio Diversification, and Trading Rules. *Quart. Rev. Econ. Bus.*, Autumn 1981, *21*(3), pp. 87–97.

Cicchetti, Paul; Dale, Charles and Vignola, Anthony

J. Usefulness of Treasury Bill Futures as Hedging Instruments. *J. Futures Markets*, Fall 1981, *1*(3), pp. 379–87. [G: U.S.]

Colletaz, Gilbert and Marois, William. L'analyse des relations dynamiques entre variables: une application au taux du marché monetaire français. (The Analysis of the Dynamic Relationships between Variables: An Application to the French Money Market Rate. With English summary.) *Revue Écon.*, January 1981, *32*(1), pp. 86–109. [G: France]

Condell, Derek. A Review of Bond Rating Systems and an Assessment of Their Likely Contribution to the Australian Capital Market: Comments. In *Jüttner, D. J., ed.*, 1981, pp. 336–38. [G: Australia; U.S.]

Cook, Timothy. Determinants of the Spread between Treasury Bill and Private Sector Money Market Rates. *J. Econ. Bus.*, Spring/Summer 1981, *33*(3), pp. 177–87. [G: U.S.]

Cornell, Bradford. A Note on Taxes and the Pricing of Treasury Bill Futures Contracts. *J. Finance*, December 1981, *36*(5), pp. 1169–76. [G: U.S.]

Cornell, Bradford. The Relationship between Volume and Price Variability in Futures Markets. *J. Futures Markets*, Fall 1981, *1*(3), pp. 303–16. [G: U.S.]

Cornell, Bradford and Reinganum, Marc R. Forward and Futures Prices: Evidence from the Foreign Exchange Markets. *J. Finance*, December 1981, *36*(5), pp. 1035–45. [G: U.S.]

Corrigan, E. Gerald. Statement to Subcommittee on Conservation, Credit and Rural Development of the House Committee on Agriculture, October 1, 1981. *Fed. Res. Bull.*, October 1981, *67*(10), pp. 778–81. [G: U.S.]

Crawford, Donald J. Current Regulatory Framework for Banks' Securities Activities as Viewed by Regulators: Comment. In *Sametz, A. W., ed.*, 1981, pp. 46–47. [G: U.S.]

Cristini, Giovanni. Il mercato dei titoli a reddito fisso negli anni '70. (The Fixed-Interest Securities Market in the 1970s. With English summary.) *Bancaria*, March 1981, *37*(3), pp. 260–69. [G: Italy]

Cummins, J. David and Westerfield, Randolph. Patterns of Concentration in Private Pension Plan Common Stock Portfolios since ERISA. *J. Risk Ins.*, June 1981, *48*(2), pp. 201–19. [G: U.S.]

Dale, Charles. Brownian Motion in the Treasury Bill Futures Market. *Bus. Econ.*, May 1981, *16*(3), pp. 47–54.

Dale, Charles. The Hedging Effectiveness of Currency Futures Markets. *J. Futures Markets*, Spring 1981, *1*(1), pp. 77–88. [G: U.S.]

Dale, Charles and Workman, Rosemarie. Measuring Patterns of Price Movements in the Treasury Bill Futures Market. *J. Econ. Bus.*, Winter 1981, *33*(2), pp. 81–87. [G: U.S.]

Dann, Larry Y. Common Stock Repurchases: An Analysis of Returns to Bondholders and Stockholders. *J. Finan. Econ.*, June 1981, *9*(2), pp. 113–38. [G: U.S.]

Davies, Rhodri and Grabiner, Anthony. Trade Financing: Legal Issues. In *Gmür, C. J., ed.*, 1981, pp. 173–86. [G: U.K.; Selected Countries]

Dew, James Kurt. "Innovation, Competition, and

New Contract Design in Futures Markets": Comment. *J. Futures Markets,* Summer 1981, *1*(2), pp. 161–67. [G: U.S.]

Dew, James Kurt. Comment on "Usefulness of Treasury Bill Futures as Hedging Instruments." *J. Futures Markets,* Fall 1981, *1*(3), pp. 389–91. [G: U.S.]

Diamond, Douglas B., Jr. Inflation and Extraordinary Returns on Owner-Occupied Housing: Some Implications for Capital Allocation: Discussion. In *Tuccillo, J. A. and Villani, K. E., eds.,* 1981, pp. 35–36. [G: U.S.]

Dotsey, Michael; Englander, Steven and Partlan, John C. Money Market Mutual Funds and Monetary Control. *Fed. Res. Bank New York Quart. Rev.,* Winter 1981–82, *6*(4), pp. 9–17. [G: U.S.]

Draper, Dennis W. Information Sets, Macroeconomic Reform, and Stock Prices: Discussion. *J. Finan. Quant. Anal.,* November 1981, *16*(4), pp. 511–13.

Dufey, Gunter and Giddy, Ian H. Innovation in the International Financial Markets. *J. Int. Bus. Stud.,* Fall 1981, *12*(2), pp. 33–51.

Dunn, Kenneth B. and McConnell, John J. Rate of Return Indexes for GNMA Securities. *J. Portfol. Manage.,* Winter 1981, *7*(2), pp. 65–74. [G: U.S.]

Dyl, Edward A. and Joehnk, Michael D. Riding the Yield Curve: Does It Work? *J. Portfol. Manage.,* Spring 1981, *7*(3), pp. 13–17. [G: U.S.]

Edwards, Franklin R. Current Regulatory Framework for Banks' Securities Activities as Viewed by Regulators: Comment. In *Sametz, A. W., ed.,* 1981, pp. 74–76. [G: U.S.]

Edwards, Franklin R. The Regulation of Futures and Forward Trading by Depository Institutions: A Legal and Economic Analysis. *J. Futures Markets,* Summer 1981, *1*(2), pp. 201–18.

Evans, William H. and Rozenstein, H. A. The Market for Commonwealth Government Securities. In *Jüttner, D. J., ed.,* 1981, pp. 144–70. [G: Australia]

Fabozzi, Frank J. and West, Richard R. Negotiated versus Competitive Underwritings of Public Utility Bonds: Just One More Time. *J. Finan. Quant. Anal.,* September 1981, *16*(3), pp. 323–39. [G: U.S.]

Farrar, Donald E. and Girton, Lance. Institutional Investors and Concentration of Financial Power: Berle and Means Revisited. *J. Finance,* May 1981, *36*(2), pp. 369–81. [G: U.S.]

Fausto, Domenicantonio. The Market for Government Securities in Italy, 1961–1971. *Econ. Notes,* 1981, *10*(2), pp. 14–34. [G: Italy]

Ferri, Michael G. and Oberhelman, H. Dennis. How Well do Money Market Funds Perform? *J. Portfol. Manage.,* Spring 1981, *7*(3), pp. 18–26. [G: U.S.]

Fieleke, Norman S. Foreign-Currency Positioning by U.S. Firms: Some New Evidence. *Rev. Econ. Statist.,* February 1981, *63*(1), pp. 35–42. [G: U.S.]

Figlewski, Stephen. Futures Trading and Volatility in the GNMA Market. *J. Finance,* May 1981, *36*(2), pp. 445–56. [G: U.S.]

Firth, Michael. The Relative Information Content of the Release of Financial Results Data by Firms.

J. Acc. Res., Autumn 1981, *19*(2), pp. 521–29. [G: U.S.]

Forbes, Ronald W. State and Local Debt. In *Altman, E. I., ed.,* 1981, pp. 3.3–30. [G: U.S.]

Foster, George. Intra-Industry Information Transfers Associated with Earnings Releases. *J. Acc. Econ.,* December 1981, *3*(3), pp. 201–32. [G: U.S.]

Frankfurter, George M. and Young, Allan. Reply [Option Spreading: Theory and an Illustration]. *J. Portfol. Manage.,* Winter 1981, *7*(2), pp. 91–92.

Freeman, Robert N. The Disclosure of Replacement Cost Accounting Data and Its Effect on Transaction Volumes: A Comment. *Accounting Rev.,* January 1981, *56*(1), pp. 177–80. [G: U.S.]

Frey, Norman E. and Labuszewski, John W. Newspaper Articles and Their Impact On Commodity Price Formation Case Study: Copper. *J. Futures Markets,* Spring 1981, *1*(1), pp. 89–91. [G: U.S.]

Fried, Dov and Schiff, Allen. CPA Switches and Associated Market Reactions. *Accounting Rev.,* April 1981, *56*(2), pp. 326–41. [G: U.S.]

Friedman, Stephen J. Rapidly Changing Financial Markets. In *Sametz, A. W., ed.,* 1981, pp. 31–34. [G: U.S.]

Froewiss, Kenneth C. "Financial Futures Markets: Is More Regulation Needed?": Comment. *J. Futures Markets,* Summer 1981, *1*(2), pp. 191–92. [G: U.S.]

Fuller, Russell J. and Petry, Glenn H. Inflation, Return on Equity, and Stock Prices. *J. Portfol. Manage.,* Summer 1981, *7*(4), pp. 19–25. [G: U.S.]

Garil, Barnard H. The Probable Impacts of Expanded Securities and Other Financing Activities of Banks and Securities Firms in the 1980s: Impacts on the Securities Industry. In *Sametz, A. W., ed.,* 1981, pp. 161–64. [G: U.S.]

Gastineau, Gary L. Options Markets and Instruments. In *Altman, E. I., ed.,* 1981, pp. 20.3–45. [G: U.S.]

Geithman, Frederick E.; Marvel, Howard P. and Weiss, Leonard W. Concentration, Price and Critical Concentration Ratios. *Rev. Econ. Statist.,* August 1981, *63*(3), pp. 346–53. [G: U.S.]

de Gelsey, William. The Lender's View of the Financial Markets in the 80's. In *Burghardt, A. M., ed.,* 1981, pp. 43–57. [G: Global]

Gemmill, Gordon. Financial Futures in London: Rational Market or New Casino? *Nat. Westminster Bank Quart. Rev.,* February 1981, pp. 2–13. [G: U.K.]

Geske, Robert. Comments on Whaley's Note [An Analytical Formula for Unprotected American Call Options on Stocks with Known Dividends]. *J. Finan. Econ.,* June 1981, *9*(2), pp. 213–15.

Gheysens, Lieven. Profitability and Risk of the Belgian Financial Sector: A Stock Market Analysis and a Comparison with Accounting Data. In *Verheirstraeten, A., ed.,* 1981, pp. 97–113. [G: Belgium]

Giles, David E. A. and Goss, Barry A. Futures Prices as Forecasts of Commodity Spot Prices: Live Cattle and Wool. *Australian J. Agr. Econ.,* April 1981, *25*(1), pp. 1–13. [G: Australia]

Gipson, James H. Investing in a Zero Sum Economy. *J. Portfol. Manage.*, Summer 1981, *7*(4), pp. 15–16. [G: U.S.]

Givoly, Dan and Palmon, Dan. Classification of Convertible Debt as Common Stock Equivalents: Some Empirical Evidence on the Effects of APB Opinion 15. *J. Acc. Res.*, Autumn 1981, *19*(2), pp. 530–43. [G: U.S.]

Gmür, Charles J. Trade Financing: Forfaiting. **In** *Gmür, C. J., ed.*, 1981, pp. 117–32.

Gorham, Michael. The Effect of Inflation on the Rules of Futures Exchanges: A Case Study of the Chicago Mercantile Exchange. *J. Futures Markets*, Fall 1981, *1*(3), pp. 337–45. [G: U.S.]

Goss, Barry A. The Forward Pricing Function of the London Metal Exchange. *Appl. Econ.*, June 1981, *13*(2), pp. 133–50.

Gouldey, Bruce K. and Gray, Gary J. Implementing Mean-Variance Theory in the Selection of U.S. Government Bond Portfolios. *J. Bank Res.*, Autumn 1981, *12*(3), pp. 161–73. [G: U.S.]

Gray, Roger W. and Peck, Anne E. The Chicago Wheat Futures Market: Recent Problems in Historical Perspective. *Food Res. Inst. Stud.*, 1981, *18*(1), pp. 89–115. [G: U.S.]

Greenblatt, Joel M.; Pzena, Richard and Newberg, Bruce L. How the Small Investor Can Beat the Market. *J. Portfol. Manage.*, Summer 1981, *7*(4), pp. 48–52. [G: U.S.]

Greenstone, Wayne D. The Coffee Cartel: Manipulation in the Public Interest. *J. Futures Markets*, Spring 1981, *1*(1), pp. 3–16. [G: U.S.]

Groenewegen, Peter D. Market Rates or Tax Exempt Rates on Semi-government Securities. **In** *Jüttner, D. J., ed.*, 1981, pp. 27–45. [G: Australia]

Gupta, Sanjeev and Mayer, Thomas. A Test of the Efficiency of Futures Markets in Commodities. *Weltwirtsch. Arch.*, 1981, *117*(4), pp. 661–71.

Guy, James R. F. and Vaughan, Closson L. International Portfolio Diversification and Foreign Capital Markets. **In** *Altman, E. I., ed.*, 1981, pp. 15.3–27. [G: Japan; U.K.; W. Germany; France]

Hadaway, Samuel C. and Hadaway, Beverly L. Inflation Protection from Multi-Asset Sector Investments: A Long-Run Examination of Correlation Relationships with Inflation Rates. *Rev. Bus. Econ. Res.*, Spring 1981, *16*(3), pp. 80–89. [G: U.S.]

Handmaker, David. Low-Frequency Filters in Seasonal Analysis. *J. Futures Markets*, Fall 1981, *1*(3), pp. 367–78. [G: U.S.]

Hanna, Jeffrey D. The Advantages of Multicurrency Diversification. **In** *Ensor, R. and Muller, P., eds.*, 1981, pp. 219–26. [G: OECD]

Hayashi, Toshihiko. The Yield on Government Bonds and the Structure of Expected Short Term Interest Rates. (In Japanese. With English summary.) *Osaka Econ. Pap.*, December 1981, *31*(2–3), pp. 132–48. [G: Japan]

Helmuth, John W. A Report on the Systematic Downward Bias in Live Cattle Futures Prices. *J. Futures Markets*, Fall 1981, *1*(3), pp. 347–58. [G: U.S.]

Hendershott, Patric H. and Hu, Sheng-Cheng. Inflation and Extraordinary Returns on Owner-Occupied Housing: Some Implications for Capital Allocation and Productivity Growth. **In** *Tuccillo, J. A. and Villani, K. E., eds.*, 1981, pp. 11–33. [G: U.S.]

Hendershott, Patric H. and Villani, Kevin E. Savings and Loan Usage of the Authority to Invest in Corporate Bonds. **In** *Federal Home Loan Bank of San Francisco.*, 1981, pp. 149–67. [G: U.S.]

Henriksson, Roy D. and Merton, Robert C. On Market Timing and Investment Performance. II. Statistical Procedures for Evaluating Forecasting Skills. *J. Bus.*, October 1981, *54*(4), pp. 513–33. [G: U.S.]

Heri, Erwin W. Eine empirische Überprüfung der Effizienzhypothese für den Schweizer-Franken-Markt. (An Empirical Test of the Market Efficiency Hypothesis for the Swiss Franc. With English summary.) *Schweiz. Z. Volkswirtsch. Statist.*, December 1981, *117*(4), pp. 563–80.

Herman, James. Inflationary Expectations and Capital Markets. *Rev. Bus. Econ. Res.*, Spring 1981, *16*(3), pp. 69–79. [G: U.S.]

Hester, Donald D. Innovations and Monetary Control. *Brookings Pap. Econ. Act.*, 1981, (1), pp. 141–89. [G: U.S.]

Hewson, John R. Official Interest Rates: Comments. **In** *Jüttner, D. J., ed.*, 1981, pp. 57–64. [G: Australia; U.S.]

Hill, Joanne M. and Schneeweis, Thomas. A Note on the Hedging Effectiveness of Foreign Currency Futures. *J. Futures Markets*, Winter 1981, *1*(4), pp. 659–64.

Hill, Joanne M. and Schneeweis, Thomas. Diversification and Portfolio Size for Fixed Income Securities. *J. Econ. Bus.*, Winter 1981, *33*(2), pp. 115–21. [G: U.S.]

Hill, Malcolm R. Bond Interest Rates. **In** *Jüttner, D. J., ed.*, 1981, pp. 3–26. [G: Australia]

Hoffmeister, J. Ronald. On the Pricing of Preferred Stock: Discussion. *J. Finan. Quant. Anal.*, November 1981, *16*(4), pp. 529–31.

Hopwood, William S.; McKeown, James C. and Newbold, Paul. Power Transformations in Time-Series Models of Quarterly Earnings per Share. *Accounting Rev.*, October 1981, *56*(4), pp. 927–33. [G: U.S.]

Jacobson, Robert. Forecasting Bank Portfolios. **In** *Maisel, S. J., ed.*, 1981, pp. 249–70. [G: U.S.]

Jain, Arvind K. International Integration of Commodity Markets. *J. Int. Bus. Stud.*, Winter 1981, *12*(3), pp. 65–88. [G: U.S.; U.K.]

Jankus, Jonathan C. Is Beta a Useful Measure of Security Risk? Comment. *J. Portfol. Manage.*, Fall 1981, *8*(1), pp. 66. [G: U.S.]

Jarrell, Gregg A. The Economic Effects of Federal Regulation of the Market for New Security Issues. *J. Law Econ.*, December 1981, *24*(3), pp. 613–75. [G: U.S.]

Johnston, H. Neil; Russell, Don E. and Freeland, B. A. The Relationship between Dividend Yields, Interest Rates and Stock Market Prices. **In** *Jüttner, D. J., ed.*, 1981, pp. 204–23. [G: Australia]

Jones, Frank J. Spreads: Tails, Turtles, and All That. *J. Futures Markets*, Winter 1981, *1*(4), pp. 565–96.

Jones, Frank J. The Integration of the Cash and Futures Markets for Treasury Securities. *J. Futures Markets*, Spring 1981, *1*(1), pp. 33–57.

Kalay, Avner. Earnings Uncertainty and the Payout Ratio: Some Empirical Evidence. *Rev. Econ. Statist.*, August 1981, *63*(3), pp. 439–43. [G: U.S.]

Kalotay, Andrew J. Long-term Debt and Equity Markets and Instruments. In *Altman, E. I., ed.*, 1981, pp. 4.3–34. [G: U.S.]

Kaufman, George G. Municipal Bond Underwriting: Market Structure. *J. Bank Res.*, Spring 1981, *12*(1), pp. 24–31. [G: U.S.]

Kaufman, P. J. Safety-adjusted Performance Evaluation. *J. Futures Markets*, Spring 1981, *1*(1), pp. 17–31. [G: U.S.]

Keating, G. R. and Sharpe, Ian G. Australian Interest Rates: A Cross Correlation Analysis. In *Jüttner, D. J., ed.*, 1981, pp. 181–203.
[G: Australia]

Keenan, Michael. The Securities Industry: Securities Trading and Investment Banking. In *Altman, E. I., ed.*, 1981, pp. 5.3–29. [G: U.S.]

Keown, Arthur J. and Pinkerton, John M. Merger Announcements and Insider Trading Activity: An Empirical Investigation. *J. Finance*, September 1981, *36*(4), pp. 855–69. [G: U.S.]

Kiernan, Eric. Australian Interest Rates: A Cross Correlation Analysis: Comment. In *Jüttner, D. J., ed.*, 1981, pp. 224–28. [G: Australia]

Koch, Timothy W. Commercial Bank Size, Relative Profitability and the Demand for Tax-Exempt Securities. *J. Bank Res.*, Autumn 1981, *12*(3), pp. 136–44. [G: U.S.]

Kolluri, Bharat R. Gold as a Hedge against Inflation: An Empirical Investigation. *Quart. Rev. Econ. Bus.*, Winter 1981, *21*(4), pp. 13–24. [G: U.S.]

Kudla, Ronald J. Strategic Planning and Risk. *Rev. Bus. Econ. Res.*, Fall 1981, *17*(1), pp. 1–14.
[G: U.S.]

Labys, Walter C.; Cohen, B. C. and Yang, Chin Wei. The Rational Cavist. *Europ. Rev. Agr. Econ.*, 1981, *8*(4), pp. 519–25. [G: U.K.]

Lakonishok, Josef and Sadan, Simcha. Information Sets, Macroeconomic Reform, and Stock Prices. *J. Finan. Quant. Anal.*, November 1981, *16*(4), pp. 495–510. [G: Israel]

Lamle, Hugh R. Ginnie Mae: Age Equals Beauty. *J. Portfol. Manage.*, Winter 1981, *7*(2), pp. 75–79. [G: U.S.]

Langohr, Herwig. Profitability and Risk of the Belgian Financial Sector: A Stock Market Analysis and a Comparison with Accounting Data: Comment. In *Verheirstraeten, A., ed.*, 1981, pp. 114–16. [G: Belgium]

Larcker, David F. Discussion of The SEC "Reversal" of FASB Statement No. 19: An Investigation of Information Effects. *J. Acc. Res.*, Supplement 1981, *19*, pp. 218–26. [G: U.S.]

LeBaron, Dean and Schulman, Evan. Trading: The Fixable Leak. *J. Portfol. Manage.*, Fall 1981, *8*(1), pp. 10–12. [G: U.S.]

Lee, Cheng Few and Zumwalt, J. Kenton. Associations between Alternative Accounting Profitability Measures and Security Returns. *J. Finan. Quant. Anal.*, March 1981, *16*(1), pp. 71–93.
[G: U.S.]

Leibowitz, Martin L. Specialized Fixed Income Security Strategies. In *Altman, E. I., ed.*, 1981, pp. 19.3–40.

Leonard, David C. and Kehr, James B. Stock Market Returns and Monetary Aggregates: Recent Evidence on the Issue of Causality. *Rev. Bus. Econ. Res.*, Fall 1981, *17*(1), pp. 40–50.
[G: U.S.]

Levitt, Arthur, Jr. The Probable Impacts of Expanded Securities and Other Financing Activities of Banks and Securities Firms in the 1980s: Impacts on the Exchanges. In *Sametz, A. W., ed.*, 1981, pp. 155–56. [G: U.S.]

Livingston, Miles. Taxation and Bond Market Equilibrium in a World of Uncertain Future Interest Rates: Reply. *J. Finan. Quant. Anal.*, December 1981, *16*(5), pp. 779–81. [G: U.S.]

Livnat, Joshua. A Generalization of the API Methodology as a Way of Measuring the Association between Income and Stock Prices. *J. Acc. Res.*, Autumn 1981, *19*(2), pp. 350–59. [G: U.S.]

Lloyd, William P. and Goldstein, Steven J. Called Bonds: How Does the Investor Fare? Comment. *J. Portfol. Manage.*, Fall 1981, *8*(1), pp. 62–63.
[G: U.S.]

Logue, Dennis E. Overseas Money and Capital Markets. In *Altman, E. I., ed.*, 1981, pp. 13.3–33.

London, Anselm. The Stability of the Interest Parity Relationship between Canada and the United States: A Note. *Rev. Econ. Statist.*, November 1981, *63*(4), pp. 625–26. [G: Canada; U.S.]

Loomis, Philip C. A Critique of Current Regulatory Procedures in the Municipal Securities Industry. In *Sametz, A. W., ed.*, 1981, pp. 65–69.
[G: U.S.]

Lybecker, Martin E. Comment [Commingled-Agency Accounts for Bank Trust Departments—An Idea Whose Time Has Come] [Preserving Barriers against Banks' Engaging in the Personal-Investment Business]. In *Sametz, A. W., ed.*, 1981, pp. 100–107. [G: U.S.]

Lynge, Morgan J., Jr. Money Supply Announcements and Stock Prices. *J. Portfol. Manage.*, Fall 1981, *8*(1), pp. 40–43. [G: U.S.]

Ma, Ronald and Whittred, G. P. Ben Graham's Last Will and Testament: An Evaluation. *Australian J. Manage.*, June 1981, *6*(1), pp. 51–65.
[G: Australia]

Madden, Gerald P. Potential Corporate Takeovers and Market Efficiency: A Note. *J. Finance*, December 1981, *36*(5), pp. 1191–97. [G: U.S.]

Maisel, Sherman J. and Jacobson, Robert. Interest Rate Changes and Commercial Bank Revenues and Costs. In *Maisel, S. J., ed.*, 1981, pp. 203–22. [G: U.S.]

Maness, Terry S. Optimal versus Naive Buy-Hedging with T-Bill Futures. *J. Futures Markets*, Fall 1981, *1*(3), pp. 393–403. [G: U.S.]

Martell, Terrence F. and Salzman, Jerrold E. Cash Settlement for Futures Contracts Based on Common Stock Indices: An Economic and Legal Perspective. *J. Futures Markets*, Fall 1981, *1*(3), pp. 291–301.

McCallum, John S. The Empirical Impact of Changes in Government on Bond Yields: The Canadian Provincial Experience. *J. Bank Res.*, Winter 1981, *11*(4), pp. 245–47. [G: Canada]

McClay, Marvin. Is the Equity Market Becoming More Volatile? *J. Portfol. Manage.*, Spring 1981,

7(3), pp. 51–54. [G: U.S.]

McEnally, Richard W. What Causes Bond Prices to Change? *J. Portfol. Manage.*, Spring 1981, 7(3), pp. 5–12. [G: U.S.]

McLeod, Robert W. and Misiolek, Walter S. The Effect of Money Market CDs on the Growth of Money Market Mutual Funds. *Bus. Econ.*, January 1981, 16(1), pp. 75–78. [G: U.S.]

Melamed, Leo. The Futures Market: Liquidity and the Technique of Spreading. *J. Futures Markets*, Fall 1981, 1(3), pp. 405–11.

Menell, Howard. Current Regulatory Framework for Banks' Securities Activities as Viewed by Regulators: Comment. In *Sametz, A. W., ed.*, 1981, pp. 76–81. [G: U.S.]

Mikkelson, Wayne H. Convertible Calls and Security Returns. *J. Finan. Econ.*, Summer 1981, 9(3), pp. 237–64. [G: U.S.]

Minarik, Joseph J. Capital Gains. In *Aaron, H. J. and Pechman, J. A., eds.*, 1981, pp. 241–77. [G: U.S.]

Modigliani, Franco and Cohn, Richard A. Inflation and the Stock Market. *Rev. Econ. Cond. Italy*, October 1981, (3), pp. 415–31. [G: U.S.]

Morrissey, Thomas F. Interest Rate Effects on the Maturity Composition of Household Portfolios of Marketable U.S. Government Securities. *Bus. Econ.*, January 1981, 16(1), pp. 30–34. [G: U.S.]

Morse, Dale. Price and Trading Volume Reaction Surrounding Earnings Announcements: A Closer Examination. *J. Acc. Res.*, Autumn 1981, 19(2), pp. 374–83. [G: U.S.]

Nardi, Paolo. Il rendimento effettivo medio di più prestiti obbligazionari. (The Average Effective Yields of a Number of Bond Loans. With English summary.) *Bancaria*, January 1981, 37(1), pp. 58–63.

Nardi, Paolo. Il risultato degli investimenti finanziari in Italia in periodi di inflazione. (The Results of Financial Investments in Italy during Periods of Inflation. With English summary.) *Bancaria*, May 1981, 37(5), pp. 498–506. [G: Italy]

Nauss, Robert M. and Keeler, Bradford R. Optimizing Municipal Bond Bids. *J. Bank Res.*, Autumn 1981, 12(3), pp. 174–81. [G: U.S.]

Newman, Maurice L. Bond Interest Rates: Comment. In *Jüttner, D. J., ed.*, 1981, pp. 46–50. [G: Australia]

Nichols, William D. and Brown, Stewart L. Assimilating Earnings and Split Information: Is the Capital Market Becoming More Efficient? *J. Finan. Econ.*, Summer 1981, 9(3), pp. 309–15. [G: U.S.]

Noreen, Eric W. and Sepe, James. Market Reactions to Accounting Policy Deliberations: The Inflation Accounting Case Revisited—A Reply. *Accounting Rev.*, October 1981, 56(4), pp. 955–58. [G: U.S.]

Noreen, Eric W. and Sepe, James. Market Reactions to Accounting Policy Deliberations: The Inflation Accounting Case. *Accounting Rev.*, April 1981, 56(2), pp. 253–69. [G: U.S.]

Noreen, Eric W. and Wolfson, Mark A. Equilibrium Warrant Pricing Models and Accounting for Executive Stock Options. *J. Acc. Res.*, Autumn 1981,

19(2), pp. 384–98. [G: U.S.]

Ølgaard, Anders. Indekslån—et supplement til traditionelle fordringer? (Introduction of Index-Linked Bonds in the Danish Capital Market as a Supplement to Traditional Bonds. With English summary.) *Nationaløkon. Tidsskr.*, 1981, 119(3), pp. 309–29. [G: Denmark]

Opper, Franz F. Current Regulatory Framework for Banks' Securities Activities as Viewed by Regulators: Comment. In *Sametz, A. W., ed.*, 1981, pp. 47–51. [G: U.S.]

Otani, Ichiro and Tiwari, Siddharth. Capital Controls and Interest Rate Parity: The Japanese Experience, 1978–81. *Int. Monet. Fund Staff Pap.*, December 1981, 28(4), pp. 793–815. [G: Japan]

Palme, Lennart A., Jr. and Graham, James. The Systematic Downward Bias in Live Cattle Futures: An Evaluation. *J. Futures Markets*, Fall 1981, 1(3), pp. 359–66. [G: U.S.]

Parker, Jack W. and Daigler, Robert T. Hedging Money Market CDs with Treasury-Bill Futures. *J. Futures Markets*, Winter 1981, 1(4), pp. 597–606. [G: U.S.]

Partee, J. Charles. Statement to Subcommittee on Telecommunications, Consumer Protection and Finance, House Committee on Energy and Commerce, February 26, 1981. *Fed. Res. Bull.*, March 1981, 67(3), pp. 241–43. [G: U.S.]

Patell, James M. and Wolfson, Mark A. The Ex Ante and Ex Post Price Effects of Quarterly Earnings Announcements Reflected in Option and Stock Prices. *J. Acc. Res.*, Autumn 1981, 19(2), pp. 434–58. [G: U.S.]

Payne, Adrian F. T. Options, Premium Contracts, and the EOE. *De Economist*, 1981, 129(2), pp. 224–40. [G: Netherlands]

Peck, Anne Elizabeth. "The Economics of Hedging and Spreading Futures Markets": Comment. *J. Futures Markets*, Summer 1981, 1(2), pp. 287–89.

Peters, Roy. Overseas Portfolio Investment—Developments since the Abolition of Exchange Controls. *Nat. Westminster Bank Quart. Rev.*, May 1981, pp. 32–39. [G: U.K.]

Petersen, John E. The Municipal Bond Market: Recent Changes and Future Prospects. In *Walzer, N. and Chicoine, D. L., eds.*, 1981, pp. 129–41. [G: U.S.]

Phillips, Willard R., Jr. Fiduciaries and Futures. *J. Futures Markets*, Fall 1981, 1(3), pp. 317–28. [G: U.S.]

Pohlman, Jerry E. Optimal Assets Choice: Comments. In *Federal Home Loan Bank of San Francisco.*, 1981, pp. 169–72. [G: U.S.]

Poole, William. Official Interest Rates: Comments. In *Jüttner, D. J., ed.*, 1981, pp. 51–56. [G: Australia; U.S.]

Poole, William. Short-term Interest Rates and Futures Markets: Comments. In *Jüttner, D. J., ed.*, 1981, pp. 373–78. [G: Australia; U.S.]

Poole, William. The Relationship between Dividend Yields, Interest Rates and Stock Market Prices: Comment. In *Jüttner, D. J., ed.*, 1981, pp. 229–32. [G: Australia]

Pozen, Robert C. A Broad Critique of the Current Regulatory Framework. In *Sametz, A. W., ed.*,

1981, pp. 55–58. [G: U.S.]

Price, Kelly. An Analysis of the Effects of a Multi-Tiered Stock Market: Discussion. *J. Finan. Quant. Anal.*, November 1981, *16*(4), pp. 577–79.

Raman, K. K. Financial Reporting and Municipal Bond Rating Changes. *Accounting Rev.*, October 1981, *56*(4), pp. 910–26. [G: U.S.]

Rana, Pradumna B. Exchange Rate Risk under Generalized Floating: Eight Asian Countries. *J. Int. Econ.*, November 1981, *11*(4), pp. 459–66. [G: Asia]

Randall, Maury R. and Greenfield, Robert L. Effects of Changes in Anticipated Inflation and Taxes on Stock Prices. *Nebr. J. Econ. Bus.*, Winter 1981, *20*(1), pp. 49–58. [G: U.S.]

Reddaway, W. B. Portfolio Selection in Practice. In *Currie, D.; Nobay, R. and Peel, D., eds.*, 1981, pp. 383–404. [G: U.K.]

Reilly, Frank K. and Drzycimski, Eugene F. An Analysis of the Effects of a Multi-Tiered Stock Market. *J. Finan. Quant. Anal.*, November 1981, *16*(4), pp. 559–75. [G: U.S.]

Ro, Byung T. The Disclosure of Replacement Cost Accounting Data and Its Effects on Transaction Volumes. *Accounting Rev.*, January 1981, *56*(1), pp. 70–84. [G: U.S.]

Ro, Byung T. The Disclosure of Replacement Cost Accounting Data and Its Effect on Transaction Volumes: A Reply. *Accounting Rev.*, January 1981, *56*(1), pp. 181–87. [G: U.S.]

Rogowski, Robert J. The Cyclical Pattern in Corporate Bond Supply: A Comment [The Cyclical Pattern in Corporate Bond Quality]. *J. Portfol. Manage.*, Winter 1981, *7*(2), pp. 94. [G: U.S.]

Roley, V. Vance. The Determinants of the Treasury Security Yield Curve. *J. Finance*, December 1981, *36*(5), pp. 1103–26. [G: U.S.]

Roll, Richard. A Possible Explanation of the Small Firm Effect. *J. Finance*, September 1981, *36*(4), pp. 879–88. [G: U.S.]

Ronen, Joshua and Livnat, Joshua. Incentives for Segment Reporting. *J. Acc. Res.*, Autumn 1981, *19*(2), pp. 459–81. [G: U.S.]

Rowen, Harvey A. The Probable Impacts of Expanded Securities and Other Financing Activities of Banks and Securities Firms in the 1980s: Impacts on the Securities Industry. In *Sametz, A. W., ed.*, 1981, pp. 164–66. [G: U.S.]

Rudd, Andrew. Using Options to Increase Reward and Decrease Risk. *J. Bank Res.*, Autumn 1981, *12*(3), pp. 182–91. [G: U.S.]

Rundfelt, Rolf. Capital Gains Taxation and Effective Rates of Return. In *Eliasson, G. and Södersten, J., eds.*, 1981, pp. 345–80. [G: Sweden; U.K.]

Rutledge, David J. S. Short-term Interest Rates and Futures Markets: Comments. In *Jüttner, D. J., ed.*, 1981, pp. 379–81. [G: U.S.; Australia]

Salkin, Harvey M. and Ritchken, Peter H. Comment: Option Spreading [Option Spreading: Theory and an Illustration]. *J. Portfol. Manage.*, Winter 1981, *7*(2), pp. 89–90.

Salkin, Harvey M. and Ritchken, Peter H. Rejoinder [Option Spreading: Theory and an Illustration]. *J. Portfol. Manage.*, Winter 1981, *7*(2), pp. 93.

Sametz, Arnold W. Background of the Controversy over Banks' Securities Activities—A Briefing. In *Sametz, A. W., ed.*, 1981, pp. 3–19. [G: U.S.]

Sandor, Richard L. and Jones, Dallas. Futures and Commodities Markets. In *Altman, E. I., ed.*, 1981, pp. 21.3–31. [G: U.S.]

Santomero, Anthony M. Comment [Commingled-Agency Accounts for Bank Trust Departments—An Idea Whose Time Has Come] [Preserving Barriers against Banks' Engaging in the Personal-Investment Business]. In *Sametz, A. W., ed.*, 1981, pp. 95–100. [G: U.S.]

Santoni, Gary J. and Stone, Courtenay C. What Really Happened to Interest Rates?: A Longer-Run Analysis. *Fed. Res. Bank St. Louis Rev.*, November 1981, *63*(9), pp. 3–14. [G: U.S.]

Sarris, Alexander H. and Schmitz, Andrew. Price Formation in International Agricultural Trade. In *McCalla, A. F. and Josling, T. E., eds.*, 1981, pp. 29–48.

Saunders, Anthony and Tress, Richard B. Inflation and Stock Market Returns: Some Australian Evidence. *Econ. Rec.*, March 1981, *57*(156), pp. 58–66. [G: Australia]

Schaefer, Jeffrey M. Current Regulatory Framework for Banks' Securities Activities as Viewed by Regulators: Comment. In *Sametz, A. W., ed.*, 1981, pp. 71–74. [G: U.S.]

Schaefer, Stephen M. Measuring a Tax-Specific Term Structure of Interest Rates in the Market for British Government Securities. *Econ. J.*, June 1981, *91*(362), pp. 415–38. [G: U.K.]

Schaefer, Stephen M. Taxation and Bond Market Equilibrium in a World of Uncertain Future Interest Rates: Comment. *J. Finan. Quant. Anal.*, December 1981, *16*(5), pp. 773–77.

Schneeweis, Thomas and Branch, Ben. Capital Market Efficiency in Fixed Income Securities. *Rev. Bus. Econ. Res.*, Winter 1981, *16*(2), pp. 34–42. [G: U.S.]

Scholes, Myron S. The Economics of Hedging and Spreading in Futures Markets. *J. Futures Markets*, Summer 1981, *1*(2), pp. 265–86. [G: U.S.]

Schwert, G. William. The Adjustment of Stock Prices to Information about Inflation. *J. Finance*, March 1981, *36*(1), pp. 15–29. [G: U.S.]

Scott, Elton and Teycock, Stefan. Published Results on Speculative Markets: Some Evidence from the Stock Market. *Bus. Econ.*, January 1981, *16*(1), pp. 67–74. [G: U.S.]

Seater, John J. The Market Value of Outstanding Government Debt, 1919–1975. *J. Monet. Econ.*, July 1981, *8*(1), pp. 85–101. [G: U.S.]

Seevers, Gary L. "Innovation, Competition, and New Contract Design in Futures Markets": Comment. *J. Futures Markets*, Summer 1981, *1*(2), pp. 157–59. [G: U.S.]

Seiders, David F. GNMA Passthrough Securities: Discussion. *J. Finance*, May 1981, *36*(2), pp. 484–86.

Sharpe, Ian G. The Market for Commonwealth Government Securities: Comment. In *Jüttner, D. J., ed.*, 1981, pp. 177–78. [G: Australia]

Sharpe, W. F. Bank Capital Adequacy, Deposit Insurance, and Security Values. In *Maisel, S. J., ed.*, 1981, *1978*, pp. 187–202.

Shevlin, Terrence J. Measuring Abnormal Performance on the Australian Securities Market. *Australian J. Manage.*, June 1981, *6*(1), pp. 67–107.
[G: Australia]

Silber, William L. Innovation, Competition, and New Contract Design in Futures Markets. *J. Futures Markets*, Summer 1981, *1*(2), pp. 123–55.
[G: U.S.]

Silver, Andrew. Original Issue Deep Discount Bonds. *Fed. Res. Bank New York Quart. Rev.*, Winter 1981–82, *6*(4), pp. 18–28. [G: U.S.]

Simonoff, Jeffrey S. Application of Statistical Methodology to the Evaluation of Timing Devices in Commodities Trading. *J. Futures Markets*, Winter 1981, *1*(4), pp. 649–56.

Sinai, Allen. New Approaches to Stabilization Policy and the Effects on U.S. Financial Markets. *Nat. Tax J.*, September 1981, *34*(3), pp. 341–72.

Singleton, J. Clay; Schmidt, James R. and Matzke, Jane. Regional Bond Yields and Economic Activity: Theory and Application. *Reg. Sci. Persp.*, 1981, *11*(2), pp. 83–93. [G: U.S.]

Slivka, Ronald T. Call Option Spreading. *J. Portfol. Manage.*, Spring 1981, *7*(3), pp. 71–76.

Smith, Abbie J. The SEC "Reversal" of FASB Statement No. 19: An Investigation of Information Effects. *J. Acc. Res.*, Supplement 1981, *19*, pp. 174–211. [G: U.S.]

Smith, Abbie J. and Dyckman, Thomas. The Impact of Accounting Regulation on the Stock Market: The Case of Oil and Gas Companies: A Comment. *Accounting Rev.*, October 1981, *56*(4), pp. 959–66. [G: U.S.]

Smith, Rodney T. The Economic Effects of Federal Regulation of the Market for New Security Issues: Comment. *J. Law Econ.*, December 1981, *24*(3), pp. 677–86. [G: U.S.]

Smith, Tildon W. Short-term Money Markets and Instruments. In *Altman, E. I., ed.*, 1981, pp. 10.3–14. [G: U.S.]

Smith, William M. The Probable Impacts of Expanded Securities and Other Financing Activities of Banks and Securities Firms in the 1980s: Impacts on the Exchanges. In *Sametz, A. W., ed.*, 1981, pp. 156–59. [G: U.S.]

Soldofsky, Robert M. The Risk–Return Performance of Convertibles. *J. Portfol. Manage.*, Winter 1981, *7*(2), pp. 80–84. [G: U.S.]

Solt, Michael E. and Swanson, Paul J. On the Efficiency of the Markets for Gold and Silver. *J. Bus.*, July 1981, *54*(3), pp. 453–78. [G: U.S.]

Sorensen, Eric H. and Hawkins, Clark A. On the Pricing of Preferred Stock. *J. Finan. Quant. Anal.*, November 1981, *16*(4), pp. 515–28.
[G: U.S.]

Sorensen, Eric H. and Wert, James E. A New Tool for Estimating New Issue Bond Yields. *J. Portfol. Manage.*, Spring 1981, *7*(3), pp. 42–45.
[G: U.S.]

Spencer, Peter D. A Model of the Demand for British Government Stocks by Non-Bank Residents, 1967–77. *Econ. J.*, December 1981, *91*(364), pp. 938–60. [G: U.K.]

Spencer, Roger W. Rationale of Current Regulatory Approaches to Banks' Securities Activities. In *Sametz, A. W., ed.*, 1981, pp. 35–43. [G: U.S.]

Spiro, Harvey M. Economic Sector Investing. *Bus. Econ.*, March 1981, *16*(2), pp. 1–5.

Stanley, Kenneth L. Measuring the Operational Costs of Dual Trading: An Analytical Framework. *J. Futures Markets*, Fall 1981, *1*(3), pp. 329–36.
[G: U.S.]

Stein, Jerome L. Speculative Price: Economic Welfare and the Idiot of Chance. *Rev. Econ. Statist.*, May 1981, *63*(2), pp. 223–32. [G: U.S.]

Stock, Duane and Robertson, Terry. Improved Techniques for Predicting Municipal Bond Ratings. *J. Bank Res.*, Autumn 1981, *12*(3), pp. 153–60. [G: U.S.]

Stoll, Hans R. Revolution in the Regulation of Securities Markets: An Examination of the Effects of Increased Competition. In *Weiss, L. W. and Klass, M. W., eds.*, 1981, pp. 12–52. [G: U.S.]

Stone, James M. Principles of the Regulation of Futures Markets. *J. Futures Markets*, Summer 1981, *1*(2), pp. 117–21.

Strong, Robert A. The Impact of Mayday on Diversification Costs: Comment. *J. Portfol. Manage.*, Spring 1981, *7*(3), pp. 77–78.

Struble, Frederick M. "Financial Futures Markets: Is More Regulation Needed?": Comment. *J. Futures Markets*, Summer 1981, *1*(2), pp. 193–99.
[G: U.S.]

Taylor, Christopher A. Current Regulatory Procedures in the Municipal Securities Industry. In *Sametz, A. W., ed.*, 1981, pp. 59–63. [G: U.S.]

Telser, Lester G. Margins and Futures Contracts. *J. Futures Markets*, Summer 1981, *1*(2), pp. 225–53.

Teriba, O. Financial Institutions, Financial Markets, and Income Distribution. In *Bienen, H. and Diejomaoh, V. P., eds.*, 1981, pp. 485–512.
[G: Nigeria]

Thygerson, Kenneth J. Futures, Options, and the Savings and Loan Business. In *Federal Home Loan Bank of San Francisco.*, 1981, pp. 119–47.
[G: U.S.]

Tinic, S. M. Impact of Regulation on Economic Behavior: Discussion. *J. Finance*, May 1981, *36*(2), pp. 395–97.

Urich, Thomas and Wachtel, Paul. Market Response to the Weekly Money Supply Announcements in the 1970s. *J. Finance*, December 1981, *36*(5), pp. 1063–72. [G: U.S.]

Vandell, Robert F. Is Beta a Useful Measure of Security Risk? Reply. *J. Portfol. Manage.*, Fall 1981, *8*(1), pp. 66. [G: U.S.]

Vandell, Robert F. Is Beta a Useful Measure of Security Risk? *J. Portfol. Manage.*, Winter 1981, *7*(2), pp. 23–31. [G: U.S.]

Vaughn, Richard; Kelly, Marvin and Hochheimer, Frank. Identifying Seasonality in Futures Prices Using X-11. *J. Futures Markets*, Spring 1981, *1*(1), pp. 93–101. [G: U.S.]

Vermaelen, Theo. Common Stock Repurchases and Market Signalling: An Empirical Study. *J. Finan. Econ.*, June 1981, *9*(2), pp. 139–83. [G: U.S.]

Verrecchia, Robert E. On the Relationship between Volume Reaction and Consensus of Investors: Implications for Interpreting Tests of Information Content. *J. Acc. Res.*, Spring 1981, *19*(1), pp. 271–83.

Vigeland, Robert L. The Market Reaction to Statement of Financial Accounting Standards No. 2. *Accounting Rev.*, April 1981, *56*(2), pp. 309–25. [G: U.S.]

Wallace, Wanda A. The Association between Municipal Market Measures and Selected Financial Reporting Practices. *J. Acc. Res.*, Autumn 1981, *19*(2), pp. 502–20. [G: U.S.]

Wallich, Henry C. The Probable Impacts of Expanded Securities and Other Financing Activities of Banks and Securities Firms in the 1980s: Impacts on the Regulatory Structure. In *Sametz, A. W., ed.*, 1981, pp. 151–54. [G: U.S.]

Watson, John and Dickinson, John P. International Diversification: An Ex Post and Ex Ante Analysis of Possible Benefits. *Australian J. Manage.*, June 1981, *6*(1), pp. 125–34. [G: Australia]

Weiner, Neil S. The Hedging Rationale for a Stock Index Futures Contract. *J. Futures Markets*, Spring 1981, *1*(1), pp. 59–76. [G: U.S.]

Weinstein, Mark. The Systematic Risk of Corporate Bonds. *J. Finan. Quant. Anal.*, September 1981, *16*(3), pp. 257–78. [G: U.S.]

Weston, C. Rae. Short-term Interest Rates and Interest-Rate Futures. In *Jüttner, D. J., ed.*, 1981, pp. 345–60. [G: Australia; U.S.]

Wetzler, James W. Capital Gains: Comments. In *Aaron, H. J. and Pechman, J. A., eds.*, 1981, pp. 277–81. [G: U.S.]

Whaley, Robert E. On the Valuation of American Call Options on Stocks with Known Dividends [An Analytical Valuation Formula for Unprotected American Call Options on Stocks with Known Dividends]. *J. Finan. Econ.*, June 1981, *9*(2), pp. 207–11.

White, Lawrence J. Current Regulatory Framework for Banks' Securities Activities as Viewed by Regulators: Comment. In *Sametz, A. W., ed.*, 1981, pp. 51–54. [G: U.S.]

Whiteside, Mary; Dukes, William P. and Dunne, Patrick. Announcement Impact on Securities of Future Option Trading. *Nebr. J. Econ. Bus.*, Spring 1981, *20*(2), pp. 63–72. [G: U.S.]

Williamson, J. Peter. Performance Measurement. In *Altman, E. I., ed.*, 1981, pp. 22.3–27.

314 Financial Intermediaries

3140 Financial Intermediaries

Aftalion, Florin. Government Intervention in the French Financial System. In *Verheirstraeten, A., ed.*, 1981, pp. 157–72. [G: France]

Aharony, Joseph and Swary, Itzhak. Effects of the 1970 Bank Holding Company Act: Evidence from Capital Markets. *J. Finance*, September 1981, *36*(4), pp. 841–53. [G: U.S.]

Angermueller, Hans H. Current Regulatory Framework for Banks' Securities Activities as Viewed by Regulators: Comment. In *Sametz, A. W., ed.*, 1981, pp. 43–45. [G: U.S.]

Arcuti, Luigi. Dalla regolamentazione alla liberalizzazione del movimento valutario. (From Control to Liberalization of Capital Movements. With English summary.) *Bancaria*, September 1981, *37*(9), pp. 891–94. [G: Italy]

Barth, James R. and Cordes, Joseph J. Nontraditional Criteria for Investing Pension Assets: An Economic Appraisal. *J. Lab. Res.*, Fall 1981, *2*(2), pp. 219–47. [G: U.S.]

Beason, Amos T. The Legal, Economic, and Social Case for Banks' Underwriting Municipal Revenue Bonds. In *Sametz, A. W., ed.*, 1981, pp. 123–27. [G: U.S.]

Beim, David O. The Public-Policy Case for Private-Placement Services by Commercial Banks. In *Sametz, A. W., ed.*, 1981, pp. 109–13. [G: U.S.]

Bellante, Don. Union Divergent Investing of Pensions: A Power, Non-Employee Relations Issue: Comment. *J. Lab. Res.*, Fall 1981, *2*(2), pp. 209–13. [G: U.S.]

Bench, Joseph. Money and Capital Markets: Institutional Framework and Federal Reserve Control. In *Altman, E. I., ed.*, 1981, pp. 1.3–33. [G: U.S.]

Bennett, James T. and Johnson, Manuel H. Union Use of Employee Pension Funds: Introduction and Overview. *J. Lab. Res.*, Fall 1981, *2*(2), pp. 181–90. [G: U.S.]

Bevan, Robert L. Current Regulatory Framework for Banks' Securities Activities as Viewed by Regulators: Comment. In *Sametz, A. W., ed.*, 1981, pp. 69–71. [G: U.S.]

Bickley, James M. An Evaluation of the Reconstruction Finance Corporation with Implications for Current Capital Needs of the Steel Industry. In *Sternlieb, G. and Listokin, D., eds.*, 1981, pp. 144–62. [G: U.S.]

Biederman, Kenneth R. Non-mortgage Lending: Panel Presentation. In *Federal Home Loan Bank of San Francisco.*, 1981, pp. 343–52. [G: U.S.]

Black, Harold A. and Dugger, Robert H. Credit Union Structure, Growth and Regulatory Problems. *J. Finance*, May 1981, *36*(2), pp. 529–38. [G: U.S.]

Black, Harold A. and Schweitzer, Robert L. An Analysis of Market Segmentation in Mortgage Lending between a Commercial Bank and a Mutual Savings Bank. *Amer. Real Estate Urban Econ. Assoc. J.*, Fall 1981, *9*(3), pp. 234–40. [G: U.S.]

Boddy, Martin. The Property Sector in Late Capitalism: The Case of Britain. In *Dear, M. and Scott, A. J., eds.*, 1981, pp. 267–86. [G: U.K.]

Bonds, W. Kenneth. Commingled-Agency Accounts for Bank Trust Departments—An Idea Whose Time Has Come. In *Sametz, A. W., ed.*, 1981, pp. 85–89. [G: U.S.]

Boyd, John H. and Kwast, Myron L. Bank Regulation and the Efficiency of Financial Intermediation. In *Federal Reserve System*, 1981, pp. 233–49. [G: U.S.]

Bradford, William D. The Cash Flow Implications of Alternative Mortgage Instruments. In *Federal Home Loan Bank of San Francisco.*, 1981, pp. 205–37. [G: U.S.]

Broadbent, John; Clements, Kenneth W. and Johnson, Lester W. Growth in Holdings of a New Financial Asset: A Logistic Analysis. *Australian J. Manage.*, December 1981, *6*(2), pp. 1–6. [G: Australia]

Cagan, Phillip. Comment [The Legal, Economic, and Social Case for Banks' Underwriting Municipal Revenue Bonds] [The Public-Policy Case against Banks' Underwriting Revenue Bonds]. In *Sametz, A. W., ed.,* 1981, pp. 136–38.
[G: U.S.]

Carney, Owen. "The Regulation of Futures and Forward Trading by Depository Institutions: A Legal and Economic Analysis": Comment. *J. Futures Markets,* Summer 1981, *1*(2), pp. 219–23.

Carr, Elliott G. The Condition of Massachusetts Savings Banks and California Savings and Loan Associations: Discussion. In *Federal Reserve Bank of Boston (II),* 1981, pp. 37–43. [G: U.S.]

Clements, Kenneth W. and Taylor, John C. The Determinants of Holdings of Financial Assets in Australia. *Australian J. Manage.,* December 1981, *6*(2), pp. 17–25. [G: Australia]

Crawford, Donald J. Current Regulatory Framework for Banks' Securities Activities as Viewed by Regulators: Comment. In *Sametz, A. W., ed.,* 1981, pp. 46–47. [G: U.S.]

Davis, Kevin. Banks, Thrifts and Interest Rates: Comments: Intermediaries and Interest Rates. In *Jüttner, D. J., ed.,* 1981, pp. 106–13.
[G: Australia]

Davis, Stuart. Deregulation and the Thrift Industry: Comments. In *Federal Home Loan Bank of San Francisco.,* 1981, pp. 61–70. [G: U.S.]

De Smet, Michel and Martin, Georges. Concentration and Economies of Scale in the Belgian Financial Sector: Comment. In *Verheirstraeten, A., ed.,* 1981, pp. 92–96. [G: Belgium]

Deihl, Richard H. Considerations of the Variable-Rate Mortgage Index: Panel Presentation. In *Federal Home Loan Bank of San Francisco.,* 1981, pp. 329–41. [G: U.S.]

Desiata, Alfonso. L'euroscudo nei rapporti assicurativi. (The E.C.U. in Insurance Business. With English summary.) *Bancaria,* March 1981, *37*(3), pp. 257–59. [G: EEC]

Dobbins, R.; Lowes, B. and Pass, Christopher L. Financial Institutions and the Ownership and Control of British Industry. *Managerial Dec. Econ.,* March 1981, *2*(1), pp. 16–24. [G: U.K.]

Dorsey, Stuart. Nontraditional Criteria for Investing Pension Assets: An Economic Appraisal: Comment. *J. Lab. Res.,* Fall 1981, *2*(2), pp. 248–51.
[G: U.S.]

Ebaugh, Dwight D. The Users and Providers of Consumer Financial Services: A Legal Framework. In *Heggestad, A. A., ed.,* 1981, pp. 62–91.
[G: U.S.]

Edwards, Franklin R. Current Regulatory Framework for Banks' Securities Activities as Viewed by Regulators: Comment. In *Sametz, A. W., ed.,* 1981, pp. 74–76. [G: U.S.]

Edwards, Franklin R. The Regulation of Futures and Forward Trading by Depository Institutions: A Legal and Economic Analysis. *J. Futures Markets,* Summer 1981, *1*(2), pp. 201–18.

Eisenmenger, Robert W. The Experience of Canadian Thrift Institutions. In *Federal Reserve Bank of Boston (II),* 1981, pp. 112–39. [G: Canada]

Elstone, Robert G. Interest Rates and Thrift Institu-

tions. In *Jüttner, D. J., ed.,* 1981, pp. 86–105.
[G: Australia]

Ettin, Edward C. The Implications for Federal Reserve Policy of Deregulation of the Thrift Industry: One View. In *Federal Home Loan Bank of San Francisco.,* 1981, pp. 73–79. [G: U.S.]

Flannery, Mark J. Credit Unions: Discussion. *J. Finance,* May 1981, *36*(2), pp. 554–56.

Forster, Edgar. Versicherung, Geld und Wirtschaftswachstum. (Insurance, Money and Economic Growth. With English summary.) *Konjunkturpolitik,* 1981, *27*(2), pp. 89–104.

Friedman, Stephen J. Rapidly Changing Financial Markets. In *Sametz, A. W., ed.,* 1981, pp. 31–34. [G: U.S.]

Gambs, Carl M. Credit Unions: Discussion. *J. Finance,* May 1981, *36*(2), pp. 552–54.

Garil, Barnard H. The Probable Impacts of Expanded Securities and Other Financing Activities of Banks and Securities Firms in the 1980s: Impacts on the Securities Industry. In *Sametz, A. W., ed.,* 1981, pp. 161–64. [G: U.S.]

Gilbert, R. Alton. Will the Removal of Regulation Q Raise Mortgage Interest Rates? *Fed. Res. Bank St. Louis Rev.,* December 1981, *63*(10), pp. 3–12. [G: U.S.]

Gramley, Lyle E. Statement to Subcommittee on Monopolies and Commercial Law, House Committee on the Judiciary, July 9, 1981. *Fed. Res. Bull.,* July 1981, *67*(7), pp. 555–60. [G: U.S.]

Guttentag, Jack M. The Conventional Passthrough Market: Trickle or Flood? In *Federal Home Loan Bank of San Francisco.,* 1981, pp. 271–313.
[G: U.S.]

Harwood, Edwin. Unions, Pensions, and Financial Responsibility: The British Experience: Comment. *J. Lab. Res.,* Fall 1981, *2*(2), pp. 299–305.
[G: U.K.]

Haywood, Charles F. Provision of Consumer Financial Services. In *Heggestad, A. A., ed.,* 1981, pp. 17–61. [G: U.S.]

Heimann, John G. The Probable Impacts of Expanded Securities and Other Financing Activities of Banks and Securities Firms in the 1980s: Impacts on the Regulatory Structure. In *Sametz, A. W., ed.,* 1981, pp. 145–47. [G: U.S.]

Heldman, Dan C. Unions, Pensions, and Financial Responsibility: The British Experience: Comment. *J. Lab. Res.,* Fall 1981, *2*(2), pp. 306–08.
[G: U.K.]

Hendershott, Patric H. and Villani, Kevin E. Savings and Loan Usage of the Authority to Invest in Corporate Bonds. In *Federal Home Loan Bank of San Francisco.,* 1981, pp. 149–67. [G: U.S.]

Hester, Donald D. Innovations and Monetary Control. *Brookings Pap. Econ. Act.,* 1981, (1), pp. 141–89. [G: U.S.]

Horvitz, Paul M. and Pettit, R. Richardson. Short-run Financial Solutions for Troubled Thrift Institutions. In *Federal Reserve Bank of Boston (II),* 1981, pp. 44–67. [G: U.S.]

Hunt, Ben F. Rate Sensitivity of Financial Flows: Comment. In *Jüttner, D. J., ed.,* 1981, pp. 171–72. [G: Australia]

Iden, George. Nontraditional Criteria for Investing Pension Assets: An Economic Appraisal: Comment. *J. Lab. Res.*, Fall 1981, *2*(2), pp. 252–57. [G: U.S.]

Janis, Jay. Dealing with Inflation: Ideology vs. Pragmatism. In *Federal Home Loan Bank of San Francisco.*, 1981, pp. 7–12. [G: U.S.]

Johnson, Paul. Unions, Pensions, and Financial Responsibility: The British Experience. *J. Lab. Res.*, Fall 1981, *2*(2), pp. 289–98. [G: U.K.]

Kalish, Lionel. Application of the "Probable Future Competition" Doctrine to the Commercial Banking and Savings and Loan Industries. *Atlantic Econ. J.*, July 1981, *9*(2), pp. 49–52. [G: U.S.]

Kane, Edward J. Reregulation, Savings and Loan Diversification, and the Flow of Housing Finance. In *Federal Home Loan Bank of San Francisco.*, 1981, pp. 81–109. [G: U.S.]

Kaplan, Donald M. and Measell, Ira D., III. Savings Institutions. In *Altman, E. I., ed.*, 1981, pp. 7.3–32. [G: U.S.]

Kaplan, Marshall A. Short-run Financial Solutions for Troubled Thrift Institutions: Discussion. In *Federal Reserve Bank of Boston (II)*, 1981, pp. 68–74. [G: U.S.]

Karmel, Roberta S. Critique of Current Regulatory Approaches to the Separation of Commercial and Investment Banking. In *Sametz, A. W., ed.*, 1981, pp. 23–30. [G: U.S.]

Kaufman, George G. Comment [The Legal, Economic, and Social Case for Banks' Underwriting Municipal Revenue Bonds] [The Public-Policy Case against Banks' Underwriting Revenue Bonds]. In *Sametz, A. W., ed.*, 1981, pp. 138–42. [G: U.S.]

Kawaller, Ira G. and Freund, James. Mortgage Lending at Savings and Loan Associations: A Further Inquiry. *Bus. Econ.*, January 1981, *16*(1), pp. 39–44. [G: U.S.]

Keefe, Harry V., Jr. Short-run Financial Solutions for Troubled Thrift Institutions: Discussion. In *Federal Reserve Bank of Boston (II)*, 1981, pp. 75–80. [G: U.S.]

Keenan, Michael. The Securities Industry: Securities Trading and Investment Banking. In *Altman, E. I., ed.*, 1981, pp. 5.3–29. [G: U.S.]

Kent, Richard J. An Analysis of Countercyclical Policies of the FHLBB. *J. Finance*, March 1981, *36*(1), pp. 61–79. [G: U.S.]

Kharadia, V. C. and Collins, Robert A. Forecasting Credit Union Failures. *J. Econ. Bus.*, Winter 1981, *33*(2), pp. 147–52. [G: U.S.]

Kidwell, David S. Optimal Asset Choice: Comments. In *Federal Home Loan Bank of San Francisco.*, 1981, pp. 239–43. [G: U.S.]

Kiernan, Eric. Interest Rate Sensitivity of Financial Flows. In *Jüttner, D. J., ed.*, 1981, pp. 127–43. [G: Australia]

Kohers, Theodor and Simpson, W. Gary. Concentration and Advertising in the United States Savings and Loan Industry. *Appl. Econ.*, March 1981, *13*(1), pp. 79–88. [G: U.S.]

Kopcke, Richard W. The Condition of Massachusetts Savings Banks and California Savings and Loan Associations. In *Federal Reserve Bank of Boston (II)*, 1981, pp. 1–32. [G: U.S.]

Kopcke, Richard W. and Woglom, Geoffrey R. H. Regulation Q and Savings Bank Solvency—The

Connecticut Experience. In *Fed. Res. Bank of Boston and National Sci. Foundation*, 1981, pp. 68–95. [G: U.S.]

Lane, David and Golen, Lawrence. Some Simulation-Based Estimates of Commercial Bank Deposit Insurance Premiums. In *Maisel, S. J., ed.*, 1981, pp. 341–65. [G: U.S.]

Levitt, Arthur, Jr. The Probable Impacts of Expanded Securities and Other Financing Activities of Banks and Securities Firms in the 1980s: Impacts on the Exchanges. In *Sametz, A. W., ed.*, 1981, pp. 155–56. [G: U.S.]

Lewis, Mervyn K. Interest Rate Sensitivity of Financial Flows: Comments: Interest Rates and Monetary Policy. In *Jüttner, D. J., ed.*, 1981, pp. 173–76. [G: Australia]

Loomis, Philip C. A Critique of Current Regulatory Procedures in the Municipal Securities Industry. In *Sametz, A. W., ed.*, 1981, pp. 65–69. [G: U.S.]

Lovell, Michael C. Unraveling the Real-Payment Twist. *Brookings Pap. Econ. Act.*, 1981, (1), pp. 283–97. [G: U.S.]

Lybecker, Martin E. Comment [Commingled-Agency Accounts for Bank Trust Departments—An Idea Whose Time Has Come] [Preserving Barriers against Banks' Engaging in the Personal-Investment Business]. In *Sametz, A. W., ed.*, 1981, pp. 100–107. [G: U.S.]

Mahajan, Y. Lal. A Macro-Econometric Model of the Credit Unions. *Atlantic Econ. J.*, July 1981, *9*(2), pp. 40–48. [G: U.S.]

Marcis, Richard G. and Kelsey, Susan E. Managing Mortgage Assets for Profit. In *Federal Home Loan Bank of San Francisco.*, 1981, pp. 247–69. [G: U.S.]

Maris, Brian A. FHLB Advances and the Cost and Availability of Funds to S&Ls: A Comment [A Note on the Impact of FHLB Advances and the Cost and Availability of Funds at S&Ls]. *J. Finance*, September 1981, *36*(4), pp. 971–74. [G: U.S.]

Marston, Garth. Short-run Structural Solutions to the Problems of Thrift Institutions: Discussion. In *Federal Reserve Bank of Boston (II)*, 1981, pp. 107–11. [G: U.S.]

Martin, Donald L. Nontraditional Criteria for Investing Pension Assets: An Economic Appraisal: Comment. *J. Lab. Res.*, Fall 1981, *2*(2), pp. 258–63. [G: U.S.]

McCulloch, J. Huston. Interest Rate Risk and Capital Adequacy for Traditional Banks and Financial Intermediaries. In *Maisel, S. J., ed.*, 1981, pp. 223–48. [G: U.S.]

McLean, Kenneth A. Legislative Background of the Depository Institutions Deregulation and Monetary Control Act of 1980. In *Federal Home Loan Bank of San Francisco.*, 1981, pp. 17–30. [G: U.S.]

McMahon, Christopher W. L'evoluzione del sistema di intermediazione finanziaria nel Regno Unito. (The Changing Pattern of Financial Intermediation in the United Kingdom during the Seventies. With English summary.) *Bancaria*, October 1981, *37*(10), pp. 1014–22. [G: U.K.]

Meadows, George Richard and Mitrisin, John. A

National Development Bank: Survey and Discussion of the Literature on Capital Shortages and Employment Changes in Distressed Areas. **In** *Sternlieb, G. and Listokin, D., eds.,* 1981, pp. 84–143. **[G: U.S.]**

Mehle, Roger W. The Public-Policy Case against Banks' Underwriting Revenue Bonds. **In** *Sametz, A. W., ed.,* 1981, pp. 129–35. **[G: U.S.]**

Melton, William C. and Roley, V. Vance. Imperfect Asset Elasticities and Financial Model Building. *J. Econometrics,* January 1981, *15*(1), pp. 139–54.

Menell, Howard. Current Regulatory Framework for Banks' Securities Activities as Viewed by Regulators: Comment. **In** *Sametz, A. W., ed.,* 1981, pp. 76–81. **[G: U.S.]**

Mingo, John J. A Comparison of European Housing Finance Systems: Discussion. **In** *Federal Reserve Bank of Boston (II),* 1981, pp. 161–63.
[G: France; W. Germany; U.K.]

Mingo, John J. Short-run Structural Solutions to the Problems of Thrift Institutions. **In** *Federal Reserve Bank of Boston (II),* 1981, pp. 81–106.
[G: U.S.]

Minsky, Hyman P. Financial Markets and Economic Instability, 1965–1980. *Nebr. J. Econ. Bus.,* Autumn 1981, *20*(4), pp. 5–16. **[G: U.S.]**

Morrison, Jay B. and Pyle, David H. Interest Rate Risk and the Regulation of Financial Institutions. **In** *Maisel, S. J., ed.,* 1981, pp. 285–314.
[G: U.S.]

Nadauld, Stephen D. Calculating the Present Value of an Asset's Uncertain Future Cash Flows. **In** *Maisel, S. J., ed.,* 1981, pp. 315–39. **[G: U.S.]**

Navratil, Frank J. An Aggregate Model of the Credit Union Industry. *J. Finance,* May 1981, *36*(2), pp. 539–49. **[G: U.S.]**

Northrup, James P. and Northrup, Herbert R. Union Divergent Investing of Pensions: A Power, Non-Employee Relations Issue. *J. Lab. Res.,* Fall 1981, *2*(2), pp. 191–208. **[G: U.S.]**

Opper, Franz F. Current Regulatory Framework for Banks' Securities Activities as Viewed by Regulators: Comment. **In** *Sametz, A. W., ed.,* 1981, pp. 47–51. **[G: U.S.]**

Ostas, James R. The Federal Home Loan Bank System: Cause or Cure for Disintermediation? *J. Monet. Econ.,* September 1981, *8*(2), pp. 231–46. **[G: U.S.]**

Pacolet, Jozef and Verheirstraeten, Albert. Concentration and Economies of Scale in the Belgian Financial Sector. **In** *Verheirstraeten, A., ed.,* 1981, pp. 55–91. **[G: Belgium]**

Peterson, Richard L. Consumer Lending by Savings and Loan Associations. **In** *Federal Home Loan Bank of San Francisco.,* 1981, pp. 175–203.
[G: U.S.]

Peterson, Richard L. Credit Unions: Discussion. *J. Finance,* May 1981, *36*(2), pp. 550–52.

Phillips, Almarin. Comment [The Public-Policy Case for Private-Placement Services by Commercial Banks] [Banks' Unfair Advantages in Private-Placement Activity]. **In** *Sametz, A. W., ed.,* 1981, pp. 121–22. **[G: U.S.]**

Phillips, Richard M. Preserving Barriers against Banks' Engaging in the Personal-Investment

Business. **In** *Sametz, A. W., ed.,* 1981, pp. 91–95. **[G: U.S.]**

Pierce, James L. The Condition of Massachusetts Savings Banks and California Savings and Loan Associations: Discussion. **In** *Federal Reserve Bank of Boston (II),* 1981, pp. 33–36. **[G: U.S.]**

Pohlman, Jerry E. Optimal Assets Choice: Comments. **In** *Federal Home Loan Bank of San Francisco.,* 1981, pp. 169–72. **[G: U.S.]**

Poole, William. Banks, Thrifts and Interest Rates: Comments. **In** *Jüttner, D. J., ed.,* 1981, pp. 120–24. **[G: Australia]**

Pozen, Robert C. A Broad Critique of the Current Regulatory Framework. **In** *Sametz, A. W., ed.,* 1981, pp. 55–58. **[G: U.S.]**

Raisian, John. Union Divergent Investing of Pensions: A Power, Non-Employee Relations Issue: Comment. *J. Lab. Res.,* Fall 1981, *2*(2), pp. 214–18. **[G: U.S.]**

Riedy, Mark J. Sale of Assets: Panel Presentation. **In** *Federal Home Loan Bank of San Francisco.,* 1981, pp. 323–27. **[G: U.S.]**

Riordan, Dale P. and Hartzog, Jerry. The Impact of the Deregulation Act on Policy Choices of the Federal Home Loan Bank Board. **In** *Federal Home Loan Bank of San Francisco.,* 1981, pp. 33–58. **[G: U.S.]**

Robinson, Thomas R. Have Pension Investment Managers Over-Emphasized the Needs of Retirees? Comment. *J. Lab. Res.,* Fall 1981, *2*(2), pp. 284–87. **[G: U.S.]**

Rose, John T. and Rutz, Roger D. Organizational Form and Risk in Bank-Affiliated Mortgage Companies: A Note. *J. Money, Credit, Banking,* August 1981, *13*(3), pp. 375–80. **[G: U.S.]**

Rosen, Kenneth T. A Comparison of European Housing Finance Systems. **In** *Federal Reserve Bank of Boston (II),* 1981, pp. 144–60.
[G: U.K.; W. Germany; France]

Rosen, Kenneth T. The Transition Problem for the Savings and Loan Industry: Comments. **In** *Federal Home Loan Bank of San Francisco.,* 1981, pp. 111–14.

Rowen, Harvey A. The Probable Impacts of Expanded Securities and Other Financing Activities of Banks and Securities Firms in the 1980s: Impacts on the Securities Industry. **In** *Sametz, A. W., ed.,* 1981, pp. 164–66. **[G: U.S.]**

Sacerdote, Peter M. Banks' Unfair Advantages in Private-Placement Activity. **In** *Sametz, A. W., ed.,* 1981, pp. 115–19. **[G: U.S.]**

Sametz, Arnold W. Background of the Controversy over Banks' Securities Activities—A Briefing. **In** *Sametz, A. W., ed.,* 1981, pp. 3–19. **[G: U.S.]**

Sametz, Arnold W. Comment [The Public-Policy Case for Private-Placement Services by Commercial Banks] [Banks' Unfair Advantages in Private-Placement Activity]. **In** *Sametz, A. W., ed.,* 1981, pp. 119–21. **[G: U.S.]**

Santomero, Anthony M. Comment [Commingled-Agency Accounts for Bank Trust Departments—An Idea Whose Time Has Come] [Preserving Barriers against Banks' Engaging in the Personal-Investment Business]. **In** *Sametz, A. W., ed.,* 1981, pp. 95–100. **[G: U.S.]**

Schaefer, Jeffrey M. Current Regulatory Framework

for Banks' Securities Activities as Viewed by Regulators: Comment. In *Sametz, A. W., ed.*, 1981, pp. 71–74. [G: U.S.]

Schotland, Roy A. Have Pension Investment Managers Over-Emphasized the Needs of Retirees? *J. Lab. Res.*, Fall 1981, *2*(2), pp. 265–83. [G: U.S.]

Schott, Francis H. The Probable Impacts of Expanded Securities and Other Financing Activities of Banks and Securities Firms in the 1980s: Impacts on Financing Nonfinancial Business. In *Sametz, A. W., ed.*, 1981, pp. 179–81. [G: U.S.]

Serbein, Oscar N. Insurance and Reinsurance. In *Altman, E. I., ed.*, 1981, pp. 8.3–38. [G: U.S.]

Siaens, Alain. Government Intervention in the French Financial System: Comment. In *Verheirstraeten, A., ed.*, 1981, pp. 173–74. [G: France]

Siebert, Muriel. The Probable Impacts of Expanded Securities and Other Financing Activities of Banks and Securities Firms in the 1980s: Impacts on the Regulatory Structure. In *Sametz, A. W., ed.*, 1981, pp. 147–51. [G: U.S.]

Smith, Donald J.; Cargill, Thomas F. and Meyer, Robert A. An Economic Theory of a Credit Union. *J. Finance*, May 1981, *36*(2), pp. 519–28.

Sobhan, Rehman and Mahmood, Syed Akhter. Repayment of Loans to Specialised Financial Institutions in Bangladesh: Issues and Constraints. *Bangladesh Devel. Stud.*, Winter 1981, *9*(1), pp. 35–75. [G: Bangladesh]

Spellman, Lewis J. Commercial Banks and the Profits of Savings and Loan Markets. *J. Bank Res.*, Spring 1981, *12*(1), pp. 32–36. [G: U.S.]

Taylor, R. G. Joint Ventures: Panel Presentation. In *Federal Home Loan Bank of San Francisco.*, 1981, pp. 355–61. [G: U.S.]

Teriba, O. Financial Institutions, Financial Markets, and Income Distribution. In *Bienen, H. and Diejomaoh, V. P., eds.*, 1981, pp. 485–512. [G: Nigeria]

Thiessen, Gordon G. The Experience of Canadian Thrift Institutions: Discussion. In *Federal Reserve Bank of Boston (II)*, 1981, pp. 140–43. [G: Canada]

Thygerson, Kenneth J. Futures, Options, and the Savings and Loan Business. In *Federal Home Loan Bank of San Francisco.*, 1981, pp. 119–47. [G: U.S.]

Tinsley, P. A.; Garrett, Bonnie and Friar, Monica. An Exposé of Disguised Deposits. *J. Econometrics*, January 1981, *15*(1), pp. 117–37. [G: U.S.]

Treadway, Peter. Sale of Assets: Comments. In *Federal Home Loan Bank of San Francisco.*, 1981, pp. 315–18. [G: U.S.]

Trebing, Michael E. The New Bank-Thrift Competition: Will It Affect Bank Acquisition and Merger Analysis? *Fed. Res. Bank St. Louis Rev.*, February 1981, *63*(2), pp. 3–11. [G: U.S.]

Tsung, Stephen. Interest Rates and Thrift Institutions: Comments. In *Jüttner, D. J., ed.*, 1981, pp. 114–19. [G: Australia]

Tucker, Donald P. Regulation Q and Savings Bank Solvency—The Connecticut Experience: Discus-

sion. In *Fed. Res. Bank of Boston and National Sci. Foundation*, 1981, pp. 96–100. [G: U.S.]

Verbrugge, James A. and Jahera, John S., Jr. Expense–Preference Behavior in the Savings and Loan Industry. *J. Money, Credit, Banking*, November 1981, *13*(4), pp. 465–76. [G: U.S.]

Volcker, Paul A. Statement to Senate Committee on Banking, Housing, and Urban Affairs, October 29, 1981. *Fed. Res. Bull.*, November 1981, *67*(11), pp. 835–45. [G: U.S.]

Volcker, Paul A. Statement to Subcommittee on Domestic Monetary Policy, House Committee on Banking, Finance and Urban Affairs, June 25, 1981. *Fed. Res. Bull.*, July 1981, *67*(7), pp. 548–55. [G: U.S.]

Volcker, Paul A. Statement to Subcommittee on Financial Institutions Supervision, Regulation and Insurance of the House Committee on Banking, Finance and Urban Affairs, October 1, 1981. *Fed. Res. Bull.*, October 1981, *67*(10), pp. 775–78. [G: U.S.]

Wallich, Henry C. The Probable Impacts of Expanded Securities and Other Financing Activities of Banks and Securities Firms in the 1980s: Impacts on the Regulatory Structure. In *Sametz, A. W., ed.*, 1981, pp. 151–54. [G: U.S.]

Weinrobe, Maurice. Savings and Loan Demand for Liquid Assets: Theory, Evidence and Implications for Policy. *Amer. Real Estate Urban Econ. Assoc. J.*, Spring 1981, *9*(1), pp. 18–37. [G: U.S.]

White, Lawrence J. Current Regulatory Framework for Banks' Securities Activities as Viewed by Regulators: Comment. In *Sametz, A. W., ed.*, 1981, pp. 51–54. [G: U.S.]

Wilson, J. Holton. A Note on Scale Economies in the Savings and Loan Industry. *Bus. Econ.*, January 1981, *16*(1), pp. 45–49.

Wolken, John D. and Navratil, Frank J. The Economic Impact of the Federal Credit Union Usury Ceiling. *J. Finance*, December 1981, *36*(5), pp. 1157–68. [G: U.S.]

315 Credit to Business, Consumer, etc.
(including mortgages)

3150 General

Aftalion, Florin. Government Intervention in the French Financial System. In *Verheirstraeten, A., ed.*, 1981, pp. 157–72. [G: France]

Backhouse, Roger E. Credit Rationing in a General Equilibrium Model. *Economica*, May 1981, *48*(190), pp. 173–79.

Biederman, Kenneth R. Non-mortgage Lending: Panel Presentation. In *Federal Home Loan Bank of San Francisco.*, 1981, pp. 343–52. [G: U.S.]

Chambers, Jay G. Cost and Price Level Adjustments to State Aid for Education: A Theoretical and Empirical Review. In *Jordan, K. F. and Cambron-McCabe, N. H., eds.*, 1981, pp. 39–85. [G: U.S.]

Ciampi, Carlo Azeglio. Discrzionalità nell'orientamento del sistema creditizio e tutela dell'imprenditorialità bancaria. (Discretionary Powers in Credit-System Guidelines and Protection of Bankers' Entrepreneurial Capabilities. With English summary.) *Bancaria*, April 1981, *37*(4), pp. 342–47. [G: Italy]

Dini, Lamberto. L'attività creditizia: problemi e metodi di controllo. (The Provision of Credit: Aspects and Methods of Control. With English summary.) *Bancaria*, July 1981, *37*(7), pp. 666–72. [G: Italy]

Gilliam, Kenneth P. and Hunter, William C. Some Normative Aspects of Bank Loan Commitment Pricing. *Econ. Notes*, 1981, *10*(3), pp. 105–13.

Goldin, Claudia Dale. Credit Merchandising in the New South: The Role of Competition and Risk. In *Walton, G. M. and Shepherd, J. F., eds.*, 1981, pp. 3–23. [G: U.S.]

Gori, A. R. Problemi specifici degli Istituti di credito di diritto pubblico e degli Istituti di credito speciale nel contesto del sistema. (Specific Aspects of Public-Law Credit Institutions and Special Credit Institutions. With English summary.) *Bancaria*, March 1981, *37*(3), pp. 294–301.
[G: Italy]

Gramley, Lyle E. Statement to Senate Forum, July 27, 1981. *Fed. Res. Bull.*, August 1981, *67*(8), pp. 623–24. [G: U.S.]

Hagihara, Yoshimi and Hagihara, Kiyoko. Project Grant Allocation Process Applied in Sewerage Planning. *Water Resources Res.*, June 1981, *17*(3), pp. 449–54.

Hekman, Christine R. The Effect of Trade Credit on Price and Price Level Comparisons. *Rev. Econ. Statist.*, November 1981, *63*(4), pp. 526–32.

Ito, Takatoshi and Ueda, Kazuo. Tests of the Equilibrium Hypothesis in Disequilibrium Econometrics: An International Comparison of Credit Rationing. *Int. Econ. Rev.*, October 1981, *22*(3), pp. 691–708. [G: U.S.; Japan]

Kaplan, Donald M. and Measell, Ira D., III. Savings Institutions. In *Altman, E. I., ed.*, 1981, pp. 7.3–32. [G: U.S.]

Maisel, Sherman J. Risk and Capital Adequacy in Banks. In *Fed. Res. Bank of Boston and National Sci. Foundation*, 1981, pp. 203–24. [G: U.S.]

Merton, Robert C. Discussion [Risk and Capital Adequacy in Banks] [Capital Requirements for Entry into Property and Liability Underwriting: An empirical Examination]. In *Fed. Res. Bank of Boston and National Sci. Foundation*, 1981, pp. 256–63. [G: U.S.]

Monti, Mario and Padoa-Schioppa, Tommaso. Structural Changes and Cyclical Behaviour of the Italian Banking System. In *Courakis, A. S., ed.*, 1981, pp. 217–31. [G: Italy]

Ransom, Roger L. and Sutch, Richard. Credit Merchandising in the Post-emancipation South: Structure, Conduct, and Performance. In *Walton, G. M. and Shepherd, J. F., eds.*, 1981, 1980, pp. 57–81. [G: U.S.]

Rudolph, Bernd. Ein dynamisches Modell der Kreditbeziehungen zwischen einer Bank und ihren Kreditnehmern. (A Dynamic Model of Credit Relations between a Bank and Its Borrowers. With English summary.) *Kredit Kapital*, 1981, *14*(1), pp. 94–113.

Sarcinelli, Mario. Stagflazione e strutture finanziarie: il caso dell'Italia. (Stagflation and Financial Struc-

tures: The Case of Italy. With English summary.) *Bancaria*, November 1981, *37*(11), pp. 1105–31.
[G: Italy]

Scholz, Franz Josef. Verbraucherschutz in der Marktwirtschaft Dargestellt am Beispiel des Konsumentenkredits. (Consumer Protection in the Market Economy. With English summary.) In *[von Haberler, G.]*, 1981, pp. 185–98.

Siaens, Alain. Government Intervention in the French Financial System: Comment. In *Verheirstraeten, A., ed.*, 1981, pp. 173–74.
[G: France]

Stiglitz, Joseph E. and Weiss, Andrew. Credit Rationing in Markets with Imperfect Information. *Amer. Econ. Rev.*, June 1981, *71*(3), pp. 393–410.

Stone, Alan. State and Market: Economic Regulation and the Great Productivity Debate. In *Ferguson, T. and Rogers, J., eds.*, 1981, pp. 232–59.
[G: U.S.]

Teeters, Nancy H. Statement to Subcommittee on Consumer Affairs and Coinage of the House Committee on Banking, Finance, and Urban Affairs, October 21, 1981. *Fed. Res. Bull.*, November 1981, *67*(11), pp. 826–28. [G: U.S.]

Teeters, Nancy H. Statement to Subcommittee on Economic Stabilization, House Committee on Banking, Finance and Urban Affairs, April 30, 1981. *Fed. Res. Bull.*, May 1981, *67*(5), pp. 424–29. [G: U.S.]

Teeters, Nancy H. Statement to Task Force on Federal Credit, Senate Committee on the Budget, December 10, 1981. *Fed. Res. Bull.*, December 1981, *67*(12), pp. 895–99. [G: U.S.]

Temin, Peter. Freedom and Coercion: Notes on the Analysis of Debt Peonage in *One Kind of Freedom*. In *Walton, G. M. and Shepherd, J. F., eds.*, 1981, *1980*, pp. 25–32. [G: U.S.]

Teriba, O. Financial Institutions, Financial Markets, and Income Distribution. In *Bienen, H. and Diejomaoh, V. P., eds.*, 1981, pp. 485–512.
[G: Nigeria]

Volcker, Paul A. Statement to Senate Committee on Banking, Housing, and Urban Affairs, October 29, 1981. *Fed. Res. Bull.*, November 1981, *67*(11), pp. 835–45. [G: U.S.]

Wallich, Henry C. Statement to Temporary Subcommittee on Industrial Growth and Productivity, Senate Committee on the Budget, January 27, 1981. *Fed. Res. Bull.*, February 1981, *67*(2), pp. 137–40. [G: U.S.]

3151 Consumer Finance

Avery, Robert B. Estimating Credit Constraints by Switching Regressions. In *Manski, C. F. and McFadden, D., eds.*, 1981, pp. 435–72.
[G: U.S.]

Batko, William. Proposals for Regulatory Reform in the Consumer Financial Services Sector. In *Heggestad, A. A., ed.*, 1981, pp. 92–123. [G: U.S.]

Black, Harold A. and Dugger, Robert H. Credit Union Structure, Growth and Regulatory Problems. *J. Finance*, May 1981, *36*(2), pp. 529–38.
[G: U.S.]

Brandt, William K. and Shay, Robert P. Consumers'

Perceptions of Discriminatory Treatment and Credit Availability, and Access to Consumer Credit Markets: Rebuttal. In *Fed. Res. Bank of Boston and National Sci. Foundation*, 1981, pp. 23. [G: U.S.]

Brandt, William K. and Shay, Robert P. Consumers' Perceptions of Discriminatory Treatment and Credit Availability, and Access to Consumer Credit Markets. In *Fed. Res. Bank of Boston and National Sci. Foundation*, 1981, pp. 1–19. [G: U.S.]

Dunkelberg, William C. and De Magistris, Robin. Measuring the Impact of Credit Regulation on Consumers. In *Fed. Res. Bank of Boston and National Sci. Foundation*, 1981, pp. 44–62. [G: U.S.]

Durkin, Thomas A. Discussion [Effects of Creditor Remedies and Rate Restrictions] [Measuring the Impact of Credit Regulation on Consumers]. In *Fed. Res. Bank of Boston and National Sci. Foundation*, 1981, pp. 63–67. [G: U.S.]

Ebaugh, Dwight D. The Users and Providers of Consumer Financial Services: A Legal Framework. In *Heggestad, A. A., ed.*, 1981, pp. 62–91. [G: U.S.]

Filkins, Jesse B., Jr. An Approach to Regulatory Simplification. *Fed. Res. Bull.*, July 1981, 67(7), pp. 535–38. [G: U.S.]

Flannery, Mark J. Credit Unions: Discussion. *J. Finance*, May 1981, 36(2), pp. 554–56.

Gambs, Carl M. Credit Unions: Discussion. *J. Finance*, May 1981, 36(2), pp. 552–54.

Grablowsky, Bernie J. and Talley, Wayne K. Probit and Discriminant Functions for Classifying Credit Applicants: A Comparison. *J. Econ. Bus.*, Spring/Summer 1981, 33(3), pp. 254–61. [G: U.S.]

Greenwald, Carol S. Consumers' Perceptions of Discriminatory Treatment and Credit Availability, and Access to Consumer Credit Markets: Discussion. In *Fed. Res. Bank of Boston and National Sci. Foundation*, 1981, pp. 20–22. [G: U.S.]

Hakala, Marcia A. The Consumer Advisory Council: The First Five Years. *Fed. Res. Bull.*, July 1981, 67(7), pp. 529–34. [G: U.S.]

Haywood, Charles F. Provision of Consumer Financial Services. In *Heggestad, A. A., ed.*, 1981, pp. 17–61. [G: U.S.]

Haywood, Charles F. Regulation, Structure, and Technological Change in the Consumer Financial Services Industry. In *Heggestad, A. A., ed.*, 1981, pp. 163–67. [G: U.S.]

Heggestad, Arnold A. An Evaluation of Interinstitutional Competition for Consumer Financial Services. In *Heggestad, A. A., ed.*, 1981, pp. 144–62. [G: U.S.]

Heggestad, Arnold A. Regulation of Consumer Financial Services: Introduction. In *Heggestad, A., ed.*, 1981, pp. 1–16. [G: U.S.]

Hurley, Evelyn M. Survey of Finance Companies, 1980. *Fed. Res. Bull.*, May 1981, 67(5), pp. 398–409. [G: U.S.]

Kharadia, V. C. and Collins, Robert A. Forecasting Credit Union Failures. *J. Econ. Bus.*, Winter 1981, 33(2), pp. 147–52. [G: U.S.]

Kidwell, David S. Optimal Asset Choice: Comments. In *Federal Home Loan Bank of San Francisco.*,

1981, pp. 239–43. [G: U.S.]

Kinsey, Jean. Determinants of Credit Card Accounts: An Application of Tobit Analysis. *J. Cons. Res.*, September 1981, 8(2), pp. 172–82. [G: U.S.]

Mahajan, Y. Lal. A Macro-Econometric Model of the Credit Unions. *Atlantic Econ. J.*, July 1981, 9(2), pp. 40–48. [G: U.S.]

Maris, Brian A. Indirect Evidence on the Efficacy of Selective Credit Controls: The Case of Consumer Credit. *J. Money, Credit, Banking*, August 1981, 13(3), pp. 388–90. [G: U.S.]

Marshall, John M. Discrimination in Consumer Credit. In *Heggestad, A. A., ed.*, 1981 1981, pp. 240–55. [G: U.S.]

Martell, Terrence F. and Fitts, Robert L. A Quadratic Discriminant Analysis of Bank Credit Card User Characteristics. *J. Econ. Bus.*, Winter 1981, 33(2), pp. 153–59. [G: U.S.]

Mathot, Fons. L'utilisation du crédit lors de l'achat d'une voiture. (The Use of Credit in the Purchase of an Automobile. With English summary.) *Ann. INSEE*, October–December 1981, (44), pp. 121–48. [G: Netherlands]

Navratil, Frank J. An Aggregate Model of the Credit Union Industry. *J. Finance*, May 1981, 36(2), pp. 539–49. [G: U.S.]

Oster, Sharon. Product Regulations: A Measure of the Benefits. *J. Ind. Econ.*, June 1981, 29(4), pp. 395–411. [G: U.S.]

Peterson, Richard L. Consumer Lending by Savings and Loan Associations. In *Federal Home Loan Bank of San Francisco.*, 1981, pp. 175–203. [G: U.S.]

Peterson, Richard L. Credit Unions: Discussion. *J. Finance*, May 1981, 36(2), pp. 550–52.

Peterson, Richard L. Effects of Creditor Remedies and Rate Restrictions. In *Fed. Res. Bank of Boston and National Sci. Foundation*, 1981, pp. 24–43. [G: U.S.]

Peterson, Richard L. Rewriting Consumer Contracts: Creditors' Remedies. In *Clarkson, K. W. and Muris, T. J., eds.*, 1981, pp. 184–203. [G: U.S.]

Peterson, Richard L. and Ginsberg, Michael D. Determinants of Commercial Bank Auto Loan Rates. *J. Bank Res.*, Spring 1981, 12(1), pp. 46–55. [G: U.S.]

Shah, Anup R. Imperfections in the Capital Markets and Consumer Behavior. *Southern Econ. J.*, April 1981, 47(4), pp. 1032–45.

Shay, Robert P. and Brandt, William K. Public Regulation of Financial Services: The Truth in Lending Act. In *Heggestad, A. A., ed.*, 1981, pp. 168–207. [G: U.S.]

Shay, Robert P.; Brandt, William K. and Sexton, Donald E., Jr. Public Regulation of Financial Services: The Equal Credit Opportunity Act. In *Heggestad, A. A., ed.*, 1981, pp. 208–39. [G: U.S.]

Smith, Donald J.; Cargill, Thomas F. and Meyer, Robert A. An Economic Theory of a Credit Union. *J. Finance*, May 1981, 36(2), pp. 519–28.

Steinberg, Edward I. Consumer Credit, 1960–80. *Surv. Curr. Bus.*, February 1981, 61(2), pp. 14–18. [G: U.S.]

Sullivan, A. Charlene. Consumer Finance. In *Alt-*

man, E. I., ed., 1981, pp. 9.3–27. [G: U.S.]

Teeters, Nancy H. Statement to Subcommittee on Consumer Affairs, House Committee on Banking, Finance and Urban Affairs, February 5, 1981. *Fed. Res. Bull.*, February 1981, *67*(2), pp. 143–44. [G: U.S.]

Teeters, Nancy H. Statement to Subcommittee on Consumer Affairs, Senate Committee on Banking, Housing, and Urban Affairs, February 18, 1981. *Fed. Res. Bull.*, March 1981, *67*(3), pp. 235–37. [G: U.S.]

Wolken, John D. and Navratil, Frank J. The Economic Impact of the Federal Credit Union Usury Ceiling. *J. Finance*, December 1981, *36*(5), pp. 1157–68. [G: U.S.]

3152 Mortgage Market

Barth, James R.; Cordes, Joseph J. and Yezer, Anthony M. J. Financial Institution Regulations, Redlining and Mortgage Markets. In *Fed. Res. Bank of Boston and National Sci. Foundation*, 1981, pp. 101–43. [G: U.S.]

Benston, George J. Mortgage Redlining Research: A Review and Critical Analysis Discussion. In *Fed. Res. Bank of Boston and National Sci. Foundation*, 1981, pp. 144–95. [G: U.S.]

Benston, George J. Mortgage Redlining Research: A Review and Critical Analysis. *J. Bank Res.*, Spring 1981, *12*(1), pp. 8–23. [G: U.S.]

Black, Deborah G.; Garbade, Kenneth D. and Silber, William L. The Impact of the GNMA Pass-through Program on FHA Mortgage Costs. *J. Finance*, May 1981, *36*(2), pp. 457–69. [G: U.S.]

Black, Harold A. and Schweitzer, Robert L. An Analysis of Market Segmentation in Mortgage Lending between a Commercial Bank and a Mutual Savings Bank. *Amer. Real Estate Urban Econ. Assoc. J.*, Fall 1981, *9*(3), pp. 234–40. [G: U.S.]

Bradford, William D. The Cash Flow Implications of Alternative Mortgage Instruments. In *Federal Home Loan Bank of San Francisco.*, 1981, pp. 205–37. [G: U.S.]

Canner, Glenn. Redlining and Mortgage Lending Patterns. In *Henderson, J. V., ed.*, 1981, pp. 67–101. [G: U.S.]

Cleary, Martin. Shopping Center: A Lender's Perspective. In *Sternlieb, G. and Hughes, J. W., eds.*, 1981, pp. 297–301. [G: U.S.]

Corgel, Jack B. Long-Term Effects of Firm Size on Life Insurer Mortgage Investment. *J. Risk Ins.*, June 1981, *48*(2), pp. 296–307. [G: U.S.]

Darden, Joe T. The Determination of Demand in Redlining Research. *Rev. Public Data Use (See J. Econ. Soc. Meas. after 4/85)*, July 1981, *9*(2), pp. 125–32. [G: U.S.]

Deihl, Richard H. Considerations of the Variable-Rate Mortgage Index: Panel Presentation. In *Federal Home Loan Bank of San Francisco.*, 1981, pp. 329–41. [G: U.S.]

Dunn, Kenneth B. and McConnell, John J. Valuation of GNMA Mortgage-Backed Securities. *J. Finance*, June 1981, *36*(3), pp. 599–616. [G: U.S.]

Guttentag, Jack M. The Conventional Passthrough Market: Trickle or Flood? In *Federal Home Loan Bank of San Francisco.*, 1981, pp. 271–313. [G: U.S.]

Hein, Scott E. and Lamb, James C., Jr. Why the Median-Priced Home Costs So Much. *Fed. Res. Bank St. Louis Rev.*, June–July 1981, *63*(6), pp. 11–19. [G: U.S.]

Hula, Richard C. Public Needs and Private Investment: The Case of Home Credit. *Soc. Sci. Quart.*, December 1981, *62*(4), pp. 685–703. [G: U.S.]

Jaffee, Dwight M. The Future Role of Thrift Institutions in Mortgage Lending. In *Federal Reserve Bank of Boston (II)*, 1981, pp. 164–80. [G: U.S.]

Kane, Edward J. Reregulation, Savings and Loan Diversification, and the Flow of Housing Finance. In *Federal Home Loan Bank of San Francisco.*, 1981, pp. 81–109. [G: U.S.]

Kaufman, Herbert M. FNMA and Its Relationship to the Mortgage Market. *J. Bank Res.*, Autumn 1981, *12*(3), pp. 145–52. [G: U.S.]

Kaufman, Herbert M. and Schlagenhauf, Don E. FNMA Auction Results as a Forecaster of Residential Mortgage Yields. *J. Money, Credit, Banking*, August 1981, *13*(3), pp. 352–64. [G: U.S.]

Kawaller, Ira G. and Freund, James. Mortgage Lending at Savings and Loan Associations: A Further Inquiry. *Bus. Econ.*, January 1981, *16*(1), pp. 39–44. [G: U.S.]

Kent, Richard J. A Disaggregated Model of the Residential Mortgage Market. *Southern Econ. J.*, January 1981, *47*(3), pp. 714–27. [G: U.S.]

Kent, Richard J. An Analysis of Countercyclical Policies of the FHLBB. *J. Finance*, March 1981, *36*(1), pp. 61–79. [G: U.S.]

Kesselman, Jonathan R. Mortgage Policies for Financial Relief in Inflationary Periods. *Can. Public Policy*, Winter 1981, *7*(1), pp. 82–93.

[G: Canada]

Kidwell, David S. Optimal Asset Choice: Comments. In *Federal Home Loan Bank of San Francisco.*, 1981, pp. 239–43. [G: U.S.]

Knox, Joan. Index-Linking of Mortgages and the Implications for Stabilization Policies. *S. Afr. J. Econ.*, December 1981, *49*(4), pp. 365–80.

Kopcke, Richard W. and Woglom, Geoffrey R. H. Regulation Q and Savings Bank Solvency—The Connecticut Experience. In *Fed. Res. Bank of Boston and National Sci. Foundation*, 1981, pp. 68–95. [G: U.S.]

Ladd, Edward H. The Future Role of Thrift Institutions in Mortgage Lending: Discussion. In *Federal Reserve Bank of Boston (II)*, 1981, pp. 181–87. [G: U.S.]

Lovell, Michael C. Unraveling the Real-Payment Twist. *Brookings Pap. Econ. Act.*, 1981, (1), pp. 283–97. [G: U.S.]

Marcis, Richard G. and Kelsey, Susan E. Managing Mortgage Assets for Profit. In *Federal Home Loan Bank of San Francisco.*, 1981, pp. 247–69. [G: U.S.]

Miles, Mike and Sears, R. Stephen. An Econometric Approach to the FNMA Free Market System Auction. *J. Finan. Quant. Anal.*, June 1981, *16*(2), pp. 177–92. [G: U.S.]

Mingo, John J. A Comparison of European Housing Finance Systems: Discussion. In *Federal Reserve*

Bank of Boston (II), 1981, pp. 161–63.
[G: France; W. Germany; U.K.]

Nadauld, Stephen D. Calculating the Present Value of an Asset's Uncertain Future Cash Flows. In *Maisel, S. J., ed.*, 1981, pp. 315–39. [G: U.S.]

Ostas, James R.; Reed, J. David and Hutchinson, Peter M. Pooled Regression Analysis of Inner City Mortgage Loan Flows. *Reg. Sci. Persp.*, 1981, *11*(1), pp. 57–70. [G: U.S.]

Phaup, E. Dwight and Hinton, John. The Distributional Effects of Usury Laws: Some Empirical Evidence. *Atlantic Econ. J.*, September 1981, *9*(3), pp. 91–98. [G: U.S.]

Pratt, Richard T. and Ricks, R. Bruce. Real Estate Finance. In *Altman, E. I., ed.*, 1981, pp. 23.3–33. [G: U.S.]

Ranney, Susan I. The Future Price of Houses, Mortgage Market Conditions, and the Returns to Homeownership. *Amer. Econ. Rev.*, June 1981, *71*(3), pp. 323–33.

Riedy, Mark J. Sale of Assets: Panel Presentation. In *Federal Home Loan Bank of San Francisco.*, 1981, pp. 323–27. [G: U.S.]

Rosen, Kenneth T. A Comparison of European Housing Finance Systems. In *Federal Reserve Bank of Boston (II)*, 1981, pp. 144–60.
[G: U.K.; W. Germany; France]

Rowe, Andy. The Financing of Residential Construction in Newfoundland. *Can. Public Policy*, Winter 1981, *7*(1), pp. 119–22. [G: Canada]

Schafer, Robert. Discussion [Financial Institution Regulations, Redlining and Mortgage Markets] [Mortgage Redlining Research: A Review and Critical Analysis Discussion]. In *Fed. Res. Bank of Boston and National Sci. Foundation*, 1981, pp. 196–202. [G: U.S.]

Seiders, David F. Changing Patterns of Housing Finance. *Fed. Res. Bull.*, June 1981, *67*(6), pp. 461–72. [G: U.S.]

Tansey, Michael M. and Tansey, Patricia Hoon. An Analysis of the Impact of Usury Ceilings on Conventional Mortgage Loans. *Amer. Real Estate Urban Econ. Assoc. J.*, Fall 1981, *9*(3), pp. 265–82. [G: U.S.]

Thygerson, Kenneth J. Futures, Options, and the Savings and Loan Business. In *Federal Home Loan Bank of San Francisco.*, 1981, pp. 119–47. [G: U.S.]

Treadway, Peter. Sale of Assets: Comments. In *Federal Home Loan Bank of San Francisco.*, 1981, pp. 315–18. [G: U.S.]

Tucker, Donald P. Regulation Q and Savings Bank Solvency—The Connecticut Experience: Discussion. In *Fed. Res. Bank of Boston and National Sci. Foundation*, 1981, pp. 96–100. [G: U.S.]

3153 Business Credit

Bagchi, Amiya Kumar. Reinforcing and Offsetting Constraints in Indian Industry. In *Bagchi, A. K. and Banerjee, N., eds.*, 1981, pp. 23–62.
[G: India]

Bannock, Graham. The Clearing Banks and Small Firms. *Lloyds Bank Rev.*, October 1981, (142), pp. 15–25. [G: U.K.]

Bates, Timothy. Effectiveness of the Small Business Administration in Financing Minority Business. *Rev. Black Polit. Econ.*, Spring 1981, *11*(3), pp. 321–36. [G: U.S.]

Beckers, Lode G. Contract Guarantees and International Bonding Practices. In *Gmür, C. J., ed.*, 1981, pp. 149–71.

Bickley, James M. An Evaluation of the Reconstruction Finance Corporation with Implications for Current Capital Needs of the Steel Industry. In *Sternlieb, G. and Listokin, D., eds.*, 1981, pp. 144–62. [G: U.S.]

Bitros, George C. The Fungibility Factor in Credit and the Question of the Efficacy of Selective Controls. *Oxford Econ. Pap.*, November 1981, *33*(3), pp. 459–77. [G: Greece]

Cappugi, Luigi. The Financing of Industrial Investment. *Rev. Econ. Cond. Italy*, February 1981, (1), pp. 41–83. [G: Italy]

Clark, K. J. Financing Exports and Imports. In *Ensor, R. and Muller, P., eds.*, 1981, pp. 243–54.

Davies, Rhodri and Grabiner, Anthony. Trade Financing: Legal Issues. In *Gmür, C. J., ed.*, 1981, pp. 173–86. [G: U.K.; Selected Countries]

Ferris, J. Stephen. A Transactions Theory of Trade Credit Use. *Quart. J. Econ.*, May 1981, *96*(2), pp. 243–70. [G: U.S.]

Gmür, Charles J. Financing Trade in Consumer Goods. In *Gmür, C. J., ed.*, 1981, pp. 73–82.
[G: Switzerland]

Gmür, Charles J. Trade Financing: Forfaiting. In *Gmür, C. J., ed.*, 1981, pp. 117–32.

Gori, A. R. Problemi del sistema creditizio, rapporti tra banca e impresa, finanziamento della spesa pubblica. (Credit-System Problems, Relations between Banks and Businesses, Financing of Public Expenditure. With English summary.) *Bancaria*, February 1981, *37*(2), pp. 179–89.

Grassman, Sven. Financial Repression and the Liberalisation Problem within Less-developed Countries: Comments. In *Grassman, S. and Lundberg, E., eds.*, 1981, pp. 387–90. [G: LDCs; MDCs]

Matthes, Heinrich. Il sistema creditizio della Germania Federale. (The West German Credit System. With English summary.) *Bancaria*, November 1981, *37*(11), pp. 1099–1104. [G: W. Germany]

McKinnon, Ronald I. Financial Repression and the Liberalisation Problem within Less-developed Countries. In *Grassman, S. and Lundberg, E., eds.*, 1981, pp. 365–86. [G: LDCs; MDCs]

Meadows, George Richard and Mitrisin, John. A National Development Bank: Survey and Discussion of the Literature on Capital Shortages and Employment Changes in Distressed Areas. In *Sternlieb, G. and Listokin, D., eds.*, 1981, pp. 84–143. [G: U.S.]

Miller, Robert H. Financing Trade in Capital Goods. In *Gmür, C. J., ed.*, 1981, pp. 83–89.
[G: W. Europe]

O'Hanlon, Paul. Documentary Collection and Letters of Credit. In *Gmür, C. J., ed.*, 1981, pp. 43–72.

Rhoades, Stephen A. Are the Big Banks Big Enough? *Antitrust Bull.*, Summer 1981, *26*(2), pp. 315–25. [G: U.S.]

Saito, Katrine Anderson and Villanueva, Delano P. Transaction Costs of Credit to the Small-Scale

Sector in the Philippines. *Econ. Develop. Cult. Change*, April 1981, *29*(3), pp. 631–40.
[G: Philippines]

Schatz, S. P. The Capital Shortage Illusion: Government Lending in Nigeria. In *Livingstone, I., ed., 1981, 1965*, pp. 21–24. [G: Nigeria]

Schultz, Frederick H. Statement to Senate Committee on Small Business, September 23, 1981. *Fed. Res. Bull.*, October 1981, *67*(10), pp. 767–69.
[G: U.S.]

Sobhan, Rehman and Mahmood, Syed Akhter. Repayment of Loans to Specialised Financial Institutions in Bangladesh: Issues and Constraints. *Bangladesh Devel. Stud.*, Winter 1981, *9*(1), pp. 35–75. [G: Bangladesh]

320 FISCAL THEORY AND POLICY; PUBLIC FINANCE

3200 General

Arestis, P. Fiscal Actions and "Crowding-Out" in the United Kingdom. *Metroecon.*, Feb.-Oct. 1981, *33*(1–2–3), pp. 205–32. [G: U.K.]

Beck, Morris. On Measuring Public Sector Shares [Diverging Trends in the Shares of Nominal and Real Government Expenditure in GDP: Implications for Policy]. *Nat. Tax J.*, December 1981, *34*(4), pp. 487–88. [G: MDCs; LDCs]

Bonus, Holger. What Can the Public Sector Contribute to Growth? In *Giersch, H., ed. (II), 1981*, pp. 359–74.

Campbell, Alan K. Government and Productivity. In *Hogan, J. D. and Craig, A. M., eds., Vol. 2*, 1981, pp. 941–52. [G: U.S.]

Chan, James L. A Selected Bibliography on Governmental Accounting, 1979–1981. *Public Budg. Finance*, Summer 1981, *1*(2), pp. 69–73.
[G: U.S.]

Charnovitz, Steve. Evaluating Sunset: What Will it Mean? In *Lynch, T. D., ed., 1981*, pp. 149–61.
[G: U.S.]

Davidson, James. Sunset—A New Challenge. In *Lynch, T. D., ed., 1981*, pp. 143–47. [G: U.S.]

DiLorenzo, Thomas J. Special Districts and Local Public Services. *Public Finance Quart.*, July 1981, *9*(3), pp. 353–67. [G: U.S.]

Elazar, Daniel J. The Evolving Federal System. In *Pious, R. M., ed., 1981*, pp. 5–19. [G: U.S.]

Forte, Francesco and Giardina, Emilio. The Crisis of the Fiscal State. In *Roskamp, K. W. and Forte, F., eds., 1981*, pp. 1–9. [G: OECD]

Frey, René L. What Can the Public Sector Contribute to Growth? Comments. In *Giersch, H., ed. (II), 1981*, pp. 375–81.

Gørtz, Erik. The Effect of Changes in Real Income and Relative Price on the Share of a Sector, with Special Reference to the Public Sector. *Scand. J. Econ.*, 1981, *83*(1), pp. 55–67. [G: Denmark]

Hatry, Harry P. The Status of Productivity Measurement in the Public Sector. In *Lynch, T. D., ed., 1981*, pp. 179–91. [G: U.S.]

Heller, Peter S. Diverging Trends in the Shares of Nominal and Real Government Expenditure in GDP: Implications for Policy. *Nat. Tax J.*, March 1981, *34*(1), pp. 61–74. [G: MDCs; LDCs]

Hood, Christopher. Axeperson, Spare that Quango ... In *Hood, C. and Wright, M., eds., 1981*, pp. 100–22. [G: U.K.]

Hood, Christopher and Wright, Maurice. From Decrementalism to Quantum Cuts? In *Hood, C. and Wright, M., eds., 1981*, pp. 199–226.
[G: U.K.]

Jonung, Lars and Wadensjö, Eskil. The Effect of Unemployment, Inflation and Real Income Growth on Government Popularity in Sweden. In *Strøm, S., ed., 1981, 1979*, pp. 202–12.
[G: Sweden]

Kau, James B. and Rubin, Paul H. The Size of Government. *Public Choice*, 1981, *37*(2), pp. 261–74.

Mark, Jerome A. Measuring Productivity in Federal, State and Local Government. In *Hogan, J. D. and Craig, A. M., eds., Vol. 2, 1981*, pp. 993–1011. [G: U.S.]

Meltzer, Allan H. and Richard, Scott F. A Rational Theory of the Size of Government. *J. Polit. Econ.*, October 1981, *89*(5), pp. 914–27.

Montmarquette, Claude. Politique budgétaire de stabilisation et taille relative des gouvernements. (Budgetary Policy of Stabilization and Relative Size of Governments. With English summary.) *Public Finance*, 1981, *36*(2), pp. 244–66.
[G: France]

Paldam, Martin. Is There an Electional Cycle? A Comparative Study of National Accounts. In *Strøm, S., ed., 1981, 1979*, pp. 182–201.
[G: OECD]

Petersen, Jørn Henrik. Decentralisering i den offentlige sektor. (Collective Decision-Making and Decentralization. With English summary.) *Nationaløkon. Tidsskr.*, 1981, *119*(3), pp. 378–91.

Pluta, Joseph E. Real Public Sector Growth and Decline in Developing Countries. *Public Finance*, 1981, *36*(3), pp. 439–54. [G: LDCs]

Polsby, Nelson W. Contemporary Transformations of American Politics: Thoughts on the Research Agendas of Political Scientists. *Polit. Sci. Quart.*, Winter 1981–82, *96*(4), pp. 551–70. [G: U.S.]

Sneath, William S. Give the Government a Chance. In *Cleveland, H., ed., 1981*, pp. 360–66.
[G: U.S.]

Staats, Elmer B. Economics and the Truman Administration: Comments. In *Heller, F. H., ed., 1981*, pp. 122–24. [G: U.S.]

Tobin, James. Reflections Inspired by Proposed Constitutional Restrictions on Fiscal Policy. In *[Nelson, J. R.], 1981*, pp. 341–67. [G: U.S.]

Weidenbaum, Murray L. The Growth of Government. In *Cleveland, H., ed., 1981*, pp. 309–29.
[G: U.S.]

Wildavsky, Aaron. Budgetary Futures: Why Politicians May Want Spending Limits in Turbulent Times. *Public Budg. Finance*, Spring 1981, *1*(1), pp. 20–27.

Wiseman, Jack. What Can the Public Sector Contribute to Growth? Comments. In *Giersch, H., ed. (II), 1981*, pp. 382–86.

Wright, Maurice. Big Government in Hard Times: The Restraint of Public Expenditure. In *Hood, C. and Wright, M., eds., 1981*, pp. 3–31.
[G: U.K.]

321 Fiscal Theory and Policy

3210 Fiscal Theory and Policy

Andic, Fuat M. and Cao-Garca, Ramon J. Trends and Functions of Tax Reforms in LDCs—Some Limiting Factors. In *Roskamp, K. W. and Forte, F., eds.*, 1981, pp. 413–24. [G: LDCs]

Baldwin, G. B. A Layman's Guide to Little–Mirrlees. In *Livingstone, I., ed.*, 1981, 1972, pp. 223–28.

Barro, Robert J. Output Effects of Government Purchases. *J. Polit. Econ.*, December 1981, *89*(6), pp. 1086–1121. [G: U.S.]

Bhagwati, Jagdish N. and Srinivasan, T. N. The Evaluation of Projects at World Prices under Trade Distortions: Quantitative Restrictions, Monopoly Power in Trade and Nontraded Goods. *Int. Econ. Rev.*, June 1981, *22*(2), pp. 385–99.

Blitzer, Charles; Dasgupta, Partha and Stiglitz, Joseph E. Project Appraisal and Foreign Exchange Constraints. *Econ. J.*, March 1981, *91*(361), pp. 58–74.

Brookshire, David S. and Crocker, Thomas D. The Advantages of Contingent Valuation Methods for Benefit-Cost Analysis. *Public Choice*, 1981, *36*(2), pp. 235–52.

Browning, Edgar K. A Theory of Paternalistic In-Kind Transfers. *Econ. Inquiry*, October 1981, *19*(4), pp. 579–97.

Burgess, David F. The Social Discount Rate for Canada: Theory and Evidence. *Can. Public Policy*, Summer 1981, *7*(3), pp. 383–94. [G: Canada]

Cairncross, Alec. The Relationship between Fiscal and Monetary Policy. *Banca Naz. Lavoro Quart. Rev.*, December 1981, (139), pp. 375–93.

Campbell, Harry F. Shadow-Prices for the Economic Appraisal of Public Sector Expenditures. *Can. Public Policy*, Summer 1981, *7*(3), pp. 395–98. [G: Canada]

Cebula, Richard J. The Positively Sloped IS Curve and Joint Balance: An Analysis in Light of Recent New Evidence on the Interest Sensitivity of Commodity Demand. *Rivista Int. Sci. Econ. Com.*, April 1981, *28*(4), pp. 366–77.

Cebula, Richard J.; Carlos, Christopher and Koch, James V. The 'Crowding Out' Effect of Federal Government Outlay Decisions: An Empirical Note [The 'Crowding Out' Effect of Government Transfers on Private Charitable Contributions]. *Public Choice*, 1981, *36*(2), pp. 329–36. [G: U.S.]

Chalmers, James A. and Threadgill, J. Randall. Evaluation of Underutilized Resources in Water Resource Development. *Water Resources Res.*, June 1981, *17*(3), pp. 455–61.

Chirinko, Robert S. A Further Comment on "Would Tax Shifting Undermine the Tax-Based Incomes Policy?" *J. Econ. Issues*, March 1981, *15*(1), pp. 177–81.

Cuzán, Alfred G. Political Profit: Taxing and Spending in Democracies and Dictatorships. *Amer. J. Econ. Soc.*, October 1981, *40*(4), pp. 329–40.

Darcy, Robert L. Value Issues in Program Evaluation. *J. Econ. Issues*, June 1981, *15*(2), pp. 449–61.

Emerson, Craig and Warr, Peter G. Economic Evaluation of Mineral Processing Projects: A Case Study of Copper Smelting in the Philippines. *Philippine Econ. J.*, 1981, *20*(2), pp. 175–97. [G: Philippines]

Epple, Dennis and Zelenitz, Allan. The Roles of Jurisdictional Competition and of Collective Choice Institutions in the Market for Local Public Goods. *Amer. Econ. Rev.*, May 1981, *71*(2), pp. 87–92.

Fayette, J. R. Appraisal of Non-independent Projects. In *Nijkamp, P. and Spronk, J., eds.*, 1981, pp. 137–50.

Feltenstein, Andrew. A General-Equilibrium Approach to the Analysis of Monetary and Fiscal Policies. *Int. Monet. Fund Staff Pap.*, December 1981, *28*(4), pp. 653–81. [G: U.S.]

Fogarty, T. M. Prisoner's Dilemma and Other Public Goods Games. *Conflict Manage. Peace Sci.*, Spring 1981, *5*(2), pp. 111–20.

Frasca, Ralph R. Instability in Voluntary Contributions Based upon Jointness in Supply. *Public Choice*, 1981, *37*(3), pp. 435–45.

Fry, Maxwell J. Government Revenue from Monopoly Supply of Currency and Deposits. *J. Monet. Econ.*, September 1981, *8*(2), pp. 261–70. [G: Turkey]

Fry, Maxwell J. Monopoly Finance and Portugal's Government Deficit. *Economia (Portugal)*, May 1981, *5*(2), pp. 315–23. [G: Portugal]

Genser, Bernd. Public Finance and Private Saving in Austria: The Effects of Saving Promotion. *Empirica*, 1981, (2), pp. 169–85. [G: Austria]

Guesnerie, Roger and Oddou, Claude. Second Best Taxation as a Game. *J. Econ. Theory*, August 1981, *25*(1), pp. 67–91.

Hanke, Steve H. and Wentworth, Roland W. Project Evaluation during Inflation, Revisited: A Solution to Turvey's Relative Price Change Problem. *Water Resources Res.*, December 1981, *17*(6), pp. 1737–38. [G: U.S.]

Harris, Robert B. Compensation for Loss of Income and Its Taxation: Comment. *Nat. Tax J.*, March 1981, *34*(1), pp. 135–36.

Heady, Christopher John. Shadow Wages and Induced Migration. *Oxford Econ. Pap.*, March 1981, *33*(1), pp. 108–21.

Henry, Claude. Criteres Simples Pour La Prise En Compte Du Risque. (With English summary.) *Econometrica*, January 1981, *49*(1), pp. 153–70.

Holandez, Patrocinio Cruz. An Inquiry into the Relationship between the Economic Rate of Return and the Internal Rate of Return of Selected DBP-Financed Projects. *Philippine Econ. J.*, 1981, *20*(3&4), pp. 337–56. [G: Philippines]

Holzmann, Robert. Public Finance and Private Saving in Austria: The Effects of Social Security. *Empirica*, 1981, (2), pp. 187–221. [G: Austria]

Hossain, Belayet. Choice of Techniques in Small Scale Irrigation in Bangladesh. *Bangladesh Devel. Stud.*, Autumn 1981, *9*(4), pp. 35–49. [G: Bangladesh]

Jenkins, Glenn P. The Public-Sector Discount Rate for Canada: Some Further Observations. *Can. Public Policy*, Summer 1981, *7*(3), pp. 399–407.

Johansson, Per-Olov. On Regional Effects of Government Policies in a Small Open Economy. *Scand. J. Econ.*, 1981, *83*(4), pp. 541–52.

Joshi, V. The Rationale and Relevance of the Little–Mirrlees Criterion. In *Livingstone, I., ed.*, 1981, 1972, pp. 229–44.

Kienzle, Edward C. Measurement of the Progressivity of Public Expenditures and Net Fiscal Incidence. *Southern Econ. J.*, July 1981, *48*(1), pp. 197–203.

Kochanowski, Paul and Hertzfeld, Henry. Often Overlooked Factors in Measuring the Rate of Return to Government R & D Expenditures. *Policy Anal.*, Spring 1981, *7*(2), pp. 153–67. [G: U.S.]

Krohn, Lawrence D. The Generational Optimum Economy: Extracting Monopoly Gains from Posterity through Taxation of Capital. *Amer. Econ. Rev.*, June 1981, *71*(3), pp. 411–20.

Looney, Robert and Frederiksen, Peter C. The Regional Impact of Infrastructure Investment in Mexico. *Reg. Stud.*, 1981, *15*(4), pp. 285–96. [G: Mexico]

Marwell, Gerald and Ames, Ruth E. Economists Free Ride, Does Anyone Else?: Experiments on the Provision of Public Goods, IV. *J. Public Econ.*, June 1981, *15*(3), pp. 295–310.

Mason, Will E. Some Negative Thoughts on Friedman's Positive Economics. *J. Post Keynesian Econ.*, Winter 1980–81, *3*(2), pp. 235–55.

McGuire, Thomas G. Budget-Maximizing Governmental Agencies: An Empirical Test. *Public Choice*, 1981, *36*(2), pp. 313–22. [G: U.S.]

Meade, James E. Fiscal Devices for the Control of Inflation. *Atlantic Econ. J.*, December 1981, *9*(4), pp. 1–11.

Mendelsohn, Robert. The Choice of Discount Rates for Public Projects. *Amer. Econ. Rev.*, March 1981, *71*(1), pp. 239–41.

Middleton, Roger. The Constant Employment Budget Balance and British Budgetary Policy, 1929–39. *Econ. Hist. Rev., 2nd Ser.*, May 1981, *34*(2), pp. 266–86. [G: U.K.]

Mishan, Ezra J. The Difficulty in Evaluating Long-lived Projects. In *Mishan, E. J.*, 1981, pp. 196–205.

Mishan, Ezra J. The Use of DPV in Public Investment Criteria: A Critique. In *Mishan, E. J.*, 1981, pp. 188–95.

Mitchell, Douglas W. Stability of the Government Budget Constraint with a Constant Exogenous Monetary Growth Rate. *Quart. Rev. Econ. Bus.*, Autumn 1981, *21*(3), pp. 15–22.

Munroe, Tapan. The Question of the Social Discount Rate. *Econ. Forum*, Summer 1981, *12*(1), pp. 26–50.

Oates, Wallace E. On Local Finance and the Tiebout Model. *Amer. Econ. Rev.*, May 1981, *71*(2), pp. 93–98.

Pasour, E. C., Jr. Pareto Optimality as a Guide to Income Redistribution. *Public Choice*, 1981, *36*(1), pp. 75–87.

Patnaik, Prabhat. An Explanatory Hypothesis on the Indian Industrial Stagnation. In *Bagchi, A. K. and Banerjee, N., eds.*, 1981, pp. 65–89. [G: India]

Peacock, Alan. Model Building and Fiscal Policy: Then and Now. *Finanzarchiv*, 1981, *39*(1), pp. 43–52.

Plotnick, Robert. A Measure of Horizontal Inequity. *Rev. Econ. Statist.*, May 1981, *63*(2),

pp. 283–88. [G: U.S.]

Powers, Terry A. An Overview of the LMST Accounting Price System. In *Powers, T. A., ed.*, 1981, pp. 1–59.

Prachowny, Martin F. J. Aggregate Supply Management in a Small Open Economy. *J. Macroecon.*, Summer 1981, *3*(3), pp. 409–21.

Sakellariou, Dimitri M. A Simple Method for Finding Shadow Prices Using Leontief Matrices. *Rev. Econ. Statist.*, May 1981, *63*(2), pp. 309–10.

Schneider, Friedrich and Pommerehne, Werner W. Free Riding and Collective Action: An Experiment in Public Microeconomics. *Quart. J. Econ.*, November 1981, *96*(4), pp. 689–704.

Sen, Amartya K. Some Notes on the Choice of Capital-Intensity in Development Planning. In *Livingstone, I., ed.*, 1981, 1957, pp. 215–22. [G: LDCs]

Shavell, Steven. A Note on Efficiency vs. Distributional Equity in Legal Rulemaking: Should Distributional Equity Matter Given Optimal Income Taxation? *Amer. Econ. Rev.*, May 1981, *71*(2), pp. 414–18.

Srinivasan, T. N. and Bhagwati, Jagdish N. Shadow Prices for Project Selection in the Presence of Distortions: Effective Rates of Protection and Domestic Resource Costs. In *Bhagwati, J. N., ed.*, 1981, 1978, pp. 243–61.

Tullio, Giuseppe. Demand Management and Exchange Rate Policy: The Italian Experience. *Int. Monet. Fund Staff Pap.*, March 1981, *28*(1), pp. 80–117. [G: Italy]

Warr, Peter G. and Wright, Brian D. The Isolation Paradox and the Discount Rate for Benefit–Cost Analysis. *Quart. J. Econ.*, February 1981, *96*(1), pp. 129–45.

Yinger, John. Capitalization and the Median Voter. *Amer. Econ. Rev.*, May 1981, *71*(2), pp. 99–103.

3212 Fiscal Theory; Empirical Studies Illustrating Fiscal Theory

Adams, E. Kathleen and Odden, Allan. Alternative Wealth Measures. In *Jordan, K. F. and Cambron-McCabe, N. H., eds.*, 1981, pp. 143–65.

Andic, Suphan. Public Expenditure Growth. *Finanzarchiv*, 1981, *39*(1), pp. 148–57.

Arnott, Richard J. and Grieson, Ronald E. Optimal Fiscal Policy for a State or Local Government. *J. Urban Econ.*, January 1981, *9*(1), pp. 23–48.

Atsumi, Hiroshi. Taxes and Subsidies in the Input–Output Model. *Quart. J. Econ.*, February 1981, *96*(1), pp. 27–45.

Auerbach, Alan J. A Note on the Efficient Design of Investment Incentives. *Econ. J.*, March 1981, *91*(361), pp. 217–23.

Auerbach, Alan J. Inflation and the Tax Treatment of Firm Behavior. *Amer. Econ. Rev.*, May 1981, *71*(2), pp. 419–23.

Bacon, Robert and Karayiannis-Bacon, Hariklia. The Growth of the Non-Market Sector and the Greek Economy: A Reply to Hadjimatheou and Skouras. *Greek Econ. Rev.*, April 1981, *3*(1), pp. 81–82. [G: Greece]

Ballentine, J. Gregory. The General Nonneutrality of Income and Consumption Taxes: Comment [A

Simple Neutrality Result for Movements between Income and Consumption Taxes]. *Amer. Econ. Rev.*, September 1981, *71*(4), pp. 770–72.

Barnett, A. H. and Bradley, James, Jr. An Extension of the Dolbear Triangle. *Southern Econ. J.*, January 1981, *47*(3), pp. 792–98.

Baron, David P. and Forsythe, Robert. Uncertainty and the Theory of Tax Incidence in a Stock Market Economy. *Int. Econ. Rev.*, October 1981, *22*(3), pp. 567–76.

Barro, Robert J. Are Government Bonds Net Wealth? In *Barro, R. J.*, 1981, *1974*, pp. 243–65.

Barro, Robert J. On the Determination of the Public Debt. In *Barro, R. J.*, 1981, *1979*, pp. 267–98. [G: U.S.]

Baumol, William J. and Fischer, Dietrich. The Output Distribution Frontier: Reply. *Amer. Econ. Rev.*, September 1981, *71*(4), pp. 800.

Baye, Michael R. and Parker, Darrell F. The Consumption Tax and Supply-Side Economics: Some Short-term Revenue Effects. *Cato J.*, Fall 1981, *1*(2), pp. 629–32. [G: U.S.]

Bennett, John. A Variable-Production Generalisation of Lerner's Theorem. *J. Public Econ.*, December 1981, *16*(3), pp. 371–76.

Berglas, Eitan and Pines, David. Clubs, Local Public Goods and Transportation Models: A Synthesis. *J. Public Econ.*, April 1981, *15*(2), pp. 141–62.

Bergstrom, Theodore C.; Cross, John G. and Porter, Richard C. Efficiency-Inducing Taxation for a Monopolistically Supplied Depletable Resource. *J. Public Econ.*, February 1981, *15*(1), pp. 23–32.

Bergström, Villy and Södersten, Jan. Double Taxation and Corporate Capital Cost. In *Eliasson, G. and Södersten, J.*, eds., 1981, pp. 163–90. [G: Sweden]

Bergström, Villy and Södersten, Jan. Inflation, Taxation and Capital Cost. In *Eliasson, G. and Södersten, J.*, eds., 1981, pp. 233–66.

Bernheim, B. Douglas. A Note on Dynamic Tax Incidence. *Quart. J. Econ.*, November 1981, *96*(4), pp. 705–23.

Bewley, Truman F. A Critique of Tiebout's Theory of Local Public Expenditures. *Econometrica*, May 1981, *49*(3), pp. 713–40.

Bhatia, Kul B. Intermediate Goods and the Incidence of the Corporation Income Tax. *J. Public Econ.*, August 1981, *16*(1), pp. 93–112. [G: U.S.]

Blake, Daniel R. Property Tax Incidence: Reply [Property Tax Incidence: An Alternative View]. *Land Econ.*, August 1981, *57*(3), pp. 473–75.

Blinder, Alan S. Thoughts on the Laffer Curve. In *Meyer, L. H.*, ed., 1981, pp. 81–92. [G: U.S.]

Bohm, Peter. Estimating Willingness to Pay: Why and How? In *Strøm, S.*, ed., 1981, *1979*, pp. 1–12.

Bohnet, A. Formen und Wirkungen der Vermögensbesteuerung. (With English summary.) In *Roskamp, K. W. and Forte, F.*, eds., 1981, pp. 173–98. [G: LDCs; OECD]

Böttger, Geert; Gretschmann, Klaus and Huppertz, Paul-Helmut. Finanzierungspotentiale kompen-
satorischer Staatsbudgets. (Financial Resources for Compensatory Budgets. With English summary.) *Konjunkturpolitik*, 1981, *27*(4), pp. 207–26. [G: W. Germany]

Braden, John B. and Bromley, Daniel W. The Economics of Cooperation over Collective Bads. *J. Environ. Econ. Manage.*, June 1981, *8*(2), pp. 134–50.

Bradford, David F. Issues in the Design of Savings and Investment Incentives. In *Hulten, C. R.*, ed., 1981, pp. 13–47.

Bradford, David F. The Incidence and Allocation Effects of a Tax on Corporate Distributions. *J. Public Econ.*, February 1981, *15*(1), pp. 1–22.

Bradford, David F. and Fullerton, Don. Pitfalls in the Construction and Use of Effective Tax Rates. In *Hulten, C. R.*, ed., 1981, pp. 251–78.

Brennan, Geoffrey. The Attribution of Public Goods Benefits. *Public Finance*, 1981, *36*(3), pp. 347–73.

Brennan, Geoffrey and Walsh, Cliff. A Monopoly Model of Public Goods Provision: The Uniform Pricing Case. *Amer. Econ. Rev.*, March 1981, *71*(1), pp. 196–206.

Bronfenbrenner, Martin. The Balanced-Budget Multiplier by the Back Door in a Tax-Revolt Context. *Kyklos*, 1981, *34*(2), pp. 178–85.

Brown, C. V. Macroeconomic Implications I: Income Taxation and Employment—An Integration of Neo-classical and Keynesian Approaches. In *Brown, C. V.*, ed., 1981, pp. 213–22.

Bruce, Neil. Some Macroeconomic Effects of Income Tax Indexation. *J. Monet. Econ.*, September 1981, *8*(2), pp. 271–75.

Bryant, W. D. A. A Note on a Generalization of a Second Best Tax Theorem. *Public Finance*, 1981, *36*(2), pp. 282–85.

Bucovetsky, Sam. Optimal Jurisdictional Fragmentation and Mobility. *J. Public Econ.*, October 1981, *16*(2), pp. 171–91.

Burness, H. Stuart; Cummings, R. G. and Paik, I. Environmental Trade-Offs with the Adoption of Cogeneration Technologies. *J. Environ. Econ. Manage.*, March 1981, *8*(1), pp. 45–58. [G: U.S.]

Butkiewicz, James L. The Impact of Debt Finance on Aggregate Demand. *J. Macroecon.*, Winter 1981, *3*(1), pp. 77–90. [G: U.S.]

Butler, James R. G. and Doessel, Darrel P. Efficiency and Equity in Natural Disaster Relief. *Public Finance*, 1981, *36*(2), pp. 193–213.

Callahan, J. The Lease versus Purchase Decision in the Public Sector. *Nat. Tax J.*, June 1981, *34*(2), pp. 235–40. [G: U.S.]

Cansier, Dieter. Vermögenseffekte der Staatsverschuldung—Multiplikatorwirkungen und Implikationen fur den "konjunkturneutralen öffentlichen Haushalt". (Wealth Effects of Government Debt. With English summary.) *Kredit Kapital*, 1981, *14*(3), pp. 390–411.

Canto, Victor A. Taxation in a Closed Economy Intertemporal Model with a Variable Supply of Labor to the Market Sector. *Public Finance*, 1981, *36*(3), pp. 374–94.

Canto, Victor A.; Joines, Douglas H. and Laffer, Arthur B. Tax Rates, Factor Employment, and

Market Production. In *Meyer, L. H., ed.*, 1981, pp. 3–32. [G: U.S.]

Chamley, Christophe. The Welfare Cost of Capital Income Taxation in a Growing Economy. *J. Polit. Econ.*, June 1981, 89(3), pp. 468–96. [G: U.S.]

Christiansen, Vidar. Evaluation of Public Projects under Optimal Taxation. *Rev. Econ. Stud.*, July 1981, 48(3), pp. 447–57.

Christiansen, Vidar. Optimization and Quantitative Assessment of Child Allowances. In *Strøm, S., ed.*, 1981, 1979, pp. 103–22. [G: Norway]

Conrad, Robert F. and Hool, Bryce. Resource Taxation with Heterogeneous Quality and Endogenous Reserves. *J. Public Econ.*, August 1981, 16(1), pp. 17–33.

Corden, W. M. Taxation, Real Wage Rigidity and Employment. *Econ. J.*, June 1981, 91(362), pp. 309–30.

Cordes, Joseph J. and Sheffrin, Steven M. Taxation and the Sectoral Allocation of Capital in the U.S. *Nat. Tax J.*, December 1981, 34(4), pp. 419–32. [G: U.S.]

Courant, Paul N. and Rubinfeld, Daniel L. On the Welfare Effects of Tax Limitation. *J. Public Econ.*, December 1981, 16(3), pp. 289–316.

Cross, Melvin L. and Ekelund, Robert B., Jr. A. T. Hadley: The American Invention of the Economics of Property Rights and Public Goods. *Rev. Soc. Econ.*, April 1981, 39(1), pp. 37–50.

Cross, R. B. and Shaw, G. K. The Evasion-Avoidance Choice: A Suggested Approach. *Nat. Tax J.*, December 1981, 34(4), pp. 489–91.

Cullison, William E. Monetarist Econometric Models and Tax Cuts: Comment [Monetarist Econometric Models and the Effects of Tax Cuts: Further Evidence]. *Econ. Inquiry*, January 1981, 19(1), pp. 173–75.

Dalamagas, Basil. A Microeconomic Analysis of VAT. *Indian Econ. J.*, April–June 1981, 28(4), pp. 89–99.

Dalrymple, Robert, et al. Quantitative Aspects of Tax Burdens—Methodology and Appraisal. In *Roskamp, K. W. and Forte, F., eds.*, 1981, pp. 309–30. [G: Netherlands; U.S.]

Davidson, Paul. Can VAT Resolve the Shortage of Savings (SOS) Distress? *J. Post Keynesian Econ.*, Fall 1981, 4(1), pp. 51–60. [G: U.S.]

De Wulf, Luc. Incidence of Budgetary Outlays: Where Do We Go from Here? *Public Finance*, 1981, 36(1), pp. 55–76.

Deaton, Angus. Optimal Taxes and the Structure of Preferences. *Econometrica*, September 1981, 49(5), pp. 1245–60.

Diewert, W. Erwin. On Measuring the Loss of Output Due to Nonneutral Business Taxation. In *Hulten, C. R., ed.*, 1981, pp. 57–80.

Diewert, W. Erwin. The Measurement of Deadweight Loss Revisited. *Econometrica*, September 1981, 49(5), pp. 1225–44.

Eaton, Jonathan. Fiscal Policy, Inflation and the Accumulation of Risky Capital. *Rev. Econ. Stud.*, July 1981, 48(3), pp. 435–45.

Edelstein, Robert H. The Impact of Proposition 13 Property Tax Reductions: A Theoretical Note. In *Kaufman, G. G. and Rosen, K. T., eds.*, 1981, pp. 207–14. [G: U.S.]

Epple, Dennis and Zelenitz, Allan. The Implications of Competition among Jurisdictions: Does Tiebout Need Politics? *J. Polit. Econ.*, December 1981, 89(6), pp. 1197–1217.

Faulhaber, Gerald R. and Levinson, Stephen B. Subsidy-Free Prices and Anonymous Equity [Cross-Subsidization: Pricing in Public Enterprises]. *Amer. Econ. Rev.*, December 1981, 71(5), pp. 1083–91.

Fausten, Dietrich K. A Partial Rehabilitation of the Policy-Mix Approach. *Kyklos*, 1981, 34(2), pp. 203–15.

Fei, John C. H. Equity Oriented Fiscal Programs. *Econometrica*, June 1981, 49(4), pp. 869–81.

Feldman, Stephen L.; Breese, John and Obeiter, Robert. The Search for Equity and Efficiency in the Pricing of a Public Service: Urban Water. *Econ. Geogr.*, January 1981, 57(1), pp. 78–93. [G: U.S.]

Feldstein, Martin S.; Green, Jerry and Sheshinski, Eytan. Corporate Financial Policy and Taxation in a Growing Economy. In *Eliasson, G. and Södersten, J., eds.*, 1981, 1979, pp. 127–62. [G: U.S.]

Fesmire, James M. and Truscott, Michael H. The Net Demand for Public Goods. *Eastern Econ. J.*, July-Oct. 1981, 7(3–4), pp. 151–56.

Folkers, Cay. Grundsatzfragen und Konzepte der dynamischen Inzidenzanalyse. (Basic Problems and Concepts of Dynamic Incidence. With English summary.) *Z. Wirtschaft. Sozialwissen.*, 1981, 101(2), pp. 127–51.

Formby, John P.; Seaks, Terry G. and Smith, W. James. A Comparison of Two New Measures of Tax Progressivity [Measurement of Tax Progressivity: An International Comparison]. [Measurement of Tax Progressivity]. *Econ. J.*, December 1981, 91(364), pp. 1015–19. [G: U.S.; U.K.; Australia; Canada]

Fralick, James S. Tax Incentives and Private Saving: Some Policy Options. In *Federal Reserve System*, 1981, pp. 143–59.

Fujigaki, Yoshifumi and Sato, Kimitoshi. Incentives in the Generalized MDP Procedure for the Provision of Public Goods. *Rev. Econ. Stud.*, July 1981, 48(3), pp. 473–85.

Gandhi, Devinder K. and Saunders, Anthony. A Stochastic Dominance Analysis of Taxation and Risk. *Public Finance*, 1981, 36(2), pp. 162–70.

Glaister, K. W. Macroeconomic Implications II: Labour Supply and Fiscal Policy in a Disequilibrium Model. In *Brown, C. V., ed.*, 1981, pp. 223–54.

Goldstein, G. S. and Pauly, Mark V. Tiebout Bias on the Demand for Local Public Goods. *J. Public Econ.*, October 1981, 16(2), pp. 131–43.

Harstad, Ronald M. and Marrese, Michael. Implementation of Mechanism by Processes: Public Good Allocation Experiments. *J. Econ. Behav. Organ.*, June 1981, 2(2), pp. 129–51.

Hein, Scott E. Deficits and Inflation. *Fed. Res. Bank St. Louis Rev.*, March 1981, 63(3), pp. 3–10. [G: U.S.]

Hendershott, Patric H. Estimates of Investment Functions and Some Implications for Productivity Growth. In *Meyer, L. H., ed.*, 1981, pp. 149–63.

Henderson, David. Limitations of the Laffer Curve as a Justification for Tax Cuts. *Cato J.*, Spring 1981, *1*(1), pp. 45–52.

Hicks, John R. The Concept of Income in Relation to Taxation and to Business Management. In *Roskamp, K. W. and Forte, F., eds.*, 1981, pp. 73–85.

Hochman, Oded. Land Rents, Optimal Taxation and Local Fiscal Independence in an Economy with Local Public Goods. *J. Public Econ.*, February 1981, *15*(1), pp. 59–85.

Holcombe, Randall G.; Jackson, John D. and Zardkoohi, Asghar. The National Debt Controversy. *Kyklos*, 1981, *34*(2), pp. 186–202.   [G: U.S.]

Holcombe, Randall G. and Meiners, Roger E. Corrective Taxes and Auctions of Rights in the Control of Externalities: A Reply. *Public Finance Quart.*, October 1981, *9*(4), pp. 479–84.

Holly, Sean. Rational Expectations and the Scope for an Optimal Fiscal Policy in a Simple Model of an Open Economy: Some Numerical Results. In *Janssen, J. M. L.; Pau, L. F. and Straszak, A. J., eds.*, 1981, pp. 91–97.

Homma, Masaaki. A Dynamic Analysis of the Differential Incidence of Capital and Labour Taxes in a Two-Class Economy. *J. Public Econ.*, June 1981, *15*(3), pp. 363–78.

Hushak, Leroy J. Property Tax Incidence: Comment [Property Tax Incidence: An Alternative View]. *Land Econ.*, August 1981, *57*(3), pp. 471–72.

Hylland, Aanund and Zeckhauser, Richard. Distributional Objectives Should Affect Taxes but Not Program Choice or Design. In *Strim, S., ed.*, 1981, *1979*, pp. 123–43.

Ikeda, Hisashi. Tax Incidence with Social Capital and Non-Shiftable Private Capital. (In Japanese. With English summary.) *Osaka Econ. Pap.*, June 1981, *31*(1), pp. 21–27.

Ito, Yozo and Kaneko, Mamoru. Linerization of Cost Functions in Public Goods Economies. *Econ. Stud. Quart.*, December 1981, *32*(3), pp. 237–46.

Jackson, Raymond. A Rejoinder [Optimal Studies for Public Transit]. *J. Transp. Econ. Policy*, January 1981, *15*(1), pp. 72–75.

Jain, M. M. Public Goods, Optimal Taxation, and Economic Efficiency. *Indian Econ. J.*, January–March 1981, *28*(3), pp. 70–85.

Jakobsson, Ulf and Normann, Göran. Welfare Effects of Changes in Income Tax Progression in Sweden. In *Eliasson, G.; Holmlund, B. and Stafford, F. P., eds.*, 1981, pp. 313–38.
     [G: Sweden]

Joines, Douglas H. Estimates of Effective Marginal Tax Rates on Factor Incomes. *J. Bus.*, April 1981, *54*(2), pp. 191–226.   [G: U.S.]

Jonsson, Ernst. On the Rationing of Public Products (Services) by Queuing vis-à-vis Rationing by Price. *Public Finance*, 1981, *36*(3), pp. 430–38.

Jorgenson, Dale W. Issues in the Design of Savings and Investment Incentives: Discussion. In *Hulten, C. R., ed.*, 1981, pp. 52–56.

Kanbur, S. M. Risk Taking and Taxation: An Alternative Perspective. *J. Public Econ.*, April 1981, *15*(2), pp. 163–84.

Kaneko, Mamoru. On the Existence of an Optimal

Income Tax Schedule. *Rev. Econ. Stud.*, October 1981, *48*(4), pp. 633–42.

Katz, Eliakim and Zilberfarb, Ben-Zion. On the Stabilizing Effects of Taxation. *Public Finance*, 1981, *36*(2), pp. 286–89.

Keenan, Donald and Rubin, Paul H. The Output Distribution Frontier: Comment. *Amer. Econ. Rev.*, September 1981, *71*(4), pp. 796–99.

Krzyaniak, Marian. Impossibility Theorems and Incidence of the Government Size: An Effort at Reconstruction of Modern Incidence Theory. *Public Finance*, 1981, *36*(3), pp. 311–36.

Laffer, Arthur B. Government Exactions and Revenue Deficiencies. *Cato J.*, Spring 1981, *1*(1), pp. 1–21.   [G: U.S.]

Laker, John F. Fiscal Proxies for Devaluation: A General Review. *Int. Monet. Fund Staff Pap.*, March 1981, *28*(1), pp. 118–43.

Lawson, G. H. and Stark, A. W. Equity Values and Inflation: A Rejoinder. *Lloyds Bank Rev.*, October 1981, (142), pp. 39–43.   [G: U.K.]

Lawson, G. H. and Stark, A. W. Equity Values and Inflation: Dividends and Debt Financing. *Lloyds Bank Rev.*, January 1981, (139), pp. 40–54.
     [G: U.K.]

Lephardt, George P. Taxes and Aggregate Supply: A Case of a Misplaced Blade. *J. Macroecon.*, Winter 1981, *3*(1), pp. 117–24.

Lewis, Tracy R. Markets and Environmental Management with a Storable Pollutant. *J. Environ. Econ. Manage.*, March 1981, *8*(1), pp. 11–18.

Lewis, Verne B. Incremental Thinking: Toward a Theory of Budgeting. *Public Budg. Finance*, Autumn 1981, *1*(3), pp. 69–82.

Lindholm, Richard W. VAT, the Third Way. *J. Post Keynesian Econ.*, Fall 1981, *4*(1), pp. 44–50.
     [G: U.S.]

Lindholm, Richard W. VAT, the Third Way: Rejoinder. *J. Post Keynesian Econ.*, Fall 1981, *4*(1), pp. 61–62.   [G: U.S.]

Lippman, Steven A. and McCall, John J. Progressive Taxation in Sequential Decisionmaking: Deterministic and Stochastic Analysis. *J. Public Econ.*, August 1981, *16*(1), pp. 35–52.

Livingston, Miles. Taxation and Bond Market Equilibrium in a World of Uncertain Future Interest Rates: Reply. *J. Finan. Quant. Anal.*, December 1981, *16*(5), pp. 779–81.

Malcomson, James M. Corporate Tax Policy and the Service Life of Capital Equipment. *Rev. Econ. Stud.*, April 1981, *48*(2), pp. 311–16.

McCaleb, Thomas S. Excess Burden and Optimal Income Taxation. *Public Finance*, 1981, *36*(3), pp. 395–410.

McElroy, F. William. Classical Misconceptions and Keynesian Innovations. *Rivista Int. Sci. Econ. Com.*, October–November 1981, *28*(10–11), pp. 1053–69.

McKee, Arnold F. What Is "Distributive" Justice? *Rev. Soc. Econ.*, April 1981, *39*(1), pp. 1–17.

McKenzie, Richard B. The Construction of the Demand for Public Goods and the Theory of Income Redistribution. *Public Choice*, 1981, *36*(2), pp. 337–44.

McMillin, W. Douglas. A Dynamic Analysis of the Impact of Fiscal Policy on the Money Supply: A

Note. *J. Money, Credit, Banking*, May 1981, *13*(2), pp. 221–26. [G: U.S.]

McMillin, W. Douglas and Beard, Thomas R. The Impact of Fiscal Policy on the Money Supply in the U.S.: Theory and Empirical Evidence. *Rivista Int. Sci. Econ. Com.*, October–November 1981, *28*(10–11), pp. 941–58. [G: U.S.]

McMullen, B. Starr. The Laffer Curve: Fact or Convenient Fantasy. *Econ. Forum*, Winter 1981–82, *12*(2), pp. 113–15. [G: U.S.]

Mestelman, Stuart. Corrective Production Subsidies in an Increasing Cost Industry: A Note on a Baumol–Oates Proposition. *Can. J. Econ.*, February 1981, *14*(1), pp. 124–30.

Mills, David E. The Non-Neutrality of Land Value Taxation. *Nat. Tax J.*, March 1981, *34*(1), pp. 125–29.

Mintz, Jack M. Some Additional Results on Investment, Risk Taking, and Full Loss Offset Corporate Taxation with Interest Deductibility. *Quart. J. Econ.*, November 1981, *96*(4), pp. 631–42.

Mirrlees, J. A. Property and Commodity taxes and Under-Provision in the Public Sector: Comment. In *Currie, D.; Peel, D. and Peters, W., eds.*, 1981, pp. 136–38.

Mishan, Ezra J. Flexibility and Consistency in Project Evaluation. In *Mishan, E. J.*, 1981, *1974*, pp. 155–64.

Mitchell, Douglas W. Deficit and Inflation in a Post Keynesian Model. *J. Post Keynesian Econ.*, Summer 1981, *3*(4), pp. 560–67.

Moore, Basil J. Equity Values and Inflation: Reply. *Lloyds Bank Rev.*, January 1981, (139), pp. 55–57.

Moore, Basil J. Equity Values and Inflation: Reply. *Lloyds Bank Rev.*, October 1981, (142), pp. 44–45. [G: U.K.]

Moore, George R. Taxes, Inflation, and Capital Formation. In *Federal Reserve System*, 1981, pp. 303–26.

Mori, Toru. On the Existence of Satisfactory Dynamic Revelation Processes for Public Good Provision. *Scand. J. Econ.*, 1981, *83*(3), pp. 429–43.

Morrison, Clarence C. and Pfouts, Ralph W. A Postscript [Harold Hotelling and Marginal Cost Pricing]. *Atlantic Econ. J.*, December 1981, *9*(4), pp. 41–42.

Morrison, Clarence C. and Pfouts, Ralph W. Hotelling's Proof of the Marginal Cost Pricing Theorem [Harold Hotelling and Marginal Cost Pricing]. *Atlantic Econ. J.*, December 1981, *9*(4), pp. 34–37.

Moszer, Max. A Comment on the Laffer Model. *Cato J.*, Spring 1981, *1*(1), pp. 23–44. [G: U.S.]

Murthy, N. R. Vasudeva. Wagner's Law of Public Expenditures: An Empirical Investigation of the Indian Economy Using the Appropriate Measure for a Valid Test. *Indian Econ. J.*, January–March 1981, *28*(3), pp. 86–93. [G: India]

Musgrave, Richard A. A Non-Existing Paradox: Response to Professor Yeh [Musgrave's Paradox and Progressive Income Taxation]. *Public Finance*, 1981, *36*(2), pp. 280–81.

Musgrave, Richard A. Tax Reform or Tax Deform? *Eastern Econ. J.*, July-Oct. 1981, *7*(3–4), pp. 143–50.

Nakatani, Iwao. A "Sample" Tâtonnement Process for Public Goods. *Osaka Econ. Pap.*, December 1981, *31*(2–3), pp. 115–20.

Neumann, Manfred J. M. Inflation und Staatsverschuldung. (Inflation and Debted Financing Deficits. With English summary.) *Z. Wirtschaft. Sozialwissen.*, 1981, *101*(2), pp. 113–26.

Noam, Eli M. Income Sensitivity of Price Elasticities: Effects on the Demand for Public Goods. *Public Finance Quart.*, January 1981, *9*(1), pp. 23–34. [G: Switzerland]

Noguchi, Yukio. On the Intertemporal Non-Neutrality of Taxes on Land: A Dynamic Market Clearing Model. *Hitotsubashi J. Econ.*, June 1981, *22*(1), pp. 20–31.

Nosse, Tetsuya. The Effects of Tax Structure Change upon Income Redistribution under Inflationary Economic Growth. *Public Finance*, 1981, *36*(2), pp. 145–61. [G: Japan]

Oates, Wallace E. Corrective Taxes and Auctions of Rights in the Control of Externalities: Some Further Thoughts. *Public Finance Quart.*, October 1981, *9*(4), pp. 471–78.

Okuno, Nobuhiro and Yakita, Akira. Public Investment and Income Distribution: A Note. *Quart. J. Econ.*, February 1981, *96*(1), pp. 171–76.

Ordover, Janusz A. Redistributing Incomes: Ex Ante or Ex Post. *Econ. Inquiry*, April 1981, *19*(2), pp. 333–49.

Ordover, Janusz A. and Schotter, Andrew. On the Political Sustainability of Taxes. *Amer. Econ. Rev.*, May 1981, *71*(2), pp. 278–82.

Pazner, Elisha and Sadka, Efraim. Welfare Criteria for Tax Reforms: Efficiency Aspects. *J. Public Econ.*, August 1981, *16*(1), pp. 113–22.

Peacock, Alan. Fiscal Theory and the "Market" for Tax Reform. In *Roskamp, K. W. and Forte, F., eds.*, 1981, pp. 11–21.

Peel, David A. On Fiscal and Monetary Stabilization Policy under Rational Expectations. *Public Finance*, 1981, *36*(2), pp. 290–96.

Peston, Maurice H. A Note on a Balanced Budget Change in Local Expenditure. *Public Finance*, 1981, *36*(3), pp. 455–59.

Peston, Maurice H. A Note on the Validation of Cost Push. *J. Public Econ.*, August 1981, *16*(1), pp. 87–91.

Peston, Maurice H. An Aspect of the Crowding Out Problem. *Oxford Econ. Pap.*, March 1981, *33*(1), pp. 19–27.

Petersen, Hans-Georg. Some Further Results on Income Tax Progression. *Z. Wirtschaft. Sozialwissen.*, 1981, *101*(1), pp. 45–59. [G: U.S.; Germany]

Pitchford, J. D. Taxation, Real Wage Rigidity and Employment: The Flexible Price Case. *Econ. J.*, September 1981, *91*(363), pp. 716–20.

Qadeer, M. A. The Nature of Urban Land. *Amer. J. Econ. Soc.*, April 1981, *40*(2), pp. 165–82.

Ramm, Wolfhard. Tax Design and Individual Saving. In *Federal Reserve System*, 1981, pp. 115–32.

Reinhard, Raymond M. Estimating Property Tax Capitalization: A Further Comment. *J. Polit. Econ.*, December 1981, *89*(6), pp. 1251–60. [G: U.S.]

Richards, Ken. Capital Gains and Interest Rate Changes—A Theoretical Correction [Capital Gains Taxation and Interest Rate Changes: An Extension of Paish's Argument]. *Nat. Tax J.*, March 1981, *34*(1), pp. 137–40.

Ricketts, Martin. Tax Theory and Tax Policy. In *Peacock, A. and Forte, F.*, eds., 1981, pp. 29–46.

Roskamp, Karl W. Lindahl Equilibrium, Tax Prices, and the Optimal Supply of Public Goods: A Non-Cooperative Differential Game Approach. *Public Finance*, 1981, *36*(3), pp. 337–46.

Rothbard, Murray N. The Myth of Neutral Taxation. *Cato J.*, Fall 1981, *1*(2), pp. 519–64.

Salter, Stephen J. and Topham, Neville. The Distribution of Local Public Goods in a Non-Tiebout World. *Manchester Sch. Econ. Soc. Stud.*, March 1981, *49*(1), pp. 51–69.

Sandmo, Agnar. Income Tax Evasion, Labour Supply, and the Equity–Efficiency Tradeoff. *J. Public Econ.*, December 1981, *16*(3), pp. 265–88.

Sandmo, Agnar. The Rate of Return and Personal Savings [The Rate of Return, Taxation and Personal Savings]. *Econ. J.*, June 1981, *91*(362), pp. 536–40.

Schaefer, Stephen M. Taxation and Bond Market Equilibrium in a World of Uncertain Future Interest Rates: Comment. *J. Finan. Quant. Anal.*, December 1981, *16*(5), pp. 773–77.

Sheffrin, Steven M. Taxation and Automatic Stabilizers. *Public Finance*, 1981, *36*(1), pp. 99–107.

Shilony, Yuval. A Methodological Note on Welfare Calculus [Optimal Subsidies for Public Transit]. *J. Transp. Econ. Policy*, January 1981, *15*(1), pp. 69–72.

Shim, Ki R. A Note on the K-M Tax Shifting Model. *Indian Econ. J.*, April–June 1981, *28*(4), pp. 29–35.   [G: Japan]

Shome, Parthasarathi. The General Equilibrium Theory and Concepts of Tax Incidence in the Presence of Third or More Factors. *Public Finance*, 1981, *36*(1), pp. 22–38.

Silberberg, Eugene. Harold Hotelling and Marginal Cost Pricing: Reply [Harold Hotelling and Marginal Cost Pricing]. *Atlantic Econ. J.*, December 1981, *9*(4), pp. 38–40.

Sinn, Hans-Werner. Capital Income Taxation, Depreciation Allowances and Economic Growth: A Perfect-Foresight General Equilibrium Model. *Z. Nationalökon.*, 1981, *41*(3–4), pp. 295–305.

Smith, Vernon L. An Experimental Comparison of Three Public Good Decision Mechanisms. In *Strm, S.*, ed., 1981, *1979*, pp. 57–74. [G: U.S.]

Snickars, F. and Granholm, A. A Multiregional Planning and Forecasting Model with Special Regard to the Public Sector. *Reg. Sci. Urban Econ.*, August 1981, *11*(3), pp. 377–404.   [G: Sweden]

Søndergaard, Jørgen. Samspillet mellem indkomstskatter og inflation. (Long-run and Short-run Interaction of Inflation and Income Taxation. With English summary.) *Nationaløkon. Tidsskr.*, 1981, *119*(3), pp. 343–61.

Spindler, Z. A. Balanced Demand and Supply-Side Fiscal Policies. *J. Econ. Stud.*, 1981, *8*(3), pp. 3–21.

Starrett, David A. Land Value Capitalization in Local Public Finance. *J. Polit. Econ.*, April 1981,

89(2), pp. 306–27.

Streeten, Paul P. Taxation and Enterprise. In *Streeten, P.*, 1981, *1958*, pp. 407–17.

Sturrock, John. Eliminating the Tax Discrimination against Income from Business Capital: A Proposal. In *Federal Reserve System*, 1981, pp. 281–302.

Summers, Lawrence H. Capital Taxation and Accumulation in a Life Cycle Growth Model. *Amer. Econ. Rev.*, September 1981, *71*(4), pp. 533–44.

Sumner, Michael T. Investment Grants. In *Currie, D.; Nobay, R. and Peel, D.*, eds., 1981, pp. 286–320.   [G: U.K.]

Sumner, Michael T. and Laing, C. J. Countercyclical Tax Changes and Consumers' Expenditure. *Oxford Bull. Econ. Statist.*, May 1981, *43*(2), pp. 131–47.   [G: U.K.]

Sumner, Michael T. and Ward, Robert. Tax Changes and Cigarette Prices [An Alternative Approach to the Analysis of Taxation]. *J. Polit. Econ.*, December 1981, *89*(6), pp. 1261–65.   [G: U.S.]

Supel, Thomas M. Macroeconomic Implications for Tax Indexing in the McCallum-Whitaker Framework. *J. Monet. Econ.*, July 1981, *8*(1), pp. 131–37.

Swan, Peter L. Durability and Taxes: Market Structure and Quasi-Capital Market Distortion. *Econometrica*, March 1981, *49*(2), pp. 425–35.

Tanzi, Vito. Inflation Accounting and the Taxation of Capital Gains of Business Enterprises. In *Roskamp, K. W. and Forte, F.*, eds., 1981, pp. 87–101.

Thurow, Lester C. Employment and Public Expenditure in USA in the 1980s. *Giorn. Econ.*, May–June 1981, *40*(5–6), pp. 371–78.   [G: U.S.]

Tideman, T. Nicolaus and Tullock, Gordon. Coalitions under Demand Revealing [A New and Superior Process of Making Social Choices]. *Public Choice*, 1981, *36*(2), pp. 323–28.

Tirole, Jean and Guesnerie, Roger. Tax Reform from the Gradient Projection Viewpoint. *J. Public Econ.*, June 1981, *15*(3), pp. 275–93.

Tobin, James. Reflections Inspired by Proposed Constitutional Restrictions on Fiscal Policy. In *[Nelson, J. R.]*, 1981, pp. 341–67.   [G: U.S.]

Topham, Neville. Property and Commodity Taxes and Under-Provision in the Public Sector. In *Currie, D.; Peel, D. and Peters, W.*, eds., 1981, pp. 107–35.

Tullock, Gordon. The Rhetoric and Reality of Redistribution. *Southern Econ. J.*, April 1981, *47*(4), pp. 895–907.

Ulph, David T. Labour Supply, Taxation and the Measurement of Inequality. In *Brown, C. V.*, ed., 1981, pp. 144–62.

Ulph, David T. and Ulph, Alistair M. Implications for Optimal Income Taxation. In *Brown, C. V.*, ed., 1981, pp. 189–212.   [G: U.K.]

Van Cott, T. Norman. Inflation as a Tax on Money: Integration into IS–LM Analysis. *Public Finance Quart.*, January 1981, *9*(1), pp. 61–74.

Vartiainen, Henri J. Progressive Income Taxation, Disincentives and Barter. In *Roskamp, K. W. and Forte, F.*, eds., 1981, pp. 103–19.

Walker, Mark. A Simple Incentive Compatible Scheme for Attaining Lindahl Allocations. *Econometrica*, January 1981, *49*(1), pp. 65–71.

Wallace, Neil. A Modigliani-Miller Theorem for Open-Market Operations. *Amer. Econ. Rev.*, June 1981, *71*(3), pp. 267–74.

Walsh, Cliff. A Reconsideration of Some Aspects of the Private Production of Public Goods. *Rev. Soc. Econ.*, April 1981, *39*(1), pp. 19–35.

Webb, David C. The Net Wealth Effect of Government Bonds When Credit Markets are Imperfect. *Econ. J.*, June 1981, *91*(362), pp. 405–14.

Wenzel, H.-Dieter. Zur Effizienz und Stabilität geldund bondfinanzierter Staatsausgabenpolitik in Makromodellen mit Government Budget Restraint. (Efficiency and Stability Aspects of Money- vs. Bond-Financed Government Expenditure Policies in Macro Models with Government Budget Restraint. With English summary.) *Z. ges. Staatswiss.*, March 1981, *137*(1), pp. 17–35.

Wenzel, H.-Dieter and Wiegard, Wolfgang. Merit Goods and Second-Best Taxation. *Public Finance*, 1981, *36*(1), pp. 125–40.

Whalley, John. Capital Gains and Interest Rate Changes: A Reply [Capital Gains Taxation and Interest Rate Changes: An Extension of Paish's Argument]. *Nat. Tax J.*, March 1981, *34*(1), pp. 141.

Whalley, John. The General Nonneutrality of Income and Consumption Taxes: Reply [A Simple Neutrality Result for Movements between Income and Consumption Taxes]. *Amer. Econ. Rev.*, September 1981, *71*(4), pp. 773.

van Winden, Frans and van Praag, Bernard M. S. A Dynamic Model of the Interaction between the State and the Private Sector. *J. Public Econ.*, August 1981, *16*(1), pp. 53–86.

Witte, John F. Tax Philosophy and Income Equality. In *Solo, R. A. and Anderson, C. W., eds.*, 1981, pp. 340–78.

Wooders, Myrna. Equilibria, the Core and Jurisdiction Structures in Economies with a Local Public Good: A Correction. *J. Econ. Theory*, August 1981, *25*(1), pp. 144–51.

Yeh, Chiou-nan. Musgrave's Paradox and Progressive Income Taxation. *Public Finance*, 1981, *36*(1), pp. 16–21.

Ysander, Bengt-Christer. Taxes and Market Stability. In *Eliasson, G. and Södersten, J., eds.*, 1981, pp. 191–231. [G: Sweden; U.S.]

Zee, Howell H. Local Income Taxation and Optimal Jurisdiction. *Public Finance*, 1981, *36*(2), pp. 267–79.

Zodrow, George. Implementing Tax Reform. *Nat. Tax J.*, December 1981, *34*(4), pp. 401–18.

3216 Fiscal Policy

Abizadeh, Sohrab and Yousefi, Mahmood. Iran: Tax Structure Changes—A Time Series Analysis. *Bull. Int. Fiscal Doc.*, May 1981, *35*(5), pp. 202–06. [G: Iran]

Allison, Theodore E. Statement to Subcommittee on Consumer Affairs, House Committee on Banking, Finance and Urban Affairs, March 31, 1981. *Fed. Res. Bull.*, April 1981, *67*(4), pp. 296–97. [G: U.S.]

Alt, James E. and Chrystal, K. Alec. Politico-economic Models of British Fiscal Policy. In *Hibbs, D. A., Jr. and Fassbender, H., eds.*, 1981, pp. 185–207. [G: U.K.]

Anderson, Paul A. A Rational Expectations Approach to "Supply-Side" Economics. *Bus. Econ.*, March 1981, *16*(2), pp. 13–16. [G: U.S.]

Andic, Fuat M. and Cao-Garca, Ramon J. Trends and Functions of Tax Reforms in LDCs—Some Limiting Factors. In *Roskamp, K. W. and Forte, F., eds.*, 1981, pp. 413–24. [G: LDCs]

Andreatta, Beniamino. Linee essenziali della politica finanziaria e monetaria. (Essential Guidelines of Financial and Monetary Policy. With English summary.) *Bancaria*, April 1981, *37*(4), pp. 348–67. [G: Italy]

Antonioli Corigliano, Magda. Sugli effetti inflazionistici della finanza pubblica in Italia negli anni '70. (On the Inflationary Effects of Public Finance in Italy during the 1970s. With English summary.) *Giorn. Econ.*, March–April 1981, *40*(3–4), pp. 167–82. [G: Italy]

Arestis, P. Fiscal Actions and "Crowding-Out" in the United Kingdom. *Metroecon.*, Feb.-Oct. 1981, *33*(1–2–3), pp. 205–32. [G: U.K.]

Artus, Patrick, et al. Economic Policy and Private Investment since the Oil Crisis: A Comparative Study of France and Germany. *Europ. Econ. Rev.*, May 1981, *16*(1), pp. 7–51. [G: France; W. Germany]

Blinder, Alan S. Temporary Income Taxes and Consumer Spending. *J. Polit. Econ.*, February 1981, *89*(1), pp. 26–53. [G: U.S.]

Blume, Marshall E.; Crockett, Jean A. and Friend, Irwin. Stimulation of Capital Formation: Ends and Means. In *Wachter, M. L. and Wachter, S. M., eds.*, 1981, pp. 41–94. [G: U.S.]

Bodkin, Ronald G. The Challenge of Inflation and Unemployment in Canada during the 1980s: Would a Tax-Based Incomes Policy Help? *Can. Public Policy*, Supplement, April 1981, *7*, pp. 204–14. [G: Canada]

Boltho, Andrea. British Fiscal Policy, 1955–71—Stabilizing or Destabilizing? *Oxford Bull. Econ. Statist.*, November 1981, *43*(4), pp. 357–62. [G: U.K.]

Brophy, Theodore F. Toward a New U.S. Industrial Policy? Capital Formation: Comment. In *Wachter, M. L. and Wachter, S. M., eds.*, 1981, pp. 152–55. [G: U.S.]

Brough, A. T. and Curtin, T. R. C. Growth and Stability: An Account of Fiscal and Monetary Policy. In *Killick, T., ed.*, 1981, pp. 37–51. [G: Kenya]

Brunner, Karl. Transition to a New Regime. In *Shadow Open Market Committee (I)*, 1981, pp. 7–15. [G: U.S.]

Buenker, John D. The Ratification of the Federal Income Tax Amendment. *Cato J.*, Spring 1981, *1*(1), pp. 183–223. [G: U.S.]

Buiter, Willem H. and Miller, Marcus. The Thatcher Experiment: The First Two Years. *Brookings Pap. Econ. Act.*, 1981, (2), pp. 315–67. [G: U.K.]

Burchell, Robert W. and Listokin, David. The Fiscal Impact of Economic-Development Programs: Case Studies of the Local Cost–Revenue Implications of HUD, EDA AND FmHA Projects. In

Sternlieb, G. and Listokin, D., eds., 1981, pp. 163–229. [G: U.S.]

Caspersen, Finn M. W. Toward a New U.S. Industrial Policy? Capital Formation: Comment. In *Wachter, M. L. and Wachter, S. M.*, eds., 1981, pp. 143–45. [G: U.S.]

Cavaco Silva, Aníbal. Enquadramento global do desenvolvimento económico português. (The Global Framework of the Portuguese Economic Development. With English summary.) *Economia (Portugal)*, May 1981, 5(2), pp. 375–88. [G: Portugal]

Choate, Pat and Walter, Susan. America in Ruins. *Challenge*, September/October 1981, 24(4), pp. 53–57. [G: U.S.]

Christ, Carl F. and Walters, Alan A. The Mythology of Tax Cuts. *Policy Rev.*, Spring 1981, (16), pp. 73–86. [G: U.S.; EEC; Sweden]

Coutts, Ken, et al. The Economic Consequences of Mrs. Thatcher. *Cambridge J. Econ.*, March 1981, 5(1), pp. 81–93. [G: U.K.]

Danziger, Sheldon and Haveman, Robert H. The Reagan Budget: A Sharp Break with the Past. *Challenge*, May/June 1981, 24(2), pp. 5–13. [G: U.S.]

Eichner, Alfred S. Reagan's Doubtful Game Plan. *Challenge*, May/June 1981, 24(2), pp. 19–27. [G: U.S.]

Ekirch, Arthur A., Jr. The Sixteenth Amendment: The Historical Background. *Cato J.*, Spring 1981, 1(1), pp. 161–82. [G: U.S.]

Fisher, Louis. Developing Fiscal Responsibility. In *Pious, R. M.*, ed., 1981, pp. 62–75. [G: U.S.]

Forte, Francesco and Peacock, Alan. Tax Planning, Tax Analysis and Tax Policy. In *Peacock, A. and Forte, F.*, eds., 1981, pp. 3–28.

Fritzsche, Michael. Mining Ventures in Developing Countries: Fiscal Regime. In *Schanze, E., et al.*, 1981, pp. 108–44.

Genetski, Robert J. The Impact of the Reagan Administration's Economic Proposals (Simulations with the Harris Monetarist–Supply Side Model). In *Shadow Open Market Committee (II)*, 1981, pp. 13–38. [G: U.S.]

Goodman, John L., Jr. Federal Funding Formulas and the 1980 Census. *Public Policy*, Spring 1981, 29(2), pp. 179–96. [G: U.S.]

Grüske, Karl-Dieter. An International Comparison of Quantitative Aspects of Tax Burdens and Specific Expenditure Benefits. In *Roskamp, K. W. and Forte, F.*, eds., 1981, pp. 331–39. [G: U.S.; W. Germany]

Hamburger, Michael J. and Zwick, Burton. Deficits, Money and Inflation. *J. Monet. Econ.*, January 1981, 7(1), pp. 141–50. [G: U.S.]

Hamowy, Ronald. The IRS and Civil Liberties: Powers of Search and Seizure. *Cato J.*, Spring 1981, 1(1), pp. 225–75. [G: U.S.]

Heller, Walter W. Kennedy's Supply-Side Economics. *Challenge*, May/June 1981, 24(2), pp. 14–18. [G: U.S.]

Herber, Bernard P. Personal Income Tax Reform and the Interaction between Budgetary Goals: A UK and USA Comparison. In *Roskamp, K. W. and Forte, F.*, eds., 1981, pp. 55–71. [G: U.S.; U.K.]

Hirschhorn, Joel S. Industrial Policy and Clusters of Innovation: Comment. *Challenge*, May/June 1981, 24(2), pp. 53–55.

Hunt, Lacy H. Toward a New U.S. Industrial Policy? Capital Formation: Comment. In *Wachter, M. L. and Wachter, S. M.*, eds., 1981, pp. 145–49. [G: U.S.]

Johnson, Darwin G. Sensitivity of Federal Expenditures to Unemployment. *Public Finance Quart.*, January 1981, 9(1), pp. 3–21. [G: U.S.]

Jorgenson, Dale W. Economic Policy and Private Investment since the Oil Crisis by Artus, et al.: Comment. *Europ. Econ. Rev.*, May 1981, 16(1), pp. 53–56.

Kapur, Basant K. Rejoinder to Mathieson's "Further Reply" [Traded Goods, Nontraded Goods, and the Balance of Payments]. *Int. Econ. Rev.*, June 1981, 22(2), pp. 485.

Kapur, Basant K. Traded Goods, Nontraded Goods, and the Balance of Payments: Further Comment. *Int. Econ. Rev.*, June 1981, 22(2), pp. 477–80.

Key, V. O., Jr. Incremental Thinking: The Lack of a Budgetary Theory. *Public Budg. Finance*, Summer 1981, 1(2), pp. 86–92.

Keyserling, Leon H. International Implications of U.S. Economic Performance and National Policies. *Atlantic Econ. J.*, December 1981, 9(4), pp. 27–33. [G: U.S.]

King, Arthur T. Economic Development Aspects of a Public Policy Program: Section 8(a) Contracts. *Rev. Black Polit. Econ.*, Spring 1981, 11(3), pp. 337–46. [G: U.S.]

Leibinger, Hans-Bodo and Rohwer, Bernd. Die Fiskalpolitik in den Jahren 1974 bis 1979: Ineffiziente Instrumente oder unzulängliche Anwendung? (Fiscal Policy from 1974 to 1979: Inefficient Instruments or Insufficient Application? With English summary.) *Konjunkturpolitik*, 1981, 27(5), pp. 261–78. [G: W. Germany]

Majumdar, Badiul Alam. Effectiveness of Indirect "Operational Control" over the Private Sector: The Case of Pakistan. *Pakistan Econ. Soc. Rev.*, Summer 1981, 19(1), pp. 69–81. [G: Pakistan]

Mathieson, Donald J. A Final Reply to Kapur [Traded Goods, Nontraded Goods and the Balance of Payments]. *Int. Econ. Rev.*, June 1981, 22(2), pp. 487.

Mathieson, Donald J. Traded Goods, Nontraded Goods, and the Balance of Payments: Further Reply. *Int. Econ. Rev.*, June 1981, 22(2), pp. 481–83.

Matthöfer, Hans. Aufgaben der deutschen Finanzpolitik in den 80er Jahren. (The Objectives of the Fiscal Policy of the Federal Republic of Germany in the 1980s. With English summary.) *Bull. Int. Fiscal Doc.*, August–September 1981, 35(8–9), pp. 343–47, 355. [G: W. Germany]

Meadows, George Richard and Mitrisin, John. A National Development Bank: Survey and Discussion of the Literature on Capital Shortages and Employment Changes in Distressed Areas. In *Sternlieb, G. and Listokin, D.*, eds., 1981, pp. 84–143. [G: U.S.]

Murthy, N. R. Vasudeva. Fiscal Policy and Government Savings in a Developing Economy: Some Empirical Evidence in the Indian Economy. *Bull.*

Int. Fiscal Doc., March 1981, 35(3), pp. 120–25. [G: India]

Musgrave, Richard A. What Will the Tax Cut Accomplish? *Challenge*, May/June 1981, 24(2), pp. 55–59. [G: U.S.]

Nickell, Stephen J. Economic Policy and Private Investment since the Oil Crisis by Artus, et al.: Comment. *Europ. Econ. Rev.*, May 1981, 16(1), pp. 57–59.

Pedone, Antonio. Payroll Taxes, Value-Added Taxes and Income Taxes. In *Roskamp, K. W. and Forte, F., eds.*, 1981, pp. 139–52.

Penner, Rudolph G. Fiscal Policy Outlook: A Report to the Shadow Open Market Committee. In *Shadow Open Market Committee (I)*, 1981, pp. 17–24. [G: U.S.]

Penner, Rudolph G. Report on Fiscal Policy for the Shadow Open Market Committee. In *Shadow Open Market Committee (II)*, 1981, pp. 49–52. [G: U.S.]

Qureshi, N. M. Pakistan's Budget for 1980–81 in Perspective—Important Fiscal Measures. *Bull. Int. Fiscal Doc.*, January 1981, 35(1), pp. 35–37. [G: Pakistan]

Reuber, G. L. Steps to Improve International Economic Policy Co-ordination. *Can. Public Policy*, Autumn 1981, 7(4), pp. 596–603.

Rezende, Fernando. Fiscal Policy, Inflation and Development. In *Roskamp, K. W. and Forte, F., eds.*, 1981, pp. 425–35. [G: LDCs]

Shadow Open Market Committee. Policy Statement, March 16, 1981. In *Shadow Open Market Committee (II)*, 1981, pp. 5–9. [G: U.S.]

Shadow Open Market Committee. Policy Statement, September 14, 1981. In *Shadow Open Market Committee (I)*, 1981, pp. 1–5. [G: U.S.]

Shaw, G. K. Leading Issues of Tax Policy in Developing Countries: The Economic Problems. In *Peacock, A. and Forte, F., eds.*, 1981, pp. 148–62. [G: LDCs]

Siaens, Alain. Plus d'impôts sur les intérêts des dépôts et obligations en FB en Belgique? (No More Taxes on "Interests" from Deposits and Bonds in Belgian Francs: A Cost Benefit Analysis from the Point of View of the Collectivity and of His Members. With English summary.) *Ann. Sci. Écon. Appl.*, 1981, 37(1), pp. 9–27. [G: Belgium]

Sinai, Allen. New Approaches to Stabilization Policy and the Effects on U.S. Financial Markets. *Nat. Tax J.*, September 1981, 34(3), pp. 341–72.

Smith, Adrian. The Informal Economy. *Lloyds Bank Rev.*, July 1981, (141), pp. 45–61. [G: EEC]

Strömberg, Dorothea. Success and Failures in Recent Swedish Tax Policy. In *Roskamp, K. W. and Forte, F., eds.*, 1981, pp. 121–34. [G: Sweden]

Sunley, Emil M. Acceleration of Tax Depreciation: Basic Issues and Major Alternatives. In *Hulten, C. R., ed.*, 1981, pp. 137–47. [G: U.S.]

Tullio, Giuseppe. Fiscal Deficits, Monetary Growth and Inflation under Flexible Exchange Rates: The Italian Experience. *Econ. Notes*, 1981, 10(3), pp. 37–57. [G: Italy]

Volcker, Paul A. Statement to House Committee on the Budget, March 27, 1981. *Fed. Res. Bull.*, April 1981, 67(4), pp. 293–96. [G: U.S.]

Volcker, Paul A. Statement to Senate Committee on Appropriations, January 27, 1981. *Fed. Res. Bull.*, February 1981, 67(2), pp. 135–37. [G: U.S.]

Wasserfallen, Walter. Die Wirkungen der Fiskalpolitik in der Schweiz. Eine empirische Untersuchung. (The Effects of Fiscal Policy in Switzerland—An Empirical Investigation. With English summary.) *Schweiz. Z. Volkswirtsch. Statist.*, December 1981, 117(4), pp. 665–78. [G: Switzerland]

Ysander, Bengt-Christer. Taxes and Market Stability. In *Eliasson, G. and Södersten, J., eds.*, 1981, pp. 191–231. [G: Sweden; U.S.]

Zayas, Edison R. Proceedings of the Seminar on Employment: Statement. In *U.S. Congress, Joint Economic Committee (I)*, 1981, pp. 119–24. [G: U.S.]

322 National Government Expenditures and Budgeting

3220 General

Arnold, R. Douglas. Legislators, Bureaucrats, and Locational Decisions. *Public Choice*, 1981, 37(1), pp. 107–32.

Blaug, Mark. Comments on M. Peston [The Finance of Recurrent Education: Some Theoretical Considerations] and H. Glennerster [The Role of the State in Financing Recurrent Education: Lessons from European Experience]. *Public Choice*, 1981, 36(3), pp. 573–77.

Bronfenbrenner, Martin. The Balanced-Budget Multiplier by the Back Door in a Tax-Revolt Context. *Kyklos*, 1981, 34(2), pp. 178–85.

Cansier, Dieter. Vermögenseffekte der Staatsverschuldung—Multiplikatorwirkungen und Implikationen fur den "konjunkturneutralen öffentlichen Haushalt". (Wealth Effects of Government Debt. With English summary.) *Kredit Kapital*, 1981, 14(3), pp. 390–411.

Carmichael, Jeffrey and Hawtrey, Kim. Social Security, Government Finance, and Savings. *Econ. Rec.*, December 1981, 57(159), pp. 332–43. [G: Australia]

Chan, James L. Standards and Issues in Governmental Accounting and Financial Reporting. *Public Budg. Finance*, Spring 1981, 1(1), pp. 55–65. [G: U.S.]

Chrystal, K. Alec and Alt, James E. Some Problems in Formulating and Testing a Politico-Economic Model of the United Kingdom. *Econ. J.*, September 1981, 91(363), pp. 730–36. [G: U.K.]

Frey, Bruno S. and Schneider, Friedrich. A Politico-Economic Model of the U.K.: New Estimates and Predictions. *Econ. J.*, September 1981, 91(363), pp. 737–40. [G: U.K.]

Glennerster, Howard. The Role of the State in Financing Recurrent Education: Lessons from European Experience. *Public Choice*, 1981, 36(3), pp. 551–71.

Holcombe, Randall G.; Jackson, John D. and Zardkoohi, Asghar. The National Debt Controversy. *Kyklos*, 1981, 34(2), pp. 186–202. [G: U.S.]

Holcombe, Randall G. and Zardkoohi, Asghar. The

Determinants of Federal Grants. *Southern Econ. J.*, October 1981, *48*(2), pp. 393–99. **[G: U.S.]**

Keller, Wouter J. Public Sector Employment and the Distribution of Income. *J. Public Econ.*, April 1981, *15*(2), pp. 235–49. **[G: Netherlands]**

Oppenheimer, Joe A. Legislators, Bureaucrats and Locational Decisions and Beyond: Some Comments. *Public Choice*, 1981, *37*(1), pp. 133–40.

Salamon, Lester M. Rethinking Public Management: Third-Party Government and the Changing Forms of Government Action. *Public Policy*, Summer 1981, *29*(3), pp. 255–75. **[G: U.S.]**

Staats, Elmer B. Financial Management Improvements: An Agenda for Federal Managers. *Public Budg. Finance*, Spring 1981, *1*(1), pp. 43–54.

Tobin, James. Reflections Inspired by Proposed Constitutional Restrictions on Fiscal Policy. In *[Nelson, J. R.]*, 1981, pp. 341–67. **[G: U.S.]**

Usilaner, Brian L. Can We Expect Productivity Improvement in the Federal Government? In *Hogan, J. D. and Craig, A. M., eds.*, Vol. 2, 1981, pp. 963–85. **[G: U.S.]**

Volcker, Paul A. Statement to House Committee on Ways and Means, March 3, 1981. *Fed. Res. Bull.*, March 1981, *67*(3), pp. 243–46. **[G: U.S.]**

Webb, James E. Economics and the Truman Administration: Comments. In *Heller, F. H., ed.*, 1981, pp. 117–22. **[G: U.S.]**

West, Edwin G. Comments on H. Glennerster [The Role of the State in Financing Recurrent Education: Lessons from European Experience]. *Public Choice*, 1981, *36*(3), pp. 579–82.

3221 National Government Expenditures

Alt, James E. and Chrystal, K. Alec. Public Sector Behaviour: The Status of the Political Business Cycle. In *Currie, D.; Nobay, R. and Peel, D., eds.*, 1981, pp. 353–76. **[G: U.K.]**

Andic, Suphan. Public Expenditure Growth. *Finanzarchiv*, 1981, *39*(1), pp. 148–57.

Anton, Thomas J.; Cawley, Jerry P. and Kramer, Kevin L. Federal Spending in States and Regions: Patterns of Stability and Change. In *Burchell, R. W. and Listokin, D., eds.*, 1981, pp. 577–616. **[G: U.S.]**

Aprile, Gianni. L'analyse de la dépense publique dans une structure fédéraliste: le cas de la Suisse. (Public Expenditure Analysis in a Federalist Context: The Swiss Case. With English summary.) *Schweiz. Z. Volkswirtsch. Statist.*, September 1981, *117*(3), pp. 281–95. **[G: Switzerland]**

Barro, Robert J. Output Effects of Government Purchases. *J. Polit. Econ.*, December 1981, *89*(6), pp. 1086–1121. **[G: U.S.]**

Bernholz, Peter. Crescente attivitá dello Stato e sue ragioni principali. (The Increasing Activity by the State: Its Main Explanations. With English summary.) *Mondo Aperto*, June–August 1981, *35*(3–4), pp. 169–75.

Bixby, Ann Kallman. Social Welfare Expenditures, Fiscal Year 1979. *Soc. Sec. Bull.*, November 1981, *44*(11), pp. 3–12. **[G: U.S.]**

Capra, James R. The National Defense Budget and Its Economic Effects. *Fed. Res. Bank New York*

Quart. Rev., Summer 1981, *6*(2), pp. 21–31. **[G: U.S.]**

Carlson, Keith M. Trends in Federal Revenues: 1955–86. *Fed. Res. Bank St. Louis Rev.*, May 1981, *63*(5), pp. 31–39. **[G: U.S.]**

Carlson, Keith M. Trends in Federal Spending: 1955–86. *Fed. Res. Bank St. Louis Rev.*, November 1981, *63*(9), pp. 15–24. **[G: U.S.]**

Carron, Andrew S. Fiscal Activities outside the Budget. In *Pechman, J. A., ed.*, 1981, pp. 261–69. **[G: U.S.]**

Crocker, Royce. Federal Government Spending and Public Opinion. *Public Budg. Finance*, Autumn 1981, *1*(3), pp. 25–35. **[G: U.S.]**

De Wulf, Luc. Incidence of Budgetary Outlays: Where Do We Go from Here? *Public Finance*, 1981, *36*(1), pp. 55–76.

Du Pasquier, Jean-Noël. Le facteur démographique en tant que déterminant des dépenses publiques. (The Demographic Factor as a Determinant of Public Expenditures. With English summary.) *Schweiz. Z. Volkswirtsch. Statist.*, September 1981, *117*(3), pp. 257–69.

Ellwood, John. Making and Enforcing Federal Spending Limitations: Issues and Options. *Public Budg. Finance*, Spring 1981, *1*(1), pp. 28–42. **[G: U.S.]**

Glennerster, Howard. Social Service Spending in a Hostile Environment. In *Hood, C. and Wright, M., eds.*, 1981, pp. 174–96. **[G: U.K.]**

Hartley, Keith. UK Defence: A Case Study of Spending Cuts. In *Hood, C. and Wright, M., eds.*, 1981, pp. 125–51. **[G: U.K.]**

Hartley, Keith and McLean, Pat. U.K. Defence Expenditure. *Public Finance*, 1981, *36*(2), pp. 171–92. **[G: U.K.]**

Hartwell, Ronald Max. Taxation in England during the Industrial Revolution. *Cato J.*, Spring 1981, *1*(1), pp. 129–53. **[G: U.K.]**

Hood, Christopher and Wright, Maurice. From Decrementalism to Quantum Cuts? In *Hood, C. and Wright, M., eds.*, 1981, pp. 199–226. **[G: U.K.]**

Horowitz, Irving Louis. Social Science and the Reagan Administration. *J. Policy Anal. Manage.*, Fall 1981, *1*(1), pp. 125–29. **[G: U.S.]**

Johnson, Darwin G. Sensitivity of Federal Expenditures to Unemployment. *Public Finance Quart.*, January 1981, *9*(1), pp. 3–21. **[G: U.S.]**

Keith, Robert A. Budget Reconciliation in 1981. *Public Budg. Finance*, Winter 1981, *1*(4), pp. 37–47. **[G: U.S.]**

Kogan, Maurice. Education in 'Hard Times.' In *Hood, C. and Wright, M., eds.*, 1981, pp. 152–73. **[G: U.K.]**

Leipert, Christian. Kompensatorische Ausgaben, Symptombekämpfung und Kontraproduktivität im Staatssektor. (Compensating Expenditures, Curing of Symptoms and Negative Productivity in the Public Sector. With English summary.) *Ifo-Studien*, 1981, *27*(1), pp. 35–51.

Martin, George T., Jr. Social Welfare Trends in the United States. In *Martin, G. T., Jr., and Zald, M. N., eds.*, 1981, pp. 505–12. **[G: U.S.]**

McCloskey, Donald N. "Taxation in England during the Industrial Revolution": A Comment. *Cato J.*,

Spring 1981, *1*(1), pp. 155–59. [G: U.K.]

O'Higgins, Michael and Ruggles, Patricia. The Distribution of Public Expenditures and Taxes among Households in the United Kingdom. *Rev. Income Wealth*, September 1981, *27*(3), pp. 298–326.
[G: U.K.]

Odufalu, Johnson O. The Distributive Impact of Public Expenditures in Nigeria. In *Bienen, H. and Diejomaoh, V. P., eds.*, 1981, pp. 455–83.
[G: Nigeria]

de Pouvourville, Gérard. Les achats publics, outils indociles d'une politique industrielle. (Public Procurement, an Unwieldy Tool in Industrial Policy Making. With English summary.) *Écon. Soc.*, October–November–December 1981, *15*(10–12), pp. 1723–55. [G: France]

Proost, Stef; Schokkaert, Erik and Van Elewijck, Paul. Enkele economische aspecten van de Belgische defensie-uitgaven. (Some Economic Aspects of the Belgian Military Spending. With English summary.) *Cah. Écon. Bruxelles*, 4th Trimestre 1981, (92), pp. 571–99. [G: Belgium]

Ruggles, Patricia and O'Higgins, Michael. The Distribution of Public Expenditure among Households in the United States. *Rev. Income Wealth*, June 1981, *27*(2), pp. 137–64. [G: U.S.; U.K.]

Scarfe, Brian L. The Federal Budget and Energy Program, October 28th, 1980: A Review. *Can. Public Policy*, Winter 1981, *7*(1), pp. 1–14.
[G: Canada]

Schott, Kerry. Public Sector Behaviour: The Status of the Political Business Cycle: Comment. In *Currie, D.; Nobay, R. and Peel, D., eds.*, 1981, pp. 377–82. [G: U.K.]

Smith, Tony E. A Representational Framework for the Joint Analysis of Regional Welfare Inequalities and National Expenditure Priorities. *J. Reg. Sci.*, May 1981, *21*(2), pp. 187–202.

Teeters, Nancy H. Statement to Task Force on Enforcement, Credit and Multi-Year Budgeting of the House Committee on the Budget, October 29, 1981. *Fed. Res. Bull.*, November 1981, *67*(11), pp. 845–49. [G: U.S.]

Teeters, Nancy H. Statement to Task Force on Federal Credit, Senate Committee on the Budget, December 10, 1981. *Fed. Res. Bull.*, December 1981, *67*(12), pp. 895–99. [G: U.S.]

Wessels, Hans. Auswirkungen des öffentlichen Verbrauchs auf die Struktur der Vorleistungen. (The Effects of the Public Sector's Consumption on the Structure of Intermediate Inputs. With English summary.) *Ifo-Studien*, 1981, *27*(1), pp. 53–74.
[G: W. Germany]

Wright, Maurice. Big Government in Hard Times: The Restraint of Public Expenditure. In *Hood, C. and Wright, M., eds.*, 1981, pp. 3–31.
[G: U.K.]

3226 National Government Budgeting and Deficits

Agarwala, Virendra. Can Budget Provide the Right Climate? *Econ. Aff.*, January–March 1981, *26*(1), pp. 33–38. [G: India]

Atkinson, P. E.; Blundell-Wignall, A. and Chouraqui, J. C. Budget Financing and Monetary Targets with Special Reference to the Seven Major OECD Countries. *Greek Econ. Rev.*, December 1981, *3*(3), pp. 245–78. [G: U.S.; EEC; Canada; Japan]

Benson, Bruce L. Why Are Congressional Committees Dominated by "High-Demand" Legislators?—A Comment on Niskanen's View of Bureaucrats and Politicians [Bureaucrats and Politicians]. *Southern Econ. J.*, July 1981, *48*(1), pp. 68–77. [G: U.S.]

Betts, Ernest C., Jr. and Miller, Richard E. More about the Impact of the Congressional Budget and Impoundment Control Act. In *Lynch, T. D., ed.*, 1981, pp. 135–41. [G: U.S.]

Bhandari, Dharmendra. Comments on and Highlights of the Indian Central Budget for 1981/82. *Bull. Int. Fiscal Doc.*, May 1981, *35*(5), pp. 214–17. [G: India]

Blandin, Nanette M. and Donahue, Arnold E. ZBB: Not a Panacea, But a Definite Plus: An OMB Perspective. In *Lynch, T. D., ed.*, 1981, pp. 79–86. [G: U.S.]

Bledsoe, Ralph C. Zero-Base Budgeting at HUD. In *Lynch, T. D., ed.*, 1981, pp. 23–64.
[G: U.S.]

Caiden, Naomi. Public Budgeting amidst Uncertainty and Instability. *Public Budg. Finance*, Spring 1981, *1*(1), pp. 6–19.

Choate, Pat. The Case for a National Capital Budget. *Public Budg. Finance*, Winter 1981, *1*(4), pp. 21–26. [G: U.S.]

Crawford, Peter. Federal Deficits are a Red Herring. *Challenge*, November–December 1981, *24*(5), p. 49. [G: U.S.]

Danziger, Sheldon and Haveman, Robert H. The Reagan Budget: A Sharp Break with the Past. *Challenge*, May/June 1981, *24*(2), pp. 5–13.
[G: U.S.]

Das, Kumar B. 1981–82 Budget: Its Strength and Weakness. *Econ. Aff.*, July–September 1981, *26*(3), pp. 209–16. [G: India]

Davis, Robert R. and Genetski, Robert J. Federal Budget Outlook and Economic Prospects through 1982. In *Shadow Open Market Committee (I)*, 1981, pp. 51–61. [G: U.S.]

Dumas, Lloyd J. Taxes and Militarism. *Cato J.*, Spring 1981, *1*(1), pp. 277–92. [G: U.S.]

Emmanuel, A. B. C. Zambia's 1981 Budget. *Bull. Int. Fiscal Doc.*, July 1981, *35*(7), pp. 301–02.
[G: Zambia]

Fisher, Louis. Developing Fiscal Responsibility. In *Pious, R. M., ed.*, 1981, pp. 62–75. [G: U.S.]

Flint, Paul. The EEC Budgetary Problem. *Quart. Rev. Rural Econ.*, February 1981, *3*(1), pp. 36–46. [G: EEC; Australia]

Franco, Giampiero and Mengarelli, Gianluigi. Debito pubblico, base monetaria e inflazione. (Public Debt, Monetary Base and Inflation. With English summary.) *Bancaria*, November 1981, *37*(11), pp. 1141–45. [G: Italy]

Gramley, Lyle E. Statement to Subcommittee on Domestic Monetary Policy of the House Committee on Banking, Finance and Urban Affairs, October 27, 1981. *Fed. Res. Bull.*, November 1981, *67*(11), pp. 832–35. [G: U.S.]

Haddon-Cave, Philip [Sir]. Hong Kong: Budget 1981/82. *Bull. Int. Fiscal Doc.*, July 1981, *35*(7), pp. 314–25. [G: Hong Kong]

Haider, Donald H. Balancing the Federal Budget: The Intergovernmental Casualty and Opportunity. In *Walzer, N. and Chicoine, D. L., eds.*, 1981, pp. 205–22. [G: U.S.]

Hamzah, Mulia Tengku Razaleigh. Malaysia: Budget 1981. *Bull. Int. Fiscal Doc.*, February 1981, 35(2), pp. 79–83. [G: Malaysia]

Hannah, S. P. A Note on Employment Subsidies and the Government Budget Constraint in a Closed Economy. *Bull. Econ. Res.*, May 1981, 33(1), pp. 3–13.

Hartman, Robert W. The Budget Outlook. In *Pechman, J. A., ed.*, 1981, pp. 185–228. [G: U.S.]

Hong, Lee Fook. Singapore's 1981 Budget: Summary. *Bull. Int. Fiscal Doc.*, June 1981, 35(6), pp. 243–53. [G: Singapore]

Kaufmann, William W. The Defense Budget. In *Pechman, J. A., ed.*, 1981, pp. 133–83. [G: U.S.]

Keith, Robert A. Budget Reconciliation in 1981. *Public Budg. Finance*, Winter 1981, 1(4), pp. 37–47. [G: U.S.]

Kopcke, Richard W. Is the Federal Budget out of Control? *New Eng. Econ. Rev.*, November/December 1981, pp. 5–15. [G: U.S.]

Lér, Leopold. The Czechoslovak State Budget for 1981. *Czech. Econ. Digest.*, March 1981, (2), pp. 24–32. [G: Czechoslovakia]

Lewis, Verne B. Incremental Thinking: Toward a Theory of Budgeting. *Public Budg. Finance*, Autumn 1981, 1(3), pp. 69–82.

Markham, Emerson. Zero-Base Budgeting in ACTION. In *Lynch, T. D., ed.*, 1981, pp. 65–70. [G: U.S.]

McDowell, Moore. Irish Budgetary Policies. *Nat. Westminster Bank Quart. Rev.*, August 1981, pp. 22–35. [G: Ireland]

McOmber, Dale. A Public Accounting: An OMB Retrospective. *Public Budg. Finance*, Spring 1981, 1(1), pp. 78–84. [G: U.S.]

Miles, Jerome A. Fundamentals of Budgeting and ZBB. In *Lynch, T. D., ed.*, 1981, pp. 71–77. [G: U.S.]

Montesano, Aldo. Inflazione e finanziamento del deficit pubblico. (Inflation and Public-Debt Financing. With English summary.) *Bancaria*, November 1981, 37(11), pp. 1146–52.

Nathan, Richard P. Field Network Evaluation of the Reagan Domestic Program. *Public Budg. Finance*, Winter 1981, 1(4), pp. 85–89. [G: U.S.]

Pechman, Joseph A. Setting National Priorities: The 1982 Budget: Introduction and Summary. In *Pechman, J. A., ed.*, 1981, pp. 1–16. [G: U.S.]

Pechman, Joseph A. and Bosworth, Barry P. The Federal Budget, Fiscal Years 1980–82. In *Pechman, J. A., ed.*, 1981, pp. 17–44. [G: U.S.]

Pechman, Joseph A., et al. The Nondefense Budget. In *Pechman, J. A., ed.*, 1981, pp. 45–132. [G: U.S.]

Pekkala, Ahti. Talousarvio vuodelle 1982. (The Budget for 1982. With English summary.) *Kansant. Aikak.*, 1981, 77(4), pp. 403–11.

Premchand, A. Government Budget Reforms: An Overview. *Public Budg. Finance*, Summer 1981, 1(2), pp. 74–85.

Premchand, A. Government Budget Reforms: Agenda for the 1980s. *Public Budg. Finance*, Autumn 1981, 1(3), pp. 16–24.

Rahman, Mohammed Saifur. Bangladesh: Budget 1980–81. *Bull. Int. Fiscal Doc.*, February 1981, 35(2), pp. 84–87. [G: Bangladesh]

Reischauer, Robert. The Economy and the Federal Budget in the 1980s: Implications for the State and Local Sector. In *Bahl, R., ed.*, 1981, pp. 13–38. [G: U.S.]

Rupley, Lawrence A. and Finucane, Brendan P. Kenya's 1980 Budget. *Bull. Int. Fiscal Doc.*, January 1981, 35(1), pp. 24–29. [G: Kenya]

Schaafsma, Joseph. A Reply [Was the 1979 Federal Budget Deficit Too Large?]. *Can. Public Policy*, Autumn 1981, 7(4), pp. 621–23. [G: Canada]

Schick, Allen. The President's Budget Problem. *Public Budg. Finance*, Winter 1981, 1(4), pp. 56–67. [G: U.S.]

Sheikh, Munir A. and Grady, Patrick. Was the 1979 Federal Budget Deficit Too Large? A Comment. *Can. Public Policy*, Autumn 1981, 7(4), pp. 617–21. [G: Canada]

Smith, Linda. The Congressional Budget Process: Why It Worked this Time. In *Lynch, T. D., ed.*, 1981, pp. 115–33. [G: U.S.]

Taylor, Graeme M. Introduction to Zero-Base Budgeting. In *Lynch, T. D., ed.*, 1981, 1979, pp. 5–22. [G: U.S.]

Volcker, Paul A. Statement to Senate Committee on the Budget, September 16, 1981. *Fed. Res. Bull.*, October 1981, 67(10), pp. 764–67. [G: U.S.]

Waite, Charles A. and Wakefield, Joseph C. Fiscal Year 1982 Federal Budget Revisions. *Surv. Curr. Bus.*, April 1981, 61(4), pp. 24–28. [G: U.S.]

Wakefield, Joseph C. Federal Budget Developments: The Omnibus Budget Reconciliation Act: The Fall Budget Program. *Surv. Curr. Bus.*, December 1981, 61(12), pp. 21–24. [G: U.S.]

White, B. Ward. Proposals for a Regulatory Budget. *Public Budg. Finance*, Autumn 1981, 1(3), pp. 46–55. [G: U.S.]

3228 National Government Debt Management

Antonioli Corigliano, Magda. Sugli effetti inflazionistici della finanza pubblica in Italia negli anni '70. (On the Inflationary Effects of Public Finance in Italy during the 1970s. With English summary.) *Giorn. Econ.*, March–April 1981, 40(3–4), pp. 167–82. [G: Italy]

Barro, Robert J. Are Government Bonds Net Wealth? In *Barro, R. J.*, 1981, 1974, pp. 243–65.

Barro, Robert J. On the Determination of the Public Debt. In *Barro, R. J.*, 1981, 1979, pp. 267–98. [G: U.S.]

Barro, Robert J. Public Debt and Taxes. In *Barro, R. J.*, 1981, 1978, pp. 227–41.

Bench, Joseph. Government Obligations: U.S. Treasury and Federal Agency Securities. In *Altman, E. I., ed.*, 1981, pp. 2.3–19. [G: U.S.]

Böttger, Geert; Gretschmann, Klaus and Huppertz, Paul-Helmut. Finanzierungspotentiale kompensatorischer Staatsbudgets. (Financial Resources for Compensatory Budgets. With English summary.) *Konjunkturpolitik,* 1981, *27*(4), pp. 207–26. **[G: W. Germany]**

Butkiewicz, James L. The Impact of Debt Finance on Aggregate Demand. *J. Macroecon.,* Winter 1981, *3*(1), pp. 77–90. **[G: U.S.]**

Giffin, Phillip E.; Macomber, James H. and Berry, Robert E. An Empirical Examination of Current Inflation and Deficit Spending. *J. Post Keynesian Econ.,* Fall 1981, *4*(1), pp. 63–67. **[G: U.S.]**

Gori, A. R. Problemi del sistema creditizio, rapporti tra banca e impresa, finanziamento della spesa pubblica. (Credit-System Problems, Relations between Banks and Businesses, Financing of Public Expenditure. With English summary.) *Bancaria,* February 1981, *37*(2), pp. 179–89.

Laidler, David. Monetary Targets and The Public Sector Borrowing Requirement: Comments. **In** *Griffiths, B. and Wood, G. E., eds.,* 1981, pp. 176–79. **[G: U.K.]**

Magnifico, Giovanni. Governo della moneta, disavanzi pubblici e inflazione: il caso italiano. (Money Management, Public Deficits and Inflation: The Italian Case. With English summary.) *Bancaria,* September 1981, *37*(9), pp. 908–17. **[G: Italy]**

Middleton, P. E., et al. Monetary Targets and the Public Sector Borrowing Requirement. **In** *Griffiths, B. and Wood, G. E., eds.,* 1981, pp. 135–75. **[G: U.K.]**

Neumann, Manfred J. M. Inflation und Staatsverschuldung. (Inflation and Debted Financing Deficits. With English summary.) *Z. Wirtschaft. Sozialwissen.,* 1981, *101*(2), pp. 113–26.

Pompili, Luigi. Le banche nel sistema valutario italiano. (Banks and the Italian Foreign Exchange Regulation. With English summary.) *Bancaria,* September 1981, *37*(9), pp. 895–907. **[G: Italy]**

Ruggeri, Giovanni. Estimating the Enlarged Public Sector Borrowing Requirement: Comments and Prospects. *Rev. Econ. Cond. Italy,* February 1981, (1), pp. 121–44. **[G: Italy]**

Seater, John J. The Market Value of Outstanding Government Debt, 1919–1975. *J. Monet. Econ.,* July 1981, *8*(1), pp. 85–101. **[G: U.S.]**

Trevithick, James. Monetary Targets and The Public Sector Borrowing Requirement: Comment. **In** *Griffiths, B. and Wood, G. E., eds.,* 1981, pp. 180–82. **[G: U.K.]**

323 National Taxation, Revenue, and Subsidies

3230 National Taxation, Revenue, and Subsidies

Aaron, Henry J. Do Housing Allowances Work? Policy Implications: A Progress Report. **In** *Bradbury, K. L. and Downs, A., eds.,* 1981, pp. 67–111. **[G: U.S.]**

Aaron, Henry J. The Value-Added Tax: Introduction and Summary. **In** *Aaron, H. J., ed.,* 1981, pp. 1–18. **[G: EEC]**

Aaron, Henry J. and Pechman, Joseph A. How Taxes Affect Economic Behavior: Introduction and Summary. **In** *Aaron, H. J. and Pechman, J. A., eds.,* 1981, pp. 1–25. **[G: U.S.]**

Abel, Andrew B. Taxes, Inflation, and the Durability of Capital. *J. Polit. Econ.,* June 1981, *89*(3),

pp. 548–60.

Abizadeh, Sohrab and Yousefi, Mahmood. Iran: Tax Structure Changes—A Time Series Analysis. *Bull. Int. Fiscal Doc.,* May 1981, *35*(5), pp. 202–06. **[G: Iran]**

Adams, Roy D. Tax Rates and Tax Collections: The Basic Analytics of Khaldun-Laffer Curves. *Public Finance Quart.,* October 1981, *9*(4), pp. 415–30.

Adams, Steven J. and Whittenburg, Gerald E. How the Energy Tax Act Affects Capital Budgeting. *Manage. Account.,* November 1981, *63*(5), pp. 34–39, 52. **[G: U.S.]**

Agarwala, Virendra. Need for an Equitable Tax Structure. *Econ. Aff.,* July–September 1981, *26*(3), pp. 207–10. **[G: India]**

Aho, Teemu and Virtanen, Ilkka. Adequacy of Depreciation Allowances under Inflation. *Liiketaloudellinen Aikak.,* 1981, *30*(4), pp. 351–79. **[G: Finland]**

Aiginger, Karl. Accelerated Depreciation Matters After All: A Note on the Effects of the Existence and the Utilization of Accelerated Depreciation on Feldstein's Extra Tax on Fictitious Profits. *Empirica,* 1981, (2), pp. 263–75.

Al-kadi, Ahmed Abdullah. Taxation of Individuals in the People's Democratic Republic of Yemen. *Bull. Int. Fiscal Doc.,* December 1981, *35*(12), pp. 556–62. **[G: Yemen, PDR]**

Alam, K. F. Taxation, Corporate Planning and Company Financial Policy: A Theoretical Exposition. *METU,* 1981, *8*(3&4), pp. 697–714. **[G: U.K.]**

Alexander, James R. Policy Design and the Impact of Federal Aid to Declining Communities. *Growth Change,* January 1981, *12*(1), pp. 35–41. **[G: U.S.]**

Allen, Garland E.; Fitts, Jerry J. and Glatt, Evelyn S. The Experimental Housing Allowance Program. **In** *Bradbury, K. L. and Downs, A., eds.,* 1981, pp. 1–31. **[G: U.S.]**

Alpert, Herbert H. and Feingold, Fred. U.S.A.: Foreign Investment in Real Property Tax Act of 1980. *Bull. Int. Fiscal Doc.,* May 1981, *35*(5), pp. 195–98. **[G: U.S.]**

Alworth, Julian. Piecemeal Corporation Tax Reform: A Survey. **In** *Peacock, A. and Forte, F., eds.,* 1981, pp. 63–77. **[G: U.K.; U.S.]**

Andel, Norbert. Corporation Taxes, Their Integration with Personal Income Taxes, and International Capital Flows. **In** *Roskamp, K. W. and Forte, F., eds.,* 1981, pp. 159–72. **[G: W. Europe]**

Andic, Suphan. Does the Personal Income Tax Discriminate against Women? *Public Finance,* 1981, *36*(1), pp. 1–15.

Arnould, Richard and Eisenstadt, David. The Effects of Provider-Controlled Blue Shield Plans: Regulatory Options. **In** *Olson, M., ed.,* 1981, pp. 339–60.

Arpan, Jeffrey S.; de la Torre, José and Toyne, Brian. International Developments and the U.S. Apparel Industry. *J. Int. Bus. Stud.,* Winter 1981, *12*(3), pp. 49–64. **[G: U.S.]**

Asher, Mukul, G. Structural Features of Sales Taxes in ASEAN Countries. *Bull. Int. Fiscal Doc.,* May 1981, *35*(5), pp. 207–13. **[G: ASEAN]**

Ashworth, J. S. and Ulph, David T. Endogeneity

I: Estimating Labour Supply with Piecewise Linear Budget Constraints. In *Brown, C. V., ed.,* 1981, pp. 53–68. [G: U.K.]

Ashworth, J. S. and Ulph, David T. Taxation and Labour Supply: Household Models. In *Brown, C. V., ed.,* 1981, pp. 117–33. [G: U.K.]

Ault, Thomas A. Federal–State Relations and Income Support Policy. In *Brown, P. G.; Johnson, C. and Vernier, P., eds.,* 1981, pp. 57–80. [G: U.S.]

Axelsson, Roger; Jacobsson, Roger and Löfgren, Karl-Gustaf. A Note on the General Equilibrium Effects of Taxes on Labor Supply in Sweden. *Scand. J. Econ.,* 1981, *83*(3), pp. 449–56. [G: Sweden]

Axelsson, Roger; Jacobsson, Roger and Löfgren, Karl-Gustaf. On the Determinants of Labor Supply in Sweden. In *Eliasson, G.; Holmlund, B. and Stafford, F. P., eds.,* 1981, pp. 269–300. [G: Sweden]

Bagchi, Amaresh. Exports Incentives in India: A Review. In *Bagchi, A. K. and Banerjee, N., eds.,* 1981, pp. 297–327. [G: India]

Baigent, Nick. Rational Choice and the Taxation of Sin: Comment. *J. Public Econ.,* October 1981, *16*(2), pp. 253–59.

Baird, Charles W. Proportionality, Justice, and the Value-Added Tax. *Cato J.,* Fall 1981, *1*(2), pp. 405–20.

Baldwin, Robert E. Trade, Growth and Income Distribution: The Korean Experience: Comment. In *Hong, W. and Krause, L. B., eds.,* 1981, pp. 287–89. [G: S. Korea]

Balladur, Jean-Pierre and Coutière, Antoine. The Value-Added Tax: France. In *Aaron, H. J., ed.,* 1981, pp. 19–29. [G: France]

Ballentine, J. Gregory. Corporation Finance: Comments. In *Aaron, H. J. and Pechman, J. A., eds.,* 1981, pp. 192–96. [G: U.S.]

Ballentine, J. Gregory. The Cost of the Intersectoral and Intertemporal Price Distortions of a Corporation Income Tax. *Southern Econ. J.,* July 1981, *48*(1), pp. 87–96.

Barnea, Amir; Haugen, Robert A. and Senbet, Lemma W. An Equilibrium Analysis of Debt Financing under Costly Tax Arbitrage and Agency Problems. *J. Finance,* June 1981, *36*(3), pp. 569–81.

Barnett, A. H. Taxation and Pollution Control: An Illustration. *Rev. Reg. Stud.,* Winter 1981, *11*(3), pp. 63–78. [G: U.S.]

Barnett, A. H. and Bradley, James, Jr. An Extension of the Dolbear Triangle. *Southern Econ. J.,* January 1981, *47*(3), pp. 792–98.

Baron, David P. and Forsythe, Robert. Uncertainty and the Theory of Tax Incidence in a Stock Market Economy. *Int. Econ. Rev.,* October 1981, *22*(3), pp. 567–76.

Barro, Robert J. Public Debt and Taxes. In *Barro, R. J.,* 1981, *1978,* pp. 227–41.

Baye, Michael R. and Parker, Darrell F. The Consumption Tax and Supply-Side Economics: Some Short-term Revenue Effects. *Cato J.,* Fall 1981, *1*(2), pp. 629–32. [G: U.S.]

Beavis, Brian and Walker, Martin. Pollution Control with Imperfect Monitoring—An Alternative For-

mulation [The Criminal Waste Discharger]. *Scot. J. Polit. Econ.,* February 1981, *28*(1), pp. 92–94.

Benavie, Arthur. Stabilization Policies Which Reverse Stagflation in a Short Run Macromodel. *Southern Econ. J.,* July 1981, *48*(1), pp. 17–25.

Bendick, Marc, Jr. and Squire, Anne D. Housing Vouchers for the Poor: The Three Experiments. In *Struyk, R. J. and Bendick, M., Jr., eds.,* 1981, pp. 51–75. [G: U.S.]

Bendick, Marc, Jr. and Struyk, Raymond J. Housing Vouchers for the Poor: Origins of an Experimental Approach. In *Struyk, R. J. and Bendick, M., Jr., eds.,* 1981, pp. 23–49. [G: U.S.]

Berglas, Eitan. Harmonization of Commodity Taxes: Destination, Origin and Restricted Origin Principles. *J. Public Econ.,* December 1981, *16*(3), pp. 377–87.

Bergsten, C. Fred. The Export Credit Policy of the United States: Meeting International Competition Effectively. In *Bergsten, C. F., ed.,* 1981, pp. 85–91. [G: OECD; U.S.]

Bergsten, C. Fred. The International Arrangement on Export Credits. In *Bergsten, C. F., ed.,* 1981, pp. 73–83. [G: OECD; U.S.]

Bergstrom, Theodore C.; Cross, John G. and Porter, Richard C. Efficiency-Inducing Taxation for a Monopolistically Supplied Depletable Resource. *J. Public Econ.,* February 1981, *15*(1), pp. 23–32.

Bergström, Villy and Södersten, Jan. Double Taxation and Corporate Capital Cost. In *Eliasson, G. and Södersten, J., eds.,* 1981, pp. 163–90. [G: Sweden]

Bergström, Villy and Södersten, Jan. Inflation, Taxation and Capital Cost. In *Eliasson, G. and Södersten, J., eds.,* 1981, pp. 233–66.

Bernard, Georges. A Drastic Proposal for Fiscal Reform. In *Roskamp, K. W. and Forte, F., eds.,* 1981, pp. 23–39. [G: MDCs]

Berndt, Ernst R.; Kesselman, Jonathan R. and Watkins, G. C. Tax Normalization, Regulation, and Economic Efficiency. In *Nemetz, P. N., ed.,* 1981, pp. 171–83. [G: Canada]

Bernheim, B. Douglas. A Note on Dynamic Tax Incidence. *Quart. J. Econ.,* November 1981, *96*(4), pp. 705–23.

Betson, David and Bishop, John. Reform of the Tax System to Stimulate Labor Supply: Efficiency and Distributional Effects. In *Dennis, B. D., ed.,* 1981, pp. 307–15. [G: U.S.]

Bhandari, Dharmendra. Comments on and Highlights of the Indian Central Budget for 1981/82. *Bull. Int. Fiscal Doc.,* May 1981, *35*(5), pp. 214–17. [G: India]

Bhandari, Dharmendra. Taxation of Non-Residents in India for Royalties and Fees for Technical Services. *Bull. Int. Fiscal Doc.,* June 1981, *35*(6), pp. 277–81. [G: India]

Bhatia, Kul B. Intermediate Goods and the Incidence of the Corporation Income Tax. *J. Public Econ.,* August 1981, *16*(1), pp. 93–112. [G: U.S.]

Bishop, John. Employment in Construction and Distribution Industries: The Impact of the New Jobs Tax Credit. In *Rosen, S., ed.,* 1981, pp. 209–46. [G: U.S.]

Bishop, John and Haveman, Robert H. Targeted Wage Subsidies: Their Rationale and Effectiveness. In *Eliasson, G. and Södersten, J., eds.,* 1981, pp. 297–343. **[G: U.S.]**

Blaich, Robert and Schuster, Walter. Did Fictitious Profits Contribute to the Decline in the Rate of Profit? *Empirica,* 1981, (2), pp. 241–54.
[G: Austria]

Blinder, Alan S. Temporary Income Taxes and Consumer Spending. *J. Polit. Econ.,* February 1981, *89*(1), pp. 26–53. **[G: U.S.]**

Blinder, Alan S. Thoughts on the Laffer Curve. In *Meyer, L. H., ed.,* 1981, pp. 81–92. **[G: U.S.]**

Blomquist, N. Sören. A Comparison of Tax Bases for a Personal Tax. *Scand. J. Econ.,* 1981, *83*(3), pp. 390–407.

Boatsman, James R. and Baskin, Elba F. Asset Valuation with Incomplete Markets. *Accounting Rev.,* January 1981, *56*(1), pp. 38–53. **[G: U.S.]**

Bohnet, A. Formen und Wirkungen der Vermögensbesteuerung. (With English summary.) In *Roskamp, K. W. and Forte, F., eds.,* 1981, pp. 173–98. **[G: LDCs; OECD]**

Boidman, Nathan. International Tax Avoidance—The Impact on Legal Systems. *Bull. Int. Fiscal Doc.,* October 1981, *35*(10), pp. 435–47.
[G: U.S.; Canada]

Bond, Eric W. Tax Holidays and Industry Behavior. *Rev. Econ. Statist.,* February 1981, *63*(1), pp. 88–95. **[G: Puerto Rico]**

Bondonio, Piervincenzo. Broad-Based Sales Taxes versus Excise Taxes in Industrialized Countries: Trends and Issues. In *Roskamp, K. W. and Forte, F., eds.,* 1981, pp. 251–67. **[G: OECD]**

Bondonio, Piervincenzo. Personal Income Taxation, Wage Differentials, and Inflation with Special Reference to Italy. In *Peacock, A. and Forte, F., eds.,* 1981, pp. 49–62. **[G: Italy]**

Boskin, Michael J. Labor Supply: Comments. In *Aaron, H. J. and Pechman, J. A., eds.,* 1981, pp. 72–75. **[G: U.S.]**

Boskin, Michael J. Some Issues in "Supply-Side" Economics. *Carnegie-Rochester Conf. Ser. Public Policy,* Spring 1981, *14,* pp. 201–20.

Boss, Alfred. Zur Reform des Systems der sozialen Sicherung in der Bundesrepublik Deutschland. (On the Reform of the System of Social Insurance in the Federal Republic of Germany. With English summary.) *Konjunkturpolitik,* 1981, *27*(2), pp. 59–88. **[G: W. Germany]**

Boyer, Kenneth D. Intermediate-Term Railroad Traffic Gains in Response to Rising Energy Costs. In *[Nelson, J. R.],* 1981, pp. 115–30.
[G: U.S.]

Bradford, David F. Issues in the Design of Savings and Investment Incentives. In *Hulten, C. R., ed.,* 1981, pp. 13–47.

Bradford, David F. The Incidence and Allocation Effects of a Tax on Corporate Distributions. *J. Public Econ.,* February 1981, *15*(1), pp. 1–22.

Bradford, David F. and Södersten, Jan. An International Comparison of Effective Corporate Tax Rates. In *Industrial Inst. for Econ. and Soc. Research,* 1981, pp. 78–82. **[G: U.S.; Sweden]**

Brancato, Carolyn Kay. An Economic Profile of Major Presidential and Congressional Initiatives to Deal with the "Energy Crisis." In *Kamrany, N. M.,* 1981, pp. 99–120. **[G: U.S.; OECD]**

Brannon, Gerard M. Charitable Contributions: Comments. In *Aaron, H. J. and Pechman, J. A., eds.,* 1981, pp. 437–41. **[G: U.S.]**

Break, George. The New Focus of Federal Fiscal Policies and Implications for State and Local Governments: Symposium Summary: Historical Perspective and Evaluation. *Nat. Tax J.,* September 1981, *34*(3), pp. 395–97.

Bridges, Benjamin, Jr. Family Social Security Taxes Compared with Federal Income Taxes, 1979. *Soc. Sec. Bull.,* December 1981, *44*(12), pp. 12–18.
[G: U.S.]

Brinner, Roger E. and Brooks, Stephen H. Stock Prices. In *Aaron, H. J. and Pechman, J. A., eds.,* 1981, pp. 199–238. **[G: U.S.]**

Brittain, John A. Charitable Contributions: Comments. In *Aaron, H. J. and Pechman, J. A., eds.,* 1981, pp. 441–46. **[G: U.S.]**

Brown, C. V. Taxation and Labour Supply: Summary of Results. In *Brown, C. V., ed.,* 1981, pp. 134–43. **[G: U.K.]**

Brown, C. V. Taxation and Labour Supply: Data Quality. In *Brown, C. V., ed.,* 1981, pp. 11–20.
[G: U.K.]

Brown, C. V. Taxation and Labour Supply: Sample Selection and Questionnaire Design. In *Brown, C. V., ed.,* 1981, pp. 5–10.

Brown, C. V. and Levin, E. Taxation and Labour Supply: The Interview Approach. In *Brown, C. V., ed.,* 1981, pp. 21–34. **[G: U.K.]**

Brown, C. V.; Levin, E. and Ulph, David T. Inflation, Taxation and Income Distribution. In *Brown, C. V., ed.,* 1981, *1977,* pp. 255–68.
[G: U.K.; Australia]

Brown, C. V.; Levin, E. and Ulph, David T. Taxation and Labour Supply: The Basic Model. In *Brown, C. V., ed.,* 1981, pp. 35–52. **[G: U.K.]**

Brown, E. Cary. The "Net" versus the "Gross" Investment Tax Credit. In *Hulten, C. R., ed.,* 1981, pp. 133–34.

Brown, Ray L. Management Accountants: Are You Ready for VAT? *Manage. Account.,* November 1981, *63*(5), pp. 40–44, 52. **[G: U.S.]**

Bruce, Neil. Some Macroeconomic Effects of Income Tax Indexation. *J. Monet. Econ.,* September 1981, *8*(2), pp. 271–75.

Brueggeman, William B. The Rental Housing Situation: Implications for Policy and Research. In *Weicher, J. C.; Villani, K. E. and Roistacher, E. A., eds.,* 1981, pp. 13–22. **[G: U.S.]**

Brueggeman, William B.; Fisher, Jeffrey D. and Stern, Jerrold J. Federal Income Taxes, Inflation and Holding Periods for Income-Producing Property. *Amer. Real Estate Urban Econ. Assoc. J.,* Summer 1981, *9*(2), pp. 148–64. **[G: U.S.]**

Bryant, W. D. A. A Note on a Generalization of a Second Best Tax Theorem. *Public Finance,* 1981, *36*(2), pp. 282–85.

Buenker, John D. The Ratification of the Federal Income Tax Amendment. *Cato J.,* Spring 1981, *1*(1), pp. 183–223. **[G: U.S.]**

Burtless, Gary. Labor Supply: Comments. In *Aaron, H. J. and Pechman, J. A., eds.,* 1981, pp. 76–83. **[G: U.S.]**

Butler, Richard J. and Sisti, Thomas R. Impact of Experience Rating and UI Benefits on Unemployment: The Neglected Firm Side. In *Dennis, B. D., ed.*, 1981, pp. 316–25.　　　　[G: U.S.]

Canto, Victor A. Taxation in a Closed Economy Intertemporal Model with a Variable Supply of Labor to the Market Sector. *Public Finance*, 1981, *36*(3), pp. 374–94.

Canto, Victor A.; Joines, Douglas H. and Laffer, Arthur B. Tax Rates, Factor Employment, and Market Production. In *Meyer, L. H., ed.*, 1981, pp. 3–32.　　　　[G: U.S.]

Cantril, Albert. American Politics, Public Opinion, and Social Security Financing: Comment. In *Skidmore, F., ed.*, 1981, pp. 274–77.　　　　[G: U.S.]

Capra, James R. and Beek, David C. Combining Decontrol of Natural Gas with a New Tax on Producer Revenues. *Fed. Res. Bank New York Quart. Rev.*, Winter 1981–82, *6*(4), pp. 61–66.　　　　[G: U.S.]

Carlson, George N. and Hufbauer, Gary Clyde. Tax Frontiers and National Frontiers. In *Eliasson, G. and Södersten, J., eds.*, 1981, pp. 33–49.

Carlson, Jack. The Economy of 1981: A Bipartisan Look: The Proceedings of a Congressional Economic Conference: Statement. In *U.S. Congress, Joint Economic Committee (I)*, 1981, pp. 580–82.　　　　[G: U.S.]

Carron, Andrew S. Fiscal Activities outside the Budget. In *Pechman, J. A., ed.*, 1981, pp. 261–69.　　　　[G: U.S.]

Carswell, Robert. The Political Response to Three Potential Major Bankruptcies: Lockheed, New York City, and Chrysler: Comment. In *Wachter, M. L. and Wachter, S. M., eds.*, 1981, pp. 487–90.　　　　[G: U.S.]

Chakraborty, Baidyanath. The Corporate Income Tax—Its Trend and Elasticity. *Indian Econ. J.*, April–June 1981, *28*(4), pp. 70–84.　　[G: India]

Chamley, Christophe. The Welfare Cost of Capital Income Taxation in a Growing Economy. *J. Polit. Econ.*, June 1981, *89*(3), pp. 468–96.　[G: U.S.]

Chen, Yung-Ping. The Growth of Fringe Benefits: Implications for Social Security. *Mon. Lab. Rev.*, November 1981, *104*(11), pp. 3–10.　　[G: U.S.]

Chiancone, Aldo. On the Taxation of Agricultural Income vs. Other Incomes. In *Roskamp, K. W. and Forte, F., eds.*, 1981, pp. 135–38.

[G: MDCs]

Christ, Carl F. and Walters, Alan A. The Mythology of Tax Cuts. *Policy Rev.*, Spring 1981, (16), pp. 73–86.　　　　[G: U.S.; EEC; Sweden]

Christman, John H. Comments [Petroleum and Mexican Economic Growth and Development in the 1980s] [The Political Economy of Mexican Oil, 1976–1979]. In *Ladman, J. R.; Baldwin, D. J. and Bergman, E., eds.*, 1981, pp. 123–28.

[G: Mexico]

Clotfelter, Charles T. and Steuerle, C. Eugene. Charitable Contributions. In *Aaron, H. J. and Pechman, J. A., eds.*, 1981, pp. 403–37.

[G: U.S.]

Cnossen, Sijbren. Dutch Experience with the Value-Added Tax. *Finanzarchiv*, 1981, *39*(2), pp. 223–54.　　　　[G: Netherlands]

Cnossen, Sijbren. Specific Issues in Excise Taxation:

The Alcohol Problem. In *Roskamp, K. W. and Forte, F., eds.*, 1981, pp. 269–86.　　[G: OECD]

Cnossen, Sijbren. The Value-Added Tax: The Netherlands. In *Aaron, H. J., ed.*, 1981, pp. 43–59.

[G: Netherlands]

Colander, David. Tax- and Market-Based Incomes Policies: The Interface of Theory and Practice. In *Claudon, M. P. and Cornwall, R. R., eds.*, 1981, pp. 79–97.

Colander, David C. New Approaches to Anti-Inflation Policy. *Public Finance*, 1981, *36*(1), pp. 39–54.

Collins, Eileen L. Tax Incentives for Innovation—Productivity Miracle or Media Hype? *J. Post Keynesian Econ.*, Fall 1981, *4*(1), pp. 68–74.

[G: U.S.]

Conrad, Robert F. and Hool, Bryce. Resource Taxation with Heterogeneous Quality and Endogenous Reserves. *J. Public Econ.*, August 1981, *16*(1), pp. 17–33.

Conrad, William E. and Cohen, Darrel S. Inflation, Taxes, and the Capital Stock: A Long-run Analysis. In *Federal Reserve System*, 1981, pp. 267–74.

Corcoran, Patrick J. Inflation, Taxes, and the Composition of Business Investment. In *Federal Reserve System*, 1981, pp. 191–200.　　[G: U.S.]

Cordes, Joseph J. and Sheffrin, Steven M. Taxation and the Sectoral Allocation of Capital in the U.S. *Nat. Tax J.*, December 1981, *34*(4), pp. 419–32.

[G: U.S.]

Cornell, Bradford. A Note on Taxes and the Pricing of Treasury Bill Futures Contracts. *J. Finance*, December 1981, *36*(5), pp. 1169–76.　[G: U.S.]

Coven, Glenn E. The Decline and Fall of Taxable Income. *Mich. Law Rev.*, August 1981, *79*(8), pp. 1525–72.　　　　[G: U.S.]

Cowell, Frank A. Income Maintenance Schemes under Wage-Rate Uncertainty. *Amer. Econ. Rev.*, September 1981, *71*(4), pp. 692–703.

Cowell, Frank A. Taxation and Labour Supply with Risky Activities. *Economica*, November 1981, *48*(192), pp. 365–79.

Crain, W. Mark, et al. Rational Choice and the Taxation of Sin: Reply. *J. Public Econ.*, October 1981, *16*(2), pp. 261–63.

Creedy, John. Taxation and National Insurance Contributions in Britain. *J. Public Econ.*, June 1981, *15*(3), pp. 379–88.　　　　[G: U.K.]

Crick, Nelson. Taxes, Lost Future Earnings, and Unexamined Assumptions. *Nat. Tax J.*, June 1981, *34*(2), pp. 271–73.　　　　[G: U.S.]

Cronin, Francis J. Household Responsiveness to Unconstrained Housing Allowances. In *Struyk, R. J. and Bendick, M., Jr., eds.*, 1981, pp. 159–76.　　　　[G: U.S.]

Cronin, Francis J. Housing Vouchers for the Poor: Consumption Responses to Constrained Programs. In *Struyk, R. J. and Bendick, M., Jr., eds.*, 1981, pp. 129–57.　　　　[G: U.S.]

Cronin, Francis J. Participation in the Experimental Housing Allowance Program. In *Struyk, R. J. and Bendick, M., Jr., eds.*, 1981, pp. 79–106.

[G: U.S.]

Cronin, Francis J. and Rasmussen, David W. Housing Vouchers for the Poor: Mobility. In *Struyk,*

R. J. and Bendick, M., Jr., eds., 1981, pp. 107–28. [G: U.S.]

Cross, R. B. and Shaw, G. K. The Evasion-Avoidance Choice: A Suggested Approach. *Nat. Tax J.*, December 1981, *34*(4), pp. 489–91.

Cullison, William E. Monetarist Econometric Models and Tax Cuts: Comment [Monetarist Econometric Models and the Effects of Tax Cuts: Further Evidence]. *Econ. Inquiry*, January 1981, *19*(1), pp. 173–75.

Cummins, J. David and Westerfield, Randolph. Patterns of Concentration in Private Pension Plan Common Stock Portfolios since ERISA. *J. Risk Ins.*, June 1981, *48*(2), pp. 201–19. [G: U.S.]

Cuzán, Alfred G. Political Profit: Taxing and Spending in Democracies and Dictatorships. *Amer. J. Econ. Soc.*, October 1981, *40*(4), pp. 329–40.

Cymrot, Donald J. Tax Incentives, Turnover Costs and Private Pensions. *Southern Econ. J.*, October 1981, *48*(2), pp. 365–76.

Dalamagas, Basil. A Microeconomic Analysis of VAT. *Indian Econ. J.*, April–June 1981, *28*(4), pp. 89–99.

Dalrymple, Robert, et al. Quantitative Aspects of Tax Burdens—Methodology and Appraisal. In *Roskamp, K. W. and Forte, F., eds.*, 1981, pp. 309–30. [G: Netherlands; U.S.]

Daly, M. and Wrage, Peter. The Effect of Income Tax Incentives on Retirement Savings: Some Canadian Evidence. *Eastern Econ. J.*, July-Oct. 1981, *7*(3–4), pp. 163–74. [G: Canada]

Daly, Michael J. The Role of Registered Retirement Savings Plans in a Life-Cycle Model. *Can. J. Econ.*, August 1981, *14*(3), pp. 409–21.

Danziger, Sheldon and Plotnick, Robert. Income Maintenance Programs and the Pursuit of Income Security. *Ann. Amer. Acad. Polit. Soc. Sci.*, January 1981, *453*, pp. 130–52. [G: U.S.]

Dasmahapatra, Rajkrishna. Black Money and the Special Bearer Bonds. *Econ. Aff.*, July–September 1981, *26*(3), pp. 161–66. [G: India]

David, Martin. The Use of Attitude Surveys in Determining Tax Policy. In *Roskamp, K. W. and Forte, F., eds.*, 1981, pp. 209–34. [G: U.S.]

Davidson, Paul. Can VAT Resolve the Shortage of Savings (SOS) Distress? *J. Post Keynesian Econ.*, Fall 1981, *4*(1), pp. 51–60. [G: U.S.]

Davies, Alun G. The Commonwealth of the Bahamas as a Center of International Business Investment. *Bull. Int. Fiscal Doc.*, April 1981, *35*(4), pp. 165–69. [G: Bahamas]

Deaton, Angus. Optimal Taxes and the Structure of Preferences. *Econometrica*, September 1981, *49*(5), pp. 1245–60.

Dennis, Geoffrey. The Harmonisation of Fiscal Systems. In *Twitchett, C. C., ed.*, 1981, pp. 33–46. [G: EEC]

Dernburg, Thomas. Issues in the Design of Savings and Investment Incentives: Discussion. In *Hulten, C. R., ed.*, 1981, pp. 48–52.

Diamond, Peter. Comment [A Reappraisal of Financing Social Security] [VAT versus the Payroll Tax]. In *Skidmore, F., ed.*, 1981, pp. 164–69. [G: U.S.]

Diejomaoh, V. P. and Anusionwu, E. C. Education and Income Distribution in Nigeria. In *Bienen,*

H. and Diejomaoh, V. P., eds., 1981, pp. 373–420. [G: Nigeria]

Diewert, W. Erwin. On Measuring the Loss of Output Due to Nonneutral Business Taxation. In *Hulten, C. R., ed.*, 1981, pp. 57–80.

Dixit, Mukund and Prasad, Kamta. Applicability of Neoclassical Model of Investment Behaviour to Industrial Corporations in India. *Indian Econ. J.*, October–December 1981, *29*(2), pp. 1–22. [G: India]

Dosser, Douglas. The Value Added Tax in the UK and the EEC. In *Peacock, A. and Forte, F., eds.*, 1981, pp. 118–30. [G: EEC]

Downs, Anthony and Bradbury, Katharine L. Do Housing Allowances Work? Conference Discussion. In *Bradbury, K. L. and Downs, A., eds.*, 1981, pp. 375–404. [G: U.S.]

Dumas, Lloyd J. Taxes and Militarism. *Cato J.*, Spring 1981, *1*(1), pp. 277–92. [G: U.S.]

Eichner, Alfred S. Reagan's Doubtful Game Plan. *Challenge*, May/June 1981, *24*(2), pp. 19–27. [G: U.S.]

Ekirch, Arthur A., Jr. The Sixteenth Amendment: The Historical Background. *Cato J.*, Spring 1981, *1*(1), pp. 161–82. [G: U.S.]

Eliasson, Gunnar and Lindberg, Thomas. Allocation and Growth Effects of Corporate Income Taxes. In *Eliasson, G. and Södersten, J., eds.*, 1981, pp. 381–435. [G: Sweden]

Eliasson, Gunnar and Södersten, Jan. Business Taxation, Rates of Return and the Allocation Process. In *Eliasson, G. and Södersten, J., eds.*, 1981, pp. 11–30. [G: U.S.; U.K.; Sweden]

Esguerra, Emmanuel F. An Assessment of the Masagana 99 Credit Subsidy as an Equity Measure. *Phillipine Rev. Econ. Bus.*, Sept. & Dec. 1981, *18*(3/4), pp. 168–91. [G: Philippines]

Evans, Paul. Why the Great Inflation Has Been a Catastrophe. In *Gale, W. A., ed.*, 1981, pp. 133–65. [G: U.S.]

Ezejelue, A. C. Impact of Residence on Tax Liability in Nigeria. *Bull. Int. Fiscal Doc.*, December 1981, *35*(12), pp. 547–54. [G: Nigeria]

Fabozzi, Frank J. and Fonfeder, Robert. Corporate Tax Rates in an Inflationary Environment: 1976 and 1977. *Bus. Econ.*, January 1981, *16*(1), pp. 55–58. [G: U.S.]

Fasci, Martha A. The Windfall Profits Tax: Panacea or Pandora's Box? *Manage. Account.*, October 1981, *63*(4), pp. 51–53. [G: U.S.]

Fausto, Domenicantonio and Leccisotti, Mario. An Interpretation of Government Intervention in Health: The Italian Case. In *van der Gaag, J. and Perlman, M., eds.*, 1981, pp. 33–43. [G: Italy]

Feenberg, Daniel. Does the Investment Interest Limitation Explain the Existence of Dividends? *J. Finan. Econ.*, Summer 1981, *9*(3), pp. 265–69. [G: U.S.]

Feigin, Paul and Landsberger, Michael. The Induced Inefficiency of Income Taxes under Conditions of Imperfect Information about Job Offers. *Can. J. Econ.*, February 1981, *14*(1), pp. 119–24.

Feldstein, Martin S. Adjusting Depreciation in an Inflationary Economy: Indexing versus Acceleration. *Nat. Tax J.*, March 1981, *34*(1), pp. 29–43. [G: U.S.]

Feldstein, Martin S. and Allison, Elisabeth. Tax Subsidies of Private Health Insurance: Distribution, Revenue Loss, and Effects. In *Feldstein, M., ed.*, 1981, *1974*, pp. 205–20. [G: U.S.]

Feldstein, Martin S. and Friedman, Bernard. Tax Subsidies, the Rational Demand for Insurance, and the Health-Care Crisis. In *Feldstein, M., ed.*, 1981, *1977*, pp. 221–44. [G: U.S.]

Feldstein, Martin S. and Friedman, Bernard. The Effect of National Health Insurance on the Price and Quantity of Medical Care. In *Feldstein, M., ed.*, 1981, *1976*, pp. 283–305.

Fibiger, John. Comment [A Reappraisal of Financing Social Security] [VAT versus the Payroll Tax]. In *Skidmore, F., ed.*, 1981, pp. 169–72. [G: U.S.]

Filosa, Vincenzo. Rivalutazione dell'oro e rivalutazione di gruppo: La problematica del Decreto Ministeriale 5–8–1980. (Revaluation of Gold and Revaluation of Group Assets. With English summary.) *Bancaria*, May 1981, *37*(5), pp. 470–84. [G: Italy]

Findlay, Christopher C. International Civil Aviation Policy Options. *Australian J. Manage.*, December 1981, *6*(2), pp. 27–42.

Fishburn, Geoffrey. Tax Evasion and Inflation. *Australian Econ. Pap.*, December 1981, *20*(37), pp. 325–32.

Fisher, Peter S. Investment Tax Credits, Capital Gains Taxation, and Reindustrialization of the U.S. Economy. *J. Econ. Issues*, September 1981, *15*(3), pp. 769–73. [G: U.S.]

Flowers, Marilyn R. Majority Voting on Tax Shares: A Simple Life-Cycle Model. *Public Finance Quart.*, January 1981, *9*(1), pp. 47–59.

Floyd, Robert H. Equivalence of Product Tax Changes and Public Enterprise Price Changes. *Int. Monet. Fund Staff Pap.*, June 1981, *28*(2), pp. 338–74.

Formby, John P.; Seaks, Terry G. and Smith, W. James. A Comparison of Two New Measures of Tax Progressivity [Measurement of Tax Progressivity: An International Comparison]. [Measurement of Tax Progressivity]. *Econ. J.*, December 1981, *91*(364), pp. 1015–19. [G: U.S.; U.K.; Australia; Canada]

Forte, Francesco and Peacock, Alan. Tax Planning, Tax Analysis and Tax Policy. In *Peacock, A. and Forte, F., eds.*, 1981, pp. 3–28.

Foster, Edward. Competitively Awarded Government Grants. *J. Public Econ.*, February 1981, *15*(1), pp. 105–11.

Foster, Francis H. Towards a Uniform Standard: The Effect of Close Corporation and Partnership Restrictive Agreements on Federal Estate Tax Valuation. *Yale Law J.*, March 1981, *90*(4), pp. 863–88. [G: U.S.]

Fralick, James S. Tax Incentives and Private Saving: Some Policy Options. In *Federal Reserve System*, 1981, pp. 143–59.

Fralick, James S. Tax Policy and the Demand for Real Capital. In *Federal Reserve System*, 1981, pp. 177–90.

Frank, Max. Le régime de taxation des agriculteurs en Belgique. (With English summary.) *Cah.*

Écon. Bruxelles, 3rd Trimestre 1981, (91), pp. 407–32. [G: Belgium]

Fratianni, Michele and Christie, Herbert. Abolishing Fiscal Frontiers within the EEC. *Public Finance*, 1981, *36*(3), pp. 411–29. [G: EEC]

Freedman, Craig and Makofsky, David. Supporting the Rich. *Calif. Manage. Rev.*, Summer 1981, *23*(4), pp. 49–54. [G: U.S.]

Freund, William C. Corporation Finance: Comments. In *Aaron, H. J. and Pechman, J. A., eds.*, 1981, pp. 197–98. [G: U.S.]

Fritzsche, Michael. Mining Ventures in Developing Countries: Fiscal Regime. In *Schanze, E., et al.*, 1981, pp. 108–44.

Fullerton, Don, et al. Corporate Tax Integration in the United States: A General Equilibrium Approach. *Amer. Econ. Rev.*, September 1981, *71*(4), pp. 677–91. [G: U.S.]

Galambos, Eva C. and Schreiber, Arthur F. The Analysis of Double Taxation. *Public Budg. Finance*, Summer 1981, *1*(2), pp. 31–40. [G: U.S.]

Galvin, Charles O. Tax Reform in the United States and Canada: A Comparison. *Law Contemp. Probl.*, Summer 1981, *44*(3), pp. 131–42. [G: U.S.; Canada]

Gardner, Bruce. Consequences of Farm Policies during the 1970s. In *Johnson, D. G., ed.*, 1981, pp. 48–72. [G: U.S.]

Gastineau, Gary L. Options Markets and Instruments. In *Altman, E. I., ed.*, 1981, pp. 20.3–45. [G: U.S.]

Gaudemet, Paul M. Les relations entre le fisc et le contribuable. (With English summary.) In *Roskamp, K. W. and Forte, F., eds.*, 1981, pp. 199–208. [G: OECD]

Georgakopoulos, Theodore A. Tax Structure Changes and the Balance of Trade. *Greek Econ. Rev.*, April 1981, *3*(1), pp. 25–32.

Gerra, Ralph A. The New Forms of Federal Fiscal Policies and Implications for State and Local Governments: Observations from Business. *Nat. Tax J.*, September 1981, *34*(3), pp. 293–302. [G: U.S.]

Gianaris, Nicholas V. Indirect Taxes: A Comparative Study of Greece and the EEC. *Europ. Econ. Rev.*, January 1981, *15*(1), pp. 111–17. [G: Greece; EEC]

Gilburn, David A. and White, Roger. Tax Planning. In *Ensor, R. and Muller, P., eds.*, 1981, pp. 63–76. [G: OECD]

Gison, Cornelio C. and Salvador, Serafin U., Jr. Philippine Taxation of Alien Individuals. *Bull. Int. Fiscal Doc.*, May 1981, *35*(5), pp. 223–29. [G: Philippines]

Giuliani, William J. Needed: Tax Reform to Save the U.S. Economy. *Manage. Account.*, November 1981, *63*(5), pp. 48–52. [G: U.S.]

Glaister, K. W.; McGlone, A. and Ruffell, R. J. Taxation and Labour Supply: Preferences. In *Brown, C. V., ed.*, 1981, pp. 69–100. [G: U.K.]

Glaister, K. W.; McGlone, A. and Ulph, David T. Labour Supply Responses to Tax Changes. In *Brown, C. V., ed.*, 1981, pp. 163–88. [G: U.K.]

Gofran, K. A. Some Aspects of Tax Laws in Bangladesh. *Bull. Int. Fiscal Doc.*, April 1981, *35*(4), pp. 181–84. [G: Bangladesh]

Goldberg, Sanford H. Foreign Investors and the United States Estate, Gift and Generation-Skipping Taxes. *Bull. Int. Fiscal Doc.*, April 1981, 35(4), pp. 147–61. [G: U.S.]

Gonedes, Nicholas J. Evidence on the "Tax Effects" of Inflation under Historical Cost Accounting Methods. *J. Bus.*, April 1981, 54(2), pp. 227–70.

Goode, Richard. Limits to Taxation. In *Roskamp, K. W. and Forte, F., eds.*, 1981, pp. 41–54.
[G: LDCs; OECD]

Goode, Richard. Some Economic Aspects of Tax Administration. *Int. Monet. Fund Staff Pap.*, June 1981, 28(2), pp. 249–74.

Gordon, Roger H. and Malkiel, Burton G. Corporation Finance. In *Aaron, H. J. and Pechman, J. A., eds.*, 1981, pp. 131–92. [G: U.S.]

Gottschalk, Peter T. A Note on Estimating Treatment Effects [The Estimation of Labor Supply Models Using Experimental Data]. *Amer. Econ. Rev.*, September 1981, 71(4), pp. 764–69.
[G: U.S.]

Gravelle, Jane G. The Social Cost of Nonneutral Taxation: Estimates for Nonresidential Capital. In *Hulten, C. R., ed.*, 1981, pp. 239–50. [G: U.S.]

Greenaway, David. Taxes on International Transactions and Economic Development. In *Peacock, A. and Forte, F., eds.*, 1981, pp. 131–47.
[G: LDCs]

Greenberg, David; Moffitt, Robert A. and Friedmann, John. Underreporting and Experimental Effects on Work Effort: Evidence from the Gary Income Maintenance Experiment. *Rev. Econ. Statist.*, November 1981, 63(4), pp. 581–89.
[G: U.S.]

Grüske, Karl-Dieter. An International Comparison of Quantitative Aspects of Tax Burdens and Specific Expenditure Benefits. In *Roskamp, K. W. and Forte, F., eds.*, 1981, pp. 331–39. [G: U.S.; W. Germany]

Gui, Benedetto. Investment Decisions in a Worker-Managed Firm. *Econ. Anal. Worker's Manage.*, 1981, 15(1), pp. 45–65.

Guthrie, Robert S. The Effect of Competition on Tax Revenues in the Casino Gaming Industry. *Nat. Tax J.*, June 1981, 34(2), pp. 261–65.
[G: U.S.]

Hadari, Yitzhak. The United States–Israel Income Tax Treaty: An Amending Protocol. *Bull. Int. Fiscal Doc.*, May 1981, 35(5), pp. 229. [G: U.S.; Israel]

Hall, Robert E. Tax Treatment of Depreciation, Capital Gains, and Interest in an Inflationary Economy. In *Hulten, C. R., ed.*, 1981, pp. 149–66.

Hamermesh, Daniel S. Transfers, Taxes and the NAIRU. In *Meyer, L. H., ed.*, 1981, pp. 203–29. [G: U.S.]

Hamilton, W. E. Consequences of Farm Policies during the 1970s: Comment. In *Johnson, D. G., ed.*, 1981, pp. 75–80. [G: U.S.]

Hansmann, Henry B. The Rationale for Exempting Nonprofit Organizations from Corporate Income Taxation. *Yale Law J.*, November 1981, 91(1), pp. 54–100. [G: U.S.]

Hanushek, Eric A. and Quigley, John M. Do Housing Allowances Work? Consumption Aspects. In

Bradbury, K. L. and Downs, A., eds., 1981, pp. 185–246. [G: U.S.]

Harberger, Arnold C. Comment on Papers by Boskin [Some Issues in "Supply-Side" Economics] and Piggott and Whalley [A Summary of Some Findings from a General Equilibrium Tax Model for the United Kingdom]. *Carnegie-Rochester Conf. Ser. Public Policy*, Spring 1981, 14, pp. 221–29.

Harris, Edwin C. Recent Canadian Income Tax Amendments: International Aspects. *Bull. Int. Fiscal Doc.*, August–September 1981, 35(8–9), pp. 368–71. [G: Canada]

Harris, Robert B. Compensation for Loss of Income and Its Taxation: Comment. *Nat. Tax J.*, March 1981, 34(1), pp. 135–36.

Harte, L. N. Farmer Taxation Equity and Incentive—A Literature Review. *Irish J. Agr. Econ. Rural Soc.*, 1981, 8(2), pp. 167–77.

Hartle, Douglas G., et al. Stagflation Consequences of the Canadian Tax/Transfer System. In *Ontario Economic Council, Vol. 1*, 1981, pp. 67–105.
[G: Canada; U.S.]

Hartwell, Ronald Max. Taxation in England during the Industrial Revolution. *Cato J.*, Spring 1981, 1(1), pp. 129–53. [G: U.K.]

Hatch, Orrin G. The Politics of Supply-Side Economics. In *Meyer, L. H., ed.*, 1981, pp. 255–62.
[G: U.S.]

Hathaway, Dale E. Agricultural Policy Alternatives for the 1980s: Comment. In *Johnson, D. G., ed.*, 1981, pp. 228–29. [G: U.S.]

Hauser, Wolfgang. International Deep Seabed Mining: Institutional and Fiscal Framework. In *Schanze, E., et al.*, 1981, pp. 145–70.

Hausman, Jerry A. Income and Payroll Tax Policy and Labor Supply. In *Meyer, L. H., ed.*, 1981, pp. 173–202. [G: U.S.]

Hausman, Jerry A. Labor Supply. In *Aaron, H. J. and Pechman, J. A., eds.*, 1981, pp. 27–72.
[G: U.S.]

Heins, A. James and Primeaux, Walter J., Jr. Regional Prices and the Conflict between Horizontal and Vertical Equity. *Public Finance Quart.*, April 1981, 9(2), pp. 235–40.

Heller, Peter S. Testing the Impact of Value-Added and Global Income Tax Reforms on Korean Tax Incidence in 1976: An Input-Output and Sensitivity Analysis. *Int. Monet. Fund Staff Pap.*, June 1981, 28(2), pp. 375–410 [G: Korea]

Hemming, Richard and Kay, John A. The Value-Added Tax: The United Kingdom. In *Aaron, H. J., ed.*, 1981, pp. 75–89. [G: U.K.]

Hendershott, Patric H. Estimates of Investment Functions and Some Implications for Productivity Growth. In *Meyer, L. H., ed.*, 1981, pp. 149–63.

Hendershott, Patric H. and Hu, Sheng-Cheng. Investment in Producers' Equipment. In *Aaron, H. J. and Pechman, J. A., eds.*, 1981, pp. 85–126. [G: U.S.]

Henderson, David. Limitations of the Laffer Curve as a Justification for Tax Cuts. *Cato J.*, Spring 1981, 1(1), pp. 45–52.

Herber, Bernard P. Personal Income Tax Reform and the Interaction between Budgetary Goals: A

UK and USA Comparison. In *Roskamp, K. W. and Forte, F., eds.*, 1981, pp. 55–71. [G: U.S.; U.K.]

Hessel, Christopher A. and Huffman, Lucy. The Effect of Taxation on Immunization Rules and Duration Estimation. *J. Finance,* December 1981, *36*(5), pp. 1127–42.

Hirsch, Werner Z. Tax Alternatives for Affecting the Environment. In *Roskamp, K. W. and Forte, F., eds.*, 1981, pp. 381–92.

Hite, Gailen L. and Sanders, Anthony B. Excess Depreciation and the Maximum Tax. *Amer. Real Estate Urban Econ. Assoc. J.,* Summer 1981, *9*(2), pp. 134–47. [G: U.S.]

Holcombe, Randall G. and Meiners, Roger E. Corrective Taxes and Auctions of Rights in the Control of Externalities: A Reply. *Public Finance Quart.,* October 1981, *9*(4), pp. 479–84.

Holcombe, Randall G. and Stecher, Edwin L. Intra-Industry Adjustment and the Correction of an Externality. *Atlantic Econ. J.,* September 1981, *9*(3), pp. 79–84.

Holcombe, Randall G. and Zardkoohi, Asghar. The Determinants of Federal Grants. *Southern Econ. J.,* October 1981, *48*(2), pp. 393–99. [G: U.S.]

Holmlund, Bertil. A Note on Changes in Payroll Taxes—Does Legal Incidence Matter? *Nat. Tax J.,* December 1981, *34*(4), pp. 479–82. [G: U.S.]

Holmlund, Bertil. Employment Subsidies and the Behavior of the Firm. In *Eliasson, G. and Södersten, J., eds.*, 1981, pp. 267–93.

Homma, Masaaki. A Dynamic Analysis of the Differential Incidence of Capital and Labour Taxes in a Two-Class Economy. *J. Public Econ.,* June 1981, *15*(3), pp. 363–78.

Hong, Lee Fook. Singapore's 1981 Budget: Summary. *Bull. Int. Fiscal Doc.,* June 1981, *35*(6), pp. 243–53. [G: Singapore]

Hong, Wontack. Export Promotion and Employment Growth in South Korea. In *Krueger, A. O., et al., eds.*, 1981, pp. 341–91. [G: S. Korea]

Hong, Wontack. Trade, Growth and Income Distribution: The Korean Experience. In *Hong, W. and Krause, L. B., eds.*, 1981, pp. 258–83. [G: S. Korea]

Honkapohja, Seppo and Kanniainen, Vesa. Corporate Taxation, Inventory Undervaluation and Neutrality. *Kansant. Aikak.,* 1981, *77*(4), pp. 435–45. [G: Finland]

Howe, Geoffrey [Sir]. United Kingdom: Budget '81–82. *Bull. Int. Fiscal Doc.,* May 1981, *35*(5), pp. 230–33. [G: U.K.]

Huber, Gérard. ICHA et accumulation de capital. (The Swiss Wholesale Sales Tax and Capital Accumulation. With English summary.) *Schweiz. Z. Volkswirtsch. Statist.,* December 1981, *117*(4), pp. 581–604. [G: Switzerland]

Huddleston, Jack R. Variations in Development Subsidies under Tax Increment Financing. *Land Econ.,* August 1981, *57*(3), pp. 373–84. [G: U.S.]

Hughes, Gordon A. The Distributional Impact of Commodity Taxes and Subsidies. *Bull. Indonesian Econ. Stud.,* November 1981, *17*(3), pp. 25–47. [G: Indonesia]

Hulten, Charles R. Depreciation, Inflation, and the Taxation of Income from Capital: Introduction. In *Hulten, C. R., ed.*, 1981, pp. 1–9. [G: U.S.]

Hulten, Charles R. and Wykoff, Frank C. Economic Depreciation and Accelerated Depreciation: An Evaluation of the Conable–Jones 10–5–3 Proposal. *Nat. Tax J.,* March 1981, *34*(1), pp. 45–60. [G: U.S.]

Hulten, Charles R. and Wykoff, Frank C. The Measurement of Economic Depreciation. In *Hulten, C. R., ed.*, 1981, pp. 81–125. [G: U.S.; Japan]

Hunt, Janet C.; DeLorme, Charles D., Jr. and Hill, R. Carter. Taxation and the Wife's Use of Time. *Ind. Lab. Relat. Rev.,* April 1981, *34*(3), pp. 426–32. [G: U.S.]

Hurd, Michael D. and Pencavel, John H. A Utility-Based Analysis of the Wage Subsidy Program. *J. Public Econ.,* April 1981, *15*(2), pp. 185–201. [G: U.S.]

Ikeda, Hisashi. Tax Incidence with Social Capital and Non-Shiftable Private Capital. (In Japanese. With English summary.) *Osaka Econ. Pap.,* June 1981, *31*(1), pp. 21–27.

Ingram, William D. and Pearson, Scott R. The Impact of Investment Concessions on the Profitability of Selected Firms in Ghana. *Econ. Develop. Cult. Change,* July 1981, *29*(4), pp. 831–39.

Ishi, Hiromitsu. Inflation Adjustment for Individual Income Tax in Japan. *Hitotsubashi J. Econ.,* February 1981, *21*(2), pp. 19–32. [G: Japan]

Isler, Morton L. Housing Vouchers for the Poor: Policy Implications: Moving from Research to Programs. In *Struyk, R. J. and Bendick, M., Jr., eds.*, 1981, pp. 267–93. [G: U.S.]

Jackson, Antony G. The Average Marginal Tax Rate. *Can. J. Econ.,* August 1981, *14*(3), pp. 496–99.

Jacobs, Susan S. and Wasylenko, Michael. Government Policy to Stimulate Economic Development: Enterprise Zones. In *Walzer, N. and Chicoine, D. L., eds.*, 1981, pp. 175–201. [G: U.S.; U.K.]

Jakobsson, Ulf and Normann, Göran. Welfare Effects of Changes in Income Tax Progression in Sweden. In *Eliasson, G.; Holmlund, B. and Stafford, F. P., eds.*, 1981, pp. 313–38. [G: Sweden]

Janis, Jay. Dealing with Inflation: Ideology vs. Pragmatism. In *Federal Home Loan Bank of San Francisco.*, 1981, pp. 7–12. [G: U.S.]

Jao, Y. C. A Further Note on Tax Developments in China. *Bull. Int. Fiscal Doc.,* April 1981, *35*(4), pp. 179–80. [G: China]

Jao, Y. C. Recent Developments in China's Tax System. *Bull. Int. Fiscal Doc.,* January 1981, *35*(1), pp. 16–23. [G: China]

Jao, Y. C. Tax Changes and Reforms in Hong Kong. *Bull. Int. Fiscal Doc.,* August–September 1981, *35*(8–9), pp. 401–07. [G: Hong Kong]

Jehle, Eugen. The Tax System of the Federal Republic of Germany—A Short Survey. *Bull. Int. Fiscal Doc.,* August–September 1981, *35*(8–9), pp. 357–67. [G: W. Germany]

Jelčić, Bozidar. Rules for the Avoidance of International and Internal Double Taxation in Yugoslavia. *Bull. Int. Fiscal Doc.,* June 1981, *35*(6), pp. 254–60. [G: Yugoslavia]

Jenkins, Glenn P.; Misir, Devendranauth and Glenday, Graham. The Taxation of Foreign Investment Income in Canada, the United States and Mexico. *Law Contemp. Probl.*, Summer 1981, *44*(3), pp. 143–59. **[G: Canada; U.S.; Mexico]**

Jetha, Nizar. Some Problems of Tax Policy in Developing Countries. *Bull. Int. Fiscal Doc.*, October 1981, *35*(10), pp. 448–55. **[G: LDCs]**

Jha, Raghbendra and Lächler, Ulrich. Optimum Taxation and Public Production in a Dynamic Harris-Todaro World. *J. Devel. Econ.*, December 1981, *9*(3), pp. 357–73.

Johnson, D. Gale. Agricultural Policy Alternatives for the 1980s. In *Johnson, D. G., ed.*, 1981, pp. 183–209. **[G: U.S.]**

Joines, Douglas H. Estimates of Effective Marginal Tax Rates on Factor Incomes. *J. Bus.*, April 1981, *54*(2), pp. 191–226. **[G: U.S.]**

Jorgenson, Dale W. Issues in the Design of Savings and Investment Incentives: Discussion. In *Hulten, C. R., ed.*, 1981, pp. 52–56.

Jorgenson, Dale W. Proceedings of the Seminar on Productivity: Statement. In *U.S. Congress, Joint Economic Committee (I)*, 1981, pp. 166–84. **[G: U.S.]**

Jorgenson, Dale W. and Sullivan, Martin A. Inflation and Corporate Capital Recovery. In *Hulten, C. R., ed.*, 1981, pp. 171–237. **[G: U.S.]**

Kaikati, Jack G. The Anti-Export Policy of the U.S. *Calif. Manage. Rev.*, Spring 1981, *23*(3), pp. 5–19. **[G: U.S.]**

Kain, John F. A Universal Housing Allowance Program. In *Bradbury, K. L. and Downs, A., eds.*, 1981, pp. 329–73. **[G: U.S.]**

Kanbur, S. M. Risk Taking and Taxation: An Alternative Perspective. *J. Public Econ.*, April 1981, *15*(2), pp. 163–84.

Kaneko, Mamoru. On the Existence of an Optimal Income Tax Schedule. *Rev. Econ. Stud.*, October 1981, *48*(4), pp. 633–42.

Kelly, John M. The New Barbarians: The Continuing Relevance of Henry George. *Amer. J. Econ. Soc.*, July 1981, *40*(3), pp. 299–308.

Kendrick, John W. Tax Treatment of Depreciation, Capital Gains, and Interest in an Inflationary Economy: Discussion. In *Hulten, C. R., ed.*, 1981, pp. 167–70.

Khan, Ghulam Ishaq. Pakistan: Budget, 1980–81. *Bull. Int. Fiscal Doc.*, January 1981, *35*(1), pp. 38–43. **[G: Pakistan]**

Kibaki, Mwai. Kenya: Budget, 1980–81. *Bull. Int. Fiscal Doc.*, January 1981, *35*(1), pp. 30–34. **[G: Kenya]**

Kiefer, David. The Interaction of Inflation and the U.S. Tax Subsidies of Housing. *Nat. Tax J.*, December 1981, *34*(4), pp. 433–46. **[G: U.S.]**

Kiefer, Donald W. The Effects of Alternative Regulatory Treatments of the Investment Tax Credit in the Public Utility Industry. *J. Bus.*, October 1981, *54*(4), pp. 549–77. **[G: U.S.]**

Kienzle, Edward C. Measurement of the Progressivity of Public Expenditures and Net Fiscal Incidence. *Southern Econ. J.*, July 1981, *48*(1), pp. 197–203.

Kiesling, H. J. Henry Simons, Equality, and the Personal Income Tax. *Nat. Tax J.*, June 1981,

34(2), pp. 257–59.

Killingsworth, Charles C. Proceedings of the Seminar on Employment: Statement. In *U.S. Congress, Joint Economic Committee (I)*, 1981, pp. 113–15. **[G: U.S.]**

Killingsworth, Charles C. Trouble in Social Insurance. *Challenge*, July/August 1981, *24*(3), pp. 50–52. **[G: U.S.]**

Kleiman, Ephraim and Pincus, Jonathan J. The Cyclical Effects of Incremental Export Subsidies. *Econ. Rec.*, June 1981, *57*(157), pp. 140–49. **[G: Australia]**

Knauthe, E. Die Zahlungen der volkseigenen Industrie an den Staatshaushalt. (With English summary.) In *Roskamp, K. W. and Forte, F., eds.*, 1981, pp. 437–57. **[G: CMEA]**

Kopcke, Richard W. Inflation, Corporate Income Taxation, and the Demand for Capital Assets. *J. Polit. Econ.*, February 1981, *89*(1), pp. 122–31. **[G: U.S.]**

Kopcke, Richard W. The Efficiency of Traditional Investment Tax Incentives. In *Federal Reserve System*, 1981, pp. 163–75. **[G: U.S.]**

Kopits, George F. Fiscal Incentives for Investment in Industrial Countries. *Bull. Int. Fiscal Doc.*, July 1981, *35*(7), pp. 291–94. **[G: EEC; U.S.; Japan]**

Kraft, John L. Local Public Policy and Tax-Exempt Financing: Is Local Initiative Preempted by Federal Control? *Nat. Tax J.*, September 1981, *34*(3), pp. 373–81. **[G: U.S.]**

Krashinsky, Michael. Subsidies to Child Care: Public Policy and Optimality. *Public Finance Quart.*, July 1981, *9*(3), pp. 243–69. **[G: U.S.]**

Laffer, Arthur B. Government Exactions and Revenue Deficiencies. *Cato J.*, Spring 1981, *1*(1), pp. 1–21. **[G: U.S.]**

Laker, John F. Fiscal Proxies for Devaluation: A General Review. *Int. Monet. Fund Staff Pap.*, March 1981, *28*(1), pp. 118–43.

Lareau, Thomas J. Alternate Stationary Source Air Pollution Control Policies: A Welfare Analysis. *Public Finance Quart.*, July 1981, *9*(3), pp. 281–307. **[G: U.S.]**

de Leeuw, Frank. The Measurement of Economic Depreciation: Discussion. In *Hulten, C. R., ed.*, 1981, pp. 126–29. **[G: U.S.; Japan]**

de Leeuw, Frank and Ozanne, Larry J. Housing. In *Aaron, H. J. and Pechman, J. A., eds.*, 1981, pp. 283–319. **[G: U.S.]**

Leffler, Keith B. and Lindsay, Cotton M. Student Discount Rates, Consumption Loans, and Subsidies to Professional Training. *J. Human Res.*, Summer 1981, *16*(3), pp. 468–76.

Lehman, Dale E. A Reexamination of the Crude Oil Windfall Profit Tax [The Incidence and Effects of the Crude Oil Windfall Profit Tax]. *Natural Res. J.*, October 1981, *21*(4), pp. 683–89. **[G: U.S.]**

Leuthold, Jane H. Taxation and the Consumption of Household Time. *J. Cons. Res.*, March 1981, *7*(4), pp. 388–94. **[G: U.S.]**

Levasseur, Michel and Olivaux, Jean-Louis. Théorie du financement des entreprises et évolution de la fiscalité française. (Theory of Capital Structure and the Evolution of the French Tax System.

With English summary.) *Revue Écon.*, May 1981, 32(3), pp. 490–512.   [G: France]

Levy, Yvonne. Crude Oil Price Controls and the Windfall Profit Tax: Deterrents to Production? *Fed. Res. Bank San Francisco Econ. Rev.*, Spring 1981, pp. 6–28.   [G: U.S.]

Lim, David. Export Instability and Revenue Instability in Less Developed Countries. *Malayan Econ. Rev. (See Singapore Econ. Rev.)*, October 1981, 26(2), pp. 46–52.   [G: Selected LDCs]

Lindberg, Thomas. Industrial Profits—Their Importance and Evaluation. In *Industrial Inst. for Econ. and Soc. Research*, 1981, pp. 66–77.
                                          [G: Sweden]

Lindholm, Richard W. VAT, the Third Way. *J. Post Keynesian Econ.*, Fall 1981, 4(1), pp. 44–50.
                                          [G: U.S.]

Lindholm, Richard W. VAT, the Third Way: Rejoinder. *J. Post Keynesian Econ.*, Fall 1981, 4(1), pp. 61–62.   [G: U.S.]

Lindsey, Lawrence B. Is the Maximum Tax on Earned Income Effective? *Nat. Tax J.*, June 1981, 34(2), pp. 249–55.   [G: U.S.]

Lippman, Steven A. and McCall, John J. Progressive Taxation in Sequential Decisionmaking: Deterministic and Stochastic Analysis. *J. Public Econ.*, August 1981, 16(1), pp. 35–52.

List, Heinrich. Recent Cases of the German Supreme Tax Court on International Tax Law. *Bull. Int. Fiscal Doc.*, August–September 1981, 35(8–9), pp. 348–55.   [G: W. Germany]

Lodin, Sven-Olof. International Enterprises and Taxation—Some Preliminary Results of an Empirical Study Concerning International Enterprises. In *Eliasson, G. and Södersten, J.*, eds., 1981, pp. 97–123.   [G: Sweden; U.K.; U.S.]

Long, David A.; Mallar, Charles D. and Thornton, Craig V. D. Evaluating the Benefits and Costs of the Job Corps. *J. Policy Anal. Manage.*, Fall 1981, 1(1), pp. 55–76.   [G: U.S.]

Longo, Carlos A. Indirect Tax Harmonization: The Case of LAIA? *Bull. Int. Fiscal Doc.*, December 1981, 35(12), pp. 533–43.   [G: LAIA]

Lowenthal, Franklin. A Decision Model for the Alternative Tax on Capital Gains. *Accounting Rev.*, April 1981, 56(2), pp. 390–94.   [G: U.S.]

Macón, Jorge. Argentina: Adjustment for Inflation in Argentine Income Tax Law. *Bull. Int. Fiscal Doc.*, July 1981, 35(7), pp. 295–300.
                                          [G: Argentina]

MacRae, C. Duncan and Turner, Margery Austin. Estimating Demand for Owner-Occupied Housing Subject to the Income Tax. *J. Urban Econ.*, November 1981, 10(3), pp. 338–56.   [G: U.S.]

Madeo, Silvia A. and Madeo, Laurence A. Some Evidence on the Equity Effects of the Minimum Tax on Individual Taxpayers. *Nat. Tax J.*, December 1981, 34(4), pp. 457–65.   [G: U.S.]

Majumdar, Badiul Alam. Effectiveness of Indirect "Operational Control" over the Private Sector: The Case of Pakistan. *Pakistan Econ. Soc. Rev.*, Summer 1981, 19(1), pp. 69–81.

                                          [G: Pakistan]

Mallar, Charles D. and Maynard, Rebecca A. The Effects of Income Maintenance on School Performance and Educational Attainment. In *Khan, A.*

and Sirageldin, I., eds., 1981, pp. 121–41.
                                          [G: U.S.]

Manser, Marilyn E. Historical and Political Issues in Social Security Financing. In *Skidmore, F.*, ed., 1981, pp. 21–43.   [G: U.S.]

Marfels, Christian. Market Concentration and Implicit Grants in the Energy Industry: Some Observations. *Z. Wirtschaft. Sozialwissen.*, 1981, 101(4), pp. 429–40.   [G: U.S.]

Massone, Pedro. Adjustment of Profits for Inflation: Part II. *Bull. Int. Fiscal Doc.*, February 1981, 35(2), pp. 51–61.   [G: Latin America]

Massone, Pedro. Adjustment of Profits for Inflation: Part I. *Bull. Int. Fiscal Doc.*, January 1981, 35(1), pp. 3–15.   [G: Latin America]

Massone, Pedro. Developments in Latin America— The Mexican Income Tax (1980). *Bull. Int. Fiscal Doc.*, August–September 1981, 35(8–9), pp. 389– 400.   [G: Mexico]

Masters, Stanley H. The Effects of Supported Work on the Earnings and Transfer Payments of Its AFDC Target Group. *J. Human Res.*, Fall 1981, 16(4), pp. 600–636.   [G: U.S.]

Mauskopf, Eileen and Conrad, William E. Taxes, Inflation, and the Allocation of Capital. In *Federal Reserve System*, 1981, pp. 201–20.   [G: U.S.]

Maynard, Alan and Ludbrook, Anne. Thirty Years of Fruitless Indeavor? An Analysis of Government Intervention in the Health Care Market. In *van der Gaag, J. and Perlman, M.*, eds., 1981, pp. 45–65.   [G: U.K.; France; Netherlands]

McCaleb, Thomas S. Excess Burden and Optimal Income Taxation. *Public Finance*, 1981, 36(3), pp. 395–410.

McCloskey, Donald N. "Taxation in England during the Industrial Revolution": A Comment. *Cato J.*, Spring 1981, 1(1), pp. 155–59.   [G: U.K.]

McClure, Charles E., Jr. VAT versus the Payroll Tax. In *Skidmore, F.*, ed., 1981, pp. 129–64.

McConnell, John J. and Schlarbaum, Gary G. Evidence on the Impact of Exchange Offers on Security Prices: The Case of Income Bonds. *J. Bus.*, January 1981, 54(1), pp. 65–85.   [G: U.S.]

McDonald, Stephen L. The Incidence and Effects of the Crude Oil Windfall Profit Tax: A Reply to Lehman. *Natural Res. J.*, October 1981, 21(4), pp. 690–91.   [G: U.S.]

McDonald, Stephen L. The Incidence and Effects of the Crude Oil Windfall Profit Tax. *Natural Res. J.*, April 1981, 21(2), pp. 331–39.   [G: U.S.]

McKenzie, Richard B. Taxation and Income Redistribution: An Unsympathetic Critique of Practice and Theory. *Cato J.*, Fall 1981, 1(2), pp. 339– 71.   [G: U.S.]

McLoughlin, Kevin and Proudfoot, Stuart B. Giving by not Taking: A Primer on Tax Expenditures. *Can. Public Policy*, Spring 1981, 7(2), pp. 328– 37.   [G: Canada]

McLure, Charles E., Jr. Tax Integration in the United States. In *Eliasson, G. and Södersten, J.*, eds., 1981, pp. 51–95.   [G: U.S.]

McLure, Charles E., Jr. The Elusive Incidence of the Corporate Income Tax: The State Case. *Public Finance Quart.*, October 1981, 9(4), pp. 395–413.

Meadows, George Richard and Mitrisin, John. A National Development Bank: Survey and Discussion of the Literature on Capital Shortages and Employment Changes in Distressed Areas. In *Sternlieb, G. and Listokin, D., eds.*, 1981, pp. 84–143. [G: U.S.]

Meister, Jürgen. Taxes, Tax Systems and Economic Growth: Comments. In *Giersch, H., ed. (II)*, 1981, pp. 354–57. [G: Selected Countries]

de Mel, Ronnie. Sri Lanka: Budget, 1980. *Bull. Int. Fiscal Doc.*, May 1981, 35(5), pp. 221–22. [G: Sri Lanka]

Messere, Carl J. and Zuckerman, Gilroy J. An Alternative Approach to Depreciation Switches. *Accounting Rev.*, July 1981, 56(3), pp. 642–52. [G: U.S.]

Meyer, Jack A. Health Care Competition: Are Tax Incentives Enough? In *Olson, M., ed.*, 1981, pp. 424–49. [G: U.S.]

Mikander, Lars. Träförädlingsindustrin och framtiden. (The Wood-processing Industry and the Future. With English summary.) *Ekon. Samfundets Tidskr.*, 1981, 34(4), pp. 271–88. [G: Finland]

Mikesell, John L. Changed Sensitivity of the Federal Individual Income Tax, 1973–1976. *Rev. Bus. Econ. Res.*, Fall 1981, 17(1), pp. 89–95. [G: U.S.]

Minarik, Joseph J. Capital Gains. In *Aaron, H. J. and Pechman, J. A., eds.*, 1981, pp. 241–77. [G: U.S.]

Minarik, Joseph J. Tax Expenditures. In *Pechman, J. A., ed.*, 1981, pp. 271–75. [G: U.S.]

Minotti, Maurizio. In tema di deducibilità delle spese generali ai fini della determinazione del reddito d'impresa. (On the Deductibility of General Expenditures in the Computation of Taxable Business Income. With English summary.) *Bancaria*, January 1981, 37(1), pp. 64–67. [G: Italy]

Mintz, Jack M. Some Additional Results on Investment, Risk Taking, and Full Loss Offset Corporate Taxation with Interest Deductibility. *Quart. J. Econ.*, November 1981, 96(4), pp. 631–42.

Mirus, Rolf and Smith, Roger S. Canada's Irregular Economy. *Can. Public Policy*, Summer 1981, 7(3), pp. 444–53. [G: Canada]

Miura, Makoto. Japan: Medium Term Tax Policy and the Tax Increase in Fiscal Year 1981. *Bull. Int. Fiscal Doc.*, May 1981, 35(5), pp. 199–201. [G: Japan]

Moeller, John F. Consumer Expenditure Responses to Income Redistribution Programs. *Rev. Econ. Statist.*, August 1981, 63(3), pp. 409–21.

Moffitt, Robert A. The Negative Income Tax: Would It Discourage Work? *Mon. Lab. Rev.*, April 1981, 104(4), pp. 23–27. [G: U.S.]

Moffitt, Robert A. and Kehrer, Kenneth C. The Effect of Tax and Transfer Programs on Labor Supply: The Evidence from the Income Maintenance Experiments. In *Ehrenberg, R. G., ed.*, 1981, pp. 103–50. [G: U.S.]

Moore, George R. Taxes, Inflation, and Capital Formation. In *Federal Reserve System*, 1981, pp. 303–26.

Moskow, Michael H. The Political Response to Three Potential Major Bankruptcies: Lockheed, New York City, and Chrysler: Comment. In *Wachter, M. L. and Wachter, S. M., eds.*, 1981, pp. 485–87. [G: U.S.]

Moszer, Max. A Comment on the Laffer Model. *Cato J.*, Spring 1981, 1(1), pp. 23–44. [G: U.S.]

Murthy, N. R. Vasudeva. Fiscal Policy and Government Savings in a Developing Economy: Some Empirical Evidence in the Indian Economy. *Bull. Int. Fiscal Doc.*, March 1981, 35(3), pp. 120–25. [G: India]

Musgrave, Peggy B. Women and Taxation. In *Roskamp, K. W. and Forte, F., eds.*, 1981, pp. 341–54. [G: OECD; U.S.]

Musgrave, Richard A. A Non-Existing Paradox: Response to Professor Yeh [Musgrave's Paradox and Progressive Income Taxation]. *Public Finance*, 1981, 36(2), pp. 280–81.

Musgrave, Richard A. A Reappraisal of Financing Social Security. In *Skidmore, F., ed.*, 1981, pp. 89–127. [G: U.S.]

Musgrave, Richard A. What Will the Tax Cut Accomplish? *Challenge*, May/June 1981, 24(2), pp. 55–59. [G: U.S.]

Mutén, Leif. Leading Issues of Tax Policy in Developing Countries: The Administrative Problems. In *Peacock, A. and Forte, F., eds.*, 1981, pp. 192–205. [G: LDCs]

Mutti, John H. Tax Incentives and the Repatriation Decisions of U.S. Multinational Corporations. *Nat. Tax J.*, June 1981, 34(2), pp. 241–48. [G: U.S.]

Neudeck, Werner. Inflation and the Taxation of Capital Income: A Note. *Empirica*, 1981, (2), pp. 255–61. [G: Austria]

Neumark, Fritz. Taxes, Tax Systems and Economic Growth: Comments. In *Giersch, H., ed. (II)*, 1981, pp. 348–53. [G: Selected Countries]

Nielsen, Niels Christian. Inflation and Taxation: Nominal and Real Rates of Return. *J. Monet. Econ.*, March 1981, 7(2), pp. 261–70.

Noguchi, Yukio. Economic Effects of Taxes on Land. (In Japanese. With English summary.) *Econ. Stud. Quart.*, December 1981, 32(3), pp. 193–200.

Nolan, Brian. Redistribution of Household Income in Ireland by Taxes and Benefits. *Econ. Soc. Rev.*, October 1981, 13(1), pp. 59–88. [G: Ireland]

Nordhaus, William D. Tax-Based Incomes Policies: A Better Mousetrap? In *Claudon, M. P. and Cornwall, R. R., eds.*, 1981, pp. 135–51. [G: U.S.]

Nordhauser, Susan L. and Kramer, John L. Repeal of the Deferral Privilege for Earnings from Direct Foreign Investments: An Analysis. *Accounting Rev.*, January 1981, 56(1), pp. 54–69. [G: U.S.]

Normann, Göran. The Value-Added Tax: Sweden. In *Aaron, H. J., ed.*, 1981, pp. 61–73. [G: Sweden]

O'Higgins, Michael and Ruggles, Patricia. The Distribution of Public Expenditures and Taxes among Households in the United Kingdom. *Rev. Income Wealth*, September 1981, 27(3), pp. 298–326. [G: U.K.]

Oates, Wallace E. Corrective Taxes and Auctions of Rights in the Control of Externalities: Some Further Thoughts. *Public Finance Quart.*, October 1981, 9(4), pp. 471–78.

Olson, Mancur. A New Approach to the Economics of Health Care: Introduction. In *Olson, M., ed.*,

1981, pp. 1–26. [G: U.S.]

Omorogiuwa, P. Ada. Personal Income Taxation and Income Distribution in Nigeria. In *Bienen, H. and Diejomaoh, V. P.*, eds., 1981, pp. 421–53. [G: Nigeria]

Ordover, Janusz A. and Schotter, Andrew. On the Political Sustainability of Taxes. *Amer. Econ. Rev.*, May 1981, *71*(2), pp. 278–82.

Osteryoung, Jerome S.; Fortin, Karen A. and McCarty, Daniel E. How the New Cost Recovery System Compares with Prior Methods. *Manage. Account.*, November 1981, *63*(5), pp. 13–20. [G: U.S.]

Osteryoung, Jerome S.; McCarty, Daniel E. and Fortin, Karen A. A Note on Optimal Depreciation Research—A Comment [A Note on the Optimal Tax Lives for Assets Qualifying for the Investment Tax Credit]. *Accounting Rev.*, July 1981, *56*(3), pp. 719–21. [G: U.S.]

Ostro, Bart D. The Distributive Effects of Public Law 92–500: Comment. *J. Environ. Econ. Manage.*, June 1981, *8*(2), pp. 196–98.

Ozanne, Larry J. and Zais, James P. Community-wide Effects of Housing Allowances. In *Struyk, R. J. and Bendick, M., Jr.*, eds., 1981, pp. 207–33. [G: U.S.]

Page, Benjamin I. Why Doesn't the Government Promote Equality? In *Solo, R. A. and Anderson, C. W.*, eds., 1981, pp. 279–319. [G: U.S.]

Paules, Edward P. Taxation and Exposure Management. In *Ensor, R. and Muller, P.*, eds., 1981, pp. 143–66. [G: U.S.]

Pazner, Elisha and Sadka, Efraim. Welfare Criteria for Tax Reforms: Efficiency Aspects. *J. Public Econ.*, August 1981, *16*(1), pp. 113–22.

Peacock, Alan. Fiscal Theory and the "Market" for Tax Reform. In *Roskamp, K. W. and Forte, F.*, eds., 1981, pp. 11–21.

Pearce, Joan. Subsidized Export Credit. In *The Royal Inst. of Internat. Affairs*, 1981, pp. 166–241. [G: France; Japan; U.K.; U.S.; W. Germany]

Pedone, Antonio. Payroll Taxes, Value-Added Taxes and Income Taxes. In *Roskamp, K. W. and Forte, F.*, eds., 1981, pp. 139–52.

Pedone, Antonio. The Value-Added Tax: Italy. In *Aaron, H. J.*, ed., 1981, pp. 31–42. [G: Italy]

Penner, Rudolph G. Discussion of the Papers by Piggott and Whalley [A Summary of Some Findings from a General Equilibrium Tax Model for the United Kingdom] and Boskin [Some Issues in "Supply-Side" Economics]. *Carnegie-Rochester Conf. Ser. Public Policy*, Spring 1981, *14*, pp. 231–35.

Pepper, H. W. T. Tax Treatment of Donations for Public Benefit. *Bull. Int. Fiscal Doc.*, February 1981, *35*(2), pp. 62–66.

Perloff, Jeffrey M. Income and Payroll Tax Policy and Labor Supply: Discussion. In *Meyer, L. H.*, ed., 1981, pp. 231–36. [G: U.S.]

Peters, W. and Langendorf, U. Direct Income Transfers for the Agricultural Sector in Less-Favoured Areas (DIT-LFA). The Council Directive No. 268/75 EEC, Title II: A Comparison between and within Member Countries. *Europ. Rev. Agr. Econ.*, 1981, *8*(1), pp. 41–55. [G: EEC]

Petersen, Hans-Georg. Some Further Results on Income Tax Progression. *Z. Wirtschaft. Sozialwissen.*, 1981, *101*(1), pp. 45–59. [G: U.S.; Germany]

Petersen, Hans-Georg. Taxes, Tax Systems and Economic Growth. In *Giersch, H.*, ed. (*II*), 1981, pp. 313–47. [G: Selected Countries]

Peterson, George E. Housing: Comments. In *Aaron, H. J. and Pechman, J. A.*, eds., 1981, pp. 319–23. [G: U.S.]

Piggott, John and Whalley, John. A Summary of Some Findings from a General Equilibrium Tax Model for the United Kingdom. *Carnegie-Rochester Conf. Ser. Public Policy*, Spring 1981, *14*, pp. 153–99. [G: U.K.]

Pires, Manuel. Portugal: Taxation of Business Profits. *Bull. Int. Fiscal Doc.*, November 1981, *35*(11), pp. 483–86. [G: Portugal]

de Pitta e Cunha, Paulo. Tax Reform in Portugal in the Context of Accession to the European Communities. *Bull. Int. Fiscal Doc.*, February 1981, *35*(2), pp. 75–78. [G: Portugal]

Pitts, Robert E. and Wittenbach, James L. Tax Credits as a Means of Influencing Consumer Behavior. *J. Cons. Res.*, December 1981, *8*(3), pp. 335–38. [G: U.S.]

Plasschaert, Sylvain R. F. The Design of Schedular and Global Systems of Income Taxation—The International Dimension. *Bull. Int. Fiscal Doc.*, August–September 1981, *35*(8–9), pp. 409–16.

Plasschaert, Sylvain R. F. The Treatment of Enterprise Profits in Schedular and Global Frameworks of Income Taxation. *Bull. Int. Fiscal Doc.*, June 1981, *35*(6), pp. 261–71.

Pohmer, Dieter. The Value-Added Tax: Germany. In *Aaron, H. J.*, ed., 1981, pp. 91–101. [G: W. Germany]

Prewitt, Kenneth. American Politics, Public Opinion, and Social Security Financing: Comment. In *Skidmore, F.*, ed., 1981, pp. 277–82. [G: U.S.]

Prindle, Allen M. Impacts of Federal Estate Taxation on Investments in Forestry: Comment. *Land Econ.*, February 1981, *57*(1), pp. 122–25. [G: U.S.]

Pucher, John and Hirschman, Ira. Distribution of the Tax Burden of Transit Subsidies in the United States. *Public Policy*, Summer 1981, *29*(3), pp. 341–67. [G: U.S.]

Raines, Fredric. Transfers, Taxes, and the NAIRU: Discussion. In *Meyer, L. H.*, ed., 1981, pp. 237–41. [G: U.S.]

Ramm, Wolfhard. Tax Design and Individual Saving. In *Federal Reserve System*, 1981, pp. 115–32.

Randall, Laura R. The Political Economy of Mexican Oil, 1976–1979. In *Ladman, J. R.; Baldwin, D. J. and Bergman, E.*, eds., 1981, pp. 87–115. [G: Mexico]

Randall, Maury R. and Greenfield, Robert L. Effects of Changes in Anticipated Inflation and Taxes on Stock Prices. *Nebr. J. Econ. Bus.*, Winter 1981, *20*(1), pp. 49–58. [G: U.S.]

Rea, Samuel A., Jr. Private Disability Insurance and Public Welfare Programs. *Public Finance*, 1981, *36*(1), pp. 84–98.

Reutlinger, Shlomo and Bigman, David. Feasibility,

Effectiveness, and Costs of Food Security Alternatives in Developing Countries. In *Valdés, A.*, 1981, pp. 185–212.

Richards, Ken. Capital Gains and Interest Rate Changes—A Theoretical Correction [Capital Gains Taxation and Interest Rate Changes: An Extension of Paish's Argument]. *Nat. Tax J.*, March 1981, *34*(1), pp. 137–40.

Ricketts, Martin. Tax Theory and Tax Policy. In *Peacock, A. and Forte, F., eds.*, 1981, pp. 29–46.

Robinson, Ray. Housing Tax-Expenditures, Subsidies and the Distribution of Income. *Manchester Sch. Econ. Soc. Stud.*, June 1981, *49*(2), pp. 91–110. **[G: U.K.]**

Rosen, Harvey S. Housing: Comments. In *Aaron, H. J. and Pechman, J. A., eds.*, 1981, pp. 323–26. **[G: U.S.]**

Rosenberg, Samuel. Incomes Policy: The "TIP" of the Iceberg. In *Claudon, M. P. and Cornwall, R. R., eds.*, 1981, pp. 175–95. **[G: U.S.]**

Roueche, Leonard. Notes on Government Subsidisation of Ferry Transport. *J. Transp. Econ. Policy*, September 1981, *15*(3), pp. 233–42. **[G: U.K.; Canada; U.S.; Norway]**

Ruffell, R. J. Endogeneity II: Direct Estimation of Labour Supply Functions with Piecewise Linear Budget Constraints. In *Brown, C. V., ed.*, 1981, pp. 101–16. **[G: U.K.]**

Ruggles, Patricia and O'Higgins, Michael. The Distribution of Public Expenditure among Households in the United States. *Rev. Income Wealth*, June 1981, *27*(2), pp. 137–64. **[G: U.S.; U.K.]**

Rundfelt, Rolf. Capital Gains Taxation and Effective Rates of Return. In *Eliasson, G. and Södersten, J., eds.*, 1981, pp. 345–80. **[G: Sweden; U.K.]**

Sackey, James A. Inflation and Government Tax Revenue: The Case of Trinidad and Tobago with Comparative Reference to Barbados and Jamaica. *Soc. Econ. Stud.*, September 1981, *30*(3), pp. 76–103. **[G: Barbados; Jamaica; Trinidad and Tobago]**

Sandford, Cedric. Economic Aspects of Compliance Costs. In *Peacock, A. and Forte, F., eds.*, 1981, pp. 163–73. **[G: U.K.]**

Sandmo, Agnar. Income Tax Evasion, Labour Supply, and the Equity–Efficiency Tradeoff. *J. Public Econ.*, December 1981, *16*(3), pp. 265–88.

Sarna, A. J. International Guidelines for Industrial Adjustment Policies. *J. World Trade Law*, November–December 1981, *15*(6), pp. 490–99.

Saunders, Peter G. The Commission of Inquiry into Poverty's Guaranteed Minimum Income Scheme: A Perspective from the 1980s. *Australian Econ. Rev.*, 1st Quarter 1981, (53), pp. 20–28. **[G: Australia]**

Schobel, Bruce D. A Comparison of Social Security Taxes and Federal Income Taxes, 1980–90. *Soc. Sec. Bull.*, December 1981, *44*(12), pp. 19–22. **[G: U.S.]**

Schrems, Edward L. The Tax Treatment of Workers Compensation Costs and Safety and Health Incentives. *J. Risk Ins.*, June 1981, *48*(2), pp. 272–85. **[G: U.S.]**

Seidman, Laurence S. Equity and Tradeoffs in a Tax-Based Incomes Policy. *Amer. Econ. Rev.*, May 1981, *71*(2), pp. 295–300. **[G: U.S.]**

Seidman, Laurence S. Insurance for Labor under a Tax-Based Incomes Policy. In *Claudon, M. P. and Cornwall, R. R., eds.*, 1981, pp. 109–33. **[G: U.S.]**

Sfligiotti, Giuseppe M. Taxation and the Regulation of Energy Supply and Consumption: Comment. In *Roskamp, K. W. and Forte, F., eds.*, 1981, pp. 297–303. **[G: U.S.]**

Shavell, Steven. A Note on Efficiency vs. Distributional Equity in Legal Rulemaking: Should Distributional Equity Matter Given Optimal Income Taxation? *Amer. Econ. Rev.*, May 1981, *71*(2), pp. 414–18.

Shaw, G. K. Leading Issues of Tax Policy in Developing Countries: The Economic Problems. In *Peacock, A. and Forte, F., eds.*, 1981, pp. 148–62. **[G: LDCs]**

Shepherd, Mark, Jr. The U.S. Corporation within the Competitive Environment. In *U.S. Congress, Joint Economic Committee (I)*, 1981, pp. 191–222. **[G: U.S.; OECD]**

Shim, Ki R. A Note on the K-M Tax Shifting Model. *Indian Econ. J.*, April–June 1981, *28*(4), pp. 29–35. **[G: Japan]**

Shome, Parthasarathi. The General Equilibrium Theory and Concepts of Tax Incidence in the Presence of Third or More Factors. *Public Finance*, 1981, *36*(1), pp. 22–38.

Short, George G. The Loan-Out Corporation in Tax Planning for Entertainers. *Law Contemp. Probl.*, Autumn 1981, *44*(4), pp. 51–78.

Shoup, Carl Sumner. Economic Limits to Taxation. *Atlantic Econ. J.*, March 1981, *9*(1), pp. 9–23.

Shoyama, T. K. Stagflation Consequences of the Canadian Tax/Transfer System: Comments. In *Ontario Economic Council, Vol. 1*, 1981, pp. 105–13. **[G: Canada; U.S.]**

Siaens, Alain. Plus d'impôts sur les intérêts des dépôts et obligations en FB en Belgique? (No More Taxes on "Interests" from Deposits and Bonds in Belgian Francs: A Cost Benefit Analysis from the Point of View of the Collectivity and of His Members. With English summary.) *Ann. Sci. Écon. Appl.*, 1981, *37*(1), pp. 9–27. **[G: Belgium]**

Silver, Andrew. Original Issue Deep Discount Bonds. *Fed. Res. Bank New York Quart. Rev.*, Winter 1981–82, *6*(4), pp. 18–28. **[G: U.S.]**

Sinai, Allen. Economic Impacts of Accelerated Capital Cost Recovery. In *U.S. Congress, Joint Economic Committee (I)*, 1981, pp. 610–28. **[G: U.S.]**

Siong, Jap Kim. Indonesia: Anti-Tax Avoidance Measures. *Bull. Int. Fiscal Doc.*, October 1981, *35*(10), pp. 456–58. **[G: Indonesia]**

Smith, Lawrence B. Canadian Housing Policy in the Seventies. *Land Econ.*, August 1981, *57*(3), pp. 338–52. **[G: Canada]**

Smith, Lawrence B. Housing Assistance: A Re-evaluation. *Can. Public Policy*, Summer 1981, *7*(3), pp. 454–63. **[G: Canada]**

Sobbrio, Giuseppe. On Some Components of the Statutory Incidence of the Personal Income Tax in Italy. In *Roskamp, K. W. and Forte, F., eds.*, 1981, pp. 153–78. **[G: Italy]**

Solo, Robert A. A Progressive Expenditure Tax Reconsidered. In *Solo, R. A. and Anderson, C. W.*, *eds.*, 1981, pp. 379–81.

Sørensen, Christen. Skattefrie pensionsordninger ved høj inflation og højt skattetryk. (Tax Free Pension Schemes with Ongoing Inflation and a High Level of Income Tax. With English summary.) *Nationaløkon. Tidsskr.*, 1981, *119*(3), pp. 339–42.
[G: Denmark]

Spiro, Erwin. The 1981 Income Tax Changes in the Republic of South Africa. *Bull. Int. Fiscal Doc.*, November 1981, *35*(11), pp. 508–10.
[G: S. Africa]

Stafford, Frank P. On the Determinants of Labor Supply in Sweden. In *Eliasson, G.; Holmlund, B. and Stafford, F. P., eds.*, 1981, pp. 301–11.
[G: Sweden]

Stein, Robert M. The Allocation of Federal Aid Monies: The Synthesis of Demand-Side and Supply-Side Explanations. *Amer. Polit. Sci. Rev.*, June 1981, *75*(2), pp. 334–43. [G: U.S.]

Sternlieb, George. Kemp–Garcia Act: An Initial Evaluation. In *Sternlieb, G. and Listokin, D., eds.*, 1981, pp. 42–83. [G: U.S.]

Steuerle, Eugene and Hartzmark, Michael. Individual Income Taxation, 1947–79. *Nat. Tax J.*, June 1981, *34*(2), pp. 145–66. [G: U.S.]

Stevens, David W. Contributed Papers: Labor Markets and Other IR Topics: Discussion. In *Dennis, B. D., ed.*, 1981, pp. 337–38. [G: U.S.]

Stewart, Frances. Taxation and the Control of Transfer Pricing. In *Murray, R., ed.*, 1981, pp. 177–84.

Stewart, Frances. Taxation and Technology Transfer. In *Sagafi-nejad, T.; Moxon, R. W. and Perlmutter, H. V., eds.*, 1981, pp. 137–72. [G: LDCs; MDCs]

Stickney, Clyde P. A Note on Optimal Tax Depreciation Research [A Note on the Optimal Tax Lives for Assets Qualifying for the Investment Tax Credit]. *Accounting Rev.*, July 1981, *56*(3), pp. 622–25. [G: U.S.]

Stout, Lynn A. The Case for Mandatory Separate Filing by Married Persons. *Yale Law J.*, December 1981, *91*(2), pp. 363–82. [G: U.S.]

Strachan, Valerie. VAT in the UK: The Tax Collector's View. In *Peacock, A. and Forte, F., eds.*, 1981, pp. 177–91. [G: U.K.]

Straf, Miron L. Revenue Allocation by Regression: National Health Service Appropriations for Teaching Hospitals. *J. Roy. Statist. Soc.*, Part 1, 1981, *144*, pp. 80–84.

Straszheim, Mahlon R. Do Housing Allowances Work? Participation. In *Bradbury, K. L. and Downs, A., eds.*, 1981, pp. 113–45. [G: U.S.]

Strichman, George A. The Economy of 1981: A Bipartisan Look: The Proceedings of a Congressional Economic Conference: Statement. In *U.S. Congress, Joint Economic Committee (1)*, 1981, pp. 590–609. [G: OECD]

Strömberg, Dorothea. Success and Failures in Recent Swedish Tax Policy. In *Roskamp, K. W. and Forte, F., eds.*, 1981, pp. 121–34. [G: Sweden]

Struyk, Raymond J. Housing Vouchers for the Poor: Policy Questions and Experimental Responses. In *Struyk, R. J. and Bendick, M., Jr., eds.*, 1981, pp. 3–20. [G: U.S.]

Struyk, Raymond J. Housing Vouchers for the Poor: Social Experimentation and Policy Research. In *Struyk, R. J. and Bendick, M., Jr., eds.*, 1981, pp. 295–310. [G: U.S.]

Stuart, Charles E. Swedish Tax Rates, Labor Supply, and Tax Revenues. *J. Polit. Econ.*, October 1981, *89*(5), pp. 1020–38. [G: Sweden]

Sturrock, John. Eliminating the Tax Discrimination against Income from Business Capital: A Proposal. In *Federal Reserve System*, 1981, pp. 281–302.

Summers, Lawrence H. Capital Taxation and Accumulation in a Life Cycle Growth Model. *Amer. Econ. Rev.*, September 1981, *71*(4), pp. 533–44.

Summers, Lawrence H. Tax Policy and Corporate Investment. In *Meyer, L. H., ed.*, 1981, pp. 115–48. [G: U.S.]

Summers, Lawrence H. Taxation and Corporate Investment: A *q*-Theory Approach. *Brookings Pap. Econ. Act.*, 1981, (1), pp. 67–127.

Sumner, Michael T. and Laing, C. J. Countercyclical Tax Changes and Consumers' Expenditure. *Oxford Bull. Econ. Statist.*, May 1981, *43*(2), pp. 131–47. [G: U.K.]

Sumner, Michael T. and Ward, Robert. Tax Changes and Cigarette Prices [An Alternative Approach to the Analysis of Taxation]. *J. Polit. Econ.*, December 1981, *89*(6), pp. 1261–65. [G: U.S.]

Sunley, Emil M. Acceleration of Tax Depreciation: Basic Issues and Major Alternatives. In *Hulten, C. R., ed.*, 1981, pp. 137–47. [G: U.S.]

Sunley, Emil M. Housing Tax Preferences: Options for Reform. In *Weicher, J. C.; Villani, K. E. and Roistacher, E. A., eds.*, 1981, pp. 65–71.
[G: U.S.]

Sunley, Emil M. Investment in Producers' Equipment: Comments. In *Aaron, H. J. and Pechman, J. A., eds.*, 1981, pp. 127–29. [G: U.S.]

Sunley, Emil M. Tax Incentives and Public Utility Regulation. In *[Nelson, J. R.]*, 1981, pp. 299–309. [G: U.S.]

Sunley, Emil M. Taxation and the Regulation of Energy Supply and Consumption. In *Roskamp, K. W. and Forte, F., eds.*, 1981, pp. 287–95.
[G: U.S.]

Supel, Thomas M. Macroeconomic Implications for Tax Indexing in the McCallum-Whitaker Framework. *J. Monet. Econ.*, July 1981, *8*(1), pp. 131–37.

Sutherland, Charles F., Jr. and Tedder, Philip L. Impacts of Federal Estate Taxation on Investments in Forestry: Reply. *Land Econ.*, February 1981, *57*(1), pp. 126–27. [G: U.S.]

Tachibanaki, Toshiaki. A Note on the Impact of Tax on Income Redistribution. *Rev. Income Wealth*, September 1981, *27*(3), pp. 327–32.
[G: OECD]

Tait, Alan. Is the Introduction of a Value-Added Tax Inflationary? *Finance Develop.*, June 1981, *18*(2), pp. 38–42. [G: Selected Countries]

Tarditi, Secondo. A More Effective Role of Public Finance in Agricultural Policy. *Econ. Notes*, 1981, *10*(3), pp. 128–37. [G: EEC]

Taubman, Paul. The Measurement of Economic Depreciation: Discussion. In *Hulten, C. R., ed.*, 1981, pp. 129–32. [G: U.S.; Japan]

Taylor, D. Garth. American Politics, Public Opinion, and Social Security Financing. In *Skidmore, F., ed.*, 1981, pp. 235–73. [G: U.S.]

Tepper, Irwin. Taxation and Corporate Pension Policy. *J. Finance*, March 1981, *36*(1), pp. 1–13.

Theret, Bruno. Un point de vue macroéconomique sur le traitement de la taxe sur la valeur ajoutée dans le système élargi de comptabilité nationale française. (A Macroeconomic View on the Treatment of the Value-Added Tax in the Extended French National Accounting System. With English summary.) *Public Finance*, 1981, *36*(1), pp. 108–24.   [G: France]

Thimmaiah, G. Perspectives in Tax Design and Tax Reform. *Bull. Int. Fiscal Doc.*, February 1981, *35*(2), pp. 67–74.

Thimmaiah, G. The New International Debate on Expenditure Tax: An Assessment. *Bull. Int. Fiscal Doc.*, November 1981, *35*(11), pp. 498–507.

Thompson, Dennis. The Ethics of Social Experimentation: The Case of the DIME. *Public Policy*, Summer 1981, *29*(3), pp. 369–98.   [G: U.S.]

Thurow, Lester C. Solving the Energy Problem. **In** *Kamrany, N. M.*, 1981, pp. 23–27.   [G: U.S.]

Tirole, Jean and Guesnerie, Roger. Tax Reform from the Gradient Projection Viewpoint. *J. Public Econ.*, June 1981, *15*(3), pp. 275–93.

Tixier, Susan. Tribal Severance Taxes—Outside the Purview of the Commerce Clause. *Natural Res. J.*, April 1981, *21*(2), pp. 405–13.   [G: U.S.]

Tkachenko, V. Highlights of the U.S. Treasury Department Report on Tax Havens and Their Use by U.S. Taxpayers. *Bull. Int. Fiscal Doc.*, August–September 1981, *35*(8–9), pp. 381–88.
[G: U.S.]

Tobin, James. Reflections Inspired by Proposed Constitutional Restrictions on Fiscal Policy. **In** *[Nelson, J. R.]*, 1981, pp. 341–67.   [G: U.S.]

de la Torre, Jose. Public Intervention Strategies in the European Clothing Industries. *J. World Trade Law*, March–April 1981, *15*(2), pp. 124–48.   [G: EEC]

Ture, Norman B. Tax Policy and Corporate Investment: Discussion. **In** *Meyer, L. H.*, *ed.*, 1981, pp. 165–70.   [G: U.S.]

Udagawa, Akihito. Taxation and Regulation of Energy Supply and Consumption: Comment. **In** *Roskamp, K. W. and Forte, F.*, *eds.*, 1981, pp. 305–08.   [G: U.S.]

Ulph, David T. Labour Supply, Taxation and the Measurement of Inequality. **In** *Brown, C. V.*, *ed.*, 1981, pp. 144–62.

Ulph, David T. and Ulph, Alistair M. Implications for Optimal Income Taxation. **In** *Brown, C. V.*, *ed.*, 1981, pp. 189–212.   [G: U.K.]

U.S. Internal Revenue Service. Multinational Companies' (MNCs) Tax Avoidance and/or Evasion Schemes and Available Methods to Curb Abuse. **In** *Murray, R.*, *ed.*, 1981, pp. 245–77.

U.S. Treasury Department. Summary Study of International Cases Involving Section 482 of the Internal Revenue Code. **In** *Murray, R.*, *ed.*, 1981, pp. 308–24.   [G: U.S.]

Vandell, Robert F. and Pontius, Marcia L. The Impact of Tax Status on Stock Selection. *J. Portfol. Manage.*, Summer 1981, *7*(4), pp. 35–42.

Vartiainen, Henri J. Progressive Income Taxation, Disincentives and Barter. **In** *Roskamp, K. W. and Forte, F.*, *eds.*, 1981, pp. 103–19.

Vaupel, James W. Free Social Security Recipients from the Social Security Tax. *Policy Anal.*, Winter 1981, *7*(1), pp. 125–29.   [G: U.S.]

Venkataraman, R. India: Budget Speech, 1981. *Bull. Int. Fiscal Doc.*, May 1981, *35*(5), pp. 218–21.
[G: India]

Volcker, Paul A. Statement to House Committee on Ways and Means, March 3, 1981. *Fed. Res. Bull.*, March 1981, *67*(3), pp. 243–46. [G: U.S.]

Waldauer, Charles. Comment on "The Variable Rate Value Added Tax as an Anti-Inflation Fiscal Stabilizer." *Nat. Tax J.*, March 1981, *34*(1), pp. 131–32.   [G: U.S.]

Walker, Charls E. Proceedings of the Seminar on Productivity: Statement. **In** *U.S. Congress, Joint Economic Committee (I)*, 1981, pp. 147–48.
[G: U.S.]

Walker, Charls E. and Bloomfield, Mark A. The Political Response to Three Potential Major Bankruptcies: Lockheed, New York City, and Chrysler. **In** *Wachter, M. L. and Wachter, S. M.*, *eds.*, 1981, pp. 423–52.   [G: U.S.]

Wallich, Henry C. Statement to Temporary Subcommittee on Industrial Growth and Productivity, Senate Committee on the Budget, January 27, 1981. *Fed. Res. Bull.*, February 1981, *67*(2), pp. 137–40.   [G: U.S.]

Watson, Peter. Inflation Accounting and Business Taxation. **In** *Peacock, A. and Forte, F.*, *eds.*, 1981, pp. 78–93.   [G: U.K.]

Watts, Harold W. A Critical Review of the Program as a Social Experiment. **In** *Bradbury, K. L. and Downs, A.*, *eds.*, 1981, pp. 33–65.   [G: U.S.]

Waverman, Leonard. The Distribution of Resource Rents: For Whom the Firm Tolls. **In** *Nemetz, P. N.*, *ed.*, 1981, pp. 255–79.   [G: Canada]

Weintraub, Sidney. The Carter Economic Council's Thalidomide TIP. *J. Post Keynesian Econ.*, Spring 1981, *3*(3), pp. 459–62.

Weintraub, Sidney. Tips Against Inflation. **In** *Claudon, M. P. and Cornwall, R. R.*, *eds.*, 1981, pp. 7–34.   [G: U.S.]

Weitzman, Martin L. Sequential R&D Strategy for Synfuels. *Bell J. Econ. (See Rand J. Econ. after 4/85)*, Autumn 1981, *12*(2), pp. 574–90.
[G: U.S.]

Wells, Louis T., Jr. Taxation and Technology Transfer: Comment. **In** *Sagafi-nejad, T.; Moxon, R. W. and Perlmutter, H. V.*, *eds.*, 1981, pp. 173–76.   [G: LDCs; MDCs]

Wells, R. J. G. Producer Subsidies in the Dairy Industry in Peninsular Malaysia. *J. Econ. Stud.*, 1981, *8*(2), pp. 57–64.

Wenglowski, Gary M. Stock Prices: Comments. **In** *Aaron, H. J. and Pechman, J. A.*, *eds.*, 1981, pp. 238–40.   [G: U.S.]

Wenzel, H.-Dieter and Wiegard, Wolfgang. Merit Goods and Second-Best Taxation. *Public Finance*, 1981, *36*(1), pp. 125–40.

West, Edwin G. and McKee, Michael. The Public Choice of Price Control and Rationing of Oil. *Southern Econ. J.*, July 1981, *48*(1), pp. 204–10.

Wetzler, James W. Capital Gains: Comments. **In** *Aaron, H. J. and Pechman, J. A.*, *eds.*, 1981, pp. 277–81.   [G: U.S.]

Weymark, John A. Undominated Directions of Tax Reform. *J. Public Econ.*, December 1981, *16*(3), pp. 343–69.

Whalley, John. Border Adjustments and Tax Harmonization: Comment on Berglas [Harmonization of Commodity Taxes: Destination, Origin, and Restricted Origin Principles]. *J. Public Econ.*, December 1981, *16*(3), pp. 389–90.

Whalley, John. Capital Gains and Interest Rate Changes: A Reply [Capital Gains Taxation and Interest Rate Changes: An Extension of Paish's Argument]. *Nat. Tax J.*, March 1981, *34*(1), pp. 141.

White, Daniel L. The Variable Rate Value Added Tax as an Anti-Inflation Fiscal Stabilizer: A Response. *Nat. Tax J.*, March 1981, *34*(1), pp. 133. [G: U.S.]

Whitman, Marina v. N. Automobiles: Turning Around on a Dime? *Challenge*, May/June 1981, *24*(2), pp. 36–44. [G: U.S.]

Yasuba, Yasukichi. Trade, Growth and Income Distribution: The Korean Experience: Comment. **In** *Hong, W. and Krause, L. B., eds.*, 1981, pp. 284–86. [G: S. Korea]

Yeh, Chiou-nan. Musgrave's Paradox and Progressive Income Taxation. *Public Finance*, 1981, *36*(1), pp. 16–21.

Yin, Robert K. Contemporary Issues in Domestic Technology Transfer. **In** *Doctors, S. I., ed.*, 1981, pp. 69–116. [G: U.S.]

Yoingco, Angel Q. Attempts to Restructure the Philippine Income Tax and Recent Developments. *Bull. Int. Fiscal Doc.*, November 1981, *35*(11), pp. 487–97. [G: Philippines]

Yoingco, Angel Q. and Sukarya, Sutadi. Study Group on Asian Tax Administration and Research (SGATAR)—An Experiment in Regional Tax Cooperation—Part II. *Bull. Int. Fiscal Doc.*, April 1981, *35*(4), pp. 173–78. [G: Asia]

Yoingco, Angel Q. and Sukarya, Sutadi. Study Group on Asian Tax Administration and Research (SGATAR)—An Experiment in Regional Tax Cooperation—Part I. *Bull. Int. Fiscal Doc.*, March 1981, *35*(3), pp. 110–18. [G: S.E. Asia; Australia; Japan; New Zealand]

Ysander, Bengt-Christer. Taxes and Market Stability. **In** *Eliasson, G. and Södersten, J., eds.*, 1981, pp. 191–231. [G: Sweden; U.S.]

Zais, James P. Administering Housing Allowances. **In** *Struyk, R. J. and Bendick, M., Jr., eds.*, 1981, pp. 235–64. [G: U.S.]

Zais, James P. Repairs and Maintenance on the Units Occupied by Allowance Recipients. **In** *Struyk, R. J. and Bendick, M., Jr., eds.*, 1981, pp. 179–206. [G: U.S.]

Zodrow, George. Implementing Tax Reform. *Nat. Tax J.*, December 1981, *34*(4), pp. 401–18.

Zoller, Elisabeth. Le statut fiscal de la femme mariée en France. (With English summary.) **In** *Roskamp, K. W. and Forte, F., eds.*, 1981, pp. 355–64. [G: France]

324 State and Local Government Finance

3240 General

Arnott, Richard J. and Grieson, Ronald E. Optimal Fiscal Policy for a State or Local Government. *J. Urban Econ.*, January 1981, *9*(1), pp. 23–48.

Bahl, Roy W. The Next Decade in State and Local Government Finance: A Period of Adjustment. **In** *Bahl, R., ed.*, 1981, pp. 191–220. [G: U.S.]

Barnard, J. R.; Dent, W. T. and Reznek, A. P. An Econometric Model of a State Government Sector. *Reg. Sci. Persp.*, 1981, *11*(1), pp. 3–21. [G: U.S.]

Barrows, Richard. Management Information Systems for Local Government: Discussion. *Amer. J. Agr. Econ.*, December 1981, *63*(5), pp. 984–85. [G: U.S.]

Berglas, Eitan and Pines, David. Clubs, Local Public Goods and Transportation Models: A Synthesis. *J. Public Econ.*, April 1981, *15*(2), pp. 141–62.

Bewley, Truman F. A Critique of Tiebout's Theory of Local Public Expenditures. *Econometrica*, May 1981, *49*(3), pp. 713–40.

Biere, Arlo and Sjo, John. Management Information Systems for Local Government. *Amer. J. Agr. Econ.*, December 1981, *63*(5), pp. 967–73. [G: U.S.]

Blaug, Mark. Comments on M. Peston [The Finance of Recurrent Education: Some Theoretical Considerations] and H. Glennerster [The Role of the State in Financing Recurrent Education: Lessons from European Experience]. *Public Choice*, 1981, *36*(3), pp. 573–77.

Bona, B.; Merighi, D. and Ostanello-Borreani, A. Financial Resource Allocation in a Decentralized Urban System. **In** *Nijkamp, P. and Spronk, J., eds.*, 1981, pp. 101–15. [G: Italy]

Broder, Josef M. Decision Aids for Local Decision Making: Discussion. *Amer. J. Agr. Econ.*, December 1981, *63*(5), pp. 988–89. [G: U.S.]

Browne, Lynn E. How Much Government Is Too Much? *New Eng. Econ. Rev.*, March–April 1981, pp. 21–34. [G: U.S.]

Bucovetsky, Sam. Optimal Jurisdictional Fragmentation and Mobility. *J. Public Econ.*, October 1981, *16*(2), pp. 171–91.

Carlson, Leonard A. and Cebula, Richard J. Voting with One's Feet: A Brief Note on the Case of Public Welfare and the American Indian. *Public Choice*, 1981, *37*(2), pp. 321–25. [G: U.S.]

Cebula, Richard J. The Tiebout Hypothesis of Voting with One's Feet: A Look at the Most Recent Evidence. *Rev. Reg. Stud.*, Winter 1981, *11*(3), pp. 47–50. [G: U.S.]

Cebula, Richard J. and Chevlin, Linda. Proposition 4, Tax Reduction Mirage: An Exploratory Note on Its Potential Spending and Tax Impacts. *Amer. J. Econ. Soc.*, October 1981, *40*(4), pp. 343–48. [G: U.S.]

Church, Albert M. The Effects of Local Government Expenditure and Property Taxes on Investment. *Amer. Real Estate Urban Econ. Assoc. J.*, Summer 1981, *9*(2), pp. 165–80. [G: U.S.]

Clark, Terry Nichols. Urban Fiscal Strain: Trends and Policy Options. **In** *Walzer, N. and Chicoine, D. L., eds.*, 1981, pp. 3–18. [G: U.S.]

Clark, Terry Nichols and Ferguson, Lorna Crowley. Fiscal Strain and American Cities: Six Basic Processes. **In** *Newton, K., ed.*, 1981, pp. 137–55. [G: U.S.]

Clark, Terry Nichols and Ferguson, Lorna Crowley.

Political Leadership and Urban Fiscal Policy. In *Clark, T. N., ed.,* 1981, pp. 81–101. [G: U.S.]

Colette, W. Arden. Decision Aids for Local Decision Making: Discussion. *Amer. J. Agr. Econ.,* December 1981, *63*(5), pp. 986–87. [G: U.S.]

Cuthbertson, K.; Foreman-Peck, James S. and Gripaios, P. A Model of Local Authority Fiscal Behaviour. *Public Finance,* 1981, *36*(2), pp. 229–43. [G: U.K.]

Doeksen, Gerald A. and Nelson, James R. Decision Aids for Local Decision Making. *Amer. J. Agr. Econ.,* December 1981, *63*(5), pp. 974–81. [G: U.S.]

Eberts, Randall W. and Gronberg, Timothy J. Jurisdictional Homogeneity and the Tiebout Hypothesis. *J. Urban Econ.,* September 1981, *10*(2), pp. 227–39.

Epple, Dennis and Schipper, Katherine. Municipal Pension Funding: A Theory and Some Evidence. *Public Choice,* 1981, *37*(1), pp. 141–78.

Epple, Dennis and Zelenitz, Allan. The Implications of Competition among Jurisdictions: Does Tiebout Need Politics? *J. Polit. Econ.,* December 1981, *89*(6), pp. 1197–1217.

Epple, Dennis and Zelenitz, Allan. The Roles of Jurisdictional Competition and of Collective Choice Institutions in the Market for Local Public Goods. *Amer. Econ. Rev.,* May 1981, *71*(2), pp. 87–92.

Feller, Irwin. Public-Sector Innovation as "Conspicuous Production." *Policy Anal.,* Winter 1981, *7*(1), pp. 1–20. [G: U.S.]

Ferguson, Lorna Crowley. Fiscal Strain in American Cities: Some Limitations to Popular Explanations. In *Newton, K., ed.,* 1981, pp. 156–78. [G: U.S.]

Fischel, William A. Is Local Government Structure in Large Urbanized Areas Monopolistic or Competitive? *Nat. Tax J.,* March 1981, *34*(1), pp. 95–104. [G: U.S.]

Fisher, Ronald C. Expenditure Incentives of Intergovernmental Grants: Revenue Sharing and Matching Grants. In *Henderson, J. V., ed.,* 1981, pp. 201–18. [G: U.S.]

Friedman, Joseph. A Conditional Logit Model of the Role of Local Public Services in Residential Choice. *Urban Stud.,* October 1981, *18*(3), pp. 347–58. [G: U.S.]

Furno, Orlando F. and Magers, Dexter A. An Analysis of State School Support Programs. In *Jordan, K. F. and Cambron-McCabe, N. H., eds.,* 1981, pp. 169–90. [G: U.S.]

Glennerster, Howard. The Role of the State in Financing Recurrent Education: Lessons from European Experience. *Public Choice,* 1981, *36*(3), pp. 551–71.

Goldberg, Kalman and Scott, Robert C. Fiscal Incidence: A Revision of Benefits Incidence Estimates. *J. Reg. Sci.,* May 1981, *21*(2), pp. 203–21. [G: U.S.]

Goldstein, G. S. and Pauly, Mark V. Tiebout Bias on the Demand for Local Public Goods. *J. Public Econ.,* October 1981, *16*(2), pp. 131–43.

Gramlich, Edward M.; Rubinfeld, Daniel L. and Swift, Deborah A. Why Voters Turn out for Tax Limitation Votes. *Nat. Tax J.,* March 1981, *34*(1), pp. 115–24. [G: U.S.]

Grossman, David A. and Hayes, Frederick O'R. Moving toward Integrated Fiscal Management. *Public Budg. Finance,* Summer 1981, *1*(2), pp. 41–46.

Groves, Sanford M. and Godsey, W. Maureen. Managing Financial Condition. In *Aronson, J. R. and Schwartz, E., eds.,* 1981, pp. 277–301. [G: U.S.]

Groves, Sanford M.; Godsey, W. Maureen and Shulman, Martha A. Financial Indicators for Local Government. *Public Budg. Finance,* Summer 1981, *1*(2), pp. 5–19.

Hack, Walter G.; Edlefson, Carla and Ogawa, Rodney T. Fiscal Accountability: The Challenge of Formulating Responsive Policy. In *Jordan, K. F. and Cambron-McCabe, N. H., eds.,* 1981, pp. 251–79. [G: U.S.]

Hancock, Scott. Supreme Court Fails to Reach Inverse Condemnation Issue. *Natural Res. J.,* January 1981, *21*(1), pp. 169–75. [G: U.S.]

Hansen, Reed R. Revenue Alternatives for State and Local Governments: Crisis-ridden Areas and Those Seeking Fiscal Equity and Stability Offered New Options. *Amer. J. Econ. Soc.,* April 1981, *40*(2), pp. 183–89. [G: U.S.]

Hicks, Alexander; Friedland, Roger and Johnson, Edwin. Class Power and State Policy. In *Martin, G. T., Jr., and Zald, M. N., eds.,* 1981, *1978,* pp. 131–46. [G: U.S.]

Hochman, Oded. Land Rents, Optimal Taxation and Local Fiscal Independence in an Economy with Local Public Goods. *J. Public Econ.,* February 1981, *15*(1), pp. 59–85.

Holder, William W. Local Government Accounting. In *Aronson, J. R. and Schwartz, E., eds.,* 1981, pp. 414–32.

Huddleston, Mark W. and Palley, Marian Lief. Shortchanging Nonmetropolitan America: Small Communities and Federal Aid. *Public Budg. Finance,* Autumn 1981, *1*(3), pp. 36–45. [G: U.S.]

Ingram, Robert W. and Copeland, Ronald M. Disclosure Practices in Audited Financial Statements of Municipalities. *Public Budg. Finance,* Summer 1981, *1*(2), pp. 47–58. [G: U.S.]

Inman, Robert P. "Municipal Pension Funding: A Theory and Some Evidence" by Dennis Epple and Katherine Schipper: A Comment. *Public Choice,* 1981, *37*(1), pp. 179–87.

Inman, Robert P. On Setting the Agenda for Pennsylvania School Finance Reform: An Exercise in Giving Policy Advice. *Public Choice,* 1981, *36*(3), pp. 449–74. [G: U.S.]

Levin, David J. State and Local Government Fiscal Position in 1980. *Surv. Curr. Bus.,* February 1981, *61*(2), pp. 19–21. [G: U.S.]

Lotz, Joergen R. Fiscal Problems and Issues in Scandinavian Cities. In *Bahl, R., ed.,* 1981, pp. 221–43. [G: Scandinavia]

Margolis, Julius. Fiscal Problems of Political Boundaries. In *Aronson, J. R. and Schwartz, E., eds.,* 1981, pp. 213–33. [G: U.S.]

Maynard, Alan. Fiscal Structure of Local Authorities in Britain. In *Aronson, J. R. and Schwartz, E., eds.,* 1981, pp. 255–73. [G: U.K.]

McFadden, Daniel. Comments on R. P. Inman [On Setting the Agenda for Pennsylvania School Fi-

nance Reform: An Exercise in Giving Policy Advice]. *Public Choice*, 1981, *36*(3), pp. 477–80.
[G: U.S.]

McGuire, Thomas G. Budget-Maximizing Governmental Agencies: An Empirical Test. *Public Choice*, 1981, *36*(2), pp. 313–22. [G: U.S.]

Merget, Astrid E. Achieving Equity in an Era of Fiscal Constraint. In *Burchell, R. W. and Listokin, D., eds.*, 1981, pp. 401–36. [G: U.S.]

Mirrlees, J. A. Comments on R. P. Inman [On Setting the Agenda for Pennsylvania School Finance Reform: An Exercise in Giving Policy Advice]. *Public Choice*, 1981, *36*(3), pp. 475–76.
[G: U.S.]

Murray, Steven W. Management Information Systems for Local Government: Discussion. *Amer. J. Agr. Econ.*, December 1981, *63*(5), pp. 982–83. [G: U.S.]

Oates, Wallace E. On Local Finance and the Tiebout Model. *Amer. Econ. Rev.*, May 1981, *71*(2), pp. 93–98.

Peston, Maurice H. A Note on a Balanced Budget Change in Local Expenditure. *Public Finance*, 1981, *36*(3), pp. 455–59.

Phares, Donald. The Fiscal Status of the State–Local Sector: A Look to the 1980s. In *Walzer, N. and Chicoine, D. L., eds.*, 1981, pp. 145–73.
[G: U.S.]

Raman, K. K. Municipal Financial Reporting: "Managing" the Numbers. *Public Budg. Finance*, Autumn 1981, *1*(3), pp. 56–61.

Reischauer, Robert. The Economy and the Federal Budget in the 1980s: Implications for the State and Local Sector. In *Bahl, R., ed.*, 1981, pp. 13–38. [G: U.S.]

Richardson, David H. and Thalheimer, Richard. Measuring the Extent of Property Tax Capitalization for Single Family Residences. *Southern Econ. J.*, January 1981, *47*(3), pp. 674–89.
[G: U.S.]

Rousmaniere, Peter F. and Guild, Nathaniel B. The Second Wave of Municipal Accounting Reform. *Public Budg. Finance*, Spring 1981, *1*(1), pp. 66–77. [G: U.S.]

Ruchelman, Leonard I. The Finance Function in Local Government. In *Aronson, J. R. and Schwartz, E., eds.*, 1981, pp. 3–24. [G: U.S.]

Salter, Stephen J. and Topham, Neville. The Distribution of Local Public Goods in a Non-Tiebout World. *Manchester Sch. Econ. Soc. Stud.*, March 1981, *49*(1), pp. 51–69.

Schroeder, Larry D. Forecasting Local Revenues and Expenditures. In *Aronson, J. R. and Schwartz, E., eds.*, 1981, pp. 66–90. [G: U.S.]

Schwartz, Eli. Inventory, Purchasing, and Risk Management. In *Aronson, J. R. and Schwartz, E., eds.*, 1981, pp. 389–413.

Shannon, John and Wallin, Bruce. Fiscal Imbalance within the Federal System: The Problem of Renewing Revenue Sharing. In *Burchell, R. W. and Listokin, D., eds.*, 1981, pp. 541–75.
[G: U.S.]

Starrett, David A. Land Value Capitalization in Local Public Finance. *J. Polit. Econ.*, April 1981, *89*(2), pp. 306–27.

Stinson, Thomas F. Fiscal Status of Local Govern-

ments. In *Hawley, A. H. and Mazie, S. M., eds.*, 1981, pp. 736–66. [G: U.S.]

Stubblebine, Wm. Craig and Kennard, David N. California School Finance: The 1970s Decade. *Public Choice*, 1981, *36*(3), pp. 391–412.
[G: U.S.]

van Suntum, Ulrich. Offentliches Finanzsystem und regionale Effizienz. (With English summary.) *Kyklos*, 1981, *34*(2), pp. 216–29.

Weinstein, Bernard L. and Clark, Robert J. The Fiscal Outlook for Growing Cities. In *Bahl, R., ed.*, 1981, pp. 105–25. [G: U.S.]

West, Edwin G. Comments on H. Glennerster [The Role of the State in Financing Recurrent Education: Lessons from European Experience]. *Public Choice*, 1981, *36*(3), pp. 579–82.
[G: U.S.]

Yinger, John. Capitalization and the Median Voter. *Amer. Econ. Rev.*, May 1981, *71*(2), pp. 99–103.

3241 State and Local Government Expenditures and Budgeting

Aiken, Michael and Depre, Roger. The Urban System, Politics, and Policy in Belgian Cities. In *Newton, K., ed.*, 1981, pp. 85–116.
[G: Belgium]

Aprile, Gianni. L'analyse de la dépense publique dans une structure fédéraliste: le cas de la Suisse. (Public Expenditure Analysis in a Federalist Context: The Swiss Case. With English summary.) *Schweiz. Z. Volkswirtsch. Statist.*, September 1981, *117*(3), pp. 281–95. [G: Switzerland]

Aronson, J. Richard and Schwartz, Eli. Capital Budgeting. In *Aronson, J. R. and Schwartz, E., eds.*, 1981, pp. 433–57.

Bahl, Roy W. and Schroeder, Larry D. Fiscal Adjustments in Declining States. In *Burchell, R. W. and Listokin, D., eds.*, 1981, pp. 301–29.
[G: U.S.]

Brueckner, Jan K. Congested Public Goods: The Case of Fire Protection. *J. Public Econ.*, February 1981, *15*(1), pp. 45–58.

Buchanan, James McGill and Flowers, Marilyn R. Local Government Expenditures. In *Aronson, J. R. and Schwartz, E., eds.*, 1981, pp. 25–43.
[G: U.S.]

Buck, Andrew J. and Hakim, Simon. Inequality Constraints, Multicollinearity and Models of Police Expenditure. *Southern Econ. J.*, October 1981, *48*(2), pp. 449–63.

Burchell, Robert W. and Listokin, David. The Fiscal Impact of Economic-Development Programs: Case Studies of the Local Cost–Revenue Implications of HUD, EDA AND FmHA Projects. In *Sternlieb, G. and Listokin, D., eds.*, 1981, pp. 163–229. [G: U.S.]

Corwin, Margaret A. and Getzels, Judith. Capital Expenditures: Causes and Controls. In *Burchell, R. W. and Listokin, D., eds.*, 1981, pp. 387–400.
[G: U.S.]

DiLorenzo, Thomas J. An Empirical Assessment of the Factor-Supplier Pressure Group Hypothesis. *Public Choice*, 1981, *37*(3), pp. 559–78.
[G: U.S.]

Doctors, Samuel I. State and Local Government

Technology Transfer. In *Doctors, S. I., ed.*, 1981, pp. 3–42. [G: U.S.]

Duncombe, Sydney and Lynch, Thomas D. Taxpayer Revolt. In *Lynch, T. D., ed.*, 1981, pp. 193–212. [G: U.S.]

Friedman, Lewis. Budgeting. In *Aronson, J. R. and Schwartz, E., eds.*, 1981, pp. 91–119. [G: U.S.]

Glassberg, Andrew D. Urban Management under Fiscal Stringency: United States and Britain. In *Newton, K., ed.*, 1981, pp. 179–99. [G: U.S.; U.K.]

Goertz, Margaret. School Finance Reform and the Cities. In *Jordan, K. F. and Cambron-McCabe, N. H., eds.*, 1981, pp. 113–42. [G: U.S.]

Gramlich, Edward M. and Ysander, Bengt-Christer. Relief Work and Grant Displacement in Sweden. In *Eliasson, G.; Holmlund, B. and Stafford, F. P., eds.*, 1981, pp. 139–66. [G: Sweden]

Greenwood, Royston. Fiscal Pressure and Local Government in England and Wales. In *Hood, C. and Wright, M., eds.*, 1981, pp. 77–99. [G: U.K.]

Greytak, David and Shepard, Donald. Tax Limits and Local Expenditure Levels. In *Burchell, R. W. and Listokin, D., eds.*, 1981, pp. 333–50. [G: U.S.]

Hansen, Tore. Transforming Needs into Expenditure Decisions. In *Newton, K., ed.*, 1981, pp. 27–47. [G: Norway]

Hodge, Michael V. Improving Finance and Governance of Education for Special Populations. In *Jordan, K. F. and Cambron-McCabe, N. H., eds.*, 1981, pp. 3–38. [G: U.S.]

Hoffman, Beatrice. Proposition 13 and the San Francisco Criminal Justice System—First Reactions to a Disaster. In *Wright, K. N., ed.*, 1981, pp. 147–71. [G: U.S.]

Huckins, Larry E. and Tolley, George S. Investments in Local Infrastructure. In *Clark, T. N., ed.*, 1981, pp. 123–31. [G: U.S.]

Jackman, Richard and Papadachi, John. Local Authority Education Expenditure in England and Wales: Why Standards Differ and the Impact of Government Grants. *Public Choice*, 1981, 36(3), pp. 425–39. [G: U.K.]

Johns, Roe L. Perspectives in State School Support Programs: Introduction. In *Jordan, K. F. and Cambron-McCabe, N. H., eds.*, 1981, pp. xvii–xxvii. [G: U.S.]

Kiefer, David. The Dynamic Behavior of Public Budgets: An Empirical Study of Australian Local Governments. *Rev. Econ. Statist.*, August 1981, 63(3), pp. 422–29. [G: Australia]

Kuhnle, Stein. Economics, Politics, and Policy in Norwegian Urban Communes. In *Newton, K., ed.*, 1981, pp. 63–81. [G: Norway]

Ladd, Helen F. Municipal Expenditures and the Rate of Population Change. In *Burchell, R. W. and Listokin, D., eds.*, 1981, pp. 351–67. [G: U.S.]

Lauth, Thomas P. Zero-Base Budgeting in Georgia State Government: Myth and Reality. In *Lynch, T. D., ed.*, 1981, 1979, pp. 87–106. [G: U.S.]

Lee, Robert D., Jr. Centralization/Decentralization in State Government Budgeting. *Public Budg. Fi-*

nance, Winter 1981, 1(4), pp. 76–79. [G: U.S.]

Levine, Charles H. and Posner, Paul L. The Centralizing Effects of Austerity on the Intergovernmental System. *Polit. Sci. Quart.*, Spring 1981, 96(1), pp. 67–85. [G: U.S.]

Link, Charles R.; Lewis, Kenneth A. and Black, David E. New Evidence on the Achievement of Wealth Neutrality in School Finance. *J. Human Res.*, Spring 1981, 16(2), pp. 260–73. [G: U.S.]

Linn, Johannes F. Urban Finances in Developing Countries. In *Bahl, R., ed.*, 1981, pp. 245–83. [G: LDCs]

Martin, George T., Jr. Social Welfare Trends in the United States. In *Martin, G. T., Jr., and Zald, M. N., eds.*, 1981, pp. 505–12. [G: U.S.]

Massey, Jane and Straussman, Jeffrey D. Budget Control Is Alive and Well: Case Study of a County Government. *Public Budg. Finance*, Winter 1981, 1(4), pp. 3–11. [G: U.S.]

Matz, Deborah. The Tax and Expenditure Limitation Movement. In *Bahl, R., ed.*, 1981, pp. 127–53. [G: U.S.]

McCaffery, Jerry. The Transformation of Zero Based Budgeting: Program Level Budgeting in Oregon. *Public Budg. Finance*, Winter 1981, 1(4), pp. 48–55. [G: U.S.]

McMillan, Melville L.; Wilson, W. Robert and Arthur, Louise M. The Publicness of Local Public Goods: Evidence from Ontario Municipalities. *Can. J. Econ.*, November 1981, 14(4), pp. 596–608. [G: Canada]

Mehay, Stephen L. The Expenditure Effects of Municipal Annexation. *Public Choice*, 1981, 36(1), pp. 53–62. [G: U.S.]

Midwinter, Arthur and Page, Edward C. Cutting Local Spending—The Scottish Experience, 1976–80. In *Hood, C. and Wright, M., eds.*, 1981, pp. 56–76. [G: U.K.]

Miller, Howard F. A Public Accounting: Behind the State Budget. *Public Budg. Finance*, Winter 1981, 1(4), pp. 68–75. [G: U.S.]

Mogull, Robert G. Jurisdictional Spending for Public Welfare. *J. Reg. Sci.*, August 1981, 21(3), pp. 403–10. [G: U.S.]

Muller, Thomas. Changing Expenditures and Service Demand Patterns of Stressed Cities. In *Burchell, R. W. and Listokin, D., eds.*, 1981, pp. 277–99. [G: U.S.]

Newton, Ken. Central Places and Urban Services. In *Newton, K., ed.*, 1981, pp. 117–33. [G: U.K.]

Petersen, John E. Tax and Expenditure Limitations: Projecting Their Impact on Big City Finances. In *Kaufman, G. G. and Rosen, K. T., eds.*, 1981, pp. 171–201. [G: U.S.]

Peterson, George E. Transmitting the Municipal Fiscal Squeeze to a New Generation of Taxpayers: Pension Obligations and Capital Investment Needs. In *Burchell, R. W. and Listokin, D., eds.*, 1981, pp. 249–76. [G: U.S.]

Pjerrou-Desrochers, Lindsay. Fiscal Role and Partisanship in California's Budgetary Process, 1962–1976. *Public Budg. Finance*, Autumn 1981, 1(3), pp. 3–15. [G: U.S.]

Roessner, J. David. The Local Government Market as a Stimulus to Industrial Innovation. In *Doctors,*

S. I., ed., 1981, pp. 193–216.   [G: U.S.]

Sacks, Seymour; Palumbo, George and Ross, Robert. The Determinants of Expenditures: A New Approach to the Role of Intergovernmental Grants. In *Burchell, R. W. and Listokin, D., eds.*, 1981, pp. 369–85.   [G: U.S.]

Sebold, Frederick D. and Dato, William. School Funding and Student Achievement: An Empirical Analysis. *Public Finance Quart.*, January 1981, 9(1), pp. 91–105.   [G: U.S.]

Shannon, John. The Slowdown in the Growth of State–Local Spending: Will It Last? In *Walzer, N. and Chicoine, D. L., eds.*, 1981, pp. 223–45.   [G: U.S.]

Sharpe, L. J. Does Politics Matter? An Interim Summary with Findings. In *Newton, K., ed.*, 1981, pp. 1–26.   [G: U.K.]

Silverman, Eli B. New York City's New Integrated Financial System. In *Lynch, T. D., ed.*, 1981, pp. 165–77.   [G: U.S.]

Skovsgaard, Carl-Johan. Party Influence on Local Spending in Denmark. In *Newton, K., ed.*, 1981, pp. 48–62.   [G: Denmark]

Toma, Eugenia Froedge. Bureaucratic Structures and Educational Spending. *Southern Econ. J.*, January 1981, 47(3), pp. 640–54.   [G: U.S.]

Van Horne, James C. Cast Management. In *Aronson, J. R. and Schwartz, E., eds.*, 1981, pp. 328–45.

Veillette, Paul T. A Public Accounting: Reflections on State Budgeting. *Public Budg. Finance*, Autumn 1981, 1(3), pp. 62–68.   [G: U.S.]

Verry, Donald W. Comments on R. Jackman and J. Papadachi [Local Authority Education Expenditure in England and Wales: Why Standards Differ and the Impact of Government Grants]. *Public Choice*, 1981, 36(3), pp. 443–45.   [G: U.K.]

Walker, Warren E., et al. The Impact of Proposition 13 on Local Criminal Justice Agencies: Emerging Patterns. In *Wright, K. N., ed.*, 1981, pp. 173–227.   [G: U.S.]

Wallin, Bruce. Tax and Expenditure Limitations: Projecting Their Impact on Big City Finances: Comment. In *Kaufman, G. G. and Rosen, K. T., eds.*, 1981, pp. 202–05.   [G: U.S.]

Wanamaker, Daniel K. ZBB is Light-Years Away from Rural America. In *Lynch, T. D., ed.*, 1981, pp. 107–12.   [G: U.S.]

Welch, W. P. Estimating School District Expenditure Functions under Conditions of Closed-End Matching Aid. *J. Urban Econ.*, July 1981, 10(1), pp. 61–75.   [G: U.S.]

Wilkerson, William R. State Participation in Financing School Facilities. In *Jordan, K. F. and Cambron-McCabe, N. H., eds.*, 1981, pp. 191–213.   [G: U.S.]

Windham, Douglas M. Comments on R. Jackman and J. Papadachi [Local Authority Education Expenditure in England and Wales: Why Standards Differ and the Impact of Government Grants]. *Public Choice*, 1981, 36(3), pp. 441–42.   [G: U.K.]

Ysander, Bengt-Christer. Local Government and Economic Growth. In *Industrial Inst. for Econ. and Soc. Research*, 1981, pp. 47–53.   [G: Sweden]

3242 State and Local Government Taxation, Subsidies, and Revenue

Adams, E. Kathleen and Odden, Allan. Alternative Wealth Measures. In *Jordan, K. F. and Cambron-McCabe, N. H., eds.*, 1981, pp. 143–65.

Arnott, Richard J. and Grieson, Ronald E. Optimal Fiscal Policy for a State or Local Government. *J. Urban Econ.*, January 1981, 9(1), pp. 23–48.

Bahl, Roy W. and Schroeder, Larry D. Fiscal Adjustments in Declining States. In *Burchell, R. W. and Listokin, D., eds.*, 1981, pp. 301–29.   [G: U.S.]

Balderston, Frederick. Proposition 13, Property Transfers, and the Real Estate Markets. In *Kaufman, G. G. and Rosen, K. T., eds.*, 1981, pp. 65–103.   [G: U.S.]

Beaton, W. Patrick. Regional Tax Base Sharing: Problems in the Distribution Function. In *Burchell, R. W. and Listokin, D., eds.*, 1981, pp. 501–26.   [G: U.S.]

Beebe, Jack H. California Bonds after Proposition 13. In *Kaufman, G. G. and Rosen, K. T., eds.*, 1981, pp. 135–63.   [G: U.S.]

Beebe, Jack H. From 13 to 4 and beyond: The Political Meaning of the Ongoing Tax Revolt in California: Comment. In *Kaufman, G. G. and Rosen, K. T., eds.*, 1981, pp. 27–30.   [G: U.S.]

Berne, Robert and Stiefel, Leanna. Measuring the Equity of School Finance Policies: A Conceptual and Empirical Analysis. *Policy Anal.*, Winter 1981, 7(1), pp. 47–69.   [G: U.S.]

Bjornstad, David J. Compensation Policy for Tax Exempt Property in Theory and Practice: Comment. *Land Econ.*, November 1981, 57(4), pp. 660.   [G: U.S.]

Blake, Daniel R. Property Tax Incidence: Reply [Property Tax Incidence: An Alternative View]. *Land Econ.*, August 1981, 57(3), pp. 473–75.

Bondonio, Piervincenzo. Broad-Based Sales Taxes versus Excise Taxes in Industrialized Countries: Trends and Issues. In *Roskamp, K. W. and Forte, F., eds.*, 1981, pp. 251–67.   [G: OECD]

Brazer, Harvey E. On Tax Limitation. In *Walzer, N. and Chicoine, D. L., eds.*, 1981, pp. 19–34.   [G: U.S.]

Brueckner, Jan K. Labor Mobility and the Incidence of the Residential Property Tax. *J. Urban Econ.*, September 1981, 10(2), pp. 173–82.

Calmus, Thomas W. Measuring the Regressivity of Gambling Taxes. *Nat. Tax J.*, June 1981, 34(2), pp. 267–70.   [G: U.S.]

Carlton, Dennis W. The Spatial Effects of a Tax on Housing and Land. *Reg. Sci. Urban Econ.*, November 1981, 11(4), pp. 509–27.

Cebula, Richard J. A Note on the Determinants of AFDC Policies [State Tax Structure and the Supply of AFDC Assistance]. *Public Choice*, 1981, 37(2), pp. 327–30.   [G: U.S.]

Citrin, Jack and Levy, Frank. From 13 to 4 and beyond: The Political Meaning of the Ongoing Tax Revolt in California. In *Kaufman, G. G. and Rosen, K. T., eds.*, 1981, pp. 1–26.   [G: U.S.]

Cnossen, Sijbren. Specific Issues in Excise Taxation: The Alcohol Problem. In *Roskamp, K. W. and Forte, F., eds.*, 1981, pp. 269–86.   [G: OECD]

Cochran, Tom and Prestidge, J. R. Growing Disparity among States in Revenues from Nonrenewable Energy Sources. In *Walzer, N. and Chicoine, D. L., eds.,* 1981, pp. 247–62. [G: U.S.]

Costa, Alan S. California Bonds after Proposition 13: Comment. In *Kaufman, G. G. and Rosen, K. T., eds.,* 1981, pp. 167–69. [G: U.S.]

Courant, Paul N. and Rubinfeld, Daniel L. On the Welfare Effects of Tax Limitation. *J. Public Econ.,* December 1981, *16*(3), pp. 289–316.

David, Martin. The Use of Attitude Surveys in Determining Tax Policy. In *Roskamp, K. W. and Forte, F., eds.,* 1981, pp. 209–34. [G: U.S.]

Davis, Charles J. and Covaleski, Mark A. Alternative Capital Reimbursement Policies for Wisconsin Nursing Homes. *Inquiry,* Summer 1981, *18*(2), pp. 165–78. [G: U.S.]

Dorf, Ronald J.; Jorgens, Thomas P. and Rose, Gordon D. Local Allocations of Payments in Lieu of Taxes and Indirect State Aids: Their Contribution to Creating Negative Fiscal Impacts Attributed to Federal and State Wildlife Lands. *Reg. Sci. Persp.,* 1981, *11*(1), pp. 83–93. [G: U.S.]

Doud, Arthur A. and Summers, Anita A. Inflation and the Philadelphia Economy. *Ann. Amer. Acad. Polit. Soc. Sci.,* July 1981, *456,* pp. 13–31. [G: U.S.]

Downing, Paul B. and DiLorenzo, Thomas J. User Charges and Special Districts. In *Aronson, J. R. and Schwartz, E., eds.,* 1981, pp. 184–210. [G: U.S.]

Duncombe, Sydney and Lynch, Thomas D. Taxpayer Revolt. In *Lynch, T. D., ed.,* 1981, pp. 193–212. [G: U.S.]

Dunford, Richard W. and Marousek, Douglas C. Sub-County Property Tax Shifts Attributable to Use-Value Assessments on Farmland. *Land Econ.,* May 1981, *57*(2), pp. 221–29. [G: U.S.]

Dusansky, Richard; Ingber, Melvin and Karatjas, Nicholas. The Impact of Property Taxation on Housing Values and Rents. *J. Urban Econ.,* September 1981, *10*(2), pp. 240–55. [G: U.S.]

Edelstein, Robert H. Regressivity and the Inequity of the Residential Property Tax: The Philadelphia Story. In *Henderson, J. V., ed.,* 1981, pp. 219–47. [G: U.S.]

Edelstein, Robert H. The Impact of Proposition 13 Property Tax Reductions: A Theoretical Note. In *Kaufman, G. G. and Rosen, K. T., eds.,* 1981, pp. 207–14. [G: U.S.]

Fisher, Glenn W. The Changing Role of Property Taxation. In *Walzer, N. and Chicoine, D. L., eds.,* 1981, pp. 37–60. [G: U.S.]

Fisher, Glenn W. What Is the Ideal Revenue Balance?—A Political View. In *Burchell, R. W. and Listokin, D., eds.,* 1981, pp. 439–57. [G: U.S.]

Fisher, Peter S. State Equalizing Aids and Metropolitan Tax Base Sharing: A Comparative Analysis. *Public Finance Quart.,* October 1981, *9*(4), pp. 449–70.

Forbes, Ronald W.; Frankle, Alan and Fischer, Philip. The Effects of Proposition 13 on Tax-Supported Municipal Bonds in California: A Case Study of Bond Market Efficiency. In *Kaufman, G. G. and Rosen, K. T., eds.,* 1981, pp. 117–33. [G: U.S.]

Fox, William F. An Evaluation of Metropolitan Area Tax Base Sharing: A Comment. *Nat. Tax J.,* June 1981, *34*(2), pp. 275–79. [G: U.S.]

Fox, William F. Fiscal Differentials and Industrial Location: Some Empirical Evidence. *Urban Stud.,* February 1981, *18*(1), pp. 105–11. [G: U.S.]

Frankena, Mark W. The Effects of Alternative Urban Transit Subsidy Formulas. *J. Public Econ.,* June 1981, *15*(3), pp. 337–48.

Galambos, Eva C. and Schreiber, Arthur F. The Analysis of Double Taxation. *Public Budg. Finance,* Summer 1981, *1*(2), pp. 31–40. [G: U.S.]

Gerking, Shelby D. and Mutti, John H. Possibilities for the Exportation of Production Taxes: A General Equilibrium Analysis. *J. Public Econ.,* October 1981, *16*(2), pp. 233–52.

Gold, Steven D. Homeowner Property Taxes, Inflation and Property Tax Relief. *Nat. Tax J.,* June 1981, *34*(2), pp. 167–84. [G: U.S.]

Gold, Steven D. Property Tax Relief Trends in the Midwest: Where It All (or Much of It) Began. In *Walzer, N. and Chicoine, D. L., eds.,* 1981, pp. 61–87. [G: U.S.]

Greenwood, Royston. Fiscal Pressure and Local Government in England and Wales. In *Hood, C. and Wright, M., eds.,* 1981, pp. 77–99. [G: U.K.]

Greytak, David and Shepard, Donald. Tax Limits and Local Expenditure Levels. In *Burchell, R. W. and Listokin, D., eds.,* 1981, pp. 333–50. [G: U.S.]

Grosskopf, Shawna. The Revenue Potential of a Site Value Tax: Extension and Update of a General Equilibrium Model with Recent Empirical Estimates of Several Key Parameters. *Amer. J. Econ. Soc.,* April 1981, *40*(2), pp. 207–15.

Gustafsson, Siv. Comments on S. C. Nelson and D. W. Breneman [An Equity Perspective on Community College Finance]. *Public Choice,* 1981, *36*(3), pp. 533–34. [G: U.S.]

Guthrie, Robert S. Taxing Horse Race Gambling: The Revenue Potential. *Public Finance Quart.,* January 1981, *9*(1), pp. 79–90.

Hare, Paul G. and Ulph, David T. Imperfect Capital Markets and the Public Provision of Education. *Public Choice,* 1981, *36*(3), pp. 481–507.

Haurin, Donald R. Local Income Taxation in an Urban Area. *J. Urban Econ.,* November 1981, *10*(3), pp. 323–37.

Haurin, Donald R. Property Taxation and the Structure of Urban Areas. In *Henderson, J. V., ed.,* 1981, pp. 263–76.

Henszey, Benjamin N. and Roadarmel, Richard L. A Comparative Analysis of State Individual Income Tax Enforcement Procedures. *Nat. Tax J.,* June 1981, *34*(2), pp. 207–16. [G: U.S.]

Hirsch, Werner Z. The Post-Proposition 13 Environment in California and Its Consequences for Education. *Public Choice,* 1981, *36*(3), pp. 413–23. [G: U.S.]

Hoffman, Beatrice. Proposition 13 and the San Francisco Criminal Justice System—First Reactions to a Disaster. In *Wright, K. N., ed.,* 1981, pp. 147–71. [G: U.S.]

Howard, Thomas P. and Johnson, Douglas A. Municipal Financial Reports for the 1980s. *Public Budg. Finance*, Winter 1981, *1*(4), pp. 80–84. [G: U.S.]

Hushak, Leroy J. Property Tax Incidence: Comment [Property Tax Incidence: An Alternative View]. *Land Econ.*, August 1981, *57*(3), pp. 471–72.

Jacobs, Susan S. and Wasylenko, Michael. Government Policy to Stimulate Economic Development: Enterprise Zones. In *Walzer, N. and Chicoine, D. L., eds.*, 1981, pp. 175–201. [G: U.S.; U.K.]

Jonish, James and Olson, Dennis. Taxation of Electricity Generation in New Mexico—Some Remaining Issues. *Natural Res. J.*, April 1981, *21*(2), pp. xi–xvi.

Kaufman, George G. Inflation, Proposition 13 Fever, and Suggested Relief. In *Kaufman, G. G. and Rosen, K. T., eds.*, 1981, pp. 215–21. [G: U.S.]

Keevey, Richard F. State Fiscal Changes: The Long Road from Planning to Implementation. *Public Budg. Finance*, Winter 1981, *1*(4), pp. 27–36. [G: U.S.]

Linn, Johannes F. Urban Finances in Developing Countries. In *Bahl, R., ed.*, 1981, pp. 245–83. [G: LDCs]

Longo, Carlos A. A Note on Local Tax Revenues: The Case of Brazilian Municipalities. *Public Finance Quart.*, July 1981, *9*(3), pp. 343–52. [G: Brazil]

Lotz, Joergen R. Local Government Taxation: Recent Trends and Issues. In *Roskamp, K. W. and Forte, F., eds.*, 1981, pp. 235–49. [G: OECD]

Lowery, David and Sigelman, Lee. Understanding the Tax Revolt: Eight Explanations. *Amer. Polit. Sci. Rev.*, December 1981, *75*(4), pp. 963–74. [G: U.S.]

Lyall, Katharine C. Regional Tax Base Sharing—Nature and Potential for Success. In *Burchell, R. W. and Listokin, D., eds.*, 1981, pp. 493–500. [G: U.S.]

Manuel, David P. Coastal State Taxation of OCS-Produced Natural Gas. *Natural Res. J.*, January 1981, *21*(1), pp. 93–105. [G: U.S.]

Matz, Deborah. The Tax and Expenditure Limitation Movement. In *Bahl, R., ed.*, 1981, pp. 127–53. [G: U.S.]

McEachern, William A. Tax-Exempt Property, Tax Capitalization, and the Cumulative-Urban-Decay Hypothesis. *Nat. Tax J.*, June 1981, *34*(2), pp. 185–92.

McHugh, Richard. Income Tax Indexation in the States: A Quantitative Appraisal of Partial Indexation. *Nat. Tax J.*, June 1981, *34*(2), pp. 193–206. [G: U.S.]

McLure, Charles E., Jr. Integration of the State Income Taxes: Economic and Administrative Factors. *Nat. Tax J.*, March 1981, *34*(1), pp. 75–94. [G: U.S.]

McLure, Charles E., Jr. Market Dominance and the Exporting of State Taxes. *Nat. Tax J.*, December 1981, *34*(4), pp. 483–85.

McLure, Charles E., Jr. The Elusive Incidence of the Corporate Income Tax: The State Case. *Public Finance Quart.*, October 1981, *9*(4), pp. 395–413.

Mikesell, John L. The Structure of State Revenue Administration. *Nat. Tax J.*, June 1981, *34*(2), pp. 217–34. [G: U.S.]

Mills, David E. The Non-Neutrality of Land Value Taxation. *Nat. Tax J.*, March 1981, *34*(1), pp. 125–29.

Mirrlees, J. A. Comments on P. G. Hare and D. T. Ulph [Imperfect Capital Markets and the Public Provision of Education]. *Public Choice*, 1981, *36*(3), pp. 511–13.

Moak, Lennox L. The Revenue Source with Vitality—A New Look at Some Ancient Concepts—Non-tax Revenues. In *Burchell, R. W. and Listokin, D., eds.*, 1981, pp. 475–92. [G: U.S.]

Morgan, James N.; Ponza, Michael and Imbruglia, Renata. Trends in Residential Property Taxes. In *Hill, M. S.; Hill, D. H. and Morgan, J. N., eds.*, 1981, pp. 391–403. [G: U.S.]

Morgan, William E. and Mutti, John H. Shifting, Incidence, and Inter-State Exportation of Production Taxes on Energy Resources. *Land Econ.*, August 1981, *57*(3), pp. 422–35. [G: U.S.]

Muller, Thomas. Changing Expenditures and Service Demand Patterns of Stressed Cities. In *Burchell, R. W. and Listokin, D., eds.*, 1981, pp. 277–99. [G: U.S.]

Nelson, Susan C. and Breneman, David W. An Equity Perspective on Community College Finance. *Public Choice*, 1981, *36*(3), pp. 515–32. [G: U.S.]

Netzer, Dick. The Property Tax in the New Environment. In *Burchell, R. W. and Listokin, D., eds.*, 1981, pp. 459–73. [G: U.S.]

Noguchi, Yukio. Economic Effects of Taxes on Land. (In Japanese. With English summary.) *Econ. Stud. Quart.*, December 1981, *32*(3), pp. 193–200.

Noragon, Jack L. Political Finance and Political Reform: The Experience with State Income Tax Checkoffs. *Amer. Polit. Sci. Rev.*, September 1981, *75*(3), pp. 667–87.

Oakland, William H. Proposition 13: Genesis and Consequences. In *Kaufman, G. G. and Rosen, K. T., eds.*, 1981, *1979*, pp. 31–63. [G: U.S.]

Olson, Irene F. State Tax Incentives for Solar Energy. *J. Energy Devel.*, Spring 1981, *6*(2), pp. 281–96. [G: U.S.]

Peston, Maurice H. The Finance of Recurrent Education: Some Theoretical Considerations. *Public Choice*, 1981, *36*(3), pp. 537–50.

Petersen, John E. Tax and Expenditure Limitations: Projecting Their Impact on Big City Finances. In *Kaufman, G. G. and Rosen, K. T., eds.*, 1981, pp. 171–201. [G: U.S.]

Pissarides, Christopher A. Comments on P. G. Hare and D. T. Ulph [Imperfect Capital Markets and the Public Provision of Education]. *Public Choice*, 1981, *36*(3), pp. 509–10.

Prud'homme, Rémy. Les fonctions de la fiscalité dans la planification des villes. (With English summary.) In *Roskamp, K. W. and Forte, F., eds.*, 1981, pp. 365–80. [G: France]

Raimondo, Henry J. Compensation Policy for Tax Exempt Property in Theory and Practice: Reply. *Land Econ.*, November 1981, *57*(4), pp. 661. [G: U.S.]

Raphaelson, Arnold H. The Property Tax. **In** *Aronson, J. R. and Schwartz, E., eds.*, 1981, pp. 123–51. [G: U.S.]

Redmond, James C. The Unitary System of Taxation: Identification of the Source of Income. *Bull. Int. Fiscal Doc.*, March 1981, 35(3), pp. 99–107. [G: U.S.]

Reinhard, Raymond M. Estimating Property Tax Capitalization: A Further Comment. *J. Polit. Econ.*, December 1981, 89(6), pp. 1251–60. [G: U.S.]

Reschovsky, Andrew. An Evaluation of Metropolitan Area Tax Base Sharing: Reply. *Nat. Tax J.*, June 1981, 34(2), pp. 281–82. [G: U.S.]

Rodgers, James D. Sales Taxes, Income Taxes, and Other Revenues. **In** *Aronson, J. R. and Schwartz, E., eds.*, 1981, pp. 152–83. [G: U.S.]

Samprone, Joseph C., Jr. and Savoian, Roy. Gasoline Conservation and Motor Fuel Taxation Policy: The Dilemma for State Government Financing. *J. Energy Devel.*, Spring 1981, 6(2), pp. 251–62. [G: U.S.]

Schroeder, Larry. Property Tax Equalization Rates: Implications of Their Use in Tax Inequality Cases in the City of New York. *Amer. J. Econ. Soc.*, January 1981, 40(1), pp. 79–95. [G: U.S.]

Shannon, John. The Slowdown in the Growth of State–Local Spending: Will It Last? **In** *Walzer, N. and Chicoine, D. L., eds.*, 1981, pp. 223–45. [G: U.S.]

Sjogren, Jane. Municipal Overburden and State Aid for Education. **In** *Jordan, K. F. and Cambron-McCabe, N. H., eds.*, 1981, pp. 87–111. [G: U.S.]

Sjoquist, David L. A Median Voter Analysis of Variations in the Use of Property Taxes among Local Governments. *Public Choice*, 1981, 36(2), pp. 273–85. [G: U.S.]

Sliger, Bernard F. and Tuckman, Barbara H. Local Government Revenues. **In** *Aronson, J. R. and Schwartz, E., eds.*, 1981, pp. 44–65. [G: U.S.]

Spain, Catherine L. and Wooldridge, Blue. Financing Local Government in the 1980s: Expansion through Diversification. **In** *Walzer, N. and Chicoine, D. L., eds.*, 1981, pp. 109–28. [G: U.S.]

Swales, J. K. The Employment Effects of a Regional Capital Subsidy. *Reg. Stud.*, 1981, 15(4), pp. 263–73.

Talley, Wayne K. and Warner, Stanley E., Jr. Energy Legislation and Gasoline Tax Revenue. *Public Finance Quart.*, January 1981, 9(1), pp. 35–46. [G: U.S.]

Tattersall, James N. California Bonds after Proposition 13: Comment. **In** *Kaufman, G. G. and Rosen, K. T., eds.*, 1981, pp. 164–66. [G: U.S.]

Thomas, Ann R. Fiscal Limitations and Municipal Debt: The Extreme Case of Proposition 13. **In** *Kaufman, G. G. and Rosen, K. T., eds.*, 1981, pp. 105–16. [G: U.S.]

Walker, Warren E., et al. The Impact of Proposition 13 on Local Criminal Justice Agencies: Emerging Patterns. **In** *Wright, K. N., ed.*, 1981, pp. 173–227. [G: U.S.]

Wallin, Bruce. Tax and Expenditure Limitations: Projecting Their Impact on Big City Finances: Comment. **In** *Kaufman, G. G. and Rosen, K. T.,*

eds., 1981, pp. 202–05. [G: U.S.]

Wasylenko, Michael. The Location of Firms: The Role of Taxes and Fiscal Incentives. **In** *Bahl, R., ed.*, 1981, pp. 155–90. [G: U.S.]

Wentzler, Nancy. Locational Variations in the Public School Teacher Supply Price. *Public Finance Quart.*, October 1981, 9(4), pp. 431–48. [G: U.S.]

Willis, Mark A. Leasing—A Financial Option for States and Localities? *Fed. Res. Bank New York Quart. Rev.*, Winter 1981–82, 6(4), pp. 42–46. [G: U.S.]

Zee, Howell H. Local Income Taxation and Optimal Jurisdiction. *Public Finance*, 1981, 36(2), pp. 267–79.

3243 State and Local Government Borrowing

Asefa, Sally A.; Adams, Roy D. and Starleaf, Dennis R. Municipal Borrowing: Some Empirical Results. *Public Finance Quart.*, July 1981, 9(3), pp. 271–80. [G: U.S.]

Beebe, Jack H. California Bonds after Proposition 13. **In** *Kaufman, G. G. and Rosen, K. T., eds.*, 1981, pp. 135–63. [G: U.S.]

Cole, Charles W. and Officer, Dennis T. The Interest Cost Effect of Private Municipal Bond Insurance. *J. Risk Ins.*, September 1981, 48(3), pp. 435–49. [G: U.S.]

Costa, Alan S. California Bonds after Proposition 13: Comment. **In** *Kaufman, G. G. and Rosen, K. T., eds.*, 1981, pp. 167–69. [G: U.S.]

Craig, Eleanor D. Impact of Federal Policies on Municipal Bond Financing. *Nat. Tax J.*, September 1981, 34(3), pp. 389–94. [G: U.S.]

Dyl, Edward A. Optimal Short-Term Financial Policies for Municipalities. *Rev. Bus. Econ. Res.*, Fall 1981, 17(1), pp. 78–83. [G: U.S.]

Forbes, Ronald W. State and Local Debt. **In** *Altman, E. I., ed.*, 1981, pp. 3.3–30. [G: U.S.]

Forbes, Ronald W.; Frankle, Alan and Fischer, Philip. The Effects of Proposition 13 on Tax-Supported Municipal Bonds in California: A Case Study of Bond Market Efficiency. **In** *Kaufman, G. G. and Rosen, K. T., eds.*, 1981, pp. 117–33. [G: U.S.]

Kaufman, George G. Debt Management. **In** *Aronson, J. R. and Schwartz, E., eds.*, 1981, pp. 302–27. [G: U.S.]

Kraft, John L. Local Public Policy and Tax-Exempt Financing: Is Local Initiative Preempted by Federal Control? *Nat. Tax J.*, September 1981, 34(3), pp. 373–81. [G: U.S.]

Petersen, John E. Big City Borrowing Costs and Credit Quality. **In** *Burchell, R. W. and Listokin, D., eds.*, 1981, pp. 231–48. [G: U.S.]

Petersen, John E. The Municipal Bond Market: Recent Changes and Future Prospects. **In** *Walzer, N. and Chicoine, D. L., eds.*, 1981, pp. 129–41. [G: U.S.]

Raman, K. K. Financial Reporting and Municipal Bond Rating Changes. *Accounting Rev.*, October 1981, 56(4), pp. 910–26. [G: U.S.]

Sbragia, Alberta. Cities, Capital, and Banks: The Politics of Debt in the United States, United Kingdom, and France. **In** *Newton, K., ed.*, 1981, pp. 200–220.   [G: U.S.; U.K.; France]

Tattersall, James N. California Bonds after Proposition 13: Comment. In *Kaufman, G. G. and Rosen, K. T., eds.*, 1981, pp. 164–66.   [G: U.S.]

Thomas, Ann R. Fiscal Limitations and Municipal Debt: The Extreme Case of Proposition 13. In *Kaufman, G. G. and Rosen, K. T., eds.*, 1981, pp. 105–16.   [G: U.S.]

325 Intergovernmental Financial Relationships

3250 Intergovernmental Financial Relationships

Alexander, James R. Policy Design and the Impact of Federal Aid to Declining Communities. *Growth Change*, January 1981, *12*(1), pp. 35–41.   [G: U.S.]

Anton, Thomas J.; Cawley, Jerry P. and Kramer, Kevin L. Federal Spending in States and Regions: Patterns of Stability and Change. In *Burchell, R. W. and Listokin, D., eds.*, 1981, pp. 577–616.   [G: U.S.]

Ault, Thomas A. Federal–State Relations and Income Support Policy. In *Brown, P. G.; Johnson, C. and Vernier, P., eds.*, 1981, pp. 57–80.   [G: U.S.]

Bahl, Roy W. The Next Decade in State and Local Government Finance: A Period of Adjustment. In *Bahl, R., ed.*, 1981, pp. 191–220.   [G: U.S.]

Beaton, W. Patrick. Regional Tax Base Sharing: Problems in the Distribution Function. In *Burchell, R. W. and Listokin, D., eds.*, 1981, pp. 501–26.   [G: U.S.]

Beck, John H. Budget-Maximizing Bureaucracy and the Effects of State Aid on School Expenditures. *Public Finance Quart.*, April 1981, *9*(2), pp. 159–82.   [G: U.S.]

Bjornstad, David J. Compensation Policy for Tax Exempt Property in Theory and Practice: Comment. *Land Econ.*, November 1981, *57*(4), pp. 660.   [G: U.S.]

Brennen, Steven R. Reforming the Federal Grant-in-Aid System for States and Localities: Response to Dr. Richard Nathan's Paper. *Nat. Tax J.*, September 1981, *34*(3), pp. 339–40.   [G: U.S.]

Burchell, Robert W. and Listokin, David. The Fiscal Impact of Economic-Development Programs: Case Studies of the Local Cost–Revenue Implications of HUD, EDA AND FmHA Projects. In *Sternlieb, G. and Listokin, D., eds.*, 1981, pp. 163–229.   [G: U.S.]

Burchell, Robert W., et al. Measuring Urban Distress: A Summary of the Major Urban Hardship Indices and Resource Allocation Systems. In *Burchell, R. W. and Listokin, D., eds.*, 1981, pp. 159–229.   [G: U.S.]

Carleson, Robert B. Changes Affecting State and Local Grants. *Nat. Tax J.*, September 1981, *34*(3), pp. 289–92.   [G: U.S.]

Chan, Arthur H. The Structure of Federal Water Resources Policy Making. *Amer. J. Econ. Soc.*, April 1981, *40*(2), pp. 115–27.   [G: U.S.]

Chang, Cyril F. Different Forms of Outside Aid: A Collective-Choice Model for Predicting Effects on Local Educational Expenditure. *Public Finance Quart.*, July 1981, *9*(3), pp. 321–41.   [G: U.S.]

Chernick, Howard A. Price Discrimination and Federal Project Grants. *Public Finance Quart.*, October 1981, *9*(4), pp. 371–94.   [G: U.S.]

Choate, Pat. Public Institutions and the Planning Process. In *Hawley, A. H. and Mazie, S. M., eds.*, 1981, pp. 767–805.   [G: U.S.]

Chubb, Judith. The Social Bases of an Urban Political Machine: The Case of Palermo. *Polit. Sci. Quart.*, Spring 1981, *96*(1), pp. 107–25.   [G: Italy]

Connock, Stuart W. Evaluating the Federal Aid Reform Options—Sorting Out, Block Grants and Tax Turnbacks: State Reaction. *Nat. Tax J.*, September 1981, *34*(3), pp. 329–33.   [G: U.S.]

Cox, Joseph C. The Interprovincial and International Impact of Federal Grants to Provincial Governments: Evidence from the Canadian Federation. *Public Finance*, 1981, *36*(2), pp. 214–28.   [G: Canada]

Dean, James M. The Appropriate Fiscal Transfer to the Northwest Territories: A Structure. *Can. Public Policy*, Summer 1981, *7*(3), pp. 408–17.   [G: Canada]

Deutsch, Antal. Three Fiscal Irritants in Confederation. *Can. Public Policy*, Spring 1981, *7*(2), pp. 343–47.   [G: Canada]

Dommel, Paul R. Trends in Intergovernmental Relations: Getting Less, but Enjoying It More (Maybe). In *Walzer, N. and Chicoine, D. L., eds.*, 1981, pp. 91–108.   [G: U.S.]

Dorf, Ronald J.; Jorgens, Thomas P. and Rose, Gordon D. Local Allocations of Payments in Lieu of Taxes and Indirect State Aids: Their Contribution to Creating Negative Fiscal Impacts Attributed to Federal and State Wildlife Lands. *Reg. Sci. Persp.*, 1981, *11*(1), pp. 83–93.   [G: U.S.]

Eapen, A. T. The Finance Commission and Fiscal Federalism Procedures: Its Role and Procedures. *Indian Econ. J.*, April–June 1981, *28*(4), pp. 60–69.   [G: India]

Eveland, J. D. Program Implementation: The New Focus of Federal Technology Transfer. In *Doctors, S. I., ed.*, 1981, pp. 117–29.   [G: U.S.]

Farber, Stephen B. Reforming and Cutting Back the Federal Aid System: Implications for State and Local Governments. *Nat. Tax J.*, September 1981, *34*(3), pp. 311–13.   [G: U.S.]

Farnham, Paul G. The Targeting of Federal Aid: Continued Ambivalence. *Public Policy*, Winter 1981, *29*(1), pp. 75–92.   [G: U.S.]

Feller, Irwin. The Diffusion and Utilization of Scientific and Technological Knowledge in State and Local Governments. In *Doctors, S. I., ed.*, 1981, pp. 131–49.   [G: U.S.]

Fisher, Ronald C. Expenditure Incentives of Intergovernmental Grants: Revenue Sharing and Matching Grants. In *Henderson, J. V., ed.*, 1981, pp. 201–l8.   [G: U.S.]

Foster, Edward. Competitively Awarded Government Grants. *J. Public Econ.*, February 1981, *15*(1), pp. 105–11.

Fox, William F. An Evaluation of Metropolitan Area Tax Base Sharing: A Comment. *Nat. Tax J.*, June 1981, *34*(2), pp. 275–79.   [G: U.S.]

Friedman, David D. and Kurth, Michael M. Revenue Sharing and Monopoly Government: A Com-

ment. *Public Choice*, 1981, 37(2), pp. 365–70.
[G: U.S.]

Gerra, Ralph A. The New Forms of Federal Fiscal Policies and Implications for State and Local Governments: Observations from Business. *Nat. Tax J.*, September 1981, 34(3), pp. 293–302.
[G: U.S.]

Gist, John R. and Hill, R. Carter. The Economics of Choice in the Allocation of Federal Grants: An Empirical Test. *Public Choice*, 1981, 36(1), pp. 63–73.
[G: U.S.]

Goodman, John L., Jr. Federal Funding Formulas and the 1980 Census. *Public Policy*, Spring 1981, 29(2), pp. 179–96.
[G: U.S.]

Gottschalk, Peter T. Regional Allocation of Federal Funds. *Policy Anal.*, Spring 1981, 7(2), pp. 183–97.
[G: U.S.]

Greenwood, Royston. Fiscal Pressure and Local Government in England and Wales. In *Hood, C. and Wright, M., eds.*, 1981, pp. 77–99.
[G: U.K.]

Groenewold, Nicolaas. The 'New Federalism' and Horizontal Equalization. *Econ. Rec.*, September 1981, 57(158), pp. 282–87. [G: Australia]

Gustely, Richard D. and Ballard, Kenneth P. Regional Macro-economic Impact of Federal Grants: An Empirical Analysis. In *Burchell, R. W. and Listokin, D., eds.*, 1981, pp. 665–91. [G: U.S.]

Haider, Donald H. Balancing the Federal Budget: The Intergovernmental Casualty and Opportunity. In *Walzer, N. and Chicoine, D. L., eds.*, 1981, pp. 205–22. [G: U.S.]

Haider, Donald H. The Intergovernmental System. In *Pious, R. M., ed.*, 1981, pp. 20–30.
[G: U.S.]

Helliwell, John F. and McRae, Robert N. The National Energy Conflict. *Can. Public Policy*, Winter 1981, 7(1), pp. 15–23. [G: Canada]

Hofgesang, Edward G. Reforming and Cutting Back the Federal Aid System: Implications for State and Local Governments. *Nat. Tax J.*, September 1981, 34(3), pp. 315–18. [G: U.S.]

Holcombe, Randall G. and Zardkoohi, Asghar. The Determinants of Federal Grants. *Southern Econ. J.*, October 1981, 48(2), pp. 393–99. [G: U.S.]

Huddleston, Mark W. and Palley, Marian Lief. Shortchanging Nonmetropolitan America: Small Communities and Federal Aid. *Public Budg. Finance*, Autumn 1981, 1(3), pp. 36–45. [G: U.S.]

James, Franklin J. Economic Distress in Central Cities. In *Burchell, R. W. and Listokin, D., eds.*, 1981, pp. 19–49. [G: U.S.]

Jones, James R. The New Focus of Federal Fiscal Policies and Implications for State and Local Governments: Luncheon Speech. *Nat. Tax J.*, September 1981, 34(3), pp. 307–09. [G: U.S.]

Killingsworth, Charles C. Trouble in Social Insurance. *Challenge*, July/August 1981, 24(3), pp. 50–52. [G: U.S.]

Kraft, John L. Local Public Policy and Tax-Exempt Financing: Is Local Initiative Preempted by Federal Control? *Nat. Tax J.*, September 1981, 34(3), pp. 373–81. [G: U.S.]

Levine, Charles H. and Posner, Paul L. The Centralizing Effects of Austerity on the Intergovernmental System. *Polit. Sci. Quart.*, Spring 1981,

96(1), pp. 67–85. [G: U.S.]

Levinson, Richard D. Interstate Taxation and Apportionment of Bank Income. *Nat. Tax J.*, December 1981, 34(4), pp. 447–55. [G: U.S.]

Lotz, Joergen R. Fiscal Problems and Issues in Scandinavian Cities. In *Bahl, R., ed.*, 1981, pp. 221–43. [G: Scandinavia]

Lyall, Katharine C. Regional Tax Base Sharing—Nature and Potential for Success. In *Burchell, R. W. and Listokin, D., eds.*, 1981, pp. 493–500.
[G: U.S.]

Markusen, Ann R.; Saxenian, Annalee and Weiss, Marc A. Who Benefits from Intergovernmental Transfers? In *Burchell, R. W. and Listokin, D., eds.*, 1981, pp. 617–64. [G: U.S.]

McKenzie, Richard B. and Staaf, Robert J. Revenue Sharing and Monopoly Government: A Reply. *Public Choice*, 1981, 37(2), pp. 371–74.
[G: U.S.]

McLure, Charles E., Jr. Integration of the State Income Taxes: Economic and Administrative Factors. *Nat. Tax J.*, March 1981, 34(1), pp. 75–94.
[G: U.S.]

Merget, Astrid E. The Fiscal Dependency of American Cities. *Public Budg. Finance*, Summer 1981, 1(2), pp. 20–30. [G: U.S.]

Midwinter, Arthur and Page, Edward C. Cutting Local Spending—The Scottish Experience, 1976–80. In *Hood, C. and Wright, M., eds.*, 1981, pp. 56–76. [G: U.K.]

Moody, Tom. Evaluating the Federal Aid Reform Options: Municipal Reaction. *Nat. Tax J.*, September 1981, 34(3), pp. 335–37. [G: U.S.]

Nathan, Richard P. "Reforming" the Federal Grant-in-Aid System for States and Localities. *Nat. Tax J.*, September 1981, 34(3), pp. 321–27.
[G: U.S.]

Nathan, Richard P. Federal Grants—How Are They Working? In *Burchell, R. W. and Listokin, D., eds.*, 1981, pp. 529–39. [G: U.S.]

Nathan, Richard P. Field Network Evaluation of the Reagan Domestic Program. *Public Budg. Finance*, Winter 1981, 1(4), pp. 85–89. [G: U.S.]

Oates, Wallace E. Fiscal Structure in the Federal System. In *Aronson, J. R. and Schwartz, E., eds.*, 1981, pp. 234–54. [G: U.S.]

Petersen, John E. Federal Fiscal Policy and Aid to State and Local Governments: An Age of Austerity. *Nat. Tax J.*, September 1981, 34(3), pp. 383–88. [G: U.S.]

Quindry, Kenneth E. and Schoening, Niles C. Administration, Control, and Finance: Changing Relationships in the American Federal System. *Growth Change*, October 1981, 12(4), pp. 33–42. [G: U.S.]

Raimondo, Henry J. Compensation Policy for Tax Exempt Property in Theory and Practice: Reply. *Land Econ.*, November 1981, 57(4), pp. 661.
[G: U.S.]

Reischauer, Robert. The Economy and the Federal Budget in the 1980s: Implications for the State and Local Sector. In *Bahl, R., ed.*, 1981, pp. 13–38. [G: U.S.]

Reschovsky, Andrew. An Evaluation of Metropolitan Area Tax Base Sharing: Reply. *Nat. Tax J.*, June 1981, 34(2), pp. 281–82. [G: U.S.]

Roemer, Arthur C. The New Focus of Federal Fiscal Policies and Implications for State and Local Governments—State Observations. *Nat. Tax J.*, September 1981, *34*(3), pp. 303–06. [G: U.S.]

Roessner, J. David. Federal Technology Policy: Innovation and Problem Solving in State and Local Governments. In *Doctors, S. I., ed.*, 1981, *1979*, pp. 151–68. [G: U.S.]

Sacks, Seymour; Palumbo, George and Ross, Robert. The Determinants of Expenditures: A New Approach to the Role of Intergovernmental Grants. In *Burchell, R. W. and Listokin, D., eds.*, 1981, pp. 369–85. [G: U.S.]

Schwartz, Gail Garfield. Urban Policy and the Inner Cities in the United States. In *Schwartz, G. G., ed.*, 1981, pp. 37–98. [G: U.S.]

Shannon, John. The Slowdown in the Growth of State–Local Spending: Will It Last? In *Walzer, N. and Chicoine, D. L., eds.*, 1981, pp. 223–45. [G: U.S.]

Shannon, John and Wallin, Bruce. Fiscal Imbalance within the Federal System: The Problem of Renewing Revenue Sharing. In *Burchell, R. W. and Listokin, D., eds.*, 1981, pp. 541–75. [G: U.S.]

Sharkansky, Ira. Intergovernmental Relations. In *Nystrom, P. C. and Starbuck, W. H., eds., Vol. 1*, 1981, pp. 456–70. [G: U.S.]

Stein, Robert M. The Allocation of Federal Aid Monies: The Synthesis of Demand-Side and Supply-Side Explanations. *Amer. Polit. Sci. Rev.*, June 1981, *75*(2), pp. 334–43. [G: U.S.]

Walker, Warren E., et al. The Impact of Proposition 13 on Local Criminal Justice Agencies: Emerging Patterns. In *Wright, K. N., ed.*, 1981, pp. 173–227. [G: U.S.]

Wickes, R. Paul. Reforming and Cutting Back the Federal Aid System: Implications for State and Local Governments. *Nat. Tax J.*, September 1981, *34*(3), pp. 319–20. [G: U.S.]

Wise, Arthur E. and Darling-Hammond, Linda. Educational Needs: Accounting for School Finance. In *Jordan, K. F. and Cambron-McCabe, N. H., eds.*, 1981, pp. 281–314. [G: U.S.]

Woolston, Susan W. Local Government Technology Transfer—Overview of Recent Research and Federal Programs. In *Doctors, S. I., ed.*, 1981, pp. 43–66. [G: U.S.]

Yadava, Gorelal. Industrialization of Bihar: Some Major Constraints and Possible Solutions. In *Karna, M. N., ed.*, 1981, pp. 45–56. [G: India]

400 International Economics

4000 General

Alker, Hayward R., Jr. Dialectical Foundations of Global Disparities. In *Hollist, W. L. and Rosenau, J. N., eds.*, 1981, pp. 80–109.

Amin, Samir. Some Thoughts of Self-reliant Development, Collective Self-reliance and the New International Economic Order. In *Grassman, S. and Lundberg, E., eds.*, 1981, pp. 534–52.

Anguiano, Eugenio. The People's Republic of China and the New International Economic Order: Relations with the Third World. In *Lozoya, J. A. and*

Bhattacharya, A. K., eds., 1981, pp. 53–89. [G: China; LDCs]

Arndt, Heinz W. Australia and the New International Economic Order. In *Lozoya, J. A. and Bhattacharya, A. K., eds.*, 1981, pp. 203–213. [G: Australia]

Arndt, Heinz W. Indonesia and the New International Economic Order. In *Lozoya, J. A. and Bhattacharya, A. K., eds.*, 1981, pp. 189–202. [G: Indonesia]

Arriola, Salvador. Access to Supplies and the Strategy of the Industrialized Countries. In *Lozoya, J. and Green, R., eds.*, 1981, pp. 181–98. [G: Global]

Barthwal, R. R. The New International Economic Order: Reality or Myth? *Econ. Aff.*, January–March 1981, *26*(1), pp. 9–16.

Bauer, P. T. Western Guilt and Third World Poverty. In *Novak, M. and Cooper, J. W., eds.*, 1981, pp. 104–23.

Baumol, William J. and Willig, Robert D. Intertemporal Failures of the Invisible Hand: Theory and Implications for International Market Dominance. *Indian Econ. Rev.*, January–June 1981, *16*(1 and 2), pp. 1–12.

Bergsten, C. Fred. North–South Relations: A Candid Appraisal. In *Bergsten, C. F., ed.*, 1981, pp. 115–25. [G: LDCs; U.S.]

Bertin, Gilles. Les nouvelles conditions d'analyse des relations internationales: Quelques réflexions sur trois domaines d'étude. (New Conditions of Analysis in International Economics: Some Comments on Three Fields of Study. With English summary.) *Revue Écon.*, March 1981, *32*(2), pp. 341–55.

Bettati, Mario and Timsit, Gérard. The Regional Institutional Requisites of the NIEO. In *Nicol, D.; Echeverria, L. and Peccei, A., eds.*, 1981, pp. 318–27.

Bettati, Mario and Timsit, Gérard. The Regional Institutional Requirements of the NIEO. In *Laszlo, E. and Kurtzman, J., eds.*, 1981, pp. 93–102. [G: LDCs]

Bhattacharya, A. K. and Hudson, Michael. A Regional Strategy to Finance the New International Economic Order. In *Nicol, D.; Echeverria, L. and Peccei, A., eds.*, 1981, pp. 299–317.

Bogomolov, Oleg. The CMEA Countries and the New International Economic Order. In *Saunders, C. T., ed. (I)*, 1981, pp. 246–56. [G: CMEA]

Boulding, Kenneth E. Cartels, Prices, and the Grants Economy. In *Reubens, E. P., ed.*, 1981, pp. 61–70.

Calcagno, Alfredo Eric and Martner, Gonzalo. International Trade and the NIEO. In *Lozoya, J. and Green, R., eds.*, 1981, pp. 1–53. [G: LDCs]

Cardoso, Fernando Henrique. Towards Another Development. In *Muñoz, H., ed.*, 1981, *1977*, pp. 295–313.

Castañeda, Jorge. Some Political Issues in the Negotiation of the New International Economic Order: The Resources of the Seabed. In *Laszlo, E. and Kurtzman, J., eds.*, 1981, pp. 30–65. [G: Global]

Chenery, Hollis B. Restructuring the World Economy: Round II. *Foreign Aff.*, Summer 1981, 59(5), pp. 1102–20.

Corden, W. Max. The NIEO Proposals: A Cool Look. In *Baldwin, R. E. and Richardson, J. D., eds.*, 1981, 1979, pp. 123–58.

Ehrlicher, Werner. Zukunftsprobleme unserer Wirtschaft. (Future Problems of Our Economy. With English summary.) *Kredit Kapital*, 1981, 14(1), pp. 3–25.

Estévez, Jaime and Puyana, Alicia. Regionalism, Nationalism, and the NIEO. In *Nicol, D.; Echeverria, L. and Peccei, A., eds.*, 1981, pp. 151–63.

Faaland, Just. Europe's Role in North–South Relations: The Role of the Research Community. In *Mauri, A., ed.*, 1981, pp. 21–34. **[G: Europe; LDCs]**

Fabnic, Ivo. The Developing Countries' Interest in East–West Relations. In *Saunders, C. T., ed. (I)*, 1981, pp. 66–74.

Faulwetter, Helmut. Improving the International Division of Labour: Comment. In *Saunders, C. T., ed. (I)*, 1981, pp. 309–12.

Foster, John. Energy for Development: Introduction. In *Foster, J., et al.*, 1981, pp. 1–4. **[G: Global]**

Galtung, Johan. Global Processes and the World in the 1980s. In *Hollist, W. L. and Rosenau, J. N., eds.*, 1981, pp. 110–38.

Galtung, Johan. The Politics of Self-reliance. In *Muñoz, H., ed.*, 1981, pp. 173–96.

Gordon, Lincoln. Changing Growth Patterns and World Order. In *Cleveland, H., ed.*, 1981, pp. 266–98.

Grassman, Sven and Lundberg, Erik. On the Nature of the International Economic Disorder: Introduction. In *Grassman, S. and Lundberg, E., eds.*, 1981, pp. 1–8.

Gregg, Robert. UN Decision-Making Structures and the Implementation of the NIEO. In *Laszlo, E. and Kurtzman, J., eds.*, 1981, pp. 103–32. **[G: Global]**

Guernier, Maurice. Regionalism and the New International Economic Order: Some Conclusions. In *Nicol, D.; Echeverria, L. and Peccei, A., eds.*, 1981, pp. 328–40.

ul Haq, Mahbub. Negotiating the Future. *Foreign Aff.*, Winter 1980/81, 59(2), pp. 398–417.

Hardin, Garrett. Proceedings of the Seminar on International Economic Problems: Statement. In *U.S. Congress, Joint Economic Committee (I)*, 1981, pp. 337–40.

Hardt, John P. East–West–South: Economic Interactions between Three Worlds: The Background: Interests and Prospects: Comment. In *Saunders, C. T., ed. (I)*, 1981, pp. 74–78.

Helleiner, Gerald K. International Economic Disorder and North–South Relations: An Introduction. In *Helleiner, G. K.*, pp. 1–21.

Helleiner, Gerald K. The Refsnes Seminar: Economic Theory and North-South Negotiations. *World Devel.*, June 1981, 9(6), pp. 539–55.

Hershlag, Zvi Y. Pitfalls of Development Strategy and Planning. *METU*, Special Issue, 1981, pp. 19–54. **[G: LDCs]**

Hollist, W. Ladd. Anticipating World System Theory Synthesis. In *Hollist, W. L. and Rosenau, J. N., eds.*, 1981, pp. 289–300.

Jankowitsch, Odette. A Round of Global Negotiations on International Economic Cooperation: A Preview. In *Saunders, C. T., ed. (I)*, 1981, pp. 257–64.

Jolly, Richard. Mutual Interests and the Implications for Reform of the International Economic Order. In *Grassman, S. and Lundberg, E., eds.*, 1981, pp. 558–81.

Kohlemy, Gunther. Improving the International Division of Labour: Comment. In *Saunders, C. T., ed. (I)*, 1981, pp. 333–36. **[G: E. Germany]**

Kojima, Kiyoshi. A New Capitalism for a New International Economic Order. *Hitotsubashi J. Econ.*, June 1981, 22(1), pp. 1–19.

Komiya, Ryutaro. Mutual Interests and the Implications for Reform of the International Economic Order: Comments. In *Grassman, S. and Lundberg, E., eds.*, 1981, pp. 582–86.

Kornai, János. Ethical Issues in Income Distribution: National and International: Comments. In *Grassman, S. and Lundberg, E., eds.*, 1981, pp. 495–97.

Krasner, Stephen D. Transforming International Regimes. In *Hollist, W. L. and Rosenau, J. N., eds.*, 1981, pp. 172–201.

Krishnamurti, R. UNCTAD as a Negotiating Institution. *J. World Trade Law*, January–February 1981, 15(1), pp. 3–40.

Labra, Armando, et al. Some Political Issues in the Negotiation of the New International Economic Order: The Sovereignty of States. In *Laszlo, E. and Kurtzman, J., eds.*, 1981, pp. 3–13. **[G: Global]**

Lagos, Gustavo. The Revolution of Being: A Preferred World Model. In *Muñoz, H., ed.*, 1981, pp. 123–60. **[G: Latin America]**

Leet, Mildred Robbins. Regionalism and Women. In *Nicol, D.; Echeverria, L. and Peccei, A., eds.*, 1981, pp. 200–209.

Lindbeck, Assar. Some Thoughts of Self-reliant Development, Collective Self-reliance and the New International Economic Order: Comments. In *Grassman, S. and Lundberg, E., eds.*, 1981, pp. 553–57.

Macesich, George. Improving the International Division of Labour: Comment. In *Saunders, C. T., ed. (I)*, 1981, pp. 331–32.

Moghbel, Zafar. The New International Economic Order: A Survey of Issues. *Osaka Econ. Pap.*, June 1981, 31(1), pp. 55–72.

Möller, Hans. The Reconstruction of the International Economic Order after the Second World War and the Integration of the Federal Republic of Germany into the World Economy. *Z. ges. Staatswiss.*, September 1981, 137(3), pp. 344–66. **[G: W. Germany]**

Moneta, Carlos. The Impact of Research on Policymaking. In *Laszlo, E. and Kurtzman, J., eds.*, 1981, pp. 133–72.

Panic, Mica. Evolution of the Concept of International Economic Order: Comments. In *[Cairncross, A.]*, 1981, pp. 182–87.

Paszynski, Marian. Improving the International Division of Labour: Comment. In *Saunders, C. T., ed. (I)*, 1981, pp. 326–29.

Reubens, Edwin P. An Overview of the NIEO. In *Reubens, E. P., ed.*, 1981, pp. 1–18.

Reubens, Edwin P. The Challenge of the New International Economic Order: Conclusions. In *Reubens, E. P., ed.*, 1981, pp. 281–88.

Rosenau, James N. Interpreting Aggregative Processes in the International Political Economy. In *Hollist, W. L. and Rosenau, J. N., eds.*, 1981, pp. 262–88.

Sakamoto, Masahiro. Japan and the New International Economic Order. In *Lozoya, J. A. and Bhattacharya, A. K., eds.*, 1981, pp. 12–27. [G: Japan]

Saunders, Christopher T. Joint Strategies for World Development. In *Saunders, C. T., ed. (I)*, 1981, pp. 1–17.

Saunders, Christopher T. The Political Economy of New and Old Industrial Countries: Introduction and Selective Summary. In *Saunders, C. T., ed. (II)*, 1981, pp. 1–24. [G: Global]

Sauvant, Karl P. The Role of Transitional Enterprises in the Establishment of the NIEO: A Critical View. In *Lozoya, J. and Green, R., eds.*, 1981, pp. 109–70. [G: LDCs; MDCs]

Sen, Amartya K. Ethical Issues in Income Distribution: National and International. In *Grassman, S. and Lundberg, E., eds.*, 1981, pp. 464–94.

Shalamanov, Stojan and Sivov, Wassil. Improving the International Division of Labour: Comment. In *Saunders, C. T., ed. (I)*, 1981, pp. 321–26.

Standke, Klaus-Heinrich. Appropriate Technology for the Third Development Decade. In *Reubens, E. P., ed.*, 1981, pp. 133–46.

Stoffaes, Christian. Quelques applications de la théorie des jeux aux relations économiques internationales. (A Game Theory Approach to International Economic Relations. With English summary.) *Revue Écon.*, March 1981, *32*(2), pp. 271–340.

Streeten, Paul P. Constructive Responses to the North–South Dialogue. In *Reubens, E. P., ed.*, 1981, pp. 71–89.

Streeten, Paul P. It *Is* a Moral Issue. In *Streeten, P.*, 1981, *1976*, pp. 232–36.

Streeten, Paul P. The New International Economic Order. In *Streeten, P.*, 1981, pp. 237–64.

Streeten, Paul P. The New International Economic Order: Development Strategy Options. In *Saunders, C. T., ed. (I)*, 1981, pp. 219–45.

Szentes, Tamás. The New International Economic Order: Redistribution or Restructuring? In *Saunders, C. T., ed. (I)*, 1981, pp. 303–08.

Tévoédjrè, Albert. Employment, Human Needs, and the NIEO. In *Lozoya, J. A. and Birgin, H., eds.*, 1981, pp. 1–28. [G: LDCs]

Timsit, Gérard. The Administrative Apparatus of States and the Implementation of the NIEO. In *Laszlo, E. and Kurtzman, J., eds.*, 1981, pp. 69–92. [G: LDCs]

Tinbergen, Jan. The Need for an Ambitious Innovation of the World Order. In *Muñoz, H., ed.*, 1981, *1977*, pp. 161–72.

Tumlir, Jan. Evolution of the Concept of International Economic Order. In *[Cairncross, A.]*, 1981, pp. 152–82.

Zevin, Leon. Concepts of Economic Development of the Developing Nations and Problems of Tripartite Cooperation. In *Saunders, C. T., ed. (I)*, 1981, pp. 295–302.

410 INTERNATIONAL TRADE THEORY

411 International Trade Theory

4110 General

Aizenman, Joshua. Devaluation and Liberalization in the Presence of Tariff and Quota Restrictions: An Equilibrium Model. *J. Int. Econ.*, May 1981, *11*(2), pp. 197–206.

Bhagwati, Jagdish N. and Srinivasan, T. N. The Evaluation of Projects at World Prices under Trade Distortions: Quantitative Restrictions, Monopoly Power in Trade and Nontraded Goods. *Int. Econ. Rev.*, June 1981, *22*(2), pp. 385–99.

Brecher, Richard A. and Bhagwati, Jagdish N. Foreign Ownership and the Theory of Trade and Welfare. *J. Polit. Econ.*, June 1981, *89*(3), pp. 497–511.

Mutti, John H. Regional Analysis from the Standpoint of International Trade: Is It a Useful Perspective? *Int. Reg. Sci. Rev.*, Winter 1981, *6*(2), pp. 95–120. [G: U.S.]

Samuelson, Paul A. To Protect Manufacturing? *Z. ges. Staatswiss.*, September 1981, *137*(3), pp. 407–14.

Schuh, G. Edward. Economics and International Relations: A Conceptual Framework. *Amer. J. Agr. Econ.*, December 1981, *63*(5), pp. 767–78.

Yamamoto, Shigenobu. Production Adjustment Policy and Protectionism. (In Japanese. With English summary.) *Osaka Econ. Pap.*, December 1981, *31*(2–3), pp. 40–52.

Yeh, Yeong-Her. A Note on Immiserizing Growth. *Atlantic Econ. J.*, December 1981, *9*(4), pp. 49–50.

4112 Theory of International Trade

Abraham-Frois, Gilbert. L'analyse de la spécialisation internationale dans une problématique "Post-Sraffaienne." (With English summary.) *Écon. Appl.*, 1981, *34*(2–3), pp. 449–68.

Aglietta, Michel; Orléan, André and Oudiz, Gilles. Des adaptations différenciées aux contraintes internationales: Les enseignements d'un modèle. (National Adjustments to International Constraints: Learning from a Model. With English summary.) *Revue Écon.*, July 1981, *32*(4), pp. 660–712. [G: W. Germany; France; U.K.]

d'Alcantara, G. and Theeuwes, J. Specification of Equations for International Bilateral Trade Flows. In *Courbis, R., ed.*, 1981, pp. 105–09.

Anderson, James E. Cross-Section Tests of the Heckscher–Ohlin Theorem: Comment [Factor Abundance and Comparative Advantage]. *Amer. Econ. Rev.*, December 1981, *71*(5), pp. 1037–39.

Anderson, James E. The Heckscher-Ohlin and Travis-Vanek Theorems under Uncertainty. *J. Int. Econ.*, May 1981, *11*(2), pp. 239–47.

Anderson, Richard K. and Takayama, Akira. Tariffs, the Terms of Trade and Domestic Prices in a Monetary Economy: A Further Analysis. *Rev. Econ. Stud.*, July 1981, *48*(3), pp. 537–39.

Arad, Ruth W. and Hirsch, Seev. Determination of Trade Flows and Choice of Trade Partners:

Reconciling the Heckscher-Ohlin and the Burenstam Linder Models of International Trade. *Weltwirtsch. Arch.*, 1981, *117*(2), pp. 276–97.
[G: OECD; EFTA; S. Africa; Middle East]

Aw, Bee Yan. An Empirical Test of the Heckscher-Ohlin Theorem Using ASEAN Data. *Malayan Econ. Rev. (See Singapore Econ. Rev.)*, April 1981, *26*(1), pp. 25–38. [G: ASEAN; Singapore]

Baldry, Jonathan C. The Effects of a Minimum Wage on Foreign Factor Rewards. *J. Int. Econ.*, August 1981, *11*(3), pp. 415–21.

Baldwin, Robert E. Determinants of the Commodity Structure of U.S. Trade. In *Baldwin, R. E. and Richardson, J. D., eds.*, 1981, *1971*, pp. 4–27.

Baldwin, Robert E. The Political Economy of Postwar United States Trade Policy. In *Baldwin, R. E. and Richardson, J. D., eds.*, 1981, *1976*, pp. 64–77. [G: U.S.]

Bhagwati, Jagdish N. Alternative Theories of Illegal Trade: Economic Consequences and Statistical Detection. *Weltwirtsch. Arch.*, 1981, *117*(3), pp. 409–27.

Bhagwati, Jagdish N. Immiserizing Growth: A Geometrical Note. In *Bhagwati, J. N., ed.*, 1981, *1956*, pp. 301–06.

Bhagwati, Jagdish N. The Generalized Theory of Distortions and Welfare. In *Bhagwati, J. N., ed.*, 1981, *1971*, pp. 171–89.

Bhagwati, Jagdish N. and Brecher, Richard A. National Welfare in an Open Economy in the Presence of Foreign-Owned Factors of Production. In *Bhagwati, J. N., ed.*, 1981, *1980*, pp. 316–28.

Bloomfield, Arthur I. Miscellany: An Early Anticipation of the Concept of Immiserizing Growth. *J. Int. Econ.*, August 1981, *11*(3), pp. 423–27.

van Bochove, C. A. Stability of International Trade Equilibrium with Import Adjustment. *De Economist*, 1981, *129*(2), pp. 262–65.

Brander, James A. Intra-Industry Trade in Identical Commodities. *J. Int. Econ.*, February 1981, *11*(1), pp. 1–14.

Calcagno, Alfredo Eric and Jakobowicz, Jean-Michel. Some Aspects of the International Distribution of Industrial Activity. *Cepal Rev.*, April 1981, (13), pp. 7–33. [G: LDCs; MDCs]

Camagni, Roberto and Tiberi-Vipraio, Patrizia. Il commercio orizzontale rivisitato: una interpretazione stocastica interregionale. (Intra-industry Trade Revisited: An Interregional Stochastic Interpretation. With English summary.) *Giorn. Econ.*, July–August 1981, *40*(7–8), pp. 465–92.

Camilleri, Joseph. The Advanced Capitalist State and the Contemporary World Crisis. *Sci. Soc.*, Summer 1981, *45*(2), pp. 130–58.

Casas, F. R. Transport Costs in the Pure Theory of International Trade: Some Comments. *Econ. J.*, September 1981, *91*(363), pp. 741–44.

Cassing, James H. On the Relationship between Commodity Price Changes and Factor Owners' Real Positions [The Relevance of the Two-Sector Production Model in Trade Theory]. *J. Polit. Econ.*, June 1981, *89*(3), pp. 593–95.

Chang, Winston W. Production Externalities, Variable Returns to Scale, and the Theory of Trade. *Int. Econ. Rev.*, October 1981, *22*(3), pp. 511–25.

Clements, Kenneth W. Changes in the Size of the Traded Goods Sector: Theory and Applications. *Empirical Econ.*, 1981, *6*(4), pp. 203–13.
[G: U.S.; Australia]

Das, Sandwip Kumar. Price Uncertainty and the Neoclassical Theory of International Trade. *Indian Econ. Rev.*, January–June 1981, *16*(1 and 2), pp. 81–93.

Deardorff, Alan V. Weak Links in the Chain of Comparative Advantage. In *Bhagwati, J. N., ed.*, 1981, *1979*, pp. 76–87.

Del Punta, Veniero. I trasferimenti di capitale alla luce della teoria pura degli scambi internazionali. (Capital Transfers and the Pure Theory of International Trade. With English summary.) *Rivista Int. Sci. Econ. Com.*, October–November 1981, *28*(10–11), pp. 1027–33.

Dervis, Kemal. Technology and International Trade: a Heckscher–Ohlin Approach: Comment. In *Grassman, S. and Lundberg, E., eds.*, 1981, pp. 230–32.

Dixit, Avinash. The Export of Capital Theory: Review Article. *J. Int. Econ.*, May 1981, *11*(2), pp. 279–94.

Dunning, John H. Trade, Location of Economic Activity and the Multinational Enterprise: Some Empirical Tests. In *Dunning, J. H.*, 1981, pp. 46–71. [G: Selected countries]

Enders, Walter and Lapan, Harvey E. The Exchange Regime, Resource Allocation, and Uncertainty. *Southern Econ. J.*, April 1981, *47*(4), pp. 924–40.

Ethier, Wilfred. A Reply to Professors Metcalfe and Steedman [The Theorems of International Trade in Time-Phased Economies]. *J. Int. Econ.*, May 1981, *11*(2), pp. 273–77.

Falvey, Rodney Edward. Commercial Policy and Intra-Industry Trade. *J. Int. Econ.*, November 1981, *11*(4), pp. 495–511.

Falvey, Rodney Edward. Comparative Advantage in a Multi-Factor World. *Int. Econ. Rev.*, June 1981, *22*(2), pp. 401–13.

Farley, Noel J. J. Outward Looking Policies and the Changing Basis of Ireland's Foreign Trade. *Econ. Soc. Rev.*, January 1981, *12*(2), pp. 73–95.
[G: Ireland]

Findlay, Ronald. Factor Proportions and Comparative Advantage in the Long Run. In *Bhagwati, J. N., ed.*, 1981, *1970*, pp. 67–75.

Findlay, Ronald. The Fundamental Determinants of the Terms of Trade. In *Grassman, S. and Lundberg, E., eds.*, 1981, pp. 425–57.

Findlay, Ronald and Grubert, Harry. Factor Intensities, Technological Progress and the Terms of Trade. In *Bhagwati, J. N., ed.*, 1981, *1959*, pp. 289–300.

Fischer, Stanley and Frenkel, Jacob A. Investment, the Two-Sector Model, and Trade in Debt and Capital Goods. In *Bhagwati, J. N., ed.*, 1981, pp. 360–74.

Gabisch, Günter. Handel—Wozu? Optimale Zeitprofile des Pro-Kopf-Konsums mit und ohne Handel. (Optimal Time Profiles for per Capita Consumption with and without Trade. With English summary. *Z. Wirtschaft. Sozialwissen.*, 1981, *101*(3), pp. 299–319.

Gardner, H. Stephen. The Embodied Factor Content of Soviet Foreign Trade: A Rejoinder [The Factor Content of Soviet Foreign Trade: A Synthesis]. *ACES Bull. (See Comp. Econ. Stud. after 8/85),* Spring 1981, *23*(1), pp. 89–101.
[G: U.S.S.R.]

Gasparetto, Marialuisa Manfredini. L'importance prépondérante de la qualité du travail dans le commerce international et l'avantage comparatif potentiel. (The Impact of Labour Quality and the Potential Comparative Advantage in International Trade. With English summary.) *Rivista Int. Sci. Econ. Com.,* January–February 1981, *28*(1–2), pp. 52–60.

Grubel, Herbert G. The Theory of Intra-industry Trade. In *Baldwin, R. E. and Richardson, J. D., eds.,* 1981, *1970,* pp. 51–60.

Hamilton, Carl and Söderström, Hans Tson. Technology and International Trade: A Heckscher–Ohlin Approach. In *Grassman, S. and Lundberg, E., eds.,* 1981, pp. 198–229.

Harkness, Jon. Cross-Section Tests of the Heckscher–Ohlin Theorem: Reply [Factor Abundance and Comparative Advantage]. *Amer. Econ. Rev.,* December 1981, *71*(5), pp. 1044–48.

Harris, Richard G. Trade and Depletable Resources: The Small Open Economy. *Can. J. Econ.,* November 1981, *14*(4), pp. 649–64.

Hartigan, James C. The U.S. Tariff and Comparative Advantage: A Survey of Method. *Weltwirtsch. Arch.,* 1981, *117*(1), pp. 65–109. **[G: U.S.]**

Hazari, Bharat R. On Specific Factors in the Non-Traded Goods Sector and Some Propositions in the Pure Theory of International Trade. *Greek Econ. Rev.,* April 1981, *3*(1), pp. 71–80.

Helpman, Elhanan. International Trade in the Presence of Product Differentiation, Economies of Scale and Monopolistic Competition: A Chamberlin-Heckscher-Ohlin Approach. *J. Int. Econ.,* August 1981, *11*(3), pp. 305–40.

Horiba, Yutaka and Kirkpatrick, Rickey C. Factor Endowments, Factor Proportions, and the Allocative Efficiency of U.S. Interregional Trade. *Rev. Econ. Statist.,* May 1981, *63*(2), pp. 178–87.
[G: U.S.]

Hufbauer, Gary Clyde. Income Levels and the Structure of Trade: Comments. In *Grassman, S. and Lundberg, E., eds.,* 1981, pp. 162–64.
[G: Global]

Ingene, Charles A. and Yu, Eden S. H. Wage Distortion and Resource Allocation under Uncertainty. *Southern Econ. J.,* October 1981, *48*(2), pp. 283–95.

Inoue, Tadashi. A Generalization of the Samuelson Reciprocity Relation, the Stolper–Samuelson Theorem and the Rybczynski Theorem under Variable Returns to Scale. *J. Int. Econ.,* February 1981, *11*(1), pp. 79–98.

Jaskold-Gabszewicz, J., et al. International Trade in Differentiated Products. *Int. Econ. Rev.,* October 1981, *22*(3), pp. 527–34.

Johnson, Harry G. The Possibility of Income Losses from Increased Efficiency or Factor Accumulation in the Presence of Tariffs. In *Bhagwati, J. N., ed.,* 1981, *1967,* pp. 307–09.

Jones, Ronald W. The Structure of Simple General Equilibrium Models. In *Bhagwati, J. N., ed.,* 1981, *1965,* pp. 30–49.

Kaldor, Nicholas. The Foundations of Free Trade Theory and their Implications for the Current World Recession. In *[Lipiński, E.],* 1981, pp. 213–21.

Kaldor, Nicholas. The Role of Increasing Returns, Technical Progress and Cumulative Causation in the Theory of International Trade and Economic Growth. *Écon. Appl.,* 1981, *34*(4), pp. 593–617.
[G: LDCs; U.K.]

Kapur, Basant K. Rejoinder to Mathieson's "Further Reply" [Traded Goods, Nontraded Goods, and the Balance of Payments]. *Int. Econ. Rev.,* June 1981, *22*(2), pp. 485.

Kapur, Basant K. Traded Goods, Nontraded Goods, and the Balance of Payments: Further Comment. *Int. Econ. Rev.,* June 1981, *22*(2), pp. 477–80.

Kemp, Murray C.; Long, Ngo Van and Okuguchi, Koji. On the Possibility of Deriving Conclusions of Stolper-Samuelson Type When Commodity Prices Are Random. *Econ. Stud. Quart.,* August 1981, *32*(2), pp. 111–16.

Khandker, A. Wahhab. Multinational Firms and the Theory of International Trade and Investment: A Correction and a Stronger Conclusion. *Amer. Econ. Rev.,* June 1981, *71*(3), pp. 515–16.

Kravis, Irving B.; Heston, Alan and Summers, Robert. New Insights into the Structure of the World Economy. *Rev. Income Wealth,* December 1981, *27*(4), pp. 339–55. **[G: Global]**

Krugman, Paul R. Increasing Returns, Monopolistic Competition, and International Trade. In *Bhagwati, J. N., ed.,* 1981, *1979,* pp. 88–99.

Krugman, Paul R. Intraindustry Specialization and the Gains from Trade. *J. Polit. Econ.,* October 1981, *89*(5), pp. 959–73.

Lafay, Gérard. La dynamique de spécialisation des pays européens. (Dynamics of Specialization in European Countries. With English summary.) *Revue Écon.,* July 1981, *32*(4), pp. 636–59.
[G: EEC]

Leamer, Edward E. and Bowen, Harry P. Cross-Section Tests of the Heckscher–Ohlin Theorem: Comment [Factor Abundance and Comparative Advantage]. *Amer. Econ. Rev.,* December 1981, *71*(5), pp. 1040–43.

Linder, Staffan Burenstam. Causes of Trade in Primary Products versus Manufactures. In *Baldwin, R. E. and Richardson, J. D., eds.,* 1981, *1961,* pp. 40–51.

Lizondo, José Saúl; Johnson, Harry G. and Yeh, Yeong-Her. Factor Intensities and the Shape of the Production Possibility Curve. *Economica,* May 1981, *48*(190), pp. 199–202.

Luciani, Sergio F. A Note on the Concept of Two Way Trade. *Weltwirtsch. Arch.,* 1981, *117*(1), pp. 136–41. **[G: U.S.]**

Manger, Gary J. The Australian Case for Protection Reconsidered. *Australian Econ. Pap.,* December 1981, *20*(37), pp. 193–204. **[G: Australia]**

Manning, R. Specialization and Dynamics in a Trade Model. *Econ. Rec.,* September 1981, *57*(158), pp. 251–60.

Markusen, James R. Trade and the Gains from Trade with Imperfect Competition. *J. Int. Econ.,* November 1981, *11*(4), pp. 531–51.

Markusen, James R. and Melvin, James R. Trade, Factor Prices, and the Gains from Trade with Increasing Returns to Scale. *Can. J. Econ.*, August 1981, *14*(3), pp. 450–69.

Mathieson, Donald J. A Final Reply to Kapur [Traded Goods, Nontraded Goods and the Balance of Payments]. *Int. Econ. Rev.*, June 1981, *22*(2), pp. 487.

Mathieson, Donald J. Traded Goods, Nontraded Goods, and the Balance of Payments: Further Reply. *Int. Econ. Rev.*, June 1981, *22*(2), pp. 481–83.

McAleese, Dermot and Carey, Patrick. Employment Coefficients for Irish Trade with Extra-EEC Countries: Measurement and Implications. *Econ. Soc. Rev.*, January 1981, *12*(2), pp. 115–32.
[G: Ireland]

Metcalfe, J. S. and Steedman, Ian W. On the Transformation of Theorems [The Theorems of International Trade in Time-Phased Economies]. *J. Int. Econ.*, May 1981, *11*(2), pp. 267–71.

Michaely, Michael. Income Levels and the Structure of Trade. In *Grassman, S. and Lundberg, E.*, eds., 1981, pp. 121–61. [G: Global]

Michalet, Charles-Albert. Une nouvelle approche de la spécialisation internationale. (A New Approach to International Specialisation. With English summary.) *Rev. Econ. Ind.*, 3rd Trimestre 1981, (17), pp. 61–75.

Mundell, Robert A. International Trade and Factor Mobility. In *Bhagwati, J. N.*, ed., 1981, *1957*, pp. 17–29.

Mussa, Michael L. The Two-Sector Model in Terms of Its Dual: A Geometric Exposition. In *Bhagwati, J. N.*, ed., 1981, *1979*, pp. 50–63.

Nandi, Sukumar. A Note on Equilibrium Theory of International Trade and Underdevelopment. *Econ. Aff.*, April–June 1981, *26*(2), pp. 117–23.

Neary, J. Peter. Dynamic Stability and the Theory of Factor-Market Distortions. In *Bhagwati, J. N.*, ed., 1981, *1978*, pp. 201–18.

Nishimura, Kazuo. Kuhn's Intensity Hypothesis Revisited. *Rev. Econ. Stud.*, April 1981, *48*(2), pp. 351–54.

Okuguchi, Koji. Joint Production and Specific Factor: A Dynamic Analysis. *Econ. Stud. Quart.*, December 1981, *32*(3), pp. 267–71.

Ølgaard, Anders. Concepts and Problems of Consistency in Terms-of-Trade Analysis. *Rev. Income Wealth*, June 1981, *27*(2), pp. 165–93.

Onida, Fabrizio. Il commercio orizzontale rivisitato: un commento. (Intra-industry Trade Revisited: A Comment. With English summary.) *Giorn. Econ.*, July–August 1981, *40*(7–8), pp. 493–500.

Palomba, Giuseppe. La disgregazione delle leggi economiche. (The Collapse of Economic Laws. With English summary.) *Rivista Int. Sci. Econ. Com.*, October–November 1981, *28*(10–11), pp. 1070–81.

Paroush, Jacob. Market Research as Self Protection of a Competitive Firm under Price Uncertainty. *Int. Econ. Rev.*, June 1981, *22*(2), pp. 365–75.

Perroux, François. Commerce entre grandes firmes ou commerce entre nations? (With English summary.) *Écon. Appl.*, 1981, *34*(4), pp. 567–91.

Perroux, François. Structure et échange dit "International." L'équilibre général reconsidéré. (Structure and the So-called "International" Exchange: The General Equilibrium Revisited. With English summary.) *Rivista Int. Sci. Econ. Com.*, December 1981, *28*(12), pp. 1116–37.

Petoussis, Emmanuel. The Aggregate Import Function within a General Equilibrium Context. *Greek Econ. Rev.*, December 1981, *3*(3), pp. 310–24.
[G: Greece]

Pigott, Charles. The Influence of Real Factors on Exchange Rates. *Fed. Res. Bank San Francisco Econ. Rev.*, Fall 1981, pp. 37–54.
[G: W. Europe; Canada; Japan]

Pitt, Mark M. Smuggling and Price Disparity. *J. Int. Econ.*, November 1981, *11*(4), pp. 447–58.
[G: Indonesia]

Pourvoyeur, Robert. Pre-Ricardiaanse theorieën over de buitenlandse handel. (Pre-Ricardian Foreign Trade Theories. With English summary.) *Econ. Soc. Tijdschr.*, October 1981, *35*(5), pp. 575–84.

Prastacos, Gregory P. and Xafa, Miranda. Optimal Decisions on Production and Export of Interrelated Products. In *Chikán, A.*, ed. *(I)*, 1981, pp. 291–300.

Pugel, Thomas A. Technology Transfer and the Neoclassical Theory of International Trade. In *Hawkins, R. G. and Prasad, A. J.*, eds., 1981, pp. 11–37.

Ramanathan, Ramu and Roberts, William W. The Impact of Monetary Expansion with Terms of Trade Effects and Trade in Securities. *J. Int. Econ.*, February 1981, *11*(1), pp. 61–77.

Rieber, William J. Tariffs as a Means of Altering Trade Patterns. *Amer. Econ. Rev.*, December 1981, *71*(5), pp. 1098–99.

Rocherieux, François. Sur la théorie des modèles inter-industriels: Quelques remarques appliquées à l'analyse de l'emploi et du commerce international. (On Input-Output Models Theory: Some Remarks Applied to Employment and International Trade Analysis. With English summary.) *Revue Écon.*, September 1981, *32*(5), pp. 887–922.
[G: France]

Rodriguez, Carlos Alfredo. The Technology Transfer Issue. In *Grassman, S. and Lundberg, E.*, eds., 1981, pp. 167–93.

Ruiz, Maria L. Trade Flows under Oligopolistic Conditions: A Supply Oriented Approach. *Econ. Notes*, 1981, *10*(1), pp. 46–66. [G: Italy]

Samuelson, Paul A. Bertil Ohlin (1899–1979). *Scand. J. Econ.*, 1981, *83*(3), pp. 355–71.

Samuelson, Paul A. Bertil Ohlin: 1899–1979. *J. Int. Econ.*, May 1981, *11*(2), pp. 147–63.

Samuelson, Paul A. International Factor-Price Equalisation Once Again. In *Bhagwati, J. N.*, ed., 1981, *1949*, pp. 3–15.

Samuelson, Paul A. The Gains from International Trade Once Again. In *Bhagwati, J. N.*, ed., 1981, *1962*, pp. 131–41.

Sarris, Alexander H. and Schmitz, Andrew. Price Formation in International Agricultural Trade. In *McCalla, A. F. and Josling, T. E.*, eds., 1981, pp. 29–48.

Savary, Julien. La France dans la division internationale du travail: Une approche par l'investissement direct international. (The International Division of Labour and the French Economy: An Approach through Foreign Direct Investment. With English summary.) *Revue Écon.*, July 1981, *32*(4), pp. 713–53.   [G: France]

Sawhney, Bansi L. and Di Pietro, William R. Monopoly Power, the Participation Theory and International Trade. *Econ. Int.*, February 1981, *34*(1), pp. 143–58.   [G: MDCs; LDCs]

Shea, Koon-lam. A Graphical Analysis of Factor Accumulation in a Three-Sector, Three-Factor Model of International Trade. *Econ. J.*, December 1981, *91*(364), pp. 1020–25.

Sheikh, Munir A. Smuggling, Production and Welfare. In *Bhagwati, J. N., ed.*, 1981, *1974*, pp. 233–42.

Shin, Chang Min. The Limit of Generalization in International Trade Models. *J. Econ. Devel.*, December 1981, *6*(2), pp. 185–203.

Södersten, Bo. The Fundamental Determinants of the Terms of Trade: Comments. In *Grassman, S. and Lundberg, E., eds.*, 1981, pp. 458–63.

Soete, Luc L. G. A General Test of Technological Gap Trade Theory. *Weltwirtsch. Arch.*, 1981, *117*(4), pp. 638–60.   [G: OECD]

Stern, Robert M. Changes in U.S. Comparative Advantage: Issues for Research and Policy. In *National Science Foundation*, 1981, pp. III81–105.   [G: U.S.]

Stern, Robert M. and Maskus, Keith E. Determinants of the Structure of U.S. Foreign Trade, 1958–76. *J. Int. Econ.*, May 1981, *11*(2), pp. 207–24.   [G: U.S.]

Svensson, Lars E. O. National Welfare in the Presence of Foreign-owned Factors of Production: An Extension. *Scand. J. Econ.*, 1981, *83*(4), pp. 497–507.

Taylor, Lance. South-North Trade and Southern Growth: Bleak Prospects from the Structuralist Point of View. *J. Int. Econ.*, November 1981, *11*(4), pp. 589–602.

Teitel, Simón. Productivity, Mechanization and Skills: A Test of the Hirschman Hypothesis for Latin American Industry. *World Devel.*, April 1981, *9*(4), pp. 355–71.   [G: Latin America]

Waelbroeck, Jean. The Technology Transfer Issue: Comments. In *Grassman, S. and Lundberg, E., eds.*, 1981, pp. 194–97.

Yu, Eden S. H. On Factor Market Distortions and Economic Growth. *Southern Econ. J.*, July 1981, *48*(1), pp. 172–78.

Yu, Eden S. H. Trade Diversion, Trade Creation and Factor Market Imperfections. *Weltwirtsch. Arch.*, 1981, *117*(3), pp. 546–61.

4113 Theory of Protection

Bhagwati, Jagdish N. The Generalized Theory of Distortions and Welfare. In *Bhagwati, J. N., ed.*, 1981, *1971*, pp. 171–89.

Bhagwati, Jagdish N. and Brecher, Richard A. National Welfare in an Open Economy in the Presence of Foreign-Owned Factors of Production. In *Bhagwati, J. N., ed.*, 1981, *1980*, pp. 316–28.

Bhagwati, Jagdish N. and Srinivasan, T. N. Optimal

Trade Policy and Compensation under Endogenous Uncertainty: The Phenomenon of Market Disruption. In *Bhagwati, J. N., ed.*, 1981, *1976*, pp. 219–32.

Bolnick, Bruce R. Recalculating the Scientific Tariff. *J. Polit. Econ.*, February 1981, *89*(1), pp. 192–95.

Brander, James A. and Spencer, Barbara J. Tariffs and the Extraction of Foreign Monopoly Rents under Potential Entry. *Can. J. Econ.*, August 1981, *14*(3), pp. 371–89.

Brecher, Richard A. Optimal Commercial Policy for a Minimum-wage Economy. In *Bhagwati, J. N., ed.*, 1981, *1974*, pp. 190–200.

Brecher, Richard A. and Díaz-Alejandro, Carlos F. Tariffs, Foreign Capital and Immiserizing Growth. In *Bhagwati, J. N., ed.*, 1981, *1977*, pp. 310–15.

Bruton, Henry J. The Import-Substitution Strategy of Economic Development: A Survey. In *Livingstone, I., ed.*, 1981, *1970*, pp. 167–76.

Corden, W. Max. The Structure of a Tariff System and the Effective Protective Rate. In *Bhagwati, J. N., ed.*, 1981, *1966*, pp. 108–28.

Cuddington, John T. Import Substitution Policies: A Two-Sector, Fix-Price Model. *Rev. Econ. Stud.*, April 1981, *48*(2), pp. 327–42.

El-Agraa, A. M. Tariff Bargaining—A Correction [On Tariff Bargaining]. *Bull. Econ. Res.*, November 1981, *33*(2), pp. 102–03.

Flanders, M. J. Prebisch on Protectionism: An Evaluation. In *Livingstone, I., ed.*, 1981, *1964*, pp. 108–16.

Fukushima, Takashi. A Dynamic Quantity Adjustment Process in a Small Open Economy, and Welfare Effects of Tariff Changes. *J. Int. Econ.*, November 1981, *11*(4), pp. 513–29.

Hillman, Arye L. Unilateral and Bilateral Trade Policies for a Minimum-Wage Economy. *J. Int. Econ.*, August 1981, *11*(3), pp. 407–13.

Jackson, Richard. Industrialization in Papua New Guinea: A Social or Economic Investment? In *Hamilton, F. E. I. and Linge, G. J. R., eds.*, 1981, pp. 549–80.   [G: Papua New Guinea]

Johansson, Per-Olov and Löfgren, Karl-Gustaf. A Note on Employment Effects of Tariffs in a Small Open Economy [The Employment Effects of Tariffs under a Free Exchange Rate Regime. A Monetary Approach]. *Weltwirtsch. Arch.*, 1981, *117*(3), pp. 578–83.

Johnson, Harry G. Optimal Trade Intervention in the Presence of Domestic Distortions. In *Bhagwati, J. N., ed.*, 1981, *1965*, pp. 142–70.

Johnson, Harry G. The Possibility of Income Losses from Increased Efficiency or Factor Accumulation in the Presence of Tariffs. In *Bhagwati, J. N., ed.*, 1981, *1967*, pp. 307–09.

Kaldor, Nicholas. A Note on Tariffs and the Terms of Trade. In *Kaldor, N.*, 1981, *1940*, pp. 147–50.

Katrak, Homi. Multi-National Firms' Exports and Host Country Commercial Policy. *Econ. J.*, June 1981, *91*(362), pp. 454–65.

Laski, Kazimierz. International Financing: Comment. In *Saunders, C. T., ed. (I)*, 1981, pp. 162–64.   [G: LDCs]

Manger, Gary J. Summing up on the Australian Case for Protection: Comment. *Quart. J. Econ.*, February 1981, *96*(1), pp. 161–67. [G: Australia]

Markusen, James R. The Distribution of Gains from Bilateral Tariff Reductions. *J. Int. Econ.*, November 1981, *11*(4), pp. 553–72.

Mayer, Wolfgang. Theoretical Considerations on Negotiated Tariff Adjustments. *Oxford Econ. Pap.*, March 1981, *33*(1), pp. 135–53.

Möschel, Wernhard. Zur wettbewerbstheoretischen Begrundbarkeit von Ausnahmebereichen. (Areas Exempt from Competition and Competition Theory. With English Summary.) In [von Haberler, G.], 1981, pp. 85–102.

Mussa, Michael. The Monetary Approach to the Balance of Payments. In *Baldwin, R. E. and Richardson, J. D., eds.*, 1981, *1976*, pp. 368–73.

Ossa, Fernando. Aspectos teóricos de la protección en economías pequeñas. (With English summary.) *Cuadernos Econ.*, August–December 1981, *18*(54–55), pp. 231–61. [G: LDCs]

Panagariya, Arvind. Quantitative Restrictions in International Trade under Monopoly. *J. Int. Econ.*, February 1981, *11*(1), pp. 15–31.

Pryor, Frederic L. Static and Dynamic Effects of Different Types of Trade Barriers: A Synthesis Using a General Equilibrium Model. *Eastern Econ. J.*, April 1981, *7*(2), pp. 59–74.

Pugel, Thomas A. Technology Transfer and the Neoclassical Theory of International Trade. In *Hawkins, R. G. and Prasad, A. J., eds.*, 1981, pp. 11–37.

Rieber, William J. Tariffs as a Means of Altering Trade Patterns. *Amer. Econ. Rev.*, December 1981, *71*(5), pp. 1098–99.

Rodriguez, Carlos Alfredo. Política comercial y salarios reales. (With English summary.) *Cuadernos Econ.*, August–December 1981, *18*(54–55), pp. 293–316. [G: Argentina]

Rodriguez, Carlos Alfredo. The Non-equivalence of Tariffs and Quotas under Retaliation. In *Bhagwati, J. N., ed.*, 1981, *1974*, pp. 103–07.

Saidi, Nasser and Srinagesh, Padmanabhan. On Non-Linear Tariff Schedules. *J. Int. Econ.*, May 1981, *11*(2), pp. 173–95.

Samuelson, Paul A. Justice to the Australians. *Quart. J. Econ.*, February 1981, *96*(1), pp. 169–70.

Samuelson, Paul A. Summing up on the Australian Case for Protection. *Quart. J. Econ.*, February 1981, *96*(1), pp. 147–60. [G: Australia]

Sjaastad, Larry A. La protección y el volumen del comercio en Chile: La evidencia. (With English summary.) *Cuadernos Econ.*, August–December 1981, *18*(54–55), pp. 263–92. [G: Chile]

Smith, M. Alasdair M. Capital Accumulation in the Open Two-Sector Economy. In *Bhagwati, J. N., ed.*, 1981, *1977*, pp. 329–41.

Srinivasan, T. N. and Bhagwati, Jagdish N. Shadow Prices for Project Selection in the Presence of Distortions: Effective Rates of Protection and Domestic Resource Costs. In *Bhagwati, J. N., ed.*, 1981, *1978*, pp. 243–61.

Szychowski, Mario L. and Perazzo, Alfredo C. Una Evaluación empírica de la eficiencia económica y de los costos de protección en el caso argentino 1973–1974. (An Empirical Evaluation of the Economic Efficiency and the Costs of Protection in the Argentine Case: 1973–1974. With English summary.) *Económica*, September–December 1981, *27*(3), pp. 223–65. [G: Argentina]

Tower, Edward. Buffer Stocks are Better Stabilizers Than Quotas. *J. Int. Econ.*, February 1981, *11*(1), pp. 113–15.

Tullock, Gordon. Lobbying and Welfare: A Comment. *J. Public Econ.*, December 1981, *16*(3), pp. 391–94.

Weinblatt, Jacob and Zilberfarb, Ben-Zion. Price Discrimination in the Exports of a Small Economy: Empirical Evidence. *Weltwirtsch. Arch.*, 1981, *117*(2), pp. 368–79. [G: Israel]

Werner, Horst. Freihandel oder internationaler "Kampf um Produktionsprivilegien"? (Free Trade or International "Fight for Production Privileges"? With English summary.) In [von Haberler, G.], 1981, pp. 51–69.

Wonnacott, Paul and Wonnacott, Ronald. Is Unilateral Tariff Reduction Preferable to a Customs Union? The Curious Case of the Missing Foreign Tariffs. *Amer. Econ. Rev.*, September 1981, *71*(4), pp. 704–14.

Yabuuchi, Shigemi and Tanaka, Kazuyoshi. Non-Traded Inputs, Interindustry Flows, Resource Allocation and the ERP Theory. *J. Int. Econ.*, February 1981, *11*(1), pp. 99–111.

4114 Theory of International Trade and Economic Development

Anderson, Kym and Smith, Ben. Changing Economic Relations between the Asian ADCs and Resource-Exporting Advanced Countries of the Pacific Basin. In *Hong, W. and Krause, L. B., eds.*, 1981, pp. 293–338. [G: Hong Kong; Singapore; S. Korea; Taiwan; Selected MDCs]

Balassa, Bela. The Process of Industrial Development and Alternative Development Strategies. In *Balassa, B.*, 1981, pp. 1–26. [G: LDCs]

Beckford, G. L. The Economics of Agricultural Resource Use and Development in Plantation Economies. In *Livingstone, I., ed.*, 1981, *1969*, pp. 277–86.

Bhagwati, Jagdish N. Immiserizing Growth: A Geometrical Note. In *Bhagwati, J. N., ed.*, 1981, *1956*, pp. 301–06.

Bruno, Michael. Short-term Policy Tradeoffs under Different Phases of Economic Development. In *Grassman, S. and Lundberg, E., eds.*, 1981, pp. 295–313.

Bruton, Henry J. The Import-Substitution Strategy of Economic Development: A Survey. In *Livingstone, I., ed.*, 1981, *1970*, pp. 167–76.

Chenery, Hollis B. Interactions between Inflation and Trade Regime Objectives in Stabilization Programs: Comment. In *Cline, W. R. and Weintraub, S., eds.*, 1981, pp. 114–16. [G: LDCs]

Chichilnisky, Graciela. Terms of Trade and Domestic Distribution: Export-Led Growth with Abundant Labour. *J. Devel. Econ.*, April 1981, *8*(2), pp. 163–92.

Datta-Chaudhuri, Mrinal. Labour-Intensive Industrialisation, Organisation of Trade and the Role of the State. *Indian Econ. Rev.*, July-Sept. 1981,

16(3), pp. 199–212.

Dos Santos, T. The Structure of Dependence. In *Livingstone, I., ed.*, 1981, *1970*, pp. 143–47.
[G: Latin America]

Ellsworth, P. T. The Terms of Trade between Primary-Producing and Industrial Countries. In *Livingstone, I., ed.*, 1981, *1961*, pp. 129–36.
[G: Global]

Eralp, Atilâ. Türkiye'de Izlenen Ithal Ikameci Kalkinma Stratejisi ve Yabanci Sermaye. (Import Substitution Strategy and Foreign Capital in Turkey. With English summary.) *METU*, Special Issue, 1981, pp. 613–33. [G: Turkey]

Evans, D. Unequal Exchange and Economic Policies: Some Implications of the Neo-Ricardian Critique of the Theory of Comparative Advantage. In *Livingstone, I., ed.*, 1981, pp. 117–28.

Findlay, Ronald. Export-Led Industrial Growth Reconsidered: Comment. In *Hong, W. and Krause, L. B., eds.*, 1981, pp. 30–33. [G: LDCs]

Findlay, Ronald. The Fundamental Determinants of the Terms of Trade. In *Grassman, S. and Lundberg, E., eds.*, 1981, pp. 425–57.

Fong, Pang Eng and Tan, Augustine. Employment and Export-led Industrialisation: The Experience of Singapore. In *Amjad, R., ed.*, 1981, pp. 141–74. [G: Singapore]

Glezakos, C. Export Instability and Economic Growth: A Statistical Verification. In *Livingstone, I., ed.*, 1981, *1973*, pp. 137–42. [G: LDCs; MDCs]

Greenaway, David. Taxes on International Transactions and Economic Development. In *Peacock, A. and Forte, F., eds.*, 1981, pp. 131–47.
[G: LDCs]

Grossman, Gene M. The Theory of Domestic Content Protection and Content Preference. *Quart. J. Econ.*, November 1981, *96*(4), pp. 583–603.

Kaldor, Nicholas. The Role of Increasing Returns, Technical Progress and Cumulative Causation in the Theory of International Trade and Economic Growth. *Écon. Appl.*, 1981, *34*(4), pp. 593–617.
[G: LDCs; U.K.]

Kim, Kwang Suk. Export-Led Industrial Growth Reconsidered: Comment. In *Hong, W. and Krause, L. B., eds.*, 1981, pp. 28–29. [G: LDCs]

Krueger, Anne O. Export-Led Industrial Growth Reconsidered. In *Hong, W. and Krause, L. B., eds.*, 1981, pp. 3–27. [G: LDCs]

Krueger, Anne O. Interactions between Inflation and Trade Regime Objectives in Stabilization Programs. In *Cline, W. R. and Weintraub, S., eds.*, 1981, pp. 83–114. [G: LDCs]

Lee, Hoe Sung. Changing Economic Relations between the Asian ADCs and Resource-Exporting Advanced Countries of the Pacific Basin: Comment. In *Hong, W. and Krause, L. B., eds.*, 1981, pp. 339–40. [G: Hong Kong; Singapore; S. Korea; Taiwan; Selected MDCs]

Lim, David. Export Instability and Revenue Instability in Less Developed Countries. *Malayan Econ. Rev. (See Singapore Econ. Rev.)*, October 1981, *26*(2), pp. 46–52. [G: Selected LDCs]

McNamara, Robert S. To the United Nations Conference on Trade and Development, Manila, Philippines, May 10, 1979. In *McNamara, R. S.,*

1981, *1979*, pp. 521–50.

de Melo, Jaime and Robinson, Sherman. Trade Policy and Resource Allocation in the Presence of Product Differentiation. *Rev. Econ. Statist.*, May 1981, *63*(2), pp. 169–77. [G: Turkey]

Michaely, Michael. Foreign Aid, Economic Structure, and Dependence. *J. Devel. Econ.*, December 1981, *9*(3), pp. 313–30.

Myint, H. The 'Classical Theory' of International Trade and Underdeveloped Countries. In *Livingstone, I., ed.*, 1981, *1958*, pp. 99–107.

Nagy, András. Growth and Trade: the Hungarian Case. In *Bornstein, M.; Gitelman, Z. and Zimmerman, W., eds.*, 1981, pp. 192–220.
[G: Hungary]

Nixson, Frederick I. State Intervention, Economic Planning and Import-Substituting Industrialisation: The Experience of the Less Developed Countries. *METU*, Special Issue, 1981, pp. 55–78. [G: LDCs]

Ognev, Alexandre P. The Role of Development Aid Facilities: Comment. In *Saunders, C. T., ed. (I)*, 1981, pp. 165–66. [G: LDCs]

Roemer, Michael. Dependence and Industrialization Strategies. *World Devel.*, May 1981, *9*(5), pp. 429–34.

Ross, Bruce J. Changing Economic Relations between the Asian ADCs and Resource-Exporting Advanced Countries of the Pacific Basin: Comment. In *Hong, W. and Krause, L. B., eds.*, 1981, pp. 340–43. [G: Hong Kong; Singapore; S. Korea; Taiwan; Selected MDCs]

Schiavo-Campo, Salvatore. Instability of Developmental Imports and Economic Growth: A Theoretical Framework. *Weltwirtsch. Arch.*, 1981, *117*(3), pp. 562–73.

Scott, Maurice FG. Short-term Policy Tradeoffs under Different Phases of Economic Development: Comments. In *Grassman, S. and Lundberg, E., eds.*, 1981, pp. 314–18.

Sercovich, Francisco Colman. The Exchange and Absorption of Technology in Brazilian Industry. In *Bruneau, T. C. and Faucher, P., eds.*, 1981, pp. 127–40. [G: Brazil]

Seton, Francis. The Role of Development Aid Facilities. In *Saunders, C. T., ed. (I)*, 1981, pp. 127–59. [G: LDCs]

Södersten, Bo. The Fundamental Determinants of the Terms of Trade: Comments. In *Grassman, S. and Lundberg, E., eds.*, 1981, pp. 458–63.

Soldaczuk, Józef. The Role of Development Aid Facilities: Comment. In *Saunders, C. T., ed. (I)*, 1981, pp. 167–71. [G: LDCs]

Stecher, Bernd. The Role of Economic Policies. In *Saunders, C. T., ed. (II)*, 1981, pp. 27–46.
[G: Selected LDCs]

Streeten, Paul P. Self-reliant Industrialization. In *Streeten, P.*, 1981, *1979*, pp. 193–212.

Tamaschke, H. U. and Duriyaprapan, C. Economic Development through Export Expansion: An Econometric Study of Thailand. *Philippine Econ. J.*, 1981, *20*(2), pp. 159–74. [G: Thailand]

Tyler, William G. Growth and Export Expansion in Developing Countries: Some Empirical Evidence. *J. Devel. Econ.*, August 1981, *9*(1), pp. 121–30. [G: LDCs]

Vernon, Raymond. International Investment and International Trade in the Product Cycle. In *Baldwin, R. E. and Richardson, J. D., eds., 1981, 1966*, pp. 27–40.

420 TRADE RELATIONS; COMMERCIAL POLICY; INTERNATIONAL ECONOMIC INTEGRATION

4200 General

Bacha, Edmar L. Comment on "Gains to Latin America from Trade Liberalization in Developed and Developing Nations" *Quart. Rev. Econ. Bus.*, Summer 1981, *21*(2), pp. 258–59.

Bagley, Bruce M. Mexico–United States Relations: A United States Perspective. In *Purcell, S. K., ed.*, 1981, pp. 13–27. **[G: Mexico; U.S.]**

Bergsten, C. Fred. The United States and Brazil: A Framework for Future Economic Relations. In *Bergsten, C. F., ed.*, 1981, pp. 159–64.
[G: Brazil; U.S.]

Borner, Silvio. Die Internationalisierung der Industrie. (With English summary.) *Kyklos*, 1981, *34*(1), pp. 14–35.

Brundell, Peter; Horn, Henrik and Svedberg, Peter. On the Causes of Instability in Export Earnings. *Oxford Bull. Econ. Statist.*, August 1981, *43*(3), pp. 301–13.

Bruton, Henry J. The Import-Substitution Strategy of Economic Development: A Survey. In *Livingstone, I., ed.*, 1981, *1970*, pp. 167–76.

Chaikin, Sol C. Toward a New U.S. Industrial Policy? International Trade: Comment. In *Wachter, M. L. and Wachter, S. M., eds.*, 1981, pp. 409–12. **[G: U.S.]**

Cline, William R. and Weintraub, Sidney. Economic Stabilization in Developing Countries: Introduction and Overview. In *Cline, W. R. and Weintraub, S., eds.*, 1981, pp. 1–42. **[G: LDCs]**

Courbis, R. Les Problèmes Internationaux a la Lumière des Modèles. (With English summary.) In *Courbis, R., ed.*, 1981, pp. 337–50.

Dobrska, Zofia. The Present World Economic Situation and Structural Changes in Developing Countries. In *[Lipiński, E.]*, 1981, pp. 165–76.
[G: LDCs]

Dornbusch, Rudiger. Comment on "Exports and Policy in Latin-American Countries" *Quart. Rev. Econ. Bus.*, Summer 1981, *21*(2), pp. 43–47.
[G: Latin America; Asia; OECD]

Finley, Murray H. Foreign Trade and United States Employment. In *Baldwin, R. E. and Richardson, J. D., eds.*, 1981, *1978*, pp. 77–87.

Hager, Wolfgang. The Strains on the International System. In *Saunders, C. T., ed. (II)*, 1981, pp. 287–309. **[G: LDCs; MDCs]**

Hardt, John P. East–West–South: Economic Interactions between Three Worlds: The Background: Interests and Prospects: Comment. In *Saunders, C. T., ed. (I)*, 1981, pp. 74–78.

Helleiner, Gerald K. International Technology Issues: Southern Needs and Northern Responses. In *Helleiner, G. K.*, 1981, pp. 166–93.

Helleiner, Gerald K. World Market Imperfections and the Developing Countries. In *Helleiner, G. K.*, 1981, pp. 22–61. **[G: LDCs]**

Hudson, Robert. The Effects of Dock Strikes on UK International Trade. *Appl. Econ.*, March 1981, *13*(1), pp. 67–77. **[G: U.K.]**

Keesing, Donald B. Exports and Policy in Latin-American Countries: Prospects for the World Economy and for Latin-American Exports, 1980-90. *Quart. Rev. Econ. Bus.*, Summer 1981, *21*(2), pp. 18–43. **[G: Latin America]**

Malmgren, Harald B. Changing Forms of Competition and World Trade Rules. In *Center for Strategic and Internat. Studies, ed. (I)*, 1981, pp. 409–50.

McBride, Robert H. The United States and Mexico. In *McBride, R. H., ed.*, 1981, pp. 1–30.
[G: U.S.; Mexico]

McCulloch, Rachel. Gains to Latin America from Trade Liberalization in Developed and Developing Nations. *Quart. Rev. Econ. Bus.*, Summer 1981, *21*(2), pp. 231–58. **[G: Latin America]**

McNamara, Robert S. To the Board of Governors, Manila, Philippines, October 4, 1976. In *McNamara, R. S.*, 1981, *1976*, pp. 337–76.
[G: OECD; LDCs]

Melchor, Alejandro, Jr. Resource Management: Some Problems and Issues in the 1980s. In *Hewett, R. B., ed.*, 1981, pp. 164–76.
[G: Pacific Basin]

Nayyar, Deepak. East–West–South: Economic Interactions between Three Worlds: The Background: Interests and Prospects: Comment. In *Saunders, C. T., ed. (I)*, 1981, pp. 78–84.
[G: CMEA; LDCs]

Pellicer de Brody, Olga. Mexico–United States Relations: A Mexican Perspective. In *Purcell, S. K., ed.*, 1981, pp. 4–12. **[G: Mexico; U.S.]**

Ranis, Gustav. Alternative Resource Transfer Mechanisms and the Development Process: Research Issues. In *National Science Foundation*, 1981, pp. II79–101.

Saunders, Christopher T. Joint Strategies for World Development. In *Saunders, C. T., ed. (I)*, 1981, pp. 1–17.

Seers, Dudley. Massive Transfers and Mutual Interests. *World Devel.*, June 1981, *9*(6), pp. 557–62.

Tovias, Alfred. Egypt's Trade Policies. *J. World Trade Law*, November–December 1981, *15*(6), pp. 471–89. **[G: Egypt]**

Vaganov, Boris. Foreign Economic Relations. In *Novosti Press Agency*, 1981, pp. 176–90.
[G: U.S.S.R.]

Wichtrich, Al R. Mexican–American Commercial Relations. In *McBride, R. H., ed.*, 1981, pp. 77–103. **[G: Mexico; U.S.]**

Yamamoto, Shigenobu. Production Adjustment Policy and Protectionism. (In Japanese. With English summary.) *Osaka Econ. Pap.*, December 1981, *31*(2–3), pp. 40–52.

421 Trade Relations

4210 Trade Relations

Adamovic, Ljubisa S. Yugoslavia and the European Economic Community. In *Inst. of Internat. Pub. Law and Internat. Relat. of Thessaloniki*, 1981, pp. 85–113. **[G: Yugoslavia; EEC]**

Adams, Darius and Haynes, Richard. U.S.–Canadian Lumber Trade: The Effect of Restrictions. In *Sedjo, R. A., ed.*, 1981, pp. 101–32.
[G: U.S.; Canada]

Adams, F. Gerard; Behrman, Jere R. and Lasaga, M. Commodity Exports and NIEO Proposals for Buffer Stocks and Compensatory Finance: Implications for Latin America. *Quart. Rev. Econ. Bus.*, Summer 1981, *21*(2), pp. 48–76.
[G: Latin America]

Adams, F. Gerard; Behrman, Jere R. and Lasaga, M. Commodity Exports and NIEO Proposals for Buffer Stocks and Compensatory Finance: Implications for Latin America. In *Baer, W. and Gillis, M., eds.*, 1981, pp. 48–76.
[G: Chile; Latin America]

Aho, C. Michael. The Economy of 1981: A Bipartisan Look: Proceedings of a Congressional Economic Conference: Statement. In *U.S. Congress, Joint Economic Committee (1)*, 1981, pp. 560–67.
[G: U.S.]

Aho, C. Michael and Orr, James A. Trade-Sensitive Employment: Who Are the Affected Workers? *Mon. Lab. Rev.*, February 1981, *104*(2), pp. 29–35.
[G: U.S.]

Akhtar, M. A. Income and Price Elasticities of Non-Oil Imports for Six Industrial Countries. *Manchester Sch. Econ. Soc. Stud.*, December 1981, *49*(4), pp. 334–47.
[G: OECD]

Akhtar, M. A. Manufacturing Import Functions for Canada, Japan and the United States. *Hitotsubashi J. Econ.*, June 1981, *22*(1), pp. 61–71.
[G: Canada; Japan; U.S.]

Akrasanee, Narongchai. ADCs' Manufactured Export Growth and OECD Adjustment: Comment. In *Hong, W. and Krause, L. B., eds.*, 1981, pp. 507–09.
[G: LDCs; OECD]

Akrasanee, Narongchai. Trade Strategy for Employment Growth in Thailand. In *Krueger, A. O., et al., eds.*, 1981, pp. 393–433.
[G: Thailand]

Alamgir, Mohiuddin. The Changing Composition of Developing Country Exports: Comments. In *Grassman, S. and Lundberg, E., eds.*, 1981, pp. 117–20.
[G: LDCs]

Allen, William A. What Can Be Rescued from the "Law of One Price"? *Jahr. Nationalökon. Statist.*, January 1981, *196*(1), pp. 47–62.
[G: OECD]

Andersen, E. S.; Dalum, B. and Villumsen, G. The Importance of the Home Market for the Development of Technology and the Export Specialization of Manufacturing Industry. In *Freeman, C., et al.*, 1981, pp. 49–102.
[G: Denmark]

Anderson, James E. Cross-Section Tests of the Heckscher–Ohlin Theorem: Comment [Factor Abundance and Comparative Advantage]. *Amer. Econ. Rev.*, December 1981, *71*(5), pp. 1037–39.

Anderson, Kym and Smith, Ben. Changing Economic Relations between the Asian ADCs and Resource-Exporting Advanced Countries of the Pacific Basin. In *Hong, W. and Krause, L. B., eds.*, 1981, pp. 293–338.
[G: Hong Kong; Singapore; S. Korea; Taiwan; Selected MDCs]

Anguiano, Eugenio. The People's Republic of China and the New International Economic Order: Relations with the Third World. In *Lozoya, J. A. and*

Bhattacharya, A. K., eds., 1981, pp. 53–89.
[G: China; LDCs]

Aquino, Antonio. Changes over Time in the Pattern of Comparative Advantage in Manufactured Goods: An Empirical Analysis for the Period 1962–1974. *Europ. Econ. Rev.*, January 1981, *15*(1), pp. 41–62.

Aquino, Antonio. The Measurement of Intra-Industry Trade When Overall Trade Is Imbalanced. *Weltwirtsch. Arch.*, 1981, *117*(4), pp. 763–66.

Arad, Ruth W. and Hirsch, Seev. Determination of Trade Flows and Choice of Trade Partners: Reconciling the Heckscher-Ohlin and the Burenstam Linder Models of International Trade. *Weltwirtsch. Arch.*, 1981, *117*(2), pp. 276–97.
[G: OECD; EFTA; S. Africa; Middle East]

Ariff, Mohamed. Trade Relations between Latin American and the Asian ADCs: Comment. In *Hong, W. and Krause, L. B., eds.*, 1981, pp. 382–85.
[G: E. Asia; Latin America]

Arpan, Jeffrey S.; de la Torre, José and Toyne, Brian. International Developments and the U.S. Apparel Industry. *J. Int. Bus. Stud.*, Winter 1981, *12*(3), pp. 49–64.
[G: U.S.]

Atkinson, Thomas R. The Role of Productivity in International Trade. In *Hogan, J. D. and Craig, A. M., eds., Vol. 1*, 1981, pp. 647–56.
[G: Selected OECD]

Ault, David E. and Meisel, John B. An Investigation into the Effects of Technology and Economies of Scale on International Trade in Basic Steel: 1955–76. *Rivista Int. Sci. Econ. Com.*, May 1981, *28*(5), pp. 461–86.
[G: OECD]

Aw, Bee Yan. An Empirical Test of the Heckscher-Ohlin Theorem Using ASEAN Data. *Malayan Econ. Rev. (See Singapore Econ. Rev.)*, April 1981, *26*(1), pp. 25–38.
[G: ASEAN; Singapore]

Aw, Bee Yan. The Short–Run Employment Impact of ASEAN–U.S. Trade. *Malayan Econ. Rev. (See Singapore Econ. Rev.)*, October 1981, *26*(2), pp. 80–91.
[G: U.S.; ASEAN]

Bach, Christopher L. U.S. International Transactions, Fourth Quarter and Year 1980. *Surv. Curr. Bus.*, March 1981, *61*(3), pp. 40–67.
[G: U.S.]

Bacha, Edmar L. Gains to Latin America from Trade Liberalization in Developed and Developing Nations: Comment. In *Baer, W. and Gillis, M., eds.*, 1981, pp. 258–59.
[G: Latin America]

Baer, Werner and Gillis, Malcolm. Preface: Changing Perspectives on Latin-American Trade. *Quart. Rev. Econ. Bus.*, Summer 1981, *21*(2), pp. 9–17.
[G: Latin America; U.S.]

Balassa, Bela. Évolution de la structure des échanges de produits manufacturés entre pays industriels et pays en développement. (Pattern of Structural Change in Trade in Manufactured Goods between Industrial and Developing Countries. With English summary.) *Revue Écon.*, July 1981, *32*(4), pp. 754–97.
[G: MDCs; LDCs]

Balassa, Bela. A 'Stages' Approach to Comparative Advantage. In *Balassa, B.*, 1981, pp. 149–67.
[G: LDCs; MDCs]

Balassa, Bela. Development Strategy and the Six Year Plan in Taiwan. In *Balassa, B.*, 1981, pp. 381–406.
[G: Taiwan]

Balassa, Bela. Incentives for Economic Growth in

Taiwan. In *Balassa, B.*, 1981, pp. 407–22.
[G: Taiwan]
Balassa, Bela. Planning and Policy Making in Greece. In *Balassa, B.*, 1981, pp. 281–96.
[G: Greece]
Balassa, Bela. Policy Responses to External Shocks in Selected Latin-American Countries. *Quart. Rev. Econ. Bus.*, Summer 1981, *21*(2), pp. 131–64.
[G: Brazil; Mexico; Uruguay]
Balassa, Bela. Policy Responses to External Shocks in Selected Latin-American Countries. In *Baer, W. and Gillis, M., eds.*, 1981, pp. 131–64.
[G: Brazil; Mexico; Uruguay]
Balassa, Bela. Prospects for Trade in Manufactured Goods between Industrial and Developing Countries, 1978–1990. In *Balassa, B.*, 1981, pp. 211–27.
[G: LDCs; MDCs; OPEC]
Balassa, Bela. The "New Protectionism" and the International Economy. In *Balassa, B.*, 1981, pp. 109–26.
Balassa, Bela. The Changing International Division of Labor in Manufactured Goods. In *Balassa, B.*, 1981, pp. 169–91.
Balassa, Bela. The Newly-Industrializing Developing Countries after the Oil Crisis. *Weltwirtsch. Arch.*, 1981, *117*(1), pp. 142–94. [G: LDCs]
Balassa, Bela. The Newly-Industrializing Developing Countries after the Oil Crisis. In *Balassa, B.*, 1981, pp. 29–81. [G: LDCs]
Balassa, Bela. The Tokyo Round and the Developing Countries. In *Balassa, B.*, 1981, pp. 127–48.
Balassa, Bela. The 15-Year Social and Economic Development Plan for Korea. In *Balassa, B.*, 1981, pp. 347–63. [G: South Korea]
Balassa, Bela. Trade in Manufactured Goods: Patterns of Change. *World Devel.*, March 1981, *9*(3), pp. 263–75.
Balassa, Bela. Trade in Manufactured Goods: Patterns of Change. In *Balassa, B.*, 1981, pp. 193–209.
Baldwin, Robert E. and Bale, Malcolm D. Policy Responses in the Old Industrial Countries: North America. In *Saunders, C. T., ed. (II)*, 1981, pp. 240–60. [G: Canada; U.S.]
Bale, Malcolm D. The Role of Export Cropping in Less Developed Countries: Discussion. *Amer. J. Agr. Econ.*, May 1981, *63*(2), pp. 396–98.
Barker, T. S. A Priori Constraints and the Analysis of British Imports. In *Courbis, R., ed.*, 1981, pp. 77–86. [G: U.K.]
Barten, Anton P. Comet in a Nutshell. In *Courbis, R., ed.*, 1981, pp. 211–19. [G: EEC]
Baum, Kenneth; Safyurtlu, Ali N. and Purcell, Wayne. Analyzing the Economic Impact of National Beef Import Level Changes on the Virginia Beef and Pork Sectors. *Southern J. Agr. Econ.*, December 1981, *13*(2), pp. 111–18. [G: U.S.]
Bautista, Romeo M. An Analysis of Structural Dependence between Korea and Japan: Comment. In *Hong, W. and Krause, L. B., eds.*, 1981, pp. 428–31. [G: Japan; S. Korea]
Bautista, Romeo M. Exchange Rate Changes and LDC Export Performance under Generalized Currency Floating. *Weltwirtsch. Arch.*, 1981, *117*(3), pp. 443–68. [G: LDCs]
Bautista, Romeo M. Exchange Rate Flexibility and

the Less Developed Countries: A Survey of Empirical Research and Policy Issues. *Philippine Econ. J.*, 1981, *20*(1), pp. 1–30. [G: LDCs]
Bautista, Romeo M. The Development of Labour Intensive Industry in the Philippines. In *Amjad, R., ed.*, 1981, pp. 29–75. [G: Philippines]
Beckers, Lode G. Contract Guarantees and International Bonding Practices. In *Gmür, C. J., ed.*, 1981, pp. 149–71.
Behrman, Jack N. and Mikesell, Raymond F. The Impact of U.S. Foreign Direct Investment on U.S. Export Competitiveness in Third World Markets. In *Center for Strategic and Internat. Studies, ed. (II)*, 1981, pp. 147–82. [G: U.S.; LDCs]
Bennett, Karl. Mobilising Foreign Exchange Reserves for Economic Growth in CARICOM. *Soc. Econ. Stud.*, December 1981, *30*(4), pp. 172–86. [G: Jamaica]
Bension, Alberto and Caumont, Jorge. Uruguay: Alternative Trade Strategies and Employment Implications. In *Krueger, A. O., et al., eds.*, 1981, pp. 499–529. [G: Uruguay]
Bergsten, C. Fred. The Economic Interests of the United States and Saudi Arabia. In *Bergsten, C. F., ed.*, 1981, pp. 147–58. [G: Saudi Arabia; U.S.]
Bergsten, C. Fred. The Growing International Competitiveness of the U.S. Economy. In *Bergsten, C. F., ed.*, 1981, pp. 63–71. [G: U.S.]
Berthelot, Yves. The Interests of the Industrial West in Relations with Developing Countries. In *Saunders, C. T., ed. (I)*, 1981, pp. 19–32. [G: OECD; LDCs]
Bhalla, Surjit S. India's Closed Economy and World Inflation. In *Cline, W. R., et al.*, 1981, pp. 136–65. [G: India]
Bhalla, Surjit S. The Transmission of Inflation into Developing Economies. In *Cline, W. R., et al.*, 1981, pp. 52–101. [G: LDCs]
Binkley, James K. and Harrer, Bruce. Major Determinants of Ocean Freight Rates for Grains: An Econometric Analysis. *Amer. J. Agr. Econ.*, February 1981, *63*(1), pp. 47–57.
Binkley, James K. and McKinzie, Lance. Alternative Methods of Estimating Export Demand: A Monte Carlo Comparison. *Can. J. Agr. Econ.*, July 1981, *29*(2), pp. 187–202. [G: Canada]
Black, Stanley W. The Impact of Changes in the World Economy on Stabilization Policies in the 1970s. In *Cline, W. R. and Weintraub, S., eds.*, 1981, pp. 43–77. [G: LDCs]
Bluma, Aleš. Le processus de décision d'achat dans le système socialiste. (The Procedure behind the Decision to Purchase in the Socialist System. With English summary.) *Ann. Sci. Écon. Appl.*, 1981, *37*(3), pp. 145–66. [G: Czechoslovakia]
Bornstein, Morris. East–West Economic Relations and Soviet–East European Economic Relations. In *Bornstein, M., ed.*, 1981, *1979*, pp. 193–215. [G: CMEA; U.S.S.R.]
Bornstein, Morris. Issues in East–West Economic Relations. In *Bornstein, M.; Gitelman, Z. and Zimmerman, W., eds.*, 1981, pp. 31–61. [G: E. Europe]
Bornstein, Morris. Soviet–East European Economic

Relations. In *Bornstein, M.; Gitelman, Z. and Zimmerman, W., eds.,* 1981, pp. 105–24.
[G: CMEA; E. Europe]

Brada, Josef C. Problems of Polish–U.S. Economic Relations: Comment. In *Marer, P. and Tabaczynski, E., eds.,* 1981, pp. 117–19. [G: Poland; U.S.]

Brada, Josef C. Technology Transfer between the United States and Communist Countries. In *Hawkins, R. G. and Prasad, A. J., eds.,* 1981, pp. 219–87. [G: CMEA; U.S.]

Bradford, Colin I., Jr. ADCs' Manufactured Export Growth and OECD Adjustment. In *Hong, W. and Krause, L. B., eds.,* 1981, pp. 476–506.
[G: LDCs; OECD]

Branson, William H. Industrial Policy and U.S. International Trade. In *Wachter, M. L. and Wachter, S. M., eds.,* 1981, pp. 378–408.
[G: U.S.]

Branson, William H. Trends in United States International Trade and Comparative Advantage: Analysis and Prospects. In *National Science Foundation,* 1981, pp. III22–48. [G: U.S.]

Brech, M. J. and Stout, D. K. The Rate of Exchange and Non-Price Competitiveness: A Provisional Study within UK Manufactured Exports. *Oxford Econ. Pap.,* Supplement July 1981, *33,* pp. 268–81. [G: U.K.]

Bredahl, Maury E. Interrelationships between Monetary Instruments and Agricultural Commodity Trade: Discussion. *Amer. J. Agr. Econ.,* December 1981, *63*(5), pp. 944–46. [G: U.S.]

Brodsky, David A. U.S. Trade Statistics and the Virgin Islands: An Anomaly. *Bus. Econ.,* January 1981, *16*(1), pp. 50–54. [G: U.S.]

Brooks, Simon. Systematic Econometric Comparisons: Exports of Manufactured Goods. *Nat. Inst. Econ. Rev.,* August 1981, (97), pp. 67–80.
[G: U.K.]

Browne, Robert S. Changing International Specialization and U.S. Imports of Manufactures. In *Reubens, E. P., ed.,* 1981, pp. 91–112. [G: U.S.]

Calcagno, Alfredo Eric and Jakobowicz, Jean-Michel. Some Aspects of the International Distribution of Industrial Activity. *Cepal Rev.,* April 1981, (13), pp. 7–33. [G: LDCs; MDCs]

Calcagno, Alfredo Eric and Martner, Gonzalo. International Trade and the NIEO. In *Lozoya, J. and Green, R., eds.,* 1981, pp. 1–53.
[G: LDCs]

Campbell, John. American Leaf Exports on Decline: Imperial Tobacco Limited Closes Its Last American Primary-Processing Plant. In *Finger, W. R., ed.,* 1981, pp. 145–49. [G: U.S.; U.K.]

Caporaso, James A. Industrialization in the Periphery: The Evolving Global Division of Labor. In *Hollist, W. L. and Rosenau, J. N., eds.,* 1981, pp. 140–71. [G: LDCs]

Carlson, Jack and Graham, Hugh. The Economic Importance of Exports to the United States. In *Center for Strategic and Internat. Studies, ed. (II),* 1981, pp. 39–146. [G: U.S.; Selected OECD]

Carter, C. A. and Kraft, D. F. An Evaluation of Pricing Performance of the Canadian Feed Grains Policy: A Comment. *Can. J. Agr. Econ.,* Novem-

ber 1981, *29*(3), pp. 349–54. [G: Canada]

Carvalho, José L. and Haddad, Cláudio, L. S. Foreign Trade Strategies and Employment in Brazil. In *Krueger, A. O., et al., eds.,* 1981, pp. 29–81.
[G: Brazil]

Cauas, Jorge and de la Cuadra, Sergio. La política económica de la apertura al exterior en Chile. (With English summary.) *Cuadernos Econ.,* August–December 1981, *18*(54–55), pp. 195–230.
[G: Chile]

Caves, Richard E. Intra-Industry Trade and Market Structure in the Industrial Countries. *Oxford Econ. Pap.,* July 1981, *33*(2), pp. 203–23.

Chambers, Robert G. Interrelationships between Monetary Instruments and Agricultural Commodity Trade. *Amer. J. Agr. Econ.,* December 1981, *63*(5), pp. 934–41. [G: U.S.]

Chambers, Robert G. and Just, Richard E. Effects of Exchange Rate Changes on U.S. Agriculture: A Dynamic Analysis. *Amer. J. Agr. Econ.,* February 1981, *63*(1), pp. 32–46. [G: U.S.]

Chambers, Robert G., et al. Estimating the Impact of Beef Import Restrictions in the U.S. Import Market. *Australian J. Agr. Econ.,* August 1981, *25*(2), pp. 123–33. [G: U.S.]

Chander, R.; Robless, C. L. and Teh, K. P. Malaysian Growth and Price Stabilization. In *Cline, W. R., et al.,* 1981, pp. 208–27. [G: Malaysia]

Chee, Peng Lim; Lee, Donald and Foo, Kok Thye. The Case for Labour Intensive Industries in Malaysia. In *Amjad, R., ed.,* 1981, pp. 235–309.
[G: Malaysia]

Chen, Edward K. Y. Adjusting to the ADCs in the Face of Structurally Depressed Industries: Japan: Comment. In *Hong, W. and Krause, L. B., eds.,* 1981, pp. 468–71. [G: Japan; E. Asia]

Chenery, Hollis B. Challenges and Opportunities Posed by Asia's Superexporters: Implications for Manufactured Exports from Latin America: Comment. In *Baer, W. and Gillis, M., eds.,* 1981, pp. 227–30. [G: East Asia; Latin America]

Chenery, Hollis B. Comments on "Challenges and Opportunities Posed by Asia's Superexporters: Implications for Manufactured Exports from Latin America" *Quart. Rev. Econ. Bus.,* Summer 1981, *21*(2), pp. 227–30. [G: Latin America; E. Asia]

Chenery, Hollis B. and Keesing, Donald B. The Changing Composition of Developing Country Exports. In *Grassman, S. and Lundberg, E., eds.,* 1981, pp. 82–116. [G: LDCs]

Chichilnisky, Graciela. Terms of Trade and Domestic Distribution: Export-Led Growth with Abundant Labour. *J. Devel. Econ.,* April 1981, *8*(2), pp. 163–92.

Chinn, Dennis L. A Calorie-Arbitrage Model of Chinese Grain Trade. *J. Devel. Stud.,* July 1981, *17*(4), pp. 357–70. [G: China]

Chipman, John S. Internal-External Price Relationships in the West German Economy, 1958–79. *Z. ges. Staatswiss.,* September 1981, *137*(3), pp. 612–37. [G: W. Germany]

Claeys, Maurice. Le commerce extérieur de l'UEBL avec les pays de l'Europe Orientale. (External Trade of UEBL (BLEU) with the Countries of Eastern Europe. With English summary.) *Ann.*

Sci. Écon. Appl., 1981, *37*(3), pp. 21–33.
[G: Belgium; Luxemburg; E. Europe]

Clark, Don P. Protection by International Transport Charges: Analysis by Stage of Fabrication. *J. Devel. Econ.*, June 1981, *8*(3), pp. 339–45.
[G: U.S.; LDCs]

Clark, K. J. Financing Exports and Imports. In *Ensor, R. and Muller, P., eds.*, 1981, pp. 243–54.

Clarke, Giles. Trade Financing: Bonds, Private Placements and Eurocredits. In *Gmür, C. J., ed.*, 1981, pp. 133–47. [G: W. Europe]

Clawson, Patrick. The Character of Soviet Economic Relations with Third World Countries. *Rev. Radical Polit. Econ.*, Spring 1981, *13*(1), pp. 76–84.
[G: U.S.S.R.]

Clements, Kenneth W. Changes in the Size of the Traded Goods Sector: Theory and Applications. *Empirical Econ.*, 1981, *6*(4), pp. 203–13.
[G: U.S.; Australia]

Cline, William R. Brazil's Aggressive Response to External Shocks. In *Cline, W. R., et al.*, 1981, pp. 102–35. [G: Brazil]

Cline, William R. Imports and Consumer Prices: A Survey Analysis. In *Baldwin, R. E. and Richardson, J. D., eds.*, 1981, *1979*, pp. 110–17.
[G: U.S.]

Cline, William R. Real Economic Effects of World Inflation and Recession. In *Cline, W. R., et al.*, 1981, pp. 10–51. [G: LDCs]

Coes, Donald V. The Crawling Peg and Exchange Rate Uncertainty. In *Williamson, J., ed.*, 1981, pp. 113–36. [G: Brazil]

Coffey, Joseph D. The Role of Food in the International Affairs of the United States. *Southern J. Agr. Econ.*, July 1981, *13*(1), pp. 29–37.
[G: U.S.]

Colucci, Mario. L'evoluzione degli scambi commerciali tra l'URSS e i paesi capitalistici industrializzati negli anni settanta. (The Development of Commercial Relations between the U.S.S.R. and the Industrialized Capitalist Countries during the Seventies. With English summary.) *Rivista Int. Sci. Econ. Com.*, April 1981, *28*(4), pp. 338–49.
[G: U.S.S.R.]

Conlon, R. M. Transport Cost and Tariff Protection of Australian and Canadian Manufacturing: A Comparative Study. *Can. J. Econ.*, November 1981, *14*(4), pp. 700–707. [G: Australia; Canada]

Corbo, Vittorio and Meller, Patricio. Alternative Trade Strategies and Employment Implications: Chile. In *Krueger, A. O., et al., eds.*, 1981, pp. 83–134. [G: Chile]

Corden, W. Max. Export Growth and the Balance of Payments in Korea, 1960–78: Comment. In *Hong, W. and Krause, L. B., eds.*, 1981, pp. 253–56. [G: S. Korea]

Corden, W. Max. Trade and Industrial Policies, and the Structure of Protection in Korea: Comment. In *Hong, W. and Krause, L. B., eds.*, 1981, pp. 212–14. [G: S. Korea]

Cracco, Etienne. Prospecter en Tchécoslovaquie. (Prospecting in Czechoslovakia. With English summary.) *Ann. Sci. Écon. Appl.*, 1981, *37*(3), pp. 129–44. [G: Belgium; Czechoslovakia]

Dale, Charles, et al. Measuring Export Prices. *Rev.*

Public Data Use (See J. Econ. Soc. Meas. after 4/85), November 1981, *9*(3), pp. 199–209.
[G: U.S.]

Darr, David R. U.S. Exports and Imports of Some Major Forest Products—The Next Fifty Years. In *Sedjo, R. A., ed.*, 1981, pp. 54–83.
[G: U.S.]

Davies, G. J. The Role of Exporter and Freight Forwarder in the United Kingdom. *J. Int. Bus. Stud.*, Winter 1981, *12*(3), pp. 99–108. [G: U.K.]

Davies, Rhodri and Grabiner, Anthony. Trade Financing: Legal Issues. In *Gmür, C. J., ed.*, 1981, pp. 173–86. [G: U.K.; Selected Countries]

De Wulf, Luc. Statistical Analysis of Under- and Overinvoicing of Imports. *J. Devel. Econ.*, June 1981, *8*(3), pp. 303–23.

Decaluwe, Bernard. La formation des prix et les industries canadiennes exposées et abritées. (Price Formation and the Canadian Exposed and Sheltered Industries. With English summary.) *L'Actual. Econ.*, October–December 1981, *57*(4), pp. 454–90. [G: Canada]

Delacollette, Jean. Exportation et transfert de technologie. (Export and Transfer of Technology. With English summary.) *Ann. Sci. Écon. Appl.*, 1981, *37*(4), pp. 167–85.

Delivanis, Dimitrios. Greece and the European Economic Community Aims and Achievements. In *Inst. of Internat. Pub. Law and Internat. Relat. of Thessaloniki*, 1981, pp. 325–31. [G: Greece; EEC]

Dell, Sidney. The Impact of Changes in the World Economy on Stabilization Policies in the 1970s: Comment. In *Cline, W. R. and Weintraub, S., eds.*, 1981, pp. 77–81. [G: LDCs]

Denison, Edward F. International Transactions in Measures of the Nation's Production. *Surv. Curr. Bus.*, May 1981, *61*(5), pp. 17–28. [G: U.S.]

DeRosa, Dean A. and Goldstein, Morris. Import Discipline in the U.S. Manufacturing Sector. *Int. Monet. Fund Staff Pap.*, September 1981, *28*(3), pp. 600–634. [G: U.S.]

DiLullo, Anthony J. Service Transactions in the U.S. International Accounts, 1970–80. *Surv. Curr. Bus.*, November 1981, *61*(11), pp. 29–46.
[G: U.S.]

DiLullo, Anthony J. U.S. International Transactions, Third Quarter 1981. *Surv. Curr. Bus.*, December 1981, *61*(12), pp. 31–35, 56. [G: U.S.]

Dimitrov, Pavel. Analysis of Import Effects on Aggregate Inventories. In *Chikán, A., ed. (I)*, 1981, pp. 99–107. [G: Bulgaria]

Dobozi, István. The Fifth Hungarian-US Economic Round-Table. *Acta Oecon.*, 1981, *26*(1–2), pp. 186–94. [G: Hungary; U.S.]

Dobozi, István and Inotai, András. Prospects of Economic Cooperation between CMEA Countries and Developing Countries. In *Saunders, C. T., ed. (I)*, 1981, pp. 48–65. [G: CMEA; LDCs]

Dopfer, Kurt. Determinants of Japan's Expansion in Western Markets. *Wirtsch. Recht*, 1981, *33*(3/4), pp. 153–59. [G: Japan]

Dornbusch, Rudiger. Exports and Policy in Latin-American Countries: Comment. In *Baer, W. and Gillis, M., eds.*, 1981, pp. 43–47.
[G: Latin America]

Dowdle, Barney. Log Export Restrictions: Causes and Consequences. In *Sedjo, R. A., ed.*, 1981, pp. 248–58.   [G: U.S.]

Drysdale, Peter. ADCs' Manufactured Export Growth and OECD Adjustment: Comment. In *Hong, W. and Krause, L. B., eds.*, 1981, pp. 509–11.   [G: LDCs; OECD]

Dunning, John H. A Note on Intra-Industry Foreign Direct Investment. *Banca Naz. Lavoro Quart. Rev.*, December 1981, (139), pp. 427–37.

Dunning, John H. Multinational Enterprises and Trade Flows of Developing Countries. In *Dunning, J. H.*, 1981, pp. 304–20.

Dunning, John H. Trade, Location of Economic Activity and the Multinational Enterprise: Some Empirical Tests. In *Dunning, J. H.*, 1981, pp. 46–71.   [G: Selected countries]

Eidem, Rolf. East, West, and South: The Role of the Centrally Planned Economies in the International Economy: Comments. In *Grassman, S. and Lundberg, E., eds.*, 1981, pp. 358–61.   [G: CMEA]

Elliott, Robert F. and Wood, Peter W. The International Transfer of Technology and Western European Integration. In *Hawkins, R. G. and Prasad, A. J., eds.*, 1981, pp. 117–50.   [G: W. Europe]

Ellis, Frank. Export Valuation and Intra-firm Transfers in the Banana Export Industry in Central America. In *Murray, R., ed.*, 1981, pp. 61–76.   [G: Costa Rica; Honduras; Guatemala; Panama]

Ellsworth, P. T. The Terms of Trade between Primary-Producing and Industrial Countries. In *Livingstone, I., ed.*, 1981, *1961*, pp. 129–36.   [G: Global]

English, H. Edward. Export-Oriented Growth and Industrial Diversification in Hong Kong: Comment. In *Hong, W. and Krause, L. B., eds.*, 1981, pp. 124–28.   [G: Hong Kong]

Ernst, Wolfgang. The Free Movement of Goods and Services within the European Economic Community in the Context of the World Economy. *Z. ges. Staatswiss.*, September 1981, *137*(3), pp. 556–74.   [G: EEC]

Etienne, Gilbert. Rural Development in China and Its Impact on Foreign Trade. *Rivista Int. Sci. Econ. Com.*, September 1981, *28*(9), pp. 831–51.   [G: China]

Ewing, A. F. Energy and East-West Co-operation. *J. World Trade Law*, May–June 1981, *15*(3), pp. 218–30.   [G: E. Europe; W. Europe]

Fajnzylber, Fernando. Some Reflections on South-East Asian Export Industrialization. *Cepal Rev.*, December 1981, (15), pp. 111–32.

     [G: S. Korea; Taiwan; Hong Kong; Singapore]

Farley, Noel J. J. Outward Looking Policies and the Changing Basis of Ireland's Foreign Trade. *Econ. Soc. Rev.*, January 1981, *12*(2), pp. 73–95.   [G: Ireland]

Figueroa, Adolfo. Effects of Changes in Consumption and Trade Patterns on Agricultural Development in Latin America. *Quart. Rev. Econ. Bus.*, Summer 1981, *21*(2), pp. 83–97.   [G: Latin America]

Figueroa, Adolfo. Effects of Changes in Consumption and Trade Patterns on Agricultural Development in Latin America. In *Baer, W. and Gillis,*

M., eds., 1981, pp. 83–97.   [G: Peru; Latin America]

Findlay, Ronald. An Analysis of Structural Dependence between Korea and Japan: Comment. In *Hong, W. and Krause, L. B., eds.*, 1981, pp. 431–32.   [G: Japan; S. Korea]

Fodella, Gianni. Economic Relations between China and Japan: Problems and Prospects. *Rivista Int. Sci. Econ. Com.*, September 1981, *28*(9), pp. 889–99.   [G: China; Japan]

Fong, Pang Eng and Tan, Augustine. Employment and Export-led Industrialisation: The Experience of Singapore. In *Amjad, R., ed.*, 1981, pp. 141–74.   [G: Singapore]

Franklin, Daniel. Bribery and Corruption in East-West Trade. *ACES Bull. (See Comp. Econ. Stud. after 8/85),* Fall–Winter 1981, 23(3–4), pp. 1–71.   [G: E. Europe]

Franko, Lawrence G. Adjusting to Export Thrusts of Newly Industrialising Countries: An Advanced Country Perspective. *Econ. J.*, June 1981, *91*(362), pp. 486–506.   [G: OECD]

Franko, Lawrence G. and Stephenson, Sherry. French Export Behavior in Third World Markets. In *Center for Strategic and Internat. Studies, ed. (I)*, 1981, pp. 171–251.   [G: France; OECD; LDCs]

Freeman, C. British Trade Performance and Technical Innovation. In *Freeman, C., et al.*, 1981, pp. 1–25.   [G: U.K.]

Froment, René. Matrices de Structure: Propriétés et Problèmes de Projection. (With English summary.) In *Courbis, R., ed.*, 1981, pp. 171–82.

Gaines, David B.; Sawyer, William C. and Sprinkle, Richard. EEC Mediterranean Policy and U.S. Trade in Citrus. *J. World Trade Law*, September–October 1981, *15*(5), pp. 431–39.   [G: U.S.; EEC]

Gardner, H. Stephen. The Embodied Factor Content of Soviet Foreign Trade: A Rejoinder [The Factor Content of Soviet Foreign Trade: A Synthesis]. *ACES Bull. (See Comp. Econ. Stud. after 8/85),* Spring 1981, *23*(1), pp. 89–101.   [G: U.S.S.R.]

Garrity, Monique P. The Assembly Industries in Haiti: Causes and Effects, 1967–1973. *Rev. Black Polit. Econ.*, Winter 1981, *11*(2), pp. 203–15.   [G: Haiti]

Gärtner, Manfred and Heri, Erwin W. Oil Imports and Inflation: A Comment [Oil Imports and Inflation: An Empirical International Analysis of the "Imported" Inflation Thesis]. *Kyklos*, 1981, *34*(3), pp. 461–67.   [G: EEC; Japan; U.S.; Australia]

Georgiou, George C. Alternative Trade Strategies and Employment in Cyprus. *J. Econ. Devel.*, December 1981, *6*(2), pp. 113–31.   [G: Cyprus]

Giersch, Herbert. Problems of Adjustment to Imports from Less-Developed Countries. In *Grassman, S. and Lundberg, E., eds.*, 1981, pp. 265–88.

Ginsburgh, V. and Waelbroeck, Jean. Some Calculations of the Impact of Tariffs on World Trade and Welfare with a General Equilibrium Model of World Economy. In *Courbis, R., ed.*, 1981, pp. 279–94.   [G: Global]

Girgis, Maurice. Foreign Trade and Development

in Egypt [Review Article]. *Weltwirtsch. Arch.*, 1981, *117*(2), pp. 389–96. [G: Egypt]

Givens, William L. International Industrial Competitiveness: The United States and Japan. In *Hogan, J. D. and Craig, A. M., eds., Vol. 1*, 1981, pp. 669–73. [G: Japan; U.S.]

Gmür, Charles J. Financing Trade in Consumer Goods. In *Gmür, C. J., ed.*, 1981, pp. 73–82. [G: Switzerland]

Gmür, Charles J. Trade Financing: Forfaiting. In *Gmür, C. J., ed.*, 1981, pp. 117–32.

Gmür, Charles J. Trade Financing: Leasing. In *Gmür, C. J., ed.*, 1981, pp. 105–16. [G: W. Europe]

Goetz, Arturo L. Beyond the Slogan of South-South Co-operation: Comment. *World Devel.*, June 1981, *9*(6), pp. 583–85.

Goldsbrough, David J. International Trade of Multinational Corporations and Its Responsiveness to Changes in Aggregate Demand and Relative Prices. *Int. Monet. Fund Staff Pap.*, September 1981, *28*(3), pp. 573–99. [G: U.S.]

Graham, Edward M. A Comment on "The Dilemmas of Technology." *J. Econ. Issues*, March 1981, *15*(1), pp. 199–204. [G: U.S.S.R.; U.S.]

Graham, Thomas R. The Impact of the Tokyo Round Agreements on U.S. Export Competitiveness. In *Center for Strategic and Internat. Studies, ed. (II)*, 1981, pp. 319–73. [G: U.S.; Selected OECD]

Graziani, Giovanni. Dependency Structures in COMECON. *Rev. Radical Polit. Econ.*, Spring 1981, *13*(1), pp. 67–75. [G: COMECON]

Greenaway, David and Milner, Chris. Trade Imbalance Effects in the Measurement of Intra-Industry Trade. *Weltwirtsch. Arch.*, 1981, *117*(4), pp. 756–62. [G: U.K.]

Grossman, Gene M. The Theory of Domestic Content Protection and Content Preference. *Quart. J. Econ.*, November 1981, *96*(4), pp. 583–603.

Guisinger, Stephen E. Trade Policies and Employment: The Case of Pakistan. In *Krueger, A. O., et al., eds.*, 1981, pp. 291–340. [G: Pakistan]

Gülalp, Haldun. Gelişme Stratejileri Tartişmasi: Bir Eleştiriye Yanit. (The Debate on Development Strategies: Reply to a Critique. With English summary.) *METU*, 1981, *8*(3&4), pp. 755–70. [G: Turkey]

Guru, D. D. Economic Relations between India and Poland. *Econ. Aff.*, January–March 1981, *26*(1), pp. 25–32. [G: India; Poland]

Gutmann, Pierre. The Measurement of Terms of Trade Effects. *Rev. Income Wealth*, December 1981, *27*(4), pp. 433–53. [G: Saudi Arabia; OECD]

Hadley, Eleanor G. Japan's Export Competitiveness in Third World Markets. In *Center for Strategic and Internat. Studies, ed. (I)*, 1981, pp. 254–330. [G: Japan; MDCs; LDCs]

Halliday, Jon. The Specificity of Japan's Re-integration into the World Capitalist Economy after 1945: Notes on Some Myths and Misconceptions. *Rivista Int. Sci. Econ. Com.*, July–August 1981, *28*(7–8), pp. 663–81. [G: Japan]

Harkness, Jon. Cross-Section Tests of the Heckscher–Ohlin Theorem: Reply [Factor Abun-

dance and Comparative Advantage]. *Amer. Econ. Rev.*, December 1981, *71*(5), pp. 1044–48.

Harley, C. K. and McCloskey, D. N. Foreign Trade: Competition and the Expanding International Economy. In *Floud, R. and McCloskey, D., eds., Vol. 2*, 1981, pp. 50–69. [G: U.K.]

Hartland-Thunberg, Penelope. Has the U.S. Export Problem Been Solved? In *Center for Strategic and Internat. Studies, ed. (II)*, 1981, pp. 267–77. [G: U.S.]

Hartland-Thunberg, Penelope. The Political and Strategic Importance of Exports. In *Center for Strategic and Internat. Studies, ed. (II)*, 1981, pp. 1–38. [G: U.S.]

Hay, D. A. and Morris, D. J. The Sterling Rate of Exchange and UK Profitability: Short Term Effects. *Oxford Econ. Pap.*, Supplement July 1981, *33*, pp. 248–67. [G: U.K.]

Haynes, Richard; Darr, David R. and Adams, Darius. U.S.–Japanese Log Trade—Effect of a Ban. In *Sedjo, R. A., ed.*, 1981, pp. 216–32. [G: U.S.; Japan]

Heady, Earl O. and Short, Cameron. Interrelationship among Export Markets, Resource Conservation, and Agricultural Productivity. *Amer. J. Agr. Econ.*, December 1981, *63*(5), pp. 840–47. [G: U.S.]

Heiss, Hertha W.; Lenz, Allen J. and Brougher, Jack. U.S.–Soviet Commercial Relations since 1972. In *Bornstein, M., ed.*, 1981, *1979*, pp. 233–52. [G: U.S.S.R.; U.S.]

Helleiner, G. K. Intra-firm Trade and the Developing Countries: An Assessment of the Data. In *Murray, R., ed.*, 1981, pp. 31–57. [G: U.S.; Global]

Helleiner, Gerald K. Adjusting to the ADCs in the Face of Structurally Depressed Industries: Japan: Comment. In *Hong, W. and Krause, L. B., eds.*, 1981, pp. 471–74. [G: Japan; E. Asia]

Helleiner, Gerald K. Devil Take the Hindmost? The Least Developed in a New International Economic Order. In *Helleiner, G. K.*, 1981, pp. 194–218. [G: LDCs]

Henry, C. Michael. U.S. Inflation and the Import Demand of Ghana and Nigeria, 1967–1976. *Rev. Black Polit. Econ.*, Winter 1981, *11*(2), pp. 217–28. [G: Ghana; Nigeria]

Hewitt, Adrian and Stevens, Christopher. The Second Lomé Convention. In *Stevens, C., ed.*, 1981, pp. 30–59. [G: EEC; LDCs]

Hillman, Jimmye S. Policy Issues Relevant to United States Agricultural Trade. In *McCalla, A. F. and Josling, T. E., eds.*, 1981, pp. 113–42. [G: U.S.]

Hillman, Jimmye S. The Role of Export Cropping in Less Developed Countries. *Amer. J. Agr. Econ.*, May 1981, *63*(2), pp. 375–83. [G: LDCs]

Hisrich, Robert D.; Peters, Michael P. and Weinstein, Arnold K. East–West Trade: The View from the United States. *J. Int. Bus. Stud.*, Winter 1981, *12*(3), pp. 109–21. [G: U.S.; E. Europe; China]

Hojman, David E. The Andean Pact: Failure of a Model of Economic Integration? *J. Common Market Stud.*, December 1981, *20*(2), pp. 139–60. [G: Andean Pact]

Holden, Merle and Holden, Paul. The Employment Effects of Different Trade Regimes in South Africa. *S. Afr. J. Econ.*, September 1981, *49*(3), pp. 232–40.

Hong, Wontack. Export Promotion and Employment Growth in South Korea. In *Krueger, A. O., et al., eds.*, 1981, pp. 341–91. [G: S. Korea]

Horwitz, Eva Christina. Swedish Export Performance: A Constant-Market-share Analysis. In *Industrial Inst. for Econ. and Soc. Research*, 1981, pp. 54–58. [G: Sweden]

Hudson, Edward A. U.S. Energy Price Decontrol: Energy, Trade and Economic Effects. *Scand. J. Econ.*, 1981, *83*(2), pp. 180–200.

Hufbauer, Gary Clyde. Income Levels and the Structure of Trade: Comments. In *Grassman, S. and Lundberg, E., eds.*, 1981, pp. 162–64. [G: Global]

Hufbauer, Gary Clyde; Smith, W. N. Harrell, IV and Vukmanic, Frank G. Mexico–United States Relations: Bilateral Trade Relations. In *Purcell, S. K., ed.*, 1981, pp. 136–45. [G: Mexico; U.S.]

Hughes, Helen. The New Industrial Countries in the World Economy: Pessimism and a Way Out. In *Saunders, C. T., ed. (II)*, 1981, pp. 97–131. [G: LDCs; MDCs]

Huguel, Catherine. Les échanges technologiques mondiaux. (The International Flows of Technology. With English summary.) *Revue Écon.*, September 1981, *32*(5), pp. 923–49. [G: OECD; Eastern Europe; Selected LDCs]

Ingersoll, Robert S. Political Aspects of American–Japanese Economic Confrontations. In *Hewett, R. B., ed.*, 1981, pp. 153–63. [G: U.S.; Japan]

Islam, Rizwanul. Some Macroeconomic Implications of Higher Oil Prices for Bangladesh. *Bangladesh Devel. Stud.*, Summer 1981, *9*(2), pp. 1–20. [G: Bangladesh]

Jarjour, Gabi. Long-Term Gas Pricing Strategy. *J. Energy Devel.*, Autumn 1981, *7*(1), pp. 89–98. [G: Global]

Jepma, Catrinus J. An Application of the Constant Market Shares Technique on Trade between the Associated African and Malagasy States and the European Community (1958–1978) *J. Common Market Stud.*, December 1981, *20*(2), pp. 175–92. [G: AAMS (W. Africa)]

Johansson, J. K. and Spich, Robert S. Trade Interdependence in the Pacific Rim Basin and the E.C.: A Comparative Analysis. *J. Common Market Stud.*, September 1981, *20*(1), pp. 41–59. [G: New Zealand; Australia; N. America; Japan; EEC]

Johnson, D. Gale. Comparative Advantage of United States Agriculture. In *Baldwin, R. E. and Richardson, J. D., eds.*, 1981, *1979*, pp. 221–30. [G: U.S.; EEC]

Johnson, D. Gale. Food and Agriculture of the Centrally Planned Economies: Implications for the World Food System. In *Fellner, W., ed.*, 1981, pp. 171–213. [G: U.S.S.R.; China; E. Europe]

Josling, Timothy. World Food Production, Consumption, and International Trade: Implications for U.S. Agriculture. In *Johnson, D. G., ed.*, 1981, pp. 83–112. [G: U.S.; Global]

Kádár, Béla. Adjustment Problems, Patterns and Policies in Small Countries. *Acta Oecon.*, 1981, *27*(1–2), pp. 125–39. [G: W. Europe]

Kaikati, Jack G. The Anti-Export Policy of the U.S. *Calif. Manage. Rev.*, Spring 1981, *23*(3), pp. 5–19. [G: U.S.]

Kairamo, Kari. Finländsk industri i hårdnande internationell konkurrens. (Finnish Industry in Growing International Competition. With English summary.) *Ekon. Samfundets Tidskr.*, 1981, *34*(1), pp. 5–15. [G: Finland]

Kaynak, Erdener and Stevenson, Lois. Conceptualizations and Methodological Framework for Export Marketing Planning. *Liiketaloudellinen Aikak.*, 1981, *30*(4), pp. 393–406. [G: Canada]

Keesing, Donald B. Exports and Policy in Latin-American Countries: Prospects for the World Economy and for Latin-American Exports, 1980–90. In *Baer, W. and Gillis, M., eds.*, 1981, pp. 18–43. [G: Latin America]

Keyserling, Leon H. International Implications of U.S. Economic Performance and National Policies. *Atlantic Econ. J.*, December 1981, *9*(4), pp. 27–33. [G: U.S.]

Kierzkowski, Henryk and Sampson, Gary P. The Multifibre Arrangement: The Approach and Setting to the Forthcoming Negotiations. *Aussenwirtschaft*, March 1981, *36*(1), pp. 41–56. [G: OECD]

Kiger, Hugh C. Open Trade and Modernized Tobacco Program: The Keys to an Expanded U.S. Flue-Cured World Market. In *Finger, W. R., ed.*, 1981, pp. 131–44. [G: Global; U.S.]

Kinney, Joseph A. Tobacco's Global Economy: Is North Carolina Losing? In *Finger, W. R., ed.*, 1981, pp. 119–29. [G: Global; U.S.]

Kisiel, Michal. Links of Polish Agriculture with the World Economy. In *Johnson, G. and Maunder, A., eds.*, 1981, pp. 338–44. [G: Poland]

Kitching, Beverly. Structural Changes in United States Foreign Trade in the 1970s. *Int. J. Soc. Econ.*, 1981, *8*(7), pp. 63–69. [G: U.S.]

Kivikari, Urpo. Problems and Prospects of an Open Economy: Finland's Case. *Acta Oecon.*, 1981, *26*(1–2), pp. 157–74. [G: Finland]

Kleiman, Ephraim and Pincus, Jonathan J. The Cyclical Effects of Incremental Export Subsidies. *Econ. Rec.*, June 1981, *57*(157), pp. 140–49. [G: Australia]

Klein, Lawrence R. International Aspects of Industrial Policy. In *Wachter, M. L. and Wachter, S. M., eds.*, 1981, pp. 361–77. [G: U.S.]

Klein, Lawrence R. The Link Project. In *Courbis, R., ed.*, 1981, pp. 197–209. [G: OECD]

Klein, Lawrence R.; Fardoust, Shahrokh and Filatov, Victor. Purchasing Power Parity in Medium Term Simulation of the World Economy. *Scand. J. Econ.*, 1981, *83*(4), pp. 479–96.

Kohlemy, Gunther. Improving the International Division of Labour: Comment. In *Saunders, C. T., ed. (I)*, 1981, pp. 333–36. [G: E. Germany]

Kohli, Ulrich R. Import Requirements of Canadian Final Output Components. *Empirical Econ.*, 1981, *6*(4), pp. 215–27. [G: Canada]

Kooyman, Jan. The Meteor Model. In *Courbis, R., ed.*, 1981, pp. 235–42. [G: OECD]

Kossut, Zygmunt. Determinants of Polish Exports

of Manufactured Products to the West and the Strategy of Industrial Cooperation: Comment. In *Marer, P. and Tabaczynski, E., eds.*, 1981, pp. 293–95. **[G: Poland; W. Germany]**

Kossut, Zygmunt. Problems of Polish–U.S. Economic Relations: A Polish Perspective. In *Marer, P. and Tabaczynski, E., eds.*, 1981, pp. 109–16. **[G: Poland; U.S.]**

Kossut, Zygmunt. Problems of Polish–U.S. Economic Relations: Reply. In *Marer, P. and Tabaczynski, E., eds.*, 1981, pp. 119–20. **[G: Poland; U.S.]**

Kreinin, Mordechai E. Static Effect of E.C. Enlargement on Trade Flows in Manufactured Products. *Kyklos*, 1981, *34*(1), pp. 60–71. **[G: EEC]**

Krishnamurti, R. UNCTAD as a Negotiating Institution. *J. World Trade Law*, January–February 1981, *15*(1), pp. 3–40.

Krueger, Anne O. Trade and Industrial Policies, and the Structure of Protection in Korea: Comment. In *Hong, W. and Krause, L. B., eds.*, 1981, pp. 214–16. **[G: S. Korea]**

Krueger, Russell C. U.S. International Transactions, Second Quarter 1981. *Surv. Curr. Bus.*, September 1981, *61*(9), pp. 42–45, 64. **[G: U.S.]**

Krueger, Russell C. U.S. International Transactions, First Quarter 1981. *Surv. Curr. Bus.*, June 1981, *61*(6), pp. 31–71.

Laarman, Jan G. World Forest Plantations—What Are the Implications for U.S. Forest Products Trade? Discussion. In *Sedjo, R. A., ed.*, 1981, pp. 40–53. **[G: U.S.; Brazil]**

Lagos, Gustavo. The Revolution of Being: A Preferred World Model. In *Muñoz, H., ed.*, 1981, pp. 123–60. **[G: Latin America]**

Lall, Sanjaya. Recent Trends in Exports of Manufactures by Newly-Industrialising Countries. In *Lall, S.*, 1981, pp. 173–227. **[G: LDCs]**

Lall, Sanjaya and Kumar, Rajiv. Firm-Level Export Performance in an Inward-Looking Economy: The Indian Engineering Industry. *World Devel.*, May 1981, *9*(5), pp. 453–63. **[G: India]**

Lam, Ngo Van. Government Responses to Export Instability in Papua New Guinea. *Malayan Econ. Rev. (See Singapore Econ. Rev.)*, October 1981, *26*(2), pp. 27–45. **[G: Papua New Guinea]**

Lamaswala, K. M. The Pricing of Unwrought Cooper in Relation to Transfer Pricing. In *Murray, R., ed.*, 1981, pp. 77–85. **[G: Zambia]**

Landau, Zbigniew and Tomaszewski, Jerzy. The International Movement of Capital in Central and South-Eastern Europe before the Second World War. In *[Lipiński, E.]*, 1981, pp. 19–37. **[G: S.E. Europe]**

de Laubier, Dominique and Richemond, Alain. Inteprénétration des capitaux et concurrence industrielle mondiale. (With English summary.) *Écon. Appl.*, 1981, *34*(2–3), pp. 469–515. **[G: U.S.; Japan; Europe; Canada]**

Lawrence, Max. Brazil's Fuel Alcohol Program: Implications for the World Sugar Market. *Quart. Rev. Rural Econ.*, November 1981, *3*(4), pp. 330–33. **[G: Brazil]**

Lawson, C. W. and Thanassoulas, C. Commodity Concentration and Export Instability: A Missing Link or Hunting a Snark? *Oxford Bull. Econ. Sta-*

tist., May 1981, *43*(2), pp. 201–06. **[G: LDCs]**

Leamer, Edward E. and Bowen, Harry P. Cross-Section Tests of the Heckscher–Ohlin Theorem: Comment [Factor Abundance and Comparative Advantage]. *Amer. Econ. Rev.*, December 1981, *71*(5), pp. 1040–43.

Lee, Hoe Sung. Changing Economic Relations between the Asian ADCs and Resource-Exporting Advanced Countries of the Pacific Basin: Comment. In *Hong, W. and Krause, L. B., eds.*, 1981, pp. 339–40. **[G: Hong Kong; Singapore; S. Korea; Taiwan; Selected MDCs]**

Levcik, Friedrich. The Prospects for East–West Trade in the 1980s. In *Bornstein, M.; Gitelman, Z. and Zimmerman, W., eds.*, 1981, pp. 62–84. **[G: CMEA; U.S.S.R.]**

Lewis, W. Arthur. The Rate of Growth of World Trade, 1830–1973. In *Grassman, S. and Lundberg, E., eds.*, 1981, pp. 11–74. **[G: Global]**

Leyva, Jesús Puente. Mexico–United States Relations: The Natural Gas Controversy. In *Purcell, S. K., ed.*, 1981, pp. 158–67. **[G: Mexico; U.S.]**

Liao, Xunzhen. Readjustment in China's Foreign Trade. *Rivista Int. Sci. Econ. Com.*, September 1981, *28*(9), pp. 823–30. **[G: China]**

Lim, Chong-Yah. The Economic Development of the Members of the Association of Southeast Asian Nations (ASEAN). In *Lozoya, J. A. and Bhattacharya, A. K., eds.*, 1981, pp. 174–88. **[G: S. E. Asia]**

Lin, Tzong Biau and Ho, Yin Ping. Export-Oriented Growth and Industrial Diversification in Hong Kong. In *Hong, W. and Krause, L. B., eds.*, 1981, pp. 69–123. **[G: Hong Kong]**

Linder, Staffan Burenstam. Causes of Trade in Primary Products versus Manufactures. In *Baldwin, R. E. and Richardson, J. D., eds.*, 1981, *1961*, pp. 40–51.

Linge, G. J. R. and Hamilton, F. E. Ian. International Industrial Systems. In *Hamilton, F. E. I. and Linge, G. J. R., eds.*, 1981, pp. 1–117. **[G: OECD; CMEA; LDCs]**

Lippke, Bruce. U.S.–Japanese Log Trade—Effect of a Ban: Discussion. In *Sedjo, R. A., ed.*, 1981, pp. 233–47. **[G: U.S.; Japan]**

Lipsey, Robert E. and Weiss, Merle Yahr. Foreign Production and Exports in Manufacturing Industries. *Rev. Econ. Statist.*, November 1981, *63*(4), pp. 488–94. **[G: U.S.]**

Loasby, B. J. Price-Cost Margins, Market Structure and International Trade: Comment. In *Currie, D.; Peel, D. and Peters, W., eds.*, 1981, pp. 296–98. **[G: U.K.]**

Long, Frank. Multinational Corporations and the Non-Primary Sector Trade of Developing Countries: A Survey of Available Data. *Econ. Int.*, May–August–November 1981, *34*(2–3–4), pp. 376–99. **[G: LDCs]**

Longo, Carlos A. Comment on "Policy Responses to External Shocks in Selected Latin-American Countries." *Quart. Rev. Econ. Bus.*, Summer 1981, *21*(2), pp. 165–67. **[G: Brazil; Mexico; Uruguay]**

Longo, Carlos A. Policy Responses to External Shocks in Selected Latin-American Countries: Comment. In *Baer, W. and Gillis, M., eds.*, 1981, pp. 165–67.   [G: Brazil; Mexico; Uruguay]

Lord, Montague J. Comment on "Commodity Exports and NIEO Proposals for Buffer Stocks and Compensatory Finance." *Quart. Rev. Econ. Bus.*, Summer 1981, *21*(2), pp. 76–82.
[G: Latin America]

Lord, Montague J. Commodity Exports and NIEO Proposals for Buffer Stocks and Compensatory Finance: Comment. In *Baer, W. and Gillis, M., eds.*, 1981, pp. 76–82.   [G: Brazil; Chile; Latin America]

Loseby, Margaret and Venzi, Lorenzo. Floating Exchange Rates and International Trade in Agricultural Commodities. In *Johnson, G. and Maunder, A., eds.*, 1981, pp. 426–36.

Love, J. Commodity Diversification: A Market Model. *J. Devel. Stud.*, October 1981, *18*(1), pp. 94–103.   [G: Latin America; Africa; Asia]

Luciani, Sergio F. A Note on the Concept of Two Way Trade. *Weltwirtsch. Arch.*, 1981, *117*(1), pp. 136–41.   [G: U.S.]

Lundberg, Erik. Problems of Adjustment to Imports from Less-Developed Countries: Comments. In *Grassman, S. and Lundberg, E., eds.*, 1981, pp. 289–94.

Lundborg, Per. The Elasticities of Supply and Demand for Swedish Exports in a Simultaneous Model. *Scand. J. Econ.*, 1981, *83*(3), pp. 444–48.   [G: Sweden]

Luttrell, Clifton B. Grain Export Agreements—No Gains, No Losses. *Fed. Res. Bank St. Louis Rev.*, August/September 1981, *63*(7), pp. 23–29.
[G: U.S.]

Luttrell, Clifton B. The Voluntary Automobile Import Agreement with Japan—More Protectionism. *Fed. Res. Bank St. Louis Rev.*, November 1981, *63*(9), pp. 25–30.   [G: U.S.; Japan]

Lyons, Bruce. Price-Cost Margins, Market Structure and International Trade. In *Currie, D.; Peel, D. and Peters, W., eds.*, 1981, pp. 276–95.
[G: U.K.]

Macbean, A. I. and Nguyen, D. T. Commodity Concentration and Export Earnings Instability: A Reply. *Econ. J.*, September 1981, *91*(363), pp. 758.

de Macedo, Jorge Braga. International Investment, Migration and Finance: Issues and Policies: Comment. *Economia (Portugal)*, January 1981, *5*(1), pp. 111–15.

Magiera, Stephen L. The Role of Wheat in the Indonesian Food Sector. *Bull. Indonesian Econ. Stud.*, November 1981, *17*(3), pp. 48–73.
[G: Indonesia]

Mahmood, Muhammad and Williams, Ross A. The World Jute Market. *Bangladesh Devel. Stud.*, Autumn 1981, *9*(4), pp. 113–23.   [G: Bangladesh; India; Thailand]

Mahmood, Zafar. Changes in Export Shares and Competitive Strength in Pakistan. *Pakistan Devel. Rev.*, Winter 1981, *20*(4), pp. 399–415.
[G: Pakistan]

Marer, Paul. The Mechanism and Performance of Hungary's Foreign Trade, 1968–79. In *Hare, P. G.; Radice, H. K. and Swain, N., eds.*, 1981, pp. 161–204.   [G: Hungary]

Markowski, Aleksander and Uggla, Magnus. Internordiskt handelsberoende. (Internordic Trade

Dependence. With English summary.) *Ekon. Samfundets Tidskr.*, 1981, *34*(2), pp. 121–46.
[G: Denmark; Sweden; Norway; Finland]

Marquenie, Erwig L. Les PME dans le commerce belge avec les pays de l'Europe de l'Est. (SME in Belgian Trade with Eastern Countries. With English summary.) *Ann. Sci. Écon. Appl.*, 1981, *37*(3), pp. 93–107.   [G: Belgium]

Martin, John P. and Evans, John M. Notes on Measuring the Employment Displacement Effects of Trade by the Accounting Procedure. *Oxford Econ. Pap.*, March 1981, *33*(1), pp. 154–64.

McAleese, Dermot and Carey, Patrick. Employment Coefficients for Irish Trade with Extra-EEC Countries: Measurement and Implications. *Econ. Soc. Rev.*, January 1981, *12*(2), pp. 115–32.
[G: Ireland]

McCloskey, Donald N. Magnanimous Albion: Free Trade and British National Income, 1841–1881. In *McCloskey, D. N.*, 1981, *1980*, pp. 155–72.
[G: U.K.]

McCulloch, Rachel. Gains to Latin America from Trade Liberalization in Developed and Developing Nations. In *Baer, W. and Gillis, M., eds.*, 1981, pp. 231–58.   [G: Latin America]

McCusker, John J. The Tonnage of Ships Engaged in British Colonial Trade during the Eighteenth Century. In *Uselding, P., ed.*, 1981, pp. 73–105.
[G: U.K.]

McKillop, William. Log Export Restrictions: Causes and Consequences: Discussion. In *Sedjo, R. A., ed.*, 1981, pp. 259–63.   [G: U.S.]

McMillan, Charles J. The Pros and Cons of a National Export Trading House. *Can. Public Policy*, Autumn 1981, *7*(4), pp. 569–83.   [G: Canada]

Meyer-Thoms, Gerold. Trade Structure and Export Instability: The Case of Ghana. In *Schmitt-Rink, G., ed.*, 1981, pp. 72–116.   [G: Ghana]

Michaely, Michael. Income Levels and the Structure of Trade. In *Grassman, S. and Lundberg, E., eds.*, 1981, pp. 121–61.   [G: Global]

Mikesell, Raymond F. and Farah, Mark G. U.S. Export Competitiveness in Manufactures in Third World Markets. In *Center for Strategic and Internat. Studies, ed. (I)*, 1981, pp. 45–169.
[G: MDCs; LDCs; U.S.]

Miller, Elisa B. Barter Trade in East-West Commerce: Extending the "Parallel Market" Concept. *ACES Bull. (See Comp. Econ. Stud. after 8/85)*, Fall–Winter 1981, *23*(3–4), pp. 81–91.
[G: E. Europe; MDCs]

Miller, Robert H. Financing Trade in Capital Goods. In *Gmür, C. J., ed.*, 1981, pp. 83–89.
[G: W. Europe]

Mölders, Peter. The Pattern of Ghanaian Exports in the Seventies. In *Schmitt-Rink, G., ed.*, 1981, pp. 117–58.   [G: Ghana]

Molitor, Bernhard. International Investment, Migration and Finance: Issues and Policies: Comment. *Economia (Portugal)*, January 1981, *5*(1), pp. 105–10.

Monke, Eric A. Toward a U.S. Agricultural Export Policy for the 1980s: Discussion. *Amer. J. Agr. Econ.*, December 1981, *63*(5), pp. 848–50.
[G: U.S.]

Monson, Terry. Trade Strategies and Employment

in the Ivory Coast. In *Krueger, A. O., et al.*, *eds.*, 1981, pp. 239–90. [G: Ivory Coast]

Müller, Jürgen. Competitive Performance and Trade within the EEC: Generalizations from Several Case Studies with Specific Reference to the West German Economy. *Z. ges. Staatswiss.*, September 1981, *137*(3), pp. 638–63.
[G: W. Germany; EEC]

Murrell, Peter. An Evaluation of the Success of the Hungarian Economic Reform: An Analysis Using International-Trade Data. *J. Compar. Econ.*, December 1981, *5*(4), pp. 352–66.
[G: Mediterranean Europe; Austria; U.K.; Hungary; E. Europe]

Mussa, Michael L. The Crawling Peg and Exchange Rate Uncertainty: Comment. In *Williamson, J.*, *ed.*, 1981, pp. 137–39. [G: Brazil]

Nabli, Mustapha K. Alternative Trade Policies and Employment in Tunisia. In *Krueger, A. O., et al., eds.*, 1981, pp. 435–98. [G: Tunisia]

Naggl, Walter. Kurzfristige Schätzfunktionen für den Warenhandel der Bundesrepublik Deutschland. (With English summary.) *Weltwirtsch. Arch.*, 1981, *117*(4), pp. 687–705. [G: W. Germany]

Nagy, András. Comment [East–West–South Patterns of Trade] [Structural Policy Issues in Production and Trade: A Western View]. In *Saunders, C. T., ed. (I)*, 1981, pp. 313–21.
[G: CMEA; LDCs; OECD]

Nagy, András. Growth and Trade: the Hungarian Case. In *Bornstein, M.; Gitelman, Z. and Zimmerman, W., eds.*, 1981, pp. 192–220.
[G: Hungary]

Nam, Chong Hyun. Trade and Industrial Policies, and the Strucure of Protection in Korea. In *Hong, W. and Krause, L. B., eds.*, 1981, pp. 187–211.
[G: S. Korea]

Nguyen, The-Hiep. Trends in Terms of Trade of LDCs. *J. Econ. Stud.*, 1981, *8*(2), pp. 46–56.

Nobel, Klaus. Development Opportunities of Ghana within the Frame of Intra-industry Trade—An Empirical Analysis on the Basis of Triangularized Trade Matrices. In *Schmitt-Rink, G., ed.*, 1981, pp. 159–213. [G: Ghana]

Nziramasanga, Mudziviri T. and Obidegwu, Chukwuma. Primary Commodity Price Fluctuations and Developing Countries: An Econometric Model of Copper and Zambia. *J. Devel. Econ.*, August 1981, *9*(1), pp. 89–119. [G: Zambia]

O'Hanlon, Paul. Documentary Collection and Letters of Credit. In *Gmür, C. J., ed.*, 1981, pp. 43–72.

Ocampo, José-Antonio. Export Growth and Capitalist Development in Colombia in the Nineteenth Century. In *Bairoch, P. and Lévy-Leboyer, M., eds.*, 1981, pp. 98–109. [G: Colombia]

Ohlin, Göran. East–West–South Patterns of Trade. In *Saunders, C. T., ed. (I)*, 1981, pp. 265–78.
[G: CMEA; OECD; OPEC]

Okumura, Ariyoshi. Policy Responses in the Old Industrial Countries: Japan and East Asia. In *Saunders, C. T., ed. (II)*, 1981, pp. 261–83.
[G: Japan; E. Asia]

Olgun, Hasan. Ithal Ikamesi Tartişmasi ve G. Özler. (The Crisis of Import Substitution: A Reply. With English summary.) *METU*, 1981, *8*(3&4),

pp. 771–76. [G: Turkey]

Olgun, Hasan. Türkiye'de Ithal Ikamesi Bunalimi ve Dişa Açilma: Ikinci Eleştiri. (The Crisis of Import Substitution: A Second Critique. With English summary.) *METU*, 1981, *8*(3&4), pp. 777–93. [G: Turkey]

Ollmann, Hartmut. Terms of Trade of Ghana, 1968–75 in Regional and Sectoral Analysis. In *Schmitt-Rink, G., ed.*, 1981, pp. 214–77. [G: Ghana]

Ozawa, Terutomo. Technology Transfer and Control Systems: The Japanese Experience. In *Sagafinejad, T.; Moxon, R. W. and Perlmutter, H. V., eds.*, 1981, pp. 376–426. [G: Japan]

Özler, Güntaç. Gülalp-Oglun Tartişmasi Üzerine. (On Gülalp-Olgun Controversy. With English summary.) *METU*, 1981, *8*(3&4), pp. 747–53.
[G: Turkey]

Page, S. A. B. The Revival of Protectionism and Its Consequences for Europe. *J. Common Market Stud.*, September 1981, *20*(1), pp. 17–40.
[G: W. Europe]

Pagoulatos, Emilio. Discussion: The Role of Food and Agriculture in the International Affairs of the United States. *Southern J. Agr. Econ.*, July 1981, *13*(1), pp. 39–42. [G: U.S.]

Pagoulatos, Emilio; Shonkwiler, J. Scott and Degner, Robert L. Foreign Competition and Trade Policy for the Florida Lime Industry. *Amer. J. Agr. Econ.*, August 1981, *63*(3), pp. 557–61.

Paine, Suzanne. International Investment, Migration and Finance: Issues and Policies. *Economia (Portugal)*, January 1981, *5*(1), pp. 63–104.

Paliwoda, Stanley J. Multinational Corporations: Trade and Investment across the East–West Divide. *Managerial Dec. Econ.*, December 1981, *2*(4), pp. 247–55. [G: CMEA; OECD]

Palócz-Németh, Éva. Exports of Manufactures of CMEA and Developing Countries to Developed Industrial Countries. *Acta Oecon.*, 1981, *26*(1–2), pp. 93–106. [G: OECD; CMEA; LDCs]

Paquay-Deghilage, Anne. Promouvoir son entreprise et ses produits en Tchécoslovaquie: organiser une campagne publicitaire. (Promoting a Company and Its Products in Czechoslovakia. With English summary.) *Ann. Sci. Écon. Appl.*, 1981, *37*(3), pp. 179–219. [G: Belgium; Czechoslovakia]

Park, Yung Chul. Export Growth and the Balance of Payments in Korea, 1960–78. In *Hong, W. and Krause, L. B., eds.*, 1981, pp. 218–51.
[G: S. Korea]

Paszynski, Marian. The Economic Interest of the CMEA Countries in Relations with Developing Countries: Reply. In *Saunders, C. T., ed. (I)*, 1981, pp. 87–89. [G: CMEA; LDCs]

Paszynski, Marian. The Economic Interest of the CMEA Countries in Relations with Developing Countries. In *Saunders, C. T., ed. (I)*, 1981, pp. 33–47. [G: CMEA; LDCs]

Pelzman, Joseph and Martin, Randolph C. Direct Employment Effects of Increased Imports: A Case Study of the Textile Industry. *Southern Econ. J.*, October 1981, *48*(2), pp. 412–26. [G: U.S.]

Perrons, D. C. The Role of Ireland in the New International Division of Labour: A Proposed Framework for Regional Analysis. *Reg. Stud.*, 1981,

15(2), pp. 81–100.   [G: Ireland]

Petoussis, Emmanuel. The Aggregate Import Function within a General Equilibrium Context. *Greek Econ. Rev.*, December 1981, *3*(3), pp. 310–24.   [G: Greece]

Phaup, E. Dwight. The Demand for Imports: Estimates of Bilateral Trade Flows. *J. Macroecon.*, Winter 1981, *3*(1), pp. 97–115.

Philip, Kjeld. Danmarks bilaterale samarbejde med udviklingslandene. (Denmarks Bilateral Co-operation with Developing Countries. With English summary.) *Nationaløkon. Tidsskr.*, 1981, *119*(1), pp. 47–63.   [G: LDCs; Denmark]

Piskulov, Jurij Vasiljevitz. De nordeuropeiska länderna i dagens världsekonomiska system. (The Nordic Countries in the World Economy. With English summary.) *Ekon. Samfundets Tidskr.*, 1981, *34*(3), pp. 183–207.   [G: Denmark; Norway; Sweden; Finland]

Pitt, Mark M. Alternative Trade Strategies and Employment in Indonesia. In *Krueger, A. O., et al., eds.*, 1981, pp. 181–237.   [G: Indonesia]

Pitt, Mark M. Smuggling and Price Disparity. *J. Int. Econ.*, November 1981, *11*(4), pp. 447–58.   [G: Indonesia]

Plessz, N. Policy Responses in the Old Industrial Countries: Western Europe. In *Saunders, C. T., ed. (II)*, 1981, pp. 217–39.   [G: W. Europe; Selected LDCs]

Plihon, D. Un Modéle Sectoriel de la Balance Commerciale Française. (With English summary.) In *Courbis, R., ed.*, 1981, pp. 47–63.   [G: France]

Pomfret, Richard. The Impact of EEC Enlargement on Non-member Mediterranean Countries' Exports to the EEC. *Econ. J.*, September 1981, *91*(363), pp. 726–29.   [G: EEC]

Porter, Roger B. The U.S.-U.S.S.R. Grain Agreement: Some Lessons for Policymakers. *Public Policy*, Fall 1981, *29*(4), pp. 527–51.

Portes, Richard. East, West, and South: The Role of the Centrally Planned Economies in the International Economy. In *Grassman, S. and Lundberg, E., eds.*, 1981, pp. 319–57.   [G: CMEA]

Pravda, Alex. East–West Interdependence and the Social Compact in Eastern Europe. In *Bornstein, M.; Gitelman, Z. and Zimmerman, W., eds.*, 1981, pp. 162–87.   [G: E. Europe]

Rácz, Lászlo. On the New Price System. *Eastern Europ. Econ.*, Fall 1981, *20*(1), pp. 49–69.   [G: Hungary]

Radcliffe, Samuel J. U.S. Forest Products Trade and the Multilateral Trade Negotiations. In *Sedjo, R. A., ed.*, 1981, pp. 136–68.   [G: U.S.]

Radice, H. K. Industrial Co-operation between Hungary and the West. In *Hare, P. G.; Radice, H. K. and Swain, N., eds.*, 1981, pp. 109–31.   [G: Hungary; W. Europe; U.S.]

Raemy-Dirks, Christine. Countertrade: Linked Purchases in International Trade. In *Gmür, C. J., ed.*, 1981, pp. 17–27.   [G: Global]

Rahman, M. Akhlaqur; Bhuyan, Rahman and Reza, Sadrel. The Trade Effects of a South Asian Customs Union: An Expository Study. *Pakistan Devel. Rev.*, Spring 1981, *20*(1), pp. 61–80.

Rahman, Sultan Hafez. Simulation of an Econometric Model to Analyze the Impact of a Buffer Stock Scheme in the Bangladesh Jute Sector. *Bangladesh Devel. Stud.*, Autumn 1981, *9*(4), pp. 1–33.   [G: Bangladesh]

Randall, Laura R. Mexican Development and Its Effects upon United States Trade. In *McBride, R. H., ed.*, 1981, pp. 49–76.   [G: Mexico; U.S.]

Ranis, Gustav. Challenges and Opportunities Posed by Asia's Superexporters: Implications for Manufactured Exports from Latin America. *Quart. Rev. Econ. Bus.*, Summer 1981, *21*(2), pp. 204–26.   [G: Latin America; E. Asia]

Ranis, Gustav. Challenges and Opportunities Posed by Asia's Superexporters: Implications for Manufactured Exports from Latin America. In *Baer, W. and Gillis, M., eds.*, 1981, pp. 204–26.   [G: East Asia; Latin America]

Rapacki, Ryszard. Poland's Exports of Licenses. *Econ. Planning*, 1981, *17*(2–3), pp. 53–63.   [G: Poland]

Ray, Edward John. Tariff and Nontariff Barriers to Trade in the United States and Abroad. *Rev. Econ. Statist.*, May 1981, *63*(2), pp. 161–68.

Reynolds, Clark W. The Structure of the Economic Relationship. In *Purcell, S. K., ed.*, 1981, pp. 125–35.   [G: Mexico; U.S.]

Ripley, Duncan. The I.M.F. World Trade Model: A Progress Report. In *Courbis, R., ed.*, 1981, pp. 123–36.

Rocherieux, François. Sur la théorie des modèles inter-industriels: Quelques remarques appliquées à l'analyse de l'emploi et du commerce international. (On Input-Output Models Theory: Some Remarks Applied to Employment and International Trade Analysis. With English summary.) *Revue Écon.*, September 1981, *32*(5), pp. 887–922.   [G: France]

Roehl, Thomas. Technology Transfer and Control Systems: The Japanese Experience: Comment. In *Sagafi-nejad, T.; Moxon, R. W. and Perlmutter, H. V., eds.*, 1981, pp. 427–29.   [G: Japan]

Root, Franklin R. and Contractor, Farok J. Negotiating Compensation in International Licensing Agreements. *Sloan Manage. Rev.*, Winter 1981, *22*(2), pp. 23–32.   [G: U.S.]

Rösch, Franz and Homann, Fritz. Thirty Years of the Berlin Agreement—Thirty Years of Inner-German Trade: Economic and Political Dimensions. *Z. ges. Staatswiss.*, September 1981, *137*(3), pp. 525–55.   [G: E. Germany; W. Germany]

Rosefielde, Steven. Comparative Advantage and the Evolving Pattern of Soviet International Commodity Specialization, 1950–1973. In *[Bergson, A.]*, 1981, pp. 185–220.   [G: U.S.S.R.; CMEA]

Ross, Bruce J. Changing Economic Relations between the Asian ADCs and Resource-Exporting Advanced Countries of the Pacific Basin: Comment. In *Hong, W. and Krause, L. B., eds.*, 1981, pp. 340–43.   [G: Hong Kong; Singapore; S. Korea; Taiwan; Selected MDCs]

Roumeliotis, Panayotis. Underinvoicing Aluminium from Greece. In *Murray, R., ed.*, 1981, pp. 86–88.   [G: Greece]

Rousslang, Donald and Parker, Stephen. The Effects of Aggregation on Estimated Import Price Elasticities: The Role of Imported Intermediate Inputs.

Rev. Econ. Statist., August 1981, *63*(3), pp. 436–39. [G: U.S.]

Rowe, Lyndon and Forster, Gavan. Measuring Australia's International Competitiveness: A Note. *Australian Bull. Lab.*, December 1981, *8*(1), pp. 21–30.

Ruiz, Maria L. Trade Flows under Oligopolistic Conditions: A Supply Oriented Approach. *Econ. Notes*, 1981, *10*(1), pp. 46–66. [G: Italy]

Russett, Bruce. United States Solar Energy Policy for Less-Developed Countries. *J. Energy Devel.*, Autumn 1981, *7*(1), pp. 39–59. [G: LDCs; U.S.]

Sallin-Kornberg, Eugenia and Fontela, Emilio. Scenarios Building with the Explor-Multitrade 85 Model. In *Courbis, R., ed.*, 1981, pp. 309–25.

Samuelson, Lee W. OECD World Trade Model: Some Recent Extensions. In *Courbis, R., ed.*, 1981, pp. 149–62. [G: OECD]

Sapir, André. European Imports of Manufactures under Trade Preferences for Developing Countries. In *Reubens, E. P., ed.*, 1981, pp. 113–31. [G: EEC]

Sapir, André. Trade Benefits under the EEC Generalized System of Preferences. *Europ. Econ. Rev.*, March 1981, *15*(3), pp. 339–55. [G: EEC]

Sarris, Alexander H. Empirical Models of International Trade in Agricultural Commodities. In *McCalla, A. F. and Josling, T. E., eds.*, 1981, pp. 87–112.

Sarris, Alexander H. and Schmitz, Andrew. Toward a U.S. Agricultural Export Policy for the 1980s. *Amer. J. Agr. Econ.*, December 1981, *63*(5), pp. 832–39. [G: U.S.]

Saulniers, Alfred. State Trading Organizations: A Bias Decision Model and Applications. *World Devel.*, July 1981, *9*(7), pp. 679–94. [G: Peru]

Sawhney, Bansi L. and Di Pietro, William R. Monopoly Power, the Participation Theory and International Trade. *Econ. Int.*, February 1981, *34*(1), pp. 143–58. [G: MDCs; LDCs]

Schneider, Jürgen. Terms of Trade between France and Latin America, 1826–1856: Causes of Increasing Economic Disparities? In *Bairoch, P. and Lévy-Leboyer, M., eds.*, 1981, pp. 110–119. [G: France; Latin America]

Schuh, G. Edward. Economics and International Relations: A Conceptual Framework. *Amer. J. Agr. Econ.*, December 1981, *63*(5), pp. 767–78.

Schultz, Siegfried; Schumacher, Dieter and Wilkens, Herbert. North-South Interdependence: The Case of the Federal Republic of Germany. *World Devel.*, May 1981, *9*(5), pp. 435–52. [G: W. Germany; LDCs]

Schweiter, Aloys and Baumer, Helen. Protezionismo in aumento commercio mondiale in regresso? (Increasing Protectionism and a Backward Trend in World Trade? With English summary.) *Mondo Aperto*, December 1981, *35*(6), pp. 359–68.

Sedjo, Roger. World Forest Plantations—What Are the Implications for U.S. Forest Products Trade? In *Sedjo, R. A., ed.*, 1981, pp. 17–39. [G: U.S.; Brazil]

Semudram, M. Relative Prices and the External Sector of the Malaysian Economy. *Malayan Econ. Rev. (See Singapore Econ. Rev.)*, April 1981, *26*(1), pp. 39–51. [G: Malaya]

Sercovich, Francisco Colman. The Exchange and Absorption of Technology in Brazilian Industry. In *Bruneau, T. C. and Faucher, P., eds.*, 1981, pp. 127–40. [G: Brazil]

Serfaty, Simon. The United States, Western Europe, and the Third World: Allies and Adversaries. In *Center for Strategic and Internat. Studies, ed. (I)*, 1981, pp. 1–44. [G: MDCs; LDCs]

Shepherd, Geoffrey. Industrial Strategies in Textiles and Clothing and Motor Cars. In *Saunders, C. T., ed. (II)*, 1981, pp. 132–56. [G: LDCs; OECD]

Shields, Roger E. and Sonksen, R. Craig. Government Financial Institutions in Support of U.S. Exports. In *Center for Strategic and Internat. Studies, ed. (II)*, 1981, pp. 183–265. [G: U.S.; Selected OECD]

Shinkai, Yoichi. Terms of Trade, Wages and Exchange Rates in Japan. (In Japanese. With English summary.) *Osaka Econ. Pap.*, December 1981, *31*(2–3), pp. 15–29. [G: Japan]

Siebert, Horst. Strategische Ansatzpunkte der Rohstoffpolitik der Industrienationen nach der Theorie des intertemporalen Ressourcenangebots. (Strategies of Natural Resource Policy for the Industrial Nations According to the Theory of Intertemporal Allocation. With English summary.) *Konjunkturpolitik*, 1981, *27*(5), pp. 297–310. [G: W. Germany]

Singh, Ajit. Third World Industrialisation and the Structure of the World Economy. In *Currie, D.; Peel, D. and Peters, W., eds.*, 1981, pp. 454–95. [G: LDCs; MDCs]

Siri, Gabriel and Domínguez, Luis Raúl. Central American Accommodation to External Disruptions. In *Cline, W. R., et al.*, 1981, pp. 166–207. [G: El Salvador; Guatemala]

Smith, Ben. Trade Relations between Latin American and the Asian ADCs: Comment. In *Hong, W. and Krause, L. B., eds.*, 1981, pp. 385–88. [G: E. Asia; Latin America]

Solís, Leopoldo. The Impact of the Float on LDCs: Latin American Experience in the 1970s: Comment. In *Williamson, J., ed.*, 1981, pp. 322–23. [G: Brazil; Chile; Costa Rica; Guatemala]

Solo, Robert. The Dilemmas of Technology: A Reply. *J. Econ. Issues*, March 1981, *15*(1), pp. 204–11. [G: U.S.S.R.; U.S.]

Sornarajah, M. The Myth of International Contract Law. *J. World Trade Law*, May–June 1981, *15*(3), pp. 187–217.

Soskin, Nikolas P. Trade Financing: Bills of Exchange. In *Gmür, C. J., ed.*, 1981, pp. 29–41. [G: Global]

Soth, Lauren. The Grain Export Boom: Should It be Tamed? *Foreign Aff.*, Spring 1981, *59*(4), pp. 895–912. [G: U.S.]

Stammati, Gaetano. Italy and Japan Facing the New Oil and Monetary Crises. *Rivista Int. Sci. Econ. Com.*, July–August 1981, *28*(7–8), pp. 755–61. [G: Japan; Italy]

Steed, Guy P. F. International Location and Comparative Advantage: The Clothing Industries and Developing Countries. In *Hamilton, F. E. I. and Linge, G. J. R., eds.*, 1981, pp. 265–303. [G: LDCs]

Steel, David [Sir]. Risks in the International Oil Trade. In *Tempest, P., ed.*, 1981, pp. 3–9.

Stein, Leslie. The Growth and Implications of LDC Manufactured Exports to Advanced Countries. *Kyklos*, 1981, *34*(1), pp. 36–59. [G: LDCs.]

Stern, Robert M. Changes in U.S. Comparative Advantage: Issues for Research and Policy. In *National Science Foundation*, 1981, pp. III81–105. [G: U.S.]

Stern, Robert M. and Maskus, Keith E. Determinants of the Structure of U.S. Foreign Trade, 1958–76. *J. Int. Econ.*, May 1981, *11*(2), pp. 207–24. [G: U.S.]

Stewart, Frances. Kenya Strategies for Development. In *Killick, T., ed.*, 1981, *1976*, pp. 75–89. [G: Kenya]

Stobaugh, Robert B. Energy Future and International Trade. *J. Int. Bus. Stud.*, Spring/Summer 1981, *12*(1), pp. 23–28. [G: U.S.]

Stoevener, Herbert H. Interrelationship among Export Markets, Resource Conservation, and Agricultural Productivity: Discussion. *Amer. J. Agr. Econ.*, December 1981, *63*(5), pp. 851–52. [G: U.S.]

Storey, Gary G. and Kulshreshtha, Surenda N. An Evaluation of Pricing Performance of the Canadian Feed Grain Policy: A Reply. *Can. J. Agr. Econ.*, November 1981, *29*(3), pp. 355–60. [G: Canada]

Storey, Gary G. and Kulshreshtha, Surendra N. An Evaluation of Pricing Performance of the Canadian Feed Grains Policy. *Can. J. Agr. Econ.*, February 1981, *29*(1), pp. 1–20. [G: Canada]

Streeten, Paul P. World Trade in Agricultural Commodities and the Terms of Trade with Industrial Goods. In *Streeten, P.*, 1981, *1974*, pp. 213–31. [G: Global]

Stromback, C. T. Aggregation in Logarithmic Models: Some Experiments with UK Export Functions: A Comment. *Oxford Bull. Econ. Statist.*, November 1981, *43*(4), pp. 363–65. [G: U.K.]

Strydom, P. D. F. Trends in World Trade (Review Note) *S. Afr. J. Econ.*, June 1981, *49*(2), pp. 166–71.

Švarc, František and Polačková, Vlasta. Czechoslovak Economic Cooperation with Developing Countries. *Czech. Econ. Digest.*, August 1981, (5), pp. 78–87. [G: LDCs]

Swedenborg, Birgitta. The Internationalization of Swedish Industry: Determinants and Effects. In *Industrial Inst. for Econ. and Soc. Research*, 1981, pp. 59–65. [G: U.S.; Sweden]

Szakolczai, György. Foreign Trade in the Hungarian Models. In *Courbis, R., ed.*, 1981, pp. 65–75. [G: Hungary]

Tambunlertchai, Somsak and Loohawenchit, Chesada. Labour Intensive and Small Scale Manufacturing in Thailand. In *Amjad, R., ed.*, 1981, pp. 175–233. [G: Thailand]

Tangermann, Stefan. Policies of the European Community and Agricultural Trade with Developing Countries. In *Johnson, G. and Maunder, A., eds.*, 1981, pp. 440–51. [G: EEC]

Tatemoto, Masahiro. Trade Conflicts between Japan and the European Countries. *Osaka Econ. Pap.*,

December 1981, *31*(2–3), pp. 30–39. [G: Japan; W. Europe]

Taylor, Lance. South-North Trade and Southern Growth: Bleak Prospects from the Structuralist Point of View. *J. Int. Econ.*, November 1981, *11*(4), pp. 589–602.

Teichman, Thomas. The Importer: Buyer Credits from the Euromarkets. In *Gmür, C. J., ed.*, 1981, pp. 91–103. [G: W. Europe]

Thomas, D. J. General Equilibrium Assessment of a Free Area between Two Small Countries: Australia and New Zealand. *Australian Econ. Pap.*, December 1981, *20*(37), pp. 283–98. [G: Australia; New Zealand]

Thomas, R. P. and McCloskey, Donald N. Overseas Trade and Empire 1700–1860. In *Floud, R. and McCloskey, D., eds.*, Vol. 1, 1981, pp. 87–102. [G: U.K.]

Thoumi, Francisco E. International Trade Strategies, Employment, and Income Distribution in Colombia. In *Krueger, A. O., et al., eds.*, 1981, pp. 135–79. [G: Colombia]

Tilley, Daniel S. and Lee, Jonq-Ying. Import and Retail Demand for Orange Juice in Canada. *Can. J. Agr. Econ.*, July 1981, *29*(2), pp. 171–86. [G: Canada]

Timmer, C. Peter. China and the World Grain Market. *Challenge*, September/October 1981, *24*(4), pp. 13–21. [G: China]

Tironi, Ernesto. Trade Relations between Latin American and the Asian ADCs. In *Hong, W. and Krause, L. B., eds.*, 1981, pp. 346–81. [G: E. Asia; Latin America]

Treml, Vladimir G. The Inferior Quality of Soviet Machinery as Reflected in Export Prices. *J. Compar. Econ.*, June 1981, *5*(2), pp. 200–221. [G: U.S.S.R.]

Troch, Rudy. La coopération et la compensation avec les pays socialistes. (Compensation and Co-operation with the Socialist Countries. With English summary.) *Ann. Sci. Écon. Appl.*, 1981, *37*(3), pp. 35–56. [G: E. Europe; W. Europe]

Trzeciakowski, Witold. Solving Poland's Foreign Trade Problems. In *Bornstein, M.; Gitelman, Z. and Zimmerman, W., eds.*, 1981, pp. 242–51. [G: Poland]

Tsegaye, Asrat. The Specification of the Foreign Trade Multiplier for a Developing Country. *Oxford Bull. Econ. Statist.*, August 1981, *43*(3), pp. 287–300. [G: LDCs]

Tsurumi, Yoshi. Export Assistance for Foreign Firms. In *Richardson, B. M. and Ueda, T., eds.*, 1981, pp. 299–303. [G: Japan]

Tsurumi, Yoshi. Exports to Japan by Small Firms. In *Richardson, B. M. and Ueda, T., eds.*, 1981, pp. 290–98. [G: Japan]

Tsurumi, Yoshi. Realities of the Japanese Consumer Imports Market. In *Richardson, B. M. and Ueda, T., eds.*, 1981, pp. 283–89. [G: Japan]

Tufarelli, Nicola. The Current International Situation and the National Restraints of Italy and Japan. *Rivista Int. Sci. Econ. Com.*, July–August 1981, *28*(7–8), pp. 762–68. [G: Italy; Japan]

Turner, Louis, et al. Living with the Newly Industrialized Countries. In *The Royal Inst. of Internat.*

Affairs, 1981, pp. 103–65.   [G: Selected LDCs; OECD]

Turner, R. E. and Lambert, P. J. Commodity Concentration and Export Earnings Instability: A Comment. *Econ. J.*, September 1981, *91*(363), pp. 755–57.

Tyler, William G. Advanced Developing Countries as Export Competitors in Third World Markets: the Brazilian Experience. In *Center for Strategic and Internat. Studies, ed. (1)*, 1981, pp. 331–408. [G: Brazil; LDCs]

Uri, Noel D. and Mixon, J. Wilson, Jr. The Effect of Exports and Imports on the Stability of Employment in Manufacturing Industries in the United States. *Appl. Econ.*, June 1981, *13*(2), pp. 193–203.   [G: U.S.]

Vaitsos, Constantine V. From a Colonial Past to Asymmetrical Interdependences: The Role of Europe in North–South Relations. In *Mauri, A., ed.*, 1981, pp. 35–81.   [G: W. Europe; LDCs]

Valdés, Alberto and Siamwalla, Ammar. Assessing Food Insecurity in LDCs—Roles of International Schemes in Relation to LDCs. In *Johnson, G. and Maunder, A., eds.*, 1981, pp. 454–64. [G: Selected LDCs]

Vargha, Louis. U.S. Forest Products Trade and the Multilateral Trade Negotiations: Discussion. In *Sedjo, R. A., ed.*, 1981, pp. 175–84. [G: U.S.]

Vartia, Pentti and Salmi, Kari. A Note on the Short-term Determinants of Finnish Export Prices. *Liiketaloudellinen Aikak.*, 1981, *30*(1), pp. 3–19.   [G: Finland]

Vernon, Raymond. State-Owned Enterprises in Latin-American Exports. In *Baer, W. and Gillis, M., eds.*, 1981, pp. 98–114. [G: Latin America]

Vollmer, Rainer. The Structure of West German Foreign Trade. *Z. ges. Staatswiss.*, September 1981, *137*(3), pp. 575–89.   [G: W. Germany]

Volpi, Vittorio. Giappone: un mercato importante. *(Japan: An Important Market. With English summary.)* *L'Impresa*, 1981, *23*(4), pp. 35–40.   [G: Japan; Italy]

Wall, David. Reply [Industrial Processing of Natural Resources]. *World Devel.*, May 1981, *9*(5), pp. 495–98.

Wallich, Henry C. Statement to Subcommittee on Trade of the House Ways and Means Committee, November 3, 1981. *Fed. Res. Bull.*, November 1981, *67*(11), pp. 850–53.   [G: U.S.]

Wallich, Henry C. Statement to Subcommittee on International Finance and Monetary Policy, Senate Committee on Banking, Housing, and Urban Affairs, February 17, 1981. *Fed. Res. Bull.*, March 1981, *67*(3), pp. 233–35.   [G: U.S.]

Ward, John. U.S. Exports and Imports of Some Major Forest Products—The Next Fifty Years: Discussion. In *Sedjo, R. A., ed.*, 1981, pp. 93–98.   [G: U.S.]

Wassermann, Ursula. Apartheid and Economic Sanctions. *J. World Trade Law*, July–August 1981, *15*(4), pp. 367–69.   [G: S. Africa]

Wassermann, Ursula. Zimbabwe's Foreign Trade. *J. World Trade Law*, March–April 1981, *15*(2), pp. 173–79.   [G: Zimbabwe]

Wassermann, Ursula. Zurich Conference on Trade with China. *J. World Trade Law*, November–December 1981, *15*(6), pp. 553–57.   [G: China]

Watanabe, Toshio. An Analysis of Structural Dependence between Korea and Japan. In *Hong, W. and Krause, L. B., eds.*, 1981, pp. 393–427.   [G: Japan; S. Korea]

Watkins, G. Campbell. Canadian Oil Exports to the USA: From Profusion to Parsimony. *Energy Econ.*, October 1981, *3*(4), pp. 219–24.   [G: U.S.; Canada]

Weeks, Peter and Turner, Bruce. Effects of the Proposed Canadian Meat Import Law. *Quart. Rev. Rural Econ.*, August 1981, *3*(3), pp. 232–39.   [G: Canada; Australia]

Weintraub, Sidney. Trade Integration of the United States, Canada, and Mexico. In *U.S. Congress, Joint Economic Committee (III)*, 1981, pp. 179–208.   [G: U.S.; Canada; Mexico]

Wigny, Pierre-Henry. Le commerce extérieur des produits chimiques entre la Belgique et la Tchécoslovaquie. (External Trade of Chemical Products between Belgium and Czechoslovakia. With English summary.) *Ann. Sci. Écon. Appl.*, 1981, *37*(3), pp. 167–75. [G: Belgium; Czechoslovakia]

Winters, L. A. Aggregation in Logarithmic Models: Some Experiments with UK Exports: A Reply. *Oxford Bull. Econ. Statist.*, November 1981, *43*(4), pp. 367–69.   [G: U.K.]

Wisdom, Harold. U.S. Forest Products Trade and the Multilateral Trade Negotiations: Discussion. In *Sedjo, R. A., ed.*, 1981, pp. 169–74.   [G: U.S.]

Wiseman, A. Clark. U.S.–Canadian Lumber Trade: The Effect of Restrictions: Discussion. In *Sedjo, R. A., ed.*, 1981, pp. 133–35. [G: U.S.; Canada]

Witte, Willard E. The Lagged Adjustment of Canadian Exports to Prices and Foreign Activity, 1973-1978. *Rev. Econ. Statist.*, May 1981, *63*(2), pp. 303–07.   [G: Canada]

Wolf, Thomas A. Determinants of Polish Exports of Manufactured Products to the West and the Strategy of Industrial Cooperation: Reply. In *Marer, P. and Tabaczynski, E., eds.*, 1981, pp. 295–97.   [G: Poland; W. Germany]

Wolf, Thomas A. Determinants of Polish Exports of Manufactured Products to the West and the Strategy of Industrial Cooperation. In *Marer, P. and Tabaczynski, E., eds.*, 1981, pp. 272–92. [G: Poland; W. Germany]

Wright, J. F. Britain's Inter-War Experience. *Oxford Econ. Pap.*, Supplement July 1981, *33*, pp. 282–305.   [G: U.K.]

Wu, Yuan-li. The Economic Impact of China's Modernization on Pacific Relationships. In *Hewett, R. B., ed.*, 1981, pp. 88–98.   [G: China; U.S.]

Wurth, P. The Arrangement Regarding International Trade in Textiles. *Aussenwirtschaft*, March 1981, *36*(1), pp. 57–69.

Yamazawa, Ippei. Adjusting to the ADCs in the Face of Structurally Depressed Industries: Japan. In *Hong, W. and Krause, L. B., eds.*, 1981, pp. 435–67.   [G: Japan; E. Asia]

Yang, Yung Y. A Comparative Analysis of the Determinants of Nontraditional Exports for Brazil, Israel, and South Korea. *Weltwirtsch. Arch.*, 1981, *117*(3), pp. 497–512.   [G: Brazil; Israel; S. Korea]

Yeats, Alexander J. The Influence of Trade and Commercial Barriers on the Industrial Processing of Natural Resources [Industrial Processing of Natural Resources]. *World Devel.*, May 1981, *9*(5), pp. 485–94.

Yeats, Alexander J. The Rate of Growth of World Trade, 1830–1973: Comments. In *Grassman, S. and Lundberg, E., eds.*, 1981, pp. 75–81.
[G: Europe; U.S.; Japan]

Yoffie, David B. Orderly Marketing Agreements as an Industrial Policy: The Case of the Footwear Industry. *Public Policy*, Winter 1981, *29*(1), pp. 93–119. [G: U.S.]

Zighera, Jacques A. Nomenclatures et Prévision des Échanges Internationaux. (With English summary.) In *Courbis, R., ed.*, 1981, pp. 41–46.
[G: EEC]

Zimmerman, William. East–West Relations and the Future of Eastern Europe: Conclusion. In *Bornstein, M.; Gitelman, Z. and Zimmerman, W., eds.*, 1981, pp. 283–96. [G: E. Europe]

Zimmerman, William. Soviet–East European Relations in the 1980s and the Changing International System. In *Bornstein, M.; Gitelman, Z. and Zimmerman, W., eds.*, 1981, pp. 87–104.
[G: U.S.S.R.; E. Europe]

Zimmermann, Rainer. Prognosis of the Ghanaian Export Values 1975–1985. In *Schmitt-Rink, G., ed.*, 1981, pp. 278–315. [G: Ghana]

Zivnuska, John. U.S. Exports and Imports of Some Major Forest Products—The Next Fifty Years: Discussion. In *Sedjo, R. A., ed.*, 1981, pp. 84–92. [G: U.S.]

422 Commercial Policy

4220 Commercial Policy and Trade Regulations; Empirical Studies

Adams, Darius and Haynes, Richard. U.S.–Canadian Lumber Trade: The Effect of Restrictions. In *Sedjo, R. A., ed.*, 1981, pp. 101–32.
[G: U.S.; Canada]

Adams, F. Gerard; Behrman, Jere R. and Lasaga, M. Commodity Exports and NIEO Proposals for Buffer Stocks and Compensatory Finance: Implications for Latin America. *Quart. Rev. Econ. Bus.*, Summer 1981, *21*(2), pp. 48–76.
[G: Latin America]

Adams, F. Gerard; Behrman, Jere R. and Lasaga, M. Commodity Exports and NIEO Proposals for Buffer Stocks and Compensatory Finance: Implications for Latin America. In *Baer, W. and Gillis, M., eds.*, 1981, pp. 48–76. [G: Chile; Latin America]

Adelman, Morris A. and Moran, Theodore H. Statements on Oil and OPEC. In *Baldwin, R. E. and Richardson, J. D., eds.*, 1981, 1977, pp. 202–20.
[G: OPEC]

Ahluwalia, Montek S. and Lysy, Frank J. Employment, Income Distribution, and Programs to Remedy Balance-of-Payments Difficulties. In *Cline, W. R. and Weintraub, S., eds.*, 1981, pp. 149–88. [G: Malaysia]

Aho, C. Michael. The Economy of 1981: A Bipartisan Look: Proceedings of a Congressional Economic Conference: Statement. In *U.S. Congress, Joint Economic Committee (I)*, 1981, pp. 560–67.
[G: U.S.]

Aho, C. Michael and Bowen, Harry P. U.S. Industrial Competitiveness in the 1980' and the Need for an Expanded Policy Horizon. In *U.S. Congress, Joint Economic Committee (I)*, 1981, pp. 567–70. [G: U.S.]

Akiba, Hiroya. Beggar Thy Neighbor, Better Thy Neighbor? Comment. *J. Post Keynesian Econ.*, Fall 1981, *4*(1), pp. 159–61.

Akrasanee, Narongchai. Trade Strategy for Employment Growth in Thailand. In *Krueger, A. O., et al., eds.*, 1981, pp. 393–433. [G: Thailand]

Alam, M. Shahid. Rentiers or Rent-Seekers? Some Clarifications. *Indian Econ. J.*, April–June 1981, *28*(4), pp. 48–54.

Alston, Julian M. A Note on the Effects of Non-Transferable Quotas on Supply Functions. *Rev. Marketing Agr. Econ.*, December 1981, *49*(3), pp. 189–97.

Alston, Philip. Commodity Agreements—As Though People Don't Matter: A Reply to "'Fair Labour Standards' in International Commodity Agreements." *J. World Trade Law*, September–October 1981, *15*(5), pp. 455–60.

Anastasopoulos, A. and Sims, W. A. Effective Protection When Demand and Employment are Endogenous: Estimates for Quebec. *Can. J. Econ.*, May 1981, *14*(2), pp. 201–15. [G: Canada]

Appleyard, Dennis R. and Field, Alfred J., Jr. Input Aggregation and the U.S. Tariff Structure. *Weltwirtsch. Arch.*, 1981, *117*(4), pp. 717–26.
[G: U.S.]

Arriola, Salvador. Access to Supplies and the Strategy of the Industrialized Countries. In *Lozoya, J. and Green, R., eds.*, 1981, pp. 181–98.
[G: Global]

Baade, Robert A. The Protectionist Sentiment in the Seventies: Its Implications for Factor Real Incomes in the U.S. *Empirical Econ.*, 1981, *6*(3), pp. 145–61. [G: U.S.]

Bacha, Edmar L. Gains to Latin America from Trade Liberalization in Developed and Developing Nations: Comment. In *Baer, W. and Gillis, M., eds.*, 1981, pp. 258–59. [G: Latin America]

Baer, Werner and Gillis, Malcolm. Preface: Changing Perspectives on Latin-American Trade. *Quart. Rev. Econ. Bus.*, Summer 1981, *21*(2), pp. 9–17. [G: Latin America; U.S.]

Baer, Werner and Samuelson, Larry. Toward a Service-oriented Growth Strategy. *World Devel.*, June 1981, *9*(6), pp. 499–514.

Bagchi, Amaresh. Exports Incentives in India: A Review. In *Bagchi, A. K. and Banerjee, N., eds.*, 1981, pp. 297–327. [G: India]

Balassa, Bela. Évolution de la structure des échanges de produits manufacturés entre pays industriels et pays en développement. (Pattern of Structural Change in Trade in Manufactured Goods between Industrial and Developing Countries. With English summary.) *Revue Écon.*, July 1981, *32*(4), pp. 754–87. [G: MDCs; LDCs]

Balassa, Bela. Development Strategy and the Six Year Plan in Taiwan. In *Balassa, B.*, 1981, pp. 381–406. [G: Taiwan]

Balassa, Bela. Incentive Policies in Brazil. In *Balassa, B.*, 1981, pp. 231–54.   [G: Brazil]

Balassa, Bela. Incentives for Economic Growth in Taiwan. In *Balassa, B.*, 1981, pp. 407–22.
          [G: Taiwan]

Balassa, Bela. Inflation and Trade Liberalization in Korea. In *Balassa, B.*, 1981, pp. 365–79.
          [G: South Korea]

Balassa, Bela. Policy Responses to External Shocks in Selected Latin American Countries. In *Balassa, B.*, 1981, pp. 83–108.

Balassa, Bela. Policy Responses to External Shocks in Selected Latin-American Countries. *Quart. Rev. Econ. Bus.*, Summer 1981, 21(2), pp. 131–64.   [G: Brazil; Mexico; Uruguay]

Balassa, Bela. Policy Responses to External Shocks in Selected Latin-American Countries. In *Baer, W. and Gillis, M., eds.*, 1981, pp. 131–64.
          [G: Brazil; Mexico; Uruguay]

Balassa, Bela. The "New Protectionism" and the International Economy. In *Balassa, B.*, 1981, pp. 109–26.

Balassa, Bela. The Economic Reform in Hungary Ten Years After. In *Balassa, B.*, 1981, pp. 329–46.   [G: Hungary]

Balassa, Bela. The Tokyo Round and the Developing Countries. In *Balassa, B.*, 1981, pp. 127–48.

Balassa, Bela. The 15-Year Social and Economic Development Plan for Korea. In *Balassa, B.*, 1981, pp. 347–63.   [G: South Korea]

Balassa, Bela. Trade in Manufactured Goods: Patterns of Change. In *Balassa, B.*, 1981, pp. 193–209.

Balassa, Bela. Trade in Manufactured Goods: Patterns of Change. *World Devel.*, March 1981, 9(3), pp. 263–75.

Balassa, Bela and Schydlowsky, Daniel M. Effective Tariffs, Domestic Cost of Foreign Exchange, and the Equilibrium Exchange Rate. In *Livingstone, I., ed.*, 1981, 1968, pp. 254–60.

Balasubramanyan, V. N. Prospects for the NICs: India. In *Saunders, C. T., ed. (II)*, 1981, pp. 183–203.   [G: India]

Baldwin, Robert E. The Political Economy of Postwar United States Trade Policy. In *Baldwin, R. E. and Richardson, J. D., eds.*, 1981, 1976, pp. 64–77.   [G: U.S.]

Baldwin, Robert E. Trade, Growth and Income Distribution: The Korean Experience: Comment. In *Hong, W. and Krause, L. B., eds.*, 1981, pp. 287–89.   [G: S. Korea]

Baldwin, Robert E. U.S. Political Pressures against Adjustment to Greater Imports. In *Hong, W. and Krause, L. B., eds.*, 1981, pp. 515–50.
          [G: U.S.]

Baldwin, Robert E. and Bale, Malcolm D. Policy Responses in the Old Industrial Countries: North America. In *Saunders, C. T., ed. (II)*, 1981, pp. 240–60.   [G: Canada; U.S.]

Bale, Malcolm D. and Lutz, Ernst. Price Distortions in Agriculture and Their Effects: An International Comparison. *Amer. J. Agr. Econ.*, February 1981, 63(1), pp. 8–22.

Bauer, P. T. Costs and Risks of Commodity Stabilization. In *Bauer, P. T.*, 1981, 1976, pp. 156–62.

Baysan, Tercan. Ithalat Kotalarinin Kaldirilmasi ve Kambiyo Kontrol Rejimi. (Removal of Import Quotas and the Foreign Exchange Controls. With English summary.) *METU*, 1981, 8(1 & 2), pp. 487–509.   [G: Turkey]

Bension, Alberto and Caumont, Jorge. Uruguay: Alternative Trade Strategies and Employment Implications. In *Krueger, A. O., et al., eds.*, 1981, pp. 499–529.   [G: Uruguay]

Bergsten, C. Fred. The Export Credit Policy of the United States: Meeting International Competition Effectively. In *Bergsten, C. F., ed.*, 1981, pp. 85–91.   [G: OECD; U.S.]

Bergsten, C. Fred. The International Arrangement on Export Credits. In *Bergsten, C. F., ed.*, 1981, pp. 73–83.   [G: OECD; U.S.]

Bergsten, C. Fred. The International Economic Policy of the United States: An Assessment and Agenda for the Future. In *Bergsten, C. F., ed.*, 1981, pp. 3–21.   [G: U.S.]

Bergsten, C. Fred. The United States and Mexico in the World Economy. In *Bergsten, C. F., ed.*, 1981, pp. 165–70.   [G: Mexico; U.S.]

Berreby, Jean-Jacques. Opec: venti anni che hanno trasformato il mondo. (OPEC: 20 Years That Have Changed the World. With English summary.) *Mondo Aperto*, April 1981, 35(2), pp. 89–97.
          [G: OPEC]

Bertsch, Gary K. U.S. Export Controls: The 1970's and Beyond. *J. World Trade Law*, January–February 1981, 15(1), pp. 67–82.   [G: U.S.]

Bhagwati, Jagdish N. and Srinivasan, T. N. Optimal Trade Policy and Compensation under Endogenous Uncertainty: The Phenomenon of Market Disruption. In *Bhagwati, J. N., ed.*, 1981, 1976, pp. 219–32.

Bird, Peter J. W. N. Reply [Beggar Thy Neighbor, Better Thy Neighbor?]. *J. Post Keynesian Econ.*, Fall 1981, 4(1), pp. 162.

Blackhurst, Richard; Marian, Nicolas and Tumlir, Jan. The Issue of Further Reductions in Barriers to International Trade. In *Baldwin, R. E. and Richardson, J. D., eds.*, 1981, 1977, pp. 94–109.

Blaisdell, Thomas C., Jr. Economics and the Truman Administration: Comments. In *Heller, F. H., ed.*, 1981, pp. 114–17.   [G: U.S.]

Bornstein, Morris. Issues in East–West Economic Relations. In *Bornstein, M.; Gitelman, Z. and Zimmerman, W., eds.*, 1981, pp. 31–61.
          [G: E. Europe]

Botchie, George. Ghanaian Industrialization and its External Linkages. In *Hamilton, F. E. I. and Linge, G. J. R., eds.*, 1981, pp. 509–27.
          [G: Ghana]

Brada, Josef C. Problems of Polish–U.S. Economic Relations: Comment. In *Marer, P. and Tabaczynski, E., eds.*, 1981, pp. 117–19.   [G: Poland; U.S.]

Brainard, Lawrence J. Foreign Economic Constraints on Soviet Economic Policy in the 1980s. In *Bornstein, M., ed.*, 1981, 1979, pp. 217–31.
          [G: U.S.S.R.]

Brander, James A. and Spencer, Barbara J. Tariffs and the Extraction of Foreign Monopoly Rents under Potential Entry. *Can. J. Econ.*, August 1981, 14(3), pp. 371–89.

Branson, William H. Industrial Policy and U.S. In-

ternational Trade. In *Wachter, M. L. and Wachter, S. M., eds.*, 1981, pp. 378–408.
[G: U.S.]

Browne, Robert S. Changing International Specialization and U.S. Imports of Manufactures. In *Reubens, E. P., ed.*, 1981, pp. 91–112. [G: U.S.]

Bruno, Michael. Short-term Policy Tradeoffs under Different Phases of Economic Development. In *Grassman, S. and Lundberg, E., eds.*, 1981, pp. 295–313.

Bulmuş, Ismail. Türkiye'de Tarimsal Taban Fiyat Politikasi ve Etkileri. (Price Support Policies in Turkey and Their Impacts. With English summary.) *METU*, Special Issue, 1981, pp. 541–73.
[G: Turkey]

Bunn, Delmar. Oil Import Limit: Pivotal Move in Solution: A Citizen's View of the Energy Problem. In *Kamrany, N. M.*, 1981, pp. 43–52. [G: U.S.]

Busch, Manfred. The Relevance of EEC Preference Politics to the EEC—Exports of Ghana and ECOWAS. In *Schmitt-Rink, G., ed.*, 1981, pp. 26–71. [G: EEC; Ghana]

Calcagno, Alfredo Eric and Martner, Gonzalo. International Trade and the NIEO. In *Lozoya, J. and Green, R., eds.*, 1981, pp. 1–53.
[G: LDCs]

Campbell, Robert W. The Foreign Trade System in Poland: Comment. In *Marer, P. and Tabaczynski, E., eds.*, 1981, pp. 92–96. [G: Poland]

Campos, Roberto de Oliveira and Valentino, Raphael. Prospects for the NICs: Brazil. In *Saunders, C. T., ed. (II)*, 1981, pp. 204–14.
[G: Brazil]

Campos, Roberto de Oliveira and Valentino, Raphael. Theories of Diffusion and Dependency. In *Saunders, C. T., ed. (II)*, 1981, pp. 71–80.
[G: LDCs; MDCs]

Capie, Forrest H. Shaping the British Tariff Structure in the 1930s. *Exploration Econ. Hist.*, April 1981, *18*(2), pp. 155–73. [G: U.K.]

Carlson, Jack and Graham, Hugh. The Economic Importance of Exports to the United States. In *Center for Strategic and Internat. Studies, ed. (II)*, 1981, pp. 39–146. [G: U.S.; Selected OECD]

Cartwright, Philip. Welfare Economics and the Log Export Policy Issue: Discussion. In *Sedjo, R. A., ed.*, 1981, pp. 209–15. [G: U.S.]

Carvalho, José L. and Haddad, Cláudio, L. S. Foreign Trade Strategies and Employment in Brazil. In *Krueger, A. O., et al., eds.*, 1981, pp. 29–81.
[G: Brazil]

Cauas, Jorge and de la Cuadra, Sergio. La política económica de la apertura al exterior en Chile. (With English summary.) *Cuadernos Econ.*, August–December 1981, *18*(54–55), pp. 195–230.
[G: Chile]

Caves, Richard E. Competitive Processes in the Open Economy: Evidence and Policy. In *[von Haberler, G.]*, 1981, pp. 71–84.

Chambers, Robert G., et al. Estimating the Impact of Beef Import Restrictions in the U.S. Import Market. *Australian J. Agr. Econ.*, August 1981, *25*(2), pp. 123–33. [G: U.S.]

Chen, Edward K. Y. Adjusting to the ADCs in the Face of Structurally Depressed Industries: Japan:

Comment. In *Hong, W. and Krause, L. B., eds.*, 1981, pp. 468–71. [G: Japan; E. Asia]

Chenery, Hollis B. Challenges and Opportunities Posed by Asia's Superexporters: Implications for Manufactured Exports from Latin America: Comment. In *Baer, W. and Gillis, M., eds.*, 1981, pp. 227–30. [G: East Asia; Latin America]

Chenery, Hollis B. Interactions between Inflation and Trade Regime Objectives in Stabilization Programs: Comment. In *Cline, W. R. and Weintraub, S., eds.*, 1981, pp. 114–16. [G: LDCs]

Chin, Rockwood Q. P. Trade Policies toward the PRC's Textile Exports. *Rivista Int. Sci. Econ. Com.*, September 1981, *28*(9), pp. 864–88.
[G: China]

Clark, Don P. On the Relative Importance of International Transport Charges as a Barrier to Trade. *Quart. Rev. Econ. Bus.*, Winter 1981, *21*(4), pp. 127–35. [G: U.S.]

Clark, Don P. Protection by International Transport Charges: Analysis by Stage of Fabrication. *J. Devel. Econ.*, June 1981, *8*(3), pp. 339–45.
[G: U.S.; LDCs]

Cline, William R. Brazil's Aggressive Response to External Shocks. In *Cline, W. R., et al.*, 1981, pp. 102–35. [G: Brazil]

Colucci, Mario. Prospettive di sviluppo degli scambi commerciali tra l'URSS e i paesi capitalistici industrializzati. (Development Perspectives of the Trade Exchanges between USSR and Capitalist Industrialized Countries. With English summary.) *Rivista Int. Sci. Econ. Com.*, May 1981, *28*(5), pp. 487–500. [G: U.S.S.R.]

Conlon, R. M. The Structure of the Australian Tariff and the Protection of the Textiles and Clothing Industries. *Australian Econ. Pap.*, June 1981, *20*(36), pp. 179–82. [G: Australia]

Conlon, R. M. Transport Cost and Tariff Protection of Australian and Canadian Manufacturing: A Comparative Study. *Can. J. Econ.*, November 1981, *14*(4), pp. 700–707. [G: Australia; Canada]

Cooper, Charles. Aspects of Transfer Pricing in Machinery Markets. In *Murray, R., ed.*, 1981, pp. 133–44.

Corbo, Vittorio and Meller, Patricio. Alternative Trade Strategies and Employment Implications: Chile. In *Krueger, A. O., et al., eds.*, 1981, pp. 83–134. [G: Chile]

Corden, W. Max. The NIEO Proposals: A Cool Look. In *Baldwin, R. E. and Richardson, J. D., eds.*, 1981, 1979, pp. 123–58.

Corden, W. Max. Trade and Industrial Policies, and the Structure of Protection in Korea: Comment. In *Hong, W. and Krause, L. B., eds.*, 1981, pp. 212–14. [G: S. Korea]

Curzon, Gerard and Price, Victoria Curzon. Protección antigua y nueva: Una revisión histórica. (With English summary.) *Cuadernos Econ.*, August–December 1981, *18*(54–55), pp. 129–40.
[G: Chile]

De Wulf, Luc. Customs Valuation and the Faking of Invoices. *Econ. Int.*, February 1981, *34*(1), pp. 13–33.

Denison, Ray. Proceedings of the Seminar on International Economic Problems: Statement. In *U.S.*

Congress, Joint Economic Committee (I), 1981, pp. 313–19. [G: U.S.]

Dennis, Geoffrey. The Harmonisation of Fiscal Systems. In *Twitchett, C. C., ed.*, 1981, pp. 33–46. [G: EEC]

Dennis, Geoffrey. The Harmonisation of Non-tariff Barriers. In *Twitchett, C. C., ed.*, 1981, pp. 18–32. [G: EEC]

Díaz-Alejandro, Carlos F. Southern Cone Stabilization Plans. In *Cline, W. R. and Weintraub, S., eds.*, 1981, pp. 119–41. [G: Argentina; Chile; Uruguay]

Dobozi, István and Inotai, András. Prospects of Economic Cooperation between CMEA Countries and Developing Countries. In *Saunders, C. T., ed. (I)*, 1981, pp. 48–65. [G: CMEA; LDCs]

Donges, Juergen B. Structural Policy Issues in Production and Trade: A Western View. In *Saunders, C. T., ed. (I)*, 1981, pp. 279–94.

Dornbusch, Rudiger. Exports and Policy in Latin-American Countries: Comment. In *Baer, W. and Gillis, M., eds.*, 1981, pp. 43–47. [G: Latin America]

Douglas, Hernán Cortés; Butelmann, Andrea and Videla, Pedro. Proteccionismo en Chile: Una vision retrospectiva. (With English summary.) *Cuadernos Econ.*, August–December 1981, 18(54–55), pp. 141–94. [G: Chile]

Douglas, Hernán Cortés and Sjaastad, Larry A. Protección y empleo. (With English summary.) *Cuadernos Econ.*, August–December 1981, 18(54–55), pp. 317–60. [G: Chile]

Dowdle, Barney. Log Export Restrictions: Causes and Consequences. In *Sedjo, R. A., ed.*, 1981, pp. 248–58. [G: U.S.]

Downer, Joseph P. Proceedings of the Seminar on Energy: Statement. In *U.S. Congress, Joint Economic Committee (I)*, 1981, pp. 505–14. [G: U.S.; Other Countries]

Eichengreen, Barry J. A Dynamic Model of Tariffs, Output and Employment under Flexible Exchange Rates. *J. Int. Econ.*, August 1981, 11(3), pp. 341–59.

Eralp, Atilâ. Türkiye'de Izlenen Ithal Ikameci Kalkinma Stratejisi ve Yabanci Sermaye. (Import Substitution Strategy and Foreign Capital in Turkey. With English summary.) *METU*, Special Issue, 1981, pp. 613–33. [G: Turkey]

Fajardo, Daniel; McCarl, Bruce A. and Thompson, Robert L. A Multicommodity Analysis of Trade Policy Effects: The Case of Nicaraguan Agriculture. *Amer. J. Agr. Econ.*, February 1981, 63(1), pp. 23–31. [G: Nicaragua]

Fajnzylber, Fernando. The Industrial Dynamic in Advanced Developing Countries. In *Hong, W. and Krause, L. B., eds.*, 1981, pp. 35–59. [G: Latin America]

Falvey, Rodney Edward. Commercial Policy and Intra-Industry Trade. *J. Int. Econ.*, November 1981, 11(4), pp. 495–511.

Fecteau, George and Mara, John. It's a Walkover for Shoe Imports. In *Baldwin, R. E. and Richardson, J. D., eds.*, 1981, 1979, pp. 87–93. [G: U.S.]

Feinberg, Richard E. Bureaucratic Organization and United States Policy toward Mexico. In *Purcell,*

S. K., ed., 1981, pp. 32–42. [G: Mexico; U.S.]

Ferreira do Amaral, João. Industrial Policy in an Enlarged Community: Comment. *Economia (Portugal)*, January 1981, 5(1), pp. 58–61. [G: EEC]

Findlay, Ronald. Export-Led Industrial Growth Reconsidered: Comment. In *Hong, W. and Krause, L. B., eds.*, 1981, pp. 30–33. [G: LDCs]

Finger, Joseph Michael. The Industry-Country Incidence of "Less Than Fair Value" Cases in US Import Trade. *Quart. Rev. Econ. Bus.*, Summer 1981, 21(2), pp. 260–79. [G: U.S.]

Finger, Joseph Michael. The Industry-Country Incidence of "Less than Fair Value" Cases in U.S. Import Trade. In *Baer, W. and Gillis, M., eds.*, 1981, pp. 260–79. [G: U.S.]

Flammang, Robert A. U.S. Programs That Impede U.S. Export Competitiveness: The Regulatory Environment. In *Center for Strategic and Internat. Studies, ed. (II)*, 1981, pp. 277–318. [G: U.S.]

Fontaine, Marcel. Les problèmes juridiques des contrats de compensation. (Legal Aspects of Compensation Contracts. With English summary.) *Ann. Sci. Écon. Appl.*, 1981, 37(3), pp. 57–70. [G: E. Europe; W. Europe]

Franko, Lawrence G. and Stephenson, Sherry. French Export Behavior in Third World Markets. In *Center for Strategic and Internat. Studies, ed. (I)*, 1981, pp. 171–251. [G: France; OECD; LDCs]

Gaines, David B.; Sawyer, William C. and Sprinkle, Richard. EEC Mediterranean Policy and U.S. Trade in Citrus. *J. World Trade Law*, September–October 1981, 15(5), pp. 431–39. [G: U.S.; EEC]

Ghoshal, Animesh. The Effect of the Embargo on Grain Exports to the Soviet Union on the Exchange Rate. *Nebr. J. Econ. Bus.*, Summer 1981, 20(3), pp. 37–46. [G: U.S.; U.S.S.R.]

Giersch, Herbert. Problems of Adjustment to Imports from Less-Developed Countries. In *Grassman, S. and Lundberg, E., eds.*, 1981, pp. 265–88.

Giezgala, Jan. The Foreign Trade System in Poland. In *Marer, P. and Tabaczynski, E., eds.*, 1981, pp. 87–91. [G: Poland]

Giezgala, Jan. The Foreign Trade System in Poland: Reply. In *Marer, P. and Tabaczynski, E., eds.*, 1981, pp. 96–97. [G: Poland]

Gill, David G. International Cartels and Their Regulation: Commentary. In *Schachter, O. and Hellawell, R., eds.*, 1981, pp. 277–82. [G: EEC; U.S.]

Ginsburgh, V. and Waelbroeck, Jean. Some Calculations of the Impact of Tariffs on World Trade and Welfare with a General Equilibrium Model of World Economy. In *Courbis, R., ed.*, 1981, pp. 279–94. [G: Global]

Glass, Walter. Restrictive Business Practices Affecting Transfer of Technology: Commentary. In *Schachter, O. and Hellawell, R., eds.*, 1981, pp. 139–42. [G: U.S.; Japan]

Goettle, Richard J., IV. An Economic Analysis of Petroleum Import Reduction Policies: Energy Conservation versus New Supply. In *Mork, K. A., ed.*, 1981 , pp. 125–55. [G: U.S.]

Goreux, Louis M. Compensatory Financing for Fluctuations in the Cost of Cereal Imports. In *Valdés, A.*, 1981, pp. 307–32. [G: LDCs]

Graham, Thomas R. The Impact of the Tokyo Round Agreements on U.S. Export Competitiveness. In *Center for Strategic and Internat. Studies, ed. (II)*, 1981, pp. 319–73. [G: U.S.; Selected OECD]

Greenaway, David. Taxes on International Transactions and Economic Development. In *Peacock, A. and Forte, F., eds.*, 1981, pp. 131–47. [G: LDCs]

Greer, Douglas F. Control of Terms and Conditions for International Transfers of Technology to Developing Countries. In *Schachter, O. and Hellawell, R., eds.*, 1981, pp. 41–83. [G: U.S.; Japan]

Grossman, Gene M. The Theory of Domestic Content Protection and Content Preference. *Quart. J. Econ.*, November 1981, *96*(4), pp. 583–603.

Guisinger, Stephen E. Trade Policies and Employment: The Case of Pakistan. In *Krueger, A. O., et al., eds.*, 1981, pp. 291–340. [G: Pakistan]

Gülalp, Haldun. Gelişme Stratejileri Tartişmasi: Bir Eleştiriye Yanit. (The Debate on Development Strategies: Reply to a Critique. With English summary.) *METU*, 1981, *8*(3&4), pp. 755–70. [G: Turkey]

Hadley, Eleanor G. Japan's Export Competitiveness in Third World Markets. In *Center for Strategic and Internat. Studies, ed. (I)*, 1981, pp. 254–330. [G: Japan; MDCs; LDCs]

Hager, Wolfgang. Industrial Policy in an Enlarged Community. *Economia (Portugal)*, January 1981, *5*(1), pp. 33–53. [G: EEC]

Hamilton, Carl. A New Approach to Estimation of the Effects of Non-Tariff Barriers to Trade: An Application to the Swedish Textile and Clothing Industry. *Weltwirtsch. Arch.*, 1981, *117*(2), pp. 298–325. [G: Sweden]

Han, Seung-Joo. Responding to the "New Protectionism": Strategies for the Advanced Developing Countries in the Pacific Basin: Comment. In *Hong, W. and Krause, L. B., eds.*, 1981, pp. 590–92. [G: E. Asia; U.S.]

Han, Seung Soo. Reform of the Tariff System in a Fast Growing Open Economy—A Suggested Methodology for Practical Problems. In *Roskamp, K. W. and Forte, F., eds.*, 1981, pp. 393–99. [G: S. Korea]

ul Haq, Mahbub. Negotiating a New Bargain with the Rich Countries. In *Muñoz, H., ed.*, 1981, 1975, pp. 117–22.

Hartigan, James C. Does Factor Content Determine Protection? *Southern Econ. J.*, July 1981, *48*(1), pp. 144–48. [G: U.S.]

Hartigan, James C. The U.S. Tariff and Comparative Advantage: A Survey of Method. *Weltwirtsch. Arch.*, 1981, *117*(1), pp. 65–109. [G: U.S.]

Hartland-Thunberg, Penelope. Has the U.S. Export Problem Been Solved? In *Center for Strategic and Internat. Studies, ed. (II)*, 1981, pp. 267–77. [G: U.S.]

Hartland-Thunberg, Penelope. The Political and Strategic Importance of Exports. In *Center for Strategic and Internat. Studies, ed. (II)*, 1981,

pp. 1–38. [G: U.S.]

Hawkins, Robert G. and Gladwin, Thomas N. Conflicts in the International Transfer of Technology: A U.S. Home Country View. In *Sagafi-nejad, T.; Moxon, R. W. and Perlmutter, H. V., eds.*, 1981, pp. 212–62. [G: U.S.]

Haynes, Richard; Darr, David R. and Adams, Darius. U.S.–Japanese Log Trade—Effect of a Ban. In *Sedjo, R. A., ed.*, 1981, pp. 216–32. [G: U.S.; Japan]

Heiss, Hertha W.; Lenz, Allen J. and Brougher, Jack. U.S.–Soviet Commercial Relations since 1972. In *Bornstein, M., ed.*, 1981, *1979*, pp. 233–52. [G: U.S.S.R.; U.S.]

Helleiner, Gerald K. Adjusting to the ADCs in the Face of Structurally Depressed Industries: Japan: Comment. In *Hong, W. and Krause, L. B., eds.*, 1981, pp. 471–74. [G: Japan; E. Asia]

Helleiner, Gerald K. The New Industrial Protectionism and the Developing Countries. In *Helleiner, G. K.*, 1981, pp. 62–103. [G: LDCs]

Helou, Angelina. Japan and the Tokyo Round. *J. World Trade Law*, September–October 1981, *15*(5), pp. 450–55. [G: Japan]

Hewitt, Adrian and Stevens, Christopher. The Second Lomé Convention. In *Stevens, C., ed.*, 1981, pp. 30–59. [G: EEC; LDCs]

Hillman, Jimmye S. A New Mode of Agricultural Protectionism. In *Johnson, G. and Maunder, A., eds.*, 1981, pp. 547–51.

Hitiris, Theodore. Protection, Concentration and Labour Intensity: Reply [The Impact of Protection and Concentration on the Labor Intensity of U.K. Industries]. *Weltwirtsch. Arch.*, 1981, *117*(2), pp. 383–84. [G: U.K.]

Hojman, David E. The Andean Pact: Failure of a Model of Economic Integration? *J. Common Market Stud.*, December 1981, *20*(2), pp. 139–60. [G: Andean Pact]

Holopainen, Kari. Suomen ja Neuvostoliiton välisen kaupan toimintaperiaatteet ja kaupan kehitys. (Operating Principles in the Trade between Finland and the Soviet Union and the Development of the Trade. With English summary.) *Kansant. Aikak.*, 1981, *77*(3), pp. 306–25. [G: Finland; U.S.S.R.]

Hong, Wontack. Export Promotion and Employment Growth in South Korea. In *Krueger, A. O., et al., eds.*, 1981, pp. 341–91. [G: S. Korea]

Hong, Wontack. Trade, Growth and Income Distribution: The Korean Experience. In *Hong, W. and Krause, L. B., eds.*, 1981, pp. 258–83. [G: S. Korea]

Huber, Jürgen. The Practice of GATT in Examining Regional Arrangements under Article XXIV. *J. Common Market Stud.*, March 1981, *19*(3), pp. 281–98.

Hufbauer, Gary Clyde. Analyzing the Effects of United States Trade Policy Instruments. In *National Science Foundation*, 1981, pp. III49–80. [G: U.S.]

Hufbauer, Gary Clyde. Economic and Political Characteristics of Cartel and Cartel-like Practices: Commentary. In *Schachter, O. and Hellawell, R., eds.*, 1981, pp. 283–85.

Hufbauer, Gary Clyde; Smith, W. N. Harrell, IV

and Vukmanic, Frank G. Mexico–United States Relations: Bilateral Trade Relations. In *Purcell, S. K., ed.*, 1981, pp. 136–45. [G: Mexico; U.S.]

Icamina, Benvenuto N. The Impact of UNCTAD Commodity Stabilization on Philippine Trade: A Simulation Analysis of Selected Commodities. *Philippine Econ. J.*, 1981, 20(3&4), pp. 277–94. [G: Philippines]

Ikemoto, Kiyoshi. The Industrial Dynamic in Advanced Developing Countries: Comment. In *Hong, W. and Krause, L. B., eds.*, 1981, pp. 60–62. [G: Latin America]

Jabara, Cathy L. Effect of Monetary Compensatory Amounts in Determining Rates of Production from EC Grain Import Levies. *Can. J. Agr. Econ.*, February 1981, 29(1), pp. 63–70. [G: EEC]

Jacquemin, Alexis. Industrial Policy in an Enlarged Community: Comment. *Economia (Portugal)*, January 1981, 5(1), pp. 54–57. [G: EEC]

Jacquemin, Alexis; Nambu, Tsuruhiko and Dewez, Isabelle. A Dynamic Analysis of Export Cartels: The Japanese Case. *Econ. J.*, September 1981, 91(363), pp. 685–96. [G: Japan]

James, John A. The Optimal Tariff in the Antebellum United States. *Amer. Econ. Rev.*, September 1981, 71(4), pp. 726–34. [G: U.S.]

Jasinowski, Jerry J. Toward a New U.S. Industrial Policy? International Trade: Comment. In *Wachter, M. L. and Wachter, S. M., eds.*, 1981, pp. 415–17. [G: U.S.]

Josling, Timothy. Price, Stock, and Trade Policies and the Functioning of International Grain Markets. In *Valdés, A.*, 1981, pp. 161–84. [G: Selected MDCs; U.S.S.R.]

Josling, Timothy E. Imperfect Markets in Agricultural Trade: Introduction. In *McCalla, A. F. and Josling, T. E., eds.*, 1981, pp. 1–8.

Kadhim, Mihssen. A Note on "Downstream" Industrialization and the Security of Oil Supplies. *J. Energy Devel.*, Autumn 1981, 7(1), pp. 99–109. [G: OAPEC; U.S.]

Kaikati, Jack G. The Anti-Export Policy of the U.S. *Calif. Manage. Rev.*, Spring 1981, 23(3), pp. 5–19. [G: U.S.]

Kanamori, Hisao. Responding to the "New Protectionism": Strategies for the Advanced Developing Countries in the Pacific Basin: Comment. In *Hong, W. and Krause, L. B., eds.*, 1981, pp. 592–93. [G: E. Asia; U.S.]

Katrak, Homi. Multi-National Firms' Exports and Host Country Commercial Policy. *Econ. J.*, June 1981, 91(362), pp. 454–65.

Keesing, Donald B. Exports and Policy in Latin-American Countries: Prospects for the World Economy and for Latin-American Exports, 1980–90. In *Baer, W. and Gillis, M., eds.*, 1981, pp. 18–43. [G: Latin America]

Kierzkowski, Henryk and Sampson, Gary P. The Multifibre Arrangement: The Approach and Setting to the Forthcoming Negotiations. *Aussenwirtschaft*, March 1981, 36(1), pp. 41–56. [G: OECD]

Kiger, Hugh C. Open Trade and Modernized Tobacco Program: The Keys to an Expanded U.S. Flue-Cured World Market. In *Finger, W. R., ed.*,

1981, pp. 131–44. [G: Global; U.S.]

Kim, Key W. Prospects for the NICs: South Korea. In *Saunders, C. T., ed. (II)*, 1981, pp. 159–82. [G: S. Korea]

Kim, Kwang Suk. Export-Led Industrial Growth Reconsidered: Comment. In *Hong, W. and Krause, L. B., eds.*, 1981, pp. 28–29. [G: LDCs]

Kim, Soo Yong. Trade Strategy and the Exchange Rate Policies in Taiwan: Comment. In *Hong, W. and Krause, L. B., eds.*, 1981, pp. 179–80. [G: Taiwan]

Klein, Lawrence R. International Aspects of Industrial Policy. In *Wachter, M. L. and Wachter, S. M., eds.*, 1981, pp. 361–77. [G: U.S.]

Klein, Lawrence R. Project Link: Policy Implications for the World Economy. In *Evan, W. M., ed.*, 1981, pp. 91–106.

Kojima, Kiyoshi. U.S. Political Pressures against Adjustment to Greater Imports: Comment. In *Hong, W. and Krause, L. B., eds.*, 1981, pp. 551–53. [G: U.S.]

Kossut, Zygmunt. Determinants of Polish Exports of Manufactured Products to the West and the Strategy of Industrial Cooperation: Comment. In *Marer, P. and Tabaczynski, E., eds.*, 1981, pp. 293–95. [G: Poland; W. Germany]

Kossut, Zygmunt. Problems of Polish–U.S. Economic Relations: Reply. In *Marer, P. and Tabaczynski, E., eds.*, 1981, pp. 119–20. [G: Poland; U.S.]

Kossut, Zygmunt. Problems of Polish–U.S. Economic Relations: A Polish Perspective. In *Marer, P. and Tabaczynski, E., eds.*, 1981, pp. 109–16. [G: Poland; U.S.]

Kostecki, M. M. State Trading. In *Vernon, R. and Aharoni, Y., eds.*, 1981, pp. 170–83.

Krishnamurti, R. UNCTAD as a Negotiating Institution. *J. World Trade Law*, January–February 1981, 15(1), pp. 3–40.

Krueger, Anne O. Alternative Trade Strategies and Employment in LDCs: An Overview. *Pakistan Devel. Rev.*, Autumn 1981, 20(3), pp. 277–301. [G: LDCs]

Krueger, Anne O. Export-Led Industrial Growth Reconsidered. In *Hong, W. and Krause, L. B., eds.*, 1981, pp. 3–27. [G: LDCs]

Krueger, Anne O. Interactions between Inflation and Trade Regime Objectives in Stabilization Programs. In *Cline, W. R. and Weintraub, S., eds.*, 1981, pp. 83–114. [G: LDCs]

Krueger, Anne O. Trade and Employment in Developing Countries: The Framework of the Country Studies. In *Krueger, A. O., et al., eds.*, 1981, pp. 1–28. [G: LDCs]

Krueger, Anne O. Trade and Industrial Policies, and the Structure of Protection in Korea: Comment. In *Hong, W. and Krause, L. B., eds.*, 1981, pp. 214–16. [G: S. Korea]

Krueger, Anne O. U.S. Economic Policy in Support of Growth in the Developing Countries. In *National Science Foundation*, 1981, pp. II41–78. [G: U.S.; LDCs]

Kullmann, Ulrich. "Fair Labour Standards" in International Commodity Agreements: Reply. *J. World Trade Law*, September–October 1981, 15(5), pp. 460–61.

Kung, Wan Chong and Carlos, Carolina R. Effective Protection of the Chemical Industry. *Phillipine Rev. Econ. Bus.*, March & June 1981, *18*(1 & 2), pp. 55–74.   [G: Philippines]

Lacarte, Julio A. Current Movements toward Regionalism: UNCTAD's Experience. In *Nicol, D.; Echeverria, L. and Peccei, A., eds.*, 1981, pp. 30–48.

Lall, Sanjaya. Recent Trends in Exports of Manufactures by Newly-Industrialising Countries. In *Lall, S.*, 1981, pp. 173–227.   [G: LDCs]

Levine, Herbert S. The Impact of New Transnational Technology Transfer Control Systems on the International Patent System: A European Perspective: Comment. In *Sagafi-nejad, T.; Moxon, R. W. and Perlmutter, H. V., eds.*, 1981, pp. 118–19.   [G: U.S.S.R.]

Liang, Kuo-Shu and Liang, Ching-ing Hou. Trade Strategy and the Exchange Rate Policies in Taiwan. In *Hong, W. and Krause, L. B., eds.*, 1981, pp. 150–78.   [G: Taiwan]

Lippke, Bruce. U.S.–Japanese Log Trade—Effect of a Ban: Discussion. In *Sedjo, R. A., ed.*, 1981, pp. 233–47.   [G: U.S.; Japan]

Longo, Carlos A. Comment on "Policy Responses to External Shocks in Selected Latin-American Countries." *Quart. Rev. Econ. Bus.*, Summer 1981, *21*(2), pp. 165–67.   [G: Brazil; Mexico; Uruguay]

Longo, Carlos A. Policy Responses to External Shocks in Selected Latin-American Countries: Comment. In *Baer, W. and Gillis, M., eds.*, 1981, pp. 165–67.   [G: Brazil; Mexico; Uruguay]

Lord, Montague J. Comment on "Commodity Exports and NIEO Proposals for Buffer Stocks and Compensatory Finance." *Quart. Rev. Econ. Bus.*, Summer 1981, *21*(2), pp. 76–82.   [G: Latin America]

Lord, Montague J. Commodity Exports and NIEO Proposals for Buffer Stocks and Compensatory Finance: Comment. In *Baer, W. and Gillis, M., eds.*, 1981, pp. 76–82.   [G: Brazil; Chile; Latin America]

Lundberg, Erik. Problems of Adjustment to Imports from Less-Developed Countries: Comments. In *Grassman, S. and Lundberg, E., eds.*, 1981, pp. 289–94.

Luttrell, Clifton B. A Bushel of Wheat for a Barrell of Oil: Can We Offset OPEC's Gains with a Grain Cartel? *Fed. Res. Bank St. Louis Rev.*, April 1981, *63*(4), pp. 13–21.   [G: U.S.]

Luttrell, Clifton B. The Voluntary Automobile Import Agreement with Japan—More Protectionism. *Fed. Res. Bank St. Louis Rev.*, November 1981, *63*(9), pp. 25–30.   [G: U.S.; Japan]

Lyet, J. Paul. Toward a New U.S. Industrial Policy? International Trade: Comment. In *Wachter, M. L. and Wachter, S. M., eds.*, 1981, pp. 412–15.   [G: U.S.]

Malan, T. Economic Sanctions as Policy Instrument to Effect Change—The Case of South Africa. *Finance Trade Rev.*, June 1981, *14*(3), pp. 87–116.   [G: S. Africa]

Manger, Gary J. Summing up on the Australian Case for Protection: Comment. *Quart. J. Econ.*, February 1981, *96*(1), pp. 161–67.   [G: Australia]

Manger, Gary J. The Australian Case for Protection Reconsidered. *Australian Econ. Pap.*, December 1981, *20*(37), pp. 193–204.   [G: Australia]

Marer, Paul. Import Protectionism in the US and Poland's Manufactures Exports: Reply. In *Marer, P. and Tabaczynski, E., eds.*, 1981, pp. 255–58.   [G: Poland; U.S.]

Marer, Paul. Import Protectionism in the US and Poland's Manufactures Exports. In *Marer, P. and Tabaczynski, E., eds.*, 1981, pp. 228–50.   [G: Poland; U.S.]

Marer, Paul. The Mechanism and Performance of Hungary's Foreign Trade, 1968–79. In *Hare, P. G.; Radice, H. K. and Swain, N., eds.*, 1981, pp. 161–204.   [G: Hungary]

Martin, John P. and Evans, John M. Notes on Measuring the Employment Displacement Effects of Trade by the Accounting Procedure. *Oxford Econ. Pap.*, March 1981, *33*(1), pp. 154–64.

Mayer, Wolfgang. Theoretical Considerations on Negotiated Tariff Adjustments. *Oxford Econ. Pap.*, March 1981, *33*(1), pp. 135–53.

McCalla, Alex F. Structural and Market Power Consideration in Imperfect Agricultural Markets. In *McCalla, A. F. and Josling, T. E., eds.*, 1981, pp. 9–28.

McCulloch, Rachel. Gains to Latin America from Trade Liberalization in Developed and Developing Nations. In *Baer, W. and Gillis, M., eds.*, 1981, pp. 231–58.   [G: Latin America]

McKillop, William. Log Export Restrictions: Causes and Consequences: Discussion. In *Sedjo, R. A., ed.*, 1981, pp. 259–63.   [G: U.S.]

McKinnon, Ronald I. Southern Cone Stabilization Plans: Comment. In *Cline, W. R. and Weintraub, S., eds.*, 1981, pp. 141–46.   [G: Argentina; Chile; Uruguay]

McNamara, Robert S. To the United Nations Conference on Trade and Development, Manila, Philippines, May 10, 1979. In *McNamara, R. S.*, 1981, *1979*, pp. 521–50.

Melton, William C. and Mahr, Jean M. Bankers' Acceptances. *Fed. Res. Bank New York Quart. Rev.*, Summer 1981, *6*(2), pp. 39–55.   [G: U.S.]

Mennis, Bernard. Conflicts in the International Transfer of Technology: A U.S. Home Country View: Comment. In *Sagafi-nejad, T.; Moxon, R. W. and Perlmutter, H. V., eds.*, 1981, pp. 263–69.   [G: U.S.]

Merciai, Patrizio. Safeguard Measures in GATT. *J. World Trade Law*, January–February 1981, *15*(1), pp. 41–66.

Messerlin, Patrick A. The Political Economy of Protectionism: The Bureaucratic Case. *Weltwirtsch. Arch.*, 1981, *117*(3), pp. 469–96.

Miguel, Urrutia M. Colombia and the Andean Group: Economic and Political Determinants of Regional Integration Policy. In *Baer, W. and Gillis, M., eds.*, 1981, pp. 182–99.   [G: Colombia; Latin America]

Mikesell, Raymond F. and Farah, Mark G. U.S. Export Competitiveness in Manufactures in Third World Markets. In *Center for Strategic and Internat. Studies, ed. (I)*, 1981, pp. 45–169.   [G: MDCs; LDCs; U.S.]

Milner, Chris and Greenaway, David. Rethinking

Trade Policy? *Nat. Westminster Bank Quart. Rev.*, February 1981, pp. 25–36. [G: U.K.]

Mishalani, Philip, et al. The Pyramid of Privilege. In *Stevens, C., ed.*, 1981, pp. 60–82. [G: EEC; Selected Countries]

Monson, Terry. Trade Strategies and Employment in the Ivory Coast. In *Krueger, A. O., et al., eds.*, 1981, pp. 239–90. [G: Ivory Coast]

Morawetz, David. Clothes for Export: Not Made in Colombia. *Finance Develop.*, March 1981, *18*(1), pp. 29–32. [G: Colombia]

Morrow, Daniel. The International Wheat Agreement and LDC Food Security. In *Valdés, A.*, 1981, pp. 213–39. [G: Global]

Mutti, John H. and Bale, Malcolm D. Output and Employment Changes in a "Trade Sensitive" Sector: Adjustment in the U.S. Footwear Industry. *Weltwirtsch. Arch.*, 1981, *117*(2), pp. 352–67. [G: U.S.]

Nabli, Mustapha K. Alternative Trade Policies and Employment in Tunisia. In *Krueger, A. O., et al., eds.*, 1981, pp. 435–98. [G: Tunisia]

Nagy, András. Comment [East–West–South Patterns of Trade] [Structural Policy Issues in Production and Trade: A Western View]. In *Saunders, C. T., ed. (1)*, 1981, pp. 313–21. [G: CMEA; LDCs; OECD]

Nam, Chong Hyun. Trade and Industrial Policies, and the Strucure of Protection in Korea. In *Hong, W. and Krause, L. B., eds.*, 1981, pp. 187–211. [G: S. Korea]

Nazarenko, Victor J. The Part Played by Agricultural Economists in State Trading Bodies. In *Johnson, G. and Maunder, A., eds.*, 1981, pp. 546–47.

Nef, Edward and Brown, Emerson. The United States and Canada: A Changing Relationship with Our Number One Trading Partner. In *U.S. Congress, Joint Economic Committee (III)*, 1981, pp. 124–47. [G: Canada; U.S.]

Neumann, George R. Adjustment Assistance for Trade-Displaced Workers. In *Baldwin, R. E. and Richardson, J. D., eds.*, 1981, *1979*, pp. 158–80. [G: U.S.]

Noreng, Øystein. State Oil Trading and the Perspective of Shortage. In *Tempest, P., ed.*, 1981, pp. 229–44. [G: OPEC]

Norman, Neville R. Policies towards Prices—The Influence of Regulation. In *Hancock, K., ed.*, 1981, pp. 349–69. [G: Australia]

O'Mara, Paul; Knopke, Philip and Roberts, Ivan. Costs of Japanese Agricultural Support Policies: Some Concepts and Estimates. *Quart. Rev. Rural Econ.*, May 1981, *3*(2), pp. 141–48. [G: Japan]

Ohara, Yoshio. Japanese Regulation of Technology Imports. *J. World Trade Law*, January–February 1981, *15*(1), pp. 83–90. [G: Japan]

Olgun, Hasan. Ithal Ikamesi Tartişmasi ve G. Özler. (The Crisis of Import Substitution: A Reply. With English summary.) *METU*, 1981, *8*(3&4), pp. 771–76. [G: Turkey]

Olgun, Hasan. Türkiye'de Ithal Ikamesi Bunalimi ve Dişa Açilma: Ikinci Eleştiri. (The Crisis of Import Substitution: A Second Critique. With English summary.) *METU*, 1981, *8*(3&4), pp. 777–93. [G: Turkey]

Ozawa, Terutomo. Technology Transfer and Control

Systems: The Japanese Experience. In *Sagafinejad, T.; Moxon, R. W. and Perlmutter, H. V., eds.*, 1981, pp. 376–426. [G: Japan]

Özler, Güntaç. Gülalp-Oglun Tartişmasi Üzerine. (On Gülalp-Olgun Controversy. With English summary.) *METU*, 1981, *8*(3&4), pp. 747–53. [G: Turkey]

Page, S. A. B. The Revival of Protectionism and Its Consequences for Europe. *J. Common Market Stud.*, September 1981, *20*(1), pp. 17–40. [G: W. Europe]

Pal, Dipti Prakas and Pal, Gunendra Prasad. Macro Measurers of Import Substitution. *Econ. Aff.*, October–December 1981, *26*(4), pp. 241–49. [G: India]

Parmenter, B. R.; Sams, D. and Vincent, D. P. Who Pays for Home Consumption Pricing Schemes? *Econ. Rec.*, June 1981, *57*(157), pp. 168–79. [G: Australia]

Patrick, Hugh. Trade Strategy and the Exchange Rate Policies in Taiwan: Comment. In *Hong, W. and Krause, L. B., eds.*, 1981, pp. 180–83. [G: Taiwan]

Pearce, Joan. Subsidized Export Credit. In *The Royal Inst. of Internat. Affairs*, 1981, pp. 166–241. [G: France; Japan; U.K.; U.S.; W. Germany]

Pearson, Charles and Takacs, Wendy E. Should the U.S. Restrict Auto Imports? *Challenge*, May/June 1981, *24*(2), pp. 45–52. [G: U.S.]

Pellicer de Brody, Olga. Oil and U.S. Policy toward Mexico. In *Ladman, J. R.; Baldwin, D. J. and Bergman, E., eds.*, 1981, pp. 185–96. [G: Mexico; U.S.]

Pelzman, Joseph and Martin, Randolph C. Direct Employment Effects of Increased Imports: A Case Study of the Textile Industry. *Southern Econ. J.*, October 1981, *48*(2), pp. 412–26. [G: U.S.]

Petersen, Donald E. Toward a New U.S. Industrial Policy? International Trade: Comment. In *Wachter, M. L. and Wachter, S. M., eds.*, 1981, pp. 417–19. [G: U.S.]

Pitt, Mark M. Alternative Trade Strategies and Employment in Indonesia. In *Krueger, A. O., et al., eds.*, 1981, pp. 181–237. [G: Indonesia]

Plessz, N. Policy Responses in the Old Industrial Countries: Western Europe. In *Saunders, C. T., ed. (II)*, 1981, pp. 217–39. [G: W. Europe; Selected LDCs]

Podbielski, Gisele. The Common Agricultural Policy and the Mezzogiorno. *J. Common Market Stud.*, June 1981, *19*(4), pp. 331–50. [G: Italy; EEC]

Porter, Michael G. U.S. Political Pressures against Adjustment to Greater Imports: Comment. In *Hong, W. and Krause, L. B., eds.*, 1981, pp. 553–58. [G: U.S.]

Radcliffe, Samuel J. U.S. Forest Products Trade and the Multilateral Trade Negotiations. In *Sedjo, R. A., ed.*, 1981, pp. 136–68. [G: U.S.]

Radice, H. K. Industrial Co-operation between Hungary and the West. In *Hare, P. G.; Radice, H. K. and Swain, N., eds.*, 1981, pp. 109–31. [G: Hungary; W. Europe; U.S.]

Rahl, James A. International Cartels and Their Regulation. In *Schachter, O. and Hellawell, R., eds.*, 1981, pp. 240–76. [G: EEC; U.S.]

Ranis, Gustav. Challenges and Opportunities Posed by Asia's Superexporters: Implications for Manufactured Exports from Latin America. In *Baer, W. and Gillis, M., eds.,* 1981, pp. 204–26.
[G: East Asia; Latin America]

Ray, Edward John. Tariff and Nontariff Barriers to Trade in the United States and Abroad. *Rev. Econ. Statist.,* May 1981, *63*(2), pp. 161–68.

Ray, Edward John. The Determinants of Tariff and Nontariff Trade Restrictions in the United States. *J. Polit. Econ.,* February 1981, *89*(1), pp. 105–21.
[G: U.S.]

Rego, Carlos. Le financement de la grande exportation. (Medium and Long Term Export Financing. With English summary.) *Ann. Sci. Écon. Appl.,* 1981, *37*(4), pp. 129–42.

Reutlinger, Shlomo and Bigman, David. Feasibility, Effectiveness, and Costs of Food Security Alternatives in Developing Countries. In *Valdés, A.,* 1981, pp. 185–212.

Richardson, Bradley M. The Contemporary Myth of Japanese Protectionism. In *Richardson, B. M. and Ueda, T., eds.,* 1981, pp. 115–23.
[G: Japan]

Roberts, Ivan; Tie, Graeme and Murphy, Susan. EEC Sugar Policies and World Market Prices. *Quart. Rev. Rural Econ.,* November 1981, *3*(4), pp. 309–19.
[G: EEC]

Rodriguez, Carlos Alfredo. Política comercial y salarios reales. (With English summary.) *Cuadernos Econ.,* August–December 1981, *18*(54–55), pp. 293–316.
[G: Argentina]

Roehl, Thomas. Technology Transfer and Control Systems: The Japanese Experience: Comment. In *Sagafi-nejad, T.; Moxon, R. W. and Perlmutter, H. V., eds.,* 1981, pp. 427–29.
[G: Japan]

Roett, Riordan. Brazilian Foreign Policy: Options in the 1980s. In *Bruneau, T. C. and Faucher, P., eds.,* 1981, pp. 179–92.
[G: Brazil]

Royon, Michel. Accord Multifibres et nouvelles fonctions du protectionnisme. (Multifibre Agreement and New Functions of Protectionism. With English summary.) *Rev. Econ. Ind.,* 1st Trimester 1981, (15), pp. 60–77.
[G: France]

Safarian, A. E. The Industrial Dynamic in Advanced Developing Countries: Comment. In *Hong, W. and Krause, L. B., eds.,* 1981, pp. 62–65.
[G: Latin America]

Saidi, Nasser and Srinagesh, Padmanabhan. On Non-Linear Tariff Schedules. *J. Int. Econ.,* May 1981, *11*(2), pp. 173–95.

Samuelson, Paul A. Justice to the Australians. *Quart. J. Econ.,* February 1981, *96*(1), pp. 169–70.

Samuelson, Paul A. Summing up on the Australian Case for Protection. *Quart. J. Econ.,* February 1981, *96*(1), pp. 147–60.
[G: Australia]

Samuelson, Paul A. To Protect Manufacturing? *Z. ges. Staatswiss.,* September 1981, *137*(3), pp. 407–14.

Sapir, André. European Imports of Manufactures under Trade Preferences for Developing Countries. In *Reubens, E. P., ed.,* 1981, pp. 113–31.
[G: EEC]

Sapir, André. Trade Benefits under the EEC Generalized System of Preferences. *Europ. Econ. Rev.,* March 1981, *15*(3), pp. 339–55.
[G: EEC]

Sarna, A. J. International Guidelines for Industrial Adjustment Policies. *J. World Trade Law,* November–December 1981, *15*(6), pp. 490–99.

Schmitz, Andrew; Firch, Robert S. and Hillman, Jimmye S. Agricultural Export Dumping: The Case of Mexican Winter Vegetables in the U.S. Market. *Amer. J. Agr. Econ.,* November 1981, *63*(4), pp. 645–54.
[G: U.S.; Mexico]

Schmitz, Andrew and McCalla, Alex F. Analysis of Imperfections in International Trade: The Case of Grain Export Cartels. In *McCalla, A. F. and Josling, T. E., eds.,* 1981, pp. 69–86.

Schuh, G. Edward. Challenges for Agricultural Economists Working in State Trading Agencies. In *Johnson, G. and Maunder, A., eds.,* 1981, pp. 544–46.

Schwartz, Louis B. The Impact of New Transnational Technology Transfer Control Systems on the International Patent System: A European Perspective: Comment. In *Sagafi-nejad, T.; Moxon, R. W. and Perlmutter, H. V., eds.,* 1981, pp. 115–17.
[G: EEC]

Schweiter, Aloys and Baumer, Helen. Protezionismo in aumento commercio mondiale in regresso? (Increasing Protectionism and a Backward Trend in World Trade? With English summary.) *Mondo Aperto,* December 1981, *35*(6), pp. 359–68.

Scott, Maurice FG. Short-term Policy Tradeoffs under Different Phases of Economic Development: Comments. In *Grassman, S. and Lundberg, E., eds.,* 1981, pp. 314–18.

Serfaty, Simon. The United States, Western Europe, and the Third World: Allies and Adversaries. In *Center for Strategic and Internat. Studies, ed. (I),* 1981, pp. 1–44.
[G: MDCs; LDCs]

Sharma, U. C. Import Substitution in Chemicals: Case Studies of Soda Ash, Caustic Soda and Bleaching Powder. *Indian Econ. J.,* October–December 1981, *29*(2), pp. 78–88.
[G: India]

Shields, Roger E. and Sonksen, R. Craig. Government Financial Institutions in Support of U.S. Exports. In *Center for Strategic and Internat. Studies, ed. (II),* 1981, pp. 183–265.
[G: U.S.; Selected OECD]

Sjaastad, Larry A. La protección y el volumen del comercio en Chile: La evidencia. (With English summary.) *Cuadernos Econ.,* August–December 1981, *18*(54–55), pp. 263–92.
[G: Chile]

Smith, Ian. EEC Sugar Policy in an International Context. *J. World Trade Law,* March–April 1981, *15*(2), pp. 95–110.
[G: EEC]

Smith, Ian. GATT: EEC Sugar Export Refunds Dispute. *J. World Trade Law,* November–December 1981, *15*(6), pp. 534–43.
[G: EEC]

Smith, Robert E. Economic and Political Characteristics of Cartel and Cartel-like Practices. In *Schachter, O. and Hellawell, R., eds.,* 1981, pp. 179–239.

Soltysinski, Stanislav J. The Impact of New Transnational Technology Transfer Control Systems on the International Patent System: A European Perspective. In *Sagafi-nejad, T.; Moxon, R. W. and Perlmutter, H. V., eds.,* 1981, pp. 89–114.
[G: CMEA; EEC]

Soltysinski, Stanislaw. U.S. Antidumping Laws and State-Controlled Economies. *J. World Trade*

Law, May–June 1981, *15*(3), pp. 251–65.
[G: U.S.]
Southard, Frank A., Jr. International Economic and Financial Policies. In *Heller, F. H., ed.*, 1981, pp. 67–77. [G: U.S.]
Stahnke, Arthur A. The West German System of Protection against Dumping by Centrally Planned Economies. *ACES Bull. (See Comp. Econ. Stud. after 8/85)*, Spring 1981, *23*(1), pp. 1–24.
[G: W. Germany; E. Europe; China]
Stecher, Bernd. The Role of Economic Policies. In *Saunders, C. T., ed. (II)*, 1981, pp. 27–46.
[G: Selected LDCs]
Steed, Guy P. F. International Location and Comparative Advantage: The Clothing Industries and Developing Countries. In *Hamilton, F. E. I. and Linge, G. J. R., eds.*, 1981, pp. 265–303.
[G: LDCs]
Stein, Leslie. The Growth and Implications of LDC Manufactured Exports to Advanced Countries. *Kyklos*, 1981, *34*(1), pp. 36–59. [G: LDCs.]
Stevens, Christopher. EEC and the Third World: The Search for Coherence. In *Stevens, C., ed.*, 1981, pp. 1–19. [G: EEC]
Streeten, Paul P. The Dynamics of the New Poor Power. In *Streeten, P.*, 1981, *1976*, pp. 175–92.
Szeworski, Adam. Import Protectionism in the US and Poland's Manufactures Exports: Comment. In *Marer, P. and Tabaczynski, E., eds.*, 1981, pp. 251–55. [G: Poland; U.S.]
Szychowski, Mario L. and Perazzo, Alfredo C. Una Evaluación empírica de la eficiencia económica y de los costos de protección en el caso argentino 1973–1974. (An Empirical Evaluation of the Economic Efficiency and the Costs of Protection in the Argentine Case: 1973–1974. With English summary.) *Económica*, September–December 1981, *27*(3), pp. 223–65. [G: Argentina]
Tabaczynski, Eugeniusz. East–West Industrial Cooperation and Specialization in Polish Production. In *Marer, P. and Tabaczynski, E., eds.*, 1981, pp. 99–103. [G: Poland]
Tabaczynski, Eugeniusz. East–West Industrial Cooperation and Specialization in Polish Production: Reply. In *Marer, P. and Tabaczynski, E., eds.*, 1981, pp. 107–08. [G: Poland]
Takacs, Wendy E. Pressures for Protectionism: An Empirical Analysis. *Econ. Inquiry*, October 1981, *19*(4), pp. 687–93. [G: U.S.]
Tanaka, Shigekazu. The Impact of Protection and Concentration on the Labour Intensity of U.K. Industries: Comment. *Weltwirtsch. Arch.*, 1981, *117*(2), pp. 380–82. [G: U.K.]
Thoumi, Francisco E. International Trade Strategies, Employment, and Income Distribution in Colombia. In *Krueger, A. O., et al., eds.*, 1981, pp. 135–79. [G: Colombia]
de la Torre, Jose. Public Intervention Strategies in the European Clothing Industries. *J. World Trade Law*, March–April 1981, *15*(2), pp. 124–48. [G: EEC]
Tower, Edward. Buffer Stocks are Better Stabilizers Than Quotas. *J. Int. Econ.*, February 1981, *11*(1), pp. 113–15.
Tsurumi, Yoshi. Export Assistance for Foreign Firms. In *Richardson, B. M. and Ueda, T., eds.*,

1981, pp. 299–303. [G: Japan]
Tsurumi, Yoshi. Exports to Japan by Small Firms. In *Richardson, B. M. and Ueda, T., eds.*, 1981, pp. 290–98. [G: Japan]
Tsurumi, Yoshi. Realities of the Japanese Consumer Imports Market. In *Richardson, B. M. and Ueda, T., eds.*, 1981, pp. 283–89. [G: Japan]
Turner, Louis, et al. Living with the Newly Industrialized Countries. In *The Royal Inst. of Internat. Affairs*, 1981, pp. 103–65. [G: Selected LDCs; OECD]
Tyler, William G. Advanced Developing Countries as Export Competitors in Third World Markets: the Brazilian Experience. In *Center for Strategic and Internat. Studies, ed. (I)*, 1981, pp. 331–408.
[G: Brazil; LDCs]
Urrutia M., Miguel. Colombia and the Andean Group: Economic and Political Determinants of Regional Integration Policy. *Quart. Rev. Econ. Bus.*, Summer 1981, *21*(2), pp. 182–99.
[G: Andean Group]
Ustor, Endre. The MFN Customs Union Exception. *J. World Trade Law*, September–October 1981, *15*(5), pp. 377–87.
Vargha, Louis. U.S. Forest Products Trade and the Multilateral Trade Negotiations: Discussion. In *Sedjo, R. A., ed.*, 1981, pp. 175–84. [G: U.S.]
Vernon, Raymond. State-Owned Enterprises in Latin-American Exports. *Quart. Rev. Econ. Bus.*, Summer 1981, *21*(2), pp. 98–114.
[G: Latin America]
Verreydt, E. and Waelbroeck, Jean. EEC Industrial Policy and the Third World. In *Stevens, C., ed.*, 1981, pp. 20–29. [G: EEC]
Villarreal, René and de Villarreal, Rocío. Mexico's Development Strategy. In *Purcell, S. K., ed.*, 1981, pp. 97–103. [G: Mexico]
Wall, David. Reply [Industrial Processing of Natural Resources]. *World Devel.*, May 1981, *9*(5), pp. 495–98.
Walter, Ingo. A Survey of International Economic Repercussions of Environmental Policy. In *Butlin, J. A., ed.*, 1981, pp. 163–82.
Walter, Ingo. Control of Terms and Conditions for International Transfers of Technology to Developing Countries: Commentary. In *Schachter, O. and Hellawell, R., eds.*, 1981, pp. 143–59.
[G: U.S.; Japan]
Warley, T. K. Panel Discussion on State Trading Agencies. In *Johnson, G. and Maunder, A., eds.*, 1981, pp. 541–44.
Wassermann, Ursula. UNCTAD: International Cocoa Agreement, 1980. *J. World Trade Law*, March–April 1981, *15*(2), pp. 149–50.
Wassermann, Ursula. UNCTAD: Sixth International Tin Agreement. *J. World Trade Law*, November–December 1981, *15*(6), pp. 557–58.
Weeks, Peter and Turner, Bruce. Effects of the Proposed Canadian Meat Import Law. *Quart. Rev. Rural Econ.*, August 1981, *3*(3), pp. 232–39.
[G: Canada; Australia]
Weinblatt, Jacob and Zilberfarb, Ben-Zion. Price Discrimination in the Exports of a Small Economy: Empirical Evidence. *Weltwirtsch. Arch.*, 1981, *117*(2), pp. 368–79. [G: Israel]
Weintraub, Sidney. Trade Integration of the United

States, Canada, and Mexico. **In** *U.S. Congress, Joint Economic Committee (III)*, 1981, pp. 179–208. **[G: U.S.; Canada; Mexico]**

Wells, Louis T., Jr. Control of Terms and Conditions for International Transfers of Technology to Developing Countries: Commentary. **In** *Schachter, O. and Hellawell, R., eds.*, 1981, pp. 160–64. **[G: U.S.; Japan]**

Werner, Horst. Freihandel oder internationaler "Kampf um Produktionsprivilegien"? (Free Trade or International "Fight for Production Privileges"? With English summary.) **In** *[von Haberler, G.]*, 1981, pp. 51–69.

Whalen, Richard J. Politics and the Export Mess. **In** *Center for Strategic and Internat. Studies, ed. (II)*, 1981, pp. 375–88. **[G: U.S.]**

Whitman, Marina v. N. Automobiles: Turning Around on a Dime? *Challenge*, May/June 1981, *24*(2), pp. 36–44. **[G: U.S.]**

Williamson, John. Colombia and the Andean Group: Comment. **In** *Baer, W. and Gillis, M., eds.*, 1981, pp. 199–203. **[G: Colombia; Latin America]**

Williamson, John. Comment on "Colombia and the Andean Group." *Quart. Rev. Econ. Bus.*, Summer 1981, *21*(2), pp. 199–203. **[G: Andean Group]**

Wisdom, Harold. U.S. Forest Products Trade and the Multilateral Trade Negotiations: Discussion. **In** *Sedjo, R. A., ed.*, 1981, pp. 169–74. **[G: U.S.]**

Wiseman, A. Clark. U.S.–Canadian Lumber Trade: The Effect of Restrictions: Discussion. **In** *Sedjo, R. A., ed.*, 1981, pp. 133–35. **[G: U.S.; Canada]**

Wiseman, A. Clark and Sedjo, Roger. Welfare Economics and the Log Export Policy Issue. **In** *Sedjo, R. A., ed.*, 1981, pp. 187–208. **[G: U.S.]**

Wiseman, A. Clark and Sedjo, Roger A. Effects of an Export Embargo on Related Goods: Logs and Lumber. *Amer. J. Agr. Econ.*, August 1981, *63*(3), pp. 423–29. **[G: U.S.]**

Wolf, Thomas A. Determinants of Polish Exports of Manufactured Products to the West and the Strategy of Industrial Cooperation: Reply. **In** *Marer, P. and Tabaczynski, E., eds.*, 1981, pp. 295–97. **[G: Poland; W. Germany]**

Wolf, Thomas A. Determinants of Polish Exports of Manufactured Products to the West and the Strategy of Industrial Cooperation. **In** *Marer, P. and Tabaczynski, E., eds.*, 1981, pp. 272–92. **[G: Poland; W. Germany]**

Wolf, Thomas A. East–West Industrial Cooperation and Specialization in Polish Production: Comment. **In** *Marer, P. and Tabaczynski, E., eds.*, 1981, pp. 104–07. **[G: Poland]**

Wonnacott, Paul and Wonnacott, Ronald. Is Unilateral Tariff Reduction Preferable to a Customs Union? The Curious Case of the Missing Foreign Tariffs. *Amer. Econ. Rev.*, September 1981, *71*(4), pp. 704–14.

Wurth, P. The Arrangement Regarding International Trade in Textiles. *Aussenwirtschaft*, March 1981, *36*(1), pp. 57–69.

Yamazawa, Ippei. Adjusting to the ADCs in the Face of Structurally Depressed Industries: Japan. **In** *Hong, W. and Krause, L. B., eds.*, 1981, pp. 435–67. **[G: Japan; E. Asia]**

Yasuba, Yasukichi. Trade, Growth and Income Distribution: The Korean Experience: Comment. **In** *Hong, W. and Krause, L. B., eds.*, 1981, pp. 284–86. **[G: S. Korea]**

Yeats, Alexander J. The Influence of Trade and Commercial Barriers on the Industrial Processing of Natural Resources [Industrial Processing of Natural Resources]. *World Devel.*, May 1981, *9*(5), pp. 485–94.

Yoffie, David B. Orderly Marketing Agreements as an Industrial Policy: The Case of the Footwear Industry. *Public Policy*, Winter 1981, *29*(1), pp. 93–119. **[G: U.S.]**

Yoffie, David B. and Keohane, Robert O. Responding to the "New Protectionism": Strategies for the Advanced Developing Countries in the Pacific Basin. **In** *Hong, W. and Krause, L. B., eds.*, 1981, pp. 560–89. **[G: E. Asia; U.S.]**

Yoingco, Angel Q. and Sukarya, Sutadi. Study Group on Asian Tax Administration and Research (SGATAR)—An Experiment in Regional Tax Cooperation—Part I. *Bull. Int. Fiscal Doc.*, March 1981, *35*(3), pp. 110–18. **[G: S.E. Asia; Australia; Japan; New Zealand]**

Yoo, Jong Youl. The Republic of Korea and the New International Economic Order. **In** *Lozoya, J. A. and Bhattacharya, A. K., eds.*, 1981, pp. 28–38. **[G: S. Korea]**

423 Economic Integration

4230 General

Bergson, Abram. The Geometry of COMECON Trade: Note. *Europ. Econ. Rev.*, June/July 1981, *16*(2/3), pp. 233.

Černý, Miroslav and Holeček, Josef. Traditionally, but with New Approaches. *Czech. Econ. Digest.*, August 1981, (5), pp. 49–62. **[G: CMEA]**

Franzmeyer, Fritz. Europäische Energiepolitik—wenig Spielraum für abgestuftes Vorgehen. (European Energy Policy—Little Scope for Two-or-Multi-Tier Integration. With English summary.) *Konjunkturpolitik*, 1981, *27*(6), pp. 337–78. **[G: EEC]**

Hetzel, Nancy K. Regionalism and the Environment. **In** *Nicol, D.; Echeverria, L. and Peccei, A., eds.*, 1981, pp. 210–17.

Hudson, Michael. The Logic of Regionalism in History and Today. **In** *Nicol, D.; Echeverria, L. and Peccei, A., eds.*, 1981, pp. 13–29.

Hurwicz, Leonid. Global Modeling and Decision-Making: Comment. **In** *Evan, W. M., ed.*, 1981, pp. 127–30.

Johansson, J. K. and Spich, Robert S. Trade Interdependence in the Pacific Rim Basin and the E.C.: A Comparative Analysis. *J. Common Market Stud.*, September 1981, *20*(1), pp. 41–59. **[G: New Zealand; Australia; N. America; Japan; EEC]**

Jones, Thomas E. Regionalism: The Problem of Public Support. **In** *Nicol, D.; Echeverria, L. and Peccei, A., eds.*, 1981, pp. 218–32.

Lacarte, Julio A. Current Movements toward Regionalism: UNCTAD's Experience. **In** *Nicol, D.;*

Echeverria, L. and Peccei, A., eds., 1981, pp. 30–48.

Laszlo, Ervin; Moneta, Carlos and Kurtzman, Joel. The Place of Regional Approaches in Current Negotiations on International Development. In *Nicol, D.; Echeverria, L. and Peccei, A., eds.,* 1981, pp. 251–61.

Moneta, Carlos. Political Obstacles to Regional Economic Cooperation. In *Nicol, D.; Echeverria, L. and Peccei, A., eds.,* 1981, pp. 164–74.

Omer, Assad U. Regional Approaches to the Transfer, Control, and Creation of Technology. In *Nicol, D.; Echeverria, L. and Peccei, A., eds.,* 1981, pp. 277–88.

Raman, K. Venkata. The Achievement of Specific NIEO Objectives by Means of Regional Approaches: Access to Markets, International Trade and Industrialization. In *Nicol, D.; Echeverria, L. and Peccei, A., eds.,* 1981, pp. 262–76.

Robson, Peter. Regional Economic Cooperation among Developing Countries: Some Further Considerations. In *Streeten, P. and Jolly, R, eds.,* 1981, pp. 331–37. **[G: LDCs; ASEAN]**

Sneider, Richard L. The Evolving Pacific Community—Reality or Rhetoric? In *Hewett, R. B., ed.,* 1981, pp. 33–43. **[G: East Asia]**

Štrougal, Lubomír. With Responsibility and Initiative at the Start of the 7th Five-Year Plan. *Czech. Econ. Digest.,* May 1981, (3), pp. 22–38. **[G: Czechoslovakia]**

Taylor, Alastair M. Regional Processes in History. In *Nicol, D.; Echeverria, L. and Peccei, A., eds.,* 1981, pp. 3–12.

Vaitsos, Constantine V. Crisis in Regional Economic Cooperation (Integration) among Developing Countries: A Survey. In *Streeten, P. and Jolly, R, eds.,* 1981, 1978, pp. 279–329. **[G: Latin America]**

Wassermann, Ursula. Zimbabwe's Foreign Trade. *J. World Trade Law,* March–April 1981, 15(2), pp. 173–79. **[G: Zimbabwe]**

Wilford, D. Sykes and Nattress, W. Dayle. Monetary and Financial Integration in North America. *Law Contemp. Probl.,* Summer 1981, 44(3), pp. 55–79. **[G: U.S.; Canada; Mexico]**

Wionczek, Miguel S. Can the Broken Humpty-Dumpty Be Put Together Again and by Whom? Comments on the Vaitsos Survey [Crisis in Regional Economic Cooperation (Integration) among Developing Countries: A Survey]. In *Streeten, P. and Jolly, R, eds.,* 1981, 1978, pp. 339–42. **[G: LDCs]**

4232 Theory of Economic Integration

Berglas, Eitan. Harmonization of Commodity Taxes: Destination, Origin and Restricted Origin Principles. *J. Public Econ.,* December 1981, 16(3), pp. 377–87.

Deiss, Joseph. Le processus d'ajustement au sein d'une union monétaire. (The Adjustment Process in a Monetary Union. With English summary.) *Rivista Int. Sci. Econ. Com.,* October–November 1981, 28(10–11), pp. 1015–26.

Estévez, Jaime and Puyana, Alicia. Regionalism, Nationalism, and the NIEO. In *Nicol, D.; Echever-*

ria, L. and Peccei, A., eds., 1981, pp. 151–63.

Fratianni, Michele and Christie, Herbert. Abolishing Fiscal Frontiers within the EEC. *Public Finance,* 1981, 36(3), pp. 411–29. **[G: EEC]**

Grinols, Earl. An Extension of the Kemp-Wan Theorem on the Formation of Customs Unions. *J. Int. Econ.,* May 1981, 11(2), pp. 259–66.

Hudson, Michael. The Objectives of Regionalism in the 1980s. In *Nicol, D.; Echeverria, L. and Peccei, A., eds.,* 1981, pp. 185–99.

Kemp, Murray C. and Wan, Henry, Jr. An Elementary Proposition Concerning the Formation of Customs Unions. In *Bhagwati, J. N., ed.,* 1981, 1976, pp. 283–86.

Kindleberger, Charles P. Optimal Economic Interdependence. In *Kindleberger, C. P.,* 1981, 1971, pp. 317–28.

Lipsey, Richard G. The Theory of Customs Unions: A General Survey. In *Bhagwati, J. N., ed.,* 1981, 1960, pp. 265–82.

McMillan, John and McCann, Ewen. Welfare Effects in Customs Unions. *Econ. J.,* September 1981, 91(363), pp. 697–703.

Miljan, Toivo. Functionalist Solutions to Political Obstacles to Regional Economic Cooperation. In *Nicol, D.; Echeverria, L. and Peccei, A., eds.,* 1981, pp. 175–84.

Orantes, Isaac Cohen. The Concept of Integration. *Cepal Rev.,* December 1981, (15), pp. 143–52.

Sheer, Alain. A Survey of the Political Economy of Customs Unions. *Law Contemp. Probl.,* Summer 1981, 44(3), pp. 33–53.

Whalley, John. Border Adjustments and Tax Harmonization: Comment on Berglas [Harmonization of Commodity Taxes: Destination, Origin, and Restricted Origin Principles]. *J. Public Econ.,* December 1981, 16(3), pp. 389–90.

Wonnacott, Paul and Wonnacott, Ronald. Is Unilateral Tariff Reduction Preferable to a Customs Union? The Curious Case of the Missing Foreign Tariffs. *Amer. Econ. Rev.,* September 1981, 71(4), pp. 704–14.

Yu, Eden S. H. Trade Diversion, Trade Creation and Factor Market Imperfections. *Weltwirtsch. Arch.,* 1981, 117(3), pp. 546–61.

4233 Economic Integration: Policy and Empirical Studies

Abdul-Karim, Tayeh. OPEC: Challenges of the Present and Strategy for the Future. In *OPEC, Public Information Dept.,* 1981, pp. 9–16. **[G: OPEC]**

Adamovic, Ljubisa S. Yugoslavia and the European Economic Community. In *Inst. of Internat. Pub. Law and Internat. Relat. of Thessaloniki,* 1981, pp. 85–113. **[G: Yugoslavia; EEC]**

Adams, F. Gerard; Behrman, Jere R. and Lasaga, M. Commodity Exports and NIEO Proposals for Buffer Stocks and Compensatory Finance: Implications for Latin America. *Quart. Rev. Econ. Bus.,* Summer 1981, 21(2), pp. 48–76. **[G: Latin America]**

Agarwala, P. N. The Need for Regional Cooperation among the Indian Ocean Basin Countries: A Case Study. In *Nicol, D.; Echeverria, L. and Peccei, A., eds.,* 1981, pp. 82–90. **[G: S. Asia]**

Akins, James E. OPEC Actions: Consumer Reactions 1970–2000. In *OPEC, Public Information Dept.*, 1981, pp. 215–38. [G: OPEC]

Al-Anbari, Abdul Amir. OPEC Actions: Consumer Reactions 1970–2000: Commentary. In *OPEC, Public Information Dept.*, 1981, pp. 239–46. [G: OPEC]

Al-Chalabi, Fadhil J. The Concept of Conservation in OPEC Member Countries. In *OPEC, Public Information Dept.*, 1981, pp. 189–200. [G: OPEC]

Alting Von Geusau, Frans A. M. The External Relations of the European Communities. In *Inst. of Internat. Pub. Law and Internat. Relat. of Thessaloniki*, 1981, pp. 19–45. [G: EEC]

Attiga, Ali A. Crossing the Energy Bridge. In *OPEC, Public Information Dept.*, 1981, pp. 29–36. [G: OPEC]

Balaam, David N. and Carey, Michael J. Agri-Policy in the Soviet Union and Eastern Europe. In *Balaam, D. N. and Carey, M. J., eds.*, 1981, pp. 48–80. [G: U.S.S.R.; E. Europe]

Balassa, Bela. Portugal in Face of the Common Market. In *Balassa, B.*, 1981, pp. 255–80. [G: Portugal]

Balažik, Milan. Joint Enterprises in the System of Organizations of the CMEA Countries. *Czech. Econ. Digest.*, August 1981, (5), pp. 63–77. [G: CMEA]

Bora, Gyula. International Division of Labour and the National Industrial System: The Case of Hungary. In *Hamilton, F. E. I. and Linge, G. J. R., eds.*, 1981, pp. 155–83. [G: Hungary; CMEA]

Borchert, Manfred. On the Efficiency of Monetary Policy in the EMS. *Z. Wirtschaft. Sozialwissen.*, 1981, *101*(4), pp. 417–28. [G: EEC]

Bornstein, Morris. East–West Economic Relations and Soviet–East European Economic Relations. In *Bornstein, M., ed.*, 1981, *1979*, pp. 193–215. [G: CMEA; U.S.S.R.]

Bornstein, Morris. Soviet–East European Economic Relations. In *Bornstein, M.; Gitelman, Z. and Zimmerman, W., eds.*, 1981, pp. 105–24. [G: CMEA; E. Europe]

Bourrinet, Jacques. A Case Study of the European Community. In *Nicol, D.; Echeverria, L. and Peccei, A., eds.*, 1981, pp. 114–21. [G: EEC]

Bredimas, Anna E. and Tzoannos, John G. In Search of a Common Shipping Policy for the E.C. *J. Common Market Stud.*, December 1981, *20*(2), pp. 95–114. [G: EEC]

Butt Philip, Alan. The Harmonisation of Industrial Policy and Practices. In *Twitchett, C. C., ed.*, 1981, pp. 47–62. [G: EEC]

Carey, Michael J. European Food Policy: Rules of the Game. In *Balaam, D. N. and Carey, M. J., eds.*, 1981, pp. 30–47. [G: W. Europe]

Carstensen, Peter C. Competition Policy for an Economically Integrated North America. *Law Contemp. Probl.*, Summer 1981, *44*(3), pp. 81–103. [G: U.S.; Canada; Mexico]

Caves, Richard E. Intra-Industry Trade and Market Structure in the Industrial Countries. *Oxford Econ. Pap.*, July 1981, *33*(2), pp. 203–23.

Coffey, Peter. Regional Disequilibria, Financial Flows and Budgetary Policy in the European Community: Comment. *Economia (Portugal)*, January 1981, *5*(1), pp. 154–57. [G: EEC]

Colitti, Marcello. The Concept of Conservation in OPEC Member Countries: Commentary. In *OPEC, Public Information Dept.*, 1981, pp. 201–07. [G: OPEC]

Cosgrove Twitchett, Carol. Harmonisation and Road Freight Transport. In *Twitchett, C. C., ed.*, 1981, pp. 63–77. [G: EEC]

Csaba, László. Planning and Finances in the Decade after the Adoption of the Comprehensive Programme in the CMEA. *Acta Oecon.*, 1981, *27*(3–4), pp. 351–71. [G: CMEA]

Dashwood, Alan. The Harmonisation Process. In *Twitchett, C. C., ed.*, 1981, pp. 7–17. [G: EEC]

De Bernardi, Bruno. L'applicazione dei principi fondamentali di bilancio al bilancio funzionale di ricerca e di investimento delle Communità Europee. (The Application of the Basic Budgetary Principles to the Functional Budget of Research and Investment of the European Communities. With English summary.) *Rivista Int. Sci. Econ. Com.*, May 1981, *28*(5), pp. 501–14. [G: EEC]

De Grauwe, Paul. Capital Movements, Financial Integration and the EMS. *Giorn. Econ.*, Sept.-Dec. 1981, *40*(9–12), pp. 649–67. [G: EEC]

Delivanis, Dimitrios. Greece and the European Economic Community Aims and Achievements. In *Inst. of Internat. Pub. Law and Internat. Relat. of Thessaloniki*, 1981, pp. 325–31. [G: Greece; EEC]

Dennis, Geoffrey. The Harmonisation of Fiscal Systems. In *Twitchett, C. C., ed.*, 1981, pp. 33–46. [G: EEC]

Dennis, Geoffrey. The Harmonisation of Non-tariff Barriers. In *Twitchett, C. C., ed.*, 1981, pp. 18–32. [G: EEC]

Dramais, A. Le Modèle Desmos. (With English summary.) In *Courbis, R., ed.*, 1981, pp. 221–34. [G: EEC]

Ebrahimzadeh, Cyrus. The Integration of the Oil Sector in Economies of OPEC Member Countries. In *OPEC, Public Information Dept.*, 1981, pp. 165–81. [G: OPEC]

Elliott, Robert F. and Wood, Peter W. The International Transfer of Technology and Western European Integration. In *Hawkins, R. G. and Prasad, A. J., eds.*, 1981, pp. 117–50. [G: W. Europe]

Ernst, Wolfgang. The Free Movement of Goods and Services within the European Economic Community in the Context of the World Economy. *Z. ges. Staatswiss.*, September 1981, *137*(3), pp. 556–74. [G: EEC]

Fáy, József and Nyers, Reszö. Specialization and Cooperation in the Hungarian Economy and the CMEA. *Acta Oecon.*, 1981, *27*(1–2), pp. 1–18. [G: CMEA; Hungary]

Ferreira do Amaral, João. Industrial Policy in an Enlarged Community: Comment. *Economia (Portugal)*, January 1981, *5*(1), pp. 58–61. [G: EEC]

Ferreira, Raquel. Decision-Making in an Enlarged Community: Comment. *Economia (Portugal)*, January 1981, *5*(1), pp. 181–86. [G: EEC]

Gianaris, Nicholas V. Indirect Taxes: A Comparative Study of Greece and the EEC. *Europ. Econ.*

Rev., January 1981, *15*(1), pp. 111–17.
[G: Greece; EEC]

González, Marta and Guerrero, Gemma Cruz. ASEAN—A Case Study of Regionalism in Southeast Asia. In *Nicol, D.; Echeverria, L. and Peccei, A., eds.*, 1981, pp. 75–81. [G: ASEAN]

Graziani, Giovanni. Dependency Structures in COMECON. *Rev. Radical Polit. Econ.*, Spring 1981, *13*(1), pp. 67–75. [G: COMECON]

Greenstone, Wayne D. The Coffee Cartel: Manipulation in the Public Interest. *J. Futures Markets*, Spring 1981, *1*(1), pp. 3–16. [G: U.S.]

Hager, Wolfgang. Industrial Policy in an Enlarged Community. *Economia (Portugal)*, January 1981, *5*(1), pp. 33–53. [G: EEC]

Hall, Kenneth and Blake, Byron. Collective Self-reliance: The Case of the Caribbean Community (CARICOM). In *Muñoz, H., ed.*, 1981, pp. 197–206. [G: Caribbean]

Henderson, W. O. The German Zollverein and the European Economic Community. *Z. ges. Staatswiss.*, September 1981, *137*(3), pp. 491–507. [G: EEC]

Hewitt, Adrian and Stevens, Christopher. The Second Lomé Convention. In *Stevens, C., ed.*, 1981, pp. 30–59. [G: EEC; LDCs]

Hirschman, Albert O. Three Uses of Political Economy in Analyzing European Integration. In *Hirschman, A. O.*, 1981, pp. 266–84. [G: Europe]

Hoffman, Kurt and Burch, David. The EEC and Energy Aid to the Third World. In *Stevens, C., ed.*, 1981, pp. 104–18. [G: EEC; LDCs]

Hojman, David E. The Andean Pact: Failure of a Model of Economic Integration? *J. Common Market Stud.*, December 1981, *20*(2), pp. 139–60. [G: Andean Pact]

Holeček, Josef. Topical Questions Concerning Management of the Process of International Socialist Economic Integration. *Czech. Econ. Digest.*, December 1981, (8), pp. 69–82. [G: CMEA]

Huber, Jürgen. The Practice of GATT in Examining Regional Arrangements under Article XXIV. *J. Common Market Stud.*, March 1981, *19*(3), pp. 281–98.

Jacquemin, Alexis. Industrial Policy in an Enlarged Community: Comment. *Economia (Portugal)*, January 1981, *5*(1), pp. 54–57. [G: EEC]

Jaidah, Ali M. OPEC Policy Options. In *OPEC, Public Information Dept.*, 1981, pp. 208–14. [G: OPEC]

Jepma, Catrinus J. An Application of the Constant Market Shares Technique on Trade between the Associated African and Malagasy States and the European Community (1958–1978) *J. Common Market Stud.*, December 1981, *20*(2), pp. 175–92. [G: AAMS (W. Africa)]

Kadhim, Sabri A. R. and Al-Janabi, Adnan A. Domestic Energy Requirements in OPEC Member Countries. In *OPEC, Public Information Dept.*, 1981, pp. 140–60. [G: OPEC]

Kent, Pendarell H. Capital Movements, Financial Integration and the EMS: Comment. *Giorn. Econ.*, Sept.-Dec. 1981, *40*(9–12), pp. 669–71. [G: EEC]

Kohler, Beate. Decision-Making in an Enlarged

Community. *Economia (Portugal)*, January 1981, *5*(1), pp. 159–72. [G: EEC]

Köves, András. Turning Inward or Turning Outward: Reflections on the Foreign Economic Strategy of CMEA Countries. *Acta Oecon.*, 1981, *26*(1–2), pp. 51–69. [G: CMEA]

Kreinin, Mordechai E. North American Economic Integration. *Law Contemp. Probl.*, Summer 1981, *44*(3), pp. 7–31. [G: N. America]

Kreinin, Mordechai E. Static Effect of E.C. Enlargement on Trade Flows in Manufactured Products. *Kyklos*, 1981, *34*(1), pp. 60–71. [G: EEC]

Lafay, Gérard. La dynamique de spécialisation des pays européens. (Dynamics of Specialization in European Countries. With English summary.) *Revue Écon.*, July 1981, *32*(4), pp. 636–59. [G: EEC]

Languetin, Pierre. The European Monetary System—Managing the External Relationships. *Banca Naz. Lavoro Quart. Rev.*, September 1981, (138), pp. 327–38. [G: EEC]

Leistner, G. M. E. Towards a Regional Development Strategy for Southern Africa. *S. Afr. J. Econ.*, December 1981, *49*(4), pp. 349–64. [G: Africa]

Lloyd, Michael. Migration in the EEC. In *Twitchett, C. C., ed.*, 1981, pp. 94–101. [G: EEC]

Longo, Carlos A. Indirect Tax Harmonization: The Case of LAIA? *Bull. Int. Fiscal Doc.*, December 1981, *35*(12), pp. 533–43. [G: LAIA]

M'Bouy-Boutzit, Edouard Alexis. The Road to Cooperation: Gabon's Standpoint. In *OPEC, Public Information Dept.*, 1981, pp. 17–21. [G: OPEC; Gabon]

Maldague, Robert. Les politiques "d'ajustement positif" *dans la Communauté européenne. (Positive Adjustment Policies in the European Community. With English summary.) Revue Écon.*, July 1981, *32*(4), pp. 625–35. [G: EEC]

Markmann, Heinz. Decision-Making in an Enlarged Community: Comment. *Economia (Portugal)*, January 1981, *5*(1), pp. 178–80. [G: EEC]

Marsh, J. The Need for New Policies: Agricultural Policy. *Economia (Portugal)*, January 1981, *5*(1), pp. 1–32. [G: EEC]

McKie, James W. An Antimonopoly Policy for North America: Opportunities and Problems. *Law Contemp. Probl.*, Summer 1981, *44*(3), pp. 105–30. [G: Mexico; Canada; U.S.]

Meissner, Werner. Strukturpolitik in marktwirtschaftlich orientierten Wirtschaftssystemen. (Industrial Policy in Market Systems. With English summary.) *Z. Wirtschaft. Sozialwissen.*, 1981, *101*(5), pp. 537–54. [G: W. Germany; U.K.; France; Sweden]

Miguel, Urrutia M. Colombia and the Andean Group: Economic and Political Determinants of Regional Integration Policy. In *Baer, W. and Gillis, M., eds.*, 1981, pp. 182–99. [G: Colombia; Latin America]

Mishalani, Philip, et al. The Pyramid of Privilege. In *Stevens, C., ed.*, 1981, pp. 60–82. [G: EEC; Selected Countries]

Monti, Mario. L'integrazione finanziaria internazionale e l'Italia: alcuni problemi da risolvere. (Italy and International Financial Integration: Some Problems Still to be Solved. With English summary.) *Bancaria*, September 1981, *37*(9), pp. 884–90. **[G: Italy]**

Morgan, Annette. Pressure Groups and Harmonisation. In *Twitchett, C. C., ed.*, 1981, pp. 102–15. **[G: EEC]**

Muir, Donald. EEC Production Subsidies for Canned Pears: Implications for World Trade. *Quart. Rev. Rural Econ.*, August 1981, *3*(3), pp. 254–60. **[G: EEC; Australia]**

Müller, Jürgen. Competitive Performance and Trade within the EEC: Generalizations from Several Case Studies with Specific Reference to the West German Economy. *Z. ges. Staatswiss.*, September 1981, *137*(3), pp. 638–63. **[G: W. Germany; EEC]**

Musto, Stefan A. Die Süderweiterung der Europäichen Gemeinschaft. (With English summary.) *Kyklos*, 1981, *34*(2), pp. 242–73. **[G: EEC]**

Musto, Stefan A. The Canary Islands and the EC—Options for Integration. *J. Common Market Stud.*, December 1981, *20*(2), pp. 115–37. **[G: Spain; EEC]**

Mutharika, B. W. A Case Study of Regionalism in Africa. In *Nicol, D.; Echeverria, L. and Peccei, A., eds.*, 1981, pp. 91–113. **[G: Africa]**

Nsouli, Saleh M. Monetary Integration in Developing Countries. *Finance Develop.*, December 1981, *18*(4), pp. 41–44.

Odell, Peter R. Energy Policies in the EEC and Their Impact on the Third World. In *Stevens, C., ed.*, 1981, pp. 84–91. **[G: EEC; LDCs]**

Olorunfemi, M. A. Structural Changes in World Oil Market: Commentary. In *OPEC, Public Information Dept.*, 1981, pp. 161–64. **[G: OPEC]**

Ortiz, René G. OPEC's Role in Future Energy Markets. In *OPEC, Public Information Dept.*, 1981, pp. 43–50. **[G: OPEC]**

Padoa-Schioppa, Tommaso. Lo scudo e il Sistema Monetario Europeo. (The E.C.U. and the European Monetary System. With English summary.) *Bancaria*, March 1981, *37*(3), pp. 245–50. **[G: EEC]**

Payne, Anthony. The Rise and Fall of Caribbean Regionalisation. *J. Common Market Stud.*, March 1981, *19*(3), pp. 255–80. **[G: CARIFTA; CARICOM]**

Pecchioli, Rinaldo. European Financial Integration: Institutional and Legal Aspects: Comment. *Giorn. Econ.*, Sept.-Dec. 1981, *40*(9–12), pp. 775–79. **[G: EEC]**

Petzina, Dietmar. The Origin of the European Coal and Steel Community: Economic Forces and Political Interests. *Z. ges. Staatswiss.*, September 1981, *137*(3), pp. 450–68. **[G: W. Europe]**

Piskulov, Jurij Vasiljevitz. De nordeuropeiska länderna i dagens världsekonomiska system. (The Nordic Countries in the World Economy. With English summary.) *Ekon. Samfundets Tidskr.*, 1981, *34*(3), pp. 183–207. **[G: Denmark; Norway; Sweden; Finland]**

Pomfret, Richard. The Impact of EEC Enlargement on Non-member Mediterranean Countries' Exports to the EEC. *Econ. J.*, September 1981, *91*(363), pp. 726–29. **[G: EEC]**

Puyana, Alicia. Latin America: Lessons of the Strength and Weakness of Regional Cooperation. In *Nicol, D.; Echeverria, L. and Peccei, A., eds.*, 1981, pp. 49–74. **[G: Latin America]**

Rahman, M. Akhlaqur; Bhuyan, Rahman and Reza, Sadrel. The Trade Effects of a South Asian Customs Union: An Expository Study. *Pakistan Devel. Rev.*, Spring 1981, *20*(1), pp. 61–80.

Rico F., Carlos. Mexico–United States Relations: Prospects for Economic Cooperation. In *Purcell, S. K., ed.*, 1981, pp. 189–94. **[G: Mexico; U.S.]**

Robinson, P. W. Medium Term Forecasting in the European Communities: The Use of the Comet Model. In *Courbis, R., ed.*, 1981, pp. 251–58.

Santa Maria, Alberto. European Financial Integration: Institutional and Legal Aspects. *Giorn. Econ.*, Sept.-Dec. 1981, *40*(9–12), pp. 747–66. **[G: EEC]**

Sapir, André. Trade Benefits under the EEC Generalized System of Preferences. *Europ. Econ. Rev.*, March 1981, *15*(3), pp. 339–55. **[G: EEC]**

Sarcinelli, Mario. Assetti monetari internazionali, movimenti di capitali, controlli amministrativi: un difficile cammino verso la libertà. (International Monetary Conditions, Capital Flows and Controls: The Difficult Path toward Freedom. With English summary.) *Bancaria*, September 1981, *37*(9), pp. 874–83. **[G: Italy]**

Sayigh, Yusif A. The Integration of the Oil Sector in Economies of OPEC Member Countries: Commentary. In *OPEC, Public Information Dept.*, 1981, pp. 182–88.

Scharrer, Hans-Eckart. Capital Movements, Financial Integration and the EMS: Comment. *Giorn. Econ.*, Sept.-Dec. 1981, *40*(9–12), pp. 673–77. **[G: EEC]**

Schweitzer, Michael. Barriers to a Common West European Economic Area: The Case of Austria. *Z. ges. Staatswiss.*, September 1981, *137*(3), pp. 508–24. **[G: Austria]**

de la Serre, Françoise. The Community's Mediterranean Policy after the Second Enlargement. *J. Common Market Stud.*, June 1981, *19*(4), pp. 377–87. **[G: EEC]**

Simai, Mihály. A Case Study of Economic Cooperation in Eastern Europe. In *Nicol, D.; Echeverria, L. and Peccei, A., eds.*, 1981, pp. 122–37. **[G: CMEA]**

Smith, Ian. EEC Sugar Policy in an International Context. *J. World Trade Law*, March–April 1981, *15*(2), pp. 95–110. **[G: EEC]**

Stevens, Christopher. EEC and the Third World: The Search for Coherence. In *Stevens, C., ed.*, 1981, pp. 1–19. **[G: EEC]**

Tangermann, Stefan. Policies of the European Community and Agricultural Trade with Developing Countries. In *Johnson, G. and Maunder, A., eds.*, 1981, pp. 440–51. **[G: EEC]**

Tarditi, Secondo. A More Effective Role of Public Finance in Agricultural Policy. *Econ. Notes*, 1981, *10*(3), pp. 128–37. **[G: EEC]**

Thomas, D. J. General Equilibrium Assessment of a Free Area between Two Small Countries: Australia and New Zealand. *Australian Econ. Pap.*, December 1981, *20*(37), pp. 283–98. **[G: Australia; New Zealand]**

Thygesen, Niels. The European Monetary System:

The First Two Years: Introduction. *Banca Naz. Lavoro Quart. Rev.*, September 1981, (138), pp. 261–69. [G: EEC]

Tokuyama, Jiro. The New Pacific Era and Japan's Role. In *Hewett, R. B., ed.*, 1981, pp. 53–63. [G: Pacific Basin; Japan]

Triffin, Robert. The European Monetary System: The First Two Years: Concluding Remarks. *Banca Naz. Lavoro Quart. Rev.*, September 1981, (138), pp. 365–70. [G: EEC]

Urrutia M., Miguel. Colombia and the Andean Group: Economic and Political Determinants of Regional Integration Policy. *Quart. Rev. Econ. Bus.*, Summer 1981, *21*(2), pp. 182–99. [G: Andean Group]

Ustor, Endre. The MFN Customs Union Exception. *J. World Trade Law*, September–October 1981, *15*(5), pp. 377–87.

Vaganov, Boris. Foreign Economic Relations. In *Novosti Press Agency*, 1981, pp. 176–90. [G: U.S.S.R.]

Válek, Vratislav. Agreed Plan of Multilateral Integration Measures for the Five-Year Period, 1981–1985. *Czech. Econ. Digest.*, December 1981, (8), pp. 55–68. [G: CMEA]

Vanden Abeele, Michel. Regional Disequilibria, Financial Flows and Budgetary Policy in the European Community. *Economia (Portugal)*, January 1981, *5*(1), pp. 117–53. [G: EEC]

Vaubel, Roland. Logische Implikationen und Anreizwirkungen des europäischen Währungssystems. (Logical Implications and Incentive Effects of the European Monetary System. With English summary.) *Z. Wirtschaft. Sozialwissen.*, 1981, *101*(1), pp. 1–23. [G: EEC]

Verreydt, E. and Waelbroeck, Jean. EEC Industrial Policy and the Third World. In *Stevens, C., ed.*, 1981, pp. 20–29. [G: EEC]

Waelbroeck, Jean. Decision-Making in an Enlarged Community: Comment. *Economia (Portugal)*, January 1981, *5*(1), pp. 173–77. [G: EEC]

Weidenfeld, Werner. Economic Factors in the Origins of European Integration after the Second World War: A Political Scientist's View. *Z. ges. Staatswiss.*, September 1981, *137*(3), pp. 434–49. [G: EEC]

Williamson, John. Colombia and the Andean Group: Comment. In *Baer, W. and Gillis, M., eds.*, 1981, pp. 199–203. [G: Colombia; Latin America]

Williamson, John. Comment on "Colombia and the Andean Group." *Quart. Rev. Econ. Bus.*, Summer 1981, *21*(2), pp. 199–203. [G: Andean Group]

Wilson, Thomas. Issues of Regional Finance: Fiscal Transfers between Regions and between Members of the European Community. In *Roskamp, K. W. and Forte, F., eds.*, 1981, pp. 401–11. [G: EEC]

Wyatt, Derrick. Freedom of Movement—An Economic and Political Right. In *Twitchett, C. C., ed.*, 1981, pp. 83–93. [G: EEC]

Zimmerman, William. Soviet–East European Relations in the 1980s and the Changing International System. In *Bornstein, M.; Gitelman, Z. and Zimmerman, W., eds.*, 1981, pp. 87–104. [G: U.S.S.R.; E. Europe]

430 INTERNATIONAL FINANCE

4300 General

Baffi, Paolo. Comment [Mobilité et mouvements de capitaux en Europe]. *Giorn. Econ.*, Sept.-Dec. 1981, *40*(9–12), pp. 621–33. [G: EEC]

Cline, William R. and Weintraub, Sidney. Economic Stabilization in Developing Countries: Introduction and Overview. In *Cline, W. R. and Weintraub, S., eds.*, 1981, pp. 1–42. [G: LDCs]

De Grauwe, Paul. Capital Movements, Financial Integration and the EMS. *Giorn. Econ.*, Sept.-Dec. 1981, *40*(9–12), pp. 649–67. [G: EEC]

Kent, Pendarell H. Capital Movements, Financial Integration and the EMS: Comment. *Giorn. Econ.*, Sept.-Dec. 1981, *40*(9–12), pp. 669–71. [G: EEC]

Micossi, Stefano. Comment [Mobilité et mouvements de capitaux en Europe]. *Giorn. Econ.*, Sept.-Dec. 1981, *40*(9–12), pp. 641–43. [G: EEC]

Palmerio, Giovanni. Tasso di cambio, ritmi di inflazione e movimenti di capitali. (Exchange Rate, Inflation Rates and Capital Movements. With English summary.) *Rivista Int. Sci. Econ. Com.*, October–November 1981, *28*(10–11), pp. 990–1000.

Scharrer, Hans-Eckart. Capital Movements, Financial Integration and the EMS: Comment. *Giorn. Econ.*, Sept.-Dec. 1981, *40*(9–12), pp. 673–77. [G: EEC]

Swoboda, Alexander K. Comment [Mobilité et mouvements de capitaux en Europe]. *Giorn. Econ.*, Sept.-Dec. 1981, *40*(9–12), pp. 635–40. [G: EEC]

Williams, Robert G. The Political Economy of Hub Currency Defense: Sterling and the Dollar. *Rev. Radical Polit. Econ.*, Fall 1981, *13*(3), pp. 1–20. [G: U.S.; U.K.]

Williamson, John. International Monetary Issues and the Developing Countries: A Survey: Comment. In *Streeten, P. and Jolly, R, eds.*, 1981, *1975*, pp. 381–82.

431 Open Economy Macroeconomics; Exchange Rates

4310 General

Aizenman, Joshua. Devaluation and Liberalization in the Presence of Tariff and Quota Restrictions: An Equilibrium Model. *J. Int. Econ.*, May 1981, *11*(2), pp. 197–206.

Artus, Jacques R. and McGuirk, Anne Kenny. A Revised Version of the Multilateral Exchange Rate Model. *Int. Monet. Fund Staff Pap.*, June 1981, *28*(2), pp. 275–309.

Berthelot, Yves. The Interests of the Industrial West in Relations with Developing Countries. In *Saunders, C. T., ed. (I)*, 1981, pp. 19–32. [G: OECD; LDCs]

Bird, Graham. International Monetary Issues and the Developing Countries: A Survey: Postscript. In *Streeten, P. and Jolly, R, eds.*, 1981, pp. 367–73. [G: LDCs]

Bloomfield, Arthur I. and Marston, Richard C. Policies for an OPEC Dollar Run. *J. Post Keynesian Econ.*, Spring 1981, *3*(3), pp. 299–311.

Brittain, Bruce. International Currency Substitution and the Apparent Instability of Velocity in Some Western European Economies and in the United States. *J. Money, Credit, Banking*, May 1981, *13*(2), pp. 135–55. [G: U.S.; W. Germany; U.K.]

Callier, Philippe. Speculation, Interest Arbitrage, and the Forward Foreign Exchange Rate and the Canadian Dollar: Updated Evidence. *J. Macroecon.*, Spring 1981, *3*(2), pp. 293–99.
[G: Canada]

Cobham, David. Definitions of Domestic Credit Expansion for the United Kingdom. *J. Econ. Stud.*, 1981, *8*(3), pp. 65–78. [G: U.K.]

Cobham, David. Sterilisation and the Exchange Equalisation Account. *Scot. J. Polit. Econ.*, November 1981, *28*(3), pp. 278–83.

Dell, Sidney. International Monetary Issues and the Developing Countries: A Survey: Comment. In *Streeten, P. and Jolly, R, eds.*, 1981, *1975*, pp. 375–79.

Demattè, Claudio. International Financial Intermediation: Implications for Bankers and Regulators. *Banca Naz. Lavoro Quart. Rev.*, March 1981, (136), pp. 91–110.

Drèze, Jacques H. and Modigliani, Franco. The Trade-off between Real Wages and Employment in an Open Economy (Belgium). *Europ. Econ. Rev.*, January 1981, *15*(1), pp. 1–40.
[G: Belgium]

Eltis, W. A. The Fundamental Problem. *Oxford Econ. Pap.*, Supplement July 1981, *33*, pp. 1–8.
[G: U.K.]

Frenkel, Jacob A. and Mussa, Michael L. Monetary and Fiscal Policies in an Open Economy. *Amer. Econ. Rev.*, May 1981, *71*(2), pp. 253–58.

Hodgson, John S. and Schneck, Ronald G. Stability of the Relationship between Monetary Variables and Exchange Market Pressure: Empirical Evidence. *Southern Econ. J.*, April 1981, *47*(4), pp. 941–58.

Kapur, Basant K. Monetary Policy in an Inside-Money, Open Economy: Comment. *Quart. J. Econ.*, May 1981, *96*(2), pp. 349–56.

Kareken, John H. and Wallace, Neil. On the Indeterminacy of Equilibrium Exchange Rates. *Quart. J. Econ.*, May 1981, *96*(2), pp. 207–22.

Khan, Mohsin S. and Knight, Malcolm D. Stabilization Programs in Developing Countries: A Formal Framework. *Int. Monet. Fund Staff Pap.*, March 1981, *28*(1), pp. 1–53. [G: LDCs]

Kindleberger, Charles P. Lessons of Floating Exchange Rates. In *Kindleberger, C. P.*, 1981, *1976*, pp. 183–206.

Kindleberger, Charles P. Measuring Equilibrium in the Balance of Payments. In *Kindleberger, C. P.*, 1981, *1969*, pp. 120–38.

Kreicher, Lawrence L. International Portfolio Capital Flows and Real Rates of Interest. *Rev. Econ. Statist.*, February 1981, *63*(1), pp. 20–28.
[G: U.K.; W. Germany; Italy; U.S.]

Laidler, David. Inflation and Unemployment in an Open Economy: A Monetarist View. *Can. Public Policy*, Supplement, April 1981, *7*, pp. 179–88.
[G: Canada]

Mathieson, Donald J. Monetary Policy in an Inside-Money, Open Economy: Reply. *Quart. J. Econ.*, May 1981, *96*(2), pp. 357–61.

Maynard, Geoffrey and Bird, Graham. International Monetary Issues and the Developing Countries: A Survey. In *Streeten, P. and Jolly, R, eds.*, 1981, *1975*, pp. 343–65. [G: LDCs]

Miles, Marc A. Currency Substitution: Some Further Results and Conclusions. *Southern Econ. J.*, July 1981, *48*(1), pp. 78–86. [G: U.S.; W. Germany]

Obstfeld, Maurice. Capital Mobility and Devaluation in an Optimizing Model with Rational Expectations. *Amer. Econ. Rev.*, May 1981, *71*(2), pp. 217–21.

Reuber, G. L. Steps to Improve International Economic Policy Co-ordination. *Can. Public Policy*, Autumn 1981, *7*(4), pp. 596–603.

Sachs, Jeffrey D. The Current Account and Macroeconomic Adjustment in the 1970s. *Brookings Pap. Econ. Act.*, 1981, (1), pp. 201–68.
[G: OECD; LDCs]

Solomon, Robert. Brunner on the State of International Monetary Policy. *Banca Naz. Lavoro Quart. Rev.*, March 1981, (136), pp. 111–13.

Tullio, Giuseppe. Demand Management and Exchange Rate Policy: The Italian Experience. *Int. Monet. Fund Staff Pap.*, March 1981, *28*(1), pp. 80–117. [G: Italy]

Weiller, Jean. L'influence des variations de change et des mouvements internationaux de capitaux dans un modèle ou scénario de rééquilibrage des balances des paiements. (The Effects of Foreign Exchange Instability and International Capital Movements on Balance of Payments Policies. With English summary.) *Rivista Int. Sci. Econ. Com.*, October–November 1981, *28*(10–11), pp. 977–89.

Williamson, John. International Monetary Issues and the Developing Countries: A Survey: Comment. In *Streeten, P. and Jolly, R, eds.*, 1981, *1975*, pp. 381–82.

Worswick, G. D. N. The Money Supply and the Exchange Rate. *Oxford Econ. Pap.*, Supplement July 1981, *33*, pp. 9–22. [G: U.K.]

4312 Open Economy Macroeconomic Theory: Balance of Payments and Adjustment Mechanisms

Aghevli, Bijan B. Monetary Control and the Crawling Peg: Comment. In *Williamson, J., ed.*, 1981, pp. 53–54. [G: OECD; LDCs]

Ahluwalia, Montek S. and Lysy, Frank J. Employment, Income Distribution, and Programs to Remedy Balance-of-Payments Difficulties. In *Cline, W. R. and Weintraub, S., eds.*, 1981, pp. 149–88. [G: Malaysia]

Aizenman, Joshua. The Use of the Balance of Payments as a Shock Absorber in Fixed Rate and Managed Float Systems. *J. Int. Econ.*, November 1981, *11*(4), pp. 479–86.

Allen, Stuart D. and Crickard, Donald L. The Impact of Demand and Cost Factors on Inflation in

Open Economies. *Southern Econ. J.*, April 1981, 47(4), pp. 1092–1104. [G: OECD]

Aspe, Pedro. Comment [Exchange Rate Rules and Macroeconomic Stability] [The Analysis of Floating Exchange Rates and the Choice between Crawl and Float]. In *Williamson, J., ed.*, 1981, pp. 82–84. [G: OECD; LDCs]

Bach, Christopher L. U.S. International Transactions, Fourth Quarter and Year 1980. *Surv. Curr. Bus.*, March 1981, 61(3), pp. 40–67. [G: U.S.]

Balassa, Bela. The Newly-Industrializing Developing Countries after the Oil Crisis. In *Balassa, B.*, 1981, pp. 29–81. [G: LDCs]

Balassa, Bela. The Newly-Industrializing Developing Countries after the Oil Crisis. *Weltwirtsch. Arch.*, 1981, 117(1), pp. 142–94. [G: LDCs]

Beenstock, Michael; Budd, Alan and Warburton, Peter. Monetary Policy, Expectations and Real Exchange Rate Dynamics. *Oxford Econ. Pap.*, Supplement July 1981, 33, pp. 85–119.
[G: U.K.]

Beenstock, Michael and Longbottom, J. Andrew. The Term Structure of Interest Rates in a Small Open Economy. *J. Money, Credit, Banking*, February 1981, 13(1), pp. 44–59. [G: U.K.]

Bernauer, Kenneth. Effectiveness of Exchange-Rate Changes on the Trade Account: The Japanese Case. *Fed. Res. Bank San Francisco Econ. Rev.*, Fall 1981, pp. 55–71. [G: Japan]

Berthélemy, Jean-Claude. La théorie des transferts: une approche en termes de déséquilibres. (The Transfer Theory: A Disequilibrium Approach. With English summary.) *Revue Écon.*, January 1981, 32(1), pp. 32–62.

Bhandari, Jagdeep S. A Simple Transnational Model of Large Open Economies. *Southern Econ. J.*, April 1981, 47(4), pp. 990–1006.

Bhandari, Jagdeep S. A Stochastic Macroequilibrium Approach to a Floating Exchange Rate Economy with Interest-Bearing Assets. *Weltwirtsch. Arch.*, 1981, 117(1), pp. 1–19.

Bhandari, Jagdeep S. A Theory of Exchange Rate Determination and Adjustment. *Weltwirtsch. Arch.*, 1981, 117(4), pp. 605–21.

Bhandari, Jagdeep S. Some Pitfalls in Open Economy Model Building. *J. Macroecon.*, Summer 1981, 3(3), pp. 423–33.

Bhandari, Jagdeep S. The Simple Macroeconomics of an Oil-Dependent Economy. *Europ. Econ. Rev.*, June/July 1981, 16(2/3), pp. 333–54.

Black, Stanley W. Inflation and Growth: Exchange Rate Alternatives for Mexico: Comment. In *Williamson, J., ed.*, 1981, pp. 349–50. [G: Mexico]

Black, Stanley W. The Analysis of Floating Exchange Rates and the Choice between Crawl and Float. In *Williamson, J., ed.*, 1981, pp. 68–81.
[G: OECD; LDCs]

Blejer, Mario I. and Leiderman, Leonardo. A Monetary Approach to the Crawling-Peg System: Theory and Evidence. *J. Polit. Econ.*, February 1981, 89(1), pp. 132–51. [G: Brazil]

Boyes, William J. and Schlagenhauf, Don E. Price Controls in an Open Economy. *J. Macroecon.*, Summer 1981, 3(3), pp. 391–408.

Brakman, S. and Jepma, Catrinus J. Purchasing Power Parity Theory and the Monetary Approach

to the Balance of Payments: A Commentary. *De Economist*, 1981, 129(3), pp. 412–15.

Branson, William H. and Katseli-Papaefstratiou, Louka. Exchange Rate Policy for Developing Countries. In *Grassman, S. and Lundberg, E., eds.*, 1981, pp. 391–419. [G: LDCs; MDCs]

Bruno, Michael. Short-term Policy Tradeoffs under Different Phases of Economic Development. In *Grassman, S. and Lundberg, E., eds.*, 1981, pp. 295–313.

Bruno, Michael and Sussman, Zvi. Floating versus Crawling: Israel 1977–9 by Hindsight. In *Williamson, J., ed.*, 1981, pp. 252–71. [G: Israel]

Buiter, Willem H. and Eaton, Jonathan. Keynesian Balance of Payments Models: Comment [On the Almost Total Inadequacy of Keynesian Balance-of-Payments Theory]. *Amer. Econ. Rev.*, September 1981, 71(4), pp. 784–95.

Buiter, Willem H. and Miller, Marcus. Monetary Policy and International Competitiveness: The Problems of Adjustment. *Oxford Econ. Pap.*, Supplement July 1981, 33, pp. 143–75.

Bürgenmeier, Beat. Kapitalströme und Zahlungsbilanz: Auswirkungen auf das Realeinkommen. (The Consequences of International Capital Movements on Real Income. With English summary.) *Schweiz. Z. Volkswirtsch. Statist.*, March 1981, 117(1), pp. 41–54.

Burton, David. Expectations and the Dynamics of Devaluation: A Comment. *Rev. Econ. Stud.*, October 1981, 48(4), pp. 659–60.

Calvo, Guillermo A. Capitalización de las reservas y tipo real de cambio. (With English summary.) *Cuadernos Econ.*, April 1981, 18(53), pp. 5–14.

Cardoso, Eliana A. The Burden of Exchange Rate Adjustment in Brazil. In *Baer, W. and Gillis, M., eds.*, 1981, pp. 168–81. [G: Brazil]

Cauas, Jorge and Desormeaux, Jorge. Equilibrio monetario, inflación y balanza de pagos: la cuenta de capitales. (With English summary.) *Cuadernos Econ.*, April 1981, 18(53), pp. 43–64.

Chen, Chau-nan and Tsaur, Tien-wang. Monetary Approaches to Devaluation: Reply [IS, LM, BT and a Simplified Synthesis of the Elasticity, Absorption and Monetary Approaches to Devaluation]. *Southern Econ. J.*, April 1981, 47(4), pp. 1147–51.

Chenery, Hollis B. Interactions between Inflation and Trade Regime Objectives in Stabilization Programs: Comment. In *Cline, W. R. and Weintraub, S., eds.*, 1981, pp. 114–16. [G: LDCs]

Clements, Kenneth W. The Monetary Approach to Exchange Rate Determination: A Geometric Analysis. *Weltwirtsch. Arch.*, 1981, 117(1), pp. 20–29.

Cuddington, John T. Import Substitution Policies: A Two-Sector, Fix-Price Model. *Rev. Econ. Stud.*, April 1981, 48(2), pp. 327–42.

Daniel, Betty C. International Transmission of a Real Shock under Flexible Exchange Rates: A Comment. *J. Polit. Econ.*, August 1981, 89(4), pp. 813–18.

Daniel, Betty C. Real Output Effects of Announced Monetary Policy in a Small Open Economy. *Weltwirtsch. Arch.*, 1981, 117(3), pp. 428–42.

Daniel, Betty C. The International Transmission of

Economic Disturbances under Flexible Exchange Rates. *Int. Econ. Rev.*, October 1981, *22*(3), pp. 491–509.

Deardorff, Alan V. Keynesian Balance of Payments Models: Comment [On the Almost Total Inadequacy of Keynesian Balance-of-Payments Theory]. *Amer. Econ. Rev.*, September 1981, *71*(4), pp. 774–77.

Dervis, Kemal. IS/LM in the Tropics: Diagrammatics of the New Structuralist Macro Critique: Comment. In *Cline, W. R. and Weintraub, S., eds.*, 1981, pp. 503–06. **[G: LDCs]**

Dervis, Kemal; de Melo, Jaime and Robinson, Sherman. A General Equilibrium Analysis of Foreign Exchange Shortages in a Developing Economy. *Econ. J.*, December 1981, *91*(364), pp. 891–906. **[G: Turkey]**

Dornbusch, Rudiger. Exchange Rate Rules and Macroeconomic Stability. In *Williamson, J., ed.*, 1981, pp. 55–67.

Eichengreen, Barry J. A Dynamic Model of Tariffs, Output and Employment under Flexible Exchange Rates. *J. Int. Econ.*, August 1981, *11*(3), pp. 341–59.

Enders, Walter and Lapan, Harvey E. The Exchange Regime, Resource Allocation, and Uncertainty. *Southern Econ. J.*, April 1981, *47*(4), pp. 924–40.

Fausten, Dietrich K. A Partial Rehabilitation of the Policy-Mix Approach. *Kyklos*, 1981, *34*(2), pp. 203–15.

Feige, Edgar L. and Johannes, James M. Testing the Causal Relationship between the Domestic Credit and Reserve Components of a Country's Monetary Base. *J. Macroecon.*, Winter 1981, *3*(1), pp. 55–76. **[G: W. Europe]**

Fellner, William. Gold and the Uneasy Case for Responsibly Managed Fiat Money. In *Fellner, W., ed.*, 1981, pp. 97–121.

Fendt, Roberto, Jr. Inflation and Growth: Exchange Rate Alternatives for Mexico: Comment. In *Williamson, J., ed.*, 1981, pp. 347–48. **[G: Mexico]**

Ffrench-Davis, Ricardo. The Crawling Peg in Historical Perspective: Comment. In *Williamson, J., ed.*, 1981, pp. 31–34. **[G: Latin America]**

Fischer, Stanley and Frenkel, Jacob A. Investment, the Two-Sector Model, and Trade in Debt and Capital Goods. In *Bhagwati, J. N., ed.*, 1981, pp. 360–74.

Fishlow, Albert. Comment [Employment, Income Distribution, and Programs to Remedy Balance-of-Payments Difficulties] [Stabilization Policies and Their Effects on Employment and Income Distribution: A Latin American Perspective]. In *Cline, W. R. and Weintraub, S., eds.*, 1981, pp. 229–32. **[G: Malaysia; Latin America]**

Florio, Ubaldo G. Optimization of Economic Targets in an Open Economy. *Econ. Notes*, 1981, *10*(1), pp. 122–31.

von Furstenberg, George M. Domestic Determinants of Net U.S. Foreign Investment. In *Hogan, J. D. and Craig, A. M., eds., Vol. 1*, 1981, pp. 115–63. **[G: U.S.]**

von Furstenberg, George M. Incentives for International Currency Diversification by U.S. Financial Investors. *Int. Monet. Fund Staff Pap.*, September 1981, *28*(3), pp. 477–94. **[G: U.S.]**

Genberg, Hans. Comment [The European Monetary System—An Approximate Implementation of the Crawling Peg?] [United States Economic Interests and Crawling Peg Systems]. In *Williamson, J., ed.*, 1981, pp. 387–90. **[G: U.S.; W. Europe]**

Georgakopoulos, Theodore A. Tax Structure Changes and the Balance of Trade. *Greek Econ. Rev.*, April 1981, *3*(1), pp. 25–32.

Girton, Lance and Roper, Don E. Theory and Implications of Currency Substitution. *J. Money, Credit, Banking*, February 1981, *13*(1), pp. 12–30.

Hacche, Graham and Townend, John C. Monetary Models of Exchange Rates and Exchange Market Pressure: Some General Limitations and an Application to Sterling's Effective Rate. *Weltwirtsch. Arch.*, 1981, *117*(4), pp. 622–37. **[G: U.K.]**

Hahn, Oswald. Financing of Raw Material Reserves by Banks of Issue. In *Chikán, A., ed. (I)*, 1981, pp. 179–87. **[G: W. Germany]**

Hara, Masayuki. Monetary, Intervention Policy and Exchange Rates—A General Asset Approach. (In Japanese. With English summary.) *Osaka Econ. Pap.*, December 1981, *31*(2–3), pp. 73–80.

Harberger, Arnold C. Comment [Employment, Income Distribution, and Programs to Remedy Balance-of-Payments Difficulties] [Stabilization Policies and Their Effects on Employment and Income Distribution: A Latin American Perspective]. In *Cline, W. R. and Weintraub, S., eds.*, 1981, pp. 226–29. **[G: Malaysia; Latin America]**

Hoel, Michael. The Domestic Demand Compensated Effects of changes in the Exchange Rate, Foreign Prices, Tariffs and Foreign Demand. *Scand. J. Econ.*, 1981, *83*(4), pp. 508–21.

Holly, Sean. Rational Expectations and the Scope for an Optimal Fiscal Policy in a Simple Model of an Open Economy: Some Numerical Results. In *Janssen, J. M. L.; Pau, L. F. and Straszak, A. J., eds.*, 1981, pp. 91–97.

Holzman, Franklyn D. Creditworthiness and Balance-of-payments Adjustment Mechanisms of Centrally Planned Economies. In *[Bergson, A.]*, 1981, pp. 163–84. **[G: E. Europe]**

Johannes, James M. Testing the Exogeneity Specification Underlying the Monetary Approach to the Balance of Payments. *Rev. Econ. Statist.*, February 1981, *63*(1), pp. 29–34. **[G: Australia; France; W. Germany; Norway; Sweden]**

Jossa, Bruno and Torrisi, Alfio. Teoria monetaria e teoria keynesiana della bilancia dei pagamenti. (Una critica a recenti contributi di Hahn, Miller e Kuska). (Monetary Theory and Keynesian Theory of the Balance of Payments. With English summary.) *Giorn. Econ.*, January–February 1981, *40*(1–2), pp. 31–49.

Kapur, Basant K. Rejoinder to Mathieson's "Further Reply" [Traded Goods, Nontraded Goods, and the Balance of Payments]. *Int. Econ. Rev.*, June 1981, *22*(2), pp. 485.

Kapur, Basant K. Traded Goods, Nontraded Goods, and the Balance of Payments: Further Comment. *Int. Econ. Rev.*, June 1981, *22*(2), pp. 477–80.

Kapur, Basant K. Traded Goods, Nontraded Goods,

and the Balance of Payments: A Steady–State Analysis. *Int. Econ. Rev.*, February 1981, 22(1), pp. 167–78.

Kawai, Masahiro. The Behaviour of an Open-Economy Firm under Flexible Exchange Rates. *Economica*, February 1981, 48(189), pp. 45–60.

Kincaid, G. Russell. Conditionality and the Use of Fund Resources: Jamaica. *Finance Develop.*, June 1981, 18(2), pp. 18–21.   [G: Jamaica]

Krueger, Anne O. Interactions between Inflation and Trade Regime Objectives in Stabilization Programs. In *Cline, W. R. and Weintraub, S., eds.,* 1981, pp. 83–114.   [G: LDCs]

Kulkarni, Kishore G. and Dhekane, Sunil G. The Monetarist Model of Imported Inflation in Small Open Economy. *Econ. Aff.*, July–September 1981, 26(3), pp. 188–92.

Laidler, David. Some Policy Implications of the Monetary Approach to Balance of Payments and Exchange Rate Analysis. *Oxford Econ. Pap.*, Supplement July 1981, 33, pp. 70–84.

Levin, Jay H. The Niehans Paradox, Flexible Exchange Rates, and Macroeconomic Stability. *J. Int. Econ.*, May 1981, 11(2), pp. 225–37.

Levy, Victor. Oil Prices, Relative Prices, and Balance-of-Payments Adjustment: The Turkish Experience. *Europ. Econ. Rev.*, March 1981, 15(3), pp. 357–72.   [G: Turkey]

Liviatan, Nissan. Monetary Expansion and Real Exchange Rate Dynamics. *J. Polit. Econ.*, December 1981, 89(6), pp. 1218–27.

Malan, Pedro S. Monetary Control and the Crawling Peg: Comment. In *Williamson, J., ed.,* 1981, pp. 50–52.   [G: OECD; LDCs]

Marczewski, Jean. La concurrence macroéconomique par les taux d'inflation et les taux de change. (With English summary.) *Écon. Appl.*, 1981, 34(4), pp. 619–37.   [G: U.S.]

Marois, William. Les interactions entre les mouvements de capitaux et la politique monétaire en systèmes de changes quasi fixes. (The Interactions between the Capital Movements and the Monetary Policy in a Quasi-Fixed Exchange Rates System. With English summary.) *Revue Écon.*, March 1981, 32(2), pp. 374–404.

Martirena-Mantel, Ana María. Crawling Peg Systems and Macroeconomic Stability: The Case of Argentina 1971–8. In *Williamson, J., ed.,* 1981, pp. 181–206.   [G: Argentina]

Mathieson, Donald J. A Final Reply to Kapur [Traded Goods, Nontraded Goods and the Balance of Payments]. *Int. Econ. Rev.*, June 1981, 22(2), pp. 487.

Mathieson, Donald J. Traded Goods, Nontraded Goods, and the Balance of Payments: Further Reply. *Int. Econ. Rev.*, June 1981, 22(2), pp. 481–83.

McCallum, John C. P. and Vines, David. Cambridge and Chicago on the Balance of Payments. *Econ. J.*, June 1981, 91(362), pp. 439–53.

McKinnon, Ronald I. Foreign Exchange Constraints in Economic Development and Efficient Aid Allocation. In *Bhagwati, J. N., ed.,* 1981, 1964, pp. 342–48.

McKinnon, Ronald I. Monetary Control and the Crawling Peg. In *Williamson, J., ed.,* 1981,

pp. 38–49.   [G: OECD; LDCs]

McKinnon, Ronald I. The Exchange Rate and Macroeconomic Policy: Changing Postwar Perceptions. *J. Econ. Lit.*, June 1981, 19(2), pp. 531–57.

Metcalfe, J. S. and Steedman, Ian W. Some Long-Run Theory of Employment, Income Distribution and the Exchange Rate. *Manchester Sch. Econ. Soc. Stud.*, March 1981, 49(1), pp. 1–20.

Miller, Norman C. Keynesian Balance of Payments Models: Comment [On the Almost Total Inadequacy of Keynesian Balance-of-Payments Theory]. *Amer. Econ. Rev.*, September 1981, 71(4), pp. 778–83.

Minford, Patrick. The Exchange Rate and Monetary Policy. *Oxford Econ. Pap.*, Supplement July 1981, 33, pp. 120–42.   [G: U.K.]

Mixon, J. Wilson, Jr.; Pratt, Lelia J. and Wallace, Myles S. The Short-Run Transmission of U.S. Price Changes under Fixed and Flexible Exchange Rates: Evidence from the U.K. *Southern Econ. J.*, April 1981, 47(4), pp. 1072–79.
          [G: U.K.; U.S.]

Mussa, Michael. The Monetary Approach to the Balance of Payments. In *Baldwin, R. E. and Richardson, J. D., eds.,* 1981, 1976, pp. 368–73.

Mussa, Michael L. Public Policy Issues in International Finance. In *National Science Foundation,* 1981, pp. I76–104.

Obstfeld, Maurice. Macroeconomic Policy, Exchange-Rate Dynamics, and Optimal Asset Accumulation. *J. Polit. Econ.*, December 1981, 89(6), pp. 1142–61.

Ortiz, Guillermo and Solís, Leopoldo. Inflation and Growth: Exchange Rate Alternatives for Mexico. In *Williamson, J., ed.,* 1981, pp. 327–46.
          [G: Mexico]

Pereira Leite, Sérgio. International Reserves in a Neo-Classical Growth Model. *Economia (Portugal)*, May 1981, 5(2), pp. 389–99.

Pikoulakis, Emmanuel. Growth, Saving, the Balance of Payments and the Neo-Classical Growth Diagram. *Bull. Econ. Res.*, November 1981, 33(2), pp. 104–14.

Prachowny, Martin F. J. Sectoral Conflict over Stabilisation Policies in Small Open Economies. *Econ. J.*, September 1981, 91(363), pp. 671–84.

Pyo, Hak K. and Yoo, Jang H. A Note on the Effects of Imported Inflation in a Small Open Economy. *J. Econ. Devel.*, July 1981, 6(1), pp. 111–23.
          [G: S. Korea]

Ramanathan, Ramu and Roberts, William W. The Impact of Monetary Expansion with Terms of Trade Effects and Trade in Securities. *J. Int. Econ.*, February 1981, 11(1), pp. 61–77.

de Ridder, Peter B. Exchange Rate Determination and the Balance of Payments, a Theoretical Framework. *De Economist*, 1981, 129(3), pp. 373–81.

de Roos, Folkert. Purchasing Power Parity Theory and the Monetary Approach to the Balance of Payments. *De Economist*, 1981, 129(1), pp. 41–57.

de Roos, Folkert. Reply to Brakman and Jepma [Purchasing Power Parity Theory and the Monetary Approach to the Balance of Payments]. *De Economist*, 1981, 129(3), pp. 414–15.

Saidi, Nasser. The Square-Root Law, Uncertainty and International Reserves under Alternative Regimes: Canadian Experience, 1950–1976. *J. Monet. Econ.*, May 1981, *7*(3), pp. 271–90. [G: Canada]

Sano, Shinsaku. The Balance of Payments, and Its Adjustments Mechanism: An Analytical Model. (In Japanese. With English summary.) *Osaka Econ. Pap.*, December 1981, *31*(2–3), pp. 59–72.

Schuh, G. Edward. Floating Exchange Rates, International Interdependence, and Agricultural Policy. In *Johnson, G. and Maunder, A., eds.*, 1981, pp. 416–23.

Scott, Maurice FG. Short-term Policy Tradeoffs under Different Phases of Economic Development: Comments. In *Grassman, S. and Lundberg, E., eds.*, 1981, pp. 314–18.

Sheahan, John. Incomes Policies in an Open Economy: Domestic and External Interactions. In *Claudon, M. P. and Cornwall, R. R., eds.*, 1981, pp. 155–74.

Shieh, Yeung-nan. Monetary Approaches to Devaluation: Comment [IS, LM, BT and a Simplified Synthesis of the Elasticity, Absorption and Monetary Approaches to Devaluation]. *Southern Econ. J.*, April 1981, *47*(4), pp. 1143–46.

Smith, M. Alasdair M. Capital Accumulation in the Open Two-Sector Economy. In *Bhagwati, J. N., ed.*, 1981, 1977, pp. 329–41.

Steedman, Ian W. and Metcalfe, J. S. On Duality and Basic Commodities in an Open Economy. *Australian Econ. Pap.*, June 1981, *20*(36), pp. 133–41.

Swoboda, Alexander K. Comment [Exchange Rate Rules and Macroeconomic Stability] [The Analysis of Floating Exchange Rates and the Choice between Crawl and Float]. In *Williamson, J., ed.*, 1981, pp. 85–87. [G: OECD; LDCs]

Swoboda, Alexander K. The Crawling Peg in Historical Perspective: Comment. In *Williamson, J., ed.*, 1981, pp. 35–37. [G: OECD; Selected LDCs]

Tarshis, Lorie. Understanding and Treating Stagflation in Canada's Open Economy. In *Ontario Economic Council, Vol. 2*, 1981, pp. 67–91. [G: Canada]

Taylor, Lance. IS/LM in the Tropics: Diagrammatics of the New Structuralist Macro Critique. In *Cline, W. R. and Weintraub, S., eds.*, 1981, pp. 465–503. [G: LDCs]

Turnovsky, Stephen J. Monetary Policy and Foreign Price Disturbances under Flexible Exchange Rates: A Stochastic Approach. *J. Money, Credit, Banking*, May 1981, *13*(2), pp. 156–76.

Turnovsky, Stephen J. Secular Inflation and Dynamics of Exchange Rates under Perfect Myopic Foresight. *Scand. J. Econ.*, 1981, *83*(4), pp. 522–40.

Turnovsky, Stephen J. The Effects of Devaluation and Foreign Price Disturbances under Rational Expectations. *J. Int. Econ.*, February 1981, *11*(1), pp. 33–60.

Weber, Warren E. Output Variability under Monetary Policy and Exchange Rate Rules. *J. Polit. Econ.*, August 1981, *89*(4), pp. 733–51.

Wellisz, Stanislaw. Exchange Rate Policy for Developing Countries: Comments. In *Grassman, S.*

and Lundberg, E., eds., 1981, pp. 420–22. [G: LDCs; MDCs]

Willett, Thomas D. Policy Research Issues in a Floating Rate World: An Assessment of Policy-relevant Research on the Effects of International Monetary Institutions and Behavior on Macroeconomic Performance. In *National Science Foundation*, 1981, pp. I24–58.

Williamson, John. The Crawling Peg in Historical Perspective. In *Williamson, J., ed.*, 1981, pp. 3–30. [G: OECD; Selected LDCs]

Witte, Willard E. Expectations, Monetary Policy Rules, and Macroeconomic Stability: Analysis of an Open Economy with Flexible Exchange Rates. *J. Int. Econ.*, August 1981, *11*(3), pp. 379–94.

Yano, Keiji. Exchange Rate Determination and Foreign Assets Accumulation. (In Japanese. With English summary.) *Osaka Econ. Pap.*, December 1981, *31*(2–3), pp. 53–58.

Zikry, Emad. Government Budget Constraint and Balance of Payments: A Reply. *Amer. Econ.*, Spring 1981, *25*(1), pp. 61–62.

4313 Open Economy Macroeconomic Studies: Balance of Payments and Adjustment Mechanisms

Abbott, George C. The Recycling of Surplus Oil Funds. *Econ. Int.*, May–August–November 1981, *34*(2–3–4), pp. 203–21. [G: OPEC; OECD]

Aghevli, Bijan B. Experiences of Asian Countries with Various Exchange Rate Policies. In *Williamson, J., ed.*, 1981, pp. 298–318. [G: Asia]

Aliber, Robert Z. Issues in U.S. International Monetary Policies. In *National Science Foundation*, 1981, pp. I59–75. [G: U.S.]

Andreatta, Beniamino. Linee essenziali della politica finanziaria e monetaria. (Essential Guidelines of Financial and Monetary Policy. With English summary.) *Bancaria*, April 1981, *37*(4), pp. 348–67. [G: Italy]

Balassa, Bela. Policy Responses to External Shocks in Selected Latin-American Countries. In *Baer, W. and Gillis, M., eds.*, 1981, pp. 131–64. [G: Brazil; Mexico; Uruguay]

Balassa, Bela. Policy Responses to External Shocks in Selected Latin-American Countries. *Quart. Rev. Econ. Bus.*, Summer 1981, *21*(2), pp. 131–64. [G: Brazil; Mexico; Uruguay]

Bennett, Karl. Mobilising Foreign Exchange Reserves for Economic Growth in CARICOM. *Soc. Econ. Stud.*, December 1981, *30*(4), pp. 172–86. [G: Jamaica]

Bergsten, C. Fred. Recycling the World's Surpluses and Deficits: Challenge and Response. In *Bergsten, C. F., ed.*, 1981, pp. 39–48. [G: LDCs; OECD; OPEC]

Bhalla, Surjit S. The Transmission of Inflation into Developing Economies. In *Cline, W. R., et al.*, 1981, pp. 52–101. [G: LDCs]

Black, Stanley W. The Impact of Changes in the World Economy on Stabilization Policies in the 1970s. In *Cline, W. R. and Weintraub, S., eds.*, 1981, pp. 43–77. [G: LDCs]

Calleo, David P. Inflation and American Power. *Foreign Aff.*, Spring 1981, *59*(4), pp. 781–812. [G: U.S.]

Cardoso, Eliana A. The Burden of Exchange Rate Adjustment in Brazil. In *Baer, W. and Gillis, M.*, eds., 1981, pp. 168–81. **[G: Brazil]**

Cardoso, Eliana A. The Burden of Exchange Rate Adjustment in Brazil. *Quart. Rev. Econ. Bus.*, Summer 1981, *21*(2), pp. 168–81. **[G: Brazil]**

Cavaco Silva, Aníbal. Enquadramento global do desenvolvimento económico português. (The Global Framework of the Portuguese Economic Development. With English summary.) *Economia (Portugal)*, May 1981, *5*(2), pp. 375–88.
[G: Portugal]

Caves, Richard E. Competitive Processes in the Open Economy: Evidence and Policy. In *[von Haberler, G.]*, 1981, pp. 71–84.

Chander, R.; Robless, C. L. and Teh, K. P. Malaysian Growth and Price Stabilization. In *Cline, W. R., et al.*, 1981, pp. 208–27. **[G: Malaysia]**

Ciampi, Carlo Azeglio. Il ricupero della stabilità della moneta quale condizione di progresso. (Recovery of Stability of the Lira as a Condition for Progress. With English summary.) *Bancaria*, July 1981, *37*(7), pp. 659–65. **[G: Italy]**

Cline, William R. Brazil's Aggressive Response to External Shocks. In *Cline, W. R., et al.*, 1981, pp. 102–35. **[G: Brazil]**

Coghlan, Richard. Money Supply in an Open Economy. *Appl. Econ.*, June 1981, *13*(2), pp. 181–91.
[G: U.K.]

Corden, W. Max. Export Growth and the Balance of Payments in Korea, 1960–78: Comment. In *Hong, W. and Krause, L. B.*, eds., 1981, pp. 253–56. **[G: S. Korea]**

Craig, Gary A. A Monetary Approach to the Balance of Trade. *Amer. Econ. Rev.*, June 1981, *71*(3), pp. 460–66. **[G: OECD]**

Decabooter, Jean-Pierre. Le financement du commerce Est–Ouest et le problème de l'endettement des pays d'Europe de l'Est. (Financing East–West Trade and the Problem of East European Insolvency. With English summary.) *Ann. Sci. Écon. Appl.*, 1981, *37*(3), pp. 71–92. **[G: COMECON]**

Dell, Sidney. The Impact of Changes in the World Economy on Stabilization Policies in the 1970s: Comment. In *Cline, W. R. and Weintraub, S.*, eds., 1981, pp. 77–81. **[G: LDCs]**

Díaz-Alejandro, Carlos F. Southern Cone Stabilization Plans. In *Cline, W. R. and Weintraub, S.*, eds., 1981, pp. 119–41. **[G: Argentina; Chile; Uruguay]**

Dunn, Robert M., Jr. Exchange Rates, Payments Adjustment, and OPEC: Why Oil Deficits Persist. In *Baldwin, R. E. and Richardson, J. D.*, eds., 1981, *1979*, pp. 487–505. **[G: OPEC; OECD]**

Eklöf, J. A. On Optimal Macro-economic Control with Inaccurate Data. In *Janssen, J. M. L.; Pau, L. F. and Straszak, A. J.*, eds., 1981, pp. 57–62. **[G: Sweden]**

El Serafy, Salah. Absorptive Capacity, the Demand for Revenue, and the Supply of Petroleum. *J. Energy Devel.*, Autumn 1981, *7*(1), pp. 73–88.
[G: OPEC]

Erös, Gyula. Some Problems of the International Monetary System. *Acta Oecon.*, 1981, *26*(1–2), pp. 107–22. **[G: W. Europe; Japan; U.S.]**

Filc, Wolfgang and Heinemann, Hans-Joachim. Leistungsbilanzdefizite in der Bundesrepublik Deutschland: Ein Problem der Anpassung oder der Finanzierung? (Current Account Deficits: Adjustment of Financing? The Case of the Federal Republic of Germany. With English summary.) *Konjunkturpolitik*, 1981, *27*(3), pp. 129–55.
[G: W. Germany]

Frowen, Stephen F. The Interaction between the International Monetary System and Financial Markets in the 1980's. In *Burghardt, A. M., ed.*, 1981, pp. 7–22. **[G: Global]**

Gafar, John. Devaluation and the Balance of Payments Adjustment in a Developing Economy: An Analysis Relating to Jamaica: 1954–72. *Appl. Econ.*, June 1981, *13*(2), pp. 151–65.
[G: Jamaica]

Grant, Wyn. The Politics of the Green Pound, 1974–79. *J. Common Market Stud.*, June 1981, *19*(4), pp. 313–29. **[G: U.K.; EEC]**

Guenther, Jack. The Outlook for the 1980s. In *Ensor, R., ed.*, 1981, pp. 155–59. **[G: Non-OPEC LDCs]**

Gutmann, Pierre. The Measurement of Terms of Trade Effects. *Rev. Income Wealth*, December 1981, *27*(4), pp. 433–53. **[G: Saudi Arabia; OECD]**

Hanselmann, Guido. Petrodollars and the Banks. In *Burghardt, A. M., ed.*, 1981, pp. 23–36.
[G: LDCs; OECD; OPEC]

Harley, C. K. and McCloskey, D. N. Foreign Trade: Competition and the Expanding International Economy. In *Floud, R. and McCloskey, D., eds.*, Vol. 2, 1981, pp. 50–69. **[G: U.K.]**

Hojman, David E. The Andean Pact: Failure of a Model of Economic Integration? *J. Common Market Stud.*, December 1981, *20*(2), pp. 139–60.
[G: Andean Pact]

Howe, James W. Oil-Importing Developing Countries. In *Foster, J., et al.*, 1981, pp. 57–95.
[G: LDCs]

Humes, Dorla. Foreign Reserves Management in Belize: An Assessment of the Liquidity Constraints in 1979. *Soc. Econ. Stud.*, December 1981, *30*(4), pp. 187–200. **[G: Belize]**

Hunter, J. S. H. and Wood, J. C. Australian Resource Development in the 1980s. *Nat. Westminster Bank Quart. Rev.*, November 1981, pp. 17–26. **[G: Australia]**

Inaba, Kazuo. The Postwar U.S. Balance of Payments. (In Japanese. With English summary.) *Econ. Stud. Quart.*, December 1981, *32*(3), pp. 217–36.

Islam, Rizwanul. Some Macroeconomic Implications of Higher Oil Prices for Bangladesh. *Bangladesh Devel. Stud.*, Summer 1981, *9*(2), pp. 1–20.
[G: Bangladesh]

Kanesa-Thasan, S. The Fund and Adjustment Policies in Africa. *Finance Develop.*, September 1981, *18*(3), pp. 20–24. **[G: Africa]**

Karatzas, George. Inflationary Forces in Fifty-Four Countries in the Past Decade: An Analysis. *Econ. Int.*, May–August–November 1981, *34*(2–3–4), pp. 322–55. **[G: Selected LDCs; Selected MDCs]**

Khan, Sakiya. India's Balance of Trade during the Sixth Plan (1980–85): An Estimation. *Econ. Aff.*,

April–June 1981, *26*(2), pp. 141–45. [G: India]
Killick, Tony. Eurocurrency Market Recycling of OPEC Surpluses to Developing Countries: Fact or Myth? In *Stevens, C., ed.*, 1981, pp. 92–104.
[G: EEC; LDCs]
Killick, Tony and Thorne, Maurice. Problems of an Open Economy: The Balance of Payments in the Nineteen-Seventies. In *Killick, T., ed.*, 1981, pp. 59–70. [G: Kenya]
Kindleberger, Charles P. Capital Movements and International Payments Adjustment. In *Kindleberger, C. P.*, 1981, *1966*, pp. 209–24.
[G: Europe; U.S.]
Kindleberger, Charles P. Germany's Persistent Balance-of-Payments Disequilibrium Revisited. In *Kindleberger, C. P.*, 1981, *1976*, pp. 139–68.
[G: U.S.; W. Germany]
Kindleberger, Charles P. The Balance of Payments as Seen in the Economic Report of the President for 1966. In *Kindleberger, C. P.*, 1981, *1967*, pp. 113–19.
Kozma, G. The Role of the Exchange Rate in Hungary's Adjustment to External Economic Disturbances. In *Hare, P. G.; Radice, H. K. and Swain, N., eds.*, 1981, pp. 205–21. [G: Hungary]
Landau, Zbigniew and Tomaszewski, Jerzy. The International Movement of Capital in Central and South-Eastern Europe before the Second World War. In *[Lipiński, E.]*, 1981, pp. 19–37.
[G: S.E. Europe]
Longo, Carlos A. Comment on "Policy Responses to External Shocks in Selected Latin-American Countries." *Quart. Rev. Econ. Bus.*, Summer 1981, *21*(2), pp. 165–67. [G: Brazil; Mexico; Uruguay]
Longo, Carlos A. Policy Responses to External Shocks in Selected Latin-American Countries: Comment. In *Baer, W. and Gillis, M., eds.*, 1981, pp. 165–67. [G: Brazil; Mexico; Uruguay]
Lopes, José da Silva. Factores explicativos da evolução do saldo da Balança de Transacçoes Correntes. (With English summary.) *Economia (Portugal)*, October 1981, *5*(3), pp. 431–62. [G: Portugal]
Magill, W. G.; Felmingham, B. S. and Wells, G. M. Cyclical Interdependencies between Nations in the Pacific Basin. *Econ. Int.*, February 1981, *34*(1), pp. 34–45. [G: U.S.; Canada; Japan; Australia; New Zealand]
Magnifico, Giovanni. "Oil Deficits, Inflation and Exchange Rates." *Econ. Notes*, 1981, *10*(1), pp. 13–28. [G: EEC; U.S.]
McCombie, J. S. L. Are International Growth Rates Constrained by the Balance of Payments? A Comment on Professor Thirlwall [The Balance of Payments Constraint as an Explanation of International Growth Rate Differences]. *Banca Naz. Lavoro Quart. Rev.*, December 1981, (139), pp. 455–58.
McKinnon, Ronald I. Southern Cone Stabilization Plans: Comment. In *Cline, W. R. and Weintraub, S., eds.*, 1981, pp. 141–46. [G: Argentina; Chile; Uruguay]
Meloe, Tor. Oil and the Transfer Problem. *J. Energy Devel.*, Autumn 1981, *7*(1), pp. 17–25.
[G: Global]
Minford, Patrick. Locomotives, Convoys or What?—

The International Adjustment Problem. In *Gaskin, M., ed.*, 1981, pp. 125–39. [G: OECD]
Monti, Mario. L'integrazione finanziaria internazionale e l'Italia: alcuni problemi da risolvere. (Italy and International Financial Integration: Some Problems Still to be Solved. With English summary.) *Bancaria*, September 1981, *37*(9), pp. 884–90. [G: Italy]
Morgan Guaranty Trust Company of New York. The Response to Higher Oil Prices: Adjustment and Financing. In *Baldwin, R. E. and Richardson, J. D., eds.*, 1981, *1980*, pp. 506–16. [G: OPEC; Non-OPEC LDCs]
Nunnenkamp, Peter. Die Auswirkungen externer Schocks auf die internationale Verschuldung von Schwellenländern nach 1973—am Beispiel Brasiliens, Südkoreas und der Türkei. (With English summary.) *Aussenwirtschaft*, December 1981, *36*(4), pp. 352–71. [G: S. Korea; Brazil; Turkey]
Page, S. A. B. The Choice of Invoicing Currency in Merchandise Trade. *Nat. Inst. Econ. Rev.*, November 1981, (98), pp. 60–72.
Park, Yung Chul. Export Growth and the Balance of Payments in Korea, 1960–78. In *Hong, W. and Krause, L. B., eds.*, 1981, pp. 218–51.
[G: S. Korea]
Plihon, D. Un Modéle Sectoriel de la Balance Commerciale Française. (With English summary.) In *Courbis, R., ed.*, 1981, pp. 47–63. [G: France]
Posta, G. and Veliczky, József. Forecasting and Simulation by Controlled Dynamic Factors of Open Economies. In *Janssen, J. M. L.; Pau, L. F. and Straszak, A. J., eds.*, 1981, pp. 279–84.
[G: Hungary]
Safarian, A. E. The Financing of Trade and Development in the ADCs: The Experience of Singapore: Comment. In *Hong, W. and Krause, L. B., eds.*, 1981, pp. 145–47. [G: Singapore]
Sarcinelli, Mario. Assetti monetari internazionali, movimenti di capitali, controlli amministrativi: un difficile cammino verso la libertà. (International Monetary Conditions, Capital Flows and Controls: The Difficult Path toward Freedom. With English summary.) *Bancaria*, September 1981, *37*(9), pp. 874–83. [G: Italy]
Schmitt, Hans O. Estabilização económica e crescimento em Portugal. (With English summary.) *Economia (Portugal)*, May 1981, *5*(2), pp. 325–73. [G: Portugal]
Schultz, Siegfried; Schumacher, Dieter and Wilkens, Herbert. North-South Interdependence: The Case of the Federal Republic of Germany. *World Devel.*, May 1981, *9*(5), pp. 435–52.
[G: W. Germany; LDCs]
Sinclair, Peter. Floating Exchange Rates: A Study of Sterling 1972–76. In *Courakis, A. S., ed.*, 1981, pp. 146–79. [G: U.K.]
Siri, Gabriel and Domínguez, Luis Raúl. Central American Accommodation to External Disruptions. In *Cline, W. R., et al.*, 1981, pp. 166–207.
[G: El Salvador; Guatemala]
St. Cyr, E. B. A. Wages, Prices and Balance of Payments: Trinidad and Tobago; 1956–1976. *Soc. Econ. Stud.*, December 1981, *30*(4), pp. 111–33.
[G: Trinidad and Tobago]

Stekler, Lois E. U.S. International Transactions in 1980. *Fed. Res. Bull.*, April 1981, *67*(4), pp. 269–76. [G: U.S.]

Stuart, Brian C. Stabilization Policy in Portugal, 1974–78. *Finance Develop.*, September 1981, *18*(3), pp. 25–29. [G: Portugal]

Tardos, Márton M. Options in Hungary's Foreign Trade. *Acta Oecon.*, 1981, *26*(1–2), pp. 29–49. [G: Hungary]

Thirlwall, A. P. A Reply to Mr. McCombie [The Balance of Payments Constraint as an Explanation of International Growth Rate Differences]. *Banca Naz. Lavoro Quart. Rev.*, December 1981, (139), pp. 458–59.

Tíkal, Svatopluk. The Balance of Forces between the U.S.A. and the European Communities. *Czech. Econ. Digest.*, March 1981, (2), pp. 55–72. [G: U.S.; EEC]

de Vries, Rimmer. Proceedings of the Seminar on International Economic Problems: Statement. In *U.S. Congress, Joint Economic Committee (I)*, 1981, pp. 319–35. [G: U.S.; Selected Countries]

Wallace, Myles S. The Dollar Exchange Rate, Oil Imports, and the Trade Balance: A Test of Causality. *Rev. Bus. Econ. Res.*, Winter 1981, *16*(2), pp. 23–33. [G: U.S.]

Wallich, Henry C. Statement to Commerce, Consumer, and Monetary Affairs Subcommittee of the House Committee on Government Operations, September 23, 1981. *Fed. Res. Bull.*, October 1981, *67*(10), pp. 769–74. [G: U.S.; OPEC]

Wanniski, Jude. The Mundell–Laffer Hypothesis— A New View of the World Economy. In *Baldwin, R. E. and Richardson, J. D., eds.*, 1981, *1975*, pp. 374–88. [G: U.S.]

Whitman, Marina v. N. International Interdependence and the U.S. Economy. In *Baldwin, R. E. and Richardson, J. D., eds.*, 1981, *1977*, pp. 389–408. [G: U.S.]

Wibulswasdi, Chaiyawat. Experiences of Asian Countries with Various Exchange Rate Policies: Comment. In *Williamson, J., ed.*, 1981, pp. 319–21. [G: Asia]

Wong, Kum Poh. The Financing of Trade and Development in the ADCs: The Experience of Singapore. In *Hong, W. and Krause, L. B., eds.*, 1981, pp. 129–44. [G: Singapore]

Worrell, Delisle. External Influences and Domestic Policies: The Economies of Barbados and Jamaica. *Soc. Econ. Stud.*, December 1981, *30*(4), pp. 134–55. [G: Barbados; Jamaica]

Wright, J. F. Britain's Inter-War Experience. *Oxford Econ. Pap.*, Supplement July 1981, *33*, pp. 282–305. [G: U.K.]

Yang, Shu-Chin. The Foreign Exchange Problem of the Philippines in the Mid-Fifties. *Philippine Econ. J.*, 1981, *20*(2), pp. 127–50. [G: Philippines]

4314 Exchange Rates and Markets: Theory and Studies

Aghevli, Bijan B. Experiences of Asian Countries with Various Exchange Rate Policies. In *Williamson, J., ed.*, 1981, pp. 298–318. [G: Asia]

Aghevli, Bijan B. Monetary Control and the Crawling Peg: Comment. In *Williamson, J., ed.*, 1981, pp. 53–54. [G: OECD; LDCs]

Aglietta, Michel; Orléan, André and Oudiz, Gilles. Des adaptations différenciées aux contraintes internationales: Les enseignements d'un modèle. (National Adjustments to International Constraints: Learning from a Model. With English summary.) *Revue Écon.*, July 1981, *32*(4), pp. 660–712. [G: W. Germany; France; U.K.]

Ahluwalia, Montek S. and Lysy, Frank J. Employment, Income Distribution, and Programs to Remedy Balance-of-Payments Difficulties. In *Cline, W. R. and Weintraub, S., eds.*, 1981, pp. 149–88. [G: Malaysia]

Aliber, Robert Z. Issues in U.S. International Monetary Policies. In *National Science Foundation*, 1981, pp. I59–75. [G: U.S.]

Arcuti, Luigi. Dalla regolamentazione alla liberalizzazione del movimento valutario. (From Control to Liberalization of Capital Movements. With English summary.) *Bancaria*, September 1981, *37*(9), pp. 891–94. [G: Italy]

Argy, V. and Semudram, M. Test of a Simple Model of the Determination of the Effective Exchange Rate for the Mark (March 1973–December 1979). *Empirical Econ.*, 1981, *6*(3), pp. 163–71. [G: W. Germany]

Artis, M. J. From Monetary to Exchange Rate Targets. *Banca Naz. Lavoro Quart. Rev.*, September 1981, (138), pp. 339–58.

Artis, M. J. and Currie, David A. Monetary Targets and the Exchange Rate: A Case for Conditional Targets. *Oxford Econ. Pap.*, Supplement July 1981, *33*, pp. 176–200. [G: U.K.]

Artus, Jacques R. and McGuirk, Anne Kenny. A New Version of the I.M.F. Multilateral Exchange Rate Model (MERM2). In *Courbis, R., ed.*, 1981, pp. 111–21.

Artus, Jacques R. and Young, John H. Fixed and Flexible Exchange Rates: A Renewal of the Debate. In *Baldwin, R. E. and Richardson, J. D., eds.*, 1981, *1979*, pp. 327–51.

Aspe, Pedro. Comment [Exchange Rate Rules and Macroeconomic Stability] [The Analysis of Floating Exchange Rates and the Choice between Crawl and Float]. In *Williamson, J., ed.*, 1981, pp. 82–84. [G: OECD; LDCs]

Aubry, Jean-Pierre and Kierzkowski, Henryk. The Transmission of Foreign Price Inflation under Alternative Exchange Rate Regimes: Some Experiments with the RDX2 and MPS Models. In *Courbis, R., ed.*, 1981, pp. 259–77. [G: Canada; U.S.]

Baade, Robert A. A Monetary (Asset) Approach to Exchange Rate Determination: The Evidence since 1973. *Kredit Kapital*, 1981, *14*(3), pp. 341–49. [G: Switzerland; EEC; Japan; Canada]

Bacha, Edmar L. The Impact of the Float on LDCs: Latin American Experience in the 1970s. In *Williamson, J., ed.*, 1981, pp. 282–97. [G: Brazil; Chile; Costa Rica; Guatemala]

Balassa, Bela and Schydlowsky, Daniel M. Effective Tariffs, Domestic Cost of Foreign Exchange, and the Equilibrium Exchange Rate. In *Livingstone, I., ed.*, 1981, *1968*, pp. 254–60.

Baltensperger, Ernst. Geldpolitik und Wechselkurs-dynamik. (Monetary Policy and Exchange Rate Dynamics. With English summary.) *Kredit Kapital*, 1981, *14*(3), pp. 320–40.

Barrett, Richard N. Purchasing Power Parity and the Equilibrium Exchange Rate: A Note. *J. Money, Credit, Banking*, May 1981, *13*(2), pp. 227–33.

Bartlett, Sarah. Transnational Banking: A Case of Transfer Parking with Money. In *Murray, R., ed.*, 1981, pp. 96–115.

Batten, Dallas S. Foreign Exchange Markets: The Dollar in 1980. *Fed. Res. Bank St. Louis Rev.*, April 1981, *63*(4), pp. 22–30. [G: U.S.]

Bauer, P. T. Economists and the Two Dollar Problems. In *Bauer, P. T.*, 1981, *1971*, pp. 214–20.

Bautista, Romeo M. Exchange Rate Changes and LDC Export Performance under Generalized Currency Floating. *Weltwirtsch. Arch.*, 1981, *117*(3), pp. 443–68. [G: LDCs]

Bautista, Romeo M. Exchange Rate Flexibility and the Less Developed Countries: A Survey of Empirical Research and Policy Issues. *Philippine Econ. J.*, 1981, *20*(1), pp. 1–30. [G: LDCs]

Beenstock, Michael. Exchange Rate Expectations and Interest Rate Differentials. *Rev. Econ. Statist.*, February 1981, *63*(1), pp. 148. [G: U.K.; Canada]

Bernauer, Kenneth. Effectiveness of Exchange-Rate Changes on the Trade Account: The Japanese Case. *Fed. Res. Bank San Francisco Econ. Rev.*, Fall 1981, pp. 55–71. [G: Japan]

Bernstein, Edward M. Perils of the Gold Standard. *Challenge*, November–December 1981, *24*(5), pp. 58–62.

Bhandari, Jagdeep S. A Theory of Exchange Rate Determination and Adjustment. *Weltwirtsch. Arch.*, 1981, *117*(4), pp. 605–21.

Bhandari, Jagdeep S. Exchange Rate Overshooting Revisited. *Manchester Sch. Econ. Soc. Stud.*, June 1981, *49*(2), pp. 165–72.

Bhandari, Jagdeep S. Expectations, Exchange Rate Volatility and Non-Neutral Disturbances. *Int. Econ. Rev.*, October 1981, *22*(3), pp. 535–40.

Bhandari, Jagdeep S. Toward a Multi-Country Model of Exchange Rage Determination. *J. Macroecon.*, Fall 1981, *3*(4), pp. 501–15.

Bilson, John F. O. The "Speculative Efficiency" Hypothesis. *J. Bus.*, July 1981, *54*(3), pp. 435–51. [G: OECD]

Bird, Graham. Reserve Currency Consolidation, Gold Policy and Financial Flows to Developing Countries: Mechanisms for an Aid-augmented Substitution Account. *World Devel.*, July 1981, *9*(7), pp. 609–19.

Black, Stanley W. Inflation and Growth: Exchange Rate Alternatives for Mexico: Comment. In *Williamson, J., ed.*, 1981, pp. 349–50. [G: Mexico]

Black, Stanley W. The Analysis of Floating Exchange Rates and the Choice between Crawl and Float. In *Williamson, J., ed.*, 1981, pp. 68–81. [G: OECD; LDCs]

Blackie, Henry and Antl, Boris. Currency Strategy in Multicurrency Portfolio Management. In *Ensor, R. and Muller, P., eds.*, 1981, pp. 227–40.

Blackman, Courtney N. The Management of Foreign Exchange Reserves in Small Developing Countries. *Soc. Econ. Stud.*, December 1981, *30*(4), pp. 156–71.

Blejer, Mario I. and Leiderman, Leonardo. A Monetary Approach to the Crawling-Peg System: Theory and Evidence. *J. Polit. Econ.*, February 1981, *89*(1), pp. 132–51. [G: Brazil]

Blejer, Mario I. and Mathieson, Donald J. The Pre-announcement of Exchange Rate Changes as a Stabilization Instrument. *Int. Monet. Fund Staff Pap.*, December 1981, *28*(4), pp. 760–92.

Blitzer, Charles; Dasgupta, Partha and Stiglitz, Joseph E. Project Appraisal and Foreign Exchange Constraints. *Econ. J.*, March 1981, *91*(361), pp. 58–74.

Boltho, Andrea. Are the British So Different from Everyone Else? Comments. In *[Cairncross, A.]*, 1981, pp. 244–47. [G: U.K.; Italy]

Booth, G. Geoffrey; Kaen, Fred R. and Koveos, Peter E. Foreign Exchange Market Behavior: 1975–1978. *Rivista Int. Sci. Econ. Com.*, April 1981, *28*(4), pp. 311–26.

Bordo, Michael David. The Classical Gold Standard: Some Lessons for Today. *Fed. Res. Bank St. Louis Rev.*, May 1981, *63*(5), pp. 2–17. [G: U.K.; U.S.]

Bowles, Roger A. and Whelan, Christopher J. International Contracts: English Law and Floating Exchange Rates. *Nat. Westminster Bank Quart. Rev.*, November 1981, pp. 27–36.

Braga de Macedo, Jorge. Portugal's Crawling Peg: Comment. In *Williamson, J., ed.*, 1981, pp. 272–78. [G: Portugal]

Brakman, S. and Jepma, Catrinus J. Purchasing Power Parity Theory and the Monetary Approach to the Balance of Payments: A Commentary. *De Economist*, 1981, *129*(3), pp. 412–15.

Branson, William H. The Collapse of Purchasing Power Parities during the 1970's by Frenkel: Comment. *Europ. Econ. Rev.*, May 1981, *16*(1), pp. 167–71.

Branson, William H. and Katseli-Papaefstratiou, Louka. Exchange Rate Policy for Developing Countries. In *Grassman, S. and Lundberg, E., eds.*, 1981, pp. 391–419. [G: LDCs; MDCs]

Brech, M. J. and Stout, D. K. The Rate of Exchange and Non-Price Competitiveness: A Provisional Study within UK Manufactured Exports. *Oxford Econ. Pap.*, Supplement July 1981, *33*, pp. 268–81. [G: U.K.]

Brown, Kathleen Hope. Effects of Changes in the Discount Rate on the Foreign Exchange Value of the Dollar: 1973 to 1978. *Quart. J. Econ.*, August 1981, *96*(3), pp. 551–58. [G: U.S.]

Bruno, Michael and Sussman, Zvi. Floating versus Crawling: Israel 1977–9 by Hindsight. In *Williamson, J., ed.*, 1981, pp. 252–71. [G: Israel]

Burton, David. Expectations and the Dynamics of Devaluation: A Comment. *Rev. Econ. Stud.*, October 1981, *48*(4), pp. 659–60.

Callier, Philippe. Covered Arbitrage Margin and Transaction Costs. *Weltwirtsch. Arch.*, 1981, *117*(2), pp. 262–75.

Callier, Philippe. One Way Arbitrage, Foreign Exchange and Securities Markets: A Note. *J. Finance*, December 1981, *36*(5), pp. 1177–86.

Calvo, Guillermo A. Capitalización de las reservas y tipo real de cambio. (With English summary.) *Cuadernos Econ.*, April 1981, *18*(53), pp. 5–14.

Calvo, Guillermo A. Devaluation: Levels versus Rates. *J. Int. Econ.*, May 1981, *11*(2), pp. 165–72.

Campbell, Robert B. Flexible and Fixed Target Stabilisation in an Open Economy. *J. Econ. Dynam. Control*, August 1981, *3*(3), pp. 235–66. [G: Australia]

Carli, Guido. Are the British So Different from Everyone Else? In *[Cairncross, A.]*, 1981, pp. 232–44. [G: U.K.; Italy]

Chen, Chau-nan and Tsaur, Tien-wang. Monetary Approaches to Devaluation: Reply [IS, LM, BT and a Simplified Synthesis of the Elasticity, Absorption and Monetary Approaches to Devaluation]. *Southern Econ. J.*, April 1981, *47*(4), pp. 1147–51.

Chittle, Charles R. Foreign-Exchange Distribution in Yugoslavia's New Planning System: An Input–Output Approach. *J. Compar. Econ.*, March 1981, *5*(1), pp. 79–86. [G: Yugoslavia]

Clements, Kenneth W. The Monetary Approach to Exchange Rate Determination: A Geometric Analysis. *Weltwirtsch. Arch.*, 1981, *117*(1), pp. 20–29.

Cline, William R. World Inflation and the Developing Countries: Policy Response to External Fluctuations. In *Cline, W. R., et al.*, 1981, pp. 228–39. [G: LDCs]

Coes, Donald V. The Crawling Peg and Exchange Rate Uncertainty. In *Williamson, J., ed.*, 1981, pp. 113–36. [G: Brazil]

Cooper, Richard N. Exchange Rate Rules: The Theory, Performance and Prospects of the Crawling Peg: Panel Discussion. In *Williamson, J., ed.*, 1981, pp. 400–403. [G: OECD]

Cooper, Richard N. United States Economic Interests and Crawling Peg Systems: Comment. In *Williamson, J., ed.*, 1981, pp. 384–86. [G: U.S.]

Corden, W. M. The Exchange Rate, Monetary Policy and North Sea Oil: The Economic Theory of the Squeeze on Tradeables. *Oxford Econ. Pap.*, Supplement July 1981, *33*, pp. 23–46. [G: U.K.]

Cornell, Bradford and Reinganum, Marc R. Forward and Futures Prices: Evidence from the Foreign Exchange Markets. *J. Finance*, December 1981, *36*(5), pp. 1035–45. [G: U.S.]

Crockett, Andrew D. Determinants of Exchange Rate Movements: A Review. *Finance Develop.*, March 1981, *18*(1), pp. 33–37.

Cross, Sam Y. Treasury and Federal Reserve Foreign Exchange Operations. *Fed. Res. Bank New York Quart. Rev.*, Autumn 1981, *6*(3), pp. 45–64. [G: U.S.]

Cross, Sam Y. Treasury and Federal Reserve Foreign Exchange Operations. *Fed. Res. Bank New York Quart. Rev.*, Winter 1981–82, *6*(4), pp. 67–69. [G: U.S.]

Cross, Sam Y. Treasury and Federal Reserve Foreign Exchange Operations: Interim Report. *Fed. Res. Bull.*, December 1981, *67*(12), pp. 888–90. [G: U.S.]

Cross, Sam Y. Treasury and Federal Reserve Foreign Exchange Operations. *Fed. Res. Bull.*, September 1981, *67*(9), pp. 687–706.

Cumby, Robert E. and Obstfeld, Maurice. A Note on Exchange-Rate Expectations and Nominal Interest Differentials: A Test of the Fisher Hypothesis. *J. Finance*, June 1981, *36*(3), pp. 697–703.

Dale, Charles. The Hedging Effectiveness of Currency Futures Markets. *J. Futures Markets*, Spring 1981, *1*(1), pp. 77–88. [G: U.S.]

Daniel, Betty C. International Transmission of a Real Shock under Flexible Exchange Rates: A Comment. *J. Polit. Econ.*, August 1981, *89*(4), pp. 813–18.

Dervis, Kemal; de Melo, Jaime and Robinson, Sherman. A General Equilibrium Analysis of Foreign Exchange Shortages in a Developing Economy. *Econ. J.*, December 1981, *91*(364), pp. 891–906. [G: Turkey]

Desai, Padma and Bhagwati, Jagdish N. Three Alternative Concepts of Foreign Exchange Difficulties in Centrally Planned Economies. In *Bhagwati, J. N., ed.*, 1981, *1979*, pp. 349–59.

Díaz-Alejandro, Carlos F. Comment [Crawling Peg Systems and Macroeconomic Stability: The Case of Argentina 1971–8] [Experience with the Crawling Peg in Colombia]. In *Williamson, J., ed.*, 1981, pp. 221–23. [G: Argentina; Chile; Colombia]

Díaz-Alejandro, Carlos F. Exchange Rate Rules: The Theory, Performance and Prospects of the Crawling Peg: Panel Discussion. In *Williamson, J., ed.*, 1981, pp. 396–97. [G: Latin America]

Dimsdale, N. H. British Monetary Policy and the Exchange Rate, 1920–1938. *Oxford Econ. Pap.*, Supplement July 1981, *33*, pp. 306–49. [G: U.K.]

Donovan, Donal J. Real Responses Associated with Exchange Rate Action in Selected Upper Credit Tranche Stabilization Programs. *Int. Monet. Fund Staff Pap.*, December 1981, *28*(4), pp. 698–727.

Dornbusch, Rudiger. Comment [From Monetary to Exchange Rate Targets]. *Banca Naz. Lavoro Quart. Rev.*, September 1981, (138), pp. 359–64.

Dornbusch, Rudiger. Monetary Policy under Exchange-Rate Flexibility. In *Baldwin, R. E. and Richardson, J. D., eds.*, 1981, *1978*, pp. 408–24.

Dornbusch, Rudiger. Portugal's Crawling Peg. In *Williamson, J., ed.*, 1981, pp. 243–51. [G: Portugal]

Driskill, Robert A. Exchange Rate Overshooting, the Trade Balance, and Rational Expectations. *J. Int. Econ.*, August 1981, *11*(3), pp. 361–77.

Driskill, Robert A. Exchange-Rate Dynamics: An Empirical Investigation. *J. Polit. Econ.*, April 1981, *89*(2), pp. 357–71. [G: U.S.; Switzerland]

Driskill, Robert A. and Sheffrin, Steven M. On the Mark: Comment [On the Mark: A Theory of Floating Exchange Rates Based on Real Interest Differential]. *Amer. Econ. Rev.*, December 1981, *71*(5), pp. 1068–74. [G: U.S.]

Dunn, Robert M., Jr. Exchange Rates, Payments Adjustment, and OPEC: Why Oil Deficits Persist. In *Baldwin, R. E. and Richardson, J. D., eds.*, 1981, *1979*, pp. 487–505. [G: OPEC; OECD]

Eaker, Mark R. The Numeraire Problem and Foreign Exchange Risk. *J. Finance*, May 1981, *36*(2),

pp. 419–26.

Enders, Walter and Lapan, Harvey E. The Exchange Regime, Resource Allocation, and Uncertainty. *Southern Econ. J.*, April 1981, 47(4), pp. 924–40.

Eun, Cheol S. Global Purchasing Power View of Exchange Risk. *J. Finan. Quant. Anal.*, December 1981, 16(5), pp. 639–50.

Feige, Edgar L. and Singleton, Kenneth J. Multinational Inflation under Fixed Exchange Rates: Some Empirical Evidence from Latent Variable Models. *Rev. Econ. Statist.*, February 1981, 63(1), pp. 11–19. **[G: W. Europe]**

Fendt, Robert, Jr. The Brazilian Experience with the Crawling Peg. In *Williamson, J., ed.*, 1981, pp. 140–51. **[G: Brazil]**

Fendt, Roberto, Jr. Inflation and Growth: Exchange Rate Alternatives for Mexico: Comment. In *Williamson, J., ed.*, 1981, pp. 347–48. **[G: Mexico]**

Ffrench-Davis, Ricardo. Exchange Rate Policies in Chile: The Experience with the Crawling Peg. In *Williamson, J., ed.*, 1981, pp. 152–74. **[G: Chile]**

Ffrench-Davis, Ricardo. The Crawling Peg in Historical Perspective: Comment. In *Williamson, J., ed.*, 1981, pp. 31–34. **[G: Latin America]**

Fieleke, Norman S. Foreign-Currency Positioning by U.S. Firms: Some New Evidence. *Rev. Econ. Statist.*, February 1981, 63(1), pp. 35–42. **[G: U.S.]**

Finnerty, Joseph E. and Schneeweis, Thomas. Determinants of Eurodollar Interest Rates under Fixed and Floating Exchange Rates. *Nebr. J. Econ. Bus.*, Autumn 1981, 20(4), pp. 51–61. **[G: U.S.]**

Fishlow, Albert. Comment [Employment, Income Distribution, and Programs to Remedy Balance-of-Payments Difficulties] [Stabilization Policies and Their Effects on Employment and Income Distribution: A Latin American Perspective]. In *Cline, W. R. and Weintraub, S., eds.*, 1981, pp. 229–32. **[G: Malaysia; Latin America]**

Flanders, M. June and Tishler, Asher. The Role of Elasticity Optimism in Choosing an Optimal Currency Basket with Applications to Israel. *J. Int. Econ.*, August 1981, 11(3), pp. 395–406. **[G: Israel]**

Flood, Robert P. Explanations of Exchange-Rate Volatility and Other Empirical Regularities in Some Popular Models of the Foreign Exchange Market. *Carnegie-Rochester Conf. Ser. Public Policy*, Autumn 1981, 15, pp. 219–49.

Fontaine, Marcel. Les problèmes juridiques des contrats de compensation. (Legal Aspects of Compensation Contracts. With English summary.) *Ann. Sci. Écon. Appl.*, 1981, 37(3), pp. 57–70. **[G: E. Europe; W. Europe]**

Frankel, Jeffrey A. On the Mark: Reply [On the Mark: A Theory of Floating Exchange Rates Based on Real Interest Differential]. *Amer. Econ. Rev.*, December 1981, 71(5), pp. 1075–82. **[G: U.S.]**

Frenkel, Jacob A. Explanations of Exchange-Rate Volatility and Other Regularities in Some Popular Models of the Foreign Exchange Market: A Comment. *Carnegie-Rochester Conf. Ser. Public Policy*, Autumn 1981, 15, pp. 251–59.

Frenkel, Jacob A. Flexible Exchange Rates, Prices, and the Role of "News": Lessons from the 1970s. *J. Polit. Econ.*, August 1981, 89(4), pp. 665–705. **[G: U.S.]**

Frenkel, Jacob A. The Collapse of Purchasing Power Parities during the 1970's. *Europ. Econ. Rev.*, May 1981, 16(1), pp. 145–65. **[G: U.S.; U.K.; France; W. Germany]**

Friedman, Daniel. Makin's MARP: A Comment [Portfolio Theory and the Problem of Foreign Exchange Risk]. *J. Finance*, June 1981, 36(3), pp. 739–41.

Gafar, John. Devaluation and the Balance of Payments Adjustment in a Developing Economy: An Analysis Relating to Jamaica: 1954–72. *Appl. Econ.*, June 1981, 13(2), pp. 151–65. **[G: Jamaica]**

Gärtner, Manfred and Ursprung, Heinrich W. An Empirical Analysis of a Scandinavian Exchange Rate Model. *Scand. J. Econ.*, 1981, 83(1), pp. 38–54. **[G: Switzerland]**

Genberg, Hans. Comment [The European Monetary System—An Approximate Implementation of the Crawling Peg?] [United States Economic Interests and Crawling Peg Systems]. In *Williamson, J., ed.*, 1981, pp. 387–90. **[G: U.S.; W. Europe]**

Genberg, Hans. Effects of Central Bank Intervention in the Foreign Exchange Market. *Int. Monet. Fund Staff Pap.*, September 1981, 28(3), pp. 451–76.

Genberg, Hans. Purchasing Power Parity as a Rule for a Crawling Peg. In *Williamson, J., ed.*, 1981, pp. 88–106. **[G: OECD]**

Ghoshal, Animesh. The Effect of the Embargo on Grain Exports to the Soviet Union on the Exchange Rate. *Nebr. J. Econ. Bus.*, Summer 1981, 20(3), pp. 37–46. **[G: U.S.; U.S.S.R.]**

Gordon, Robert J. International Monetarism, Wage Push, and Monetary Accommodation. In *Courakis, A. S., ed.*, 1981, pp. 1–63. **[G: OECD]**

Granziol, Markus. Devisenterminkurse als Prognosen zukünftiger Kassakurse: Lassen systematische Abweichungen der Terminkurse von den später realisierten Kassakursen auf unausgenützte Gewinnchancen und nicht rationale Erwartungen der Marktteilnehmer schliessen? Systematic Deviations of Forward Exchange Rates from Future Spot Rates—Unexploited Profits. With English summary.) *Z. Wirtschaft. Sozialwissen.*, 1981, 101(6), pp. 627–50.

Gupta, Sanjeev. A Note on the Efficiency of Black Markets in Foreign Currencies. *J. Finance*, June 1981, 36(3), pp. 705–10. **[G: India; S. Korea; Taiwan]**

Hacche, Graham and Townend, John C. Exchange Rates and Monetary Policy: Modelling Sterling's Effective Exchange Rate, 1972–80. *Oxford Econ. Pap.*, Supplement July 1981, 33, pp. 201–47. **[G: U.K.]**

Hacche, Graham and Townend, John C. Monetary Models of Exchange Rates and Exchange Market Pressure: Some General Limitations and an Application to Sterling's Effective Rate. *Weltwirtsch. Arch.*, 1981, 117(4), pp. 622–37. **[G: U.K.]**

Hakkio, Craig S. Expectations and the Forward Exchange Rate. *Int. Econ. Rev.*, October 1981, *22*(3), pp. 663–78.

Hakkio, Craig S. The Term Structure of the Forward Premium. *J. Monet. Econ.*, July 1981, *8*(1), pp. 41–58.   **[G: U.S.; Canada]**

Hamaui, Rony. La determinazione del tasso di cambio nel breve periodo: una rassegna della letteratura empirica. (Exchange Rate Determination in the Short Run: A Survey of Empirical Literature. With English summary.) *Giorn. Econ.*, July–August 1981, *40*(7–8), pp. 501–20.

Hanna, Jeffrey D. The Advantages of Multicurrency Diversification. In *Ensor, R. and Muller, P., eds.*, 1981, pp. 219–26.   **[G: OECD]**

Hara, Masayuki. Monetary, Intervention Policy and Exchange Rates—A General Asset Approach. (In Japanese. With English summary.) *Osaka Econ. Pap.*, December 1981, *31*(2–3), pp. 73–80.

Harberger, Arnold C. Comment [Employment, Income Distribution, and Programs to Remedy Balance-of-Payments Difficulties] [Stabilization Policies and Their Effects on Employment and Income Distribution: A Latin American Perspective]. In *Cline, W. R. and Weintraub, S., eds.*, 1981, pp. 226–29. **[G: Malaysia; Latin America]**

Harris, Richard G. and Purvis, Douglas D. Diverse Information and Market Efficiency in a Monetary Model of the Exchange Rate. *Econ. J.*, December 1981, *91*(364), pp. 829–47.

Haseltine, John B. A Longer-term Approach. In *Ensor, R. and Muller, P., eds.*, 1981, pp. 139–42.   **[G: U.S.]**

Hay, D. A. and Morris, D. J. The Sterling Rate of Exchange and UK Profitability: Short Term Effects. *Oxford Econ. Pap.*, Supplement July 1981, *33*, pp. 248–67.   **[G: U.K.]**

Haynes, Stephen E. and Stone, Joe A. On the Mark: Comment [On the Mark: A Theory of Floating Exchange Rates Based on Real Interest Differential]. *Amer. Econ. Rev.*, December 1981, *71*(5), pp. 1060–67.   **[G: U.S.]**

Healy, James P. and Piderit, John J. The Time Series Properties of the Spot Exchange Rate: A Multiple Input Transfer Function. *J. Econ. Devel.*, July 1981, *6*(1), pp. 47–76.   **[G: U.S.]**

Hekman, Christine R. Foreign Exchange Risk: Relevance and Management. *Managerial Dec. Econ.*, December 1981, *2*(4), pp. 256–62.

Hekman, Christine R. The Effect of Trade Credit on Price and Price Level Comparisons. *Rev. Econ. Statist.*, November 1981, *63*(4), pp. 526–32.

Helpman, Elhanan. An Exploration in the Theory of Exchange-Rate Regimes. *J. Polit. Econ.*, October 1981, *89*(5), pp. 865–90.

Heri, Erwin W. Eine empirische Überprüfung der Effizienzhypothese für den Schweizer-Franken-Markt. (An Empirical Test of the Market Efficiency Hypothesis for the Swiss Franc. With English summary.) *Schweiz. Z. Volkswirtsch. Statist.*, December 1981, *117*(4), pp. 563–80.

Heri, Erwin W. Foreign Exchange Market Efficiency: Some Caveats. *Rivista Int. Sci. Econ. Com.*, October–November 1981, *28*(10–11), pp. 1034–43.

Hill, Joanne M. and Schneeweis, Thomas. A Note

on the Hedging Effectiveness of Foreign Currency Futures. *J. Futures Markets*, Winter 1981, *1*(4), pp. 659–64.

Hill, Joanne M. and Schneeweis, Thomas. Forecasting Effectiveness of Foreign Currency Futures. *Bus. Econ.*, May 1981, *16*(3), pp. 42–46.
[G: U.K.; Switzerland; W. Germany; Canada; Japan]

Hodrick, Robert J. International Asset Pricing with Time-Varying Risk Premia. *J. Int. Econ.*, November 1981, *11*(4), pp. 573–87.

Holden, Merle; Holden, Paul and Suss, Esther. Policy Objectives, Country Characteristics and the Choice of Exchange Rate Regime. *Rivista Int. Sci. Econ. Com.*, October–November 1981, *28*(10–11), pp. 1001–14.

Horne, Jocelyn. Beggar-My-Neighbour Devaluation: The Case of Ireland, 1967. *Europ. Econ. Rev.*, March 1981, *15*(3), pp. 327–38.   **[G: Ireland]**

Huang, Roger D. The Monetary Approach to Exchange Rate in an Efficient Foreign Exchange Market: Tests Based on Volatility. *J. Finance*, March 1981, *36*(1), pp. 31–41.   **[G: U.S.; U.K.; Germany]**

Ip, Pui C. International Interest-rate Linkages and Speculative Behaviour: Comments. In *Jüttner, D. J., ed.*, 1981, pp. 397.

Itagaki, Takao. The Theory of the Multinational Firm under Exchange Rate Uncertainty. *Can. J. Econ.*, May 1981, *14*(2), pp. 276–97.

Jacque, Laurent L. Management of Foreign Exchange Risk: A Review Article. *J. Int. Bus. Stud.*, Spring/Summer 1981, *12*(1), pp. 81–101.

Jenner, Stephen R. Inflation, Exchange Rates, and the Location of Automobile Manufacturing. *Bus. Econ.*, January 1981, *16*(1), pp. 26–29.
[G: EEC; U.S.; Japan]

Johansson, Per-Olov and Löfgren, Karl-Gustaf. A Note on Employment Effects of Tariffs in a Small Open Economy [The Employment Effects of Tariffs under a Free Exchange Rate Regime. A Monetary Approach]. *Weltwirtsch. Arch.*, 1981, *117*(3), pp. 578–83.

Keinath, Karl. Die Bedeutung der Einkommenskreislaufgeschwindigkeit des Geldes für die Effizienz der Geldpolitik bei festen und flexiblen Wechselkursen. (The Significance of the Income-Velocity of Monetary for the Efficiency of Monetary Policy with Fixed and Flexible Exchange Rates. With English summary.) *Kredit Kapital*, 1981, *14*(2), pp. 180–85.

Kemp, Donald S. Hedging Long-term Financings. In *Ensor, R. and Muller, P., eds.*, 1981, pp. 115–21.

Kim, Soo Yong. Trade Strategy and the Exchange Rate Policies in Taiwan: Comment. In *Hong, W. and Krause, L. B., eds.*, 1981, pp. 179–80.
[G: Taiwan]

Kindleberger, Charles P. International Financial Intermediation for Developing Countries. In *Kindleberger, C. P., 1981, 1976*, pp. 269–78.

Kindleberger, Charles P. Money Illusion and Foreign Exchange. In *Kindleberger, C. P., 1981, 1973*, pp. 87–99.

Kindleberger, Charles P. Quantity and Price, Especially in Financial Markets. In *Kindleberger,*

C. P., 1981, *1975*, pp. 256–68.

Kindleberger, Charles P. The Benefits of International Money. In *Kindleberger, C. P.*, 1981, *1972*, pp. 9–23.

Kindleberger, Charles P. The Case for Fixed Exchange Rates, 1969. In *Kindleberger, C. P.*, 1981, *1969*, pp. 169–82.

Kindleberger, Charles P. The Dollar and World Liquidity: A Minority View. In *Kindleberger, C. P.*, 1981, *1966*, pp. 42–52.

Kindleberger, Charles P. The Eurodollar and the Internationalization of United States Monetary Policy. In *Kindleberger, C. P.*, 1981, *1969*, pp. 100–110.

Kindleberger, Charles P. The Price of Gold and the N–1 Problem. In *Kindleberger, C. P.*, 1981, *1970*, pp. 76–86.

Kindleberger, Charles P. Time and Money. In *Kindleberger, C. P.*, 1981, *1969*, pp. 35–41.

Korteweg, Pieter. Comment [The First Two Years of the EMS: The Exchange-Rate Experience]. *Banca Naz. Lavoro Quart. Rev.*, September 1981, (138), pp. 290–95. **[G: U.S.; EEC]**

Kozma, G. The Role of the Exchange Rate in Hungary's Adjustment to External Economic Disturbances. In *Hare, P. G.; Radice, H. K. and Swain, N., eds.*, 1981, pp. 205–21. **[G: Hungary]**

Kudoh, Kazuhisa. Formation of Expectations and Exchange Rate Dynamics. *Econ. Stud. Quart.*, August 1981, *32*(2), pp. 135–45.

Laker, John F. Fiscal Proxies for Devaluation: A General Review. *Int. Monet. Fund Staff Pap.*, March 1981, *28*(1), pp. 118–43.

Lara-Resende, André. Comment [The Brazilian Experience with the Crawling Peg] [Exchange Rate Policies in Chile: The Experience with the Crawling Peg]. In *Williamson, J., ed.*, 1981, pp. 178–80. **[G: Chile; Brazil]**

Levich, Richard M. Exchange Rates and Currency Exposure. In *Altman, E. I., ed.*, 1981, pp. 12.3–41.

Levich, Richard M. Tests of Forecasting Models and Market Efficiency in the International Money Market. In *Baldwin, R. E. and Richardson, J. D., eds.*, 1981, *1978*, pp. 362–68.

Levy, Haim. Optimal Portfolio of Foreign Currencies with Borrowing and Lending. *J. Money, Credit, Banking*, August 1981, *13*(3), pp. 325–41. **[G: U.S.]**

Liang, Kuo-Shu and Liang, Ching-ing Hou. Trade Strategy and the Exchange Rate Policies in Taiwan. In *Hong, W. and Krause, L. B., eds.*, 1981, pp. 150–78. **[G: Taiwan]**

London, Anselm. Bank Rate Changes and Exchange Rate Movements: A Test for Anticipations and Announcement Effects. *Can. J. Econ.*, February 1981, *14*(1), pp. 115–19. **[G: Canada]**

Longworth, David. Testing the Efficiency of the Canadian–U.S. Exchange Market under the Assumption of no Risk Premium. *J. Finance*, March 1981, *36*(1), pp. 43–49. **[G: U.S.; Canada]**

Loseby, Margaret and Venzi, Lorenzo. Floating Exchange Rates and International Trade in Agricultural Commodities. In *Johnson, G. and Maunder, A., eds.*, 1981, pp. 426–36.

Loubergé, Henri. Le rôle des anticipations dans la formation du cours de change à terme: Quelques réflexions et résultats supplémentaires. (Expectations and Forward Exchange Pricing: Some Additional Thoughts and Results. With English summary.) *Revue Écon.*, November 1981, *32*(6), pp. 1045–73.

Magnifico, Giovanni. "Oil Deficits, Inflation and Exchange Rates." *Econ. Notes*, 1981, *10*(1), pp. 13–28. **[G: EEC; U.S.]**

Makin, John H. International Finance: Discussion. *J. Finance*, May 1981, *36*(2), pp. 440–42.

Makin, John H. Portfolio Theory and the Problem of Foreign Exchange Risk: Reply. *J. Finance*, June 1981, *36*(3), pp. 743–45.

Malan, Pedro S. Monetary Control and the Crawling Peg: Comment. In *Williamson, J., ed.*, 1981, pp. 50–52. **[G: OECD; LDCs]**

Marion, Nancy Peregrim. Insulation Properties of a Two-Tier Exchange Market in a Portfolio Balance Model. *Economica*, February 1981, *48*(189), pp. 61–70.

Martirena-Mantel, Ana María. Crawling Peg Systems and Macroeconomic Stability: The Case of Argentina 1971–8. In *Williamson, J., ed.*, 1981, pp. 181–206. **[G: Argentina]**

Martirena-Mantel, Ana María. Minidevaluaciones y estabilidad macroeconómica. El caso Argentino: 1971–1978. (Crawling Peg System and Macroeconomic Stability: The Argentine Case, 1971/78. With English summary.) *Económica*, January–August 1981, *27*(1–2), pp. 3–49. **[G: Argentina]**

Marzetti, Silva. Sul ruolo internazionale dell'oro e il regime dei cambi. (The International Role of Gold and the Exchange Rate System. With English summary.) *Rivista Int. Sci. Econ. Com.*, January–February 1981, *28*(1–2), pp. 90–109.

Masera, Rainer Stefano. The First Two Years of the EMS: The Exchange-Rate Experience. *Banca Naz. Lavoro Quart. Rev.*, September 1981, (138), pp. 271–89. **[G: U.S.; EEC]**

Masera, Rainer Stefano. The Interaction between Money, the Exchange Rate and Prices: The Italian Experience in the 1970s. In *Courakis, A. S., ed.*, 1981, pp. 234–47. **[G: Italy]**

Masson, Paul R. Dynamic Stability of Portfolio Balance Models of the Exchange Rate. *J. Int. Econ.*, November 1981, *11*(4), pp. 467–77.

McCloskey, Donald N. and Zecher, J. Richard. How the Gold Standard Worked, 1880–1913. In *McCloskey, D. N.*, 1981, *1976*, pp. 184–208. **[G: U.K.; U.S.; Sweden; Germany]**

McCrickard, Donald L. Macroeconomic Stability and the Initiation of Exchange-Rate Adjustments. *Southern Econ. J.*, January 1981, *47*(3), pp. 655–63.

McGregor, Peter G. The Portfolio Selection Approach and Short-Run Econometric Models of Capital Flows and the Foreign Exchange Market: A Theoretical Analysis. *J. Econ. Stud.*, 1981, *8*(2), pp. 3–24.

McKinnon, Ronald I. Monetary Control and the Crawling Peg. In *Williamson, J., ed.*, 1981, pp. 38–49. **[G: OECD; LDCs]**

McKinnon, Ronald I. The Exchange Rate and Macroeconomic Policy: Changing Postwar Perceptions. *J. Econ. Lit.*, June 1981, *19*(2), pp. 531–57.

Meierjohann, Freidrich W. An Index-controlled Hedging Programme. In *Ensor, R. and Muller, P., eds.*, 1981, pp. 131–37.

Minford, Patrick. The Exchange Rate and Monetary Policy. *Oxford Econ. Pap.*, Supplement July 1981, *33*, pp. 120–42. **[G: U.K.]**

Mirus, Rolf. Arbitrage, Speculation, and Official Forward Intervention: The Cases of Sterling and the Canadian Dollar: A Comment. *Rev. Econ. Statist.*, February 1981, *63*(1), p. 147. **[G: U.K.; Canada]**

Modeste, Nelson C. Exchange Market Pressure during the 1970s in Argentina: An Application of the Girton-Roper Monetary Model: A Note. *J. Money, Credit, Banking*, May 1981, *13*(2), pp. 234–40. **[G: Argentina]**

Monti, Mario. L'integrazione finanziaria internazionale e l'Italia: alcuni problemi da risolvere. (Italy and International Financial Integration: Some Problems Still to be Solved. With English summary.) *Bancaria*, September 1981, *37*(9), pp. 884–90. **[G: Italy]**

Mussa, Michael L. Exchange Rate Rules: The Theory, Performance and Prospects of the Crawling Peg: Panel Discussion. In *Williamson, J., ed.*, 1981, pp. 394–96. **[G: OECD; LDCs]**

Mussa, Michael L. Public Policy Issues in International Finance. In *National Science Foundation*, 1981, pp. I76–104.

Mussa, Michael L. Purchasing Power Parity as a Rule for a Crawling Peg: Comment. In *Williamson, J., ed.*, 1981, pp. 107–09. **[G: OECD]**

Mussa, Michael L. The Crawling Peg and Exchange Rate Uncertainty: Comment. In *Williamson, J., ed.*, 1981, pp. 137–39. **[G: Brazil]**

Nars, Kari. Finland och de internationella konjunkturerna. (Finland and International Economic Prospects. With English summary.) *Ekon. Samfundets Tidskr.*, 1981, *34*(1), pp. 35–36.

Niehans, Jürg. Static Deviations from Purchasing-Power Parity. *J. Monet. Econ.*, January 1981, *7*(1), pp. 57–68.

Nyiri, Iván. Gold—Gold Price—Currency Reserves. *Acta Oecon.*, 1981, *26*(1–2), pp. 123–32.

Officer, Lawrence H. The Floating Dollar in the Greenback Period: A Test of Theories of Exchange-Rate Determination. *J. Econ. Hist.*, September 1981, *41*(3), pp. 629–50. **[G: U.S.]**

Ortiz, Guillermo and Solís, Leopoldo. Inflation and Growth: Exchange Rate Alternatives for Mexico. In *Williamson, J., ed.*, 1981, pp. 327–46. **[G: Mexico]**

Otani, Ichiro and Tiwari, Siddharth. Capital Controls and Interest Rate Parity: The Japanese Experience, 1978–81. *Int. Monet. Fund Staff Pap.*, December 1981, *28*(4), pp. 793–815. **[G: Japan]**

de Pablo, Juan Carlos. Crawling Peg Systems and Macroeconomic Stability: The Case of Argentina 1971–8: Comment. In *Williamson, J., ed.*, 1981, pp. 228–29. **[G: Argentina]**

Page, S. A. B. The Choice of Invoicing Currency in Merchandise Trade. *Nat. Inst. Econ. Rev.*, November 1981, (98), pp. 60–72.

Pardee, Scott. Commentary on the Rutledge Paper [The Foreign Exchange Market under Flexible Exchange Rates: Comment]. In *Baldwin, R. E.*

and Richardson, J. D., eds., 1981, *1978*, pp. 357–60.

Pardee, Scott E. Treasury and Federal Reserve Foreign Exchange Operations. *Fed. Res. Bank New York Quart. Rev.*, Spring 1981, *6*(1), pp. 54–74. **[G: U.S.]**

Pardee, Scott E. Treasury and Federal Reserve Foreign Exchange Operations. *Fed. Res. Bank New York Quart. Rev.*, Summer 1981, *6*(2), pp. 76–78. **[G: U.S.]**

Pardee, Scott E. Treasury and Federal Reserve Foreign Exchange Operations: Interim Report. *Fed. Res. Bull.*, June 1981, *67*(6), pp. 486–87. **[G: U.S.]**

Patrick, Hugh. Trade Strategy and the Exchange Rate Policies in Taiwan: Comment. In *Hong, W. and Krause, L. B., eds.*, 1981, pp. 180–83. **[G: Taiwan]**

Phaup, E. Dwight. A Reinterpretation of the Modern Theory of Forward Exchange Rates. *J. Money, Credit, Banking*, November 1981, *13*(4), pp. 477–84.

Pigott, Charles. The Influence of Real Factors on Exchange Rates. *Fed. Res. Bank San Francisco Econ. Rev.*, Fall 1981, pp. 37–54. **[G: W. Europe; Canada; Japan]**

Pompili, Luigi. Le banche nel sistema valutario italiano. (Banks and the Italian Foreign Exchange Regulation. With English summary.) *Bancaria*, September 1981, *37*(9), pp. 895–907. **[G: Italy]**

Quadrio-Curzio, Alberto. Un diagramma dell'oro tra demonetizzazione e rimonetizzazione. (A Diagram of Gold between Demonetization and Remonetization. With English summary.) *Rivista Int. Sci. Econ. Com.*, October–November 1981, *28*(10–11), pp. 915–40.

Rana, Pradumna B. Exchange Rate Risk under Generalized Floating: Eight Asian Countries. *J. Int. Econ.*, November 1981, *11*(4), pp. 459–66. **[G: Asia]**

Redman, Milton B. and Stronge, William B. An Analysis of the Futures Rate as a Predictor of the Spot Rate: The Case of the Mexican Peso. *Rev. Bus. Econ. Res.*, Winter 1981, *16*(2), pp. 89–97. **[G: Mexico]**

Revey, Patricia A. Evolution and Growth of the United States Foreign Exchange Market. *Fed. Res. Bank New York Quart. Rev.*, Autumn 1981, *6*(3), pp. 32–44. **[G: U.S.]**

de Ridder, Peter B. Exchange Rate Determination and the Balance of Payments, a Theoretical Framework. *De Economist*, 1981, *129*(3), pp. 373–81.

Rodriguez, Carlos Alfredo. Comment [Crawling Peg Systems and Macroeconomic Stability: The Case of Argentina 1971–8] [Experience with the Crawling Peg in Colombia]. In *Williamson, J., ed.*, 1981, pp. 224–27. **[G: Argentina; Colombia]**

Rodriguez, Carlos Alfredo. Managed Float: An Evaluation of Alternative Rules in the Presence of Speculative Capital Flows. *Amer. Econ. Rev.*, March 1981, *71*(1), pp. 256–60.

de Roos, Folkert. Purchasing Power Parity Theory and the Monetary Approach to the Balance of Payments. *De Economist*, 1981, *129*(1), pp. 41–57.

de Roos, Folkert. Reply to Brakman and Jepma [Purchasing Power Parity Theory and the Monetary Approach to the Balance of Payments]. *De Economist*, 1981, *129*(3), pp. 414–15.

Ruck, Adam. Using the Market. In *Ensor, R. and Muller, P., eds.*, 1981, pp. 167–73.

Ruof, Peter. Comment[Exchange Rate Policies in Peru, 1971–9] [Portugal's Crawling Peg] [Floating versus Crawling: Israel 1977–9 by Hindsight]. In *Williamson, J., ed.*, 1981, pp. 279–81.
[G: Israel; Peru; Portugal]

Rutledge, John. An Economist's View of the Foreign Exchange Market: Report on Interviews with West Coast Foreign Exchange Dealers. In *Baldwin, R. E. and Richardson, J. D., eds.*, 1981, *1978*, pp. 351–57.

Sarcinelli, Mario. Aggiustamento o finanziamento del disavanzo esterno: ragioni, compatibilità, politiche. (Motives, Consistency and Policies for Adjusting or Financing the External Deficit. With English summary.) *Bancaria*, December 1981, *37*(12), pp. 1226–34. [G: Italy]

Sarcinelli, Mario. Assetti monetari internazionali, movimenti di capitali, controlli amministrativi: un difficile cammino verso la libertà. (International Monetary Conditions, Capital Flows and Controls: The Difficult Path toward Freedom. With English summary.) *Bancaria*, September 1981, *37*(9), pp. 874–83. [G: Italy]

Sauernheimer, Karlhans. Beschäftigungseffekte in makroökonomischen Modellen offener Volkswirtschaften mit flexiblen Wechselkursen. (Macroeconomic Policy under Flexible Exchange Rates and Flexible Wages. With English summary.) *Z. Wirtschaft. Sozialwissen.*, 1981, *101*(1), pp. 61–81.

Shieh, Yeung-nan. Monetary Approaches to Devaluation: Comment [IS, LM, BT and a Simplified Synthesis of the Elasticity, Absorption and Monetary Approaches to Devaluation]. *Southern Econ. J.*, April 1981, *47*(4), pp. 1143–46.

Shinkai, Yoichi. Terms of Trade, Wages and Exchange Rates in Japan. (In Japanese. With English summary.) *Osaka Econ. Pap.*, December 1981, *31*(2–3), pp. 15–29. [G: Japan]

Sinclair, Peter. Floating Exchange Rates: A Study of Sterling 1972–76. In *Courakis, A. S., ed.*, 1981, pp. 146–79. [G: U.K.]

Smyslov, D. V. The Crisis of Bourgeois Concepts of International Monetary Relations and Balance-of-Payments Regulation. In *Mileikovsky, A. G., et al.*, 1981, pp. 283–333.

Solís, Leopoldo. The Impact of the Float on LDCs: Latin American Experience in the 1970s: Comment. In *Williamson, J., ed.*, 1981, pp. 322–23.
[G: Brazil; Chile; Costa Rica; Guatemala]

Steigmann, A. J. What Next for the Dollar? *Bus. Econ.*, September 1981, *16*(4), pp. 62–63.
[G: U.S.]

Steinherr, Alfred. Effectiveness of Exchange Rate Policy for Trade Account Adjustment. *Int. Monet. Fund Staff Pap.*, March 1981, *28*(1), pp. 199–224.

Suhar, V. Victor. Managing Translation and Transaction Exposure. In *Ensor, R. and Muller, P., eds.*, 1981, pp. 89–99.

Swoboda, Alexander K. Comment [Exchange Rate Rules and Macroeconomic Stability] [The Analysis of Floating Exchange Rates and the Choice between Crawl and Float]. In *Williamson, J., ed.*, 1981, pp. 85–87. [G: OECD; LDCs]

Swoboda, Alexander K. Exchange-Rate Flexibility in Practice: A Selective Survey of Experience from 1973 to 1979. In *Giersch, H, ed. (I)*, 1981, pp. 143–79. [G: Selected OECD]

Swoboda, Alexander K. The Crawling Peg in Historical Perspective: Comment. In *Williamson, J., ed.*, 1981, pp. 35–37. [G: OECD; Selected LDCs]

Thursby, Marie. The Resource Reallocation Costs of Fixed and Flexible Exchange Rates: A Multi-Country Extension. *J. Int. Econ.*, November 1981, *11*(4), pp. 487–93.

Thygesen, Niels. Exchange Rate Rules: The Theory, Performance and Prospects of the Crawling Peg: Panel Discussion. In *Williamson, J., ed.*, 1981, pp. 397–400. [G: OECD; LDCs]

Thygesen, Niels. The European Monetary System—An Approximate Implementation of the Crawling Peg? In *Williamson, J., ed.*, 1981, pp. 351–70.
[G: W. Europe]

Troch, Rudy. La coopération et la compensation avec les pays socialistes. (Compensation and Cooperation with the Socialist Countries. With English summary.) *Ann. Sci. Écon. Appl.*, 1981, *37*(3), pp. 35–56. [G: E. Europe; W. Europe]

Tronzano, Marco. Exchange-Rate Dynamics in a Stock-Flow Model: The Lira/Dollar Case (1972–1980). *Econ. Notes*, 1981, *10*(3), pp. 118–27.
[G: Italy; U.S.]

Turnovsky, Stephen J. The Asset Market Approach to Exchange Rate Determination: Some Short-Run, Stability, and Steady-State Properties. *J. Macroecon.*, Winter 1981, *3*(1), pp. 1–32.

Turnovsky, Stephen J. The Effects of Devaluation and Foreign Price Disturbances under Rational Expectations. *J. Int. Econ.*, February 1981, *11*(1), pp. 33–60.

Turnovsky, Stephen J. and Eaton, Jonathan. International Interest Rate Linkages and Speculative Behaviour. In *Jüttner, D. J., ed.*, 1981, pp. 385–96.

Tyler, William G. Comment [The Brazilian Experience with the Crawling Peg] [Exchange Rate Policies in Chile: The Experience with the Crawling Peg]. In *Williamson, J., ed.*, 1981, pp. 175–77.
[G: Brazil; Chile]

Urrutia M., Miguel. Experience with the Crawling Peg in Colombia. In *Williamson, J., ed.*, 1981, pp. 207–20. [G: Colombia]

Vaubel, Roland. The Collapse of Purchasing Power Parities during the 1970's by Frenkel: Comment. *Europ. Econ. Rev.*, May 1981, *16*(1), pp. 173–75.

Wallace, Myles S. The Dollar Exchange Rate, Oil Imports, and the Trade Balance: A Test of Causality. *Rev. Bus. Econ. Res.*, Winter 1981, *16*(2), pp. 23–33. [G: U.S.]

Wanniski, Jude. The Mundell–Laffer Hypothesis—A New View of the World Economy. In *Baldwin, R. E. and Richardson, J. D., eds.*, 1981, *1975*, pp. 374–88. [G: U.S.]

Weatherstone, Dennis. Commentary on the Rutledge Paper [The Foreign Exchange Market under Flexible Exchange Rates: Comment]. In *Baldwin, R. E. and Richardson, J. D., eds., 1981, 1978*, pp. 360–62.

Weintraub, Sidney. Flexible Exchange Rates: Old Vinegar in New Wine? *J. Post Keynesian Econ.*, Summer 1981, *3*(4), pp. 467–78.

Wellisz, Stanislaw. Exchange Rate Policy for Developing Countries: Comments. In *Grassman, S. and Lundberg, E., eds.*, 1981, pp. 420–22. [G: LDCs; MDCs]

Wibulswasdi, Chaiyawat. Experiences of Asian Countries with Various Exchange Rate Policies: Comment. In *Williamson, J., ed.*, 1981, pp. 319–21. [G: Asia]

Willett, Thomas D. Alternative Approaches to International Surveillance of Exchange-Rate Policies. In *Baldwin, R. E. and Richardson, J. D., eds., 1981, 1978*, pp. 432–49.

Willett, Thomas D. Macroeconomic Instability and Exchange-rate Volatility. In *[von Haberler, G.]*, 1981, pp. 35–50.

Willett, Thomas D. Policy Research Issues in a Floating Rate World: An Assessment of Policy-relevant Research on the Effects of International Monetary Institutions and Behavior on Macroeconomic Performance. In *National Science Foundation*, 1981, pp. 124–58.

Willett, Thomas D. United States Economic Interests and Crawling Peg Systems. In *Williamson, J., ed.*, 1981, pp. 371–83. [G: U.S.]

Williamson, Denise. Exchange Rate Policies in Peru, 1971–9. In *Williamson, J., ed.*, 1981, pp. 230–42. [G: Peru]

Williamson, John. The Crawling Peg in Historical Perspective. In *Williamson, J., ed.*, 1981, pp. 3–30. [G: OECD; Selected LDCs]

Yano, Keiji. Exchange Rate Determination and Foreign Assets Accumulation. (In Japanese. With English summary.) *Osaka Econ. Pap.*, December 1981, *31*(2–3), pp. 53–58.

Zippel, Wulfdiether. Zur langfristigen Instabilität einer Gold-Reservewährungs-Ordnung. (On the Long-Term Instability of a Gold-Reserve Currency System. With English summary.) *Kredit Kapital*, 1981, *14*(1), pp. 32–51.

432 International Monetary Arrangements

4320 International Monetary Arrangements

Agnew, Jonathan G. The Yankee Bond Market. In *Burghardt, A. M., ed.*, 1981, pp. 65–72. [G: U.S.]

Alessandroni, Alessandro. L'intermediazione bancaria internazionale: evoluzione del passato e prospettive attuali. (International Banking Intermediation: Retrospect and Current Prospects. With English summary.) *Bancaria*, February 1981, *37*(2), pp. 132–39.

Andreatta, Beniamino. Problemi dello sviluppo nel mondo e del suo finanziamento. (World Economic Development and Its Financing. With English summary.) *Bancaria*, February 1981, *37*(2), pp. 129–31. [G: LDCs]

Askari, Hossein and Mustafa, Ahmad. The Distributional Aspects of Special Drawing Rights: An LDC

Compromise. *Econ. Int.*, May–August–November 1981, *34*(2–3–4), pp. 242–60. [G: LDCs]

Baan, Jan Willem and Kleinheyer, Norbert. Zur monetären Relevanz der Euromärkte. (On the Monetary Relevance of the Euromarkets. With English summary.) *Kredit Kapital*, 1981, *14*(3), pp. 423–33. [G: Switzerland; Japan; U.S.; Canada; EEC]

Baffi, Paolo. L'euroscudo in taluni rapporti finanziari. (The Role of the E.C.U. in Certain Financial Relations. With English summary.) *Bancaria*, March 1981, *37*(3), pp. 251–53. [G: EEC]

Baker, S. A. European Monetary Union and the Demand for International Reserves: A Reply. *Bull. Econ. Res.*, May 1981, *33*(1), pp. 47. [G: Europe]

Bennett, Karl. Mobilising Foreign Exchange Reserves for Economic Growth in CARICOM. *Soc. Econ. Stud.*, December 1981, *30*(4), pp. 172–86. [G: Jamaica]

Bergsten, C. Fred. Recycling the World's Surpluses and Deficits: Challenge and Response. In *Bergsten, C. F., ed.*, 1981, pp. 39–48. [G: LDCs; OECD; OPEC]

Bergsten, C. Fred. The International Economic Policy of the United States: An Assessment and Agenda for the Future. In *Bergsten, C. F., ed.*, 1981, pp. 3–21. [G: U.S.]

Bergsten, C. Fred. The International Monetary System in the 1980s. In *Bergsten, C. F., ed.*, 1981, pp. 25–37. [G: OECD; U.S.]

Bergsten, C. Fred. The Role of the International Monetary Fund. In *Bergsten, C. F., ed.*, 1981, pp. 49–60.

Bernstein, Edward M. Perils of the Gold Standard. *Challenge*, November–December 1981, *24*(5), pp. 58–62.

Bhattacharya, A. K. and Hudson, Michael. A Regional Strategy to Finance the New International Economic Order. In *Nicol, D.; Echeverria, L. and Peccei, A., eds.*, 1981, pp. 299–317.

Bird, Graham. Acerca del uso de la reforma monetaria internacional en beneficio de los países en desarrollo. (On Using International Monetary Reform for the Benefit of Developing Countries. With English summary.) *Económica*, September–December 1981, *27*(3), pp. 143–61. [G: LDCs]

Bird, Graham. International Monetary Issues and the Developing Countries: A Survey: Postscript. In *Streeten, P. and Jolly, R, eds.*, 1981, pp. 367–73. [G: LDCs]

Bird, Graham. On Using International Monetary Reform for the Benefit of Developing Countries. *Econ. Notes*, 1981, *10*(1), pp. 29–45.

Bird, Graham. Reserve Currency Consolidation, Gold Policy and Financial Flows to Developing Countries: Mechanisms for an Aid-augmented Substitution Account. *World Devel.*, July 1981, *9*(7), pp. 609–19.

Bird, Graham and Orme, Timothy. An Analysis of Drawings on the International Monetary Fund by Developing Countries. *World Devel.*, June 1981, *9*(6), pp. 563–68. [G: LDCs]

Blackman, Courtney N. The Management of Foreign Exchange Reserves in Small Developing Countries. *Soc. Econ. Stud.*, December 1981, *30*(4),

pp. 156–71.

Bordo, Michael David. The Classical Gold Standard: Some Lessons for Today. *Fed. Res. Bank St. Louis Rev.*, May 1981, *63*(5), pp. 2–17.   [G: U.K.; U.S.]

Brau, Eduard. The Consultation Process of the Fund. *Finance Develop.*, December 1981, *18*(4), pp. 13–16.

Brodsky, David A. and Sampson, Gary P. Implications of the Effective Revaluation of Reserve Asset Gold: The Case for a Gold Account for Development. *World Devel.*, July 1981, *9*(7), pp. 589–608.

Brown, Adlith. Economic Policy and the IMF in Jamaica. *Soc. Econ. Stud.*, December 1981, *30*(4), pp. 1–51.   [G: Jamaica]

Buira Seira, Ariel. Recession, Inflation and the International Monetary System. *World Devel.*, November/December 1981, *9*(11/12), pp. 1115–28.   [G: MDCs; LDCs]

Burki, Shahid Javed and Haq, Mahbub. Meeting Basic Needs: An Overview. *World Devel.*, February 1981, *9*(2), pp. 167–82.

Burtle, James L. The International Monetary System. In *Altman, E. I., ed.*, 1981, pp. 11.3–28.

Casari, Mario. La moneta come strumento di cooperazione internazionale. (Money as an Instrument of International Cooperation. With English summary.) *Rivista Int. Sci. Econ. Com.*, March 1981, *28*(3), pp. 226–40.

Ciampi, Carlo Azeglio. Incontro con la Banca Mondiale. (Meeting with the World Bank. With English summary.) *Bancaria*, February 1981, *37*(2), pp. 119–22.

Cingano, Francesco. L'euroscudo nei rapporti bancari. (The E.C.U. in Banking Business. With English summary.) *Bancaria*, March 1981, *37*(3), pp. 254–56.   [G: EEC]

Clark, William. Robert McNamara at the World Bank. *Foreign Aff.*, Fall 1981, *60*(1), pp. 167–84.

Clark, William. The McNamara Years. *Finance Develop.*, June 1981, *18*(2), pp. 6–9.

Clarke, Giles. Trade Financing: Bonds, Private Placements and Eurocredits. In *Gmür, C. J., ed.*, 1981, pp. 133–47.   [G: W. Europe]

Coats, Warren L., Jr. The Weekend Eurodollar Game. *J. Finance*, June 1981, *36*(3), pp. 649–59.   [G: U.S.]

Cooke, Peter. Sviluppi nella cooperazione fra le autorità di vigilanza bancaria. (Developments in Cooperation among Banking Supervisory Authorities. With English summary.) *Bancaria*, June 1981, *37*(6), pp. 578–86.   [G: EEC]

Coussement, André M. Developments in Financing Institutions, Instruments and Banking. In *Ensor, R. and Muller, P., eds.*, 1981, pp. 25–30.

Csaba, László. Planning and Finances in the Decade after the Adoption of the Comprehensive Programme in the CMEA. *Acta Oecon.*, 1981, *27*(3–4), pp. 351–71.   [G: CMEA]

D'Aroma, Antonio. L'ultimo ventennio della Banca dei Regolamenti Internazionali di Basilea. (The Past Twenty Years of the Bank for International Settlements. With English summary.) *Bancaria*, January 1981, *37*(1), pp. 37–45.

Dale, Richard S. Prudential Regulation of Multina-tional Banking: The Problem Outlined. *Nat. Westminster Bank Quart. Rev.*, February 1981, pp. 14–24.

Davies, Alun G. The Commonwealth of the Bahamas as a Center of International Business Investment. *Bull. Int. Fiscal Doc.*, April 1981, *35*(4), pp. 165–69.   [G: Bahamas]

Dell, Sidney. International Monetary Issues and the Developing Countries: A Survey: Comment. In *Streeten, P. and Jolly, R, eds.*, 1981, *1975*, pp. 375–79.

Desiata, Alfonso. L'euroscudo nei rapporti assicurativi. (The E.C.U. in Insurance Business. With English summary.) *Bancaria*, March 1981, *37*(3), pp. 257–59.   [G: EEC]

Dini, Lamberto. Liquidity Creation and Risk in the International Monetary System. *Banca Naz. Lavoro Quart. Rev.*, December 1981, (139), pp. 395–402.

Dufey, Gunter and Giddy, Ian H. Innovation in the International Financial Markets. *J. Int. Bus. Stud.*, Fall 1981, *12*(2), pp. 33–51.

Dufey, Gunter and Giddy, Ian H. The International Money Market: Perspective and Prognosis. In *Baldwin, R. E. and Richardson, J. D., eds.*, 1981, *1978*, pp. 533–43.

Earley, James S. What Caused Worldwide Inflation: Excess Liquidity, Excessive Credit, or Both? *Weltwirtsch. Arch.*, 1981, *117*(2), pp. 213–43.

Eidem, Rolf. East, West, and South: The Role of the Centrally Planned Economies in the International Economy: Comments. In *Grassman, S. and Lundberg, E., eds.*, 1981, pp. 358–61.   [G: CMEA]

El-Agraa, A. M. European Monetary Union and the Demand for International Reserves: A Comment. *Bull. Econ. Res.*, May 1981, *33*(1), pp. 45–46.   [G: Europe]

Erb, Richard D. The IMF and World Economic Stability. *Challenge*, September/October 1981, *24*(4), pp. 22–27.

Erös, Gyula. Some Problems of the International Monetary System. *Acta Oecon.*, 1981, *26*(1–2), pp. 107–22.   [G: W. Europe; Japan; U.S.]

Falchi, Giannandrea. Considerazioni di due esperti sul Sistema monetario europeo. (Two Experts' Views on the EMS. With English summary.) *Bancaria*, June 1981, *37*(6), pp. 625–28.   [G: EEC]

Fellner, William. Gold and the Uneasy Case for Responsibly Managed Fiat Money. In *Fellner, W., ed.*, 1981, pp. 97–121.

Fellner, William. On the Merits of Gradualism and on a Fall-back Position if It Should Nevertheless Fail: Introductory Remarks. In *Fellner, W., ed.*, 1981, pp. 3–18.   [G: U.S.]

Finnerty, Joseph E. and Schneeweis, Thomas. Determinants of Eurodollar Interest Rates under Fixed and Floating Exchange Rates. *Nebr. J. Econ. Bus.*, Autumn 1981, *20*(4), pp. 51–61.   [G: U.S.]

de Fontenay, Patrick. Portugal and the IMF: The Political Economy of Stabilization: Comment. In *Braga de Macedo, J. and Serfaty, S., eds.*, 1981, pp. 137–42.   [G: Portugal]

Fordwor, Kwame D. Some Unresolved Problems of the African Development Bank. *World Devel.*,

November/December 1981, 9(11/12), pp. 1129–39. [G: Africa]

Frenkel, Jacob A. and Jovanovic, Boyan. Optimal International Reserves: A Stochastic Framework. *Econ. J.*, June 1981, 91(362), pp. 507–14.

Frowen, Stephen F. The Interaction between the International Monetary System and Financial Markets in the 1980's. In *Burghardt, A. M., ed.*, 1981, pp. 7–22. [G: Global]

von Furstenberg, George M. Price Deflators for Special Drawing Rights over the Past Decade. *Rev. Public Data Use (See J. Econ. Soc. Meas. after 4/85)*, April 1981, 9(1), pp. 1–20.

Fusfeld, Daniel R. Response to Professor Gurley [The Next Great Depression II: The Impending Financial Collapse]. *J. Econ. Issues*, March 1981, 15(1), pp. 181–83. [G: U.S.; Europe]

Garcha, Belwant S. Channeling Limited Resources for the Greatest Impact. *Finance Develop.*, December 1981, 18(4), pp. 6–8. [G: LDCs]

de Gelsey, William. The Lender's View of the Financial Markets in the 80's. In *Burghardt, A. M., ed.*, 1981, pp. 43–57. [G: Global]

Genberg, Hans. Comment [The European Monetary System—An Approximate Implementation of the Crawling Peg?] [United States Economic Interests and Crawling Peg Systems]. In *Williamson, J., ed.*, 1981, pp. 387–90. [G: U.S.; W. Europe]

Giddy, Ian H. Risk and Return in the Eurocurrency Interbank Market. *Greek Econ. Rev.*, August 1981, 3(2), pp. 158–86. [G: Europe]

Gmür, Charles J. Trade Financing: Forfaiting. In *Gmür, C. J., ed.*, 1981, pp. 117–32.

Gold, Joseph. Keynes and the Articles of the Fund: Review Article. *Finance Develop.*, September 1981, 18(3), pp. 38–42.

Gold, Joseph. The Fund Agreement in the Courts—XVII. *Int. Monet. Fund Staff Pap.*, December 1981, 28(4), pp. 728–59.

Gold, Joseph. The Fund Agreement in the Courts—XVI. *Int. Monet. Fund Staff Pap.*, June 1981, 28(2), pp. 411–36.

Gold, Joseph. The Origins of Weighted Voting Power in the Fund. *Finance Develop.*, March 1981, 18(1), pp. 25–28.

Guitián, Manuel. Fund Conditionality and the International Adjustment Process: The Changing Environment of the 1970s. *Finance Develop.*, March 1981, 18(1), pp. 8–11.

Guitián, Manuel. Fund Conditionality and the International Adjustment Process: A Look into the 1980s. *Finance Develop.*, June 1981, 18(2), pp. 14–17.

Haegele, Monroe J. Using a Market Determined Spread as a Guide. In *Ensor, R., ed.*, 1981, pp. 75–79. [G: Selected MDCs; Selected LDCs]

Hazlitt, Henry. Gold Prospects. *Policy Rev.*, Spring 1981, (16), pp. 107–14.

Helleiner, Gerald K. The Less Developed Countries and the International Monetary System. In *Helleiner, G. K.*, 1981, pp. 130–65. [G: LDCs]

Heller, H. Robert. International Reserves and World-Wide Inflation: Further Analysis. *Int. Monet. Fund Staff Pap.*, March 1981, 28(1), pp. 230–33.

Hinshaw, Randall. Global Monetary Anarchy: Background. In *Hinshaw, R., ed.*, 1981, pp. 13–25. [G: OECD]

Hooke, Augustus W. The Brandt Commission and International Monetary Issues. *Finance Develop.*, June 1981, 18(2), pp. 22–24.

Humes, Dorla. Foreign Reserves Management in Belize: An Assessment of the Liquidity Constraints in 1979. *Soc. Econ. Stud.*, December 1981, 30(4), pp. 187–200. [G: Belize]

Hürni, Bettina. Die Sonderfazilitäten im Internationalen Währungsfonds (IWF): Verwendung und Nutzen. (The IMF Special Financing Facilities: Applicability and Benefit. With English summary.) *Schweiz. Z. Volkswirtsch. Statist.*, March 1981, 117(1), pp. 55–74.

Hürni, Bettina. IFC: The New Five-Year Programme. *J. World Trade Law*, September–October 1981, 15(5), pp. 461–65.

Hurwicz, Leonid. Global Modeling and Decision-Making: Comment. In *Evan, W. M., ed.*, 1981, pp. 127–30.

James, Emile. Il Sistema monetario europeo ha due anni di vita. (The European Monetary System: Two Years After. With English summary.) *Bancaria*, June 1981, 37(6), pp. 555–60. [G: EEC]

Johnson, Harry G. Networks of Economists: Their Role in International Monetary Reforms. In *Evan, W. M., ed.*, 1981, pp. 79–90.

Kanesa-Thasan, S. The Fund and Adjustment Policies in Africa. *Finance Develop.*, September 1981, 18(3), pp. 20–24. [G: Africa]

Karlik, John R. Some Questions and Brief Answers about the Eurodollar Market. In *Baldwin, R. E. and Richardson, J. D., eds.*, 1981, 1977, pp. 516–33.

Kaul, P. N. Technical Assistance from the Fund: Central Banking Department. *Finance Develop.*, June 1981, 18(2), pp. 34–37.

Kenen, Peter B. The Analytics of a Substitution Account. *Banca Naz. Lavoro Quart. Rev.*, December 1981, (139), pp. 403–26. [G: U.S.]

Kern, David. The Eurocurrency Markets. *Irish Banking Rev.*, December 1981, pp. 24–30. [G: W. Europe]

Killick, Tony. Eurocurrency Market Recycling of OPEC Surpluses to Developing Countries: Fact or Myth? In *Stevens, C., ed.*, 1981, pp. 92–104. [G: EEC; LDCs]

Kincaid, G. Russell. Conditionality and the Use of Fund Resources: Jamaica. *Finance Develop.*, June 1981, 18(2), pp. 18–21. [G: Jamaica]

Kindleberger, Charles P. An Economist's View of the Eurodollar Market: Two Puzzles. In *Kindleberger, C. P.*, 1981, 1970, pp. 53–62.

Kindleberger, Charles P. International Financial Intermediation for Developing Countries. In *Kindleberger, C. P.*, 1981, 1976, pp. 269–78.

Kindleberger, Charles P. Less Developed Countries and the International Capital Market. In *Kindleberger, C. P.*, 1981, 1970, pp. 243–55. [G: LDCs]

Kindleberger, Charles P. Quantity and Price, Especially in Financial Markets. In *Kindleberger, C. P.*, 1981, 1975, pp. 256–68.

Kindleberger, Charles P. Systems of International Economic Organization. In *Kindleberger, C. P.*, 1981, 1976, pp. 301–16.

Kindleberger, Charles P. The Benefits of International Money. In *Kindleberger, C. P.*, 1981, *1972*, pp. 9–23.

Kindleberger, Charles P. The Dollar and World Liquidity: A Minority View. In *Kindleberger, C. P.*, 1981, *1966*, pp. 42–52.

Kindleberger, Charles P. The Eurodollar and the Internationalization of United States Monetary Policy. In *Kindleberger, C. P.*, 1981, *1969*, pp. 100–110.

Kindleberger, Charles P. The International Monetary System. In *Kindleberger, C. P.*, 1981, *1976*, pp. 281–300.

Kindleberger, Charles P. The Politics of International Money and World Language. In *Kindleberger, C. P.*, 1981, *1967*, pp. 24–34.

Kindleberger, Charles P. The Price of Gold and the N–1 Problem. In *Kindleberger, C. P.*, 1981, *1970*, pp. 76–86.

Kindleberger, Charles P. The Pros and Cons of an International Capital Market. In *Kindleberger, C. P.*, 1981, *1967*, pp. 225–42.

Kindleberger, Charles P. The SDR as International Money. In *Kindleberger, C. P.*, 1981, *1975*, pp. 63–75.

Kindleberger, Charles P. Time and Money. In *Kindleberger, C. P.*, 1981, *1969*, pp. 35–41.

Korteweg, Pieter. Comment [The First Two Years of the EMS: The Exchange-Rate Experience]. *Banca Naz. Lavoro Quart. Rev.*, September 1981, (138), pp. 290–95. [G: U.S.; EEC]

Kouri, Pentti J. K. The Political Economy of Stabilization: Comment. In *Braga de Macedo, J. and Serfaty, S., eds.*, 1981, pp. 143–52. [G: Portugal]

Landell-Mills, Pierre M. Structural Adjustment Lending: Early Experience. *Finance Develop.*, December 1981, *18*(4), pp. 17–21.

Languetin, Pierre. The European Monetary System—Managing the External Relationships. *Banca Naz. Lavoro Quart. Rev.*, September 1981, (138), pp. 327–38. [G: EEC]

de Larosière, Jacques. Compiti del Fondo Monetario Internazionale nel quadro della lotta all'inflazione e di una politica di sviluppo stabile. (The Tasks of the International Monetary Fund in the Context of the Fight against Inflation and of a Steady Development Policy. With English summary.) *Bancaria*, January 1981, *37*(1), pp. 30–36.

de Larosière, Jacques. The Role of the Fund in Recycling. *Finance Develop.*, March 1981, *18*(1), pp. 12–13.

Lockhart, James B., III. Gulf Oil: A Case History. In *Ensor, R. and Muller, P., eds.*, 1981, pp. 47–53.

Logue, Dennis E. Overseas Money and Capital Markets. In *Altman, E. I., ed.*, 1981, pp. 13.3–33.

Magnifico, Giovanni. Il Sistema monetario europea verso il terzo anno. (The European Monetary System Towards the Third Year. With English summary.) *Bancaria*, June 1981, *37*(6), pp. 561–65. [G: EEC]

Marzetti, Silva. Sul ruolo internazionale dell'oro e il regime dei cambi. (The International Role of Gold and the Exchange Rate System. With English summary.) *Rivista Int. Sci. Econ. Com.*, January–February 1981, *28*(1–2), pp. 90–109.

Masera, Rainer Stefano. Riforma monetaria internazionale e Sistema monetario europeo: Problemi e prospettive. (European Monetary System and International Monetary Reform: Problems and Perspectives. With English summary.) *Bancaria*, June 1981, *37*(6), pp. 566–71. [G: EEC]

Masera, Rainer Stefano. The Behaviour of the Euromarkets and the Problem of Monetary Control in Europe: Comment. *Giorn. Econ.*, Sept.-Dec. 1981, *40*(9–12), pp. 723–31. [G: EEC]

Masera, Rainer Stefano. The First Two Years of the EMS: The Exchange-Rate Experience. *Banca Naz. Lavoro Quart. Rev.*, September 1981, (138), pp. 271–89. [G: U.S.; EEC]

Mayer, Helmut W. The Behaviour of the Euro-markets and the Problem of Monetary Control in Europe. *Giorn. Econ.*, Sept.-Dec. 1981, *40*(9–12), pp. 681–721. [G: EEC]

Maynard, Geoffrey and Bird, Graham. International Monetary Issues and the Developing Countries: A Survey. In *Streeten, P. and Jolly, R, eds.*, 1981, *1975*, pp. 343–65. [G: LDCs]

Micossi, Stefano and Saccomanni, Fabrizio. The Substitution Account: The Problem, the Techniques and the Politics. *Banca Naz. Lavoro Quart. Rev.*, June 1981, (137), pp. 171–89.

Miles, Marc A. Currency Substitution: Some Further Results and Conclusions. *Southern Econ. J.*, July 1981, *48*(1), pp. 78–86. [G: U.S.; W. Germany]

Moggridge, D. E. Financial Crises and Lenders of Last Resort: Policy in the Crises of 1920 and 1929. *J. Europ. Econ. Hist.*, Spring 1981, *10*(1), pp. 47–69.

Murphy, Robert G. and Furstenberg, George M. An Analysis of Factors Influencing the Level of SDR Holdings in Non-Oil Developing Countries. *Int. Monet. Fund Staff Pap.*, June 1981, *28*(2), pp. 310–37. [G: LDCs]

Nsouli, Saleh M. Monetary Integration in Developing Countries. *Finance Develop.*, December 1981, *18*(4), pp. 41–44.

Nyiri, Iván. Gold—Gold Price—Currency Reserves. *Acta Oecon.*, 1981, *26*(1–2), pp. 123–32.

Ossola, Rinaldo. A Modest Step towards Fixed Parities. *Banca Naz. Lavoro Quart. Rev.*, March 1981, (136), pp. 69–74.

Padoa-Schioppa, Tommaso. Lo scudo e il Sistema Monetario Europeo. (The E.C.U. and the European Monetary System. With English summary.) *Bancaria*, March 1981, *37*(3), pp. 245–50. [G: EEC]

Pecchioli, Rinaldo. European Financial Integration: Institutional and Legal Aspects: Comment. *Giorn. Econ.*, Sept.-Dec. 1981, *40*(9–12), pp. 775–79. [G: EEC]

Portes, Richard. East, West, and South: The Role of the Centrally Planned Economies in the International Economy. In *Grassman, S. and Lundberg, E., eds.*, 1981, pp. 319–57. [G: CMEA]

Quadrio-Curzio, Alberto. Un diagramma dell'oro tra demonetizzazione e rimonetizzazione. (A Diagram of Gold between Demonetization and Remonetization. With English summary.) *Rivista Int. Sci. Econ. Com.*, October–November 1981, *28*(10–11), pp. 915–40.

Rabin, Alan and Pratt, Leila J. A Note on Heller's

Use of Regression Analysis [International Reserves and World-Wide Inflation]. *Int. Monet. Fund Staff Pap.*, March 1981, *28*(1), pp. 225–29.

Reserve Assets Study Group of the Group of Thirty. Reserve Assets and a Substitution Account: Towards a Less Unstable International Monetary System. In *Baldwin, R. E. and Richardson, J. D., eds.*, 1981, *1980*, pp. 450–65.

Robbins, Lionel. Global Monetary Anarchy: Concluding Reactions. In *Hinshaw, R., ed.*, 1981, pp. 161–76. **[G: OECD]**

Robbins, Lionel. Global Monetary Anarchy: Questions and Options. In *Hinshaw, R., ed.*, 1981, pp. 27–47. **[G: OECD]**

von Rosen, Rüdiger. IWF weiterhin auf Stabilitätskurs. (IMF Still on a Stability Path. With English summary.) *Kredit Kapital*, 1981, *14*(4), pp. 574–89.

Ruding, H. O. Co-ordinating IMF and Commercial Bank Policies. In *Ensor, R., ed.*, 1981, pp. 149–52.

Russell, Robert W. Global Modeling and Decision-Making: Comment. In *Evan, W. M., ed.*, 1981, pp. 121–26.

Salop, Joanne. The Divergence Indicator: A Technical Note. *Int. Monet. Fund Staff Pap.*, December 1981, *28*(4), pp. 682–97. **[G: EEC]**

Santa Maria, Alberto. European Financial Integration: Institutional and Legal Aspects. *Giorn. Econ.*, Sept.-Dec. 1981, *40*(9–12), pp. 747–66. **[G: EEC]**

Shenayev, V. N. The Crisis of Neoliberalism and the Evolution of the "Social Market Economy" Theory. In *Mileikovsky, A. G., et al.*, 1981, pp. 253–82.

Siegman, Charles J. Developing Countries and the International Financial System: A Survey of Trends and Selected Issues. In *Reubens, E. P., ed.*, 1981, pp. 179–213. **[G: LDCs]**

Sobol, Dorothy Meadow. The SDR in Private International Finance. *Fed. Res. Bank New York Quart. Rev.*, Winter 1981–82, *6*(4), pp. 29–41.

Solomon, Robert. Brunner on the State of International Monetary Policy. *Banca Naz. Lavoro Quart. Rev.*, March 1981, (136), pp. 11–13.

Southard, Frank A., Jr. International Economic and Financial Policies. In *Heller, F. H., ed.*, 1981, pp. 67–77. **[G: U.S.]**

Stallings, Barbara. Portugal and the IMF: The Political Economy of Stabilization. In *Braga de Macedo, J. and Serfaty, S., eds.*, 1981, pp. 101–35. **[G: Portugal; U.K.; Italy]**

Stuart, Brian C. Stabilization Policy in Portugal, 1974–78. *Finance Develop.*, September 1981, *18*(3), pp. 25–29. **[G: Portugal]**

Sumner, Michael T. and Zis, G. Whither European Monetary Union? *Nat. Westminster Bank Quart. Rev.*, February 1981, pp. 49–61. **[G: EEC]**

Teichman, Thomas. The Importer: Buyer Credits from the Euromarkets. In *Gmür, C. J., ed.*, 1981, pp. 91–103. **[G: W. Europe]**

Thygesen, Niels. The European Monetary System—An Approximate Implementation of the Crawling Peg? In *Williamson, J., ed.*, 1981, pp. 351–70. **[G: W. Europe]**

Thygesen, Niels. The European Monetary System:

The First Two Years: Introduction. *Banca Naz. Lavoro Quart. Rev.*, September 1981, (138), pp. 261–69. **[G: EEC]**

Triffin, Robert. The American Response to the European Monetary System. In *Baldwin, R. E. and Richardson, J. D., eds.*, 1981, *1979*, pp. 477–86.

Triffin, Robert. The European Monetary System: The First Two Years: Concluding Remarks. *Banca Naz. Lavoro Quart. Rev.*, September 1981, (138), pp. 365–70. **[G: EEC]**

Türel, Oktar. Planlama ve Ulusararasi Örgütler: Turkiye'nin Dünya Bankasi ile Ilişkileri Örnek Olayi. (Planning and International Organizations: The Case of Turkey's Relations with the World Bank. With English summary.) *METU*, Special Issue, 1981, pp. 635–54. **[G: Turkey]**

Vanhala, Matti. Kansainvälisen valuuttayhteistyön näkymät 1980-luvulla. (Prospects for Monetary Co-operation in the 80's. With English summary.) *Kansant. Aikak.*, 1981, *77*(2), pp. 172–84.

Vaubel, Roland. Logische Implikationen und Anreizwirkungen des europäischen Währungssystems. (Logical Implications and Incentive Effects of the European Monetary System. With English summary.) *Z. Wirtschaft. Sozialwissen.*, 1981, *101*(1), pp. 1–23. **[G: EEC]**

de Vries, Rimmer. Proceedings of the Seminar on International Economic Problems: Statement. In *U.S. Congress, Joint Economic Committee (I)*, 1981, pp. 319–35. **[G: U.S.; Selected Countries]**

Welcker, Johannes. Der Eurodollarmarkt: Tatsächliche und vermeintliche Probleme. (The Euro-Dollar Market—Actual and Alleged Problems. With English summary.) *Konjunkturpolitik*, 1981, *27*(5), pp. 279–96. **[G: W. Germany]**

Wilson, Thomas. Issues of Regional Finance: Fiscal Transfers between Regions and between Members of the European Community. In *Roskamp, K. W. and Forte, F., eds.*, 1981, pp. 401–11. **[G: EEC]**

Wright, John Winthrop. Proceedings of the Seminar on International Economic Problems: Statement. In *U.S. Congress, Joint Economic Committee (I)*, 1981, pp. 295–312. **[G: U.S.]**

Yoshida, Taroichi. L'Asia negli anni Ottanta: il ruolo della Banca Asiatica di Sviluppo. (Asia in the '80s: The Role of the Asian Development Bank. With English summary.) *Bancaria*, January 1981, *37*(1), pp. 46–48. **[G: Asia]**

van Ypersele de Strihou, Jacques. Operating Principles and Procedures of the European Monetary System. In *Baldwin, R. E. and Richardson, J. D., eds.*, 1981, *1979*, pp. 465–77.

Zippel, Wulfdiether. Zur langfristigen Instabilität einer Gold-Reservewährungs-Ordnung. (On the Long-Term Instability of a Gold-Reserve Currency System. With English summary.) *Kredit Kapital*, 1981, *14*(1), pp. 32–51.

433 Private International Lending

4330 Private International Lending

Abbott, George C. International Indebtedness of Less Developed Countries: Structure, Growth, Indicators. *Aussenwirtschaft*, December 1981,

36(4), pp. 340–51. [G: LDCs]

Bakó, Ede. Credits to the South and International Financial Relations: Comment. In *Saunders, C. T., ed. (I),* 1981, pp. 160–62. [G: Hungary; LDCs]

Bartlett, Sarah. Transnational Banking: A Case of Transfer Parking with Money. In *Murray, R., ed.,* 1981, pp. 96–115.

Bhaduri, Amit. Credits to the South and International Financial Relations. In *Saunders, C. T., ed. (I),* 1981, pp. 91–102. [G: OECD; OPEC; LDCs]

Brainard, Lawrence J. Bankers Trust's Approach to International Risk Assessment. In *Ensor, R., ed.,* 1981, pp. 93–98. [G: S. Korea; Brazil; Ecuador]

Caldwell, J. Alexander and Villamil, J. Antonio. Factors Affecting Creditworthiness. In *Ensor, R., ed.,* 1981, pp. 19–25. [G: Iran; Nicaragua; Bolivia; Turkey; Zaire]

Cline, William R. Economic Stabilization in Peru, 1975–78. In *Cline, W. R. and Weintraub, S., eds.,* 1981, pp. 297–326. [G: Peru]

Davis, Christopher. Financing Third World Debt. In *The Royal Inst. of Internat. Affairs,* 1981, pp. 59–102. [G: LDCs]

Devlin, Robert. Transnational Banks, External Debt and Peru: Results of a Recent Study. *Cepal Rev.,* August 1981, (14), pp. 153–84. [G: Peru]

Dod, David P. Bank Lending to Developing Countries: Recent Developments in Historical Perspective. *Fed. Res. Bull.,* September 1981, 67(9), pp. 647–56. [G: LDCs]

Friedman, Irving S. The Evolution of Country Risk Assessment. In *Ensor, R., ed.,* 1981, pp. 9–15.

Friedman, Irving S. The Role of Private Banks in Stabilization Programs. In *Cline, W. R. and Weintraub, S., eds.,* 1981, pp. 235–65. [G: LDCs]

Frowen, Stephen F. The Interaction between the International Monetary System and Financial Markets in the 1980's. In *Burghardt, A. M., ed.,* 1981, pp. 7–22. [G: Global]

de Gelsey, William. The Lender's View of the Financial Markets in the 80's. In *Burghardt, A. M., ed.,* 1981, pp. 43–57. [G: Global]

Giddy, Ian H. International Commercial Banking. In *Altman, E. I., ed.,* 1981, pp. 14.3–52.

Goodman, Laurie S. Bank Lending to Non-OPEC LDCs: Are Risks Diversifiable? *Fed. Res. Bank New York Quart. Rev.,* Summer 1981, 6(2), pp. 10–20. [G: Non-Oil LDCs]

Green, María del Rosario. Mexico's Economic Dependence. In *Purcell, S. K., ed.,* 1981, pp. 104–14. [G: Mexico]

Heller, H. Robert. The Role of Private Banks in Stabilization Programs: Comment. In *Cline, W. R. and Weintraub, S., eds.,* 1981, pp. 265–68. [G: LDCs]

Kubarych, Roger M. Country Risk Analysis for Supervisory Purposes. In *Ensor, R., ed.,* 1981, pp. 117–19. [G: U.S.]

Long, Millard F. and Veneroso, Frank. The Debt-related Problems of the Non-Oil Less Developed Countries. *Econ. Develop. Cult. Change,* April 1981, 29(3), pp. 501–16. [G: LDCs]

Masera, Francesco. Regolamentazione della posizione sull'estero delle aziende di credito italiane.

(Italian Regulations Governing International Banking Relations. With English summary.) *Rivista Int. Sci. Econ. Com.,* October–November 1981, 28(10–11), pp. 1044–52. [G: Italy]

Mortimore, Michael D. The State and Transnational Banks: Lessons from the Bolivian Crisis of External Public Indebtedness. *Cepal Rev.,* August 1981, (14), pp. 127–51. [G: Bolivia]

Nagy, Pancras. Economic Development, Debt Profiles and Country Risk. In *Ensor, R., ed.,* 1981, pp. 27–30. [G: Selected LDCs]

Nagy, Pancras. The Use of Quantified Country Risk in Decision Making in Banks. In *Ensor, R., ed.,* 1981, pp. 103–10. [G: Selected Countries]

O'Brien, Richard. Country Risk and Bank Lending Risk. In *Ensor, R., ed.,* 1981, pp. 87–91. [G: OECD]

Ruding, H. O. Co-ordinating IMF and Commercial Bank Policies. In *Ensor, R., ed.,* 1981, pp. 149–52.

Tunney, Joseph J. Bank Perspectives in Measuring Risk. In *Ensor, R., ed.,* 1981, pp. 83–85.

Weinert, Richard S. Foreign Capital in Mexico. In *Purcell, S. K., ed.,* 1981, pp. 115–24. [G: Mexico]

Weinert, Richard S. Nicaragua's Debt Renegotiation. *Cambridge J. Econ.,* June 1981, 5(2), pp. 187–94. [G: Nicaragua]

440 INTERNATIONAL INVESTMENT AND FOREIGN AID

441 International Investment and Long-term Capital Movements

4410 Theory of International Investment and Long-term Capital Movements

Brecher, Richard A. and Díaz-Alejandro, Carlos F. Tariffs, Foreign Capital and Immiserizing Growth. In *Bhagwati, J. N., ed.,* 1981, 1977, pp. 310–15.

Buckley, Peter J. and Casson, Mark. The Optimal Timing of a Foreign Direct Investment. *Econ. J.,* March 1981, 91(361), pp. 75–87.

Buiter, Willem H. Time Preference and International Lending and Borrowing in an Overlapping-Generations Model. *J. Polit. Econ.,* August 1981, 89(4), pp. 769–97.

Bürgenmeier, Beat. Kapitalströme und Zahlungsbilanz: Auswirkungen auf das Realeinkommen. (The Consequences of International Capital Movements on Real Income. With English summary.) *Schweiz. Z. Volkswirtsch. Statist.,* March 1981, 117(1), pp. 41–54.

Calvet, A. L. A Synthesis of Foreign Direct Investment Theories and Theories of the Multinational Firm. *J. Int. Bus. Stud.,* Spring/Summer 1981, 12(1), pp. 43–59.

Camilleri, Joseph. The Advanced Capitalist State and the Contemporary World Crisis. *Sci. Soc.,* Summer 1981, 45(2), pp. 130–58.

Das, Satya P. Effects of Foreign Investment in the Presence of Unemployment. *J. Int. Econ.,* May 1981, 11(2), pp. 249–57.

Dunning, John H. Explaining Outward Direct Investment of Developing Countries: In Support of the Eclectic Theory of International Production. In *Kumar, K. and McLeod, M. G., eds.,* 1981, pp. 1–22. [G: LDCs]

von Furstenberg, George M. Domestic Determinants of Net U.S. Foreign Investment. In *Hogan, J. D. and Craig, A. M., eds., Vol. 1,* 1981, pp. 115–63. [G: U.S.]

Garavello, Oscar. processi di sviluppo e dipendenza dai flussi esterni di capitale. (Growth: The L.D.C. Dependency on Foreign Capital Inflows. With English summary.) *Rivista Int. Sci. Econ. Com.,* October–November 1981, *28*(10–11), pp. 959–76. [G: LDCs]

Hemmings, Dan B. Exchange Controls, Security Prices and Exchange Rates. *Bull. Econ. Res.,* November 1981, *33*(2), pp. 82–90. [G: U.K.]

Jacobs, Klaas Peter. The Probable Impacts of Expanded Securities and Other Financing Activities of Banks and Securities Firms in the 1980s: Impacts on International Banking and Finance. In *Sametz, A. W., ed.,* 1981, pp. 171–78. [G: U.S.; W. Europe]

Kindleberger, Charles P. The Pros and Cons of an International Capital Market. In *Kindleberger, C. P.,* 1981, *1967,* pp. 225–42.

Lall, Sanjaya. Developing Countries and Foreign Investment. In *Lall, S.,* 1981, *1974,* pp. 53–67.

Maged, Mark J. The Probable Impacts of Expanded Securities and Other Financing Activities of Banks and Securities Firms in the 1980s: Impacts on International Banking and Finance. In *Sametz, A. W., ed.,* 1981, pp. 167–71. [G: U.S.; W. Europe]

Magee, Stephen P. Information and the Multinational Corporation: An Appropriability Theory of Direct Foreign Investment. In *Baldwin, R. E. and Richardson, J. D., eds.,* 1981, *1977,* pp. 180–201.

Minabe, Nobuo. Tariffs, Capital Export and Immiserizing Growth. *J. Int. Econ.,* February 1981, *11*(1), pp. 117–21.

Pereira Leite, Sérgio. International Reserves in a Neo-Classical Growth Model. *Economia (Portugal),* May 1981, *5*(2), pp. 389–99.

Quibria, M. G. Foreign Dependence, Domestic Policies, and Economic Development in a Poor Labour Surplus Economy. *Bangladesh Devel. Stud.,* Summer 1981, *9*(2), pp. 21–41.

Saudi, Abdulla A. Investment Strategies for OPEC in the 80's. In *Burghardt, A. M., ed.,* 1981, pp. 37–41. [G: OPEC]

Shawky, Hany A. and Ricks, David A. Capital Budgeting for Multinational Firms: A Theoretical Analysis. *Southern Econ. J.,* January 1981, *47*(3), pp. 703–13.

Vernon, Raymond. International Investment and International Trade in the Product Cycle. In *Baldwin, R. E. and Richardson, J. D., eds.,* 1981, *1966,* pp. 27–40.

4412 International Investment and Long-term Capital Movements: Studies

Allsopp, Chris. Changing Attitudes towards Capital Movements: Comments. In *[Cairncross, A.],*

1981, pp. 217–23.

Arpan, Jeffrey S.; Flowers, Edward B. and Ricks, David A. Foreign Direct Investment in the United States: The State of Knowledge in Research. *J. Int. Bus. Stud.,* Spring/Summer 1981, *12*(1), pp. 137–54.

Behrman, Jack N. and Mikesell, Raymond F. The Impact of U.S. Foreign Direct Investment on U.S. Export Competitiveness in Third World Markets. In *Center for Strategic and Internat. Studies, ed. (II),* 1981, pp. 147–82. [G: U.S.; LDCs]

Belli, R. David. U.S. Business Enterprises Acquired or Established by Foreign Direct Investors in 1980. *Surv. Curr. Bus.,* August 1981, *61*(8), pp. 58–71.

Bergsten, C. Fred. Foreign Investment in the United States. In *Bergsten, C. F., ed.,* 1981, pp. 107–12. [G: U.S.]

Bergsten, C. Fred. Toward Greater Cooperation in International Investment Policies. In *Bergsten, C. F., ed.,* 1981, pp. 95–105. [G: OECD; U.S.]

Bond, Eric W. Tax Holidays and Industry Behavior. *Rev. Econ. Statist.,* February 1981, *63*(1), pp. 88–95. [G: Puerto Rico]

Calcagno, Alfredo Eric and Kñakal, Jan. Transnational Companies and Direct Private Investment in Developing Countries. In *Saunders, C. T., ed. (I),* 1981, pp. 103–26. [G: LDCs; U.S.]

Chia, Siow Yue. Foreign Direct Investment in Manufacturing in Developing Countries: The Case of Singapore. In *Hamilton, F. E. I. and Linge, G. J. R., eds.,* 1981, pp. 439–64. [G: Singapore]

Chung, William K. and Fouch, Gregory G. Foreign Direct Investment in the United States in 1980. *Surv. Curr. Bus.,* August 1981, *61*(8), pp. 40–51. [G: U.S.]

Cohen, Robert B. and Frieden, Jeffry. The Impact of Multinational Corporations on Developing Nations. In *Reubens, E. P., ed.,* 1981, pp. 147–77. [G: Selected LDCs]

Connor, John M. Foreign Food Firms: Their Participation in and Competitive Impact on the US Food and Tobacco Manufacturing Sector. In *Johnson, G. and Maunder, A., eds.,* 1981, pp. 552–67. [G: U.S.]

Davies, Alun G. The Commonwealth of the Bahamas as a Center of International Business Investment. *Bull. Int. Fiscal Doc.,* April 1981, *35*(4), pp. 165–69. [G: Bahamas]

Davis, Robert R. Alternative Techniques for Country Risk Evaluation. *Bus. Econ.,* May 1981, *16*(3), pp. 34–41.

Degefe, Befekadu. Ethiopia. In *Adedeji, A., ed.,* 1981, pp. 238–77. [G: Ethiopia]

Devlin, Robert. Transnational Banks, External Debt and Peru: Results of a Recent Study. *Cepal Rev.,* August 1981, (14), pp. 153–84. [G: Peru]

Dufey, Gunter. International Capital Markets: Structure and Response in an Era of Instability. *Sloan Manage. Rev.,* Spring 1981, *22*(3), pp. 35–45.

Dunning, John H. A Note on Intra-Industry Foreign Direct Investment. *Banca Naz. Lavoro Quart. Rev.,* December 1981, (139), pp. 427–37.

Dunning, John H. Explaining the International Di-

rect Investment Position of Countries: Towards a Dynamic or Developmental Approach. *Welt-wirtsch. Arch.*, 1981, *117*(1), pp. 30–64.
[G: Selected Countries]

Dunning, John H. Explaining the International Direct Investment Position of Countries: Towards a Dynamic or Developmental Approach. In *Dunning, J. H.*, 1981, *1981*, pp. 109–41.

Dunning, John H. Explaining Changing Patterns of International Production: In Support of the Eclectic Theory. In *Dunning, J. H.*, 1981, *1980*, pp. 72–108. [G: OECD]

Dunning, John H. Multinational Enterprises and Domestic Capital Formation. In *Dunning, J. H.*, 1981, pp. 221–48. [G: U.S.]

Dunning, John H. The Consequences of International Transfer of Technology by MNEs: Some Home Country Implications. In *Dunning, J. H.*, 1981, pp. 321–53. [G: Selected LDCs]

Dunning, John H. The UK's International Direct Investment Position in the Mid-1970s. In *Dunning, J. H.*, 1981, pp. 142–75. [G: U.K.]

Edelstein, M. Foreign Investment and Empire 1860–1914. In *Floud, R. and McCloskey, D., eds., Vol. 2*, 1981, pp. 70–98. [G: U.K.]

Ehrlich, Edna E. International Diversification by United States Pension Funds. *Fed. Res. Bank New York Quart. Rev.*, Autumn 1981, *6*(3), pp. 1–14. [G: U.S.]

Eraydin, Ayda. Foreign Investment, International Labour Migration and the Turkish Economy. In *Hamilton, F. E. I. and Linge, G. J. R., eds.*, 1981, pp. 225–64. [G: Turkey]

Ezeife, Emeka. Nigeria. In *Adedeji, A., ed.*, 1981, pp. 164–86. [G: Nigeria]

Green, Reginald Herbold. Foreign Direct Investment and African Political Economy. In *Adedeji, A., ed.*, 1981, pp. 331–52. [G: Africa]

Gulcz, Mieczyslaw and Gruchman, Bohdan. Industrial Investment Assistance: The Socialist Countries' Approach to the Third World. In *Hamilton, F. E. I. and Linge, G. J. R., eds.*, 1981, pp. 215–23. [G: CMEA; LDCs]

Guy, James R. F. and Vaughan, Closson L. International Portfolio Diversification and Foreign Capital Markets. In *Altman, E. I., ed.*, 1981, pp. 15.3–27. [G: Japan; U.K.; W. Germany; France]

Hanselmann, Guido. Petrodollars and the Banks. In *Burghardt, A. M., ed.*, 1981, pp. 23–36. [G: LDCs; OECD; OPEC]

Hara, Masayuki. Foreign Direct Investment and Japan. (In Japanese. With English summary.) *Osaka Econ. Pap.*, March 1981, *30*(4), pp. 1–15. [G: Japan]

Hood, Neil; Reeves, Alan and Young, Stephen. Foreign Direct Investment in Scotland: The European Dimension. *Scot. J. Polit. Econ.*, June 1981, *28*(2), pp. 165–85. [G: U.K.]

Jenkins, Glenn P.; Misir, Devendranauth and Glenday, Graham. The Taxation of Foreign Investment Income in Canada, the United States and Mexico. *Law Contemp. Probl.*, Summer 1981, *44*(3), pp. 143–59. [G: Canada; U.S.; Mexico]

Jo, Sung-Hwan. Overseas Direct Investment by South Korean Firms: Direction and Pattern. In *Kumar, K. and McLeod, M. G., eds.*, 1981,

pp. 53–77. [G: S. Korea]

Kindleberger, Charles P. Capital Movements and International Payments Adjustment. In *Kindleberger, C. P.*, 1981, *1966*, pp. 209–24.
[G: Europe; U.S.]

Kindleberger, Charles P. Less Developed Countries and the International Capital Market. In *Kindleberger, C. P.*, 1981, *1970*, pp. 243–55.
[G: LDCs]

Kreicher, Lawrence L. International Portfolio Capital Flows and Real Rates of Interest. *Rev. Econ. Statist.*, February 1981, *63*(1), pp. 20–28.
[G: U.K.; W. Germany; Italy; U.S.]

Lagos, Gustavo. The Revolution of Being: A Preferred World Model. In *Muñoz, H., ed.*, 1981, pp. 123–60. [G: Latin America]

Lamfalussy, Alexandre. Changing Attitudes towards Capital Movements. In *[Cairncross, A.]*, 1981, pp. 194–217.

Landau, Zbigniew and Tomaszewski, Jerzy. The International Movement of Capital in Central and South-Eastern Europe before the Second World War. In *[Lipiński, E.]*, 1981, pp. 19–37.
[G: S.E. Europe]

Liao, Xunzhen. Readjustment in China's Foreign Trade. *Rivista Int. Sci. Econ. Com.*, September 1981, *28*(9), pp. 823–30. [G: China]

Little, Jane Sneddon. The Financial Health of U.S. Manufacturing Firms Acquired by Foreigners. *New Eng. Econ. Rev.*, July/August 1981, pp. 5–18. [G: U.S.]

Lowe, Jeffrey H. Capital Expenditures by Majority-Owned Foreign Affiliates of U.S. Companies, 1981. *Surv. Curr. Bus.*, March 1981, *61*(3), pp. 34–39. [G: U.S.]

de Macedo, Jorge Braga. International Investment, Migration and Finance: Issues and Policies: Comment. *Economia (Portugal)*, January 1981, *5*(1), pp. 111–15.

McBain, Helen. The Political Economy of Capital Flows: The Case of Jamaica. *Soc. Econ. Stud.*, December 1981, *30*(4), pp. 75–110.
[G: Jamaica]

McNamara, Robert S. To the Board of Governors, Washington, D.C., September 25, 1978. In *McNamara, R. S.*, 1981, *1978*, pp. 479–518.
[G: OECD; LDCs]

Molitor, Bernhard. International Investment, Migration and Finance: Issues and Policies: Comment. *Economia (Portugal)*, January 1981, *5*(1), pp. 105–10.

Muñoz, Heraldo. The Strategic Dependency of the Centers and the Economic Importance of the Latin American Periphery. In *Muñoz, H., ed.*, 1981, pp. 59–92. [G: U.S.; Latin America]

Neersø, Peter. Peru, Andes-pagten og de transnationale selskaber. (Peru, the Andean Pact and the Transnationals. With English summary.) *Nationaløkon. Tidsskr.*, 1981, *119*(1), pp. 64–77.
[G: Peru]

Okumura, Ariyoshi. Policy Responses in the Old Industrial Countries: Japan and East Asia. In *Saunders, C. T., ed. (II)*, 1981, pp. 261–83.
[G: Japan; E. Asia]

Paine, Suzanne. International Investment, Migration and Finance: Issues and Policies. *Economia*

(Portugal), January 1981, 5(1), pp. 63–104.

Paszynski, Marian. Transnational Companies and Direct Private Investment in Developing Countries: Comment. In *Saunders, C. T., ed. (I)*, 1981, pp. 174–75. **[G: LDCs]**

Safarian, A. E. The Financing of Trade and Development in the ADCs: The Experience of Singapore: Comment. In *Hong, W. and Krause, L. B., eds.*, 1981, pp. 145–47. **[G: Singapore]**

Sahlgren, Klaus A. Trends and Features of Foreign Direct Investment. *Ifo-Studien*, 1981, 27(2/3), pp. 133–41.

Scholl, Russell B. The International Investment Position of the United States: Developments in 1980. *Surv. Curr. Bus.*, August 1981, 61(8), pp. 52–57.

Siegman, Charles J. Developing Countries and the International Financial System: A Survey of Trends and Selected Issues. In *Reubens, E. P., ed.*, 1981, pp. 179–213. **[G: LDCs]**

Stockmayer, Albrecht. Financing Mining Projects in Developing Countries. In *Schanze, E., et al.*, 1981, pp. 171–97.

Svedberg, Peter. Colonial Enforcement of Foreign Direct Investment. *Manchester Sch. Econ. Soc. Stud.*, March 1981, 49(1), pp. 21–38.

Taylor, Michael and Thrift, Nigel. British Capital Overseas: Direct Investment and Corporate Development in Australia. *Reg. Stud.*, 1981, 15(3), pp. 183–212. **[G: U.K.; Australia]**

Vaitsos, Constantine V. From a Colonial Past to Asymmetrical Interdependences: The Role of Europe in North–South Relations. In *Mauri, A., ed.*, 1981, pp. 35–81. **[G: W. Europe; LDCs]**

Watson, John and Dickinson, John P. International Diversification: An Ex Post and Ex Ante Analysis of Possible Benefits. *Australian J. Manage.*, June 1981, 6(1), pp. 125–34. **[G: Australia]**

Weinert, Richard S. Foreign Capital in Mexico. In *Purcell, S. K., ed.*, 1981, pp. 115–24. **[G: Mexico]**

Whichard, Obie G. Trends in the U.S. Direct Investment Position Abroad, 1950–79. *Surv. Curr. Bus.*, February 1981, 61(2), pp. 39–56. **[G: U.S.]**

Whichard, Obie G. U.S. Direct Investment Abroad in 1980. *Surv. Curr. Bus.*, August 1981, 61(8), pp. 20–39. **[G: U.S.]**

White, Eduardo. The International Projection of Firms from Latin American Countries. In *Kumar, K. and McLeod, M. G., eds.*, 1981, pp. 155–86. **[G: Latin America]**

Wong, Kum Poh. The Financing of Trade and Development in the ADCs: The Experience of Singapore. In *Hong, W. and Krause, L. B., eds.*, 1981, pp. 129–44. **[G: Singapore]**

442 International Business and Multinational Enterprises

4420 International Business and Multinational Enterprises

Adedeji, Adebayo. Historical and Theoretical Background. In *Adedeji, A., ed.*, 1981, pp. 29–41. **[G: Africa]**

Adedeji, Adebayo. Indigenization of African Economies: Introduction to the Case Studies. In *Adedeji, A., ed.*, 1981, pp. 45–48. **[G: Africa]**

Adler, Michael. Investor Recognition of Corporation International Diversification: Comment. *J. Finance*, March 1981, 36(1), pp. 187–90.

Agmon, Tamir and Lessard, Donald R. Investor Recognition of Corporate International Diversification: Reply. *J. Finance*, March 1981, 36(1), pp. 191–92.

Agrawal, Ram Gopal. Third-World Joint Ventures: Indian Experience. In *Kumar, K. and McLeod, M. G., eds.*, 1981, pp. 115–31. **[G: India; LDCs]**

Ajami, Riad A. and Ricks, David A. Motives of Non-American Firms Investing in the United States. *J. Int. Bus. Stud.*, Winter 1981, 12(3), pp. 25–34. **[G: U.S.; W. Europe; Japan; Canada]**

Ake, Claude. Kenya. In *Adedeji, A., ed.*, 1981, pp. 187–203. **[G: Kenya]**

Alam, Ghayur and Langrish, John. Non-Multinational Firms and Transfer of Technology to Less Developed Countries. *World Devel.*, April 1981, 9(4), pp. 383–87. **[G: India]**

Alessandroni, Alessandro. L'intermediazione bancaria internazionale: evoluzione del passato e prospettive attuali. (International Banking Intermediation: Retrospect and Current Prospects. With English summary.) *Bancaria*, February 1981, 37(2), pp. 132–39.

Alpert, Herbert H. and Feingold, Fred. U.S.A.: Foreign Investment in Real Property Tax Act of 1980. *Bull. Int. Fiscal Doc.*, May 1981, 35(5), pp. 195–98. **[G: U.S.]**

Andel, Norbert. Corporation Taxes, Their Integration with Personal Income Taxes, and International Capital Flows. In *Roskamp, K. W. and Forte, F., eds.*, 1981, pp. 159–72. **[G: W. Europe]**

Anusz, Jan. Technology Transfer by Means of Industrial Cooperation: A Theoretical Appraisal: Comment. In *Marer, P. and Tabaczynski, E., eds.*, 1981, pp. 224–26. **[G: Poland; U.S.]**

Arpan, Jeffrey S.; Flowers, Edward B. and Ricks, David A. Foreign Direct Investment in the United States: The State of Knowledge in Research. *J. Int. Bus. Stud.*, Spring/Summer 1981, 12(1), pp. 137–54.

Artemiev, Igor E. Alternative Channels and Modes of International Resource Transmission: Comment. In *Sagafi-nejad, T.; Moxon, R. W. and Perlmutter, H. V., eds.*, 1981, pp. 37–41.

Atkeson, Timothy. The Seeking of a World Competition Code: Quixotic Quest? Commentary. In *Schachter, O. and Hellawell, R., eds.*, 1981, pp. 416–21.

Aydin, Nizam and Terpstra, Vern. Marketing Know-How Transfers by Multinationals: A Case Study in Turkey. *J. Int. Bus. Stud.*, Winter 1981, 12(3), pp. 35–48. **[G: Turkey]**

Bagchi, Amiya Kumar and Dasgupta, Subhendu. Imported Technology and the Legal Process. In *Bagchi, A. K. and Banerjee, N., eds.*, 1981, pp. 393–416. **[G: India]**

Balažik, Milan. Joint Enterprises in the System of Organizations of the CMEA Countries. *Czech.*

Econ. Digest., August 1981, (5), pp. 63–77.
[G: CMEA]

Bardsley, R. Geoffrey. Management Procedures for Investing Surplus Cash. In *Ensor, R. and Muller, P., eds.*, 1981, pp. 217–18. [G: OECD]

Barker, Betty L. A Profile of U.S. Multinational Companies in 1977. *Surv. Curr. Bus.*, October 1981, *61*(10), pp. 38–57. [G: U.S.]

Bartels, Martin. Mining Ventures in Developing Countries: Localization of Labor. In *Schanze, E., et al.*, 1981, pp. 198–211. [G: Selected LDCs]

Bartlett, Christopher A. Multinational Structural Change: Evolution Versus Reorganization. In *Otterbeck, L., ed.*, 1981, pp. 121–45. [G: U.S.]

Basak, Aroon K. Tripartite Industrial Cooperation and Third Countries: Comment. In *Saunders, C. T., ed. (I)*, 1981, pp. 369–71. [G: CMEA; OECD; LDCs]

Bavishi, Vinod B. Capital Budgeting Practices at Multinationals. *Manage. Account.*, August 1981, *63*(2), pp. 32–35.

Behrman, Jack N. Transnational Corporations in the New International Economic Order. *J. Int. Bus. Stud.*, Spring/Summer 1981, *12*(1), pp. 29–42. [G: LDCs]

Belli, R. David. U.S. Business Enterprises Acquired or Established by Foreign Direct Investors in 1980. *Surv. Curr. Bus.*, August 1981, *61*(8), pp. 58–71.

Bergsten, C. Fred; Horst, Thomas and Moran, Theodore H. Home-Country Policy toward Multinationals. In *Baldwin, R. E. and Richardson, J. D., eds.*, 1981, 1978, pp. 267–95. [G: U.S.; OECD]

Berreby, Jean-Jacques. Opec: venti anni che hanno trasformato il mondo. (OPEC: 20 Years That Have Changed the World. With English summary.) *Mondo Aperto*, April 1981, *35*(2), pp. 89–97. [G: OPEC]

Berry, Maureen H. Why International Cost Accounting Practices Should be Harmonized. *Manage. Account.*, August 1981, *63*(2), pp. 36–42.

Bhandari, Dharmendra. Taxation of Non-Residents in India for Royalties and Fees for Technical Services. *Bull. Int. Fiscal Doc.*, June 1981, *35*(6), pp. 277–81. [G: India]

Bishara, Halim I. An Empirical Study of the Canadian Multinational Corporations and Canadian Conglomerate Firms with Regard to Performance Evaluation. *Nebr. J. Econ. Bus.*, Autumn 1981, *20*(4), pp. 33–50. [G: Canada]

Blachford, J. Technology Transfer through Licensing: The Experience of a Small Canadian-Owned Chemical Company. In *Science Council of Canada, Industrial Policies Committee*, 1981, pp. 123–30. [G: Canada]

Blake, David H. Headquarters and Subsidiary Roles in Managing International Public Affairs—A Preliminary Investigation. In *Otterbeck, L., ed.*, 1981, pp. 319–36. [G: U.S.]

Bloch, Gérard. Approche Pratique des Marchés Extérieurs D'une Entreprise de Biens D'Équipement Industriels. (With English summary.) In *Courbis, R., ed.*, 1981, pp. 93–102. [G: France]

Bloom, L. H. Analysis of Restrictive Business Practices by Transnational Corporations and Their Impact on Trade and Development: Commentary. In *Schachter, O. and Hellawell, R., eds.*, 1981, pp. 22–26.

Bloomfield, Gerald T. The Changing Spatial Organization of Multinational Corporations in the World Automotive Industry. In *Hamilton, F. E. I. and Linge, G. J. R., eds.*, 1981, pp. 357–94. [G: Global]

Bluma, Aleš. Sources d'information les clefs de la réussite. (Information Source—The Key to Success. With English summary.) *Ann. Sci. Écon. Appl.*, 1981, *37*(4), pp. 63–93.

Bookstaber, Richard M. Corporate Production and Sales Decisions in Achieving International Diversification. *Rev. Bus. Econ. Res.*, Winter 1981, *16*(2), pp. 68–75.

Borner, Silvio. Die Internationalisierung der Industrie. (With English summary.) *Kyklos*, 1981, *34*(1), pp. 14–35.

Borowski, Jerzy. Marketing Polish Industrial Goods in the United States: Comment. In *Marer, P. and Tabaczynski, E., eds.*, 1981, pp. 266–70. [G: Poland; U.S.]

Brada, Josef C. Problems of Polish–U.S. Economic Relations: Comment. In *Marer, P. and Tabaczynski, E., eds.*, 1981, pp. 117–19. [G: Poland; U.S.]

Brada, Josef C. Technology Transfer by Means of Industrial Cooperation: A Theoretical Appraisal. In *Marer, P. and Tabaczynski, E., eds.*, 1981, pp. 207–24. [G: Poland; U.S.]

Brada, Josef C. Technology Transfer by Means of Industrial Cooperation: A Theoretical Appraisal: Reply. In *Marer, P. and Tabaczynski, E., eds.*, 1981, pp. 226–27. [G: Poland; U.S.]

Brada, Josef C., et al. International Harvester–Bumar Cooperation. In *Marer, P. and Tabaczynski, E., eds.*, 1981, pp. 41–83. [G: Poland; U.S.]

Brada, Josef C., et al. Polish–U.S. Industrial Cooperation in the 1980s: Summary, Conclusions, Recommendations. In *Marer, P. and Tabaczynski, E., eds.*, 1981, pp. 1–39. [G: U.S.; Poland]

Bradley, Keith. International Perspectives of Industrial Relations: Review Article. *Brit. J. Ind. Relat.*, March 1981, *19*(1), pp. 106–11.

Brewer, H. L. Investor Benefits from Corporate International Diversification. *J. Finan. Quant. Anal.*, March 1981, *16*(1), pp. 113–26. [G: U.S.]

Britton, J. N. Industrial Patterns in Early and Late Adoption of New Products in Canada: Commentary. In *Science Council of Canada, Industrial Policies Committee*, 1981, pp. 55–59. [G: Canada]

Brooke, Michael Z. and Holly, Joseph. International Management Contracts. In *Otterbeck, L., ed.*, 1981, pp. 297–317. [G: U.K.]

Brown, Shannon R. Technology Transfer and Economic Systems: The Case of China in the Nineteenth Century. *ACES Bull. (See Comp. Econ. Stud. after 8/85)*, Spring 1981, *23*(1), pp. 79–88. [G: China]

Buckley, Peter J. A Critical Review of Theories of the Multinational Enterprise. *Aussenwirtschaft*, March 1981, *36*(1), pp. 70–87.

Buckley, Peter J. and Davies, Howard. Foreign Licensing in Overseas Operations: Theory and Evidence from the U.K. In *Hawkins, R. G. and Prasad, A. J., eds.*, 1981, pp. 75–89. [G: U.K.]

Buckley, Peter J. and Pearce, Robert D. Market Servicing by Multinational Manufacturing Firms: Exporting versus Foreign Production. *Managerial Dec. Econ.*, December 1981, 2(4), pp. 229–46. [G: Selected Countries]

Bueno, G. M. A New Order in Financial and Technological Relations with the Third World? *Tijdschrift Econ. Manage.*, 1981, 26(1), pp. 95–116.

Calcagno, Alfredo Eric and Jakobowicz, Jean-Michel. Some Aspects of the International Distribution of Industrial Activity. *Cepal Rev.*, April 1981, (13), pp. 7–33. [G: LDCs; MDCs]

Calcagno, Alfredo Eric and Kñakal, Jan. Transnational Companies and Direct Private Investment in Developing Countries. In *Saunders, C. T., ed. (I)*, 1981, pp. 103–26. [G: LDCs; U.S.]

Calvet, A. L. A Synthesis of Foreign Direct Investment Theories and Theories of the Multinational Firm. *J. Int. Bus. Stud.*, Spring/Summer 1981, 12(1), pp. 43–59.

Campbell, Robert W. Technology Transfer in U.S.–Polish Industrial Cooperation: Comment. In *Marer, P. and Tabaczynski, E., eds.*, 1981, pp. 154–57. [G: Poland; U.S.]

Carman, J. K. Technology Transfer within a Multinational: The Case of Westinghouse Canada Ltd. In *Science Council of Canada, Industrial Policies Committee*, 1981, pp. 111–22. [G: Canada]

Cavalcanti, Leonardo; Geiger, Pedro P. and de Andrade, Thompson. Multinationals, the New International Economic Order and the Spatial Industrial Structure of Brazil. In *Hamilton, F. E. I. and Linge, G. J. R., eds.*, 1981, pp. 423–38. [G: Brazil]

Caves, Richard E. Competitive Processes in the Open Economy: Evidence and Policy. In *[von Haberler, G.]*, 1981, pp. 71–84.

Chen, Edward K. Y. Hong Kong Multinationals in Asia: Characteristics and Objectives. In *Kumar, K. and McLeod, M. G., eds.*, 1981, pp. 79–99. [G: Hong Kong; East Asia]

Chia, Siow Yue. Foreign Direct Investment in Manufacturing in Developing Countries: The Case of Singapore. In *Hamilton, F. E. I. and Linge, G. J. R., eds.*, 1981, pp. 439–64. [G: Singapore]

Chudnovsky, Daniel. Pricing of Intra-firm Technological Transactions. In *Murray, R., ed.*, 1981, pp. 119–32. [G: U.S.; Argentina; Selected Countries]

Chudson, Walter A. Intra-firm Trade and Transfer Pricing. In *Murray, R., ed.*, 1981, pp. 17–30. [G: U.K.]

Chung, William K. and Fouch, Gregory G. Foreign Direct Investment in the United States in 1980. *Surv. Curr. Bus.*, August 1981, 61(8), pp. 40–51. [G: U.S.]

Clairmonte, Frederick F. World Tobacco: A Portrait of Corporate Power. In *Finger, W. R., ed.*, 1981, pp. 203–19. [G: U.S.; U.K.]

Cobbe, James. Enclave Development of Minerals: An Argument and an Illustration. *J. Econ. Devel.*, December 1981, 6(2), pp. 93–112. [G: Botswana]

Coburn, David L.; Ellis, Joseph K., III and Milano, Duane R. Dilemmas in MNC Transfer Pricing. *Manage. Account.*, November 1981, 63(5), pp. 53–58, 69. [G: U.S.]

Cohen, Robert B. Brave New World of the Global Car. *Challenge*, May/June 1981, 24(2), pp. 28–35.

Cohen, Robert B. The New International Division of Labor, Multinational Corporations and Urban Hierarchy. In *Dear, M. and Scott, A. J., eds.*, 1981, pp. 287–315. [G: U.S.]

Cohen, Robert B. and Frieden, Jeffry. The Impact of Multinational Corporations on Developing Nations. In *Reubens, E. P., ed.*, 1981, pp. 147–77. [G: Selected LDCs]

da Conceição Tavares, María and Teixeira, Aloisia. Transnational Enterprises and the Internationalization of Capital in Brazilian Industry. *Cepal Rev.*, August 1981, (14), pp. 85–105. [G: Brazil]

Connor, John M. Foreign Food Firms: Their Participation in and Competitive Impact on the US Food and Tobacco Manufacturing Sector. In *Johnson, G. and Maunder, A., eds.*, 1981, pp. 552–67. [G: U.S.]

Constas, Kimon J. and Vichas, Robert P. Patterns and Performance of Multinational and Domestic Food Wholesale Firms. *Managerial Dec. Econ.*, March 1981, 2(1), pp. 25–31. [G: Puerto Rico]

Contractor, Farok J. and Sagafi-Nejad, Tagi. International Technology Transfer: Major Issues and Policy Responses. *J. Int. Bus. Stud.*, Fall 1981, 12(2), pp. 113–35.

Cooper, Charles. Aspects of Transfer Pricing in Machinery Markets. In *Murray, R., ed.*, 1981, pp. 133–44.

Coussement, André M. Developments in Financing Institutions, Instruments and Banking. In *Ensor, R. and Muller, P., eds.*, 1981, pp. 25–30.

Cracco, Etienne. Un processus de selection de marchés: la méthode de l'entonnoir. (A Market Selection Process: The "Funnel" Method. With English summary.) *Ann. Sci. Écon. Appl.*, 1981, 37(4), pp. 45–62.

Cromarty, William A. Challenges for Agricultural Economists Working for Multi-national Firms. In *Johnson, G. and Maunder, A., eds.*, 1981, pp. 509–17.

Davidow, Joel. The Seeking of a World Competition Code: Quixotic Quest? In *Schachter, O. and Hellawell, R., eds.*, 1981, pp. 361–415.

Davidson, William H. Trends in the Transfer of U.S. Technology to Canada: Commentary. In *Science Council of Canada, Industrial Policies Committee*, 1981, pp. 25–38. [G: U.S.; Canada; Selected Countries]

Davidson, William H. Trends in the Transfer of U.S. Technology to Canada. In *Science Council of Canada, Industrial Policies Committee*, 1981, pp. 9–24. [G: U.S.; Canada; Selected Countries]

Davies, Warnock. SMR Forum: Unsticking the State of the Art of Political Risk Management. *Sloan Manage. Rev.*, Summer 1981, 22(4), pp. 59–63.

Davis, Robert R. Alternative Techniques for Country Risk Evaluation. *Bus. Econ.*, May 1981, *16*(3), pp. 34–41.

De Smet, Monique. Recommendations pour l'efficacité d'une étude de marché à l'étranger. (How to Achieve Efficiency in Conducting Market Research Abroad? With English summary.) *Ann. Sci. Écon. Appl.*, 1981, *37*(4), pp. 113–26.

Dean, James W. and Giddy, Ian H. Strangers and Neighbors: Cross-Border Banking in North America. *Banca Naz. Lavoro Quart. Rev.*, June 1981, (137), pp. 191–211.

DeBresson, Chris. Industrial Patterns in Early and Late Adoption of New Products in Canada. In *Science Council of Canada, Industrial Policies Committee*, 1981, pp. 41–50.   [G: Canada]

Degefe, Befekadu. Ethiopia. In *Adedeji, A., ed.*, 1981, pp. 238–77.   [G: Ethiopia]

Demelto, Dennis. Technology Acquisition: Licence Agreement or Joint Venture: Commentary. In *Science Council of Canada, Industrial Policies Committee*, 1981, pp. 97–103.   [G: U.S.; Canada; Sweden]

Díaz-Alejandro, Carlos F. The Less-Developed Countries and Transnational Enterprises. In *Grassman, S. and Lundberg, E., eds.*, 1981, pp. 233–56.

Doz, Yves L.; Bartlett, Christopher A. and Prahalad, C. K. Global Competitive Pressures and Host Country Demands: Managing Tensions in MNCs. *Calif. Manage. Rev.*, Spring 1981, *23*(3), pp. 63–74.

Doz, Yves L. and Prahalad, C. K. Headquarters Influence and Strategic Control in MNCs. *Sloan Manage. Rev.*, Fall 1981, *23*(1), pp. 15–29.

Driscoll, Robert E. and Wallender, Harvey W., III. Control and Incentives for Technology Transfer: A Multinational Perspective. In *Sagafi-nejad, T.; Moxon, R. W. and Perlmutter, H. V., eds.*, 1981, pp. 273–86.

Dunning, John H. Alternative Channels and Modes of International Resource Transmission. In *Sagafi-nejad, T.; Moxon, R. W. and Perlmutter, H. V., eds.*, 1981, pp. 3–26.

Dunning, John H. Employee Compensation in US Multinationals and Indigenous Firms: An Exploratory Micro/Macro Analysis. In *Dunning, J. H.*, 1981, pp. 272–303.

Dunning, John H. Evaluating the Costs and Benefits of Multinational Enterprises to Host Countries: A 'Tool-Kit' Approach. In *Dunning, J. H.*, 1981, pp. 357–84.   [G: U.S.; U.K.; LDCs]

Dunning, John H. Explaining the International Direct Investment Position of Countries: Towards a Dynamic or Developmental Approach. *Weltwirtsch. Arch.*, 1981, *117*(1), pp. 30–64.   [G: Selected Countries]

Dunning, John H. Explaining Changing Patterns of International Production: In Support of the Eclectic Theory. In *Dunning, J. H.*, 1981, *1980*, pp. 72–108.   [G: OECD]

Dunning, John H. Multinational Enterprises and Domestic Capital Formation. In *Dunning, J. H.*, 1981, pp. 221–48.   [G: U.S.]

Dunning, John H. Multinational Enterprises and the Challenge of the 1980s. In *Dunning, J. H.*, 1981, pp. 409–25.

Dunning, John H. Multinational Enterprises, Locational Strategies and Regional Development. In *Dunning, J. H.*, 1981, pp. 249–71.   [G: U.K.; Belgium]

Dunning, John H. Multinational Enterprises, Market Structure, Economic Power and Industrial Policy. In *Dunning, J. H.*, 1981, pp. 179–220.   [G: U.S.; U.K.]

Dunning, John H. Multinational Enterprises and Trade Flows of Developing Countries. In *Dunning, J. H.*, 1981, pp. 304–20.

Dunning, John H. Technology Exports and Technology Transfer Controls. In *Sagafi-nejad, T.; Moxon, R. W. and Perlmutter, H. V., eds.*, 1981, pp. 331–61.   [G: LDCs; MDCs]

Dunning, John H. The Consequences of International Transfer of Technology by MNEs: Some Home Country Implications. In *Dunning, J. H.*, 1981, pp. 321–53.   [G: Selected LDCs]

Dunning, John H. The Distinctive Nature of the Multinational Enterprise. In *Dunning, J. H.*, 1981, pp. 1–20.

Dunning, John H. Trade, Location of Economic Activity and the Multinational Enterprise: A Search for an Eclectic Approach. In *Dunning, J. H.*, 1981, pp. 21–45.

Dunning, John H. Trade, Location of Economic Activity and the Multinational Enterprise: Some Empirical Tests. In *Dunning, J. H.*, 1981, pp. 46–71.   [G: Selected countries]

Dunning, John H. and Gilman, M. Alternative Policy Prescriptions and the Multinational Enterprise. In *Dunning, J. H.*, 1981, *1976*, pp. 385–408.

Dunning, John H. and McQueen, Matthew. The Eclectic Theory of International Production: A Case Study of the International Hotel Industry. *Managerial Dec. Econ.*, December 1981, *2*(4), pp. 197–210.   [G: Selected Countries]

Ellis, Frank. Export Valuation and Intra-firm Transfers in the Banana Export Industry in Central America. In *Murray, R., ed.*, 1981, pp. 61–76.   [G: Costa Rica; Honduras; Guatemala; Panama]

Eralp, Atilâ. Türkiye'de Izlenen Ithal Ikameci Kalkinma Stratejisi ve Yabanci Sermaye. (Import Substitution Strategy and Foreign Capital in Turkey. With English summary.) *METU*, Special Issue, 1981, pp. 613–33.   [G: Turkey]

Eraydin, Ayda. Foreign Investment, International Labour Migration and the Turkish Economy. In *Hamilton, F. E. I. and Linge, G. J. R., eds.*, 1981, pp. 225–64.   [G: Turkey]

Errunza, Vihang R. and Senbet, Lemma W. The Effects of International Operations on the Market Value of the Firm: Theory and Evidence. *J. Finance*, May 1981, *36*(2), pp. 401–17.   [G: U.S.]

Eschbach, Eugene. Technology Exports and Technology Transfer Controls: Comment. In *Sagafi-nejad, T.; Moxon, R. W. and Perlmutter, H. V., eds.*, 1981, pp. 362–72.   [G: MDCs]

Evans, Peter. Collectivized Capitalism: Integrated Petrochemical Complexes and Capital Accumulation in Brazil. In *Bruneau, T. C. and Faucher, P., eds.*, 1981, pp. 85–125.   [G: Brazil]

Ezeife, Emeka. Nigeria. In *Adedeji, A., ed.*, 1981,

pp. 164–86. [G: Nigeria]

Feder, Gershon; Just, Richard E. and Ross, Knud. Projecting Debt Servicing Capacity of Developing Countries. *J. Finan. Quant. Anal.*, December 1981, *16*(5), pp. 651–69.

Fieldhouse, D. K. Decolonisation and the Multinational Company: Unilever in India, 1917–65. In *Bairoch, P. and Lévy-Leboyer, M., eds.*, 1981, pp. 58–64. [G: India]

Fitzpatrick, Peter. Two Legal Models in the Control of Transfer Pricing. In *Murray, R., ed.*, 1981, pp. 197–206.

Fodella, Gianni. Economic Relations between China and Japan: Problems and Prospects. *Rivista Int. Sci. Econ. Com.*, September 1981, *28*(9), pp. 889–99. [G: China; Japan]

Fonteyne, Françoise and Sauboin, Michel. Orientations pour réussir l'expatriation du personnel. (Guidelines for Successful Personnel Expatriation. With English summary.) *Ann. Sci. Écon. Appl.*, 1981, *37*(4), pp. 143–66.

Fritzsche, Michael. Mining Ventures in Developing Countries: Fiscal Regime. In *Schanze, E., et al.*, 1981, pp. 108–44.

Gammaldi, Domenico and Lanciotti, Giulio. Misure alternative dell' "attività internazionale" del sistema bancario italiano 1975–1979. (Alternative Measures for the International Activity of the Italian Banking System, 1975–1979. With English summary.) *Bancaria*, February 1981, *37*(2), pp. 146–51. [G: Italy]

Ganiatsos, Tom. The Control of Transfer Pricing in Greece: A Progress Report. In *Murray, R., ed.*, 1981, pp. 286–303. [G: Greece]

Garland, John. Organizational Constraints on Industrial Cooperation. In *Marer, P. and Tabaczynski, E., eds.*, 1981, pp. 298–311. [G: Poland]

Garland, John. Organizational Constraints on Industrial Cooperation: Reply. In *Marer, P. and Tabaczynski, E., eds.*, 1981, pp. 316–17. [G: Poland]

Garland, John. The International Harvester–BUMAR Cooperation Experience: Practical Problems and their Solutions: Comment. In *Marer, P. and Tabaczynski, E., eds.*, 1981, pp. 171–74. [G: Poland; U.S.]

Gèze, François. Le redéploiement international des grands groupes industriels français et ses conséquences sur l'emploi en France. (International Redeployment of Major French Industrial Companies and Its Impact on Employment in France. With English summary.) *Rev. Econ. Ind.*, 1st Trimester 1981, (15), pp. 1–18. [G: France]

Giddy, Ian H. The Cost of Capital in the International Firm. *Managerial Dec. Econ.*, December 1981, *2*(4), pp. 263–71.

Gilburn, David A. and White, Roger. Tax Planning. In *Ensor, R. and Muller, P., eds.*, 1981, pp. 63–76. [G: OECD]

Glass, Walter. Restrictive Business Practices Affecting Transfer of Technology: Commentary. In *Schachter, O. and Hellawell, R., eds.*, 1981, pp. 139–42. [G: U.S.; Japan]

Gmür, Charles J. Trade Financing: Leasing. In *Gmür, C. J., ed.*, 1981, pp. 105–16. [G: W. Europe]

Godano, Giuseppe. L'evoluzione della normativa sulle banche estere negli Stati Uniti. (Evolution of Regulations of Foreign Banks in the United States. With English summary.) *Bancaria*, July 1981, *37*(7), pp. 716–25. [G: U.S.]

Goldberg, Ray. The Role of the Multinational Corporation. *Amer. J. Agr. Econ.*, May 1981, *63*(2), pp. 367–74.

Goldsbrough, David J. International Trade of Multinational Corporations and Its Responsiveness to Changes in Aggregate Demand and Relative Prices. *Int. Monet. Fund Staff Pap.*, September 1981, *28*(3), pp. 573–99. [G: U.S.]

Goodman, Stephen H. Corporate Attitudes. In *Ensor, R., ed.*, 1981, pp. 111–15.

Goss, Richard T. An Introduction: Risk Definition, Strategy and Techniques. In *Ensor, R. and Muller, P., eds.*, 1981, pp. 79–88.

Goudswaard, J. M. How to Become a "Profound Person." *Ifo-Studien*, 1981, *27*(2/3), pp. 121–32.

Goulet, Denis. Technology-Importing National Perspectives: Comment. In *Sagafi-nejad, T.; Moxon, R. W. and Perlmutter, H. V., eds.*, 1981, pp. 321–25. [G: LDCs]

Graham, Edward M. International Technology Transfer: Issues and Policy Options: Comment. In *Streeten, P. and Jolly, R, eds.*, 1981, pp. 111–14. [G: Selected LDCs]

Gray, S. J.; Shaw, J. C. and McSweeney, L. B. Accounting Standards and Multinational Corporations. *J. Int. Bus. Stud.*, Spring/Summer 1981, *12*(1), pp. 121–36.

von Grebmer, K. International Pharmaceutical Supply Prices: Definitions–Problems–Policy Implications. *Managerial Dec. Econ.*, June 1981, *2*(2), pp. 74–81. [G: OECD]

Green, Charles. La banca degli anni novanta. (The Bank in Its Nineties. With English summary.) *Mondo Aperto*, February 1981, *35*(1), pp. 11–23. [G: U.K.]

Green, Reginald Herbold. Foreign Direct Investment and African Political Economy. In *Adedeji, A., ed.*, 1981, pp. 331–52. [G: Africa]

Green, Reginald Herbold. Transfer Pricing, Its Relatives and Their Control in Developing Countries: Notes toward an Operational Definition and Approach. In *Murray, R., ed.*, 1981, pp. 221–44.

Green, Stephen; Mack, Christopher and Turner, William D. The Role of the Treasury Function. In *Ensor, R. and Muller, P., eds.*, 1981, pp. 1–12.

Greenhill, C. R. and Herbolzheimer, E. O. Control of Transfer Prices in International Transactions: The Restrictive Business Practices Approach. In *Murray, R., ed.*, 1981, pp. 185–94. [G: LDCs; MDCs]

Greer, Charles R. and Shearer, John C. Do Foreign-Owned U.S. Firms Practice Unconventional Labor Relations? *Mon. Lab. Rev.*, January 1981, *104*(1), pp. 44–48. [G: U.S.]

Greer, Charles R. and Shearer, John C. Foreign Ownership Effects on NLRB Representation Elections. *J. Int. Bus. Stud.*, Winter 1981, *12*(3), pp. 9–23. [G: U.S.]

Greer, Douglas F. Control of Terms and Conditions for International Transfers of Technology to Developing Countries. In *Schachter, O. and Hella-*

well, R., eds., 1981, pp. 41–83.   [G: U.S.; Japan]

Guertin, Donald L. The Pricing of International Technology Transfers via Nonaffiliate Licensing Arrangements: Comment. In *Sagafi-nejad, T.; Moxon, R. W. and Perlmutter, H. V., eds.*, 1981, pp. 134–36.   [G: U.S.]

Gutman, Patrick. Tripartite Industrial Cooperation and Third Countries. In *Saunders, C. T., ed. (1)*, 1981, pp. 337–64.   [G: CMEA; OECD; LDCs]

Gutman, Patrick and Arkwright, Francis. Tripartite Industrial Cooperation between East, West, and South. In *Hamilton, F. E. I. and Linge, G. J. R., eds.*, 1981, pp. 185–214.   [G: France; OECD; CMEA; LDCs]

Hadley, Eleanor G. Japan's Export Competitiveness in Third World Markets. In *Center for Strategic and Internat. Studies, ed. (1)*, 1981, pp. 254–330.   [G: Japan; MDCs; LDCs]

Hanafi, Mohammed N. Egypt. In *Adedeji, A., ed.*, 1981, pp. 49–80.   [G: Egypt]

Handlin, Oscar. The Taxonomy of the Corporation. In *Novak, M. and Cooper, J. W., eds.*, 1981, pp. 17–26.   [G: U.S.]

Hara, Masayuki. Foreign Direct Investment and Japan. (In Japanese. With English summary.) *Osaka Econ. Pap.*, March 1981, *30*(4), pp. 1–15.   [G: Japan]

Harris, Edwin C. Recent Canadian Income Tax Amendments: International Aspects. *Bull. Int. Fiscal Doc.*, August–September 1981, *35*(8–9), pp. 368–71.   [G: Canada]

Haseltine, John B. A Longer-term Approach. In *Ensor, R. and Muller, P., eds.*, 1981, pp. 139–42.   [G: U.S.]

Hauser, Wolfgang. International Deep Seabed Mining: Institutional and Fiscal Framework. In *Schanze, E., et al.*, 1981, pp. 145–70.

Hawkins, R. G. International Finance: Discussion. *J. Finance*, May 1981, *36*(2), pp. 442–44.

Hawkins, Robert G. Control and Incentives for Technology Transfer: A Multinational Perspective: Comment. In *Sagafi-nejad, T.; Moxon, R. W. and Perlmutter, H. V., eds.*, 1981, pp. 287–90.

Hawkins, Robert G. and Walter, Ingo. Planning Multinational Operations. In *Nystrom, P. C. and Starbuck, W. H., eds., Vol. 1*, 1981, pp. 253–67.

Hedlund, Gunnar. Autonomy of Subsidiaries and Formalization of Headquarters-Subsidiary Relationships in Swedish MNCs. In *Otterbeck, L., ed.*, 1981, pp. 25–78.   [G: Sweden]

Helleiner, G. K. Intra-firm Trade and the Developing Countries: An Assessment of the Data. In *Murray, R., ed.*, 1981, pp. 31–57.   [G: U.S.; Global]

Helleiner, G. K. The International Economics of the Information Industry and the Developing Countries. In *Murray, R., ed.*, 1981, pp. 207–20.

Helleiner, Gerald K. Analysis of Restrictive Business Practices by Transnational Corporations and Their Impact on Trade and Development: Commentary. In *Schachter, O. and Hellawell, R., eds.*, 1981, pp. 27–33.

Hirschey, Robert C. and Caves, Richard E. Re-search and Transfer of Technology by Multinational Enterprises. *Oxford Bull. Econ. Statist.*, May 1981, *43*(2), pp. 115–30.   [G: U.S.]

Hirschman, Albert O. On Hegel, Imperialism, and Structural Stagnation. In *Hirschman, A. O., 1981, 1976*, pp. 167–76.

Holton, Richard H. Making International Joint Ventures Work. In *Otterbeck, L., ed.*, 1981, pp. 255–67.

Hood, Neil; Reeves, Alan and Young, Stephen. Foreign Direct Investment in Scotland: The European Dimension. *Scot. J. Polit. Econ.*, June 1981, *28*(2), pp. 165–85.   [G: U.K.]

Hood, Neil and Young, Stephen. British Policy and Inward Direct Investment. *J. World Trade Law*, May–June 1981, *15*(3), pp. 231–50.   [G: U.K.]

Houpt, James V. Performance and Characteristics of Edge Corporations. *Fed. Res. Bull.*, January 1981, *67*(1), pp. 13–14.   [G: U.S.]

Howenstine, Ned G. Selected Data on the Operations of U.S. Affiliates of Foreign Companies, 1978 and 1979. *Surv. Curr. Bus.*, May 1981, *61*(5), pp. 35–52.   [G: U.S.]

Huebner, Albert. Making the Third-World Marlboro Country. In *Finger, W. R., ed., 1981, 1979*, pp. 151–56.   [G: LDCs]

Hughes, Helen. The Transfer of Resources to Developing Countries: Policy Implications and Research Priorities. In *National Science Foundation*, 1981, pp. II23–40.

Hume, James. Basic Principles of Surplus Cash Management. In *Ensor, R. and Muller, P., eds.*, 1981, pp. 213–16.

Hymer, Stephen. The Efficiency (Contradictions) of Multinational Corporations. In *Baldwin, R. E. and Richardson, J. D., eds., 1981, 1970*, pp. 296–308.

Irvin, G. W. Bargaining Asymmetry in Technology Transfer: A Games Theoretical Approach. *J. Devel. Stud.*, October 1981, *18*(1), pp. 85–93.

Itagaki, Takao. The Theory of the Multinational Firm under Exchange Rate Uncertainty. *Can. J. Econ.*, May 1981, *14*(2), pp. 276–97.

Jacque, Laurent L. Management of Foreign Exchange Risk: A Review Article. *J. Int. Bus. Stud.*, Spring/Summer 1981, *12*(1), pp. 81–101.

Janiszewski, Hubert A. Technology-Importing National Perspectives. In *Sagafi-nejad, T.; Moxon, R. W. and Perlmutter, H. V., eds.*, 1981, pp. 306–20.   [G: LDCs]

Jiménez de Lucio, Alberto. The East, the South and the Transnational Corporations. *Cepal Rev.*, August 1981, (14), pp. 51–61.   [G: Latin America]

Jo, Sung-Hwan. Overseas Direct Investment by South Korean Firms: Direction and Pattern. In *Kumar, K. and McLeod, M. G., eds.*, 1981, pp. 53–77.   [G: S. Korea]

Joelson, Mark R. Merger Control in Western Europe: National and International Aspects: Commentary. In *Schachter, O. and Hellawell, R., eds.*, 1981, pp. 335–43.   [G: U.S.]

Johnson, Howard C. An Actuarial Analysis. In *Ensor, R., ed.*, 1981, pp. 31–48.   [G: Selected Countries]

Jones, Reginald H. The Transnational Enterprise and World Economic Development. In *Novak,*

M. and Cooper, J. W., eds., 1981, pp. 129–41.

Kagono, Tadao. Structural Design of Headquarters-Division Relationships and Economic Performance: An Analysis of Japanese Firms. In *Otterbeck, L., ed.*, 1981, pp. 147–85. [G: Japan]

Kaikati, Jack G. The Anti-Export Policy of the U.S. *Calif. Manage. Rev.*, Spring 1981, 23(3), pp. 5–19. [G: U.S.]

Karpeles, Jean-Claude. L'Approche du Commerce Extérieur par L'Entreprise. (With English summary.) In *Courbis, R., ed.*, 1981, pp. 87–91. [G: France]

Katrak, Homi. Multi-National Firms' Exports and Host Country Commercial Policy. *Econ. J.*, June 1981, 91(362), pp. 454–65.

Kemp, Donald S. Hedging Long-term Financings. In *Ensor, R. and Muller, P., eds.*, 1981, pp. 115–21.

Khandker, A. Wahhab. Multinational Firms and the Theory of International Trade and Investment: A Correction and a Stronger Conclusion. *Amer. Econ. Rev.*, June 1981, 71(3), pp. 515–16.

Killing, Peter. Technology Acquisition: Licence Agreement or Joint Venture. In *Science Council of Canada, Industrial Policies Committee*, 1981, pp. 71–92. [G: Sweden; Canada; U.S.]

Kirchner, Christian. Mining Ventures in Developing Countries: Information Disclosure. In *Schanze, E., et al.*, 1981, pp. 68–107.

Kirkpatrick, Colin H. and Yamin, M. The Determinants of Export Subsidiary Formation by US Transnationals in Developing Countries: An Inter-Industry Analysis. *World Devel.*, April 1981, 9(4), pp. 373–82. [G: U.S.]

Kňakal, Jan. Transnationals and Mining Development in Bolivia, Chile and Peru. *Cepal Rev.*, August 1981, (14), pp. 63–83. [G: Bolivia; Chile; Peru]

Kolde, Endel-Jakob. Control and Incentives for Technology Transfer: A Multinational Perspective: Comment. In *Sagafi-nejad, T.; Moxon, R. W. and Perlmutter, H. V., eds.*, 1981, pp. 291–301.

Kortus, Bronislaw and Kaczorowski, Wojciech. Polish Industry Forges External Links. In *Hamilton, F. E. I. and Linge, G. J. R., eds.*, 1981, pp. 119–53. [G: Poland; CMEA]

Kossut, Zygmunt. Problems of Polish–U.S. Economic Relations: Reply. In *Marer, P. and Tabaczynski, E., eds.*, 1981, pp. 119–20. [G: Poland; U.S.]

Kossut, Zygmunt. Problems of Polish–U.S. Economic Relations: A Polish Perspective. In *Marer, P. and Tabaczynski, E., eds.*, 1981, pp. 109–16. [G: Poland; U.S.]

Koutsoyiannis, A. The Impact of Multinational Firms on Prices and Costs in Host-Country Markets: The Case of Canadian Manufacturing Industry. *Econ. Int.*, May–August–November 1981, 34(2–3–4), pp. 356–75. [G: Canada]

Kozinski, Janusz. Technology Transfer in U.S.–Polish Industrial Cooperation. In *Marer, P. and Tabaczynski, E., eds.*, 1981, pp. 140–54. [G: Poland; U.S.]

Kozinski, Janusz. Technology Transfer in U.S.–Polish Industrial Cooperation: Reply. In *Marer, P.*

and Tabaczynski, E., eds., 1981, pp. 157–58. [G: Poland; U.S.]

Kreye, Otto. Dependency in the 1980s. In *Saunders, C. T., ed. (II)*, 1981, pp. 81–93. [G: LDCs]

Krumme, Günter. Making it Abroad: The Evolution of Volkswagen's North American Production Plans. In *Hamilton, F. E. I. and Linge, G. J. R., eds.*, 1981, pp. 329–56. [G: U.S.; W. Germany]

Kujawa, Duane. U.S. Manufacturing Investment in the Developing Countries: American Labour's Concerns and the Enterprise Environment in the Decade Ahead. *Brit. J. Ind. Relat.*, March 1981, 19(1), pp. 38–48. [G: U.S.]

Kumar, Krishna. Multinationalization of Third-World Public-Sector Enterprises. In *Kumar, K. and McLeod, M. G., eds.*, 1981, pp. 187–201. [G: LDCs]

Lahera, Eugenio. The Transnational Corporations in the Chilean Economy. *Cepal Rev.*, August 1981, (14), pp. 107–25. [G: Chile]

Lall, Sanjaya. Dependence and Underdevelopment. In *Lall, S.*, 1981, 1975, pp. 3–23.

Lall, Sanjaya. Developing Countries as Exporters of Industrial Technology. In *Lall, S.*, 1981, 1980, pp. 228–56. [G: LDCs]

Lall, Sanjaya. Food Transnationals and Developing Countries. In *Lall, S.*, 1981, 1979, pp. 68–120. [G: LDCs; U.K.; U.S.]

Lall, Sanjaya. Transnationals, Domestic Enterprises, and Industrial Structure in Host LDCs: A Survey. In *Livingstone, I., ed.*, 1981, 1978, pp. 148–63. [G: LDCs]

Lamaswala, K. M. The Pricing of Unwrought Cooper in Relation to Transfer Pricing. In *Murray, R., ed.*, 1981, pp. 77–85. [G: Zambia]

Laski, Kazimierz. International Financing: Comment. In *Saunders, C. T., ed. (I)*, 1981, pp. 162–64. [G: LDCs]

de Laubier, Dominique and Richemond, Alain. Inteprénétration des capitaux et concurrence industrielle mondiale. (With English summary.) *Écon. Appl.*, 1981, 34(2–3), pp. 469–515. [G: U.S.; Japan; Europe; Canada]

Lax, David A. and Sebenius, James K. Insecure Contracts and Resource Development. *Public Policy*, Fall 1981, 29(4), pp. 417–36. [G: LDCs]

Lecraw, Donald J. Internationalization of Firms from LDCs: Evidence from the ASEAN Region. In *Kumar, K. and McLeod, M. G., eds.*, 1981, pp. 37–51. [G: S. E. Asia]

Leksell, Laurent. The Design and Function of the Financial Reporting System in Multinational Companies. In *Otterbeck, L., ed.*, 1981, pp. 205–32. [G: Sweden]

Liao, Xunzhen. Readjustment in China's Foreign Trade. *Rivista Int. Sci. Econ. Com.*, September 1981, 28(9), pp. 823–30. [G: China]

Lindgren, Ulf and Spangberg, Kjell. Management of the Post-Acquisition Process in Diversified MNCs. In *Otterbeck, L., ed.*, 1981, pp. 233–53. [G: Sweden]

Linge, G. J. R. and Hamilton, F. E. Ian. International Industrial Systems. In *Hamilton, F. E. I. and Linge, G. J. R., eds.*, 1981, pp. 1–117. [G: OECD; CMEA; LDCs]

Lipsey, Robert E. and Weiss, Merle Yahr. Foreign Production and Exports in Manufacturing Industries. *Rev. Econ. Statist.*, November 1981, *63*(4), pp. 488–94. [G: U.S.]

List, Heinrich. Recent Cases of the German Supreme Tax Court on International Tax Law. *Bull. Int. Fiscal Doc.*, August–September 1981, *35*(8–9), pp. 348–55. [G: W. Germany]

Lister, Neil. International Project Financing. In *Ensor, R. and Muller, P., eds.*, 1981, pp. 31–46.

Little, Jane Sneddon. The Financial Health of U.S. Manufacturing Firms Acquired by Foreigners. *New Eng. Econ. Rev.*, July/August 1981, pp. 5–18. [G: U.S.]

Lockhart, James B., III. International Liquidity Management at Gulf Oil. In *Ensor, R. and Muller, P., eds.*, 1981, pp. 195–99.

Lodin, Sven-Olof. International Enterprises and Taxation—Some Preliminary Results of an Empirical Study Concerning International Enterprises. In *Eliasson, G. and Södersten, J., eds.*, 1981, pp. 97–123. [G: Sweden; U.K.; U.S.]

Logue, Dennis E. International Finance: Discussion. *J. Finance*, May 1981, *36*(2), pp. 439–40.

Long, Frank. Multinational Corporations and the Non-Primary Sector Trade of Developing Countries: A Survey of Available Data. *Econ. Int.*, May–August–November 1981, *34*(2–3–4), pp. 376–99. [G: LDCs]

Lord, Peter. Financing the International Corporation. In *Ensor, R. and Muller, P., eds.*, 1981, pp. 15–24.

Lowe, Jeffrey H. Capital Expenditures by Majority-Owned Foreign Affiliates of U.S. Companies, 1981. *Surv. Curr. Bus.*, March 1981, *61*(3), pp. 34–39. [G: U.S.]

Magee, Stephen P. Information and the Multinational Corporation: An Appropriability Theory of Direct Foreign Investment. In *Baldwin, R. E. and Richardson, J. D., eds.*, 1981, *1977*, pp. 180–201.

Maher, Michael W. The Impact of Regulation on Controls: Firms' Response to the Foreign Corrupt Practices Act. *Accounting Rev.*, October 1981, *56*(4), pp. 751–70. [G: U.S.]

Mancke, Richard B. Competition and Monopoly in World Oil Markets: The Role of the International Oil Companies. *Cato J.*, Spring 1981, *1*(1), pp. 107–27. [G: U.S.]

Manser, W. A. P. and Webley, Simon. Technology Transfer to Developing Countries. In *The Royal Inst. of Internat. Affairs*, 1981, pp. 1–58. [G: LDCs; MDCs]

Mansour, Mohamed B. Definitional Issues in Technology Transfer: Channels, Mechanisms and Sources. In *Hawkins, R. G. and Prasad, A. J., eds.*, 1981, pp. 1–9. [G: LDCs]

Marer, Paul. U.S.–Polish Industrial Cooperation: Achievements, Problems, Prospects: Comment. In *Marer, P. and Tabaczynski, E., eds.*, 1981, pp. 131–36. [G: Poland; U.S.]

Marinho, Luiz Claudio. The Transnational Corporations and Latin America's Present Form of Economic Growth. *Cepal Rev.*, August 1981, (14), pp. 9–34. [G: Latin America; Brazil; Mexico]

Markert, Kurt. Merger Control in Western Europe: National and International Aspects. In *Schachter, O. and Hellawell, R., eds.*, 1981, pp. 293–334. [G: EEC]

Marois, Bernard and Behar, Michel. La prévision du risque politique liée aux investissements à l'étranger. (Forecasting the Political Risks of Foreign Investments. With English summary.) *Rev. Econ. Ind.*, 2nd Trimester 1981, (16), pp. 34–43.

Mason, R. Hal. Alternative Channels and Modes of International Resource Transmission: Comment. In *Sagafi-nejad, T.; Moxon, R. W. and Perlmutter, H. V., eds.*, 1981, pp. 27–36.

Mason, R. Hal. Technology Transfer Control Systems: The Case of East and Southeast Asian Developing Countries. In *Sagafi-nejad, T.; Moxon, R. W. and Perlmutter, H. V., eds.*, 1981, pp. 430–66. [G: S. Korea; Taiwan; S.E. Asia]

Maule, C. J. Technology Acquisition: Licence Agreement or Joint Venture: Commentary. In *Science Council of Canada, Industrial Policies Committee*, 1981, pp. 93–96. [G: U.S.; Canada; Sweden]

McCann, Joseph. Technology Transfer Control Systems: The Case of East and Southeast Asian Developing Countries: Comment. In *Sagafi-nejad, T.; Moxon, R. W. and Perlmutter, H. V., eds.*, 1981, pp. 474–77. [G: S. Korea; Taiwan; S.E. Asia]

McMillan, Carl H. Trends in East-West Industrial Cooperation. *J. Int. Bus. Stud.*, Fall 1981, *12*(2), pp. 53–67. [G: CMEA; OECD]

McMillan, Carl H. Tripartite Industrial Cooperation and Third Countries: Comment. In *Saunders, C. T., ed. (I)*, 1981, pp. 365–68. [G: CMEA; OECD; LDCs]

Mees, Philip. Using Computerized Information Systems. In *Ensor, R. and Muller, P., eds.*, 1981, pp. 201–10.

Meierjohann, Freidrich W. An Index-controlled Hedging Programme. In *Ensor, R. and Muller, P., eds.*, 1981, pp. 131–37.

Mennis, Bernard. Technology-Importing National Perspectives: Comment. In *Sagafi-nejad, T.; Moxon, R. W. and Perlmutter, H. V., eds.*, 1981, pp. 326–30. [G: LDCs]

Micallef, Joseph V. Political Risk Assessment and the Multinational. In *Ensor, R., ed.*, 1981, pp. 123–27.

Miller, Joseph C. Marketing Polish Industrial Goods in the United States: Reply. In *Marer, P. and Tabaczynski, E., eds.*, 1981, pp. 270–71. [G: Poland; U.S.]

Miller, Joseph C. Marketing Polish Industrial Goods in the United States. In *Marer, P. and Tabaczynski, E., eds.*, 1981, pp. 259–66. [G: Poland; U.S.]

Miscimarra, Philip A. The Entertainment Industry: Inroads in Multinational Collective Bargaining. *Brit. J. Ind. Relat.*, March 1981, *19*(1), pp. 49–65.

Moldelski, George. Technology Exports and Technology Transfer Controls: Comment. In *Sagafi-nejad, T.; Moxon, R. W. and Perlmutter, H. V., eds.*, 1981, pp. 373–75.

Mueller, W. F. Merger Control in Western Europe:

National and International Aspects: Commentary. In *Schachter, O. and Hellawell, R., eds.*, 1981, pp. 344–51. [G: EEC]

Muller, Peter J. Cash Management—A Definition. In *Ensor, R. and Muller, P., eds.*, 1981, pp. 177–81.

Muller, Peter J. Organization of the Exposure Management Function. In *Ensor, R. and Muller, P., eds.*, 1981, pp. 101–13.

Muñoz, Heraldo. The Strategic Dependency of the Centers and the Economic Importance of the Latin American Periphery. In *Muñoz, H., ed.*, 1981, pp. 59–92. [G: U.S.; Latin America]

Murray, Robin. Multinationals beyond the Market: Introduction. In *Murray, R., ed.*, 1981, pp. 1–14.

Murray, Robin. Transfer Pricing and Its Control: Alternative Approaches. In *Murray, R., ed.*, 1981, pp. 147–76.

Mushi, S. S. Tanzania. In *Adedeji, A., ed.*, 1981, pp. 204–37. [G: Tanzania]

Mutti, John H. Tax Incentives and the Repatriation Decisions of U.S. Multinational Corporations. *Nat. Tax J.*, June 1981, *34*(2), pp. 241–48. [G: U.S.]

Nambudiri, C. N. S.; Iyanda, Olukunle and Akinnusi, D. M. Third-World-Country Firms in Nigeria. In *Kumar, K. and McLeod, M. G., eds.*, 1981, pp. 145–53. [G: Nigeria]

Neersø, Peter. Peru, Andes-pagten og de transnationale selskaber. (Peru, the Andean Pact and the Transnationals. With English summary.) *Nationaløkon. Tidsskr.*, 1981, *119*(1), pp. 64–77. [G: Peru]

Negandhi, Anant R. and Baliga, B. R. Internal Functioning of American, German and Japanese Multinational Corporations. In *Otterbeck, L., ed.*, 1981, pp. 107–20. [G: Japan; U.S.; W. Germany]

Newfarmer, Richard S. and Marsh, Lawrence C. Foreign Ownership, Market Structure and Industrial Performance: Brazil's Electrical Industry. *J. Devel. Econ.*, February 1981, *8*(1), pp. 47–75. [G: Brazil]

Nordhauser, Susan L. and Kramer, John L. Repeal of the Deferral Privilege for Earnings from Direct Foreign Investments: An Analysis. *Accounting Rev.*, January 1981, *56*(1), pp. 54–69. [G: U.S.]

Novoa, Eduardo. Some Political Issues in the Negotiation of the New International Economic Order: The Policies of Nationalization. In *Laszlo, E. and Kurtzman, J., eds.*, 1981, pp. 14–29. [G: LDCs]

Núñez del Prado, Arturo. The Transnational Corporations in a New Planning Process. *Cepal Rev.*, August 1981, (14), pp. 35–50. [G: Latin America]

Okochi, Akio. Automobiles and International Markets: Comment. In *Okochi, A. and Shimokawa, K., eds.*, 1981, pp. 212–13.

Okumura, Ariyoshi. Policy Responses in the Old Industrial Countries: Japan and East Asia. In *Saunders, C. T., ed. (II)*, 1981, pp. 261–83. [G: Japan; E. Asia]

Otterbeck, Lars. The Management of Headquarters-Subsidiary Relationships in Multinational Corporations: Concluding Remarks—And a Review of Subsidiary Autonomy. In *Otterbeck, L., ed.*, 1981, pp. 337–43. [G: Japan; Sweden; U.K.; U.S.; W. Germany]

Otterbeck, Lars. The Mangement of Joint Ventures. In *Otterbeck, L., ed.*, 1981, pp. 269–96. [G: Sweden]

Overton, James. Diversification and International Expansion: The Future of the American Tobacco Manufacturing Industry with Corporate Profiles of the "Big Six." In *Finger, W. R., ed.*, 1981, pp. 159–95. [G: U.S.]

Ozawa, Terutomo. Technology Transfer and Japanese Economic Growth in the Postwar Period. In *Hawkins, R. G. and Prasad, A. J., eds.*, 1981, pp. 91–116. [G: Japan]

Ozawa, Terutomo. The Role of the Multinational Corporation: Discussion. *Amer. J. Agr. Econ.*, May 1981, *63*(2), pp. 393–95.

Pack, Stirling. Performance Component Evolution in the Multiplant Corporate Sector: The Integrated Oil Industry Example. In *Rees, J.; Hewings, G. J. D. and Stafford, H. A., eds.*, 1981, pp. 59–71.

Paliwoda, Stanley J. Multinational Corporations: Trade and Investment across the East–West Divide. *Managerial Dec. Econ.*, December 1981, *2*(4), pp. 247–55. [G: CMEA; OECD]

Parry, Thomas G. Australian and New Zealand Investment in the Pacific Island Region. *J. World Trade Law*, July–August 1981, *15*(4), pp. 345–51. [G: Papua New Guinea; Australia; New Zealand; Fiji]

Parry, Thomas G. The Multinational Enterprise and Two-stage Technology Transfer to Developing Nations. In *Hawkins, R. G. and Prasad, A. J., eds.*, 1981, pp. 175–92. [G: Australia; LDCs]

Partee, J. Charles. Statement to Subcommittee on Telecommunications, Consumer Protection and Finance, House Committee on Energy and Commerce, February 26, 1981. *Fed. Res. Bull.*, March 1981, *67*(3), pp. 241–43. [G: U.S.]

Paszynski, Marian. Transnational Companies and Direct Private Investment in Developing Countries: Comment. In *Saunders, C. T., ed. (I)*, 1981, pp. 174–75. [G: LDCs]

Patel, Meena. A Note on Transfer Pricing by Transnational Corporations. *Indian Econ. Rev.*, January–June 1981, *16*(1 and 2), pp. 139–52.

Paules, Edward P. Taxation and Exposure Management. In *Ensor, R. and Muller, P., eds.*, 1981, pp. 143–66. [G: U.S.]

Perlmutter, Howard V. The Future of East–West Industrial Cooperation: A Social Architectural Perspective. In *Marer, P. and Tabaczynski, E., eds.*, 1981, pp. 187–204. [G: Poland; U.S.]

Perlmutter, Howard V. The Future of East–West Industrial Cooperation: A Social Architectural Perspective: Reply. In *Marer, P. and Tabaczynski, E., eds.*, 1981, pp. 206. [G: Poland; U.S.]

Perrons, D. C. The Role of Ireland in the New International Division of Labour: A Proposed Framework for Regional Analysis. *Reg. Stud.*, 1981, *15*(2), pp. 81–100. [G: Ireland]

Peterson, Graham. Cash Forecasting at Unilever, Australia. In *Ensor, R. and Muller, P., eds.*, 1981, pp. 189–94. [G: Australia]

Plasschaert, Sylvain R. F. The Design of Schedular and Global Systems of Income Taxation—The International Dimension. *Bull. Int. Fiscal Doc.*, August–September 1981, 35(8–9), pp. 409–16.

Plasschaert, Sylvain R. F. The Treatment of Enterprise Profits in Schedular and Global Frameworks of Income Taxation. *Bull. Int. Fiscal Doc.*, June 1981, 35(6), pp. 261–71.

Porter, Andrew. Britain, the Cape Colony, and Natal, 1870–1914: Capital, Shipping, and the Imperial Connexion. *Econ. Hist. Rev.*, 2nd Ser., November 1981, 34(4), pp. 554–77. **[G: U.K.; S. Africa]**

Prahalad, C. K. and Doz, Yves L. An Approach to Strategic Control in MNCs. *Sloan Manage. Rev.*, Summer 1981, 22(4), pp. 5–13.

Prahalad, C. K. and Doz, Yves L. Strategic Control—The Dilemma in Headquarters-Subsidiary Relationship. In *Otterbeck, L., ed.*, 1981, pp. 187–203.

Prasad, A. J. Licensing as an Alternative to Foreign Investment for Technology Transfer. In *Hawkins, R. G. and Prasad, A. J., eds.*, 1981, pp. 193–218. **[G: LDCs; MDCs; U.S.]**

Prasad, A. J. Technology Transfer to Developing Countries through Multinational Corporations. In *Hawkins, R. G. and Prasad, A. J., eds.*, 1981, pp. 151–73. **[G: LDCs]**

Pugel, Thomas A. The Determinants of Foreign Direct Investment: An Analysis of U.S. Manufacturing Industries. *Managerial Dec. Econ.*, December 1981, 2(4), pp. 220–28. **[G: U.S.]**

Radice, H. K. Industrial Co-operation between Hungary and the West. In *Hare, P. G.; Radice, H. K. and Swain, N., eds.*, 1981, pp. 109–31. **[G: Hungary; W. Europe; U.S.]**

Rayfield, Gordon. General Motor's Approach to Country Risk. In *Ensor, R., ed.*, 1981, pp. 129–33. **[G: Latin America]**

Redmond, James C. The Unitary System of Taxation: Identification of the Source of Income. *Bull. Int. Fiscal Doc.*, March 1981, 35(3), pp. 99–107. **[G: U.S.]**

Reid, Stan D. The Decision-Maker and Export Entry and Expansion. *J. Int. Bus. Stud.*, Fall 1981, 12(2), pp. 101–12.

Richards, Stewart F. Industrial Activities in the Periphery: Hong Kong. In *Hamilton, F. E. I. and Linge, G. J. R., eds.*, 1981, pp. 465–80. **[G: Hong Kong]**

Richardson, P. Industrial Patterns in Early and Late Adoption of New Products in Canada: Commentary. In *Science Council of Canada, Industrial Policies Committee*, 1981, pp. 51–54. **[G: Canada]**

Ripoll, José. Transfer Prices in the Insurance Sector. In *Murray, R., ed.*, 1981, pp. 91–95.

Robinson, Richard D. Background Concepts and Philosophy of International Business from World War II to the Present. *J. Int. Bus. Stud.*, Spring/Summer 1981, 12(1), pp. 13–21.

Rodriguez, Rita M. Corporate Exchange Risk Management: Theme and Aberrations. *J. Finance*, May 1981, 36(2), pp. 427–38. **[G: U.S.]**

Romeril, Barry. ICI's Approach to Currency Exposure and Cash Management. In *Ensor, R. and*

Muller, P., eds., 1981, pp. 123–29.

Root, Franklin R. The Pricing of International Technology Transfers via Nonaffiliate Licensing Arrangements. In *Sagafi-nejad, T.; Moxon, R. W. and Perlmutter, H. V., eds.*, 1981, pp. 120–33. **[G: U.S.]**

Rosser, J. Barkley, Jr. The Emergence of the Megacorpstate and the Acceleration of Global Inflation. *J. Post Keynesian Econ.*, Spring 1981, 3(3), pp. 429–39.

Roumeliotis, Panayotis. A Blueprint for a Transfer Pricing Commando Unit. In *Murray, R., ed.*, 1981, pp. 278–84.

Roussakis, Emmanuel N. Il processo di "internazionalizzazione" delle banche americane. (The Internationalization of U.S. Commercial Banks. With English summary.) *Bancaria*, July 1981, 37(7), pp. 698–715. **[G: U.S.; W. Europe; Japan; Canada]**

Rousseau, P. Réflexions sur un système d'informations commerciales. (Information Systems Related to International Markets (SIRMI). With English summary.) *Ann. Sci. Écon. Appl.*, 1981, 37(4), pp. 95–112.

Rugman, Alan M. A Test of Internalization Theory. *Managerial Dec. Econ.*, December 1981, 2(4), pp. 211–19. **[G: Canada; U.S.]**

Rugman, Alan M. Research and Development by Multinational and Domestic Firms in Canada. *Can. Public Policy*, Autumn 1981, 7(4), pp. 604–16. **[G: Canada]**

Sauvant, Karl P. The Role of Transitional Enterprises in the Establishment of the NIEO: A Critical View. In *Lozoya, J. and Green, R., eds.*, 1981, pp. 109–70. **[G: LDCs; MDCs]**

Savary, Julien. La France dans la division internationale du travail: Une approche par l'investissement direct international. (The International Division of Labour and the French Economy: An Approach through Foreign Direct Investment. With English summary.) *Revue Écon.*, July 1981, 32(4), pp. 713–53. **[G: France]**

Savary, Julien. Taille et multinationalisation des entreprises françaises. (Size of the French Corporations and Their Foreign Production. With English summary.) *Rev. Econ. Ind.*, 1st Trimester 1981, (15), pp. 78–91. **[G: France]**

Savey, Suzane. Pechiney Ugine Kuhlmann: A Frence Multinational Corporation. In *Hamilton, F. E. I. and Linge, G. J. R., eds.*, 1981, pp. 305–27. **[G: France]**

Schanze, Erich. Mining Ventures in Developing Countries: Forms of Agreement and the Joint Venture Practice. In *Schanze, E., et al.*, 1981, pp. 20–67. **[G: Selected LDCs]**

Schatz, Sayre P. Assertive Pragmatism and the Multinational Enterprise. *World Devel.*, January 1981, 9(1), pp. 93–105.

von Schlabrendorff, Fabian. Mining Ventures in Developing Countries: Environmental Provisions. In *Schanze, E., et al.*, 1981, pp. 212–35.

Schoenfeld, Hanns-Martin W. International Accounting: Development, Issues, and Future Directions. *J. Int. Bus. Stud.*, Fall 1981, 12(2), pp. 83–100.

Schweikart, James A. We Must End Consolidation

of Foreign Subsidiaries. *Manage. Account.*, August 1981, *63*(2), pp. 15–18. [G: U.S.]

de Schweinitz, Karl, Jr. What Is Economic Imperialism? *J. Econ. Issues*, September 1981, *15*(3), pp. 675–701.

Shapiro, Alan C. and Goeltz, Richard Karl. Financial Decisions for Multinational Enterprises. In *Altman, E. I., ed.*, 1981, pp. 38.3–52.

Shawky, Hany A. and Ricks, David A. Capital Budgeting for Multinational Firms: A Theoretical Analysis. *Southern Econ. J.*, January 1981, *47*(3), pp. 703–13.

Shepherd, Geoffrey. Industrial Strategies in Textiles and Clothing and Motor Cars. In *Saunders, C. T., ed. (II)*, 1981, pp. 132–56. [G: LDCs; OECD]

Sierra, Oscar Hernandes. Incomex and Transfer Pricing Control in Colombia. In *Murray, R., ed.*, 1981, pp. 304–07. [G: Colombia]

Singh, Mahinder Santokh and Chi, Seck Choo. Spatial Dynamics in the Growth and Development of Multinational Corporations in Malaysia. In *Hamilton, F. E. I. and Linge, G. J. R., eds.*, 1981, pp. 481–507. [G: Malaysia]

Singh, Rana K. D. N. Policy Issues and Trends in Parent-Affiliate Relationships in Developing Countries. In *Otterbeck, L., ed.*, 1981, pp. 11–24. [G: LDCs]

Slaybaugh, Clifford W. Factors in Technology Transfer: A Multinational Firm Perspective. In *Hawkins, R. G. and Prasad, A. J., eds.*, 1981, pp. 289–305. [G: U.S.]

Sornarajah, M. The Myth of International Contract Law. *J. World Trade Law*, May–June 1981, *15*(3), pp. 187–217.

Stanley, Marjorie Thines. Capital Structure and Cost-of-Capital for the Multinational Firm. *J. Int. Bus. Stud.*, Spring/Summer 1981, *12*(1), pp. 103–20.

Steed, Guy P. F. International Location and Comparative Advantage: The Clothing Industries and Developing Countries. In *Hamilton, F. E. I. and Linge, G. J. R., eds.*, 1981, pp. 265–303. [G: LDCs]

Stewart, Frances. International Technology Transfer: Issues and Policy Options. In *Streeten, P. and Jolly, R, eds.*, 1981, pp. 67–110. [G: Selected LDCs]

Stewart, Frances. Taxation and the Control of Transfer Pricing. In *Murray, R., ed.*, 1981, pp. 177–84.

Stewart, Frances. Taxation and Technology Transfer. In *Sagafi-nejad, T.; Moxon, R. W. and Perlmutter, H. V., eds.*, 1981, pp. 137–72. [G: LDCs; MDCs]

Stockmayer, Albrecht. Financing Mining Projects in Developing Countries. In *Schanze, E., et al.*, 1981, pp. 171–97.

Stockmayer, Albrecht. Mining Ventures in Developing Countries: Investor Consortia: Antitrust Considerations. In *Schanze, E., et al.*, 1981, pp. 236–59. [G: U.S.; EEC]

Streeten, Paul P. Bargaining with Multi-nationals. In *Streeten, P.*, 1981, *1975*, pp. 298–302.

Streeten, Paul P. Multi-nationals Revisited. In *Streeten, P.*, 1981, *1979*, pp. 311–19.

Streeten, Paul P. Multinationals Revisited. In *Baldwin, R. E. and Richardson, J. D., eds.*, 1981, *1979*, pp. 308–15.

Streeten, Paul P. Policies towards Multi-nationals. In *Streeten, P.*, 1981, *1975*, pp. 303–10.

Streeten, Paul P. The Multi-national Enterprise and the Theory of Development Policy. In *Streeten, P.*, 1981, *1973*, pp. 267–97.

Streeten, Paul P. Trans-national Corporations and Basic Needs. In *Streeten, P.*, 1981, pp. 398–404.

Suhar, V. Victor. Managing Translation and Transaction Exposure. In *Ensor, R. and Muller, P., eds.*, 1981, pp. 89–99.

Sunkel, Osvaldo. Development Styles and the Environment: An Interpretation of the Latin American Case. In *Muñoz, H., ed.*, 1981, pp. 93–114. [G: Latin America]

Svedberg, Peter. Colonial Enforcement of Foreign Direct Investment. *Manchester Sch. Econ. Soc. Stud.*, March 1981, *49*(1), pp. 21–38.

Svedberg, Peter. The Less-Developed Countries and Transnational Enterprises: Comments. In *Grassman, S. and Lundberg, E., eds.*, 1981, pp. 257–61.

Swedenborg, Birgitta. The Internationalization of Swedish Industry: Determinants and Effects. In *Industrial Inst. for Econ. and Soc. Research*, 1981, pp. 59–65. [G: U.S.; Sweden]

Szumski, Jerzy. The International Harvester–BUMAR Cooperation Experience: Practical Problems and Their Solutions: Reply. In *Marer, P. and Tabaczynski, E., eds.*, 1981, pp. 174. [G: Poland; U.S.]

Szumski, Jerzy. The International Harvester–BUMAR Cooperation Experience: Practical Problems and their Solutions. In *Marer, P. and Tabaczynski, E., eds.*, 1981, pp. 158–71. [G: Poland; U.S.]

Tabaczynski, Eugeniusz. The Future of East–West Industrial Cooperation: A Social Architectural Perspective: Comment. In *Marer, P. and Tabaczynski, E., eds.*, 1981, pp. 204–06. [G: Poland; U.S.]

Tabaczynski, Eugeniusz. Today's Approach to Joint Ventures in Poland. In *Marer, P. and Tabaczynski, E., eds.*, 1981, pp. 341–48. [G: Poland]

Taylor, Graham D. Management Relations in a Multinational Enterprise: The Case of Canadian Industries Limited, 1928–1948. *Bus. Hist. Rev.*, Autumn 1981, *55*(3), pp. 337–58. [G: Canada]

Taylor, Michael and Thrift, Nigel. British Capital Overseas: Direct Investment and Corporate Development in Australia. *Reg. Stud.*, 1981, *15*(3), pp. 183–212. [G: U.K.; Australia]

Teece, David J. Technology Transfer and R and D Activities of Multinational Firms: Some Theory and Evidence. In *Hawkins, R. G. and Prasad, A. J., eds.*, 1981, pp. 39–74. [G: LDCs]

Teece, David J. The Multinational Enterprise: Market Failure and Market Power Considerations. *Sloan Manage. Rev.*, Spring 1981, *22*(3), pp. 3–17.

Thee, Kian-Wie. Indonesia as a Host Country to Indian Joint Ventures. In *Kumar, K. and McLeod, M. G., eds.*, 1981, pp. 133–44. [G: India; Indonesia]

Timberg, Sigmund. Restrictive Business Practices in the International Transfer and Diffusion of Technology. In *Schachter, O. and Hellawell, R.,* eds., 1981, pp. 84–138.

Ting, Wen-Lee and Schive, Chi. Direct Investment and Technology Transfer from Taiwan. In *Kumar, K. and McLeod, M. G.,* eds., 1981, pp. 101–14. [G: Taiwan]

Toba, Kin'ichiro. Automobiles and International Markets: Comment. In *Okochi, A. and Shimokawa, K.,* eds., 1981, pp. 210–12.

Tobi, Niki. The Nigerian Enterprises Promotion Act. *J. World Trade Law,* November–December 1981, *15*(6), pp. 543–53. [G: Nigeria]

de la Torre, José. Foreign Investment and Economic Development: Conflict and Negotiation. *J. Int. Bus. Stud.,* Fall 1981, *12*(2), pp. 9–32. [G: LDCs]

U.S. Internal Revenue Service. Multinational Companies' (MNCs) Tax Avoidance and/or Evasion Schemes and Available Methods to Curb Abuse. In *Murray, R.,* ed., 1981, pp. 245–77.

U.S. Treasury Department. Summary Study of International Cases Involving Section 482 of the Internal Revenue Code. In *Murray, R.,* ed., 1981, pp. 308–24. [G: U.S.]

Van der Wees, Gerrit. Multinational Corporations, Transfer of Technology, and the Socialist Strategy of a Developing Nation: Perspectives from Tanzania. In *Hamilton, F. E. I. and Linge, G. J. R.,* eds., 1981, pp. 529–47. [G: Tanzania]

Walter, Ingo. Control of Terms and Conditions for International Transfers of Technology to Developing Countries: Commentary. In *Schachter, O. and Hellawell, R.,* eds., 1981, pp. 143–59. [G: U.S.; Japan]

Wang, N. T. Analysis of Restrictive Business Practices by Transnational Corporations and Their Impact on Trade and Development. In *Schachter, O. and Hellawell, R.,* eds., 1981, pp. 3–21.

Watanabe, Susumu. Multinational Enterprises, Employment and Technology Adaptations. *Int. Lab. Rev.,* November–December 1981, *120*(6), pp. 693–710. [G: LDCs]

Welge, Martin K. The Effective Design of Headquarter-Subsidiary Relationships in German MNCs. In *Otterbeck, L.,* ed., 1981, pp. 79–106. [G: W. Germany]

Wells, Louis T., Jr. Control of Terms and Conditions for International Transfers of Technology to Developing Countries: Commentary. In *Schachter, O. and Hellawell, R.,* eds., 1981, pp. 160–64. [G: U.S.; Japan]

Wells, Louis T., Jr. Foreign Investors from the Third World. In *Kumar, K. and McLeod, M. G.,* eds., 1981, pp. 23–36. [G: LDCs]

Wells, Louis T., Jr. Taxation and Technology Transfer: Comment. In *Sagafi-nejad, T.; Moxon, R. W. and Perlmutter, H. V.,* eds., 1981, pp. 173–76. [G: LDCs; MDCs]

Wells, Louis T., Jr. Technology Transfer Control Systems: The Case of East and Southeast Asian Developing Countries: Comment. In *Sagafi-nejad, T.; Moxon, R. W. and Perlmutter, H. V.,* eds., 1981, pp. 467–73. [G: S. Korea; Taiwan; S.E. Asia]

Wex, Samuel. The Seeking of a World Competition Code: Quixotic Quest? Commentary. In *Schachter, O. and Hellawell, R.,* eds., 1981, pp. 422–25.

Whichard, Obie G. Trends in the U.S. Direct Investment Position Abroad, 1950–79. *Surv. Curr. Bus.,* February 1981, *61*(2), pp. 39–56. [G: U.S.]

Whichard, Obie G. U.S. Direct Investment Abroad in 1980. *Surv. Curr. Bus.,* August 1981, *61*(8), pp. 20–39. [G: U.S.]

White, Eduardo. The International Projection of Firms from Latin American Countries. In *Kumar, K. and McLeod, M. G.,* eds., 1981, pp. 155–86. [G: Latin America]

Whitman, Marina v. N. Automobiles: Turning Around on a Dime? *Challenge,* May/June 1981, *24*(2), pp. 36–44. [G: U.S.]

Wilkins, Mira. Automobiles and International Markets. In *Okochi, A. and Shimokawa, K.,* eds., 1981, pp. 193–209.

Wilkins, Mira. The Internationalization of Japanese Manufacturing Firms: Comment. In *Okochi, A. and Shimokawa, K.,* eds., 1981, pp. 230–32. [G: Japan]

Wilner, Gabriel. Control and Incentives for Technology Transfer: A Multinational Perspective: Comment. In *Sagafi-nejad, T.; Moxon, R. W. and Perlmutter, H. V.,* eds., 1981, pp. 302–05.

Wind, Yoram and Douglas, Susan. International Portfolio Analysis and Strategy: The Challenge of the 80s. *J. Int. Bus. Stud.,* Fall 1981, *12*(2), pp. 69–82.

Wojciechowski, Bronislaw. Organizational Constraints on Industrial Cooperation: Comment. In *Marer, P. and Tabaczynski, E.,* eds., 1981, pp. 312–16. [G: Poland]

Yamazaki, Kiyoshi. The Internationalization of Japanese Manufacturing Firms. In *Okochi, A. and Shimokawa, K.,* eds., 1981, pp. 215–29. [G: Japan]

Yoingco, Angel Q. and Sukarya, Sutadi. Study Group on Asian Tax Administration and Research (SGATAR)—An Experiment in Regional Tax Cooperation—Part I. *Bull. Int. Fiscal Doc.,* March 1981, *35*(3), pp. 110–18. [G: S.E. Asia; Australia; Japan; New Zealand]

Zagorski, Edwin. U.S.–Polish Industrial Cooperation: Achievements, Problems, Prospects. In *Marer, P. and Tabaczynski, E.,* eds., 1981, pp. 121–31. [G: Poland; U.S.]

Zagorski, Edwin. U.S.–Polish Industrial Cooperation: Achievements, Problems, Prospects: Reply. In *Marer, P. and Tabaczynski, E.,* eds., 1981, pp. 136–39. [G: Poland; U.S.]

443 International Lending and Aid (Public)

4430 International Lending and Aid (Public)

Abbott, George C. International Indebtedness of Less Developed Countries: Structure, Growth, Indicators. *Aussenwirtschaft,* December 1981, *36*(4), pp. 340–51. [G: LDCs]

Abbott, John C. Technical Assistance in Marketing: A View over Time. In *Johnson, G. and Maunder,*

A., eds., 1981, pp. 115–27.

Andreatta, Beniamino. Problemi dello sviluppo nel mondo e del suo finanziamento. (World Economic Development and Its Financing. With English summary.) *Bancaria*, February 1981, *37*(2), pp. 129–31. [G: LDCs]

Anguiano, Eugenio. The People's Republic of China and the New International Economic Order: Relations with the Third World. In *Lozoya, J. A. and Bhattacharya, A. K., eds.*, 1981, pp. 53–89. [G: China; LDCs]

Bakó, Ede. Credits to the South and International Financial Relations: Comment. In *Saunders, C. T., ed. (I)*, 1981, pp. 160–62. [G: Hungary; LDCs]

Bauer, P. T. Background to Aid. In *Bauer, P. T.*, 1981, pp. 138–50.

Bauer, P. T. Foreign Aid and Its Hydra-Headed Rationalization. In *Bauer, P. T.*, 1981, pp. 86–137. [G: LDCs]

Bauer, P. T. The Link Scheme of Aid. In *Bauer, P. T.*, 1981, pp. 151–55.

Bauer, P. T. The Third World, Foreign Aid, and Global Redistribution. In *Novak, M. and Cooper, J. W., eds.*, 1981, pp. 83–95.

Bauer, Peter and Yamey, Basil S. The Political Economy of Foreign Aid. *Lloyds Bank Rev.*, October 1981, (142), pp. 1–14. [G: LDCs]

Bell, Carl. Promoting Private Investment: The Role of the International Finance Corporation. *Finance Develop.*, September 1981, *18*(3), pp. 16–19. [G: LDCs]

Bergsten, C. Fred. The Role of the Multilateral Development Banks. In *Bergsten, C. F., ed.*, 1981, pp. 127–45. [G: LDCs; U.S.]

Bergsten, C. Fred. The United States and Mexico in the World Economy. In *Bergsten, C. F., ed.*, 1981, pp. 165–70. [G: Mexico; U.S.]

Bhaduri, Amit. Credits to the South and International Financial Relations. In *Saunders, C. T., ed. (I)*, 1981, pp. 91–102. [G: OECD; OPEC; LDCs]

Bird, Graham. Acerca del uso de la reforma monetaria internacional en beneficio de los países en desarrollo. (On Using International Monetary Reform for the Benefit of Developing Countries. With English summary.) *Económica*, September–December 1981, *27*(3), pp. 143–61. [G: LDCs]

Bird, Graham. International Monetary Issues and the Developing Countries: A Survey: Postscript. In *Streeten, P. and Jolly, R, eds.*, 1981, pp. 367–73. [G: LDCs]

Bird, Graham and Gutmann, Peter. Foreign Aid—The Issues. *Nat. Westminster Bank Quart. Rev.*, August 1981, pp. 36–51. [G: OECD; OPEC]

Bornstein, Morris. Issues in East–West Economic Relations. In *Bornstein, M.; Gitelman, Z. and Zimmerman, W., eds.*, 1981, pp. 31–61. [G: E. Europe]

Bourne, Compton. Government Foreign Borrowing and Economic Growth: The Jamaican Experience. *Soc. Econ. Stud.*, December 1981, *30*(4), pp. 52–74. [G: Jamaica]

Brainard, Lawrence J. Bankers Trust's Approach to International Risk Assessment. In *Ensor, R., ed.*, 1981, pp. 93–98. [G: S. Korea; Brazil; Ecuador]

Bueno, G. M. A New Order in Financial and Technological Relations with the Third World? *Tijdschrift Econ. Manage.*, 1981, *26*(1), pp. 95–116.

Burki, Shahid Javed and Haq, Mahbub. Meeting Basic Needs: An Overview. *World Devel.*, February 1981, *9*(2), pp. 167–82.

Cline, William R. Economic Stabilization in Peru, 1975–78. In *Cline, W. R. and Weintraub, S., eds.*, 1981, pp. 297–326. [G: Peru]

Cline, William R. Real Economic Effects of World Inflation and Recession. In *Cline, W. R., et al.*, 1981, pp. 10–51. [G: LDCs]

Cohn, Steven; Wood, Robert and Haag, Richard. U.S. Aid and Third World Women: The Impact of Peace Corps Programs. *Econ. Develop. Cult. Change*, July 1981, *29*(4), pp. 795–811. [G: U.S.; LDCs]

Cooper, Orah and Fogarty, Carol. Soviet Military and Economic Aid to the Less Developed Countries, 1954–78. In *Bornstein, M., ed.*, 1981, *1979*, pp. 253–66. [G: U.S.S.R.; LDCs]

Coverdale, A. G. and Healey, J. M. The Real Resource Cost of Untying Bilateral Aid. *Oxford Bull. Econ. Statist.*, May 1981, *43*(2), pp. 185–99. [G: France; W. Germany; U.K.; U.S.; Japan]

Crosswell, Michael J. Growth, Poverty Alleviation, and Foreign Assistance. In *Leipziger, D. M., ed.*, 1981, pp. 181–218. [G: LDCs]

Davis, Christopher. Financing Third World Debt. In *The Royal Inst. of Internat. Affairs*, 1981, pp. 59–102. [G: LDCs]

Dell, Sidney. International Monetary Issues and the Developing Countries: A Survey: Comment. In *Streeten, P. and Jolly, R, eds.*, 1981, *1975*, pp. 375–79.

Devlin, Robert. Transnational Banks, External Debt and Peru: Results of a Recent Study. *Cepal Rev.*, August 1981, (14), pp. 153–84. [G: Peru]

Dos Santos, T. The Structure of Dependence. In *Livingstone, I., ed.*, 1981, *1970*, pp. 143–47. [G: Latin America]

Due, Jean M. and Due, John F. Donor Finances of Agricultural Development in Southern Sudan—Development or Dependency? *J. Econ. Devel.*, December 1981, *6*(2), pp. 71–91. [G: Sudan]

Eaton, Jonathan and Gersovitz, Mark. Debt with Potential Repudiation: Theoretical and Empirical Analysis. *Rev. Econ. Stud.*, April 1981, *48*(2), pp. 289–309.

Faaland, Just. Aid and Dependence: The Lessons. In *Faaland, J., ed.*, 1981, pp. 179–193. [G: Bangladesh]

Faaland, Just. Aid and Influence: The Case of Bangladesh: The Story. In *Faaland, J., ed.*, 1981, pp. 3–13. [G: Bangladesh]

Faaland, Just. The Bangladesh Aid Group. In *Faaland, J., ed.*, 1981, pp. 105–27. [G: Bangladesh]

Faaland, Just. The Debt Liability of Pakistan. In *Faaland, J., ed.*, 1981, pp. 128–46. [G: Bangladesh; Pakistan]

Feder, Gershon. Growth and External Borrowing in Trade Gap Economies of Less Developed

Countries. *Aussenwirtschaft*, December 1981, *36*(4), pp. 381–95. **[G: LDCs]**

Fishlow, Albert. Latin America's Debt: Problem or Solution? In *U.S. Congress, Joint Economic Committee (III)*, 1981, pp. 149–65.
[G: Latin America]

Friedman, Irving S. The Role of Private Banks in Stabilization Programs. In *Cline, W. R. and Weintraub, S., eds.*, 1981, pp. 235–65. **[G: LDCs]**

Garavello, Oscar. processi di sviluppo e dipendenza dai flussi esterni di capitale. (Growth: The L.D.C. Dependency on Foreign Capital Inflows. With English summary.) *Rivista Int. Sci. Econ. Com.*, October–November 1981, *28*(10–11), pp. 959–76.
[G: LDCs]

Graham, John A. Third World Dynamics in the 1980s. In *Ensor, R., ed.*, 1981, pp. 161–68.
[G: Selected MDCs; Selected LDCs]

Green, María del Rosario. Mexico's Economic Dependence. In *Purcell, S. K., ed.*, 1981, pp. 104–14. **[G: Mexico]**

Guenther, Jack. The Outlook for the 1980s. In *Ensor, R., ed.*, 1981, pp. 155–59. **[G: Non-OPEC LDCs]**

Gulcz, Mieczyslaw and Gruchman, Bohdan. Industrial Investment Assistance: The Socialist Countries' Approach to the Third World. In *Hamilton, F. E. I. and Linge, G. J. R., eds.*, 1981, pp. 215–23. **[G: CMEA; LDCs]**

Haegele, Monroe J. Using a Market Determined Spread as a Guide. In *Ensor, R., ed.*, 1981, pp. 75–79. **[G: Selected MDCs; Selected LDCs]**

Harding, Harry. China and the Third World: From Revolution to Containment. In *Solomon, R. H., ed.*, 1981, pp. 257–95. **[G: China]**

Harriman, W. Averell. Economics and the Truman Administration: Comments. In *Heller, F. H., ed.*, 1981, pp. 111–14. **[G: U.S.; Europe]**

Haschek, Helmut H. Piani di credito alle esportazioni per i paesi in via di sviluppo. (Export Credit Plans for Developing Countries. With English summary.) *Mondo Aperto*, February 1981, *35*(1), pp. 1–10.

Haschek, Helmut H. The Borrower's View of the Financial Markets in the 80's. In *Burghardt, A. M., ed.*, 1981, pp. 59–64. **[G: OECD]**

Helleiner, Gerald K. Aid and Dependence: Issues for Recipients. In *Helleiner, G. K.*, 1981, pp. 219–38.

Helleiner, Gerald K. Relief and Reform in Third World Debt. In *Helleiner, G. K.*, 1981, pp. 104–29.

Heller, H. Robert. The Role of Private Banks in Stabilization Programs: Comment. In *Cline, W. R. and Weintraub, S., eds.*, 1981, pp. 265–68. **[G: LDCs]**

Hoffman, Kurt and Burch, David. The EEC and Energy Aid to the Third World. In *Stevens, C., ed.*, 1981, pp. 25–44. **[G: EEC; LDCs]**

Holzman, Franklyn D. Creditworthiness and Balance-of-payments Adjustment Mechanisms of Centrally Planned Economies. In *[Bergson, A.]*, 1981, pp. 163–84. **[G: E. Europe]**

Huddleston, Barbara. Responsiveness of Food Aid to Variable Import Requirements. In *Valdés, A.*, 1981, pp. 287–306. **[G: LDCs]**

Huddleston, Barbara and Konandreas, Panos. Insurance Approach to Food Security: Simulation of Benefits for 1970/71–1975/76 and for 1978–1982. In *Valdés, A.*, 1981, pp. 241–54.
[G: LDCs]

Hughes, Helen. The New Industrial Countries in the World Economy: Pessimism and a Way Out. In *Saunders, C. T., ed. (II)*, 1981, pp. 97–131.
[G: LDCs; MDCs]

Hughes, Helen. The Transfer of Resources to Developing Countries: Policy Implications and Research Priorities. In *National Science Foundation*, 1981, pp. II23–40.

Hunt, Cecil. Insuring for Political Risk. In *Ensor, R., ed.*, 1981, pp. 137–42.

Ishimine, Tomotaka. Japan's Economic Cooperation in Latin America in the Perspective of the Second Development Decade. *Rivista Int. Sci. Econ. Com.*, July–August 1981, *28*(7–8), pp. 711–30.
[G: Japan; Latin America]

Islam, Nurul. Aid and Influence: The Case of Bangladesh: The Debate. In *Faaland, J., ed.*, 1981, pp. 14–24. **[G: Bangladesh]**

Islam, Nurul. Aid Requirements and Donor Preferences. In *Faaland, J., ed.*, 1981, pp. 37–52.
[G: Bangladesh]

Islam, Nurul. Interest Groups and Aid Conditionality. In *Faaland, J., ed.*, 1981, pp. 53–72.
[G: Bangladesh]

Islam, Nurul. Relationships to Donors: Commodity Aid. In *Faaland, J., ed.*, 1981, pp. 73–84.
[G: Bangladesh]

Johnson, D. Gale. Grain Insurance, Reserves, and Trade: Contributions to Food Security for LDCs. In *Valdés, A.*, 1981, pp. 255–86. **[G: LDCs]**

Kaul, P. N. Technical Assistance from the Fund: Central Banking Department. *Finance Develop.*, June 1981, *18*(2), pp. 34–37.

Killick, Tony. Eurocurrency Market Recycling of OPEC Surpluses to Developing Countries: Fact or Myth? In *Stevens, C., ed.*, 1981, pp. 92–104.
[G: EEC; LDCs]

Kincaid, G. Russell. Inflation and the External Debt of Developing Countries. *Finance Develop.*, December 1981, *18*(4), pp. 45–48. **[G: Non-Oil LDCs]**

Kindleberger, Charles P. Debt Situation of the Developing Countries in Historical Perspective (1800–1945) *Aussenwirtschaft*, December 1981, *36*(4), pp. 372–80.

Kindleberger, Charles P. Less Developed Countries and the International Capital Market. In *Kindleberger, C. P.*, 1981, *1970*, pp. 243–55.
[G: LDCs]

Knapp, Manfred. Reconstruction and West-Integration: The Impact of the Marshall Plan on Germany. *Z. ges. Staatswiss.*, September 1981, *137*(3), pp. 415–33. **[G: W. Germany]**

Koch, Walter A. S. and Lang, Eva. Die Finanzierung von Folgekosten als Instrument der Entwicklungshilfepolitik. (Financing of Recurrent Costs as Investment of Development Policy. With English summary.) *Z. Wirtschaft. Sozialwissen.*, 1981, *101*(3), pp. 321–47. **[G: LDCs]**

Krueger, Anne O. U.S. Economic Policy in Support of Growth in the Developing Countries. In *Na-*

tional Science Foundation, 1981, pp. II41–78.
[G: U.S.; LDCs]

Landell-Mills, Pierre M. Structural Adjustment Lending: Early Experience. *Finance Develop.*, December 1981, *18*(4), pp. 17–21.

de Larosière, Jacques. Compiti del Fondo Monetario Internazionale nel quadro della lotta all'inflazione e di una politica di sviluppo stabile. (The Tasks of the International Monetary Fund in the Context of the Fight against Inflation and of a Steady Development Policy. With English summary.) *Bancaria*, January 1981, *37*(1), pp. 30–36.

Laski, Kazimierz. International Financing: Comment. In *Saunders, C. T., ed. (I)*, 1981, pp. 162–64. [G: LDCs]

Leipziger, Danny M. The Basic Human Needs Approach and North–South Relations. In *Reubens, E. P., ed.*, 1981, pp. 255–79.

Long, Millard F. External Debt and the Trade Imperative in Latin America. In *Baer, W. and Gillis, M., eds.*, 1981, pp. 280–301.
[G: Latin America]

Long, Millard F. External Debt and the Trade Imperative in Latin America. *Quart. Rev. Econ. Bus.*, Summer 1981, *21*(2), pp. 280–301.
[G: Latin America]

Long, Millard F. and Veneroso, Frank. The Debt-related Problems of the Non-Oil Less Developed Countries. *Econ. Develop. Cult. Change*, April 1981, *29*(3), pp. 501–16. [G: LDCs]

Manfredi, Eileen M. Predicting Debt Reschedulings in Developing Countries. *Agr. Econ. Res.*, April 1981, *33*(2), pp. 26–30. [G: LDCs]

Maxwell, S. J. and Singer, H. W. Food Aid to Developing Countries: A Survey. In *Streeten, P. and Jolly, R, eds.*, 1981, pp. 219–40. [G: LDCs]

Maynard, Geoffrey and Bird, Graham. International Monetary Issues and the Developing Countries: A Survey. In *Streeten, P. and Jolly, R, eds.*, 1981, *1975*, pp. 343–65. [G: LDCs]

McBain, Helen. External Financing of the Water Commission of Jamaica. *Soc. Econ. Stud.*, March 1981, *30*(1), pp. 171–96. [G: Jamaica]

McKinnon, Ronald I. Foreign Exchange Constraints in Economic Development and Efficient Aid Allocation. In *Bhagwati, J. N., ed.*, 1981, *1964*, pp. 342–48.

McNamara, Robert S. Lo sviluppo del Terzo Mondo e il ruolo della Banca Mondiale negli anni Ottanta. (Third World Development and the Role of the World Bank in the '70s. With English summary.) *Bancaria*, January 1981, *37*(1), pp. 7–29.
[G: LDCs]

McNamara, Robert S. To the Board of Governors, Nairobi, Kenya, September 24, 1973. In *McNamara, R. S.*, 1981, *1973*, pp. 233–63.
[G: OECD]

McNamara, Robert S. To the Board of Governors, Washington, D.C., September 30, 1980. In *McNamara, R. S.*, 1981, *1980*, pp. 613–60.
[G: LDCs; OECD]

McNamara, Robert S. To the Board of Governors, Washington, D.C., September 25, 1978. In *McNamara, R. S.*, 1981, *1978*, pp. 479–518.
[G: OECD; LDCs]

McNamara, Robert S. To the Board of Governors,

Manila, Philippines, October 4, 1976. In *McNamara, R. S.*, 1981, *1976*, pp. 337–76.
[G: OECD; LDCs]

McNamara, Robert S. To the Board of Governors, Washington, D.C., September 29, 1969. In *McNamara, R. S.*, 1981, *1969*, pp. 69–94.

McNamara, Robert S. To the Board of Governors, Washington, D.C., September 26, 1977. In *McNamara, R. S.*, 1981, *1977*, pp. 437–75.
[G: OECD; LDCs]

McNamara, Robert S. To the Board of Governors, Washington, D.C., September 25, 1972. In *McNamara, R. S.*, 1981, *1972*, pp. 209–29.
[G: OECD]

McNamara, Robert S. To the Board of Governors, Belgrade, Yugoslavia, October 2, 1979. In *McNamara, R. S.*, 1981, *1979*, pp. 565–610.
[G: OECD; LDCs]

McNamara, Robert S. To the Board of Governors, Washington, D.C., September 30, 1974. In *McNamara, R. S.*, 1981, *1974*, pp. 267–93.
[G: OECD; LDCs]

McNamara, Robert S. To the Board of Governors, Copenhagen, Denmark, September 21, 1970. In *McNamara, R. S.*, 1981, *1970*, pp. 111–34.
[G: Selected LDCs]

McNamara, Robert S. To the Board of Governors, Washington, D.C., September 30, 1968. In *McNamara, R. S.*, 1981, *1968*, pp. 3–15.

McNamara, Robert S. To the Board of Governors, Washington, D.C., September 1, 1975. In *McNamara, R. S.*, 1981, *1975*, pp. 297–334.
[G: OECD; LDCs]

McNamara, Robert S. To the Bond Club of New York, New York, New York, May 14, 1969. In *McNamara, R. S.*, 1981, *1969*, pp. 55–66.

McNamara, Robert S. To the Columbia University Conference on International Economic Development, New York, New York, February 20, 1970. In *McNamara, R. S.*, 1981, *1970*, pp. 97–108.

McNamara, Robert S. To the Inter-American Press Association, Buenos Aires, Argentina, October 18, 1968. In *McNamara, R. S.*, 1981, *1986*, pp. 19–29. [G: Latin America]

McNamara, Robert S. To the United Nations Conference on Trade and Development, Santiago, Chile, April 14, 1972. In *McNamara, R. S.*, 1981, *1972*, pp. 171–89. [G: OECD; LDCs]

Michaely, Michael. Foreign Aid, Economic Structure, and Dependence. *J. Devel. Econ.*, December 1981, *9*(3), pp. 313–30.

Montgomery, Douglas L. An Approach to LDC Risk Assessment. In *Ensor, R., ed.*, 1981, pp. 99–102.

Morgan Guaranty Trust Company of New York. The Response to Higher Oil Prices: Adjustment and Financing. In *Baldwin, R. E. and Richardson, J. D., eds.*, 1981, *1980*, pp. 506–16. [G: OPEC; Non-OPEC LDCs]

Mortimore, Michael D. The State and Transnational Banks: Lessons from the Bolivian Crisis of External Public Indebtedness. *Cepal Rev.*, August 1981, (14), pp. 127–51. [G: Bolivia]

Mosley, Paul. Aid for the Poorest: Some Early Lessons of UK Experience. *J. Devel. Stud.*, January 1981, *17*(2), pp. 214–25. [G: U.K.]

Mushi, S. S. Tanzania. In *Adedeji, A., ed.*, 1981, pp. 204–37. [G: Tanzania]

Nagy, Pancras. Economic Development, Debt Profiles and Country Risk. In *Ensor, R., ed.*, 1981, pp. 27–30. [G: Selected LDCs]

Nunnenkamp, Peter. Die Auswirkungen externer Schocks auf die internationale Verschuldung von Schwellenländern nach 1973—am Beispiel Brasiliens, Südkoreas und der Türkei. (With English summary.) *Aussenwirtschaft*, December 1981, 36(4), pp. 352–71. [G: S. Korea; Brazil; Turkey]

O'Brien, Richard. Country Risk and Bank Lending Risk. In *Ensor, R., ed.*, 1981, pp. 87–91. [G: OECD]

Ognev, Alexandre P. The Role of Development Aid Facilities: Comment. In *Saunders, C. T., ed. (I)*, 1981, pp. 165–66. [G: LDCs]

Parkinson, Jack. Aid and Influence: The Case of Bangladesh: The Needs. In *Faaland, J., ed.*, 1981, pp. 25–34. [G: Bangladesh]

Parkinson, Jack. Donor Co-ordination and Collective Leverage: The Role of the World Bank. In *Faaland, J., ed.*, 1981, pp. 147–64. [G: Bangladesh]

Parkinson, Jack. Donor Co-ordination and Collective Leverage: The Role of the Fund. In *Faaland, J., ed.*, 1981, pp. 165–76. [G: Bangladesh]

Parkinson, Jack. Relationships to Donors: Food Aid. In *Faaland, J., ed.*, 1981, pp. 82–101. [G: Bangladesh]

Philip, Kjeld. Danmarks bilaterale samarbejde med udviklingslandene. (Denmarks Bilateral Co-operation with Developing Countries. With English summary.) *Nationaløkon. Tidsskr.*, 1981, 119(1), pp. 47–63. [G: LDCs; Denmark]

Quibria, M. G. Domestic Policies and Foreign Resource Requirements. *Quart. J. Econ.*, February 1981, 96(1), pp. 17–26.

Ranis, Gustav. Alternative Resource Transfer Mechanisms and the Development Process: Research Issues. In *National Science Foundation*, 1981, pp. II79–101.

Roberts, David. The LDC Debt Burden. *Fed. Res. Bank New York Quart. Rev.*, Spring 1981, 6(1), pp. 33–41. [G: LDCs]

Seton, Francis. The Role of Development Aid Facilities. In *Saunders, C. T., ed. (I)*, 1981, pp. 127–59. [G: LDCs]

Siegman, Charles J. Developing Countries and the International Financial System: A Survey of Trends and Selected Issues. In *Reubens, E. P., ed.*, 1981, pp. 179–213. [G: LDCs]

Sofia, A. Zuheir. Rationalizing Country Risk Ratios. In *Ensor, R., ed.*, 1981, pp. 49–68. [G: LDCs]

Soldaczuk, Józef. The Role of Development Aid Facilities: Comment. In *Saunders, C. T., ed. (I)*, 1981, pp. 167–71. [G: LDCs]

Solomon, Robert. The Debt of Developing Countries: Another Look. *Brookings Pap. Econ. Act.*, 1981, (2), pp. 592–606. [G: LDCs]

Takagi, Yasuoki. Aid and Debt Problems in Less–Developed Countries. *Oxford Econ. Pap.*, July 1981, 33(2), pp. 323–37. [G: LDCs]

Thompson, John K. An Index of Economic Risk. In *Ensor, R., ed.*, 1981, pp. 69–74.

Trejo Reyes, Saúl. Case Study of Economic Stabilization: Mexico: Comment. In *Cline, W. R. and Weintraub, S., eds.*, 1981, pp. 292–95. [G: Mexico]

Trouvain, Franz-J. Längerfristige Aspekte der Auslandsverschuldung der Entwicklungsländer. (With English summary.) *Aussenwirtschaft*, December 1981, 36(4), pp. 318–39. [G: LDCs]

Tumlir, Jan and La Haye, Laura. The Two Attempts at European Economic Reconstruction after 1945. *Z. ges. Staatswiss.*, September 1981, 137(3), pp. 367–89. [G: W. Europe]

Türel, Oktar. Planlama ve Ulusararasi Örgütler: Turkiye'nin Dünya Bankasi ile Ilişkileri Örnek Olayi. (Planning and International Organizations: The Case of Turkey's Relations with the World Bank. With English summary.) *METU*, Special Issue, 1981, pp. 635–54. [G: Turkey]

Upadhyay, J. and Shrestha, B. R. External Assistance for Nepal's Hill Agriculture. In *Nepal, Ministry of Food and Agriculture*, 1981, pp. 135–43. [G: Nepal]

de Vries, Barend A. Public Policy and the Private Sector. *Finance Develop.*, September 1981, 18(3), pp. 11–15. [G: LDCs]

de Vries, Rimmer. Proceedings of the Seminar on International Economic Problems: Statement. In *U.S. Congress, Joint Economic Committee (I)*, 1981, pp. 319–35. [G: U.S.; Selected Countries]

Wallich, Henry C. LDC Debt . . . to Worry or not to Worry. *Challenge*, September/October 1981, 24(4), pp. 28–34. [G: LDCs; U.S.]

Weiner, Mervyn L. Evaluating the Bank's Development Projects. *Finance Develop.*, March 1981, 18(1), pp. 38–40.

Weinert, Richard S. Foreign Capital in Mexico. In *Purcell, S. K., ed.*, 1981, pp. 115–24. [G: Mexico]

Weinert, Richard S. Nicaragua's Debt Renegotiation. *Cambridge J. Econ.*, June 1981, 5(2), pp. 187–94. [G: Nicaragua]

Weintraub, Sidney. Case Study of Economic Stabilization: Mexico. In *Cline, W. R. and Weintraub, S., eds.*, 1981, pp. 271–92. [G: Mexico]

Williams, Gavin. The World Bank and the Peasant Problem. In *Heyer, J.; Roberts, P. and Williams, G., eds.*, 1981, pp. 16–51.

Williamson, John. International Monetary Issues and the Developing Countries: A Survey: Comment. In *Streeten, P. and Jolly, R, eds.*, 1981, 1975, pp. 381–82.

500 Administration; Business Finance; Marketing; Accounting

5000 General

Frazer, Timothy and Frazer, June. Fairfax Cone: Foote, Cone and Belding. *J. Behav. Econ.*, Winter 1981, 10(2), pp. 127–36. [G: U.S.]

Frazer, Timothy and Frazer, June. Harry Barber and William B. Greene: The Barber-Greene Corporation. *J. Behav. Econ.*, Winter 1981, 10(2), pp. 107–17. [G: U.S.]

Frazer, Timothy and Frazer, June. Leo Burnett: Leo Burnett, Inc. *J. Behav. Econ.*, Winter 1981, *10*(2), pp. 97–105. [G: U.S.]

Frazer, Timothy and Frazer, June. Wes Loomis: General Directory Telephone Company. *J. Behav. Econ.*, Winter 1981, *10*(2), pp. 119–26. [G: U.S.]

Hattwick, Richard E. Eugene F. McDonald, Jr.: Zenith Radio Corporation. *J. Behav. Econ.*, Winter 1981, *10*(2), pp. 29–55. [G: U.S.]

Hattwick, Richard E. Irl Martin—A Study in Business Ethics. *J. Behav. Econ.*, Summer 1981, *10*(1), pp. 115–31.

Hattwick, Richard E. John M. Cotter: Cotter and Company. *J. Behav. Econ.*, Winter 1981, *10*(2), pp. 83–95. [G: U.S.]

Hattwick, Richard E. Paul Galvin: Motorola. *J. Behav. Econ.*, Winter 1981, *10*(2), pp. 17–28. [G: U.S.]

Hattwick, Richard E. R. J. Frisby. *J. Behav. Econ.*, Winter 1981, *10*(2), pp. 137–54. [G: U.S.]

Hattwick, Richard E. Richard Sears, Julius Rosenwald and Robert Wood: Sears, Roebuck and Company. *J. Behav. Econ.*, Winter 1981, *10*(2), pp. 57–81. [G: U.S.]

Hattwick, Richard E. William A. Patterson: United Airlines. *J. Behav. Econ.*, Winter 1981, *10*(2), pp. 1–15. [G: U.S.]

Honko, Jaakko. Kauppatieteellisen tutkimuksen ongelma- alueista 1980 -luvulla. (Problem Areas for Management and Business Research in the 1980s. With English summary.) *Liiketaloudellinen Aikak.*, 1981, *30*(3), pp. 309–24. [G: Finland]

Marks, Robert; Watt, Peter and Yetton, Philip W. GMAT Scores and Performance: Selecting Students into a Graduate Management School. *Australian J. Manage.*, December 1981, *6*(2), pp. 81–102. [G: Australia]

510 Administration

511 Organization and Decision Theory

5110 Organization and Decision Theory

Akoka, Jacky. Centralisation ou décentralisation des systèmes d'information un modèle d'aide à la décision. (Centralization versus Decentralization of Information Systems. A Decision Support Model. With English summary.) *Écon. Soc.*, October–November–December 1981, *15*(10–12), pp. 1759–73.

Aldrich, Howard E. and Whetten, David A. Organization-sets, Action-sets, and Networks: Making the Most of Simplicity. In *Nystrom, P. C. and Starbuck, W. H., eds.*, Vol. 1, 1981, pp. 385–408.

Arthur, Jeffrey L. and Lawrence, Kenneth D. Produce or Purchase—A Multiple Goal Linear Programming Model. In *Morse, J. N., ed.*, 1981, pp. 1–9.

Ashton, Robert H. A Descriptive Study of Information Evaluation. *J. Acc. Res.*, Spring 1981, *19*(1), pp. 42–61.

Baetge, Jörg and Fischer, Thomas. Substitution des Markt-Preis-Mechanismus durch Steuerungs- und Regelungsmechanismen im Unternehmen. (Managerial Control Strategies Instead of Price Mechanism. With English summary.) *Z. ges. Staatswiss.*, December 1981, *137*(4), pp. 723–32.

Bartlett, Christopher A. Multinational Structural Change: Evolution Versus Reorganization. In *Otterbeck, L., ed.*, 1981, pp. 121–45. [G: U.S.]

Baum, Sanford; Terry, W. Robert and Parekh, Uday N. Random Sampling Approach to MCDM. In *Morse, J. N., ed.*, 1981, pp. 10–27.

Belkin, M. I., et al. Modeling the Impact of the Economic Mechanism on the Indicators of Enterprise Activity. *Matekon*, Winter 1981–82, *18*(2), pp. 32–52. [G: U.S.S.R.]

Biţă, V. Objectives for the Informatic Systems. *Econ. Computat. Cybern. Stud. Res.*, 1981, *15*(2), pp. 41–49. [G: Romania]

Bloom, Barry M. The Pharmaceutical Research and Development Decision Process: Comment. In *Helms, R. B., ed.*, 1981, pp. 114–17.

Bluma, Aleš. Sources d'information les clefs de la réussite. (Information Source—The Key to Success. With English summary.) *Ann. Sci. Écon. Appl.*, 1981, *37*(4), pp. 63–93.

Bod, Péter. Strategic Decisions on the Development of the Aluminum Industry. *Matekon*, Winter 1981–82, *18*(2), pp. 3–18. [G: Hungary]

Bodily, Samuel E. Stability, Equality, Balance, and Multivariate Risk. In *Morse, J. N., ed.*, 1981, pp. 40–55.

Brownell, Peter. Participation in Budgeting, Locus of Control and Organizational Effectiveness. *Accounting Rev.*, October 1981, *56*(4), pp. 844–60. [G: U.S.]

de Bruyne, Paul. L'écologie des organisations: Modèles d'adaptation, de régulation, de sélection. (The Ecology of Organization: Models of Adaptation, Regulation, Selection. With English summary.) *Ann. Sci. Écon. Appl.*, 1981, *37*(1), pp. 61–98.

Burness, H. Stuart. Risk: Accounting for an Uncertain Future. *Natural Res. J.*, October 1981, *21*(4), pp. 723–34. [G: U.S.]

Campion, William M. and Jackson, John H. Research for Strategic Decisions: Beginning to Put Humpty Dumpty Together Again. *J. Behav. Econ.*, Summer 1981, *10*(1), pp. 33–46.

Candau, Pierre. Pour une taxonomie de l'hypofirme. (With English summary.) *Rev. Econ. Ind.*, 2nd Trimester 1981, (16), pp. 16–33.

Carlsson, C. Solving Complex and Ill-Structured Problems: An MCDM-Approach. In *Nijkamp, P. and Spronk, J., eds.*, 1981, pp. 53–83.

Cartoccio, Achille. Perché servono i consulenti interni. (The Utility of Internal Consultants. With English summary.) *L'Impresa*, 1981, *23*(2), pp. 35–43.

Chalmet, L. G. and Lawphongpanich, S. Efficient Solutions for Point-Objective Discrete Facility Location Problems. In *Morse, J. N., ed.*, 1981, pp. 56–71.

Child, John and Kieser, Alfred. Development of Organizations over Time. In *Nystrom, P. C. and Starbuck, W. H., eds.*, Vol. 1, 1981, pp. 28–64.

Christensen, John. Communication in Agencies. *Bell J. Econ. (See Rand J. Econ. after 4/85)*, Autumn

1981, *12*(2), pp. 661–74.

Cohen, Michael D. The Power of Parallel Thinking. *J. Econ. Behav. Organ.*, December 1981, *2*(4), pp. 285–306.

Cracco, Etienne. Un processus de selection de marchés: la méthode de l'entonnoir. (A Market Selection Process: The "Funnel" Method. With English summary.) *Ann. Sci. Écon. Appl.*, 1981, *37*(4), pp. 45–62.

van Dam, André. The Pause That Refreshes. *Rivista Int. Sci. Econ. Com.*, January–February 1981, *28*(1–2), pp. 170–76.

Degroof, Jean-Jacques. Jeux et enjeux des bilans sociaux étude de cas. (Strategic Analysis of Social Audit Experiments. With English summary.) *Ann. Sci. Écon. Appl.*, 1981, *37*(1), pp. 99–117. [G: Belgium]

Demski, Joel S. and Swieringa, Robert J. Discussion of Behavioral Decision Theory: Processes of Judgment and Choice. *J. Acc. Res.*, Spring 1981, *19*(1), pp. 32–41.

Dong, Yusheng. Instituting an Intrafactory Economic Contract System Is a Good Device to Strengthen Business Management. *Chinese Econ. Stud.*, Fall 1981, *15*(1), pp. 38–46. [G: China]

Dorward, Neil and Wiedemann, Paul. Robustness as a Corporate Objective under Uncertainty. *Managerial Dec. Econ.*, September 1981, *2*(3), pp. 186–91.

Duckstein, L. and Kempf, J. Multicriteria Q-Analysis for Plan Evaluation. In *Nijkamp, P. and Spronk, J., eds.*, 1981, pp. 87–99. [G: Hungary]

Dunbar, Roger L. M. Designs for Organizational Control. In *Nystrom, P. C. and Starbuck, W. H., eds., Vol. 2*, 1981, pp. 85–115.

Einhorn, Hillel J. and Hogarth, Robin M. Behavioral Decision Theory: Processes of Judgment and Choice. *J. Acc. Res.*, Spring 1981, *19*(1), pp. 1–31.

Ekern, Steinar. Time Dominance Efficiency Analysis. *J. Finance*, December 1981, *36*(5), pp. 1023–34.

Elden, J. Maxwell. Political Efficacy at Work: The Connection between More Autonomous Forms of Workplace Organization and a More Participatory Politics. *Amer. Polit. Sci. Rev.*, March 1981, *75*(1), pp. 43–58. [G: U.S.]

Fandel, Günter. Decision Concepts for Organizations. In *Morse, J. N., ed.*, 1981, pp. 91–109.

Fáy, József and Nyers, Reszö. Specialization and Cooperation in the Hungarian Economy and the CMEA. *Acta Oecon.*, 1981, *27*(1–2), pp. 1–18. [G: CMEA; Hungary]

Fernandes, Manuel C. C. Objectivos múltiplos em programaçao. (With English summary.) *Economia (Portugal)*, October 1981, *5*(3), pp. 471–87.

Fisher, Steven B. Recent Developments in Team Decision Theory. *Amer. Econ.*, Fall 1981, *25*(2), pp. 30–34.

Frantz, Roger S. On the Existence of X-Efficiency: A Reply. *J. Post Keynesian Econ.*, Fall 1981, *4*(1), pp. 149–51. [G: U.S.]

Franz, L. S. and Lee, S. M. A Goal Programming Based Interactive Decision Support System. In *Morse, J. N., ed.*, 1981, pp. 110–15.

Friesz, Terry L. Multiobjective Optimization in Transportation: The Case of Equilibrium Network Design. In *Morse, J. N., ed.*, 1981, pp. 116–27.

Gasparotti, Giorgio. Quali vantaggi per l'analisi transazionale. (Which Advantages for the Transactional Analysis. With English summary.) *L'Impresa*, 1981, *23*(4), pp. 29–33.

Gerwin, Donald. Relationships between Structure and Technology. In *Nystrom, P. C. and Starbuck, W. H., eds., Vol. 2*, 1981, pp. 3–38.

Glazer, Herbert. Com'è, come funziona il management giapponese. (The Management Made in Japan. With English summary.) *L'Impresa*, 1981, *23*(6), pp. 29–39. [G: Japan]

Gligorov, Kiro. The Social and Economic Basis of Socialist Self-Management in Yugoslavia. *Eastern Europ. Econ.*, Winter 1981–82, *20*(2), pp. 3–22.

Green, Paul E.; Carroll, J. Douglas and DeSarbo, Wayne S. Estimating Choice Probabilities in Multiattribute Decision Making. *J. Cons. Res.*, June 1981, *8*(1), pp. 76–84.

Green, Stephen; Mack, Christopher and Turner, William D. The Role of the Treasury Function. In *Ensor, R. and Muller, P., eds.*, 1981, pp. 1–12.

Greiner, Larry E. and Schein, Virginia E. The Paradox of Managing a Project-Oriented Matrix: Establishing Coherence within Chaos. *Sloan Manage. Rev.*, Winter 1981, *22*(2), pp. 17–22.

Guran, M., et al. Multilevel Approach to Real Time Management and Control Systems. *Econ. Computat. Cybern. Stud. Res.*, 1981, *15*(1), pp. 22–33.

Guth, Wilfried. The Change in Leadership and Continuity in an Enterprise. In *Engels, W. and Pohl, H., eds.*, 1981, pp. 1–9.

Haimes, Y. Y. and Tarvainen, K. Hierarchical-Multiobjective Framework for Large Scale Systems. In *Nijkamp, P. and Spronk, J., eds.*, 1981, pp. 201–32.

Hedberg, Bo. How Organizations Learn and Unlearn. In *Nystrom, P. C. and Starbuck, W. H., eds., Vol. 1*, 1981, pp. 3–27.

Hefftner, Susann. A. H. Maslows Lehre von der Bedürfnishierarchie und Bedurfnisentwicklung. Überlegungen zu ihrem Inhalt und Erkenntniswert. (A. H. Maslow's Theory about the Needs-Hierarchy and Needs Development—Preflections on Its Content and Perception Value. With English summary.) *Z. Wirtschaft. Sozialwissen.*, 1981, *101*(5), pp. 479–505.

Hemming, Tom. Some Modifications of a Large Step Gradient Method for Interactive Multicriterion Optimization. In *Morse, J. N., ed.*, 1981, pp. 128–39.

Hey, John D. Are Optimal Search Rules Reasonable? And Vice Versa? (And Does It Matter Anyway?) *J. Econ. Behav. Organ.*, March 1981, *2*(1), pp. 47–70.

Ho, James K. An Experiment in Multiple Criteria Energy Policy Analysis. In *Morse, J. N., ed.*, 1981, pp. 145–56. [G: U.S.]

Horwitch, Mel and Prahalad, C. K. Managing Multi-Organization Enterprises: The Emerging Strategic Frontier. *Sloan Manage. Rev.*, Winter 1981, *22*(2), pp. 3–16.

Jansen, M. J. M. and Tijs, S. H. Arbitration Games. A Survey. In *Fandel, G., et al., eds.*, 1981, pp. 116–26.

Joyce, Edward J. and Libby, Robert. Some Accounting Implications of "Behavioral Decision Theory: Processes of Judgment and Choice." *J. Acc. Res.*, Autumn 1981, *19*(2), pp. 544–50.

Kagono, Tadao. Structural Design of Headquarters-Division Relationships and Economic Performance: An Analysis of Japanese Firms. In *Otterbeck, L., ed.*, 1981, pp. 147–85. **[G: Japan]**

Kallio, Markku. Sovelletusta systeemianalyysista. (On Applied Systems Analysis. With English summary.) *Liiketaloudellinen Aikak.*, 1981, *30*(2), pp. 157–67.

Keen, Peter G. W. Decision Support Systems and Managerial Productivity Analysis. In *Hogan, J. D. and Craig, A. M., eds., Vol. 1*, 1981, pp. 571–601. **[G: U.S.]**

Kessler, Lawrence and Ashton, Robert H. Feedback and Prediction Achievement in Financial Analysis. *J. Acc. Res.*, Spring 1981, *19*(1), pp. 146–62.

Kimberly, John R. Managerial Innovation. In *Nystrom, P. C. and Starbuck, W. H., eds., Vol. 1*, 1981, pp. 84–104.

Kornbluth, J. S. H. Multiple Objective Linear Fractional Programming Algorithms: Some Computational Experience. In *Morse, J. N., ed.*, 1981, pp. 173–98.

Kudla, Ronald J. Strategic Planning and Risk. *Rev. Bus. Econ. Res.*, Fall 1981, *17*(1), pp. 1–14. **[G: U.S.]**

Lawrence, Kenneth D. and Reeves, Gary R. Consensus Time Series Forecasting. In *Morse, J. N., ed.*, 1981, pp. 199–204.

Lawrence, Sheila M.; Lawrence, Kenneth D. and Reeves, Gary R. A Multiple Goal Model for Allocation of Teaching Personnel. In *Morse, J. N., ed.*, 1981, pp. 222–31.

Leibkind, A. R.; Rudnik, B. L. and Chukhnov, A. I. Models for Forming Organizational Structures—A Survey. *Matekon*, Spring 1981, *17*(3), pp. 102–35.

Levinthal, Daniel and March, James G. A Model of Adaptive Organizational Search. *J. Econ. Behav. Organ.*, December 1981, *2*(4), pp. 307–33.

Lockett, A. G.; Muhlemann, A. P. and Gear, A. E. Group Decision Making and Multiple Criteria—A Documented Application. In *Morse, J. N., ed.*, 1981, pp. 205–21.

Mackenzie, Kenneth D. Concepts and Measures in Organizational Development. In *Hogan, J. D. and Craig, A. M., eds., Vol. 1*, 1981, pp. 233–301.

Mali, Paul. Managerial Strategies for Productivity Improvement. In *Hogan, J. D. and Craig, A. M., eds., Vol. 1*, 1981, pp. 477–90. **[G: U.S.]**

Mănescu, Manea. The System of Scientific Research and Technological Development: Cybernetic—Economic Models of the system. *Econ. Computat. Cybern. Stud. Res.*, 1981, *15*(1), pp. 7–12.

Máriás, Antal, et al. Organization of Large Industrial Enterprises in Hungary: A Comparative Analysis. *Acta Oecon.*, 1981, *27*(3–4), pp. 327–42. **[G: Hungary]**

McNally, Mary. On X-Efficiency: Comment [On the Existence of X-Efficiency]. *J. Post Keynesian Econ.*, Fall 1981, *4*(1), pp. 145–48. **[G: U.S.]**

Metcalfe, Les. Designing Precarious Partnerships. In *Nystrom, P. C. and Starbuck, W. H., eds., Vol. 1*, 1981, pp. 503–30.

Michalowski, Wojciech. The Choice of Final Compromise Solution in Multiple Criteria Linear Programming Problem. In *Morse, J. N., ed.*, 1981, pp. 233–38.

Miller, Jeffrey B. and Murrell, Peter. Limitations on the Use of Information-Revealing Incentive Schemes in Economic Organizations. *J. Compar. Econ.*, September 1981, *5*(3), pp. 251–71.

Moch, Michael and Seashore, Stanley E. How Norms Affect Behaviors in and of Corporations. In *Nystrom, P. C. and Starbuck, W. H., eds., Vol. 1*, 1981, pp. 210–37.

Negoiţă, C. V. On the Fundamental Research in Modelling Decision-Making Processes. *Econ. Computat. Cybern. Stud. Res.*, 1981, *15*(1), pp. 35–42.

Nelson, Richard R. Assessing Private Enterprise: An Exegesis of Tangled Doctrine. *Bell J. Econ. (See Rand J. Econ. after 4/85)*, Spring 1981, *12*(1), pp. 93–111.

Niculescu-Mizil, E. Informatics on Industrial Platforms. *Econ. Computat. Cybern. Stud. Res.*, 1981, *15*(2), pp. 25–30.

Niculescu-Mizil, E. Information Processing for Managing Economic Units. *Econ. Computat. Cybern. Stud. Res.*, 1981, *15*(1), pp. 13–22.

Nijkamp, Peter and Spronk, Jaap. Multiple Criteria Analysis: Theory and Reality. In *Nijkamp, P. and Spronk, J., eds.*, 1981, pp. 1–8.

Nowakowska, Maria. A Model of Internal Decisions in Answering Questions. In *Morse, J. N., ed.*, 1981, pp. 265–82.

Peterson, Richard A. Entrepreneurship and Organization. In *Nystrom, P. C. and Starbuck, W. H., eds., Vol. 1*, 1981, pp. 65–83.

Petrović-Lazarević, Sonja. Some Aspects of the Importance of Information in the Process of Decision-Making in the Self-Management Society. *Econ. Anal. Worker's Manage.*, 1981, *15*(4), pp. 517–25. **[G: Yugoslavia]**

Prahalad, C. K. and Doz, Yves L. Strategic Control—The Dilemma in Headquarters-Subsidiary Relationship. In *Otterbeck, L., ed.*, 1981, pp. 187–203.

Priewasser, Erich. Implementation of OR/MS Models in German Banks. *J. Bank Res.*, Summer 1981, *12*(2), pp. 124–27. **[G: W. Germany]**

Pun, Lucas. Trilogical Coherence in Multicriteria Decision-Aid Making—A Methodological Approach to Computer-Aid Management. In *Morse, J. N., ed.*, 1981, pp. 283–95.

Putterman, Louis. The Organization of Work: Comment. *J. Econ. Behav. Organ.*, September 1981, *2*(3), pp. 273–79.

Quiggin, John C. Risk Perception and the Analysis of Risk Attitudes. *Australian J. Agr. Econ.*, August 1981, *25*(2), pp. 160–69. **[G: Australia]**

Raiffa, Howard. Decision Making in the State-

Owned Enterprise. In *Vernon, R. and Aharoni, Y., eds.*, 1981, pp. 54–62.

Ratick, Samuel J.; Cohon, Jared L. and ReVelle, Charles S. Multiobjective Programming Solutions to N-Person Bargaining Games. In *Morse, J. N., ed.*, 1981, pp. 296–319.

ReVelle, Charles S.; Cohon, Jared L. and Shobrys, Donald. Multiple Objectives in Facility Location: A Review. In *Morse, J. N., ed.*, 1981, pp. 320–37.

Revsine, Lawrence. The Theory and Measurement of Business Income: A Review Article. *Accounting Rev.*, April 1981, 56(2), pp. 342–54.

Richardson, James A. Organizational Conditions for Improving Human Productivity: Definition, Diagnosis and Change. In *Hogan, J. D. and Craig, A. M., eds., Vol. 1*, 1981, pp. 361–91.

Richman, Eugene and Coleman, Denis. Monte Carlo Simulation for Management. *Calif. Manage. Rev.*, Spring 1981, 23(3), pp. 82–91.

Roos, Leslie L., Jr. and Starke, Frederick A. Organizational Roles. In *Nystrom, P. C. and Starbuck, W. H., eds., Vol. 1*, 1981, pp. 290–308.

Rousseau, P. Réflexions sur un système d'informations commerciales. (Information Systems Related to International Markets (SIRMI). With English summary.) *Ann. Sci. Écon. Appl.*, 1981, 37(4), pp. 95–112.

Routamaa, Vesa. Toward a Systematic Understanding of the Relationship between Organizational Structure and Performance. *Liiketaloudellinen Aikak.*, 1981, 30(4), pp. 422–34.   [G: Finland]

Roy, B. A Multicriteria Analysis for Trichotomic Segmentation Problems. In *Nijkamp, P. and Spronk, J., eds.*, 1981, pp. 245–57.

Sage, Andrew P. Designs for Optimal Information Filters. In *Nystrom, P. C. and Starbuck, W. H., eds., Vol. 1*, 1981, pp. 105–21.

Schanze, Erich. Der Beitrag von Coase zu Recht und Ökonomie des Unternehmens. (Coase's Contribution to Law and Economics of Business Organizations. With English summary.) *Z. ges. Staatswiss.*, December 1981, 137(4), pp. 694–701.

Schoemaker, Paul J. H. Behavioral Issues in Multiattribute Utility Modeling and Decision Analysis. In *Morse, J. N., ed.*, 1981, pp. 338–62.

Seashore, Stanley E. Organizational Effectiveness: Productivity and What Else? In *Hogan, J. D. and Craig, A. M., eds., Vol. 1*, 1981, pp. 495–504.

Seo, Fumiko. Organizational Aspects of Multicriteria Decision Making. In *Morse, J. N., ed.*, 1981, pp. 363–79.

Shen, T. Y. Technology and Organizational Economics. In *Nystrom, P. C. and Starbuck, W. H., eds., Vol. 1*, 1981, pp. 268–89.

Spronk, Jaap. Capital Budgeting and Financial Planning with Multiple Goals. In *Nijkamp, P. and Spronk, J., eds.*, 1981, pp. 25–36.

Starbuck, William H. and Nystrom, Paul C. Designing and Understanding Organizations. In *Nystrom, P. C. and Starbuck, W. H., eds., Vol. 1*, 1981, pp. ix–xxii.

Stephenson, Robert W. and Stephenson, Matilde K. Design Requirements for an Investment Strategy Decision System for Training and Personnel Technology RDT&E. In *Morse, J. N., ed.*, 1981, pp. 388–408.

Street, David. Welfare Administration and Organizational Theory. In *Martin, G. T., Jr., and Zald, M. N., eds.*, 1981, pp. 285–300.

Tarvainen, K. and Haimes, Yacov Y. Hierarchical-Multiobjective Framework for Energy Storage Systems. In *Morse, J. N., ed.*, 1981, pp. 424–46.

Taylor, Ronald N. and Vertinsky, Ilan. Experimenting with Organizational Behavior. In *Nystrom, P. C. and Starbuck, W. H., eds., Vol. 1*, 1981, pp. 139–66.

Tichy, Noel M. Networks in Organizations. In *Nystrom, P. C. and Starbuck, W. H., eds., Vol. 2*, 1981, pp. 225–49.

Tomer, John F. Organizational Change, Organization Capital and Economic Growth. *Eastern Econ. J.*, January 1981, 7(1), pp. 1–14.   [G: U.S.]

Tomlinson, R. Intervention—The Interface between Reality and Thought. In *Fandel, G., et al., eds.*, 1981, pp. 25–40.

Tsurumi, Yoshi. The Japanese Corporation. In *Richardson, B. M. and Ueda, T., eds.*, 1981, pp. 5–14.   [G: Japan]

Waid, C. Carter and Schoemaker, Paul J. H. On the Fidelity of Multiattribute Preference Representations: Some Analytical Considerations. In *Morse, J. N., ed.*, 1981, pp. 447–64.

Walton, Richard E. Planned Changes to Improve Organizational Effectiveness. In *Hogan, J. D. and Craig, A. M., eds., Vol. 1*, 1981, pp. 203–31.   [G: U.S.]

Warner, Malcolm. Organizational Experiments and Social Innovations. In *Nystrom, P. C. and Starbuck, W. H., eds., Vol. 1*, 1981, pp. 167–84.

Wierzbicki, Andrzej P. A Mathematical Basis for Satisficing Decision Making. In *Morse, J. N., ed.*, 1981, pp. 465–85.

Wiggins, Steven N. The Pharmaceutical Research and Development Decision Process. In *Helms, R. B., ed.*, 1981, pp. 55–83.   [G: U.S.]

Williams, H. P. Reallocating the Cost of Dependent Decisions. *Appl. Econ.*, March 1981, 13(1), pp. 89–98.

Williamson, Oliver E. The Organization of Work: Reply. *J. Econ. Behav. Organ.*, September 1981, 2(3), pp. 281–83.

Wrather, C. and Yu, P. L. Probability Dominance in Random Outcomes—An Introduction. In *Morse, J. N., ed.*, 1981, pp. 486–89.

Yokoyama, Tamotsu. On Knowledge Utilization Method—Database Search. (In Japanese. With English summary.) *Osaka Econ. Pap.*, December 1981, 31(2–3), pp. 209–14.

Yu, P. L. and Seiford, L. Multistage Decision Problems with Multiple Criteria. In *Nijkamp, P. and Spronk, J., eds.*, 1981, pp. 235–44.

Zanakis, S. H. A Method for Large-Scale Integer Goal Programming with an Application to a Facility Location/Allocation Problem. In *Morse, J. N., ed.*, 1981, pp. 490–98.

Zeleny, M. A Case Study in Multiobjective Design: de Novo Programming. In *Nijkamp, P. and Spronk, J., eds.*, 1981, pp. 37–52.

512 Managerial Economics

5120 Managerial Economics

Allard, Richard. Factors Affecting the Growth of the Firm—Theory and Practice: Comment. In *Currie, D.; Peel, D. and Peters, W., eds.*, 1981, pp. 357–60. **[G: U.K.]**

Andersson, John. A Framework for Distributed Computerized Inventory Control Systems. In *Chikán, A., ed. (II)*, 1981, pp. 23–33.

Ashton, D. J. and Atkins, D. R. Multicriteria Programming for Financial Planning: Some Second Thoughts. In *Nijkamp, P. and Spronk, J., eds.*, 1981, pp. 11–23.

Balachandran, K. R.; Maschmeyer, Richard A. and Livingstone, J. Leslie. Product Warranty Period: A Markovian Approach to Estimation and Analysis of Repair and Replacement Costs. *Accounting Rev.*, January 1981, *56*(1), pp. 115–24.

Balaton, Károly. Using Contingency Approach in the Analysis of Company Level Inventory Systems. In *Chikán, A., ed. (II)*, 1981, pp. 35–44.

Barancsi, E., et al. Analysis of a System of Inventory Models. In *Chikán, A., ed. (II)*, 1981, pp. 297–308.

Beasley, Wm. Howard, III. Can Managerial Economics Aid the Chief Executive Officer? *Managerial Dec. Econ.*, September 1981, *2*(3), pp. 129–32. **[G: U.S.]**

Benninga, Simon and Muller, Eitan. Majority Choice and the Objective Function of the Firm under Uncertainty: Reply. *Bell J. Econ. (See Rand J. Econ. after 4/85)*, Spring 1981, *12*(1), pp. 338–39.

Berács, József. Inventory Control—A Logistics Approach. In *Chikán, A., ed. (II)*, 1981, pp. 45–55.

Bettis, Richard A. and Hall, William K. Strategic Portfolio Management in the Multibusiness Firm. *Calif. Manage. Rev.*, Fall 1981, *24*(1), pp. 23–38.

Blackburn, Joseph D. and Millen, Robert A. Guidelines for Lot-Sizing Selection in Multi-echelon Requirements Planning Systems. In *Chikán, A., ed. (II)*, 1981, pp. 57–66.

Britt, Gisela. Methods for Long-term Planning of Stocks of Semi-finished Goods within an Extended Mass Production Process. In *Chikán, A., ed. (II)*, 1981, pp. 67–75.

Buell, Stephen G. and Schwartz, Eli. Increasing Leverage, Potential Failure Rates and Possible Effects on the Macro-Economy. *Oxford Econ. Pap.*, November 1981, *33*(3), pp. 442–58. **[G: U.S.]**

Bulinskaya, E. V. Some Inventory Models. In *Chikán, A., ed. (II)*, 1981, pp. 309–17.

Bylka, Stanislaw. Policies of (Multi-S) Type in Dynamic Inventory Problem. In *Chikán, A., ed. (II)*, 1981, pp. 319–29.

Camacho, Antonio and White, William D. A Note on Loss of Control and the Optimum Size of the Firm [Supervision, Loss of Control, and the Optimum Size of the Firm]. *J. Polit. Econ.*, April 1981, *89*(2), pp. 407–10.

Cantani, Gianni. Marketing e pianificazione nelle PMI. (Marketing and Planning in Small and Me-

dium-Sized Firms. With English summary.) *L'Impresa*, 1981, *23*(6), pp. 53–56.

Carlson, Robert C. and Kropp, Dean H. Inventory Planning Using Rolling Production Scheduling. In *Chikán, A., ed. (II)*, 1981, pp. 331–40.

Carter, E. Eugene. Resource Allocation. In *Nystrom, P. C. and Starbuck, W. H., eds., Vol. 2*, 1981, pp. 152–65.

di Castri, Gianluca. Quando i contratti devono essere flessibili. (When Contracts Must Be Flexible. With English summary.) *L'Impresa*, 1981, *23*(4), pp. 47–53.

Chillemi, Ottorino. Sul regime del capitale nell'impresa autogestita. (Property Rights and the Labour-managed Firm. With English summary.) *Rivista Int. Sci. Econ. Com.*, January–February 1981, *28*(1–2), pp. 151–69.

Claycamp, Henry J. and Liddy, Lucien E. Prediction of New-Product Performance: An Analytical Approach. In *Wind, Y.; Mahajan, V. and Cardozo, R. N., eds.*, 1981, *1969*, pp. 357–69. **[G: U.S.]**

Coburn, David L.; Ellis, Joseph K., III and Milano, Duane R. Dilemmas in MNC Transfer Pricing. *Manage. Account.*, November 1981, *63*(5), pp. 53–58, 69. **[G: U.S.]**

Davies, G. J. The Role of Exporter and Freight Forwarder in the United Kingdom. *J. Int. Bus. Stud.*, Winter 1981, *12*(3), pp. 99–108. **[G: U.K.]**

Degroof, Jean-Jacques. Jeux et enjeux des bilans sociaux étude de cas. (Strategic Analysis of Social Audit Experiments. With English summary.) *Ann. Sci. Écon. Appl.*, 1981, *37*(1), pp. 99–117. **[G: Belgium]**

Delhaye, Guy and Sturbois, Georges. Les étudiants et la gestion sociale: perception de la dimension socio-gestionnaire du management chez de futurs cadres en Hainaut. (Students and Social Management: Perception of the Socio-Managerial Dimension of Management by Future Executives in the Province of Hainaut (Belgium). With English summary.) *Ann. Sci. Écon. Appl.*, 1981, *37*(2), pp. 57–88. **[G: Belgium]**

Desenzani, Leonardo. Marketing e progettazione: un'intervista. (Marketing and Planning: An Interview. With English summary.) *L'Impresa*, 1981, *23*(6), pp. 57–60. **[G: Italy]**

Di Stefano, Guido. L'industria giapponese: tre giornate di studio. (Japanese Industry: A 3-Day Meeting. With English summary.) *L'Impresa*, 1981, *23*(5), pp. 51–55. **[G: Japan]**

Dirickx, Yvo M. I. and Koevoets, Danielle. Continuous Review Inventory Models with Stochastic Lead-Time. In *Chikán, A., ed. (II)*, 1981, pp. 341–49.

Donkersloot, Richard, Jr. Productivity through Manufacturing Control. *Manage. Account.*, December 1981, *63*(6), pp. 25–32.

Doyle, P.; Fenwick, I. and Savage, G. P. A Model for Evaluating Branch Location and Performance. *J. Bank Res.*, Summer 1981, *12*(2), pp. 90–95. **[G: U.K.]**

Eppen, G. D. Mathematics and Managers. *Tijdschrift Econ. Manage.*, 1981, *26*(2), pp. 251–60.

Eschenbach, Rolf. Efficiency and Efficiency Measurement in Materials Management. In *Chikán,*

A., ed. (II), 1981, pp. 77–84.

Farkas, Katalin. The Changing Role of Inventories in the Enterprise. An Example for the Adaptation of the Management. In *Chikán, A., ed. (II)*, 1981, pp. 85–98. **[G: Hungary]**

Federwisch, Jacques. Etat et perspective des modèles intégrés de gestion. (Status of Progress and Prospects of Management Integrated Models. With English summary.) *Cah. Écon. Bruxelles*, 2nd Trimestre 1981, (90), pp. 269–79.

Gerencsér, L; Gyepesi, Gy. and Urbánszki, F. A Spare Parts Inventory Problem with Seasonal Fluctuations. In *Chikán, A., ed. (II)*, 1981, pp. 351–53. **[G: Hungary]**

Giannone, Antonio. Il controllo di gestione nelle imprese di impiantistica. (Management Control in Plant Construction Firms. With English summary.) *L'Impresa*, 1981, 23(6), pp. 21–28.

Girin, Jacques. Quel paradigme pour la recherche en gestion? (What Paradigm for Management Research? With English summary.) *Écon. Soc.*, October–November–December 1981, 15(10–12), pp. 1871–89.

Girlich, H.-J. and Küenle, H.-U. Reliability Type Inventory Models with Ordering Time Limit. In *Chikán, A., ed. (II)*, 1981, pp. 355–64.

Glazer, Herbert. Com'è, come funziona il management giapponese. (The Management Made in Japan. With English summary.) *L'Impresa*, 1981, 23(6), pp. 29–39. **[G: Japan]**

Gold, Bela. Frontiers of Productivity Analysis for Management: With Special Reference to Steel and Other Manufacturing Industries. In *Hogan, J. D. and Craig, A. M., eds.*, Vol. 2, 1981, pp. 1159–76. **[G: U.S.]**

Goyal, Suresh Kumar. A Simple Method of Determining Nearly Optimum Order Quantities for a Multi-product Single-Supplier System. In *Chikán, A., ed. (II)*, 1981, pp. 365–71.

Grubbström, Robert W. and Thorstenson, Anders. An Improved Procedure for Determining Inventory Holding Costs. In *Chikán, A., ed. (II)*, 1981, pp. 373–83.

Hansen, Terje. Analysing the Demand for Fishmeal by a Linear Programming Model. In *Haley, K. B., ed.*, 1981, pp. 247–60. **[G: Global]**

ter Haseborg, F. Optimale Programmpolitik für Produkte mit Deckungsbeitragssprüngen bei einem gegebenen Engpass. (With English summary.) In *Fandel, G., et al., eds.*, 1981, pp. 345–53.

Haugen, Robert A. and Senbet, Lemma W. Resolving the Agency Problems of External Capital through Options. *J. Finance*, June 1981, 36(3), pp. 629–47.

Hey, John D. Goodwill—Investment in the Intangible. In *Currie, D.; Peel, D. and Peters, W., eds.*, 1981, pp. 196–229.

Hodgson, Thomas J. and Lowe, Timothy J. Lotsizing in an Automated Warehouse. In *Chikán, A., ed. (II)*, 1981, pp. 99–108.

Horsman, H. M. and Wharton, F. A Comparison of Multi-echelon Inventory Control Systems. In *Chikán, A., ed. (II)*, 1981, pp. 109–20.

Kelle, Péter. Reliability Type Inventory Models for Random Delivery Process. In *Chikán, A., ed. (II)*, 1981, pp. 385–95.

Kimberly, John R. Managerial Innovation. In *Nys-trom, P. C. and Starbuck, W. H., eds., Vol. 1*, 1981, pp. 84–104.

Klemm, Hermann. Inventory Models with Ordering Time Limit. Analysis of the Problem. In *Chikán, A., ed. (II)*, 1981, pp. 397–414.

Klinger, Harry; Przyborowski, Claus-Jürgen and Wilhelm, Klaus. Centralization of Material Stocks Justified by Economic Reasons. Decision Aids and Results in Their Application. In *Chikán, A., ed. (II)*, 1981, pp. 121–34.

Kloock, J. Erfolgsrechnungen auf der Basis produktionsanalytischer Kostenrechnungen. (With English summary.) In *Fandel, G., et al., eds.*, 1981, pp. 502–20.

König, Heinz; Nerlove, Marc and Oudiz, Gilles. Micro-analysis of Realizations, Plans, and Expectations in the IFO and INSEE Business Texts by Multivariate Log-Linear Probability Models. In *[Valavanis, S.]*, 1981, pp. 393–420. **[G: W. Germany]**

Kudo, Hideyuki. L'evoluzione del management. (Gradual Modification of Japanese Management. With English summary.) *L'Impresa*, 1981, 23(5), pp. 31–37. **[G: Japan]**

Kulcsár, Tamás. An Analytical Inventory Model with Stochastic Lead Time. In *Chikán, A., ed. (II)*, 1981, pp. 415–25.

Kyläkoski, Kalevi. Yrityksen strategiasuunnittelu systeeminä ja prosessina. (Corporate Strategic Planning—as a System and as a Process. With English summary.) *Liiketaloudellinen Aikak.*, 1981, 30(3), pp. 335–42. **[G: Finland]**

Laitinen, Erkki K. A Life-Cycle Approach to Business Pricing with Empirical Evidence from Finnish Industrial Firms. *Liiketaloudellinen Aikak.*, 1981, 30(4), pp. 407–21. **[G: Finland]**

Leman, Christopher K. and Nelson, Robert H. Ten Commandments for Policy Economists. *J. Policy Anal. Manage.*, Fall 1981, 1(1), pp. 97–117. **[G: U.S.]**

Lott, R. and Klibor, H.-U. Planung der Produktion und Lagerhaltung für ein Unternehmen der Konsumgüterindustrie. (With English summary.) In *Fandel, G., et al., eds.*, 1981, pp. 333–41.

Makridakis, Spyros and Wheelwright, Steven C. Forecasting an Organization's Futures. In *Nys-trom, P. C. and Starbuck, W. H., eds., Vol. 1*, 1981, pp. 122–38.

Marchi, Luciano. Role of Computers in Inventory Management. The Retailing Case. In *Chikán, A., ed. (II)*, 1981, pp. 155–66.

Märcz, Henrik. Inter-company Relations from the Point of View of Inventory Control. In *Chikán, A., ed. (II)*, 1981, pp. 145–53.

Martin, James R. Segment Planning and Reporting for Firms with Reciprocal Intersegment Transfers. *Bus. Econ.*, May 1981, 16(3), pp. 25–29.

Megyeri, Endre. Control of Multi-location Inventory System. In *Chikán, A., ed. (II)*, 1981, pp. 167–81.

Meunier, Marc. MBO: management-perspectieven voor de toekomst. (MBO (Management by Objectives): Management Perspectives for the Future. With English summary.) *Econ. Soc. Tijdschr.*, August 1981, 35(4), pp. 425–45.

Mikovsky, Vasil. Approach to Data Processing in Rating Inventory in Supply Enterprises. In *Chikán, A., ed. (II),* 1981, pp. 183–94.

Montironi, Marina. Organizzazione del lavoro e retribuzione, un rapporto che cambia. (Labour Organisation and Remuneration, a Changing Relationship. With English summary.) *L'Impresa,* 1981, 23(1), pp. 27–34. [G: Switzerland; W. Germany; U.K.; France; Italy]

Müller, Johann-Adolf. About the Optimum Execution of Stock Keeping Processes by Means of Planned Model Tests. In *Chikán, A., ed. (II),* 1981, pp. 427–36.

Naddor, Eliezer. A Framework for Evaluating Scheduling Algorithms in Multi-level Production Systems. In *Chikán, A., ed. (II),* 1981, pp. 437–47.

Nahmias, Steven. Queueing Models for Controlling Perishable Inventories. In *Chikán, A., ed. (II),* 1981, pp. 449–57.

Negoiţă, C. V. On the Fundamental Research in Modelling Decision-Making Processes. *Econ. Computat. Cybern. Stud. Res.,* 1981, 15(1), pp. 35–42.

Neuhäuser, Christine. Legal Regulations for the Implementation of Efficient Inventory Control at Combines and Enterprises. In *Chikán, A., ed. (II),* 1981, pp. 195–203. [G: E. Germany]

Niculescu-Mizil, E. Informatics on Industrial Platforms. *Econ. Computat. Cybern. Stud. Res.,* 1981, 15(2), pp. 25–30.

O'Grady, P. J. and Bonney, M. C. Optimal Estimation of Inter-machining Inventory Levels Using Discrete State Variable Control Theory. In *Chikán, A., ed. (II),* 1981, pp. 459–68.

Odle, Curt; Koshal, Rajindar K. and Shukla, Vishwa. Unfilled Orders and Price Changes: A Simultaneous Equations System. *Managerial Dec. Econ.,* June 1981, 2(2), pp. 97–105. [G: U.S.]

Papathanassiou, Byron. Production Smoothing. Stock Level Middle-Term Planning of Preconstruction Elements. In *Chikán, A., ed. (II),* 1981, pp. 205–14.

Papps, Ivy. Goodwill—Investment in the Intangible: Comment. In *Currie, D.; Peel, D. and Peters, W., eds.,* 1981, pp. 230–32.

Pearce, John A., II. An Executive-Level Perspective on the Strategic Management Process. *Calif. Manage. Rev.,* Fall 1981, 24(1), pp. 39–48. [G: U.S.]

Pegels, C. Carl. A Batch Size Model for the Hospital Pharmacy. In *Chikán, A., ed. (II),* 1981, pp. 469–76.

Perry, Martin K. The Manager and the Competitive Firm's Supply. *Southern Econ. J.,* January 1981, 47(3), pp. 630–39.

Pompéry, Béla. Function Oriented Distribution of Data Processing for Material Management. In *Chikán, A., ed. (II),* 1981, pp. 215–26. [G: Hungary Bu]

Pras, Bernard. Essai d'analyse du comportement des responsables des grandes entreprises envers le risque. (An Attempt to Analyse the Risk Behavior of Major Firms Top Managers. With English summary.) *Écon. Soc.,* October–November–December 1981, 15(10–12), pp. 1421–41. [G: U.S.]

Prékopa, András. Reliability Type Inventory Mod-

els. A Survey. In *Chikán, A., ed. (II),* 1981, pp. 477–90.

Proth, Jean-Marie. Gestion de stocks avec coûts concaves. Notion d'horizon de planification. (Inventory Control with Concave Cost Functions: The Notion of Planning Horizons. With English summary.) *Écon. Soc.,* October–November–December 1981, 15(10–12), pp. 1811–32.

Reichmann, Thomas. Economic Inventory Management Based on Demand Plans. In *Chikán, A., ed. (II),* 1981, pp. 227–37.

Rempala, Ryszarda. On the Multicommodity Arrow–Karlin Inventory Model. In *Chikán, A., ed. (II),* 1981, pp. 491–99.

Revsine, Lawrence. A Capital Maintenance Approach to Income Measurement. *Accounting Rev.,* April 1981, 56(2), pp. 383–89.

Richter, Knut. Solving a Capacity Constrained Deterministic Dynamic Inventory Problem. In *Chikán, A., ed. (II),* 1981, pp. 501–09.

Ritchie, E. Practical Inventory Policies for the Stocking of Spare Parts. In *Chikán, A., ed. (II),* 1981, pp. 511–21.

Saldaña, Cesar G. Cost Allocations and the Management Control Problem. *Phillipine Rev. Econ. Bus.,* March & June 1981, 18(1 & 2), pp. 23–44.

Saldaña, Cesar G. Information and Incentives Issues in Management Control. *Phillipine Rev. Econ. Bus.,* Sept. & Dec. 1981, 18(3/4), pp. 154–67.

Sandras, William A., Jr. and Bolander, Steven F. Zone Defense Improves Stockroom Record Accuracy. In *Chikán, A., ed. (II),* 1981, pp. 239–54.

Sárai, József. Practical Approach to the ABC Analysis. Its Extension and Application. In *Chikán, A., ed. (II),* 1981, pp. 255–61. [G: Hungary]

Sarjusz Wolski, Zdzislaw. Inventory Control of Spare Parts in Supplying Organizations. In *Chikán, A., ed. (II),* 1981, pp. 263–72.

Schneider, Helmut. On Obtaining a Required Service-Level in a Periodic Inventory Model. In *Chikán, A., ed. (II),* 1981, pp. 523–33.

Shone, Robert [Sir]. Technical Change, Inflation and Pricing Decisions. *Managerial Dec. Econ.,* September 1981, 2(3), pp. 169–78. [G: U.K.]

Siegel, Klaus. Simulation Experiments in Inventory Control. In *Chikán, A., ed. (II),* 1981, pp. 535–51.

Silberston, Aubrey. Factors Affecting the Growth of the Firm—Theory and Practice. In *Currie, D.; Peel, D. and Peters, W., eds.,* 1981, pp. 329–56. [G: U.K.]

Silver, Edward A. and Massard, Neal E. Setting of Parameter Values in Coordinated Inventory Control by Means of Graphical and Hand Calculator Methods. In *Chikán, A., ed. (II),* 1981, pp. 553–66.

Soom, Erich. Optimal Planning of Inventories. A Method for the Improvement of Liquidity and Efficiency of Enterprises. In *Chikán, A., ed. (II),* 1981, pp. 273–85.

Stanton, Robert and Drury, Edward A. Forecasting at Hewlett-Packard: Finding a Better Way. *Manage. Account.,* June 1981, 62(12), pp. 45–49. [G: U.S.]

Stern, Gary. Productivity and Division Profitability. In *Hogan, J. D. and Craig, A. M., eds., Vol. 1,*

1981, pp. 391–401.

Teplitz, Charles J. Warehouse Replenishment Using the Cost-Service Transportation Model. In *Chikán, A., ed. (II)*, 1981, pp. 567–73.

Thirlby, G. F. Economists' Cost Rules and Equilibrium Theory. In *Buchanan, J. M. and Thirlby, G. F., eds.*, 1981, *1960*, pp. 273–87.

Thirlby, G. F. The Economist's Description of Business Behaviour. In *Buchanan, J. M. and Thirlby, G. F., eds.*, 1981, *1952*, pp. 201–24.

Tomek, Gustav. Utilization of Computer Technics in Inventory Control. In *Chikán, A., ed. (II)*, 1981, pp. 287–94.

Trotman, K. T.; Yetton, Philip W. and Zimmer, I. Group Size and Performance: Prediction of Failure by Loan Officers. *Australian J. Manage.*, June 1981, *6*(1), pp. 137–43. [G: Australia]

Trotman, K. T.; Yetton, Philip W. and Zimmer, I. Group Size and Performance: Prediction of Failure by Loan Officers [Correction]. *Australian J. Manage.*, December 1981, *6*(2), pp. 127–36. [G: Australia]

Unčovský, Ladislav. Approximative Methods of Multi-item Inventory Management. In *Chikán, A., ed. (II)*, 1981, pp. 575–82.

Vander Eecken, Jacques. Aggregate Inventory Management. A Case Study. In *Chikán, A., ed. (II)*, 1981, pp. 583–96. [G: U.S.]

de Vio, Sergio. Recupero di efficienza e governabilità di impresa. (Business Managing Ability and Efficiency Recovery. With English summary.) *L'Impresa*, 1981, *23*(4), pp. 21–28.

Vrat, Prem and Subash Babu, A. Optimal Policies for Spares in Multi-echelon Repair Inventory Systems. In *Chikán, A., ed. (II)*, 1981, pp. 597–610.

Wagner, Harvey M. Research Portfolio for Inventory Management and Production Planning Systems. In *Chikán, A., ed. (II)*, 1981, pp. 611–21.

Waldmann, Karl-Heinz. On Optimal Inventory Control with Varying Stochastic Demands. In *Chikán, A., ed. (II)*, 1981, pp. 623–29.

Warner, Malcolm. Organizational Experiments and Social Innovations. In *Nystrom, P. C. and Starbuck, W. H., eds., Vol. 1*, 1981, pp. 167–84.

Winter, Ralph A. Majority Choice and the Objective Function of the Firm under Uncertainty: Note. *Bell J. Econ. (See Rand J. Econ. after 4/85)*, Spring 1981, *12*(1), pp. 335–37.

Winter, Sidney G. Attention Allocation and Input Proportions. *J. Econ. Behav. Organ.*, March 1981, *2*(1), pp. 31–46.

Yefimov, Vladimir M. Gaming-Simulation of the Functioning of Economic Systems. *J. Econ. Behav. Organ.*, June 1981, *2*(2), pp. 187–200.

Zmijewski, Mark E. and Hagerman, Robert L. An Income Strategy Approach to the Positive Theory of Accounting Standard Setting/Choice. *J. Acc. Econ.*, August 1981, *3*(2), pp. 129–49. [G: U.S.]

513 Business and Public Administration

5130 General

Baldini, Vittorio. Come gestire la creatività in azienda. (Managing Creativity. With English summary.) *L'Impresa*, 1981, *23*(3), pp. 37–42.

Brown, Montague. Contract Management: Legal and Policy Implications. *Inquiry*, Spring 1981, *18*(1), pp. 8–17. [G: U.S.]

Candau, Pierre. Pour une approche stratégique de la fonction personnel. (For a Strategic Approach to the Personnel Function. With English summary.) *Écon. Soc.*, October–November–December 1981, *15*(10–12), pp. 1555–92.

Candau, Pierre. Pour une taxonomie de l'hypofirme. (With English summary.) *Rev. Econ. Ind.*, 2nd Trimester 1981, (16), pp. 16–33.

Cartoccio, Achille. Perché servono i consulenti interni. (The Utility of Internal Consultants. With English summary.) *L'Impresa*, 1981, *23*(2), pp. 35–43.

Cauvin, Pierre. Un modèle pour gérer les organismes de service à but non lucratif: la théorie des quatre corps. (A Management Model for Nonprofit Organizations: The Four Constituencies Theory. With English summary.) *Écon. Soc.*, October–November–December 1981, *15*(10–12), pp. 1593–1639.

van Dam, André. The Pause That Refreshes. *Rivista Int. Sci. Econ. Com.*, January–February 1981, *28*(1–2), pp. 170–76.

Delhaye, Guy and Sturbois, Georges. Les étudiants et la gestion sociale: perception de la dimension socio-gestionnaire du management chez de futurs cadres en Hainaut. (Students and Social Management: Perception of the Socio-Managerial Dimension of Management by Future Executives in the Province of Hainaut (Belgium). With English summary.) *Ann. Sci. Écon. Appl.*, 1981, *37*(2), pp. 57–88. [G: Belgium]

Dunbar, Roger L. M. Designs for Organizational Control. In *Nystrom, P. C. and Starbuck, W. H., eds., Vol. 2*, 1981, pp. 85–115.

Edmunds, Stahrl W. Organizational Size and Efficiency in the U.S. *Antitrust Bull.*, Fall 1981, *26*(3), pp. 507–19. [G: U.S.]

Edokpayi, S. I. Administrative and Managerial Implications. In *Adedeji, A., ed.*, 1981, pp. 353–80. [G: Africa]

Glazer, Herbert. Com'è, come funziona il management giapponese. (The Management Made in Japan. With English summary.) *L'Impresa*, 1981, *23*(6), pp. 29–39. [G: Japan]

Gray, Lois S. Unions Implementing Managerial Techniques. *Mon. Lab. Rev.*, June 1981, *104*(6), pp. 3–13. [G: U.S.]

Gros Pietro, Gian Maria. Qualità dello sviluppo economico e sviluppo della consulenza. (The Quality of Economic Development and the Consultancy Development. With English summary.) *L'Impresa*, 1981, *23*(2), pp. 19–22.

Halal, William E. and Brown, Bob S. Participative Management: Myth and Reality. *Calif. Manage. Rev.*, Summer 1981, *23*(4), pp. 20–32. [G: U.S.]

Horwitch, Mel and Prahalad, C. K. Managing Multi-Organization Enterprises: The Emerging Strategic Frontier. *Sloan Manage. Rev.*, Winter 1981, *22*(2), pp. 3–16.

Jacur, Roberto Romanin. Affidabilità e protezione dei sistemi informativi. (Reliability and Protection of Information Systems. With English summary.) *L'Impresa*, 1981, 23(3), pp. 53–59.

Keim, Gerald D. Foundations of a Political Strategy for Business. *Calif. Manage. Rev.*, Spring 1981, 23(3), pp. 41–48. [G: U.S.]

Kerr, Steven and Slocum, John W., Jr. Controlling the Performances of People in Organization. In *Nystrom, P. C. and Starbuck, W. H., eds., Vol. 2*, 1981, pp. 116–34.

Koenig, Thomas and Gogel, Robert. Interlocking Corporate Directorships as a Social Network. *Amer. J. Econ. Soc.*, January 1981, 40(1), pp. 37–50. [G: U.S.]

Kónya, Lajos. Conditions of Setting Up Simple Forms of Cooperatives in the Hungarian Industry. *Acta Oecon.*, 1981, 27(1–2), pp. 77–92. [G: Hungary]

Mayer, Paul. Techniques de gestion et analyse des institutions l'exemple des règlements de sécurité. (Management Techniques and Analysis of Institutions: The Example of Safety Regulations. With English summary.) *Écon. Soc.*, October–November–December 1981, 15(10–12), pp. 1641–67.

McCann, Joseph and Galbraith, Jay R. Interdepartmental Relations. In *Nystrom, P. C. and Starbuck, W. H., eds., Vol. 2*, 1981, pp. 60–84.

Merlino, Massimo and Zamparo, Roberto. L'organizzazione delle staff di produzione in un'ottica logistica. (The Organization of Production Staff in View of Logistics. With English summary.) *L'Impresa*, 1981, 23(4), pp. 41–45.

Niitamo, Olavi E. Johtajaan eli "vetäjään" kohdistettavia odotuksia. (What I Expect of the Chiefs of the CSO. With English summary.) *Liiketaloudellinen Aikak.*, 1981, 30(2), pp. 182–92.

Puffer, Sheila M. Inside a Soviet Management Institute. *Calif. Manage. Rev.*, Fall 1981, 24(1), pp. 90–96. [G: U.S.S.R.]

Randolph, W. Alan. Matching Technology and the Design of Organization Units. *Calif. Manage. Rev.*, Summer 1981, 23(4), pp. 39–48.

Ren, Tao. Why Did the Four Hundred Pilot Experiment Enterprises in Sichuan Achieve Swift Results? *Chinese Econ. Stud.*, Fall 1981, 15(1), pp. 72–86. [G: China]

Roberts, Edward B. and Fusfeld, Alan R. Staffing the Innovative Technology-Base Organization. *Sloan Manage. Rev.*, Spring 1981, 22(3), pp. 19–34.

Schein, Edgar H. Does Japanese Management Style Have a Message for American Managers? *Sloan Manage. Rev.*, Fall 1981, 23(1), pp. 55–68. [G: U.S.; Japan]

Schein, Edgar H. SMR Forum: Improving Face-to-Face Relationships. *Sloan Manage. Rev.*, Winter 1981, 22(2), pp. 43–52.

Scott, William G.; Mitchell, Terence R. and Peery, Newman S. Organizational Governance. In *Nystrom, P. C. and Starbuck, W. H., eds., Vol. 2*, 1981, pp. 135–51.

Sloan, Frank A. and Becker, Edmund R. Internal Organization of Hospitals and Hospital Costs. *Inquiry*, Fall 1981, 18(3), pp. 224–39. [G: U.S.]

Štrougal, Lubomír. With Responsibility and Initiative at the Start of the 7th Five-Year Plan. *Czech.*

Econ. Digest., May 1981, (3), pp. 22–38. [G: Czechoslovakia]

Tinbergen, Jan. Skill Scarcity, Monopoloid and Hierarchical Incomes in Some Western Countries. In *[Lipiński, E.]*, 1981, pp. 155–62. [G: U.S.; W. Germany; Netherlands]

Tsuda, Masumi. Le ragioni dell'unicità del modello. (The Roots of the Uniqueness of Japanese Management. With English summary.) *L'Impresa*, 1981, 23(5), pp. 25–29. [G: Japan]

Varga, György. Management—In a Fast Changing Environment. *Acta Oecon.*, 1981, 27(3–4), pp. 301–26. [G: Hungary]

Varvelli, Maria Ludovica Lombardi and Varelli, Riccardo. È sempre utile verificare il clima aziendale. (It Is Always Useful to Take Soundings of Company Climate. With English summary.) *L'Impresa*, 1981, 23(2), pp. 45–52. [G: Italy]

de Vio, Sergio. Recupero di efficienza e governabilità di impresa. (Business Managing Ability and Efficiency Recovery. With English summary.) *L'Impresa*, 1981, 23(4), pp. 21–28.

Zhang, Zhuoyuan. Le recenti riforme nella struttura dell'economia cinese. (Recent Reforms in the Structure of Chinese Economy. With English summary.) *Rivista Int. Sci. Econ. Com.*, September 1981, 28(9), pp. 799–810. [G: China]

5131 Business Administration

Agarwal, Naresh C. Determinants of Executive Compensation. *Ind. Relat.*, Winter 1981, 20(1), pp. 36–46. [G: U.S.]

Beasley, Wm. Howard, III. Can Managerial Economics Aid the Chief Executive Officer? *Managerial Dec. Econ.*, September 1981, 2(3), pp. 129–32. [G: U.S.]

Bourgeois, L. J., III and Boltvinik, Manuel. OD in Cross-Cultural Settings: Latin America. *Calif. Manage. Rev.*, Spring 1981, 23(3), pp. 75–81.

del Castillo, Achille and Papetti, Sergio. Verso una matrice prodotto/mercato per la consulenza. (Towards a Product/Market Matrix for Consultancy. With English summary.) *L'Impresa*, 1981, 23(3), pp. 15–19.

Darling, John R. and Santalainen, Timo J. Keys to Successful Management: A Results Orientation in Developing Leadership Qualities. *Liiketaloudellinen Aikak.*, 1981, 30(4), pp. 380–92.

Di Stefano, Guido. L'industria giapponese: tre giornate di studio. (Japanese Industry: A 3-Day Meeting. With English summary.) *L'Impresa*, 1981, 23(5), pp. 51–55. [G: Japan]

Dockson, Robert R. and Vance, Jack O. Retirement in Peril: Inflation and the Executive Compensation Program. *Calif. Manage. Rev.*, Summer 1981, 23(4), pp. 87–94. [G: U.S.]

Doz, Yves L. and Prahalad, C. K. Headquarters Influence and Strategic Control in MNCs. *Sloan Manage. Rev.*, Fall 1981, 23(1), pp. 15–29.

Dubinsky, Alan J. and Hansen, Richard W. The Sales Force Management Audit. *Calif. Manage. Rev.*, Winter 1981, 24(2), pp. 86–95.

Dunham, Constance. Commercial Bank Costs and Correspondent Banking. *New Eng. Econ. Rev.*, September–October 1981, pp. 22–36. [G: U.S.]

Fonteyne, Françoise and Sauboin, Michel. Orientations pour réussir l'expatriation du personnel. (Guidelines for Successful Personnel Expatriation. With English summary.) *Ann. Sci. Écon. Appl.*, 1981, *37*(4), pp. 143–66.

Greenfield, Sidney M. and Strickon, Arnold. A New Paradigm for the Study of Entrepreneurship and Social Change. *Econ. Develop. Cult. Change*, April 1981, *29*(3), pp. 467–99.

Guasch, J. Luis and Weiss, Andrew. Self-Selection in the Labor Market. *Amer. Econ. Rev.*, June 1981, *71*(3), pp. 275–84.

Haft, Robert J. Business Decisions by the New Board: Behavioral Science and Corporate Law. *Mich. Law Rev.*, November 1981, *80*(1), pp. 1–67. **[G: U.S.]**

Haywood, K. H. and Ruckes, E. A Business Management Game for Training of Fish Marketing Personnel. In *Haley, K. B., ed.*, 1981, pp. 261–72. **[G: Sri Lanka]**

Jennergren, L. Peter. Decentralization in Organizations. In *Nystrom, P. C. and Starbuck, W. H., eds., Vol. 2*, 1981, pp. 39–59.

Kudo, Hideyuki. L'evoluzione del management. (Gradual Modification of Japanese Management. With English summary.) *L'Impresa*, 1981, *23*(5), pp. 31–37. **[G: Japan]**

Levinthal, Daniel and March, James G. A Model of Adaptive Organizational Search. *J. Econ. Behav. Organ.*, December 1981, *2*(4), pp. 307–33.

Lindgren, Ulf and Spangberg, Kjell. Management of the Post-Acquisition Process in Diversified MNCs. In *Otterbeck, L., ed.*, 1981, pp. 233–53. **[G: Sweden]**

Mitchell, Olivia S. and Andrews, Emily S. Scale Economies in Private Multi-Employer Pension Systems. *Ind. Lab. Relat. Rev.*, July 1981, *34*(4), pp. 522–30. **[G: U.S.]**

Möller, Kristian and Åberg, Leif. Factors Affecting the Perception of Managerial Concepts. *Liiketaloudellinen Aikak.*, 1981, *30*(2), pp. 125–44. **[G: Finland]**

Murray, R. Stuart. Managerial Perceptions of Two Appraisal Systems. *Calif. Manage. Rev.*, Spring 1981, *23*(3), pp. 92–96.

Nielsen, Richard P. Toward a Method for Building Consensus during Strategic Planning. *Sloan Manage. Rev.*, Summer 1981, *22*(4), pp. 29–40.

Pearce, John A., II. An Executive-Level Perspective on the Strategic Management Process. *Calif. Manage. Rev.*, Fall 1981, *24*(1), pp. 39–48. **[G: U.S.]**

Prahalad, C. K. and Doz, Yves L. An Approach to Strategic Control in MNCs. *Sloan Manage. Rev.*, Summer 1981, *22*(4), pp. 5–13.

Rolland, Ian and Janson, Robert. Total Involvement as a Productivity Strategy. *Calif. Manage. Rev.*, Winter 1981, *24*(2), pp. 40–48. **[G: U.S.]**

Rones, Philip L. Response to Recession: Reduce Hours or Jobs? *Mon. Lab. Rev.*, October 1981, *104*(10), pp. 3–11. **[G: U.S.]**

Sloan, Stephen B. How Milliken Measures Training Program Effectiveness. *Manage. Account.*, July 1981, *63*(1), pp. 37–41. **[G: U.S.]**

Stout, Roy G. Organizing Marketing Research to Impact Management. *Sloan Manage. Rev.*, Fall

1981, *23*(1), pp. 77–79.

Swartz, Katherine. Information in the Hiring Process: A Case Study. *J. Econ. Behav. Organ.*, March 1981, *2*(1), pp. 71–94. **[G: U.S.]**

Tanaka, Fujio John. Lifetime Employment in Japan. *Challenge*, July/August 1981, *24*(3), pp. 23–29. **[G: Japan]**

Taylor, Graham D. Management Relations in a Multinational Enterprise: The Case of Canadian Industries Limited, 1928–1948. *Bus. Hist. Rev.*, Autumn 1981, *55*(3), pp. 337–58. **[G: Canada]**

Toba, Kin'ichiro. Confronto con l'Occidente. (How Japanese and Western Managements Differ. With English summary.) *L'Impresa*, 1981, *23*(5), pp. 45–49. **[G: W. Europe; N. America; Japan]**

Woronoff, Jon. Può essere trasferibile il modello giapponese? (Japanese Management System Cannot be Transplanted. With English summary.) *L'Impresa*, 1981, *23*(5), pp. 39–43. **[G: Japan]**

5132 Public Administration

Benson, Bruce L. Why Are Congressional Committees Dominated by "High-Demand" Legislators?—A Comment on Niskanen's View of Bureaucrats and Politicians [Bureaucrats and Politicians]. *Southern Econ. J.*, July 1981, *48*(1), pp. 68–77. **[G: U.S.]**

Berkman, Ali Ümit. Planlı Dönemde Idari Reform Anlayişi ve Uygulamasi: idari Reformun "Yönetilmesi" Açisidan bir Değerlendirme. (Conception and Implementation of Administrative Reform in the Planned Period: An Evaluation with Respect to "Administration" of Administrative Reform. With English summary.) *METU*, Special Issue, 1981, pp. 207–25. **[G: Turkey]**

Campbell, Alan K. Government and Productivity. In *Hogan, J. D. and Craig, A. M., eds., Vol. 2*, 1981, pp. 941–52. **[G: U.S.]**

Clarkson, Kenneth W. The Federal Trade Commission since 1970: Economic Regulation and Bureaucratic Behavior: Legislative Constraints. In *Clarkson, K. W. and Muris, T. J., eds.*, 1981, pp. 18–34. **[G: U.S.]**

Clarkson, Kenneth W. The Federal Trade Commission since 1970: Economic Regulation and Bureaucratic Behavior: Executive Constraints. In *Clarkson, K. W. and Muris, T. J., eds.*, 1981, pp. 50–58. **[G: U.S.]**

Gligorov, Kiro. The Social and Economic Basis of Socialist Self-Management in Yugoslavia. *Eastern Europ. Econ.*, Winter 1981–82, *20*(2), pp. 3–22.

Holmes, A. S. The Good Fight. *Econ. Rec.*, March 1981, *57*(156), pp. 1–11. **[G: Australia]**

Jones, Edwin. Class and Administrative Development Doctrines in Jamaica. *Soc. Econ. Stud.*, September 1981, *30*(3), pp. 1–20. **[G: Jamaica]**

Joskow, Paul L. The Effects of FTC Advertising Regulation: Comment. *J. Law Econ.*, December 1981, *24*(3), pp. 449–55. **[G: U.S.]**

Kershaw, David N. and Williams, Roberton C., Jr. Do Housing Allowances Work? Administrative Lessons. In *Bradbury, K. L. and Downs, A., eds.*, 1981, pp. 285–337. **[G: U.S.]**

Li, Yinglu. The Management System of Material Must be Reformed. *Chinese Econ. Stud.*, Summer 1981, *14*(4), pp. 38–47. [G: China]

Luo, Jingfen. The Administrative System of the Economy Should be Separated from the Administrative System of State Power. *Chinese Econ. Stud.*, Summer 1981, *14*(4), pp. 17–29.
[G: China]

Mikesell, John L. The Structure of State Revenue Administration. *Nat. Tax J.*, June 1981, *34*(2), pp. 217–34. [G: U.S.]

Nelson, Phillip. The Effects of FTC Advertising Regulation: Comment. *J. Law Econ.*, December 1981, *24*(3), pp. 457–59. [G: U.S.]

Parks, Roger B. and Ostrom, Elinor. Complex Models of Urban Service Systems. In *Clark, T. N., ed.*, 1981, pp. 171–99.

Peltzman, Sam. The Effects of FTC Advertising Regulation. *J. Law Econ.*, December 1981, *24*(3), pp. 403–48. [G: U.S.]

Plumlee, John P. Professional Training and Policy Dominance in the Higher Civil Service. *Soc. Sci. Quart.*, September 1981, *62*(3), pp. 569–75.
[G: U.S.]

Porter, Grover. Management Information Systems. *Manage. Account.*, February 1981, *62*(8), pp. 53, 62.

Rosenthal, Stephen R. and Levine, Edith S. Executing Public Policy by Caseload Control. In *Crecine, J. P., ed.*, 1981, pp. 135–60.

Saari, David J. On Rationing Justice and Liberty in a Declining Economy. In *Wright, K. N., ed.*, 1981, pp. 257–72. [G: U.S.]

Sanderson, Paul W. Scientific–Technical Innovation in East Germany. *Polit. Sci. Quart.*, Winter 1981–82, *96*(4), pp. 571–89. [G: E. Germany]

Savas, E. S. Alternative Institutional Models for the Delivery of Public Services. *Public Budg. Finance*, Winter 1981, *1*(4), pp. 12–20. [G: U.S.]

Schobel, Bruce D. Administrative Expenses under OASDI. *Soc. Sec. Bull.*, March 1981, *44*(3), pp. 21–28. [G: U.S.]

Timsit, Gérard. The Administrative Apparatus of States and the Implementation of the NIEO. In *Laszlo, E. and Kurtzman, J., eds.*, 1981, pp. 69–92. [G: LDCs]

Upham, Frank K. Business and the Bureaucracy. In *Richardson, B. M. and Ueda, T., eds.*, 1981, pp. 194–99. [G: Japan]

Usilaner, Brian L. Can We Expect Productivity Improvement in the Federal Government? In *Hogan, J. D. and Craig, A. M., eds., Vol. 2*, 1981, pp. 963–85. [G: U.S.]

Wallace, Wanda A. Internal Control Reporting Practices in the Municipal Sector. *Accounting Rev.*, July 1981, *56*(3), pp. 666–89. [G: U.S.]

Weiss, Janet A. Substance vs. Symbol in Administrative Reform: The Case of Human Services Coordination. *Policy Anal.*, Winter 1981, *7*(1), pp. 21–45.

West, William F. Judicial Rulemaking Procedures in the FTC: A Case Study of Their Causes and Effects. *Public Policy*, Spring 1981, *29*(2), pp. 197–217. [G: U.S.]

Zimbalist, Andrew. On the Role of Management in Socialist Development. *World Devel.*, September/October 1981, *9*(9/10), pp. 971–77.
[G: Yugoslavia; U.S.S.R.; Cuba; Chile]

514 Goals and Objectives of Firms

5140 Goals and Objectives of Firms

Alam, K. F. Taxation, Corporate Planning and Company Financial Policy: A Theoretical Exposition. *METU*, 1981, *8*(3&4), pp. 697–714. [G: U.K.]

Albach, Horst. The Nature of the Firm—A Production-Theoretical Viewpoint. *Z. ges. Staatswiss.*, December 1981, *137*(4), pp. 717–22.

Amihud, Yakov and Lev, Baruch. Risk Reduction as a Managerial Motive for Conglomerate Mergers. *Bell J. Econ. (See Rand J. Econ. after 4/85)*, Autumn 1981, *12*(2), pp. 605–17. [G: U.S.]

Bauer, Michel and Cohen, Elie. Autoproduction de la grande entreprise et transformation de son univers marchand. (The Self Production of the Large Company and the Conversion of Its Merchant Universe. With English summary.) *Revue Écon.*, May 1981, *32*(3), pp. 513–62.

Beyer, Janice M. Ideologies, Values, and Decision Making in Organizations. In *Nystrom, P. C. and Starbuck, W. H., eds., Vol. 2*, 1981, pp. 166–202.

Brandis, Royall. An Alarmist View of Corporate Influence. In *Hessen, R., ed.*, 1981, pp. 17–22.

Buchan, P. Bruce. Boards of Directors: Adversaries or Advisers. *Calif. Manage. Rev.*, Winter 1981, *24*(2), pp. 31–39. [G: U.S.]

Champagne, Anthony; Neef, Marian and Nagel, Stuart. Laws, Organizations, and the Judiciary. In *Nystrom, P. C. and Starbuck, W. H., eds., Vol. 1*, 1981, pp. 187–209.

Child, John and Kieser, Alfred. Development of Organizations over Time. In *Nystrom, P. C. and Starbuck, W. H., eds., Vol. 1*, 1981, pp. 28–64.

Childers, Sloan K. The Work Ethic in the Context of the Community. In *Hoffman, W. M. and Wyly, T. J., eds.*, 1981, pp. 173–76. [G: U.S.]

Coffee, John C., Jr. "No Soul to Damn: No Body to Kick": An Unscandalized Inquiry into the Problem of Corporate Punishment. *Mich. Law Rev.*, January 1981, *79*(3), pp. 386–459. [G: U.S.]

Dorward, Neil and Wiedemann, Paul. Robustness as a Corporate Objective under Uncertainty. *Managerial Dec. Econ.*, September 1981, *2*(3), pp. 186–91.

Eisenstadt, David and Kennedy, Thomas E. Control and Behavior of Nonprofit Firms: The Case of Blue Shield. *Southern Econ. J.*, July 1981, *48*(1), pp. 26–36. [G: U.S.]

Eisenstadt, Shmuel N. Interactions between Organizations and Societal Stratification. In *Nystrom, P. C. and Starbuck, W. H., eds., Vol. 1*, 1981, pp. 309–22.

Fasching, Darrell J. A Case for Corporate and Management Ethics. *Calif. Manage. Rev.*, Summer 1981, *23*(4), pp. 62–76. [G: U.S.]

Ford, Robert and McLaughlin, Frank. Defining Corporate Social Responsibility: A Three-Group Survey. *Rev. Bus. Econ. Res.*, Fall 1981, *17*(1), pp. 72–77. [G: U.S.]

Foulkes, Fred K. A Conceptual Framework for Business-Community Relations. In *Hoffman, W. M. and Wyly, T. J., eds.*, 1981, pp. 181–84.
[G: U.S.]

Frederick, William C. Free Market vs. Social Responsibility: Decision Time at the CED. *Calif. Manage. Rev.*, Spring 1981, *23*(3), pp. 20–28. [G: U.S.]

Freedman, Martin and Jaggi, Bikki. The SEC's Pollution Disclosure Requirements: Are They Meaningful? *Calif. Manage. Rev.*, Winter 1981, *24*(2), pp. 60–67. [G: U.S.]

Frost, Frederick G., III. Small Business Involvement in the Community. In *Hoffman, W. M. and Wyly, T. J., eds.*, 1981, pp. 177–80. [G: U.S.]

Fuller, Stephen H. Becoming the Organization of the Future. In *Hoffman, W. M. and Wyly, T. J., eds.*, 1981, pp. 67–73. [G: U.S.]

Furubotn, Eirik G. Codetermination and the Efficient Partitioning of Ownership Rights in the Firm. *Z. ges. Staatswiss.*, December 1981, *137*(4), pp. 702–09.

Haft, Robert J. Business Decisions by the New Board: Behavioral Science and Corporate Law. *Mich. Law Rev.*, November 1981, *80*(1), pp. 1–67. [G: U.S.]

Handlin, Oscar. The Taxonomy of the Corporation. In *Novak, M. and Cooper, J. W., eds.*, 1981, pp. 17–26. [G: U.S.]

Haugen, Robert A. and Senbet, Lemma W. Resolving the Agency Problems of External Capital through Options. *J. Finance*, June 1981, *36*(3), pp. 629–47.

Hedberg, Bo. How Organizations Learn and Unlearn. In *Nystrom, P. C. and Starbuck, W. H., eds., Vol. 1*, 1981, pp. 3–27.

Hirschey, Mark and Pappas, James L. Regulatory and Life Cycle Influences on Managerial Incentives. *Southern Econ. J.*, October 1981, *48*(2), pp. 327–34.

Jönsson, Berth. The Quality of Work Life—the Volvo Experience. In *Hoffman, W. M. and Wyly, T. J., eds.*, 1981, pp. 74–86. [G: Sweden]

Keim, Gerald D. Foundations of a Political Strategy for Business. *Calif. Manage. Rev.*, Spring 1981, *23*(3), pp. 41–48. [G: U.S.]

Khan, M. Y. and Singh, Preeti. Life Insurance Corporation and Corporate Control in India. *Indian Econ. J.*, October–December 1981, *29*(2), pp. 51–64.

Knauss, Robert L. Corporate Governance—A Moving Target. *Mich. Law Rev.*, January 1981, *79*(3), pp. 478–500. [G: U.S.]

Louderback, Joseph G. and Manners, George E., Jr. Integrating ROI and CVP. *Manage. Account.*, April 1981, *62*(10), pp. 33–39.

Manne, Henry G. The Publicly Held Corporation as a Market Creation. *Z. ges. Staatswiss.*, December 1981, *137*(4), pp. 689–93.

McCracken, Paul W. The Corporation and the Liberal Order. In *Novak, M. and Cooper, J. W., eds.*, 1981, pp. 34–46. [G: U.S.]

Moch, Michael and Seashore, Stanley E. How Norms Affect Behaviors in and of Corporations. In *Nystrom, P. C. and Starbuck, W. H., eds., Vol. 1*, 1981, pp. 210–37.

Mulkern, John R.; Handler, Edward and Godtfredsen, Lawrence. Corporate PACs as Fundraisers. *Calif. Manage. Rev.*, Spring 1981, *23*(3), pp. 49–55. [G: U.S.]

Nelson, Richard R. Assessing Private Enterprise: An Exegesis of Tangled Doctrine. *Bell J. Econ. (See Rand J. Econ. after 4/85)*, Spring 1981, *12*(1), pp. 93–111.

Novak, Michael. A Theology of the Corporation. In *Novak, M. and Cooper, J. W., eds.*, 1981, pp. 203–24.

Pomeranz, Felix. Social Measurement: Concepts and Practices. In *Hogan, J. D. and Craig, A. M., eds., Vol. 1*, 1981, pp. 403–12. [G: U.S.]

Preston, Lee E. and Post, James E. Private Management and Public Policy [Corporate Social Responsibility Revisited, Redefined]. *Calif. Manage. Rev.*, Spring 1981, *23*(3), pp. 56–62. [G: U.S.]

Reed, Rex R. Work Itself and Its Aftermath at AT&T. In *Hoffman, W. M. and Wyly, T. J., eds.*, 1981, pp. 87–91. [G: U.S.]

Reid, Stan D. The Decision-Maker and Export Entry and Expansion. *J. Int. Bus. Stud.*, Fall 1981, *12*(2), pp. 101–12.

Rudd, Andrew. Social Responsibility and Portfolio Performance. *Calif. Manage. Rev.*, Summer 1981, *23*(4), pp. 55–61.

Scaramuzzi, Maurizio. Qual è il costo migliore per decidere il prezzo? (What Is the Best Way for Fixing a Price? With English summary.) *L'Impresa*, 1981, *23*(3), pp. 45–50.

Schreuder, Hein. Employees and the Corporate Social Report: The Dutch Case. *Accounting Rev.*, April 1981, *56*(2), pp. 294–308. [G: Netherlands]

Smith, Timothy. Churches and Corporate Responsibility. In *Novak, M. and Cooper, J. W., eds.*, 1981, pp. 56–61. [G: U.S.]

de Sola Pool, Ithiel. How Powerful is Business? In *Hessen, R., ed.*, 1981, pp. 23–34.

Soulage, Bernard. L'Evolution des politiques sociales des groupes industriels français avec la crise. (Social Policies of Industrial Conglomerates through the Crisis. With English summary.) *Rev. Econ. Ind.*, 2nd Trimester 1981, (16), pp. 57–75. [G: France]

Sproull, Lee S. Beliefs in Organizations. In *Nystrom, P. C. and Starbuck, W. H., eds., Vol. 2*, 1981, pp. 203–24.

Tamminen, Rauno. Yrityksen persoonallisuus ja kannattavuus. (Personality Characteristics and the Profitability of a Firm. With English summary.) *Liiketaloudellinen Aikak.*, 1981, *30*(2), pp. 222–35.

Taylor, Ronald N. and Vertinsky, Ilan. Experimenting with Organizational Behavior. In *Nystrom, P. C. and Starbuck, W. H., eds., Vol. 1*, 1981, pp. 139–66.

Tichy, Noel M. Networks in Organizations. In *Nystrom, P. C. and Starbuck, W. H., eds., Vol. 2*, 1981, pp. 225–49.

Tinsley, Dillard B. Business Organizations in the Sustainable Society. In *Coomer, J. C., ed.*, 1981, pp. 164–82.

Todd, Jerry D. and Goldstein, David N. A Computerized Simulation Model for Analyzing Profit Sharing Plans. *J. Risk Ins.*, December 1981, *48*(4), pp. 662–73.

Williamson, Oliver E. The Modern Corporation: Origins, Evolution, Attributes. *J. Econ. Lit.*, De-

cember 1981, *19*(4), pp. 1537–68.
Wood, Leonard A. Changing Attitudes and the Work Ethic. In *Hoffman, W. M. and Wyly, T. J., eds.,* 1981, pp. 1–17.   [G: U.S.]

520 BUSINESS FINANCE AND INVESTMENT

5200 Business Finance and Investment

Ashton, D. J. and Atkins, D. R. Multicriteria Programming for Financial Planning: Some Second Thoughts. In *Nijkamp, P. and Spronk, J., eds.,* 1981, pp. 11–23.

Bavishi, Vinod B. Capital Budgeting Practices at Multinationals. *Manage. Account.,* August 1981, *63*(2), pp. 32–35.

Bowen, Robert M.; Noreen, Eric W. and Lacey, John M. Determinants of the Corporate Decision to Capitalize Interest. *J. Acc. Econ.,* August 1981, *3*(2), pp. 151–79.   [G: U.S.]

Evans, Peter. Collectivized Capitalism: Integrated Petrochemical Complexes and Capital Accumulation in Brazil. In *Bruneau, T. C. and Faucher, P., eds.,* 1981, pp. 85–125.   [G: Brazil]

Green, Stephen; Mack, Christopher and Turner, William D. The Role of the Treasury Function. In *Ensor, R. and Muller, P., eds.,* 1981, pp. 1–12.

Hellwig, Martin F. Bankruptcy, Limited Liability, and the Modigliani–Miller Theorem. *Amer. Econ. Rev.,* March 1981, *71*(1), pp. 155–70.

Kim, Suk H. and Farragher, Edward J. Current Capital Budgeting Practices. *Manage. Account.,* June 1981, *62*(12), pp. 26–30.   [G: U.S.]

Rosenblatt, Mier J. A Note on "Who Needs a Discount Rate?" *Eng. Econ.,* Winter 1981, *26*(2), pp. 158–60.

Shawky, Hany A. and Ricks, David A. Capital Budgeting for Multinational Firms: A Theoretical Analysis. *Southern Econ. J.,* January 1981, *47*(3), pp. 703–13.

Smith, Gary N. Investment and *q* in a Stock Valuation Model. *Southern Econ. J.,* April 1981, *47*(4), pp. 1007–20.

Spronk, Jaap. Capital Budgeting and Financial Planning with Multiple Goals. In *Nijkamp, P. and Spronk, J., eds.,* 1981, pp. 25–36.

Weiss, Stanley and McCarthy, Phillip A. Summary of Final Regulations on Treatment of Certain Interests in Corporations as Stock or Debt. *Bull. Int. Fiscal Doc.,* June 1981, *35*(6), pp. 272–76.
                    [G: U.S.]

521 Business Finance

5210 Business Finance

Agmon, Tamir; Ofer, A. R. and Tamir, A. Variable Rate Debt Instruments and Corporate Debt Policy. *J. Finance,* March 1981, *36*(1), pp. 113–25.

Aho, Teemu and Virtanen, Ilkka. Analysis of Lease Financing under Inflation. *Liiketaloudellinen Aikak.,* 1981, *30*(3), pp. 239–77.

Aiginger, Karl. Accelerated Depreciation Matters After All: A Note on the Effects of the Existence and the Utilization of Accelerated Depreciation

on Feldstein's Extra Tax on Fictitious Profits. *Empirica,* 1981, (2), pp. 263–75.

Alam, K. F. Taxation, Corporate Planning and Company Financial Policy: A Theoretical Exposition. *METU,* 1981, *8*(3&4), pp. 697–714.   [G: U.K.]

Allen, Franklin. The Prevention of Default. *J. Finance,* May 1981, *36*(2), pp. 271–76.

Altman, Edward I. Bankruptcy and Reorganization. In *Altman, E. I., ed.,* 1981, pp. 35.3–47.
                    [G: U.S.]

Andel, Norbert. Corporation Taxes, Their Integration with Personal Income Taxes, and International Capital Flows. In *Roskamp, K. W. and Forte, F., eds.,* 1981, pp. 159–72.
                    [G: W. Europe]

Andersen, Arne Geel. Hvad er overskuddet af en virksomhed? (Measurement of Business Income. With English summary.) *Nationaløkon. Tidsskr.,* 1981, *119*(3), pp. 362–77.

Arcuti, Luigi. Dalla regolamentazione alla liberalizzazione del movimento valutario. (From Control to Liberalization of Capital Movements. With English summary.) *Bancaria,* September 1981, *37*(9), pp. 891–94.   [G: Italy]

Arthur, Jeffrey L. and Lawrence, Kenneth D. Produce or Purchase—A Multiple Goal Linear Programming Model. In *Morse, J. N., ed.,* 1981, pp. 1–9.

Arzac, Enrique R.; Schwartz, Robert A. and Whitcomb, David K. A Theory and Test of Credit Rationing: Some Further Results. *Amer. Econ. Rev.,* September 1981, *71*(4), pp. 735–37.

Ballentine, J. Gregory. Corporation Finance: Comments. In *Aaron, H. J. and Pechman, J. A., eds.,* 1981, pp. 192–96.   [G: U.S.]

Barnea, Amir; Haugen, Robert A. and Senbet, Lemma W. An Equilibrium Analysis of Debt Financing under Costly Tax Arbitrage and Agency Problems. *J. Finance,* June 1981, *36*(3), pp. 569–81.

Ben-Horim, Moshe and Levy, Haim. Financial Management in an Inflationary Environment. In *Altman, E. I., ed.,* 1981, pp. 37.3–40.

Beranek, William. Research Directions in Finance. *Quart. Rev. Econ. Bus.,* Spring 1981, *21*(1), pp. 6–24.

Bernanke, Ben S. Bankruptcy, Liquidity, and Recession. *Amer. Econ. Rev.,* May 1981, *71*(2), pp. 155–59.

Black, Fischer and Dewhurst, Moray P. A New Investment Strategy for Pension Funds. *J. Portfol. Manage.,* Summer 1981, *7*(4), pp. 26–34.
                    [G: U.S.]

Blackie, Henry and Antl, Boris. Currency Strategy in Multicurrency Portfolio Management. In *Ensor, R. and Muller, P., eds.,* 1981, pp. 227–40.

Blaich, Robert and Schuster, Walter. Did Fictitious Profits Contribute to the Decline in the Rate of Profit? *Empirica,* 1981, (2), pp. 241–54.
                    [G: Austria]

Boatsman, James R. and Baskin, Elba F. Asset Valuation with Incomplete Markets. *Accounting Rev.,* January 1981, *56*(1), pp. 38–53.   [G: U.S.]

Boer, Germain B. and Barcus, Sam W., III. How a Small Company Evaluates Acquisition of a Minicomputer. *Manage. Account.,* March 1981, *62*(9),

pp. 13–23.

Bowen, Robert M. Valuation of Earnings Components in the Electric Utility Industry. *Accounting Rev.*, January 1981, *56*(1), pp. 1–22.   [G: U.S.]

Bowman, Robert G. The Theoretical Relationship between Systematic Risk and Financial (Accounting) Variables: Reply. *J. Finance*, June 1981, *36*(3), pp. 749–50.

Breit, William and Elzinga, Kenneth G. Information for Antitrust and Business Activity: Line-of-Business Reporting. In *Clarkson, K. W. and Muris, T. J., eds.*, 1981, pp. 98–120.   [G: U.S.]

Brinner, Roger E. and Brooks, Stephen H. Stock Prices. In *Aaron, H. J. and Pechman, J. A., eds.*, 1981, pp. 199–238.   [G: U.S.]

Bruse, Helmut and Fuhrmann, Gregor H. Capital Stocks of Firms—Calculation on a Microeconomic Basis. *Z. Nationalökon.*, 1981, *41*(3–4), pp. 361–83.   [G: W. Germany]

Buell, Stephen G. and Schwartz, Eli. Increasing Leverage, Potential Failure Rates and Possible Effects on the Macro-Economy. *Oxford Econ. Pap.*, November 1981, *33*(3), pp. 442–58.   [G: U.S.]

Callahan, J. The Lease versus Purchase Decision in the Public Sector. *Nat. Tax J.*, June 1981, *34*(2), pp. 235–40.   [G: U.S.]

Cappugi, Luigi. The Financing of Industrial Investment. *Rev. Econ. Cond. Italy*, February 1981, (1), pp. 41–83.   [G: Italy]

Caprara, Giordano. Una interpretazione dei rapporti tra dati di bilancio caratteristici delle imprese industriali. (How the Characteristic Items on Balance Sheets of Industrial Firms Are Related to Each Other. With English summary.) *Rivista Int. Sci. Econ. Com.*, December 1981, *28*(12), pp. 1181–88.

Carter, E. Eugene. Resource Allocation. In *Nystrom, P. C. and Starbuck, W. H., eds., Vol. 2*, 1981, pp. 152–65.

Castagna, A. D. and Matolcsy, Z. P. The Prediction of Corporate Failure: Testing the Australian Experience. *Australian J. Manage.*, June 1981, *6*(1), pp. 23–50.   [G: Australia]

Chance, Don M. Leverage and the Valuation of Risk Assets: A Comment. *Quart. Rev. Econ. Bus.*, Spring 1981, *21*(1), pp. 125–27.   [G: U.S.]

Chaudhary, Mohammad Ali and Iqbal, Nuzhat. Economic Analysis of Firm Size and Saving Rate. *Pakistan Econ. Soc. Rev.*, Winter 1981, *19*(2), pp. 115–22.   [G: Pakistan]

Clark, K. J. Financing Exports and Imports. In *Ensor, R. and Muller, P., eds.*, 1981, pp. 243–54.

Cogger, Kenneth O. and Emery, Gary W. A Determination of the Risk of Ruin: Comment. *J. Finan. Quant. Anal.*, December 1981, *16*(5), pp. 759–64.   [G: U.S.]

Cohen, David L. Small Business Capital Formation. In *Federal Reserve System*, 1981, pp. 251–64.   [G: U.S.]

Copeland, Thomas E. Long-term Sources of Funds and the Cost of Capital. In *Altman, E. I., ed.*, 1981, pp. 31.3–54.

Cordes, Joseph J. and Sheffrin, Steven M. Taxation and the Sectoral Allocation of Capital in the U.S. *Nat. Tax J.*, December 1981, *34*(4), pp. 419–32.   [G: U.S.]

DeAngelo, Harry. Competition and Unanimity. *Amer. Econ. Rev.*, March 1981, *71*(1), pp. 18–27.

Drukarczyk, Jochen. Verschuldung, Konkursrisiko, Kreditverträge und Marktwert von Aktiengesellschaften. (Debts, Risks of Bankruptcy, Credit Contracts Market Value of Limited Companies. With English summary.) *Kredit Kapital*, 1981, *14*(3), pp. 287–319.

Edmunds, Stahrl W. Organizational Size and Efficiency in the U.S. *Antitrust Bull.*, Fall 1981, *26*(3), pp. 507–19.   [G: U.S.]

Elton, Edwin J.; Gruber, Martin J. and Lightstone, John B. The Impact of Bankruptcy on the Firm's Capital Structure, the Reasonableness of Mergers, and the Risk Independence of Projects. In *Levy, H., ed.*, 1981, pp. 143–56.

Feenberg, Daniel. Does the Investment Interest Limitation Explain the Existence of Dividends? *J. Finan. Econ.*, Summer 1981, *9*(3), pp. 265–69.   [G: U.S.]

Feldstein, Martin S.; Green, Jerry and Sheshinski, Eytan. Corporate Financial Policy and Taxation in a Growing Economy. In *Eliasson, G. and Södersten, J., eds.*, 1981, *1979*, pp. 127–62.   [G: U.S.]

Feldstein, Martin S. and Seligman, Stephanie. Pension Funding, Share Prices, and National Savings. *J. Finance*, September 1981, *36*(4), pp. 801–24.   [G: U.S.]

Flaherty, M. Therese. Prices versus Quantities and Vertical Financial Integration. *Bell J. Econ. (See Rand J. Econ. after 4/85)*, Autumn 1981, *12*(2), pp. 507–25.

Fornasari, Franco. The Effects of Inflation on Company Profits: A Comment on the Application of Inflation Accounting Techniques to the Italian Case. *Rev. Econ. Cond. Italy*, October 1981, (3), pp. 455–78.   [G: Italy]

Frankfurter, George M. and Hill, Joanne M. A Normative Approach to Pension Fund Management. *J. Finan. Quant. Anal.*, November 1981, *16*(4), pp. 533–55.

Freedman, Craig and Makofsky, David. Supporting the Rich. *Calif. Manage. Rev.*, Summer 1981, *23*(4), pp. 49–54.   [G: U.S.]

Freund, William C. Corporation Finance: Comments. In *Aaron, H. J. and Pechman, J. A., eds.*, 1981, pp. 197–98.   [G: U.S.]

Friedlaender, Ann F. Saving: Comments. In *Aaron, H. J. and Pechman, J. A., eds.*, 1981, pp. 390–96.

Fuller, Russell J. and Kerr, Halbert S. Estimating the Divisional Cost of Capital: An Analysis of the Pure-Play Technique. *J. Finance*, December 1981, *36*(5), pp. 997–1009.

von Furstenberg, George M. Saving. In *Aaron, H. J. and Pechman, J. A., eds.*, 1981, pp. 327–90.   [G: U.S.]

Gastineau, Gary L. Options Markets and Instruments. In *Altman, E. I., ed.*, 1981, pp. 20.3–45.   [G: U.S.]

Gilburn, David A. and White, Roger. Tax Planning. In *Ensor, R. and Muller, P., eds.*, 1981, pp. 63–76.   [G: OECD]

Gmür, Charles J. Trade Financing: Leasing. In

Gmür, C. J., ed., 1981, pp. 105–16.
[G: W. Europe]

Golbe, Devra L. The Effects of Imminent Bankruptcy on Stockholder Risk Preferences and Behavior [The Bankruptcy Decision]. *Bell J. Econ. (See Rand J. Econ. after 4/85),* Spring 1981, *12*(1), pp. 321–28.

Goldschmitt, Y. and Shashua, L. The Real Cost of Debt during Inflation. *Eng. Econ.,* Winter 1981, *26*(2), pp. 161–66.

Gordon, Myron J. and Yagil, Joseph. Financial Gain from Conglomerate Mergers. In *Levy, H., ed.,* 1981, pp. 103–42. [G: U.S.]

Gordon, Roger H. and Malkiel, Burton G. Corporation Finance. In *Aaron, H. J. and Pechman, J. A., eds.,* 1981, pp. 131–92. [G: U.S.]

Goss, Richard T. An Introduction: Risk Definition, Strategy and Techniques. In *Ensor, R. and Muller, P., eds.,* 1981, pp. 79–88.

Greenberg, Edward; Marshall, William J. and Yawitz, Jess B. The Technology of Risk and Return: Reply. *Amer. Econ. Rev.,* June 1981, *71*(3), pp. 491–92.

Greenwald, Eleanor. Why Doesn't Business Float Indexed Bonds? *Bus. Econ.,* May 1981, *16*(3), pp. 62. [G: U.S.]

Grossman, Sanford J. and Hart, Oliver D. The Allocational Role of Takeover Bids in Situations of Asymmetric Information. *J. Finance,* May 1981, *36*(2), pp. 253–70.

Hackett, John T. Dividend Policy. In *Altman, E. I., ed.,* 1981, pp. 32.3–26.

Hagin, Robert L. Financial Statement Analysis. In *Altman, E. I., ed.,* 1981, pp. 24.3–31.

Hammond, J. D. and Shapiro, Arnold F. Capital Requirements for Entry into Property and Liability Underwriting: An Empirical Examination. In *Fed. Res. Bank of Boston and National Sci. Foundation,* 1981, pp. 225–55. [G: U.S.]

Harrington, Scott E. Stock Life Insurer Shareholder Dividend Policy and Holding Company Affiliation. *J. Risk Ins.,* December 1981, *48*(4), pp. 550–76. [G: U.S.]

Harris, Richard G. The Consequences of Costly Default: A Reply. *Econ. Inquiry,* July 1981, *19*(3), pp. 526–27.

Haseltine, John B. A Longer-term Approach. In *Ensor, R. and Muller, P., eds.,* 1981, pp. 139–42. [G: U.S.]

Haugen, Robert A. and Senbet, Lemma W. Resolving the Agency Problems of External Capital through Options. *J. Finance,* June 1981, *36*(3), pp. 629–47.

Hawanini, Gabriel A. and Vora, Ashok. The Capital Asset Pricing Model and the Investment Horizon: Comment. *Rev. Econ. Statist.,* November 1981, *63*(4), pp. 633–36.

Hekman, Christine R. Foreign Exchange Risk: Relevance and Management. *Managerial Dec. Econ.,* December 1981, *2*(4), pp. 256–62.

Hicks, John R. The Concept of Income in Relation to Taxation and to Business Management. In *Roskamp, K. W. and Forte, F., eds.,* 1981, pp. 73–85.

Hill, Ned C. Planning and Control Techniques. In *Altman, E. I., ed.,* 1981, pp. 25.3–25.

Hinna, Luciano. Marketing e controllo (Marketing and Control. With English summary.) *L'Impresa,* 1981, *23*(6), pp. 43–46.

Holland, J. B. Problems in the Development and Use of Managerial Financial Models. *Managerial Dec. Econ.,* March 1981, *2*(1), pp. 40–48.

Holthausen, Robert W. Evidence on the Effect of Bond Covenants and Management Compensation Contracts on the Choice of Accounting Techniques: The Case of the Depreciation Switch-Back. *J. Acc. Econ.,* March 1981, *3*(1), pp. 73–109. [G: U.S.]

Honkapohja, Seppo and Kanniainen, Vesa. Corporate Taxation, Inventory Undervaluation and Neutrality. *Kansant. Aikak.,* 1981, *77*(4), pp. 435–45. [G: Finland]

Horvitz, Paul M. and Pettit, R. Richardson. Short-run Financial Solutions for Troubled Thrift Institutions. In *Federal Reserve Bank of Boston (II),* 1981, pp. 44–67. [G: U.S.]

Horwitz, Bertrand and Kolodny, Richard. The Relationship between Firm Characteristics and the Choice of Financial Measurement Methods: An Application to R&D. *Quart. Rev. Econ. Bus.,* Winter 1981, *21*(4), pp. 75–86. [G: U.S.]

Imhoff, Eugene A., Jr. Income Smoothing: An Analysis of Critical Issues. *Quart. Rev. Econ. Bus.,* Autumn 1981, *21*(3), pp. 23–42.

Jacobson, Robert. Forecasting Bank Portfolios. In *Maisel, S. J., ed.,* 1981, pp. 249–70. [G: U.S.]

James, Christopher. The Technology of Risk and Return: Comment. *Amer. Econ. Rev.,* June 1981, *71*(3), pp. 485–90.

Johnson, Dana J. and Deckro, Richard F. The Role of Economic Variables in Relating Changes in a Firm's Earnings to Changes in the Price of Its Common Stock. *Rev. Bus. Econ. Res.,* Fall 1981, *17*(1), pp. 27–39. [G: U.S.]

Johnson, Robert W. Management of Accounts Receivable and Payable. In *Altman, E. I., ed.,* 1981, pp. 28.3–28.

Joy, O. Maurice and Grube, R. Corwin. Cash Flows That Require Negative Discount Rates. *Eng. Econ.,* Winter 1981, *26*(2), pp. 154–58.

Kalay, Avner. Earnings Uncertainty and the Payout Ratio: Some Empirical Evidence. *Rev. Econ. Statist.,* August 1981, *63*(3), pp. 439–43. [G: U.S.]

Kaplan, Marshall A. Short-run Financial Solutions for Troubled Thrift Institutions: Discussion. In *Federal Reserve Bank of Boston (II),* 1981, pp. 68–74. [G: U.S.]

Keefe, Harry V., Jr. Short-run Financial Solutions for Troubled Thrift Institutions: Discussion. In *Federal Reserve Bank of Boston (II),* 1981, pp. 75–80. [G: U.S.]

Keenan, Michael. A Normative Approach to Pension Fund Management: Discussion. *J. Finan. Quant. Anal.,* November 1981, *16*(4), pp. 557–58.

Kemp, Donald S. Hedging Long-term Financings. In *Ensor, R. and Muller, P., eds.,* 1981, pp. 115–21.

Kim, Kee S. The Theoretical Relationship between Systematic Risk and Financial (Accounting) Variables: Comment. *J. Finance,* June 1981, *36*(3), pp. 747–48.

Kolb, Robert W. Predicting Dividend Changes. *J.*

Econ. Bus., Spring/Summer 1981, *33*(3), pp. 218–30. **[G: U.S.]**

Kudla, Ronald J. and McInish, Thomas H. The Microeconomic Consequences of an Involuntary Corporate Spin-off. *Sloan Manage. Rev.*, Summer 1981, *22*(4), pp. 41–46. **[G: U.S.]**

Kunreuther, Howard. Theory of Solvency Regulation in the Property and Casualty Insurance Industry: Comment. In *Fromm, G., ed.*, 1981, pp. 168–72.

Kurz, William C. F. Documentation. In *Ensor, R. and Muller, P., eds.*, 1981, pp. 55–62.

Kyd, Charles W. Managing the Financial Demands of Growth. *Manage. Account.*, December 1981, *63*(6), pp. 33–41.

Laitinen, Erkki K. Taseanalyysin tunnusluvut ja yritysten kannattavuuden mittaaminen. (Financial Ratios and the Measurement of the Profitability of the Firm. With English summary.) *Liiketaloudellinen Aikak.*, 1981, *30*(2), pp. 168–76.

Landskroner, Yoram and Liviatan, Nissan. Risk Premia and the Sources of Inflation. *J. Money, Credit, Banking*, May 1981, *13*(2), pp. 205–14.

Larsen, Norma L. Policy Loan Utilization Factors in Dividend Distribution Formulas. *J. Risk Ins.*, March 1981, *48*(1), pp. 80–94. **[G: U.S.]**

Lawson, G. H. and Stark, A. W. Equity Values and Inflation: A Rejoinder. *Lloyds Bank Rev.*, October 1981, (142), pp. 39–43. **[G: U.K.]**

Lawson, G. H. and Stark, A. W. Equity Values and Inflation: Dividends and Debt Financing. *Lloyds Bank Rev.*, January 1981, (139), pp. 40–54. **[G: U.K.]**

Leftwich, Richard W. Evidence of the Impact of Mandatory Changes in Accounting Principles on Corporate Loan Agreements. *J. Acc. Econ.*, March 1981, *3*(1), pp. 3–36. **[G: U.S.]**

Leigh, L. H. Crimes in Bankruptcy. In *Leigh, L. H., ed.*, 1981, pp. 106–208. **[G: U.K.]**

LeRoy, Stephen F. and Porter, Richard D. The Present-Value Relation: Tests Based on Implied Variance Bounds. *Econometrica*, May 1981, *49*(3), pp. 555–74. **[G: U.S.]**

Levasseur, Michel and Olivaux, Jean-Louis. Théorie du financement des entreprises et évolution de la fiscalité française. (Theory of Capital Structure and the Evolution of the French Tax System. With English summary.) *Revue Écon.*, May 1981, *32*(3), pp. 490–512. **[G: France]**

Levhari, David and Levy, Haim. The Capital Asset Pricing Model and the Investment Horizon: Reply. *Rev. Econ. Statist.*, November 1981, *63*(4), pp. 637–38.

Levine, Paul and Aaronovitch, Sam. The Financial Characteristics of Firms and Theories of Merger Activity. *J. Ind. Econ.*, December 1981, *30*(2), pp. 149–72. **[G: U.K.]**

Levy, Haim. Optimal Portfolio of Foreign Currencies with Borrowing and Lending. *J. Money, Credit, Banking*, August 1981, *13*(3), pp. 325–41. **[G: U.S.]**

Lewellen, Wilbur G. and Emery, Douglas R. On the Matter of Parity among Financial Obligations. *J. Finance*, March 1981, *36*(1), pp. 97–111.

Lintner, John. Economic Theory and Financial Management. In *Vernon, R. and Aharoni, Y., eds.*, 1981, pp. 23–53.

Lister, Neil. International Project Financing. In *Ensor, R. and Muller, P., eds.*, 1981, pp. 31–46.

Little, Jane Sneddon. The Financial Health of U.S. Manufacturing Firms Acquired by Foreigners. *New Eng. Econ. Rev.*, July/August 1981, pp. 5–18. **[G: U.S.]**

Livingston, Miles. Taxation and Bond Market Equilibrium in a World of Uncertain Future Interest Rates: Reply. *J. Finan. Quant. Anal.*, December 1981, *16*(5), pp. 779–81.

Lockhart, James B., III. Gulf Oil: A Case History. In *Ensor, R. and Muller, P., eds.*, 1981, pp. 47–53.

Lockhart, James B., III. International Liquidity Management at Gulf Oil. In *Ensor, R. and Muller, P., eds.*, 1981, pp. 195–99.

Lodin, Sven-Olof. International Enterprises and Taxation—Some Preliminary Results of an Empirical Study Concerning International Enterprises. In *Eliasson, G. and Södersten, J., eds.*, 1981, pp. 97–123. **[G: Sweden; U.K.; U.S.]**

Lord, Peter. Financing the International Corporation. In *Ensor, R. and Muller, P., eds.*, 1981, pp. 15–24.

Lorek, Kenneth S.; Kee, Robert and Vass, William H. Time-Series Properties of Annual Earnings Data: The State of the Art. *Quart. Rev. Econ. Bus.*, Spring 1981, *21*(1), pp. 97–113.

Lucatti, Riccardo. Una proposta per la gestione dei finanziamenti a breve. (A Proposal for Loan Management. With English summary.) *L'Impresa*, 1981, *23*(2), pp. 59–62.

Lumby, Stephen. New Ways of Financing Nationalized Industries. *Lloyds Bank Rev.*, July 1981, (141), pp. 34–44. **[G: U.K.]**

Lye, Stephen and Silberston, Aubrey. Merger Activity and Sales of Subsidiaries between Company Groups. *Oxford Bull. Econ. Statist.*, August 1981, *43*(3), pp. 257–72. **[G: U.S.]**

Lynch, Michael P. Theory of Solvency Regulation in the Property and Casualty Insurance Industry: Comment. In *Fromm, G., ed.*, 1981, pp. 173–79.

Maisel, Sherman J. Risk and Capital Adequacy in Banks. In *Fed. Res. Bank of Boston and National Sci. Foundation*, 1981, pp. 203–24. **[G: U.S.]**

Maisel, Sherman J. Risk and Capital Adequacy in Commercial Banks: Introduction. In *Maisel, S. J., ed.*, 1981, pp. 1 —16. **[G: U.S.]**

Maisel, Sherman J. The Theory and Measurement of Risk and Capital Adequacy. In *Maisel, S. J., ed.*, 1981, pp. 17–183. **[G: U.S.]**

Maisel, Sherman J. and Jacobson, Robert. Interest Rate Changes and Commercial Bank Revenues and Costs. In *Maisel, S. J., ed.*, 1981, pp. 203–22. **[G: U.S.]**

Malécot, Jean-François. La défaillance d'une entreprise est-elle une catastrophe? (The Firm's Bankruptcy: A Catastrophe? With English summary.) *Ann. Sci. Écon. Appl.*, 1981, *37*(2), pp. 9–23.

Martin, John D. Leasing. In *Altman, E. I., ed.*, 1981, pp. 30.3–33.

McConnell, John J. and Schlarbaum, Gary G. Evidence on the Impact of Exchange Offers on Security Prices: The Case of Income Bonds. *J. Bus.*,

January 1981, *54*(1), pp. 65–85.   [G: U.S.]

McConnell, John J. and Schlarbaum, Gary G. Returns, Risks, and Pricing of Income Bonds, 1956–76 (Does Money Have an Odor?) *J. Bus.*, January 1981, *54*(1), pp. 33–63.   [G: U.S.]

McCulloch, J. Huston. Interest Rate Risk and Capital Adequacy for Traditional Banks and Financial Intermediaries. In *Maisel, S. J., ed.*, 1981, pp. 223–48.   [G: U.S.]

Mees, Philip. Using Computerized Information Systems. In *Ensor, R. and Muller, P., eds.*, 1981, pp. 201–10.

Meierjohann, Freidrich W. An Index-controlled Hedging Programme. In *Ensor, R. and Muller, P., eds.*, 1981, pp. 131–37.

Merchant, Kenneth A. The Design of the Corporate Budgeting System: Influences on Managerial Behavior and Performance. *Accounting Rev.*, October 1981, *56*(4), pp. 813–29.

Merton, Robert C. Discussion [Risk and Capital Adequacy in Banks] [Capital Requirements for Entry into Property and Liability Underwriting: An empirical Examination]. In *Fed. Res. Bank of Boston and National Sci. Foundation*, 1981, pp. 256–63.   [G: U.S.]

Michel, Allen. The Inflation Audit. *Calif. Manage. Rev.*, Winter 1981, *24*(2), pp. 68–74.

Monroe, Margaret. Conglomerate Mergers: Financial Theory and Evidence. In *Blair, R. D. and Lanzillotti, R. F., eds.*, 1981, pp. 113–35.
     [G: U.S.]

Moore, Basil J. Equity Values and Inflation: Reply. *Lloyds Bank Rev.*, October 1981, (142), pp. 44–45.   [G: U.K.]

Moore, Basil J. Equity Values and Inflation: Reply. *Lloyds Bank Rev.*, January 1981, (139), pp. 55–57.

Muller, Peter J. Cash Management—A Definition. In *Ensor, R. and Muller, P., eds.*, 1981, pp. 177–81.

Muller, Peter J. Organization of the Exposure Management Function. In *Ensor, R. and Muller, P., eds.*, 1981, pp. 101–13.

Munch, Patricia and Smallwood, Dennis. Theory of Solvency Regulation in the Property and Casualty Insurance Industry. In *Fromm, G., ed.*, 1981, pp. 119–67.

Murray, Roger F. Pension and Profit-sharing Plans. In *Altman, E. I., ed.*, 1981, pp. 34.3–25.

Mutti, John H. Tax Incentives and the Repatriation Decisions of U.S. Multinational Corporations. *Nat. Tax J.*, June 1981, *34*(2), pp. 241–48.
     [G: U.S.]

Nakamura, Toru. Productivity Losses through Capital Misallocation in the U.S., Japan, and West Germany. *Quart. Rev. Econ. Bus.*, Autumn 1981, *21*(3), pp. 65–76.   [G: W. Germany; Japan; U.S.]

Neudeck, Werner. Inflation and the Taxation of Capital Income: A Note. *Empirica*, 1981, (2), pp. 255–61.   [G: Austria]

Panton, Don B. and Verdini, William A. A Fortran Program for Applying Sturm's Theorem in Counting Internal Rates of Return. *J. Finan. Quant. Anal.*, September 1981, *16*(3), pp. 381–88.

Parker, George G. C. Financial Forecasting. In *Alt-*

man, E. I., ed., 1981, pp. 26.3–39.

Paules, Edward P. Taxation and Exposure Management. In *Ensor, R. and Muller, P., eds.*, 1981, pp. 143–66.   [G: U.S.]

Peterson, Graham. Cash Forecasting at Unilever, Australia. In *Ensor, R. and Muller, P., eds.*, 1981, pp. 189–94.   [G: Australia]

Racette, George A. The Consequences of Costly Default: A Comment. *Econ. Inquiry*, July 1981, *19*(3), pp. 522–25.

Ram, Rati. Business Demand for Money in India: A Suggestion for Inferential Caution. *Indian Econ. J.*, July–September 1981, *29*(1), pp. 37–40.   [G: India]

Rao, V. G. Corporate Level Demand for Bank Loans. *Indian Econ. J.*, July–September 1981, *29*(1), pp. 97–110.   [G: India]

Roberts, Gordon S. and Viscione, Jerry A. Captive Finance Subsidiaries and the M-Form Hypothesis. *Bell J. Econ. (See Rand J. Econ. after 4/85)*, Spring 1981, *12*(1), pp. 285–95.   [G: U.S.]

Rodriguez, Rita M. Corporate Exchange Risk Management: Theme and Aberrations. *J. Finance*, May 1981, *36*(2), pp. 427–38.   [G: U.S.]

Romeril, Barry. ICI's Approach to Currency Exposure and Cash Management. In *Ensor, R. and Muller, P., eds.*, 1981, pp. 123–29.

Rosenberg, Barr and Perry, Philip R. The Fundamental Determinants of Risk in Banking. In *Maisel, S. J., ed.*, 1981, pp. 367–407.   [G: U.S.]

Saxena, Umesh and Garg, Arun. Equivalence of Cash Flows When Compounding Occurs Less Frequently Than the Cash Flows. *Eng. Econ.*, Winter 1981, *26*(2), pp. 148–52.

Schaefer, Stephen M. Taxation and Bond Market Equilibrium in a World of Uncertain Future Interest Rates: Comment. *J. Finan. Quant. Anal.*, December 1981, *16*(5), pp. 773–77.

Schmidt, Reinhard H. Grundformen der Finanzierung: Eine Anwendung des neo-institutionalistischen Ansatzes der Finanzierungstheorie. (Basic Forms of Financing: An Application of the Neo-Institutionalist Approach to Financing Theory. With English summary.) *Kredit Kapital*, 1981, *14*(2), pp. 186–221.

Shelton, Judy. Equal Access and Miller's Equilibrium. *J. Finan. Quant. Anal.*, November 1981, *16*(4), pp. 603–23.

Sherlock, Anthony G. A Total Approach. In *Ensor, R. and Muller, P., eds.*, 1981, pp. 183–88.

Shim, Jae K. Forecasting Cash Inflows for Better Budgeting. *Bus. Econ.*, January 1981, *16*(1), pp. 35–38.   [G: U.S.]

Shirley, Tim. The Leveraged ESOT as a Financial Tool. *Manage. Account.*, July 1981, *63*(1), pp. 49–52.   [G: U.S.]

Shrieves, Ronald E. Uncertainty, the Theory of Production, and Optimal Operating Leverage. *Southern Econ. J.*, January 1981, *47*(3), pp. 690–702.

Sick, Gordon. Asymmetric Information, Signaling, and Optimal Corporate Financial Decisions: Discussion. *J. Finan. Quant. Anal.*, November 1981, *16*(4), pp. 437–38.

Soom, Erich. Optimal Planning of Inventories. A Method for the Improvement of Liquidity and Efficiency of Enterprises. In *Chikán, A., ed. (II)*,

1981, pp. 273–85.

Stanley, Marjorie Thines. Capital Structure and Cost-of-Capital for the Multinational Firm. *J. Int. Bus. Stud.*, Spring/Summer 1981, *12*(1), pp. 103–20.

Stockmayer, Albrecht. Financing Mining Projects in Developing Countries. In *Schanze, E., et al.*, 1981, pp. 171–97.

Stone, Bernell K. Cash Management. In *Altman, E. I., ed.*, 1981, pp. 27.3–33.

Stone, Bernell K. and Hill, Ned C. The Design of a Cash Concentration System. *J. Finan. Quant. Anal.*, September 1981, *16*(3), pp. 301–22.

Subrahmanyam, Marti G. Mathematics of Finance. In *Altman, E. I., ed.*, 1981, pp. A3–50.

Suhar, V. Victor. Managing Translation and Transaction Exposure. In *Ensor, R. and Muller, P., eds.*, 1981, pp. 89–99.

Talmor, Eli. Asymmetric Information, Signaling, and Optimal Corporate Financial Decisions. *J. Finan. Quant. Anal.*, November 1981, *16*(4), pp. 413–35.

Tanzi, Vito. Inflation Accounting and the Taxation of Capital Gains of Business Enterprises. In *Roskamp, K. W. and Forte, F., eds.*, 1981, pp. 87–101.

Teece, David J. Internal Organization and Economic Performance: An Empirical Analysis of the Profitability of Principal Firms. *J. Ind. Econ.*, December 1981, *30*(2), pp. 173–99. [G: U.S.]

Tepper, Irwin. Taxation and Corporate Pension Policy. *J. Finance*, March 1981, *36*(1), pp. 1–13.

Thompson, A. Frank, Jr. Immunization of Pension Funds and Sensitivity to Actuarial Assumptions: Comment. *J. Risk Ins.*, March 1981, *48*(1), pp. 148–53.

Thompson, R. S. Internal Organization and Profit: A Note [Internal Organization and Profit: An Empirical Analysis of Large UK Companies]. *J. Ind. Econ.*, December 1981, *30*(2), pp. 201–11. [G: U.K.]

Todd, Jerry D. and Goldstein, David N. A Computerized Simulation Model for Analyzing Profit Sharing Plans. *J. Risk Ins.*, December 1981, *48*(4), pp. 662–73.

Vander Weele, Ray. Is This Merger Right for You? *Manage. Account.*, March 1981, *62*(9), pp. 35–39, 47.

Vinso, Joseph D. A Determination of the Risk of Ruin: Reply. *J. Finan. Quant. Anal.*, December 1981, *16*(5), pp. 765–72. [G: U.S.]

Walton, John. Capital Maintenance and the Measurement of Corporate Income. *Rev. Income Wealth*, June 1981, *27*(2), pp. 109–35. [G: U.K.]

Watson, Peter. Inflation Accounting and Business Taxation. In *Peacock, A. and Forte, F., eds.*, 1981, pp. 78–93. [G: U.K.]

Weber, Warren E. Saving: Comments. In *Aaron, H. J. and Pechman, J. A., eds.*, 1981, pp. 396–402. [G: U.S.]

Wenglowski, Gary M. Stock Prices: Comments. In *Aaron, H. J. and Pechman, J. A., eds.*, 1981, pp. 238–40. [G: U.S.]

Wolff, M. R. A Control-Theoretic Approach to the Portfolio Selection Problem Including Cash Bal-

ance. In *Fandel, G., et al., eds.*, 1981, pp. 594–600.

Yli-Olli, Paavo. Leverage, the Cost of Capital and the Value of the Firm: Empirical Evidence on Finnish Industrial Firms. *Liiketaloudellinen Aikak.*, 1981, *30*(4), pp. 435–46. [G: Finland]

522 Business Investment

5220 Business Investment

Abel, Andrew B. A Dynamic Model of Investment and Capacity Utilization. *Quart. J. Econ.*, August 1981, *96*(3), pp. 379–403.

Aho, Teemu and Virtanen, Ilkka. Adequacy of Depreciation Allowances under Inflation. *Liiketaloudellinen Aikak.*, 1981, *30*(4), pp. 351–79. [G: Finland]

Alho, Kari. Pääoman tuotto Suomessa. (The Rate of Return in Finland. With English summary.) *Kansant. Aikak.*, 1981, *77*(2), pp. 151–61. [G: Finland]

Anderson, G. J. A New Approach to the Empirical Investigation of Investment Expenditures. *Econ. J.*, March 1981, *91*(361), pp. 88–103. [G: U.K.]

Anderson, G. J. An Econometric Model of Manufacturing Investment in the U.K.: A Comment. *Econ. J.*, March 1981, *91*(361), pp. 122–23.

Artus, Patrick, et al. Economic Policy and Private Investment since the Oil Crisis: A Comparative Study of France and Germany. *Europ. Econ. Rev.*, May 1981, *16*(1), pp. 7–51. [G: France; W. Germany]

Arzac, Enrique R. and Marcus, Matityahu. Flotation Cost Allowance in Rate of Return Regulation: A Note. *J. Finance*, December 1981, *36*(5), pp. 1199–1202.

Atkinson, Sherry S. An Analysis of Finished Goods Inventory Behavior: A Microtheoretic Approach. *Southern Econ. J.*, October 1981, *48*(2), pp. 312–26.

Auerbach, Alan J. A Note on the Efficient Design of Investment Incentives. *Econ. J.*, March 1981, *91*(361), pp. 217–23.

Baillie, Richard T. and McMahon, Patrick C. Interest Rates and Investment in West Germany. *Empirical Econ.*, 1981, *6*(1), pp. 1–9. [G: W. Germany]

Bardsley, R. Geoffrey. Management Procedures for Investing Surplus Cash. In *Ensor, R. and Muller, P., eds.*, 1981, pp. 217–18. [G: OECD]

Bean, Charles R. A New Approach to the Empirical Investigation of Investment Expenditures: A Comment. *Econ. J.*, March 1981, *91*(361), pp. 104–05.

Bean, Charles R. An Econometric Model of Manufacturing Investment in the UK. *Econ. J.*, March 1981, *91*(361), pp. 106–21. [G: U.K.]

Bergström, Villy and Södersten, Jan. Double Taxation and Corporate Capital Cost. In *Eliasson, G. and Södersten, J., eds.*, 1981, pp. 163–90. [G: Sweden]

Bergström, Villy and Södersten, Jan. Inflation, Taxation and Capital Cost. In *Eliasson, G. and Södersten, J., eds.*, 1981, pp. 233–66.

Bernhard, Richard H. On the Park-Thuesen Index

and the Value of Earlier Uncertainty Resolution. *Eng. Econ.*, Winter 1981, *26*(2), pp. 113–22.

Bhattacharya, Prodyot K., et al. Variable Wages and Prices and the Demand for Capital with Discrete and Continuous Adjustments. *Int. Econ. Rev.*, June 1981, *22*(2), pp. 295–307.

Bierman, Harold, Jr. Capital Budgeting. In *Altman, E. I., ed.*, 1981, pp. 29.3–35.

Bitros, George C. The Fungibility Factor in Credit and the Question of the Efficacy of Selective Controls. *Oxford Econ. Pap.*, November 1981, *33*(3), pp. 459–77.   [G: Greece]

Blair, Peter; Cassel, Thomas and Edelstein, Robert H. Optimal Investments in Geothermal Electricity Facilities: A Theoretic Note. In *Nemetz, P. N., ed.*, 1981, pp. 197–212.

Blinder, Alan S. Retail Inventory Behavior and Business Fluctuations. *Brookings Pap. Econ. Act.*, 1981, (2), pp. 443–505.   [G: U.S.]

Blume, Marshall E.; Crockett, Jean A. and Friend, Irwin. Stimulation of Capital Formation: Ends and Means. In *Wachter, M. L. and Wachter, S. M., eds.*, 1981, pp. 41–94.   [G: U.S.]

Boatsman, James R. and Baskin, Elba F. Asset Valuation with Incomplete Markets. *Accounting Rev.*, January 1981, *56*(1), pp. 38–53.   [G: U.S.]

Boddy, Martin. The Property Sector in Late Capitalism: The Case of Britain. In *Dear, M. and Scott, A. J., eds.*, 1981, pp. 267–86.   [G: U.K.]

Bradford, David F. Issues in the Design of Savings and Investment Incentives. In *Hulten, C. R., ed.*, 1981, pp. 13–47.

Bradford, David F. and Fullerton, Don. Pitfalls in the Construction and Use of Effective Tax Rates. In *Hulten, C. R., ed.*, 1981, pp. 251–78.

Braun, Steven. The Inventory Stock-Adjustment Model Reconsidered. *Rev. Econ. Statist.*, August 1981, *63*(3), pp. 452–54.   [G: U.S.]

van Breda, Michael F. Capital Budgeting Using Terminal Values. *Manage. Account.*, July 1981, *63*(1), pp. 42–48.

Brigham, Eugene F. Public Utility Finance. In *Altman, E. I., ed.*, 1981, pp. 36.3–31.

Brown, E. Cary. The "Net" versus the "Gross" Investment Tax Credit. In *Hulten, C. R., ed.*, 1981, pp. 133–34.

Brush, Brian C. What Do Labor Productivity Data Show about Economies of Scale: Comment. *Southern Econ. J.*, January 1981, *47*(3), pp. 839–46.   [G: U.S.]

Cappugi, Luigi. The Financing of Industrial Investment. *Rev. Econ. Cond. Italy*, February 1981, (1), pp. 41–83.   [G: Italy]

Church, Albert M. The Effects of Local Government Expenditure and Property Taxes on Investment. *Amer. Real Estate Urban Econ. Assoc. J.*, Summer 1981, *9*(2), pp. 165–80.   [G: U.S.]

Ciravegna, Daniele. Metodi di scelta degli investimenti. (Methods for Investment Selection. With English summary.) *L'Impresa*, 1981, *23*(5), pp. 11–20.

Cohen, David L. Small Business Capital Formation. In *Federal Reserve System*, 1981, pp. 251–64.   [G: U.S.]

Copeland, Thomas E. Long-term Sources of Funds and the Cost of Capital. In *Altman, E. I., ed.*, 1981, pp. 31.3–54.

Corcoran, Patrick J. Inflation, Taxes, and the Composition of Business Investment. In *Federal Reserve System*, 1981, pp. 191–200.   [G: U.S.]

Davidson, Russell and Harris, Richard G. Non-Convexities in Continuous-Time Investment Theory. *Rev. Econ. Stud.*, April 1981, *48*(2), pp. 235–53.

Dernburg, Thomas. Issues in the Design of Savings and Investment Incentives: Discussion. In *Hulten, C. R., ed.*, 1981, pp. 48–52.

Diewert, W. Erwin. On Measuring the Loss of Output Due to Nonneutral Business Taxation. In *Hulten, C. R., ed.*, 1981, pp. 57–80.

Dixit, Mukund and Prasad, Kamta. Applicability of Neoclassical Model of Investment Behaviour to Industrial Corporations in India. *Indian Econ. J.*, October–December 1981, *29*(2), pp. 1–22.   [G: India]

Dorfman, Robert. The Meaning of Internal Rates of Return. *J. Finance*, December 1981, *36*(5), pp. 1011–21.

Ekern, Steinar. Time Dominance Efficiency Analysis. *J. Finance*, December 1981, *36*(5), pp. 1023–34.

Eliasson, Gunnar and Lindberg, Thomas. Allocation and Growth Effects of Corporate Income Taxes. In *Eliasson, G. and Södersten, J., eds.*, 1981, pp. 381–435.   [G: Sweden]

Eliasson, Gunnar and Södersten, Jan. Business Taxation, Rates of Return and the Allocation Process. In *Eliasson, G. and Södersten, J., eds.*, 1981, pp. 11–30.   [G: U.S.; U.K.; Sweden]

Enzler, Jared J.; Conrad, William E. and Johnson, Lewis. Public Policy and Capital Formation: Introduction. In *Federal Reserve System*, 1981, pp. 1–44.   [G: U.S.; OECD]

Errunza, Vihang R. and Senbet, Lemma W. The Effects of International Operations on the Market Value of the Firm: Theory and Evidence. *J. Finance*, May 1981, *36*(2), pp. 401–17.   [G: U.S.]

Feldstein, Martin S. Adjusting Depreciation in an Inflationary Economy: Indexing versus Acceleration. *Nat. Tax J.*, March 1981, *34*(1), pp. 29–43.   [G: U.S.]

Fiebig, D. G. A Bayesian Analysis of Inventory Investment. *Empirical Econ.*, 1981, *6*(4), pp. 229–37.   [G: Australia]

Fralick, James S. Tax Policy and the Demand for Real Capital. In *Federal Reserve System*, 1981, pp. 177–90.

Friedman, Benjamin M. Financing Capital Formation in the 1980s: Issues for Public Policy. In *Wachter, M. L. and Wachter, S. M., eds.*, 1981, pp. 95–126.   [G: U.S.]

von Furstenberg, George M. Domestic Determinants of Net U.S. Foreign Investment. In *Hogan, J. D. and Craig, A. M., eds.*, Vol. 1, 1981, pp. 115–63.

Gerra, Ralph A. The New Forms of Federal Fiscal Policies and Implications for State and Local Governments: Observations from Business. *Nat. Tax J.*, September 1981, *34*(3), pp. 293–302.   [G: U.S.]

Ghali, Moheb A. Production Smoothing and Inventory Behaviour: A Simple Model. In *Chikán, A., ed. (1)*, 1981, pp. 157–66.   [G: U.S.]

Giddy, Ian H. The Cost of Capital in the International Firm. *Managerial Dec. Econ.*, December 1981, *2*(4), pp. 263–71.

Grant, R. M. The Relationship between Risk and Rate of Return on Capital in UK Industry. *Appl. Econ.*, June 1981, *13*(2), pp. 205–14. [G: U.K.]

Grossman, Sanford J. and Hart, Oliver D. The Allocational Role of Takeover Bids in Situations of Asymmetric Information. *J. Finance*, May 1981, *36*(2), pp. 253–70.

Gui, Benedetto. Investment Decisions in a Worker-Managed Firm. *Econ. Anal. Worker's Manage.*, 1981, *15*(1), pp. 45–65.

Gürmann, Klaus. Complex Stock Planning by the Improvement of Plan Indicators. In *Chikán, A., ed. (1)*, 1981, pp. 167–78. [G: E. Germany]

Hall, Robert E. Tax Treatment of Depreciation, Capital Gains, and Interest in an Inflationary Economy. In *Hulten, C. R., ed.*, 1981, pp. 149–66.

Hawkins, R. G. International Finance: Discussion. *J. Finance*, May 1981, *36*(2), pp. 442–44.

Hendershott, Patric H. Estimates of Investment Functions and Some Implications for Productivity Growth. In *Meyer, L. H., ed.*, 1981, pp. 149–63.

Hendershott, Patric H. and Hu, Sheng-Cheng. Investment in Producers' Equipment. In *Aaron, H. J. and Pechman, J. A., eds.*, 1981, pp. 85–126. [G: U.S.]

Hill, Stephen and Gough, Julian. Discounting Inflation—A Note. *Managerial Dec. Econ.*, June 1981, *2*(2), pp. 121–23. [G: U.K.]

Holandez, Patrocinio Cruz. An Inquiry into the Relationship between the Economic Rate of Return and the Internal Rate of Return of Selected DBP-Financed Projects. *Philippine Econ. J.*, 1981, *20*(3&4), pp. 337–56. [G: Philippines]

Homan, John E. Utility Depreciation: An Inequity. *Calif. Manage. Rev.*, Fall 1981, *24*(1), pp. 5–13. [G: U.S.]

Hulten, Charles R. and Wykoff, Frank C. Economic Depreciation and Accelerated Depreciation: An Evaluation of the Conable–Jones 10–5–3 Proposal. *Nat. Tax J.*, March 1981, *34*(1), pp. 45–60. [G: U.S.]

Hulten, Charles R. and Wykoff, Frank C. The Estimation of Economic Depreciation Using Vintage Asset Prices: An Application of the Box-Cox Power Transformation. *J. Econometrics*, April 1981, *15*(3), pp. 367–96. [G: U.S.]

Hume, James. Basic Principles of Surplus Cash Management. In *Ensor, R. and Muller, P., eds.*, 1981, pp. 213–16.

Hymans, Saul H. Saving, Investment, and Social Security. *Nat. Tax J.*, March 1981, *34*(1), pp. 1–8. [G: U.S.]

Ingram, William D. and Pearson, Scott R. The Impact of Investment Concessions on the Profitability of Selected Firms in Ghana. *Econ. Develop. Cult. Change*, July 1981, *29*(4), pp. 831–39.

Irvine, F. Owen, Jr. A Study of Automobile Inventory Investment. *Econ. Inquiry*, July 1981, *19*(3), pp. 353–79. [G: U.S.]

Irvine, F. Owen, Jr. Merchant Wholesaler Inventory Investment and the Cost of Capital. *Amer. Econ. Rev.*, May 1981, *71*(2), pp. 23–29. [G: U.S.]

Irvine, F. Owen, Jr. Retail Inventory Investment and the Cost of Capital. *Amer. Econ. Rev.*, September 1981, *71*(4), pp. 633–48. [G: U.S.]

Irvine, F. Owen, Jr. The Dependence of Aggregate Inventory Investment on Inventory Carrying Costs. A Critique of Recent Research. In *Chikán, A., ed. (1)*, 1981, pp. 199–208.

Irvine, F. Owen, Jr. The Influence of Capital Costs on Inventory Investment: Time-Series Evidence for a Department Store. *Quart. Rev. Econ. Bus.*, Winter 1981, *21*(4), pp. 25–44. [G: U.S.]

Jorgenson, Dale W. Economic Policy and Private Investment since the Oil Crisis by Artus, et al.: Comment. *Europ. Econ. Rev.*, May 1981, *16*(1), pp. 53–56.

Jorgenson, Dale W. Issues in the Design of Savings and Investment Incentives: Discussion. In *Hulten, C. R., ed.*, 1981, pp. 52–56.

Jorgenson, Dale W. and Sullivan, Martin A. Inflation and Corporate Capital Recovery. In *Hulten, C. R., ed.*, 1981, pp. 171–237. [G: U.S.]

Kania, John J. and McKean, John R. Profit, Growth, and the Marris Theory of the Firm: A Short Run Empirical Test. *Amer. Econ.*, Spring 1981, *25*(1), pp. 63–66. [G: U.S.]

Kendrick, John W. Tax Treatment of Depreciation, Capital Gains, and Interest in an Inflationary Economy: Discussion. In *Hulten, C. R., ed.*, 1981, pp. 167–70.

Ketterer, Karl-Heinz and Vollmer, Rainer. Tobin's q und private Investitionsausgaben. Einige analytische Aspekte und empirische Ergebnisse. (Tobin's q and Private Investment Expenditures—Some Analytical and Empirical Issues. With English summary.) *Z. Wirtschaft. Sozialwissen.*, 1981, *101*(2), pp. 153–80. [G: W. Germany]

Kopcke, Richard W. Inflation, Corporate Income Taxation, and the Demand for Capital Assets. *J. Polit. Econ.*, February 1981, *89*(1), pp. 122–31. [G: U.S.]

Kopcke, Richard W. The Efficiency of Traditional Investment Tax Incentives. In *Federal Reserve System*, 1981, pp. 163–75. [G: U.S.]

Kopits, George F. Fiscal Incentives for Investment in Industrial Countries. *Bull. Int. Fiscal Doc.*, July 1981, *35*(7), pp. 291–94. [G: EEC; U.S.; Japan]

Kumar, Manmohan S. Do Mergers Reduce Corporate Investment? Evidence from United Kingdom Experience. *Cambridge J. Econ.*, June 1981, *5*(2), pp. 107–18. [G: U.K.]

Larcker, David F. The Perceived Importance of Selected Information Characteristics for Strategic Capital Budgeting Decisions. *Accounting Rev.*, July 1981, *56*(3), pp. 519–38.

de Leeuw, Frank and McKelvey, Michael J. The Realization of Plans Reported in the BEA Plant and Equipment Survey. *Surv. Curr. Bus.*, October 1981, *61*(10), pp. 28–37. [G: U.S.]

Levin, Richard C. Regulation, Barriers to Exit, and the Investment Behavior of Railroads. In *Fromm, G., ed.*, 1981, pp. 181–224. [G: U.S.]

Levy, Nino S. On the Ranking of Economic Alternatives by the Total Opportunity ROR and B/C Ratios—A Note [Modified Rates of Return for Investment Project Evaluation—A Comparison and

Critique]. *Eng. Econ.*, Winter 1981, *26*(2), pp. 166–71.

Lindberg, Thomas. Industrial Profits—Their Importance and Evaluation. **In** *Industrial Inst. for Econ. and Soc. Research*, 1981, pp. 66–77. [G: Sweden]

Logue, Dennis E. International Finance: Discussion. *J. Finance*, May 1981, *36*(2), pp. 439–40.

Louderback, Joseph G. and Manners, George E., Jr. Integrating ROI and CVP. *Manage. Account.*, April 1981, *62*(10), pp. 33–39.

Lowe, Jeffrey H. Capital Expenditures by Majority-Owned Foreign Affiliates of U.S. Companies, 1981 and 1982. *Surv. Curr. Bus.*, October 1981, *61*(10), pp. 58–68. [G: U.S.]

Lowenthal, Franklin. A Decision Model for the Alternative Tax on Capital Gains. *Accounting Rev.*, April 1981, *56*(2), pp. 390–94. [G: U.S.]

Lucas, Robert E., Jr. Distributed Lags and Optimal Investment Policy. **In** *Lucas, R. E. and Sargent, T. J., eds.*, 1981, pp. 39–54.

Lucas, Robert E., Jr. Optimal Investment with Rational Expectations. **In** *Lucas, R. E. and Sargent, T. J., eds.*, 1981, pp. 55–66.

Lucas, Robert E., Jr. and Prescott, Edward C. Investment under Uncertainty. **In** *Lucas, R. E. and Sargent, T. J., eds.*, 1981, *1971*, pp. 67–90.

Lütkepohl, Helmut. A Model for Non-Negative and Non-Positive Distributed Lag Functions. *J. Econometrics*, June 1981, *16*(2), pp. 211–19. [G: U.S.]

Maccini, Louis J. Return-to-Normal Expectations and Investment Demand Functions. *J. Macroecon.*, Summer 1981, *3*(3), pp. 317–34.

Maccini, Louis J. and Rossana, Robert J. Investment in Finished Goods Inventories: An Analysis of Adjustment Speeds. *Amer. Econ. Rev.*, May 1981, *71*(2), pp. 17–22. [G: U.S.]

Malcomson, James M. Corporate Tax Policy and the Service Life of Capital Equipment. *Rev. Econ. Stud.*, April 1981, *48*(2), pp. 311–16.

Mangiameli, Paul M.; Banks, Jerry and Schwarzbach, Henry. Static Inventory Models and Inflationary Cost Increases. *Eng. Econ.*, Winter 1981, *26*(2), pp. 91–112.

Mauskopf, Eileen and Conrad, William E. Taxes, Inflation, and the Allocation of Capital. **In** *Federal Reserve System*, 1981, pp. 201–20. [G: U.S.]

McBride, Richard D. Finding the Integer Efficient Frontier for Quadratic Capital Budgeting Problems. *J. Finan. Quant. Anal.*, June 1981, *16*(2), pp. 247–53.

McGowan, John J. Regulation, Barriers to Exit, and the Investment Behavior of Railroads: Comment. **In** *Fromm, G., ed.*, 1981, pp. 225–27. [G: U.S.]

McKelvey, Michael J. Constant-Dollar Estimates of New Plant and Equipment Expenditures in the United States, 1947–80. *Surv. Curr. Bus.*, September 1981, *61*(9), pp. 26–41. [G: U.S.]

Menssen, M. D. Eliminating Low Profit Product Lines. *Manage. Account.*, March 1981, *62*(9), pp. 24–25, 33.

Messere, Carl J. and Zuckerman, Gilroy J. An Alternative Approach to Depreciation Switches. *Accounting Rev.*, July 1981, *56*(3), pp. 642–52. [G: U.S.]

Miller, Edward M. What Do Labor Productivity Data Show about Economies of Scale: Reply. *Southern Econ. J.*, January 1981, *47*(3), pp. 847–51. [G: U.S.]

Mintz, Jack M. Some Additional Results on Investment, Risk Taking, and Full Loss Offset Corporate Taxation with Interest Deductibility. *Quart. J. Econ.*, November 1981, *96*(4), pp. 631–42.

Nakamura, Alice and Nakamura, Masao. Valuation, Debt Financing and the Cost of Capital: Japanese Firms, 1962–1976. *Econ. Stud. Quart.*, August 1981, *32*(2), pp. 97–110. [G: Japan]

Nickell, Stephen J. Economic Policy and Private Investment since the Oil Crisis by Artus, et al.: Comment. *Europ. Econ. Rev.*, May 1981, *16*(1), pp. 57–59.

Nicol, David J. A Note on Capital Budgeting Techniques and the Reinvestment Rate: Comment. *J. Finance*, March 1981, *36*(1), pp. 193–95.

Osteryoung, Jerome S.; Fortin, Karen A. and McCarty, Daniel E. How the New Cost Recovery System Compares with Prior Methods. *Manage. Account.*, November 1981, *63*(5), pp. 13–20. [G: U.S.]

Osteryoung, Jerome S.; McCarty, Daniel E. and Fortin, Karen A. A Note on Optimal Depreciation Research—A Comment [A Note on the Optimal Tax Lives for Assets Qualifying for the Investment Tax Credit]. *Accounting Rev.*, July 1981, *56*(3), pp. 719–21. [G: U.S.]

Oswald, Rudolph A. Toward a New U.S. Industrial Policy? Capital Formation: Comment. **In** *Wachter, M. L. and Wachter, S. M., eds.*, 1981, pp. 149–52. [G: U.S.]

Oulton, Nicholas. Aggregate Investment and Tobin's Q: The Evidence from Britain. *Oxford Econ. Pap.*, July 1981, *33*(2), pp. 177–202. [G: U.K.]

Pagano, Marcello and Hartley, Michael J. On Fitting Distributed Lag Models Subject to Polynomial Restrictions. *J. Econometrics*, June 1981, *16*(2), pp. 171–98. [G: U.S.]

Palterovich, D. The Actual Effectiveness of New Technology. *Prob. Econ.*, February 1981, *23*(10), pp. 25–46. [G: U.S.S.R.]

Penson, John B., Jr.; Romain, Robert F. J. and Hughes, Dean W. Net Investment in Farm Tractors: An Econometric Analysis. *Amer. J. Agr. Econ.*, November 1981, *63*(4), pp. 629–35. [G: U.S.]

Pew, Robert C. Capital and Productivity: A Firm View. **In** *Hogan, J. D. and Craig, A. M., eds.*, Vol. 1, 1981, pp. 165–68. [G: U.S.]

Phillips, Almarin. Regulation, Barriers to Exit, and the Investment Behavior of Railroads: Comment. **In** *Fromm, G., ed.*, 1981, pp. 228–29.

Podshivalenko, P. Strengthening the Role of Financial and Credit Levers in Increasing the Effectiveness of Capital Investments. *Prob. Econ.*, February 1981, *23*(10), pp. 78–95. [G: U.S.S.R.]

Portney, Paul R. The Macroeconomic Impacts of Federal Environmental Regulation. **In** *Peskin, H. M.; Portney, P. R. and Kneese, A. V., eds.*, 1981, pp. 25–54. [G: U.S.]

Rappaport, Alfred. Mergers and Acquisitions. **In** *Altman, E. I., ed.*, 1981, pp. 33.3–24.

Rees, R. D. and Miall, R. H. C. The Effect of Regional Policy on Manufacturing Investment and Capital Stock within the U.K. between 1959 and 1978. *Reg. Stud.*, 1981, *15*(6), pp. 413–24.
[G: U.K.]

Roulac, Stephen E. How to Structure Real Estate Investment Management. *J. Portfol. Manage.*, Fall 1981, *8*(1), pp. 32–35. [G: U.S.]

Rutledge, Gary L. and O'Connor, Betsy D. Plant and Equipment Expenditures by Business for Pollution Abatement, 1973–80, and Planned 1981. *Surv. Curr. Bus.*, June 1981, *61*(6), pp. 19–25, 30, 72. [G: U.S.]

Sarantis, Nicholas C. On Optimal Dynamic Adjustment of Capital and Labour under Non-Stationary Expectations. *Greek Econ. Rev.*, April 1981, *3*(1), pp. 46–58.

Sarnat, Marshall and Engelhardt, Annerose. The Pattern of Risk and Return in Germany, Selected Industries, 1928–1976. *Konjunkturpolitik*, 1981, *27*(2), pp. 105–25. [G: W. Germany]

Scanlon, Martha S. Postwar Trends in Corporate Rates of Return. In *Federal Reserve System*, 1981, pp. 75–87. [G: U.S.]

Sheffrin, Steven M. Dynamics of Investment in a Perfect Foresight Model. *J. Econ. Bus.*, Winter 1981, *33*(2), pp. 160–65.

Shelton, Judy. Equal Access and Miller's Equilibrium. *J. Finan. Quant. Anal.*, November 1981, *16*(4), pp. 603–23.

Shone, Robert [Sir]. Technical Change, Inflation and Pricing Decisions. *Managerial Dec. Econ.*, September 1981, *2*(3), pp. 169–78. [G: U.K.]

Sinai, Allen. Economic Impacts of Accelerated Capital Cost Recovery. In *U.S. Congress, Joint Economic Committee (I)*, 1981, pp. 610–28.
[G: U.S.]

Smith, Richard L., II. Efficiency Gains from Strategic Investment. *J. Ind. Econ.*, September 1981, *30*(1), pp. 1–23. [G: U.S.]

Spiller, Earl A., Jr. Capital Expenditure Analysis: An Incident Process Case. *Accounting Rev.*, January 1981, *56*(1), pp. 158–65.

Stephenson, Robert W. and Stephenson, Matilde K. Design Requirements for an Investment Strategy Decision System for Training and Personnel Technology RDT&E. In *Morse, J. N., ed.*, 1981, pp. 388–408.

Stickney, Clyde P. A Note on Optimal Tax Depreciation Research [A Note on the Optimal Tax Lives for Assets Qualifying for the Investment Tax Credit]. *Accounting Rev.*, July 1981, *56*(3), pp. 622–25. [G: U.S.]

Strichman, George A. The Economy of 1981: A Bipartisan Look: The Proceedings of a Congressional Economic Conference: Statement. In *U.S. Congress, Joint Economic Committee (I)*, 1981, pp. 590–609. [G: OECD]

Sturrock, John. Eliminating the Tax Discrimination against Income from Business Capital: A Proposal. In *Federal Reserve System*, 1981, pp. 281–302.

Summers, Lawrence H. Tax Policy and Corporate Investment. In *Meyer, L. H., ed.*, 1981, pp. 115–48. [G: U.S.]

Sumner, Michael T. Investment Grants. In *Currie,*

D.; Nobay, R. and Peel, D., eds., 1981, pp. 286–320. [G: U.K.]

Sunley, Emil M. Acceleration of Tax Depreciation: Basic Issues and Major Alternatives. In *Hulten, C. R., ed.*, 1981, pp. 137–47. [G: U.S.]

Sunley, Emil M. Investment in Producers' Equipment: Comments. In *Aaron, H. J. and Pechman, J. A., eds.*, 1981, pp. 127–29. [G: U.S.]

Taylor, Michael and Thrift, Nigel. British Capital Overseas: Direct Investment and Corporate Development in Australia. *Reg. Stud.*, 1981, *15*(3), pp. 183–212. [G: U.K.; Australia]

Ture, Norman B. Tax Policy and Corporate Investment: Discussion. In *Meyer, L. H., ed.*, 1981, pp. 165–70. [G: U.S.]

Varaiya, Pravin and Wiseman, Michael. Investment and Employment in Manufacturing in U.S. Metropolitan Areas, 1960–1976. *Reg. Sci. Urban Econ.*, November 1981, *11*(4), pp. 431–69.
[G: U.S.]

Woodward, John T. Plant and Equipment Expenditures, First and Second Quarters and Second Half of 1981. *Surv. Curr. Bus.*, March 1981, *61*(3), pp. 28–33. [G: U.S.]

Woodward, John T. Plant and Equipment Expenditures, the Four Quarters of 1981. *Surv. Curr. Bus.*, June 1981, *61*(6), pp. 26–30. [G: U.S.]

Woodward, John T. Plant and Equipment Expenditures, the Four Quarters of 1981. *Surv. Curr. Bus.*, September 1981, *61*(9), pp. 21–25, 41.
[G: U.S.]

Woodward, John T. Plant and Equipment Expenditures, Quarters of 1981 and First and Second Quarters of 1982. *Surv. Curr. Bus.*, December 1981, *61*(12), pp. 25–30.

Woodward, John T. Plant and Equipment Expenditures: 1981. *Surv. Curr. Bus.*, January 1981, *61*(1), pp. 24–25. [G: U.S.]

Zimmer, Michael A. Firm Valuation in the Electric Utility Industry: Alternative Expectations Hypotheses. *Quart. Rev. Econ. Bus.*, Winter 1981, *21*(4), pp. 136–46. [G: U.S.]

530 MARKETING

531 Marketing and Advertising

5310 Marketing and Advertising

Alcaly, Roger E. Consumer Information and Advertising: Comments. In *Galatin, M. and Leiter, R. D., eds .*, 1981, pp. 78–82. [G: U.S.]

Arterburn, Alfred and Woodbury, John. Advertising, Price Competition and Market Structure. *Southern Econ. J.*, January 1981, *47*(3), pp. 763–75. [G: U.S.]

Aydin, Nizam and Terpstra, Vern. Marketing Know-How Transfers by Multinationals: A Case Study in Turkey. *J. Int. Bus. Stud.*, Winter 1981, *12*(3), pp. 35–48. [G: Turkey]

Balcer, Yves. Equilibrium Distributions of Sales and Advertising Prices over Space. *J. Econ. Theory*, October 1981, *25*(2), pp. 196–218.

Bass, Frank M. A New-Product Growth Model for Consumer Durables. In *Wind, Y.; Mahajan, V.*

and Cardozo, R. N., eds., 1981, *1969*, pp. 457–74. [G: U.S.]

Baye, Michael R. Optimal Adjustments to Changes in the Price of Advertising. *J. Ind. Econ.*, September 1981, *30*(1), pp. 95–103.

Blaich, Fritz. Japan's Automobile Marketing: Its Introduction, Consolidation, Development and Characteristics: Comment. In *Okochi, A. and Shimokawa, K., eds.*, 1981, pp. 188–90. [G: Japan]

Blaich, Fritz. The Development of the Distribution Sector in the German Car Industry. In *Okochi, A. and Shimokawa, K., eds.*, 1981, pp. 93–117. [G: Germany]

Blattberg, Robert and Golanty, John. TRACKER: An Early Test-Market Forecasting and Diagnostic Model for New-Product Planning. In *Wind, Y.; Mahajan, V. and Cardozo, R. N., eds.*, 1981, *1978*, pp. 387–409.

Bloch, Gérard. Approche Pratique des Marchés Extérieurs D'une Entreprise de Biens D'Équipement Industriels. (With English summary.) In *Courbis, R., ed.*, 1981, pp. 93–102. [G: France]

Boddewyn, Jean J. Comparative Marketing: The First Twenty-Five Years. *J. Int. Bus. Stud.*, Spring/Summer 1981, *12*(1), pp. 61–79.

Bookstaber, Richard M. Corporate Production and Sales Decisions in Achieving International Diversification. *Rev. Bus. Econ. Res.*, Winter 1981, *16*(2), pp. 68–75.

Borowski, Jerzy. Marketing Polish Industrial Goods in the United States: Comment. In *Marer, P. and Tabaczynski, E., eds.*, 1981, pp. 266–70. [G: Poland; U.S.]

Bourguignon, Francoise and Sethi, Suresh P. Dynamic Optimal Pricing and (Possibly) Advertising in the Face of Various Kinds of Potential Entrants. *J. Econ. Dynam. Control*, May 1981, *3*(2), pp. 119–40.

Brick, Ivan E. and Jagpal, Harsharanjeet S. Monopoly Price-Advertising Decision-Making under Uncertainty. *J. Ind. Econ.*, March 1981, *29*(3), pp. 279–85.

Brown, Marilyn A. Spatial Diffusion Aspects of Marketing Strategies. *Rev. Reg. Stud.*, Fall 1981, *11*(2), pp. 54–73. [G: U.S.]

Burger, Philip C.; Gundee, Howard and Lavidge, Robert. COMP: A Comprehensive System for the Evaluation of New Products. In *Wind, Y.; Mahajan, V. and Cardozo, R. N., eds.*, 1981, pp. 269–83.

Cantani, Gianni. Marketing e pianificazione nelle PMI. (Marketing and Planning in Small and Medium-Sized Firms. With English summary.) *L'Impresa*, 1981, *23*(6), pp. 53–56.

Carlson, Roger D. Advertising and Sales Relationships for Toothpaste. *Bus. Econ.*, September 1981, *16*(4), pp. 36–39. [G: U.S.]

Church, Roy. French Automobile Marketing, 1890–1979: Comment. In *Okochi, A. and Shimokawa, K., eds.*, 1981, pp. 155–60. [G: France]

Church, Roy. The Marketing of Automobiles in Britain and the United States before 1939. In *Okochi, A. and Shimokawa, K., eds.*, 1981, pp. 59–87. [G: U.K.; U.S.]

Claycamp, Henry J. and Liddy, Lucien E. Predic-

tion of New-Product Performance: An Analytical Approach. In *Wind, Y.; Mahajan, V. and Cardozo, R. N., eds.*, 1981, *1969*, pp. 357–69. [G: U.S.]

Comanor, William S.; Kover, Arthur J. and Smiley, Robert H. Advertising and its Consequences. In *Nystrom, P. C. and Starbuck, W. H., eds., Vol. 2*, 1981, pp. 429–39.

Connor, John M. Advertising, Promotion, and Competition: A Survey with Special Reference to Food. *Agr. Econ. Res.*, January 1981, *33*(1), pp. 19–27. [G: U.S.]

Crosby, Lawrence A. and Taylor, James R. Effects of Consumer Information and Education on Cognition and Choice. *J. Cons. Res.*, June 1981, *8*(1), pp. 43–56. [G: U.S.]

Cubbin, John S. Advertising and the Theory of Entry Barriers. *Economica*, August 1981, *48*(191), pp. 289–98.

D'Alfonso, Edmondo and Santoro, Gaetano Maria. Marketing e personale. (Marketing and Personnel. With English summary.) *L'Impresa*, 1981, *23*(6), pp. 47–51.

Daito, Eisuke. Marketing History in the Automobile Industry: The United States and Japan: Comment. In *Okochi, A. and Shimokawa, K., eds.*, 1981, pp. 33–35. [G: U.S.; Japan]

Darling, John R. and Lipson, Harry A. Export Marketing Systems and Their Environments. *Liiketaloudellinen Aikak.*, 1981, *30*(2), pp. 111–24.

De Smet, Monique. Recommendations pour l'efficacité d'une étude de marché à l'étranger. (How to Achieve Efficiency in Conducting Market Research Abroad? With English summary.) *Ann. Sci. Écon. Appl.*, 1981, *37*(4), pp. 113–26.

Deangeli, Giorgio. La via di scampo: innovare il prodotto. (Escape Route: Updating the Product. With English summary.) *L'Impresa*, 1981, *23*(6), pp. 15–20.

Debeer-Laperche, Claudine. L'image de marque des restaurants universitaires à Louvain-la-Neuve. (A Brand Image Study of University Restaurants in Louvain-la-Neuve. With English summary.) *Ann. Sci. Écon. Appl.*, 1981, *37*(1), pp. 29–59. [G: Belgium]

Desenzani, Leonardo. Marketing e progettazione: un'intervista. (Marketing and Planning: An Interview. With English summary.) *L'Impresa*, 1981, *23*(6), pp. 57–60. [G: Italy]

Dewbre, Joe H. Interrelationships between Spot and Futures Markets: Some Implications of Rational Expectations. *Amer. J. Agr. Econ.*, December 1981, *63*(5), pp. 926–33.

Dodson, Joe A. Application and Utilization of Test-Market-Based New-Product Forecasting Models. In *Wind, Y.; Mahajan, V. and Cardozo, R. N., eds.*, 1981, pp. 411–21.

Dubinsky, Alan J. and Hansen, Richard W. The Sales Force Management Audit. *Calif. Manage. Rev.*, Winter 1981, *24*(2), pp. 86–95.

Erickson, Gary M. Using Ridge Regression to Estimate Directly Lagged Effects in Marketing. *J. Amer. Statist. Assoc.*, December 1981, *76*(376), pp. 766–73. [G: U.S.]

Farley, John U.; Lehmann, Donald R. and Ryan, Michael J. Generalizing from "Imperfect" Replication. *J. Bus.*, October 1981, *54*(4), pp. 597–610.

Favotto, Francesco. Marketing anni '80 in USA: La scuola instituzionalista. (Marketing in the '80s in the USA. With English summary.) *L'Impresa,* 1981, *23*(1), pp. 15–18. **[G: U.S.; Italy]**

Flath, David and Leonard, E. W. A Comparison of Two Logit Models in the Analysis of Qualitative Marketing Data. In *Wind, Y.; Mahajan, V. and Cardozo, R. N., eds.,* 1981, *1979*, pp. 155–67.

Fridenson, Patrick. French Automobile Marketing, 1890–1979. In *Okochi, A. and Shimokawa, K., eds.,* 1981, pp. 127–54. **[G: France]**

Fridenson, Patrick. The Marketing of Automobiles in Britain and the United States before 1939: Comment. In *Okochi, A. and Shimokawa, K., eds.,* 1981, pp. 88–90. **[G: U.K.; U.S.]**

Geurts, Michael D. and Buchman, Thomas A. Accounting for 'Shocks' in Forecasts. *Manage. Account.,* April 1981, *62*(10), pp. 21–26, 39.

Glazer, Amihai. Advertising, Information, and Prices—A Case Study. *Econ. Inquiry,* October 1981, *19*(4), pp. 661–71. **[G: U.S.]**

Globerman, Steven. Returns to Industrial R & D and Industrial Marketing and Administration Activities. *J. Econ. Bus.,* Spring/Summer 1981, *33*(3), pp. 231–37. **[G: U.S.]**

Grady, Mark F. Regulating Information: Advertising Overview. In *Clarkson, K. W. and Muris, T. J., eds.,* 1981, pp. 222–45. **[G: U.S.]**

Green, Paul E. and Carroll, J. Douglas. New Computer Tools for Product Strategy. In *Wind, Y.; Mahajan, V. and Cardozo, R. N., eds.,* 1981, pp. 109–54. **[G: U.S.]**

Green, Paul E. and Wind, Yoram. New Way to Measure Consumers' Judgments. In *Wind, Y.; Mahajan, V. and Cardozo, R. N., eds.,* 1981, *1975*, pp. 89–108.

Gröonroos, Christian. Resultatinriktad företagsledning genom bättre marknadsorientering eller effektivare marknadsföring. (Result-Oriented Management by Better Market-Orientation or Better Marketing. With English summary.) *Liiketaloudellinen Aikak.,* 1981, *30*(4), pp. 447–58. **[G: Finland]**

Haahti, Antti and van den Heuvel, Rob. Positioning: Some Conceptual Observations with an Illustration. *Liiketaloudellinen Aikak.,* 1981, *30*(1), pp. 61–73. **[G: Finland]**

Hansen, Flemming. Hemispheral Lateralization: Implications for Understanding Consumer Behavior. *J. Cons. Res.,* June 1981, *8*(1), pp. 23–36.

Hara, Terushi. French Automobile Marketing, 1890–1979: Comment. In *Okochi, A. and Shimokawa, K., eds.,* 1981, pp. 160–62. **[G: France]**

Harris, Frederick H. deB. Value-Maximizing Price and Advertising with Stochastic Demand. *Southern Econ. J.,* October 1981, *48*(2), pp. 296–311.

Hinna, Luciano. Marketing e controllo (Marketing and Control. With English summary.) *L'Impresa,* 1981, *23*(6), pp. 43–46.

Hirschey, Mark. The Effect of Advertising on Industrial Mobility, 1947–72. *J. Bus.,* April 1981, *54*(2), pp. 329–39. **[G: U.S.]**

Hornik, Jacob and Schlinger, Mary Jane. Allocation of Time to the Mass Media. *J. Cons. Res.,* March 1981, *7*(4), pp. 343–55. **[G: U.S.]**

Huebner, Albert. Making the Third-World Marlboro Country. In *Finger, W. R., ed.,* 1981, *1979*, pp. 151–56. **[G: LDCs]**

Ishikawa, Kenjiro. Development of Marketing in the Course of Industrialization in Korea: Comment. In *Okochi, A. and Shimokawa, K., eds.,* 1981, pp. 264. **[G: S. Korea]**

Jolibert, Alain J. P. L'économie du consommateur: les nouvelles approches théoriques et commerciales sont-elles conciliables? (Consumer Economy: Are the New Theoretical and Commercial Approaches Reconcilable? With English summary.) *Écon. Soc.,* October–November–December 1981, *15*(10–12), pp. 1457–80.

Kaldor, Nicholas. The Economic Aspects of Advertising. In *Kaldor, N.,* 1981, *1949*, pp. 96–140.

Kalwani, Manohar U. and Silk, Alvin J. Structure of Repeat Buying for New Packaged Goods. In *Wind, Y.; Mahajan, V. and Cardozo, R. N., eds.,* 1981, *1980*, pp. 371–85. **[G: U.S.]**

Karpeles, Jean-Claude. L'Approche du Commerce Extérieur par L'Entreprise. (With English summary.) In *Courbis, R., ed.,* 1981, pp. 87–91. **[G: France]**

Katahira, Hotaka. Brand Similarity and Market Share. (In Japanese. With English summary.) *Osaka Econ. Pap.,* December 1981, *31*(2–3), pp. 247–60.

Kaynak, Erdener and Stevenson, Lois. Conceptualizations and Methodological Framework for Export Marketing Planning. *Liiketaloudellinen Aikak.,* 1981, *30*(4), pp. 393–406. **[G: Canada]**

Kohers, Theodor and Simpson, W. Gary. Concentration and Advertising in the United States Savings and Loan Industry. *Appl. Econ.,* March 1981, *13*(1), pp. 79–88. **[G: U.S.]**

Lancaster, Kelvin J. Advertising and Consumer Choice. *Greek Econ. Rev.,* April 1981, *3*(1), pp. 3–17.

Lawrence, Kenneth D. and Lawton, William H. Applications of Diffusion Models: Some Empirical Results. In *Wind, Y.; Mahajan, V. and Cardozo, R. N., eds.,* 1981, pp. 529–41. **[G: U.S.]**

Lean, David F. The Market for Research and Development: Physician Demand and Drug Company Supply: Comment. In *Helms, R. B., ed.,* 1981, pp. 227–31. **[G: U.S.]**

Lee, Jonq-Ying. Generic Advertising, FOB Price Promotion, and FOB Revenue: A Case Study of the Florida Grapefruit Juice Industry. *Southern J. Agr. Econ.,* December 1981, *13*(2), pp. 69–78. **[G: U.S.]**

Leffler, Keith B. Persuasion or Information? The Economics of Prescription Drug Advertising. *J. Law Econ.,* April 1981, *24*(1), pp. 45–74. **[G: U.S.]**

Levine, Joel. Pre-test-market Research of New Packaged-Goods Products—A User Orientation. In *Wind, Y.; Mahajan, V. and Cardozo, R. N., eds.,* 1981, pp. 285–90.

Lim, Jong Won. Development of Marketing in the Course of Industrialization in Korea. In *Okochi, A. and Shimokawa, K., eds.,* 1981, pp. 235–60. **[G: S. Korea]**

Livesay, Harold C. Marketing History in the Automobile Industry: The United States and Japan:

Comment. In *Okochi, A. and Shimokawa, K.,* eds., 1981, pp. 31–33. [G: U.S.; Japan]

Livesay, Harold C. Nineteenth Century Precursors to Automobile Marketing in the United States. In *Okochi, A. and Shimokawa, K., eds.*, 1981, pp. 39–52. [G: U.S.]

Luksetich, William A. Advertising Intensity and Antitrust Activity. *J. Behav. Econ.*, Summer 1981, *10*(1), pp. 101–09. [G: U.S.]

Lynk, William J. Information, Advertising, and the Structure of the Market. *J. Bus.*, April 1981, *54*(2), pp. 271–303. [G: U.S.]

Mahajan, Vijay and Muller, Eitan. Innovation Diffusion and New-Product Growth Models in Marketing. In *Wind, Y.; Mahajan, V. and Cardozo, R. N., eds.*, 1981, 1979, pp. 425–56.

McLendon, Teresa Gaines. An Economic Approach to Deception in Advertising: Definition and Remedies. *Amer. Econ.*, Fall 1981, *25*(2), pp. 49–54. [G: U.S.]

Metwally, M. M. and Tamaschke, H. U. Advertising and the Propensity to Consume. *Oxford Bull. Econ. Statist.*, August 1981, *43*(3), pp. 273–85. [G: Australia]

Midgley, David F. A Simple Mathematical Theory of Innovative Behavior. In *Wind, Y.; Mahajan, V. and Cardozo, R. N., eds.*, 1981, 1976, pp. 475–98. [G: U.S.]

Miller, Joseph C. Marketing Polish Industrial Goods in the United States. In *Marer, P. and Tabaczynski, E., eds.*, 1981, pp. 259–66. [G: Poland; U.S.]

Miller, Joseph C. Marketing Polish Industrial Goods in the United States: Reply. In *Marer, P. and Tabaczynski, E., eds.*, 1981, pp. 270–71. [G: Poland; U.S.]

Miyamoto, Matao. Development of Marketing in the Course of Industrialization in Korea: Comment. In *Okochi, A. and Shimokawa, K., eds.*, 1981, pp. 261–63. [G: S. Korea]

Moulton, Kirby S. Market Reporting and its Public Policy Implications. In *[Grether, E. T.]*, 1981, pp. 190–200.

Nagle, Thomas T. Do Advertising-Profitability Studies Really Show That Advertising Creates a Barrier to Entry? *J. Law Econ.*, October 1981, *24*(2), pp. 333–49. [G: U.S.]

Narasimhan, Chakravarthi and Sen, Subrata K. Test-Market Models for New-Product Introduction. In *Wind, Y.; Mahajan, V. and Cardozo, R. N., eds.*, 1981, pp. 293–321.

Nelson, Phillip J. Consumer Information and Advertising. In *Galatin, M. and Leiter, R. D., eds.*, 1981, pp. 42–77. [G: U.S.]

Okochi, Akio. Automobiles and International Markets: Comment. In *Okochi, A. and Shimokawa, K., eds.*, 1981, pp. 212–13.

Ong, Nai-Pew. Target Pricing, Competition, and Growth. *J. Post Keynesian Econ.*, Fall 1981, *4*(1), pp. 101–16.

Pagoulatos, Emilio and Sorensen, Robert. A Simultaneous Equation Analysis of Advertising, Concentration and Profitability. *Southern Econ. J.*, January 1981, *47*(3), pp. 728–41. [G: U.S.]

Paquay-Deghilage, Anne. Promouvoir son entreprise et ses produits en Tchécoslovaquie: organ-

iser une campagne publicitaire. (Promoting a Company and Its Products in Czechoslovakia. With English summary.) *Ann. Sci. Écon. Appl.*, 1981, *37*(3), pp. 179–219. [G: Belgium; Czechoslovakia]

Parfitt, J. H. and Collins, B. J. K. Use of Consumer Panels for Brand-Share Prediction. In *Wind, Y.; Mahajan, V. and Cardozo, R. N., eds.*, 1981, 1968, pp. 323–56. [G: U.K.]

Patterson, Perry. Advertising and Profitability. *Bus. Econ.*, January 1981, *16*(1), pp. 92–93. [G: U.S.]

Primeaux, Walter J., Jr. An Assessment of the Effect of Competition on Advertising Intensity. *Econ. Inquiry*, October 1981, *19*(4), pp. 613–25. [G: U.S.]

Rao, Vithala R. New-Product Sales Forecasting Using the Hendry System. In *Wind, Y.; Mahajan, V. and Cardozo, R. N., eds.*, 1981, pp. 499–527.

Rayburn, Gayle L. Marketing Costs—Accountants to the Rescue. *Manage. Account.*, January 1981, *62*(7), pp. 32–41. [G: U.S.]

Reekie, W. Duncan and Bhoyrub, Pat. Profitability and Intangible Assets: Another Look at Advertising and Entry Barriers. *Appl. Econ.*, March 1981, *13*(1), pp. 99–107.

Resnik, Alan J.; Sand, Harold E. and Mason, J. Barry. Marketing Dilemma: Change in the '80s. *Calif. Manage. Rev.*, Fall 1981, *24*(1), pp. 49–57. [G: U.S.]

Riecken, Glen and Samli, A. Coskun. Measuring Children's Attitudes toward Television Commercials: Extension and Replication. *J. Cons. Res.*, June 1981, *8*(1), pp. 57–61. [G: U.S.]

Robinson, Patrick J. Comparison of Pre-test-market New-Product Forecasting Models. In *Wind, Y.; Mahajan, V. and Cardozo, R. N., eds.*, 1981, pp. 181–204.

Roedder, Deborah L. Age Differences in Children's Responses to Television Advertising: An Information–Processing Approach. *J. Cons. Res.*, September 1981, *8*(2), pp. 144–53. [G: U.S.]

Rousseau, P. Réflexions sur un système d'informations commerciales. (Information Systems Related to International Markets (SIRMI). With English summary.) *Ann. Sci. Écon. Appl.*, 1981, *37*(4), pp. 95–112.

Ryans, Adrian B. and Weinberg, Charles B. Sales Force Management: Integrating Research Advances. *Calif. Manage. Rev.*, Fall 1981, *24*(1), pp. 75–89.

Savitt, Ronald. Marketing anni '80 in USA: Quali sviluppi e quali tendenze nella teoria del marketing. (Marketing in the '80s in the USA. With English summary.) *L'Impresa*, 1981, *23*(1), pp. 19–26. [G: U.S.]

Savitt, Ronald. The Theory of Interregional Marketing. In *[Grether, E. T.]*, 1981, pp. 229–38.

Selby, Edward B., Jr. and Beranek, William. Sweepstakes Contests: Analysis, Strategies, and Survey. *Amer. Econ. Rev.*, March 1981, *71*(1), pp. 189–95. [G: U.S.]

Shapiro, Nina. Pricing and the Growth of the Firm. *J. Post Keynesian Econ.*, Fall 1981, *4*(1), pp. 85–100.

Shimokawa, Koichi. Marketing History in the Automobile Industry: The United States and Japan. In *Okochi, A. and Shimokawa, K., eds.*, 1981, pp. 3–30. [G: U.S.; Japan]

Shimokawa, Koichi. The Development of the Distribution Sector in the German Car Industry: Comment. In *Okochi, A. and Shimokawa, K., eds.*, 1981, pp. 118–21. [G: Germany]

Shocker, Allan D. and Srinivasan, V. Multiattribute Approaches for Product Concept Evaluation and Generation: A Critical Review. In *Wind, Y.; Mahajan, V. and Cardozo, R. N., eds.*, 1981, *1979*, pp. 47–88.

Silk, Alvin J. and Urban, Glen L. Pre-test-market Evaluation of New Packaged Goods: A Model and Measurement Methodology. In *Wind, Y.; Mahajan, V. and Cardozo, R. N., eds.*, 1981, *1978*, pp. 205–48.

Simon, Hermann. Informationstransfer und Marketing. Ein Survey. (Transfer of Information and Marketing: A Survey. With English summary.) *Z. Wirtschaft. Sozialwissen.*, 1981, *101*(6), pp. 589–608.

Smead, Raymond J.; Wilcox, James B. and Wilkes, Robert E. How Valid are Product Descriptions and Protocols in Choice Experiments? *J. Cons. Res.*, June 1981, *8*(1), pp. 37–42.

Sturgess, Brian and Young, Robert. The Sales Response to Advertising: A Reconsideration. *Managerial Dec. Econ.*, September 1981, *2*(3), pp. 133–38.

Sullivan, James D. Interrelationships between Spot and Futures Markets: Some Implications of Rational Expectations: Discussion. *Amer. J. Agr. Econ.*, December 1981, *63*(5), pp. 942–43. [G: U.S.]

Tauber, Edward M. Utilization of Concept Testing for New-Product Forecasting: Traditional versus Multiattribute Approaches. In *Wind, Y.; Mahajan, V. and Cardozo, R. N., eds.*, 1981, pp. 169–78.

Telser, Lester G. The Market for Research and Development: Physician Demand and Drug Company Supply. In *Helms, R. B., ed.*, 1981, pp. 183–221. [G: U.S.]

Thorelli, Hans B. and Thorelli, Sarah V. Consumer Information Systems of the Future. In *[Grether, E. T.]*, 1981, pp. 155–73.

Thurston, William R. SMR Forum: The Revitalization of GenRad. *Sloan Manage. Rev.*, Summer 1981, *22*(4), pp. 53–57. [G: U.S.]

Toba, Kin'ichiro. Automobiles and International Markets: Comment. In *Okochi, A. and Shimokawa, K., eds.*, 1981, pp. 210–12.

Toba, Kin'ichiro. Nineteenth Century Precursors to Automobile Marketing in the United States: Comment. In *Okochi, A. and Shimokawa, K., eds.*, 1981, pp. 53–55. [G: U.S.]

Udagawa, Masaru. Japan's Automobile Marketing: Its Introduction, Consolidation, Development and Characteristics. In *Okochi, A. and Shimokawa, K., eds.*, 1981, pp. 163–87. [G: Japan]

Wahlroos, Björn. Advertising and Market Structure: Evidence for Finland. *Liiketaloudellinen Aikak.*, 1981, *30*(3), pp. 296–308. [G: Finland]

Watanabe, Hisashi. The Development of the Distribution Sector in the German Car Industry: Com-

ment. In *Okochi, A. and Shimokawa, K., eds.*, 1981, pp. 121–25. [G: Germany]

Wilkins, Mira. Automobiles and International Markets. In *Okochi, A. and Shimokawa, K., eds.*, 1981, pp. 193–209.

Wilton, Peter C. and Pessemier, Edgar A. Forecasting the Ultimate Acceptance of an Innovation: The Effects of Information. *J. Cons. Res.*, September 1981, *8*(2), pp. 162–71.

Wind, Yoram. A Framework for Classifying New-Product Forecasting Models. In *Wind, Y.; Mahajan, V. and Cardozo, R. N., eds.*, 1981, *1981*, pp. 3–42.

Wind, Yoram and Douglas, Susan. International Portfolio Analysis and Strategy: The Challenge of the 80s. *J. Int. Bus. Stud.*, Fall 1981, *12*(2), pp. 69–82.

Yamada, Makiko. Nineteenth Century Precursors to Automobile Marketing in the United States: Comment. In *Okochi, A. and Shimokawa, K., eds.*, 1981, pp. 55–57. [G: U.S.]

Yankelovich, Skelly and White, Inc. LTM Estimating Procedures. In *Wind, Y.; Mahajan, V. and Cardozo, R. N., eds.*, 1981, pp. 249–67.

Yuzawa, Takeshi. The Marketing of Automobiles in Britain and the United States before 1939: Comment. In *Okochi, A. and Shimokawa, K., eds.*, 1981, pp. 90–92. [G: U.K.; U.S.]

540 ACCOUNTING

541 Accounting

5410 Accounting

Alderman, C. Wayne. The Effect of Changes in Accounting Techniques on Systematic Risk. *Rev. Bus. Econ. Res.*, Winter 1981, *16*(2), pp. 12–22. [G: U.S.]

Alexander, Michael O. Discussion of The SEC "Reversal" of FASB Statement No. 19: An Investigation of Information Effects. *J. Acc. Res.*, Supplement 1981, *19*, pp. 212–17. [G: U.S.]

Arcady, Alex T. and Rosen, Bruce J. 1980 Review—FASB Developments. In *Weinstein, S. and Walker, M. A., eds.*, 1981, pp. 1–16. [G: U.S.]

Ashton, Robert H. A Descripitive Study of Information Evaluation. *J. Acc. Res.*, Spring 1981, *19*(1), pp. 42–61.

Bailey, William T. The Effects of Audit Reports on Chartered Financial Analysts' Perceptions of the Sources of Financial-Statement and Audit-Report Messages. *Accounting Rev.*, October 1981, *56*(4), pp. 882–96. [G: U.S.]

Balachandran, Bala V. and Ramakrishnan, Ram T. S. Joint Cost Allocation: A Unified Approach. *Accounting Rev.*, January 1981, *56*(1), pp. 85–96.

Balachandran, Bala V. and Zoltners, Andris A. An Interactive Audit-Staff Scheduling Decision Support System. *Accounting Rev.*, October 1981, *56*(4), pp. 801–12.

Balachandran, K. R.; Maschmeyer, Richard A. and Livingstone, J. Leslie. Product Warranty Period: A Markovian Approach to Estimation and Analysis of Repair and Replacement Costs. *Accounting Rev.*, January 1981, *56*(1), pp. 115–24.

Barkman, Arnold I. Testing the Markov Chain Approach on Accounts Receivable. *Manage. Account.*, January 1981, 62(7), pp. 48–50.

Basu, S. Market Reactions to Accounting Policy Deliberations: The Inflation Accounting Case Revisited. *Accounting Rev.*, October 1981, 56(4), pp. 942–54. [G: U.S.]

Bejan, Mary. On the Application of Rational Choice Theory to Financial Reporting Controversies: A Comment on Cushing [On the Possibility of Optimal Accounting Principles]. *Accounting Rev.*, July 1981, 56(3), pp. 704–12.

Benke, Ralph L., Jr. and Edwards, James Don. Should You Use Transfer Pricing to Create Pseudo-Profit Centers? *Manage. Account.*, February 1981, 62(8), pp. 36–39, 43.

Beranek, William and Selby, Edward B., Jr. Accelerated Depreciation and Income Growth. *Amer. Real Estate Urban Econ. Assoc. J.*, Spring 1981, 9(1), pp. 67–73. [G: U.S.]

Berry, Maureen H. Why International Cost Accounting Practices Should be Harmonized. *Manage. Account.*, August 1981, 63(2), pp. 36–42.

Billera, Louis J.; Heath, David C. and Verrecchia, Robert E. A Unique Procedure for Allocating Common Costs from a Production Process. *J. Acc. Res.*, Spring 1981, 19(1), pp. 185–96.

Black, Thomas G. Usefulness of Constant Dollar Accounting Information. *Rev. Bus. Econ. Res.*, Spring 1981, 16(3), pp. 58–68. [G: U.S.]

Bloom, Robert and Debessay, Araya. A Critique of FAS No. 33. *Manage. Account.*, May 1981, 62(11), pp. 48–53. [G: U.S.]

Boatsman, James R. and Baskin, Elba F. Asset Valuation with Incomplete Markets. *Accounting Rev.*, January 1981, 56(1), pp. 38–53. [G: U.S.]

Bowen, Robert M. Valuation of Earnings Components in the Electric Utility Industry. *Accounting Rev.*, January 1981, 56(1), pp. 1–22. [G: U.S.]

Bowen, Robert M.; Noreen, Eric W. and Lacey, John M. Determinants of the Corporate Decision to Capitalize Interest. *J. Acc. Econ.*, August 1981, 3(2), pp. 151–79. [G: U.S.]

Brackney, William O. and Anderson, Henry R. Regulation of Cost Accounting: The Answer or the Abyss. *Manage. Account.*, October 1981, 63(4), pp. 24–31. [G: U.S.]

van Breda, Michael F. Accounting Rates of Return under Inflation. *Sloan Manage. Rev.*, Summer 1981, 22(4), pp. 15–28.

Brown, Clifton. Human Information Processing for Decisions to Investigate Cost Variances. *J. Acc. Res.*, Spring 1981, 19(1), pp. 62–85.

Brown, Paul R. A Descriptive Analysis of Select Input Bases of the Financial Accounting Standards Board. *J. Acc. Res.*, Spring 1981, 19(1), pp. 232–46.

Brown, Ray L. Management Accountants: Are You Ready for VAT? *Manage. Account.*, November 1981, 63(5), pp. 40–44, 52. [G: U.S.]

Brownell, Peter. Participation in Budgeting, Locus of Control and Organizational Effectiveness. *Accounting Rev.*, October 1981, 56(4), pp. 844–60. [G: U.S.]

Bryant, Murray J. and Mahaney, Mary Claire. The Politics of Standard Setting. *Manage. Account.*, March 1981, 62(9), pp. 26–33. [G: U.S.]

Burggraaff, J. A. The Case for International Accounting Standards. In *Weinstein, S. and Walker, M. A., eds.*, 1981, pp. 79–96.

Burton, John C. Discussion of Voluntary Corporate Disclosure: The Case of Interim Reporting. *J. Acc. Res.*, Supplement 1981, 19, pp. 78–84. [G: U.S.]

Caprara, Giordano. Una interpretazione dei rapporti tra dati di bilancio caratteristici delle imprese industriali. (How the Characteristic Items on Balance Sheets of Industrial Firms Are Related to Each Other. With English summary.) *Rivista Int. Sci. Econ. Com.*, December 1981, 28(12), pp. 1181–88.

Carlson, Marvin L. and Lamb, James W. Constructing a Theory of Accounting—An Axiomatic Approach. *Accounting Rev.*, July 1981, 56(3), pp. 554–73.

Carter, William K. A Benefits Approach to Certain Accounting Policy Choices. *Accounting Rev.*, January 1981, 56(1), pp. 108–14.

Chambers, A. D. The State of the Art of Computer Auditing within an Organisation. *Tijdschrift Econ. Manage.*, 1981, 26(3), pp. 385–402. [G: U.S.; Canada]

Chan, James L. Standards and Issues in Governmental Accounting and Financial Reporting. *Public Budg. Finance*, Spring 1981, 1(1), pp. 55–65. [G: U.S.]

Choi, Frederick D. S. A Cluster Approach to Accounting Harmonization. *Manage. Account.*, August 1981, 63(2), pp. 27–31.

Clark, Myrtle W.; Gibbs, Thomas E. and Schroeder, Richard G. CPAs Judge Internal Audit Department Objectivity. *Manage. Account.*, February 1981, 62(8), pp. 40–43.

Coase, R. H. Business Organization and the Accountant. In *Buchanan, J. M. and Thirlby, G. F., eds.*, 1981, pp. 95–132.

Cogger, Kenneth O. A Time-Series Analytic Approach to Aggregation Issues in Accounting Data. *J. Acc. Res.*, Autumn 1981, 19(2), pp. 285–98.

Collins, Daniel W.; Rozeff, Michael S. and Dhaliwal, Dan S. The Economic Determinants of the Market Reaction to Proposed Mandatory Accounting Changes in the Oil and Gas Industry: A Cross-Sectional Analysis. *J. Acc. Econ.*, March 1981, 3(1), pp. 37–71.

Copeland, Ronald M.; Taylor, Ronald L. and Brown, Shari H. Observation Error and Bias in Accounting Research. *J. Acc. Res.*, Spring 1981, 19(1), pp. 197–207.

Crosby, Michael A. Bayesian Statistics in Auditing: A Comparison of Probability Elicitation Techniques. *Accounting Rev.*, April 1981, 56(2), pp. 355–65.

Cushing, Barry E. On the Possibility of Optimal Accounting Principles: A Restatement. *Accounting Rev.*, July 1981, 56(3), pp. 713–18.

Davis, Harry Zvi. The Effects of LIFO Inventory Costing on Resource Allocation: A Comment. *Accounting Rev.*, October 1981, 56(4), pp. 975–76.

DeAngelo, Linda Elizabeth. Auditor Independence, 'Low Balling', and Disclosure Regulation. *J. Acc. Econ.*, August 1981, 3(2), pp. 113–27. [G: U.S.]

Del Treppo, Mario. Federigo Melis and the Renaissance Economy. *J. Europ. Econ. Hist.*, Winter 1981, *10*(3), pp. 709–42.

Dernburg, Thomas. Issues in the Design of Savings and Investment Incentives: Discussion. In *Hulten, C. R., ed.*, 1981, pp. 48–52.

Dillon, Gadis J. The Business Combination Process. *Accounting Rev.*, April 1981, *56*(2), pp. 395–99.

Douglas, David V. LIFO: Big Benefits for a Small Company. *Manage. Account.*, April 1981, *62*(10), pp. 40–42.   [G: U.S.]

Doyle, James J. and Rosen, Bruce J. 1980 Review—SEC Developments. In *Weinstein, S. and Walker, M. A., eds.*, 1981, pp. 47–62.
                                                        [G: U.S.]

Dykxhoorn, Hans J. and Sinning, Kathleen E. Wirtschaftsprüfer Perception of Auditor Independence. *Accounting Rev.*, January 1981, *56*(1), pp. 97–107.   [G: W. Germany; U.S.]

Edwards, James B.; Ingram, Robert W. and Sanders, Howard P. Developing Teaching Skills in Doctoral Programs: The Current Status and Perceived Needs. *Accounting Rev.*, January 1981, *56*(1), pp. 144–57.   [G: U.S.]

Edwards, R. S. The Rationale of Cost Accounting. In *Buchanan, J. M. and Thirlby, G. F., eds.*, 1981, *1937*, pp. 71–92.

Ferran, Bernardo. Corporate and Social Accounting for Petroleum. *Rev. Income Wealth*, March 1981, *27*(1), pp. 97–105.

Ferrara, William L. A Cash Flow Model for the Future. *Manage. Account.*, June 1981, *62*(12), pp. 12–17.

Fess, Philip E. Forecasts by Management and the Independent Accountant's Review. In *Weinstein, S. and Walker, M. A., eds.*, 1981, pp. 63–77.
                                                        [G: U.S.]

Finley, D. R. and Liao, Woody M. A General Decision Model for Cost–Volume–Profit Analysis under Uncertainty: A Comment. *Accounting Rev.*, April 1981, *56*(2), pp. 400–403.

Fornasari, Franco. The Effects of Inflation on Company Profits: A Comment on the Application of Inflation Accounting Techniques to the Italian Case. *Rev. Econ. Cond. Italy*, October 1981, (3), pp. 455–78.   [G: Italy]

Franz, K.-P. Die Formen der Verrechnung von Zinsen in Entscheidungsrechnungen über kurzfristig mittelbindende Projekte—Darstellung und kritischer Vergleich. (With English summary.) In *Fandel, G., et al., eds.*, 1981, pp. 521–29.

Freeman, Robert N. The Disclosure of Replacement Cost Accounting Data and Its Effect on Transaction Volumes: A Comment. *Accounting Rev.*, January 1981, *56*(1), pp. 177–80.   [G: U.S.]

Fried, Dov and Livnat, Joshua. Interim Statements: An Analytical Examination of Alternative Accounting Techniques. *Accounting Rev.*, July 1981, *56*(3), pp. 493–509.

Fried, Dov and Schiff, Allen. CPA Switches and Associated Market Reactions. *Accounting Rev.*, April 1981, *56*(2), pp. 326–41.   [G: U.S.]

Friedlob, George T. Federal Tax Management: A Disclosure Problem. *Manage. Account.*, November 1981, *63*(5), pp. 28–33.   [G: U.S.]

Friedman, Mark E. The Effect on Achievement of Using the Computer as a Problem-Solving Tool in the Intermediate Accounting Course. *Accounting Rev.*, January 1981, *56*(1), pp. 137–43.
                                                        [G: U.S.]

Fukuba, Yo and Miyamoto, Masaaki. Initial Wealth Problems: From Descriptive and Normative Point of View. *Osaka Econ. Pap.*, December 1981, *31*(2–3), pp. 226–39.

Gambino, Anthony J. and Reardon, Thomas J. Financial Planning and Evaluation for the Nonprofit Organization. *Manage. Account.*, June 1981, *62*(12), pp. 50.   [G: U.S.]

Gangolly, Jagdish S. On Joint Cost Allocation: Independent Cost Proportional Scheme (ICPS) and Its Properties. *J. Acc. Res.*, Autumn 1981, *19*(2), pp. 299–312.

Gillespie, Jackson F. An Application of Learning Curves to Standard Costing. *Manage. Account.*, September 1981, *63*(3), pp. 63–65.

Giovinazzo, Vincent J. Speeding up Interim Closings. *Manage. Account.*, December 1981, *63*(6), pp. 51–59.   [G: U.S.]

Giroux, Gary; Grossman, Steven and Kratchman, Stanley. What FAS No. 33 Does to Bank Financial Statements. *Manage. Account.*, January 1981, *62*(7), pp. 42–47.   [G: U.S.]

Gjesdal, Frøystein. Accounting for Stewardship. *J. Acc. Res.*, Spring 1981, *19*(1), pp. 208–31.

Gray, S. J.; Shaw, J. C. and McSweeney, L. B. Accounting Standards and Multinational Corporations. *J. Int. Bus. Stud.*, Spring/Summer 1981, *12*(1), pp. 121–36.

Groomer, S. Michael. An Experiment in Computer-Assisted Instruction for Introductory Accounting. *Accounting Rev.*, October 1981, *56*(4), pp. 934–41.

Guinan, John M. Management Reports in the Era of Voluntary Reporting on Internal Accounting Controls. In *Weinstein, S. and Walker, M. A., eds.*, 1981, pp. 121–43.   [G: U.S.]

Hagerman, Robert L. and Zmijewski, Mark E. A Test of Accounting Bias and Market Structure: Some Additional Evidence. *Rev. Bus. Econ. Res.*, Fall 1981, *17*(1), pp. 84–88.   [G: U.S.]

Hagin, Robert L. Financial Statement Analysis. In *Altman, E. I., ed.*, 1981, pp. 24.3–31.

Hakansson, Nils H. On the Politics of Accounting Disclosure and Measurement: An Analysis of Economic Incentives: A Reply. *J. Acc. Res.*, Supplement 1981, *19*, pp. 48–49.   [G: U.S.]

Hakansson, Nils H. On the Politics of Accounting Disclosure and Measurement: An Analysis of Economic Incentives. *J. Acc. Res.*, Supplement 1981, *19*, pp. 1–35.   [G: U.S.]

Hall, Robert E. Tax Treatment of Depreciation, Capital Gains, and Interest in an Inflationary Economy. In *Hulten, C. R., ed.*, 1981, pp. 149–66.

Halperin, Robert. The Effects of LIFO Inventory Costing on Resource Allocation: A Reply. *Accounting Rev.*, October 1981, *56*(4), pp. 977–79.

Hartman, Bart P. and Lee, Johng Y. Influence of Company Debt Burden on Reported Replacement Cost Values. *J. Bank Res.*, Spring 1981, *12*(1), pp. 56–59.   [G: U.S.]

Hicks, John R. The Concept of Income in Relation to Taxation and to Business Management. In *Ros-*

kamp, K. W. and Forte, F., eds., 1981, pp. 73–85.

Hilton, Ronald W. and Swieringa, Robert J. Perception of Initial Uncertainty as a Determinant of Information Value. *J. Acc. Res.*, Spring 1981, *19*(1), pp. 109–19.

Hilton, Ronald W.; Swieringa, Robert J. and Hoskin, Robert E. Perception of Accuracy as a Determinant of Information Value. *J. Acc. Res.*, Spring 1981, *19*(1), pp. 86–108.

Hirst, Mark K. Accounting Information and the Evaluation of Subordinate Performance: A Situational Approach. *Accounting Rev.*, October 1981, *56*(4), pp. 771–84.

Holthausen, Robert W. Evidence on the Effect of Bond Covenants and Management Compensation Contracts on the Choice of Accounting Techniques: The Case of the Depreciation Switch-Back. *J. Acc. Econ.*, March 1981, *3*(1), pp. 73–109. [G: U.S.]

Hopwood, William S. and McKeown, James C. An Evaluation of Univariate Time-Series Earnings Models and Their Generalization to a Single Input Transfer Function. *J. Acc. Res.*, Autumn 1981, *19*(2), pp. 313–22. [G: U.S.]

Horwitz, Bertrand and Kolodny, Richard. The FASB, the SEC, and R&D. *Bell J. Econ. (See Rand J. Econ. after 4/85)*, Spring 1981, *12*(1), pp. 249–62. [G: U.S.]

Horwitz, Bertrand and Kolodny, Richard. The Relationship between Firm Characteristics and the Choice of Financial Measurement Methods: An Application to R&D. *Quart. Rev. Econ. Bus.*, Winter 1981, *21*(4), pp. 75–86. [G: U.S.]

Howard, Thomas P. Attitude Measurement: Some Further Considerations. *Accounting Rev.*, July 1981, *56*(3), pp. 613–21.

Imhoff, Eugene A., Jr. Evaluating Accounting Alternatives. *Manage. Account.*, October 1981, *63*(4), pp. 56–62, 71.

Imhoff, Eugene A., Jr. Income Smoothing: An Analysis of Critical Issues. *Quart. Rev. Econ. Bus.*, Autumn 1981, *21*(3), pp. 23–42.

Ingram, Robert W. and Copeland, Ronald M. Disclosure Practices in Audited Financial Statements of Municipalities. *Public Budg. Finance*, Summer 1981, *1*(2), pp. 47–58. [G: U.S.]

Ingram, Robert W. and Copeland, Ronald M. Municipal Accounting Information and Voting Behavior. *Accounting Rev.*, October 1981, *56*(4), pp. 830–43. [G: U.S.]

Ishikawa, Junji. Mathematical Models of Overhead Cost Allocation: From Matrix Models to LP Models. (In Japanese. With English summary.) *Osaka Econ. Pap.*, March 1981, *30*(4), pp. 36–55.

Johnson, Johnny R.; Leitch, Robert A. and Neter, John. Characteristics of Errors in Accounts Receivable and Inventory Audits. *Accounting Rev.*, April 1981, *56*(2), pp. 270–93. [G: U.S.]

Johnson, Orace. Some Implications of the United States Constitution for Accounting Institution Alternatives. *J. Acc. Res.*, Supplement 1981, *19*, pp. 129–33. [G: U.S.]

Johnson, Orace. Some Implications of the United States Constitution for Accounting Institution Alternatives. *J. Acc. Res.*, Supplement 1981, *19*,

pp. 89–119. [G: U.S.]

Jorgenson, Dale W. and Sullivan, Martin A. Inflation and Corporate Capital Recovery. In *Hulten, C. R., ed.*, 1981, pp. 171–237. [G: U.S.]

Joskow, Paul L. The Effects of FTC Advertising Regulation: Comment. *J. Law Econ.*, December 1981, *24*(3), pp. 449–55. [G: U.S.]

Joyce, Edward J. and Biddle, Gary C. Anchoring and Adjustment in Probabilistic Inference in Auditing. *J. Acc. Res.*, Spring 1981, *19*(1), pp. 120–45.

Joyce, Edward J. and Biddle, Gary C. Are Auditors' Judgments Sufficiently Regressive? *J. Acc. Res.*, Autumn 1981, *19*(2), pp. 323–49.

Karmel, Roberta S. Discussion of Some Implications of the United States Constitution for Accounting Institution Alternatives. *J. Acc. Res.*, Supplement 1981, *19*, pp. 120–22. [G: U.S.]

Kellens, Jean-Pierre. A Fresh Look at Inflation Accounting. *Cah. Écon. Bruxelles*, 1st Trimestre 1981, (89), pp. 109–22.

Kellens, Jean-Pierre. The Foundations of a Real Life Approach to Business Accounting. *Cah. Écon. Bruxelles*, 3rd Trimestre 1981, (91), pp. 503–20.

Kendrick, John W. Tax Treatment of Depreciation, Capital Gains, and Interest in an Inflationary Economy: Discussion. In *Hulten, C. R., ed.*, 1981, pp. 167–70.

Kessler, Lawrence and Ashton, Robert H. Feedback and Prediction Achievement in Financial Analysis. *J. Acc. Res.*, Spring 1981, *19*(1), pp. 146–62.

Kirchner, Christian. Mining Ventures in Developing Countries: Information Disclosure. In *Schanze, E., et al.*, 1981, pp. 68–107.

Kitch, Edmund W. Discussion of Some Implications of the United States Constitution for Accounting Institution Alternatives. *J. Acc. Res.*, Supplement 1981, *19*, pp. 123–28. [G: U.S.]

Koch, Bruce S. Income Smoothing: An Experiment. *Accounting Rev.*, July 1981, *56*(3), pp. 574–86.

Kosiol, Erich E. Some Remarks on Accounting. *Int. J. Soc. Econ.*, 1981, *8*(7), pp. 50–55.

Kraus, Jerome. Adapting Accounting Systems for Productivity Analysis. In *Hogan, J. D. and Craig, A. M., eds., Vol. 1*, 1981, pp. 551–69. [G: U.S.]

Kucic, A. Ronald and Battaglia, Samuel T. Matrix Accounting for the Statement of Changes in Financial Position. *Manage. Account.*, April 1981, *62*(10), pp. 27–32.

Larcker, David F. Discussion of The SEC "Reversal" of FASB Statement No. 19: An Investigation of Information Effects. *J. Acc. Res.*, Supplement 1981, *19*, pp. 218–26. [G: U.S.]

Lau, Amy Hing-Ling and Lau, Hon-Shiang. A Comment on Shih's General Decision Model for CVP Analysis. *Accounting Rev.*, October 1981, *56*(4), pp. 980–83.

Lee, Cheng Few and Zumwalt, J. Kenton. Associations between Alternative Accounting Profitability Measures and Security Returns. *J. Finan. Quant. Anal.*, March 1981, *16*(1), pp. 71–93. [G: U.S.]

Lee, Geoffrey A. The Francis Willughby Executorship Accounts, 1672–1682: An Early Double-Entry System in England. *Accounting Rev.*, July 1981, *56*(3), pp. 539–53. [G: U.K.]

Leftwich, Richard W. Evidence of the Impact of Mandatory Changes in Accounting Principles on Corporate Loan Agreements. *J. Acc. Econ.*, March 1981, *3*(1), pp. 3–36. [G: U.S.]

Leftwich, Richard W.; Watts, Ross L. and Zimmerman, Jerold L. Voluntary Corporate Disclosure: The Case of Interim Reporting. *J. Acc. Res.*, Supplement 1981, *19*, pp. 50–77. [G: U.S.]

Leisenring, James J. Auditing Developments. **In** *Weinstein, S. and Walker, M. A., eds.*, 1981, pp. 17–33. [G: U.S.]

Leksell, Laurent. The Design and Function of the Financial Reporting System in Multinational Companies. **In** *Otterbeck, L., ed.*, 1981, pp. 205–32. [G: Sweden]

Lilien, Steven and Pastena, Victor. Intramethod Comparability: The Case of the Oil and Gas Industry. *Accounting Rev.*, July 1981, *56*(3), pp. 690–703. [G: U.S.]

Lillestøl, Jostein. A Note on Computing Upper Error Limits in Dollar-Unit Sampling. *J. Acc. Res.*, Spring 1981, *19*(1), pp. 263–67.

Livnat, Joshua. A Generalization of the API Methodology as a Way of Measuring the Association between Income and Stock Prices. *J. Acc. Res.*, Autumn 1981, *19*(2), pp. 350–59.

Lorek, Kenneth S.; Kee, Robert and Vass, William H. Time-Series Properties of Annual Earnings Data: The State of the Art. *Quart. Rev. Econ. Bus.*, Spring 1981, *21*(1), pp. 97–113.

Lowenthal, Franklin. A Decision Model for the Alternative Tax on Capital Gains. *Accounting Rev.*, April 1981, *56*(2), pp. 390–94. [G: U.S.]

Lucas, William H. and Morrison, Thomas L. Management Accounting for Construction Contracts. *Manage. Account.*, November 1981, *63*(5), pp. 59–65. [G: U.S.]

Maher, Michael W. The Impact of Regulation on Controls: Firms' Response to the Foreign Corrupt Practices Act. *Accounting Rev.*, October 1981, *56*(4), pp. 751–70. [G: U.S.]

Manegold, James G. Time-Series Properties of Earnings: A Comparison of Extrapolative and Component Models. *J. Acc. Res.*, Autumn 1981, *19*(2), pp. 360–73. [G: U.S.]

Martin, James R. Segment Planning and Reporting for Firms with Reciprocal Intersegment Transfers. *Bus. Econ.*, May 1981, *16*(3), pp. 25–29.

Mathur, Ike and Loy, David. Foreign Currency Translation: Survey of Corporate Treasurers. *Manage. Account.*, September 1981, *63*(3), pp. 33–38. [G: U.S.]

Mayer-Sommer, Alan P. and Loeb, Stephen E. Fostering More Successful Professional Socialization among Accounting Students. *Accounting Rev.*, January 1981, *56*(1), pp. 125–36. [G: U.S.]

Merchant, Kenneth A. The Design of the Corporate Budgeting System: Influences on Managerial Behavior and Performance. *Accounting Rev.*, October 1981, *56*(4), pp. 813–29.

Merten, Alan G.; Severance, Dennis G. and White, Bernard J. Internal Control and the Foreign Corrupt Practices Act. *Sloan Manage. Rev.*, Spring 1981, *22*(3), pp. 47–54. [G: U.S.]

Messere, Carl J. and Zuckerman, Gilroy J. An Alternative Approach to Depreciation Switches. *Accounting Rev.*, July 1981, *56*(3), pp. 642–52. [G: U.S.]

Morpeth, Douglas [Sir]. Inflation Accounting. **In** *Weinstein, S. and Walker, M. A., eds.*, 1981, pp. 177–91.

Morse, Dale. Discussion of On the Politics of Accounting Disclosure and Measurement: An Analysis of Economic Incentives. *J. Acc. Res.*, Supplement 1981, *19*, pp. 36–42.

Murray, Daniel R. How Management Accountants Can Make a Manufacturing Control System More Effective. *Manage. Account.*, July 1981, *63*(1), pp. 25–31, 48.

Nagahama, Bokuryo. A Note on Management Accounting. (In Japanese. With English summary.) *Osaka Econ. Pap.*, December 1981, *31*(2–3), pp. 240–46.

Nakano, Isao. Current Cost Accounting and the Concept of Specific Purchasing Power Capital. *Kobe Econ. Bus. Rev.*, 1981, (27), pp. 37–48.

Nakayama, Mie; Lilien, Steven and Benis, Martin. Due Process and FAS No. 13. *Manage. Account.*, April 1981, *62*(10), pp. 49–53. [G: U.S.]

Nelson, Phillip. The Effects of FTC Advertising Regulation: Comment. *J. Law Econ.*, December 1981, *24*(3), pp. 457–59. [G: U.S.]

Nelson, W. Dale. A Guide to Accounting for Costs of Discontinued Operations. *Manage. Account.*, April 1981, *62*(10), pp. 43–48.

Newman, D. Paul. An Investigation of the Distribution of Power in the APB and FASB. *J. Acc. Res.*, Spring 1981, *19*(1), pp. 247–62. [G: U.S.]

Newman, D. Paul. Coalition Formation in the APB and the FASB: Some New Evidence on the Size Principle. *Accounting Rev.*, October 1981, *56*(4), pp. 897–909. [G: U.S.]

Newman, D. Paul. The SEC's Influence on Accounting Standards: The Power of the Veto: A Reply. *J. Acc. Res.*, Supplement 1981, *19*, pp. 170–73. [G: U.S.]

Newman, D. Paul. The SEC's Influence on Accounting Standards: The Power of the Veto. *J. Acc. Res.*, Supplement 1981, *19*, pp. 134–56. [G: U.S.]

Nobes, C. W. An Empirical Analysis of International Accounting Principles: A Comment. *J. Acc. Res.*, Spring 1981, *19*(1), pp. 268–70.

Noreen, Eric W. and Sepe, James. Market Reactions to Accounting Policy Deliberations: The Inflation Accounting Case. *Accounting Rev.*, April 1981, *56*(2), pp. 253–69. [G: U.S.]

Noreen, Eric W. and Sepe, James. Market Reactions to Accounting Policy Deliberations: The Inflation Accounting Case Revisited—A Reply. *Accounting Rev.*, October 1981, *56*(4), pp. 955–58. [G: U.S.]

Noreen, Eric W. and Wolfson, Mark A. Equilibrium Warrant Pricing Models and Accounting for Executive Stock Options. *J. Acc. Res.*, Autumn 1981, *19*(2), pp. 384–98. [G: U.S.]

Ohlson, James A. and Buckman, A. G. Toward a Theory of Financial Accounting: Welfare and Public Information. *J. Acc. Res.*, Autumn 1981, *19*(2), pp. 399–433.

Parker, R. H. The Third International Congress of Accounting Historians. *J. Europ. Econ. Hist.*, Winter 1981, *10*(3), pp. 743–54.

Peltzman, Sam. The Effects of FTC Advertising Regulation. *J. Law Econ.*, December 1981, *24*(3), pp. 403–48. [G: U.S.]

Pihlanto, Pekka. Laskentatoimen tutkimuksen uusia näkökulmia. (New Orientations in Accounting Research. With English summary.) *Liiketaloudellinen Aikak.*, 1981, *30*(1), pp. 91–108.

Pihlanto, Pekka. Yrityksen mikropoliittiset prosessit ja laskentatoimi. (The Micropolitical Processes of a Firm and Accounting. With English summary.) *Liiketaloudellinen Aikak.*, 1981, *30*(4), pp. 459–70.

Plott, Charles R. and Sunder, Shyam. Studies on Standardization of Accounting Practices: An Assessment of Alternative Institutional Arrangements: A Synthesis. *J. Acc. Res.*, Supplement 1981, *19*, pp. 227–39. [G: U.S.]

Raman, K. K. Financial Reporting and Municipal Bond Rating Changes. *Accounting Rev.*, October 1981, *56*(4), pp. 910–26. [G: U.S.]

Ratcliffe, Thomas A. and Munter, Paul. Implementing FAS No. 33: A Case Example. *Manage. Account.*, February 1981, *62*(8), pp. 44–49, 52. [G: U.S.]

Rayburn, Gayle L. Marketing Costs—Accountants to the Rescue. *Manage. Account.*, January 1981, *62*(7), pp. 32–41. [G: U.S.]

Revsine, Lawrence. *The Theory and Measurement of Business Income:* A Review Article. *Accounting Rev.*, April 1981, *56*(2), pp. 342–54.

Revsine, Lawrence. A Capital Maintenance Approach to Income Measurement. *Accounting Rev.*, April 1981, *56*(2), pp. 383–89.

Rice, Edward M. Discussion of On the Politics of Accounting Disclosure and Measurement: An Analysis of Economic Incentives. *J. Acc. Res.*, Supplement 1981, *19*, pp. 43–47. [G: U.S.]

Ro, Byung T. The Disclosure of Replacement Cost Accounting Data and Its Effects on Transaction Volumes. *Accounting Rev.*, January 1981, *56*(1), pp. 70–84. [G: U.S.]

Ro, Byung T. The Disclosure of Replacement Cost Accounting Data and Its Effect on Transaction Volumes: A Reply. *Accounting Rev.*, January 1981, *56*(1), pp. 181–87. [G: U.S.]

Ronen, Joshua. Discussion of The SEC's Influence on Accounting Standards: The Power of the Veto. *J. Acc. Res.*, Supplement 1981, *19*, pp. 157–64. [G: U.S.]

Rousmaniere, Peter F. and Guild, Nathaniel B. The Second Wave of Municipal Accounting Reform. *Public Budg. Finance*, Spring 1981, *1*(1), pp. 66–77. [G: U.S.]

Rutteman, Paul J. Accounting Developments in the EEC—The Community's Company Law Harmonization Programme. In *Weinstein, S. and Walker, M. A.*, eds., 1981, pp. 193–222. [G: EEC]

Ryder, Paul A. Comments on Wolf's "The Nature of Managerial Work"—The Case for Unobtrusive Measures Revisited. *Accounting Rev.*, October 1981, *56*(4), pp. 967–70. [G: Canada]

Saldaña, Cesar G. Cost Allocations and the Management Control Problem. *Phillipine Rev. Econ. Bus.*, March & June 1981, *18*(1 & 2), pp. 23–44.

Saldaña, Cesar G. Information and Incentives Issues in Management Control. *Phillipine Rev. Econ. Bus.*, Sept. & Dec. 1981, *18*(3/4), pp. 154–67.

Salmi, Timo and Luoma, Martti. Deriving the Internal Rate of Return from the Accountant's Rate of Profit: Analysis and Empirical Estimation. *Liiketaloudellinen Aikak.*, 1981, *30*(1), pp. 20–45.

Santesso, Erasmo. Il futuro è molto incerto: conviene ancora fare il budget? (The Future is Highly Uncertain: Is It Still Worth Preparing a Budget? With English summary.) *L'Impresa*, 1981, *23*(2), pp. 53–58.

Scheiner, James H. Income Smoothing: An Analysis in the Banking Industry. *J. Bank Res.*, Summer 1981, *12*(2), pp. 119–23. [G: U.S.]

Schiedler, Patricia L. Using Accounting Information to Assess Risk. *Manage. Account.*, June 1981, *62*(12), pp. 38–42.

Schipper, Katherine. Discussion of Voluntary Corporate Disclosure: The Case of Interim Reporting. *J. Acc. Res.*, Supplement 1981, *19*, pp. 85–88. [G: U.S.]

Schoenfeld, Hanns-Martin W. International Accounting: Development, Issues, and Future Directions. *J. Int. Bus. Stud.*, Fall 1981, *12*(2), pp. 83–100.

Schultz, Joseph J., Jr. and Reckers, Philip M. J. The Impact of Group Processing on Selected Audit Disclosure Decisions. *J. Acc. Res.*, Autumn 1981, *19*(2), pp. 482–501.

Schweikart, James A. We Must End Consolidation of Foreign Subsidiaries. *Manage. Account.*, August 1981, *63*(2), pp. 15–18. [G: U.S.]

Shih, Wei. A Comment on Shih's General Decision Model for CVP Analysis—A Reply. *Accounting Rev.*, October 1981, *56*(4), pp. 984–85.

Shih, Wei. A General Decision Model for Cost–Volume–Profit Analysis under Uncertainty: A Reply. *Accounting Rev.*, April 1981, *56*(2), pp. 404–08.

Shockley, Randolph A. Perceptions of Auditors' Independence: An Empirical Analysis. *Accounting Rev.*, October 1981, *56*(4), pp. 785–800. [G: U.S.]

Siedel, George J. Corporate Governance under the Foreign Corrupt Practices Act. *Quart. Rev. Econ. Bus.*, Autumn 1981, *21*(3), pp. 43–48. [G: U.S.]

Sinai, Allen. Economic Impacts of Accelerated Capital Cost Recovery. In *U.S. Congress, Joint Economic Committee (I)*, 1981, pp. 610–28. [G: U.S.]

Smith, Abbie J. The SEC "Reversal" of FASB Statement No. 19: An Investigation of Information Effects. *J. Acc. Res.*, Supplement 1981, *19*, pp. 174–211. [G: U.S.]

Smith, Abbie J. and Dyckman, Thomas. The Impact of Accounting Regulation on the Stock Market: The Case of Oil and Gas Companies: A Comment. *Accounting Rev.*, October 1981, *56*(4), pp. 959–66. [G: U.S.]

Sprouse, Robert T. Discussion of The SEC's Influence on Accounting Standards: The Power of the Veto. *J. Acc. Res.*, Supplement 1981, *19*, pp. 165–69. [G: U.S.]

Staats, Elmer B. Financial Management Improvements: An Agenda for Federal Managers. *Public Budg. Finance*, Spring 1981, *1*(1), pp. 43–54.

Sunley, Emil M. Acceleration of Tax Depreciation: Basic Issues and Major Alternatives. In *Hulten, C. R., ed.*, 1981, pp. 137–47. [G: U.S.]

Swieringa, Robert J. The Silver-Lined Bonds of Sunshine Mining. *Accounting Rev.*, January 1981, *56*(1), pp. 166–76.

Tamminen, Rauno. Valmistevaraston arvostus ja perioditulos. (Stabilization of Profit by Inventory Valuation. With English summary.) *Liiketaloudellinen Aikak.*, 1981, *30*(3), pp. 325–34.

Tanzi, Vito. Inflation Accounting and the Taxation of Capital Gains of Business Enterprises. In *Roskamp, K. W. and Forte, F., eds.*, 1981, pp. 87–101.

Thirlby, G. F. The Ruler. In *Buchanan, J. M. and Thirlby, G. F., eds.*, 1981, *1946*, pp. 163–98.

Thirlby, G. F. The Subjective Theory of Value and Accounting 'Cost.' In *Buchanan, J. M. and Thirlby, G. F., eds.*, 1981, *1946*, pp. 135–61.

Thomas, W. E. On the Integrated Flow Report. *Tijdschrift Econ. Manage.*, 1981, *26*(4), pp. 463–72.

Tritschler, Ch. A. Accounting Standardization and Analytical Review. *Tijdschrift Econ. Manage.*, 1981, *26*(2), pp. 189–207. [G: U.S.]

Uecker, Wilfred C. Behavioral Accounting Research as a Source for Experimental Teaching Aids: An Example. *Accounting Rev.*, April 1981, *56*(2), pp. 366–82.

Uecker, Wilfred C.; Brief, Arthur P. and Kinney, William R., Jr. Perception of the Internal and External Auditor as a Deterrent to Corporate Irregularities. *Accounting Rev.*, July 1981, *56*(3), pp. 465–78. [G: U.S.]

Vander Weele, Ray. Is This Merger Right for You? *Manage. Account.*, March 1981, *62*(9), pp. 35–39, 47.

Vangermeersch, Richard. Let's Recognize Dissent in Standard-Making. *Manage. Account.*, September 1981, *63*(3), pp. 53–59. [G: U.S.]

Verrecchia, Robert E. On the Relationship between Volume Reaction and Consensus of Investors: Implications for Interpreting Tests of Information Content. *J. Acc. Res.*, Spring 1981, *19*(1), pp. 271–83.

Vigeland, Robert L. The Market Reaction to Statement of Financial Accounting Standards No. 2. *Accounting Rev.*, April 1981, *56*(2), pp. 309–25. [G: U.S.]

Wallace, Wanda A. Internal Control Reporting Practices in the Municipal Sector. *Accounting Rev.*, July 1981, *56*(3), pp. 666–89. [G: U.S.]

Wallace, Wanda A. The Association between Municipal Market Measures and Selected Financial Reporting Practices. *J. Acc. Res.*, Autumn 1981, *19*(2), pp. 502–20. [G: U.S.]

Walter, Herbert E., II and Sale, J. Timothy. Financial Reporting: A Two-Perspective Issue. *Manage. Account.*, June 1981, *62*(12), pp. 33–37.

Walton, John. Capital Maintenance and the Measurement of Corporate Income. *Rev. Income Wealth*, June 1981, *27*(2), pp. 109–35. [G: U.K.]

Watson, Peter. Inflation Accounting and Business Taxation. In *Peacock, A. and Forte, F., eds.*, 1981, pp. 78–93. [G: U.K.]

Weber, Richard P. and Stevenson, W. C. Evaluations of Accounting Journal and Department Quality. *Accounting Rev.*, July 1981, *56*(3), pp. 596–612.

Williams, John J. Designing a Budgeting System with Planned Confusion. *Calif. Manage. Rev.*, Winter 1981, *24*(2), pp. 75–85.

Windal, Floyd W. Publishing for a Varied Public: An Empirical Study. *Accounting Rev.*, July 1981, *56*(3), pp. 653–58. [G: U.S.]

Wolf, Frank M. "The Nature of Managerial Work—The Case for Unobtrusive Measures Revisited"—A Reply. *Accounting Rev.*, October 1981, *56*(4), pp. 971–74. [G: Canada]

Wolf, Frank M. The Nature of Managerial Work: An Investigation of the Work of the Audit Manager. *Accounting Rev.*, October 1981, *56*(4), pp. 861–81. [G: Canada]

Yamaji, Hidetoshi. The Function of Modern Corporate Financial Reporting in a Mass Democratic Society. *Kobe Econ. Bus. Rev.*, 1981, (27), pp. 69–87. [G: U.S.]

Yang, Chi-liang. 'Mass Line' Accounting in China. *Manage. Account.*, May 1981, *62*(11), pp. 13–17. [G: China]

Yavas, Ugar. Attitudinal Orientations as Inputs for Improving Images of Educational Fields. *Liiketaloudellinen Aikak.*, 1981, *30*(2), pp. 145–56. [G: Turkey]

Zéghal, Daniel. L'effet de l'information non comptable sur la valeur informationnelle des états financiers dans le marché des capitaux. (The Effect of Non-Accounting Information on the Informational Value of Financial Statements. With English summary.) *Can. J. Econ.*, May 1981, *14*(2), pp. 298–312.

Ziegler, Donald R. Some Thoughts on Auditors' Responsibility for False and Misleading Financial Statements. In *Weinstein, S. and Walker, M. A., eds.*, 1981, pp. 241–56. [G: U.S.]

Zmijewski, Mark E. and Hagerman, Robert L. An Income Strategy Approach to the Positive Theory of Accounting Standard Setting/Choice. *J. Acc. Econ.*, August 1981, *3*(2), pp. 129–49. [G: U.S.]

600 Industrial Organization; Technological Change; Industry Studies

610 INDUSTRIAL ORGANIZATION AND PUBLIC POLICY

611 Market Structure: Industrial Organization and Corporate Strategy

6110 Market Structure: Industrial Organization and Corporate Strategy

Aaronovitch, Sam and Sawyer, Malcolm C. Price Change and Oligopoly. *J. Ind. Econ.*, December 1981, *30*(2), pp. 137–47. [G: U.K.]

Ait-Laoussine, Nordine. Structural Changes in World Oil Market. In *OPEC, Public Information Dept.*, 1981, pp. 112–32.

Alcaly, Roger E. Consumer Information and Advertising: Comments. In *Galatin, M. and Leiter, R. D., eds.*, 1981, pp. 78–82. [G: U.S.]

Allard, Richard. Factors Affecting the Growth of the Firm—Theory and Practice: Comment. In *Currie, D.; Peel, D. and Peters, W., eds.*, 1981, pp. 357–60. [G: U.K.]

Allen, Bruce T. Structure and Stability in Gasoline Markets. *J. Econ. Issues*, March 1981, *15*(1), pp. 73–94. [G: U.S.]

Alpander, G. G.; Botter, C. and Marchesnay, Michael. An Enlarged Product-Process Matrix for Industrial Organisations. *Écon. Soc.*, October–November–December 1981, *15*(10–12), pp. 1689–1719.

Amato, Louis; Ryan, J. Michael and Wilder, Ronald P. Market Structure and Dynamic Performance in U.S. Manufacturing. *Southern Econ. J.*, April 1981, *47*(4), pp. 1105–10. [G: U.S.]

Amihud, Yakov and Lev, Baruch. Risk Reduction as a Managerial Motive for Conglomerate Mergers. *Bell J. Econ. (See Rand J. Econ. after 4/85)*, Autumn 1981, *12*(2), pp. 605–17. [G: U.S.]

Arterburn, Alfred and Woodbury, John. Advertising, Price Competition and Market Structure. *Southern Econ. J.*, January 1981, *47*(3), pp. 763–75. [G: U.S.]

Artle, Roland A. Competitive Behavior: Comments. In *[Grether, E. T.]*, 1981, pp. 128–30.

Avinger, Robert L., Jr. Product Durability and Market Structure: Some Evidence. *J. Ind. Econ.*, June 1981, *29*(4), pp. 357–74. [G: U.S.]

Babe, Robert E. Vertical Integration and Productivity: Canadian Telecommunications. *J. Econ. Issues*, March 1981, *15*(1), pp. 1–31. [G: Canada]

Barnes, P. A. and Dodds, J. C. Building Society Mergers and the Size-Efficiency Relationship: A Comment. *Appl. Econ.*, December 1981, *13*(4), pp. 531–34. [G: U.K.]

Bartlett, Randall. Property Rights and the Pricing of Real Estate Brokerage. *J. Ind. Econ.*, September 1981, *30*(1), pp. 79–94. [G: U.S.]

Bauer, Michel and Cohen, Elie. Autoproduction de la grande entreprise et transformation de son univers marchand. (The Self Production of the Large Company and the Conversion of Its Merchant Universe. With English summary.) *Revue Écon.*, May 1981, *32*(3), pp. 513–62.

Beck, Roger L. Concentration and Performance: The New Thinking and Some Canadian Evidence. *Managerial Dec. Econ.*, March 1981, *2*(1), pp. 9–15. [G: Canada]

Ben-Zion, Uri and Fixler, Dennis J. Market Structure and Product Innovation. *Southern Econ. J.*, October 1981, *48*(2), pp. 437–48.

Benson, Bruce L. The Optimal Size and Number of Market Areas. *Southern Econ. J.*, April 1981, *47*(4), pp. 1080–85.

Berg, Sanford V. and Friedman, Philip. Impacts of Domestic Joint Ventures on Industrial Rates of Return: A Pooled Cross-Section Analysis, 1964–1975. *Rev. Econ. Statist.*, May 1981, *63*(2), pp. 293–98. [G: U.S.]

Bernhardt, Irwin. Sources of Productivity Differences among Canadian Manufacturing Industries. *Rev. Econ. Statist.*, November 1981, *63*(4), pp. 503–12. [G: U.S.; Canada]

Bettis, Richard A. and Hall, William K. Strategic Portfolio Management in the Multibusiness Firm. *Calif. Manage. Rev.*, Fall 1981, *24*(1), pp. 23–38.

Bishara, Halim I. An Empirical Study of the Canadian Multinational Corporations and Canadian Conglomerate Firms with Regard to Performance Evaluation. *Nebr. J. Econ. Bus.*, Autumn 1981, *20*(4), pp. 33–50. [G: Canada]

Blair, Roger D. and Peles, Yoram C. Conglomerate Mergers: Efficiency Considerations. In *Blair, R. D. and Lanzillotti, R. F., eds.*, 1981, pp. 99–111. [G: U.S.]

Bloch, Harry. Concentration and Profitability in Canadian Manufacturing: An Indirect Test of the Effect of Aggregation. *Can. J. Econ.*, February 1981, *14*(1), pp. 130–35. [G: Canada]

Bloch, Harry. Determinants of the Variance in Market Shares in Canadian Manufacturing. *J. Ind. Econ.*, June 1981, *29*(4), pp. 385–93. [G: Canada]

Bock, Betty. The Conglomerate Corporation: Remarks. In *Blair, R. D. and Lanzillotti, R. F., eds.*, 1981, pp. 349–58. [G: U.S.]

Bolch, Ben W. and Damon, William W. The Windfall Profit Tax and Vertical Integration in the Petroleum Industry. *Southern Econ. J.*, January 1981, *47*(3), pp. 788–91. [G: U.S.]

Boyer, Kenneth D. Testing the Applicability of the Natural Monopoly Concept. In *Sichel, W. and Gies, T. G., eds.*, 1981, pp. 1–15.

Braeutigam, Ronald R. The Deregulation of Natural Gas. In *Weiss, L. W. and Klass, M. W., eds.*, 1981, pp. 142–86. [G: U.S.]

Bresnahan, Timothy F. Departures from Marginal-Cost Pricing in the American Automobile Industry: Estimates for 1977–1978. *J. Econometrics*, November 1981, *17*(2), pp. 201–27. [G: U.S.]

Bressler, Barry. Search, Information, and Market Structure: Comments. In *Galatin, M. and Leiter, R. D., eds.*, 1981, pp. 98–103.

Brockhoff, Klaus. Competition, Innovation, Productivity Growth, and Public Policy: Comments. In *Giersch, H., ed. (II)*, 1981, pp. 180–86.

Bruch, Mathias. X-Efficiency Theory, Productivity and Growth: Comments. In *Giersch, H., ed. (II)*, 1981, pp. 217–19.

Brush, Brian C. On the Use of Principal Component Analysis in the Measurement of Concentration [A Note on Principal Component Analysis of Census Concentration Ratios]. *Rev. Bus. Econ. Res.*, Spring 1981, *16*(3), pp. 102–05. [G: U.S.]

Brush, Brian C. What Do Labor Productivity Data Show about Economies of Scale: Comment. *Southern Econ. J.*, January 1981, *47*(3), pp. 839–46. [G: U.S.]

Cable, John. "Merger Control Remains the Priority": The Third Report of the German Monopolies Commission: A Review Article. *Z. ges. Staatswiss.*, June 1981, *137*(2), pp. 302–08.

Cain, Louis P. and Neumann, George R. Planning for Peace: The Surplus Property Act of 1944. *J.*

Econ. Hist., March 1981, *41*(1), pp. 129–35.
[G: U.S.]

Camagni, Roberto and Tiberi-Vipraio, Patrizia. Il commercio orizzontale rivisitato: una interpretazione stocastica interregionale. (Intra-industry Trade Revisited: An Interregional Stochastic Interpretation. With English summary.) *Giorn. Econ.*, July–August 1981, *40*(7–8), pp. 465–92.

Carter, E. Eugene. Resource Allocation. In *Nystrom, P. C. and Starbuck, W. H., eds.*, Vol. 2, 1981, pp. 152–65.

Cavalcanti, Leonardo; Geiger, Pedro P. and de Andrade, Thompson. Multinationals, the New International Economic Order and the Spatial Industrial Structure of Brazil. In *Hamilton, F. E. I. and Linge, G. J. R., eds.*, 1981, pp. 423–38. [G: Brazil]

Caves, Richard E. Diversification and Seller Concentration: Evidence from Changes, 1963–72. *Rev. Econ. Statist.*, May 1981, *63*(2), pp. 289–93. [G: U.S.]

Chandra, Nirmal K. Monopoly Capital, Private Corporate Sector and the Indian Economy: A Study in Relative Growth, 1931–1976. In *Bagchi, A. K. and Banerjee, N., eds.*, 1981, pp. 329–81. [G: India]

Chaudhary, Mohammad Ali and Iqbal, Nuzhat. Economic Analysis of Firm Size and Saving Rate. *Pakistan Econ. Soc. Rev.*, Winter 1981, *19*(2), pp. 115–22. [G: Pakistan]

Chowdhury, Nuimuddin. On the Structure of Input and Product Markets in Cotton Weaving Industry of Bangladesh: A Case Study Using Firm Level Data. *Bangladesh Devel. Stud.*, Summer 1981, *9*(2), pp. 43–74. [G: Bangladesh]

Comanor, William S. Conglomerate Mergers: Considerations for Public Policy. In *Blair, R. D. and Lanzillotti, R. F., eds.*, 1981, pp. 13–24. [G: U.S.]

Comanor, William S.; Kover, Arthur J. and Smiley, Robert H. Advertising and its Consequences. In *Nystrom, P. C. and Starbuck, W. H., eds., Vol. 2*, 1981, pp. 429–39.

Connor, John M. Food Product Proliferation: A Market Structure Analysis. *Amer. J. Agr. Econ.*, November 1981, *63*(4), pp. 607–17. [G: U.S.]

Cooper, Edward H. The Case against a New Presumptive Approach to Conglomerate Mergers. In *Blair, R. D. and Lanzillotti, R. F., eds.*, 1981, pp. 283–345. [G: U.S.]

Cornell, Bradford and Roll, Richard. Strategies for Pairwise Competitions in Markets and Organizations. *Bell J. Econ. (See Rand J. Econ. after 4/85)*, Spring 1981, *12*(1), pp. 201–13.

Cory, Peter F. A Technique for Obtaining Improved Proxy Estimates of Minimum Optimal Scale. *Rev. Econ. Statist.*, February 1981, *63*(1), pp. 96–106. [G: U.S.]

Cosimano, Thomas F. The Incentive to Adopt Cost Reducing Innovation in the Presence of a Non-Linear Demand Curve. *Southern Econ. J.*, July 1981, *48*(1), pp. 97–102.

Cox, Charles C. Monopoly Explanations of the Great Depression and Public Policies toward Business. In *Brunner, K., ed.*, 1981, pp. 174–207. [G: U.S.]

Cox, Reavis. Establishments, Firms, and Channels as Units of Competition. In *[Grether, E. T.]*, 1981, pp. 214–28.

Craver, Theodore F. The Conglomerate Corporation: Remarks. In *Blair, R. D. and Lanzillotti, R. F., eds.*, 1981, pp. 359–63. [G: U.S.]

Cubbin, John S. Advertising and the Theory of Entry Barriers. *Economica*, August 1981, *48*(191), pp. 289–98.

Dalton, James A. and Esposito, Louis. The Traditional and Strategy Formulation Models of Industry Analysis: Implications for Public Policy. *Eastern Econ. J.*, January 1981, *7*(1), pp. 15–25.

Damus, Sylvester. Two-Part Tariffs and Optimum Taxation: The Case of Railway Rates. *Amer. Econ. Rev.*, March 1981, *71*(1), pp. 65–79. [G: U.S.]

Dasgupta, Partha and Stiglitz, Joseph E. Entry, Innovation, Exit: Towards a Dynamic Theory of Oligopolistic Industrial Structure. *Europ. Econ. Rev.*, February 1981, *15*(2), pp. 137–58.

Davidow, Joel. Extraterritorial Antitrust and the Concept of Comity. *J. World Trade Law*, November–December 1981, *15*(6), pp. 500–520. [G: U.S.; OECD]

De Smet, Michel and Martin, Georges. Concentration and Economies of Scale in the Belgian Financial Sector: Comment. In *Verheirstraeten, A., ed.*, 1981, pp. 92–96. [G: Belgium]

DeAngelo, Harry. Competition and Unanimity. *Amer. Econ. Rev.*, March 1981, *71*(1), pp. 18–27.

DeRosa, Dean A. and Goldstein, Morris. Import Discipline in the U.S. Manufacturing Sector. *Int. Monet. Fund Staff Pap.*, September 1981, *28*(3), pp. 600–634. [G: U.S.]

Dillon, Gadis J. The Business Combination Process. *Accounting Rev.*, April 1981, *56*(2), pp. 395–99.

DiLorenzo, Thomas J. Corporate Management, Property Rights and the X–istence of X-inefficiency. *Southern Econ. J.*, July 1981, *48*(1), pp. 116–23.

Dirlam, Joel B. Marginal Cost Pricing Tests for Predation: Naive Welfare Economics and Public Policy. *Antitrust Bull.*, Winter 1981, *26*(4), pp. 769–814. [G: U.S.]

Dobbins, R.; Lowes, B. and Pass, Christopher L. Financial Institutions and the Ownership and Control of British Industry. *Managerial Dec. Econ.*, March 1981, *2*(1), pp. 16–24. [G: U.K.]

Domberger, Simon. Price Adjustment and Market Structure: A Reply. *Econ. J.*, December 1981, *91*(364), pp. 1031–35. [G: U.K.]

Donkin, George L. Competition and the Rate-making Process: The Case of the Trans-Alaska Oil Pipeline. In *Sichel, W. and Gies, T. G., eds.*, 1981, pp. 87–101. [G: U.S.]

Dopfer, Kurt. Determinants of Japan's Expansion in Western Markets. *Wirtsch. Recht*, 1981, *33*(3/4), pp. 153–59. [G: Japan]

Dorward, Neil and Walker, Mike. Stochastic Processes and Industrial Concentration. *Brit. Rev. Econ. Issues*, Spring 1981, *2*(8), pp. 21–43. [G: U.K.]

Dunning, John H. Multinational Enterprises, Market Structure, Economic Power and Industrial

Policy. In *Dunning, J. H.*, 1981, pp. 179–220.
[G: U.S.; U.K.]

Eccles, Robert G. The Quasifirm in the Construction Industry. *J. Econ. Behav. Organ.*, December 1981, *2*(4), pp. 335–57. [G: U.S.]

Eckard, E. Woodrow, Jr. Antitrust and the Concentration Doctrine: A Rejoinder. *Bus. Econ.*, March 1981, *16*(2), pp. 22–25.

Eckard, E. Woodrow, Jr. Concentration Changes and Inflation: Some Evidence [A Note on Inflation and Concentration]. *J. Polit. Econ.*, October 1981, *89*(5), pp. 1044–51. [G: U.S.]

Eckard, E. Woodrow, Jr. Industrial Concentration, Plant Scale Economies, and Multi-Plant Operations: Further Evidence. *Rev. Bus. Econ. Res.*, Spring 1981, *16*(3), pp. 90–97. [G: U.S.]

Edmunds, Stahrl W. Organizational Size and Efficiency in the U.S. *Antitrust Bull.*, Fall 1981, *26*(3), pp. 507–19. [G: U.S.]

Eichenseher, John W. and Danos, Paul. The Analysis of Industry-Specific Auditor Concentration: Towards an Explanatory Model. *Accounting Rev.*, July 1981, *56*(3), pp. 479–92. [G: U.S.]

Elton, Edwin J.; Gruber, Martin J. and Lightstone, John B. The Impact of Bankruptcy on the Firm's Capital Structure, the Reasonableness of Mergers, and the Risk Independence of Projects. In *Levy, H., ed.*, 1981, pp. 143–56.

Elzinga, Kenneth G. Defining Geographic Market Boundaries [The Problem of Geographic Market Definition in Antimerger Suits]. *Antitrust Bull.*, Winter 1981, *26*(4), pp. 739–52. [G: U.S.]

Engwall, Lars. Newspaper Competition: A Case for Theories of Oligopoly: Review Article. *Scand. Econ. Hist. Rev.*, 1981, *29*(2), pp. 145–54.
[G: Sweden]

Evans, R. G. Incomplete Vertical Integration: The Distinctive Structure of the Health-Care Industry. In *van der Gaag, J. and Perlman, M., eds.*, 1981, pp. 329–54.

Evraert, Serge. La relation entre la taille et la croissance des entreprises et la loi de l'effet proportionnel. (The Relation between Size and the Growth of Business Firms and the Law of Proportionate Effect. With English summary.) *Écon. Soc.*, October–November–December 1981, *15*(10–12), pp. 1775–1810.

Farber, Stephen C. Buyer Market Structure and R&D Effort: A Simultaneous Equations Model. *Rev. Econ. Statist.*, August 1981, *63*(3), pp. 336–45. [G: U.S.]

Feinberg, Robert M. On the Measurement of Aggregate Concentration [What Has Been Happening to Aggregate Concentration in the United States?]. *J. Ind. Econ.*, December 1981, *30*(2), pp. 217–22. [G: U.S.]

Flaherty, M. Therese. Prices versus Quantities and Vertical Financial Integration. *Bell J. Econ. (See Rand J. Econ. after 4/85)*, Autumn 1981, *12*(2), pp. 507–25.

Friedlaender, Ann F. Equity, Efficiency, and Regulation in the Rail and Trucking Industries. In *Weiss, L. W. and Klass, M. W., eds.*, 1981, pp. 102–41. [G: U.S.]

Friedland, Thomas S. and Simon, Julian L. Strategies of Oligopolistic Competition. In *Nystrom,*

P. C. and Starbuck, W. H., eds., Vol. 2, 1981, pp. 454–63. [G: U.S.]

Friedman, James W. Limit Pricing and Entry. *J. Econ. Dynam. Control*, August 1981, *3*(3), pp. 319–23.

Fuss, Melvyn A. and Gupta, Vinod K. A Cost Function Approach to the Estimation of Minimum Efficient Scale, Returns to Scale, and Suboptimal Capacity: With an Application to Canadian Manufacturing. *Europ. Econ. Rev.*, February 1981, *15*(2), pp. 123–35. [G: Canada]

Galatin, Malcolm. Search, Information, and Market Structure. In *Galatin, M. and Leiter, R. D., eds.*, 1981, pp. 83–97.

Geithman, Frederick E.; Marvel, Howard P. and Weiss, Leonard W. Concentration, Price and Critical Concentration Ratios. *Rev. Econ. Statist.*, August 1981, *63*(3), pp. 346–53. [G: U.S.]

Geroski, P. A. On the Nature of Industrial Market Power in the U.K.: Comment. In *Currie, D.; Peel, D. and Peters, W., eds.*, 1981, pp. 325–28.
[G: U.K.]

Geroski, P. A. Specification and Testing the Profits–Concentration Relationship: Some Experiments for the UK. *Economica*, August 1981, *48*(191), pp. 279–88. [G: U.K.]

Gill, David G. International Cartels and Their Regulation: Commentary. In *Schachter, O. and Hellawell, R., eds.*, 1981, pp. 277–82. [G: EEC; U.S.]

Golbe, Devra L. The Effects of Imminent Bankruptcy on Stockholder Risk Preferences and Behavior [The Bankruptcy Decision]. *Bell J. Econ. (See Rand J. Econ. after 4/85)*, Spring 1981, *12*(1), pp. 321–28.

Gold, Bela. Changing Perspectives on Size, Scale, and Returns: An Interpretive Survey. *J. Econ. Lit.*, March 1981, *19*(1), pp. 5–33.

Gordon, Myron J. and Yagil, Joseph. Financial Gain from Conglomerate Mergers. In *Levy, H., ed.*, 1981, pp. 103–42. [G: U.S.]

Goto, Akira. Statistical Evidence on the Diversification of Japanese Large Firms. *J. Ind. Econ.*, March 1981, *29*(3), pp. 271–78. [G: Japan]

Gottfredson, Linda S. and White, Paul E. Interorganizational Agreements. In *Nystrom, P. C. and Starbuck, W. H., eds., Vol. 1*, 1981, pp. 471–86.

Gough, T. J. Building Society Mergers and the Size-Efficiency Relationship: A Reply. *Appl. Econ.*, December 1981, *13*(4), pp. 535–38. [G: U.K.]

Greer, Douglas F. Control of Terms and Conditions for International Transfers of Technology to Developing Countries. In *Schachter, O. and Hellawell, R., eds.*, 1981, pp. 41–83. [G: U.S.; Japan]

Greer, Douglas F. The Causes of Concentration in the U.S. Brewing Industry. *Quart. Rev. Econ. Bus.*, Winter 1981, *21*(4), pp. 87–106.
[G: U.S.]

Grether, David M. Research and Development Expenditures as a Competitive Strategy. In *[Grether, E. T.]*, 1981, pp. 30–59.

Guesnier, Bernard. Analyse et prévision de la démographie des entreprises à l'aide d'un processus markovien: Application à l'industrie de la chaussure. (Demographic Analysis and Forecast of Firms with a Stochastic Model: Markov Chain. Application to Boot and Shoe Industry. With English summary.) *Rev. Econ. Ind.*, 1st Trimester 1981, (15), pp. 19–43. **[G: France]**

Gupta, Vinod K. Minimum Efficient Scale as a Determinant of Concentration: A Reappraisal. *Manchester Sch. Econ. Soc. Stud.*, June 1981, 49(2), pp. 153–64. **[G: Canada]**

Hagerman, Robert L. and Zmijewski, Mark E. A Test of Accounting Bias and Market Structure: Some Additional Evidence. *Rev. Bus. Econ. Res.*, Fall 1981, 17(1), pp. 84–88. **[G: U.S.]**

Handlin, Oscar. The Taxonomy of the Corporation. In *Novak, M. and Cooper, J. W., eds.*, 1981, pp. 17–26. **[G: U.S.]**

Hannah, L. and Kay, John A. The Contribution of Mergers to Concentration Growth: A Reply to Professor Hart [On Bias and Concentration]. *J. Ind. Econ.*, March 1981, 29(3), pp. 305–13. **[G: U.K.]**

Hannah, L. and Kay, John A. The Contribution of Mergers to Industrial Concentration: A Reply to Professor Prais [The Contribution of Mergers to Concentration Growth]. *J. Ind. Econ.*, March 1981, 29(3), pp. 331–32. **[G: U.K.]**

Hannan, Timothy H. Mutual Awareness among Potential Entrants: An Empirical Examination. *Southern Econ. J.*, January 1981, 47(3), pp. 805–08.

Harris, Milton and Raviv, Artur. A Theory of Monopoly Pricing Schemes with Demand Uncertainty. *Amer. Econ. Rev.*, June 1981, 71(3), pp. 347–65.

Hart, P. E. The Effects of Mergers on Industrial Concentration [On Bias and Concentration]. *J. Ind. Econ.*, March 1981, 29(3), pp. 315–20. **[G: U.K.]**

Hay, George and Untiet, Charles. Statistical Measurement of the Conglomerate Problem. In *Blair, R. D. and Lanzillotti, R. F., eds.*, 1981, pp. 163–91. **[G: U.S.]**

Hazledine, Tim. On the Nature of Industrial Market Power in the U.K. In *Currie, D.; Peel, D. and Peters, W., eds.*, 1981, pp. 299–324. **[G: U.K.]**

Heinkel, Robert. Uncertain Product Quality: The Market for Lemons with an Imperfect Testing Technology. *Bell J. Econ. (See Rand J. Econ. after 4/85)*, Autumn 1981, 12(2), pp. 625–36.

Helmberger, Peter G.; Campbell, Gerald R. and Dobson, William D. Organization and Performance of Agricultural Markets. In *Martin, L. R., ed.*, 1981 cat kp22a, pp. 503–653. **[G: U.S.]**

Henning, J. A. and Mann, H. M. An Appraisal of Model Building in Industrial Organization. In *Zerbe, R. O., Jr., ed.*, 1981, pp. 1–14.

Hey, John D. A Unified Theory of the Behaviour of Profit-Maximising, Labour-Managed and Joint-Stock Firms Operating under Uncertainty. *Econ. J.*, June 1981, 91(362), pp. 364–74.

Hilke, John and Nelson, Philip. Antitrust Policy and the Market Concentration Doctrine: A Response. *Bus. Econ.*, March 1981, 16(2), pp. 17–21.

Hill, Hal. Subcontracting and Inter-Firm Linkages in Philippine Manufacturing. *Philippine Econ. J.*, 1981, 20(1), pp. 58–79. **[G: Philippines]**

Hirschey, Mark. The Effect of Advertising on Industrial Mobility, 1947–72. *J. Bus.*, April 1981, 54(2), pp. 329–39. **[G: U.S.]**

Hirschey, Mark and Pappas, James L. Market Power and Manufacturer Leasing. *J. Ind. Econ.*, September 1981, 30(1), pp. 39–47. **[G: U.S.]**

Hirschey, Mark and Pappas, James L. Regulatory and Life Cycle Influences on Managerial Incentives. *Southern Econ. J.*, October 1981, 48(2), pp. 327–34.

Hitiris, Theodore. Protection, Concentration and Labour Intensity: Reply [The Impact of Protection and Concentration on the Labor Intensity of U.K. Industries]. *Weltwirtsch. Arch.*, 1981, 117(2), pp. 383–84. **[G: U.K.]**

Hoffmann, Lutz. X-Efficiency Theory, Productivity and Growth: Comments. In *Giersch, H., ed. (II)*, 1981, pp. 213–16.

Hornbrook, Mark C. Price and Quality Competition in Drug Markets: Evidence from the United States and the Netherlands: Comment. In *Helms, R. B., ed.*, 1981, pp. 152–66. **[G: U.S.; Netherlands]**

Horowitz, Ira. The Relevance of the Relevant Market in a Section 7 Analysis of Conglomerate Mergers (Whatever Those Are). In *Blair, R. D. and Lanzillotti, R. F., eds.*, 1981, pp. 137–61. **[G: U.S.]**

Horwitch, Mel and Prahalad, C. K. Managing Multi-Organization Enterprises: The Emerging Strategic Frontier. *Sloan Manage. Rev.*, Winter 1981, 22(2), pp. 3–16.

House, William J. Industrial Performance and Market Structure. In *Killick, T., ed.*, 1981, pp. 339–45. **[G: Kenya]**

Hufbauer, Gary Clyde. Economic and Political Characteristics of Cartel and Cartel-like Practices: Commentary. In *Schachter, O. and Hellawell, R., eds.*, 1981, pp. 283–85.

Huppert, Rémi. Stratégies de développement des P.M.I. françaises. (Strategies and Growth of French Small Businesses. With English summary.) *Rev. Econ. Ind.*, 3rd Trimestre 1981, (17), pp. 26–41. **[G: France]**

Hutchinson, R. W. Price-Cost Margins and Manufacturing Industry Structure: The Case of a Small Economy with Bilateral Trade in Manufactured Goods. *Europ. Econ. Rev.*, June/July 1981, 16(2/3), pp. 247–67. **[G: Ireland]**

Ilmakunnas, Pekka. Giffen Phenomena for Normal Inputs: The Multiproduct, Sales-Maximizing Firm. *Southern Econ. J.*, January 1981, 47(3), pp. 598–605.

Isaac, Barry L. Price, Competition, and Profits among Hawkers and Shopkeepers in Pendembu, Sierra Leone: An Inventory Approach. *Econ. Develop. Cult. Change*, January 1981, 29(2), pp. 353–73. **[G: Sierra Leone]**

Isaac, R. Mark and Plott, Charles R. The Opportunity for Conspiracy in Restraint of Trade: An Experimental Study. *J. Econ. Behav. Organ.*, March 1981, 2(1), pp. 1–30.

Jacquemin, Alexis; Nambu, Tsuruhiko and Dewez, Isabelle. A Dynamic Analysis of Export Cartels: The Japanese Case. *Econ. J.*, September 1981, 91(363), pp. 685–96. **[G: Japan]**

Jadlow, Joseph M. New Evidence on Innovation and Market Structure. *Managerial Dec. Econ.*, June 1981, *2*(2), pp. 91–96. [G: U.S.]

Jennergren, L. Peter. Decentralization in Organizations. In *Nystrom, P. C. and Starbuck, W. H., eds., Vol. 2,* 1981, pp. 39–59.

Jovanovic, Boyan. Entry with Private Information. *Bell J. Econ. (See Rand J. Econ. after 4/85),* Autumn 1981, *12*(2), pp. 649–60.

Kairamo, Kari. Finländsk industri i hårdnande internationell konkurrens. (Finnish Industry in Growing International Competition. With English summary.) *Ekon. Samfundets Tidskr.*, 1981, *34*(1), pp. 5–15. [G: Finland]

Kania, John J. and McKean, John R. Profit, Growth, and the Marris Theory of the Firm: A Short Run Empirical Test. *Amer. Econ.*, Spring 1981, *25*(1), pp. 63–66. [G: U.S.]

Kaserman, David L. and Rice, Patricia L. A Note on Predatory Vertical Integration in the U.S. Petroleum Industry. *J. Econ. Bus.*, Spring/Summer 1981, *33*(3), pp. 262–66. [G: U.S.]

Keeler, Theodore E. The Revolution in Airline Regulation. In *Weiss, L. W. and Klass, M. W., eds.,* 1981, pp. 53–85. [G: U.S.]

Keeler, Theodore E. and Abrahams, Michael. Market Structure, Pricing, and Service Quality in the Airline Industry under Deregulation. In *Sichel, W. and Gies, T. G., eds.,* 1981, pp. 103–19. [G: U.S.]

Keidel, Albert. Patterns in Economic Organization. In *Richardson, B. M. and Ueda, T., eds.,* 1981, pp. 21–28. [G: Japan]

Kelly, William A., Jr. A Generalized Interpretation of the Herfindahl Index. *Southern Econ. J.*, July 1981, *48*(1), pp. 50–57.

Khandwalla, Pradip N. Properties of Competing Organizations. In *Nystrom, P. C. and Starbuck, W. H., eds., Vol. 1,* 1981, pp. 409–32. [G: U.S.]

Koenig, Thomas and Gogel, Robert. Interlocking Corporate Directorships as a Social Network. *Amer. J. Econ. Soc.*, January 1981, *40*(1), pp. 37–50. [G: U.S.]

Kohers, Theodor and Simpson, W. Gary. Concentration and Advertising in the United States Savings and Loan Industry. *Appl. Econ.*, March 1981, *13*(1), pp. 79–88. [G: U.S.]

Kónya, Lajos. Conditions of Setting Up Simple Forms of Cooperatives in the Hungarian Industry. *Acta Oecon.*, 1981, *27*(1–2), pp. 77–92. [G: Hungary]

Kumar, Manmohan S. Do Mergers Reduce Corporate Investment? Evidence from United Kingdom Experience. *Cambridge J. Econ.*, June 1981, *5*(2), pp. 107–18. [G: U.K.]

Kwoka, John E., Jr. Does the Choice of Concentration Measure Really Matter? *J. Ind. Econ.*, June 1981, *29*(4), pp. 445–53. [G: U.S.]

Kyläkoski, Kalevi. Yrityksen strategiasuunnittelu systeeminä ja prosessina. (Corporate Strategic Planning—as a System and as a Process. With English summary.) *Liiketaloudellinen Aikak.*, 1981, *30*(3), pp. 335–42. [G: Finland]

Lall, Sanjaya. Transnationals, Domestic Enterprises, and Industrial Structure in Host LDCs: A Survey. In *Livingstone, I., ed.,* 1981, *1978,* pp. 148–63. [G: LDCs]

Lamm, Ray McFall. Prices and Concentration in the Food Retailing Industry. *J. Ind. Econ.*, September 1981, *30*(1), pp. 67–78. [G: U.S.]

Larson, David. On the Use of Principal Component Analysis in the Measurement of Concentration: Reply [A Note on Principal Component Analysis of Census Concentration Ratios]. *Rev. Bus. Econ. Res.*, Spring 1981, *16*(3), pp. 106. [G: U.S.]

Lazonick, William H. Competition, Specialization, and Industrial Decline. *J. Econ. Hist.*, March 1981, *41*(1), pp. 31–38. [G: U.K.]

Lecler, Yveline. Les petites et moyennes entreprises japonaises et la régulation de l'activité des grandes entreprises. (The Japanese Small and Medium Enterprises and the Regulation of Big Enterprises Activity. With English summary.) *Rev. Econ. Ind.*, 3rd Trimestre 1981, (17), pp. 42–60. [G: Japan]

Lee, Dwight R. Least-Cost Pollution Abatement, Effluent Charges, and Monopoly Power. *Amer. Econ.*, Spring 1981, *25*(1), pp. 57–60.

Leibenstein, Harvey. X-Efficiency Theory, Productivity and Growth. In *Giersch, H., ed. (II),* 1981, pp. 187–212.

Levin, Richard C. Vertical Integration and Profitability in the Oil Industry. *J. Econ. Behav. Organ.*, September 1981, *2*(3), pp. 215–35. [G: U.S.]

Levine, Paul and Aaronovitch, Sam. The Financial Characteristics of Firms and Theories of Merger Activity. *J. Ind. Econ.*, December 1981, *30*(2), pp. 149–72. [G: U.K.]

Lindenberg, Eric B. and Ross, Stephen A. Tobin's *q* Ratio and Industrial Organization. *J. Bus.*, January 1981, *54*(1), pp. 1–32. [G: U.S.]

Lindsey, Charles W. Firm Size and Profit Rate in Philippine Manufacturing. *J. Devel. Areas*, April 1981, *15*(3), pp. 445–56. [G: Philippines]

Littlechild, S. C. Misleading Calculations of the Social Costs of Monopoly Power. *Econ. J.*, June 1981, *91*(362), pp. 348–63. [G: U.S.; U.K.]

Loasby, B. J. Price-Cost Margins, Market Structure and International Trade: Comment. In *Currie, D.; Peel, D. and Peters, W., eds.,* 1981, pp. 296–98. [G: U.K.]

Lorch, Brian J. Mergers and Acquisitions and the Geographic Transfer of Corporate Control: Canada's Manufacturing Industry. In *Rees, J.; Hewings, G. J. D. and Stafford, H. A., eds.,* 1981, pp. 123–34. [G: Canada]

Luksetich, William A. Advertising Intensity and Antitrust Activity. *J. Behav. Econ.*, Summer 1981, *10*(1), pp. 101–09. [G: U.S.]

Luksetich, William A. Market Power and Discrimination in White-Collar Employment: 1969–1975. *Rev. Soc. Econ.*, October 1981, *39*(2), pp. 145–64. [G: U.S.]

Lye, Stephen and Silberston, Aubrey. Merger Activity and Sales of Subsidiaries between Company Groups. *Oxford Bull. Econ. Statist.*, August 1981, *43*(3), pp. 257–72. [G: U.S.]

Lyons, Bruce. Price-Cost Margins, Market Structure and International Trade. In *Currie, D.; Peel, D. and Peters, W., eds.,* 1981, pp. 276–95. [G: U.K.]

Maddigan, Ruth J. The Measurement of Vertical Integration. *Rev. Econ. Statist.*, August 1981, *63*(3), pp. 328–35.

Makepeace, Gerald H. Measuring the Effects of Monopolies in a Partial Monopoly Model. *Scot. J. Polit. Econ.*, November 1981, *28*(3), pp. 236–55.

Manne, Henry G. The Publicly Held Corporation as a Market Creation. *Z. ges. Staatswiss.*, December 1981, *137*(4), pp. 689–93.

Mansfield, Edwin. Composition of R and D Expenditures: Relationship to Size of Firm, Concentration, and Innovative Output. *Rev. Econ. Statist.*, November 1981, *63*(4), pp. 610–15. [G: U.S.]

Marfels, Christian. Market Concentration and Implicit Grants in the Energy Industry: Some Observations. *Z. Wirtschaft. Sozialwissen.*, 1981, *101*(4), pp. 429–40. [G: U.S.]

Máriás, Antal, et al. Organization of Large Industrial Enterprises in Hungary: A Comparative Analysis. *Acta Oecon.*, 1981, *27*(3–4), pp. 327–42. [G: Hungary]

Marsden, Keith. Creating the Right Environment for Small Firms. *Finance Develop.*, December 1981, *18*(4), pp. 33–36. [G: LDCs]

Martinet, Alain. Externalitiés et comportements stratégiques à la recherche de nouvelles équilibrations. (With English summary.) *Écon. Appl.*, 1981, *34*(1), pp. 61–88.

Mayer, Thomas. Monopoly Explanations of the Great Depression and Public Policies toward Business: Comments. In *Brunner, K., ed.*, 1981, pp. 211–19.

McCraw, Thomas K. Rethinking the Trust Question. In *McCraw, T. K., ed.*, 1981, pp. 1–55. [G: U.S.]

McGraw, Thomas K. Discussion [The Response of the Giant Corporations to Wage and Price Controls in World War II] [Planning for Peace: The Surplus Property Act of 1944]. *J. Econ. Hist.*, March 1981, *41*(1), pp. 136–37. [G: U.S.]

Meehan, James W., Jr. and Larner, Robert J. A Proposed Rule of Reason for Vertical Restraints on Competition. *Antitrust Bull.*, Summer 1981, *26*(2), pp. 195–225. [G: U.S.]

Meeks, G. and Meeks, J. G. Profitability Measures as Indicators of Post-merger Efficiency. *J. Ind. Econ.*, June 1981, *29*(4), pp. 335–44.

Meisel, John B. Entry, Multiple-Brand Firms and Market Share Instability. *J. Ind. Econ.*, June 1981, *29*(4), pp. 375–84. [G: U.S.]

Meissner, Werner and Fassing, Werner. Concentration and Inflation. *Konjunkturpolitik*, 1981, *27*(4), pp. 247–59. [G: W. Germany]

Miller, Edward M. Large Firms are Good for Their Workers: Manufacturing Wages as a Function of Firm Size and Concentration. *Antitrust Bull.*, Spring 1981, *26*(1), pp. 145–54. [G: U.S.]

Miller, Edward M. What Do Labor Productivity Data Show about Economies of Scale: Reply. *Southern Econ. J.*, January 1981, *47*(3), pp. 847–51. [G: U.S.]

Millsaps, Steven W. and Ott, Mack. Information and Bidding Behavior by Major Oil Companies for Outer Continental Shelf Leases: Is the Joint Bidding Ban Justified? *Energy J.*, July 1981, *2*(3), pp. 71–90. [G: U.S.]

Monroe, Margaret. Conglomerate Mergers: Financial Theory and Evidence. In *Blair, R. D. and Lanzillotti, R. F., eds.*, 1981, pp. 113–35. [G: U.S.]

de Montaigu, Roland. Structural Changes in World Oil Market: Commentary. In *OPEC, Public Information Dept.*, 1981, pp. 133–39.

Moss, S. J. Technology and Market Structure in the Analysis of Exchange. *Managerial Dec. Econ.*, June 1981, *2*(2), pp. 106–20.

Mueller, Dennis C. The Case against Conglomerate Mergers. In *Blair, R. D. and Lanzillotti, R. F., eds.*, 1981, pp. 71–95. [G: OECD]

Mueller, Dennis C. and Cowling, Keith. The Social Costs of Monopoly Power Revisited. *Econ. J.*, September 1981, *91*(363), pp. 721–25. [G: U.S.; U.K.]

Muliere, Pietro. Sull'invarianza del rapporto di concentrazione R di gini. (On the Invariance of Gini's Concentration Ratio R. With English summary.) *Statistica*, April–June 1981, *41*(2), pp. 333–44.

Nagle, Thomas T. Do Advertising-Profitability Studies Really Show That Advertising Creates a Barrier to Entry? *J. Law Econ.*, October 1981, *24*(2), pp. 333–49. [G: U.S.]

Narver, John C. On the Unresponsiveness of Market Price. In *[Grether, E. T.]*, 1981, pp. 14–29.

Nelson, Phillip J. Consumer Information and Advertising. In *Galatin, M. and Leiter, R. D., eds.*, 1981, pp. 42–77. [G: U.S.]

Nelson, Richard R. Assessing Private Enterprise: An Exegesis of Tangled Doctrine. *Bell J. Econ. (See Rand J. Econ. after 4/85)*, Spring 1981, *12*(1), pp. 93–111.

Nelson, Richard R. Competition, Innovation, Productivity Growth, and Public Policy. In *Giersch, H., ed. (II)*, 1981, pp. 151–79.

Nelson, Richard R. X-Efficiency Theory, Productivity and Growth: Comments. In *Giersch, H., ed. (II)*, 1981, pp. 220.

Neumann, Manfred; Böbel, I. and Haid, A. Market Structure and the Labour Market in West German Industries—A Contribution towards Interpreting the Structure-Performance Relationship. *Z. Nationalökon.*, 1981, *41*(1–2), pp. 97–109. [G: W. Germany]

Newbery, David M. G. Oil Prices, Cartels, and the Problem of Dynamic Inconsistency. *Econ. J.*, September 1981, *91*(363), pp. 617–46.

Newfarmer, Richard S. and Marsh, Lawrence C. Foreign Ownership, Market Structure and Industrial Performance: Brazil's Electrical Industry. *J. Devel. Econ.*, February 1981, *8*(1), pp. 47–75. [G: Brazil]

O'Rourke, A. Desmond and Greig, W. Smith. Estimates of Consumer Loss Due to Monopoly in the U.S. Food-Manufacturing Industries: Comment. *Amer. J. Agr. Econ.*, May 1981, *63*(2), pp. 285–89. [G: U.S.]

Oi, Walter Y. Slack Capacity: Productive or Wasteful? *Amer. Econ. Rev.*, May 1981, *71*(2), pp. 64–69.

Ong, Nai-Pew. Target Pricing, Competition, and Growth. *J. Post Keynesian Econ.*, Fall 1981, *4*(1), pp. 101–16.

Onida, Fabrizio. Il commercio orizzontale rivisitato:

un commento. (Intra-industry Trade Revisited: A Comment. With English summary.) *Giorn. Econ.*, July–August 1981, *40*(7–8), pp. 493–500.

Ornstein, Stanley I. Antitrust Policy and Market Forces as Determinants of Industry Structure: Case Histories in Beer and Distilled Spirits. *Antitrust Bull.*, Summer 1981, *26*(2), pp. 281–313. [G: U.S.]

Ortiz, René G. 1982 Realities of the Oil Market: Can OPEC Retain Its Ability to Fix Oil Prices? *J. Energy Devel.*, Autumn 1981, *7*(1), pp. 13–15. [G: OPEC]

Osano, Hiroshi. Nonprice Competition in the Newspaper Industry, and the Incentive Effects of 'ABC BUSUU'. (In Japanese. With English summary.) *Osaka Econ. Pap.*, June 1981, *31*(1), pp. 10–20. [G: Japan]

Pacolet, Jozef and Verheirstraeten, Albert. Concentration and Economies of Scale in the Belgian Financial Sector. In *Verheirstraeten, A., ed.*, 1981, pp. 55–91. [G: Belgium]

Pagoulatos, Emilio and Sorensen, Robert. A Simultaneous Equation Analysis of Advertising, Concentration and Profitability. *Southern Econ. J.*, January 1981, *47*(3), pp. 728–41. [G: U.S.]

Pakravan, Karim. Exhaustible Resource Models and Predictions of Crude Oil Prices—Some Preliminary Results. *Energy Econ.*, July 1981, *3*(3), pp. 169–77. [G: OPEC]

Parker, Russell C. and Connor, John M. Estimates of Consumer Loss Due to Monopoly in the U.S. Food-Manufacturing Industries: Reply. *Amer. J. Agr. Econ.*, May 1981, *63*(2), pp. 293–97. [G: U.S.]

Paturel, Robert. Délimitation des concepts de croissance interne et de croissance externe. (Delimiting the Concepts of Internal versus External Growth. With English summary.) *Écon. Soc.*, October–November–December 1981, *15*(10–12), pp. 1393–1420.

Pennings, Johannes M. Strategically Interdependent Organizations. In *Nystrom, P. C. and Starbuck, W. H., eds., Vol. 1*, 1981, pp. 433–55.

Perroux, François. Commerce entre grandes firmes ou commerce entre nations? (With English summary.) *Écon. Appl.*, 1981, *34*(4), pp. 567–91.

Perry, Martin K. The Manager and the Competitive Firm's Supply. *Southern Econ. J.*, January 1981, *47*(3), pp. 630–39.

Ponssard, Jean-Pierre. Marchés publics et innovation: concurrence ou régulation? (The Governance of Contractual Relations: Competition or Regulation? With English summary.) *Revue Écon.*, January 1981, *32*(1), pp. 163–79. [G: France]

Poole, William. Monopoly Explanations of the Great Depression and Public Policies toward Business: Comments. In *Brunner, K., ed.*, 1981, pp. 208–10.

Prahalad, C. K. and Doz, Yves L. An Approach to Strategic Control in MNCs. *Sloan Manage. Rev.*, Summer 1981, *22*(4), pp. 5–13.

Prais, S. J. The Contribution of Mergers to Industrial Concentration: What Do We Know? [The Contribution of Mergers to Concentration Growth]. *J. Ind. Econ.*, March 1981, *29*(3), pp. 321–29. [G: U.K.]

Pras, Bernard. Essai d'analyse du comportement des responsables des grandes entreprises envers le risque. (An Attempt to Analyse the Risk Behavior of Major Firms Top Managers. With English summary.) *Écon. Soc.*, October–November–December 1981, *15*(10–12), pp. 1421–41. [G: U.S.]

Primeaux, Walter J., Jr. An Assessment of the Effect of Competition on Advertising Intensity. *Econ. Inquiry*, October 1981, *19*(4), pp. 613–25. [G: U.S.]

Pugel, Thomas A. The Determinants of Foreign Direct Investment: An Analysis of U.S. Manufacturing Industries. *Managerial Dec. Econ.*, December 1981, *2*(4), pp. 220–28. [G: U.S.]

Putterman, Louis. The Organization of Work: Comment. *J. Econ. Behav. Organ.*, September 1981, *2*(3), pp. 273–79.

Qualls, P. David. Cyclical Wage Flexibility, Inflation, and Industrial Structure: An Alternative View and Some Empirical Evidence. *J. Ind. Econ.*, June 1981, *29*(4), pp. 345–56. [G: U.S.]

Radice, H. K. Industrial Co-operation between Hungary and the West. In *Hare, P. G.; Radice, H. K. and Swain, N., eds.*, 1981, pp. 109–31. [G: Hungary; W. Europe; U.S.]

Rahl, James A. International Cartels and Their Regulation. In *Schachter, O. and Hellawell, R., eds.*, 1981, pp. 240–76. [G: EEC; U.S.]

Rappaport, Alfred. Mergers and Acquisitions. In *Altman, E. I., ed.*, 1981, pp. 33.3–24.

Reekie, W. Duncan. Innovation and Pricing in the Dutch Drug Industry. *Managerial Dec. Econ.*, March 1981, *2*(1), pp. 49–56. [G: Netherlands]

Reekie, W. Duncan. Price and Quality Competition in Drug Markets: Evidence from the United States and the Netherlands. In *Helms, R. B., ed.*, 1981, pp. 123–39. [G: U.S.; Netherlands]

Reid, Stan D. The Decision-Maker and Export Entry and Expansion. *J. Int. Bus. Stud.*, Fall 1981, *12*(2), pp. 101–12.

Reinganum, Jennifer F. Market Structure and the Diffusion of New Technology. *Bell J. Econ. (See Rand J. Econ. after 4/85)*, Autumn 1981, *12*(2), pp. 618–24.

Roberts, Gordon S. and Viscione, Jerry A. Captive Finance Subsidiaries and the M-Form Hypothesis. *Bell J. Econ. (See Rand J. Econ. after 4/85)*, Spring 1981, *12*(1), pp. 285–95. [G: U.S.]

Rockoff, Hugh. The Response of the Giant Corporations to Wage and Price Controls in World War II. *J. Econ. Hist.*, March 1981, *41*(1), pp. 123–28. [G: U.S.]

Rothschild, R. Cartel Problems: Note. *Amer. Econ. Rev.*, March 1981, *71*(1), pp. 179–81.

Round, David K. Concentration, Plant Size, and Multiple Plant Operations of Large Firms in Australian Manufacturing Industries. *Nebr. J. Econ. Bus.*, Winter 1981, *20*(1), pp. 19–29. [G: Australia]

Routamaa, Vesa. Toward a Systematic Understanding of the Relationship between Organizational Structure and Performance. *Liiketaloudellinen Aikak.*, 1981, *30*(4), pp. 422–34. [G: Finland]

Savary, Julien. Taille et multinationalisation des entreprises françaises. (Size of the French Corporations and Their Foreign Production. With English summary.) *Rev. Econ. Ind.*, 1st Trimester 1981, (15), pp. 78–91. [G: France]

Scheps, Howard Barry. Effects of Concentration on the Wage–Sales Ratio. *Amer. Econ.*, Fall 1981, 25(2), pp. 55–58.

Schifrin, Leonard. The Effect of Patent Expiration on the Market Position of Drugs: Comment. In *Helms, R. B., ed.*, 1981, pp. 166–70. [G: U.S.]

Schmalensee, Richard. The Conglomerate Corporation: Remarks. In *Blair, R. D. and Lanzillotti, R. F., eds.*, 1981, pp. 365–68. [G: U.S.]

Schmitz, Andrew and McCalla, Alex F. Analysis of Imperfections in International Trade: The Case of Grain Export Cartels. In *McCalla, A. F. and Josling, T. E., eds.*, 1981, pp. 69–86.

Schönwitz, Dietrich. Aggregierte Unternehmenskonzentration und privatwirtschaftliche Wirtschaftslenkung. (Aggregate Concentration and Private Coordination of Economic Processes. With English summary.) *Konjunkturpolitik*, 1981, 27(6), pp. 311–27. [G: W. Germany]

Schönwitz, Dietrich. Zunehmende Unternehmenskonzentration in der Bundesrepublik Deutschland: Zur bankbetrieblichen Bedeutung des dritten Hauptgutachtens der Monopolkommission. (Increasing Business Concentration in the Federal Republic of Germany: On the Significance of the Third Major Opinion of the Monopoly Commission for Banking. With English summary.) *Kredit Kapital*, 1981, 14(2), pp. 222–35. [G: W. Germany]

Schönwitz, Dietrich and Weber, Hans-Jürgen. Indirekte personelle Verflechtungen zwischen Grossunternehmen über Organe der Geschäftsführungskontrolle. (Indirect Interlocking Directorates among German Major Firms. With English summary.) *Konjunkturpolitik*, 1981, 27(1), pp. 12–37. [G: W. Germany]

Schweitzer, Iván. Some Interrelations between Enterprise Organization and the Economic Mechanism in Hungary. *Acta Oecon.*, 1981, 27(3–4), pp. 289–300. [G: Hungary]

Scott, John T. The Pure Capital-Cost Barrier to Entry. *Rev. Econ. Statist.*, August 1981, 63(3), pp. 444–46.

Shaanan, Joseph. The Adoption of Limit Pricing by the Courts: Paradoxical Inferences. *Antitrust Bull.*, Fall 1981, 26(3), pp. 541–65. [G: U.S.]

Shaked, Avner and Sutton, John. Heterogeneous Consumers and Product Differentiation in a Market for Professional Services. *Europ. Econ. Rev.*, February 1981, 15(2), pp. 159–77.

Shaked, Avner and Sutton, John. The Self-Regulating Profession. *Rev. Econ. Stud.*, April 1981, 48(2), pp. 217–34.

Sharkey, William W. Existence of Sustainable Prices for Natural Monopoly Outputs. *Bell J. Econ. (See Rand J. Econ. after 4/85)*, Spring 1981, 12(1), pp. 144–54.

Shipley, David D. Pricing Objectives in British Manufacturing Industry. *J. Ind. Econ.*, June 1981, 29(4), pp. 429–43. [G: U.K.]

Siegfried, John J. The Effects of Conglomerate Mergers on Political Democracy: A Survey. In *Blair, R. D. and Lanzillotti, R. F., eds.*, 1981, pp. 25–52. [G: U.S.]

Siegfried, John J. and Wheeler, Edwin H. Cost Efficiency and Monopoly Power: A Survey. *Quart. Rev. Econ. Bus.*, Spring 1981, 21(1), pp. 25–46.

Silberston, Aubrey. Factors Affecting the Growth of the Firm—Theory and Practice. In *Currie, D.; Peel, D. and Peters, W., eds.*, 1981, pp. 329–56. [G: U.K.]

Smith, Richard L., II. Efficiency Gains from Strategic Investment. *J. Ind. Econ.*, September 1981, 30(1), pp. 1–23. [G: U.S.]

Smith, Robert E. Economic and Political Characteristics of Cartel and Cartel-like Practices. In *Schachter, O. and Hellawell, R., eds.*, 1981, pp. 179–239.

Spence, A. Michael. The Learning Curve and Competition. *Bell J. Econ. (See Rand J. Econ. after 4/85)*, Spring 1981, 12(1), pp. 49–70.

Spulber, Daniel F. Capacity, Output, and Sequential Entry. *Amer. Econ. Rev.*, June 1981, 71(3), pp. 503–14.

Statman, Meir. The Effect of Patent Expiration on the Market Position of Drugs. In *Helms, R. B., ed.*, 1981, pp. 140–51. [G: U.S.]

Steele, Henry and Daly, George. Vertical Divestiture of the US Oil Industry and US–OPEC Relations. *Energy Econ.*, January 1981, 3(1), pp. 43–56. [G: U.S.; OPEC]

Steiner, Peter O. The Conglomerate Corporation: Remarks. In *Blair, R. D. and Lanzillotti, R. F., eds.*, 1981, pp. 369–71. [G: U.S.]

Stiglitz, Joseph E. Ownership, Control, and Efficient Markets: Some Paradoxes in the Theory of Capital Markets. In *[Nelson, J. R.]*, 1981, pp. 311–40.

Stiglitz, Joseph E. and Dasgupta, Partha. Market Structure and Resource Extraction under Uncertainty. *Scand. J. Econ.*, 1981, 83(2), pp. 318–33.

Stoll, Hans R. Revolution in the Regulation of Securities Markets: An Examination of the Effects of Increased Competition. In *Weiss, L. W. and Klass, M. W., eds.*, 1981, pp. 12–52. [G: U.S.]

Sumner, Daniel A. Measurement of Monopoly Behavior: An Application to the Cigarette Industry. *J. Polit. Econ.*, October 1981, 89(5), pp. 1010–19. [G: U.S.]

Sutton, C. J. Merger Cycles: An Exploratory Discussion. *Brit. Rev. Econ. Issues*, Spring 1981, 2(8), pp. 89–97. [G: U.K.]

Swan, Peter L. Durability and Taxes: Market Structure and Quasi-Capital Market Distortion. *Econometrica*, March 1981, 49(2), pp. 425–35.

Tanaka, Shigekazu. The Impact of Protection and Concentration on the Labour Intensity of U.K. Industries: Comment. *Weltwirtsch. Arch.*, 1981, 117(2), pp. 380–82. [G: U.K.]

Tarondeau, Jean-Claude. Analyse des couples produits-processus de production. (Analysis of Product/Production Process Relationships. With English summary.) *Écon. Soc.*, October–November–December 1981, 15(10–12), pp. 1671–88.

Taylor, R. G. Joint Ventures: Panel Presentation. In *Federal Home Loan Bank of San Francisco.*, 1981, pp. 355–61. [G: U.S.]

Teece, David J. Internal Organization and Economic Performance: An Empirical Analysis of the Profitability of Principal Firms. *J. Ind. Econ.*, December 1981, *30*(2), pp. 173–99. **[G: U.S.]**

Teece, David J. The Multinational Enterprise: Market Failure and Market Power Considerations. *Sloan Manage. Rev.*, Spring 1981, *22*(3), pp. 3–17.

Thiétart, Raymond-Alain. La stratégie: aujourd'hui et demain. (Strategy Today and Tomorrow. With English summary.) *Écon. Soc.*, October–November–December 1981, *15*(10–12), pp. 1443–54.

Thomas, Christopher R. A Theory of the Vertically Integrated Input Monopolist with a Depletion Allowance. *Southern Econ. J.*, January 1981, *47*(3), pp. 799–804.

Thompson, Donald N. The Experience Curve Effect on Costs and Prices: Implications for Public Policy. In *[Grether, E. T.]*, 1981, pp. 60–80. **[G: U.S.; Canada; Japan; U.K.]**

Thompson, R. S. Internal Organization and Profit: A Note [Internal Organization and Profit: An Empirical Analysis of Large UK Companies]. *J. Ind. Econ.*, December 1981, *30*(2), pp. 201–11. **[G: U.K.]**

Tsurumi, Yoshi. The Japanese Corporation. In *Richardson, B. M. and Ueda, T., eds.*, 1981, pp. 5–14. **[G: Japan]**

Turner, Donald. The Need for Rules and the Difficulty in Formulating Them. In *[Grether, E. T.]*, 1981, pp. 7–13.

Tyabji, Nasir. Stratification of Indian Business. In *Bagchi, A. K. and Banerjee, N., eds.*, 1981, pp. 149–71. **[G: India]**

Urban, Sabine. L'organisation de la compétitivité internationale en France et en R.F.A. (With English summary.) *Écon. Appl.*, 1981, *34*(4), pp. 639–66. **[G: France; W. Germany]**

Vander Weele, Ray. Is This Merger Right for You? *Manage. Account.*, March 1981, *62*(9), pp. 35–39, 47.

Varga, György. Management—In a Fast Changing Environment. *Acta Oecon.*, 1981, *27*(3–4), pp. 301–26. **[G: Hungary]**

Wahlroos, Björn. Advertising and Market Structure: Evidence for Finland. *Liiketaloudellinen Aikak.*, 1981, *30*(3), pp. 296–308. **[G: Finland]**

Wahlroos, Björn. On the Economics of Multiplant Operation: Some Concepts and an Example. *J. Ind. Econ.*, March 1981, *29*(3), pp. 231–45. **[G: N. America; U.K.; W. Europe; Japan; India]**

Walter, Ingo. Control of Terms and Conditions for International Transfers of Technology to Developing Countries: Commentary. In *Schachter, O. and Hellawell, R., eds.*, 1981, pp. 143–59. **[G: U.S.; Japan]**

Waterson, Michael. On the Definition and Meaning of Barriers to Entry. *Antitrust Bull.*, Fall 1981, *26*(3), pp. 521–39.

Weiss, Leo A. Start-up Businesses: A Comparison of Performances. *Sloan Manage. Rev.*, Fall 1981, *23*(1), pp. 37–53. **[G: U.S.]**

Wells, Louis T., Jr. Control of Terms and Conditions for International Transfers of Technology to Developing Countries: Commentary. In *Schachter, O. and Hellawell, R., eds.*, 1981, pp. 160–64. **[G: U.S.; Japan]**

Werden, Gregory J. The Use and Misuse of Shipments Data in Defining Geographic Markets [The Problem of Geographic Market Definition in Antimerger Suits]. *Antitrust Bull.*, Winter 1981, *26*(4), pp. 719–37. **[G: U.S.]**

West, Douglas S. Tests of Two Locational Implications of a Theory of Market Pre-Emption. *Can. J. Econ.*, May 1981, *14*(2), pp. 313–26. **[G: Canada]**

Westfield, Fred M. Vertical Integration: Does Product Price Rise or Fall? *Amer. Econ. Rev.*, June 1981, *71*(3), pp. 334–46.

White, Alice P. The Dominant Firm Structure: Theoretical Myth or Empirical Reality? *Southern Econ. J.*, October 1981, *48*(2), pp. 427–36. **[G: U.S.]**

White, Lawrence J. How Organizations use Exchange Media and Agreements. In *Nystrom, P. C. and Starbuck, W. H., eds., Vol. 2*, 1981, pp. 440–53. **[G: U.S.]**

White, Lawrence J. On Measuring Aggregate Concentration: A Reply [What Has Been Happening to Aggregate Concentration in the United States?]. *J. Ind. Econ.*, December 1981, *30*(2), pp. 223–24. **[G: U.S.]**

White, Lawrence J. Vertical Restraints in Antitrust Law: A Coherent Model. *Antitrust Bull.*, Summer 1981, *26*(2), pp. 327–45. **[G: U.S.]**

White, Lawrence J. What Has Been Happening to Aggregate Concentration in the United States? *J. Ind. Econ.*, March 1981, *29*(3), pp. 223–30. **[G: U.S.]**

Wiggins, Steven N. A Theoretical Analysis of Conglomerate Mergers. In *Blair, R. D. and Lanzillotti, R. F., eds.*, 1981, pp. 53–70.

Williamson, Oliver E. On the Nature of the Firm: Some Recent Developments. *Z. ges. Staatswiss.*, December 1981, *137*(4), pp. 675–80.

Williamson, Oliver E. The Modern Corporation: Origins, Evolution, Attributes. *J. Econ. Lit.*, December 1981, *19*(4), pp. 1537–68.

Williamson, Oliver E. The Organization of Work: Reply. *J. Econ. Behav. Organ.*, September 1981, *2*(3), pp. 281–83.

Wind, Yoram and Douglas, Susan. International Portfolio Analysis and Strategy: The Challenge of the 80s. *J. Int. Bus. Stud.*, Fall 1981, *12*(2), pp. 69–82.

Winters, L. A. Price Adjustment and Market Structure: A Comment. *Econ. J.*, December 1981, *91*(364), pp. 1026–30. **[G: U.K.]**

612 Public Policy Toward Monopoly and Competition

6120 Public Policy Toward Monopoly and Competition

Adams, John. Franchising and Antitrust in the United Kingdom and European Community. *Antitrust Bull.*, Winter 1981, *26*(4), pp. 815–37. **[G: EEC]**

Aduddell, Robert M. and Cain, Louis P. Public Policy toward "The Greatest Trust in the World." *Bus. Hist. Rev.*, Summer 1981, *55*(2), pp. 217–42. **[G: U.S.]**

Aduddell, Robert M. and Cain, Louis P. The Consent Decree in the Meatpacking Industry, 1920–1956. *Bus. Hist. Rev.*, Autumn 1981, *55*(3), pp. 359–78. [G: U.S.]

Aguilar, Enrique. Restrictive Business Practices and International Controls on Transfer of Technology: Comment. In *Sagafi-nejad, T.; Moxon, R. W. and Perlmutter, H. V., eds.*, 1981, pp. 205–11. [G: Mexico]

Allen, Robert F. Oligopoly, Tacit Collusion and the Problem of Proof under the Antitrust Laws. *Antitrust Bull.*, Fall 1981, *26*(3), pp. 487–506. [G: U.S.]

Ariga, Michiko. Restrictive Business Practices and International Controls on Transfer of Technology. In *Sagafi-nejad, T.; Moxon, R. W. and Perlmutter, H. V., eds.*, 1981, pp. 177–200. [G: Japan]

Armentano, D. T. The Petroleum Industry: A Historical Study in Power. *Cato J.*, Spring 1981, *1*(1), pp. 53–85. [G: U.S.]

Artle, Roland A. Competitive Behavior: Comments. In *[Grether, E. T.]*, 1981, pp. 128–30.

Atkeson, Timothy. The Seeking of a World Competition Code: Quixotic Quest? Commentary. In *Schachter, O. and Hellawell, R., eds.*, 1981, pp. 416–21.

Bagchi, Amiya Kumar and Dasgupta, Subhendu. Imported Technology and the Legal Process. In *Bagchi, A. K. and Banerjee, N., eds.*, 1981, pp. 393–416. [G: India]

Bailey, Elizabeth E. Contestability and the Design of Regulatory and Antitrust Policy. *Amer. Econ. Rev.*, May 1981, *71*(2), pp. 178–83. [G: U.S.]

Beck, Roger L. Competition for Patent Monopolies. In *Zerbe, R. O., Jr., ed.*, 1981, pp. 91–110.

Bellico, Russell. An Indictment of Monopoly Power. *Econ. Forum*, Summer 1981, *12*(1), pp. 51–64. [G: U.S.]

Bethell, Tom. Breakfastgate: The FTC vs. the Cereal Companies. *Policy Rev.*, Spring 1981, (16), pp. 13–32. [G: U.S.]

Block, Michael Kent and Nold, Frederick Carl. The Deterrent Effect of Antitrust Enforcement. *J. Polit. Econ.*, June 1981, *89*(3), pp. 429–45. [G: U.S.]

Bloom, L. H. Analysis of Restrictive Business Practices by Transnational Corporations and Their Impact on Trade and Development: Commentary. In *Schachter, O. and Hellawell, R., eds.*, 1981, pp. 22–26.

Bock, Betty. The Conglomerate Corporation: Remarks. In *Blair, R. D. and Lanzillotti, R. F., eds.*, 1981, pp. 349–58. [G: U.S.]

Breit, William and Elzinga, Kenneth G. Information for Antitrust and Business Activity: Line-of-Business Reporting. In *Clarkson, K. W. and Muris, T. J., eds.*, 1981, pp. 98–120. [G: U.S.]

Brodley, Joseph F. In Defense of Presumptive Rules: An Approach to Legal Rulemaking for Conglomerate Mergers. In *Blair, R. D. and Lanzillotti, R. F., eds.*, 1981, pp. 249–81. [G: U.S.]

Cable, John. "Merger Control Remains the Priority": The Third Report of the German Monopolies Commission: A Review Article. *Z. ges. Staatswiss.*, June 1981, *137*(2), pp. 302–08.

Carey, Robin. The Toehold Acquisition Doctrine: Economic Theory and Judicial Application. In *Sirkin, G., ed.*, 1981, pp. 195–240. [G: U.S.]

Carstensen, Peter C. Competition Policy for an Economically Integrated North America. *Law Contemp. Probl.*, Summer 1981, *44*(3), pp. 81–103. [G: U.S.; Canada; Mexico]

Chatov, Robert. Cooperation between Government and Business. In *Nystrom, P. C. and Starbuck, W. H., eds., Vol. 1*, 1981, pp. 487–502. [G: U.S.]

Clarkson, Kenneth W. The Federal Trade Commission since 1970: Economic Regulation and Bureaucratic Behavior: Executive Constraints. In *Clarkson, K. W. and Muris, T. J., eds.*, 1981, pp. 50–58. [G: U.S.]

Clarkson, Kenneth W. The Federal Trade Commission since 1970: Economic Regulation and Bureaucratic Behavior: Legislative Constraints. In *Clarkson, K. W. and Muris, T. J., eds.*, 1981, pp. 18–34. [G: U.S.]

Clarkson, Kenneth W. and Muris, Timothy J. The Federal Trade Commission since 1970: Economic Regulation and Bureaucratic Behavior: Commission Performance, Incentives, and Behavior. In *Clarkson, K. W. and Muris, T. J., eds.*, 1981, pp. 280–306. [G: U.S.]

Clarkson, Kenneth W.; Muris, Timothy J. and Martin, Donald L. Exclusionary Practices: Shopping Center Restrictive Covenants. In *Clarkson, K. W. and Muris, T. J., eds.*, 1981, pp. 141–60. [G: U.S.]

Conant, Michael. The Paramount Decrees Reconsidered. *Law Contemp. Probl.*, Autumn 1981, *44*(4), pp. 79–107. [G: U.S.]

Cooper, Edward H. The Case against a New Presumptive Approach to Conglomerate Mergers. In *Blair, R. D. and Lanzillotti, R. F., eds.*, 1981, pp. 283–345. [G: U.S.]

Craver, Theodore F. The Conglomerate Corporation: Remarks. In *Blair, R. D. and Lanzillotti, R. F., eds.*, 1981, pp. 359–63. [G: U.S.]

Dalton, James A. and Esposito, Louis. The Traditional and Strategy Formulation Models of Industry Analysis: Implications for Public Policy. *Eastern Econ. J.*, January 1981, *7*(1), pp. 15–25.

Davidow, Joel. International Antitrust Codes: The Post-Acceptance Phase. *Antitrust Bull.*, Fall 1981, *26*(3), pp. 567–91. [G: U.N.]

Davidow, Joel. The Seeking of a World Competition Code: Quixotic Quest? In *Schachter, O. and Hellawell, R., eds.*, 1981, pp. 361–415.

Dirlam, Joel B. Marginal Cost Pricing Tests for Predation: Naive Welfare Economics and Public Policy. *Antitrust Bull.*, Winter 1981, *26*(4), pp. 769–814. [G: U.S.]

Dirlam, Joel B. Predatory Pricing and Antitrust Policy: Economic Theory and the Quest for Certainty. In *[Nelson, J. R.]*, 1981, pp. 197–222. [G: U.S.]

Eckard, E. Woodrow, Jr. Antitrust and the Concentration Doctrine: A Rejoinder. *Bus. Econ.*, March 1981, *16*(2), pp. 22–25.

Einhorn, Henry A.; Rosenthal, H. Arthur and Smith, William Paul. Merger Litigation: Two Strategic Alternatives. *Antitrust Bull.*, Winter 1981, *26*(4), pp. 669–96. [G: U.S.]

Ekelund, Robert B., Jr. and Hébert, Robert F. The Proto-History of Franchise Bidding. *Southern Econ. J.*, October 1981, *48*(2), pp. 464–74.

Elzinga, Kenneth G. Defining Geographic Market Boundaries [The Problem of Geographic Market Definition in Antimerger Suits]. *Antitrust Bull.*, Winter 1981, *26*(4), pp. 739–52. **[G: U.S.]**

Farrar, Donald E. and Girton, Lance. Institutional Investors and Concentration of Financial Power: Berle and Means Revisited. *J. Finance*, May 1981, *36*(2), pp. 369–81. **[G: U.S.]**

Faustman, David F. and Goldman, Roger S. Criminal Prosecution for Vertical Price Fixing: Antitrust Division Aiming for the Waterline. *Antitrust Bull.*, Summer 1981, *26*(2), pp. 227–46. **[G: U.S.]**

Finsinger, Jörg and Vogelsang, Ingo. Alternative Institutional Frameworks for Price Incentive Mechanism. *Kyklos*, 1981, *34*(3), pp. 388–404.

Fitzpatrick, Peter. Two Legal Models in the Control of Transfer Pricing. In *Murray, R., ed.*, 1981, pp. 197–206.

Flynn, John J. Monopolization under the Sherman Act: The Third Wave and Beyond. *Antitrust Bull.*, Spring 1981, *26*(1), pp. 1–131. **[G: U.S.]**

Gill, David G. International Cartels and Their Regulation: Commentary. In *Schachter, O. and Hellawell, R., eds.*, 1981, pp. 277–82. **[G: EEC; U.S.]**

Glass, Walter. Restrictive Business Practices Affecting Transfer of Technology: Commentary. In *Schachter, O. and Hellawell, R., eds.*, 1981, pp. 139–42. **[G: U.S.; Japan]**

Goetz, Charles J. and Schwartz, Warren F. Industry Structure Investigation: Xerox's Multiple Patents and Competition. In *Clarkson, K. W. and Muris, T. J., eds.*, 1981, pp. 121–40. **[G: U.S.]**

Gorecki, Paul K. and Henderson, Ida. Compulsory Patent Licensing of Drugs in Canada: A Comment on the Debate. *Can. Public Policy*, Autumn 1981, *7*(4), pp. 559–68. **[G: Canada]**

Grant, R. M. Recent Developments in the Control of Price Discrimination in Countries outside North America. *Antitrust Bull.*, Fall 1981, *26*(3), pp. 593–632. **[G: Australia; W. Germany; France; Ireland]**

Green, C. Canadian Competition Policy at a Crossroads. *Can. Public Policy*, Summer 1981, *7*(3), pp. 418–32. **[G: Canada]**

Greenhill, C. R. and Herbolzheimer, E. O. Control of Transfer Prices in International Transactions: The Restrictive Business Practices Approach. In *Murray, R., ed.*, 1981, pp. 185–94. **[G: LDCs; MDCs]**

Grether, David M.; Isaac, R. Mark and Plott, Charles R. The Allocation of Landing Rights by Unanimity among Competitors. *Amer. Econ. Rev.*, May 1981, *71*(2), pp. 166–71. **[G: U.S.]**

Havighurst, Clark C. and Hackbarth, Glenn M. Enforcing the Rules of Free Enterprise in an Imperfect Market: The Case of Individual Practice Associations. In *Olson, M., ed.*, 1981, pp. 377–406.

Hays, Samuel P. Political Choice in Regulatory Administration. In *McCraw, T. K., ed.*, 1981, pp. 124–54.

Helleiner, Gerald K. Analysis of Restrictive Business Practices by Transnational Corporations and Their Impact on Trade and Development: Commentary. In *Schachter, O. and Hellawell, R., eds.*, 1981, pp. 27–33.

Hilke, John and Nelson, Philip. Antitrust Policy and the Market Concentration Doctrine: A Response. *Bus. Econ.*, March 1981, *16*(2), pp. 17–21.

Horowitz, Ira. Market Definition in Antitrust Analysis: A Regression-Based Approach. *Southern Econ. J.*, July 1981, *48*(1), pp. 1–16.

Horowitz, Ira. The Perceived Potential Competitor: Antitrust Sinner or Saint? *Antitrust Bull.*, Summer 1981, *26*(2), pp. 247–79. **[G: U.S.]**

Horowitz, Ira. The Relevance of the Relevant Market in a Section 7 Analysis of Conglomerate Mergers (Whatever Those Are). In *Blair, R. D. and Lanzillotti, R. F., eds.*, 1981, pp. 137–61. **[G: U.S.]**

Jenny, F. From Price Controls to Competition Policy in France: The Uneasy Alliance of Economical and Political Considerations. *Ann. Pub. Co-op. Econ.*, December 1981, *52*(4), pp. 477–90. **[G: France]**

Joelson, Mark R. Merger Control in Western Europe: National and International Aspects: Commentary. In *Schachter, O. and Hellawell, R., eds.*, 1981, pp. 335–43. **[G: U.S.]**

Kaikati, Jack G. The Anti-Export Policy of the U.S. *Calif. Manage. Rev.*, Spring 1981, *23*(3), pp. 5–19. **[G: U.S.]**

Kareken, John H. Commercial Banking as a Line of Commerce: An Appraisal. *Fed. Res. Bank Minn. Rev.*, Winter 1981, *5*(1), pp. 7–13. **[G: U.S.]**

Keller, Morton. The Pluralist State: American Economic Regulation in Comparative Perspective, 1900–1930. In *McCraw, T. K., ed.*, 1981, pp. 56–94. **[G: U.S.]**

Keyes, Lucile S. A Non-Paretian Approach to Market Regulation. *J. Post Keynesian Econ.*, Spring 1981, *3*(3), pp. 440–51.

Klebaner, Benjamin J. The Toehold Acquisition Doctrine: Comments. In *Sirkin, G., ed.*, 1981, pp. 241–56. **[G: U.S.]**

Lefever, J. Timothy. Predatory Pricing Rules: A Comment on Williamson's Output Restriction Rule [Predatory Pricing: A Strategic and Welfare Analysis]. *Yale Law J.*, June 1981, *90*(7), pp. 1639–45. **[G: U.S.]**

Liebeler, Wesley J. Bureau of Competition: Antitrust Enforcement Activities. In *Clarkson, K. W. and Muris, T. J., eds.*, 1981, pp. 65–97. **[G: U.S.]**

Lindenberg, Eric B. and Ross, Stephen A. Tobin's q Ratio and Industrial Organization. *J. Bus.*, January 1981, *54*(1), pp. 1–32. **[G: U.S.]**

Littlechild, S. C. Misleading Calculations of the Social Costs of Monopoly Power. *Econ. J.*, June 1981, *91*(362), pp. 348–63. **[G: U.S.; U.K.]**

Luksetich, William A. Advertising Intensity and Antitrust Activity. *J. Behav. Econ.*, Summer 1981, *10*(1), pp. 101–09. **[G: U.S.]**

Lurie, Howard R. The Burger Court and Conglomerate Mergers. In *Blair, R. D. and Lanzillotti, R. F., eds.*, 1981, pp. 195–229. **[G: U.S.]**

Lynk, William J. Regulatory Control of the Membership of Corporate Boards of Directors: The Blue Shield Case. *J. Law Econ.*, April 1981, *24*(1), pp. 159–73. [G: U.S.]

Mandelker, Daniel R. Commentary on Legal Aspects of Controlling Shopping Center Competition. In *Sternlieb, G. and Hughes, J. W., eds.*, 1981, pp. 109–12. [G: U.S.]

Markert, Kurt. Merger Control in Western Europe: National and International Aspects. In *Schachter, O. and Hellawell, R., eds.*, 1981, pp. 293–334. [G: EEC]

McCraw, Thomas K. Rethinking the Trust Question. In *McCraw, T. K., ed.*, 1981, pp. 1–55. [G: U.S.]

McKie, James W. An Antimonopoly Policy for North America: Opportunities and Problems. *Law Contemp. Probl.*, Summer 1981, *44*(3), pp. 105–30. [G: Mexico; Canada; U.S.]

Meehan, James W., Jr. and Larner, Robert J. A Proposed Rule of Reason for Vertical Restraints on Competition. *Antitrust Bull.*, Summer 1981, *26*(2), pp. 195–225. [G: U.S.]

Millsaps, Steven W. and Ott, Mack. Information and Bidding Behavior by Major Oil Companies for Outer Continental Shelf Leases: Is the Joint Bidding Ban Justified? *Energy J.*, July 1981, *2*(3), pp. 71–90. [G: U.S.]

Mueller, W. F. Merger Control in Western Europe: National and International Aspects: Commentary. In *Schachter, O. and Hellawell, R., eds.*, 1981, pp. 344–51. [G: EEC]

Muris, Timothy J. The Federal Trade Commission since 1970: Economic Regulation and Bureaucratic Behavior: What Can be Done? In *Clarkson, K. W. and Muris, T. J., eds.*, 1981, pp. 307–15. [G: U.S.]

Muris, Timothy J. The Federal Trade Commission since 1970: Economic Regulation and Bureaucratic Behavior: Judicial Constraints. In *Clarkson, K. W. and Muris, T. J., eds.*, 1981, pp. 35–49. [G: U.S.]

Muris, Timothy J. The Federal Trade Commission since 1970: Economic Regulation and Bureaucratic Behavior: Statutory Powers. In *Clarkson, K. W. and Muris, T. J., eds.*, 1981, pp. 13–17. [G: U.S.]

Muris, Timothy J. and Clarkson, Kenneth W. The Federal Trade Commission since 1970: Economic Regulation and Bureaucratic Behavior: Introduction. In *Clarkson, K. W. and Muris, T. J., eds.*, 1981, pp. 1–7. [G: U.S.]

Nakao, Takeo. The Effects of Demonopolization on the Aggregate Stock of Capital and the Welfare of a Society. *Southern Econ. J.*, October 1981, *48*(2), pp. 358–64.

Noll, Roger G. and Joskow, Paul L. Regulation in Theory and Practice: An Overview. In *Fromm, G., ed.*, 1981, pp. 1–65. [G: U.S.]

Norman, Neville R. Policies towards Prices—The Influence of Regulation. In *Hancock, K., ed.*, 1981, pp. 349–69. [G: Australia]

Ordover, Janusz A. and Weiss, Andrew. Information and the Law: Evaluating Legal Restrictions on Competitive Contracts. *Amer. Econ. Rev.*, May 1981, *71*(2), pp. 399–404.

Ordover, Janusz A. and Willig, Robert D. An Economic Definition of Predation: Pricing and Product Innovation. *Yale Law J.*, November 1981, *91*(1), pp. 8–53. [G: U.S.]

Ornstein, Stanley I. Antitrust Policy and Market Forces as Determinants of Industry Structure: Case Histories in Beer and Distilled Spirits. *Antitrust Bull.*, Summer 1981, *26*(2), pp. 281–313. [G: U.S.]

Pass, Christopher L. and Sparkes, J. R. Control of Tacit Collusion in Britain. *J. World Trade Law*, November–December 1981, *15*(6), pp. 521–33. [G: U.K.]

Perrakis, Stylianos and Zerbinis, John. An Empirical Analysis of Monopoly Regulation under Uncertainty. *Appl. Econ.*, March 1981, *13*(1), pp. 109–25. [G: U.S.]

Phillips, Almarin. Predation and Antitrust Rules: The Complications When Quality is Considered. In *[Grether, E. T.]*, 1981, pp. 113–27.

Phillips, Almarin. Theory and Practice in Public Utility Regulation: The Case of Telecommunications. In *[Nelson, J. R.]*, 1981, pp. 181–96. [G: U.S.]

Preston, Lee E. Predatory Marketing. In *[Grether, E. T.]*, 1981, pp. 81–112.

Rahl, James A. International Cartels and Their Regulation. In *Schachter, O. and Hellawell, R., eds.*, 1981, pp. 240–76. [G: EEC; U.S.]

Reschenthaler, G. B. and Stanbury, W. T. Recent Conspiracy Decisions in Canada: New Legislation Needed. *Antitrust Bull.*, Winter 1981, *26*(4), pp. 839–69. [G: Canada]

Rice, Edward M. and Ulen, Thomas S. Rent-Seeking and Welfare Loss. In *Zerbe, R. O., Jr., ed.*, 1981, pp. 53–65.

Riegel, Quentin. The FTC in the 1980's: An Analysis of the FTC Improvements Act of 1980. *Antitrust Bull.*, Fall 1981, *26*(3), pp. 449–86. [G: U.S.]

Rubin, Stephen. Antitrust Presumptions: Some History about Prophecy. In *Blair, R. D. and Lanzillotti, R. F., eds.*, 1981, pp. 231–48. [G: U.S.]

Scherer, F. M. Regulatory Dynamics and Economic Growth. In *Wachter, M. L. and Wachter, S. M., eds.*, 1981, pp. 289–320. [G: U.S.]

Schlag, Pierre. A Theoretical Analysis of Knowhow Licensing under EEC Competition Law: Territorial Restrictions. *Antitrust Bull.*, Summer 1981, *26*(2), pp. 347–445. [G: EEC]

Schmalensee, Richard. The Conglomerate Corporation: Remarks. In *Blair, R. D. and Lanzillotti, R. F., eds.*, 1981, pp. 365–68. [G: U.S.]

Schmidt, Ingo. Price Control in Germany. *Ann. Pub. Co-op. Econ.*, December 1981, *52*(4), pp. 491–503. [G: W. Germany]

Shaanan, Joseph. The Adoption of Limit Pricing by the Courts: Paradoxical Inferences. *Antitrust Bull.*, Fall 1981, *26*(3), pp. 541–65. [G: U.S.]

Smiley, Robert. The Effect of State Securities Statutes on Tender Offer Activity. *Econ. Inquiry*, July 1981, *19*(3), pp. 426–35.

Steiner, Peter O. The Conglomerate Corporation: Remarks. In *Blair, R. D. and Lanzillotti, R. F., eds.*, 1981, pp. 369–71. [G: U.S.]

Stiglitz, Joseph E. Potential Competition May Reduce Welfare. *Amer. Econ. Rev.*, May 1981, *71*(2), pp. 184–89.

Stockmayer, Albrecht. Mining Ventures in Developing Countries: Investor Consortia: Antitrust Considerations. In *Schanze, E., et al.*, 1981, pp. 236–59. [G: U.S.; EEC]

Thomas, R. Keith. The New U.S. Antidumping Law: Some Advice to Exporters. *J. World Trade Law*, July–August 1981, *15*(4), pp. 323–36. [G: U.S.]

Thompson, Dennis. West Germany: Monopolies Commission. *J. World Trade Law*, March–April 1981, *15*(2), pp. 159–73. [G: W. Germany]

Tiedemann, K. Antitrust Law and Criminal Law Policy in Western Europe. In *Leigh, L. H., ed.*, 1981, pp. 39–56. [G: W. Europe]

Timberg, Sigmund. Restrictive Business Practices in the International Transfer and Diffusion of Technology. In *Schachter, O. and Hellawell, R., eds.*, 1981, pp. 84–138.

Tinic, S. M. Impact of Regulation on Economic Behavior: Discussion. *J. Finance*, May 1981, *36*(2), pp. 395–97.

Turner, R. W. and Pepperell, H. C. Barriers to Entry: Antitrust's Search for a New Look. *Calif. Manage. Rev.*, Spring 1981, *23*(3), pp. 29–40. [G: U.S.]

Wang, N. T. Analysis of Restrictive Business Practices by Transnational Corporations and Their Impact on Trade and Development. In *Schachter, O. and Hellawell, R., eds.*, 1981, pp. 3–21.

Weaver, Clifford L. and Hejna, David T. Antitrust Liability and Commercial Zoning Litigation. In *Sternlieb, G. and Hughes, J. W., eds.*, 1981, pp. 113–28.

von Weizsäcker, Carl Christian. Rechte und Verhältnisse in der Modernen Wirtschaftslehre. (Rights and Relations in Modern Economic Theory. With English summary.) *Kyklos*, 1981, *34*(3), pp. 345–76. [G: U.S.]

Werden, Gregory J. The Use and Misuse of Shipments Data in Defining Geographic Markets [The Problem of Geographic Market Definition in Antimerger Suits]. *Antitrust Bull.*, Winter 1981, *26*(4), pp. 719–37. [G: U.S.]

Wex, Samuel. The Seeking of a World Competition Code: Quixotic Quest? Commentary. In *Schachter, O. and Hellawell, R., eds.*, 1981, pp. 422–25.

White, Lawrence J. Vertical Restraints in Antitrust Law: A Coherent Model. *Antitrust Bull.*, Summer 1981, *26*(2), pp. 327–45. [G: U.S.]

Williamson, Oliver E. Reply to Lefever [Predatory Pricing: A Strategic and Welfare Analysis]. *Yale Law J.*, June 1981, *90*(7), pp. 1646–49. [G: U.S.]

Wionczek, Miguel S. Restrictive Business Practices and International Controls on Transfer of Technology: Comment. In *Sagafi-nejad, T.; Moxon, R. W. and Perlmutter, H. V., eds.*, 1981, pp. 201–04.

Wolf, Charles, Jr. A Non-Paretian Approach to Market Regulation: Comment. *J. Post Keynesian Econ.*, Spring 1981, *3*(3), pp. 457–58.

Zanon, Lucio. Price Discrimination and Hoffmann-La Roche. *J. World Trade Law*, July–August 1981, *15*(4), pp. 305–22. [G: EEC]

613 Public Utilities; Costs of Government Regulation of Other Industries in the Private Sector

6130 General

Amit, Eilon. On Quality and Price Regulation under Competition and under Monopoly. *Southern Econ. J.*, April 1981, *47*(4), pp. 1056–62.

Aranson, Peter H. and Ordeshook, Peter C. Regulation, Redistribution, and Public Choice. *Public Choice*, 1981, *37*(1), pp. 69–100.

Babe, Robert E. Vertical Integration and Productivity: Canadian Telecommunications. *J. Econ. Issues*, March 1981, *15*(1), pp. 1–31. [G: Canada]

Bailey, Elizabeth E. Contestability and the Design of Regulatory and Antitrust Policy. *Amer. Econ. Rev.*, May 1981, *71*(2), pp. 178–83. [G: U.S.]

Baron, David P. Price Regulation, Product Quality, and Asymmetric Information. *Amer. Econ. Rev.*, March 1981, *71*(1), pp. 212–20.

Baron, David P. and De Bondt, Raymond R. On the Design of Regulatory Price Adjustment Mechanisms. *J. Econ. Theory*, February 1981, *24*(1), pp. 70–94.

Bartlett, Randall K. Information, Uncertainty, and Regulation. In *Ferguson, A. R., ed.*, 1981, pp. 19–37.

Berk, Gerald P. Approaches to the History of Regulation. In *McCraw, T. K., ed.*, 1981, pp. 187–204. [G: U.S.]

Black, Charles L., Jr. Perspectives on the American Common Market [Regulation and the American Common Market]. In *Tarlock, A. D., ed.*, 1981, pp. 59–66. [G: U.S.]

Blankart, Charles B. Towards an Economic Theory of Advice and Its Application to the Deregulation Issue. *Kyklos*, 1981, *34*(1), pp. 95–105.

Bolwell, Harry J. A New Threat to Freedom: The Challenge of the 1980s. In *Gatti, J. F., ed.*, 1981, pp. 25–33. [G: U.S.]

Boyer, Kenneth D. Testing the Applicability of the Natural Monopoly Concept. In *Sichel, W. and Gies, T. G., eds.*, 1981, pp. 1–15.

Brown, Clarence J. The Servility of Business. In *Hessen, R., ed.*, 1981, pp. 50–54. [G: U.S.]

Chatov, Robert. Cooperation between Government and Business. In *Nystrom, P. C. and Starbuck, W. H., eds., Vol. 1*, 1981, pp. 487–502. [G: U.S.]

Christainsen, Gregory B. and Haveman, Robert H. Public Regulations and the Slowdown in Productivity Growth. *Amer. Econ. Rev.*, May 1981, *71*(2), pp. 320–25. [G: U.S.]

Cole, Lawrence P. A Note on Fully Distributed Cost Prices [An Analysis of Fully Distributed Cost Pricing in Regulated Industries]. *Bell J. Econ. (See Rand J. Econ. after 4/85)*, Spring 1981, *12*(1), pp. 329–34. [G: U.S.]

Cowing, Thomas G. and Stevenson, Rodney E. Productivity Measurement and Regulated Industries: Introduction. In *Cowing, T. G. and Stevenson, R. E., eds.*, 1981, pp. 3–14.

Crandall, Robert W. Regulation and Productivity Growth. In *Federal Reserve Bank of Boston (I)*, 1981, pp. 93–111. [G: U.S.]

Crandall, Robert W. and Lave, Lester B. The Scientific Basis of Health and Safety Regulation: Introduction and Summary. In *Crandall, R. W. and Lave, L. B., eds.*, 1981, pp. 1–17.   [G: U.S.]

Denison, Edward F. Research Concerning the Effect of Regulation on Productivity. In *Hogan, J. D. and Craig, A. M., eds., Vol. 2*, 1981, pp. 1015–25.   [G: U.S.]

Diewert, W. Erwin. The Theory of Total Factor Productivity Measurement in Regulated Industries. In *Cowing, T. G. and Stevenson, R. E., eds.*, 1981, pp. 17–44.

Eads, George C. Research in Regulation: Past Contributions and Future Needs. In *Ferguson, A. R., ed.*, 1981, pp. 1–17.

Eckert, Ross D. The Life Cycle of Regulatory Commissioners. *J. Law Econ.*, April 1981, *24*(1), pp. 113–20.   [G: U.S.]

Ekelund, Robert B., Jr. and Saba, Richard P. A Note on Politics and Franchise Bidding. *Public Choice*, 1981, *37*(2), pp. 343–48.

El-Hodiri, Mohamed and Takayama, Akira. Dynamic Behavior of the Firm with Adjustment Costs, under Regulatory Constraint. *J. Econ. Dynam. Control*, February 1981, *3*(1), pp. 29–41.

Epple, Dennis. Petroleum Product Price Regulations: Output and Efficiency Effects: A Comment. *Carnegie-Rochester Conf. Ser. Public Policy*, Spring 1981, *14*, pp. 147–51.   [G: U.S.]

Faith, Roger L. and Tollison, Robert D. The Allocative Equivalence of Contracting and Regulation. *Atlantic Econ. J.*, July 1981, *9*(2), pp. 57–59.

Finsinger, Jörg and Vogelsang, Ingo. Alternative Institutional Frameworks for Price Incentive Mechanism. *Kyklos*, 1981, *34*(3), pp. 388–404.

Fisher, Anthony C.; Krupnick, Alan J. and Ferguson, Allen R. Setting Regulatory Priorities. In *Ferguson, A. R., ed.*, 1981, pp. 145–65.

Fuller, Stephen and Shanmugham, C. V. Effectiveness of Competition to Limit Rail Rate Increases under Deregulation: The Case of Wheat Exports from the Southern Plains. *Southern J. Agr. Econ.*, December 1981, *13*(2), pp. 11–19.   [G: U.S.]

Gaskins, Darius W., Jr. and Voytko, James M. Managing the Transition to Deregulation. *Law Contemp. Probl.*, Winter 1981, *44*(1), pp. 9–32.   [G: U.S.]

Gatti, James F. An Overview of the Problem of Government Regulation. In *Gatti, J. F., ed.*, 1981, pp. 1–8.   [G: U.S.]

Goldberg, Victor P. Pigou on Complex Contracts and Welfare Economics. In *Zerbe, R. O., Jr., ed.*, 1981, pp. 39–51.

Harvey, Scott and Roush, Calvin T., Jr. Petroleum Product Price Regulations: Output and Efficiency Effects. *Carnegie-Rochester Conf. Ser. Public Policy*, Spring 1981, *14*, pp. 109–45. [G: U.S.]

Hawley, Ellis. Three Facets of Hooverian Associationalism: Lumber, Aviation, and Movies, 1921–1930. In *McCraw, T. K., ed.*, 1981, pp. 95–123.   [G: U.S.]

Hays, Samuel P. Political Choice in Regulatory Administration. In *McCraw, T. K., ed.*, 1981, pp. 124–54.   [G: U.S.]

Helms, Robert B. Drugs and Health: Preface. In *Helms, R. B., ed.*, 1981, pp. xix–xxvi. [G: U.S.]

Hirschey, Mark and Pappas, James L. Regulatory and Life Cycle Influences on Managerial Incentives. *Southern Econ. J.*, October 1981, *48*(2), pp. 327–34.

Houthakker, Hendrik S. Regulation and Productivity Growth: Discussion. In *Federal Reserve Bank of Boston (1)*, 1981, pp. 112–14.   [G: U.S.]

Kahn, Alfred E. Regulation in Theory and Practice: An Overview: Comment. In *Fromm, G., ed.*, 1981, pp. 66–72.   [G: U.S.]

Kelman, Steven. Regulation and Paternalism. *Public Policy*, Spring 1981, *29*(2), pp. 219–54.

Kelvorick, Alvin K. Regulation and Cost Containment in the Delivery of Mental Health Services. In *McGuire, T. G. and Weisbrod, B. A., eds.*, 1981, pp. 62–71.

Kemp, Kathleen. Symbolic and Strict Regulation in the American States. *Soc. Sci. Quart.*, September 1981, *62*(3), pp. 516–26.   [G: U.S.]

Keyes, Lucile S. A Non-Paretian Approach to Market Regulation. *J. Post Keynesian Econ.*, Spring 1981, *3*(3), pp. 440–51.

Kimm, Victor J.; Kuzmack, Arnold M. and Schnare, David W. Waterborne Carcinogens: A Regulator's View. In *Crandall, R. W. and Lave, L. B., eds.*, 1981, pp. 229–49.   [G: U.S.]

Kitch, Edmund W. Regulation and the American Common Market. In *Tarlock, A. D., ed.*, 1981, pp. 9–55.   [G: U.S.]

Koenker, Roger W. and Perry, Martin K. Product Differentiation, Monopolistic Competition, and Public Policy. *Bell J. Econ. (See Rand J. Econ. after 4/85)*, Spring 1981, *12*(1), pp. 217–31.

Kosters, Marvin H. Government Regulation: Present Status and Need for Reform. In *Wachter, M. L. and Wachter, S. M., eds.*, 1981, pp. 321–45.   [G: U.S.]

Kunreuther, Howard. Theory of Solvency Regulation in the Property and Casualty Insurance Industry: Comment. In *Fromm, G., ed.*, 1981, pp. 168–72.

Laurie, Dennis. What Should We Do about Government Regulation? In *Hoffman, W. M. and Wyly, T. J., eds.*, 1981, pp. 150–59.   [G: U.S.]

Lucy, William. Toward a New U.S. Industrial Policy? Regulation: Comment. In *Wachter, M. L. and Wachter, S. M., eds.*, 1981, pp. 353–57.   [G: U.S.]

Lynch, Michael P. Theory of Solvency Regulation in the Property and Casualty Insurance Industry: Comment. In *Fromm, G., ed.*, 1981, pp. 173–79.

Magat, Wesley A. Managing the Transistion to Deregulation: Introduction. *Law Contemp. Probl.*, Winter 1981, *44*(1), pp. 1–7.   [G: U.S.]

Marino, Anthony M. Optimal Departures from Marginal Cost Pricing: The Case of a Rate of Return Constraint. *Southern Econ. J.*, July 1981, *48*(1), pp. 37–49.

Marquard, William A. Toward a New U.S. Industrial Policy? Regulation: Comment. In *Wachter, M. L. and Wachter, S. M., eds.*, 1981, pp. 346–49.   [G: U.S.]

Marshall, William J.; Yawitz, Jess B. and Greenberg, Edward. Optimal Regulation under Uncertainty. *J. Finance*, September 1981, *36*(4), pp. 909–21.

McBain, Helen. External Financing of the Water Commission of Jamaica. *Soc. Econ. Stud.*, March 1981, *30*(1), pp. 171–96.   [G: Jamaica]

McGregor, Stephen E. Government Policy and the Petroleum Industry. In *Hogan, J. D. and Craig, A. M., eds.*, Vol. 2, 1981, pp. 1147–51.
[G: U.S.]

Merrill, Richard A. Saccharin: A Regulator's View. In *Crandall, R. W. and Lave, L. B., eds.*, 1981, pp. 153–70.   [G: U.S.]

Middleton, John T. Sulfur Dioxide: A Regulator's View. In *Crandall, R. W. and Lave, L. B., eds.*, 1981, pp. 279–88.   [G: U.S.]

Mishan, Ezra J. Distributive Implications of Economic Controls. In *Ferguson, A. R. and LeVeen, E. P., eds.*, 1981, pp. 155–75.

Moore, Thomas Gale. Comments on Aranson & Ordershook's Regulation, Redistribution, and Public Choice. *Public Choice*, 1981, *37*(1), pp. 101–05.

Munch, Patricia and Smallwood, Dennis. Theory of Solvency Regulation in the Property and Casualty Insurance Industry. In *Fromm, G., ed.*, 1981, pp. 119–67.

Murphy, Thomas A. The Distressing Relationship between Government and Business. In *Gatti, J. F., ed.*, 1981, pp. 133–42.   [G: U.S.]

Noll, Roger G. and Joskow, Paul L. Regulation in Theory and Practice: An Overview. In *Fromm, G., ed.*, 1981, pp. 1–65.   [G: U.S.]

North, Douglass C. An Economist's Perspective on the American Common Market [Regulation and the American Common Market]. In *Tarlock, A. D., ed.*, 1981, pp. 77–81.   [G: U.S.]

Ordover, Janusz A. and Weiss, Andrew. Information and the Law: Evaluating Legal Restrictions on Competitive Contracts. *Amer. Econ. Rev.*, May 1981, *71*(2), pp. 399–404.

Owen, Bruce M. The Rise and Fall of Cable Television Regulation. In *Weiss, L. W. and Klass, M. W., eds.*, 1981, pp. 86–101.   [G: U.S.]

Payton, Sallyanne. The Duty of a Public Utility to Serve in the Presence of New Competition. In *Sichel, W. and Gies, T. G., eds.*, 1981, pp. 121–52.   [G: U.S.]

Peltzman, Sam. Current Developments in the Economics of Regulation. In *Fromm, G., ed.*, 1981, pp. 371–84.

Peterson, Esther. Toward a New U.S. Industrial Policy? Regulation: Comment. In *Wachter, M. L. and Wachter, S. M., eds.*, 1981, pp. 349–51.
[G: U.S.]

Phillips, Almarin. Toward a New U.S. Industrial Policy? Regulation: Comment. In *Wachter, M. L. and Wachter, S. M., eds.*, 1981, pp. 351–53.
[G: U.S.]

Platts, A. R. Traditional Peak-Load Pricing Theory: A Synthesis. *J. Econ. Stud.*, 1981, *8*(1), pp. 47–51.

Plott, Charles R. Experimental Methods in Political Economy: A Tool for Regulatory Research. In *Ferguson, A. R., ed.*, 1981, pp. 117–43.

Ponssard, Jean-Pierre. Marchés publics et innovation: concurrence ou régulation? (The Governance of Contractual Relations: Competition or Regulation? With English summary.) *Revue Écon.*, January 1981, *32*(1), pp. 163–79.
[G: France]

Potter, David S. The Scientific Basis of Health and Safety Regulation: Comments. In *Crandall, R. W. and Lave, L. B., eds.*, 1981, pp. 291–95.

Pozen, Robert C. A Broad Critique of the Current Regulatory Framework. In *Sametz, A. W., ed.*, 1981, pp. 55–58.   [G: U.S.]

Pratt, Michael D. Firm Behavior under Regulatory Constraint: An Immanent Criticism [Depreciation, Tax Policy and Firm Behavior under Regulatory Constraint]. *Southern Econ. J.*, July 1981, *48*(1), pp. 235–38.   [G: U.S.]

Quirk, James and Terasawa, Katsuaki. Nuclear Regulation: An Historical Perspective. *Natural Res. J.*, October 1981, *21*(4), pp. 833–55.   [G: U.S.]

Reynolds, Larry. Foundations of an Institutional Theory of Regulation. *J. Econ. Issues*, September 1981, *15*(3), pp. 641–56.   [G: U.S.]

Scherer, F. M. Regulatory Dynamics and Economic Growth. In *Wachter, M. L. and Wachter, S. M., eds.*, 1981, pp. 289–320.   [G: U.S.]

Schneider, Lynne; Klein, Benjamin and Murphy, Kevin M. Governmental Regulation of Cigarette Health Information. *J. Law Econ.*, December 1981, *24*(3), pp. 575–612.   [G: U.S.]

Schneiderman, Marvin. The Scientific Basis of Health and Safety Regulation: Comments. In *Crandall, R. W. and Lave, L. B., eds.*, 1981, pp. 297–99.

Sherman, Roger. Pricing Inefficiency under Profit Regulation. *Southern Econ. J.*, October 1981, *48*(2), pp. 475–89.

Shreiber, Chanoch. The Economic Reasons for Price and Entry Regulation of Taxicabs: A Rejoinder. *J. Transp. Econ. Policy*, January 1981, *15*(1), pp. 81–83.   [G: U.S.]

Simon, Michael E. Measuring Regulation Impacts: The Firm View. In *Hogan, J. D. and Craig, A. M., eds.*, Vol. 2, 1981, pp. 1027–34.
[G: U.S.]

Simon, William E. Government Regulation and a Free Society. In *Gatti, J. F., ed.*, 1981, pp. 11–24.

Spencer, Roger W. Rationale of Current Regulatory Approaches to Banks' Securities Activities. In *Sametz, A. W., ed.*, 1981, pp. 35–43. [G: U.S.]

Stigler, George J. Regulation in Theory and Practice: An Overview: Comment. In *Fromm, G., ed.*, 1981, pp. 73–77.   [G: U.S.]

Stone, Alan. State and Market: Economic Regulation and the Great Productivity Debate. In *Ferguson, T. and Rogers, J., eds.*, 1981, pp. 232–59.
[G: U.S.]

Sweeney, George. Adoption of Cost-Saving Innovations by a Regulated Firm. *Amer. Econ. Rev.*, June 1981, *71*(3), pp. 437–47.

Thompson, Fred and Jones, L. R. SMR Forum: Reforming Regulatory Decision Making—The Regulatory Budget. *Sloan Manage. Rev.*, Winter 1981, *22*(2), pp. 53–61.   [G: U.S.]

Thomson, Norm and Walsh, Cliff. Cross-subsidisation of Rural Areas via Utility Pricing Policies. *Australian J. Agr. Econ.*, December 1981, *25*(3), pp. 221–32.   [G: Australia]

Trebing, Harry M. Motivations and Barriers to Superior Performance under Public Utility Regulation. In *Cowing, T. G. and Stevenson, R. E.*, eds., 1981, pp. 369–94. [G: U.S.]

Upham, Frank K. Business and the Bureaucracy. In *Richardson, B. M. and Ueda, T.*, eds., 1981, pp. 194–99. [G: Japan]

Vander Weide, James H. and Zalkind, Julie H. Deregulation and Oligopolistic Price–Quality Rivalry. *Amer. Econ. Rev.*, March 1981, *71*(1), pp. 144–54.

Voytko, James M. The Business-Government Problem. *J. Policy Anal. Manage.*, Fall 1981, *1*(1), pp. 140–42. [G: U.S.]

Weidenbaum, Murray L. An Overview of Government Regulation. In *Gatti, J. F.*, ed., 1981, pp. 87–94. [G: U.S.]

Weidenbaum, Murray L. The New Regulation and the American Common Market [Regulation and the American Common Market]. In *Tarlock, A. D.*, ed., 1981, pp. 83–92. [G: U.S.]

Weidenbaum, Murray L. The Power of Negative Thinking: Government Regulation and Economic Performance. In *Meyer, L. H.*, ed., 1981, pp. 245–54. [G: U.S.]

Weingast, Barry R. Regulation, Reregulation, and Deregulation: The Political Foundations of Agency Clientele Relationships. *Law Contemp. Probl.*, Winter 1981, *44*(1), pp. 147–77. [G: U.S.]

Weingast, Barry R. and Hall, Kent S. Congress, Regulation, and the Courts: Economic Perspectives on Political Choice. In *Ferguson, A. R.*, ed., 1981, pp. 55–93. [G: U.S.]

Weiss, Leonard W. The Regulatory Reform Movement. In *Weiss, L. W. and Klass, M. W.*, eds., 1981, pp. 1–11. [G: U.S.]

West, William F. Judicial Rulemaking Procedures in the FTC: A Case Study of Their Causes and Effects. *Public Policy*, Spring 1981, *29*(2), pp. 197–217. [G: U.S.]

White, B. Ward. Proposals for a Regulatory Budget. *Public Budg. Finance*, Autumn 1981, *1*(3), pp. 46–55. [G: U.S.]

Wolf, Charles, Jr. A Non-Paretian Approach to Market Regulation: Comment. *J. Post Keynesian Econ.*, Spring 1981, *3*(3), pp. 457–58.

Ylä-Liedenpohja, Jouka. Public Pricing under Different Behavioural Postulates. *Liiketaloudellinen Aikak.*, 1981, *30*(1), pp. 46–60.

6131 Regulation of Public Utilities

Acton, Jan Paul. Planning, Processing, and Analyzing Data for Residential Load Studies. In *U.S. Dept. of Energy*, 1981, pp. 137–51. [G: U.S.]

Aivazian, Varouj A. and Callen, Jeffrey L. Capacity Expansion in the U.S. Natural-Gas Pipeline Industry. In *Cowing, T. G. and Stevenson, R. E.*, eds., 1981, pp. 145–59. [G: U.S.]

Arzac, Enrique R. and Marcus, Matityahu. Flotation Cost Allowance in Rate of Return Regulation: A Note. *J. Finance*, December 1981, *36*(5), pp. 1199–1202.

Atkinson, Scott E. and Halvorsen, Robert. Automatic Price Adjustment Clauses and Input Choice

in Regulated Utilities. In *Nemetz, P. N.*, ed., 1981, pp. 185–96.

Barry, Leo. Interprovincial Electrical Energy Transfers: The Constitutional Background. In *Nemetz, P. N.*, ed., 1981, pp. 213–53. [G: Canada]

Baseman, Kenneth C. Open Entry and Cross-Subsidization in Regulated Markets. In *Fromm, G.*, ed., 1981, pp. 329–60. [G: U.S.]

Baumol, William J. Open Entry and Cross-Subsidization in Regulated Markets: Comment. In *Fromm, G.*, ed., 1981, pp. 361–64. [G: U.S.]

Beals, Ralph E. Elasticity Estimates for Domestic Electricity Consumption under Time-of-Day Pricing: An Analysis of British Data. In *[Nelson, J. R.]*, 1981, pp. 277–97. [G: U.K.]

Bennis, Jerome. Developing and Maintaining a Load Research Data Base: Comment. In *U.S. Dept. of Energy*, 1981, pp. 118–21. [G: U.S.]

Berndt, Ernst R.; Kesselman, Jonathan R. and Watkins, G. C. Tax Normalization, Regulation, and Economic Efficiency. In *Nemetz, P. N.*, ed., 1981, pp. 171–83. [G: Canada]

Berry, Sandra H. Contacting and Interviewing Residential Electricity Customers. In *U.S. Dept. of Energy*, 1981, pp. 60–72.

Besen, Stanley M. and Crandall, Robert W. The Deregulation of Cable Television. *Law Contemp. Probl.*, Winter 1981, *44*(1), pp. 77–124. [G: U.S.]

Bishop, Lane. Considerations in Analysing and Generalizing from Time-of-Use Electricity Pricing Studies. In *U.S. Dept. of Energy*, 1981, pp. 158–65.

Bowen, Robert M. Valuation of Earnings Components in the Electric Utility Industry. *Accounting Rev.*, January 1981, *56*(1), pp. 1–22. [G: U.S.]

Bower, R. S. Impact of Regulation on Economic Behavior: Discussion. *J. Finance*, May 1981, *36*(2), pp. 397–99.

Boyer, Kenneth D. and Wirth, Michael O. The Economics of Regulation by Policy Directive: FCC Public-Interest Requirements. *Quart. Rev. Econ. Bus.*, Spring 1981, *21*(1), pp. 77–96. [G: U.S.]

Braeutigam, Ronald R. Regulation and the Multiproduct Firm: The Case of Telecommunications in Canada: Comment. In *Fromm, G.*, ed., 1981, pp. 314–20. [G: Canada]

Brigham, Eugene F. Public Utility Finance. In *Altman, E. I.*, ed., 1981, pp. 36.3–31.

Burgess, Giles and Paglin, Morton. Lifeline Electricity Rates as an Income Transfer Device. *Land Econ.*, February 1981, *57*(1), pp. 41–47. [G: U.S.]

Caves, Douglas W. Effects on the Residential Load Curve from Time-of-Use Pricing of Electricity: Econometric Inferences from the Wisconsin Experiment for Summer System Peak Days. In *U.S. Dept. of Energy*, 1981, pp. 249–74. [G: U.S.]

Clark, Robert M. and Stevie, Richard G. A Water Supply Cost Model Incorporating Spatial Variables. *Land Econ.*, February 1981, *57*(1), pp. 18–32.

Clayton, C. Andrew. Drawing a Sample and Allocating Customers to Design Points. In *U.S. Dept. of Energy*, 1981, pp. 32–48.

Cowing, Thomas G.; Stevenson, Rodney E. and

Small, Jeffrey. Comparative Measures of Total Factor Productivity in the Regulated Sector: The Electric Utility Industry. In *Cowing, T. G. and Stevenson, R. E., eds.*, 1981, pp. 161–77.
[G: U.S.]

Crano, William D. Variables Affecting Treatment Perception in an Electric Time-of-Use Rate Demonstration: Analytic and Interpretative Implications. In *U.S. Dept. of Energy*, 1981, pp. 287–304.
[G: U.S.]

Crew, Michael A. and Kleindorfer, Paul R. Regulation and Diverse Technology in the Peak Load Problem. *Southern Econ. J.*, October 1981, *48*(2), pp. 335–43.

Daniel, Coldwell, III. The New Theory of Public Utilities: The Case of the Natural Monopoly. *Antitrust Bull.*, Spring 1981, *26*(1), pp. 133–43.
[G: U.S.]

Denny, Michael; Fuss, Melvyn A. and Waverman, Leonard. The Measurement and Interpretation of Total Factor Productivity in Regulated Industries, with an Application to Canadian Telecommunications. In *Cowing, T. G. and Stevenson, R. E., eds.*, 1981, pp. 179–218.
[G: Canada]

Dikeman, Neil J., Jr. A Summary of the Edmond Electric Utility Demonstration Project and Its Findings. In *U.S. Dept. of Energy*, 1981, pp. 205–11.
[G: U.S.]

Dimopoulos, Dionissis. Pricing Schemes for Regulated Enterprises and Their Welfare Implications in the Case of Electricity. *Bell J. Econ. (See Rand J. Econ. after 4/85)*, Spring 1981, *12*(1), pp. 185–200.
[G: U.S.]

Downing, Paul B. Policy Consequences of Indirect Regulatory Costs. *Public Policy*, Fall 1981, *29*(4), pp. 507–26.
[G: U.S.]

Dugger, William M. Entrenched Corporate Power and Our Options for Dealing with It. *Rev. Soc. Econ.*, October 1981, *39*(2), pp. 133–44.
[G: U.S.]

Famadas, Nelson. The Role of Survey Data in Load Research. In *U.S. Dept. of Energy*, 1981, pp. 49–52.

Feiler, David and Zahavi, Jacob. Marginal Generating Costs of Multi-Block Power Systems with and without Partial Outages. *Energy Econ.*, April 1981, *3*(2), pp. 91–101.

Feldman, Stephen L.; Breese, John and Obeiter, Robert. The Search for Equity and Efficiency in the Pricing of a Public Service: Urban Water. *Econ. Geogr.*, January 1981, *57*(1), pp. 78–93.
[G: U.S.]

Fuss, Melvyn A. and Waverman, Leonard. Regulation and the Multiproduct Firm: The Case of Telecommunications in Canada. In *Fromm, G., ed.*, 1981, pp. 276–313.
[G: Canada]

Goyco, Osvaldo C. Procedures for Collecting, Translating, and Editing Meter Data: Comment. In *U.S. Dept. of Energy*, 1981, pp. 81–92.
[G: U.S.]

Groves, Robert M. Definition of the Population and Formation and Use of Strata. In *U.S. Dept. of Energy*, 1981, pp. 23–31.

Heberlein, Thomas A. Electric Rate Demonstration Conference: Questionnaire Development. In *U.S. Dept. of Energy*, 1981, pp. 53–59.

Hendricks, Wallace E. Evaluation and Future Uses of the DOE Sponsored Demonstration Data. In *U.S. Dept. of Energy*, 1981, pp. 279–86.
[G: U.S.]

Hill, Daniel H. Electric Rate Demonstration Conference: Limitations on Analysis. In *U.S. Dept. of Energy*, 1981, pp. 152–57.
[G: U.S.]

Homan, John E. Utility Depreciation: An Inequity. *Calif. Manage. Rev.*, Fall 1981, *24*(1), pp. 5–13.
[G: U.S.]

James, Richard E. Procedures for Collecting, Translating, and Editing Meter Data. In *U.S. Dept. of Energy*, 1981, pp. 73–80.

Jonish, James and Olson, Dennis. Taxation of Electricity Generation in New Mexico—Some Remaining Issues. *Natural Res. J.*, April 1981, *21*(2), pp. xi–xvi.

Kiefer, Donald W. The Effects of Alternative Regulatory Treatments of the Investment Tax Credit in the Public Utility Industry. *J. Bus.*, October 1981, *54*(4), pp. 549–77.
[G: U.S.]

Klevorick, Alvin K. Income-Distribution Concerns in Regulatory Policymaking: Comment. In *Fromm, G., ed.*, 1981, pp. 108–11.
[G: U.S.]

Latham, Robert J. Implementing Pricing Reforms in the Presence of Underutilized Capital Assets. In *Sichel, W. and Gies, T. G., eds.*, 1981, pp. 73–85.

Levy, Roger. Developing and Maintaining a Load Research Data Base. In *U.S. Dept. of Energy*, 1981, pp. 93–117.
[G: U.S.]

Lifson, Dale P. Practical Considerations in Modelling the Demand for Electricity. In *U.S. Dept. of Energy*, 1981, pp. 166–86.
[G: U.S.]

Lillard, Lee A. and Acton, Jan Paul. Seasonal Electricity Demand and Pricing Analysis with a Variable Response Model. *Bell J. Econ. (See Rand J. Econ. after 4/85)*, Spring 1981, *12*(1), pp. 71–92.
[G: U.S.]

Main, Robert S. A New Approach to Peak Load Pricing. *Managerial Dec. Econ.*, September 1981, *2*(3), pp. 139–44.

Malko, J. Robert; Ray, Dennis J. and Hassig, Nancy L. Time-of-Day Pricing of Electricity Activities in Some Midwestern States. In *Nemetz, P. N., ed.*, 1981, pp. 143–70.

Metcalf, Charles E. Sample Design for Rate Demonstrations and Load Research. In *U.S. Dept. of Energy*, 1981, pp. 15–22.

Miedema, Allen K. North Carolina Rate Demonstration Project—Preliminary Results. In *U.S. Dept. of Energy*, 1981, pp. 228–48.
[G: U.S.]

Miedema, Allen K. Overview of DOE Analyses of Residential TOU Data. In *U.S. Dept. of Energy*, 1981, pp. 193–204.
[G: U.S.]

Mitchell, Bridger M. Regulation and the Multiproduct Firm: The Case of Telecommunications in Canada: Comment. In *Fromm, G., ed.*, 1981, pp. 321–27.
[G: Canada]

Mitchell, Bridger M. The Effect of Time-of-Day Rates in the Los Angeles Electricity Rate Study. In *U.S. Dept. of Energy*, 1981, pp. 212–27.
[G: U.S.]

Munasinghe, Mohan and Jahangir, Muhammad. Determining Marginal Cost-Based Electricity Tariffs: Case Study of the WAPDA System. *Paki-*

stan Econ. Soc. Rev., Summer 1981, *19*(1), pp. 50–68. [G: Pakistan]

Murray, Barbara B. Capital Budgeting Decisions for Load Management Equipment by Industrial Electric Users. *Nebr. J. Econ. Bus.*, Winter 1981, *20*(1), pp. 31–47. [G: U.S.]

Navarro, Peter; Petersen, Bruce C. and Stauffer, Thomas R. A Critical Comparison of Utility-Type Ratemaking Methodologies in Oil Pipeline Regulation. *Bell J. Econ. (See Rand J. Econ. after 4/85)*, Autumn 1981, *12*(2), pp. 392–412. [G: U.S.]

Nufeld, John L. and Watts, James M. Inverted Block or Lifeline Rates and Micro-Efficiency in the Consumption of Electricity. *Energy Econ.*, April 1981, *3*(2), pp. 113–21. [G: U.S.]

Panzar, John C. Open Entry and Cross-Subsidization in Regulated Markets: Comment. In *Fromm, G., ed.*, 1981, pp. 365–69. [G: U.S.]

Peles, Yoram C. A Proposal for Peak Load Pricing of Public Utilities. *Energy Econ.*, July 1981, *3*(3), pp. 187–90.

Pfannenstiel, Jackalyne. Implementing Marginal Cost Pricing in the Electric Utility Industry. In *Sichel, W. and Gies, T. G., eds.*, 1981, pp. 53–72. [G: U.S.]

Phillips, Almarin. Theory and Practice in Public Utility Regulation: The Case of Telecommunications. In *[Nelson, J. R.]*, 1981, pp. 181–96. [G: U.S.]

Rashid, Salim. Public Utilities in Egalitarian LDC's: The Role of Bribery in Achieving Pareto Efficiency. *Kyklos*, 1981, *34*(3), pp. 448–60. [G: LDCs]

Rowse, John. Economic Benefits of Cooperative Power Supply Expansion. *J. Reg. Sci.*, August 1981, *21*(3), pp. 389–402. [G: Canada]

Sackey, James A. The Case of Guyana Electricity Corporation. *Soc. Econ. Stud.*, March 1981, *30*(1), pp. 146–70. [G: Guyana]

Saving, T. R. and De Vany, Arthur S. Uncertain Markets, Reliability and Peak-Load Pricing. *Southern Econ. J.*, April 1981, *47*(4), pp. 908–23.

Schmalensee, Richard. Income-Distribution Concerns in Regulatory Policymaking: Comment. In *Fromm, G., ed.*, 1981, pp. 112–17. [G: U.S.]

Schmidt, Ingo. Price Control in Germany. *Ann. Pub. Co-op. Econ.*, December 1981, *52*(4), pp. 491–503. [G: W. Germany]

Scott, Frank A., Jr. Estimating Recipient Benefits and Waste from Lifeline Electricity Rates. *Land Econ.*, November 1981, *57*(4), pp. 536–43. [G: U.S.]

Sharkey, William W. Existence of Sustainable Prices for Natural Monopoly Outputs. *Bell J. Econ. (See Rand J. Econ. after 4/85)*, Spring 1981, *12*(1), pp. 144–54.

Stevenson, Rodney E. Establishing Objectives for Residential Load Research. In *U.S. Dept. of Energy*, 1981, pp. 8–14.

Sunley, Emil M. Tax Incentives and Public Utility Regulation. In *[Nelson, J. R.]*, 1981, pp. 299–309. [G: U.S.]

Swaby, Raphael A. The Rationale for State Ownership of Public Utilities in Jamaica. *Soc. Econ.*

Stud., March 1981, *30*(1), pp. 75–107. [G: Jamaica]

Taggart, Robert A., Jr. Rate-of-Return Regulation and Utility Capital Structure Decisions. *J. Finance*, May 1981, *36*(2), pp. 383–93. [G: U.S.]

Trebing, Harry M. Equity, Efficiency, and the Viability of Public Utility Regulation. In *Sichel, W. and Gies, T. G., eds.*, 1981, pp. 17–52.

Trebing, Harry M. Regulatory Reform in the Public Utility Industries. In *[Nelson, J. R.]*, 1981, pp. 155–79. [G: U.S.]

Weingast, Barry R. Regulation, Reregulation, and Deregulation: The Political Foundations of Agency Clientele Relationships. *Law Contemp. Probl.*, Winter 1981, *44*(1), pp. 147–77. [G: U.S.]

Weiss, Leonard W. State Regulation of Public Utilities and Marginal-Cost Pricing. In *Weiss, L. W. and Klass, M. W., eds.*, 1981, pp. 262–91. [G: U.S.]

Wenders, John T. The Welfare Economics of Optional Seasonal Time-of-Day Electricity Tariffs. *Energy Econ.*, April 1981, *3*(2), pp. 102–04.

Willig, Robert D. and Bailey, Elizabeth E. Income-Distribution Concerns in Regulatory Policymaking. In *Fromm, G., ed.*, 1981, pp. 79–107. [G: U.S.]

Wiseman, Jack. The Theory of Public Utility Price—An Empty Box. In *Buchanan, J. M. and Thirlby, G. F., eds.*, 1981, *1957*, pp. 245–71.

Zayas, Edison R. Motor Carrier Regulation and Small Truckers. *Bus. Econ.*, January 1981, *16*(1), pp. 59–66. [G: U.S.]

6132 Effects of Intervention on Market Structure, Costs, and Efficiency

Armstrong, Alan G. Consumer Safety and the Regulation of Industry. *Managerial Dec. Econ.*, June 1981, *2*(2), pp. 67–73.

Atkinson, Graham and Cook, Jack. Regulation: Incentives Rather than Command and Control. In *Olson, M., ed.*, 1981, pp. 211–18. [G: U.S.]

Boucher, Michel. La réglementation de l'industrie québécoise du camionnage: aperçu et considérations analytiques. (Regulation of the Quebec Trucking Industry: Institutions, Practices and Analytical Considerations. With English summary.) *L'Actual. Econ.*, January–March 1981, *57*(1), pp. 87–112. [G: Canada]

Braeutigam, Ronald R. Regulation of Multiproduct Enterprises by Rate of Return, Markup, and Operating Ratio. In *Zerbe, R. O., Jr., ed.*, 1981, pp. 15–38.

Clague, Christopher. Regulation: Can It Improve Incentives? Commentary. In *Olson, M., ed.*, 1981, pp. 313–17. [G: U.S.]

Clarkson, Kenneth W. and MacLeod, William C. Reducing the Drug Lag: Entrepreneurship in Pharmaceutical Clinical Testing. In *Helms, R. B., ed.*, 1981, pp. 84–113. [G: U.S.]

Cocks, Douglas L. Company Total Factor Productivity: Refinements, Production Functions, and Certain Effects of Regulation. *Bus. Econ.*, May 1981, *16*(3), pp. 5–14.

Cohen, Harold A. and Schramm, Carl J. A Design

for Resolving the Conflicts Resulting from Separate Regulation of Hospital Rates and Hospital Capacity. In *Olson, M., ed.*, 1981, pp. 258–73.
[G: U.S.]

Crout, J. Richard. Reducing the Drug Lag: Entrepreneurship in Pharmaceutical Clinical Testing: Comment. In *Helms, R. B., ed.*, 1981, pp. 117–19.

Desprairies, Pierre. The Role of Government in Regulating Energy Markets: Commentary. In *OPEC, Public Information Dept.*, 1981, pp. 106–11.

Dorfman, Robert. Transition Costs of Changing Regulations. In *Ferguson, A. R., ed.*, 1981, pp. 39–54.

Felton, John Richard. The Impact of Rate Regulation upon ICC-Regulated Truck Back Hauls. *J. Transp. Econ. Policy*, September 1981, *15*(3), pp. 253–67. [G: U.S.; U.K.; Australia]

Ferguson, Allen R. and Weidenbaum, Murray L. The Problem of Balancing the Costs and Benefits of Regulation: Two Views. In *Gatti, J. F., ed.*, 1981, pp. 143–66. [G: U.S.]

Frech, H. E., III. The Long-Lost Free Market in Health Care: Government and Professional Regulation of Medicine. In *Olson, M., ed.*, 1981, pp. 44–66. [G: U.S.]

Frew, James R. The Existence of Monopoly Profits in the Motor Carrier Industry. *J. Law Econ.*, October 1981, *24*(2), pp. 289–315. [G: U.S.]

Fuller, John W. Inflationary Effects on Transportation. *Ann. Amer. Acad. Polit. Soc. Sci.*, July 1981, *456*, pp. 112–22. [G: U.S.]

Gordon, Kenneth. Deregulation, Rights, and the Compensation of Losers. In *[Nelson, J. R.]*, 1981, pp. 223–44. [G: U.S.]

Graglia, Lino A. The Supreme Court and the American Common Market [Regulation and the American Common Market]. In *Tarlock, A. D., ed.*, 1981, pp. 67–75. [G: U.S.]

Guttmann, J. Michele. Pennsylvania's Technologically Impossible Air Pollution Standards Upheld. *Natural Res. J.*, April 1981, *21*(2), pp. 395–404. [G: U.S.]

Hall, George R. Natural Gas Curtailment Policy: Where Do We Go from Here? *Energy J.*, October 1981, *2*(4), pp. 43–61. [G: U.S.]

Harrison, David, Jr. Regulation and Distribution. In *Ferguson, A. R., ed.*, 1981, pp. 185–208. [G: U.S.]

Hartley, Keith and Watt, Peter A. Profits, Regulation and the UK Aerospace Industry. *J. Ind. Econ.*, June 1981, *29*(4), pp. 413–28. [G: U.K.]

Hartman, Raymond S. An Analysis of Department of Energy Residential Appliance Efficiency Standards. *Energy J.*, July 1981, *2*(3), pp. 49–70. [G: U.S.]

Haveman, Robert H. and Christainsen, Gregory B. Environmental Regulations and Productivity Growth. *Natural Res. J.*, July 1981, *21*(3), pp. 489–509. [G: U.S.]

Jadlow, Joseph M. The Economic Effects of Generic Substitution. *Rivista Int. Sci. Econ. Com.*, January–February 1981, *28*(1–2), pp. 110–20. [G: U.S.]

Jarrell, Gregg A. The Economic Effects of Federal Regulation of the Market for New Security Issues. *J. Law Econ.*, December 1981, *24*(3), pp. 613–75. [G: U.S.]

Joskow, Paul L. Alternative Regulatory Mechanisms for Controlling Hospital Costs. In *Olson, M., ed.*, 1981, pp. 219–57. [G: U.S.]

Klausner, Michael D. Uncertainty over Adverse Government Action and the Law of Just Compensation. *Yale Law J.*, June 1981, *90*(7), pp. 1670–93. [G: U.S.]

Kühner, Jochen and Bower, Blair T. Water Quality Management in the Ruhr Area of the Federal Republic of Germany, with Special Emphasis on Charge Systems. In *Bower, B. T., et al., eds.*, 1981, pp. 213–301. [G: W. Germany]

Leone, Robert A. and Jackson, John E. The Political Economy of Federal Regulatory Activity: The Case of Water-Pollution Controls. In *Fromm, G., ed.*, 1981, pp. 231–71. [G: U.S.]

Levin, Richard C. Regulation, Barriers to Exit, and the Investment Behavior of Railroads. In *Fromm, G., ed.*, 1981, pp. 181–224. [G: U.S.]

Levy, Yvonne. Crude Oil Price Controls and the Windfall Profit Tax: Deterrents to Production? *Fed. Res. Bank San Francisco Econ. Rev.*, Spring 1981, pp. 6–28. [G: U.S.]

Lower, Milton D. Decontrol déjà vu. *J. Post Keynesian Econ.*, Summer 1981, *3*(4), pp. 597–601. [G: U.S.]

Mabro, Robert. The Role of Government in Regulating Energy Markets. In *OPEC, Public Information Dept.*, 1981, pp. 92–105.

McCarthy, Thomas R. Regulation: Can It Improve Incentives? Commentary. In *Olson, M., ed.*, 1981, pp. 309–13. [G: U.S.]

McGowan, John J. Regulation, Barriers to Exit, and the Investment Behavior of Railroads: Comment. In *Fromm, G., ed.*, 1981, pp. 225–27. [G: U.S.]

McKenzie, Richard B. The Case for Plant Closures. *Policy Rev.*, Winter 1981, (15), pp. 119–33. [G: U.S.]

O'Hara, Maureen. Property Rights and the Financial Firm. *J. Law Econ.*, October 1981, *24*(2), pp. 317–32. [G: U.S.]

Odell, Peter R. Lower Oil Prices—Dangers to the North Sea. *Lloyds Bank Rev.*, October 1981, (142), pp. 26–38. [G: U.K.; EEC]

Oster, Sharon. Product Regulations: A Measure of the Benefits. *J. Ind. Econ.*, June 1981, *29*(4), pp. 395–411. [G: U.S.]

Pauly, Mark V. Paying the Piper and Calling the Tune: The Relationship between Public Financing and Public Regulation of Health Care. In *Olson, M., ed.*, 1981, pp. 67–86. [G: U.S.]

Peskin, Henry M.; Portney, Paul R. and Kneese, Allen V. Regulation and the Economy: Concluding Thoughts. *Natural Res. J.*, July 1981, *21*(3), pp. 589–91. [G: U.S.]

Piette, Michael J. and Desvousges, William H. Behavior of the Firm: The U.S. Petroleum Pipeline Industry under Regulatory Constraint. *Growth Change*, April 1981, *12*(2), pp. 17–22. [G: U.S.]

Pittman, Russell W. Issue in Pollution Control: Interplant Cost Differences and Economies of Scale. *Land Econ.*, February 1981, *57*(1), pp. 1–17. [G: U.S.]

Portney, Paul R. The Macroeconomic Impacts of Federal Environmental Regulation. *Natural Res. J.*, July 1981, *21*(3), pp. 459–88. [G: U.S.]

Reza, Ali M. The Impact of President Reagan's Sudden Decontrol of Petroleum Prices on Petroleum Consumption. *Energy J.*, July 1981, *2*(3), pp. 129–33. [G: U.S.]

Ridker, Ronald G. and Watson, William D. Long–Run Effects of Environmental Regulation. *Natural Res. J.*, July 1981, *21*(3), pp. 565–87. [G: U.S.]

Robinson, Colin. The Errors of North Sea Policy. *Lloyds Bank Rev.*, July 1981, (141), pp. 14–33. [G: U.K.]

Rosenberg, Morton. Beyond the Limits of Executive Power: Presidential Control of Agency Rulemaking under Executive Order 12,291. *Mich. Law Rev.*, December 1981, *80*(2), pp. 193–247. [G: U.S.]

Schwert, G. William. Using Financial Data to Measure Effects of Regulation. *J. Law Econ.*, April 1981, *24*(1), pp. 121–58. [G: U.S.]

Smith, Rodney T. The Economic Effects of Federal Regulation of the Market for New Security Issues: Comment. *J. Law Econ.*, December 1981, *24*(3), pp. 677–86. [G: U.S.]

Starr, Paul. Inherent Difficulties Compounded by Mistaken Principles: Commentary. In *Olson, M., ed.*, 1981, pp. 119–28. [G: U.S.]

Steinwald, Bruce and Sloan, Frank A. Regulatory Approaches to Hospital Cost Containment: A Synthesis of the Empirical Evidence. In *Olson, M., ed.*, 1981, pp. 274–308. [G: U.S.]

The Business Roundtable and Arthur Anderson & Co. Cost of Government Regulation Study. In *Gatti, J. F., ed.*, 1981, *1979*, pp. 95–129. [G: U.S.]

Weidenbaum, Murray L. Proceedings of the Seminar on Inflation: Statement. In *U.S. Congress, Joint Economic Committee (I)*, 1981, pp. 92–100. [G: U.S.]

Zeckhauser, Richard. The Political Economy of Federal Regulatory Activity: The Case of Water-Pollution Controls: Comment. In *Fromm, G., ed.*, 1981, pp. 273–76. [G: U.S.]

Zeckhauser, Richard and Zook, Christopher. Failures to Control Health Costs: Departures from First Principles. In *Olson, M., ed.*, 1981, pp. 87–116. [G: U.S.]

614 Public Enterprises

6140 Public Enterprises

Aharoni, Yair. Managerial Discretion. In *Vernon, R. and Aharoni, Y., eds.*, 1981, pp. 184–93.

Anastassopoulos, Jean-Pierre C. The French Experience: Conflicts with Government. In *Vernon, R. and Aharoni, Y., eds.*, 1981, pp. 99–116. [G: France]

Anastassopoulos, Jean-Pierre C. The French Experience: Conflicts with Government. In *Vernon, R. and Aharoni, Y., eds.*, 1981, pp. 99–116. [G: France]

Arrow, Kenneth J. On Finance and Decision Making. In *Vernon, R. and Aharoni, Y., eds.*, 1981, pp. 63–69.

Baer, Werner and Figueroa, Adolfo. State Enterprise and the Distribution of Income: Brazil and Peru. In *Bruneau, T. C. and Faucher, P., eds.*, 1981, pp. 59–83. [G: Brazil; Peru]

Bagchi, Amiya Kumar. Reinforcing and Offsetting Constraints in Indian Industry. In *Bagchi, A. K. and Banerjee, N., eds.*, 1981, pp. 23–62. [G: India]

Beesley, Michael and Evans, Tom. The British Experience: The Case of British Rail. In *Vernon, R. and Aharoni, Y., eds.*, 1981, pp. 117–32. [G: U.K.]

Bourne, Compton. Issues of Public Financial Enterprise in Jamaica: The Case of the Jamaica Development Bank. *Soc. Econ. Stud.*, March 1981, *30*(1), pp. 197–208. [G: Jamaica]

Brown, Adlith. Issues of Public Enterprise. *Soc. Econ. Stud.*, March 1981, *30*(1), pp. 1–16. [G: Caribbean]

Cabral, Nuno. Criteria for the Control of Public Enterprises. *Ann. Pub. Co-op. Econ.*, January–June 1981, *52*(1/2), pp. 27–47.

Cassese, Sabino. Public Control and Corporate Efficiency. In *Vernon, R. and Aharoni, Y., eds.*, 1981, pp. 145–56.

Chesshire, John. Public Enterprises and Consumers. *Ann. Pub. Co-op. Econ.*, January–June 1981, *52*(1/2), pp. 157–62.

Chileshe, Jonathan H. Zambia. In *Adedeji, A., ed.*, 1981, pp. 81–132. [G: Zambia]

Christman, John H. Comments [Petroleum and Mexican Economic Growth and Development in the 1980s] [The Political Economy of Mexican Oil, 1976–1979]. In *Ladman, J. R.; Baldwin, D. J. and Bergman, E., eds.*, 1981, pp. 123–28. [G: Mexico]

Davies, David G. Property Rights and Economic Behavior in Private and Government Enterprises: The Case of Australia's Banking System. In *Zerbe, R. O., Jr., ed.*, 1981, pp. 111–42. [G: Australia]

Edokpayi, S. I. Administrative and Managerial Implications. In *Adedeji, A., ed.*, 1981, pp. 353–80. [G: Africa]

Ekzen, Aykut. Kamu Iktisadi Kuruluşlarinin Yeniden Düzenlenmesi Yaklaşimlari ve Dördüncü Beş Yillik Plan'in Politikalari. (Approaches to the Reorganization of the State Economic Enterprises and the Policies of the Fourth Plan. With English summary.) *METU*, Special Issue, 1981, pp. 227–60. [G: Turkey]

Evans, Peter. Collectivized Capitalism: Integrated Petrochemical Complexes and Capital Accumulation in Brazil. In *Bruneau, T. C. and Faucher, P., eds.*, 1981, pp. 85–125. [G: Brazil]

Falkena, H. B. Public and Private Enterprise (Review Note). *S. Afr. J. Econ.*, September 1981, *49*(3), pp. 289–94.

Faulhaber, Gerald R. and Levinson, Stephen B. Subsidy-Free Prices and Anonymous Equity [Cross-Subsidization: Pricing in Public Enterprises]. *Amer. Econ. Rev.*, December 1981, *71*(5), pp. 1083–91.

Floyd, Robert H. Equivalence of Product Tax Changes and Public Enterprise Price Changes. *Int. Monet. Fund Staff Pap.*, June 1981, *28*(2), pp. 338–74.

Foster, J. Fagg. The Institutionalist Theory of Government Ownership. *J. Econ. Issues*, December 1981, *15*(4), pp. 915–22.

Grassini, Franco A. The Italian Enterprises: The Political Constraints. **In** *Vernon, R. and Aharoni, Y., eds.*, 1981, pp. 70–84. [G: Italy]

Haar, Ernst. Public Enterprises and Their Employees: The Case of the German Federal Railways. *Ann. Pub. Co-op. Econ.*, January–June 1981, *52*(1/2), pp. 145–55. [G: W. Germany]

Heald, David and Steel, David. The Privatisation of UK Public Enterprises. *Ann. Pub. Co-op. Econ.*, September 1981, *52*(3), pp. 351–67. [G: U.K.]

Jones, Edwin. Role of the State in Public Enterprise. *Soc. Econ. Stud.*, March 1981, *30*(1), pp. 17–44. [G: Caribbean]

Kim, Kwan S. Enterprise Performances in the Public and Private Sectors: Tanzanian Experience, 1970–75. *J. Devel. Areas*, April 1981, *15*(3), pp. 471–84. [G: Tanzania]

Kñakal, Jan. Transnationals and Mining Development in Bolivia, Chile and Peru. *Cepal Rev.*, August 1981, (14), pp. 63–83. [G: Bolivia; Chile; Peru]

Kostecki, M. M. State Trading. **In** *Vernon, R. and Aharoni, Y., eds.*, 1981, pp. 170–83.

Kumar, Krishna. Multinationalization of Third-World Public-Sector Enterprises. **In** *Kumar, K. and McLeod, M. G., eds.*, 1981, pp. 187–201. [G: LDCs]

Leveson, Sidney M. Comments [Possible Dimensions of Mexican Petroleum] [PEMEX in a Dependent Society]. **In** *Ladman, J. R.; Baldwin, D. J. and Bergman, E., eds.*, 1981, pp. 117–21. [G: Mexico; U.S.]

Levy, Victor. On Estimating Efficiency Differentials between the Public and Private Sectors in a Developing Economy—Iraq. *J. Compar. Econ.*, September 1981, *5*(3), pp. 235–50. [G: Iraq]

Lintner, John. Economic Theory and Financial Management. **In** *Vernon, R. and Aharoni, Y., eds.*, 1981, pp. 23–53.

Lumby, Stephen. New Ways of Financing Nationalized Industries. *Lloyds Bank Rev.*, July 1981, (141), pp. 34–44. [G: U.K.]

Mallon, Richard D. Performance Evaluation and Compensation of the Social Burdens of Public Enterprise in Less Developed Countries. *Ann. Pub. Co-op. Econ.*, September 1981, *52*(3), pp. 281–300. [G: LDCs]

Martinelli, Alberto. The Italian Experience: A Historical Perspective. **In** *Vernon, R. and Aharoni, Y., eds.*, 1981, pp. 85–98. [G: Italy]

Martinelli, Alberto. The Italian Experience: A Historical Perspective. **In** *Vernon, R. and Aharoni, Y., eds.*, 1981, pp. 85–98. [G: Italy]

McBain, Helen. External Financing of the Water Commission of Jamaica. *Soc. Econ. Stud.*, March 1981, *30*(1), pp. 171–96. [G: Jamaica]

Mills, G. E. The Administration of Public Enterprise: Jamaica and Trinidad–Tobago. *Soc. Econ. Stud.*, March 1981, *30*(1), pp. 45–74. [G: Jamaica; Trinidad and Tobago; Guyana]

Nelson, Robert J. Mitterand's Nationalization Plans. *Challenge*, November–December 1981, *24*(5), pp. 54–56. [G: France]

Noreng, Øystein. State-Owned Oil Companies:

Western Europe. **In** *Vernon, R. and Aharoni, Y., eds.*, 1981, pp. 133–44. [G: U.K.; France; Italy; Norway]

Normanton, E. Leslie. Accountability and Audit. **In** *Vernon, R. and Aharoni, Y., eds.*, 1981, pp. 157–69. [G: U.K.; U.S.; France]

O'Hara, Maureen. Property Rights and the Financial Firm. *J. Law Econ.*, October 1981, *24*(2), pp. 317–32. [G: U.S.]

Parris, Carl D. Joint Venture I: The Trinidad–Tobago Telephone Company, 1968–1972. *Soc. Econ. Stud.*, March 1981, *30*(1), pp. 108–26. [G: Trinidad and Tobago]

Parris, Carl D. Joint Venture II: The National Flour Mill of Trinidad–Tobago, 1972–1979. *Soc. Econ. Stud.*, March 1981, *30*(1), pp. 127–45. [G: Trinidad and Tobago]

Pitkänen, Eero. Julkisyhteiöst liiketaloustieteen tutkimuskohteina. (Public Organizations as Research Objectives in Business Economics. With English summary.) *Liiketaloudellinen Aikak.*, 1981, *30*(2), pp. 193–221.

Posner, Michael. Running Public Enterprises: Theory and Practice. *Ann. Pub. Co-op. Econ.*, January–June 1981, *52*(1/2), pp. 17–25.

Rai, Khemraj. Worker Participation in Public Enterprise in Guyana. *Soc. Econ. Stud.*, March 1981, *30*(1), pp. 209–44. [G: Guyana]

Raiffa, Howard. Decision Making in the State-Owned Enterprise. **In** *Vernon, R. and Aharoni, Y., eds.*, 1981, pp. 54–62.

Rand, Adam. Public and Social Enterprises and Consumers. *Ann. Pub. Co-op. Econ.*, January–June 1981, *52*(1/2), pp. 163–69. [G: Israel]

Randall, Laura E. The Political Economy of Mexican Oil, 1976–1979. **In** *Ladman, J. R.; Baldwin, D. J. and Bergman, E., eds.*, 1981, pp. 87–115. [G: Mexico]

Saulniers, Alfred. State Trading Organizations: A Bias Decision Model and Applications. *World Devel.*, July 1981, *9*(7), pp. 679–94. [G: Peru]

Sepúlveda, Isidro. PEMEX in a Dependent Society. **In** *Ladman, J. R.; Baldwin, D. J. and Bergman, E., eds.*, 1981, pp. 45–68. [G: Mexico]

Sobhan, Rehman and Mahmood, Syed Akhter. Repayment of Loans to Specialised Financial Institutions in Bangladesh: Issues and Constraints. *Bangladesh Devel. Stud.*, Winter 1981, *9*(1), pp. 35–75. [G: Bangladesh]

Stefani, Giorgio. Control Mechanisms of Public Enterprises. *Ann. Pub. Co-op. Econ.*, January–June 1981, *52*(1/2), pp. 49–71. [G: Italy]

Swaby, Raphael A. The Rationale for State Ownership of Public Utilities in Jamaica. *Soc. Econ. Stud.*, March 1981, *30*(1), pp. 75–107. [G: Jamaica]

Taher, Abdulhady Hassan. The Future Role of the National Oil Companies. **In** *OPEC, Public Information Dept.*, 1981, pp. 76–87. [G: OPEC]

Trebat, Thomas J. Public Enterprises in Brazil and Mexico: A Comparison of Origins and Performance. **In** *Bruneau, T. C. and Faucher, P., eds.*, 1981, pp. 41–58. [G: Brazil; Mexico]

Türel, Oktar. 1970'li Yillarda Mühendislik Sanayilerindeki Kamu Yatirimlari: Gözlem ve Değerlendirmeler. (Public Investments in Engineering Industries in the '70's: Some Observations and

Comments. With English summary.) *METU*, Special Issue, 1981, pp. 575–612.   [G: Turkey]

Uca, Mehmet Nezir. Some Considerations on the Transition to a Self-Managed Economy in Turkey. *Econ. Anal. Worker's Manage.*, 1981, *15*(2), pp. 259–69.   [G: Turkey]

Van der Bellen, Alexander. The Control of Public Enterprises: The Case of Austria. *Ann. Pub. Coop. Econ.*, January–June 1981, *52*(1/2), pp. 73–100.   [G: Austria]

Vandebosch, Jacques. The Public Enterprise and Its Personnel. *Ann. Pub. Co-op. Econ.*, January–June 1981, *52*(1/2), pp. 127–44.

Vernon, Raymond. State-Owned Enterprise in the Western Economies: Introduction. In *Vernon, R. and Aharoni, Y., eds.*, 1981, pp. 7–22.

Vernon, Raymond. State-Owned Enterprises in Latin-American Exports. In *Baer, W. and Gillis, M., eds.*, 1981, pp. 98–114. [G: Latin America]

Vernon, Raymond. State-Owned Enterprises in Latin-American Exports. *Quart. Rev. Econ. Bus.*, Summer 1981, *21*(2), pp. 98–114.
[G: Latin America]

Viezca, Juan Aizpuru. The Future Role of the National Oil Companies: Commentary. In *OPEC, Public Information Dept.*, 1981, pp. 88–91.
[G: OPEC]

Ylä-Liedenpohja, Jouka. Public Pricing under Different Behavioural Postulates. *Liiketaloudellinen Aikak.*, 1981, *30*(1), pp. 46–60.

615 Economics of Transportation

6150 Economics of Transportation

Adler, Thomas J. Disaggregate Models for Decisions Other than Travel-Mode Choices. In *Stopher, P. R.; Meyburg, A. H. and Brög, W., eds.*, 1981, pp. 695–99.

Allen, Benjamin J. The Nature, Effectiveness, and Importance of Motor Common Carrier Service Obligations. *Amer. Econ. Rev.*, May 1981, *71*(2), pp. 110–15.   [G: U.S.]

Anderson, James E. and Kraus, Marvin. Quality of Service and the Demand for Air Travel. *Rev. Econ. Statist.*, November 1981, *63*(4), pp. 533–40.   [G: U.S.]

Arnott, Richard J. and Stiglitz, Joseph E. Aggregate Land Rents and Aggregate Transport Costs. *Econ. J.*, June 1981, *91*(362), pp. 331–47.

Ashley, David J. Uncertainty in Interurban Highway-Scheme Appraisal. In *Stopher, P. R.; Meyburg, A. H. and Brög, W., eds.*, 1981, pp. 599–615.   [G: U.K.]

Bailey, Elizabeth E. and Panzar, John C. The Contestability of Airline Markets during the Transition to Deregulation. *Law Contemp. Probl.*, Winter 1981, *44*(1), pp. 125–45.   [G: U.S.]

Barrocas, José Manuel. Significado dos valores duais e sensibilidade nos modelos de transportes. (With English summary.) *Economia (Portugal)*, October 1981, *5*(3), pp. 489–96.

Baxter, Mike and Ewing, Gordon. Models of Recreational Trip Distribution. *Reg. Stud.*, 1981, *15*(5), pp. 327–44.

Beesley, Michael and Evans, Tom. The British Ex-

perience: The Case of British Rail. In *Vernon, R. and Aharoni, Y., eds.*, 1981, pp. 117–32.
[G: U.K.]

Ben-Akiva, Moshe and Watanatada, Thawat. Application of a Continuous Spatial Choice Logit Model. In *Manski, C. F. and McFadden, D., eds.*, 1981, pp. 320–43.

Ben-Akiva, Moshe E. Issues in Transferring and Updating Travel-Behavior Models. In *Stopher, P. R.; Meyburg, A. H. and Brög, W., eds.*, 1981, pp. 665–86.   [G: U.S.]

Bending, Richard. Data Collection Methodologies—Transport and Commercial Sectors. In *Amman, F. and Wilson, R., eds.*, 1981, pp. 119–28.

Benjamin, Les and Richards, Darrell. Electrification Is the Way to Move Canada in the 1980s. *Can. Public Policy*, Summer 1981, *7*(3), pp. 472–75.

Bernard, Martin J., III. Problems in Predicting Market Response to New Transportation Technology. In *Stopher, P. R.; Meyburg, A. H. and Brög, W., eds.*, 1981, pp. 465–87.   [G: U.S.]

Bieber, Alain and Matalon, Benjamin. Urban Travel Behavior, Uncertainty, and Conceptual Framework in Models: Some Questions Raised by Recent Research. In *Stopher, P. R.; Meyburg, A. H. and Brög, W., eds.*, 1981, pp. 503–09.

Binkley, James K. and Harrer, Bruce. Major Determinants of Ocean Freight Rates for Grains: An Econometric Analysis. *Amer. J. Agr. Econ.*, February 1981, *63*(1), pp. 47–57.

Blaich, Fritz. Japan's Automobile Marketing: Its Introduction, Consolidation, Development and Characteristics: Comment. In *Okochi, A. and Shimokawa, K., eds.*, 1981, pp. 188–90. [G: Japan]

Blaich, Fritz. The Development of the Distribution Sector in the German Car Industry. In *Okochi, A. and Shimokawa, K., eds.*, 1981, pp. 93–117.
[G: Germany]

Blomquist, Glenn C. and Peltzman, Sam. Passive Restraints: An Economist's View. In *Crandall, R. W. and Lave, L. B., eds.*, 1981, pp. 37–52.
[G: U.S.]

Bolyard, Joan E. International Travel and Passenger Fares, 1980. *Surv. Curr. Bus.*, May 1981, *61*(5), pp. 29–34.   [G: U.S.]

Boncher, William. A Comparative Engineering-Economic Analysis of the Evolution of the Soviet Mainline Freight Locomotive. *J. Compar. Econ.*, June 1981, *5*(2), pp. 149–68.   [G: U.S.; U.S.S.R.]

de Borger, B. and Nonneman, W. Statistical Cost Functions for Dry Bulk Carriers. *J. Transp. Econ. Policy*, May 1981, *15*(2), pp. 155–65.

Borins, Sandford F. Mieszkowski and Saper's Estimate of the Effects of Airport Noise on Property Values: A Comment. *J. Urban Econ.*, January 1981, *9*(1), pp. 125–28.   [G: Canada]

Borins, Sandford F. The Effect of Pricing Policy on the Optimal Timing of Investments in Transport Facilities. *J. Transp. Econ. Policy*, May 1981, *15*(2), pp. 121–33.

Boucher, Michel. La réglementation de l'industrie québécoise du camionnage: aperçu et considérations analytiques. (Regulation of the Quebec Trucking Industry: Institutions, Practices and Analytical Considerations. With English summary.) *L'Actual. Econ.*, January–March 1981, 57(1), pp. 87–112. [G: Canada]

Bourgin, Christian and Godard, Xavier. Structural and Threshold Effects in the Use of Transportation Modes. In *Stopher, P. R.; Meyburg, A. H. and Brög, W., eds.*, 1981, pp. 353–68.

Boyd, Colin W. Cost Savings from One-Man Operation of Buses: A Re-Evaluation. *J. Transp. Econ. Policy*, January 1981, 15(1), pp. 59–66.
[G: U.K.]

Boyd, Colin W. The Impact of Reduced Service Quality on Demand for Bus Travel: The Case of One-Man Operation. *J. Transp. Econ. Policy*, May 1981, 15(2), pp. 167–77. [G: U.K.]

Boyer, Kenneth D. Equalizing Discrimination and Cartel Pricing in Transport Rate Regulation. *J. Polit. Econ.*, April 1981, 89(2), pp. 270–86.
[G: U.S.]

Boyer, Kenneth D. Intermediate-Term Railroad Traffic Gains in Response to Rising Energy Costs. In *[Nelson, J. R.]*, 1981, pp. 115–30. [G: U.S.]

Brand, Daniel and Cheslow, Melvin D. Spatial, Temporal, and Cultural Transferability of Travel-Choice Models. In *Stopher, P. R.; Meyburg, A. H. and Brög, W., eds.*, 1981, pp. 687–91.

Bredimas, Anna E. and Tzoannos, John G. In Search of a Common Shipping Policy for the E.C. *J. Common Market Stud.*, December 1981, 20(2), pp. 95–114. [G: EEC]

Burnett, K. Patricia. Spatial Transferability of Travel-Demand Models. In *Stopher, P. R.; Meyburg, A. H. and Brög, W., eds.*, 1981, pp. 623–28.

Burnett, Pat. Theoretical Advances in Modeling Economic and Social Behaviors: Applications to Geographical, Policy-Oriented Models. *Econ. Geogr.*, October 1981, 57(4), pp. 291–303.

Businaro, Ugo Lucio and Fedrighini, Aldo. Prospects of Energy Conservation in Transportation. In *Amman, F. and Wilson, R., eds.*, 1981, pp. 139–256. [G: Selected Countries]

Cairns, Malcolm B. The Automatic Interaction Detector Algorithm and the Measurement of Transport Output. *J. Transp. Econ. Policy*, September 1981, 15(3), pp. 277–82. [G: Canada]

Carnes, Richard B. Productivity Trends for Intercity Bus Carriers. *Mon. Lab. Rev.*, May 1981, 104(5), pp. 23–27. [G: U.S.]

Caves, Douglas W.; Christensen, Laurits R. and Swanson, Joseph A. Economic Performance in Regulated and Unregulated Environments: A Comparison of U.S. and Canadian Railroads. *Quart. J. Econ.*, November 1981, 96(4), pp. 559–81. [G: U.S.; Canada]

Caves, Douglas W.; Christensen, Laurits R. and Swanson, Joseph A. Productivity Growth, Scale Economies, and Capacity Utilization in U.S. Railroads, 1955–74. *Amer. Econ. Rev.*, December 1981, 71(5), pp. 994–1002. [G: U.S.]

Caves, Douglas W.; Christensen, Laurits R. and Thretheway, Michael W. U.S. Trunk Air Carriers, 1972–1977: A Multilateral Comparison of Total Factor Productivity. In *Cowing, T. G. and Stevenson, R. E., eds.*, 1981, pp. 47–76.
[G: U.S.]

Channon, Geoffrey. The Great Western Railway un-

der the British Railways Act of 1921. *Bus. Hist. Rev.*, Summer 1981, 55(2), pp. 188–216.
[G: U.K.]

Chappell, Henry W., Jr. Campaign Contributions and Voting on the Cargo Preference Bill: A Comparison of Simultaneous Models. *Public Choice*, 1981, 36(2), pp. 301–12. [G: U.S.]

Cherry, Russell C. and Backman, Carl. Market Structure and Concentration in the Regulated Trucking Industry. *Amer. Econ. Rev.*, May 1981, 71(2), pp. 385–88. [G: U.S.]

Chung, Jae Wan. The Price of Gasoline, the Oil Crisis, and the Choice of Transportation Mode. *Quart. Rev. Econ. Bus.*, Autumn 1981, 21(3), pp. 77–86. [G: U.S.]

Church, Roy. French Automobile Marketing, 1890–1979: Comment. In *Okochi, A. and Shimokawa, K., eds.*, 1981, pp. 155–60. [G: France]

Church, Roy. The Marketing of Automobiles in Britain and the United States before 1939. In *Okochi, A. and Shimokawa, K., eds.*, 1981, pp. 59–87.
[G: U.K.; U.S.]

Clark, David and Unwin, Kathryn I. Telecommunications and Travel: Potential Impact in Rural Areas. *Reg. Stud.*, 1981, 15(1), pp. 47–56.
[G: U.K.]

Clark, Don P. On the Relative Importance of International Transport Charges as a Barrier to Trade. *Quart. Rev. Econ. Bus.*, Winter 1981, 21(4), pp. 127–35. [G: U.S.]

Clark, Don P. Protection by International Transport Charges: Analysis by Stage of Fabrication. *J. Devel. Econ.*, June 1981, 8(3), pp. 339–45.
[G: U.S.; LDCs]

Conley, Dennis M. and Heady, Earl O. The Interregional Impacts of Improved Truck Transportation on Farm Income from Rice in Thailand. *J. Devel. Areas*, July 1981, 15(4), pp. 549–59.
[G: Thailand]

Cosgrove Twitchett, Carol. Harmonisation and Road Freight Transport. In *Twitchett, C. C., ed.*, 1981, pp. 63–77. [G: EEC]

Daganzo, Carlos F. Calibration and Prediction with Random-Utility Models: Some Recent Advances and Unresolved Questions. In *Stopher, P. R.; Meyburg, A. H. and Brög, W., eds.*, 1981, pp. 35–53.

Daito, Eisuke. Marketing History in the Automobile Industry: The United States and Japan: Comment. In *Okochi, A. and Shimokawa, K., eds.*, 1981, pp. 33–35. [G: U.S.; Japan]

Daly, Andrew J. Some Issues in the Application of Disaggregate Choice Models. In *Stopher, P. R.; Meyburg, A. H. and Brög, W., eds.*, 1981, pp. 55–72.

Damus, Sylvester. Two-Part Tariffs and Optimum Taxation: The Case of Railway Rates. *Amer. Econ. Rev.*, March 1981, 71(1), pp. 65–79. [G: U.S.]

Daughety, Andrew F. and Inaba, Frederick S. An Analysis of Regulatory Change in the Transportation Industry. *Rev. Econ. Statist.*, May 1981, 63(2), pp. 246–55. [G: U.S.]

Dix, Martin C. Structuring Our Understanding of Travel Choices: The Use of Psychometric and Social-Science Research Techniques. In *Stopher, P. R.; Meyburg, A. H. and Brög, W., eds.*, 1981,

pp. 89–109.

de Donnea, François-Xavier and Herz, Raimund K. The Conceptual Context of Uncertainty in Modeling Travel Behavior. In *Stopher, P. R.; Meyburg, A. H. and Brög, W., eds.*, 1981, pp. 517–20.

Drinka, Thomas P. and Prescott, James R. Optimal Roadway Tolls and Operating Costs in Urbanized Regions. *Reg. Sci. Persp.*, 1981, *11*(2), pp. 15–28. **[G: U.S.]**

Due, John F. Railroads: An Endangered Species and the Possibility of a Fatal Mistake. *Quart. Rev. Econ. Bus.*, Spring 1981, *21*(1), pp. 58–76. **[G: U.S.]**

Dunn, Kenneth B. and McConnell, John J. Valuation of GNMA Mortgage-Backed Securities. *J. Finance*, June 1981, *36*(3), pp. 599–616. **[G: U.S.]**

Ehrnrooth, Robert G. Rederierna och konjunkturutvecklingen. (The Shipping Trade and Economic Prospects. With English summary.) *Ekon. Samfundets Tidskr.*, 1981, *34*(1), pp. 29–31.
[G: Finland]

Else, P. K. A Reformulation of the Theory of Optimal Congestion Taxes. *J. Transp. Econ. Policy*, September 1981, *15*(3), pp. 217–32.

Felton, John Richard. The Impact of Rate Regulation upon ICC-Regulated Truck Back Hauls. *J. Transp. Econ. Policy*, September 1981, *15*(3), pp. 253–67. **[G: U.S.; U.K.; Australia]**

Findlay, Christopher C. International Civil Aviation Policy Options. *Australian J. Manage.*, December 1981, *6*(2), pp. 27–42.

Foerster, James F. Nonlinear and Noncompensatory Perceptual Functions of Evaluation and Choice. In *Stopher, P. R.; Meyburg, A. H. and Brög, W., eds.*, 1981, pp. 335–51.

Forsyth, P. J. Urban Transportation Pricing. In *Ballabon, M. B., ed.*, 1981, pp. 195–228.

Frank, Robert H. Productivity Gains since Deregulation in the Airline Industry: A Survey of Research in Progress. In *Hogan, J. D. and Craig, A. M., eds., Vol. 2*, 1981, pp. 1035–54.
[G: U.S.]

Frederiksen, Peter C. Further Evidence on the Relationship between Population Density and Infrastructure: The Philippines and Electrification. *Econ. Develop. Cult. Change*, July 1981, *29*(4), pp. 749–58. **[G: Philippines]**

Frew, James R. The Existence of Monopoly Profits in the Motor Carrier Industry. *J. Law Econ.*, October 1981, *24*(2), pp. 289–315. **[G: U.S.]**

Fridenson, Patrick. French Automobile Marketing, 1890–1979. In *Okochi, A. and Shimokawa, K., eds.*, 1981, pp. 127–54. **[G: France]**

Fridenson, Patrick. The Marketing of Automobiles in Britain and the United States before 1939: Comment. In *Okochi, A. and Shimokawa, K., eds.*, 1981, pp. 88–90. **[G: U.K.; U.S.]**

Friedlaender, Ann F. Equity, Efficiency, and Regulation in the Rail and Trucking Industries. In *Weiss, L. W. and Klass, M. W., eds.*, 1981, pp. 102–41. **[G: U.S.]**

Friedlaender, Ann F. Price Distortions and Second Best Investment Rules in the Transportation Industries. *Amer. Econ. Rev.*, May 1981, *71*(2), pp. 389–93. **[G: U.S.]**

Friedlaender, Ann F.; Chiang, S. J. Wang and Spady, Richard H. Regulation and the Structure of Technology in the Trucking Industry. In *Cowing, T. G. and Stevenson, R. E., eds.*, 1981, pp. 77–106. **[G: U.S.]**

Friesz, Terry L. Multiobjective Optimization in Transportation: The Case of Equilibrium Network Design. In *Morse, J. N., ed.*, 1981, pp. 116–27.

Fruin, Jerry E. Impacts on Agriculture of Deregulating the Transportation System: Discussion. *Amer. J. Agr. Econ.*, December 1981, *63*(5), pp. 923–25.

Fuller, John W. Inflationary Effects on Transportation. *Ann. Amer. Acad. Polit. Soc. Sci.*, July 1981, *456*, pp. 112–22. **[G: U.S.]**

Fuller, Stephen and Shanmugham, C. V. Effectiveness of Competition to Limit Rail Rate Increases under Deregulation: The Case of Wheat Exports from the Southern Plains. *Southern J. Agr. Econ.*, December 1981, *13*(2), pp. 11–19. **[G: U.S.]**

Garbrecht, Dietrich. Walking—Facts, Assertions, and Propositions. In *Molt, W.; Hartmann, H. A. and Stringer, P., eds.*, 1981, pp. 403–12.
[G: W. Germany]

Garden, Jackie. Applications of Behavioral Models to Travel and Activity Needs of the Mobility Limited. In *Stopher, P. R.; Meyburg, A. H. and Brög, W., eds.*, 1981, pp. 455–61.

Gendell, David S. and Garden, Jackie. The Effect of Future Options on Travel Behavior. In *Stopher, P. R.; Meyburg, A. H. and Brög, W., eds.*, 1981, pp. 489–500.

Gensch, Dennis H. Choice-Modeling Process Assumptions. In *Stopher, P. R.; Meyburg, A. H. and Brög, W., eds.*, 1981, pp. 514–17.

Gibson, J. G. A Rational Alternative Fare Structure for British Rail's London and South-East Commuter Passengers. *J. Transp. Econ. Policy*, September 1981, *15*(3), pp. 269–75. **[G: U.K.]**

Glazer, Amihai. Congestion Tolls and Consumer Welfare. *Public Finance*, 1981, *36*(1), pp. 77–83.

Glen, D.; Owen, M. and van der Meer, R. Spot and Time Charter Rates for Tankers, 1970–77. *J. Transp. Econ. Policy*, January 1981, *15*(1), pp. 45–58.

Golob, Thomas F. and Richardson, Anthony J. Noncompensatory and Discontinuous Constructs in Travel-Behavior Models. In *Stopher, P. R.; Meyburg, A. H. and Brög, W., eds.*, 1981, pp. 369–84.

Graglia, Lino A. The Supreme Court and the American Common Market [Regulation and the American Common Market]. In *Tarlock, A. D., ed.*, 1981, pp. 67–75. **[G: U.S.]**

Greschner, G. Modifiziertes Verfahren des "Dynamic Programming" zur Lösung eines speziellen Travelling Salesman Problems bei der optimalen Routenberechnung Bedarfsgesteuerter Busse. (With English summary.) In *Fandel, G., et al., eds.*, 1981, pp. 372–81.

Grether, David M.; Isaac, R. Mark and Plott, Charles R. The Allocation of Landing Rights by Unanimity among Competitors. *Amer. Econ. Rev.*, May 1981, *71*(2), pp. 166–71. **[G: U.S.]**

Gronberg, Timothy J. and Meyer, Jack. Transport Inefficiency and the Choice of Spatial Pricing

Mode. *J. Reg. Sci.*, November 1981, *21*(4), pp. 541–49.

Guandolo, John. The Role of the Interstate Commerce Commission in the 1980's. *Amer. Econ. Rev.*, May 1981, *71*(2), pp. 116–21. **[G: U.S.]**

Haar, Ernst. Public Enterprises and Their Employees: The Case of the German Federal Railways. *Ann. Pub. Co-op. Econ.*, January–June 1981, *52*(1/2), pp. 145–55. **[G: W. Germany]**

Halsey, Harlan I. The Choice between High-Pressure and Low-Pressure Steam Power in America in the Early Nineteenth Century. *J. Econ. Hist.*, December 1981, *41*(4), pp. 723–44. **[G: U.S.]**

Hansen, Stein. In Favor of Cross-Cultural Transferability of Travel-Demand Models. In *Stopher, P. R.; Meyburg, A. H. and Brög, W., eds.*, 1981, pp. 637–51.

Hanson, Susan and Burnett, K. Patricia. Understanding Complex Travel Behavior: Measurement Issues. In *Stopher, P. R.; Meyburg, A. H. and Brög, W., eds.*, 1981, pp. 207–30.

Hara, Terushi. French Automobile Marketing, 1890–1979: Comment. In *Okochi, A. and Shimokawa, K., eds.*, 1981, pp. 160–62. **[G: France]**

Harmatuck, Donald J. A Motor Carrier Joint Cost Function: A Flexible Functional Form with Activity Prices. *J. Transp. Econ. Policy*, May 1981, *15*(2), pp. 135–53. **[G: U.S.]**

Harris, Robert G. and Keeler, Theodore E. Determinants of Railroad Profitability: An Econometric Study. In *[Nelson, J. R.]*, 1981, pp. 37–53. **[G: U.S.]**

Harrison, A. J. M. and Stabler, M. J. An Analysis of Journeys for Canal-based Recreation. *Reg. Stud.*, 1981, *15*(5), pp. 345–58. **[G: U.K.]**

Hartgen, David T. Uncertainty in the Application of Travel-Behavior Models. In *Stopher, P. R.; Meyburg, A. H. and Brög, W., eds.*, 1981, pp. 617–20.

Hartmann, Hans A. Causes and Cures of Traffic Behavior: Facts—Myths—Research—Planning. In *Molt, W.; Hartmann, H. A. and Stringer, P., eds.*, 1981, pp. 319–55. **[G: W. Germany]**

Havens, John J. New Approaches to Understanding Travel Behavior: Role, Life-Style, and Adaptation. In *Stopher, P. R.; Meyburg, A. H. and Brög, W., eds.*, 1981, pp. 269–87.

Hawke, G. R. and Higgins, J. P. P. Transport and Social Overhead Capital. In *Floud, R. and McCloskey, D., eds., Vol. 1*, 1981, pp. 227–52. **[G: U.K.]**

Hayut, Yehuda. Containerization and the Load Center Concept. *Econ. Geogr.*, April 1981, *57*(2), pp. 160–76.

Haywood, Richard Mowbray. The Development of Steamboats on the Volga River and Its Tributaries, 1817–1856. In *Uselding, P., ed.*, 1981, pp. 127–92. **[G: U.S.S.R.]**

Heidemann, Claus. Spatial-Behavior Studies: Concepts and Contexts. In *Stopher, P. R.; Meyburg, A. H. and Brög, W., eds.*, 1981, pp. 289–315.

Held, Martin. Some Thoughts about the Individual's Choice among Alternative Travel Modes and Its Determinants. In *Stopher, P. R.; Meyburg, A. H. and Brög, W., eds.*, 1981, pp. 155–69.

Hensher, David A. Two Contentions Related to Conceptual Context in Behavioral Travel Modeling. In *Stopher, P. R.; Meyburg, A. H. and Brög, W., eds.*, 1981, pp. 509–14. **[G: U.S.]**

Hensher, David A. and Johnson, Lester W. Behavioural Response and Form of the Representative Component of the Indirect Utility Function in Travel Choice Models. *Reg. Sci. Urban Econ.*, November 1981, *11*(4), pp. 559–72. **[G: Australia]**

Higgins, Thomas J. Road Pricing: A Clash of Analysis and Politics. *Policy Anal.*, Winter 1981, *7*(1), pp. 71–89. **[G: U.S.]**

Hill, Daniel H. The Gasoline Price Responsiveness of Personal Transportation Demand. In *Hill, M. S.; Hill, D. H. and Morgan, J. N., eds.*, 1981, pp. 269–96. **[G: U.S.]**

Hills, Peter J. and Mitchell, Christopher G. B. New Approaches to Understanding Travel Behavior. In *Stopher, P. R.; Meyburg, A. H. and Brög, W., eds.*, 1981, pp. 317–32.

Hoch, Irving. Energy and Location. In *Hawley, A. H. and Mazie, S. M., eds.*, 1981, pp. 285–356. **[G: U.S.]**

Horowitz, Joel L. Sources of Error and Uncertainty in Behavioral Travel-Demand Models. In *Stopher, P. R.; Meyburg, A. H. and Brög, W., eds.*, 1981, pp. 543–58.

Höttler, Rainer. Some Issues of Policy Sensitivity in Behavioral Travel Models. In *Stopher, P. R.; Meyburg, A. H. and Brög, W., eds.*, 1981, pp. 399–412.

Huelke, Donald F. and O'Day, James. Passive Restraints: A Scientist's View. In *Crandall, R. W. and Lave, L. B., eds.*, 1981, pp. 21–35. **[G: U.S.]**

Ippolito, Richard A. Estimating Airline Demand with Quality of Service Variables. *J. Transp. Econ. Policy*, January 1981, *15*(1), pp. 7–15. **[G: U.S.]**

Islam, Nurul. Interest Groups and Aid Conditionality. In *Faaland, J., ed.*, 1981, pp. 53–72. **[G: Bangladesh]**

Jech, Otto. Social Consumption of the Population and Its Expected Trends. *Czech. Econ. Digest.*, February 1981, (1), pp. 18–37. **[G: Czechoslovakia]**

Johnson, Marc A. Current and Developing Issues in Interregional Competition and Agricultural Transportation. *Southern J. Agr. Econ.*, July 1981, *13*(1), pp. 59–68. **[G: U.S.]**

Johnson, Marc A. Impacts on Agriculture of Deregulating the Transportation System. *Amer. J. Agr. Econ.*, December 1981, *63*(5), pp. 913–20. **[G: U.S.]**

Jones, Peter M. Activity Approaches to Understanding Travel Behavior. In *Stopher, P. R.; Meyburg, A. H. and Brög, W., eds.*, 1981, pp. 253–66.

Kahn, Alfred E. Regulation in Theory and Practice: An Overview: Comment. In *Fromm, G., ed.*, 1981, pp. 66–72. **[G: U.S.]**

Keeler, Theodore E. The Revolution in Airline Regulation. In *Weiss, L. W. and Klass, M. W., eds.*, 1981, pp. 53–85. **[G: U.S.]**

Keeler, Theodore E. and Abrahams, Michael. Market Structure, Pricing, and Service Quality in the Airline Industry under Deregulation. In *Sichel,*

W. and Gies, T. G., eds., 1981, pp. 103–19. [G: U.S.]

Kobrin, Paul. Fuel Switching, Gasoline Price Controls, and the Leaded-Unleaded Gasoline Price Differential. *J. Environ. Econ. Manage.*, September 1981, 8(3), pp. 287–302. [G: U.S.]

Koppelman, Frank S. Uncertainty in Methods and Measurements for Travel-Behavior Models. In *Stopher, P. R.; Meyburg, A. H. and Brög, W.,* eds., 1981, pp. 577–83.

Kraus, Marvin. Indivisibilities, Economies of Scale, and Optimal Subsidy Policy for Freeways. *Land Econ.*, February 1981, 57(1), pp. 115–21. [G: U.S.]

Kraus, Marvin. The Problem of Optimal Resource Allocation in Urban Transportation. In *Ballabon, M. B.,* ed., 1981, pp. 229–61.

Kutter, Eckhard. Some Remarks on Activity-Pattern Analysis in Transportation Planning. In *Stopher, P. R.; Meyburg, A. H. and Brög, W.,* eds., 1981, pp. 231–51.

Lackman, Conway L. and Heinzelmann, Raymond G. Marine Preference Cargo Market: Opportunities for Minority Shippers. *Rev. Black Polit. Econ.*, Spring 1981, 11(3), pp. 365–74. [G: U.S.]

Lacoste, Louis. The Structure of Railroad Fares and Rates in a Highly Competitive Freight Transportation Market. In *[Nelson, J. R.],* 1981, pp. 83–91.

Lago, Armando M.; Mayworm, Patrick and McEnroe, J. Matthew. Transit Service Elasticities: Evidence from Demonstrations and Demand Models. *J. Transp. Econ. Policy*, May 1981, 15(2), pp. 99–119. [G: U.S.; U.K.; Canada]

Lang, A. Scheffer. The Great Economic Leveling-out of the Intercity Freight Transportation Market. In *[Nelson, J. R.],* 1981, pp. 55–64. [G: U.S.]

Larson, Donald W. and Vogel, Robert C. Railroad Abandonment: Optimal Solutions and Policy Outcomes. In *[Nelson, J. R.],* 1981, pp. 65–82. [G: U.S.]

Lerman, Steven R. A Comment on Interspatial, Intraspatial, and Temporal Transferability. In *Stopher, P. R.; Meyburg, A. H. and Brög, W.,* eds., 1981, pp. 628–32.

Levin, Irwin P. Laboratory Simulation of Transportation Mode Choice: Methods, Models, and Validity Tests. In *Molt, W.; Hartmann, H. A. and Stringer, P.,* eds., 1981, pp. 357–66.

Levin, Irwin P. New Applications of Attitude-Measurement and Attitudinal-Modeling Techniques in Transportation Research. In *Stopher, P. R.; Meyburg, A. H. and Brög, W.,* eds., 1981, pp. 171–88.

Levin, Richard C. Railroad Rates, Profitability, and Welfare under Deregulation. *Bell J. Econ. (See Rand J. Econ. after 4/85)*, Spring 1981, 12(1), pp. 1–26. [G: U.S.]

Levin, Richard C. Railroad Regulation, Deregulation, and Workable Competition. *Amer. Econ. Rev.*, May 1981, 71(2), pp. 394–98. [G: U.S.]

Levin, Richard C. Regulation, Barriers to Exit, and the Investment Behavior of Railroads. In *Fromm, G.,* ed., 1981, pp. 181–224. [G: U.S.]

Levine, Michael E. Revisionism Revised? Airline Deregulation and the Public Interest. *Law Contemp. Probl.*, Winter 1981, 44(1), pp. 179–95. [G: U.S.]

Liang, Ernest P. L. Market Accessibility and Agricultural Development in Prewar China. *Econ. Develop. Cult. Change*, October 1981, 30(1), pp. 77–105. [G: China]

Lincoln, Edward J. Regulation of Rates on the Japanese National Railways. In *[Nelson, J. R.],* 1981, pp. 131–49. [G: Japan]

Livesay, Harold C. Marketing History in the Automobile Industry: The United States and Japan: Comment. In *Okochi, A. and Shimokawa, K.,* eds., 1981, pp. 31–33. [G: U.S.; Japan]

Livesay, Harold C. Nineteenth Century Precursors to Automobile Marketing in the United States. In *Okochi, A. and Shimokawa, K.,* eds., 1981, pp. 39–52. [G: U.S.]

Louviere, Jordan J. A Conceptual and Analytical Framework for Understanding Spatial and Travel Choices. *Econ. Geogr.*, October 1981, 57(4), pp. 304–14.

Louviere, Jordan J. Some Comments on Premature Expectations Regarding Spatial, Temporal, and Cultural Transferability of Travel-Choice Models. In *Stopher, P. R.; Meyburg, A. H. and Brög, W.,* eds., 1981, pp. 653–63.

Lutz, James M.; Miller, Philip L. and Reddy, Y. V. Optimized Steam Coal Transportation Patterns for the United States. *J. Energy Devel.*, Spring 1981, 6(2), pp. 297–314. [G: U.S.]

Lyon, Kenneth S. Mining of the Forest and the Time Path of the Price of Timber. *J. Environ. Econ. Manage.*, December 1981, 8(4), pp. 330–44.

Mäcke, Paul A. Reflections on Transferability. In *Stopher, P. R.; Meyburg, A. H. and Brög, W.,* eds., 1981, pp. 632–36.

Magat, Wesley A. and Estomin, Steven. The Behavior of Regulatory Agencies. In *Ferguson, A. R.,* ed., 1981, pp. 95–116. [G: U.S.]

Manheim, L. Marvin and Sobel, Kenneth L. Modeling Individual Choice in Nontransportation Contexts. In *Stopher, P. R.; Meyburg, A. H. and Brög, W.,* eds., 1981, pp. 706–13.

Manski, Charles F. Recent Advances in and New Directions for Behavioral Travel Modeling. In *Stopher, P. R.; Meyburg, A. H. and Brög, W.,* eds., 1981, pp. 73–86.

McCusker, John J. The Tonnage of Ships Engaged in British Colonial Trade during the Eighteenth Century. In *Uselding, P.,* ed., 1981, pp. 73–105. [G: U.K.]

McGowan, John J. Regulation, Barriers to Exit, and the Investment Behavior of Railroads: Comment. In *Fromm, G.,* ed., 1981, pp. 225–27. [G: U.S.]

McRae, James J. An Empirical Measure of the Influence on Transportation Costs on Regional Income. *Can. J. Econ.*, February 1981, 14(1), pp. 155–63. [G: Canada]

Melcher, Thomas R. State Pupil Transportation Programs. In *Jordan, K. F. and Cambron-McCabe, N. H.,* eds., 1981, pp. 215–47. [G: U.S.]

Meyer, H. R. Bundesbahnpolitik auf verfehltem Kurs. (Wrong Solution for the Swiss Federal Railways. With English summary.) *Schweiz. Z. Volks-wirtsch. Statist.*, December 1981, *117*(4), pp. 617–32. [G: Switzerland]

Meyer, John R. and Tye, William B. On the Problems of Maintaining Competition in International Air Transportation. In *[Nelson, J. R.]*, 1981, pp. 263–76. [G: U.S.]

Michaels, Richard M. and Allaman, Peter M. Research in Psychometrics: Potential for Applications and New Directions for Travel Modeling. In *Stopher, P. R.; Meyburg, A. H. and Brög, W., eds.*, 1981, pp. 139–51.

Michon, John A. and Benwell, Mary. Travelers' Attitudes and Judgments: Application of Fundamental Concepts of Psychology. In *Stopher, P. R.; Meyburg, A. H. and Brög, W., eds.*, 1981, pp. 189–203.

Mishan, Ezra J. Interpretation of the Benefits of Private Transport. In *Mishan, E. J.*, 1981, *1967*, pp. 100–104.

Mishan, Ezra J. What Is Wrong with Roskill? In *Mishan, E. J.*, 1981, *1970*, pp. 209–18. [G: U.K.]

Mitaishvili, A. The Development of the Transport System of the USSR. *Prob. Econ.*, February 1981, *23*(10), pp. 47–63. [G: U.S.S.R.]

Molt, Walter. Traffic as an Economic and Psychological Problem. In *Molt, W.; Hartmann, H. A. and Stringer, P., eds.*, 1981, pp. 315–18.

Morash, Edward A. Regulatory Policy and Industry Structure: The Case of Interstate Household Goods Carriers. *Land Econ.*, November 1981, *57*(4), pp. 544–57. [G: U.S.]

Mount, Randall I. and Williams, Harold R. Energy Conservation, Motor Gasoline Demand and the OECD Countries. *Rev. Bus. Econ. Res.*, Spring 1981, *16*(3), pp. 48–57. [G: OECD]

Nachane, D. M., et al. Forecasting Freight and Passenger Traffic on Indian Railways: A Generalized Adaptive-Filtering Approach. *Indian Econ. J.*, October–December 1981, *29*(2), pp. 98–116. [G: India]

Nash, C. A. and Brown, R. H. A Rejoinder [Cost Savings from One-Man Operation of Buses]. *J. Transp. Econ. Policy*, January 1981, *15*(1), pp. 66–67. [G: U.K.]

Nash, Carl E. Passive Restraints: A Regulator's View. In *Crandall, R. W. and Lave, L. B., eds.*, 1981, pp. 53–67. [G: U.S.]

Nelson, James C. British Freight Transport Deregulation and U.S. Transport Policy. In *[Nelson, J. R.]*, 1981, pp. 93–114. [G: U.K.; U.S.]

Norton, Roger D. Policy Issues in the Routing of Radioactive Materials Shipments. *Natural Res. J.*, October 1981, *21*(4), pp. 735–55. [G: U.S.]

Okyay, Vildan. Bati Anadolu Bölgesinde Ulaşim Sistemindeki Değişikliğin Merkezler Kademelenmesi Üzerindeki Etkileri (1844–1914). (With English summary.) *METU*, 1981, *8*(3&4), pp. 649–82. [G: Turkey]

Olson, C. Vincent and Trapani, John M., III. Who Has Benefited from Regulation of the Airline Industry? *J. Law Econ.*, April 1981, *24*(1), pp. 75–93. [G: U.S.]

Paaswell, Robert E. Travel and Activity Needs of the Mobility Limited. In *Stopher, P. R.; Mey-*

burg, A. H. and Brög, W., eds., 1981, pp. 425–54. [G: U.S.]

Phillips, Almarin. Regulation, Barriers to Exit, and the Investment Behavior of Railroads: Comment. In *Fromm, G., ed.*, 1981, pp. 228–29.

Pisarski, Alan E. Transportation. *Ann. Amer. Acad. Polit. Soc. Sci.*, January 1981, *453*, pp. 70–95. [G: U.S.]

Pucher, John and Hirschman, Ira. Distribution of the Tax Burden of Transit Subsidies in the United States. *Public Policy*, Summer 1981, *29*(3), pp. 341–67. [G: U.S.]

Rachlin, Marjorie B. Labor Education for Women Workers: Training Rank and File Leaders: A Case Study. In *Wertheimer, B. M., ed.*, 1981, pp. 62–70. [G: U.S.]

Rahou, Ghazi Ibrahim. Aspects of Organization and Efficiency of Oil Products Transport in Irak. *Econ. Computat. Cybern. Stud. Res.*, 1981, *15*(2), pp. 85–88. [G: Iraq]

Richards, Martin G. Issues in Policy Sensitivity of Behavioral Models. In *Stopher, P. R.; Meyburg, A. H. and Brög, W., eds.*, 1981, pp. 413–22.

Rosenberg, William G. The Democratization of Russia's Railroads in 1917. *Amer. Hist. Rev.*, December 1981, *86*(5), pp. 983–1008. [G: U.S.S.R.]

Rosengren, Eric and Webb, George. The Australian Road Freight Industry: Is There a Need for Government Regulation? *Australian Econ. Pap.*, December 1981, *20*(37), pp. 299–308. [G: Australia]

Roueche, Leonard. Notes on Government Subsidisation of Ferry Transport. *J. Transp. Econ. Policy*, September 1981, *15*(3), pp. 233–42. [G: U.K.; Canada; U.S.; Norway]

Rowse, John. Solving the Generalized Transportation Problem. *Reg. Sci. Urban Econ.*, February 1981, *11*(1), pp. 57–68.

Saltzman, Arthur and Newlin, Lawrence W. The Availability of Passenger Transportation. In *Hawley, A. H. and Mazie, S. M., eds.*, 1981, pp. 255–84. [G: U.S.]

Sargious, Michel; Szplett, David and Janarthanan, N. Potential Price-Induced Fuel Conservation with Changes in the Canadian Urban Transportation System. *J. Energy Devel.*, Autumn 1981, *7*(1), pp. 61–71. [G: Canada]

Serafetinidis, M., et al. The Development of Greek Shipping Capital and Its Implications for the Political Economy of Greece. *Cambridge J. Econ.*, September 1981, *5*(3), pp. 289–310. [G: Greece]

Shimojo, Tetsuji. An Input–Output Table for Evaluation of the Shipping Activities. *Kobe Econ. Bus. Rev.*, 1981, (27), pp. 49–68.

Shimokawa, Koichi. Marketing History in the Automobile Industry: The United States and Japan. In *Okochi, A. and Shimokawa, K., eds.*, 1981, pp. 3–30. [G: U.S.; Japan]

Shimokawa, Koichi. The Development of the Distribution Sector in the German Car Industry: Comment. In *Okochi, A. and Shimokawa, K., eds.*, 1981, pp. 118–21. [G: Germany]

Shneerson, Dan. Investment in Port Systems: A Case Study of the Nigerian Ports. *J. Transp.*

Econ. Policy, September 1981, *15*(3), pp. 201–16. [G: Nigeria]

Simpson, James R. and Stegelin, Forrest E. The Effect of Increasing Transportation Costs on Florida's Cattle Feeding Industry: An Extension Application. *Southern J. Agr. Econ.*, December 1981, *13*(2), pp. 141–48. [G: U.S.]

Spear, Bruce D. Travel-Behavior Research: The Need and Potential for Policy Relevance. In *Stopher, P. R.; Meyburg, A. H. and Brög, W., eds.*, 1981, pp. 387–97.

Spychalski, John C. Antitrust Standards and Railway Freight Pricing: New Round in an Old Debate. *Amer. Econ. Rev.*, May 1981, *71*(2), pp. 104–09. [G: U.S.]

Stopher, Peter R.; Meyburg, Arnim H. and Brög, Werner. Travel-Behavior Research: Summary of Findings and Recommendations. In *Stopher, P. R.; Meyburg, A. H. and Brög, W., eds.*, 1981, pp. 717–31.

Stopher, Peter R.; Meyburg, Arnim H. and Brög, Werner. Travel-Behavior Research: A Perspective. In *Stopher, P. R.; Meyburg, A. H. and Brög, W., eds.*, 1981, pp. 3–32.

Talvitie, Antti P. Inaccurate or Incomplete Data as a Source of Uncertainty in Econometric or Attitudinal Models of Travel Behavior. In *Stopher, P. R.; Meyburg, A. H. and Brög, W., eds.*, 1981, pp. 559–75. [G: U.S.]

Teplitz, Charles J. Warehouse Replenishment Using the Cost-Service Transportation Model. In *Chikán, A., ed. (II)*, 1981, pp. 567–73.

Theophanides, Stavros M. The Consumer Firm: The Popular Shipping Companies in Greece—A Case-Study of Consumer Participation in the Creation of Firms. *Econ. Anal. Worker's Manage.*, 1981, *15*(2), pp. 231–50. [G: Greece]

Till, Thomas A. Productivity and the Railroad Industry. In *Hogan, J. D. and Craig, A. M., eds., Vol. 2*, 1981, pp. 1109–13. [G: U.S.]

Tinhofer, G. Über ein Problem der diskreten Optimierung aus dem Bereich der StraBenplanung. (With English summary.) In *Fandel, G., et al., eds.*, 1981, pp. 282–85.

Tischer, Mary Lynn. Attitude Measurement: Psychometric Modeling. In *Stopher, P. R.; Meyburg, A. H. and Brög, W., eds.*, 1981, pp. 111–38.

Toba, Kin'ichiro. Nineteenth Century Precursors to Automobile Marketing in the United States: Comment. In *Okochi, A. and Shimokawa, K., eds.*, 1981, pp. 53–55. [G: U.S.]

Udagawa, Masaru. Japan's Automobile Marketing: Its Introduction, Consolidation, Development and Characteristics. In *Okochi, A. and Shimokawa, K., eds.*, 1981, pp. 163–87. [G: Japan]

Udall, Alan T. Transport Improvements and Rural Outmigration in Colombia. *Econ. Develop. Cult. Change*, April 1981, *29*(3), pp. 613–29. [G: Colombia]

Vermet-Desroches, Bernard. Interactions humaines et théorie des catastrophes: une application au comportement du vacancier. (Human Interaction and the Theory of Catastrophes: An Application to the Behaviour of the Holiday-Maker. With English summary.) *L'Actual. Econ.*, January–March 1981, *57*(1), pp. 54–69. [G: Canada]

Vickerman, Roger W. Travel-Choice Models and the Limit of Their Applicability in Other Choice Situations. In *Stopher, P. R.; Meyburg, A. H. and Brög, W., eds.*, 1981, pp. 700–706.

Walters, A. A. A Rejoinder [The Benefits of Minibuses: The Case of Kuala Lumpur]. *J. Transp. Econ. Policy*, January 1981, *15*(1), pp. 79–80. [G: Malaysia]

Warner, Stanley L. Balanced Information: The Pickering Airport Experiment. *Rev. Econ. Statist.*, May 1981, *63*(2), pp. 256–62. [G: Canada]

Watanabe, Hisashi. The Development of the Distribution Sector in the German Car Industry: Comment. In *Okochi, A. and Shimokawa, K., eds.*, 1981, pp. 121–25. [G: Germany]

Weber, Hans Peter. Uncertainty in Application: A German Case Study. In *Stopher, P. R.; Meyburg, A. H. and Brög, W., eds.*, 1981, pp. 587–98. [G: W. Germany]

Wei, jia ju. UN Multimodal Transport Convention. *J. World Trade Law*, July–August 1981, *15*(4), pp. 283–304.

Weigand, W. Planungshilfe für Betriebsleitsysteme in zeitabhängigen Verkehrsnetzen. (With English summary.) In *Fandel, G., et al., eds.*, 1981, pp. 366–71.

Wermuth, Manfred J. Effects of Survey Methods and Measurement Techniques on the Accuracy of Household Travel-Behavior Surveys. In *Stopher, P. R.; Meyburg, A. H. and Brög, W., eds.*, 1981, pp. 523–41. [G: W. Germany]

White, Peter R. The Benefits of Minibuses: A Comment [The Benefits of Minibuses: The Case of Kuala Lumpur]. *J. Transp. Econ. Policy*, January 1981, *15*(1), pp. 77–79. [G: Malaysia]

Williams, D. J. Labour Costs and Taxi Supply in Melbourne. *J. Transp. Econ. Policy*, May 1981, *15*(2), pp. 179–84. [G: Australia]

Williams, Martin and Hall, Carol. Returns to Scale in the United States Intercity Bus Industry. *Reg. Sci. Urban Econ.*, November 1981, *11*(4), pp. 573–84. [G: U.S.]

Wilson, George W. The Relative Importance of Economic Regulation of Transportation Vis-à-Vis Everything Else. In *[Nelson, J. R.]*, 1981, pp. 9–35. [G: U.S.]

Winsberg, Morton D. Agriculture and the Interstate: A Note on Locational Impacts in the South. *Growth Change*, July 1981, *12*(3), pp. 41–46. [G: U.S.]

Winston, Clifford. A Disaggregate Model of the Demand for Intercity Freight Transportation. *Econometrica*, June 1981, *49*(4), pp. 981–1006. [G: U.S.]

Winston, Clifford. A Multinomial Probit Prediction of the Demand for Domestic Ocean Container Service. *J. Transp. Econ. Policy*, September 1981, *15*(3), pp. 243–52.

Winston, Clifford. The Welfare Effects of ICC Rate Regulation Revisited. *Bell J. Econ. (See Rand J. Econ. after 4/85)*, Spring 1981, *12*(1), pp. 232–44. [G: U.S.]

Wright, Charles L.; Meyer, Richard L. and Walker, Francis E. Analyzing Bottlenecks in Grain Transportation and Storage Systems: A Brazilian Case Study. *J. Devel. Stud.*, October 1981, *18*(1), pp. 68–84. [G: Brazil]

Yamada, Makiko. Nineteenth Century Precursors to

Automobile Marketing in the United States: Comment. In *Okochi, A. and Shimokawa, K., eds.*, 1981, pp. 55–57. [G: U.S.]

Yuzawa, Takeshi. The Marketing of Automobiles in Britain and the United States before 1939: Comment. In *Okochi, A. and Shimokawa, K., eds.*, 1981, pp. 90–92. [G: U.K.; U.S.]

Zayas, Edison R. Motor Carrier Regulation and Small Truckers. *Bus. Econ.*, January 1981, 16(1), pp. 59–66. [G: U.S.]

Ziderman, Adrian. The Valuation of Accident Cost Savings: A Comment. *J. Transp. Econ. Policy*, May 1981, 15(2), pp. 185–87. [G: U.K.]

616 Industrial Policy

6160 Industrial Policy

Adedeji, Adebayo. Indigenization of African Economies: Introduction to the Case Studies. In *Adedeji, A., ed.*, 1981, pp. 45–48. [G: Africa]

Ake, Claude. Kenya. In *Adedeji, A., ed.*, 1981, pp. 187–203. [G: Kenya]

Allen, G. C. Industrial Policy and Innovation in Japan. In *Carter, C., ed.*, 1981, pp. 68–87. [G: Japan; U.K.]

Amin, Samir. Senegal. In *Adedeji, A., ed.*, 1981, pp. 309–27. [G: Senegal]

Anderson, Bernard E. Toward a New U.S. Industrial Policy? Political Experience: Comment. In *Wachter, M. L. and Wachter, S. M., eds.*, 1981, pp. 483–85. [G: U.S.]

Archer, R. W. Industrial Policy and Innovation: Comment. In *Carter, C., ed.*, 1981, pp. 179–81. [G: U.K.]

Baffoe, Frank. Southern Africa. In *Adedeji, A., ed.*, 1981, pp. 278–308. [G: S. Africa]

Balassa, Bela. Portugal in Face of the Common Market. In *Balassa, B.*, 1981, pp. 255–80. [G: Portugal]

Ball, R. James. Industrial Policy in the United Kingdom. In *Wachter, M. L. and Wachter, S. M., eds.*, 1981, pp. 501–08. [G: U.K.]

Banerjee, Nirmala. Change and Choice in Indian Industry: Is Small Beautiful? In *Bagchi, A. K. and Banerjee, N., eds.*, 1981, pp. 277–95. [G: India]

Berend, Iván T. Continuity and Changes of Industrialization in Hungary after the Turn of 1956/57. *Acta Oecon.*, 1981, 27(3–4), pp. 221–50. [G: Hungary]

Branson, William H. Industrial Policy and U.S. International Trade. In *Wachter, M. L. and Wachter, S. M., eds.*, 1981, pp. 378–408. [G: U.S.]

Bueno, G. M. Regional Policy in EC Countries and Community Regional Policy: A Note on Problems and Perspectives in Developing Depressed Rural Regions: Comment. *Europ. Rev. Agr. Econ.*, 1981, 8(2–3), pp. 247–49. [G: EEC]

Butt Philip, Alan. The Harmonisation of Industrial Policy and Practices. In *Twitchett, C. C., ed.*, 1981, pp. 47–62. [G: EEC]

Cagan, Phillip. Some Macroeconomic Impacts of the National Industrial Recovery Act, 1933–35: Comments. In *Brunner, K., ed.*, 1981, pp. 282–85. [G: U.S.]

Cantor, Arnold. Proceedings of the Seminar on Employment: Statement. In *U.S. Congress, Joint Economic Committee (I)*, 1981, pp. 116–19. [G: U.S.]

Carswell, Robert. The Political Response to Three Potential Major Bankruptcies: Lockheed, New York City, and Chrysler: Comment. In *Wachter, M. L. and Wachter, S. M., eds.*, 1981, pp. 487–90. [G: U.S.]

Chee, Peng Lim; Lee, Donald and Foo, Kok Thye. The Case for Labour Intensive Industries in Malaysia. In *Amjad, R., ed.*, 1981, pp. 235–69. [G: Malaysia]

Chen, Edward K. Y. Adjusting to the ADCs in the Face of Structurally Depressed Industries: Japan: Comment. In *Hong, W. and Krause, L. B., eds.*, 1981, pp. 468–71. [G: Japan; E. Asia]

Chileshe, Jonathan H. Zambia. In *Adedeji, A., ed.*, 1981, pp. 81–132. [G: Zambia]

Corden, W. Max. Trade and Industrial Policies, and the Structure of Protection in Korea: Comment. In *Hong, W. and Krause, L. B., eds.*, 1981, pp. 212–14. [G: S. Korea]

Dalal, S. N. and Lahiri, A. Some Observations on Industrial Investment in India with Special Reference to the Private Corporate Sector. In *Bagchi, A. K. and Banerjee, N., eds.*, 1981, pp. 119–27. [G: India]

Dosi, Giovanni. Institutions and Markets in High Technology: Government Support for Micro-electronics in Europe. In *Carter, C., ed.*, 1981, pp. 182–202. [G: EEC]

Drucker, Peter F. Demographics and American Economic Policy. In *Wachter, M. L. and Wachter, S. M., eds.*, 1981, pp. 237–56. [G: U.S.]

Dunlop, John T. The Consensus: Process and Substance. In *Wachter, M. L. and Wachter, S. M., eds.*, 1981, pp. 497–500. [G: U.S.]

Dunning, John H. Multinational Enterprises, Market Structure, Economic Power and Industrial Policy. In *Dunning, J. H.*, 1981, pp. 179–220. [G: U.S.; U.K.]

Eads, George C. The Political Experience in Allocating Investment: Lessons from the United States and Elsewhere. In *Wachter, M. L. and Wachter, S. M., eds.*, 1981, pp. 453–82. [G: U.S.; Japan; W. Europe]

Edokpayi, S. I. Administrative and Managerial Implications. In *Adedeji, A., ed.*, 1981, pp. 353–80. [G: Africa]

El Mehdawi, Mohammed. The Industrialization of Libya. In *[Fisher, W. B.]*, 1981, pp. 252–63. [G: Libya]

English, H. Edward. Export-Oriented Growth and Industrial Diversification in Hong Kong: Comment. In *Hong, W. and Krause, L. B., eds.*, 1981, pp. 124–28. [G: Hong Kong]

Fajnzylber, Fernando. The Industrial Dynamic in Advanced Developing Countries. In *Hong, W. and Krause, L. B., eds.*, 1981, pp. 35–59. [G: Latin America]

Hanafi, Mohammed N. Egypt. In *Adedeji, A., ed.*, 1981, pp. 49–80. [G: Egypt]

Helleiner, Gerald K. Adjusting to the ADCs in the Face of Structurally Depressed Industries: Japan: Comment. In *Hong, W. and Krause, L. B., eds.*, 1981, pp. 471–74. [G: Japan; E. Asia]

Henderson, P. D. Industrial Policy and Innovation: Comment. In *Carter, C., ed.*, 1981, pp. 170–78. [G: U.K.]

Ietto Gillies, Grazia. The De-Industrialisation of the UK: Some Issues and Hypotheses. *Brit. Rev. Econ. Issues*, Spring 1981, *2*(8), pp. 1–20. [G: U.K.]

Ikemoto, Kiyoshi. The Industrial Dynamic in Advanced Developing Countries: Comment. In *Hong, W. and Krause, L. B., eds.*, 1981, pp. 60–62. [G: Latin America]

Jackson, Richard. Industrialization in Papua New Guinea: A Social or Economic Investment? In *Hamilton, F. E. I. and Linge, G. J. R., eds.*, 1981, pp. 549–80. [G: Papua New Guinea]

Jacobs, Susan S. and Wasylenko, Michael. Government Policy to Stimulate Economic Development: Enterprise Zones. In *Walzer, N. and Chicoine, D. L., eds.*, 1981, pp. 175–201. [G: U.S.; U.K.]

Jasinowski, Jerry J. Toward a New U.S. Industrial Policy? International Trade: Comment. In *Wachter, M. L. and Wachter, S. M., eds.*, 1981, pp. 415–17. [G: U.S.]

Jones, D. T. Catching up with Our Competitors: The Role of Industrial Policy. In *Carter, C., ed.*, 1981, pp. 146–56. [G: U.K.]

Jones, Reginald H. Toward a New Industrial Policy. In *Wachter, M. L. and Wachter, S. M., eds.*, 1981, pp. 9–16. [G: U.S.]

King, Arthur T. Economic Development Aspects of a Public Policy Program: Section 8(a) Contracts. *Rev. Black Polit. Econ.*, Spring 1981, *11*(3), pp. 337–46. [G: U.S.]

Kirkland, Lane. Labor's View of Reindustrializing America. In *Wachter, M. L. and Wachter, S. M., eds.*, 1981, pp. 30–37. [G: U.S.]

Klein, Lawrence R. International Aspects of Industrial Policy. In *Wachter, M. L. and Wachter, S. M., eds.*, 1981, pp. 361–77. [G: U.S.]

Knight, Arthur [Sir]. Industrial Policy. In *[Cairncross, A.]*, 1981, pp. 114–37. [G: U.K.]

Krueger, Anne O. Trade and Industrial Policies, and the Structure of Protection in Korea: Comment. In *Hong, W. and Krause, L. B., eds.*, 1981, pp. 214–16. [G: S. Korea]

Likierman, Andrew. Industrial Policy; Comments. In *[Cairncross, A.]*, 1981, pp. 137–39. [G: U.K.]

Lin, Tzong Biau and Ho, Yin Ping. Export-Oriented Growth and Industrial Diversification in Hong Kong. In *Hong, W. and Krause, L. B., eds.*, 1981, pp. 69–123. [G: Hong Kong]

Lovell, Malcolm R., Jr. Toward a New U.S. Industrial Policy? Strategies for Training and Retraining: Comment. In *Wachter, M. L. and Wachter, S. M., eds.*, 1981, pp. 281–82. [G: U.S.]

Marer, Paul. U.S.–Polish Industrial Cooperation: Achievements, Problems, Prospects: Comment. In *Marer, P. and Tabaczynski, E., eds.*, 1981, pp. 131–36. [G: Poland; U.S.]

Meissner, Werner. Strukturpolitik in marktwirtschaftlich orientierten Wirtschaftssystemen. (Industrial Policy in Market Systems. With English summary.) *Z. Wirtschaft. Sozialwissen.*, 1981, *101*(5), pp. 537–54. [G: W. Germany; U.K.; France; Sweden]

Mills, D. Quinn. The Human Resource Consequences of Industrial Revitalization. In *Wachter, M. L. and Wachter, S. M., eds.*, 1981, pp. 257–80. [G: U.S.]

Moskow, Michael H. The Political Response to Three Potential Major Bankruptcies: Lockheed, New York City, and Chrysler: Comment. In *Wachter, M. L. and Wachter, S. M., eds.*, 1981, pp. 485–87. [G: U.S.]

Mushi, S. S. Tanzania. In *Adedeji, A., ed.*, 1981, pp. 204–37. [G: Tanzania]

Nam, Chong Hyun. Trade and Industrial Policies, and the Strucure of Protection in Korea. In *Hong, W. and Krause, L. B., eds.*, 1981, pp. 187–211. [G: S. Korea]

Orlando, Giuseppe and Antonelli, Gervasio. Regional Policy in EC Countries and Community Regional Policy: A Note on Problems and Perspectives in Developing Depressed Rural Regions. *Europ. Rev. Agr. Econ.*, 1981, *8*(2–3), pp. 213–46. [G: EEC]

Owusu-Ansah, K. A. Ghana. In *Adedeji, A., ed.*, 1981, pp. 133–63. [G: Ghana]

Pindyck, Robert S. Energy, Productivity, and the New U.S. Industrial Policy. In *Wachter, M. L. and Wachter, S. M., eds.*, 1981, pp. 176–201. [G: U.S.]

Pitkänen, Eero. Julkisyhteisöt liiketaloustieteen tutkimuskohteina. (Public Organizations as Research Objectives in Business Economics. With English summary.) *Liiketaloudellinen Aikak.*, 1981, *30*(2), pp. 193–221.

Pogge von Strandmann, Hartmut. Industrial Primacy in German Foreign Policy? Myths and Realities in German-Russian Relations at the End of the Weimar Republic. In *Bessel, R. and Feuchtwanger, E. J., eds.*, 1981, pp. 241–67. [G: U.S.S.R.; Germany]

de Pouvourville, Gérard. Les achats publics, outils indociles d'une politique industrielle. (Public Procurement, an Unwieldy Tool in Industrial Policy Making. With English summary.) *Écon. Soc.*, October–November–December 1981, *15*(10–12), pp. 1723–55. [G: France]

Reuss, Henry S. Can American Industry Be Born Again? In *Wachter, M. L. and Wachter, S. M., eds.*, 1981, pp. 23–29. [G: U.S.]

Rosa, Giuseppe. Italian Industry in the Seventies: Dimensional Aspects. *Rivista Polit. Econ.*, Supplement December 1981, *71*, pp. 149–79. [G: Italy]

Safarian, A. E. The Industrial Dynamic in Advanced Developing Countries: Comment. In *Hong, W. and Krause, L. B., eds.*, 1981, pp. 62–65. [G: Latin America]

Schatz, S. P. The Capital Shortage Illusion: Government Lending in Nigeria. In *Livingstone, I., ed.*, 1981, *1965*, pp. 21–24. [G: Nigeria]

Silberston, Aubrey. Industrial Policies in Britain 1960–80. In *Carter, C., ed.*, 1981, pp. 39–51. [G: U.K.]

Tabaczynski, Eugeniusz. East–West Industrial Cooperation and Specialization in Polish Production. In *Marer, P. and Tabaczynski, E., eds.*, 1981, pp. 99–103. [G: Poland]

Tabaczynski, Eugeniusz. East–West Industrial Cooperation and Specialization in Polish Production:

Reply. In *Marer, P. and Tabaczynski, E., eds.*, 1981, pp. 107–08. [G: Poland]

Tambunlertchai, Somsak and Loohawenchit, Chesada. Labour Intensive and Small Scale Manufacturing in Thailand. In *Amjad, R., ed.*, 1981, pp. 175–233. [G: Thailand]

Verreydt, E. and Waelbroeck, Jean. EEC Industrial Policy and the Third World. In *Stevens, C., ed.*, 1981, pp. 20–29. [G: EEC]

Villarreal, René and de Villarreal, Rocío. Mexico's Development Strategy. In *Purcell, S. K., ed.*, 1981, pp. 97–103. [G: Mexico]

Wachter, Michael L. and Wachter, Susan M. Toward a New U.S. Industrial Policy? Introduction. In *Wachter, M. L. and Wachter, S. M., eds.*, 1981, pp. 1–5. [G: U.S.]

Walker, Charls E. and Bloomfield, Mark A. The Political Response to Three Potential Major Bankruptcies: Lockheed, New York City, and Chrysler. In *Wachter, M. L. and Wachter, S. M., eds.*, 1981, pp. 423–52. [G: U.S.]

Walker, David F. Regional Industrial Development Policy in Canada since 1973. In *Rees, J.; Hewings, G. J. D. and Stafford, H. A., eds.*, 1981, pp. 239–55. [G: Canada]

Weinstein, Michael M. Some Macroeconomic Impacts of the National Industrial Recovery Act, 1933–1935. In *Brunner, K., ed.*, 1981, pp. 262–81. [G: U.S.]

Wescott, Clay G. Industrial Policy: A Case Study of Incentives for Industrial Dispersion. In *Killick, T., ed.*, 1981, pp. 346–56. [G: Kenya]

Wolf, Thomas A. East–West Industrial Cooperation and Specialization in Polish Production: Comment. In *Marer, P. and Tabaczynski, E., eds.*, 1981, pp. 104–07. [G: Poland]

Wright, Kevin N. Economic Adversity, Reindustrialization, and Criminality. In *Wright, K. N., ed.*, 1981, pp. 51–68. [G: U.S.]

Yamazawa, Ippei. Adjusting to the ADCs in the Face of Structurally Depressed Industries: Japan. In *Hong, W. and Krause, L. B., eds.*, 1981, pp. 435–67. [G: Japan; E. Asia]

Yap, K. H. Basic Materials Industries: Aspects of Technology Choice and Industrial Location. In *U.N. Industrial Development Organization*, 1981, pp. 23–27.

Zagorski, Edwin. U.S.–Polish Industrial Cooperation: Achievements, Problems, Prospects. In *Marer, P. and Tabaczynski, E., eds.*, 1981, pp. 121–31. [G: Poland; U.S.]

Zagorski, Edwin. U.S.–Polish Industrial Cooperation: Achievements, Problems, Prospects: Reply. In *Marer, P. and Tabaczynski, E., eds.*, 1981, pp. 136–39. [G: Poland; U.S.]

620 ECONOMICS OF TECHNOLOGICAL CHANGE

621 Technological Change; Innovation; Research and Development

6210 General

Alam, Ghayur and Langrish, John. Non-Multinational Firms and Transfer of Technology to Less Developed Countries. *World Devel.*, April 1981,

9(4), pp. 383–87. [G: India]

Baruch, Jordon. The Role of Government in Promoting Research and Development. In *Hogan, J. D. and Craig, A. M., eds., Vol. 1*, 1981, pp. 87–92. [G: U.S.]

Biggs, Stephen D. and Clay, Edward J. Sources of Innovation in Agricultural Technology. *World Devel.*, April 1981, 9(4), pp. 321–36.

Boncher, William. A Comparative Engineering-Economic Analysis of the Evolution of the Soviet Mainline Freight Locomotive. *J. Compar. Econ.*, June 1981, 5(2), pp. 149–68. [G: U.S.; U.S.S.R.]

Boyer, Robert and Petit, Pascal. Progrès technique, croissance et emploi: Un modèle d'inspiration kaldorienne pour six industries européennes. (Technical Progress, Growth and Employment: A Kaldorian Model for Six European Industries. With English summary.) *Revue Écon.*, November 1981, 32(6), pp. 1113–53. [G: W. Europe; U.K.]

Brockhoff, Klaus. Competition, Innovation, Productivity Growth, and Public Policy: Comments. In *Giersch, H., ed. (II)*, 1981, pp. 180–86.

Brown, Thomas G. Changing Delivery Systems for Agricultural Extension: The Extension Teacher—Changing Roles and Competencies. *Amer. J. Agr. Econ.*, December 1981, 63(5), pp. 859–62. [G: U.S.]

Busch, Lawrence and Lacy, William B. Sources of Influence on Problem Choice in the Agricultural Sciences: The New Atlantis Revisited. In *Busch, L., ed.*, 1981, pp. 113–28.

Cantley, Mark and Sargeant, Ken. Biotechnology: The Challenge to Europe. *Rev. Econ. Ind.*, 4th Trimester 1981, (18), pp. 323–34. [G: W. Europe]

Carmichael, Jeffrey. The Effects of Mission-Oriented Public R&D Spending on Private Industry. *J. Finance*, June 1981, 36(3), pp. 617–27. [G: U.S.]

Chianese, Robert L. New Metaphors, Myths, and Values for a Steady-State Future. In *Coomer, J. C., ed.*, 1981, pp. 89–102.

Collins, Eileen L. Tax Incentives for Innovation—Productivity Miracle or Media Hype? *J. Post Keynesian Econ.*, Fall 1981, 4(1), pp. 68–74. [G: U.S.]

Coomer, James C. The Nature of the Quest for a Sustainable Society. In *Coomer, J. C., ed.*, 1981, pp. 1–9.

Davenport, Paul. Unemployment and Technology in a Model of Steady Growth. *Australian Econ. Pap.*, June 1981, 20(36), pp. 115–32.

Davis, Jeffrey S. A Comparison of Procedures for Estimating Returns to Research Using Production Functions. *Australian J. Agr. Econ.*, April 1981, 25(1), pp. 60–72. [G: Australia]

Dervis, Kemal. Technology and International Trade: a Heckscher–Ohlin Approach: Comment. In *Grassman, S. and Lundberg, E., eds.*, 1981, pp. 230–32.

Diesslin, H. G. The Computer—Extension's Delivery System of the Future. *Amer. J. Agr. Econ.*, December 1981, 63(5), pp. 863–67.

Doctors, Samuel I. Facilitating Technological Innovation and Transfer: The National Innovation Network and the Role of Private Sector Firms. **In** *Doctors, S. I., ed.,* 1981, pp. 217–28. **[G: U.S.]**

Drabek, Zdenek. The Product Substitution and Technological Change in Czechoslovakia and Austria: The RAS Approach. *Greek Econ. Rev.,* December 1981, *3*(3), pp. 325–46.
[G: Czechoslovakia; Austria]

Ellis, Gene. Development Planning and Appropriate Technology: A Dilemma and a Proposal. *World Devel.,* March 1981, *9*(3), pp. 251–62.

Eveland, J. D. Program Implementation: The New Focus of Federal Technology Transfer. **In** *Doctors, S. I., ed.,* 1981, pp. 117–29. **[G: U.S.]**

Ewing, A. F. Energy and East-West Co-operation. *J. World Trade Law,* May–June 1981, *15*(3), pp. 218–30. **[G: E. Europe; W. Europe]**

Farber, Stephen C. Buyer Market Structure and R&D Effort: A Simultaneous Equations Model. *Rev. Econ. Statist.,* August 1981, *63*(3), pp. 336–45. **[G: U.S.]**

Feller, Irwin. The Diffusion and Utilization of Scientific and Technological Knowledge in State and Local Governments. **In** *Doctors, S. I., ed.,* 1981, pp. 131–49. **[G: U.S.]**

Fodella, Gianni. Narrowing the Gap among the Pure Research, Applied Research and Technological Diffusion: The Japanese Experience. *Rivista Int. Sci. Econ. Com.,* July–August 1981, *28*(7–8), pp. 769–79. **[G: Japan]**

Gerster, Richard. Switzerland and the Revision of the Paris Convention. *J. World Trade Law,* March–April 1981, *15*(2), pp. 111–23.
[G: Switzerland]

Glass, Walter. Restrictive Business Practices Affecting Transfer of Technology: Commentary. **In** *Schachter, O. and Hellawell, R., eds.,* 1981, pp. 139–42. **[G: U.S.; Japan]**

Globerman, Steven. Returns to Industrial R & D and Industrial Marketing and Administration Activities. *J. Econ. Bus.,* Spring/Summer 1981, *33*(3), pp. 231–37. **[G: U.S.]**

Gold, Bela. Changing Perspectives on Size, Scale, and Returns: An Interpretive Survey. *J. Econ. Lit.,* March 1981, *19*(1), pp. 5–33.

Graham, Edward M. A Comment on "The Dilemmas of Technology." *J. Econ. Issues,* March 1981, *15*(1), pp. 199–204. **[G: U.S.S.R.; U.S.]**

Greer, Douglas F. Control of Terms and Conditions for International Transfers of Technology to Developing Countries. **In** *Schachter, O. and Hellawell, R., eds.,* 1981, pp. 41–83. **[G: U.S.; Japan]**

Hamilton, Carl and Söderström, Hans Tson. Technology and International Trade: A Heckscher–Ohlin Approach. **In** *Grassman, S. and Lundberg, E., eds.,* 1981, pp. 198–229.

Hastings, Trevor. The Impact of Scientific Research on Australian Rural Productivity. *Australian J. Agr. Econ.,* April 1981, *25*(1), pp. 48–59.
[G: Australia]

Herrera, Amilcar O. The Generation of Technologies in Rural Areas. *World Devel.,* January 1981, *9*(1), pp. 21–35. **[G: LDCs]**

Hildreth, R. J. and Armbruster, Walter J. Extension Program Delivery—Past, Present, and Future: An Overview. *Amer. J. Agr. Econ.,*

December 1981, *63*(5), pp. 853–58. **[G: U.S.]**

Hirschey, Robert C. and Caves, Richard E. Research and Transfer of Technology by Multinational Enterprises. *Oxford Bull. Econ. Statist.,* May 1981, *43*(2), pp. 115–30. **[G: U.S.]**

Holt, John. Changing Delivery Systems for Agricultural Extension: Discussion. *Amer. J. Agr. Econ.,* December 1981, *63*(5), pp. 868–69. **[G: U.S.]**

Horwitz, Bertrand and Kolodny, Richard. The FASB, the SEC, and R&D. *Bell J. Econ. (See Rand J. Econ. after 4/85),* Spring 1981, *12*(1), pp. 249–62. **[G: U.S.]**

Horwitz, Bertrand and Kolodny, Richard. The Relationship between Firm Characteristics and the Choice of Financial Measurement Methods: An Application to R&D. *Quart. Rev. Econ. Bus.,* Winter 1981, *21*(4), pp. 75–86. **[G: U.S.]**

Huffman, Wallace E. and Miranowski, John A. An Economic Analysis of Expenditures on Agricultural Experiment Station Research. *Amer. J. Agr. Econ.,* February 1981, *63*(1), pp. 104–18.
[G: U.S.]

Hughes, Harlan. Changing Delivery Systems for Agricultural Extension: Discussion. *Amer. J. Agr. Econ.,* December 1981, *63*(5), pp. 870.
[G: U.S.]

Kjeldsen-Kragh, S. The Specialization Pattern in the Danish Machinery Sector. **In** *Freeman, C., et al.,* 1981, pp. 27–46. **[G: Denmark]**

Klein, K. K. and Kehrberg, E. W. The Use of an Innovation Possibility Frontier to Evaluate an Applied Animal Breeding Research Project. *Can. J. Agr. Econ.,* July 1981, *29*(2), pp. 141–58.
[G: Canada]

Kul'bovskaia, N. The Evaluation of the Social Results of Scientific–Technical Progress. *Prob. Econ.,* March 1981, *23*(11), pp. 16–30. **[G: U.S.S.R.]**

Kushlin, V. Development of the Production Apparatus. *Prob. Econ.,* June 1981, *24*(2), pp. 13–31.

Leffler, Keith B. Industry Equilibrium in New Product Research and Development: A Simple Approach. *Econ. Inquiry,* January 1981, *19*(1), pp. 60–76.

Levy, Victor. On Estimating Efficiency Differentials between the Public and Private Sectors in a Developing Economy—Iraq. *J. Compar. Econ.,* September 1981, *5*(3), pp. 235–50. **[G: Iraq]**

Link, Albert N. Basic Research and Productivity Increase in Manufacturing: Additional Evidence. *Amer. Econ. Rev.,* December 1981, *71*(5), pp. 1111–12. **[G: U.S]**

Mănescu, Manea. The System of Scientific Research and Technological Development: Cybernetic—Economic Models of the system. *Econ. Computat. Cybern. Stud. Res.,* 1981, *15*(1), pp. 7–12.

Mansfield, Edwin. Composition of R and D Expenditures: Relationship to Size of Firm, Concentration, and Innovative Output. *Rev. Econ. Statist.,* November 1981, *63*(4), pp. 610–15. **[G: U.S.]**

Mansfield, Edwin; Schwartz, Mark and Wagner, Samuel. Imitation Costs and Patents: An Empirical Study. *Econ. J.,* December 1981, *91*(364), pp. 907–18. **[G: U.S.]**

Mayhew, Anne. Ayresian Technology, Technological Reasoning, and Doomsday. *J. Econ. Issues,* June 1981, *15*(2), pp. 513–20.

McCain, Roger A. Tradition and Innovation: Some Economics of the Creative Arts, Science, Scholarship, and Technical Development. In *Galatin, M. and Leiter, R. D., eds.*, 1981, pp. 173–204.

Nelson, Richard R. Competition, Innovation, Productivity Growth, and Public Policy. In *Giersch, H., ed. (II)*, 1981, pp. 151–79.

Nelson, Richard R. Research on Productivity Growth and Productivity Differences: Dead Ends and New Departures. *J. Econ. Lit.*, September 1981, *19*(3), pp. 1029–64.

Ohara, Yoshio. Japanese Regulation of Technology Imports. *J. World Trade Law*, January–February 1981, *15*(1), pp. 83–90. [G: Japan]

Ordover, Janusz A. and Willig, Robert D. An Economic Definition of Predation: Pricing and Product Innovation. *Yale Law J.*, November 1981, *91*(1), pp. 8–53. [G: U.S.]

Paarlberg, Don. The Land Grant Colleges and the Structure Issue. *Amer. J. Agr. Econ.*, February 1981, *63*(1), pp. 129–34. [G: U.S.]

Paine, Thomas O. The Impact of New Technology on the Pacific Region. In *Hewett, R. B., ed.*, 1981, pp. 177–89. [G: Pacific Basin]

Prais, S. J. Comment [Innovation: Does Government Have a Role?] [Reasons for Not Innovating]. In *Carter, C., ed.*, 1981, pp. 32–38.

Reinganum, Jennifer F. Dynamic Games of Innovation. *J. Econ. Theory*, August 1981, *25*(1), pp. 21–41.

Reubens, Edwin P. Tradition and Innovation: Some Economics of the Creative Arts, Science, Scholarship, and Technical Development: Comments. In *Galatin, M. and Leiter, R. D., eds.*, 1981, pp. 205–08.

Roberts, Kevin and Weitzman, Martin L. Funding Criteria for Research, Development, and Exploration Projects. *Econometrica*, September 1981, *49*(5), pp. 1261–88.

Rodriguez, Carlos Alfredo. The Technology Transfer Issue. In *Grassman, S. and Lundberg, E., eds.*, 1981, pp. 167–93.

Roessner, J. David. Federal Technology Policy: Innovation and Problem Solving in State and Local Governments. In *Doctors, S. I., ed.*, 1981, *1979*, pp. 151–68. [G: U.S.]

Sharma, Brij Mohan. Technology and Economic Growth. *Econ. Aff.*, July–September 1981, *26*(3), pp. 174–81. [G: India]

Shonfield, Andrew. Innovation: Does Government have a Role? In *Carter, C., ed.*, 1981, pp. 4–20.

Shumway, C. Richard. Subjectivity in *Ex Ante* Research Evaluation. *Amer. J. Agr. Econ.*, February 1981, *63*(1), pp. 169–73.

Siggel, Eckhard. Immizerizing Technical Progress: The Effect of Product Innovations on Consumption and Welfare of the Poor in Less Developed Countries: Theoretical Analysis and Empirical Observations in Zaire. *J. Econ. Devel.*, July 1981, *6*(1), pp. 7–31. [G: Zaire]

Singh, R. B. and Shrestha, G. R. Delivery of Agricultural Input to Hill Farmers: Issues and Problems. In *Nepal, Ministry of Food and Agriculture*, 1981, pp. 93–99. [G: Nepal]

Solo, Robert. The Dilemmas of Technology: A Reply. *J. Econ. Issues*, March 1981, *15*(1), pp. 204–11. [G: U.S.S.R.; U.S.]

Stonier, Tom. Science, Technology, and the Emerging Postindustrial Society. In *Coomer, J. C., ed.*, 1981, pp. 70–85.

Stonier, Tom. Technological Change and the Future. In *Gaskin, M., ed.*, 1981, pp. 140–51. [G: U.K.]

Sveikauskas, Leo. Technological Inputs and Multifactor Productivity Growth. *Rev. Econ. Statist.*, May 1981, *63*(2), pp. 275–82. [G: U.S.]

Timberg, Sigmund. Restrictive Business Practices in the International Transfer and Diffusion of Technology. In *Schachter, O. and Hellawell, R., eds.*, 1981, pp. 84–138.

Walter, Ingo. Control of Terms and Conditions for International Transfers of Technology to Developing Countries: Commentary. In *Schachter, O. and Hellawell, R., eds.*, 1981, pp. 143–59. [G: U.S.; Japan]

Wells, Louis T., Jr. Control of Terms and Conditions for International Transfers of Technology to Developing Countries: Commentary. In *Schachter, O. and Hellawell, R., eds.*, 1981, pp. 160–64. [G: U.S.; Japan]

Woolston, Susan W. Local Government Technology Transfer—Overview of Recent Research and Federal Programs. In *Doctors, S. I., ed.*, 1981, pp. 43–66. [G: U.S.]

Yin, Robert K. Contemporary Issues in Domestic Technology Transfer. In *Doctors, S. I., ed.*, 1981, pp. 69–116. [G: U.S.]

6211 Technological Change and Innovation

Abonyi, A. Imported Technology, Hungarian Industrial Development and Factors Impeding the Emergence of Innovative Capability. In *Hare, P. G.; Radice, H. K. and Swain, N., eds.*, 1981, pp. 132–57. [G: Hungary]

Ackermann, Werner. Cultural Values and Social Choice of Technology. *Int. Soc. Sci. J.*, 1981, *33*(3), pp. 447–65.

Adams, Alvin P. The Role of the International Patent System in the International Transfer and Control of Technology: Comment. In *Sagafi-nejad, T.; Moxon, R. W. and Perlmutter, H. V., eds.*, 1981, pp. 85–88.

Agarwal, Bina. Agricultural Mechanisation and Labour Use: A Disaggregated Approach. *Int. Lab. Rev.*, January–February 1981, *120*(1), pp. 115–27. [G: India]

Aguilar, Enrique. Restrictive Business Practices and International Controls on Transfer of Technology: Comment. In *Sagafi-nejad, T.; Moxon, R. W. and Perlmutter, H. V., eds.*, 1981, pp. 205–11. [G: Mexico]

Alberro, José and Persky, Joseph. The Dynamics of Fixed Capital Revaluation and Scrapping. *Rev. Radical Polit. Econ.*, Summer 1981, *13*(2), pp. 32–37.

Allen, G. C. Industrial Policy and Innovation in Japan. In *Carter, C., ed.*, 1981, pp. 68–87. [G: Japan; U.K.]

Andersen, E. S.; Dalum, B. and Villumsen, G. The

Importance of the Home Market for the Development of Technology and the Export Specialization of Manufacturing Industry. **In** *Freeman, C., et al.*, 1981, pp. 49–102. **[G: Denmark]**

Anusz, Jan. Technology Transfer by Means of Industrial Cooperation: A Theoretical Appraisal: Comment. **In** *Marer, P. and Tabaczynski, E., eds.*, 1981, pp. 224–26. **[G: Poland; U.S.]**

Apostolakis, Bobby. A Transcendental Logarithmic Cost Function: An Empirical Case. *Metroecon.*, Feb.-Oct. 1981, *33*(1–2–3), pp. 193–204. **[G: Italy]**

Ariga, Michiko. Restrictive Business Practices and International Controls on Transfer of Technology. **In** *Sagafi-nejad, T.; Moxon, R. W. and Perlmutter, H. V., eds.*, 1981, pp. 177–200. **[G: Japan]**

Artemiev, Igor E. Alternative Channels and Modes of International Resource Transmission: Comment. **In** *Sagafi-nejad, T.; Moxon, R. W. and Perlmutter, H. V., eds.*, 1981, pp. 37–41.

Ault, David E. and Meisel, John B. An Investigation into the Effects of Technology and Economies of Scale on International Trade in Basic Steel: 1955–76. *Rivista Int. Sci. Econ. Com.*, May 1981, *28*(5), pp. 461–86. **[G: OECD]**

Bagchi, Amiya Kumar. Reinforcing and Offsetting Constraints in Indian Industry. **In** *Bagchi, A. K. and Banerjee, N., eds.*, 1981, pp. 23–62. **[G: India]**

Bagchi, Amiya Kumar and Dasgupta, Subhendu. Imported Technology and the Legal Process. **In** *Bagchi, A. K. and Banerjee, N., eds.*, 1981, pp. 393–416. **[G: India]**

Baily, Mary Ann. Brick Manufacturing in Colombia: A Case Study of Alternative Technologies. *World Devel.*, February 1981, *9*(2), pp. 201–13. **[G: Colombia]**

Banta, David. Public Policy and Medical Technology: Critical Issues Reconsidered. **In** *Altenstetter, C., ed.*, 1981, pp. 57–86. **[G: U.S.]**

Barbiroli, Giancarlo; Ballini, Vladimiro and Savio, Giorgio. The Effect of Technological Development on Renewable Raw Materials. A Look at the International Situation. *Econ. Notes*, 1981, *10*(1), pp. 104–21. **[G: Selected Countries]**

Baron, C. G. Sugar Processing Techniques in India. **In** *Bhalla, A. S., ed.*, 1981, *1975*, pp. 181–208. **[G: India]**

Baumol, William J. Technological Change and the New Urban Equilibrium. **In** *Burchell, R. W. and Listokin, D., eds.*, 1981, pp. 3–17. **[G: U.S.]**

Bergman, Lars and Mäler, Karl-Göran. Efficiency–flexibility Trade-off and the Cost of Unexpected Oil Price Increases. *Scand. J. Econ.*, 1981, *83*(2), pp. 253–68. **[G: Sweden]**

Berliner, Joseph S. Technological Progress and the Evolution of Soviet Pricing Policy. **In** *[Bergson, A.]*, 1981, pp. 105–25.

Berliner, Joseph S. The Prospects for Technological Progress. **In** *Bornstein, M., ed.*, 1981, *1976*, pp. 293–311.

Bernard, Martin J., III. Problems in Predicting Market Response to New Transportation Technology. **In** *Stopher, P. R.; Meyburg, A. H. and Brög, W., eds.*, 1981, pp. 465–87. **[G: U.S.]**

Bhalla, A. S. Technology and Employment in Indus-

try: Lessons from the Case Studies. **In** *Bhalla, A. S., ed.*, 1981, *1975*, pp. 357–80. **[G: LDCs]**

Blachford, J. Technology Transfer through Licensing: The Experience of a Small Canadian-Owned Chemical Company. **In** *Science Council of Canada, Industrial Policies Committee*, 1981, pp. 123–30. **[G: Canada]**

Blattner, Niklaus. Labour Displacement by Technological Change? A Preliminary Survey of the Case of Microelectronics. *Rivista Int. Sci. Econ. Com.*, May 1981, *28*(5), pp. 422–48.

Blume, Stuart S. Technology in Medical Diagnosis: Aspects of Its Dynamic and Impact. **In** *Altenstetter, C., ed.*, 1981, pp. 107–24.

Blumenthal, Tuvia. Factor Proportions and Choice of Technology: The Japanese Experience: Reply. *Econ. Develop. Cult. Change*, July 1981, *29*(4), pp. 845–48. **[G: Japan]**

Boon, G. K. Technological Choice in Metalworking, with Special Reference to Mexico. **In** *Bhalla, A. S., ed.*, 1981, *1975*, pp. 303–21. **[G: Mexico]**

Bowles, Samuel. Technical Change and the Profit Rate: A Simple Proof of the Okishio Theorem: Note [Technical Change and the Rate of Profit]. *Cambridge J. Econ.*, June 1981, *5*(2), pp. 183–86.

Boyle, G. Input Substitution and Technical Change in Irish Agriculture—1953–1977. *Econ. Soc. Rev.*, April 1981, *12*(3), pp. 149–61. **[G: Ireland]**

Brada, Josef C. Technology Transfer between the United States and Communist Countries. **In** *Hawkins, R. G. and Prasad, A. J., eds.*, 1981, pp. 219–87. **[G: CMEA; U.S.]**

Brada, Josef C. Technology Transfer by Means of Industrial Cooperation: A Theoretical Appraisal. **In** *Marer, P. and Tabaczynski, E., eds.*, 1981, pp. 207–24. **[G: Poland; U.S.]**

Brada, Josef C. Technology Transfer by Means of Industrial Cooperation: A Theoretical Appraisal: Reply. **In** *Marer, P. and Tabaczynski, E., eds.*, 1981, pp. 226–27. **[G: Poland; U.S.]**

Britton, J. N. Industrial Patterns in Early and Late Adoption of New Products in Canada: Commentary. **In** *Science Council of Canada, Industrial Policies Committee*, 1981, pp. 55–59. **[G: Canada]**

Brown, Shannon R. Technology Transfer and Economic Systems: The Case of China in the Nineteenth Century. *ACES Bull. (See Comp. Econ. Stud. after 8/85)*, Spring 1981, *23*(1), pp. 79–88. **[G: China]**

Cain, Louis P. and Paterson, Donald G. Factor Biases and Technical Change in Manufacturing: The American System, 1850–1919. *J. Econ. Hist.*, June 1981, *41*(2), pp. 341–60. **[G: U.S.]**

Caire, Guy. Automation: technologie, travail, relations sociales (Sur quelques travaux récents relatifs à l'automation: réponses et questions). (Automation, Technology, Labour, Social Relations. Answers and Questions on Recent Studies on Automation. With English summary.) *Consommation*, January–March 1981, *28*(1), pp. 51–84.

Campbell, Robert W. Technology Transfer in U.S.–Polish Industrial Cooperation: Comment. **In**

Marer, P. and Tabaczynski, E., eds., 1981, pp. 154–57. [G: Poland; U.S.]

Caravani, Paolo. Technology and Technical Change in a Dynamic Production Model. *Reg. Sci. Urban Econ.*, August 1981, *11*(3), pp. 335–49.

Carman, J. K. Technology Transfer within a Multinational: The Case of Westinghouse Canada Ltd. In *Science Council of Canada, Industrial Policies Committee*, 1981, pp. 111–22. [G: Canada]

Carter, Charles. Reasons for Not Innovating. In *Carter, C.*, ed., 1981, pp. 21–31.

Carter, Michael. Technological Change in Australia: A Review of the Myers Report. *Australian Econ. Rev.*, 2nd Quarter 1981, (54), pp. 55–64. [G: Australia]

Cassing, James H. and Hillman, Arye L. A Social Safety Net for the Impact of Technical Change: An Evaluation of the Myers Committee's Adjustment Assistance Proposal. *Econ. Rec.*, September 1981, *57*(158), pp. 232–37. [G: Australia]

Chee, Peng Lim. Manufacture of Leather Shoes and Bricks in Malaysia. In *Bhalla, A. S.*, ed., 1981, pp. 247–88. [G: Malaysia]

Chevalier, Jean-Marie. Les nouvelles technologies énergétiques: leur impact sur l'évolution des prix de l'énergie. (New Energy Technologies: Their Impact on the Evolution on the Future Energy Prices. With English summary.) *Rev. Econ. Ind.*, 3rd Trimestre 1981, (17), pp. 1–25.

Chiang, Alpha C. Hicks-Neutral and Harrod-Neutral Technological Progress: The Solution of a Puzzle [Neutrality of Technological Progress: A Synthetic View and a Puzzle]. *Rivista Int. Sci. Econ. Com.*, April 1981, *28*(4), pp. 304–10.

Cieślik, Jerzy and Rapacki, Ryszard. Restrictive Clauses in East-West Licensing Trade: The Case of Poland. *Econ. Planning*, 1981, *17*(1), pp. 37–51. [G: Poland]

Claffey, Barbara A. Patenting Life Forms: Issues Surrounding the Plant Variety Protection Act. *Southern J. Agr. Econ.*, December 1981, *13*(2), pp. 29–37. [G: U.S.]

Contractor, Farok J. and Sagafi-Nejad, Tagi. International Technology Transfer: Major Issues and Policy Responses. *J. Int. Bus. Stud.*, Fall 1981, *12*(2), pp. 113–35.

Cooper, Charles and Kaplinsky, R. Second-hand Equipment in Developing Countries: Jute Processing Machinery in Kenya. In *Bhalla, A. S.*, ed., 1981, *1975*, pp. 129–57. [G: Kenya; U.K.]

Cooper, Charles, et al. Choice of Techniques for Can Making in Kenya, Tanzania and Thailand. In *Bhalla, A. S.*, ed., 1981, *1975*, pp. 91–127. [G: Kenya; Tanzania; Thailand]

Correa, Carlos M. Transfer of Technology in Latin America: A Decade of Control. *J. World Trade Law*, September–October 1981, *15*(5), pp. 388–409. [G: Latin America]

Cortés, Julio A. Appropriate Technology: Obstacles and Strategies. In *Lozoya, J. and Green, R.*, eds., 1981, pp. 171–80. [G: LDCs]

Cosimano, Thomas F. The Incentive to Adopt Cost Reducing Innovation in the Presence of a Non-Linear Demand Curve. *Southern Econ. J.*, July 1981, *48*(1), pp. 97–102.

Currie, W. M. The Application of Technology for Energy Conservation in Industry. In *Amman, F. and Wilson, R.*, eds., 1981, pp. 257–347. [G: U.K.]

Dasgupta, Partha. Resource Pricing and Technological Innovations under Oligopoly: A Theoretical Exploration. *Scand. J. Econ.*, 1981, *83*(2), pp. 289–317.

Dasgupta, Partha and Stiglitz, Joseph E. Resource Depletion under Technological Uncertainty. *Econometrica*, January 1981, *49*(1), pp. 85–104.

Davidson, William H. Trends in the Transfer of U.S. Technology to Canada. In *Science Council of Canada, Industrial Policies Committee*, 1981, pp. 9–24. [G: U.S.; Canada; Selected Countries]

Davidson, William H. Trends in the Transfer of U.S. Technology to Canada: Commentary. In *Science Council of Canada, Industrial Policies Committee*, 1981, pp. 25–38. [G: U.S.; Canada; Selected Countries]

DeBresson, Chris. Industrial Patterns in Early and Late Adoption of New Products in Canada. In *Science Council of Canada, Industrial Policies Committee*, 1981, pp. 41–50. [G: Canada]

Delacollette, Jean. Exportation et transfert de technologie. (Export and Transfer of Technology. With English summary.) *Ann. Sci. Écon. Appl.*, 1981, *37*(4), pp. 167–85.

Demelto, Dennis. Technology Acquisition: Licence Agreement or Joint Venture: Commentary. In *Science Council of Canada, Industrial Policies Committee*, 1981, pp. 97–103. [G: U.S.; Canada; Sweden]

Denny, M., et al. Estimating the Effects of Diffusion of Technological Innovations in Telecommunications: The Production Structure of Bell Canada. *Can. J. Econ.*, February 1981, *14*(1), pp. 24–43. [G: Canada]

Dickson, David and Noble, David. By Force of Reason: The Politics of Science and Technology Policy. In *Ferguson, T. and Rogers, J.*, eds., 1981, pp. 260–312. [G: U.S.]

Doctors, Samuel I. State and Local Government Technology Transfer. In *Doctors, S. I.*, ed., 1981, pp. 3–42. [G: U.S.]

Donaldson, Loraine. Efficiency Ranges for Intermediate Technology: A General Equilibrium Approach. *Greek Econ. Rev.*, April 1981, *3*(1), pp. 59–70.

Driscoll, Robert E. and Wallender, Harvey W., III. Control and Incentives for Technology Transfer: A Multinational Perspective. In *Sagafi-nejad, T.; Moxon, R. W. and Perlmutter, H. V.*, eds., 1981, pp. 273–86.

Dunning, John H. Alternative Channels and Modes of International Resource Transmission. In *Sagafi-nejad, T.; Moxon, R. W. and Perlmutter, H. V.*, eds., 1981, pp. 3–26.

Dunning, John H. Technology Exports and Technology Transfer Controls. In *Sagafi-nejad, T.; Moxon, R. W. and Perlmutter, H. V.*, eds., 1981, pp. 331–61. [G: LDCs; MDCs]

Dunning, John H. The Consequences of International Transfer of Technology by MNEs: Some Home Country Implications. In *Dunning, J. H.*, 1981, pp. 321–53. [G: Selected LDCs]

Easterlin, Richard A. Why Isn't the Whole World Developed? *J. Econ. Hist.*, March 1981, *41*(1), pp. 1–19.

Ebel, Karl-H. The Microelectronics Training Gap in the Metal Trades. *Int. Lab. Rev.*, November–December 1981, *120*(6), pp. 727–39.

Egberts, G. and Voss, A. Energy Models and Technology Assessment. In *Bayraktar, B. A., et al., eds.*, 1981, pp. 159–72.

Elliott, Robert F. and Wood, Peter W. The International Transfer of Technology and Western European Integration. In *Hawkins, R. G. and Prasad, A. J., eds.*, 1981, pp. 117–50. **[G: W. Europe]**

Ernst, Dieter. Technology Policy for Self-Reliance: Some Major Issues. *Int. Soc. Sci. J.*, 1981, *33*(3), pp. 466–80. **[G: LDCs]**

Eschbach, Eugene. Technology Exports and Technology Transfer Controls: Comment. In *Sagafi-nejad, T.; Moxon, R. W. and Perlmutter, H. V., eds.*, 1981, pp. 362–72. **[G: MDCs]**

Fatouros, A. A. International Controls of Technology Transfer. In *Sagafi-nejad, T.; Moxon, R. W. and Perlmutter, H. V., eds.*, 1981, pp. 478–505.

Feder, Gershon and O'Mara, Gerald T. Farm Size and the Diffusion of Green Revolution Technology. *Econ. Develop. Cult. Change*, October 1981, *30*(1), pp. 59–76.

Fei, John C. H. and Ranis, Gustav. Factor Proportions and Choice of Technology: The Japanese Experience: Comment. *Econ. Develop. Cult. Change*, July 1981, *29*(4), pp. 841–44. **[G: Japan]**

Feller, Irwin. Public-Sector Innovation as "Conspicuous Production." *Policy Anal.*, Winter 1981, *7*(1), pp. 1–20. **[G: U.S.]**

Field, Barry C. and Berndt, Ernst R. An Introductory Review of Research on the Economics of Natural Resource Substitution. In *Berndt, E. R. and Field, B. C., eds.*, 1981, pp. 1–14.

Findlay, Ronald and Grubert, Harry. Factor Intensities, Technological Progress and the Terms of Trade. In *Bhagwati, J. N., ed.*, 1981, *1959*, pp. 289–300.

Foster, J. Fagg. The Effect of Technology on Institutions. *J. Econ. Issues*, December 1981, *15*(4), pp. 907–13.

Freeman, C. British Trade Performance and Technical Innovation. In *Freeman, C., et al.*, 1981, pp. 1–25. **[G: U.K.]**

Frey, Luigi. Verso nuove ricerche in tema di produttività, costi e prezzi nel settore bancario. (Further Research into Banking Productivity, Costs and Prices. With English summary.) *Bancaria*, August 1981, *37*(8), pp. 784–90. **[G: W. Europe]**

Geweke, John F. and Weisbrod, Burton A. Some Economic Consequences of Technological Advance in Medical Care: The Case of a New Drug. In *Helms, R. B., ed.*, 1981, pp. 235–71. **[G: U.S.]**

Ghatak, Subrata. The Impact of the Fertilizer Technology Transfer on the Environment of Developing Countries. In *Chatterji, M., ed.*, 1981, pp. 71–87. **[G: LDCs]**

Ghodake, R. D.; Ryan, James G. and Sarin, R. Human Labour Use with Existing and Prospective Technologies in the Semi-Arid Tropics of South India. *J. Devel. Stud.*, October 1981, *18*(1), pp. 25–46. **[G: India]**

Giannini, Carlo. Una nota sul cambiamento tecnologico nei sistemi input-output. (A Note on Technological Change in Input-Output Systems. With English summary.) *Giorn. Econ.*, January–February 1981, *40*(1–2), pp. 101–09.

Giral B., J. Appropriate Technology for the Chemical Industry. In *U.N. Industrial Development Organization*, 1981, pp. 56–73. **[G: Mexico]**

Gold, Bela. Technological Diffusion in Industry: Research Needs and Shortcomings. *J. Ind. Econ.*, March 1981, *29*(3), pp. 247–69.

Gollop, Frank M. Scale Effects and Technical Change as Sources of Productivity Growth. In *Hogan, J. D. and Craig, A. M., eds., Vol. 2*, 1981, pp. 805–38. **[G: U.S.]**

Gorecki, Paul K. and Henderson, Ida. Compulsory Patent Licensing of Drugs in Canada: A Comment on the Debate. *Can. Public Policy*, Autumn 1981, *7*(4), pp. 559–68. **[G: Canada]**

Goulet, Denis. Technology-Importing National Perspectives: Comment. In *Sagafi-nejad, T.; Moxon, R. W. and Perlmutter, H. V., eds.*, 1981, pp. 321–25. **[G: LDCs]**

Grabowski, Richard. Induced Innovation, Green Revolution, and Income Distribution: Reply [The Implications of an Induced Innovation Model]. *Econ. Develop. Cult. Change*, October 1981, *30*(1), pp. 177–81. **[G: Asia]**

Graham, Edward M. International Technology Transfer: Issues and Policy Options: Comment. In *Streeten, P. and Jolly, R, eds.*, 1981, pp. 111–14. **[G: Selected LDCs]**

Guertin, Donald L. The Pricing of International Technology Transfers via Nonaffiliate Licensing Arrangements: Comment. In *Sagafi-nejad, T.; Moxon, R. W. and Perlmutter, H. V., eds.*, 1981, pp. 134–36. **[G: U.S.]**

Gupta, Suraj B. The Productivity of Workers' Consumption and the Choice of Techniques. *Indian Econ. Rev.*, Oct.-Dec. 1981, *16*(4), pp. 279–96.

Hamburg, David A. More Judicious Use of Biomedical Technology. In *Gleason, H. P., ed.*, 1981, pp. 33–46. **[G: U.S.]**

Haselbach, Arne. Adapting R and D Programmes to the Needs of Less Developed Countries. In *Saunders, C. T., ed. (I)*, 1981, pp. 196–211. **[G: LDCs]**

Haustein, Heinz-Dieter and Maier, Harry. Appropriate Technology and the National Economy of Developing Countries. In *Saunders, C. T., ed. (I)*, 1981, pp. 177–95. **[G: LDCs]**

Hawkins, Robert G. Control and Incentives for Technology Transfer: A Multinational Perspective: Comment. In *Sagafi-nejad, T.; Moxon, R. W. and Perlmutter, H. V., eds.*, 1981, pp. 287–90.

Hawkins, Robert G. and Gladwin, Thomas N. Conflicts in the International Transfer of Technology: A U.S. Home Country View. In *Sagafi-nejad, T.; Moxon, R. W. and Perlmutter, H. V., eds.*, 1981, pp. 212–62. **[G: U.S.]**

Hayami, Yujiro. Induced Innovation, Green Revolution, and Income Distribution: Comment [The Implications of an Induced Innovation Model].

Econ. Develop. Cult. Change, October 1981, *30*(1), pp. 169–76. [G: Asia]

Haywood, Charles F. Regulation, Structure, and Technological Change in the Consumer Financial Services Industry. In *Heggestad, A. A., ed.,* 1981, pp. 163–67. [G: U.S.]

Haywood, Charles F. Regulation, Technological Change, and Productivity in Commercial Banking. In *Cowing, T. G. and Stevenson, R. E., eds.,* 1981, pp. 283–307. [G: U.S.]

Heiba, Farouk I. International Controls of Technology Transfer: Comment. In *Sagafi-nejad, T.; Moxon, R. W. and Perlmutter, H. V., eds.,* 1981, pp. 506–09.

Helleiner, Gerald K. International Technology Issues: Southern Needs and Northern Responses. In *Helleiner, G. K.,* 1981, pp. 166–93.

Herdt, Robert W. and Mandac, A. M. Modern Technology and Economic Efficiency of Philippine Rice Farmers. *Econ. Develop. Cult. Change,* January 1981, *29*(2), pp. 375–99. [G: Philippines]

Hirschhorn, Joel S. Industrial Policy and Clusters of Innovation: Comment. *Challenge,* May/June 1981, *24*(2), pp. 53–55.

Hossain, Belayet. Choice of Techniques in Small Scale Irrigation in Bangladesh. *Bangladesh Devel. Stud.,* Autumn 1981, *9*(4), pp. 35–49. [G: Bangladesh]

Hughes, James J.; Perlman, Richard and Das, Satya P. Technological Progress and the Skill Differential. *Econ. J.,* December 1981, *91*(364), pp. 998–1005.

Hughes, Thomas P. Transfer and Style: A Historical Account. In *Sagafi-nejad, T.; Moxon, R. W. and Perlmutter, H. V., eds.,* 1981, pp. 42–54. [G: U.S.; U.K.]

Huguel, Catherine. Les échanges technologiques mondiaux. (The International Flows of Technology. With English summary.) *Revue Écon.,* September 1981, *32*(5), pp. 923–49. [G: OECD; Eastern Europe; Selected LDCs]

Institute of Technological Research, Bogotá. Capacity of the Engineering Industry in Colombia. In *Bhalla, A. S., ed.,* 1981, *1975*, pp. 289–301. [G: Colombia]

Irvin, G. W. Bargaining Asymmetry in Technology Transfer: A Games Theoretical Approach. *J. Devel. Stud.,* October 1981, *18*(1), pp. 85–93.

Iyengar, R. K. and Ramachandran, S. Appropriate Technology for the Iron and Steel Industry. In *U.N. Industrial Development Organization,* 1981, pp. 33–42. [G: India]

Jackson, K. R. and Yerbury, D. Introducing Technological Change: A Case Study. *Australian J. Manage.,* December 1981, *6*(2), pp. 59–79. [G: Australia]

Jadlow, Joseph M. New Evidence on Innovation and Market Structure. *Managerial Dec. Econ.,* June 1981, *2*(2), pp. 91–96. [G: U.S.]

James, Jeffrey. Growth, Technology and the Environment in Less Developed Countries: A Survey. In *Streeten, P. and Jolly, R, eds.,* 1981, *1978,* pp. 115–43. [G: LDCs]

James, John A. Some Evidence on Relative Labor Scarcity in 19th-Century American Manufactur-

ing. *Exploration Econ. Hist.,* October 1981, *18*(4), pp. 376–88. [G: U.S.]

Janiszewski, Hubert A. Technology-Importing National Perspectives. In *Sagafi-nejad, T.; Moxon, R. W. and Perlmutter, H. V., eds.,* 1981, pp. 306–20. [G: LDCs]

Jarvis, Lovell S. Predicting the Diffusion of Improved Pastures in Uruguay. *Amer. J. Agr. Econ.,* August 1981, *63*(3), pp. 495–502. [G: Uruguay]

Jonas, Hans. Reflections on Technology, Progress, and Utopia. *Soc. Res.,* Autumn 1981, *48*(3), pp. 411–55.

Jones, Philip C. A Remark on Economic Response to Technological Innovation [Division of Labor—Simon Revisited]. *Reg. Sci. Urban Econ.,* May 1981, *11*(2), pp. 255–66.

Jorgenson, Dale W. Proceedings of the Seminar on Productivity: Statement. In *U.S. Congress, Joint Economic Committee (I),* 1981, pp. 166–84. [G: U.S.]

Jorgenson, Dale W. and Fraumeni, Barbara M. Relative Prices and Technical Change. In *Berndt, E. R. and Field, B. C., eds.,* 1981, pp. 17–47. [G: U.S.]

Kabanoff, Boris. Technological Change—Employee Attitudes to the Issue. *Australian Bull. Lab.,* December 1981, *8*(1), pp. 45–51.

Kaldor, Nicholas. The Role of Increasing Returns, Technical Progress and Cumulative Causation in the Theory of International Trade and Economic Growth. *Écon. Appl.,* 1981, *34*(4), pp. 593–617. [G: LDCs; U.K.]

Kalirajan, K. P. and Flinn, J. C. Comparative Technical Efficiency in Rice Production. *Philippine Econ. J.,* 1981, *20*(1), pp. 31–43. [G: Philippines]

Keen, Peter G. W. Decision Support Systems and Managerial Productivity Analysis. In *Hogan, J. D. and Craig, A. M., eds., Vol. 1,* 1981, pp. 571–601. [G: U.S.]

Khan, Amir U. Small Scale Machinery Development for Labour Surplus Economies. In *Johnson, G. and Maunder, A., eds.,* 1981, pp. 88–98. [G: Asia]

Killing, Peter. Technology Acquisition: Licence Agreement or Joint Venture. In *Science Council of Canada, Industrial Policies Committee,* 1981, pp. 71–92. [G: Sweden; Canada; U.S.]

Kislev, Yoav and Peterson, Willis. Induced Innovations and Farm Mechanization. *Amer. J. Agr. Econ.,* August 1981, *63*(3), pp. 562–65. [G: U.S.]

Kochanowski, Paul and Hertzfeld, Henry. Often Overlooked Factors in Measuring the Rate of Return to Government R & D Expenditures. *Policy Anal.,* Spring 1981, *7*(2), pp. 153–67. [G: U.S.]

Kohli, Ulrich R. Nonjointness and Factor Intensity in U.S. Production. *Int. Econ. Rev.,* February 1981, *22*(1), pp. 3–18. [G: U.S.]

Kohli, Ulrich R. Valeur adoutée et progrès technique en Suisse, 1948–1976. (Value Added and Technological Change in Switzerland, 1948–1976. With English summary.) *Schweiz. Z. Volkswirtsch. Statist.,* March 1981, *117*(1), pp. 11–24. [G: Switzerland]

Kolde, Endel-Jakob. Control and Incentives for

Technology Transfer: A Multinational Perspective: Comment. In *Sagafi-nejad, T.; Moxon, R. W. and Perlmutter, H. V., eds.,* 1981, pp. 291–301.

Kopp, Raymond J. The Measurement of Productive Efficiency: A Reconsideration. *Quart. J. Econ.,* August 1981, *96*(3), pp. 477–503.

Kopp, Raymond J. and Smith, V. Kerry. Measuring the Prospects for Resource Substitution under Input and Technology Aggregations. In *Berndt, E. R. and Field, B. C., eds.,* 1981, pp. 145–73.

Kozinski, Janusz. Technology Transfer in U.S.–Polish Industrial Cooperation. In *Marer, P. and Tabaczynski, E., eds.,* 1981, pp. 140–54.
[G: Poland; U.S.]

Kozinski, Janusz. Technology Transfer in U.S.–Polish Industrial Cooperation: Reply. In *Marer, P. and Tabaczynski, E., eds.,* 1981, pp. 157–58.
[G: Poland; U.S.]

Krueger, Anne O. U.S. Economic Policy in Support of Growth in the Developing Countries. In *National Science Foundation,* 1981, pp. II41–78.
[G: U.S.; LDCs]

Lacronique, Jean François and Sandier, Simone. Technological Innovation: Cause or Effect of Increasing Expenditures for Health? In *Altenstetter, C., ed.,* 1981, pp. 87–105.

Laibman, David. Two-Sector Growth with Endogenous Technical Change: A Marxian Simulation Model. *Quart. J. Econ.,* February 1981, *96*(1), pp. 47–75.

Lall, Sanjaya. Developing Countries as Exporters of Industrial Technology. In *Lall, S.,* 1981, *1980,* pp. 228–56.
[G: LDCs]

Lall, Sanjaya. Technology and Developing Countries: A Review and an Agenda for Research. In *Lall, S.,* 1981, pp. 123–52.
[G: LDCs]

Lall, Sanjaya. The Patent System and the Transfer of Technology to Less-Developed Countries. In *Lall, S.,* 1981, *1976,* pp. 153–70.
[G: LDCs]

Lazonick, William H. Factor Costs and the Diffusion of Ring Spinning in Britain Prior to World War I. *Quart. J. Econ.,* February 1981, *96*(1), pp. 89–109.
[G: U.K.]

Lele, Uma and Mellor, John W. Technological Change, Distributive Bias and Labor Transfer in a Two-Sector Economy. *Oxford Econ. Pap.,* November 1981, *33*(3), pp. 426–41.

Levine, Herbert S. The Impact of New Transnational Technology Transfer Control Systems on the International Patent System: A European Perspective: Comment. In *Sagafi-nejad, T.; Moxon, R. W. and Perlmutter, H. V., eds.,* 1981, pp. 118–19.
[G: U.S.S.R.]

Levy, Victor. Total Factor Productivity, Non-Neutral Technical Change and Economic Growth: A Parametric Study of a Developing Economy. *J. Devel. Econ.,* February 1981, *8*(1), pp. 93–109.
[G: Iraq]

Lukaszewicz, Aleksander. The Transfer of Technology: Comment. In *Saunders, C. T., ed. (I),* 1981, pp. 212–26.
[G: LDCs]

Luo, Rucheng and Shu, Jinzhong. Give Full Play to the Active Role of Loans for Minor Technological Innovation. *Chinese Econ. Stud.,* Fall 1981, *15*(1), pp. 87–94.
[G: China]

Luukkainen, Pecca A. Debatten om den svenska industrins strukturproblem. (The Debate on the Structural Problem of Swedish Industry: A Survey. With English summary.) *Ekon. Samfundets Tidskr.,* 1981, *34*(2), pp. 147–62.
[G: Sweden]

Lynn, Leonard. New Data on the Diffusion of the Basic Oxygen Furnace in the U.S. and Japan. *J. Ind. Econ.,* December 1981, *30*(2), pp. 123–35.
[G: U.S.; Japan]

Ma'Rafi, M. J. Technology for Oil and Gas Based Industries: The Case of Kuwait. In *U.N. Industrial Development Organization,* 1981, pp. 74–76.
[G: Kuwait]

MacDonald, J. D. Canadian Innovation: A National Imperative. In *Science Council of Canada, Industrial Policies Committee,* 1981, pp. 131–37.
[G: Canada]

Maitra, Priyatosh. Technology Transfer, Population Growth and the Development Gap since the Industrial Revolution. In *Bairoch, P. and Lévy-Leboyer, M., eds.,* 1981, pp. 78–85.
[G: LDCs; W. Europe]

Manser, W. A. P. and Webley, Simon. Technology Transfer to Developing Countries. In *The Royal Inst. of Internat. Affairs,* 1981, pp. 1–58.
[G: LDCs; MDCs]

Mansour, Mohamed B. Definitional Issues in Technology Transfer: Channels, Mechanisms and Sources. In *Hawkins, R. G. and Prasad, A. J., eds.,* 1981, pp. 1–9.
[G: LDCs]

Mason, R. Hal. Alternative Channels and Modes of International Resource Transmission: Comment. In *Sagafi-nejad, T.; Moxon, R. W. and Perlmutter, H. V., eds.,* 1981, pp. 27–36.

Mason, R. Hal. Technology Transfer Control Systems: The Case of East and Southeast Asian Developing Countries. In *Sagafi-nejad, T.; Moxon, R. W. and Perlmutter, H. V., eds.,* 1981, pp. 430–66.
[G: S. Korea; Taiwan; S.E. Asia]

Maule, C. J. Technology Acquisition: Licence Agreement or Joint Venture: Commentary. In *Science Council of Canada, Industrial Policies Committee,* 1981, pp. 93–96.
[G: U.S.; Canada; Sweden]

McCann, Joseph. Technology Transfer Control Systems: The Case of East and Southeast Asian Developing Countries: Comment. In *Sagafi-nejad, T.; Moxon, R. W. and Perlmutter, H. V., eds.,* 1981, pp. 474–77.
[G: S. Korea; Taiwan; S.E. Asia]

Mehta, Balraj. Foreign Technology—Adaptation and Development: The Experience in the Fertilizer Industry. In *Bagchi, A. K. and Banerjee, N., eds.,* 1981, pp. 389–91.
[G: India]

Meir, Avinoam. Innovation Diffusion and Regional Economic Development: The Spatial Diffusion of Automobiles in Ohio. *Reg. Stud.,* 1981, *15*(2), pp. 111–22.
[G: U.S.]

Mennis, Bernard. Conflicts in the International Transfer of Technology: A U.S. Home Country View: Comment. In *Sagafi-nejad, T.; Moxon, R. W. and Perlmutter, H. V., eds.,* 1981, pp. 263–69.
[G: U.S.]

Mennis, Bernard. Technology-Importing National Perspectives: Comment. In *Sagafi-nejad, T.;*

Moxon, R. W. and Perlmutter, H. V., eds., 1981, pp. 326–30. **[G: LDCs]**

Miller, Debra Lynn. An Economic Appraisal of the Proposed Code of Conduct for Technology Transfer. *Aussenwirtschaft*, June 1981, 36(2), pp. 121–42.

Miloslavskii, N. On Uniform Principles in Determining the Economic Effectiveness of New Technology and Capital Investments. *Prob. Econ.*, July 1981, 24(3), pp. 55–72. **[G: U.S.S.R.]**

Moldelski, George. Technology Exports and Technology Transfer Controls: Comment. In *Sagafinejad, T.; Moxon, R. W. and Perlmutter, H. V., eds.*, 1981, pp. 373–75.

Moore, John H. Agency Costs, Technological Change, and Soviet Central Planning. *J. Law Econ.*, October 1981, 24(2), pp. 189–214. **[G: U.S.S.R.]**

Moroney, John R. and Trapani, John M., III. Alternative Models of Substitution and Technical Change in Natural Resource Intensive Industries. In *Berndt, E. R. and Field, B. C., eds.*, 1981, pp. 48–69. **[G: U.S.]**

Mubayi, Vinod; Palmedo, Philip F. and Doernberg, Andres B. A Framework for Energy Policy and Technology Assessment in Developing Countries: A Case Study of Peru. In *Chatterji, M., ed.*, 1981, pp. 289–314. **[G: Peru]**

Murrell, Peter. Endogenous Technological Change and Optimal Growth. *Eastern Econ. J.*, April 1981, 7(2), pp. 97–109.

Musoke, Moses S. Mechanizing Cotton Production in the American South: The Tractor, 1915–1960. *Exploration Econ. Hist.*, October 1981, 18(4), pp. 347–75. **[G: U.S.]**

Nadiri, M. Ishaq and Schankerman, Mark A. Technical Change, Returns to Scale, and the Productivity Slowdown. *Amer. Econ. Rev.*, May 1981, 71(2), pp. 314–19. **[G: U.S.]**

Nadiri, M. Ishaq and Schankerman, Mark A. The Structure of Production, Technological Change, and the Rate of Growth of Total Factor Productivity in the U.S. Bell System. In *Cowing, T. G. and Stevenson, R. E., eds.*, 1981, pp. 219–47. **[G: U.S.]**

National Industrial Development Corporation Ltd. The Role of the Engineering Industry. In *U.N. Industrial Development Organization*, 1981, pp. 48–55. **[G: India]**

Neary, J. Peter. On the Short-Run Effects of Technological Progress. *Oxford Econ. Pap.*, July 1981, 33(2), pp. 224–33.

Nepali, S. B. and Regmi, I. R. Technological Innovations for Hill Agricultural Development. In *Nepal, Ministry of Food and Agriculture*, 1981, pp. 123–29. **[G: Nepal]**

Newcombe, Ken. Technology Assessment and Policy: Examples from Papua New Guinea. *Int. Soc. Sci. J.*, 1981, 33(3), pp. 495–507.

Nijhawan, B. R. Choice and Adaptation of Alternative Technology for the Iron and Steel Industry. In *U.N. Industrial Development Organization*, 1981, pp. 28–32.

Northcott, Jim. Policies for Micro-electronic Applications in Industry. In *Carter, C., ed.*, 1981, pp. 213–24. **[G: U.K.]**

Okuguchi, Koji. Population Growth, Costly Innovation and Modified Hartwick's Rule [Costly Innovation and Natural Resources]. *Int. Econ. Rev.*, October 1981, 22(3), pp. 657–61.

Omer, Assad U. Regional Approaches to the Transfer, Control, and Creation of Technology. In *Nicol, D.; Echeverria, L. and Peccei, A., eds.*, 1981, pp. 277–88.

Ono, Akira. Borrowed Technology in the Iron and Steel Industry: A Comparison between Brazil, India and Japan. *Hitotsubashi J. Econ.*, February 1981, 21(2), pp. 1–18. **[G: India; Brazil; Japan]**

Ozawa, Terutomo. Technology Transfer and Control Systems: The Japanese Experience. In *Sagafinejad, T.; Moxon, R. W. and Perlmutter, H. V., eds.*, 1981, pp. 376–80. **[G: Japan]**

Ozawa, Terutomo. Technology Transfer and Japanese Economic Growth in the Postwar Period. In *Hawkins, R. G. and Prasad, A. J., eds.*, 1981, pp. 91–116. **[G: Japan]**

Pack, Howard. The Choice of Technique and Employment in the Textile Industry. In *Bhalla, A. S., ed.*, 1981, pp. 159–79. **[G: U.K.]**

Pack, Howard. The Substitution of Labour for Capital in Kenyan Manufacturing. In *Killick, T., ed.*, 1981, 1976, pp. 254–62. **[G: Kenya]**

Packer, Arnold and Steger, Wilbur. Energy/Employment Policy Analysis: International Impacts of Alternative Energy Technologies. In *Tempest, P., ed.*, 1981, pp. 99–117.

Palterovich, D. The Actual Effectiveness of New Technology. *Prob. Econ.*, February 1981, 23(10), pp. 25–46. **[G: U.S.S.R.]**

Papola, T. S. Industrialization, Technological Choices and Urban Labour Markets. In *Bagchi, A. K. and Banerjee, N., eds.*, 1981, pp. 249–57. **[G: India]**

Paris, Quirino. On the Estimation of Biased Technological Progress. *Statistica*, July–September 1981, 41(3), pp. 395–409. **[G: U.S.]**

Parry, Thomas G. The Multinational Enterprise and Two-stage Technology Transfer to Developing Nations. In *Hawkins, R. G. and Prasad, A. J., eds.*, 1981, pp. 175–92. **[G: Australia; LDCs]**

Pastré, Olivier. Informatisation et emploi: de faux débats autour d'un vrai problème. (The Computer Revolution and Employment: False Debates about Real Problems. With English summary.) *Rev. Econ. Ind.*, 2nd Trimester 1981, (16), pp. 44–56.

Patil, S. M. Appropriate Technology for the Capital Goods Industry (Machine Tools) in Developing Countries. In *U.N. Industrial Development Organization*, 1981, pp. 43–47.

Pitt, Mark M. and Lee, Lung-Fei. The Measurement and Sources of Technical Inefficiency in the Indonesian Weaving Industry. *J. Devel. Econ.*, August 1981, 9(1), pp. 43–64. **[G: Indonesia]**

Polyakov, Michail; Kuhlmann, Friedrich and Ohlmer, Bo. Computerization of Farm Management Decision Aids. In *Johnson, G. and Maunder, A., eds.*, 1981, pp. 102–13.

Popov, Todor. Scientific and Technical Collaboration between the CMEA Member Countries in the Sphere of Agriculture. In *Johnson, G. and Maunder, A., eds.*, 1981, pp. 467–75. **[G: CMEA]**

Potter, Harry R. and Norville, Heather J. Social Values Inherent in Policy Statements: An Evaluation of an Energy Technology Assessment. In *Mann, D. E., ed.*, 1981, pp. 177–89. [G: U.S.]

Prasad, A. J. Licensing as an Alternative to Foreign Investment for Technology Transfer. In *Hawkins, R. G. and Prasad, A. J., eds.*, 1981, pp. 193–218. [G: LDCs; MDCs; U.S.]

Prasad, A. J. Technology Transfer to Developing Countries through Multinational Corporations. In *Hawkins, R. G. and Prasad, A. J., eds.*, 1981, pp. 151–73. [G: LDCs]

Pugel, Thomas A. Technology Transfer and the Neoclassical Theory of International Trade. In *Hawkins, R. G. and Prasad, A. J., eds.*, 1981, pp. 11–37.

Qadir, A. and Qadir, K. Inflation in a Growing Economy. *Pakistan Econ. Soc. Rev.*, Winter 1981, 19(2), pp. 149–56.

Rahman, A. The Interaction between Science, Technology and Society: Historical and Comparative Perspectives. *Int. Soc. Sci. J.*, 1981, 33(3), pp. 508–21.

Ranis, Gustav. Transfer and Style: A Historical Account: Comment. In *Sagafi-nejad, T.; Moxon, R. W. and Perlmutter, H. V., eds.*, 1981, pp. 55–63. [G: Selected Countries; U.K.; U.S.]

Rapacki, Ryszard. Poland's Exports of Licenses. *Econ. Planning*, 1981, 17(2–3), pp. 53–63. [G: Poland]

Ravasz, Károly. The Role of Technology Transfer in Cooperation Agreements. *Acta Oecon.*, 1981, 27(1–2), pp. 19–39. [G: Hungary]

Reddy, Amulya Kumar N. An Alternative Pattern of Indian Industrialization. In *Bagchi, A. K. and Banerjee, N., eds.*, 1981, pp. 221–47. [G: India]

Reinganum, Jennifer F. Market Structure and the Diffusion of New Technology. *Bell J. Econ. (See Rand J. Econ. after 4/85)*, Autumn 1981, 12(2), pp. 618–24.

Reinganum, Jennifer F. On the Diffusion of New Technology: A Game Theoretic Approach. *Rev. Econ. Stud.*, July 1981, 48(3), pp. 395–405.

Resnikoff, Howard L. and Weiss, Edward C. Adapting Use of Information and Knowledge to Enhance Productivity: Productivity, Information and Energy. In *Hogan, J. D. and Craig, A. M., eds.*, Vol. 1, 1981, pp. 507–49. [G: U.S.]

Richardson, P. Industrial Patterns in Early and Late Adoption of New Products in Canada: Commentary. In *Science Council of Canada, Industrial Policies Committee*, 1981, pp. 51–54. [G: Canada]

Riddiough, Michael A. Some Economic Consequences of Technological Advance in Medical Care: The Case of a New Drug: Comment. In *Helms, R. B., ed.*, 1981, pp. 290–93. [G: U.S.]

Roberts, Deborah D. and Wilemon, David L. Industry's Innovation Role in Urban Technology Transfer. In *Doctors, S. I., ed.*, 1981, pp. 169–92. [G: U.S.]

Roberts, Edward B. and Fusfeld, Alan R. Staffing the Innovative Technology-Base Organization. *Sloan Manage. Rev.*, Spring 1981, 22(3), pp. 19–34.

Roberts, Markley. The Workers' Stake in Adjust-

ments to Technological Change. In *Hogan, J. D. and Craig, A. M., eds.*, Vol. 1, 1981, pp. 467–73. [G: U.S.]

Robertson, Andrew. Introduction: Technological Innovations and Their Social Impacts. *Int. Soc. Sci. J.*, 1981, 33(3), pp. 431–46. [G: U.K.]

Roehl, Thomas. Technology Transfer and Control Systems: The Japanese Experience: Comment. In *Sagafi-nejad, T.; Moxon, R. W. and Perlmutter, H. V., eds.*, 1981, pp. 427–29. [G: Japan]

Roessner, J. David. The Local Government Market as a Stimulus to Industrial Innovation. In *Doctors, S. I., ed.*, 1981, pp. 193–216. [G: U.S.]

Root, Franklin R. The Pricing of International Technology Transfers via Nonaffiliate Licensing Arrangements. In *Sagafi-nejad, T.; Moxon, R. W. and Perlmutter, H. V., eds.*, 1981, pp. 120–33. [G: U.S.]

Root, Franklin R. and Contractor, Farok J. Negotiating Compensation in International Licensing Agreements. *Sloan Manage. Rev.*, Winter 1981, 22(2), pp. 23–32. [G: U.S.]

Rosenberg, N. Capital Goods, Technology, and Economic Growth. In *Livingstone, I., ed.*, 1981, 1963, pp. 188–93. [G: LDCs]

Russett, Bruce. United States Solar Energy Policy for Less-Developed Countries. *J. Energy Devel.*, Autumn 1981, 7(1), pp. 39–59. [G: LDCs; U.S.]

Ruttan, Vernon W. Three Cases of Induced Institutional Innovation. In *Russell, C. S. and Nicholson, N. K., eds.*, 1981, pp. 239–70. [G: Argentina; Philippines; Thailand]

Sachs, Ignacy. Ecodevelopment: A Paradigm for Strategic Planning? Comment on James [Growth, Technology and the Environment in Less Developed Countries: A Survey]. In *Streeten, P. and Jolly, R, eds.*, 1981, 1978, pp. 145–47. [G: LDCs]

Salanti, Andrea. L'analisi del progresso tecnico in termini di curve salario-profitto. (The Analysis of Technical Progress through Wage-Profit Curves: An Appraisal. With English summary.) *Econ. Int.*, February 1981, 34(1), pp. 124–42.

Sandberg, Lars G. The Entrepreneur and Technological Change. In *Floud, R. and McCloskey, D., eds.*, Vol. 2, 1981, pp. 99–120. [G: U.K.]

Sanderson, Paul W. Scientific–Technical Innovation in East Germany. *Polit. Sci. Quart.*, Winter 1981–82, 96(4), pp. 571–89. [G: E. Germany]

Schifrin, Leonard. The Effect of Patent Expiration on the Market Position of Drugs: Comment. In *Helms, R. B., ed.*, 1981, pp. 166–70. [G: U.S.]

Schlag, Pierre. A Theoretical Analysis of Knowhow Licensing under EEC Competition Law: Territorial Restrictions. *Antitrust Bull.*, Summer 1981, 26(2), pp. 347–445. [G: EEC]

Schwartz, Louis B. The Impact of New Transnational Technology Transfer Control Systems on the International Patent System: A European Perspective: Comment. In *Sagafi-nejad, T.; Moxon, R. W. and Perlmutter, H. V., eds.*, 1981, pp. 115–17. [G: EEC]

Shah, Anup R. and Desai, Meghnad. Growth Cycles with Induced Technical Change. *Econ. J.*, December 1981, 91(364), pp. 1006–10.

Shen, T. Y. Technology and Organizational Economics. **In** *Nystrom, P. C. and Starbuck, W. H., eds.,* Vol. 1, 1981, pp. 268–89.

Silverman, Barry G. Multimarket, Multitechnology, Multiattribute Technological Forecasting. *Energy J.,* April 1981, *2*(2), pp. 119–22.

Simos, Evangelos O. Learning-by-Doing or Doing-by-Learning? Evidence on Factor Learning and Biased Factor Efficiency Growth in the United States. *Rev. Bus. Econ. Res.,* Spring 1981, *16*(3), pp. 14–25. **[G: U.S.]**

Sinclair, Peter J. N. When Will Technical Progress Destroy Jobs? *Oxford Econ. Pap.,* March 1981, *33*(1), pp. 1–18.

Skott, Peter. Technological Advance with Depletion of Innovation Possibilities: A Comment and Some Extensions. *Econ. J.,* December 1981, *91*(364), pp. 977–87.

Slavin, M. and Ben'iash, G. The Effectiveness of Scientific and Technical Progress in Health Care. *Prob. Econ.,* July 1981, *24*(3), pp. 3–19. **[G: U.S.S.R.]**

Slaybaugh, Clifford W. Factors in Technology Transfer: A Multinational Firm Perspective. **In** *Hawkins, R. G. and Prasad, A. J., eds.,* 1981, pp. 289–305. **[G: U.S.]**

Soete, Luc L. G. A General Test of Technological Gap Trade Theory. *Weltwirtsch. Arch.,* 1981, *117*(4), pp. 638–60. **[G: OECD]**

Soltysinski, Stanislav J. The Impact of New Transnational Technology Transfer Control Systems on the International Patent System: A European Perspective. **In** *Sagafi-nejad, T.; Moxon, R. W. and Perlmutter, H. V., eds.,* 1981, pp. 89–114. **[G: CMEA; EEC]**

Standke, Klaus-Heinrich. Appropriate Technology for the Third Development Decade. **In** *Reubens, E. P., ed.,* 1981, pp. 133–46.

Stark, Oded. On the Optimal Choice of Capital Intensity in LDCs with Migration. *J. Devel. Econ.,* August 1981, *9*(1), pp. 31–41. **[G: LDCs]**

Statman, Meir. The Effect of Patent Expiration on the Market Position of Drugs. **In** *Helms, R. B., ed.,* 1981, pp. 140–51. **[G: U.S.]**

Stewart, Frances. International Technology Transfer: Issues and Policy Options. **In** *Streeten, P. and Jolly, R, eds.,* 1981, pp. 67–110. **[G: Selected LDCs]**

Stewart, Frances. Manufacture of Cement Blocks in Kenya. **In** *Bhalla, A. S., ed.,* 1981, *1975,* pp. 209–46. **[G: Kenya]**

Stewart, Frances. Taxation and Technology Transfer. **In** *Sagafi-nejad, T.; Moxon, R. W. and Perlmutter, H. V., eds.,* 1981, pp. 137–72. **[G: LDCs; MDCs]**

Stoneman, Patrick. Intra-Firm Diffusion, Bayesian Learning and Profitability. *Econ. J.,* June 1981, *91*(362), pp. 375–88.

Stoneman, Patrick. L'impact d'une nouvelle technologie sur l'emploi. (The Impact of New Technology of Employment Levels. With English summary.) *Rev. Econ. Ind.,* 3rd Trimestre 1981, (17), pp. 76–91.

Stubbs, P. C. Technological Change in Australia: A Review of the Myers Report. *Econ. Rec.,* September 1981, *57*(158), pp. 224–31. **[G: Australia]**

Sweeney, George. Adoption of Cost-Saving Innova-

tions by a Regulated Firm. *Amer. Econ. Rev.,* June 1981, *71*(3), pp. 437–47.

Tardos, Márton M. Importing Western Technology into Hungary. **In** *Bornstein, M.; Gitelman, Z. and Zimmerman, W., eds.,* 1981, pp. 221–41. **[G: Hungary]**

Teece, David J. Technology Transfer and R and D Activities of Multinational Firms: Some Theory and Evidence. **In** *Hawkins, R. G. and Prasad, A. J., eds.,* 1981, pp. 39–74. **[G: LDCs]**

Teece, David J. The Multinational Enterprise: Market Failure and Market Power Considerations. *Sloan Manage. Rev.,* Spring 1981, *22*(3), pp. 3–17.

Timberg, Sigmund. The Role of the International Patent System in the International Transfer and Control of Technology. **In** *Sagafi-nejad, T.; Moxon, R. W. and Perlmutter, H. V., eds.,* 1981, pp. 64–84.

Ting, Wen-Lee and Schive, Chi. Direct Investment and Technology Transfer from Taiwan. **In** *Kumar, K. and McLeod, M. G., eds.,* 1981, pp. 101–14. **[G: Taiwan]**

von Tunzelmann, G. N. Technical Progress during the Industrial Revolution. **In** *Floud, R. and McCloskey, D., eds., Vol. 1,* 1981, pp. 143–63. **[G: U.K.]**

Underwood, Daniel August. Thermodynamics and Genetic Engineering: An Alternative Conception of Optimal Resource Pricing and Production. *Econ. Forum,* Summer 1981, *12*(1), pp. 10–25.

Valle, P. Della. Productivity and Employment in the Copper and Aluminium Industries. **In** *Bhalla, A. S., ed.,* 1981, *1975,* pp. 323–55. **[G: Selected LDCs; U.S.]**

Van der Wees, Gerrit. Multinational Corporations, Transfer of Technology, and the Socialist Strategy of a Developing Nation: Perspectives from Tanzania. **In** *Hamilton, F. E. I. and Linge, G. J. R., eds.,* 1981, pp. 529–47. **[G: Tanzania]**

Vanderslice, Thomas A. Closing the Technology–Productivity Gap. **In** *Hogan, J. D. and Craig, A. M., eds., Vol. 2,* 1981, pp. 1231–38. **[G: U.S.]**

Waelbroeck, Jean. The Technology Transfer Issue: Comments. **In** *Grassman, S. and Lundberg, E., eds.,* 1981, pp. 194–97.

Watanabe, Susumu. Multinational Enterprises, Employment and Technology Adaptations. *Int. Lab. Rev.,* November–December 1981, *120*(6), pp. 693–710. **[G: LDCs]**

Wells, Louis T., Jr. Taxation and Technology Transfer: Comment. **In** *Sagafi-nejad, T.; Moxon, R. W. and Perlmutter, H. V., eds.,* 1981, pp. 173–76. **[G: LDCs; MDCs]**

Wells, Louis T., Jr. Technology Transfer Control Systems: The Case of East and Southeast Asian Developing Countries: Comment. **In** *Sagafi-nejad, T.; Moxon, R. W. and Perlmutter, H. V., eds.,* 1981, pp. 467–73. **[G: S. Korea; Taiwan; S.E. Asia]**

Wills, Hugh R. Estimating Input Demand Equations by Direct and Indirect Methods. *Rev. Econ. Stud.,* April 1981, *48*(2), pp. 255–70. **[G: U.S.]**

Wilner, Gabriel. Control and Incentives for Technology Transfer: A Multinational Perspective: Comment. In *Sagafi-nejad, T.; Moxon, R. W. and Perlmutter, H. V., eds.*, 1981, pp. 302–05.

Wilton, Peter C. and Pessemier, Edgar A. Forecasting the Ultimate Acceptance of an Innovation: The Effects of Information. *J. Cons. Res.*, September 1981, *8*(2), pp. 162–71.

Wionczek, Miguel S. International Controls of Technology Transfer: Comment. In *Sagafi-nejad, T.; Moxon, R. W. and Perlmutter, H. V., eds.*, 1981, pp. 510–13.

Wionczek, Miguel S. Restrictive Business Practices and International Controls on Transfer of Technology: Comment. In *Sagafi-nejad, T.; Moxon, R. W. and Perlmutter, H. V., eds.*, 1981, pp. 201–04.

Wisnosky, Dennis E. The Factory of the Future. In *Hogan, J. D. and Craig, A. M., eds.*, Vol. 1, 1981, pp. 101–06. [G: U.S.]

Wizarat, Shahida. Technological Change in Pakistan's Agriculture: 1953–54 to 1978–79. *Pakistan Devel. Rev.*, Winter 1981, *20*(4), pp. 427–45.
[G: Pakistan]

Yap, K. H. Basic Materials Industries: Aspects of Technology Choice and Industrial Location. In *U.N. Industrial Development Organization*, 1981, pp. 23–27.

Yassour, Joseph; Zilberman, David and Rausser, Gordon C. Optimal Choices among Alternative Technologies with Stochastic Yield. *Amer. J. Agr. Econ.*, November 1981, *63*(4), pp. 718–23.

You, Jong S. Money, Technology, and the Production Function: An Empirical Study. *Can. J. Econ.*, August 1981, *14*(3), pp. 515–24.
[G: Canada]

Yu, Ben T. Potential Competition and Contracting in Innovation. *J. Law Econ.*, October 1981, *24*(2), pp. 215–38.

Yu, Eden S. H. On Factor Market Distortions and Economic Growth. *Southern Econ. J.*, July 1981, *48*(1), pp. 172–78.

Zhan, Wu. Take the Road of Agricultural Modernization the Chinese Way. *Chinese Econ. Stud.*, Summer 1981, *14*(4), pp. 48–89. [G: China]

Zind, Richard G. Modèle d'estimation de l'élasticité de substitution et du progrès technologique. (Estimation of the Elasticity of Substitution and Technological Change: A Model. With English summary.) *L'Actual. Econ.*, April–June 1981, *57*(2), pp. 148–59.

6212 Research and Development

Abonyi, A. Imported Technology, Hungarian Industrial Development and Factors Impeding the Emergence of Innovative Capability. In *Hare, P. G.; Radice, H. K. and Swain, N., eds.*, 1981, pp. 132–57. [G: Hungary]

Andersson, Åke E. Structural Change and Technological Development. *Reg. Sci. Urban Econ.*, August 1981, *11*(3), pp. 351–61.

Archer, R. W. Industrial Policy and Innovation: Comment. In *Carter, C., ed.*, 1981, pp. 179–81.
[G: U.K.]

Barker, Randolph. Establishing Priorities for Allocating Funds to Rice Research. In *Johnson, G. and Maunder, A., eds.*, 1981, pp. 493–504.

Bashin, M. The Economics of Practical Utilization of Basic Research. *Prob. Econ.*, December 1981, *24*(8), pp. 24–43. [G: U.S.S.R.]

Beck, Roger L. Competition for Patent Monopolies. In *Zerbe, R. O., Jr., ed.*, 1981, pp. 91–110.

Bloom, Barry M. The Pharmaceutical Research and Development Decision Process: Comment. In *Helms, R. B., ed.*, 1981, pp. 114–17.

Busch, Lawrence and Sachs, Carolyn. The Agricultural Sciences and the Modern World System. In *Busch, L., ed.*, 1981, pp. 131–56.
[G: Selected Countries]

Chudnovsky, Daniel. Pricing of Intra-firm Technological Transactions. In *Murray, R., ed.*, 1981, pp. 119–32. [G: U.S.; Argentina; Selected Countries]

Clarkson, Kenneth W. and MacLeod, William C. Reducing the Drug Lag: Entrepreneurship in Pharmaceutical Clinical Testing. In *Helms, R. B., ed.*, 1981, pp. 84–113. [G: U.S.]

Crout, J. Richard. Reducing the Drug Lag: Entrepreneurship in Pharmaceutical Clinical Testing: Comment. In *Helms, R. B., ed.*, 1981, pp. 117–19.

Cruickshank, Andrew and Walker, William. Energy Research, Development and Demonstration in the European Communities. *J. Common Market Stud.*, September 1981, *20*(1), pp. 61–90.
[G: EEC]

Dale, Christopher. Agricultural Research as State Intervention. In *Busch, L., ed.*, 1981, pp. 69–82. [G: U.S.]

Daly, Anne. Government Support for Innovation in the British Machine Tool Industry: A Case Study. In *Carter, C., ed.*, 1981, pp. 52–67. [G: U.K.]

Davis, Jeffrey. The Relationship between the Economic Surplus and Production Function Approaches for Estimating Ex-Post Returns to Agricultural Research. *Rev. Marketing Agr. Econ.*, August 1981, *49*(2), pp. 95–105.

Day, Lee M. Research and the Family Farm: Implications for Agricultural Economics Research. *Amer. J. Agr. Econ.*, December 1981, *63*(5), pp. 997–1004. [G: U.S.]

De Bernardi, Bruno. L'applicazione dei principi fondamentali di bilancio al bilancio funzionale di ricerca e di investimento delle Communità Europee. (The Application of the Basic Budgetary Principles to the Functional Budget of Research and Investment of the European Communities. With English summary.) *Rivista Int. Sci. Econ. Com.*, May 1981, *28*(5), pp. 501–14. [G: EEC]

Dosi, Giovanni. Institutions and Markets in High Technology: Government Support for Micro-electronics in Europe. In *Carter, C., ed.*, 1981, pp. 182–202. [G: EEC]

Doyle, James J. and Navratil, Frank J. The Effects of Expectations on Industrial R & D Activity: Evidence Based on the Efficient Market Hypothesis. *Nebr. J. Econ. Bus.*, Autumn 1981, *20*(4), pp. 17–32. [G: U.S.]

Gibbons, Michael. Some Implications of Law Economic Growth Rates for the Development of Science and Technology in the United Kingdom. In *Coomer, J. C., ed.*, 1981, pp. 53–69.
[G: U.K.]

Gorman, Lyn. The Funding of Development Research. *World Devel.*, May 1981, 9(5), pp. 465–83. **[G: OECD]**

Grabowski, Henry G. and Vernon, John. The Determinants of Research and Development Expenditures in the Pharmaceutical Industry. In *Helms, R. B., ed.*, 1981, pp. 3–20. **[G: U.S.]**

Greig, I. D. Agricultural Research Management and the Ex Ante Evaluation of Research Proposals: A Review. *Rev. Marketing Agr. Econ.*, August 1981, 49(2), pp. 73–94.

Grether, David M. Research and Development Expenditures as a Competitive Strategy. In *[Grether, E. T.]*, 1981, pp. 30–59.

Hall, Richard H. Technological Policies and their Consequences. In *Nystrom, P. C. and Starbuck, W. H., eds., Vol. 2*, 1981, pp. 320–35.

Hansen, Ronald W. Pharmaceutical Innovation, Product Imitation, and Public Policy: Comment. In *Helms, R. B., ed.*, 1981, pp. 293–99.

Haselbach, Arne. Adapting R and D Programmes to the Needs of Less Developed Countries. In *Saunders, C. T., ed. (I)*, 1981, pp. 196–211. **[G: LDCs]**

Havlicek, Joseph, Jr. Funding for Agricultural Economics: Discussion. *Amer. J. Agr. Econ.*, December 1981, 63(5), pp. 806–07.

Henderson, P. D. Industrial Policy and Innovation: Comment. In *Carter, C., ed.*, 1981, pp. 170–78. **[G: U.K.]**

Kedrova, K. Financial Provision for the Scientific and Technical Development of the Branch. *Prob. Econ.*, May 1981, 24(1), pp. 61–77. **[G: U.S.S.R.]**

Kendrick, John W. International Comparisons of Recent Productivity Trends. In *Fellner, W., ed.*, 1981, pp. 125–70. **[G: OECD]**

Lall, Sanjaya and Kumar, Rajiv. Firm-Level Export Performance in an Inward-Looking Economy: The Indian Engineering Industry. *World Devel.*, May 1981, 9(5), pp. 453–63. **[G: India]**

Lambright, W. Henry and Teich, Albert H. The Organizational Context of Scientific Research. In *Nystrom, P. C. and Starbuck, W. H., eds., Vol. 2*, 1981, pp. 305–19.

Lean, David F. The Market for Research and Development: Physician Demand and Drug Company Supply: Comment. In *Helms, R. B., ed.*, 1981, pp. 227–31. **[G: U.S.]**

Link, Albert N. and Long, James E. The Simple Economics of Basic Scientific Research: A Test of Nelson's Diversification Hypothesis. *J. Ind. Econ.*, September 1981, 30(1), pp. 105–09. **[G: U.S.]**

Lukaszewicz, Aleksander. The Transfer of Technology: Comment. In *Saunders, C. T., ed. (I)*, 1981, pp. 212–26. **[G: LDCs]**

MacDonald, J. D. Canadian Innovation: A National Imperative. In *Science Council of Canada, Industrial Policies Committee*, 1981, pp. 131–37. **[G: Canada]**

Malecki, Edward J. Recent Trends in the Location of Industrial Research and Development: Regional Development Implications for the United States. In *Rees, J.; Hewings, G. J. D. and Stafford, H. A., eds.*, 1981, pp. 217–37. **[G: U.S.]**

Norton, George W. and Davis, Jeffrey S. Evaluating Returns to Agricultural Research: A Review. *Amer. J. Agr. Econ.*, November 1981, 63(4), pp. 685–99. **[G: U.S.]**

Pavitt, Keith. Technology in British Industry: A Suitable Case for Improvement. In *Carter, C., ed.*, 1981, pp. 88–115. **[G: U.K.; OECD]**

Phillips, Michael J. and Dalrymple, Dana G. U.S. Food and Agricultural Research Assessment: Implications for Agricultural Economists. *Amer. J. Agr. Econ.*, December 1981, 63(5), pp. 990–96. **[G: U.S.]**

Purcell, Joseph C. U.S. Food and Agricultural Research Assessment: Implications for Agricultural Economists: Discussion. *Amer. J. Agr. Econ.*, December 1981, 63(5), pp. 1005–07. **[G: U.S.]**

Randolph, S. Randi and Sachs, Carolyn. The Establishment of Applies Sciences: Medicine and Agriculture Compared. In *Busch, L., ed.*, 1981, pp. 83–111. **[G: U.S.]**

Ranftl, R. M. Role of R and D in Productivity: Microeconomic Issues. In *Hogan, J. D. and Craig, A. M., eds., Vol. 1*, 1981, pp. 93–100. **[G: U.S.]**

Říha, Ladislav. Plan-Based Management of Science and Research in Czechoslovakia. *Czech. Econ. Digest.*, February 1981, (1), pp. 54–70. **[G: Czechoslovakia]**

Rugman, Alan M. A Test of Internalization Theory. *Managerial Dec. Econ.*, December 1981, 2(4), pp. 211–19. **[G: Canada; U.S.]**

Rugman, Alan M. Research and Development by Multinational and Domestic Firms in Canada. *Can. Public Policy*, Autumn 1981, 7(4), pp. 604–16. **[G: Canada]**

Schankerman, Mark A. The Effects of Double-Counting and Expensing on the Measured Returns to R&D. *Rev. Econ. Statist.*, August 1981, 63(3), pp. 454–58. **[G: U.S.]**

Scherer, F. M. The Determinants of Research and Development Expenditures in the Pharmaceutical Industry: Comment. In *Helms, R. B., ed.*, 1981, pp. 46–48. **[G: U.S.]**

Stanton, Bernard F. and Farrell, Kenneth R. Funding for Agricultural Economics: Needs and Strategies for the 1980s. *Amer. J. Agr. Econ.*, December 1981, 63(5), pp. 796–805.

Statman, Meir. The Effect of Patent Expiration on the Market Position of Drugs. *Managerial Dec. Econ.*, June 1981, 2(2), pp. 61–66. **[G: U.S.]**

Stout, D. K. The Case for Government Support of R and D and Innovation. In *Carter, C., ed.*, 1981, pp. 116–28. **[G: U.K.]**

Teece, David J. Technology Transfer and R and D Activities of Multinational Firms: Some Theory and Evidence. In *Hawkins, R. G. and Prasad, A. J., eds.*, 1981, pp. 39–74. **[G: LDCs]**

Telser, Lester G. The Market for Research and Development: Physician Demand and Drug Company Supply. In *Helms, R. B., ed.*, 1981, pp. 183–221. **[G: U.S.]**

Toussaint, W. D. Funding for Agricultural Economics: Discussion. *Amer. J. Agr. Econ.*, December 1981, 63(5), pp. 808–09.

Tsurumi, Yoshi. Japan's Trade Competitiveness: Research and Development. In *Richardson, B. M.*

and Ueda, T., eds., 1981, pp. 101–08.
[G: Japan]

Virts, John R. and Weston, J. Fred. Expectations and the Allocation of Research and Development Resources. In *Helms, R. B., ed.*, 1981, pp. 21–45. [G: U.S.]

Weeks, Eldon E. Research on the Family Farm: Implications for Agricultural Economics Research: Discussion. *Amer. J. Agr. Econ.*, December 1981, 63(5), pp. 1008–09. [G: U.S.]

White, G. M. The Adoption and Transfer of Technology and the Role of Government. In *Carter, C., ed.*, 1981, pp. 157–69.

Wiggins, Steven N. The Pharmaceutical Research and Development Decision Process. In *Helms, R. B., ed.*, 1981, pp. 55–83. [G: U.S.]

Willott, W. B. Industrial Innovation and the Role of Bodies Like the National Enterprise Board. In *Carter, C., ed.*, 1981, pp. 129–45. [G: U.K.]

Woltman, Harry R. Expectations and the Allocation of Research and Development Resources: Comment. In *Helms, R. B., ed.*, 1981, pp. 49–52.
[G: U.S.]

Wu, S. Y. Pharmaceutical Innovation, Product Imitation, and Public Policy. In *Helms, R. B., ed.*, 1981, pp. 272–89.

630 INDUSTRY STUDIES

6300 General

Abonyi, A. Imported Technology, Hungarian Industrial Development and Factors Impeding the Emergence of Innovative Capability. In *Hare, P. G.; Radice, H. K. and Swain, N., eds.*, 1981, pp. 132–57. [G: Hungary]

Aldrich, Howard E., et al. Business Development and Self-segregation: Asian Enterprise in Three British Cities. In *Peach, C.; Robinson, V. and Smith, S., eds.*, 1981, pp. 170–90. [G: U.K.]

Anastasopoulos, A. and Sims, W. A. Effective Protection When Demand and Employment are Endogenous: Estimates for Quebec. *Can. J. Econ.*, May 1981, 14(2), pp. 201–15. [G: Canada]

Aquino, Antonio. The Measurement of Intra-Industry Trade When Overall Trade Is Imbalanced. *Weltwirtsch. Arch.*, 1981, 117(4), pp. 763–66.

Arterburn, Alfred and Woodbury, John. Advertising, Price Competition and Market Structure. *Southern Econ. J.*, January 1981, 47(3), pp. 763–75. [G: U.S.]

Aujac, Henri. Cultures and Growth. In *Saunders, C. T., ed. (II)*, 1981, pp. 47–70. [G: Brazil; France; Ivory Coast; Japan]

Bagchi, Amiya Kumar. Reinforcing and Offsetting Constraints in Indian Industry. In *Bagchi, A. K. and Banerjee, N., eds.*, 1981, pp. 23–62.
[G: India]

Banerjee, Nirmala. Change and Choice in Indian Industry: Is Small Beautiful? In *Bagchi, A. K. and Banerjee, N., eds.*, 1981, pp. 277–95.
[G: India]

Basak, Aroon K. Tripartite Industrial Cooperation and Third Countries: Comment. In *Saunders, C. T., ed. (I)*, 1981, pp. 369–71. [G: CMEA; OECD; LDCs]

Bautista, Romeo M. An Analysis of Structural Dependence between Korea and Japan: Comment. In *Hong, W. and Krause, L. B., eds.*, 1981, pp. 428–31. [G: Japan; S. Korea]

Berg, Sanford V. and Friedman, Philip. Impacts of Domestic Joint Ventures on Industrial Rates of Return: A Pooled Cross-Section Analysis, 1964–1975. *Rev. Econ. Statist.*, May 1981, 63(2), pp. 293–98. [G: U.S.]

Berlinck, Manuel Tosta; Bovo, José Murari and Cintra, Luiz Carlos. The Urban Informal Sector and Industrial Development in a Small City: The Case of Campinas (Brazil). In *Sethuraman, S. V., ed.*, 1981, pp. 159–67. [G: Brazil]

Bhalla, A. S. The Concept and Measurement of Labour Intensity. In *Bhalla, A. S., ed.*, 1981, 1975, pp. 17–39. [G: Selected LDCs]

Bora, Gyula. International Division of Labour and the National Industrial System: The Case of Hungary. In *Hamilton, F. E. I. and Linge, G. J. R., eds.*, 1981, pp. 155–83.
[G: Hungary; CMEA]

Botchie, George. Ghanaian Industrialization and its External Linkages. In *Hamilton, F. E. I. and Linge, G. J. R., eds.*, 1981, pp. 509–27.
[G: Ghana]

Boyer, Robert and Petit, Pascal. Employment and Productivity in the EEC. *Cambridge J. Econ.*, March 1981, 5(1), pp. 47–58. [G: EEC]

Cavalcanti, Leonardo; Geiger, Pedro P. and de Andrade, Thompson. Multinationals, the New International Economic Order and the Spatial Industrial Structure of Brazil. In *Hamilton, F. E. I. and Linge, G. J. R., eds.*, 1981, pp. 423–38. [G: Brazil]

Chandra, Nirmal K. The New International Economic Order and Industrialization in India. In *Lozoya, J. A. and Bhattacharya, A. K., eds.*, 1981, pp. 90–140. [G: India]

Chapman, D. R. and Junor, C. W. Profits, Variability of Profits and the Prices Justification Tribunal. *Econ. Rec.*, June 1981, 57(157), pp. 128–39.
[G: Australia]

Chew, Soon-Beng. Incomes Policy and Wage Inflation in the UK: An Empirical Study. *Malayan Econ. Rev. (See Singapore Econ. Rev.)*, April 1981, 26(1), pp. 52–73. [G: U.K.]

Chittle, Charles R. Foreign-Exchange Distribution in Yugoslavia's New Planning System: An Input–Output Approach. *J. Compar. Econ.*, March 1981, 5(1), pp. 79–86. [G: Yugoslavia]

Clark, Don P. Protection by International Transport Charges: Analysis by Stage of Fabrication. *J. Devel. Econ.*, June 1981, 8(3), pp. 339–45.
[G: U.S.; LDCs]

Cole, Lawrence P. A Note on Fully Distributed Cost Prices [An Analysis of Fully Distributed Cost Pricing in Regulated Industries]. *Bell J. Econ. (See Rand J. Econ. after 4/85)*, Spring 1981, 12(1), pp. 329–34. [G: U.S.]

Cole, W. A. Factors in Demand 1700–80. In *Floud, R. and McCloskey, D., eds., Vol. 1*, 1981, pp. 36–65. [G: U.K.]

Coquery-Vidrovitch, Catherine. Industry and Empire: The Beginnings of French Industrial Politics in the Colonies under the Vichy Regime. In *Bair-*

och, P. and Lévy-Leboyer, M., eds., 1981, pp. 29–33. **[G: France; Selected LDCs]**

Corden, W. Max. Trade and Industrial Policies, and the Structure of Protection in Korea: Comment. In *Hong, W. and Krause, L. B., eds.*, 1981, pp. 212–14. **[G: S. Korea]**

Cory, Peter F. A Technique for Obtaining Improved Proxy Estimates of Minimum Optimal Scale. *Rev. Econ. Statist.*, February 1981, *63*(1), pp. 96–106. **[G: U.S.]**

Cripps, Francis. Government Planning as a Means to Economic Recovery in the UK. *Cambridge J. Econ.*, March 1981, *5*(1), pp. 95–106. **[G: U.K.]**

Dalal, S. N. and Lahiri, A. Some Observations on Industrial Investment in India with Special Reference to the Private Corporate Sector. In *Bagchi, A. K. and Banerjee, N., eds.*, 1981, pp. 119–27. **[G: India]**

Decaluwe, Bernard. La formation des prix et les industries canadiennes exposées et abritées. (Price Formation and the Canadian Exposed and Sheltered Industries. With English summary.) *L'Actual. Econ.*, October–December 1981, *57*(4), pp. 454–90. **[G: Canada]**

Degamo, Julia Thelma Y. The Rediscount Policy and Its Impact on the Lending Patterns of Commercial Banks and on the Economy. *Philippine Econ. J.*, 1981, *20*(3&4), pp. 311–36. **[G: Philippines]**

Di Stefano, Guido. L'industria giapponese: tre giornate di studio. (Japanese Industry: A 3-Day Meeting. With English summary.) *L'Impresa*, 1981, *23*(5), pp. 51–55. **[G: Japan]**

Diejomaoh, V. P. and Anusionwu, E. C. The Structure of Income Inequality in Nigeria: a Macro Analysis. In *Bienen, H. and Diejomaoh, V. P., eds.*, 1981, pp. 89–125. **[G: Nigeria]**

Drabek, Zdenek. The Product Substitution and Technological Change in Czechoslovakia and Austria: The RAS Approach. *Greek Econ. Rev.*, December 1981, *3*(3), pp. 325–46. **[G: Czechoslovakia; Austria]**

El Mehdawi, Mohammed. The Industrialization of Libya. In *[Fisher, W. B.]*, 1981, pp. 252–63. **[G: Libya]**

English, H. Edward. Export-Oriented Growth and Industrial Diversification in Hong Kong: Comment. In *Hong, W. and Krause, L. B., eds.*, 1981, pp. 124–28. **[G: Hong Kong]**

Fajana, Olufemi. Aspects of Income Distribution in the Nigerian Urban Sector. In *Bienen, H. and Diejomaoh, V. P., eds.*, 1981, pp. 193–236. **[G: Nigeria]**

Fajnzylber, Fernando. The Industrial Dynamic in Advanced Developing Countries. In *Hong, W. and Krause, L. B., eds.*, 1981, pp. 35–59. **[G: Latin America]**

Fapohunda, O. J. Human Resources and the Lagos Informal Sector. In *Sethuraman, S. V., ed.*, 1981, pp. 70–82. **[G: Nigeria]**

Feinberg, Robert M. On the Measurement of Aggregate Concentration [What Has Been Happening to Aggregate Concentration in the United States?]. *J. Ind. Econ.*, December 1981, *30*(2), pp. 217–22. **[G: U.S.]**

Ferreira do Amaral, João. Industrial Policy in an Enlarged Community: Comment. *Economia (Por-*

tugal), January 1981, *5*(1), pp. 58–61. **[G: EEC]**

Findlay, Ronald. An Analysis of Structural Dependence between Korea and Japan: Comment. In *Hong, W. and Krause, L. B., eds.*, 1981, pp. 431–32. **[G: Japan; S. Korea]**

Fox, William F. Fiscal Differentials and Industrial Location: Some Empirical Evidence. *Urban Stud.*, February 1981, *18*(1), pp. 105–11. **[G: U.S.]**

Gillula, James W. Selected Problems of Regional Development in the USSR: The Growth and Structure of Fixed Capital. In *Koropeckyj, I. S. and Schroeder, G. E., eds.*, 1981, pp. 157–93. **[G: U.S.S.R.]**

Girgis, Maurice. Growth Patterns and Structural Changes in Output and Employment in the Arab World. In *Sherbiny, N. A., ed.*, 1981, pp. 21–54. **[G: Arab Countries]**

Givens, William L. International Industrial Competitiveness: The United States and Japan. In *Hogan, J. D. and Craig, A. M., eds., Vol. 1*, 1981, pp. 669–73. **[G: Japan; U.S.]**

Gordon, Robert J. Comment on Rasche and Tatom, "Energy Price Shocks, Aggregate Supply and Monetary Policy: The Theory and the International Evidence." *Carnegie-Rochester Conf. Ser. Public Policy*, Spring 1981, *14*, pp. 95–102. **[G: U.S.]**

Greenaway, David and Milner, Chris. Trade Imbalance Effects in the Measurement of Intra-Industry Trade. *Weltwirtsch. Arch.*, 1981, *117*(4), pp. 756–62. **[G: U.K.]**

Griffin, James M. The Energy–Capital Complementarity Controversy: A Progress Report on Reconciliation. In *Berndt, E. R. and Field, B. C., eds.*, 1981, pp. 70–80. **[G: Selected Countries]**

Gulcz, Mieczyslaw and Gruchman, Bohdan. Industrial Investment Assistance: The Socialist Countries' Approach to the Third World. In *Hamilton, F. E. I. and Linge, G. J. R., eds.*, 1981, pp. 215–23. **[G: CMEA; LDCs]**

Gutman, Patrick. Tripartite Industrial Cooperation and Third Countries. In *Saunders, C. T., ed. (1)*, 1981, pp. 337–64. **[G: CMEA; OECD; LDCs]**

Gutman, Patrick and Arkwright, Francis. Tripartite Industrial Cooperation between East, West, and South. In *Hamilton, F. E. I. and Linge, G. J. R., eds.*, 1981, pp. 185–214. **[G: France; OECD; CMEA; LDCs]**

Hager, Wolfgang. Industrial Policy in an Enlarged Community. *Economia (Portugal)*, January 1981, *5*(1), pp. 33–53. **[G: EEC]**

Helleiner, G. K. Intra-firm Trade and the Developing Countries: An Assessment of the Data. In *Murray, R., ed.*, 1981, pp. 31–57. **[G: U.S.; Global]**

Herman, Arthur S. Productivity Slows or Drops in 1979 in More Than Half of Industries Measured. *Mon. Lab. Rev.*, April 1981, *104*(4), pp. 58–61. **[G: U.S.]**

Hitiris, Theodore. Protection, Concentration and Labour Intensity: Reply [The Impact of Protection and Concentration on the Labor Intensity of U.K. Industries]. *Weltwirtsch. Arch.*, 1981, *117*(2), pp. 383–84. **[G: U.K.]**

Hoselitz, B. F. Small Industry in Underdeveloped

Countries. In *Livingstone, I., ed.*, 1981, *1959*, pp. 203–11.   [G: LDCs; Japan; W. Europe]

Hufbauer, Gary Clyde. Income Levels and the Structure of Trade: Comments. In *Grassman, S. and Lundberg, E., eds.*, 1981, pp. 162–64.
     [G: Global]

Ikemoto, Kiyoshi. The Industrial Dynamic in Advanced Developing Countries: Comment. In *Hong, W. and Krause, L. B., eds.*, 1981, pp. 60–62.   [G: Latin America]

Jackson, Richard. Industrialization in Papua New Guinea: A Social or Economic Investment? In *Hamilton, F. E. I. and Linge, G. J. R., eds.*, 1981, pp. 549–80.   [G: Papua New Guinea]

Jacquemin, Alexis. Industrial Policy in an Enlarged Community: Comment. *Economia (Portugal)*, January 1981, *5*(1), pp. 54–57.   [G: EEC]

Jorgenson, Dale W. Energy Prices and Productivity Growth. *Scand. J. Econ.*, 1981, *83*(2), pp. 165–79.   [G: U.S.]

Jorgenson, Dale W. U.S. Productivity Growth: Retrospect and Prospect. In *Hogan, J. D. and Craig, A. M., eds., Vol. 1*, 1981, pp. 5–25.   [G: U.S.]

Jorgenson, Dale W. and Fraumeni, Barbara M. Relative Prices and Technical Change. In *Berndt, E. R. and Field, B. C., eds.*, 1981, pp. 17–47.
     [G: U.S.]

Jurado, Gonzalo M., et al. The Manila Informal Sector: In Transition? In *Sethuraman, S. V., ed.*, 1981, pp. 121–43.   [G: Philippines]

Kendrick, John W. Survey of the Factors Contributing to the Decline in U.S. Productivity Growth. In *Federal Reserve Bank of Boston (I)*, 1981, pp. 1–21.   [G: U.S.]

Kheinman, S. A. Organizational–Structural Factors in Economic Growth [Part II]. *Prob. Econ.*, January 1981, *23*(9), pp. 25–52.   [G: U.S.S.R.]

Kheinman, S. A. Organizational–Structural Factors in Economic Growth [Part I]. *Prob. Econ.*, January 1981, *23*(9), pp. 3–24.   [G: U.S.S.R.]

Kirkpatrick, Colin H. and Yamin, M. The Determinants of Export Subsidiary Formation by US Transnationals in Developing Countries: An Inter-Industry Analysis. *World Devel.*, April 1981, *9*(4), pp. 373–82.   [G: U.S.]

Kohli, Ulrich R. Nonjointness and Factor Intensity in U.S. Production. *Int. Econ. Rev.*, February 1981, *22*(1), pp. 3–18.   [G: U.S.]

König, Heinz; Nerlove, Marc and Oudiz, Gilles. Micro-analysis of Realizations, Plans, and Expectations in the IFO and INSEE Business Texts by Multivariate Log-Linear Probability Models. In *[Valavanis, S.]*, 1981, pp. 393–420.
     [G: W. Germany]

Kort, John R. Regional Economic Instability and Industrial Diversification in the U.S. *Land Econ.*, November 1981, *57*(4), pp. 596–608. [G: U.S.]

Krishnaswamy, K. S. Change and Choice in Indian Industry: Inaugural Address. In *Bagchi, A. K. and Banerjee, N., eds.*, 1981, pp. 17–22.
     [G: India]

Krueger, Anne O. Trade and Industrial Policies, and the Structure of Protection in Korea: Comment. In *Hong, W. and Krause, L. B., eds.*, 1981, pp. 214–16.   [G: S. Korea]

Lall, Sanjaya. Transnationals, Domestic Enterprises,

and Industrial Structure in Host LDCs: A Survey. In *Livingstone, I., ed.*, 1981, *1978*, pp. 148–63.
     [G: LDCs]

Li, Yinglu. The Management System of Material Must be Reformed. *Chinese Econ. Stud.*, Summer 1981, *14*(4), pp. 38–47.   [G: China]

Lin, Tzong Biau and Ho, Yin Ping. Export-Oriented Growth and Industrial Diversification in Hong Kong. In *Hong, W. and Krause, L. B., eds.*, 1981, pp. 69–123.   [G: Hong Kong]

Lindenberg, Eric B. and Ross, Stephen A. Tobin's *q* Ratio and Industrial Organization. *J. Bus.*, January 1981, *54*(1), pp. 1–32.   [G: U.S.]

Linge, G. J. R. and Hamilton, F. E. Ian. International Industrial Systems. In *Hamilton, F. E. I. and Linge, G. J. R., eds.*, 1981, pp. 1–117.
     [G: OECD; CMEA; LDCs]

Maitha, J. K. and Manundu, M. Production Techniques, Factor Proportions and Elasticities of Substitution. In *Killick, T., ed.*, 1981, pp. 245–53.
     [G: Kenya]

Marer, Paul. U.S.–Polish Industrial Cooperation: Achievements, Problems, Prospects: Comment. In *Marer, P. and Tabaczynski, E., eds.*, 1981, pp. 131–36.   [G: Poland; U.S.]

Marga Institute. Informal Sector without Migration: The Case of Colombo. In *Sethuraman, S. V., ed.*, 1981, pp. 101–08.   [G: Sri Lanka]

Markwalder, Don. The Potential for Black Business. *Rev. Black Polit. Econ.*, Spring 1981, *11*(3), pp. 303–12.   [G: U.S.]

Mazzoni, Riccardo. An Analysis of the Changes in the Distribution of Employment between Industry and Services. *Rev. Econ. Cond. Italy*, February 1981, (1), pp. 87–117.   [G: Italy]

McMillan, Carl H. Tripartite Industrial Cooperation and Third Countries: Comment. In *Saunders, C. T., ed. (1)*, 1981, pp. 365–68.   [G: CMEA; OECD; LDCs]

Meller, Patricio and Marfán, Manuel. Small and Large Industry: Employment Generation, Linkages, and Key Sectors. *Econ. Develop. Cult. Change*, January 1981, *29*(2), pp. 263–74.
     [G: Chile]

Michaely, Michael. Income Levels and the Structure of Trade. In *Grassman, S. and Lundberg, E., eds.*, 1981, pp. 121–61.   [G: Global]

Miller, Edward M. Differences in Productivity by Size of Firm and Region. In *Hogan, J. D. and Craig, A. M., eds., Vol. 2*, 1981, pp. 839–53.
     [G: U.S.]

Mori, Giorgio. The Process of Industrialisation in General and the Process of Industrialisation in Italy: Some Suggestions, Problems and Questions. In *Bairoch, P. and Lévy-Leboyer, M., eds.*, 1981, pp. 151–64.   [G: Italy]

Nam, Chong Hyun. Trade and Industrial Policies, and the Strucure of Protection in Korea. In *Hong, W. and Krause, L. B., eds.*, 1981, pp. 187–211.
     [G: S. Korea]

Nayyar, Deepak. Industrial Development in India: Growth or Stagnation? In *Bagchi, A. K. and Banerjee, N., eds.*, 1981, pp. 91–117.   [G: India]

Nelson, Richard R. Research on Productivity Growth and Productivity Differences: Dead Ends and New Departures. *J. Econ. Lit.*, September

1981, *19*(3), pp. 1029–64.

Nurul Amin, A. T. M. Marginalisation vs. Dynamism: A Study of the Informal Sector in Dhaka City. *Bangladesh Devel. Stud.*, Autumn 1981, *9*(4), pp. 77–112. **[G: Bangladesh]**

Ong, Paul M. Factors Influencing the Size of the Black Business Community. *Rev. Black Polit. Econ.*, Spring 1981, *11*(3), pp. 313–19.
[G: U.S.]

Özhan, H. Gazi. An Evaluation of the 1973 Soviet Industrial Reorganization. *METU*, 1981, *8*(3&4), pp. 715–46. **[G: U.S.S.R.]**

Papola, T. S. Industrialization, Technological Choices and Urban Labour Markets. In *Bagchi, A. K. and Banerjee, N., eds.*, 1981, pp. 249–57.
[G: India]

Patnaik, Prabhat. An Explanatory Hypothesis on the Indian Industrial Stagnation. In *Bagchi, A. K. and Banerjee, N., eds.*, 1981, pp. 65–89. **[G: India]**

Personick, Valerie A. The Outlook for Industry Output and Employment through 1990. *Mon. Lab. Rev.*, August 1981, *104*(8), pp. 28–41. **[G: U.S.]**

Potier, M. The Role of International Organisations in the Control of Transfrontier Natural Resources and Environmental Issues. In *Butlin, J. A., ed.*, 1981, pp. 183–200. **[G: OECD]**

Powers, Terry A. Estimating Accounting Prices for Project Appraisal: Summary of Results. In *Powers, T. A., ed.*, 1981, pp. 123–45.
[G: Barbados; Paraguay; Ecuador; El Salvador]

Ránki, György. On the Economic Development of the Habsburg Monarchy. In *Bairoch, P. and Lévy-Leboyer, M., eds.*, 1981, pp. 165–74.
[G: Austria; Hungary]

Rao, S. Subba, et al. Determination of Energy Costs and Intensities of Goods and Services in the Indian Economy—An Input–Output Approach. In *Chatterji, M., ed.*, 1981, pp. 205–221.
[G: India]

Rasche, Robert H. and Tatom, John A. Energy Price Shocks, Aggregate Supply and Monetary Policy: The Theory and the International Evidence. *Carnegie-Rochester Conf. Ser. Public Policy*, Spring 1981, *14*, pp. 9–93. **[G: N. America; U.K.; Germany; France; Japan]**

Rasche, Robert H. and Tatom, John A. Reply to Gordon [Energy Price Shocks, Aggregate Supply and Monetary Policy: The Theory and the International Evidence]. *Carnegie-Rochester Conf. Ser. Public Policy*, Spring 1981, *14*, pp. 103–07.

Reddy, Amulya Kumar N. An Alternative Pattern of Indian Industrialization. In *Bagchi, A. K. and Banerjee, N., eds.*, 1981, pp. 221–47. **[G: India]**

Rogerson, Christian M. Industrialization in the Shadows of Apartheid: A World-Systems Analysis. In *Hamilton, F. E. I. and Linge, G. J. R., eds.*, 1981, pp. 395–421. **[G: Southern Africa]**

Rosefielde, Steven. Comparative Advantage and the Evolving Pattern of Soviet International Commodity Specialization, 1950–1973. In *[Bergson, A.]*, 1981, pp. 185–220. **[G: U.S.S.R.; CMEA]**

Rousslang, Donald and Parker, Stephen. The Effects of Aggregation on Estimated Import Price Elasticities: The Role of Imported Intermediate Inputs. *Rev. Econ. Statist.*, August 1981, *63*(3), pp. 436–39. **[G: U.S.]**

Safarian, A. E. The Industrial Dynamic in Advanced Developing Countries: Comment. In *Hong, W. and Krause, L. B., eds.*, 1981, pp. 62–65.
[G: Latin America]

Sandesara, J. C. The Small Industry Question: Issues, Evidence and Suggestions. In *Bagchi, A. K. and Banerjee, N., eds.*, 1981, pp. 135–47.
[G: India]

Schim van der Loeff, Sybrand and Harkema, Rins. Estimation and Testing of Alternative Production Function Models. *J. Macroecon.*, Winter 1981, *3*(1), pp. 33–53. **[G: Netherlands]**

Singh, Ajit. Third World Industrialisation and the Structure of the World Economy. In *Currie, D.; Peel, D. and Peters, W., eds.*, 1981, pp. 454–95.
[G: LDCs; MDCs]

Steiner, Michael. Zur Aussagekraft von Normalstrukturmodellen: Eine Note. (With English summary.) *Empirica*, 1981, (1), pp. 111–27.
[G: Austria]

Tabaczynski, Eugeniusz. East–West Industrial Cooperation and Specialization in Polish Production: Reply. In *Marer, P. and Tabaczynski, E., eds.*, 1981, pp. 107–08. **[G: Poland]**

Tabaczynski, Eugeniusz. East–West Industrial Cooperation and Specialization in Polish Production. In *Marer, P. and Tabaczynski, E., eds.*, 1981, pp. 99–103. **[G: Poland]**

Tanaka, Shigekazu. The Impact of Protection and Concentration on the Labour Intensity of U.K. Industries: Comment. *Weltwirtsch. Arch.*, 1981, *117*(2), pp. 380–82. **[G: U.K.]**

Teichova, Alice. Structural Change and Industrialisation in Inter-war Central-East Europe. In *Bairoch, P. and Lévy-Leboyer, M., eds.*, 1981, pp. 175–86. **[G: E. Europe]**

Thomas, D. J. General Equilibrium Assessment of a Free Area between Two Small Countries: Australia and New Zealand. *Australian Econ. Pap.*, December 1981, *20*(37), pp. 283–98.
[G: Australia; New Zealand]

Thurow, Lester C. Survey of the Factors Contributing to the Decline in U.S. Productivity Growth: Discussion. In *Federal Reserve Bank of Boston (I)*, 1981, pp. 22–25. **[G: U.S.]**

Vilensky, Matvey A.; Loginov, Viktor P. and Tushunov, Yuri A. Industry. In *Novosti Press Agency*, 1981, pp. 77–133. **[G: U.S.S.R.]**

Watanabe, Toshio. An Analysis of Structural Dependence between Korea and Japan. In *Hong, W. and Krause, L. B., eds.*, 1981, pp. 393–427.
[G: Japan; S. Korea]

Wenban-Smith, G. C. A Study of the Movements of Productivity in Individual Industries in the United Kingdom, 1968–79. *Nat. Inst. Econ. Rev.*, August 1981, (97), pp. 57–66. **[G: U.K.]**

White, Lawrence J. On Measuring Aggregate Concentration: A Reply [What Has Been Happening to Aggregate Concentration in the United States?]. *J. Ind. Econ.*, December 1981, *30*(2), pp. 223–24. **[G: U.S.]**

White, Lawrence J. What Has Been Happening to Aggregate Concentration in the United States? *J. Ind. Econ.*, March 1981, *29*(3), pp. 223–30.
[G: U.S.]

Wolf, Thomas A. East–West Industrial Cooperation

and Specialization in Polish Production: Comment. In *Marer, P. and Tabaczynski, E., eds.*, 1981, pp. 104–07. **[G: Poland]**

Woodward, John T. Plant and Equipment Expenditures: 1981. *Surv. Curr. Bus.*, January 1981, *61*(1), pp. 24–25. **[G: U.S.]**

Yadava, Gorelal. Industrialization of Bihar: Some Major Constraints and Possible Solutions. In *Karna, M. N., ed.*, 1981, pp. 45–56. **[G: India]**

Zagorski, Edwin. U.S.–Polish Industrial Cooperation: Achievements, Problems, Prospects: Reply. In *Marer, P. and Tabaczynski, E., eds.*, 1981, pp. 136–39. **[G: Poland; U.S.]**

Zagorski, Edwin. U.S.–Polish Industrial Cooperation: Achievements, Problems, Prospects. In *Marer, P. and Tabaczynski, E., eds.*, 1981, pp. 121–31. **[G: Poland; U.S.]**

631 Industry Studies: Manufacturing

6310 General

Aaronovitch, Sam and Sawyer, Malcolm C. Price Change and Oligopoly. *J. Ind. Econ.*, December 1981, *30*(2), pp. 137–47. **[G: U.K.]**

Aglietta, Michel; Orléan, André and Oudiz, Gilles. Des adaptations différenciées aux contraintes internationales: Les enseignements d'un modèle. (National Adjustments to International Constraints: Learning from a Model. With English summary.) *Revue Écon.*, July 1981, *32*(4), pp. 660–712. **[G: W. Germany; France; U.K.]**

Alford, B. W. E. New Industries for Old? British Industry between the Wars. In *Floud, R. and McCloskey, D., eds., Vol. 2*, 1981, pp. 308–31. **[G: U.K.]**

Amato, Louis; Ryan, J. Michael and Wilder, Ronald P. Market Structure and Dynamic Performance in U.S. Manufacturing. *Southern Econ. J.*, April 1981, *47*(4), pp. 1105–10. **[G: U.S.]**

Amjad, Rashid. The Development of Labour Intensive Industry in ASEAN Countries—An Overview. In *Amjad, R., ed.*, 1981, pp. 1–28. **[G: ASEAN]**

Amsden, Alice H. An International Comparison of the Rate of Surplus Value in Manufacturing Industry. *Cambridge J. Econ.*, September 1981, *5*(3), pp. 229–49.

Andersen, E. S.; Dalum, B. and Villumsen, G. The Importance of the Home Market for the Development of Technology and the Export Specialization of Manufacturing Industry. In *Freeman, C., et al.*, 1981, pp. 49–102. **[G: Denmark]**

Anderson, G. J. An Econometric Model of Manufacturing Investment in the U.K.: A Comment. *Econ. J.*, March 1981, *91*(361), pp. 122–23.

Anderson, Richard G. On the Specification of Conditional Factor Demand Functions in Recent Studies of U.S. Manufacturing. In *Berndt, E. R. and Field, B. C., eds.*, 1981, pp. 119–44. **[G: U.S.]**

Aryee, George. The Informal Manufacturing Sector in Kumasi. In *Sethuraman, S. V., ed.*, 1981, pp. 90–100. **[G: Ghana]**

Balassa, Bela. A 'Stages' Approach to Comparative Advantage. In *Balassa, B.*, 1981, pp. 149–67. **[G: LDCs; MDCs]**

Balassa, Bela. Prospects for Trade in Manufactured Goods between Industrial and Developing Countries, 1978–1990. In *Balassa, B.*, 1981, pp. 211–27. **[G: LDCs; MDCs; OPEC]**

Balassa, Bela. The Changing International Division of Labor in Manufactured Goods. In *Balassa, B.*, 1981, pp. 169–91.

Balassa, Bela. Trade in Manufactured Goods: Patterns of Change. In *Balassa, B.*, 1981, pp. 193–209.

Barsky, Carl B. and Personick, Martin E. Measuring Wage Dispersion: Pay Ranges Reflect Industry Traits. *Mon. Lab. Rev.*, April 1981, *104*(4), pp. 35–41. **[G: U.S.]**

Bautista, Romeo M. The Development of Labour Intensive Industry in the Philippines. In *Amjad, R., ed.*, 1981, pp. 29–75. **[G: Philippines]**

Bean, Charles R. An Econometric Model of Manufacturing Investment in the UK. *Econ. J.*, March 1981, *91*(361), pp. 106–21. **[G: U.K.]**

Bending, Richard. Data Collection Methodologies—Industry. In *Amman, F. and Wilson, R., eds.*, 1981, pp. 109–18. **[G: U.K.]**

Berend, Iván T. Continuity and Changes of Industrialization in Hungary after the Turn of 1956/57. *Acta Oecon.*, 1981, *27*(3–4), pp. 221–50. **[G: Hungary]**

Berndt, Ernst R. Energy Price Increases and the Productivity Slowdown in United States Manufacturing. In *Federal Reserve Bank of Boston (I)*, 1981, pp. 60–89. **[G: U.S.]**

Berndt, Ernst R.; Morrison, Catherine J. and Watkins, G. Campbell. Dynamic Models of Energy Demand: An Assessment and Comparison. In *Berndt, E. R. and Field, B. C., eds.*, 1981, pp. 259–89. **[G: U.S.]**

Bernhardt, Irwin. Sources of Productivity Differences among Canadian Manufacturing Industries. *Rev. Econ. Statist.*, November 1981, *63*(4), pp. 503–12. **[G: U.S.; Canada]**

Bhatia, S. L. Short-Run Employment Functions in the Indian Manufacturing Sector. *Indian Econ. J.*, April–June 1981, *28*(4), pp. 18–28. **[G: India]**

Bloch, Harry. Concentration and Profitability in Canadian Manufacturing: An Indirect Test of the Effect of Aggregation. *Can. J. Econ.*, February 1981, *14*(1), pp. 130–35. **[G: Canada]**

Bloch, Harry. Determinants of the Variance in Market Shares in Canadian Manufacturing. *J. Ind. Econ.*, June 1981, *29*(4), pp. 385–93. **[G: Canada]**

Boyer, Robert and Petit, Pascal. Progrès technique, croissance et emploi: Un modèle d'inspiration kaldorienne pour six industries européennes. (Technical Progress, Growth and Employment: A Kaldorian Model for Six European Industries. With English summary.) *Revue Écon.*, November 1981, *32*(6), pp. 1113–53. **[G: W. Europe; U.K.]**

Brech, M. J. and Stout, D. K. The Rate of Exchange and Non-Price Competitiveness: A Provisional Study within UK Manufactured Exports. *Oxford Econ. Pap.*, Supplement July 1981, *33*, pp. 268–81. **[G: U.K.]**

Buckley, Peter J. and Pearce, Robert D. Market

Servicing by Multinational Manufacturing Firms: Exporting versus Foreign Production. *Managerial Dec. Econ.*, December 1981, 2(4), pp. 229–46. [G: Selected Countries]

Cain, Louis P. and Paterson, Donald G. Factor Biases and Technical Change in Manufacturing: The American System, 1850–1919. *J. Econ. Hist.*, June 1981, 41(2), pp. 341–60. [G: U.S.]

Calcagno, Alfredo Eric and Jakobowicz, Jean-Michel. Some Aspects of the International Distribution of Industrial Activity. *Cepal Rev.*, April 1981, (13), pp. 7–33. [G: LDCs; MDCs]

Caporaso, James A. Industrialization in the Periphery: The Evolving Global Division of Labor. In *Hollist, W. L. and Rosenau, J. N., eds.*, 1981, pp. 140–71. [G: LDCs]

Caves, Richard E. Diversification and Seller Concentration: Evidence from Changes, 1963–72. *Rev. Econ. Statist.*, May 1981, 63(2), pp. 289–93. [G: U.S.]

Chang, Hui S. and Chern, Wen S. A Study on the Demand for Electricity and the Variation in the Price Elasticities for Manufacturing Industries. *J. Econ. Bus.*, Winter 1981, 33(2), pp. 122–31. [G: U.S.]

Chatterji, M. and Wickens, Michael R. Verdoorn's Law—The Externalities Hypothesis and Economic Growth in the U.K. In *Currie, D.; Nobay, R. and Peel, D., eds.*, 1981, pp. 405–29. [G: U.K.]

Chee, Peng Lim; Lee, Donald and Foo, Kok Thye. The Case for Labour Intensive Industries in Malaysia. In *Amjad, R., ed.*, 1981, pp. 235–309. [G: Malaysia]

Chenery, Hollis B. Comments on "Challenges and Opportunities Posed by Asia's Superexporters: Implications for Manufactured Exports from Latin America" *Quart. Rev. Econ. Bus.*, Summer 1981, 21(2), pp. 227–30. [G: Latin America; E. Asia]

Chenery, Hollis B. and Keesing, Donald B. The Changing Composition of Developing Country Exports. In *Grassman, S. and Lundberg, E., eds.*, 1981, pp. 82–116. [G: LDCs]

Chia, Siow Yue. Foreign Direct Investment in Manufacturing in Developing Countries: The Case of Singapore. In *Hamilton, F. E. I. and Linge, G. J. R., eds.*, 1981, pp. 439–64. [G: Singapore]

Christensen, Sandra and Maki, Dennis. The Union Wage Effect in Canadian Manufacturing Industries. *J. Lab. Res.*, Fall 1981, 2(2), pp. 355–67. [G: Canada]

Clark, Don P. On the Relative Importance of International Transport Charges as a Barrier to Trade. *Quart. Rev. Econ. Bus.*, Winter 1981, 21(4), pp. 127–35. [G: U.S.]

Corcione, Frank P. and Thornton, Robert J. The Economic Determinants of Strike Activity: An Industry Approach. *Rev. Bus. Econ. Res.*, Fall 1981, 17(1), pp. 15–26. [G: U.S.]

Crandall, Robert W. Pollution Controls and Productivity Growth in Basic Industries. In *Cowing, T. G. and Stevenson, R. E., eds.*, 1981, pp. 347–68. [G: U.S.]

Defeyt, Ph. and Houard, J. Restructuration industrielle: La Belgique face à ses concurrents europeens (1970–1979). (Industrial Restructuring:

Belgium Facing Its European Competitors (1970–1979). With English summary.) *Ann. Sci. Écon. Appl.*, 1981, 37(4), pp. 23–41. [G: Belgium]

Denny, Melvyn A.; Fuss, M. and May, J. D. Intertemporal Changes in Regional Productivity in Canadian Manufacturing. *Can. J. Econ.*, August 1981, 14(3), pp. 390–408. [G: Canada]

Denny, Michael; Fuss, Melvyn A. and Waverman, Leonard. Substitution Possibilities for Energy: Evidence from U.S. and Canadian Manufacturing Industries. In *Berndt, E. R. and Field, B. C., eds.*, 1981, pp. 230–58. [G: U.S.; Canada]

DeRosa, Dean A. and Goldstein, Morris. Import Discipline in the U.S. Manufacturing Sector. *Int. Monet. Fund Staff Pap.*, September 1981, 28(3), pp. 600–634. [G: U.S.]

Dixit, Mukund and Prasad, Kamta. Applicability of Neoclassical Model of Investment Behaviour to Industrial Corporations in India. *Indian Econ. J.*, October–December 1981, 29(2), pp. 1–22. [G: India]

Domberger, Simon. Price Adjustment and Market Structure: A Reply. *Econ. J.*, December 1981, 91(364), pp. 1031–35. [G: U.K.]

Dunning, John H. A Note on Intra-Industry Foreign Direct Investment. *Banca Naz. Lavoro Quart. Rev.*, December 1981, (139), pp. 427–37.

Dunning, John H. Explaining Changing Patterns of International Production: In Support of the Eclectic Theory. In *Dunning, J. H.*, 1981, *1980*, pp. 72–108. [G: OECD]

Dunning, John H. Multinational Enterprises and Domestic Capital Formation. In *Dunning, J. H.*, 1981, pp. 221–48. [G: U.S.]

Ebel, Karl-H. The Microelectronics Training Gap in the Metal Trades. *Int. Lab. Rev.*, November–December 1981, 120(6), pp. 727–39.

Edwards, P. K. The Strike-Proneness of British Manufacturing Establishments. *Brit. J. Ind. Relat.*, July 1981, 19(2), pp. 135–48. [G: U.K.]

Eliasson, Gunnar and Lindberg, Thomas. Allocation and Growth Effects of Corporate Income Taxes. In *Eliasson, G. and Södersten, J., eds.*, 1981, pp. 381–435. [G: Sweden]

Erickson, Rodney A. Corporations, Branch Plants, and Employment Stability in Nonmetropolitan Areas. In *Rees, J.; Hewings, G. J. D. and Stafford, H. A., eds.*, 1981, pp. 135–53. [G: U.S.]

Felli, Ernesto. Labour Productivity, Returns to Scale and Capital Accumulation in Italian Manufacturing Industry (1954–1978). *Rivista Polit. Econ.*, Supplement December 1981, 71, pp. 61–107. [G: Italy]

Fong, Pang Eng and Tan, Augustine. Employment and Export-led Industrialisation: The Experience of Singapore. In *Amjad, R., ed.*, 1981, pp. 141–74. [G: Singapore]

Foss, Murray F. Long-Run Changes in the Workweek of Fixed Capital. *Amer. Econ. Rev.*, May 1981, 71(2), pp. 58–63.

Franko, Lawrence G. and Stephenson, Sherry. French Export Behavior in Third World Markets. In *Center for Strategic and Internat. Studies, ed. (1)*, 1981, pp. 171–251. [G: France; OECD; LDCs]

Fuss, Melvyn A. and Gupta, Vinod K. A Cost Function Approach to the Estimation of Minimum Efficient Scale, Returns to Scale, and Suboptimal Capacity: With an Application to Canadian Manufacturing. *Europ. Econ. Rev.*, February 1981, *15*(2), pp. 123–35. [G: Canada]

Ghali, Moheb A. Production Smoothing and Inventory Behaviour: A Simple Model. In *Chikán, A., ed. (I)*, 1981, pp. 157–66. [G: U.S.]

Globerman, Steven. Returns to Industrial R & D and Industrial Marketing and Administration Activities. *J. Econ. Bus.*, Spring/Summer 1981, *33*(3), pp. 231–37. [G: U.S.]

Golladay, Fredrick L. Productivity Problems in Developing Countries. In *Hogan, J. D. and Craig, A. M., eds., Vol. 1*, 1981, pp. 737–49.
[G: LDCs]

Grant, R. M. The Relationship between Risk and Rate of Return on Capital in UK Industry. *Appl. Econ.*, June 1981, *13*(2), pp. 205–14. [G: U.K.]

Greenhut, Melvin L. Spatial Pricing in the United States, West Germany and Japan. *Economica*, February 1981, *48*(189), pp. 79–86. [G: U.S.; W. Germany; Japan]

Gregory, Paul R. Energy Price Increases and the Productivity Slowdown in United States Manufacturing: Discussion. In *Federal Reserve Bank of Boston (1)*, 1981, pp. 90–92. [G: U.S.]

Hall, P. H. Patterns of Energy Use in Australian Manufacturing Industry. *Australian J. Manage.*, December 1981, *6*(2), pp. 43–58. [G: Australia]

Hay, George and Untiet, Charles. Statistical Measurement of the Conglomerate Problem. In *Blair, R. D. and Lanzillotti, R. F., eds.*, 1981, pp. 163–91. [G: U.S.]

Hekman, John S. and Strong, John S. The Evolution of New England Industry. *New Eng. Econ. Rev.*, March–April 1981, pp. 35–46. [G: U.S.]

Hill, Hal. Subcontracting and Inter-Firm Linkages in Philippine Manufacturing. *Philippine Econ. J.*, 1981, *20*(1), pp. 58–79. [G: Philippines]

Hjorth-Andersen, Christian. Price and Quality of Industrial Products: Some Results of an Empirical Investigation. *Scand. J. Econ.*, 1981, *83*(3), pp. 372–89. [G: Denmark]

Hodge, James H. A Study of Regional Investment Decisions. In *Henderson, J. V., ed.*, 1981, pp. 1–65. [G: U.S.]

Horiba, Yutaka and Kirkpatrick, Rickey C. Factor Endowments, Factor Proportions, and the Allocative Efficiency of U.S. Interregional Trade. *Rev. Econ. Statist.*, May 1981, *63*(2), pp. 178–87.
[G: U.S.]

House, William J. Industrial Performance and Market Structure. In *Killick, T., ed.*, 1981, pp. 339–45. [G: Kenya]

Hutchinson, R. W. Price-Cost Margins and Manufacturing Industry Structure: The Case of a Small Economy with Bilateral Trade in Manufactured Goods. *Europ. Econ. Rev.*, June/July 1981, *16*(2/3), pp. 247–67. [G: Ireland]

Jacquemin, Alexis; Nambu, Tsuruhiko and Dewez, Isabelle. A Dynamic Analysis of Export Cartels: The Japanese Case. *Econ. J.*, September 1981, *91*(363), pp. 685–96. [G: Japan]

Kaldor, Nicholas. Verdoorn's Law—The Externalities Hypothesis and Economic Growth in the U.K.: Comment. In *Currie, D.; Nobay, R. and Peel, D., eds.*, 1981, pp. 430–433. [G: U.K.]

Kale, Steven. Industrial Development Trends in the Northern Plains States. In *Lawson, M. P. and Baker, M. E., eds.*, 1981, pp. 205–19. [G: U.S]

Kang, Heejoon and Brown, Gardner M. Partial and Full Elasticities of Substitution and the Energy–Capital Complementarity Controversy. In *Berndt, E. R. and Field, B. C., eds.*, 1981, pp. 81–89. [G: U.S.]

Keeble, David. Manufacturing Dispersion and Government Policy in a Declining Industrial System: The United Kingdom Case, 1971–76. In *Rees, J.; Hewings, G. J. D. and Stafford, H. A., eds.*, 1981, pp. 197–215. [G: U.K.]

Kemal, A. R. Substitution Elasticities in the Large-Scale Manufacturing Industries of Pakistan. *Pakistan Devel. Rev.*, Spring 1981, *20*(1), pp. 1–36.
[G: Pakistan]

Khan, Omar Asghar. Inter-Industry Wage Differentials in the Manufacturing Sector of the Punjab (1970–71—1975–76). *Pakistan Econ. Soc. Rev.*, Winter 1981, *19*(2), pp. 131–47. [G: Pakistan]

Kim, Kwan S. Enterprise Performances in the Public and Private Sectors: Tanzanian Experience, 1970–75. *J. Devel. Areas*, April 1981, *15*(3), pp. 471–84. [G: Tanzania]

Kirkpatrick, Grant. Further Results on the Time Series Analysis of Real Wages and Employment for U.S. Manufacturing, 1948–1977. *Weltwirtsch. Arch.*, 1981, *117*(2), pp. 326–51. [G: U.S.]

Koutsoyiannis, A. The Impact of Multinational Firms on Prices and Costs in Host-Country Markets: The Case of Canadian Manufacturing Industry. *Econ. Int.*, May–August–November 1981, *34*(2–3–4), pp. 356–75. [G: Canada]

Kushlin, V. Development of the Production Apparatus. *Prob. Econ.*, June 1981, *24*(2), pp. 13–31.

Lall, Sanjaya. Recent Trends in Exports of Manufactures by Newly-Industrialising Countries. In *Lall, S.*, 1981, pp. 173–227. [G: LDCs]

Laumas, Prem S. and Williams, Martin. The Elasticity of Substitution in India's Manufacturing Sector. *J. Devel. Econ.*, June 1981, *8*(3), pp. 325–37. [G: India]

Laurie, Bruce and Schmitz, Mark. Manufacture and Productivity: The Making of an Industrial Base, Philadelphia, 1850–1880. In *Hershberg, T., ed.*, 1981, pp. 43–92. [G: U.S.]

Levy, Victor. On Estimating Efficiency Differentials between the Public and Private Sectors in a Developing Economy—Iraq. *J. Compar. Econ.*, September 1981, *5*(3), pp. 235–50. [G: Iraq]

Lim, David. Another Look at the Effect of Capital Subsidies on Capital-Intensity. *Australian Econ. Pap.*, December 1981, *20*(37), pp. 376–82.
[G: Malaysia]

Lindberg, Thomas. Industrial Profits—Their Importance and Evaluation. In *Industrial Inst. for Econ. and Soc. Research*, 1981, pp. 66–77.
[G: Sweden]

Lindsey, Charles W. Firm Size and Profit Rate in Philippine Manufacturing. *J. Devel. Areas*, April 1981, *15*(3), pp. 445–56. [G: Philippines]

Link, Albert N. Basic Research and Productivity Increase in Manufacturing: Additional Evidence. *Amer. Econ. Rev.*, December 1981, *71*(5), pp. 1111–12. [G: U.S]

Lipsey, Robert E. and Weiss, Merle Yahr. Foreign Production and Exports in Manufacturing Industries. *Rev. Econ. Statist.*, November 1981, *63*(4), pp. 488–94. [G: U.S.]

Little, Jane Sneddon. The Financial Health of U.S. Manufacturing Firms Acquired by Foreigners. *New Eng. Econ. Rev.*, July/August 1981, pp. 5–18. [G: U.S.]

Loasby, B. J. Price-Cost Margins, Market Structure and International Trade: Comment. In *Currie, D.; Peel, D. and Peters, W., eds.*, 1981, pp. 296–98. [G: U.K.]

Lorch, Brian J. Mergers and Acquisitions and the Geographic Transfer of Corporate Control: Canada's Manufacturing Industry. In *Rees, J.; Hewings, G. J. D. and Stafford, H. A., eds.*, 1981, pp. 123–34. [G: Canada]

Lynk, William J. Information, Advertising, and the Structure of the Market. *J. Bus.*, April 1981, *54*(2), pp. 271–303. [G: U.S.]

Lyons, Bruce. Price-Cost Margins, Market Structure and International Trade. In *Currie, D.; Peel, D. and Peters, W., eds.*, 1981, pp. 276–95. [G: U.K.]

Maccini, Louis J. and Rossana, Robert J. Investment in Finished Goods Inventories: An Analysis of Adjustment Speeds. *Amer. Econ. Rev.*, May 1981, *71*(2), pp. 17–22. [G: U.S.]

MacDonald, Glenn M. and Evans, John C. The Size and Structure of Union-Non-Union Wage Differentials in Canadian Industry. *Can. J. Econ.*, May 1981, *14*(2), pp. 216–31. [G: Canada]

Mangan, John. Labour Hoarding in Australian Manufacturing: An Inter-Industry Analysis. *Australian Bull. Lab.*, September 1981, *7*(4), pp. 219–35. [G: Australia]

Mansfield, Edwin; Schwartz, Mark and Wagner, Samuel. Imitation Costs and Patents: An Empirical Study. *Econ. J.*, December 1981, *91*(364), pp. 907–18. [G: U.S.]

Manzetti, Fabio A. On the Stability Implications of Inventory Cycles: An Econometric Analysis of Some Italian Sectors. In *Chikán, A., ed. (I)*, 1981, pp. 241–53. [G: Italy]

Marais, G. Structural Changes in Manufacturing Industry, 1916 to 1975. *S. Afr. J. Econ.*, March 1981, *49*(1), pp. 26–45. [G: S. Africa]

McAvinchey, Ian D. Generalized Adjustment, Stability and Functional Form with Reference to the UK Manufacturing Sector. *Appl. Econ.*, March 1981, *13*(1), pp. 51–65. [G: U.K.]

McCloskey, Donald N. The Industrial Revolution 1780–1860: A Survey. In *Floud, R. and McCloskey, D., eds., Vol. 1*, 1981, pp. 103–27. [G: U.K.]

McCombie, J. S. L. What Still Remains of Kaldor's Laws? *Econ. J.*, March 1981, *91*(361), pp. 206–16.

Miller, E. Willard. Spatial Organization of Manufacturing in Nonmetropolitan Pennsylvania. In *Rees, J.; Hewings, G. J. D. and Stafford, H. A., eds.*, 1981, pp. 155–69. [G: U.S.]

Moroney, John R. and Trapani, John M., III. Alternative Models of Substitution and Technical Change in Natural Resource Intensive Industries. In *Berndt, E. R. and Field, B. C., eds.*, 1981, pp. 48–69. [G: U.S.]

Moroney, John R. and Trapani, John M., III. Factor Demand and Substitution in Mineral-Intensive Industries. *Bell J. Econ. (See Rand J. Econ. after 4/85)*, Spring 1981, *12*(1), pp. 272–84. [G: U.S.]

Morrison, Catherine J. and Berndt, Ernst R. Short-Run Labor Productivity in a Dynamic Model. *J. Econometrics*, August 1981, *16*(3), pp. 339–65.

Murray, Barbara B. Capital Budgeting Decisions for Load Management Equipment by Industrial Electric Users. *Nebr. J. Econ. Bus.*, Winter 1981, *20*(1), pp. 31–47. [G: U.S.]

Nadiri, M. Ishaq and Schankerman, Mark A. Technical Change, Returns to Scale, and the Productivity Slowdown. *Amer. Econ. Rev.*, May 1981, *71*(2), pp. 314–19. [G: U.S.]

Naples, Michele I. Industrial Conflict and Its Implications for Productivity Growth. *Amer. Econ. Rev.*, May 1981, *71*(2), pp. 36–41. [G: U.S.]

Nicholson, B. M.; Brinkley, Ian and Evans, Alan W. The Role of the Inner City in the Development of Manufacturing Industry. *Urban Stud.*, February 1981, *18*(1), pp. 57–71. [G: U.K.]

Nobel, Klaus. Development Opportunities of Ghana within the Frame of Intra-industry Trade—An Empirical Analysis on the Basis of Triangularized Trade Matrices. In *Schmitt-Rink, G., ed.*, 1981, pp. 159–213. [G: Ghana]

Norsworthy, J. R. and Harper, Michael J. Dynamic Models of Energy Substitution in U.S. Manufacturing. In *Berndt, E. R. and Field, B. C., eds.*, 1981, pp. 177–208. [G: U.S.]

O'Farrell, P. N. and O'Loughlin, B. The Impact of New Industry Enterprises in Ireland: An Analysis of Service Linkages. *Reg. Stud.*, 1981, *15*(6), pp. 439–58. [G: Ireland]

Odle, Curt; Koshal, Rajindar K. and Shukla, Vishwa. Unfilled Orders and Price Changes: A Simultaneous Equations System. *Managerial Dec. Econ.*, June 1981, *2*(2), pp. 97–105. [G: U.S.]

Pack, Howard. Fostering the Capital–Goods Sector in LDCs. *World Devel.*, March 1981, *9*(3), pp. 227–50. [G: LDCs]

Pack, Howard. The Substitution of Labour for Capital in Kenyan Manufacturing. In *Killick, T., ed.*, 1981, *1976*, pp. 254–62. [G: Kenya]

Poot, H. The Development of Labour Intensive Industries in Indonesia. In *Amjad, R., ed.*, 1981, pp. 77–140. [G: Indonesia]

Portney, Paul R. The Macroeconomic Impacts of Federal Environmental Regulation. *Natural Res. J.*, July 1981, *21*(3), pp. 459–88. [G: U.S.]

Ranis, Gustav. Challenges and Opportunities Posed by Asia's Superexporters: Implications for Manufactured Exports from Latin America. *Quart. Rev. Econ. Bus.*, Summer 1981, *21*(2), pp. 204–26. [G: Latin America; E. Asia]

Rao, P. Someshwar. Factor Prices and Labour Productivity in the Canadian Manufacturing Industries. *Empirical Econ.*, 1981, *6*(4), pp. 187–202. [G: Canada]

Rayment, P. B. W. Structural Change in Manufacturing Industry and the Stability of the Verdoorn Law. *Econ. Int.*, February 1981, *34*(1), pp. 104–23. [G: W. Europe]

Reati, Angelo. A propos de la baisse tendancielle

du taux de profit: Analyse désagrégée de l'industrie italienne 1951–1971: Deuxième Partie. (On the Law of the Falling Rate of Profit: A Disaggregated Analysis of Italian Industry, 1951–1971 (Second Part). With English summary.) *Cah. Écon. Bruxelles*, 1st Trimestre 1981, (89), pp. 75–108. [G: Italy]

Rees, R. D. and Miall, R. H. C. The Effect of Regional Policy on Manufacturing Investment and Capital Stock within the U.K. between 1959 and 1978. *Reg. Stud.*, 1981, 15(6), pp. 413–24. [G: U.K.]

Richards, Stewart F. Industrial Activities in the Periphery: Hong Kong. In *Hamilton, F. E. I. and Linge, G. J. R., eds.*, 1981, pp. 465–80. [G: Hong Kong]

Robinson, J. F. F. and Storey, D. J. Employment Change in Manufacturing Industry in Cleveland, 1965-1976. *Reg. Stud.*, 1981, 15(3), pp. 161–72. [G: U.K.]

Rosa, Giuseppe. Italian Industry in the Seventies: Dimensional Aspects. *Rivista Polit. Econ.*, Supplement December 1981, 71, pp. 149–79. [G: Italy]

Rosefielde, Steven. Are Soviet Industrial-Production Statistics Significantly Distorted by Hidden Inflation? *J. Compar. Econ.*, June 1981, 5(2), pp. 185–99. [G: U.S.S.R.]

Round, David K. Concentration, Plant Size, and Multiple Plant Operations of Large Firms in Australian Manufacturing Industries. *Nebr. J. Econ. Bus.*, Winter 1981, 20(1), pp. 19–29. [G: Australia]

Samuelson, Paul A. To Protect Manufacturing? *Z. ges. Staatswiss.*, September 1981, 137(3), pp. 407–14.

Sandberg, Lars G. The Entrepreneur and Technological Change. In *Floud, R. and McCloskey, D., eds., Vol. 2*, 1981, pp. 99–120. [G: U.K.]

Sarantis, Nicholas C. Employment, Labor Supply and Real Wages in Market Disequilibrium. *J. Macroecon.*, Summer 1981, 3(3), pp. 335–54. [G: U.S.]

Saunders, Peter G. Price Determination in Australian Manufacturing Firms: A Cross-Section Study. *Australian Econ. Pap.*, December 1981, 20(37), pp. 359–75. [G: Australia]

Shipley, David D. Pricing Objectives in British Manufacturing Industry. *J. Ind. Econ.*, June 1981, 29(4), pp. 429–43. [G: U.K.]

Soete, Luc L. G. A General Test of Technological Gap Trade Theory. *Weltwirtsch. Arch.*, 1981, 117(4), pp. 638–60. [G: OECD]

Soza, Héctor. The Industrialization Debate in Latin America. *Cepal Rev.*, April 1981, (13), pp. 35–64. [G: Latin America]

Stein, Leslie. The Growth and Implications of LDC Manufactured Exports to Advanced Countries. *Kyklos*, 1981, 34(1), pp. 36–59. [G: LDCs.]

Sveikauskas, Leo. Technological Inputs and Multifactor Productivity Growth. *Rev. Econ. Statist.*, May 1981, 63(2), pp. 275–82. [G: U.S.]

Tambunlertchai, Somsak and Loohawenchit, Chesada. Labour Intensive and Small Scale Manufacturing in Thailand. In *Amjad, R., ed.*, 1981, pp. 175–233. [G: Thailand]

Tarling, R. and Wilkinson, F. Regional Earnings Determination in the United Kingdom Engineering Industry, 1964–1979. In *Martin, R. L., ed.*, 1981, pp. 60–74. [G: U.K.]

Thomas, Morgan D. Industry Perspectives on Growth and Change in the Manufacturing Sector. In *Rees, J.; Hewings, G. J. D. and Stafford, H. A., eds.*, 1981, pp. 41–58.

Thomson, Lydia. Industrial Employment Performance and Regional Policy, 1952–71: A Cross-Sectional Approach. *Urban Stud.*, June 1981, 18(2), pp. 231–38. [G: U.K.]

Thoroe, Carsten S. Changes in the Regional Growth Pattern in the European Community. In *Giersch, H., ed. (II)*, 1981, pp. 283–311. [G: W. Germany; France; Italy; U.K.]

Till, Thomas E. Manufacturing Industry: Trends and Impacts. In *Hawley, A. H. and Mazie, S. M., eds.*, 1981, pp. 194–230. [G: U.S.]

Tyler, William G. Advanced Developing Countries as Export Competitors in Third World Markets: the Brazilian Experience. In *Center for Strategic and Internat. Studies, ed. (I)*, 1981, pp. 331–408. [G: Brazil; LDCs]

Uri, Noel D. and Mixon, J. Wilson, Jr. The Effect of Exports and Imports on the Stability of Employment in Manufacturing Industries in the United States. *Appl. Econ.*, June 1981, 13(2), pp. 193–203. [G: U.S.]

Varaiya, Pravin and Wiseman, Michael. Investment and Employment in Manufacturing in U.S. Metropolitan Areas, 1960–1976. *Reg. Sci. Urban Econ.*, November 1981, 11(4), pp. 431–69. [G: U.S.]

Vernon, Raymond. State-Owned Enterprises in Latin-American Exports. In *Baer, W. and Gillis, M., eds.*, 1981, pp. 98–114. [G: Latin America]

Wabe, J. S. Energy Expenditure in Sectors of Manufacturing. *Energy Econ.*, July 1981, 3(3), pp. 178–81. [G: Yugoslavia; France; India; Japan; Mexico]

Walton, A. L. Variations in the Substitutability of Energy and Nonenergy Inputs: The Case of the Middle Atlantic Region. *J. Reg. Sci.*, August 1981, 21(3), pp. 411–20. [G: U.S.]

Wheeler, James O. Effects of Geographical Scale on Location Decisions in Manufacturing: The Atlanta Example. *Econ. Geogr.*, April 1981, 57(2), pp. 134–45. [G: U.S.]

Williams, Martin and Laumas, Prem S. The Relation between Energy and Non-Energy Inputs in India's Manufacturing Industries. *J. Ind. Econ.*, December 1981, 30(2), pp. 113–22. [G: India]

Winters, L. A. Price Adjustment and Market Structure: A Comment. *Econ. J.*, December 1981, 91(364), pp. 1026–30. [G: U.K.]

Yli-Olli, Paavo. Leverage, the Cost of Capital and the Value of the Firm: Empirical Evidence on Finnish Industrial Firms. *Liiketaloudellinen Aikak.*, 1981, 30(4), pp. 435–46. [G: Finland]

6312 Metals (iron, steel, and other)

Allen, Robert C. Accounting for Price Changes: American Steel Rails, 1879–1910. *J. Polit. Econ.*, June 1981, 89(3), pp. 512–28. [G: U.S.]

Allen, Robert C. Entrepreneurship and Technical Progress in the Northeast Coast Pig Iron Industry: 1850–1913. In *Uselding, P., ed.*, 1981, pp. 35–71. [G: U.K.]

Ault, David E. and Meisel, John B. An Investigation into the Effects of Technology and Economies of Scale on International Trade in Basic Steel: 1955–76. *Rivista Int. Sci. Econ. Com.*, May 1981, *28*(5), pp. 461–86. [G: OECD]

Baldwin, Robert E. U.S. Political Pressures against Adjustment to Greater Imports. In *Hong, W. and Krause, L. B., eds.*, 1981, pp. 515–50. [G: U.S.]

Bickley, James M. An Evaluation of the Reconstruction Finance Corporation with Implications for Current Capital Needs of the Steel Industry. In *Sternlieb, G. and Listokin, D., eds.*, 1981, pp. 144–62. [G: U.S.]

Bod, Péter. Strategic Decisions on the Development of the Aluminum Industry. *Matekon*, Winter 1981–82, *18*(2), pp. 3–18. [G: Hungary]

Boon, G. K. Technological Choice in Metalworking, with Special Reference to Mexico. In *Bhalla, A. S., ed.*, 1981, *1975*, pp. 303–21. [G: Mexico]

Emerson, Craig and Warr, Peter G. Economic Evaluation of Mineral Processing Projects: A Case Study of Copper Smelting in the Philippines. *Philippine Econ. J.*, 1981, *20*(2), pp. 175–97. [G: Philippines]

Feldenkirchen, Wilfried. The Banks and the Steel Industry in the Ruhr: Developments in Relations from 1873 to 1914. In *Engels, W. and Pohl, H., eds.*, 1981, pp. 27–51. [G: W. Germany]

Gold, Bela. Frontiers of Productivity Analysis for Management: With Special Reference to Steel and Other Manufacturing Industries. In *Hogan, J. D. and Craig, A. M., eds., Vol. 2*, 1981, pp. 1159–76. [G: U.S.]

Iyengar, R. K. and Ramachandran, S. Appropriate Technology for the Iron and Steel Industry. In *U.N. Industrial Development Organization*, 1981, pp. 33–42. [G: India]

Kojima, Kiyoshi. U.S. Political Pressures against Adjustment to Greater Imports: Comment. In *Hong, W. and Krause, L. B., eds.*, 1981, pp. 551–53. [G: U.S.]

Kopp, Raymond J. and Smith, V. Kerry. Productivity Measurement and Environmental Regulation: An Engineering–Econometric Analysis. In *Cowing, T. G. and Stevenson, R. E., eds.*, 1981, pp. 248–81.

Li, Bingquan. The Application of Input–Output Analysis to Steel and Iron Combined Enterprises. *Chinese Econ. Stud.*, Fall 1981, *15*(1), pp. 3–19. [G: China]

Lim, Manuel T. An Evaluation of the Performance of the Steel and Cement Industries in the 1960s and 1970s. *Philippine Econ. J.*, 1981, *20*(3&4), pp. 295–310. [G: Philippines]

Lynn, Leonard. New Data on the Diffusion of the Basic Oxygen Furnace in the U.S. and Japan. *J. Ind. Econ.*, December 1981, *30*(2), pp. 123–35. [G: U.S.; Japan]

McCloskey, Donald N. International Differences in Productivity? Coal and Steel in America and Britain before World War I. In *McCloskey, D. N.*, 1981, *1973*, pp. 73–93. [G: U.K.; U.S.]

Nijhawan, B. R. Choice and Adaptation of Alternative Technology for the Iron and Steel Industry. In *U.N. Industrial Development Organization*, 1981, pp. 28–32.

Ono, Akira. Borrowed Technology in the Iron and Steel Industry: A Comparison between Brazil, India and Japan. *Hitotsubashi J. Econ.*, February 1981, *21*(2), pp. 1–18. [G: India; Brazil; Japan]

Petzina, Dietmar. The Origin of the European Coal and Steel Community: Economic Forces and Political Interests. *Z. ges. Staatswiss.*, September 1981, *137*(3), pp. 450–68. [G: W. Europe]

Piette, Michael J. and Desvousges, William H. Behavior of the Firm: The U.S. Petroleum Pipeline Industry under Regulatory Constraint. *Growth Change*, April 1981, *12*(2), pp. 17–22. [G: U.S.]

Plessz, N. Policy Responses in the Old Industrial Countries: Western Europe. In *Saunders, C. T., ed. (II)*, 1981, pp. 217–39. [G: W. Europe; Selected LDCs]

Porter, Michael G. U.S. Political Pressures against Adjustment to Greater Imports: Comment. In *Hong, W. and Krause, L. B., eds.*, 1981, pp. 553–58. [G: U.S.]

Raddock, Richard D. Cyclical and Secular Developments in the U.S. Steel Industry. *Fed. Res. Bull.*, February 1981, *67*(2), pp. 117–26. [G: U.S.]

Roumeliotis, Panayotis. Underinvoicing Aluminium from Greece. In *Murray, R., ed.*, 1981, pp. 86–88. [G: Greece]

Savey, Suzane. Pechiney Ugine Kuhlmann: A Frence Multinational Corporation. In *Hamilton, F. E. I. and Linge, G. J. R., eds.*, 1981, pp. 305–27. [G: France]

Sengupta, Jati K. and Sfeir, Raymond I. Short-Term Industry Output Behaviour: An Econometric Analysis. *Appl. Econ.*, March 1981, *13*(1), pp. 1–18. [G: U.S.]

Sengupta, Ram Prasad. Measurement of Steel Capacity: Bhilai Steel Plant—A Case Study. In *Bagchi, A. K. and Banerjee, N., eds.*, 1981, pp. 173–214. [G: India]

Signora, André. Les Leçons D'Une Expérience D'Application De Modèles Mondiaux au Niveau Sectoriel. (With English summary.) In *Courbis, R., ed.*, 1981, pp. 163–70.

6313 Machinery (tools, electrical equipment, computers, and appliances)

Anusz, Jan. Technology Transfer by Means of Industrial Cooperation: A Theoretical Appraisal: Comment. In *Marer, P. and Tabaczynski, E., eds.*, 1981, pp. 224–26. [G: Poland; U.S.]

Artle, Roland A. Competitive Behavior: Comments. In *[Grether, E. T.]*, 1981, pp. 128–30.

Avinger, Robert L., Jr. Product Durability and Market Structure: Some Evidence. *J. Ind. Econ.*, June 1981, *29*(4), pp. 357–74. [G: U.S.]

Blattner, Niklaus. Labour Displacement by Technological Change? A Preliminary Survey of the Case of Microelectronics. *Rivista Int. Sci. Econ. Com.*, May 1981, *28*(5), pp. 422–48.

Brada, Josef C. Technology Transfer by Means of Industrial Cooperation: A Theoretical Appraisal:

Reply. In *Marer, P. and Tabaczynski, E., eds.*, 1981, pp. 226–27.   [G: Poland; U.S.]

Brada, Josef C. Technology Transfer by Means of Industrial Cooperation: A Theoretical Appraisal. In *Marer, P. and Tabaczynski, E., eds.*, 1981, pp. 207–24.   [G: Poland; U.S.]

Brada, Josef C., et al. International Harvester–BUMAR Cooperation. In *Marer, P. and Tabaczynski, E., eds.*, 1981, pp. 41–83.   [G: Poland; U.S.]

Cooper, Charles. Aspects of Transfer Pricing in Machinery Markets. In *Murray, R., ed.*, 1981, pp. 133–44.

Curran, James and Stanworth, John. Size of Workplace and Attitudes to Industrial Relations in the Printing and Electronics Industries. *Brit. J. Ind. Relat.*, March 1981, *19*(1), pp. 14–25. [G: U.K.]

Daly, Anne. Government Support for Innovation in the British Machine Tool Industry: A Case Study. In *Carter, C., ed.*, 1981, pp. 52–67.   [G: U.K.]

Das, Subir Kumar. Economies of Scale and Implications for Policy: A Study of the Electrical Ceiling Fan Industry. In *Bagchi, A. K. and Banerjee, N., eds.*, 1981, pp. 259–68.   [G: India]

Dosi, Giovanni. Institutions and Markets in High Technology: Government Support for Micro-electronics in Europe. In *Carter, C., ed.*, 1981, pp. 182–202.   [G: EEC]

Duke, John and Brand, Horst. Cyclical Behavior of Productivity in the Machine Tool Industry. *Mon. Lab. Rev.*, November 1981, *104*(11), pp. 27–34.   [G: U.S.]

Garland, John. The International Harvester–BUMAR Cooperation Experience: Practical Problems and their Solutions: Comment. In *Marer, P. and Tabaczynski, E., eds.*, 1981, pp. 171–74.   [G: Poland; U.S.]

Goetz, Charles J. and Schwartz, Warren F. Industry Structure Investigation: Xerox's Multiple Patents and Competition. In *Clarkson, K. W. and Muris, T. J., eds.*, 1981, pp. 121–40.   [G: U.S.]

Gorbunov, E. The Construction Complex as a Part of the Investment Potential. *Prob. Econ.*, August 1981, *24*(4), pp. 57–75.   [G: U.S.S.R.]

Harmer, D. Richard. The Work Ethic is Alive, Well, and Living in Cleveland: The Lincoln Electric Company. In *Hoffman, W. M. and Wyly, T. J., eds.*, 1981, pp. 283–336.   [G: U.S.]

Hirschey, Mark and Pappas, James L. Market Power and Manufacturer Leasing. *J. Ind. Econ.*, September 1981, *30*(1), pp. 39–47.   [G: U.S.]

Institute of Technological Research, Bogotá. Capacity of the Engineering Industry in Colombia. In *Bhalla, A. S., ed.*, 1981, *1975*, pp. 289–301.   [G: Colombia]

Karpeles, Jean-Claude. L'Approche du Commerce Extérieur par L'Entreprise. (With English summary.) In *Courbis, R., ed.*, 1981, pp. 87–91.   [G: France]

Kirk, Robert and Simmons, Colin. Engineering and the First World War: A Case Study of the Lancashire Cotton Spinning Machine Industry. *World Devel.*, August 1981, *9*(8), pp. 773–91.   [G: U.K.]

Kjeldsen-Kragh, S. The Specialization Pattern in the Danish Machinery Sector. In *Freeman, C., et al.,* 1981, pp. 27–46.   [G: Denmark]

Kohlemy, Gunther. Improving the International Division of Labour: Comment. In *Saunders, C. T., ed. (I)*, 1981, pp. 333–36.   [G: E. Germany]

Lall, Sanjaya and Kumar, Rajiv. Firm-Level Export Performance in an Inward-Looking Economy: The Indian Engineering Industry. *World Devel.*, May 1981, *9*(5), pp. 453–63.   [G: India]

Leggett, Robert E. Measuring Inflation in the Soviet Machinebuilding Sector, 1960–1973. *J. Compar. Econ.*, June 1981, *5*(2), pp. 169–84.   [G: U.S.S.R.]

Massey, Doreen. The UK Electrical Engineering and Electronics Industries: The Implications of the Crisis for the Restructuring of Capital and Locational Change. In *Dear, M. and Scott, A. J., eds.*, 1981, pp. 199–230.   [G: U.K.]

National Industrial Development Corporation Ltd. The Role of the Engineering Industry. In *U.N. Industrial Development Organization*, 1981, pp. 48–55.   [G: India]

Otto, Phyllis Flohr. Transformer Industry Productivity Slows. *Mon. Lab. Rev.*, November 1981, *104*(11), pp. 35–39.   [G: U.S.]

Patil, S. M. Appropriate Technology for the Capital Goods Industry (Machine Tools) in Developing Countries. In *U.N. Industrial Development Organization*, 1981, pp. 43–47.

Preston, Lee E. Predatory Marketing. In *[Grether, E. T.]*, 1981, pp. 81–112.   [G: U.S.]

Rapelius, Eckhard and Weber, Adolf. The World Agricultural Input Industries as Factors of Rural Change. In *Johnson, G. and Maunder, A., eds.*, 1981, pp. 570–83.   [G: Selected Countries]

Richardson, Sue. Skilled Metal Tradesmen: Shortage or Surplus? *Australian Bull. Lab.*, September 1981, *7*(4), pp. 195–204.   [G: Australia]

Sengupta, Jati K. and Sfeir, Raymond I. Short-Term Industry Output Behaviour: An Econometric Analysis. *Appl. Econ.*, March 1981, *13*(1), pp. 1–18.   [G: U.S.]

Stoneman, Patrick. L'impact d'une nouvelle technologie sur l'emploi. (The Impact of New Technology of Employment Levels. With English summary.) *Rev. Econ. Ind.*, 3rd Trimestre 1981, (17), pp. 76–91.

Szumski, Jerzy. The International Harvester–BUMAR Cooperation Experience: Practical Problems and their Solutions. In *Marer, P. and Tabaczynski, E., eds.*, 1981, pp. 158–71. [G: Poland; U.S.]

Szumski, Jerzy. The International Harvester–BUMAR Cooperation Experience: Practical Problems and Their Solutions: Reply. In *Marer, P. and Tabaczynski, E., eds.*, 1981, pp. 174.   [G: Poland; U.S.]

Treml, Vladimir G. The Inferior Quality of Soviet Machinery as Reflected in Export Prices. *J. Compar. Econ.*, June 1981, *5*(2), pp. 200–221.   [G: U.S.S.R.]

Türel, Oktar. 1970'li Yillarda Mühendislik Sanayilerindeki Kamu Yatirimlari: Gözlem ve Değerlendirmeler. (Public Investments in Engineering Industries in the '70's: Some Observations and Comments. With English summary.) *METU*, Special Issue, 1981, pp. 575–612.   [G: Turkey]

Walker, Jill. Markets, Industrial Processes and Class Struggle: The Evolution of the Labor Process in the U.K. Engineering Industry. *Rev. Radical Polit. Econ.*, Winter 1981, *12*(4), pp. 46–59.
[G: U.K.]

Willott, W. B. The NEB Involvement in Electronics and Information Technology. In *Carter, C., ed.*, 1981, pp. 202–12. [G: U.K.]

York, James D. and Persigehl, Elmer S. Productivity Trends in the Ball and Roller Bearing Industry. *Mon. Lab. Rev.*, January 1981, *104*(1), pp. 40–43. [G: U.S.]

6314 Transportation and Communication Equipment

Arnould, Richard J. and Grabowski, Henry. Auto Safety Regulation: An Analysis of Market Failure. *Bell J. Econ. (See Rand J. Econ. after 4/85),* Spring 1981, *12*(1), pp. 27–48. [G: U.S.]

Atkinson, Thomas R. The Role of Productivity in International Trade. In *Hogan, J. D. and Craig, A. M., eds., Vol. 1,* 1981, pp. 647–56.
[G: Selected OECD]

Beggs, S.; Cardell, S. and Hausman, Jerry A. Assessing the Potential Demand for Electric Cars. *J. Econometrics*, September 1981, *17*(1), pp. 1–19. [G: U.S.]

Blaich, Fritz. Japan's Automobile Marketing: Its Introduction, Consolidation, Development and Characteristics: Comment. In *Okochi, A. and Shimokawa, K., eds.,* 1981, pp. 188–90.
[G: Japan]

Blaich, Fritz. The Development of the Distribution Sector in the German Car Industry. In *Okochi, A. and Shimokawa, K., eds.,* 1981, pp. 93–117.
[G: Germany]

Blomquist, Glenn C. and Peltzman, Sam. Passive Restraints: An Economist's View. In *Crandall, R. W. and Lave, L. B., eds.,* 1981, pp. 37–52.
[G: U.S.]

Bloomfield, Gerald T. The Changing Spatial Organization of Multinational Corporations in the World Automotive Industry. In *Hamilton, F. E. I. and Linge, G. J. R., eds.,* 1981, pp. 357–94.
[G: Global]

Boncher, William. A Comparative Engineering-Economic Analysis of the Evolution of the Soviet Mainline Freight Locomotive. *J. Compar. Econ.,* June 1981, *5*(2), pp. 149–68. [G: U.S.; U.S.S.R.]

Bresnahan, Timothy F. Departures from Marginal-Cost Pricing in the American Automobile Industry: Estimates for 1977–1978. *J. Econometrics,* November 1981, *17*(2), pp. 201–27. [G: U.S.]

Carmichael, Jeffrey. The Effects of Mission-Oriented Public R&D Spending on Private Industry. *J. Finance*, June 1981, *36*(3), pp. 617–27.
[G: U.S.]

Church, Roy. French Automobile Marketing, 1890–1979: Comment. In *Okochi, A. and Shimokawa, K., eds.,* 1981, pp. 155–60. [G: France]

Church, Roy. The Marketing of Automobiles in Britain and the United States before 1939. In *Okochi, A. and Shimokawa, K., eds.,* 1981, pp. 59–87.
[G: U.K.; U.S.]

Cohen, Robert B. Brave New World of the Global Car. *Challenge*, May/June 1981, *24*(2), pp. 28–35.

Crafton, Steven M. and Hoffer, George E. Estimating a Transaction Price for New Automobiles. *J. Bus.*, October 1981, *54*(4), pp. 611–21.
[G: U.S.]

Crafton, Steven M.; Hoffer, George E. and Reilly, Robert J. Testing the Impact of Recalls on the Demand for Automobiles. *Econ. Inquiry*, October 1981, *19*(4), pp. 694–703. [G: U.S.]

Daito, Eisuke. Marketing History in the Automobile Industry: The United States and Japan: Comment. In *Okochi, A. and Shimokawa, K., eds.,* 1981, pp. 33–35. [G: U.S.; Japan]

De Alessi, Louis. Regulating Postpurchase Relations: Mobile Homes. In *Clarkson, K. W. and Muris, T. J., eds.,* 1981, pp. 204–21. [G: U.S.]

Doyle, James J. and Navratil, Frank J. The Effects of Expectations on Industrial R & D Activity: Evidence Based on the Efficient Market Hypothesis. *Nebr. J. Econ. Bus.*, Autumn 1981, *20*(4), pp. 17–32. [G: U.S.]

Ehrnrooth, Robert G. Rederierna och konjunkturutvecklingen. (The Shipping Trade and Economic Prospects. With English summary.) *Ekon. Samfundets Tidskr.*, 1981, *34*(1), pp. 29–31.
[G: Finland]

Ephlin, Donald F. Quality of Work Life in the Auto Industry. In *Hoffman, W. M. and Wyly, T. J., eds.,* 1981, pp. 227–33. [G: U.S.]

Fieleke, Norman S. Challenge and Response in the Automobile Industry. *New Eng. Econ. Rev.*, July/August 1981, pp. 37–48. [G: U.S.]

Foreman-Peck, James S. The Effect of Market Failure on the British Motor Industry before 1939. *Exploration Econ. Hist.*, July 1981, *18*(3), pp. 257–89. [G: U.K.]

Fox, Douglas R. Motor Vehicles, Model Year 1981. *Surv. Curr. Bus.*, October 1981, *61*(10), pp. 22–25. [G: U.S.]

Fridenson, Patrick. French Automobile Marketing, 1890–1979. In *Okochi, A. and Shimokawa, K., eds.,* 1981, pp. 127–54. [G: France]

Fridenson, Patrick. The Marketing of Automobiles in Britain and the United States before 1939: Comment. In *Okochi, A. and Shimokawa, K., eds.,* 1981, pp. 88–90. [G: U.K.; U.S.]

Garrity, Monique P. The Assembly Industries in Haiti: Causes and Effects, 1967–1973. *Rev. Black Polit. Econ.*, Winter 1981, *11*(2), pp. 203–15.
[G: Haiti]

Hara, Terushi. French Automobile Marketing, 1890–1979: Comment. In *Okochi, A. and Shimokawa, K., eds.,* 1981, pp. 160–62. [G: France]

Hartley, Keith and Watt, Peter A. Profits, Regulation and the UK Aerospace Industry. *J. Ind. Econ.*, June 1981, *29*(4), pp. 413–28. [G: U.K.]

Hawkesworth, Richard I. The Rise of Spain's Automobile Industry. *Nat. Westminster Bank Quart. Rev.*, February 1981, pp. 37–48. [G: Spain]

Huelke, Donald F. and O'Day, James. Passive Restraints: A Scientist's View. In *Crandall, R. W. and Lave, L. B., eds.,* 1981, pp. 21–35.
[G: U.S.]

Husbands, Harry. The Impact of Harmonisation on the British Motor Industry. In *Twitchett, C. C.,* *ed.*, 1981, pp. 78–82. [G: U.K.]

Irvine, F. Owen, Jr. A Study of Automobile Inventory Investment. *Econ. Inquiry*, July 1981, *19*(3), pp. 353–79. [G: U.S.]

Jenner, Stephen R. Inflation, Exchange Rates, and the Location of Automobile Manufacturing. *Bus. Econ.*, January 1981, *16*(1), pp. 26–29. [G: EEC; U.S.; Japan]

Kortus, Bronislaw and Kaczorowski, Wojciech. Polish Industry Forges External Links. In *Hamilton, F. E. I. and Linge, G. J. R., eds.*, 1981, pp. 119–53. [G: Poland; CMEA]

Krumme, Günter. Making it Abroad: The Evolution of Volkswagen's North American Production Plans. In *Hamilton, F. E. I. and Linge, G. J. R., eds.*, 1981, pp. 329–56. [G: U.S.; W. Germany]

Lall, Sanjaya and Kumar, Rajiv. Firm-Level Export Performance in an Inward-Looking Economy: The Indian Engineering Industry. *World Devel.*, May 1981, *9*(5), pp. 453–63. [G: India]

Livesay, Harold C. Marketing History in the Automobile Industry: The United States and Japan: Comment. In *Okochi, A. and Shimokawa, K., eds.*, 1981, pp. 31–33. [G: U.S.; Japan]

Livesay, Harold C. Nineteenth Century Precursors to Automobile Marketing in the United States. In *Okochi, A. and Shimokawa, K., eds.*, 1981, pp. 39–52. [G: U.S.]

Luttrell, Clifton B. The Voluntary Automobile Import Agreement with Japan—More Protectionism. *Fed. Res. Bank St. Louis Rev.*, November 1981, *63*(9), pp. 25–30. [G: U.S.; Japan]

McCrohan, Kevin F. and Finkelman, Jay M. Social Character and the New Automobile Industry. *Calif. Manage. Rev.*, Fall 1981, *24*(1), pp. 58–68. [G: U.S.]

Morris, David and Jepson, David. Coventry and the Motor Vehicle Industry. *Nat. Westminster Bank Quart. Rev.*, May 1981, pp. 51–62. [G: U.K.]

Nash, Carl E. Passive Restraints: A Regulator's View. In *Crandall, R. W. and Lave, L. B., eds.*, 1981, pp. 53–67. [G: U.S.]

National Industrial Development Corporation Ltd. The Role of the Engineering Industry. In *U.N. Industrial Development Organization*, 1981, pp. 48–55. [G: India]

Okochi, Akio. Automobiles and International Markets: Comment. In *Okochi, A. and Shimokawa, K., eds.*, 1981, pp. 212–13.

Pearson, Charles and Takacs, Wendy E. Should the U.S. Restrict Auto Imports? *Challenge*, May/June 1981, *24*(2), pp. 45–52. [G: U.S.]

Petersen, Donald E. Toward a New U.S. Industrial Policy? International Trade: Comment. In *Wachter, M. L. and Wachter, S. M., eds.*, 1981, pp. 417–19. [G: U.S.]

Shepherd, Geoffrey. Industrial Strategies in Textiles and Clothing and Motor Cars. In *Saunders, C. T., ed. (II)*, 1981, pp. 132–56. [G: LDCs; OECD]

Shimokawa, Koichi. Marketing History in the Automobile Industry: The United States and Japan. In *Okochi, A. and Shimokawa, K., eds.*, 1981, pp. 3–30. [G: U.S.; Japan]

Shimokawa, Koichi. The Development of the Distribution Sector in the German Car Industry: Comment. In *Okochi, A. and Shimokawa, K., eds.*, 1981, pp. 118–21. [G: Germany]

Stillwell, J. W. Productivity and the Commercial Aircraft Industry. In *Hogan, J. D. and Craig, A. M., eds., Vol. 2*, 1981, pp. 1121–24. [G: U.S.]

Toba, Kin'ichiro. Automobiles and International Markets: Comment. In *Okochi, A. and Shimokawa, K., eds.*, 1981, pp. 210–12.

Toba, Kin'ichiro. Nineteenth Century Precursors to Automobile Marketing in the United States: Comment. In *Okochi, A. and Shimokawa, K., eds.*, 1981, pp. 53–55. [G: U.S.]

Udagawa, Masaru. Japan's Automobile Marketing: Its Introduction, Consolidation, Development and Characteristics. In *Okochi, A. and Shimokawa, K., eds.*, 1981, pp. 163–87. [G: Japan]

Walker, Charls E. and Bloomfield, Mark A. The Political Response to Three Potential Major Bankruptcies: Lockheed, New York City, and Chrysler. In *Wachter, M. L. and Wachter, S. M., eds.*, 1981, pp. 423–52. [G: U.S.]

Watanabe, Hisashi. The Development of the Distribution Sector in the German Car Industry: Comment. In *Okochi, A. and Shimokawa, K., eds.*, 1981, pp. 121–25. [G: Germany]

Whitman, Marina v. N. Automobiles: Turning Around on a Dime? *Challenge*, May/June 1981, *24*(2), pp. 36–44. [G: U.S.]

Wilkins, Mira. Automobiles and International Markets. In *Okochi, A. and Shimokawa, K., eds.*, 1981, pp. 193–209.

Wilkins, Mira. The Internationalization of Japanese Manufacturing Firms: Comment. In *Okochi, A. and Shimokawa, K., eds.*, 1981, pp. 230–32. [G: Japan]

Yamada, Makiko. Nineteenth Century Precursors to Automobile Marketing in the United States: Comment. In *Okochi, A. and Shimokawa, K., eds.*, 1981, pp. 55–57. [G: U.S.]

Yamazaki, Kiyoshi. The Internationalization of Japanese Manufacturing Firms. In *Okochi, A. and Shimokawa, K., eds.*, 1981, pp. 215–29. [G: Japan]

Yuzawa, Takeshi. The Marketing of Automobiles in Britain and the United States before 1939: Comment. In *Okochi, A. and Shimokawa, K., eds.*, 1981, pp. 90–92. [G: U.K.; U.S.]

6315 Chemicals, Drugs, Plastics, Ceramics, Glass, Cement, and Rubber

Al-Zamil, Abdulaziz. The Petrochemical Industry in the Kingdom of Saudi Arabia. *J. Energy Devel.*, Spring 1981, *6*(2), pp. 205–12. [G: Saudi Arabia]

Anusz, Jan. Technology Transfer by Means of Industrial Cooperation: A Theoretical Appraisal: Comment. In *Marer, P. and Tabaczynski, E., eds.*, 1981, pp. 224–26. [G: Poland; U.S.]

Belkin, M. I., et al. Modeling the Impact of the Economic Mechanism on the Indicators of Enterprise Activity. *Matekon*, Winter 1981–82, *18*(2), pp. 32–52. [G: U.S.S.R.]

Brada, Josef C. Technology Transfer by Means of Industrial Cooperation: A Theoretical Appraisal: Reply. In *Marer, P. and Tabaczynski, E., eds.*, 1981, pp. 226–27. [G: Poland; U.S.]

Brada, Josef C. Technology Transfer by Means of Industrial Cooperation: A Theoretical Appraisal. In *Marer, P. and Tabaczynski, E., eds.*, 1981, pp. 207–24. [G: Poland; U.S.]

Bruse, Helmut and Fuhrmann, Gregor H. Capital Stocks of Firms—Calculation on a Microeconomic Basis. *Z. Nationalökon.*, 1981, *41*(3–4), pp. 361–83. [G: W. Germany]

Cantley, Mark and Sargeant, Ken. Biotechnology: The Challenge to Europe. *Rev. Econ. Ind.*, 4th Trimester 1981, (18), pp. 323–34.
[G: W. Europe]

Chee, Peng Lim. Manufacture of Leather Shoes and Bricks in Malaysia. In *Bhalla, A. S., ed.*, 1981, pp. 247–88. [G: Malaysia]

Clarkson, Kenneth W. and MacLeod, William C. Reducing the Drug Lag: Entrepreneurship in Pharmaceutical Clinical Testing. In *Helms, R. B., ed.*, 1981, pp. 84–113. [G: U.S.]

Crout, J. Richard. Reducing the Drug Lag: Entrepreneurship in Pharmaceutical Clinical Testing: Comment. In *Helms, R. B., ed.*, 1981, pp. 117–19.

Doyle, James J. and Navratil, Frank J. The Effects of Expectations on Industrial R & D Activity: Evidence Based on the Efficient Market Hypothesis. *Nebr. J. Econ. Bus.*, Autumn 1981, *20*(4), pp. 17–32. [G: U.S.]

Evans, Peter. Collectivized Capitalism: Integrated Petrochemical Complexes and Capital Accumulation in Brazil. In *Bruneau, T. C. and Faucher, P., eds.*, 1981, pp. 85–125. [G: Brazil]

Fertilizer India Ltd. The Fertilizer Industry in India. In *U.N. Industrial Development Organization*, 1981, pp. 77–78. [G: India]

Geweke, John F. and Weisbrod, Burton A. Some Economic Consequences of Technological Advance in Medical Care: The Case of a New Drug. In *Helms, R. B., ed.*, 1981, pp. 235–71.
[G: U.S.]

Ghatak, Subrata. The Impact of the Fertilizer Technology Transfer on the Environment of Developing Countries. In *Chatterji, M., ed.*, 1981, pp. 71–87. [G: LDCs]

Giral B., J. Appropriate Technology for the Chemical Industry. In *U.N. Industrial Development Organization*, 1981, pp. 56–73. [G: Mexico]

Gorecki, Paul K. and Henderson, Ida. Compulsory Patent Licensing of Drugs in Canada: A Comment on the Debate. *Can. Public Policy*, Autumn 1981, *7*(4), pp. 559–68. [G: Canada]

Grabowski, Henry G. and Vernon, John. The Determinants of Research and Development Expenditures in the Pharmaceutical Industry. In *Helms, R. B., ed.*, 1981, pp. 3–20. [G: U.S.]

von Grebmer, K. International Pharmaceutical Supply Prices: Definitions–Problems–Policy Implications. *Managerial Dec. Econ.*, June 1981, *2*(2), pp. 74–81. [G: OECD]

Hambleton, H. G. L'essor de l'industrie pétrochimique en Arabie Saoudite. (The Growth of Petrochemical Industry in Saudi Arabia. With English

summary.) *L'Actual. Econ.*, October–December 1981, *57*(4), pp. 589–98. [G: Saudi Arabia]

Hansen, Ronald W. Pharmaceutical Innovation, Product Imitation, and Public Policy: Comment. In *Helms, R. B., ed.*, 1981, pp. 293–99.

Helms, Robert B. Drugs and Health: Preface. In *Helms, R. B., ed.*, 1981, pp. xix–xxvi. [G: U.S.]

Hornbrook, Mark C. Price and Quality Competition in Drug Markets: Evidence from the United States and the Netherlands: Comment. In *Helms, R. B., ed.*, 1981, pp. 152–66. [G: U.S.; Netherlands]

Kadhim, Mihssen. A Note on "Downstream" Industrialization and the Security of Oil Supplies. *J. Energy Devel.*, Autumn 1981, *7*(1), pp. 99–109.
[G: OAPEC; U.S.]

Kerton, Robert R. and Chowdhury, Tapan K. The Impact of the PARCOST Program on Prescription Drug Prices in Ontario. *Can. Public Policy*, Spring 1981, *7*(2), pp. 306–17. [G: Canada]

Kung, Wan Chong and Carlos, Carolina R. Effective Protection of the Chemical Industry. *Phillipine Rev. Econ. Bus.*, March & June 1981, *18*(1 & 2), pp. 55–74. [G: Philippines]

Lean, David F. The Market for Research and Development: Physician Demand and Drug Company Supply: Comment. In *Helms, R. B., ed.*, 1981, pp. 227–31. [G: U.S.]

Leffler, Keith B. Persuasion or Information? The Economics of Prescription Drug Advertising. *J. Law Econ.*, April 1981, *24*(1), pp. 45–74.
[G: U.S.]

Lim, Manuel T. An Evaluation of the Performance of the Steel and Cement Industries in the 1960s and 1970s. *Philippine Econ. J.*, 1981, *20*(3&4), pp. 295–310. [G: Philippines]

Massam, A. D. W. Product Liability: The Specialty Problem of Medicines. *Managerial Dec. Econ.*, September 1981, *2*(3), pp. 160–68. [G: EEC]

McBride, Mark E. The Nature and Source of Economies of Scale in Cement Production. *Southern Econ. J.*, July 1981, *48*(1), pp. 105–15.
[G: U.S.]

Mehta, Balraj. Foreign Technology—Adaptation and Development: The Experience in the Fertilizer Industry. In *Bagchi, A. K. and Banerjee, N., eds.*, 1981, pp. 389–91. [G: India]

Moir, Brian. Phosphatic Fertilisers: Issues in the 1980s. *Quart. Rev. Rural Econ.*, May 1981, *3*(2), pp. 149–56. [G: Australia]

Parkinson, Jack. Donor Co-ordination and Collective Leverage: The Role of the World Bank. In *Faaland, J., ed.*, 1981, pp. 147–64.
[G: Bangladesh]

Pyndt, P. E. The Causes and Development of Health Care System Costs: The Danish Experience. *Managerial Dec. Econ.*, September 1981, *2*(3), pp. 179–85. [G: Denmark; Selected Countries]

Rapelius, Eckhard and Weber, Adolf. The World Agricultural Input Industries as Factors of Rural Change. In *Johnson, G. and Maunder, A., eds.*, 1981, pp. 570–83. [G: Selected Countries]

Reekie, W. Duncan. Innovation and Pricing in the Dutch Drug Industry. *Managerial Dec. Econ.*, March 1981, *2*(1), pp. 49–56. [G: Netherlands]

Reekie, W. Duncan. Price and Quality Competition

in Drug Markets: Evidence from the United States and the Netherlands. In *Helms, R. B., ed.*, 1981, pp. 123–39.   [G: U.S.; Netherlands]

Roze, Janis A. The Competitiveness of Natural Resources with Synthetic Substances. In *Lozoya, J. and Green, R., eds.*, 1981, pp. 54–65.
[G: Global]

Scherer, F. M. The Determinants of Research and Development Expenditures in the Pharmaceutical Industry: Comment. In *Helms, R. B., ed.*, 1981, pp. 46–48.   [G: U.S.]

Schifrin, Leonard. The Effect of Patent Expiration on the Market Position of Drugs: Comment. In *Helms, R. B., ed.*, 1981, pp. 166–70.   [G: U.S.]

Sharma, U. C. Import Substitution in Chemicals: Case Studies of Soda Ash, Caustic Soda and Bleaching Powder. *Indian Econ. J.*, October–December 1981, 29(2), pp. 78–88.   [G: India]

Statman, Meir. The Effect of Patent Expiration on the Market Position of Drugs. *Managerial Dec. Econ.*, June 1981, 2(2), pp. 61–66.   [G: U.S.]

Statman, Meir. The Effect of Patent Expiration on the Market Position of Drugs. In *Helms, R. B., ed.*, 1981, pp. 140–51.   [G: U.S.]

Stewart, Frances. Manufacture of Cement Blocks in Kenya. In *Bhalla, A. S., ed.*, 1981, 1975, pp. 209–46.   [G: Kenya]

Telser, Lester G. The Market for Research and Development: Physician Demand and Drug Company Supply. In *Helms, R. B., ed.*, 1981, pp. 183–221.   [G: U.S.]

Todd, Douglas. Synthetic Rubber in the German War Economy: A Case of Economic Dependence. *J. Europ. Econ. Hist.*, Spring 1981, 10(1), pp. 153–65.   [G: Germany]

Virts, John R. and Weston, J. Fred. Expectations and the Allocation of Research and Development Resources. In *Helms, R. B., ed.*, 1981, pp. 21–45.   [G: U.S.]

Wiederhorn, Robert. Productivity and the Petrochemical Industry. In *Hogan, J. D. and Craig, A. M., eds., Vol. 2*, 1981, pp. 1153–57.
[G: U.S.]

Wigny, Pierre-Henry. Le commerce extérieur des produits chimiques entre la Belgique et la Tchécoslovaquie. (External Trade of Chemical Products between Belgium and Czechoslovakia. With English summary.) *Ann. Sci. Écon. Appl.*, 1981, 37(3), pp. 167–75.
[G: Belgium; Czechoslovakia]

Woltman, Harry R. Expectations and the Allocation of Research and Development Resources: Comment. In *Helms, R. B., ed.*, 1981, pp. 49–52.
[G: U.S.]

Wu, S. Y. Pharmaceutical Innovation, Product Imitation, and Public Policy. In *Helms, R. B., ed.*, 1981, pp. 272–89.

Zanon, Lucio. Price Discrimination and Hoffmann-La Roche. *J. World Trade Law*, July–August 1981, 15(4), pp. 305–22.   [G: EEC]

6316 Textiles, Leather, and Clothing

Alessandroni, A.; Leporelli, C. and Rey, G. M. Economic Industry Model Building: The Synthetic Fibres Case. In *Janssen, J. M. L.; Pau, L. F.*

and Straszak, A. J., eds., 1981, pp. 169–75.
[G: Italy]

Anderson, Jock R., et al. A Dynamic Simulation Model of the World Jute Economy. *Europ. Econ. Rev.*, June/July 1981, 16(2/3), pp. 303–31.

Arpan, Jeffrey S.; de la Torre, José and Toyne, Brian. International Developments and the U.S. Apparel Industry. *J. Int. Bus. Stud.*, Winter 1981, 12(3), pp. 49–64.   [G: U.S.]

Barkin, Solomon. Management and Ownership in the New England Cotton Textile Industry. *J. Econ. Issues*, June 1981, 15(2), pp. 463–75.
[G: U.S.]

Blewett, Mary H. Discussion [Mechanization and Work in the American Shoe Industry: Lynn, Massachusetts, 1852–1883]. *J. Econ. Hist.*, March 1981, 41(1), pp. 64.   [G: U.S.]

Bond, Eric W. Tax Holidays and Industry Behavior. *Rev. Econ. Statist.*, February 1981, 63(1), pp. 88–95.   [G: Puerto Rico]

Carlson, Leonard A. Labor Supply, the Acquisition of Skills, and the Location of Southern Textile Mills, 1880–1900. *J. Econ. Hist.*, March 1981, 41(1), pp. 65–71.   [G: U.S.]

Chee, Peng Lim. Manufacture of Leather Shoes and Bricks in Malaysia. In *Bhalla, A. S., ed.*, 1981, pp. 247–88.   [G: Malaysia]

Chen, Edward K. Y. Adjusting to the ADCs in the Face of Structurally Depressed Industries: Japan: Comment. In *Hong, W. and Krause, L. B., eds.*, 1981, pp. 468–71.   [G: Japan; E. Asia]

Chin, Rockwood Q. P. Trade Policies toward the PRC's Textile Exports. *Rivista Int. Sci. Econ. Com.*, September 1981, 28(9), pp. 864–88.
[G: China]

Chowdhury, Nuimuddin. An Enquiry into the Nature and Determinants of Polarisation in Personal Wealth: A Case Study Using Handloom Industry Data. *Bangladesh Devel. Stud.*, Autumn 1981, 9(4), pp. 51–76.   [G: Bangladesh]

Chowdhury, Nuimuddin. On the Structure of Input and Product Markets in Cotton Weaving Industry of Bangladesh: A Case Study Using Firm Level Data. *Bangladesh Devel. Stud.*, Summer 1981, 9(2), pp. 43–74.   [G: Bangladesh]

Chowdhury, Nuimuddin. Relative Efficiency of Alternative Techniques in the Cotton Weaving Industry of Bangladesh: A Case Study. *Bangladesh Devel. Stud.*, Monsoon 1981, 9(3), pp. 45–66.
[G: Bangladesh]

Ciriacono, Salvatore. Silk Manufacturing in France and Italy in the XVIIth Century: Two Models Compared. *J. Europ. Econ. Hist.*, Spring 1981, 10(1), pp. 167–99.   [G: France; Italy]

Conlon, R. M. The Structure of the Australian Tariff and the Protection of the Textiles and Clothing Industries. *Australian Econ. Pap.*, June 1981, 20(36), pp. 179–82.   [G: Australia]

Cooper, Charles and Kaplinsky, R. Second-hand Equipment in Developing Countries: Jute Processing Machinery in Kenya. In *Bhalla, A. S., ed.*, 1981, 1975, pp. 129–57.   [G: Kenya; U.K.]

Corn, Morton. Cotton Dust: A Regulator's View. In *Crandall, R. W. and Lave, L. B., eds.*, 1981, pp. 109–14.   [G: U.S.]

Dattatreyulu, M. India: The Jute Industry's Need

for Viability. *J. World Trade Law*, July–August 1981, *15*(4), pp. 351–58. [G: India]

Fecteau, George and Mara, John. It's a Walkover for Shoe Imports. In *Baldwin, R. E. and Richardson, J. D.*, eds., 1981, 1979, pp. 87–93. [G: U.S.]

Guesnier, Bernard. Analyse et prévision de la démographie des entreprises à l'aide d'un processus markovien: Application à l'industrie de la chaussure. (Demographic Analysis and Forecast of Firms with a Stochastic Model: Markov Chain. Application to Boot and Shoe Industry. With English summary.) *Rev. Econ. Ind.*, 1st Trimester 1981, (15), pp. 19–43. [G: France]

Hamilton, Carl. A New Approach to Estimation of the Effects of Non-Tariff Barriers to Trade: An Application to the Swedish Textile and Clothing Industry. *Weltwirtsch. Arch.*, 1981, *117*(2), pp. 298–325. [G: Sweden]

Helleiner, Gerald K. Adjusting to the ADCs in the Face of Structurally Depressed Industries: Japan: Comment. In *Hong, W. and Krause, L. B.*, eds., 1981, pp. 471–74. [G: Japan; E. Asia]

Heywood, Colin Michael. The Launching of an "Infant Industry"? The Cotton Industry of Troyes under Protectionism, 1793–1860. *J. Europ. Econ. Hist.*, Winter 1981, *10*(3), pp. 553–81. [G: France]

Jung, Yojin. Comparative Advantage and Productive Efficiency of Korea in the Textiles, Clothing and Footwear Industries. *J. Econ. Devel.*, December 1981, *6*(2), pp. 133–64. [G: S. Korea]

Kierzkowski, Henryk and Sampson, Gary P. The Multifibre Arrangement: The Approach and Setting to the Forthcoming Negotiations. *Aussenwirtschaft*, March 1981, *36*(1), pp. 41–56. [G: OECD]

Kiesewetter, Hubert. Regional Disparities in Wages: The Cotton Industry in Nineteenth-century Germany—Some Methodological Considerations. In *Bairoch, P. and Lévy-Leboyer, M.*, eds., 1981, pp. 248–58. [G: Germany]

Kisch, Herbert. The Textile Industries in Silesia and the Rhineland: A Comparative Study in Industrialization. In *Kriedte, P.; Medick, H. and Schlumbohm, J.*, 1981, pp. 178–200. [G: Germany; Poland]

Lazonick, William H. Competition, Specialization, and Industrial Decline. *J. Econ. Hist.*, March 1981, *41*(1), pp. 31–38. [G: U.K.]

Lazonick, William H. Factor Costs and the Diffusion of Ring Spinning in Britain Prior to World War I. *Quart. J. Econ.*, February 1981, *96*(1), pp. 89–109. [G: U.K.]

Likierman, Andrew. Pricing Policy in the Texturising Industry, 1958–71. *J. Ind. Econ.*, September 1981, *30*(1), pp. 25–38. [G: U.K.]

Merchant, James A. Cotton Dust: A Scientist's View. In *Crandall, R. W. and Lave, L. B.*, eds., 1981, pp. 71–91. [G: U.S.]

Morawetz, David. Clothes for Export: Not Made in Colombia. *Finance Develop.*, March 1981, *18*(1), pp. 29–32. [G: Colombia]

Morrall, John F., III. Cotton Dust: An Economist's View. In *Crandall, R. W. and Lave, L. B.*, eds., 1981, pp. 93–108. [G: U.S.]

Mulligan, William H., Jr. Mechanization and Work in the American Shoe Industry: Lynn, Massachusetts, 1852–1883. *J. Econ. Hist.*, March 1981, *41*(1), pp. 59–63. [G: U.S.]

Mutti, John H. and Bale, Malcolm D. Output and Employment Changes in a "Trade Sensitive" Sector: Adjustment in the U.S. Footwear Industry. *Weltwirtsch. Arch.*, 1981, *117*(2), pp. 352–67. [G: U.S.]

Oates, Mary J. Discussion [Labor Supply, the Acquisition of Skills, and the Location of Southern Textile Mills, 1880–1900]. *J. Econ. Hist.*, March 1981, *41*(1), pp. 72–73. [G: U.S.]

Okumura, Ariyoshi. Policy Responses in the Old Industrial Countries: Japan and East Asia. In *Saunders, C. T.*, ed. *(II)*, 1981, pp. 261–83. [G: Japan; E. Asia]

Pack, Howard. The Choice of Technique and Employment in the Textile Industry. In *Bhalla, A. S.*, ed., 1981, pp. 159–79. [G: U.K.]

Pelzman, Joseph and Martin, Randolph C. Direct Employment Effects of Increased Imports: A Case Study of the Textile Industry. *Southern Econ. J.*, October 1981, *48*(2), pp. 412–26. [G: U.S.]

Pitt, Mark M. and Lee, Lung-Fei. The Measurement and Sources of Technical Inefficiency in the Indonesian Weaving Industry. *J. Devel. Econ.*, August 1981, *9*(1), pp. 43–64. [G: Indonesia]

Plessz, N. Policy Responses in the Old Industrial Countries: Western Europe. In *Saunders, C. T.*, ed. *(II)*, 1981, pp. 217–39. [G: W. Europe; Selected LDCs]

Routamaa, Vesa. Toward a Systematic Understanding of the Relationship between Organizational Structure and Performance. *Liiketaloudellinen Aikak.*, 1981, *30*(4), pp. 422–34. [G: Finland]

Royon, Michel. Accord Multifibres et nouvelles fonctions du protectionnisme. (Multifibre Agreement and New Functions of Protectionism. With English summary.) *Rev. Econ. Ind.*, 1st Trimester 1981, (15), pp. 60–77. [G: France]

Schilirò, Daniele. An Econometric Study of Lags in the Cost–Price Relation: The Textiles Case in the U.K. *Econ. Notes*, 1981, *10*(2), pp. 81–91. [G: U.K.]

Shepherd, Geoffrey. Industrial Strategies in Textiles and Clothing and Motor Cars. In *Saunders, C. T.*, ed. *(II)*, 1981, pp. 132–56. [G: LDCs; OECD]

Steed, Guy P. F. International Location and Comparative Advantage: The Clothing Industries and Developing Countries. In *Hamilton, F. E. I. and Linge, G. J. R.*, eds., 1981, pp. 265–303. [G: LDCs]

de la Torre, Jose. Public Intervention Strategies in the European Clothing Industries. *J. World Trade Law*, March–April 1981, *15*(2), pp. 124–48. [G: EEC]

Trivedi, P. K. Dynamics of Output and Inventory in the Japanese Wool Textile Industry: A Further Analysis of the Carland-Pagan Model [A Short-Run Econometric Model of the Japanese Wool Textile Industry]. *Econ. Rec.*, March 1981, *57*(156), pp. 91–94. [G: Japan]

Tucker, Barbara M. The Merchant, the Manufacturer, and the Factory Manager: The Case of Samuel Slater. *Bus. Hist. Rev.*, Autumn 1981, 55(3), pp. 297–313. [G: U.S.]

Watkins, G. Campbell and Berndt, Ernst R. Energy Output Coefficients: Complex Realities behind Simple Ratios. In *Tempest, P., ed.*, 1981, pp. 93–98. [G: Canada]

Wurth, P. The Arrangement Regarding International Trade in Textiles. *Aussenwirtschaft*, March 1981, 36(1), pp. 57–69.

Yamazawa, Ippei. Adjusting to the ADCs in the Face of Structurally Depressed Industries: Japan. In *Hong, W. and Krause, L. B., eds.*, 1981, pp. 435–67. [G: Japan; E. Asia]

Yoffie, David B. Orderly Marketing Agreements as an Industrial Policy: The Case of the Footwear Industry. *Public Policy*, Winter 1981, 29(1), pp. 93–119. [G: U.S.]

6317 Forest Products, Lumber, Paper, Printing and Publishing

Adams, Darius and Haynes, Richard. U.S.–Canadian Lumber Trade: The Effect of Restrictions. In *Sedjo, R. A., ed.*, 1981, pp. 101–32. [G: U.S.; Canada]

Allen, Steven G. Compensation, Safety, and Absenteeism: Evidence from the Paper Industry. *Ind. Lab. Relat. Rev.*, January 1981, 34(2), pp. 207–18. [G: U.S.]

Baily, Mary Ann. Brick Manufacturing in Colombia: A Case Study of Alternative Technologies. *World Devel.*, February 1981, 9(2), pp. 201–13. [G: Colombia]

Barsky, Carl B. Occupational Wage Variation in Wood Household Furniture Plants. *Mon. Lab. Rev.*, July 1981, 104(7), pp. 37–39. [G: U.S.]

Cartwright, Philip. Welfare Economics and the Log Export Policy Issue: Discussion. In *Sedjo, R. A., ed.*, 1981, pp. 209–15. [G: U.S.]

Curran, James and Stanworth, John. Size of Workplace and Attitudes to Industrial Relations in the Printing and Electronics Industries. *Brit. J. Ind. Relat.*, March 1981, 19(1), pp. 14–25. [G: U.K.]

Darr, David R. U.S. Exports and Imports of Some Major Forest Products—The Next Fifty Years. In *Sedjo, R. A., ed.*, 1981, pp. 54–83. [G: U.S.]

Deadman, Derek and Turner, R. K. Modeling the Supply of Wastepaper: Comment [Price Expectations and the Supply of Wastepaper]. *J. Environ. Econ. Manage.*, March 1981, 8(1), pp. 100–103. [G: U.S.; U.K.]

Dowdle, Barney. Log Export Restrictions: Causes and Consequences. In *Sedjo, R. A., ed.*, 1981, pp. 248–58. [G: U.S.]

Evenson, Robert E. Tropical Forests in Economic Development. In *Mergen, F., ed.*, 1981, pp. 126–42. [G: LDCs]

Haynes, Richard; Darr, David R. and Adams, Darius. U.S.–Japanese Log Trade—Effect of a Ban. In *Sedjo, R. A., ed.*, 1981, pp. 216–32. [G: U.S.; Japan]

House, William J. Redistribution, Consumer Demand and Employment in Kenyan Furniture-Making. *J. Devel. Stud.*, July 1981, 17(4), pp. 336–56. [G: Kenya]

Lippke, Bruce. U.S.–Japanese Log Trade—Effect of

a Ban: Discussion. In *Sedjo, R. A., ed.*, 1981, pp. 233–47. [G: U.S.; Japan]

McKillop, William. Log Export Restrictions: Causes and Consequences: Discussion. In *Sedjo, R. A., ed.*, 1981, pp. 259–63. [G: U.S.]

Mikander, Lars. Träförädlingsindustrin och framtiden. (The Wood-processing Industry and the Future. With English summary.) *Ekon. Samfundets Tidskr.*, 1981, 34(4), pp. 271–88. [G: Finland]

Radcliffe, Samuel J. U.S. Forest Products Trade and the Multilateral Trade Negotiations. In *Sedjo, R. A., ed.*, 1981, pp. 136–68. [G: U.S.]

Sengupta, Jati K. and Sfeir, Raymond I. Short-Term Industry Output Behaviour: An Econometric Analysis. *Appl. Econ.*, March 1981, 13(1), pp. 1–18. [G: U.S.]

Smith, M. G. Forests and Forestry Programs in Tropical Countries: Some Observations and Comments. In *Mergen, F., ed.*, 1981, pp. 144–53.

Suokko, Seppo. Träförädlingsindustrins framtid. (The Future of the Wood-processing Industry. With English summary.) *Ekon. Samfundets Tidskr.*, 1981, 34(4), pp. 289–94. [G: Finland]

Vargha, Louis. U.S. Forest Products Trade and the Multilateral Trade Negotiations: Discussion. In *Sedjo, R. A., ed.*, 1981, pp. 175–84. [G: U.S.]

Ward, John. U.S. Exports and Imports of Some Major Forest Products—The Next Fifty Years: Discussion. In *Sedjo, R. A., ed.*, 1981, pp. 93–98. [G: U.S.]

Wisdom, Harold. U.S. Forest Products Trade and the Multilateral Trade Negotiations: Discussion. In *Sedjo, R. A., ed.*, 1981, pp. 169–74. [G: U.S.]

Wiseman, A. Clark. U.S.–Canadian Lumber Trade: The Effect of Restrictions: Discussion. In *Sedjo, R. A., ed.*, 1981, pp. 133–35. [G: U.S.; Canada]

Wiseman, A. Clark and Sedjo, Roger. Welfare Economics and the Log Export Policy Issue. In *Sedjo, R. A., ed.*, 1981, pp. 187–208. [G: U.S.]

Zivnuska, John. U.S. Exports and Imports of Some Major Forest Products—The Next Fifty Years: Discussion. In *Sedjo, R. A., ed.*, 1981, pp. 84–92. [G: U.S.]

6318 Food Processing, Tobacco, and Beverages

Aduddell, Robert M. and Cain, Louis P. Public Policy toward "The Greatest Trust in the World." *Bus. Hist. Rev.*, Summer 1981, 55(2), pp. 217–42. [G: U.S.]

Aduddell, Robert M. and Cain, Louis P. The Consent Decree in the Meatpacking Industry, 1920–1956. *Bus. Hist. Rev.*, Autumn 1981, 55(3), pp. 359–78. [G: U.S.]

Baron, C. G. Sugar Processing Techniques in India. In *Bhalla, A. S., ed.*, 1981, 1975, pp. 181–208. [G: India]

Bethell, Tom. Breakfastgate: The FTC *vs.* the Cereal Companies. *Policy Rev.*, Spring 1981, (16), pp. 13–32. [G: U.S.]

Bjørndal, Trond. A Multi-objective Simulation Model for the Norwegian Fish-Meal Industry. In *Haley, K. B., ed.*, 1981, pp. 295–308. [G: Norway]

Block, Michael Kent and Nold, Frederick Carl. The

Deterrent Effect of Antitrust Enforcement. *J. Polit. Econ.*, June 1981, *89*(3), pp. 429–45.
[G: U.S.]

Boyle, G. A Time Series Forecast of Pigs Received at Irish Bacon Factories. *Irish J. Agr. Econ. Rural Soc.*, 1981, *8*(2), pp. 179–89. [G: Ireland]

Broder, Josef M. and Booth, John T. Energy Efficiency in Food Processing in the Southern Region. *Southern J. Agr. Econ.*, December 1981, *13*(2), pp. 53–59. [G: U.S.]

Bullock, J. Bruce. Estimates of Consumer Loss Due to Monopoly in the U.S. Food-Manufacturing Industries: Comment. *Amer. J. Agr. Econ.*, May 1981, *63*(2), pp. 290–92. [G: U.S.]

Bullock, J. Bruce and Ward, Clement E. Economic Welfare and Food Safety Regulation: The Case of Mechanically Deboned Meat: Comment. *Amer. J. Agr. Econ.*, November 1981, *63*(4), pp. 738–41. [G: U.S.]

Campbell, John. American Leaf Exports on Decline: Imperial Tobacco Limited Closes Its Last American Primary-Processing Plant. In *Finger, W. R., ed.*, 1981, pp. 145–49. [G: U.S.; U.K.]

Clairmonte, Frederick F. World Tobacco: A Portrait of Corporate Power. In *Finger, W. R., ed.*, 1981, pp. 203–19. [G: U.S.; U.K.]

Connor, John M. Foreign Food Firms: Their Participation in and Competitive Impact on the US Food and Tobacco Manufacturing Sector. In *Johnson, G. and Maunder, A., eds.*, 1981, pp. 552–67.
[G: U.S.]

Davis, J. The Structure and Performance of the Northern Ireland Beef Sector. *Irish J. Agr. Econ. Rural Soc.*, 1981, *8*(2), pp. 153–65. [G: U.K.]

Greer, Douglas F. The Causes of Concentration in the U.S. Brewing Industry. *Quart. Rev. Econ. Bus.*, Winter 1981, *21*(4), pp. 87–106. [G: U.S.]

Grobstein, Clifford. Saccharin: A Scientist's View. In *Crandall, R. W. and Lave, L. B., eds.*, 1981, pp. 117–29. [G: U.S.]

Hall, Anthony. Innovation and Social Structure: The Sugar Industry of Northeast Brazil. In *Mitchell, S., ed.*, 1981, pp. 143–56. [G: Brazil]

Hansen, Terje. Analysing the Demand for Fishmeal by a Linear Programming Model. In *Haley, K. B., ed.*, 1981, pp. 247–60. [G: Global]

Helmberger, Peter G.; Campbell, Gerald R. and Dobson, William D. Organization and Performance of Agricultural Markets. In *Martin, L. R., ed.*, 1981 cat kp22a, pp. 503–653. [G: U.S.]

Higgins, J. Factor Demand and Factor Substitution in Selected Sectors of the Irish Food Industry. *Econ. Soc. Rev.*, July 1981, *12*(4), pp. 253–66.
[G: Ireland]

Huebner, Albert. Making the Third-World Marlboro Country. In *Finger, W. R., ed.*, 1981, *1979*, pp. 151–56. [G: LDCs]

Jaeger, Elizabeth. To Save or Savor: The Rate of Return to Storing Wine: Comment. *J. Polit. Econ.*, June 1981, *89*(3), pp. 584–92. [G: U.S.]

Jakeš, Miloš. Efforts at Self-Sufficiency in Foodstuffs—The Joint Task of Farmers, Workers of the Food Industry and the Supplier Branches. *Czech. Econ. Digest.*, December 1981, (8), pp. 3–18. [G: Czechoslovakia]

Keane, Michael. An Analysis of Seasonal Pricing

Schemes for Manufacturing Milk. *Irish J. Agr. Econ. Rural Soc.*, 1981, *8*(2), pp. 213–33.
[G: Ireland]

Kitchin, Paul Duncan. Some Socio-Economic Determinants of Alcohol Consumption: A Research Note. *Int. J. Soc. Econ.*, 1981, *8*(5), pp. 31–35.
[G: U.K.]

Lall, Sanjaya. Food Transnationals and Developing Countries. In *Lall, S.*, 1981, *1979*, pp. 68–120.
[G: LDCs; U.K.; U.S.]

Mathiesen, Lars. A Multi-Criteria Model for Assessing Industrial Structure in the Norwegian Fish-Meal Industry. In *Haley, K. B., ed.*, 1981, pp. 281–94. [G: Norway]

Maxwell, John. Valuable Vehicles for Long-term Gains. In *Finger, W. R., ed.*, 1981, pp. 229–31.
[G: U.S.]

McNiel, Douglas W. Economic Welfare and Food Safety Regulation: The Case of Mechanically Deboned Meat: Reply. *Amer. J. Agr. Econ.*, November 1981, *63*(4), pp. 742–45. [G: U.S.]

Merrill, Richard A. Saccharin: A Regulator's View. In *Crandall, R. W. and Lave, L. B., eds.*, 1981, pp. 153–70. [G: U.S.]

Mikalsen, Bjørnar and Vassdal, Terje. A Short Term Production Planning Model in Fish Processing. In *Haley, K. B., ed.*, 1981, pp. 223–32.

Muir, Donald. EEC Production Subsidies for Canned Pears: Implications for World Trade. *Quart. Rev. Rural Econ.*, August 1981, *3*(3), pp. 254–60. [G: EEC; Australia]

O'Mara, L. P. Some Economic Implications of Minimum Pricing: The Case of Wine Grapes in Australia. *Rev. Marketing Agr. Econ.*, August 1981, *49*(2), pp. 107–23. [G: Australia]

O'Rourke, A. Desmond and Greig, W. Smith. Estimates of Consumer Loss Due to Monopoly in the U.S. Food-Manufacturing Industries: Comment. *Amer. J. Agr. Econ.*, May 1981, *63*(2), pp. 285–89. [G: U.S.]

Ornstein, Stanley I. Antitrust Policy and Market Forces as Determinants of Industry Structure: Case Histories in Beer and Distilled Spirits. *Antitrust Bull.*, Summer 1981, *26*(2), pp. 281–313.
[G: U.S.]

Overton, James. Diversification and International Expansion: The Future of the American Tobacco Manufacturing Industry with Corporate Profiles of the "Big Six." In *Finger, W. R., ed.*, 1981, pp. 159–95. [G: U.S.]

Pagoulatos, Emilio and Sorensen, Robert. A Simultaneous Equation Analysis of Advertising, Concentration and Profitability. *Southern Econ. J.*, January 1981, *47*(3), pp. 728–41. [G: U.S.]

Parker, Russell C. and Connor, John M. Estimates of Consumer Loss Due to Monopoly in the U.S. Food-Manufacturing Industries: Reply. *Amer. J. Agr. Econ.*, May 1981, *63*(2), pp. 293–97.
[G: U.S.]

Parris, Carl D. Joint Venture II: The National Flour Mill of Trinidad–Tobago, 1972–1979. *Soc. Econ. Stud.*, March 1981, *30*(1), pp. 127–45.
[G: Trinidad and Tobago]

Porter, Richard C. Further Analysis of the Impact of Mandatory Bottle Deposit Legislation: Comment. *Soc. Sci. Quart.*, June 1981, *62*(2),

pp. 367–73. [G: U.S.]

Santoni, Gary J. and Van Cott, T. Norman. Bottle Deposit Legislation: A Reply [The Impact of Mandatory Bottle Deposit Legislation]. *Soc. Sci. Quart.*, June 1981, *62*(2), pp. 374–76. [G: U.S.]

Schluter, Gerald and Beeson, Patty. Components of Labor Productivity Growth in the Food System, 1958–67. *Rev. Econ. Statist.*, August 1981, *63*(3), pp. 378–84. [G: U.S.]

Schneider, Lynne; Klein, Benjamin and Murphy, Kevin M. Governmental Regulation of Cigarette Health Information. *J. Law Econ.*, December 1981, *24*(3), pp. 575–612. [G: U.S.]

Siceloff, Bruce. Tobacco for Protein: A Revolutionary Upheaval? In *Finger, W. R., ed.*, 1981, pp. 109–15. [G: U.S.]

Sticht, J. Paul. R. J. Reynolds Industries: A Hundred Years of Progress in North Carolina. In *Finger, W. R., ed.*, 1981, pp. 197–98. [G: U.S.]

Sumner, Daniel A. Measurement of Monopoly Behavior: An Application to the Cigarette Industry. *J. Polit. Econ.*, October 1981, *89*(5), pp. 1010–19. [G: U.S.]

Tornquist, Elizabeth. Labor Displacement in Tobacco Manufacturing: Some Policy Considerations. In *Finger, W. R., ed.*, 1981, pp. 221–28. [G: U.S.]

Weissman, George. A Future of Great Promise—for Tobacco and for Philip Morris. In *Finger, W. R., ed.*, 1981, pp. 199–202. [G: U.S.]

Williamson, Oliver E. Saccharin: An Economist's View. In *Crandall, R. W. and Lave, L. B., eds.*, 1981, pp. 131–51. [G: U.S.]

6319 Other Industries

Cooper, Charles, et al. Choice of Techniques for Can Making in Kenya, Tanzania and Thailand. In *Bhalla, A. S., ed.*, 1981, *1975*, pp. 91–127. [G: Kenya; Tanzania; Thailand]

Pew, Robert C. Capital and Productivity: A Firm View. In *Hogan, J. D. and Craig, A. M., eds.*, Vol. 1, 1981, pp. 165–68. [G: U.S.]

Russett, Bruce. United States Solar Energy Policy for Less-Developed Countries. *J. Energy Devel.*, Autumn 1981, *7*(1), pp. 39–59. [G: LDCs; U.S.]

632 Industry Studies: Extractive Industries

6320 General

Barber, William J. Energy Policy in Perspective: Studied Inaction in the Kennedy Years. In *Goodwin, C. D., ed.*, 1981, pp. 287–335. [G: U.S.]

Barber, William J. The Eisenhower Energy Policy: Reluctant Intervention. In *Goodwin, C. D., ed.*, 1981, pp. 205–86. [G: U.S.]

Cochrane, James L. Carter Energy Policy and the Ninety-fifth Congress. In *Goodwin, C. D., ed.*, 1981, pp. 547–600. [G: U.S.]

Cochrane, James L. Energy Policy in the Johnson Administration: Logical Order versus Economic Pluralism. In *Goodwin, C. D., ed.*, 1981, pp. 337–93. [G: U.S.]

Cochrane, James L. and Griepentrog, Gary L. U.S. Energy: A Quantitative Review of the Past Three Decades. In *Goodwin, C. D., ed.*, 1981, pp. 685–705. [G: U.S.]

Conrad, Robert F. and Hool, Bryce. Resource Taxation with Heterogeneous Quality and Endogenous Reserves. *J. Public Econ.*, August 1981, *16*(1), pp. 17–33. [G: U.S.]

Hunter, J. S. H. and Wood, J. C. Australian Resource Development in the 1980s. *Nat. Westminster Bank Quart. Rev.*, November 1981, pp. 17–26. [G: Australia]

Schwartz, Samuel. Productivity in the Energy Producing Industries. In *Hogan, J. D. and Craig, A. M., eds.*, Vol. 1, 1981, pp. 191–97. [G: U.S.]

Vernon, Raymond. State-Owned Enterprises in Latin-American Exports. In *Baer, W. and Gillis, M., eds.*, 1981, pp. 98–114. [G: Latin America]

6322 Mining (metal, coal, and other nonmetallic minerals)

Ackerman, Bruce A. and Hassler, William T. Beyond the New Deal: Reply [Beyond the New Deal: Coal and the Clean Air Act]. *Yale Law J.*, May 1981, *90*(6), pp. 1412–34.

Adams, F. Gerard; Behrman, Jere R. and Lasaga, M. Commodity Exports and NIEO Proposals for Buffer Stocks and Compensatory Finance: Implications for Latin America. *Quart. Rev. Econ. Bus.*, Summer 1981, *21*(2), pp. 48–76. [G: Latin America]

Alacchi, Georges and Todradzé, Constantin. Safety in Mines and the Role of Training. *Int. Lab. Rev.*, September–October 1981, *120*(5), pp. 615–29. [G: EEC]

Anderson, Kym and Smith, Ben. Changing Economic Relations between the Asian ADCs and Resource-Exporting Advanced Countries of the Pacific Basin. In *Hong, W. and Krause, L. B., eds.*, 1981, pp. 293–338. [G: Hong Kong; Singapore; S. Korea; Taiwan; Selected MDCs]

Angelier, Jean-Pierre. Le charbon, industrie nouvelle. (Coal, a New Industry. With English summary.) *Rev. Econ. Ind.*, 2nd Trimester 1981, (16), pp. 1–15.

Attanasi, E. D. Exploration Decisions and Firms in the Mineral Industries. *Energy Econ.*, April 1981, *3*(2), pp. 105–12. [G: U.S.]

Attanasi, E. D. and Green, E. K. Economics and Coal Resource Appraisal: Strippable Coal in the Illinois Basin. *Southern Econ. J.*, January 1981, *47*(3), pp. 742–52. [G: U.S.]

Baker, Joe G. Sources of Deep Coal Mine Productivity Change, 1962–1975. *Energy J.*, April 1981, *2*(2), pp. 95–106. [G: U.S.]

Barsky, Carl B. and Personick, Martin E. Measuring Wage Dispersion: Pay Ranges Reflect Industry Traits. *Mon. Lab. Rev.*, April 1981, *104*(4), pp. 35–41. [G: U.S.]

Bartels, Martin. Mining Ventures in Developing Countries: Localization of Labor. In *Schanze, E., et al.*, 1981, pp. 198–211. [G: Selected LDCs]

Bird, Thomas C. Coal Leases Held Real Property. *Natural Res. J.*, April 1981, *21*(2), pp. 415–17. [G: U.S.]

Brennan, Joseph. Productivity and the Coal Industry. In *Hogan, J. D. and Craig, A. M., eds., Vol. 2*, 1981, pp. 1125–32. [G: U.S.]

Cairns, Robert D. A Reconsideration of Ontario Nickel Policy. *Can. Public Policy*, Autumn 1981, *7*(4), pp. 526–33. [G: Canada]

Cairns, Robert D. An Application of Depletion Theory to a Base Metal: Canadian Nickel. *Can. J. Econ.*, November 1981, *14*(4), pp. 635–48. [G: Canada]

Davies, Christopher S. Policy Implications for the Banking of Lignite Leases, Bastrop County, Texas: 1954–1979. *Econ. Geogr.*, July 1981, *57*(3), pp. 238–56. [G: U.S.]

DeSouza, Glenn. Electric Utility Coal Demand: A Critical Review of Recent Forecasts. *Bus. Econ.*, May 1981, *16*(3), pp. 15–24. [G: U.S.]

Edgmon, Terry D. and Menzel, Donald C. The Regulation of Coal Surface Mining in a Federal System. *Natural Res. J.*, April 1981, *21*(2), pp. 245–65. [G: U.S.]

Frey, Norman E. and Labuszewski, John W. Newspaper Articles and Their Impact On Commodity Price Formation Case Study: Copper. *J. Futures Markets*, Spring 1981, *1*(1), pp. 89–91. [G: U.S.]

Fritzsche, Michael. Mining Ventures in Developing Countries: Fiscal Regime. In *Schanze, E., et al.*, 1981, pp. 108–44.

Georgianna, Thomas D. and Haynes, Kingsley E. Competition for Water Resources: Coal and Agriculture in the Yellowstone Basin. *Econ. Geogr.*, July 1981, *57*(3), pp. 225–37. [G: U.S.]

Goodwin, Craufurd D. Truman Administration Policies toward Particular Energy Sources. In *Goodwin, C. D., ed.*, 1981, pp. 63–203. [G: U.S.]

Howes, Candace and Markusen, Ann R. Poverty: A Regional Political Economy Perspective. In *Hawley, A. H. and Mazie, S. M., eds.*, 1981, pp. 437–63. [G: U.S.]

Huff, David L. and Moyer, Reed. Relevant Geographic Markets in Coal: Analysis and Delineation. In *[Grether, E. T.]*, 1981, pp. 239–59. [G: U.S.]

Kirchner, Christian. Mining Ventures in Developing Countries: Information Disclosure. In *Schanze, E., et al.*, 1981, pp. 68–107.

Kñakal, Jan. Transnationals and Mining Development in Bolivia, Chile and Peru. *Cepal Rev.*, August 1981, (14), pp. 63–83. [G: Bolivia; Chile; Peru]

Lamaswala, K. M. The Pricing of Unwrought Cooper in Relation to Transfer Pricing. In *Murray, R., ed.*, 1981, pp. 77–85. [G: Zambia]

Lee, Hoe Sung. Changing Economic Relations between the Asian ADCs and Resource-Exporting Advanced Countries of the Pacific Basin: Comment. In *Hong, W. and Krause, L. B., eds.*, 1981, pp. 339–40. [G: Hong Kong; Singapore; S. Korea; Taiwan; Selected MDCs]

Lord, Montague J. Comment on "Commodity Exports and NIEO Proposals for Buffer Stocks and Compensatory Finance." *Quart. Rev. Econ. Bus.*, Summer 1981, *21*(2), pp. 76–82. [G: Latin America]

Lutz, James M.; Miller, Philip L. and Reddy, Y. V. Optimized Steam Coal Transportation Pat-

terns for the United States. *J. Energy Devel.*, Spring 1981, *6*(2), pp. 297–314. [G: U.S.]

McCloskey, Donald N. International Differences in Productivity? Coal and Steel in America and Britain before World War I. In *McCloskey, D. N.*, 1981, *1973*, pp. 73–93. [G: U.K.; U.S.]

Moroney, John R. and Trapani, John M., III. Factor Demand and Substitution in Mineral-Intensive Industries. *Bell J. Econ. (See Rand J. Econ. after 4/85)*, Spring 1981, *12*(1), pp. 272–84. [G: U.S.]

Naples, Michele I. Industrial Conflict and Its Implications for Productivity Growth. *Amer. Econ. Rev.*, May 1981, *71*(2), pp. 36–41. [G: U.S.]

Petzina, Dietmar. The Origin of the European Coal and Steel Community: Economic Forces and Political Interests. *Z. ges. Staatswiss.*, September 1981, *137*(3), pp. 450–68. [G: W. Europe]

Ross, Bruce J. Changing Economic Relations between the Asian ADCs and Resource-Exporting Advanced Countries of the Pacific Basin: Comment. In *Hong, W. and Krause, L. B., eds.*, 1981, pp. 340–43. [G: Hong Kong; Singapore; S. Korea; Taiwan; Selected MDCs]

Schanze, Erich. Mining Ventures in Developing Countries: Forms of Agreement and the Joint Venture Practice. In *Schanze, E., et al.*, 1981, pp. 20–67. [G: Selected LDCs]

von Schlabrendorff, Fabian. Mining Ventures in Developing Countries: Environmental Provisions. In *Schanze, E., et al.*, 1981, pp. 212–35.

Simmons, Colin. Imperial Dictate: The Effect of the Two World Wars on the Indian Coal Industry. *World Devel.*, August 1981, *9*(8), pp. 749–71. [G: India]

Smith, Lowell and Randle, Russell V. Comment on Beyond the New Deal [Beyond the New Deal: Coal and the Clean Air Act]. *Yale Law J.*, May 1981, *90*(6), pp. 1398–1411. [G: U.S.]

Stockmayer, Albrecht. Financing Mining Projects in Developing Countries. In *Schanze, E., et al.*, 1981, pp. 171–97.

Valle, P. Della. Productivity and Employment in the Copper and Aluminium Industries. In *Bhalla, A. S., ed.*, 1981, *1975*, pp. 323–55. [G: Selected LDCs; U.S.]

Vernon, Raymond. State-Owned Enterprises in Latin-American Exports. *Quart. Rev. Econ. Bus.*, Summer 1981, *21*(2), pp. 98–114. [G: Latin America]

Wool, Harold. Coal Industry Resurgence Attracts Variety of New Workers. *Mon. Lab. Rev.*, January 1981, *104*(1), pp. 3–8. [G: U.S.]

Yang, Chin Wei and Labys, Walter C. Stability of Appalachian Coal Shipments under Policy Variation. *Energy J.*, July 1981, *2*(3), pp. 111–28. [G: U.S.]

6323 Oil, Gas, and Other Fuels

Aivazian, Varouj A. and Callen, Jeffrey L. Capacity Expansion in the U.S. Natural-Gas Pipeline Industry. In *Cowing, T. G. and Stevenson, R. E., eds.*, 1981, pp. 145–59. [G: U.S.]

Allen, Bruce T. Structure and Stability in Gasoline Markets. *J. Econ. Issues*, March 1981, *15*(1), pp. 73–94. [G: U.S.]

Armentano, D. T. The Petroleum Industry: A Historical Study in Power. *Cato J.*, Spring 1981, *1*(1), pp. 53–85. [G: U.S.]

Bailey, Richard. North Sea Oil—The Norwegian Alternative. *Nat. Westminster Bank Quart. Rev.*, May 1981, pp. 11–19. [G: U.K.; Norway]

Balas, Egon. The Strategic Petroleum Reserve: How Large Should It Be? In *Bayraktar, B. A., et al., eds.*, 1981, pp. 335–86.

Barker, Terry. Depletion Policy and the De-Industrialization of the UK Economy. *Energy Econ.*, April 1981, *3*(2), pp. 71–82. [G: U.K.]

Bennett, Paul and Kuenstner, Deborah. Natural Gas Controls and Decontrol. *Fed. Res. Bank New York Quart. Rev.*, Winter 1981–82, *6*(4), pp. 50–60. [G: U.S.]

Berreby, Jean-Jacques. Opec: venti anni che hanno trasformato il mondo. (OPEC: 20 Years That Have Changed the World. With English summary.) *Mondo Aperto*, April 1981, *35*(2), pp. 89–97. [G: OPEC]

Bolch, Ben W. and Damon, William W. The Windfall Profit Tax and Vertical Integration in the Petroleum Industry. *Southern Econ. J.*, January 1981, *47*(3), pp. 788–91. [G: U.S.]

Braeutigam, Ronald R. The Deregulation of Natural Gas. In *Weiss, L. W. and Klass, M. W., eds.*, 1981, pp. 142–86. [G: U.S.]

Brodman, John and Moore, Jack. The Outlook for World Oil Supply and Demand through 1983. *J. Energy Devel.*, Autumn 1981, *7*(1), pp. 1–12. [G: OPEC]

Capra, James R. and Beek, David C. Combining Decontrol of Natural Gas with a New Tax on Producer Revenues. *Fed. Res. Bank New York Quart. Rev.*, Winter 1981–82, *6*(4), pp. 61–66. [G: U.S.]

Christman, John H. Comments [Petroleum and Mexican Economic Growth and Development in the 1980s] [The Political Economy of Mexican Oil, 1976–1979]. In *Ladman, J. R.; Baldwin, D. J. and Bergman, E., eds.*, 1981, pp. 123–28. [G: Mexico]

Colombatto, Enrico. Il negoziato petrolifero: una proposta di analisi. (Oil Pricing: A Proposal of Analysis. With English summary.) *Rivista Int. Sci. Econ. Com.*, December 1981, *28*(12), pp. 1189–1200.

Dahl, Carol A. Refinery Mix in the U.S., Canada and the E.E.C. *Europ. Econ. Rev.*, June/July 1981, *16*(2/3), pp. 235–46. [G: U.S.; Canada; EEC]

Dahl, Carol A. and Laumas, G. S. Stability of U.S. Petroleum Refinery Response to Relative Product Prices. *Energy Econ.*, January 1981, *3*(1), pp. 30–35. [G: U.S.]

Donkin, George L. Competition and the Rate-making Process: The Case of the Trans-Alaska Oil Pipeline. In *Sichel, W. and Gies, T. G., eds.*, 1981, pp. 87–101. [G: U.S.]

El Serafy, Salah. Absorptive Capacity, the Demand for Revenue, and the Supply of Petroleum. *J. Energy Devel.*, Autumn 1981, *7*(1), pp. 73–88. [G: OPEC]

Epple, Dennis. Petroleum Product Price Regulations: Output and Efficiency Effects: A Comment.

Carnegie-Rochester Conf. Ser. Public Policy, Spring 1981, *14*, pp. 147–51. [G: U.S.]

Fasci, Martha A. The Windfall Profits Tax: Panacea or Pandora's Box? *Manage. Account.*, October 1981, *63*(4), pp. 51–53. [G: U.S.]

Fieleke, Norman S. Rising Oil Prices and the Industrial Countries. *New Eng. Econ. Rev.*, January/February 1981, pp. 17–28. [G: U.S.]

Fried, Jerome F. Western Hemisphere Oil and Gas: No Relief for the United States in the 1980's? In *U.S. Congress, Joint Economic Committee (III)*, 1981, pp. 166–78. [G: Canada; Venezuela; Mexico]

Golovin, A. P.; Kitaigorodskii, V. I. and Fainshtein, I. Ia. Forecasting Gas Reserves and Optimizing Regional Production Levels within the Fuel and Energy Complex. *Matekon*, Fall 1981, *18*(1), pp. 43–59. [G: U.S.S.R.]

Goodwin, Craufurd D. Truman Administration Policies toward Particular Energy Sources. In *Goodwin, C. D., ed.*, 1981, pp. 63–203. [G: U.S.]

Greene, Richard. Employment Trends in Energy Extraction. *Mon. Lab. Rev.*, May 1981, *104*(5), pp. 3–8. [G: U.S.]

Harvey, Scott and Roush, Calvin T., Jr. Petroleum Product Price Regulations: Output and Efficiency Effects. *Carnegie-Rochester Conf. Ser. Public Policy*, Spring 1981, *14*, pp. 109–45. [G: U.S.]

Hawkins, Robert G. and Gladwin, Thomas N. Conflicts in the International Transfer of Technology: A U.S. Home Country View. In *Sagafi-nejad, T.; Moxon, R. W. and Perlmutter, H. V., eds.*, 1981, pp. 212–62. [G: U.S.]

Helliwell, John F. and McRae, Robert N. The National Energy Conflict. *Can. Public Policy*, Winter 1981, *7*(1), pp. 15–23. [G: Canada]

Hudson, Edward A. U.S. Energy Price Decontrol: Energy, Trade and Economic Effects. *Scand. J. Econ.*, 1981, *83*(2), pp. 180–200.

Jarjour, Gabi. Long-Term Gas Pricing Strategy. *J. Energy Devel.*, Autumn 1981, *7*(1), pp. 89–98. [G: Global]

Kaserman, David L. and Rice, Patricia L. A Note on Predatory Vertical Integration in the U.S. Petroleum Industry. *J. Econ. Bus.*, Spring/Summer 1981, *33*(3), pp. 262–66. [G: U.S.]

Kaufman, Alvin and Bodilly, Susan J. Supplemental Sources of Natural Gas: An Economic Comparison. *Energy J.*, October 1981, *2*(4), pp. 63–83. [G: U.S.]

Knelman, Fred H. The Geopolitics of Oil. In *Nemetz, P. N., ed.*, 1981, pp. 41–60. [G: Canada]

Leveson, Sidney M. Comments [Possible Dimensions of Mexican Petroleum] [PEMEX in a Dependent Society]. In *Ladman, J. R.; Baldwin, D. J. and Bergman, E., eds.*, 1981, pp. 117–21. [G: Mexico; U.S.]

Levin, Richard C. Vertical Integration and Profitability in the Oil Industry. *J. Econ. Behav. Organ.*, September 1981, *2*(3), pp. 215–35. [G: U.S.]

Levy, Walter J. Oil: An Agenda for the 1980s. *Foreign Aff.*, Summer 1981, *59*(5), pp. 1079–1101.

Leyva, Jesús Puente. Mexico–United States Relations: The Natural Gas Controversy. In *Purcell, S. K., ed.*, 1981, pp. 158–67. [G: Mexico; U.S.]

Lower, Milton D. Decontrol déjà vu. *J. Post*

Keynesian Econ., Summer 1981, 3(4), pp. 597–601. [G: U.S.]

Ma'Rafi, M. J. Technology for Oil and Gas Based Industries: The Case of Kuwait. In *U.N. Industrial Development Organization*, 1981, pp. 74–76. [G: Kuwait]

Maksimov, Iu. I. Modeling the Development of the Gas Industry. *Matekon*, Fall 1981, 18(1), pp. 35–42. [G: U.S.S.R.]

Mancke, Richard B. Competition and Monopoly in World Oil Markets: The Role of the International Oil Companies. *Cato J.*, Spring 1981, 1(1), pp. 107–27. [G: U.S.]

de Marchi, Neil. Energy Policy under Nixon: Mainly Putting Out Fires. In *Goodwin, C. D., ed.*, 1981, pp. 395–473. [G: U.S.]

de Marchi, Neil. The Ford Administration: Energy as a Political Good. In *Goodwin, C. D., ed.*, 1981, pp. 475–545. [G: U.S.]

Marfels, Christian. Market Concentration and Implicit Grants in the Energy Industry: Some Observations. *Z. Wirtschaft. Sozialwissen.*, 1981, 101(4), pp. 429–40. [G: U.S.]

McGregor, Stephen E. Government Policy and the Petroleum Industry. In *Hogan, J. D. and Craig, A. M., eds., Vol. 2*, 1981, pp. 1147–51. [G: U.S.]

McLachlan, Keith. The Oil Industry in the Middle East. In *[Fisher, W. B.]*, 1981, pp. 95–112. [G: Middle East]

Meisner, J. and Demirmen, F. The Creaming Method: A Bayesian Procedure to Forecast Future Oil and Gas Discoveries in Mature Exploration Provinces. *J. Roy. Statist. Soc.*, Part 1, 1981, 144, pp. 1–22. [G: U.K.]

Mennis, Bernard. Conflicts in the International Transfer of Technology: A U.S. Home Country View: Comment. In *Sagafi-nejad, T.; Moxon, R. W. and Perlmutter, H. V., eds.*, 1981, pp. 263–69. [G: U.S.]

Montgomery, W. David. Decontrol of Crude Oil Prices. In *Weiss, L. W. and Klass, M. W., eds.*, 1981, pp. 187–201. [G: U.S.]

Mueller, R. K.; Eggert, D. J. and Swanson, H. S. Petroleum Decline Analysis Using Time Series. *Energy Econ.*, October 1981, 3(4), pp. 256–67. [G: U.S.]

Navarro, Peter; Petersen, Bruce C. and Stauffer, Thomas R. A Critical Comparison of Utility-Type Ratemaking Methodologies in Oil Pipeline Regulation. *Bell J. Econ. (See Rand J. Econ. after 4/85)*, Autumn 1981, 12(2), pp. 392–412. [G: U.S.]

Newbery, David M. G. Oil Prices, Cartels, and the Problem of Dynamic Inconsistency. *Econ. J.*, September 1981, 91(363), pp. 617–46.

Noreng, Øystein. State-Owned Oil Companies: Western Europe. In *Vernon, R. and Aharoni, Y., eds.*, 1981, pp. 133–44. [G: U.K.; France; Italy; Norway]

Ortiz, René G. 1982 Realities of the Oil Market: Can OPEC Retain Its Ability to Fix Oil Prices? *J. Energy Devel.*, Autumn 1981, 7(1), pp. 13–15. [G: OPEC]

Pack, Stirling. Performance Component Evolution in the Multiplant Corporate Sector: The Integrated Oil Industry Example. In *Rees, J.; Hewings, G. J. D. and Stafford, H. A., eds.*, 1981, pp. 59–71.

Parra, Francisco Ramon. Development of Oil and Gas in the OIDCs. In *Foster, J., et al.*, 1981, pp. 161–73. [G: LDCs]

Piette, Michael J. and Desvousges, William H. Behavior of the Firm: The U.S. Petroleum Pipeline Industry under Regulatory Constraint. *Growth Change*, April 1981, 12(2), pp. 17–22. [G: U.S.]

Pindyck, Robert S. The Optimal Production of an Exhaustible Resource When Price is Exogenous and Stochastic. *Scand. J. Econ.*, 1981, 83(2), pp. 277–88.

Porter, Ed and Huskey, Lee. The Regional Economic Effect of Federal OCS Leasing: The Case of Alaska. *Land Econ.*, November 1981, 57(4), pp. 583–95. [G: U.S.]

Prasad, C. R. and Bhat, Kisan. Prospects for Ethanol as Automobile Fuel in India. In *Chatterji, M., ed.*, 1981, pp. 89–102. [G: India]

Prato, Anthony A. and Miller, Ronald R. Evaluating the Energy Production Potential of the United States Outer Continental Shelf. *Land Econ.*, February 1981, 57(1), pp. 77–90. [G: U.S.]

Rahou, Ghazi Ibrahim. Aspects of Organization and Efficiency of Oil Products Transport in Irak. *Econ. Computat. Cybern. Stud. Res.*, 1981, 15(2), pp. 85–88. [G: Iraq]

Randall, Laura R. The Political Economy of Mexican Oil, 1976–1979. In *Ladman, J. R.; Baldwin, D. J. and Bergman, E., eds.*, 1981, pp. 87–115. [G: Mexico]

Reza, Ali M. An Analysis of the Supply of Oil. *Energy J.*, April 1981, 2(2), pp. 77–94.

Rueter, Theodore and Enholm, Gregory. A Proposal for Gasoline Rationing. *J. Post Keynesian Econ.*, Winter 1980–81, 3(2), pp. 287–93. [G: U.S.]

Sepúlveda, Isidro. PEMEX in a Dependent Society. In *Ladman, J. R.; Baldwin, D. J. and Bergman, E., eds.*, 1981, pp. 45–68. [G: Mexico]

Sigmon, Brent, et al. An Evaluation of Natural Gas Consumption Data. *Rev. Public Data Use (See J. Econ. Soc. Meas. after 4/85)*, November 1981, 9(3), pp. 189–97. [G: U.S.]

Smith, Abbie J. and Dyckman, Thomas. The Impact of Accounting Regulation on the Stock Market: The Case of Oil and Gas Companies: A Comment. *Accounting Rev.*, October 1981, 56(4), pp. 959–66. [G: U.S.]

Smith, Rodney T. In Search of the "Just" U.S. Oil Policy: A Review of Arrow and Kalt and More. *J. Bus.*, January 1981, 54(1), pp. 87–116. [G: U.S.]

Steele, Henry and Daly, George. Vertical Divestiture of the US Oil Industry and US–OPEC Relations. *Energy Econ.*, January 1981, 3(1), pp. 43–56. [G: U.S.; OPEC]

Taher, Abdulhady Hassan. The Future Role of the National Oil Companies. In *OPEC, Public Information Dept.*, 1981, pp. 76–87. [G: OPEC]

Ulph, Alistair M. and Folie, G. Michael. An Economic Analysis of Oil Self-sufficiency in Australia. In *Nemetz, P. N., ed.*, 1981, pp. 1–23. [G: Australia]

Vastola, S. J., Jr. Productivity and the Petroleum

Industry. In *Hogan, J. D. and Craig, A. M., eds.,* Vol. 2, 1981, pp. 1133–46.   [G: U.S.]

Viezca, Juan Aizpuru. The Future Role of the National Oil Companies: Commentary. In *OPEC, Public Information Dept.,* 1981, pp. 88–91.
[G: OPEC]

Watkins, G. Campbell and Kirkby, R. Bidding for Petroleum Leases: Recent Canadian Experience. *Energy Econ.,* July 1981, *3*(3), pp. 182–86.
[G: Canada]

Weitzman, Martin L. Sequential R&D Strategy for Synfuels. *Bell J. Econ. (See Rand J. Econ. after 4/85),* Autumn 1981, *12*(2), pp. 574–90.
[G: U.S.]

633 Industry Studies: Distributive Trades

6330 General

Dannhaeuser, Norbert. Evolution and Devolution of Downward Channel Integration in the Philippines. *Econ. Develop. Cult. Change,* April 1981, *29*(3), pp. 577–95.   [G: Philippines]

Graglia, Lino A. The Supreme Court and the American Common Market [Regulation and the American Common Market]. In *Tarlock, A. D., ed.,* 1981, pp. 67–75.   [G: U.S.]

Ishikawa, Kenjiro. Development of Marketing in the Course of Industrialization in Korea: Comment. In *Okochi, A. and Shimokawa, K., eds.,* 1981, pp. 264.   [G: S. Korea]

Lim, Jong Won. Development of Marketing in the Course of Industrialization in Korea. In *Okochi, A. and Shimokawa, K., eds.,* 1981, pp. 235–60.   [G: S. Korea]

McClean, A. Wendell A. Pricing Policy in the Distributive Sector in Barbados. *Soc. Econ. Stud.,* September 1981, *30*(3), pp. 63–75.
[G: Barbados]

Mittendorf, H. J. Useful Strategies for Developing Countries Striving to Improve Food Marketing Systems. In *Johnson, G. and Maunder, A., eds.,* 1981, pp. 131–42.

Miyamoto, Matao. Development of Marketing in the Course of Industrialization in Korea: Comment. In *Okochi, A. and Shimokawa, K., eds.,* 1981, pp. 261–63.   [G: S. Korea]

Plott, Charles R. and Uhl, Jonathan T. Competitive Equilibrium with Middlemen: An Empirical Study. *Southern Econ. J.,* April 1981, *47*(4), pp. 1063–71.

Seger, Ronald. Productivity and Physical Distribution. In *Hogan, J. D. and Craig, A. M., eds.,* Vol. 2, 1981, pp. 1103–07.   [G: U.S.]

Tsurumi, Yoshi. The Sᴏɢᴏsʜᴏsʜᴀ. In *Richardson, B. M. and Ueda, T., eds.,* 1981, pp. 14–20.
[G: Japan]

6332 Wholesale Trade

Bishop, John. Employment in Construction and Distribution Industries: The Impact of the New Jobs Tax Credit. In *Rosen, S., ed.,* 1981, pp. 209–46.
[G: U.S.]

Constas, Kimon J. and Vichas, Robert P. Patterns and Performance of Multinational and Domestic

Food Wholesale Firms. *Managerial Dec. Econ.,* March 1981, *2*(1), pp. 25–31.   [G: Puerto Rico]

Irvine, F. Owen, Jr. Merchant Wholesaler Inventory Investment and the Cost of Capital. *Amer. Econ. Rev.,* May 1981, *71*(2), pp. 23–29.   [G: U.S.]

6333 Retail Trade

Ballard, Claude. Trends in Retail Development: The 1980s and Beyond. In *Sternlieb, G. and Hughes, J. W., eds.,* 1981, pp. 275–90.   [G: U.S.]

Beaumont, J. R.; Clarke, M. and Wilson, A. G. Changing Energy Parameters and the Evolution of Urban Spatial Structure. *Reg. Sci. Urban Econ.,* August 1981, *11*(3), pp. 287–315.

Berry, Brian J. L. Conceptual Lags in Retail Development Policy or Can the Carter White House Save the CBD? In *Sternlieb, G. and Hughes, J. W., eds.,* 1981, pp. 29–40.   [G: U.S.]

Blinder, Alan S. Retail Inventory Behavior and Business Fluctuations. *Brookings Pap. Econ. Act.,* 1981, (2), pp. 443–505.   [G: U.S.]

Breheny, Michael J.; Green, Jacqueline and Roberts, Anthony J. A Practical Approach to the Assessment of Hypermarket Impact. *Reg. Stud.,* 1981, *15*(6), pp. 459–74.   [G: U.K.]

Brous, Philip. The Chain Store Looks at the Future. In *Sternlieb, G. and Hughes, J. W., eds.,* 1981, pp. 245–50.   [G: U.S.]

Clarkson, Kenneth W.; Muris, Timothy J. and Martin, Donald L. Exclusionary Practices: Shopping Center Restrictive Covenants. In *Clarkson, K. W. and Muris, T. J., eds.,* 1981, pp. 141–60.
[G: U.S.]

Cleary, Martin. Shopping Center: A Lender's Perspective. In *Sternlieb, G. and Hughes, J. W., eds.,* 1981, pp. 297–301.   [G: U.S.]

Cowen, Stephen H. Overlooked Opportunities in Shopping Center Development. In *Sternlieb, G. and Hughes, J. W., eds.,* 1981, pp. 311–15.
[G: U.S.]

Crafton, Steven M. and Hoffer, George E. Estimating a Transaction Price for New Automobiles. *J. Bus.,* October 1981, *54*(4), pp. 611–21.
[G: U.S.]

Fix, Michael. Addressing the Issue of the Economic Impact of Regional Malls in Legal Proceedings. In *Sternlieb, G. and Hughes, J. W., eds.,* 1981, pp. 141–66.   [G: U.S.]

Fleisher, Belton M. Minimum Wage Regulation in Retail Trade. *Eastern Econ. J.,* April 1981, *7*(2), pp. 75–96.   [G: U.S.]

Geithman, Frederick E.; Marvel, Howard P. and Weiss, Leonard W. Concentration, Price and Critical Concentration Ratios. *Rev. Econ. Statist.,* August 1981, *63*(3), pp. 346–53.   [G: U.S.]

Gould, Jack. Shopping Centers: U.S.A.: Emerging Markets in the 1980s. In *Sternlieb, G. and Hughes, J. W., eds.,* 1981, pp. 49–53. [G: U.S.]

Green, Howard L. and Huntoon, David L. Regional Shopping Center Issues in the 1980s. In *Sternlieb, G. and Hughes, J. W., eds.,* 1981, pp. 55–61.   [G: U.S.]

Haar, Charles M. Shopping Center Location Decisions: National Competitive Policies and Local Zoning Regulations. In *Sternlieb, G. and Hughes,*

J. W., eds., 1981, pp. 97–107. [G: U.S.]

Hayden, Bruce P. Shopping Centers: U.S.A.: Are We Overbuilding? Is Large Gobbling Up Small? In *Sternlieb, G. and Hughes, J. W., eds.*, 1981, pp. 291–96. [G: U.S.]

Ingene, Charles A. and Yu, Eden S. H. Determinants of Retail Sales in SMSAs. *Reg. Sci. Urban Econ.*, November 1981, *11*(4), pp. 529–47. [G: U.S.]

Irvine, F. Owen, Jr. The Influence of Capital Costs on Inventory Investment: Time-Series Evidence for a Department Store. *Quart. Rev. Econ. Bus.*, Winter 1981, *21*(4), pp. 25–44. [G: U.S.]

Isaac, Barry L. Price, Competition, and Profits among Hawkers and Shopkeepers in Pendembu, Sierra Leone: An Inventory Approach. *Econ. Develop. Cult. Change*, January 1981, *29*(2), pp. 353–73. [G: Sierra Leone]

Kaplan, Marshall. Shopping Centers: U.S.A.: Community Conservation Guidance: A Promising Initiative. In *Sternlieb, G. and Hughes, J. W., eds.*, 1981, pp. 71–82. [G: U.S.]

Kelly, Michael F. Shopping Centers: U.S.A.: Are We Overbuilding? In *Sternlieb, G. and Hughes, J. W., eds.*, 1981, pp. 303–10. [G: U.S.]

Lamm, Ray McFall, Jr. Prices and Concentration in the Food Retailing Industry. *J. Ind. Econ.*, September 1981, *30*(1), pp. 67–78. [G: U.S.]

Lamm, Ray McFall, Jr. The Impact of the Voluntary Anti-Inflation Program on Retail Food Prices. *Agr. Econ. Res.*, January 1981, *33*(1), pp. 28–33. [G: U.S.]

Leibowits, Peter D. Shopping Centers: U.S.A.: Appraising the Central City Option: The Preliminary Track Record. In *Sternlieb, G. and Hughes, J. W., eds.*, 1981, pp. 219–27. [G: U.S.]

Lim, Jong Won. The Evolution of Retailing Industries in Japan: Comment. In *Okochi, A. and Shimokawa, K., eds.*, 1981, pp. 290–92. [G: Japan]

Maeda, Kazutoshi. The Evolution of Retailing Industries in Japan. In *Okochi, A. and Shimokawa, K., eds.*, 1981, pp. 265–89. [G: Japan]

Mandelker, Daniel R. Commentary on Legal Aspects of Controlling Shopping Center Competition. In *Sternlieb, G. and Hughes, J. W., eds.*, 1981, pp. 109–12. [G: U.S.]

Marchi, Luciano. Role of Computers in Inventory Management. The Retailing Case. In *Chikán, A., ed. (II)*, 1981, pp. 155–66.

Möller, Kristian and van den Heuvel, Rob. Contribution of Store Attributes to Retail Store Image and Preference. *Liiketaloudellinen Aikak.*, 1981, *30*(3), pp. 278–95. [G: Finland]

Muller, Thomas. Regional Malls and Central City Retail Sales: An Overview. In *Sternlieb, G. and Hughes, J. W., eds.*, 1981, pp. 177–99. [G: U.S.]

Robbins, Lynn W. and Haas, Thomas P. Simulated Behavior of Fast Food Restaurants under Alternative Cost/Volume Conditions. *Amer. J. Agr. Econ.*, February 1981, *63*(1), pp. 146–52. [G: U.S.]

Samson, Peter. The Department Store, Its Past and Its Future: A Review Article. *Bus. Hist. Rev.*, Spring 1981, *55*(1), pp. 26–34. [G: U.S.]

Schiller, Russell. A Model of Retail Branch Distribu-

tion. *Reg. Stud.*, 1981, *15*(1), pp. 15–22.

Sears, Foster E. Retail Economics of the 1980s. In *Sternlieb, G. and Hughes, J. W., eds.*, 1981, pp. 251–55. [G: U.S.]

Spink, Frank H., Jr. Downtown Malls: Prospects, Design, Constraints. In *Sternlieb, G. and Hughes, J. W., eds.*, 1981, pp. 201–18. [G: U.S.]

Sternlieb, George and Hughes, James W. The Uncertain Future of Shopping Centers. In *Sternlieb, G. and Hughes, J. W., eds.*, 1981, pp. 1–16. [G: U.S.]

Sussman, Albert. Shopping Centers: U.S.A.: Community Conservation Guidelines: A Failure. In *Sternlieb, G. and Hughes, J. W., eds.*, 1981, pp. 63–69. [G: U.S.]

Trieger, Raymond. The Department Store Perspective. In *Sternlieb, G. and Hughes, J. W., eds.*, 1981, pp. 257–63. [G: U.S.]

Tucker, Grady. The New Economics of Shopping Center Location and Scale. In *Sternlieb, G. and Hughes, J. W., eds.*, 1981, pp. 41–47. [G: U.S.]

Walzer, Norman and Stablein, Ralph. Small Towns and Regional Centers. *Growth Change*, July 1981, *12*(3), pp. 2–8. [G: U.S.]

West, Douglas S. Tests of Two Locational Implications of a Theory of Market Pre-Emption. *Can. J. Econ.*, May 1981, *14*(2), pp. 313–26. [G: Canada]

Wirtenberg, Margaret S. Downtown Pedestrian Malls. In *Sternlieb, G. and Hughes, J. W., eds.*, 1981, pp. 229–36. [G: U.S.]

634 Industry Studies: Construction

6340 Construction

Ahmed, Ehsan. Production Functions and Input Elasticities in the Construction of Low-Cost Housing: A Comparison of Building Firms in Pakistan with Firms in Five Other Countries. *Pakistan Devel. Rev.*, Winter 1981, *20*(4), pp. 417–26. [G: Pakistan; Colombia; Sri Lanka; Kenya; Tunisia]

Alfeld, Louis E. Productivity and the Construction Industry. In *Hogan, J. D. and Craig, A. M., eds.*, Vol. 2, 1981, pp. 1099–1102. [G: U.S.]

Ball, Robert. Employment Created by Construction Expenditures. *Mon. Lab. Rev.*, December 1981, *104*(12), pp. 38–44. [G: U.S.]

Bingham, Barbara. Labor and Material Requirements for Commercial Office Building Projects. *Mon. Lab. Rev.*, May 1981, *104*(5), pp. 41–48. [G: U.S.]

Bishop, John. Employment in Construction and Distribution Industries: The Impact of the New Jobs Tax Credit. In *Rosen, S., ed.*, 1981, pp. 209–46. [G: U.S.]

Clemhout, Simone. The Impact of Housing Cyclicality on the Construction of Residential Units and Housing Costs. *Land Econ.*, November 1981, *57*(4), pp. 609–23. [G: U.S.]

Clemhout, Simone and Neftci, Salih N. Policy Evaluation of Housing Cyclicality: A Spectral Analysis. *Rev. Econ. Statist.*, August 1981, *63*(3), pp. 385–94. [G: U.S.]

Codrington, Caroline and Henley, John S. The Industrial Relations of Injury and Death: Safety Representatives in the Construction Industry. *Brit. J. Ind. Relat.*, November 1981, *19*(3), pp. 297–315. [G: U.K.]

Cohen, Linda and Noll, Roger. The Economics of Building Codes to Resist Seismic Shock. *Public Policy*, Winter 1981, *29*(1), pp. 1–29. [G: U.S.]

Eccles, Robert G. The Quasifirm in the Construction Industry. *J. Econ. Behav. Organ.*, December 1981, *2*(4), pp. 335–57. [G: U.S.]

Goldfarb, Robert S. and Morrall, John F., III. The Davis–Bacon Act: An Appraisal of Recent Studies. *Ind. Lab. Relat. Rev.*, January 1981, *34*(2), pp. 191–206. [G: U.S.]

Gorbunov, E. The Construction Complex as a Part of the Investment Potential. *Prob. Econ.*, August 1981, *24*(4), pp. 57–75. [G: U.S.S.R.]

Keating, Barry P. Standards: Implicit, Explicit and Mandatory. *Econ. Inquiry*, July 1981, *19*(3), pp. 449–58. [G: U.S.]

Lawler, John. Reply to Professor Mitchell [Wage Spillover: The Impact of Landrum-Griffin]. *Ind. Relat.*, Fall 1981, *20*(3), pp. 347–49. [G: U.S.]

Lawler, John. Wage Spillover: The Impact of Landrum–Griffin. *Ind. Relat.*, Winter 1981, *20*(1), pp. 85–97. [G: U.S.]

Merkies, Arnold H. Q. M. and Bikker, Jacob A. Aggregation of Lag Patterns with an Application in the Construction Industry. *Europ. Econ. Rev.*, March 1981, *15*(3), pp. 385–405. [G: Netherlands]

Mitchell, Daniel J. B. Wage Spillover: The Impact of Landrum-Griffin: Comment. *Ind. Relat.*, Fall 1981, *20*(3), pp. 342–46. [G: U.S.]

Olsen, John G. Labor and Material Requirements for Federal Building Construction. *Mon. Lab. Rev.*, December 1981, *104*(12), pp. 47–51. [G: U.S.]

Oster, Sharon. Product Regulations: A Measure of the Benefits. *J. Ind. Econ.*, June 1981, *29*(4), pp. 395–411. [G: U.S.]

Paik, Soon and Hall, Gary A. Craft Requirements for Construction of Electric Power Plants. *Growth Change*, October 1981, *12*(4), pp. 16–21. [G: U.S.]

Perloff, Jeffrey M. Labor Market Adjustments in the Unionized Contract Construction Industry. *J. Lab. Res.*, Fall 1981, *2*(2), pp. 337–53. [G: U.S.]

Rabeau, Yves. Le comportement des salaires chez les travailleurs syndiqués de l'industrie de la construction au Canada. (Behaviour of Wages of the Unionized Workers of the Construction Industry in Canada. With English summary.) *L'Actual. Econ.*, October–December 1981, *57*(4), pp. 491–506. [G: Canada]

Stokes, H. Kemble, Jr. An Examination of the Productivity Decline in the Construction Industry. *Rev. Econ. Statist.*, November 1981, *63*(4), pp. 459–502. [G: U.S.]

Stretton, A. W. The Building Industry and Urbanization in Third World Countries: A Philippine Case Study. *Econ. Develop. Cult. Change*, January 1981, *29*(2), pp. 325–39. [G: Philippines]

Yevstigneyev, Viktor P. Construction. **In** *Novosti Press Agency*, 1981, pp. 134–42. [G: U.S.S.R.]

635 Industry Studies: Services and Related Industries

6350 General

Baer, Werner and Samuelson, Larry. Toward a Service-oriented Growth Strategy. *World Devel.*, June 1981, *9*(6), pp. 499–514.

Leveson, Irving. Productivity in Services: Issues for Analysis. **In** *Hogan, J. D. and Craig, A. M., eds.,* Vol. 2, 1981, pp. 765–803. [G: U.S.]

Menchik, Mark David. The Service Sector. **In** *Hawley, A. H. and Mazie, S. M., eds.,* 1981, pp. 231–54. [G: U.S.]

Mollenkopf, John H. Paths toward the Post Industrial Service City: The Northeast and the Southwest. **In** *Burchell, R. W. and Listokin, D., eds.,* 1981, pp. 77–112. [G: U.S.]

Novikova, E. E.; Iazykova, V. S. and Iankova, Z. A. Women's Work and the Family. *Prob. Econ.*, Sept.–Oct.–Nov. 1981, *24*(5–6–7), pp. 165–90. [G: U.S.S.R.]

Urquhart, Michael. The Services Industry: Is It Recession-Proof? *Mon. Lab. Rev.*, October 1981, *104*(10), pp. 12–18. [G: U.S.]

6352 Electrical, Gas, Communication, and Information Services

Abler, Ronald and Falk, Thomas. Public Information Services and the Changing Role of Distance in Human Affairs. *Econ. Geogr.*, January 1981, *57*(1), pp. 10–22.

Acton, Jan Paul. Planning, Processing, and Analyzing Data for Residential Load Studies. **In** *U.S. Dept. of Energy,* 1981, pp. 137–51. [G: U.S.]

Antsyshkin, S. V. and Polianskaia, T. M. On Possible Ways of Using Optimal Branch Plans to Improve the Price System—The Case of Power Station Coals. *Matekon*, Fall 1981, *18*(1), pp. 15–34. [G: U.S.S.R.]

Aquino, Rosemary M. The Philippines: Talomo River and Baliguian River Mini Hydroelectric Projects. **In** *Goodman, L. J.; Hawkins, J. N. and Love, R. N., eds.,* 1981, pp. 61–96. [G: Philippines]

Atkinson, Scott E. and Halvorsen, Robert. Automatic Price Adjustment Clauses and Input Choice in Regulated Utilities. **In** *Nemetz, P. N., ed.,* 1981, pp. 185–96.

Babe, Robert E. Vertical Integration and Productivity: Canadian Telecommunications. *J. Econ. Issues*, March 1981, *15*(1), pp. 1–31. [G: Canada]

Barry, Leo. Interprovincial Electrical Energy Transfers: The Constitutional Background. **In** *Nemetz, P. N., ed.,* 1981, pp. 213–53. [G: Canada]

Baseman, Kenneth C. Open Entry and Cross-Subsidization in Regulated Markets. **In** *Fromm, G., ed.,* 1981, pp. 329–60. [G: U.S.]

Baumol, William J. Open Entry and Cross-Subsidization in Regulated Markets: Comment. **In** *Fromm, G., ed.,* 1981, pp. 361–64. [G: U.S.]

Beals, Ralph E. Elasticity Estimates for Domestic

Electricity Consumption under Time-of-Day Pricing: An Analysis of British Data. In *[Nelson, J. R.]*, 1981, pp. 277–97. **[G: U.K.]**

Bennis, Jerome. Developing and Maintaining a Load Research Data Base: Comment. In *U.S. Dept. of Energy*, 1981, pp. 118–21. **[G: U.S.]**

Bernard, Pierre. The Development of Electricity in the Future French Energy Balance: An Example of Readjustment. In *Bayraktar, B. A., et al., eds.*, 1981, pp. 173–81. **[G: France]**

Berry, Sandra H. Contacting and Interviewing Residential Electricity Customers. In *U.S. Dept. of Energy*, 1981, pp. 60–72.

Besen, Stanley M. and Crandall, Robert W. The Deregulation of Cable Television. *Law Contemp. Probl.*, Winter 1981, *44*(1), pp. 77–124.
[G: U.S.]

Betancourt, Roger R. An Econometric Analysis of Peak Electricity Demand in the Short Run. *Energy Econ.*, January 1981, *3*(1), pp. 14–29.
[G: U.S.]

Bhatt, Durga Nath. Capacity-Expansion Model for Telephone Feeder Plant. *Eng. Econ.*, Winter 1981, *26*(2), pp. 123–35.

Bishop, Lane. Considerations in Analysing and Generalizing from Time-of-Use Electricity Pricing Studies. In *U.S. Dept. of Energy*, 1981, pp. 158–65.

Blair, Peter; Cassel, Thomas and Edelstein, Robert H. Optimal Investments in Geothermal Electricity Facilities: A Theoretic Note. In *Nemetz, P. N., ed.*, 1981, pp. 197–212.

Boyer, Kenneth D. and Wirth, Michael O. The Economics of Regulation by Policy Directive: FCC Public-Interest Requirements. *Quart. Rev. Econ. Bus.*, Spring 1981, *21*(1), pp. 77–96. **[G: U.S.]**

Braeutigam, Ronald R. Regulation and the Multiproduct Firm: The Case of Telecommunications in Canada: Comment. In *Fromm, G., ed.*, 1981, pp. 314–20. **[G: Canada]**

Braeutigam, Ronald R. The Deregulation of Natural Gas. In *Weiss, L. W. and Klass, M. W., eds.*, 1981, pp. 142–86. **[G: U.S.]**

Brandon, Belinda B. The Effect of the Demographics of Individual Households on Their Telephone Usage: The Questionnaire, Calling, and Billing Data. In *Brandon, B. B., ed.*, 1981, pp. 29–55.
[G: U.S.]

Brandon, Belinda B. and Ancmon, Elsa M. The Association of Distance with Calling Frequencies and Conversation Times. In *Brandon, B. B., ed.*, 1981, pp. 219–73.

Brandon, Belinda B. and Brandon, Paul S. The Effect of the Demographics of Individual Households on Their Telephone Usage: Introduction and Summary. In *Brandon, B. B., ed.*, 1981, pp. 1–18. **[G: U.S.]**

Brandon, Belinda B.; Brandon, Paul S. and Ancmon, Elsa M. The Effects of Time of Day on Local and Suburban Calling Frequencies and Conversation Times. In *Brandon, B. B., ed.*, 1981, pp. 165–218. **[G: U.S.]**

Brandon, Belinda B.; Brandon, Paul S. and Williams, Wm. H. The Effect of the Demographics of Individual Households on Their Telephone Usage: Other Studies and Suggestions for Future Research. In *Brandon, B. B., ed.*, 1981, pp. 355–93.

Brandon, Belinda B., et al. Box Plot Analysis of Local and Suburban Calling Frequencies and Conversation Times. In *Brandon, B. B., ed.*, 1981, pp. 75–131. **[G: U.S.]**

Brandon, Paul S. The Effect of the Demographics of Individual Households on Their Telephone Usage: Regression Analysis of Local and Suburban Usage. In *Brandon, B. B., ed.*, 1981, pp. 133–64. **[G: U.S.]**

Burgess, Giles and Paglin, Morton. Lifeline Electricity Rates as an Income Transfer Device. *Land Econ.*, February 1981, *57*(1), pp. 41–47.
[G: U.S.]

Caves, Douglas W. Effects on the Residential Load Curve from Time-of-Use Pricing of Electricity: Econometric Inferences from the Wisconsin Experiment for Summer System Peak Days. In *U.S. Dept. of Energy*, 1981, pp. 249–74. **[G: U.S.]**

Chang, Hui S. and Chern, Wen S. A Study on the Demand for Electricity and the Variation in the Price Elasticities for Manufacturing Industries. *J. Econ. Bus.*, Winter 1981, *33*(2), pp. 122–31.
[G: U.S.]

Chung, Chinbang and Aigner, Dennis J. Industrial and Commercial Demand for Electricity by Time-of-Day: A California Case Study. *Energy J.*, July 1981, *2*(3), pp. 91–110. **[G: U.S.]**

Clark, David and Unwin, Kathryn I. Telecommunications and Travel: Potential Impact in Rural Areas. *Reg. Stud.*, 1981, *15*(1), pp. 47–56.
[G: U.K.]

Clark, Robert M. and Stevie, Richard G. A Regional Water Supply Cost Model. *Growth Change*, July 1981, *12*(3), pp. 9–16. **[G: U.S.]**

Clayton, C. Andrew. Drawing a Sample and Allocating Customers to Design Points. In *U.S. Dept. of Energy*, 1981, pp. 32–48.

Cochrane, James L. Carter Energy Policy and the Ninety-fifth Congress. In *Goodwin, C. D., ed.*, 1981, pp. 547–600. **[G: U.S.]**

Cochrane, James L. Energy Policy in the Johnson Administration: Logical Order versus Economic Pluralism. In *Goodwin, C. D., ed.*, 1981, pp. 337–93. **[G: U.S.]**

Cochrane, James L. and Griepentrog, Gary L. U.S. Energy: A Quantitative Review of the Past Three Decades. In *Goodwin, C. D., ed.*, 1981, pp. 685–705. **[G: U.S.]**

Cowing, Thomas G.; Stevenson, Rodney E. and Small, Jeffrey. Comparative Measures of Total Factor Productivity in the Regulated Sector: The Electric Utility Industry. In *Cowing, T. G. and Stevenson, R. E., eds.*, 1981, pp. 161–77.
[G: U.S.]

Crano, William D. Variables Affecting Treatment Perception in an Electric Time-of-Use Rate Demonstration: Analytic and Interpretative Implications. In *U.S. Dept. of Energy*, 1981, pp. 287–304. **[G: U.S.]**

Denny, M., et al. Estimating the Effects of Diffusion of Technological Innovations in Telecommunications: The Production Structure of Bell Canada. *Can. J. Econ.*, February 1981, *14*(1), pp. 24–43.
[G: Canada]

Denny, Michael; Fuss, Melvyn A. and Waverman, Leonard. The Measurement and Interpretation of Total Factor Productivity in Regulated Industries, with an Application to Canadian Telecommunications. In *Cowing, T. G. and Stevenson, R. E., eds.*, 1981, pp. 179–218. [G: Canada]

DeSouza, Glenn. Electric Utility Coal Demand: A Critical Review of Recent Forecasts. *Bus. Econ.*, May 1981, *16*(3), pp. 15–24. [G: U.S.]

Devlin, Susan J. and Patterson, I. Lester. The Effect of the Demographics of Individual Households on Their Telephone Usage: Toll Usage. In *Brandon, B. B., ed.*, 1981, pp. 303–53. [G: U.S.]

Dikeman, Neil J., Jr. A Summary of the Edmond Electric Utility Demonstration Project and Its Findings. In *U.S. Dept. of Energy*, 1981, pp. 205–11. [G: U.S.]

Donovan, Maureen. The Media in Japan. In *Richardson, B. M. and Ueda, T., eds.*, 1981, pp. 258–68. [G: Japan]

Eldor, D.; Sudit, E. F. and Vinod, H. D. Economies of Scale in Telecommunications: A Further Reply. *Appl. Econ.*, June 1981, *13*(2), pp. 255–56.

Engwall, Lars. Newspaper Competition: A Case for Theories of Oligopoly: Review Article. *Scand. Econ. Hist. Rev.*, 1981, *29*(2), pp. 145–54. [G: Sweden]

Evans, A. C. Data Protection in Europe. *J. World Trade Law*, March–April 1981, *15*(2), pp. 151–58. [G: Europe]

Famadas, Nelson. The Role of Survey Data in Load Research. In *U.S. Dept. of Energy*, 1981, pp. 49–52.

Ferrari, A. France's Nuclear Power Programme. In *Tempest, P., ed.*, 1981, pp. 159–64. [G: France]

Fishelson, Gideon. Telecommunications, CES Production Function—A Rejoinder. *Appl. Econ.*, March 1981, *13*(1), pp. 127–32. [G: U.S.]

Fuss, Melvyn A. and Waverman, Leonard. Regulation and the Multiproduct Firm: The Case of Telecommunications in Canada. In *Fromm, G., ed.*, 1981, pp. 276–313. [G: Canada]

Gollop, Frank M. Scale Effects and Technical Change as Sources of Productivity Growth. In *Hogan, J. D. and Craig, A. M., eds., Vol. 2*, 1981, pp. 805–38. [G: U.S.]

Gollop, Frank M. and Roberts, Mark J. The Sources of Economic Growth in the U.S. Electric Power Industry. In *Cowing, T. G. and Stevenson, R. E., eds.*, 1981, pp. 107–43. [G: U.S.]

Goodman, Louis J.; Hawkins, John N. and Love, Ralph N. An Introduction to Small Hydroelectric Systems. In *Goodman, L. J.; Hawkins, J. N. and Love, R. N., eds.*, 1981, pp. 1–20.

Goodman, Louis J., et al. Small Hydroelectric Projects for Rural Development Planning and Management: Policy and Research Issues. In *Goodman, L. J.; Hawkins, J. N. and Love, R. N., eds.*, 1981, pp. 184–94. [G: China; New Zealand; Philippines; U.S.]

Goodwin, Craufurd D. Truman Administration Policies toward Particular Energy Sources. In *Goodwin, C. D., ed.*, 1981, pp. 63–203. [G: U.S.]

Goyco, Osvaldo C. Procedures for Collecting, Translating, and Editing Meter Data: Comment. In *U.S. Dept. of Energy*, 1981, pp. 81–92. [G: U.S.]

Groff, Robert H. The Effect of the Demographics of Individual Households on Their Telephone Usage: Analysis of Billing Data. In *Brandon, B. B., ed.*, 1981, pp. 275–301. [G: U.S.]

Groves, Robert M. Definition of the Population and Formation and Use of Strata. In *U.S. Dept. of Energy*, 1981, pp. 23–31.

Hawkins, John N. The People's Republic of China: Energy for Rural Development. In *Goodman, L. J.; Hawkins, J. N. and Love, R. N., eds.*, 1981, pp. 21–60. [G: China]

Heberlein, Thomas A. Electric Rate Demonstration Conference: Questionnaire Development. In *U.S. Dept. of Energy*, 1981, pp. 53–59.

van Helden, G. Jan and Muysken, Joan. Economies of Scale and Technological Change in Electricity Generation in the Netherlands. *De Economist*, 1981, *129*(4), pp. 476–503. [G: Netherlands]

Hendricks, Wallace E. Evaluation and Future Uses of the DOE Sponsored Demonstration Data. In *U.S. Dept. of Energy*, 1981, pp. 279–86. [G: U.S.]

Highton, Nicolas H. and Webb, Michael G. Pollution Abatement Costs in the Electricity Supply Industry in England and Wales. *J. Ind. Econ.*, September 1981, *30*(1), pp. 49–65. [G: U.K.]

Hill, Daniel H. Electric Rate Demonstration Conference: Limitations on Analysis. In *U.S. Dept. of Energy*, 1981, pp. 152–57. [G: U.S.]

Houdek, Karel. Electric Energy in the 6th and 7th Five-Year Plans. *Czech. Econ. Digest.*, February 1981, (1), pp. 71–78. [G: Czechoslovakia]

Hughes, Thomas P. Transfer and Style: A Historical Account. In *Sagafi-nejad, T.; Moxon, R. W. and Perlmutter, H. V., eds.*, 1981, pp. 42–54. [G: U.S.; U.K.]

Hutber, F. W. Energy Policy Planning: Comments on the Papers Presented in the Session on Supply Modeling. In *Bayraktar, B. A., et al., eds.*, 1981, pp. 183–86.

Jackson, K. R. and Yerbury, D. Introducing Technological Change: A Case Study. *Australian J. Manage.*, December 1981, *6*(2), pp. 59–79. [G: Australia]

James, Richard E. Procedures for Collecting, Translating, and Editing Meter Data. In *U.S. Dept. of Energy*, 1981, pp. 73–80.

Jones, Mary Gardiner. The New Telecommunication Technologies: Answer to Consumer Needs? In *[Grether, E. T.]*, 1981, pp. 174–89.

Keith, Charles A. and Love, Ralph N. New Zealand: Wairoa River Hydroelectric Project. In *Goodman, L. J.; Hawkins, J. N. and Love, R. N., eds.*, 1981, pp. 97–160. [G: New Zealand]

Lee, K. D. and McCutchan, D. A. What Is the Worth of Baseload Availability? *Eng. Econ.*, Winter 1981, *26*(2), pp. 137–47. [G: U.S.]

Levi, Isaac. Assessing Accident Risks in U.S. Commercial Nuclear Power Plants: Scientific Method and the Rasmussen Report. *Soc. Res.*, Summer 1981, *48*(2), pp. 395–408. [G: U.S.]

Levy, Roger. Developing and Maintaining a Load Research Data Base. In *U.S. Dept. of Energy*, 1981, pp. 93–117. [G: U.S.]

Lifson, Dale P. Practical Considerations in Modelling the Demand for Electricity. In *U.S. Dept. of Energy*, 1981, pp. 166–86.   [G: U.S.]

Lilien, Steven and Pastena, Victor. Intramethod Comparability: The Case of the Oil and Gas Industry. *Accounting Rev.*, July 1981, *56*(3), pp. 690–703.   [G: U.S.]

Lioukas, S. K. The Order–Delivery Lag in Electricity Investment. *Appl. Econ.*, March 1981, *13*(1), pp. 35–49.   [G: U.K.]

Lovins, Amory B. Electric Utility Investments: *Excelsior* or Confetti? In *Nemetz, P. N., ed.*, 1981, pp. 91–114.   [G: U.S.]

Malko, J. Robert; Ray, Dennis J. and Hassig, Nancy L. Time-of-Day Pricing of Electricity Activities in Some Midwestern States. In *Nemetz, P. N., ed.*, 1981, pp. 143–70.   [G: U.S.]

McGill, Robert. The Effect of the Demographics of Individual Households on Their Telephone Usage: The Data Base Design and Implementation. In *Brandon, B. B., ed.*, 1981, pp. 57–74.   [G: U.S.]

Metcalf, Charles E. Sample Design for Rate Demonstrations and Load Research. In *U.S. Dept. of Energy*, 1981, pp. 15–22.

Miedema, Allen K. North Carolina Rate Demonstration Project—Preliminary Results. In *U.S. Dept. of Energy*, 1981, pp. 228–48.   [G: U.S.]

Miedema, Allen K. Overview of DOE Analyses of Residential TOU Data. In *U.S. Dept. of Energy*, 1981, pp. 193–204.   [G: U.S.]

Militzer, Kenneth H. Productivity Measures at the Firm Level. In *Hogan, J. D. and Craig, A. M., eds., Vol. 1*, 1981, pp. 305–18.   [G: U.S.]

Milon, J. Walter. An Economic and Energetic Framework for Evaluating Dispersed Energy Technologies. *Land Econ.*, February 1981, *57*(1), pp. 63–76.

Mitchell, Bridger M. Regulation and the Multiproduct Firm: The Case of Telecommunications in Canada: Comment. In *Fromm, G., ed.*, 1981, pp. 321–27.   [G: Canada]

Mitchell, Bridger M. The Effect of Time-of-Day Rates in the Los Angeles Electricity Rate Study. In *U.S. Dept. of Energy*, 1981, pp. 212–27.   [G: U.S.]

Miyabara, Tetsuo and Goodman, Louis J. Hawaii, U.S.A.: Hydroelectric Development. In *Goodman, L. J.; Hawkins, J. N. and Love, R. N., eds.*, 1981, pp. 161–83.   [G: U.S.]

Mountain, Dean C. The Spatial Distribution of Electricity Demand: Its Impact upon Input Usage. *Land Econ.*, February 1981, *57*(1), pp. 48–62.   [G: Canada]

Munasinghe, Mohan. Optimal Electricity Supply: Reliability, Pricing and System Planning. *Energy Econ.*, July 1981, *3*(3), pp. 140–52.   [G: Brazil]

Munasinghe, Mohan and Jahangir, Muhammad. Determining Marginal Cost-Based Electricity Tariffs: Case Study of the WAPDA System. *Pakistan Econ. Soc. Rev.*, Summer 1981, *19*(1), pp. 50–68.   [G: Pakistan]

Nadiri, M. Ishaq and Schankerman, Mark A. The Structure of Production, Technological Change, and the Rate of Growth of Total Factor Productivity in the U.S. Bell System. In *Cowing, T. G.*

and Stevenson, R. E., eds., 1981, pp. 219–47.   [G: U.S.]

Newfarmer, Richard S. and Marsh, Lawrence C. Foreign Ownership, Market Structure and Industrial Performance: Brazil's Electrical Industry. *J. Devel. Econ.*, February 1981, *8*(1), pp. 47–75.   [G: Brazil]

Nufeld, John L. and Watts, James M. Inverted Block or Lifeline Rates and Micro-Efficiency in the Consumption of Electricity. *Energy Econ.*, April 1981, *3*(2), pp. 113–21.   [G: U.S.]

Oren, Shmuel S. and Smith, Stephen A. Critical Mass and Tariff Structure in Electronic Communications Markets. *Bell J. Econ. (See Rand J. Econ. after 4/85)*, Autumn 1981, *12*(2), pp. 467–87.

Osano, Hiroshi. Nonprice Competition in the Newspaper Industry, and the Incentive Effects of 'ABC BUSUU'. (In Japanese. With English summary.) *Osaka Econ. Pap.*, June 1981, *31*(1), pp. 10–20.   [G: Japan]

Owen, Bruce M. The Rise and Fall of Cable Television Regulation. In *Weiss, L. W. and Klass, M. W., eds.*, 1981, pp. 86–101.   [G: U.S.]

Paik, Soon and Hall, Gary A. Craft Requirements for Construction of Electric Power Plants. *Growth Change*, October 1981, *12*(4), pp. 16–21.   [G: U.S.]

Panzar, John C. Open Entry and Cross-Subsidization in Regulated Markets: Comment. In *Fromm, G., ed.*, 1981, pp. 365–69.   [G: U.S.]

Parkman, Allen. The Growth of CATV and the Value of TV Stations. *Quart. Rev. Econ. Bus.*, Winter 1981, *21*(4), pp. 64–74.

Parris, Carl D. Joint Venture I: The Trinidad–Tobago Telephone Company, 1968–1972. *Soc. Econ. Stud.*, March 1981, *30*(1), pp. 108–26.   [G: Trinidad and Tobago]

Pfannenstiel, Jackalyne. Implementing Marginal Cost Pricing in the Electric Utility Industry. In *Sichel, W. and Gies, T. G., eds.*, 1981, pp. 53–72.   [G: U.S.]

Phillips, Almarin. Theory and Practice in Public Utility Regulation: The Case of Telecommunications. In *[Nelson, J. R.]*, 1981, pp. 181–96.   [G: U.S.]

Ranis, Gustav. Transfer and Style: A Historical Account: Comment. In *Sagafi-nejad, T.; Moxon, R. W. and Perlmutter, H. V., eds.*, 1981, pp. 55–63.   [G: Selected Countries; U.K.; U.S.]

Roth, Timothy P. Average and Marginal Price Changes and the Demand for Electricity: An Econometric Study. *Appl. Econ.*, September 1981, *13*(3), pp. 377–88.

Sandler, Todd and Schulze, William D. The Economics of Outer Space. *Natural Res. J.*, April 1981, *21*(2), pp. 371–93.   [G: U.S.]

Soutar, Geoffrey N. and Clarke, Yvonne. Life Style and Television Viewing Behaviour in Perth, Western Australia. *Australian J. Manage.*, June 1981, *6*(1), pp. 109–23.   [G: Australia]

Starr, Chauncey. Energy at the Crossroads: Abundance or Shortage? In *Tempest, P., ed.*, 1981, pp. 11–19.   [G: U.S.]

Stevenson, Rodney E. Establishing Objectives for Residential Load Research. In *U.S. Dept. of Energy*, 1981, pp. 8–14.

Sullivan, Brian and Siemon, Donna. Interfuel Substitution—Upper Bound Estimates. *Energy J.*, April 1981, *2*(2), pp. 107–18.   [G: U.S.]

Uri, Noel D. Regional Forecasting of the Demand for Fossil Fuels by Electric Utilities in the United States. *Reg. Sci. Urban Econ.*, February 1981, *11*(1), pp. 87–100.   [G: U.S.]

Wagner, Karin. The Newspaper Industry in Britain, Germany and the United States. *Nat. Inst. Econ. Rev.*, February 1981, (95), pp. 81–88.
     [G: U.K.; W. Germany; U.S.]

Williams, Wm. H. and Goodman, Michael L. The Effect of the Demographics of Individual Households on Their Telephone Usage: The Development of the Customer Sample. In *Brandon, B. B., ed.*, 1981, pp. 19–28.   [G: U.S.]

Wills, Hugh R. Estimating Input Demand Equations by Direct and Indirect Methods. *Rev. Econ. Stud.*, April 1981, *48*(2), pp. 255–70. [G: U.S.]

Wills, John. Residential Demand for Electricity. *Energy Econ.*, October 1981, *3*(4), pp. 249–55.
     [G: U.S.]

Zimmer, Michael A. Firm Valuation in the Electric Utility Industry: Alternative Expectations Hypotheses. *Quart. Rev. Econ. Bus.*, Winter 1981, *21*(4), pp. 136–46.   [G: U.S.]

6353 Personal Services

Carroll, Sidney L. and Gaston, Robert J. Occupational Restrictions and the Quality of Service Received: Some Evidence. *Southern Econ. J.*, April 1981, *47*(4), pp. 959–76.   [G: U.S.]

Greene, Vernon L. and Monahan, Deborah J. Structural and Operational Factors Affecting Quality of Patient Care in Nursing Homes. *Public Policy*, Fall 1981, *29*(4), pp. 399–415. [G: U.S.]

Maurizi, Alex R.; Moore, Ruth L. and Shepard, Lawrence. Competing for Professional Control: Professional Mix in the Eyeglasses Industry. *J. Law Econ.*, October 1981, *24*(2), pp. 351–64.
     [G: U.S.]

6354 Business and Legal Services

Boucher, Michel. La réglementation de l'industrie québécoise du camionnage: aperçu et considérations analytiques. (Regulation of the Quebec Trucking Industry: Institutions, Practices and Analytical Considerations. With English summary.) *L'Actual. Econ.*, January–March 1981, *57*(1), pp. 87–112.   [G: Canada]

Carroll, Sidney L. and Gaston, Robert J. A Note on the Quality of Legal Services: Peer Review and Disciplinary Service. In *Zerbe, R. O., Jr., ed.*, 1981, pp. 251–60.   [G: U.S.]

DeAngelo, Linda Elizabeth. Auditor Size and Audit Quality. *J. Acc. Econ.*, December 1981, *3*(3), pp. 183–99.   [G: U.S.]

Eichenseher, John W. and Danos, Paul. The Analysis of Industry-Specific Auditor Concentration: Towards an Explanatory Model. *Accounting Rev.*, July 1981, *56*(3), pp. 479–92.   [G: U.S.]

Kwon, Jene K. A Model of the Law Firm: Reply. *Southern Econ. J.*, July 1981, *48*(1), pp. 231–34.

O'Farrell, P. N. and O'Loughlin, B. The Impact of New Industry Enterprises in Ireland: An Analysis

of Service Linkages. *Reg. Stud.*, 1981, *15*(6), pp. 439–58.   [G: Ireland]

Rotella, Elyce J. The Transformation of the American Office: Changes in Employment and Technology. *J. Econ. Hist.*, March 1981, *41*(1), pp. 51–57.
     [G: U.S.]

Sisk, David E. A Model of the Law Firm: Comment. *Southern Econ. J.*, July 1981, *48*(1), pp. 227–30.

6355 Repair Services

Oster, Sharon. Product Regulations: A Measure of the Benefits. *J. Ind. Econ.*, June 1981, *29*(4), pp. 395–411.   [G: U.S.]

6356 Insurance

Altenstetter, Christa. National Health Initiatives and Local Health-Insurance Carriers: The Case of the Federal Republic of Germany. In *Altenstetter, C., ed.*, 1981, pp. 227–63.   [G: W. Germany]

Arnould, Richard and Eisenstadt, David. The Effects of Provider-Controlled Blue Shield Plans: Regulatory Options. In *Olson, M., ed.*, 1981, pp. 339–60.   [G: U.S.]

Babbel, David F. Inflation, Indexation, and Life Insurance Sales in Brazil. *J. Risk Ins.*, March 1981, *48*(1), pp. 111–35.   [G: Brazil]

Barzel, Yoram. Competitive Tying Arrangements: The Case of Medical Insurance. *Econ. Inquiry*, October 1981, *19*(4), pp. 598–612.   [G: U.S.]

Bellhouse, David R. and Panjer, Harry H. Stochastic Modelling of Interest Rates with Applications to Life Contingencies—Part II. *J. Risk Ins.*, December 1981, *48*(4), pp. 628–37.   [G: U.S.]

Berekson, Leonard L. and Severns, Roger E. Insurance Executives' Perceptions of Insurance Instruction at the College and University Level. *J. Risk Ins.*, June 1981, *48*(2), pp. 322–33.
     [G: U.S.]

Blicksilver, Jack. Vicissitudes of a Family-Controlled Firm in an Expanding Regional Economy: Life Insurance Company of Georgia. In *Bateman, F., ed.*, 1981, pp. 100–10.   [G: U.S.]

Blostin, Allan P. Is Employer-Sponsored Life Insurance Declining Relative to Other Benefits? *Mon. Lab. Rev.*, September 1981, *104*(9), pp. 31–33.
     [G: U.S.]

Bovbjerg, Randall R. and Feder, Judith. A Cure for Cancer Insurance. *J. Policy Anal. Manage.*, Fall 1981, *1*(1), pp. 135–39.   [G: U.S.]

Cameron, Norman E. The Effect of Mutual Status on Life Insurer Behaviour in Canada. *Can. J. Econ.*, February 1981, *14*(1), pp. 145–55.
     [G: Canada]

Childers, Terry L. and Ferrell, O. C. Husband–Wife Decision Making in Purchasing and Renewing Auto Insurance. *J. Risk Ins.*, September 1981, *48*(3), pp. 482–93.   [G: U.S.]

Cole, Charles W. and Officer, Dennis T. The Interest Cost Effect of Private Municipal Bond Insurance. *J. Risk Ins.*, September 1981, *48*(3), pp. 435–49.   [G: U.S.]

Corgel, Jack B. Long-Term Effects of Firm Size on Life Insurer Mortgage Investment. *J. Risk Ins.*, June 1981, *48*(2), pp. 296–307.   [G: U.S.]

Dahlby, B. G. Adverse Selection and Pareto Improvements through Compulsory Insurance. *Public Choice*, 1981, *37*(3), pp. 547–58.

Dionne, Georges. Le risque moral et la sélection adverse: une revue critique de la littérature. (Moral Hazard and Adverse Selection: A Survey. With English summary.) *L'Actual. Econ.*, April–June 1981, *57*(2), pp. 193–224.

Dionne, Georges. Moral Hazard and Search Activity. *J. Risk Ins.*, September 1981, *48*(3), pp. 422–34.

Doherty, Neil A. Is Rate Classification Profitable? *J. Risk Ins.*, June 1981, *48*(2), pp. 286–95.

Doherty, Neil A. The Measurement of Output and Economies of Scale in Property–Liability Insurance. *J. Risk Ins.*, September 1981, *48*(3), pp. 390–402. [G: Canada]

Downing, Harry F., Jr. Productivity and the Insurance Industry. In *Hogan, J. D. and Craig, A. M., eds., Vol. 2*, 1981, pp. 1115–20. [G: U.S.]

Enthoven, Alain C. Supply-Side Economics of Health Care and Consumer Choice Health Plan. In *Olson, M., ed.*, 1981, pp. 467–89. [G: U.S.]

Fairley, William B.; Tomberlin, Thomas J. and Weisberg, Hebert I. Pricing Automobile Insurance under a Cross-Classification of Risks: Evidence from New Jersey. *J. Risk Ins.*, September 1981, *48*(3), pp. 505–14. [G: U.S.]

Feldman, Roger and Greenberg, Warren. The Relation between the Blue Cross Market Share and the Blue Cross "Discount" on Hospital Charges. *J. Risk Ins.*, June 1981, *48*(2), pp. 235–46. [G: U.S.]

Feldstein, Martin S. A New Approach to National Health Insurance. In *Feldstein, M., ed.*, 1981, *1971*, pp. 247–59. [G: U.S.]

Feldstein, Martin S. Econometric Studies of Health Economics. In *Feldstein, M., ed.*, 1981, *1974*, pp. 57–103. [G: U.S.]

Feldstein, Martin S. The Welfare Loss of Excess Health Insurance. In *Feldstein, M., ed.*, 1981, *1973*, pp. 175–204. [G: U.S.]

Feldstein, Martin S. and Allison, Elisabeth. Tax Subsidies of Private Health Insurance: Distribution, Revenue Loss, and Effects. In *Feldstein, M., ed.*, 1981, *1974*, pp. 205–20. [G: U.S.]

Feldstein, Martin S. and Friedman, Bernard. Tax Subsidies, the Rational Demand for Insurance, and the Health-Care Crisis. In *Feldstein, M., ed.*, 1981, *1977*, pp. 221–44. [G: U.S.]

Feldstein, Martin S.; Friedman, Bernard and Luft, Harold. Distributional Aspects of National Health Insurance Benefits and Finance. In *Feldstein, M., ed.*, 1981, *1972*, pp. 260–82. [G: U.S.]

Feldstein, Martin S. and Taylor, Amy. The Rapid Rise of Hospital Costs. In *Feldstein, M., ed.*, 1981, *1977*, pp. 19–56. [G: U.S.]

Formisano, Roger A. The NAIC Model Life Insurance Solicitation Regulation: Measuring the Consumer Impact in New Jersey. *J. Risk Ins.*, March 1981, *48*(1), pp. 59–79. [G: U.S.]

Frech, H. E., III and Ginsburg, Paul B. Property Rights and Competition in Health Insurance: Multiple Objectives for Nonprofit Firms. In *Zerbe, R. O., Jr., ed.*, 1981, pp. 155–71. [G: U.S.]

Graham, John D. and Vaupel, James W. The Value of a Life: What Difference Does It Make? In *Haimes, Y. Y., ed.*, 1981, pp. 233–43. [G: U.S.]

Greenberg, Warren. Provider-Influenced Insurance Plans and their Impact on Competition: Lessons from Dentistry. In *Olson, M., ed.*, 1981, pp. 361–76. [G: U.S.]

Greene, Mark R. Life Care Centers—A New Concept in Insurance. *J. Risk Ins.*, September 1981, *48*(3), pp. 403–21.

Gregory, Douglas D. Risk Analysis of an Employee Health Benefit Decision under Hospital Reimbursement. *J. Risk Ins.*, December 1981, *48*(4), pp. 577–95. [G: U.S.]

Hammond, J. D. and Shapiro, Arnold F. Capital Requirements for Entry into Property and Liability Underwriting: An Empirical Examination. In *Fed. Res. Bank of Boston and National Sci. Foundation*, 1981, pp. 225–55. [G: U.S.]

Harrington, Scott E. Stock Life Insurer Shareholder Dividend Policy and Holding Company Affiliation. *J. Risk Ins.*, December 1981, *48*(4), pp. 550–76. [G: U.S.]

Hedges, Bob A. On Positive Correlation between Means and Standard Deviations of Claims Ratios: Commentary. *J. Risk Ins.*, December 1981, *48*(4), pp. 649–52. [G: U.S.]

Hitchens, D. M. W. N. Life Insurance and Asset Holding in the United Kingdom: Comment. In *Currie, D.; Peel, D. and Peters, W., eds.*, 1981, pp. 165–68. [G: U.K.]

Holton, Richard H. Public Regulation of Consumer Information: The Life Insurance Industry Case. In *[Grether, E. T.]*, 1981, pp. 143–54.

Howard, Ronald A. The Risks of Benefit-Cost-Risk Analysis. In *Haimes, Y. Y., ed.*, 1981, pp. 135–47. [G: U.S.]

Hunt, Cecil. Insuring for Political Risk. In *Ensor, R., ed.*, 1981, pp. 137–42.

Johnson, Joseph E.; Flanigan, George B. and Weisbart, Steven N. Returns to Scale in the Property and Liability Insurance Industry. *J. Risk Ins.*, March 1981, *48*(1), pp. 18–45. [G: U.S.]

Kamath, Ravindra R. and Lin, Cheyeh. Factors Affecting the Cost of Participating Whole Life Insurance. *Nebr. J. Econ. Bus.*, Summer 1981, *20*(3), pp. 55–69. [G: U.S.]

Kass, David I. and Pautler, Paul A. Physician and Medical Society Influence on Blue Shield Plans: Effects on Physician Reimbursement. In *Olson, M., ed.*, 1981, pp. 321–38. [G: U.S.]

Khan, M. Y. and Singh, Preeti. Life Insurance Corporation and Corporate Control in India. *Indian Econ. J.*, October–December 1981, *29*(2), pp. 51–64.

Klevorick, Alvin K. The Health Professions: "The Dog that Didn't Bark?" Commentary. In *Olson, M., ed.*, 1981, pp. 407–13. [G: U.S.]

Kotlikoff, Laurence J. and Spivak, Avia. The Family as an Incomplete Annuities Market. *J. Polit. Econ.*, April 1981, *89*(2), pp. 372–91.

Kunreuther, Howard. Theory of Solvency Regulation in the Property and Casualty Insurance Industry: Comment. In *Fromm, G., ed.*, 1981, pp. 168–72.

Lane, David and Golen, Lawrence. Some Simulation-Based Estimates of Commercial Bank Deposit Insurance Premiums. In *Maisel, S. J., ed.*, 1981, pp. 341–65. [G: U.S.]

Larsen, Norma L. Policy Loan Utilization Factors in Dividend Distribution Formulas. *J. Risk Ins.*, March 1981, 48(1), pp. 80–94. [G: U.S.]

Larsen, Norma L. and Martin, Gerald D. Income Growth Factors: Error Introduced through the Application of Cohort Data. *J. Risk Ins.*, March 1981, 48(1), pp. 143–47.

Loubergé, Henri. The Management of Research in Risk and Insurance at the Geneva Association. *J. Risk Ins.*, June 1981, 48(2), pp. 309–21.

Lynch, Michael P. Theory of Solvency Regulation in the Property and Casualty Insurance Industry: Comment. In *Fromm, G., ed.*, 1981, pp. 173–79.

Lynk, William J. Regulatory Control of the Membership of Corporate Boards of Directors: The Blue Shield Case. *J. Law Econ.*, April 1981, 24(1), pp. 159–73. [G: U.S.]

Mayers, David and Smith, Clifford W., Jr. Contractual Provisions, Organizational Structure, and Conflict Control in Insurance Markets. *J. Bus.*, July 1981, 54(3), pp. 407–34.

McEwin, R. Ian. Liability Rules, Insurance and the Coase Theorem. *Australian J. Manage.*, December 1981, 6(2), pp. 103–17.

Merton, Robert C. Discussion [Risk and Capital Adequacy in Banks] [Capital Requirements for Entry into Property and Liability Underwriting: An empirical Examination]. In *Fed. Res. Bank of Boston and National Sci. Foundation*, 1981, pp. 256–63. [G: U.S.]

Munch, Patricia and Smallwood, Dennis. Theory of Solvency Regulation in the Property and Casualty Insurance Industry. In *Fromm, G., ed.*, 1981, pp. 119–67.

Oates, Wallace E. The Health Professions: "The Dog that Didn't Bark?": Commentary. In *Olson, M., ed.*, 1981, pp. 413–18. [G: U.S.]

Pinedo, Michael and Shpilberg, David. Stochastic Models with Memory for Seismic Risk Evaluation. *J. Risk Ins.*, March 1981, 48(1), pp. 46–58.

Praetz, Peter D. Returns to Scale in the Australian Life Insurance Industry. *Econ. Rec.*, September 1981, 57(158), pp. 269–76. [G: Australia]

Pupp, Roger L. Community Rating and Cross Subsidies in Health Insurance. *J. Risk Ins.*, December 1981, 48(4), pp. 610–27. [G: U.S.]

Rea, Samuel A., Jr. Consumption Stabilizing Annuities with Uncertain Inflation. *J. Risk Ins.*, December 1981, 48(4), pp. 596–609.

Ripoll, José. Transfer Prices in the Insurance Sector. In *Murray, R., ed.*, 1981, pp. 91–95.

Rolph, John E. Some Statistical Evidence on Merit Rating in Medical Malpractice Insurance. *J. Risk Ins.*, June 1981, 48(2), pp. 247–60. [G: U.S.]

Rose, Terry L. and Hand, John H. The Effects of Risk Reduction Inherent in Universal Life Insurance: Further Comment. *J. Risk Ins.*, December 1981, 48(4), pp. 682–89.

Ross, Stephen A. Some Stronger Measures of Risk Aversion in the Small and the Large with Applications. *Econometrica*, May 1981, 49(3), pp. 621–38.

Roussel, H. Lee and Rosenberg, Moses K. The High Price of "Reform": Title Insurance Rates and the Benefits of Rating Bureaus. *J. Risk Ins.*, December 1981, 48(4), pp. 638–48. [G: U.S.]

Schanz, Gerhard. Wäre die Einbeziehung der Versicherungswirtschaft in die Mindestreservepolitik kredittheoretisch gerechtfertigt? (Can Credit Theory Justify the Inclusion of the Insurance Business in Minimum Reserves Policy? With English summary.) *Kredit Kapital*, 1981, 14(1), pp. 52–73. [G: W. Germany]

Scheel, William C. The Effects of Risk Reduction Inherent in Universal Life Insurance: Author's Reply. *J. Risk Ins.*, December 1981, 48(4), pp. 690–93.

Schlesinger, Harris. The Optimal Level of Deductibility in Insurance Contracts. *J. Risk Ins.*, September 1981, 48(3), pp. 465–81.

Seidman, Laurence S. Consumer Choice Health Plan and the Patient Cost-Sharing Strategy: Can they be Reconciled? In *Olson, M., ed.*, 1981, pp. 450–66. [G: U.S.]

Serbein, Oscar N. Insurance and Reinsurance. In *Altman, E. I., ed.*, 1981, pp. 8.3–38. [G: U.S.]

Shorrocks, A. F. Life Insurance and Asset Holding in the United Kingdom. In *Currie, D.; Peel, D. and Peters, W., eds.*, 1981, pp. 139–64. [G: U.K.]

Silver, Murray. An Approximate Solution for the Unknown Rate of Interest: For an Annuity Certain. *J. Risk Ins.*, March 1981, 48(1), pp. 136–42.

Smith, Michael L. The Effects of Risk Reduction Inherent in Universal Life Insurance: Comment. *J. Risk Ins.*, December 1981, 48(4), pp. 674–81.

Smith, Michael L. Three Views of Life Insurance. *J. Risk Ins.*, June 1981, 48(2), pp. 334–50.

Smith, Michael L. and Bickelhaupt, David L. Is Coinsurance Becoming Obsolete? *J. Risk Ins.*, March 1981, 48(1), pp. 95–110. [G: U.S.]

Squires, Gregory D. and DeWolfe, Ruthanne. Insurance Redlining in Minority Communities. *Rev. Black Polit. Econ.*, Spring 1981, 11(3), pp. 347–64. [G: U.S.]

Tezel, Ahmet. Optimal Insurance Coverage. *Amer. Econ.*, Spring 1981, 25(1), pp. 70–71.

van de Ven, Wynand P. M. M. and van Praag, Bernard M. S. Risk Aversion and Deductibles in Private Health Insurance: Application of an Adjusted Tobit Model to Family Health Care Expenditures. In *van der Gaag, J. and Perlman, M., eds.*, 1981, pp. 125–48. [G: Netherlands]

van de Ven, Wynand P. M. M. and van Praag, Bernard M. S. The Demand for Deductibles in Private Health Insurance: A Probit Model with Sample Selection. *J. Econometrics*, November 1981, 17(2), pp. 229–52. [G: Netherlands]

Winter, Ralph A. On the Rate Structure of the American Life Insurance Market. *J. Finance*, March 1981, 36(1), pp. 81–96. [G: U.S.]

Witt, Robert C. On Positive Correlation between Means and Standard Deviations of Claims Ratios: Author's Reply: Underwriting Risk and Return: Some Additional Comments. *J. Risk Ins.*, December 1981, 48(4), pp. 653–61. [G: U.S.]

Wood, William C. Nuclear Liability after Three Mile

Island. *J. Risk Ins.*, September 1981, *48*(3), pp. 450–64. [G: U.S.]

6357 Real Estate

Barry, Peter J. Capital Asset Pricing and Farm Real Estate: Reply. *Amer. J. Agr. Econ.*, August 1981, *63*(3), pp. 580–81. [G: U.S.]

Bartlett, Randall. Property Rights and the Pricing of Real Estate Brokerage. *J. Ind. Econ.*, September 1981, *30*(1), pp. 79–94. [G: U.S.]

Beranek, William and Selby, Edward B., Jr. Accelerated Depreciation and Income Growth. *Amer. Real Estate Urban Econ. Assoc. J.*, Spring 1981, *9*(1), pp. 67–73. [G: U.S.]

Boddy, Martin. The Property Sector in Late Capitalism: The Case of Britain. In *Dear, M. and Scott, A. J.*, *eds.*, 1981, pp. 267–86. [G: U.K.]

Borins, Sandford F. Mieszkowski and Saper's Estimate of the Effects of Airport Noise on Property Values: A Comment. *J. Urban Econ.*, January 1981, *9*(1), pp. 125–28. [G: Canada]

Brueggeman, William B.; Fisher, Jeffrey D. and Stern, Jerrold J. Federal Income Taxes, Inflation and Holding Periods for Income-Producing Property. *Amer. Real Estate Urban Econ. Assoc. J.*, Summer 1981, *9*(2), pp. 148–64. [G: U.S.]

Carter, Colin. Capital Asset Pricing and Farm Real Estate: Comment. *Amer. J. Agr. Econ.*, August 1981, *63*(3), pp. 578–79. [G: U.S.]

Hite, Gailen L. and Sanders, Anthony B. Excess Depreciation and the Maximum Tax. *Amer. Real Estate Urban Econ. Assoc. J.*, Summer 1981, *9*(2), pp. 134–47. [G: U.S.]

Noguchi, Yukio. Economic Effects of Taxes on Land. (In Japanese. With English summary.) *Econ. Stud. Quart.*, December 1981, *32*(3), pp. 193–200.

Noguchi, Yukio. On the Intertemporal Non-Neutrality of Taxes on Land: A Dynamic Market Clearing Model. *Hitotsubashi J. Econ.*, June 1981, *22*(1), pp. 20–31.

Pratt, Richard T. and Ricks, R. Bruce. Real Estate Finance. In *Altman, E. I.*, *ed.*, 1981, pp. 23.3–33. [G: U.S.]

Roulac, Stephen E. How to Structure Real Estate Investment Management. *J. Portfol. Manage.*, Fall 1981, *8*(1), pp. 32–35. [G: U.S.]

Simons, Lawrence. Rental Housing: A Developer's Perspective. In *Weicher, J. C.; Villani, K. E. and Roistacher, E. A.*, *eds.*, 1981, pp. 49–53. [G: U.S.]

Yinger, John. A Search Model of Real Estate Broker Behavior. *Amer. Econ. Rev.*, September 1981, *71*(4), pp. 591–605.

6358 Entertainment, Recreation, Tourism

Ashman, Richard T. Proceedings of the Seminar on Energy: Statement. In *U.S. Congress, Joint Economic Committee (I)*, 1981, pp. 499–501. [G: U.S.]

Bartholomew, James. Leisure and Entertainment. In *Richardson, B. M. and Ueda, T.*, *eds.*, 1981, pp. 251–58. [G: Japan]

Bassett, Gilbert W., Jr. Point Spreads versus Odds.

J. Polit. Econ., August 1981, *89*(4), pp. 752–68.

Baumol, William J. and Baumol, Hilda. A Rejoinder to Schwarz [On Finances of the Performing Arts during Stagflation: Some Recent Data]. *J. Cult. Econ.*, December 1981, *5*(2), pp. 89–90. [G: U.S.]

Bolyard, Joan E. International Travel and Passenger Fares, 1980. *Surv. Curr. Bus.*, May 1981, *61*(5), pp. 29–34. [G: U.S.]

Brunk, Gregory G. A Test of the Friedman–Savage Gambling Model. *Quart. J. Econ.*, May 1981, *96*(2), pp. 341–48. [G: U.S.]

Chelius, James R. and Dworkin, James B. Arbitration and Salary Determination in Baseball. In *Dennis, B. D.*, *ed.*, 1981, pp. 105–12. [G: U.S.]

Cobb, William B. Tourism as a Positive Factor in the Mexican Economy and in Mexican Foreign Relations. In *McBride, R. H.*, *ed.*, 1981, pp. 178–91. [G: Mexican]

Conant, Michael. The Paramount Decrees Reconsidered. *Law Contemp. Probl.*, Autumn 1981, *44*(4), pp. 79–107. [G: U.S.]

Cooper, C. P. Spatial and Temporal Patterns of Tourist Behaviour. *Reg. Stud.*, 1981, *15*(5), pp. 359–71. [G: U.K.]

Cottle, Rex L. Economics of the Professional Golfers' Association Tour. *Soc. Sci. Quart.*, December 1981, *62*(4), pp. 721–34. [G: U.S.]

Currim, Imran S.; Weinberg, Charles B. and Wittink, Dick R. Design of Subscription Programs for a Performing Arts Series. *J. Cons. Res.*, June 1981, *8*(1), pp. 67–75. [G: U.S.]

Daly, George and Moore, William J. Externalities, Property Rights and the Allocation of Resources in Major League Baseball. *Econ. Inquiry*, January 1981, *19*(1), pp. 77–95. [G: U.S.]

DeBrock, Lawrence M. and Roth, Alvin E. Strike Two: Labor-Management Negotiations in Major League Baseball. *Bell J. Econ. (See Rand J. Econ. after 4/85)*, Autumn 1981, *12*(2), pp. 413–25. [G: U.S.]

Dunning, John H. and McQueen, Matthew. The Eclectic Theory of International Production: A Case Study of the International Hotel Industry. *Managerial Dec. Econ.*, December 1981, *2*(4), pp. 197–210. [G: Selected Countries]

Gapinski, James H. Economics, Demographics, and Attendance at the Symphony. *J. Cult. Econ.*, December 1981, *5*(2), pp. 79–83. [G: U.S.]

Garvin, David A. Blockbusters: The Economics of Mass Entertainment. *J. Cult. Econ.*, June 1981, *5*(1), pp. 1–20. [G: U.S.]

Gratton, Chris and Lisewski, Bernard. The Economics of Sport in Britain: A Case of Market Failure? *Brit. Rev. Econ. Issues*, Spring 1981, *2*(8), pp. 63–75. [G: U.K.]

Guthrie, Robert S. Taxing Horse Race Gambling: The Revenue Potential. *Public Finance Quart.*, January 1981, *9*(1), pp. 79–90.

Guthrie, Robert S. The Effect of Competition on Tax Revenues in the Casino Gaming Industry. *Nat. Tax J.*, June 1981, *34*(2), pp. 261–65. [G: U.S.]

Haahti, Antti and van den Heuvel, Rob. Positioning: Some Conceptual Observations with an Illustration. *Liiketaloudellinen Aikak.*, 1981, *30*(1), pp. 61–73.   [G: Finland]

Hansmann, Henry B. Nonprofit Enterprise in the Performing Arts. *Bell J. Econ. (See Rand J. Econ. after 4/85)*, Autumn 1981, *12*(2), pp. 341–61.

Hay, Michael J. and McConnell, Kenneth E. An Analysis of Participation in Nonconsumptive Wildlife Recreation: Reply. *Land Econ.*, May 1981, *57*(2), pp. 288–92.   [G: U.S.]

Henry, Louis H. The Economic Benefits of the Arts: A Neuropsychological Comment. *J. Cult. Econ.*, June 1981, *5*(1), pp. 52–60.

Horowitz, Harold. The UNESCO Framework for Cultural Statistics and a Cultural Data Bank for Europe. *J. Cult. Econ.*, December 1981, *5*(2), pp. 1–17.   [G: Europe]

Mabry, Mary C. and Mabry, Bevars D. The Left-Right Brain Controversy and Misinterpreted Authority. *J. Cult. Econ.*, December 1981, *5*(2), pp. 59–77.   [G: U.S.]

McConnell, Kenneth E. and Strand, Ivar E., Jr. Measuring the Cost of Time in Recreation Demand Analysis: An Application to Sportfishing. *Amer. J. Agr. Econ.*, February 1981, *63*(1), pp. 153–56.   [G: U.S.]

McFate, Patricia A. The Effects of Inflation on the Arts. *Ann. Amer. Acad. Polit. Soc. Sci.*, July 1981, *456*, pp. 70–87.   [G: U.S.]

Miller, Jon R. and Hay, Michael J. Determinants of Hunter Participation: Duck Hunting in the Mississippi Flyway. *Amer. J. Agr. Econ.*, November 1981, *63*(4), pp. 677–84.   [G: U.S.]

Miscimarra, Philip A. The Entertainment Industry: Inroads in Multinational Collective Bargaining. *Brit. J. Ind. Relat.*, March 1981, *19*(1), pp. 49–65.

Mokhov, N. The Economics, Planning, and Organization of Culture. *Prob. Econ.*, July 1981, *24*(3), pp. 36–54.   [G: U.S.S.R.]

Montias, J. M. Reflections on Historical Materialism, Economic Theory, and the History of Art in the Context of Renaissance and 17th Century Painting. *J. Cult. Econ.*, December 1981, *5*(2), pp. 19–38.

Morey, Edward R. The Demand for Site-Specific Recreational Activities: A Characteristics Approach. *J. Environ. Econ. Manage.*, December 1981, *8*(4), pp. 345–71.   [G: U.S.]

Richardson, James F. Vocal Recitals in Smaller Cities: Changes in Supply, Demand and Content since the 1920's. *J. Cult. Econ.*, June 1981, *5*(1), pp. 21–35.   [G: U.S.]

Schwarz, Samuel. The Facts First: A Reply to Baumol & Baumol [On Finances of the Performing Arts during Stagflation: Some Recent Data]. *J. Cult. Econ.*, December 1981, *5*(2), pp. 85–87.   [G: U.S.]

Seaman, Bruce A. An Assessment of Recent Applications of Economic Theory to the Arts. *J. Cult. Econ.*, June 1981, *5*(1), pp. 36–51.

Seaman, Bruce A. Economic Theory and the Positive Economics of Arts Financing. *Amer. Econ. Rev.*, May 1981, *71*(2), pp. 335–40.

Seow, Greg. Economic Significance of Tourism in Singapore. *Malayan Econ. Rev. (See Singapore Econ. Rev.)*, October 1981, *26*(2), pp. 64–79.   [G: Singapore]

Singer, Leslie P. Rivalry and Externalities in Secondary Art Markets. *J. Cult. Econ.*, December 1981, *5*(2), pp. 39–57.

Throckmorton, H. Bruce. A Bibliographical Note on Energy Conservation and Historic Preservation. *J. Cult. Econ.*, December 1981, *5*(2), pp. 91–94.   [G: U.S.]

Vaughan, William J. and Russell, Clifford S. An Analysis of Participation in Nonconsumptive Wildlife Recreation: Comment. *Land Econ.*, May 1981, *57*(2), pp. 279–87.   [G: U.S.]

Vermet-Desroches, Bernard. Interactions humaines et théorie des catastrophes: une application au comportement du vacancier. (Human Interaction and the Theory of Catastrophes: An Application to the Behaviour of the Holiday-Maker. With English summary.) *L'Actual. Econ.*, January–March 1981, *57*(1), pp. 54–69.   [G: Canada]

Wellington, Donald C. and Gallo, Joseph C. The March of the Toy Soldier: The Market for a Collectible. *J. Cult. Econ.*, June 1981, *5*(1), pp. 69–75.

Zech, Charles E. An Empirical Estimation of a Production Function: The Case of Major League Baseball. *Amer. Econ.*, Fall 1981, *25*(2), pp. 19–23.   [G: U.S.]

636 Nonprofit Industries: Theory and Studies

6360 Nonprofit Industries: Theory and Studies

Baumol, William J. and Baumol, Hilda. A Rejoinder to Schwarz [On Finances of the Performing Arts during Stagflation: Some Recent Data]. *J. Cult. Econ.*, December 1981, *5*(2), pp. 89–90.   [G: U.S.]

Berresford, Susan Vail. How Foundations View Funding Proposals on Working Women. In *Wertheimer, B. M., ed.*, 1981, pp. 233–40.   [G: U.S.]

Brannon, Gerard M. Charitable Contributions: Comments. In *Aaron, H. J. and Pechman, J. A., eds.*, 1981, pp. 437–41.   [G: U.S.]

Brittain, John A. Charitable Contributions: Comments. In *Aaron, H. J. and Pechman, J. A., eds.*, 1981, pp. 441–46.   [G: U.S.]

Cauvin, Pierre. Un modèle pour gérer les organismes de service à but non lucratif: la théorie des quatre corps. (A Management Model for Nonprofit Organizations: The Four Constituencies Theory. With English summary.) *Écon. Soc.*, October–November–December 1981, *15*(10–12), pp. 1593–1639.

Clotfelter, Charles T. and Steuerle, C. Eugene. Charitable Contributions. In *Aaron, H. J. and Pechman, J. A., eds.*, 1981, pp. 403–37.   [G: U.S.]

Cuninggim, Merrimon. The Foundation as a Nonbusiness Corporation. In *Novak, M. and Cooper, J. W., eds.*, 1981, pp. 181–92.

Eisenstadt, David and Kennedy, Thomas E. Control and Behavior of Nonprofit Firms: The Case of Blue Shield. *Southern Econ. J.*, July 1981, *48*(1), pp. 26–36.   [G: U.S.]

Frech, H. E., III and Ginsburg, Paul B. Property Rights and Competition in Health Insurance: Multiple Objectives for Nonprofit Firms. **In** *Zerbe, R. O., Jr., ed.,* 1981, pp. 155–71.
[G: U.S.]

Gambino, Anthony J. and Reardon, Thomas J. Financial Planning and Evaluation for the Nonprofit Organization. *Manage. Account.,* June 1981, *62*(12), pp. 50. [G: U.S.]

Greene, Vernon L. and Monahan, Deborah J. Structural and Operational Factors Affecting Quality of Patient Care in Nursing Homes. *Public Policy,* Fall 1981, *29*(4), pp. 399–415. [G: U.S.]

Hansmann, Henry B. Consumer Perceptions of Nonprofit Enterprise: Reply [The Role of Nonprofit Enterprise]. *Yale Law J.,* June 1981, *90*(7), pp. 1633–38.

Hansmann, Henry B. Nonprofit Enterprise in the Performing Arts. *Bell J. Econ. (See Rand J. Econ. after 4/85),* Autumn 1981, *12*(2), pp. 341–61.

Hansmann, Henry B. The Rationale for Exempting Nonprofit Organizations from Corporate Income Taxation. *Yale Law J.,* November 1981, *91*(1), pp. 54–100. [G: U.S.]

Hunter, Laurie. Comments on E. James and E. Neuberger [The University Department as a Non-Profit Labor Cooperative]. *Public Choice,* 1981, *36*(3), pp. 613–17.

James, Estelle and Neuberger, Egon. The University Department as a Non-Profit Labor Cooperative. *Public Choice,* 1981, *36*(3), pp. 585–612.

Kass, David I. and Pautler, Paul A. The Administrative Costs of Non-Profit Health Insurers. *Econ. Inquiry,* July 1981, *19*(3), pp. 515–21. [G: U.S.]

Keating, Barry P.; Pitts, Robert E. and Appel, David. United Way Contributions: Coercion, Charity or Economic Self-Interest? *Southern Econ. J.,* January 1981, *47*(3), pp. 816–23. [G: U.S.]

Kovner, Anthony R. Hospital Governance and Market Share. *Inquiry,* Fall 1981, *18*(3), pp. 255–65. [G: U.S.]

McEachern, William A. Tax-Exempt Property, Tax Capitalization, and the Cumulative-Urban-Decay Hypothesis. *Nat. Tax J.,* June 1981, *34*(2), pp. 185–92.

McFate, Patricia A. The Effects of Inflation on the Arts. *Ann. Amer. Acad. Polit. Soc. Sci.,* July 1981, *456*, pp. 70–87. [G: U.S.]

Permut, Steven E. Consumer Perceptions of Nonprofit Enterprise: A Comment on Hansmann [The Role of Nonprofit Enterprise]. *Yale Law J.,* June 1981, *90*(7), pp. 1623–32.

Pfeffer, Jeffrey and Leong, Anthony. Resource Allocations in United Funds: Examination of Power and Dependence. **In** *Martin, G. T., Jr., and Zald, M. N., eds.,* 1981, *1977,* pp. 246–62. [G: U.S.]

Reiner, Thomas A. and Wolpert, Julian. The Non-Profit Sector in the Metropolitan Economy. *Econ. Geogr.,* January 1981, *57*(1), pp. 23–33.
[G: U.S.]

Schwarz, Samuel. The Facts First: A Reply to Baumol & Baumol [On Finances of the Performing Arts during Stagflation: Some Recent Data]. *J. Cult. Econ.,* December 1981, *5*(2), pp. 85–87.
[G: U.S.]

Seaman, Bruce A. Economic Theory and the Positive Economics of Arts Financing. *Amer. Econ. Rev.,* May 1981, *71*(2), pp. 335–40.

Throckmorton, H. Bruce. A Bibliographical Note on Energy Conservation and Historic Preservation. *J. Cult. Econ.,* December 1981, *5*(2), pp. 91–94. [G: U.S.]

640 ECONOMIC CAPACITY

641 Economic Capacity

6410 Economic Capacity

Aivazian, Varouj A. and Callen, Jeffrey L. Capacity Expansion in the U.S. Natural-Gas Pipeline Industry. **In** *Cowing, T. G. and Stevenson, R. E., eds.,* 1981, pp. 145–59. [G: U.S.]

Berndt, Ernst R. and Morrison, Catherine J. Capacity Utilization Measures: Underlying Economic Theory and an Alternative Approach. *Amer. Econ. Rev.,* May 1981, *71*(2), pp. 48–52.
[G: U.S.]

Christiano, Lawrence J. A Survey of Measures of Capacity Utilization. *Int. Monet. Fund Staff Pap.,* March 1981, *28*(1), pp. 144–98. [G: U.S.]

De Vany, Arthur S. and Frey, N. G. Stochastic Equilibrium and Capacity Utilization. *Amer. Econ. Rev.,* May 1981, *71*(2), pp. 53–57.

Fal'tsman, V. The Capacity Equivalent of Fixed Capital. *Prob. Econ.,* May 1981, *24*(1), pp. 39–60.
[G: U.S.S.R.]

Foss, Murray F. Long-Run Changes in the Workweek of Fixed Capital. *Amer. Econ. Rev.,* May 1981, *71*(2), pp. 58–63.

Institute of Technological Research, Bogotá. Capacity of the Engineering Industry in Colombia. **In** *Bhalla, A. S., ed.,* 1981, *1975,* pp. 289–301.
[G: Colombia]

Oi, Walter Y. Slack Capacity: Productive or Wasteful? *Amer. Econ. Rev.,* May 1981, *71*(2), pp. 64–69.

Sengupta, Ram Prasad. Measurement of Steel Capacity: Bhilai Steel Plant—A Case Study. **In** *Bagchi, A. K. and Banerjee, N., eds.,* 1981, pp. 173–214. [G: India]

Spulber, Daniel F. Capacity, Output, and Sequential Entry. *Amer. Econ. Rev.,* June 1981, *71*(3), pp. 503–14.

Tatom, John A. Capital Utilization and Okun's Law. *Rev. Econ. Statist.,* February 1981, *63*(1), pp. 155–58. [G: U.S.]

You, Jong Keun. Capital Utilization and Okun's Law: A Reply. *Rev. Econ. Statist.,* February 1981, *63*(1), pp. 158–60. [G: U.S.]

700 Agriculture; Natural Resources

710 AGRICULTURE

7100 Agriculture

Abey, Arun; Booth, Anne and Sundrum, R. M. Labour Absorption in Indonesian Agriculture. *Bull. Indonesian Econ. Stud.,* March 1981, *17*(1), pp. 36–65. [G: Indonesia]

Ali, Karamat. Impact of Agricultural Modernization on Crude Birth Rate in Indian Punjab. *Pakistan*

Devel. Rev., Summer 1981, *20*(2), pp. 247–67.
[G: India]

Anderson, Walton J. Western Canadian Agriculture to 1990: A Review. *Can. J. Agr. Econ.*, July 1981, *29*(2), pp. 109–16. [G: Canada]

Auffret, Marc; Hau, Michel and Lévy-Leboyer, Maurice. Regional Inequalities and Economic Development: French Agriculture in the Nineteenth and Twentieth Centuries. In *Bairoch, P. and Lévy-Leboyer, M., eds.*, 1981, pp. 273–89.
[G: France]

Barbosa, Túlio. The Farm/Non-farm Interface with Special Reference to Rural Brazil. In *Johnson, G. and Maunder, A., eds.*, 1981, pp. 200–12.
[G: Brazil]

Barker, Randolph. Establishing Priorities for Allocating Funds to Rice Research. In *Johnson, G. and Maunder, A., eds.*, 1981, pp. 493–504.

Barnett, Tony. Evaluating the Gezira Scheme: Black Box or Pandora's Box. In *Heyer, J.; Roberts, P. and Williams, G., eds.*, 1981, pp. 306–24.
[G: Sudan]

Beckman, Bjorn. Ghana, 1951–78: The Agrarian Basis of the Post-colonial State. In *Heyer, J.; Roberts, P. and Williams, G., eds.*, 1981, pp. 143–67. [G: Ghana]

Beets, W. C. Towards a Strategy for Hill Agricultural Development in Nepal. In *Nepal, Ministry of Food and Agriculture*, 1981, pp. 209–15.
[G: Nepal]

Biggs, Stephen D. and Clay, Edward J. Sources of Innovation in Agricultural Technology. *World Devel.*, April 1981, *9*(4), pp. 321–36.

Bjarnason, Harold F. Accomplishments of and Opportunities for Agricultural Economists in Parastatal Organizations. In *Johnson, G. and Maunder, A., eds.*, 1981, pp. 520–27.

Boev, Vasily. Food Production for New Industrial Development Regions of the USSR. *Int. Lab. Rev.*, May–June 1981, *120*(3), pp. 351–60.
[G: U.S.S.R.]

Bolin, Olof. Regional Disparities in Agriculture: Comment. *Europ. Rev. Agr. Econ.*, 1981, *8*(2–3), pp. 211–12. [G: Europe]

Boulding, Kenneth E. Agricultural Economics in an Evolutionary Perspective. *Amer. J. Agr. Econ.*, December 1981, *63*(5), pp. 788–95.

Brandão, Antonio. Alternative Agricultural Development Models Commonly Advocated in Latin America. In *Johnson, G. and Maunder, A., eds.*, 1981, pp. 346–55. [G: Latin America]

Britton, Denis K. Fifty Years of Agricultural Economics—and What Next? In *Johnson, G. and Maunder, A., eds.*, 1981, pp. 3–11.

Bryson, Judy C. Women and Agriculture in sub-Saharan Africa: Implications for Development (An Exploratory Study) *J. Devel. Stud.*, April 1981, *17*(3), pp. 29–46. [G: sub-Saharan Africa]

Bullock, J. Bruce. Some Concepts for Measuring the Economic Value of Rural Data. *Amer. J. Agr. Econ.*, May 1981, *63*(2), pp. 346–52.

Busch, Lawrence and Sachs, Carolyn. The Agricultural Sciences and the Modern World System. In *Busch, L., ed.*, 1981, pp. 131–56.
[G: Selected Countries]

Cavaco, Carminda. A agricultura a tempo parcial: expansão, diversidade e significado económico, social e geográfico. (With English summary.) *Economia (Portugal)*, May 1981, *5*(2), pp. 271–313.
[G: Portugal]

Chan, M. W. Luke. An Econometric Model of the Canadian Agricultural Economy. *Can. J. Agr. Econ.*, November 1981, *29*(3), pp. 265–82.

Coffin, H. Garth. Western Canadian Agriculture to 1990: Blueprint or Mirage? *Can. J. Agr. Econ.*, July 1981, *29*(2), pp. 117–30. [G: Canada]

Collinson, Michael P. Micro-Level Accomplishments and Challenges for the Less Developed World. In *Johnson, G. and Maunder, A., eds.*, 1981, pp. 43–53.

Coyle, Barry T. and Lopez, Ramon E. A Comment on Bollman's "Off-Farm Work by Farmers: . . ." *Can. J. Agr. Econ.*, February 1981, *29*(1), pp. 93–99.

Cromarty, William A. Challenges for Agricultural Economists Working for Multi-national Firms. In *Johnson, G. and Maunder, A., eds.*, 1981, pp. 509–17.

Dabrowski, P. H. Regional Disparities in Agriculture. *Europ. Rev. Agr. Econ.*, 1981, *8*(2–3), pp. 199–209. [G: Europe]

Dahiphale, M. V. and Khadgi, P. P. Crop Care Service with Crop Insurance in Maharashtra. *Artha-Vikas*, January–December 1981, *17*(1–2), pp. 154–70. [G: India]

Davis, Jeffrey. The Relationship between the Economic Surplus and Production Function Approaches for Estimating Ex-Post Returns to Agricultural Research. *Rev. Marketing Agr. Econ.*, August 1981, *49*(2), pp. 95–105.

Day, Richard H. Understanding the Development of World Agriculture: Insights from Adaptive Economics. In *Johnson, G. and Maunder, A., eds.*, 1981, pp. 686–94.

Dewdney, John C. Agricultural Development in Turkey. In *[Fisher, W. B.]*, 1981, pp. 213–23.
[G: Turkey]

Due, Jean M. and Due, John F. Donor Finances of Agricultural Development in Southern Sudan—Development or Dependency? *J. Econ. Devel.*, December 1981, *6*(2), pp. 71–91.
[G: Sudan]

Elstrand, Eivind. Sub-Arctic Farming. In *Johnson, G. and Maunder, A., eds.*, 1981, pp. 57–73.
[G: N. America; N. Europe; U.S.S.R.]

Engerman, Stanley L. Agriculture as Business: The Southern Context. In *Bateman, F., ed.*, 1981, pp. 17–26. [G: U.S.]

Etienne, Gilbert. Rural Development in China and Its Impact on Foreign Trade. *Rivista Int. Sci. Econ. Com.*, September 1981, *28*(9), pp. 831–51.
[G: China]

Fako, Thabo. Development in Sub-Saharan Africa and the Decline of Folk Knowledge in Agriculture. In *Busch, L., ed.*, 1981, pp. 157–66.
[G: Africa]

Fedorova, M. The Utilization of Female Labor in Agriculture. *Prob. Econ.*, Sept.–Oct.–Nov. 1981, *24*(5–6–7), pp. 131–46. [G: U.S.S.R.]

Fekete, Ferenc. Accomplishments of and Challenges for Agricultural Economists Working at the National Level of Centrally Managed Economies.

In *Johnson, G. and Maunder, A., eds.*, 1981, pp. 285–94.

Fényes, Tamás I. Potential Applicability of Certain Socialistic Farming Practices for Rural Development in Non-Socialist Less Developed Countries. In *Johnson, G. and Maunder, A., eds.*, 1981, pp. 659–69.

Fienup, Darrell F. and Riley, Harold M. Training Agricultural Economists to Serve the Needs of a Changing World. In *Johnson, G. and Maunder, A., eds.*, 1981, pp. 632–42.   [G: U.S.; LDCs]

Figueroa, Adolfo. Effects of Changes in Consumption and Trade Patterns on Agricultural Development in Latin America. In *Baer, W. and Gillis, M., eds.*, 1981, pp. 83–97.   [G: Peru; Latin America]

Figueroa, Adolfo. Effects of Changes in Consumption and Trade Patterns on Agricultural Development in Latin America. *Quart. Rev. Econ. Bus.*, Summer 1981, *21*(2), pp. 83–97.
[G: Latin America]

Frankel, F. R. India's New Strategy of Agricultural Development: Political Costs of Agrarian Modernization. In *Livingstone, I., ed.*, 1981, *1969*, pp. 287–92.   [G: India]

Freebairn, J. W. Assessing Some Effects of Inflation on the Agricultural Sector. *Australian J. Agr. Econ.*, August 1981, *25*(2), pp. 107–22.
[G: Australia]

Fruin, Jerry E. Impacts on Agriculture of Deregulating the Transportation System: Discussion. *Amer. J. Agr. Econ.*, December 1981, *63*(5), pp. 923–25.   [G: U.S.]

Gardner, Bruce. On the Power of Macroeconomic Linkages to Explain Events in U.S. Agriculture. *Amer. J. Agr. Econ.*, December 1981, *63*(5), pp. 871–78.   [G: U.S.]

Ghodake, R. D.; Ryan, James G. and Sarin, R. Human Labour Use with Existing and Prospective Technologies in the Semi-Arid Tropics of South India. *J. Devel. Stud.*, October 1981, *18*(1), pp. 25–46.   [G: India]

Goodman, D. E. Rural Structure, Surplus Mobilisation and Modes of Production in a Peripheral Region: The Brazilian Northeast. In *Mitchell, S., ed.*, 1981, pp. 10–40.   [G: Brazil]

Grabowski, Richard. Induced Innovation, Green Revolution, and Income Distribution: Reply [The Implications of an Induced Innovation Model]. *Econ. Develop. Cult. Change*, October 1981, *30*(1), pp. 177–81.   [G: Asia]

Greig, I. D. Agricultural Research Management and the Ex Ante Evaluation of Research Proposals: A Review. *Rev. Marketing Agr. Econ.*, August 1981, *49*(2), pp. 73–94.

Guichaoua, André and Majerès, Jean. Agrarian Structure, Technology and Employment: Agricultural Development in Chile, 1955–65. *Int. Lab. Rev.*, September–October 1981, *120*(5), pp. 597–614.   [G: Chile]

Gusev, P. Trends in the Development of Collective and Cooperative Farm Property. *Prob. Econ.*, August 1981, *24*(4), pp. 76–96.   [G: U.S.S.R.]

Halliday, S. P.; Hill, P. J. and Stevenson, J. B. Early Agriculture in Scotland. In *Mercer, R., ed.*, 1981, pp. 55–65.   [G: U.K.]

Hardin, Lowell S. Emerging Roles of Agricultural Economists Working in International Research Institutions such as IRRI and CIMMYT. In *Johnson, G. and Maunder, A., eds.*, 1981, pp. 479–90.   [G: Selected LDCs]

Harte, L. N. Farmer Taxation Equity and Incentive—A Literature Review. *Irish J. Agr. Econ. Rural Soc.*, 1981, *8*(2), pp. 167–77.

Hayami, Yujiro. Induced Innovation, Green Revolution, and Income Distribution: Comment [The Implications of an Induced Innovation Model]. *Econ. Develop. Cult. Change*, October 1981, *30*(1), pp. 169–76.   [G: Asia]

Heady, Earl O. Micro-Level Accomplishments and Challenges for the Developed World. In *Johnson, G. and Maunder, A., eds.*, 1981, pp. 29–40.

Heyer, Judith. Agricultural Development Policy in Kenya from the Colonial Period to 1975. In *Heyer, J.; Roberts, P. and Williams, G., eds.*, 1981, pp. 90–120.   [G: Kenya]

Hirashima, S. Some Issues in Indian Agriculture Viewed from the Japanese Experience. In *Sarma, J. S.*, 1981, pp. 59–69.   [G: India; Japan]

Ignatovsky, Pavel A. Agriculture. In *Novosti Press Agency*, 1981, pp. 143–75.   [G: U.S.S.R.]

Jewell, Peter. A Summing-Up. In *Mercer, R., ed.*, 1981, pp. 223–30.   [G: U.K.]

Johnson, Marc A. Impacts on Agriculture of Deregulating the Transportation System. *Amer. J. Agr. Econ.*, December 1981, *63*(5), pp. 913–20.
[G: U.S.]

Johnston, Bruce F. Criteria for the Design of Agricultural Development Strategies. In *Livingstone, I., ed.*, 1981, *1972*, pp. 297–304.

Kao, C. H. C.; Anschel, K. R. and Eicher, C. K. Disguised Unemployment in Agriculture: A Survey. In *Livingstone, I., ed.*, 1981, *1964*, pp. 59–66.   [G: Greece; India; Italy; Thailand]

Kennedy, John O. S. Applications of Dynamic Programming to Agriculture, Forestry and Fisheries: Review and Prognosis. *Rev. Marketing Agr. Econ.*, December 1981, *49*(3), pp. 141–73.

Kisiel, Michal. Links of Polish Agriculture with the World Economy. In *Johnson, G. and Maunder, A., eds.*, 1981, pp. 338–44.   [G: Poland]

Kost, William E. The Agricultural Component in Macroeconomic Models. *Agr. Econ. Res.*, July 1981, *33*(3), pp. 1–10.   [G: LDCs; MDCs]

Ladejinsky, W. Ironies of India's Green Revolution. In *Livingstone, I., ed.*, 1981, *1970*, pp. 293–96.
[G: India]

Lechi, F. Agricultural Policies and Their Regional Impact in Western Europe: Comment. *Europ. Rev. Agr. Econ.*, 1981, *8*(2–3), pp. 283–85.
[G: EEC]

Lerohl, M. L. The Canada West Report—Recipe for Western Agriculture? *Can. J. Agr. Econ.*, July 1981, *29*(2), pp. 131–40.   [G: Canada]

Lewis, W. Arthur. Development Strategy in a Limping World Economy. In *Johnson, G. and Maunder, A., eds.*, 1981, pp. 12–26. [G: U.S.; LDCs]

Liang, Ernest P. L. Market Accessibility and Agricultural Development in Prewar China. *Econ. Develop. Cult. Change*, October 1981, *30*(1), pp. 77–105.   [G: China]

Maggard, Sally. From Farmers to Miners: The Decline of Agriculture in Eastern Kentucky. In *Busch, L., ed.*, 1981, pp. 25–66. **[G: U.S.]**

Malingreau, J. P. Use of Remote Sensing for Agricultural Planning in Upland Areas. In *Nepal, Ministry of Food and Agriculture*, 1981, pp. 203–08.

Mandle, Jay R. The Economic Underdevelopment of the United States South in the Post-Bellum Era. In *Bairoch, P. and Lévy-Leboyer, M., eds.*, 1981, pp. 86–97. **[G: U.S.]**

Mazoyer, Marcel L. Origins and Mechanisms of Reproduction of the Regional Discrepancies in Agricultural Development in Europe. *Europ. Rev. Agr. Econ.*, 1981, 8(2–3), pp. 177–96.
[G: Europe]

McGuire, Robert A. Economic Causes of Late-Nineteenth Century Agrarian Unrest: New Evidence. *J. Econ. Hist.*, December 1981, 41(4), pp. 835–52. **[G: U.S.]**

McLean, Ian W. The Analysis of Agricultural Productivity: Alternative Views and Victorian Evidence. *Australian Econ. Hist. Rev.*, March 1981, 21(1), pp. 6–28. **[G: Australia]**

McPherson, W. W. and Langham, Max R. Commercial Agriculture in Historical Perspective. *Amer. J. Agr. Econ.*, December 1981, 63(5), pp. 894–901. **[G: U.S.]**

Mellor, John W. World Food Production, Consumption, and International Trade: Implications for U.S. Agriculture: Comment. In *Johnson, D. G., ed.*, 1981, pp. 147–49.

Menzie, Elmer L. and Anderson, Teresa. Agricultural Economists in Canada: Graduates and Prospects. *Can. J. Agr. Econ.*, February 1981, 29(1), pp. 87–92. **[G: Canada]**

Mercer, Roger. Farming Practice in British Prehistory: Introduction. In *Mercer, R., ed.*, 1981, pp. ix–xxvi. **[G: U.K.]**

Millar, James R. The Prospects for Soviet Agriculture. In *Bornstein, M., ed.*, 1981, 1977, pp. 273–91. **[G: U.S.S.R.]**

Miller, Thomas A. Some Concepts for Measuring the Economic Value of Rural Data: Discussion. *Amer. J. Agr. Econ.*, May 1981, 63(2), pp. 363–64.

Mohammadi, S. Buik. American Capitalism and Agricultural Development. In *Busch, L., ed.*, 1981, pp. 9–24. **[G: U.S.]**

Mundlak, Yair. Agricultural Growth—Formulation, Evaluation and Policy Consequences. In *Johnson, G. and Maunder, A., eds.*, 1981, pp. 672–84.

Murray, J.; Gandrie, D. and Jowett, D. Corporate Farm Laws and Farm Size: A Case Study. *Reg. Sci. Persp.*, 1981, 11(1), pp. 71–82. **[G: U.S.]**

Nazarenko, Victor J. Accomplishments and Challenges for the Future for Agricultural Economists Working in COMECON. In *Johnson, G. and Maunder, A., eds.*, 1981, pp. 407–13.
[G: CMEA]

Nazarenko, Victor J. Origins and Mechanisms of Reproduction of the Regional Discrepancies in Agricultural Development in Europe: Comment. *Europ. Rev. Agr. Econ.*, 1981, 8(2–3), pp. 197–98. **[G: Europe]**

Nicol, Kenneth J. Farm Sector Data: Presentation and Improvement. *Amer. J. Agr. Econ.*, May 1981, 63(2), pp. 353–60. **[G: U.S.]**

Norgaard, Richard B. Sociosystem and Ecosystem Coevolution in the Amazon. *J. Environ. Econ. Manage.*, September 1981, 8(3), pp. 238–54.
[G: Brazil]

Norton, George W. and Davis, Jeffrey S. Evaluating Returns to Agricultural Research: A Review. *Amer. J. Agr. Econ.*, November 1981, 63(4), pp. 685–99. **[G: U.S.]**

O'Connor, Robert. The Current Agricultural Situation. *Irish Banking Rev.*, June 1981, pp. 10–16.
[G: Ireland]

Ojala, Eric M. Accomplishments and Opportunities of Agricultural Economists Working in International Agencies. In *Johnson, G. and Maunder, A., eds.*, 1981, pp. 391–403.

Ong, S. E. Nepal's Experience in Hill Agricultural Development: A Seminar Summary. In *Nepal, Ministry of Food and Agriculture*, 1981, pp. 1–15. **[G: Nepal]**

Paarlberg, Don. The Land Grant Colleges and the Structure Issue. *Amer. J. Agr. Econ.*, February 1981, 63(1), pp. 129–34. **[G: U.S.]**

Pant, T. N. and Thapa, G. B. Development Potentials of Nepal's Hill Agriculture. In *Nepal, Ministry of Food and Agriculture*, 1981, pp. 19–28.
[G: Nepal]

Perkins, J. A. The Agricultural Revolution in Germany, 1850–1914. *J. Europ. Econ. Hist.*, Spring 1981, 10(1), pp. 71–118. **[G: Germany]**

Petit, Michel. Agriculture and Regional Development in Europe—The Role of Agricultural Economists. *Europ. Rev. Agr. Econ.*, 1981, 8(2–3), pp. 137–53. **[G: Europe]**

Petit, Michel. Teaching Marxist Economics to Agricultural Economics Students in non-Marxist Countries. In *Johnson, G. and Maunder, A., eds.*, 1981, pp. 645–56.

Pinstrup-Andersen, Per. Economic Theory Needed in Studying the Economics of Getting Poorer While Redistributing. In *Johnson, G. and Maunder, A., eds.*, 1981, pp. 369–78.

Pollard, H. J. The Personal Factor in the Success of Planned Agricultural Development Schemes. *J. Devel. Areas*, July 1981, 15(4), pp. 561–83.
[G: Trinidad]

Renborg, Ulf. Energy Analysis of Agriculture, Biology or Economics—A Survey of Approaches, Problems and Traps. In *Johnson, G. and Maunder, A., eds.*, 1981, pp. 231–41. **[G: Sweden]**

Ritson, Christopher. Accomplishments and Opportunities for Agricultural Economists on the Theoretical Front. In *Johnson, G. and Maunder, A., eds.*, 1981, pp. 605–17.

Rodefeld, Richard D. Farm Sector Data: Presentation and Improvement: Discussion. *Amer. J. Agr. Econ.*, May 1981, 63(2), pp. 365–66. **[G: U.S.]**

Ruttan, Vernon W. Three Cases of Induced Institutional Innovation. In *Russell, C. S. and Nicholson, N. K., eds.*, 1981, pp. 239–70. **[G: Argentina; Philippines; Thailand]**

Sain, Inder; Singh, A. J. and Joshi, A. S. Inter-Temporal Shifts in Income, Expenditure and Investment Pattern in the Punjab Agriculture. *Econ. Aff.*, October–December 1981, 26(4), pp. 257–60. **[G: India]**

Schultz, Frederick H. Statement to Subcommittee

on Agriculture and Transportation, Joint Economic Committee, December 1, 1981. *Fed. Res. Bull.*, December 1981, 67(12), pp. 893–95.
[G: U.S.]

Sebestyén, Joseph. Accomplishments, Opportunities and Needs of Agricultural Economists vis-à-vis Quantitative Techniques. In *Johnson, G. and Maunder, A., eds.,* 1981, pp. 620–28.

Sen, Abhijit. Market Failure and Control of Labour Power: Towards an Explanation of 'Structure' and Change in Indian Agriculture: Part 1. *Cambridge J. Econ.,* September 1981, 5(3), pp. 201–28.

Sen, Abhijit. Market Failure and Control of Labour Power: Towards an Explanation of 'Structure' and Change in Indian Agriculture. Part 2. *Cambridge J. Econ.,* December 1981, 5(4), pp. 327–50.
[G: India]

Shah, C. H. Accomplishments, Present Status and Future Opportunities for Agricultural Economists in the Planning Processes in Less Developed Economies. In *Johnson, G. and Maunder, A., eds.,* 1981, pp. 247–57.

Shah, S. L. Agricultural Planning and Development in the North-western Himalayas, India. In *Nepal, Ministry of Food and Agriculture,* 1981, pp. 160–68.
[G: India]

Shepherd, Andrew. Agrarian Change in Northern Ghana: Public Investment, Capitalist Farming and Famine. In *Heyer, J.; Roberts, P. and Williams, G., eds.,* 1981, pp. 168–92. [G: Ghana]

Sinclair, Sol. The Function of the CAES Workshop: Past Performance and Suggestions for the Future. *Can. J. Agr. Econ.,* November 1981, 29(3), pp. 257–64. [G: Canada]

Soubeyroux, Nicole. The Spread of Agricultural Growth over the Departments of France from the Mid-nineteenth to the Mid-twentieth Century. In *Bairoch, P. and Lévy-Leboyer, M., eds.,* 1981, pp. 290–301. [G: France]

Stark, Oded. The Asset Demand for Children during Agricultural Modernization. *Population Devel. Rev.,* December 1981, 7(4), pp. 671–75.

Thimm, Heinz-Ulrich. The Challenges for Western European Teachers of Agricultural Economics in Educating for Agrarian Change in their Own and Developing Countries. In *Johnson, G. and Maunder, A., eds.,* 1981, pp. 589–601.

Thirlwall, A. P. The Valuation of Labour in Surplus Labour Economies: A Synoptic View. In *Livingstone, I., ed.,* 1981, *1971,* pp. 245–53.

Thompson, Robert L. On the Power of Macroeconomic Linkages to Explain Events in U.S. Agriculture: Discussion. *Amer. J. Agr. Econ.,* December 1981, 63(5), pp. 888–90. [G: U.S.]

Tomic, Dušan. The Regional Economic Development and Political Aims, Methods and Measures in the Regional Development of Agriculture: The Yugoslav Example. *Europ. Rev. Agr. Econ.,* 1981, 8(2–3), pp. 287–314. [G: Yugoslavia]

de Veer, Jan. Theory, Analysis and Methodology. *Europ. Rev. Agr. Econ.,* 1981, 8(2–3), pp. 409–24. [G: W. Europe]

Weinschenck, Günther and Kemper, Jutta. Agricultural Policies and Their Regional Impact in Western Europe. *Europ. Rev. Agr. Econ.,* 1981, 8(2–3), pp. 251–81. [G: EEC]

Wong, C. T. and Tse, K. L. Hill Agricultural Development in Hongkong. In *Nepal, Ministry of Food and Agriculture,* 1981, pp. 153–59.
[G: Hong Kong]

Woodman, Harold D. Agriculture and Business in the Postbellum South: The Transformation of a Slave Society. In *Bateman, F., ed.,* 1981, pp. 51–61. [G: U.S.]

Wu, Zhan. The Development of Socialist Agriculture in China. In *Johnson, G. and Maunder, A., eds.,* 1981, pp. 273–80. [G: China]

Wyeth, Peter. Economic Development in Kenyan Agriculture. In *Killick, T., ed.,* 1981, pp. 299–310. [G: Kenya]

Zapata, Juan Antonio and Siamwalla, Ammar. Un esquema para el análisis de la distribución de beneficios de proyectos de riego. (With English summary.) *Cuadernos Econ.,* April 1981, 18(53), pp. 89–95.

711 Agricultural Supply and Demand Analysis

7110 Agricultural Supply and Demand Analysis

Abouchar, Alan. The Weakness of Soviet Agriculture. *Challenge,* July/August 1981, 24(3), pp. 53–55. [G: U.S.S.R.]

Adrian, John L.; Dunkelberger, John E. and Molnar, Joseph J. Agricultural Economics Students at Southern Land Grant Universities. *Southern J. Agr. Econ.,* July 1981, 13(1), pp. 133–38.
[G: U.S.]

Ahn, Choong Yong; Singh, Inderjit and Squire, Lyn. A Model of an Agricultural Household in a Multi-Crop Economy: The Case of Korea. *Rev. Econ. Statist.,* November 1981, 63(4), pp. 520–25.
[G: Korea]

Anatskov, Vasil. Problems of Management of Production Stocks at Agricultural Organizations in the Bulgarian People's Republic. In *Chikán, A., ed. (II),* 1981, pp. 11–21. [G: Bulgaria]

Anderson, Jock R. and Griffiths, William E. Production Risk and Input Use: Pastoral Zone of Eastern Australia. *Australian J. Agr. Econ.,* August 1981, 25(2), pp. 149–59. [G: Australia]

Anderson, Jock R., et al. A Dynamic Simulation Model of the World Jute Economy. *Europ. Econ. Rev.,* June/July 1981, 16(2/3), pp. 303–31.

Balaam, David N. East and Southeast Asian Food Systems: Structural Constraints, Political Arenas, and Appropriate Food Strategies. In *Balaam, D. N. and Carey, M. J., eds.,* 1981, pp. 106–42.
[G: Asia]

Bale, Malcolm D. The Role of Export Cropping in Less Developed Countries: Discussion. *Amer. J. Agr. Econ.,* May 1981, 63(2), pp. 396–98.

Barbiroli, Giancarlo; Ballini, Vladimiro and Savio, Giorgio. The Effect of Technological Development on Renewable Raw Materials. A Look at the International Situation. *Econ. Notes,* 1981, 10(1), pp. 104–21. [G: Selected Countries]

Barker, Randolph; Gabler, Eric C. and Winkelmann, Donald. Long-term Consequences of Technological Change on Crop Yield Stability: The Case for Cereal Grain. In *Valdés, A.,* 1981, pp. 53–78.   [G: Selected Countries]

Barrett, Greg. Contraction of the New South Wales Dairy Industry: 1970–80. *Quart. Rev. Rural Econ.*, November 1981, *3*(4), pp. 345–50.
[G: Australia]

Baum, Kenneth; Safyurtlu, Ali N. and Purcell, Wayne. Analyzing the Economic Impact of National Beef Import Level Changes on the Virginia Beef and Pork Sectors. *Southern J. Agr. Econ.*, December 1981, *13*(2), pp. 111–18.   [G: U.S.]

Belongia, Mike. A Note on the Specification of Wage Rates in Cost-Push Models of Food Price Determination. *Southern J. Agr. Econ.*, December 1981, *13*(2), pp. 119–24.   [G: U.S.]

Bentley, Ernest and Shumway, C. Richard. Adaptive Planning over the Cattle Price Cycle. *Southern J. Agr. Econ.*, July 1981, *13*(1), pp. 139–48.
[G: U.S.]

Berck, Peter. Portfolio Theory and the Demand for Futures: The Case of California Cotton. *Amer. J. Agr. Econ.*, August 1981, *63*(3), pp. 466–74.
[G: U.S.]

Bigman, David. Buffer Stocks and Domestic Price Policies. In *Chikán, A., ed. (1)*, 1981, pp. 49–61.

Blanks, Robert and Jones, Harvey. Horticultural Industries: Survey Results for 1978–79 and Income Estimates for 1979–80 and 1980–81. *Quart. Rev. Rural Econ.*, February 1981, *3*(1), pp. 58–66.
[G: Australia]

Boserup, Ester. Indian Agriculture from the Perspective of Western Europe. In *Sarma, J. S.*, 1981, pp. 55–58.   [G: India; W. Europe]

Bourke, I. J. Forecasting Beef Prices: A Reply [Comparing the Box–Jenkins and Econometric Techniques for Forecasting Beef Prices]. *Rev. Marketing Agr. Econ.*, August 1981, *49*(2), pp. 125–26.

Boyle, G. Input Substitution and Technical Change in Irish Agriculture—1953–1977. *Econ. Soc. Rev.*, April 1981, *12*(3), pp. 149–61.
[G: Ireland]

Brown, Randall S. and Christensen, Laurits R. Estimating Elasticities of Substitution in a Model of Partial Static Equilibrium: An Application to U.S. Agriculture, 1947 to 1974. In *Berndt, E. R. and Field, B. C., eds.*, 1981, pp. 209–29.   [G: U.S.]

Calkins, Peter. Small Farm Structure and Output in Selected Regions of Nepal, Taiwan and the United States. In *Johnson, G. and Maunder, A., eds.*, 1981, pp. 75–85. [G: U.S.; Nepal; Taiwan]

Campbell, John. American Leaf Exports on Decline: Imperial Tobacco Limited Closes Its Last American Primary-Processing Plant. In *Finger, W. R., ed.*, 1981, pp. 145–49.   [G: U.S.; U.K.]

de Castro Andrade, Regis. On the Relationship between the Subsistence Sector and the Market Economy in the Parnaíba Valley. In *Mitchell, S., ed.*, 1981, pp. 109–32.   [G: Brazil]

Chadha, G. K. Farm Size, Tenancy and Output Gains of Modern Wheat Technology: Case Study of Punjab (India) *Pakistan Econ. Soc. Rev.*, Summer 1981, *19*(1), pp. 1–23.   [G: India]

Chambers, Robert G. and Just, Richard E. Effects of Exchange Rate Changes on U.S. Agriculture: A Dynamic Analysis. *Amer. J. Agr. Econ.*, February 1981, *63*(1), pp. 32–46.   [G: U.S.]

Chan, M. W. Luke. A Markovian Approach to the Study of the Canadian Cattle Industry. *Rev. Econ. Statist.*, February 1981, *63*(1), pp. 107–16.
[G: Canada]

Chang, T. Y. Developing Agricultural Production in Tibet, China. In *Nepal, Ministry of Food and Agriculture*, 1981, pp. 147–52.   [G: China]

Chaudhury, Rafiqul Huda. Population Pressure and Agricultural Productivity in Bangladesh. *Bangladesh Devel. Stud.*, Monsoon 1981, *9*(3), pp. 67–88.   [G: Bangladesh]

Chavas, Jean-Paul and Johnson, S. R. An Econometric Model of the US Egg Industry. *Appl. Econ.*, September 1981, *13*(3), pp. 321–35.   [G: U.S.]

Chinn, Dennis L. A Calorie-Arbitrage Model of Chinese Grain Trade. *J. Devel. Stud.*, July 1981, *17*(4), pp. 357–70.   [G: China]

Chotigeat, Tosporn. Crop Diversification, Factor Substitution, and Relative Factor Shares in Thai Agriculture. *Indian Econ. Rev.*, January–June 1981, *16*(1 and 2), pp. 117–37.   [G: Thailand]

Coffey, Joseph D. The Role of Food in the International Affairs of the United States. *Southern J. Agr. Econ.*, July 1981, *13*(1), pp. 29–37.
[G: U.S.]

Collins, Keith J. and Glade, Edward H., Jr. Regional and Functional Disaggregation of the Cotton Industry in a National Input–Output Model. *Southern J. Agr. Econ.*, July 1981, *13*(1), pp. 111–18.   [G: U.S.]

Craven, Kathryn and Tuluy, A. Hasan. Rice Policy in Senegal. In *Pearson, S. R.; Stryker, J. D. and Humphreys, C. P., et al.*, 1981, pp. 229–62.
[G: Senegal]

Crellin, Ian. White Grape Supply to 1985: Implications for the Wine Industry. *Quart. Rev. Rural Econ.*, November 1981, *3*(4), pp. 336–44.
[G: Australia]

Dams, Theodor. Synoptic View. In *Johnson, G. and Maunder, A., eds.*, 1981, pp. 710–27.

Davis, Jeffrey S. A Comparison of Procedures for Estimating Returns to Research Using Production Functions. *Australian J. Agr. Econ.*, April 1981, *25*(1), pp. 60–72.   [G: Australia]

Dey, Jennie. Gambian Women: Unequal Partners in Rice Development Projects? *J. Devel. Stud.*, April 1981, *17*(3), pp. 109–22.   [G: Gambia]

Ellman, Michael. Agricultural Productivity under Socialism. *World Devel.*, September/October 1981, *9*(9/10), pp. 979–89. [G: China; U.S.S.R.]

Elstrand, Eivind. Sub-Arctic Farming. In *Johnson, G. and Maunder, A., eds.*, 1981, pp. 57–73.
[G: N. America; N. Europe; U.S.S.R.]

Emerson, Peter M. Prospective Changes in U.S. Agricultural Structure: Comment. In *Johnson, D. G., ed.*, 1981, pp. 149–53.   [G: U.S.]

Engler, Joaquim J. C. Small Farm Structure and Output in Selected Regions of Nepal, Taiwan and the United States: Discussion. In *Johnson, G. and Maunder, A., eds.*, 1981, pp. 85–87.
[G: Taiwan; Nepal; U.S.]

Felix, F. The Effect of Rainfall on Sugar Cane Yields at Frome. *Soc. Econ. Stud.*, September 1981, *30*(3), pp. 104–18.   [G: Jamaica]

Franco, G. Robert. The Optimal Producer Price of Cocoa in Ghana. *J. Devel. Econ.*, February 1981,

8(1), pp. 77–92. [G: Ghana]

Furtan, W. Hartley and Gray, Richard S. The Translog Production Function: Application to Saskatchewan Agriculture. *Can. J. Agr. Econ.*, February 1981, 29(1), pp. 82–86. [G: Canada]

Ganzel, Richard. Regionalism, Food Policy, and Domestic Political Economy: Lessons from Latin America. In *Balaam, D. N. and Carey, M. J.*, *eds.*, 1981, pp. 83–105. [G: Latin America]

García, Jorge García. The Nature of Food Insecurity in Colombia. In *Valdés, A.*, 1981, pp. 123–42. [G: Colombia]

Gellatly, Colin. Forecasting N.S.W. Beef Production: A Reply [Forecasting N.S.W. Beef Production: An Evaluation of Alternative Techniques]. *Rev. Marketing Agr. Econ.*, August 1981, 49(2), pp. 127–30.

Gessner, Dieter. The Dilemma of German Agriculture during the Weimar Republic. In *Bessel, R. and Feuchtwanger, E. J.*, *eds.*, 1981, pp. 134–54. [G: Germany]

Ghatak, Subrata; Turner, Kerry and Ghatak, Anita. Benefits and Costs of Pesticide Use and Some Policy Implications for Less Developed Countries. In *Chatterji, M.*, *ed.*, 1981, pp. 103–24. [G: LDCs]

Ghoshal, Animesh. The Effect of the Embargo on Grain Exports to the Soviet Union on the Exchange Rate. *Nebr. J. Econ. Bus.*, Summer 1981, 20(3), pp. 37–46. [G: U.S.; U.S.S.R.]

Gill, Gerard J. Is There a 'Draught Power Constraint' on Bangladesh Agriculture? *Bangladesh Devel. Stud.*, Monsoon 1981, 9(3), pp. 1–20. [G: Bangladesh]

Goldin, Claudia Dale. Credit Merchandising in the New South: The Role of Competition and Risk. In *Walton, G. M. and Shepherd, J. F.*, *eds.*, 1981, pp. 3–23. [G: U.S.]

Goldman, Richard H. and Overholt, Catherine A. Agricultural Production, Technical Change, and Nutritional Goals. In *Austin, J. E. and Zeitlin, M. F.*, *eds.*, 1981, pp. 111–21.

Golladay, Fredrick L. Productivity Problems in Developing Countries. In *Hogan, J. D. and Craig, A. M.*, *eds.*, *Vol. 1*, 1981, pp. 737–49. [G: LDCs]

Goreux, Louis M. Compensatory Financing for Fluctuations in the Cost of Cereal Imports. In *Valdés, A.*, 1981, pp. 307–32. [G: LDCs]

Goueli, Ahmed A. Food Security Program in Egypt. In *Valdés, A.*, 1981, pp. 143–57. [G: Egypt]

Gray, H. Peter. Oil-Push Inflation: A Broader Examination. *Banca Naz. Lavoro Quart. Rev.*, March 1981, (136), pp. 49–67.

Gray, Kenneth R. Soviet Consumption of Food: Is the Bottle "Half-Full," "Half-Empty," "Half-Water," or "Too Expensive"? *ACES Bull. (See Comp. Econ. Stud. after 8/85)*, Summer 1981, 23(2), pp. 31–50. [G: U.S.S.R.]

Grewal, S. S. and Chatha, I. S. Prospects of Foodgrain Production in Punjab. *Econ. Aff.*, January–March 1981, 26(1), pp. 17–24. [G: India]

Grogan, C. O. Prospects for Plant Genetics on the Great Plains. In *Lawson, M. P. and Baker, M. E.*, *eds.*, 1981, pp. 157–68. [G: U.S.]

Harper-Fender, Ann. Discouraging the Use of a Common Resource: The Crees of Saskatchewan. *J. Econ. Hist.*, March 1981, 41(1), pp. 163–70. [G: Canada]

Heady, Earl O. and Short, Cameron. Interrelationship among Export Markets, Resource Conservation, and Agricultural Productivity. *Amer. J. Agr. Econ.*, December 1981, 63(5), pp. 840–47. [G: U.S.]

Herer, W. and Sadowski, WL. Costs of Accelerating Agricultural Expansion. In *[Lipiński, E.]*, 1981, pp. 195–212. [G: Poland]

Hill, R. Carter; Ziemer, Rod F. and White, Fred C. Mitigating the Effects of Multicollinearity Using Exact and Stochastic Restrictions: The Case of an Aggregate Agricultural Production Function in Thailand: Comment. *Amer. J. Agr. Econ.*, May 1981, 63(2), pp. 298–300. [G: Thailand]

Hillman, Gordon. Reconstructing Crop Husbandry Practices from Charred Remains of Crops. In *Mercer, R.*, *ed.*, 1981, pp. 123–62. [G: U.K.]

Hillman, Jimmye S. Policy Issues Relevant to United States Agricultural Trade. In *McCalla, A. F. and Josling, T. E.*, *eds.*, 1981, pp. 113–42. [G: U.S.]

Hillman, Jimmye S. The Role of Export Cropping in Less Developed Countries. *Amer. J. Agr. Econ.*, May 1981, 63(2), pp. 375–83. [G: LDCs]

Hopcraft, David. Nature's Technology. In *Coomer, J. C.*, *ed.*, 1981, pp. 211–24.

Huddleston, Barbara and Konandreas, Panos. Insurance Approach to Food Security: Simulation of Benefits for 1970/71–1975/76 and for 1978–1982. In *Valdés, A.*, 1981, pp. 241–54. [G: LDCs]

Hueckel, G. Agriculture during Industrialisation. In *Floud, R. and McCloskey, D.*, *eds.*, *Vol. 1*, 1981, pp. 182–203. [G: U.K.]

Humphreys, Charles P. Rice Production in the Ivory Coast. In *Pearson, S. R.; Stryker, J. D. and Humphreys, C. P.*, *et al.*, 1981, pp. 61–105. [G: Ivory Coast]

Humphreys, Charles P. and Rader, Patricia L. Rice Policy in the Ivory Coast. In *Pearson, S. R.; Stryker, J. D. and Humphreys, C. P.*, *et al.*, 1981, pp. 15–60. [G: Ivory Coast]

Hunter, Richard. Broiler Production: A Spectacular Growth Industry. *Quart. Rev. Rural Econ.*, August 1981, 3(3), pp. 246–53. [G: Australia]

Hunter, Richard. The Commercial Egg Industry: Few Farms Supply Our Eggs. *Quart. Rev. Rural Econ.*, November 1981, 3(4), pp. 351–58. [G: Australia]

Hunter, Richard and Gargett, David. Dairy Industry: Preliminary Survey Results for 1979–80 and Projections for 1980–81. *Quart. Rev. Rural Econ.*, February 1981, 3(1), pp. 67–69. [G: Australia]

Jabara, Cathy L. Effect of Monetary Compensatory Amounts in Determining Rates of Production from EC Grain Import Levies. *Can. J. Agr. Econ.*, February 1981, 29(1), pp. 63–70. [G: EEC]

Jain, Arvind K. International Integration of Commodity Markets. *J. Int. Bus. Stud.*, Winter 1981, 12(3), pp. 65–88. [G: U.S.; U.K.]

Jenkins, Sarah. Structural Change in the Beef Industry in the 1970s. *Quart. Rev. Rural Econ.*, May

1981, 3(2), pp. 166–72. [G: Australia]

Johnson, D. Gale. Food and Agriculture of the Centrally Planned Economies: Implications for the World Food System. In *Fellner, W., ed.*, 1981, pp. 171–213. [G: U.S.S.R.; China; E. Europe]

Johnson, D. Gale. Grain Insurance, Reserves, and Trade: Contributions to Food Security for LDCs. In *Valdés, A.*, 1981, pp. 255–86. [G: LDCs]

Jones, E. L. Agriculture, 1700–80. In *Floud, R. and McCloskey, D., eds., Vol. 1*, 1981, pp. 66–86. [G: U.K.]

Josling, Timothy. Price, Stock, and Trade Policies and the Functioning of International Grain Markets. In *Valdés, A.*, 1981, pp. 161–84. [G: Selected MDCs; U.S.S.R.]

Josling, Timothy. World Food Production, Consumption, and International Trade: Implications for U.S. Agriculture. In *Johnson, D. G., ed.*, 1981, pp. 83–112. [G: U.S.; Global]

Junankar, P. N. Estimation of Cross Section Production Functions under Structural Change in Indian Agriculture: Comment. In *Currie, D.; Peel, D. and Peters, W., eds.*, 1981, pp. 450–53. [G: India]

Just, Richard E. and Rausser, Gordon C. Commodity Price Forecasting with Large-Scale Econometric Models and the Futures Market. *Amer. J. Agr. Econ.*, May 1981, 63(2), pp. 197–208. [G: U.S.]

Kahn, Herman and Schneider, Ernest. Globaloney 2000. *Policy Rev.*, Spring 1981, (16), pp. 129–47.

Kalirajan, K. P. An Econometric Analysis of Yield Variability in Paddy Production. *Can. J. Agr. Econ.*, November 1981, 29(3), pp. 283–94. [G: India]

Kassirov, L. and Nikitina, M. On Determining the Share of Agriculture in the Social Product. *Prob. Econ.*, June 1981, 24(2), pp. 46–65. [G: U.S.S.R.]

Khadka, B. B. and Gautam, J. C. Demand and Production of Food Grains in the Hills. In *Nepal, Ministry of Food and Agriculture*, 1981, pp. 29–42. [G: Nepal]

Kiger, Hugh C. Open Trade and Modernized Tobacco Program: The Keys to an Expanded U.S. Flue-Cured World Market. In *Finger, W. R., ed.*, 1981, pp. 131–44. [G: Global; U.S.]

Kinney, Joseph A. Tobacco's Global Economy: Is North Carolina Losing? In *Finger, W. R., ed.*, 1981, pp. 119–29. [G: Global; U.S.]

Kislev, Yoav. International Farm Prices and the Social Cost of Cheap Food Policies: Comment. *Amer. J. Agr. Econ.*, May 1981, 63(2), pp. 280. [G: LDCs]

Kite, R. C. and Roop, J. M. Changing Agricultural Prices and Their Impact on Food Prices under Inflation. *Amer. J. Agr. Econ.*, December 1981, 63(5), pp. 956–61.

Kornai, Gábor. Has the Hog Cycle Ceased to Exist? (An Econometric Model of the Hungarian Pig Farming) *Acta Oecon.*, 1981, 26(3–4), pp. 369–88. [G: Hungary]

Kranjec, Marko. Empirijska analiza tržišta pilećeg mesa u Jugoslaviji. (The Poultry Industry of Yugoslavia—An Empirical Investigation. With English summary.) *Econ. Anal. Worker's Manage.*, 1981, 15(3), pp. 335–51. [G: Yugoslavia]

Krishna, Raj and Raychaudhuri, G. S. Agricultural Price Policy in India—A Case Study of Rice. *Indian Econ. J.*, January–March 1981, 28(3), pp. 16–34. [G: India]

Kulshreshtha, Surendra N. and Bamford, John A. Feeder Cattle Price Determination in Saskatchewan. *Can. J. Agr. Econ.*, February 1981, 29(1), pp. 49–62. [G: Canada]

Lamm, Ray McFall, Jr. and Westcott, Paul C. The Effects of Changing Input Costs on Food Prices. *Amer. J. Agr. Econ.*, May 1981, 63(2), pp. 187–96. [G: U.S.]

Lang, Mahlon G. and Rosa, Franco. Price Variation in Direct and Terminal Markets for Cattle and Hogs: An Illinois Case. *Amer. J. Agr. Econ.*, November 1981, 63(4), pp. 704–07. [G: U.S.]

Langham, Max R. and Lanier, Ray. Public Mosquito Abatement: Comment. *J. Environ. Econ. Manage.*, March 1981, 8(1), pp. 97–99. [G: U.S.]

Legge, A. J. Aspects of Cattle Husbandry. In *Mercer, R., ed.*, 1981, pp. 169–81. [G: U.K.]

Lele, Uma and Candler, Wilfred. Food Security: Some East African Considerations. In *Valdés, A.*, 1981, pp. 101–21. [G: E. Africa]

Libecap, Gary D. Bureaucratic Opposition to the Assignment of Property Rights: Overgrazing on the Western Range. *J. Econ. Hist.*, March 1981, 41(1), pp. 151–58. [G: U.S.]

Loseby, Margaret and Venzi, Lorenzo. Floating Exchange Rates and International Trade in Agricultural Commodities. In *Johnson, G. and Maunder, A., eds.*, 1981, pp. 426–36.

Low, A. R. C. The Effect of Off-Farm Employment on Farm Incomes and Production: Taiwan Contrasted with Southern Africa. *Econ. Develop. Cult. Change*, July 1981, 29(4), pp. 741–47. [G: Taiwan; Swaziland; Lesotho]

Magiera, Stephen L. The Role of Wheat in the Indonesian Food Sector. *Bull. Indonesian Econ. Stud.*, November 1981, 17(3), pp. 48–73. [G: Indonesia]

Mammen, Thampy. A Note on the Foodgrain Surplus. *Indian Econ. J.*, April–June 1981, 28(4), pp. 85–88. [G: India]

Mănescu, B.; Frăţilă, G. and Bindea, M. Optimizing the Technology of Setting up Viticultural Plantations. *Econ. Computat. Cybern. Stud. Res.*, 1981, 15(3), pp. 51–58.

Martin, Larry J. Quadratic Single and Multi-Commodity Models of Spatial Equilibrium: A Simplified Exposition. *Can. J. Agr. Econ.*, February 1981, 29(1), pp. 21–48.

Martin, Larry J. and Garcia, Philip. The Price-Forecasting Performance of Futures Markets for Live Cattle and Hogs: A Disaggregated Analysis. *Amer. J. Agr. Econ.*, May 1981, 63(2), pp. 209–15. [G: U.S.]

Mathur, P. N. and Prakash, S. Inventory Behaviour of Indian Agriculture and Its Effect on General Price Level. In *Chikán, A., ed. (I)*, 1981, pp. 255–67. [G: India]

Matuska, Tony. Sheep, Beef and Wheat Industries: Preliminary Survey Results for 1979–80 and 1980–81. *Quart. Rev. Rural Econ.*, February 1981, 3(1), pp. 70–75. [G: Australia]

Maxwell, S. J. and Singer, H. W. Food Aid to Developing Countries: A Survey. In *Streeten, P. and*

Jolly, R, eds., 1981, pp. 219–40.   [G: LDCs]
Mayer, Thomas and Junginger-Dittel, Klaus-Otto.
Risk Response in Kenyan Agriculture: The Case
of Major Export Crops. *Europ. Rev. Agr. Econ.*,
1981, *8*(1), pp. 27–39.   [G: Kenya]
McIntire, John. Rice Policy in Mali. In *Pearson, S.
R.; Stryker, J. D. and Humphreys, C. P., et al.*,
1981, pp. 299–330.   [G: Mali]
McIntire, John. Rice Production in Mali. In *Pearson,
S. R.; Stryker, J. D. and Humphreys, C. P., et
al.*, 1981, pp. 331–60.   [G: Mali]
Meilke, Karl D. and Griffith, G. R. An Application
of the Market Share Approach to the Demand
for Soybean and Rapeseed Oil. *Europ. Rev. Agr.
Econ.*, 1981, *8*(1), pp. 85–97.   [G: OECD]
Mészáros, S. Econometric Forecasting by a Fertiliser
Sectoral Model. In *Janssen, J. M. L.; Pau, L. F.
and Straszak, A. J., eds.*, 1981, pp. 163–68.
Mittelhammer, Ron C. and Young, Douglas L. Mitigating the Effects of Multicollinearity Using Exact
and Stochastic Restrictions: The Case of an Aggregate Agricultural Production Function in Thailand: Reply. *Amer. J. Agr. Econ.*, May 1981,
63(2), pp. 301–04.   [G: Thailand]
Moffitt, L. Joe and Farnsworth, Richard L. Bioeco-
nomic Analysis of Pesticide Demand. *Agr. Econ.
Res.*, October 1981, *33*(4), pp. 12–18. [G: U.S.]
Mokyr, Joel. Discussion [The Organization of Ex-
change in Early Christian Ireland] [Discouraging
the Use of a Common Resource: The Crees of
Saskatchewan]. *J. Econ. Hist.*, March 1981, *41*(1),
pp. 177–78.   [G: Canada; Ireland]
Monke, Eric A. Rice Policy in Liberia. In *Pearson,
S. R.; Stryker, J. D. and Humphreys, C. P., et
al.*, 1981, pp. 109–40.   [G: Liberia]
Monke, Eric A. The Economics of Rice in Liberia.
In *Pearson, S. R.; Stryker, J. D. and Humphreys,
C. P., et al.*, 1981, pp. 141–72.   [G: Liberia]
Montgomery, Roger. Maize Yield Increases in East
Java. *Bull. Indonesian Econ. Stud.*, November
1981, *17*(3), pp. 74–85.   [G: Indonesia]
Moock, Peter R. Education and Technical Efficiency
in Small-Farm Production. *Econ. Develop. Cult.
Change*, July 1981, *29*(4), pp. 723–39.
    [G: Kenya]
Morrow, Daniel. The International Wheat Agree-
ment and LDC Food Security. In *Valdés, A.*,
1981, pp. 213–39.   [G: Global]
Muqtada, M. Poverty and Famines in Bangladesh.
Bangladesh Devel. Stud., Winter 1981, *9*(1), pp.
1–34.   [G: Bangladesh]
Musoke, Moses S. Mechanizing Cotton Production
in the American South: The Tractor, 1915–1960.
Exploration Econ. Hist., October 1981, *18*(4), pp.
347–75.   [G: U.S.]
**Musser, Wesley N.; Tew, Bernard V. and Epper-
son, James E.** An Economic Examination of an
Integrated Pest Management Production System
with a Contrast between E-V and Stochastic Dom-
inance Analysis. *Southern J. Agr. Econ.*, July
1981, *13*(1), pp. 119–24.   [G: U.S.]
Negi, Y. S. and Grewal, M. S. Trends in Inter-State
Sugarcane and Sugar Production in India. *Econ.
Aff.*, April–June 1981, *26*(2), pp. 129–33.
    [G: India]
Nepali, S. B. and Regmi, I. R. Technological Innova-
tions for Hill Agricultural Development. In *Ne-

pal, Ministry of Food and Agriculture*, 1981, pp.
123–29.   [G: Nepal]
Nguyen, D. T. Mexican Land Reform, 1959–1969:
A Reply [The Effects of Land Reform on Agricultural Production, Employment and Income Distribution: A Statistical Study of Mexican States,
1959–69]. *Econ. J.*, September 1981, *91*(363), pp.
253–54.   [G: Mexico]
Ó Gráda, Cormac. Agricultural Decline 1860–1914.
In *Floud, R. and McCloskey, D., eds., Vol. 2*,
1981, pp. 175–97.   [G: U.K.]
O'Mara, L. P. Some Economic Implications of Minimum Pricing: The Case of Wine Grapes in Australia. *Rev. Marketing Agr. Econ.*, August 1981,
49(2), pp. 107–23.   [G: Australia]
Ospina, Enrique and Shumway, C. Richard. Impact
of Corn Prices on Slaughter Beef Composition
and Prices. *Amer. J. Agr. Econ.*, November 1981,
63(4), pp. 700–703.   [G: U.S.]
Page, John M., Jr. and Stryker, J. Dirck. Methodology for Estimating Comparative Costs and Incentives. In *Pearson, S. R.; Stryker, J. D. and
Humphreys, C. P., et al.*, 1981, pp. 435–54.
    [G: W. Africa]
Pagoulatos, Emilio. Discussion: The Role of Food
and Agriculture in the International Affairs of the
United States. *Southern J. Agr. Econ.*, July 1981,
13(1), pp. 39–42.   [G: U.S.]
Parikh, A. and Trivedi, P. K. Estimation of Cross
Section Production Functions Under Structural
Change in Indian Agriculture. In *Currie, D.; Peel,
D. and Peters, W., eds.*, 1981, pp. 413–49.
    [G: India]
Pearce, William R. U.S. Agriculture in an Interde-
pendent World Economy: Policy Alternatives for
the 1980s: Comment. In *Johnson, D. G., ed.*,
1981, pp. 219–23.   [G: U.S.]
Pemberton, Carlisle A. Resource Productivity in Agriculture in Developing Countries: A Comment
[A Study of Resource Productivity in Cooperative
Group Farming in Imo State in Nigeria]. *Can.
J. Agr. Econ.*, November 1981, *29*(3), pp. 361–
63.   [G: Tobago]
Penn, J. B. Economic Developments in U.S. Agriculture during the 1970s. In *Johnson, D. G., ed.*,
1981, pp. 3–47.   [G: U.S.]
Pincus, Jonathan J. Discussion [Government Policy
and Economic Development in Germany and Ja-
pan: A Skeptical Reevaluation] [Bureaucratic Op-
position to the Assignment of Property Rights:
Overgrazing on the Western Range]. *J. Econ.
Hist.*, March 1981, *41*(1), pp. 159–61.
    [G: Germany; Japan; U.S.]
Podbielski, Gisele. The Common Agricultural Policy
and the Mezzogiorno. *J. Common Market Stud.*,
June 1981, *19*(4), pp. 331–50.   [G: Italy; EEC]
Pope, Rulon D. Supply Response and the Dispersion
of Price Expectations. *Amer. J. Agr. Econ.*, Feb-
ruary 1981, *63*(1), pp. 161–63.
Quibria, M. G. A Layman's Geometric Proof of the
Nonexistence of "Marshallian" Sharecropping
Contracts. *Bangladesh Devel. Stud.*, Winter
1981, *9*(1), pp. 97–99.
Quizon, Jaime B. Factor Input Demand and Output
Supply Elasticities in Philippine Agriculture.
Philippine Econ. J., 1981, *20*(2), pp. 103–26.
    [G: Philippines]

Rahman, Sultan Hafez. Simulation of an Econometric Model to Analyze the Impact of a Buffer Stock Scheme in the Bangladesh Jute Sector. *Bangladesh Devel. Stud.*, Autumn 1981, *9*(4), pp. 1–33. [G: Bangladesh]

Rajbhandary, H. B. and Shah, S. G. Trends and Projections of Livestock Production in the Hills. In *Nepal, Ministry of Food and Agriculture*, 1981, pp. 43–58. [G: Nepal]

Rana, P. N. and Mathema, S. B. Potential Impact of Desirable Changes in Relation to Productivity and Income in Hill Farming Systems. In *Nepal, Ministry of Food and Agriculture*, 1981, pp. 59–78. [G: Nepal]

Ransom, Roger L. and Sutch, Richard. Growth and Welfare in the American South in the Nineteenth Century. In *Walton, G. M. and Shepherd, J. F., eds.*, 1981, pp. 127–53. [G: U.S.]

Rapelius, Eckhard and Weber, Adolf. The World Agricultural Input Industries as Factors of Rural Change. In *Johnson, G. and Maunder, A., eds.*, 1981, pp. 570–83. [G: Selected Countries]

Ray, S. K. Weather, Prices and Fluctuations in Agricultural Production. *Indian Econ. Rev.*, Oct.-Dec. 1981, *16*(4), pp. 251–77. [G: India]

Ray, Siddheswar. Impact of Rainfall on Crop Yield in West Bengal. *Econ. Aff.*, April–June 1981, *26*(2), pp. 89–92. [G: India]

Reed, Michael R. and Riggins, Steven K. A Disaggregated Analysis of Corn Acreage Response in Kentucky. *Amer. J. Agr. Econ.*, November 1981, *63*(4), pp. 708–11. [G: U.S.]

Reutlinger, Shlomo and Bigman, David. Feasibility, Effectiveness, and Costs of Food Security Alternatives in Developing Countries. In *Valdés, A.*, 1981, pp. 185–212.

Revell, B. J. Box–Jenkins Forecasting Models: Comment [Forecasting NSW Beef Production: An Evaluation of Alternative Techniques] [Comparing the Box–Jenkins and Econometric Techniques for Forecasting Beef Prices]. *Rev. Marketing Agr. Econ.*, April 1981, *49*(1), pp. 61–64.

Reynolds, Peter. Deadstock and Livestock. In *Mercer, R., ed.*, 1981, pp. 97–122. [G: U.K.]

Roberts, Walter Orr and Slater, Lloyd E. The Interaction of Food, Climate, and Population. In *Cleveland, H., ed.*, 1981, pp. 239–65.

Rowley-Conwy, P. Slash and Burn in the Temperate European Neolithic. In *Mercer, R., ed.*, 1981, pp. 85–96. [G: U.K.]

Roze, Janis A. The Competitiveness of Natural Resources with Synthetic Substances. In *Lozoya, J. and Green, R., eds.*, 1981, pp. 54–65. [G: Global]

Ryder, Michael J. Livestock Products: Skins and Fleeces. In *Mercer, R., ed.*, 1981, pp. 182–209. [G: U.K.]

Sabadell, J. Eleonora. Risk Assessment: Arid and Semiarid Lands Perspective. In *Haimes, Y. Y., ed.*, 1981, pp. 219–31. [G: U.S.]

Sadhu, A. N. and Mahajan, R. K. Disguised Unemployment and Zero Marginal Productivity of Labor: (An Empirical Test) *Econ. Aff.*, January–March 1981, *26*(1), pp. 70–76. [G: India]

Sahota, Gian S. and Rocca, Carlos A. Process of Production and Distribution in Brazilian Agriculture. *Econ. Develop. Cult. Change*, July 1981, *29*(4), pp. 683–721. [G: Brazil]

Salam, Abdul. Farm Tractorization, Fertilizer Use and Productivity of Mexican Wheat in Pakistan. *Pakistan Devel. Rev.*, Autumn 1981, *20*(3), pp. 323–45. [G: Pakistan]

Salam, Abdul; Hussain, M. Afzal and Ghayur, Sabur. Farm Mechanization, Employment and Productivity in Pakistan's Agriculture. *Pakistan Econ. Soc. Rev.*, Winter 1981, *19*(2), pp. 95–114. [G: Pakistan]

Sarris, Alexander H. Empirical Models of International Trade in Agricultural Commodities. In *McCalla, A. F. and Josling, T. E., eds.*, 1981, pp. 87–112.

Sarris, Alexander H. and Schmitz, Andrew. Price Formation in International Agricultural Trade. In *McCalla, A. F. and Josling, T. E., eds.*, 1981, pp. 29–48.

Scarlett, Lynn. Tropical Africa: Food or Famine? In *Balaam, D. N. and Carey, M. J., eds.*, 1981, pp. 166–88. [G: Africa]

Schluter, Gerald and Beeson, Patty. Components of Labor Productivity Growth in the Food System, 1958–67. *Rev. Econ. Statist.*, August 1981, *63*(3), pp. 378–84. [G: U.S.]

Schluter, Gerald and Lee, Gene K. Effects of Relative Price Changes on U.S. Food Sectors, 1967–78. *Agr. Econ. Res.*, January 1981, *33*(1), pp. 1–12. [G: U.S.]

Schmitz, Andrew and McCalla, Alex F. Analysis of Imperfections in International Trade: The Case of Grain Export Cartels. In *McCalla, A. F. and Josling, T. E., eds.*, 1981, pp. 69–86.

Schuh, G. Edward. U.S. Agriculture in an Interdependence World Economy: Policy Alternatives for the 1980s. In *Johnson, D. G., ed.*, 1981, pp. 157–82. [G: U.S.]

Sen, Amartya. Ingredients of Famine Analysis: Availability and Entitlements. *Quart. J. Econ.*, August 1981, *96*(3), pp. 433–64. [G: India; Bangladesh]

Sen, S. R. Food Security—Issues and Approaches. *Indian Econ. Rev.*, July-Sept. 1981, *16*(3), pp. 213–19.

Shahabuddin, Quazi. Estimation of Regional Production Function: An Application to Survey Data in Bangladesh Agriculture. *Bangladesh Devel. Stud.*, Monsoon 1981, *9*(3), pp. 89–94. [G: Bangladesh]

Sharples, Jerry A. and Holland, Forrest D. Impact on the Farmer-Owned Reserve on Privately Owned Wheat Stocks. *Amer. J. Agr. Econ.*, August 1981, *63*(3), pp. 538–43. [G: U.S.]

Sharpley, Jennifer. Resource Transfers between the Agricultural and Non-agricultural Sectors: 1964–1977. In *Killick, T., ed.*, 1981, pp. 311–19. [G: Kenya]

Shearer, Georgia, et al. Crop Production Costs and Returns on Midwestern Organic Farms: 1977 and 1978. *Amer. J. Agr. Econ.*, May 1981, *63*(2), pp. 264–69.

Shepherd, Andrew. Agrarian Change in Northern Ghana: Public Investment, Capitalist Farming and Famine. In *Heyer, J.; Roberts, P. and Williams, G., eds.*, 1981, pp. 168–92. [G: Ghana]

Siamwalla, Ammar. Security of Rice Supplies in the

ASEAN Region. In *Valdés, A.*, 1981, pp. 79–99. [G: ASEAN]

Sidhu, Surjit S. and Baanante, Carlos A. Estimating Farm-Level Input Demand and Wheat Supply in the Indian Punjab Using a Translog Profit Function. *Amer. J. Agr. Econ.*, May 1981, *63*(2), pp. 237–46. [G: India]

Simpson, James R. and Stegelin, Forrest E. The Effect of Increasing Transportation Costs on Florida's Cattle Feeding Industry: An Extension Application. *Southern J. Agr. Econ.*, December 1981, *13*(2), pp. 141–48. [G: U.S.]

Singh, A. J. Performance and Prospects of Indian Agriculture. *Econ. Aff.*, January–March 1981, *26*(1), pp. 8, 77–80. [G: India]

Singh, R. B.; Dey, B. K. and Roy, N. D. Demand–Supply Balance of Foodgrains in Bihar in 1982–83 and 1988–89—A Study. In *Karna, M. N., ed.*, 1981, pp. 29–44. [G: India]

Sisson, Phillip F. Economic Developments in U.S. Agriculture during the 1970s: Comment. In *Johnson, D. G., ed.*, 1981, pp. 73–75. [G: U.S.]

Smith, A. W. and Smith, Rhonda L. The Impact of Changing Economic Conditions on the Australian Agricultural Sector. In *Johnson, G. and Maunder, A., eds.*, 1981, pp. 326–37. [G: Australia]

Smith, Ian. GATT: EEC Sugar Export Refunds Dispute. *J. World Trade Law*, November–December 1981, *15*(6), pp. 534–43. [G: EEC]

Soewardi, B. and Mustari, K. Upland Agriculture in Indonesia. In *Nepal, Ministry of Food and Agriculture*, 1981, pp. 169–79. [G: Indonesia]

Soth, Lauren. The Grain Export Boom: Should It be Tamed? *Foreign Aff.*, Spring 1981, *59*(4), pp. 895–912. [G: U.S.]

Spencer, Dunstan S. C. Rice Policy in Sierra Leone. In *Pearson, S. R.; Stryker, J. D. and Humphreys, C. P., et al.*, 1981, pp. 175–200. [G: Sierra Leone]

Spencer, Dunstan S. C. Rice Production in Sierra Leone. In *Pearson, S. R.; Stryker, J. D. and Humphreys, C. P., et al.*, 1981, pp. 201–25. [G: Sierra Leone]

Stein, Jerome L. Speculative Price: Economic Welfare and the Idiot of Chance. *Rev. Econ. Statist.*, May 1981, *63*(2), pp. 223–32. [G: U.S.]

Stoevener, Herbert H. Interrelationship among Export Markets, Resource Conservation, and Agricultural Productivity: Discussion. *Amer. J. Agr. Econ.*, December 1981, *63*(5), pp. 851–52. [G: U.S.]

Stolbov, A. Prices on Agricultural Products and the Stimulation of Production. *Prob. Econ.*, June 1981, *24*(2), pp. 66–77. [G: U.S.S.R.]

Streeten, Paul P. World Trade in Agricultural Commodities and the Terms of Trade with Industrial Goods. In *Streeten, P.*, 1981, *1974*, pp. 213–31. [G: Global]

Stryker, J. Dirck. Comparative Advantage and Public Policy in West African Rice. In *Pearson, S. R.; Stryker, J. D. and Humphreys, C. P., et al.*, 1981, pp. 396–431. [G: Ivory Coast; Liberia; Mali; Senegal; Sierra Leone]

Stryker, J. Dirck; Page, John M., Jr. and Humphreys, Charles P. Shadow Price Estimation. In *Pearson, S. R.; Stryker, J. D. and Humphreys,*

C. P., et al., 1981, pp. 455–82. [G: W. Africa]

Sunkel, Osvaldo. Development Styles and the Environment: An Interpretation of the Latin American Case. In *Muñoz, H., ed.*, 1981, pp. 93–114. [G: Latin America]

Swain, N. The Evolution of Hungary's Agricultural System since 1967. In *Hare, P. G.; Radice, H. K. and Swain, N., eds.*, 1981, pp. 225–51. [G: Hungary]

Szumilak, J. and Wasik, B. Simulation Analysis of Goods Flows Stability in the Food Products Distribution System. In *Janssen, J. M. L.; Pau, L. F. and Straszak, A. J., eds.*, 1981, pp. 177–85.

Timmer, C. Peter. China and the World Grain Market. *Challenge*, September/October 1981, *24*(4), pp. 13–21. [G: China]

Todd, Mike C. and Cowell, M. D. Within-Sale Price Variation at Cattle and Carcass Auctions. *Australian J. Agr. Econ.*, April 1981, *25*(1), pp. 30–47. [G: Australia]

Trapp, James N. Forecasting Short-Run Fed Beef Supplies with Estimated Data. *Amer. J. Agr. Econ.*, August 1981, *63*(3), pp. 457–65. [G: U.S.]

Treml, Vladimir G. Losses in Soviet National Income and Agriculture: A Puzzle. *ACES Bull.* (See *Comp. Econ. Stud. after 8/85*), Spring 1981, *23*(1), pp. 103–09. [G: U.S.S.R.]

Tuluy, A. Hasan. Costs and Incentives in Rice Production in Senegal. In *Pearson, S. R.; Stryker, J. D. and Humphreys, C. P., et al.*, 1981, pp. 263–95. [G: Senegal]

Tweeten, Luther. Prospective Changes in U.S. Agricultural Structure. In *Johnson, D. G., ed.*, 1981, pp. 113–46. [G: U.S.]

Tyagi, D. S. Growth of Agricultural Output and Labour Absorption in India. *J. Devel. Stud.*, October 1981, *18*(1), pp. 104–14. [G: India]

Valdés, Alberto and Konandreas, Panos. Assessing Food Insecurity Based on National Aggregates in Developing Countries. In *Valdés, A.*, 1981, pp. 25–51. [G: Selected LDCs]

Valdés, Alberto and Siamwalla, Ammar. Assessing Food Insecurity in LDCs—Roles of International Schemes in Relation to LDCs. In *Johnson, G. and Maunder, A., eds.*, 1981, pp. 454–64. [G: Selected LDCs]

Valdés, Alberto and Siamwalla, Ammar. Food Security for Developing Countries: Introduction. In *Valdés, A.*, 1981, pp. 1–21.

Vertessen, J. Influence of Butter and Margarine Prices on the Demand for Butter in Belgium. *Europ. Rev. Agr. Econ.*, 1981, *8*(1), pp. 99–109. [G: Belgium]

Voronin, V. Personal Household Plots and Trade. *Prob. Econ.*, March 1981, *23*(11), pp. 3–15. [G: U.S.S.R.]

Waghmare, P. R. and Garule, J. H. Growth Analysis of Groundnut in India. *Econ. Aff.*, October–December 1981, *26*(4), pp. 289–92. [G: India]

Walden, Michael L. Microeconomic Impacts of Inflation on the Food and Agriculture Sector: Discussion. *Amer. J. Agr. Econ.*, December 1981, *63*(5), pp. 965–66. [G: U.S.]

Ward, Clement E. Short-Period Pricing Models for

Fed Cattle and Impacts of Wholesale Carcass Beef and Live Cattle Futures Market Prices. *Southern J. Agr. Econ.*, July 1981, *13*(1), pp. 125–32. [G: U.S.]

Warrick, Richard A. and Bowden, Martyn J. The Changing Impacts of Droughts in the Great Plains. In *Lawson, M. P. and Baker, M. E., eds.*, 1981, pp. 111–37. [G: U.S.]

Weeks, Peter and Turner, Bruce. Effects of the Proposed Canadian Meat Import Law. *Quart. Rev. Rural Econ.*, August 1981, *3*(3), pp. 232–39. [G: Canada; Australia]

Weiler, Edward M. and Tyner, Wallace E. Social Cost-Benefit Analysis of the Nianga Irrigation Pilot Project, Senegal. *J. Devel. Areas*, July 1981, *15*(4), pp. 655–69. [G: Senegal]

Weinbaum, Marvin G. Agricultural Constraints and Bureaucratic Politics in the Middle East. In *Balaam, D. N. and Carey, M. J., eds.*, 1981, pp. 143–65. [G: Middle East]

Wizarat, Shahida. Technological Change in Pakistan's Agriculture: 1953–54 to 1978–79. *Pakistan Devel. Rev.*, Winter 1981, *20*(4), pp. 427–45. [G: Pakistan]

Wu, Zhan. The Development of Socialist Agriculture in China. In *Johnson, G. and Maunder, A., eds.*, 1981, pp. 273–80. [G: China]

Wyzan, Michael L. Empirical Analysis of Soviet Agricultural Production and Policy. *Amer. J. Agr. Econ.*, August 1981, *63*(3), pp. 475–83. [G: U.S.S.R.]

Yanagida, John F. and Conway, Roger K. The Effect of Energy Price Increases on the U.S. Livestock Sector. *Can. J. Agr. Econ.*, November 1981, *29*(3), pp. 295–302. [G: U.S.]

Yates, P. Lammartine. Mexican Land Reform, 1959–1969: A Comment [The Effects of Land Reform on Agricultural Production, Employment and Income Distribution: A Statistical Study of Mexican States, 1959–69]. *Econ. J.*, September 1981, *91*(363), pp. 745–52. [G: Mexico]

Zel'dner, A. The Creation of a Stable Food Base in the Far East. *Prob. Econ.*, June 1981, *24*(2), pp. 78–91. [G: U.S.S.R.]

712 Agricultural Situation and Outlook

7120 Agricultural Situation and Outlook

Arroyo, Gonzalo; Gómez-de-Almeida, Silvio and Van der Weld, Jean-Marc. A World Food Program within the NIEO. In *Lozoya, J. and Green, R., eds.*, 1981, pp. 75–108. [G: Global]

Bain, Robert. Changes in the International Grain Trade in the 1980s. *Quart. Rev. Rural Econ.*, November 1981, *3*(4), pp. 370.

Balaam, David N. The Regional Approach Reconciling Food Policies and Policy Recommendations: Conclusion. In *Balaam, D. N. and Carey, M. J., eds.*, 1981, pp. 207–37. [G: Global]

Barbiroli, Giancarlo; Ballini, Vladimiro and Savio, Giorgio. The Effect of Technological Development on Renewable Raw Materials. A Look at the International Situation. *Econ. Notes*, 1981, *10*(1), pp. 104–21. [G: Selected Countries]

Bardhan, Pranab and Rudra, Ashok. Terms and Conditions of Labour Contracts in Agriculture: Results of a Survey in West Bengal, 1979. *Oxford Bull. Econ. Statist.*, February 1981, *43*(1), pp. 89–111. [G: W. Bengal]

Borrelli, John. Future of Irrigated Agriculture in the Great Plains. In *Lawson, M. P. and Baker, M. E., eds.*, 1981, pp. 181–91. [G: U.S.]

Breimyer, Harold F. Outlook for the Food Supply. *Challenge*, July/August 1981, *24*(3), pp. 55–59. [G: U.S.]

Busch, Lawrence and Lacy, William B. Sources of Influence on Problem Choice in the Agricultural Sciences: The New Atlantis Revisited. In *Busch, L., ed.*, 1981, pp. 113–28.

Campbell, Keith. The Risks of New Technology and their Agricultural Implications. In *Johnson, G. and Maunder, A., eds.*, 1981, pp. 261–70.

Ehrlich, Anne H. Feeding the Transitional Society. In *Coomer, J. C., ed.*, 1981, pp. 124–41.

Fekete, Ferenc; Benet, Iván and Sebestyén, Katalin. Energy Problems in the Hungarian Agriculture and Food Industry. *Acta Oecon.*, 1981, *27* (3–4), pp. 373–82. [G: Hungary]

Frank, Max and Praet, Peter. Trois optiques du concept de parité des revenus en agriculture. (With English summary.) *Cah. Écon. Bruxelles*, 3rd Trimestre 1981, (91), pp. 375–89. [G: Belgium]

Hathaway, Dale E. Agricultural Policy Alternatives for the 1980s: Comment. In *Johnson, D. G., ed.*, 1981, pp. 228–29. [G: U.S.]

Herer, W. and Sadowski, WL. Costs of Accelerating Agricultural Expansion. In *[Lipiński, E.]*, 1981, pp. 195–212. [G: Poland]

Hoover, Dale M. A Framework for Food and Agricultural Policy for the 1980s: Comment. In *Johnson, D. G., ed.*, 1981, pp. 224–28. [G: U.S.]

Johnson, D. Gale. Agricultural Policy Alternatives for the 1980s. In *Johnson, D. G., ed.*, 1981, pp. 183–209. [G: U.S.]

Johnson, D. Gale. Food and Agriculture of the Centrally Planned Economies: Implications for the World Food System. In *Fellner, W., ed.*, 1981, pp. 171–213. [G: U.S.S.R.; China; E. Europe]

Kazee, Donald K. Four Decisions Facing Latin American Extension. In *Busch, L., ed.*, 1981, pp. 167–78. [G: Latin America]

Millar, James R. The Prospects for Soviet Agriculture. In *Bornstein, M., ed.*, 1981, 1977, pp. 273–91. [G: U.S.S.R.]

Pearce, William R. U.S. Agriculture in an Interdependent World Economy: Policy Alternatives for the 1980s: Comment. In *Johnson, D. G., ed.*, 1981, pp. 219–23. [G: U.S.]

Popov, Todor. Scientific and Technical Collaboration between the CMEA Member Countries in the Sphere of Agriculture. In *Johnson, G. and Maunder, A., eds.*, 1981, pp. 467–75. [G: CMEA]

Randolph, S. Randi and Sachs, Carolyn. The Establishment of Applies Sciences: Medicine and Agriculture Compared. In *Busch, L., ed.*, 1981, pp. 83–111. [G: U.S.]

Rosenfeld, Arnoldo. The Food Crisis and the NIEO. In *Lozoya, J. and Green, R., eds.*, 1981, pp. 66–74. [G: Global]

Schnittker, John A. A Framework for Food and Agricultural Policy for the 1980s. In *Johnson, D. G.,* *ed.*, 1981, pp. 210–18. [G: U.S.]

Schuh, G. Edward. U.S. Agriculture in an Interdependence World Economy: Policy Alternatives for the 1980s. In *Johnson, D. G., ed.*, 1981, pp. 157–82. [G: U.S.]

Sen, S. R. Food Security—Issues and Approaches. *Indian Econ. Rev.*, July-Sept. 1981, *16*(3), pp. 213–19.

Simatupang, B. Polish Agriculture in the 1970s and the Prospects for the Early 1980s. *Europ. Rev. Agr. Econ.*, 1981, *8*(4), pp. 453–73. [G: Poland]

Stevens, Neil A. Outlook for Food and Agriculture in 1981. *Fed. Res. Bank St. Louis Rev.*, January 1981, *63*(1), pp. 27–32. [G: U.S.]

Tan, B. T. Prospects and Problems of Hill Agriculture in Malaysia. In *Nepal, Ministry of Food and Agriculture*, 1981, pp. 180–89. [G: Malaysia]

Thompson, Seth B. International Organizations and the Improbability of a Global Food Regime. In *Balaam, D. N. and Carey, M. J., eds.*, 1981, pp. 191–206.

Tucker, John. Comparison of Industries in the Agricultural and Grazing Industries Survey. *Quart. Rev. Rural Econ.*, November 1981, *3*(4), pp. 359–64. [G: Australia]

Webb, Steven B. The Impact of Increased Alcohol Production on Agriculture: A Simulation Study. *Amer. J. Agr. Econ.*, August 1981, *63*(3), pp. 532–37. [G: U.S.]

Zidar, Milovan. Regional Development in the Economic Policy of Yugoslavia. *Europ. Rev. Agr. Econ.*, 1981, *8*(2–3), pp. 131–36. [G: Yugoslavia]

713 Agricultural Policy, Domestic and International

7130 Agricultural Policy, Domestic and International

Adams, Dale W. and Graham, Douglas H. A Critique of Traditional Agricultural Credit Projects and Policies. *J. Devel. Econ.*, June 1981, *8*(3), pp. 347–66. [G: LDCs]

Adams, F. Gerard; Behrman, Jere R. and Lasaga, M. Commodity Exports and NIEO Proposals for Buffer Stocks and Compensatory Finance: Implications for Latin America. In *Baer, W. and Gillis, M., eds.*, 1981, pp. 48–76. [G: Chile; Latin America]

Adams, F. Gerard; Behrman, Jere R. and Lasaga, M. Commodity Exports and NIEO Proposals for Buffer Stocks and Compensatory Finance: Implications for Latin America. *Quart. Rev. Econ. Bus.*, Summer 1981, *21*(2), pp. 48–76. [G: Latin America]

Afshar, Haleh. An Assessment of Agricultural Development Policies in Iran. *World Devel.*, November/December 1981, *9*(11/12), pp. 1097–1108. [G: Iran]

Agarwal, Bina. Agricultural Mechanisation and Labour Use: A Disaggregated Approach. *Int. Lab. Rev.*, January–February 1981, *120*(1), pp. 115–27. [G: India]

Ahmad, Nesar. Agrarian Causes of the Iranian Crisis. In *Rubinson, R., ed.*, 1981, pp. 101–20. [G: Iran]

Albegov, M. M., et al. Regional Agricultural Policy Design on the Basis of a Detailed Linear Economic and Agrotechnical Model. In *Janssen, J. M. L.; Pau, L. F. and Straszak, A. J., eds.*, 1981, pp. 221–29.

Alston, Julian M. A Note on the Effects of Non-Transferable Quotas on Supply Functions. *Rev. Marketing Agr. Econ.*, December 1981, *49*(3), pp. 189–97.

Alston, Philip. Commodity Agreements—As Though People Don't Matter: A Reply to "'Fair Labour Standards' in International Commodity Agreements." *J. World Trade Law*, September–October 1981, *15*(5), pp. 455–60.

Arroyo, Gonzalo; Gómez-de-Almeida, Silvio and Van der Weld, Jean-Marc. A World Food Program within the NIEO. In *Lozoya, J. and Green, R., eds.*, 1981, pp. 75–108. [G: Global]

Balaam, David N. East and Southeast Asian Food Systems: Structural Constraints, Political Arenas, and Appropriate Food Strategies. In *Balaam, D. N. and Carey, M. J., eds.*, 1981, pp. 106–42. [G: Asia]

Balaam, David N. The Regional Approach Reconciling Food Policies and Policy Recommendations: Conclusion. In *Balaam, D. N. and Carey, M. J., eds.*, 1981, pp. 207–37. [G: Global]

Balaam, David N. and Carey, Michael J. Agri-Policy in the Soviet Union and Eastern Europe. In *Balaam, D. N. and Carey, M. J., eds.*, 1981, pp. 48–80. [G: U.S.S.R.; E. Europe]

Balassa, Bela. Portugal in Face of the Common Market. In *Balassa, B.*, 1981, pp. 255–80. [G: Portugal]

Bale, Malcolm D. and Lutz, Ernst. Price Distortions in Agriculture and Their Effects: An International Comparison. *Amer. J. Agr. Econ.*, February 1981, *63*(1), pp. 8–22.

Barbosa, Túlio. The Farm/Non-farm Interface with Special Reference to Rural Brazil. In *Johnson, G. and Maunder, A., eds.*, 1981, pp. 200–12. [G: Brazil]

Barrows, Richard. Management Information Systems for Local Government: Discussion. *Amer. J. Agr. Econ.*, December 1981, *63*(5), pp. 984–85. [G: U.S.]

Beckman, Bjorn. Ghana, 1951–78: The Agrarian Basis of the Post-colonial State. In *Heyer, J.; Roberts, P. and Williams, G., eds.*, 1981, pp. 143–67. [G: Ghana]

Berardi, Gigi. Can Tobacco Farmers Adjust to Mechanization? A Look at Allotment Holders in Two North Carolina Counties. In *Finger, W. R., ed.*, 1981, pp. 47–61. [G: U.S.]

Bergland, Robert. In the Public Interest ... Not a Constitutional Birthright: An Interview with Former U.S. Secretary of Agriculture Robert Bergland. In *Finger, W. R., ed.*, 1981, pp. 319–23. [G: U.S.]

Biere, Arlo and Sjo, John. Management Information Systems for Local Government. *Amer. J. Agr. Econ.*, December 1981, *63*(5), pp. 967–73. [G: U.S.]

Bigman, David. Buffer Stocks and Domestic Price

Policies. In *Chikán, A., ed. (I)*, 1981, pp. 49–61.

Bjarnason, Harold F. Accomplishments of and Opportunities for Agricultural Economists in Parastatal Organizations. In *Johnson, G. and Maunder, A., eds.*, 1981, pp. 520–27.

Boehm, William T. Agricultural Policy: Some Hard Choices Ahead. *Southern J. Agr. Econ.*, July 1981, *13*(1), pp. 1–9. [G: U.S.]

Boggess, William G. and Heady, Earl O. A Sector Analysis of Alternative Income Support and Soil Conservation Policies. *Amer. J. Agr. Econ.*, November 1981, *63*(4), pp. 618–28. [G: U.S.]

Brannan, Charles F. The Economics of Agriculture. In *Heller, F. H., ed.*, 1981, pp. 51–58. [G: U.S.]

Breimyer, Harold F. Outlook for the Food Supply. *Challenge*, July/August 1981, *24*(3), pp. 55–59. [G: U.S.]

Broder, Josef M. Decision Aids for Local Decision Making: Discussion. *Amer. J. Agr. Econ.*, December 1981, *63*(5), pp. 988–89. [G: U.S.]

Brown, Thomas G. Changing Delivery Systems for Agricultural Extension: The Extension Teacher—Changing Roles and Competencies. *Amer. J. Agr. Econ.*, December 1981, *63*(5), pp. 859–62. [G: U.S.]

Bullock, J. Bruce and Ward, Clement E. Economic Welfare and Food Safety Regulation: The Case of Mechanically Deboned Meat: Comment. *Amer. J. Agr. Econ.*, November 1981, *63*(4), pp. 738–41. [G: U.S.]

Bulmuş, Ismail. Türkiye'de Tarimsal Taban Fiyat Politikasi ve Etkileri. (Price Support Policies in Turkey and Their Impacts. With English summary.) *METU*, Special Issue, 1981, pp. 541–73. [G: Turkey]

Candler, Wilfred; Fortuny-Amat, Jose and McCarl, Bruce A. The Potential Role of Multilevel Programming in Agricultural Economics. *Amer. J. Agr. Econ.*, August 1981, *63*(3), pp. 521–31.

Cañete, Constancio C. The Income Level and Income Distribution Impacts of Masagana 99 Program in Central Luzon, Philippines. *Philippine Econ. J.*, 1981, *20*(3&4), pp. 238–56. [G: Philippines]

Carey, Michael J. European Food Policy: Rules of the Game. In *Balaam, D. N. and Carey, M. J., eds.*, 1981, pp. 30–47. [G: W. Europe]

Carey, Michael J. The Political Economy of Food—The Regional Approach: Introduction. In *Balaam, D. N. and Carey, M. J., eds.*, 1981, pp. 1–8.

Carter, C. A. and Kraft, D. F. An Evaluation of Pricing Performance of the Canadian Feed Grains Policy: A Comment. *Can. J. Agr. Econ.*, November 1981, *29*(3), pp. 349–54. [G: Canada]

de las Casas, P. Lizardo. Central Planning, National Policies and Local Rural Development Programmes: The Planning Process in Latin America and the Caribbean. In *Johnson, G. and Maunder, A., eds.*, 1981, pp. 167–83. [G: Latin America; Caribbean]

Chambers, Robert G., et al. Estimating the Impact of Beef Import Restrictions in the U.S. Import Market. *Australian J. Agr. Econ.*, August 1981, *25*(2), pp. 123–33. [G: U.S.]

Chan, M. W. Luke. A Markovian Approach to the Study of the Canadian Cattle Industry. *Rev. Econ. Statist.*, February 1981, *63*(1), pp. 107–16. [G: Canada]

Chassagne, M. E. Strong Agricultures but Weak Rural Economies—The Undue Emphasis on Agriculture in European Rural Development: Comment. *Europ. Rev. Agr. Econ.*, 1981, *8*(2–3), pp. 171–76. [G: Europe]

Clayton, Eric S. Kenya's Agriculture and the ILO Report—Six Years After. In *Killick, T., ed.*, 1981, *1978*, pp. 145–49. [G: Kenya]

Colette, W. Arden. Decision Aids for Local Decision Making: Discussion. *Amer. J. Agr. Econ.*, December 1981, *63*(5), pp. 986–87. [G: U.S.]

Conner, J. Richard. Discussion: The New Food and Agricultural Bill—Where Is It Headed? Potential Impacts on Southern Agriculture. *Southern J. Agr. Econ.*, July 1981, *13*(1), pp. 21–23. [G: U.S.]

Coulson, Andrew. Agricultural Policies in Mainland Tanzania, 1946–76. In *Heyer, J.; Roberts, P. and Williams, G., eds.*, 1981, pp. 52–89. [G: Tanzania]

Cowen, Michael. Commodity Production in Kenya's Central Province. In *Heyer, J.; Roberts, P. and Williams, G., eds.*, 1981, pp. 121–42. [G: Kenya]

Craven, Kathryn and Tuluy, A. Hasan. Rice Policy in Senegal. In *Pearson, S. R.; Stryker, J. D. and Humphreys, C. P., et al.*, 1981, pp. 229–62. [G: Senegal]

Csaki, Csaba. National Agricultural Sector Models for Centrally Planned Economies. In *Johnson, G. and Maunder, A., eds.*, 1981, pp. 312–23. [G: Hungary; CMEA]

Dale, Christopher. Agricultural Research as State Intervention. In *Busch, L., ed.*, 1981, pp. 69–82. [G: U.S.]

Dalton, Robert. Resources on Tobacco Production and Marketing. In *Finger, W. R., ed.*, 1981, pp. 75–89. [G: U.S.]

Dandekar, V. M. Crop Insurance in India. *Artha-Vikas*, January–December 1981, *17*(1–2), pp. 73–124. [G: India]

Day, Lee M. Research and the Family Farm: Implications for Agricultural Economics Research. *Amer. J. Agr. Econ.*, December 1981, *63*(5), pp. 997–1004. [G: U.S.]

Deere, Carmen Diana. Nicaraguan Agricultural Policy: 1979–81. *Cambridge J. Econ.*, June 1981, *5*(2), pp. 195–200. [G: Nicaragua]

Dickens, Robert E. and Moore, Richard K. Food Policy in North America: The Bread Basket. In *Balaam, D. N. and Carey, M. J., eds.*, 1981, pp. 11–29. [G: U.S.]

Diesslin, H. G. The Computer—Extension's Delivery System of the Future. *Amer. J. Agr. Econ.*, December 1981, *63*(5), pp. 863–67.

Doeksen, Gerald A. and Nelson, James R. Decision Aids for Local Decision Making. *Amer. J. Agr. Econ.*, December 1981, *63*(5), pp. 974–81. [G: U.S.]

Esguerra, Emmanuel F. An Assessment of the Masagana 99 Credit Subsidy as an Equity Measure. *Phillipine Rev. Econ. Bus.*, Sept. & Dec. 1981,

18(3/4), pp. 168–91.   [G: Philippines]

Fajardo, Daniel; McCarl, Bruce A. and Thompson, Robert L. A Multicommodity Analysis of Trade Policy Effects: The Case of Nicaraguan Agriculture. *Amer. J. Agr. Econ.*, February 1981, *63*(1), pp. 23–31.   [G: Nicaragua]

Falcon, Walter P. Reflections on the Presidential Commission on World Hunger. *Amer. J. Agr. Econ.*, December 1981, *63*(5), pp. 819–26.
[G: U.S.]

Fáy, József and Nyers, Reszö. Specialization and Cooperation in the Hungarian Economy and the CMEA. *Acta Oecon.*, 1981, *27*(1–2), pp. 1–18.
[G: CMEA; Hungary]

Flint, Paul. The EEC Budgetary Problem. *Quart. Rev. Rural Econ.*, February 1981, *3*(1), pp. 36–46.   [G: EEC; Australia]

Forrest, Tom. Agricultural Policies in Nigeria 1900–78. In *Heyer, J.; Roberts, P. and Williams, G., eds.*, 1981, pp. 222–58.   [G: Nigeria]

Franco, G. Robert. The Optimal Producer Price of Cocoa in Ghana. *J. Devel. Econ.*, February 1981, *8*(1), pp. 77–92.   [G: Ghana]

Frankel, F. R. India's New Strategy of Agricultural Development: Political Costs of Agrarian Modernization. In *Livingstone, I., ed.*, 1981, *1969*, pp. 287–92.   [G: India]

Ganzel, Richard. Regionalism, Food Policy, and Domestic Political Economy: Lessons from Latin America. In *Balaam, D. N. and Carey, M. J., eds.*, 1981, pp. 83–105.   [G: Latin America]

Garcia, Marcelo. Agrobusiness and Food in the Context of Regional Cooperation. In *Nicol, D.; Echeverria, L. and Peccei, A., eds.*, 1981, pp. 289–98.

Gardner, Bruce. Consequences of Farm Policies during the 1970s. In *Johnson, D. G., ed.*, 1981, pp. 48–72.   [G: U.S.]

Goreux, Louis M. Compensatory Financing for Fluctuations in the Cost of Cereal Imports. In *Valdés, A.*, 1981, pp. 307–32.   [G: LDCs]

Goueli, Ahmed A. Food Security Program in Egypt. In *Valdés, A.*, 1981, pp. 143–57.   [G: Egypt]

Grant, Wyn. The Politics of the Green Pound, 1974–79. *J. Common Market Stud.*, June 1981, *19*(4), pp. 313–29.   [G: U.K.; EEC]

Gray, Kenneth R. Soviet Agricultural Prices, Rent and Land Cadastres. *J. Compar. Econ.*, March 1981, *5*(1), pp. 43–59.   [G: U.S.S.R.]

Grommet, Allen. Reconciling Agricultural Pricing, Environmental, Conservation, Energy, and Structural Concerns: Discussion. *Amer. J. Agr. Econ.*, May 1981, *63*(2), pp. 333–34. [G: U.S.]

Guillory, Ferrel. The Politics of Tobacco in North Carolina: "A Load Not Easy to be Borne." In *Finger, W. R., ed.*, 1981, pp. 313–18. [G: U.S.]

Gupta, Sanjeev and Mayer, Thomas. A Test of the Efficiency of Futures Markets in Commodities. *Weltwirtsch. Arch.*, 1981, *117*(4), pp. 661–71.

Guttman, Joel M. The Political Economy of Agricultural Extension Services in India. In *Russell, C. S. and Nicholson, N. K., eds.*, 1981, pp. 183–202.   [G: India]

de Haen, Hartwig. The Use of Quantitative Sector Analysis in Agricultural Policy: Potentials and Limitations. In *Johnson, G. and Maunder, A., eds.*, 1981, pp. 299–311.

Hamilton, W. E. Consequences of Farm Policies during the 1970s: Comment. In *Johnson, D. G., ed.*, 1981, pp. 75–80.   [G: U.S.]

Hathaway, Dale E. Agricultural Policy Alternatives for the 1980s: Comment. In *Johnson, D. G., ed.*, 1981, pp. 228–29.   [G: U.S.]

Hathaway, Dale E. Government and Agriculture Revisited: A Review of Two Decades of Change. *Amer. J. Agr. Econ.*, December 1981, *63*(5), pp. 779–87.   [G: U.S.]

Hazell, Peter B. R. and Pomareda, Carlos. Evaluating Price Stabilization Schemes with Mathematical Programming. *Amer. J. Agr. Econ.*, August 1981, *63*(3), pp. 550–56.

Heyer, Judith. Agricultural Development Policy in Kenya from the Colonial Period to 1975. In *Heyer, J.; Roberts, P. and Williams, G., eds.*, 1981, pp. 90–120.   [G: Kenya]

Hildreth, R. J. and Armbruster, Walter J. Extension Program Delivery—Past, Present, and Future: An Overview. *Amer. J. Agr. Econ.*, December 1981, *63*(5), pp. 853–58.   [G: U.S.]

Hillman, Jimmye S. A New Mode of Agricultural Protectionism. In *Johnson, G. and Maunder, A., eds.*, 1981, pp. 547–51.

Hillman, Jimmye S. Policy Issues Relevant to United States Agricultural Trade. In *McCalla, A. F. and Josling, T. E., eds.*, 1981, pp. 113–42.
[G: U.S.]

Hirashima, S. Some Issues in Indian Agriculture Viewed from the Japanese Experience. In *Sarma, J. S.*, 1981, pp. 59–69.   [G: India; Japan]

Holt, John. Changing Delivery Systems for Agricultural Extension: Discussion. *Amer. J. Agr. Econ.*, December 1981, *63*(5), pp. 868–69.   [G: U.S.]

Hoover, Dale M. A Framework for Analyzing Agricultural and Food Policy in the 1980s. *Amer. J. Agr. Econ.*, May 1981, *63*(2), pp. 328–32.
[G: U.S.]

Hoover, Dale M. A Framework for Food and Agricultural Policy for the 1980s: Comment. In *Johnson, D. G., ed.*, 1981, pp. 224–28.   [G: U.S.]

Huddleston, Barbara. Responsiveness of Food Aid to Variable Import Requirements. In *Valdés, A.*, 1981, pp. 287–306.   [G: LDCs]

Huddleston, Barbara and Konandreas, Panos. Insurance Approach to Food Security: Simulation of Benefits for 1970/71–1975/76 and for 1978–1982. In *Valdés, A.*, 1981, pp. 241–54.
[G: LDCs]

Huffman, Wallace E. and Miranowski, John A. An Economic Analysis of Expenditures on Agricultural Experiment Station Research. *Amer. J. Agr. Econ.*, February 1981, *63*(1), pp. 104–18.
[G: U.S.]

Hughes, Harlan. Changing Delivery Systems for Agricultural Extension: Discussion. *Amer. J. Agr. Econ.*, December 1981, *63*(5), pp. 870.
[G: U.S.]

Humphreys, Charles P. Rice Production in the Ivory Coast. In *Pearson, S. R.; Stryker, J. D. and Humphreys, C. P., et al.*, 1981, pp. 61–105.
[G: Ivory Coast]

Humphreys, Charles P. and Rader, Patricia L. Rice Policy in the Ivory Coast. In *Pearson, S. R.; Stryker, J. D. and Humphreys, C. P., et al.*, 1981, pp. 15–60. [G: Ivory Coast]

Icamina, Benvenuto N. The Impact of UNCTAD Commodity Stabilization on Philippine Trade: A Simulation Analysis of Selected Commodities. *Philippine Econ. J.*, 1981, *20*(3&4), pp. 277–94. [G: Philippines]

Jabara, Cathy L. Interaction of Japanese Rice and Wheat Policy and the Impact on Trade. *Southern J. Agr. Econ.*, December 1981, *13*(2), pp. 133–39. [G: Japan]

Johnson, D. Gale. Agricultural Policy Alternatives for the 1980s. In *Johnson, D. G., ed.*, 1981, pp. 183–209. [G: U.S.]

Johnson, D. Gale. Comparative Advantage of United States Agriculture. In *Baldwin, R. E. and Richardson, J. D., eds.*, 1981, 1979, pp. 221–30. [G: U.S.; EEC]

Johnson, D. Gale. Food and Agricultural Policy for the 1980s: Foreword. In *Johnson, D. G., ed.*, 1981, pp. xi–xxi. [G: U.S.]

Johnson, D. Gale. Grain Insurance, Reserves, and Trade: Contributions to Food Security for LDCs. In *Valdés, A.*, 1981, pp. 255–86. [G: LDCs]

Johnson, Ruth T. and McManus, B. R. Reply: A Theoretical Framework for Analyzing Social Costs of the Tobacco Program. *Southern J. Agr. Econ.*, December 1981, *13*(2), pp. 159. [G: U.S.]

Josling, Timothy. Price, Stock, and Trade Policies and the Functioning of International Grain Markets. In *Valdés, A.*, 1981, pp. 161–84. [G: Selected MDCs; U.S.S.R.]

Josling, Timothy E. Domestic Agricultural Price Policies and Their Interaction through Trade. In *McCalla, A. F. and Josling, T. E., eds.*, 1981, pp. 49–68.

Josling, Timothy E. Imperfect Markets in Agricultural Trade: Introduction. In *McCalla, A. F. and Josling, T. E., eds.*, 1981, pp. 1–8.

Josling, Timothy E. International Agricultural Policy Issues in Relation to Research Needs. In *McCalla, A. F. and Josling, T. E., eds.*, 1981, pp. 143–66.

Kazee, Donald K. Four Decisions Facing Latin American Extension. In *Busch, L., ed.*, 1981, pp. 167–78. [G: Latin America]

Keeler, John T. S. Corporatism and Official Union Hegemony: The Case of French Agricultural Syndicalism. In *Berger, S., ed.*, 1981, pp. 185–208. [G: France]

Kiger, Hugh C. Open Trade and Modernized Tobacco Program: The Keys to an Expanded U.S. Flue-Cured World Market. In *Finger, W. R., ed.*, 1981, pp. 131–44. [G: Global; U.S.]

Kihl, Young Whan and Bark, Dong Suh. Food Policies in a Rapidly Developing Country: The Case of South Korea, 1960–1978. *J. Devel. Areas*, October 1981, *16*(1), pp. 47–70. [G: S. Korea]

Kisiel, Michal. Links of Polish Agriculture with the World Economy. In *Johnson, G. and Maunder, A., eds.*, 1981, pp. 338–44. [G: Poland]

Kislev, Yoav. International Farm Prices and the Social Cost of Cheap Food Policies: Comment. *Amer. J. Agr. Econ.*, May 1981, *63*(2), pp. 280. [G: LDCs]

Knutson, Ronald D. Discussion: Economic and Political Factors Influencing the Outcome of the 1981

Farm Bill. *Southern J. Agr. Econ.*, July 1981, *13*(1), pp. 25–28. [G: U.S.]

Kramer, Randall A. and Pope, Rulon D. Participation in Farm Commodity Programs: A Stochastic Dominance Analysis. *Amer. J. Agr. Econ.*, February 1981, *63*(1), pp. 119–28. [G: U.S.]

Kriesel, Herbert C. The Need to Co-ordinate Central and Local Rural Development Planning and Administration. In *Johnson, G. and Maunder, A., eds.*, 1981, pp. 187–98.

Krishna, Raj and Raychaudhuri, G. S. Agricultural Price Policy in India—A Case Study of Rice. *Indian Econ. J.*, January–March 1981, *28*(3), pp. 16–34. [G: India]

Kullmann, Ulrich. "Fair Labour Standards" in International Commodity Agreements: Reply. *J. World Trade Law*, September–October 1981, *15*(5), pp. 460–61.

Lanfranco, Sam. Mexican Oil, Export-led Development and Agricultural Neglect. *J. Econ. Devel.*, July 1981, *6*(1), pp. 125–51. [G: Mexico]

Langworthy, Mark; Pearson, Scott R. and Josling, Timothy. Macroeconomic Influences on Future Agricultural Prices in the European Community. *Europ. Rev. Agr. Econ.*, 1981, *8*(1), pp. 5–26. [G: EEC]

Larson, Olaf F. Agricultural Policies for Growth and Equity: The Perspective of the American Experience. In *Sarma, J. S.*, 1981, pp. 70–76. [G: U.S.]

Lechi, F. Agricultural Policies and Their Regional Impact in Western Europe: Comment. *Europ. Rev. Agr. Econ.*, 1981, *8*(2–3), pp. 283–85. [G: EEC]

Ledesma, Antonio J. Landless Workers and Rice Farmers: Peasant Subclasses under Agrarian Reform in Two Philippine Villages. *Philippine Econ. J.*, 1981, *20*(3&4), pp. 201–26. [G: Philippines]

Lord, Montague J. Comment on "Commodity Exports and NIEO Proposals for Buffer Stocks and Compensatory Finance." *Quart. Rev. Econ. Bus.*, Summer 1981, *21*(2), pp. 76–82. [G: Latin America]

Lord, Montague J. Commodity Exports and NIEO Proposals for Buffer Stocks and Compensatory Finance: Comment. In *Baer, W. and Gillis, M., eds.*, 1981, pp. 76–82. [G: Brazil; Chile; Latin America]

Love, J. Commodity Diversification: A Market Model. *J. Devel. Stud.*, October 1981, *18*(1), pp. 94–103. [G: Latin America; Africa; Asia]

Luttrell, Clifton B. A Bushel of Wheat for a Barrel of Oil: Can We Offset OPEC's Gains with a Grain Cartel? *Fed. Res. Bank St. Louis Rev.*, April 1981, *63*(4), pp. 13–21. [G: U.S.]

Luttrell, Clifton B. Grain Export Agreements—No Gains, No Losses. *Fed. Res. Bank St. Louis Rev.*, August/September 1981, *63*(7), pp. 23–29. [G: U.S.]

Maggard, Sally. From Farmers to Miners: The Decline of Agriculture in Eastern Kentucky. In *Busch, L., ed.*, 1981, pp. 25–66. [G: U.S.]

Magiera, Stephen L. The Role of Wheat in the Indonesian Food Sector. *Bull. Indonesian Econ. Stud.*, November 1981, *17*(3), pp. 48–73. [G: Indonesia]

Mammen, Thampy. A Note on the Foodgrain Surplus. *Indian Econ. J.*, April–June 1981, *28*(4), pp. 85–88. [G: India]

Mann, Charles K. The Tobacco Franchise for Whom? In *Finger, W. R., ed.*, 1981, pp. 37–46. [G: U.S.]

Marsh, J. The Need for New Policies: Agricultural Policy. *Economia (Portugal)*, January 1981, *5*(1), pp. 1–32. [G: EEC]

Martin, Marshall A. Reconciling Agricultural Pricing, Environmental, Conservation, Energy, and Structural Concerns. *Amer. J. Agr. Econ.*, May 1981, *63*(2), pp. 309–15. [G: U.S.]

Maxwell, S. J. and Singer, H. W. Food Aid to Developing Countries: A Survey. In *Streeten, P. and Jolly, R, eds.*, 1981, pp. 219–40. [G: LDCs]

McCalla, Alex F. Structural and Market Power Consideration in Imperfect Agricultural Markets. In *McCalla, A. F. and Josling, T. E., eds.*, 1981, pp. 9–28.

McCloskey, Donald N. Peasant Behavior and Social Change—Cooperatives and Individual Holdings: Comment. In *Russell, C. S. and Nicholson, N. K., eds.*, 1981, pp. 226–31. [G: Peru]

McIntire, John. Rice Policy in Mali. In *Pearson, S. R.; Stryker, J. D. and Humphreys, C. P., et al.*, 1981, pp. 299–330. [G: Mali]

McIntire, John. Rice Production in Mali. In *Pearson, S. R.; Stryker, J. D. and Humphreys, C. P., et al.*, 1981, pp. 331–60. [G: Mali]

Meyers, William H. and Ryan, Mary E. The Farmer-Owned Reserve: How Is the Experiment Working? *Amer. J. Agr. Econ.*, May 1981, *63*(2), pp. 316–23. [G: U.S.]

Monke, Eric A. Rice Policy in Liberia. In *Pearson, S. R.; Stryker, J. D. and Humphreys, C. P., et al.*, 1981, pp. 109–40. [G: Liberia]

Monke, Eric A. The Economics of Rice in Liberia. In *Pearson, S. R.; Stryker, J. D. and Humphreys, C. P., et al.*, 1981, pp. 141–72. [G: Liberia]

Monke, Eric A. Toward a U.S. Agricultural Export Policy for the 1980s: Discussion. *Amer. J. Agr. Econ.*, December 1981, *63*(5), pp. 848–50. [G: U.S.]

Morrow, Daniel. The International Wheat Agreement and LDC Food Security. In *Valdés, A.*, 1981, pp. 213–39. [G: Global]

Murray, Steven W. Management Information Systems for Local Government: Discussion. *Amer. J. Agr. Econ.*, December 1981, *63*(5), pp. 982–83. [G: U.S.]

Musser, Wesley N. and Stamoulis, Kostas G. Evaluating the Food and Agriculture Act of 1977 with Firm Quadratic Risk Programming. *Amer. J. Agr. Econ.*, August 1981, *63*(3), pp. 447–56. [G: U.S.]

Naylor, E. L. Farm Structure Policy in North-East Scotland. *Scot. J. Polit. Econ.*, November 1981, *28*(3), pp. 266–72. [G: U.K.]

Nazarenko, Victor J. The Part Played by Agricultural Economists in State Trading Bodies. In *Johnson, G. and Maunder, A., eds.*, 1981, pp. 546–47.

Nieuwoudt, W. L. An Economic Evaluation of Alternative Peanut Policies: Delayed Reply. *Amer. J. Agr. Econ.*, May 1981, *63*(2), pp. 305–08. [G: U.S.]

O'Mara, L. P. Some Economic Implications of Minimum Pricing: The Case of Wine Grapes in Australia. *Rev. Marketing Agr. Econ.*, August 1981, *49*(2), pp. 107–23. [G: Australia]

O'Mara, Paul; Knopke, Philip and Roberts, Ivan. Costs of Japanese Agricultural Support Policies: Some Concepts and Estimates. *Quart. Rev. Rural Econ.*, May 1981, *3*(2), pp. 141–48. [G: Japan]

Pagoulatos, Emilio; Shonkwiler, J. Scott and Degner, Robert L. Foreign Competition and Trade Policy for the Florida Lime Industry. *Amer. J. Agr. Econ.*, August 1981, *63*(3), pp. 557–61. [G: U.S.]

Parkinson, Jack. Relationships to Donors: Food Aid. In *Faaland, J., ed.*, 1981, pp. 82–101. [G: Bangladesh]

Parmenter, B. R.; Sams, D. and Vincent, D. P. Who Pays for Home Consumption Pricing Schemes? *Econ. Rec.*, June 1981, *57*(157), pp. 168–79. [G: Australia]

Parsons, Kenneth H. The Challenge of Agrarian Reform. In *Johnson, G. and Maunder, A., eds.*, 1981, pp. 358–66.

Pearce, William R. U.S. Agriculture in an Interdependent World Economy: Policy Alternatives for the 1980s: Comment. In *Johnson, D. G., ed.*, 1981, pp. 219–23. [G: U.S.]

Pearson, Scott R.; Humphreys, Charles P. and Monke, Eric A. A Comparative Analysis of Rice Policies in Five West African Countries. In *Pearson, S. R.; Stryker, J. D. and Humphreys, C. P., et al.*, 1981, pp. 363–95. [G: Ivory Coast; Liberia; Mali; Senegal; Sierra Leone]

Perrin, Richard K. and Scobie, Grant M. Market Intervention Policies for Increasing the Consumption of Nutrients by Low Income Households. *Amer. J. Agr. Econ.*, February 1981, *63*(1), pp. 73–82. [G: Colombia]

Persson, Lars Olof and Bolin, Olof. Agricultural Planning for Regional Balance. *Europ. Rev. Agr. Econ.*, 1981, *8*(4), pp. 499–518. [G: Sweden]

Peters, W. and Langendorf, U. Direct Income Transfers for the Agricultural Sector in Less-Favoured Areas (DIT-LFA). The Council Directive No. 268/75 EEC, Title II: A Comparison between and within Member Countries. *Europ. Rev. Agr. Econ.*, 1981, *8*(1), pp. 41–55. [G: EEC]

Petras, James and Havens, Eugene. Peasant Behavior and Social Change—Cooperatives and Individual Holdings. In *Russell, C. S. and Nicholson, N. K., eds.*, 1981, pp. 203–25. [G: Peru]

Phillips, Michael J. and Dalrymple, Dana G. U.S. Food and Agricultural Research Assessment: Implications for Agricultural Economists. *Amer. J. Agr. Econ.*, December 1981, *63*(5), pp. 990–96. [G: U.S.]

Podbielski, Gisele. The Common Agricultural Policy and the Mezzogiorno. *J. Common Market Stud.*, June 1981, *19*(4), pp. 331–50. [G: Italy; EEC]

Porter, Roger B. The U.S.-U.S.S.R. Grain Agreement: Some Lessons for Policymakers. *Public Policy*, Fall 1981, *29*(4), pp. 527–51.

Pugh, Charles. Landmarks in the Tobacco Program. In *Finger, W. R., ed.*, 1981, pp. 31–36. [G: U.S.]

Pugh, Charles. The Federal Tobacco Program: How

it Works and Alternatives for Change. In *Finger, W. R., ed.*, 1981, pp. 13–29. [G: U.S.]

Purcell, Joseph C. U.S. Food and Agricultural Research Assessment: Implications for Agricultural Economists: Discussion. *Amer. J. Agr. Econ.*, December 1981, 63(5), pp. 1005–07. [G: U.S.]

Quiggin, John C. and Anderson, Jock R. Price Bands and Buffer Funds. *Econ. Rec.*, March 1981, 57(156), pp. 67–73.

Rahman, Sultan Hafez. Simulation of an Econometric Model to Analyze the Impact of a Buffer Stock Scheme in the Bangladesh Jute Sector. *Bangladesh Devel. Stud.*, Autumn 1981, 9(4), pp. 1–33. [G: Bangladesh]

Rasmussen, Wayne D. and Porter, Jane M. Strategies for Dealing with World Hunger: Post-World War II Policies. *Amer. J. Agr. Econ.*, December 1981, 63(5), pp. 810–18.

Rausser, Gordon C. and Yassour, Joseph. Multiattribute Utility Analysis: The Case of Filipino Rice Policy. *Amer. J. Agr. Econ.*, August 1981, 63(3), pp. 484–94. [G: Philippines]

Reutlinger, Shlomo and Bigman, David. Feasibility, Effectiveness, and Costs of Food Security Alternatives in Developing Countries. In *Valdés, A.*, 1981, pp. 185–212.

Rich, M. M. The Policy Implications of Possible New Zealand Wheat Pricing Schemes. *Australian J. Agr. Econ.*, December 1981, 25(3), pp. 266–74. [G: New Zealand]

Roberts, Ivan; Tie, Graeme and Murphy, Susan. EEC Sugar Policies and World Market Prices. *Quart. Rev. Rural Econ.*, November 1981, 3(4), pp. 309–19. [G: EEC]

Rosegrant, Mark W. and Herdt, Robert W. Simulating the Impacts of Credit Policy and Fertilizer Subsidy on Central Luzon Rice Farms, the Philippines. *Amer. J. Agr. Econ.*, November 1981, 63(4), pp. 655–65. [G: Philippines]

Sain, K. Agricultural Price Policy of the Sixth Five Year Plan. *Econ. Aff.*, July–September 1981, 26(3), pp. 193–200. [G: India]

Sarma, M. T. R. Food, Natural Resources, and the New International Economic Order: The Case of India. In *Lozoya, J. A. and Bhattacharya, A. K., eds.*, 1981, pp. 141–63. [G: India]

Sarris, Alexander H. and Schmitz, Andrew. Toward a U.S. Agricultural Export Policy for the 1980s. *Amer. J. Agr. Econ.*, December 1981, 63(5), pp. 832–39. [G: U.S.]

Scarlett, Lynn. Tropical Africa: Food or Famine? In *Balaam, D. N. and Carey, M. J., eds.*, 1981, pp. 166–88. [G: Africa]

Schiefer, G. Agricultural Policy Planning with Programming Models: Problems of Centralized Planning in Decentralized Decision Situations. In *Janssen, J. M. L.; Pau, L. F. and Straszak, A. J., eds.*, 1981, pp. 157–62. [G: LDCs]

Schluter, Gerald and Lee, Gene K. Effects of Relative Price Changes on U.S. Food Sectors, 1967–78. *Agr. Econ. Res.*, January 1981, 33(1), pp. 1–12. [G: U.S.]

Schmitz, Andrew; Firch, Robert S. and Hillman, Jimmye S. Agricultural Export Dumping: The Case of Mexican Winter Vegetables in the U.S. Market. *Amer. J. Agr. Econ.*, November 1981,

63(4), pp. 645–54. [G: U.S.; Mexico]

Schnittker, John A. A Framework for Food and Agricultural Policy for the 1980s. In *Johnson, D. G., ed.*, 1981, pp. 210–18. [G: U.S.]

Schnittker, John A. A Framework for Food and Agricultural Policy for the 1980s. *Amer. J. Agr. Econ.*, May 1981, 63(2), pp. 324–27. [G: U.S.]

Schuh, G. Edward. Challenges for Agricultural Economists Working in State Trading Agencies. In *Johnson, G. and Maunder, A., eds.*, 1981, pp. 544–46.

Schuh, G. Edward. Floating Exchange Rates, International Interdependence, and Agricultural Policy. In *Johnson, G. and Maunder, A., eds.*, 1981, pp. 416–23.

Schuh, G. Edward. U.S. Agriculture in an Interdependence World Economy: Policy Alternatives for the 1980s. In *Johnson, D. G., ed.*, 1981, pp. 157–82. [G: U.S.]

Schultz, Theodore W. Knowledge is Power in Agriculture. *Challenge*, September/October 1981, 24(4), pp. 4–12.

Selowsky, Marcelo. Reflections on the Presidential Commission on World Hunger: Discussion. *Amer. J. Agr. Econ.*, December 1981, 63(5), pp. 827–28. [G: U.S.]

Sharples, Jerry A. and Holland, Forrest D. Impact on the Farmer-Owned Reserve on Privately Owned Wheat Stocks. *Amer. J. Agr. Econ.*, August 1981, 63(3), pp. 538–43. [G: U.S.]

Shepherd, Andrew. Agrarian Change in Northern Ghana: Public Investment, Capitalist Farming and Famine. In *Heyer, J.; Roberts, P. and Williams, G., eds.*, 1981, pp. 168–92. [G: Ghana]

Simatupang, B. Polish Agriculture in the 1970s and the Prospects for the Early 1980s. *Europ. Rev. Agr. Econ.*, 1981, 8(4), pp. 453–73. [G: Poland]

Smith, Ian. EEC Sugar Policy in an International Context. *J. World Trade Law*, March–April 1981, 15(2), pp. 95–110. [G: EEC]

Spencer, Dunstan S. C. Rice Policy in Sierra Leone. In *Pearson, S. R.; Stryker, J. D. and Humphreys, C. P., et al.*, 1981, pp. 175–200. [G: Sierra Leone]

Spencer, Dunstan S. C. Rice Production in Sierra Leone. In *Pearson, S. R.; Stryker, J. D. and Humphreys, C. P., et al.*, 1981, pp. 201–25. [G: Sierra Leone]

Spitze, Robert G. F. Future Agricultural and Food Policy. *Southern J. Agr. Econ.*, July 1981, 13(1), pp. 11–19. [G: U.S.]

Srinivasan, T. N. Peasant Behavior and Social Change—Cooperatives and Individual Holdings: Comment. In *Russell, C. S. and Nicholson, N. K., eds.*, 1981, pp. 231–37. [G: Peru]

Srinivasan, T. N. Reflections on the Presidential Commission on World Hunger: Discussion. *Amer. J. Agr. Econ.*, December 1981, 63(5), pp. 829–31. [G: U.S.]

Steele, W. Scott. The Farmer-Owned Reserve: How Is the Experiment Working?: Discussion. *Amer. J. Agr. Econ.*, May 1981, 63(2), pp. 335–36. [G: U.S.]

Stennis, Earl A. and Fuller, M. J. Comment: A Theoretical Framework for Analyzing Social Costs of the Tobacco Program. *Southern J. Agr. Econ.*,

December 1981, *13*(2), pp. 157–58. [G: U.S.]

Stier, J. C. and Bishop, R. C. Crop Depredation by Waterfowl: Is Compensation the Solution? *Can. J. Agr. Econ.*, July 1981, *29*(2), pp. 159–70. [G: Canada]

Storey, Gary G. and Kulshreshtha, Surenda N. An Evaluation of Pricing Performance of the Canadian Feed Grain Policy: A Reply. *Can. J. Agr. Econ.*, November 1981, *29*(3), pp. 355–60. [G: Canada]

Storey, Gary G. and Kulshreshtha, Surendra N. An Evaluation of Pricing Performance of the Canadian Feed Grains Policy. *Can. J. Agr. Econ.*, February 1981, *29*(1), pp. 1–20. [G: Canada]

Strickland, Roger. Accounting for Commodity Credit Corporation Loans in Farm Income. *Agr. Econ. Res.*, October 1981, *33*(4), pp. 19–20. [G: U.S.]

Stryker, J. Dirck. Comparative Advantage and Public Policy in West African Rice. In *Pearson, S. R.; Stryker, J. D. and Humphreys, C. P., et al.*, 1981, pp. 396–431. [G: Ivory Coast; Liberia; Mali; Senegal; Sierra Leone]

Swain, N. The Evolution of Hungary's Agricultural System since 1967. In *Hare, P. G.; Radice, H. K. and Swain, N., eds.*, 1981, pp. 225–51. [G: Hungary]

Tarditi, Secondo. A More Effective Role of Public Finance in Agricultural Policy. *Econ. Notes*, 1981, *10*(3), pp. 128–37. [G: EEC]

Thomson, K. J. and Harvey, D. R. The Efficiency of the Common Agricultural Policy. *Europ. Rev. Agr. Econ.*, 1981, *8*(1), pp. 57–83. [G: EEC]

Timmer, C. Peter. China and the World Grain Market. *Challenge*, September/October 1981, *24*(4), pp. 13–21. [G: China]

Tolwinski, B. and Sosnowski, J. Planning Model with Decentralized Structure of Decision Making. In *Janssen, J. M. L.; Pau, L. F. and Straszak, A. J., eds.*, 1981, pp. 367–74.

Tomic, Dušan. The Regional Economic Development and Political Aims, Methods and Measures in the Regional Development of Agriculture: The Yugoslav Example. *Europ. Rev. Agr. Econ.*, 1981, *8*(2–3), pp. 287–314. [G: Yugoslavia]

Tracy, Michael. General Report on Policy Aspects. *Europ. Rev. Agr. Econ.*, 1981, *8*(2–3), pp. 425–34.

Tuluy, A. Hasan. Costs and Incentives in Rice Production in Senegal. In *Pearson, S. R.; Stryker, J. D. and Humphreys, C. P., et al.*, 1981, pp. 263–95. [G: Senegal]

Warley, T. K. Panel Discussion on State Trading Agencies. In *Johnson, G. and Maunder, A., eds.*, 1981, pp. 541–44.

Wassermann, Ursula. UNCTAD: International Cocoa Agreement, 1980. *J. World Trade Law*, March–April 1981, *15*(2), pp. 149–50.

Weeks, Eldon E. Research on the Family Farm: Implications for Agricultural Economics Research: Discussion. *Amer. J. Agr. Econ.*, December 1981, *63*(5), pp. 1008–09. [G: U.S.]

Weinbaum, Marvin G. Agricultural Constraints and Bureaucratic Politics in the Middle East. In *Balaam, D. N. and Carey, M. J., eds.*, 1981, pp. 143–65. [G: Middle East]

Weinschenck, Günther and Kemper, Jutta. Agricultural Policies and Their Regional Impact in Western Europe. *Europ. Rev. Agr. Econ.*, 1981, *8*(2–3), pp. 251–81. [G: EEC]

Wells, R. J. G. Producer Subsidies in the Dairy Industry in Peninsular Malaysia. *J. Econ. Stud.*, 1981, *8*(2), pp. 57–64.

Wibberley, Gerald. Strong Agricultures but Weak Rural Economies—The Undue Emphasis on Agriculture in European Rural Development. *Europ. Rev. Agr. Econ.*, 1981, *8*(2–3), pp. 155–70. [G: Europe]

Wiseman, A. Clark and Sedjo, Roger A. Effects of an Export Embargo on Related Goods: Logs and Lumber. *Amer. J. Agr. Econ.*, August 1981, *63*(3), pp. 423–29. [G: U.S.]

Wyzan, Michael L. Empirical Analysis of Soviet Agricultural Production and Policy. *Amer. J. Agr. Econ.*, August 1981, *63*(3), pp. 475–83. [G: U.S.S.R.]

Yadav, R. P. and Rawal, T. Institutional Innovations for Hill Agricultural Development. In *Nepal, Ministry of Food and Agriculture*, 1981, pp. 130–34. [G: Nepal]

Zhan, Wu. Take the Road of Agricultural Modernization the Chinese Way. *Chinese Econ. Stud.*, Summer 1981, *14*(4), pp. 48–89. [G: China]

714 Agricultural Finance

7140 Agricultural Finance

Adams, Dale W. and Graham, Douglas H. A Critique of Traditional Agricultural Credit Projects and Policies. *J. Devel. Econ.*, June 1981, *8*(3), pp. 347–66. [G: LDCs]

Adams, Dale W. and Pablo Romero, Alfredo Antonio. Group Lending to the Rural Poor in the Dominican Republic: A Stunted Innovation. *Can. J. Agr. Econ.*, July 1981, *29*(2), pp. 217–24. [G: Dominican Republic]

Agarwal, D. K. and Rajagopalan, M. Problem of Crop Insurance Scheme under Indian Conditions. *Artha-Vikas*, January–December 1981, *17*(1–2), pp. 241–50. [G: India; U.S.; Japan]

Bandyopadhyay, Alok Kumar. Village Panchayet—A Bird's Eye View. *Econ. Aff.*, July–September 1981, *26*(3), pp. 169–73. [G: India]

Barraclough, Solon. Agricultural Finance and Rural Credit in Poor Countries: Comment. In *Streeten, P. and Jolly, R, eds.*, 1981, *1976*, pp. 215–17. [G: LDCs]

Barry, Peter J. Capital Asset Pricing and Farm Real Estate: Reply. *Amer. J. Agr. Econ.*, August 1981, *63*(3), pp. 580–81. [G: U.S.]

Barry, Peter J. Impacts of Regulatory Change on Financial Markets for Agriculture. *Amer. J. Agr. Econ.*, December 1981, *63*(5), pp. 905–12. [G: U.S.]

Barry, Peter J.; Baker, Chester B. and Sanint, Luis R. Farmers' Credit Risks and Liquidity Management. *Amer. J. Agr. Econ.*, May 1981, *63*(2), pp. 216–27.

Carter, Colin. Capital Asset Pricing and Farm Real Estate: Comment. *Amer. J. Agr. Econ.*, August 1981, *63*(3), pp. 578–79. [G: U.S.]

Chandrakanth, M. G. and Rebello, N. S. P. Crop Insurance for Rainfed Potatoes. *Artha-Vikas*, January–December 1981, *17*(1–2), pp. 184–95.
[G: India]

Choudhary, K. M. Crop Insurance Scheme for Hybrid-4 Cotton in Gujarat: Field Problems and Prospects. *Artha-Vikas*, January–December 1981, *17*(1–2), pp. 137–53. [G: India]

Chowdhury, A. K.; Singh, R. K. and Singh, R. P. Role of the State Bank of India in Raising Income in Agriculture—District Purnea, Bihar. *Econ. Aff.*, October–December 1981, *26*(4), pp. 273–77. [G: India]

Dandekar, V. M. Crop Insurance in India. *Artha-Vikas*, January–December 1981, *17*(1–2), pp. 73–124. [G: India]

David, Martin. The Transition in Smallholder Banking in Kenya: Evidence from Rural Branch Bank Loans. *J. Devel. Areas*, October 1981, *16*(1), pp. 71–85. [G: Kenya]

Davis, L. Harlan and Weisenborn, David E. Small Farmer Market Development: The El Salvador Experience. *J. Devel. Areas*, April 1981, *15*(3), pp. 407–15. [G: El Salvador]

Errunza, Vihang R., et al. Rural Credit: A Micro Synthesis of the Salvadorean Experience. *J. Devel. Econ.*, April 1981, *8*(2), pp. 227–39. [G: El Salvador]

Esguerra, Emmanuel F. An Assessment of the Masagana 99 Credit Subsidy as an Equity Measure. *Phillipine Rev. Econ. Bus.*, Sept. & Dec. 1981, *18*(3/4), pp. 168–91. [G: Philippines]

Gardner, Bruce. Consequences of Farm Policies during the 1970s. In *Johnson, D. G., ed.*, 1981, pp. 48–72. [G: U.S.]

Gilboa, Devid and Maurice, Nelson. The Reinsurance of Crop Insurance Programme. *Artha-Vikas*, January–December 1981, *17*(1–2), pp. 55–62.

Hamilton, W. E. Consequences of Farm Policies during the 1970s: Comment. In *Johnson, D. G., ed.*, 1981, pp. 75–80. [G: U.S.]

Hughes, Dean W. Impacts of Regulatory Change on Financial Markets for Agriculture: Discussion. *Amer. J. Agr. Econ.*, December 1981, *63*(5), pp. 921–22. [G: U.S.]

Ladman, Jerry R. and Tinnermeier, Ronald L. The Political Economy of Agricultural Credit: The Case of Bolivia. *Amer. J. Agr. Econ.*, February 1981, *63*(1), pp. 66–72. [G: Bolivia]

Lele, Uma. Co-operatives and the Poor: A Comparative Perspective. *World Devel.*, January 1981, *9*(1), pp. 55–72.

Lipton, Michael. Agricultural Finance and Rural Credit in Poor Countries. In *Streeten, P. and Jolly, R, eds.*, 1981, *1976*, pp. 201–11.
[G: LDCs]

Maurice, Nelson. Exploiting Crop-Credit Insurance for Development Purposes in Developing Nations. *Artha-Vikas*, January–December 1981, *17*(1–2), pp. 5–54. [G: India]

Rahman, Md. Lutfor and Barry, Peter J. Financial Control and Variable Amortization under Uncertainty: An Application to Texas Rice Farms. *Southern J. Agr. Econ.*, July 1981, *13*(1), pp. 99–103. [G: U.S.]

Ray, P. K. Crop Insurance in India: Major Policy Issues. *Artha-Vikas*, January–December 1981, *17*(1–2), pp. 63–72. [G: India]

Rosegrant, Mark W. and Herdt, Robert W. Simulating the Impacts of Credit Policy and Fertilizer Subsidy on Central Luzon Rice Farms, the Philippines. *Amer. J. Agr. Econ.*, November 1981, *63*(4), pp. 655–65. [G: Philippines]

Schultz, Frederick H. Statement to Subcommittee on Conservation, Credit, and Rural Development, House Committee on Agriculture, June 23, 1981. *Fed. Res. Bull.*, July 1981, *67*(7), pp. 545–48. [G: U.S.]

Shah, V. B. and Maharaja, Madhukar H. Crop Insurance Scheme in Gujarat: An Account of Past Experiences and Likely Response from Farmers to Specific Proposals. *Artha-Vikas*, January–December 1981, *17*(1–2), pp. 125–36. [G: India]

Singh, R. K.; Singh, R. P. and Chowdhury, A. K. The State Bank of India and Agricultural Production. *Econ. Aff.*, October–December 1981, *26*(4), pp. 261–65. [G: India]

Srivastava, R. N.; Singh, D. K. and Singh, R. P. Impact of C.K.G.B. on Rural Economy. *Econ. Aff.*, October–December 1981, *26*(4), pp. 266–72. [G: India]

Strickland, Roger. Accounting for Commodity Credit Corporation Loans in Farm Income. *Agr. Econ. Res.*, October 1981, *33*(4), pp. 19–20.
[G: U.S.]

Suhag, K. S.; Hasija, R. C. and Pandey, U. K. Crop Yield Instability and Crop Insurance in Punjab. *Artha-Vikas*, January–December 1981, *17*(1–2), pp. 226–40. [G: India]

Tarditi, Secondo. A More Effective Role of Public Finance in Agricultural Policy. *Econ. Notes*, 1981, *10*(3), pp. 128–37. [G: EEC]

Upadhyay, J. and Shrestha, B. R. External Assistance for Nepal's Hill Agriculture. In *Nepal, Ministry of Food and Agriculture*, 1981, pp. 135–43. [G: Nepal]

Vogel, Robert C. Rural Financial Market Performance: Implications of Low Delinquency Rates. *Amer. J. Agr. Econ.*, February 1981, *63*(1), pp. 58–65. [G: Costa Rica]

Yudelman, Montague. Agricultural Finance and Rural Credit in Poor Countries: Comment. In *Streeten, P. and Jolly, R, eds.*, 1981, *1976*, pp. 213–14. [G: LDCs]

715 Agricultural Markets and Marketing

7150 Agricultural Markets and Marketing; Cooperatives

Abbott, John C. Technical Assistance in Marketing: A View over Time. In *Johnson, G. and Maunder, A., eds.*, 1981, pp. 115–27.

Adams, Frank. Vegetable and Fruit Crops: Viable Alternatives for Tobacco Farmers. In *Finger, W. R., ed.*, 1981, pp. 93–102. [G: U.S.]

Alston, Julian M. A Note on the Effects of Non-Transferable Quotas on Supply Functions. *Rev. Marketing Agr. Econ.*, December 1981, *49*(3), pp. 189–97.

Badger, Anthony J. The Tobacco Program and the

Farmer: Early Efforts to Control the Market—and Why they Failed. In *Finger, W. R., ed.*, 1981, pp. 3–12. **[G: U.S.]**

Berck, Peter. Portfolio Theory and the Demand for Futures: The Case of California Cotton. *Amer. J. Agr. Econ.*, August 1981, *63*(3), pp. 466–74. **[G: U.S.]**

Bessler, David A. and Brandt, Jon A. Forecasting Livestock Prices with Individual and Composite Methods. *Appl. Econ.*, December 1981, *13*(4), pp. 513–22. **[G: U.S.]**

Binkley, James K. and Harrer, Bruce. Major Determinants of Ocean Freight Rates for Grains: An Econometric Analysis. *Amer. J. Agr. Econ.*, February 1981, *63*(1), pp. 47–57.

Blakley, Leo V. Regional Markets for Agricultural and Food Products: Needed Research. *Southern J. Agr. Econ.*, July 1981, *13*(1), pp. 69–78. **[G: U.S.]**

Brandt, Jon A. and Bessler, David A. Composite Forecasting: An Application with U.S. Hog Prices. *Amer. J. Agr. Econ.*, February 1981, *63*(1), pp. 135–40. **[G: U.S.]**

Bredahl, Maury E. Interrelationships between Monetary Instruments and Agricultural Commodity Trade: Discussion. *Amer. J. Agr. Econ.*, December 1981, *63*(5), pp. 944–46. **[G: U.S.]**

Buccola, Steven T. The Supply and Demand of Marketing Contracts under Risk. *Amer. J. Agr. Econ.*, August 1981, *63*(3), pp. 503–09.

Buccola, Steven T. and Chieruzzi, Alice M. Costs of Marketing Slaughter Cattle: Computerized versus Conventional Auction Systems. *Agr. Econ. Res.*, July 1981, *33*(3), pp. 31–35. **[G: U.S.]**

Bullock, J. Bruce. Estimates of Consumer Loss Due to Monopoly in the U.S. Food-Manufacturing Industries: Comment. *Amer. J. Agr. Econ.*, May 1981, *63*(2), pp. 290–92. **[G: U.S.]**

Chambers, Robert G. Interrelationships between Monetary Instruments and Agricultural Commodity Trade. *Amer. J. Agr. Econ.*, December 1981, *63*(5), pp. 934–41. **[G: U.S.]**

Conley, Dennis M. and Heady, Earl O. The Interregional Impacts of Improved Truck Transportation on Farm Income from Rice in Thailand. *J. Devel. Areas*, July 1981, *15*(4), pp. 549–59. **[G: Thailand]**

Connor, John M. Food Product Proliferation: A Market Structure Analysis. *Amer. J. Agr. Econ.*, November 1981, *63*(4), pp. 607–17. **[G: U.S.]**

Dalton, Robert. Resources on Tobacco Production and Marketing. In *Finger, W. R., ed.*, 1981, pp. 75–89. **[G: U.S.]**

Davis, J. The Structure and Performance of the Northern Ireland Beef Sector. *Irish J. Agr. Econ. Rural Soc.*, 1981, *8*(2), pp. 153–65. **[G: U.K.]**

Davis, L. Harlan and Weisenborn, David E. Small Farmer Market Development: The El Salvador Experience. *J. Devel. Areas*, April 1981, *15*(3), pp. 407–15. **[G: El Salvador]**

Dewbre, Joe H. Interrelationships between Spot and Futures Markets: Some Implications of Rational Expectations. *Amer. J. Agr. Econ.*, December 1981, *63*(5), pp. 926–33.

Ellis, Frank. Export Valuation and Intra-firm Transfers in the Banana Export Industry in Central

America. In *Murray, R., ed.*, 1981, pp. 61–76. **[G: Costa Rica; Honduras; Guatemala; Panama]**

Fisher, B. S. The Impact of Changing Marketing Margins on Farm Prices. *Amer. J. Agr. Econ.*, May 1981, *63*(2), pp. 261–63. **[G: U.S.]**

Franco, G. Robert. The Optimal Producer Price of Cocoa in Ghana. *J. Devel. Econ.*, February 1981, *8*(1), pp. 77–92. **[G: Ghana]**

Giles, David E. A. and Goss, Barry A. Futures Prices as Forecasts of Commodity Spot Prices: Live Cattle and Wool. *Australian J. Agr. Econ.*, April 1981, *25*(1), pp. 1–13. **[G: Australia]**

Gray, Roger W. and Peck, Anne E. The Chicago Wheat Futures Market: Recent Problems in Historical Perspective. *Food Res. Inst. Stud.*, 1981, *18*(1), pp. 89–115. **[G: U.S.]**

Handmaker, David. Low-Frequency Filters in Seasonal Analysis. *J. Futures Markets*, Fall 1981, *1*(3), pp. 367–78. **[G: U.S.]**

Helmberger, Peter G.; Campbell, Gerald R. and Dobson, William D. Organization and Performance of Agricultural Markets. In *Martin, L. R., ed.*, 1981 cat kp22a, pp. 503–653. **[G: U.S.]**

Helmuth, John W. A Report on the Systematic Downward Bias in Live Cattle Futures Prices. *J. Futures Markets*, Fall 1981, *1*(3), pp. 347–58. **[G: U.S.]**

Izraeli, Oded and Groll, Shalom. Implications of an Ideological Constraint: The Case of Hired Labor in the Kibbutz. *Econ. Develop. Cult. Change*, January 1981, *29*(2), pp. 341–51. **[G: Israel]**

Johnson, Marc A. Current and Developing Issues in Interregional Competition and Agricultural Transportation. *Southern J. Agr. Econ.*, July 1981, *13*(1), pp. 59–68. **[G: U.S.]**

King, Roger. Cooperative Policy and Village Development in Northern Nigeria. In *Heyer, J.; Roberts, P. and Williams, G., eds.*, 1981, pp. 259–80. **[G: Nigeria]**

Ladipo, Patricia. Developing Women's Cooperatives: An Experiment in Rural Nigeria. *J. Devel. Stud.*, April 1981, *17*(3), pp. 123–36. **[G: Nigeria]**

Lawrence, Max. Brazil's Fuel Alcohol Program: Implications for the World Sugar Market. *Quart. Rev. Rural Econ.*, November 1981, *3*(4), pp. 330–33. **[G: Brazil]**

Lee, Jonq-Ying. Generic Advertising, FOB Price Promotion, and FOB Revenue: A Case Study of the Florida Grapefruit Juice Industry. *Southern J. Agr. Econ.*, December 1981, *13*(2), pp. 69–78. **[G: U.S.]**

Lele, Uma. Co-operatives and the Poor: A Comparative Perspective. *World Devel.*, January 1981, *9*(1), pp. 55–72.

Liang, Ernest P. L. Market Accessibility and Agricultural Development in Prewar China. *Econ. Develop. Cult. Change*, October 1981, *30*(1), pp. 77–105. **[G: China]**

Mahmood, Muhammad and Williams, Ross A. The World Jute Market. *Bangladesh Devel. Stud.*, Autumn 1981, *9*(4), pp. 113–23. **[G: Bangladesh; India; Thailand]**

McCalla, Alex F. Structural and Market Power Consideration in Imperfect Agricultural Markets. In *McCalla, A. F. and Josling, T. E., eds.*, 1981,

pp. 9–28.

Misra, I. R. and Satyal, M. R. Development of Agricultural Marketing and the Improvements of Rural Markets in Hill Areas. In *Nepal, Ministry of Food and Agriculture,* 1981, pp. 84–92.

[G: Nepal]

Mittendorf, H. J. Useful Strategies for Developing Countries Striving to Improve Food Marketing Systems. In *Johnson, G. and Maunder, A., eds.,* 1981, pp. 131–42.

Monke, Eric A. Toward a U.S. Agricultural Export Policy for the 1980s: Discussion. *Amer. J. Agr. Econ.,* December 1981, *63*(5), pp. 848–50.

[G: U.S.]

Myers, Lester H. Discussion: Regional Markets for Food and Interregional Competition: Implication for Southern Agriculture. *Southern J. Agr. Econ.,* July 1981, *13*(1), pp. 79–81.

Nziramasanga, Mudziviri T. and Obidegwu, Chukwuma. Primary Commodity Price Fluctuations and Developing Countries: An Econometric Model of Copper and Zambia. *J. Devel. Econ.,* August 1981, *9*(1), pp. 89–119. [G: Zambia]

O'Rourke, A. Desmond and Greig, W. Smith. Estimates of Consumer Loss Due to Monopoly in the U.S. Food-Manufacturing Industries: Comment. *Amer. J. Agr. Econ.,* May 1981, *63*(2), pp. 285–89. [G: U.S.]

Palme, Lennart A., Jr. and Graham, James. The Systematic Downward Bias in Live Cattle Futures: An Evaluation. *J. Futures Markets,* Fall 1981, *1*(3), pp. 359–66. [G: U.S.]

Parker, Russell C. and Connor, John M. Estimates of Consumer Loss Due to Monopoly in the U.S. Food-Manufacturing Industries: Reply. *Amer. J. Agr. Econ.,* May 1981, *63*(2), pp. 293–97.

[G: U.S.]

Petzel, Todd E. A New Look at Some Old Evidence: The Wheat Market Scandal of 1925. *Food Res. Inst. Stud.,* 1981, *18*(1), pp. 117–28. [G: U.S.]

Piggott, R. R. Agricultural Selling Cartels: Relative Co-operator and Non-Co-operator Gains. *Australian J. Agr. Econ.,* April 1981, *25*(1), pp. 14–29.

[G: Australia]

Proulx, Yvon. Marketing Boards in Canada: Role, Impacts and Some Elements of Performance. In *Johnson, G. and Maunder, A., eds.,* 1981, pp. 530–40. [G: Canada]

Reinschmiedt, Lynn L. and Murray, Steven W. Transportation Alternatives in Rural Communities: A Feasibility Analysis. *Southern J. Agr. Econ.,* December 1981, *13*(2), pp. 99–104.

[G: U.S.]

Rich, M. M. The Policy Implications of Possible New Zealand Wheat Pricing Schemes. *Australian J. Agr. Econ.,* December 1981, *25*(3), pp. 266–74.

[G: New Zealand]

Roy, Himansu. Tea Board in Tea Auction. *Econ. Aff.,* January–March 1981, *26*(1), pp. 5–7.

[G: India]

Sarris, Alexander H. and Schmitz, Andrew. Toward a U.S. Agricultural Export Policy for the 1980s. *Amer. J. Agr. Econ.,* December 1981, *63*(5), pp. 832–39. [G: U.S.]

Shakow, Don. The Municipal Farmer's Market as an Urban Service. *Econ. Geogr.,* January 1981,

57(1), pp. 68–77. [G: U.S.]

Sikder, Firoze Shah. An Evaluation of the Poultry Marketing System in Bangladesh. *Econ. Aff.,* April–June 1981, *26*(2), pp. 124–28, 87–88.

[G: Bangladesh]

Singhal, R. C. Market Regulation—Key for Rural Reconstruction. *Econ. Aff.,* October–December 1981, *26*(4), pp. 278–82, 288. [G: India]

Strong, S. M. and Wolanowski, A. M. A Queueing Model for Egg Price Determination. *Australian J. Agr. Econ.,* August 1981, *25*(2), pp. 170–75.

[G: Australia]

Sullivan, Gregory M. and Linton, Daniel A. Economic Evaluation of an Alternative Marketing System for Feeder Cattle in Alabama. *Southern J. Agr. Econ.,* December 1981, *13*(2), pp. 85–89. [G: U.S.]

Sullivan, James D. Interrelationships between Spot and Futures Markets: Some Implications of Rational Expectations: Discussion. *Amer. J. Agr. Econ.,* December 1981, *63*(5), pp. 942–43.

[G: U.S.]

Todd, Mike C. and Cowell, M. D. Within-Sale Price Variation at Cattle and Carcass Auctions. *Australian J. Agr. Econ.,* April 1981, *25*(1), pp. 30–47.

[G: Australia]

Todd, Mike C.; Reeves, George and Robinson, Chris. Structural Changes in the Livestock Slaughtering Industry. *Quart. Rev. Rural Econ.,* November 1981, *3*(4), pp. 320–29.

[G: Australia]

Voronin, V. Personal Household Plots and Trade. *Prob. Econ.,* March 1981, *23*(11), pp. 3–15.

[G: U.S.S.R.]

Wilson, T. D. and Wissemann, A. F. A Note on the Attitudes of Retailers to Beef Carcass Classification. *Rev. Marketing Agr. Econ.,* April 1981, *49*(1), pp. 47–60. [G: Australia]

Winsberg, Morton D. Agriculture and the Interstate: A Note on Locational Impacts in the South. *Growth Change,* July 1981, *12*(3), pp. 41–46.

[G: U.S.]

7151 Corporate Agriculture

Goldberg, Ray. The Role of the Multinational Corporation. *Amer. J. Agr. Econ.,* May 1981, *63*(2), pp. 367–74.

Helmberger, Peter G.; Campbell, Gerald R. and Dobson, William D. Organization and Performance of Agricultural Markets. In *Martin, L. R., ed.,* 1981 cat kp22a, pp. 503–653. [G: U.S.]

Mohammadi, S. Buik. American Capitalism and Agricultural Development. In *Busch, L., ed.,* 1981, pp. 9–24. [G: U.S.]

Ozawa, Terutomo. The Role of the Multinational Corporation: Discussion. *Amer. J. Agr. Econ.,* May 1981, *63*(2), pp. 393–95.

716 Farm Management

7160 Farm Management; Allocative Efficiency

Adams, Frank. Vegetable and Fruit Crops: Viable Alternatives for Tobacco Farmers. In *Finger, W. R., ed.,* 1981, pp. 93–102. [G: U.S.]

Ahmed, Iqbal. Farm Size and Labour Use: Some Alternative Explanations. *Oxford Bull. Econ. Statist.*, February 1981, *43*(1), pp. 73–88.

Ahn, C. Y.; Singh, Inderjit and Squire, Lyn. A Model of an Agricultural Household in a Multi-Crop Economy: The Case of Korea. In *Johnson, G. and Maunder, A., eds.*, 1981, pp. 697– 708. [G: S. Korea]

Angirasa, Aditi K., et al. Integration, Risk, and Supply Response: A Simulation and Linear Programming Analysis of an East Texas Cow-Calf Producer. *Southern J. Agr. Econ.*, July 1981, *13*(1), pp. 89–98. [G: U.S.]

Archer, André. L'éducation des fermiers, leur âge et la productivité des intrants agricoles selon la dimension des fermes laitières: le cas de la région "04", Québec. (Farmer's Education, Their Age and the Productivity of Agricultural Inputs According to Milk Farm Sizes: The Case of Region "04", Quebec. With English summary.) *L'Actual. Econ.*, January–March 1981, *57*(1), pp. 113–27. [G: Canada]

Avrămiţă, G. M.; Fomin, P. and Păduraru, I. A Dynamic Model for Population Structure Planning in Sheep Farms. *Econ. Computat. Cybern. Stud. Res.*, 1981, *15*(2), pp. 75–84.

Bagi, Faqir S. "Economics of Share-Cropping in Haryana (India) Agriculture"—Rejoinder. *Pakistan Devel. Rev.*, Winter 1981, *20*(4), pp. 453– 64. [G: India]

Bagi, Faqir S. Economic Efficiency of Share-Cropping in Indian Agriculture. *Malayan Econ. Rev. (See Singapore Econ. Rev.)*, April 1981, *26*(1), pp. 15–24. [G: India]

Bagi, Faqir S. Economics of Share-Cropping in Haryana (India) Agriculture. *Pakistan Devel. Rev.*, Spring 1981, *20*(1), pp. 95–119. [G: India]

Bagi, Faqir S. Relationship between Farm Size and Economic Efficiency: An Analysis of Farm-Level Data from Haryana (India). *Can. J. Agr. Econ.*, November 1981, *29*(3), pp. 317–26. [G: India]

Banerjee, Biswa Nath. Impact of Consolidation of Holdings on Small Farms of District Varanasi (U.P.) *Econ. Aff.*, July–September 1981, *26*(3), pp. 201–06. [G: India]

Bartholomaeus, M. K. and Hardaker, J. B. Farm Syndication and Risk Sharing: A Case Study. *Australian J. Agr. Econ.*, December 1981, *25*(3), pp. 233–47. [G: Australia]

Beckford, G. L. The Economics of Agricultural Resource Use and Development in Plantation Economies. In *Livingstone, I., ed.*, 1981, *1969*, pp. 277–86.

Ben-Zion, Uri and Spiegel, Menahem. Cropsharing, Competition and Efficiency—Reconsidered. *Can. J. Agr. Econ.*, July 1981, *29*(2), pp. 233– 42.

Bennett, John W. Farm Management as Cultural Style: Studies of Adaptive Process in the North American Agrifamily. In *Dalton, G., ed.*, 1981, pp. 275–309. [G: U.S.; Canada]

Berardi, Gigi. Can Tobacco Farmers Adjust to Mechanization? A Look at Allotment Holders in Two North Carolina Counties. In *Finger, W. R., ed.*, 1981, pp. 47–61. [G: U.S.]

Berck, Peter. Portfolio Theory and the Demand for Futures: The Case of California Cotton. *Amer. J. Agr. Econ.*, August 1981, *63*(3), pp. 466–74. [G: U.S.]

Bond, Gary and Wonder, Bernard. Risk Attitudes amongst Australian Farmers: Reply. *Australian J. Agr. Econ.*, April 1981, *25*(1), pp. 77–82. [G: Australia]

Boserup, Ester. Indian Agriculture from the Perspective of Western Europe. In *Sarma, J. S.*, 1981, pp. 55–58. [G: India; W. Europe]

Boyle, G. Input Substitution and Technical Change in Irish Agriculture—1953–1977. *Econ. Soc. Rev.*, April 1981, *12*(3), pp. 149–61. [G: Ireland]

Bradford, Garnett L. Comment: Energy Accounting: The Case of Farm Machinery in Maryland. *Southern J. Agr. Econ.*, July 1981, *13*(1), pp. 155–57. [G: U.S.]

Brown, D. J. and Atkinson, J. H. Cash and Share Renting: An Empirical Test of the Link between Entrepreneurial Ability and Contractual Choice. *Bell J. Econ. (See Rand J. Econ. after 4/85)*, Spring 1981, *12*(1), pp. 296–99. [G: U.S.]

Buccola, Steven T. The Supply and Demand of Marketing Contracts under Risk. *Amer. J. Agr. Econ.*, August 1981, *63*(3), pp. 503–09.

Burt, Oscar R. Farm Level Economics of Soil Conservation in the Palouse Area of the Northwest. *Amer. J. Agr. Econ.*, February 1981, *63*(1), pp. 83–92. [G: U.S.]

Calkins, Peter. Small Farm Structure and Output in Selected Regions of Nepal, Taiwan and the United States. In *Johnson, G. and Maunder, A., eds.*, 1981, pp. 75–85. [G: U.S.; Nepal; Taiwan]

Calkins, Peter H. Nutritional Adaptations of Linear Programming for Planning Rural Development. *Amer. J. Agr. Econ.*, May 1981, *63*(2), pp. 247– 54. [G: Nepal]

Campbell, David. Some Issues in the Assessment of Farm Performance. *Quart. Rev. Rural Econ.*, February 1981, *3*(1), pp. 47–57. [G: Australia]

Chadha, G. K. Farm Size, Tenancy and Output Gains of Modern Wheat Technology: Case Study of Punjab (India) *Pakistan Econ. Soc. Rev.*, Summer 1981, *19*(1), pp. 1–23. [G: India]

Chase, Linda and Lerohl, M. L. On Measuring Farmers' Economic Well-Being. *Can. J. Agr. Econ.*, July 1981, *29*(2), pp. 225–32. [G: Canada]

Chowdhury, A. K.; Singh, R. K. and Singh, R. P. Role of the State Bank of India in Raising Income in Agriculture—District Purnea, Bihar. *Econ. Aff.*, October–December 1981, *26*(4), pp. 273–77. [G: India]

Comolli, Paul M. Principles and Policy in Forestry Economics. *Bell J. Econ. (See Rand J. Econ. after 4/85)*, Spring 1981, *12*(1), pp. 300–309.

Connell, Peter and Johnston, Jim. Costs of Alternative Methods of Grain Insect Control. *Quart. Rev. Rural Econ.*, November 1981, *3*(4), pp. 371–75.

Dalton, Robert. Changes in the Structure of the Flue-Cured Tobacco Farm: A Compilation of Available Data Sources. In *Finger, W. R., ed.*, 1981, pp. 63–74. [G: U.S.]

Debertin, David L., et al. Impacts on Farmers of a

Computerized Management Decision-Making Model. *Amer. J. Agr. Econ.*, May 1981, 63(2), pp. 270–74. [G: U.S.]

Deolalikar, Anil B. The Inverse Relationship between Productivity and Farm Size: A Test Using Regional Data from India. *Amer. J. Agr. Econ.*, May 1981, 63(2), pp. 275–79. [G: India]

Doll, John P. and Widdows, Richard. Capital Gains versus Current Income in the Farming Sector: Comment. *Amer. J. Agr. Econ.*, November 1981, 63(4), pp. 730–33. [G: U.S.]

Dove, Michael R. Household Composition and Intensity of Labour: A Case Study of the Kantu' of West Kalimantan. *Bull. Indonesian Econ. Stud.*, November 1981, 17(3), pp. 86–93. [G: Indonesia]

Drynan, Ross G. Risk Attitudes amongst Australian Farmers: A Comment. *Australian J. Agr. Econ.*, April 1981, 25(1), pp. 73–76. [G: Australia]

Dudek, Daniel J. and Horner, Gerald L. Return Flow Control Policy and Income Distribution among Irrigators. *Amer. J. Agr. Econ.*, August 1981, 63(3), pp. 438–46. [G: U.S.]

Emerson, Peter M. Prospective Changes in U.S. Agricultural Structure: Comment. In *Johnson, D. G., ed.*, 1981, pp. 149–53. [G: U.S.]

Engler, Joaquim J. C. Small Farm Structure and Output in Selected Regions of Nepal, Taiwan and the United States: Discussion. In *Johnson, G. and Maunder, A., eds.*, 1981, pp. 85–87. [G: Taiwan; Nepal; U.S.]

Faas, Ronald C.; Holland, David and Young, Douglas L. Variations in Farm Size, Irrigation Technology and After-Tax Income: Implications for Local Economic Development. *Land Econ.*, May 1981, 57(2), pp. 213–20. [G: U.S.]

Feder, Gershon and O'Mara, Gerald T. Farm Size and the Diffusion of Green Revolution Technology. *Econ. Develop. Cult. Change*, October 1981, 30(1), pp. 59–76.

Fenton, Alexander J. Early Manuring Techniques. In *Mercer, R., ed.*, 1981, pp. 210–17. [G: U.K.]

Filippucci, Carlo. Gli impieghi intermedi dei settori agricoli: il caso dell'Emilia Romagna. (Agriculture's Inputs: A Case Study. With English summary.) *Statistica*, January–March 1981, 41(1), pp. 95–113. [G: Italy]

Fisher, B. S. and Lee, R. R. A Dynamic Programming Approach to the Economic Control of Weed and Disease Infestations in Wheat. *Rev. Marketing Agr. Econ.*, December 1981, 49(3), pp. 175–87. [G: Australia]

Foster, Phillips and Wichelns, Dennis. Reply: Energy Accounting: The Case of Farm Machinery in Maryland. *Southern J. Agr. Econ.*, July 1981, 13(1), pp. 159–60. [G: U.S.]

Frank, Max. Le régime de taxation des agriculteurs en Belgique. (With English summary.) *Cah. Écon. Bruxelles*, 3rd Trimestre 1981, (91), pp. 407–32. [G: Belgium]

Freire, Maria E. Education and Agricultural Efficiency. In *Balderston, J. B., et al., eds.*, 1981, pp. 107–45. [G: Guatemala]

Furtan, W. Hartley and Clark, J. S. Decision Making Criteria for Purchasing Milk Quota at the Indi-

vidual Farm Level: A Comment. *Can. J. Agr. Econ.*, November 1981, 29(3), pp. 364–65.

Ghatak, Subrata; Turner, Kerry and Ghatak, Anita. Benefits and Costs of Pesticide Use and Some Policy Implications for Less Developed Countries. In *Chatterji, M., ed.*, 1981, pp. 103–24. [G: LDCs]

Gill, Gerard J. Is There a 'Draught Power Constraint' on Bangladesh Agriculture? *Bangladesh Devel. Stud.*, Monsoon 1981, 9(3), pp. 1–20. [G: Bangladesh]

Guillet, David. Surplus Extraction, Risk Management and Economic Change among Peruvian Peasants. *J. Devel. Stud.*, October 1981, 18(1), pp. 3–24. [G: Peru]

Hall, Nigel. Adjustment in the Australian Wheat-Growing Industry. *Quart. Rev. Rural Econ.*, May 1981, 3(2), pp. 163–65. [G: Australia]

Hardaker, J. B. and Anderson, Jock R. Why Farm Recording Systems Are Doomed to Failure. *Rev. Marketing Agr. Econ.*, December 1981, 49(3), pp. 199–202. [G: Australia]

Hastings, Trevor. The Impact of Scientific Research on Australian Rural Productivity. *Australian J. Agr. Econ.*, April 1981, 25(1), pp. 48–59. [G: Australia]

Herdt, Robert W. and Mandac, A. M. Modern Technology and Economic Efficiency of Philippine Rice Farmers. *Econ. Develop. Cult. Change*, January 1981, 29(2), pp. 375–99. [G: Philippines]

Huffman, Wallace E. Black–White Human Capital Differences: Impact on Agricultural Productivity in the U.S. South. *Amer. Econ. Rev.*, March 1981, 71(1), pp. 94–107. [G: U.S.]

Humphreys, Charles P. Rice Production in the Ivory Coast. In *Pearson, S. R.; Stryker, J. D. and Humphreys, C. P., et al.*, 1981, pp. 61–105. [G: Ivory Coast]

Hunter, Richard. The Commercial Egg Industry: Few Farms Supply Our Eggs. *Quart. Rev. Rural Econ.*, November 1981, 3(4), pp. 351–58. [G: Australia]

Jakeš, Miloš. Efforts at Self-Sufficiency in Foodstuffs—The Joint Task of Farmers, Workers of the Food Industry and the Supplier Branches. *Czech. Econ. Digest.*, December 1981, (8), pp. 3–18. [G: Czechoslovakia]

Jayasuriya, S.; Barlow, C. and Shand, R. T. Farmers' Long-Term Investment Decisions: A Study of Sri Lankan Rubber Smallholders. *J. Devel. Stud.*, October 1981, 18(1), pp. 47–67. [G: Sri Lanka]

Johnson, Marc A. and Pasour, E. C., Jr. An Opportunity Cost View of Fixed Asset Theory and the Overproduction Trap. *Amer. J. Agr. Econ.*, February 1981, 63(1), pp. 1–7.

Johnson, Sam H., III and Charoenwatana, Terd. Economics of Rainfed Cropping Systems: Northeast Thailand. *Water Resources Res.*, June 1981, 17(3), pp. 462–68. [G: Thailand]

Jones, E. L. Agriculture, 1700–80. In *Floud, R. and McCloskey, D., eds., Vol. 1*, 1981, pp. 66–86. [G: U.K.]

Kalirajan, K. P. An Econometric Analysis of Yield Variability in Paddy Production. *Can. J. Agr.*

Econ., November 1981, *29*(3), pp. 283–94.
[G: India]
Kalirajan, K. P. Testing the Hypothesis of Equal Relative Economic Efficiency Using Restricted Aitken's Least Squares Estimation. *J. Devel. Stud.*, July 1981, *17*(4), pp. 307–16. [G: India]
Kalirajan, K. P. The Economic Efficiency of Farmers Growing High-Yielding, Irrigated Rice in India. *Amer. J. Agr. Econ.*, August 1981, *63*(3), pp. 566–70. [G: India]
Kalirajan, K. P. and Flinn, J. C. Comparative Technical Efficiency in Rice Production. *Philippine Econ. J.*, 1981, *20*(1), pp. 31–43.
[G: Philippines]
Kennedy, John O. S. An Alternative Method for Deriving Optimal Fertilizer Rates: Comment and Extension. *Rev. Marketing Agr. Econ.*, December 1981, *49*(3), pp. 203–09.
Khan, Amir U. Small Scale Machinery Development for Labour Surplus Economies. In *Johnson, G. and Maunder, A.*, eds., 1981, pp. 88–98.
[G: Asia]
Khan, Mahmood Hasan. The Political Economy of Agricultural Research in Pakistan. *Pakistan Devel. Rev.*, Summer 1981, *20*(2), pp. 191–213.
[G: Pakistan]
King, Robert P. and Robison, Lindon J. An Interval Approach to Measuring Decision Maker Preferences. *Amer. J. Agr. Econ.*, August 1981, *63*(3), pp. 510–20.
Kislev, Yoav and Peterson, Willis. Induced Innovations and Farm Mechanization. *Amer. J. Agr. Econ.*, August 1981, *63*(3), pp. 562–65.
[G: U.S.]
Klein, K. K.; Salmon, R. E. and Gardiner, E. E. Economic Analysis of the Use of Canola Meal in Diets for Broiler Chickens. *Can. J. Agr. Econ.*, November 1981, *29*(3), pp. 327–38.
[G: Canada]
Lanzer, Edgar A. and Paris, Quirino. A New Analytical Framework for the Fertilization Problem. *Amer. J. Agr. Econ.*, February 1981, *63*(1), pp. 93–103. [G: Brazil]
Larson, Olaf F. Agriculture and the Community. In *Hawley, A. H. and Mazie, S. M.*, eds., 1981, pp. 147–93. [G: U.S.]
Lawrence, Denis and Hone, Phillip. Relative Economic Efficiency in the Australian Grazing Industry. *Rev. Marketing Agr. Econ.*, April 1981, *49*(1), pp. 7–23. [G: Australia]
Lewis, Jack. The Economics of Dryland Farming. *Quart. Rev. Rural Econ.*, May 1981, *3*(2), pp. 157. [G: Australia]
Livingstone, Ian. Supply Responses of Peasant Producers: The Effect of Own-Account Consumption on the Supply of Marketed Output. In *Livingstone, I.*, ed., 1981, 1977, pp. 272–76.
Mahmood, Moazam and Nadeem-ul-Haque. Farm Size and Productivity Revisited. *Pakistan Devel. Rev.*, Summer 1981, *20*(2), pp. 151–90.
[G: Pakistan]
Masud, Sharif M., et al. Economic Impact of Integrated Pest Management Strategies for Cotton Production in the Coastal Bend Region of Texas. *Southern J. Agr. Econ.*, December 1981, *13*(2), pp. 47–52. [G: U.S.]

Mayer, Thomas and Junginger-Dittel, Klaus-Otto. Risk Response in Kenyan Agriculture: The Case of Major Export Crops. *Europ. Rev. Agr. Econ.*, 1981, *8*(1), pp. 27–39. [G: Kenya]
McCloskey, Donald N. Peasant Behavior and Social Change—Cooperatives and Individual Holdings: Comment. In *Russell, C. S. and Nicholson, N. K.*, eds., 1981, pp. 226–31. [G: Peru]
McIntire, John. Rice Production in Mali. In *Pearson, S. R.; Stryker, J. D. and Humphreys, C. P., et al.*, 1981, pp. 331–60. [G: Mali]
Meier, Ueli. A Closed-Cycle Energy System for Rural Dairy Industry in Nepal: The Pauwa Energy System. In *Chatterji, M.*, ed., 1981, pp. 275–88. [G: Nepal]
Melichar, Emanuel. Capital Gains versus Current Income in the Farming Sector: Reply. *Amer. J. Agr. Econ.*, November 1981, *63*(4), pp. 734–37. [G: U.S.]
Monke, Eric A. The Economics of Rice in Liberia. In *Pearson, S. R.; Stryker, J. D. and Humphreys, C. P., et al.*, 1981, pp. 141–72. [G: Liberia]
Moock, Peter R. Education and Technical Efficiency in Small-Farm Production. *Econ. Develop. Cult. Change*, July 1981, *29*(4), pp. 723–39.
[G: Kenya]
Murray, J.; Gandrie, D. and Jowett, D. Corporate Farm Laws and Farm Size: A Case Study. *Reg. Sci. Persp.*, 1981, *11*(1), pp. 71–82. [G: U.S.]
Musser, Wesley N. and Stamoulis, Kostas G. Evaluating the Food and Agriculture Act of 1977 with Firm Quadratic Risk Programming. *Amer. J. Agr. Econ.*, August 1981, *63*(3), pp. 447–56.
[G: U.S.]
Obern, Catheryn C. and Jones, Steven D. Critical Factors Affecting Agricultural Production Cooperatives: A Review. *Ann. Pub. Co-op. Econ.*, September 1981, *52*(3), pp. 317–49.
Ockwell, Anthony and Stoneham, Gary. Machinery Costs for the Australian Wheat-Growing Industry. *Quart. Rev. Rural Econ.*, May 1981, *3*(2), pp. 158–60. [G: Australia]
Ohri, V. K. Rainwater, Acreage and Commercial Crops: A Revisit to Subsistance Agriculture. *Indian Econ. Rev.*, January–June 1981, *16*(1 and 2), pp. 95–116. [G: India]
Ole, Trevor. The Economic Potential of Oilseed and Grain-Legume Crops in New South Wales. *Quart. Rev. Rural Econ.*, May 1981, *3*(2), pp. 161–63. [G: Australia]
Olfert, O. O., et al. Economic Considerations in Grasshopper Control for Protection of Small Grain Crops. *Can. J. Agr. Econ.*, November 1981, *29*(3), pp. 303–16. [G: Canada]
Ospina, Enrique and Shumway, C. Richard. Impact of Corn Prices on Slaughter Beef Composition and Prices. *Amer. J. Agr. Econ.*, November 1981, *63*(4), pp. 700–703. [G: U.S.]
Page, John M., Jr. and Stryker, J. Dirck. Methodology for Estimating Comparative Costs and Incentives. In *Pearson, S. R.; Stryker, J. D. and Humphreys, C. P., et al.*, 1981, pp. 435–54.
[G: W. Africa]
Pemberton, Carlisle A. Resource Productivity in Agriculture in Developing Countries: A Comment [A Study of Resource Productivity in Cooperative

Group Farming in Imo State in Nigeria]. *Can. J. Agr. Econ.*, November 1981, *29*(3), pp. 361–63. [G: Tobago]

Penn, J. B. Economic Developments in U.S. Agriculture during the 1970s. In *Johnson, D. G., ed.*, 1981, pp. 3–47. [G: U.S.]

Penson, John B., Jr.; Romain, Robert F. J. and Hughes, Dean W. Net Investment in Farm Tractors: An Econometric Analysis. *Amer. J. Agr. Econ.*, November 1981, *63*(4), pp. 629–35. [G: U.S.]

Petras, James and Havens, Eugene. Peasant Behavior and Social Change—Cooperatives and Individual Holdings. In *Russell, C. S. and Nicholson, N. K., eds.*, 1981, pp. 203–25. [G: Peru]

Plain, Ronald L. and Williams, Joseph E. Adaptive Planning under Price Uncertainty in Pork Production. *Southern J. Agr. Econ.*, December 1981, *13*(2), pp. 39–46. [G: U.S.]

Pollard, H. J. The Personal Factor in the Success of Planned Agricultural Development Schemes. *J. Devel. Areas*, July 1981, *15*(4), pp. 561–83. [G: Trinidad]

Polyakov, Michail; Kuhlmann, Friedrich and Ohlmer, Bo. Computerization of Farm Management Decision Aids. In *Johnson, G. and Maunder, A., eds.*, 1981, pp. 102–13.

Quiggin, John C. Risk Perception and the Analysis of Risk Attitudes. *Australian J. Agr. Econ.*, August 1981, *25*(2), pp. 160–69. [G: Australia]

Ramaswamy, N. S. Notes Towards the Management of Animal Energy Utilization in India. In *Chatterji, M., ed.*, 1981, pp. 255–74. [G: India]

Rao, Vaman and Chotigeat, Tosporn. The Inverse Relationship between Size of Land Holdings and Agricultural Productivity. *Amer. J. Agr. Econ.*, August 1981, *63*(3), pp. 571–74. [G: India]

Rees, Sian. Agricultural Tools: Function and Use. In *Mercer, R., ed.*, 1981, pp. 66–84. [G: U.K.]

Richardson, James W. and Condra, Gary D. Farm Size Evaluation in the El Paso Valley: A Survival/Success Approach. *Amer. J. Agr. Econ.*, August 1981, *63*(3), pp. 430–37. [G: U.S.]

Robinson, Chris; McMahon, Pat and Gibbs, Melissa. Farmers' Attitudes to Rural Adjustment Assistance: Results of a Survey in Jemalong Shire, N.S.W. *Australian J. Agr. Econ.*, December 1981, *25*(3), pp. 248–65. [G: Australia]

Rosegrant, Mark W. and Herdt, Robert W. Simulating the Impacts of Credit Policy and Fertilizer Subsidy on Central Luzon Rice Farms, the Philippines. *Amer. J. Agr. Econ.*, November 1981, *63*(4), pp. 655–65. [G: Philippines]

Roumasset, James R. and Smith, Joyotee. Population, Technological Change, and the Evolution of Labor Markets. *Population Devel. Rev.*, September 1981, *7*(3), pp. 401–19. [G: Philippines]

Sahota, Gian S. and Rocca, Carlos A. Process of Production and Distribution in Brazilian Agriculture. *Econ. Develop. Cult. Change*, July 1981, *29*(4), pp. 683–721. [G: Brazil]

Sain, Inder; Singh, Tirath and Saini, J. S. A Study of Economic and Technical Efficiency in Raising Raya Crop in Punjab. *Econ. Aff.*, April–June 1981, *26*(2), pp. 146–51. [G: India]

Salam, Abdul. "Economics of Share-Cropping in

Haryana (India) Agriculture"—A Comment. *Pakistan Devel. Rev.*, Winter 1981, *20*(4), pp. 447–52. [G: India]

Salam, Abdul. Farm Tractorization, Fertilizer Use and Productivity of Mexican Wheat in Pakistan. *Pakistan Devel. Rev.*, Autumn 1981, *20*(3), pp. 323–45. [G: Pakistan]

Salam, Abdul; Hussain, M. Afzal and Ghayur, Sabur. Farm Mechanization, Employment and Productivity in Pakistan's Agriculture. *Pakistan Econ. Soc. Rev.*, Winter 1981, *19*(2), pp. 95–114. [G: Pakistan]

Shearer, Georgia, et al. Crop Production Costs and Returns on Midwestern Organic Farms: 1977 and 1978. *Amer. J. Agr. Econ.*, May 1981, *63*(2), pp. 264–69.

Singh, R. K.; Singh, R. P. and Chowdhury, A. K. The State Bank of India and Agricultural Production. *Econ. Aff.*, October–December 1981, *26*(4), pp. 261–65. [G: India]

Sisson, Phillip F. Economic Developments in U.S. Agriculture during the 1970s: Comment. In *Johnson, D. G., ed.*, 1981, pp. 73–75. [G: U.S.]

Spencer, Dunstan S. C. Rice Production in Sierra Leone. In *Pearson, S. R.; Stryker, J. D. and Humphreys, C. P., et al.*, 1981, pp. 201–25. [G: Sierra Leone]

Spreen, Thomas H. and Shonkwiler, J. Scott. Causal Relationships in the Fed Cattle Market. *Southern J. Agr. Econ.*, July 1981, *13*(1), pp. 149–53. [G: U.S.]

Srinivasan, T. N. Peasant Behavior and Social Change—Cooperatives and Individual Holdings: Comment. In *Russell, C. S. and Nicholson, N. K., eds.*, 1981, pp. 231–37. [G: Peru]

Srivastava, R. N.; Singh, D. K. and Singh, R. P. Impact of C.K.G.B. on Rural Economy. *Econ. Aff.*, October–December 1981, *26*(4), pp. 266–72. [G: India]

Stokes, Kenneth W.; Farris, Donald E. and Cartwright, Thomas C. Economics of Alternative Beef Cattle Genotype and Management/Marketing Systems. *Southern J. Agr. Econ.*, December 1981, *13*(2), pp. 1–10. [G: U.S.]

Stonehouse, D. Peter and MacGregor, Murray A. Decision-making Criteria for Purchasing Milk Quota at the Individual Farm Level. *Can. J. Agr. Econ.*, July 1981, *29*(2), pp. 203–16. [G: Canada]

Stryker, J. Dirck. Comparative Advantage and Public Policy in West African Rice. In *Pearson, S. R.; Stryker, J. D. and Humphreys, C. P., et al.*, 1981, pp. 396–431. [G: Ivory Coast; Liberia; Mali; Senegal; Sierra Leone]

Stryker, J. Dirck; Page, John M., Jr. and Humphreys, Charles P. Shadow Price Estimation. In *Pearson, S. R.; Stryker, J. D. and Humphreys, C. P., et al.*, 1981, pp. 455–82. [G: W. Africa]

Tan, B. T. Prospects and Problems of Hill Agriculture in Malaysia. In *Nepal, Ministry of Food and Agriculture*, 1981, pp. 180–89. [G: Malaysia]

Tchir, Robert J.; Hawkins, Murray H. and Westra, Robert. Shrinkage Losses in Alberta Hog Deliveries. *Can. J. Agr. Econ.*, February 1981, *29*(1), pp. 71–81. [G: Canada]

Tuluy, A. Hasan. Costs and Incentives in Rice Production in Senegal. **In** *Pearson, S. R.; Stryker, J. D. and Humphreys, C. P., et al.,* 1981, pp. 263–95. **[G: Senegal]**

Tweeten, Luther. Prospective Changes in U.S. Agricultural Structure. **In** *Johnson, D. G., ed.,* 1981, pp. 113–46. **[G: U.S.]**

Upadhyay, S. K. and Koirala, G. P. Production Incentives for Hill Agricultural Development. **In** *Nepal, Ministry of Food and Agriculture,* 1981, pp. 100–110. **[G: Nepal]**

Vasilevskii, V. The Use of Small Machinery on Personal Household Plots. *Prob. Econ.,* April 1981, 23(12), pp. 67–76. **[G: U.S.S.R.]**

Walker, Thomas Steven. Risk and Adoption of Hybrid Maize in El Salvador. *Food Res. Inst. Stud.,* 1981, 18(1), pp. 59–88. **[G: El Salvador]**

Wang, Y. T. The Roles of Farmers' Associations and Agricultural Development Programmes in Taiwan. **In** *Johnson, G. and Maunder, A., eds.,* 1981, pp. 158–65. **[G: Taiwan]**

Wetzstein, Michael E. Pest Information Markets and Integrated Pest Management. *Southern J. Agr. Econ.,* December 1981, 13(2), pp. 79–83.

Wonder, Bernard and Simpson, David. Economics of Large-Scale and On-Farm Production of Fuel from Crops. *Quart. Rev. Rural Econ.,* November 1981, 3(4), pp. 333–35.

Yassour, Joseph; Zilberman, David and Rausser, Gordon C. Optimal Choices among Alternative Technologies with Stochastic Yield. *Amer. J. Agr. Econ.,* November 1981, 63(4), pp. 718–23.

Zhan, Wu. Take the Road of Agricultural Modernization the Chinese Way. *Chinese Econ. Stud.,* Summer 1981, 14(4), pp. 48–89. **[G: China]**

717 Land Reform and Land Use

7170 General

Ahmad, Nesar. Agrarian Causes of the Iranian Crisis. **In** *Rubinson, R., ed.,* 1981, pp. 101–20. **[G: Iran]**

Beckford, G. L. The Economics of Agricultural Resource Use and Development in Plantation Economies. **In** *Livingstone, I., ed.,* 1981, *1969,* pp. 277–86.

Braverman, Avishay and Srinivasan, T. N. Credit and Sharecropping in Agrarian Societies. *J. Devel. Econ.,* December 1981, 9(3), pp. 289–312.

Brewer, Michael F. and Boxley, Robert F. Agricultural Land: Adequacy of Acres, Concepts, and Information. *Amer. J. Agr. Econ.,* December 1981, 63(5), pp. 879–87. **[G: U.S.]**

Castle, Emery N., et al. Natural Resource Economics, 1946–75. **In** *Martin, L. R., ed.,* 1981, pp. 393–500. **[G: U.S.]**

Dunford, Richard W. and Marousek, Douglas C. Sub-County Property Tax Shifts Attributable to Use-Value Assessments on Farmland. *Land Econ.,* May 1981, 57(2), pp. 221–29. **[G: U.S.]**

Le, Thanh Khoi. A Contribution to the Study of the AMP: The Case of Ancient Vietnam. **In** *Bailey, A. M. and Llobera, J. R., eds.,* 1981, *1973,* pp. 281–89. **[G: Vietnam]**

Needham, Barrie. A Neo-Classical Supply-Based Approach to Land Prices. *Urban Stud.,* February 1981, 18(1), pp. 91–104.

Raup, Philip M. Agricultural Land: Adequacy of Acres, Concepts, and Information: Discussion. *Amer. J. Agr. Econ.,* December 1981, 63(5), pp. 891–93. **[G: U.S.]**

7171 Land Ownership and Tenure; Land Reform

Alston, Lee J. Tenure Choice in Southern Agriculture, 1930–1960. *Exploration Econ. Hist.,* July 1981, 18(3), pp. 211–32. **[G: U.S.]**

Bagi, Faqir S. "Economics of Share-Cropping in Haryana (India) Agriculture"—Rejoinder. *Pakistan Devel. Rev.,* Winter 1981, 20(4), pp. 453–64. **[G: India]**

Bagi, Faqir S. Economic Efficiency of Share-Cropping in Indian Agriculture. *Malayan Econ. Rev. (See Singapore Econ. Rev.),* April 1981, 26(1), pp. 15–24. **[G: India]**

Bagi, Faqir S. Economics of Share-Cropping in Haryana (India) Agriculture. *Pakistan Devel. Rev.,* Spring 1981, 20(1), pp. 95–119. **[G: India]**

Baker-Lampe, Anita B. Discussion [The Development of the Peasant Commune in Russia]. *J. Econ. Hist.,* March 1981, 41(1), pp. 185–86. **[G: U.S.S.R.]**

Banerjee, Biswa Nath. Impact of Consolidation of Holdings on Small Farms of District Varanasi (U.P.) *Econ. Aff.,* July–September 1981, 26(3), pp. 201–06. **[G: India]**

Ben-Zion, Uri and Spiegel, Menahem. Cropsharing, Competition and Efficiency—Reconsidered. *Can. J. Agr. Econ.,* July 1981, 29(2), pp. 233–42.

Bhagwati, Jagdish N. Need for Reforms in Underdeveloped Countries: Comments. **In** *Grassman, S. and Lundberg, E., eds.,* 1981, pp. 526–33.

Bromley, Daniel W. The Role of Land Reform in Economic Development: Policies and Politics: Discussion. *Amer. J. Agr. Econ.,* May 1981, 63(2), pp. 399–400.

Brown, D. J. and Atkinson, J. H. Cash and Share Renting: An Empirical Test of the Link between Entrepreneurial Ability and Contractual Choice. *Bell J. Econ. (See Rand J. Econ. after 4/85),* Spring 1981, 12(1), pp. 296–99. **[G: U.S.]**

Cain, Mead. Risk and Insurance: Perspectives on Fertility and Agrarian Change in India and Bangladesh. *Population Devel. Rev.,* September 1981, 7(3), pp. 435–74. **[G: India; Bangladesh]**

Chadha, G. K. Farm Size, Tenancy and Output Gains of Modern Wheat Technology: Case Study of Punjab (India) *Pakistan Econ. Soc. Rev.,* Summer 1981, 19(1), pp. 1–23. **[G: India]**

Gray, Kenneth R. Soviet Agricultural Prices, Rent and Land Cadastres. *J. Compar. Econ.,* March 1981, 5(1), pp. 43–59. **[G: U.S.S.R.]**

Heath, J. R. Peasants or Proletarians? Rural Labour in a Brazilian Plantation Economy. *J. Devel. Stud.,* July 1981, 17(4), pp. 268–81. **[G: Brazil]**

Hirashima, S. Some Issues in Indian Agriculture Viewed from the Japanese Experience. **In** *Sarma, J. S.,* 1981, pp. 59–69. **[G: India; Japan]**

de Janvry, Alain. The Role of Land Reform in Economic Development: Policies and Politics. *Amer. J. Agr. Econ.,* May 1981, 63(2), pp. 384–92.

Khan, Mahmood Hasan. The Political Economy of Agricultural Research in Pakistan. *Pakistan Devel. Rev.*, Summer 1981, *20*(2), pp. 191–213. [G: Pakistan]

Koo, Anthony Y. C. Toward a More General Model of Land Tenancy and Reform: Reply. *Quart. J. Econ.*, November 1981, *96*(4), pp. 731.

Ledesma, Antonio J. Landless Workers and Rice Farmers: Peasant Subclasses under Agrarian Reform in Two Philippine Villages. *Philippine Econ. J.*, 1981, *20*(3&4), pp. 201–26. [G: Philippines]

McCloskey, Donald N. Peasant Behavior and Social Change—Cooperatives and Individual Holdings: Comment. In *Russell, C. S. and Nicholson, N. K., eds.*, 1981, pp. 226–31. [G: Peru]

Myrdal, Gunnar. Need for Reforms in Underdeveloped Countries. In *Grassman, S. and Lundberg, E., eds.*, 1981, pp. 501–25.

Nguyen, D. T. Mexican Land Reform, 1959–1969: A Reply [The Effects of Land Reform on Agricultural Production, Employment and Income Distribution: A Statistical Study of Mexican States, 1959–69]. *Econ. J.*, September 1981, *91*(363), pp. 253–54. [G: Mexico]

Okoth-Ogendo, H. W. O. Land Ownership and Land Distribution in Kenya's Large-Farm Areas. In *Killick, T., ed.*, 1981, pp. 329–38. [G: Kenya]

Parsons, Kenneth H. The Challenge of Agrarian Reform. In *Johnson, G. and Maunder, A., eds.*, 1981, pp. 358–66.

Pemberton, Carlisle A. Resource Productivity in Agriculture in Developing Countries: A Comment [A Study of Resource Productivity in Cooperative Group Farming in Imo State in Nigeria]. *Can. J. Agr. Econ.*, November 1981, *29*(3), pp. 361–63. [G: Tobago]

Petras, James and Havens, Eugene. Peasant Behavior and Social Change—Cooperatives and Individual Holdings. In *Russell, C. S. and Nicholson, N. K., eds.*, 1981, pp. 203–25. [G: Peru]

Putterman, Louis. On Optimality in Collective Institutional Choice. *J. Compar. Econ.*, December 1981, *5*(4), pp. 392–403.

Quibria, M. G. A Layman's Geometric Proof of the Nonexistence of "Marshallian" Sharecropping Contracts. *Bangladesh Devel. Stud.*, Winter 1981, *9*(1), pp. 97–99.

Quibria, M. G. and Rashid, Salim. Toward a More General Model of Land Tenancy and Reform: Comment. *Quart. J. Econ.*, November 1981, *96*(4), pp. 725–30.

Rao, Vaman and Chotigeat, Tosporn. The Inverse Relationship between Size of Land Holdings and Agricultural Productivity. *Amer. J. Agr. Econ.*, August 1981, *63*(3), pp. 571–74. [G: India]

Reid, Joseph D., Jr. White Land, Black Labor, and Agricultural Stagnation: The Causes and Effects of Sharecropping in the Postbellum South. In *Walton, G. M. and Shepherd, J. F., eds.*, 1981, *1980*, pp. 33–55. [G: U.S.]

Sahota, Gian S. and Rocca, Carlos A. Process of Production and Distribution in Brazilian Agriculture. *Econ. Develop. Cult. Change*, July 1981, *29*(4), pp. 683–721. [G: Brazil]

Salam, Abdul. "Economics of Share-Cropping in Haryana (India) Agriculture"—A Comment. *Paki-*stan Devel. Rev.*, Winter 1981, *20*(4), pp. 447–52. [G: India]

Salmanzadeh, Cyrus and Jones, Gwyn E. Transformations in the Agrarian Structure of Southwestern Iran. *J. Devel. Areas*, January 1981, *15*(2), pp. 199–213. [G: Iran]

Schmedemann, Ivan W. Issues of Ownership and Control of Agricultural Land in the Great Plains. In *Lawson, M. P. and Baker, M. E., eds.*, 1981, pp. 193–202. [G: U.S.]

Solow, Barbara Lewis. A New Look at the Irish Land Question. *Econ. Soc. Rev.*, July 1981, *12*(4), pp. 301–14. [G: Ireland]

Srinivasan, T. N. Peasant Behavior and Social Change—Cooperatives and Individual Holdings: Comment. In *Russell, C. S. and Nicholson, N. K., eds.*, 1981, pp. 231–37. [G: Peru]

Steele, John and Kanel, Don. Land Tenure in a Brazilian Rural Community: Life Cycle Patterns and Intergenerational Changes. In *Dalton, G., ed.*, 1981, pp. 215–31. [G: Brazil]

Toumanoff, Peter. The Development of the Peasant Commune in Russia. *J. Econ. Hist.*, March 1981, *41*(1), pp. 179–84. [G: U.S.S.R.]

Wordie, J. R. Rent Movements and the English Tenant Farmer, 1700–1839. In *Uselding, P., ed.*, 1981, pp. 193–243. [G: U.K.]

Yates, P. Lammartine. Mexican Land Reform, 1959–1969: A Comment [The Effects of Land Reform on Agricultural Production, Employment and Income Distribution: A Statistical Study of Mexican States, 1959–69]. *Econ. J.*, September 1981, *91*(363), pp. 745–52. [G: Mexico]

Zemanian, Armen H. Dynamic Adjustment of Labor Allocation between Collective, State, or Cooperative Farming and Private Farming in a Planned Economy. *J. Compar. Econ.*, September 1981, *5*(3), pp. 292–317.

7172 Land Development; Land Use; Irrigation Policy

Ake, Claude. Kenya. In *Adedeji, A., ed.*, 1981, pp. 187–203. [G: Kenya]

Ali, M., et al. Hill Farming Systems in Azad Jammu and Kashmir, Pakistan. In *Nepal, Ministry of Food and Agriculture*, 1981, pp. 190–98. [G: Pakistan]

Asabere, Paul Kwadwo. The Price of Urban Land in a Chiefdom: Empirical Evidence on a Traditional African City, Kumasi. *J. Reg. Sci.*, November 1981, *21*(4), pp. 529–39. [G: Ghana]

Barnett, Tony. Evaluating the Gezira Scheme: Black Box or Pandora's Box. In *Heyer, J.; Roberts, P. and Williams, G., eds.*, 1981, pp. 306–24. [G: Sudan]

Beaumont, Peter. Water Resources and Their Management in the Middle East. In *[Fisher, W. B.]*, 1981, pp. 40–72. [G: Middle East]

Belloit, Jerry D. and Smith, Halbert C. The Coastal Construction Control Line: A Cost-Benefit Analysis. *Amer. Real Estate Urban Econ. Assoc. J.*, Winter 1981, *9*(4), pp. 367–83. [G: U.S.]

Bobylev, S. Means of Improving the Utilization of Land Resources. *Prob. Econ.*, May 1981, *24*(1), pp. 78–95. [G: U.S.S.R.]

Boggess, William G. and Heady, Earl O. A Sector Analysis of Alternative Income Support and Soil Conservation Policies. *Amer. J. Agr. Econ.*, November 1981, *63*(4), pp. 618–28. [G: U.S.]

Borrelli, John. Future of Irrigated Agriculture in the Great Plains. In *Lawson, M. P. and Baker, M. E., eds.*, 1981, pp. 181–91. [G: U.S.]

Boyer, M. Christine. National Land Use Policy: Instrument and Product of the Economic Cycle. In *de Neufville, J. I., ed.*, 1981, pp. 109–25. [G: U.S.]

Bras, Rafael L. and Cordova, Jose R. Intraseasonal Water Allocation in Deficit Irrigation. *Water Resources Res.*, August 1981, *17*(4), pp. 866–74. [G: U.S.]

Brown, Ralph J. Simulating the Impact of an Irrigation Project on a Small Regional Economy. *Growth Change*, April 1981, *12*(2), pp. 23–30. [G: U.S.]

Burbridge, Peter; Dixon, John A. and Soewardi, Bedju. Land Allocation for Transmigration. *Bull. Indonesian Econ. Stud.*, March 1981, *17*(1), pp. 108–13. [G: Indonesia]

Burt, Oscar R. Farm Level Economics of Soil Conservation in the Palouse Area of the Northwest. *Amer. J. Agr. Econ.*, February 1981, *63*(1), pp. 83–92. [G: U.S.]

Carlson, Leonard A. Land Allotment and the Decline of American Indian Farming. *Exploration Econ. Hist.*, April 1981, *18*(2), pp. 128–54. [G: U.S.]

Chicoine, David L. Farmland Values at the Urban Fringe: An Analysis of Sale Prices. *Land Econ.*, August 1981, *57*(3), pp. 353–62. [G: U.S.]

Clawson, Marion. Land-Use Trends. In *Hawley, A. H. and Mazie, S. M., eds.*, 1981, pp. 645–67. [G: U.S.]

Daroesman, Ruth. Vegetative Elimination of Alang-Alang. *Bull. Indonesian Econ. Stud.*, March 1981, *17*(1), pp. 83–107. [G: Indonesia]

Drynan, Ross G. and Hodge, Ian D. The Value of Unrealized Farm Land Capital Gains: Comment. *Amer. J. Agr. Econ.*, May 1981, *63*(2), pp. 281–82.

Dudek, Daniel J. and Horner, Gerald L. Return Flow Control Policy and Income Distribution among Irrigators. *Amer. J. Agr. Econ.*, August 1981, *63*(3), pp. 438–46. [G: U.S.]

Edel, Matthew. Land Policy, Economic Cycles, and Social Conflict. In *de Neufville, J. I., ed.*, 1981, pp. 127–39.

Faas, Ronald C.; Holland, David and Young, Douglas L. Variations in Farm Size, Irrigation Technology and After-Tax Income: Implications for Local Economic Development. *Land Econ.*, May 1981, *57*(2), pp. 213–20. [G: U.S.]

Foster, J. Fagg. The Approach to Land Use Planning in a Changing Technology. *J. Econ. Issues*, December 1981, *15*(4), pp. 985–1007.

Fowler, Peter. Wildscape to Landscape: 'Enclosure' in Prehistoric Britain. In *Mercer, R., ed.*, 1981, pp. 9–54. [G: U.K.]

Frederiksen, Peter C. Further Evidence on the Relationship between Population Density and Infrastructure: The Philippines and Electrification. *Econ. Develop. Cult. Change*, July 1981, *29*(4),
pp. 749–58. [G: Philippines]

Freeman, David M. and Lowdermilk, Max K. Sociological Analysis of Irrigation Water Management—A Perspective and Approach to Assist Decision Making. In *Russell, C. S. and Nicholson, N. K., eds.*, 1981, pp. 153–73. [G: Pakistan]

Furuseth, Owen J. Update on Oregon's Agricultural Protection Program: A Land Use Perspective. *Natural Res. J.*, January 1981, *21*(1), pp. 57–70. [G: U.S.]

Georgianna, Thomas D. and Haynes, Kingsley E. Competition for Water Resources: Coal and Agriculture in the Yellowstone Basin. *Econ. Geogr.*, July 1981, *57*(3), pp. 225–37. [G: U.S.]

Gorkhaly, P. P. and Shrestha, M. M. Irrigation Water Management and Use at the Farm Level in the Hills. In *Nepal, Ministry of Food and Agriculture*, 1981, pp. 79–83. [G: Nepal]

Guariso, Giorgio, et al. Nile Water for Sinai: Framework for Analysis. *Water Resources Res.*, December 1981, *17*(6), pp. 1585–93. [G: Egypt]

Hall, Anthony. Irrigation in the Brazilian Northeast: Anti-Drought or Anti-Peasant? In *Mitchell, S., ed.*, 1981, pp. 157–69. [G: Brazil]

Heady, Earl O. and Short, Cameron. Interrelationship among Export Markets, Resource Conservation, and Agricultural Productivity. *Amer. J. Agr. Econ.*, December 1981, *63*(5), pp. 840–47. [G: U.S.]

Hite, J. C. and Dillman, B. L. Protection of Agricultural Land: An Institutionalist Perspective. *Southern J. Agr. Econ.*, July 1981, *13*(1), pp. 43–53. [G: U.S.]

Hopkins, Lewis D., et al. Analyzing Foodplain Policies Using an Interdependent Land Use Allocation Model. *Water Resources Res.*, June 1981, *17*(3), pp. 469–77. [G: U.S.]

Hossain, Belayet. Choice of Techniques in Small Scale Irrigation in Bangladesh. *Bangladesh Devel. Stud.*, Autumn 1981, *9*(4), pp. 35–49. [G: Bangladesh]

Hulett, G. K. The Future of the Grasslands. In *Lawson, M. P. and Baker, M. E., eds.*, 1981, pp. 141–56. [G: U.S.]

Jackson, Kathleen O. Sociological Analysis of Irrigation Water Management: Discussion. In *Russell, C. S. and Nicholson, N. K., eds.*, 1981, pp. 174–82. [G: Pakistan]

Jarvis, Lovell S. Predicting the Diffusion of Improved Pastures in Uruguay. *Amer. J. Agr. Econ.*, August 1981, *63*(3), pp. 495–502. [G: Uruguay]

Kiker, Clyde and Lynne, Gary D. Areas of Critical State Concern: Florida's Experience with the Green Swamp. *Southern J. Agr. Econ.*, December 1981, *13*(2), pp. 149–55. [G: U.S.]

Lockeretz, William. The Dust Bowl: Its Relevance to Contemporary Environmental Problems. In *Lawson, M. P. and Baker, M. E., eds.*, 1981, pp. 11–31. [G: U.S.]

Maki, Wilbur R. Regional Economic Forecast System for Resource Development Planning. *Reg. Sci. Persp.*, 1981, *11*(1), pp. 22–31.

Mandl, Christoph E. A Survey of Mathematical Optimization Models and Algorithms for Designing and Extending Irrigation and Wastewater Networks. *Water Resources Res.*, August 1981, *17*(4),

pp. 769–75.

Miller, Jon R. Irreversible Land Use and the Preservation of Endangered Species. *J. Environ. Econ. Manage.*, March 1981, *8*(1), pp. 19–26.

Nash, Michael J. British Farming Today: A Bird's-Eye View. In *Mercer, R., ed.*, 1981, pp. 1–6. [G: U.K.]

Nicholas, James C. Housing Costs and Prices under Regional Regulation. *Amer. Real Estate Urban Econ. Assoc. J.*, Winter 1981, *9*(4), pp. 384–96. [G: U.S.]

Ohri, V. K. Rainwater, Acreage and Commercial Crops: A Revisit to Subsistance Agriculture. *Indian Econ. Rev.*, January–June 1981, *16*(1 and 2), pp. 95–116. [G: India]

Oron, Gideon and Walker, Wynn R. Optimal Design and Operation of Permanent Irrigation Systems. *Water Resources Res.*, February 1981, *17*(1), pp. 11–17.

Plaxico, James S. and Kletke, Darrel D. The Value of Unrealized Farm Land Capital Gains: Reply. *Amer. J. Agr. Econ.*, May 1981, *63*(2), pp. 283–84.

Price, Barbara. Irrigation: Sociopolitical Dynamics and the Growth of Civilization. In *Bailey, A. M. and Llobera, J. R., eds.*, 1981, *1973*, pp. 216–32.

Randall, Alan. Property Entitlements and Pricing Policies for a Maturing Water Economy. *Australian J. Agr. Econ.*, December 1981, *25*(3), pp. 195–220. [G: Australia]

Reed, Michael R. and Riggins, Steven K. A Disaggregated Analysis of Corn Acreage Response in Kentucky. *Amer. J. Agr. Econ.*, November 1981, *63*(4), pp. 708–11. [G: U.S.]

Rhenals, Alonso E. and Bras, Rafael L. The Irrigation Scheduling Problem and Evapotranspiration Uncertainty. *Water Resources Res.*, October 1981, *17*(5), pp. 1328–38.

Runge, Carlisle Ford. Common Property Externalities: Isolation, Assurance, and Resource Depletion in a Traditional Grazing Context. *Amer. J. Agr. Econ.*, November 1981, *63*(4), pp. 595–606.

Sabadell, J. Eleonora. Risk Assessment: Arid and Semiarid Lands Perspective. In *Haimes, Y. Y., ed.*, 1981, pp. 219–31. [G: U.S.]

Schmidt, Elsa T. Key Issues of Land Use Planning in West Germany. *Growth Change*, April 1981, *12*(2), pp. 44–52. [G: W. Germany]

Short, Cameron; Turhollow, Anthony F., Jr. and Heady, Earl O. A Regional Problem in a National Context: The Ogallala Aquifer. *Reg. Sci. Persp.*, 1981, *11*(2), pp. 70–82. [G: U.S.]

Spears, John S. Small Farmers—or the Tropical Forest Ecosystem? A Review of Sustainable Land Use Systems for Tropical Forest Areas. In *Mergen, F., ed.*, 1981, pp. 15–47. [G: Selected LDCs]

Stevens, John H. Irrigation in the Arab Countries of the Middle East. In *[Fisher, W. B.]*, 1981, pp. 73–81. [G: Middle East]

Steward, Julian H. Wittfogel's Irrigation Hypothesis. In *Bailey, A. M. and Llobera, J. R., eds.*, 1981, *1977*, pp. 195–206.

Stoevener, Herbert H. Interrelationship among Export Markets, Resource Conservation, and Agricultural Productivity: Discussion. *Amer. J. Agr.*

Econ., December 1981, *63*(5), pp. 851–52. [G: U.S.]

Vandeveer, Lonnie R. Discussion: Protection of Agricultural Land: An Institutionalist Perspective. *Southern J. Agr. Econ.*, July 1981, *13*(1), pp. 55–57. [G: U.S.]

Wallace, Tina. The Kano River Project, Nigeria: The Impact of an Irrigation Scheme on Productivity and Welfare. In *Heyer, J.; Roberts, P. and Williams, G., eds.*, 1981, pp. 281–305. [G: Nigeria]

Whitaker, David. Bidding for Land Development. *Amer. Real Estate Urban Econ. Assoc. J.*, Fall 1981, *9*(3), pp. 223–33.

Winter, John R. and Whittaker, James K. The Relationship between Private Ranchland Prices and Public-Land Grazing Permits. *Land Econ.*, August 1981, *57*(3), pp. 414–21. [G: U.S.]

Wittfogel, Karl. The Theory of Oriental Society. In *Bailey, A. M. and Llobera, J. R., eds.*, 1981, *1968*, pp. 141–57.

Wolfram, Gary. The Sale of Development Rights and Zoning in the Preservation of Open Space: Lindahl Equilibrium and a Case Study. *Land Econ.*, August 1981, *57*(3), pp. 398–413. [G: U.S.]

Zapata, Juan Antonio and Siamwalla, Ammar. Un esquema para el análisis de la distribución de beneficios de proyectos de riego. (With English summary.) *Cuadernos Econ.*, April 1981, *18*(53), pp. 89–95.

Ziemer, Rod F. and White, Fred C. A Tobit Model of the Demand for Farmland. *Southern J. Agr. Econ.*, December 1981, *13*(2), pp. 105–09. [G: U.S.]

Ziemer, Rod F.; White, Fred C. and Clifton, Ivery D. An Analysis of Factors Affecting Differential Assessment Legislation. *Public Choice*, 1981, *36*(1), pp. 43–52. [G: U.S.]

718 Rural Economics

7180 Rural Economics

Adams, Adrian. The Senegal River Valley. In *Heyer, J.; Roberts, P. and Williams, G., eds.*, 1981, pp. 325–53. [G: Senegal]

Adelman, Alan H. Colombian Friendship Groups: Constraints on a Rural Development Acquisition System. *J. Devel. Areas*, April 1981, *15*(3), pp. 457–69. [G: Colombia]

Ahn, C. Y.; Singh, Inderjit and Squire, Lyn. A Model of an Agricultural Household in a Multi-Crop Economy: The Case of Korea. In *Johnson, G. and Maunder, A., eds.*, 1981, pp. 697–708. [G: S. Korea]

Ali, M., et al. Hill Farming Systems in Azad Jammu and Kashmir, Pakistan. In *Nepal, Ministry of Food and Agriculture*, 1981, pp. 190–98. [G: Pakistan]

Ali, M. Shaukat. Rural Urban Consumption Patterns in Pakistan. *Pakistan Econ. Soc. Rev.*, Winter 1981, *19*(2), pp. 85–94. [G: Pakistan]

Amin, Samir. Senegal. In *Adedeji, A., ed.*, 1981, pp. 309–27. [G: Senegal]

Balderston, Judith B. Synthesis of Findings and Policy Implications. In *Balderston, J. B., et al., eds.*,

1981, pp. 177–98.   [G: Guatemala]

Barbosa, Túlio. The Farm/Non-farm Interface with Special Reference to Rural Brazil. **In** *Johnson, G. and Maunder, A., eds.,* 1981, pp. 200–12.
          [G: Brazil]

Beeley, Brian W. A Fieldscape in Transition: The Case of a Turkish Orchard. **In** *[Fisher, W. B.],* 1981, pp. 224–32.   [G: Turkey]

Bekombo, M. The Child in Africa: Socialisation, Education and Work. **In** *Rodgers, G. and Standing, G., eds.,* 1981, pp. 113–29.   [G: Africa]

Bhaduri, Amit. Class Relations and the Pattern of Accumulation in an Agrarian Economy. *Cambridge J. Econ.,* March 1981, 5(1), pp. 33–46.
          [G: India]

Birks, J. Stace. The Impact of Economic Development on Pastoral Nomadism in the Middle East: An Inevitable Eclipse? **In** *[Fisher, W. B.],* 1981, pp. 82–94.   [G: Middle East]

Bonnen, James T. and Nelson, Glenn L. Changing Rural Development Data Needs. *Amer. J. Agr. Econ.,* May 1981, 63(2), pp. 337–45.   [G: U.S.]

Braverman, Avishay and Srinivasan, T. N. Credit and Sharecropping in Agrarian Societies. *J. Devel. Econ.,* December 1981, 9(3), pp. 289–312.

Broder, Josef M. Decision Aids for Local Decision Making: Discussion. *Amer. J. Agr. Econ.,* December 1981, 63(5), pp. 988–89.   [G: U.S.]

Bryant, W. Keith; Bawden, D. L. and Saupe, W. E. The Economics of Rural Poverty—A Review of the post-World War II United States and Canadian Literature. **In** *Martin, L. R., ed.,* 1981, pp. 3–150.   [G: Canada; U.S.]

Bryden, John. Appraising a Regional Development Programme—The Case of the Scottish Highlands and Islands. *Europ. Rev. Agr. Econ.,* 1981, 8(4), pp. 475–97.   [G: U.K.]

Bullock, J. Bruce. Some Concepts for Measuring the Economic Value of Rural Data. *Amer. J. Agr. Econ.,* May 1981, 63(2), pp. 346–52.

Cadeliña, Rowe V. Food Management under Scarce Resources by Philippine Marginal Agriculturalists. *Philippine Econ. J.,* 1981, 20(1), pp. 80–100.
          [G: Philippines]

Cain, Mead. Risk and Insurance: Perspectives on Fertility and Agrarian Change in India and Bangladesh. *Population Devel. Rev.,* September 1981, 7(3), pp. 435–74.   [G: India; Bangladesh]

Cain, Mead and Mozumder, A. B. M. Khorshed Alam. Labour Market Structure and Reproductive Behaviour in Rural South Asia. **In** *Rodgers, G. and Standing, G., eds.,* 1981, pp. 245–87.
          [G: S. Asia]

Calkins, Peter H. Nutritional Adaptations of Linear Programming for Planning Rural Development. *Amer. J. Agr. Econ.,* May 1981, 63(2), pp. 247–54.   [G: Nepal]

Campbell, David. Some Issues in the Assessment of Farm Performance. *Quart. Rev. Rural Econ.,* February 1981, 3(1), pp. 47–57.   [G: Australia]

Cañete, Constancio C. The Income Level and Income Distribution Impacts of Masagana 99 Program in Central Luzon, Philippines. *Philippine Econ. J.,* 1981, 20(3&4), pp. 238–56.
          [G: Philippines]

Carter, Ian. The Scottish Peasantry. **In** *Samuel, R.,*

ed., 1981, pp. 85–92.   [G: U.K.]

de las Casas, P. Lizardo. Central Planning, National Policies and Local Rural Development Programmes: The Planning Process in Latin America and the Caribbean. **In** *Johnson, G. and Maunder, A., eds.,* 1981, pp. 167–83.   [G: Latin America; Caribbean]

Castro, Alfonso Peter; Hakansson, N. Thomas and Brokensha, David. Indicators of Rural Inequality. *World Devel.,* May 1981, 9(5), pp. 401–27.

de Castro Andrade, Regis. On the Relationship between the Subsistence Sector and the Market Economy in the Parnaíba Valley. **In** *Mitchell, S., ed.,* 1981, pp. 109–32.   [G: Brazil]

Cavaco, Carminda. A agricultura a tempo parcial: expansão, diversidade e significado económico, social e geográfico. (With English summary.) *Economia (Portugal),* May 1981, 5(2), pp. 271–313.
          [G: Portugal]

Chambers, Robert. Rural Poverty Unperceived: Problems and Remedies. *World Devel.,* January 1981, 9(1), pp. 1–19.

Chassagne, M. E. Strong Agricultures but Weak Rural Economies—The Undue Emphasis on Agriculture in European Rural Development: Comment. *Europ. Rev. Agr. Econ.,* 1981, 8(2–3), pp. 171–76.   [G: Europe]

Chowdhury, Nuimuddin. An Enquiry into the Nature and Determinants of Polarisation in Personal Wealth: A Case Study Using Handloom Industry Data. *Bangladesh Devel. Stud.,* Autumn 1981, 9(4), pp. 51–76.   [G: Bangladesh]

Christianson, Jon B. and Faulkner, Lee. The Contributions of Rural Hospitals to Local Economies. *Inquiry,* Spring 1981, 18(1), pp. 46–60.
          [G: U.S.]

Clark, David and Unwin, Kathryn I. Telecommunications and Travel: Potential Impact in Rural Areas. *Reg. Stud.,* 1981, 15(1), pp. 47–56.
          [G: U.K.]

Clayton, Eric S. Programming Rural Employment Opportunities in Kenya. **In** *Killick, T., ed.,* 1975, pp. 238–44.   [G: Kenya]

Cohen, John M., et al. Development from Below: Local Development Associations in the Yemen Arab Republic. *World Devel.,* November/December 1981, 9(11/12), pp. 1039–61.
          [G: Yemen Arab Republic]

Colette, W. Arden. Decision Aids for Local Decision Making: Discussion. *Amer. J. Agr. Econ.,* December 1981, 63(5), pp. 986–87.   [G: U.S]

Collier, Valerie G. and Rempel, Henry. The Divergence of Private from Social Costs in Rural–Urban Migration: A Case Study of Nairobi. **In** *Killick, T., ed.,* 1977, pp. 228–37.   [G: Kenya]

Coulson, Andrew. Agricultural Policies in Mainland Tanzania, 1946–76. **In** *Heyer, J.; Roberts, P. and Williams, G., eds.,* 1981, pp. 52–89.
          [G: Tanzania]

Cowen, Michael. Commodity Production in Kenya's Central Province. **In** *Heyer, J.; Roberts, P. and Williams, G., eds.,* 1981, pp. 121–42.
          [G: Kenya]

Dalton, George. Economic Anthropology and History: The Work of Karl Polanyi: Comment. **In** *Dalton, G., ed.,* 1974, pp. 69–93.

Daly, Patricia A. Agricultural Employment: Has the Decline Ended? *Mon. Lab. Rev.*, November 1981, *104*(11), pp. 11–17. [G: U.S.]

Doeksen, Gerald A. and Nelson, James R. Decision Aids for Local Decision Making. *Amer. J. Agr. Econ.*, December 1981, *63*(5), pp. 974–81. [G: U.S.]

Dove, Michael R. Household Composition and Intensity of Labour: A Case Study of the Kantu' of West Kalimantan. *Bull. Indonesian Econ. Stud.*, November 1981, *17*(3), pp. 86–93. [G: Indonesia]

Dube, Leela. The Economic Roles of Children in India: Methodological Issues. In *Rodgers, G. and Standing, G., eds.,* 1981, pp. 179–213. [G: India]

Dunford, Richard W. and Marousek, Douglas C. Sub-County Property Tax Shifts Attributable to Use-Value Assessments on Farmland. *Land Econ.*, May 1981, *57*(2), pp. 221–29. [G: U.S.]

Dutton, Roderic W. A Rural Community Development Project in Oman. In *[Fisher, W. B.],* 1981, pp. 199–212. [G: Oman]

Edwards, C. J. W. Structural Underemployment on Full-Time Farms in Northern Ireland. *Irish J. Agr. Econ. Rural Soc.*, 1981, *8*(2), pp. 235–42. [G: U.K.]

Edwards, Clark. Spatial Aspects of Rural Development. *Agr. Econ. Res.*, July 1981, *33*(3), pp. 11–24.

Eidman, Vernon R. Microeconomic Impacts of Inflation on the Food and Agriculture Sector: Discussion. *Amer. J. Agr. Econ.*, December 1981, *63*(5), pp. 962–64. [G: U.S.]

Emerson, Peter M. Changing Rural Development Data Needs: Discussion. *Amer. J. Agr. Econ.*, May 1981, *63*(2), pp. 361–62. [G: U.S.]

Etienne, Gilbert. Rural Development in China and Its Impact on Foreign Trade. *Rivista Int. Sci. Econ. Com.*, September 1981, *28*(9), pp. 831–51. [G: China]

Faas, Ronald C.; Holland, David and Young, Douglas L. Variations in Farm Size, Irrigation Technology and After-Tax Income: Implications for Local Economic Development. *Land Econ.*, May 1981, *57*(2), pp. 213–20. [G: U.S.]

Fényes, Tamás I. Potential Applicability of Certain Socialistic Farming Practices for Rural Development in Non-Socialist Less Developed Countries. In *Johnson, G. and Maunder, A., eds.,* 1981, pp. 659–69.

Figueroa, Adolfo. Agricultural Price Policy and Rural Income in Peru. *Quart. Rev. Econ. Bus.*, Autumn 1981, *21*(3), pp. 49–64. [G: Peru]

Fioravanti-Molinié, Antoinette. Reciprocity and the INCA State: From Karl Polanyi to John V. Murra: Discussion. In *Dalton, G., ed.,* 1981, *1974*, pp. 54–58.

Flores Rodas, Marco A. Forestry for Rural Development: A New Approach. In *Mergen, F., ed.,* 1981, pp. 4–13.

Forman, Shepard. Life Paradigms: Makassae (East Timor) Views on Production, Reproduction, and Exchange. In *Dalton, G., ed.,* 1981, pp. 95–110. [G: Indonesia]

Fort, Rodney D. and Christianson, Jon B. Determi-

nants of Public Services Provision in Rural Communities: Evidence from Voting on Hospital Referenda. *Amer. J. Agr. Econ.*, May 1981, *63*(2), pp. 228–36. [G: U.S.]

Frank, Max and Praet, Peter. Trois optiques du concept de parité des revenus en agriculture. (With English summary.) *Cah. Écon. Bruxelles*, 3rd Trimestre 1981, (91), pp. 375–89. [G: Belgium]

Freeman, David M. and Lowdermilk, Max K. Sociological Analysis of Irrigation Water Management—A Perspective and Approach to Assist Decision Making. In *Russell, C. S. and Nicholson, N. K., eds.,* 1981, pp. 153–73. [G: Pakistan]

Freire, Maria E. Education and Agricultural Efficiency. In *Balderston, J. B., et al., eds.,* 1981, pp. 107–45. [G: Guatemala]

Friedmann, John. The Active Community: Toward a Political–Territorial Framework for Rural Development in Asia. *Econ. Develop. Cult. Change*, January 1981, *29*(2), pp. 235–61. [G: Asia]

Gaiha, Raghav and Kazmi, N. A. Aspects of Poverty in Rural India. *Econ. Planning*, 1981, *17*(2–3), pp. 74–112. [G: India]

Ghosh, M. G. An Evaluation of the Working of the Marginal Farmers and Agricultural Labourers' Development Agency in the District of Bankura, West Bengal. *Econ. Aff.*, January–March 1981, *26*(1), pp. 59–69. [G: India]

Goodman, D. E. Rural Structure, Surplus Mobilisation and Modes of Production in a Peripheral Region: The Brazilian Northeast. In *Mitchell, S., ed.,* 1981, pp. 10–40. [G: Brazil]

Green, G. D. Training for Self-Reliance in Rural Areas. *Int. Lab. Rev.*, July–August 1981, *120*(4), pp. 411–23. [G: E. Africa; S. Africa]

Grindle, Merilee S. Anticipating Failure: The Implementation of Rural Development Programs. *Public Policy*, Winter 1981, *29*(1), pp. 51–74.

Guess, George M. Technical and Financial Policy Options for Development Forestry. *Natural Res. J.*, January 1981, *21*(1), pp. 37–55. [G: LDCs]

Guha, Sunil. Income Redistribution through Labour-Intensive Rural Public Works: Some Policy Issues. *Int. Lab. Rev.*, January–February 1981, *120*(1), pp. 67–82. [G: LDCs]

Guttman, Joel M. The Political Economy of Agricultural Extension Services in India. In *Russell, C. S. and Nicholson, N. K., eds.,* 1981, pp. 183–202. [G: India]

Hastings, Trevor. The Impact of Scientific Research on Australian Rural Productivity. *Australian J. Agr. Econ.*, April 1981, *25*(1), pp. 48–59. [G: Australia]

Hawkins, John N. The People's Republic of China: Energy for Rural Development. In *Goodman, L. J.; Hawkins, J. N. and Love, R. N., eds.,* 1981, pp. 21–60. [G: China]

Heath, J. R. Peasants or Proletarians? Rural Labour in a Brazilian Plantation Economy. *J. Devel. Stud.*, July 1981, *17*(4), pp. 268–81. [G: Brazil]

Herrera, Amilcar O. The Generation of Technologies in Rural Areas. *World Devel.*, January 1981, *9*(1), pp. 21–35. [G: LDCs]

Heyer, Judith. Agricultural Development Policy in Kenya from the Colonial Period to 1975. In *Heyer, J.; Roberts, P. and Williams, G., eds.,*

1981, pp. 90–120. [G: Kenya]

Heyer, Judith. Rural Development Programmes and Impoverishment: Some Experiences in Tropical Africa. In *Johnson, G. and Maunder, A., eds.,* 1981, pp. 215–26. [G: Africa]

Heyer, Judith; Roberts, Pepe and Williams, Gavin. Rural Development. In *Heyer, J.; Roberts, P. and Williams, G., eds.,* 1981, pp. 1–15.

Himes, James R. The Impact in Peru of the Vicos Project. In *Dalton, G., ed.,* 1981, pp. 141–213. [G: Peru]

Hodsdon, Dennis F. The Federation of Free Farmers of the Philippines. *Int. Lab. Rev.,* January–February 1981, *120*(1), pp. 97–113. [G: Philippines]

Hope, Kempe R. Poverty in Rural America—Analytical View of the Dilemma. *Econ. Anal. Worker's Manage.,* 1981, *15*(2), pp. 177–95. [G: U.S.]

House, William J. and Killick, Tony. Inequality and Poverty in the Rural Economy, and the Influence of Some Aspects of Policy. In *Killick, T., ed.,* 1981, pp. 157–79. [G: Kenya]

Hugo, Graeme J. Village-Community Ties, Village Norms, and Ethnic and Social Networks: A Review of Evidence from the Third World. In *De Jong, G. F. and Gardner, R. W., eds.,* 1981, pp. 186–224.

Hull, Terence M. Perspectives and Data Requirements for the Study of Children's Work. In *Rodgers, G. and Standing, G., eds.,* 1981, pp. 47–79.

Jackson, Kathleen O. Sociological Analysis of Irrigation Water Management: Discussion. In *Russell, C. S. and Nicholson, N. K., eds.,* 1981, pp. 174–82. [G: Pakistan]

Jansma, J. Dean, et al. Rural Development: A Review of Conceptual and Empirical Studies. In *Martin, L. R., ed.,* 1981, pp. 285–361. [G: U.S.; Selected Countries]

Jha, Raghbendra and Lächler, Ulrich. Optimum Taxation and Public Production in a Dynamic Harris-Todaro World. *J. Devel. Econ.,* December 1981, *9*(3), pp. 357–73.

Johnston, Bruce F. Reply to the Ness Critique of Johnston and Meyer [Nutrition, Health, and Population in Strategies for Rural Development]. *Econ. Develop. Cult. Change,* January 1981, *29*(2), pp. 407–08.

Johnston, Joe; Matuska, Tony and Andrews, Leith. Bovine Brucellosis and Tuberculosis Eradication in Remote Pastoral Regions. *Quart. Rev. Rural Econ.,* November 1981, *3*(4), pp. 365–69. [G: Australia]

Kahk, J. and Koval'chenko, I. D. Regional Differences in the Position of Peasants in the European Part of Russia in the Nineteenth Century. In *Bairoch, P. and Lévy-Leboyer, M., eds.,* 1981, pp. 244–47. [G: U.S.S.R.]

Kanbur, S. M. Short Run Growth Effects in a Model of Costly Migration with Borrowing Constraints: Will Rural Development Work? In *Currie, D.; Peel, D. and Peters, W., eds.,* 1981, pp. 386–412.

King, Roger. Cooperative Policy and Village Development in Northern Nigeria. In *Heyer, J.; Roberts, P. and Williams, G., eds.,* 1981, pp. 259–80. [G: Nigeria]

Klindt, Thomas H.; Deaton, Brady J. and Landes, Maurice R. The Determinants of Wage Increases in New Manufacturing Plants in Rural Areas. *Southern J. Agr. Econ.,* July 1981, *13*(1), pp. 83–88. [G: U.S.]

Köhler, Ulrich. Integrated Community Development: Vicos in Peru. In *Dalton, G., ed.,* 1981, pp. 111–40. [G: Peru]

Kriesel, Herbert C. The Need to Co-ordinate Central and Local Rural Development Planning and Administration. In *Johnson, G. and Maunder, A., eds.,* 1981, pp. 187–98.

Ladipo, O. O. and Adesimi, A. A. Income Distribution in the Rural Sector. In *Bienen, H. and Diejomaoh, V. P., eds.,* 1981, pp. 299–321. [G: Nigeria]

Larson, Olaf F. Agriculture and the Community. In *Hawley, A. H. and Mazie, S. M., eds.,* 1981, pp. 147–93. [G: U.S.]

Lipton, Michael. The Theory of the Optimising Peasant. In *Livingstone, I., ed.,* 1981, *1968,* pp. 263–71.

Livingstone, Ian. Experimentation in Rural Development: Kenya's Special Rural Development Programme. In *Killick, T., ed.,* 1981, *1976,* pp. 320–28. [G: Kenya]

Livingstone, Ian. On the Concept of 'Integrated Rural Development Planning' in Less Developed Countries. In *Livingstone, I., ed.,* 1981, *1979,* pp. 305–07. [G: LDCs]

Low, A. R. C. The Effect of Off-Farm Employment on Farm Incomes and Production: Taiwan Contrasted with Southern Africa. *Econ. Develop. Cult. Change,* July 1981, *29*(4), pp. 741–47. [G: Taiwan; Swaziland; Lesotho]

MacMillan, J. A. and Winter, G. R. Income Improvement versus Efficiency in Canadian Rural Development Programmes. In *Johnson, G. and Maunder, A., eds.,* 1981, pp. 381–88. [G: Canada]

Matlon, Peter. The Structure of Production and Rural Incomes in Northern Nigeria: Results of Three Village Case Studies. In *Bienen, H. and Diejomaoh, V. P., eds.,* 1981, pp. 323–72. [G: Nigeria]

McNamara, Robert S. To the Board of Governors, Nairobi, Kenya, September 24, 1973. In *McNamara, R. S.,* 1981, *1973,* pp. 233–63. [G: OECD]

McNicoll, I. H. Intertemporal Changes in a Rural Economy: A Case Study. *Econ. Develop. Cult. Change,* October 1981, *30*(1), pp. 107–16. [G: U.K.]

Medick, Hans. The Proto-Industrial Family Economy. In *Kriedte, P.; Medick, H. and Schlumbohm, J.,* 1981, pp. 38–73. [G: Europe]

Mendels, Franklin F. Agriculture and Peasant Industry in Eighteenth-Century Flanders. In *Kriedte, P.; Medick, H. and Schlumbohm, J.,* 1981, pp. 161–77. [G: Belgium; France; Netherlands]

Merrick, Thomas W. Land Availability and Rural Fertility in Northeastern Brazil. In *Simon, J. L. and Lindert, P. H., eds.,* 1981, pp. 93–121. [G: Brazil]

Miller, Thomas A. Some Concepts for Measuring the Economic Value of Rural Data: Discussion.

Amer. J. Agr. Econ., May 1981, *63*(2), pp. 363–64.

Misra, I. R. and Satyal, M. R. Development of Agricultural Marketing and the Improvements of Rural Markets in Hill Areas. In *Nepal, Ministry of Food and Agriculture*, 1981, pp. 84–92.
[G: Nepal]

Morice, Alain. The Exploitation of Children in the "Informal Sector": Proposals for Research. In *Rodgers, G. and Standing, G., eds.*, 1981, pp. 131–58.

Murra, John V. Reciprocity and the Inca State: From Karl Polanyi to John V. Murra: Discussion. In *Dalton, G., ed.*, 1981, *1974*, pp. 51–54.
[G: Peru]

Naidu, R. Chinnaswamy. Role of Agricultural Development in Reduction in Fertility. *Econ. Aff.*, October–December 1981, *26*(4), pp. 283–88.
[G: India]

Nelson, Nici. Mobilising Village Women: Some Organisational and Management Considerations. *J. Devel. Stud.*, April 1981, *17*(3), pp. 47–58.

Ness, Gayl D. The Political Economy of Integration in Development Strategies: Comment on Johnston and Meyer [Nutrition, Health, and Population in Strategies for Rural Development]. *Econ. Develop. Cult. Change*, January 1981, *29*(2), pp. 401–05.

Nicholson, Norman K. Applications of Public Choice Theory to Rural Development—A Statement of the Problem. In *Russell, C. S. and Nicholson, N. K., eds.*, 1981, pp. 17–41.

O'Carroll, Francis X. The Differential Impacts of Inflation on Southern Plains Farms by Selected Farm Characteristics. *Amer. J. Agr. Econ.*, December 1981, *63*(5), pp. 947–55. [G: U.S.]

Oppenheimer, Joe. Does the Route to Development Pass through Public Choice? In *Russell, C. S. and Nicholson, N. K., eds.*, 1981, pp. 271–99.
[G: LDCs]

Park, Jin Hwan. The Work of Agricultural Economists at Community, Village and Local Governmental Levels—Accomplishments and Challenges. In *Johnson, G. and Maunder, A., eds.*, 1981, pp. 147–55. [G: S. Korea]

Park, Siyoung. Rural Development in Korea: The Role of Periodic Markets. *Econ. Geogr.*, April 1981, *57*(2), pp. 113–26. [G: S. Korea]

Parsons, Kenneth H. The Challenge of Agrarian Reform. In *Johnson, G. and Maunder, A., eds.*, 1981, pp. 358–66.

Peacock, Frank. Rural Poverty and Development in West Malaysia (1957–70). *J. Devel. Areas*, July 1981, *15*(4), pp. 639–54. [G: Malaysia]

Popkin, Samuel L. Public Choice and Rural Development—Free Riders, Lemons, and Institutional Design. In *Russell, C. S. and Nicholson, N. K., eds.*, 1981, pp. 43–80.

Powell, David E. The Rural Exodus. In *Bornstein, M., ed.*, 1981, *1974*, pp. 149–63. [G: U.S.S.R.]

Pratschke, John L. Rural and Farm Dwellings in the European Community. *Irish J. Agr. Econ. Rural Soc.*, 1981, *8*(2), pp. 191–211. [G: EEC]

Purcell, John F. H. Mexican Social Issues. In *Purcell, S. K., ed.*, 1981, pp. 43–54. [G: Mexico]

Putterman, Louis. Is a Democratic Collective Agri-

culture Possible? Theoretical Considerations and Evidence from Tanzania. *J. Devel. Econ.*, December 1981, *9*(3), pp. 375–403. [G: Tanzania]

Rahman, Atiqur. Variations in Terms of Exchange and Their Impact on Farm Households in Bangladesh. *J. Devel. Stud.*, July 1981, *17*(4), pp. 317–35. [G: Bangladesh]

Rahman, Rushidan Islam. Implications of Seasonality of Rural Labour Use Pattern: Evidences from Two Villages in Bangladesh. *Bangladesh Devel. Stud.*, Winter 1981, *9*(1), pp. 77–96.
[G: Bangladesh]

Rajani, B. The Royal Northern Project of Thailand. In *Nepal, Ministry of Food and Agriculture*, 1981, pp. 199–202. [G: Thailand]

Ramsay, William and Shue, Elizabeth. Infrastructure Problems for Rural New and Renewable Energy Systems. *J. Energy Devel.*, Spring 1981, *6*(2), pp. 232–50. [G: LDCs]

Rana, P. N. and Mathema, S. B. Potential Impact of Desirable Changes in Relation to Productivity and Income in Hill Farming Systems. In *Nepal, Ministry of Food and Agriculture*, 1981, pp. 59–78. [G: Nepal]

Reinschmiedt, Lynn L. and Murray, Steven W. Transportation Alternatives in Rural Communities: A Feasibility Analysis. *Southern J. Agr. Econ.*, December 1981, *13*(2), pp. 99–104.
[G: U.S.]

Ro, Y. K.; Adams, Dale W. and Hushak, Leroy J. Income Instability and Consumption-Savings in South Korean Farm Households, 1965–1970. *World Devel.*, February 1981, *9*(2), pp. 183–91.
[G: S. Korea]

Roberts, Pepe. 'Rural Development' and the Rural Economy in Niger, 1900–75. In *Heyer, J.; Roberts, P. and Williams, G., eds.*, 1981, pp. 193–221. [G: Niger]

Robinson, Chris and McMahon, Pat. Off-Farm Investment and Employment in the Australian Grazing Industry: A Preliminary Analysis. *Rev. Marketing Agr. Econ.*, April 1981, *49*(1), pp. 25–45. [G: Australia]

Robinson, Chris; McMahon, Pat and Gibbs, Melissa. Farmers' Attitudes to Rural Adjustment Assistance: Results of a Survey in Jemalong Shire, N.S.W. *Australian J. Agr. Econ.*, December 1981, *25*(3), pp. 248–65. [G: Australia]

Rodgers, Gerry and Standing, Guy. The Economic Roles of Children: Issues for Analysis. In *Rodgers, G. and Standing, G., eds.*, 1981, pp. 1–45.
[G: LDCs]

Rosenzweig, Mark R. Household and Non-household Activities of Youths: Issues of Modelling, Data and Estimation Strategies. In *Rodgers, G. and Standing, G., eds.*, 1981, pp. 215–43.
[G: India]

Russell, Clifford S. Public Choice and Rural Development: Introduction. In *Russell, C. S. and Nicholson, N. K., eds.*, 1981, pp. 1–15.

Russell, John. Adapting Extension Work to Poorer Agricultural Areas. *Finance Develop.*, June 1981, *18*(2), pp. 30–33.

Saadat, Owaise and van Gigch, Francis. Lessons from the Field: Rural Development in West Africa. *Finance Develop.*, December 1981, *18*(4), pp. 37–40. [G: W. Africa]

Sainju, M. M. and Ram, B. K. C. Hill Labour Migration: Issues and Problems. In *Nepal, Ministry of Food and Agriculture*, 1981, pp. 111–22.
[G: Nepal]

Saith, Ashwani. Production, Prices and Poverty in Rural India. *J. Devel. Stud.*, January 1981, *17*(2), pp. 196–213. [G: India]

Schlesinger, Lee I. Agriculture and Community in Maharashtra, India. In *Dalton, G., ed.*, 1981, pp. 233–74. [G: India]

Scott, C. D. Agrarian Reform and Seasonal Employment in Coastal Peruvian Agriculture. *J. Devel. Stud.*, July 1981, *17*(4), pp. 282–306. [G: Peru]

Simonen, Mari S. Education, Family Economic Production, and Fertility: The Case of Rural and Semi-Urban Guatemala. In *Balderston, J. B., et al., eds.*, 1981, pp. 147–76. [G: Guatemala]

Singh, Bhagwan Prasad. Commercial Banks in Rural India: Bihar's Relative Position. In *Karna, M. N., ed.*, 1981, pp. 57–85. [G: India]

Singh, R. B. and Shrestha, G. R. Delivery of Agricultural Input to Hill Farmers: Issues and Problems. In *Nepal, Ministry of Food and Agriculture*, 1981, pp. 93–99. [G: Nepal]

Singh, Surendra P. and Williamson, Handy, Jr. Part-Time Farming: Productivity and Some Implications of Off-Farm Work by Farmers. *Southern J. Agr. Econ.*, December 1981, *13*(2), pp. 61–67. [G: U.S.]

Steele, John and Kanel, Don. Land Tenure in a Brazilian Rural Community: Life Cycle Patterns and Intergenerational Changes. In *Dalton, G., ed.*, 1981, pp. 215–31. [G: Brazil]

Steward, Julian H. Wittfogel's Irrigation Hypothesis. In *Bailey, A. M. and Llobera, J. R., eds.*, 1981, 1977, pp. 195–206.

Sumner, Daniel A. Wage Functions and Occupational Selection in a Rural Less Developed Country Setting. *Rev. Econ. Statist.*, November 1981, *63*(4), pp. 513–19. [G: Guatemala]

Taimni, K. K. Employment Generation through Handicraft Co-operatives: The Indian Experience. *Int. Lab. Rev.*, July–August 1981, *120*(4), pp. 505–17. [G: India]

Tan, B. T. Prospects and Problems of Hill Agriculture in Malaysia. In *Nepal, Ministry of Food and Agriculture*, 1981, pp. 180–89. [G: Malaysia]

Thomson, James T. Public Choice Analysis of Institutional Constraints on Firewood Production Strategies in the West African Sahel. In *Russell, C. S. and Nicholson, N. K., eds.*, 1981, pp. 119–52. [G: W. Africa]

Thomson, Norm and Walsh, Cliff. Cross-subsidisation of Rural Areas via Utility Pricing Policies. *Australian J. Agr. Econ.*, December 1981, *25*(3), pp. 221–32. [G: Australia]

Thurmeier, Margie. The Determinants of Off-Farm Employment of Saskatchewan Farmers. *Can. J. Agr. Econ.*, November 1981, *29*(3), pp. 339–48. [G: Canada]

Tienda, Marta and Aborampah, Osei-Mensah. Energy-Related Adaptation in Low-Income Nonmetropolitan Wisconsin Counties. *J. Cons. Res.*, December 1981, *8*(3), pp. 265–70. [G: U.S.]

Tolley, George S. Rural People, Communities, and

Regions: Introduction. In *Martin, L. R., ed.*, 1981, pp. 153–58.

Troeller, Ruth R. The Future of Energy Procurement with Special Reference to Rural Areas of Third World Countries. In *Lozoya, J. and Green, R., eds.*, 1981, pp. 199–218. [G: LDCs]

Udall, Alan T. Transport Improvements and Rural Outmigration in Colombia. *Econ. Develop. Cult. Change*, April 1981, *29*(3), pp. 613–29.
[G: Colombia]

Vogel, Robert C. Rural Financial Market Performance: Implications of Low Delinquency Rates. *Amer. J. Agr. Econ.*, February 1981, *63*(1), pp. 58–65. [G: Costa Rica]

Wachtel, N. Reciprocity and the Inca State: From Karl Polanyi to John V. Murra. In *Dalton, G., ed.*, 1981, 1974, pp. 38–50. [G: Peru]

Walker, Thomas Steven. Risk and Adoption of Hybrid Maize in El Salvador. *Food Res. Inst. Stud.*, 1981, *18*(1), pp. 59–88. [G: El Salvador]

Wallace, Tina. The Kano River Project, Nigeria: The Impact of an Irrigation Scheme on Productivity and Welfare. In *Heyer, J.; Roberts, P. and Williams, G., eds.*, 1981, pp. 281–305. [G: Nigeria]

Wibberley, Gerald. Strong Agricultures but Weak Rural Economies—The Undue Emphasis on Agriculture in European Rural Development. *Europ. Rev. Agr. Econ.*, 1981, *8*(2–3), pp. 155–70.
[G: Europe]

Williams, Gavin. The World Bank and the Peasant Problem. In *Heyer, J.; Roberts, P. and Williams, G., eds.*, 1981, pp. 16–51.

Wittfogel, Karl. The Theory of Oriental Society. In *Bailey, A. M. and Llobera, J. R., eds.*, 1981, 1968, pp. 141–57.

Worsley, Peter. Village Economies. In *Samuel, R., ed.*, 1981, pp. 80–85. [G: U.K.]

720 NATURAL RESOURCES

721 Natural Resources

7210 General

Adams, F. Gerard; Behrman, Jere R. and Lasaga, M. Commodity Exports and NIEO Proposals for Buffer Stocks and Compensatory Finance: Implications for Latin America. In *Baer, W. and Gillis, M., eds.*, 1981, pp. 48–76. [G: Chile; Latin America]

Allan, J. A. Renewable Natural Resources in the Middle East. In *[Fisher, W. B.]*, 1981, pp. 24–39. [G: Middle East]

Alston, Philip. Commodity Agreements—As Though People Don't Matter: A Reply to "'Fair Labour Standards' in International Commodity Agreements." *J. World Trade Law*, September–October 1981, *15*(5), pp. 455–60.

Amaria, P. J., et al. Systems Dynamic Models of Newfoundland Fisheries. In *Haley, K. B., ed.*, 1981, pp. 55–66. [G: Canada]

Amble, Arnt. Multiobjective Optimization of a Local Fishing Fleet—A Goal Programming Approach. In *Haley, K. B., ed.*, 1981, pp. 309–19.
[G: Norway]

Ames, Glenn C. W. and Baxter, Harold O. Wood

Fuel: An Alternative Energy Source for Agribusiness and Industry. *Southern J. Agr. Econ.*, December 1981, *13*(2), pp. 91–97. [G: U.S.]

Andersen, Peder. Nogle grundtraek i fiskeriøkonomi. (Some Fundamentals in Economics of Fisheries. With English summary.) *Nationaløkon. Tidsskr.*, 1981, *119*(1), pp. 1–20.

Anderson, F. J. Optimum Forest Rotation: Comment. *Land Econ.*, May 1981, *57*(2), pp. 293–94.

Anderson, Kym and Smith, Ben. Changing Economic Relations between the Asian ADCs and Resource-Exporting Advanced Countries of the Pacific Basin. In *Hong, W. and Krause, L. B., eds.*, 1981, pp. 293–338. [G: Hong Kong; Singapore; S. Korea; Taiwan; Selected MDCs]

Anderson, Lee G., et al. Modeling and Simulation of Interdependent Fisheries, and Optimal Effort Allocation Using Mathematical Programming. In *Haley, K. B., ed.*, 1981, pp. 421–38. [G: U.S.]

Baden, John; Stroup, Richard and Thurman, Walter N. Myths, Admonitions and Rationality: The American Indian as a Resource Manager. *Econ. Inquiry*, January 1981, *19*(1), pp. 132–43. [G: U.S.]

Bailey, Richard. North Sea Oil—The Norwegian Alternative. *Nat. Westminster Bank Quart. Rev.*, May 1981, pp. 11–19. [G: U.K.; Norway]

Barker, Terry. Depletion Policy and the De-Industrialization of the UK Economy. *Energy Econ.*, April 1981, *3*(2), pp. 71–82. [G: U.K.]

Barré, Rémi and Bower, Blair T. Water Management in France, with Special Emphasis on Water Quality Management and Effluent Charges. In *Bower, B. T., et al., eds.*, 1981, pp. 33–209. [G: France]

Bath, C. Richard. Mexico–United States Relations: Resolving Water Disputes. In *Purcell, S. K., ed.*, 1981, pp. 181–88. [G: Mexico; U.S.]

Batten, Charles R. Toward a Free Market in Forest Resources. *Cato J.*, Fall 1981, *1*(2), pp. 501–17. [G: U.S.]

Beaumont, Peter. Water Resources and Their Management in the Middle East. In *[Fisher, W. B.]*, 1981, pp. 40–72. [G: Middle East]

Beckwith, James P., Jr. Parks, Property Rights, and the Possibilities of the Private Law. *Cato J.*, Fall 1981, *1*(2), pp. 473–99.

Berck, Peter. Optimal Management of Renewable Resources with Growing Demand for Stock Externalities. *J. Environ. Econ. Manage.*, June 1981, *8*(2), pp. 105–17.

Bergstrom, Theodore C.; Cross, John G. and Porter, Richard C. Efficiency-Inducing Taxation for a Monopolistically Supplied Depletable Resource. *J. Public Econ.*, February 1981, *15*(1), pp. 23–32.

Biswas, Asit K. Water for the Third World. *Foreign Aff.*, Fall 1981, *60*(1), pp. 148–66. [G: LDCs]

Blake, Gerald H. Offshore Politics and Resources in the Middle East. In *[Fisher, W. B.]*, 1981, pp. 113–29. [G: Middle East]

Boggess, William G. and Heady, Earl O. A Sector Analysis of Alternative Income Support and Soil Conservation Policies. *Amer. J. Agr. Econ.*, November 1981, *63*(4), pp. 618–28. [G: U.S.]

Bøjlund, Thorkil; Kolind, Lars and Aagaard-Svendsen, Rolf. A Strategic Planning Model for the Fisheries Sector. In *Haley, K. B., ed.*, 1981, pp. 363–73. [G: Denmark]

Braeutigam, Ronald R. The Workback Method and the Value of Helium. *Public Policy*, Winter 1981, *29*(1), pp. 31–49. [G: U.S.]

Breyer, Friedrich and Reiss, Winfried. Probleme des Konzepts preisabhängiger Ressourcenausstattungen. (Problems with the Conception of Price-Dependent Resource Endowments. With English summary.) *Z. Wirtschaft. Sozialwissen.*, 1981, *101*(1), pp. 83–98.

Bruvold, William H. Community Evaluation of Adopted Uses of Reclaimed Water. *Water Resources Res.*, June 1981, *17*(3), pp. 487–90. [G: U.S.]

Buchholz, Wolfgang. Zur Bedeutung des Durchschnittsnutzens für das Cake-Eating-Problem. (The Average Utility on Optimal Cake-Eating Paths. With English summary.) *Z. ges. Staatswiss.*, March 1981, *137*(1), pp. 97–107.

Budowski, Gerardo. The Place of Agro-Forestry in Managing Tropical Forests. In *Mergen, F., ed.*, 1981, pp. 182–94. [G: Costa Rica]

Bulkley, I. G. Property Rights and the Efficient Development of Minerals on the Ocean Floor. In *Zerbe, R. O., Jr., ed.*, 1981, pp. 143–53.

Burness, H. Stuart and Quirk, James P. The Theory of the Dam: An Application to the Colorado River. In *[Weiler, E. T.]*, 1981, pp. 107–30. [G: U.S.]

Butterworth, D. S. The Value of Catch-Statistics-Based Management Techniques for Heavily Fished Pelagic Stocks with Special Reference to the Recent Decline of the Southwest African Pilchard Stock. In *Haley, K. B., ed.*, 1981, pp. 441–64. [G: Southwest Africa]

Cadeliña, Rowe V. Food Management under Scarce Resources by Philippine Marginal Agriculturalists. *Philippine Econ. J.*, 1981, *20*(1), pp. 80–100. [G: Philippines]

Cairns, Robert D. The Constitution as Regulation: The Case of Natural Resources. *Can. Public Policy*, Winter 1981, *7*(1), pp. 66–74. [G: Canada]

Campbell, David C. Application of Risk and Uncertainty Analysis in the Principles, Standards, and Procedures of the U.S. Water Resources Council. In *Haimes, Y. Y., ed.*, 1981, pp. 157–61. [G: U.S.]

Cartwright, Philip. Welfare Economics and the Log Export Policy Issue: Discussion. In *Sedjo, R. A., ed.*, 1981, pp. 209–15. [G: U.S.]

Castañeda, Jorge. Some Political Issues in the Negotiation of the New International Economic Order: The Resources of the Seabed. In *Laszlo, E. and Kurtzman, J., eds.*, 1981, pp. 30–65. [G: Global]

Castle, Emery N., et al. Natural Resource Economics, 1946–75. In *Martin, L. R., ed.*, 1981, pp. 393–500. [G: U.S.]

Chalmers, James A. and Threadgill, J. Randall. Evaluation of Underutilized Resources in Water Resource Development. *Water Resources Res.*, June 1981, *17*(3), pp. 455–61.

Chan, Arthur H. The Structure of Federal Water Resources Policy Making. *Amer. J. Econ. Soc.*,

April 1981, *40*(2), pp. 115–27. [G: U.S.]

Chaturvedi, M. C. and Srivastava, D. K. Study of a Complex Water Resources System with Screening and Simulation Models. *Water Resources Res.*, August 1981, *17*(4), pp. 783–94.
[G: India]

Cheng, Kuo-Shung; Lin, Chau-Jy and Wang, Ar-Young. Analysis of Modified Model for Commercial Fishing with Possible Extinctive Fishery Resources. *J. Environ. Econ. Manage.*, June 1981, *8*(2), pp. 151–55.

Cigno, Alessandro. Growth with Exhaustible Resources and Endogenous Population. *Rev. Econ. Stud.*, April 1981, *48*(2), pp. 281–87.

Clark, Robert M. and Stevie, Richard G. A Regional Water Supply Cost Model. *Growth Change*, July 1981, *12*(3), pp. 9–16. [G: U.S.]

Clark, Robert M. and Stevie, Richard G. A Water Supply Cost Model Incorporating Spatial Variables. *Land Econ.*, February 1981, *57*(1), pp. 18–32.

Clawson, Marion. Land-Use Trends. In *Hawley, A. H. and Mazie, S. M., eds.*, 1981, pp. 645–67. [G: U.S.]

Clawson, Marion. Natural Resources of the Great Plains in Historical Perspective. In *Lawson, M. P. and Baker, M. E., eds.*, 1981, pp. 3–10.
[G: U.S.]

Cohon, Jared L.; ReVelle, Charles S. and Palmer, Richard N. Multiobjective Generating Techniques for Risk/Benefit Analysis. In *Haimes, Y. Y., ed.*, 1981, pp. 123–34. [G: U.S.]

Comolli, Paul M. Principles and Policy in Forestry Economics. *Bell J. Econ. (See Rand J. Econ. after 4/85)*, Spring 1981, *12*(1), pp. 300–309.

Conrad, Robert F. and Hool, Bryce. Resource Taxation with Heterogeneous Quality and Endogenous Reserves. *J. Public Econ.*, August 1981, *16*(1), pp. 17–33.

Copes, Parzival. Rational Resource Management and Institutional Constraints: The Case of the Fishery. In *Butlin, J. A., ed.*, 1981, pp. 113–28.

Cortner, Hanna J. and Schweitzer, Dennis L. Institutional Limits to National Public Planning for Forest Resources: The Resources Planning Act. *Natural Res. J.*, April 1981, *21*(2), pp. 203–22.
[G: U.S.]

Cousins, Kathryn. Lessons from the Coastline of America: Management Strategies for a Sustainable Society. In *Coomer, J. C., ed.*, 1981, pp. 225–44. [G: U.S.]

Cross, Melvin L. and Ekelund, Robert B., Jr. A. T. Hadley: The American Invention of the Economics of Property Rights and Public Goods. *Rev. Soc. Econ.*, April 1981, *39*(1), pp. 37–50.

Cuddington, John T.; Johnson, F. Reed and Knetsch, Jack L. Valuing Amenity Resources in the Presence of Substitutes. *Land Econ.*, November 1981, *57*(4), pp. 526–35.

Curr, C. T. W. A Mathematical Model Used for Pre-feasibility Studies of Fishing Operations. In *Haley, K. B., ed.*, 1981, pp. 161–72.
[G: Poland]

Dahle, Emil Aall. A Review of Models of Fishing Operations. In *Haley, K. B., ed.*, 1981, pp. 213–22.

Dasgupta, Partha. "The Economics of Common Property Resources: A Dynamic Formulation of the Fisheries Problem." *Indian Econ. Rev.*, July-Sept. 1981, *16*(3), pp. 169–97.

Dasgupta, Partha. Resource Pricing and Technological Innovations under Oligopoly: A Theoretical Exploration. *Scand. J. Econ.*, 1981, *83*(2), pp. 289–317.

Dasgupta, Partha and Stiglitz, Joseph E. Resource Depletion under Technological Uncertainty. *Econometrica*, January 1981, *49*(1), pp. 85–104.

Daubert, John T. and Young, Robert A. Recreational Demands for Maintaining Instream Flows: A Contingent Valuation Approach. *Amer. J. Agr. Econ.*, November 1981, *63*(4), pp. 666–76.
[G: U.S.]

Davidson, C. Girard. Conservation, Public Power, and Natural Resources. In *Heller, F. H., ed.*, 1981, pp. 59–66. [G: U.S.]

Dennis, William C. The Public and Private Interest in Wilderness Protection. *Cato J.*, Fall 1981, *1*(2), pp. 373–90.

Devarajan, Shantayanan and Fisher, Anthony C. Hotelling's "Economics of Exhaustible Resources": Fifty Years Later. *J. Econ. Lit.*, March 1981, *19*(1), pp. 65–73.

Digernes, Torbjørn. Simple Computation Models for Calculating Profitability of Fishing Vessels. In *Haley, K. B., ed.*, 1981, pp. 173–86. [G: Norway]

Donaldson, William J. Fisheries of the Arabian Peninsula. In *[Fisher, W. B.]*, 1981, pp. 189–98.
[G: Middle East]

Dowdle, Barney. Log Export Restrictions: Causes and Consequences. In *Sedjo, R. A., ed.*, 1981, pp. 248–58. [G: U.S.]

Duckstein, L. and Kempf, J. Multicriteria Q-Analysis for Plan Evaluation. In *Nijkamp, P. and Spronk, J., eds.*, 1981, pp. 87–99.
[G: Hungary]

Edgmon, Terry D. and Menzel, Donald C. The Regulation of Coal Surface Mining in a Federal System. *Natural Res. J.*, April 1981, *21*(2), pp. 245–65. [G: U.S.]

Ehrlicher, Werner. Zukunftsprobleme unserer Wirtschaft. (Future Problems of Our Economy. With English summary.) *Kredit Kapital*, 1981, *14*(1), pp. 3–25.

Eisel, Leo M. Uncertainty: The Water Resources Decisionmaking Dilemma. In *Haimes, Y. Y., ed.*, 1981, pp. 5–11.

Ervik, Leif K.; Flam, Sjur D. and Olsen, Trond E. Comprehensive Modelling of Fisheries: Comments and a Case Study. In *Haley, K. B., ed.*, 1981, pp. 3–21. [G: Norway]

Evenson, Robert E. Tropical Forests in Economic Development. In *Mergen, F., ed.*, 1981, pp. 126–42. [G: LDCs]

Feitel'man, N. The Economic Evaluation of Natural Resources. *Prob. Econ.*, August 1981, *24*(4), pp. 39–56.

Field, Barry C. and Berndt, Ernst R. An Introductory Review of Research on the Economics of Natural Resource Substitution. In *Berndt, E. R. and Field, B. C., eds.*, 1981, pp. 1–14.

Flores Rodas, Marco A. Forestry for Rural Development: A New Approach. In *Mergen, F., ed.*, 1981,

pp. 4–13.

Fonteneau, Alain and L'Hostis, Denez. Towards a Unified Structure of the French Fishery System. In *Haley, K. B., ed.,* 1981, pp. 23–37.
[G: France]

Foster, Henry S., Jr. and Beattie, Bruce R. Urban Residental Demand for Water in the United States: Reply. *Land Econ.,* May 1981, 57(2), pp. 257–65.
[G: U.S.]

Foster, John. The Global Energy Scene. In *Foster, J., et al.,* 1981, pp. 5–55.
[G: Global]

Garrod, D. J. and Shepherd, J. G. On the Relationship between Fishing Capacity and Resource Allocations. In *Haley, K. B., ed.,* 1981, pp. 321–36.
[G: U.K.]

Gatto, M., et al. A Study on the Demand Functions of the Sacca Degli Scardovari Fishery. In *Haley, K. B., ed.,* 1981, pp. 233–45.
[G: Italy]

Georgianna, Thomas D. and Haynes, Kingsley E. Competition for Water Resources: Coal and Agriculture in the Yellowstone Basin. *Econ. Geogr.,* July 1981, 57(3), pp. 225–37.
[G: U.S.]

Gofman, K. G. Financial Accountability and the Right to Use Resources. *Matekon,* Fall 1981, 18(1), pp. 80–86.

Golabi, Kamal and Scherer, Charles R. Extraction Timing and Economic Incentives for Geothermal Reservoir Management. *J. Environ. Econ. Manage.,* June 1981, 8(2), pp. 156–74.

Goss, Barry A. The Forward Pricing Function of the London Metal Exchange. *Appl. Econ.,* June 1981, 13(2), pp. 133–50.

Gregersen, Hans M. Environmental Constraints versus Economic Gains in Tropical Forestry. In *Mergen, F., ed.,* 1981, pp. 109–24.

Greig, P. J. and Devonshire, P. G. Tree Removals and Saline Seepage in Victorian Catchments: Some Hydrologic and Economic Results. *Australian J. Agr. Econ.,* August 1981, 25(2), pp. 134–48.
[G: Australia]

Griffin, Adrian H.; Martin, William E. and Wade, James C. Urban Residential Demand for Water in the United States: Comment. *Land Econ.,* May 1981, 57(2), pp. 252–56.
[G: U.S.]

Grilli, Enzo R. Natural Rubber: A Better Future? *Finance Develop.,* June 1981, 18(2), pp. 25–29.

Guariso, Giorgio, et al. Supply–Demand Coordination in Water Resources Management. *Water Resources Res.,* August 1981, 17(4), pp. 776–82.
[G: Mexico]

Guess, George M. Technical and Financial Policy Options for Development Forestry. *Natural Res. J.,* January 1981, 21(1), pp. 37–55.
[G: LDCs]

Gulland, J. A. An Overview of Applications of Operations Research in Fishery Management. In *Haley, K. B., ed.,* 1981, pp. 125–35.

Gupta, Sanjeev and Mayer, Thomas. A Test of the Efficiency of Futures Markets in Commodities. *Weltwirtsch. Arch.,* 1981, 117(4), pp. 661–71.

Hall, Warren A. Risk/Benefit Trade-off Analysis in Water Resources Planning. In *Haimes, Y. Y., ed.,* 1981, pp. 31–40.

Hamlin, Cyrus. Applications of Operations Research in Fisheries. In *Haley, K. B., ed.,* 1981, pp. 141–59.
[G: Jamaica; U.S.]

Hanke, Steve H. and Wentworth, Roland W. Proj-

ect Evaluation during Inflation, Revisited: A Solution to Turvey's Relative Price Change Problem. *Water Resources Res.,* December 1981, 17(6), pp. 1737–38.
[G: U.S.]

Hannesson, Røgnvaldur; Hansen, Olav R. and Dale, Svein Age. A Frontier Production Function for the Norwegian: Cod Fisheries. In *Haley, K. B., ed.,* 1981, pp. 337–360.
[G: Norway]

Hanson, R. J. and Millham, C. B. Estimating the Costs in Lost Power of Alternative Snake-Columbia Basin Management Policies. *Water Resources Res.,* October 1981, 17(5), pp. 1295–1303.
[G: U.S.]

Harris, Richard G. Trade and Depletable Resources: The Small Open Economy. *Can. J. Econ.,* November 1981, 14(4), pp. 649–64.

Hauser, Wolfgang. International Deep Seabed Mining: Institutional and Fiscal Framework. In *Schanze, E., et al.,* 1981, pp. 145–70.

Hay, Michael J. and McConnell, Kenneth E. An Analysis of Participation in Nonconsumptive Wildlife Recreation: Reply. *Land Econ.,* May 1981, 57(2), pp. 288–92.
[G: U.S.]

Haynes, Richard; Darr, David R. and Adams, Darius. U.S.–Japanese Log Trade—Effect of a Ban. In *Sedjo, R. A., ed.,* 1981, pp. 216–32.
[G: U.S.; Japan]

Heal, Geoffrey M. Economics and Resources. In *Butlin, J. A., ed.,* 1981, pp. 62–73.

Heal, Geoffrey M. Scarcity, Efficiency and Disequilibrium in Resource Markets. *Scand. J. Econ.,* 1981, 83(2), pp. 334–51.

Heaps, Terry. The Qualitative Theory of Optimal Rotations. *Can. J. Econ.,* November 1981, 14(4), pp. 686–99.

Heffernan, Patrick H. Mexico–United States Relations: Conflict over Marine Resources. In *Purcell, S. K., ed.,* 1981, pp. 168–80. [G: Mexico; U.S.]

Henderson, Emma M. and Marchesseault, Guy D. A Biological Predictor Model Developed in Support of an Operations Research Approach to the Management of the New England Groundfish Fishery. In *Haley, K. B., ed.,* 1981, pp. 465–79.
[G: U.S.]

Henry, Mark S. and Bowen, Ernie. A Method for Estimating the Value of Water among Sectors of a Regional Economy. *Southern J. Agr. Econ.,* December 1981, 13(2), pp. 125–32.
[G: U.S.]

Hochman, Harold M. California Law and Its Economic Effects on Southern California: Comments. In *Sirkin, G., ed.,* 1981, pp. 58–61.
[G: U.S.]

Hoel, Michael. Resource Extraction by a Monopolist with Influence over the Rate of Return on Non-Resource Assets. *Int. Econ. Rev.,* February 1981, 22(1), pp. 147–57.

Hoppensteadt, Frank C. and Sohn, Ira. A Multiple Species Fishery Model: An Input-Output Approach. In *Haley, K. B., ed.,* 1981, pp. 115–24.

Howe, Charles W. Guidelines for a Responsible Natural Resources Policy. In *[Weiler, E. T.],* 1981, pp. 131–51.
[G: U.S.]

Huang, C. C. and Redlack, A. R. On Methodologies which Bridge the Gap between Fish Population Models and Fishery Management. In *Haley, K. B., ed.,* 1981, pp. 39–53.
[G: Canada]

Hulett, G. K. The Future of the Grasslands. In *Law-*

son, M. P. and Baker, M. E., eds., 1981, pp. 141–56. [G: U.S.]

Hung, N. M. L'instabilité structurelle dans le modèle de croissance avec ressource non renouvelable. (Structural Instability in the Growth Model with Exhaustible Resources. With English summary.) *L'Actual. Econ.*, July–September 1981, 57(3), pp. 387–406.

Hyde, William F. Timber Economics in the Rockies: Efficiency and Management Options. *Land Econ.*, November 1981, 57(4), pp. 630–38. [G: U.S.]

Icamina, Benvenuto N. The Impact of UNCTAD Commodity Stabilization on Philippine Trade: A Simulation Analysis of Selected Commodities. *Philippine Econ. J.*, 1981, 20(3&4), pp. 277–94. [G: Philippines]

Jensson, Pall. A Simulation Model of the Capelin Fishing in Iceland. In *Haley, K. B., ed.*, 1981, pp. 187–98. [G: Iceland]

Joeres, Erhard; Seus, Günther J. and Engelmann, Herbert M. The Linear Decision Rule (LDR) Reservoir Problem with Correlated Inflows: 1. Model Development. *Water Resources Res.*, February 1981, 17(1), pp. 18–24.

Johnson, Ronald N. Economic Trade-Offs and the North Carolina Shrimp Fishery: Comment. *Amer. J. Agr. Econ.*, November 1981, 63(4), pp. 746. [G: U.S.]

Johnson, Ronald N. and Gisser, Micha. The Definition of a Surface Water Right and Transferability. *J. Law Econ.*, October 1981, 24(2), pp. 273–88. [G: U.S.]

Kamien, Morton I. and Schwartz, Nancy L. Technical Change Inclinations of a Resource Monopolist. In *[Weiler, E. T.]*, 1981, pp. 41–53.

Kaplan, E. and Thode, H. C., Jr. Water Quality, Energy, and Socioeconomics: Path Analyses for Studies of Causality. *Water Resources Res.*, June 1981, 17(3), pp. 491–503. [G: U.S.]

Kaser, Michael C. East–West Factors in International Energy Production and Trade. In *Tempest, P., ed.*, 1981, pp. 49–52. [G: E. Europe]

Keidel, Albert. Resource Dependency and Energy Problems. In *Richardson, B. M. and Ueda, T., eds.*, 1981, pp. 89–98. [G: Japan]

Kennedy, John O. S. Applications of Dynamic Programming to Agriculture, Forestry and Fisheries: Review and Prognosis. *Rev. Marketing Agr. Econ.*, December 1981, 49(3), pp. 141–73.

Kheinman, S. A. Organizational–Structural Factors in Economic Growth [Part II]. *Prob. Econ.*, January 1981, 23(9), pp. 25–52. [G: U.S.S.R.]

Kiker, Clyde and Lynne, Gary D. Areas of Critical State Concern: Florida's Experience with the Green Swamp. *Southern J. Agr. Econ.*, December 1981, 13(2), pp. 149–55. [G: U.S.]

Kopp, Raymond J. and Smith, V. Kerry. Measuring the Prospects for Resource Substitution under Input and Technology Aggregations. In *Berndt, E. R. and Field, B. C., eds.*, 1981, pp. 145–73.

Krutilla, John V. Reflections of an Applied Welfare Economist. *J. Environ. Econ. Manage.*, March 1981, 8(1), pp. 1–10.

Kullmann, Ulrich. "Fair Labour Standards" in International Commodity Agreements: Reply. *J.*

World Trade Law, September–October 1981, 15(5), pp. 460–61.

Laarman, Jan G. World Forest Plantations—What Are the Implications for U.S. Forest Products Trade? Discussion. In *Sedjo, R. A., ed.*, 1981, pp. 40–53. [G: U.S.; Brazil]

Lax, David A. and Sebenius, James K. Insecure Contracts and Resource Development. *Public Policy*, Fall 1981, 29(4), pp. 417–36. [G: LDCs]

Lee, Dwight R. Monopoly, Price Controls, and the Exploitation of Nonrenewable Resources. *J. Energy Devel.*, Autumn 1981, 7(1), pp. 111–20.

Lee, Hoe Sung. Changing Economic Relations between the Asian ADCs and Resource-Exporting Advanced Countries of the Pacific Basin: Comment. In *Hong, W. and Krause, L. B., eds.*, 1981, pp. 339–40. [G: Hong Kong; Singapore; S. Korea; Taiwan; Selected MDCs]

Leman, Christopher K. and Nelson, Robert H. Ten Commandments for Policy Economists. *J. Policy Anal. Manage.*, Fall 1981, 1(1), pp. 97–117. [G: U.S.]

Levhari, David; Michener, Ron and Mirman, Leonard J. Dynamic Programming Models of Fishing: Competition. *Amer. Econ. Rev.*, September 1981, 71(4), pp. 649–61.

Levhari, David and Pindyck, Robert S. The Pricing of Durable Exhaustible Resources. *Quart. J. Econ.*, August 1981, 96(3), pp. 365–77.

Lewis, Tracy R. Energy vs. the Environment. *J. Environ. Econ. Manage.*, March 1981, 8(1), pp. 59–71.

Lewis, Tracy R. Exploitation of a Renewable Resource under Uncertainty. *Can. J. Econ.*, August 1981, 14(3), pp. 422–39.

Libecap, Gary D. Competing for the Rental Value of Federal Land: The Assignment of Use Rights and Their Regulation. *Cato J.*, Fall 1981, 1(2), pp. 391–404. [G: U.S.]

Lierens, G. E. Planning Model for Small-Scale Fisheries Development. In *Haley, K. B., ed.*, 1981, pp. 409–20. [G: Sri Lanka]

Lippke, Bruce. U.S.–Japanese Log Trade—Effect of a Ban: Discussion. In *Sedjo, R. A., ed.*, 1981, pp. 233–47. [G: U.S.; Japan]

Lippman, Steven A. and McCall, John J. Progressive Taxation in Sequential Decisionmaking: Deterministic and Stochastic Analysis. *J. Public Econ.*, August 1981, 16(1), pp. 35–52.

Long, Alan and Johnson, Norman. Forest Plantations in Kalimantan, Indonesia. In *Mergen, F., ed.*, 1981, pp. 78–92. [G: Indonesia]

Lord, Montague J. Commodity Exports and NIEO Proposals for Buffer Stocks and Compensatory Finance: Comment. In *Baer, W. and Gillis, M., eds.*, 1981, pp. 76–82. [G: Brazil; Chile; Latin America]

Love, J. Commodity Diversification: A Market Model. *J. Devel. Stud.*, October 1981, 18(1), pp. 94–103. [G: Latin America; Africa; Asia]

Lynne, Gary D.; Conroy, Patricia and Prochaska, Frederick J. Economic Valuation of Marsh Areas for Marine Production Processes. *J. Environ. Econ. Manage.*, June 1981, 8(2), pp. 175–86.

Lyon, Kenneth S. Mining of the Forest and the Time Path of the Price of Timber. *J. Environ. Econ.*

Manage., December 1981, *8*(4), pp. 330–44.

Marchesseault, Guy D., et al. Bio-Economic Simulation of the Atlantic Sea Scallop Fishery: A Preliminary Report. In *Haley, K. B., ed.*, 1981, pp. 375–92. [G: U.S.]

Marks, David H. Comment on 'An Evaluation of Marginal Waters as a Natural Resource in Israel' by N. Buras and P. Darr. *Water Resources Res.*, February 1981, *17*(1), pp. 253. [G: Israel]

McGaw, Richard L. The Supply of Effort in a Fishery. *Appl. Econ.*, June 1981, *13*(2), pp. 245–53. [G: Canada]

McGuckin, J. Thomas and Young, Robert A. On the Economics of Desalination of Brackish Household Water Supplies. *J. Environ. Econ. Manage.*, March 1981, *8*(1), pp. 79–91. [G: U.S.]

McGuinness, Maureen. Navigable Water not Always Subject to Free Public Access. *Natural Res. J.*, January 1981, *21*(1), pp. 161–68. [G: U.S.]

McInerney, John. Natural Resource Economics: The Basic Analytical Principles. In *Butlin, J. A., ed.*, 1981, pp. 30–58.

McKillop, William. Log Export Restrictions: Causes and Consequences: Discussion. In *Sedjo, R. A., ed.*, 1981, pp. 259–63. [G: U.S.]

Meade, James E. Economic Policy and the Threat of Doom. In *Butlin, J. A., ed.*, 1981, pp. 9–29.

Miller, Jon R. and Hay, Michael J. Determinants of Hunter Participation: Duck Hunting in the Mississippi Flyway. *Amer. J. Agr. Econ.*, November 1981, *63*(4), pp. 677–84. [G: U.S.]

Mitchell, Simon. Stagnant Peasant Capitalism: The Case of Inshore Fishermen in Northeastern Brazil. In *Mitchell, S., ed.*, 1981, pp. 133–42. [G: Brazil]

Mitra, Tapan. Some Results on the Optimal Depletion of Exhaustible Resources under Negative Discounting. *Rev. Econ. Stud.*, July 1981, *48*(3), pp. 521–32.

Moroney, John R. and Trapani, John M., III. Factor Demand and Substitution in Mineral-Intensive Industries. *Bell J. Econ. (See Rand J. Econ. after 4/85)*, Spring 1981, *12*(1), pp. 272–84. [G: U.S.]

Moses, Raphael J. Water-Law Institutions of the Plains. In *Lawson, M. P. and Baker, M. E., eds.*, 1981, pp. 169–79.

Müller, Frank G. Zur Kontroverse über die Verfügbarkeit der natürlichen Ressourcen: Ressourcenknappheit und Ressourcenknappheitsindikatoren. (A Contribution to the Controversies on the Availability of Natural Resources: Scarcity of Resources and Indicators of Scarcity of Resources. With English summary.) *Schweiz. Z. Volkswirtsch. Statist.*, December 1981, *117*(4), pp. 633–64.

Mundy, P. R. and Mathisen, O. A. Abundance Estimation in a Feedback Control System Applied to the Management of a Commercial Salmon Fishery. In *Haley, K. B., ed.*, 1981, pp. 81–98. [G: U.S.]

Munro, Gordon R. The Economics of Fishing: An Introduction. In *Butlin, J. A., ed.*, 1981, pp. 129–40.

Myers, Norman. Conversion Rates in Tropical Moist Forests: Review of a Recent Survey. In *Mergen, F., ed.*, 1981, pp. 49–66. [G: Selected LDCs]

Nautiyal, Jagdish C. Optimum Forest Rotation: Re-

ply. *Land Econ.*, May 1981, *57*(2), pp. 295.

Newbery, David M. G. Dominant Firm Models of Resource Depletion: Comment. In *Currie, D.; Peel, D. and Peters, W., eds.*, 1981, pp. 101–06.

Newbery, David M. G. Oil Prices, Cartels, and the Problem of Dynamic Inconsistency. *Econ. J.*, September 1981, *91*(363), pp. 617–46.

Nijkamp, Peter and Lojenga, Frans Kutsch. Natural Resources as Spatial Development Potentials in Developing Countries: A Case Study of Surinam. In *Chatterji, M., ed.*, 1981, pp. 245–54. [G: Surinam]

North, Ronald M. Risk Analyses Applicable to Water Resources Program and Project Planning and Evaluation. In *Haimes, Y. Y., ed.*, 1981, pp. 163–74. [G: U.S.]

Ocanas, Gerardo and Mays, Larry W. A Model for Water Reuse Planning. *Water Resources Res.*, February 1981, *17*(1), pp. 25–32.

Ocanas, Gerardo and Mays, Larry W. Water Reuse Planning Models: Extensions and Applications. *Water Resources Res.*, October 1981, *17*(5), pp. 1311–27. [G: U.S.]

Okuguchi, Koji. Innovation and Intergenerational Equity in a Model with Many Exhaustible and Renewable Resources. *Econ. Stud. Quart.*, December 1981, *32*(3), pp. 272–75.

Okuguchi, Koji. Population Growth, Costly Innovation and Modified Hartwick's Rule [Costly Innovation and Natural Resources]. *Int. Econ. Rev.*, October 1981, *22*(3), pp. 657–61.

Ott, Mack. Bureaucratic Incentives, Social Efficiency, and the Conflict in Federal Land Policy. *Cato J.*, Fall 1981, *1*(2), pp. 585–607. [G: U.S.]

Page, E. A Review of Models of Harbours, Storage, Processing, Transportation and Distribution. In *Haley, K. B., ed.*, 1981, pp. 273–78.

Pepper, D. A. and Urion, H. Public Expenditure and Cost-Recovery in Fisheries: Modelling the B.C. Salmon Industry for Policy Analysis and Government Investment Decisions. In *Haley, K. B., ed.*, 1981, pp. 393–407. [G: Canada]

Pindyck, Robert S. Models of Resource Markets and the Explanation of Resource Price Behaviour. *Energy Econ.*, July 1981, *3*(3), pp. 130–39.

Pindyck, Robert S. The Optimal Production of an Exhaustible Resource When Price is Exogenous and Stochastic. *Scand. J. Econ.*, 1981, *83*(2), pp. 277–88.

na Pombhejara, Vitchitrong. Natural Resources and Raw Materials in Southeast Asia. In *Lozoya, J. A. and Bhattacharya, A. K., eds.*, 1981, pp. 164–73. [G: S. E. Asia]

Porter, Ed and Huskey, Lee. The Regional Economic Effect of Federal OCS Leasing: The Case of Alaska. *Land Econ.*, November 1981, *57*(4), pp. 583–95. [G: U.S.]

Prato, Anthony A. and Miller, Ronald R. Evaluating the Energy Production Potential of the United States Outer Continental Shelf. *Land Econ.*, February 1981, *57*(1), pp. 77–90. [G: U.S.]

Prattis, J. I. The Author's Ideology: A Dilemma for Maritime Studies: Review Article. *Econ. Develop. Cult. Change*, October 1981, *30*(1), pp. 183–92.

Prindle, Allen M. Impacts of Federal Estate Taxation

on Investments in Forestry: Comment. *Land Econ.*, February 1981, *57*(1), pp. 122–25. [G: U.S.]

Randall, Alan. Property Entitlements and Pricing Policies for a Maturing Water Economy. *Australian J. Agr. Econ.*, December 1981, *25*(3), pp. 195–220. [G: Australia]

Reed, Mark; Spaulding, Malcolm L. and Cornillon, Peter. A Fishery-Oilspill Interaction Model: Simulated Consequences of a Blowout. In *Haley, K. B., ed.*, 1981, pp. 99–114. [G: U.S.]

Reed, William J. Effects of Environmental Variability as they Relate to Fisheries Management. In *Haley, K. B., ed.*, 1981, pp. 69–80.

Ross, Bruce J. Changing Economic Relations between the Asian ADCs and Resource-Exporting Advanced Countries of the Pacific Basin: Comment. In *Hong, W. and Krause, L. B., eds.*, 1981, pp. 340–43. [G: Hong Kong; Singapore; S. Korea; Taiwan; Selected MDCs]

Roze, Janis A. The Competitiveness of Natural Resources with Synthetic Substances. In *Lozoya, J. and Green, R., eds.*, 1981, pp. 54–65. [G: Global]

Runge, Carlisle Ford. Common Property Externalities: Isolation, Assurance, and Resource Depletion in a Traditional Grazing Context. *Amer. J. Agr. Econ.*, November 1981, *63*(4), pp. 595–606.

Sabadell, J. Eleonora. Risk Assessment: Arid and Semiarid Lands Perspective. In *Haimes, Y. Y., ed.*, 1981, pp. 219–31. [G: U.S.]

Sandler, Todd and Schulze, William D. The Economics of Outer Space. *Natural Res. J.*, April 1981, *21*(2), pp. 371–93. [G: U.S.]

Sarma, M. T. R. Food, Natural Resources, and the New International Economic Order: The Case of India. In *Lozoya, J. A. and Bhattacharya, A. K., eds.*, 1981, pp. 141–63. [G: India]

Schulze, William D.; d'Arge, Ralph C. and Brookshire, David S. Valuing Environmental Commodities: Some Recent Experiments. *Land Econ.*, May 1981, *57*(2), pp. 151–72. [G: U.S.]

Sedjo, Roger. World Forest Plantations—What Are the Implications for U.S. Forest Products Trade? In *Sedjo, R. A., ed.*, 1981, pp. 17–39. [G: U.S.; Brazil]

Shapiro, David L. California Water Law and Its Economic Effects on Southern California. In *Sirkin, G., ed.*, 1981, pp. 14–57. [G: U.S.]

Short, Cameron; Turhollow, Anthony F., Jr. and Heady, Earl O. A Regional Problem in a National Context: The Ogallala Aquifer. *Reg. Sci. Persp.*, 1981, *11*(2), pp. 70–82. [G: U.S.]

Siebert, Horst. Ökonomische Theorie natürlicher Ressourcen. Ein Uberblick. (The Economic Theory of Natural Resources: A Survey. With English summary.) *Z. Wirtschaft. Sozialwissen.*, 1981, *101*(3), pp. 267–98.

Siffin, William J. Bureaucracy, Entrepreneurship, and Natural Resources: Witless Policy and the Barrier Islands. *Cato J.*, Spring 1981, *1*(1), pp. 293–311. [G: U.S.]

Simmons, Malcolm. Minimizing Risk of Flood Loss in the National Flood Insurance Program. In *Haimes, Y. Y., ed.*, 1981, pp. 41–52. [G: U.S.]

Sinn, Hans-Werner. Stock-Dependent Extraction

Costs and the Technological Efficiency of Resource Depletion. *Z. Wirtschaft. Sozialwissen.*, 1981, *101*(5), pp. 507–17.

Sinn, Hans-Werner. The Theory of Exhaustible Resources. *Z. Nationalökon.*, 1981, *41*(1–2), pp. 183–92.

Šmíd, Ladislav and Součková, Natalja. International Cooperation in Rational Utilization of Material Resources. *Czech. Econ. Digest.*, February 1981, (1), pp. 3–17. [G: CMEA]

Smith, Courtland L. Satisfaction Bonus from Salmon Fishing: Implications for Economic Evaluation. *Land Econ.*, May 1981, *57*(2), pp. 181–96. [G: U.S.]

Smith, Robert J. Resolving the Tragedy of the Commons by Creating Private Property Rights in Wildlife. *Cato J.*, Fall 1981, *1*(2), pp. 439–68.

Smith, V. Kerry. Increasing Resource Scarcity: Another Perspective: Comment [Increasing Resource Scarcity: Further Evidence]. *Quart. Rev. Econ. Bus.*, Spring 1981, *21*(1), pp. 120–25. [G: U.S.]

Soderstrom, Jon. Boomtown Analysis Disputed [Adjustment Issues of Impacted Communities or, Are Boomtowns Bad?]. *Natural Res. J.*, April 1981, *21*(2), pp. ix–x.

Sornarajah, M. The Myth of International Contract Law. *J. World Trade Law*, May–June 1981, *15*(3), pp. 187–217.

Spears, John S. Small Farmers—or the Tropical Forest Ecosystem? A Review of Sustainable Land Use Systems for Tropical Forest Areas. In *Mergen, F., ed.*, 1981, pp. 15–47. [G: Selected LDCs]

Spurr, Stephen H. Clearcutting on National Forests. *Natural Res. J.*, April 1981, *21*(2), pp. 223–43. [G: U.S.]

Stiglitz, Joseph E. and Dasgupta, Partha. Market Structure and Resource Extraction under Uncertainty. *Scand. J. Econ.*, 1981, *83*(2), pp. 318–33.

Stockman, David. How the Market Outwits the Planners. In *Hessen, R., ed.*, 1981, pp. 57–74.

Stokes, Robert L. The New Approach to Foreign Fisheries Allocation: An Economic Appraisal. *Land Econ.*, November 1981, *57*(4), pp. 568–82. [G: U.S.]

Stollery, Kenneth R. Price Controls on Nonrenewable Resources When Capacity Is Constrained [Price Controls on Non-Renewable Resources: An Intertemporal Analysis]. *Southern Econ. J.*, October 1981, *48*(2), pp. 490–98.

Sutherland, Charles F., Jr. and Tedder, Philip L. Impacts of Federal Estate Taxation on Investments in Forestry: Reply. *Land Econ.*, February 1981, *57*(1), pp. 126–27. [G: U.S.]

Thomson, James T. Public Choice Analysis of Institutional Constraints on Firewood Production Strategies in the West African Sahel. In *Russell, C. S. and Nicholson, N. K., eds.*, 1981, pp. 119–52. [G: W. Africa]

Thurman, Walter N. "Resolving the Tragedy of the Commons": A Comment. *Cato J.*, Fall 1981, *1*(2), pp. 469–71.

Tixier, Susan. Tribal Severance Taxes—Outside the Purview of the Commerce Clause. *Natural Res. J.*, April 1981, *21*(2), pp. 405–13. [G: U.S.]

Udovenko, Vitaly. Natural Conditions and Population. In *Novosti Press Agency*, 1981, pp. 17–41. [G: U.S.S.R.]

Ulph, Alistair M. and Folie, G. Michael. Dominant Firm Models of Resource Depletion. In *Currie, D.; Peel, D. and Peters, W., eds.*, 1981, pp. 77–100.

Underwood, Daniel August. Thermodynamics and Genetic Engineering: An Alternative Conception of Optimal Resource Pricing and Production. *Econ. Forum*, Summer 1981, *12*(1), pp. 10–25.

Vanderpool, Christopher K. Environmental Policy and Social-Impact-Assessment Ideology: Fishery Conservation and Management. In *Mann, D. E., ed.*, 1981, pp. 161–75. [G: U.S.]

Vastrup, Claus. Monopoler og udtømmelige ressourcer. (The Extraction of Exhaustible Resources by a Monopoly. With English summary.) *Nationaløkon. Tidsskr.*, 1981, *119*(1), pp. 21–31.

Vaughan, William J. and Russell, Clifford S. An Analysis of Participation in Nonconsumptive Wildlife Recreation: Comment. *Land Econ.*, May 1981, *57*(2), pp. 279–87. [G: U.S.]

Wadsworth, Frank H. Management of Forest Lands in the Humid Tropics under Sound Ecological Principles. In *Mergen, F., ed.*, 1981, pp. 169–80.

Wall, David. Reply [Industrial Processing of Natural Resources]. *World Devel.*, May 1981, *9*(5), pp. 495–98.

Walton, A. L. Intergenerational Equity and Resource Use. *Amer. J. Econ. Soc.*, July 1981, *40*(3), pp. 239–48.

Wassermann, Ursula. UNCTAD: Sixth International Tin Agreement. *J. World Trade Law*, November–December 1981, *15*(6), pp. 557–58.

Waters, James R.; Easley, J. E., Jr. and Danielson, Leon E. Economic Trade-Offs and the North Carolina Shrimp Fishery: Reply. *Amer. J. Agr. Econ.*, November 1981, *63*(4), pp. 747. [G: U.S.]

Waverman, Leonard. The Distribution of Resource Rents: For Whom the Firm Tolls. In *Nemetz, P. N., ed.*, 1981, pp. 255–79. [G: Canada]

Weaver, Robert C. The Politics of Scarcity. In *Pious, R. M., ed.*, 1981, pp. 233–48. [G: U.S.]

Weiler, Edward M. and Tyner, Wallace E. Social Cost-Benefit Analysis of the Nianga Irrigation Pilot Project, Senegal. *J. Devel. Areas*, July 1981, *15*(4), pp. 655–69. [G: Senegal]

Wheeler, Carl D. The Risks and Rewards of Investments in Tropical Forests. In *Mergen, F., ed.*, 1981, pp. 67–76. [G: Selected LDCs]

Wihlborg, Clas G. and Wijkman, Per Magnus. Outer Space Resources in Efficient and Equitable Use: New Frontiers for Old Principles. *J. Law Econ.*, April 1981, *24*(1), pp. 23–43.

Winje, D. Systemsimulation der Wasserwirtschaft. Ein Prognosemodell der Wasserwirtschaft der Bundesrepublik Deutschland. (With English summary.) In *Fandel, G., et al., eds.*, 1981, pp. 264–70.

Wiseman, A. Clark and Sedjo, Roger. Welfare Economics and the Log Export Policy Issue. In *Sedjo, R. A., ed.*, 1981, pp. 187–208. [G: U.S.]

Withagen, C. The Optimal Exploitation of Exhaustible Resources, A Survey. *De Economist*, 1981,

129(4), pp. 504–31.

Yeats, Alexander J. The Influence of Trade and Commercial Barriers on the Industrial Processing of Natural Resources [Industrial Processing of Natural Resources]. *World Devel.*, May 1981, *9*(5), pp. 485–94.

Zeckhauser, Richard. Preferred Policies When There Is a Concern for Probability of Adoption. *J. Environ. Econ. Manage.*, September 1981, *8*(3), pp. 215–37. [G: U.S.]

7211 Recreational Aspects of Natural Resources

Allen, P. Geoffrey; Stevens, Thomas H. and Barrett, Scott A. The Effects of Variable Omission in the Travel Cost Technique. *Land Econ.*, May 1981, *57*(2), pp. 173–80. [G: U.S.]

Bockstael, Nancy E. and McConnell, Kenneth E. Theory and Estimation of the Household Production Function for Wildlife Recreation. *J. Environ. Econ. Manage.*, September 1981, *8*(3), pp. 199–214.

Greenley, Douglas A.; Walsh, Richard G. and Young, Robert A. Option Value: Empirical Evidence from a Case Study of Recreation and Water Quality. *Quart. J. Econ.*, November 1981, *96*(4), pp. 657–73. [G: U.S.]

McConnell, Kenneth E. and Strand, Ivar E., Jr. Measuring the Cost of Time in Recreation Demand Analysis: An Application to Sportfishing. *Amer. J. Agr. Econ.*, February 1981, *63*(1), pp. 153–56. [G: U.S.]

Menz, Fredric C. and Mullen, John K. Expected Encounters and Willingness to Pay for Outdoor Recreation. *Land Econ.*, February 1981, *57*(1), pp. 33–40. [G: U.S.]

Miller, Jon R. and Higgins, Kevin C. Comment on 'Monetizing Benefits under Alternative River Recreation Use Allocation Systems' by John B. Loomis. *Water Resources Res.*, April 1981, *17*(2), pp. 446. [G: U.S.]

Morey, Edward R. The Demand for Site-Specific Recreational Activities: A Characteristics Approach. *J. Environ. Econ. Manage.*, December 1981, *8*(4), pp. 345–71. [G: U.S.]

Pigram, John J. Outdoor Recreation and Access to Countryside: Focus on the Australian Experience. *Natural Res. J.*, January 1981, *21*(1), pp. 107–23. [G: Australia]

Shechter, M., et al. Evaluation of Landscape Resources for Recreation Planning. *Reg. Stud.*, 1981, *15*(5), pp. 373–90. [G: Israel]

Sinden, J. A. and O'Hanlon, P. W. A Market Simulation Game to Value Unpriced Goods and Services. *Reg. Sci. Urban Econ.*, February 1981, *11*(1), pp. 101–19. [G: Australia]

Smith, V. Kerry. Congestion, Travel Cost Recreational Demand Models, and Benefit Evaluation [Estimating the Benefits of Recreation under Conditions of Congestion]. *J. Environ. Econ. Manage.*, March 1981, *8*(1), pp. 92–96.

Steinnes, Donald and Raab, Raymond. The Economics of a "Happening": Spring Smelt Fishing on Lake Superior. *Reg. Sci. Persp.*, 1981, *11*(1), pp. 32–41. [G: U.S.]

Thayer, Mark A. Contingent Valuation Techniques

for Assessing Environmental Impacts: Further Evidence. *J. Environ. Econ. Manage.*, March 1981, *8*(1), pp. 27–44. **[G: U.S.]**

Vaughan, Roger J. The Value of Urban Open Space. In *Henderson, J. V., ed.*, 1981, pp. 103–30.
[G: U.S]

Wetzel, James N. Congestion and Economic Valuation: A Reconsideration: Comment [Estimating the Benefits of Recreation under Conditions of Congestion]. *J. Environ. Econ. Manage.*, June 1981, *8*(2), pp. 192–95.

722 Conservation and Pollution

7220 Conservation and Pollution

Ackerman, Bruce A. and Hassler, William T. Beyond the New Deal: Reply [Beyond the New Deal: Coal and the Clean Air Act]. *Yale Law J.*, May 1981, *90*(6), pp. 1412–34.

Al-Chalabi, Fadhil J. The Concept of Conservation in OPEC Member Countries. In *OPEC, Public Information Dept.*, 1981, pp. 189–200.
[G: OPEC]

Anderson, Robert and Berry, Donna. Regulating Corrosive Water. *Water Resources Res.*, December 1981, *17*(6), pp. 1571–77. **[G: U.S.]**

Anderson, Robert O. Environmental Trade-offs: A Need for Balance. In *Brunner, D. L.; Miller, W. and Stockholm, N., eds.*, 1981, pp. 27–33.

Andrews, Richard N. L. Values Analysis in Environmental Policy. In *Mann, D. E., ed.*, 1981, pp. 137–47. **[G: U.S.]**

Arrow, Kenneth J. Energy, Economics, and the Environment: The Response of Orthodox Economics. In *Daly, H. E. and Umana, A. F., eds.*, 1981, pp. 109–113.

Banerjee, Tridib. Land Use Policy and Value Choice: An Environmental Design Perspective. In *de Neufville, J. I., ed.*, 1981, pp. 83–89.

Barnett, A. H. Taxation and Pollution Control: An Illustration. *Rev. Reg. Stud.*, Winter 1981, *11*(3), pp. 63–78. **[G: U.S.]**

Barré, Rémi and Bower, Blair T. Water Management in France, with Special Emphasis on Water Quality Management and Effluent Charges. In *Bower, B. T., et al., eds.*, 1981, pp. 33–209.
[G: France]

Beavis, Brian and Walker, Martin. Long-Run Efficiency and Property Rights Sharing for Pollution Control: A Comment. *Public Choice*, 1981, *37*(3), pp. 607–08.

Beavis, Brian and Walker, Martin. Pollution Control with Imperfect Monitoring—An Alternative Formulation [The Criminal Waste Discharger]. *Scot. J. Polit. Econ.*, February 1981, *28*(1), pp. 92–94.

Beckwith, James P., Jr. Parks, Property Rights, and the Possibilities of the Private Law. *Cato J.*, Fall 1981, *1*(2), pp. 473–99.

Belloit, Jerry D. and Smith, Halbert C. The Coastal Construction Control Line: A Cost-Benefit Analysis. *Amer. Real Estate Urban Econ. Assoc. J.*, Winter 1981, *9*(4), pp. 367–83. **[G: U.S.]**

Berck, Peter. Optimal Management of Renewable Resources with Growing Demand for Stock Externalities. *J. Environ. Econ. Manage.*, June 1981,

8(2), pp. 105–17.

Bobylev, S. Means of Improving the Utilization of Land Resources. *Prob. Econ.*, May 1981, *24*(1), pp. 78–95. **[G: U.S.S.R.]**

Bopp, Anthony, et al. Air Quality Implications of a Nuclear Moratorium: An Alternative Analysis. *Energy J.*, July 1981, *2*(3), pp. 33–48. **[G: U.S.]**

Borins, Sandford F. Mieszkowski and Saper's Estimate of the Effects of Airport Noise on Property Values: A Comment. *J. Urban Econ.*, January 1981, *9*(1), pp. 125–28. **[G: Canada]**

Bosworth, Barry P. The Economic Environment for Regulation in the 1980s. In *Peskin, H. M.; Portney, P. R. and Kneese, A. V., eds.*, 1981, pp. 7–24. **[G: U.S.]**

Bosworth, Barry P. The Economic Environment for Regulation in the 1980s. *Natural Res. J.*, July 1981, *21*(3), pp. 441–58. **[G: U.S.]**

Braden, John B. and Bromley, Daniel W. The Economics of Cooperation over Collective Bads. *J. Environ. Econ. Manage.*, June 1981, *8*(2), pp. 134–50.

Brady, Gordon L. Fee Shifting: An Institutional Change to Decrease the Benefits from Free Riding. In *Sirkin, G., ed.*, 1981, pp. 95–140.
[G: U.S.]

Brewer, Garry D. The State's Responsibilities for the Protection and Preservation of Forestry Resources. In *Mergen, F., ed.*, 1981, pp. 104–7.

Brickman, Ronald and Jasanoff, Sheila. Concepts of Risk and Safety in Toxic-Substances Regulation: A Comparison of France and the United States. In *Mann, D. E., ed.*, 1981, pp. 203–13.
[G: France; U.S.]

Brower, David R. The Urgency of Environmental Problems: A Case for Concern. In *Brunner, D. L.; Miller, W. and Stockholm, N., eds.*, 1981, pp. 13–25.

Brown, Susan. International-United States Air Pollution Control and the Acid Rain Phenomenon. *Natural Res. J.*, July 1981, *21*(3), pp. 631–45.
[G: U.S.]

Burch, William R., Jr. Toward a Social Forestry for the Tropics. In *Mergen, F., ed.*, 1981, pp. 196–9.

Burnell, James D. The Effect of Air Pollution on Residential Location Decisions in Metropolitan Areas. *Reg. Sci. Persp.*, 1981, *11*(2), pp. 3–14.
[G: U.S.]

Burness, H. Stuart. Risk: Accounting for an Uncertain Future. *Natural Res. J.*, October 1981, *21*(4), pp. 723–34. **[G: U.S.]**

Burness, H. Stuart; Cummings, R. G. and Paik, I. Environmental Trade-Offs with the Adoption of Cogeneration Technologies. *J. Environ. Econ. Manage.*, March 1981, *8*(1), pp. 45–58.
[G: U.S.]

Burrows, Paul. Controlling the Monopolistic Polluter: Nihilism or Eclecticism? *J. Environ. Econ. Manage.*, December 1981, *8*(4), pp. 372–80.

Businaro, Ugo Lucio and Fedrighini, Aldo. Prospects of Energy Conservation in Transportation. In *Amman, F. and Wilson, R., eds.*, 1981, pp. 139–256. **[G: Selected Countries]**

Butlin, J. A. Environmental Quality and Resource Use under Laissez-faire. In *Butlin, J. A., ed.*,

1981, pp. 3–8.

Butlin, J. A. The Contribution of Economic Instruments to Solid Waste Management. In *Butlin, J. A., ed.*, 1981, pp. 144–52.

Buttel, Frederick H. Environmental Quality and Protection. In *Hawley, A. H. and Mazie, S. M., eds.*, 1981, pp. 668–703. [G: U.S.]

Cahn, Robert. An Environmental Ethic in Business. In *Brunner, D. L.; Miller, W. and Stockholm, N., eds.*, 1981, pp. 121–26.

Campbell, Keith. The Risks of New Technology and their Agricultural Implications. In *Johnson, G. and Maunder, A., eds.*, 1981, pp. 261–70.

Case, Fred E. and Gale, Jeffrey. The Impact on Housing Costs of the California Coastal Zone Conservation Act. *Amer. Real Estate Urban Econ. Assoc. J.*, Winter 1981, *9*(4), pp. 345–66. [G: U.S.]

Castle, Emery N., et al. Natural Resource Economics, 1946–75. In *Martin, L. R., ed.*, 1981, pp. 393–500. [G: U.S.]

Cheng, Kuo-Shung; Lin, Chau-Jy and Wang, Ar-Young. Analysis of Modified Model for Commercial Fishing with Possible Extinctive Fishery Resources. *J. Environ. Econ. Manage.*, June 1981, *8*(2), pp. 151–55.

Christiansen, Gregory B. and Haveman, Robert H. The Contribution of Environmental Regulations to the Slowdown in Productivity Growth. *J. Environ. Econ. Manage.*, December 1981, *8*(4), pp. 381–90. [G: U.S.]

Church, Albert M. and Norton, Roger D. Issues in Emergency Preparedness for Radiological Transportation Accidents. *Natural Res. J.*, October 1981, *21*(4), pp. 757–71. [G: U.S.]

Clark, John. The Search for Natural Limits to Growth. In *de Neufville, J. I., ed.*, 1981, pp. 65–82. [G: U.S.]

Cohen, Bernard L. High Level Radioactive Waste. *Natural Res. J.*, October 1981, *21*(4), pp. 703–21.

Cohen, Linda. Who Pays the Bill: Insuring against the Risks from Low Level Nuclear Waste Disposal. *Natural Res. J.*, October 1981, *21*(4), pp. 773–87. [G: U.S.]

Colitti, Marcello. The Concept of Conservation in OPEC Member Countries: Commentary. In *OPEC, Public Information Dept.*, 1981, pp. 201–07. [G: OPEC]

Cook, Earl. The Tragedy of Turfdom [Environmental Disruption: Implications for the Social Sciences]. *Soc. Sci. Quart.*, March 1981, *62*(1), pp. 23–29.

Cooper, Charles. Professor Pearce on 'The Limits of Cost-Benefit Analysis as a Guide to Environmental Policy': A Comment. *Kyklos*, 1981, *34*(2), pp. 274–78.

Corash, Michele B. Government Regulation: a Consensual Alternative. In *Brunner, D. L.; Miller, W. and Stockholm, N., eds.*, 1981, pp. 57–77. [G: U.S.]

Costanza, Robert. Embodied Energy, Energy Analysis, and Economics: Reply: An Embodied Energy Theory of Value. In *Daly, H. E. and Umana, A. F., eds.*, 1981, pp. 187–91.

Courant, Paul N. and Porter, Richard C. Averting Expenditure and the Cost of Pollution. *J. Environ. Econ. Manage.*, December 1981, *8*(4),

pp. 321–29.

Cousins, Kathryn. Lessons from the Coastline of America: Management Strategies for a Sustainable Society. In *Coomer, J. C., ed.*, 1981, pp. 225–44. [G: U.S.]

Covello, Vincent T. Technological Hazards, Risk, and Society: A Perspective on Risk Analysis Research. In *Haimes, Y. Y., ed.*, 1981, pp. 13–30.

Crandall, Robert W. Pollution Controls and Productivity Growth in Basic Industries. In *Cowing, T. G. and Stevenson, R. E., eds.*, 1981, pp. 347–68. [G: U.S.]

Crandall, Robert W. Regulation and Productivity Growth. In *Federal Reserve Bank of Boston (1)*, 1981, pp. 93–111. [G: U.S.]

Crandall, Robert W. and Lave, Lester B. The Scientific Basis of Health and Safety Regulation: Introduction and Summary. In *Crandall, R. W. and Lave, L. B., eds.*, 1981, pp. 1–17. [G: U.S.]

Crocker, Thomas D. and Horst, Robert L., Jr. Hours of Work, Labor Productivity, and Environmental Conditions: A Case Study. *Rev. Econ. Statist.*, August 1981, *63*(3), pp. 361–68. [G: U.S.]

Cropper, M. L. Measuring the Benefits from Reduced Morbidity. *Amer. Econ. Rev.*, May 1981, *71*(2), pp. 235–40. [G: U.S.]

Cuddington, John T.; Johnson, F. Reed and Knetsch, Jack L. Valuing Amenity Resources in the Presence of Substitutes. *Land Econ.*, November 1981, *57*(4), pp. 526–35.

Cummings, R. G. and Utton, Albert E. Managing Nuclear Wastes: An Overview of the Issues. *Natural Res. J.*, October 1981, *21*(4), pp. 693–701. [G: U.S.]

Cupper, Les and Hearn, June. Unions and the Environment: Recent Australian Experience. *Ind. Relat.*, Spring 1981, *20*(2), pp. 221–31. [G: Australia]

Currie, J. William, et al. The Importance of Viewing Alternative Closed-Cycle-Cooling Systems on Nuclear Power-Plant Landscapes. In *Mann, D. E., ed.*, 1981, pp. 215–30. [G: U.S.]

Currie, W. M. The Application of Technology for Energy Conservation in Industry. In *Amman, F. and Wilson, R., eds.*, 1981, pp. 257–347. [G: U.K.]

Daly, Herman E. Energy, Economics, and the Environment: Postscript: Unresolved Problems and Issues for Further Research. In *Daly, H. E. and Umana, A. F., eds.*, 1981, pp. 165–85.

Davidson, C. Girard. Conservation, Public Power, and Natural Resources. In *Heller, F. H., ed.*, 1981, pp. 59–66. [G: U.S.]

Davies, Christopher S. Policy Implications for the Banking of Lignite Leases, Bastrop County, Texas: 1954–1979. *Econ. Geogr.*, July 1981, *57*(3), pp. 238–56. [G: U.S.]

DeLorme, Charles D., Jr. and Wood, Norman J. Quantifying Environmental Losses from a Regional Water Development Program. *Growth Change*, January 1981, *12*(1), pp. 21–26. [G: U.S.]

Dennis, William C. The Public and Private Interest in Wilderness Protection. *Cato J.*, Fall 1981, *1*(2), pp. 373–90.

Devarajan, Shantayanan and Fisher, Anthony C. Hotelling's "Economics of Exhaustible Resources": Fifty Years Later. *J. Econ. Lit.*, March 1981, *19*(1), pp. 65–73.

Dnes, A. W. The Case of Monopoly and Pollution [Monopoly Power as a Means to Pollution Control]. *J. Ind. Econ.*, December 1981, *30*(2), pp. 213–16.

Dorf, Ronald J.; Jorgens, Thomas P. and Rose, Gordon D. Local Allocations of Payments in Lieu of Taxes and Indirect State Aids: Their Contribution to Creating Negative Fiscal Impacts Attributed to Federal and State Wildlife Lands. *Reg. Sci. Persp.*, 1981, *11*(1), pp. 83–93. [G: U.S.]

Downing, Paul B. A Political Economy Model of Implementing Pollution Laws. *J. Environ. Econ. Manage.*, September 1981, *8*(3), pp. 255–71. [G: U.S.]

Edgmon, Terry D. and Menzel, Donald C. The Regulation of Coal Surface Mining in a Federal System. *Natural Res. J.*, April 1981, *21*(2), pp. 245–65. [G: U.S.]

Edmunds, Stahrl W. Environmental Policy: Bounded Rationality Applied to Unbounded Ecological Problems. In *Mann, D. E., ed.*, 1981, pp. 191–201.

Ehrlich, Paul R. An Economist in Wonderland [Environmental Disruption: Implications for the Social Sciences]. *Soc. Sci. Quart.*, March 1981, *62*(1), pp. 44–49.

Ehrlich, Paul R. Environmental Disruption: Implications for the Social Sciences. *Soc. Sci. Quart.*, March 1981, *62*(1), pp. 7–22.

Ewel, John. Environmental Implications of Tropical Forest Utilization. In *Mergen, F., ed.*, 1981, pp. 158–67.

Ferris, Benjamin G., Jr. Sulfur Dioxide: A Scientist's View. In *Crandall, R. W. and Lave, L. B., eds.*, 1981, pp. 253–66. [G: U.S.]

Few, Arthur A., Jr. Social, Environmental and Economic Implications of Widespread Conversion to Biomass-based Fuels. In *Coomer, J. C., ed.*, 1981, pp. 32–52.

Fisher, Anthony C.; Krupnick, Alan J. and Ferguson, Allen R. Setting Regulatory Priorities. In *Ferguson, A. R., ed.*, 1981, pp. 145–65.

Forster, Bruce A. Environmental Regulation and the Distribution of Income in Simple General Equilibrium Models. In *Ballabon, M. B., ed.*, 1981, pp. 105–29.

Forster, Bruce A. Separability, Functional Structure and Aggregation for a Class of Models in Environmental Economics. *J. Environ. Econ. Manage.*, June 1981, *8*(2), pp. 118–33.

Foster, J. Fagg. Environment Control. *J. Econ. Issues*, December 1981, *15*(4), pp. 1009–12.

Foster, John and Howe, James W. Energy Efficiency and Conservation. In *Foster, J., et al.*, 1981, pp. 173–83. [G: OECD; LDCs]

Freeman, A. Myrick, III. Hedonic Prices, Property Values and Measuring Environmental Benefits: A Survey of the Issues. In *Strøm, S., ed.*, 1981, 1979, pp. 13–32.

Gabel, H. Landis. Reform of the Clean Air Act—Another Decade of Waste? *Sloan Manage. Rev.*, Fall 1981, *23*(1), pp. 69–75.

Garcia, Mary Ann Louise. USDI's Outer Continental Shelf Lease Sale in the Beaufort Sea Contested. *Natural Res. J.*, October 1981, *21*(4),

pp. 943–59. [G: U.S.]

Georgescu-Roegen, Nicholas. Energy, Matter, and Economic Valuation: Where Do We Stand? Reply. In *Daly, H. E. and Umana, A. F., eds.*, 1981, pp. 193–200.

Georgescu-Roegen, Nicholas. Energy, Matter, and Economic Valuation: Where Do We Stand? In *Daly, H. E. and Umana, A. F., eds.*, 1981, pp. 43–79.

Gerking, Shelby D. and Schulze, William D. What Do We Know about Benefits of Reduced Mortality from Air Pollution Control? *Amer. Econ. Rev.*, May 1981, *71*(2), pp. 228–34. [G: U.S.]

Ghatak, Subrata. The Impact of the Fertilizer Technology Transfer on the Environment of Developing Countries. In *Chatterji, M., ed.*, 1981, pp. 71–87. [G: LDCs]

Ghatak, Subrata; Turner, Kerry and Ghatak, Anita. Benefits and Costs of Pesticide Use and Some Policy Implications for Less Developed Countries. In *Chatterji, M., ed.*, 1981, pp. 103–24. [G: LDCs]

Gianessi, Leonard P. and Peskin, Henry M. Analysis of National Water Pollution Control Policies, 2. Agricultural Sediment Control. *Water Resources Res.*, August 1981, *17*(4), pp. 803–21. [G: U.S.]

Gianessi, Leonard P.; Peskin, Henry M. and Young, G. K. Analysis of National Water Pollution Control Policies, 1. A National Network Model. *Water Resources Res.*, August 1981, *17*(4), pp. 796–802. [G: U.S.]

Grant, Douglas L. Reasonable Groundwater Pumping Levels under the Appropriation Doctrine: The Law and Underlying Economic Goals. *Natural Res. J.*, January 1981, *21*(1), pp. 1–36. [G: U.S.]

Gregersen, Hans M. Environmental Constraints versus Economic Gains in Tropical Forestry. In *Mergen, F., ed.*, 1981, pp. 109–24.

Griffin, Ronald C. Property Rights and Welfare Economics: Miller et al. v. Schoene Revisited: Comment. *Land Econ.*, November 1981, *57*(4), pp. 645–51. [G: U.S.]

Guess, George M. Technical and Financial Policy Options for Development Forestry. *Natural Res. J.*, January 1981, *21*(1), pp. 37–55. [G: LDCs]

Guttmann, J. Michele. Pennsylvania's Technologically Impossible Air Pollution Standards Upheld. *Natural Res. J.*, April 1981, *21*(2), pp. 395–404. [G: U.S.]

Haefele, Edwin T. A Plea for More Representative Government. In *de Neufville, J. I., ed.*, 1981, pp. 209–13.

Hageman, Ronda K. Nuclear Waste Disposal: Potential Property Value Impacts. *Natural Res. J.*, October 1981, *21*(4), pp. 789–810.

Hagihara, Yoshimi and Hagihara, Kiyoko. Project Grant Allocation Process Applied in Sewerage Planning. *Water Resources Res.*, June 1981, *17*(3), pp. 449–54.

Haimes, Yacov Y. Risk-benefit Analysis in a Multiobjective Framework. In *Haimes, Y. Y., ed.*, 1981, pp. 89–122.

Handl, Günther. Managing Nuclear Wastes: The International Connection. *Natural Res. J.*, April 1981, *21*(2), pp. 267–314. [G: U.S.; EEC; CMEA]

Hanke, Steve H. and Wentworth, Roland W. On the Marginal Cost of Wastewater Services. *Land Econ.*, November 1981, 57(4), pp. 558–67. [G: U.S.]

Hannon, Bruce. The Energy Cost of Energy. In *Daly, H. E. and Umana, A. F., eds.*, 1981, pp. 81–107. [G: U.S.]

Hardin, Garrett. Ending the Squanderarchy. In *Daly, H. E. and Umana, A. F., eds.*, 1981, pp. 147–64.

Harned, D. A.; Daniel, C. C., III and Crawford, J. K. Methods of Discharge Compensation as an Aid to the Evaluation of Water Quality Trends. *Water Resources Res.*, October 1981, 17(5), pp. 1389–1400. [G: U.S.]

Harrington, Winston. The Endangered Species Act and the Search for Balance. *Natural Res. J.*, January 1981, 21(1), pp. 71–92. [G: U.S.]

Harrington, Winston and Krupnick, Alan J. Stationary Source Pollution Policy and Choices for Reform. *Natural Res. J.*, July 1981, 21(3), pp. 539–64. [G: U.S.]

Harrington, Winston and Krupnick, Alan J. Stationary Source Pollution Policy and Choices for Reform. In *Peskin, H. M.; Portney, P. R. and Kneese, A. V., eds.*, 1981, pp. 105–30. [G: U.S.]

Harrison, David, Jr. Distributional Objectives in Health and Safety Regulation. In *Ferguson, A. R. and LeVeen, E. P., eds.*, 1981, pp. 177–201. [G: U.S.]

Haveman, Robert H. and Christainsen, Gregory B. Environmental Regulations and Productivity Growth. *Natural Res. J.*, July 1981, 21(3), pp. 489–509. [G: U.S.]

Haveman, Robert H. and Christainsen, Gregory B. Environmental Regulations and Productivity Growth. In *Peskin, H. M.; Portney, P. R. and Kneese, A. V., eds.*, 1981, pp. 55–75. [G: U.S.]

Henderson, Hazel. The Challenge of Decision Making in the Solar Age. In *Brunner, D. L.; Miller, W. and Stockholm, N., eds.*, 1981, pp. 35–54.

Hetzel, Nancy K. Regionalism and the Environment. In *Nicol, D.; Echeverria, L. and Peccei, A., eds.*, 1981, pp. 210–17.

Higgins, Mary Ramczyk. Oklahoma Industrial Waste Statute Held Unconstitutional. *Natural Res. J.*, January 1981, 21(1), pp. 185–88. [G: U.S.]

Higgins, Mary Ramczyk. Supreme Court Clarifies Water Act Requirement. *Natural Res. J.*, July 1981, 21(3), pp. 607–16. [G: U.S.]

Highton, Nicolas H. and Webb, Michael G. On the Economics of Pollution Control for Sulphur Dioxide Emissions. *Energy Econ.*, April 1981, 3(2), pp. 83–90. [G: U.K.]

Highton, Nicolas H. and Webb, Michael G. Pollution Abatement Costs in the Electricity Supply Industry in England and Wales. *J. Ind. Econ.*, September 1981, 30(1), pp. 49–65. [G: U.K.]

Hirsch, Werner Z. Tax Alternatives for Affecting the Environment. In *Roskamp, K. W. and Forte, F., eds.*, 1981, pp. 381–92.

Hoel, David G. and Crump, Kenny S. Waterborne Carcinogens: A Scientist's View. In *Crandall, R. W. and Lave, L. B., eds.*, 1981, pp. 173–95. [G: U.S.]

Honnold, Julie A. Predictors of Public Environmental Concern in the 1970s. In *Mann, D. E., ed.*, 1981, pp. 63–75. [G: U.S.]

Hopcraft, David. Nature's Technology. In *Coomer, J. C., ed.*, 1981, pp. 211–24.

Houthakker, Hendrik S. Regulation and Productivity Growth: Discussion. In *Federal Reserve Bank of Boston (1)*, 1981, pp. 112–14. [G: U.S.]

Humphrey, Craig R. and Buttel, Frederick H. The Sociology of the Growth/No-Growth Debate. In *Mann, D. E., ed.*, 1981, pp. 125–35.

Inoue, K., et al. A Trial towards Group Decisions in Structuring Environmental Science. In *Morse, J. N., ed.*, 1981, pp. 157–70.

James, Jeffrey. Growth, Technology and the Environment in Less Developed Countries: A Survey. In *Streeten, P. and Jolly, R, eds.*, 1981, 1978, pp. 115–43. [G: LDCs]

Jeanneret-Grosjean, Charles A. The Environment as Viewed within the Context of the NIEO. In *Lozoya, J. A. and Birgin, H., eds.*, 1981, pp. 173–92. [G: Global]

Jessen, Peter J. The Role of Energy Ideologies in Developing Environmental Policy. In *Mann, D. E., ed.*, 1981, pp. 103–23.

Johnson, Manuel H. and Bennett, James T. Regional Environmental and Economic Impact Evaluation: An Input-Output Approach. *Reg. Sci. Urban Econ.*, May 1981, 11(2), pp. 215–30.

Kemrer, Sandra. The Protection of American Antiquities: 1906–1981. *Natural Res. J.*, October 1981, 21(4), pp. 935–42. [G: U.S.]

Kimm, Victor J.; Kuzmack, Arnold M. and Schnare, David W. Waterborne Carcinogens: A Regulator's View. In *Crandall, R. W. and Lave, L. B., eds.*, 1981, pp. 229–49. [G: U.S.]

Kneese, Allen V. and d'Arge, Ralph C. Benefit Analysis and Today's Regulatory Problems. In *Ferguson, A. R. and LeVeen, E. P., eds.*, 1981, pp. 65–90. [G: U.S.]

Kobrin, Paul. Fuel Switching, Gasoline Price Controls, and the Leaded-Unleaded Gasoline Price Differential. *J. Environ. Econ. Manage.*, September 1981, 8(3), pp. 287–302. [G: U.S.]

Kopp, Raymond J. and Smith, V. Kerry. Productivity Measurement and Environmental Regulation: An Engineering–Econometric Analysis. In *Cowing, T. G. and Stevenson, R. E., eds.*, 1981, pp. 248–81.

Kosters, Marvin H. Government Regulation: Present Status and Need for Reform. In *Wachter, M. L. and Wachter, S. M., eds.*, 1981, pp. 321–45. [G: U.S.]

Krutilla, John V. Reflections of an Applied Welfare Economist. *J. Environ. Econ. Manage.*, March 1981, 8(1), pp. 1–10.

Kühner, Jochen and Bower, Blair T. Water Quality Management in the Ruhr Area of the Federal Republic of Germany, with Special Emphasis on Charge Systems. In *Bower, B. T., et al., eds.*, 1981, pp. 213–301. [G: W. Germany]

Langham, Max R. and Lanier, Ray. Public Mosquito Abatement: Comment. *J. Environ. Econ. Manage.*, March 1981, 8(1), pp. 97–99. [G: U.S.]

Lareau, Thomas J. Alternate Stationary Source Air Pollution Control Policies: A Welfare Analysis.

Public Finance Quart., July 1981, *9*(3), pp. 281–307. [G: U.S.]

Lave, Lester B. Sulfur Dioxide: An Economist's View. In *Crandall, R. W. and Lave, L. B.*, *eds.*, 1981, pp. 267–78. [G: U.S.]

Lee, Albert Yin-Po. Voluntary Conservation and Electricity Peak Demand: A Case Study of the Modesto Irrigation District. *Land Econ.*, August 1981, *57*(3), pp. 436–47. [G: U.S.]

Lee, Dwight R. Least-Cost Pollution Abatement, Effluent Charges, and Monopoly Power. *Amer. Econ.*, Spring 1981, *25*(1), pp. 57–60.

Leone, Robert A. and Jackson, John E. The Political Economy of Federal Regulatory Activity: The Case of Water-Pollution Controls. In *Fromm, G.*, *ed.*, 1981, pp. 231–71. [G: U.S.]

Levi, Isaac. Assessing Accident Risks in U.S. Commercial Nuclear Power Plants: Scientific Method and the Rasmussen Report. *Soc. Res.*, Summer 1981, *48*(2), pp. 395–408. [G: U.S.]

Lewis, Tracy R. Energy vs. the Environment. *J. Environ. Econ. Manage.*, March 1981, *8*(1), pp. 59–71.

Lewis, Tracy R. Markets and Environmental Management with a Storable Pollutant. *J. Environ. Econ. Manage.*, March 1981, *8*(1), pp. 11–18.

Liroff, Richard A. NEPA Litigation in the 1970s: A Deluge or a Dribble? *Natural Res. J.*, April 1981, *21*(2), pp. 315–30. [G: U.S.]

Lockeretz, William. The Dust Bowl: Its Relevance to Contemporary Environmental Problems. In *Lawson, M. P. and Baker, M. E.*, *eds.*, 1981, pp. 11–31. [G: U.S.]

Lohani, B. N. and Tyagi, U. N. Systems Dynamo Modelling of Environmental Pollution Control. In *Chatterji, M.*, *ed.*, 1981, pp. 193–204.

Magat, Wesley A. and Estomin, Steven. The Behavior of Regulatory Agencies. In *Ferguson, A. R.*, *ed.*, 1981, pp. 95–116. [G: U.S.]

Mandl, Christoph E. A Survey of Mathematical Optimization Models and Algorithms for Designing and Extending Irrigation and Wastewater Networks. *Water Resources Res.*, August 1981, *17*(4), pp. 769–75.

Mann, Dean E. Environmental Policy Formation: Introduction. In *Mann, D. E.*, *ed.*, 1981, pp. 1–27. [G: U.S.]

Manuel, David P. Coastal State Taxation of OCS-Produced Natural Gas. *Natural Res. J.*, January 1981, *21*(1), pp. 93–105. [G: U.S.]

Marquand, J. M. An Economist's View of Pollution Charges as Regulatory Instruments. In *Butlin, J. A.*, *ed.*, 1981, pp. 153–60.

Martellaro, Joseph A. Toward a Better Energy Policy. *Rivista Int. Sci. Econ. Com.*, January–February 1981, *28*(1–2), pp. 33–51. [G: U.S.]

Matthews, William H. and Siddiqi, Toufiq A. Energy and Environmental Issues in the Developing Countries. In *Chatterji, M.*, *ed.*, 1981, pp. 53–67. [G: LDCs]

McGuckin, J. Thomas and Young, Robert A. On the Economics of Desalination of Brackish Household Water Supplies. *J. Environ. Econ. Manage.*, March 1981, *8*(1), pp. 79–91. [G: U.S.]

McMillan, Melville L. Estimates of Households' Preferences for Environmental Quality and Other

Housing Characteristics from a System of Demand Equations. In *Strmm, S.*, *ed.*, 1981, *1979*, pp. 33–46. [G: Canada]

McNamara, Robert S. To the United Nations Conference on the Human Environment, Stockholm, Sweden, June 8, 1972. In *McNamara, R. S.*, 1981, *1972*, pp. 193–206.

Meade, James E. Economic Policy and the Threat of Doom. In *Butlin, J. A.*, *ed.*, 1981, pp. 9–29.

Mercuro, Nicholas and Ryan, Timothy. Property Rights and Welfare Economics: Miller et al. v. Schoene Revisited: Reply. *Land Econ.*, November 1981, *57*(4), pp. 657–59. [G: U.S.]

Michelman, Frank I. Localism and Political Freedom. In *de Neufville, J. I.*, *ed.*, 1981, pp. 239–43. [G: U.S.]

Middleton, John T. Sulfur Dioxide: A Regulator's View. In *Crandall, R. W. and Lave, L. B.*, *eds.*, 1981, pp. 279–88. [G: U.S.]

Milbrath, Lester W. Environmental Values and Beliefs of the General Public and Leaders in the United States, England, and Germany. In *Mann, D. E.*, *ed.*, 1981, pp. 43–61. [G: U.K.; U.S.; W. Germany]

Miller, J. Irwin. The Role of Individual Leadership. In *Brunner, D. L.; Miller, W. and Stockholm, N.*, *eds.*, 1981, pp. 147–61.

Miller, Jon R. Irreversible Land Use and the Preservation of Endangered Species. *J. Environ. Econ. Manage.*, March 1981, *8*(1), pp. 19–26.

Mishan, Ezra J. What Is the Optimal Level of Pollution? In *Mishan, E. J.*, 1981, *1974*, pp. 125–31.

Moore, Stuart A. Environmental Repercussions and the Economic Structure: Some Further Comments. *Rev. Econ. Statist.*, February 1981, *63*(1), pp. 139–42.

Mumy, Gene E. Long-Run Efficiency and Property Rights Sharing for Pollution Control: A Reply. *Public Choice*, 1981, *37*(3), p. 609.

Musser, Wesley N.; Tew, Bernard V. and Epperson, James E. An Economic Examination of an Integrated Pest Management Production System with a Contrast between E-V and Stochastic Dominance Analysis. *Southern J. Agr. Econ.*, July 1981, *13*(1), pp. 119–24. [G: U.S.]

Myers, Norman. Conversion Rates in Tropical Moist Forests: Review of a Recent Survey. In *Mergen, F.*, *ed.*, 1981, pp. 49–66. [G: Selected LDCs]

Nainis, W. Scott. Methods for Determining the Value of Model Development in Cost/Benefit/Risk Analysis. In *Haimes, Y. Y.*, *ed.*, 1981, pp. 149–56. [G: U.S.]

Nakamura, Masahisa; Brill, E. Downey, Jr. and Liebman, Jon C. Multiperiod Design of Regional Wastewater Systems: Generating and Evaluating Alternative Plans. *Water Resources Res.*, October 1981, *17*(5), pp. 1339–48.

Navarro, Peter. The 1977 Clean Air Act Amendments: Energy, Environmental, Economic, and Distributional Impacts. *Public Policy*, Spring 1981, *29*(2), pp. 121–46. [G: U.S.]

Nelson, Jon P. Three Mile Island and Residential Property Values: Empirical Analysis and Policy Implications. *Land Econ.*, August 1981, *57*(3), pp. 363–72. [G: U.S.]

de Neufville, Judith Innes. Conceptions of the Environment. In *de Neufville, J. I.*, ed., 1981, pp. 59–63.

Nicholas, James C. Housing Costs and Prices under Regional Regulation. *Amer. Real Estate Urban Econ. Assoc. J.*, Winter 1981, *9*(4), pp. 384–96. [G: U.S.]

Nijkamp, Peter and Rietveld, Piet. Multi-Objective Multi-Level Policy Models: An Application to Regional and Environmental Planning. *Europ. Econ. Rev.*, January 1981, *15*(1), pp. 63–89. [G: Netherlands]

Noll, Roger G. and Joskow, Paul L. Regulation in Theory and Practice: An Overview. In *Fromm, G.*, ed., 1981, pp. 1–65. [G: U.S.]

Norgaard, Richard B. Sociosystem and Ecosystem Coeveolution in the Amazon. *J. Environ. Econ. Manage.*, September 1981, *8*(3), pp. 238–54. [G: Brazil]

Norton, Roger D. Policy Issues in the Routing of Radioactive Materials Shipments. *Natural Res. J.*, October 1981, *21*(4), pp. 735–55. [G: U.S.]

O'Brien, John N. International Auspices for the Storage of Spent Nuclear Fuel as a Nonproliferation Measure. *Natural Res. J.*, October 1981, *21*(4), pp. 857–94. [G: U.S.]

Okrent, David. What Kind of Water will our Children Drink? In *Haimes, Y. Y.*, ed., 1981, pp. 53–58.

Ostro, Bart D. The Distributive Effects of Public Law 92–500: Comment. *J. Environ. Econ. Manage.*, June 1981, *8*(2), pp. 196–98.

Page, Talbot. Economics of a Throwaway Society; the One-way Economy. In *Butlin, J. A.*, ed., 1981, pp. 74–87.

Page, Talbot; Harris, Robert A. and Bruser, Judith. Waterborne Carcinogens: An Economist's View. In *Crandall, R. W. and Lave, L. B.*, eds., 1981, pp. 197–228. [G: U.S.]

Parasuraman, A. and Futrell, Charles M. Executives' Views about Energy Conservation: Problems and Prospects. *J. Energy Devel.*, Spring 1981, *6*(2), pp. 225–31. [G: U.S.]

Parvin, Manoucher and Grammas, Gus W. Capacity, Energy, and Environment Planning in Developing Industries. In *Chatterji, M.*, ed., 1981, pp. 153–66. [G: LDCs]

Peskin, Henry M. National Income Accounts and the Environment. In *Peskin, H. M.; Portney, P. R. and Kneese, A. V.*, eds., 1981, pp. 77–103. [G: U.S.]

Peskin, Henry M. National Income Accounts and the Environment. *Natural Res. J.*, July 1981, *21*(3), pp. 511–37. [G: U.S.]

Peskin, Henry M.; Portney, Paul R. and Kneese, Allen V. Regulation and the Economy: Concluding Thoughts. *Natural Res. J.*, July 1981, *21*(3), pp. 589–91. [G: U.S.]

Pittman, Russell W. Issue in Pollution Control: Interplant Cost Differences and Economies of Scale. *Land Econ.*, February 1981, *57*(1), pp. 1–17. [G: U.S.]

Popkin, Alice B. State Responsibility for Protection and Preservation of Forestry Resources. In *Mergen, F.*, ed., 1981, pp. 96–102.

Portney, Paul R. Housing Prices, Health Effects, and Valuing Reductions in Risk of Death. *J. Envi-*

ron. Econ. Manage., March 1981, *8*(1), pp. 72–78. [G: U.S.]

Portney, Paul R. The Macroeconomic Impacts of Federal Environmental Regulation. In *Peskin, H. M.; Portney, P. R. and Kneese, A. V.*, eds., 1981, pp. 25–54. [G: U.S.]

Portney, Paul R. The Macroeconomic Impacts of Federal Environmental Regulation. *Natural Res. J.*, July 1981, *21*(3), pp. 459–88. [G: U.S.]

Potier, M. The Role of International Organisations in the Control of Transfrontier Natural Resources and Environmental Issues. In *Butlin, J. A.*, ed., 1981, pp. 183–200. [G: OECD]

Potter, Harry R. and Norville, Heather J. Social Values Inherent in Policy Statements: An Evaluation of an Energy Technology Assessment. In *Mann, D. E.*, ed., 1981, pp. 177–89. [G: U.S.]

Pryor, C. Anthony. Environmental Impact of Renewable Energy and Alternative Development Strategies. In *Chatterji, M.*, ed., 1981, pp. 125–37. [G: LDCs]

Raiatskas, R. L. and Sutkaitis, V. P. A System of Ecological and Economic Models for Environmental Planning and Control. *Matekon*, Fall 1981, *18*(1), pp. 60–79.

Randle, Russell V. Coastal Energy Siting Dilemmas. *Natural Res. J.*, January 1981, *21*(1), pp. 125–59. [G: U.S.]

Reed, Mark; Spaulding, Malcolm L. and Cornillon, Peter. A Fishery-Oilspill Interaction Model: Simulated Consequences of a Blowout. In *Haley, K. B.*, ed., 1981, pp. 99–114. [G: U.S.]

Repetto, Robert. The Economics of Visibility Protection: On a Clear Day You Can See a Policy. *Natural Res. J.*, April 1981, *21*(2), pp. 355–70. [G: U.S.]

Ridker, Ronald G. and Watson, William D. Longrun Effects of Environmental Regulation. In *Peskin, H. M.; Portney, P. R. and Kneese, A. V.*, eds., 1981, pp. 131–53. [G: U.S.]

Ridker, Ronald G. and Watson, William D. Long-Run Effects of Environmental Regulation. *Natural Res. J.*, July 1981, *21*(3), pp. 565–87. [G: U.S.]

Ruckelshaus, William D. Corporations and the Environment: How Should Decisions Be Made? Afterword. In *Brunner, D. L.; Miller, W. and Stockholm, N.*, eds., 1981, pp. 163–67.

Ruff, Larry E. Federal Environmental Regulation. In *Weiss, L. W. and Klass, M. W.*, eds., 1981, pp. 235–61. [G: U.S.]

Russell, Clifford S. and Bower, Blair T. Incentives in Water Quality Management: France and the Ruhr Area: Introduction. In *Bower, B. T., et al.*, eds., 1981, pp. 1–30. [G: France; W. Germany]

Rutledge, Gary L. and Trevathan, Susan L. Pollution Abatement and Control Expenditures, 1972–79. *Surv. Curr. Bus.*, March 1981, *61*(3), pp. 19–27. [G: U.S.]

Ryan, Donald R. Transferable Discharge Permits and the Control of Stationary Source Air Pollution: A Survey and Synthesis: Comment. *Land Econ.*, November 1981, *57*(4), pp. 639–41. [G: U.S.]

Sachs, Ignacy. Ecodevelopment: A Paradigm for Strategic Planning? Comment on James [Growth,

Technology and the Environment in Less Developed Countries: A Survey]. In *Streeten, P. and Jolly, R, eds.*, 1981, *1978*, pp. 145–47.
[G: LDCs]

Sagoff, Mark. Economic Theory and Environmental Law. *Mich. Law Rev.*, June 1981, *79*(7), pp. 1393–1419.

Samprone, Joseph C., Jr. and Savoian, Roy. Gasoline Conservation and Motor Fuel Taxation Policy: The Dilemma for State Government Financing. *J. Energy Devel.*, Spring 1981, *6*(2), pp. 251–62.
[G: U.S.]

Sanchez-de-Carmona, Luis. Environmental and Urban Policies for the Human Habitat. In *Lozoya, J. A. and Birgin, H., eds.*, 1981, pp. 160–72.
[G: LDCs]

von Schlabrendorff, Fabian. Mining Ventures in Developing Countries: Environmental Provisions. In *Schanze, E., et al.*, 1981, pp. 212–35.

Schmidt, Elsa T. Key Issues of Land Use Planning in West Germany. *Growth Change*, April 1981, *12*(2), pp. 44–52.
[G: W. Germany]

Schulze, William D.; Brookshire, David S. and Sandler, Todd. The Social Rate of Discount for Nuclear Waste Storage: Economics or Ethics? *Natural Res. J.*, October 1981, *21*(4), pp. 811–32.

Seidl-Hohenveldern, Ignaz. Community Law Procedures against Transfrontier Environmental Hazards and Damages. In *Inst. of Internat. Pub. Law and Internat. Relat. of Thessaloniki*, 1981, pp. 336–59.
[G: EEC]

Shibata, Hirofumi. Choice of Fiscal Measures against Pollution: Effluent Charges vs. Pollution Abatement Subsidies. (In Japanese. With English summary.) *Osaka Econ. Pap.*, December 1981, *31*(2–3), pp. 106–14.
[G: Japan]

Siddall, Ernest. Uranium and Coal as Low-Cost Energy Sources—The Safety Issue. In *Nemetz, P. N., ed.*, 1981, pp. 83–90.
[G: U.S.]

Siffin, William J. Bureaucracy, Entrepreneurship, and Natural Resources: Witless Policy and the Barrier Islands. *Cato J.*, Spring 1981, *1*(1), pp. 293–311.
[G: U.S.]

Simmons, Malcolm. Minimizing Risk of Flood Loss in the National Flood Insurance Program. In *Haimes, Y. Y., ed.*, 1981, pp. 41–52.
[G: U.S.]

Simon, Julian L. Environmental disruption or Environmental Improvement? [Environmental Disruption: Implications for the Social Sciences]. *Soc. Sci. Quart.*, March 1981, *62*(1), pp. 30–43.

Sims, W. A. The Short-Run Asymmetry of Pollution Subsidies and Charges: Note. *J. Environ. Econ. Manage.*, December 1981, *8*(4), pp. 395–99.

Slovic, Paul; Fischhoff, Baruch and Lichtenstein, Sarah. Rating the Risks. In *Haimes, Y. Y., ed.*, 1981, *1980*, pp. 193–217.
[G: U.S.]

Smith, Lowell and Randle, Russell V. Comment on Beyond the New Deal [Beyond the New Deal: Coal and the Clean Air Act]. *Yale Law J.*, May 1981, *90*(6), pp. 1398–1411.
[G: U.S.]

Smith, M. G. Forests and Forestry Programs in Tropical Countries: Some Observations and Comments. In *Mergen, F., ed.*, 1981, pp. 144–53.

Smith, Robert J. Resolving the Tragedy of the Commons by Creating Private Property Rights in Wildlife. *Cato J.*, Fall 1981, *1*(2), pp. 439–68.

Smith, V. Kerry. CO_2, Climate, and Statistical Inference: A Note on Asking the Right Questions. *J. Environ. Econ. Manage.*, December 1981, *8*(4), pp. 391–94.

Sommer, Eric M. Federal Common Law of Nuisance Expands. *Natural Res. J.*, April 1981, *21*(2), pp. 419–23.
[G: U.S.]

Stier, J. C. and Bishop, R. C. Crop Depredation by Waterfowl: Is Compensation the Solution? *Can. J. Agr. Econ.*, July 1981, *29*(2), pp. 159–70.
[G: Canada]

Strong, Ann L. Land as a Public Good: An Idea Whose Time Has Come Again. In *de Neufville, J. I., ed.*, 1981, pp. 217–32.
[G: U.S.]

Sunkel, Osvaldo. Development Styles and the Environment: An Interpretation of the Latin American Case. In *Muñoz, H., ed.*, 1981, pp. 93–114.
[G: Latin America]

Suzuki, K. and Takenaka, H. The Role of Investment for Energy Conservation: Future Japanese Economic Growth. *Energy Econ.*, October 1981, *3*(4), pp. 233–43.
[G: Japan]

Swartz, David G. and Strand, Ivar E., Jr. Avoidance Costs Associated with Imperfect Information: The Case of Kepone. *Land Econ.*, May 1981, *57*(2), pp. 139–50.
[G: U.S.]

The Business Roundtable and Arthur Anderson & Co. Cost of Government Regulation Study. In *Gatti, J. F., ed.*, 1981, *1979*, pp. 95–129.
[G: U.S.]

Thurman, Walter N. "Resolving the Tragedy of the Commons": A Comment. *Cato J.*, Fall 1981, *1*(2), pp. 469–71.

Tietenberg, Thomas H. Economic Analysis and Air Pollution Control Policy: Recent Developments. In *Ballabon, M. B., ed.*, 1981, pp. 71–103.
[G: U.S.]

Tietenberg, Thomas H. Transferable Discharge Permits and the Control of Stationary Source Air Pollution: A Survey and Synthesis: Reply. *Land Econ.*, November 1981, *57*(4), pp. 642–44.
[G: U.S.]

Trilling, Julia. Land Use Policy and the Symbolic Politics of Environmental Conflict. In *de Neufville, J. I., ed.*, 1981, pp. 91–99.

Tybout, Richard A. Social Accounting for Pollution. *Land Econ.*, November 1981, *57*(4), pp. 507–25.
[G: U.S.]

Umaña, Alvaro F. Energy, Economics, and the Environment: Introduction. In *Daly, H. E. and Umana, A. F., eds.*, 1981, pp. 1–19.

Umaña, Alvaro F. Toward a Biophysical Foundation for Economics. In *Daly, H. E. and Umana, A. F., eds.*, 1981, pp. 21–41.

Upham, Frank K. Pollution Problems and Response. In *Richardson, B. M. and Ueda, T., eds.*, 1981, pp. 185–94.
[G: Japan]

Vanderpool, Christopher K. Environmental Policy and Social-Impact-Assessment Ideology: Fishery Conservation and Management. In *Mann, D. E., ed.*, 1981, pp. 161–75.
[G: U.S.]

Vaupel, James W. Priorities for Research on the Benefits of Health, Safety, and Environmental Regulation. In *Ferguson, A. R., ed.*, 1981, pp. 167–83.
[G: U.S.]

Vogel, David. The "New" Social Regulation in Historical and Comparative Perspective. In *McCraw*,

T. K., ed., 1981, pp. 155–85.   [G: U.S.]

Walter, Ingo. A Survey of International Economic Repercussions of Environmental Policy. In *Butlin, J. A., ed.*, 1981, pp. 163–82.

Warkov, Seymour. Environmental Orientations and Solar Adoption. In *Mann, D. E., ed.*, 1981, pp. 77–86.   [G: U.S.]

Warrick, Richard A. and Bowden, Martyn J. The Changing Impacts of Droughts in the Great Plains. In *Lawson, M. P. and Baker, M. E., eds.*, 1981, pp. 111–37.   [G: U.S.]

Wassermann, Ursula. Attempts at Control over Toxic Waste. *J. World Trade Law*, September–October 1981, *15*(5), pp. 410–30.

Watson, William D. and Ridker, Ronald G. Revising Water Pollution Standards in an Uncertain World. *Land Econ.*, November 1981, *57*(4), pp. 485–506.   [G: U.S.]

Watts, Nicholas and Wandesforde-Smith, Geoffrey. Postmaterial Values and Environmental Policy Change. In *Mann, D. E., ed.*, 1981, pp. 29–42.   [G: U.S.]

Webb, Michael G. and Woodfield, Robert. Standards and Charges in the Control of Trade Effluent Discharges to Public Sewers in England and Wales. *J. Environ. Econ. Manage.*, September 1981, *8*(3), pp. 272–86.   [G: U.K.]

Wetzel, James N. Congestion and Economic Valuation: A Reconsideration: Comment [Estimating the Benefits of Recreation under Conditions of Congestion]. *J. Environ. Econ. Manage.*, June 1981, *8*(2), pp. 192–95.

White, Michelle J. Fee Shifting: An Institutional Change to Decrease the Benefits from Free Riding: Comments. In *Sirkin, G., ed.*, 1981, pp. 141–44.   [G: U.S.]

Whitney, Gerald. Property Rights and Welfare Economics: Miller et al. v. Schoene Revisited: Comment. *Land Econ.*, November 1981, *57*(4), pp. 652–56.   [G: U.S.]

Williams, David G. T. Environmental Protection in the United Kingdom. In *Nemetz, P. N., ed.*, 1981, pp. 281–98.   [G: U.K.]

Wright, Ann Finley. Federal Penalties Apply to Pollution of Intermittent Streams. *Natural Res. J.*, January 1981, *21*(1), pp. 181–83.   [G: U.S.]

Yohe, Gary W. Should Sliding Controls be the Next Generation of Pollution Controls? *J. Public Econ.*, April 1981, *15*(2), pp. 251–67.

Zeckhauser, Richard. Preferred Policies When There Is a Concern for Probability of Adoption. *J. Environ. Econ. Manage.*, September 1981, *8*(3), pp. 215–37.   [G: U.S.]

Zeckhauser, Richard. The Political Economy of Federal Regulatory Activity: The Case of Water-Pollution Controls: Comment. In *Fromm, G., ed.*, 1981, pp. 273–76.   [G: U.S.]

723 Energy

7230 Energy

Abdul-Karim, Tayeh. OPEC: Challenges of the Present and Strategy for the Future. In *OPEC, Public Information Dept.*, 1981, pp. 9–16. [G: OPEC]

Adams, F. Gerard. Toward a New U.S. Industrial Policy? Energy: Comment. In *Wachter, M. L. and Wachter, S. M., eds.*, 1981, pp. 230–33.   [G: U.S.]

Adams, Steven J. and Whittenburg, Gerald E. How the Energy Tax Act Affects Capital Budgeting. *Manage. Account.*, November 1981, *63*(5), pp. 34–39, 52.   [G: U.S.]

Adelman, Morris A. The Realities of the Energy Market, an Agenda for the 1980s: Decisions and Research. In *Tempest, P., ed.*, 1981, pp. 263–75.

Adelman, Morris A. and Moran, Theodore H. Statements on Oil and OPEC. In *Baldwin, R. E. and Richardson, J. D., eds.*, 1981, 1977, pp. 202–20.   [G: OPEC]

Ait-Laoussine, Nordine. Structural Changes in World Oil Market. In *OPEC, Public Information Dept.*, 1981, pp. 112–32.

Akarca, Ali T. and Long, Thomas Veach, II. Advanced Time Series Techniques and Public Policy Analysis. In *Crecine, J. P., ed.*, 1981, pp. 39–51.   [G: U.S.]

Akkina, Krishna R. and Malhotra, Devinder M. Rapidly Rising Prices of Crude Oil and Natural Gas and Their Impact on Production out of the Existing Reserves. *Nebr. J. Econ. Bus.*, Spring 1981, *20*(2), pp. 47–62.   [G: U.S.]

Al-Anbari, Abdul Amir. OPEC Actions: Consumer Reactions 1970–2000: Commentary. In *OPEC, Public Information Dept.*, 1981, pp. 239–46.   [G: OPEC]

Al-Chalabi, Fadhil J. The Concept of Conservation in OPEC Member Countries. In *OPEC, Public Information Dept.*, 1981, pp. 189–200.   [G: OPEC]

Aler, Bo. Energy Options in Perspective. In *Atlantic Inst. for Internat. Affairs and Amer. Nucl. Society*, 1981, pp. 17–18.

Allen, Edward L. and Edmonds, James A. Energy Demand and Population Changes. *Atlantic Econ. J.*, September 1981, *9*(3), pp. 10–19.

Allen, Edward L.; Edmonds, James A. and Kuenne, Robert E. A Comparative Analysis of Global Energy Models. *Energy Econ.*, January 1981, *3*(1), pp. 2–13.

Allen, Edward L.; Edmonds, James A. and Kuenne, Robert E. Authors Reply [A Comparative Analysis of Global Models]. *Energy Econ.*, October 1981, *3*(4), pp. 268–69.

Ames, Glenn C. W. and Baxter, Harold O. Wood Fuel: An Alternative Energy Source for Agribusiness and Industry. *Southern J. Agr. Econ.*, December 1981, *13*(2), pp. 91–97.   [G: U.S.]

Anderson, Richard G. On the Specification of Conditional Factor Demand Functions in Recent Studies of U.S. Manufacturing. In *Berndt, E. R. and Field, B. C., eds.*, 1981, pp. 119–44.   [G: U.S.]

Anderson, Terry L. and Hill, Peter J. Establishing Property Rights in Energy: Efficient vs. Inefficient Processes. *Cato J.*, Spring 1981, *1*(1), pp. 87–105.   [G: U.S.; U.K.]

Archibald, Robert and Gillingham, Robert. A Decomposition of the Price and Income Elasticities of the Consumer Demand for Gasoline. *Southern*

Econ. J., April 1981, 47(4), pp. 1021–31.
[G: U.S.]

Archibald, Robert and Gillingham, Robert. The Distributional Impact of Alternative Gasoline Conservation Policies. *Bell J. Econ. (See Rand J. Econ. after 4/85)*, Autumn 1981, 12(2), pp. 426–44. [G: U.S.]

Arrow, Kenneth J. Energy, Economics, and the Environment:The Response of Orthodox Economics. In *Daly, H. E. and Umana, A. F., eds.*, 1981, pp. 109–113.

Artus, Patrick and Peyroux, Claude. Fonctions de production avec facteur énergie: estimations pour les grands pays de l'OCDE. (Production Functions with the Energy Factor: Estimates for the Large OECD Countries. With English summary.) *Ann. INSEE*, October–December 1981, (44), pp. 3–39. [G: OECD]

Atkinson, Scott E. and Halvorsen, Robert. Automatic Price Adjustment Clauses and Input Choice in Regulated Utilities. In *Nemetz, P. N., ed.*, 1981, pp. 185–96.

Attanasi, E. D. and Green, E. K. Economics and Coal Resource Appraisal: Strippable Coal in the Illinois Basin. *Southern Econ. J.*, January 1981, 47(3), pp. 742–52. [G: U.S.]

Attiga, Ali A. Crossing the Energy Bridge. In *OPEC, Public Information Dept.*, 1981, pp. 29–36.
[G: OPEC]

Attiga, Ali A. General Observations Regarding Governmental Response to Energy Problems and Issues. In *Tempest, P., ed.*, 1981, pp. 31–34.

Ayres, Robert L. U.S.–Mexican Energy Relationships: Comments. In *Ladman, J. R.; Baldwin, D. J. and Bergman, E., eds.*, 1981, pp. 215–18.
[G: Mexico; U.S.]

Baer, Walter S. Responses to Oil Supply Vulnerability. In *Kamrany, N. M.*, 1981, pp. 141–50.
[G: U.S.; OECD]

Bagley, Bruce M. Mexico–United States Relations: A United States Perspective. In *Purcell, S. K., ed.*, 1981, pp. 13–27. [G: Mexico; U.S.]

Balas, Egon. The Strategic Petroleum Reserve: How Large Should It Be? In *Bayraktar, B. A., et al., eds.*, 1981, pp. 335–86.

Bambas, Karl J. Potential for Meeting IAEA Safeguards Goals for Reprocessing. In *Atlantic Inst. for Internat. Affairs and Amer. Nucl. Society*, 1981, pp. 71–73.

Barber, William J. Energy Policy in Perspective: Studied Inaction in the Kennedy Years. In *Goodwin, C. D., ed.*, 1981, pp. 287–335. [G: U.S.]

Barber, William J. The Eisenhower Energy Policy: Reluctant Intervention. In *Goodwin, C. D., ed.*, 1981, pp. 205–86. [G: U.S.]

Barker, Terry. Depletion Policy and the De-Industrialization of the UK Economy. *Energy Econ.*, April 1981, 3(2), pp. 71–82. [G: U.K.]

Barnes, Roberta; Gillingham, Robert and Hagemann, Robert P. The Short-run Residential Demand for Electricity. *Rev. Econ. Statist.*, November 1981, 63(4), pp. 541–52. [G: U.S.]

Barry, Leo. Interprovincial Electrical Energy Transfers: The Constitutional Background. In *Nemetz, P. N., ed.*, 1981, pp. 213–53. [G: Canada]

Basile, Paul S. An Integrated Energy Modeling Approach: Experience at IIASA. In *Bayraktar, B. A., et al., eds.*, 1981, pp. 287–305.

Basile, Paul S. Balancing Energy Supply and Demand: A Fifty-Year Global Perspective. *Energy J.*, July 1981, 2(3), pp. 1–15.

Basu, D. R. A Multisectoral Stochastic Optimal Control Model for UK to Derive Future Energy Policies. In *Janssen, J. M. L.; Pau, L. F. and Straszak, A. J., eds.*, 1981, pp. 129–39. [G: U.K.]

Baumann, Harry; Irvine, Russell and Paquet, Bertrand. The Impact of Higher Energy Prices in Canada: Comment. *Can. Public Policy*, Winter 1981, 7(1), pp. 39–41. [G: Canada]

Baumol, William J. and Wolff, Edward N. Subsidies to New Energy Sources: Do They Add to Energy Stocks? *J. Polit. Econ.*, October 1981, 89(5), pp. 891–913.

Beenstock, Michael and Willcocks, P. Energy Consumption and Economic Activity in Industrialized Countries: The Dynamic Aggregate Time Series Relationship. *Energy Econ.*, October 1981, 3(4), pp. 225–32. [G: MDCs]

Begg, Iain; Cripps, Francis and Ward, Terry. The European Community: Problems and Prospects. *Cambridge Econ. Pol. Rev.*, December 1981, 7(2), pp. 1–65. [G: EEC]

Behling, David J., Jr. Use of Energy Models for Business Decisions. In *Bayraktar, B. A., et al., eds.*, 1981, pp. 215–20.

Beierlein, James G.; Dunn, James W. and McConnon, James C., Jr. The Demand for Electricity and Natural Gas in the Northeastern United States. *Rev. Econ. Statist.*, August 1981, 63(3), pp. 403–08. [G: U.S.]

Beijdorff, A. F. International Energy Options: The Route to Increased Efficiency. In *Tempest, P., ed.*, 1981, pp. 121–32. [G: EEC]

Belk, Russell; Painter, John and Semenik, Richard. Preferred Solutions to the Energy Crisis as a Function of Causal Attributions. *J. Cons. Res.*, December 1981, 8(3), pp. 306–12. [G: U.S.]

Beltran del Rio, Abel. The Mexican Oil Syndrome: Early Symptoms, Preventive Efforts, and Prognosis. In *Baer, W. and Gillis, M., eds.*, 1981, pp. 115–30. [G: Mexico; OPEC]

Bending, Richard. Data Collection Methodologies—Introduction. In *Amman, F. and Wilson, R., eds.*, 1981, pp. 99–108.

Bending, Richard. Data Collection Methodologies—Transport and Commercial Sectors. In *Amman, F. and Wilson, R., eds.*, 1981, pp. 119–28.

Bending, Richard. Data Collection Methodologies—Industry. In *Amman, F. and Wilson, R., eds.*, 1981, pp. 109–18. [G: U.K.]

Bending, Richard. The Domestic Sector—Data, History and Prospects. In *Amman, F. and Wilson, R., eds.*, 1981, pp. 129–38. [G: U.K.]

Benjamin, Les and Richards, Darrell. Electrification Is the Way to Move Canada in the 1980s. *Can. Public Policy*, Summer 1981, 7(3), pp. 472–75.

Bennett, Paul and Kuenstner, Deborah. Natural Gas Controls and Decontrol. *Fed. Res. Bank New York Quart. Rev.*, Winter 1981–82, 6(4), pp. 50–60. [G: U.S.]

Bennett, Peter D. and Moore, Noreen Klein. Consumers' Preferences for Alternative Energy Conservation Policies: A Trade-Off Analysis. *J. Cons. Res.*, December 1981, 8(3), pp. 313–21. [G: U.S.]

Bergendahl, Per-Anders and Bergström, Clas. Long-term Oil Substitution—The IEA-MARKAL Model and Some Simulation Results for Sweden. *Scand. J. Econ.*, 1981, 83(2), pp. 237–52. [G: Sweden]

Bergman, Lars. The Impact of Nuclear Power Discontinuation in Sweden: A General Equilibrium Analysis. *Reg. Sci. Urban Econ.*, August 1981, 11(3), pp. 269–86.

Bergman, Lars and Mäler, Karl-Göran. Efficiency–flexibility Trade-off and the Cost of Unexpected Oil Price Increases. *Scand. J. Econ.*, 1981, 83(2), pp. 253–68. [G: Sweden]

Bergsten, C. Fred. The Economic Interests of the United States and Saudi Arabia. **In** *Bergsten, C. F., ed.*, 1981, pp. 147–58. [G: Saudi Arabia; U.S.]

Berkowitz, Norbert. Missing Elements in Canadian Energy Policy. **In** *Nemetz, P. N., ed.*, 1981, pp. 25–39. [G: Canada]

Bernard, Pierre. The Development of Electricity in the Future French Energy Balance: An Example of Readjustment. **In** *Bayraktar, B. A., et al., eds.*, 1981, pp. 173–81. [G: France]

Berndt, Ernst R. Energy Price Increases and the Productivity Slowdown in United States Manufacturing. **In** *Federal Reserve Bank of Boston (1)*, 1981, pp. 60–89. [G: U.S.]

Berndt, Ernst R.; Morrison, Catherine J. and Watkins, G. Campbell. Dynamic Models of Energy Demand: An Assessment and Comparison. **In** *Berndt, E. R. and Field, B. C., eds.*, 1981, pp. 259–89. [G: U.S.]

Berndt, Ernst R. and Wood, David O. Engineering and Econometric Interpretations of Energy–Capital Complementarity: Reply and Further Results. *Amer. Econ. Rev.*, December 1981, 71(5), pp. 1105–10. [G: U.S.]

Bird, Thomas C. Coal Leases Held Real Property. *Natural Res. J.*, April 1981, 21(2), pp. 415–17. [G: U.S.]

Bjornerud, E. Kristopher. Technical Concepts for International Spent Fuel Storage. **In** *Atlantic Inst. for Internat. Affairs and Amer. Nucl. Society*, 1981, pp. 69–71.

Blair, Peter; Cassel, Thomas and Edelstein, Robert H. Optimal Investments in Geothermal Electricity Facilities: A Theoretic Note. **In** *Nemetz, P. N., ed.*, 1981, pp. 197–212.

Blau, Thomas. Comments [Mexican Energy Resources and U.S. Energy Requirements] [Impact of Alternatives to Petroleum on U.S.–Mexican Relations]. **In** *Ladman, J. R.; Baldwin, D. J. and Bergman, E., eds.*, 1981, pp. 171–73. [G: Mexico; U.S.]

Bornstein, Morris. Soviet–East European Economic Relations. **In** *Bornstein, M.; Gitelman, Z. and Zimmerman, W., eds.*, 1981, pp. 105–24. [G: CMEA; E. Europe]

Bourque, Philip J. Embodied Energy Trade Balances among Regions. *Int. Reg. Sci. Rev.*, Winter 1981, 6(2), pp. 121–36. [G: U.S.]

Bradford, Garnett L. Comment: Energy Account-

ing: The Case of Farm Machinery in Maryland. *Southern J. Agr. Econ.*, July 1981, 13(1), pp. 155–57. [G: U.S.]

Braeutigam, Ronald R. The Deregulation of Natural Gas. **In** *Weiss, L. W. and Klass, M. W., eds.*, 1981, pp. 142–86. [G: U.S.]

Brancato, Carolyn Kay. An Economic Profile of Major Presidential and Congressional Initiatives to Deal with the "Energy Crisis." **In** *Kamrany, N. M.*, 1981, pp. 99–120. [G: U.S.; OECD]

Brem, Walter V., Jr. Mexican Oil: A Guide to Source Materials. **In** *Ladman, J. R.; Baldwin, D. J. and Bergman, E., eds.*, 1981, pp. 221–22. [G: Mexico]

Broder, Josef M. and Booth, John T. Energy Efficiency in Food Processing in the Southern Region. *Southern J. Agr. Econ.*, December 1981, 13(2), pp. 53–59. [G: U.S.]

Brodman, John and Moore, Jack. The Outlook for World Oil Supply and Demand through 1983. *J. Energy Devel.*, Autumn 1981, 7(1), pp. 1–12. [G: OPEC]

Brookes, L. G. Postscript: Energy Elasticities and Energy Ratios [Energy-Income Coefficients and Ratios: Their Abuse and Use]. *Energy Econ.*, April 1981, 3(2), pp. 122. [G: U.S.]

Brookes, L. G. The Nuclear Route to Renewed Growth. **In** *Tempest, P., ed.*, 1981, pp. 253–61. [G: U.K.; U.S.]

Bunn, Delmar. Oil Import Limit: Pivotal Move in Solution: A Citizen's View of the Energy Problem. **In** *Kamrany, N. M.*, 1981, pp. 43–52. [G: U.S.]

Burness, H. Stuart. Risk: Accounting for an Uncertain Future. *Natural Res. J.*, October 1981, 21(4), pp. 723–34. [G: U.S.]

Burness, H. Stuart; Cummings, R. G. and Paik, I. Environmental Trade-Offs with the Adoption of Cogeneration Technologies. *J. Environ. Econ. Manage.*, March 1981, 8(1), pp. 45–58. [G: U.S.]

Businaro, Ugo Lucio and Fedrighini, Aldo. Prospects of Energy Conservation in Transportation. **In** *Amman, F. and Wilson, R., eds.*, 1981, pp. 139–256. [G: Selected Countries]

Button, Dave. Observations Concerning an Optimal Solution of the Energy Crisis. **In** *Kamrany, N. M.*, 1981, pp. 155–60. [G: U.S.]

Caramanis, Michael C. Capital, Energy, and Labor Cross-Substitution Elasticities in a Developing Country: The Case of Greek Manufacturing. **In** *Bayraktar, B. A., et al., eds.*, 1981, pp. 307–16. [G: Greece]

Carhart, Steven C. Energy Demand Analysis and Modeling. **In** *Bayraktar, B. A., et al., eds.*, 1981, pp. 221–32.

Carlough, Edward J. Toward a New U.S. Industrial Policy? Energy: Comment. **In** *Wachter, M. L. and Wachter, S. M., eds.*, 1981, pp. 222–24. [G: U.S.]

Carter, Anne P. International Effects of Energy Conservation. *Scand. J. Econ.*, 1981, 83(2), pp. 147–64.

Cazalet, Edward G. A Progress Report on the Development of Generalized Equilibrium Modeling. **In** *Bayraktar, B. A., et al., eds.*, 1981, pp. 321–34.

Chalker, Durwood. Proceedings of the Seminar on

Energy: Statement. **In** *U.S. Congress, Joint Economic Committee (1)*, 1981, pp. 501–03.

[G: U.S.]

Chang, Hui S. and Chern, Wen S. A Study on the Demand for Electricity and the Variation in the Price Elasticities for Manufacturing Industries. *J. Econ. Bus.*, Winter 1981, *33*(2), pp. 122–31.

[G: U.S.]

Chatterji, Manas. Energy and Environment in the Developing Countries: Retrospect and Prospects for Further Research. **In** *Chatterji, M., ed.*, 1981, pp. 329–47.

[G: LDCs]

Chatterji, Manas. Energy and Environment in the Developing Countries: An Overall Perspective and Plans for Action. **In** *Chatterji, M., ed.*, 1981, pp. 3–25.

[G: LDCs]

Chatterji, Manas and DeWitt, R. Peter, Jr. Problems of Latin American Energy. **In** *Chatterji, M., ed.*, 1981, pp. 315–27.

[G: Latin America]

Chenery, Hollis B. Restructuring the World Economy: Round II. *Foreign Aff.*, Summer 1981, *59*(5), pp. 1102–20.

Cherene, L. J. The Energy Crisis and the American Life Style. **In** *Kamrany, N. M.*, 1981, pp. 151–54.

[G: U.S.]

Cherif, M'hamed. Note sur l'impact cumulé des mesures de conservation de l'énergie sur les principales grandeurs macro-économiques. (With English summary.) *Cah. Écon. Bruxelles*, 4th Trimestre 1981, (92), pp. 527–37.

Cherniavsky, E. A. Multiobjective Energy Analysis. **In** *Bayraktar, B. A., et al., eds.*, 1981, pp. 399–420.

Chevalier, Jean-Marie. Les nouvelles technologies énergétiques: leur impact sur l'évolution des prix de l'énergie. (New Energy Technologies: Their Impact on the Evolution on the Future Energy Prices. With English summary.) *Rev. Econ. Ind.*, 3rd Trimestre 1981, (17), pp. 1–25.

Christman, John H. Comments [Petroleum and Mexican Economic Growth and Development in the 1980s] [The Political Economy of Mexican Oil, 1976–1979]. **In** *Ladman, J. R.; Baldwin, D. J. and Bergman, E., eds.*, 1981, pp. 123–28.

[G: Mexico]

Chung, Jae Wan. The Price of Gasoline, the Oil Crisis, and the Choice of Transportation Mode. *Quart. Rev. Econ. Bus.*, Autumn 1981, *21*(3), pp. 77–86.

[G: U.S.]

Cochran, Tom and Prestidge, J. R. Growing Disparity among States in Revenues from Nonrenewable Energy Sources. **In** *Walzer, N. and Chicoine, D. L., eds.*, 1981, pp. 247–62.

[G: U.S.]

Cochrane, James L. Carter Energy Policy and the Ninety-fifth Congress. **In** *Goodwin, C. D., ed.*, 1981, pp. 547–600.

[G: U.S.]

Cochrane, James L. Energy Policy in the Johnson Administration: Logical Order versus Economic Pluralism. **In** *Goodwin, C. D., ed.*, 1981, pp. 337–93.

[G: U.S.]

Cochrane, James L. and Griepentrog, Gary L. U.S. Energy: A Quantitative Review of the Past Three Decades. **In** *Goodwin, C. D., ed.*, 1981, pp. 685–705.

[G: U.S.]

Cohen, Jane C. Ban on Advertising Promoting Energy Usage Violates First Amendment. *Natural Res. J.*, January 1981, *21*(1), pp. 177–80.

[G: U.S.]

Cohen, Linda. Who Pays the Bill: Insuring against the Risks from Low Level Nuclear Waste Disposal. *Natural Res. J.*, October 1981, *21*(4), pp. 773–87.

[G: U.S.]

Colitti, Marcello. The Concept of Conservation in OPEC Member Countries: Commentary. **In** *OPEC, Public Information Dept.*, 1981, pp. 201–07.

[G: OPEC]

Colombatto, Enrico. Il negoziato petrolifero: una proposta di analisi. (Oil Pricing: A Proposal of Analysis. With English summary.) *Rivista Int. Sci. Econ. Com.*, December 1981, *28*(12), pp. 1189–1200.

Colombo, Umberto. Energy in Europe in the 1980s. *Giorn. Econ.*, May–June 1981, *40*(5–6), pp. 319–51.

[G: EEC]

Common, M. S. Implied Elasticities in Some UK Energy Projections. *Energy Econ.*, July 1981, *3*(3), pp. 153–58.

[G: U.K.]

Conant, Melvin. Key International Energy Problems of the 1980s. **In** *Tempest, P., ed.*, 1981, pp. 45–47.

Conrad, K. Energy Policy Planning: Discussion of the Session on Demand Modeling. **In** *Bayraktar, B. A., et al., eds.*, 1981, pp. 233–43.

Copper, John Franklin. National Energy Profiles: Taiwan. **In** *Stunkel, K. R., ed.*, 1981, pp. 359–88.

[G: Taiwan]

Costanza, Robert. Embodied Energy, Energy Analysis, and Economics: Reply: An Embodied Energy Theory of Value. **In** *Daly, H. E. and Umana, A. F., eds.*, 1981, pp. 187–91.

Costanza, Robert. Embodied Energy, Energy Analysis, and Economics. **In** *Daly, H. E. and Umana, A. F., eds.*, 1981, pp. 119–45.

[G: U.S.]

Courville, Léon; Dagenais, Marcel and Taghvaï, Hassan. La demande d'énergie au Québec. (The Demand for Energy in Quebec. With English summary.) *Can. J. Econ.*, February 1981, *14*(1), pp. 1–23.

[G: Canada]

Cruickshank, Andrew and Walker, William. Energy Research, Development and Demonstration in the European Communities. *J. Common Market Stud.*, September 1981, *20*(1), pp. 61–90.

[G: EEC]

Currie, J. William, et al. The Importance of Viewing Alternative Closed-Cycle-Cooling Systems on Nuclear Power-Plant Landscapes. **In** *Mann, D. E., ed.*, 1981, pp. 215–30. **[G: U.S.]**

Currie, W. M. The Application of Technology for Energy Conservation in Industry. **In** *Amman, F. and Wilson, R., eds.*, 1981, pp. 257–347.

[G: U.K.]

D'Hoop, H. and Laughton, M. A. Survey of Present Energy Models with Particular Reference to the European Community. **In** *Bayraktar, B. A., et al., eds.*, 1981, pp. 245–58.

Daly, Herman E. Energy, Economics, and the Environment: Postscript: Unresolved Problems and Issues for Further Research. **In** *Daly, H. E. and Umana, A. F., eds.*, 1981, pp. 165–85.

van Dam, André. Energy Transition: Plenty of Opportunities. *Indian Econ. J.*, October–December 1981, *29*(2), pp. 89–97. **[G: LDCs]**

Denny, Michael; Fuss, Melvyn A. and Waverman, Leonard. Substitution Possibilities for Energy: Evidence from U.S. and Canadian Manufacturing Industries. In *Berndt, E. R. and Field, B. C., eds.*, 1981, pp. 230–58. [G: U.S.; Canada]

Derrick, Stephen; McDonald, Daina and Rosendale, Phyllis. The Development of Energy Resources in Australia: 1981 to 1990. *Australian Econ. Rev.*, 3rd Quarter 1981, (55), pp. 13–55. [G: Australia]

Desprairies, Pierre. The Role of Government in Regulating Energy Markets: Commentary. In *OPEC, Public Information Dept.*, 1981, pp. 106–11.

Dewees, Donald N. Energy Policy and Consumer Energy Consumption. In *Nemetz, P. N., ed.*, 1981, pp. 115–41. [G: Canada]

Dienes, Leslie. An Energy Crunch Ahead in the Soviet Union? In *Bornstein, M.*, 1981, 1977, pp. 313–43. [G: U.S.S.R.]

Dingman, Michael D. Proceedings of the Seminar on Energy: Statement. In *U.S. Congress, Joint Economic Committee (I)*, 1981, pp. 503–05. [G: U.S.]

Dobozi, István. Policy Responses to the Energy Crisis: East and West. *ACES Bull. (See Comp. Econ. Stud. after 8/85)*, Spring 1981, 23(1), pp. 25–66. [G: W. Europe; CMEA; U.K.]

Dohner, Robert S. Energy Prices, Economic Activity, and Inflation: A Survey of Issues and Results. In *Mork, K. A., ed.*, 1981, pp. 7–41. [G: U.S.]

Dorfman, Nancy S. Gasoline Distribution Policies in a Shortage: Welfare Impacts on Rich and Poor. *Public Policy*, Fall 1981, 29(4), pp. 473–505. [G: U.S.]

Downer, Joseph P. Proceedings of the Seminar on Energy: Statement. In *U.S. Congress, Joint Economic Committee (I)*, 1981, pp. 505–14. [G: U.S.; Other Countries]

Drummond, Don and Grady, Patrick. The Impact of Higher Energy Prices in Canada: Comment. *Can. Public Policy*, Winter 1981, 7(1), pp. 42–49. [G: Canada]

Ebel, Robert E. U.S.–Mexican Energy Relationships: The U.S. Perspective: Comments. In *Ladman, J. R.; Baldwin, D. J. and Bergman, E., eds.*, 1981, pp. 175–79. [G: Mexico; U.S.; China; U.S.S.R.; Middle East]

Ebrahimzadeh, Cyrus. The Integration of the Oil Sector in Economies of OPEC Member Countries. In *OPEC, Public Information Dept.*, 1981, pp. 165–81. [G: OPEC]

Eckstein, Otto. Shock Inflation, Core Inflation, and Energy Disturbances in the DRI Model. In *Mork, K. A., ed.*, 1981, pp. 63–98. [G: U.S.]

Edelman, David J. A Macroeconomic Policy Simulation of the Energy Crisis and the Development of Low-Income Countries. In *Chatterji, M., ed.*, 1981, pp. 167–92. [G: LDCs]

Egberts, G. and Voss, A. Energy Models and Technology Assessment. In *Bayraktar, B. A., et al., eds.*, 1981, pp. 159–72.

Eibenschutz, Juan. Energy Issues in Mexico. In *McBride, R. H., ed.*, 1981, pp. 31–48. [G: Mexico]

Empey, W. F. The Impact of Higher Energy Prices in Canada. *Can. Public Policy*, Winter 1981, 7(1), pp. 28–35. [G: Canada]

English, Burton C.; Short, Cameron and Heady, Earl O. The Economic Feasibility of Crop Residues as Auxiliary Fuel in Coal-Fired Power Plants. *Amer. J. Agr. Econ.*, November 1981, 63(4), pp. 636–44. [G: U.S.]

Erickson, Edward W. United States Energy Policy: The Translucent Hand and the Art of Muddling Through. *Cato J.*, Fall 1981, 1(2), pp. 609–27. [G: U.S.]

Erickson, Kenneth Paul. National Energy Profiles: Brazil. In *Stunkel, K. R., ed.*, 1981, pp. 219–69. [G: Brazil]

Erickson, Kenneth Paul. State Entrepreneurship, Energy Policy, and the Political Order in Brazil. In *Bruneau, T. C. and Faucher, P., eds.*, 1981, pp. 141–77. [G: Brazil]

Evans, A. C. The International Energy Agency. *J. World Trade Law*, September–October 1981, 15(5), pp. 440–50. [G: EEC]

Ewing, A. F. Energy and East-West Co-operation. *J. World Trade Law*, May–June 1981, 15(3), pp. 218–30. [G: E. Europe; W. Europe]

Fabritius, Jan F. R. and Petersen, Christian Ettrup. OPEC Responding and the Economic Impact of an Increase in the Price of Oil. *Scand. J. Econ.*, 1981, 83(2), pp. 220–36. [G: OPEC]

Farley, Philip J. The International Nuclear Fuel Cycle Evaluation: Et Sequitur. In *Atlantic Inst. for Internat. Affairs and Amer. Nucl. Society*, 1981, pp. 27–29.

Farrag, Nureddin. Basic Issues of Energy and Development: I. *J. Energy Devel.*, Autumn 1981, 7(1), pp. 27–33. [G: LDCs; MDCs]

Feith, Douglas J. The Oil Weapon De-Mystified. *Policy Rev.*, Winter 1981, (15), pp. 19–39.

Fekete, Ferenc; Benet, Iván and Sebestyén, Katalin. Energy Problems in the Hungarian Agriculture and Food Industry. *Acta Oecon.*, 1981, 27(3–4), pp. 373–82. [G: Hungary]

Fendt, H. Modellgestützte Planung regionaler Energiesysteme. (With English summary.) In *Fandel, G., et al., eds.*, 1981, pp. 538–44.

Ferrari, A. France's Nuclear Power Programme. In *Tempest, P., ed.*, 1981, pp. 159–64. [G: France]

Few, Arthur A., Jr. Social, Environmental and Economic Implications of Widespread Conversion to Biomass-based Fuels. In *Coomer, J. C., ed.*, 1981, pp. 32–52.

Fischer, C. William. Use of Models in Decision Making: A Policy Maker's View. In *Bayraktar, B. A., et al., eds.*, 1981, pp. 47–55.

Foster, John. Comment on "Balancing Energy Supply and Demand." *Energy J.*, July 1981, 2(3), pp. 29–32.

Foster, John. Energy for Development: Introduction. In *Foster, J., et al.*, 1981, pp. 1–4. [G: Global]

Foster, John. Industrialised Countries. In *Foster, J., et al.*, 1981, pp. 120–42. [G: OECD]

Foster, John. The Global Energy Scene. In *Foster, J., et al.*, 1981, pp. 5–55. [G: Global]

Foster, John and Howe, James W. Energy Efficiency

and Conservation. In *Foster, J., et al.*, 1981, pp. 173–83.   [G: OECD; LDCs]

Foster, John and Howe, James W. Managing the Transition from Oil to Other Sources. In *Foster, J., et al.*, 1981, pp. 183–92. [G: OECD; LDCs]

Foster, Phillips and Wichelns, Dennis. Reply: Energy Accounting: The Case of Farm Machinery in Maryland. *Southern J. Agr. Econ.*, July 1981, *13*(1), pp. 159–60.   [G: U.S.]

Franssen, Herman. Energy Demand and Supply in the 1980s. *J. Energy Devel.*, Spring 1981, *6*(2), pp. 213–24.

Franzmeyer, Fritz. Europäische Energiepolitik—wenig Spielraum für abgestuftes Vorgehen. (European Energy Policy—Little Scope for Two-or-Multi-Tier Integration. With English summary.) *Konjunkturpolitik*, 1981, *27*(6), pp. 337–78.
[G: EEC]

Freedman, David. Some Pitfalls in Large Econometric Models: A Case Study. *J. Bus.*, July 1981, *54*(3), pp. 479–500.   [G: U.S.]

Fried, Jerome F. Western Hemisphere Oil and Gas: No Relief for the United States in the 1980's? In *U.S. Congress, Joint Economic Committee (III)*, 1981, pp. 166–78.   [G: Canada; Venezuela; Mexico]

Friedmann, Efrain. A Framework for Energy Policies in Oil Importing Developing Countries. In *Foster, J., et al.*, 1981, pp. 205–40. [G: LDCs]

Garcia, Mary Ann Louise. USDI's Outer Continental Shelf Lease Sale in the Beaufort Sea Contested. *Natural Res. J.*, October 1981, *21*(4), pp. 943–59.   [G: U.S.]

Gass, Saul I. Validation and Assessment Issues of Energy Models. In *Bayraktar, B. A., et al., eds.*, 1981, pp. 421–41.

Geller, E. Scott. Evaluating Energy Conservation Programs: Is Verbal Report Enough? *J. Cons. Res.*, December 1981, *8*(3), pp. 331–35.
[G: U.S.]

Georgescu-Roegen, Nicholas. Energy, Matter, and Economic Valuation: Where Do We Stand? Reply. In *Daly, H. E. and Umana, A. F., eds.*, 1981, pp. 193–200.

Georgescu-Roegen, Nicholas. Energy, Matter, and Economic Valuation: Where Do We Stand? In *Daly, H. E. and Umana, A. F., eds.*, 1981, pp. 43–79.

Gheorghe, A. V. Topical Problems in the Cybernetics of Energy Systems. *Econ. Computat. Cybern. Stud. Res.*, 1981, *15*(2), pp. 89–95.

Goettle, Richard J., IV. An Economic Analysis of Petroleum Import Reduction Policies: Energy Conservation versus New Supply. In *Mork, K. A., ed.*, 1981 , pp. 125–55. [G: U.S.]

Golabi, Kamal and Scherer, Charles R. Extraction Timing and Economic Incentives for Geothermal Reservoir Management. *J. Environ. Econ. Manage.*, June 1981, *8*(2), pp. 156–74.

Golabi, Kamal, et al. Optimal Energy Extraction from a Hot Water Geothermal Reservoir. *Water Resources Res.*, February 1981, *17*(1), pp. 1–10.

Goldemberg, José. Energy Problems in the Third World. In *Amman, F. and Wilson, R., eds.*, 1981, pp. 395–450.   [G: LDCs]

Goldman, Steven C. and Schroeder, Wayne A. The

Geopolitics of Energy. *Policy Rev.*, Summer 1981, (17), pp. 95–113.

Goldmuntz, Lawrence. Impact of Alternatives to Petroleum on U.S.–Mexican Relations. In *Ladman, J. R.; Baldwin, D. J. and Bergman, E., eds.*, 1981, pp. 145–53.   [G: U.S.]

Goldschmidt, Bertrand. Non-proliferation and Safeguards: Prospects for "New" International Arrangements and Institutions: Remarks. In *Atlantic Inst. for Internat. Affairs and Amer. Nucl. Society*, 1981, pp. 64–66.

Golovin, A. P.; Kitaigorodskii, V. I. and Fainshtein, I. Ia. Forecasting Gas Reserves and Optimizing Regional Production Levels within the Fuel and Energy Complex. *Matekon*, Fall 1981, *18*(1), pp. 43–59.   [G: U.S.S.R.]

Goodwin, Craufurd D. Energy Policy in Perspective: The Lessons of History. In *Goodwin, C. D., ed.*, 1981, pp. 665–84.   [G: U.S.]

Goodwin, Craufurd D. The Truman Administration: Toward a National Energy Policy. In *Goodwin, C. D., ed.*, 1981, pp. 1–62. [G: U.S.]

Goodwin, Craufurd D. Truman Administration Policies toward Particular Energy Sources. In *Goodwin, C. D., ed.*, 1981, pp. 63–203. [G: U.S.]

Gorbet, Frederick W. Energy Supply Security in the 1980s. In *Atlantic Inst. for Internat. Affairs and Amer. Nucl. Society*, 1981, pp. 19–21.

Gordon, Robert J. Comment on Rasche and Tatom, "Energy Price Shocks, Aggregate Supply and Monetary Policy: The Theory and the International Evidence." *Carnegie-Rochester Conf. Ser. Public Policy*, Spring 1981, *14*, pp. 95–102.
[G: U.S.]

Gowdy, John M. Radical Economics and Resource Scarcity. *Rev. Soc. Econ.*, October 1981, *39*(2), pp. 165–80.

Gray, H. Peter. Oil-Push Inflation: A Broader Examination. *Banca Naz. Lavoro Quart. Rev.*, March 1981, (136), pp. 49–67.

Grayson, George W. The Mexican Oil Boom. In *Purcell, S. K., ed.*, 1981, pp. 146–57.
[G: Mexico]

Gregory, Paul R. Energy Price Increases and the Productivity Slowdown in United States Manufacturing: Discussion. In *Federal Reserve Bank of Boston (I)*, 1981, pp. 90–92. [G: U.S.]

Griffin, James M. Engineering and Econometric Interpretations of Energy–Capital Complementarity: Comment. *Amer. Econ. Rev.*, December 1981, *71*(5), pp. 1100–1104. [G: U.S.]

Griffin, James M. Statistical Cost Analysis Re-Revisited: Reply. *Quart. J. Econ.*, February 1981, *96*(1), pp. 183–87.

Griffin, James M. The Energy–Capital Complementarity Controversy: A Progress Report on Reconciliation. In *Berndt, E. R. and Field, B. C., eds.*, 1981, pp. 70–80.   [G: Selected Countries]

Grossling, Bernardo F. Possible Dimensions of Mexican Petroleum. In *Ladman, J. R.; Baldwin, D. J. and Bergman, E., eds.*, 1981, pp. 37–43.
[G: Mexico]

Gruen, F. H. and Hillman, Arye L. A Review of Issues Pertinent to Liquid Fuel Policy. *Econ. Rec.*, June 1981, *57*(157), pp. 111–27.
[G: Australia]

Grümm, Hans J. Non-proliferation and Safeguards in the 1980s. In *Atlantic Inst. for Internat. Affairs and Amer. Nucl. Society*, 1981, pp. 21–25.

Häfele, Wolf. Energy in a Finite World—Expansio ad Absurdum? A Rebuttal. *Energy J.*, October 1981, 2(4), pp. 35–42. [G: LDCs]

Hafer, R. W. The Impact of Energy Prices and Money Growth on Five Industrial Countries. *Fed. Res. Bank St. Louis Rev.*, March 1981, 63(3), pp. 19–26. [G: W. Germany; U.S.; U.K.; Japan; Canada]

Hall, George R. Natural Gas Curtailment Policy: Where Do We Go from Here? *Energy J.*, October 1981, 2(4), pp. 43–61. [G: U.S.]

Hall, P. H. Patterns of Energy Use in Australian Manufacturing Industry. *Australian J. Manage.*, December 1981, 6(2), pp. 43–58. [G: Australia]

Halvorsen, Robert and Pollakowski, Henry O. The Effects of Fuel Prices on House Prices. *Urban Stud.*, June 1981, 18(2), pp. 205–11.

Hannon, Bruce. Energy, Economics, and the Environment: The Response of Orthodox Economics: Reply. In *Daly, H. E. and Umana, A. F., eds.*, 1981, pp. 115–17. [G: U.S.]

Hannon, Bruce. The Energy Cost of Energy. In *Daly, H. E. and Umana, A. F., eds.*, 1981, pp. 81–107. [G: U.S.]

Harris, John and Davies, Brian. The Fifth Fuel—Energy Conservation. *Lloyds Bank Rev.*, April 1981, (140), pp. 20–35. [G: U.K.]

Harrison, Selig S. China, Oil, and Asia: The Potential for Conflict or Cooperation. In *Hewett, R. B., ed.*, 1981, pp. 99–126. [G: China]

Hartigan, J. A. Estimating Volumes of Remaining Fossil Fuel Resources: A Critical Review: Comment. *J. Amer. Statist. Assoc.*, September 1981, 76(375), pp. 548. [G: U.S.]

Hartman, Raymond S. An Analysis of Department of Energy Residential Appliance Efficiency Standards. *Energy J.*, July 1981, 2(3), pp. 49–70. [G: U.S.]

Havrylyshyn, O. and Munasinghe, Mohan. Interactions among Alternative Modes of Household Energy Production: A Case Study of Colombo, Sri Lanka. *J. Econ. Devel.*, December 1981, 6(2), pp. 165–83. [G: Sri Lanka]

Hayes, Denis. Energy for Development: Third World Options. In *Chatterji, M., ed.*, 1981, pp. 27–52. [G: LDCs]

Helliwell, John F. Canadian Energy Pricing. *Can. J. Econ.*, November 1981, 14(4), pp. 577–95. [G: Canada]

Helliwell, John F. The Stagflationary Effects of Higher Energy Prices in an Open Economy. *Can. Public Policy*, Supplement, April 1981, 7, pp. 155–64. [G: Canada]

Helliwell, John F. and McRae, Robert N. The National Energy Conflict. *Can. Public Policy*, Winter 1981, 7(1), pp. 15–23. [G: Canada]

Henion, Karl E., II. Energy Usage and the Conserver Society: Review of the 1979 AMA Conference on Ecological Marketing. *J. Cons. Res.*, December 1981, 8(3), pp. 339–42.

Heslop, Louise A.; Moran, Lori and Cousineau, Amy. "Consciousness" in Energy Conservation Behavior: An Exploratory Study. *J. Cons. Res.*, December 1981, 8(3), pp. 299–305. [G: U.S.]

Hietarinta, Kai. Oljans föränderliga roll. (The Changing Role of Oil. With English summary.) *Ekon. Samfundets Tidskr.*, 1981, 34(2), pp. 105–19. [G: Finland]

Hirst, Eric and Blue, Jackalie L. Federal-State Cooperation on Managing Disaggregate Energy Consumption Data. *Rev. Public Data Use (See J. Econ. Soc. Meas. after 4/85)*, November 1981, 9(3), pp. 175–88. [G: U.S.]

Ho, James K. An Experiment in Multiple Criteria Energy Policy Analysis. In *Morse, J. N., ed.*, 1981, pp. 145–56. [G: U.S.]

Hoch, Irving. Energy and Location. In *Hawley, A. H. and Mazie, S. M., eds.*, 1981, pp. 285–356. [G: U.S.]

Hoel, Michael. Employment Effects of an Increased Oil Price in an Economy with Short-run Labor Immobility. *Scand. J. Econ.*, 1981, 83(2), pp. 269–76.

Hoffman, Kurt and Burch, David. The EEC and Energy Aid to the Third World. In *Stevens, C., ed.*, 1981, pp. 104–18. [G: EEC; LDCs]

Hogan, William W. Energy and Security Policy. In *Wachter, M. L. and Wachter, S. M., eds.*, 1981, pp. 202–21. [G: U.S.; Selected Countries]

Honea, R. B. The Southeast's Energy Prospects: A Realistic Appraisal. *Rev. Reg. Stud.*, Fall 1981, 11(2), pp. 74–87. [G: U.S.]

Houdek, Karel. Electric Energy in the 6th and 7th Five-Year Plans. *Czech. Econ. Digest.*, February 1981, (1), pp. 71–78. [G: Czechoslovakia]

Houthakker, Hendrik S. Energy Considerations in United States Foreign Policy. *Cato J.*, Fall 1981, 1(2), pp. 313–37. [G: U.S.; OPEC]

Howe, James W. Improved International Cooperation on Energy. In *Foster, J., et al.*, 1981, pp. 202–03. [G: Global]

Howe, James W. Meeting the Energy Needs of Developing Countries. In *Foster, J., et al.*, 1981, pp. 193–202. [G: LDCs]

Howe, James W. Oil-Importing Developing Countries. In *Foster, J., et al.*, 1981, pp. 57–95. [G: LDCs]

Hudson, Edward A. Modeling Production and Pricing within an Interindustry Framework. In *Bayraktar, B. A., et al., eds.*, 1981, pp. 201–14.

Hudson, Edward A. U.S. Energy Price Decontrol: Energy, Trade and Economic Effects. *Scand. J. Econ.*, 1981, 83(2), pp. 180–200.

Huettner, David A. Energy, Entropy, and Economic Analysis: Some New Directions. *Energy J.*, April 1981, 2(2), pp. 123–30.

Hunter, James E. Critique of U.S. Energy Policy. In *U.S. Congress, Joint Economic Committee (I)*, 1981, pp. 539–51. [G: U.S.; OECD]

Hutber, F. W. Energy Policy Planning: Comments on the Papers Presented in the Session on Supply Modeling. In *Bayraktar, B. A., et al., eds.*, 1981, pp. 183–86.

Hutber, F. W. Use of Models in Decision Making: A Policy Maker's View. In *Bayraktar, B. A., et al., eds.*, 1981, pp. 57–62.

Hutton, R. Bruce and McNeill, Dennis L. The Value of Incentives in Stimulating Energy Conservation. *J. Cons. Res.*, December 1981, *8*(3), pp. 291–98. [G: U.S.]

Intriligator, Michael D. The National Energy Dividend: A Proposal for a U.S. Energy Policy. **In** *Kamrany, N. M.*, 1981, pp. 77–89. [G: U.S.]

Irving, R. A. Rejoinder [A Comparative Analysis of Global Energy Models]. *Energy Econ.*, October 1981, *3*(4), pp. 268.

Islam, Rizwanul. Some Macroeconomic Implications of Higher Oil Prices for Bangladesh. *Bangladesh Devel. Stud.*, Summer 1981, *9*(2), pp. 1–20. [G: Bangladesh]

Jaidah, Ali M. OPEC Policy Options. **In** *OPEC, Public Information Dept.*, 1981, pp. 208–14. [G: OPEC]

Jessen, Peter J. The Role of Energy Ideologies in Developing Environmental Policy. **In** *Mann, D. E., ed.*, 1981, pp. 103–23.

Johannson, P. Roff and Thomas, J. C. A Dilemma of Nuclear Regulation in Canada: Political Control and Public Confidence. *Can. Public Policy*, Summer 1981, *7*(3), pp. 433–43. [G: Canada]

Johnson, Christopher. International Energy Options: The Growth Imperative. **In** *Tempest, P., ed.*, 1981, pp. 247–51.

Jones, Peter and Pearce, David. The Economics of Nuclear Fuel Reprocessing: A Case Study of the Windscale THORP Plant. *Energy Econ.*, October 1981, *3*(4), pp. 202–18. [G: U.K.]

Jorgenson, Dale W. Energy Prices and Productivity Growth. *Scand. J. Econ.*, 1981, *83*(2), pp. 165–79. [G: U.S.]

Jorgenson, Dale W. Energy Prices and Productivity Growth. **In** *Tempest, P., ed.*, 1981, pp. 75–92. [G: U.S.]

Jump, Gregory V. On Interpreting Simulations with a Macroeconometric Model: Comment [The Impact of Higher Enery Prices in Canada]. *Can. Public Policy*, Winter 1981, *7*(1), pp. 35–38. [G: Canada]

Kadhim, Sabri A. R. and Al-Janabi, Adnan A. Domestic Energy Requirements in OPEC Member Countries. **In** *OPEC, Public Information Dept.*, 1981, pp. 140–60. [G: OPEC]

Kamrany, Nake M. The Vicious Circle of the United States' Energy Problem. **In** *Kamrany, N. M.*, 1981, pp. 1–16. [G: U.S.]

Kamrany, Nake M. and Morgner, Aurelius. Energy Independence!! How? **In** *Kamrany, N. M.*, 1981, pp. 161–73. [G: U.S.]

Kang, Heejoon and Brown, Gardner M. Partial and Full Elasticities of Substitution and the Energy–Capital Complementarity Controversy. **In** *Berndt, E. R. and Field, B. C., eds.*, 1981, pp. 81–89. [G: U.S.]

Karunaratne, Neil Dias. An Input-Output Analysis of Australian Energy Planning Issues. *Energy Econ.*, July 1981, *3*(3), pp. 159–68.

[G: Australia]

Kasulis, Jack J.; Huettner, David A. and Dikeman, Neil J. The Feasibility of Changing Electricity Consumption Patterns. *J. Cons. Res.*, December 1981, *8*(3), pp. 279–90. [G: U.S.]

Kauffmann, Howard C. SMR Forum: Realizing the Potential of Synthetic Fuels. *Sloan Manage. Rev.*, Spring 1981, *22*(3), pp. 55–57. [G: U.S.]

Kaufman, Alvin and Bodilly, Susan J. Supplemental Sources of Natural Gas: An Economic Comparison. *Energy J.*, October 1981, *2*(4), pp. 63–83. [G: U.S.]

Kaufman, Gordon M. Estimating Volumes of Remaining Fossil Fuel Resources: A Critical Review: Comment. *J. Amer. Statist. Assoc.*, September 1981, *76*(375), pp. 549–50. [G: U.S.]

Keidel, Albert. Resource Dependency and Energy Problems. **In** *Richardson, B. M. and Ueda, T., eds.*, 1981, pp. 89–98. [G: Japan]

Kelley, Donald R. National Energy Profiles: The Soviet Union. **In** *Stunkel, K. R., ed.*, 1981, pp. 82–119. [G: U.S.S.R.]

Kendrick, Hugh. NASAP: Some Lessons Learned. **In** *Atlantic Inst. for Internat. Affairs and Amer. Nucl. Society*, 1981, pp. 32–34. [G: U.S.]

Khazzoom, J. Daniel. The Dilemma of Economic versus Statistical Models of Energy (and Some Results of Forecasting Monthly Peak Electricity Demand Using a Transfer Function Model) *Energy J.*, July 1981, *2*(3), pp. 134–37.

Kim, Samuel S. National Energy Profiles: The People's Republic of China. **In** *Stunkel, K. R., ed.*, 1981, pp. 171–218. [G: China]

Knelman, Fred H. The Geopolitics of Oil. **In** *Nemetz, P. N., ed.*, 1981, pp. 41–60. [G: Canada]

Kopecki, Kazimierz. The Case for Nuclear Energy. *Int. Soc. Sci. J.*, 1981, *33*(3), pp. 481–94.

Koukios, E. G. and Mavrokoukoulakis, J. G. The Energy Value of Agricultural Residues—Utilization through Briquetting. **In** *Chatterji, M., ed.*, 1981, pp. 139–49. [G: Greece]

Kouris, George. Elasticities—Science or Fiction? *Energy Econ.*, April 1981, *3*(2), pp. 66–70.

[G: U.K.]

Kozmetsky, George. Proceedings of the Seminar on Inflation: Statement. **In** *U.S. Congress, Joint Economic Committee (I)*, 1981, pp. 59–72.

[G: U.S.]

Krasts, Aivars. Proceedings of the Seminar on Energy: Statement. **In** *U.S. Congress, Joint Economic Committee (I)*, 1981, pp. 531–38.

[G: U.S.]

Kuleshov, V. V. and Sokolov, V. M. Saving Fuel: Potential and Actual. *Prob. Econ.*, June 1981, *24*(2), pp. 3–12. [G: U.S.S.R.]

Labay, Duncan G. and Kinnear, Thomas C. Exploring the Consumer Decision Process in the Adoption of Solar Energy Systems. *J. Cons. Res.*, December 1981, *8*(3), pp. 271–78. [G: U.S.]

Lakshmanan, T. R. Regional Growth and Energy Determinants: Implications for the Future. *Energy J.*, April 1981, *2*(2), pp. 1–24. [G: U.S.]

Lall, Upmanu and Mays, Larry W. Model for Planning Water-Energy Systems. *Water Resources Res.*, August 1981, *17*(4), pp. 853–65. [G: U.S.]

Lambsdorff, Otto Graf. Basic Issues of Energy and Development: II. *J. Energy Devel.*, Autumn 1981, *7*(1), pp. 35–38.

Lamont, Norman. International Energy Options: A U.K. Government View. **In** *Tempest, P., ed.*, 1981, pp. 35–41.

Lanfranco, Sam. Mexican Oil, Export-led Development and Agricultural Neglect. *J. Econ. Devel.*, July 1981, *6*(1), pp. 125–51. [G: Mexico]

Laumas, Prem S. and Williams, Martin. Energy and Economic Development. *Weltwirtsch. Arch.*, 1981, *117*(4), pp. 706–16. **[G: India]**

Lawrence, Max. Brazil's Fuel Alcohol Program: Implications for the World Sugar Market. *Quart. Rev. Rural Econ.*, November 1981, *3*(4), pp. 330–33. **[G: Brazil]**

Lee, Albert Yin-Po. Voluntary Conservation and Electricity Peak Demand: A Case Study of the Modesto Irrigation District. *Land Econ.*, August 1981, *57*(3), pp. 436–47. **[G: U.S.]**

Lehman, Dale E. A Reexamination of the Crude Oil Windfall Profit Tax [The Incidence and Effects of the Crude Oil Windfall Profit Tax]. *Natural Res. J.*, October 1981, *21*(4), pp. 683–89. **[G: U.S.]**

Lehman, Dale E. Conservation and OPEC Pricing [Effect of Conservation on Oil Prices]. *J. Energy Devel.*, Autumn 1981, *7*(1), pp. 121–24. **[G: OPEC]**

Leistritz, F. Larry and Murdock, Steve H. Implications of Energy Development for Economic Growth and Social Change in the Great Plains. In *Lawson, M. P. and Baker, M. E., eds.*, 1981, pp. 247–64. **[G: U.S.]**

Lesourd, Jean-Baptiste and Gousty, Yvon. Bases économiques et thermodynamiques des techniques de comptabilité de l'énergie. (Economic and Thermodynamic Foundations of Energy Aggregation Methods. With English summary.) *Rev. Econ. Ind.*, 1st Trimester 1981, (15), pp. 44–59.

Lester, John. The Impact of Higher Energy Prices in Canada: Comment. *Can. Public Policy*, Winter 1981, *7*(1), pp. 52–58. **[G: Canada]**

Leveson, Sidney M. Comments [Possible Dimensions of Mexican Petroleum] [PEMEX in a Dependent Society]. In *Ladman, J. R.; Baldwin, D. J. and Bergman, E., eds.*, 1981, pp. 117–21. **[G: Mexico; U.S.]**

Levy, Walter J. Oil: An Agenda for the 1980s. *Foreign Aff.*, Summer 1981, *59*(5), pp. 1079–1101. **[G: U.S.]**

Levy, Yvonne. Crude Oil Price Controls and the Windfall Profit Tax: Deterrents to Production? *Fed. Res. Bank San Francisco Econ. Rev.*, Spring 1981, pp. 6–28. **[G: U.S.]**

Leyva, Jesús Puente. Mexico–United States Relations: The Natural Gas Controversy. In *Purcell, S. K., ed.*, 1981, pp. 158–67. **[G: Mexico; U.S.]**

Leyva, Jesús Puente. Mexico: Petroleum and Perspectives. In *Ladman, J. R.; Baldwin, D. J. and Bergman, E., eds.*, 1981, pp. 17–31. **[G: Mexico]**

Lienert, Ian. The Macroeconomic Effects of the 1979/80 Oil Price Rise on Four Nordic Economies. *Scand. J. Econ.*, 1981, *83*(2), pp. 201–19. **[G: Denmark; Finland; Sweden; Norway]**

Lovins, Amory B. Electric Utility Investments: *Excelsior* or Confetti? In *Nemetz, P. N., ed.*, 1981, pp. 91–114. **[G: U.S.]**

Lovins, Amory B. Expansio ad Absurdum. *Energy J.*, October 1981, *2*(4), pp. 25–34. **[G: LDCs]**

Lücke, Fritz. Institutions for Managing Energy Shortages. In *Tempest, P., ed.*, 1981, pp. 225–28. **[G: W. Germany]**

Luttrell, Clifton B. A Bushel of Wheat for a Barrell of Oil: Can We Offset OPEC's Gains with a Grain

Cartel? *Fed. Res. Bank St. Louis Rev.*, April 1981, *63*(4), pp. 13–21. **[G: U.S.]**

M'Bouy-Boutzit, Edouard Alexis. The Road to Cooperation: Gabon's Standpoint. In *OPEC, Public Information Dept.*, 1981, pp. 17–21. **[G: OPEC; Gabon]**

Mabro, Robert. Aspects of the Oil Supply Problem. In *Courakis, A. S., ed.*, 1981, pp. 360–73. **[G: U.S.; OPEC]**

Mabro, Robert. The Role of Government in Regulating Energy Markets. In *OPEC, Public Information Dept.*, 1981, pp. 92–105.

Maddala, G. S. and Roberts, R. Blaine. Statistical Cost Analysis Re-Revisited: Comment. *Quart. J. Econ.*, February 1981, *96*(1), pp. 177–81.

Mahler, Walter R. Japan's Adjustment to the Increased Cost of Energy. *Finance Develop.*, December 1981, *18*(4), pp. 26–29. **[G: Japan]**

Manuel, David P. Coastal State Taxation of OCS-Produced Natural Gas. *Natural Res. J.*, January 1981, *21*(1), pp. 93–105. **[G: U.S.]**

de Marchi, Neil. Energy Policy under Nixon: Mainly Putting out Fires. In *Goodwin, C. D., ed.*, 1981, pp. 395–473. **[G: U.S.]**

de Marchi, Neil. The Ford Administration: Energy as a Political Good. In *Goodwin, C. D., ed.*, 1981, pp. 475–545. **[G: U.S.]**

Marlowe, Howard. Proceedings of the Seminar on Energy: Statement. In *U.S. Congress, Joint Economic Committee (I)*, 1981, pp. 551–55. **[G: U.S.]**

Martellaro, Joseph A. Soviet Energy Resources: Present and Prospective. *Econ. Int.*, February 1981, *34*(1), pp. 46–69. **[G: U.S.S.R.]**

Martellaro, Joseph A. Toward a Better Energy Policy. *Rivista Int. Sci. Econ. Com.*, January–February 1981, *28*(1–2), pp. 33–51. **[G: U.S.]**

Martin, Jean-Marie. Energy Demand Control in Energy Policy. In *Amman, F. and Wilson, R., eds.*, 1981, pp. 1–22. **[G: OECD]**

Matthews, William H. and Siddiqi, Toufiq A. Energy and Environmental Issues in the Developing Countries. In *Chatterji, M., ed.*, 1981, pp. 53–67. **[G: LDCs]**

Mattsson, C. and Bubenko, J. A. Regional Energy Modelling. In *Janssen, J. M. L.; Pau, L. F. and Straszak, A. J., eds.*, 1981, pp. 201–06. **[G: Sweden]**

Mayer, Lawrence S. Estimating Volumes of Remaining Fossil Fuel Resources: A Critical Review: Comment. *J. Amer. Statist. Assoc.*, September 1981, *76*(375), pp. 551–54. **[G: U.S.]**

McClements, Robert, Jr. Toward a New U.S. Industrial Policy? Energy: Comment. In *Wachter, M. L. and Wachter, S. M., eds.*, 1981, pp. 227–30. **[G: U.S.]**

McCracken, M. C. and Jarvis, W. D. What Is the Impact of Higher Energy Prices? Comment [The Impact of Higher Energy Prices in Canada]. *Can. Public Policy*, Winter 1981, *7*(1), pp. 50–52. **[G: Canada]**

McDaniel, Bruce A. Solar Energy and Social Economy. *Rev. Soc. Econ.*, October 1981, *39*(2), pp. 181–95. **[G: U.S.]**

McDonald, Stephen L. The Incidence and Effects of the Crude Oil Windfall Profit Tax: A Reply to

Lehman. *Natural Res. J.*, October 1981, *21*(4), pp. 690–91. [G: U.S.]

McDonald, Stephen L. The Incidence and Effects of the Crude Oil Windfall Profit Tax. *Natural Res. J.*, April 1981, *21*(2), pp. 331–39. [G: U.S.]

McDougall, Gordon H. G., et al. Consumer Energy Research: A Review. *J. Cons. Res.*, December 1981, *8*(3), pp. 343–54.

McGoldrick, Frederick F. International Plutonium Storage. In *Atlantic Inst. for Internat. Affairs and Amer. Nucl. Society*, 1981, pp. 66–69.

McGregor, Stephen E. Government Policy and the Petroleum Industry. In *Hogan, J. D. and Craig, A. M., eds., Vol. 2*, 1981, pp. 1147–51. [G: U.S.]

McIntyre, Robert J. and Thornton, James R. Energy Systems and Comparative Systems: A Reply to Ryding [Urban Design and Energy Utilization: A Comparative Analysis of Soviet Practice]. *J. Compar. Econ.*, December 1981, *5*(4), pp. 414–17. [G: U.S.S.R.]

Meadows, Dennis. A Critique of the IIASA Energy Models. *Energy J.*, July 1981, *2*(3), pp. 17–28.

Meier, Ueli. A Closed-Cycle Energy System for Rural Dairy Industry in Nepal: The Pauwa Energy System. In *Chatterji, M., ed.*, 1981, pp. 275–88. [G: Nepal]

Meloe, Tor. Oil and the Transfer Problem. *J. Energy Devel.*, Autumn 1981, *7*(1), pp. 17–25. [G: Global]

Melvin, John G. Energy: The Future Has Come. In *Nemetz, P. N., ed.*, 1981, pp. 61–81. [G: Canada]

Miller, Morris. The U.N. Conference on New and Renewable Sources of Energy: Response to the Challenge of the Global Energy Transition. *Energy J.*, July 1981, *2*(3), pp. 138–41.

Milon, J. Walter. An Economic and Energetic Framework for Evaluating Dispersed Energy Technologies. *Land Econ.*, February 1981, *57*(1), pp. 63–76.

Mitchell, John. Use of Models in Decision Making: A Policy Maker's View. In *Bayraktar, B. A., et al., eds.*, 1981, pp. 35–45.

Mitropoulos, C. S.; Samouilidis, J. E. and Protonotarios, E. N. Using Kalman Filtering for Energy Forecasting. In *Janssen, J. M. L.; Pau, L. F. and Straszak, A. J., eds.*, 1981, pp. 317–24. [G: Greece]

de Montaigu, Roland. Structural Changes in World Oil Market: Commentary. In *OPEC, Public Information Dept.*, 1981, pp. 133–39.

Montgomery, W. David. Decontrol of Crude Oil Prices. In *Weiss, L. W. and Klass, M. W., eds.*, 1981, pp. 187–201. [G: U.S.]

Morgan Guaranty Trust Company of New York. The Response to Higher Oil Prices: Adjustment and Financing. In *Baldwin, R. E. and Richardson, J. D., eds.*, 1981, *1980*, pp. 506–16. [G: OPEC; Non-OPEC LDCs]

Morgan, William E. and Mutti, John H. Shifting, Incidence, and Inter-State Exportation of Production Taxes on Energy Resources. *Land Econ.*, August 1981, *57*(3), pp. 422–35. [G: U.S.]

Mork, Knut Anton and Hall, Robert E. Macroeconomic Analysis of Energy Price Shocks and Offset-

ting Policies: An Integrated Approach. In *Mork, K. A., ed.*, 1981, pp. 43–62. [G: U.S.]

Morlan, Terry H. Modeling Energy Demand in the Short Term and the Midterm: The EIA Experience. In *Bayraktar, B. A., et al., eds.*, 1981, pp. 187–99.

Moses, Lincoln E. One Statistician's Observations Concerning Energy Modeling. In *Bayraktar, B. A., et al., eds.*, 1981, pp. 17–33.

Moss, Marvin K. U.S. Energy Security and Nonproliferation. In *Atlantic Inst. for Internat. Affairs and Amer. Nucl. Society*, 1981, pp. 29–32. [G: U.S.]

Mount, Randall I. and Williams, Harold R. Energy Conservation, Motor Gasoline Demand and the OECD Countries. *Rev. Bus. Econ. Res.*, Spring 1981, *16*(3), pp. 48–57. [G: OECD]

Mubayi, Vinod; Palmedo, Philip F. and Doernberg, Andres B. A Framework for Energy Policy and Technology Assessment in Developing Countries: A Case Study of Peru. In *Chatterji, M., ed.*, 1981, pp. 289–314. [G: Peru]

Mukherjee, Shishir K. Energy-Economic Planning in the Developing Countries: A Conceptual Model for India. In *Chatterji, M., ed.*, 1981, pp. 223–241. [G: India]

Muller, Patrice and White, W. R. The Impact of Higher Energy Prices in Canada: Comment. *Can. Public Policy*, Winter 1981, *7*(1), pp. 59–65. [G: Canada]

Murray, Barbara B. Capital Budgeting Decisions for Load Management Equipment by Industrial Electric Users. *Nebr. J. Econ. Bus.*, Winter 1981, *20*(1), pp. 31–47. [G: U.S.]

Mylander, W. Charles. Energy Policy Planning: Discussion of Papers Presented in Comprehensive/Integrated Modeling Systems Session. In *Bayraktar, B. A., et al., eds.*, 1981, pp. 317–19.

Nash, Gerald D. Energy Crises in Historical Perspective. *Natural Res. J.*, April 1981, *21*(2), pp. 341–54. [G: U.S.]

Nathan, Robert R. Policies for Energy Independence. In *Wachter, M. L. and Wachter, S. M., eds.*, 1981, pp. 158–75. [G: U.S.]

Navarro, Peter. The 1977 Clean Air Act Amendments: Energy, Environmental, Economic, and Distributional Impacts. *Public Policy*, Spring 1981, *29*(2), pp. 121–46. [G: U.S.]

Nelkin, Dorothy. Some Social and Political Dimensions of Nuclear Power: Examples from Three Mile Island. *Amer. Polit. Sci. Rev.*, March 1981, *75*(1), pp. 132–42. [G: U.S.]

Netschert, Bruce C. Mexican Energy Resources and U.S. Energy Requirements. In *Ladman, J. R.; Baldwin, D. J. and Bergman, E., eds.*, 1981, pp. 133–44. [G: Mexico; U.S.]

Noll, Roger G. Looking for Villains in the Energy Crisis. In *Kamrany, N. M.*, 1981, pp. 17–22.

Noreng, Øystein. State Oil Trading and the Perspective of Shortage. In *Tempest, P., ed.*, 1981, pp. 229–44. [G: OPEC]

Norsworthy, J. R. Capital, Energy and Productivity Research. In *Hogan, J. D. and Craig, A. M., eds., Vol. 1*, 1981, pp. 171–81. [G: U.S.]

Norsworthy, J. R. and Harper, Michael J. Dynamic Models of Energy Substitution in U.S. Manufacturing. In *Berndt, E. R. and Field, B. C., eds.*, 1981, pp. 177–208. **[G: U.S.]**

O'Brien, John N. International Auspices for the Storage of Spent Nuclear Fuel as a Nonproliferation Measure. *Natural Res. J.*, October 1981, 21(4), pp. 857–94. **[G: U.S.]**

Odell, Peter R. Energy Policies in the EEC and Their Impact on the Third World. In *Stevens, C., ed.*, 1981, pp. 84–91. **[G: EEC; LDCs]**

Odell, Peter R. International Energy Issues: The Next Ten Years. In *Tempest, P., ed.*, 1981, pp. 187–202.

Odell, Peter R. Lower Oil Prices—Dangers to the North Sea. *Lloyds Bank Rev.*, October 1981, (142), pp. 26–38. **[G: U.K.; EEC]**

Ojeda, Mario. The Negotiating Power of Oil: The Mexican Case. In *Ladman, J. R.; Baldwin, D. J. and Bergman, E., eds.*, 1981, pp. 197–213. **[G: Mexico]**

Olorunfemi, M. A. Structural Changes in World Oil Market: Commentary. In *OPEC, Public Information Dept.*, 1981, pp. 161–64. **[G: OPEC]**

Olson, Irene F. State Tax Incentives for Solar Energy. *J. Energy Devel.*, Spring 1981, 6(2), pp. 281–96. **[G: U.S.]**

Orrison, Eileen Alannah and Kamrany, Nake M. A Comparison of Major Studies of Energy Policy. In *Kamrany, N. M.*, 1981, pp. 91–98.

Ortiz, René G. OPEC's Role in Future Energy Markets. In *OPEC, Public Information Dept.*, 1981, pp. 43–50. **[G: OPEC]**

Pace, Norma. Toward a New U.S. Industrial Policy? Energy: Comment. In *Wachter, M. L. and Wachter, S. M., eds.*, 1981, pp. 224–27. **[G: U.S.]**

Pachauri, R. K. Financing Energy Developments in the Third World. In *Tempest, P., ed.*, 1981, pp. 55–66. **[G: LDCs]**

Packer, Arnold and Steger, Wilbur. Energy/Employment Policy Analysis: International Impacts of Alternative Energy Technologies. In *Tempest, P., ed.*, 1981, pp. 99–117.

Pakravan, Karim. Exhaustible Resource Models and Predictions of Crude Oil Prices—Some Preliminary Results. *Energy Econ.*, July 1981, 3(3), pp. 169–77. **[G: OPEC]**

Parasuraman, A. and Futrell, Charles M. Executives' Views about Energy Conservation: Problems and Prospects. *J. Energy Devel.*, Spring 1981, 6(2), pp. 225–31. **[G: U.S.]**

Parra, Alirio. The Orinoco Petroleum Belt. In *Tempest, P., ed.*, 1981, pp. 153–58. **[G: Venezuela]**

Parra, Francisco Ramon. Development of Oil and Gas in the OIDCs. In *Foster, J., et al.*, 1981, pp. 161–73. **[G: LDCs]**

Parra, Francisco Ramon. Oil-Exporting Developing Countries. In *Foster, J., et al.*, 1981, pp. 96–120. **[G: LDCs]**

Parra, Francisco Ramon. World Energy Balances: Looking to 2020: Commentary. In *OPEC, Public Information Dept.*, 1981, pp. 73–75.

Parvin, Manoucher and Grammas, Gus W. Capacity, Energy, and Environment Planning in Developing Industries. In *Chatterji, M., ed.*, 1981, pp. 153–66. **[G: LDCs]**

Patermann, Christian. Non-proliferation and Safe-

guards: Prospects for "New" Arrangements. In *Atlantic Inst. for Internat. Affairs and Amer. Nucl. Society*, 1981, pp. 75–77.

Pelaez, Rolando F. The Price Elasticity for Gasoline Revisited [Dynamic Demand Analyses for Gasoline and Residential Electricity]. *Energy J.*, October 1981, 2(4), pp. 85–89. **[G: U.S.]**

Pellicer de Brody, Olga. Mexico–United States Relations: A Mexican Perspective. In *Purcell, S. K., ed.*, 1981, pp. 4–12. **[G: Mexico; U.S.]**

Pellicer de Brody, Olga. Oil and U.S. Policy toward Mexico. In *Ladman, J. R.; Baldwin, D. J. and Bergman, E., eds.*, 1981, pp. 185–96. **[G: Mexico; U.S.]**

Pindyck, Robert S. Energy Policy and the American Economy. In *Kamrany, N. M.*, 1981, pp. 67–76. **[G: U.S.]**

Pindyck, Robert S. Energy, Productivity, and the New U.S. Industrial Policy. In *Wachter, M. L. and Wachter, S. M., eds.*, 1981, pp. 176–201. **[G: U.S.]**

Pitts, Robert E.; Willenborg, John F. and Sherrell, Daniel L. Consumer Adaptation to Gasoline Price Increases. *J. Cons. Res.*, December 1981, 8(3), pp. 322–30. **[G: U.S.]**

Pitts, Robert E. and Wittenbach, James L. Tax Credits as a Means of Influencing Consumer Behavior. *J. Cons. Res.*, December 1981, 8(3), pp. 335–38. **[G: U.S.]**

Plaut, Steven E. OPEC Is not a Cartel. *Challenge*, November–December 1981, 24(5), pp. 18–24. **[G: OPEC]**

Plummer, James L. Policy Implications of Energy Vulnerability. *Energy J.*, April 1981, 2(2), pp. 25–36.

Pollock, David H. and Howe, James W. Energy for Development: Convergences and Conflicts. In *Foster, J., et al.*, 1981, pp. 142–59. **[G: Global]**

Potter, Harry R. and Norville, Heather J. Social Values Inherent in Policy Statements: An Evaluation of an Energy Technology Assessment. In *Mann, D. E., ed.*, 1981, pp. 177–89. **[G: U.S.]**

Prasad, C. R. and Bhat, Kisan. Prospects for Ethanol as Automobile Fuel in India. In *Chatterji, M., ed.*, 1981, pp. 89–102. **[G: India]**

Prato, Anthony A. and Miller, Ronald R. Evaluating the Energy Production Potential of the United States Outer Continental Shelf. *Land Econ.*, February 1981, 57(1), pp. 77–90. **[G: U.S.]**

Provenzano, George and Walasek, Richard A. Regional Variation in Electric Energy: Demand Responsiveness in the Residential Sector in Illinois. *Reg. Sci. Persp.*, 1981, 11(2), pp. 56–69. **[G: U.S.]**

Pryor, C. Anthony. Environmental Impact of Renewable Energy and Alternative Development Strategies. In *Chatterji, M., ed.*, 1981, pp. 125–37. **[G: LDCs]**

Quirk, James and Terasawa, Katsuaki. Nuclear Regulation: An Historical Perspective. *Natural Res. J.*, October 1981, 21(4), pp. 833–55. **[G: U.S.]**

Ramaswamy, N. S. Notes Towards the Management of Animal Energy Utilization in India. In *Chatterji, M., ed.*, 1981, pp. 255–74. **[G: India]**

Ramsay, William and Shue, Elizabeth. Infrastructure Problems for Rural New and Renewable Energy Systems. *J. Energy Devel.*, Spring 1981, 6(2), pp. 232–50. **[G: LDCs]**

Randall, Laura R. National Energy Profiles: Mexico. In *Stunkel, K. R., ed.*, 1981, pp. 270–314.
[G: Mexico]

Randall, Laura R. The Political Economy of Mexican Oil, 1976–1979. In *Ladman, J. R.; Baldwin, D. J. and Bergman, E., eds.*, 1981, pp. 87–115.
[G: Mexico]

Randle, Russell V. Coastal Energy Siting Dilemmas. *Natural Res. J.*, January 1981, 21(1), pp. 125–59. **[G: U.S.]**

Rao, S. Subba, et al. Determination of Energy Costs and Intensities of Goods and Services in the Indian Economy—An Input–Output Approach. In *Chatterji, M., ed.*, 1981, pp. 205–221.
[G: India]

Rasche, Robert H. and Tatom, John A. Energy Price Shocks, Aggregate Supply and Monetary Policy: The Theory and the International Evidence. *Carnegie-Rochester Conf. Ser. Public Policy*, Spring 1981, 14, pp. 9–93. **[G: N. America; U.K.; Germany; France; Japan]**

Rasche, Robert H. and Tatom, John A. Reply to Gordon [Energy Price Shocks, Aggregate Supply and Monetary Evidence: The Theory and the International Evidence]. *Carnegie-Rochester Conf. Ser. Public Policy*, Spring 1981, 14, pp. 103–07.

Renborg, Ulf. Energy Analysis of Agriculture, Biology or Economics—A Survey of Approaches, Problems and Traps. In *Johnson, G. and Maunder, A., eds.*, 1981, pp. 231–41. **[G: Sweden]**

Renshaw, Edward F. Energy Efficiency and the Slump in Labour Productivity in the USA. *Energy Econ.*, January 1981, 3(1), pp. 36–42. **[G: U.S.]**

Reza, Ali M. An Analysis of the Supply of Oil. *Energy J.*, April 1981, 2(2), pp. 77–94.

Reza, Ali M. The Impact of President Reagan's Sudden Decontrol of Petroleum Prices on Petroleum Consumption. *Energy J.*, July 1981, 2(3), pp. 129–33. **[G: U.S.]**

Riaz, T. A Long-Range Energy Sector Plan for Pakistan. *Pakistan Devel. Rev.*, Autumn 1981, 20(3), pp. 303–22. **[G: Pakistan]**

Riaz, T. Energy Policy Formulation for Pakistan: An Optimization Approach. *Energy Econ.*, July 1981, 3(3), pp. 191–97. **[G: Pakistan]**

Ritchie, J. R. Brent; McDougall, Gordon H. G. and Claxton, John D. Complexities of Household Energy Consumption and Conservation. *J. Cons. Res.*, December 1981, 8(3), pp. 233–42.
[G: Canada]

Robinson, Colin. North Sea Oil: A Chance to Change? In *Gaskin, M., ed.*, 1981, pp. 98–124.
[G: U.K.]

Robinson, Colin. The Errors of North Sea Policy. *Lloyds Bank Rev.*, July 1981, (141), pp. 14–33.
[G: U.K.]

Rodekohr, Mark. An Examination of Econometric Energy Modeling and Comparison with Alternative Methodologies. In *Bayraktar, B. A., et al., eds.*, 1981, pp. 387–97.

Rodriguez Elizarraras, Gustavo. Latin American Energy Panorama. In *OPEC, Public Information Dept.*, 1981, pp. 39–42. **[G: Latin America]**

Roett, Riordan. Brazilian Foreign Policy: Options in the 1980s. In *Bruneau, T. C. and Faucher, P., eds.*, 1981, pp. 179–92. **[G: Brazil]**

Rometsch, Rudolf. International Spent Fuel Storage. In *Atlantic Inst. for Internat. Affairs and Amer. Nucl. Society*, 1981, pp. 73–75.

Romig, Frederic and O'Sullivan, Patrick. Interfuel Substitution in European Countries. In *Tempest, P., ed.*, 1981, pp. 133–50. **[G: U.K.; Europe]**

Rosen, David J. National Energy Profiles: The United States. In *Stunkel, K. R., ed.*, 1981, pp. 39–81. **[G: U.S.]**

Rostow, Walt W. Energy and the Economy. In *U.S. Congress, Joint Economic Committee (1), 1981, 1980*, pp. 348–434. **[G: U.S.; Selected Countries]**

Roth, Timothy P. Average and Marginal Price Changes and the Demand for Electricity: An Econometric Study. *Appl. Econ.*, September 1981, 13(3), pp. 377–88.

Rowen, Henry S. and Weyant, John P. Will Oil Prices Collapse? *Challenge*, November–December 1981, 24(5), pp. 11–17.

Rueter, Theodore and Enholm, Gregory. A Proposal for Gasoline Rationing. *J. Post Keynesian Econ.*, Winter 1980–81, 3(2), pp. 287–93. **[G: U.S.]**

Russell, Milton. The Energy Problem in the 1980s. *Giorn. Econ.*, May–June 1981, 40(5–6), pp. 353–61.

Russett, Bruce. United States Solar Energy Policy for Less-Developed Countries. *J. Energy Devel.*, Autumn 1981, 7(1), pp. 39–59. **[G: LDCs; U.S.]**

Ruttley, E. World Energy Balances: Looking to 2020. In *OPEC, Public Information Dept.*, 1981, pp. 51–71. **[G: Global]**

Ryding, Helene. Municipal Energy Supply and District Heating: A Comment on Robert J. McIntyre and James R. Thornton, "Urban Design and Energy Utilization: A Comparative Analysis of Soviet Practice." *J. Compar. Econ.*, December 1981, 5(4), pp. 404–13. **[G: U.S.S.R.]**

Samouilidis, J. E. A Planning Model for the Optimal Development of the Greek Energy Sector. In *Janssen, J. M. L.; Pau, L. F. and Straszak, A. J., eds.*, 1981, pp. 141–49. **[G: Greece]**

Sandler, Todd and Schulze, William D. The Economics of Outer Space. *Natural Res. J.*, April 1981, 21(2), pp. 371–93. **[G: U.S.]**

Sant, Roger W. Energy Productivity: Its Role in the Growth of the American Economy. In *Hogan, J. D. and Craig, A. M., eds., Vol. 1*, 1981, pp. 183–90. **[G: U.S.]**

Sargious, Michel; Szplett, David and Janarthanan, N. Potential Price-Induced Fuel Conservation with Changes in the Canadian Urban Transportation System. *J. Energy Devel.*, Autumn 1981, 7(1), pp. 61–71. **[G: Canada]**

Sawhill, John C. International Energy Options: International Comparison of Governmental Responses. In *Tempest, P., ed.*, 1981, pp. 23–29.
[G: U.S.]

Sayigh, Yusif A. The Integration of the Oil Sector in Economies of OPEC Member Countries: Commentary. In *OPEC, Public Information Dept.*, 1981, pp. 182–88.

Scarfe, Brian L. The Federal Budget and Energy

Program, October 28th, 1980: A Review. *Can. Public Policy,* Winter 1981, 7(1), pp. 1–14. [G: Canada]

Schelling, Thomas C. Thinking through the Energy Problem. In *U.S. Congress, Joint Economic Committee (I),* 1981, *1979,* pp. 435–98.

Schuenemeyer, John H. Estimating Volumes of Remaining Fossil Fuel Resources: A Critical Review: Comment. *J. Amer. Statist. Assoc.,* September 1981, 76(375), pp. 554–58. [G: U.S.]

Seers, Dudley. Massive Transfers and Mutual Interests. *World Devel.,* June 1981, 9(6), pp. 557–62.

Sfligiotti, Giuseppe M. Taxation and the Regulation of Energy Supply and Consumption: Comment. In *Roskamp, K. W. and Forte, F., eds.,* 1981, pp. 297–303. [G: U.S.]

Shaw, Robert W., Jr. SMR Forum: A Skeptic's View of Synfuels. *Sloan Manage. Rev.,* Spring 1981, 22(3), pp. 59–62.

Shihab-Eldin, Adnan and Al-Qudsi, Sulayman S. Energy Needs of the Less Developed Countries (LDCs). In *Amman, F. and Wilson, R., eds.,* 1981, pp. 349–93. [G: LDCs]

Shin, Euisoon. Inter-Energy Substitution in Korea, 1962–1975. *J. Econ. Devel.,* July 1981, 6(1), pp. 33–46. [G: Korea]

Siddall, Ernest. Uranium and Coal as Low-Cost Energy Sources—The Safety Issue. In *Nemetz, P. N., ed.,* 1981, pp. 83–90. [G: U.S.]

Siebert, Horst. Strategische Ansatzpunkte der Rohstoffpolitik der Industrienationen nach der Theorie des intertemporalen Ressourcenangebots. (Strategies of Natural Resource Policy for the Industrial Nations According to the Theory of Intertemporal Allocation. With English summary.) *Konjunkturpolitik,* 1981, 27(5), pp. 297–310. [G: W. Germany]

Sigmon, Brent, et al. An Evaluation of Natural Gas Consumption Data. *Rev. Public Data Use (See J. Econ. Soc. Meas. after 4/85),* November 1981, 9(3), pp. 189–97. [G: U.S.]

Sills, David L. A Comment on Dorothy Nelkin's "Some Social and Political Dimensions of Nuclear Power: Examples from Three Mile Island." *Amer. Polit. Sci. Rev.,* March 1981, 75(1), pp. 143–45. [G: U.S.]

Šmíd, Ladislav and Součková, Natalja. International Cooperation in Rational Utilization of Material Resources. *Czech. Econ. Digest.,* February 1981, (1), pp. 3–17. [G: CMEA]

Smith, Rodney T. In Search of the "Just" U.S. Oil Policy: A Review of Arrow and Kalt and More. *J. Bus.,* January 1981, 54(1), pp. 87–116. [G: U.S.]

Solo, Robert. Policy Options: Regional Building Codes Formulated and Enforced by the Federal Bureau of Standards. *J. Econ. Issues,* March 1981, 15(1), pp. 173–75. [G: U.S.]

Stammati, Gaetano. Italy and Japan Facing the New Oil and Monetary Crises. *Rivista Int. Sci. Econ. Com.,* July–August 1981, 28(7–8), pp. 755–61. [G: Japan; Italy]

Starr, Chauncey. Energy at the Crossroads: Abundance or Shortage? In *Tempest, P., ed.,* 1981, pp. 11–19. [G: U.S.]

Steel, David [Sir]. Risks in the International Oil

Trade. In *Tempest, P., ed.,* 1981, pp. 3–9.

Stegemeier, Richard J. Supply Solutions to the Energy Problem. In *Kamrany, N. M.,* 1981, pp. 29–41. [G: U.S.]

Stiglitz, Joseph E. and Dasgupta, Partha. Market Structure and Resource Extraction under Uncertainty. *Scand. J. Econ.,* 1981, 83(2), pp. 318–33.

Stitt, William C. Resource Modeling: Problems in the State of the Art. In *Bayraktar, B. A., et al., eds.,* 1981, pp. 127–58.

Stivers, William. International Politics and Iraqi Oil, 1918–1928: A Study in Anglo–American Diplomacy. *Bus. Hist. Rev.,* Winter 1981, 55(4), pp. 517–40. [G: Iraq; U.S.; U.K.]

Stobaugh, Robert B. Energy Future and International Trade. *J. Int. Bus. Stud.,* Spring/Summer 1981, 12(1), pp. 23–28. [G: U.S.]

Stone, Richard J. Toward a Secure Energy Future. In *Kamrany, N. M.,* 1981, pp. 121–40.

Stroup, Richard and Baden, John. Responsible Individuals and the Nation's Energy Future. *Cato J.,* Fall 1981, 1(2), pp. 421–38. [G: U.S.]

Stunkel, Kenneth R. Energy and the Future of Nations. In *Stunkel, K. R., ed.,* 1981, pp. 1–36.

Stunkel, Kenneth R. National Energy Profiles: Japan. In *Stunkel, K. R., ed.,* 1981, pp. 120–70. [G: Japan]

Sullivan, Brian and Siemon, Donna. Interfuel Substitution—Upper Bound Estimates. *Energy J.,* April 1981, 2(2), pp. 107–18. [G: U.S.]

Sunley, Emil M. Taxation and the Regulation of Energy Supply and Consumption. In *Roskamp, K. W. and Forte, F., eds.,* 1981, pp. 287–95. [G: U.S.]

Suzuki, K. and Takenaka, H. The Role of Investment for Energy Conservation: Future Japanese Economic Growth. *Energy Econ.,* October 1981, 3(4), pp. 233–43. [G: Japan]

Sweeney, James L. Model Comparison for Energy Policy and Planning. In *Bayraktar, B. A., et al., eds.,* 1981, pp. 259–85. [G: U.S.]

Sweeney, James L. The Relationship between Energy Use and the Economy. In *Kamrany, N. M.,* 1981, pp. 53–66. [G: U.S.]

Taher, Abdulhady Hassan. The Future Role of the National Oil Companies. In *OPEC, Public Information Dept.,* 1981, pp. 76–87. [G: OPEC]

Talley, Wayne K. and Warner, Stanley E., Jr. Energy Legislation and Gasoline Tax Revenue. *Public Finance Quart.,* January 1981, 9(1), pp. 35–46. [G: U.S.]

Tarvainen, K. and Haimes, Yacov Y. Hierarchical-Multiobjective Framework for Energy Storage Systems. In *Morse, J. N., ed.,* 1981, pp. 424–46.

Tatom, John A. Energy Prices and Short-Run Economic Performance. *Fed. Res. Bank St. Louis Rev.,* January 1981, 63(1), pp. 3–17. [G: U.S.]

Tatom, John A. Investment and the New Energy Regime. In *Federal Reserve System,* 1981, pp. 221–30. [G: U.S.]

Teisberg, Thomas J. A Dynamic Programming Model of the U.S. Strategic Petroleum Reserve. *Bell J. Econ. (See Rand J. Econ. after 4/85),* Autumn 1981, 12(2), pp. 526–46. [G: U.S.]

Telson, Michael L. Managing Oil Contingencies: The

United States Experience and Choices for the Future. In *Tempest, P., ed.*, 1981, pp. 205–23.
[G: U.S.]

Tempest, Paul. Financing Energy Development in the Industrialised Countries. In *Tempest, P., ed.*, 1981, pp. 67–72.
[G: OECD]

Thurman, Stephan and Berner, Richard. Analysis of Oil Price Shocks in the MPS Model. In *Mork, K. A., ed.*, 1981, pp. 99–124.
[G: U.S.]

Thurow, Lester C. Solving the Energy Problem. In *Kamrany, N. M.*, 1981, pp. 23–27.
[G: U.S.]

Tienda, Marta and Aborampah, Osei-Mensah. Energy-Related Adaptation in Low-Income Nonmetropolitan Wisconsin Counties. *J. Cons. Res.*, December 1981, 8(3), pp. 265–70.
[G: U.S.]

Tixier, Susan. Tribal Severance Taxes—Outside the Purview of the Commerce Clause. *Natural Res. J.*, April 1981, 21(2), pp. 405–13.
[G: U.S.]

Troeller, Ruth R. The Future of Energy Procurement with Special Reference to Rural Areas of Third World Countries. In *Lozoya, J. and Green, R., eds.*, 1981, pp. 199–218.
[G: LDCs]

Tyner, Wallace E. The Potential of Using Biomass for Energy in the United States. In *Tempest, P., ed.*, 1981, pp. 165–83.
[G: U.S.]

Udagawa, Akihito. Taxation and Regulation of Energy Supply and Consumption: Comment. In *Roskamp, K. W. and Forte, F., eds.*, 1981, pp. 305–08.
[G: U.S.]

Ulph, Alistair M. and Folie, G. Michael. An Economic Analysis of Oil Self-sufficiency in Australia. In *Nemetz, P. N., ed.*, 1981, pp. 1–23.
[G: Australia]

Umaña, Alvaro F. Energy, Economics, and the Environment: Introduction. In *Daly, H. E. and Umana, A. F., eds.*, 1981, pp. 1–19.

Verhallen, Theo M. M. and Raaij, W. Fred. Household Behavior and the Use of Natural Gas for Home Heating. *J. Cons. Res.*, December 1981, 8(3), pp. 253–57.
[G: U.S.]

Viezca, Juan Aizpuru. The Future Role of the National Oil Companies: Commentary. In *OPEC, Public Information Dept.*, 1981, pp. 88–91.
[G: OPEC]

Villarreal, René. Petroleum and Mexican Economic Growth and Development in the 1980s. In *Ladman, J. R.; Baldwin, D. J. and Bergman, E., eds.*, 1981, pp. 69–85.
[G: Mexico]

Villarreal, René and de Villarreal, Rocío. Mexico's Development Strategy. In *Purcell, S. K., ed.*, 1981, pp. 97–103.
[G: Mexico]

de Vries, Rimmer. Proceedings of the Seminar on International Economic Problems: Statement. In *U.S. Congress, Joint Economic Committee (I)*, 1981, pp. 319–35.
[G: U.S.; Selected Countries]

Wabe, J. S. Energy Expenditure in Sectors of Manufacturing. *Energy Econ.*, July 1981, 3(3), pp. 178–81.
[G: Yugoslavia; France; India; Japan; Mexico]

Wagner, H. F. Energy in Europe: Demand, Forecast, Control and Supply. In *Amman, F. and Wilson, R., eds.*, 1981, pp. 23–97.
[G: W. Europe]

Waidelich, C. J. Proceedings of the Seminar on Energy: Statement. In *U.S. Congress, Joint Eco-*

nomic Committee (I), 1981, pp. 555–59.
[G: U.S.]

Warkov, Seymour. Environmental Orientations and Solar Adoption. In *Mann, D. E., ed.*, 1981, pp. 77–86.
[G: U.S.]

Warriner, G. Keith. Electricity Consumption by the Elderly: Policy Implications. *J. Cons. Res.*, December 1981, 8(3), pp. 258–64.
[G: U.S.]

Watkins, G. Campbell. Canadian Oil Exports to the USA: From Profusion to Parsimony. *Energy Econ.*, October 1981, 3(4), pp. 219–24.
[G: U.S.; Canada]

Watkins, G. Campbell and Berndt, Ernst R. Energy Output Coefficients: Complex Realities behind Simple Ratios. In *Tempest, P., ed.*, 1981, pp. 93–98.
[G: Canada]

Waverman, Leonard. The Distribution of Resource Rents: For Whom the Firm Tolls. In *Nemetz, P. N., ed.*, 1981, pp. 255–79.
[G: Canada]

Weaver, Robert C. The Politics of Scarcity. In *Pious, R. M., ed.*, 1981, pp. 233–48.
[G: U.S.]

Webb, Steven B. The Impact of Increased Alcohol Production on Agriculture: A Simulation Study. *Amer. J. Agr. Econ.*, August 1981, 63(3), pp. 532–37.
[G: U.S.]

Weisz, George. Non-proliferation and Safeguards: National Views: Views from the United States. In *Atlantic Inst. for Internat. Affairs and Amer. Nucl. Society*, 1981, pp. 60–63.
[G: U.S.]

Weitzman, Martin L. Sequential R&D Strategy for Synfuels. *Bell J. Econ. (See Rand J. Econ. after 4/85)*, Autumn 1981, 12(2), pp. 574–90.
[G: U.S.]

West, Edwin G. and McKee, Michael. The Public Choice of Price Control and Rationing of Oil. *Southern Econ. J.*, July 1981, 48(1), pp. 204–10.

Williams, Edward J. U.S.–Mexican Energy Relations: Ambiguity and Fragility. In *Ladman, J. R.; Baldwin, D. J. and Bergman, E., eds.*, 1981, pp. 3–16.
[G: Mexico; U.S.]

Williams, Martin and Laumas, Prem S. The Relation between Energy and Non-Energy Inputs in India's Manufacturing Industries. *J. Ind. Econ.*, December 1981, 30(2), pp. 113–22.
[G: India]

Wilson, Ernest J., III. National Energy Profiles: Nigeria. In *Stunkel, K. R., ed.*, 1981, pp. 315–58.
[G: Nigeria]

Winger, John G. Financing U.S. Petroleum Supply: Need vs. Reality. In *U.S. Congress, Joint Economic Committee (I)*, 1981, 1980, pp. 515–30.
[G: U.S.]

Wiorkowski, John J. Estimating Volumes of Remaining Fossil Fuel Resources: A Critical Review. *J. Amer. Statist. Assoc.*, September 1981, 76(375), pp. 534–48.
[G: U.S.]

Wolf, Charles, Jr.; Relles, Daniel A. and Navarro, Jaime. Oil and Energy Demand in Developing Countries in 1990. *Energy J.*, October 1981, 2(4), pp. 1–24.
[G: non OPEC LDCs]

Wolf, Thomas A. Modelling Energy in the Soviet Economy: Differences between SOVMOD and SOVSIM. *ACES Bull. (See Comp. Econ. Stud. after 8/85)*, Fall–Winter 1981, 23(3–4), pp. 73–79.
[G: U.S.S.R.]

Wonder, Bernard and Simpson, David. Economics of Large-Scale and On-Farm Production of Fuel from Crops. *Quart. Rev. Rural Econ.*, November 1981, *3*(4), pp. 333–35.

Yager, Joseph A. Energy in America's Future: The Difficult Transition. In *Goodwin, C. D., ed.*, 1981, pp. 637–63. **[G: U.S.]**

Yager, Joseph A. The Energy Battles of 1979. In *Goodwin, C. D., ed.*, 1981, pp. 601–36.
[G: U.S.]

Yanagida, John F. and Conway, Roger K. The Effect of Energy Price Increases on the U.S. Livestock Sector. *Can. J. Agr. Econ.*, November 1981, *29*(3), pp. 295–302. **[G: U.S.]**

Zausner, Eric R. Energy: A Time for Choices. In *Cleveland, H., ed.*, 1981, pp. 153–65. **[G: U.S.]**

Zilberfarb, Ben-Zion and Adams, F. Gerard. The Energy-GDP Relationship in Developing Countries: Empirical Evidence and Stability Tests. *Energy Econ.*, October 1981, *3*(4), pp. 244–48.
[G: LDCs]

Zionts, S. and Deshpande, D. Energy Planning Using a Multiple Criteria Decision Method. In *Nijkamp, P. and Spronk, J., eds.*, 1981, pp. 153–62. **[G: U.S.]**

Akins, James E. OPEC Actions: Consumer Reactions 1970–2000. In *OPEC, Public Information Dept.*, 1981, pp. 215–38. **[G: OPEC]**

730 ECONOMIC GEOGRAPHY

731 Economic Geography

7310 Economic Geography

Abler, Ronald and Falk, Thomas. Public Information Services and the Changing Role of Distance in Human Affairs. *Econ. Geogr.*, January 1981, *57*(1), pp. 10–22.

Agnew, J. A. Homeownership and the Capitalist Social Order. In *Dear, M. and Scott, A. J., eds.*, 1981, pp. 457–80. **[G: U.K.; U.S.]**

Beyers, William B. Alternative Spatial Linkage Structures in Multiregional Economic Systems. In *Rees, J.; Hewings, G. J. D. and Stafford, H. A., eds.*, 1981, pp. 73–90.

Bolin, Olof. Regional Disparities in Agriculture: Comment. *Europ. Rev. Agr. Econ.*, 1981, *8*(2–3), pp. 211–12. **[G: Europe]**

Breheny, Michael J.; Green, Jacqueline and Roberts, Anthony J. A Practical Approach to the Assessment of Hypermarket Impact. *Reg. Stud.*, 1981, *15*(6), pp. 459–74. **[G: U.K.]**

Burnett, Pat. Theoretical Advances in Modeling Economic and Social Behaviors: Applications to Geographical, Policy-Oriented Models. *Econ. Geogr.*, October 1981, *57*(4), pp. 291–303.

Chisholm, Michael; Devereux, Bernard and Versey, Roy. The Myth of Non-partisan Cartography: The Tale Continued. *Urban Stud.*, June 1981, *18*(2), pp. 213–18. **[G: U.K.]**

Cox, Kevin R. Capitalism and Conflict Around the Communal Living Space. In *Dear, M. and Scott, A. J., eds.*, 1981, pp. 432–55.

Dabrowski, P. H. Regional Disparities in Agriculture. *Europ. Rev. Agr. Econ.*, 1981, *8*(2–3), pp. 199–209. **[G: Europe]**

Daniels, P. W. Transport Changes Generated by De-

centralized Offices: A Second Survey. *Reg. Stud.*, 1981, *15*(6), pp. 507–20. **[G: U.K.]**

Dear, Michael. Social and Spatial Reproduction of the Mentally Ill. In *Dear, M. and Scott, A. J., eds.*, 1981, pp. 481–97.

Gauthier, Howard L. and Mitchelson, Ronald L. Attribute Importance and Mode Satisfaction in Travel Mode Choice Research. *Econ. Geogr.*, October 1981, *57*(4), pp. 348–61. **[G: Canada]**

Hanson, Susan and Hanson, Perry. The Travel-Activity Patterns of Urban Residents: Dimensions and Relationships to Sociodemographic Characteristics. *Econ. Geogr.*, October 1981, *57*(4), pp. 332–47. **[G: Sweden]**

Harvey, David. The Urban Process under Capitalism: A Framework for Analysis. In *Dear, M. and Scott, A. J., eds.*, 1981, pp. 91–121.

Hay, Alan M. The Economic Basis of Spontaneous Home Improvement: A Graphical Analysis. *Urban Stud.*, October 1981, *18*(3), pp. 359–64.

Hodgson, M. John. A Location-Allocation Model Maximizing Consumers' Welfare. *Reg. Stud.*, 1981, *15*(6), pp. 493–506. **[G: Canada]**

Huff, James O. Rich Man-Poor Man in von Thünen's Isolated State. *Econ. Geogr.*, April 1981, *57*(2), pp. 127–33.

Johnston, R. J. and Rossiter, D. J. Shape and the Definition of Parliamentary Constituencies. *Urban Stud.*, June 1981, *18*(2), pp. 219–23.
[G: U.K.]

Kwon, Won-Yong. A Study of the Economic Impact of Industrial Relocation: The Case of Seoul. *Urban Stud.*, February 1981, *18*(1), pp. 73–90.
[G: S. Korea]

Lentnek, Barry; Harwitz, Mitchell and Narula, Subhash C. Spatial Choice in Consumer Behavior: Towards a Contextual Theory of Demand. *Econ. Geogr.*, October 1981, *57*(4), pp. 362–72.

Louviere, Jordan J. A Conceptual and Analytical Framework for Understanding Spatial and Travel Choices. *Econ. Geogr.*, October 1981, *57*(4), pp. 304–14.

Martin, R. L. Regional Wage Inflation and Unemployment: Introduction. In *Martin, R. L., ed.*, 1981, pp. 1–16. **[G: OECD]**

Massey, Doreen. The UK Electrical Engineering and Electronics Industries: The Implications of the Crisis for the Restructuring of Capital and Locational Change. In *Dear, M. and Scott, A. J., eds.*, 1981, pp. 199–230. **[G: U.K.]**

Meir, Avinoam. Innovation Diffusion and Regional Economic Development: The Spatial Diffusion of Automobiles in Ohio. *Reg. Stud.*, 1981, *15*(2), pp. 111–22. **[G: U.S.]**

Mulligan, Gordon F. The Urbanization Ratio and the Rank-Size Distribution: A Comment [Additional Properties of a Hierarchical City-Size Model]. *J. Reg. Sci.*, May 1981, *21*(2), pp. 283–85.

Nader, George A. The Delineation of a Hierarchy of Nodal Regions by Means of Higher-order Factor Analysis. *Reg. Stud.*, 1981, *15*(6), pp. 475–92. **[G: Canada]**

Pack, Stirling. Performance Component Evolution in the Multiplant Corporate Sector: The Integrated Oil Industry Example. In *Rees, J.; Hew-*

ings, G. J. D. and Stafford, H. A., eds., 1981, pp. 59–71.

Paine, Suzanne. Spatial Aspects of Chinese Development: Issues, Outcomes and Policies, 1949–79. *J. Devel. Stud.*, January 1981, *17*(2), pp. 135–95. **[G: China]**

Pipkin, J. S. The Concept of Choice and Cognitive Explanations of Spatial Behavior. *Econ. Geogr.*, October 1981, *57*(4), pp. 315–31.

Recker, Wilfred and Schuler, Harry J. Destination Choice and Processing Spatial Information: Some Empirical Tests with Alternative Constructs. *Econ. Geogr.*, October 1981, *57*(4), pp. 373–83.

Rose, Damaris. Accumulation versus Reproduction in the Inner City: *The Recurrent Crisis of London Revisited.* In *Dear, M. and Scott, A. J., eds.,* 1981, pp. 339–81. **[G: U.K.]**

Seley, John E. New Directions in Public Services: Introduction. *Econ. Geogr.*, January 1981, *57*(1), pp. 1–9. **[G: U.S.]**

Stephens, John D. and Holly, Brian P. City System Behaviour and Corporate Influence: The Headquarters Location of US Industrial Firms, 1955–75. *Urban Stud.*, October 1981, *18*(3), pp. 285–300. **[G: U.S.]**

Walker, Richard A. A Theory of Suburbanization: Capitalism and the Construction of Urban Space in the United States. In *Dear, M. and Scott, A. J., eds.,* 1981, pp. 383–429.

Wheeler, James O. Effects of Geographical Scale on Location Decisions in Manufacturing: The Atlanta Example. *Econ. Geogr.*, April 1981, *57*(2), pp. 134–45. **[G: U.S.]**

Whitmore, Harland William, Jr. Plant Location and the Demand for Investment: A Theoretical Analysis. *J. Reg. Sci.*, February 1981, *21*(1), pp. 89–101.

800 Manpower; Labor; Population

8000 General

Ramstad, Yngve. Institutional Economics: How Prevalent in the Labor Literature? *J. Econ. Issues*, June 1981, *15*(2), pp. 339–50. **[G: U.S.]**

Soltow, Martha Jane. Twenty Year Cumulative Index to Labor History: Vol. 1, No. 1 (Spring, 1960)—Vol. 20, No. 4 (Fall, 1979). *Labor Hist.*, Winter 1981, *22*(1), pp. 57–135.

Voronin, E. Utilize Labor Resources More Completely. *Prob. Econ.*, July 1981, *24*(3), pp. 20–35. **[G: U.S.S.R.]**

Weber, Arnold R. The Changing Labor Market Environment in the 1980s. *Nebr. J. Econ. Bus.*, Winter 1981, *20*(1), pp. 5–17. **[G: U.S.]**

810 MANPOWER TRAINING AND ALLOCATION; LABOR FORCE AND SUPPLY

811 Manpower Training and Development

8110 Manpower Training and Development

Bartels, Martin. Mining Ventures in Developing Countries: Localization of Labor. In *Schanze, E.,*

et al., 1981, pp. 198–211. **[G: Selected LDCs]**

Bertrand, Olivier; Timár, János and Achio, Françoise. The Planning of Training in the Third World. *Int. Lab. Rev.*, September–October 1981, *120*(5), pp. 531–44. **[G: LDCs]**

Caire, Guy. Automation: technologie, travail, relations sociales (Sur quelques travaux récents relatifs à l'automation: réponses et questions). (Automation, Technology, Labour, Social Relations. Answers and Questions on Recent Studies on Automation. With English summary.) *Consommation*, January–March 1981, *28*(1), pp. 51–84.

Ciscel, David H. and Tuckman, Barbara H. The Peripheral Worker: CETA Training as Imperfect Job Socialization. *J. Econ. Issues*, June 1981, *15*(2), pp. 489–500. **[G: U.S.]**

Coates, Mary Lou. Manpower and Labour Markets: Summary Outline. In *Wood, W. D. and Kumar, P., eds.,* 1981, pp. 27–94. **[G: Canada]**

Danziger, Sandra K. Postprogram Changes in the Lives of AFDC Supported Work Participants: A Qualitative Assessment. *J. Human Res.*, Fall 1981, *16*(4), pp. 637–48. **[G: U.S.]**

Dement, Edward F. North Carolina Balance-of-State Decentralization and Discontinuity. In *Levitan, S. A. and Mangum, G. L., eds.,* 1981, pp. 263–93. **[G: U.S.]**

Denton, Frank T. Comment on 'Diagnosing Labour Market Imbalances in Canada.' *Can. Public Policy*, Spring 1981, *7*(2), pp. 338–42. **[G: Canada]**

Dickinson, Katherine P. Supported Work for Ex-Addicts: An Exploration of Endogenous Tastes. *J. Human Res.*, Fall 1981, *16*(4), pp. 551–99. **[G: U.S.]**

Doran, Howard E. and Deen, Rozany R. The Use of Linear Difference Equations in Manpower Planning: A Criticism. *J. Devel. Econ.*, April 1981, *8*(2), pp. 193–204.

Ebel, Karl-H. The Microelectronics Training Gap in the Metal Trades. *Int. Lab. Rev.*, November–December 1981, *120*(6), pp. 727–39.

Ghosh, Ranen. An Empirically Testable Mathematical Model of Manpower for the Sixth Five Year Plan of India. *Econ. Aff.*, July–September 1981, *26*(3), pp. 182–87. **[G: India]**

Green, G. D. Training for Self-Reliance in Rural Areas. *Int. Lab. Rev.*, July–August 1981, *120*(4), pp. 411–23. **[G: E. Africa; S. Africa]**

Harris, G. T. Job Creation Schemes: Some Lessons from the New Zealand Experience. *Australian Bull. Lab.*, March 1981, *7*(2), pp. 67–87. **[G: New Zealand]**

Hill, Michael. Unemployment and Government Manpower Policy. In *Showler, B. and Sinfield, A., eds.,* 1981, pp. 89–121. **[G: U.K.]**

Hinckley, Robert. Black Teenage Unemployment. *J. Econ. Issues*, June 1981, *15*(2), pp. 501–12. **[G: U.S.]**

Hoffman, Saul D. On-the-Job Training: Differences by Race and Sex. *Mon. Lab. Rev.*, July 1981, *104*(7), pp. 34–36. **[G: U.S.]**

Horowitz, Morris A. and Loscalzo, Joanne. Worcester, Massachusetts: Decentralization in a Tight Labor Market. In *Levitan, S. A. and Mangum, G. L., eds.,* 1981, pp. 411–30. **[G: U.S.]**

Johannesson, Jan. On the Composition of Swedish Labor Market Policy. In *Eliasson, G.; Holmlund, B. and Stafford, F. P., eds.*, 1981, pp. 67–137. [G: Sweden]

Joyce, John T. Toward a New U.S. Industrial Policy? Strategies for Training and Retraining: Comment. In *Wachter, M. L. and Wachter, S. M., eds.*, 1981, pp. 282–85. [G: U.S.]

Karabín, Stefan. For a More Effective Use of Manpower. *Czech. Econ. Digest.*, February 1981, (1), pp. 38–53. [G: Czechoslovakia]

Kubursi, Atif A. Vocational and Technical Education and Development Needs in the Arab World. In *Sherbiny, N. A., ed.*, 1981, pp. 91–108. [G: Arab Countries]

Levitan, Sar A. and Mangum, Garth L. The T in CETA: Summary of Findings and Recommendations. In *Levitan, S. A. and Mangum, G. L., eds.*, 1981, pp. 1–91. [G: U.S.]

Long, David A.; Mallar, Charles D. and Thornton, Craig V. D. Evaluating the Benefits and Costs of the Job Corps. *J. Policy Anal. Manage.*, Fall 1981, *1*(1), pp. 55–76. [G: U.S.]

Lovell, Malcolm R., Jr. Toward a New U.S. Industrial Policy? Strategies for Training and Retraining: Comment. In *Wachter, M. L. and Wachter, S. M., eds.*, 1981, pp. 281–82. [G: U.S.]

Mangum, Garth L. San Francisco: The Politics of Race and Sex. In *Levitan, S. A. and Mangum, G. L., eds.*, 1981, pp. 323–43. [G: U.S.]

Mangum, Garth L. Tucson, Arizona: Orchestrated Decentralization. In *Levitan, S. A. and Mangum, G. L., eds.*, 1981, pp. 365–85. [G: U.S.]

Masters, Stanley H. The Effects of Supported Work on the Earnings and Transfer Payments of Its AFDC Target Group. *J. Human Res.*, Fall 1981, *16*(4), pp. 600–636. [G: U.S.]

McPherson, Robert. Dallas, Texas: The Burdens of Prosperity. In *Levitan, S. A. and Mangum, G. L., eds.*, 1981, pp. 177–206. [G: U.S.]

Mills, D. Quinn. The Human Resource Consequences of Industrial Revitalization. In *Wachter, M. L. and Wachter, S. M., eds.*, 1981, pp. 257–80. [G: U.S.]

Newton, Keith; Betcherman, Gordon and Meltz, Noah. Diagnosing Labour Market Imbalances in Canada. *Can. Public Policy*, Winter 1981, *7*(1), pp. 94–102. [G: Canada]

Paik, Soon and Hall, Gary A. Craft Requirements for Construction of Electric Power Plants. *Growth Change*, October 1981, *12*(4), pp. 16–21. [G: U.S.]

Pines, Marion W. Montgomery County, Maryland: A Born-Again Prime Sponsor. In *Levitan, S. A. and Mangum, G. L., eds.*, 1981, pp. 235–61. [G: U.S.]

Robson, R. Thayne. Seattle, Washington: A CBO Delivery System. In *Levitan, S. A. and Mangum, G. L., eds.*, 1981, pp. 345–63. [G: U.S.]

Robson, R. Thayne. Utah: The Perils of Pioneering. In *Levitan, S. A. and Mangum, G. L., eds.*, 1981, pp. 387–409. [G: U.S.]

Sadowski, Dieter. Finance and Governance of the German Apprenticeship System: Some Considerations on Market Failure and Its Efficient Corrections. *Z. ges. Staatswiss.*, June 1981, *137*(2),

pp. 234–51.

Sahaya, R. and Verma, R. P. Man-Power Planning—A Study on the Five Year Plan. *Econ. Aff.*, April–June 1981, *26*(2), pp. 110–16. [G: India]

Schlicht, Ekkehart. Training Costs and Wage Differentials in the Theory of Job Competition. *Z. ges. Staatswiss.*, June 1981, *137*(2), pp. 212–21.

Serageldin, M. Ismail. The Modeling and Methodology of Manpower Planning in the Arab Countries. In *Sherbiny, N. A., ed.*, 1981, pp. 55–90. [G: Arab Countries]

Shapiro, Edward. Wage Inflation, Manpower Training, and the Phillips Curve: A Graphic Integration. *Amer. Econ.*, Spring 1981, *25*(1), pp. 17–21.

Shaw, R. Paul. Manpower and Educational Shortages in the Arab World: An Interim Strategy. *World Devel.*, July 1981, *9*(7), pp. 637–55. [G: Arab Countries]

Showler, Brian and Sinfield, Adrian. A Most Unequal Tax. In *Showler, B. and Sinfield, A., eds.*, 1981, pp. 215–40. [G: U.K.]

Sloan, Stephen B. How Milliken Measures Training Program Effectiveness. *Manage. Account.*, July 1981, *63*(1), pp. 37–41. [G: U.S.]

Sorrentino, Constance. Unemployment in International Perspective. In *Showler, B. and Sinfield, A., eds.*, 1981, pp. 167–214. [G: OECD]

Sum, Andrew M. and Harrington, Paul E. Penobscot Consortium, Maine: Orientation for Change and Growth. In *Levitan, S. A. and Mangum, G. L., eds.*, 1981, pp. 295–322. [G: U.S.]

Taggart, Robert. A Review of CETA Training. In *Levitan, S. A. and Mangum, G. L., eds.*, 1981, pp. 93–144. [G: U.S.]

Tesař, Vladimír. Training and Incentives to Training in the Czechoslovak Engineering Industry. *Int. Lab. Rev.*, March–April 1981, *120*(2), pp. 201–14. [G: Czechoslovakia]

Voronin, E. Utilize Labor Resources More Completely. *Prob. Econ.*, July 1981, *24*(3), pp. 20–35. [G: U.S.S.R.]

Wright, E. Earl. Indianapolis, Indiana: Recovering from Troubles. In *Levitan, S. A. and Mangum, G. L., eds.*, 1981, pp. 207–33. [G: U.S.]

Wurzburg, Gregory. Baltimore, Maryland: The Rewards of Sound Management and Planning. In *Levitan, S. A. and Mangum, G. L., eds.*, 1981, pp. 147–75. [G: U.S.]

Zhamin, Vitali A. and Popov, Grigori M. Public Education and Training of the Labor Force. In *Novosti Press Agency*, 1981, pp. 230–47. [G: U.S.S.R.]

812 Occupation

8120 Occupation

Abed, George T. and Kubursi, Atif A. A Macroeconomic Simulation Model of High Level Manpower Requirements in Iraq. In *Sherbiny, N. A., ed.*, 1981, pp. 145–71. [G: Iraq]

Ake, Claude. Kenya. In *Adedeji, A., ed.*, 1981, pp. 187–203. [G: Kenya]

Atwater, Donald M.; Niehaus, Richard J. and Sheridan, James A. Labor Pool for Antibias Program

Varies by Occupation and Job Market. *Mon. Lab. Rev.*, September 1981, *104*(9), pp. 43–45. [G: U.S.]

Benson, Susan Porter. The Cinderalla of Occupations: Managing the Work of Department Store Saleswomen, 1900–1940. *Bus. Hist. Rev.*, Spring 1981, *55*(1), pp. 1–25. [G: U.S.]

Bergmann, Barbara R. The Economic Risks of Being a Housewife. *Amer. Econ. Rev.*, May 1981, *71*(2), pp. 81–86. [G: U.S.]

Betson, David and Bishop, John. Reform of the Tax System to Stimulate Labor Supply: Efficiency and Distributional Effects. **In** *Dennis, B. D., ed.*, 1981, pp. 307–15. [G: U.S.]

Bosworth, Derek L. The Demand for Qualified Scientists and Engineers. *Appl. Econ.*, December 1981, *13*(4), pp. 411–29. [G: U.K.]

Brenner, Reuven and Kiefer, Nicholas M. The Economics of the Diaspora: Discrimination and Occupational Structure. *Econ. Develop. Cult. Change*, April 1981, *29*(3), pp. 517–34. [G: U.S.; Middle East]

Burns, Leland S. and Van Ness, Kathy. The Decline of the Metropolitan Economy. *Urban Stud.*, June 1981, *18*(2), pp. 169–80. [G: U.S.]

Cabral, Robert; Ferber, Marianne A. and Green, Carole A. Men and Women in Fiduciary Institutions: A Study of Sex Differences in Career Development. *Rev. Econ. Statist.*, November 1981, *63*(4), pp. 573–80.

Carey, Max L. Occupational Employment Growth through 1990. *Mon. Lab. Rev.*, August 1981, *104*(8), pp. 42–55. [G: U.S.]

Carroll, Sidney L. and Gaston, Robert J. Occupational Restrictions and the Quality of Service Received: Some Evidence. *Southern Econ. J.*, April 1981, *47*(4), pp. 959–76. [G: U.S.]

Coates, Mary Lou. Manpower and Labour Markets: Summary Outline. **In** *Wood, W. D. and Kumar, P., eds.*, 1981, pp. 27–94. [G: Canada]

Collier, Paul and Bigsten, Arne. A Model of Educational Expansion and Labour Market Adjustment Applied to Kenya. *Oxford Bull. Econ. Statist.*, February 1981, *43*(1), pp. 31–49. [G: Kenya]

Corcoran, Mary and Datcher, Linda P. Intergenerational Status Transmission and the Process of Individual Attainment. **In** *Hill, M. S.; Hill, D. H. and Morgan, J. N., eds.*, 1981, pp. 169–206. [G: U.S.]

Cottle, Rex L. and Lawson, Rodger S. Leisure as Work: A Case in Professional Sports. *Atlantic Econ. J.*, September 1981, *9*(3), pp. 50–59.

De Freitas, Gregory E. What is the Occupational Mobility of Black Immigrants? *Mon. Lab. Rev.*, April 1981, *104*(4), pp. 44–45. [G: U.S.]

DeFreitas, Gregory E. Occupational Mobility Among Recent Black Immigrants. **In** *Dennis, B. D., ed.*, 1981, pp. 41–47. [G: U.S.]

Denton, Frank T. Comment on 'Diagnosing Labour Market Imbalances in Canada.' *Can. Public Policy*, Spring 1981, *7*(2), pp. 338–42. [G: Canada]

Fajana, Olufemi. Aspects of Income Distribution in the Nigerian Urban Sector. **In** *Bienen, H. and Diejomaoh, V. P., eds.*, 1981, pp. 193–236. [G: Nigeria]

Feldstein, Martin S. and Taylor, Amy. The Rapid Rise of Hospital Costs. **In** *Feldstein, M., ed.*, 1981, *1977*, pp. 19–56. [G: U.S.]

Fieleke, Norman S. Productivity and Labor Mobility in Japan, the United Kingdom, and the United States. *New Eng. Econ. Rev.*, November/December 1981, pp. 27–36. [G: Japan; U.K.; U.S.]

Fox, Karl A. and Ghosh, Syamal K. A Behavior Setting Approach to Social Accounts Combining Concepts and Data from Ecological Psychology, Economics, and Studies of Time Use. **In** *Juster, F. T. and Land, K. C., eds.*, 1981, pp. 131–217. [G: U.S.]

Johnson, Paul M. Changing Social Structure and the Political Role of Manual Workers. **In** *Triska, J. F. and Gati, C., eds.*, 1981, pp. 29–42. [G: E. Europe]

Jusenius, Carol L. and Scheffler, Richard M. Earnings Differentials among Academic Economists: Empirical Evidence on Race and Sex. *J. Econ. Bus.*, Winter 1981, *33*(2), pp. 88–96. [G: U.S.]

Kanbur, S. M. Risk Taking and Taxation: An Alternative Perspective. *J. Public Econ.*, April 1981, *15*(2), pp. 163–84.

Kostakov, V. G. Features of the Development of Female Employment. *Prob. Econ.*, Sept.–Oct.–Nov. 1981, *24*(5–6–7), pp. 33–68. [G: U.S.S.R.]

Kotliar, A. E. and Turchaninova, S. Ia. The Educational and Occupational Skill Level of Industrial Workers. *Prob. Econ.*, Sept.–Oct.–Nov. 1981, *24*(5–6–7), pp. 69–120. [G: U.S.S.R.]

Kutscher, Ronald E. New Economic Projections through 1900—An Overview. *Mon. Lab. Rev.*, August 1981, *104*(8), pp. 9–17. [G: U.S.]

Ladipo, O. O. and Adesimi, A. A. Income Distribution in the Rural Sector. **In** *Bienen, H. and Diejomaoh, V. P., eds.*, 1981, pp. 299–321. [G: Nigeria]

Lapidus, Gail W. The Female Industrial Labor Force: Dilemmas, Reassessments, and Options. **In** *Bornstein, M., ed.*, 1981, *1979*, pp. 119–48. [G: U.S.S.R.]

Latta, Geoffrey W. Union Organization among Engineers: A Current Assessment. *Ind. Lab. Relat. Rev.*, October 1981, *35*(1), pp. 29–42. [G: U.S.]

Lee, Linda K. A Comparison of the Rank and Salary of Male and Female Agricultural Economists. *Amer. J. Agr. Econ.*, December 1981, *63*(5), pp. 1013–18. [G: U.S.]

Leigh, J. Paul. Occupational Choice under Earnings Uncertainty. *Nebr. J. Econ. Bus.*, Winter 1981, *20*(1), pp. 59–71.

Lima, Anthony K. An Economic Model of Teaching Effectiveness. *Amer. Econ. Rev.*, December 1981, *71*(5), pp. 1056–59. [G: U.S.]

Link, Charles R. and Settle, Russell F. Wage Incentives and Married Professional Nurses: A Case of Backward-Bending Supply? *Econ. Inquiry*, January 1981, *19*(1), pp. 144–56. [G: U.S.]

Lundeen, Ardelle A. and Clauson, Annette L. The Conduct of the Survey on the Opportunities for and Status of Women in Agricultural Economics. *Amer. J. Agr. Econ.*, December 1981, *63*(5), pp. 1010–12. [G: U.S.]

Lyon, Larry and Rector-Owen, Holley. Labor Market Mobility among Young Black and White Women: Longitudinal Models of Occupational

Prestige and Income. *Soc. Sci. Quart.*, March 1981, *62*(1), pp. 64–78. [G: U.S.]

Mayhew, Ken and Rosewell, Bridget. Occupational Mobility in Britain. *Oxford Bull. Econ. Statist.*, August 1981, *43*(3), pp. 225–55. [G: U.K.]

Menzie, Elmer L. and Anderson, Teresa. Agricultural Economists in Canada: Graduates and Prospects. *Can. J. Agr. Econ.*, February 1981, *29*(1), pp. 87–92. [G: Canada]

Mills, D. Quinn. The Human Resource Consequences of Industrial Revitalization. In *Wachter, M. L. and Wachter, S. M., eds.*, 1981, pp. 257–80. [G: U.S.]

Moir, Hazel. Occupational Mobility and the Informal Sector in Jakarta. In *Sethuraman, S. V., ed.*, 1981, pp. 109–20. [G: Indonesia]

Moore, William J.; Pearce, Douglas K. and Wilson, R. Mark. The Regulation of Occupations and the Earnings of Women. *J. Human Res.*, Summer 1981, *16*(3), pp. 366–83. [G: U.S.]

Murnane, Richard J. Teacher Mobility Revisited. *J. Human Res.*, Winter 1981, *16*(1), pp. 3–19. [G: U.S.]

Newton, Keith; Betcherman, Gordon and Meltz, Noah. Diagnosing Labour Market Imbalances in Canada. *Can. Public Policy*, Winter 1981, *7*(1), pp. 94–102. [G: Canada]

Ofer, Gur and Vinokur, Aaron. Earning Differentials by Sex in the Soviet Union: A First Look. In *[Bergson, A.]*, 1981, pp. 127–62. [G: U.S.S.R.]

Parnes, Herbert S.; Gagen, Mary G. and King, Randall H. Job Loss among Long-Service Workers. In *Parnes, H. S., ed.*, 1981, pp. 65–92. [G: U.S.]

Payne, Geoff; Ford, Graeme and Ulas, Marion. Occupational Change and Social Mobility in Scotland Since the First World War. In *Gaskin, M., ed.*, 1981, pp. 200–17. [G: U.K.]

Polachek, Solomon William. Occupational Self-Selection: A Human Capital Approach to Sex Differences in Occupational Structure. *Rev. Econ. Statist.*, February 1981 *63*(1), pp. 60–69. [G: U.S.]

Redman, Barbara J. The Women Who Become Agricultural Economists. *Amer. J. Agr. Econ.*, December 1981, *63*(5), pp. 1019–24. [G: U.S.]

Reid, Frank and Smith, Douglas A. The Impact of Demographic Changes on Unemployment. *Can. Public Policy*, Spring 1981, *7*(2), pp. 348–51.

Rumberger, Russell W. The Changing Skill Requirements of Jobs in the U.S. Economy. *Ind. Lab. Relat. Rev.*, July 1981, *34*(4), pp. 578–90. [G: U.S.]

Sada, P. O. Urbanization and Income Distribution in Nigeria. In *Bienen, H. and Diejomaoh, V. P., eds.*, 1981, pp. 269–98. [G: Nigeria]

Schotzko, Ralph T. Projected Replacement Needs for Agricultural Economists: Reply. *Amer. J. Agr. Econ.*, November 1981, *63*(4), pp. 751–52. [G: U.S.]

Schrimper, R. A. Projected Replacement Needs for Agricultural Economists: Comment. *Amer. J. Agr. Econ.*, November 1981, *63*(4), pp. 748–50. [G: U.S.]

Serow, William J. Alternative Demographic Futures and the Composition of the Demand for Labor, by Industry and by Occupation. In *Simon, J. L.*

and Lindert, P. H., eds., 1981, pp. 209–23. [G: U.S.]

Shaked, Avner and Sutton, John. The Self-Regulating Profession. *Rev. Econ. Stud.*, April 1981, *48*(2), pp. 217–34.

Shishkan, N. M. Raising the Skill Level of Women Workers. *Prob. Econ.*, Sept.–Oct.–Nov. 1981, *24*(5–6–7), pp. 121–30. [G: U.S.S.R.]

Shulman, Steven. Race, Class and Occupational Stratification: A Critique of William J. Wilson's *The Declining Significance of Race*. *Rev. Radical Polit. Econ.*, Fall 1981, *13*(3), pp. 21–31. [G: U.S.]

Simms, Margaret C. and Swinton, David H. A Report on the Supply of Black Economists. *Rev. Black Polit. Econ.*, Winter 1981, *11*(2), pp. 181–202. [G: U.S.]

Singer, Leslie P. Supply Decisions of Professional Artists. *Amer. Econ. Rev.*, May 1981, *71*(2), pp. 341–46.

Smock, Audrey Chapman. Women's Economic Roles. In *Killick, T., ed.*, 1981, pp. 219–27. [G: Kenya]

Sonin, M. Ia. Socioeconomic Problems of Female Employment. *Prob. Econ.*, Sept.–Oct.–Nov. 1981, *24*(5–6–7), pp. 22–32. [G: U.S.S.R.]

Steele, G. R. University Salaries in the U.K.: A Study of Local Variations within a National Pay Structure. *Bull. Econ. Res.*, May 1981, *33*(1), pp. 14–36. [G: U.K.]

Sumner, Daniel A. Wage Functions and Occupational Selection in a Rural Less Developed Country Setting. *Rev. Econ. Statist.*, November 1981, *63*(4), pp. 513–19. [G: Guatemala]

Thompson, John. BLS Job Cross-Classification System Relates Information from Six Sources. *Mon. Lab. Rev.*, November 1981, *104*(11), pp. 40–44. [G: U.S.]

Trotter, G. J. The Supply of Economists. *S. Afr. J. Econ.*, September 1981, *49*(3), pp. 256–68. [G: S. Africa]

Van Regemorter, Denise. Evolution du nombre et du revenu des commerçants et des artisans de 1953 à 1977. (Evolution of the Number of Self Employed Tradesmen and Craftsmen and of Their Income in Belgium [1953–1977.] With English summary.) *Cah. Écon. Bruxelles*, 1st Trimestre 1981, (89), pp. 3–23. [G: Belgium]

White, Rudolph A.; Billings, C. David and Brown, Robert D., Jr. Assessing the Role of Business Schools in the Market for New Economics Ph.D.'s. *J. Econ. Educ.*, Summer 1981, *12*(2), pp. 34–44. [G: U.S.]

Whitehead, A. K. Competition in the Market for Chemists. *Appl. Econ.*, June 1981, *13*(2), pp. 267–78. [G: U.S.]

Williams, Lynne S. A Demographic Analysis of Australian Occupational Mobility. *Australian Bull. Lab.*, June 1981, *7*(3), pp. 139–73. [G: Australia]

813 Labor Force

8130 General

Abed, George T. and Kubursi, Atif A. A Macroeconomic Simulation Model of High Level Manpower Requirements in Iraq. In *Sherbiny, N. A., ed.*, 1981, pp. 145–71.   [G: Iraq]

Adams, Avril V. The American Work Force in the Eighties: New Problems and Policy Interests Require Improved Labor Force Data. *Ann. Amer. Acad. Polit. Soc. Sci.*, January 1981, *453*, pp. 123–29.   [G: U.S.]

Ashworth, J. S. and Ulph, David T. Endogeneity I: Estimating Labour Supply with Piecewise Linear Budget Constraints. In *Brown, C. V., ed.*, 1981, pp. 53–68.   [G: U.K.]

Ashworth, J. S. and Ulph, David T. Taxation and Labour Supply: Household Models. In *Brown, C. V., ed.*, 1981, pp. 117–33.   [G: U.K.]

Baines, D. E. The Labour Supply and the Labour Market 1860–1914. In *Floud, R. and McCloskey, D., eds., Vol. 2*, 1981, pp. 144–74.   [G: U.K.]

Barron, John M. and Mellow, Wesley S. Changes in Labor Force Status among the Unemployed. *J. Human Res.*, Summer 1981, *16*(3), pp. 427–41.   [G: U.S.]

Beneria, Lourdes. Conceptualizing the Labor Force: The Underestimation of Women's Economic Activities. *J. Devel. Stud.*, April 1981, *17*(3), pp. 10–28.

Bieker, Richard F. Work and Welfare: An Analysis of AFDC Participation Rates in Delaware. *Soc. Sci. Quart.*, March 1981, *62*(1), pp. 169–76.   [G: U.S.]

Blundell, Richard W. Estimating Continuous Consumer Equivalence Scales in an Expenditure Model with Labour Supply. In *Currie, D.; Nobay, R. and Peel, D., eds.*, 1981, pp. 111–35.   [G: U.K.]

Boskin, Michael J. Labor Supply: Comments. In *Aaron, H. J. and Pechman, J. A., eds.*, 1981, pp. 72–75.   [G: U.S.]

Bowers, Norman. Youth Labor Force Activity: Alternative Surveys Compared. *Mon. Lab. Rev.*, March 1981, *104*(3), pp. 3–17.   [G: U.S.]

Brown, C. V. Taxation and Labour Supply: Data Quality. In *Brown, C. V., ed.*, 1981, pp. 11–20.   [G: U.K.]

Brown, C. V. Taxation and Labour Supply: Sample Selection and Questionnaire Design. In *Brown, C. V., ed.*, 1981, pp. 5–10.

Brown, C. V. Taxation and Labour Supply: Summary of Results. In *Brown, C. V., ed.*, 1981, pp. 134–43.   [G: U.K.]

Brown, C. V. and Levin, E. Taxation and Labour Supply: The Interview Approach. In *Brown, C. V., ed.*, 1981, pp. 21–34.   [G: U.K.]

Brown, C. V.; Levin, E. and Ulph, David T. Inflation, Taxation and Income Distribution. In *Brown, C. V., ed.*, 1981, *1977*, pp. 255–68.   [G: U.K.; Australia]

Brown, C. V.; Levin, E. and Ulph, David T. Taxation and Labour Supply: The Basic Model. In *Brown, C. V., ed.*, 1981, pp. 35–52.   [G: U.K.]

Browne, Lynn E. A Quality Labor Supply. *New Eng. Econ. Rev.*, July/August 1981, pp. 19–36.   [G: U.S.]

Burtless, Gary. Labor Supply: Comments. In *Aaron, H. J. and Pechman, J. A., eds.*, 1981, pp. 76–83.   [G: U.S.]

Coates, Mary Lou. Manpower and Labour Markets: Summary Outline. In *Wood, W. D. and Kumar, P., eds.*, 1981, pp. 27–94.   [G: Canada]

Cogan, John F. Fixed Costs and Labor Supply. *Econometrica*, June 1981, *49*(4), pp. 945–63.   [G: U.S.]

Corcoran, Mary and MacKenzie, Abigail. Expected Wages and Men's Labor Supply. In *Hill, M. S.; Hill, D. H. and Morgan, J. N., eds.*, 1981, pp. 245–68.   [G: U.S.]

Creedy, John and Disney, Richard. Changes in Labour Market States in Great Britain. *Scot. J. Polit. Econ.*, February 1981, *28*(1), pp. 76–85.   [G: U.K.]

Dugger, William M. The Administered Labor Market: An Institutional Analysis. *J. Econ. Issues*, June 1981, *15*(2), pp. 397–407.   [G: U.S.]

Eason, Warren W. Selected Problems of Regional Development in the USSR: Population and Labor Force. In *Koropeckyj, I. S. and Schroeder, G. E., eds.*, 1981, pp. 11–91.   [G: U.S.S.R.]

Ellis, Gene. The Backward-bending Supply Curve of Labor in Africa: Models, Evidence, and Interpretation—and Why It Makes a Difference. *J. Devel. Areas*, January 1981, *15*(2), pp. 251–73.   [G: Africa]

Farkas, George; Olsen, Randall J. and Stromsdorfer, Ernst W. Youth Labor Supply During the Summer: Evidence for Youths from Low-Income Households. In *Ehrenberg, R. G., ed.*, 1981, pp. 151–90.   [G: U.S.]

Fedorova, M. The Utilization of Female Labor in Agriculture. *Prob. Econ.*, Sept.–Oct.–Nov. 1981, *24*(5–6–7), pp. 131–46.   [G: U.S.S.R.]

Ferber, Marianne A. and Birnbaum, Bonnie G. Labor Force Participation Patterns and Earnings of Women Clerical Workers. *J. Human Res.*, Summer 1981, *16*(3), pp. 416–26.   [G: U.S.]

Finegan, T. Aldrich. Discouraged Workers and Economic Fluctuations. *Ind. Lab. Relat. Rev.*, October 1981, *35*(1), pp. 88–102.   [G: U.S.]

Foster, William. Gross Flows in the Australian Labour Market: A First Look. *Australian Econ. Rev.*, 4th Quarter 1981, (56), pp. 57–64.   [G: Australia]

Franz, Wolfgang and Kawasaki, S. Labor Supply of Married Women in the Federal Republic of Germany: Theory and Empirical Results from a New Estimation Procedure. *Empirical Econ.*, 1981, *6*(2), pp. 129–43.   [G: W. Germany]

Freedman, David H. Work in Nigeria: A Cornerstone of Meeting the Needs of the People. *Int. Lab. Rev.*, November–December 1981, *120*(6), pp. 751–63.   [G: Nigeria]

Freeman, Richard B. Black Economic Progress after 1964: Who Has Gained and Why? In *Rosen, S., ed.*, 1981, pp. 247–94.   [G: U.S.]

Glaister, K. W.; McGlone, A. and Ruffell, R. J. Taxation and Labour Supply: Preferences. In *Brown, C. V., ed.*, 1981, pp. 69–100.   [G: U.K.]

Glaister, K. W.; McGlone, A. and Ulph, David T. Labour Supply Responses to Tax Changes. In *Brown, C. V., ed.*, 1981, pp. 163–88.   [G: U.K.]

Grant, James H. and Hamermesh, Daniel S. Labor Market Competition among Youths, White Women and Others. *Rev. Econ. Statist.*, August 1981, *63*(3), pp. 354–60.   [G: U.S.]

Gustman, Alan L. and Steinmeier, Thomas L. The Impact of Wages and Unemployment on Youth Enrollment and Labor Supply. *Rev. Econ. Statist.*, November 1981, *63*(4), pp. 553–60. [G: U.S.]

Hausman, Jerry A. Income and Payroll Tax Policy and Labor Supply. In *Meyer, L. H., ed.*, 1981, pp. 173–202. [G: U.S.]

Hausman, Jerry A. Labor Supply. In *Aaron, H. J. and Pechman, J. A., eds.*, 1981, pp. 27–72. [G: U.S.]

Heckman, James J. Heterogeneity and State Dependence. In *Rosen, S., ed.*, 1981, pp. 91–139. [G: U.S.]

Heckman, James J. and MaCurdy, Thomas E. New Methods for Estimating Labor Supply Functions: A Survey. In *Ehrenberg, R. G., ed.*, 1981, pp. 65–102. [G: U.S.]

Heggade, O. D. Development of Women Entrepreneurship in India—Problems and Prospects. *Econ. Aff.*, January–March 1981, *26*(1), pp. 39–50. [G: India]

Ingham, A. Estimating Continuous Consumer Equivalence Scales in an Expenditure Model with Labour Supply: Comment. In *Currie, D.; Nobay, R. and Peel, D., eds.*, 1981, pp. 136–38. [G: U.K.]

Joshi, Heather E. Secondary Workers in the Employment Cycle: Great Britain, 1961–1974. *Economica*, February 1981, *48*(189), pp. 29–44. [G: U.K.]

Killingsworth, Mark R. A Survey of Labor Supply Models: Theoretical Analyses and First-Generation Empirical Results. In *Ehrenberg, R. G., ed.*, 1981, pp. 1–53. [G: U.S]

Koç, Yildirim. Planli Dönemde Işçh Hareketini Belirleyen Etkenler. (Factors Determining the Labor Movement in Turkey in the Planned Period. With English summary.) *METU*, Special Issue, 1981, pp. 287–348. [G: Turkey]

Kutscher, Ronald E. New Economic Projections through 1900—An Overview. *Mon. Lab. Rev.*, August 1981, *104*(8), pp. 9–17. [G: U.S.]

Lapidus, Gail W. The Female Industrial Labor Force: Dilemmas, Reassessments, and Options. In *Bornstein, M., ed.*, 1981, *1979*, pp. 119–48. [G: U.S.S.R.]

Lapidus, Gail W. Women, Work, and Family: New Soviet Perspectives: Introduction. *Prob. Econ.*, Sept.–Oct.–Nov. 1981, *24*(5–6–7), pp. ix–xlvi. [G: U.S.S.R.]

Lehrer, Evelyn and Nerlove, Marc. The Labor Supply and Fertility Behavior of Married Women: A Three-Period Model. In *Simon, J. L. and Lindert, P. H., eds.*, 1981, pp. 123–45. [G: U.S.]

Lemennicier, Bertrand and Lévy-Garboua, Louis. L'arbitrage autarcie-marché: Une explication du travail féminin. (The Autarky/Market Trade-off: An Explanation of Female Labor. With English summary.) *Consommation*, April–June 1981, *28*(2), pp. 41–74. [G: France]

Leon, Carol Boyd. The Employment–Population Ratio: Its Value in Labor Force Analysis. *Mon. Lab. Rev.*, February 1981, *104*(2), pp. 36–45. [G: U.S.]

Lever, William F. The Inner City Employment Problem in Great Britain, 1952–76: A Shift–Share Approach. In *Rees, J.; Hewings, G. J. D. and Stafford, H. A., eds.*, 1981, pp. 171–96. [G: U.K.]

Levitan, Sar A. and Belous, Richard S. Working Wives and Mothers: What Happens to Family Life? *Mon. Lab. Rev.*, September 1981, *104*(9), pp. 26–30. [G: U.S.]

de la Luz Silva, Maria. Urban Poverty and Child Work: Elements for the Analysis of Child Work in Chile. In *Rodgers, G. and Standing, G., eds.*, 1981, pp. 159–77. [G: Chile]

Marmor, Theodore R. Political Perspective on Social Security Financing: Comment. In *Skidmore, F., ed.*, 1981, pp. 224–29. [G: U.S.]

Marzouk, M. Shokri. An Econometric/Input–Output Approach for Projecting Sectoral Manpower Requirements: The Case of Kuwait. In *Sherbiny, N. A., ed.*, 1981, pp. 111–44. [G: Kuwait]

Mayhew, Ken. Incomes Policy and the Private Sector. In *Fallick, J. L. and Elliott, R. F., eds.*, 1981, pp. 72–99. [G: U.K.]

McElroy, Marjorie B. A Survey of Labor Supply Models: Theoretical Analyses and First-Generation Empirical Results: Appendix: Empirical Results from Estimates of Joint Labor Supply Functions of Husbands and Wives. In *Ehrenberg, R. G., ed.*, 1981, pp. 53–64. [G: U.S.]

Mills, D. Quinn. The Human Resource Consequences of Industrial Revitalization. In *Wachter, M. L. and Wachter, S. M., eds.*, 1981, pp. 257–80. [G: U.S.]

Mills, Wilbur. Political Perspective on Social Security Financing: Comment. In *Skidmore, F., ed.*, 1981, pp. 229–33. [G: U.S.]

Moffitt, Robert A. and Kehrer, Kenneth C. The Effect of Tax and Transfer Programs on Labor Supply: The Evidence from the Income Maintenance Experiments. In *Ehrenberg, R. G., ed.*, 1981, pp. 103–50. [G: U.S.]

Moy, Joyanna and Sorrentino, Constance. Unemployment, Labor Force Trends, and Layoff Practices in 10 Countries. *Mon. Lab. Rev.*, December 1981, *104*(12), pp. 3–13. [G: N. America; Australia; Japan; EEC; Sweden]

Murphy, Terence. Aspects of High-Level Manpower Forecasting and University Development in Papua New Guinea. *J. Devel. Areas*, April 1981, *15*(3), pp. 417–33. [G: New Guinea]

Niemi, Beth T. and Lloyd, Cynthia B. Female Labor Supply in the Context of Inflation. *Amer. Econ. Rev.*, May 1981, *71*(2), pp. 70–75. [G: U.S.]

Novikova, E. E.; Iazykova, V. S. and Iankova, Z. A. Women's Work and the Family. *Prob. Econ.*, Sept.–Oct.–Nov. 1981, *24*(5–6–7), pp. 165–90. [G: U.S.S.R.]

O'Neill, June A. A Time-Series Analysis of Women's Labor Force Participation. *Amer. Econ. Rev.*, May 1981, *71*(2), pp. 76–80. [G: U.S.]

O'Riordan, William K. A Note on the Sectoral Employment Pattern. *Econ. Soc. Rev.*, January 1981, *12*(2), pp. 133–39. [G: Ireland]

Parnes, Herbert S. An Overview of Results from the National Longitudinal Surveys. *Rev. Public Data Use (See J. Econ. Soc. Meas. after 4/85)*, April 1981, *9*(1), pp. 31–38. [G: U.S.]

Parnes, Herbert S. Inflation and Early Retirement: Recent Longitudinal Findings. *Mon. Lab. Rev.*, July 1981, *104*(7), pp. 27–30. [G: U.S.]

Parsons, Donald O. Black–White Differences in Labor Force Participation of Older Males. In *Parnes, H. S., ed.*, 1981, pp. 132–54. [G: U.S.]

Perloff, Jeffrey M. Income and Payroll Tax Policy and Labor Supply: Discussion. In *Meyer, L. H., ed.*, 1981, pp. 231–36. [G: U.S.]

Pissarides, Christopher A. Staying-on at School in England and Wales. *Economica*, November 1981, *48*(192), pp. 345–63. [G: U.K.]

Pitt, Mark M. Alternative Trade Strategies and Employment in Indonesia. In *Krueger, A. O., et al., eds.*, 1981, pp. 181–237. [G: Indonesia]

Prais, S. J. Vocational Qualifications of the Labour Force in Britain and Germany. *Nat. Inst. Econ. Rev.*, November 1981, (98), pp. 47–59. [G: U.K.; W. Germany]

Reid, Frank and Smith, Douglas A. The Impact of Demographic Changes on Unemployment. *Can. Public Policy*, Spring 1981, 7(2), pp. 348–51.

Ruffell, R. J. Endogeneity II: Direct Estimation of Labour Supply Functions with Piecewise Linear Budget Constraints. In *Brown, C. V., ed.*, 1981, pp. 101–16. [G: U.K.]

Rzhanitsyna, L. Current Problems of Female Labor in the USSR. *Prob. Econ.*, Sept.–Oct.–Nov. 1981, *24*(5–6–7), pp. 3–21. [G: U.S.S.R.]

Sahaya, R. and Verma, R. P. Man-Power Planning—A Study on the Five Year Plan. *Econ. Aff.*, April–June 1981, *26*(2), pp. 110–16. [G: India]

Sánchez, Carlos E.; Palmiero, Horacio and Ferrero, Fernando. The Informal and Quasi-formal Sectors in Córdoba. In *Sethuraman, S. V., ed.*, 1981, pp. 144–58. [G: Argentina]

Santiago, Carlos E. Male–Female Labor Force Participation and Rapid Industrialization. *J. Econ. Devel.*, December 1981, *6*(2), pp. 7–40. [G: Puerto Rico]

Serageldin, M. Ismail. The Modeling and Methodology of Manpower Planning in the Arab Countries. In *Sherbiny, N. A., ed.*, 1981, pp. 55–90. [G: Arab Countries]

Sharir, Shmuel. On Labor Supply When Wants are "Limited." *Atlantic Econ. J.*, September 1981, 9(3), pp. 34–43.

Sherbiny, Naiem A. Sectoral Employment Projections with Minimum Data: The Case of Saudi Arabia. In *Sherbiny, N. A., ed.*, 1981, pp. 173–206. [G: Saudi Arabia]

Siegers, J. J. and Zandanel, R. A Simultaneous Analysis of the Labour Force Participation of Married Women and the Presence of Young Children in the Family. *De Economist*, 1981, *129*(3), pp. 382–93. [G: Netherlands]

Sinclair, W. A. Women at Work in Melbourne and Adelaide since 1871. *Econ. Rec.*, December 1981, *57*(159), pp. 344–53. [G: Australia]

Smith, Eric Owen. Trade Unions in the Developed Economies: West Germany. In *Smith, E. O., ed.*, 1981, pp. 178–207. [G: W. Germany]

Smith, Stanley K. Determinants of Female Labor Force Participation and Family Size in Mexico City. *Econ. Develop. Cult. Change*, October 1981, *30*(1), pp. 129–52. [G: Mexico]

Smith, Stanley K. Women's Work, Fertility, and Competing Time Use in Mexico City. In *Simon, J. L. and Lindert, P. H., eds.*, 1981, pp. 167–87. [G: Mexico]

Smyth, David J. and Holmes, James M. The Employment Ratio and the Potential Labor Surplus in Phillips-Type Relationships: A Note. *J. Post Keynesian Econ.*, Fall 1981, *4*(1), pp. 75–80.

Solberg, Eric J. The Supply of Labor Time for Mature Females. *Atlantic Econ. J.*, September 1981, 9(3), pp. 20–33. [G: U.S.]

Spitze, Glenna D. and Waite, Linda J. Young Women's Preferences for Market Work: Responses to Marital Events. In *Simon, J. L. and Lindert, P. H., eds.*, 1981, pp. 147–66. [G: U.S.]

Standing, Guy. The Notion of Voluntary Unemployment. *Int. Lab. Rev.*, September–October 1981, *120*(5), pp. 563–79.

Stearns, Peter N. Political Perspective on Social Security Financing. In *Skidmore, F., ed.*, 1981, pp. 173–224. [G: U.S.]

Steel, William F. Female and Small-Scale Employment under Modernization in Ghana. *Econ. Develop. Cult. Change*, October 1981, *30*(1), pp. 153–67. [G: Ghana]

Stuart, Charles E. Swedish Tax Rates, Labor Supply, and Tax Revenues. *J. Polit. Econ.*, October 1981, *89*(5), pp. 1020–38. [G: Sweden]

Summers, Lawrence H. Measuring Unemployment. *Brookings Pap. Econ. Act.*, 1981, (2), pp. 609–20. [G: U.S.]

Theeuwes, J. Family Labour Force Participation: Multinomial Logit Estimates. *Appl. Econ.*, December 1981, *13*(4), pp. 481–98. [G: U.S.]

Thomson, Andrew W. J. Trade Unions in the Developed Economies: The United States of America. In *Smith, E. O., ed.*, 1981, pp. 155–77. [G: U.S.]

Thoumi, Francisco E. International Trade Strategies, Employment, and Income Distribution in Colombia. In *Krueger, A. O., et al., eds.*, 1981, pp. 135–79. [G: Colombia]

Tranter, N. L. The Labour Supply 1780–1860. In *Floud, R. and McCloskey, D., eds., Vol. 1*, 1981, pp. 204–26. [G: U.K.]

Ubaidullaeva, R. A. The Twenty-fifth Congress of the CPSU and Current Problems of Employment of Female Labor in the Republics of Central Asia. *Prob. Econ.*, Sept.–Oct.–Nov. 1981, *24*(5–6–7), pp. 147–55. [G: U.S.S.R.]

Ulph, David T. and Ulph, Alistair M. Implications for Optimal Income Taxation. In *Brown, C. V., ed.*, 1981, pp. 189–212. [G: U.K.]

Walsh, Brendan M. Population, Employment and Economic Growth in Ireland. *Irish Banking Rev.*, June 1981, pp. 17–23. [G: Ireland]

Westcott, Diane N. The Youngest Workers: 14- and 15-Year-Olds. *Mon. Lab. Rev.*, February 1981, *104*(2), pp. 65–69. [G: U.S.]

Wolozin, Harold. Earlier Retirement and the Older Worker. *J. Econ. Issues*, June 1981, *15*(2), pp. 477–87. [G: U.S.]

Zabalza, A. and Piachaud, D. Social Security and the Elderly: A Simulation of Policy Changes. *J. Public Econ.*, October 1981, *16*(2), pp. 145–69. [G: U.K.]

8131 Agriculture

Abey, Arun; Booth, Anne and Sundrum, R. M. Labour Absorption in Indonesian Agriculture. *Bull. Indonesian Econ. Stud.*, March 1981, *17*(1), pp. 36–65. [G: Indonesia]

Agarwal, Bina. Agricultural Mechanisation and Labour Use: A Disaggregated Approach. *Int. Lab. Rev.*, January–February 1981, *120*(1), pp. 115–27. [G: India]

Bardhan, Pranab and Rudra, Ashok. Terms and Conditions of Labour Contracts in Agriculture: Results of a Survey in West Bengal, 1979. *Oxford Bull. Econ. Statist.*, February 1981, *43*(1), pp. 89–111. [G: W. Bengal]

Corson, Walter and Nicholson, Walter. Trade Adjustment Assistance for Workers: Results of a Survey of Recipients under the Trade Act of 1974. In *Ehrenberg, R. G., ed.*, 1981, pp. 417–69. [G: U.S.]

Daly, Patricia A. Agricultural Employment: Has the Decline Ended? *Mon. Lab. Rev.*, November 1981, *104*(11), pp. 11–17. [G: U.S.]

Heath, J. R. Peasants or Proletarians? Rural Labour in a Brazilian Plantation Economy. *J. Devel. Stud.*, July 1981, *17*(4), pp. 268–81. [G: Brazil]

Knopke, Philip and Watson, Bill. Australian Shearing Industry—Producer Survey. *Quart. Rev. Rural Econ.*, August 1981, *3*(3), pp. 262–64. [G: Australia]

O'Rourke, Felim. The Use of Life-Tables to Predict the Agricultural Work Force in County Leitrim in 1991. *Irish J. Agr. Econ. Rural Soc.*, 1981, *8*(2), pp. 243–45. [G: Ireland]

Roumasset, James R. and Smith, Joyotee. Population, Technological Change, and the Evolution of Labor Markets. *Population Devel. Rev.*, September 1981, *7*(3), pp. 401–19. [G: Philippines]

Scott, C. D. Agrarian Reform and Seasonal Employment in Coastal Peruvian Agriculture. *J. Devel. Stud.*, July 1981, *17*(4), pp. 282–306. [G: Peru]

Singh, Surendra P. and Williamson, Handy, Jr. Part-Time Farming: Productivity and Some Implications of Off-Farm Work by Farmers. *Southern J. Agr. Econ.*, December 1981, *13*(2), pp. 61–67. [G: U.S.]

Thirlwall, A. P. The Valuation of Labour in Surplus Labour Economies: A Synoptic View. In *Livingstone, I., ed.*, 1981, 1971, pp. 245–53.

Tyagi, D. S. Growth of Agricultural Output and Labour Absorption in India. *J. Devel. Stud.*, October 1981, *18*(1), pp. 104–14. [G: India]

8132 Manufacturing

Drucker, Peter F. Demographics and American Economic Policy. In *Wachter, M. L. and Wachter, S. M., eds.*, 1981, pp. 237–56. [G: U.S.]

Guisinger, Stephen E. Trade Policies and Employment: The Case of Pakistan. In *Krueger, A. O., et al., eds.*, 1981, pp. 291–340. [G: Pakistan]

Richardson, Sue. Skilled Metal Tradesmen: Shortage or Surplus? *Australian Bull. Lab.*, September 1981, *7*(4), pp. 195–204. [G: Australia]

Thomson, Lydia. Industrial Employment Performance and Regional Policy, 1952–71: A Cross-Sectional Approach. *Urban Stud.*, June 1981, *18*(2), pp. 231–38. [G: U.K.]

Van Regemorter, Denise. Evolution du nombre et du revenu des commerçants et des artisans de 1953 à 1977. (Evolution of the Number of Self Employed Tradesmen and Craftsmen and of Their Income in Belgium [1953–1977.] With English summary.) *Cah. Écon. Bruxelles*, 1st Trimestre 1981, (89), pp. 3–23. [G: Belgium]

8133 Service

Cabral, Robert; Ferber, Marianne A. and Green, Carole A. Men and Women in Fiduciary Institutions: A Study of Sex Differences in Career Development. *Rev. Econ. Statist.*, November 1981, *63*(4), pp. 573–80.

Chui, Kwai-Fong and Black, Robert A. Comparing Schemes to Rank Areas According to Degree of Health Manpower Shortage. *Inquiry*, Fall 1981, *18*(3), pp. 274–80. [G: U.S.]

Fuchs, Victor R. Economic Growth and the Rise of Service Employment. In *Giersch, H., ed. (II)*, 1981, pp. 221–42. [G: U.S.; OECD]

Kuznets, Simon. Economic Growth and the Rise of Service Employment: Comments. In *Giersch, H., ed. (II)*, 1981, pp. 249–52. [G: U.S.; OECD]

Peacock, Alan. Economic Growth and the Rise of Service Employment: Comments. In *Giersch, H., ed. (II)*, 1981, pp. 243–48. [G: U.S.; OECD]

Van Regemorter, Denise. Evolution du nombre et du revenu des commerçants et des artisans de 1953 à 1977. (Evolution of the Number of Self Employed Tradesmen and Craftsmen and of Their Income in Belgium [1953–1977.] With English summary.) *Cah. Écon. Bruxelles*, 1st Trimestre 1981, (89), pp. 3–23. [G: Belgium]

8134 Professional

Ambirajan, S. India: The Aftermath of Empire. In *Coats, A. W., ed.*, 1981, pp. 98–132. [G: India]

Barber, William J. The United States: Economists in a Pluralistic Polity. In *Coats, A. W., ed.*, 1981, pp. 175–209. [G: U.S.]

Bergh, Trond. Norway: The Powerful Servants. In *Coats, A. W., ed.*, 1981, pp. 133–74. [G: Norway]

Berkley, Thomas L. Black Lawyers: Struggling to Survive. In *Inst. for Contemp. Studies*, 1981, pp. 107–11. [G: U.S.]

Bowen, William G. Market Prospects for Ph.D.s in the United States. *Population Devel. Rev.*, September 1981, *7*(3), pp. 475–88. [G: U.S.]

Bracey, John. Black Studies Tenure and Promotion: A Reply to Davidson. *Rev. Black Polit. Econ.*, Spring 1981, *11*(3), pp. 375–82. [G: U.S.]

Carroll, Sidney L. and Gaston, Robert J. A Note on the Quality of Legal Services: Peer Review and Disciplinary Service. In *Zerbe, R. O., Jr., ed.*, 1981, pp. 251–60. [G: U.S.]

Chui, Kwai-Fong and Black, Robert A. Comparing Schemes to Rank Areas According to Degree of Health Manpower Shortage. *Inquiry*, Fall 1981, *18*(3), pp. 274–80. [G: U.S.]

Coats, A. W. Britain: The Rise of the Specialists.

In *Coats, A. W., ed.*, 1981, pp. 27–66.
[G: U.K.]

Coats, A. W. Economists in Government: Conclusions. In *Coats, A. W., ed.*, 1981, pp. 343–56.

Coats, A. W. Economists in Government: Introduction. In *Coats, A. W., ed.*, 1981, pp. 3–26.

Conrad, Douglas A. and Watts, Carolyn A. A Note on Measuring the Extent of Competition in the Physicians' Services Market: An Alternative Approach. In *Zerbe, R. O., Jr., ed.*, 1981, pp. 241–49.
[G: U.S.]

Enthoven, Alain C. The Behavior of Health Care Agents: Provider Behavior. In *van der Gaag, J. and Perlman, M., eds.*, 1981, pp. 173–88.
[G: U.S.]

Feldstein, Martin S. Econometric Studies of Health Economics. In *Feldstein, M., ed.*, 1981, *1974*, pp. 57–103.
[G: U.S.]

Ferraresi, Franco and Ferrari, Giuseppe. Italy: Economists in a Weak Political System. In *Coats, A. W., ed.*, 1981, pp. 291–317.
[G: Italy]

Fienup, Darrell F. and Riley, Harold M. Training Agricultural Economists to Serve the Needs of a Changing World. In *Johnson, G. and Maunder, A., eds.*, 1981, pp. 632–42.
[G: U.S.; LDCs]

Flynn, Ralph J. The Climate for Local Government Collective Bargaining in the 1980s: Discussion. In *Dennis, B. D., ed.*, 1981, pp. 299–303.

Haddad, Paulo Roberto. Brazil: Economists in a Bureaucratic-Authoritarian System. In *Coats, A. W., ed.*, 1981, pp. 318–42.
[G: Brazil]

Hansen, W. Lee. The Supply of Mental Health Manpower. In *McGuire, T. G. and Weisbrod, B. A., eds.*, 1981, pp. 85–98.
[G: U.S.]

Jonsson, Anita and Klevmarken, Anders. Disequilibrium and Non-Neutral Market Effects on Age-Earnings Profiles. In *Eliasson, G.; Holmlund, B. and Stafford, F. P., eds.*, 1981, pp. 357–92.
[G: Sweden]

Kahn, Lawrence M. Sex Discrimination in Professional Employment: A Case Study: Comment. *Ind. Lab. Relat. Rev.*, January 1981, *34*(2), pp. 273–75.
[G: U.S.]

Kemenes, Egon. Hungary: Economists in a Socialist Planning System. In *Coats, A. W., ed.*, 1981, pp. 242–61.
[G: Hungary]

Kleiman, Ephraim. Israel: Economists in a New State. In *Coats, A. W., ed.*, 1981, pp. 210–41.
[G: Israel]

Komiya, Ryutaro and Yamamoto, Kozo. Japan: The Officer in Charge of Economic Affairs. In *Coats, A. W., ed.*, 1981, pp. 262–90.
[G: Japan]

Link, Charles R. and Settle, Russell F. A Simultaneous-Equation Model of Labor Supply, Fertility and Earnings of Married Women: The Case of Registered Nurses. *Southern Econ. J.*, April 1981, *47*(4), pp. 977–89.
[G: U.S.]

Osterman, Paul. Sex Discrimination in Professional Employment: A Case Study: Reply. *Ind. Lab. Relat. Rev.*, January 1981, *34*(2), pp. 275–76.
[G: U.S.]

Petridis, A. Australia: Economists in a Federal System. In *Coats, A. W., ed.*, 1981, pp. 67–97.
[G: Australia]

Ponak, Allen M. Unionized Professionals and the Scope of Bargaining: A Study of Nurses. *Ind. Lab.*

Relat. Rev., April 1981, *34*(3), pp. 396–407.
[G: Canada]

Redisch, Michael; Gabel, Jon and Blaxall, Martha. Physician Pricing, Costs, and Income. In *Scheffler, R. M., ed.*, 1981, pp. 197–228.
[G: U.S.]

Richardson, J. The Inducement Hypothesis: That Doctors Generate Demand for their Own Services. In *van der Gaag, J. and Perlman, M., eds.*, 1981, pp. 189–214.
[G: Australia]

Rose, Harold M. The Black Professional and Residential Segregation in the American City. In *Peach, C.; Robinson, V. and Smith, S., eds.*, 1981, pp. 127–48.
[G: U.S.]

Rosenblatt, Roger A. Health and Health Services. In *Hawley, A. H. and Mazie, S. M., eds.*, 1981, pp. 614–42.
[G: U.S.]

Schaafsma, Joseph and Walsh, William D. The Supply of Canadian Physicians and Per Capita Expenditures for Their Services. *Inquiry*, Summer 1981, *18*(2), pp. 185–90.
[G: Canada]

Shaked, Avner and Sutton, John. The Self-Regulating Profession. *Rev. Econ. Stud.*, April 1981, *48*(2), pp. 217–34.

Smith, Kenneth R. and Over, A. Mead, Jr. The Effect of Health Manpower Regulations on Productivity in Medical Practices. In *Cowing, T. G. and Stevenson, R. E., eds.*, 1981, pp. 309–343.
[G: U.S.]

Trotter, G. J. The Supply of Economists. *S. Afr. J. Econ.*, September 1981, *49*(3), pp. 256–68.
[G: S. Africa]

Wilensky, Gail Roggin and Rossiter, Louis F. The Magnitude and Determinants of Physician-initiated Visits in the United States. In *van der Gaag, J. and Perlman, M., eds.*, 1981, pp. 215–43.
[G: U.S]

Woudenberg, Henry W. and McKee, David L. Musical Chairs and Revolving Doors: The Transmigration of Economists North American Style. *Eastern Econ. J.*, January 1981, *7*(1), pp. 35–38.
[G: Canada; U.S.]

Zweifel, Peter. 'Supplier-Induced Demand' in a Model of Physician Behavior. In *van der Gaag, J. and Perlman, M., eds.*, 1981, pp. 245–67.
[G: Switzerland]

8135 Government Employees

Ambirajan, S. India: The Aftermath of Empire. In *Coats, A. W., ed.*, 1981, pp. 98–132. [G: India]

Baird, Charles W. Unionism and the Public Sector. *Managerial Dec. Econ.*, June 1981, *2*(2), pp. 82–90.
[G: U.S.]

Barber, William J. The United States: Economists in a Pluralistic Polity. In *Coats, A. W., ed.*, 1981, pp. 175–209.
[G: U.S.]

Bergh, Trond. Norway: The Powerful Servants. In *Coats, A. W., ed.*, 1981, pp. 133–74.
[G: Norway]

Campbell, Alan K. Government and Productivity. In *Hogan, J. D. and Craig, A. M., eds., Vol. 2*, 1981, pp. 941–52.
[G: U.S.]

Capozzola, John M. The Impact of Government Employee Unions. In *Pious, R. M., ed.*, 1981, pp. 153–66.
[G: U.S.]

Coats, A. W. Britain: The Rise of the Specialists.

In *Coats, A. W., ed.*, 1981, pp. 27–66.
[G: U.K.]

Coats, A. W. Economists in Government: Introduction. In *Coats, A. W., ed.*, 1981, pp. 3–26.

Coats, A. W. Economists in Government: Conclusions. In *Coats, A. W., ed.*, 1981, pp. 343–56.

Culus, Martine and Praet, Peter. Evolution du nombre et du revenu des fonctionnaires de 1953 à 1977. (Evolution of the Number of Civil Servants and of Their Income in Belgium (1953–77). With English summary.) *Cah. Écon. Bruxelles*, 2nd Trimestre 1981, (90), pp. 173–86. [G: Belgium]

Ferraresi, Franco and Ferrari, Giuseppe. Italy: Economists in a Weak Political System. In *Coats, A. W., ed.*, 1981, pp. 291–317. [G: Italy]

Haddad, Paulo Roberto. Brazil: Economists in a Bureaucratic-Authoritarian System. In *Coats, A. W., ed.*, 1981, pp. 318–42. [G: Brazil]

Hutchins, Matthew and Sigelman, Lee. Black Employment in State and Local Governments: A Comparative Analysis. *Soc. Sci. Quart.*, March 1981, *62*(1), pp. 79–87. [G: U.S]

Keller, Wouter J. Public Sector Employment and the Distribution of Income. *J. Public Econ.*, April 1981, *15*(2), pp. 235–49. [G: Netherlands]

Kemenes, Egon. Hungary: Economists in a Socialist Planning System. In *Coats, A. W., ed.*, 1981, pp. 242–61. [G: Hungary]

Kleiman, Ephraim. Israel: Economists in a New State. In *Coats, A. W., ed.*, 1981, pp. 210–41. [G: Israel]

Komiya, Ryutaro and Yamamoto, Kozo. Japan: The Officer in Charge of Economic Affairs. In *Coats, A. W., ed.*, 1981, pp. 262–90. [G: Japan]

Lentz, Bernard F. Political and Economic Determinants of County Government Pay. *Public Choice*, 1981, *36*(2), pp. 253–71. [G: U.S.]

Petridis, A. Australia: Economists in a Federal System. In *Coats, A. W., ed.*, 1981, pp. 67–97. [G: Australia]

Stinson, Thomas F. Fiscal Status of Local Governments. In *Hawley, A. H. and Mazie, S. M., eds.*, 1981, pp. 736–66. [G: U.S.]

Thornton, Robert J. Collective Bargaining, Wages, and Local Government Finance. In *Aronson, J. R. and Schwartz, E., eds.*, 1981, pp. 346–66. [G: U.S.]

Whitehead, A. K. Competition in the Market for Chemists. *Appl. Econ.*, June 1981, *13*(2), pp. 267–78. [G: U.S.]

820 LABOR MARKETS; PUBLIC POLICY

821 Labor Economics

8210 Labor Economics: Theory and Empirical Studies Illustrating Theory

Abowd, John M. and Ashenfelter, Orley. Anticipated Unemployment, Temporary Layoffs, and Compensating Wage Differentials. In *Rosen, S., ed.*, 1981, pp. 141–70. [G: U.S.]

Addison, John T. and Burton, John. On Institutions and Wage Determination. *J. Lab. Res.*, Spring 1981, *2*(1), pp. 99–109.

Ahmed, Iqbal. Wage Determination in Bangladesh

Agriculture. *Oxford Econ. Pap.*, July 1981, *33*(2), pp. 298–322. [G: Bangladesh]

Akerlof, George A. Jobs as Dam Sites. *Rev. Econ. Stud.*, January 1981, *48*(1), pp. 37–49.

Akerlof, George A. and Main, Brian G. M. An Experience-Weighted Measure of Employment and Unemployment Durations. *Amer. Econ. Rev.*, December 1981, *71*(5), pp. 1003–11. [G: U.S.]

Akerlof, George A. and Main, Brian G. M. Pitfalls in Markov Modeling of Labor Market Stocks and Flows. *J. Human Res.*, Winter 1981, *16*(1), pp. 141–51.

Alberro, José. The Lucas Hypothesis on the Phillips Curve: Further International Evidence. *J. Monet. Econ.*, March 1981, *7*(2), pp. 239–50.

Albrecht, James W. A Procedure for Testing the Signalling Hypothesis. In *Eliasson, G.; Holmlund, B. and Stafford, F. P., eds.*, 1981, pp. 339–54. [G: Sweden]

Allen, Steven G. An Empirical Model of Work Attendance. *Rev. Econ. Statist.*, February 1981, *63*(1), pp. 77–87. [G: U.S.]

Amacher, Ryan C. and Sweeney, Richard James. On the Integration of Labor Markets: A Definition and Test of the Radical-Segmentation Hypothesis. *J. Lab. Res.*, Spring 1981, *2*(1), pp. 25–37. [G: U.S.]

Amendola, Adalgiso and Jossa, Bruno. Italian Economic Development: Comment on an Interpretation. *Rev. Econ. Cond. Italy*, October 1981, (3), pp. 481–512. [G: Italy]

Amihud, Yakov. Price-Level Uncertainty, Indexation and Employment. *Southern Econ. J.*, January 1981, *47*(3), pp. 776–87. [G: U.S.]

Anderson, Richard K.; House, Donald and Ormiston, Michael B. A Theory of Physician Behavior with Supplier-Induced Demand. *Southern Econ. J.*, July 1981, *48*(1), pp. 124–33.

Armstrong, H. and Taylor, J. The Measurement of Different Types of Unemployment. In *Creedy, J., ed.*, 1981, pp. 99–127. [G: U.K.]

Artis, Michael J. Is there a Wage Equation? In *Courakis, A. S., ed.*, 1981, pp. 65–80. [G: U.K.]

Asako, Kazumi. Heterogeneity of Labor, the Phillips Curve, and Stagflation. *Econ. Stud. Quart.*, August 1981, *32*(2), pp. 117–34.

Ashworth, J. S. Wages, Prices and Unemployment. In *Creedy, J., ed.*, 1981, pp. 186–234.

Ashworth, J. S. and Ulph, David T. Endogeneity I: Estimating Labour Supply with Piecewise Linear Budget Constraints. In *Brown, C. V., ed.*, 1981, pp. 53–68. [G: U.K.]

Ashworth, J. S. and Ulph, David T. Taxation and Labour Supply: Household Models. In *Brown, C. V., ed.*, 1981, pp. 117–33. [G: U.K.]

Assenmacher, Walter. Tarifpolitik, Kapitalstock und konjunkturelle Entwicklung. Ein Jahrgangsmodell. (Negotiated Wages, Capital Stock and the Business Cycle: A Vintage Approach. With English summary.) *Jahr. Nationalökon. Statist.*, March 1981, *196*(2), pp. 119–36.

Atkinson, A. B. and Stern, N. H. On Labour Supply and Commodity Demands. In *[Stone, R.]*, 1981, pp. 265–96. [G: U.K.]

Axelsson, Roger; Jacobsson, Roger and Löfgren, Karl-Gustaf. A Note on the General Equilibrium

Effects of Taxes on Labor Supply in Sweden. *Scand. J. Econ.*, 1981, *83*(3), pp. 449–56.
[G: Sweden]

Axelsson, Roger; Jacobsson, Roger and Löfgren, Karl-Gustaf. On the Determinants of Labor Supply in Sweden. In *Eliasson, G.; Holmlund, B. and Stafford, F. P., eds.*, 1981, pp. 269–300.
[G: Sweden]

Barbash, Jack. Labor Movement Theory and the Institutional Setting. *Mon. Lab. Rev.*, September 1981, *104*(9), pp. 34–37.

Barro, Robert J. Long-term Contracting, Sticky Prices, and Monetary Policy. In *Barro, R. J.*, 1981, *1977*, pp. 213–24.

Barron, John M. and Gilley, Otis W. Job Search and Vacancy Contacts: Note. *Amer. Econ. Rev.*, September 1981, *71*(4), pp. 747–52. [G: U.S.]

Bartel, Ann P. and Borjas, George J. Wage Growth and Job Turnover: An Empirical Analysis. In *Rosen, S., ed.*, 1981, pp. 65–84. [G: U.S.]

Battalio, Raymond C.; Green, Leonard and Kagel, John H. Income–Leisure Tradeoffs of Animal Workers. *Amer. Econ. Rev.*, September 1981, *71*(4), pp. 621–32.

Beigie, Carl E. Stagflation and Relative-wage Rates: Comments. In *Ontario Economic Council, Vol. 1*, 1981, pp. 50–56. [G: Canada]

Bell, Carolyn Shaw. Demand, Supply, and Labor Market Analysis. *J. Econ. Issues*, June 1981, *15*(2), pp. 423–34. [G: U.S.]

Benz, George A. The Theoretical Background of John M. Clark and His Theory of Wages. *Rev. Soc. Econ.*, December 1981, *39*(3), pp. 307–21.

Berry, A. and Sabot, R. H. Labour Market Performance in Developing Countries: A Survey. In *Streeten, P. and Jolly, R, eds.*, 1981, *1978*, pp. 149–92.

Bhatia, S. L. Short-Run Employment Functions in the Indian Manufacturing Sector. *Indian Econ. J.*, April–June 1981, *28*(4), pp. 18–28.
[G: India]

Bieker, Richard F. Work and Welfare: An Analysis of AFDC Participation Rates in Delaware. *Soc. Sci. Quart.*, March 1981, *62*(1), pp. 169–76.
[G: U.S.]

Björklund, Anders and Holmlund, Bertil. The Structure and Dynamics of Unemployment: Sweden and the United States. In *Eliasson, G.; Holmlund, B. and Stafford, F. P., eds.*, 1981, pp. 183–226.
[G: Sweden; U.S.]

Black, Matthew. An Empirical Test of the Theory of On-the-Job Search. *J. Human Res.*, Winter 1981, *16*(1), pp. 129–40. [G: U.S.]

Blatt, John M. Classical Economics of Involuntary Unemployment. *J. Post Keynesian Econ.*, Summer 1981, *3*(4), pp. 552–59.

Boskin, Michael J. Labor Supply: Comments. In *Aaron, H. J. and Pechman, J. A., eds.*, 1981, pp. 72–75. [G: U.S.]

Boskin, Michael J. Some Issues in "Supply-Side" Economics. *Carnegie-Rochester Conf. Ser. Public Policy*, Spring 1981, *14*, pp. 201–20.

Bosworth, Barry P. Stagflation and Relative-wage Rates. In *Ontario Economic Council, Vol. 1*, 1981, pp. 31–49. [G: U.S.]

Bosworth, Derek L. Specification of Factor Demand

Models and Shiftworking. *Scot. J. Polit. Econ.*, November 1981, *28*(3), pp. 256–65.

Bosworth, Derek L.; Dawkins, Peter J. and Westaway, Anthony J. The Causes of Shiftworking in Great Britain. In *Currie, D.; Peel, D. and Peters, W., eds.*, 1981, pp. 361–82. [G: U.K.]

Bourguignon, François. Participation, emploi et travail domestiques des femmes mariées: Un modèle micro-économique appliqué aux pays en développement. (Participation, Domestic Employment and Domestic Work by Married Women: A Micro-Economic Model Applied to Developing Countries. With English summary.) *Consommation*, April–June 1981, *28*(2), pp. 75–98.
[G: France]

Bowles, Samuel and Gintis, Herbert. Labour Heterogeneity and the Labour Theory of Value: A Reply [The Marxian Theory of Value and Heterogeneous Labour: A Critique and Reformulation]. *Cambridge J. Econ.*, September 1981, *5*(3), pp. 285–88.

Brechling, Frank. Layoffs and Unemployment Insurance. In *Rosen, S., ed.*, 1981, pp. 187–202.
[G: U.S.]

Brown, C. V. Macroeconomic Implications I: Income Taxation and Employment—An Integration of Neo-classical and Keynesian Approaches. In *Brown, C. V., ed.*, 1981, pp. 213–22.

Brown, C. V. Taxation and Labour Supply: Summary of Results. In *Brown, C. V., ed.*, 1981, pp. 134–43. [G: U.K.]

Brown, C. V.; Levin, E. and Ulph, David T. Inflation, Taxation and Income Distribution. In *Brown, C. V., ed.*, 1981, *1977*, pp. 255–68.
[G: U.K.; Australia]

Brown, C. V.; Levin, E. and Ulph, David T. Taxation and Labour Supply: The Basic Model. In *Brown, C. V., ed.*, 1981, pp. 35–52. [G: U.K.]

Bruton, Henry J. Labour Market Performance in Developing Countries: A Survey: Comment. In *Streeten, P. and Jolly, R, eds.*, 1981, *1978*, pp. 197–200. [G: LDCs]

Buiter, Willem H. and Jewitt, Ian. Staggered Wage Setting with Real Wage Relativities: Variations on a Theme of Taylor. *Manchester Sch. Econ. Soc. Stud.*, September 1981, *49*(3), pp. 211–28.

Burdett, Kenneth. A Useful Restriction on the Offer Distribution in Job Search Models. In *Eliasson, G.; Holmlund, B. and Stafford, F. P., eds.*, 1981, pp. 169–82.

Burdett, Kenneth and Mortensen, Dale T. Testing for Ability in a Competitive Labor Market. *J. Econ. Theory*, August 1981, *25*(1), pp. 42–66.

Burkhauser, Richard V. and Turner, John A. Life-Cycle Welfare Costs of Social Security. *Public Finance Quart.*, April 1981, *9*(2), pp. 123–42.
[G: U.S.]

Burtless, Gary. Labor Supply: Comments. In *Aaron, H. J. and Pechman, J. A., eds.*, 1981, pp. 76–83. [G: U.S.]

Butterfield, David W. and Kubursi, Atif A. Wage Indexation and the Unemployment-Inflation Trade-Off. *J. Macroecon.*, Spring 1981, *3*(2), pp. 227–45.

Campbell, David C. and Tobal, Carlos. The Efficiency Price of Labor in Developed and Developing Nations. *J. Econ. Issues*, June 1981, *15*(2), pp. 435–47.

Carlton, Dennis W. Risk Shifting, Statistical Discrimination, and the Stability of Earnings: Comment. In *Rosen, S., ed.*, 1981, pp. 315–17. [G: U.S.]

Carruth, Alan A. and Oswald, Andrew J. The Determination of Union and Non-Union Wage Rates. *Europ. Econ. Rev.*, June/July 1981, *16*(2/3), pp. 285–302.

Casson, M. C. Unemployment and the New Macroeconomics. In *Creedy, J., ed.*, 1981, pp. 48–98.

Catephores, George. On Heterogeneous Labour and the Labour Theory of Value [The Marxian Theory of Value and Heterogeneous Labour: A Critique and Reformulation]. *Cambridge J. Econ.*, September 1981, *5*(3), pp. 273–80.

Cayatte, Jean-Louis. Méthode de calcul du degré de complexité de la force de travail. (A Method of Calculating the Degree of Complexity of Labour Power. With English summary.) *Revue Écon.*, May 1981, *32*(3), pp. 563–80.

Cebula, Richard J., et al. On the Responsiveness of Money Wages to Anticipated Inflation and the Unemployment-Inflation Trade-Off: The Case of the United States. *Econ. Int.*, February 1981, *34*(1), pp. 1–12. [G: U.S.]

Chaikin, Sol C. Proceedings of the Seminar on Employment: Statement. In *U.S. Congress, Joint Economic Committee (1)*, 1981, pp. 106–09. [G: U.S.]

Chapman, P. G. The Johnston Wage Bargaining Model and Trade Union Objectives. *Manchester Sch. Econ. Soc. Stud.*, December 1981, *49*(4), pp. 310–18.

Cherry, Robert D. What Is So Natural about the Natural Rate of Unemployment? *J. Econ. Issues*, September 1981, *15*(3), pp. 729–43.

Cheshire, Paul C. Labour-Market Theory and Spatial Unemployment: The Role of Demand Reconsidered. In *Martin, R. L., ed.*, 1981, pp. 189–207. [G: U.K.]

Cheshire, Paul C. The Regional Demand for Labour Services: A Suggested Explanation for Observed Differences. *Scot. J. Polit. Econ.*, February 1981, *28*(1), pp. 95–98. [G: U.K.]

Chisari, Omar. La tasa de desempleo como argumento de la función de oferta de trabajo. (The Unemployment Rate as a Variable of the Labour Supply Function. With English summary.) *Económica*, September–December 1981, *27*(3), pp. 163–74.

Chu, Ke-young and Feltenstein, Andrew. The Welfare Implications of Relative Price Distortions and Inflation: An Analysis of the Recent Argentine Experience. In *Khan, A. and Sirageldin, I., eds.*, 1981, pp. 181–223. [G: Argentina]

Cifarelli, Giulio. Some Econometric Implications of the Natural Rate of Unemployment with Rational Expectations Model. *Econ. Notes*, 1981, *10*(2), pp. 92–115.

Clayton, Eric S. Programming Rural Employment Opportunities in Kenya. In *Killick, T., ed.*, 1981, 1975, pp. 238–44. [G: Kenya]

Cogan, John F. Fixed Costs and Labor Supply. *Eco-*

nometrica, June 1981, *49*(4), pp. 945–63. [G: U.S.]

Collier, Paul and Bigsten, Arne. A Model of Educational Expansion and Labour Market Adjustment Applied to Kenya. *Oxford Bull. Econ. Statist.*, February 1981, *43*(1), pp. 31–49. [G: Kenya]

Contini, Bruno B. Labor Market Segmentation and the Development of the Parallel Economy—The Italian Experience. *Oxford Econ. Pap.*, November 1981, *33*(3), pp. 401–12. [G: Italy]

Corden, W. M. Taxation, Real Wage Rigidity and Employment. *Econ. J.*, June 1981, *91*(362), pp. 309–30.

Cornwall, John. Do We Need Separate Theories of Inflation and Unemployment? *Can. Public Policy*, Supplement, April 1981, 7, pp. 165–78.

Cornwall, John. Unemployment and Inflation: Institutionalist and Structuralist Views: A Review Article. *J. Econ. Issues*, March 1981, *15*(1), pp. 113–27.

Costabile, Lilia. Keynesian Unemployment in Patinkin and in the "Rationing Models." *Econ. Notes*, 1981, *10*(2), pp. 64–80.

Cotterman, Robert F. The Role of Assets in Labor Supply Functions. *Econ. Inquiry*, July 1981, *19*(3), pp. 495–505.

Cowell, Frank A. Income Maintenance Schemes under Wage-Rate Uncertainty. *Amer. Econ. Rev.*, September 1981, *71*(4), pp. 692–703.

Cowell, Frank A. Taxation and Labour Supply with Risky Activities. *Economica*, November 1981, *48*(192), pp. 365–79.

Coyle, Barry T. and Lopez, Ramon E. A Comment on Bollman's "Off-Farm Work by Farmers: . . ." *Can. J. Agr. Econ.*, February 1981, *29*(1), pp. 93–99.

Crawford, Vincent P. and Knoer, Elsie Marie. Job Matching with Heterogeneous Firms and Workers. *Econometrica*, March 1981, *49*(2), pp. 437–50.

Creedy, J. The Economics of Unemployment in Britain: Introduction. In *Creedy, J., ed.*, 1981, pp. 1–16. [G: U.K.]

Daniel, Betty C. International Transmission of a Real Shock under Flexible Exchange Rates: A Comment. *J. Polit. Econ.*, August 1981, *89*(4), pp. 813–18.

Danziger, Sheldon; Haveman, Robert H. and Plotnick, Robert. How Income Transfer Programs Affect Work, Savings, and the Income Distribution: A Critical Review. *J. Econ. Lit.*, September 1981, *19*(3), pp. 975–1028. [G: U.S.]

Danziger, Sheldon and Plotnick, Robert. Income Maintenance Programs and the Pursuit of Income Security. *Ann. Amer. Acad. Polit. Soc. Sci.*, January 1981, *453*, pp. 130–52. [G: U.S.]

Das, Satya P. Effects of Foreign Investment in the Presence of Unemployment. *J. Int. Econ.*, May 1981, *11*(2), pp. 249–57.

Davenport, Paul. Unemployment and Technology in a Model of Steady Growth. *Australian Econ. Pap.*, June 1981, *20*(36), pp. 115–32.

Dawson, Alistair. Sargan's Wage Equation: A Theoretical and Empirical Reconstruction. *Appl. Econ.*, September 1981, *13*(3), pp. 351–63. [G: U.S.]

Deaton, Angus and Muellbauer, John. Functional Forms for Labor Supply and Commodity Demands with and without Quantity Restrictions. *Econometrica*, November 1981, *49*(6), pp. 1521–32.

Dertouzos, James N. and Pencavel, John H. Wage and Employment Determination under Trade Unionism: The International Typographical Union. *J. Polit. Econ.*, December 1981, *89*(6), pp. 1162–81. [G: U.S.]

Desai, Meghnad. Inflation, Unemployment and Monetary Policy—The UK Experience. *Brit. Rev. Econ. Issues*, Autumn 1981, *3*(9), pp. 1–18. [G: U.K.]

Deutschmann, Christoph. Labour Market Segmentation and Wage Dynamics. *Managerial Dec. Econ.*, September 1981, *2*(3), pp. 145–59. [G: W. Germany]

Diamond, Peter A. Mobility Costs, Frictional Unemployment, and Efficiency. *J. Polit. Econ.*, August 1981, *89*(4), pp. 798–812.

Dorsey, Stuart. Comparative Advantage and the Welfare Effects of Uniform Wage Policies. *J. Lab. Res.*, Spring 1981, *2*(1), pp. 147–56.

Drèze, Jacques H. and Modigliani, Franco. The Trade-off between Real Wages and Employment in an Open Economy (Belgium). *Europ. Econ. Rev.*, January 1981, *15*(1), pp. 1–40. [G: Belgium]

Dugger, William M. The Administered Labor Market: An Institutional Analysis. *J. Econ. Issues*, June 1981, *15*(2), pp. 397–407. [G: U.S.]

Easton, Stephen T. More on the Emigration of the Peasantry. *World Devel.*, March 1981, *9*(3), pp. 315–18.

Eden, Benjamin and Pakes, Ariél. On Measuring the Variance-Age Profile of Lifetime Earnings. *Rev. Econ. Stud.*, July 1981, *48*(3), pp. 385–94.

Ekelund, Robert B., Jr.; Higgins, Richard S. and Smithson, Charles W. Can Discrimination Increase Employment: A Neoclassical Perspective. *Southern Econ. J.*, January 1981, *47*(3), pp. 664–73.

Ekelund, Robert B., Jr. and Kordsmeier, William F. J. S. Mill, Unions, and the Wages Fund Recantation: A Reinterpretation—Comment. *Quart. J. Econ.*, August 1981, *96*(3), pp. 531–41.

Ellis, Gene. The Backward-bending Supply Curve of Labor in Africa: Models, Evidence, and Interpretation—and Why It Makes a Difference. *J. Devel. Areas*, January 1981, *15*(2), pp. 251–73. [G: Africa]

Estrup, Hector. Teorier om produktiv beskæftigelse. (A Historical Review of Doctrines of Productive Labour. With English summary.) *Nationaløkon. Tidsskr.*, 1981, *119*(2), pp. 182–98.

Eygelshoven, P. J. and Kuipers, Simon K. A Note on Pasinetti's "Ricardian System" [A Mathematical Formulation of the Ricardian System]. *Rev. Econ. Stud.*, January 1981, *48*(1), pp. 185–86.

Farkas, George; Olsen, Randall J. and Stromsdorfer, Ernst W. Youth Labor Supply During the Summer: Evidence for Youths from Low-Income Households. In *Ehrenberg, R. G., ed.*, 1981, pp. 151–90. [G: U.S.]

Faurot, David J. and Sellon, Gordon H., Jr. Analyz-

ing Labor Supply without Considering Income from Assets. *Rev. Econ. Statist.*, August 1981, *63*(3), pp. 458–62. [G: U.S.]

Fautz, Wolfgang. A Simple Dynamic Model of Autonomous Wage Policy, Price Expectations, and Monetary Accommodation. *Schweiz. Z. Volkswirtsch. Statist.*, March 1981, *117*(1), pp. 25–40.

Feigin, Paul and Landsberger, Michael. The Existence and Properties of a Stationary Distribution for Unemployment When Job Search Is Sequential. *J. Econ. Dynam. Control*, November 1981, *3*(4), pp. 329–41.

Feigin, Paul and Landsberger, Michael. The Induced Inefficiency of Income Taxes under Conditions of Imperfect Information about Job Offers. *Can. J. Econ.*, February 1981, *14*(1), pp. 119–24.

Fields, T. Windsor and Noble, Nicholas R. Testing the Friedman-Phelps Natural Rate Hypothesis Using Survey Data: An Instrumental Variable Approach. *J. Monet. Econ.*, March 1981, *7*(2), pp. 251–59. [G: U.S.]

Fischer, Stanley. Long-term Contracts, Rational Expectations, and the Optimal Money Supply Rule. In *Lucas, R. E. and Sargent, T. J., eds.*, 1981, pp. 261–75.

FitzRoy, Felix R. Work-Sharing and Insurance Policy: A Cure for Stagflation. *Kyklos*, 1981, *34*(3), pp. 432–47.

Fratianni, Michele and Spinelli, F. Sylos Labini on Spinelli and Fratianni on Inflation: A Reply [Money, Prices and Wages in Italy] [Wage Inflation in Italy: A Reappraisal]. *Banca Naz. Lavoro Quart. Rev.*, December 1981, (139), pp. 466–69.

Frenkel, Jacob A. Adjustment Lags versus Information Lags: A Test of Alternative Explanations of the Phillips Curve Phenomenon: A Comment. *J. Money, Credit, Banking*, November 1981, *13*(4), pp. 490–93.

Friedlander, Stanley L. The Cost of Labor Market Information: Male Youth Job Search Behavior: Comments. In *Galatin, M. and Leiter, R. D., eds.*, 1981, pp. 141–45. [G: U.S.]

Gal, Shmuel; Landsberger, Michael and Levykson, Benny. A Compound Strategy for Search in the Labor Market. *Int. Econ. Rev.*, October 1981, *22*(3), pp. 597–608.

Garbarino, Joseph W. Collective Bargaining under Adverse Conditions, or Hard Times in the Mill: Discussion. In *Dennis, B. D., ed.*, 1981, pp. 143–46.

Gärtner, Manfred. A Politicoeconomic Model of Wage Inflation. *De Economist*, 1981, *129*(2), pp. 183–205. [G: W. Germany]

Gärtner, Manfred. Legislative Profits and the Rate of Change of Money Wages: A Reply. *Public Choice*, 1981, *37*(3), pp. 589–93. [G: W. Germany]

Gärtner, Manfred. Politik und Arbeitsmarkt. Eine Übersicht über ausgewählte Makrotheorien. (Politics and the Labour Market: A Survey of Selected Macro Models. With English summary.) *Z. ges. Staatswiss.*, June 1981, *137*(2), pp. 252–83.

Gelber, Frank. The Inter-Industry Effect of Cumulative Wage Indexation—A Critical Comment. *Aus-*

tralian Econ. Pap., June 1981, *20*(36), pp. 186–88.

Gerson, J. The Question of Structural Unemployment in South Africa. *S. Afr. J. Econ.*, March 1981, *49*(1), pp. 10–25. [G: S. Africa]

Ghez, Gilbert R. Wage Growth and Job Turnover: An Empirical Analysis: Comment. **In** *Rosen, S., ed.*, 1981, pp. 84–90. [G: U.S.]

Gintis, Herbert and Bowles, Samuel. Structure and Practice in the Labor Theory of Value. *Rev. Radical Polit. Econ.*, Winter 1981, *12*(4), pp. 1–26.

Glaister, K. W. Macroeconomic Implications II: Labour Supply and Fiscal Policy in a Disequilibrium Model. **In** *Brown, C. V., ed.*, 1981, pp. 223–54.

Glaister, K. W.; McGlone, A. and Ruffell, R. J. Taxation and Labour Supply: Preferences. **In** *Brown, C. V., ed.*, 1981, pp. 69–100. [G: U.K.]

Glaister, K. W.; McGlone, A. and Ulph, David T. Labour Supply Responses to Tax Changes. **In** *Brown, C. V., ed.*, 1981, pp. 163–88. [G: U.K.]

Goodrich, Chris. Legislative Profits and the Rate of Change of Money Wages: A Comment. *Public Choice*, 1981, *37*(3), pp. 585–88. [G: W. Germany]

Gordon, Robert J. International Monetarism, Wage Push, and Monetary Accommodation. **In** *Courakis, A. S., ed.*, 1981, pp. 1–63. [G: OECD]

Gottschalk, Peter T. A Note on Estimating Treatment Effects [The Estimation of Labor Supply Models Using Experimental Data]. *Amer. Econ. Rev.*, September 1981, *71*(4), pp. 764–69. [G: U.S.]

Gottschalk, Peter T. A Synthesis of Contour and Flexible Wage Hypotheses. *J. Econ. Issues*, September 1981, *15*(3), pp. 629–40.

Gramlich, Edward M. The Structure and Dynamics of Unemployment: Sweden and the United States. **In** *Eliasson, G.; Holmlund, B. and Stafford, F. P., eds.*, 1981, pp. 227–32. [G: Sweden; U.S.]

Granick, David. Soviet Use of Fixed Prices: Hypothesis of a Job-Right Constraint. **In** *[Bergson, A.]*, 1981, pp. 85–103.

Greenberg, David; Moffitt, Robert A. and Friedmann, John. Underreporting and Experimental Effects on Work Effort: Evidence from the Gary Income Maintenance Experiment. *Rev. Econ. Statist.*, November 1981, *63*(4), pp. 581–89. [G: U.S.]

Gregory, R. G. and Duncan, R. C. Segmented Labor Market Theories and the Australian Experience of Equal Pay for Women. *J. Post Keynesian Econ.*, Spring 1981, *3*(3), pp. 403–28. [G: Australia]

Grossman, Herschel I. Incomplete Information, Risk Shifting, and Employment Fluctuations. *Rev. Econ. Stud.*, April 1981, *48*(2), pp. 189–97.

Grossman, Herschel I. and Happy, Kenneth. Fixed Wages, Layoffs, Unemployment Compensation, and Welfare: Note. *Amer. Econ. Rev.*, June 1981, *71*(3), pp. 483–84.

Grossman, Herschel I. and Trepeta, Warren T. Risk Shifting, Statistical Discrimination, and the Stability of Earnings. **In** *Rosen, S., ed.*, 1981, pp. 295–315. [G: U.S.]

Grossman, Sanford J. and Hart, Oliver D. Implicit Contracts, Moral Hazard, and Unemployment. *Amer. Econ. Rev.*, May 1981, *71*(2), pp. 301–07.

Grünbaum, Isi. On Wage Increases as a means to check Oversaving-Unemployment. **In** *Grünbaum, I.*, 1981, *1939*, pp. 11–56.

Guasch, J. Luis and Weiss, Andrew. Self-Selection in the Labor Market. *Amer. Econ. Rev.*, June 1981, *71*(3), pp. 275–84.

Gupta, Suraj B. The Productivity of Workers' Consumption and the Choice of Techniques. *Indian Econ. Rev.*, Oct.-Dec. 1981, *16*(4), pp. 279–96.

Hamermesh, Daniel S. Layoffs and Unemployment Insurance: Comment. **In** *Rosen, S., ed.*, 1981, pp. 203–07. [G: U.S.]

Hannah, S. P. A Note on Employment Subsidies and the Government Budget Constraint in a Closed Economy. *Bull. Econ. Res.*, May 1981, *33*(1), pp. 3–13.

Hanushek, Eric A. Alternative Models of Earnings Determination and Labor Market Structures. *J. Human Res.*, Spring 1981, *16*(2), pp. 238–59. [G: U.S.]

Harberger, Arnold C. Comment on Papers by Boskin [Some Issues in "Supply-Side" Economics] and Piggott and Whalley [A Summary of Some Findings from a General Equilibrium Tax Model for the United Kingdom]. *Carnegie-Rochester Conf. Ser. Public Policy*, Spring 1981, *14*, pp. 221–29.

Harris, Donald J. On the Timing of Wage Payments. *Cambridge J. Econ.*, December 1981, *5*(4), pp. 369–81.

Harris, John R. and Todaro, Michael P. Migration, Unemployment and Development: A Two-Sector Analysis. **In** *Livingstone, I., ed.*, 1981, *1970*, pp. 89–96.

Hart, R. A. Regional Wage-Change Transmission and the Structure of Regional Wages and Unemployment. **In** *Martin, R. L., ed.*, 1981, pp. 17–45.

Hartog, Joop. Wages and Allocation under Imperfect Information. *De Economist*, 1981, *129*(3), pp. 311–23.

Hashimoto, Masanori. Firm-Specific Human Capital as a Shared Investment. *Amer. Econ. Rev.*, June 1981, *71*(3), pp. 475–82.

Hausman, Jerry A. Income and Payroll Tax Policy and Labor Supply. **In** *Meyer, L. H., ed.*, 1981, pp. 173–202. [G: U.S.]

Hausman, Jerry A. Labor Supply. **In** *Aaron, H. J. and Pechman, J. A., eds.*, 1981, pp. 27–72. [G: U.S.]

Heckman, James J. Heterogeneity and State Dependence. **In** *Rosen, S., ed.*, 1981, pp. 91–139. [G: U.S.]

Heckman, James J. and MaCurdy, Thomas E. New Methods for Estimating Labor Supply Functions: A Survey. **In** *Ehrenberg, R. G., ed.*, 1981, pp. 65–102. [G: U.S.]

Henry, S. G. B. Incomes Policy and Aggregate Pay. **In** *Fallick, J. L. and Elliott, R. F., eds.*, 1981, pp. 23–44. [G: U.K.]

Hess, James D. The Terms of Authority. *J. Econ. Behav. Organ.*, September 1981, *2*(3), pp. 237–55.

Heubes, J. Alternative Beschäftigungssituationen im Rahmen der Ungleichgewichtstheorie. (Alternative Employment Situations in the Disequilibrium Theory. With English summary.) *Jahr. Nationalökon. Statist.*, January 1981, *196*(1), pp. 33–45.

Hey, John D. Contract Theory, Temporary Layoffs and Unemployment: A Critical Assessment: Comment. In *Currie, D.; Peel, D. and Peters, W.*, eds., 1981, pp. 72–76.

Hey, John D. and Mavromaras, Kostas Gr. The Effect of Unemployment Insurance on the Riskiness of Occupational Choice. *J. Public Econ.*, December 1981, *16*(3), pp. 317–41.

Hicks, John R. The Mainspring of Economic Growth. *Amer. Econ. Rev.*, Special Issue December 1981, *71*(6), pp. 23–29.

Hirsch, Werner Z. and Rufolo, Anthony M. Monitoring Costs and Labor Productivity in Municipal Labor Markets. In *Ballabon, M. B.*, ed., 1981, pp. 175–94. [G: U.S.]

Hoa, Tran Van. A Bivariate Model of Wages and Money for West Germany [Causality and Wage Price Inflation in West Germany, 1964–1979]. *Weltwirtsch. Arch.*, 1981, *117*(4), pp. 752–55. [G: W. Germany]

Hoa, Tran Van. Causality and Wage Price Inflation in West Germany, 1964–1979. *Weltwirtsch. Arch.*, 1981, *117*(1), pp. 110–24.

Hoel, Michael. Employment Effects of an Increased Oil Price in an Economy with Short-run Labor Immobility. *Scand. J. Econ.*, 1981, *83*(2), pp. 269–76.

Holmlund, Bertil. A Note on Changes in Payroll Taxes—Does Legal Incidence Matter? *Nat. Tax J.*, December 1981, *34*(4), pp. 479–82. [G: U.S.]

Holmlund, Bertil. Employment Subsidies and the Behavior of the Firm. In *Eliasson, G. and Södersten, J.*, eds., 1981, pp. 267–93.

Holmstrom, Bengt. Contractual Models of the Labor Market. *Amer. Econ. Rev.*, May 1981, *71*(2), pp. 308–13.

Homma, Masaaki and Osano, Hiroshi. The General Equilibrium Approach of Implicit Labor Contracts. (In Japanese. With English summary.) *Osaka Econ. Pap.*, December 1981, *31*(2–3), pp. 163–78.

Hughes, James J.; Perlman, Richard and Das, Satya P. Technological Progress and the Skill Differential. *Econ. J.*, December 1981, *91*(364), pp. 998–1005.

Hung, N. M. and Lefebvre, P. Sur l'impact de l'assurance-chômage dans une économie keynésienne. (On the Impact of Unemployment Insurance in a Keynesian Economy. With English summary.) *L'Actual. Econ.*, October–December 1981, *57*(4), pp. 525–52.

Hunt, Janet C.; DeLorme, Charles D., Jr. and Hill, R. Carter. Taxation and the Wife's Use of Time. *Ind. Lab. Relat. Rev.*, April 1981, *34*(3), pp. 426–32. [G: U.S.]

Hvidding, James M. Policy Implications of a Non-Linear Phillips Curve in a Stochastic Environment. *J. Macroecon.*, Winter 1981, *3*(1), pp. 125–28.

Immink, Maarten D. C. and Viteri, Fernando E. Energy Intake and Productivity of Guatemalan Sugarcane Cutters: An Empirical Test of the Efficiency Wage Hypothesis—Part II. *J. Devel. Econ.*, October 1981, *9*(2), pp. 273–87. [G: Guatemala]

Immink, Maarten D. C. and Viteri, Fernando E. Energy Intake and Productivity of Guatemalan Sugarcane Cutters: An Empirical Test of the Efficiency Wage Hypothesis—Part I. *J. Devel. Econ.*, October 1981, *9*(2), pp. 251–71. [G: Guatemala]

Ioannides, Yannis M. Job Search, Unemployment and Savings. *J. Monet. Econ.*, May 1981, *7*(3), pp. 355–70.

Ip, Pui Chi. A General Equilibrium Analysis in the Phillips Space. *J. Macroecon.*, Summer 1981, *3*(3), pp. 355–67.

Ireland, Norman J. The Behaviour of the Labour Managed Firm and Disutility from Supplying Factor Services. *Econ. Anal. Worker's Manage.*, 1981, *15*(1), pp. 21–43.

Ireland, Norman J. and Law, Peter J. Efficiency, Incentives, and Individual Labor Supply in the Labor-Managed Firm. *J. Compar. Econ.*, March 1981, *5*(1), pp. 1–23.

Ishikawa, Tsuneo. Dual Labor Market Hypothesis and Long-Run Income Distribution. *J. Devel. Econ.*, August 1981, *9*(1), pp. 1–30. [G: U.S.]

Iugai, T. The Economic Mechanism of the Formation of Employment Structure. *Prob. Econ.*, July 1981, *24*(3), pp. 86–98. [G: U.S.S.R.]

Jakobsson, Ulf and Normann, Göran. Welfare Effects of Changes in Income Tax Progression in Sweden. In *Eliasson, G.; Holmlund, B. and Stafford, F. P.*, eds., 1981, pp. 313–38. [G: Sweden]

Jarsulic, Marc. Unemployment in a Flexible Price Competitive Model. *J. Post Keynesian Econ.*, Fall 1981, *4*(1), pp. 32–43.

Jenkins, Glenn P. and Kuo, Chun-Yan. On Measuring the Social Opportunity Cost of Permanent and Temporary Employment: A Reply. *Can. J. Econ.*, November 1981, *14*(4), pp. 708–12. [G: Canada]

Jetzer, Martin. Causality and Wage Price Inflation in West Germany, 1964–1979: A Note [Causality and Wage Price Inflation in West Germany, 1964–1979]. *Weltwirtsch. Arch.*, 1981, *117*(4), pp. 749–51. [G: W. Germany]

Jones, Ethel B. and Long, James E. Part-Week Work and Women's Unemployment. *Rev. Econ. Statist.*, February 1981, *63*(1), pp. 70–76. [G: U.S.]

Jonsson, Anita and Klevmarken, Anders. Disequilibrium and Non-Neutral Market Effects on Age-Earnings Profiles. In *Eliasson, G.; Holmlund, B. and Stafford, F. P.*, eds., 1981, pp. 357–92. [G: Sweden]

Jonung, Lars. Ricardo on Machinery and the Present Unemployment: An Unpublished Manuscript by Knut Wicksell. *Econ. J.*, March 1981, *91*(361), pp. 195–205.

Kaliski, S. F. Inflation, Stagflation and Macroeconomics: Does Received Macro-Theory Explain Our Economic Circumstances? *Can. Public Pol-*

icy, Supplement, April 1981, 7, pp. 189–203.
[G: Canada]

Kiefer, Nicholas M. and Neumann, George R. Individual Effects in a Nonlinear Model: Explicit Treatment of Heterogeneity in the Empirical Job-Search Model. *Econometrica*, June 1981, 49(4), pp. 965–79. [G: U.S.]

Kiefer, Nicholas M. and Neumann, George R. Structural and Reduced Form Approaches to Analyzing Unemployment Durations. In *Rosen, S., ed.*, 1981, pp. 171–85. [G: U.S.]

Killingsworth, Mark R. A Survey of Labor Supply Models: Theoretical Analyses and First-Generation Empirical Results. In *Ehrenberg, R. G., ed.*, 1981, pp. 1–53. [G: U.S]

Kirby, Michael G. A Variable Expectations Coefficient Model of the Australian Phillips Curve. *Australian Econ. Pap.*, December 1981, 20(37), pp. 351–58. [G: Australia]

Kirby, Michael G. An Investigation of the Specification and Stability of the Australian Aggregate Wage Equation. *Econ. Rec.*, March 1981, 57(156), pp. 35–46. [G: Australia]

Koizumi, Susumu. The Theory of Unemployment— A Survey. (In Japanese. With English summary.) *Osaka Econ. Pap.*, December 1981, 31(2–3), pp. 81–92.

Krause, Ulrich. Heterogeneous Labour and the Fundamental Marxian Theorem. *Rev. Econ. Stud.*, January 1981, 48(1), pp. 173–78.

Krause, Ulrich. Marxian Inequalities in a von Neumann Setting. *Z. Nationalökon.*, 1981, 41(1–2), pp. 59–67.

Lahiri, Kajal and Lee, Jung Soo. Inflationary Expectations and the Wage–Price Dynamics: An Econometric Analysis. In *[Valavanis, S.]*, 1981, pp. 421–36. [G: U.S.]

Laidler, David. Inflation and Unemployment in an Open Economy: A Monetarist View. *Can. Public Policy*, Supplement, April 1981, 7, pp. 179–88. [G: Canada]

Lambrinos, James. Health: A Source of Bias in Labor Supply Models. *Rev. Econ. Statist.*, May 1981, 63(2), pp. 206–12.

Larson, Donald A. Labor Supply Adjustment over the Business Cycle [The Determination of Labor Supply: A Dynamic Model]. *Ind. Lab. Relat. Rev.*, July 1981, 34(4), pp. 591–95. [G: U.S.]

Layard, Richard. Measuring the Duration of Unemployment: A Note. *Scot. J. Polit. Econ.*, November 1981, 28(3), pp. 273–77.

Lazear, Edward P. Agency, Earnings Profiles, Productivity, and Hours Restrictions. *Amer. Econ. Rev.*, September 1981, 71(4), pp. 606–20.

Lazear, Edward P. and Rosen, Sherwin. Rank-Order Tournaments as Optimum Labor Contracts. *J. Polit. Econ.*, October 1981, 89(5), pp. 841–64.

Leigh, J. Paul. Compensating Wages for Occupational Injuries and Diseases. *Soc. Sci. Quart.*, December 1981, 62(4), pp. 772–78. [G: U.S.]

Leigh, J. Paul. Occupational Choice under Earnings Uncertainty. *Nebr. J. Econ. Bus.*, Winter 1981, 20(1), pp. 59–71.

Lele, Uma and Mellor, John W. Technological Change, Distributive Bias and Labor Transfer in a Two-Sector Economy. *Oxford Econ. Pap.*, November 1981, 33(3), pp. 426–41.

Lemennicier, Bertrand and Lévy-Garboua, Louis. L'arbitrage autarcie-marché: Une explication du travail féminin. (The Autarky/Market Trade-off: An Explanation of Female Labor. With English summary.) *Consommation*, April–June 1981, 28(2), pp. 41–74. [G: France]

Leroy, Robert. Le marché du travail: une approche hors paradigmes. (The Labor Market: Beyond Paradigms! With English summary.) *Revue Écon.*, March 1981, 32(2), pp. 237–70.

Leslie, D. G. The Causes of Shiftworking in Great Britain: Comment. In *Currie, D.; Peel, D. and Peters, W., eds.*, 1981, pp. 383–85. [G: U.K.]

Levenstein, Charles. The Political Economy of Suburbanization: In Pursuit of a Class Analysis. *Rev. Radical Polit. Econ.*, Summer 1981, 13(2), pp. 23–31.

Lewis, P. E. T. and Makepeace, Gerald H. The Estimation of Aggregate Demand and Supply Curves for Labour in the UK. *Appl. Econ.*, September 1981, 13(3), pp. 389–98. [G: U.K.]

Lippman, Steven A. and McCall, John J. The Economics of Belated Information. *Int. Econ. Rev.*, February 1981, 22(1), pp. 135–46.

Lorenzen, Gunter. Hierarchische Strukturen und die Verteilung der Lohn- und Gehaltseinkommen. (Hierarchical Structures of Earnings and the Distribution of Wage and Salary Incomes. With English summary.) *Z. ges. Staatswiss.*, March 1981, 137(1), pp. 36–44.

Lorie, Henri R. Asset Prices and Temporary Equilibrium with Rationing. *Scand. J. Econ.*, 1981, 83(3), pp. 457–62.

Loury, Glenn C. Intergenerational Transfers and the Distribution of Earnings. *Econometrica*, June 1981, 49(4), pp. 843–67.

Lovett, William A. Teamwork, Markets, and Regulation: Distortions Arising from Legal Parochialism. *J. Econ. Issues*, June 1981, 15(2), pp. 409–22. [G: U.S.]

Lucas, Robert E., Jr. Econometric Policy Evaluation: A Critique. In *Lucas, R. E., Jr.*, 1981, 1976, pp. 104–30.

Lucas, Robert E., Jr. Econometric Testing of the Natural Rate Hypothesis. In *Lucas, R. E., Jr.*, 1981, 1972, pp. 90–103.

Lucas, Robert E., Jr. Equilibrium Search and Unemployment. In *Lucas, R. E., Jr.*, 1981, 1974, pp. 156–78.

Lucas, Robert E., Jr. Real Wages, Employment, and Inflation. In *Lucas, R. E., Jr.*, 1981, 1969, pp. 19–58. [G: U.S.]

Lucas, Robert E., Jr. Unemployment in the Great Depression: Is There a Full Explanation? In *Lucas, R. E., Jr.*, 1981, 1972, pp. 59–65. [G: U.S]

Lucas, Robert E., Jr. Unemployment Policy. In *Lucas, R. E., Jr.*, 1981, 1978, pp. 240–47.

MacDonald, Glenn M. The Impact of Schooling on Wages. *Econometrica*, September 1981, 49(5), pp. 1349–59.

MacCurdy, Thomas E. An Empirical Model of Labor Supply in a Life-Cycle Setting. *J. Polit. Econ.*, December 1981, 89(6), pp. 1059–85. [G: U.S.]

Madden, Janice Fanning. Why Women Work Closer to Home. *Urban Stud.*, June 1981, *18*(2), pp. 181–94. **[G: U.S.]**

Madden, P. Unemployment Equilibrium when Production is a Function of Average Hours and Number of Workers. In *Currie, D.; Peel, D. and Peters, W., eds.*, 1981, pp. 169–93.

Malcomson, James M. Unemployment and the Efficiency Wage Hypothesis. *Econ. J.*, December 1981, *91*(364), pp. 848–66.

Mangan, John. Labour Hoarding in Australian Manufacturing: An Inter-Industry Analysis. *Australian Bull. Lab.*, September 1981, *7*(4), pp. 219–35. **[G: Australia]**

Martin, R. L. Wage-change Interdependence Amongst Regional Labour Markets: Conceptual Issues and Some Empirical Evidence for the United States. In *Martin, R. L., ed.*, 1981, pp. 96–135. **[G: U.S.]**

Masters, Stanley H. The Effects of Supported Work on the Earnings and Transfer Payments of Its AFDC Target Group. *J. Human Res.*, Fall 1981, *16*(4), pp. 600–636. **[G: U.S.]**

McCallum, Bennett T. The Current State of the Policy-Ineffectiveness Debate. In *Lucas, R. E. and Sargent, T. J., eds.*, 1981, *1979*, pp. 285–92. **[G: U.S.]**

McCallum, John C. P. Modigliani on Flexible Wages and Prices: Comment. *J. Post Keynesian Econ.*, Winter 1980–81, *3*(2), pp. 281–84. **[G: Canada]**

McDonald, Ian M. and Solow, Robert M. Wage Bargaining and Employment. *Amer. Econ. Rev.*, December 1981, *71*(5), pp. 896–908.

McElroy, Marjorie B. A Survey of Labor Supply Models: Theoretical Analyses and First-Generation Empirical Results: Appendix: Empirical Results from Estimates of Joint Labor Supply Functions of Husbands and Wives. In *Ehrenberg, R. G., ed.*, 1981, pp. 53–64. **[G: U.S.]**

McKenna, Edward J. A Comment on Bowles and Gintis' Marxian Theory of Value [The Marxian Theory of Value and Heterogeneous Labour: A Critique and Reformulation]. *Cambridge J. Econ.*, September 1981, *5*(3), pp. 281–84.

McNabb, Robert and Psacharopoulos, George. Further Evidence on the Relevance of the Dual Labor Market Hypothesis for the U.K. *J. Human Res.*, Summer 1981, *16*(3), pp. 442–48. **[G: U.K.]**

Meade, James E. Note on the Inflationary Implications of the Wage-Fixing Assumption of the Cambridge Economic Policy Group. *Oxford Econ. Pap.*, March 1981, *33*(1), pp. 28–41. **[G: U.K.]**

Mezzera, Jaime. Segmented Labour Markets without Policy-induced Labour Market Distortions. *World Devel.*, November/December 1981, *9*(11/12), pp. 1109–14.

Mincer, Jacob and Jovanovic, Boyan. Labor Mobility and Wages. In *Rosen, S., ed.*, 1981, pp. 21–63. **[G: U.S.]**

Moffitt, Robert A. The Negative Income Tax: Would It Discourage Work? *Mon. Lab. Rev.*, April 1981, *104*(4), pp. 23–27. **[G: U.S.]**

Moffitt, Robert A. and Kehrer, Kenneth C. The Effect of Tax and Transfer Programs on Labor Supply: The Evidence from the Income Maintenance Experiments. In *Ehrenberg, R. G., ed.*, 1981, pp. 103–50. **[G: U.S.]**

Mooney, Marta. Wives' Permanent Employment and Husbands' Hours of Work. *Ind. Relat.*, Spring 1981, *20*(2), pp. 205–11. **[G: U.S.]**

Mori, Pier Angelo. Economie concorrenziali, banditore e disoccupazione. (Competitive Economies, Auctioneer and Unemployment. With English summary.) *Giorn. Econ.*, March–April 1981, *40*(3–4), pp. 231–38.

Morrison, Donald G. and Schmittlein, David C. A Model of Careers in a Simple Hierarchy: Generalizing the Junior Professional's Decision Rule [A Closed Model of Careers in a Simple Hierarchy]. *Bell J. Econ. (See Rand J. Econ. after 4/85)*, Spring 1981, *12*(1), pp. 310–20.

Muellbauer, John. Are Employment Decisions Based on Rational Expectations? *J. Econometrics*, May 1981, *16*(1), pp. 156.

Muellbauer, John. Linear Aggregation in Neoclassical Labour Supply. *Rev. Econ. Stud.*, January 1981, *48*(1), pp. 21–36.

Neary, J. Peter. On the Harris–Todaro Model with Intersectoral Capital Mobility. *Economica*, August 1981, *48*(191), pp. 219–34. **[G: LDCs]**

Nelson, Charles R. Adjustment Lags versus Information Lags: A Test of Alternative Explanations of the Phillips Curve Phenomenon: A Reply. *J. Money, Credit, Banking*, November 1981, *13*(4), pp. 494–96.

Nelson, Charles R. Adjustment Lags versus Information Lags: A Test of Alternative Explanations of the Phillips Curve Phenomenon. *J. Money, Credit, Banking*, February 1981, *13*(1), pp. 1–11.

Neri, Fabio. On the Inflationary Consequences of a Keynesian Model: Variations on a Theme of Meade. *Metroecon.*, Feb.-Oct. 1981, *33*(1–2–3), pp. 159–73.

Ordover, Janusz A. Redistributing Incomes: Ex Ante or Ex Post. *Econ. Inquiry*, April 1981, *19*(2), pp. 333–49.

Oshima, Harry T. A. Lewis' Dualistic Theory and Its Relevance for Postwar Asian Growth. *Malayan Econ. Rev. (See Singapore Econ. Rev.)*, October 1981, *26*(2), pp. 1–26. **[G: Asia]**

Oswald, Andrew J. The Theory of Internal Wage and Employment Structure. *Bell J. Econ. (See Rand J. Econ. after 4/85)*, Spring 1981, *12*(1), pp. 263–71.

Oswald, Andrew J. Threat and Morale Effects in the Theory of Wages. *Europ. Econ. Rev.*, June/July 1981, *16*(2/3), pp. 269–83.

Oswald, Andrew J. Unemployment Benefit and the Supply of Labour. *Greek Econ. Rev.*, April 1981, *3*(1), pp. 33–45.

Otani, Ichiro. Real Wages, Business Cycles, and the Speed of Adjustment: A Reply [Real Wages and Business Cycles Revisited]. *Rev. Econ. Statist.*, May 1981, *63*(2), pp. 312–13. **[G: W. Europe; Japan; U.K.; U.S.]**

Papademos, Lucas. Maximum Employment and Anti-Inflation Policy. *Greek Econ. Rev.*, August 1981, *3*(2), pp. 93–127.

Pasinetti, Luigi L. On the Ricardian Theory of Value: A Note [A Mathematical Formulation of Ricardian System]. *Rev. Econ. Stud.*, October 1981, *48*(4),

pp. 673–75.

Patinkin, Don. Involuntary Unemployment and the Keynesian Supply Function. In *Patinkin, D., 1981, 1949,* pp. 155–75.

Paunio, Jouko and Suvanto, Antti. Wage Inflation, Expectations and Indexation. *J. Monet. Econ.,* September 1981, *8*(2), pp. 165–82.
[G: Finland]

Penner, Rudolph G. Discussion of the Papers by Piggott and Whalley [A Summary of Some Findings from a General Equilibrium Tax Model for the United Kingdom] and Boskin [Some Issues in "Supply-Side" Economics]. *Carnegie-Rochester Conf. Ser. Public Policy,* Spring 1981, *14,* pp. 231–35.

Perloff, Jeffrey M. Income and Payroll Tax Policy and Labor Supply: Discussion. In *Meyer, L. H., ed.,* 1981, pp. 231–36. [G: U.S.]

Pertot, Nada. Integracijski procesi v našem gospodarstvu: Modeli in metode za ugotavljanje smiselnosti in učinkovitosti takih povezovanj. (Integration Models in Yugoslav Economy: Models and Methods to Prove the Rationale and Efficiency of Merging. With English summary.) *Econ. Anal. Worker's Manage.,* 1981, *15*(3), pp. 365–81.
[G: Yugoslavia]

Petrović, Pavle. Income Distribution, Prices and Choice of Technique in the Labour-Managed Economy. *Econ. Anal. Worker's Manage.,* 1981, *15*(4), pp. 433–44.

Pissarides, Christopher A. Contract Theory, Temporary Layoffs and Unemployment: A Critical Assessment. In *Currie, D.; Peel, D. and Peters, W., eds.,* 1981, pp. 51–71.

Pissarides, Christopher A. Uncertainty and the Demand for Labour by Dynamically-Monopsonistic Firms. *Greek Econ. Rev.,* December 1981, *3*(3), pp. 279–94.

Pitchford, J. D. A Consistent Model of the Expectations-Augmented Phillips Curve and Inflation. *J. Macroecon.,* Fall 1981, *3*(4), pp. 489–99.

Pitchford, J. D. Taxation, Real Wage Rigidity and Employment: The Flexible Price Case. *Econ. J.,* September 1981, *91*(363), pp. 716–20.

Poulin Simon, Lise. Une théorie économique du loisir industriel; le cas du Canada. (An Economic Theory of Industrial Leisure. With English summary.) *L'Actual. Econ.,* January–March 1981, *57*(1), pp. 33–53. [G: Canada]

Power, Thomas M. Urban Size (Dis)amenities Revisited. *J. Urban Econ.,* January 1981, *9*(1), pp. 85–89. [G: U.S.]

Prosperetti, Luigi. A Phillips Curve for the Italian Economy? A Comment on Modigliani and Tarantelli [Market Forces, Trade Union Action and the Phillips Curve in Italy]. *Banca Naz. Lavoro Quart. Rev.,* December 1981, (139), pp. 447–54.
[G: Italy]

Putterman, Louis. On Optimality in Collective Institutional Choice. *J. Compar. Econ.,* December 1981, *5*(4), pp. 392–403.

Rader, Trout. Utility over Time: The Homothetic Case. *J. Econ. Theory,* October 1981, *25*(2), pp. 219–36.

Ramser, Hans J. Arbeitslosigkeit aufgrund unvollständiger Information. (Unemployment Due to

Imperfect Information. With English summary.) *Z. ges. Staatswiss.,* June 1981, *137*(2), pp. 163–86.

Riddell, W. Craig. Bargaining under Uncertainty. *Amer. Econ. Rev.,* September 1981, *71*(4), pp. 579–90.

Riley, John G. Learning by Observing and the Distribution of Wages: Comment. In *Rosen, S., ed.,* 1981, pp. 371–76.

Risch, Bodo. "Phillips-Loops" und endogener Konjunkturzyklus. (Phillips-Loops and Endogenous Cycles. With English summary.) *Z. ges. Staatswiss.,* March 1981, *137*(1), pp. 108–24.

Romer, David. Rosen and Quandt's Disequilibrium Model of the Labor Market: A Revision. *Rev. Econ. Statist.,* February 1981, *63*(1), pp. 145–46.
[G: U.S.]

Rosen, Sherwin. The Economics of Superstars. *Amer. Econ. Rev.,* December 1981, *71*(5), pp. 845–58.

Rosenbaum, Sonia and Wright, James D. Income Maintenance and Work Behavior. In *Martin, G. T., Jr., and Zald, M. N., eds.,* 1981, pp. 412–27. [G: U.S.]

Ross, Stephen; Taubman, Paul and Wachter, Michael L. Learning by Observing and the Distribution of Wages. In *Rosen, S., ed.,* 1981, pp. 359–71.

Roumasset, James R. and Smith, Joyotee. Population, Technological Change, and the Evolution of Labor Markets. *Population Devel. Rev.,* September 1981, *7*(3), pp. 401–19. [G: Philippines]

Ruffell, R. J. Endogeneity II: Direct Estimation of Labour Supply Functions with Piecewise Linear Budget Constraints. In *Brown, C. V., ed.,* 1981, pp. 101–16. [G: U.K.]

Saks, Daniel H. Wage Determination During Periods of High Inflation. In *Dennis, B. D., ed.,* 1981, pp. 128–34. [G: U.S.]

Sandmo, Agnar. Income Tax Evasion, Labour Supply, and the Equity–Efficiency Tradeoff. *J. Public Econ.,* December 1981, *16*(3), pp. 265–88.

Santiago, Carlos E. Male–Female Labor Force Participation and Rapid Industrialization. *J. Econ. Devel.,* December 1981, *6*(2), pp. 7–40.
[G: Puerto Rico]

Sarantis, Nicholas C. Employment, Labor Supply and Real Wages in Market Disequilibrium. *J. Macroecon.,* Summer 1981, *3*(3), pp. 335–54.
[G: U.S.]

Sargent, Thomas J. A Classical Macroeconomic Model for the United States. In *Lucas, R. E. and Sargent, T. J., eds.,* 1981, *1976,* pp. 521–51.
[G: U.S.]

Sargent, Thomas J. A Note on the "Accelerationist" Controversy. In *Lucas, R. E. and Sargent, T. J., eds.,* 1981, *1971,* pp. 33–38.

Sargent, Thomas J. Estimation of Dynamic Labor Demand Schedules under Rational Expectations. In *Lucas, R. E. and Sargent, T. J., eds.,* 1981, *1978,* pp. 463–99. [G: U.S.]

Sargent, Thomas J. Rational Expectations, the Real Rate of Interest, and the Natural Rate of Unemployment. In *Lucas, R. E. and Sargent, T. J., eds.,* 1981, *1973,* pp. 159–98. [G: U.S.]

Sawhill, Isabel V. Labor Market Policies and Inflation. **In** *Claudon, M. P. and Cornwall, R. R.,* *eds.,* 1981, pp. 217–31. **[G: U.S.]**

Schager, Nils Henrik. The Duration of Vacancies as a Measure of the State of Demand in the Labor Market. The Swedish Wage Drift Equation Reconsidered. **In** *Eliasson, G.; Holmlund, B. and Stafford, F. P., eds.,* 1981, pp. 393–442. **[G: Sweden]**

Schlicht, Ekkehart. Training Costs and Wage Differentials in the Theory of Job Competition. *Z. ges. Staatswiss.,* June 1981, *137*(2), pp. 212–21.

Schotter, Andrew and Braunstein, Yale M. Economic Search: An Experimental Study. *Econ. Inquiry,* January 1981, *19*(1), pp. 1–25.

Scott, C. D. Agrarian Reform and Seasonal Employment in Coastal Peruvian Agriculture. *J. Devel. Stud.,* July 1981, *17*(4), pp. 282–306. **[G: Peru]**

Seoka, Yoshihiko. The Effectiveness of Monetary Policy in the Keynesian Model with Rational Expectations: A Comment on Mr. Yoshikawa. *Econ. Stud. Quart.,* August 1981, *32*(2), pp. 181–87.

Serageldin, M. Ismail. The Modeling and Methodology of Manpower Planning in the Arab Countries. **In** *Sherbiny, N. A., ed.,* 1981, pp. 55–90. **[G: Arab Countries]**

Shapiro, Edward. Wage Inflation, Manpower Training, and the Phillips Curve: A Graphic Integration. *Amer. Econ.,* Spring 1981, *25*(1), pp. 17–21.

Sharir, Shmuel. On Labor Supply When Wants are "Limited." *Atlantic Econ. J.,* September 1981, *9*(3), pp. 34–43.

Shostak, E. The Natural Rate Hypothesis: An Econometric Test for the South African Economy. *S. Afr. J. Econ.,* March 1981, *49*(1), pp. 1–9. **[G: S. Africa]**

Showler, Brian. Political Economy and Unemployment. **In** *Showler, B. and Sinfield, A., eds.,* 1981, pp. 27–58. **[G: U.K.]**

Siegers, J. J. and Zandanel, R. A Simultaneous Analysis of the Labour Force Participation of Married Women and the Presence of Young Children in the Family. *De Economist,* 1981, *129*(3), pp. 382–93. **[G: Netherlands]**

Simon, D. Informal Sector Research: Note and Comment. *S. Afr. J. Econ.,* September 1981, *49*(3), pp. 295–98.

Sinclair, Peter J. N. When Will Technical Progress Destroy Jobs? *Oxford Econ. Pap.,* March 1981, *33*(1), pp. 1–18.

Smith, Robert Stewart. Compensating Differentials for Pensions and Underfunding in the Public Sector. *Rev. Econ. Statist.,* August 1981, *63*(3), pp. 463–68. **[G: U.S.]**

Smyth, David J. Real Wages, Business Cycles and the Speed of Adjustment of Employment in Manufacturing Sectors of Industrialized Countries [Real Wages and Business Cycles Revisited]. *Rev. Econ. Statist.,* May 1981, *63*(2), pp. 311–12. **[G: W. Europe; Japan; U.K.; U.S.]**

Smyth, David J. and Holmes, James M. The Employment Ratio and the Potential Labor Surplus in Phillips-Type Relationships: A Note. *J. Post Keynesian Econ.,* Fall 1981, *4*(1), pp. 75–80.

Sørensen, Troels Østergaard. Nyere arbejdsmarkedsteorier og den generaliserede Phillipskurve. (A Survey of Recent Development in Labour Market

and Inflation Theory. With English summary.) *Nationaløkon. Tidsskr.,* 1981, *119*(2), pp. 199–219.

Spence, A. Michael. Signaling, Screening, and Information. **In** *Rosen, S., ed.,* 1981, pp. 319–57.

Stafford, Frank P. On the Determinants of Labor Supply in Sweden. **In** *Eliasson, G.; Holmlund, B. and Stafford, F. P., eds.,* 1981, pp. 301–11. **[G: Sweden]**

Stephenson, Stanley P., Jr. The Cost of Labor Market Information: Male Youth Job Search Behavior. **In** *Galatin, M. and Leiter, R. D., eds.,* 1981, pp. 123–40. **[G: U.S.]**

Sutton, John. A Formal Model of the Long-run Phillips Curve Trade-off. *Economica,* November 1981, *48*(192), pp. 329–43.

Sylos Labini, Paolo. Spinelli and Fratianni on Inflation: A Comment [Money, Prices and Wages in Italy] [Wage Inflation in Italy: A Reappraisal]. *Banca Naz. Lavoro Quart. Rev.,* December 1981, (139), pp. 461–66.

Tauchen, George E. Some Evidence on Cross-Sector Effects of the Minimum Wage. *J. Polit. Econ.,* June 1981, *89*(3), pp. 529–47. **[G: U.S.]**

Theeuwes, J. Family Labour Force Participation: Multinomial Logit Estimates. *Appl. Econ.,* December 1981, *13*(4), pp. 481–98. **[G: U.S.]**

Thirlwall, A. P. The Valuation of Labour in Surplus Labour Economies: A Synoptic View. **In** *Livingstone, I., ed.,* 1981, *1971*, pp. 245–53.

Thomas, R. B. Labour Market Adjustments. **In** *Creedy, J., ed.,* 1981, pp. 17–47. **[G: U.K.]**

Todaro, Michael P. Labour Market Performance in Developing Countries: A Survey: Comment. **In** *Streeten, P. and Jolly, R, eds.,* 1981, *1978*, pp. 193–95. **[G: LDCs]**

Tomer, John F. Worker Motivation: A Neglected Element in Micro-Micro Theory. *J. Econ. Issues,* June 1981, *15*(2), pp. 351–62.

Torr, C. S. W. A Geometric Derivation of the Phillips Curve. *Amer. Econ.,* Fall 1981, *25*(2), pp. 59–62.

Tuchscherer, Thomas. The Unnatural "Natural" Rate of Unemployment. *J. Post Keynesian Econ.,* Fall 1981, *4*(1), pp. 25–31.

Turnovsky, Stephen J. The Optimal Intertemporal Choice of Inflation and Unemployment: An Analysis of the Steady State and Transitional Dynamics. *J. Econ. Dynam. Control,* November 1981, *3*(4), pp. 357–84.

Ulph, David T. Labour Supply, Taxation and the Measurement of Inequality. **In** *Brown, C. V., ed.,* 1981, pp. 144–62.

Ulph, David T. Unemployment Equilibrium when Production is a Function of Average Hours and Number of Workers: Comment. **In** *Currie, D.; Peel, D. and Peters, W., eds.,* 1981, pp. 194–95.

Ulph, David T. and Ulph, Alistair M. Implications for Optimal Income Taxation. **In** *Brown, C. V., ed.,* 1981, pp. 189–212. **[G: U.K.]**

Vint, John. A Two Sector Model of the Wages Fund: Mill's Recantation Revisited. *Brit. Rev. Econ. Issues,* Autumn 1981, *3*(9), pp. 71–88.

Waldo, Douglas G. Sticky Nominal Wages and the Optimal Employment Rule. *J. Monet. Econ.,* May 1981, *7*(3), pp. 339–53.

Wallace, Myles S. A Backward Bending Supply of Labor Schedule and the Short Run Phillips Curve. *Southern Econ. J.*, October 1981, *48*(2), pp. 502–05.

Watson, Donald. The Inter-Industry Effect of Cumulative Wage Indexation—A Critical Comment. *Australian Econ. Pap.*, June 1981, *20*(36), pp. 189–90.

Weinstein, Robert I. Union–Nonunion Wage Differentials over the Business Cycle: A Bilateral Monopoly Model. *Atlantic Econ. J.*, September 1981, *9*(3), pp. 44–49.

Weiss, Yoram and Gronau, Reuben. Expected Interruptions in Labour Force Participation and Sex-Related Differences in Earnings Growth. *Rev. Econ. Stud.*, October 1981, *48*(4), pp. 607–19.

Wells, Paul. Modigliani on Flexible Wages and Prices: Reply. *J. Post Keynesian Econ.*, Winter 1980–81, *3*(2), pp. 284–86.

West, Edwin G. and Hafer, R. W. J. S. Mill, Unions, and the Wages Fund Recantation: A Reinterpretation—Reply. *Quart. J. Econ.*, August 1981, *96*(3), pp. 543–49.

Whitehead, A. K. Screening and Education: A Theoretical and Empirical Survey. *Brit. Rev. Econ. Issues*, Spring 1981, *2*(8), pp. 44–62.

Whitehead, Donald and Bonnell, Sheila. What Ails the Lucky Country: The Debate about Diagnosis. In *Hancock, K.*, ed., 1981, pp. 89–140.
[G: Australia]

Wilde, Louis L. Information Costs, Duration of Search, and Turnover: Theory and Applications. *J. Polit. Econ.*, December 1981, *89*(6), pp. 1122–41.

Wilder, Ronald P. and Singh, Davinder. Determinants of Changes in the Wage Hierarchy: A Note. *Brit. J. Ind. Relat.*, November 1981, *19*(3), pp. 376–79.
[G: U.K.]

Wilson, Charles A. Learning by Observing and the Distribution of Wages: Comment. In *Rosen, S.*, ed., 1981, pp. 376–86.

Yatchew, Adonis J. Further Evidence on "Estimation of a Disequilibrium Aggregate Labor Market." *Rev. Econ. Statist.*, February 1981, *63*(1), pp. 142–44.
[G: U.S.]

Yoon, Bong Joon. A Model of Unemployment Duration with Variable Search Intensity. *Rev. Econ. Statist.*, November 1981, *63*(4), pp. 599–609.
[G: U.S.]

Yu, Eden S. H. On Factor Market Distortions and Economic Growth. *Southern Econ. J.*, July 1981, *48*(1), pp. 172–78.

Zylberberg, André. Flexibilité, incertain et théorie de la demande de travail. (Flexibility, Incertitude, and Theory of the Demand for Labor. With English summary.) *Ann. INSEE*, April–June 1981, (42), pp. 31–52.

822 Public Policy; Role of Government

8220 General

Alexander, Robert J. Brazil. In *Blum, A. A.*, ed., 1981, pp. 49–70.
[G: Brazil]

Bartels, Martin. Mining Ventures in Developing Countries: Localization of Labor. In *Schanze, E., et al.*, 1981, pp. 198–211. [G: Selected LDCs]

Brown, William. Labour Market Policy: Comments. In *[Cairncross, A.]*, 1981, pp. 96–100.

Bryner, Gary. Congress, Courts, and Agencies: Equal Employment and the Limits of Policy Implementation. *Polit. Sci. Quart.*, Fall 1981, *96*(3), pp. 411–30.
[G: U.S.]

Ciscel, David H. and Tuckman, Barbara H. The Peripheral Worker: CETA Training as Imperfect Job Socialization. *J. Econ. Issues*, June 1981, *15*(2), pp. 489–500.
[G: U.S.]

Coates, Mary Lou. Manpower and Labour Markets: Summary Outline. In *Wood, W. D. and Kumar, P.*, eds., 1981, pp. 27–94. [G: Canada]

Davidson, Naomi Berger. Special Groups in the Labor Market: Discussion. In *Dennis, B. D.*, ed., 1981, pp. 72–75.
[G: U.S.]

DeLorme, Charles D., Jr.; Hill, R. Carter and Wood, Norman J. The Determinants of Voting by the National Labor Relations Board on Unfair Labor Practice Cases: 1955–1975. *Public Choice*, 1981, *37*(2), pp. 207–18.
[G: U.S.]

Feuille, Peter and Lewin, David. Equal Employment Opportunity Bargaining. *Ind. Relat.*, Fall 1981, *20*(3), pp. 322–34.
[G: U.S.]

Hanami, Tadashi. The Influence of ILO Standards on Law and Practice in Japan. *Int. Lab. Rev.*, November–December 1981, *120*(6), pp. 765–79.
[G: Japan]

Koskimies, Jaakko. Finland. In *Blum, A. A.*, ed., 1981, pp. 144–67.
[G: Finland]

Kosters, Marvin H. Government and Productivity Improvement: Solution or Problem? In *Hogan, J. D. and Craig, A. M.*, eds., Vol. 2, 1981, pp. 953–59.
[G: U.S.]

Ledgerwood, Donna E. and Johnson-Dietz, Sue. Sexual Harassment: Implications for Employer Liability. *Mon. Lab. Rev.*, April 1981, *104*(4), pp. 45–47.
[G: U.S.]

Ledgerwood, Donna E. and Johnson-Dietz, Sue. The EEOC's Bold Foray into Sexual Harassment on the Job: New Implications for Employer Liability. In *Dennis, B. D.*, ed., 1981, pp. 55–61.
[G: U.S.]

Lovett, William A. Teamwork, Markets, and Regulation: Distortions Arising from Legal Parochialism. *J. Econ. Issues*, June 1981, *15*(2), pp. 409–22.
[G: U.S.]

McMurray, David. Labour Legislation and Policy: Summary Outline. In *Wood, W. D. and Kumar, P.*, eds., 1981, pp. 95–191. [G: Canada]

Morse, David A. The Role of the Labor Department. In *Heller, F. H.*, ed., 1981, pp. 37–49.
[G: U.S.]

Mounts, Gregory J. Labor and the Supreme Court: Significant Decisions of 1979–80. *Mon. Lab. Rev.*, April 1981, *104*(4), pp. 13–22. [G: U.S.]

Nelson, Richard R. State Labor Legislation Enacted in 1980. *Mon. Lab. Rev.*, January 1981, *104*(1), pp. 21–34. [G: U.S.]

Phelps Brown, Henry. Labour Market Policy. In *[Cairncross, A.]*, 1981, pp. 68–96. [G: U.K.]

Pierre, Marcel. Recent Developments in the Humanisation of Working Conditions in Belgium. *Int. Lab. Rev.*, May–June 1981, *120*(3), pp. 279–90.
[G: Belgium]

Roomkin, Myron. A Quantitative Study of Unfair Labor Practice Cases. *Ind. Lab. Relat. Rev.*, January 1981, *34*(2), pp. 245–56.   [G: U.S.]

Sagardoy Bengoechea, Juan A. The Spanish Workers' Statute. *Int. Lab. Rev.*, March–April 1981, *120*(2), pp. 215–29.   [G: Spain]

Séguret, M.-C. Child-Care Services for Working Parents. *Int. Lab. Rev.*, November–December 1981, *120*(6), pp. 711–25.   [G: Europe; LDCs]

Sheptulina, N. N. Protection of Female Labor. *Prob. Econ.*, Sept.–Oct.–Nov. 1981, *24*(5–6–7), pp. 156–62.   [G: U.S.S.R.]

Wallace, Phyllis A. and Driscoll, James W. Social Issues in Collective Bargaining. In *Stieber, J.; McKersie, R. B. and Mills, D. Q., eds.*, 1981, pp. 199–254.   [G: U.S.]

Wessels, Walter J. Economic Effects of Right to Work Laws. *J. Lab. Res.*, Spring 1981, *2*(1), pp. 55–75.   [G: U.S.]

8221 Wages and Hours

Anderson, Bernard E. Economic Growth: The Central Issue: A Partial Dissent: Fiddling with the Economy is Not Enough. In *Inst. for Contemp. Studies*, 1981, pp. 47–51.   [G: U.S.]

Betsey, Charles L. and Dunson, Bruce H. Federal Minimum Wage Laws and the Employment of Minority Youth. *Amer. Econ. Rev.*, May 1981, *71*(2), pp. 379–84.   [G: U.S.]

Fleisher, Belton M. Minimum Wage Regulation in Retail Trade. *Eastern Econ. J.*, April 1981, *7*(2), pp. 75–96.   [G: U.S.]

Goldfarb, Robert S. and Morrall, John F., III. The Davis–Bacon Act: An Appraisal of Recent Studies. *Ind. Lab. Relat. Rev.*, January 1981, *34*(2), pp. 191–206.   [G: U.S.]

Görres, Peter Anselm. Mindestlohnarbeitslosigkeit—eine wenig nützliche Vokabel. (Minimum Wage Unemployment—A Concept of Dubious Value. With English summary.) *Konjunkturpolitik*, 1981, *27*(3), pp. 156–75.

Gunn, Wendell Wilkie. Black Lawyers: Struggling to Survive: Thinking about Private Investment. In *Inst. for Contemp. Studies*, 1981, pp. 111–13.

Marrese, M. The Evolution of Wage Regulation in Hungary. In *Hare, P. G.; Radice, H. K. and Swain, N., eds.*, 1981, pp. 54–80. [G: Hungary]

Mills, D. Quinn and Frobes, Shirley. Impact of Increases in the Federal Minimum Wage on Target Groups in Urban Areas. *Public Policy*, Summer 1981, *29*(3), pp. 277–97.   [G: U.S.]

Sgro, Pasquale M. and Takayama, Akira. On the Long-Run Growth Effects of a Minimum Wage for a Two-Sector Economy. *Econ. Rec.*, June 1981, *57*(157), pp. 180–85.

Starr, Gerald. Minimum Wage Fixing: International Experience with Alternative Roles. *Int. Lab. Rev.*, September–October 1981, *120*(5), pp. 545–62.   [G: LDCs; MDCs]

Tauchen, George E. Some Evidence on Cross-Sector Effects of the Minimum Wage. *J. Polit. Econ.*, June 1981, *89*(3), pp. 529–47.   [G: U.S.]

8222 Workmen's Compensation and Vocational Rehabilitation

Elson, Martin W. and Burton, John F., Jr. Workers' Compensation Insurance: Recent Trends in Em-

ployer Costs. *Mon. Lab. Rev.*, March 1981, *104*(3), pp. 45–50.   [G: U.S.]

Halberstadt, V. and Haveman, Robert H. Public Policies for Disabled Workers: Cross National Evidence on Efficiency and Redistributive Effects. In *[Pen, J.]*, 1981, pp. 79–110. [G: Israel; U.S.; W. Europe]

Leigh, J. Paul. Compensating Wages for Occupational Injuries and Diseases. *Soc. Sci. Quart.*, December 1981, *62*(4), pp. 772–78.   [G: U.S.]

Manning, Ian. Social Security and the Future. *Australian Econ. Rev.*, 1st Quarter 1981, (53), pp. 29–34.   [G: Australia]

Price, Daniel N. Workers' Compensation: Coverage, Benefits and Costs, 1979. *Soc. Sec. Bull.*, September 1981, *44*(9), pp. 9–13.   [G: U.S.]

Rea, Samuel A., Jr. Workmen's Compensation and Occupational Safety under Imperfect Information. *Amer. Econ. Rev.*, March 1981, *71*(1), pp. 80–93.

Schrems, Edward L. The Tax Treatment of Workers Compensation Costs and Safety and Health Incentives. *J. Risk Ins.*, June 1981, *48*(2), pp. 272–85.   [G: U.S.]

Sunshine, Jonathan. Disability Payments Stabilizing after Era of Accelerating Growth. *Mon. Lab. Rev.*, May 1981, *104*(5), pp. 17–22.   [G: U.S.]

Tinsley, La Verne C. Workers' Compensation in 1980: Summary of Major Enactments. *Mon. Lab. Rev.*, March 1981, *104*(3), pp. 51–57. [G: U.S.]

8223 Factory Act and Safety Legislation

Alacchi, Georges and Todradzé, Constantin. Safety in Mines and the Role of Training. *Int. Lab. Rev.*, September–October 1981, *120*(5), pp. 615–29.   [G: EEC]

Allen, Steven G. Compensation, Safety, and Absenteeism: Evidence from the Paper Industry. *Ind. Lab. Relat. Rev.*, January 1981, *34*(2), pp. 207–18.   [G: U.S.]

Baker, Joe G. Sources of Deep Coal Mine Productivity Change, 1962–1975. *Energy J.*, April 1981, *2*(2), pp. 95–106.   [G: U.S.]

Bertinuson, Janet and Hricko, Andrea M. Occupational Health and Safety for Women Workers: Some Teaching Models. In *Wertheimer, B. M., ed.*, 1981, pp. 194–203.   [G: U.S.]

Bingham, Eula. Ethics and the Workplace. In *Hoffman, W. M. and Wyly, T. J., eds.*, 1981, pp. 145–49.   [G: U.S.]

Chambers, Ian. The Applicability of International Labour Conventions Offshore: An Approach. *Int. Lab. Rev.*, July–August 1981, *120*(4), pp. 395–049.

Codrington, Caroline and Henley, John S. The Industrial Relations of Injury and Death: Safety Representatives in the Construction Industry. *Brit. J. Ind. Relat.*, November 1981, *19*(3), pp. 297–315.   [G: U.K.]

Cooke, William N. and Gautschi, Frederick H., III. OSHA, Plant Safety Programs, and Injury Reduction. *Ind. Relat.*, Fall 1981, *20*(3), pp. 245–57.   [G: U.S.]

Corn, Morton. Cotton Dust: A Regulator's View. In *Crandall, R. W. and Lave, L. B., eds.*, 1981, pp. 109–14.   [G: U.S.]

Crandall, Robert W. and Lave, Lester B. The Scientific Basis of Health and Safety Regulation: Introduction and Summary. In *Crandall, R. W. and Lave, L. B.*, eds., 1981, pp. 1–17. [G: U.S.]

Eads, George C. The Benefits of Better Benefits Estimation. In *Ferguson, A. R. and LeVeen, E. P.*, eds., 1981, pp. 43–52. [G: U.S.]

Harris, George. Occupational Health Risks and the Worker's Right to Know. *Yale Law J.*, July 1981, *90*(8), pp. 1792–1810. [G: U.S.]

Harrison, David, Jr. Distributional Objectives in Health and Safety Regulation. In *Ferguson, A. R. and LeVeen, E. P.*, eds., 1981, pp. 177–201. [G: U.S.]

Hilaski, Harvey J. Understanding Statistics on Occupational Illnesses. *Mon. Lab. Rev.*, March 1981, *104*(3), pp. 25–29. [G: U.S.]

Kosters, Marvin H. Cost-Benefit Analysis of Government Safety and Health Regulation. In *Hoffman, W. M. and Wyly, T. J.*, eds., 1981, pp. 160–66. [G: U.S.]

MacLaury, Judson. The Job Safety Law of 1970: Its Passage was Perilous. *Mon. Lab. Rev.*, March 1981, *104*(3), pp. 18–24. [G: U.S.]

Magat, Wesley A. and Estomin, Steven. The Behavior of Regulatory Agencies. In *Ferguson, A. R.*, ed., 1981, pp. 95–116. [G: U.S.]

Marlow, Michael L. The Impact of Different Government Units in the Regulation of the Workplace Environment. *Public Choice*, 1981, *37*(2), pp. 349–56.

Merchant, James A. Cotton Dust: A Scientist's View. In *Crandall, R. W. and Lave, L. B.*, eds., 1981, pp. 71–91. [G: U.S.]

Morrall, John F., III. Cotton Dust: An Economist's View. In *Crandall, R. W. and Lave, L. B.*, eds., 1981, pp. 93–108. [G: U.S.]

Naschold, Frieder. Two Roads toward Innovation in Occupational Safety and Health in Western Countries. In *Altenstetter, C.*, ed., 1981, pp. 145–59. [G: U.S.; Sweden; W. Germany]

Nichols, Albert and Zeckhauser, Richard. OSHA after a Decade: A Time for Reason. In *Weiss, L. W. and Klass, M. W.*, eds., 1981, pp. 202–34. [G: U.S.]

Noll, Roger G. and Joskow, Paul L. Regulation in Theory and Practice: An Overview. In *Fromm, G.*, ed., 1981, pp. 1–65. [G: U.S.]

Potter, David S. The Scientific Basis of Health and Safety Regulation: Comments. In *Crandall, R. W. and Lave, L. B.*, eds., 1981, pp. 291–95. [G: U.S.]

Rea, Samuel A., Jr. Workmen's Compensation and Occupational Safety under Imperfect Information. *Amer. Econ. Rev.*, March 1981, *71*(1), pp. 80–93.

Root, Norman. Injuries at Work Are Fewer among Older Employees. *Mon. Lab. Rev.*, March 1981, *104*(3), pp. 30–34. [G: U.S.]

Root, Norman and Sebastian, Deborah. BLS Develops Measure of Job Risk by Occupation. *Mon. Lab. Rev.*, October 1981, *104*(10), pp. 26–30. [G: U.S.]

Ruben, George. Industrial Relations in 1980 Influenced by Inflation and Recession. *Mon. Lab. Rev.*, January 1981, *104*(1), pp. 15–20. [G: U.S.]

Schrems, Edward L. The Tax Treatment of Workers Compensation Costs and Safety and Health Incentives. *J. Risk Ins.*, June 1981, *48*(2), pp. 272–85. [G: U.S.]

Stigler, George J. Regulation in Theory and Practice: An Overview: Comment. In *Fromm, G.*, ed., 1981, pp. 73–77. [G: U.S.]

The Business Roundtable and Arthur Anderson & Co. Cost of Government Regulation Study. In *Gatti, J. F.*, ed., 1981, *1979*, pp. 95–129. [G: U.S.]

Vaupel, James W. On the Benefits of Health and Safety Regulation. In *Ferguson, A. R. and LeVeen, E. P.*, eds., 1981, pp. 1–22. [G: U.S.]

Vaupel, James W. Priorities for Research on the Benefits of Health, Safety, and Environmental Regulation. In *Ferguson, A. R.*, ed., 1981, pp. 167–83. [G: U.S.]

Workman, Philip A. Using Statistics to Manage a State Safety and Health Program. *Mon. Lab. Rev.*, March 1981, *104*(3), pp. 42–44. [G: U.S.]

8224 Unemployment Insurance

Arpan, Jeffrey S.; de la Torre, José and Toyne, Brian. International Developments and the U.S. Apparel Industry. *J. Int. Bus. Stud.*, Winter 1981, *12*(3), pp. 49–64. [G: U.S.]

Atkinson, A. B. Unemployment Benefits and Incentives. In *Creedy, J.*, ed., 1981, pp. 128–49. [G: U.K.]

Barron, John M. and Mellow, Wesley S. Interstate Differences in Unemployment Insurance. *Nat. Tax J.*, March 1981, *34*(1), pp. 105–13. [G: U.S.]

Barron, John M. and Mellow, Wesley S. Unemployment Insurance: The Recipients and Its Impact. *Southern Econ. J.*, January 1981, *47*(3), pp. 606–16. [G: U.S.]

Brechling, Frank. Layoffs and Unemployment Insurance. In *Rosen, S.*, ed., 1981, pp. 187–202. [G: U.S.]

Burgess, Paul L. and Kingston, Jerry L. UI Benefit Effects on Compensated Unemployment. *Ind. Relat.*, Fall 1981, *20*(3), pp. 258–70. [G: U.S.]

Butler, Richard J. and Sisti, Thomas R. Impact of Experience Rating and UI Benefits on Unemployment: The Neglected Firm Side. In *Dennis, B. D.*, ed., 1981, pp. 316–25. [G: U.S.]

Cooke, William N. The Behavior of Unemployment Insurance Recipients under Adverse Market Conditions. *Ind. Lab. Relat. Rev.*, April 1981, *34*(3), pp. 386–95. [G: U.S.]

Corson, Walter and Nicholson, Walter. Trade Adjustment Assistance for Workers: Results of a Survey of Recipients under the Trade Act of 1974. In *Ehrenberg, R. G.*, ed., 1981, pp. 417–69. [G: U.S.]

Creedy, John and Disney, Richard. Eligibility for Unemployment Benefits in Great Britain. *Oxford Econ. Pap.*, July 1981, *33*(2), pp. 256–73. [G: U.K.]

Danziger, Sheldon; Haveman, Robert H. and Plotnick, Robert. How Income Transfer Programs Affect Work, Savings, and the Income Distribution:

A Critical Review. *J. Econ. Lit.*, September 1981, 19(3), pp. 975–1028. [G: U.S.]

Disney, R. Unemployment Insurance in Britain. In *Creedy, J., ed.*, 1981, pp. 150–85. [G: U.K.]

Faust, A. State and Unemployment in Germany 1890–1918 (Labour Exchanges, Job Creation and Unemployment Insurance). In *Mommsen, W. J., ed.*, 1981, pp. 150–63. [G: Germany]

Gutierrez-Rieger, Hannah and Podczek, Konrad. On the Nonexistence of Temporary Layoff Unemployment in Austria. *Empirica*, 1981, (2), pp. 277–89. [G: Austria]

Hamermesh, Daniel S. Layoffs and Unemployment Insurance: Comment. In *Rosen, S., ed.*, 1981, pp. 203–07. [G: U.S.]

Hamermesh, Daniel S. Transfers, Taxes and the NAIRU. In *Meyer, L. H., ed.*, 1981, pp. 203–29. [G: U.S.]

Hassenkam, Henrik. Aktuel arbejdsmarkedspolitik. (Danish Labour Market Policy. With English summary.) *Nationaløkon. Tidsskr.*, 1981, 119(2), pp. 166–81. [G: Denmark]

Hey, John D. and Mavromaras, Kostas Gr. The Effect of Unemployment Insurance on the Riskiness of Occupational Choice. *J. Public Econ.*, December 1981, 16(3), pp. 317–41.

Hutchens, Robert M. Distributional Equity in the Unemployment Insurance System. *Ind. Lab. Relat. Rev.*, April 1981, 34(3), pp. 377–85. [G: U.S.]

Johnson, Darwin G. Sensitivity of Federal Expenditures to Unemployment. *Public Finance Quart.*, January 1981, 9(1), pp. 3–21. [G: U.S.]

Kiefer, Nicholas M. and Neumann, George R. Structural and Reduced Form Approaches to Analyzing Unemployment Durations. In *Rosen, S., ed.*, 1981, pp. 171–85. [G: U.S.]

Killingsworth, Charles C. Proceedings of the Seminar on Employment: Statement. In *U.S. Congress, Joint Economic Committee (I)*, 1981, pp. 113–15. [G: U.S.]

Killingsworth, Charles C. Trouble in Social Insurance. *Challenge*, July/August 1981, 24(3), pp. 50–52. [G: U.S.]

Manning, Ian. The 1970s: A Decade of Social Security Policy. *Australian Econ. Rev.*, 1st Quarter 1981, (53), pp. 13–19. [G: Australia]

Nicholson, Walter. A Statistical Model of Exhaustion of Unemployment Insurance Benefits. *J. Human Res.*, Winter 1981, 16(1), pp. 117–28. [G: U.S.]

Oswald, Andrew J. Unemployment Benefit and the Supply of Labour. *Greek Econ. Rev.*, April 1981, 3(1), pp. 33–45.

Padilla, Arthur. The Unemployment Insurance System: Its Financial Structure. *Mon. Lab. Rev.*, December 1981, 104(12), pp. 32–37. [G: U.S.]

Price, Daniel N. Report of the National Commission on Unemployment Compensation. *Soc. Sec. Bull.*, October 1981, 44(10), pp. 37–39. [G: U.S.]

Raines, Fredric. Transfers, Taxes, and the NAIRU: Discussion. In *Meyer, L. H., ed.*, 1981, pp. 237–41. [G: U.S.]

Risch, Bodo. Gewerkschaftseigene Arbeitslosenversicherung vor 1914. (Trade Union Unemployment Insurance before 1914. With English summary.)

Weltwirtsch. Arch., 1981, 117(3), pp. 513–45. [G: Germany]

Runner, Diana. Legislative Revisions of Unemployment Insurance in 1980. *Mon. Lab. Rev.*, January 1981, 104(1), pp. 35–39. [G: U.S.]

Stevens, David W. Contributed Papers: Labor Markets and Other IR Topics: Discussion. In *Dennis, B. D., ed.*, 1981, pp. 337–38. [G: U.S.]

Weisbrod, Bernd. The Crisis of German Unemployment Insurance in 1928/1929 and its Political Repercussions. In *Mommsen, W. J., ed.*, 1981, pp. 188–204. [G: Germany]

8225 Government Employment Policy (including Employment Services)

Balkenhol, Bernd. Direct Job Creation in Industrialised Countries. *Int. Lab. Rev.*, July–August 1981, 120(4), pp. 425–38. [G: Scandinavia; EEC; U.S.; Canada]

Bishop, John. Employment in Construction and Distribution Industries: The Impact of the New Jobs Tax Credit. In *Rosen, S., ed.*, 1981, pp. 209–46. [G: U.S.]

Bishop, John and Haveman, Robert H. Targeted Wage Subsidies: Their Rationale and Effectiveness. In *Eliasson, G. and Södersten, J., eds.*, 1981, pp. 297–343. [G: U.S.]

Cantor, Arnold. Proceedings of the Seminar on Employment: Statement. In *U.S. Congress, Joint Economic Committee (1)*, 1981, pp. 116–19. [G: U.S.]

Farkas, George; Olsen, Randall J. and Stromsdorfer, Ernst W. Youth Labor Supply During the Summer: Evidence for Youths from Low-Income Households. In *Ehrenberg, R. G., ed.*, 1981, pp. 151–90. [G: U.S.]

Faust, A. State and Unemployment in Germany 1890–1918 (Labour Exchanges, Job Creation and Unemployment Insurance). In *Mommsen, W. J., ed.*, 1981, pp. 150–63. [G: Germany]

Gibson, N. J. and Spencer, J. E. Unemployment and Wages in Northern Ireland. In *Crick, B., ed.*, 1981, 1981, pp. 100–14. [G: U.K.]

Goossens, Karel and Vuchelen, Jozef. Het bedrijfseconomische karakter van het Plan De Wulf. (The Business Economic Nature of the "Plan De Wulf." With English summary.) *Cah. Écon. Bruxelles*, 2nd Trimestre 1981, (90), pp. 203–28. [G: Belgium]

Gramlich, Edward M. and Ysander, Bengt-Christer. Relief Work and Grant Displacement in Sweden. In *Eliasson, G.; Holmlund, B. and Stafford, F. P., eds.*, 1981, pp. 139–66. [G: Sweden]

Guha, Sunil. Income Redistribution through Labour-Intensive Rural Public Works: Some Policy Issues. *Int. Lab. Rev.*, January–February 1981, 120(1), pp. 67–82. [G: LDCs]

Hannah, S. P. A Note on Employment Subsidies and the Government Budget Constraint in a Closed Economy. *Bull. Econ. Res.*, May 1981, 33(1), pp. 3–13.

Hassenkam, Henrik. Aktuel arbejdsmarkedspolitik. (Danish Labour Market Policy. With English summary.) *Nationaløkon. Tidsskr.*, 1981, 119(2), pp. 166–81. [G: Denmark]

Hill, Michael. Unemployment and Government Manpower Policy. In *Showler, B. and Sinfield, A., eds.*, 1981, pp. 89–121. [G: U.K.]

Holland, Robert. Proceedings of the Seminar on Employment: Statement. In *U.S. Congress, Joint Economic Committee (I)*, 1981, pp. 109–10. [G: U.S.]

Holmlund, Bertil. Employment Subsidies and the Behavior of the Firm. In *Eliasson, G. and Södersten, J., eds.*, 1981, pp. 267–93.

Howson, S. Slump and Unemployment. In *Floud, R. and McCloskey, D., eds.*, Vol. 2, 1981, pp. 265–85. [G: U.K.]

Johannesson, Jan. On the Composition of Swedish Labor Market Policy. In *Eliasson, G.; Holmlund, B. and Stafford, F. P., eds.*, 1981, pp. 67–137. [G: Sweden]

Killingsworth, Charles C. The Development of Employment Policy. In *Carter, M. J. and Leahy, W. H., eds.*, 1981, pp. 1–60. [G: U.S.]

Lizano Fait, Eduardo. Towards a National Employment Policy: The Case of Costa Rica. *Int. Lab. Rev.*, May–June 1981, *120*(3), pp. 361–74. [G: Costa Rica]

Lucas, Robert E., Jr. Rules, Discretion, and the Role of the Economic Advisor. In *Lucas, R. E., Jr.*, 1981, *1980*, pp. 248–61.

Lucas, Robert E., Jr. Unemployment Policy. In *Lucas, R. E., Jr.*, 1981, *1978*, pp. 240–47.

Martin, Randolph C. A Note on the Cost per Job Created by Federal Regional Development Programs. *Reg. Sci. Persp.*, 1981, *11*(2), pp. 49–55. [G: U.S.]

Middlemas, Keith. Unemployment: The Past and Future of a Political Problem. In *Crick, B., ed.*, 1981, *1981*, pp. 135–51. [G: U.K.]

Mitchell, Parren J. Proceedings of the Seminar on Employment: Statement. In *U.S. Congress, Joint Economic Committee (I)*, 1981, pp. 104–06. [G: U.S.]

Mueller, Charles F. Migration of the Unemployed: A Relocation Assistance Program. *Mon. Lab. Rev.*, April 1981, *104*(4), pp. 62–64. [G: U.S.]

Reynolds, Clark W. Mexican Economic Development and the United States. In *Ladman, J. R.; Baldwin, D. J. and Bergman, E., eds.*, 1981, pp. 155–69. [G: Mexico; U.S.]

Rosenstein-Rodan, P. M. Planning for Full Employment. In *[Lipiński, E.]*, 1981, pp. 223–34.

Sawhill, Isabel V. Labor Market Policies and Inflation. In *Claudon, M. P. and Cornwall, R. R., eds.*, 1981, pp. 217–31. [G: U.S.]

Showler, Brian and Sinfield, Adrian. A Most Unequal Tax. In *Showler, B. and Sinfield, A., eds.*, 1981, pp. 215–40. [G: U.K.]

Sorrentino, Constance. Unemployment in International Perspective. In *Showler, B. and Sinfield, A., eds.*, 1981, pp. 167–214. [G: OECD]

Stafford, Frank P. Unemployment and Labor Market Policy in Sweden and the United States. In *Eliasson, G.; Holmlund, B. and Stafford, F. P., eds.*, 1981, pp. 21–65. [G: U.S.; Sweden]

Sternlieb, George. Kemp–Garcia Act: An Initial Evaluation. In *Sternlieb, G. and Listokin, D., eds.*, 1981, pp. 42–83. [G: U.S.]

Tokman, Víctor E. The Development Strategy and Employment in the 1980s. *Cepal Rev.*, December 1981, (15), pp. 133–41. [G: Latin America]

Wolffsohn, M. Creation of Employment as a Welfare Policy. The Final Phase of the Weimar Republic. In *Mommsen, W. J., ed.*, 1981, pp. 205–44.

8226 Employment in the Public Sector

Bellante, Don and Link, Albert N. Are Public Sector Workers More Risk Averse Than Private Sector Workers? *Ind. Lab. Relat. Rev.*, April 1981, *34*(3), pp. 408–12. [G: U.S.]

Cassing, James H. and Hillman, Arye L. A Social Safety Net for the Impact of Technical Change: An Evaluation of the Myers Committee's Adjustment Assistance Proposal. *Econ. Rec.*, September 1981, *57*(158), pp. 232–37. [G: Australia]

Cayer, N. Joseph and Schaefer, Roger C. Affirmative Action and Municipal Employees. *Soc. Sci. Quart.*, September 1981, *62*(3), pp. 487–94. [G: U.S.]

Daub, Peter M. and Jacobson, Hugh H. Title VII and Congressional Employees: The "Chilling Effect" and the Speech or Debate Clause. *Yale Law J.*, May 1981, *90*(6), pp. 1458–85. [G: U.S.]

David, Lily Mary. Experience under the Federal Pay Comparability Act of 1970. In *Dennis, B. D., ed.*, 1981, pp. 76–81. [G: U.S.]

Dean, Andrew. Public and Private Sector Pay and the Economy. In *Fallick, J. L. and Elliott, R. F., eds.*, 1981, pp. 45–71. [G: U.K.]

Diejomaoh, V. P. and Anusionwu, E. C. Education and Income Distribution in Nigeria. In *Bienen, H. and Diejomaoh, V. P., eds.*, 1981, pp. 373–420. [G: Nigeria]

Douglas, Hernán Cortés and Sjaastad, Larry A. Protección y empleo. (With English summary.) *Cuadernos Econ.*, August–December 1981, *18*(54–55), pp. 317–60. [G: Chile]

Dye, Thomas R. and Renick, James. Political Power and City Jobs: Determinants of Minority Employment. *Soc. Sci. Quart.*, September 1981, *62*(3), pp. 475–86. [G: U.S.]

Görzig, Bernd. The Influence of Public Demand on Sectoral Employment: The Case of the Federal Republic of Germany. *Konjunkturpolitik*, 1981, *27*(1), pp. 47–57. [G: W. Germany]

Grosskopf, Shawna. Public Employment's Impact on the Future of Urban Economies. In *Bahl, R., ed.*, 1981, pp. 39–62. [G: U.S.]

Hartman, Robert W. Retirement for Federal Civil Servants: Down from the Incomparable. In *Dennis, B. D., ed.*, 1981, pp. 82–89. [G: U.S.]

Hildebrand, George H. The Prevailing Wage Concept in the Public Sector: Discussion. In *Dennis, B. D., ed.*, 1981, pp. 102–04. [G: U.S.]

Katz, Harry C. and Lewin, David. Efficiency and Equity Considerations in State and Local Government Wage Determination. In *Dennis, B. D., ed.*, 1981, pp. 90–98. [G: U.S.]

Keller, Berndt K. Determinants of the Wage Rate in the Public Sector: The Case of Civil Servants in the Federal Republic of Germany. *Brit. J. Ind. Relat.*, November 1981, *19*(3), pp. 345–60. [G: W. Germany]

Manning, Ian. The 1970s: A Decade of Social Security Policy. *Australian Econ. Rev.*, 1st Quarter 1981, (53), pp. 13–19.   [G: Australia]

Odufalu, Johnson O. The Distributive Impact of Public Expenditures in Nigeria. In *Bienen, H. and Diejomaoh, V. P., eds.*, 1981, pp. 455–83.
[G: Nigeria]

Petersen, John E. Pension Fund Management. In *Aronson, J. R. and Schwartz, E., eds.*, 1981, pp. 367–88.   [G: U.S.]

Porter, Felice and Keller, Richard L. Public and Private Pay Levels: A Comparison in Large Labor Markets. *Mon. Lab. Rev.*, July 1981, *104*(7), pp. 22–26.   [G: U.S.]

Price, Daniel N. Federal Civil Service Adult Survivor Annuitants and Social Security, December 1975. *Soc. Sec. Bull.*, August 1981, *44*(8), pp. 3–14.   [G: U.S.]

Smith, Robert Stewart. Compensating Differentials for Pensions and Underfunding in the Public Sector. *Rev. Econ. Statist.*, August 1981, *63*(3), pp. 463–68.   [G: U.S.]

Smith, Sharon P. The Prevailing Wage Concept in the Public Sector: Discussion. In *Dennis, B. D., ed.*, 1981, pp. 99–101.   [G: U.S.]

Thornton, Robert J. Collective Bargaining, Wages, and Local Government Finance. In *Aronson, J. R. and Schwartz, E., eds.*, 1981, pp. 346–66.
[G: U.S.]

Tucker, John T. Government Employment: An Era of Slow Growth. *Mon. Lab. Rev.*, October 1981, *104*(10), pp. 19–25.   [G: U.S.]

Wolozin, Harold. Earlier Retirement and the Older Worker. *J. Econ. Issues*, June 1981, *15*(2), pp. 477–87.   [G: U.S.]

823 Labor Mobility; National and International Migration

8230 Labor Mobility; National and International Migration

Akder, A. Halis and Gitmez, Ali S. Yurt Dişindan Dönen Işçiler Üzerine Gözlemler. (With English summary.) *METU*, 1981, *8*(3&4), pp. 683–96.
[G: Turkey]

Atkinson, Anthony B. On Intergenerational Income Mobility in Britain. *J. Post Keynesian Econ.*, Winter 1980–81, *3*(2), pp. 194–218.   [G: U.K.]

Ba, Cheikh. The Uprooted of the Western Sahel: Northern Senegal. In *Colvin, L. G., et al.*, 1981, pp. 113–35.   [G: Senegal]

Bagley, Bruce M. Mexico–United States Relations: A United States Perspective. In *Purcell, S. K., ed.*, 1981, pp. 13–27.   [G: Mexico; U.S.]

Ballard, Kenneth P. and Clark, Gordon L. The Short-run Dynamics of Inter-state Migration: A Space-Time Economic Adjustment Model of In-migration to Fast Growing States. *Reg. Stud.*, 1981, *15*(3), pp. 213–28.   [G: U.S.]

Belsasso, Guido. Undocumented Mexican Workers in the U.S. In *McBride, R. H., ed.*, 1981, pp. 128–57.   [G: U.S.; Mexico]

Bhandari, Dharmendra. Taxation of Non-Residents in India for Royalties and Fees for Technical Services. *Bull. Int. Fiscal Doc.*, June 1981, *35*(6), pp. 277–81.   [G: India]

Boadway, Robin W. and Flatters, Frank R. The Efficiency Basis for Regional Employment Policy. *Can. J. Econ.*, February 1981, *14*(1), pp. 58–77.

Böhning, W. R. Estimating the Propensity of Guest-workers to Leave. *Mon. Lab. Rev.*, May 1981, *104*(5), pp. 37–40.   [G: W. Germany]

Borjas, George J. Job Mobility and Earnings over the Life Cycle. *Ind. Lab. Relat. Rev.*, April 1981, *34*(3), pp. 365–76.   [G: U.S.]

Brown, David L. Spatial Aspects of Post-1970 Work Force Migration in the United States. *Growth Change*, January 1981, *12*(1), pp. 9–20.
[G: U.S.]

Brown, Lawrence A. and Sanders, Rickie L. Toward a Development Paradigm of Migration, with Particular Reference to Third World Settings. In *De Jong, G. F. and Gardner, R. W., eds.*, 1981, pp. 149–85.

Chiswick, Barry R. Guidelines for the Reform of Immigration Policy. In *Fellner, W., ed.*, 1981, pp. 309–47.   [G: U.S.]

Collier, Paul and Bigsten, Arne. A Model of Educational Expansion and Labour Market Adjustment Applied to Kenya. *Oxford Bull. Econ. Statist.*, February 1981, *43*(1), pp. 31–49.   [G: Kenya]

Collier, Valerie G. and Rempel, Henry. The Divergence of Private from Social Costs in Rural–Urban Migration: A Case Study of Nairobi. In *Killick, T., ed.*, 1981, 1977, pp. 228–37.   [G: Kenya]

Colvin, Lucie Gallistel. Labor and Migration in Colonial Senegambia. In *Colvin, L. G., et al.*, 1981, pp. 58–80.   [G: W. Africa]

Colvin, Lucie Gallistel. Migration and Public Policy in the Senegambia. In *Colvin, L. G., et al.*, 1981, pp. 317–43.   [G: W. Africa]

Colvin, Lucie Gallistel. The Uprooted of the Western Sahel: Senegal. In *Colvin, L. G., et al.*, 1981, pp. 83–112.   [G: Senegal]

Colvin, Lucie Gallistel. The Uprooted of the Western Sahel: Mali. In *Colvin, L. G., et al.*, 1981, pp. 260–86.   [G: Mali]

Colvin, Lucie Gallistel. The Uprooted of the Western Sahel: The Gambia. In *Colvin, L. G., et al.*, 1981, pp. 287–313.   [G: Gambia]

Conk, Margo A. Immigrant Workers in the City, 1870–1930: Agents of Growth or Threats to Democracy. *Soc. Sci. Quart.*, December 1981, *62*(4), pp. 704–20.   [G: U.S.]

Cornelius, Wayne A. Mexican Migration to the United States. In *Purcell, S. K., ed.*, 1981, pp. 67–77.   [G: Mexico; U.S.]

DaVanzo, Julie. Microeconomic Approaches to Studying Migration Decisions. In *De Jong, G. F. and Gardner, R. W., eds.*, 1981, pp. 90–129.   [G: U.S.]

De Freitas, Gregory E. What is the Occupational Mobility of Black Immigrants? *Mon. Lab. Rev.*, April 1981, *104*(4), pp. 44–45.   [G: U.S.]

De Jong, Gordon F. and Fawcett, James T. Motivations for Migration: An Assessment and a Value-Expectancy Research Model. In *De Jong, G. F. and Gardner, R. W., eds.*, 1981, pp. 13–58.
[G: Selected Countries]

DeFreitas, Gregory E. Occupational Mobility Among Recent Black Immigrants. In *Dennis, B. D., ed.*, 1981, pp. 41–47.   [G: U.S.]

Degefe, Befekadu. Ethiopia. In *Adedeji, A., ed.*, 1981, pp. 238–77. [G: Ethiopia]

Easton, Stephen T. More on the Emigration of the Peasantry. *World Devel.*, March 1981, *9*(3), pp. 315–18.

Eraydin, Ayda. Foreign Investment, International Labour Migration and the Turkish Economy. In *Hamilton, F. E. I. and Linge, G. J. R., eds.*, 1981, pp. 225–64. [G: Turkey]

Faye, Jacques. Zonal Approach to Migration in the Senegalese Peanut Basin. In *Colvin, L. G., et al.*, 1981, pp. 136–60. [G: Senegal]

Fieleke, Norman S. Productivity and Labor Mobility in Japan, the United Kingdom, and the United States. *New Eng. Econ. Rev.*, November/December 1981, pp. 27–36. [G: Japan; U.K.; U.S.]

Findlay, Allan M. Labour Mobility and Manpower Planning in Tunisia. In *[Fisher, W. B.]*, 1981, pp. 242–51. [G: Tunisia]

Fowler, D. A. The Informal Sector in Freetown: Opportunities for Self-employment. In *Sethuraman, S. V., ed.*, 1981, pp. 51–69. [G: Sierre Leone]

Franz, Wolfgang. Employment Policy and Labor Supply of Foreign Workers in the Federal Republic of Germany: A Theoretical and Empirical Analysis. *Z. ges. Staatswiss.*, September 1981, *137*(3), pp. 590–611. [G: W. Germany]

Fujii, Edwin T. and Mak, James. The Effect of Acculturation and Assimilation on the Income of Immigrant Filipino Men in Hawaii. *Phillipine Rev. Econ. Bus.*, March & June 1981, *18*(1 & 2), pp. 75–85. [G: U.S.]

Gardner, Robert W. Macrolevel Influences on the Migration Decision Process. In *De Jong, G. F. and Gardner, R. W., eds.*, 1981, pp. 59–89.

Gehrels, Franz. Allokative und Wohlfahrtseffekte der Arbeitszuwanderung. (Allocative and Welfare Effects of Labor Immigration. With English summary.) *Z. Wirtschaft. Sozialwissen.*, 1981, *101*(6), pp. 573–88.

Ghosh, B. N. Brain Drain vis-à-vis Brain Overflow: A Conceptual Note. *Malayan Econ. Rev. (See Singapore Econ. Rev.)*, April 1981, *26*(1), pp. 74–78.

Ghosh, B. N. Typology of Brain Migration and Some Policy Implications. *Rivista Int. Sci. Econ. Com.*, April 1981, *28*(4), pp. 350–65. [G: LDCs]

Gison, Cornelio C. and Salvador, Serafin U., Jr. Philippine Taxation of Alien Individuals. *Bull. Int. Fiscal Doc.*, May 1981, *35*(5), pp. 223–29. [G: Philippines]

Goodman, John L. Information, Uncertainty, and the Microeconomic Model of Migration Decision Making. In *De Jong, G. F. and Gardner, R. W., eds.*, 1981, pp. 130–48.

Gordon, Elizabeth. Easing the Plight of Migrant Workers' Families in Lesotho. In *Böhning, W. R., ed.*, 1981, pp. 113–30. [G: S. Africa]

Gregory, David D. A U.S.-Mexican Temporary Workers Program. In *McBride, R. H., ed.*, 1981, pp. 158–77. [G: Mexico; U.S.]

Hamer, Alice. Diola Women and Migration: A Case Study. In *Colvin, L. G., et al.*, 1981, pp. 183–203. [G: Senegal]

Harris, John R. and Todaro, Michael P. Migration,

Unemployment and Development: A Two-Sector Analysis. In *Livingstone, I., ed.*, 1981, *1970*, pp. 89–96.

Harris, Richard J. Rewards of Migration for Income Change and Income Attainment, 1968–73. *Soc. Sci. Quart.*, June 1981, *62*(2), pp. 275–93. [G: U.S.]

Hughes, Gordon A. and McCormick, Barry. Do Council Housing Policies Reduce Migration between Regions? *Econ. J.*, December 1981, *91*(364), pp. 919–37. [G: U.K.]

Hugo, Graeme J. Village-Community Ties, Village Norms, and Ethnic and Social Networks: A Review of Evidence from the Third World. In *De Jong, G. F. and Gardner, R. W., eds.*, 1981, pp. 186–224.

Inoki, Takenori and Suruga, Terukazu. Migration and Income Distribution in the Post-War Japan—A Note on the Concept of Efficiency of Migration. (In Japanese. With English summary.) *Osaka Econ. Pap.*, December 1981, *31*(2–3), pp. 192–98. [G: Japan]

Inoki, Takenori and Suruga, Terukazu. Migration, Age, and Education: A Cross-Sectional Analysis of Geographic Labor Mobility in Japan. *J. Reg. Sci.*, November 1981, *21*(4), pp. 507–17. [G: Japan]

Jenkins, Glenn P. and Kuo, Chun-Yan. On Measuring the Social Opportunity Cost of Permanent and Temporary Employment: A Reply. *Can. J. Econ.*, November 1981, *14*(4), pp. 708–12. [G: Canada]

Jones, Philip C. A Remark on Economic Response to Technological Innovation [Division of Labor—Simon Revisited]. *Reg. Sci. Urban Econ.*, May 1981, *11*(2), pp. 255–66.

Kanbur, S. M. Short Run Growth Effects in a Model of Costly Migration with Borrowing Constraints: Will Rural Development Work? In *Currie, D.; Peel, D. and Peters, W., eds.*, 1981, pp. 386–412.

Keenan, J. G. Irish Migration, All or Nothing Resolved? *Econ. Soc. Rev.*, April 1981, *12*(3), pp. 169–86. [G: Ireland; U.K.]

Kim, Dae Young and Sloboda, John E. Migration and Korean Development. In *Repetto, R., et al.*, 1981, pp. 36–138. [G: S. Korea]

Knowles, James C. and Anker, Richard. An Analysis of Income Transfers in a Developing Country: The Case of Kenya. *J. Devel. Econ.*, April 1981, *8*(2), pp. 205–26. [G: Kenya]

Laurie, Bruce; Alter, George and Hershberg, Theodore. Immigrants and Industry: The Philadelphia Experience, 1850–1880. In *Hershberg, T., ed.*, 1981, *1975*, pp. 93–119. [G: U.S.]

Lefelmann, Gerd. Zum "Brain drain" ausländischer Humanmediziner in die Bundesrepublik Deutschland. (On the Brain Drain of Foreign Medical Graduates into the Federal Republic of Germany. With English summary.) *Konjunkturpolitik*, 1981, *27*(3), pp. 176–206. [G: W. Germany]

Lloyd, Michael. Migration in the EEC. In *Twitchett, C. C., ed.*, 1981, pp. 94–101. [G: EEC]

de Macedo, Jorge Braga. International Investment, Migration and Finance: Issues and Policies: Comment. *Economia (Portugal)*, January 1981, *5*(1),

pp. 111–15.

Marr, William L.; McCready, Douglas and Millerd, Frank. Canadian Internal Migration of Medical Personnel. *Growth Change*, July 1981, *12*(3), pp. 32–40. **[G: Canada]**

Martin, Philip L. Germany's Guestworkers. *Challenge*, July/August 1981, *24*(3), pp. 34–42. **[G: W. Germany]**

Mayhew, Ken and Rosewell, Bridget. Occupational Mobility in Britain. *Oxford Bull. Econ. Statist.*, August 1981, *43*(3), pp. 225–55. **[G: U.K.]**

McBride, Robert H. The United States and Mexico. In *McBride, R. H., ed.*, 1981, pp. 1–30. **[G: U.S.; Mexico]**

Moir, Hazel. Occupational Mobility and the Informal Sector in Jakarta. In *Sethuraman, S. V., ed.*, 1981, pp. 109–20. **[G: Indonesia]**

Molitor, Bernhard. International Investment, Migration and Finance: Issues and Policies: Comment. *Economia (Portugal)*, January 1981, *5*(1), pp. 105–10.

Morrill, Richard L. How Migration and Regional Development Affect Organizations. In *Nystrom, P. C. and Starbuck, W. H., eds., Vol. 1*, 1981, pp. 238–52.

Mueller, Charles F. Migration of the Unemployed: A Relocation Assistance Program. *Mon. Lab. Rev.*, April 1981, *104*(4), pp. 62–64. **[G: U.S.]**

Murnane, Richard J. Teacher Mobility Revisited. *J. Human Res.*, Winter 1981, *16*(1), pp. 3–19. **[G: U.S.]**

Nghiep, Nguyen huu; Herzog, Henry W., Jr. and Schlottmann, Alan M. Earnings Expectations and the Role of Human Captial in the Migration Decision: An Empirical Analysis. *Rev. Reg. Stud.*, Winter 1981, *11*(3), pp. 38–46. **[G: U.S.]**

Oberai, A. S. State Policies and Internal Migration in Asia. *Int. Lab. Rev.*, March–April 1981, *120*(2), pp. 231–44. **[G: Asia]**

Paine, Suzanne. International Investment, Migration and Finance: Issues and Policies. *Economia (Portugal)*, January 1981, *5*(1), pp. 63–104.

Pellicer de Brody, Olga. Oil and U.S. Policy toward Mexico. In *Ladman, J. R.; Baldwin, D. J. and Bergman, E., eds.*, 1981, pp. 185–96. **[G: Mexico; U.S.]**

Polese, Mario. Regional Disparity, Migration and Economic Adjustment: A Reappraisal. *Can. Public Policy*, Autumn 1981, *7*(4), pp. 519–25. **[G: Canada]**

Puig, Jean-Pierre. La migration régionale de la population active. (Regional Migration of the Labor Force. With English summary.) *Ann. INSEE*, October–December 1981, (44), pp. 41–79. **[G: France]**

Reubens, Edwin P. International Migration in North–South Relations. In *Reubens, E. P., ed.*, 1981, pp. 215–54.

Reynolds, Clark W. Mexican Economic Development and the United States. In *Ladman, J. R.; Baldwin, D. J. and Bergman, E., eds.*, 1981, pp. 155–69. **[G: Mexico; U.S.]**

Rivera-Batiz, Francisco L. The Effects of Immigration in a Distorted Two-Sector Economy. *Econ. Inquiry*, October 1981, *19*(4), pp. 626–39.

Rolfe, Philip H. The Causes of Inter-Regional La-

bour Force Migration in Great Britain. *Bull. Econ. Res.*, November 1981, *33*(2), pp. 74–81. **[G: U.K.]**

Sada, P. O. Urbanization and Income Distribution in Nigeria. In *Bienen, H. and Diejomaoh, V. P., eds.*, 1981, pp. 269–98. **[G: Nigeria]**

Sainju, M. M. and Ram, B. K. C. Hill Labour Migration: Issues and Problems. In *Nepal, Ministry of Food and Agriculture*, 1981, pp. 111–22. **[G: Nepal]**

Salanti, Andrea. L'analisi del progresso tecnico in termini di curve salario-profitto. (The Analysis of Technical Progress through Wage-Profit Curves: An Appraisal. With English summary.) *Econ. Int.*, February 1981, *34*(1), pp. 124–42.

Salvatore, Dominick. A Theoretical and Empirical Evaluation and Extension of the Todaro Migration Model. *Reg. Sci. Urban Econ.*, November 1981, *11*(4), pp. 499–508. **[G: Italy]**

Sandefur, Gary D. and Scott, Wilbur J. A Dynamic Analysis of Migration: An Assessment of the Effects of Age, Family and Career Variables. *Demography*, August 1981, *18*(3), pp. 355–68. **[G: U.S.]**

Schlottmann, Alan M. and Herzog, Henry W., Jr. Employment Status and the Decision to Migrate. *Rev. Econ. Statist.*, November 1981, *63*(4), pp. 590–98. **[G: U.S.]**

Schultz, Siegfried; Schumacher, Dieter and Wilkens, Herbert. North-South Interdependence: The Case of the Federal Republic of Germany. *World Devel.*, May 1981, *9*(5), pp. 435–52. **[G: W. Germany; LDCs]**

Serageldin, M. Ismail. Labor Adaptation in the Oil Exporting Countries. In *Sherbiny, N. A., ed.*, 1981, pp. 209–27. **[G: OPEC]**

Sherbiny, Naiem A. Labor and Capital Flows in the Arab World: A Policy Perspective. In *Sherbiny, N. A., ed.*, 1981, pp. 229–49. **[G: Arab Countries]**

Sherbiny, Naiem A. Sectoral Employment Projections with Minimum Data: The Case of Saudi Arabia. In *Sherbiny, N. A., ed.*, 1981, pp. 173–206. **[G: Saudi Arabia]**

Smith, Terence R. and Slater, Paul B. A Family of Spatial Interaction Models Incorporating Information Flows and Choice Set Constraints Applied to U.S. Interstate Labor Flows. *Int. Reg. Sci. Rev.*, Fall 1981, *6*(1), pp. 15–31. **[G: U.S.]**

Soumah, Moussa. Regional Migrations in Southeastern Senegal, Internal and International. In *Colvin, L. G., et al.*, 1981, pp. 161–82. **[G: Senegal]**

Sow, Fatou. Migration to Dakar. In *Colvin, L. G., et al.*, 1981, pp. 204–43. **[G: Senegal]**

Stahl, C. W. Migrant Labour Supplies, Past, Present and Future; with Special Reference to the Gold-Mining Industry. In *Böhning, W. R., ed.*, 1981, pp. 7–44. **[G: S. Africa]**

Stahl, C. W. and Böhning, W. R. Reducing Dependence on Migration in Southern Africa. In *Böhning, W. R., ed.*, 1981, pp. 147–78. **[G: S. Africa]**

Tweed, Dan L., et al. Labor Force Deconcentration in the United States: An Examination of the Relative Impacts of Intrasystemic and Intersystemic

Movement. *Rev. Public Data Use (See J. Econ. Soc. Meas. after 4/85)*, July 1981, *9*(2), pp. 133–42. [G: U.S.]

Vialet, Joyce. U.S. Immigration Policy. In *U.S. Congress, Joint Economic Committee (III)*, 1981, pp. 209–23. [G: U.S.]

Villars, C. Social Security for Migrant Workers in the Framework of the Council of Europe. *Int. Lab. Rev.*, May–June 1981, *120*(3), pp. 291–302.

de Vletter, F. Conditions Affecting Black Migrant Workers in South Africa: a Case Study of the Gold-Mines. In *Böhning, W. R., ed.*, 1981, pp. 91–112. [G: S. Africa]

de Vletter, F. Labour Migration in Swaziland. In *Böhning, W. R., ed.*, 1981, pp. 45–89.
[G: S. Africa]

Wasow, Bernard. The Working Age Sex Ratio and Job Search Migration in Kenya. *J. Devel. Areas*, April 1981, *15*(3), pp. 435–44. [G: Kenya]

Williams, Peter. The Overseas Student Question: Studies for a Policy: The Emergence of the Problem: Editorial Introduction. In *Williams, P., ed.*, 1981, pp. 1–21. [G: U.K.]

Woods, W. Computer Simulation and Migration Planning. In *Böhning, W. R., ed.*, 1981, pp. 131–46. [G: S. Africa]

Woudenberg, Henry W. and McKee, David L. Musical Chairs and Revolving Doors: The Transmigration of Economists North American Style. *Eastern Econ. J.*, January 1981, *7*(1), pp. 35–38.
[G: Canada; U.S.]

Wrage, Peter. The Effects of Internal Migration on Regional Wage and Unemployment Disparities in Canada. *J. Reg. Sci.*, February 1981, *21*(1), pp. 51–63. [G: Canada]

Wyatt, Derrick. Freedom of Movement—An Economic and Political Right. In *Twitchett, C. C., ed.*, 1981, pp. 83–93. [G: EEC]

824 Labor Market Studies, Wages, Employment

8240 General

Akerlof, George A. Jobs as Dam Sites. *Rev. Econ. Stud.*, January 1981, *48*(1), pp. 37–49.

Amacher, Ryan C. and Sweeney, Richard James. On the Integration of Labor Markets: A Definition and Test of the Radical-Segmentation Hypothesis. *J. Lab. Res.*, Spring 1981, *2*(1), pp. 25–37.
[G: U.S.]

Axelsson, Roger; Jacobsson, Roger and Löfgren, Karl-Gustaf. A Note on the General Equilibrium Effects of Taxes on Labor Supply in Sweden. *Scand. J. Econ.*, 1981, *83*(3), pp. 449–56.
[G: Sweden]

Bellante, Don and Link, Albert N. Are Public Sector Workers More Risk Averse Than Private Sector Workers? *Ind. Lab. Relat. Rev.*, April 1981, *34*(3), pp. 408–12. [G: U.S.]

Berry, A. and Sabot, R. H. Labour Market Performance in Developing Countries: A Survey. In *Streeten, P. and Jolly, R, eds.*, 1981, *1978*, pp. 149–92.

Bishop, John and Haveman, Robert H. Targeted Wage Subsidies: Their Rationale and Effective-

ness. In *Eliasson, G. and Södersten, J., eds.*, 1981, pp. 297–343. [G: U.S.]

Blattner, Niklaus, et al. Arbeitsmarktliche Anpassungsprozesse: Problemstellung, Lösungsansatze, Datenbasis und erste Ergebnisse. (Labor Market Adjustment Processes: Issues, Solution Approaches, Data Base and Preliminary Results. With English summary.) *Schweiz. Z. Volkswirtsch. Statist.*, September 1981, *117*(3), pp. 407–44. [G: Switzerland]

Bonnell, Sheila. Real Wages and Employment in the Great Depression. *Econ. Rec.*, September 1981, *57*(158), pp. 277–81. [G: U.K.; U.S.; Sweden; Germany]

Bowen, William G. Market Prospects for Ph.D.s in the United States. *Population Devel. Rev.*, September 1981, *7*(3), pp. 475–88. [G: U.S.]

Bruton, Henry J. Labour Market Performance in Developing Countries: A Survey: Comment. In *Streeten, P. and Jolly, R, eds.*, 1981, *1978*, pp. 197–200. [G: LDCs]

Cabral, Robert; Ferber, Marianne A. and Green, Carole A. Men and Women in Fiduciary Institutions: A Study of Sex Differences in Career Development. *Rev. Econ. Statist.*, November 1981, *63*(4), pp. 573–80.

Coates, Mary Lou. Manpower and Labour Markets: Summary Outline. In *Wood, W. D. and Kumar, P., eds.*, 1981, pp. 27–94. [G: Canada]

Collier, Paul and Bigsten, Arne. A Model of Educational Expansion and Labour Market Adjustment Applied to Kenya. *Oxford Bull. Econ. Statist.*, February 1981, *43*(1), pp. 31–49. [G: Kenya]

Contini, Bruno B. Labor Market Segmentation and the Development of the Parallel Economy—The Italian Experience. *Oxford Econ. Pap.*, November 1981, *33*(3), pp. 401–12. [G: Italy]

Cornelius, Wayne A. Immigration, Mexican Development Policy, and the Future of U.S.–Mexican Relations. In *McBride, R. H., ed.*, 1981, pp. 104–27. [G: Mexico; U.S.]

Covick, Owen. The Australian Labour Market, March 1981. *Australian Bull. Lab.*, March 1981, *7*(2), pp. 51–66. [G: Australia]

Drèze, Jacques H. and Modigliani, Franco. The Trade-off between Real Wages and Employment in an Open Economy (Belgium). *Europ. Econ. Rev.*, January 1981, *15*(1), pp. 1–40.
[G: Belgium]

Eliasson, Gunnar; Holmlund, Bertil and Stafford, Frank P. Labor Market Behavior in Sweden and the U.S. In *Eliasson, G.; Holmlund, B. and Stafford, F. P., eds.*, 1981, pp. 9–17. [G:sm n; U.S.]

Fapohunda, O. J. Human Resources and the Lagos Informal Sector. In *Sethuraman, S. V., ed.*, 1981, pp. 70–82. [G: Nigeria]

Fowler, D. A. The Informal Sector in Freetown: Opportunities for Self-employment. In *Sethuraman, S. V., ed.*, 1981, pp. 51–69.
[G: Sierre Leone]

Freeman, Richard B. Black Economic Progress after 1964: Who Has Gained and Why? In *Rosen, S., ed.*, 1981, pp. 247–94. [G: U.S.]

Gábor, I. and Galasi, P. The Labour Market in Hungary since 1968. In *Hare, P. G.; Radice, H. K.*

and Swain, N., eds., 1981, pp. 41–53.
[G: Hungary]

Greenberg, David; Moffitt, Robert A. and Friedmann, John. Underreporting and Experimental Effects on Work Effort: Evidence from the Gary Income Maintenance Experiment. *Rev. Econ. Statist.*, November 1981, *63*(4), pp. 581–89.
[G: U.S.]

Gustman, Alan L. and Steinmeier, Thomas L. The Impact of Wages and Unemployment on Youth Enrollment and Labor Supply. *Rev. Econ. Statist.*, November 1981, *63*(4), pp. 553–60.
[G: U.S.]

Killingsworth, Charles C. The Development of Employment Policy. In *Carter, M. J. and Leahy, W. H., eds.*, 1981, pp. 1–60. [G: U.S.]

Laurie, Bruce; Alter, George and Hershberg, Theodore. Immigrants and Industry: The Philadelphia Experience, 1850–1880. In *Hershberg, T., ed.*, 1981, *1975*, pp. 93–119. [G: U.S.]

Link, Charles R. and Settle, Russell F. A Simultaneous-Equation Model of Labor Supply, Fertility and Earnings of Married Women: The Case of Registered Nurses. *Southern Econ. J.*, April 1981, *47*(4), pp. 977–89. [G: U.S.]

Lucas, Robert E., Jr. Real Wages, Employment, and Inflation. In *Lucas, R. E., Jr.*, 1981, *1969*, pp. 19–58. [G: U.S.]

Morgan, James N. Child Care when Parents are Employed. In *Hill, M. S.; Hill, D. H. and Morgan, J. N., eds.*, 1981, pp. 441–56. [G: U.S.]

Pendleton, Clarence M., Jr. Legal Barriers to Black Economic Gain: Employment and Transportation: Self-Help at Work: The Urban League in San Diego. In *Inst. for Contemp. Studies*, 1981, pp. 35–37. [G: U.S.]

Perloff, Jeffrey M. Labor Market Adjustments in the Unionized Contract Construction Industry. *J. Lab. Res.*, Fall 1981, *2*(2), pp. 337–53.
[G: U.S.]

Rempel, Henry. The Labour Market. In *Killick, T., ed.*, 1981, pp. 208–18. [G: Kenya]

Rodgers, Gerry B. An Analysis of Education, Employment, and Income Distribution Using an Economic-Demographic Model of the Philippines. In *Khan, A. and Sirageldin, I., eds.*, 1981, pp. 143–80. [G: Philippines]

Sirageldin, M. Ismail. Labor Adaptation in the Oil Exporting Countries. In *Sherbiny, N. A., ed.*, 1981, pp. 209–27. [G: OPEC]

Todaro, Michael P. Labour Market Performance in Developing Countries: A Survey: Comment. In *Streeten, P. and Jolly, R, eds.*, 1981, *1978*, pp. 193–95. [G: LDCs]

Van Regemorter, Denise. Evolution du nombre et du revenu des commerçants et des artisans de 1953 à 1977. (Evolution of the Number of Self Employed Tradesmen and Craftsmen and of Their Income in Belgium [1953–1977.] With English summary.) *Cah. Écon. Bruxelles*, 1st Trimestre 1981, (89), pp. 3–23. [G: Belgium]

8241 Geographic Labor Market Studies

Blandy, Richard and Sloan, Judith. The Australian Labour Market. *Australian Bull. Lab.*, Septem-

ber 1981, 7(4), pp. 179–94. [G: Australia]

Brown, David L. and Beale, Calvin L. Diversity in Post-1970 Population Trends. In *Hawley, A. H. and Mazie, S. M., eds.*, 1981, pp. 27–71.
[G: U.S.]

Cheshire, Paul C. Inner Areas as Spatial Labour Markets: A Rejoinder. *Urban Stud.*, June 1981, *18*(2), pp. 227–29. [G: U.K.]

Cheshire, Paul C. The Regional Demand for Labour Services: A Suggested Explanation for Observed Differences. *Scot. J. Polit. Econ.*, February 1981, *28*(1), pp. 95–98. [G: U.K.]

Clapier, Patrick and Tabard, Nicole. Transformation de la morphologie sociale des communes et variation des consommations: Un essai pour la région parisienne. (The Change in the Social Morphology of Districts and the Variations of Consumption: An Attempt for the Paris Region. With English summary.) *Consommation*, April–June 1981, *28*(2), pp. 3–40. [G: France]

Gibson, N. J. and Spencer, J. E. Unemployment and Wages in Northern Ireland. In *Crick, B., ed.*, 1981, *1981*, pp. 100–14. [G: U.K.]

Needham, Barrie. Inner Areas as Spatial Labour Markets: A Comment. *Urban Stud.*, June 1981, *18*(2), pp. 225–26. [G: U.K.]

Singelmann, Joachim. The Population of the South: Southern Industrialization. In *Poston, D. L., Jr. and Weller, R. H., eds.*, 1981, pp. 175–97.
[G: U.S.]

Till, Thomas E. Manufacturing Industry: Trends and Impacts. In *Hawley, A. H. and Mazie, S. M., eds.*, 1981, pp. 194–230. [G: U.S.]

Yu, Eden S. H. Regional Factor Specificity, Wage Differential and Resource Allocation. *Reg. Sci. Urban Econ.*, February 1981, *11*(1), pp. 69–79.

8242 Wage, Hours, and Fringe Benefit Studies

Abowd, John M. and Ashenfelter, Orley. Anticipated Unemployment, Temporary Layoffs, and Compensating Wage Differentials. In *Rosen, S., ed.*, 1981, pp. 141–70. [G: U.S.]

Abramovitz, Mimi. Funding Worker Education through Tuition Refund Plans. In *Wertheimer, B. M., ed.*, 1981, pp. 241–51. [G: U.S.]

Addison, John T. Incomes Policy: The Recent European Experience. In *Fallick, J. L. and Elliott, R. F., eds.*, 1981, pp. 187–245.
[G: W. Europe]

Addison, John T. and Burton, John. On Institutions and Wage Determination. *J. Lab. Res.*, Spring 1981, *2*(1), pp. 99–109.

Ahmed, Iqbal. Wage Determination in Bangladesh Agriculture. *Oxford Econ. Pap.*, July 1981, *33*(2), pp. 298–322. [G: Bangladesh]

Allen, Steven G. An Empirical Model of Work Attendance. *Rev. Econ. Statist.*, February 1981, *63*(1), pp. 77–87. [G: U.S.]

Allen, Steven G. Compensation, Safety, and Absenteeism: Evidence from the Paper Industry. *Ind. Lab. Relat. Rev.*, January 1981, *34*(2), pp. 207–18. [G: U.S.]

Amacher, Ryan C. and Sweeney, Richard James. On the Integration of Labor Markets: A Definition and Test of the Radical-Segmentation Hypothesis.

J. Lab. Res., Spring 1981, *2*(1), pp. 25–37.
[G: U.S.]

Andorka, Rudolf and Falussy, Béla. The Way of Life of the Hungarian Society as Reflected by the Time Budget Survey of 1976–1977. *Acta Oecon.*, 1981, *26*(3–4), pp. 243–73. [G: Hungary]

Artis, Michael J. Is there a Wage Equation? In *Courakis, A. S., ed.*, 1981, pp. 65–80. [G: U.K.]

Aryee, George. The Informal Manufacturing Sector in Kumasi. In *Sethuraman, S. V., ed.*, 1981, pp. 90–100. [G: Ghana]

Atkinson, Anthony B. On Intergenerational Income Mobility in Britain. *J. Post Keynesian Econ.*, Winter 1980–81, *3*(2), pp. 194–218. [G: U.K.]

Augustyniak, Sue. Some Econometric Advantages of Panel Data. In *Hill, M. S.; Hill, D. H. and Morgan, J. N., eds.*, 1981, pp. 405–20.

Auld, D. A. L., et al. The Effect of Settlement Stage on Negotiated Wage Settlements in Canada. *Ind. Lab. Relat. Rev.*, January 1981, *34*(2), pp. 234–44. [G: Canada]

Ayeni, Bola. Spatial Aspects of Urbanization and Effects on the Distribution of Income in Nigeria. In *Bienen, H. and Diejomaoh, V. P., eds.*, 1981, pp. 237–68. [G: Nigeria]

Barsky, Carl B. Occupational Wage Variation in Wood Household Furniture Plants. *Mon. Lab. Rev.*, July 1981, *104*(7), pp. 37–39. [G: U.S.]

Barsky, Carl B. and Personick, Martin E. Measuring Wage Dispersion: Pay Ranges Reflect Industry Traits. *Mon. Lab. Rev.*, April 1981, *104*(4), pp. 35–41. [G: U.S.]

Bartel, Ann P. and Borjas, George J. Wage Growth and Job Turnover: An Empirical Analysis. In *Rosen, S., ed.*, 1981, pp. 65–84. [G: U.S.]

Bartel, Ann P. and Lewin, David. Wages and Unionism in the Public Sector: The Case of Police. *Rev. Econ. Statist.*, February 1981, *63*(1), pp. 53–59. [G: U.S.]

Barth, James R. and Cordes, Joseph J. Nontraditional Criteria for Investing Pension Assets: An Economic Appraisal. *J. Lab. Res.*, Fall 1981, *2*(2), pp. 219–47. [G: U.S.]

Beigie, Carl E. Stagflation and Relative-wage Rates: Comments. In *Ontario Economic Council, Vol. 1*, 1981, pp. 50–56. [G: Canada]

Bellante, Don. Union Divergent Investing of Pensions: A Power, Non-Employee Relations Issue: Comment. *J. Lab. Res.*, Fall 1981, *2*(2), pp. 209–13. [G: U.S.]

Bellante, Don and Long, James E. The Political Economy of the Rent-Seeking Society: The Case of Public Employees and Their Unions. *J. Lab. Res.*, Spring 1981, *2*(1), pp. 1–14. [G: U.S.]

Beller, Daniel J. Coverage Patterns of Full-Time Employees under Private Retirement Plans. *Soc. Sec. Bull.*, July 1981, *44*(7), pp. 3–11, 47–53. [G: U.S.]

Belongia, Mike. A Note on the Specification of Wage Rates in Cost-Push Models of Food Price Determination. *Southern J. Agr. Econ.*, December 1981, *13*(2), pp. 119–24. [G: U.S.]

Bennett, James T. and Johnson, Manuel H. Union Use of Employee Pension Funds: Introduction and Overview. *J. Lab. Res.*, Fall 1981, *2*(2), pp. 181–90. [G: U.S.]

Black, Fischer and Dewhurst, Moray P. A New Investment Strategy for Pension Funds. *J. Portfol. Manage.*, Summer 1981, *7*(4), pp. 26–34. [G: U.S.]

Blackorby, Charles; Donaldson, David and Auersperg, Maria. A New Procedure for the Measurement of Inequality within and among Population Subgroups. *Can. J. Econ.*, November 1981, *14*(4), pp. 665–85. [G: Canada]

Blair, Roger D. ERISA and the Prudent Man Rule: Avoiding Perverse Results. In *Sirkin, G., ed.*, 1981, pp. 62–84. [G: U.S.]

Blejer, Mario I. Strike Activity and Wage Determination under Rapid Inflation: The Chilean Case. *Ind. Lab. Relat. Rev.*, April 1981, *34*(3), pp. 356–64. [G: Chile]

Block, Walter and Williams, Walter E. Male–Female Earnings Differentials: A Critical Reappraisal. *J. Lab. Res.*, Fall 1981, *2*(2), pp. 385–87. [G: Canada]

Blostin, Allan P. Is Employer-Sponsored Life Insurance Declining Relative to Other Benefits? *Mon. Lab. Rev.*, September 1981, *104*(9), pp. 31–33. [G: U.S.]

Bondonio, Piervincenzo. Personal Income Taxation, Wage Differentials, and Inflation with Special Reference to Italy. In *Peacock, A. and Forte, F., eds.*, 1981, pp. 49–62. [G: Italy]

Borjas, George J. Job Mobility and Earnings over the Life Cycle. *Ind. Lab. Relat. Rev.*, April 1981, *34*(3), pp. 365–76. [G: U.S.]

Borum, Joan D. Wage Increases in 1980 Outpaced by Inflation. *Mon. Lab. Rev.*, May 1981, *104*(5), pp. 55–57. [G: U.S.]

Bosworth, Barry P. Stagflation and Relative-wage Rates. In *Ontario Economic Council, Vol. 1*, 1981, pp. 31–49. [G: U.S.]

Brown, C. V.; Levin, E. and Ulph, David T. Taxation and Labour Supply: The Basic Model. In *Brown, C. V., ed.*, 1981, pp. 35–52. [G: U.K.]

Bruno, Michael and Sachs, Jeffrey. Supply versus Demand Approaches to the Problem of Stagflation. In *Giersch, H, ed. (1)*, 1981, pp. 15–60.
[G: Selected OECD]

Brush, Brian C. What Do Labor Productivity Data Show about Economies of Scale: Comment. *Southern Econ. J.*, January 1981, *47*(3), pp. 839–46. [G: U.S.]

Bunich, P. G. Wages as an Economic Incentive. *Prob. Econ.*, May 1981, *24*(1), pp. 3–18.
[G: U.S.S.R.]

Burns, Leland S. and Van Ness, Kathy. The Decline of the Metropolitan Economy. *Urban Stud.*, June 1981, *18*(2), pp. 169–80. [G: U.S.]

Cain, Glen G., et al. The Effect of Unions on Wages in Hospitals. In *Ehrenberg, R. G., ed.*, 1981, pp. 191–320. [G: U.S.]

Cain, Mead and Mozumder, A. B. M. Khorshed Alam. Labour Market Structure and Reproductive Behaviour in Rural South Asia. In *Rodgers, G. and Standing, G., eds.*, 1981, pp. 245–87.
[G: S. Asia]

Cantril, Albert. American Politics, Public Opinion, and Social Security Financing: Comment. In *Skidmore, F., ed.*, 1981, pp. 274–77. [G: U.S.]

Capian, Alain. La socialisation du salaire. (The Socialization of Wages. With English summary.) *Revue Écon.*, November 1981, *32*(6), pp. 1087–1112.

Carliner, Geoffrey. Wage Differences by Language Group and the Market for Language Skills in Canada. *J. Human Res.*, Summer 1981, *16*(3), pp. 384–99. [G: Canada]

Chen, Yung-Ping. The Growth of Fringe Benefits: Implications for Social Security. *Mon. Lab. Rev.*, November 1981, *104*(11), pp. 3–10. [G: U.S.]

Chew, Soon-Beng. Incomes Policy and Wage Inflation in the UK: An Empirical Study. *Malayan Econ. Rev. (See Singapore Econ. Rev.)*, April 1981, *26*(1), pp. 52–73. [G: U.K.]

Chirikos, Thomas N. and Nestel, Gilbert. Impairment and Labor Market Outcomes: A Cross-Sectional and Longitudinal Analysis. In *Parnes, H. S., ed.*, 1981, pp. 93–131. [G: U.S.]

Chu, Ke-young and Feltenstein, Andrew. The Welfare Implications of Relative Price Distortions and Inflation: An Analysis of the Recent Argentine Experience. In *Khan, A. and Sirageldin, I., eds.*, 1981, pp. 181–223. [G: Argentina]

Clark, Gordon L. and Ballard, Kenneth P. The Demand and Supply of Labor and Interstate Relative Wages: An Empirical Analysis. *Econ. Geogr.*, April 1981, *57*(2), pp. 95–112. [G: U.S.]

Collat, Donald S. Discrimination in the Coverage of Retirement Plans. *Yale Law J.*, March 1981, *90*(4), pp. 817–39. [G: U.S.]

Corcoran, Mary and MacKenzie, Abigail. Expected Wages and Men's Labor Supply. In *Hill, M. S.; Hill, D. H. and Morgan, J. N., eds.*, 1981, pp. 245–68. [G: U.S.]

Cowell, Frank A. Income Maintenance Schemes under Wage-Rate Uncertainty. *Amer. Econ. Rev.*, September 1981, *71*(4), pp. 692–703.

Crocker, Thomas D. and Horst, Robert L., Jr. Hours of Work, Labor Productivity, and Environmental Conditions: A Case Study. *Rev. Econ. Statist.*, August 1981, *63*(3), pp. 361–68. [G: U.S.]

Cropper, M. L. The Value of Urban Amenities. *J. Reg. Sci.*, August 1981, *21*(3), pp. 359–74. [G: U.S.]

Culus, Martine and Praet, Peter. Evolution du nombre et du revenu des fonctionnaires de 1953 à 1977. (Evolution of the Number of Civil Servants and of Their Income in Belgium (1953–77). With English summary.) *Cah. Écon. Bruxelles*, 2nd Trimestre 1981, (90), pp. 173–86. [G: Belgium]

Cummins, J. David and Westerfield, Randolph. Patterns of Concentration in Private Pension Plan Common Stock Portfolios since ERISA. *J. Risk Ins.*, June 1981, *48*(2), pp. 201–19. [G: U.S.]

Cymrot, Donald J. Tax Incentives, Turnover Costs and Private Pensions. *Southern Econ. J.*, October 1981, *48*(2), pp. 365–76. [G: U.S.]

Dahlby, B. G. Monopsony and the Shortage of School Teachers in England and Wales, 1948–73. *Appl. Econ.*, September 1981, *13*(3), pp. 303–19. [G: U.K.]

Daly, M. and Wrage, Peter. The Effect of Income Tax Incentives on Retirement Savings: Some Canadian Evidence. *Eastern Econ. J.*, July-Oct. 1981, *7*(3–4), pp. 163–74. [G: Canada]

Daly, Michael J. Reforming Canada's Retirement In-

come System: The Potential Role of RRSPs. *Can. Public Policy*, Autumn 1981, *7*(4), pp. 550–58. [G: Canada]

Daly, Michael J. The Role of Registered Retirement Savings Plans in a Life-Cycle Model. *Can. J. Econ.*, August 1981, *14*(3), pp. 409–21.

Datcher, Linda P. Race/Sex Differences in the Effects of Background on Achievement. In *Hill, M. S.; Hill, D. H. and Morgan, J. N., eds.*, 1981, pp. 359–90. [G: U.S.]

David, Lily Mary. Experience under the Federal Pay Comparability Act of 1970. In *Dennis, B. D., ed.*, 1981, pp. 76–81. [G: U.S.]

Daymont, Thomas N. Changes in Black–White Labor Market Opportunities, 1966–76. In *Parnes, H. S., ed.*, 1981, pp. 42–64. [G: U.S.]

Dean, Andrew. Public and Private Sector Pay and the Economy. In *Fallick, J. L. and Elliott, R. F., eds.*, 1981, pp. 45–71. [G: U.K.]

Deutschmann, Christoph. Labour Market Segmentation and Wage Dynamics. *Managerial Dec. Econ.*, September 1981, *2*(3), pp. 145–59. [G: W. Germany]

Diejomaoh, V. P. and Anusionwu, E. C. Education and Income Distribution in Nigeria. In *Bienen, H. and Diejomaoh, V. P., eds.*, 1981, pp. 373–420. [G: Nigeria]

Donsimoni, Marie-Paule. Union Power and the American Labour Movement. *Appl. Econ.*, December 1981, *13*(4), pp. 449–64. [G: U.S.]

Dorsey, Stuart. Nontraditional Criteria for Investing Pension Assets: An Economic Appraisal: Comment. *J. Lab. Res.*, Fall 1981, *2*(2), pp. 248–51. [G: U.S.]

Dror, David M. Flexible Indexation: A Proposal to Improve Wage Indexation Made in the Light of Israeli Experience. *Int. Lab. Rev.*, March–April 1981, *120*(2), pp. 183–200. [G: Israel]

Dubin, Robert and Aharoni, Yair. Ideology and Reality: Work and Pay in Israel. *Ind. Relat.*, Winter 1981, *20*(1), pp. 18–35. [G: Israel]

Duffy, Norman F. Australia. In *Blum, A. A., ed.*, 1981, pp. 3–36. [G: Australia]

Duncan, Greg J. and Hoffman, Saul D. Dynamics of Wage Change. In *Hill, M. S.; Hill, D. H. and Morgan, J. N., eds.*, 1981, pp. 45–92. [G: U.S.]

Dunning, John H. Employee Compensation in US Multinationals and Indigenous Firms: An Exploratory Micro/Macro Analysis. In *Dunning, J. H.*, 1981, pp. 272–303.

Eberts, Randall W. An Empirical Investigation of Intraurban Wage Gradients. *J. Urban Econ.*, July 1981, *10*(1), pp. 50–60. [G: U.S.]

Eden, Benjamin and Pakes, Ariél. On Measuring the Variance-Age Profile of Lifetime Earnings. *Rev. Econ. Stud.*, July 1981, *48*(3), pp. 385–94. [G: U.S.]

Elliott, Robert F. Some Further Observations on the Importance of National Wage Agreements. *Brit. J. Ind. Relat.*, November 1981, *19*(3), pp. 370–75. [G: U.K.]

Engle, Robert and Watson, Mark. A One-Factor Multivariate Time Series Model of Metropolitan Wage Rates. *J. Amer. Statist. Assoc.*, December 1981, *76*(376), pp. 774–81. [G: U.S.]

Epple, Dennis and Schipper, Katherine. Municipal Pension Funding: A Theory and Some Evidence.

Public Choice, 1981, *37*(1), pp. 141–78.

Estenson, David. Relative Price Variability and Indexed Labor Agreements. *Ind. Relat.*, Winter 1981, *20*(1), pp. 71–84. [G: U.S.]

Fajana, Olufemi. Aspects of Income Distribution in the Nigerian Urban Sector. In *Bienen, H. and Diejomaoh, V. P., eds.*, 1981, pp. 193–236. [G: Nigeria]

Fallick, J. L. and Elliott, Robert F. Incomes Policy and the Public Sector. In *Fallick, J. L. and Elliott, R. F., eds.*, 1981, pp. 100–27. [G: U.K.]

Fazio, Antonio. Inflation and Wage Indexation in Italy. *Banca Naz. Lavoro Quart. Rev.*, June 1981, (137), pp. 147–70. [G: Italy]

Feinberg, Robert M. Earnings-Risk as a Compensating Differential. *Southern Econ. J.*, July 1981, *48*(1), pp. 156–63. [G: U.S.]

Feinberg, Robert M. Employment Instability, Earnings and Market Structure. *Appl. Econ.*, June 1981, *13*(2), pp. 257–65. [G: U.S.]

Feldstein, Martin. Private Pensions and Inflation. *Amer. Econ. Rev.*, May 1981, *71*(2), pp. 424–28.

Feldstein, Martin S. and Taylor, Amy. The Rapid Rise of Hospital Costs. In *Feldstein, M., ed.*, 1981, *1977*, pp. 19–56. [G: U.S.]

Fels, Allan and Hoa, Tran Van. Causal Relationships in Australian Wage Inflation and Minimum Award Rates. *Econ. Rec.*, March 1981, *57*(156), pp. 23–34. [G: Australia]

Ferber, Marianne A. and Birnbaum, Bonnie G. Labor Force Participation Patterns and Earnings of Women Clerical Workers. *J. Human Res.*, Summer 1981, *16*(3), pp. 416–26. [G: U.S.]

Filer, Randall Keith. The Influence of Affective Human Capital on the Wage Equation. In *Ehrenberg, R. G., ed.*, 1981, pp. 367–416. [G: U.S.]

Flanagan, Robert J. Equal Opportunity: Current Industrial Relations Perspectives: Discussion. In *Dennis, B. D., ed.*, 1981, pp. 163–67.

Fleisher, Belton M. Minimum Wage Regulation in Retail Trade. *Eastern Econ. J.*, April 1981, *7*(2), pp. 75–96. [G: U.S.]

Fogarty, M. P.; Egan, D. and Ryan, W. J. L. Pay Policy for the 1980s. *Irish Banking Rev.*, September 1981, pp. 2–14. [G: Ireland]

Fox, Karl A. and Ghosh, Syamal K. A Behavior Setting Approach to Social Accounts Combining Concepts and Data from Ecological Psychology, Economics, and Studies of Time Use. In *Juster, F. T. and Land, K. C., eds.*, 1981, pp. 131–217. [G: U.S.]

Foxley, Alejandro. Stabilization Policies and Their Effects on Employment and Income Distribution: A Latin American Perspective. In *Cline, W. R. and Weintraub, S., eds.*, 1981, pp. 191–225. [G: Argentina; Brazil; Chile; Uruguay]

Freedman, David H. Work in Nigeria: A Cornerstone of Meeting the Needs of the People. *Int. Lab. Rev.*, November–December 1981, *120*(6), pp. 751–63. [G: Nigeria]

Freeman, Richard B. The Effect of Unionism on Fringe Benefits. *Ind. Lab. Relat. Rev.*, July 1981, *34*(4), pp. 489–509. [G: U.S.]

Freeman, Richard B. and Medoff, James L. The Impact of the Percentage Organized on Union and Nonunion Wages. *Rev. Econ. Statist.*, No-

vember 1981, *63*(4), pp. 561–72. [G: U.S.]

Freeman, Richard B. and Medoff, James L. The Impact of Collective Bargaining: Illusion or Reality? In *Stieber, J.; McKersie, R. B. and Mills, D. Q., eds.*, 1981, pp. 47–97. [G: U.S.]

Freiden, Alan and Leimer, Dean R. The Earnings of College Students. *J. Human Res.*, Winter 1981, *16*(1), pp. 152–56. [G: U.S.]

Gaetani-d'Aragona, Gabriele. The Hidden Economy: Concealed Labor Markets in Italy. *Rivista Int. Sci. Econ. Com.*, March 1981, *28*(3), pp. 270–80. [G: Italy]

Ghez, Gilbert R. Wage Growth and Job Turnover: An Empirical Analysis: Comment. In *Rosen, S., ed.*, 1981, pp. 84–90. [G: U.S.]

Gibson, N. J. and Spencer, J. E. Unemployment and Wages in Northern Ireland. In *Crick, B., ed.*, 1981, *1981*, pp. 100–14. [G: U.K.]

Goodwin, William B. and Carlson, John A. Job-Advertising and Wage Control Spillovers. *J. Human Res.*, Winter 1981, *16*(1), pp. 80–93. [G: U.S.]

Greer, Charles R. Contributed Papers: Labor Markets and Other IR Topics: Discussion. In *Dennis, B. D., ed.*, 1981, pp. 334–37.

Gregory, Mary B. and Thomson, Andrew W. J. The Coverage Mark-up, Bargaining Structure and Earnings in Britain, 1973 and 1978. *Brit. J. Ind. Relat.*, March 1981, *19*(1), pp. 26–37. [G: U.K.]

Gregory, R. G. and Duncan, R. C. Employment, Unemployment and Income Effects of Relative Wage Changes. In *Hancock, K., ed.*, 1981, pp. 297–318. [G: Australia]

Gregory, R. G. and Duncan, R. C. Segmented Labor Market Theories and the Australian Experience of Equal Pay for Women. *J. Post Keynesian Econ.*, Spring 1981, *3*(3), pp. 403–28. [G: Australia]

Griliches, Zvi and Yatchew, Adonis J. Sample Selection Bias and Endogeneity in the Estimation of a Wage Equation: An Alternative Specification. *Ann. INSEE*, July–September 1981, (43), pp. 35–46.

Grosse, Scott and Morgan, James N. Intertemporal Variability in Income and the Interpersonal Distribution of Economic Welfare. In *Hill, M. S.; Hill, D. H. and Morgan, J. N., eds.*, 1981, pp. 297–315. [G: U.S.]

Grosskopf, Shawna. Public Employment's Impact on the Future of Urban Economies. In *Bahl, R., ed.*, 1981, pp. 39–62. [G: U.S.]

Gustafsson, Siv. Male–Female Lifetime Earnings Differentials and Labor Force History. In *Eliasson, G.; Holmlund, B. and Stafford, F. P., eds.*, 1981, pp. 235–68. [G: Sweden; U.S.]

Hancock, Keith. The Economics of Retirement Provision in Australia. *Australian Econ. Pap.*, June 1981, *20*(36), pp. 1–23. [G: Australia]

Hanham, R. Q. and Chang, H. Wage Inflation in a Growth Region: The American Sun Belt. In *Martin, R. L., ed.*, 1981, pp. 75–95. [G: U.S.]

Hansen, Richard B. The Sensitivity of Variable Measurement in Faculty Salary Studies. *J. Behav. Econ.*, Summer 1981, *10*(1), pp. 1–12. [G: U.S.]

Hansen, W. Lee. The Decline of Real Faculty Salaries in the 1970s. *Quart. Rev. Econ. Bus.*, Winter

1981, *21*(4), pp. 7–12.   [G: U.S.]

Hanushek, Eric A. Alternative Models of Earnings Determination and Labor Market Structures. *J. Human Res.*, Spring 1981, *16*(2), pp. 238–59.
                                        [G: U.S.]

Harrison, Alan. Earnings by Size: A Tale of Two Distributions. *Rev. Econ. Stud.*, October 1981, *48*(4), pp. 621–31.   [G: U.K.]

Hartman, Robert W. Retirement for Federal Civil Servants: Down from the Incomparable. In *Dennis, B. D., ed.*, 1981, pp. 82–89.   [G: U.S.]

Harwood, Edwin. Unions, Pensions, and Financial Responsibility: The British Experience: Comment. *J. Lab. Res.*, Fall 1981, *2*(2), pp. 299–305.
                                        [G: U.K.]

Hausman, Jerry A. and Taylor, William E. Panel Data and Unobservable Individual Effects. *Econometrica*, November 1981, *49*(6), pp. 1377–98.   [G: U.S.]

Heckman, James J. and MaCurdy, Thomas E. New Methods for Estimating Labor Supply Functions: A Survey. In *Ehrenberg, R. G., ed.*, 1981, pp. 65–102.   [G: U.S.]

Heldman, Dan C. Unions, Pensions, and Financial Responsibility: The British Experience: Comment. *J. Lab. Res.*, Fall 1981, *2*(2), pp. 306–08.
                                        [G: U.K.]

Hendricks, Wallace E. Unionism, Oligopoly and Rigid Wages. *Rev. Econ. Statist.*, May 1981, *63*(2), pp. 198–205.   [G: U.S.]

Hodne, Fritz and Gjølberg, Ole. Market Integration during the Period of Industrialisation in Norway. In *Bairoch, P. and Lévy-Leboyer, M., eds.*, 1981, pp. 216–25.   [G: Norway]

Hunt, Janet C.; DeLorme, Charles D., Jr. and Hill, R. Carter. Taxation and the Wife's Use of Time. *Ind. Lab. Relat. Rev.*, April 1981, *34*(3), pp. 426–32.   [G: U.S.]

Iden, George. Nontraditional Criteria for Investing Pension Assets: An Economic Appraisal: Comment. *J. Lab. Res.*, Fall 1981, *2*(2), pp. 252–57.
                                        [G: U.S.]

Inman, Robert P. "Municipal Pension Funding: A Theory and Some Evidence" by Dennis Epple and Katherine Schipper: A Comment. *Public Choice*, 1981, *37*(1), pp. 179–87.

Irvine, I. J. The Use of Cross-Section Microdata in Life Cycle Models: An Application to Inequality Theory in Nonstationary Economies. *Quart. J. Econ.*, May 1981, *96*(2), pp. 301–16.   [G: U.S.]

Johnson, Paul. Unions, Pensions, and Financial Responsibility: The British Experience. *J. Lab. Res.*, Fall 1981, *2*(2), pp. 289–98.   [G: U.K.]

Jones, Ethel B. and Long, James E. Part-Week Work and Women's Unemployment. *Rev. Econ. Statist.*, February 1981, *63*(1), pp. 70–76.
                                        [G: U.S.]

Jonsson, Anita and Klevmarken, Anders. Disequilibrium and Non-Neutral Market Effects on Age-Earnings Profiles. In *Eliasson, G.; Holmlund, B. and Stafford, F. P., eds.*, 1981, pp. 357–92.
                                        [G: Sweden]

Jörberg, Lennart and Bengtsson, Tommy. Regional Wages in Sweden during the Nineteenth Century. In *Bairoch, P. and Lévy-Leboyer, M., eds.*, 1981, pp. 226–43.   [G: Sweden]

Jusenius, Carol L. and Scheffler, Richard M. Earnings Differentials among Academic Economists: Empirical Evidence on Race and Sex. *J. Econ. Bus.*, Winter 1981, *33*(2), pp. 88–96.   [G: U.S.]

Keller, Berndt K. Determinants of the Wage Rate in the Public Sector: The Case of Civil Servants in the Federal Republic of Germany. *Brit. J. Ind. Relat.*, November 1981, *19*(3), pp. 345–60.
                                        [G: W. Germany]

Keyfitz, Nathan. Equity between the Sexes: The Pension Problem. *J. Policy Anal. Manage.*, Fall 1981, *1*(1), pp. 133–35.   [G: U.S.]

Khan, Omar Asghar. Inter-Industry Wage Differentials in the Manufacturing Sector of the Punjab (1970–71—1975–76). *Pakistan Econ. Soc. Rev.*, Winter 1981, *19*(2), pp. 131–47.   [G: Pakistan]

Kheifets, L. Material Rewards for the Work Force and the Improvement of the Economic Mechanism. *Prob. Econ.*, June 1981, *24*(2), pp. 32–45.
                                        [G: U.S.S.R.]

Kiesewetter, Hubert. Regional Disparities in Wages: The Cotton Industry in Nineteenth-century Germany—Some Methodological Considerations. In *Bairoch, P. and Lévy-Leboyer, M., eds.*, 1981, pp. 248–58.   [G: Germany]

Kiker, B. F. and Condon, C. M. The Influence of Socioeconomic Background on the Earnings of Young Men. *J. Human Res.*, Winter 1981, *16*(1), pp. 94–105.   [G: U.S.]

Kimura, Yoko. An Empirical Study on the Earning Profile in Japan. (In Japanese. With English summary.) *Osaka Econ. Pap.*, March 1981, *30*(4), pp. 70–79.   [G: Japan]

Kirby, Michael G. An Investigation of the Specification and Stability of the Australian Aggregate Wage Equation. *Econ. Rec.*, March 1981, *57*(156), pp. 35–46.   [G: Australia]

Kirkpatrick, Grant. Further Results on the Time Series Analysis of Real Wages and Employment for U.S. Manufacturing, 1948–1977. *Weltwirtsch. Arch.*, 1981, *117*(2), pp. 326–51.   [G: U.S.]

Klindt, Thomas H.; Deaton, Brady J. and Landes, Maurice R. The Determinants of Wage Increases in New Manufacturing Plants in Rural Areas. *Southern J. Agr. Econ.*, July 1981, *13*(1), pp. 83–88.   [G: U.S.]

Knight, J. B. and Sabot, R. H. The Returns to Education: Increasing with Experience or Decreasing with Expansion? *Oxford Bull. Econ. Statist.*, February 1981, *43*(1), pp. 51–71.   [G: Tanzania]

Kochan, Thomas A. and Helfman, David E. The Effects of Collective Bargaining on Economic and Behavioral Job Outcomes. In *Ehrenberg, R. G., ed.*, 1981, pp. 321–65.   [G: U.S.]

Kornhauser, Lewis A. ERISA and the Prudent Man Rule: Comments. In *Sirkin, G., ed.*, 1981, pp. 85–94.   [G: U.S.]

Kumar, Pradeep. Wages, Productivity and Labour Costs: Summary Outline. In *Wood, W. D. and Kumar, P., eds.*, 1981, pp. 385–461.
                                        [G: Canada]

Lage, Gerald M. and Greer, Charles R. Adjusting Salaries for the Effects of Inflation. *Rev. Bus. Econ. Res.*, Spring 1981, *16*(3), pp. 1–13.

Lapidus, Gail W. The Female Industrial Labor Force: Dilemmas, Reassessments, and Options.

In *Bornstein, M., ed.*, 1981, *1979*, pp. 119–48.
[G: U.S.S.R.]

Larsen, Norma L. and Martin, Gerald D. Income Growth Factors: Error Introduced through the Application of Cohort Data. *J. Risk Ins.*, March 1981, *48*(1), pp. 143–47.

Lawler, John. Reply to Professor Mitchell [Wage Spillover: The Impact of Landrum-Griffin]. *Ind. Relat.*, Fall 1981, *20*(3), pp. 347–49. [G: U.S.]

Lawler, John. Wage Spillover: The Impact of Landrum–Griffin. *Ind. Relat.*, Winter 1981, *20*(1), pp. 85–97. [G: U.S.]

Lazear, Edward P. and Rosen, Sherwin. Rank-Order Tournaments as Optimum Labor Contracts. *J. Polit. Econ.*, October 1981, *89*(5), pp. 841–64.

Lee, Linda K. A Comparison of the Rank and Salary of Male and Female Agricultural Economists. *Amer. J. Agr. Econ.*, December 1981, *63*(5), pp. 1013–18. [G: U.S.]

Leigh, Duane E. Do Union Members Receive Compensating Wage Differentials? Note. *Amer. Econ. Rev.*, December 1981, *71*(5), pp. 1049–55.
[G: U.S.]

Leigh, Duane E. The Effect of Unionism on Workers' Valuation of Future Pension Benefits. *Ind. Lab. Relat. Rev.*, July 1981, *34*(4), pp. 510–21.
[G: U.S.]

Leigh, J. Paul. Racial Differences in Compensating Wages for Job Risks. *Ind. Relat.*, Fall 1981, *20*(3), pp. 318–21. [G: U.S.]

Leigh, J. Paul. The Economic Returns to Personal Values. *J. Behav. Econ.*, Summer 1981, *10*(1), pp. 13–32. [G: U.S.]

Leigh, J. Paul. The Effects of Union Membership on Absence from Work Due to Illness. *J. Lab. Res.*, Fall 1981, *2*(2), pp. 329–36. [G: U.S.]

Lentz, Bernard F. Political and Economic Determinants of County Government Pay. *Public Choice*, 1981, *36*(2), pp. 253–71. [G: U.S.]

Leon, Carol Boyd. Employed But Not at Work: A Review of Unpaid Absences. *Mon. Lab. Rev.*, November 1981, *104*(11), pp. 18–22. [G: U.S.]

LeRoy, Douglas R. Scheduled Wage Increases and Cost-of-Living Provisions in 1981. *Mon. Lab. Rev.*, January 1981, *104*(1), pp. 9–14. [G: U.S.]

Levine, Solomon B. Japan's Trade Competitiveness: Cheap Labor. In *Richardson, B. M. and Ueda, T., eds.*, 1981, pp. 108–14. [G: Japan]

Lipas, Tauno. Palkan muutos ja ostovoima. (Change in Wages and Buying Power. With English summary.) *Liiketaloudellinen Aikak.*, 1981, *30*(2), pp. 177–81. [G: Finland]

Liu, Pak-wai and Wong, Yue-chim. Human Capital and Inequality in Singapore. *Econ. Develop. Cult. Change*, January 1981, *29*(2), pp. 275–93.
[G: Singapore]

Lovell, Michael C. Unraveling the Real-Payment Twist. *Brookings Pap. Econ. Act.*, 1981, (1), pp. 283–97. [G: U.S.]

MacDonald, Glenn M. and Evans, John C. The Size and Structure of Union-Non-Union Wage Differentials in Canadian Industry. *Can. J. Econ.*, May 1981, *14*(2), pp. 216–31. [G: Canada]

Manning, Ian. Social Security and the Future. *Australian Econ. Rev.*, 1st Quarter 1981, (53), pp. 29–34. [G: Australia]

Marks, Mitchell Lee and Mirvis, Philip H. Wage Guidelines: Impact on Job Attitudes and Behavior. *Ind. Relat.*, Fall 1981, *20*(3), pp. 286–96.
[G: U.S.]

Marrese, M. The Evolution of Wage Regulation in Hungary. In *Hare, P. G.; Radice, H. K. and Swain, N., eds.*, 1981, pp. 54–80. [G: Hungary]

Marsden, David. The Evolution of Household Income for Different Social Groups in the UK since 1966. *Cah. Écon. Bruxelles*, 2nd Trimestre 1981, (90), pp. 187–201. [G: U.K.]

Martin, Donald L. Nontraditional Criteria for Investing Pension Assets: An Economic Appraisal: Comment. *J. Lab. Res.*, Fall 1981, *2*(2), pp. 258–63.
[G: U.S.]

Martin, R. L. Wage-change Interdependence Amongst Regional Labour Markets: Conceptual Issues and Some Empirical Evidence for the United States. In *Martin, R. L., ed.*, 1981, pp. 96–135. [G: U.S.]

Mayhew, Ken. Incomes Policy and the Private Sector. In *Fallick, J. L. and Elliott, R. F., eds.*, 1981, pp. 72–99. [G: U.K.]

McNabb, Robert and Psacharopoulos, George. Racial Earnings Differentials in the U.K. *Oxford Econ. Pap.*, November 1981, *33*(3), pp. 413–25.
[G: U.K.]

Medoff, James L. and Abraham, Katharine G. Are Those Paid More Really More Productive? The Case of Experience. *J. Human Res.*, Spring 1981, *16*(2), pp. 186–216. [G: U.S.]

Meeker, Suzanne E. Equal Pay, Comparable Work, and Job Evaluation. *Yale Law J.*, January 1981, *90*(3), pp. 657–80. [G: U.S.]

Mellow, Wesley S. Unionism and Wages: A Longitudinal Analysis. *Rev. Econ. Statist.*, February 1981, *63*(1), pp. 43–52. [G: U.S.]

Mennis, Edmund A.; Valentine, Jerome L. and Mennis, Daniel L. New Perspectives on Pension Fund Management. *J. Portfol. Manage.*, Spring 1981, *7*(3), pp. 46–50.

Merrilees, William J. Interindustry Variations in Job Tenure. *Ind. Relat.*, Spring 1981, *20*(2), pp. 200–204. [G: U.S.]

Milkovich, George T. Pay Inequalities and Comparable Worth. In *Dennis, B. D., ed.*, 1981, pp. 147–54.

Milkovich, George T. The Male–Female Pay Gap: Need for Reevaluation. *Mon. Lab. Rev.*, April 1981, *104*(4), pp. 42–44. [G: U.S.]

Miller, Edward M. Large Firms are Good for Their Workers: Manufacturing Wages as a Function of Firm Size and Concentration. *Antitrust Bull.*, Spring 1981, *26*(1), pp. 145–54. [G: U.S.]

Miller, Edward M. What Do Labor Productivity Data Show about Economies of Scale: Reply. *Southern Econ. J.*, January 1981, *47*(3), pp. 847–51. [G: U.S.]

Minford, Patrick and Brech, Michael. The Wage Equation and Rational Expectations. In *Currie, D.; Nobay, R. and Peel, D., eds.*, 1981, pp. 434–59. [G: OECD; U.K.]

Mitchell, Daniel J. B. Collective Bargaining and Wage Determination in the 1970s. In *Dennis, B. D., ed.*, 1981, pp. 135–42. [G: U.S.]

Mitchell, Daniel J. B. Collective Bargaining and the

Economy. In *Stieber, J.; McKersie, R. B. and Mills, D. Q., eds.*, 1981, pp. 1–46. [G: U.S.]

Mitchell, Daniel J. B. Wage Spillover: The Impact of Landrum-Griffin: Comment. *Ind. Relat.*, Fall 1981, *20*(3), pp. 342–46. [G: U.S.]

Mitchell, Olivia S. and Andrews, Emily S. Scale Economies in Private Multi-Employer Pension Systems. *Ind. Lab. Relat. Rev.*, July 1981, *34*(4), pp. 522–30. [G: U.S.]

Mogull, Robert G. Salary Discrimination in Professional Sports. *Atlantic Econ. J.*, September 1981, *9*(3), pp. 106–10. [G: U.S.]

Montinaro, Mario. Un modello markoviano per la distribuzione dei redditi da secondo lavoro: dinamica dei redditi complessivi e dei redditi specifici per professioni. (A Markovian Model for the Distribution of Incomes Deriving from a Second Job: The Dynamics of Overall Incomes and of Incomes Specific to Professions. With English summary.) *Statistica*, July–September 1981, *41*(3), pp. 459–73. [G: Italy]

Montironi, Marina. Organizzazione del lavoro e retribuzione, un rapporto che cambia. (Labour Organisation and Remuneration, a Changing Relationship. With English summary.) *L'Impresa*, 1981, *23*(1), pp. 27–34. [G: Switzerland; W. Germany; U.K.; France; Italy]

Moomaw, Ronald L. Productivity and City Size? A Critique of the Evidence [Are There Returns to Scale in City Size?]. [Bias in the Cross Section Estimates of the Elasticity of Substitution]. *Quart. J. Econ.*, November 1981, *96*(4), pp. 675–88. [G: U.S.]

Moore, B. and Rhodes, J. The Convergence of Earnings in the Regions of the United Kingdom. In *Martin, R. L., ed.*, 1981, pp. 46–59. [G: U.K.]

Morgan, James N. Consistency of Reports of Hourly Earnings. In *Hill, M. S.; Hill, D. H. and Morgan, J. N., eds.*, 1981, pp. 427–39. [G: U.S.]

Morgan, James N. Some Tests of Wage Trade-off Hypotheses. In *Hill, M. S.; Hill, D. H. and Morgan, J. N., eds.*, 1981, pp. 421–26. [G: U.S.]

Morgan, James N. Trends in Non-money Income Through Do-It-Yourself Activities, 1971 to 1978. In *Hill, M. S.; Hill, D. H. and Morgan, J. N., eds.*, 1981, pp. 317–58. [G: U.S.]

Moszer, Max. A Comment on the Laffer Model. *Cato J.*, Spring 1981, *1*(1), pp. 23–44. [G: U.S.]

Mott, Frank L. and Haurin, R. Jean. The Impact of Health Problems and Mortality on Family Well-Being. In *Parnes, H. S., ed.*, 1981, pp. 198–253. [G: U.S.]

Munnell, Alicia H. Social Security, Private Pensions, and Saving. *New Eng. Econ. Rev.*, May/June 1981, pp. 31–47. [G: U.S.]

Murray, Roger F. Pension and Profit-sharing Plans. In *Altman, E. I., ed.*, 1981, pp. 34.3–25.

Nabli, M. K. Inter-Industry Wage Differentials and Distortions in Developing Countries: The Case of Tunisia. *Tijdschrift Econ. Manage.*, 1981, *26*(2), pp. 209–26. [G: Tunisia]

Neumann, Manfred; Böbel, I. and Haid, A. Market Structure and the Labour Market in West German Industries—A Contribution towards Interpreting the Structure-Performance Relationship.

Z. Nationalökon., 1981, *41*(1–2), pp. 97–109. [G: W. Germany]

Northrup, James P. and Northrup, Herbert R. Union Divergent Investing of Pensions: A Power, Non-Employee Relations Issue. *J. Lab. Res.*, Fall 1981, *2*(2), pp. 191–208. [G: U.S.]

Nurul Amin, A. T. M. Marginalisation vs. Dynamism: A Study of the Informal Sector in Dhaka City. *Bangladesh Devel. Stud.*, Autumn 1981, *9*(4), pp. 77–112. [G: Bangladesh]

Ofer, Gur and Vinokur, Aaron. Earning Differentials by Sex in the Soviet Union: A First Look. In *[Bergson, A.]*, 1981, pp. 127–62. [G: U.S.S.R.]

Olson, Craig A. An Analysis of Wage Differentials Received by Workers on Dangerous Jobs. *J. Human Res.*, Spring 1981, *16*(2), pp. 167–85. [G: U.S.]

Petersen, John E. Pension Fund Management. In *Aronson, J. R. and Schwartz, E., eds.*, 1981, pp. 367–88. [G: U.S.]

Peterson, George E. Transmitting the Municipal Fiscal Squeeze to a New Generation of Taxpayers: Pension Obligations and Capital Investment Needs. In *Burchell, R. W. and Listokin, D., eds.*, 1981, pp. 249–76. [G: U.S.]

Pfeffer, Jeffrey and Ross, Jerry. Unionization and Female Wage and Status Attainment. *Ind. Relat.*, Spring 1981, *20*(2), pp. 179–85. [G: U.S.]

Phelps Brown, Henry. The Economic Consequences of Collective Bargaining. In *Phelps Brown, H. and Hopkins, S. V.*, 1981, *1966*, pp. 191–214. [G: OECD]

Phelps Brown, Henry and Hopkins, Sheila V. Seven Centuries of the Prices of Consumables Compared with Builders' Wage-rates. In *Phelps Brown, H. and Hopkins, S. V.*, 1981, *1956*, pp. 13–59. [G: U.K.]

Phelps Brown, Henry and Hopkins, Sheila V. Seven Centuries of Building Wages. In *Phelps Brown, H. and Hopkins, S. V.*, 1981, *1955*, pp. 1–12. [G: U.K.]

Phelps Brown, Henry and Hopkins, Sheila V. Seven Centuries of Wages and Prices: Some Earlier Estimates. In *Phelps Brown, H. and Hopkins, S. V.*, 1981, *1961*, pp. 99–105. [G: U.K.]

Phelps Brown, Henry and Hopkins, Sheila V. Wage-rates and Prices: Evicence for Population Pressure in the Sixteenth Century. In *Phelps Brown, H. and Hopkins, S. V.*, 1981, *1957*, pp. 60–77. [G: U.K.; France]

Phipps, A. J. The Impact of Wage Indexation on Wage Inflation in Australia: 1975(2)–1980(2) *Australian Econ. Pap.*, December 1981, *20*(37), pp. 333–50. [G: Australia]

Popov, Sofija. Međunarodna analiza efekata diferencijacija zarada na njihov opšti rast. (An International Analysis of the Effects of Differentiation of Earnings on Their General Growth. With English summary.) *Econ. Anal. Worker's Manage.*, 1981, *15*(2), pp. 163–76. [G: E. Europe; MDCs]

Porter, Felice and Keller, Richard L. Public and Private Pay Levels: A Comparison in Large Labor Markets. *Mon. Lab. Rev.*, July 1981, *104*(7), pp. 22–26. [G: U.S.]

Predetti, Adalberto. La retribuzione operaia ad incentivo in Germania, Regno Unito Svezia e Francia. (Wage Incentive Systems in West Germany, United Kingdom, France and Sweden. With English summary.) *Giorn. Econ.*, March–April 1981, *40*(3–4), pp. 131–44. **[G: W. Germany; U.K.; Sweden; France]**

Prewitt, Kenneth. American Politics, Public Opinion, and Social Security Financing: Comment. In *Skidmore, F., ed.*, 1981, pp. 277–82. **[G: U.S.]**

Price, Daniel N. Federal Civil Service Adult Survivor Annuitants and Social Security, December 1975. *Soc. Sec. Bull.*, August 1981, *44*(8), pp. 3–14. **[G: U.S.]**

Pupp, Roger L. Smoking, Disabilities and Health: Their Effect on Labor Market Experience. *J. Behav. Econ.*, Summer 1981, *10*(1), pp. 66–100. **[G: U.S.]**

Qualls, P. David. Cyclical Wage Flexibility, Inflation, and Industrial Structure: An Alternative View and Some Empirical Evidence. *J. Ind. Econ.*, June 1981, *29*(4), pp. 345–56. **[G: U.S.]**

Quinn, Joseph F. and McCormick, Karen. Wage Rates and City Size. *Ind. Relat.*, Spring 1981, *20*(2), pp. 193–99.

Ragan, James F., Jr. and Smith, Sharon P. The Impact of Differences in Turnover Rates on Male/Female Pay Differentials. *J. Human Res.*, Summer 1981, *16*(3), pp. 343–65. **[G: U.S.]**

Raisian, John. Union Divergent Investing of Pensions: A Power, Non-Employee Relations Issue: Comment. *J. Lab. Res.*, Fall 1981, *2*(2), pp. 214–18. **[G: U.S.]**

Riddell, W. Craig. Contemporaneous Correlation in Wage Contract Studies. *Econometrica*, March 1981, *49*(2), pp. 515–16.

Robinson, Olive and Wallace, John. Relative Pay and Part-Time Employment in Great Britain. *Oxford Bull. Econ. Statist.*, May 1981, *43*(2), pp. 149–71. **[G: U.K.]**

Robinson, Thomas R. Have Pension Investment Managers Over-Emphasized the Needs of Retirees? Comment. *J. Lab. Res.*, Fall 1981, *2*(2), pp. 284–87. **[G: U.S.]**

Rodgers, Gerry and Standing, Guy. The Economic Roles of Children: Issues for Analysis. In *Rodgers, G. and Standing, G., eds.*, 1981, pp. 1–45. **[G: LDCs]**

Rogers, Gayle Thompson. Vesting of Private Pension Benefits in 1979 and Change from 1972. *Soc. Sec. Bull.*, July 1981, *44*(7), pp. 12–29. **[G: U.S.]**

Rumberger, Russell W. The Changing Skill Requirements of Jobs in the U.S. Economy. *Ind. Lab. Relat. Rev.*, July 1981, *34*(4), pp. 578–90. **[G: U.S.]**

Sánchez, Carlos E.; Palmiero, Horacio and Ferrero, Fernando. The Informal and Quasi-formal Sectors in Córdoba. In *Sethuraman, S. V., ed.*, 1981, pp. 144–58. **[G: Argentina]**

Sargent, Thomas J. Estimation of Dynamic Labor Demand Schedules under Rational Expectations. In *Lucas, R. E. and Sargent, T. J., eds.*, 1981, 1978, pp. 463–99. **[G: U.S.]**

Schlieper, Ulrich and McMahon, Patrick C. Behaviour of the Real Wage Rate in the Trade Cycle in West Germany and the U.K. *Kyoto Univ. Econ. Rev.*, April–October 1981, *51*(1–2), pp. 52–58. **[G: W. Germany; U.K.]**

Schotland, Roy A. Have Pension Investment Managers Over-Emphasized the Needs of Retirees? *J. Lab. Res.*, Fall 1981, *2*(2), pp. 265–83. **[G: U.S.]**

Seidman, Laurence S. Insurance for Labor under a Tax-Based Incomes Policy. In *Claudon, M. P. and Cornwall, R. R., eds.*, 1981, pp. 109–33. **[G: U.S.]**

Sekscenski, Edward S. The Health Services Industry: A Decade of Expansion. *Mon. Lab. Rev.*, May 1981, *104*(5), pp. 9–16. **[G: U.S.]**

Serow, William J. Demographic and Economic Considerations for Future Retirement Policy. *Policy Anal.*, Spring 1981, *7*(2), pp. 143–51. **[G: U.S.]**

Shapiro, Daniel M. and Stelcner, Morton. Male-Female Earnings Differentials and the Role of Language in Canada, Ontario, and Quebec, 1970. *Can. J. Econ.*, May 1981, *14*(2), pp. 341–48. **[G: Canada]**

Sheehan, Peter. Wages Policy and the Economy in the Seventies and Beyond. In *Hancock, K., ed.*, 1981, pp. 141–70. **[G: Australia]**

Siebert, W. Stanley and Sloane, P. J. The Measurement of Sex and Marital Status Discrimination at the Workplace. *Economica*, May 1981, *48*(190), pp. 125–41. **[G: U.K.]**

Smith, Marvin M. A Note on Tests of Significance and Wage Discrimination. *Amer. Econ.*, Spring 1981, *25*(1), pp. 72–75.

Smith, Patricia B. The Employment Cost Index in 1980: A First Look at Total Compensation. *Mon. Lab. Rev.*, June 1981, *104*(6), pp. 22–26. **[G: U.S.]**

Smith, Robert Stewart. Compensating Differentials for Pensions and Underfunding in the Public Sector. *Rev. Econ. Statist.*, August 1981, *63*(3), pp. 463–68. **[G: U.S.]**

Smith, Sharon P. The Prevailing Wage Concept in the Public Sector: Discussion. In *Dennis, B. D., ed.*, 1981, pp. 99–101. **[G: U.S.]**

Snape, Richard H. Wages Policy and the Economy in the Seventies and Beyond. In *Hancock, K., ed.*, 1981, pp. 170–93. **[G: Australia]**

Srinivasan, T. N. and Bhagwati, Jagdish N. Shadow Prices for Project Selection in the Presence of Distortions: Effective Rates of Protection and Domestic Resource Costs. In *Bhagwati, J. N., ed.*, 1981, 1978, pp. 243–61.

St. Cyr, E. B. A. Wages, Prices and Balance of Payments: Trinidad and Tobago; 1956–1976. *Soc. Econ. Stud.*, December 1981, *30*(4), pp. 111–33. **[G: Trinidad and Tobago]**

Stafford, Frank P. Unemployment and Labor Market Policy in Sweden and the United States. In *Eliasson, G.; Holmlund, B. and Stafford, F. P., eds.*, 1981, pp. 21–65. **[G: U.S.; Sweden]**

Stamas, George D. The Puzzling Lag in Southern Earnings. *Mon. Lab. Rev.*, June 1981, *104*(6), pp. 27–36. **[G: U.S.]**

Steele, G. R. University Salaries in the U.K.: A Study of Local Variations within a National Pay Structure. *Bull. Econ. Res.*, May 1981, *33*(1), pp. 14–36. **[G: U.K.]**

Steele, R. Incomes Policies and Low Pay. In *Fallick, J. L. and Elliott, R. F., eds.*, 1981, pp. 128–54. **[G: U.K.]**

Stephenson, Stanley P., Jr. In-School Labour Force Status and Post-School Wage Rates of Young Men. *Appl. Econ.*, September 1981, *13*(3), pp. 279–302. [G: U.S.]

Sumner, Daniel A. Wage Functions and Occupational Selection in a Rural Less Developed Country Setting. *Rev. Econ. Statist.*, November 1981, *63*(4), pp. 513–19. [G: Guatemala]

Svejnar, Jan. Relative Wage Effects of Unions, Dictatorship and Codetermination: Econometric Evidence from Germany. *Rev. Econ. Statist.*, May 1981, *63*(2), pp. 188–97. [G: W. Germany]

Tanner, Lucretia Dewey and Converse, Mary. The 1978–80 Pay Guidelines: Meeting the Need for Flexibility. *Mon. Lab. Rev.*, July 1981, *104*(7), pp. 16–21. [G: U.S.]

Tarling, R. and Wilkinson, F. Regional Earnings Determination in the United Kingdom Engineering Industry, 1964–1979. In *Martin, R. L.*, ed., 1981, pp. 60–74. [G: U.K.]

Tauber, Ronald S. Is Gold a Prudent Investment under ERISA? *J. Portfol. Manage.*, Fall 1981, *8*(1), pp. 28–31. [G: U.S.]

Taylor, D. Garth. American Politics, Public Opinion, and Social Security Financing. In *Skidmore, F.*, ed., 1981, pp. 235–73. [G: U.S.]

Taylor, Daniel E. Education, On–the–Job Training, and the Black–White Earnings Gap. *Mon. Lab. Rev.*, April 1981, *104*(4), pp. 28–34. [G: U.S.]

Thompson, A. Frank, Jr. Immunization of Pension Funds and Sensitivity to Actuarial Assumptions: Comment. *J. Risk Ins.*, March 1981, *48*(1), pp. 148–53.

Trinder, Chris. Pay of Employees in the Public and Private Sector. *Nat. Inst. Econ. Rev.*, August 1981, (97), pp. 48–56. [G: U.K.]

Turner, John A. Inflation and the Accumulation of Assets in Private Pension Funds. *Econ. Inquiry*, July 1981, *19*(3), pp. 410–25.

Wesolowski, Wlodzimierz and Krauze, Tadeusz. Socialist Society and the Meritocratic Principle of Remuneration. In *Berreman, G. D.*, ed., 1981, pp. 337–49. [G: Poland]

Wessels, Walter J. Economic Effects of Right to Work Laws. *J. Lab. Res.*, Spring 1981, *2*(1), pp. 55–75. [G: U.S.]

White, Halbert and Olson, Lawrence. Conditional Distributions of Earnings, Wages and Hours for Blacks and Whites. *J. Econometrics*, December 1981, *17*(3), pp. 263–85. [G: U.S.]

Whitehead, Donald and Bonnell, Sheila. What Ails the Lucky Country: The Debate about Diagnosis. In *Hancock, K.*, ed., 1981, pp. 89–140. [G: Australia]

Zemanian, Armen H. Dynamic Adjustment of Labor Allocation between Collective, State, or Cooperative Farming and Private Farming in a Planned Economy. *J. Compar. Econ.*, September 1981, *5*(3), pp. 292–317.

8243 Employment Studies; Unemployment and Vacancies; Retirements and Quits

Abed, George T. and Kubursi, Atif A. A Macroeconomic Simulation Model of High Level Manpower Requirements in Iraq. In *Sherbiny, N. A.*, ed., 1981, pp. 145–71. [G: Iraq]

Abey, Arun; Booth, Anne and Sundrum, R. M. Labour Absorption in Indonesian Agriculture. *Bull. Indonesian Econ. Stud.*, March 1981, *17*(1), pp. 36–65. [G: Indonesia]

Abowd, John M. and Ashenfelter, Orley. Anticipated Unemployment, Temporary Layoffs, and Compensating Wage Differentials. In *Rosen, S.*, ed., 1981, pp. 141–70. [G: U.S.]

Adams, Avril V. The American Work Force in the Eighties: New Problems and Policy Interests Require Improved Labor Force Data. *Ann. Amer. Acad. Polit. Soc. Sci.*, January 1981, *453*, pp. 123–29. [G: U.S.]

Agarwal, Bina. Agricultural Mechanisation and Labour Use: A Disaggregated Approach. *Int. Lab. Rev.*, January–February 1981, *120*(1), pp. 115–27. [G: India]

Ahmed, Iqbal. Farm Size and Labour Use: Some Alternative Explanations. *Oxford Bull. Econ. Statist.*, February 1981, *43*(1), pp. 73–88.

Aho, C. Michael and Orr, James A. Trade-Sensitive Employment: Who Are the Affected Workers? *Mon. Lab. Rev.*, February 1981, *104*(2), pp. 29–35. [G: U.S.]

Aislabie, C. J. The Sectoral Impact on Employment of Some Economic Policies: An Australian Case Study. *Metroecon.*, Feb.-Oct. 1981, *33*(1–2–3), pp. 175–91. [G: Australia]

Akarca, Ali T. and Long, Thomas Veach, II. Advanced Time Series Techniques and Public Policy Analysis. In *Crecine, J. P.*, ed., 1981, pp. 39–51. [G: U.S.]

Akerlof, George A. and Main, Brian G. M. An Experience-Weighted Measure of Employment and Unemployment Durations. *Amer. Econ. Rev.*, December 1981, *71*(5), pp. 1003–11. [G: U.S.]

Akrasanee, Narongchai. Trade Strategy for Employment Growth in Thailand. In *Krueger, A. O., et al.*, eds., 1981, pp. 393–433. [G: Thailand]

Albrecht, James W. A Procedure for Testing the Signalling Hypothesis. *J. Public Econ.*, February 1981, *15*(1), pp. 123–32. [G: Sweden; U.S.]

Amjad, Rashid. The Development of Labour Intensive Industry in ASEAN Countries—An Overview. In *Amjad, R.*, ed., 1981, pp. 1–28. [G: ASEAN]

Arellano, José-Pablo. Do More Jobs in the Modern Sector Increase Urban Unemployment? *J. Devel. Econ.*, April 1981, *8*(2), pp. 241–47.

Armstrong, H. and Taylor, J. The Measurement of Different Types of Unemployment. In *Creedy, J.*, ed., 1981, pp. 99–127. [G: U.K.]

Aryee, George. The Informal Manufacturing Sector in Kumasi. In *Sethuraman, S. V.*, ed., 1981, pp. 90–100. [G: Ghana]

Atkinson, A. B. Unemployment Benefits and Incentives. In *Creedy, J.*, ed., 1981, pp. 128–49. [G: U.K.]

Aw, Bee Yan. The Short–Run Employment Impact of ASEAN–U.S. Trade. *Malayan Econ. Rev. (See Singapore Econ. Rev.)*, October 1981, *26*(2), pp. 80–91. [G: U.S.; ASEAN]

Baker, David G. and Colby, David C. The Politics of Municipal Employment Policy: A Comparative Study of U.S. Cities. *Amer. J. Econ. Soc.*, July

1981, *40*(3), pp. 249–63. [G: U.S.]

Ball, Robert. Employment Created by Construction Expenditures. *Mon. Lab. Rev.*, December 1981, *104*(12), pp. 38–44. [G: U.S.]

Barro, Robert J. Unanticipated Money Growth and Economic Activity in the United States. In *Barro, R. J.*, 1981, pp. 137–69.

Barro, Robert J. Unanticipated Money Growth and Unemployment in the United States. In *Lucas, R. E. and Sargent, T. J.*, eds., 1981, *1977*, pp. 563–84. [G: U.S.]

Barron, John M. and Mellow, Wesley S. Changes in Labor Force Status among the Unemployed. *J. Human Res.*, Summer 1981, *16*(3), pp. 427–41. [G: U.S.]

Barron, John M. and Mellow, Wesley S. Unemployment Insurance: The Recipients and Its Impact. *Southern Econ. J.*, January 1981, *47*(3), pp. 606–16. [G: U.S.]

Bartel, Ann P. and Borjas, George J. Wage Growth and Job Turnover: An Empirical Analysis. In *Rosen, S.*, ed., 1981, pp. 65–84. [G: U.S.]

Bautista, Romeo M. The Development of Labour Intensive Industry in the Philippines. In *Amjad, R.*, ed., 1981, pp. 29–75. [G: Philippines]

Becker, Brian E. and Hills, Stephen M. Youth Attitudes and Adult Labor Market Activity. *Ind. Relat.*, Winter 1981, *20*(1), pp. 60–70. [G: U.S.]

Begg, Iain; Cripps, Francis and Ward, Terry. The European Community: Problems and Prospects. *Cambridge Econ. Pol. Rev.*, December 1981, *7*(2), pp. 1–65. [G: EEC]

Bell, David N. F. Regional Output: Employment and Unemployment Fluctuations. *Oxford Econ. Pap.*, March 1981, *33*(1), pp. 42–60. [G: U.K.]

Bension, Alberto and Caumont, Jorge. Uruguay: Alternative Trade Strategies and Employment Implications. In *Krueger, A. O., et al.*, eds., 1981, pp. 499–529. [G: Uruguay]

Berlinck, Manuel Tosta; Bovo, José Murari and Cintra, Luiz Carlos. The Urban Informal Sector and Industrial Development in a Small City: The Case of Campinas (Brazil). In *Sethuraman, S. V.*, ed., 1981, pp. 159–67. [G: Brazil]

Berry, Roger. Redistribution, Demand Structure and Factor Requirements: The Case of India. *World Devel.*, July 1981, *9*(7), pp. 621–35. [G: India]

Betsey, Charles L. and Dunson, Bruce H. Federal Minimum Wage Laws and the Employment of Minority Youth. *Amer. Econ. Rev.*, May 1981, *71*(2), pp. 379–84. [G: U.S.]

Bhalla, A. S. Technology and Employment in Industry: Lessons from the Case Studies. In *Bhalla, A. S.*, ed., 1981, *1975*, pp. 357–80. [G: LDCs]

Bishop, John. Employment in Construction and Distribution Industries: The Impact of the New Jobs Tax Credit. In *Rosen, S.*, ed., 1981, pp. 209–46. [G: U.S.]

Björklund, Anders and Holmlund, Bertil. The Duration of Unemployment and Unexpected Inflation: An Empirical Analysis. *Amer. Econ. Rev.*, March 1981, *71*(1), pp. 121–31. [G: U.S.; Sweden]

Björklund, Anders and Holmlund, Bertil. The Structure and Dynamics of Unemployment: Sweden and the United States. In *Eliasson, G.; Holmlund, B. and Stafford, F. P.*, eds., 1981, pp. 183–226. [G: Sweden; U.S.]

Black, Matthew. An Empirical Test of the Theory of On-the-Job Search. *J. Human Res.*, Winter 1981, *16*(1), pp. 129–40. [G: U.S.]

Blattner, Niklaus. Labour Displacement by Technological Change? A Preliminary Survey of the Case of Microelectronics. *Rivista Int. Sci. Econ. Com.*, May 1981, *28*(5), pp. 422–48.

Blau, Francine D. and Kahn, Lawrence M. Causes and Consequences of Layoffs. *Econ. Inquiry*, April 1981, *19*(2), pp. 270–96. [G: U.S.]

Blau, Francine D. and Kahn, Lawrence M. Race and Sex Differences in Quits by Young Workers. *Ind. Lab. Relat. Rev.*, July 1981, *34*(4), pp. 563–77. [G: U.S.]

Bloch, Howard R. and Pennington, Robert Leroy. An Econometric Analysis of Affirmative Action. *Rev. Black Polit. Econ.*, Winter 1981, *11*(2), pp. 267–76. [G: U.S.]

Blyton, Paul and Hill, Stephen. The Economics of Worksharing. *Nat. Westminster Bank Quart. Rev.*, November 1981, pp. 37–45. [G: U.K.]

Borus, Michael E. Special Groups in the Labor Market: Discussion. In *Dennis, B. D.*, ed., 1981, pp. 69–71. [G: U.S.]

Bosworth, Derek L. Specification of Factor Demand Models and Shiftworking. *Scot. J. Polit. Econ.*, November 1981, *28*(3), pp. 256–65.

Bosworth, Derek L.; Dawkins, Peter J. and Westaway, Anthony J. The Causes of Shiftworking in Great Britain. In *Currie, D.; Peel, D. and Peters, W.*, eds., 1981, pp. 361–82. [G: U.K.]

Bosworth, Derek L.; Dawkins, Peter J. and Westaway, Anthony J. Explaining the Incidence of Shiftworking in Great Britain. *Econ. J.*, March 1981, *91*(361), pp. 145–57. [G: U.K.]

Bowers, Norman. Have Employment Patterns in Recessions Changed? *Mon. Lab. Rev.*, February 1981, *104*(2), pp. 15–28. [G: U.S.]

Boyer, Robert and Petit, Pascal. Employment and Productivity in the EEC. *Cambridge J. Econ.*, March 1981, *5*(1), pp. 47–58. [G: EEC]

Brechling, Frank. Layoffs and Unemployment Insurance. In *Rosen, S.*, ed., 1981, pp. 187–202. [G: U.S.]

Briggs, Vernon M., Jr. Unemployment and Underemployment. In *Hawley, A. H. and Mazie, S. M.*, eds., 1981, pp. 359–81. [G: U.S.]

de Broucker, Patrice. Sensibilité du chômage et caractéristiques de l'offre et de la demande sur le marché du travail. (Sensitivity of Unemployment and Characteristics of Supply and Demand in the Labor Market. With English summary.) *L'Actual. Econ.*, July–September 1981, *57*(3), pp. 359–75. [G: Canada]

Burridge, Peter and Gordon, Ian Richard. Unemployment in the British Metropolitan Labour Areas. *Oxford Econ. Pap.*, July 1981, *33*(2), pp. 274–97. [G: U.K.]

Butler, Richard J. and Sisti, Thomas R. Impact of Experience Rating and UI Benefits on Unemployment: The Neglected Firm Side. In *Dennis, B. D.*, ed., 1981, pp. 316–25. [G: U.S.]

Button, James. The Quest for Economic Equality:

Factors Related to Black Employment in the South. *Soc. Sci. Quart.*, September 1981, *62*(3), pp. 461–74. [G: U.S.]

Caire, Guy. Automation: technologie, travail, relations sociales (Sur quelques travaux récents relatifs à l'automation: réponses et questions). (Automation, Technology, Labour, Social Relations. Answers and Questions on Recent Studies on Automation. With English summary.) *Consommation*, January–March 1981, *28*(1), pp. 51–84.

Carmichael, C. L. The Labour-Market Behaviour of Employers: A Framework for Analysis and a Case Study of a Local Labour Market. In *Martin, R. L., ed.*, 1981, pp. 160–88. [G: U.K.]

Carvalho, José L. and Haddad, Cláudio, L. S. Foreign Trade Strategies and Employment in Brazil. In *Krueger, A. O., et al., eds.*, 1981, pp. 29–81. [G: Brazil]

Chaikin, Sol C. Toward a New U.S. Industrial Policy? International Trade: Comment. In *Wachter, M. L. and Wachter, S. M., eds.*, 1981, pp. 409–12. [G: U.S.]

Chatterji, M. and Wickens, Michael R. Verdoorn's Law—The Externalities Hypothesis and Economic Growth in the U.K. In *Currie, D.; Nobay, R. and Peel, D., eds.*, 1981, pp. 405–29. [G: U.K.]

Chee, Peng Lim; Lee, Donald and Foo, Kok Thye. The Case for Labour Intensive Industries in Malaysia. In *Amjad, R., ed.*, 1981, pp. 235–309. [G: Malaysia]

Cheshire, Paul C. Labour-Market Theory and Spatial Unemployment: The Role of Demand Reconsidered. In *Martin, R. L., ed.*, 1981, pp. 189–207. [G: U.K.]

Chirikos, Thomas N. and Nestel, Gilbert. Impairment and Labor Market Outcomes: A Cross-Sectional and Longitudinal Analysis. In *Parnes, H. S., ed.*, 1981, pp. 93–131. [G: U.S.]

Clark, Gordon L. The Regional Impact of Stagflation: A Conceptual Model and Empirical Evidence for Canada. In *Martin, R. L., ed.*, 1981, pp. 136–59. [G: Canada]

Clark, Kim B. and Summers, Lawrence H. Demographic Differences in Cyclical Employment Variation. *J. Human Res.*, Winter 1981, *16*(1), pp. 61–79. [G: U.S.]

Clarke, James J. An Analysis of Unemployment across Industrial Sectors, 1965–1977. *Rev. Soc. Econ.*, October 1981, *39*(2), pp. 197–203. [G: U.S.]

Cole, Robert E. Permanent Employment. In *Richardson, B. M. and Ueda, T., eds.*, 1981, pp. 31–36. [G: Japan]

Colvin, Lucie Gallistel. The Uprooted of the Western Sahel: Mauritania. In *Colvin, L. G., et al.*, 1981, pp. 244–59. [G: Mauritania]

Cooke, William N. Permanent Layoffs: What's Implicit in the Contract? *Ind. Relat.*, Spring 1981, *20*(2), pp. 186–92. [G: U.S.]

Cooke, William N. The Behavior of Unemployment Insurance Recipients under Adverse Market Conditions. *Ind. Lab. Relat. Rev.*, April 1981, *34*(3), pp. 386–95. [G: U.S.]

Corbo, Vittorio and Meller, Patricio. Alternative Trade Strategies and Employment Implications: Chile. In *Krueger, A. O., et al., eds.*, 1981, pp. 83–134. [G: Chile]

Corcoran, Mary and MacKenzie, Abigail. Expected Wages and Men's Labor Supply. In *Hill, M. S.; Hill, D. H. and Morgan, J. N., eds.*, 1981, pp. 245–68. [G: U.S.]

Corson, Walter and Nicholson, Walter. Trade Adjustment Assistance for Workers: Results of a Survey of Recipients under the Trade Act of 1974. In *Ehrenberg, R. G., ed.*, 1981, pp. 417–69. [G: U.S.]

Covick, Owen. The Australian Labour Market, June, 1981. *Australian Bull. Lab.*, June 1981, *7*(3), pp. 109–21. [G: Australia]

Crawford, Vincent P. and Lilien, David M. Social Security and the Retirement Decision. *Quart. J. Econ.*, August 1981, *96*(3), pp. 505–29. [G: U.S.]

Creedy, J. The Economics of Unemployment in Britain: Introduction. In *Creedy, J., ed.*, 1981, pp. 1–16. [G: U.K.]

Creedy, John and Disney, Richard. Changes in Labour Market States in Great Britain. *Scot. J. Polit. Econ.*, February 1981, *28*(1), pp. 76–85. [G: U.K.]

Cromley, Robert G. and Leinbach, Thomas R. The Pattern and Impact of the Filter Down Process in Nonmetropolitan Kentucky. *Econ. Geogr.*, July 1981, *57*(3), pp. 208–24. [G: U.S.]

Cunningham, Edward. Regional Development and the Changing Economy. In *Gaskin, M., ed.*, 1981, pp. 152–64. [G: U.K.; OECD]

Curran, Margaret M. Inter-Industry Variations in Male Labour Turnover. *Brit. J. Ind. Relat.*, July 1981, *19*(2), pp. 201–10. [G: U.K.]

Daymont, Thomas N. Changes in Black–White Labor Market Opportunities, 1966–76. In *Parnes, H. S., ed.*, 1981, pp. 42–64. [G: U.S.]

Deacon, Alan. Unemployment and Politics in Britain since 1945. In *Showler, B. and Sinfield, A., eds.*, 1981, pp. 59–88. [G: U.K.]

Denton, Frank T. Comment on 'Diagnosing Labour Market Imbalances in Canada.' *Can. Public Policy*, Spring 1981, *7*(2), pp. 338–42. [G: Canada]

Deutschmann, Christoph. Labour Market Segmentation and Wage Dynamics. *Managerial Dec. Econ.*, September 1981, *2*(3), pp. 145–59. [G: W. Germany]

Devens, Richard M., Jr. Testing an Hypothesis of Institutional Change: Welfare Work Registration, Aggregate Demand, and the Unemployment Rate. *J. Monet. Econ.*, May 1981, *7*(3), pp. 387–93. [G: U.S.]

Disney, R. Unemployment Insurance in Britain. In *Creedy, J., ed.*, 1981, pp. 150–85. [G: U.K.]

Douglas, Hernán Cortés and Sjaastad, Larry A. Protección y empleo. (With English summary.) *Cuadernos Econ.*, August–December 1981, *18*(54–55), pp. 317–60. [G: Chile]

Eason, Warren W. Selected Problems of Regional Development in the USSR: Population and Labor Force. In *Koropeckyj, I. S. and Schroeder, G. E., eds.*, 1981, pp. 11–91. [G: U.S.S.R.]

Edwards, C. J. W. Structural Underemployment on Full-Time Farms in Northern Ireland. *Irish J.*

Agr. Econ. Rural Soc., 1981, *8*(2), pp. 235–42. [G: U.K.]

Eliasson, Gunnar and Lindberg, Thomas. Allocation and Growth Effects of Corporate Income Taxes. In *Eliasson, G. and Södersten, J., eds.,* 1981, pp. 381–435. [G: Sweden]

Erickson, Rodney A. Corporations, Branch Plants, and Employment Stability in Nonmetropolitan Areas. In *Rees, J.; Hewings, G. J. D. and Stafford, H. A., eds.,* 1981, pp. 135–53. [G: U.S.]

Evans, Alan W. and Richardson, Ray. Urban Unemployment: Interpretation and Additional Evidence. *Scot. J. Polit. Econ.,* June 1981, *28*(2), pp. 107–24. [G: U.K.]

Favereau, Olivier and Mouillart, Michel. La stabilité du lien emploi-croissance et la loi d'Okun: Une application à l'économie française. (The Stability of the Relationship between Employment and Growth in Okun's Law: An Application to the French Economy. With English summary.) *Consommation,* January–March 1981, *28*(1), pp. 85–117. [G: France]

Feinberg, Robert M. Employment Instability, Earnings and Market Structure. *Appl. Econ.,* June 1981, *13*(2), pp. 257–65. [G: U.S.]

Fenn, Paul T. Sickness Duration, Residual Disability, and Income Replacement: An Empirical Analysis. *Econ. J.,* March 1981, *91*(361), pp. 158–73. [G: U.K.]

Findlay, Allan M. Labour Mobility and Manpower Planning in Tunisia. In *[Fisher, W. B.],* 1981, pp. 242–51. [G: Tunisia]

Finegan, T. Aldrich. Discouraged Workers and Economic Fluctuations. *Ind. Lab. Relat. Rev.,* October 1981, *35*(1), pp. 88–102. [G: U.S.]

Fleisher, Belton M. Minimum Wage Regulation in Retail Trade. *Eastern Econ. J.,* April 1981, *7*(2), pp. 75–96. [G: U.S.]

Fong, Pang Eng and Tan, Augustine. Employment and Export-led Industrialisation: The Experience of Singapore. In *Amjad, R., ed.,* 1981, pp. 141–74. [G: Singapore]

Foster, William. Gross Flows in the Australian Labour Market: A First Look. *Australian Econ. Rev.,* 4th Quarter 1981, (56), pp. 57–64. [G: Australia]

Foxley, Alejandro. Stabilization Policies and Their Effects on Employment and Income Distribution: A Latin American Perspective. In *Cline, W. R. and Weintraub, S., eds.,* 1981, pp. 191–225. [G: Argentina; Brazil; Chile; Uruguay]

Frankena, Mark W. Intrametropolitan Location of Employment. *J. Urban Econ.,* September 1981, *10*(2), pp. 256–69. [G: Canada]

Frost, M. and Spence, N. The Timing of Unemployment Response in British Regional Labour Markets, 1963–76. In *Martin, R. L., ed.,* 1981, pp. 208–31. [G: U.K.]

Fuchs, Victor R. Economic Growth and the Rise of Service Employment. In *Giersch, H., ed. (II),* 1981, pp. 221–42. [G: U.S.; OECD]

Gaskin, Maxwell. The Political Economy of Tolerable Survival. In *Gaskin, M., ed.,* 1981, pp. 15–33. [G: U.K.]

Georgiou, George C. Alternative Trade Strategies and Employment in Cyprus. *J. Econ. Devel.,* December 1981, *6*(2), pp. 113–31. [G: Cyprus]

Gèze, François. Le redéploiement international des grands groupes industriels français et ses conséquences sur l'emploi en France. (International Redeployment of Major French Industrial Companies and Its Impact on Employment in France. With English summary.) *Rev. Econ. Ind.,* 1st Trimester 1981, (15), pp. 1–18. [G: France]

Ghez, Gilbert R. Wage Growth and Job Turnover: An Empirical Analysis: Comment. In *Rosen, S., ed.,* 1981, pp. 84–90. [G: U.S.]

Ghodake, R. D.; Ryan, James G. and Sarin, R. Human Labour Use with Existing and Prospective Technologies in the Semi-Arid Tropics of South India. *J. Devel. Stud.,* October 1981, *18*(1), pp. 25–46. [G: India]

Gibson, N. J. and Spencer, J. E. Unemployment and Wages in Northern Ireland. In *Crick, B., ed.,* 1981, *1981,* pp. 100–14. [G: U.K.]

van Ginneken, W. Unemployment: Some Trends, Causes and Policy Implications: Evidence from the Federal Republic of Germany, France and the Netherlands. *Int. Lab. Rev.,* March–April 1981, *120*(2), pp. 165–81. [G: W. Germany; Netherlands; France]

Girgis, Maurice. Growth Patterns and Structural Changes in Output and Employment in the Arab World. In *Sherbiny, N. A., ed.,* 1981, pp. 21–54. [G: Arab Countries]

Glynn, Sean and Shaw, Stephen. Wage Bargaining and Unemployment. In *Crick, B., ed.,* 1981, *1981,* pp. 115–26. [G: U.K.]

Görres, Peter Anselm. Mindestlohnarbeitslosigkeit—eine wenig nützliche Vokabel. (Minimum Wage Unemployment—A Concept of Dubious Value. With English summary.) *Konjunkturpolitik,* 1981, *27*(3), pp. 156–75.

Görzig, Bernd. The Influence of Public Demand on Sectoral Employment: The Case of the Federal Republic of Germany. *Konjunkturpolitik,* 1981, *27*(1), pp. 47–57. [G: W. Germany]

Gramlich, Edward M. The Structure and Dynamics of Unemployment: Sweden and the United States. In *Eliasson, G.; Holmlund, B. and Stafford, F. P., eds.,* 1981, pp. 227–32. [G: Sweden; U.S.]

Greene, Richard. Employment Trends in Energy Extraction. *Mon. Lab. Rev.,* May 1981, *104*(5), pp. 3–8. [G: U.S.]

Gregory, R. G. and Duncan, R. C. Employment, Unemployment and Income Effects of Relative Wage Changes. In *Hancock, K., ed.,* 1981, pp. 297–318. [G: Australia]

Grosskopf, Shawna. Public Employment's Impact on the Future of Urban Economies. In *Bahl, R., ed.,* 1981, pp. 39–62. [G: U.S.]

Grossman, Allyson Sherman. The Employment Situation for Military Wives. *Mon. Lab. Rev.,* February 1981, *104*(2), pp. 60–64. [G: U.S.]

Guisinger, Stephen E. Trade Policies and Employment: The Case of Pakistan. In *Krueger, A. O., et al., eds.,* 1981, pp. 291–340. [G: Pakistan]

Gutierrez-Camara, José L. and Vaubel, Roland. Reducing the Cost of Reducing Inflation through Gradualism, Preannouncement or Indexation? The International Evidence. *Weltwirtsch. Arch.,*

1981, *117*(2), pp. 244–61.

Gutierrez-Rieger, Hannah and Podczek, Konrad. On the Nonexistence of Temporary Layoff Unemployment in Austria. *Empirica*, 1981, (2), pp. 277–89. **[G: Austria]**

Hamermesh, Daniel S. Layoffs and Unemployment Insurance: Comment. In *Rosen, S., ed.*, 1981, pp. 203–07. **[G: U.S.]**

Hamermesh, Daniel S. Transfers, Taxes and the NAIRU. In *Meyer, L. H., ed.*, 1981, pp. 203–29. **[G: U.S.]**

Hamilton, Carl. A New Approach to Estimation of the Effects of Non-Tariff Barriers to Trade: An Application to the Swedish Textile and Clothing Industry. *Weltwirtsch. Arch.*, 1981, *117*(2), pp. 298–325. **[G: Sweden]**

Hart, Keith. Informal Income Opportunities and Urban Employment in Ghana. In *Livingstone, I., ed.*, 1981, *1973*, pp. 75–84. **[G: Ghana]**

Hassenkam, Henrik. Aktuel arbejdsmarkedspolitik. (Danish Labour Market Policy. With English summary.) *Nationaløkon. Tidsskr.*, 1981, *119*(2), pp. 166–81. **[G: Denmark]**

Heer, David. Fertility and Female Work Status in the USSR. In *Desfosses, H., ed.*, 1981, pp. 62–94. **[G: U.S.S.R.]**

Hill, Michael. Unemployment and Government Manpower Policy. In *Showler, B. and Sinfield, A., eds.*, 1981, pp. 89–121. **[G: U.K.]**

Hinckley, Robert. Black Teenage Unemployment. *J. Econ. Issues*, June 1981, *15*(2), pp. 501–12. **[G: U.S.]**

Hong, Wontack. Export Promotion and Employment Growth in South Korea. In *Krueger, A. O., et al., eds.*, 1981, pp. 341–91. **[G: S. Korea]**

House, William J. Redistribution, Consumer Demand and Employment in Kenyan Furniture-Making. *J. Devel. Stud.*, July 1981, *17*(4), pp. 336–56. **[G: Kenya]**

Howson, S. Slump and Unemployment. In *Floud, R. and McCloskey, D., eds.*, Vol. 2, 1981, pp. 265–85. **[G: U.K.]**

Isard, W. and Reiner, Th. A. Megalopolitan Decline and Urban Redevelopment in the United States, an Analysis of Evolutionary Forces. In *Klaassen, L. H.; Molle, W. T. M. and Paelinck, J. H. P., eds.*, 1981, pp. 225–48. **[G: U.S.]**

Iugai, T. The Economic Mechanism of the Formation of Employment Structure. *Prob. Econ.*, July 1981, *24*(3), pp. 86–98. **[G: U.S.S.R.]**

Izraeli, Oded and Groll, Shalom. Implications of an Ideological Constraint: The Case of Hired Labor in the Kibbutz. *Econ. Develop. Cult. Change*, January 1981, *29*(2), pp. 341–51. **[G: Israel]**

James, Franklin J. Economic Distress in Central Cities. In *Burchell, R. W. and Listokin, D., eds.*, 1981, pp. 19–49. **[G: U.S.]**

Jenkins, Glenn P. and Kuo, Chun-Yan. On Measuring the Social Opportunity Cost of Permanent and Temporary Employment: A Reply. *Can. J. Econ.*, November 1981, *14*(4), pp. 708–12.

[G: Canada]

Johannesson, Jan. On the Composition of Swedish Labor Market Policy. In *Eliasson, G.; Holmlund, B. and Stafford, F. P., eds.*, 1981, pp. 67–137. **[G: Sweden]**

Johnson, Paul M. Changing Social Structure and the Political Role of Manual Workers. In *Triska, J. F. and Gati, C., eds.*, 1981, pp. 29–42.

[G: E. Europe]

Jones, Ethel B. and Long, James E. Part-Week Work and Women's Unemployment. *Rev. Econ. Statist.*, February 1981, *63*(1), pp. 70–76.

[G: U.S.]

Joshi, Heather E. Secondary Workers in the Employment Cycle: Great Britain, 1961–1974. *Economica*, February 1981, *48*(189), pp. 29–44.

[G: U.K.]

Junankar, P. N. An Econometric Analysis of Unemployment in Great Britain, 1952–75. *Oxford Econ. Pap.*, November 1981, *33*(3), pp. 387–400.

[G: U.K.]

Kahn, Lawrence M. Sex Discrimination in Professional Employment: A Case Study: Comment. *Ind. Lab. Relat. Rev.*, January 1981, *34*(2), pp. 273–75. **[G: U.S.]**

Kaldor, Nicholas. Verdoorn's Law—The Externalities Hypothesis and Economic Growth in the U.K.: Comment. In *Currie, D.; Nobay, R. and Peel, D., eds.*, 1981, pp. 430–433. **[G: U.K.]**

Kao, C. H. C.; Anschel, K. R. and Eicher, C. K. Disguised Unemployment in Agriculture: A Survey. In *Livingstone, I., ed.*, 1981, *1964*, pp. 59–66. **[G: Greece; India; Italy; Thailand]**

Keeble, David. Manufacturing Dispersion and Government Policy in a Declining Industrial System: The United Kingdom Case, 1971–76. In *Rees, J.; Hewings, G. J. D. and Stafford, H. A., eds.*, 1981, pp. 197–215. **[G: U.K.]**

Keyfitz, Nathan. Paradoxes of Work and Consumption in Late Twentieth Century America. In *Khan, A. and Sirageldin, I., eds.*, 1981, pp. 31–54. **[G: U.S.]**

Kiefer, Nicholas M. and Neumann, George R. Individual Effects in a Nonlinear Model: Explicit Treatment of Heterogeneity in the Empirical Job-Search Model. *Econometrica*, June 1981, *49*(4), pp. 965–79. **[G: U.S.]**

Kiefer, Nicholas M. and Neumann, George R. Structural and Reduced Form Approaches to Analyzing Unemployment Durations. In *Rosen, S., ed.*, 1981, pp. 171–85. **[G: U.S.]**

Kiewiet, D. Roderick. Policy-Oriented Voting in Response to Economic Issues. *Amer. Polit. Sci. Rev.*, June 1981, *75*(2), pp. 448–59. **[G: U.S.]**

Kirkpatrick, Grant. Further Results on the Time Series Analysis of Real Wages and Employment for U.S. Manufacturing, 1948–1977. *Weltwirtsch. Arch.*, 1981, *117*(2), pp. 326–51. **[G: U.S.]**

Krishnamurty, J. Indirect Employment Effects of Investment. In *Bhalla, A. S., ed.*, 1981, *1975*, pp. 65–87. **[G: LDCs]**

Krueger, Anne O. Alternative Trade Strategies and Employment in LDCs: An Overview. *Pakistan Devel. Rev.*, Autumn 1981, *20*(3), pp. 277–301.

[G: LDCs]

Krueger, Anne O. Trade and Employment in Developing Countries: The Framework of the Country Studies. In *Krueger, A. O., et al., eds.*, 1981, pp. 1–28. **[G: LDCs]**

Kujawa, Duane. U.S. Manufacturing Investment in the Developing Countries: American Labour's

Concerns and the Enterprise Environment in the Decade Ahead. *Brit. J. Ind. Relat.*, March 1981, *19*(1), pp. 38–48. [G: U.S.]

Kuleshova, L. M. and Mamontova, T. I. Part-time Employment of Women. *Prob. Econ.*, Sept.–Oct.–Nov. 1981, *24*(5–6–7), pp. 277–81.

Kutscher, Ronald E. New Economic Projections through 1900—An Overview. *Mon. Lab. Rev.*, August 1981, *104*(8), pp. 9–17. [G: U.S.]

Kuznets, Simon. Economic Growth and the Rise of Service Employment: Comments. In *Giersch, H., ed. (II)*, 1981, pp. 249–52. [G: U.S.; OECD]

Layard, Richard. Measuring the Duration of Unemployment: A Note. *Scot. J. Polit. Econ.*, November 1981, *28*(3), pp. 273–77.

Leon, Carol Boyd. The Employment–Population Ratio: Its Value in Labor Force Analysis. *Mon. Lab. Rev.*, February 1981, *104*(2), pp. 36–45. [G: U.S.]

Leslie, D. G. The Causes of Shiftworking in Great Britain: Comment. In *Currie, D.; Peel, D. and Peters, W., eds.*, 1981, pp. 383–85. [G: U.K.]

Lever, William F. The Inner City Employment Problem in Great Britain, 1952–76: A Shift–Share Approach. In *Rees, J.; Hewings, G. J. D. and Stafford, H. A., eds.*, 1981, pp. 171–96. [G: U.K.]

Leys, Colin. A Critique of the ILO Report. In *Killick, T., ed.*, 1981, pp. 136–41. [G: Kenya]

Long, James E. and Jones, Ethel B. Married Women in Part-Time Employment. *Ind. Lab. Relat. Rev.*, April 1981, *34*(3), pp. 413–25. [G: U.S.]

Lord, J. S. Unemployment Statistics in Britain. In *Creedy, J., ed.*, 1981, pp. 235–54. [G: U.K.]

Lucas, Robert E., Jr. Unemployment in the Great Depression: Is There a Full Explanation? In *Lucas, R. E., Jr.*, 1981, *1972*, pp. 59–65. [G: U.S.]

Luksetich, William A. Market Power and Discrimination in White-Collar Employment: 1969–1975. *Rev. Soc. Econ.*, October 1981, *39*(2), pp. 145–64. [G: U.S.]

Lutz, Mark A. Stagflation as an Institutional Problem. *J. Econ. Issues*, September 1981, *15*(3), pp. 745–68. [G: MDCs]

Luukkainen, Pecca A. Debatten om den svenska industrins strukturproblem. (The Debate on the Structural Problem of Swedish Industry: A Survey. With English summary.) *Ekon. Samfundets Tidskr.*, 1981, *34*(2), pp. 147–62. [G: Sweden]

Madsen, Henrik Jess. Partisanship and Macroeconomic Outcomes: A Reconsideration. In *Hibbs, D. A., Jr. and Fassbender, H., eds.*, 1981, pp. 269–82. [G: Norway; OECD]

Main, Brian G. M. The Length of Employment and Unemployment in Great Britain. *Scot. J. Polit. Econ.*, June 1981, *28*(2), pp. 146–64. [G: U.K.]

Mair, Douglas. Urban Unemployment: A Comment [Urban Unemployment in England]. *Econ. J.*, March 1981, *91*(361), pp. 224–30. [G: U.K.]

Martin, John P. and Evans, John M. Notes on Measuring the Employment Displacement Effects of Trade by the Accounting Procedure. *Oxford Econ. Pap.*, March 1981, *33*(1), pp. 154–64.

Martin, R. L. Regional Wage Inflation and Unemployment: Introduction. In *Martin, R. L., ed.*, 1981, pp. 1–16. [G: OECD]

Marzouk, M. Shokri. An Econometric/Input–Output Approach for Projecting Sectoral Manpower Requirements: The Case of Kuwait. In *Sherbiny, N. A., ed.*, 1981, pp. 111–44. [G: Kuwait]

Massey, Doreen. The UK Electrical Engineering and Electronics Industries: The Implications of the Crisis for the Restructuring of Capital and Locational Change. In *Dear, M. and Scott, A. J., eds.*, 1981, pp. 199–230. [G: U.K.]

Mattsson, Lars-Göran and Weibull, Jörgen W. Competition and Accessibility on a Regional Labour Market. *Reg. Sci. Urban Econ.*, November 1981, *11*(4), pp. 471–97. [G: Sweden]

Maxwell, Stephen. The Politics of Unemployment in Scotland. In *Crick, B., ed.*, 1981, *1981*, pp. 88–99. [G: U.K.]

Mazzocchi, Giancarlo. Unemployment in Italy and Europe in the 1980s. *Giorn. Econ.*, May–June 1981, *40*(5–6), pp. 363–70. [G: Italy; W. Europe]

Mazzoni, Riccardo. An Analysis of the Changes in the Distribution of Employment between Industry and Services. *Rev. Econ. Cond. Italy*, February 1981, (1), pp. 87–117. [G: Italy]

McAleese, Dermot and Carey, Patrick. Employment Coefficients for Irish Trade with Extra-EEC Countries: Measurement and Implications. *Econ. Soc. Rev.*, January 1981, *12*(2), pp. 115–32. [G: Ireland]

McGavin, P. A. School Participation of Australians Aged Sixteen: An Analysis of Youth Unemployment. *Econ. Rec.*, December 1981, *57*(159), pp. 379–81. [G: Australia]

McKenzie, Richard B. The Case for Plant Closures. *Policy Rev.*, Winter 1981, (15), pp. 119–33. [G: U.S.]

Meller, Patricio and Marfán, Manuel. Small and Large Industry: Employment Generation, Linkages, and Key Sectors. *Econ. Develop. Cult. Change*, January 1981, *29*(2), pp. 263–74. [G: Chile]

Menchik, Mark David. The Service Sector. In *Hawley, A. H. and Mazie, S. M., eds.*, 1981, pp. 231–54. [G: U.S.]

Merrilees, William J. Interindustry Variations in Job Tenure. *Ind. Relat.*, Spring 1981, *20*(2), pp. 200–204. [G: U.S.]

Merrilees, William J. The Effect of Labour Market Conditions on School Enrolment Rates. *Australian Econ. Rev.*, 3rd Quarter 1981, (55), pp. 56–60. [G: Australia]

Middlemas, Keith. Unemployment: The Past and Future of a Political Problem. In *Crick, B., ed.*, 1981, *1981*, pp. 135–51. [G: U.K.]

Miller, E. Willard. Spatial Organization of Manufacturing in Nonmetropolitan Pennsylvania. In *Rees, J.; Hewings, G. J. D. and Stafford, H. A., eds.*, 1981, pp. 155–69. [G: U.S.]

Mills, D. Quinn. The Human Resource Consequences of Industrial Revitalization. In *Wachter, M. L. and Wachter, S. M., eds.*, 1981, pp. 257–80. [G: U.S.]

Mitchell, Austin. Political Aspects of Unemployment: The Alternative Policy. In *Crick, B., ed.*, 1981, *1981*, pp. 38–50. [G: U.K.]

Monson, Terry. Trade Strategies and Employment

in the Ivory Coast. In *Krueger, A. O., et al., eds.*, 1981, pp. 239–90. [G: Ivory Coast]

Moore, Geoffrey H. A New Leading Index of Employment and Unemployment. *Mon. Lab. Rev.*, June 1981, *104*(6), pp. 44–47. [G: U.S.]

Morse, Laurence C. Increasing Unemployment and Changing Labor Market Expectations among Black Male Teenagers. *Amer. Econ. Rev.*, May 1981, *71*(2), pp. 374–78. [G: U.S.]

Mott, Frank L. and Haurin, R. Jean. The Impact of Health Problems and Mortality on Family Well-Being. In *Parnes, H. S., ed.*, 1981, pp. 198–253. [G: U.S.]

Moy, Joyanna and Sorrentino, Constance. Unemployment, Labor Force Trends, and Layoff Practices in 10 Countries. *Mon. Lab. Rev.*, December 1981, *104*(12), pp. 3–13. [G: N. America; Australia; Japan; EEC; Sweden]

Nabli, Mustapha K. Alternative Trade Policies and Employment in Tunisia. In *Krueger, A. O., et al., eds.*, 1981, pp. 435–98. [G: Tunisia]

Newton, Keith; Betcherman, Gordon and Meltz, Noah. Diagnosing Labour Market Imbalances in Canada. *Can. Public Policy*, Winter 1981, *7*(1), pp. 94–102. [G: Canada]

Novikova, E. E. and Kutyrev, B. P. The Quantity and Quality of Work: A Round Table. *Prob. Econ.*, Sept.–Oct.–Nov. 1981, *24*(5–6–7), pp. 253–66. [G: U.S.S.R.]

Nurul Amin, A. T. M. Marginalisation vs. Dynamism: A Study of the Informal Sector in Dhaka City. *Bangladesh Devel. Stud.*, Autumn 1981, *9*(4), pp. 77–112. [G: Bangladesh]

O'Riordan, William K. A Note on the Sectoral Employment Pattern. *Econ. Soc. Rev.*, January 1981, *12*(2), pp. 133–39. [G: Ireland]

Ogle, George. South Korea. In *Blum, A. A., ed.*, 1981, pp. 499–514. [G: S. Korea]

Osmond, John. Wales: Will Unemployment Breed Unrest or Apathy? In *Crick, B., ed.*, 1981, *1981*, pp. 127–34. [G: U.K.]

Osterman, Paul. Sex Discrimination in Professional Employment: A Case Study: Reply. *Ind. Lab. Relat. Rev.*, January 1981, *34*(2), pp. 275–76. [G: U.S.]

Ostojić, Slobodan. Interna alokacija rada i razlike u ličnim dohocima izmedu OOUR-a U SOUR-ima. (Inter-boal Personal Income Differences and the Internal Allocation of Labour in Large Yugoslav Enterprises [COALs]. With English summary.) *Econ. Anal. Worker's Manage.*, 1981, *15*(4), pp. 481–500. [G: Yugoslavia]

Pack, Howard. The Choice of Technique and Employment in the Textile Industry. In *Bhalla, A. S., ed.*, 1981, pp. 159–79. [G: U.K.]

Parnes, Herbert S. Inflation and Early Retirement: Recent Longitudinal Findings. *Mon. Lab. Rev.*, July 1981, *104*(7), pp. 27–30. [G: U.S.]

Parnes, Herbert S. Work and Retirement: Introduction and Overview. In *Parnes, H. S., ed.*, 1981, pp. 1–41. [G: U.S.]

Parnes, Herbert S.; Gagen, Mary G. and King, Randall H. Job Loss among Long-Service Workers. In *Parnes, H. S., ed.*, 1981, pp. 65–92. [G: U.S.]

Parnes, Herbert S. and Nestel, Gilbert. The Retire-

ment Experience. In *Parnes, H. S., ed.*, 1981, pp. 155–97. [G: U.S.]

Pastré, Olivier. Informatisation et emploi: de faux débats autour d'un vrai problème. (The Computer Revolution and Employment: False Debates about Real Problems. With English summary.) *Rev. Econ. Ind.*, 2nd Trimester 1981, (16), pp. 44–56.

Peacock, Alan. Economic Growth and the Rise of Service Employment: Comments. In *Giersch, H., ed. (II)*, 1981, pp. 243–48. [G: U.S.; OECD]

Peel, David A. Some Empirical Evidence on the Influence of Political Parties on the Behaviour of the Unemployment Rate. *Empirical Econ.*, 1981, *6*(1), pp. 67–73. [G: U.K.]

Perloff, Jeffrey M. The Duration of Unemployment in the Construction Industry. *J. Lab. Res.*, Spring 1981, *2*(1), pp. 111–31. [G: U.S.]

Personick, Valerie A. The Outlook for Industry Output and Employment through 1990. *Mon. Lab. Rev.*, August 1981, *104*(8), pp. 28–41. [G: U.S.]

Peston, Maurice. Economic Aspects of Unemployment. In *Crick, B., ed.*, 1981, *1981*, pp. 28–37. [G: U.K.]

Pimlott, Ben. The North East: Back to the 1930s? In *Crick, B., ed.*, 1981, *1981*, pp. 51–63. [G: U.K.]

Pitt, Mark M. Alternative Trade Strategies and Employment in Indonesia. In *Krueger, A. O., et al., eds.*, 1981, pp. 181–237. [G: Indonesia]

Pleeter, Saul and Trotta, Joseph. An Evaluation of the Bureau of Labor Statistics Methodology for Calculating Local Unemployment Rates: A Case Study of Cincinnati. *Rev. Public Data Use (See J. Econ. Soc. Meas. after 4/85)*, July 1981, *9*(2), pp. 115–22. [G: U.S.]

Plunkert, Lois. BLS Tests Feasibility of a New Job Openings Survey. *Mon. Lab. Rev.*, December 1981, *104*(12), pp. 52–54. [G: U.S.]

Poot, H. The Development of Labour Intensive Industries in Indonesia. In *Amjad, R., ed.*, 1981, pp. 77–140. [G: Indonesia]

Powell, David E. Labor Turnover in the Soviet Union. In *Bornstein, M., ed.*, 1981, *1977*, pp. 101–17. [G: U.S.S.R.]

Pursell, Donald E. Natural Population Decrease: Its Origins and Implications on the Great Plains. In *Lawson, M. P. and Baker, M. E., eds.*, 1981, pp. 53–66. [G: U.S.]

Rahman, Rushidan Islam. Implications of Seasonality of Rural Labour Use Pattern: Evidences from Two Villages in Bangladesh. *Bangladesh Devel. Stud.*, Winter 1981, *9*(1), pp. 77–96. [G: Bangladesh]

Raines, Fredric. Transfers, Taxes, and the NAIRU: Discussion. In *Meyer, L. H., ed.*, 1981, pp. 237–41. [G: U.S.]

Rattinger, Hans. Unemployment and the 1976 Election in Germany: Some Findings at the Aggregate and the Individual Level of Analysis. In *Hibbs, D. A., Jr. and Fassbender, H., eds.*, 1981, pp. 121–35.

Reid, Frank and Smith, Douglas A. The Impact of Demographic Changes on Unemployment. *Can. Public Policy*, Spring 1981, *7*(2), pp. 348–51.

Ridley, F. F. View from a Disaster Area: Unemployed Youth in Merseyside. **In** *Crick, B., ed.,* 1981, *1981,* pp. 16–27. **[G: U.K.]**

Robinson, Chris and McMahon, Pat. Off-Farm Investment and Employment in the Australian Grazing Industry: A Preliminary Analysis. *Rev. Marketing Agr. Econ.,* April 1981, *49*(1), pp. 25–45. **[G: Australia]**

Robinson, J. F. F. and Storey, D. J. Employment Change in Manufacturing Industry in Cleveland, 1965-1976. *Reg. Stud.,* 1981, *15*(3), pp. 161–72. **[G: U.K.]**

Rocherieux, François. Sur la théorie des modèles inter-industriels: Quelques remarques appliquées à l'analyse de l'emploi et du commerce international. (On Input-Output Models Theory: Some Remarks Applied to Employment and International Trade Analysis. With English summary.) *Revue Écon.,* September 1981, *32*(5), pp. 887–922. **[G: France]**

Romer, David. Rosen and Quandt's Disequilibrium Model of the Labor Market: A Revision. *Rev. Econ. Statist.,* February 1981, *63*(1), pp. 145–46. **[G: U.S.]**

Rones, Philip L. Can the Current Population Survey be Used to Identify the Disabled? *Mon. Lab. Rev.,* June 1981, *104*(6), pp. 37–39. **[G: U.S.]**

Rones, Philip L. Response to Recession: Reduce Hours or Jobs? *Mon. Lab. Rev.,* October 1981, *104*(10), pp. 3–11. **[G: U.S.]**

Rosenzweig, Mark R. Household and Non-household Activities of Youths: Issues of Modelling, Data and Estimation Strategies. **In** *Rodgers, G. and Standing, G., eds.,* 1981, pp. 215–43. **[G: India]**

Sadhu, A. N. and Mahajan, R. K. Disguised Unemployment and Zero Marginal Productivity of Labor: (An Empirical Test) *Econ. Aff.,* January–March 1981, *26*(1), pp. 70–76. **[G: India]**

Salam, Abdul; Hussain, M. Afzal and Ghayur, Sabur. Farm Mechanization, Employment and Productivity in Pakistan's Agriculture. *Pakistan Econ. Soc. Rev.,* Winter 1981, *19*(2), pp. 95–114. **[G: Pakistan]**

Salisbury, Robert H. and Shepsle, Kenneth A. Congressional Staff Turnover and the Ties-That-Bind. *Amer. Polit. Sci. Rev.,* June 1981, *75*(2), pp. 381–96. **[G: U.S.]**

Santos, Richard. Measuring the Employment Status of Youth: A Comparison of the Current Population Survey and the National Longitudinal Survey. **In** *Dennis, B. D., ed.,* 1981, pp. 62–68. **[G: U.S.]**

Sargent, Thomas J. Estimation of Dynamic Labor Demand Schedules under Rational Expectations. **In** *Lucas, R. E. and Sargent, T. J., eds.,* 1981, *1978,* pp. 463–99. **[G: U.S.]**

Schager, Nils Henrik. The Duration of Vacancies as a Measure of the State of Demand in the Labor Market. The Swedish Wage Drift Equation Reconsidered. **In** *Eliasson, G.; Holmlund, B. and Stafford, F. P., eds.,* 1981, pp. 393–442. **[G: Sweden]**

Schechter, Evan S. Commitment to Work and the Self-Perception of Disability. *Soc. Sec. Bull.,* June 1981, *44*(6), pp. 22–30. **[G: U.S.]**

Schotzko, Ralph T. Projected Replacement Needs for Agricultural Economists: Reply. *Amer. J. Agr.*

Econ., November 1981, *63*(4), pp. 751–52. **[G: U.S.]**

Schrimper, R. A. Projected Replacement Needs for Agricultural Economists: Comment. *Amer. J. Agr. Econ.,* November 1981, *63*(4), pp. 748–50. **[G: U.S.]**

Scull, Robert W. SMR Forum: Planned Renewal—Preparing Workers for Competitive Jobs. *Sloan Manage. Rev.,* Summer 1981, *22*(4), pp. 47–51. **[G: U.S.]**

Seabrook, Jeremy. Unemployment Now and in the 1930s. **In** *Crick, B., ed.,* 1981, *1981,* pp. 7–15. **[G: U.S.]**

Sekscenski, Edward S. The Health Services Industry: A Decade of Expansion. *Mon. Lab. Rev.,* May 1981, *104*(5), pp. 9–16. **[G: U.S.]**

Serow, William J. Alternative Demographic Futures and the Composition of the Demand for Labor, by Industry and by Occupation. **In** *Simon, J. L. and Lindert, P. H., eds.,* 1981, pp. 209–23. **[G: U.S.]**

Serow, William J. Demographic and Economic Considerations for Future Retirement Policy. *Policy Anal.,* Spring 1981, *7*(2), pp. 143–51. **[G: U.S.]**

Sethuraman, S. V. Implications for Environment and Development Policies. **In** *Sethuraman, S. V., ed.,* 1981, pp. 171–208. **[G: Selected LDCs]**

Sherbiny, Naiem A. Sectoral Employment Projections with Minimum Data: The Case of Saudi Arabia. **In** *Sherbiny, N. A., ed.,* 1981, pp. 173–206. **[G: Saudi Arabia]**

Showler, Brian and Sinfield, Adrian. A Most Unequal Tax. **In** *Showler, B. and Sinfield, A., eds.,* 1981, pp. 215–40. **[G: U.K.]**

Sinfield, Adrian. Unemployment in an Unequal Society. **In** *Showler, B. and Sinfield, A., eds.,* 1981, pp. 122–66. **[G: U.K.]**

Sinfield, Adrian and Showler, Brian. Unemployment and the Unemployed in 1980. **In** *Showler, B. and Sinfield, A., eds.,* 1981, pp. 1–26. **[G: U.K.]**

Singh, H. Nabakihore. The Problem of Unemployment in Manipur. *Econ. Aff.,* October–December 1981, *26*(4), pp. 233–34, 250–56. **[G: India]**

Smith, Adrian. The Informal Economy. *Lloyds Bank Rev.,* July 1981, (141), pp. 45–61. **[G: EEC]**

Smock, Audrey Chapman. Women's Economic Roles. **In** *Killick, T., ed.,* 1981, pp. 219–27. **[G: Kenya]**

Snape, Richard H. Wages Policy and the Economy in the Seventies and Beyond. **In** *Hancock, K., ed.,* 1981, pp. 170–93. **[G: Australia]**

Solberg, Eric J. The Supply of Labor Time for Mature Females. *Atlantic Econ. J.,* September 1981, *9*(3), pp. 20–33. **[G: U.S.]**

Sorrentino, Constance. Unemployment in International Perspective. **In** *Showler, B. and Sinfield, A., eds.,* 1981, pp. 167–214. **[G: OECD]**

Sorrentino, Constance. Youth Unemployment: An International Perspective. *Mon. Lab. Rev.,* July 1981, *104*(7), pp. 3–15. **[G: MDCs]**

Stafford, Frank P. Unemployment and Labor Market Policy in Sweden and the United States. **In** *Eliasson, G.; Holmlund, B. and Stafford, F. P., eds.,* 1981, pp. 21–65. **[G: U.S.; Sweden]**

Stahl, C. W. Migrant Labour Supplies, Past, Present

and Future; with Special Reference to the Gold-Mining Industry. In *Böhning, W. R., ed.*, 1981, pp. 7–44. [G: S. Africa]

Standing, Guy. The Notion of Voluntary Unemployment. *Int. Lab. Rev.*, September–October 1981, *120*(5), pp. 563–79.

Steel, William F. Female and Small-Scale Employment under Modernization in Ghana. *Econ. Develop. Cult. Change*, October 1981, *30*(1), pp. 153–67. [G: Ghana]

Stevens, David W. Contributed Papers: Labor Markets and Other IR Topics: Discussion. In *Dennis, B. D., ed.*, 1981, pp. 337–38. [G: U.S.]

Stinson, Thomas F. Fiscal Status of Local Governments. In *Hawley, A. H. and Mazie, S. M., eds.*, 1981, pp. 736–66. [G: U.S.]

Stoneman, Patrick. L'impact d'une nouvelle technologie sur l'emploi. (The Impact of New Technology of Employment Levels. With English summary.) *Rev. Econ. Ind.*, 3rd Trimestre 1981, (17), pp. 76–91.

Stonier, Tom. Technological Change and the Future. In *Gaskin, M., ed.*, 1981, pp. 140–51. [G: U.K.]

Storey, D. J. New Firm Formation, Employment Change and the Small Firm: The Case of Cleveland County. *Urban Stud.*, October 1981, *18*(3), pp. 335–45. [G: U.K.]

Summers, Lawrence H. Measuring Unemployment. *Brookings Pap. Econ. Act.*, 1981, (2), pp. 609–20. [G: U.S.]

Swales, J. K. The Employment Effects of a Regional Capital Subsidy. *Reg. Stud.*, 1981, *15*(4), pp. 263–73.

Swartz, Katherine. Information in the Hiring Process: A Case Study. *J. Econ. Behav. Organ.*, March 1981, *2*(1), pp. 71–94. [G: U.S.]

Taimni, K. K. Employment Generation through Handicraft Co-operatives: The Indian Experience. *Int. Lab. Rev.*, July–August 1981, *120*(4), pp. 505–17. [G: India]

Tambunlertchai, Somsak and Loohawenchit, Chesada. Labour Intensive and Small Scale Manufacturing in Thailand. In *Amjad, R., ed.*, 1981, pp. 175–233. [G: Thailand]

Tanaka, Fujio John. Lifetime Employment in Japan. *Challenge*, July/August 1981, *24*(3), pp. 23–29. [G: Japan]

Tauchen, George E. Some Evidence on Cross-Sector Effects of the Minimum Wage. *J. Polit. Econ.*, June 1981, *89*(3), pp. 529–47. [G: U.S.]

Taylor, Daniel E. Absences from Work among Full-Time Employees. *Mon. Lab. Rev.*, March 1981, *104*(3), pp. 68–70. [G: U.S.]

Taylor, Stan. De-industrialisation and Unemployment in the West Midlands. In *Crick, B., ed.*, 1981, *1981*, pp. 64–73. [G: U.K.]

Terry, Sylvia Lazos. Involuntary Part-Time Work: New Information from the CPS. *Mon. Lab. Rev.*, February 1981, *104*(2), pp. 70–74. [G: U.S.]

Terry, Sylvia Lazos. Work Experience of the Population in 1979. *Mon. Lab. Rev.*, June 1981, *104*(6), pp. 48–53. [G: U.S.]

Tévoédjrè, Albert. Employment, Human Needs, and the NIEO. In *Lozoya, J. A. and Birgin, H., eds.*, 1981, pp. 1–28. [G: LDCs]

Thomas, R. B. Labour Market Adjustments. In *Creedy, J., ed.*, 1981, pp. 17–47. [G: U.K.]

Thomas, T. Aggregate Demand in the United Kingdom 1918–45. In *Floud, R. and McCloskey, D., eds., Vol. 2*, 1981, pp. 332–46. [G: U.K.]

Thomson, Lydia. Industrial Employment Performance and Regional Policy, 1952–71: A Cross-Sectional Approach. *Urban Stud.*, June 1981, *18*(2), pp. 231–38. [G: U.K.]

Thoumi, Francisco E. International Trade Strategies, Employment, and Income Distribution in Colombia. In *Krueger, A. O., et al., eds.*, 1981, pp. 135–79. [G: Colombia]

Thurow, Lester C. Employment and Public Expenditure in USA in the 1980s. *Giorn. Econ.*, May–June 1981, *40*(5–6), pp. 371–78. [G: U.S.]

Till, Thomas E. Manufacturing Industry: Trends and Impacts. In *Hawley, A. H. and Mazie, S. M., eds.*, 1981, pp. 194–230. [G: U.S.]

Tornquist, Elizabeth. Labor Displacement in Tobacco Manufacturing: Some Policy Considerations. In *Finger, W. R., ed.*, 1981, pp. 221–28. [G: U.S.]

de la Torre, Jose. Public Intervention Strategies in the European Clothing Industries. *J. World Trade Law*, March–April 1981, *15*(2), pp. 124–48. [G: EEC]

Uri, Noel D. and Mixon, J. Wilson, Jr. The Effect of Exports and Imports on the Stability of Employment in Manufacturing Industries in the United States. *Appl. Econ.*, June 1981, *13*(2), pp. 193–203. [G: U.S.]

Valle, P. Della. Productivity and Employment in the Copper and Aluminium Industries. In *Bhalla, A. S., ed.*, 1981, *1975*, pp. 323–55. [G: Selected LDCs; U.S.]

Van Poeck, André. Tewerkstelling en internationale concurrentiepositie. (Employment and International Competition. With English summary.) *Econ. Soc. Tijdschr.*, June 1981, *35*(3), pp. 287–97. [G: U.S.; U.K.; Europe; Japan; Canada]

Varaiya, Pravin and Wiseman, Michael. Investment and Employment in Manufacturing in U.S. Metropolitan Areas, 1960–1976. *Reg. Sci. Urban Econ.*, November 1981, *11*(4), pp. 431–69. [G: U.S.]

Visaria, Pravin. Poverty and Unemployment in India: An Analysis of Recent Evidence. *World Devel.*, March 1981, *9*(3), pp. 277–300. [G: India]

Walker, Alan. South Yorkshire: The Economic and Social Impact of Unemployment. In *Crick, B., ed.*, 1981, *1981*, pp. 74–87. [G: U.K.]

Walker, Warren E., et al. The Impact of Proposition 13 on Local Criminal Justice Agencies: Emerging Patterns. In *Wright, K. N., ed.*, 1981, pp. 173–227. [G: U.S.]

Warren, Ronald S., Jr. The Behavior of Unemployment and Vacancies in Sweden: An Alternative Test. *Scand. J. Econ.*, 1981, *83*(1), pp. 109–14. [G: Sweden]

Watts, Glenn E. Productivity and Employment: The Social Gains and Costs. In *Hogan, J. D. and Craig, A. M., eds., Vol. 1*, 1981, pp. 77–83. [G: U.S.]

Wescott, Diane N. and Bednarzik, Robert W. Employment and Unemployment: A Report on 1980. *Mon. Lab. Rev.*, February 1981, *104*(2), pp. 4–14. [G: U.S.]

Westcott, Diane N. Employment and Unemployment in the First Half of 1981. *Mon. Lab. Rev.*, August 1981, *104*(8), pp. 3–8. [G: U.S.]

Windolf, Paul. Strategies of Enterprises in the German Labour Market. *Cambridge J. Econ.*, December 1981, *5*(4), pp. 351–67. [G: W. Germany]

Wolozin, Harold. Earlier Retirement and the Older Worker. *J. Econ. Issues*, June 1981, *15*(2), pp. 477–87. [G: U.S.]

Wright, Gavin. Black and White Labor in the Old New South. In *Bateman, F., ed.*, 1981, pp. 35–50. [G: U.S.]

Yatchew, Adonis J. Further Evidence on "Estimation of a Disequilibrium Aggregate Labor Market." *Rev. Econ. Statist.*, February 1981, *63*(1), pp. 142–44. [G: U.S.]

Young, Anne McDougall. Labor Force Activity among Students, Graduates, and Dropouts in 1980. *Mon. Lab. Rev.*, July 1981, *104*(7), pp. 31–33. [G: U.S.]

825 Productivity Studies: Labor, Capital, and Total Factor

8250 Productivity Studies: Labor, Capital, and Total Factor

Aivazian, Varouj A. and Callen, Jeffrey L. Capacity Expansion in the U.S. Natural-Gas Pipeline Industry. In *Cowing, T. G. and Stevenson, R. E., eds.*, 1981, pp. 145–59. [G: U.S.]

Alexander, Kenneth O. Scientists, Engineers and the Organization of Work. *Amer. J. Econ. Soc.*, January 1981, *40*(1), pp. 51–66.

Alfeld, Louis E. Productivity and the Construction Industry. In *Hogan, J. D. and Craig, A. M., eds., Vol. 2*, 1981, pp. 1099–1102. [G: U.S.]

Amjad, Rashid. The Development of Labour Intensive Industry in ASEAN Countries—An Overview. In *Amjad, R., ed.*, 1981, pp. 1–28. [G: ASEAN]

Ando, Albert. An Econometric Model Incorporating the Supply-Side Effects of Economic Policy: Discussion. In *Meyer, L. H., ed.*, 1981, pp. 103–11. [G: U.S.]

Atkinson, Thomas R. The Role of Productivity in International Trade. In *Hogan, J. D. and Craig, A. M., eds., Vol. 1*, 1981, pp. 647–56. [G: Selected OECD]

Baily, Martin Neil. Productivity and the Services of Capital and Labor. *Brookings Pap. Econ. Act.*, 1981, (1), pp. 1–50. [G: U.S.]

Baily, Martin Neil. The Productivity Growth Slowdown and Capital Accumulation. *Amer. Econ. Rev.*, May 1981, *71*(2), pp. 326–31. [G: U.S.]

Baker, Joe G. Sources of Deep Coal Mine Productivity Change, 1962–1975. *Energy J.*, April 1981, *2*(2), pp. 95–106. [G: U.S.]

Baranenkova, T. Reserves for Economizing the Work Force. *Prob. Econ.*, February 1981, *23*(10), pp. 3–24. [G: U.S.S.R.]

Baruch, Jordon. The Role of Government in Promoting Research and Development. In *Hogan, J. D. and Craig, A. M., eds., Vol. 1*, 1981, pp. 87–92. [G: U.S.]

Benarey, Henry A. International Productivity: A European View. In *Hogan, J. D. and Craig, A. M., eds., Vol. 1*, 1981, pp. 639–44. [G: W. Europe]

Bergmann, Barbara R. and Darity, William A., Jr. Social Relations, Productivity, and Employer Discrimination. *Mon. Lab. Rev.*, April 1981, *104*(4), pp. 47–49. [G: U.S.]

Berndt, Ernst R. Energy Price Increases and the Productivity Slowdown in United States Manufacturing. In *Federal Reserve Bank of Boston (1)*, 1981, pp. 60–89. [G: U.S.]

Bernhardt, Irwin. Sources of Productivity Differences among Canadian Manufacturing Industries. *Rev. Econ. Statist.*, November 1981, *63*(4), pp. 503–12. [G: U.S.; Canada]

Bernolak, Imre. The Whole and Its Parts: Micro and Macro Productivity Research. In *Hogan, J. D. and Craig, A. M., eds., Vol. 2*, 1981, pp. 755–64. [G: Canada]

Bhalla, A. S. The Concept and Measurement of Labour Intensity. In *Bhalla, A. S., ed.*, 1981, *1975*, pp. 17–39. [G: Selected LDCs]

Bingham, Barbara. Labor and Material Requirements for Commercial Office Building Projects. *Mon. Lab. Rev.*, May 1981, *104*(5), pp. 41–48. [G: U.S.]

Bowen, William. Productivity: A Journalist's Perspective. In *Hogan, J. D. and Craig, A. M., eds., Vol. 1*, 1981, pp. 725–36. [G: U.S.]

Braun, Steven. An Econometric Model Incorporating the Supply-Side Effects of Economic Policy: Discussion. In *Meyer, L. H., ed.*, 1981, pp. 93–101. [G: U.S.]

Brennan, Joseph. Productivity and the Coal Industry. In *Hogan, J. D. and Craig, A. M., eds., Vol. 2*, 1981, pp. 1125–32. [G: U.S.]

Brown, Clarence J. Proceedings of the Seminar on Productivity: Statement. In *U.S. Congress, Joint Economic Committee (1)*, 1981, pp. 125–26. [G: U.S.]

Browne, Lynn E. A Quality Labor Supply. *New Eng. Econ. Rev.*, July/August 1981, pp. 19–36. [G: U.S.]

Bruch, Mathias. X-Efficiency Theory, Productivity and Growth: Comments. In *Giersch, H., ed. (II)*, 1981, pp. 217–19.

Brush, Brian C. What Do Labor Productivity Data Show about Economies of Scale: Comment. *Southern Econ. J.*, January 1981, *47*(3), pp. 839–46. [G: U.S.]

Bullock, R. J. and Lawler, Edward E., III. Incentives and Gain-Sharing: Stimuli for Productivity. In *Hogan, J. D. and Craig, A. M., eds., Vol. 1*, 1981, pp. 453–66. [G: U.S.]

Campbell, Alan K. Government and Productivity. In *Hogan, J. D. and Craig, A. M., eds., Vol. 2*, 1981, pp. 941–52. [G: U.S.]

Capdevielle, Patricia and Alvarez, Donato. International Comparisons of Trends in Productivity and Labor Costs. *Mon. Lab. Rev.*, December 1981, *104*(12), pp. 14–20. [G: N. America; Japan; Sweden; EEC]

Carlsson, Bo. The Content of Productivity Growth

in Swedish Manufacturing. In *Industrial Inst. for Econ. and Soc. Research*, 1981, pp. 33–46. [G: Sweden]

Carnes, Richard B. Productivity Trends for Intercity Bus Carriers. *Mon. Lab. Rev.*, May 1981, *104*(5), pp. 23–27. [G: U.S.]

Caves, Douglas W.; Christensen, Laurits R. and Thretheway, Michael W. U.S. Trunk Air Carriers, 1972–1977: A Multilateral Comparison of Total Factor Productivity. In *Cowing, T. G. and Stevenson, R. E., eds.*, 1981, pp. 47–76. [G: U.S.]

Christainsen, Gregory B. and Haveman, Robert H. Public Regulations and the Slowdown in Productivity Growth. *Amer. Econ. Rev.*, May 1981, *71*(2), pp. 320–25. [G: U.S.]

Christiansen, Gregory B. and Haveman, Robert H. The Contribution of Environmental Regulations to the Slowdown in Productivity Growth. *J. Environ. Econ. Manage.*, December 1981, *8*(4), pp. 381–90. [G: U.S.]

Cocks, Douglas L. Company Total Factor Productivity: Refinements, Production Functions, and Certain Effects of Regulation. *Bus. Econ.*, May 1981, *16*(3), pp. 5–14.

Cowing, Thomas G. and Stevenson, Rodney E. Productivity Measurement and Regulated Industries: Introduction. In *Cowing, T. G. and Stevenson, R. E., eds.*, 1981, pp. 3–14.

Cowing, Thomas G.; Stevenson, Rodney E. and Small, Jeffrey. Comparative Measures of Total Factor Productivity in the Regulated Sector: The Electric Utility Industry. In *Cowing, T. G. and Stevenson, R. E., eds.*, 1981, pp. 161–77. [G: U.S.]

Crandall, Robert W. Pollution Controls and Productivity Growth in Basic Industries. In *Cowing, T. G. and Stevenson, R. E., eds.*, 1981, pp. 347–68. [G: U.S.]

Crandall, Robert W. Regulation and Productivity Growth. In *Federal Reserve Bank of Boston (1)*, 1981, pp. 93–111. [G: U.S.]

Crocker, Thomas D. and Horst, Robert L., Jr. Hours of Work, Labor Productivity, and Environmental Conditions: A Case Study. *Rev. Econ. Statist.*, August 1981, *63*(3), pp. 361–68. [G: U.S.]

Davenport, Paul. The Productivity Problem: Comment. In *Ontario Economic Council, Vol. 2*, 1981, pp. 35–43. [G: U.S.; Canada]

Denison, Edward F. Capital Accumulation and Potential Growth: Discussion. In *Federal Reserve Bank of Boston (1)*, 1981, pp. 54–59. [G: U.S.]

Denison, Edward F. Research Concerning the Effect of Regulation on Productivity. In *Hogan, J. D. and Craig, A. M., eds., Vol. 2*, 1981, pp. 1015–25. [G: U.S.]

Denny, Melvyn A.; Fuss, M. and May, J. D. Intertemporal Changes in Regional Productivity in Canadian Manufacturing. *Can. J. Econ.*, August 1981, *14*(3), pp. 390–408. [G: Canada]

Denny, Michael; Fuss, Melvyn A. and Waverman, Leonard. The Measurement and Interpretation of Total Factor Productivity in Regulated Industries, with an Application to Canadian Telecommunications. In *Cowing, T. G. and Stevenson, R. E., eds.*, 1981, pp. 179–218. [G: Canada]

Diewert, W. Erwin. On Measuring the Loss of Output Due to Nonneutral Business Taxation. In *Hulten, C. R., ed.*, 1981, pp. 57–80.

Diewert, W. Erwin. The Theory of Total Factor Productivity Measurement in Regulated Industries. In *Cowing, T. G. and Stevenson, R. E., eds.*, 1981, pp. 17–44.

Downing, Harry F., Jr. Productivity and the Insurance Industry. In *Hogan, J. D. and Craig, A. M., eds., Vol. 2*, 1981, pp. 1115–20. [G: U.S.]

Duke, John and Brand, Horst. Cyclical Behavior of Productivity in the Machine Tool Industry. *Mon. Lab. Rev.*, November 1981, *104*(11), pp. 27–34. [G: U.S.]

Eads, George C. and McClain, David. The Role of Government Policy in Productivity. In *Hogan, J. D. and Craig, A. M., eds., Vol. 1*, 1981, pp. 41–51. [G: U.S.]

Eccles, Mary E. Productivity Research Needs: The Congressional Viewpoint. In *Hogan, J. D. and Craig, A. M., eds., Vol. 2*, 1981, pp. 987–91. [G: U.S.]

Ellman, Michael. Agricultural Productivity under Socialism. *World Devel.*, September/October 1981, *9*(9/10), pp. 979–89. [G: China; U.S.S.R.]

Evans, Michael K. An Econometric Model Incorporating the Supply-Side Effects of Economic Policy. In *Meyer, L. H., ed.*, 1981, pp. 33–80. [G: U.S.]

Favereau, Olivier and Mouillart, Michel. La stabilité du lien emploi-croissance et la loi d'Okun: Une application à l'économie française. (The Stability of the Relationship between Employment and Growth in Okun's Law: An Application to the French Economy. With English summary.) *Consommation*, January–March 1981, *28*(1), pp. 85–117. [G: France]

Feinstein, C. H. Capital Accumulation and the Industrial Revolution. In *Floud, R. and McCloskey, D., eds., Vol. 1*, 1981, pp. 128–42. [G: U.K.]

Felli, Ernesto. Labour Productivity, Returns to Scale and Capital Accumulation in Italian Manufacturing Industry (1954–1978). *Rivista Polit. Econ.*, Supplement December 1981, *71*, pp. 61–107. [G: Italy]

Fisk, Donald M. Pilot Study Measures Productivity of State, Local Electric Utilities. *Mon. Lab. Rev.*, December 1981, *104*(12), pp. 45–47. [G: U.S.]

Frank, Robert H. Productivity Gains since Deregulation in the Airline Industry: A Survey of Research in Progress. In *Hogan, J. D. and Craig, A. M., eds., Vol. 2*, 1981, pp. 1035–54. [G: U.S.]

Freund, William C. and Manchester, Paul B. Productivity and Inflation. In *Hogan, J. D. and Craig, A. M., eds., Vol. 1*, 1981, pp. 53–75. [G: U.S.]

Frey, Luigi. Verso nuove ricerche in tema di produttività, costi e prezzi nel settore bancario. (Further Research into Banking Productivity, Costs and Prices. With English summary.) *Bancaria*, August 1981, *37*(8), pp. 784–90. [G: W. Europe]

Friedlaender, Ann F.; Chiang, S. J. Wang and Spady, Richard H. Regulation and the Structure of Technology in the Trucking Industry. In *Cow-*

ing, T. G. and Stevenson, R. E., eds., 1981, pp. 77–106. [G: U.S.]

Fromm, Gary. Research on Capital and Productivity. In *Hogan, J. D. and Craig, A. M., eds., Vol. 1,* 1981, pp. 109–14. [G: U.S.]

Fulco, Lawrence J. Long Nonfarm Productivity Slide Ends during the Third Quarter. *Mon. Lab. Rev.,* March 1981, *104*(3), pp. 66–67. [G: U.S.]

Gillespie, Jackson F. An Application of Learning Curves to Standard Costing. *Manage. Account.,* September 1981, *63*(3), pp. 63–65.

Givens, William L. International Industrial Competitiveness: The United States and Japan. In *Hogan, J. D. and Craig, A. M., eds., Vol. 1,* 1981, pp. 669–73. [G: Japan; U.S.]

Globerman, Steven. Returns to Industrial R & D and Industrial Marketing and Administration Activities. *J. Econ. Bus.,* Spring/Summer 1981, *33*(3), pp. 231–37. [G: U.S.]

Gold, Bela. Frontiers of Productivity Analysis for Management: With Special Reference to Steel and Other Manufacturing Industries. In *Hogan, J. D. and Craig, A. M., eds., Vol. 2,* 1981, pp. 1159–76. [G: U.S.]

Golladay, Fredrick L. Productivity Problems in Developing Countries. In *Hogan, J. D. and Craig, A. M., eds., Vol. 1,* 1981, pp. 737–49.
[G: LDCs]

Gollop, Frank M. and Roberts, Mark J. The Sources of Economic Growth in the U.S. Electric Power Industry. In *Cowing, T. G. and Stevenson, R. E., eds.,* 1981, pp. 107–43. [G: U.S.]

Gordon, David M. Capital–Labor Conflict and the Productivity Slowdown. *Amer. Econ. Rev.,* May 1981, *71*(2), pp. 30–35. [G: U.S.]

Goshi, Kohei. The Productivity Movement in Japan. In *Hogan, J. D. and Craig, A. M., eds., Vol. 1,* 1981, pp. 677–83. [G: Japan]

Grayson, C. Jackson, Jr. Proceedings of the Seminar on Productivity: Statement. In *U.S. Congress, Joint Economic Committee (I),* 1981, pp. 127–44.
[G: U.S.; OECD]

Greenberg, David; Moffitt, Robert A. and Friedmann, John. Underreporting and Experimental Effects on Work Effort: Evidence from the Gary Income Maintenance Experiment. *Rev. Econ. Statist.,* November 1981, *63*(4), pp. 581–89.
[G: U.S.]

Gregory, Paul R. Energy Price Increases and the Productivity Slowdown in United States Manufacturing: Discussion. In *Federal Reserve Bank of Boston (I),* 1981, pp. 90–92. [G: U.S.]

Gupta, Suraj B. The Productivity of Workers' Consumption and the Choice of Techniques. *Indian Econ. Rev.,* Oct.-Dec. 1981, *16*(4), pp. 279–96.

Haggerty, Patrick E. Technology, People and Productivity. In *Hogan, J. D. and Craig, A. M., eds., Vol. 2,* 1981, pp. 1197–1209. [G: U.S.]

Hall, P. H. Patterns of Energy Use in Australian Manufacturing Industry. *Australian J. Manage.,* December 1981, *6*(2), pp. 43–58. [G: Australia]

Hatry, Harry P. The Status of Productivity Measurement in the Public Sector. In *Lynch, T. D., ed.,* 1981, pp. 179–91. [G: U.S.]

Haywood, Charles F. Regulation, Technological Change, and Productivity in Commercial Bank-

ing. In *Cowing, T. G. and Stevenson, R. E., eds.,* 1981, pp. 283–307. [G: U.S.]

Herman, Arthur S. Productivity Slows or Drops in 1979 in More Than Half of Industries Measured. *Mon. Lab. Rev.,* April 1981, *104*(4), pp. 58–61.
[G: U.S.]

Hirsch, Werner Z. and Rufolo, Anthony M. Monitoring Costs and Labor Productivity in Municipal Labor Markets. In *Ballabon, M. B., ed.,* 1981, pp. 175–94. [G: U.S.]

Hoffmann, Lutz. X-Efficiency Theory, Productivity and Growth: Comments. In *Giersch, H., ed. (II),* 1981, pp. 213–16.

Hogan, John D. Interfirm Comparisons: Current State and Future Prospects. In *Hogan, J. D. and Craig, A. M., eds., Vol. 1,* 1981, pp. 319–37.
[G: U.S.; Selected Countries]

Houthakker, Hendrik S. Regulation and Productivity Growth: Discussion. In *Federal Reserve Bank of Boston (I),* 1981, pp. 112–14. [G: U.S.]

Huffman, Wallace E. Black–White Human Capital Differences: Impact on Agricultural Productivity in the U.S. South. *Amer. Econ. Rev.,* March 1981, *71*(1), pp. 94–107. [G: U.S.]

Ibielski, Dieter. Productivity Research in the Federal Republic of Germany. In *Hogan, J. D. and Craig, A. M., eds., Vol. 1,* 1981, pp. 685–98.
[G: W. Germany]

Immink, Maarten D. C. and Viteri, Fernando E. Energy Intake and Productivity of Guatemalan Sugarcane Cutters: An Empirical Test of the Efficiency Wage Hypothesis—Part I. *J. Devel. Econ.,* October 1981, *9*(2), pp. 251–71.
[G: Guatemala]

Immink, Maarten D. C. and Viteri, Fernando E. Energy Intake and Productivity of Guatemalan Sugarcane Cutters: An Empirical Test of the Efficiency Wage Hypothesis—Part II. *J. Devel. Econ.,* October 1981, *9*(2), pp. 273–87.
[G: Guatemala]

Kallek, Shirley. Government Statistics for Productivity Research. In *Hogan, J. D. and Craig, A. M., eds., Vol. 2,* 1981, pp. 1071–84. [G: U.S.]

Karabín, Štefan. For a More Effective Use of Manpower. *Czech. Econ. Digest.,* February 1981, (1), pp. 38–53. [G: Czechoslovakia]

Keen, Peter G. W. Decision Support Systems and Managerial Productivity Analysis. In *Hogan, J. D. and Craig, A. M., eds., Vol. 1,* 1981, pp. 571–601. [G: U.S.]

Kendrick, John W. International Comparisons of Recent Productivity Trends. In *Fellner, W., ed.,* 1981, pp. 125–70. [G: OECD]

Kendrick, John W. Survey of the Factors Contributing to the Decline in U.S. Productivity Growth. In *Federal Reserve Bank of Boston (I),* 1981, pp. 1–21. [G: U.S.]

Kendrick, John W. Why Productivity Growth Rates Change and Differ. In *Giersch, H., ed. (II),* 1981, pp. 111–40. [G: U.S.]

Kirkland, Lane. Productivity: A Labor View. In *Hogan, J. D. and Craig, A. M., eds., Vol. 2,* 1981, pp. 1211–19. [G: U.S.]

Kopcke, Richard W. Capital Accumulation and Potential Growth. In *Federal Reserve Bank of Boston (I),* 1981, pp. 26–53. [G: U.S.]

Kopp, Raymond J. and Smith, V. Kerry. Productivity Measurement and Environmental Regulation: An Engineering–Econometric Analysis. In *Cowing, T. G. and Stevenson, R. E., eds.*, 1981, pp. 248–81.

Koropeckyj, I. S. Selected Problems of Regional Development in the USSR: Growth and Productivity. In *Koropeckyj, I. S. and Schroeder, G. E., eds.*, 1981, pp. 92–117. [G: U.S.S.R.]

Kosters, Marvin H. Government and Productivity Improvement: Solution or Problem? In *Hogan, J. D. and Craig, A. M., eds., Vol. 2*, 1981, pp. 953–59. [G: U.S.]

Kostin, L. A. Labor Productivity in the Present Stage. *Prob. Econ.*, August 1981, *24*(4), pp. 3–19. [G: U.S.S.R.]

Kraus, Jerome. Adapting Accounting Systems for Productivity Analysis. In *Hogan, J. D. and Craig, A. M., eds., Vol. 1*, 1981, pp. 551–69. [G: U.S.]

Kumar, Pradeep. Wages, Productivity and Labour Costs: Summary Outline. In *Wood, W. D. and Kumar, P., eds.*, 1981, pp. 385–461. [G: Canada]

Kuznets, Simon. A Note on Production Structure and Aggregate Growth. In *[Bergson, A.]*, 1981, pp. 289–303. [G: Global]

Landen, D. L. Labor-Management Cooperation in Productivity Improvement. In *Hogan, J. D. and Craig, A. M., eds., Vol. 1*, 1981, pp. 415–51. [G: U.S.]

Laurie, Bruce and Schmitz, Mark. Manufacture and Productivity: The Making of an Industrial Base, Philadelphia, 1850–1880. In *Hershberg, T., ed.*, 1981, pp. 43–92. [G: U.S.]

Lazear, Edward P. Agency, Earnings Profiles, Productivity, and Hours Restrictions. *Amer. Econ. Rev.*, September 1981, *71*(4), pp. 606–20.

Leibenstein, Harvey. X-Efficiency Theory, Productivity and Growth. In *Giersch, H., ed. (II)*, 1981, pp. 187–212.

Leveson, Irving. Productivity in Services: Issues for Analysis. In *Hogan, J. D. and Craig, A. M., eds., Vol. 2*, 1981, pp. 765–803. [G: U.S.]

Lewin, Wayne B. Productivity and the Banking Industry. In *Hogan, J. D. and Craig, A. M., eds., Vol. 2*, 1981, pp. 1177–83. [G: U.S.]

Mackenzie, Kenneth D. Concepts and Measures in Organizational Development. In *Hogan, J. D. and Craig, A. M., eds., Vol. 1*, 1981, pp. 233–301.

Maddison, Angus. International Productivity Comparisons: National Differentials. In *Hogan, J. D. and Craig, A. M., eds., Vol. 1*, 1981, pp. 607–37. [G: OECD]

Maitha, J. K. and Manundu, M. Production Techniques, Factor Proportions and Elasticities of Substitution. In *Killick, T., ed.*, 1981, pp. 245–53. [G: Kenya]

Mali, Paul. Managerial Strategies for Productivity Improvement. In *Hogan, J. D. and Craig, A. M., eds., Vol. 1*, 1981, pp. 477–90. [G: U.S.]

Mansfield, Edwin. Why Productivity Growth Rates Change and Differ: Comments. In *Giersch, H., ed. (II)*, 1981, pp. 141–48. [G: U.S.]

Mark, Jerome A. Measuring Productivity in Federal, State and Local Government. In *Hogan, J. D. and Craig, A. M., eds., Vol. 2*, 1981, pp. 993–1011. [G: U.S.]

Mazzoni, Riccardo. An Analysis of the Changes in the Distribution of Employment between Industry and Services. *Rev. Econ. Cond. Italy*, February 1981, (1), pp. 87–117. [G: Italy]

McCarthy, John F. Proceedings of the Seminar on International Economic Problems: Statement. In *U.S. Congress, Joint Economic Committee (I)*, 1981, pp. 340–43. [G: U.S.]

McCloskey, Donald N. International Differences in Productivity? Coal and Steel in America and Britain before World War I. In *McCloskey, D. N.*, 1981, 1973, pp. 73–93. [G: U.K.; U.S.]

Medoff, James L. and Abraham, Katharine G. Are Those Paid More Really More Productive? The Case of Experience. *J. Human Res.*, Spring 1981, *16*(2), pp. 186–216. [G: U.S.]

Militzer, Kenneth H. Productivity Measures at the Firm Level. In *Hogan, J. D. and Craig, A. M., eds., Vol. 1*, 1981, pp. 305–18. [G: U.S.]

Miller, Edward M. Differences in Productivity by Size of Firm and Region. In *Hogan, J. D. and Craig, A. M., eds., Vol. 2*, 1981, pp. 839–53. [G: U.S.]

Miller, Edward M. What Do Labor Productivity Data Show about Economies of Scale: Reply. *Southern Econ. J.*, January 1981, *47*(3), pp. 847–51. [G: U.S.]

Mohr, Michael F. Concepts in the Theory and Measurement of Productivity. In *Hogan, J. D. and Craig, A. M., eds., Vol. 2*, 1981, pp. 855–934. [G: U.S.]

Moomaw, Ronald L. Productive Efficiency and Region. *Southern Econ. J.*, October 1981, *48*(2), pp. 344–57. [G: U.S.]

Moomaw, Ronald L. Productivity and City Size? A Critique of the Evidence [Are There Returns to Scale in City Size?]. [Bias in the Cross Section Estimates of the Elasticity of Substitution]. *Quart. J. Econ.*, November 1981, *96*(4), pp. 675–88. [G: U.S.]

Morrison, Catherine J. and Berndt, Ernst R. Short-Run Labor Productivity in a Dynamic Model. *J. Econometrics*, August 1981, *16*(3), pp. 339–65.

Nadiri, M. Ishaq and Schankerman, Mark A. Technical Change, Returns to Scale, and the Productivity Slowdown. *Amer. Econ. Rev.*, May 1981, *71*(2), pp. 314–19. [G: U.S.]

Nadiri, M. Ishaq and Schankerman, Mark A. The Structure of Production, Technological Change, and the Rate of Growth of Total Factor Productivity in the U.S. Bell System. In *Cowing, T. G. and Stevenson, R. E., eds.*, 1981, pp. 219–47. [G: U.S.]

Naples, Michele I. Industrial Conflict and Its Implications for Productivity Growth. *Amer. Econ. Rev.*, May 1981, *71*(2), pp. 36–41. [G: U.S.]

Nelson, Richard R. Research on Productivity Growth and Productivity Differences: Dead Ends and New Departures. *J. Econ. Lit.*, September 1981, *19*(3), pp. 1029–64.

Nelson, Richard R. Why Productivity Growth Rates Change and Differ: Comment. In *Giersch, H.,* *ed. (II)*, 1981, pp. 149–50. [G: U.S.]

Nelson, Richard R. X-Efficiency Theory, Productivity and Growth: Comments. In *Giersch, H., ed. (II)*, 1981, pp. 220.

Nordhaus, William D. Policy Responses to the Productivity Slowdown. In *Federal Reserve Bank of Boston (I)*, 1981, pp. 147–72. [G: U.S.]

Norsworthy, J. R. Capital, Energy and Productivity Research. In *Hogan, J. D. and Craig, A. M., eds., Vol. 1*, 1981, pp. 171–81. [G: U.S.]

Norsworthy, J. R. The Productivity Slowdown: A Labor Problem? Discussion. In *Federal Reserve Bank of Boston (I)*, 1981, pp. 143–46. [G: U.S.]

Olsen, John G. Labor and Material Requirements for Federal Building Construction. *Mon. Lab. Rev.*, December 1981, *104*(12), pp. 47–51. [G: U.S.]

Otto, Phyllis Flohr. Transformer Industry Productivity Slows. *Mon. Lab. Rev.*, November 1981, *104*(11), pp. 35–39. [G: U.S.]

Pack, Howard. The Substitution of Labour for Capital in Kenyan Manufacturing. In *Killick, T., ed., 1981, 1976*, pp. 254–62. [G: Kenya]

Perloff, Jeffrey M. and Wachter, Michael L. The Productivity Slowdown: A Labor Problem? In *Federal Reserve Bank of Boston (I)*, 1981, pp. 115–42. [G: U.S.]

Pew, Robert C. Capital and Productivity: A Firm View. In *Hogan, J. D. and Craig, A. M., eds., Vol. 1*, 1981, pp. 165–68. [G: U.S.]

Pfeiffer, Ralph A., Jr. Productivity: A Multinational View. In *Hogan, J. D. and Craig, A. M., eds., Vol. 2*, 1981, pp. 1221–29. [G: U.S.]

Pomeranz, Felix. Social Measurement: Concepts and Practices. In *Hogan, J. D. and Craig, A. M., eds., Vol. 1*, 1981, pp. 403–12. [G: U.S.]

Pratten, C. F. International Productivity Comparisons. In *Hogan, J. D. and Craig, A. M., eds., Vol. 1*, 1981, pp. 657–67. [G: U.K.; Selected OECD]

Predetti, Adalberto. La retribuzione operaia ad incentivo in Germania, Regno Unito Svezia e Francia. (Wage Incentive Systems in West Germany, United Kingdom, France and Sweden. With English summary.) *Giorn. Econ.*, March–April 1981, *40*(3–4), pp. 131–44. [G: W. Germany; U.K.; Sweden; France]

Ranftl, R. M. Role of R and D in Productivity: Microeconomic Issues. In *Hogan, J. D. and Craig, A. M., eds., Vol. 1*, 1981, pp. 93–100. [G: U.S.]

Rao, P. Someshwar. Factor Prices and Labour Productivity in the Canadian Manufacturing Industries. *Empirical Econ.*, 1981, *6*(4), pp. 187–202. [G: Canada]

Rayment, P. B. W. Structural Change in Manufacturing Industry and the Stability of the Verdoorn Law. *Econ. Int.*, February 1981, *34*(1), pp. 104–23. [G: W. Europe]

Renshaw, Edward F. Energy Efficiency and the Slump in Labour Productivity in the USA. *Energy Econ.*, January 1981, *3*(1), pp. 36–42. [G: U.S.]

Resnikoff, Howard L. and Weiss, Edward C. Adapting Use of Information and Knowledge to Enhance Productivity: Productivity, Information and Energy. In *Hogan, J. D. and Craig, A. M., eds.,*

Vol. 1, 1981, pp. 507–49. [G: U.S.]

Richardson, James A. Organizational Conditions for Improving Human Productivity: Definition, Diagnosis and Change. In *Hogan, J. D. and Craig, A. M., eds., Vol. 1*, 1981, pp. 361–91.

Roberts, Markley. The Workers' Stake in Adjustments to Technological Change. In *Hogan, J. D. and Craig, A. M., eds., Vol. 1*, 1981, pp. 467–73. [G: U.S.]

Ruch, William A. Measuring Knowledge Worker Productivity. In *Hogan, J. D. and Craig, A. M., eds., Vol. 1*, 1981, pp. 339–58. [G: U.S.]

Schlicht, Ekkehart. Reference Group Behaviour and Economic Incentives: A Further Remark. *Z. ges. Staatswiss.*, December 1981, *137*(4), pp. 733–36.

Schlicht, Ekkehart. Reference Group Behaviour and Economic Incentives: A Remark. *Z. ges. Staatswiss.*, March 1981, *137*(1), pp. 125–27.

Schluter, Gerald and Beeson, Patty. Components of Labor Productivity Growth in the Food System, 1958–67. *Rev. Econ. Statist.*, August 1981, *63*(3), pp. 378–84. [G: U.S.]

Schwartz, Samuel. Productivity in the Energy Producing Industries. In *Hogan, J. D. and Craig, A. M., eds., Vol. 1*, 1981, pp. 191–97. [G: U.S.]

Seashore, Stanley E. Organizational Effectiveness: Productivity and What Else? In *Hogan, J. D. and Craig, A. M., eds., Vol. 1*, 1981, pp. 495–504. [G: U.S.]

Seger, Ronald. Productivity and Physical Distribution. In *Hogan, J. D. and Craig, A. M., eds., Vol. 2*, 1981, pp. 1103–07. [G: U.S.]

Shepherd, Mark, Jr. The U.S. Corporation within the Competitive Environment. In *U.S. Congress, Joint Economic Committee (I)*, 1981, pp. 191–222. [G: U.S.; OECD]

Sherbiny, Naiem A. Sectoral Employment Projections with Minimum Data: The Case of Saudi Arabia. In *Sherbiny, N. A., ed.*, 1981, pp. 173–206. [G: Saudi Arabia]

Siegel, Irving H. Need for Improvement in Government Productivity Information. In *Hogan, J. D. and Craig, A. M., eds., Vol. 2*, 1981, pp. 1057–69. [G: U.S.]

Smith, Kenneth R. and Over, A. Mead, Jr. The Effect of Health Manpower Regulations on Productivity in Medical Practices. In *Cowing, T. G. and Stevenson, R. E., eds.*, 1981, pp. 309–343. [G: U.S.]

Solow, Robert M. Policy Responses to the Productivity Slowdown: Discussion. In *Federal Reserve Bank of Boston (I)*, 1981, pp. 173–77. [G: U.S.]

Stern, Gary. Productivity and Division Profitability. In *Hogan, J. D. and Craig, A. M., eds., Vol. 1*, 1981, pp. 391–401.

Stieber, Jack and Block, Richard N. U.S. Industrial Relations 1950–1980: Summary and Conclusions. In *Stieber, J.; McKersie, R. B. and Mills, D. Q., eds.*, 1981, pp. 343–61. [G: U.S.]

Stillwell, J. W. Productivity and the Commercial Aircraft Industry. In *Hogan, J. D. and Craig, A. M., eds., Vol. 2*, 1981, pp. 1121–24. [G: U.S.]

Stokes, H. Kemble, Jr. An Examination of the Productivity Decline in the Construction Industry.

Rev. Econ. Statist., November 1981, *63*(4), pp. 459–502. [G: U.S.]

Stone, Alan. State and Market: Economic Regulation and the Great Productivity Debate. In *Ferguson, T. and Rogers, J., eds.*, 1981, pp. 232–59. [G: U.S.]

Tatom, John A. Capital Utilization and Okun's Law. *Rev. Econ. Statist.*, February 1981, *63*(1), pp. 155–58. [G: U.S.]

Terleckyj, Nestor E. Contribution of Government to the Quality of Life. In *Hogan, J. D. and Craig, A. M., eds., Vol. 2*, 1981, pp. 1085–93. [G: U.S.]

Thurow, Lester C. Stagflation, Productivity, and the Labor Market. In *Carter, M. J. and Leahy, W. H., eds.*, 1981, pp. 61–106. [G: U.S.]

Thurow, Lester C. Survey of the Factors Contributing to the Decline in U.S. Productivity Growth: Discussion. In *Federal Reserve Bank of Boston (I)*, 1981, pp. 22–25. [G: U.S.]

Thurow, Lester C. The Productivity Problem. In *Ontario Economic Council, Vol. 2*, 1981, pp. 11–35. [G: U.S.]

Till, Thomas A. Productivity and the Railroad Industry. In *Hogan, J. D. and Craig, A. M., eds., Vol. 2*, 1981, pp. 1109–13. [G: U.S.]

Tomer, John F. Worker Motivation: A Neglected Element in Micro-Micro Theory. *J. Econ. Issues*, June 1981, *15*(2), pp. 351–62.

Usilaner, Brian L. Can We Expect Productivity Improvement in the Federal Government? In *Hogan, J. D. and Craig, A. M., eds., Vol. 2*, 1981, pp. 963–85. [G: U.S.]

Valle, P. Della. Productivity and Employment in the Copper and Aluminium Industries. In *Bhalla, A. S., ed.*, 1981, *1975*, pp. 323–55. [G: Selected LDCs; U.S.]

Vanderslice, Thomas A. Closing the Technology–Productivity Gap. In *Hogan, J. D. and Craig, A. M., eds., Vol. 2*, 1981, pp. 1231–38. [G: U.S.]

Vastola, S. J., Jr. Productivity and the Petroleum Industry. In *Hogan, J. D. and Craig, A. M., eds., Vol. 2*, 1981, pp. 1133–46. [G: U.S.]

Vetter, Edward O. The Role of the Manager in Productivity Improvement. In *Hogan, J. D. and Craig, A. M., eds., Vol. 1*, 1981, pp. 491–94. [G: U.S.]

Visser, Jan H. Productivity Research in the Republic of South Africa. In *Hogan, J. D. and Craig, A. M., eds., Vol. 1*, 1981, pp. 699–711. [G: S. Africa]

Wallich, Henry C. Statement to Temporary Subcommittee on Industrial Growth and Productivity, Senate Committee on the Budget, January 27, 1981. *Fed. Res. Bull.*, February 1981, *67*(2), pp. 137–40. [G: U.S.]

Watts, Glenn E. Productivity and Employment: The Social Gains and Costs. In *Hogan, J. D. and Craig, A. M., eds., Vol. 1*, 1981, pp. 77–83. [G: U.S.]

Wiederhorn, Robert. Productivity and the Petrochemical Industry. In *Hogan, J. D. and Craig, A. M., eds., Vol. 2*, 1981, pp. 1153–57. [G: U.S.]

York, James D. and Persigehl, Elmer S. Productivity Trends in the Ball and Roller Bearing Industry. *Mon. Lab. Rev.*, January 1981, *104*(1), pp. 40–43. [G: U.S.]

You, Jong Keun. Capital Utilization and Okun's Law: A Reply. *Rev. Econ. Statist.*, February 1981, *63*(1), pp. 158–60. [G: U.S.]

826 Labor Markets: Demographic Characteristics

8260 Labor Markets: Demographic Characteristics

Acton, Norman. Employment of Disabled Persons: Where Are We Going? *Int. Lab. Rev.*, January–February 1981, *120*(1), pp. 1–14.

Aho, C. Michael and Orr, James A. Trade-Sensitive Employment: Who Are the Affected Workers? *Mon. Lab. Rev.*, February 1981, *104*(2), pp. 29–35. [G: U.S.]

Anderson, Bernard E. Economic Growth: The Central Issue: A Partial Dissent: Fiddling with the Economy is Not Enough. In *Inst. for Contemp. Studies*, 1981, pp. 47–51. [G: U.S.]

Andrisani, Paul J. Internal–External Attitudes, Sense of Efficacy, and Labor Market Experience: A Reply to Duncan and Morgan [Internal–External Attitudes, Personal Initiative, and the Labor Market Experience of Black and White Men]. *J. Human Res.*, Fall 1981, *16*(4), pp. 658–66. [G: U.S.]

Bannon, Robert. Dual-Earner Families: An Annotated Bibliography. *Mon. Lab. Rev.*, February 1981, *104*(2), pp. 53–59.

Bartel, Ann P. Race Differences in Job Satisfaction: A Reappraisal. *J. Human Res.*, Spring 1981, *16*(2), pp. 294–303. [G: U.S.]

Becker, Brian E. and Hills, Stephen M. Youth Attitudes and Adult Labor Market Activity. *Ind. Relat.*, Winter 1981, *20*(1), pp. 60–70. [G: U.S.]

Bekombo, M. The Child in Africa: Socialisation, Education and Work. In *Rodgers, G. and Standing, G., eds.*, 1981, pp. 113–29. [G: Africa]

Betsey, Charles L. and Dunson, Bruce H. Federal Minimum Wage Laws and the Employment of Minority Youth. *Amer. Econ. Rev.*, May 1981, *71*(2), pp. 379–84. [G: U.S.]

Blau, Francine D. and Kahn, Lawrence M. Causes and Consequences of Layoffs. *Econ. Inquiry*, April 1981, *19*(2), pp. 270–96. [G: U.S.]

Blau, Francine D. and Kahn, Lawrence M. Race and Sex Differences in Quits by Young Workers. *Ind. Lab. Relat. Rev.*, July 1981, *34*(4), pp. 563–77. [G: U.S.]

Borus, Michael E. Special Groups in the Labor Market: Discussion. In *Dennis, B. D., ed.*, 1981, pp. 69–71. [G: U.S.]

Bourguignon, François. Participation, emploi et travail domestiques des femmes mariées: Un modèle micro-économique appliqué aux pays en développement. (Participation, Domestic Employment and Domestic Work by Married Women: A Micro-Economic Model Applied to Developing Countries. With English summary.) *Consommation*, April–June 1981, *28*(2), pp. 75–98. [G: France]

Bowers, Norman. Have Employment Patterns in Recessions Changed? *Mon. Lab. Rev.*, February 1981, *104*(2), pp. 15–28. [G: U.S.]

Bowers, Norman. Youth Labor Force Activity: Alternative Surveys Compared. *Mon. Lab. Rev.*, March 1981, *104*(3), pp. 3–17. [G: U.S.]

de Broucker, Patrice. Sensibilité du chômage et caractéristiques de l'offre et de la demande sur le marché du travail. (Sensitivity of Unemployment and Characteristics of Supply and Demand in the Labor Market. With English summary.) *L'Actual. Econ.*, July–September 1981, *57*(3), pp. 359–75. [G: Canada]

Brown, C. V. and Levin, E. Taxation and Labour Supply: The Interview Approach. **In** *Brown, C. V., ed.*, 1981, pp. 21–34. [G: U.K.]

Brulhardt, Marie-Claude and Bassand, Michel. La mobilité spatiale en tant que système. (Spatial Mobility as a System. With English summary.) *Schweiz. Z. Volkswirtsch. Statist.*, September 1981, *117*(3), pp. 505–19.

Cain, Mead and Mozumder, A. B. M. Khorshed Alam. Labour Market Structure and Reproductive Behaviour in Rural South Asia. **In** *Rodgers, G. and Standing, G., eds.*, 1981, pp. 245–87. [G: S. Asia]

Carliner, Geoffrey. Female Labor Force Participation Rates for Nine Ethnic Groups. *J. Human Res.*, Spring 1981, *16*(2), pp. 286–93. [G: U.S.]

Chirikos, Thomas N. and Nestel, Gilbert. Impairment and Labor Market Outcomes: A Cross-Sectional and Longitudinal Analysis. **In** *Parnes, H. S., ed.*, 1981, pp. 93–131. [G: U.S.]

Clark, Kim B. and Summers, Lawrence H. Demographic Differences in Cyclical Employment Variation. *J. Human Res.*, Winter 1981, *16*(1), pp. 61–79. [G: U.S.]

Daymont, Thomas N. Changes in Black–White Labor Market Opportunities, 1966–76. **In** *Parnes, H. S., ed.*, 1981, pp. 42–64. [G: U.S.]

Dube, Leela. The Economic Roles of Children in India: Methodological Issues. **In** *Rodgers, G. and Standing, G., eds.*, 1981, pp. 179–213. [G: India]

Duncan, Greg J. and Morgan, James N. Sense of Efficacy and Subsequent Change in Earnings— A Replication [Internal–External Attitudes, Personal Initiative, and the Labor Market Experience of Black and White Men]. *J. Human Res.*, Fall 1981, *16*(4), pp. 649–57. [G: U.S.]

Farkas, George; Olsen, Randall J. and Stromsdorfer, Ernst W. Youth Labor Supply During the Summer: Evidence for Youths from Low-Income Households. **In** *Ehrenberg, R. G., ed.*, 1981, pp. 151–90. [G: U.S.]

Firth, Michael. Racial Discrimination in the British Labor Market. *Ind. Lab. Relat. Rev.*, January 1981, *34*(2), pp. 265–72. [G: U.K.]

Foster, Ann C. Wives' Earnings as a Factor in Family Net Worth Accumulation. *Mon. Lab. Rev.*, January 1981, *104*(1), pp. 53–57. [G: U.S.]

Franz, Wolfgang and Kawasaki, S. Labor Supply of Married Women in the Federal Republic of Germany: Theory and Empirical Results from a New Estimation Procedure. *Empirical Econ.*, 1981, *6*(2), pp. 129–43. [G: W. Germany]

Friedlander, Stanley L. The Cost of Labor Market Information: Male Youth Job Search Behavior: Comments. **In** *Galatin, M. and Leiter, R. D., eds.*, 1981, pp. 141–45. [G: U.S.]

Gastwirth, Joseph L. Estimating the Demographic Mix of the Available Labor Force. *Mon. Lab. Rev.*, April 1981, *104*(4), pp. 50–57. [G: U.S.]

Glaister, K. W.; McGlone, A. and Ruffell, R. J. Taxation and Labour Supply: Preferences. **In** *Brown, C. V., ed.*, 1981, pp. 69–100. [G: U.K.]

Grant, James H. and Hamermesh, Daniel S. Labor Market Competition among Youths, White Women and Others. *Rev. Econ. Statist.*, August 1981, *63*(3), pp. 354–60. [G: U.S.]

Gregory, R. G. and Duncan, R. C. Employment, Unemployment and Income Effects of Relative Wage Changes. **In** *Hancock, K., ed.*, 1981, pp. 297–318. [G: Australia]

Grossman, Allyson Sherman. The Employment Situation for Military Wives. *Mon. Lab. Rev.*, February 1981, *104*(2), pp. 60–64. [G: U.S.]

Grossman, Allyson Sherman. Working Mothers and Their Children. *Mon. Lab. Rev.*, May 1981, *104*(5), pp. 49–54. [G: U.S.]

Haber, Sheldon E. The Mobility of Professional Workers and Fair Hiring. *Ind. Lab. Relat. Rev.*, January 1981, *34*(2), pp. 257–64. [G: U.S.]

Hayghe, Howard. Husbands and Wives as Earners: An Analysis of Family Data. *Mon. Lab. Rev.*, February 1981, *104*(2), pp. 46–53. [G: U.S.]

Hull, Terence M. Perspectives and Data Requirements for the Study of Children's Work. **In** *Rodgers, G. and Standing, G., eds.*, 1981, pp. 47–79.

Hyclak, Thomas and Stewart, James. A Note on the Relative Earnings of Central City Black Males. *J. Human Res.*, Spring 1981, *16*(2), pp. 304–13. [G: U.S.]

Janjić, Marion. Diversifying Women's Employment: The Only Road to Genuine Equality of Opportunity. *Int. Lab. Rev.*, March–April 1981, *120*(2), pp. 149–63. [G: U.S.]

Johnson, Beverly L. and Waldman, Elizabeth. Marital and Family Patterns of the Labor Force. *Mon. Lab. Rev.*, October 1981, *104*(10), pp. 36–38. [G: U.S.]

Keyfitz, Nathan. The Limits of Population Forecasting. *Population Devel. Rev.*, December 1981, *7*(4), pp. 579–93.

Kiker, B. F. and Condon, C. M. The Influence of Socioeconomic Background on the Earnings of Young Men. *J. Human Res.*, Winter 1981, *16*(1), pp. 94–105. [G: U.S.]

Lapidus, Gail W. The Female Industrial Labor Force: Dilemmas, Reassessments, and Options. **In** *Bornstein, M., ed.*, 1981, 1979, pp. 119–48. [G: U.S.S.R.]

Lehrer, Evelyn and Nerlove, Marc. The Impact of Female Work on Family Income Distribution in the United States: Black-White Differentials. *Rev. Income Wealth*, December 1981, *27*(4), pp. 423–31. [G: U.S.]

Lemennicier, Bertrand and Lévy-Garboua, Louis. L'arbitrage autarcie-marché: Une explication du travail féminin. (The Autarky/Market Trade-off: An Explanation of Female Labor. With English summary.) *Consommation*, April–June 1981, 28(2), pp. 41–74. [G: France]

Leon, Carol Boyd. The Employment–Population Ratio: Its Value in Labor Force Analysis. *Mon. Lab. Rev.*, February 1981, 104(2), pp. 36–45. [G: U.S.]

Long, James E. and Jones, Ethel B. Married Women in Part-Time Employment. *Ind. Lab. Relat. Rev.*, April 1981, 34(3), pp. 413–25. [G: U.S.]

de la Luz Silva, Maria. Urban Poverty and Child Work: Elements for the Analysis of Child Work in Chile. In *Rodgers, G. and Standing, G., eds.*, 1981, pp. 159–77. [G: Chile]

Lyon, Larry and Rector-Owen, Holley. Labor Market Mobility among Young Black and White Women: Longitudinal Models of Occupational Prestige and Income. *Soc. Sci. Quart.*, March 1981, 62(1), pp. 64–78. [G: U.S.]

Mair, Douglas. Urban Unemployment: A Comment [Urban Unemployment in England]. *Econ. J.*, March 1981, 91(361), pp. 224–30. [G: U.K.]

Marmor, Theodore R. Political Perspective on Social Security Financing: Comment. In *Skidmore, F., ed.*, 1981, pp. 224–29. [G: U.S.]

McGavin, P. A. School Participation of Australians Aged Sixteen: An Analysis of Youth Unemployment. *Econ. Rec.*, December 1981, 57(159), pp. 379–81. [G: Australia]

Mills, Wilbur. Political Perspective on Social Security Financing: Comment. In *Skidmore, F., ed.*, 1981, pp. 229–33. [G: U.S.]

Morice, Alain. The Exploitation of Children in the "Informal Sector": Proposals for Research. In *Rodgers, G. and Standing, G., eds.*, 1981, pp. 131–58.

Nakamura, Alice and Nakamura, Masao. A Comparison of the Labor Force Behavior of Married Women in the United States and Canada, with Special Attention to the Impact of Income Taxes. *Econometrica*, March 1981, 49(2), pp. 451–89. [G: U.S.; Canada]

Nakamura, Jirou. A Quantitative Study on the Male and Female Labor Market in Macroeconometric Models. (In Japanese. With English summary.) *Econ. Stud. Quart.*, December 1981, 32(3), pp. 201–16. [G: Japan]

Niemi, Beth T. and Lloyd, Cynthia B. Female Labor Supply in the Context of Inflation. *Amer. Econ. Rev.*, May 1981, 71(2), pp. 70–75. [G: U.S.]

O'Neill, June A. A Time-Series Analysis of Women's Labor Force Participation. *Amer. Econ. Rev.*, May 1981, 71(2), pp. 76–80. [G: U.S.]

Parnes, Herbert S. Work and Retirement: Introduction and Overview. In *Parnes, H. S., ed.*, 1981, pp. 1–41. [G: U.S.]

Parnes, Herbert S. Work and Retirement: Summary and Conclusions. In *Parnes, H. S., ed.*, 1981, pp. 254–70. [G: U.S.]

Parnes, Herbert S.; Gagen, Mary G. and King, Randall H. Job Loss among Long-Service Workers. In *Parnes, H. S., ed.*, 1981, pp. 65–92. [G: U.S.]

Parnes, Herbert S. and Nestel, Gilbert. The Retirement Experience. In *Parnes, H. S., ed.*, 1981, pp. 155–97. [G: U.S.]

Parsons, Donald O. Black–White Differences in La-

bor Force Participation of Older Males. In *Parnes, H. S., ed.*, 1981, pp. 132–54. [G: U.S.]

Perloff, Jeffrey M. The Duration of Unemployment in the Construction Industry. *J. Lab. Res.*, Spring 1981, 2(1), pp. 111–31. [G: U.S.]

Polachek, Solomon William. Occupational Self-Selection: A Human Capital Approach to Sex Differences in Occupational Structure. *Rev. Econ. Statist.*, February 1981, 63(1), pp. 60–69. [G: U.S.]

Redman, Barbara J. The Women Who Become Agricultural Economists. *Amer. J. Agr. Econ.*, December 1981, 63(5), pp. 1019–24. [G: U.S.]

Ridley, F. F. View from a Disaster Area: Unemployed Youth in Merseyside. In *Crick, B., ed.*, 1981, 1981, pp. 16–27. [G: U.K.]

Rodgers, Gerry and Standing, Guy. Economic Roles of Children in Low-Income Countries. *Int. Lab. Rev.*, January–February 1981, 120(1), pp. 31–47.

Rodgers, Gerry and Standing, Guy. The Economic Roles of Children: Issues for Analysis. In *Rodgers, G. and Standing, G., eds.*, 1981, pp. 1–45. [G: LDCs]

Rones, Philip L. Can the Current Population Survey be Used to Identify the Disabled? *Mon. Lab. Rev.*, June 1981, 104(6), pp. 37–39. [G: U.S.]

Rosenzweig, Mark R. Household and Non-household Activities of Youths: Issues of Modelling, Data and Estimation Strategies. In *Rodgers, G. and Standing, G., eds.*, 1981, pp. 215–43. [G: India]

Rotella, Elyce J. The Transformation of the American Office: Changes in Employment and Technology. *J. Econ. Hist.*, March 1981, 41(1), pp. 51–57. [G: U.S.]

Rytina, Nancy F. Occupational Segregation and Earnings Differences by Sex. *Mon. Lab. Rev.*, January 1981, 104(1), pp. 49–53. [G: U.S.]

Sánchez, Carlos E.; Palmiero, Horacio and Ferrero, Fernando. The Informal and Quasi-formal Sectors in Córdoba. In *Sethuraman, S. V., ed.*, 1981, pp. 144–58. [G: Argentina]

Santiago, Carlos E. Male–Female Labor Force Participation and Rapid Industrialization. *J. Econ. Devel.*, December 1981, 6(2), pp. 7–40. [G: Puerto Rico]

Santos, Richard. Measuring the Employment Status of Youth: A Comparison of the Current Population Survey and the National Longitudinal Survey. In *Dennis, B. D., ed.*, 1981, pp. 62–68. [G: U.S.]

Schildkrout, Enid. The Employment of Children in Kano (Nigeria). In *Rodgers, G. and Standing, G., eds.*, 1981, pp. 81–112. [G: Nigeria]

Shapiro, Daniel M. and Stelcner, Morton. Male-Female Earnings Differentials and the Role of Language in Canada, Ontario, and Quebec, 1970. *Can. J. Econ.*, May 1981, 14(2), pp. 341–48. [G: Canada]

Sinclair, W. A. Women at Work in Melbourne and Adelaide since 1871. *Econ. Rec.*, December 1981, 57(159), pp. 344–53. [G: Australia]

Stafford, Frank P. Unemployment and Labor Market Policy in Sweden and the United States. In *Eliasson, G.; Holmlund, B. and Stafford, F. P., eds.*, 1981, pp. 21–65. [G: U.S.; Sweden]

Stearns, Peter N. Political Perspective on Social Security Financing. In *Skidmore, F., ed.*, 1981, pp. 173–224. **[G: U.S.]**

Stephenson, Stanley P., Jr. The Cost of Labor Market Information: Male Youth Job Search Behavior. In *Galatin, M. and Leiter, R. D., eds.*, 1981, pp. 123–40. **[G: U.S.]**

Terry, Sylvia Lazos. Involuntary Part-Time Work: New Information from the CPS. *Mon. Lab. Rev.*, February 1981, *104*(2), pp. 70–74. **[G: U.S.]**

Tienda, Marta. The Mexican-American Population. In *Hawley, A. H. and Mazie, S. M., eds.*, 1981, pp. 503–48. **[G: U.S.]**

Tranter, N. L. The Labour Supply 1780–1860. In *Floud, R. and McCloskey, D., eds., Vol. 1*, 1981, pp. 204–26. **[G: U.K.]**

Wasow, Bernard. The Working Age Sex Ratio and Job Search Migration in Kenya. *J. Devel. Areas*, April 1981, *15*(3), pp. 435–44. **[G: Kenya]**

Westcott, Diane N. The Youngest Workers: 14- and 15-Year-Olds. *Mon. Lab. Rev.*, February 1981, *104*(2), pp. 65–69. **[G: U.S.]**

Williams, Lynne S. A Demographic Analysis of Australian Occupational Mobility. *Australian Bull. Lab.*, June 1981, *7*(3), pp. 139–73.
[G: Australia]

Williams, Walter E. Economic Growth: The Central Issue: Answers: A Culprit is a Culprit. In *Inst. for Contemp. Studies*, 1981, pp. 51–53.

Wool, Harold. Coal Industry Resurgence Attracts Variety of New Workers. *Mon. Lab. Rev.*, January 1981, *104*(1), pp. 3–8. **[G: U.S.]**

830 TRADE UNIONS; COLLECTIVE BARGAINING; LABOR–MANAGEMENT RELATIONS

8300 General

Brüggemeier, Franz-Josef. Ruhr Miners and Their Historians. In *Samuel, R., ed.*, 1981, pp. 326–32. **[G: W. Germany]**

Christiansen, Niels Finn and Rasmussen, Jens Rahbek. 'To Be or Not to Be': Socialist Historians in Denmark. In *Samuel, R., ed.*, 1981, pp. 278–83.
[G: Denmark]

Davin, Anna. Feminism and Labour History. In *Samuel, R., ed.*, 1981, pp. 176–81.

Gramm, Warren S. Property Rights in Work: Capitalism, Industrialism, and Democracy. *J. Econ. Issues*, June 1981, *15*(2), pp. 363–75.

Johnson, Paul M. Changing Social Structure and the Political Role of Manual Workers. In *Triska, J. F. and Gati, C., eds.*, 1981, pp. 29–42.
[G: E. Europe]

Joyce, John T. Toward a New U.S. Industrial Policy? Strategies for Training and Retraining: Comment. In *Wachter, M. L. and Wachter, S. M., eds.*, 1981, pp. 282–85. **[G: U.S.]**

Kumar, Pradeep. The Current Industrial Relations Scene in Canada 1981: Technical Notes. In *Wood, W. D. and Kumar, P., eds.*, 1981, pp. 465–76.
[G: Canada]

Pescarolo, Sandra. From Gramsci to 'Workerism': Notes on Italian Working-Class History. In *Samuel, R., ed.*, 1981, pp. 273–78. **[G: Italy]**

Pravda, Alex. Political Attitudes and Activity. In

Triska, J. F. and Gati, C., eds., 1981, pp. 43–69. **[G: E. Europe]**

Rancière, Jacques. 'Le Socail': The Lost Tradition in French Labour History. In *Samuel, R., ed.*, 1981, pp. 267–72. **[G: France]**

Sagardoy Bengoechea, Juan A. The Spanish Workers' Statute. *Int. Lab. Rev.*, March–April 1981, *120*(2), pp. 215–29. **[G: Spain]**

Sellier, François. Les transformations sociales du système économique capitaliste. (With English summary.) *Écon. Appl.*, 1981, *34*(2–3), pp. 279–318.

Svejnar, Jan. Relative Wage Effects of Unions, Dictatorship and Codetermination: Econometric Evidence from Germany. *Rev. Econ. Statist.*, May 1981, *63*(2), pp. 188–97. **[G: W. Germany]**

Walker, Jill. Markets, Industrial Processes and Class Struggle: The Evolution of the Labor Process in the U.K. Engineering Industry. *Rev. Radical Polit. Econ.*, Winter 1981, *12*(4), pp. 46–59.
[G: U.K.]

Wiehahn, Nic. Some Aspects of Industrial Relations at the In-House Level. *Finance Trade Rev.*, December 1981, *14*(4), pp. 136–47. **[G: S. Africa]**

831 Trade Unions

8310 Trade Unions

Adelman, William. Labor History through Field Trips. In *Wertheimer, B. M., ed.*, 1981, pp. 159–70. **[G: U.S.]**

Alba, Victor. Spain. In *Blum, A. A., ed.*, 1981, pp. 515–37. **[G: Spain]**

Alexander, Robert J. Brazil. In *Blum, A. A., ed.*, 1981, pp. 49–70. **[G: Brazil]**

Allen, G. C. Trade Unions in the Developed Economies: Japan. In *Smith, E. O., ed.*, 1981, pp. 73–96. **[G: Japan]**

Alston, Philip. Commodity Agreements—As Though People Don't Matter: A Reply to '"Fair Labour Standards' in International Commodity Agreements." *J. World Trade Law*, September–October 1981, *15*(5), pp. 455–60.

Baird, Charles W. Unionism and the Public Sector. *Managerial Dec. Econ.*, June 1981, *2*(2), pp. 82–90. **[G: U.S.]**

Barbash, Jack. Theories of the Labor Movement in an Institutional Setting. *J. Econ. Issues*, June 1981, *15*(2), pp. 299–309.

Bartel, Ann P. and Lewin, David. Wages and Unionism in the Public Sector: The Case of Police. *Rev. Econ. Statist.*, February 1981, *63*(1), pp. 53–59.
[G: U.S.]

Baseo, Sahadeo. The Role of the British Labour Movement in the Development of Labour Organisation in Trinidad 1919–1929. *Soc. Econ. Stud.*, September 1981, *30*(3), pp. 21–41.
[G: Trinidad and Tobago; U.K.]

Beaumont, P. B. Time Delays, Employer Opposition and White Collar Recognition Claims: The Section 12 Results. *Brit. J. Ind. Relat.*, July 1981, *19*(2), pp. 238–42. **[G: U.K.]**

Becker, Brian E. and Miller, Richard U. Patterns and Determinants of Union Growth in the Hospital Industry. *J. Lab. Res.*, Fall 1981, *2*(2), pp. 309–28. [G: U.S.]

Bentley, Philip. The Industrial Relations Consequences of Incomes Policies. In *Hancock, K., ed.*, 1981, pp. 235–58. [G: Australia]

Blum, Albert A. United States. In *Blum, A. A., ed.*, 1981, pp. 621–45. [G: U.S.]

Bolweg, Joep F. The Quality of Working Life: An Industrial Relations Perspective. In *Dennis, B. D., ed.*, 1981, pp. 174–84. [G: OECD]

Brown, William. Labour Market Policy: Comments. In *[Cairncross, A.]*, 1981, pp. 96–100.

Brown, William A. British Collective Bargaining: A Decade of Reformation. *Mon. Lab. Rev.*, July 1981, *104*(7), pp. 40–43. [G: U.K.]

Buchanan, R. T. Union Concentration and the Largest Unions. *Brit. J. Ind. Relat.*, July 1981, *19*(2), pp. 232–37. [G: U.K.]

Cain, Glen G., et al. The Effect of Unions on Wages in Hospitals. In *Ehrenberg, R. G., ed.*, 1981, pp. 191–320. [G: U.S.]

Capozzola, John M. The Impact of Government Employee Unions. In *Pious, R. M., ed.*, 1981, pp. 153–66. [G: U.S.]

Carroll, Thomas M. Achieving Cartel Profits through Unionization: Comment. *Southern Econ. J.*, April 1981, *47*(4), pp. 1152–61.

Carruth, Alan A. and Oswald, Andrew J. The Determination of Union and Non-Union Wage Rates. *Europ. Econ. Rev.*, June/July 1981, *16*(2/3), pp. 285–302.

Chaison, Gary N. Union Growth and Union Mergers. *Ind. Relat.*, Winter 1981, *20*(1), pp. 98–108. [G: U.S.]

Chapman, P. G. The Johnston Wage Bargaining Model and Trade Union Objectives. *Manchester Sch. Econ. Soc. Stud.*, December 1981, *49*(4), pp. 310–18.

Christensen, Sandra and Maki, Dennis. The Union Wage Effect in Canadian Manufacturing Industries. *J. Lab. Res.*, Fall 1981, *2*(2), pp. 355–67. [G: Canada]

Coates, Mary Lou and Longmore, Janet. Trade Unionism: Summary Outline. In *Wood, W. D. and Kumar, P., eds.*, 1981, pp. 193–273. [G: Canada; U.S.]

Conrad, Wolfgang. Federal Republic of Germany. In *Blum, A. A., ed.*, 1981, pp. 209–38. [G: W. Germany]

Cook, Alice H. and Till-Retz, Roberta. Labor Education and Women Workers: An International Comparison. In *Wertheimer, B. M., ed.*, 1981, pp. 255–64. [G: Sweden; U.K.; Austria; W. Germany]

Craypo, Charles. The Decline of Union Bargaining Power. In *Carter, M. J. and Leahy, W. H., eds.*, 1981, pp. 107–66. [G: U.S]

Cupper, Les and Hearn, June M. Unions and the Environment: Recent Australian Experience. *Ind. Relat.*, Spring 1981, *20*(2), pp. 221–31. [G: Australia]

Cupper, Les and Hearn, June M. Trade Unions in the Developed Economies: Australia. In *Smith, E. O., ed.*, 1981, pp. 13–42. [G: Australia]

Delaney, John Thomas. Union Success in Hospital Representation Elections. *Ind. Relat.*, Spring

1981, *20*(2), pp. 149–61. [G: U.S.]

Dereli, Toker. Turkey. In *Blum, A. A., ed.*, 1981, pp. 547–92. [G: Turkey]

Dertouzos, James N. and Pencavel, John H. Wage and Employment Determination under Trade Unionism: The International Typographical Union. *J. Polit. Econ.*, December 1981, *89*(6), pp. 1162–81. [G: U.S.]

Desolre, Guy G. Belgium. In *Blum, A. A., ed.*, 1981, pp. 37–48. [G: Belgium]

Dickenson, Mary. The Effects of Parties and Factions on Trade Union Elections. *Brit. J. Ind. Relat.*, July 1981, *19*(2), pp. 190–200. [G: U.K.]

Donsimoni, Marie-Paule. Union Power and the American Labour Movement. *Appl. Econ.*, December 1981, *13*(4), pp. 449–64. [G: U.S.]

Dorsey, Stuart. Comparative Advantage and the Welfare Effects of Uniform Wage Policies. *J. Lab. Res.*, Spring 1981, *2*(1), pp. 147–56.

Duffy, Norman F. Australia. In *Blum, A. A., ed.*, 1981, pp. 3–36. [G: Australia]

Dufty, N. F. Conscripts and Volunteers. *Australian Bull. Lab.*, March 1981, *7*(2), pp. 88–107. [G: Australia]

Edwards, P. K. The Strike-Proneness of British Manufacturing Establishments. *Brit. J. Ind. Relat.*, July 1981, *19*(2), pp. 135–48. [G: U.K.]

Fallenbuchl, Zbigniew M. Poland: Command Planning in Crisis. *Challenge*, July/August 1981, *24*(3), pp. 5–12. [G: Poland]

Fones-Wolf, Elizabeth and Fones-Wolf, Kenneth. Voluntarism and Factional Disputes in the AFL: The Painters' Split in 1894–1900. *Ind. Lab. Relat. Rev.*, October 1981, *35*(1), pp. 58–69.

Fong, Pang Eng. Singapore. In *Blum, A. A., ed.*, 1981, pp. 481–97. [G: Singapore]

Freeman, John. Competitive Processes and Patterns of Selection in Union Mergers. In *Dennis, B. D., ed.*, 1981, pp. 203–10. [G: U.S.]

Freeman, Richard B. The Effect of Unionism on Fringe Benefits. *Ind. Lab. Relat. Rev.*, July 1981, *34*(4), pp. 489–509. [G: U.S.]

Freeman, Richard B. and Medoff, James L. The Impact of the Percentage Organized on Union and Nonunion Wages. *Rev. Econ. Statist.*, November 1981, *63*(4), pp. 561–72. [G: U.S.]

Freeman, Richard B. and Medoff, James L. The Impact of Collective Bargaining: Illusion or Reality? In *Stieber, J.; McKersie, R. B. and Mills, D. Q., eds.*, 1981, pp. 47–97.

Garbarino, Joseph W. Collective Bargaining under Adverse Conditions, or Hard Times in the Mill: Discussion. In *Dennis, B. D., ed.*, 1981, pp. 143–46.

Gärtner, Manfred. Legislative Profits and the Rate of Change of Money Wages: A Reply. *Public Choice*, 1981, *37*(3), pp. 589–93. [G: W. Germany]

Gati, Charles. Workers' Assertiveness, Western Dilemmas. In *Triska, J. F. and Gati, C., eds.*, 1981, pp. 283–94. [G: E. Europe]

Glynn, Sean and Shaw, Stephen. Wage Bargaining and Unemployment. In *Crick, B., ed.*, 1981, 1981, pp. 115–26. [G: U.K.]

Goodman, John F. B. United Kingdom. In *Blum, A. A., ed.*, 1981, pp. 593–620. [G: U.K.]

Goodrich, Chris. Legislative Profits and the Rate of Change of Money Wages: A Comment. *Public Choice*, 1981, 37(3), pp. 585–88.
[G: W. Germany]

Gordon, David M. The Best Defense is a Good Defense: Toward a Marxian Theory of Labor Union Structure and Behavior. In *Carter, M. J. and Leahy, W. H., eds.*, 1981, pp. 167–214.

Gordon, Michael E. and Long, Larry N. Demographic and Attitudinal Correlates of Union Joining. *Ind. Relat.*, Fall 1981, 20(3), pp. 306–11.
[G: U.S.]

Gray, Lois S. Unions Implementing Managerial Techniques. *Mon. Lab. Rev.*, June 1981, 104(6), pp. 3–13.
[G: U.S.]

Greer, Charles R. Contributed Papers: Labor Markets and Other IR Topics: Discussion. In *Dennis, B. D., ed.*, 1981, pp. 334–37.

Gruchy, Allan G. Organized Labor and Institutional Economics. *J. Econ. Issues*, June 1981, 15(2), pp. 311–24.
[G: U.S.]

Harrison, Royden. The Webbs as Historians of Trade Unionism. In *Samuel, R., ed.*, 1981, pp. 322–23.
[G: U.K.]

Harwood, Edwin. Unions, Pensions, and Financial Responsibility: The British Experience: Comment. *J. Lab. Res.*, Fall 1981, 2(2), pp. 299–305.
[G: U.K.]

Heldman, Dan C. Unions, Pensions, and Financial Responsibility: The British Experience: Comment. *J. Lab. Res.*, Fall 1981, 2(2), pp. 306–08.
[G: U.K.]

Hendricks, Wallace E. Unionism, Oligopoly and Rigid Wages. *Rev. Econ. Statist.*, May 1981, 63(2), pp. 198–205.
[G: U.S.]

Henley, John S. and Chen, Peter K. N. A Note on the Appearance, Disappearance and Re-Appearance of Dual Functioning Trade Unions in the People's Republic of China: Comment [Dual Functioning Trade Unions in the U.S.S.R.]. *Brit. J. Ind. Relat.*, March 1981, 19(1), pp. 87–93.
[G: China]

Héthy, L. Trade Unions, Shop Stewards and Participation in Hungary. *Int. Lab. Rev.*, July–August 1981, 120(4), pp. 491–503. [G: Hungary]

Hicks, Alexander; Friedland, Roger and Johnson, Edwin. Class Power and State Policy. In *Martin, G. T., Jr., and Zald, M. N., eds.*, 1981, 1978, pp. 131–46.
[G: U.S.]

Hillery, Brian J. Ireland. In *Blum, A. A., ed.*, 1981, pp. 283–301. [G: Ireland]

Hodsdon, Dennis F. The Federation of Free Farmers of the Philippines. *Int. Lab. Rev.*, January–February 1981, 120(1), pp. 97–113.
[G: Philippines]

Hough, J. R. Trade Unions in the Developed Economies: France. In *Smith, E. O., ed.*, 1981, pp. 43–72. [G: France]

Işikli, Alpaslan. Planli Dönemde Sendikal Örgütlenme. (Organization of Labour in the Planned Period. With English summary.) *METU*, Special Issue, 1981, pp. 349–67. [G: Turkey]

Iwuji, Eleazar C. Nigeria. In *Blum, A. A., ed.*, 1981, pp. 417–42. [G: Nigeria]

Johnson, Gloria T. and Komer, Odessa. Education for Affirmative Action: Two Union Approaches.

In *Wertheimer, B. M., ed.*, 1981, pp. 204–16.
[G: U.S.]

Johnson, Paul. Unions, Pensions, and Financial Responsibility: The British Experience. *J. Lab. Res.*, Fall 1981, 2(2), pp. 289–98. [G: U.K.]

Johnston, T. L. Trade Unions in the Developed Economies: Sweden. In *Smith, E. O., ed.*, 1981, pp. 97–122. [G: Sweden]

Kau, James B. and Rubin, Paul H. The Impact of Labor Unions on the Passage of Economic Legislation. *J. Lab. Res.*, Spring 1981, 2(1), pp. 133–45. [G: U.S.]

Kaufman, Stuart Bruce. Birth of a Federation: Mr. Gompers Endeavors 'Not to Build a Bubble.' *Mon. Lab. Rev.*, November 1981, 104(11), pp. 23–36. [G: U.S.]

Keeler, John T. S. Corporatism and Official Union Hegemony: The Case of French Agricultural Syndicalism. In *Berger, S., ed.*, 1981, pp. 185–208. [G: France]

Kirkland, Lane. Productivity: A Labor View. In *Hogan, J. D. and Craig, A. M., eds., Vol. 2*, 1981, pp. 1211–19. [G: U.S.]

Koç, Yildirim. Planli Dönemde Işçh Hareketini Belirleyen Etkenler. (Factors Determining the Labor Movement in Turkey in the Planned Period. With English summary.) *METU*, Special Issue, 1981, pp. 287–348. [G: Turkey]

Kochan, Thomas A. and Helfman, David E. The Effects of Collective Bargaining on Economic and Behavioral Job Outcomes. In *Ehrenberg, R. G., ed.*, 1981, pp. 321–65. [G: U.S.]

Kolankiewicz, George. Poland, 1980: The Working Class under 'Anomic Socialism.' In *Triska, J. F. and Gati, C., eds.*, 1981, pp. 136–56.
[G: Poland]

Kornbluh, Joyce L. and Kornbluh, Hy. Labor Education for Women Workers: Conferences: The One-Day Model. In *Wertheimer, B. M., ed.*, 1981, pp. 54–61. [G: U.S.]

Koskimies, Jaakko. Finland. In *Blum, A. A., ed.*, 1981, pp. 144–67. [G: Finland]

Koziara, Karen S. and Pierson, David A. Barriers to Women Becoming Union Leaders. In *Dennis, B. D., ed.*, 1981, pp. 48–54. [G: U.S.]

Krishnan, V. N. India. In *Blum, A. A., ed.*, 1981, pp. 239–54. [G: India]

Kujawa, Duane. U.S. Manufacturing Investment in the Developing Countries: American Labour's Concerns and the Enterprise Environment in the Decade Ahead. *Brit. J. Ind. Relat.*, March 1981, 19(1), pp. 38–48. [G: U.S.]

Lange, Peter. Unions, Parties, the State, and Liberal Corporatism. In *Denitch, B., ed.*, 1981, pp. 82–103. [G: Italy]

Lansbury, Russell D. and Prideaux, Geoffrey J. Industrial Democracy: Toward an Analytical Framework. *J. Econ. Issues*, June 1981, 15(2), pp. 325–38.

Latta, Geoffrey W. Union Organization among Engineers: A Current Assessment. *Ind. Lab. Relat. Rev.*, October 1981, 35(1), pp. 29–42. [G: U.S.]

Leigh, Duane E. Do Union Members Receive Compensating Wage Differentials? Note. *Amer. Econ. Rev.*, December 1981, 71(5), pp. 1049–55.
[G: U.S.]

Leigh, Duane E. The Effect of Unionism on Workers' Valuation of Future Pension Benefits. *Ind. Lab. Relat. Rev.*, July 1981, *34*(4), pp. 510–21. [G: U.S.]

Leigh, J. Paul. The Effects of Union Membership on Absence from Work Due to Illness. *J. Lab. Res.*, Fall 1981, *2*(2), pp. 329–36. [G: U.S.]

Levine, Solomon B. Japan. In *Blum, A. A., ed.*, 1981, pp. 323–50. [G: Japan]

Livernash, E. Robert and Argheyd, Kamal. Iran. In *Blum, A. A., ed.*, 1981, pp. 255–82. [G: Iran]

Loveman, Brian. Chile. In *Blum, A. A., ed.*, 1981, pp. 93–116. [G: Chile]

MacDonald, Glenn M. and Evans, John C. The Size and Structure of Union-Non-Union Wage Differentials in Canadian Industry. *Can. J. Econ.*, May 1981, *14*(2), pp. 216–31. [G: Canada]

Maloney, Michael T.; McCormick, Robert E. and Tollison, Robert D. Achieving Cartel Profits through Unionization. *Southern Econ. J.*, April 1981, *47*(4), pp. 1162–64.

Maxey, Charles and Mohrman, Susan Albers. Worker Attitudes toward Unions: A Study Integrating Industrial Relations and Organizational Behavior Perspectives. In *Dennis, B. D., ed.*, 1981, pp. 326–33. [G: U.S.]

Meidner, Rudolf. Collective Asset Formation through Wage-Earner Funds. *Int. Lab. Rev.*, May–June 1981, *120*(3), pp. 303–17. [G: Europe]

Mellow, Wesley S. Unionism and Wages: A Longitudinal Analysis. *Rev. Econ. Statist.*, February 1981, *63*(1), pp. 43–52. [G: U.S.]

Meyers, Frederic. France. In *Blum, A. A., ed.*, 1981, pp. 169–208. [G: France]

Mills, D. Quinn. Management Performance. In *Stieber, J.; McKersie, R. B. and Mills, D. Q., eds.*, 1981, pp. 99–128. [G: U.S.]

Minford, Patrick and Brech, Michael. The Wage Equation and Rational Expectations. In *Currie, D.; Nobay, R. and Peel, D., eds.*, 1981, pp. 434–59. [G: OECD; U.K.]

Mitchell, Daniel J. B. Collective Bargaining and the Economy. In *Stieber, J.; McKersie, R. B. and Mills, D. Q., eds.*, 1981, pp. 1–46. [G: U.S.]

Mitchell, Daniel J. B. Collective Bargaining and Wage Determination in the 1970s. In *Dennis, B. D., ed.*, 1981, pp. 135–42. [G: U.S.]

Myrdal, Hans-Göran. Collective Wage-Earner Funds in Sweden: A Road to Socialism and the End of Freedom of Association. *Int. Lab. Rev.*, May–June 1981, *120*(3), pp. 319–34. [G: Sweden]

Naschold, Frieder. Two Roads toward Innovation in Occupational Safety and Health in Western Countries. In *Altenstetter, C., ed.*, 1981, pp. 145–59. [G: U.S.; Sweden; W. Germany]

Nicholson, Nigel; Ursell, Gill and Lubbock, Jackie. Membership Participation in a White-Collar Union. *Ind. Relat.*, Spring 1981, *20*(2), pp. 162–78. [G: U.K.]

Nolan, P. I. Incomes Policies: A Trade Union Perspective. In *Hancock, K., ed.*, 1981, pp. 273–95. [G: Australia]

Ogle, George. South Korea. In *Blum, A. A., ed.*, 1981, pp. 499–514. [G: S. Korea]

Oswald, Andrew J. Threat and Morale Effects in the Theory of Wages. *Europ. Econ. Rev.*, June/July 1981, *16*(2/3), pp. 269–83.

Paul, Chris W., II and Rubin, Paul H. Union Membership and Campaign Contributions. *Atlantic Econ. J.*, September 1981, *9*(3), pp. 99–105. [G: U.S.]

Pegnetter, Richard. Majority Voting Requirements in Public–Employee Bargaining Unit Elections. In *Dennis, B. D., ed.*, 1981, pp. 234–40. [G: U.S.]

Perloff, Jeffrey M. The Duration of Unemployment in the Construction Industry. *J. Lab. Res.*, Spring 1981, *2*(1), pp. 111–31. [G: U.S.]

Pfeffer, Jeffrey and Ross, Jerry. Unionization and Female Wage and Status Attainment. *Ind. Relat.*, Spring 1981, *20*(2), pp. 179–85. [G: U.S.]

Pfeffer, Jeffrey and Ross, Jerry. Unionization and Income Inequality. *Ind. Relat.*, Fall 1981, *20*(3), pp. 271–85. [G: U.S.]

Phelps Brown, Henry. Labour Market Policy. In *[Cairncross, A.]*, 1981, pp. 68–96. [G: U.K.]

Ponak, Allen M. Unionized Professionals and the Scope of Bargaining: A Study of Nurses. *Ind. Lab. Relat. Rev.*, April 1981, *34*(3), pp. 396–407. [G: Canada]

Rabeau, Yves. Le comportement des salaires chez les travailleurs syndiqués de l'industrie de la construction au Canada. (Behaviour of Wages of the Unionized Workers of the Construction Industry in Canada. With English summary.) *L'Actual. Econ.*, October–December 1981, *57*(4), pp. 491–506. [G: Canada]

Rachlin, Marjorie B. Labor Education for Women Workers: Training Rank and File Leaders: A Case Study. In *Wertheimer, B. M., ed.*, 1981, pp. 62–70. [G: U.S.]

Ramondt, Joop. Netherlands. In *Blum, A. A., ed.*, 1981, pp. 394–416. [G: Netherlands]

Ramos, Elias. Philippines. In *Blum, A. A., ed.*, 1981, pp. 441–60. [G: Philippines]

Rawson, D. W. Changes in Union Membership in the 1970s and Beyond. *Australian Bull. Lab.*, December 1981, *8*(1), pp. 31–41. [G: Australia]

Reynolds, Morgan O. Whatever Happened to the Monopoly Theory of Labor Unions? *J. Lab. Res.*, Spring 1981, *2*(1), pp. 163–73.

Richman, Jonathan E. Facial Adjudication of Disciplinary Provisions in Union Constitutions. *Yale Law J.*, November 1981, *91*(1), pp. 144–67. [G: U.S.]

Risch, Bodo. Gewerkschaftseigene Arbeitslosenversicherung vor 1914. (Trade Union Unemployment Insurance before 1914. With English summary.) *Weltwirtsch. Arch.*, 1981, *117*(3), pp. 513–45. [G: Germany]

Rogin, Lawrence. Labor Education for Women Workers: A Summary Discussion. In *Wertheimer, B. M., ed.*, 1981, pp. 265–68.

Rozen, Frieda Shoenberg. Labor Education for Women Workers: Promoting and Recruiting: Reaching the Target Audience. In *Wertheimer, B. M., ed.*, 1981, pp. 32–41. [G: U.S.]

Ruben, George. Industrial Relations in 1980 Influenced by Inflation and Recession. *Mon. Lab.*

Rev., January 1981, *104*(1), pp. 15–20.
[G: U.S.]

Sabel, Charles F. The Internal Politics of Trade Unions. In *Berger, S., ed.*, 1981, pp. 209–44.

Saks, Daniel H. Wage Determination During Periods of High Inflation. In *Dennis, B. D., ed.*, 1981, pp. 128–34.
[G: U.S.]

Samper, Maria-Luz D. and Rosen, Stanley. Evaluating Programs for Working Adults. In *Wertheimer, B. M., ed.*, 1981, pp. 98–108.

Sandver, Marcus H. and Heneman, Herbert G., III. Union Growth through the Election Process. *Ind. Relat.*, Winter 1981, *20*(1), pp. 109–16.
[G: U.S.]

Schregle, Johannes. Comparative Industrial Relations: Pitfalls and Potential. *Int. Lab. Rev.*, January–February 1981, *120*(1), pp. 15–30.

Schrier, Katherine. Credit Programs for Working Women. In *Wertheimer, B. M., ed.*, 1981, pp. 71–82.
[G: U.S.]

Semel, Rochelle. Labor Education for Women Workers: The Short Course. In *Wertheimer, B. M., ed.*, 1981, pp. 42–53.
[G: U.S.]

Sheflin, Neil; Troy, Leo and Koeller, C. Timothy. Structural Stability in Models of American Trade Union Growth. *Quart. J. Econ.*, February 1981, *96*(1), pp. 77–88.
[G: U.S.]

Siebert, W. Stanley and Addison, John T. Are Strikes Accidential? *Econ. J.*, June 1981, *91*(362), pp. 389–404.

Smith, Eric Owen. Trade Unions in the Developed Economies: West Germany. In *Smith, E. O., ed.*, 1981, pp. 178–207.
[G: W. Germany]

Smith, Eric Owen. Trade Unions in the Developed Economies: The United Kingdom. In *Smith, E. O., ed.*, 1981, pp. 123–54.
[G: U.K.]

St. Antoine, Theodore J. U.S. Industrial Relations 1950–1980: The Role of Law. In *Stieber, J.; McKersie, R. B. and Mills, D. Q., eds.*, 1981, pp. 159–97.
[G: U.S.]

Stieber, Jack and Block, Richard N. U.S. Industrial Relations 1950–1980: Summary and Conclusions. In *Stieber, J.; McKersie, R. B. and Mills, D. Q., eds.*, 1981, pp. 343–61.
[G: U.S.]

Swanson, Dorothy. Annual Bibliography on American Labor History, 1980: Periodicals, Dissertations, and Research in Progress. *Labor Hist.*, Fall 1981, *22*(4), pp. 545–72.
[G: U.S.]

Taha, Abdel-Rahman E. Ali. Sudan. In *Blum, A. A., ed.*, 1981, pp. 539–46.
[G: Sudan]

Thompson, Mark. Canada. In *Blum, A. A., ed.*, 1981, pp. 71–91.
[G: Canada]

Thomson, Andrew W. J. Trade Unions in the Developed Economies: The United States of America. In *Smith, E. O., ed.*, 1981, pp. 155–77.
[G: U.S.]

Thomson, Andrew W. J. U.S. Industrial Relations 1950–1980: A View from Abroad. In *Stieber, J.; McKersie, R. B. and Mills, D. Q., eds.*, 1981, pp. 297–342.
[G: U.S.; W. Europe]

Valenta, Jiri. Czechoslovakia: A 'Prolétariat Embourgeoisé'? In *Triska, J. F. and Gati, C., eds.*, 1981, pp. 209–23.
[G: Czechoslovakia]

Veneziani, Bruno. Italy. In *Blum, A. A., ed.*, 1981, pp. 303–21.
[G: Italy]

Wallace, Phyllis A. and Driscoll, James W. Social Issues in Collective Bargaining. In *Stieber, J.;*

McKersie, R. B. and Mills, D. Q., eds., 1981, pp. 199–254.
[G: U.S.]

Weinstein, Robert I. Union–Nonunion Wage Differentials over the Business Cycle: A Bilateral Monopoly Model. *Atlantic Econ. J.*, September 1981, *9*(3), pp. 44–49.

Wertheimer, Barbara M. Labor Education for Women Workers: Residential Schools. In *Wertheimer, B. M., ed.*, 1981, pp. 83–97. [G: U.S.]

Wessels, Walter J. Economic Effects of Right to Work Laws. *J. Lab. Res.*, Spring 1981, *2*(1), pp. 55–75.
[G: U.S.]

Windmuller, John P. Concentration Trends in Union Structure: An International Comparison. *Ind. Lab. Relat. Rev.*, October 1981, *35*(1), pp. 43–57.
[G: W. Europe; U.S.]

Wright, Michael. Unionisation in Australia and Coverage of the Closed Shop. *Australian Bull. Lab.*, June 1981, *7*(3), pp. 122–38.
[G: Australia]

Zapata, Francisco. Mexico. In *Blum, A. A., ed.*, 1981, pp. 351–91.
[G: Mexico]

Zupanov, Josip and Adizes, Ichak. Yugoslavia. In *Blum, A. A., ed.*, 1981, pp. 647–72.
[G: Yugoslavia]

832 Collective Bargaining

8320 General

Alexander, Robert J. Brazil. In *Blum, A. A., ed.*, 1981, pp. 49–70.
[G: Brazil]

Auld, D. A. L., et al. The Effect of Settlement Stage on Negotiated Wage Settlements in Canada. *Ind. Lab. Relat. Rev.*, January 1981, *34*(2), pp. 234–44.
[G: Canada]

Bacharach, Samuel B. and Lawler, Edward J. Power and Tactics in Bargaining. *Ind. Lab. Relat. Rev.*, January 1981, *34*(2), pp. 219–33.

Bentley, Philip. The Industrial Relations Consequences of Incomes Policies. In *Hancock, K., ed.*, 1981, pp. 235–58.
[G: Australia]

Berthelot, Yves. The Interests of the Industrial West in Relations with Developing Countries. In *Saunders, C. T., ed. (I)*, 1981, pp. 19–32.
[G: OECD; LDCs]

Bloom, David E. Is Arbitration Really Compatible with Bargaining? *Ind. Relat.*, Fall 1981, *20*(3), pp. 233–44.

Brett, Jeanne M.; Goldberg, Stephen B. and Ury, William. Mediation and Organizational Development: Models for Conflict Management. In *Dennis, B. D., ed.*, 1981, pp. 195–202.

Brown, Gary and Krislov, Joseph. The Determinants of Mediation Activity: A Two-Country Comparison. *J. Lab. Res.*, Spring 1981, *2*(1), pp. 157–62.
[G: U.S.; U.K.]

Brown, William A. British Collective Bargaining: A Decade of Reformation. *Mon. Lab. Rev.*, July 1981, *104*(7), pp. 40–43.
[G: U.K.]

Chapman, P. G. The Johnston Wage Bargaining Model and Trade Union Objectives. *Manchester Sch. Econ. Soc. Stud.*, December 1981, *49*(4), pp. 310–18.

Crowley, R. W. Income Control Policies and Industrial Relations in Canada. *Can. Public Policy*, Autumn 1981, *7*(4), pp. 534–49.
[G: Canada]

DeLorme, Charles D., Jr.; Hill, R. Carter and

Wood, Norman J. The Determinants of Voting by the National Labor Relations Board on Unfair Labor Practice Cases: 1955–1975. *Public Choice,* 1981, *37*(2), pp. 207–18. [G: U.S.]

DeNisi, Angelo S. and Dworkin, James B. Final-Offer Arbitration and the Naive Negotiator. *Ind. Lab. Relat. Rev.,* October 1981, *35*(1), pp. 78–87.

Farber, Henry S. Splitting-the-Difference in Interest Arbitration. *Ind. Lab. Relat. Rev.,* October 1981, *35*(1), pp. 70–77.

Fels, Allan and Hoa, Tran Van. Causal Relationships in Australian Wage Inflation and Minimum Award Rates. *Econ. Rec.,* March 1981, *57*(156), pp. 23–34. [G: Australia]

Feuille, Peter and Lewin, David. Equal Employment Opportunity Bargaining. *Ind. Relat.,* Fall 1981, *20*(3), pp. 322–34. [G: U.S.]

Flora, P. Solution or Source of Crises? The Welfare State in Historical Perspective. In *Mommsen, W. J., ed.,* 1981, pp. 343–89. [G: Europe]

Fogarty, M. P.; Egan, D. and Ryan, W. J. L. Pay Policy for the 1980s. *Irish Banking Rev.,* September 1981, pp. 2–14. [G: Ireland]

Freeman, Richard B. and Medoff, James L. The Impact of Collective Bargaining: Illusion or Reality? In *Stieber, J.; McKersie, R. B. and Mills, D. Q., eds.,* 1981, pp. 47–97. [G: U.S.]

Fulmer, William E. Decertification: Is the Current Trend a Threat to Collective Bargaining? *Calif. Manage. Rev.,* Fall 1981, *24*(1), pp. 14–22. [G: U.S.]

Gärtner, Manfred. A Politicoeconomic Model of Wage Inflation. *De Economist,* 1981, *129*(2), pp. 183–205. [G: W. Germany]

Gennard, John. The Effects of Strike Activity on Households. *Brit. J. Ind. Relat.,* November 1981, *19*(3), pp. 327–44. [G: U.K.]

Glynn, Sean and Shaw, Stephen. Wage Bargaining and Unemployment. In *Crick, B., ed.,* 1981, 1981, pp. 115–26. [G: U.K.]

Goodman, John F. B. United Kingdom. In *Blum, A. A., ed.,* 1981, pp. 593–620. [G: U.K.]

Hatano, Daryl G. Employee Rights and Corporate Restrictions: A Balancing of Liberties. *Calif. Manage. Rev.,* Winter 1981, *24*(2), pp. 5–13. [G: U.S.]

Héthy, L. Trade Unions, Shop Stewards and Participation in Hungary. *Int. Lab. Rev.,* July–August 1981, *120*(4), pp. 491–503. [G: Hungary]

Hillery, Brian J. Ireland. In *Blum, A. A., ed.,* 1981, pp. 283–301. [G: Ireland]

Horvitz, Wayne. Confrontation Politics and Fundamental Issues in the Collective Bargaining Process. In *Hoffman, W. M. and Wyly, T. J., eds.,* 1981, pp. 239–43. [G: U.S.]

Hough, J. R. Trade Unions in the Developed Economies: France. In *Smith, E. O., ed.,* 1981, pp. 43–72. [G: France]

Isaac, J. E. Equity and Wage Determination. *Australian Bull. Lab.,* September 1981, *7*(4), pp. 205–18. [G: Australia]

Kolb, Deborah M. Roles Mediators Play: State and Federal Practice. *Ind. Relat.,* Winter 1981, *20*(1), pp. 1–17. [G: U.S.]

Koskimies, Jaakko. Finland. In *Blum, A. A., ed.,* 1981, pp. 144–67. [G: Finland]

Krishnan, V. N. India. In *Blum, A. A., ed.,* 1981, pp. 239–54. [G: India]

Kumar, Pradeep. Wages, Productivity and Labour Costs: Summary Outline. In *Wood, W. D. and Kumar, P., eds.,* 1981, pp. 385–461. [G: Canada]

Levine, Solomon B. Japan. In *Blum, A. A., ed.,* 1981, pp. 323–50. [G: Japan]

Loveman, Brian. Chile. In *Blum, A. A., ed.,* 1981, pp. 93–116. [G: Chile]

McDonald, Ian M. and Solow, Robert M. Wage Bargaining and Employment. *Amer. Econ. Rev.,* December 1981, *71*(5), pp. 896–908.

McMurray, David. Labour Legislation and Policy: Summary Outline. In *Wood, W. D. and Kumar, P., eds.,* 1981, pp. 95–191. [G: Canada]

Meyers, Frederic. France. In *Blum, A. A., ed.,* 1981, pp. 169–208. [G: France]

Mitchell, Daniel J. B. Collective Bargaining and Wage Determination in the 1970s. In *Dennis, B. D., ed.,* 1981, pp. 135–42. [G: U.S.]

Mounts, Gregory J. Labor and the Supreme Court: Significant Decisions of 1979–80. *Mon. Lab. Rev.,* April 1981, *104*(4), pp. 13–22. [G: U.S.]

Munck, Ronaldo. The Labor Movement and the Crisis of the Dictatorship in Brazil. In *Bruneau, T. C. and Faucher, P., eds.,* 1981, pp. 219–38. [G: Brazil]

Nelson, Nels E. and Curry, Earl M., Jr. Arbitrator Characteristics and Arbitral Decisions. *Ind. Relat.,* Fall 1981, *20*(3), pp. 312–17.

Perry, James L. and Angle, Harold L. Bargaining Unit Structure and Organizational Outcomes. *Ind. Relat.,* Winter 1981, *20*(1), pp. 47–59. [G: U.S.]

Ponak, Allen M. Unionized Professionals and the Scope of Bargaining: A Study of Nurses. *Ind. Lab. Relat. Rev.,* April 1981, *34*(3), pp. 396–407. [G: Canada]

Rimlinger, G. V. Comments on Professor Peter Flora's Analytical Perspective of the Welfare State [Solution or Source of Crises? The Welfare State in Historical Perspective]. In *Mommsen, W. J., ed.,* 1981, pp. 390–94. [G: Europe]

Roomkin, Myron. A Quantitative Study of Unfair Labor Practice Cases. *Ind. Lab. Relat. Rev.,* January 1981, *34*(2), pp. 245–56. [G: U.S.]

Siebert, W. Stanley and Addison, John T. Are Strikes Accidental? *Econ. J.,* June 1981, *91*(362), pp. 389–404.

Smith, David F. and Turkington, Don J. Testing a Behavioural Theory of Bargaining: An International Comparative Study. *Brit. J. Ind. Relat.,* November 1981, *19*(3), pp. 361–69.

Smith, Eric Owen. Trade Unions in the Developed Economies: The United Kingdom. In *Smith, E. O., ed.,* 1981, pp. 123–54. [G: U.K.]

Smith, Eric Owen. Trade Unions in the Developed Economies: West Germany. In *Smith, E. O., ed.,* 1981, pp. 178–207. [G: W. Germany]

St. Antoine, Theodore J. U.S. Industrial Relations 1950–1980: The Role of Law. In *Stieber, J.; McKersie, R. B. and Mills, D. Q., eds.,* 1981, pp. 159–97. [G: U.S.]

Stone, Katherine Van Wezel. The Post-War Paradigm in American Labor Law. *Yale Law J.,* June

1981, *90*(7), pp. 1509–80.   [G: U.S.]

Thompson, Mark. Canada. In *Blum, A. A., ed.,* 1981, pp. 71–91.   [G: Canada]

Wallace, Phyllis A. and Driscoll, James W. Social Issues in Collective Bargaining. In *Stieber, J.; McKersie, R. B. and Mills, D. Q., eds.,* 1981, pp. 199–254.   [G: U.S.]

Whitehead, Donald and Bonnell, Sheila. What Ails the Lucky Country: The Debate about Diagnosis. In *Hancock, K., ed.,* 1981, pp. 89–140.
          [G: Australia]

Wilder, Ronald P. and Singh, Davinder. Determinants of Changes in the Wage Hierarchy: A Note. *Brit. J. Ind. Relat.,* November 1981, *19*(3), pp. 376–79.   [G: U.K.]

Yerbury, D. The Government, the Arbitration Commission and Wages Policy: The Role of the 'Supporting Mechanisms' under the Whitlam Government. In *Hancock, K., ed.,* 1981, pp. 195–234.   [G: Australia]

Zupanov, Josip and Adizes, Ichak. Yugoslavia. In *Blum, A. A., ed.,* 1981, pp. 647–72.
          [G: Yugoslavia]

8321 Collective Bargaining in the Private Sector

Andrews, Mary Anne and Schlein, David. Bargaining Calendar Will be Heavy in 1982. *Mon. Lab. Rev.,* December 1981, *104*(12), pp. 21–31.
          [G: U.S.]

Bellante, Don. Union Divergent Investing of Pensions: A Power, Non-Employee Relations Issue: Comment. *J. Lab. Res.,* Fall 1981, *2*(2), pp. 209–13.   [G: U.S.]

Bennett, James T. and Johnson, Manuel H. Union Use of Employee Pension Funds: Introduction and Overview. *J. Lab. Res.,* Fall 1981, *2*(2), pp. 181–90.   [G: U.S.]

Blejer, Mario I. Strike Activity and Wage Determination under Rapid Inflation: The Chilean Case. *Ind. Lab. Relat. Rev.,* April 1981, *34*(3), pp. 356–64.   [G: Chile]

Bradley, Keith. International Perspectives of Industrial Relations: Review Article. *Brit. J. Ind. Relat.,* March 1981, *19*(1), pp. 106–11.

Chelius, James R. and Dworkin, James B. Arbitration and Salary Determination in Baseball. In *Dennis, B. D., ed.,* 1981, pp. 105–12. [G: U.S.]

Churnside, R. J. and Creigh, S. W. Strike Activity and Plant Size: A Note. *J. Roy. Statist. Soc.,* Part 1, 1981, *144*, pp. 104–11.   [G: U.K.]

Clarke, Oliver. The Development of Industrial Relations in European Market Economies. In *Dennis, B. D., ed.,* 1981, pp. 167–73.   [G: EEC]

Coates, Mary Lou and Wood, W. Donald. Collective Bargaining: Summary Outline. In *Wood, W. D. and Kumar, P., eds.,* 1981, pp. 275–384.
          [G: Canada; U.S.]

Codrington, Caroline and Henley, John S. The Industrial Relations of Injury and Death: Safety Representatives in the Construction Industry. *Brit. J. Ind. Relat.,* November 1981, *19*(3), pp. 297–315.   [G: U.K.]

Conrad, Wolfgang. Federal Republic of Germany. In *Blum, A. A., ed.,* 1981, pp. 209–38.
          [G: W. Germany]

Corcione, Frank P. and Thornton, Robert J. The Economic Determinants of Strike Activity: An Industry Approach. *Rev. Bus. Econ. Res.,* Fall 1981, *17*(1), pp. 15–26.   [G: U.S.]

Craypo, Charles. The Decline of Union Bargaining Power. In *Carter, M. J. and Leahy, W. H., eds.,* 1981, pp. 107–66.   [G: U.S]

Cupper, Les and Hearn, June M. Trade Unions in the Developed Economies: Australia. In *Smith, E. O., ed.,* 1981, pp. 13–42.   [G: Australia]

Daunton, Martin James. Down the Pit: Work in the Great Northern and South Wales Coalfields, 1870–1914. *Econ. Hist. Rev., 2nd Ser.,* November 1981, *34*(4), pp. 578–97.   [G: U.K.]

DeBrock, Lawrence M. and Roth, Alvin E. Strike Two: Labor-Management Negotiations in Major League Baseball. *Bell J. Econ. (See Rand J. Econ. after 4/85),* Autumn 1981, *12*(2), pp. 413–25.
          [G: U.S.]

Dereli, Toker. Turkey. In *Blum, A. A., ed.,* 1981, pp. 547–92.   [G: Turkey]

Desolre, Guy G. Belgium. In *Blum, A. A., ed.,* 1981, pp. 37–48.   [G: Belgium]

Dunn, Stephen. The Growth of the Post-Entry Closed Shop in Britain since the 1960s: Some Theoretical Considerations. *Brit. J. Ind. Relat.,* November 1981, *19*(3), pp. 275–96.   [G: U.K.]

Edwards, P. K. The Strike-Proneness of British Manufacturing Establishments. *Brit. J. Ind. Relat.,* July 1981, *19*(2), pp. 135–48.   [G: U.K.]

Estenson, David. Relative Price Variability and Indexed Labor Agreements. *Ind. Relat.,* Winter 1981, *20*(1), pp. 71–84.   [G: U.S.]

Feuille, Peter; Hendricks, Wallace E. and Kahn, Lawrence M. Wage and Nonwage Outcomes in Collective Bargaining: Determinants and Tradeoffs. *J. Lab. Res.,* Spring 1981, *2*(1), pp. 39–53.
          [G: U.S.]

Feuille, Peter and Wheeler, Hoyt N. Will the Real Industrial Conflict Please Stand Up? In *Stieber, J.; McKersie, R. B. and Mills, D. Q., eds.,* 1981, pp. 255–95.   [G: U.S.]

Fong, Pang Eng. Singapore. In *Blum, A. A., ed.,* 1981, pp. 481–97.   [G: Singapore]

Garbarino, Joseph W. Collective Bargaining under Adverse Conditions, or Hard Times in the Mill: Discussion. In *Dennis, B. D., ed.,* 1981, pp. 143–46.

Greer, Charles R. and Shearer, John C. Foreign Ownership Effects on NLRB Representation Elections. *J. Int. Bus. Stud.,* Winter 1981, *12*(3), pp. 9–23.   [G: U.S.]

Gregory, Mary B. and Thomson, Andrew W. J. The Coverage Mark-up, Bargaining Structure and Earnings in Britain, 1973 and 1978. *Brit. J. Ind. Relat.,* March 1981, *19*(1), pp. 26–37. [G: U.K.]

Hudson, Robert. The Effects of Dock Strikes on UK International Trade. *Appl. Econ.,* March 1981, *13*(1), pp. 67–77.   [G: U.K.]

Iwuji, Eleazar C. Nigeria. In *Blum, A. A., ed.,* 1981, pp. 417–42.   [G: Nigeria]

Kassalow, Everett M. Collective Bargaining: In the Grip of Structural Change. In *Dennis, B. D., ed.,* 1981, pp. 118–27.   [G: U.S.]

Kaufman, Bruce E. Bargaining Theory, Inflation, and Cyclical Strike Activity in Manufacturing.

Ind. Lab. Relat. Rev., April 1981, *34*(3), pp. 333–55. **[G: U.S.]**

Kochan, Thomas A. and Helfman, David E. The Effects of Collective Bargaining on Economic and Behavioral Job Outcomes. In *Ehrenberg, R. G., ed.*, 1981, pp. 321–65. **[G: U.S.]**

Korpi, Walter. Unofficial Strikes in Sweden. *Brit. J. Ind. Relat.*, March 1981, *19*(1), pp. 66–86. **[G: Sweden; U.K.]**

Lawler, John. Reply to Professor Mitchell [Wage Spillover: The Impact of Landrum-Griffin]. *Ind. Relat.*, Fall 1981, *20*(3), pp. 347–49. **[G: U.S.]**

Lawler, John. Wage Spillover: The Impact of Landrum–Griffin. *Ind. Relat.*, Winter 1981, *20*(1), pp. 85–97. **[G: U.S.]**

LeRoy, Douglas R. Scheduled Wage Increases and Cost-of-Living Provisions in 1981. *Mon. Lab. Rev.*, January 1981, *104*(1), pp. 9–14. **[G: U.S.]**

Levine, Solomon B. Labor Conflict. In *Richardson, B. M. and Ueda, T., eds.*, 1981, pp. 42–52. **[G: Japan]**

Levine, Solomon B. Labor Regulations. In *Richardson, B. M. and Ueda, T., eds.*, 1981, pp. 52–61. **[G: Japan]**

Lewis, Paul. An Analysis of Why Legislation Has Failed to Provide Employment Protection for Unfairly Dismissed Employees. *Brit. J. Ind. Relat.*, November 1981, *19*(3), pp. 316–26. **[G: U.K.]**

Livernash, E. Robert and Argheyd, Kamal. Iran. In *Blum, A. A., ed.*, 1981, pp. 255–82. **[G: Iran]**

Lund, Reinhard. Scandinavia. In *Blum, A. A., ed.*, 1981, pp. 461–79. **[G: Scandinavia]**

Miscimarra, Philip A. The Entertainment Industry: Inroads in Multinational Collective Bargaining. *Brit. J. Ind. Relat.*, March 1981, *19*(1), pp. 49–65.

Mitchell, Daniel J. B. A Note on Strike Propensities and Wage Developments. *Ind. Relat.*, Winter 1981, *20*(1), pp. 123–27. **[G: U.S.]**

Mitchell, Daniel J. B. Collective Bargaining and the Economy. In *Stieber, J.; McKersie, R. B. and Mills, D. Q., eds.*, 1981, pp. 1–46. **[G: U.S.]**

Mitchell, Daniel J. B. Wage Spillover: The Impact of Landrum-Griffin: Comment. *Ind. Relat.*, Fall 1981, *20*(3), pp. 342–46. **[G: U.S.]**

Naples, Michele I. Industrial Conflict and Its Implications for Productivity Growth. *Amer. Econ. Rev.*, May 1981, *71*(2), pp. 36–41. **[G: U.S.]**

Northrup, James P. and Northrup, Herbert R. Union Divergent Investing of Pensions: A Power, Non-Employee Relations Issue. *J. Lab. Res.*, Fall 1981, *2*(2), pp. 191–208. **[G: U.S.]**

Ogle, George. South Korea. In *Blum, A. A., ed.*, 1981, pp. 499–514. **[G: S. Korea]**

Parsons, Drew. Labor Management Relations and Conflict Resolutions. *Econ. Forum*, Summer 1981, *12*(1), pp. 104–08. **[G: U.S.]**

Perloff, Jeffrey M. Labor Market Adjustments in the Unionized Contract Construction Industry. *J. Lab. Res.*, Fall 1981, *2*(2), pp. 337–53. **[G: U.S.]**

Phelps Brown, Henry. The Economic Consequences of Collective Bargaining. In *Phelps Brown, H. and Hopkins, S. V.*, 1981, *1966*, pp. 191–214. **[G: OECD]**

Prachowny, Martin F. J. Wage Indexation: Social Benefits and Private Incentives. *J. Lab. Res.*, Spring 1981, *2*(1), pp. 15–24. **[G: Canada; U.S.]**

Raisian, John. Union Divergent Investing of Pensions: A Power, Non-Employee Relations Issue: Comment. *J. Lab. Res.*, Fall 1981, *2*(2), pp. 214–18. **[G: U.S.]**

Ramos, Elias. Philippines. In *Blum, A. A., ed.*, 1981, pp. 441–60. **[G: Philippines]**

Reich, Michael. Changes in the Distribution of Benefits from Racism in the 1960s. *J. Human Res.*, Spring 1981, *16*(2), pp. 314–21. **[G: U.S.]**

Ruben, George. Industrial Relations in 1980 Influenced by Inflation and Recession. *Mon. Lab. Rev.*, January 1981, *104*(1), pp. 15–20. **[G: U.S.]**

Stieber, Jack and Block, Richard N. U.S. Industrial Relations 1950–1980: Summary and Conclusions. In *Stieber, J.; McKersie, R. B. and Mills, D. Q., eds.*, 1981, pp. 343–61. **[G: U.S.]**

Taha, Abdel-Rahman E. Ali. Sudan. In *Blum, A. A., ed.*, 1981, pp. 539–46. **[G: Sudan]**

Thomson, Andrew W. J. U.S. Industrial Relations 1950–1980: A View from Abroad. In *Stieber, J.; McKersie, R. B. and Mills, D. Q., eds.*, 1981, pp. 297–342. **[G: U.S.; W. Europe]**

Torres, Ida. Grievance Handling for Women Stewards. In *Wertheimer, B. M., ed.*, 1981, pp. 182–93. **[G: U.S.]**

Tyrväinen, Timo. Työtaistelujen takoudellisesta taustasta Suomessa. (The Economic Background of Strike Behaviour in Finland. With English summary.) *Kansant. Aikak.*, 1981, *77*(2), pp. 192–203. **[G: Finland]**

Vartia, Pentti. Wage and Price Changes in Indexed and Non-Indexed Wage Agreements. *Ekon. Samfundets Tidskr.*, 1981, *34*(3), pp. 223–48.

Veneziani, Bruno. Italy. In *Blum, A. A., ed.*, 1981, pp. 303–21. **[G: Italy]**

Wessels, Walter J. Economic Effects of Right to Work Laws. *J. Lab. Res.*, Spring 1981, *2*(1), pp. 55–75. **[G: U.S.]**

Willman, Paul. The Growth of Combined Committees: A Reconsideration. *Brit. J. Ind. Relat.*, March 1981, *19*(1), pp. 1–13. **[G: U.K.]**

Wolters, Roger S. Union–Management Ideological Frames of Reference in Bargaining. In *Dennis, B. D., ed.*, 1981, pp. 211–18. **[G: U.S.]**

8322 Collective Bargaining in the Public Sector

Anderson, John C. The Impact of Arbitration: A Methodological Assessment. *Ind. Relat.*, Spring 1981, *20*(2), pp. 129–48. **[G: U.S.]**

Baird, Charles W. Unionism and the Public Sector. *Managerial Dec. Econ.*, June 1981, *2*(2), pp. 82–90. **[G: U.S.]**

Bartel, Ann P. and Lewin, David. Wages and Unionism in the Public Sector: The Case of Police. *Rev. Econ. Statist.*, February 1981, *63*(1), pp. 53–59. **[G: U.S.]**

Bellante, Don and Long, James E. The Political Economy of the Rent-Seeking Society: The Case of Public Employees and Their Unions. *J. Lab. Res.*, Spring 1981, *2*(1), pp. 1–14. **[G: U.S.]**

Bloom, David E. Collective Bargaining, Compulsory

Arbitration, and Salary Settlements in the Public Sector: The Case of New Jersey's Municipal Police Officers. *J. Lab. Res.*, Fall 1981, 2(2), pp. 369–84. [G: U.S.]

Bornstein, Tim L. Taxpayer and Other Third-Party Intervention in Local Government Collective Bargaining. **In** *Dennis, B. D., ed.*, 1981, pp. 278–83. [G: U.S.]

Butler, Richard J. and Ehrenberg, Ronald G. Estimating the Narcotic Effect of Public Sector Impasse Procedures. *Ind. Lab. Relat. Rev.*, October 1981, 35(1), pp. 3–20. [G: U.S.]

Christensen, Sandra. Reply [Pay Boards versus Collective Bargaining in the Public Sector]. *Can. Public Policy*, Summer 1981, 7(3), pp. 469–71. [G: Canada]

Coates, Mary Lou and Wood, W. Donald. Collective Bargaining: Summary Outline. **In** *Wood, W. D. and Kumar, P., eds.*, 1981, pp. 275–384. [G: Canada; U.S.]

Connor, Walter D. Workers and Power. **In** *Triska, J. F. and Gati, C., eds.*, 1981, pp. 157–72. [G: E. Europe]

Crawford, Vincent P. Arbitration and Conflict Resolution in Labor–Management Bargaining. *Amer. Econ. Rev.*, May 1981, 71(2), pp. 205–10. [G: U.S.]

Cunningham, W. B. Pay Boards versus Collective Bargaining in the Public Sector: A Dissent. *Can. Public Policy*, Summer 1981, 7(3), pp. 464–68. [G: Canada]

Dahl, Roger E. The Climate for Local Government Collective Bargaining in the 1980s: Discussion. **In** *Dennis, B. D., ed.*, 1981, pp. 296–98.

Eiger, Norman. The Expanding Scope of Public Bargaining in Sweden. *Ind. Relat.*, Fall 1981, 20(3), pp. 335–41. [G: Sweden]

Fallick, J. L. and Elliott, Robert F. Incomes Policy and the Public Sector. **In** *Fallick, J. L. and Elliott, R. F., eds.*, 1981, pp. 100–27. [G: U.K.]

Farber, Henry S. Does Final-offer Arbitration Encourage Bargaining? **In** *Dennis, B. D., ed.*, 1981, pp. 219–26.

Feuille, Peter. Contributed Papers: Public-sector Bargaining: Discussion. **In** *Dennis, B. D., ed.*, 1981, pp. 252–56.

Flynn, Ralph J. The Climate for Local Government Collective Bargaining in the 1980s: Discussion. **In** *Dennis, B. D., ed.*, 1981, pp. 299–303.

Haluška, Ivan. Workers' Participation in the Management of the Economy. *Czech. Econ. Digest.*, May 1981, (3), pp. 39–53. [G: Czechoslovakia]

Hanna, Chris. The Climate for Local Government Collective Bargaining in the 1980s: Discussion. **In** *Dennis, B. D., ed.*, 1981, pp. 304–06.

Hildebrand, George H. The Prevailing Wage Concept in the Public Sector: Discussion. **In** *Dennis, B. D., ed.*, 1981, pp. 102–04. [G: U.S.]

Jackson, K. R. and Yerbury, D. Introducing Technological Change: A Case Study. *Australian J. Manage.*, December 1981, 6(2), pp. 59–79. [G: Australia]

Katz, Harry C. and Lewin, David. Efficiency and Equity Considerations in State and Local Government Wage Determination. **In** *Dennis, B. D., ed.*, 1981, pp. 90–98. [G: U.S.]

Kochan, Thomas A. and Baderschneider, Jean. Estimating the Narcotic Effect: Choosing Techniques that Fit the Problem. *Ind. Lab. Relat. Rev.*, October 1981, 35(1), pp. 21–28. [G: U.S.]

Kolankiewicz, George. Poland, 1980: The Working Class under 'Anomic Socialism.' **In** *Triska, J. F. and Gati, C., eds.*, 1981, pp. 136–56. [G: Poland]

Lewin, David and McCormick, Mary. Coalition Bargaining in Municipal Government: The New York City Experience. *Ind. Lab. Relat. Rev.*, January 1981, 34(2), pp. 175–90. [G: U.S.]

McCollum, James K. Local Government Initiated Collective Bargaining: The Northern Virginia Case. **In** *Dennis, B. D., ed.*, 1981, pp. 227–33. [G: U.S.]

Montias, J. M. Observations on Strikes, Riots and Other Disturbances. **In** *Triska, J. F. and Gati, C., eds.*, 1981, pp. 173–86.

Nelson, William B.; Stone, Gerald W., Jr. and Swint, J. Michael. An Economic Analysis of Public Sector Collective Bargaining and Strike Activity. *J. Lab. Res.*, Spring 1981, 2(1), pp. 77–98. [G: U.S.]

Overton, Craig E. The Climate for Collective Bargaining in General Purpose Local Government in the 1980s. **In** *Dennis, B. D., ed.*, 1981, pp. 290–95.

Pegnetter, Richard. Majority Voting Requirements in Public–Employee Bargaining Unit Elections. **In** *Dennis, B. D., ed.*, 1981, pp. 234–40. [G: U.S.]

Peterson, Andrew A. Deterring Strikes by Public Employees: New York's Two-for-One Salary Penalty and the 1979 Prison Guard Strike. *Ind. Lab. Relat. Rev.*, July 1981, 34(4), pp. 545–62. [G: U.S.]

Rodgers, Robert C. A Replication of the Burton–Krider Model of Public–Employee Strike Activity. **In** *Dennis, B. D., ed.*, 1981, pp. 241–51. [G: U.S.]

Sarthory, Joseph A. The Climate for Collective Bargaining in Public Education in the 1980s. **In** *Dennis, B. D., ed.*, 1981, pp. 284–89. [G: U.S.]

Thornton, Robert J. Collective Bargaining, Wages, and Local Government Finance. **In** *Aronson, J. R. and Schwartz, E., eds.*, 1981, pp. 346–66. [G: U.S.]

Zimmer, Lynn and Jacobs, James B. Challenging the Taylor Law: Prison Guards on Strike. *Ind. Lab. Relat. Rev.*, July 1981, 34(4), pp. 531–44. [G: U.S.]

833 Labor–Management Relations

8330 General

Alexander, Kenneth O. Scientists, Engineers and the Organization of Work. *Amer. J. Econ. Soc.*, January 1981, 40(1), pp. 51–66.

Alexander, Robert J. Brazil. **In** *Blum, A. A., ed.*, 1981, pp. 49–70. [G: Brazil]

Barbash, Jack. Values in Industrial Relations: The Case of the Adversary Principle. **In** *Dennis, B. D., ed.*, 1981, pp. 1–7.

Bergmann, Barbara R. and Darity, William A., Jr.

Social Relations in the Workplace and Employer Discrimination. In *Dennis, B. D.*, *ed.*, 1981, pp. 155–62.

Bingham, Eula. Ethics and the Workplace. In *Hoffman, W. M. and Wyly, T. J.*, *eds.*, 1981, pp. 145–49. [G: U.S.]

Blankenship, L. Vaughn. The National Science Foundation's Role in Labor–Management Research. In *Dennis, B. D.*, *ed.*, 1981, pp. 26–40. [G: U.S.]

Boratav, Korkut. The Market, Self-Management and Socialism. *Econ. Anal. Worker's Manage.*, 1981, 15(2), pp. 197–206.

Bowie, Norman E. The Moral Contract between Employer and Employee. In *Hoffman, W. M. and Wyly, T. J.*, *eds.*, 1981, pp. 195–202.

Brower, Michael and Balzer, Richard. Joint Labor/Management Activities: A Workshop Discussion. In *Hoffman, W. M. and Wyly, T. J.*, *eds.*, 1981, pp. 269–71. [G: U.S.]

Carroll, Thomas M. Achieving Cartel Profits through Unionization: Comment. *Southern Econ. J.*, April 1981, 47(4), pp. 1152–61.

Childers, Sloan K. The Work Ethic in the Context of the Community. In *Hoffman, W. M. and Wyly, T. J.*, *eds.*, 1981, pp. 173–76. [G: U.S.]

Cole, Robert E. Enterprise Unions. In *Richardson, B. M. and Ueda, T.*, *eds.*, 1981, pp. 36–42. [G: Japan]

Cole, Robert E. Permanent Employment. In *Richardson, B. M. and Ueda, T.*, *eds.*, 1981, pp. 31–36. [G: Japan]

Cummings, Thomas G. Designing Effective Work Groups. In *Nystrom, P. C. and Starbuck, W. H.*, *eds.*, Vol. 2, 1981, pp. 250–71.

Delaney, John Thomas. Union Success in Hospital Representation Elections. *Ind. Relat.*, Spring 1981, 20(2), pp. 149–61. [G: U.S.]

Duffy, Norman F. Australia. In *Blum, A. A.*, *ed.*, 1981, pp. 3–36. [G: Australia]

Dunbar, Roger L. M. Designs for Organizational Control. In *Nystrom, P. C. and Starbuck, W. H.*, *eds.*, Vol. 2, 1981, pp. 85–115.

Finn, Peter. The Effects of Shift Work on the Lives of Employees. *Mon. Lab. Rev.*, October 1981, 104(10), pp. 31–35. [G: U.S.]

Flanagan, Robert J. Equal Opportunity: Current Industrial Relations Perspectives: Discussion. In *Dennis, B. D.*, *ed.*, 1981, pp. 163–67.

Freedman, Audrey. A User's Agenda for Labor Relations Research. In *Dennis, B. D.*, *ed.*, 1981, pp. 22–25.

Fürstenberg, Friedrich. Co-determination and Its Contribution to Industrial Democracy: A Critical Evaluation. In *Dennis, B. D.*, *ed.*, 1981, pp. 185–90. [G: W. Germany]

Furubotn, Eirik G. Codetermination and the Efficient Partitioning of Ownership Rights in the Firm. *Z. ges. Staatswiss.*, December 1981, 137(4), pp. 702–09.

Gardell, Bertil. Stress Research and its Implications: Sweden. In *Dennis, B. D.*, *ed.*, 1981, pp. 268–75. [G: Sweden]

Gerwin, Donald. Relationships between Structure and Technology. In *Nystrom, P. C. and Starbuck, W. H.*, *eds.*, Vol. 2, 1981, pp. 3–38.

Goodman, John F. B. United Kingdom. In *Blum, A. A.*, *ed.*, 1981, pp. 593–620. [G: U.K.]

Goshi, Kohei. The Productivity Movement in Japan. In *Hogan, J. D. and Craig, A. M.*, *eds.*, Vol. 1, 1981, pp. 677–83. [G: Japan]

Hall, John R. A Business View of the Work Ethic. In *Hoffman, W. M. and Wyly, T. J.*, *eds.*, 1981, pp. 234–38. [G: U.S.]

Hanami, Tadashi. The Influence of ILO Standards on Law and Practice in Japan. *Int. Lab. Rev.*, November–December 1981, 120(6), pp. 765–79. [G: Japan]

Harman, Sydney. A Peace Plan for Workers and Bosses. In *Hoffman, W. M. and Wyly, T. J.*, *eds.*, 1981, pp. 215–19. [G: U.S.]

Hulin, Charles L. and Triandis, Harry C. Meanings of Work in Different Organizational Environments. In *Nystrom, P. C. and Starbuck, W. H.*, *eds.*, Vol. 2, 1981, pp. 336–57.

Kabanoff, Boris. Technological Change—Employee Attitudes to the Issue. *Australian Bull. Lab.*, December 1981, 8(1), pp. 45–51.

Kahn, Robert L. Work, Stress, and Health. In *Dennis, B. D.*, *ed.*, 1981, pp. 257–67.

Kanawaty, George and Thorsrud, Einar. Field Experiences with New Forms of Work Organisation. *Int. Lab. Rev.*, May–June 1981, 120(3), pp. 263–77. [G: India; Tanzania]

Kerr, Steven and Slocum, John W., Jr. Controlling the Performances of People in Organization. In *Nystrom, P. C. and Starbuck, W. H.*, *eds.*, Vol. 2, 1981, pp. 116–34.

Kitano, Toshinobu. Industrialization and the Work Group. (In Japanese. With English summary.) *Osaka Econ. Pap.*, December 1981, 31(2–3), pp. 215–25.

Kochan, Thomas A. Labor–Management Relations Research: The Role of the Department of Labor. In *Dennis, B. D.*, *ed.*, 1981, pp. 8–15. [G: U.S.]

Kocka, Jürgen. Class Formation, Interest Articulation, and Public Policy: The Origins of the German White-Collar Class in the Late Nineteenth and Early Twentieth Centuries. In *Berger, S.*, *ed.*, 1981, pp. 63–81. [G: Germany]

Kolb, Deborah M. Roles Mediators Play: State and Federal Practice. *Ind. Relat.*, Winter 1981, 20(1), pp. 1–17. [G: U.S.]

Kosters, Marvin H. Cost-Benefit Analysis of Government Safety and Health Regulation. In *Hoffman, W. M. and Wyly, T. J.*, *eds.*, 1981, pp. 160–66. [G: U.S.]

Krishnan, V. N. India. In *Blum, A. A.*, *ed.*, 1981, pp. 239–54. [G: India]

Landen, D. L. Labor-Management Cooperation in Productivity Improvement. In *Hogan, J. D. and Craig, A. M.*, *eds.*, Vol. 1, 1981, pp. 415–51. [G: U.S.]

Landen, D. L. Stress in the Workplace: An Emerging Industrial Relations Issue: Discussion. In *Dennis, B. D.*, *ed.*, 1981, pp. 276–77.

Ledgerwood, Donna E. and Johnson-Dietz, Sue. The EEOC's Bold Foray into Sexual Harassment on the Job: New Implications for Employer Liability. In *Dennis, B. D.*, *ed.*, 1981, pp. 55–61. [G: U.S.]

Maccoby, Michael and Terzi, Katherine A. What Happened to the Work Ethic? In *Hoffman, W. M. and Wyly, T. J., eds.*, 1981, pp. 19–58. [G: U.S.]

Maloney, Michael T.; McCormick, Robert E. and Tollison, Robert D. Achieving Cartel Profits through Unionization: Reply. *Southern Econ. J.*, April 1981, 47(4), pp. 1162–64.

Marks, Mitchell Lee and Mirvis, Philip H. Wage Guidelines: Impact on Job Attitudes and Behavior. *Ind. Relat.*, Fall 1981, 20(3), pp. 286–96. [G: U.S.]

McCann, Joseph and Galbraith, Jay R. Interdepartmental Relations. In *Nystrom, P. C. and Starbuck, W. H., eds., Vol. 2*, 1981, pp. 60–84.

McMurray, David. Labour Legislation and Policy: Summary Outline. In *Wood, W. D. and Kumar, P., eds.*, 1981, pp. 95–191. [G: Canada]

Meidner, Rudolf. Collective Asset Formation through Wage-Earner Funds. *Int. Lab. Rev.*, May–June 1981, 120(3), pp. 303–17. [G: Europe]

Myrdal, Hans-Göran. Collective Wage-Earner Funds in Sweden: A Road to Socialism and the End of Freedom of Association. *Int. Lab. Rev.*, May–June 1981, 120(3), pp. 319–34. [G: Sweden]

Nystrom, Paul C. Designing Jobs and Assigning Employees. In *Nystrom, P. C. and Starbuck, W. H., eds., Vol. 2*, 1981, pp. 272–301.

O'Toole, James. Work in an Era of Slow Economic Growth. In *Cleveland, H., ed.*, 1981, pp. 195–235. [G: U.S.]

Oswald, Rudolph A. Labor's Agenda for 1980s' Research. In *Dennis, B. D., ed.*, 1981, pp. 16–21. [G: U.S.]

Pellegrini, Claudio. Industrial Relations in Western Europe: Discussion. In *Dennis, B. D., ed.*, 1981, pp. 191–94.

Perryman, M. Ray. A Neglected Institutional Feature of the Labor Sector of the U.S. Economy. *J. Econ. Issues*, June 1981, 15(2), pp. 387–95. [G: U.S.]

Pierre, Marcel. Recent Developments in the Humanisation of Working Conditions in Belgium. *Int. Lab. Rev.*, May–June 1981, 120(3), pp. 279–90. [G: Belgium]

Powers, Charles W. Individual Dignity and Institutional Identity: The Paradoxical Needs of the Corporate Employee. In *Hoffman, W. M. and Wyly, T. J., eds.*, 1981, pp. 203–09.

Roca, Santiago. An Approach towards Differentiating Self-Managed from Non-Selfmanaged Enterprises. *Econ. Anal. Worker's Manage.*, 1981, 15(1), pp. 1–19.

Schein, Edgar H. SMR Forum: Improving Face-to-Face Relationships. *Sloan Manage. Rev.*, Winter 1981, 22(2), pp. 43–52.

Schienstock, G. Towards a Theory of Industrial Relations. *Brit. J. Ind. Relat.*, July 1981, 19(2), pp. 170–89. [G: U.K.]

Scott, William G.; Mitchell, Terence R. and Peery, Newman S. Organizational Governance. In *Nystrom, P. C. and Starbuck, W. H., eds., Vol. 2*, 1981, pp. 135–51.

Smith, Howard R. The Uphill Struggle for Job En-

richment. *Calif. Manage. Rev.*, Summer 1981, 23(4), pp. 33–38. [G: U.S.]

Takagi, Tadao. Labour Relations in Japan and Italy. *Rivista Int. Sci. Econ. Com.*, July–August 1981, 28(7–8), pp. 689–710. [G: Japan; Italy]

Tanaka, Fujio John. Lifetime Employment in Japan. *Challenge*, July/August 1981, 24(3), pp. 23–29. [G: Japan]

Thimm, Alfred L. How Far Should German Codetermination Go? *Challenge*, July/August 1981, 24(3), pp. 13–22. [G: W. Germany]

Thompson, Mark. Canada. In *Blum, A. A., ed.*, 1981, pp. 71–91. [G: Canada]

Tomer, John F. Worker Motivation: A Neglected Element in Micro-Micro Theory. *J. Econ. Issues*, June 1981, 15(2), pp. 351–62.

Tsongas, Paul E. Work Ethics in an Era of Limited Resources. In *Hoffman, W. M. and Wyly, T. J., eds.*, 1981, pp. 337–40. [G: U.S.]

Uca, Mehmet Nezir. Some Considerations on the Transition to a Self-Managed Economy in Turkey. *Econ. Anal. Worker's Manage.*, 1981, 15(2), pp. 259–69. [G: Turkey]

Vogt, Roy. Property Rights and Employee Decision Making in West Germany. *J. Econ. Issues*, June 1981, 15(2), pp. 377–86. [G: W. Germany]

Warner, Malcolm. Organizational Experiments and Social Innovations. In *Nystrom, P. C. and Starbuck, W. H., eds., Vol. 1*, 1981, pp. 167–84.

Wood, Leonard A. Changing Attitudes and the Work Ethic. In *Hoffman, W. M. and Wyly, T. J., eds.*, 1981, pp. 1–17. [G: U.S.]

Wurf, Jerry. Labor's View of Quality of Working Life Programs. In *Hoffman, W. M. and Wyly, T. J., eds.*, 1981, pp. 101–07. [G: U.S.]

8331 Labor–Management Relations in Private Sector

Bolweg, Joep F. The Quality of Working Life: An Industrial Relations Perspective. In *Dennis, B. D., ed.*, 1981, pp. 174–84. [G: OECD]

Clarke, Oliver. The Development of Industrial Relations in European Market Economies. In *Dennis, B. D., ed.*, 1981, pp. 167–73. [G: EEC]

Conrad, Wolfgang. Federal Republic of Germany. In *Blum, A. A., ed.*, 1981, pp. 209–38. [G: W. Germany]

Curran, James and Stanworth, John. Size of Workplace and Attitudes to Industrial Relations in the Printing and Electronics Industries. *Brit. J. Ind. Relat.*, March 1981, 19(1), pp. 14–25. [G: U.K.]

Dugger, William M. Entrenched Corporate Power and Our Options for Dealing with It. *Rev. Soc. Econ.*, October 1981, 39(2), pp. 133–44. [G: U.S.]

Elden, J. Maxwell. Political Efficacy at Work: The Connection between More Autonomous Forms of Workplace Organization and a More Participatory Politics. *Amer. Polit. Sci. Rev.*, March 1981, 75(1), pp. 43–58. [G: U.S.]

Ephlin, Donald F. Quality of Work Life in the Auto Industry. In *Hoffman, W. M. and Wyly, T. J., eds.*, 1981, pp. 227–33. [G: U.S.]

Foulkes, Fred K. Large Nonunionized Employers. In *Stieber, J.; McKersie, R. B. and Mills, D. Q.,* *eds.*, 1981, pp. 129–57. [G: U.S.]

Fraser, Douglas A. Labor on Corporate Boards: Interview. *Challenge*, July/August 1981, *24*(3), pp. 30–33. [G: U.S.]

Fuller, Stephen H. Becoming the Organization of the Future. In *Hoffman, W. M. and Wyly, T. J., eds.*, 1981, pp. 67–73. [G: U.S.]

Giglioni, Giovanni B.; Giglioni, Joyce B. and Bryant, James A. Performance Appraisal: Here Comes the Judge. *Calif. Manage. Rev.*, Winter 1981, *24*(2), pp. 14–23. [G: U.S.]

Gordon, David M. Capital–Labor Conflict and the Productivity Slowdown. *Amer. Econ. Rev.*, May 1981, *71*(2), pp. 30–35. [G: U.S.]

Greenberg, Edward S. Industrial Self-Management and Political Attitudes. *Amer. Polit. Sci. Rev.*, March 1981, *75*(1), pp. 29–42. [G: U.S.]

Greer, Charles R. and Shearer, John C. Do Foreign-Owned U.S. Firms Practice Unconventional Labor Relations? *Mon. Lab. Rev.*, January 1981, *104*(1), pp. 44–48. [G: U.S.]

Harmer, D. Richard. The Work Ethic is Alive, Well, and Living in Cleveland: The Lincoln Electric Company. In *Hoffman, W. M. and Wyly, T. J., eds.*, 1981, pp. 283–336. [G: U.S.]

Hillery, Brian J. Ireland. In *Blum, A. A., ed.*, 1981, pp. 283–301. [G: Ireland]

Ishikawa, Akihiro. Experiments in Self-Management in Japan. *Econ. Anal. Worker's Manage.*, 1981, *15*(1), pp. 115–24. [G: Japan]

Iwuji, Eleazar C. Nigeria. In *Blum, A. A., ed.*, 1981, pp. 417–42. [G: Nigeria]

Jönsson, Berth. The Quality of Work Life—the Volvo Experience. In *Hoffman, W. M. and Wyly, T. J., eds.*, 1981, pp. 74–86. [G: Sweden]

Kochan, Thomas A. and Helfman, David E. The Effects of Collective Bargaining on Economic and Behavioral Job Outcomes. In *Ehrenberg, R. G., ed.*, 1981, pp. 321–65. [G: U.S.]

Koskimies, Jaakko. Finland. In *Blum, A. A., ed.*, 1981, pp. 144–67. [G: Finland]

Levine, Solomon B. Labor Conflict. In *Richardson, B. M. and Ueda, T., eds.*, 1981, pp. 42–52. [G: Japan]

Levine, Solomon B. Labor Regulations. In *Richardson, B. M. and Ueda, T., eds.*, 1981, pp. 52–61. [G: Japan]

Lewis, Paul. An Analysis of Why Legislation Has Failed to Provide Employment Protection for Unfairly Dismissed Employees. *Brit. J. Ind. Relat.*, November 1981, *19*(3), pp. 316–26. [G: U.K.]

Livernash, E. Robert and Argheyd, Kamal. Iran. In *Blum, A. A., ed.*, 1981, pp. 255–82. [G: Iran]

Loveman, Brian. Chile. In *Blum, A. A., ed.*, 1981, pp. 93–116. [G: Chile]

Lund, Reinhard. Scandinavia. In *Blum, A. A., ed.*, 1981, pp. 461–79. [G: Scandinavia]

Meyers, Frederic. France. In *Blum, A. A., ed.*, 1981, pp. 169–208. [G: France]

Mills, D. Quinn. Management Performance. In *Stieber, J.; McKersie, R. B. and Mills, D. Q., eds.*, 1981, pp. 99–128. [G: U.S.]

Moberg, Dennis J. Job Enrichment through Symbol Management. *Calif. Manage. Rev.*, Winter 1981,

24(2), pp. 24–30.

Naples, Michele I. Industrial Conflict and Its Implications for Productivity Growth. *Amer. Econ. Rev.*, May 1981, *71*(2), pp. 36–41. [G: U.S.]

Neffa, Julio César. Improvement of Working Conditions and Environment: A Peruvian Experiment with New Forms of Work Organisation. *Int. Lab. Rev.*, July–August 1981, *120*(4), pp. 473–90. [G: Peru]

Ramondt, Joop. Netherlands. In *Blum, A. A., ed.*, 1981, pp. 394–416. [G: Netherlands]

Ramos, Elias. Philippines. In *Blum, A. A., ed.*, 1981, pp. 441–60. [G: Philippines]

Reed, Rex R. Work Itself and Its Aftermath at AT&T. In *Hoffman, W. M. and Wyly, T. J., eds.*, 1981, pp. 87–91. [G: U.S.]

Reich, Michael and Devine, James. The Microeconomics of Conflict and Hierarchy in Capitalist Production. *Rev. Radical Polit. Econ.*, Winter 1981, *12*(4), pp. 27–45.

Schregle, Johannes. Comparative Industrial Relations: Pitfalls and Potential. *Int. Lab. Rev.*, January–February 1981, *120*(1), pp. 15–30.

Schreuder, Hein. Employees and the Corporate Social Report: The Dutch Case. *Accounting Rev.*, April 1981, *56*(2), pp. 294–308. [G: Netherlands]

Seashore, Stanley E. Humanization of Work: Ethical Issues in Converting Ideology to Practice. In *Hoffman, W. M. and Wyly, T. J., eds.*, 1981, pp. 253–64. [G: U.S.]

Streeck, Wolfgang. Qualitative Demands and the Neo-Corporatist Manageability of Industrial Relations. *Brit. J. Ind. Relat.*, July 1981, *19*(2), pp. 149–69. [G: W. Germany]

Thomson, Andrew W. J. U.S. Industrial Relations 1950–1980: A View from Abroad. In *Stieber, J.; McKersie, R. B. and Mills, D. Q., eds.*, 1981, pp. 297–342. [G: U.S.; W. Europe]

Todd, Jerry D. and Goldstein, David N. A Computerized Simulation Model for Analyzing Profit Sharing Plans. *J. Risk Ins.*, December 1981, *48*(4), pp. 662–73.

de Vletter, F. Conditions Affecting Black Migrant Workers in South Africa: a Case Study of the Gold-Mines. In *Böhning, W. R., ed.*, 1981, pp. 91–112. [G: S. Africa]

8332 Labor–Management Relations in Public Sector

Bielasiak, Jack. Workers and Mass Participation in 'Socialist Democracy.' In *Triska, J. F. and Gati, C., eds.*, 1981, pp. 88–107. [G: E. Europe]

Boyd, William L. Comments on E. G. West and R. J. Staaf [Extra-Governmental Powers in Public Schooling: The Unions and the Courts]. *Public Choice*, 1981, *36*(3), pp. 639–40.

Comisso, Ellen T. The Logic of Worker (Non) Participation in Yugoslav Self-Management. *Rev. Radical Polit. Econ.*, Summer 1981, *13*(2), pp. 11–22. [G: Yugoslavia]

Comisso, Ellen Turkish. Can a Party of the Working Class Be a Working-Class Party? In *Triska, J. F. and Gati, C., eds.*, 1981, pp. 70–87. [G: Yugoslavia; Italy]

Denitch, Bogdan. Yugoslav Exceptionalism. In

Triska, J. F. and Gati, C., eds., 1981, pp. 253–67. [G: Yugoslavia]

Ehrenberg, Ronald G. Comments on E. G. West and R. J. Staaf [Extra-Governmental Powers in Public Schooling: The Unions and the Courts]. *Public Choice*, 1981, *36*(3), pp. 641–45.

Hoffman, Charles. People's Republic of China. In *Blum, A. A., ed.*, 1981, pp. 117–41. [G: China]

Holesovsky, Vaclav. Ideas of Industrial Democracy in Eastern Europe: Dilemmas and Blind Alleys. *ACES Bull. (See Comp. Econ. Stud. after 8/85)*, Summer 1981, *23*(2), pp. 71–79. [G: E. Europe]

Ireland, Norman J. and Law, Peter J. Efficiency, Incentives, and Individual Labor Supply in the Labor-Managed Firm. *J. Compar. Econ.*, March 1981, *5*(1), pp. 1–23.

Kosta, Jiří. Decentral Planning and Workers' Participation in Decision-Making: The Polish and the Czechoslovak Experience. *Econ. Anal. Worker's Manage.*, 1981, *15*(3), pp. 383–96. [G: Poland; Czechoslovakia]

Kul'bovskaia, N. The Evaluation of the Social Results of Scientific–Technical Progress. *Prob. Econ.*, March 1981, *23*(11), pp. 16–30. [G: U.S.S.R.]

Lockett, Martin. Self-Management in China? *Econ. Anal. Worker's Manage.*, 1981, *15*(1), pp. 85–114. [G: China]

McKersie, Robert B.; Greenhalgh, Leonard and Jick, Todd D. The CEC: Labor-Management Cooperation in New York. *Ind. Relat.*, Spring 1981, *20*(2), pp. 212–20. [G: U.S.]

Montias, J. M. Observations on Strikes, Riots and Other Disturbances. In *Triska, J. F. and Gati, C., eds.*, 1981, pp. 173–86.

Nardi, Angelo. Il sistema di informazioni nell'industria metalmeccanica. Riflessioni economiche sulle clausole contrattuali. (The Information System in the Metal-Mechanical Industry: Decisional Constraints of the Contract Clauses. With English summary.) *Rivista Int. Sci. Econ. Com.*, January–February 1981, *28*(1–2), pp. 129–50. [G: Italy]

Nelson, Daniel. Romania: Participatory Dynamics in 'Developed Socialism.' In *Triska, J. F. and Gati, C., eds.*, 1981, pp. 236–52. [G: Romania]

Perry, James L. and Angle, Harold L. Bargaining Unit Structure and Organizational Outcomes. *Ind. Relat.*, Winter 1981, *20*(1), pp. 47–59. [G: U.S.]

Triska, Jan F. Workers' Assertiveness and Soviet Policy Choices. In *Triska, J. F. and Gati, C., eds.*, 1981, pp. 268–82.

Valenta, Jiri. Czechoslovakia: A 'Prolétariat Embourgeoisé'? In *Triska, J. F. and Gati, C., eds.*, 1981, pp. 209–23. [G: Czechoslovakia]

West, Edwin G. and Staaf, Robert J. Extra-Governmental Powers in Public Schooling: The Unions and the Courts. *Public Choice*, 1981, *36*(3), pp. 619–37.

West, Edwin G. and Staaf, Robert J. Extra-Governmental Powers in Public Schooling: The Unions and the Courts: Rejoinder. *Public Choice*, 1981, *36*(3), pp. 647–50.

de Weydenthal, Jan B. Poland: Workers and Politics. In *Triska, J. F. and Gati, C., eds.*, 1981, pp. 187–208. [G: Poland]

Yang, Chi-liang. 'Mass Line' Accounting in China. *Manage. Account.*, May 1981, *62*(11), pp. 13–17. [G: China]

Zimbalist, Andrew. On the Role of Management in Socialist Development. *World Devel.*, September/October 1981, *9*(9/10), pp. 971–77. [G: Yugoslavia; U.S.S.R.; Cuba; Chile]

Zupanov, Josip and Adizes, Ichak. Yugoslavia. In *Blum, A. A., ed.*, 1981, pp. 647–72. [G: Yugoslavia]

840 DEMOGRAPHIC ECONOMICS

841 Demographic Economics

8410 Demographic Economics

Abad, Ricardo G. The Utility of Microlevel Approaches to Migration: A Philippine Perspective. In *De Jong, G. F. and Gardner, R. W., eds.*, 1981, pp. 291–302. [G: Philippines]

Abumere, S. I. Population Distribution Policies and Measures in Africa South of the Sahara: A Review. *Population Devel. Rev.*, September 1981, *7*(3), pp. 421–33. [G: Africa]

Akder, A. Halis and Gitmez, Ali S. Yurt Dişindan Dönen İşçiler Üzerine Gözlemler. (With English summary.) *METU*, 1981, *8*(3&4), pp. 683–96. [G: Turkey]

Akin, John, et al. The Determinants of Breast-Feeding in Sri Lanka. *Demography*, August 1981, *18*(3), pp. 287–307. [G: Sri Lanka]

Ali, Karamat. Impact of Agricultural Modernization on Crude Birth Rate in Indian Punjab. *Pakistan Devel. Rev.*, Summer 1981, *20*(2), pp. 247–67. [G: India]

Allen, Edward L. and Edmonds, James A. Energy Demand and Population Changes. *Atlantic Econ. J.*, September 1981, *9*(3), pp. 10–19.

Ata-Mirzaev, O. Women with Large Families: A Sociodemographic Analysis. *Prob. Econ.*, Sept.–Oct.–Nov. 1981, *24*(5–6–7), pp. 240–49. [G: U.S.S.R.]

Austen-Smith, David. Society and Economy: A Review Article. *Scot. J. Polit. Econ.*, November 1981, *28*(3), pp. 291–96.

Baines, D. E. The Labour Supply and the Labour Market 1860–1914. In *Floud, R. and McCloskey, D., eds., Vol. 2*, 1981, pp. 144–74. [G: U.K.]

Baldassare, Mark. Local Perspectives on Community Growth. In *Hawley, A. H. and Mazie, S. M., eds.*, 1981, pp. 116–43. [G: U.S.]

Ballard, Kenneth P. and Clark, Gordon L. The Short-run Dynamics of Inter-state Migration: A Space-Time Economic Adjustment Model of In-migration to Fast Growing States. *Reg. Stud.*, 1981, *15*(3), pp. 213–28. [G: U.S.]

Banerjee, Biswajit. Rural–Urban Migration and Family Ties: An Analysis of Family Considerations in Migration Behaviour in India. *Oxford Bull. Econ. Statist.*, November 1981, *43*(4), pp. 321–55. [G: India]

Banerjee, Biswajit and Kanbur, S. M. On the Specification and Estimation of Macro Rural–Urban Migration Functions: With an Application to Indian Data. *Oxford Bull. Econ. Statist.*, February 1981,

43(1), pp. 7–29. **[G: India]**

Banister, Judith and Preston, Samuel H. Mortality in China. *Population Devel. Rev.*, March 1981, *7*(1), pp. 98–110. **[G: China]**

Bauer, P. T. and Yamey, Basil S. The Population Explosion: Myths and Realities. In *Bauer, P. T.*, 1981, pp. 42–65. **[G: LDCs]**

Becker, Gary S. An Equilibrium Theory of the Distribution of Income and Intergenerational Mobility. In *Currie, D.; Peel, D. and Peters, W.*, eds., 1981, *1979*, pp. 1–33.

Becker, Stan. Seasonal Patterns of Fertility Measures: Theory and Data. *J. Amer. Statist. Assoc.*, June 1981, *76*(374), pp. 249–59.

Bell, David N. F. and Kirwan, F. X. Further Thoughts on Return Migration: A Rejoinder to Gordon (1981) [Return Migration in a Scottish Context]. *Reg. Stud.*, 1981, *15*(1), pp. 63–66.
[G: U.K.]

van den Berg, L. and van der Meer, J. Urban Change in the Netherlands. In *Klaassen, L. H.; Molle, W. T. M. and Paelinck, J. H. P.*, eds., 1981, pp. 137–69. **[G: Netherlands]**

Bernard, Frank E. and Thom, Derrick J. Population Pressure and Human Carrying Capacity in Selected Locations of Machakos and Kitui Districts. *J. Devel. Areas*, April 1981, *15*(3), pp. 381–406.
[G: Kenya]

Berry, Brian J. L. Inner-City Futures: An American Dilemma Revisited. In *Stave, B. M.*, ed., 1981, *1980*, pp. 187–219. **[G: U.S.]**

Blackwood, Larry. Alaska Native Fertility Trends, 1950–1978. *Demography*, May 1981, *18*(2), pp. 173–79. **[G: U.S.]**

Blake, Judith. Family Size and the Quality of Children. *Demography*, November 1981, *18*(4), pp. 421–42. **[G: U.S.]**

Blake, Judith. The Only Child in America: Prejudice versus Performance. *Population Devel. Rev.*, March 1981, *7*(1), pp. 43–54. **[G: U.S.]**

Bourgeois-Pichat, Jean. Recent Demographic Change in Western Europe: An Assessment. *Population Devel. Rev.*, March 1981, *7*(1), pp. 19–42. **[G: W. Europe]**

Bridges, Benjamin, Jr. and Packard, Michael D. Price and Income Changes for the Elderly. *Soc. Sec. Bull.*, January 1981, *44*(1), pp. 3–15.
[G: U.S.]

Brown, David L. Potential Impacts of Changing Population Size and Composition of the Plains. In *Lawson, M. P. and Baker, M. E.*, eds., 1981, pp. 35–51. **[G: U.S.]**

Brown, David L. and Beale, Calvin L. Diversity in Post-1970 Population Trends. In *Hawley, A. H. and Mazie, S. M.*, eds., 1981, pp. 27–71.
[G: U.S.]

Brown, Lawrence A. and Sanders, Rickie L. Toward a Development Paradigm of Migration, with Particular Reference to Third World Settings. In *De Jong, G. F. and Gardner, R. W.*, eds., 1981, pp. 149–85.

Browne, Lynn E. Why the Mini-Skirt Won't Come Back. *New Eng. Econ. Rev.*, November/December 1981, pp. 16–26. **[G: U.S.]**

Brulhardt, Marie-Claude and Bassand, Michel. La mobilité spatiale en tant que système. (Spatial Mobility as a System. With English summary.) *Schweiz. Z. Volkswirtsch. Statist.*, September 1981, *117*(3), pp. 505–19.

Bulatao, Rodolfo A. Values and Disvalues of Children in Successive Childbearing Decisions. *Demography*, February 1981, *18*(1), pp. 1–25.
[G: Philippines; Korea; U.S.]

Burke, Fred G. Bilingualism/Biculturalism in American Education: An Adventure in Wonderland. *Ann. Amer. Acad. Polit. Soc. Sci.*, March 1981, *454*, pp. 164–77. **[G: U.S.]**

Burns, Leland S. The Metropolitan Population of the United States: Historical and Emerging Trends. In *Klaassen, L. H.; Molle, W. T. M. and Paelinck, J. H. P.*, eds., 1981, pp. 197–224.
[G: U.S.]

Burns, Leland S. and Van Ness, Kathy. The Decline of the Metropolitan Economy. *Urban Stud.*, June 1981, *18*(2), pp. 169–80. **[G: U.S.]**

Burstein, Alan N. Immigrants and Residential Mobility: The Irish and Germans in Philadelphia, 1850–1880. In *Hershberg, T.*, ed., 1981, pp. 174–203.
[G: U.S.]

Butz, William P. The Changing Role of Breastfeeding in Economic Development: A Theoretical Exposition. In *Khan, A. and Sirageldin, I.*, eds., 1981, pp. 95–117.

Cain, Mead. Risk and Insurance: Perspectives on Fertility and Agrarian Change in India and Bangladesh. *Population Devel. Rev.*, September 1981, *7*(3), pp. 435–74. **[G: India; Bangladesh]**

Caldwell, J. C. The Mechanisms of Demographic Change in Historical Perspective. *Population Stud.*, March 1981, *35*(1), pp. 5–27.

Canlas, Dante B. An Economic Analysis of Marital Fertility: Some Notes. *Philippine Econ. J.*, 1981, *20*(3&4), pp. 227–37.

Card, Josefina J. Long-Term Consequences for Children of Teenage Parents. *Demography*, May 1981, *18*(2), pp. 137–56. **[G: U.S.]**

Carmon, Naomi. Economic Integration of Immigrants. *Amer. J. Econ. Soc.*, April 1981, *40*(2), pp. 149–63. **[G: Israel]**

Cassen, Robert H. Population and Development: A Survey. In *Streeten, P. and Jolly, R*, eds., 1981, *1976*, pp. 1–46.

Catsiapis, George and Robinson, Chris. The Theory of the Family and Intergenerational Mobility: An Empirical Test. *J. Human Res.*, Winter 1981, *16*(1), pp. 106–16. **[G: U.S.]**

Cebula, Richard J. "Money Illusion" and Migration Decisions: An International Comparison of the United States and Canadian Experiences. *Reg. Stud.*, 1981, *15*(4), pp. 241–46. **[G: U.S.; Canada]**

Cebula, Richard J. Differential White-Nonwhite Migration Sensitivities to Income Differentials: An Exploratory Note. *Amer. Econ.*, Spring 1981, *25*(1), pp. 67–69.

Cebula, Richard J. The Tiebout Hypothesis of Voting with One's Feet: A Look at the Most Recent Evidence. *Rev. Reg. Stud.*, Winter 1981, *11*(3), pp. 47–50. **[G: U.S.]**

Cebula, Richard J. and Koch, James V. A Further Note on Welfare Outlays and Nonwhite Migration [A Note on Welfare Outlays and Nonwhite Migration: An Analysis for SMSA's, 1965–1970]. *Rev. Bus. Econ. Res.*, Spring 1981, *16*(3), pp. 98–101. [G: U.S.]

Chan, Tuck Hoong Paul. A Review of Micro Migration Research in the Third World Context. In *De Jong, G. F. and Gardner, R. W., eds.*, 1981, pp. 303–27.

Chaudhury, Rafiqul Huda. Population Pressure and Agricultural Productivity in Bangladesh. *Bangladesh Devel. Stud.*, Monsoon 1981, *9*(3), pp. 67–88. [G: Bangladesh]

Chen, Lincoln C.; Huq, Emdadul and D'Souza, Stan. Sex Bias in the Family Allocation of Food and Health Care in Rural Bangladesh. *Population Devel. Rev.*, March 1981, *7*(1), pp. 55–70. [G: Bangladesh]

Chesnais, Jean-Claude. Génération et gain: une simulation de bilans financiers individuels par classe sociale. (Generation and Earnings: A Simulation of Individual Financial Balances per Social Group. With English summary.) *Consommation*, January–March 1981, *28*(1), pp. 37–50. [G: France]

Chidambaram, V. C. and Pullum, T. W. Estimating Fertility Trends from Retrospective Birth Histories: Sensitivity to Imputation of Missing Dates. *Population Stud.*, July 1981, *35*(2), pp. 307–20.

Chinn, Jeff. The Aging Soviet Society. In *Desfosses, H., ed.*, 1981, pp. 44–61. [G: U.S.S.R.]

Chiswick, Barry R. Guidelines for the Reform of Immigration Policy. In *Fellner, W., ed.*, 1981, pp. 309–47. [G: U.S.]

Chorney, Harold. Amnesia, Integration and repression: The Roots of Canadian Urban Political Culture. In *Dear, M. and Scott, A. J., eds.*, 1981, pp. 536–63. [G: Canada]

Chowdhury, Tawfiq-e-Elahi. Fertility Behaviour under Uncertainty—A Mathematical Model. *Bangladesh Devel. Stud.*, Summer 1981, *9*(2), pp. 97–101.

Cigno, Alessandro. Growth with Exhaustible Resources and Endogenous Population. *Rev. Econ. Stud.*, April 1981, *48*(2), pp. 281–87.

Clarke, John I. Contemporary Urban Growth in the Middle East. In *[Fisher, W. B.]*, 1981, *1980*, pp. 154–70. [G: Middle East]

Clarke, Susan E. A Political Perspective on Population Change in the South. In *Poston, D. L., Jr. and Weller, R. H., eds.*, 1981, pp. 227–67. [G: U.S.]

Coale, Ansley J. A Further Note on Chinese Population Statistics. *Population Devel. Rev.*, September 1981, *7*(3), pp. 512–18. [G: China]

Coale, Ansley J. Population Trends, Population Policy, and Population Studies in China. *Population Devel. Rev.*, March 1981, *7*(1), pp. 85–97. [G: China]

Collier, Valerie G. and Rempel, Henry. The Divergence of Private from Social Costs in Rural–Urban Migration: A Case Study of Nairobi. In *Killick, T., ed.*, 1981, *1977*, pp. 228–37. [G: Kenya]

Colvin, Lucie Gallistel. Labor and Migration in Colonial Senegambia. In *Colvin, L. G., et al.*, 1981, pp. 58–80. [G: W. Africa]

Colvin, Lucie Gallistel. Migration and Public Policy in the Senegambia. In *Colvin, L. G., et al.*, 1981, pp. 317–43. [G: W. Africa]

Colvin, Lucie Gallistel. The Uprooted of the Western Sahel: Senegal. In *Colvin, L. G., et al.*, 1981, pp. 83–112. [G: Senegal]

Colvin, Lucie Gallistel. The Uprooted of the Western Sahel: The Gambia. In *Colvin, L. G., et al.*, 1981, pp. 287–313. [G: Gambia]

Colvin, Lucie Gallistel. The Uprooted of the Western Sahel: Introduction and Regional Historical Background. In *Colvin, L. G., et al.*, 1981, pp. 3–26. [G: W. Africa]

Colvin, Lucie Gallistel. The Uprooted of the Western Sahel: Mali. In *Colvin, L. G., et al.*, 1981, pp. 260–86. [G: Mali]

Colvin, Lucie Gallistel. The Uprooted of the Western Sahel: Mauritania. In *Colvin, L. G., et al.*, 1981, pp. 244–59. [G: Mauritania]

Corcoran, Mary and Datcher, Linda P. Intergenerational Status Transmission and the Process of Individual Attainment. In *Hill, M. S.; Hill, D. H. and Morgan, J. N., eds.*, 1981, pp. 169–206. [G: U.S.]

Cornelius, Wayne A. Immigration, Mexican Development Policy, and the Future of U.S.–Mexican Relations. In *McBride, R. H., ed.*, 1981, pp. 104–27. [G: Mexico; U.S.]

Crawford, Vincent P. and Lilien, David M. Social Security and the Retirement Decision. *Quart. J. Econ.*, August 1981, *96*(3), pp. 505–29. [G: U.S.]

Crimmins, Eileen M. The Changing Pattern of American Mortality Decline, 1940–77, and Its Implications for the Future. *Population Devel. Rev.*, June 1981, *7*(2), pp. 229–54. [G: U.S.]

Czarkowski, Jan. Elements of the Theory of Prognosticating the Development of World Demographic Relations. In *[Lipiński, E.]*, 1981, pp. 3–17.

DaVanzo, Julie. Microeconomic Approaches to Studying Migration Decisions. In *De Jong, G. F. and Gardner, R. W., eds.*, 1981, pp. 90–129. [G: U.S.]

DaVanzo, Julie S. and Morrison, Peter A. Return and Other Sequences of Migration in the United States. *Demography*, February 1981, *18*(1), pp. 85–101. [G: U.S.]

Davis, Kingsley and van den Oever, Pietronella. Age Relations and Public Policy in Advanced Industrial Societies. *Population Devel. Rev.*, March 1981, *7*(1), pp. 1–18.

De Jong, Gordon F. The Impact of Regional Population Redistribution Policies on Internal Migration: What We Learn from the Netherlands and Great Britain. *Soc. Sci. Quart.*, June 1981, *62*(2), pp. 313–22. [G: U.K.; Netherlands]

De Jong, Gordon F. and Fawcett, James T. Motivations for Migration: An Assessment and a Value-Expectancy Research Model. In *De Jong, G. F. and Gardner, R. W., eds.*, 1981, pp. 13–58. [G: Selected Countries]

De Jong, Gordon F. and Gardner, Robert W. Migration Decision Making: Introduction and Overview. In *De Jong, G. F. and Gardner, R. W., eds.*, 1981, pp. 1–10.

De Jong, Gordon F. and Harbison, Sarah F. Policy Intervention Consideration: The Relationship of Theoretical Models to Planning. In *De Jong,*

G. F. and Gardner, R. W., eds., 1981, pp. 281–90.

Deloria, Vine, Jr. Native Americans: The American Indian Today. *Ann. Amer. Acad. Polit. Soc. Sci.*, March 1981, *454*, pp. 139–49.

Demeny, Paul. The North–South Income Gap: A Demographic Perspective. *Population Devel. Rev.*, June 1981, *7*(2), pp. 297–310.

Desfosses, Helen. Population as a Global Issue: The Soviet Prism. In *Desfosses, H., ed.*, 1981, pp. 179–201. [G: U.S.S.R.]

Desfosses, Helen. Pro-Natalism in Soviet Law and Propaganda. In *Desfosses, H., ed.*, 1981, pp. 95–123. [G: U.S.S.R.]

Díaz-Briquets, S. Determinants of Mortality Transition in Developing Countries before and after the Second World War: Some Evidence from Cuba. *Population Stud.*, November 1981, *35*(3), pp. 399–411. [G: Cuba]

DiMaio, Alfred J., Jr. Contemporary Soviet Population Problems. In *Desfosses, H., ed.*, 1981, pp. 16–43. [G: U.S.S.R.]

DiMaio, Alfred J., Jr. Evolution of Soviet Population Thought: From Marxism-Leninism to the *Literaturnaya Gazeta* Debate. In *Desfosses, H., ed.*, 1981, pp. 157–78. [G: U.S.S.R.]

Domanski, R. Development of the Urban System of Poland. In *Klaassen, L. H.; Molle, W. T. M. and Paelinck, J. H. P., eds.*, 1981, pp. 90–116. [G: Poland]

Donaldson, Peter J. Evolution of the Family-Planning System. In *Repetto, R., et al.*, 1981, pp. 222–58. [G: S. Korea]

Drewett, R. and Rossi, A. General Urbanisation Trends in Western Europe. In *Klaassen, L. H.; Molle, W. T. M. and Paelinck, J. H. P., eds.*, 1981, pp. 119–36. [G: W. Europe]

Drucker, Peter F. Demographics and American Economic Policy. In *Wachter, M. L. and Wachter, S. M., eds.*, 1981, pp. 237–56. [G: U.S.]

Du Pasquier, Jean-Noël. Le facteur démographique en tant que déterminant des dépenses publiques. (The Demographic Factor as a Determinant of Public Expenditures. With English summary.) *Schweiz. Z. Volkswirtsch. Statist.*, September 1981, *117*(3), pp. 257–69.

Duncan, Greg J. and Morgan, James N. Persistence and Change in Economic Status and the Role of Changing Family Composition. In *Hill, M. S.; Hill, D. H. and Morgan, J. N., eds.*, 1981, pp. 1–44. [G: U.S.]

Eason, Warren W. Selected Problems of Regional Development in the USSR: Population and Labor Force. In *Koropeckyj, I. S. and Schroeder, G. E., eds.*, 1981, pp. 11–91. [G: U.S.S.R.]

Easton, Stephen T. More on the Emigration of the Peasantry. *World Devel.*, March 1981, *9*(3), pp. 315–18.

Edlefsen, Lee E. An Investigation of the Timing Pattern of Childbearing. *Population Stud.*, November 1981, *35*(3), pp. 375–86. [G: Philippines]

Edlefsen, Lee E. The Effect of Sample Truncation on Estimates of Fertility Relationships. In *Simon, J. L. and Lindert, P. H., eds.*, 1981, pp. 41–66. [G: U.S.]

Ehrlich, Anne H. Feeding the Transitional Society.

In *Coomer, J. C., ed.*, 1981, pp. 124–41.

Ehrlicher, Werner. Zukunftsprobleme unserer Wirtschaft. (Future Problems of Our Economy. With English summary.) *Kredit Kapital*, 1981, *14*(1), pp. 3–25.

Enderle, Georges. Wanderungen und sozio-ökonomische Entwicklung, Korreferat. (Migration and Socio-Economic Development—A Rejoinder. With English summary.) *Schweiz. Z. Volkswirtsch. Statist.*, September 1981, *117*(3), pp. 393–406. [G: Switzerland]

Entwisle, Barbara. CBR versus TFR in Cross-National Fertility Research. *Demography*, November 1981, *18*(4), pp. 635–43.

Ermisch, John F. An Economic Theory of Household Formation: Theory and Evidence from the General Household Survey. *Scot. J. Polit. Econ.*, February 1981, *28*(1), pp. 1–19. [G: U.K.]

Ermisch, John F. An Emerging Secular Rise in the Western World's Fertility? *Population Devel. Rev.*, December 1981, *7*(4), pp. 677–84.

Ermisch, John F. Economic Opportunities, Marriage Squeezes and the Propensity to Marry: An Economic Analysis of Period Marriage Rates in England and Wales. *Population Stud.*, November 1981, *35*(3), pp. 347–56. [G: U.K.]

Espenshade, Thomas J.; Hobbs, Frank B. and Pol, Louis G. An Experiment in Estimating Postcensal Age Distributions of State Populations from Death Registration Data. *Rev. Public Data Use (See J. Econ. Soc. Meas. after 4/85)*, July 1981, *9*(2), pp. 97–114. [G: U.S.]

Farooq, Ghazi M. Population, Human Resources and Development Planning: Towards an Integrated Approach. *Int. Lab. Rev.*, May–June 1981, *120*(3), pp. 335–49.

Ferguson, Lorna Crowley. Fiscal Strain in American Cities: Some Limitations to Popular Explanations. In *Newton, K., ed.*, 1981, pp. 156–78. [G: U.S.]

Feshbach, Murray. Development of the Soviet Census. In *Desfosses, H., ed.*, 1981, pp. 3–15. [G: U.S.S.R.]

Fitzpatrick, Joseph P. and Parker, Lourdes Travieso. Hispanic–Americans in the Eastern United States. *Ann. Amer. Acad. Polit. Soc. Sci.*, March 1981, *454*, pp. 98–110. [G: U.S.]

Frederiksen, Peter C. Further Evidence on the Relationship between Population Density and Infrastructure: The Philippines and Electrification. *Econ. Develop. Cult. Change*, July 1981, *29*(4), pp. 749–58. [G: Philippines]

Frejka, Tomas. Long-Term Prospects for World Population Growth. *Population Devel. Rev.*, September 1981, *7*(3), pp. 489–511.

Friedman, David D. What Does "Optimum Population" Mean? In *Simon, J. L. and Lindert, P. H., eds.*, 1981, pp. 273–87.

Friedman, Joseph and Sjogren, Jane. Assets of the Elderly as They Retire. *Soc. Sec. Bull.*, January 1981, *44*(1), pp. 16–31. [G: U.S.]

Frisch, Helmut and Hof, Franz. A "Textbook"—Model of Inflation and Unemployment. *Kredit Kapital*, 1981, *14*(2), pp. 159–76.

Fuller, Theodore D. Migrant Evaluations of the Quality of Urban Life in Northeast Thailand. *J.*

Devel. Areas, October 1981, *16*(1), pp. 87–104. [G: Thailand]

Fuller, Theodore D. Migrant–Native Socioeconomic Differentials in Thailand. *Demography*, February 1981, *18*(1), pp. 55–66. [G: Thailand]

Fulop, Marcel. A Dynamic Macroeconomic Model of Fertility Rate for the United States. *Amer. Econ.*, Spring 1981, *25*(1), pp. 22–27. [G: U.S.]

Furstenberg, Frank F., Jr.; Modell, John and Hershberg, Theodore. The Origins of the Female-Headed Black Family: The Impact of the Urban Experience. In *Hershberg, T., ed.*, 1981, *1975*, pp. 435–54.

Galenson, David W. Literacy and Age in Preindustrial England: Quantitative Evidence and Implications. *Econ. Develop. Cult. Change*, July 1981, *29*(4), pp. 813–29. [G: U.K.]

Galle, Omer R. and Stern, Robert N. The Metropolitan System in the South: Continuity and Change. In *Poston, D. L., Jr. and Weller, R. H., eds.*, 1981, pp. 155–74. [G: U.S.]

Gardner, Robert W. Macrolevel Influences on the Migration Decision Process. In *De Jong, G. F. and Gardner, R. W., eds.*, 1981, pp. 59–89.

Ghayur, M. Arif. Muslims in the United States: Settlers and Visitors. *Ann. Amer. Acad. Polit. Soc. Sci.*, March 1981, *454*, pp. 150–63. [G: U.S.]

Goldbeck, Amanda L. A Probability Mixture Model of Completed Parity. *Demography*, November 1981, *18*(4), pp. 645–58. [G: Mexico]

Goldman, Noreen. Dissolution of First Unions in Colombia, Panama, and Peru. *Demography*, November 1981, *18*(4), pp. 659–79. [G: Colombia; Panama; Peru]

Goldstein, Sidney and Goldstein, Alice. The Impact of Migration on Fertility: An 'Own Children' Analysis for Thailand. *Population Stud.*, July 1981, *35*(2), pp. 265–84. [G: Thailand]

Goldstein, Sidney and Goldstein, Alice. The Use of the Multiplicity Survey to Identify Migrants. *Demography*, February 1981 *18*(1), pp. 67–83. [G: U.S.]

Goodman, John L. Information, Uncertainty, and the Microeconomic Model of Migration Decision Making. In *De Jong, G. F. and Gardner, R. W., eds.*, 1981, pp. 130–48.

Goodman, John L., Jr. Demographic Trends and Housing Prices. In *Tuccillo, J. A. and Villani, K. E., eds.*, 1981, pp. 81–86. [G: U.S.]

Gordon, Ian Richard. Balance and Stability in Return Migration: A Comment on Bell and Kirwan's (1979) Scottish Study [Return Migration in a Scottish Context]. *Reg. Stud.*, 1981, *15*(1), pp. 57–61.

Gordon, Peter and Ledent, Jacques. Towards an Interregional Demoeconomic Model. *J. Reg. Sci.*, February 1981, *21*(1), pp. 79–87.

Gordon, Peter and Theobald, Peter. Migration and Spatial Development in the Republic of Mexico. *J. Devel. Areas*, January 1981, *15*(2), pp. 239–50. [G: Mexico]

Graves, Philip E. and Clawson, Marion. Rural to Urban Migration: Population Distribution Patterns. In *Martin, L. R., ed.*, 1981, pp. 363–90. [G: U.S.]

Greenwood, Michael J.; Ladman, Jerry R. and Sie-

gel, **Barry S.** Long-Term Trends in Migratory Behavior in a Developing Country: The Case of Mexico. *Demography*, August 1981, *18*(3), pp. 369–88. [G: Mexico]

Grossman, Michael and Jacobowitz, Steven. Variations in Infant Mortality Rates among Counties of the United States: The Roles of Public Policies and Programs. *Demography*, November 1981, *18*(4), pp. 695–713. [G: U.S.]

Guest, Avery M. Social Structure and U.S. Inter-State Fertility Differentials in 1900. *Demography*, November 1981, *18*(4), pp. 465–86. [G: U.S.]

Haberkorn, Gerald. The Migration Decision-Making Process: Some Social-Psychological Considerations. In *De Jong, G. F. and Gardner, R. W., eds.*, 1981, pp. 252–78.

Harbison, Sarah F. Family Structure and Family Strategy in Migration Decision Making. In *De Jong, G. F. and Gardner, R. W., eds.*, 1981, pp. 225–51.

Hashimoto, Masanori and Hongladarom, Chira. Effects of Child Mortality on Fertility in Thailand. *Econ. Develop. Cult. Change*, July 1981, *29*(4), pp. 781–94.

Hawley, Amos H. and Mazie, Sarah Mills. Nonmetropolitan America in Transition: An Overview. In *Hawley, A. H. and Mazie, S. M., eds.*, 1981, pp. 3–23.

Hayghe, Howard. Husbands and Wives as Earners: An Analysis of Family Data. *Mon. Lab. Rev.*, February 1981, *104*(2), pp. 46–53. [G: U.S.]

Hazledine, Tim and Moreland, R. Scott. Population and Economic Growth: A Rejoinder. *Rev. Econ. Statist.*, February 1981, *63*(1), pp. 153–55.

Heady, Christopher John. Shadow Wages and Induced Migration. *Oxford Econ. Pap.*, March 1981, *33*(1), pp. 108–21.

Heer, David. Fertility and Female Work Status in the USSR. In *Desfosses, H., ed.*, 1981, pp. 62–94. [G: U.S.S.R.]

Heer, David. Soviet Population Policy: Four Model Futures. In *Desfosses, H., ed.*, 1981, pp. 124–54. [G: U.S.S.R.]

Henin, R. A. The Characteristics and Development Implications of a Fast Growing Population. In *Killick, T., ed.*, 1981, pp. 193–207. [G: Kenya]

Hernandez, Donald J. A Note on Measuring the Independent Impact of Family Planning Programs on Fertility Declines. *Demography*, November 1981, *18*(4), pp. 627–34. [G: LDCs]

Herrin, Alejandro N., et al. Demographic Development in ASEAN: A Comparative Overview. *Phillipine Rev. Econ. Bus.*, Sept. & Dec. 1981, *18*(3/4), pp. 132–53. [G: ASEAN Countries]

Hershberg, Theodore and Williams, Henry. Mulattoes and Blacks: Intra-group Color Differences and Social Stratification in Nineteenth-Century Philadelphia. In *Hershberg, T., ed.*, 1981, pp. 392–434. [G: U.S.]

Hershberg, Theodore, et al. A Tale of Three Cities: Blacks, Immigrants, and Opportunity in Philadelphia, 1850–1880, 1930, 1970. In *Hershberg, T., ed.*, 1981, pp. 461–91. [G: U.S.]

Herzog, Henry W., Jr. and Schlottmann, Alan M. Labor Force Migration and Allocative Efficiency in the United States: The Roles of Information and Psychic Costs. *Econ. Inquiry*, July 1981, *19*(3), pp. 459–75. **[G: U.S.]**

Hill, Allan G. Population Growth in the Middle East since 1945 with Special Reference to the Arab Countries of West Asia. In *[Fisher, W. B.]*, 1981, pp. 130–53. **[G: Middle East]**

Hirschman, Charles. The Uses of Demography in Development Planning. *Econ. Develop. Cult. Change*, April 1981, *29*(3), pp. 561–75.

Hogan, Dennis P. and Frenzen, Paul D. Antecedents to Contraceptive Innovation: Evidence from Rural Northern Thailand. *Demography*, November 1981, *18*(4), pp. 597–614. **[G: Thailand]**

Höpflinger, François. Neuere Veränderungen der Familienbildung in der Schweiz. (Recent Trends in Family-Formation in Switzerland. With English summary.) *Schweiz. Z. Volkswirtsch. Statist.*, September 1981, *117*(3), pp. 479–89. **[G: Switzerland]**

Hornik, Jacob and Schlinger, Mary Jane. Allocation of Time to the Mass Media. *J. Cons. Res.*, March 1981, *7*(4), pp. 343–55. **[G: U.S.]**

Hughes, Gordon A. and McCormick, Barry. Do Council Housing Policies Reduce Migration between Regions? *Econ. J.*, December 1981, *91*(364), pp. 919–37. **[G: U.K.]**

Hughes, J. G. The Relationship between Alternative Population and Migration Series: A Comment. *Econ. Soc. Rev.*, January 1981, *12*(2), pp. 141–44. **[G: Ireland]**

Hugo, Graeme J. Village-Community Ties, Village Norms, and Ethnic and Social Networks: A Review of Evidence from the Third World. In *De Jong, G. F. and Gardner, R. W., eds.*, 1981, pp. 186–224.

Hull, Terence H. Indonesian Population Growth, 1971–1980. *Bull. Indonesian Econ. Stud.*, March 1981, *17*(1), pp. 114–20. **[G: Indonesia]**

Hunt, Janet C. and Kiker, B. F. The Effect of Fertility on the Time Use of Working Wives. *J. Cons. Res.*, March 1981, *7*(4), pp. 380–87. **[G: U.S.]**

Ingram, Gregory K. and Carroll, Alan. Symposium on Urbanization and Development: The Spatial Structure of Latin American Cities. *J. Urban Econ.*, March 1981, *9*(2), pp. 257–73. **[G: Latin America; U.S.; Canada]**

Inoki, Takenori and Suruga, Terukazu. Migration and Income Distribution in the Post-War Japan—A Note on the Concept of Efficiency of Migration. (In Japanese. With English summary.) *Osaka Econ. Pap.*, December 1981, *31*(2–3), pp. 192–98. **[G: Japan]**

Isard, W. and Reiner, Th. A. Megalopolitan Decline and Urban Redevelopment in the United States, an Analysis of Evolutionary Forces. In *Klaassen, L. H.; Molle, W. T. M. and Paelinck, J. H. P., eds.*, 1981, pp. 225–48. **[G: U.S.]**

Ishitani, H., et al. Modelling of Geographical Distribution of Population in a Region and Its Application for Regional Planning. In *Janssen, J. M. L.; Pau, L. F. and Straszak, A. J., eds.*, 1981, pp. 213–20. **[G: Japan]**

Jain, Anrudh K. The Effect of Female Education on Fertility: A Simple Explanation. *Demography*, November 1981, *18*(4), pp. 577–95. **[G: Latin America; Asia]**

Jansen, J. C. and Paelinck, J. H. P. The Urbanisation Phenomenon in the Process of Development: Some Statistical Evidence. In *Klaassen, L. H.; Molle, W. T. M. and Paelinck, J. H. P., eds.*, 1981, pp. 31–46. **[G: Selected LDCs]**

Janssen, Martin and Müller, Heinz. Der Einfluss der Demographie auf die Aktivitäten des Staates: die Finanzierung der 1. und 2. Säule der Altersvorsorge. (The Influence of Demography on the Activities of the State: Financing of the First and Second Pillars of the Old Age Security Scheme. With English summary.) *Schweiz. Z. Volkswirtsch. Statist.*, September 1981, *117*(3), pp. 297–314.

Janssen, Susan G. and Hauser, Robert M. Religion, Socialization, and Fertility. *Demography*, November 1981, *18*(4), pp. 511–28. **[G: U.S.]**

Johansen, Hans Chr. Slave Demography of the Danish West Indian Islands. *Scand. Econ. Hist. Rev.*, 1981, *29*(1), pp. 1–20. **[G: W. Indies]**

Johnston, Bruce F. Reply to the Ness Critique of Johnston and Meyer [Nutrition, Health, and Population in Strategies for Rural Development]. *Econ. Develop. Cult. Change*, January 1981, *29*(2), pp. 407–08.

Jones, Elise F. The Impact of Women's Employment on Marital Fertility in the U.S., 1970–75. *Population Stud.*, July 1981, *35*(2), pp. 161–73. **[G: U.S.]**

Jones, Philip C. A Remark on Economic Response to Technological Innovation [Division of Labor—Simon Revisited]. *Reg. Sci. Urban Econ.*, May 1981, *11*(2), pp. 255–66.

Kadane, Joseph B. Modeling Demographic Relationships: An Analysis of Forecast Functions for Australian Births: Comment. *J. Amer. Statist. Assoc.*, December 1981, *76*(376), pp. 792–93. **[G: Australia]**

Kâgitçibaşi, Çigdem. The Value of Children: Motivations for Childbearing in Turkey. In *Molt, W.; Hartmann, H. A. and Stringer, P., eds.*, 1981, pp. 243–53. **[G: Turkey]**

Kahn, Herman and Schneider, Ernest. Globaloney 2000. *Policy Rev.*, Spring 1981, (16), pp. 129–47.

Kasarda, John D. Population and Economic Base Changes in Metropolitan Areas. In *Clark, T. N., ed.*, 1981, pp. 247–56. **[G: U.S.]**

Kasun, Jacqueline. The International Politics of Contraception. *Policy Rev.*, Winter 1981, (15), pp. 135–52.

Katzman, Martin T. An Ecology of Family Decisions: Suburbanization, Schooling, and Fertility in Philadelphia, 1880–1920: Comment. In *Stave, B. M., ed.*, 1981, pp. 61–67. **[G: U.S.]**

Keenan, J. G. Irish Migration, All or Nothing Resolved? *Econ. Soc. Rev.*, April 1981, *12*(3), pp. 169–86. **[G: Ireland; U.K.]**

Kelley, Allen C. Demographic Impacts on Demand Patterns in the Low-Income Setting. *Econ. Develop. Cult. Change*, October 1981, *30*(1), pp. 1–16. **[G: Kenya]**

Keyfitz, Nathan. Equity between the Sexes: The Pension Problem. *J. Policy Anal. Manage.*, Fall 1981, *1*(1), pp. 133–35. **[G: U.S.]**

Keyfitz, Nathan. The Limits of Population Forecasting. *Population Devel. Rev.*, December 1981, 7(4), pp. 579–93.

Khan, M. Ali and Sirageldin, Ismail. Intrafamily Interaction and Desired Additional Fertility in Pakistan: A Simultaneous-Equation Model with Dichotomous Dependent Variables. *Pakistan Devel. Rev.*, Spring 1981, 20(1), pp. 37–60.
[G: Pakistan]

Kim, Dae Young and Sloboda, John E. Migration and Korean Development. In *Repetto, R., et al.*, 1981, pp. 36–138. [G: S. Korea]

Kim, Son-Ung. Population Policies in Korea. In *Repetto, R., et al.*, 1981, pp. 196–221.
[G: S. Korea]

Kingson, Eric R. and Scheffler, Richard M. Aging: Issues and Economic Trends for the 1980s. *Inquiry*, Fall 1981, 18(3), pp. 197–213. [G: U.S.]

Kiseleva, G. The Position of Women and Demographic Policy. *Prob. Econ.*, Sept.–Oct.–Nov. 1981, 24(5–6–7), pp. 282–95. [G: U.S.S.R.]

Kitagawa, Evelyn M. New Life-Styles: Marriage Patterns, Living Arrangements, and Fertility Outside of Marriage. *Ann. Amer. Acad. Polit. Soc. Sci.*, January 1981, 453, pp. 1–27. [G: U.S.]

Kitano, Harry H. L. Asian–Americans: The Chinese, Japanese, Koreans, Philippinos, and Southeast Asians. *Ann. Amer. Acad. Polit. Soc. Sci.*, March 1981, 454, pp. 125–38. [G: U.S.]

Klep, Paul M. M. Regional Disparities in Brabantine Urbanisation before and after the Industrial Revolution (1374–1970): Some Aspects of Measurement and Explanation. In *Bairoch, P. and Lévy-Leboyer, M., eds.*, 1981, pp. 259–69.
[G: Belgium]

Klinger, András. Population, Demographic Policy and Its Instruments in Hungary. *Acta Oecon.*, 1981, 27(1–2), pp. 93–109. [G: Hungary]

Knodel, J. and Wilson, C. The Secular Increase in Fecundity in German Village Populations: An Analysis of Reproductive Histories of Couples Married, 1750–1899. *Population Stud.*, March 1981, 35(1), pp. 53–84. [G: Germany]

Kosobud, Richard F. and O'Neill, William D. On the Dependence of Population Growth on Income: New Results in a Ricardian-Malthus Model. *De Economist*, 1981, 129(2), pp. 206–23.

Kotlikoff, Laurence J. and Spivak, Avia. The Family as an Incomplete Annuities Market. *J. Polit. Econ.*, April 1981, 89(2), pp. 372–91.

Krashinsky, Michael. Subsidies to Child Care: Public Policy and Optimality. *Public Finance Quart.*, July 1981, 9(3), pp. 243–69. [G: U.S.]

Kubat, Daniel and Hoffman-Nowotny, Hans-Joachim. Migration: Towards a New Paradigm. *Int. Soc. Sci. J.*, 1981, 33(2), pp. 307–29.

Kwon, Tai Hwan. The Historical Background to Korea's Demographic Transition. In *Repetto, R., et al.*, 1981, pp. 10–35. [G: S. Korea]

Ladd, Helen F. Municipal Expenditures and the Rate of Population Change. In *Burchell, R. W. and Listokin, D., eds.*, 1981, pp. 351–67.
[G: U.S.]

Land, Kenneth C. and McMillen, Marilyn M. Demographic Accounts and the Study of Social Change, with Applications to the Post-World War II United States. In *Juster, F. T. and Land,*

K. C., eds., 1981, pp. 241–306. [G: U.S.]

Langford, C. M. Fertility Change in Sri Lanka since the War: An Analysis of the Experience of Different Districts. *Population Stud.*, July 1981, 35(2), pp. 285–306. [G: Sri Lanka]

Langsten, Ray. The Effects of Crises on Differential Mortality by Sex in Bangladesh. *Bangladesh Devel. Stud.*, Summer 1981, 9(2), pp. 75–96.
[G: Bangladesh]

Lapidus, Gail W. Women, Work, and Family: New Soviet Perspectives: Introduction. *Prob. Econ.*, Sept.–Oct.–Nov. 1981, 24(5–6–7), pp. ix–xlvi.
[G: U.S.S.R.]

Leach, Donald. Re-evaluation of the Logistic Curve for Human Populations. *J. Roy. Statist. Soc.*, Part 1, 1981, 144, pp. 94–103. [G: U.K.]

Ledent, Jacques and Gordon, Peter. A Framework for Modeling Interregional Population Distribution and Economic Growth. *Int. Reg. Sci. Rev.*, Fall 1981, 6(1), pp. 85–90.

Lee, R. D. and Schofield, R. S. British Population in the Eighteenth Century. In *Floud, R. and McCloskey, D., eds., Vol. 1*, 1981, pp. 17–35.
[G: U.K.]

Lee, Ronald. A Stock Adjustment Model of U.S. Marital Fertility. In *Simon, J. L. and Lindert, P. H., eds.*, 1981, pp. 67–93. [G: U.S.]

Lee, Ronald. Modeling Demographic Relationships: An Analysis of Forecast Functions for Australian Births: Comment. *J. Amer. Statist. Assoc.*, December 1981, 76(376), pp. 793–95.
[G: Australia]

Lehrer, Evelyn and Nerlove, Marc. The Labor Supply and Fertility Behavior of Married Women: A Three-Period Model. In *Simon, J. L. and Lindert, P. H., eds.*, 1981, pp. 123–45. [G: U.S.]

Leibenstein, Harvey. Economic Decision Theory and Human Fertility Behavior: A Speculative Essay. *Population Devel. Rev.*, September 1981, 7(3), pp. 381–400.

Leontief, Wassily W. Population Growth and Economic Development: Illustrative Projections. In *Reubens, E. P., ed.*, 1981, 1979, pp. 39–60.

Lesthaeghe, Ron J. Demographic Change, Social Security and Economic Growth: Inferences from the Belgian Example. *Schweiz. Z. Volkswirtsch. Statist.*, September 1981, 117(3), pp. 225–55.
[G: Belgium]

Levitan, Sar A. and Belous, Richard S. Working Wives and Mothers: What Happens to Family Life? *Mon. Lab. Rev.*, September 1981, 104(9), pp. 26–30. [G: U.S.]

Lewis, Maureen A. Sectoral Aspects of a Basic Human Needs Approach: The Linkages among Population, Nutrition, and Health. In *Leipziger, D. M., ed.*, 1981, pp. 29–105. [G: LDCs]

Lithwick, N. H. and Cohen, Gad. The Israeli Experience: Some Economic Aspects of Population Distribution Policies. *Growth Change*, July 1981, 12(3), pp. 23–31. [G: Israel]

Little, Roderick J. A. Modeling Demographic Relationships: An Analysis of Forecast Functions for Australian Births: Comment. *J. Amer. Statist. Assoc.*, December 1981, 76(376), pp. 795–96.
[G: Australia]

von Loesch, Heinrich. Economistic Theories of Fertility Motivation and Rich and Poor Populations; a Critical Evaluation and Proposals for Socio-Psychology Approaches. In *Molt, W.; Hartmann, H. A. and Stringer, P., eds.*, 1981, pp. 233–42.

Long, John F. Modeling Demographic Relationships: An Analysis of Forecast Functions for Australian Births: Comment. *J. Amer. Statist. Assoc.*, December 1981, *76*(376), pp. 796–98.
[G: Australia]

Long, John F. Survey of Federally Produced National Level Demographic Projections. *Rev. Public Data Use (See J. Econ. Soc. Meas. after 4/85)*, December 1981, *9*(4), pp. 309–19.
[G: U.S.]

MacDonald, Maurice M. and Rindfuss, Ronald R. Earnings, Relative Income, and Family Formation. *Demography*, May 1981, *18*(2), pp. 123–36.
[G: U.S.]

Maitra, Priyatosh. Malthus Revisited—Population, Poverty and Pollution. *Int. J. Soc. Econ.*, 1981, *8*(3), pp. 47–61.

Maitra, Priyatosh. Technology Transfer, Population Growth and the Development Gap since the Industrial Revolution. In *Bairoch, P. and Lévy-Leboyer, M., eds.*, 1981, pp. 78–85. [G: LDCs; W. Europe]

Mandelbaum, Seymour J. The Economy of Cities: Comment. In *Stave, B. M., ed.*, 1981, pp. 251–57. [G: U.S.]

Manton, Kenneth G.; Stallard, Eric and Vaupel, James W. Methods for Comparing the Mortality Experience of Heterogeneous Populations. *Demography*, August 1981, *18*(3), pp. 389–410.
[G: Sweden; U.S.]

Marini, Margaret Mooney and Hodsdon, Peter J. Effects of the Timing of Marriage and First Birth on the Spacing of Subsequent Births. *Demography*, November 1981, *18*(4), pp. 529–48.

Mason, Andrew and Suits, Daniel B. Computing the Level and Distribution of Gains from Fertility Reduction. In *Simon, J. L. and Lindert, P. H., eds.*, 1981, pp. 255–72.

Mason, Karen Oppenheim and Palan, V. T. Female Employment and Fertility in Peninsular Malaysia: The Maternal Role Incompatibility Hypothesis Reconsidered. *Demography*, November 1981, *18*(4), pp. 549–75. [G: Malaysia]

McDonald, John. Modeling Demographic Relationships: An Analysis of Forecast Functions for Australian Births. *J. Amer. Statist. Assoc.*, December 1981, *76*(376), pp. 782–92. [G: Australia]

McDonald, John. Modeling Demographic Relationships: An Analysis of Forecast Functions for Australian Births: Rejoinder. *J. Amer. Statist. Assoc.*, December 1981, *76*(376), pp. 799–801.
[G: Australia]

McDonald, John and Morgan, Peter. Forecasting Australian Marriage Rates. *Econ. Rec.*, March 1981, *57*(156), pp. 47–57. [G: Australia]

McIntosh, C. Alison. Low Fertility and Liberal Democracy in Western Europe. *Population Devel. Rev.*, June 1981, *7*(2), pp. 181–207.
[G: W. Europe]

McNamara, Robert S. To the Board of Governors, Copenhagen, Denmark, September 21, 1970. In

McNamara, R. S., 1981, *1970*, pp. 111–34.
[G: Selected LDCs]

McNamara, Robert S. To the Board of Governors, Washington, D.C., September 27, 1971. In *McNamara, R. S.*, 1981, *1971*, pp. 137–67.

McNamara, Robert S. To the Massachusetts Institute of Technology, Cambridge, Massachusetts, April 28, 1977. In *McNamara, R. S.*, 1981, *1977*, pp. 379–433.

McNamara, Robert S. To the University of Notre Dame, Notre Dame, Indiana, May 1, 1969. In *McNamara, R. S.*, 1981, *1969*, pp. 33–52.

McPheters, Lee R. and Schlagenhauf, Don E. Macroeconomic Determinants of the Flow of Undocumented Aliens in North America. *Growth Change*, January 1981, *12*(1), pp. 2–8.
[G: U.S.]

Medick, Hans. The Structures and Function of Population-Development under the Protoindustrial System. In *Kriedte, P.; Medick, H. and Schlumbohm, J.*, 1981, pp. 74–93. [G: Europe]

Meidinger, Claude. La théorie économique de la famille: Une critique méthodologique. (The Economic Theory of Family Decisions. With English summary.) *Consommation*, July–September 1981, *28*(3), pp. 75–93.

Méng-Try, EA. Kampuchea: A Country Adrift. *Population Devel. Rev.*, June 1981, *7*(2), pp. 209–28. [G: Kampuchea]

Menken, Jane, et al. Proportional Hazards Life Table Models: An Illustrative Analysis of Socio-Demographic Influences on Marriage Dissolution in the United States. *Demography*, May 1981, *18*(2), pp. 181–200. [G: U.S.]

Menthonnex, Jacques. Modèle explicatif de la fécondité en analyse longitudinale. (A Model Explaining Fertility Behaviour over Time. With English summary.) *Schweiz. Z. Volkswirtsch. Statist.*, September 1981, *117*(3), pp. 491–504.
[G: Switzerland]

Merrick, Thomas W. Land Availability and Rural Fertility in Northeastern Brazil. In *Simon, J. L. and Lindert, P. H., eds.*, 1981, pp. 93–121.
[G: Brazil]

Milne, William J. Migration in an Interregional Macroeconometric Model of the United States: Will Net Outmigration from the Northeast Continue? *Int. Reg. Sci. Rev.*, Fall 1981, *6*(1), pp. 71–83.
[G: U.S.]

Modell, John. An Ecology of Family Decisions: Suburbanization, Schooling, and Fertility in Philadelphia, 1880–1920. In *Stave, B. M., ed.*, 1981, *1980*, pp. 39–59. [G: U.S.]

Modell, John; Hershberg, Theodore and Furstenberg, Frank F., Jr. Social Change and Transitions to Adulthood in Historical Perspective. In *Hershberg, T., ed.*, 1981, *1975*, pp. 311–41.
[G: U.S.]

Modell, John and Lees, Lynn H. The Irish Countryman Urbanized: A Comparative Perspective on the Famine Migration. In *Hershberg, T., ed.*, 1981, *1977*, pp. 351–67. [G: U.S.; U.K.]

Moland, John, Jr. The Black Population. In *Hawley, A. H. and Mazie, S. M., eds.*, 1981, pp. 464–501. [G: U.S.]

Morgan, Barrie S. and Norbury, John. Some Further Observations on the Index of Residential Differentiation. *Demography*, May 1981, *18*(2), pp. 251–56. [G: U.S.]

Morgan, James N. Child Care when Parents are Employed. In *Hill, M. S.; Hill, D. H. and Morgan, J. N., eds.*, 1981, pp. 441–56. [G: U.S.]

Morgan, S. Philip. Intention and Uncertainty at Later Stages of Childbearing: The United States, 1965 and 1970. *Demography*, August 1981, *18*(3), pp. 267–85. [G: U.S.]

Morley, Samuel A. The Effect of Changes in the Population on Several Measures of Income Distribution. *Amer. Econ. Rev.*, June 1981, *71*(3), pp. 285–94. [G: Brazil]

Mosk, Carl. The Evolution of the Pre-modern Demographic Regime in Japan. *Population Stud.*, March 1981, *35*(1), pp. 28–52. [G: Japan]

Mosk, Carl. The Evolution of Premodern Demographic Regimes: A Research Note. *Exploration Econ. Hist.*, April 1981, *18*(2), pp. 199–208. [G: Sweden; Japan]

Murnane, Richard J.; Maynard, Rebecca A. and Ohls, James C. Home Resources and Children's Achievement. *Rev. Econ. Statist.*, August 1981, *63*(3), pp. 369–77. [G: U.S.]

Myers, George C. The Demographically Emergent South. In *Poston, D. L., Jr. and Weller, R. H., eds.*, 1981, pp. 268–82. [G: U.S.]

Naidu, D. Audikesavulu. Unmet Needs of Indian Children and the Alternative Strategies for Potential Human Resource Development. *Econ. Aff.*, April–June 1981, *26*(2), pp. 93–103. [G: India]

Naidu, R. Chinnaswamy. Role of Agricultural Development in Reduction in Fertility. *Econ. Aff.*, October–December 1981, *26*(4), pp. 283–88. [G: India]

Nam, Duck-Woo and Ro, Kong-Kyun. Population Research and Population Policy in Korea in the 1970s. *Population Devel. Rev.*, December 1981, *7*(4), pp. 651–69. [G: S. Korea]

Nerlove, Marc and Razin, Assaf. Child Spacing and Numbers: An Empirical Analysis. In *[Stone, R.]*, 1981, pp. 297–324. [G: Canada]

Ness, Gayl D. The Political Economy of Integration in Development Strategies: Comment on Johnston and Meyer [Nutrition, Health, and Population in Strategies for Rural Development]. *Econ. Develop. Cult. Change*, January 1981, *29*(2), pp. 401–05.

Neun, Gabi. Workshop Reproductive Behavior. In *Molt, W.; Hartmann, H. A. and Stringer, P., eds.*, 1981, pp. 265–67.

Newman, Allen R. A Test of the Okun–Richardson Model of Internal Migration. *Econ. Develop. Cult. Change*, January 1981, *29*(2), pp. 295–307. [G: Germany]

Nolan, Michael F., et al. A Note on Ozark Migrants and Nonmigrants. *Growth Change*, July 1981, *12*(3), pp. 47–52. [G: U.S.]

Nosse, Nobuko. Accounting Systems of Non-Market Oriented Activities. *Kobe Econ. Bus. Rev.*, 1981, (27), pp. 1–10.

O'Connell, Martin. Regional Fertility Patterns in the United States: Convergence or Divergence? *Int. Reg. Sci. Rev.*, Fall 1981, *6*(1), pp. 1–14. [G: U.S.]

Oberai, A. S. State Policies and Internal Migration in Asia. *Int. Lab. Rev.*, March–April 1981, *120*(2), pp. 231–44. [G: Asia]

Pachon, Harry P. and Moore, Joan W. Mexican Americans. *Ann. Amer. Acad. Polit. Soc. Sci.*, March 1981, *454*, pp. 111–24. [G: U.S.]

Palloni, Alberto. A Review of Infant Mortality Trends in Selected Underdeveloped Countries: Some New Estimates. *Population Stud.*, March 1981, *35*(1), pp. 100–119. [G: LDCs]

Palloni, Alberto. Mortality in Latin America: Emerging Patterns. *Population Devel. Rev.*, December 1981, *7*(4), pp. 623–49. [G: Latin America?]

Paqueo, Vicente B. Economic-Demographic Interactions and the Impact of Investments in Population Control. *Philippine Econ. J.*, 1981, *20*(3&4), pp. 257–76. [G: Philippines]

Parkinson, Jack. Donor Co-ordination and Collective Leverage: The Role of the World Bank. In *Faaland, J., ed.*, 1981, pp. 147–64. [G: Bangladesh]

Pebley, Anne R. The Age at First Birth and Timing of the Second in Costa Rica and Guatemala. *Population Stud.*, November 1981, *35*(3), pp. 387–97. [G: Costa Rica; Guatemala]

Perlman, Mark. Population and Economic Change in Developing Countries: A Review Article. *J. Econ. Lit.*, March 1981, *19*(1), pp. 74–82.

Perlman, Mark. Some Economic Consequences of the New Patterns of Population Growth. In *Fellner, W., ed.*, 1981, pp. 247–79. [G: U.S.]

Pernia, Ernesto M. On the Relationship between Migration and Fertility. *Phillipine Rev. Econ. Bus.*, Sept. & Dec. 1981, *18*(3/4), pp. 192–202. [G: Philippines]

Pillet, Gonzague, et al. Démographie et système d'éducation. (Demography and Educational System. With English summary.) *Schweiz. Z. Volkswirtsch. Statist.*, September 1981, *117*(3), pp. 337–61. [G: Switzerland]

Pittenger, Donald B. On the Persistence of U.S. Net Migration Rates in the 20th Century. *Growth Change*, October 1981, *12*(4), pp. 43–49. [G: U.S.]

Plane, David A. Estimation of Place-to-Place Migration Flows from Net Migration Totals: A Minimum Information Approach. *Int. Reg. Sci. Rev.*, Fall 1981, *6*(1), pp. 33–51. [G: U.S.]

Plaut, Thomas R. An Econometric Model for Forecasting Regional Population Growth. *Int. Reg. Sci. Rev.*, Fall 1981, *6*(1), pp. 53–70. [G: U.S.]

Pollak, Robert A. and Wales, Terence J. Demographic Variables in Demand Analysis. *Econometrica*, November 1981, *49*(6), pp. 1533–51. [G: U.K.]

Pope, David H. Modelling the Peopling of Australia: 1900–1930. *Australian Econ. Pap.*, December 1981, *20*(37), pp. 258–82. [G: Australia]

Porell, Frank W. and Hua, Chang-I. An Econometric Procedure for Estimation of a Generalized Systemic Gravity Model under Incomplete Information about the System. *Reg. Sci. Urban Econ.*, November 1981, *11*(4), pp. 585–606. [G: U.S.]

Poston, Dudley L., Jr. An Ecological Explanation of Southern Population Redistribution, 1970–1975. In *Poston, D. L., Jr. and Weller, R. H.,* eds., 1981, pp. 137–54. [G: U.S.]

Poston, Dudley L., Jr.; Serow, William J. and Weller, Robert H. Demographic Change in the South. In *Poston, D. L., Jr. and Weller, R. H., eds.*, 1981, pp. 3–22. [G: U.S.]

Powell, David E. The Rural Exodus. In *Bornstein, M., ed.*, 1981, *1974*, pp. 149–63. [G: U.S.S.R.]

Pursell, Donald E. Natural Population Decrease: Its Origins and Implications on the Great Plains. In *Lawson, M. P. and Baker, M. E., eds.*, 1981, pp. 53–66. [G: U.S.]

Ram, Rati. Population and Economic Growth: A Critical Note. *Rev. Econ. Statist.*, February 1981, *63*(1), pp. 149–53.

Reimers, David M. Post-World War II Immigration to the United States: America's Latest Newcomers. *Ann. Amer. Acad. Polit. Soc. Sci.*, March 1981, *454*, pp. 1–12. [G: U.S.]

Repetto, Robert. Socio-economic Influences on the Fertility Decline in Korea. In *Repetto, R., et al.*, 1981, pp. 139–95. [G: S. Korea]

Reubens, Edwin P. International Migration in North–South Relations. In *Reubens, E. P., ed.*, 1981, pp. 215–54.

Rindfuss, Ronald R. The Population of the South: Fertility. In *Poston, D. L., Jr. and Weller, R. H., eds.*, 1981, pp. 23–54. [G: U.S.]

Roberts, Walter Orr and Slater, Lloyd E. The Interaction of Food, Climate, and Population. In *Cleveland, H., ed.*, 1981, pp. 239–65.

Robinson, W. C. Population Control and Development Strategy. In *Livingstone, I., ed.*, 1981, *1972*, pp. 51–58. [G: LDCs]

Rodgers, Gerry and Standing, Guy. Economic Roles of Children in Low-Income Countries. *Int. Lab. Rev.*, January–February 1981, *120*(1), pp. 31–47.

Rodgers, Gerry B. An Analysis of Education, Employment, and Income Distribution Using an Economic-Demographic Model of the Philippines. In *Khan, A. and Sirageldin, I., eds.*, 1981, pp. 143–80. [G: Philippines]

Rodriguez, G. and Trussell, T. J. A Note on Synthetic Cohort Estimates of Average Desired Family Size. *Population Stud.*, July 1981, *35*(2), pp. 321–28.

Rolfe, Philip H. The Causes of Inter-Regional Labour Force Migration in Great Britain. *Bull. Econ. Res.*, November 1981, *33*(2), pp. 74–81. [G: U.K.]

Romaniuk, A. Increase in Natural Fertility during the Early Stages of Modernization: Canadian Indians Case Study. *Demography*, May 1981, *18*(2), pp. 157–72. [G: Canada]

Rosenberg, Harry M. and Burnham, Drusilla. The Population of the South: Mortality. In *Poston, D. L., Jr. and Weller, R. H., eds.*, 1981, pp. 55–108. [G: U.S.]

von Rosenstiel, Lutz. Regarding Psychology of Reproductive Behavior—An Introduction. In *Molt, W.; Hartmann, H. A. and Stringer, P., eds.*, 1981, pp. 191–96.

Ross, J. A. and Madhavan, Shantha. A Gompertz Model for Birth Interval Analysis. *Population Stud.*, November 1981, *35*(3), pp. 439–54. [G: Korea]

Rotherham, James A. Impact of Future Social and Demographic Change on Programs for Reducing Economic Dependency. In *Brown, P. G.; Johnson, C. and Vernier, P., eds.*, 1981, pp. 337–62. [G: U.S.]

Ruggles, Richard. The Conceptual and Empirical Strengths and Limitations of Demographic and Time-Based Accounts. In *Juster, F. T. and Land, K. C., eds.*, 1981, pp. 453–76.

Russett, Bruce, et al. Health and Population Patterns as Indicators of Income Inequality. *Econ. Develop. Cult. Change*, July 1981, *29*(4), pp. 759–79. [G: LDCs]

Ryder, N. B. A Time Series of Instrumental Fertility Variables. *Demography*, November 1981, *18*(4), pp. 487–509. [G: U.S.]

Salvatore, Dominick. A Theoretical and Empirical Evaluation and Extension of the Todaro Migration Model. *Reg. Sci. Urban Econ.*, November 1981, *11*(4), pp. 499–508. [G: Italy]

Sandefur, Gary D. and Scott, Wilbur J. A Dynamic Analysis of Migration: An Assessment of the Effects of Age, Family and Career Variables. *Demography*, August 1981, *18*(3), pp. 355–68. [G: U.S.]

Sapir, André. Economic Reform and Migration in Yugoslavia: An Econometric Model. *J. Devel. Econ.*, October 1981, *9*(2), pp. 149–81. [G: Yugoslavia]

Sauvy, Alfred. Population Changes: Contemporary Models and Theories. In *Simon, J. L. and Lindert, P. H., eds.*, 1981, pp. 225–38.

Schapiro, Morton Owen and Easterlin, Richard A. Educational Attainment by Sex and Age, 1980–2000. *Rev. Public Data Use (See J. Econ. Soc. Meas. after 4/85)*, December 1981, *9*(4), pp. 323–39. [G: U.S.]

Schram, Vicki R. and Dunsing, Marilyn M. Influences on Married Women's Volunteer Work Participation. *J. Cons. Res.*, March 1981, *7*(4), pp. 372–79. [G: U.S.]

Schuler, Martin. Mobilitätsentwicklung und Substitutionsformen der räumlichen Mobilität. (The Development of Mobility and the Substitution of Spatial Mobility. With English summary.) *Schweiz. Z. Volkswirtsch. Statist.*, September 1981, *117*(3), pp. 445–52. [G: Switzerland]

Serow, William J. Alternative Demographic Futures and the Composition of the Demand for Labor, by Industry and by Occupation. In *Simon, J. L. and Lindert, P. H., eds.*, 1981, pp. 209–23. [G: U.S.]

Serow, William J. An Economic Approach to Population Change in the South. In *Poston, D. L., Jr. and Weller, R. H., eds.*, 1981, pp. 198–226. [G: U.S.]

Serow, William J. Demographic and Economic Considerations for Future Retirement Policy. *Policy Anal.*, Spring 1981, *7*(2), pp. 143–51. [G: U.S.]

Serow, William J. Population and Other Policy Responses to an Era of Sustained Low Fertility. *Soc. Sci. Quart.*, June 1981, *62*(2), pp. 323–32.

Simon, Julian L. and Steinmann, Gunter. Population Growth and Phelps' Technical Progress Model: Interpretation and Generalization. In *Simon, J. L. and Lindert, P. H., eds.*, 1981, pp. 239–54.

Simonen, Mari S. Education, Family Economic Production, and Fertility: The Case of Rural and Semi-Urban Guatemala. In *Balderston, J. B., et al., eds.*, 1981, pp. 147–76.   [G: Guatemala]

Singh, J. P. Patterns of Urbanization in a Developing Region: A Demographic Perspective. In *Karna, M. N., ed.*, 1981, pp. 87–103.   [G: India]

Sinha, Amareshwar Prasad. Economic Backwardness of Bihar and Certain Relevant Aspects of Census Data. In *Karna, M. N., ed.*, 1981, pp. 15–27.   [G: India]

Slovic, Paul; Fischhoff, Baruch and Lichtenstein, Sarah. Rating the Risks. In *Haimes, Y. Y., ed.*, 1981, *1980*, pp. 193–217.   [G: U.S.]

Sly, David F. The Population of the South: Migration. In *Poston, D. L., Jr. and Weller, R. H., eds.*, 1981, pp. 109–36.   [G: U.S.]

Smith, David P. A Reconsideration of Easterlin Cycles. *Population Stud.*, July 1981, *35*(2), pp. 247–64.   [G: U.S.]

Smith, James P. and Welch, Finis. No Time to Be Young: The Economic Prospects for Large Cohorts in the United States. *Population Devel. Rev.*, March 1981, *7*(1), pp. 71–83.   [G: U.S.]

Smith, Richard M. Fertility, Economy, and Household Formation in England over Three Centuries. *Population Devel. Rev.*, December 1981, *7*(4), pp. 595–622.   [G: U.K.]

Smith, Stanley K. Determinants of Female Labor Force Participation and Family Size in Mexico City. *Econ. Develop. Cult. Change*, October 1981, *30*(1), pp. 129–52.   [G: Mexico]

Smith, Stanley K. Women's Work, Fertility, and Competing Time Use in Mexico City. In *Simon, J. L. and Lindert, P. H., eds.*, 1981, pp. 167–87.   [G: Mexico]

Smith, Terence R. and Slater, Paul B. A Family of Spatial Interaction Models Incorporating Information Flows and Choice Set Constraints Applied to U.S. Interstate Labor Flows. *Int. Reg. Sci. Rev.*, Fall 1981, *6*(1), pp. 15–31.   [G: U.S.]

Sommers, Paul M. Analysis of Net Interstate Migration Revisited. *Soc. Sci. Quart.*, June 1981, *62*(2), pp. 294–302.   [G: U.S.]

Southwick, Lawrence, Jr. Public Welfare Programs and Recipient Migration. *Growth Change*, October 1981, *12*(4), pp. 22–32.   [G: U.S.]

Sow, Fatou. Migration to Dakar. In *Colvin, L. G., et al.*, 1981, pp. 204–43.   [G: Senegal]

Spitze, Glenna D. and Waite, Linda J. Young Women's Preferences for Market Work: Responses to Marital Events. In *Simon, J. L. and Lindert, P. H., eds.*, 1981, pp. 147–66.   [G: U.S.]

Srinivasan, T. N. Malnutrition: Some Measurement and Policy Issues. *J. Devel. Econ.*, February 1981, *8*(1), pp. 3–19.   [G: India; Sri Lanka]

Stark, Oded. The Asset Demand for Children during Agricultural Modernization. *Population Devel. Rev.*, December 1981, *7*(4), pp. 671–75.

Steel, William F. Female and Small-Scale Employment under Modernization in Ghana. *Econ. Develop. Cult. Change*, October 1981, *30*(1), pp. 153–67.   [G: Ghana]

Sternlieb, George and Hughes, James W. New Dimensions of the Urban Crisis. In *Burchell,*

R. W. *and Listokin, D., eds.*, 1981, pp. 51–75.   [G: U.S.]

Sternlieb, George and Hughes, James W. Some Economic Effects of Recent Migration Patterns on Central Cities. In *Simon, J. L. and Lindert, P. H., eds.*, 1981, pp. 189–207.   [G: U.S.]

Stinner, William F. and Bacol-Montilla, Melinda. Population Deconcentration in Metropolitan Manila in the Twentieth Century. *J. Devel. Areas*, October 1981, *16*(1), pp. 3–16. [G: Philippines]

Stone, Richard. The Relationship of Demographic Accounts to National Income and Product Accounts. In *Juster, F. T. and Land, K. C., eds.*, 1981, pp. 307–76.   [G: U.S.; U.K.]

Suyker, W. B. C. An Analysis of Interprovincial Migration in the Netherlands. *De Economist*, 1981, *129*(3), pp. 394–411.   [G: Netherlands]

Syed, Sabiha Hasan. Acceptors of Population Programme in Pakistan. *Pakistan Devel. Rev.*, Spring 1981, *20*(1), pp. 81–93.

Szymanski, Albert. On the Uses of Disinformation to Legitimize the Revival of the Cold War: Health in the U.S.S.R. *Sci. Soc.*, Winter 1981–1982, *45*(4), pp. 453–74.   [G: U.S.S.R.]

Taeuber, Karl E., et al. A Demographic Perspective on School Desegregation in the USA. In *Peach, C.; Robinson, V. and Smith, S., eds.*, 1981, pp. 83–105.   [G: U.S.]

Tarascio, Vincent J. Cantillon's Theory of Population Size and Distribution. *Atlantic Econ. J.*, July 1981, *9*(2), pp. 12–18.

Teitelbaum, Michael S. Population and Development: A Survey: Comment. In *Streeten, P. and Jolly, R, eds.*, 1981, *1976*, pp. 47–51.

Thornton, Arland. The Influence of Income and Aspirations on Childbearing: Evidence from Research Using Multiple Indicators from Mutiple Data Sets. In *Molt, W.; Hartmann, H. A. and Stringer, P., eds.*, 1981, pp. 211–31.   [G: U.S.]

Tienda, Marta. The Mexican-American Population. In *Hawley, A. H. and Mazie, S. M., eds.*, 1981, pp. 503–48.   [G: U.S.]

Tissue, Thomas and McCoy, John L. Income and Living Arrangements among Poor Aged Singles. *Soc. Sec. Bull.*, April 1981, *44*(4), pp. 3–13.   [G: U.S.]

Tolnay, Stewart E. Trends in Total and Marital Fertility for Black Americans, 1886–1899. *Demography*, November 1981, *18*(4), pp. 443–63.   [G: U.S.]

Tomes, Nigel. A Model of Fertility and Children's Schooling. *Econ. Inquiry*, April 1981, *19*(2), pp. 209–34.

Treas, Judith. Postwar Trends in Family Size. *Demography*, August 1981, *18*(3), pp. 321–34.   [G: U.S.]

Tsui, Amy Ong, et al. Community Availability of Contraceptives and Family Limitation. *Demography*, November 1981, *18*(4), pp. 615–25.   [G: Bangladesh; Korea; Mexico]

Tucker, C. Jack. Age and Educational Dimensions of Recent U.S. Migration Reversal. *Growth Change*, April 1981, *12*(2), pp. 31–36. [G: U.S.]

Turchi, Boone A. A Comprehensive Micro Theory of Fertility. In *Molt, W.; Hartmann, H. A. and*

Stringer, P., eds., 1981, pp. 197–210.

Udall, Alan T. Transport Improvements and Rural Outmigration in Colombia. *Econ. Develop. Cult. Change*, April 1981, 29(3), pp. 613–29.
[G: Colombia]

Udovenko, Vitaly. Natural Conditions and Population. In *Novosti Press Agency*, 1981, pp. 17–41.
[G: U.S.S.R.]

Urzúa, Raúl. Priorities for Fundamental Research Relevant to Population Policy: A Summary Report from the International Review Group. *Rev. Public Data Use (See J. Econ. Soc. Meas. after 4/85)*, April 1981, 9(1), pp. 21–30.

Vaessen, M. Knowledge of Contraceptives: An Assessment of World Fertility Survey Data Collection Procedures. *Population Stud.*, November 1981, 35(3), pp. 357–73.
[G: Colombia; Sri Lanka; Thailand; LDCs]

Vaillancourt, François and Lefebvre, Lise. Antecédénts familiaux et connaissance de l'anglais chez les francophones du Québec. (Family Background and the Knowledge of English by Quebec Francophones. With English summary.) *L'Actual. Econ.*, July–September 1981, 57(3), pp. 343–58.
[G: Canada]

Vialet, Joyce. U.S. Immigration Policy. In *U.S. Congress, Joint Economic Committee (III)*, 1981, pp. 209–23.
[G: U.S.]

Volkov, A. G. Changes in the Status of Women and the Demographic Development of the Family. *Prob. Econ.*, Sept.–Oct.–Nov. 1981, 24(5–6–7), pp. 218–29.
[G: U.S.S.R.]

Waite, Linda J. and Spitze, Glenna D. Young Women's Transition to Marriage. *Demography*, November 1981, 18(4), pp. 681–94.
[G: U.S.]

Walsh, Brendan M. Population, Employment and Economic Growth in Ireland. *Irish Banking Rev.*, June 1981, pp. 17–23.
[G: Ireland]

Waxman, Chaim I. The Fourth Generation Grows Up: The Contemporary America Jewish Community. *Ann. Amer. Acad. Polit. Soc. Sci.*, March 1981, 454, pp. 70–85.
[G: U.S.]

Weber, Cynthia and Goodman, Ann. The Demographic Policy Debate in the USSR. *Population Devel. Rev.*, June 1981, 7(2), pp. 279–95.
[G: U.S.S.R.]

Westoff, C. F. Another Look at Fertility and Social Mobility [The Impact of Social Mobility on Fertility]. *Population Stud.*, March 1981, 35(1), pp. 132–35.
[G: U.K.]

White, Lynn K. A Note on Racial Differences in the Effect of Female Economic Opportunity on Marriage Rates. *Demography*, August 1981, 18(3), pp. 349–54.

Wiesler, Hans. Nouveaux coéfficients pour le calcul d'une table de mortalité abrégée. (New Coefficients for the Calculation of an Abridged Life Table. With English summary.) *Schweiz. Z. Volkswirtsch. Statist.*, March 1981, 117(1), pp. 75–85.

Wilde, Louis L. Information Costs, Duration of Search, and Turnover: Theory and Applications. *J. Polit. Econ.*, December 1981, 89(6), pp. 1122–41.

Williams, Lynne S. A Demographic Analysis of Australian Occupational Mobility. *Australian Bull.*

Lab., June 1981, 7(3), pp. 139–73.
[G: Australia]

Williams, Wm. H. and Goodman, Michael L. The Effect of the Demographics of Individual Households on Their Telephone Usage: The Development of the Customer Sample. In *Brandon, B. B., ed.*, 1981, pp. 19–28.
[G: U.S.]

Wilson, William Julius. The Black Community in the 1980s: Questions of Race, Class, and Public Policy. *Ann. Amer. Acad. Polit. Soc. Sci.*, March 1981, 454, pp. 26–41.
[G: U.S.]

Wiltgen, Richard J. Marx and Engels on Malthus and Population: A Reconstruction and Reconsideration. *Quart. Rev. Econ. Bus.*, Winter 1981, 21(4), pp. 107–26.

Wrage, Peter. The Effects of Internal Migration on Regional Wage and Unemployment Disparities in Canada. *J. Reg. Sci.*, February 1981, 21(1), pp. 51–63.
[G: Canada]

Yusuf, F. and Rockett, I. Immigrant Fertility Patterns and Differentials in Australia, 1971–1976. *Population Stud.*, November 1981, 35(3), pp. 413–24.
[G: Australia]

Ziegler, Joseph A. and Britton, Charles R. A Comparative Analysis of Socioeconomic Variations in Measuring the Quality of Life. *Soc. Sci. Quart.*, June 1981, 62(2), pp. 303–12.
[G: U.S.]

Zimmer, B. G. A Rejoinder [The Impact of Social Mobility on Fertility]. *Population Stud.*, March 1981, 35(1), pp. 136.
[G: U.K.]

Zimmer, B. G. The Impact of Social Mobility on Fertility: A Reconsideration. *Population Stud.*, March 1981, 35(1), pp. 120–31.
[G: U.K.]

Zlotnik, Hania and Hill, Kenneth. The Use of Hypothetical Cohorts in Estimating Demographic Parameters under Conditions of Changing Fertility and Mortality. *Demography*, February 1981, 18(1), pp. 103–22.

Zuiches, James J. Residential Preferences in the United States. In *Hawley, A. H. and Mazie, S. M., eds.*, 1981, pp. 72–115.
[G: U.S.]

850 HUMAN CAPITAL; VALUE OF HUMAN LIFE

851 Human Capital; Value of Human Life

8510 Human Capital; Value of Human Life

Akerlof, George A. Jobs as Dam Sites. *Rev. Econ. Stud.*, January 1981, 48(1), pp. 37–49.

Albrecht, James W. A Procedure for Testing the Signalling Hypothesis. In *Eliasson, G.; Holmlund, B. and Stafford, F. P., eds.*, 1981, pp. 39–54.
[G: Sweden]

Albrecht, James W. A Procedure for Testing the Signalling Hypothesis. *J. Public Econ.*, February 1981, 15(1), pp. 123–32.
[G: Sweden; U.S.]

Archer, André. L'éducation des fermiers, leur âge et la productivité des intrants agricoles selon la dimension des fermes laitières: le cas de la région "04", Québec. (Farmer's Education, Their Age and the Productivity of Agricultural Inputs According to Milk Farm Sizes: The Case of Region "04", Quebec. With English summary.) *L'Actual. Econ.*, January–March 1981, 57(1), pp. 113–27.
[G: Canada]

Arthur, W. B. The Economics of Risks to Life. *Amer. Econ. Rev.*, March 1981, *71*(1), pp. 54–64.

Balogh, T. and Streeten, Paul P. The Coefficient of Ignorance. In *Livingstone, I., ed.*, 1981, *1963*, pp. 25–29.

Bartel, Ann P. and Borjas, George J. Wage Growth and Job Turnover: An Empirical Analysis. In *Rosen, S., ed.*, 1981, pp. 65–84. [G: U.S.]

Becker, Gary S. An Equilibrium Theory of the Distribution of Income and Intergenerational Mobility. In *Currie, D.; Peel, D. and Peters, W., eds.*, 1981, *1979*, pp. 1–33.

Blair, Larry M.; Finn, Michael G. and Stevenson, Wayne L. The Returns to the Associate Degree for Technicians. *J. Human Res.*, Summer 1981, *16*(3), pp. 449–58. [G: U.S.]

Blomquist, Glenn. The Value of Human Life: An Empirical Perspective. *Econ. Inquiry*, January 1981, *19*(1), pp. 157–64.

Bolino, Paul. A Century of Human Capital Development by On-the-Job Training. *Int. J. Soc. Econ.*, 1981, *8*(7), pp. 24–41. [G: U.S.]

Cheng, Benjamin S. Differences in White-non-White Returns to Schooling: Theory and Policy. *Rev. Black Polit. Econ.*, Winter 1981, *11*(2), pp. 251–66. [G: U.S.]

Civelek, Mehmet A. Education and Economic Growth Revisited: The Evidence from the Turkish Development Experience. *Rivista Int. Sci. Econ. Com.*, March 1981, *28*(3), pp. 257–69. [G: Turkey]

Corcoran, Mary and Datcher, Linda P. Intergenerational Status Transmission and the Process of Individual Attainment. In *Hill, M. S.; Hill, D. H. and Morgan, J. N., eds.*, 1981, pp. 169–206. [G: U.S.]

Creedy, John. Education versus Cash Redistribution: A Comment. *J. Public Econ.*, April 1981, *15*(2), pp. 269–72.

Datcher, Linda P. Race/Sex Differences in the Effects of Background on Achievement. In *Hill, M. S.; Hill, D. H. and Morgan, J. N., eds.*, 1981, pp. 359–90. [G: U.S.]

Daymont, Thomas N. Changes in Black–White Labor Market Opportunities, 1966–76. In *Parnes, H. S., ed.*, 1981, pp. 42–64. [G: U.S.]

Diejomaoh, V. P. and Anusionwu, E. C. Education and Income Distribution in Nigeria. In *Bienen, H. and Diejomaoh, V. P., eds.*, 1981, pp. 373–420. [G: Nigeria]

Dietz, James L. and Leigh, J. Paul. Investment in Education in the Absence of Capital Markets. *Atlantic Econ. J.*, September 1981, *9*(3), pp. 60–68.

Dothan, Uri and Williams, Joseph. Education as an Option. *J. Bus.*, January 1981, *54*(1), pp. 117–39.

Dugger, William M. The Administered Labor Market: An Institutional Analysis. *J. Econ. Issues*, June 1981, *15*(2), pp. 397–407. [G: U.S.]

Edwards, E. O. Investment in Education in Developing Nations: Policy Responses When Private and Social Signals Conflict. In *Livingstone, I., ed.*, 1981, *1975*, pp. 85–88. [G: U.S.]

Etzioni, Amitai. Productivity: The Human Factor. In *Hogan, J. D. and Craig, A. M., eds.*, Vol. 1,

1981, pp. 27–38. [G: U.S.]

Filer, Randall Keith. The Influence of Affective Human Capital on the Wage Equation. In *Ehrenberg, R. G., ed.*, 1981, pp. 367–416. [G: U.S.]

Findlay, Ronald and Rodriguez, Carlos Alfredo. A Model of Economic Growth with Investment in Human Capital. In *Khan, A. and Sirageldin, I., eds.*, 1981, pp. 57–72.

Fiorito, Jack. The School-to-Work Transition of College Graduates. *Ind. Lab. Relat. Rev.*, October 1981, *35*(1), pp. 103–14. [G: U.S.]

Fraser, Clive D. The Value of Non-Marginal Changes in Physical Risk: Comment. In *Currie, D.; Peel, D. and Peters, W., eds.*, 1981, pp. 269–75.

Freire, Maria E. Education and Agricultural Efficiency. In *Balderston, J. B., et al., eds.*, 1981, pp. 107–45. [G: Guatemala]

Fujii, Edwin T. and Mak, James. The Effect of Acculturation and Assimilation on the Income of Immigrant Filipino Men in Hawaii. *Phillipine Rev. Econ. Bus.*, March & June 1981, *18*(1 & 2), pp. 75–85. [G: U.S.]

Galenson, David W. The Market Evaluation of Human Capital: The Case of Indentured Servitude. *J. Polit. Econ.*, June 1981, *89*(3), pp. 446–67. [G: U.S.]

Graham, John. The Influence of Nonhuman Wealth on the Accumulation of Human Capital. In *Khan, A. and Sirageldin, I., eds.*, 1981, pp. 73–94. [G: U.S.]

Graham, John D. and Vaupel, James W. The Value of a Life: What Difference Does It Make? In *Haimes, Y. Y., ed.*, 1981, pp. 233–43. [G: U.S.]

Graham, John W. An Explanation for the Correlation of Stocks of Nonhuman Capital with Investment in Human Capital. *Amer. Econ. Rev.*, March 1981, *71*(1), pp. 248–55.

Griliches, Zvi and Yatchew, Adonis J. Sample Selection Bias and Endogeneity in the Estimation of a Wage Equation: An Alternative Specification. *Ann. INSEE*, July–September 1981, (43), pp. 35–46.

Gustafsson, Siv. Male–Female Lifetime Earnings Differentials and Labor Force History. In *Eliasson, G.; Holmlund, B. and Stafford, F. P., eds.*, 1981, pp. 235–68. [G: Sweden; U.S.]

Hashimoto, Masanori. Firm-Specific Human Capital as a Shared Investment. *Amer. Econ. Rev.*, June 1981, *71*(3), pp. 475–82.

Howard, Ronald A. The Risks of Benefit-Cost-Risk Analysis. In *Haimes, Y. Y., ed.*, 1981, pp. 135–47. [G: U.S.]

Huffman, Wallace E. Black–White Human Capital Differences: Impact on Agricultural Productivity in the U.S. South. *Amer. Econ. Rev.*, March 1981, *71*(1), pp. 94–107. [G: U.S.]

Jones, Ethel B. and Long, James E. Part-Week Work and Women's Unemployment. *Rev. Econ. Statist.*, February 1981, *63*(1), pp. 70–76. [G: U.S.]

Jones-Lee, M. The Value of Non-Marginal Changes in Physical Risk. In *Currie, D.; Peel, D. and Peters, W., eds.*, 1981, pp. 232–68.

Jonsson, Anita and Klevmarken, Anders. Disequilibrium and Non-Neutral Market Effects on Age-

Earnings Profiles. **In** *Eliasson, G.; Holmlund, B. and Stafford, F. P., eds.*, 1981, pp. 357–92.
[G: Sweden]

Knight, J. B. and Sabot, R. H. The Returns to Education: Increasing with Experience or Decreasing with Expansion? *Oxford Bull. Econ. Statist.*, February 1981, *43*(1), pp. 51–71. [G: Tanzania]

Kopelyushnikov, R. I. The Concept of "Human Capital." **In** *Mileikovsky, A. G., et al.*, 1981, pp. 492–513.

Kotliar, A. E. and Turchaninova, S. Ia. The Educational and Occupational Skill Level of Industrial Workers. *Prob. Econ.*, Sept.–Oct.–Nov. 1981, *24*(5–6–7), pp. 69–120. [G: U.S.S.R.]

Lambrinos, James. Health: A Source of Bias in Labor Supply Models. *Rev. Econ. Statist.*, May 1981, *63*(2), pp. 206–12.

Layard, Richard. Reply to John Creedy's Comment [Education versus Cash Redistribution: The Lifetime Context]. *J. Public Econ.*, April 1981, *15*(2), pp. 273.

Leffler, Keith B. and Lindsay, Cotton M. Student Discount Rates, Consumption Loans, and Subsidies to Professional Training. *J. Human Res.*, Summer 1981, *16*(3), pp. 468–76.

Lehrer, Evelyn and Nerlove, Marc. The Labor Supply and Fertility Behavior of Married Women: A Three-Period Model. **In** *Simon, J. L. and Lindert, P. H., eds.*, 1981, pp. 123–45. [G: U.S.]

Leigh, J. Paul. The Economic Returns to Personal Values. *J. Behav. Econ.*, Summer 1981, *10*(1), pp. 13–32. [G: U.S.]

Liu, Pak-wai and Wong, Yue-chim. Human Capital and Inequality in Singapore. *Econ. Develop. Cult. Change*, January 1981, *29*(2), pp. 275–93.
[G: Singapore]

Lorenzen, Gunter. Hierarchische Strukturen und die Verteilung der Lohn- und Gehaltseinkommen. (Hierarchical Structures of Earnings and the Distribution of Wage and Salary Incomes. With English summary.) *Z. ges. Staatswiss.*, March 1981, *137*(1), pp. 36–44.

Mallar, Charles D. and Maynard, Rebecca A. The Effects of Income Maintenance on School Performance and Educational Attainment. **In** *Khan, A. and Sirageldin, I., eds.*, 1981, pp. 121–41.
[G: U.S.]

McMahon, Walter W. and Wagner, Alan P. Expected Returns to Investment in Higher Education. *J. Human Res.*, Spring 1981, *16*(2), pp. 274–85. [G: U.S.]

Medoff, James L. and Abraham, Katharine G. Are Those Paid More Really More Productive? The Case of Experience. *J. Human Res.*, Spring 1981, *16*(2), pp. 186–216. [G: U.S.]

Mincer, Jacob and Jovanovic, Boyan. Labor Mobility and Wages. **In** *Rosen, S., ed.*, 1981, pp. 21–63. [G: U.S.]

Mishan, Ezra J. Evaluation of Life and Limb: A Theoretical Approach. **In** *Mishan, E. J.*, 1981, *1971*, pp. 89–99.

Mishan, Ezra J. The Value of Trying to Value Life [Trying to Value a Life]. *J. Public Econ.*, February 1981, *15*(1), pp. 133–37.

Moore, William J.; Pearce, Douglas K. and Wilson, R. Mark. The Regulation of Occupations and the

Earnings of Women. *J. Human Res.*, Summer 1981, *16*(3), pp. 366–83. [G: U.S.]

Nghiep, Nguyen huu; Herzog, Henry W., Jr. and Schlottmann, Alan M. Earnings Expectations and the Role of Human Captial in the Migration Decision: An Empirical Analysis. *Rev. Reg. Stud.*, Winter 1981, *11*(3), pp. 38–46. [G: U.S.]

Piñera, Sebastian and Selowsky, Marcelo. The Optimal Ability–Education Mix and the Misallocation of Resources within Education Magnitude for Developing Countries. *J. Devel. Econ.*, February 1981, *8*(1), pp. 111–31. [G: Latin America; Asia; Africa]

Polachek, Solomon William. Occupational Self-Selection: A Human Capital Approach to Sex Differences in Occupational Structure. *Rev. Econ. Statist.*, February 1981, *63*(1), pp. 60–69.
[G: U.S.]

Prais, S. J. Vocational Qualifications of the Labour Force in Britain and Germany. *Nat. Inst. Econ. Rev.*, November 1981, (98), pp. 47–59.
[G: U.K.; W. Germany]

Psacharopoulos, George. Education and the Structure of Earnings in Portugal. *De Economist*, 1981, *129*(4), pp. 532–45. [G: Portugal]

Ram, Rati. Inequalities in Income and Schooling: A Different Point of View. *De Economist*, 1981, *129*(2), pp. 253–61.

Riley, John G. Learning by Observing and the Distribution of Wages: Comment. **In** *Rosen, S., ed.*, 1981, pp. 371–76.

Rodgers, Gerry B. An Analysis of Education, Employment, and Income Distribution Using an Economic-Demographic Model of the Philippines. **In** *Khan, A. and Sirageldin, I., eds.*, 1981, pp. 143–80. [G: Philippines]

Ross, Stephen; Taubman, Paul and Wachter, Michael L. Learning by Observing and the Distribution of Wages. **In** *Rosen, S., ed.*, 1981, pp. 359–71.

Rumberger, Russell W. The Changing Skill Requirements of Jobs in the U.S. Economy. *Ind. Lab. Relat. Rev.*, July 1981, *34*(4), pp. 578–90.
[G: U.S.]

Schultz, Theodore W. Knowledge is Power in Agriculture. *Challenge*, September/October 1981, *24*(4), pp. 4–12.

Selowsky, Marcelo. Nutrition, Health and Education: The Economic Significance of Complementarities at Early Age. *J. Devel. Econ.*, December 1981, *9*(3), pp. 331–46.

Shaw, R. Paul. Manpower and Educational Shortages in the Arab World: An Interim Strategy. *World Devel.*, July 1981, *9*(7), pp. 637–55.
[G: Arab Countries]

Shishkan, N. M. Raising the Skill Level of Women Workers. *Prob. Econ.*, Sept.–Oct.–Nov. 1981, *24*(5–6–7), pp. 121–30. [G: U.S.S.R.]

Simonen, Mari S. Education, Family Economic Production, and Fertility: The Case of Rural and Semi-Urban Guatemala. **In** *Balderston, J. B., et al., eds.*, 1981, pp. 147–76. [G: Guatemala]

Simos, Evangelos O. Learning-by-Doing or Doing-by-Learning? Evidence on Factor Learning and Biased Factor Efficiency Growth in the United States. *Rev. Bus. Econ. Res.*, Spring 1981, *16*(3),

pp. 14–25. [G: U.S.]

Spence, A. Michael. Signaling, Screening, and Information. In *Rosen, S., ed.*, 1981, pp. 319–57.

Stephenson, Stanley P., Jr. In-School Labour Force Status and Post-School Wage Rates of Young Men. *Appl. Econ.*, September 1981, *13*(3), pp. 279–302. [G: U.S.]

Taubman, Paul. On Heritability. *Economica*, November 1981, *48*(192), pp. 417–20.

Taylor, Daniel E. Education, On–the–Job Training, and the Black–White Earnings Gap. *Mon. Lab. Rev.*, April 1981, *104*(4), pp. 28–34. [G: U.S.]

Tinbergen, Jan. Optimal Education, Occupation, and Income Distribution in a Simplist Model. In *[Bergson, A.]*, 1981, pp. 305–10.
[G: Netherlands]

Tomer, John F. Organizational Change, Organization Capital and Economic Growth. *Eastern Econ. J.*, January 1981, *7*(1), pp. 1–14.
[G: U.S.]

Tomes, Nigel. A Model of Fertility and Children's Schooling. *Econ. Inquiry*, April 1981, *19*(2), pp. 209–34.

Trivellato, Ugo. Modelli di misura della riuscita scolastica e loro invarianza fra maschi e femmine. (Measurement Models of Educational Achievement and Their Invariance between Boys and Girls. With English summary.) *Statistica*, October–December 1981, *41*(4), pp. 575–97.
[G: Italy]

Trost, Robert P. Interpretation of Error Covariances with Nonrandom Data: An Empirical Illustration of Returns to College Education. *Atlantic Econ. J.*, September 1981, *9*(3), pp. 85–90. [G: U.S.]

Vaillancourt, François and Lefebvre, Lise. Antecédénts familiaux et connaissance de l'anglais chez les francophones du Québec. (Family Background and the Knowledge of English by Quebec Francophones. With English summary.) *L'Actual. Econ.*, July–September 1981, *57*(3), pp. 343–58.
[G: Canada]

Whitehead, A. K. Screening and Education: A Theoretical and Empirical Survey. *Brit. Rev. Econ. Issues*, Spring 1981, *2*(8), pp. 44–62.

Wilson, Charles A. Learning by Observing and the Distribution of Wages: Comment. In *Rosen, S., ed.*, 1981, pp. 376–86.

Wirtz, Willard. Growth, Education, and Work. In *Cleveland, H., ed.*, 1981, pp. 169–94. [G: U.S.]

Zeckhauser, Richard and Shepard, Donald S. Principles for Saving and Valuing Lives. In *Ferguson, A. R. and LeVeen, E. P., eds.*, 1981, pp. 91–130.

900 Welfare Programs; Consumer Economics; Urban and Regional Economics

910 WELFARE, HEALTH, AND EDUCATION

9100 General

Abramovitz, Moses. Welfare Quandaries and Productivity Concerns. *Amer. Econ. Rev.*, March 1981, *71*(1), pp. 1–17. [G: U.S.]

Bhagwati, Jagdish N. Need for Reforms in Underde-

veloped Countries: Comments. In *Grassman, S. and Lundberg, E., eds.*, 1981, pp. 526–33.

Bixby, Ann Kallman. Social Welfare Expenditures, Fiscal Year 1979. *Soc. Sec. Bull.*, November 1981, *44*(11), pp. 3–12. [G: U.S.]

Burchell, Robert W., et al. Measuring Urban Distress: A Summary of the Major Urban Hardship Indices and Resource Allocation Systems. In *Burchell, R. W. and Listokin, D., eds.*, 1981, pp. 159–229. [G: U.S.]

Garden, Jackie. Applications of Behavioral Models to Travel and Activity Needs of the Mobility Limited. In *Stopher, P. R.; Meyburg, A. H. and Brög, W., eds.*, 1981, pp. 455–61.

Glazer, Nathan. The Limits of Social Policy. In *Martin, G. T., Jr., and Zald, M. N., eds.*, 1981, 1971, pp. 147–63. [G: U.S.]

Glennerster, Howard. Social Service Spending in a Hostile Environment. In *Hood, C. and Wright, M., eds.*, 1981, pp. 174–96. [G: U.K.]

Hancock, Keith. The Economics of Retirement Provision in Australia. *Australian Econ. Pap.*, June 1981, *20*(36), pp. 1–23. [G: Australia]

Hannesson, Rögnvaldur. Stagflation: A Problem of the Aging Welfare State? A Comment on the Baumol-Oates "Cost-Disease" Model. *Scand. J. Econ.*, 1981, *83*(1), pp. 104–08.

Jech, Otto. Social Consumption of the Population and Its Expected Trends. *Czech. Econ. Digest.*, February 1981, (1), pp. 18–37.
[G: Czechoslovakia]

Kahn, Alfred J. and Kamerman, Sheila B. Social Services for All? In *Martin, G. T., Jr., and Zald, M. N., eds.*, 1981, 1978, pp. 513–22. [G: U.S.]

Komarov, V. and Ulanovskaia, V. The Service Sector and Increasing the Effectiveness of Production. *Prob. Econ.*, May 1981, *24*(1), pp. 19–38.
[G: U.S.S.R.]

Marmor, Theodore R. The North American Welfare State: Social Science and Evaluation. In *Solo, R. A. and Anderson, C. W., eds.*, 1981, pp. 320–39. [G: Canada; U.S.]

Martin, George T., Jr. Historical Overview of Social Welfare. In *Martin, G. T., Jr., and Zald, M. N., eds.*, 1981, pp. 11–17. [G: Europe; U.S.]

Myrdal, Gunnar. Need for Reforms in Underdeveloped Countries. In *Grassman, S. and Lundberg, E., eds.*, 1981, pp. 501–25.

Painton, Frederick. I guai dello stato assistenziale in Europa. (Woes of the Welfare State. With English summary.) *Mondo Aperto*, December 1981, *35*(6), pp. 345–57. [G: W. Europe]

Purcell, John F. H. Mexican Social Issues. In *Purcell, S. K., ed.*, 1981, pp. 43–54. [G: Mexico]

Richards, Peter J. Target Setting for Basic-Needs Services: Some Possible Approaches. *Int. Lab. Rev.*, September–October 1981, *120*(5), pp. 645–57. [G: Madagascar; India]

Scitovsky, Tibor. The Desire for Excitement in Modern Society. *Kyklos*, 1981, *34*(1), pp. 3–13.

Seers, Dudley. What Needs Are Really Basic in Nigeria: Some Thoughts Prompted by an ILO Mission. *Int. Lab. Rev.*, November–December 1981, *120*(6), pp. 741–50. [G: Nigeria]

Sellier, François. Les transformations sociales du système économique capitaliste. (With English summary.) *Écon. Appl.*, 1981, *34*(2–3), pp. 279–318.

Thursz, Daniel and Vigilante, Joseph L. Current Social Service Architecture: A Retrospective Appraisal. In *Martin, G. T., Jr., and Zald, M. N., eds.*, 1981, *1976*, pp. 55–63.
[G: Selected Countries]

Tropman, John E. Societal Values and Social Policy: Implications for Social Work. In *Martin, G. T., Jr., and Zald, M. N., eds.*, 1981, *1976*, pp. 87–104. [G: U.S.]

Wilson, Thomas. The Finance of the Welfare State. In *Peacock, A. and Forte, F., eds.*, 1981, pp. 94–117. [G: U.S.; U.K.; W. Europe]

911 General Welfare Programs

9110 General Welfare Programs

Aaron, Henry J. Do Housing Allowances Work? Policy Implications: A Progress Report. In *Bradbury, K. L. and Downs, A., eds.*, 1981, pp. 67–111.
[G: U.S.]

Aaron, Henry J. Welfare Reform: What Kind and When? In *Brown, P. G.; Johnson, C. and Vernier, P., eds.*, 1981, pp. 323–35. [G: U.S.]

Allen, Garland E.; Fitts, Jerry J. and Glatt, Evelyn S. The Experimental Housing Allowance Program. In *Bradbury, K. L. and Downs, A., eds.*, 1981, pp. 1–31. [G: U.S.]

Allen, Jodie T. The Concept of Vertical Equity and Its Application to Social Program Design. In *Brown, P. G.; Johnson, C. and Vernier, P., eds.*, 1981, pp. 87–107. [G: U.S.]

Anderson, Mary Ann, et al. Supplementary Feeding. In *Austin, J. E. and Zeitlin, M. F., eds.*, 1981, pp. 25–48.

Ault, Thomas A. Federal–State Relations and Income Support Policy. In *Brown, P. G.; Johnson, C. and Vernier, P., eds.*, 1981, pp. 57–80.
[G: U.S.]

Barr, Nicholas A. and Hall, Robert E. The Probability of Dependence on Public Assistance. *Economica*, May 1981, *48*(190), pp. 109–23. [G: U.S.]

Berfenstam, Ragnar and Placht, Ragnhild. Toward Coordination of Health and Social Services: Substance and Means in Cooperation. In *Altenstetter, C., ed.*, 1981, pp. 179–92. [G: Sweden]

Bergmann, Barbara R. The Economic Support of "Fatherless" Children. In *Brown, P. G.; Johnson, C. and Vernier, P., eds.*, 1981, pp. 195–211.
[G: U.S.]

Bieker, Richard F. Work and Welfare: An Analysis of AFDC Participation Rates in Delaware. *Soc. Sci. Quart.*, March 1981, *62*(1), pp. 169–76.
[G: U.S.]

Campbell, John Creighton. Japan's Social Welfare System. In *Richardson, B. M. and Ueda, T., eds.*, 1981, pp. 207–14. [G: Japan]

Carlson, Leonard A. and Cebula, Richard J. Voting with One's Feet: A Brief Note on the Case of Public Welfare and the American Indian. *Public Choice*, 1981, *37*(2), pp. 321–25. [G: U.S.]

Cebula, Richard J. A Note on the Determinants of AFDC Policies [State Tax Structure and the Supply of AFDC Assistance]. *Public Choice*, 1981,

37(2), pp. 327–30. [G: U.S.]

Cebula, Richard J.; Carlos, Christopher and Koch, James V. The 'Crowding Out' Effect of Federal Government Outlay Decisions: An Empirical Note [The 'Crowding Out' Effect of Government Transfers on Private Charitable Contributions]. *Public Choice*, 1981, *36*(2), pp. 329–36.
[G: U.S.]

Cebula, Richard J. and Koch, James V. A Further Note on Welfare Outlays and Nonwhite Migration [A Note on Welfare Outlays and Nonwhite Migration: An Analysis for SMSA's, 1965–1970]. *Rev. Bus. Econ. Res.*, Spring 1981, *16*(3), pp. 98–101.
[G: U.S.]

Cebula, Richard J. and Smith, Lisa K. An Empirical Note on the Determinants of Welfare Levels in the United States, 1961 and 1971. *Econ. Notes*, 1981, *10*(2), pp. 59–63. [G: U.S.]

Christiansen, Vidar. Optimization and Quantitative Assessment of Child Allowances. In *Strøm, S., ed.*, 1981, *1979*, pp. 103–22. [G: Norway]

Ciscel, David H. and Tuckman, Barbara H. The Peripheral Worker: CETA Training as Imperfect Job Socialization. *J. Econ. Issues*, June 1981, *15*(2), pp. 489–500. [G: U.S.]

Coe, Richard D. A Preliminary Empirical Examination of the Dynamics of Welfare Use. In *Hill, M. S.; Hill, D. H. and Morgan, J. N., eds.*, 1981, pp. 121–68. [G: U.S.]

Cowell, Frank A. Income Maintenance Schemes under Wage-Rate Uncertainty. *Amer. Econ. Rev.*, September 1981, *71*(4), pp. 692–703.

Cronin, Francis J. Household Responsiveness to Unconstrained Housing Allowances. In *Struyk, R. J. and Bendick, M., Jr., eds.*, 1981, pp. 159–76. [G: U.S.]

Cronin, Francis J. Participation in the Experimental Housing Allowance Program. In *Struyk, R. J. and Bendick, M., Jr., eds.*, 1981, pp. 79–106. [G: U.S.]

Cutright, Phillips. Income Redistribution: A Cross-National Analysis. In *Martin, G. T., Jr., and Zald, M. N., eds.*, 1981, *1967*, pp. 38–54. [G: LDCs; MDCs]

Daniels, Norman. Conflicting Objectives and the Priorities Problem. In *Brown, P. G.; Johnson, C. and Vernier, P., eds.*, 1981, pp. 147–64.

Danziger, Sandra K. Postprogram Changes in the Lives of AFDC Supported Work Participants: A Qualitative Assessment. *J. Human Res.*, Fall 1981, *16*(4), pp. 637–48. [G: U.S.]

Danziger, Sheldon and Haveman, Robert H. The Reagan Budget: A Sharp Break with the Past. *Challenge*, May/June 1981, *24*(2), pp. 5–13.
[G: U.S.]

Danziger, Sheldon; Haveman, Robert H. and Plotnick, Robert. How Income Transfer Programs Affect Work, Savings, and the Income Distribution: A Critical Review. *J. Econ. Lit.*, September 1981, *19*(3), pp. 975–1028. [G: U.S.]

Danziger, Sheldon and Plotnick, Robert. Income Maintenance Programs and the Pursuit of Income Security. *Ann. Amer. Acad. Polit. Soc. Sci.*, January 1981, *453*, pp. 130–52. [G: U.S.]

Davidson, R. and Lowe, R. Bureaucracy and Innovation in British Welfare Policy 1870-1945. In

Mommsen, W. J., ed., 1981, pp. 263–95.
[G: U.K.]

Davis, Kingsley and van den Oever, Pietronella. Age Relations and Public Policy in Advanced Industrial Societies. *Population Devel. Rev.*, March 1981, 7(1), pp. 1–18.

Devens, Richard M., Jr. Testing an Hypothesis of Institutional Change: Welfare Work Registration, Aggregate Demand, and the Unemployment Rate. *J. Monet. Econ.*, May 1981, 7(3), pp. 387–93.
[G: U.S.]

Downs, Anthony and Bradbury, Katharine L. Do Housing Allowances Work? Conference Discussion. In *Bradbury, K. L. and Downs, A., eds.*, 1981, pp. 375–404.
[G: U.S.]

Fersh, Robert J. An Assessment of Major Welfare Reform Proposals of the 95th Congress. In *Brown, P. G.; Johnson, C. and Vernier, P., eds.*, 1981, pp. 305–21.
[G: U.S.]

Fraser, Derek. The English Poor Law and the Origins of the British Welfare State. In *Mommsen, W. J., ed.*, 1981, pp. 9–31.
[G: U.K.]

Gottschalk, Peter T. A Note on Estimating Treatment Effects [The Estimation of Labor Supply Models Using Experimental Data]. *Amer. Econ. Rev.*, September 1981, 71(4), pp. 764–69.
[G: U.S.]

Gottschalk, Peter T. Transfer Scenarios and Projections of Poverty into the 1980s. *J. Human Res.*, Winter 1981, 16(1), pp. 41–60.

Gramlich, Edward M. and Ysander, Bengt-Christer. Relief Work and Grant Displacement in Sweden. In *Eliasson, G.; Holmlund, B. and Stafford, F. P., eds.*, 1981, pp. 139–66.
[G: Sweden]

Greenberg, David; Moffitt, Robert A. and Friedmann, John. Underreporting and Experimental Effects on Work Effort: Evidence from the Gary Income Maintenance Experiment. *Rev. Econ. Statist.*, November 1981, 63(4), pp. 581–89.
[G: U.S.]

Guesnerie, Roger. La gratuité, outil de politique économique? (Could Giving out Freely a Private Good be a Tool of Economic Policy? With English summary.) *Can. J. Econ.*, May 1981, 14(2), pp. 232–60.

Hamermesh, Daniel S. Transfers, Taxes and the NAIRU. In *Meyer, L. H., ed.*, 1981, pp. 203–29.
[G: U.S.]

Hanushek, Eric A. and Quigley, John M. Do Housing Allowances Work? Consumption Aspects. In *Bradbury, K. L. and Downs, A., eds.*, 1981, pp. 185–246.
[G: U.S.]

Harris, José. Some Aspects of Social Policy in Britain During the Second World War. In *Mommsen, W. J., ed.*, 1981, pp. 247–62.
[G: U.K.]

Hausman, Jerry A. and Wise, David A. AFDC Participation: Measured Variables or Unobserved Characteristics, Permanent or Transitory. In *[Valavanis, S.]*, 1981, pp. 321–39.
[G: U.S.]

Hausman, Jerry A. and Wise, David A. Stratification on Endogenous Variables and Estimation: The Gary Income Maintenance Experiment. In *Manski, C. F. and McFadden, D., eds.*, 1981, pp. 365–91.
[G: U.S.]

Hauver, James H.; Goodman, John A. and Grainer, Marc A. The Federal Poverty Thresholds: Appearance and Reality. *J. Cons. Res.*, June 1981, 8(1), pp. 1–10.
[G: U.S.]

HeB, Jurgen C. The Social Policy of the Attlee Government. In *Mommsen, W. J., ed.*, 1981, pp. 296–314.
[G: U.K.]

Hemming, Richard. Market Failure and Superannuation—A Reply [The Economic Impact of the Proposed National Superannuation Scheme for Australia]. *Econ. Rec.*, March 1981, 57(156), pp. 89–90.
[G: Australia]

Higa, Teruyuki. An Analysis of Structural Changes in the Food Stamp Program. *Amer. Econ.*, Fall 1981, 25(2), pp. 24–29.
[G: U.S.]

Hockerts, H. G. German Post-War Social Policies against the Background of the Beveridge Plan. Some Observations Preparatory to a Comparative Analysis. In *Mommsen, W. J., ed.*, 1981, pp. 315–39.
[G: Germany]

Huang, Chung-Liang; Fletcher, Stanley M. and Raunikar, Robert. Modeling the Effects of the Food Stamp Program on Participating Households' Purchases: An Empirical Application. *Southern J. Agr. Econ.*, December 1981, 13(2), pp. 21–28.
[G: U.S.]

Hutchens, Robert M. Entry and Exit Transitions in a Government Transfer Program: The Case of Aid to Families with Dependent Children. *J. Human Res.*, Spring 1981, 16(2), pp. 217–37.
[G: U.S.]

Johnson, Darwin G. Sensitivity of Federal Expenditures to Unemployment. *Public Finance Quart.*, January 1981, 9(1), pp. 3–21.
[G: U.S.]

Jones, R. L. and Page, K. R. Market Failure and Superannuation—A Comment [The Economic Impact of the Proposed National Superannuation Scheme for Australia]. *Econ. Rec.*, March 1981, 57(156), pp. 86–88.
[G: Australia]

Kain, John F. A Universal Housing Allowance Program. In *Bradbury, K. L. and Downs, A., eds.*, 1981, pp. 329–73.
[G: U.S.]

Knaub, Norman L. The Impact of Food Stamps and Cash Welfare on Food Expenditures, 1971–1975. *Policy Anal.*, Spring 1981, 7(2), pp. 169–82.
[G: U.S.]

Kulcsár, Kálmán. Social Policy in Today's Hungarian Society. *Acta Oecon.*, 1981, 27(1–2), pp. 183–89.
[G: Hungary]

Lindeman, David. The Concept of Horizontal Equity and Its Application to Social Program Design. In *Brown, P. G.; Johnson, C. and Vernier, P., eds.*, 1981, pp. 108–24.
[G: U.S.]

Macarov, D. Welfare as Work's Handmaiden. *Int. J. Soc. Econ.*, 1981, 8(5), pp. 21–30.

Mallar, Charles D. and Maynard, Rebecca A. The Effects of Income Maintenance on School Performance and Educational Attainment. In *Khan, A. and Sirageldin, I., eds.*, 1981, pp. 121–41.
[G: U.S.]

Manning, Ian. Social Security and the Future. *Australian Econ. Rev.*, 1st Quarter 1981, (53), pp. 29–34.
[G: Australia]

Manning, Ian. The 1970s: A Decade of Social Security Policy. *Australian Econ. Rev.*, 1st Quarter 1981, (53), pp. 13–19.
[G: Australia]

Martin, George T., Jr. Social Welfare Trends in the United States. In *Martin, G. T., Jr., and Zald, M. N., eds.*, 1981, pp. 505–12.
[G: U.S.]

Masters, Stanley H. The Effects of Supported Work on the Earnings and Transfer Payments of Its AFDC Target Group. *J. Human Res.*, Fall 1981, *16*(4), pp. 600–636. [G: U.S.]

McKenzie, Richard B. Taxation and Income Redistribution: An Unsympathetic Critique of Practice and Theory. *Cato J.*, Fall 1981, *1*(2), pp. 339–71. [G: U.S.]

de Melo, Martha. Modeling the Effects of Alternative Approaches to Basic Human Needs: Case Study of Sri Lanka. In *Leipziger, D. M., ed.*, 1981, pp. 137–80. [G: Sri Lanka]

Menefee, John A.; Edwards, Bea and Schieber, Sylvester J. Analysis of Nonparticipation in the SSI Program. *Soc. Sec. Bull.*, June 1981, *44*(6), pp. 3–21. [G: U.S.]

Metcalf, David. Poverty in the United Kingdom by Peter Townsend: Review Article. *Brit. J. Ind. Relat.*, March 1981, *19*(1), pp. 112–16. [G: U.K.]

Mills, Edwin S. and Sullivan, Arthur. Do Housing Allowances Work? Market Effects. In *Bradbury, K. L. and Downs, A., eds.*, 1981, pp. 247–83. [G: U.S.]

Moeller, John F. Consumer Expenditure Responses to Income Redistribution Programs. *Rev. Econ. Statist.*, August 1981, *63*(3), pp. 409–21. [G: U.S.]

Moffitt, Robert A. Participation in the AFDC Program and the Stigma of Welfare Receipt: Estimation of a Choice-Theoretic Model. *Southern Econ. J.*, January 1981, *47*(3), pp. 753–62. [G: U.S.]

Moffitt, Robert A. The Negative Income Tax: Would It Discourage Work? *Mon. Lab. Rev.*, April 1981, *104*(4), pp. 23–27. [G: U.S.]

Moffitt, Robert A. and Kehrer, Kenneth C. The Effect of Tax and Transfer Programs on Labor Supply: The Evidence from the Income Maintenance Experiments. In *Ehrenberg, R. G., ed.*, 1981, pp. 103–50. [G: U.S.]

Mogull, Robert G. Jurisdictional Spending for Public Welfare. *J. Reg. Sci.*, August 1981, *21*(3), pp. 403–10. [G: U.S.]

Nyers, Reszö. Problems of People in Disadvantageous Social Situation from the Viewpoint of Economic Policy. *Acta Oecon.*, 1981, *27*(1–2), pp. 178–83. [G: Hungary]

Olsen, Edgar O. and Reeder, William J. Does HUD Pay Too Much for Section 8 Existing Housing? *Land Econ.*, May 1981, *57*(2), pp. 243–51. [G: U.S.]

Page, Benjamin I. Why Doesn't the Government Promote Equality? In *Solo, R. A. and Anderson, C. W., eds.*, 1981, pp. 279–319. [G: U.S.]

Perrin, Richard K. and Scobie, Grant M. Market Intervention Policies for Increasing the Consumption of Nutrients by Low Income Households. *Amer. J. Agr. Econ.*, February 1981, *63*(1), pp. 73–82. [G: Colombia]

Pfeffer, Jeffrey and Leong, Anthony. Resource Allocations in United Funds: Examination of Power and Dependence. In *Martin, G. T., Jr., and Zald, M. N., eds.*, 1981, *1977*, pp. 246–62. [G: U.S.]

Phillips, Martha H. Favorable Family Impact as an Objective of Income Support Policy. In *Brown, P. G.; Johnson, C. and Vernier, P., eds.*, 1981, pp. 165–94. [G: U.S.]

Plotnick, Robert. A Measure of Horizontal Inequity. *Rev. Econ. Statist.*, May 1981, *63*(2), pp. 283–88. [G: U.S.]

Ponce, Elsa Orley and Rigby, Donald. SSI Recipients in Medicaid Institutions, December 1979. *Soc. Sec. Bull.*, April 1981, *44*(4), pp. 32–37, 47. [G: U.S.]

Raines, Fredric. Transfers, Taxes, and the NAIRU: Discussion. In *Meyer, L. H., ed.*, 1981, pp. 237–41. [G: U.S.]

Rea, Samuel A., Jr. Private Disability Insurance and Public Welfare Programs. *Public Finance*, 1981, *36*(1), pp. 84–98.

Reulecke, J. English Social Policy around the Middle of the Nineteenth Century as Seen by German Social Reformers. In *Mommsen, W. J., ed.*, 1981, pp. 32–49. [G: U.K.]

Rodgers, Charles S. Work Tests for Welfare Recipients: The Gap between the Goal and the Reality. *J. Policy Anal. Manage.*, Fall 1981, *1*(1), pp. 5–17. [G: U.S.]

Rogers, Beatrice Lorge, et al. Consumer Food Price Subsidies. In *Austin, J. E. and Zeitlin, M. F., eds.*, 1981, pp. 99–110.

Rose, M. E. The Crisis of Poor Relief in England, 1860–1890. In *Mommsen, W. J., ed.*, 1981, pp. 50–70. [G: U.K.]

Rosenbaum, Sonia and Wright, James D. Income Maintenance and Work Behavior. In *Martin, G. T., Jr., and Zald, M. N., eds.*, 1981, pp. 412–27. [G: U.S.]

Rossi, Peter H. Do Housing Allowances Work? Residential Mobility. In *Bradbury, K. L. and Downs, A., eds.*, 1981, pp. 147–83. [G: U.S.]

Rotherham, James A. Impact of Future Social and Demographic Change on Programs for Reducing Economic Dependency. In *Brown, P. G.; Johnson, C. and Vernier, P., eds.*, 1981, pp. 337–62. [G: U.S.]

Saunders, Peter G. The Commission of Inquiry into Poverty's Guaranteed Minimum Income Scheme: A Perspective from the 1980s. *Australian Econ. Rev.*, 1st Quarter 1981, (53), pp. 20–28. [G: Australia]

Scott, Robert A. The Factory as a Social Service Organization: Goal Displacement in Workshops for the Blind. In *Martin, G. T., Jr., and Zald, M. N., eds.*, 1981, *1967*, pp. 264–84. [G: U.S.]

Séguret, M.-C. Child-Care Services for Working Parents. *Int. Lab. Rev.*, November–December 1981, *120*(6), pp. 711–25. [G: Europe; LDCs]

Sosin, Michael. Study of Emergency Assistance and Special Needs Programs. *Soc. Sec. Bull.*, September 1981, *44*(9), pp. 3–8. [G: U.S.]

Southwick, Lawrence, Jr. Public Welfare Programs and Recipient Migration. *Growth Change*, October 1981, *12*(4), pp. 22–32. [G: U.S.]

Straszheim, Mahlon R. Do Housing Allowances Work? Participation. In *Bradbury, K. L. and Downs, A., eds.*, 1981, pp. 113–45. [G: U.S.]

Street, David. Welfare Administration and Organizational Theory. In *Martin, G. T., Jr., and Zald, M. N., eds.*, 1981, pp. 285–300.

Takayama, Noriyuki and Hamada, Koichi. Measures of Poverty and Their Policy Implications. In

Khan, A. and Sirageldin, I., eds., 1981, pp. 3–
30. [G: Japan]
Tampke, J. Bismarck's Social Legislation: A Genuine
Breakthrough? In Mommsen, W. J., ed., 1981,
pp. 71–83. [G: Germany]
Thompson, Dennis. The Ethics of Social Experimen-
tation: The Case of the DIME. Public Policy,
Summer 1981, 29(3), pp. 369–98. [G: U.S.]
Thon, Dominique. Income Inequality and Poverty:
Some Problems. Rev. Income Wealth, June 1981,
27(2), pp. 207–10.
Thurow, Lester C. The Illusion of Economic Neces-
sity. In Solo, R. A. and Anderson, C. W., eds.,
1981, pp. 250–75. [G: U.S.]
Vasey, Wayne. Recurring Themes in the Income
Support Policy Debate— Obstacles to Change.
In Brown, P. G.; Johnson, C. and Vernier, P.,
eds., 1981, pp. 283–303. [G: U.S.]
Vernier, Paul. Rights to Welfare as an Issue in In-
come Support Policy. In Brown, P. G.; Johnson,
C. and Vernier, P., eds., 1981, pp. 219–32.
[G: U.S.]
Wallis, John Joseph and Benjamin, Daniel K. Public
Relief and Private Employment in the Great De-
pression. J. Econ. Hist., March 1981, 41(1), pp.
97–102. [G: U.S.]
Watts, Harold W. A Critical Review of the Program
as a Social Experiment. In Bradbury, K. L. and
Downs, A., eds., 1981, pp. 33–65. [G: U.S.]
Weiss, Janet A. Substance vs. Symbol in Administra-
tive Reform: The Case of Human Services Coordi-
nation. Policy Anal., Winter 1981, 7(1), pp. 21–
45.
Zais, James P. Administering Housing Allowances.
In Struyk, R. J. and Bendick, M., Jr., eds., 1981,
pp. 235–64. [G: U.S.]
Zald, Mayer N. The Structure of Society and Social
Service Integration. In Martin, G. T., Jr., and
Zald, M. N., eds., 1981, 1969, pp. 233–45.
[G: U.S.]

912 Economics of Education

9120 Economics of Education

Abramovitz, Mimi. Funding Worker Education
through Tuition Refund Plans. In Wertheimer,
B. M., ed., 1981, pp. 241–51. [G: U.S.]
Adams, E. Kathleen and Odden, Allan. Alternative
Wealth Measures. In Jordan, K. F. and Cambron-
McCabe, N. H., eds., 1981, pp. 143–65.
Ahlburg, Dennis; Crimmins, Eileen M. and Easter-
lin, Richard A. The Outlook for Higher Educa-
tion: A Cohort Size Model of Enrollment of the
College Age Population, 1948–2000. Rev. Public
Data Use (See J. Econ. Soc. Meas. after 4/85),
November 1981, 9(3), pp. 211–27. [G: U.S.]
Anthony, William P. Business School Management
by Objectives. Rev. Bus. Econ. Res., Spring 1981,
16(3), pp. 38–47.
Ayeni, Bola. Spatial Aspects of Urbanization and Ef-
fects on the Distribution of Income in Nigeria.
In Bienen, H. and Diejomaoh, V. P., eds., 1981,
pp. 237–68. [G: Nigeria]
Balderston, Judith B. Determinants of Children's
School Participation. In Balderston, J. B., et al.,
eds., 1981, pp. 83–105. [G: Guatemala]

Bedford, Leslie. Japan's Educational System. In
Richardson, B. M. and Ueda, T., eds., 1981, pp.
236–44. [G: Japan]
Berg, Ivar. The Effects of Inflation on and in Higher
Education. Ann. Amer. Acad. Polit. Soc. Sci.,
July 1981, 456, pp. 99–111.
Berne, Robert and Stiefel, Leanna. Measuring the
Equity of School Finance Policies: A Conceptual
and Empirical Analysis. Policy Anal., Winter
1981, 7(1), pp. 47–69. [G: U.S.]
Bilciu, C. and Brad, St. The Concept of a Data-
Processing System for Scientific Documentation
in Education. Econ. Computat. Cybern. Stud.
Res., 1981, 15(2), pp. 21–24.
Blaug, Mark. Comments on M. Peston [The Finance
of Recurrent Education: Some Theoretical Con-
siderations] and H. Glennerster [The Role of the
State in Financing Recurrent Education: Lessons
from European Experience]. Public Choice, 1981,
36(3), pp. 573–77.
Blaug, Mark. The Economic Costs and Benefits of
Overseas Students. In Williams, P., ed., 1981,
pp. 47–90. [G: U.K.]
Blaug, Mark and Woodhall, Maureen. A Survey of
Overseas Students in British Higher Education
1980. In Williams, P., ed., 1981, pp. 239–63.
[G: U.K.]
Bowen, Howard R. Observations on the Costs of
Higher Education. Quart. Rev. Econ. Bus.,
Spring 1981, 21(1), pp. 47–57. [G: U.S.]
Boyd, William L. Comments on E. G. West and
R. J. Staaf [Extra-Governmental Powers in Public
Schooling: The Unions and the Courts]. Public
Choice, 1981, 36(3), pp. 639–40.
Chambers, Jay G. Cost and Price Level Adjustments
to State Aid for Education: A Theoretical and Em-
pirical Review. In Jordan, K. F. and Cambron-
McCabe, N. H., eds., 1981, pp. 39–85.
[G: U.S.]
Chang, Cyril F. Different Forms of Outside Aid: A
Collective-Choice Model for Predicting Effects on
Local Educational Expenditure. Public Finance
Quart., July 1981, 9(3), pp. 321–41. [G: U.S.]
Cook, Alice H. and Till-Retz, Roberta. Labor Edu-
cation and Women Workers: An International
Comparison. In Wertheimer, B. M., ed., 1981,
pp. 255–64. [G: Sweden; U.K.; Austria;
W. Germany]
Cook, Earl. The Tragedy of Turfdom [Environmental
Disruption: Implications for the Social Sciences].
Soc. Sci. Quart., March 1981, 62(1), pp. 23–29.
Court, David. The Education System as a Response
to Inequality. In Killick, T., ed., 1981, pp. 287–
91. [G: Kenya]
Dahlby, B. G. Monopsony and the Shortage of
School Teachers in England and Wales, 1948–73.
Appl. Econ., September 1981, 13(3), pp. 303–
19. [G: U.K.]
Datcher, Linda P. Race/Sex Differences in the Ef-
fects of Background on Achievement. In Hill,
M. S.; Hill, D. H. and Morgan, J. N., eds., 1981,
pp. 359–90. [G: U.S.]
Diejomaoh, V. P. and Anusionwu, E. C. Education
and Income Distribution in Nigeria. In Bienen,
H. and Diejomaoh, V. P., eds., 1981, pp. 373–
420. [G: Nigeria]
Dietz, James L. and Leigh, J. Paul. Investment in

Education in the Absence of Capital Markets. *Atlantic Econ. J.*, September 1981, *9*(3), pp. 60–68.

Dothan, Uri and Williams, Joseph. Education as an Option. *J. Bus.*, January 1981, *54*(1), pp. 117–39.

Edwards, E. O. Investment in Education in Developing Nations: Policy Responses When Private and Social Signals Conflict. In *Livingstone, I., ed.*, 1981, *1975*, pp. 85–88. **[G: U.S.]**

Ehrenberg, Ronald G. Comments on E. G. West and R. J. Staaf [Extra-Governmental Powers in Public Schooling: The Unions and the Courts]. *Public Choice*, 1981, *36*(3), pp. 641–45.

Freire, Maria E. Education and Agricultural Efficiency. In *Balderston, J. B., et al., eds.*, 1981, pp. 107–45. **[G: Guatemala]**

Furno, Orlando F. and Magers, Dexter A. An Analysis of State School Support Programs. In *Jordan, K. F. and Cambron-McCabe, N. H., eds.*, 1981, pp. 169–90. **[G: U.S.]**

Glennerster, Howard. The Role of the State in Financing Recurrent Education: Lessons from European Experience. *Public Choice*, 1981, *36*(3), pp. 551–71.

Goertz, Margaret. School Finance Reform and the Cities. In *Jordan, K. F. and Cambron-McCabe, N. H., eds.*, 1981, pp. 113–42. **[G: U.S.]**

Gustafsson, Siv. Comments on S. C. Nelson and D. W. Breneman [An Equity Perspective on Community College Finance]. *Public Choice*, 1981, *36*(3), pp. 533–34. **[G: U.S.]**

Gustman, Alan L. and Steinmeier, Thomas L. The Impact of Wages and Unemployment on Youth Enrollment and Labor Supply. *Rev. Econ. Statist.*, November 1981, *63*(4), pp. 553–60. **[G: U.S.]**

Hack, Walter G.; Edlefson, Carla and Ogawa, Rodney T. Fiscal Accountability: The Challenge of Formulating Responsive Policy. In *Jordan, K. F. and Cambron-McCabe, N. H., eds.*, 1981, pp. 251–79. **[G: U.S.]**

Hansen, Richard B. The Sensitivity of Variable Measurement in Faculty Salary Studies. *J. Behav. Econ.*, Summer 1981, *10*(1), pp. 1–12. **[G: U.S.]**

Hansen, W. Lee. The Decline of Real Faculty Salaries in the 1970s. *Quart. Rev. Econ. Bus.*, Winter 1981, *21*(4), pp. 7–12. **[G: U.S.]**

Hanushek, Eric A. The Continuing Hope: A Rejoinder [Throwing Money at Schools]. *J. Policy Anal. Manage.*, Fall 1981, *1*(1), pp. 53–54. **[G: U.S.]**

Hanushek, Eric A. Throwing Money at Schools. *J. Policy Anal. Manage.*, Fall 1981, *1*(1), pp. 19–41. **[G: U.S.]**

Hare, Paul G. and Ulph, David T. Imperfect Capital Markets and the Public Provision of Education. *Public Choice*, 1981, *36*(3), pp. 481–507.

Hildebrandt, Gregory G. and Tregarthen, Timothy D. Observing Preferences for Educational Quality: The Weak Complementarity Approach. In *Strim, S., ed.*, 1981, *1979*, pp. 47–56. **[G: U.S.]**

Hodge, Michael V. Improving Finance and Governance of Education for Special Populations. In *Jordan, K. F. and Cambron-McCabe, N. H., eds.*, 1981, pp. 3–38. **[G: U.S.]**

Hogan, Timothy D. Faculty Research Activity and the Quality of Graduate Training. *J. Human Res.*, Summer 1981, *16*(3), pp. 400–415. **[G: U.S.]**

Huang, Chung-Liang; Fletcher, Stanley M. and Raunikar, Robert. Modeling the Effects of the Food Stamp Program on Participating Households' Purchases: An Empirical Application. *Southern J. Agr. Econ.*, December 1981, *13*(2), pp. 21–28. **[G: U.S.]**

Hunter, Guy. The Needs and Desires of Developing Countries for Foreign Student Facilities: Some Reflections. In *Williams, P., ed.*, 1981, pp. 135–49. **[G: LDCs; U.K.]**

Hunter, Laurie. Comments on E. James and E. Neuberger [The University Department as a Non-Profit Labor Cooperative]. *Public Choice*, 1981, *36*(3), pp. 613–17.

Inman, Robert P. On Setting the Agenda for Pennsylvania School Finance Reform: An Exercise in Giving Policy Advice. *Public Choice*, 1981, *36*(3), pp. 449–74. **[G: U.S.]**

Jackman, Richard and Papadachi, John. Local Authority Education Expenditure in England and Wales: Why Standards Differ and the Impact of Government Grants. *Public Choice*, 1981, *36*(3), pp. 425–39. **[G: U.K.]**

James, Estelle and Neuberger, Egon. The University Department as a Non-Profit Labor Cooperative. *Public Choice*, 1981, *36*(3), pp. 585–612.

Johns, Roe L. Perspectives in State School Support Programs: Introduction. In *Jordan, K. F. and Cambron-McCabe, N. H., eds.*, 1981, pp. xvii–xxvii. **[G: U.S.]**

Jud, G. Donald and Watts, James M. Schools and Housing Values. *Land Econ.*, August 1981, *57*(3), pp. 459–70. **[G: U.S.]**

Katzman, Martin T. An Ecology of Family Decisions: Suburbanization, Schooling, and Fertility in Philadelphia, 1880–1920: Comment. In *Stave, B. M., ed.*, 1981, pp. 61–67. **[G: U.S.]**

Killick, Tony. The Economics of Education: Introduction. In *Killick, T., ed.*, 1981, pp. 265–68. **[G: Kenya]**

Kirp, David L. The Academic as Would-Be Analyst: A Cautionary Tale. *Policy Anal.*, Winter 1981, *7*(1), pp. 91–102. **[G: U.S.]**

Kogan, Maurice. Education in 'Hard Times.' In *Hood, C. and Wright, M., eds.*, 1981, pp. 152–73. **[G: U.K.]**

Lassibille, Gérard and Navarro-Gomez, Lucia. La production d'enseignement supérieur dans les établissements français. (The Production of Education in French Academic Institution. With English summary.) *Consommation*, October–December 1981, *28*(4), pp. 3–38. **[G: France]**

Lawrence, Sheila M.; Lawrence, Kenneth D. and Reeves, Gary R. A Multiple Goal Model for Allocation of Teaching Personnel. In *Morse, J. N., ed.*, 1981, pp. 222–31.

Leffler, Keith B. and Lindsay, Cotton M. Student Discount Rates, Consumption Loans, and Subsidies to Professional Training. *J. Human Res.*, Summer 1981, *16*(3), pp. 468–76.

Lima, Anthony K. An Economic Model of Teaching Effectiveness. *Amer. Econ. Rev.*, December 1981, *71*(5), pp. 1056–59. **[G: U.S.]**

Link, Charles R.; Lewis, Kenneth A. and Black, David E. New Evidence on the Achievement of

Wealth Neutrality in School Finance. *J. Human Res.*, Spring 1981, *16*(2), pp. 260–73. **[G: U.S.]**

Lockhart, Lawrence. The Economics of Nine Years Education for All. In *Killick, T., ed.*, 1981, pp. 279–86. **[G: Kenya]**

MacDonald, Glenn M. The Impact of Schooling on Wages. *Econometrica*, September 1981, *49*(5), pp. 1349–59.

Mare, Robert D. Trends in Schooling: Demography, Performance, and Organization. *Ann. Amer. Acad. Polit. Soc. Sci.*, January 1981, *453*, pp. 96–122. **[G: U.S.]**

McCarthy, Martha M. Adequacy in Educational Programs: A Legal Perspective. In *Jordan, K. F. and Cambron-McCabe, N. H., eds.*, 1981, pp. 315–51. **[G: U.S.]**

McFadden, Daniel. Comments on R. P. Inman [On Setting the Agenda for Pennsylvania School Finance Reform: An Exercise in Giving Policy Advice]. *Public Choice*, 1981, *36*(3), pp. 477–80. **[G: U.S.]**

McGavin, P. A. School Participation of Australians Aged Sixteen: An Analysis of Youth Unemployment. *Econ. Rec.*, December 1981, *57*(159), pp. 379–81. **[G: Australia]**

McMahon, Walter W. and Wagner, Alan P. Expected Returns to Investment in Higher Education. *J. Human Res.*, Spring 1981, *16*(2), pp. 274–85. **[G: U.S.]**

Melcher, Thomas R. State Pupil Transportation Programs. In *Jordan, K. F. and Cambron-McCabe, N. H., eds.*, 1981, pp. 215–47. **[G: U.S.]**

Merrilees, William J. The Effect of Labour Market Conditions on School Enrolment Rates. *Australian Econ. Rev.*, 3rd Quarter 1981, (55), pp. 56–60. **[G: Australia]**

Miller, Leonard S. College Admissions and Financial Aid Policies as Revealed by Institutional Practices. *Econ. Inquiry*, January 1981, *19*(1), pp. 117–31. **[G: U.S.]**

Mirrlees, J. A. Comments on P. G. Hare and D. T. Ulph [Imperfect Capital Markets and the Public Provision of Education]. *Public Choice*, 1981, *36*(3), pp. 511–13.

Mirrlees, J. A. Comments on R. P. Inman [On Setting the Agenda for Pennsylvania School Finance Reform: An Exercise in Giving Policy Advice]. *Public Choice*, 1981, *36*(3), pp. 475–76. **[G: U.S.]**

Modell, John. An Ecology of Family Decisions: Suburbanization, Schooling, and Fertility in Philadelphia, 1880–1920. In *Stave, B. M., ed.*, 1980, pp. 39–59. **[G: U.S.]**

Murnane, Richard J. Teacher Mobility Revisited. *J. Human Res.*, Winter 1981, *16*(1), pp. 3–19. **[G: U.S.]**

Murnane, Richard J.; Maynard, Rebecca A. and Ohls, James C. Home Resources and Children's Achievement. *Rev. Econ. Statist.*, August 1981, *63*(3), pp. 369–77. **[G: U.S.]**

Murphy, Terence. Aspects of High-Level Manpower Forecasting and University Development in Papua New Guinea. *J. Devel. Areas*, April 1981, *15*(3), pp. 417–33. **[G: New Guinea]**

Murray, Steven W. and Tweeten, Luther. Some Trade-Offs: Culture, Education, and Economic Progress on Federal Indian Reservations. *Growth*

Change, April 1981, *12*(2), pp. 10–16. **[G: U.S.]**

Nelson, Susan C. and Breneman, David W. An Equity Perspective on Community College Finance. *Public Choice*, 1981, *36*(3), pp. 515–32. **[G: U.S.]**

Nicolau, Ed. The Educational System—A Cybernetic System. *Econ. Computat. Cybern. Stud. Res.*, 1981, *15*(4), pp. 41–46.

Olmstead, Alan L. and Sheffrin, Steven M. Affirmative Action in Medical Schools: Econometric Evidence and Legal Doctrine. In *Zerbe, R. O., Jr., ed.*, 1981, pp. 207–23. **[G: U.S.]**

Olmstead, Alan L. and Sheffrin, Steven M. The Medical School Admission Process: An Empirical Investigation. *J. Human Res.*, Summer 1981, *16*(3), pp. 459–67. **[G: U.S.]**

Oxenham, John. Study Abroad and Development Policy: An Enquiry. In *Williams, P., ed.*, 1981, pp. 150–64. **[G: LDCs; U.K.]**

Peston, Maurice H. The Finance of Recurrent Education: Some Theoretical Considerations. *Public Choice*, 1981, *36*(3), pp. 537–50.

Piñera, Sebastian and Selowsky, Marcelo. The Optimal Ability–Education Mix and the Misallocation of Resources within Education Magnitude for Developing Countries. *J. Devel. Econ.*, February 1981, *8*(1), pp. 111–31. **[G: Latin America; Asia; Africa]**

Pissarides, Christopher A. Comments on P. G. Hare and D. T. Ulph [Imperfect Capital Markets and the Public Provision of Education]. *Public Choice*, 1981, *36*(3), pp. 509–10.

Pissarides, Christopher A. Staying-on at School in England and Wales. *Economica*, November 1981, *48*(192), pp. 345–63. **[G: U.K.]**

Psacharopoulos, George. Education, Employment and Inequality in LDCs. *World Devel.*, January 1981, *9*(1), pp. 37–54. **[G: LDCs]**

Ram, Rati. Inequalities in Income and Schooling: A Different Point of View. *De Economist*, 1981, *129*(2), pp. 253–61.

Rogin, Lawrence. Labor Education for Women Workers: A Summary Discussion. In *Wertheimer, B. M., ed.*, 1981, pp. 265–68.

Rozen, Frieda Shoenberg. Labor Education for Women Workers: Promoting and Recruiting: Reaching the Target Audience. In *Wertheimer, B. M., ed.*, 1981, pp. 32–41. **[G: U.S.]**

Samper, Maria-Luz D. and Rosen, Stanley. Evaluating Programs for Working Adults. In *Wertheimer, B. M., ed.*, 1981, pp. 98–108.

Sarthory, Joseph A. The Climate for Collective Bargaining in Public Education in the 1980s. In *Dennis, B. D., ed.*, 1981, pp. 284–89. **[G: U.S.]**

Schapiro, Morton Owen and Easterlin, Richard A. Educational Attainment by Sex and Age, 1980–2000. *Rev. Public Data Use (See J. Econ. Soc. Meas. after 4/85)*, December 1981, *9*(4), pp. 323–39. **[G: U.S.]**

Schrier, Katherine. Credit Programs for Working Women. In *Wertheimer, B. M., ed.*, 1981, pp. 71–82. **[G: U.S.]**

Sebold, Frederick D. and Dato, William. School Funding and Student Achievement: An Empirical Analysis. *Public Finance Quart.*, January 1981, *9*(1), pp. 91–105. **[G: U.S.]**

Selowsky, Marcelo. Nutrition, Health and Education: The Economic Significance of Complementarities at Early Age. *J. Devel. Econ.*, December 1981, *9*(3), pp. 331–46.

Semel, Rochelle. Labor Education for Women Workers: The Short Course. In *Wertheimer, B. M., ed.*, 1981, pp. 42–53. [G: U.S.]

Shaw, R. Paul. Manpower and Educational Shortages in the Arab World: An Interim Strategy. *World Devel.*, July 1981, *9*(7), pp. 637–55. [G: Arab Countries]

Simonen, Mari S. Education, Family Economic Production, and Fertility: The Case of Rural and Semi-Urban Guatemala. In *Balderston, J. B., et al., eds.*, 1981, pp. 147–76. [G: Guatemala]

Sisk, David E. A Theory of Government Enterprise: University Ph.D. Production. *Public Choice*, 1981, *37*(2), pp. 357–63. [G: U.S.]

Sjogren, Jane. Municipal Overburden and State Aid for Education. In *Jordan, K. F. and Cambron-McCabe, N. H., eds.*, 1981, pp. 87–111. [G: U.S.]

Smith, Alan; Woesler de Panafieu, Christine and Jarousse, Jean-Pierre. Foreign Student Flows and Policies in an International Perspective. In *Williams, P., ed.*, 1981, pp. 165–222. [G: Global]

Spencer, Bruce D. and Wiley, David E. The Sense and the Nonsense of School Effectiveness [Throwing Money at Schools]. *J. Policy Anal. Manage.*, Fall 1981, *1*(1), pp. 43–52. [G: U.S.]

Steele, G. R. University Salaries in the U.K.: A Study of Local Variations within a National Pay Structure. *Bull. Econ. Res.*, May 1981, *33*(1), pp. 14–36. [G: U.K.]

Stubblebine, Wm. Craig and Kennard, David N. California School Finance: The 1970s Decade. *Public Choice*, 1981, *36*(3), pp. 391–412. [G: U.S.]

Taeuber, Karl E., et al. A Demographic Perspective on School Desegregation in the USA. In *Peach, C.; Robinson, V. and Smith, S., eds.*, 1981, pp. 83–105. [G: U.S.]

Taubman, Paul. On Heritability. *Economica*, November 1981, *48*(192), pp. 417–20.

Thompson, Fred. Utility-Maximizing Behavior in Organized Anarchies: An Empirical Investigation of the Breneman Thesis. *Public Choice*, 1981, *36*(1), pp. 17–32. [G: U.S.]

Todaro, Michael P. Education and National Economic Development in Kenya. In *Killick, T., ed.*, 1981, pp. 269–78. [G: Kenya]

Toma, Eugenia Froedge. Bureaucratic Structures and Educational Spending. *Southern Econ. J.*, January 1981, *47*(3), pp. 640–54. [G: U.S.]

Tomes, Nigel. A Model of Fertility and Children's Schooling. *Econ. Inquiry*, April 1981, *19*(2), pp. 209–34.

Weis, Lois. The Reproduction of Social Inequality: Closure in the Ghanaian University. *J. Devel. Areas*, October 1981, *16*(1), pp. 17–29. [G: Ghana]

Wentzler, Nancy. Locational Variations in the Public School Teacher Supply Price. *Public Finance Quart.*, October 1981, *9*(4), pp. 431–48. [G: U.S.]

Wertheimer, Barbara M. Labor Education for Women Workers: Introduction. In *Wertheimer,*

B. M., ed., 1981, pp. 3–11.

Wertheimer, Barbara M. Labor Education for Women Workers: Residential Schools. In *Wertheimer, B. M., ed.*, 1981, pp. 83–97. [G: U.S.]

West, Edwin G. Choice or Monopoly in Education. *Policy Rev.*, Winter 1981, (15), pp. 103–17. [G: U.S.]

West, Edwin G. Comments on H. Glennerster [The Role of the State in Financing Recurrent Education: Lessons from European Experience]. *Public Choice*, 1981, *36*(3), pp. 579–82.

West, Edwin G. and Staaf, Robert J. Extra-Governmental Powers in Public Schooling: The Unions and the Courts: Rejoinder. *Public Choice*, 1981, *36*(3), pp. 647–50.

West, Edwin G. and Staaf, Robert J. Extra-Governmental Powers in Public Schooling: The Unions and the Courts. *Public Choice*, 1981, *36*(3), pp. 619–37.

White, Gordon. Higher Education and Social Redistribution in a Socialist Society: The Chinese Case. *World Devel.*, February 1981, *9*(2), pp. 149–66. [G: China]

Wilkerson, William R. State Participation in Financing School Facilities. In *Jordan, K. F. and Cambron-McCabe, N. H., eds.*, 1981, pp. 191–213. [G: U.S.]

Williams, Peter. Overseas Students in Britain: The Background. In *Williams, P., ed.*, 1981, pp. 22–46. [G: U.K.]

Williams, Peter. The Overseas Student Question: Studies for a Policy: Conclusion: The Way Ahead. In *Williams, P., ed.*, 1981, pp. 223–38. [G: U.K.]

Williams, Peter. The Overseas Student Question: Studies for a Policy: The Emergence of the Problem: Editorial Introduction. In *Williams, P., ed.*, 1981, pp. 1–21. [G: U.K.]

Windham, Douglas M. Comments on R. Jackman and J. Papadachi [Local Authority Education Expenditure in England and Wales: Why Standards Differ and the Impact of Government Grants]. *Public Choice*, 1981, *36*(3), pp. 441–42. [G: U.K.]

Wirtz, Willard. Growth, Education, and Work. In *Cleveland, H., ed.*, 1981, pp. 169–94. [G: U.S.]

Wise, Arthur E. and Darling-Hammond, Linda. Educational Needs: Accounting for School Finance. In *Jordan, K. F. and Cambron-McCabe, N. H., eds.*, 1981, pp. 281–314. [G: U.S.]

Zhamin, Vitali A. and Popov, Grigori M. Public Education and Training of the Labor Force. In *Novosti Press Agency*, 1981, pp. 230–47. [G: U.S.S.R.]

913 Economics of Health (including medical subsidy programs)

9130 Economics of Health (including medical subsidy programs)

Aaron, Henry J. Economic Aspects of the Role of Government in Health Care. In *van der Gaag, J. and Perlman, M., eds.*, 1981, pp. 15–32.

Albert, Michel. Liberté ou planification en matière de recherche médicale. (Liberty or Plannification for Medical Research. With English summary.)

Consommation, July–September 1981, *28*(3), pp. 3–16. [G: France]

Albou, Paul. Automedication. In *Molt, W.; Hartmann, H. A. and Stringer, P., eds.*, 1981, pp. 433–55. [G: France]

Altenstetter, Christa. National Health Initiatives and Local Health-Insurance Carriers: The Case of the Federal Republic of Germany. In *Altenstetter, C., ed.*, 1981, pp. 227–63. [G: W. Germany]

Anderson, Mary Ann, et al. Supplementary Feeding. In *Austin, J. E. and Zeitlin, M. F., eds.*, 1981, pp. 25–48.

Anderson, Richard K.; House, Donald and Ormiston, Michael B. A Theory of Physician Behavior with Supplier-Induced Demand. *Southern Econ. J.*, July 1981, *48*(1), pp. 124–33.

Arnould, Richard and Eisenstadt, David. The Effects of Provider-Controlled Blue Shield Plans: Regulatory Options. In *Olson, M., ed.*, 1981, pp. 339–60. [G: U.S.]

Arnould, Richard J. and Grabowski, Henry. Auto Safety Regulation: An Analysis of Market Failure. *Bell J. Econ. (See Rand J. Econ. after 4/85)*, Spring 1981, *12*(1), pp. 27–48. [G: U.S.]

Arthur, W. B. The Economics of Risks to Life. *Amer. Econ. Rev.*, March 1981, *71*(1), pp. 54–64.

Atkinson, Graham and Cook, Jack. Regulation: Incentives Rather than Command and Control. In *Olson, M., ed.*, 1981, pp. 211–18. [G: U.S.]

Auster, Richard D. and Oaxaca, Ronald L. Identification of Supplier Induced Demand in the Health Care Sector. *J. Human Res.*, Summer 1981, *16*(3), pp. 327–42. [G: U.S.]

Austin, Charles J. and Carter, Harrison S. National Hospital Information Resource Center: A Model. *Inquiry*, Winter 1981, *18*(4), pp. 291–99.

Austin, James E. and Zeitlin, Marian F. Concluding Observations. In *Austin, J. E. and Zeitlin, M. F., eds.*, 1981, pp. 137–45.

Austin, James E. and Zeitlin, Marian F. Evaluation. In *Austin, J. E. and Zeitlin, M. F., eds.*, 1981, pp. 15–24.

Austin, James E. and Zeitlin, Marian F. Nutrition Interventions: A Conceptual Framework. In *Austin, J. E. and Zeitlin, M. F., eds.*, 1981, pp. 5–14.

Austin, James E., et al. Fortification. In *Austin, J. E. and Zeitlin, M. F., eds.*, 1981, pp. 73–84.

Austin, James E., et al. Integrated Nutrition and Primary Health Care Programs. In *Austin, J. E. and Zeitlin, M. F., eds.*, 1981, pp. 123–35.

Bair, C. William; Anderson, Michael C. and McNamara, Michael J. A Comparison of Diagnostic Costs for Hospitalized and Ambulatory Hypertension Patients. *Inquiry*, Spring 1981, *18*(1), pp. 37–45. [G: U.S.]

Balderston, Judith B. Investigating the Web of Poverty—The Need for Research. In *Balderston, J. B., et al., eds.*, 1981, pp. 1–22.

Balderston, Judith B. Synthesis of Findings and Policy Implications. In *Balderston, J. B., et al., eds.*, 1981, pp. 177–98. [G: Guatemala]

Banta, David. Public Policy and Medical Technology: Critical Issues Reconsidered. In *Altenstetter, C., ed.*, 1981, pp. 57–86. [G: U.S.]

Barzel, Yoram. Competitive Tying Arrangements:

The Case of Medical Insurance. *Econ. Inquiry*, October 1981, *19*(4), pp. 598–612. [G: U.S.]

Beck, Glen and Horne, John. Medical Fee Determination. *Can. Public Policy*, Winter 1981, *7*(1), pp. 108–14. [G: Canada]

Beck, John H. Budget-Maximizing Bureaucracy and the Effects of State Aid on School Expenditures. *Public Finance Quart.*, April 1981, *9*(2), pp. 159–82. [G: U.S.]

Becker, Brian E. and Miller, Richard U. Patterns and Determinants of Union Growth in the Hospital Industry. *J. Lab. Res.*, Fall 1981, *2*(2), pp. 309–28. [G: U.S.]

Benham, Lee. The Effects of Government Regulation on Teenage Smoking: Comment. *J. Law Econ.*, December 1981, *24*(3), pp. 571–73. [G: U.S.]

Berfenstam, Ragnar and Placht, Ragnhild. Toward Coordination of Health and Social Services: Substance and Means in Cooperation. In *Altenstetter, C., ed.*, 1981, pp. 179–92. [G: Sweden]

Bertorelli, Linda M. A Survey of Recent Research in Health Economics. *Amer. Econ.*, Spring 1981, *25*(1), pp. 5–9.

Bice, Thomas W. Regulation of Capital Investments of Hospitals in the United States: Certificate-of-Need Controls. In *Altenstetter, C., ed.*, 1981, pp. 43–54. [G: U.S.]

Blomquist, Glenn. The Value of Human Life: An Empirical Perspective. *Econ. Inquiry*, January 1981, *19*(1), pp. 157–64.

Blume, Stuart S. Technology in Medical Diagnosis: Aspects of Its Dynamic and Impact. In *Altenstetter, C., ed.*, 1981, pp. 107–24.

Bojanczyk, M. An Optimal Management in Health Care System. In *Janssen, J. M. L.; Pau, L. F. and Straszak, A. J., eds.*, 1981, pp. 151–56.

Brown, Montague. Contract Management: Legal and Policy Implications. *Inquiry*, Spring 1981, *18*(1), pp. 8–17. [G: U.S.]

Brown, R. G. S. Priorities in the English National Health Service. In *Altenstetter, C., ed.*, 1981, pp. 193–209. [G: U.K.]

Butler, James R. G. and Doessel, Darrel P. Measuring Benefits in Health: A Clarification. *Scot. J. Polit. Econ.*, June 1981, *28*(2), pp. 196–205.

Butz, William P. The Changing Role of Breastfeeding in Economic Development: A Theoretical Exposition. In *Khan, A. and Sirageldin, I., eds.*, 1981, pp. 95–117.

Cain, Glen G., et al. The Effect of Unions on Wages in Hospitals. In *Ehrenberg, R. G., ed.*, 1981, pp. 191–320. [G: U.S.]

Cantril, Albert. American Politics, Public Opinion, and Social Security Financing: Comment. In *Skidmore, F., ed.*, 1981, pp. 274–77. [G: U.S.]

Carroll, Sidney L. and Gaston, Robert J. Occupational Restrictions and the Quality of Service Received: Some Evidence. *Southern Econ. J.*, April 1981, *47*(4), pp. 959–76. [G: U.S.]

Chester, T. E. Market Forces and Health Economics: A Case Study of Switzerland. *Nat. Westminster Bank Quart. Rev.*, November 1981, pp. 2–16. [G: Switzerland]

Chirikos, Thomas N. and Nestel, Gilbert. Impairment and Labor Market Outcomes: A Cross-Sectional and Longitudinal Analysis. In *Parnes,*

H. S., ed., 1981, pp. 93–131.   [G: U.S.]
Christianson, Jon B. and Faulkner, Lee. The Contributions of Rural Hospitals to Local Economies. *Inquiry*, Spring 1981, *18*(1), pp. 46–60.
[G: U.S.]
Chui, Kwai-Fong and Black, Robert A. Comparing Schemes to Rank Areas According to Degree of Health Manpower Shortage. *Inquiry*, Fall 1981, *18*(3), pp. 274–80.   [G: U.S.]
Clague, Christopher. Regulation: Can It Improve Incentives? Commentary. In *Olson, M., ed.,* 1981, pp. 313–17.   [G: U.S.]
Cohen, Harold A. and Schramm, Carl J. A Design for Resolving the Conflicts Resulting from Separate Regulation of Hospital Rates and Hospital Capacity. In *Olson, M., ed.,* 1981, pp. 258–73.
[G: U.S.]
Cole, Joan and Pilisuk, Marc. Differences in the Provision of Mental Health Services by Race. In *Martin, G. T., Jr., and Zald, M. N., eds.,* 1981, 1976, pp. 368–89.
Conrad, Douglas A. and Watts, Carolyn A. A Note on Measuring the Extent of Competition in the Physicians' Services Market: An Alternative Approach. In *Zerbe, R. O., Jr., ed.,* 1981, pp. 241–49.   [G: U.S.]
Copeland, Lois S. International Trends in Disability Program Growth. *Soc. Sec. Bull.,* October 1981, *44*(10), pp. 25–36.   [G: Belgium; Finland; W. Germany; Netherlands; France]
Corn, Richard F. The Sensitivity of Prospective Hospital Reimbursement to Errors in Patient Data. *Inquiry*, Winter 1981, *18*(4), pp. 351–60.
[G: U.S.]
Crandall, Robert W. The Impossibility of Finding a Mechanism to Ration Health Care Resources Efficiently. In *Olson, M., ed.,* 1981, pp. 29–43.
Crick, Nelson. Taxes, Lost Future Earnings, and Unexamined Assumptions. *Nat. Tax J.,* June 1981, *34*(2), pp. 271–73.   [G: U.S.]
Crile, George, Jr. How to Keep down the Risk and Cost of Surgery. *Inquiry*, Summer 1981, *18*(2), pp. 99–101.   [G: U.S.]
Cromwell, Jerry and Mitchell, Janet B. High Income Medicaid Practices. *Inquiry*, Spring 1981, *18*(1), pp. 18–27.   [G: U.S.]
Cropper, M. L. Measuring the Benefits from Reduced Morbidity. *Amer. Econ. Rev.,* May 1981, *71*(2), pp. 235–40.   [G: U.S.]
Culyer, A. J. Health, Economics, and Health Economics. In *van der Gaag, J. and Perlman, M., eds.,* 1981, pp. 3–11.
Culyer, A. J.; Maynard, Alan and Williams, Alan. Alternative Systems of Health Care Provision: An Essay on Motes and Beams. In *Olson, M., ed.,* 1981, pp. 131–50.   [G: OECD]
Curtis, W. Robert and Neuhauser, Duncan. Reorganizing Human Services in Massachusetts. In *Altenstetter, C., ed.,* 1981, pp. 161–77.
[G: U.S.]
Davis, Charles J. and Covaleski, Mark A. Alternative Capital Reimbursement Policies for Wisconsin Nursing Homes. *Inquiry*, Summer 1981, *18*(2), pp. 165–78.   [G: U.S.]
Dear, Michael. Social and Spatial Reproduction of the Mentally Ill. In *Dear, M. and Scott, A. J.,*

eds., 1981, pp. 481–97.
Dickinson, Katherine P. Supported Work for Ex-Addicts: An Exploration of Endogenous Tastes. *J. Human Res.,* Fall 1981, *16*(4), pp. 551–99.
[G: U.S.]
Dittman, David A. and Morey, Richard C. Optimal Pricing of Hospital Services. *Inquiry*, Winter 1981, *18*(4), pp. 311–21.   [G: U.S.]
Doron, Haim R. The Organization of Primary Care in Israel. In *Gleason, H. P., ed.,* 1981, pp. 85–102.   [G: Israel]
Drummond, M. F. Welfare Economics and Cost Benefit Analysis in Health Care. *Scot. J. Polit. Econ.,* June 1981, *28*(2), pp. 125–45.
Eastaugh, Steven R. Teaching the Principles of Cost-Effective Clinical Decisionmaking to Medical Students. *Inquiry*, Spring 1981, *18*(1), pp. 28–36.
[G: U.S.]
Edwards, Linda N. and Grossman, Michael. Children's Health and the Family. In *Scheffler, R. M., ed.,* 1981, pp. 35–84.   [G: U.S.]
Eisenstadt, David and Kennedy, Thomas E. Control and Behavior of Nonprofit Firms: The Case of Blue Shield. *Southern Econ. J.,* July 1981, *48*(1), pp. 26–36.   [G: U.S.]
Enthoven, Alain C. A Brief Outline of the Competition Strategy for Health Services Delivery System Reform. In *Olson, M., ed.,* 1981, pp. 421–23.
Enthoven, Alain C. Supply-Side Economics of Health Care and Consumer Choice Health Plan. In *Olson, M., ed.,* 1981, pp. 467–89.   [G: U.S.]
Enthoven, Alain C. The Behavior of Health Care Agents: Provider Behavior. In *van der Gaag, J. and Perlman, M., eds.,* 1981, pp. 173–88.
[G: U.S.]
Evans, R. G. Incomplete Vertical Integration: The Distinctive Structure of the Health-Care Industry. In *van der Gaag, J. and Perlman, M., eds.,* 1981, pp. 329–54.
Fausto, Domenicantonio and Leccisotti, Mario. An Interpretation of Government Intervention in Health: The Italian Case. In *van der Gaag, J. and Perlman, M., eds.,* 1981, pp. 33–43.
[G: Italy]
Feldman, Roger and Greenberg, Warren. The Relation between the Blue Cross Market Share and the Blue Cross "Discount" on Hospital Charges. *J. Risk Ins.,* June 1981, *48*(2), pp. 235–46.
[G: U.S.]
Feldman, Roger; Sloan, Frank A. and Paringer, Lynn. Compensation Arrangements between Hospitals and Physicians. *Bell J. Econ. (See Rand J. Econ. after 4/85),* Spring 1981, *12*(1), pp. 155–70.   [G: U.S.]
Feldman, Roger D. and Ballard, David J. The Role of Waiting Time in a Prepaid Health Care System: Evidence from the British National Health Service. *Eastern Econ. J.,* July-Oct. 1981, *7*(3–4), pp. 175–85.   [G: U.K.]
Feldman, Roger, et al. Physician Choice of Patient Load and Mode of Treatment. *Atlantic Econ. J.,* September 1981, *9*(3), pp. 69–78.
Feldstein, Martin S. A New Approach to National Health Insurance. In *Feldstein, M., ed.,* 1981, 1971, pp. 247–59.   [G: U.S.]
Feldstein, Martin S. Econometric Studies of Health

Economics. In *Feldstein, M., ed.*, 1981, *1974*, pp. 57–103. [G: U.S.]

Feldstein, Martin S. Hospital Cost Inflation: A Study of Nonprofit Price Dynamics. In *Feldstein, M., ed.*, 1981, *1971*, pp. 104–32. [G: U.S.]

Feldstein, Martin S. Hospital Costs and Health Insurance: Introduction. In *Feldstein, M., ed.*, 1981, pp. 1–15. [G: U.S.]

Feldstein, Martin S. Quality Change and the Demand for Hospital Care. In *Feldstein, M., ed.*, 1981, *1977*, pp. 133–55. [G: U.S.]

Feldstein, Martin S. The Quality of Hospital Services: An Analysis of Geographic Variation and Intertemporal Change. In *Feldstein, M., ed.*, 1981, *1974*, pp. 156–72. [G: U.S.]

Feldstein, Martin S. The Welfare Loss of Excess Health Insurance. In *Feldstein, M., ed.*, 1981, *1973*, pp. 175–204. [G: U.S.]

Feldstein, Martin S. and Allison, Elisabeth. Tax Subsidies of Private Health Insurance: Distribution, Revenue Loss, and Effects. In *Feldstein, M., ed.*, 1981, *1974*, pp. 205–20. [G: U.S.]

Feldstein, Martin S. and Friedman, Bernard. Tax Subsidies, the Rational Demand for Insurance, and the Health-Care Crisis. In *Feldstein, M., ed.*, 1981, *1977*, pp. 221–44. [G: U.S.]

Feldstein, Martin S. and Friedman, Bernard. The Effect of National Health Insurance on the Price and Quantity of Medical Care. In *Feldstein, M., ed.*, 1981, *1976*, pp. 283–305.

Feldstein, Martin S.; Friedman, Bernard and Luft, Harold. Distributional Aspects of National Health Insurance Benefits and Finance. In *Feldstein, M., ed.*, 1981, *1972*, pp. 260–82. [G: U.S.]

Feldstein, Martin S. and Taylor, Amy. The Rapid Rise of Hospital Costs. In *Feldstein, M., ed.*, 1981, *1977*, pp. 19–56. [G: U.S.]

Fenn, Paul T. Sickness Duration, Residual Disability, and Income Replacement: An Empirical Analysis. *Econ. J.*, March 1981, *91*(361), pp. 158–73. [G: U.K.]

Flynn, Ralph J. The Climate for Local Government Collective Bargaining in the 1980s: Discussion. In *Dennis, B. D., ed.*, 1981, pp. 299–303.

Fort, Rodney D. and Christianson, Jon B. Determinants of Public Services Provision in Rural Communities: Evidence from Voting on Hospital Referenda. *Amer. J. Agr. Econ.*, May 1981, *63*(2), pp. 228–36. [G: U.S.]

Frech, H. E., III. The Long-Lost Free Market in Health Care: Government and Professional Regulation of Medicine. In *Olson, M., ed.*, 1981, pp. 44–66. [G: U.S.]

Frech, H. E., III and Ginsburg, Paul B. Property Rights and Competition in Health Insurance: Multiple Objectives for Nonprofit Firms. In *Zerbe, R. O., Jr., ed.*, 1981, pp. 155–71. [G: U.S.]

Frech, H. E., III and Ginsburg, Paul B. The Cost of Nursing Home Care in the United States: Government Financing, Ownership, and Efficiency. In *van der Gaag, J. and Perlman, M., eds.*, 1981, pp. 67–81.

Freiden, Alan and Leimer, Dean R. The Earnings of College Students. *J. Human Res.*, Winter 1981, *16*(1), pp. 152–56. [G: U.S.]

Frey, René L. and Leu, Robert E. Demographie und Inzidenz der öffentlichen Ausgaben im Gesundheitswesen. (Demography and the Incidence of Public Expenditures in the Health Sector. With English summary.) *Schweiz. Z. Volkswirtsch. Statist.*, September 1981, *117*(3), pp. 319–36.

Friedman, Bernard and Pauly, Mark V. Cost Functions for a Service Firm with Variable Quality and Stochastic Demand: The Case of Hospitals. *Rev. Econ. Statist.*, November 1981, *63*(4), pp. 620–24. [G: U.S.]

Gardell, Bertil. Stress Research and its Implications: Sweden. In *Dennis, B. D., ed.*, 1981, pp. 268–75. [G: Sweden]

Gerking, Shelby D. and Schulze, William D. What Do We Know about Benefits of Reduced Mortality from Air Pollution Control? *Amer. Econ. Rev.*, May 1981, *71*(2), pp. 228–34. [G: U.S.]

Geweke, John F. and Weisbrod, Burton A. Some Economic Consequences of Technological Advance in Medical Care: The Case of a New Drug. In *Helms, R. B., ed.*, 1981, pp. 235–71. [G: U.S.]

Gleason, Herbert P. Consumer Participation in Formulating Health Policy. In *Gleason, H. P., ed.*, 1981, pp. 103–11.

Godber, George [Sir]. Disease Prevention and Health Promotion. In *Gleason, H. P., ed.*, 1981, pp. 47–62.

Godber, George [Sir]. Enabling the Elderly to Continue Functionally Independent. In *Gleason, H. P., ed.*, 1981, pp. 63–74.

Goldman, Mitchell, et al. Account of Proceedings at the Salzburg Seminar. In *Gleason, H. P., ed.*, 1981, pp. 119–35.

Goldman, Richard H. and Overholt, Catherine A. Agricultural Production, Technical Change, and Nutritional Goals. In *Austin, J. E. and Zeitlin, M. F., eds.*, 1981, pp. 111–21.

Gottinger, Hans W. Application of a Multi-Criteria Evaluation Procedure to Health Care Delivery. *Z. Nationalökon.*, 1981, *41*(1–2), pp. 79–95.

Greenberg, Michael R. A Note on the Changing Geography of Cancer Mortality within Metropolitan Regions of the United States. *Demography*, August 1981, *18*(3), pp. 411–20. [G: U.S.]

Greenberg, Warren. Provider-Influenced Insurance Plans and their Impact on Competition: Lessons from Dentistry. In *Olson, M., ed.*, 1981, pp. 361–76. [G: U.S.]

Greene, Mark R. Life Care Centers—A New Concept in Insurance. *J. Risk Ins.*, September 1981, *48*(3), pp. 403–21.

Greene, Vernon L. and Monahan, Deborah J. Structural and Operational Factors Affecting Quality of Patient Care in Nursing Homes. *Public Policy*, Fall 1981, *29*(4), pp. 399–415. [G: U.S.]

Gregory, Douglas D. Risk Analysis of an Employee Health Benefit Decision under Hospital Reimbursement. *J. Risk Ins.*, December 1981, *48*(4), pp. 577–95. [G: U.S.]

Grossman, Michael and Jacobowitz, Steven. Variations in Infant Mortality Rates among Counties of the United States: The Roles of Public Policies and Programs. *Demography*, November 1981, *18*(4), pp. 695–713. [G: U.S.]

Halberstam, Michael. Physician Prescribing Behavior: Is There Learning by Doing? Comment. In *Helms, R. B., ed.*, 1981, pp. 222–27.

Hamburg, David A. More Judicious Use of Biomedical Technology. In *Gleason, H. P., ed.*, 1981, pp. 33–46. [G: U.S.]

Hansen, W. Lee. The Supply of Mental Health Manpower. In *McGuire, T. G. and Weisbrod, B. A., eds.*, 1981, pp. 85–98. [G: U.S.]

Härö, A. S. Innovative Policy for Central-Local Government Cooperation in the Finnish Health System. In *Altenstetter, C., ed.*, 1981, pp. 211–26. [G: Finland]

Harrison, David, Jr. Distributional Objectives in Health and Safety Regulation. In *Ferguson, A. R. and LeVeen, E. P., eds.*, 1981, pp. 177–201. [G: U.S.]

Hattinga-Verschure, John C. M. A Systems Approach to Delivery of Care in Health and Disease: Its Impact on Clients. In *Altenstetter, C., ed.*, 1981, pp. 125–39. [G: Netherlands]

Havelka, Jaroslav. Care for Handicapped Citizens. *Czech. Econ. Digest.*, September 1981, (6), pp. 76–84. [G: Czechoslovakia]

Havighurst, Clark C. Health Planning for Deregulation: Implementing the 1979 Amendments. *Law Contemp. Probl.*, Winter 1981, *44*(1), pp. 33–76. [G: U.S.]

Havighurst, Clark C. and Hackbarth, Glenn M. Enforcing the Rules of Free Enterprise in an Imperfect Market: The Case of Individual Practice Associations. In *Olson, M., ed.*, 1981, pp. 377–406.

Heimendinger, Jerianne; Zeitlin, Marian F. and Austin, James E. Formulated Foods. In *Austin, J. E. and Zeitlin, M. F., eds.*, 1981, pp. 85–98.

Hilaski, Harvey J. Understanding Statistics on Occupational Illnesses. *Mon. Lab. Rev.*, March 1981, *104*(3), pp. 25–29. [G: U.S.]

Hochban, Jacquelyn, et al. The Hill-Burton Program and Changes in Health Services Delivery. *Inquiry*, Spring 1981, *18*(1), pp. 61–69. [G: U.S.]

Hollingsworth, J. Rogers. Experience Abroad: Is It So Different? Commentary. In *Olson, M., ed.*, 1981, pp. 196–201. [G: OECD]

Hu, Teh-wei. The Demand for Dental Care Services, by Income and Insurance Status. In *Scheffler, R. M., ed.*, 1981, pp. 143–95. [G: U.S.]

Intriligator, Michael D. Major Policy Issues in the Economics of Health Care in the United States. In *van der Gaag, J. and Perlman, M., eds.*, 1981, pp. 355–68. [G: U.S.]

Ippolito, Pauline M. Information and the Life Cycle Consumption of Hazardous Goods. *Econ. Inquiry*, October 1981, *19*(4), pp. 529–58.

Jadlow, Joseph M. The Economic Effects of Generic Substitution. *Rivista Int. Sci. Econ. Com.*, January–February 1981, *28*(1–2), pp. 110–20. [G: U.S.]

Jarrett, Jeffrey E. Rising Hospital Costs and Service Intensity. *J. Risk Ins.*, June 1981, *48*(2), pp. 261–71. [G: U.S.]

Johnston, Bruce F. Reply to the Ness Critique of Johnston and Meyer [Nutrition, Health, and Population in Strategies for Rural Development]. *Econ. Develop. Cult. Change*, January 1981,

29(2), pp. 407–08.

Joskow, Paul L. Alternative Regulatory Mechanisms for Controlling Hospital Costs. In *Olson, M., ed.*, 1981, pp. 219–57. [G: U.S.]

Kahn, Alfred E. Health Care Economics: Paths to Structural Reform. In *Olson, M., ed.*, 1981, pp. 493–502. [G: U.S.]

Kahn, Robert L. Work, Stress, and Health. In *Dennis, B. D., ed.*, 1981, pp. 257–67.

Karna, M. N. Caste and Concepts of Health in a North Bihar Village. In *Karna, M. N., ed.*, 1981, pp. 113–26. [G: India]

Karsch, Christian. An Estimation of Feldstein's Dynamic Adjustment Model for Physicians' Services with Austrian Data. *Empirica*, 1981, (2), pp. 301–24. [G: Austria]

Kass, David I. and Pautler, Paul A. Physician and Medical Society Influence on Blue Shield Plans: Effects on Physician Reimbursement. In *Olson, M., ed.*, 1981, pp. 321–38. [G: U.S.]

Kass, David I. and Pautler, Paul A. The Administrative Costs of Non-Profit Health Insurers. *Econ. Inquiry*, July 1981, *19*(3), pp. 515–21. [G: U.S.]

Kay, Bonnie J.; Whitted, Nancy A. and Hardin, Saundra S. An Economic Interpretation of the Distribution and Organization of Abortion Services. *Inquiry*, Winter 1981, *18*(4), pp. 322–31. [G: U.S.]

Kelvorick, Alvin K. Regulation and Cost Containment in the Delivery of Mental Health Services. In *McGuire, T. G. and Weisbrod, B. A., eds.*, 1981, pp. 62–71.

Kerton, Robert R. and Chowdhury, Tapan K. The Impact of the PARCOST Program on Prescription Drug Prices in Ontario. *Can. Public Policy*, Spring 1981, 7(2), pp. 306–17. [G: Canada]

de Kervasdoué, Jean. Are Health Policies Adapted to the Practice of Medical Care? In *Altenstetter, C., ed.*, 1981, pp. 11–33.

Kingson, Eric R. and Scheffler, Richard M. Aging: Issues and Economic Trends for the 1980s. *Inquiry*, Fall 1981, *18*(3), pp. 197–213. [G: U.S.]

Klein, Rudolf. Prospects and Problems in the Comparative Study of Health-Services Innovation. In *Altenstetter, C., ed.*, 1981, pp. 267–76.

Klevorick, Alvin K. The Health Professions: "The Dog that Didn't Bark?" Commentary. In *Olson, M., ed.*, 1981, pp. 407–13. [G: U.S.]

Kneese, Allen V. and d'Arge, Ralph C. Benefit Analysis and Today's Regulatory Problems. In *Ferguson, A. R. and LeVeen, E. P., eds.*, 1981, pp. 65–90. [G: U.S.]

Kobrinski, Edward J. and Matteson, Ann L. Characteristics of High-Cost Treatment in Acute Care Facilities. *Inquiry*, Summer 1981, *18*(2), pp. 179–84. [G: U.S.]

Kompa, Ain. Motivational Analysis of Health-Related Life-Style: Preliminary Results and Propositions for Further Research. In *Molt, W.; Hartmann, H. A. and Stringer, P., eds.*, 1981, pp. 475–92. [G: W. Germany]

Kovanov, Vladimir V. Public Health Service. In *Novosti Press Agency*, 1981, pp. 248–62. [G: U.S.S.R.]

Kovner, Anthony R. Hospital Governance and Market Share. *Inquiry*, Fall 1981, *18*(3), pp. 255–65. [G: U.S.]

Krämer, Walter. Eine ökonometrische Untersuchung des Marktes fur ambulante kassenärztliche Leistungen. (An Econometric Investigation of the Market for Physicians' Services. With English summary.) *Z. ges. Staatswiss.*, March 1981, *137*(1), pp. 45–61. [G: W. Germany]

Lacronique, Jean François and Sandier, Simone. Technological Innovation: Cause or Effect of Increasing Expenditures for Health? In *Altenstetter, C., ed.*, 1981, pp. 87–105.

Lambrinos, James. Health: A Source of Bias in Labor Supply Models. *Rev. Econ. Statist.*, May 1981, *63*(2), pp. 206–12.

Langham, Max R. and Lanier, Ray. Public Mosquito Abatement: Comment. *J. Environ. Econ. Manage.*, March 1981, *8*(1), pp. 97–99. [G: U.S.]

Lawlor, Ann C. and Reid, Jack T. Hierarchical Patterns in the Location of Physician Specialists among Counties. *Inquiry*, Spring 1981, *18*(1), pp. 79–90. [G: U.S.]

Lazarus, Maurice. Controlling Hospital Costs. In *Gleason, H. P., ed.*, 1981, pp. 113–18.

Lefelmann, Gerd. Zum "Brain drain" ausländischer Humanmediziner in die Bundesrepublik Deutschland. (On the Brain Drain of Foreign Medical Graduates into the Federal Republic of Germany. With English summary.) *Konjunkturpolitik*, 1981, *27*(3), pp. 176–206. [G: W. Germany]

Leffler, Keith B. Persuasion or Information? The Economics of Prescription Drug Advertising. *J. Law Econ.*, April 1981, *24*(1), pp. 45–74. [G: U.S.]

Leffler, Keith B. and Lindsay, Cotton M. Markets for Medical Care and Medical Education: An Integrated Long-Run Structural Approach. *J. Human Res.*, Winter 1981, *16*(1), pp. 20–40. [G: U.S.]

Lewis, Maureen A. Sectoral Aspects of a Basic Human Needs Approach: The Linkages among Population, Nutrition, and Health. In *Leipziger, D. M., ed.*, 1981, pp. 29–105. [G: LDCs]

Lewit, Eugene M.; Coate, Douglas and Grossman, Michael. The Effects of Government Regulation on Teenage Smoking. *J. Law Econ.*, December 1981, *24*(3), pp. 545–69. [G: U.S.]

Link, Charles R. and Settle, Russell F. A Simultaneous-Equation Model of Labor Supply, Fertility and Earnings of Married Women: The Case of Registered Nurses. *Southern Econ. J.*, April 1981, *47*(4), pp. 977–89. [G: U.S.]

Link, Charles R. and Settle, Russell F. Wage Incentives and Married Professional Nurses: A Case of Backward-Bending Supply? *Econ. Inquiry*, January 1981, *19*(1), pp. 144–56. [G: U.S.]

Long, Michael J. The Role of Consumer Location in the Demand for Inpatient Care. *Inquiry*, Fall 1981, *18*(3), pp. 266–73. [G: U.S.]

Lozoya, Xavier and Zolla, Carlos. Traditional Medicine as an Alternative for Health in Third World Countries. In *Lozoya, J. A. and Birgin, H., eds.*, 1981, pp. 147–59. [G: Mexico; Latin America]

Ludbrook, Anne. A Cost-Effective Analysis of the Treatment of Chronic Renal Failure. *Appl. Econ.*, September 1981, *13*(3), pp. 337–50. [G: U.K.]

Lunde, Anders Steen. Health in the United States. *Ann. Amer. Acad. Polit. Soc. Sci.*, January 1981, *453*, pp. 28–69. [G: U.S.]

Lynk, William J. Regulatory Control of the Membership of Corporate Boards of Directors: The Blue Shield Case. *J. Law Econ.*, April 1981, *24*(1), pp. 159–73. [G: U.S.]

MacStravic, Robin E. Scott. Admissions Scheduling and Capacity Pooling: Minimizing Hospital Bed Requirements. *Inquiry*, Winter 1981, *18*(4), pp. 345–50. [G: U.S.]

Manning, Willard G., et al. A Two-Part Model of the Demand for Medical Care: Preliminary Results from the Health Insurance Study. In *van der Gaag, J. and Perlman, M., eds.*, 1981, pp. 103–23. [G: U.S.]

Marmor, Theodore R. and Morone, James A. Innovation and the Health Services Sector: Notes on the United States. In *Altenstetter, C., ed.*, 1981, pp. 35–42. [G: U.S.]

Marr, William L.; McCready, Douglas and Millerd, Frank. Canadian Internal Migration of Medical Personnel. *Growth Change*, July 1981, *12*(3), pp. 32–40. [G: Canada]

Mausner, Bernard and Mausner, Judith S. The Use of an Ecological Model in the Analysis of Health-Related Behavior. In *Molt, W.; Hartmann, H. A. and Stringer, P., eds.*, 1981, pp. 457–73.

Maxwell, Robert. Health Systems: an Overview. In *Gleason, H. P., ed.*, 1981, pp. 11–22.

Maxwell, Robert. Toward Regionalization in Health Services. In *Gleason, H. P., ed.*, 1981, pp. 75–84. [G: OECD]

Mayers, David and Smith, Clifford W., Jr. Contractual Provisions, Organizational Structure, and Conflict Control in Insurance Markets. *J. Bus.*, July 1981, *54*(3), pp. 407–34.

Maynard, Alan and Ludbrook, Anne. Thirty Years of Fruitless Indeavor? An Analysis of Government Intervention in the Health Care Market. In *van der Gaag, J. and Perlman, M., eds.*, 1981, pp. 45–65. [G: U.K.; France; Netherlands]

McCaffrey, David P. Work–Related Amputations by Type and Prevalence. *Mon. Lab. Rev.*, March 1981, *104*(3), pp. 35–41. [G: U.S.]

McCarthy, Thomas R. Regulation: Can It Improve Incentives? Commentary. In *Olson, M., ed.*, 1981, pp. 309–13. [G: U.S.]

McGuire, Thomas G. Financing and Demand for Mental Health Services. *J. Human Res.*, Fall 1981, *16*(4), pp. 501–22. [G: U.S.]

McGuire, Thomas G. Financing and Demand for Mental Health Services. In *McGuire, T. G. and Weisbrod, B. A., eds.*, 1981, pp. 29–61. [G: U.S.]

McGuire, Thomas G. National Health Insurance for Private Psychiatric Care: A Study in Distribution of Income. *Public Finance Quart.*, April 1981, *9*(2), pp. 183–96. [G: U.S.]

McGuire, Thomas G. and Weisbrod, Burton A. NIMH Conference of Economics and Mental Health: Introduction. In *McGuire, T. G. and Weisbrod, B. A., eds.*, 1981, pp. 1–7.

Meier, Gitta. HMO Experiences with Mental Health Services to the Long-Term Emotionally Disabled.

Inquiry, Summer 1981, *18*(2), pp. 125–38.
[G: U.S.]

Melnick, Glenn A.; Wheeler, John R. C. and Feldstein, Paul J. Effects of Rate Regulation on Selected Components of Hospital Expenses. *Inquiry,* Fall 1981, *18*(3), pp. 240–46. [G: U.S.]

Meyer, Jack A. Health Care Competition: Are Tax Incentives Enough? In *Olson, M., ed.,* 1981, pp. 424–49. [G: U.S.]

Miners, Laurence A. The Family's Demand for Health: Evidence from a Rural Community. In *Scheffler, R. M., ed.,* 1981, pp. 85–142.
[G: U.S.]

Mott, Frank L. and Haurin, R. Jean. The Impact of Health Problems and Mortality on Family Well-Being. In *Parnes, H. S., ed.,* 1981, pp. 198–253. [G: U.S.]

Muller, Charlotte F. Economic Aspects of Information on Health and Health Care. In *Galatin, M. and Leiter, R. D., eds.,* 1981, pp. 146–70.

Mullner, Ross. The American Hospital Association's Hospital Data Center: An Overview. *Rev. Public Data Use (See J. Econ. Soc. Meas. after 4/85),* November 1981, *9*(3), pp. 231–33. [G: U.S.]

Mullner, Ross; Byre, Calvin S. and Kralovec, Peter. Data on U.S. Hospitals: A Comparison of the Two Principal Sources. *Rev. Public Data Use (See J. Econ. Soc. Meas. after 4/85),* December 1981, *9*(4), pp. 301–07. [G: U.S.]

Naidu, D. Audikesavulu. Unmet Needs of Indian Children and the Alternative Strategies for Potential Human Resource Development. *Econ. Aff.,* April–June 1981, *26*(2), pp. 93–103. [G: India]

Naschold, Frieder. Two Roads toward Innovation in Occupational Safety and Health in Western Countries. In *Altenstetter, C., ed.,* 1981, pp. 145–59. [G: U.S.; Sweden; W. Germany]

Neale, R. S., et al. Life and Death in Hillgrove, 1870–1914. *Australian Econ. Hist. Rev.,* September 1981, *21*(2), pp. 91–113. [G: Australia]

Ness, Gayl D. The Political Economy of Integration in Development Strategies: Comment on Johnston and Meyer [Nutrition, Health, and Population in Strategies for Rural Development]. *Econ. Develop. Cult. Change,* January 1981, *29*(2), pp. 401–05.

Newhouse, Joseph P. Experience Abroad: Is It So Different? Commentary. In *Olson, M., ed.,* 1981, pp. 202–08. [G: U.S.]

Newhouse, Joseph P. The Demand for Medical Care Services: A Retrospect and Prospect. In *van der Gaag, J. and Perlman, M., eds.,* 1981, pp. 85–102.

Newhouse, Joseph P. The Erosion of the Medical Marketplace. In *Scheffler, R. M., ed.,* 1981, pp. 1–34. [G: U.S.]

Nishimura, Shuzo. Physician Manpower Allocation and the Rising Cost of Health Care—A Comparative Study of Three Countries: the United States, The United Kingdom, and Japan. *Kyoto Univ. Econ. Rev.,* April-October 1981, *51*(1–2), pp. 36–51. [G: Japan; U.K.; U.S.]

Nutt, Paul C. and Hurley, Robert. Factors That Influence Capital Expenditure Review Decisions. *Inquiry,* Summer 1981, *18*(2), pp. 151–64.
[G: U.S.]

Oates, Wallace E. The Health Professions: "The Dog that Didn't Bark?": Commentary. In *Olson, M., ed.,* 1981, pp. 413–18. [G: U.S.]

Olmstead, Alan L. and Sheffrin, Steven M. The Medical School Admission Process: An Empirical Investigation. *J. Human Res.,* Summer 1981, *16*(3), pp. 459–67. [G: U.S.]

Olson, Craig A. An Analysis of Wage Differentials Received by Workers on Dangerous Jobs. *J. Human Res.,* Spring 1981, *16*(2), pp. 167–85.
[G: U.S.]

Olson, Mancur. A New Approach to the Economics of Health Care: Introduction. In *Olson, M., ed.,* 1981, pp. 1–26. [G: U.S.]

Pauly, Mark V. Paying the Piper and Calling the Tune: The Relationship between Public Financing and Public Regulation of Health Care. In *Olson, M., ed.,* 1981, pp. 67–86. [G: U.S.]

Pauly, Mark V. and Satterthwaite, Mark A. The Pricing of Primary Care Physicians' Services: A Test of the Role of Consumer Information. *Bell J. Econ. (See Rand J. Econ. after 4/85),* Autumn 1981, *12*(2), pp. 488–506. [G: U.S.]

Pegels, C. Carl. A Batch Size Model for the Hospital Pharmacy. In *Chikán, A., ed. (II),* 1981, pp. 469–76.

Perrin, Richard K. and Scobie, Grant M. Market Intervention Policies for Increasing the Consumption of Nutrients by Low Income Households. *Amer. J. Agr. Econ.,* February 1981, *63*(1), pp. 73–82. [G: Colombia]

Pfaff, Martin and Bäuerle, Eberhard U. The Utilization of Public Health Services by Socio-Economic Groups: The Case of the Federal Republic of Germany. In *Molt, W.; Hartmann, H. A. and Stringer, P., eds.,* 1981, pp. 415–32.
[G: W. Germany]

Poirier, Dale J. A Switching Simultaneous Equations Model of Physician Behaviour in Ontario. In *Manski, C. F. and McFadden, D., eds.,* 1981, pp. 392–421. [G: Canada]

Poleman, Thomas T. Quantifying the Nutrition Situation in Developing Countries. *Food Res. Inst. Stud.,* 1981, *18*(1), pp. 1–58. [G: LDCs]

Ponce, Elsa Orley and Rigby, Donald. SSI Recipients in Medicaid Institutions, December 1979. *Soc. Sec. Bull.,* April 1981, *44*(4), pp. 32–37, 47.
[G: U.S.]

Portney, Paul R. Housing Prices, Health Effects, and Valuing Reductions in Risk of Death. *J. Environ. Econ. Manage.,* March 1981, *8*(1), pp. 72–78. [G: U.S.]

Prewitt, Kenneth. American Politics, Public Opinion, and Social Security Financing: Comment. In *Skidmore, F., ed.,* 1981, pp. 277–82. [G: U.S.]

Price, Daniel N. Income Replacement during Sickness, 1948–78. *Soc. Sec. Bull.,* May 1981, *44*(5), pp. 18–32. [G: U.S.]

Pupp, Roger L. Smoking, Disabilities and Health: Their Effect on Labor Market Experience. *J. Behav. Econ.,* Summer 1981, *10*(1), pp. 66–100.
[G: U.S.]

Pyndt, P. E. The Causes and Development of Health Care System Costs: The Danish Experience. *Managerial Dec. Econ.,* September 1981, *2*(3), pp. 179–85. [G: Denmark; Selected Countries]

Rand, Adam. Public and Social Enterprises and Consumers. *Ann. Pub. Co-op. Econ.*, January–June 1981, *52*(1/2), pp. 163–69. [G: Israel]

Randolph, S. Randi and Sachs, Carolyn. The Establishment of Applies Sciences: Medicine and Agriculture Compared. In *Busch, L., ed.*, 1981, pp. 83–111. [G: U.S.]

Rea, Samuel A., Jr. Workmen's Compensation and Occupational Safety under Imperfect Information. *Amer. Econ. Rev.*, March 1981, *71*(1), pp. 80–93.

Redisch, Michael; Gabel, Jon and Blaxall, Martha. Physician Pricing, Costs, and Income. In *Scheffler, R. M., ed.*, 1981, pp. 197–228.
[G: U.S.]

Reinhardt, Uwe E. Health Insurance and Cost Containment Policies: The Experience Abroad. In *Olson, M., ed.*, 1981, pp. 151–71. [G: Canada; France; W. Germany]

Reis, Jaime. Hunger in the Northeast: Some Historical Aspects. In *Mitchell, S., ed.*, 1981, pp. 41–57. [G: Brazil]

Richardson, J. The Inducement Hypothesis: That Doctors Generate Demand for their Own Services. In *van der Gaag, J. and Perlman, M., eds.*, 1981, pp. 189–214. [G: Australia]

Riddiough, Michael A. Some Economic Consequences of Technological Advance in Medical Care: The Case of a New Drug: Comment. In *Helms, R. B., ed.*, 1981, pp. 290–93. [G: U.S.]

Rodwin, Victor G. On the Separation of Health Planning and Provider Reimbursement: The U.S. and France. *Inquiry*, Summer 1981, *18*(2), pp. 139–50. [G: U.S.; France]

Rogers, Beatrice Lorge, et al. Consumer Food Price Subsidies. In *Austin, J. E. and Zeitlin, M. F., eds.*, 1981, pp. 99–110.

Rolph, John E. Some Statistical Evidence on Merit Rating in Medical Malpractice Insurance. *J. Risk Ins.*, June 1981, *48*(2), pp. 247–60. [G: U.S.]

Rones, Philip L. Can the Current Population Survey be Used to Identify the Disabled? *Mon. Lab. Rev.*, June 1981, *104*(6), pp. 37–39. [G: U.S.]

Root, Norman. Injuries at Work Are Fewer among Older Employees. *Mon. Lab. Rev.*, March 1981, *104*(3), pp. 30–34. [G: U.S.]

Root, Norman and Sebastian, Deborah. BLS Develops Measure of Job Risk by Occupation. *Mon. Lab. Rev.*, October 1981, *104*(10), pp. 26–30.
[G: U.S.]

Rosen, Sherwin. Valuing Health Risk. *Amer. Econ. Rev.*, May 1981, *71*(2), pp. 241–45.

Rosenblatt, Roger A. Health and Health Services. In *Hawley, A. H. and Mazie, S. M., eds.*, 1981, pp. 614–42. [G: U.S.]

Ruchlin, Hirsch S. and Rosen, Harry M. The Process of Hospital Rate Regulation: The New York Experience. *Inquiry*, Spring 1981, *18*(1), pp. 70–78. [G: U.S.]

Russett, Bruce, et al. Health and Population Patterns as Indicators of Income Inequality. *Econ. Develop. Cult. Change*, July 1981, *29*(4), pp. 759–79. [G: LDCs]

Sandier, Simone. Les soins médicaux en France et aux U.S.A. (Medical Care in France and in the U.S.A. With English summary.) *Consommation*,

January–March 1981, *28*(1), pp. 3–36.
[G: France; U.S.]

Saward, Ernest W. International Escalation of Health Care Expenditures. In *Gleason, H. P., ed.*, 1981, pp. 1–10.

Schaafsma, Joseph and Walsh, William D. The Supply of Canadian Physicians and Per Capita Expenditures for Their Services. *Inquiry*, Summer 1981, *18*(2), pp. 185–90. [G: Canada]

Schechter, Evan S. Commitment to Work and the Self-Perception of Disability. *Soc. Sec. Bull.*, June 1981, *44*(6), pp. 22–30. [G: U.S.]

Segal, Elliot A. and Gardner, Kenneth D. Preadmission Certification and Denied Hospital Stays: Two Surveys of PSROs. *Inquiry*, Summer 1981, *18*(2), pp. 120–24. [G: U.S.]

Seidman, Laurence S. Consumer Choice Health Plan and the Patient Cost-Sharing Strategy: Can they be Reconciled? In *Olson, M., ed.*, 1981, pp. 450–66. [G: U.S.]

Sekscenski, Edward S. The Health Services Industry: A Decade of Expansion. *Mon. Lab. Rev.*, May 1981, *104*(5), pp. 9–16. [G: U.S.]

Selowsky, Marcelo. Nutrition, Health and Education: The Economic Significance of Complementarities at Early Age. *J. Devel. Econ.*, December 1981, *9*(3), pp. 331–46.

Sen, Amartya. Ingredients of Famine Analysis: Availability and Entitlements. *Quart. J. Econ.*, August 1981, *96*(3), pp. 433–64. [G: India; Bangladesh]

Shakotko, Robert A.; Edwards, Linda N. and Grossman, Michael. An Exploration of the Dynamic Relationship between Health and Cognitive Development in Adolescence. In *van der Gaag, J. and Perlman, M., eds.*, 1981, pp. 305–35.
[G: U.S.]

Simon, Marilyn J. Imperfect Information, Costly Litigation, and Product Quality. *Bell J. Econ. (See Rand J. Econ. after 4/85)*, Spring 1981, *12*(1), pp. 171–84.

Sirkin, Gerald. Economic Aspects of Information on Health and Health Care: Comments. In *Galatin, M. and Leiter, R. D., eds.*, 1981, pp. 171–72.

Slack, Paul. The Disappearance of Plague: An Alternative View: Comment. *Econ. Hist. Rev.*, 2nd Ser., August 1981, *34*(3), pp. 469–76.
[G: Europe]

Slavin, M. and Ben'iash, G. The Effectiveness of Scientific and Technical Progress in Health Care. *Prob. Econ.*, July 1981, *24*(3), pp. 3–19.
[G: U.S.S.R.]

Sloan, Frank A. Regulation and the Rising Cost of Hospital Care. *Rev. Econ. Statist.*, November 1981, *63*(4), pp. 479–87. [G: U.S.]

Sloan, Frank A. and Becker, Edmund R. Internal Organization of Hospitals and Hospital Costs. *Inquiry*, Fall 1981, *18*(3), pp. 224–39. [G: U.S.]

Smith, Kenneth R. and Over, A. Mead, Jr. The Effect of Health Manpower Regulations on Productivity in Medical Practices. In *Cowing, T. G. and Stevenson, R. E., eds.*, 1981, pp. 309–343.
[G: U.S.]

Soderstrom, Lee. Extra-Billing and Cost-Sharing. *Can. Public Policy*, Winter 1981, *7*(1), pp. 103–07. [G: Canada]

Srinivasan, T. N. Malnutrition: Some Measurement

and Policy Issues. *J. Devel. Econ.*, February 1981, *8*(1), pp. 3–19. [G: India; Sri Lanka]

Stahl, Ingemar. Can Equality and Efficiency be Combined? The Experience of the Planned Swedish Health Care System. In *Olson, M., ed.*, 1981, pp. 172–95. [G: Sweden]

Starr, Paul. Inherent Difficulties Compounded by Mistaken Principles: Commentary. In *Olson, M., ed.*, 1981, pp. 119–28. [G: U.S.]

Steele, R. Marginal Met Need and Geographical Equity in Health Care. *Scot. J. Polit. Econ.*, June 1981, *28*(2), pp. 186–95. [G: U.K.]

Steinwald, Bruce and Sloan, Frank A. Regulatory Approaches to Hospital Cost Containment: A Synthesis of the Empirical Evidence. In *Olson, M., ed.*, 1981, pp. 274–308. [G: U.S.]

Stoddart, Greg L. and Barer, Morris L. Analyses of Demand and Utilization through Episodes of Medical Service. In *van der Gaag, J. and Perlman, M., eds.*, 1981, pp. 149–70. [G: Canada]

Straf, Miron L. Revenue Allocation by Regression: National Health Service Appropriations for Teaching Hospitals. *J. Roy. Statist. Soc.*, Part 1, 1981, *144*, pp. 80–84.

Sukhatme, P. V. and Margen, S. Relationship between Under-Nutrition and Poverty. *Indian Econ. Rev.*, January–June 1981, *16*(1 and 2), pp. 13–39. [G: LDCs]

Sunshine, Jonathan. Disability Payments Stabilizing after Era of Accelerating Growth. *Mon. Lab. Rev.*, May 1981, *104*(5), pp. 17–22. [G: U.S.]

Svahn, John A. Omnibus Reconciliation Act of 1981: Legislative History and Summary of OASDI and Medicare Provisions. *Soc. Sec. Bull.*, October 1981, *44*(10), pp. 3–24. [G: U.S.]

Szymanski, Albert. On the Uses of Disinformation to Legitimize the Revival of the Cold War: Health in the U.S.S.R. *Sci. Soc.*, Winter 1981–1982, *45*(4), pp. 453–74. [G: U.S.S.R.]

Taylor, D. Garth. American Politics, Public Opinion, and Social Security Financing. In *Skidmore, F., ed.*, 1981, pp. 235–73. [G: U.S.]

Temin, Peter. Physician Prescribing Behavior: Is There Learning by Doing? In *Helms, R. B., ed.*, 1981, pp. 173–82. [G: U.S.]

Thomas, J. William and Lowery, Julie. Determining Information Needs of Hospital Managers: The Critical-Success-Factor Approach. *Inquiry*, Winter 1981, *18*(4), pp. 300–310. [G: U.S.]

Vaupel, James W. On the Benefits of Health and Safety Regulation. In *Ferguson, A. R. and LeVeen, E. P., eds.*, 1981, pp. 1–22. [G: U.S.]

van de Ven, Wynand P. M. M. and van Praag, Bernard M. S. Risk Aversion and Deductibles in Private Health Insurance: Application of an Adjusted Tobit Model to Family Health Care Expenditures. In *van der Gaag, J. and Perlman, M., eds.*, 1981, pp. 125–48. [G: Netherlands]

van de Ven, Wynand P. M. M. and van Praag, Bernard M. S. The Demand for Deductibles in Private Health Insurance: A Probit Model with Sample Selection. *J. Econometrics*, November 1981, *17*(2), pp. 229–52. [G: Netherlands]

Veney, James E. Thoughts of a Former Editor. *Inquiry*, Spring 1981, *18*(1), pp. 3–7. [G: U.S.]

Wallack, Stanley S. Financing Care for the Chroni-

cally Mentally Ill: The Implications of the Various Approaches. In *McGuire, T. G. and Weisbrod, B. A., eds.*, 1981, pp. 72–84. [G: U.S.]

Warner, Michael; Steinberg, Joan S. and Brown, Montague. A Strategic Planning Model for Multihospital Systems. *Inquiry*, Fall 1981, *18*(3), pp. 214–23. [G: U.S.]

Wassermann, Ursula. Attempts at Control over Toxic Waste. *J. World Trade Law*, September–October 1981, *15*(5), pp. 410–30.

Weigel, Wolfgang. On the Rising Costs of Hospital Care. *Empirica*, 1981, (2), pp. 325–43. [G: Austria]

Weisbrod, Burton A. Benefit–Cost Analysis of a Controlled Experiment: Treating the Mentally Ill. *J. Human Res.*, Fall 1981, *16*(4), pp. 523–48. [G: U.S.]

Weisbrod, Burton A. and Schlesinger, Mark. Benefit–Cost Analysis in the Mental Health Area: Issues and Directions for Research. In *McGuire, T. G. and Weisbrod, B. A., eds.*, 1981, pp. 8–28.

Weissert, William G. Toward a Continuum of Care for the Elderly: A Note of Caution. *Public Policy*, Summer 1981, *29*(3), pp. 331–40.

Whipple, David. Incentives and Organizational Structure in Health Maintenance Organizations. In *Scheffler, R. M., ed.*, 1981, pp. 229–67. [G: U.S.]

White, William D. Inherent Difficulties Compounded by Mistaken Principles: Commentary. In *Olson, M., ed.*, 1981, pp. 117–19. [G: U.S.]

Wiggins, Steven N. Product Quality Regulation and New Drug Introductions: Some New Evidence from the 1970s. *Rev. Econ. Statist.*, November 1981, *63*(4), pp. 615–19. [G: U.S.]

Wilensky, Gail Roggin and Rossiter, Louis F. The Magnitude and Determinants of Physician-initiated Visits in the United States. In *van der Gaag, J. and Perlman, M., eds.*, 1981, pp. 215–43. [G: U.S]

Williams, Alan. Welfare Economics and Health Status Measurement. In *van der Gaag, J. and Perlman, M., eds.*, 1981, pp. 271–81.

Wilson, Alan B. Longitudinal Analysis of Diet, Physical Growth, Verbal Development, and School Performance. In *Balderston, J. B., et al., eds.*, 1981, pp. 39–81. [G: Guatemala]

Wilson, Peter A. Hospital Use by the Aging Population. *Inquiry*, Winter 1981, *18*(4), pp. 332–44. [G: U.S.]

Witt, Stephen F. and Pass, Christopher L. The Effects of Health Warnings and Advertising on the Demand for Cigarettes. *Scot. J. Polit. Econ.*, February 1981, *28*(1), pp. 86–91. [G: U.K.]

Wolfe, Barbara and van der Gaag, Jacques. A New Health Status Index for Children. In *van der Gaag, J. and Perlman, M., eds.*, 1981, pp. 283–304. [G: U.S.]

Wood, Walter R.; Ament, Richard P. and Kobrinski, Edward J. A Foundation for Hospital Case Mix Measurement. *Inquiry*, Fall 1981, *18*(3), pp. 247–54. [G: U.S.]

Wood, William C. Nuclear Liability after Three Mile Island. *J. Risk Ins.*, September 1981, *48*(3), pp. 450–64. [G: U.S.]

Workman, Philip A. Using Statistics to Manage a State Safety and Health Program. *Mon. Lab. Rev.*, March 1981, *104*(3), pp. 42–44. [G: U.S.]

Zeckhauser, Richard and Zook, Christopher. Failures to Control Health Costs: Departures from First Principles. In *Olson, M., ed.*, 1981, pp. 87–116. [G: U.S.]

Zeitlin, Marian F. and Formacion, Candelaria S. Nutrition Education. In *Austin, J. E. and Zeitlin, M. F., eds.*, 1981, pp. 49–72.

Ziderman, Adrian. The Valuation of Accident Cost Savings: A Comment. *J. Transp. Econ. Policy*, May 1981, *15*(2), pp. 185–87. [G: U.K.]

Zweifel, Peter. 'Supplier-Induced Demand' in a Model of Physician Behavior. In *van der Gaag, J. and Perlman, M., eds.*, 1981, pp. 245–67. [G: Switzerland]

Zweifel, Peter. Demande médicale induite par l'offre: chimère ou réalité. (Supplier Induced Demand in a Model of Physician Behaviour. With English summary.) *Consommation*, October–December 1981, *28*(4), pp. 39–62. [G: Switzerland]

914 Economics of Poverty

9140 Economics of Poverty

Altimir, Oscar. Poverty in Latin America: A Review of Concepts and Data. *Cepal Rev.*, April 1981, (13), pp. 65–91. [G: Latin America]

Aquilanti, Augusto. Defining Poverty: A Survey of American and English Economic Literature of the Sixties and Seventies. *Econ. Notes*, 1981, *10*(1), pp. 83–103. [G: U.S.; U.K.]

Atkinson, Anthony B., et al. Poverty in York: A Re-Analysis of Rowntree's 1950 Survey. *Bull. Econ. Res.*, November 1981, *33*(2), pp. 59–71. [G: U.K.]

Balderston, Judith B. Investigating the Web of Poverty—The Need for Research. In *Balderston, J. B., et al., eds.*, 1981, pp. 1–22.

Balderston, Judith B. Synthesis of Findings and Policy Implications. In *Balderston, J. B., et al., eds.*, 1981, pp. 177–98. [G: Guatemala]

Barr, Nicholas A. and Hall, Robert E. The Probability of Dependence on Public Assistance. *Economica*, May 1981, *48*(190), pp. 109–23. [G: U.S.]

Bauer, P. T. The Vicious Circle of Poverty. In *Livingstone, I., ed.*, 1981, *1965*, pp. 3–9. [G: LDCs]

Bauer, P. T. Western Guilt and Third World Poverty. In *Bauer, P. T.*, 1981, pp. 66–85.

Bose, S. K. Bihar's Backwardness—An Enigma? In *Karna, M. N., ed.*, 1981, pp. 7–13. [G: India]

Brown, Michael K. and Erie, Steven P. Blacks and the Legacy of the Great Society: The Economic and Political Impact of Federal Social Policy. *Public Policy*, Summer 1981, *29*(3), pp. 299–330. [G: U.S.]

Bryant, W. Keith; Bawden, D. L. and Saupe, W. E. The Economics of Rural Poverty—A Review of the post-World War II United States and Canadian Literature. In *Martin, L. R., ed.*, 1981, pp. 3–150. [G: Canada; U.S.]

Burkhauser, Richard V. and Smeeding, Timothy M. The Net Impact of the Social Security System on the Poor. *Public Policy*, Spring 1981, *29*(2), pp. 159–78. [G: U.S.]

Castro, Alfonso Peter; Hakansson, N. Thomas and Brokensha, David. Indicators of Rural Inequality. *World Devel.*, May 1981, *9*(5), pp. 401–27.

Clark, Stephen; Hemming, Richard and Ulph, David T. On Indices for the Measurement of Poverty. *Econ. J.*, June 1981, *91*(362), pp. 515–26. [G: U.K.]

Crosswell, Michael J. Growth, Poverty Alleviation, and Foreign Assistance. In *Leipziger, D. M., ed.*, 1981, pp. 181–218. [G: LDCs]

Curtis, Lynn A. Inflation, Economic Policy, and the Inner City. *Ann. Amer. Acad. Polit. Soc. Sci.*, July 1981, *456*, pp. 46–59. [G: U.S.]

Danziger, Sheldon; Haveman, Robert H. and Plotnick, Robert. How Income Transfer Programs Affect Work, Savings, and the Income Distribution: A Critical Review. *J. Econ. Lit.*, September 1981, *19*(3), pp. 975–1028. [G: U.S.]

Danziger, Sheldon and Plotnick, Robert. Income Maintenance Programs and the Pursuit of Income Security. *Ann. Amer. Acad. Polit. Soc. Sci.*, January 1981, *453*, pp. 130–52. [G: U.S.]

Duncan, Greg J. and Morgan, James N. Persistence and Change in Economic Status and the Role of Changing Family Composition. In *Hill, M. S.; Hill, D. H. and Morgan, J. N., eds.*, 1981, pp. 1–44. [G: U.S.]

Evers, H. D. The Contribution of Urban Subsistence Production to Incomes in Jakarta. *Bull. Indonesian Econ. Stud.*, July 1981, *17*(2), pp. 89–96. [G: Indonesia]

Farley, Rawle. Poverty and Enterprise: Towards the Sixth Stage of Economic Growth. *Rev. Black Polit. Econ.*, Winter 1981, *11*(2), pp. 229–50. [G: U.S.; LDCs]

Friedman, Joseph and Sjogren, Jane. Assets of the Elderly as They Retire. *Soc. Sec. Bull.*, January 1981, *44*(1), pp. 16–31. [G: U.S.]

Gaiha, Raghav and Kazmi, N. A. Aspects of Poverty in Rural India. *Econ. Planning*, 1981, *17*(2–3), pp. 74–112. [G: India]

Gist, John R. and Hill, R. Carter. The Economics of Choice in the Allocation of Federal Grants: An Empirical Test. *Public Choice*, 1981, *36*(1), pp. 63–73. [G: U.S.]

Gmelch, George and Bennett, Don. Interpreting the Research on Poverty in the Irish Republic. *Growth Change*, January 1981, *12*(1), pp. 27–34. [G: Ireland]

Gottschalk, Peter T. Transfer Scenarios and Projections of Poverty into the 1980s. *J. Human Res.*, Winter 1981, *16*(1), pp. 41–60. [G: U.S.]

Gregory, Mary B., et al. Urban Poverty and Some Policy Options: An Analysis for India. *Urban Stud.*, June 1981, *18*(2), pp. 155–67. [G: India]

Haines, Michael R. Poverty, Economic Stress, and the Family in a Late Nineteenth-Century American City: Whites in Philadelphia, 1880. In *Hershberg, T., ed.*, 1981, pp. 240–76. [G: U.S.]

Hauver, James H.; Goodman, John A. and Grainer, Marc A. The Federal Poverty Thresholds: Appearance and Reality. *J. Cons. Res.*, June 1981,

8(1), pp. 1–10.   [G: U.S.]

Hazlewood, Arthur. Income Distribution and Poverty—An Unfashionable View. In *Killick, T., ed.*, 1981, *1978*, pp. 150–56.   [G: Kenya]

Hicks, Alexander; Friedland, Roger and Johnson, Edwin. Class Power and State Policy. In *Martin, G. T., Jr., and Zald, M. N., eds.*, 1981, *1978*, pp. 131–46.   [G: U.S.]

Hill, Martha S. Some Dynamic Aspects of Poverty. In *Hill, M. S.; Hill, D. H. and Morgan, J. N., eds.*, 1981, pp. 93–120.   [G: U.S.]

House, William J. and Killick, Tony. Inequality and Poverty in the Rural Economy, and the Influence of Some Aspects of Policy. In *Killick, T., ed.*, 1981, pp. 157–79.   [G: Kenya]

Howes, Candace and Markusen, Ann R. Poverty: A Regional Political Economy Perspective. In *Hawley, A. H. and Mazie, S. M., eds.*, 1981, pp. 437–63.   [G: U.S.]

Hurd, Michael D. and Pencavel, John H. A Utility-Based Analysis of the Wage Subsidy Program. *J. Public Econ.*, April 1981, *15*(2), pp. 185–201.
                    [G: U.S.]

Huszár, István. People in Disadvantageous (Handicapped) Situation in Hungary. *Acta Oecon.*, 1981, *27*(1–2), pp. 163–78.   [G: Hungary]

Kakwani, Nanak. Note on a New Measure of Poverty. *Econometrica*, March 1981, *49*(2), pp. 525–26.

Kapsalis, Constantine. Poverty Lines: An Alternative Method of Estimation. *J. Human Res.*, Summer 1981, *16*(3), pp. 477–80.   [G: Netherlands]

Kulcsár, Kálmán. Social Policy in Today's Hungarian Society. *Acta Oecon.*, 1981, *27*(1–2), pp. 183–89.
                    [G: Hungary]

de la Luz Silva, Maria. Urban Poverty and Child Work: Elements for the Analysis of Child Work in Chile. In *Rodgers, G. and Standing, G., eds.*, 1981, pp. 159–77.   [G: Chile]

Metcalf, David. Poverty in the United Kingdom by Peter Townsend: Review Article. *Brit. J. Ind. Relat.*, March 1981, *19*(1), pp. 112–16.
                    [G: U.K.]

Mitchell, Simon. The Logic of Poverty: Introduction. In *Mitchell, S., ed.*, 1981, pp. 1–9. [G: Brazil]

Molina, Sergio and Piñera, Sebastian. Extreme Poverty in Latin America. In *Novak, M., ed.*, 1981, pp. 82–88.   [G: Latin America]

Muqtada, M. Poverty and Famines in Bangladesh. *Bangladesh Devel. Stud.*, Winter 1981, *9*(1), pp. 1–34.   [G: Bangladesh]

Musgrove, Philip. The Oil Price Increases and the Alleviation of Poverty: Income Distribution in Caracas, Venezuela, in 1966 and 1975. *J. Devel. Econ.*, October 1981, *9*(2), pp. 229–50.

Nyers, Reszö. Problems of People in Disadvantageous Social Situation from the Viewpoint of Economic Policy. *Acta Oecon.*, 1981, *27*(1–2), pp. 178–83.   [G: Hungary]

Poleman, Thomas T. Quantifying the Nutrition Situation in Developing Countries. *Food Res. Inst. Stud.*, 1981, *18*(1), pp. 1–58. [G: LDCs]

Rao, V. V. Bhanoji. Measurement of Deprivation and Poverty Based on the Proportion Spent on Food: An Exploratory Exercise. *World Devel.*, April 1981, *9*(4), pp. 337–53.   [G: India]

Reis, Jaime. Hunger in the Northeast: Some Historical Aspects. In *Mitchell, S., ed.*, 1981, pp. 41–57.   [G: Brazil]

Rosenbaum, Sonia and Wright, James D. Income Maintenance and Work Behavior. In *Martin, G. T., Jr., and Zald, M. N., eds.*, 1981, pp. 412–27.   [G: U.S.]

Selowsky, Marcelo. Income Distribution, Basic Needs and Trade-Offs with Growth: The Case of Semi-Industrialized Latin American Countries. *World Devel.*, January 1981, *9*(1), pp. 73–92.
                    [G: Latin America]

Sen, Amartya K. Issues in the Measurement of Poverty. In *Strøm, S., ed.*, 1981, *1979*, pp. 144–66.

Seninger, Stephen F. and Smeeding, Timothy M. Poverty: A Human Resource–Income Maintenance Perspective. In *Hawley, A. H. and Mazie, S. M., eds.*, 1981, pp. 382–436. [G: U.S.]

Sinha, Amareshwar Prasad. Economic Backwardness of Bihar and Certain Relevant Aspects of Census Data. In *Karna, M. N., ed.*, 1981, pp. 15–27.   [G: India]

Sowell, Thomas. Poverty, the Distribution of Income, and Social Policy: Some Thoughts. In *Gatti, J. F., ed.*, 1981, pp. 35–56. [G: U.S.]

Sowell, Thomas. Thoughts and Details on Poverty. *Policy Rev.*, Summer 1981, (17), pp. 11–25.
                    [G: U.S.]

Streeten, Paul P. How Have the Poor Fared? In *Streeten, P.*, 1981, pp. 135–39.

Sukhatme, P. V. and Margen, S. Relationship between Under-Nutrition and Poverty. *Indian Econ. Rev.*, January–June 1981, *16*(1 and 2), pp. 13–39.   [G: LDCs]

Takayama, Noriyuki and Hamada, Koichi. Measures of Poverty and Their Policy Implications. In *Khan, A. and Sirageldin, I., eds.*, 1981, pp. 3–30.   [G: Japan]

Tévoédjrè, Albert. Employment, Human Needs, and the NIEO. In *Lozoya, J. A. and Birgin, H., eds.*, 1981, pp. 1–28.   [G: LDCs]

Thon, Dominique. Income Inequality and Poverty: Some Problems. *Rev. Income Wealth*, June 1981, *27*(2), pp. 207–10.

Tissue, Thomas and McCoy, John L. Income and Living Arrangements among Poor Aged Singles. *Soc. Sec. Bull.*, April 1981, *44*(4), pp. 3–13.
                    [G: U.S.]

Vernier, Paul. Rights to Welfare as an Issue in Income Support Policy. In *Brown, P. G.; Johnson, C. and Vernier, P., eds.*, 1981, pp. 219–32.
                    [G: U.S.]

Verry, Donald W. Comments on R. Jackman and J. Papadachi [Local Authority Education Expenditure in England and Wales: Why Standards Differ and the Impact of Government Grants]. *Public Choice*, 1981, *36*(3), pp. 443–45. [G: U.K.]

Visaria, Pravin. Poverty and Unemployment in India: An Analysis of Recent Evidence. *World Devel.*, March 1981, *9*(3), pp. 277–300.
                    [G: India]

Wilson, Alan B. Longitudinal Analysis of Diet, Physical Growth, Verbal Development, and School Performance. In *Balderston, J. B., et al., eds.*, 1981, pp. 39–81.   [G: Guatemala]

915 Social Security

9150 Social Security

Aaron, Henry J. Social Security Can be Saved. *Challenge*, November–December 1981, *24*(5), pp. 4–10. [G: U.S.]

Aaron, Henry J. The Economic Effects of the OASI Program: Comment. In *Skidmore, F., ed.*, 1981, pp. 81–84. [G: U.S.]

Blinder, Alan S.; Gordon, Roger H. and Wise, Donald E. Rhetoric and Reality in Social Security Analysis—A Rejoinder [Reconsidering the Work Disincentive Effects of Social Security]. *Nat. Tax J.*, December 1981, *34*(4), pp. 473–78. [G: U.S.]

Boss, Alfred. Zur Reform des Systems der sozialen Sicherung in der Bundesrepublik Deutschland. (On the Reform of the System of Social Insurance in the Federal Republic of Germany. With English summary.) *Konjunkturpolitik*, 1981, *27*(2), pp. 59–88. [G: W. Germany]

Break, George F. The Economic Effects of the OASI Program. In *Skidmore, F., ed.*, 1981, pp. 45–81. [G: U.S.]

Bridges, Benjamin, Jr. Family Social Security Taxes Compared with Federal Income Taxes, 1979. *Soc. Sec. Bull.*, December 1981, *44*(12), pp. 12–18. [G: U.S.]

Bridges, Benjamin, Jr. and Packard, Michael D. Price and Income Changes for the Elderly. *Soc. Sec. Bull.*, January 1981, *44*(1), pp. 3–15. [G: U.S.]

Burkhauser, Richard V. and Smeeding, Timothy M. The Net Impact of the Social Security System on the Poor. *Public Policy*, Spring 1981, *29*(2), pp. 159–78. [G: U.S.]

Burkhauser, Richard V. and Turner, John A. Can Twenty-Five Million Americans Be Wrong?—A Response to Blinder, Gordon, and Wise [Reconsidering the Work Disincentive Effects of Social Security]. *Nat. Tax J.*, December 1981, *34*(4), pp. 467–72. [G: U.S.]

Burkhauser, Richard V. and Turner, John A. Life-Cycle Welfare Costs of Social Security. *Public Finance Quart.*, April 1981, *9*(2), pp. 123–42. [G: U.S.]

Burkhauser, Richard V. and Warlick, Jennifer L. Disentangling the Annuity from the Redistributive Aspects of Social Security in the United States. *Rev. Income Wealth*, December 1981, *27*(4), pp. 401–21. [G: U.S.]

Burkhauser, Richard V. and Warlick, Jennifer L. L'effet redistributif du régime de retraite de la sécurité sociale des États-Unis. (Measuring Income Redistribution under U.S. Social Security Retirement Program. With English summary.) *Consommation*, July–September 1981, *28*(3), pp. 51–74. [G: U.S.]

Busch, Georg and Wüger, Michael. Social Security and Saving—A Critical Note on the Feldstein Hypothesis. *Empirica*, 1981, (2), pp. 223–40.

Campbell, Colin D. The Exploding Cost of Social Security. In *Fellner, W., ed.*, 1981, pp. 281–308. [G: U.S.]

Campbell, John Creighton. Japan's Social Welfare

System. In *Richardson, B. M. and Ueda, T., eds.*, 1981, pp. 207–14. [G: Japan]

Cantril, Albert. American Politics, Public Opinion, and Social Security Financing: Comment. In *Skidmore, F., ed.*, 1981, pp. 274–77. [G: U.S.]

Carmichael, Jeffrey and Hawtrey, Kim. Social Security, Government Finance, and Savings. *Econ. Rec.*, December 1981, *57*(159), pp. 332–43. [G: Australia]

Castellino, Onorato. Social Security in Italy: Is It Really Social and Is It Secure? *Rivista Polit. Econ.*, Supplement December 1981, *71*, pp. 3–38. [G: Italy]

Chen, Yung-Ping. The Growth of Fringe Benefits: Implications for Social Security. *Mon. Lab. Rev.*, November 1981, *104*(11), pp. 3–10. [G: U.S.]

Copeland, Lois S. International Trends in Disability Program Growth. *Soc. Sec. Bull.*, October 1981, *44*(10), pp. 25–36. [G: Belgium; Finland; W. Germany; Netherlands; France]

Crawford, Vincent P. and Lilien, David M. Social Security and the Retirement Decision. *Quart. J. Econ.*, August 1981, *96*(3), pp. 505–29. [G: U.S.]

Creutz, Helmut. The New Agreement on Social Security for Rhine Boatmen. *Int. Lab. Rev.*, January–February 1981, *120*(1), pp. 83–96. [G: W. Europe]

Cutright, Phillips. Income Redistribution: A Cross-National Analysis. In *Martin, G. T., Jr., and Zald, M. N., eds.*, 1981, *1967*, pp. 38–54. [G: LDCs; MDCs]

Daly, Michael J. Reforming Canada's Retirement Income System: The Potential Role of RRSPs. *Can. Public Policy*, Autumn 1981, *7*(4), pp. 550–58. [G: Canada]

Danziger, Sheldon; Haveman, Robert H. and Plotnick, Robert. How Income Transfer Programs Affect Work, Savings, and the Income Distribution: A Critical Review. *J. Econ. Lit.*, September 1981, *19*(3), pp. 975–1028. [G: U.S.]

Danziger, Sheldon and Plotnick, Robert. Income Maintenance Programs and the Pursuit of Income Security. *Ann. Amer. Acad. Polit. Soc. Sci.*, January 1981, *453*, pp. 130–52. [G: U.S.]

Denton, Frank T. and Spencer, Byron G. A Macro-Economic Analysis of the Effects of a Public Pension Plan. *Can. J. Econ.*, November 1981, *14*(4), pp. 609–34. [G: Canada]

Diamond, Peter. Comment [A Reappraisal of Financing Social Security] [VAT versus the Payroll Tax]. In *Skidmore, F., ed.*, 1981, pp. 164–69. [G: U.S.]

Eldred, Gary W. Social Security: A Conceptual Alternative. *J. Risk Ins.*, June 1981, *48*(2), pp. 220–34. [G: U.S.]

Feldstein, Martin S. The Effect of Social Security on Saving. In *Currie, D.; Nobay, R. and Peel, D., eds.*, 1981, pp. 1–23. [G: U.S.]

Fibiger, John. Comment [A Reappraisal of Financing Social Security] [VAT versus the Payroll Tax]. In *Skidmore, F., ed.*, 1981, pp. 169–72. [G: U.S.]

Frey, René L. and Leu, Robert E. Demographie und Inzidenz der öffentlichen Ausgaben im Gesundheitswesen. (Demography and the Incidence of Public Expenditures in the Health Sector. With

English summary.) *Schweiz. Z. Volkswirtsch. Statist.*, September 1981, *117*(3), pp. 319–36.

Fujita, Sei. National Pension and Its Finance. (In Japanese. With English summary.) *Osaka Econ. Pap.*, December 1981, *31*(2–3), pp. 93–105.
[G: Japan]

Grad, Susan. Impact on Widows of Proposed Changes in OASI Mother's Benefits. *Soc. Sec. Bull.*, February 1981, *44*(2), pp. 3–18.
[G: U.S.]

Halberstadt, V. and Haveman, Robert H. Public Policies for Disabled Workers: Cross National Evidence on Efficiency and Redistributive Effects. In *[Pen, J.]*, 1981, pp. 79–110. [G: Israel; U.S.; W. Europe]

Hamm, Walter. An den Grenzen des Wohlfahrtsstaats. (The Welfare State at its Limits. With English Summary.) In *[von Haberler, G.]*, 1981, pp. 117–39. [G: W. Germany]

Hanami, Tadashi. The Influence of ILO Standards on Law and Practice in Japan. *Int. Lab. Rev.*, November–December 1981, *120*(6), pp. 765–79.
[G: Japan]

Hay, J. R. The British Business Community, Social Insurance and the German Example. In *Mommsen, W. J., ed.*, 1981, pp. 107–32.
[G: U.K.; Germany]

Hemming, Richard. Market Failure and Superannuation—A Reply [The Economic Impact of the Proposed National Superannuation Scheme for Australia]. *Econ. Rec.*, March 1981, *57*(156), pp. 89–90. [G: Australia]

Hennock, E. P. The Origins of British National Insurance and the German Precedent 1880–1914. In *Mommsen, W. J., ed.*, 1981, pp. 84–106.
[G: U.K.; Germany]

Hockerts, H. G. German Post-War Social Policies against the Background of the Beveridge Plan. Some Observations Preparatory to a Comparative Analysis. In *Mommsen, W. J., ed.*, 1981, pp. 315–39. [G: Germany]

Holzmann, Robert. Public Finance and Private Saving in Austria: The Effects of Social Security. *Empirica*, 1981, (2), pp. 187–221. [G: Austria]

Hymans, Saul H. Saving, Investment, and Social Security. *Nat. Tax J.*, March 1981, *34*(1), pp. 1–8. [G: U.S.]

Janssen, Martin and Müller, Heinz. Der Einfluss der Demographie auf die Aktivitäten des Staates: die Finanzierung der 1. und 2. Säule der Altersvorsorge. (The Influence of Demography on the Activities of the State: Financing of the First and Second Pillars of the Old Age Security Scheme. With English summary.) *Schweiz. Z. Volkswirtsch. Statist.*, September 1981, *117*(3), pp. 297–314.

Jenkins, Michael. Social Security Trends in the English-Speaking Caribbean. *Int. Lab. Rev.*, September–October 1981, *120*(5), pp. 631–43.
[G: Caribbean]

Johnson, Darwin G. Sensitivity of Federal Expenditures to Unemployment. *Public Finance Quart.*, January 1981, *9*(1), pp. 3–21. [G: U.S.]

Johnson, Lewis. Life-cycle Saving, Social Security, and the Long-run Capital Stock. In *Federal Reserve System*, 1981, pp. 275–79.

Jones, R. L. and Page, K. R. Market Failure and Superannuation—A Comment [The Economic Impact of the Proposed National Superannuation Scheme for Australia]. *Econ. Rec.*, March 1981, *57*(156), pp. 86–88. [G: Australia]

Killingsworth, Charles C. Trouble in Social Insurance. *Challenge*, July/August 1981, *24*(3), pp. 50–52. [G: U.S.]

Kimura, Yoko. The Rates of Return to Pensioners under the Kosei Pension Scheme. (In Japanese. With English summary.) *Osaka Econ. Pap.*, June 1981, *31*(1), pp. 28–41. [G: Japan]

Kritzer, Barbara E. Chile Changes Social Security. *Soc. Sec. Bull.*, May 1981, *44*(5), pp. 33–37.
[G: Chile]

Leeds, Morton. Inflation and the Elderly: A Housing Perspective. *Ann. Amer. Acad. Polit. Soc. Sci.*, July 1981, *456*, pp. 60–69. [G: U.S.]

Leimer, Dean R. and Petri, Peter A. Cohort-Specific Effects of Social Security Policy. *Nat. Tax J.*, March 1981, *34*(1), pp. 9–28. [G: U.S.]

Lesthaeghe, Ron J. Demographic Change, Social Security and Economic Growth: Inferences from the Belgian Example. *Schweiz. Z. Volkswirtsch. Statist.*, September 1981, *117*(3), pp. 225–55.
[G: Belgium]

Manning, Ian. Social Security and the Future. *Australian Econ. Rev.*, 1st Quarter 1981, (53), pp. 29–34. [G: Australia]

Manning, Ian. The 1970s: A Decade of Social Security Policy. *Australian Econ. Rev.*, 1st Quarter 1981, (53), pp. 13–19. [G: Australia]

Manser, Marilyn E. Historical and Political Issues in Social Security Financing. In *Skidmore, F., ed.*, 1981, pp. 21–43. [G: U.S.]

Marmor, Theodore R. Political Perspective on Social Security Financing: Comment. In *Skidmore, F., ed.*, 1981, pp. 224–29. [G: U.S.]

Martin, Linda Gray. The Social Security System: Should You Withdraw? *New Eng. Econ. Rev.*, September–October 1981, pp. 37–42. [G: U.S.]

McManus, Leo A. Evaluation of Disability Insurance Savings Due to Beneficiary Rehabilitation. *Soc. Sec. Bull.*, February 1981, *44*(2), pp. 19–26.
[G: U.S.]

McMurray, David. Labour Legislation and Policy: Summary Outline. In *Wood, W. D. and Kumar, P., eds.*, 1981, pp. 95–191. [G: Canada]

Menefee, John A.; Edwards, Bea and Schieber, Sylvester J. Analysis of Nonparticipation in the SSI Program. *Soc. Sec. Bull.*, June 1981, *44*(6), pp. 3–21. [G: U.S.]

Mills, Wilbur. Political Perspective on Social Security Financing: Comment. In *Skidmore, F., ed.*, 1981, pp. 229–33. [G: U.S.]

Motylyov, Leonid. Social Security and Social Insurance. In *Novosti Press Agency*, 1981, pp. 216–29. [G: U.S.S.R.]

Munnell, Alicia H. Social Security, Private Pensions, and Saving. *New Eng. Econ. Rev.*, May/June 1981, pp. 31–47. [G: U.S.]

Musgrave, Richard A. A Reappraisal of Financing Social Security. In *Skidmore, F., ed.*, 1981, pp. 89–127. [G: U.S.]

Perelman, Sergio. Evaluation patrimoniale des droits a la pension en Belgique. (With English summary.) *Cah. Écon. Bruxelles*, 1st Trimestre 1981, (89), pp. 25–52. [G: Belgium]

Pfaff, Martin. Redistribution, Social Security and Growth: Comments. In *Giersch, H., ed. (II)*, 1981, pp. 426–45. [G: W. Germany; LDCs]

Prewitt, Kenneth. American Politics, Public Opinion, and Social Security Financing: Comment. In *Skidmore, F., ed.*, 1981, pp. 277–82. [G: U.S.]

Price, Daniel N. Federal Civil Service Adult Survivor Annuitants and Social Security, December 1975. *Soc. Sec. Bull.*, August 1981, 44(8), pp. 3–14. [G: U.S.]

Reischauer, Robert. The Economic Effects of the OASI Program: Comment. In *Skidmore, F., ed.*, 1981, pp. 84–88.

Rogers, Gayle Thompson. Aged Widows and OASDI: Age at and Economic Status before and after Receipt of Benefits. *Soc. Sec. Bull.*, March 1981, 44(3), pp. 3–19. [G: U.S.]

Schobel, Bruce D. A Comparison of Social Security Taxes and Federal Income Taxes, 1980–90. *Soc. Sec. Bull.*, December 1981, 44(12), pp. 19–22. [G: U.S.]

Schobel, Bruce D. Administrative Expenses under OASDI. *Soc. Sec. Bull.*, March 1981, 44(3), pp. 21–28. [G: U.S.]

Serow, William J. Demographic and Economic Considerations for Future Retirement Policy. *Policy Anal.*, Spring 1981, 7(2), pp. 143–51. [G: U.S.]

Sheshinski, Eytan and Weiss, Yoram. Uncertainty and Optimal Social Security Systems. *Quart. J. Econ.*, May 1981, 96(2), pp. 189–206.

Skidmore, Felicity. Social Security Financing: Overview of the Symposium. In *Skidmore, F., ed.*, 1981, pp. 1–19.

Smith, Stanley D. and Stanley, Kenneth L. Social Security Retirement Age: Alternatives and Cost Comparisons. *J. Risk Ins.*, December 1981, 48(4), pp. 694–99. [G: U.S.]

Stearns, Peter N. Political Perspective on Social Security Financing. In *Skidmore, F., ed.*, 1981, pp. 173–224. [G: U.S.]

Stevens, Neil A. Indexation of Social Security Benefits—A Reform in Need of Reform. *Fed. Res. Bank St. Louis Rev.*, June–July 1981, 63(6), pp. 3–10. [G: U.S.]

Stiglin, Laura E. A Classic Case of Overreaction: Women and Social Security. *New Eng. Econ. Rev.*, January/February 1981, pp. 29–40.

Svahn, John A. Omnibus Reconciliation Act of 1981: Legislative History and Summary of OASDI and Medicare Provisions. *Soc. Sec. Bull.*, October 1981, 44(10), pp. 3–24. [G: U.S.]

Taylor, D. Garth. American Politics, Public Opinion, and Social Security Financing. In *Skidmore, F., ed.*, 1981, pp. 235–73. [G: U.S.]

Townley, Peter G. C. Public Choice and the Social Insurance Paradox: A Note. *Can. J. Econ.*, November 1981, 14(4), pp. 712–17.

Ullmann, H.-P. German Industry and Bismarck's Social Security System. In *Mommsen, W. J., ed.*, 1981, pp. 133–49. [G: Germany]

Vasey, Wayne. Recurring Themes in the Income Support Policy Debate— Obstacles to Change. In *Brown, P. G.; Johnson, C. and Vernier, P., eds.*, 1981, pp. 283–303. [G: U.S.]

Vaubel, Roland. Redistribution, Social Security and Growth. In *Giersch, H., ed. (II)*, 1981, pp. 387–425.

Vaupel, James W. Free Social Security Recipients from the Social Security Tax. *Policy Anal.*, Winter 1981, 7(1), pp. 125–29. [G: U.S.]

Villars, C. Social Security for Migrant Workers in the Framework of the Council of Europe. *Int. Lab. Rev.*, May–June 1981, 120(3), pp. 291–302.

Wolozin, Harold. Earlier Retirement and the Older Worker. *J. Econ. Issues*, June 1981, 15(2), pp. 477–87. [G: U.S.]

Zabalza, A. and Piachaud, D. Social Security and the Elderly: A Simulation of Policy Changes. *J. Public Econ.*, October 1981, 16(2), pp. 145–69. [G: U.K.]

916 Economics of Law and Crime

9160 Economics of Law and Crime

Balkin, Steven and McDonald, John F. The Market for Street Crime: An Economic Analysis of Victim—Offender Interaction. *J. Urban Econ.*, November 1981, 10(3), pp. 390–405.

Belsasso, Guido. Undocumented Mexican Workers in the U.S. In *McBride, R. H., ed.*, 1981, pp. 128–57. [G: U.S.; Mexico]

Bhagwati, Jagdish N. Alternative Theories of Illegal Trade: Economic Consequences and Statistical Detection. *Weltwirtsch. Arch.*, 1981, 117(3), pp. 409–27.

Black, Charles L., Jr. Perspectives on the American Common Market [Regulation and the American Common Market]. In *Tarlock, A. D., ed.*, 1981, pp. 59–66. [G: U.S.]

Blumstein, Alfred; Cohen, Jacqueline and Miller, Harold D. Demographically Disaggregated Projections of Prison Populations. In *Crecine, J. P., ed.*, 1981, pp. 3–37. [G: U.S.]

Brady, Gordon L. Fee Shifting: An Institutional Change to Decrease the Benefits from Free Riding. In *Sirkin, G., ed.*, 1981, pp. 95–140. [G: U.S.]

Buchanan, James McGill and Faith, Roger L. Entrepreneurship and the Internalization of Externalities. *J. Law Econ.*, April 1981, 24(1), pp. 95–111.

Buck, Andrew J. and Hakim, Simon. A Simultaneous Equations System of Crime and Police. *Statistica*, July–September 1981, 41(3), pp. 449–57.

Buck, Andrew J. and Hakim, Simon. Appropriate Roles for Statistical Decision Theory and Hypothesis Testing in Model Selection: An Exposition. *Reg. Sci. Urban Econ.*, February 1981, 11(1), pp. 135–47. [G: U.S.]

Buck, Andrew J. and Hakim, Simon. Inequality Constraints, Multicollinearity and Models of Police Expenditure. *Southern Econ. J.*, October 1981, 48(2), pp. 449–63.

Carroll, William J. The Effect of Crime on Residential Rents and Property Values: A Comment. *Amer. Econ.*, Spring 1981, 25(1), pp. 76–77. [G: U.S.]

Champagne, Anthony; Neef, Marian and Nagel,

Stuart. Laws, Organizations, and the Judiciary. In *Nystrom, P. C. and Starbuck, W. H., eds.,* Vol. 1, 1981, pp. 187–209.

Cloninger, Dale O. Risk, Arson and Abandonment. *J. Risk Ins.,* September 1981, *48*(3), pp. 494–504. [G: U.S.]

Coffee, John C., Jr. "No Soul to Damn: No Body to Kick": An Unscandalized Inquiry into the Problem of Corporate Punishment. *Mich. Law Rev.,* January 1981, *79*(3), pp. 386–459. [G: U.S.]

Conley, John A. Revising Conceptions about the Origin of Prisons: The Importance of Economic Considerations. *Soc. Sci. Quart.,* June 1981, *62*(2), pp. 247–58. [G: U.S.]

Conybeare, John A. C. The Private and Social Utility of Extortion. *Amer. Econ. Rev.,* December 1981, *71*(5), pp. 1028–30.

Corman, Hope. Criminal Deterrence in New York: The Relationship between Court Activities and Crime. *Econ. Inquiry,* July 1981, *19*(3), pp. 476–87. [G: U.S.]

Davies, Rhodri and Grabiner, Anthony. Trade Financing: Legal Issues. In *Gmür, C. J., ed.,* 1981, pp. 173–86. [G: U.K.; Selected Countries]

Delmas-Marty, Mireille. White-collar Crime and the EEC. In *Leigh, L. H., ed.,* 1981, pp. 78–105. [G: EEC]

Dickinson, Katherine P. Supported Work for Ex-Addicts: An Exploration of Endogenous Tastes. *J. Human Res.,* Fall 1981, *16*(4), pp. 551–99. [G: U.S.]

Duffee, David E. Changes in Penal Goals and Structure in a Downward Economy. In *Wright, K. N., ed.,* 1981, pp. 273–86. [G: U.S.]

Ehrlich, Isaac. On the Usefulness of Controlling Individuals: An Economic Analysis of Rehabilitation, Incapacitation, and Deterrence. *Amer. Econ. Rev.,* June 1981, *71*(3), pp. 307–22.

Eskridge, Chris W. The Futures of Crime in America: An Economic Perspective. In *Wright, K. N., ed.,* 1981, pp. 305–23. [G: U.S.]

Fabrikant, Richard S. Police Allocation in the Presence of Crime Spillover. In *Hakim, S. and Rengert, G. F., eds.,* 1981, pp. 97–118. [G: U.S.]

Fishburn, Geoffrey. Tax Evasion and Inflation. *Australian Econ. Pap.,* December 1981, *20*(37), pp. 325–32.

Franklin, Daniel. Bribery and Corruption in East-West Trade. *ACES Bull. (See Comp. Econ. Stud. after 8/85),* Fall–Winter 1981, *23*(3–4), pp. 1–71. [G: E. Europe]

Friedman, David D. Reflections on Optimal Punishment, or: Should the Rich Pay Higher Fines? In *Zerbe, R. O., Jr., ed.,* 1981, pp. 185–205.

Furlong, William J. and Mehay, Stephen L. Urban Law Enforcement in Canada: An Empirical Analysis. *Can. J. Econ.,* February 1981, *14*(1), pp. 44–57. [G: Canada]

Gaetani-d'Aragona, Gabriele. The Hidden Economy: Concealed Labor Markets in Italy. *Rivista Int. Sci. Econ. Com.,* March 1981, *28*(3), pp. 270–80. [G: Italy]

Galatin, Malcolm. The Optimal Size of the Criminal Court System: Comments. In *Sirkin, G., ed.,* 1981, pp. 162–64. [G: U.S.]

Greene, Jack R. Changes in the Conception of Police

Work: Crime Control versus Collective Goods. In *Wright, K. N., ed.,* 1981, pp. 233–56. [G: U.S.]

Greffe, Xavier. L'économie non officielle. (The Unofficial Economy. With English summary.) *Consommation,* July–September 1981, *28*(3), pp. 95–118.

Hakim, Simon and Rengert, George F. Crime Spillover: Introduction. In *Hakim, S. and Rengert, G. F., eds.,* 1981, pp. 7–19.

Hamowy, Ronald. The IRS and Civil Liberties: Powers of Search and Seizure. *Cato J.,* Spring 1981, *1*(1), pp. 225–75. [G: U.S.]

Hannan, Timothy H. On the Optimality of Legalizing Heroin Sales. In *Henderson, J. V., ed.,* 1981, pp. 249–61.

Hellman, Daryl A. Criminal Mobility and Policy Recommendations. In *Hakim, S. and Rengert, G. F., eds.,* 1981, pp. 135–50. [G: U.S.]

Hochman, Harold M. California Law and Its Economic Effects on Southern California: Comments. In *Sirkin, G., ed.,* 1981, pp. 58–61. [G: U.S.]

Hoffman, Beatrice. Proposition 13 and the San Francisco Criminal Justice System—First Reactions to a Disaster. In *Wright, K. N., ed.,* 1981, pp. 147–71. [G: U.S.]

Holzman, Franklyn D. The Second Economy in CMEA: A Terminological Note. *ACES Bull. (See Comp. Econ. Stud. after 8/85),* Spring 1981, *23*(1), pp. 111–14. [G: CMEA]

Hughes, Michael and Carter, Timothy J. A Declining Economy and Sociological Theories of Crime: Predictions and Explications. In *Wright, K. N., ed.,* 1981, pp. 5–25. [G: U.S.]

Katzman, Martin T. The Supply of Criminals: A Geo-Economic Examination. In *Hakim, S. and Rengert, G. F., eds.,* 1981, pp. 119–34. [G: U.S.]

Keto, David B. The Corporation and the Constitution: Economic Due Process and Corporate Speech. *Yale Law J.,* July 1981, *90*(8), pp. 1833–60. [G: U.S.]

Kitch, Edmund W. Regulation and the American Common Market. In *Tarlock, A. D., ed.,* 1981, pp. 9–55. [G: U.S.]

Klein, Benjamin and Leffler, Keith B. The Role of Market Forces in Assuring Contractual Performance. *J. Polit. Econ.,* August 1981, *89*(4), pp. 615–41.

Landa, Janet and Grofman, Bernard. Games of Breach and the Role of Contract Law in Protecting the Expectation Interest. In *Zerbe, R. O., Jr., ed.,* 1981, pp. 67–90.

Leigh, L. H. Aspects of the Control of Economic Crime in the United Kingdom. In *Leigh, L. H., ed.,* 1981, pp. 15–38. [G: U.K.]

Leigh, L. H. Crimes in Bankruptcy. In *Leigh, L. H., ed.,* 1981, pp. 106–208. [G: U.K.]

Levi, Michael. The Sentencing of Long-firm Frauds. In *Leigh, L. H., ed.,* 1981, pp. 57–77. [G: U.K.]

Long, Sharon K. and Witte, Ann D. Current Economic Trends: Implications for Crime and Criminal Justice. In *Wright, K. N., ed.,* 1981, pp. 69–143. [G: U.S.]

Martell, Terrence F. and Salzman, Jerrold E. Cash Settlement for Futures Contracts Based on Common Stock Indices: An Economic and Legal Perspective. *J. Futures Markets*, Fall 1981, *1*(3), pp. 291–301.

Martino, Antonio. Measuring Italy's Underground Economy. *Policy Rev.*, Spring 1981, (16), pp. 87–106. [G: Italy]

McIver, John P. Criminal Mobility: A Review of Empirical Studies. In *Hakim, S. and Rengert, G. F., eds.*, 1981, pp. 20–47. [G: U.S.]

McPheters, Lee R. and Schlagenhauf, Don E. Macroeconomic Determinants of the Flow of Undocumented Aliens in North America. *Growth Change*, January 1981, *12*(1), pp. 2–8. [G: U.S.]

McPheters, Lee R. and Stronge, William B. Crime Spillover in the Boston Area. In *Hakim, S. and Rengert, G. F., eds.*, 1981, pp. 83–96. [G: U.S.]

Mehay, Stephen L. Burglary Spillover in Los Angeles. In *Hakim, S. and Rengert, G. F., eds.*, 1981, pp. 67–82. [G: U.S.]

Meyer, Peter B. "Survival" in Economic Downturns: Some Implications for the Criminal Justice System. In *Wright, K. N., ed.*, 1981, pp. 39–50. [G: U.S.]

Mishan, Ezra J. Pareto Optimality and the Law. In *Mishan, E. J.*, 1981, *1967*, pp. 105–24.

Montias, J. M. and Rose-Ackerman, Susan. Corruption in a Soviet-type Economy: Theoretical Considerations. In *[Bergson, A.]*, 1981, pp. 53–83.

Noam, Eli M. A Cost–Benefit Model of Criminal Courts. In *Zerbe, R. O., Jr., ed.*, 1981, pp. 173–83. [G: U.S.]

Noam, Eli M. The Optimal Size of the Criminal Court System. In *Sirkin, G., ed.*, 1981, pp. 145–61. [G: U.S.]

North, Douglass C. An Economist's Perspective on the American Common Market [Regulation and the American Common Market]. In *Tarlock, A. D., ed.*, 1981, pp. 77–81. [G: U.S.]

Olmstead, Alan L. and Sheffrin, Steven M. Affirmative Action in Medical Schools: Econometric Evidence and Legal Doctrine. In *Zerbe, R. O., Jr., ed.*, 1981, pp. 207–23. [G: U.S.]

Pejovich, Svetozar. Law as a Capital Good. In *Sirkin, G., ed.*, 1981, pp. 257–67.

Perryman, M. Ray. A Neglected Institutional Feature of the Labor Sector of the U.S. Economy. *J. Econ. Issues*, June 1981, *15*(2), pp. 387–95. [G: U.S.]

Peterson, Andrew A. Deterring Strikes by Public Employees: New York's Two-for-One Salary Penalty and the 1979 Prison Guard Strike. *Ind. Lab. Relat. Rev.*, July 1981, *34*(4), pp. 545–62. [G: U.S.]

Pitt, Mark M. Smuggling and Price Disparity. *J. Int. Econ.*, November 1981, *11*(4), pp. 447–58. [G: Indonesia]

Reiman, Jeffrey H. and Headlee, Sue. Crime and Crisis. In *Wright, K. N., ed.*, 1981, pp. 27–38. [G: U.S.]

Reiss, Albert J., Jr. Public Safety: Marshaling Crime Statistics. *Ann. Amer. Acad. Polit. Soc. Sci.*, January 1981, *453*, pp. 222–36. [G: U.S.]

Ryan, John E. Statement to House Select Committee on Narcotics Abuse and Control, October 9,

1981. *Fed. Res. Bull.*, October 1981, *67*(10), pp. 781–84. [G: U.S.]

Saari, David J. On Rationing Justice and Liberty in a Declining Economy. In *Wright, K. N., ed.*, 1981, pp. 257–72. [G: U.S.]

Schanze, Erich. Der Beitrag von Coase zu Recht und Ökonomie des Unternehmens. (Coase's Contribution to Law and Economics of Business Organizations. With English summary.) *Z. ges. Staatswiss.*, December 1981, *137*(4), pp. 694–701.

Schwartz, Gary T. Tort Law and the Economy in Nineteenth-Century America: A Reinterpretation. *Yale Law J.*, July 1981, *90*(8), pp. 1717–75. [G: U.S.]

Shapiro, David L. California Water Law and Its Economic Effects on Southern California. In *Sirkin, G., ed.*, 1981, pp. 14–57. [G: U.S.]

Silver, Morris. Law as a Capital Good: Comments. In *Sirkin, G., ed.*, 1981, pp. 268–71.

Sirkin, Gerald. Lexeconics: The Interaction of Law and Economics: Introduction. In *Sirkin, G., ed.*, 1981, pp. 9–13.

Sirkin, Gerald. Rent Seeking: Comments. In *Sirkin, G., ed.*, 1981, pp. 191–94.

Sorrentino, John A., Jr. An Economic Theory of Criminal Externalities. In *Hakim, S. and Rengert, G. F., eds.*, 1981, pp. 54–66.

Spiegel, Uriel. Economic Theoretical View of Criminal Spillover. In *Hakim, S. and Rengert, G. F., eds.*, 1981, pp. 48–53.

St. Antoine, Theodore J. U.S. Industrial Relations 1950–1980: The Role of Law. In *Stieber, J.; McKersie, R. B. and Mills, D. Q., eds.*, 1981, pp. 159–97. [G: U.S.]

Stone, Katherine Van Wezel. The Post-War Paradigm in American Labor Law. *Yale Law J.*, June 1981, *90*(7), pp. 1509–80. [G: U.S.]

Sykes, Alan O. An Efficiency Analysis of Vicarious Liability under the Law of Agency. *Yale Law J.*, November 1981, *91*(1), pp. 168–206. [G: U.S.]

Tiedemann, K. Antitrust Law and Criminal Law Policy in Western Europe. In *Leigh, L. H., ed.*, 1981, pp. 39–56. [G: W. Europe]

Tullock, Gordon. Rent Seeking. In *Sirkin, G., ed.*, 1981, pp. 165–90.

Upham, Frank K. Crime in Japan. In *Richardson, B. M. and Ueda, T., eds.*, 1981, pp. 155–61. [G: Japan]

Upham, Frank K. Litigation in Japan. In *Richardson, B. M. and Ueda, T., eds.*, 1981, pp. 149–55. [G: Japan]

Upham, Frank K. The Japanese Legal System. In *Richardson, B. M. and Ueda, T., eds.*, 1981, pp. 143–49. [G: Japan]

Viladás Jené, Carlos. Business Crime in Spain. In *Leigh, L. H., ed.*, 1981, pp. 1–14. [G: Spain]

Wahlroos, Björn. On Finnish Property Criminality: An Empirical Analysis of the Postwar Era Using an Ehrlich Model. *Scand. J. Econ.*, 1981, *83*(4), pp. 553–62. [G: Finland]

Walker, Warren E., et al. The Impact of Proposition 13 on Local Criminal Justice Agencies: Emerging Patterns. In *Wright, K. N., ed.*, 1981, pp. 173–227. [G: U.S.]

Weidenbaum, Murray L. The New Regulation and

the American Common Market [Regulation and the American Common Market]. In *Tarlock, A. D., ed.*, 1981, pp. 83–92. [G: U.S.]

White, Michelle J. Fee Shifting: An Institutional Change to Decrease the Benefits from Free Riding: Comments. In *Sirkin, G., ed.*, 1981, pp. 141–44. [G: U.S.]

Wright, Kevin N. Crime and Criminal Justice in a Declining Economy: Introduction. In *Wright, K. N., ed.*, 1981, pp. xi–xv. [G: U.S.]

Wright, Kevin N. Economic Adversity, Reindustrialization, and Criminality. In *Wright, K. N., ed.*, 1981, pp. 51–68. [G: U.S.]

Zimmer, Lynn and Jacobs, James B. Challenging the Taylor Law: Prison Guards on Strike. *Ind. Lab. Relat. Rev.*, July 1981, *34*(4), pp. 531–44. [G: U.S.]

917 Economics of Minorities; Economics of Discrimination

9170 Economics of Minorities; Economics of Discrimination

Abramovitz, Mimi. Funding Worker Education through Tuition Refund Plans. In *Wertheimer, B. M., ed.*, 1981, pp. 241–51. [G: U.S.]

Acton, Norman. Employment of Disabled Persons: Where Are We Going? *Int. Lab. Rev.*, January–February 1981, *120*(1), pp. 1–14.

Aho, C. Michael and Orr, James A. Trade-Sensitive Employment: Who Are the Affected Workers? *Mon. Lab. Rev.*, February 1981, *104*(2), pp. 29–35. [G: U.S.]

Aldrich, Howard E., et al. Business Development and Self-segregation: Asian Enterprise in Three British Cities. In *Peach, C.; Robinson, V. and Smith, S., eds.*, 1981, pp. 170–90. [G: U.K.]

Anders, Gary C. The Reduction of a Self-Sufficient People to Poverty and Welfare Dependence: An Analysis of the Causes of Cherokee Indian Underdevelopment. *Amer. J. Econ. Soc.*, July 1981, *40*(3), pp. 225–37. [G: U.S.]

Anderson, Bernard E. Economic Growth: The Central Issue: A Partial Dissent: Fiddling with the Economy is Not Enough. In *Inst. for Contemp. Studies*, 1981, pp. 47–51. [G: U.S.]

Andic, Suphan. Does the Personal Income Tax Discriminate against Women? *Public Finance*, 1981, *36*(1), pp. 1–15.

Baden, John; Stroup, Richard and Thurman, Walter N. Myths, Admonitions and Rationality: The American Indian as a Resource Manager. *Econ. Inquiry*, January 1981, *19*(1), pp. 132–43. [G: U.S.]

Barth, James R.; Cordes, Joseph J. and Yezer, Anthony M. J. Financial Institution Regulations, Redlining and Mortgage Markets. In *Fed. Res. Bank of Boston and National Sci. Foundation*, 1981, pp. 101–43. [G: U.S.]

Bates, Timothy. Effectiveness of the Small Business Administration in Financing Minority Business. *Rev. Black Polit. Econ.*, Spring 1981, *11*(3), pp. 321–36. [G: U.S.]

Becker, Brian E. and Hills, Stephen M. Youth Attitudes and Adult Labor Market Activity. *Ind.*

Relat., Winter 1981, *20*(1), pp. 60–70. [G: U.S.]

Beneria, Lourdes. Conceptualizing the Labor Force: The Underestimation of Women's Economic Activities. *J. Devel. Stud.*, April 1981, *17*(3), pp. 10–28.

Benston, George J. Mortgage Redlining Research: A Review and Critical Analysis Discussion. In *Fed. Res. Bank of Boston and National Sci. Foundation*, 1981, pp. 144–95. [G: U.S.]

Bergmann, Barbara R. The Economic Risks of Being a Housewife. *Amer. Econ. Rev.*, May 1981, *71*(2), pp. 81–86. [G: U.S.]

Bergmann, Barbara R. and Darity, William A., Jr. Social Relations in the Workplace and Employer Discrimination. In *Dennis, B. D., ed.*, 1981, pp. 155–62.

Bergmann, Barbara R. and Darity, William A., Jr. Social Relations, Productivity, and Employer Discrimination. *Mon. Lab. Rev.*, April 1981, *104*(4), pp. 47–49. [G: U.S.]

Berkley, Thomas L. Black Lawyers: Struggling to Survive. In *Inst. for Contemp. Studies*, 1981, pp. 107–11. [G: U.S.]

Berresford, Susan Vail. How Foundations View Funding Proposals on Working Women. In *Wertheimer, B. M., ed.*, 1981, pp. 233–40. [G: U.S.]

Bertinuson, Janet and Hricko, Andrea M. Occupational Health and Safety for Women Workers: Some Teaching Models. In *Wertheimer, B. M., ed.*, 1981, pp. 194–203. [G: U.S.]

Betsey, Charles L. and Dunson, Bruce H. Federal Minimum Wage Laws and the Employment of Minority Youth. *Amer. Econ. Rev.*, May 1981, *71*(2), pp. 379–84. [G: U.S.]

Birgin, Haydee. The Condition of Women and the Exercise of Political Power. In *Lozoya, J. A. and Birgin, H., eds.*, 1981, pp. 90–114. [G: LDCs]

Blau, Francine D. and Kahn, Lawrence M. Causes and Consequences of Layoffs. *Econ. Inquiry*, April 1981, *19*(2), pp. 270–96. [G: U.S.]

Blewett, Mary H. Discussion [Mechanization and Work in the American Shoe Industry: Lynn, Massachusetts, 1852–1883]. *J. Econ. Hist.*, March 1981, *41*(1), pp. 64. [G: U.S.]

Bloch, Howard R. and Pennington, Robert Leroy. An Econometric Analysis of Affirmative Action. *Rev. Black Polit. Econ.*, Winter 1981, *11*(2), pp. 267–76. [G: U.S.]

Block, Walter and Williams, Walter E. Male–Female Earnings Differentials: A Critical Reappraisal. *J. Lab. Res.*, Fall 1981, *2*(2), pp. 385–87. [G: Canada]

Boal, F. W. Ethnic Residential Segregation, Ethnic Mixing and Resource Conflict: A Study in Belfast, Northern Ireland. In *Peach, C.; Robinson, V. and Smith, S., eds.*, 1981, pp. 235–51. [G: U.K.]

Boskin, Michael. Economic Growth: The Central Issue: Answers: Economic Reforms are Important. In *Inst. for Contemp. Studies*, 1981, pp. 53–55. [G: U.S.]

Boskin, Michael J. Economic Growth: The Central Issue. In *Inst. for Contemp. Studies*, 1981, pp. 39–47. [G: U.S.]

Bracey, John. Black Studies Tenure and Promotion:

A Reply to Davidson. *Rev. Black Polit. Econ.*, Spring 1981, *11*(3), pp. 375–82. [G: U.S.]

Brandt, William K. and Shay, Robert P. Consumers' Perceptions of Discriminatory Treatment and Credit Availability, and Access to Consumer Credit Markets. In *Fed. Res. Bank of Boston and National Sci. Foundation*, 1981, pp. 1–19. [G: U.S.]

Brandt, William K. and Shay, Robert P. Consumers' Perceptions of Discriminatory Treatment and Credit Availability, and Access to Consumer Credit Markets: Rebuttal. In *Fed. Res. Bank of Boston and National Sci. Foundation*, 1981, pp. 23. [G: U.S.]

Brenner, Reuven and Kiefer, Nicholas M. The Economics of the Diaspora: Discrimination and Occupational Structure. *Econ. Develop. Cult. Change*, April 1981, *29*(3), pp. 517–34. [G: U.S.; Middle East]

Brown, Michael K. and Erie, Steven P. Blacks and the Legacy of the Great Society: The Economic and Political Impact of Federal Social Policy. *Public Policy*, Summer 1981, *29*(3), pp. 299–330. [G: U.S.]

Bryner, Gary. Congress, Courts, and Agencies: Equal Employment and the Limits of Policy Implementation. *Polit. Sci. Quart.*, Fall 1981, *96*(3), pp. 411–30. [G: U.S.]

Buckles, Vivian. Affirmative Action and the Progress of Women in the American Work Force. In *Hoffman, W. M. and Wyly, T. J., eds.*, 1981, pp. 119–23. [G: U.S.]

Burke, Fred G. Bilingualism/Biculturalism in American Education: An Adventure in Wonderland. *Ann. Amer. Acad. Polit. Soc. Sci.*, March 1981, *454*, pp. 164–77. [G: U.S.]

Burkitt, Brian and Rose, Hilary. Towards a Theory of Capitalist Exploitation Incorporating Domestic Labour. *Indian Econ. J.*, January–March 1981, *28*(3), pp. 94–104.

Button, James. The Quest for Economic Equality: Factors Related to Black Employment in the South. *Soc. Sci. Quart.*, September 1981, *62*(3), pp. 461–74. [G: U.S.]

Cabral, Robert; Ferber, Marianne A. and Green, Carole A. Men and Women in Fiduciary Institutions: A Study of Sex Differences in Career Development. *Rev. Econ. Statist.*, November 1981, *63*(4), pp. 573–80.

Caccavallo, Frank M. Racial Discrimination: The Housing Market. *Amer. Econ.*, Spring 1981, *25*(1), pp. 43–52. [G: U.S.]

Canner, Glenn. Redlining and Mortgage Lending Patterns. In *Henderson, J. V., ed.*, 1981, pp. 67–101. [G: U.S.]

Carliner, Geoffrey. Female Labor Force Participation Rates for Nine Ethnic Groups. *J. Human Res.*, Spring 1981, *16*(2), pp. 286–93. [G: U.S.]

Carlson, Leonard A. and Cebula, Richard J. Voting with One's Feet: A Brief Note on the Case of Public Welfare and the American Indian. *Public Choice*, 1981, *37*(2), pp. 321–25. [G: U.S.]

Carlton, Dennis W. Risk Shifting, Statistical Discrimination, and the Stability of Earnings: Comment. In *Rosen, S., ed.*, 1981, pp. 315–17. [G: U.S.]

Caulfield, Mina Davis. Equality, Sex, and Mode of Production. In *Berreman, G. D., ed.*, 1981, pp. 201–19.

Cayer, N. Joseph and Schaefer, Roger C. Affirmative Action and Municipal Employees. *Soc. Sci. Quart.*, September 1981, *62*(3), pp. 487–94. [G: U.S.]

Cebula, Richard J. Differential White-Nonwhite Migration Sensitivities to Income Differentials: An Exploratory Note. *Amer. Econ.*, Spring 1981, *25*(1), pp. 67–69. [G: U.S.]

Cebula, Richard J. and Koch, James V. A Further Note on Welfare Outlays and Nonwhite Migration [A Note on Welfare Outlays and Nonwhite Migration: An Analysis for SMSA's, 1965–1970]. *Rev. Bus. Econ. Res.*, Spring 1981, *16*(3), pp. 98–101. [G: U.S.]

Cheng, Benjamin S. Differences in White-nonWhite Returns to Schooling: Theory and Policy. *Rev. Black Polit. Econ.*, Winter 1981, *11*(2), pp. 251–66. [G: U.S.]

Chiplin, Brian. An Alternative Approach to the Measurement of Sex Discrimination: An Illustration from University Entrance. *Econ. J.*, December 1981, *91*(364), pp. 988–97. [G: U.K.]

Cohn, Steven; Wood, Robert and Haag, Richard. U.S. Aid and Third World Women: The Impact of Peace Corps Programs. *Econ. Develop. Cult. Change*, July 1981, *29*(4), pp. 795–811. [G: U.S.; LDCs]

Cole, Joan and Pilisuk, Marc. Differences in the Provision of Mental Health Services by Race. In *Martin, G. T., Jr., and Zald, M. N., eds.*, 1981, *1976*, pp. 368–89. [G: U.S.]

Collat, Donald S. Discrimination in the Coverage of Retirement Plans. *Yale Law J.*, March 1981, *90*(4), pp. 817–39. [G: U.S.]

Cook, Alice H. and Till-Retz, Roberta. Labor Education and Women Workers: An International Comparison. In *Wertheimer, B. M., ed.*, 1981, pp. 255–64. [G: Sweden; U.K.; Austria; W. Germany]

Cronin, Francis J. and Rasmussen, David W. Housing Vouchers for the Poor: Mobility. In *Struyk, R. J. and Bendick, M., Jr., eds.*, 1981, pp. 107–28. [G: U.S.]

Datcher, Linda P. Race/Sex Differences in the Effects of Background on Achievement. In *Hill, M. S.; Hill, D. H. and Morgan, J. N., eds.*, 1981, pp. 359–90. [G: U.S.]

Daub, Peter M. and Jacobson, Hugh H. Title VII and Congressional Employees: The "Chilling Effect" and the Speech or Debate Clause. *Yale Law J.*, May 1981, *90*(6), pp. 1458–85. [G: U.S.]

Davidson, Naomi Berger. Special Groups in the Labor Market: Discussion. In *Dennis, B. D., ed.*, 1981, pp. 72–75. [G: U.S.]

Davin, Anna. Feminism and Labour History. In *Samuel, R., ed.*, 1981, pp. 176–81.

Daymont, Thomas N. Changes in Black–White Labor Market Opportunities, 1966–76. In *Parnes, H. S., ed.*, 1981, pp. 42–64. [G: U.S.]

DeCanio, Stephen J. Accumulation and Discrimination in the Postbellum South. In *Walton, G. M. and Shepherd, J. F., eds.*, 1981, *1980*, pp. 103–25. [G: U.S.]

DeFreitas, Gregory E. Occupational Mobility Among Recent Black Immigrants. In *Dennis, B. D., ed.,* 1981, pp. 41–47. **[G: U.S.]**

Deloria, Vine, Jr. Native Americans: The American Indian Today. *Ann. Amer. Acad. Polit. Soc. Sci.,* March 1981, *454,* pp. 139–49.

Dey, Jennie. Gambian Women: Unequal Partners in Rice Development Projects? *J. Devel. Stud.,* April 1981, *17*(3), pp. 109–22. **[G: Gambia]**

Dillingham, Alan E. Sex Differences in Labor Market Injury Risk. *Ind. Relat.,* Winter 1981, *20*(1), pp. 117–22. **[G: U.S.]**

Duncan, Greg J. and Hoffman, Saul D. Dynamics of Wage Change. In *Hill, M. S.; Hill, D. H. and Morgan, J. N., eds.,* 1981, pp. 45–92. **[G: U.S.]**

Dye, Thomas R. and Renick, James. Political Power and City Jobs: Determinants of Minority Employment. *Soc. Sci. Quart.,* September 1981, *62*(3), pp. 475–86. **[G: U.S.]**

Ekelund, Robert B., Jr.; Higgins, Richard S. and Smithson, Charles W. Can Discrimination Increase Employment: A Neoclassical Perspective. *Southern Econ. J.,* January 1981, *47*(3), pp. 664–73.

England, Richard and Greene, Michael. A Comment on John Roemer's Theory of Differentially Exploited Labor. *Rev. Radical Polit. Econ.,* Winter 1981, *12*(4), pp. 71–74.

Fareed, A. E. and Riggs, G. D. Racial Differences in Consumer Expenditure Patterns, 1972–73. *Rev. Black Polit. Econ.,* Spring 1981, *11*(3), pp. 293–301. **[G: U.S.]**

Farkas, George; Olsen, Randall J. and Stromsdorfer, Ernst W. Youth Labor Supply During the Summer: Evidence for Youths from Low-Income Households. In *Ehrenberg, R. G., ed.,* 1981, pp. 151–90. **[G: U.S.]**

Fedorova, M. The Utilization of Female Labor in Agriculture. *Prob. Econ.,* Sept.–Oct.–Nov. 1981, *24*(5–6–7), pp. 131–46. **[G: U.S.S.R.]**

Ferber, Marianne A. and Birnbaum, Bonnie G. Labor Force Participation Patterns and Earnings of Women Clerical Workers. *J. Human Res.,* Summer 1981, *16*(3), pp. 416–26. **[G: U.S.]**

Feuille, Peter and Lewin, David. Equal Employment Opportunity Bargaining. *Ind. Relat.,* Fall 1981, *20*(3), pp. 322–34. **[G: U.S.]**

Firth, Michael. Racial Discrimination in the British Labor Market. *Ind. Lab. Relat. Rev.,* January 1981, *34*(2), pp. 265–72. **[G: U.K.]**

Fitzpatrick, Joseph P. and Parker, Lourdes Travieso. Hispanic–Americans in the Eastern United States. *Ann. Amer. Acad. Polit. Soc. Sci.,* March 1981, *454,* pp. 98–110. **[G: U.S.]**

Flanagan, Robert J. Equal Opportunity: Current Industrial Relations Perspectives: Discussion. In *Dennis, B. D., ed.,* 1981, pp. 163–67.

Follain, James R., Jr. and Malpezzi, Stephen. Another Look at Racial Differences in Housing Prices. *Urban Stud.,* June 1981, *18*(2), pp. 195–203. **[G: U.S.]**

Freeman, Richard B. Black Economic Progress after 1964: Who Has Gained and Why? In *Rosen, S., ed.,* 1981, pp. 247–94. **[G: U.S.]**

Fried, Marlene Gerber. Affirmative Action in a De-

clining Economy. In *Hoffman, W. M. and Wyly, T. J., eds.,* 1981, pp. 124–27. **[G: U.S.]**

Gann, L. H. and Rabushka, Alvin. Racial Classification: Politics of the Future? *Policy Rev.,* Summer 1981, (17), pp. 87–94. **[G: U.S.]**

Garcia-Chafardet, Irma. Sexism as an Obstacle to Development. In *Lozoya, J. A. and Birgin, H., eds.,* 1981, pp. 115–46. **[G: LDCs]**

Gastwirth, Joseph L. Estimating the Demographic Mix of the Available Labor Force. *Mon. Lab. Rev.,* April 1981, *104*(4), pp. 50–57. **[G: U.S.]**

Ghayur, M. Arif. Muslims in the United States: Settlers and Visitors. *Ann. Amer. Acad. Polit. Soc. Sci.,* March 1981, *454,* pp. 150–63. **[G: U.S.]**

Giglioni, Giovanni B.; Giglioni, Joyce B. and Bryant, James A. Performance Appraisal: Here Comes the Judge. *Calif. Manage. Rev.,* Winter 1981, *24*(2), pp. 14–23. **[G: U.S.]**

Giunipero, Larry C. Developing Effective Minority Purchasing Programs. *Sloan Manage. Rev.,* Winter 1981, *22*(2), pp. 33–42. **[G: U.S.]**

Gordon, Milton M. Models of Pluralism: The New American Dilemma. *Ann. Amer. Acad. Polit. Soc. Sci.,* March 1981, *454,* pp. 178–88. **[G: U.S.]**

Greenwald, Carol S. Consumers' Perceptions of Discriminatory Treatment and Credit Availability, and Access to Consumer Credit Markets: Discussion. In *Fed. Res. Bank of Boston and National Sci. Foundation,* 1981, pp. 20–22. **[G: U.S.]**

Gregory, R. G. and Duncan, R. C. Segmented Labor Market Theories and the Australian Experience of Equal Pay for Women. *J. Post Keynesian Econ.,* Spring 1981, *3*(3), pp. 403–28. **[G: Australia]**

Grossman, Herschel I. and Trepeta, Warren T. Risk Shifting, Statistical Discrimination, and the Stability of Earnings. In *Rosen, S., ed.,* 1981, pp. 295–315. **[G: U.S.]**

Gunn, Wendell Wilkie. Black Lawyers: Struggling to Survive: Thinking about Private Investment. In *Inst. for Contemp. Studies,* 1981, pp. 111–13.

Guscott, Kenneth I. Affirmative Action as a Human Resource Tool. In *Hoffman, W. M. and Wyly, T. J., eds.,* 1981, pp. 128–31. **[G: U.S.]**

Gustafsson, Siv. Male–Female Lifetime Earnings Differentials and Labor Force History. In *Eliasson, G.; Holmlund, B. and Stafford, F. P., eds.,* 1981, pp. 235–68. **[G: Sweden; U.S.]**

Haber, Sheldon E. The Mobility of Professional Workers and Fair Hiring. *Ind. Lab. Relat. Rev.,* January 1981, *34*(2), pp. 257–64. **[G: U.S.]**

Hall, Catherine. Gender Divisions and Class Formation in the Birmingham Middle Class, 1780–1850. In *Samuel, R., ed.,* 1981, pp. 164–75. **[G: U.K.]**

Hamer, Alice. Diola Women and Migration: A Case Study. In *Colvin, L. G., et al.,* 1981, pp. 183–203. **[G: Senegal]**

Harris, William H. Federal Intervention in Union Discrimination: FEPC and West Coast Shipyards during World War II. *Labor Hist.,* Summer 1981, *22*(3), pp. 325–47. **[G: U.S.]**

Heckman, James J. Heterogeneity and State Dependence. In *Rosen, S., ed.,* 1981, pp. 91–139. **[G: U.S.]**

Heer, David. Fertility and Female Work Status in

the USSR. **In** *Desfosses, H., ed.*, 1981, pp. 62–94. [G: U.S.S.R.]

Heggade, O. D. Development of Women Entrepreneurship in India—Problems and Prospects. *Econ. Aff.*, January–March 1981, *26*(1), pp. 39–50. [G: India]

Hershberg, Theodore. Free Blacks in Antebellum Philadelphia: A Study of Ex-Slaves, Freeborn, and Socioeconomic Decline. **In** *Hershberg, T., ed.*, 1981, *1971*, pp. 368–91. [G: U.S.]

Hershberg, Theodore and Williams, Henry. Mulattoes and Blacks: Intra-group Color Differences and Social Stratification in Nineteenth-Century Philadelphia. **In** *Hershberg, T., ed.*, 1981, pp. 392–434. [G: U.S.]

Hershberg, Theodore, et al. A Tale of Three Cities: Blacks, Immigrants, and Opportunity in Philadelphia, 1850–1880, 1930, 1970. **In** *Hershberg, T., ed.*, 1981, pp. 461–91. [G: U.S.]

Hinckley, Robert. Black Teenage Unemployment. *J. Econ. Issues*, June 1981, *15*(2), pp. 501–12. [G: U.S.]

Huffman, Wallace E. Black–White Human Capital Differences: Impact on Agricultural Productivity in the U.S. South. *Amer. Econ. Rev.*, March 1981, *71*(1), pp. 94–107. [G: U.S.]

Hula, Richard C. Public Needs and Private Investment: The Case of Home Credit. *Soc. Sci. Quart.*, December 1981, *62*(4), pp. 685–703. [G: U.S.]

Hutchins, Matthew and Sigelman, Lee. Black Employment in State and Local Governments: A Comparative Analysis. *Soc. Sci. Quart.*, March 1981, *62*(1), pp. 79–87. [G: U.S]

Hyclak, Thomas and Stewart, James. A Note on the Relative Earnings of Central City Black Males. *J. Human Res.*, Spring 1981, *16*(2), pp. 304–13. [G: U.S.]

Janjić, Marion. Diversifying Women's Employment: The Only Road to Genuine Equality of Opportunity. *Int. Lab. Rev.*, March–April 1981, *120*(2), pp. 149–63. [G: U.S.]

Johnson, Gloria T. and Komer, Odessa. Education for Affirmative Action: Two Union Approaches. **In** *Wertheimer, B. M., ed.*, 1981, pp. 204–16. [G: U.S.]

Johnson, Maria Lucia. Legal Barriers to Black Economic Gains: Employment and Transportation: More Legal Barriers: Housing. **In** *Inst. for Contemp. Studies*, 1981, pp. 31–35.

Jones, James E. "Reverse Discrimination" in Employment: Judicial Treatment of Affirmative Action Programmes in the United States. *Int. Lab. Rev.*, July–August 1981, *120*(4), pp. 453–72. [G: U.S.]

Jusenius, Carol L. and Scheffler, Richard M. Earnings Differentials among Academic Economists: Empirical Evidence on Race and Sex. *J. Econ. Bus.*, Winter 1981, *33*(2), pp. 88–96. [G: U.S.]

Kahn, Lawrence M. Sex Discrimination in Professional Employment: A Case Study: Comment. *Ind. Lab. Relat. Rev.*, January 1981, *34*(2), pp. 273–75. [G: U.S.]

Kern, Clifford R. Racial Prejudice and Residential Segregation: The Yinger Model Revisited. *J. Urban Econ.*, September 1981, *10*(2), pp. 164–72.

Killian, Lewis M. Black Power and White Reactions:

The Revitalization of Race-thinking in the United States. *Ann. Amer. Acad. Polit. Soc. Sci.*, March 1981, *454*, pp. 42–54. [G: U.S.]

King, Arthur T. Economic Development Aspects of a Public Policy Program: Section 8(a) Contracts. *Rev. Black Polit. Econ.*, Spring 1981, *11*(3), pp. 337–46. [G: U.S.]

Kirp, David L. The Academic as Would-Be Analyst: A Cautionary Tale. *Policy Anal.*, Winter 1981, *7*(1), pp. 91–102. [G: U.S.]

Kitano, Harry H. L. Asian–Americans: The Chinese, Japanese, Koreans, Philippinos, and Southeast Asians. *Ann. Amer. Acad. Polit. Soc. Sci.*, March 1981, *454*, pp. 125–38. [G: U.S.]

Kornbluh, Joyce L. and Goldfarb, Lyn. Labor Education and Women Workers: An Historical Perspective. **In** *Wertheimer, B. M., ed.*, 1981, pp. 15–31. [G: U.S.]

Kornbluh, Joyce L. and Kornbluh, Hy. Labor Education for Women Workers: Conferences: The One-Day Model. **In** *Wertheimer, B. M., ed.*, 1981, pp. 54–61. [G: U.S.]

Kostakov, V. G. Features of the Development of Female Employment. *Prob. Econ.*, Sept.–Oct.–Nov. 1981, *24*(5–6–7), pp. 33–68. [G: U.S.S.R.]

Kotliar, A. E. and Turchaninova, S. Ia. The Educational and Occupational Skill Level of Industrial Workers. *Prob. Econ.*, Sept.–Oct.–Nov. 1981, *24*(5–6–7), pp. 69–120. [G: U.S.S.R.]

Kuleshova, L. M. and Mamontova, T. I. Part-time Employment of Women. *Prob. Econ.*, Sept.–Oct.–Nov. 1981, *24*(5–6–7), pp. 277–81.

Kwast, Myron L. New Minority-Owned Commercial Banks: A Statistical Analysis. *J. Bank Res.*, Spring 1981, *12*(1), pp. 37–45. [G: U.S.]

Lackman, Conway L. and Heinzelmann, Raymond G. Marine Preference Cargo Market: Opportunities for Minority Shippers. *Rev. Black Polit. Econ.*, Spring 1981, *11*(3), pp. 365–74. [G: U.S.]

Ladipo, Patricia. Developing Women's Cooperatives: An Experiment in Rural Nigeria. *J. Devel. Stud.*, April 1981, *17*(3), pp. 123–36. [G: Nigeria]

Lamb, Charles M. Legal Foundations of Civil Rights and Pluralism in America. *Ann. Amer. Acad. Polit. Soc. Sci.*, March 1981, *454*, pp. 13–25. [G: U.S.]

Lambert, Richard D. Ethnic/Racial Relations in the United States in Comparative Perspective. *Ann. Amer. Acad. Polit. Soc. Sci.*, March 1981, *454*, pp. 189–205. [G: U.S.]

Lane, Sylvia. Evidence on Barriers to the Parallel Advancement of Male and Female Agricultural Economists. *Amer. J. Agr. Econ.*, December 1981, *63*(5), pp. 1025–31. [G: U.S.]

Lapidus, Gail W. The Female Industrial Labor Force: Dilemmas, Reassessments, and Options. **In** *Bornstein, M., ed.*, 1981, *1979*, pp. 119–48. [G: U.S.S.R.]

Lapidus, Gail W. Women, Work, and Family: New Soviet Perspectives: Introduction. *Prob. Econ.*, Sept.–Oct.–Nov. 1981, *24*(5–6–7), pp. ix–xlvi. [G: U.S.S.R.]

Ledgerwood, Donna E. and Johnson-Dietz, Sue. Sexual Harassment: Implications for Employer

Liability. *Mon. Lab. Rev.*, April 1981, *104*(4), pp. 45–47. [G: U.S.]

Ledgerwood, Donna E. and Johnson-Dietz, Sue. The EEOC's Bold Foray into Sexual Harassment on the Job: New Implications for Employer Liability. In *Dennis, B. D., ed.*, 1981, pp. 55–61. [G: U.S.]

Lee, Linda K. A Comparison of the Rank and Salary of Male and Female Agricultural Economists. *Amer. J. Agr. Econ.*, December 1981, *63*(5), pp. 1013–18. [G: U.S.]

Leeds, Morton. Inflation and the Elderly: A Housing Perspective. *Ann. Amer. Acad. Polit. Soc. Sci.*, July 1981, *456*, pp. 60–69. [G: U.S.]

Leet, Mildred Robbins. Regionalism and Women. In *Nicol, D.; Echeverria, L. and Peccei, A., eds.*, 1981, pp. 200–209.

Lehrer, Evelyn and Nerlove, Marc. The Impact of Female Work on Family Income Distribution in the United States: Black-White Differentials. *Rev. Income Wealth*, December 1981, *27*(4), pp. 423–31. [G: U.S.]

Leigh, J. Paul. Racial Differences in Compensating Wages for Job Risks. *Ind. Relat.*, Fall 1981, *20*(3), pp. 318–21. [G: U.S.]

Levitan, Sar A. and Belous, Richard S. Working Wives and Mothers: What Happens to Family Life? *Mon. Lab. Rev.*, September 1981, *104*(9), pp. 26–30. [G: U.S.]

Lopez, Manuel Mariano. Patterns of Interethnic Residential Segregation in the Urban Southwest, 1960 and 1970. *Soc. Sci. Quart.*, March 1981, *62*(1), pp. 50–63. [G: U.S.]

Lorenz, James. Expanding Choice and Opportunities for Entrepreneurship. In *Inst. for Contemp. Studies*, 1981, pp. 93–97. [G: U.S.]

Loury, Glenn C. Is Equal Opportunity Enough? *Amer. Econ. Rev.*, May 1981, *71*(2), pp. 122–26. [G: U.S.]

Luksetich, William A. Market Power and Discrimination in White-Collar Employment: 1969–1975. *Rev. Soc. Econ.*, October 1981, *39*(2), pp. 145–64. [G: U.S.]

Lundeen, Ardelle A. and Clauson, Annette L. The Conduct of the Survey on the Opportunities for and Status of Women in Agricultural Economics. *Amer. J. Agr. Econ.*, December 1981, *63*(5), pp. 1010–12. [G: U.S.]

Lyon, Larry and Rector-Owen, Holley. Labor Market Mobility among Young Black and White Women: Longitudinal Models of Occupational Prestige and Income. *Soc. Sci. Quart.*, March 1981, *62*(1), pp. 64–78. [G: U.S.]

Magubane, Bernard. Social Inequality: The South Africa Case. In *Berreman, G. D., ed.*, 1981, pp. 257–76. [G: S. Africa]

Malan, T. Economic Sanctions as Policy Instrument to Effect Change—The Case of South Africa. *Finance Trade Rev.*, June 1981, *14*(3), pp. 87–116. [G: S. Africa]

Markwalder, Don. The Potential for Black Business. *Rev. Black Polit. Econ.*, Spring 1981, *11*(3), pp. 303–12. [G: U.S.]

Marshall, John M. Discrimination in Consumer Credit. In *Heggestad, A. A., ed.*, 1981 1981, pp. 240–55. [G: U.S.]

McDougall, Gerald and Bunce, Harold. Evaluating the Distributional Consequences of Local Service Delivery Systems—An Alternative Perspective. *Rev. Reg. Stud.*, Fall 1981, *11*(2), pp. 25–40. [G: U.S.]

McNabb, Robert and Psacharopoulos, George. Racial Earnings Differentials in the U.K. *Oxford Econ. Pap.*, November 1981, *33*(3), pp. 413–25. [G: U.K.]

Meeker, Suzanne E. Equal Pay, Comparable Work, and Job Evaluation. *Yale Law J.*, January 1981, *90*(3), pp. 657–80. [G: U.S.]

Milkovich, George T. Pay Inequalities and Comparable Worth. In *Dennis, B. D., ed.*, 1981, pp. 147–54.

Milkovich, George T. The Male–Female Pay Gap: Need for Reevaluation. *Mon. Lab. Rev.*, April 1981, *104*(4), pp. 42–44. [G: U.S.]

Mogull, Robert G. Salary Discrimination in Professional Sports. *Atlantic Econ. J.*, September 1981, *9*(3), pp. 106–10. [G: U.S.]

Moland, John, Jr. The Black Population. In *Hawley, A. H. and Mazie, S. M., eds.*, 1981, pp. 464–501. [G: U.S.]

Molyneux, Maxine. Women's Emancipation under Socialism: A Model for the Third World? *World Devel.*, September/October 1981, *9*(9/10), pp. 1019–37. [G: LDCs; E. Europe; U.S.S.R.; China]

Mooney, Marta. Wives' Permanent Employment and Husbands' Hours of Work. *Ind. Relat.*, Spring 1981, *20*(2), pp. 205–11. [G: U.S.]

Moore, William J.; Pearce, Douglas K. and Wilson, R. Mark. The Regulation of Occupations and the Earnings of Women. *J. Human Res.*, Summer 1981, *16*(3), pp. 366–83. [G: U.S.]

Morgan, James N. Child Care when Parents are Employed. In *Hill, M. S.; Hill, D. H. and Morgan, J. N., eds.*, 1981, pp. 441–56. [G: U.S.]

Morse, Laurence C. Increasing Unemployment and Changing Labor Market Expectations among Black Male Teenagers. *Amer. Econ. Rev.*, May 1981, *71*(2), pp. 374–78. [G: U.S.]

Mott, Frank L. and Haurin, R. Jean. The Impact of Health Problems and Mortality on Family Well-Being. In *Parnes, H. S., ed.*, 1981, pp. 198–253. [G: U.S.]

Mounts, Gregory J. Labor and the Supreme Court: Significant Decisions of 1979–80. *Mon. Lab. Rev.*, April 1981, *104*(4), pp. 13–22. [G: U.S.]

Murray, Steven W. and Tweeten, Luther. Some Trade-Offs: Culture, Education, and Economic Progress on Federal Indian Reservations. *Growth Change*, April 1981, *12*(2), pp. 10–16. [G: U.S.]

Musgrave, Peggy B. Women and Taxation. In *Roskamp, K. W. and Forte, F., eds.*, 1981, pp. 341–54. [G: OECD; U.S.]

Nakamura, Alice and Nakamura, Masao. A Comparison of the Labor Force Behavior of Married Women in the United States and Canada, with Special Attention to the Impact of Income Taxes. *Econometrica*, March 1981, *49*(2), pp. 451–89. [G: U.S.; Canada]

Nelson, Nici. African Women in the Development Process: Introduction. *J. Devel. Stud.*, April 1981, *17*(3), pp. 1–9. [G: sub-Saharan Africa]

Novikova, E. E. and Kutyrev, B. P. The Quantity and Quality of Work: A Round Table. *Prob. Econ.*, Sept.–Oct.–Nov. 1981, *24*(5–6–7), pp. 253–66. [G: U.S.S.R.]

Ofer, Gur and Vinokur, Aaron. Earning Differentials by Sex in the Soviet Union: A First Look. **In** *[Bergson, A.]*, 1981, pp. 127–62. [G: U.S.S.R.]

Ogbu, John U. Education, Clientage, and Social Mobility: Caste and Social Change in the United States and Nigeria. **In** *Berreman, G. D., ed.*, 1981, pp. 277–306. [G: Nigeria; U.S.]

Olmstead, Alan L. and Sheffrin, Steven M. Affirmative Action in Medical Schools: Econometric Evidence and Legal Doctrine. **In** *Zerbe, R. O., Jr., ed.*, 1981, pp. 207–23. [G: U.S.]

Ong, Paul M. Factors Influencing the Size of the Black Business Community. *Rev. Black Polit. Econ.*, Spring 1981, *11*(3), pp. 313–19. [G: U.S.]

Osterman, Paul. Sex Discrimination in Professional Employment: A Case Study: Reply. *Ind. Lab. Relat. Rev.*, January 1981, *34*(2), pp. 275–76. [G: U.S.]

Pachon, Harry P. and Moore, Joan W. Mexican Americans. *Ann. Amer. Acad. Polit. Soc. Sci.*, March 1981, *454*, pp. 111–24. [G: U.S.]

Parsons, Donald O. Black–White Differences in Labor Force Participation of Older Males. **In** *Parnes, H. S., ed.*, 1981, pp. 132–54. [G: U.S.]

Pendleton, Clarence M., Jr. Legal Barriers to Black Economic Gain: Employment and Transportation: Self-Help at Work: The Urban League in San Diego. **In** *Inst. for Contemp. Studies*, 1981, pp. 35–37. [G: U.S.]

Peterson, Richard L. An Investigation of Sex Discrimination in Commercial Banks' Direct Consumer Lending. *Bell J. Econ. (See Rand J. Econ. after 4/85)*, Autumn 1981, *12*(2), pp. 547–61. [G: U.S.]

Pfeffer, Jeffrey and Ross, Jerry. Unionization and Female Wage and Status Attainment. *Ind. Relat.*, Spring 1981, *20*(2), pp. 179–85. [G: U.S.]

Pharr, Susan. The Status of Women. **In** *Richardson, B. M. and Ueda, T., eds.*, 1981, pp. 268–77. [G: Japan]

Polachek, Solomon William. Occupational Self-Selection: A Human Capital Approach to Sex Differences in Occupational Structure. *Rev. Econ. Statist.*, February 1981, *63*(1), pp. 60–69. [G: U.S.]

Rachlin, Marjorie B. Labor Education for Women Workers: Training Rank and File Leaders: A Case Study. **In** *Wertheimer, B. M., ed.*, 1981, pp. 62–70. [G: U.S.]

Ragan, James F., Jr. and Smith, Sharon P. The Impact of Differences in Turnover Rates on Male/Female Pay Differentials. *J. Human Res.*, Summer 1981, *16*(3), pp. 343–65. [G: U.S.]

Ransom, Roger L. and Sutch, Richard. Credit Merchandising in the Post-emancipation South: Structure, Conduct, and Performance. **In** *Walton, G. M. and Shepherd, J. F., eds.*, 1981, *1980*, pp. 57–81. [G: U.S.]

Reich, Michael. Changes in the Distribution of Benefits from Racism in the 1960s. *J. Human Res.*, Spring 1981, *16*(2), pp. 314–21. [G: U.S.]

Reid, Joseph D., Jr. White Land, Black Labor, and Agricultural Stagnation: The Causes and Effects of Sharecropping in the Postbellum South. **In** *Walton, G. M. and Shepherd, J. F., eds.*, 1981, *1980*, pp. 33–55. [G: U.S.]

Rex, John. Urban Segregation and Inner City Policy in Great Britain. **In** *Peach, C.; Robinson, V. and Smith, S., eds.*, 1981, pp. 25–42. [G: U.K.]

Robinson, Vaughan. The Development of South Asian Settlement in Britain and the Myth of Return. **In** *Peach, C.; Robinson, V. and Smith, S., eds.*, 1981, pp. 149–69. [G: U.K.]

Roemer, John E. Reply to England and Greene [Differentially Exploited Labor: A Marxian Theory of Discrimination]. *Rev. Radical Polit. Econ.*, Winter 1981, *12*(4), pp. 75.

Rogerson, Christian M. Industrialization in the Shadows of Apartheid: A World-Systems Analysis. **In** *Hamilton, F. E. I. and Linge, G. J. R., eds.*, 1981, pp. 395–421. [G: Southern Africa]

Rogin, Lawrence. Labor Education for Women Workers: A Summary Discussion. **In** *Wertheimer, B. M., ed.*, 1981, pp. 265–68.

Rose, Harold M. The Black Professional and Residential Segregation in the American City. **In** *Peach, C.; Robinson, V. and Smith, S., eds.*, 1981, pp. 127–48. [G: U.S.]

Rose, Peter I. Blacks and Jews: The Strained Alliance. *Ann. Amer. Acad. Polit. Soc. Sci.*, March 1981, *454*, pp. 55–69. [G: U.S.]

Rozen, Frieda Shoenberg. Labor Education for Women Workers: Promoting and Recruiting: Reaching the Target Audience. **In** *Wertheimer, B. M., ed.*, 1981, pp. 32–41. [G: U.S.]

Rytina, Nancy F. Occupational Segregation and Earnings Differences by Sex. *Mon. Lab. Rev.*, January 1981, *104*(1), pp. 49–53. [G: U.S.]

Rzhanitsyna, L. Current Problems of Female Labor in the USSR. *Prob. Econ.*, Sept.–Oct.–Nov. 1981, *24*(5–6–7), pp. 3–21. [G: U.S.S.R.]

Samper, Maria-Luz D. and Rosen, Stanley. Evaluating Programs for Working Adults. **In** *Wertheimer, B. M., ed.*, 1981, pp. 98–108.

Schafer, Robert. Discussion [Financial Institution Regulations, Redlining and Mortgage Markets] [Mortgage Redlining Research: A Review and Critical Analysis Discussion]. **In** *Fed. Res. Bank of Boston and National Sci. Foundation*, 1981, pp. 196–202. [G: U.S.]

Schrier, Katherine. Credit Programs for Working Women. **In** *Wertheimer, B. M., ed.*, 1981, pp. 71–82. [G: U.S.]

Scott, Robert A. The Factory as a Social Service Organization: Goal Displacement in Workshops for the Blind. **In** *Martin, G. T., Jr., and Zald, M. N., eds.*, 1981, *1967*, pp. 264–84. [G: U.S.]

Séguret, M.-C. Child-Care Services for Working Parents. *Int. Lab. Rev.*, November–December 1981, *120*(6), pp. 711–25. [G: Europe; LDCs]

Semel, Rochelle. Labor Education for Women Workers: The Short Course. **In** *Wertheimer, B. M., ed.*, 1981, pp. 42–53. [G: U.S.]

Shapiro, Daniel M. and Stelcner, Morton. Male-Female Earnings Differentials and the Role of Language in Canada, Ontario, and Quebec, 1970.

Can. J. Econ., May 1981, *14*(2), pp. 341–48.
[G: Canada]

Shay, Robert P.; Brandt, William K. and Sexton, Donald E., Jr. Public Regulation of Financial Services: The Equal Credit Opportunity Act. In *Heggestad, A. A., ed.*, 1981, pp. 208–39. [G: U.S.]

Sheptulina, N. N. Protection of Female Labor. *Prob. Econ.*, Sept.–Oct.–Nov. 1981, *24*(5–6–7), pp. 156–62. [G: U.S.S.R.]

Shishkan, N. M. Raising the Skill Level of Women Workers. *Prob. Econ.*, Sept.–Oct.–Nov. 1981, *24*(5–6–7), pp. 121–30. [G: U.S.S.R.]

Shulman, Steven. Race, Class and Occupational Stratification: A Critique of William J. Wilson's *The Declining Significance of Race*. *Rev. Radical Polit. Econ.*, Fall 1981, *13*(3), pp. 21–31.
[G: U.S.]

Siebert, W. Stanley and Sloane, P. J. The Measurement of Sex and Marital Status Discrimination at the Workplace. *Economica*, May 1981, *48*(190), pp. 125–41. [G: U.K.]

Simms, Margaret C. and Swinton, David H. A Report on the Supply of Black Economists. *Rev. Black Polit. Econ.*, Winter 1981, *11*(2), pp. 181–202. [G: U.S.]

Sinfield, Adrian. Unemployment in an Unequal Society. In *Showler, B. and Sinfield, A., eds.*, 1981, pp. 122–66. [G: U.K.]

Smith, Barton A. A Study of Racial Discrimination in Housing. In *Henderson, J. V., ed.*, 1981, pp. 131–99. [G: U.S.]

Smith, Dan J. Five Policy Proposals. In *Inst. for Contemp. Studies*, 1981, pp. 99–104. [G: U.S.]

Smith, Marvin M. A Note on Tests of Significance and Wage Discrimination. *Amer. Econ.*, Spring 1981, *25*(1), pp. 72–75.

Smock, Audrey Chapman. Women's Economic Roles. In *Killick, T., ed.*, 1981, pp. 219–27.
[G: Kenya]

Sonin, M. Ia. Socioeconomic Problems of Female Employment. *Prob. Econ.*, Sept.–Oct.–Nov. 1981, *24*(5–6–7), pp. 22–32. [G: U.S.S.R.]

Spalter-Roth, Roberta M. and Zeitz, Eileen. Production and Reproduction of Everyday Life. In *Rubinson, R., ed.*, 1981, pp. 193–209.
[G: Philippines]

Squires, Gregory D. and DeWolfe, Ruthanne. Insurance Redlining in Minority Communities. *Rev. Black Polit. Econ.*, Spring 1981, *11*(3), pp. 347–64. [G: U.S.]

Stiglin, Laura E. A Classic Case of Overreaction: Women and Social Security. *New Eng. Econ. Rev.*, January/February 1981, pp. 29–40.

Sutton, Percy E. A Skeptic Persuaded? In *Inst. for Contemp. Studies*, 1981, pp. 153–57. [G: U.S.]

Taeuber, Karl E., et al. A Demographic Perspective on School Desegregation in the USA. In *Peach, C.; Robinson, V. and Smith, S., eds.*, 1981, pp. 83–105. [G: U.S.]

Taubman, Paul. On Heritability. *Economica*, November 1981, *48*(192), pp. 417–20.

Taylor, Barbara. Socialist Feminism: Utopian or Scientific? In *Samuel, R., ed.*, 1981, pp. 158–63.

Taylor, D. Garth. Racial Preferences, Housing Segregation, and the Causes of School Segregation: Recent Evidence from a Social Survey Used in Civil Litigation. *Rev. Public Data Use (See J. Econ. Soc. Meas. after 4/85)*, December 1981, *9*(4), pp. 267–82. [G: U.S.]

Taylor, Daniel E. Education, On–the–Job Training, and the Black–White Earnings Gap. *Mon. Lab. Rev.*, April 1981, *104*(4), pp. 28–34. [G: U.S.]

Temin, Peter. Freedom and Coercion: Notes on the Analysis of Debt Peonage in *One Kind of Freedom*. In *Walton, G. M. and Shepherd, J. F., eds.*, 1981, *1980*, pp. 25–32. [G: U.S.]

Tienda, Marta. The Mexican-American Population. In *Hawley, A. H. and Mazie, S. M., eds.*, 1981, pp. 503–48. [G: U.S.]

Torres, Ida. Grievance Handling for Women Stewards. In *Wertheimer, B. M., ed.*, 1981, pp. 182–93. [G: U.S.]

Tullock, Gordon. The Rhetoric and Reality of Redistribution. *Southern Econ. J.*, April 1981, *47*(4), pp. 895–907.

Ubaidullaeva, R. A. The Twenty-fifth Congress of the CPSU and Current Problems of Employment of Female Labor in the Republics of Central Asia. *Prob. Econ.*, Sept.–Oct.–Nov. 1981, *24*(5–6–7), pp. 147–55. [G: U.S.S.R.]

Vandell, Kerry D. The Effects of Racial Composition on Neighbourhood Succession. *Urban Stud.*, October 1981, *18*(3), pp. 315–33. [G: U.S.]

Wall, Paul L. Changes in the Black Community. *Amer. J. Agr. Econ.*, December 1981, *63*(5), pp. 902–04. [G: U.S.]

Wallace, Phyllis A. and Driscoll, James W. Social Issues in Collective Bargaining. In *Stieber, J.; McKersie, R. B. and Mills, D. Q., eds.*, 1981, pp. 199–254. [G: U.S.]

Ward, Robin and Sims, Ronald. Social Status, the Market and Ethnic Segregation. In *Peach, C.; Robinson, V. and Smith, S., eds.*, 1981, pp. 217–34. [G: U.K.]

Waxman, Chaim I. The Fourth Generation Grows Up: The Contemporary America Jewish Community. *Ann. Amer. Acad. Polit. Soc. Sci.*, March 1981, *454*, pp. 70–85. [G: U.S.]

Weiss, Yoram and Gronau, Reuben. Expected Interruptions in Labour Force Participation and Sex-Related Differences in Earnings Growth. *Rev. Econ. Stud.*, October 1981, *48*(4), pp. 607–19.

Welch, Finis. Affirmative Action and Its Enforcement. *Amer. Econ. Rev.*, May 1981, *71*(2), pp. 127–33. [G: U.S.]

Wertheimer, Barbara M. Labor Education for Women Workers: Introduction. In *Wertheimer, B. M., ed.*, 1981, pp. 3–11.

Wertheimer, Barbara M. Labor Education for Women Workers: Residential Schools. In *Wertheimer, B. M., ed.*, 1981, pp. 83–97. [G: U.S.]

White, Lynn K. A Note on Racial Differences in the Effect of Female Economic Opportunity on Marriage Rates. *Demography*, August 1981, *18*(3), pp. 349–54.

Wiegersma, Nancy. Women in the Transition to Capitalism: Nineteenth to Mid-twentieth Century Vietnam. In *Zarembka, P., ed.*, 1981, pp. 1–28.
[G: Vietnam]

Williams, Walter E. Economic Growth: The Central Issue: Answers: A Culprit is a Culprit. In *Inst. for Contemp. Studies*, 1981, pp. 51–53.

Williams, Walter E. Five Policy Proposals: Reply. In *Inst. for Contemp. Studies*, 1981, pp. 104–06. [G: U.S.]

Williams, Walter E. Legal Barriers to Black Economic Gains: Employment and Transportation. In *Inst. for Contemp. Studies*, 1981, pp. 23–30.

Wilson, William Julius. The Black Community in the 1980s: Questions of Race, Class, and Public Policy. *Ann. Amer. Acad. Polit. Soc. Sci.*, March 1981, *454*, pp. 26–41. [G: U.S.]

Wright, Gavin. Black and White Labor in the Old New South. In *Bateman, F., ed.*, 1981, pp. 35–50. [G: U.S.]

Wright, Gavin. Freedom and the Southern Economy. In *Walton, G. M. and Shepherd, J. F., eds.*, 1981, *1980*, pp. 85–102. [G: U.S.]

Yinger, John. A Search Model of Real Estate Broker Behavior. *Amer. Econ. Rev.*, September 1981, *71*(4), pp. 591–605.

Zoller, Elisabeth. Le statut fiscal de la femme mariée en France. (With English summary.) In *Roskamp, K. W. and Forte, F., eds.*, 1981, pp. 355–64. [G: France]

918 Economics of Aging

9180 Economics of Aging

Bridges, Benjamin, Jr. and Packard, Michael D. Price and Income Changes for the Elderly. *Soc. Sec. Bull.*, January 1981, *44*(1), pp. 3–15. [G: U.S.]

Chinn, Jeff. The Aging Soviet Society. In *Desfosses, H., ed.*, 1981, pp. 44–61. [G: U.S.S.R.]

Daly, M. and Wrage, Peter. The Effect of Income Tax Incentives on Retirement Savings: Some Canadian Evidence. *Eastern Econ. J.*, July-Oct. 1981, *7*(3–4), pp. 163–74. [G: Canada]

Davis, Charles J. and Covaleski, Mark A. Alternative Capital Reimbursement Policies for Wisconsin Nursing Homes. *Inquiry*, Summer 1981, *18*(2), pp. 165–78. [G: U.S.]

Godber, George [Sir]. Enabling the Elderly to Continue Functionally Independent. In *Gleason, H. P., ed.*, 1981, pp. 63–74.

Greene, Vernon L. and Monahan, Deborah J. Structural and Operational Factors Affecting Quality of Patient Care in Nursing Homes. *Public Policy*, Fall 1981, *29*(4), pp. 399–415. [G: U.S.]

Harmston, Floyd K. A Study of the Economic Relationships of Retired People and a Small Community. *Reg. Sci. Persp.*, 1981, *11*(1), pp. 42–56.

Kingson, Eric R. and Scheffler, Richard M. Aging: Issues and Economic Trends for the 1980s. *Inquiry*, Fall 1981, *18*(3), pp. 197–213. [G: U.S.]

Leeds, Morton. Inflation and the Elderly: A Housing Perspective. *Ann. Amer. Acad. Polit. Soc. Sci.*, July 1981, *456*, pp. 60–69. [G: U.S.]

Marsh, Robert E. The Income and Resources of the Elderly in 1978. *Soc. Sec. Bull.*, December 1981, *44*(12), pp. 3–11. [G: U.S.]

Morgan, James N. Antecedents and Consequences of Retirement. In *Hill, M. S.; Hill, D. H. and Morgan, J. N., eds.*, 1981, pp. 207–244. [G: U.S.]

Parnes, Herbert S. Work and Retirement: Introduc-

tion and Overview. In *Parnes, H. S., ed.*, 1981, pp. 1–41. [G: U.S.]

Parnes, Herbert S. Work and Retirement: Summary and Conclusions. In *Parnes, H. S., ed.*, 1981, pp. 254–70. [G: U.S.]

Parnes, Herbert S. and Nestel, Gilbert. The Retirement Experience. In *Parnes, H. S., ed.*, 1981, pp. 155–97. [G: U.S.]

Rea, Samuel A., Jr. Consumption Stabilizing Annuities with Uncertain Inflation. *J. Risk Ins.*, December 1981, *48*(4), pp. 596–609.

Reilly, Donald F. The Economy of 1981: A Bipartisan Look: The Proceedings of a Congressional Economic Conference: Statement. In *U.S. Congress, Joint Economic Committee (I)*, 1981, pp. 582–89. [G: U.S.]

Rogers, Gayle Thompson. Aged Widows and OASDI: Age at and Economic Status before and after Receipt of Benefits. *Soc. Sec. Bull.*, March 1981, *44*(3), pp. 3–19. [G: U.S.]

Stearns, Peter N. Retirement Policy: The Case for an Applied History Approach. In *Crecine, J. P., ed.*, 1981, pp. 259–75. [G: U.S.]

Weissert, William G. Toward a Continuum of Care for the Elderly: A Note of Caution. *Public Policy*, Summer 1981, *29*(3), pp. 331–40.

Wilson, Peter A. Hospital Use by the Aging Population. *Inquiry*, Winter 1981, *18*(4), pp. 332–44. [G: U.S.]

Wolozin, Harold. Earlier Retirement and the Older Worker. *J. Econ. Issues*, June 1981, *15*(2), pp. 477–87. [G: U.S.]

Zabalza, A. and Piachaud, D. Social Security and the Elderly: A Simulation of Policy Changes. *J. Public Econ.*, October 1981, *16*(2), pp. 145–69. [G: U.K.]

920 CONSUMER ECONOMICS

921 Consumer Economics; Levels and Standards of Living

9210 General

Andorka, Rudolf and Falussy, Béla. The Way of Life of the Hungarian Society as Reflected by the Time Budget Survey of 1976–1977. *Acta Oecon.*, 1981, *26*(3–4), pp. 243–73. [G: Hungary]

Arthur, W. B. The Economics of Risks to Life. *Amer. Econ. Rev.*, March 1981, *71*(1), pp. 54–64.

Barro, Robert J. and Santomero, Anthony M. Household Money Holdings and the Demand Deposit Rate. In *Barro, R. J.*, 1981, *1972*, pp. 337–53. [G: U.S.]

Baxter, Mike and Ewing, Gordon. Models of Recreational Trip Distribution. *Reg. Stud.*, 1981, *15*(5), pp. 327–44.

Behrend, Hilde. Research into Public Accounting Attitudes and the Attitudes of the Public to Inflation. *Managerial Dec. Econ.*, March 1981, *2*(1), pp. 1–8. [G: U.K.]

Belk, Russell; Painter, John and Semenik, Richard. Preferred Solutions to the Energy Crisis as a Function of Causal Attributions. *J. Cons. Res.*, December 1981, *8*(3), pp. 306–12. [G: U.S.]

Bennett, John W. Farm Management as Cultural Style: Studies of Adaptive Process in the North American Agrifamily. In *Dalton, G., ed.*, 1981, pp. 275–309. [G: U.S.; Canada]

Bennett, Peter D. and Moore, Noreen Klein. Consumers' Preferences for Alternative Energy Conservation Policies: A Trade-Off Analysis. *J. Cons. Res.*, December 1981, 8(3), pp. 313–21. [G: U.S.]

Bernardo, John J. A Programming Approach to Measure Attributes Utilities. *J. Econ. Bus.*, Spring/ Summer 1981, 33(3), pp. 239–45.

Binswanger, Hans P. Attitudes toward Risk: Theoretical Implications of an Experiment in Rural India. *Econ. J.*, December 1981, 91(364), pp. 867–90. [G: India]

Brandstätter, Hermann. Time Sampling of Subjective Well-being. In *Molt, W.; Hartmann, H. A. and Stringer, P., eds.*, 1981, pp. 63–76. [G: W. Germany]

Brodsky, David A. and Rodrik, Dani. Indicators of Development and Data Availability: The Case of the PQLI. *World Devel.*, July 1981, 9(7), pp. 695–99. [G: LDCs]

Bullock, J. Bruce. Estimates of Consumer Loss Due to Monopoly in the U.S. Food-Manufacturing Industries: Comment. *Amer. J. Agr. Econ.*, May 1981, 63(2), pp. 290–92. [G: U.S.]

Calder, Bobby J.; Phillips, Lynn W. and Tybout, Alice M. Designing Research for Application. *J. Cons. Res.*, September 1981, 8(2), pp. 197–207.

Cherif, M'hamed. Indices d'utilité pour la consommation d'énergie dans le secteur résidentiel. (With English summary.) *Cah. Écon. Bruxelles,* 4th Trimestre 1981, (92), pp. 557–70.

Cooper, C. P. Spatial and Temporal Patterns of Tourist Behaviour. *Reg. Stud.*, 1981, 15(5), pp. 359–71. [G: U.K.]

Cottle, Rex L. and Lawson, Rodger S. Leisure as Work: A Case in Professional Sports. *Atlantic Econ. J.*, September 1981, 9(3), pp. 50–59.

Dionne, Georges. Moral Hazard and Search Activity. *J. Risk Ins.*, September 1981, 48(3), pp. 422–34.

Etgar, Michael and Malhotra, Naresh K. Determinants of Price Dependency: Personal and Perceptual Factors. *J. Cons. Res.*, September 1981, 8(2), pp. 217–22.

Evers, H. D. The Contribution of Urban Subsistence Production to Incomes in Jakarta. *Bull. Indonesian Econ. Stud.*, July 1981, 17(2), pp. 89–96. [G: Indonesia]

Feldman, Laurence P. and Hornik, Jacob. The Use of Time: An Integrated Conceptual Model. *J. Cons. Res.*, March 1981, 7(4), pp. 407–19.

Filgueira, Carlos. Consumption in the new Latin American Models. *Cepal Rev.*, December 1981, (15), pp. 71–110. [G: Latin America]

Forman, Shepard. Life Paradigms: Makassae (East Timor) Views on Production, Reproduction, and Exchange. In *Dalton, G., ed.*, 1981, pp. 95–110. [G: Indonesia]

Foster, Ann C. Wives' Earnings as a Factor in Family Net Worth Accumulation. *Mon. Lab. Rev.*, January 1981, 104(1), pp. 53–57. [G: U.S.]

Francken, Dick A.; van Raaij, W. Fred and Verhallen, Theo M. M. Satisfaction with Leisure Activi-

ties. In *Molt, W.; Hartmann, H. A. and Stringer, P., eds.*, 1981, pp. 119–33. [G: Netherlands]

Gallant, A. Ronald. On the Bias in Flexible Functional Forms and an Essentially Unbiased Form: The Fourier Flexible Form. *J. Econometrics*, February 1981, 15(2), pp. 211–45. [G: U.S.]

Gauthier, Howard L. and Mitchelson, Ronald L. Attribute Importance and Mode Satisfaction in Travel Mode Choice Research. *Econ. Geogr.*, October 1981, 57(4), pp. 348–61. [G: Canada]

Gleason, Herbert P. Consumer Participation in Formulating Health Policy. In *Gleason, H. P., ed.*, 1981, pp. 103–11.

Glyptis, Susan A. Leisure Life-styles. *Reg. Stud.*, 1981, 15(5), pp. 311–26. [G: U.K.]

Goldin, Claudia Dale. Family Strategies and the Family Economy in the Late Nineteenth Century: The Role of Secondary Workers. In *Hershberg, T., ed.*, 1981, pp. 277–310. [G: U.S.]

Graham, Robert J. The Role of Perception of Time in Consumer Research. *J. Cons. Res.*, March 1981, 7(4), pp. 335–42.

Hagemann, Robert P. The Determinants of Household Vacation Travel: Some Empirical Evidence. *Appl. Econ.*, June 1981, 13(2), pp. 225–34. [G: U.S.]

Hansen, Flemming. Hemispheral Lateralization: Implications for Understanding Consumer Behavior. *J. Cons. Res.*, June 1981, 8(1), pp. 23–36.

Harrison, A. J. M. and Stabler, M. J. An Analysis of Journeys for Canal-based Recreation. *Reg. Stud.*, 1981, 15(5), pp. 345–58. [G: U.K.]

Heinkel, Robert. Uncertain Product Quality: The Market for Lemons with an Imperfect Testing Technology. *Bell J. Econ. (See Rand J. Econ. after 4/85)*, Autumn 1981, 12(2), pp. 625–36.

van Herwaarden, Floor G. and Kapteyn, Arie. Empirical Comparison of the Shape of Welfare Functions. *Europ. Econ. Rev.*, March 1981, 15(3), pp. 261–86. [G: Netherlands]

Hjorth-Andersen, Christian. Price and Quality of Industrial Products: Some Results of an Empirical Investigation. *Scand. J. Econ.*, 1981, 83(3), pp. 372–89. [G: Denmark]

Holbrook, Morris B. and Lehmann, Donald R. Allocating Discretionary Time: Complementarity among Activities. *J. Cons. Res.*, March 1981, 7(4), pp. 395–406. [G: U.S.]

Holbrook, Morris B. and Moore, William L. Feature Interactions in Consumer Judgments of Verbal versus Pictorial Presentations. *J. Cons. Res.*, June 1981, 8(1), pp. 103–13. [G: U.S.]

Hornik, Jacob and Schlinger, Mary Jane. Allocation of Time to the Mass Media. *J. Cons. Res.*, March 1981, 7(4), pp. 343–55. [G: U.S.]

Hunt, Janet C. and Kiker, B. F. The Effect of Fertility on the Time Use of Working Wives. *J. Cons. Res.*, March 1981, 7(4), pp. 380–87. [G: U.S.]

Jackson-Beeck, Marilyn and Robinson, John P. Television Nonviewers: An Endangered Species? *J. Cons. Res.*, March 1981, 7(4), pp. 356–59. [G: U.S.]

Jolibert, Alain J. P. L'économie du consommateur: les nouvelles approches théoriques et commerciales sont-elles conciliables? (Consumer Economy: Are the New Theoretical and Commercial

Approaches Reconcilable? With English summary.) *Écon. Soc.*, October–November–December 1981, *15*(10–12), pp. 1457–80.

Keating, Barry P.; Pitts, Robert E. and Appel, David. United Way Contributions: Coercion, Charity or Economic Self-Interest? *Southern Econ. J.*, January 1981, *47*(3), pp. 816–23. **[G: U.S.]**

Labay, Duncan G. and Kinnear, Thomas C. Exploring the Consumer Decision Process in the Adoption of Solar Energy Systems. *J. Cons. Res.*, December 1981, *8*(3), pp. 271–78. **[G: U.S.]**

Laluha, Ivan. Higher Quality of Living Conditions—An Essential Prerequisite of Development of the Socialist Way of Life. *Czech. Econ. Digest.*, December 1981, (8), pp. 39–54.

[G: Czechoslovakia]

Lancaster, Kelvin J. Advertising and Consumer Choice. *Greek Econ. Rev.*, April 1981, *3*(1), pp. 3–17.

Larsen, Norma L. and Martin, Gerald D. Income Growth Factors: Error Introduced through the Application of Cohort Data. *J. Risk Ins.*, March 1981, *48*(1), pp. 143–47.

Leonard-Barton, Dorothy. Voluntary Simplicity Lifestyles and Energy Conservation. *J. Cons. Res.*, December 1981, *8*(3), pp. 243–52.

[G: U.S.]

Leuthold, Jane H. Taxation and the Consumption of Household Time. *J. Cons. Res.*, March 1981, *7*(4), pp. 388–94. **[G: U.S.]**

McCain, Roger A. Cultivation of Taste, Catastrophe Theory, and the Demand for Works of Art. *Amer. Econ. Rev.*, May 1981, *71*(2), pp. 332–34.

Metwally, M. M. and Tamaschke, H. U. Advertising and the Propensity to Consume. *Oxford Bull. Econ. Statist.*, August 1981, *43*(3), pp. 273–85.

[G: Australia]

Midgley, David F. A Simple Mathematical Theory of Innovative Behavior. In *Wind, Y.; Mahajan, V. and Cardozo, R. N.*, eds., 1981, *1976*, pp. 475–98. **[G: U.S.]**

Molt, Walter. The Function of Needs for Planning in the Public Sector. In *Molt, W.; Hartmann, H. A. and Stringer, P.*, eds., 1981, pp. 273–79.

Montes, Manuel F. Truncation Bias in Household Money Demand Tests. *Phillipine Rev. Econ. Bus.*, March & June 1981, *18*(1 & 2), pp. 1–21.

[G: Philippines]

Moon, Marilyn. Measuring Economic Status: Recent Contributions and Future Directions. In *Ballabon, M. B.*, ed., 1981, pp. 131–53.

Morgan, James N. Trends in Non-money Income Through Do-It-Yourself Activities, 1971 to 1978. In *Hill, M. S.; Hill, D. H. and Morgan, J. N.*, eds., 1981, pp. 317–58. **[G: U.S.]**

Noam, Eli M. The Valuation of Legal Rights. *Quart. J. Econ.*, August 1981, *96*(3), pp. 465–76.

[G: Switzerland]

O'Rourke, A. Desmond and Greig, W. Smith. Estimates of Consumer Loss Due to Monopoly in the U.S. Food-Manufacturing Industries: Comment. *Amer. J. Agr. Econ.*, May 1981, *63*(2), pp. 285–89. **[G: U.S.]**

Olshavsky, Richard W. and Jaffee, Bruce L. Responsiveness of Consumer Expectations and Intentions to Economic Forecasts: An Experimental

Approach. *Rev. Econ. Statist.*, May 1981, *63*(2), pp. 298–302. **[G: U.S.]**

Park, C. Whan and Lessig, V. Parker. Familiarity and Its Impact on Consumer Decision Biases and Heuristics. *J. Cons. Res.*, September 1981, *8*(2), pp. 223–30.

Parker, Russell C. and Connor, John M. Estimates of Consumer Loss Due to Monopoly in the U.S. Food-Manufacturing Industries: Reply. *Amer. J. Agr. Econ.*, May 1981, *63*(2), pp. 293–97.

[G: U.S.]

Pipkin, J. S. The Concept of Choice and Cognitive Explanations of Spatial Behavior. *Econ. Geogr.*, October 1981, *57*(4), pp. 315–31.

Pollard, Sidney. Sheffield and Sweet Auburn—Amenities and Living Standards in the British Industrial Revolution: A Comment. *J. Econ. Hist.*, December 1981, *41*(4), pp. 902–04. **[G: U.K.]**

Pudney, Stephen E. Instrumental Variable Estimation of a Characteristics Model of Demand. *Rev. Econ. Stud.*, July 1981, *48*(3), pp. 417–33.

Rahman, Atiqur. Variations in Terms of Exchange and Their Impact on Farm Households in Bangladesh. *J. Devel. Stud.*, July 1981, *17*(4), pp. 317–35. **[G: Bangladesh]**

Rea, Samuel A., Jr. Consumption Stabilizing Annuities with Uncertain Inflation. *J. Risk Ins.*, December 1981, *48*(4), pp. 596–609.

Recker, Wilfred and Schuler, Harry J. Destination Choice and Processing Spatial Information: Some Empirical Tests with Alternative Constructs. *Econ. Geogr.*, October 1981, *57*(4), pp. 373–83.

Rigaux-Bricmont, B.; Sayegh, E. and Vlahopoulos, P. Pour un modèle du rôle de l'information et du risque perçu dans la prise de decision de consommation. (Building a Model of Consumer Decision-Making Emphasizing the Use of Information for Perceived Risk Reduction. With English summary.) *Ann. Sci. Écon. Appl.*, 1981, *37*(2), pp. 25–55.

Schaninger, Charles M. and Sciglimpaglia, Donald. The Influence of Cognitive Personality Traits and Demographics on Consumer Information Acquisition. *J. Cons. Res.*, September 1981, *8*(2), pp. 208–16. **[G: U.S.]**

Schiffman, Leon G.; Dillon, William R. and Ngumah, Festus E. The Influence of Subcultural and Personality Factors on Consumer Acculturation. *J. Int. Bus. Stud.*, Fall 1981, *12*(2), pp. 137–43.

[G: Nigeria]

Scitovsky, Tibor. The Desire for Excitement in Modern Society. *Kyklos*, 1981, *34*(1), pp. 3–13.

Selby, Edward B., Jr. and Beranek, William. Sweepstakes Contests: Analysis, Strategies, and Survey. *Amer. Econ. Rev.*, March 1981, *71*(1), pp. 189–95. **[G: U.S.]**

Shah, Anup R. Imperfections in the Capital Markets and Consumer Behavior. *Southern Econ. J.*, April 1981, *47*(4), pp. 1032–45.

Shatalin, S. Methodological Problems in the Analysis of the People's Well-Being. *Prob. Econ.*, August 1981, *24*(4), pp. 20–38. **[G: U.S.S.R.]**

Shechter, M., et al. Evaluation of Landscape Resources for Recreation Planning. *Reg. Stud.*, 1981, *15*(5), pp. 373–90. **[G: Israel]**

Skurski, Roger. Socialism and the Consumer in the

U.S.S.R. *Rev. Radical Polit. Econ.*, Spring 1981, *13*(1), pp. 22–30. **[G: U.S.S.R.]**

Smith, Gary N. The Systematic Specification of a Full Prior Covariance Matrix for Asset Demand Equations. *Quart. J. Econ.*, May 1981, *96*(2), pp. 317–39.

Soutar, Geoffrey N. and Clarke, Yvonne. Life Style and Television Viewing Behaviour in Perth, Western Australia. *Australian J. Manage.*, June 1981, *6*(1), pp. 109–23. **[G: Australia]**

Sumner, Michael T. and Laing, C. J. Countercyclical Tax Changes and Consumers' Expenditure. *Oxford Bull. Econ. Statist.*, May 1981, *43*(2), pp. 131–47. **[G: U.K.]**

Suranyi-Unger, Theodore, Jr. Consumer Behavior and Consumer Well-Being: An Economist's Digest. *J. Cons. Res.*, September 1981, *8*(2), pp. 132–43.

Swartz, David G. and Strand, Ivar E., Jr. Avoidance Costs Associated with Imperfect Information: The Case of Kepone. *Land Econ.*, May 1981, *57*(2), pp. 139–50. **[G: U.S.]**

Thaler, Richard H. and Shefrin, Hersh M. An Economic Theory of Self-Control. *J. Polit. Econ.*, April 1981, *89*(2), pp. 392–406.

Thélot, Claude. Note sur la loi logistique et l'imitation. (A Note on the Logistic Law and Imitation. With English summary.) *Ann. INSEE*, April–June 1981, (42), pp. 111–26.

Thornton, Arland. The Influence of Income and Aspirations on Childbearing: Evidence from Research Using Multiple Indicators from Mutiple Data Sets. In *Molt, W.; Hartmann, H. A. and Stringer, P., eds.*, 1981, pp. 211–31. **[G: U.S.]**

Vaughan, Roger J. The Value of Urban Open Space. In *Henderson, J. V., ed.*, 1981, pp. 103–30. **[G: U.S]**

Voronin, V. Personal Household Plots and Trade. *Prob. Econ.*, March 1981, *23*(11), pp. 3–15. **[G: U.S.S.R.]**

Wellington, Donald C. and Gallo, Joseph C. The March of the Toy Soldier: The Market for a Collectible. *J. Cult. Econ.*, June 1981, *5*(1), pp. 69–75.

Williamson, Jeffrey G. Some Myths Die Hard—Urban Disamenities One More Time: A Reply. *J. Econ. Hist.*, December 1981, *41*(4), pp. 905–07. **[G: U.K.]**

Williamson, Jeffrey G. Urban Disamenities, Dark Satanic Mills, and the British Standard of Living Debate. *J. Econ. Hist.*, March 1981, *41*(1), pp. 75–83. **[G: U.K.]**

Yankelovich, Daniel and Lefkowitz, Bernard. The Public Debate about Growth. In *Cleveland, H., ed.*, 1981, pp. 16–78. **[G: U.S.]**

Zeckhauser, Richard and Shepard, Donald S. Principles for Saving and Valuing Lives. In *Ferguson, A. R. and LeVeen, E. P., eds.*, 1981, pp. 91–130.

9211 Living Standards, Composition of Overall Expenditures, and Empirical Consumption and Savings Studies

Ahn, C. Y.; Singh, Inderjit and Squire, Lyn. A Model of an Agricultural Household in a Multi-Crop Economy: The Case of Korea. In *Johnson,*

G. and Maunder, A., eds., 1981, pp. 697– 708. **[G: S. Korea]**

Ali, M. Shaukat. Rural Urban Consumption Patterns in Pakistan. *Pakistan Econ. Soc. Rev.*, Winter 1981, *19*(2), pp. 85–94. **[G: Pakistan]**

Alogoskoufis, George S. and Nissim, John. Consumption–Income Dynamics under Rational Expectations: Theory and Evidence. *Greek Econ. Rev.*, August 1981, *3*(2), pp. 128–47. **[G: Greece]**

Barnett, William A. and Kopecky, Kenneth J. Estimation of Implicit Utility Models. *Europ. Econ. Rev.*, March 1981, *15*(3), pp. 247–59.

Binkley, James K. The Relationship between Elasticity and Least Squares Bias. *Rev. Econ. Statist.*, May 1981, *63*(2), pp. 307–09.

Blinder, Alan S. Temporary Income Taxes and Consumer Spending. *J. Polit. Econ.*, February 1981, *89*(1), pp. 26–53. **[G: U.S.]**

Blundell, Richard W. Estimating Continuous Consumer Equivalence Scales in an Expenditure Model with Labour Supply. In *Currie, D.; Nobay, R. and Peel, D., eds.*, 1981, pp. 111–35. **[G: U.K.]**

Bollino, Carlo Andrea. Domanda di beni di consumo in Italia: una analisi econometrica. (On the Demand of Consumer Goods in Italy: An Econometric Analysis. With English summary.) *Giorn. Econ.*, March–April 1981, *40*(3–4), pp. 145–65. **[G: Italy]**

Brannon, Gerard M. Charitable Contributions: Comments. In *Aaron, H. J. and Pechman, J. A., eds.*, 1981, pp. 437–41. **[G: U.S.]**

Bridges, Benjamin, Jr. and Packard, Michael D. Price and Income Changes for the Elderly. *Soc. Sec. Bull.*, January 1981, *44*(1), pp. 3–15. **[G: U.S.]**

Brittain, John A. Charitable Contributions: Comments. In *Aaron, H. J. and Pechman, J. A., eds.*, 1981, pp. 441–46. **[G: U.S.]**

Bulkley, George. Personal Savings and Anticipated Inflation. *Econ. J.*, March 1981, *91*(361), pp. 124–35.

Carmichael, Jeffrey and Hawtrey, Kim. Social Security, Government Finance, and Savings. *Econ. Rec.*, December 1981, *57*(159), pp. 332–43. **[G: Australia]**

Cebula, Richard J. and Smith, Lisa Karen. An Exploratory Empirical Note on Determinants of Inter-Regional Living-Cost Differentials in the United States, 1970 and 1975. *Reg. Sci. Urban Econ.*, February 1981, *11*(1), pp. 81–85. **[G: U.S.]**

Chrystal, K. Alec. The 'New Cambridge' Aggregate Expenditure Function: The Emperor's Old Clothes? *J. Monet. Econ.*, May 1981, *7*(3), pp. 395–402. **[G: U.K.]**

Clotfelter, Charles T. and Steuerle, C. Eugene. Charitable Contributions. In *Aaron, H. J. and Pechman, J. A., eds.*, 1981, pp. 403–37. **[G: U.S.]**

Cooper, Russell J. and McLaren, Keith R. Specification and Estimation of ELES. *Econ. Rec.*, March 1981, *57*(156), pp. 74–79. **[G: Australia]**

Cox, Donald. The Decline in Personal Saving. *Fed. Res. Bank New York Quart. Rev.*, Spring 1981,

6(1), pp. 25–32. [G: U.S.]

Dahlhoff, Hans-Dieter. Unplanned and Impulse Purchasing Behavior: Revisited and Extended. In *Molt, W.; Hartmann, H. A. and Stringer, P., eds.,* 1981, pp. 175–84. [G: W. Germany]

Daly, M. and Wrage, Peter. The Effect of Income Tax Incentives on Retirement Savings: Some Canadian Evidence. *Eastern Econ. J.,* July-Oct. 1981, 7(3–4), pp. 163–74. [G: Canada]

Daly, Michael J. The Role of Registered Retirement Savings Plans in a Life-Cycle Model. *Can. J. Econ.,* August 1981, 14(3), pp. 409–21.

Daly, Vince and Hadjimatheou, George. Stochastic Implications of the Life Cycle-Permanent Income Hypothesis: Evidence for the U.K. Economy: Comment. *J. Polit. Econ.,* June 1981, 89(3), pp. 596–99. [G: U.K.]

Danziger, Sheldon; Haveman, Robert H. and Plotnick, Robert. How Income Transfer Programs Affect Work, Savings, and the Income Distribution: A Critical Review. *J. Econ. Lit.,* September 1981, 19(3), pp. 975–1028. [G: U.S.]

Davidson, James E. H. and Hendry, David F. Interpreting Econometric Evidence: The Behaviour of Consumers' Expenditure in the UK. *Europ. Econ. Rev.,* May 1981, 16(1), pp. 177–92. [G: U.K.]

Davies, James B. Uncertain Lifetime, Consumption, and Dissaving in Retirement. *J. Polit. Econ.,* June 1981, 89(3), pp. 561–77.

Dellacasa, Giorgio. Level of Living and National Product per Capita—Some Empirical Results. *Konjunkturpolitik,* 1981, 27(1), pp. 38–46.

Denton, M. Elizabeth. Soviet Consumer Policy: Trends and Prospects. In *Bornstein, M., ed.,* 1981, 1979, pp. 165–85. [G: U.S.S.R.]

Diamond, Peter. Comment [A Reappraisal of Financing Social Security] [VAT versus the Payroll Tax]. In *Skidmore, F., ed.,* 1981, pp. 164–69. [G: U.S.]

Duncan, Greg J. and Morgan, James N. Persistence and Change in Economic Status and the Role of Changing Family Composition. In *Hill, M. S.; Hill, D. H. and Morgan, J. N., eds.,* 1981, pp. 1–44. [G: U.S.]

Fareed, A. E. and Riggs, G. D. Racial Differences in Consumer Expenditure Patterns, 1972–73. *Rev. Black Polit. Econ.,* Spring 1981, 11(3), pp. 293–301. [G: U.S.]

Feldstein, Martin S. The Effect of Social Security on Saving. In *Currie, D.; Nobay, R. and Peel, D., eds.,* 1981, pp. 1–23. [G: U.S.]

Ferris, Tom. Comparisons of Productivity on Living Standards: Ireland and other EEC Countries. *Irish Banking Rev.,* March 1981, pp. 7–15. [G: Ireland; U.K.; Denmark; Benelux]

Fibiger, John. Comment [A Reappraisal of Financing Social Security] [VAT versus the Payroll Tax]. In *Skidmore, F., ed.,* 1981, pp. 169–72. [G: U.S.]

Figueroa, Adolfo. Effects of Changes in Consumption and Trade Patterns on Agricultural Development in Latin America. In *Baer, W. and Gillis, M., eds.,* 1981, pp. 83–97. [G: Peru; Latin America]

Friedlaender, Ann F. Saving: Comments. In *Aaron, H. J. and Pechman, J. A., eds.,* 1981, pp. 390–96. [G: U.S.]

Fry, Maxwell J. The Permanent Income Hypothesis in Underdeveloped Countries: Mea Culpa. *J. Devel. Econ.,* April 1981, 8(2), pp. 263–68. [G: Asia; LDCs]

von Furstenberg, George M. Saving. In *Aaron, H. J. and Pechman, J. A., eds.,* 1981, pp. 327–90. [G: U.S.]

Gamaletsos, Theodore. A Dynamic Generalized Linear Expenditure System of the Demand for Consumer Goods in Greece. In *[Valavanis, S.],* 1981, pp. 379–89. [G: Greece]

Genser, Bernd. Public Finance and Private Saving in Austria: The Effects of Saving Promotion. *Empirica,* 1981, (2), pp. 169–85. [G: Austria]

Geweke, John F. and Singleton, Kenneth J. Latent Variable Models for Time Series: A Frequency Domain Approach with an Application to the Permanent Income Hypothesis. *J. Econometrics,* December 1981, 17(3), pp. 287–304. [G: U.S.]

Grabicke, Klaus. The Information Level of Consumers and the Measurement of Its Changes. In *Molt, W.; Hartmann, H. A. and Stringer, P., eds.,* 1981, pp. 185–90.

Gray, Kenneth R. Soviet Consumption of Food: Is the Bottle "Half-Full," "Half-Empty," "Half-Water," or "Too Expensive"? *ACES Bull. (See Comp. Econ. Stud. after 8/85),* Summer 1981, 23(2), pp. 31–50. [G: U.S.S.R.]

Green, Francis G. The Effect of Occupational Pension Schemes on Saving in the United Kingdom: A Test of the Life Cycle Hypothesis. *Econ. J.,* March 1981, 91(361), pp. 136–44. [G: U.K.]

Gregory, Mary B., et al. Urban Poverty and Some Policy Options: An Analysis for India. *Urban Stud.,* June 1981, 18(2), pp. 155–67. [G: India]

Gylfason, Thorvaldur. Interest Rates, Inflation, and the Aggregate Consumption Function. *Rev. Econ. Statist.,* May 1981, 63(2), pp. 233–45.

Haines, Michael R. Poverty, Economic Stress, and the Family in a Late Nineteenth-Century American City: Whites in Philadelphia, 1880. In *Hershberg, T., ed.,* 1981, pp. 240–76. [G: U.S.]

Hall, Robert E. Interpreting Econometric Evidence by Davidson and Hendry: Comment. *Europ. Econ. Rev.,* May 1981, 16(1), pp. 193–94.

Hall, Robert E. Stochastic Implications of the Life Cycle–Permanent Income Hypothesis: Theory and Evidence. In *Lucas, R. E. and Sargent, T. J., eds.,* 1981, 1978, pp. 501–17. [G: U.S.]

Hartle, Douglas G., et al. Stagflation Consequences of the Canadian Tax/Transfer System. In *Ontario Economic Council, Vol. 1,* 1981, pp. 67–105. [G: Canada; U.S.]

Holzmann, Robert. Public Finance and Private Saving in Austria: The Effects of Social Security. *Empirica,* 1981, (2), pp. 187–221. [G: Austria]

Hughes, Gordon A. The Distributional Impact of Commodity Taxes and Subsidies. *Bull. Indonesian Econ. Stud.,* November 1981, 17(3), pp. 25–47. [G: Indonesia]

Hymans, Saul H. Saving, Investment, and Social Security. *Nat. Tax J.,* March 1981, 34(1), pp. 1–8. [G: U.S.]

Ichimura, Shinichi. Economic Growth, Savings and Housing Finance in Japan. *J. Econ. Stud.,* 1981, 8(3), pp. 41–64. [G: Japan]

Ingham, A. Estimating Continuous Consumer Equivalence Scales in an Expenditure Model with Labour Supply: Comment. In *Currie, D.; Nobay, R. and Peel, D., eds.,* 1981, pp. 136–38. [G: U.K.]

Jorgenson, Dale W.; Lau, L. J. and Stoker, T. M. Aggregate Consumer Behaviour and Individual Welfare. In *Currie, D.; Nobay, R. and Peel, D., eds.,* 1981, pp. 35–61. [G: U.S.]

Keidel, Albert. Income Distribution in Contemporary Japan. In *Richardson, B. M. and Ueda, T., eds.,* 1981, pp. 125–33. [G: Japan]

Kelley, Allen C. Demographic Impacts on Demand Patterns in the Low-Income Setting. *Econ. Develop. Cult. Change,* October 1981, *30*(1), pp. 1–16. [G: Kenya]

Keyfitz, Nathan. Paradoxes of Work and Consumption in Late Twentieth Century America. In *Khan, A. and Sirageldin, I., eds.,* 1981, pp. 31–54. [G: U.S.]

Knoll, O. and Ondrchka, P. An Empirical Analysis of Consumption Based on Family Budget Studies. *Matekon,* Winter 1981–82, *18*(2), pp. 19–31. [G: Czechoslovakia]

Kravis, Irving B. An Approximation of the Relative Real per Capita GDP of the People's Republic of China. *J. Compar. Econ.,* March 1981, *5*(1), pp. 60–78. [G: China]

Krishnamurty, K. and Saibaba, P. Determinants of Saving Rate in India. *Indian Econ. Rev.,* Oct.-Dec. 1981, *16*(4), pp. 225–49. [G: India]

Kuznets, Simon. Size of Households and Income Disparities. In *Simon, J. L. and Lindert, P. H., eds.,* 1981, pp. 1–40. [G: Selected Countries]

Landsburg, Steven E. Taste Change in the United Kingdom, 1900–1955. *J. Polit. Econ.,* February 1981, *89*(1), pp. 92–104. [G: U.K.]

Laumas, Prem S. and Mohabbat, Khan A. A Note on the Two Concepts of Permanent Income. *Eastern Econ. J.,* July-Oct. 1981, *7*(3–4), pp. 187–91. [G: U.S.]

Leipziger, Danny M. The Basic Human Needs Approach and North–South Relations. In *Reubens, E. P., ed.,* 1981, pp. 255–79.

Lindqvist, Alf and Julander, Claes-Robert. Indicators of Household Saving in Sweden: Some Results from the Empirical Studies. In *Molt, W.; Hartmann, H. A. and Stringer, P., eds.,* 1981, pp. 135–48. [G: Sweden]

MacMillan, J. A. and Winter, G. R. Income Improvement versus Efficiency in Canadian Rural Development Programmes. In *Johnson, G. and Maunder, A., eds.,* 1981, pp. 381–88. [G: Canada]

Marsden, David. The Evolution of Household Income for Different Social Groups in the UK since 1966. *Cah. Écon. Bruxelles,* 2nd Trimestre 1981, (90), pp. 187–201. [G: U.K.]

McClure, Charles E., Jr. VAT versus the Payroll Tax. In *Skidmore, F., ed.,* 1981, pp. 129–64.

Milanović, Branko. Godišnje potrošne funkcije za Jugoslaviju 1952–78. (Yearly Consumption Functions for Yugoslavia, 1952–1978. With English summary.) *Econ. Anal. Worker's Manage.,* 1981, *15*(3), pp. 291–334. [G: Yugoslavia]

Moeller, John F. Consumer Expenditure Responses to Income Redistribution Programs. *Rev. Econ. Statist.,* August 1981, *63*(3), pp. 409–21.

Morrison, Donald G. Inequalities of Social Rewards: Realities and Perceptions in Nigeria. In *Bienen, H. and Diejomaoh, V. P., eds.,* 1981, pp. 173–92. [G: Nigeria]

Munnell, Alicia H. Pensions and Capital Accumulation. In *Federal Reserve System,* 1981, pp. 133–42. [G: U.S.]

Munnell, Alicia H. Social Security, Private Pensions, and Saving. *New Eng. Econ. Rev.,* May/June 1981, pp. 31–47. [G: U.S.]

Norwood, Janet L. Two Consumer Price Index Issues: Weighting and Homeownership. *Mon. Lab. Rev.,* March 1981, *104*(3), pp. 58–59. [G: U.S.]

Ölander, Folke. The Effects of Income Level upon the Efficiency of Buying, or Do the Poor Pay More? In *Molt, W.; Hartmann, H. A. and Stringer, P., eds.,* 1981, pp. 149–59.

Ouliaris, Sam. Household Saving and the Rate of Interest. *Econ. Rec.,* September 1981, *57*(158), pp. 205–14. [G: Australia]

Panov, Vladimir P. The Supreme Goal of Social Production. In *Novosti Press Agency,* 1981, pp. 191–215. [G: U.S.S.R.]

Perrin, Richard K. and Scobie, Grant M. Market Intervention Policies for Increasing the Consumption of Nutrients by Low Income Households. *Amer. J. Agr. Econ.,* February 1981, *63*(1), pp. 73–82. [G: Colombia]

Phelps Brown, Henry and Hopkins, Sheila V. Seven Centuries of Wages and Prices: Some Earlier Estimates. In *Phelps Brown, H. and Hopkins, S. V.,* 1981, *1961,* pp. 99–105. [G: U.K.]

Pollak, Robert A. The Social Cost of Living Index. *J. Public Econ.,* June 1981, *15*(3), pp. 311–36.

Pollak, Robert A. and Wales, Terence J. Demographic Variables in Demand Analysis. *Econometrica,* November 1981, *49*(6), pp. 1533–51. [G: U.K.]

Qureshi, Zia M. Household Saving in Pakistan: Some Findings from Time-Series Data. *Pakistan Devel. Rev.,* Winter 1981, *20*(4), pp. 375–97. [G: Pakistan]

Ram, Rati. Applicability of the Permanent Income Hypothesis to Underdeveloped Economies: A Comment [The Permanent Income Hypothesis in Underdeveloped Economies: Additional Evidence]. *J. Devel. Econ.,* April 1981, *8*(2), pp. 259–62. [G: Asia; LDCs]

Randall, Maury R. Inflation, Income, and Erosion of Household Wealth. *Bus. Econ.,* September 1981, *16*(4), pp. 20–23. [G: U.S.]

Ro, Y. K.; Adams, Dale W. and Hushak, Leroy J. Income Instability and Consumption-Savings in South Korean Farm Households, 1965–1970. *World Devel.,* February 1981, *9*(2), pp. 183–91. [G: S. Korea]

Sada, P. O. Urbanization and Income Distribution in Nigeria. In *Bienen, H. and Diejomaoh, V. P., eds.,* 1981, pp. 269–98. [G: Nigeria]

Schaafsma, Joseph. Inflation and the Standard of Living of Pensioners: A Case Study. *Can. Public Policy,* Winter 1981, *7*(1), pp. 115–18. [G: Canada]

Schaninger, Charles M. and Allen, Chris T. Wife's Occupational Status as a Consumer Behavior Construct. *J. Cons. Res.,* September 1981, *8*(2), pp. 189–96. [G: U.S.]

Schroeder, Gertrude E. Selected Problems of Regional Development in the USSR: Regional Living Standards. In *Koropeckyj, I. S. and Schroeder, G. E., eds.,* 1981, pp. 118–56.
[G: U.S.S.R.]

Shepherd, W. F. and Prasada Rao, D. S. A Comparison of Purchasing Power Parity between the Pound Sterling and the Australian Dollar in 1979. *Econ. Rec.,* September 1981, 57(158), pp. 215–23.
[G: U.K.; Australia]

Shoyama, T. K. Stagflation Consequences of the Canadian Tax/Transfer System: Comments. In *Ontario Economic Council, Vol. 1,* 1981, pp. 105–13.
[G: Canada; U.S.]

Simmons, P. Consistent Estimation of a Large Generalised Strongly Separable Demand System. In *Currie, D.; Nobay, R. and Peel, D., eds.,* 1981, pp. 139–73.
[G: U.K.]

Slifman, Lawrence. A Dissection of Personal Saving Behavior. *Bus. Econ.,* September 1981, 16(4), pp. 5–14.
[G: U.S.]

Song, Byung-Nak. Empirical Research on Consumption Behavior: Evidence from Rich and Poor LDCs. *Econ. Develop. Cult. Change,* April 1981, 29(3), pp. 597–611.
[G: S. Korea; Italy]

Sørensen, Christen. Skattefrie pensionsordninger ved høj inflation og højt skattetryk. (Tax Free Pension Schemes with Ongoing Inflation and a High Level of Income Tax. With English summary.) *Nationaløkon. Tidsskr.,* 1981, 119(3), pp. 339–42.
[G: Denmark]

Spencer, J. E. Consistent Estimation of a Large Generalised Strongly Separable Demand System: Comment. In *Currie, D.; Nobay, R. and Peel, D., eds.,* 1981, pp. 174–77.
[G: U.K.]

Spinnewyn, Frans. Rational Habit Formation. *Europ. Econ. Rev.,* January 1981, 15(1), pp. 91–109.

Steindel, Charles. The Determinants of Private Saving. In *Federal Reserve System,* 1981, pp. 101–14.
[G: U.S.]

Terleckyj, Nestor E. A Social Production Framework for Resource Accounting. In *Juster, F. T. and Land, K. C., eds.,* 1981, pp. 95–129. [G: U.S.]

Thomas, R. Leighton. Wealth and Aggregate Consumption. *Manchester Sch. Econ. Soc. Stud.,* June 1981, 49(2), pp. 129–52.

Trognon, Alain. Composition des ménages et système linéaire de dépenses. (Household Composition and Linear System of Expenditures. With English summary.) *Ann. INSEE,* January–March 1981, (41), pp. 3–40. [G: France]

Tyson, Laura D'Andrea. Aggregate Economic Difficulties and Workers' Welfare. In *Triska, J. F. and Gati, C., eds.,* 1981, pp. 108–35.
[G: Hungary; Poland]

von Ungern-Sternberg, Thomas. Inflation and Savings: International Evidence on Inflation-Induced Income Losses. *Econ. J.,* December 1981, 91(364), pp. 961–76. [G: W. Germany; U.K.]

Weber, Warren E. Saving: Comments. In *Aaron, H. J. and Pechman, J. A., eds.,* 1981, pp. 396–402. [G: U.S.]

Westphal, Uwe. Interpreting Econometric Evidence by Davidson and Hendry: Comment. *Europ. Econ. Rev.,* May 1981, 16(1), pp. 195–97.

Wijnholds, Heiko de B. Market Forecasting for Dual

Economies: The Application and Accuracy of Income Elasticities. *J. Int. Bus. Stud.,* Winter 1981, 12(3), pp. 89–98. [G: S. Africa]

Wolff, Edward N. The Accumulation of Household Wealth over the Life-Cycle: A Microdata Analysis. *Rev. Income Wealth,* March 1981, 27(1), pp. 75–96. [G: U.S.]

Zaitsev, A. The Personal Savings of the Working People under Developed Socialism. *Prob. Econ.,* February 1981, 23(10), pp. 64–77.
[G: U.S.S.R.]

Ziegler, Joseph A. and Britton, Charles R. A Comparative Analysis of Socioeconomic Variations in Measuring the Quality of Life. *Soc. Sci. Quart.,* June 1981, 62(2), pp. 303–12. [G: U.S.]

9212 Patterns of Expenditure and Consumption of Specific Items

Alcaly, Roger E. Consumer Information and Advertising: Comments. In *Galatin, M. and Leiter, R. D., eds.,* 1981, pp. 78–82. [G: U.S.]

Allen, P. Geoffrey; Stevens, Thomas H. and Barrett, Scott A. The Effects of Variable Omission in the Travel Cost Technique. *Land Econ.,* May 1981, 57(2), pp. 173–80. [G: U.S.]

Archibald, Robert and Gillingham, Robert. A Decomposition of the Price and Income Elasticities of the Consumer Demand for Gasoline. *Southern Econ. J.,* April 1981, 47(4), pp. 1021–31.
[G: U.S.]

Archibald, Robert and Gillingham, Robert. The Distributional Impact of Alternative Gasoline Conservation Policies. *Bell J. Econ. (See Rand J. Econ. after 4/85),* Autumn 1981, 12(2), pp. 426–44. [G: U.S.]

Ashley, David J. Uncertainty in Interurban Highway-Scheme Appraisal. In *Stopher, P. R.; Meyburg, A. H. and Brög, W., eds.,* 1981, pp. 599–615. [G: U.K.]

Atkinson, A. B. and Stern, N. H. On Labour Supply and Commodity Demands. In *[Stone, R.],* 1981, pp. 265–96. [G: U.K.]

Barnes, Roberta; Gillingham, Robert and Hagemann, Robert P. The Short-run Residential Demand for Electricity. *Rev. Econ. Statist.,* November 1981, 63(4), pp. 541–52. [G: U.S.]

Bass, Frank M. A New-Product Growth Model for Consumer Durables. In *Wind, Y.; Mahajan, V. and Cardozo, R. N., eds.,* 1981, 1969, pp. 457–74. [G: U.S.]

Battese, George E. and Bonyhady, Bruce P. Estimation of Household Expenditure Functions: An Application of a Class of Heteroscedastic Regression Models. *Econ. Rec.,* March 1981, 57(156), pp. 80–85. [G: Australia]

Beals, Ralph E. Elasticity Estimates for Domestic Electricity Consumption under Time-of-Day Pricing: An Analysis of British Data. In *[Nelson, J. R.],* 1981, pp. 277–97. [G: U.K.]

Beckmann, Martin J. Binary Choice and the Demand for Durables. In *[Lipiński, E.],* 1981, pp. 87–92. [G: U.S.]

Beenstock, Michael and Willcocks, P. Energy Consumption and Economic Activity in Industrialized Countries: The Dynamic Aggregate Time Series

Relationship. *Energy Econ.*, October 1981, *3*(4), pp. 225–32. [G: MDCs]

Beggs, S.; Cardell, S. and Hausman, Jerry A. Assessing the Potential Demand for Electric Cars. *J. Econometrics*, September 1981, *17*(1), pp. 1–19. [G: U.S.]

Beierlein, James G.; Dunn, James W. and McConnon, James C., Jr. The Demand for Electricity and Natural Gas in the Northeastern United States. *Rev. Econ. Statist.*, August 1981, *63*(3), pp. 403–08. [G: U.S.]

Bending, Richard. The Domestic Sector—Data, History and Prospects. In *Amman, F. and Wilson, R., eds.*, 1981, pp. 129–38. [G: U.K.]

Benham, Lee. The Effects of Government Regulation on Teenage Smoking: Comment. *J. Law Econ.*, December 1981, *24*(3), pp. 571–73. [G: U.S.]

Betancourt, Roger R. An Econometric Analysis of Peak Electricity Demand in the Short Run. *Energy Econ.*, January 1981, *3*(1), pp. 14–29. [G: U.S.]

Billings, R. Bruce and Agthe, Donald E. Price Elasticities for Water: A Case of Increasing Block Rates: Reply. *Land Econ.*, May 1981, *57*(2), pp. 276–78. [G: U.S.]

Biørn, Erik. Estimating Economic Relations from Incomplete Cross-Section/Time-Series Data. *J. Econometrics*, June 1981, *16*(2), pp. 221–36.

Blanciforti, Laura; Green, Richard D. and Lane, Sylvia. Income and Expenditure for Relatively More versus Relatively Less Nutritious Food over the Life Cycle. *Amer. J. Agr. Econ.*, May 1981, *63*(2), pp. 255–60. [G: U.S.]

Blomgren-Hansen, Niels and Rode, Christian B. O. En model for efterspørgselen efter personbiler i Danmark. (The Demand for Cars in Denmark. With English summary.) *Nationaløkon. Tidsskr.*, 1981, *119*(1), pp. 78–94.

Bohm, Peter. Estimating Willingness to Pay: Why and How? In *Strøm, S., ed.*, 1981, *1979*, pp. 1–12.

Bourgin, Christian and Godard, Xavier. Structural and Threshold Effects in the Use of Transportation Modes. In *Stopher, P. R.; Meyburg, A. H. and Brög, W., eds.*, 1981, pp. 353–68.

Brandon, Belinda B. The Effect of the Demographics of Individual Households on Their Telephone Usage: The Questionnaire, Calling, and Billing Data. In *Brandon, B. B., ed.*, 1981, pp. 29–55. [G: U.S.]

Brandon, Belinda B. and Ancmon, Elsa M. The Association of Distance with Calling Frequencies and Conversation Times. In *Brandon, B. B., ed.*, 1981, pp. 219–73. [G: U.S.]

Brandon, Belinda B. and Brandon, Paul S. The Effect of the Demographics of Individual Households on Their Telephone Usage: Introduction and Summary. In *Brandon, B. B., ed.*, 1981, pp. 1–18. [G: U.S.]

Brandon, Belinda B.; Brandon, Paul S. and Ancmon, Elsa M. The Effects of Time of Day on Local and Suburban Calling Frequencies and Conversation Times. In *Brandon, B. B., ed.*, 1981, pp. 165–218. [G: U.S.]

Brandon, Belinda B.; Brandon, Paul S. and Williams, Wm. H. The Effect of the Demographics

of Individual Households on Their Telephone Usage: Other Studies and Suggestions for Future Research. In *Brandon, B. B., ed.*, 1981, pp. 355–93.

Brandon, Belinda B., et al. Box Plot Analysis of Local and Suburban Calling Frequencies and Conversation Times. In *Brandon, B. B., ed.*, 1981, pp. 75–131. [G: U.S.]

Brandon, Paul S. The Effect of the Demographics of Individual Households on Their Telephone Usage: Regression Analysis of Local and Suburban Usage. In *Brandon, B. B., ed.*, 1981, pp. 133–64. [G: U.S.]

Brookes, L. G. Postscript: Energy Elasticities and Energy Ratios [Energy-Income Coefficients and Ratios: Their Abuse and Use]. *Energy Econ.*, April 1981, *3*(2), p. 122. [G: U.S.]

Brunk, Gregory G. A Test of the Friedman–Savage Gambling Model. *Quart. J. Econ.*, May 1981, *96*(2), pp. 341–48. [G: U.S.]

Bryant, W. Keith and Gerner, Jennifer L. Television Use by Adults and Children: A Multivariate Analysis. *J. Cons. Res.*, September 1981, *8*(2), pp. 154–61. [G: U.S.]

Carlson, Roger D. Advertising and Sales Relationships for Toothpaste. *Bus. Econ.*, September 1981, *16*(4), pp. 36–39. [G: U.S.]

Caves, Douglas W. Effects on the Residential Load Curve from Time-of-Use Pricing of Electricity: Econometric Inferences from the Wisconsin Experiment for Summer System Peak Days. In *U.S. Dept. of Energy*, 1981, pp. 249–74. [G: U.S.]

Clapier, Patrick and Tabard, Nicole. Transformation de la morphologie sociale des communes et variation des consommations: Un essai pour la région parisienne. (The Change in the Social Morphology of Districts and the Variations of Consumption: An Attempt for the Paris Region. With English summary.) *Consommation*, April–June 1981, *28*(2), pp. 3–40. [G: France]

Claycamp, Henry J. and Liddy, Lucien E. Prediction of New-Product Performance: An Analytical Approach. In *Wind, Y.; Mahajan, V. and Cardozo, R. N., eds.*, 1981, *1969*, pp. 357–69. [G: U.S.]

Cnossen, Sijbren. Specific Issues in Excise Taxation: The Alcohol Problem. In *Roskamp, K. W. and Forte, F., eds.*, 1981, pp. 269–86. [G: OECD]

Crafton, Steven M.; Hoffer, George E. and Reilly, Robert J. Testing the Impact of Recalls on the Demand for Automobiles. *Econ. Inquiry*, October 1981, *19*(4), pp. 694–703. [G: U.S.]

Cronin, Francis J. Household Responsiveness to Unconstrained Housing Allowances. In *Struyk, R. J. and Bendick, M., Jr., eds.*, 1981, pp. 159–76. [G: U.S.]

Cronin, Francis J. Housing Vouchers for the Poor: Consumption Responses to Constrained Programs. In *Struyk, R. J. and Bendick, M., Jr., eds.*, 1981, pp. 129–57. [G: U.S.]

Currim, Imran S.; Weinberg, Charles B. and Wittink, Dick R. Design of Subscription Programs for a Performing Arts Series. *J. Cons. Res.*, June 1981, *8*(1), pp. 67–75. [G: U.S.]

Deaton, Angus. Theoretical and Empirical Approaches to Consumer Demand under Rationing.

In *[Stone, R.]*, 1981, pp. 55–72. [G: U.K.]

Debeer-Laperche, Claudine. L'image de marque des restaurants universitaires à Louvain-la-Neuve. (A Brand Image Study of University Restaurants in Louvain-la-Neuve. With English summary.) *Ann. Sci. Écon. Appl.*, 1981, *37*(1), pp. 29–59. [G: Belgium]

Devlin, Susan J. and Patterson, I. Lester. The Effect of the Demographics of Individual Households on Their Telephone Usage: Toll Usage. In *Brandon, B. B., ed.*, 1981, pp. 303–53. [G: U.S.]

Dewees, Donald N. Energy Policy and Consumer Energy Consumption. In *Nemetz, P. N., ed.*, 1981, pp. 115–41. [G: Canada]

Dikeman, Neil J., Jr. A Summary of the Edmond Electric Utility Demonstration Project and Its Findings. In *U.S. Dept. of Energy*, 1981, pp. 205–11. [G: U.S.]

Doti, James L. and Sharir, Shmuel. Households' Grocery Shopping Behavior in the Short-Run: Theory and Evidence. *Econ. Inquiry*, April 1981, *19*(2), pp. 196–208. [G: U.S.]

Eastwood, David B. and Craven, John A. Food Demand and Savings in a Complete, Extended, Linear Expenditure System. *Amer. J. Agr. Econ.*, August 1981, *63*(3), pp. 544–49. [G: U.S.]

Federenko, N. P. and Rimashevskaya, N. M. The Analysis of Consumption and Demand in the USSR. In *[Stone, R.]*, 1981, pp. 113–28.

Figueroa, Adolfo. Agricultural Price Policy and Rural Income in Peru. *Quart. Rev. Econ. Bus.*, Autumn 1981, *21*(3), pp. 49–64. [G: Peru]

Figueroa, Adolfo. Effects of Changes in Consumption and Trade Patterns on Agricultural Development in Latin America. *Quart. Rev. Econ. Bus.*, Summer 1981, *21*(2), pp. 83–97.
  [G: Latin America]

Fisher, Gordon R.; McAleer, Michael and Whistler, Diana. Interest Rates and Durability in the Linear Expenditure Family. *Can. J. Econ.*, May 1981, *14*(2), pp. 331–41. [G: Australia]

Fortune, J. Neill. Voluntary (Dis) Saving and Expected Inflation. *Southern Econ. J.*, July 1981, *48*(1), pp. 134–43. [G: U.S.]

Foster, Henry S., Jr. and Beattie, Bruce R. On the Specification of Price in Studies of Consumer Demand under Block Price Scheduling. *Land Econ.*, November 1981, *57*(4), pp. 624–29.
  [G: U.S.]

Foster, Henry S., Jr. and Beattie, Bruce R. Urban Residental Demand for Water in the United States: Reply. *Land Econ.*, May 1981, *57*(2), pp. 257–65. [G: U.S.]

Fox, Douglas R. Motor Vehicles, Model Year 1981. *Surv. Curr. Bus.*, October 1981, *61*(10), pp. 22–25. [G: U.S.]

Gapinski, James H. Economics, Demographics, and Attendance at the Symphony. *J. Cult. Econ.*, December 1981, *5*(2), pp. 79–83. [G: U.S.]

García, Jorge García. The Nature of Food Insecurity in Colombia. In *Valdés, A.*, 1981, pp. 123–42.
  [G: Colombia]

Goueli, Ahmed A. Food Security Program in Egypt. In *Valdés, A.*, 1981, pp. 143–57. [G: Egypt]

Green, Paul E. and Carroll, J. Douglas. New Computer Tools for Product Strategy. In *Wind, Y.;*

Mahajan, V. and Cardozo, R. N., eds., 1981, pp. 109–54. [G: U.S.]

Green, Richard D.; Pope, Rulon D. and Phipps, Tim T. Discriminating among Alternative Habit Formation Schemes in Single-Equation Demand Models. *Appl. Econ.*, September 1981, *13*(3), pp. 399–409. [G: U.S.]

Griffin, Adrian H. and Martin, William E. Price Elasticities for Water: A Case of Increasing Block Rates: Comment. *Land Econ.*, May 1981, *57*(2), pp. 266–75. [G: U.S.]

Groff, Robert H. The Effect of the Demographics of Individual Households on Their Telephone Usage: Analysis of Billing Data. In *Brandon, B. B., ed.*, 1981, pp. 275–301. [G: U.S.]

Hanson, Susan and Burnett, K. Patricia. Understanding Complex Travel Behavior: Measurement Issues. In *Stopher, P. R.; Meyburg, A. H. and Brög, W., eds.*, 1981, pp. 207–30.

Hanushek, Eric A. and Quigley, John M. Do Housing Allowances Work? Consumption Aspects. In *Bradbury, K. L. and Downs, A., eds.*, 1981, pp. 185–246. [G: U.S.]

Hartman, Raymond S. and Werth, Alix. Short-Run Residential Demand for Fuels: A Disaggregated Approach. *Land Econ.*, May 1981, *57*(2), pp. 197–212. [G: U.S.]

Havrylyshyn, O. and Munasinghe, Mohan. Interactions among Alternative Modes of Household Energy Production: A Case Study of Colombo, Sri Lanka. *J. Econ. Devel.*, December 1981, *6*(2), pp. 165–83. [G: Sri Lanka]

Hendry, David F. and von Ungern-Sternberg, Thomas. Liquidity and Inflation Effects on Consumers' Expenditure. In *[Stone, R.]*, 1981, pp. 237–60. [G: U.K.]

Hill, Daniel H. The Gasoline Price Responsiveness of Personal Transportation Demand. In *Hill, M. S.; Hill, D. H. and Morgan, J. N., eds.*, 1981, pp. 269–96. [G: U.S.]

Hoch, Irving. Energy and Location. In *Hawley, A. H. and Mazie, S. M., eds.*, 1981, pp. 285–356. [G: U.S.]

House, William J. Redistribution, Consumer Demand and Employment in Kenyan Furniture-Making. *J. Devel. Stud.*, July 1981, *17*(4), pp. 336–56. [G: Kenya]

Hu, Teh-wei. The Demand for Dental Care Services, by Income and Insurance Status. In *Scheffler, R. M., ed.*, 1981, pp. 143–95. [G: U.S.]

Huang, Chung-Liang and Raunikar, Robert. Spline Functions: An Alternative to Estimating Income-Expenditure Relationships for Beef. *Southern J. Agr. Econ.*, July 1981, *13*(1), pp. 105–10.
  [G: U.S.]

Kalwani, Manohar U. and Silk, Alvin J. Structure of Repeat Buying for New Packaged Goods. In *Wind, Y.; Mahajan, V. and Cardozo, R. N., eds.*, 1981, *1980*, pp. 371–85. [G: U.S.]

Kasulis, Jack J.; Huettner, David A. and Dikeman, Neil J. The Feasibility of Changing Electricity Consumption Patterns. *J. Cons. Res.*, December 1981, *8*(3), pp. 279–90. [G: U.S.]

Kau, James B. and Keenan, Donald. On the Theory of Interest Rates, Consumer Durables, and the Demand for Housing. *J. Urban Econ.*, September

1981, *10*(2), pp. 183–200.

Kearl, James R. Inflation and Extraordinary Returns on Owner-Occupied Housing: Some Implications for Capital Allocation: Discussion. In *Tuccillo, J. A. and Villani, K. E., eds.*, 1981, pp. 37–42. **[G: U.S.]**

Kitchin, Paul Duncan. Some Socio-Economic Determinants of Alcohol Consumption: A Research Note. *Int. J. Soc. Econ.*, 1981, *8*(5), pp. 31–35. **[G: U.K.]**

Knaub, Norman L. The Impact of Food Stamps and Cash Welfare on Food Expenditures, 1971–1975. *Policy Anal.*, Spring 1981, *7*(2), pp. 169–82. **[G: U.S.]**

Kobrin, Paul. Fuel Switching, Gasoline Price Controls, and the Leaded-Unleaded Gasoline Price Differential. *J. Environ. Econ. Manage.*, September 1981, *8*(3), pp. 287–302. **[G: U.S.]**

Kolankiewicz, George. Poland, 1980: The Working Class under 'Anomic Socialism.' In *Triska, J. F. and Gati, C., eds.*, 1981, pp. 136–56. **[G: Poland]**

Kompa, Ain. Motivational Analysis of Health-Related Life-Style: Preliminary Results and Propositions for Further Research. In *Molt, W.; Hartmann, H. A. and Stringer, P., eds.*, 1981, pp. 475–92. **[G: W. Germany]**

Lamm, Ray McFall, Jr. and Westcott, Paul C. The Effects of Changing Input Costs on Food Prices. *Amer. J. Agr. Econ.*, May 1981, *63*(2), pp. 187–96. **[G: U.S.]**

Lawrence, Kenneth D. and Lawton, William H. Applications of Diffusion Models: Some Empirical Results. In *Wind, Y.; Mahajan, V. and Cardozo, R. N., eds.*, 1981, pp. 529–41. **[G: U.S.]**

Leamer, Edward E. Is It a Demand Curve, or Is It a Supply Curve? Partial Identification through Inequality Constraints. *Rev. Econ. Statist.*, August 1981, *63*(3), pp. 319–27. **[G: U.S.]**

Levin, Irwin P. Laboratory Simulation of Transportation Mode Choice: Methods, Models, and Validity Tests. In *Molt, W.; Hartmann, H. A. and Stringer, P., eds.*, 1981, pp. 357–66.

Lewit, Eugene M.; Coate, Douglas and Grossman, Michael. The Effects of Government Regulation on Teenage Smoking. *J. Law Econ.*, December 1981, *24*(3), pp. 545–69. **[G: U.S.]**

Lillard, Lee A. and Acton, Jan Paul. Seasonal Electricity Demand and Pricing Analysis with a Variable Response Model. *Bell J. Econ. (See Rand J. Econ. after 4/85)*, Spring 1981, *12*(1), pp. 71–92. **[G: U.S.]**

Maddox, R. Neil. Two-factor Theory and Consumer Satisfaction: Replication and Extension. *J. Cons. Res.*, June 1981, *8*(1), pp. 97–102. **[G: U.S.]**

Main, Brian G. M. An Engel Curve for the Direct and Indirect Consumption of Oil. *Rev. Econ. Statist.*, February 1981, *63*(1), pp. 132–36. **[G: U.S.]**

Manning, Willard G., et al. A Two-Part Model of the Demand for Medical Care: Preliminary Results from the Health Insurance Study. In *van der Gaag, J. and Perlman, M., eds.*, 1981, pp. 103–23. **[G: U.S.]**

Maris, Brian A. Indirect Evidence on the Efficacy of Selective Credit Controls: The Case of Consumer Credit. *J. Money, Credit, Banking*, August 1981, *13*(3), pp. 388–90. **[G: U.S.]**

Mark, John; Brown, Frank and Pierson, B. J. Consumer Demand Theory, Goods and Characteristics: Breathing Empirical Content into the Lancastrian Approach. *Managerial Dec. Econ.*, March 1981, *2*(1), pp. 32–39. **[G: U.K.]**

Mathot, Fons. L'utilisation du crédit lors de l'achat d'une voiture. (The Use of Credit in the Purchase of an Automobile. With English summary.) *Ann. INSEE*, October–December 1981, (44), pp. 121–48. **[G: Netherlands]**

Mayo, Stephen K. Theory and Estimation in the Economics of Housing Demand. *J. Urban Econ.*, July 1981, *10*(1), pp. 95–116. **[G: U.S.]**

McAleer, Michael, et al. Estimation of the Consumption Function: A Systems Approach to Employment Effects on the Purchase of Durables. In *[Valavanis, S.]*, 1981, pp. 169–97. **[G: Australia]**

McCarthy, F. Desmond. Quality Effects in Consumer Behaviour. *Pakistan Devel. Rev.*, Summer 1981, *20*(2), pp. 133–50. **[G: Pakistan]**

McCrohan, Kevin F. and Finkelman, Jay M. Social Character and the New Automobile Industry. *Calif. Manage. Rev.*, Fall 1981, *24*(1), pp. 58–68. **[G: U.S.]**

McGill, Robert. The Effect of the Demographics of Individual Households on Their Telephone Usage: The Data Base Design and Implementation. In *Brandon, B. B., ed.*, 1981, pp. 57–74. **[G: U.S.]**

McMillan, Melville L. Estimates of Households' Preferences for Environmental Quality and Other Housing Characteristics from a System of Demand Equations. In *Strøm, S., ed.*, 1981, *1979*, pp. 33–46. **[G: Canada]**

Miedema, Allen K. North Carolina Rate Demonstration Project—Preliminary Results. In *U.S. Dept. of Energy*, 1981, pp. 228–48. **[G: U.S.]**

Miedema, Allen K. Overview of DOE Analyses of Residential TOU Data. In *U.S. Dept. of Energy*, 1981, pp. 193–204. **[G: U.S.]**

Miners, Laurence A. The Family's Demand for Health: Evidence from a Rural Community. In *Scheffler, R. M., ed.*, 1981, pp. 85–142. **[G: U.S.]**

Mitchell, Bridger M. The Effect of Time-of-Day Rates in the Los Angeles Electricity Rate Study. In *U.S. Dept. of Energy*, 1981, pp. 212–27. **[G: U.S.]**

Mount, Randall I. and Williams, Harold R. Energy Conservation, Motor Gasoline Demand and the OECD Countries. *Rev. Bus. Econ. Res.*, Spring 1981, *16*(3), pp. 48–57. **[G: OECD]**

Muellbauer, John. Testing Neoclassical Models of the Demand for Consumer Durables. In *[Stone, R.]*, 1981, pp. 213–35. **[G: U.K.]**

Murty, K. N. Analysis of Food Consumption in the Federal Republic of Germany. *Empirical Econ.*, 1981, *6*(2), pp. 75–86. **[G: W. Germany]**

Nelson, Phillip J. Consumer Information and Advertising. In *Galatin, M. and Leiter, R. D., eds.*, 1981, pp. 42–77. **[G: U.S.]**

Noam, Eli M. Income Sensitivity of Price Elasticities: Effects on the Demand for Public Goods.

Public Finance Quart., January 1981, 9(1), pp. 23–34. [G: Switzerland]

Nufeld, John L. and Watts, James M. Inverted Block or Lifeline Rates and Micro-Efficiency in the Consumption of Electricity. *Energy Econ.*, April 1981, 3(2), pp. 113–21. [G: U.S.]

Odland, John. A Household Production Approach to Destination Choice. *Econ. Geogr.*, July 1981, 57(3), pp. 257–69.

Paaswell, Robert E. Travel and Activity Needs of the Mobility Limited. In *Stopher, P. R.; Meyburg, A. H. and Brög, W., eds.*, 1981, pp. 425–54. [G: U.S.]

Parfitt, J. H. and Collins, B. J. K. Use of Consumer Panels for Brand-Share Prediction. In *Wind, Y.; Mahajan, V. and Cardozo, R. N., eds.*, 1981, 1968, pp. 323–56. [G: U.K.]

Park, C. Whan and Lessig, V. Parker. Familiarity and Its Impact on Consumer Decision Biases and Heuristics. *J. Cons. Res.*, September 1981, 8(2), pp. 223–30.

Pelaez, Rolando F. The Price Elasticity for Gasoline Revisited [Dynamic Demand Analyses for Gasoline and Residential Electricity]. *Energy J.*, October 1981, 2(4), pp. 85–89. [G: U.S.]

Pfaff, Martin and Bäuerle, Eberhard U. The Utilization of Public Health Services by Socio-Economic Groups: The Case of the Federal Republic of Germany. In *Molt, W.; Hartmann, H. A. and Stringer, P., eds.*, 1981, pp. 415–32.
[G: W. Germany]

Pitts, Robert E.; Willenborg, John F. and Sherrell, Daniel L. Consumer Adaptation to Gasoline Price Increases. *J. Cons. Res.*, December 1981, 8(3), pp. 322–30. [G: U.S.]

Prasad, C. R. and Bhat, Kisan. Prospects for Ethanol as Automobile Fuel in India. In *Chatterji, M., ed.*, 1981, pp. 89–102. [G: India]

Provenzano, George and Walasek, Richard A. Regional Variation in Electric Energy: Demand Responsiveness in the Residential Sector in Illinois. *Reg. Sci. Persp.*, 1981, 11(2), pp. 56–69.
[G: U.S.]

Pudney, Stephen E. An Empirical Method of Approximating the Separable Structure of Consumer Preferences. *Rev. Econ. Stud.*, October 1981, 48(4), pp. 561–77. [G: U.K.]

Rao, V. V. Bhanoji. Measurement of Deprivation and Poverty Based on the Proportion Spent on Food: An Exploratory Exercise. *World Devel.*, April 1981, 9(4), pp. 337–53. [G: India]

Rao, Vithala R. and Sabavala, Darius Jal. Inference in Hierarchical Choice Processes from Panel Data. *J. Cons. Res.*, June 1981, 8(1), pp. 85–96.

Reza, Ali M. The Impact of President Reagan's Sudden Decontrol of Petroleum Prices on Petroleum Consumption. *Energy J.*, July 1981, 2(3), pp. 129–33. [G: U.S.]

Richardson, James F. Vocal Recitials in Smaller Cities: Changes in Supply, Demand and Content since the 1920's. *J. Cult. Econ.*, June 1981, 5(1), pp. 21–35. [G: U.S.]

Ritchie, J. R. Brent; McDougall, Gordon H. G. and Claxton, John D. Complexities of Household Energy Consumption and Conservation. *J. Cons.*

Res., December 1981, 8(3), pp. 233–42.
[G: Canada]

Rosenhek, Walter. Segmenten in de markt voor personenwagens. (Segments in the Market for Family Cars. With English summary.) *Cah. Écon. Bruxelles*, 1st Trimestre 1981, (89), pp. 123–39.
[G: Belgium]

Sands, Saul and Warwick, Kenneth. What Product Benefits to Offer to Whom: An Application of Conjoint Segmentation. *Calif. Manage. Rev.*, Fall 1981, 24(1), pp. 69–74.

Schulze, William D.; d'Arge, Ralph C. and Brookshire, David S. Valuing Environmental Commodities: Some Recent Experiments. *Land Econ.*, May 1981, 57(2), pp. 151–72. [G: U.S.]

Shaked, Avner and Sutton, John. Heterogeneous Consumers and Product Differentiation in a Market for Professional Services. *Europ. Econ. Rev.*, February 1981, 15(2), pp. 159–77.

Shihab-Eldin, Adnan and Al-Qudsi, Sulayman S. Energy Needs of the Less Developed Countries (LDCs). In *Amman, F. and Wilson, R., eds.*, 1981, pp. 349–93. [G: LDCs]

Sigmon, Brent, et al. An Evaluation of Natural Gas Consumption Data. *Rev. Public Data Use (See J. Econ. Soc. Meas. after 4/85)*, November 1981, 9(3), pp. 189–97. [G: U.S.]

Sinden, J. A. and O'Hanlon, P. W. A Market Simulation Game to Value Unpriced Goods and Services. *Reg. Sci. Urban Econ.*, February 1981, 11(1), pp. 101–19. [G: Australia]

Skopal, Zdeněk. Private Car Ownership in Czechoslovakia. *Czech. Econ. Digest.*, September 1981, (6), pp. 85–99. [G: Czechoslovakia]

Small, Kenneth A. A Comment on Gasoline Prices and Urban Structure [Urban Structure, Gas Prices, and the Demand for Transportation]. *J. Urban Econ.*, November 1981, 10(3), pp. 311–22.

Smith, Courtland L. Satisfaction Bonus from Salmon Fishing: Implications for Economic Evaluation. *Land Econ.*, May 1981, 57(2), pp. 181–96.
[G: U.S.]

Stoddart, Greg L. and Barer, Morris L. Analyses of Demand and Utilization through Episodes of Medical Service. In *van der Gaag, J. and Perlman, M., eds.*, 1981, pp. 149–70. [G: Canada]

Supple, B. E. Income and Demand 1860–1914. In *Floud, R. and McCloskey, D., eds., Vol. 2*, 1981, pp. 121–43. [G: U.K.]

Talvitie, Antti P. Inaccurate or Incomplete Data as a Source of Uncertainty in Econometric or Attitudinal Models of Travel Behavior. In *Stopher, P. R.; Meyburg, A. H. and Brög, W., eds.*, 1981, pp. 559–75. [G: U.S.]

Theil, Henri. The Quality of Consumption in the U.S. and Abroad. *Sloan Manage. Rev.*, Fall 1981, 23(1), pp. 31–36. [G: U.S.]

Theil, Henri and Laitinen, Kenneth. The Independence Transformation: A Review and Some Further Explorations. In *[Stone, R.]*, 1981, pp. 73–112. [G: U.S.]

Tilley, Daniel S. and Lee, Jonq-Ying. Import and Retail Demand for Orange Juice in Canada. *Can. J. Agr. Econ.*, July 1981, 29(2), pp. 171–86.
[G: Canada]

Timmer, C. Peter. Is There "Curvature" in the Slutsky Matrix? *Rev. Econ. Statist.*, August 1981, *63*(3), pp. 395–402. [G: U.S.]

Tsolakis, Dimitris and Riethmuller, Paul. Some Characteristics of Alcohol Consumption in Australia. *Quart. Rev. Rural Econ.*, August 1981, *3*(3), pp. 240–45.

Tsui, Amy Ong, et al. Community Availability of Contraceptives and Family Limitation. *Demography*, November 1981, *18*(4), pp. 615–25. [G: Bangladesh; Korea; Mexico]

Tsurumi, Yoshi. Consumer Spending in Japan. In *Richardson, B. M. and Ueda, T., eds.*, 1981, pp. 134–38. [G: Japan]

Val'tukh, K. K. Optimization and Balance of National Economy Models. In *Janssen, J. M. L.; Pau, L. F. and Straszak, A. J., eds.*, 1981, pp. 21–30. [G: W. Germany]

Val'tukh, K. K. and Ryzhenkov, A. V. An Analysis of Personal Consumption Structure in Austria Using a Theoretical Utility Function. *Empirical Econ.*, 1981, *6*(1), pp. 11–65. [G: Austria]

van de Ven, Wynand P. M. M. and van Praag, Bernard M. S. Risk Aversion and Deductibles in Private Health Insurance: Application of an Adjusted Tobit Model to Family Health Care Expenditures. In *van der Gaag, J. and Perlman, M., eds.*, 1981, pp. 125–48. [G: Netherlands]

Verhallen, Theo M. M. and Raaij, W. Fred. Household Behavior and the Use of Natural Gas for Home Heating. *J. Cons. Res.*, December 1981, *8*(3), pp. 253–57. [G: U.S.]

Vertessen, J. Influence of Butter and Margarine Prices on the Demand for Butter in Belgium. *Europ. Rev. Agr. Econ.*, 1981, *8*(1), pp. 99–109. [G: Belgium]

Ward, A. V. and Pickering, J. F. Preliminary Testing of the Explanatory Power of the EEC Consumer Attitudes Survey in the United Kingdom. *Appl. Econ.*, March 1981, *13*(1), pp. 19–34. [G: U.K.]

Warriner, G. Keith. Electricity Consumption by the Elderly: Policy Implications. *J. Cons. Res.*, December 1981, *8*(3), pp. 258–64. [G: U.S.]

Weber, Hans Peter. Uncertainty in Application: A German Case Study. In *Stopher, P. R.; Meyburg, A. H. and Brög, W., eds.*, 1981, pp. 587–98. [G: W. Germany]

Wermuth, Manfred J. Effects of Survey Methods and Measurement Techniques on the Accuracy of Household Travel-Behavior Surveys. In *Stopher, P. R.; Meyburg, A. H. and Brög, W., eds.*, 1981, pp. 523–41. [G: W. Germany]

Williams, Wm. H. and Goodman, Michael L. The Effect of the Demographics of Individual Households on Their Telephone Usage: The Development of the Customer Sample. In *Brandon, B. B., ed.*, 1981, pp. 19–28. [G: U.S.]

Wills, John. Residential Demand for Electricity. *Energy Econ.*, October 1981, *3*(4), pp. 249–55. [G: U.S.]

Witt, Stephen F. and Pass, Christopher L. The Effects of Health Warnings and Advertising on the Demand for Cigarettes. *Scot. J. Polit. Econ.*, February 1981, *28*(1), pp. 86–91. [G: U.K.]

9213 Consumer Protection

Armstrong, Alan G. Consumer Safety and the Regulation of Industry. *Managerial Dec. Econ.*, June 1981, *2*(2), pp. 67–73.

Arnould, Richard J. and Grabowski, Henry. Auto Safety Regulation: An Analysis of Market Failure. *Bell J. Econ. (See Rand J. Econ. after 4/85)*, Spring 1981, *12*(1), pp. 27–48. [G: U.S.]

Balachandran, K. R.; Maschmeyer, Richard A. and Livingstone, J. Leslie. Product Warranty Period: A Markovian Approach to Estimation and Analysis of Repair and Replacement Costs. *Accounting Rev.*, January 1981, *56*(1), pp. 115–24.

Beales, Howard; Craswell, Richard and Salop, Steven C. Information Remedies for Consumer Protection. *Amer. Econ. Rev.*, May 1981, *71*(2), pp. 410–13.

Beales, Howard; Craswell, Richard and Salop, Steven C. The Efficient Regulation of Consumer Information. *J. Law Econ.*, December 1981, *24*(3), pp. 491–539. [G: U.S.]

Beales, Howard, et al. Consumer Search and Public Policy. *J. Cons. Res.*, June 1981, *8*(1), pp. 11–22. [G: U.S.]

Blomquist, Glenn C. and Peltzman, Sam. Passive Restraints: An Economist's View. In *Crandall, R. W. and Lave, L. B., eds.*, 1981, pp. 37–52. [G: U.S.]

Brandt, William K. and Shay, Robert P. Consumers' Perceptions of Discriminatory Treatment and Credit Availability, and Access to Consumer Credit Markets. In *Fed. Res. Bank of Boston and National Sci. Foundation*, 1981, pp. 1–19. [G: U.S.]

Brandt, William K. and Shay, Robert P. Consumers' Perceptions of Discriminatory Treatment and Credit Availability, and Access to Consumer Credit Markets: Rebuttal. In *Fed. Res. Bank of Boston and National Sci. Foundation*, 1981, pp. 23. [G: U.S.]

Brickman, Ronald and Jasanoff, Sheila. Concepts of Risk and Safety in Toxic-Substances Regulation: A Comparison of France and the United States. In *Mann, D. E., ed.*, 1981, pp. 203–13. [G: France; U.S.]

Carlton, Dennis W. Product Quality and Value in the New Home Market: Implications for Consumer Protection Regulation: Comment. *J. Law Econ.*, December 1981, *24*(3), pp. 399–400. [G: U.S.]

Chesshire, John. Public Enterprises and Consumers. *Ann. Pub. Co-op. Econ.*, January–June 1981, *52*(1/2), pp. 157–62.

Clarkson, Kenneth W. The Federal Trade Commission since 1970: Economic Regulation and Bureaucratic Behavior: Executive Constraints. In *Clarkson, K. W. and Muris, T. J., eds.*, 1981, pp. 50–58. [G: U.S.]

Clarkson, Kenneth W. The Federal Trade Commission since 1970: Economic Regulation and Bureaucratic Behavior: Legislative Constraints. In *Clarkson, K. W. and Muris, T. J., eds.*, 1981, pp. 18–34. [G: U.S.]

Clarkson, Kenneth W. and Muris, Timothy J. The Federal Trade Commission since 1970: Economic

Regulation and Bureaucratic Behavior: Commission Performance, Incentives, and Behavior. In *Clarkson, K. W. and Muris, T. J.*, eds., 1981, pp. 280–306. [G: U.S.]

Crandall, Robert W. and Lave, Lester B. The Scientific Basis of Health and Safety Regulation: Introduction and Summary. In *Crandall, R. W. and Lave, L. B.*, eds., 1981, pp. 1–17. [G: U.S.]

Crosby, Lawrence A. and Taylor, James R. Effects of Consumer Information and Education on Cognition and Choice. *J. Cons. Res.*, June 1981, *8*(1), pp. 43–56. [G: U.S.]

De Alessi, Louis. Regulating Postpurchase Relations: Mobile Homes. In *Clarkson, K. W. and Muris, T. J.*, eds., 1981, pp. 204–21. [G: U.S.]

Durkin, Thomas A. Discussion [Effects of Creditor Remedies and Rate Restrictions] [Measuring the Impact of Credit Regulation on Consumers]. In *Fed. Res. Bank of Boston and National Sci. Foundation*, 1981, pp. 63–67. [G: U.S.]

Eads, George C. The Benefits of Better Benefits Estimation. In *Ferguson, A. R. and LeVeen, E. P.*, eds., 1981, pp. 43–52. [G: U.S.]

Ebaugh, Dwight D. The Users and Providers of Consumer Financial Services: A Legal Framework. In *Heggestad, A. A.*, ed., 1981, pp. 62–91. [G: U.S.]

Eekhoff, Johann. Zur Kontroverse um die ökonomischen Auswirkungen des Zweiten Wohnraumkündigungsschutzgesetzes. (The Economic Effects of Tenants' Protection against Arbitrary Notice. With English summary.) *Z. ges. Staatswiss.*, March 1981, *137*(1), pp. 62–77. [G: W. Germany]

Ellis, Dorsey D., Jr. Legislative Powers: FTC Rule Making. In *Clarkson, K. W. and Muris, T. J.*, eds., 1981, pp. 161–83. [G: U.S.]

Ferris, Benjamin G., Jr. Sulfur Dioxide: A Scientist's View. In *Crandall, R. W. and Lave, L. B.*, eds., 1981, pp. 253–66. [G: U.S.]

Fisher, Anthony C.; Krupnick, Alan J. and Ferguson, Allen R. Setting Regulatory Priorities. In *Ferguson, A. R.*, ed., 1981, pp. 145–65.

Goldstein, G. S. Product Quality and Value in the New Home Market: Implications for Consumer Protection Regulation: Comment. *J. Law Econ.*, December 1981, *24*(3), pp. 401–02. [G: U.S.]

Grady, Mark F. Regulating Information: Advertising Overview. In *Clarkson, K. W. and Muris, T. J.*, eds., 1981, pp. 222–45. [G: U.S.]

Greenwald, Carol S. Consumers' Perceptions of Discriminatory Treatment and Credit Availability, and Access to Consumer Credit Markets: Discussion. In *Fed. Res. Bank of Boston and National Sci. Foundation*, 1981, pp. 20–22. [G: U.S.]

Grobstein, Clifford. Saccharin: A Scientist's View. In *Crandall, R. W. and Lave, L. B.*, eds., 1981, pp. 117–29. [G: U.S.]

Grossman, Sanford J. The Informational Role of Warranties and Private Disclosure about Product Quality. *J. Law Econ.*, December 1981, *24*(3), pp. 461–83.

Hakala, Marcia A. The Consumer Advisory Council: The First Five Years. *Fed. Res. Bull.*, July 1981, *67*(7), pp. 529–34. [G: U.S.]

Heggestad, Arnold A. Regulation of Consumer Fi-

nancial Services: Introduction. In *Heggestad, A. A.*, ed., 1981, pp. 1–16. [G: U.S.]

Hirsch, Werner Z. Habitability Laws and the Welfare of Indigent Tenants. *Rev. Econ. Statist.*, May 1981, *63*(2), pp. 263–74. [G: U.S.]

Hoel, David G. and Crump, Kenny S. Waterborne Carcinogens: A Scientist's View. In *Crandall, R. W. and Lave, L. B.*, eds., 1981, pp. 173–95. [G: U.S.]

Holton, Richard H. Public Regulation of Consumer Information: The Life Insurance Industry Case. In *[Grether, E. T.]*, 1981, pp. 143–54.

Huelke, Donald F. and O'Day, James. Passive Restraints: A Scientist's View. In *Crandall, R. W. and Lave, L. B.*, eds., 1981, pp. 21–35. [G: U.S.]

Ippolito, Pauline M. Information and the Life Cycle Consumption of Hazardous Goods. *Econ. Inquiry*, October 1981, *19*(4), pp. 529–58.

Jolibert, Alain J. P. and Baumgartner, Gary. Toward a Definition of the Consumerist Segment in France. *J. Cons. Res.*, June 1981, *8*(1), pp. 114–17. [G: France]

Jones, Mary Gardiner. The New Telecommunication Technologies: Answer to Consumer Needs? In *[Grether, E. T.]*, 1981, pp. 174–89.

Kimm, Victor J.; Kuzmack, Arnold M. and Schnare, David W. Waterborne Carcinogens: A Regulator's View. In *Crandall, R. W. and Lave, L. B.*, eds., 1981, pp. 229–49. [G: U.S.]

Kleindorfer, Paul R. and Kunreuther, Howard. Descriptive and Prescriptive Aspects of Health and Safety Regulation. In *Ferguson, A. R. and LeVeen, E. P.*, eds., 1981, pp. 25–42.

Lave, Lester B. Sulfur Dioxide: An Economist's View. In *Crandall, R. W. and Lave, L. B.*, eds., 1981, pp. 267–78. [G: U.S.]

Leland, Hayne E. The Informational Role of Warranties and Private Disclosure about Product Quality: Comment. *J. Law Econ.*, December 1981, *24*(3), pp. 485–89.

Magat, Wesley A. and Estomin, Steven. The Behavior of Regulatory Agencies. In *Ferguson, A. R.*, ed., 1981, pp. 95–116. [G: U.S.]

Mantell, Edmund H. Inefficacy of the Truth-in-Lending Act. *Bus. Econ.*, September 1981, *16*(4), pp. 60–61. [G: U.S.]

Massam, A. D. W. Product Liability: The Specialty Problem of Medicines. *Managerial Dec. Econ.*, September 1981, *2*(3), pp. 160–68. [G: EEC]

McLendon, Teresa Gaines. An Economic Approach to Deception in Advertising: Definition and Remedies. *Amer. Econ.*, Fall 1981, *25*(2), pp. 49–54. [G: U.S.]

McNiel, Douglas W. Economic Welfare and Food Safety Regulation: The Case of Mechanically Deboned Meat: Reply. *Amer. J. Agr. Econ.*, November 1981, *63*(4), pp. 742–45. G: U.S.]

Merrill, Richard A. Saccharin: A Regulator's View. In *Crandall, R. W. and Lave, L. B.*, eds., 1981, pp. 153–70. [G: U.S.]

Middleton, John T. Sulfur Dioxide: A Regulator's View. In *Crandall, R. W. and Lave, L. B.*, eds., 1981, pp. 279–88. [G: U.S.]

Moulton, Kirby S. Market Reporting and its Public Policy Implications. In *[Grether, E. T.]*, 1981,

pp. 190–200.

Muris, Timothy J. The Federal Trade Commission since 1970: Economic Regulation and Bureaucratic Behavior: Statutory Powers. In *Clarkson, K. W. and Muris, T. J., eds.*, 1981, pp. 13–17. [G: U.S.]

Muris, Timothy J. The Federal Trade Commission since 1970: Economic Regulation and Bureaucratic Behavior: What Can be Done? In *Clarkson, K. W. and Muris, T. J., eds.*, 1981, pp. 307–15. [G: U.S.]

Muris, Timothy J. The Federal Trade Commission since 1970: Economic Regulation and Bureaucratic Behavior: Judicial Constraints. In *Clarkson, K. W. and Muris, T. J., eds.*, 1981, pp. 35–49. [G: U.S.]

Muris, Timothy J. and Clarkson, Kenneth W. The Federal Trade Commission since 1970: Economic Regulation and Bureaucratic Behavior: Introduction. In *Clarkson, K. W. and Muris, T. J., eds.*, 1981, pp. 1–7. [G: U.S.]

Nash, Carl E. Passive Restraints: A Regulator's View. In *Crandall, R. W. and Lave, L. B., eds.*, 1981, pp. 53–67. [G: U.S.]

Norman, Neville R. Policies towards Prices—The Influence of Regulation. In *Hancock, K., ed.*, 1981, pp. 349–69. [G: Australia]

Oster, Sharon. Product Regulations: A Measure of the Benefits. *J. Ind. Econ.*, June 1981, 29(4), pp. 395–411. [G: U.S.]

Page, Talbot; Harris, Robert A. and Bruser, Judith. Waterborne Carcinogens: An Economist's View. In *Crandall, R. W. and Lave, L. B., eds.*, 1981, pp. 197–228. [G: U.S.]

Peterson, Richard L. Effects of Creditor Remedies and Rate Restrictions. In *Fed. Res. Bank of Boston and National Sci. Foundation*, 1981, pp. 24–43. [G: U.S.]

Peterson, Richard L. Rewriting Consumer Contracts: Creditors' Remedies. In *Clarkson, K. W. and Muris, T. J., eds.*, 1981, pp. 184–203. [G: U.S.]

Pinney, John M. Warning Citizens about the Hazards of Smoking: Where we are in 1981. In *Finger, W. R., ed.*, 1981, pp. 241–45. [G: U.S.]

Porter, Richard C. Further Analysis of the Impact of Mandatory Bottle Deposit Legislation: Comment. *Soc. Sci. Quart.*, June 1981, 62(2), pp. 367–73. [G: U.S.]

Priest, George L. A Theory of the Consumer Product Warranty. *Yale Law J.*, May 1981, 90(6), pp. 1297–52.

Priest, George L. Special Statutes: The Structure and Operation of the Magnuson–Moss Warranty Act. In *Clarkson, K. W. and Muris, T. J., eds.*, 1981, pp. 246–75. [G: U.S.]

Russo, J. Edward; Metcalf, Barbara L. and Stephens, Debra. Identifying Misleading Advertising. *J. Cons. Res.*, September 1981, 8(2), pp. 119–31.

Santoni, Gary J. and Van Cott, T. Norman. Bottle Deposit Legislation: A Reply [The Impact of Mandatory Bottle Deposit Legislation]. *Soc. Sci. Quart.*, June 1981, 62(2), pp. 374–76. [G: U.S.]

Schmalensee, Richard. The Efficient Regulation of Consumer Information: Comment. *J. Law Econ.*, December 1981, 24(3), pp. 541–44. [G: U.S.]

Schneider, Lynne; Klein, Benjamin and Murphy, Kevin M. Governmental Regulation of Cigarette Health Information. *J. Law Econ.*, December 1981, 24(3), pp. 575–612. [G: U.S.]

Scholz, Franz Josef. Verbraucherschutz in der Marktwirtschaft Dargestellt am Beispiel des Konsumentenkredits. (Consumer Protection in the Market Economy. With English summary.) In *[von Haberler, G.]*, 1981, pp. 185–98.

Shay, Robert P. and Brandt, William K. Public Regulation of Financial Services: The Truth in Lending Act. In *Heggestad, A. A., ed.*, 1981, pp. 168–207. [G: U.S.]

Shay, Robert P.; Brandt, William K. and Sexton, Donald E., Jr. Public Regulation of Financial Services: The Equal Credit Opportunity Act. In *Heggestad, A. A., ed.*, 1981, pp. 208–39. [G: U.S.]

Simon, Marilyn J. Imperfect Information, Costly Litigation, and Product Quality. *Bell J. Econ. (See Rand J. Econ. after 4/85)*, Spring 1981, 12(1), pp. 171–84.

Slovic, Paul; Fischhoff, Baruch and Lichtenstein, Sarah. Rating the Risks. In *Haimes, Y. Y., ed.*, 1981, 1980, pp. 193–217. [G: U.S.]

Stuart, Charles E. Consumer Protection in Markets with Informationally Weak Buyers. *Bell J. Econ. (See Rand J. Econ. after 4/85)*, Autumn 1981, 12(2), pp. 562–73.

Thomson, Judith Jarvis. Some Ruminations on Rights. In *Paul, J., ed.*, 1981, 1977, pp. 130–47.

Thorelli, Hans B. and Thorelli, Sarah V. Consumer Information Systems of the Future. In *[Grether, E. T.]*, 1981, pp. 155–73.

Tinsley, Dillard B. Business Organizations in the Sustainable Society. In *Coomer, J. C., ed.*, 1981, pp. 164–82.

Vaupel, James W. On the Benefits of Health and Safety Regulation. In *Ferguson, A. R. and Leveen, E. P., eds.*, 1981, pp. 1–22. [G: U.S.]

Vaupel, James W. Priorities for Research on the Benefits of Health, Safety, and Environmental Regulation. In *Ferguson, A. R., ed.*, 1981, pp. 167–83. [G: U.S.]

Vogel, David. The "New" Social Regulation in Historical and Comparative Perspective. In *McCraw, T. K., ed.*, 1981, pp. 155–85. [G: U.S.]

Weicher, John C. Product Quality and Value in the New Home Market: Implications for Consumer Protection Regulation. *J. Law Econ.*, December 1981, 24(3), pp. 365–97. [G: U.S.]

Williamson, Oliver E. Saccharin: An Economist's View. In *Crandall, R. W. and Lave, L. B., eds.*, 1981, pp. 131–51. [G: U.S.]

930 Urban Economics

9300 General

Abler, Ronald and Falk, Thomas. Public Information Services and the Changing Role of Distance in Human Affairs. *Econ. Geogr.*, January 1981, 57(1), pp. 10–22.

Altmann, James L. Analysis and Comparison of the Mills–Muth Urban Residential Land-Use Simulation Models. *J. Urban Econ.*, May 1981, 9(3),

pp. 365–80. [G: U.S.]

Brueckner, Jan K. and von Rabenau, Burkhard. Dynamics of Land-Use for a Closed City. *Reg. Sci. Urban Econ.*, February 1981, *11*(1), pp. 1–17.

Buck, Andrew J. and Hakim, Simon. Appropriate Roles for Statistical Decision Theory and Hypothesis Testing in Model Selection: An Exposition. *Reg. Sci. Urban Econ.*, February 1981, *11*(1), pp. 135–47. [G: U.S.]

Chorney, Harold. Amnesia, Integration and repression: The Roots of Canadian Urban Political Culture. In *Dear, M. and Scott, A. J., eds.*, 1981, pp. 536–63. [G: Canada]

Cohen, Robert B. The New International Division of Labor, Multinational Corporations and Urban Hierarchy. In *Dear, M. and Scott, A. J., eds.*, 1981, pp. 287–315. [G: U.S.]

Cox, Kevin R. Capitalism and Conflict Around the Communal Living Space. In *Dear, M. and Scott, A. J., eds.*, 1981, pp. 432–55.

Dear, Michael. Social and Spatial Reproduction of the Mentally Ill. In *Dear, M. and Scott, A. J., eds.*, 1981, pp. 481–97.

Dear, Michael and Scott, Allen J. Towards a Framework for Analysis. In *Dear, M. and Scott, A. J., eds.*, 1981, pp. 3–16.

Edel, Matthew. Capitalism, Accumulation and the Explanation of Urban Phenomena. In *Dear, M. and Scott, A. J., eds.*, 1981, pp. 19–44.

Frankena, Mark W. and Scheffman, David T. A Theory of Development Controls in a 'Small' City. *J. Public Econ.*, April 1981, *15*(2), pp. 203–34.

Furstenberg, Frank F., Jr.; Modell, John and Hershberg, Theodore. The Origins of the Female-Headed Black Family: The Impact of the Urban Experience. In *Hershberg, T., ed.*, 1981, *1975*, pp. 435–54. [G: U.S.]

Goldfield, David R. An Ecology of Family Decisions: Suburbanization, Schooling, and Fertility in Philadelphia, 1880–1920: Comment. In *Stave, B. M., ed.*, 1981, pp. 67–74.

Harloe, Michael. Notes on Comparative Urban Research. In *Dear, M. and Scott, A. J., eds.*, 1981, pp. 179–95.

Harvey, David. The Urban Process under Capitalism: A Framework for Analysis. In *Dear, M. and Scott, A. J., eds.*, 1981, pp. 91–121.

Hershberg, Theodore. Free Blacks in Antebellum Philadelphia: A Study of Ex-Slaves, Freeborn, and Socioeconomic Decline. In *Hershberg, T., ed.*, 1981, *1971*, pp. 368–91. [G: U.S.]

Hershberg, Theodore. The New Urban History: Toward an Interdisciplinary History of the City. In *Hershberg, T., ed.*, 1981, *1978*, pp. 3–35.

Hirsch, Joachim. The Apparatus of the State, the Reproduction of Capital and Urban Conflicts. In *Dear, M. and Scott, A. J., eds.*, 1981, pp. 593–607.

Ingram, Gregory K. and Carroll, Alan. Symposium on Urbanization and Development: The Spatial Structure of Latin American Cities. *J. Urban Econ.*, March 1981, *9*(2), pp. 257–73.
[G: Latin America; U.S.; Canada]

Lampard, Eric E. Modern Industrial Cities: History, Policy, and Survival: Comment. In *Stave, B. M.,*

ed., 1981, pp. 267–82. [G: U.S.]

Laurie, Bruce; Alter, George and Hershberg, Theodore. Immigrants and Industry: The Philadelphia Experience, 1850–1880. In *Hershberg, T., ed.*, 1981, *1975*, pp. 93–119. [G: U.S.]

Lee, Kyu Sik. Symposium on Urbanization and Development: Intra–urban Location of Manufacturing Employment in Colombia. *J. Urban Econ.*, March 1981, *9*(2), pp. 222–41. [G: Colombia; U.S.]

Madden, Janice Fanning. Why Women Work Closer to Home. *Urban Stud.*, June 1981, *18*(2), pp. 181–94. [G: U.S.]

Piccinato, Giorgio. Modern Industrial Cities: History, Policy, and Survival: Comment. In *Stave, B. M., ed.*, 1981, pp. 282–85.

Pines, David and Sadka, Efraim. Optimum, Second-Best, and Market Allocations of Resources within an Urban Area. *J. Urban Econ.*, March 1981, *9*(2), pp. 173–89.

Rodwin, Lloyd. Great and Terrible Cities. In *Rodwin, L.*, 1981, pp. 8–18.

Rodwin, Lloyd. The Profession of City Planning. In *Rodwin, L.*, 1981, pp. 256–71.

Rodwin, Lloyd. Training City Planners in Third World Countries. In *Rodwin, L.*, 1981, pp. 210–26.

Sanchez-de-Carmona, Luis. Environmental and Urban Policies for the Human Habitat. In *Lozoya, J. A. and Birgin, H., eds.*, 1981, pp. 160–72.
[G: LDCs]

Sharpless, John B. The Economy of Cities: Comment. In *Stave, B. M., ed.*, 1981, pp. 258–62.

Szelenyi, Ivan. The Relative Autonomy of the State or State Mode of Production? In *Dear, M. and Scott, A. J., eds.*, 1981, pp. 565–91.

Tilly, Charles. Modern Industrial Cities: History, Policy, and Survival: Comment. In *Stave, B. M., ed.*, 1981, pp. 285–90.

Tucci, Gianrocco. Il legame fra trasporto e uso del suolo: una riflessione su alcune ricerche. (Land Use and Transport Systems: Some Considerations on a Ten-year Research. With English summary.) *Rivista Int. Sci. Econ. Com.*, May 1981, *28*(5), pp. 449–60.

Warner, Sam Bass, Jr. Modern Industrial Cities: History, Policy, and Survival: Comment. In *Stave, B. M., ed.*, 1981, pp. 290–96.

931 Urban Economics and Public Policy

9310 Urban Economics and Public Policy

Aiken, Michael and Alford, Robert R. Community Structure and Innovation: The Case of Urban Renewal. In *Martin, G. T., Jr., and Zald, M. N., eds.*, 1981, *1970*, pp. 208–32. [G: U.S.]

Aiken, Michael and Depre, Roger. The Urban System, Politics, and Policy in Belgian Cities. In *Newton, K., ed.*, 1981, pp. 85–116.
[G: Belgium]

Ali, M. Shaukat. Rural Urban Consumption Patterns in Pakistan. *Pakistan Econ. Soc. Rev.*, Winter 1981, *19*(2), pp. 85–94. [G: Pakistan]

Altmann, James L. and DeSalvo, Joseph S. Tests and Extensions of the Mills–Muth Simulation

Model of Urban Residential Land Use. *J. Reg. Sci.*, February 1981, *21*(1), pp. 1–21. [G: U.S.]

Appleyard, Donald. Place and Nonplace: The New Search for Roots. In *de Neufville, J. I., ed.*, 1981, pp. 49–55.

Archer, Wayne R. Determinants of Location for General Purpose Office Firms within Medium Size Cities. *Amer. Real Estate Urban Econ. Assoc. J.*, Fall 1981, *9*(3), pp. 283–97. [G: U.S.]

Arellano, José-Pablo. Do More Jobs in the Modern Sector Increase Urban Unemployment? *J. Devel. Econ.*, April 1981, *8*(2), pp. 241–47.

Arnott, Richard J. and Stiglitz, Joseph E. Aggregate Land Rents and Aggregate Transport Costs. *Econ. J.*, June 1981, *91*(362), pp. 331–47.

Asabere, Paul Kwadwo. The Determinants of Land Values in an African City: The Case of Accra, Ghana. *Land Econ.*, August 1981, *57*(3), pp. 385–97. [G: Ghana]

Asabere, Paul Kwadwo. The Price of Urban Land in a Chiefdom: Empirical Evidence on a Traditional African City, Kumasi. *J. Reg. Sci.*, November 1981, *21*(4), pp. 529–39. [G: Ghana]

Ayeni, Bola. Spatial Aspects of Urbanization and Effects on the Distribution of Income in Nigeria. In *Bienen, H. and Diejomaoh, V. P., eds.*, 1981, pp. 237–68. [G: Nigeria]

Baker, David G. and Colby, David C. The Politics of Municipal Employment Policy: A Comparative Study of U.S. Cities. *Amer. J. Econ. Soc.*, July 1981, *40*(3), pp. 249–63. [G: U.S.]

Baldassare, Mark. Local Perspectives on Community Growth. In *Hawley, A. H. and Mazie, S. M., eds.*, 1981, pp. 116–43. [G: U.S.]

Ballard, Claude. Trends in Retail Development: The 1980s and Beyond. In *Sternlieb, G. and Hughes, J. W., eds.*, 1981, pp. 275–90. [G: U.S.]

Baumol, William J. Technological Change and the New Urban Equilibrium. In *Burchell, R. W. and Listokin, D., eds.*, 1981, pp. 3–17. [G: U.S.]

Beaumont, J. R.; Clarke, M. and Wilson, A. G. Changing Energy Parameters and the Evolution of Urban Spatial Structure. *Reg. Sci. Urban Econ.*, August 1981, *11*(3), pp. 287–315.

Bédarida, François and Sutcliffe, Anthony R. The Street in the Structure and Life of the City: Reflections on Nineteenth-Century London and Paris. In *Stave, B. M., ed.*, 1981, *1980*, pp. 21–38. [G: U.K.; France]

Beguin, Hubert and Peeters, Dominique. Urbanization in Some Hierarchical Urban Models. *Reg. Sci. Urban Econ.*, February 1981, *11*(1), pp. 19–37.

Bekombo, M. The Child in Africa: Socialisation, Education and Work. In *Rodgers, G. and Standing, G., eds.*, 1981, pp. 113–29. [G: Africa]

van den Berg, L. and van der Meer, J. Urban Change in the Netherlands. In *Klaassen, L. H.; Molle, W. T. M. and Paelinck, J. H. P., eds.*, 1981, pp. 137–69. [G: Netherlands]

van den Berg, L., et al. Dynamics of Urban Development: Synthesis and Conclusions. In *Klaassen, L. H.; Molle, W. T. M. and Paelinck, J. H. P., eds.*, 1981, pp. 251–67.

Berlinck, Manuel Tosta; Bovo, José Murari and Cintra, Luiz Carlos. The Urban Informal Sector and Industrial Development in a Small City: The Case of Campinas (Brazil). In *Sethuraman, S. V., ed.*, 1981, pp. 159–67. [G: Brazil]

Berry, Brian J. L. Conceptual Lags in Retail Development Policy or Can the Carter White House Save the CBD? In *Sternlieb, G. and Hughes, J. W., eds.*, 1981, pp. 29–40. [G: U.S.]

Boeckhout, I. J. and Molle, W. T. M. Some Forces Underlying the Change in the Dutch Urban System. In *Klaassen, L. H.; Molle, W. T. M. and Paelinck, J. H. P., eds.*, 1981, pp. 170–93. [G: Netherlands]

Boehm, Thomas P. Tenure Choice and Expected Mobility: A Synthesis. *J. Urban Econ.*, November 1981, *10*(3), pp. 375–89. [G: U.S.]

Bona, B.; Merighi, D. and Ostanello-Borreani, A. Financial Resource Allocation in a Decentralized Urban System. In *Nijkamp, P. and Spronk, J., eds.*, 1981, pp. 101–15. [G: Italy]

Brueckner, Jan K. Testing a Vintage Model of Urban Growth. *J. Reg. Sci.*, February 1981, *21*(1), pp. 23–35. [G: U.S.]

Brueckner, Jan K. Zoning and Property Taxation in a System of Local Governments: Further Analysis. *Urban Stud.*, February 1981, *18*(1), pp. 113–20.

Buck, N. H. The Analysis of State Intervention in Nineteenth-Century Cities: The Case of Municipal Labour Policy in East London, 1886–1914. In *Dear, M. and Scott, A. J., eds.*, 1981, pp. 501–33. [G: U.K.]

Bullamore, Henry W. Job Change as a Motivation for Intraurban Residential Mobility. *Growth Change*, January 1981, *12*(1), pp. 42–49. [G: U.S.]

Burchell, Robert W. and Listokin, David. The Fiscal Impact of Economic-Development Programs: Case Studies of the Local Cost–Revenue Implications of HUD, EDA AND FmHA Projects. In *Sternlieb, G. and Listokin, D., eds.*, 1981, pp. 163–229. [G: U.S.]

Burchell, Robert W., et al. Measuring Urban Distress: A Summary of the Major Urban Hardship Indices and Resource Allocation Systems. In *Burchell, R. W. and Listokin, D., eds.*, 1981, pp. 159–229. [G: U.S.]

Burnell, James D. The Effect of Air Pollution on Residential Location Decisions in Metropolitan Areas. *Reg. Sci. Persp.*, 1981, *11*(2), pp. 3–14. [G: U.S.]

Burnett, Pat. Theoretical Advances in Modeling Economic and Social Behaviors: Applications to Geographical, Policy-Oriented Models. *Econ. Geogr.*, October 1981, *57*(4), pp. 291–303.

Burns, Leland S. The Metropolitan Population of the United States: Historical and Emerging Trends. In *Klaassen, L. H.; Molle, W. T. M. and Paelinck, J. H. P., eds.*, 1981, pp. 197–224. [G: U.S.]

Burns, Leland S. and Van Ness, Kathy. The Decline of the Metropolitan Economy. *Urban Stud.*, June 1981, *18*(2), pp. 169–80. [G: U.S.]

Butler, Stuart M. Enterprise Zones: Pioneering in the Inner City. In *Sternlieb, G. and Listokin, D., eds.*, 1981, pp. 25–41. [G: U.S.; U.K.]

Büttler, Hans-Jürg. Equilibrium of a Residential

City, Attributes of Housing, and Land-Use Zoning. *Urban Stud.*, February 1981, *18*(1), pp. 23–39.

Carlton, Dennis W. The Spatial Effects of a Tax on Housing and Land. *Reg. Sci. Urban Econ.*, November 1981, *11*(4), pp. 509–27.

Case, Fred E. and Gale, Jeffrey. The Impact on Housing Costs of the California Coastal Zone Conservation Act. *Amer. Real Estate Urban Econ. Assoc. J.*, Winter 1981, *9*(4), pp. 345–66.
　　　　　　　　　　　　　　　　[G: U.S.]

Cebula, Richard J. The Tiebout Hypothesis of Voting with One's Feet: A Look at the Most Recent Evidence. *Rev. Reg. Stud.*, Winter 1981, *11*(3), pp. 47–50.　　　　　　　　　　[G: U.S.]

Cheshire, Paul C. Inner Areas as Spatial Labour Markets: A Rejoinder. *Urban Stud.*, June 1981, *18*(2), pp. 227–29.　　　　　[G: U.K.]

Chicoine, David L. Farmland Values at the Urban Fringe: An Analysis of Sale Prices. *Land Econ.*, August 1981, *57*(3), pp. 353–62.　[G: U.S.]

Clark, Brian D. Urban Planning in Iran. In *[Fisher, W. B.]*, 1981, pp. 280–88.　　　　[G: Iran]

Clark, Terry Nichols. Urban Fiscal Strain: Trends and Policy Options. In *Walzer, N. and Chicoine, D. L., eds.*, 1981, pp. 3–18.　　[G: U.S.]

Clark, Terry Nichols and Ferguson, Lorna Crowley. Fiscal Strain and American Cities: Six Basic Processes. In *Newton, K., ed.*, 1981, pp. 137–55.
　　　　　　　　　　　　　　　　[G: U.S.]

Clark, Terry Nichols and Ferguson, Lorna Crowley. Political Leadership and Urban Fiscal Policy. In *Clark, T. N., ed.*, 1981, pp. 81–101.　[G: U.S.]

Clark, Terry Nichols, et al. Urban Policy Analysis: A New Research Agenda. In *Clark, T. N., ed.*, 1981, pp. 23–77.　　　　　[G: U.S.]

Clarke, John I. Contemporary Urban Growth in the Middle East. In *[Fisher, W. B.]*, 1981, *1980*, pp. 154–70.　　　　　[G: Middle East]

Coelen, Stephen P. and Fox, William F. The Provision of Community Services. In *Hawley, A. H. and Mazie, S. M., eds.*, 1981, pp. 589–613.

Collier, Valerie G. and Rempel, Henry. The Divergence of Private from Social Costs in Rural–Urban Migration: A Case Study of Nairobi. In *Killick, T., ed.*, 1981, *1977*, pp. 228–37.　[G: Kenya]

Cowen, Stephen H. Overlooked Opportunities in Shopping Center Development. In *Sternlieb, G. and Hughes, J. W., eds.*, 1981, pp. 311–15.
　　　　　　　　　　　　　　　　[G: U.S.]

Cropper, M. L. The Value of Urban Amenities. *J. Reg. Sci.*, August 1981, *21*(3), pp. 359–74.
　　　　　　　　　　　　　　　　[G: U.S.]

Davies, H. W. E. The Inner City in Britain. In *Schwartz, G. G., ed.*, 1981, pp. 1–36.
　　　　　　　　　　　　　　　　[G: U.K.]

Dendrinos, Dimitrios S. Individual Lot and Neighborhood Competitive Equilibria: Some Extensions from the Theory of Structural Stability. *J. Reg. Sci.*, February 1981, *21*(1), pp. 37–49.

Domanski, R. Development of the Urban System of Poland. In *Klaassen, L. H.; Molle, W. T. M. and Paelinck, J. H. P., eds.*, 1981, pp. 90–116.
　　　　　　　　　　　　　　　　[G: Poland]

Doud, Arthur A. and Summers, Anita A. Inflation and the Philadelphia Economy. *Ann. Amer. Acad.*

Polit. Soc. Sci., July 1981, *456*, pp. 13–31.
　　　　　　　　　　　　　　　　[G: U.S.]

Dowall, David E. The Effects of Economic Policy on Patterns of Land Use. In *de Neufville, J. I., ed.*, 1981, pp. 17–28.　　　[G: U.S.]

Drewett, R. and Rossi, A. General Urbanisation Trends in Western Europe. In *Klaassen, L. H.; Molle, W. T. M. and Paelinck, J. H. P., eds.*, 1981, pp. 119–36.　　　[G: W. Europe]

Eberts, Randall W. An Empirical Investigation of Intraurban Wage Gradients. *J. Urban Econ.*, July 1981, *10*(1), pp. 50–60.　　[G: U.S.]

Eberts, Randall W. and Gronberg, Timothy J. Jurisdictional Homogeneity and the Tiebout Hypothesis. *J. Urban Econ.*, September 1981, *10*(2), pp. 227–39.

Evans, Alan W. and Richardson, Ray. Urban Unemployment: Interpretation and Additional Evidence. *Scot. J. Polit. Econ.*, June 1981, *28*(2), pp. 107–24.　　　　　[G: U.K.]

Feldman, Stephen L.; Breese, John and Obeiter, Robert. The Search for Equity and Efficiency in the Pricing of a Public Service: Urban Water. *Econ. Geogr.*, January 1981, *57*(1), pp. 78–93.
　　　　　　　　　　　　　　　　[G: U.S.]

Ferguson, Lorna Crowley. Fiscal Strain in American Cities: Some Limitations to Popular Explanations. In *Newton, K., ed.*, 1981, pp. 156–78.
　　　　　　　　　　　　　　　　[G: U.S.]

Fischel, William A. Is Local Government Structure in Large Urbanized Areas Monopolistic or Competitive? *Nat. Tax J.*, March 1981, *34*(1), pp. 95–104.　　　　　　　　　　[G: U.S.]

Fisher, Peter S. State Equalizing Aids and Metropolitan Tax Base Sharing: A Comparative Analysis. *Public Finance Quart.*, October 1981, *9*(4), pp. 449–70.

Fix, Michael. Addressing the Issue of the Economic Impact of Regional Malls in Legal Proceedings. In *Sternlieb, G. and Hughes, J. W., eds.*, 1981, pp. 141–66.

Fossett, James W. and Nathan, Richard P. The Prospects for Urban Revival. In *Bahl, R., ed.*, 1981, pp. 63–104.　　　[G: U.S.]

Foster, Henry S., Jr. and Beattie, Bruce R. Urban Residential Demand for Water in the United States: Reply. *Land Econ.*, May 1981, *57*(2), pp. 257–65.　　　　　[G: U.S.]

Fowler, D. A. The Informal Sector in Freetown: Opportunities for Self-employment. In *Sethuraman, S. V., ed.*, 1981, pp. 51–69.
　　　　　　　　　　　　　[G: Sierre Leone]

Frankena, Mark W. Intrametropolitan Location of Employment. *J. Urban Econ.*, September 1981, *10*(2), pp. 256–69.　　　[G: Canada]

Friedland, Roger and Bielby, William T. The Power of Business in the City. In *Clark, T. N., ed.*, 1981, pp. 133–51.　　　[G: U.S.]

Fuller, Theodore D. Migrant–Native Socioeconomic Differentials in Thailand. *Demography*, February 1981, *18*(1), pp. 55–66.　[G: Thailand]

Galle, Omer R. and Stern, Robert N. The Metropolitan System in the South: Continuity and Change. In *Poston, D. L., Jr. and Weller, R. H., eds.*, 1981, pp. 155–74.　　　　[G: U.S.]

Gist, John R. and Hill, R. Carter. The Economics

of Choice in the Allocation of Federal Grants: An Empirical Test. *Public Choice*, 1981, *36*(1), pp. 63–73. [G: U.S.]

Glassberg, Andrew D. Urban Management under Fiscal Stringency: United States and Britain. In *Newton, K., ed.*, 1981, pp. 179–99. [G: U.S.; U.K.]

Goertz, Margaret. School Finance Reform and the Cities. In *Jordan, K. F. and Cambron-McCabe, N. H., eds.*, 1981, pp. 113–42. [G: U.S.]

Goldberg, Kalman and Scott, Robert C. Fiscal Incidence: A Revision of Benefits Incidence Estimates. *J. Reg. Sci.*, May 1981, *21*(2), pp. 203–21. [G: U.S.]

Goldin, Claudia Dale. Family Strategies and the Family Economy in the Late Nineteenth Century: The Role of Secondary Workers. In *Hershberg, T., ed.*, 1981, pp. 277–310. [G: U.S.]

Gould, Jack. Shopping Centers: U.S.A.: Emerging Markets in the 1980s. In *Sternlieb, G. and Hughes, J. W., eds.*, 1981, pp. 49–53. [G: U.S.]

Green, Howard L. and Huntoon, David L. Regional Shopping Center Issues in the 1980s. In *Sternlieb, G. and Hughes, J. W., eds.*, 1981, pp. 55–61. [G: U.S.]

Greenberg, Michael R. A Note on the Changing Geography of Cancer Mortality within Metropolitan Regions of the United States. *Demography*, August 1981, *18*(3), pp. 411–20. [G: U.S.]

Greer, William and White, Michelle J. The Effects of City Size and Moving Costs on Public Project Benefits. *J. Urban Econ.*, March 1981, *9*(2), pp. 149–64.

Gregory, Mary B., et al. Urban Poverty and Some Policy Options: An Analysis for India. *Urban Stud.*, June 1981, *18*(2), pp. 155–67. [G: India]

Griffin, Adrian H.; Martin, William E. and Wade, James C. Urban Residential Demand for Water in the United States: Comment. *Land Econ.*, May 1981, *57*(2), pp. 252–56. [G: U.S.]

Griffith, Daniel A. Modelling Urban Population Density in a Multi-Centered City. *J. Urban Econ.*, May 1981, *9*(3), pp. 298–310.
[G: Canada]

Gude, Sigmar; Heinz, Werner and Rothammer, Peter. Urban Policy in the Federal Republic of Germany. In *Schwartz, G. G., ed.*, 1981, pp. 99–140. [G: W. Germany]

Haar, Charles M. Shopping Center Location Decisions: National Competitive Policies and Local Zoning Regulations. In *Sternlieb, G. and Hughes, J. W., eds.*, 1981, pp. 97–107. [G: U.S.]

Hansen, Tore. Transforming Needs into Expenditure Decisions. In *Newton, K., ed.*, 1981, pp. 27–47. [G: Norway]

Hart, Keith. Informal Income Opportunities and Urban Employment in Ghana. In *Livingstone, I., ed.*, 1981, *1973*, pp. 75–84. [G: Ghana]

Haurin, Donald R. Local Income Taxation in an Urban Area. *J. Urban Econ.*, November 1981, *10*(3), pp. 323–37.

Hawley, Amos H. and Mazie, Sarah Mills. Nonmetropolitan America in Transition: An Overview. In *Hawley, A. H. and Mazie, S. M., eds.*, 1981, pp. 3–23.

Haworth, C. T.; Long, James E. and Rasmussen,

David W. Income Distribution, City Size and Urban Growth: A Final Word. *Urban Stud.*, February 1981, *18*(1), pp. 123.

Hembd, Jerry and Infanger, Craig L. An Application of Trend Surface Analysis to a Rural–Urban Land Market. *Land Econ.*, August 1981, *57*(3), pp. 303–22. [G: U.S.]

Henderson, J. Vernon and Ioannides, Yannis M. Aspects of Growth in a System of Cities. *J. Urban Econ.*, July 1981, *10*(1), pp. 117–39.

Hochman, Harold M. The Over-Regulated City: A Perspective on Regulatory Procedures in the City of New York. *Public Finance Quart.*, April 1981, *9*(2), pp. 197–219. [G: U.S.]

Holleb, Doris B. Housing and the Environment: Shooting at Moving Targets. *Ann. Amer. Acad. Polit. Soc. Sci.*, January 1981, *453*, pp. 180–221.
[G: U.S.]

Hörcher, N. and Schubert, U. Urban Development and Policy in Eastern Europe. In *Klaassen, L. H.; Molle, W. T. M. and Paelinck, J. H. P., eds.*, 1981, pp. 75–89. [G: E. Europe]

House, William J. Nairobi's Informal Sector: An Exploratory Study. In *Killick, T., ed.*, 1981, pp. 357–68. [G: Kenya]

Howe, Geoffrey [Sir]. Liberating Free Enterprise: A New Experiment. In *Sternlieb, G. and Listokin, D., eds.*, 1981, pp. 13–24. [G: U.K.]

Huckins, Larry E. and Tolley, George S. Investments in Local Infrastructure. In *Clark, T. N., ed.*, 1981, pp. 123–31. [G: U.S.]

Huddleston, Jack R. Variations in Development Subsidies under Tax Increment Financing. *Land Econ.*, August 1981, *57*(3), pp. 373–84.
[G: U.S.]

Ingene, Charles A. and Yu, Eden S. H. Determinants of Retail Sales in SMSAs. *Reg. Sci. Urban Econ.*, November 1981, *11*(4), pp. 529–47.
[G: U.S.]

Isard, W. and Reiner, Th. A. Megalopolitan Decline and Urban Redevelopment in the United States, an Analysis of Evolutionary Forces. In *Klaassen, L. H.; Molle, W. T. M. and Paelinck, J. H. P., eds.*, 1981, pp. 225–48. [G: U.S.]

Ishitani, H., et al. Modelling of Geographical Distribution of Population in a Region and Its Application for Regional Planning. In *Janssen, J. M. L.; Pau, L. F. and Straszak, A. J., eds.*, 1981, pp. 213–20. [G: Japan]

Jacobs, Susan S. and Wasylenko, Michael. Government Policy to Stimulate Economic Development: Enterprise Zones. In *Walzer, N. and Chicoine, D. L., eds.*, 1981, pp. 175–201.
[G: U.S.; U.K.]

James, Franklin J. Economic Distress in Central Cities. In *Burchell, R. W. and Listokin, D., eds.*, 1981, pp. 19–49. [G: U.S.]

Jansen, J. C. and Paelinck, J. H. P. The Urbanisation Phenomenon in the Process of Development: Some Statistical Evidence. In *Klaassen, L. H.; Molle, W. T. M. and Paelinck, J. H. P., eds.*, 1981, pp. 31–46. [G: Selected LDCs]

Jha, Raghbendra and Lächler, Ulrich. Optimum Taxation and Public Production in a Dynamic Harris-Todaro World. *J. Devel. Econ.*, December 1981, *9*(3), pp. 357–73.

Jonas, Stephan. Future Organization of the European Industrial City: "Urban Alternatives." In *Stave, B. M., ed.*, 1981, pp. 221–49.
[G: Europe]

Jones, Bryan D. Party and Bureaucracy: The Influence of Intermediary Groups on Urban Public Service Delivery. *Amer. Polit. Sci. Rev.*, September 1981, *75*(3), pp. 688–70. [G: U.S.]

Jurado, Gonzalo M., et al. The Manila Informal Sector: In Transition? In *Sethuraman, S. V., ed.*, 1981, pp. 121–43. [G: Philippines]

Kane, Howard E. and Belkin, Elizabeth H. Legal and Land Use Issues: Suburb versus Central City. In *Sternlieb, G. and Hughes, J. W., eds.*, 1981, pp. 129–39. [G: U.S.]

Kaplan, Marshall. Shopping Centers: U.S.A.: Community Conservation Guidance: A Promising Initiative. In *Sternlieb, G. and Hughes, J. W., eds.*, 1981, pp. 71–82. [G: U.S.]

Kasarda, John D. Population and Economic Base Changes in Metropolitan Areas. In *Clark, T. N., ed.*, 1981, pp. 247–56. [G: U.S.]

Katzman, Martin T. An Ecology of Family Decisions: Suburbanization, Schooling, and Fertility in Philadelphia, 1880–1920: Comment. In *Stave, B. M., ed.*, 1981, pp. 61–67. [G: U.S.]

Keith, John P. Cities of the Future. In *Pious, R. M., ed.*, 1981, pp. 222–32.

Klaassen, Leo H. Infrastructure Design and Urban Form: An Exercise in Geometry. *De Economist*, 1981, *129*(1), pp. 105–26.

Klaassen, Leo H. and Scimemi, G. Theoretical Issues in Urban Dynamics. In *Klaassen, L. H.; Molle, W. T. M. and Paelinck, J. H. P., eds.*, 1981, pp. 8–28.

Klep, Paul M. M. Regional Disparities in Brabantine Urbanisation before and after the Industrial Revolution (1374–1970): Some Aspects of Measurement and Explanation. In *Bairoch, P. and Lévy-Leboyer, M., eds.*, 1981, pp. 259–69.
[G: Belgium]

Kort, John R. Regional Economic Instability and Industrial Diversification in the U.S. *Land Econ.*, November 1981, *57*(4), pp. 596–608. [G: U.S.]

Kuhnle, Stein. Economics, Politics, and Policy in Norwegian Urban Communes. In *Newton, K., ed.*, 1981, pp. 63–81. [G: Norway]

Kwon, Won-Yong. A Study of the Economic Impact of Industrial Relocation: The Case of Seoul. *Urban Stud.*, February 1981, *18*(1), pp. 73–90.
[G: S. Korea]

Laurie, Bruce and Schmitz, Mark. Manufacture and Productivity: The Making of an Industrial Base, Philadelphia, 1850–1880. In *Hershberg, T., ed.*, 1981, pp. 43–92. [G: U.S.]

Lawless, Paul. The Role of Some Central Government Agencies in Urban Economic Regeneration. *Reg. Stud.*, 1981, *15*(1), pp. 1–14. [G: U.K.]

Lawless, Richard I. Social and Economic Change in North African Medinas: The Case of Tunis. In *[Fisher, W. B.]*, 1981, pp. 264–79.
[G: Tunisia]

Leibowits, Peter D. Shopping Centers: U.S.A.: Appraising the Central City Option: The Preliminary Track Record. In *Sternlieb, G. and Hughes, J. W., eds.*, 1981, pp. 219–27. [G: U.S.]

Levenstein, Charles. The Political Economy of Suburbanization: In Pursuit of a Class Analysis. *Rev. Radical Polit. Econ.*, Summer 1981, *13*(2), pp. 23–31.

Lever, William F. The Inner City Employment Problem in Great Britain, 1952–76: A Shift–Share Approach. In *Rees, J.; Hewings, G. J. D. and Stafford, H. A., eds.*, 1981, pp. 171–96.
[G: U.K.]

Linn, Johannes F. Urban Finances in Developing Countries. In *Bahl, R., ed.*, 1981, pp. 245–83.
[G: LDCs]

Linthorst, Joop M. and van Praag, Bernard M. S. Interaction-Patterns and Service-Areas of Local Public Services in the Netherlands. *Reg. Sci. Urban Econ.*, February 1981, *11*(1), pp. 39–56.
[G: Netherlands]

Lopez, Manuel Mariano. Patterns of Interethnic Residential Segregation in the Urban Southwest, 1960 and 1970. *Soc. Sci. Quart.*, March 1981, *62*(1), pp. 50–63. [G: U.S.]

Lotz, Joergen R. Fiscal Problems and Issues in Scandinavian Cities. In *Bahl, R., ed.*, 1981, pp. 221–43. [G: Scandinavia]

de la Luz Silva, Maria. Urban Poverty and Child Work: Elements for the Analysis of Child Work in Chile. In *Rodgers, G. and Standing, G., eds.*, 1981, pp. 159–77. [G: Chile]

Mabogunje, A. L. and Filani, M. O. The Informal Sector in a Small City: The Case of Kano (Nigeria). In *Sethuraman, S. V., ed.*, 1981, pp. 83–89.
[G: Nigeria]

Maclennan, Duncan. Tolerable Survival in the City: The Realities for Urban Policy. In *Gaskin, M., ed.*, 1981, pp. 165–89. [G: U.K.]

Mair, Douglas. Urban Unemployment: A Comment [Urban Unemployment in England]. *Econ. J.*, March 1981, *91*(361), pp. 224–30. [G: U.K.]

Mandelker, Daniel R. Commentary on Legal Aspects of Controlling Shopping Center Competition. In *Sternlieb, G. and Hughes, J. W., eds.*, 1981, pp. 109–12. [G: U.S.]

Marga Institute. Informal Sector without Migration: The Case of Colombo. In *Sethuraman, S. V., ed.*, 1981, pp. 101–08. [G: Sri Lanka]

Margolis, Julius. Fiscal Problems of Political Boundaries. In *Aronson, J. R. and Schwartz, E., eds.*, 1981, pp. 213–33. [G: U.S.]

Mark, Jonathan H. and Goldberg, Michael A. Land Use Controls: The Case of Zoning in the Vancouver Area. *Amer. Real Estate Urban Econ. Assoc. J.*, Winter 1981, *9*(4), pp. 418–35. [G: Canada]

Mayer, Neil S. Rehabilitation Decisions in Rental Housing: An Empirical Analysis. *J. Urban Econ.*, July 1981, *10*(1), pp. 76–94. [G: U.S.]

McEachern, William A. Tax-Exempt Property, Tax Capitalization, and the Cumulative-Urban-Decay Hypothesis. *Nat. Tax J.*, June 1981, *34*(2), pp. 185–92.

McIntyre, Robert J. and Thornton, James R. Energy Systems and Comparative Systems: A Reply to Ryding [Urban Design and Energy Utilization: A Comparative Analysis of Soviet Practice]. *J. Compar. Econ.*, December 1981, *5*(4), pp. 414–17. [G: U.S.S.R.]

Meadows, George Richard and Mitrisin, John. A

National Development Bank: Survey and Discussion of the Literature on Capital Shortages and Employment Changes in Distressed Areas. In *Sternlieb, G. and Listokin, D., eds.*, 1981, pp. 84–143. [G: U.S.]

Mehay, Stephen L. The Expenditure Effects of Municipal Annexation. *Public Choice*, 1981, *36*(1), pp. 53–62. [G: U.S.]

Merget, Astrid E. Achieving Equity in an Era of Fiscal Constraint. In *Burchell, R. W. and Listokin, D., eds.*, 1981, pp. 401–36. [G: U.S.]

Mills, David E. Growth, Speculation and Sprawl in a Monocentric City. *J. Urban Econ.*, September 1981, *10*(2), pp. 201–26.

Mills, David E. The Non-Neutrality of Land Value Taxation. *Nat. Tax J.*, March 1981, *34*(1), pp. 125–29.

Modell, John. An Ecology of Family Decisions: Suburbanization, Schooling, and Fertility in Philadelphia, 1880–1920. In *Stave, B. M., ed.*, 1981, *1980*, pp. 39–59. [G: U.S.]

Modell, John and Lees, Lynn H. The Irish Countryman Urbanized: A Comparative Perspective on the Famine Migration. In *Hershberg, T., ed.*, 1981, *1977*, pp. 351–67. [G: U.S.; U.K.]

Moir, Hazel. Occupational Mobility and the Informal Sector in Jakarta. In *Sethuraman, S. V., ed.*, 1981, pp. 109–20. [G: Indonesia]

Mollenkopf, John H. Community and Accumulation. In *Dear, M. and Scott, A. J., eds.*, 1981, pp. 319–37. [G: U.S.]

Mollenkopf, John H. Paths toward the Post Industrial Service City: The Northeast and the Southwest. In *Burchell, R. W. and Listokin, D., eds.*, 1981, pp. 77–112. [G: U.S.]

Moomaw, Ronald L. Productivity and City Size? A Critique of the Evidence [Are There Returns to Scale in City Size?]. [Bias in the Cross Section Estimates of the Elasticity of Substitution]. *Quart. J. Econ.*, November 1981, *96*(4), pp. 675–88. [G: U.S.]

Muller, Thomas. Changing Expenditures and Service Demand Patterns of Stressed Cities. In *Burchell, R. W. and Listokin, D., eds.*, 1981, pp. 277–99. [G: U.S.]

Muller, Thomas. Regional Malls and Central City Retail Sales: An Overview. In *Sternlieb, G. and Hughes, J. W., eds.*, 1981, pp. 177–99. [G: U.S.]

Mulligan, Gordon F. The Urbanization Ratio and the Rank-Size Distribution: A Comment [Additional Properties of a Hierarchical City-Size Model]. *J. Reg. Sci.*, May 1981, *21*(2), pp. 283–85.

Nathan, Richard P. Federal Grants—How Are They Working? In *Burchell, R. W. and Listokin, D., eds.*, 1981, pp. 529–39. [G: U.S.]

Nechemias, Carol. The Impact of Soviet Housing Policy on Housing Conditions in Soviet Cities: The Uneven Push from Moscow. *Urban Stud.*, February 1981, *18*(1), pp. 1–8. [G: U.S.S.R.]

Needham, Barrie. A Neo-Classical Supply-Based Approach to Land Prices. *Urban Stud.*, February 1981, *18*(1), pp. 91–104.

Needham, Barrie. Inner Areas as Spatial Labour Markets: A Comment. *Urban Stud.*, June 1981, *18*(2), pp. 225–26. [G: U.K.]

de Neufville, Judith Innes. Conclusion: Disentangling the Debate. In *de Neufville, J. I., ed.*, 1981, pp. 245–55.

de Neufville, Judith Innes. Land Use: A Tool for Social Policies. In *de Neufville, J. I., ed.*, 1981, pp. 31–47. [G: U.S.]

Newton, Ken. Central Places and Urban Services. In *Newton, K., ed.*, 1981, pp. 117–33. [G: U.K.]

Nicholson, B. M.; Brinkley, Ian and Evans, Alan W. The Role of the Inner City in the Development of Manufacturing Industry. *Urban Stud.*, February 1981, *18*(1), pp. 57–71. [G: U.K.]

Parker, Carl, III. Trend Surface and the Spatio-Temporal Analysis of Residential Land-Use Intensity and Household Housing Expenditure. *Land Econ.*, August 1981, *57*(3), pp. 323–37. [G: U.S.]

Parks, Roger B. and Ostrom, Elinor. Complex Models of Urban Service Systems. In *Clark, T. N., ed.*, 1981, pp. 171–99.

Peirce, Neal R. and Hagstrom, Jerry. Inner City in Three Countries. In *Schwartz, G. G., ed.*, 1981, pp. 141–55. [G: U.K.; U.S.; W. Germany]

Peiser, Richard B. Land Development Regulation: A Case Study of Dallas and Houston, Texas. *Amer. Real Estate Urban Econ. Assoc. J.*, Winter 1981, *9*(4), pp. 397–417. [G: U.S.]

Petersen, John E. Tax and Expenditure Limitations: Projecting Their Impact on Big City Finances. In *Kaufman, G. G. and Rosen, K. T., eds.*, 1981, pp. 171–201. [G: U.S.]

Porell, Frank W. and Hua, Chang-I. An Econometric Procedure for Estimation of a Generalized Systemic Gravity Model under Incomplete Information about the System. *Reg. Sci. Urban Econ.*, November 1981, *11*(4), pp. 585–606. [G: U.S.]

Power, Thomas M. Urban Size (Dis)amenities Revisited. *J. Urban Econ.*, January 1981, *9*(1), pp. 85–89. [G: U.S.]

Prud'homme, Rémy. Les fonctions de la fiscalité dans la planification des villes. (With English summary.) In *Roskamp, K. W. and Forte, F., eds.*, 1981, pp. 365–80. [G: France]

Qadeer, M. A. The Nature of Urban Land. *Amer. J. Econ. Soc.*, April 1981, *40*(2), pp. 165–82.

Quinn, Joseph F. and McCormick, Karen. Wage Rates and City Size. *Ind. Relat.*, Spring 1981, *20*(2), pp. 193–99.

Reiner, Thomas A. and Wolpert, Julian. The Non-Profit Sector in the Metropolitan Economy. *Econ. Geogr.*, January 1981, *57*(1), pp. 23–33. [G: U.S.]

Remolona, Eli M. Two Empirical Notes on the Urban Economy. *Phillipine Rev. Econ. Bus.*, March & June 1981, *18*(1 & 2), pp. 87–93. [G: Philippines]

Richardson, Harry W. National Urban Development Strategies in Developing Countries. *Urban Stud.*, October 1981, *18*(3), pp. 267–83. [G: LDCs]

Rodwin, Lloyd. Four Approaches to Urban Studies. In *Rodwin, L.*, 1981, pp. 189–209.

Rodwin, Lloyd. On the Illusions of City Planners.

In *Rodwin, L.*, 1981, pp. 229–55.

Rodwin, Lloyd. Problems of the Metropolis: Changing Images and Realities. In *Rodwin, L.*, 1981, pp. 81–101. **[G: U.S.]**

Rodwin, Lloyd. Realism and Utopianism in City Planning: A Retrospective View. In *Rodwin, L.*, 1981, *1978*, pp. 139–59.

Rodwin, Lloyd and Evans, Hugh. The New Communities Program and Why It Failed. In *Rodwin, L.*, 1981, *1979*, pp. 115–36. **[G: U.S.]**

Rodwin, Lloyd and Hollister, Robert. Images of the City in the Social Sciences. In *Rodwin, L.*, 1981, pp. 61–78.

Rodwin, Lloyd and Lynch, Kevin. The Form of the City. In *Rodwin, L.*, 1981, pp. 30–60.

Rodwin, Lloyd and Southworth, Michael. The Educative City. In *Rodwin, L.*, 1981, *1972*, pp. 19–29.

Rodwin, Lloyd and Susskind, Lawrence. Conditions for a Successful New Communities Program. In *Rodwin, L.*, 1981, *1973*, pp. 102–14. **[G: U.S.]**

Rose, Damaris. Accumulation versus Reproduction in the Inner City: *The Recurrent Crisis of London* Revisited. In *Dear, M. and Scott, A. J.*, *eds.*, 1981, pp. 339–81. **[G: U.K.]**

Rosen, Kenneth T. and Katz, Lawrence F. Growth Management and Land Use Controls: The San Francisco Bay Area Experience. *Amer. Real Estate Urban Econ. Assoc. J.*, Winter 1981, *9*(4), pp. 321–44. **[G: U.S.]**

Rossi, Angelo. Décentralisation de la population en milieu urbain et activité du secteur public local. (Decentralization of Population in Urban Areas and the Activity of the Local Public Sector. With English summary.) *Schweiz. Z. Volkswirtsch. Statist.*, September 1981, *117*(3), pp. 271–80. **[G: Switzerland]**

Roweis, Shoukry T. Urban Planning in Early and Late Capitalist Societies: Outline of a Theoretical Perspective. In *Dear, M. and Scott, A. J.*, *eds.*, 1981, pp. 159–77.

Rugg, Dean S. and Rundquist, Donald C. Urbanization in the Great Plains: Trends and Prospects. In *Lawson, M. P. and Baker, M. E.*, *eds.*, 1981, pp. 221–46. **[G: U.S.]**

Ryding, Helene. Municipal Energy Supply and District Heating: A Comment on Robert J. McIntyre and James R. Thornton, "Urban Design and Energy Utilization: A Comparative Analysis of Soviet Practice." *J. Compar. Econ.*, December 1981, *5*(4), pp. 404–13. **[G: U.S.S.R.]**

Sada, P. O. Urbanization and Income Distribution in Nigeria. In *Bienen, H. and Diejomaoh, V. P.*, *eds.*, 1981, pp. 269–98. **[G: Nigeria]**

Sánchez, Carlos E.; Palmiero, Horacio and Ferrero, Fernando. The Informal and Quasi-formal Sectors in Córdoba. In *Sethuraman, S. V.*, *ed.*, 1981, pp. 144–58. **[G: Argentina]**

Sbragia, Alberta. Cities, Capital, and Banks: The Politics of Debt in the United States, United Kingdom, and France. In *Newton, K.*, *ed.*, 1981, pp. 200–220. **[G: U.S.; U.K.; France]**

Schiller, Russell. A Model of Retail Branch Distribution. *Reg. Stud.*, 1981, *15*(1), pp. 15–22.

Schlichting, Kurt. Decentralization and the Decline of the Central City: A Case Study of Demographic and Economic Change in Bridgeport, Conn. *Amer. J. Econ. Soc.*, October 1981, *40*(4), pp. 353–66. **[G: U.S.]**

Schmenner, Roger W. The Rent Gradient for Manufacturing. *J. Urban Econ.*, January 1981, *9*(1), pp. 90–96. **[G: U.S.]**

Schumaker, Paul D. Citizen Preferences and Policy Responsiveness. In *Clark, T. N.*, *ed.*, 1981, pp. 227–43.

Schwartz, Gail Garfield. Urban Policy and the Inner Cities in the United States. In *Schwartz, G. G.*, *ed.*, 1981, pp. 37–98. **[G: U.S.]**

Schwartz, Seymour I.; Hansen, David E. and Green, Richard D. Suburban Growth Controls and the Price of New Housing. *J. Environ. Econ. Manage.*, December 1981, *8*(4), pp. 303–20. **[G: U.S.]**

Seley, John E. New Directions in Public Services: Introduction. *Econ. Geogr.*, January 1981, *57*(1), pp. 1–9. **[G: U.S.]**

Seley, John E. Targeting Economic Development: An Examination of the Needs of Small Businesses. *Econ. Geogr.*, January 1981, *57*(1), pp. 34–51. **[G: U.S.]**

Sethuraman, S. V. Implications for Environment and Development Policies. In *Sethuraman, S. V.*, *ed.*, 1981, pp. 171–208. **[G: Selected LDCs]**

Sethuraman, S. V. The Role of the Urban Informal Sector. In *Sethuraman, S. V.*, *ed.*, 1981, pp. 1–47.

Shakow, Don. The Municipal Farmer's Market as an Urban Service. *Econ. Geogr.*, January 1981, *57*(1), pp. 68–77. **[G: U.S.]**

Sharpe, L. J. Does Politics Matter? An Interim Summary with Findings. In *Newton, K.*, *ed.*, 1981, pp. 1–26. **[G: U.K.]**

Shedd, Peter J. Land Use Controls: Can Landowners Force Governmental Bodies to Pay? *Amer. Real Estate Urban Econ. Assoc. J.*, Winter 1981, *9*(4), pp. 457–73. **[G: U.S.]**

Shlay, Anne B. and Rossi, Peter H. Putting Politics into Urban Ecology: Estimating Net Effects of Zoning. In *Clark, T. N.*, *ed.*, 1981, pp. 257–86. **[G: U.S.]**

Singh, J. P. Patterns of Urbanization in a Developing Region: A Demographic Perspective. In *Karna, M. N.*, *ed.*, 1981, pp. 87–103. **[G: India]**

Skovsgaard, Carl-Johan. Party Influence on Local Spending in Denmark. In *Newton, K.*, *ed.*, 1981, pp. 48–62. **[G: Denmark]**

Small, Kenneth A. A Comment on Gasoline Prices and Urban Structure [Urban Structure, Gas Prices, and the Demand for Transportation]. *J. Urban Econ.*, November 1981, *10*(3), pp. 311–22.

Soderstrom, Jon. Boomtown Analysis Disputed [Adjustment Issues of Impacted Communities or, Are Boomtowns Bad?]. *Natural Res. J.*, April 1981, *21*(2), pp. ix–x.

Spink, Frank H., Jr. Downtown Malls: Prospects, Design, Constraints. In *Sternlieb, G. and Hughes, J. W.*, *eds.*, 1981, pp. 201–18. **[G: U.S.]**

Stefani, Giorgio. Finanza locale, investimenti e servizi urbani in Cina. (Local Finance, Investment and Urban Services in China. With English sum-

mary.) *Bancaria*, May 1981, *37*(5), pp. 454–69.
[G: China]

Stein, Rona B. New York City's Economy in 1980. *Fed. Res. Bank New York Quart. Rev.*, Spring 1981, *6*(1), pp. 1–7. [G: U.S.]

Sternlieb, George. Kemp–Garcia Act: An Initial Evaluation. In *Sternlieb, G. and Listokin, D., eds.*, 1981, pp. 42–83. [G: U.S.]

Sternlieb, George and Hughes, James W. New Dimensions of the Urban Crisis. In *Burchell, R. W. and Listokin, D., eds.*, 1981, pp. 51–75. [G: U.S.]

Sternlieb, George and Hughes, James W. Some Economic Effects of Recent Migration Patterns on Central Cities. In *Simon, J. L. and Lindert, P. H., eds.*, 1981, pp. 189–207. [G: U.S.]

Sternlieb, George and Hughes, James W. The Uncertain Future of Shopping Centers. In *Sternlieb, G. and Hughes, J. W., eds.*, 1981, pp. 1–16. [G: U.S.]

Sternlieb, George and Listokin, David. New Tools for Economic Development: The Enterprise Zone, Development Bank, and RFC: Introduction. In *Sternlieb, G. and Listokin, D., eds.*, 1981, pp. 1–9. [G: U.S.]

Stinner, William F. and Bacol-Montilla, Melinda. Population Deconcentration in Metropolitan Manila in the Twentieth Century. *J. Devel. Areas*, October 1981, *16*(1), pp. 3–16. [G: Philippines]

Sussman, Albert. Shopping Centers: U.S.A.: Community Conservation Guidelines: A Failure. In *Sternlieb, G. and Hughes, J. W., eds.*, 1981, pp. 63–69. [G: U.S.]

Tannian, Francis and Stapleford, John. Community Preference and Urban Public Policy. *Growth Change*, April 1981, *12*(2), pp. 37–43. [G: U.S.]

Tucker, Grady. The New Economics of Shopping Center Location and Scale. In *Sternlieb, G. and Hughes, J. W., eds.*, 1981, pp. 41–47. [G: U.S.]

Upton, Charles. An Equilibrium Model of City Size. *J. Urban Econ.*, July 1981, *10*(1), pp. 15–36.

Varaiya, Pravin and Wiseman, Michael. Investment and Employment in Manufacturing in U.S. Metropolitan Areas, 1960–1976. *Reg. Sci. Urban Econ.*, November 1981, *11*(4), pp. 431–69. [G: U.S.]

Vitali, Ornello. Lo sviluppo dell'urbanizzazione in Emilia-Romagna (1951–1977). (The Development of Urbanization in Emilia-Romagna (1951–1977). With English summary.) *Statistica*, April–June 1981, *41*(2), pp. 285–99. [G: Italy]

Vousden, Neil. Market Power in a Non-Malleable City. *Rev. Econ. Stud.*, January 1981, *48*(1), pp. 3–19.

Walker, Bruce. Income Distribution, City Size and Urban Growth: A Rejoinder. *Urban Stud.*, February 1981, *18*(1), pp. 121–22.

Wallin, Bruce. Tax and Expenditure Limitations: Projecting Their Impact on Big City Finances: Comment. In *Kaufman, G. G. and Rosen, K. T., eds.*, 1981, pp. 202–05. [G: U.S.]

Walton, John. The New Urban Sociology. *Int. Soc. Sci. J.*, 1981, *33*(2), pp. 374–90.

Ward, Sally K. Economic Ownership in U.S. Communities: Corporate Change, 1961–75. *Soc. Sci.*

Quart., March 1981, *62*(1), pp. 139–50.
[G: U.S.]

Webman, Jerry A. UDAG: Targeting Urban Economic Development. *Polit. Sci. Quart.*, Summer 1981, *96*(2), pp. 189–207. [G: U.S.]

Weinstein, Bernard L. and Clark, Robert J. The Fiscal Outlook for Growing Cities. In *Bahl, R., ed.*, 1981, pp. 105–25. [G: U.S.]

Wellbelove, D.; Woods, A. and Zafiris, N. Survival and Success of the Inner City Economy: The Performance of Manufacturing and Services in Islington. *Urban Stud.*, October 1981, *18*(3), pp. 301–13. [G: U.K.]

Wheaton, William C. and Shishido, Hisanobu. Urban Concentration, Agglomeration Economies, and the Level of Economic Development. *Econ. Develop. Cult. Change*, October 1981, *30*(1), pp. 17–30.

Whitaker, David. Bidding for Land Development. *Amer. Real Estate Urban Econ. Assoc. J.*, Fall 1981, *9*(3), pp. 223–33.

White, Michelle J. Optimal Inequality in Systems of Cities or Regions. *J. Reg. Sci.*, August 1981, *21*(3), pp. 375–87.

Wirtenberg, Margaret S. Downtown Pedestrian Malls. In *Sternlieb, G. and Hughes, J. W., eds.*, 1981, pp. 229–36. [G: U.S.]

932 Housing Economics

9320 Housing Economics (including nonurban housing)

Aaron, Henry J. Do Housing Allowances Work? Policy Implications: A Progress Report. In *Bradbury, K. L. and Downs, A., eds.*, 1981, pp. 67–111. [G: U.S.]

Agnew, J. A. Homeownership and the Capitalist Social Order. In *Dear, M. and Scott, A. J., eds.*, 1981, pp. 457–80. [G: U.K.; U.S.]

Ahmed, Ehsan. Production Functions and Input Elasticities in the Construction of Low-Cost Housing: A Comparison of Building Firms in Pakistan with Firms in Five Other Countries. *Pakistan Devel. Rev.*, Winter 1981, *20*(4), pp. 417–26. [G: Pakistan; Colombia; Sri Lanka; Kenya; Tunisia]

Akbar Zaki, M. Javed. Housing Conditions in Pakistan: 1960–80. *Pakistan Devel. Rev.*, Summer 1981, *20*(2), pp. 215–46. [G: Pakistan]

Alberts, William W. and Kerr, Halbert S. The Rate of Return from Investing in Single-Family Housing. *Land Econ.*, May 1981, *57*(2), pp. 230–42. [G: U.S.]

Allen, Garland E.; Fitts, Jerry J. and Glatt, Evelyn S. The Experimental Housing Allowance Program. In *Bradbury, K. L. and Downs, A., eds.*, 1981, pp. 1–31. [G: U.S.]

Altmann, James L. and DeSalvo, Joseph S. Tests and Extensions of the Mills–Muth Simulation Model of Urban Residential Land Use. *J. Reg. Sci.*, February 1981, *21*(1), pp. 1–21. [G: U.S.]

Anas, Alex. The Estimation of Multinomial Logit Models of Joint Location and Travel Mode Choice from Aggregated Data. *J. Reg. Sci.*, May 1981, *21*(2), pp. 223–42. [G: U.S.]

Anderson, John E. Ridge Estimation of House Value Determinants. *J. Urban Econ.*, May 1981, *9*(3), pp. 286–97. [G: U.S.]

Ault, Richard W. The Presumed Advantages and Real Disadvantages of Rent Control. In *Block, W. and Olsen, E., eds.*, 1981, pp. 55–81. [G: U.S.]

Badcock, B. A. and Cloher, D. U. Urlich. Neighbourhood Change in Inner Adelaide, 1966–76. *Urban Stud.*, February 1981, *18*(1), pp. 41–55. [G: Australia]

Baldassare, Mark. Local Perspectives on Community Growth. In *Hawley, A. H. and Mazie, S. M., eds.*, 1981, pp. 116–43. [G: U.S.]

Balderston, Frederick. Proposition 13, Property Transfers, and the Real Estate Markets. In *Kaufman, G. G. and Rosen, K. T., eds.*, 1981, pp. 65–103. [G: U.S.]

Barth, James R.; Cordes, Joseph J. and Yezer, Anthony M. J. Financial Institution Regulations, Redlining and Mortgage Markets. In *Fed. Res. Bank of Boston and National Sci. Foundation*, 1981, pp. 101–43. [G: U.S.]

Bender, Bruce. Urban Housing Density and the Price of Housing Services. *J. Urban Econ.*, January 1981, *9*(1), pp. 80–84.

Bendick, Marc, Jr. and Squire, Anne D. Housing Vouchers for the Poor: The Three Experiments. In *Struyk, R. J. and Bendick, M., Jr., eds.*, 1981, pp. 51–75. [G: U.S.]

Bendick, Marc, Jr. and Struyk, Raymond J. Housing Vouchers for the Poor: Origins of an Experimental Approach. In *Struyk, R. J. and Bendick, M., Jr., eds.*, 1981, pp. 23–49. [G: U.S.]

Benston, George J. Mortgage Redlining Research: A Review and Critical Analysis Discussion. In *Fed. Res. Bank of Boston and National Sci. Foundation*, 1981, pp. 144–95. [G: U.S.]

Berry, Brian J. L. Inner-City Futures: An American Dilemma Revisited. In *Stave, B. M., ed.*, 1981, *1980*, pp. 187–219. [G: U.S.]

Block, Walter. Rent Control: Postscript: A Reply to the Critics. In *Block, W. and Olsen, E., eds.*, 1981, pp. 285–319. [G: Canada]

Blomquist, Glenn and Worley, Lawrence. Hedonic Prices, Demands for Urban Housing Amenities, and Benefit Estimates. *J. Urban Econ.*, March 1981, *9*(2), pp. 212–21.

Boal, F. W. Ethnic Residential Segregation, Ethnic Mixing and Resource Conflict: A Study in Belfast, Northern Ireland. In *Peach, C.; Robinson, V. and Smith, S., eds.*, 1981, pp. 235–51. [G: U.K.]

Boehm, Thomas P. Tenure Choice and Expected Mobility: A Synthesis. *J. Urban Econ.*, November 1981, *10*(3), pp. 375–89. [G: U.S.]

Borins, Sandford F. Mieszkowski and Saper's Estimate of the Effects of Airport Noise on Property Values: A Comment. *J. Urban Econ.*, January 1981, *9*(1), pp. 125–28. [G: Canada]

Boyer, M. Christine. National Land Use Policy: Instrument and Product of the Economic Cycle. In *de Neufville, J. I., ed.*, 1981, pp. 109–25. [G: U.S.]

Braid, Ralph M. The Short-Run Comparative Statics of a Rental Housing Market. *J. Urban Econ.*, November 1981, *10*(3), pp. 286–310.

Brown, H. James. Market Failure: Efficiency or Equity? In *de Neufville, J. I., ed.*, 1981, pp. 143–47.

Brueckner, Jan K. A Dynamic Model of Housing Production. *J. Urban Econ.*, July 1981, *10*(1), pp. 1–14.

Brueckner, Jan K. Labor Mobility and the Incidence of the Residential Property Tax. *J. Urban Econ.*, September 1981, *10*(2), pp. 173–82.

Brueckner, Jan K. Testing a Vintage Model of Urban Growth. *J. Reg. Sci.*, February 1981, *21*(1), pp. 23–35. [G: U.S.]

Brueckner, Jan K. and von Rabenau, Burkhard. Dynamics of Land-Use for a Closed City. *Reg. Sci. Urban Econ.*, February 1981, *11*(1), pp. 1–17.

Brueggeman, William B. The Rental Housing Situation: Implications for Policy and Research. In *Weicher, J. C.; Villani, K. E. and Roistacher, E. A., eds.*, 1981, pp. 13–22. [G: U.S.]

Buckley, Robert M. and Ermisch, John F. A Financial Model of House Price Behavior in the United Kingdom. In *Tuccillo, J. A. and Villani, K. E., eds.*, 1981, pp. 43–68. [G: U.K.]

Bullamore, Henry W. Job Change as a Motivation for Intraurban Residential Mobility. *Growth Change*, January 1981, *12*(1), pp. 42–49. [G: U.S.]

Burnell, James D. The Effect of Air Pollution on Residential Location Decisions in Metropolitan Areas. *Reg. Sci. Persp.*, 1981, *11*(2), pp. 3–14. [G: U.S.]

Burns, Leland S. and Shoup, Donald C. Effects of Resident Control and Ownership in Self-Help Housing. *Land Econ.*, February 1981, *57*(1), pp. 106–14. [G: El Salvador]

Burstein, Alan N. Immigrants and Residential Mobility: The Irish and Germans in Philadelphia, 1850–1880. In *Hershberg, T., ed.*, 1981, pp. 174–203. [G: U.S.]

Büttler, Hans-Jürg. Equilibrium of a Residential City, Attributes of Housing, and Land-Use Zoning. *Urban Stud.*, February 1981, *18*(1), pp. 23–39.

Caccavallo, Frank M. Racial Discrimination: The Housing Market. *Amer. Econ.*, Spring 1981, *25*(1), pp. 43–52. [G: U.S.]

Canner, Glenn. Redlining and Mortgage Lending Patterns. In *Henderson, J. V., ed.*, 1981, pp. 67–101. [G: U.S.]

Canner, Glenn. The Community Reinvestment Act: A Second Progress Report. *Fed. Res. Bull.*, November 1981, *67*(11), pp. 813–23. [G: U.S.]

Carlson, Jack. The Economy of 1981: A Bipartisan Look: The Proceedings of a Congressional Economic Conference: Statement. In *U.S. Congress, Joint Economic Committee (I)*, 1981, pp. 580–82. [G: U.S.]

Carlton, Dennis W. Product Quality and Value in the New Home Market: Implications for Consumer Protection Regulation: Comment. *J. Law Econ.*, December 1981, *24*(3), pp. 399–400. [G: U.S.]

Carlton, Dennis W. The Spatial Effects of a Tax on Housing and Land. *Reg. Sci. Urban Econ.*, November 1981, *11*(4), pp. 509–27.

Case, Fred E. and Gale, Jeffrey. The Impact on Housing Costs of the California Coastal Zone Conservation Act. *Amer. Real Estate Urban Econ. Assoc. J.*, Winter 1981, *9*(4), pp. 345–66. [G: U.S.]

Chan, S. J.; Park, C. W. and Yu, P. L. High-Stake Decision Making—An Empirical Study Based on House Purchase Process—An Introduction. **In** *Morse, J. N., ed.,* 1981, pp. 72–76.

Cherunilam, Francis. Housing in India—Problem and Policy. *Econ. Aff.*, April–June 1981, *26*(2), pp. 134–40. [G: India]

Church, Albert M. The Effects of Local Government Expenditure and Property Taxes on Investment. *Amer. Real Estate Urban Econ. Assoc. J.*, Summer 1981, *9*(2), pp. 165–80. [G: U.S.]

Clapp, John M. The Impact of Inclusionary Zoning on the Location and Type of Construction Activity. *Amer. Real Estate Urban Econ. Assoc. J.*, Winter 1981, *9*(4), pp. 436–56. [G: U.S.]

Clark, John. The Search for Natural Limits to Growth. **In** *de Neufville, J. I., ed.,* 1981, pp. 65–82. [G: U.S.]

Clemhout, Simone. The Impact of Housing Cyclicity on the Construction of Residential Units and Housing Costs. *Land Econ.*, November 1981, *57*(4), pp. 609–23. [G: U.S.]

Clemhout, Simone and Neftci, Salih N. Policy Evaluation of Housing Cyclicality: A Spectral Analysis. *Rev. Econ. Statist.*, August 1981, *63*(3), pp. 385–94. [G: U.S.]

Cronin, Francis J. Household Responsiveness to Unconstrained Housing Allowances. **In** *Struyk, R. J. and Bendick, M., Jr., eds.,* 1981, pp. 159–76. [G: U.S.]

Cronin, Francis J. Housing Vouchers for the Poor: Consumption Responses to Constrained Programs. **In** *Struyk, R. J. and Bendick, M., Jr., eds.,* 1981, pp. 129–57. [G: U.S.]

Cronin, Francis J. Participation in the Experimental Housing Allowance Program. **In** *Struyk, R. J. and Bendick, M., Jr., eds.,* 1981, pp. 79–106. [G: U.S.]

Cronin, Francis J. and Rasmussen, David W. Housing Vouchers for the Poor: Mobility. **In** *Struyk, R. J. and Bendick, M., Jr., eds.,* 1981, pp. 107–28. [G: U.S.]

Cullingworth, J. Barry. Rental Housing in Industrialized Countries: Issues and Policies: Comment. **In** *Weicher, J. C.; Villani, K. E. and Roistacher, E. A., eds.,* 1981, pp. 109–10. [G: OECD]

Dahmann, Donald C. Subjective Indicators of Neighborhood Quality. **In** *Johnston, D. F., ed.,* 1981, pp. 97–117. [G: U.S.]

Darden, Joe T. The Determination of Demand in Redlining Research. *Rev. Public Data Use (See J. Econ. Soc. Meas. after 4/85)*, July 1981, *9*(2), pp. 125–32. [G: U.S.]

DeMilner, Lawrence. Discussion [Inflation and Housing Costs] [Expanding and Improving the CPI Rent Component] [Measuring the Cost of Shelter for Homeowners]. **In** *Tuccillo, J. A. and Villani, K. E., eds.,* 1981, pp. 131–33. [G: U.S.]

Diamond, Douglas B., Jr. Inflation and Extraordinary Returns on Owner-Occupied Housing: Some Implications for Capital Allocation: Discussion. **In** *Tuccillo, J. A. and Villani, K. E., eds.,* 1981, pp. 35–36. [G: U.S.]

Diamond, Douglas B., Jr. The Rental Housing Crisis: Comment. **In** *Weicher, J. C.; Villani, K. E. and Roistacher, E. A., eds.,* 1981, pp. 81–83. [G: U.S.]

Dienstfrey, Ted. The Politics of Rent Control in the United States: A Program at the Yellow Light. **In** *Block, W. and Olsen, E., eds.,* 1981, pp. 5–31. [G: U.S.]

Dougherty, Ann and Van Order, Robert. Inflation and Housing Costs. **In** *Tuccillo, J. A. and Villani, K. E., eds.,* 1981, pp. 87–108. [G: U.S.]

Dowall, David E. The Effects of Economic Policy on Patterns of Land Use. **In** *de Neufville, J. I., ed.,* 1981, pp. 17–28. [G: U.S.]

Downs, Anthony. Some Aspects of the Future of Rental Housing. **In** *Weicher, J. C.; Villani, K. E. and Roistacher, E. A., eds.,* 1981, pp. 85–94. [G: U.S.]

Downs, Anthony and Bradbury, Katharine L. Do Housing Allowances Work? Conference Discussion. **In** *Bradbury, K. L. and Downs, A., eds.,* 1981, pp. 375–404. [G: U.S.]

Durez-Demal, Martine; Lux, Bernard and Vandeville, Victor. Pour une réorientation de la politique économique dans le secteur logement. (For a Reorientation of the Economic Policy in the Private Housing Sector. With English summary.) *Cah. Écon. Bruxelles*, 2nd Trimestre 1981, (90), pp. 229–51. [G: Belgium]

Dusansky, Richard; Ingber, Melvin and Karatjas, Nicholas. The Impact of Property Taxation on Housing Values and Rents. *J. Urban Econ.*, September 1981, *10*(2), pp. 240–55. [G: U.S.]

Dusansky, Richard and Kalman, Peter J. Regional Multi-Objective Planning under Uncertainty: Optimal Housing Supply over Time. *Reg. Sci. Urban Econ.*, February 1981, *11*(1), pp. 121–34.

Edel, Matthew. Land Policy, Economic Cycles, and Social Conflict. **In** *de Neufville, J. I., ed.,* 1981, pp. 127–39.

Edelstein, Robert H. Regressivity and the Inequity of the Residential Property Tax: The Philadelphia Story. **In** *Henderson, J. V., ed.,* 1981, pp. 219–47. [G: U.S.]

Eekhoff, Johann. Zur Kontroverse um die ökonomischen Auswirkungen des Zweiten Wohnraumkündigungsschutzgesetzes. (The Economic Effects of Tenants' Protection against Arbitrary Notice. With English summary.) *Z. ges. Staatswiss.*, March 1981, *137*(1), pp. 62–77. [G: W. Germany]

Ellickson, Bryan. An Alternative Test of the Hedonic Theory of Housing Markets. *J. Urban Econ.*, January 1981, *9*(1), pp. 56–79. [G: U.S.]

Elliott, Michael. The Impact of Growth Control Regulations on Housing Prices in California. *Amer. Real Estate Urban Econ. Assoc. J.*, Summer 1981, *9*(2), pp. 115–33. [G: U.S.]

Evans, Richard D. Residential Construction Volatility: A Seasonal and Cyclical Inventory Adjustment Analysis. *Amer. Real Estate Urban Econ. Assoc. J.*, Spring 1981, *9*(1), pp. 74–82. [G: U.S.]

Färe, Rolf and Yoon, Bong Joon. Variable Elasticity

of Substitution in Urban Housing Production. *J. Urban Econ.*, November 1981, *10*(3), pp. 369–74.

Fisher, Glenn W. The Changing Role of Property Taxation. In *Walzer, N. and Chicoine, D. L., eds.*, 1981, pp. 37–60. [G: U.S.]

Fleming, M. C. and Nellis, Joseph G. The Inflation of House Prices in Northern Ireland in the 1970s. *Econ. Soc. Rev.*, October 1981, *13*(1), pp. 1–19. [G: U.K.]

Follain, James R., Jr. and Malpezzi, Stephen. Another Look at Racial Differences in Housing Prices. *Urban Stud.*, June 1981, *18*(2), pp. 195–203. [G: U.S.]

Follain, James R., Jr. and Malpezzi, Stephen. The Flight to the Suburbs: Insights Gained from an Analysis of Central-City vs Suburban Housing Costs. *J. Urban Econ.*, May 1981, *9*(3), pp. 381–98.

Freeman, A. Myrick, III. Hedonic Prices, Property Values and Measuring Environmental Benefits: A Survey of the Issues. In *Strøm, S., ed.*, 1981, *1979*, pp. 13–32.

Friedman, Joseph. A Conditional Logit Model of the Role of Local Public Services in Residential Choice. *Urban Stud.*, October 1981, *18*(3), pp. 347–58. [G: U.S.]

Friedman, Joseph and Weinberg, Daniel H. The Demand for Rental Housing: Evidence from the Housing Allowance Demand Experiment. *J. Urban Econ.*, May 1981, *9*(3), pp. 311–31. [G: U.S.]

Friedman, Milton and Stigler, George J. Roofs or Ceilings? The Current Housing Problem. In *Block, W. and Olsen, E., eds.*, 1981, pp. 87–103. [G: U.S.]

Galster, George C. A Neighborhood Interaction Model of Housing Maintenance and Quality Changes by Owner Occupants. *Reg. Sci. Persp.*, 1981, *11*(2), pp. 29–48.

Gilbert, Alan. Pirates and Invaders: Land Acquisition in Urban Colombia and Venezuela. *World Devel.*, July 1981, *9*(7), pp. 657–78. [G: Colombia; Venezuela]

Giles, Michael W.; Wright, Gerald C. and Dantico, Marilyn K. Social Status and Political Behavior: The Impact of Residential Context. *Soc. Sci. Quart.*, September 1981, *62*(3), pp. 453–60. [G: U.S.]

Gillingham, Robert and Greenlees, John S. Estimating Inter-city Differences in the Price of Housing Services: Further Evidence. *Urban Stud.*, October 1981, *18*(3), pp. 365–69. [G: U.K.]

Gillingham, Robert; Greenlees, John S. and Reece, William S. Measuring the Cost of Shelter for Homeowners. In *Tuccillo, J. A. and Villani, K. E., eds.*, 1981, pp. 123–30. [G: U.S.]

Gold, Steven D. Property Tax Relief Trends in the Midwest: Where It All (or Much of It) Began. In *Walzer, N. and Chicoine, D. L., eds.*, 1981, pp. 61–87. [G: U.S.]

Goldstein, G. S. Product Quality and Value in the New Home Market: Implications for Consumer Protection Regulation: Comment. *J. Law Econ.*, December 1981, *24*(3), pp. 401–02. [G: U.S.]

Goodman, Allen C. Housing Submarkets within Urban Areas: Definitions and Evidence. *J. Reg. Sci.*,

May 1981, *21*(2), pp. 175–85. [G: U.S.]

Goodman, John L., Jr. Demographic Trends and Housing Prices. In *Tuccillo, J. A. and Villani, K. E., eds.*, 1981, pp. 81–86. [G: U.S.]

Greenberg, Stephanie W. Industrial Location and Ethnic Residential Patterns in an Industrializing City: Philadelphia, 1880. In *Hershberg, T., ed.*, 1981, pp. 204–32. [G: U.S.]

Greer, William and White, Michelle J. The Effects of City Size and Moving Costs on Public Project Benefits. *J. Urban Econ.*, March 1981, *9*(2), pp. 149–64.

Grieson, Ronald E. and Murray, Michael P. On the Possibility and Optimality of Positive Rent Gradients: Comment. *J. Urban Econ.*, May 1981, *9*(3), pp. 275–85.

Grieson, Ronald E. and White, James R. The Effects of Zoning on Structure and Land Markets. *J. Urban Econ.*, November 1981, *10*(3), pp. 271–85.

Griffith, Daniel A. Modelling Urban Population Density in a Multi-Centered City. *J. Urban Econ.*, May 1981, *9*(3), pp. 298–310. [G: Canada]

Haefele, Edwin T. A Plea for More Representative Government. In *de Neufville, J. I., ed.*, 1981, pp. 209–13.

Halvorsen, Robert and Pollakowski, Henry O. Choice of Functional Form for Hedonic Price Equations. *J. Urban Econ.*, July 1981, *10*(1), pp. 37–49.

Halvorsen, Robert and Pollakowski, Henry O. The Effects of Fuel Prices on House Prices. *Urban Stud.*, June 1981, *18*(2), pp. 205–11.

Hamilton, Bruce W. and Cooke, Timothy W. The Price of Housing, 1950–1975: Synopsis. In *Tuccillo, J. A. and Villani, K. E., eds.*, 1981, pp. 69–71. [G: U.S.]

Hanushek, Eric A. and Quigley, John M. Do Housing Allowances Work? Consumption Aspects. In *Bradbury, K. L. and Downs, A., eds.*, 1981, pp. 185–246. [G: U.S.]

Hardoy, J. A Particularly Acute Problem: Housing. In *Klaassen, L. H.; Molle, W. T. M. and Paelinck, J. H. P., eds.*, 1981, pp. 47–64.

Hartman, Chester. The Limits of Consensus Building. In *de Neufville, J. I., ed.*, 1981, pp. 205–07. [G: U.S.]

Haurin, Donald R. Property Taxation and the Structure of Urban Areas. In *Henderson, J. V., ed.*, 1981, pp. 263–76.

Hay, Alan M. The Economic Basis of Spontaneous Home Improvement: A Graphical Analysis. *Urban Stud.*, October 1981, *18*(3), pp. 359–64.

Hein, Scott E. and Lamb, James C., Jr. Why the Median-Priced Home Costs So Much. *Fed. Res. Bank St. Louis Rev.*, June–July 1981, *63*(6), pp. 11–19. [G: U.S.]

Hendershott, Patric H. The Rental Housing Crisis. In *Weicher, J. C.; Villani, K. E. and Roistacher, E. A., eds.*, 1981, pp. 75–80. [G: U.S.]

Hendershott, Patric H. and Hu, Sheng-Cheng. Inflation and Extraordinary Returns on Owner-Occupied Housing: Some Implications for Capital Allocation and Productivity Growth. *J. Macroecon.*, Spring 1981, *3*(2), pp. 177–203. [G: U.S.]

Hendershott, Patric H. and Hu, Sheng-Cheng. Inflation and Extraordinary Returns on Owner-Occupied Housing: Some Implications for Capital Allocation and Productivity Growth. In *Tuccillo, J. A. and Villani, K. E., eds.*, 1981, pp. 11–33. [G: U.S.]

Hildebrandt, Gregory G. and Tregarthen, Timothy D. Observing Preferences for Educational Quality: The Weak Complementarity Approach. In *Strim, S., ed.*, 1981, *1979*, pp. 47–56. [G: U.S.]

Hirsch, Werner Z. Habitability Laws and the Welfare of Indigent Tenants. *Rev. Econ. Statist.*, May 1981, *63*(2), pp. 263–74. [G: U.S.]

Holleb, Doris B. Housing and the Environment: Shooting at Moving Targets. *Ann. Amer. Acad. Polit. Soc. Sci.*, January 1981, *453*, pp. 180–221. [G: U.S.]

Howenstine, E. Jay. Private Rental Housing Abroad: Dwindling Supply Stirs Concern. *Mon. Lab. Rev.*, September 1981, *104*(9), pp. 38–42. [G: W. Europe; N. America; Japan]

Howenstine, E. Jay. Rental Housing in Industrialized Countries: Issues and Policies. In *Weicher, J. C.; Villani, K. E. and Roistacher, E. A., eds.*, 1981, pp. 99–108. [G: OECD]

Hughes, Gordon A. and McCormick, Barry. Do Council Housing Policies Reduce Migration between Regions? *Econ. J.*, December 1981, *91*(364), pp. 919–37. [G: U.K.]

Hula, Richard C. Public Needs and Private Investment: The Case of Home Credit. *Soc. Sci. Quart.*, December 1981, *62*(4), pp. 685–703. [G: U.S.]

Ihlanfeldt, Keith Ray. An Empirical Investigation of Alternative Approaches to Estimating the Equilibrium Demand for Housing. *J. Urban Econ.*, January 1981, *9*(1), pp. 97–105. [G: U.S.]

Isler, Morton L. Housing Vouchers for the Poor: Policy Implications: Moving from Research to Programs. In *Struyk, R. J. and Bendick, M., Jr., eds.*, 1981, pp. 267–93. [G: U.S.]

Jackson, Kenneth T. The Spatial Dimensions of Social Control: Race, Ethnicity, and Government Housing Policy in the United States, 1918–1968. In *Stave, B. M., ed.*, 1981, pp. 79–128. [G: U.S.]

Jaffee, Dwight M. The Future Role of Thrift Institutions in Mortgage Lending. In *Federal Reserve Bank of Boston (II)*, 1981, pp. 164–80. [G: U.S.]

Jech, Otto. Social Consumption of the Population and Its Expected Trends. *Czech. Econ. Digest.*, February 1981, (1), pp. 18–37. [G: Czechoslovakia]

Jenkis, Helmut W. Die Mietenpolitik zwischen Ökonomie und Ideologie. (Rental Policy between Economics and Idealogy. With English Summary.) In *[von Haberler, G.]*, 1981, pp. 141–84. [G: W. Germany]

Johnson, Maria Lucia. Legal Barriers to Black Economic Gains: Employment and Transportation: More Legal Barriers: Housing. In *Inst. for Contemp. Studies*, 1981, pp. 31–35.

Johnson, Michael S. A Cash Flow Model of Rational Housing Tenure Choice. *Amer. Real Estate Urban Econ. Assoc. J.*, Spring 1981, *9*(1), pp. 1–17.

Jones, Colin A. Residential Mobility: An Economic Model. *Scot. J. Polit. Econ.*, February 1981,

28(1), pp. 62–75. [G: U.K.]

Jones, Wesley H.; Ferri, Michael G. and McGee, L. Randolph. A Competitive Testing Approach to Models of Depreciation in Housing. *J. Econ. Bus.*, Spring/Summer 1981, *33*(3), pp. 202–11. [G: U.S.]

de Jouvenel, Bertrand. Rent Control: No Vacancies. In *Block, W. and Olsen, E., eds.*, 1981, *1948*, pp. 189–97. [G: France]

Jud, G. Donald and Watts, James M. Schools and Housing Values. *Land Econ.*, August 1981, *57*(3), pp. 459–70. [G: U.S.]

Kain, John F. A Universal Housing Allowance Program. In *Bradbury, K. L. and Downs, A., eds.*, 1981, pp. 329–73. [G: U.S.]

Kaish, Stanley. What Is 'Just and Reasonable' in Rent Control? Why Historic Cost Is More Rational Than Current Value. *Amer. J. Econ. Soc.*, April 1981, *40*(2), pp. 129–37. [G: U.S.]

Kalymon, Basil A. Apartment Shortages and Rent Control. In *Block, W. and Olsen, E., eds.*, 1981, pp. 233–45. [G: Canada]

Kau, James B. and Keenan, Donald. On the Theory of Interest Rates, Consumer Durables, and the Demand for Housing. *J. Urban Econ.*, September 1981, *10*(2), pp. 183–200. [G: U.S.]

Kau, James B. and Sirmans, C. F. The Demand for Urban Residential Land. *J. Reg. Sci.*, November 1981, *21*(4), pp. 519–28. [G: U.S.]

Kawaller, Ira G. and Koch, Timothy W. Housing as a Monetary Phenomenon: Forecasting Housing Starts Using the Monetary Aggregate Targets. *Bus. Econ.*, September 1981, *16*(4), pp. 30–35. [G: U.S.]

Kearl, James R. Inflation and Extraordinary Returns on Owner-Occupied Housing: Some Implications for Capital Allocation: Discussion. In *Tuccillo, J. A. and Villani, K. E., eds.*, 1981, pp. 37–42. [G: U.S.]

Kern, Clifford R. Racial Prejudice and Residential Segregation: The Yinger Model Revisited. *J. Urban Econ.*, September 1981, *10*(2), pp. 164–72. [G: U.S.]

Kern, Clifford R. Upper-Income Renaissance in the City: Its Sources and Implications for the City's Future. *J. Urban Econ.*, January 1981, *9*(1), pp. 106–24. [G: U.S.]

Kershaw, David N. and Williams, Roberton C., Jr. Do Housing Allowances Work? Administrative Lessons. In *Bradbury, K. L. and Downs, A., eds.*, 1981, pp. 285–337. [G: U.S.]

Kiefer, David. The Interaction of Inflation and U.S. Tax Subsidies of Housing. *Nat. Tax J.*, December 1981, *34*(4), pp. 433–46. [G: U.S.]

Kristof, Frank S. The Effects of Rent Control and Rent Stabilization in New York City. In *Block, W. and Olsen, E., eds.*, 1981, pp. 125–47. [G: U.S.]

Ladd, Edward H. The Future Role of Thrift Institutions in Mortgage Lending: Discussion. In *Federal Reserve Bank of Boston (II)*, 1981, pp. 181–87. [G: U.S.]

Lee, Douglass B., Jr. Land Use Planning as a Response to Market Failure. In *de Neufville, J. I., ed.*, 1981, pp. 149–64.

Leeds, Morton. Inflation and the Elderly: A Housing Perspective. *Ann. Amer. Acad. Polit. Soc. Sci.*, July 1981, *456*, pp. 60–69. [G: U.S.]

de Leeuw, Frank. A Synthesis of Views on Rental Housing. In *Weicher, J. C.; Villani, K. E. and Roistacher, E. A., eds.*, 1981, pp. 61–64.
[G: U.S.]

de Leeuw, Frank. Discussion [Inflation and Housing Costs] [Expanding and Improving the CPI Rent Component] [Measuring the Cost of Shelter for Homeowners]. In *Tuccillo, J. A. and Villani, K. E., eds.*, 1981, pp. 133–36.   [G: U.S.]

de Leeuw, Frank and Ozanne, Larry J. Housing. In *Aaron, H. J. and Pechman, J. A., eds.*, 1981, pp. 283–319.   [G: U.S.]

Lefcoe, George. A Case for Local Governance and Private Property. In *de Neufville, J. I., ed.*, 1981, pp. 233–38.

Linneman, Peter. The Demand for Residence Site Characteristics. *J. Urban Econ.*, March 1981, 9(2), pp. 129–48.   [G: U.S.]

Lowry, Ira S. Rental Housing in the 1970s: Searching for the Crisis. In *Weicher, J. C.; Villani, K. E. and Roistacher, E. A., eds.*, 1981, pp. 23–38.
[G: U.S.]

MacRae, C. Duncan and Turner, Margery Austin. Estimating Demand for Owner-Occupied Housing Subject to the Income Tax. *J. Urban Econ.*, November 1981, 10(3), pp. 338–56.   [G: U.S.]

Mandelbaum, Seymour J. The Economy of Cities: Comment. In *Stave, B. M., ed.*, 1981, pp. 251–57.   [G: U.S.]

Mandelker, Daniel R. The Taking Issue in Land Use Regulation. In *de Neufville, J. I., ed.*, 1981, pp. 167–80.

Marcuse, Peter A. Class Tension and the Mechanisms of Social Control: The Housing Experience: Comment. In *Stave, B. M., ed.*, 1981, pp. 175–81.   [G: Europe; U.S.]

Margolis, Stephen E. Depreciation and Maintenance of Houses. *Land Econ.*, February 1981, 57(1), pp. 91–105.

Mark, Jonathan H. and Goldberg, Michael A. Land Use Controls: The Case of Zoning in the Vancouver Area. *Amer. Real Estate Urban Econ. Assoc. J.*, Winter 1981, 9(4), pp. 418–35. [G: Canada]

Mayer, Neil S. Rehabilitation Decisions in Rental Housing: An Empirical Analysis. *J. Urban Econ.*, July 1981, 10(1), pp. 76–94.   [G: U.S.]

Mayo, Stephen K. Theory and Estimation in the Economics of Housing Demand. *J. Urban Econ.*, July 1981, 10(1), pp. 95–116.   [G: U.S.]

McDonald, John F. Capital–Land Substitution in Urban Housing: A Survey of Empirical Estimates. *J. Urban Econ.*, March 1981, 9(2), pp. 190–211.
[G: U.S.]

McMillan, Melville L. Estimates of Households' Preferences for Environmental Quality and Other Housing Characteristics from a System of Demand Equations. In *Strøm, S., ed.*, 1981, 1979, pp. 33–46.   [G: Canada]

Mennes, L. B. M. and Mulder, E. H. Alternative Views on Urbanisation and Housing in Developing Countries. In *Klaassen, L. H.; Molle, W. T. M. and Paelinck, J. H. P., eds.*, 1981, pp. 65–72.

Michelman, Frank I. Localism and Political Freedom. In *de Neufville, J. I., ed.*, 1981, pp. 239–43.

Mills, David E. Urban Residential Development Timing. *Reg. Sci. Urban Econ.*, May 1981, 11(2), pp. 239–54.

Mills, Edwin S. and Sullivan, Arthur. Do Housing Allowances Work? Market Effects. In *Bradbury, K. L. and Downs, A., eds.*, 1981, pp. 247–83.
[G: U.S.]

Mingo, John J. A Comparison of European Housing Finance Systems: Discussion. In *Federal Reserve Bank of Boston (II)*, 1981, pp. 161–63.
[G: France; W. Germany; U.K.]

Morgan, Barrie S. and Norbury, John. Some Further Observations on the Index of Residential Differentiation. *Demography*, May 1981, 18(2), pp. 251–56.   [G: U.S.]

Morgan, James N.; Ponza, Michael and Imbruglia, Renata. Trends in Residential Property Taxes. In *Hill, M. S.; Hill, D. H. and Morgan, J. N., eds.*, 1981, pp. 391–403.   [G: U.S.]

Nechemias, Carol. The Impact of Soviet Housing Policy on Housing Conditions in Soviet Cities: The Uneven Push from Moscow. *Urban Stud.*, February 1981, 18(1), pp. 1–8.
[G: U.S.S.R.]

Nellis, Joseph G. and Longbottom, J. Andrew. An Empirical Analysis of the Determination of House Prices in the United Kingdom. *Urban Stud.*, February 1981, 18(1), pp. 9–21.   [G: U.K.]

Nelson, Jon P. Three Mile Island and Residential Property Values: Empirical Analysis and Policy Implications. *Land Econ.*, August 1981, 57(3), pp. 363–72.   [G: U.S.]

de Neufville, Judith Innes. Conclusion: Disentangling the Debate. In *de Neufville, J. I., ed.*, 1981, pp. 245–55.

de Neufville, Judith Innes. Land Use: A Tool for Social Policies. In *de Neufville, J. I., ed.*, 1981, pp. 31–47.   [G: U.S.]

Newman, Sandra J. and Ponza, Michael. The Characteristics of Housing Demand in the 1970s: A Research Note. In *Hill, M. S.; Hill, D. H. and Morgan, J. N., eds.*, 1981, pp. 467–96.
[G: U.S.]

Nicholas, James C. Housing Costs and Prices under Regional Regulation. *Amer. Real Estate Urban Econ. Assoc. J.*, Winter 1981, 9(4), pp. 384–96.
[G: U.S.]

Niethammer, Lutz. Some Elements of the Housing Reform Debate in Nineteenth-Century Europe: Or, On the Making of a New Paradigm of Social Control. In *Stave, B. M., ed.*, 1981, pp. 129–64.   [G: Europe]

O'Hare, Michael. Improvement of Owner-Occupied Rental Housing: A Game-theoretic Study of the Decision to Invest. *Amer. Real Estate Urban Econ. Assoc. J.*, Spring 1981, 9(1), pp. 54–66.

Olsen, Edgar O. Questions and Some Answers about Rent Control: An Empirical Analysis of New York's Experience. In *Block, W. and Olsen, E., eds.*, 1981, pp. 107–21.   [G: U.S.]

Olsen, Edgar O. and Reeder, William J. Does HUD Pay Too Much for Section 8 Existing Housing? *Land Econ.*, May 1981, 57(2), pp. 243–51.
[G: U.S.]

Olsen, Edgar O. and Walker, M. A. Rent Control:

Alternatives. In *Block, W. and Olsen, E., eds.*, 1981, pp. 267–82. [G: U.S.]

Ozanne, Larry J. Double Vision in the Rental Housing Market and a Prescription for Correcting It. In *Weicher, J. C.; Villani, K. E. and Roistacher, E. A., eds.*, 1981, pp. 39–48. [G: U.S.]

Ozanne, Larry J. Expanding and Improving the CPI Rent Component. In *Tuccillo, J. A. and Villani, K. E., eds.*, 1981, pp. 109–21. [G: U.S.]

Ozanne, Larry J. and Zais, James P. Community-wide Effects of Housing Allowances. In *Struyk, R. J. and Bendick, M., Jr., eds.*, 1981, pp. 207–33. [G: U.S.]

Paish, F. W. The Economics of Rent Restriction. In *Block, W. and Olsen, E., eds.*, 1981, pp. 151–60. [G: U.K.]

Parker, Carl, III. Trend Surface and the Spatio-Temporal Analysis of Residential Land-Use Intensity and Household Housing Expenditure. *Land Econ.*, August 1981, 57(3), pp. 323–37. [G: U.S.]

Peiser, Richard B. Land Development Regulation: A Case Study of Dallas and Houston, Texas. *Amer. Real Estate Urban Econ. Assoc. J.*, Winter 1981, 9(4), pp. 397–417. [G: U.S.]

Peterson, George E. Housing: Comments. In *Aaron, H. J. and Pechman, J. A., eds.*, 1981, pp. 319–23. [G: U.S.]

Phillips, Robyn Swaim. A Note on the Determinants of Residential Succession. *J. Urban Econ.*, January 1981, 9(1), pp. 49–55. [G: U.S.]

Portney, Paul R. Housing Prices, Health Effects, and Valuing Reductions in Risk of Death. *J. Environ. Econ. Manage.*, March 1981, 8(1), pp. 72–78. [G: U.S.]

Pratschke, John L. Rural and Farm Dwellings in the European Community. *Irish J. Agr. Econ. Rural Soc.*, 1981, 8(2), pp. 191–211. [G: EEC]

Ranney, Susan I. The Future Price of Houses, Mortgage Market Conditions, and the Returns to Homeownership. *Amer. Econ. Rev.*, June 1981, 71(3), pp. 323–33.

Rex, John. Urban Segregation and Inner City Policy in Great Britain. In *Peach, C.; Robinson, V. and Smith, S., eds.*, 1981, pp. 25–42. [G: U.K.]

Robinson, Ray. Housing Tax-Expenditures, Subsidies and the Distribution of Income. *Manchester Sch. Econ. Soc. Stud.*, June 1981, 49(2), pp. 91–110. [G: U.K.]

Robinson, Vaughan. The Development of South Asian Settlement in Britain and the Myth of Return. In *Peach, C.; Robinson, V. and Smith, S., eds.*, 1981, pp. 149–69. [G: U.K.]

Rose, Damaris. Accumulation versus Reproduction in the Inner City: *The Recurrent Crisis of London* Revisited. In *Dear, M. and Scott, A. J., eds.*, 1981, pp. 339–81. [G: U.K.]

Rose, Harold M. The Black Professional and Residential Segregation in the American City. In *Peach, C.; Robinson, V. and Smith, S., eds.*, 1981, pp. 127–48. [G: U.S.]

Rosen, Christine M. Class Tension and the Mechanisms of Social Control: The Housing Experience: Comment. In *Stave, B. M., ed.*, 1981, pp. 165–75.

Rosen, Harvey S. Housing: Comments. In *Aaron, H. J. and Pechman, J. A., eds.*, 1981, pp. 323–26. [G: U.S.]

Rosen, Harvey S. Reply to Gillingham and Greenlees [Estimating Inter-city Differences in the Price of Housing Services]. *Urban Stud.*, October 1981, 18(3), pp. 371.

Rosen, Kenneth T. A Comparison of European Housing Finance Systems. In *Federal Reserve Bank of Boston (II)*, 1981, pp. 144–60.
[G: U.K.; W. Germany; France]

Rosen, Kenneth T. and Katz, Lawrence F. Growth Management and Land Use Controls: The San Francisco Bay Area Experience. *Amer. Real Estate Urban Econ. Assoc. J.*, Winter 1981, 9(4), pp. 321–44. [G: U.S.]

Rossi, Peter H. Do Housing Allowances Work? Residential Mobility. In *Bradbury, K. L. and Downs, A., eds.*, 1981, pp. 147–83.

Rowe, Andy. The Financing of Residential Construction in Newfoundland. *Can. Public Policy*, Winter 1981, 7(1), pp. 119–22. [G: Canada]

Roweis, Shoukry T. and Scott, Allen J. The Urban Land Question. In *Dear, M. and Scott, A. J., eds.*, 1981, pp. 123–57.

Rydenfelt, Sven. The Rise, Fall, and Revival of Swedish Rent Control. In *Block, W. and Olsen, E., eds.*, 1981, pp. 201–30. [G: Sweden]

Sandelin, Bo. Price Behavior and Capital Gains on Residential Real Estate: The Case of Sweden. *Amer. Real Estate Urban Econ. Assoc. J.*, Fall 1981, 9(3), pp. 241–64.

Schafer, Robert. Discussion [Financial Institution Regulations, Redlining and Mortgage Markets] [Mortgage Redlining Research: A Review and Critical Analysis Discussion]. In *Fed. Res. Bank of Boston and National Sci. Foundation*, 1981, pp. 196–202. [G: U.S.]

Schall, Lawrence D. Commodity Chain Systems and the Housing Market. *J. Urban Econ.*, September 1981, 10(2), pp. 141–63.

Schwartz, Seymour I.; Hansen, David E. and Green, Richard D. Suburban Growth Controls and the Price of New Housing. *J. Environ. Econ. Manage.*, December 1981, 8(4), pp. 303–20. [G: U.S.]

Schweizer, Urs. Eine neoklassische Erklärung urbaner Wohnstrukturen. (A Neoclassical Model of a Residential Economy. With English summary.) *Z. ges. Staatswiss.*, June 1981, 137(2), pp. 222–33.

Seiders, David F. Changing Patterns of Housing Finance. *Fed. Res. Bull.*, June 1981, 67(6), pp. 461–72. [G: U.S.]

Shlay, Anne B. and Rossi, Peter H. Putting Politics into Urban Ecology: Estimating Net Effects of Zoning. In *Clark, T. N., ed.*, 1981, pp. 257–86. [G: U.S.]

Shulman, David. Real Estate Valuation under Rent Control: The Case of Santa Monica. *Amer. Real Estate Urban Econ. Assoc. J.*, Spring 1981, 9(1), pp. 38–53. [G: U.S.]

Simons, Lawrence. Rental Housing: A Developer's Perspective. In *Weicher, J. C.; Villani, K. E. and Roistacher, E. A., eds.*, 1981, pp. 49–53. [G: U.S.]

Skaburskis, A. Determinants of Canadian Housing

Stock Losses. *Amer. Real Estate Urban Econ. Assoc. J.*, Summer 1981, 9(2), pp. 181–84.
[G: Canada]

Smith, Barton A. A Study of Racial Discrimination in Housing. In *Henderson, J. V., ed.*, 1981, pp. 131–99. [G: U.S.]

Smith, Lawrence B. Canadian Housing Policy in the Seventies. *Land Econ.*, August 1981, 57(3), pp. 338–52. [G: Canada]

Smith, Lawrence B. Housing Assistance: A Re-evaluation. *Can. Public Policy*, Summer 1981, 7(3), pp. 454–63. [G: Canada]

Smith, Lawrence B. and Tomlinson, Peter. Rent Controls in Ontario: Roofs or Ceilings? *Amer. Real Estate Urban Econ. Assoc. J.*, Summer 1981, 9(2), pp. 93–114. [G: Canada]

Solo, Robert. Policy Options: Regional Building Codes Formulated and Enforced by the Federal Bureau of Standards. *J. Econ. Issues*, March 1981, 15(1), pp. 173–75. [G: U.S.]

Spellman, Lewis J. Inflation and Housing Prices. *Amer. Real Estate Urban Econ. Assoc. J.*, Fall 1981, 9(3), pp. 205–22. [G: U.S.]

Sternlieb, George. The Future of Rental Housing. In *Weicher, J. C.; Villani, K. E. and Roistacher, E. A., eds.*, 1981, pp. 55–60. [G: U.S.]

Straszheim, Mahlon R. Do Housing Allowances Work? Participation. In *Bradbury, K. L. and Downs, A., eds.*, 1981, pp. 113–45. [G: U.S.]

Strong, Ann L. Land as a Public Good: An Idea Whose Time Has Come Again. In *de Neufville, J. I., ed.*, 1981, pp. 217–32. [G: U.S.]

Struyk, Raymond J. Housing Vouchers for the Poor: Policy Questions and Experimental Responses. In *Struyk, R. J. and Bendick, M., Jr., eds.*, 1981, pp. 3–20. [G: U.S.]

Struyk, Raymond J. Housing Vouchers for the Poor: Social Experimentation and Policy Research. In *Struyk, R. J. and Bendick, M., Jr., eds.*, 1981, pp. 295–310. [G: U.S.]

Sulvetta, Anthony J. The Price of Housing, 1950–1975: Synopsis: Discussion. In *Tuccillo, J. A. and Villani, K. E., eds.*, 1981, pp. 76–79. [G: U.S.]

Summers, Lawrence H. Inflation, the Stock Market, and Owner-Occupied Housing. *Amer. Econ. Rev.*, May 1981, 71(2), pp. 429–34. [G: U.S.]

Sunley, Emil M. Housing Tax Preferences: Options for Reform. In *Weicher, J. C.; Villani, K. E. and Roistacher, E. A., eds.*, 1981, pp. 65–71.
[G: U.S.]

Susskind, Lawrence. Citizen Participation and Consensus Building in Land Use Planning: A Case Study. In *de Neufville, J. I., ed.*, 1981, pp. 183–204. [G: U.S.]

Swan, Craig. The Price of Housing, 1950–1975: Synopsis: Discussion. In *Tuccillo, J. A. and Villani, K. E., eds.*, 1981, pp. 73–76. [G: U.S.]

Tauchen, Helen. The Possibility of Positive Rent Gradients Reconsidered. *J. Urban Econ.*, March 1981, 9(2), pp. 165–72.

Taylor, D. Garth. Racial Preferences, Housing Segregation, and the Causes of School Segregation: Recent Evidence from a Social Survey Used in Civil Litigation. *Rev. Public Data Use (See J. Econ. Soc. Meas. after 4/85)*, December 1981, 9(4), pp. 267–82. [G: U.S.]

Thompson, Wilbur R. and Mikesell, James J. Housing Supply and Demand. In *Hawley, A. H. and Mazie, S. M., eds.*, 1981, pp. 551–88. [G: U.S.]

Tuccillo, John A. and Villani, Kevin E. House Prices and Inflation: Introduction. In *Tuccillo, J. A. and Villani, K. E., eds.*, 1981, pp. 1–9.

Vandell, Kerry D. The Effects of Racial Composition on Neighbourhood Succession. *Urban Stud.*, October 1981, 18(3), pp. 315–33. [G: U.S.]

Vaughan, Roger J. The Value of Urban Open Space. In *Henderson, J. V., ed.*, 1981, pp. 103–30.
[G: U.S]

Vousden, Neil. Market Power in a Non-Malleable City. *Rev. Econ. Stud.*, January 1981, 48(1), pp. 3–19.

Walden, Michael L. A Note on Benefit and Cost Estimates in Publicly Assisted Housing. *J. Reg. Sci.*, August 1981, 21(3), pp. 421–23. [G: U.S.]

Walker, M. A. A Short Course in Housing Economics. In *Block, W. and Olsen, E., eds.*, 1981, pp. 37–52.

Walker, M. A. Rent Control: Decontrol. In *Block, W. and Olsen, E., eds.*, 1981, pp. 249–61.
[G: Canada]

Walker, P. A. and Davis, J. R. Reconciling Dwelling Stock Estimates with Census Data. *Rev. Public Data Use (See J. Econ. Soc. Meas. after 4/85)*, November 1981, 9(3), pp. 167–74. [G: U.S.]

Walker, Richard A. A Theory of Suburbanization: Capitalism and the Construction of Urban Space in the United States. In *Dear, M. and Scott, A. J., eds.*, 1981, pp. 383–429.

Wallich, Henry C. The High Cost of Trying to Help Housing. In *Tuccillo, J. A. and Villani, K. E., eds.*, 1981, pp. 163–67. [G: U.S.]

Walsh, P. K., et al. Models for Forecasting Residential Populations—The Geometric Programming Approach. *Reg. Stud.*, 1981, 15(6), pp. 521–31.
[G: Australia]

Ward, Robin and Sims, Ronald. Social Status, the Market and Ethnic Segregation. In *Peach, C.; Robinson, V. and Smith, S., eds.*, 1981, pp. 217–34. [G: U.K.]

Watts, Harold W. A Critical Review of the Program as a Social Experiment. In *Bradbury, K. L. and Downs, A., eds.*, 1981, pp. 33–65. [G: U.S.]

Weaver, Clifford L. and Hejna, David T. Antitrust Liability and Commercial Zoning Litigation. In *Sternlieb, G. and Hughes, J. W., eds.*, 1981, pp. 113–28. [G: U.S.]

Weicher, John C. Product Quality and Value in the New Home Market: Implications for Consumer Protection Regulation. *J. Law Econ.*, December 1981, 24(3), pp. 365–97. [G: U.S.]

Weicher, John C. Some Aspects of the Future of Rental Housing: Comment. In *Weicher, J. C.; Villani, K. E. and Roistacher, E. A., eds.*, 1981, pp. 95–98. [G: U.S.]

Weinberg, Daniel H.; Friedman, Joseph and Mayo, Stephen K. Intraurban Residential Mobility: The Role of Transactions Costs, Market Imperfections, and Household Disequilibrium. *J. Urban Econ.*, May 1981, 9(3), pp. 332–48. [G: U.S.]

Wheaton, William C. Symposium on Urbanization and Development: Housing Policies and Urban "Markets" in Developing Countries: The Egyptian Experience. *J. Urban Econ.*, March 1981, 9(2), pp. 242–56. **[G: Egypt]**

Wolch, Jennifer R. The Location of Service-Dependent Households in Urban Areas. *Econ. Geogr.*, January 1981, 57(1), pp. 52–67.

Yates, Judith N. The Demand for Owner-Occupied Housing. *Australian Econ. Pap.*, December 1981, 20(37), pp. 309–24. **[G: Australia]**

Yinger, John. A Search Model of Real Estate Broker Behavior. *Amer. Econ. Rev.*, September 1981, 71(4), pp. 591–605.

Zais, James P. Administering Housing Allowances. In *Struyk, R. J. and Bendick, M., Jr., eds.*, 1981, pp. 235–64. **[G: U.S.]**

Zais, James P. Repairs and Maintenance on the Units Occupied by Allowance Recipients. In *Struyk, R. J. and Bendick, M., Jr., eds.*, 1981, pp. 179–206. **[G: U.S.]**

Zuiches, James J. Residential Preferences in the United States. In *Hawley, A. H. and Mazie, S. M., eds.*, 1981, pp. 72–115. **[G: U.S.]**

933 Urban Transportation Economics

9330 Urban Transportation Economics

Anas, Alex. The Estimation of Multinomial Logit Models of Joint Location and Travel Mode Choice from Aggregated Data. *J. Reg. Sci.*, May 1981, 21(2), pp. 223–42. **[G: U.S.]**

Ashley, David J. Uncertainty in Interurban Highway-Scheme Appraisal. In *Stopher, P. R.; Meyburg, A. H. and Brög, W., eds.*, 1981, pp. 599–615. **[G: U.K.]**

Ben-Akiva, Moshe E. Issues in Transferring and Updating Travel-Behavior Models. In *Stopher, P. R.; Meyburg, A. H. and Brög, W., eds.*, 1981, pp. 665–86. **[G: U.S.]**

Bonsall, Peter. Car Sharing in the United Kingdom: A Policy Appraisal. *J. Transp. Econ. Policy*, January 1981, 15(1), pp. 35–44. **[G: U.K.]**

Bourgin, Christian and Godard, Xavier. Structural and Threshold Effects in the Use of Transportation Modes. In *Stopher, P. R.; Meyburg, A. H. and Brög, W., eds.*, 1981, pp. 353–68.

Brand, Daniel and Cheslow, Melvin D. Spatial, Temporal, and Cultural Transferability of Travel-Choice Models. In *Stopher, P. R.; Meyburg, A. H. and Brög, W., eds.*, 1981, pp. 687–91.

Burnett, K. Patricia. Spatial Transferability of Travel-Demand Models. In *Stopher, P. R.; Meyburg, A. H. and Brög, W., eds.*, 1981, pp. 623–28.

Carnes, Richard B. Productivity Trends for Intercity Bus Carriers. *Mon. Lab. Rev.*, May 1981, 104(5), pp. 23–27. **[G: U.S.]**

Chall, Daniel E. The Economic Costs of Subway Deterioration. *Fed. Res. Bank New York Quart. Rev.*, Spring 1981, 6(1), pp. 8–14. **[G: U.S.]**

Cherlow, Jay R. Measuring Values of Travel Time Savings. *J. Cons. Res.*, March 1981, 7(4), pp. 360–71. **[G: U.S.]**

D'Este, Glen. A Technique for Estimating the Average Duration of Commuter Trips. *J. Urban Econ.*, November 1981, 10(3), pp. 357–68. **[G: U.K.]**

Daniels, P. W. Transport Changes Generated by De-

centralized Offices: A Second Survey. *Reg. Stud.*, 1981, 15(6), pp. 507–20. **[G: U.K.]**

Dick, H. W. Urban Public Transport—Part II. *Bull. Indonesian Econ. Stud.*, July 1981, 17(2), pp. 72–88. **[G: Indonesia]**

Dick, H. W. Urban Public Transport: Jakarta, Surabaya and Malang: Part I. *Bull. Indonesian Econ. Stud.*, March 1981, 17(1), pp. 66–82. **[G: Indonesia]**

Drinka, Thomas P. and Prescott, James R. Optimal Roadway Tolls and Operating Costs in Urbanized Regions. *Reg. Sci. Persp.*, 1981, 11(2), pp. 15–28. **[G: U.S.]**

Fisher, James S. and Mitchelson, Ronald L. Extended and Internal Commuting in the Transformation of the Intermetropolitan Periphery. *Econ. Geogr.*, July 1981, 57(3), pp. 189–207. **[G: U.S.]**

Forsyth, P. J. Urban Transportation Pricing. In *Ballabon, M. B., ed.*, 1981, pp. 195–228.

Frankena, Mark W. The Effects of Alternative Urban Transit Subsidy Formulas. *J. Public Econ.*, June 1981, 15(3), pp. 337–48.

Gauthier, Howard L. and Mitchelson, Ronald L. Attribute Importance and Mode Satisfaction in Travel Mode Choice Research. *Econ. Geogr.*, October 1981, 57(4), pp. 348–61. **[G: Canada]**

Hansen, Stein. In Favor of Cross-Cultural Transferability of Travel-Demand Models. In *Stopher, P. R.; Meyburg, A. H. and Brög, W., eds.*, 1981, pp. 637–51.

Hanson, Susan and Hanson, Perry. The Travel-Activity Patterns of Urban Residents: Dimensions and Relationships to Sociodemographic Characteristics. *Econ. Geogr.*, October 1981, 57(4), pp. 332–47. **[G: Sweden]**

Hartgen, David T. Uncertainty in the Application of Travel-Behavior Models. In *Stopher, P. R.; Meyburg, A. H. and Brög, W., eds.*, 1981, pp. 617–20.

Havens, John J. New Approaches to Understanding Travel Behavior: Role, Life-Style, and Adaptation. In *Stopher, P. R.; Meyburg, A. H. and Brög, W., eds.*, 1981, pp. 269–87.

Held, Martin. The Motivation of Using Alternative Modes of Transportation in Urban Areas. In *Molt, W.; Hartmann, H. A. and Stringer, P., eds.*, 1981, pp. 383–98. **[G: W. Germany]**

Henderson, J. Vernon. The Economics of Staggered Work Hours. *J. Urban Econ.*, May 1981, 9(3), pp. 349–64. **[G: U.S.]**

Hensher, David A. and Johnson, Lester W. Behavioural Response and Form of the Representative Component of the Indirect Utility Function in Travel Choice Models. *Reg. Sci. Urban Econ.*, November 1981, 11(4), pp. 559–72. **[G: Australia]**

Hershberg, Theodore, et al. The "Journey-to-Work": An Empirical Investigation of Work, Residence and Transportation, Philadelphia, 1850 and 1880. In *Hershberg, T., ed.*, 1981, pp. 128–73. **[G: U.S.]**

Jackson, Raymond. A Rejoinder [Optimal Studies for Public Transit]. *J. Transp. Econ. Policy*, January 1981, 15(1), pp. 72–75.

Jones, Peter M. Activity Approaches to Understanding Travel Behavior. In *Stopher, P. R.; Meyburg, A. H. and Brög, W., eds.*, 1981, pp. 253–66.

Klaassen, Leo H. Infrastructure Design and Urban Form: An Exercise in Geometry. *De Economist*, 1981, 129(1), pp. 105–26.

Kraus, Marvin. Indivisibilities, Economies of Scale, and Optimal Subsidy Policy for Freeways. *Land Econ.*, February 1981, 57(1), pp. 115–21. **[G: U.S.]**

Kraus, Marvin. Scale Economies Analysis for Urban Highway Networks. *J. Urban Econ.*, January 1981, 9(1), pp. 1–22. **[G: U.K.]**

Kraus, Marvin. The Problem of Optimal Resource Allocation in Urban Transportation. In *Ballabon, M. B., ed.*, 1981, pp. 229–61.

Kutter, Eckhard. Some Remarks on Activity-Pattern Analysis in Transportation Planning. In *Stopher, P. R.; Meyburg, A. H. and Brög, W., eds.*, 1981, pp. 231–51.

Lerman, Steven R. A Comment on Interspatial, Intraspatial, and Temporal Transferability. In *Stopher, P. R.; Meyburg, A. H. and Brög, W., eds.*, 1981, pp. 628–32.

Mäcke, Paul A. Reflections on Transferability. In *Stopher, P. R.; Meyburg, A. H. and Brög, W., eds.*, 1981, pp. 632–36.

Martens, Gerd and Verron, Hedwig. Acceptance of Public Transportation Systems. In *Molt, W.; Hartmann, H. A. and Stringer, P., eds.*, 1981, pp. 399–402. **[G: W. Germany]**

Nash, C. A. The Allocation of Investment to Interurban Road and Rail—A Comment. *Reg. Stud.*, 1981, 15(2), pp. 143–44. **[G: U.S.]**

Paaswell, Robert E. Travel and Activity Needs of the Mobility Limited. In *Stopher, P. R.; Meyburg, A. H. and Brög, W., eds.*, 1981, pp. 425–54. **[G: U.S.]**

Pipkin, J. S. The Concept of Choice and Cognitive Explanations of Spatial Behavior. *Econ. Geogr.*, October 1981, 57(4), pp. 315–31.

Saltzman, Arthur and Newlin, Lawrence W. The Availability of Passenger Transportation. In *Hawley, A. H. and Mazie, S. M., eds.*, 1981, pp. 255–84. **[G: U.S.]**

Shilony, Yuval. A Methodological Note on Welfare Calculus [Optimal Subsidies for Public Transit]. *J. Transp. Econ. Policy*, January 1981, 15(1), pp. 69–72.

Shreiber, Chanoch. The Economic Reasons for Price and Entry Regulation of Taxicabs: A Rejoinder. *J. Transp. Econ. Policy*, January 1981, 15(1), pp. 81–83. **[G: U.S.]**

Small, Kenneth A. A Comment on Gasoline Prices and Urban Structure [Urban Structure, Gas Prices, and the Demand for Transportation]. *J. Urban Econ.*, November 1981, 10(3), pp. 311–22.

Spear, Bruce D. Travel-Behavior Research: The Need and Potential for Policy Relevance. In *Stopher, P. R.; Meyburg, A. H. and Brög, W., eds.*, 1981, pp. 387–97.

St. Clair, David J. The Motorization and Decline of Urban Public Transit, 1935–1950. *J. Econ. Hist.*, September 1981, 41(3), pp. 579–600. **[G: U.S.]**

Starkie, D. N. M. Rejoinder to C. A. Nash [Alloca-

tion of Investment to Interurban Road and Rail]. *Reg. Stud.*, 1981, 15(2), pp. 145–46. **[G: U.S.]**

Stringer, Peter. Time, Cost and Other Factors in Inter-urban Travel Mode Choice. In *Molt, W.; Hartmann, H. A. and Stringer, P., eds.*, 1981, pp. 367–81. **[G: U.K.]**

Talley, Wayne K. and French, Gary L. The Redistributive Impact of the Atlanta Mass Transit System: A Comment. *Southern Econ. J.*, January 1981, 47(3), pp. 831–38. **[G: U.S.]**

Talvitie, Antti P. Inaccurate or Incomplete Data as a Source of Uncertainty in Econometric or Attitudinal Models of Travel Behavior. In *Stopher, P. R.; Meyburg, A. H. and Brög, W., eds.*, 1981, pp. 559–75. **[G: U.S.]**

Tucci, Gianrocco. Il legame fra trasporto e uso del suolo: una riflessione su alcune ricerche. (Land Use and Transport Systems: Some Considerations on a Ten-year Research. With English summary.) *Rivista Int. Sci. Econ. Com.*, May 1981, 28(5), pp. 449–60.

Viton, Philip A. A Translog Cost Function for Urban Bus Transit. *J. Ind. Econ.*, March 1981, 29(3), pp. 287–304. **[G: U.S.]**

Viton, Philip A. On Competition and Product Differentiation in Urban Transportation: The San Francisco Bay Area. *Bell J. Econ. (See Rand J. Econ. after 4/85)*, Autumn 1981, 12(2), pp. 362–79. **[G: U.S.]**

Walters, A. A. A Rejoinder [The Benefits of Minibuses: The Case of Kuala Lumpur]. *J. Transp. Econ. Policy*, January 1981, 15(1), pp. 79–80. **[G: Malaysia]**

Weber, Hans Peter. Uncertainty in Application: A German Case Study. In *Stopher, P. R.; Meyburg, A. H. and Brög, W., eds.*, 1981, pp. 587–98. **[G: W. Germany]**

White, Peter R. "Travelcard" Tickets in Urban Public Transport. *J. Transp. Econ. Policy*, January 1981, 15(1), pp. 17–34. **[G: U.K.; W. Europe]**

White, Peter R. The Benefits of Minibuses: A Comment [The Benefits of Minibuses: The Case of Kuala Lumpur]. *J. Transp. Econ. Policy*, January 1981, 15(1), pp. 77–79. **[G: Malaysia]**

Williams, Martin and Dalal, Ardeshir. Estimation of the Elasticities of Factor Substitution in Urban Bus Transportation: A Cost Function Approach. *J. Reg. Sci.*, May 1981, 21(2), pp. 263–75.

940 REGIONAL ECONOMICS

941 Regional Economics

9410 General

Bagchi, A.; Olsder, G. J. and Strijobs, R. C. W. Regional Allocation of Investment as a Hierarchical Optimization Problem. *Reg. Sci. Urban Econ.*, May 1981, 11(2), pp. 205–13.

Beebe, W. T. Southern Business: The Future. In *Bateman, F., ed.*, 1981, pp. 113–15. **[G: U.S.]**

Bell, David N. F. Regional Output: Employment and Unemployment Fluctuations. *Oxford Econ. Pap.*, March 1981, 33(1), pp. 42–60. **[G: U.K.]**

Boisier, Sergio. Towards a Social and Political Dimension of Regional Planning. *Cepal Rev.*, April

1981, (13), pp. 93–123.   [G: Latin America]

Delp, Peter. District Planning in Kenya. In *Killick, T., ed.*, 1981, pp. 117–26.   [G: Kenya]

Edwards, Clark. Spatial Aspects of Rural Development. *Agr. Econ. Res.*, July 1981, *33*(3), pp. 11–24.

Geck, Hinrich-Matthias and Petry, Günther. Zur Eignung der Exportbasis-Theorie als Grundlage der regionalen Wirtschaftsförderung. (The Suitability of Economic Base Theory for Regional Policy. With English summary.) *Jahr. Nationalökon. Statist.*, September 1981, *196*(5), pp. 421–42.   [G: W. Germany]

Gerking, Shelby D. and Isserman, Andrew M. Bifurcation and the Time Pattern of Impacts in the Economic Base Model. *J. Reg. Sci.*, November 1981, *21*(4), pp. 451–67.   [G: U.S.]

Goodrich, Henry C. Southern Business: the Future. In *Bateman, F., ed.*, 1981, pp. 116–18.   [G: U.S.]

Howell, Paul N. Southern Business: The Future. In *Bateman, F., ed.*, 1981, pp. 119–22.   [G: U.S.]

Martin, R. L. Regional Wage Inflation and Unemployment: Introduction. In *Martin, R. L., ed.*, 1981, pp. 1–16.   [G: OECD]

Mazoyer, Marcel L. Origins and Mechanisms of Reproduction of the Regional Discrepancies in Agricultural Development in Europe. *Europ. Rev. Agr. Econ.*, 1981, *8*(2–3), pp. 177–96.   [G: Europe]

Menchik, Mark David. The Service Sector. In *Hawley, A. H. and Mazie, S. M., eds.*, 1981, pp. 231–54.   [G: U.S.]

Monaghan, Bernard A. Southern Business: the Future. In *Bateman, F., ed.*, 1981, pp. 123–26.   [G: U.S.]

Nazarenko, Victor J. Origins and Mechanisms of Reproduction of the Regional Discrepancies in Agricultural Development in Europe: Comment. *Europ. Rev. Agr. Econ.*, 1981, *8*(2–3), pp. 197–98.   [G: Europe]

Nijkamp, Peter and Rietveld, P. Hierarchical Multiobjective Models in a Spatial System. In *Nijkamp, P. and Spronk, J., eds.*, 1981, pp. 163–86.

de Oliveira, Francisco. State and Society in Northeastern Brazil: Sudene and the Role of Regional Planning. In *Mitchell, S., ed.*, 1981, pp. 170–89.   [G: Brazil]

Petit, Michel. Agriculture and Regional Development in Europe—The Role of Agricultural Economists. *Europ. Rev. Agr. Econ.*, 1981, *8*(2–3), pp. 137–53.   [G: Europe]

Rabevazaha, C. Control of Development by the People: Regional Planning and Basic Needs in Madagascar. *Int. Lab. Rev.*, July–August 1981, *120*(4), pp. 439–52.   [G: Madagascar]

Rodwin, Lloyd. Training City Planners in Third World Countries. In *Rodwin, L.*, 1981, pp. 210–26.

Tolley, George S. Rural People, Communities, and Regions: Introduction. In *Martin, L. R., ed.*, 1981, pp. 153–58.

Tracy, Michael. General Report on Policy Aspects. *Europ. Rev. Agr. Econ.*, 1981, *8*(2–3), pp. 425–34.

de Veer, Jan. Theory, Analysis and Methodology. *Europ. Rev. Agr. Econ.*, 1981, *8*(2–3), pp. 409–24.   [G: W. Europe]

9411 Theory of Regional Economics

Arnott, Richard J. and Stiglitz, Joseph E. Aggregate Land Rents and Aggregate Transport Costs. *Econ. J.*, June 1981, *91*(362), pp. 331–47.

Benson, Bruce L. The Optimal Size and Number of Market Areas. *Southern Econ. J.*, April 1981, *47*(4), pp. 1080–85.

Beyers, William B. Alternative Spatial Linkage Structures in Multiregional Economic Systems. In *Rees, J.; Hewings, G. J. D. and Stafford, H. A., eds.*, 1981, pp. 73–90.

Bigsten, Arne. A Note on the Estimation of Interregional Input–Output Coefficients. *Reg. Sci. Urban Econ.*, February 1981, *11*(1), pp. 149–53.

Black, Philip A. Injection Leakages, Trade Repercussions and the Regional Income Multiplier. *Scot. J. Polit. Econ.*, November 1981, *28*(3), pp. 227–35.   [G: U.K.]

Boadway, Robin W. and Flatters, Frank R. The Efficiency Basis for Regional Employment Policy. *Can. J. Econ.*, February 1981, *14*(1), pp. 58–77.

Bourque, Philip J. Embodied Energy Trade Balances among Regions. *Int. Reg. Sci. Rev.*, Winter 1981, *6*(2), pp. 121–36.   [G: U.S.]

Cadwallader, Martin. Towards a Cognitive Gravity Model: The Case of Consumer Spatial Behaviour. *Reg. Stud.*, 1981, *15*(4), pp. 275–84.   [G: U.S.]

Camagni, Roberto and Tiberi-Vipraio, Patrizia. Il commercio orizzontale rivisitato: una interpretazione stocastica interregionale. (Intra-industry Trade Revisited: An Interregional Stochastic Interpretation. With English summary.) *Giorn. Econ.*, July–August 1981, *40*(7–8), pp. 465–92.

Carlberg, Michael. A Neoclassical Model of Interregional Economic Growth. *Reg. Sci. Urban Econ.*, May 1981, *11*(2), pp. 191–203.

Carruthers, Norman. Central Place Theory and the Problem of Aggregating Individual Location Choices. *J. Reg. Sci.*, May 1981, *21*(2), pp. 243–61.

Clark, Gordon L. Regional Economic Systems, Spatial Interdependence and the Role of Money. In *Rees, J.; Hewings, G. J. D. and Stafford, H. A., eds.*, 1981, pp. 91–105.

Clark, Gordon L. The Regional Impact of Stagflation: A Conceptual Model and Empirical Evidence for Canada. In *Martin, R. L., ed.*, 1981, pp. 136–59.   [G: Canada]

Dorward, Neil. "Impacts of Distance on Microeconomic Theory": A Critique. *Manchester Sch. Econ. Soc. Stud.*, September 1981, *49*(3), pp. 245–58.

Edwards, Clark. The Bases for Regional Growth: A Review. In *Martin, L. R., ed.*, 1981, pp. 159–282.   [G: U.S.]

Eswaran, Mukesh; Kanemoto, Yoshitsugu and Ryan, David. A Dual Approach to the Locational Decision of the Firm. *J. Reg. Sci.*, November 1981, *21*(4), pp. 469–90.

Fisch, Oscar. Contributions to the General Theory of Movement. *Reg. Sci. Urban Econ.*, May 1981,

11(2), pp. 157–73. [G: Canada]

Freudenberger, Herman and Mensch, Gerhard. Regional Differences, Differential Development and Generative Regional Growth. In *Bairoch, P. and Lévy-Leboyer, M.*, eds., 1981, pp. 199–209. [G: Czechoslovakia]

Genosko, Joachim and Hasl, Rainer. Reconsidering the Theory of Social Gravity: A Comment. *J. Reg. Sci.*, November 1981, *21*(4), pp. 551–53.

Greenhut, Melvyn L. Mr. Dorward and Impacts of Distance on Microeconomic Theory. *Manchester Sch. Econ. Soc. Stud.*, September 1981, *49*(3), pp. 259–65.

Griesinger, Donald W. Reconsidering the Theory of Social Gravity: A Reply. *J. Reg. Sci.*, November 1981, *21*(4), pp. 555–56.

Gronberg, Timothy J. and Meyer, Jack. Competitive Equilibria in Uniform Delivered Pricing Models. *Amer. Econ. Rev.*, September 1981, *71*(4), pp. 758–63.

Gronberg, Timothy J. and Meyer, Jack. Transport Inefficiency and the Choice of Spatial Pricing Mode. *J. Reg. Sci.*, November 1981, *21*(4), pp. 541–49.

Hansen, Pierre; Peeters, Dominique and Thisse, Jacques-François. Some Localization Theorems for a Constrained Weber Problem. *J. Reg. Sci.*, February 1981, *21*(1), pp. 103–15.

Hart, R. A. Regional Wage-Change Transmission and the Structure of Regional Wages and Unemployment. In *Martin, R. L.*, ed., 1981, pp. 17–45.

Henderson, J. Vernon and Ioannides, Yannis M. Aspects of Growth in a System of Cities. *J. Urban Econ.*, July 1981, *10*(1), pp. 117–39.

Henry, Mark S. and Nyankori, J. C. O. The Existence of Short-Run Economic Base Multipliers: Some New Empirical Evidence. *Land Econ.*, August 1981, *57*(3), pp. 448–58. [G: U.S.]

Holahan, William L. and Schuler, Richard E. Competitive Entry in a Spatial Economy: Market Equilibrium and Welfare Implications. *J. Reg. Sci.*, August 1981, *21*(3), pp. 341–57.

Holahan, William L. and Schuler, Richard E. The Welfare Effects of Market Shapes in the Löschian Location Model: Squares vs. Hexagons [The Non-Uniqueness of Equilibrium in the Löschian Location Model]. *Amer. Econ. Rev.*, September 1981, *71*(4), pp. 738–46.

Huff, James O. Rich Man-Poor Man in von Thünen's Isolated State. *Econ. Geogr.*, April 1981, *57*(2), pp. 127–33.

Johansson, Börje and Strömquist, Ulf. Regional Rigidities in the Process of Economic Structural Development. *Reg. Sci. Urban Econ.*, August 1981, *11*(3), pp. 363–75.

Johansson, Per-Olov. On Regional Effects of Government Policies in a Small Open Economy. *Scand. J. Econ.*, 1981, *83*(4), pp. 541–52.

Jones, Philip C. A Network Model of Economic Growth: A Regional Analysis. *Reg. Sci. Urban Econ.*, May 1981, *11*(2), pp. 231–37.

Jones, Philip C. A Remark on Economic Response to Technological Innovation [Division of Labor—Simon Revisited]. *Reg. Sci. Urban Econ.*, May 1981, *11*(2), pp. 255–66.

Jovanovic, Boyan. Entry with Private Information. *Bell J. Econ. (See Rand J. Econ. after 4/85)*, Autumn 1981, *12*(2), pp. 649–60.

Juel, Henrik. Bounds in the Location-Allocation Problem. *J. Reg. Sci.*, May 1981, *21*(2), pp. 277–82.

Klaassen, Leo H. Infrastructure Design and Urban Form: An Exercise in Geometry. *De Economist*, 1981, *129*(1), pp. 105–26.

Krumme, Günter. Flexibility Views in Industrial Location and Location Decision Theory. In *Rees, J.; Hewings, G. J. D. and Stafford, H. A.*, eds., 1981, pp. 107–21.

Lentnek, Barry; Harwitz, Mitchell and Narula, Subhash C. Spatial Choice in Consumer Behavior: Towards a Contextual Theory of Demand. *Econ. Geogr.*, October 1981, *57*(4), pp. 362–72.

Looney, Robert and Frederiksen, Peter C. The Regional Impact of Infrastructure Investment in Mexico. *Reg. Stud.*, 1981, *15*(4), pp. 285–96. [G: Mexico]

Mai, Chao-cheng. Optimum Location and the Theory of the Firm under Demand Uncertainty. *Reg. Sci. Urban Econ.*, November 1981, *11*(4), pp. 549–57.

Martin, R. L. Wage-change Interdependence Amongst Regional Labour Markets: Conceptual Issues and Some Empirical Evidence for the United States. In *Martin, R. L.*, ed., 1981, pp. 96–135. [G: U.S.]

Matthews, Ralph. Two Alternative Explanations of the Problem of Regional Dependency in Canada. *Can. Public Policy*, Spring 1981, *7*(2), pp. 268–83. [G: Canada]

Miron, John R. and Skarke, Peter. Non-Price Information and Price Sustainability in the Koopmans–Beckmann Problem. *J. Reg. Sci.*, February 1981, *21*(1), pp. 117–22.

Mulligan, Gordon F. The Urbanization Ratio and the Rank-Size Distribution: A Comment [Additional Properties of a Hierarchical City-Size Model]. *J. Reg. Sci.*, May 1981, *21*(2), pp. 283–85.

Mutti, John H. Regional Analysis from the Standpoint of International Trade: Is It a Useful Perspective? *Int. Reg. Sci. Rev.*, Winter 1981, *6*(2), pp. 95–120. [G: U.S.]

Nijkamp, Peter and Spronk, Jaap. Multidimensional Locational Decisions and Interactive Programming. In *Morse, J. N.*, ed., 1981, pp. 248–64.

Norman, George. Spatial Competition and Spatial Price Discrimination. *Rev. Econ. Stud.*, January 1981, *48*(1), pp. 97–111.

Norman, George. Uniform Pricing as an Optimal Spatial Pricing Policy. *Economica*, February 1981, *48*(189), pp. 87–91.

Odland, John. A Household Production Approach to Destination Choice. *Econ. Geogr.*, July 1981, *57*(3), pp. 257–69.

Ohta, Hiroshi. The Price Effects of Spatial Competition. *Rev. Econ. Stud.*, April 1981, *48*(2), pp. 317–25.

Onida, Fabrizio. Il commercio orizzontale rivisitato: un commento. (Intra-industry Trade Revisited: A Comment. With English summary.) *Giorn. Econ.*, July–August 1981, *40*(7–8), pp. 493–500.

Perroux, F. Note on the Concept of 'Growth Poles.' In *Livingstone, I., ed.*, 1981, *1955*, pp. 182–87.

Puu, Tönu. Catastrophic Structural Change in a Continuous Regional Model. *Reg. Sci. Urban Econ.*, August 1981, *11*(3), pp. 317–33.

ReVelle, Charles S.; Cohon, Jared L. and Shobrys, Donald. Multiple Objectives in Facility Location: A Review. In *Morse, J. N., ed.*, 1981, pp. 320–37.

Richardson, Harry W. National Urban Development Strategies in Developing Countries. *Urban Stud.*, October 1981, *18*(3), pp. 267–83. **[G: LDCs]**

Rodwin, Lloyd. Changing Perspectives on Area Development Strategies. In *Rodwin, L.*, 1981, pp. 160–85.

Rodwin, Lloyd. Four Approaches to Urban Studies. In *Rodwin, L.*, 1981, pp. 189–209.

Savitt, Ronald. The Theory of Interregional Marketing. In *[Grether, E. T.]*, 1981, pp. 229–38.

de Smith, Michael J. Optimum Location Theory— Generalizations of Some Network Problems and Some Heuristic Solutions. *J. Reg. Sci.*, November 1981, *21*(4), pp. 491–505.

Spulber, Daniel F. Spatial Nonlinear Pricing. *Amer. Econ. Rev.*, December 1981, *71*(5), pp. 923–33.

Steiner, Michael. Zur Aussagekraft von Normalstrukturmodellen: Eine Note. (With English summary.) *Empirica*, 1981, (1), pp. 111–27. **[G: Austria]**

Storper, Michael. Toward a Structural Theory of Industrial Location. In *Rees, J.; Hewings, G. J. D. and Stafford, H. A., eds.*, 1981, pp. 17–40.

van Suntum, Ulrich. Öffentliches Finanzsystem und regionale Effizienz. (With English summary.) *Kyklos*, 1981, *34*(2), pp. 216–29.

Swales, J. K. The Employment Effects of a Regional Capital Subsidy. *Reg. Stud.*, 1981, *15*(4), pp. 263–73.

Upton, Charles. An Equilibrium Model of City Size. *J. Urban Econ.*, July 1981, *10*(1), pp. 15–36.

Veendorp, E. C. H. Instability in Competition: Two Variations on a Hotelling Theme. *Atlantic Econ. J.*, July 1981, *9*(2), pp. 30–34.

West, Douglas S. Testing for Market Preemption Using Sequential Location Data. *Bell J. Econ.* (*See Rand J. Econ. after 4/85*), Spring 1981, *12*(1), pp. 129–43. **[G: Canada]**

Whitmore, Harland William, Jr. Plant Location and the Demand for Investment: A Theoretical Analysis. *J. Reg. Sci.*, February 1981, *21*(1), pp. 89–101.

Wolch, Jennifer R. The Location of Service-Dependent Households in Urban Areas. *Econ. Geogr.*, January 1981, *57*(1), pp. 52–67.

Yu, Eden S. H. Regional Factor Specificity, Wage Differential and Resource Allocation. *Reg. Sci. Urban Econ.*, February 1981, *11*(1), pp. 69–79.

9412 Regional Economic Studies

Abumere, S. I. Population Distribution Policies and Measures in Africa South of the Sahara: A Review. *Population Devel. Rev.*, September 1981, *7*(3), pp. 421–33. **[G: Africa]**

Albegov, M. M., et al. Regional Agricultural Policy Design on the Basis of a Detailed Linear Economic and Agrotechnical Model. In *Janssen, J. M. L.; Pau, L. F. and Straszak, A. J., eds.*, 1981, pp. 221–29.

Alexander, James R. Policy Design and the Impact of Federal Aid to Declining Communities. *Growth Change*, January 1981, *12*(1), pp. 35–41. **[G: U.S.]**

Archer, Wayne R. Determinants of Location for General Purpose Office Firms within Medium Size Cities. *Amer. Real Estate Urban Econ. Assoc. J.*, Fall 1981, *9*(3), pp. 283–97. **[G: U.S.]**

Auffret, Marc; Hau, Michel and Lévy-Leboyer, Maurice. Regional Inequalities and Economic Development: French Agriculture in the Nineteenth and Twentieth Centuries. In *Bairoch, P. and Lévy-Leboyer, M., eds.*, 1981, pp. 273–89. **[G: France]**

Avadhani, V. A. Small Scale Industries in East and North-East Region. *Indian Econ. J.*, October–December 1981, *29*(2), pp. 35–50. **[G: India]**

Ayeni, Bola. Spatial Aspects of Urbanization and Effects on the Distribution of Income in Nigeria. In *Bienen, H. and Diejomaoh, V. P., eds.*, 1981, pp. 237–68. **[G: Nigeria]**

Ba, Cheikh. The Uprooted of the Western Sahel: Northern Senegal. In *Colvin, L. G., et al.*, 1981, pp. 113–35. **[G: Senegal]**

Bade, Franz-Josef. Die Standortstruktur grosser Industrieunternehmen: Eine explorative Studie zum Einfluss von Grossunternehmen auf die regionale Wirtschaftsentwicklung. (The Spatial Organization of Large Industrial Enterprises: An Explorative Study about the Influence of Large Enterprises on Regional Development. With English summary.) *Jahr. Nationalökon. Statist.*, July 1981, *196*(4), pp. 341–66. **[G: W. Germany]**

Bahl, Roy W. and Schroeder, Larry D. Fiscal Adjustments in Declining States. In *Burchell, R. W. and Listokin, D., eds.*, 1981, pp. 301–29. **[G: U.S.]**

Ballard, Kenneth P. and Clark, Gordon L. The Short-run Dynamics of Inter-state Migration: A Space-Time Economic Adjustment Model of Inmigration to Fast Growing States. *Reg. Stud.*, 1981, *15*(3), pp. 213–28. **[G: U.S.]**

Bateman, Fred. Business in the New South: The Interaction between History and Economics. In *Bateman, F., ed.*, 1981, pp. 8–13. **[G: U.S.]**

Beierlein, James G.; Dunn, James W. and McConnon, James C., Jr. The Demand for Electricity and Natural Gas in the Northeastern United States. *Rev. Econ. Statist.*, August 1981, *63*(3), pp. 403–08. **[G: U.S.]**

Bigsten, Arne. Regional Inequality in Kenya. In *Killick, T., ed.*, 1981, pp. 180–88. **[G: Kenya]**

Bolin, Olof. Regional Disparities in Agriculture: Comment. *Europ. Rev. Agr. Econ.*, 1981, *8*(2–3), pp. 211–12. **[G: Europe]**

Bose, S. K. Bihar's Backwardness—An Enigma? In *Karna, M. N., ed.*, 1981, pp. 7–13. **[G: India]**

Breheny, Michael J.; Green, Jacqueline and Roberts, Anthony J. A Practical Approach to the Assessment of Hypermarket Impact. *Reg. Stud.*, 1981, *15*(6), pp. 459–74. **[G: U.K.]**

Briggs, Vernon M., Jr. Unemployment and Underemployment. In *Hawley, A. H. and Mazie,*

S. M., eds., 1981, pp. 359–81. [G: U.S.]

Brown, David L. Potential Impacts of Changing Population Size and Composition of the Plains. In Lawson, M. P. and Baker, M. E., eds., 1981, pp. 35–51. [G: U.S.]

Brown, David L. Spatial Aspects of Post-1970 Work Force Migration in the United States. Growth Change, January 1981, 12(1), pp. 9–20. [G: U.S.]

Brown, David L. and Beale, Calvin L. Diversity in Post-1970 Population Trends. In Hawley, A. H. and Mazie, S. M., eds., 1981, pp. 27–71. [G: U.S.]

Brown, Marilyn A. Spatial Diffusion Aspects of Marketing Strategies. Rev. Reg. Stud., Fall 1981, 11(2), pp. 54–73. [G: U.S.]

Browne, Lynn E. and Hekman, John S. New England's Economy in the 1980s. New Eng. Econ. Rev., January/February 1981, pp. 5–16. [G: U.S.]

Bryden, John. Appraising a Regional Development Programme—The Case of the Scottish Highlands and Islands. Europ. Rev. Agr. Econ., 1981, 8(4), pp. 475–97. [G: U.K.]

Bueno, G. M. Regional Policy in EC Countries and Community Regional Policy: A Note on Problems and Perspectives in Developing Depressed Rural Regions: Comment. Europ. Rev. Agr. Econ., 1981, 8(2–3), pp. 247–49. [G: EEC]

Buescu, Mircea. Regional Inequalities in Brazil during the Second Half of the Nineteenth Century. In Bairoch, P. and Lévy-Leboyer, M., eds., 1981, pp. 349–58. [G: Brazil]

Burchell, Robert W. and Listokin, David. The Fiscal Impact of Economic-Development Programs: Case Studies of the Local Cost–Revenue Implications of HUD, EDA AND FmHA Projects. In Sternlieb, G. and Listokin, D., eds., 1981, pp. 163–229. [G: U.S.]

Burns, Leland S. The Metropolitan Population of the United States: Historical and Emerging Trends. In Klaassen, L. H.; Molle, W. T. M. and Paelinck, J. H. P., eds., 1981, pp. 197–224. [G: U.S.]

Burridge, Peter and Gordon, Ian Richard. Unemployment in the British Metropolitan Labour Areas. Oxford Econ. Pap., July 1981, 33(2), pp. 274–97. [G: U.K.]

Cameron, David M. Regional Economic Disparities: The Challenge to Federalism and Public Policy. Can. Public Policy, Autumn 1981, 7(4), pp. 500–505. [G: Canada]

de Castro Andrade, Regis. On the Relationship between the Subsistence Sector and the Market Economy in the Parnaíba Valley. In Mitchell, S., ed., 1981, pp. 109–32. [G: Brazil]

Cavalcanti, Leonardo; Geiger, Pedro P. and de Andrade, Thompson. Multinationals, the New International Economic Order and the Spatial Industrial Structure of Brazil. In Hamilton, F. E. I. and Linge, G. J. R., eds., 1981, pp. 423–38. [G: Brazil]

Cebula, Richard J. and Smith, Lisa Karen. An Exploratory Empirical Note on Determinants of Inter-Regional Living-Cost Differentials in the United States, 1970 and 1975. Reg. Sci. Urban

Econ., February 1981, 11(1), pp. 81–85. [G: U.S.]

Cheshire, Paul C. Labour-Market Theory and Spatial Unemployment: The Role of Demand Reconsidered. In Martin, R. L., ed., 1981, pp. 189–207. [G: U.K.]

Cheshire, Paul C. The Regional Demand for Labour Services: A Suggested Explanation for Observed Differences. Scot. J. Polit. Econ., February 1981, 28(1), pp. 95–98. [G: U.K.]

Choate, Pat. Public Institutions and the Planning Process. In Hawley, A. H. and Mazie, S. M., eds., 1981, pp. 767–805. [G: U.S.]

Clapier, Patrick and Tabard, Nicole. Transformation de la morphologie sociale des communes et variation des consommations: Un essai pour la région parisienne. (The Change in the Social Morphology of Districts and the Variations of Consumption: An Attempt for the Paris Region. With English summary.) Consommation, April–June 1981, 28(2), pp. 3–40. [G: France]

Clapp, John M. The Elasticity of Substitution of Nonland for Land: A Reconciliation of Diverse Estimates. J. Reg. Sci., February 1981, 21(1), pp. 123–25.

Clark, Gordon L. The Regional Impact of Stagflation: A Conceptual Model and Empirical Evidence for Canada. In Martin, R. L., ed., 1981, pp. 136–59. [G: Canada]

Clark, Gordon L. and Ballard, Kenneth P. The Demand and Supply of Labor and Interstate Relative Wages: An Empirical Analysis. Econ. Geogr., April 1981, 57(2), pp. 95–112. [G: U.S.]

Clarke, Susan E. A Political Perspective on Population Change in the South. In Poston, D. L., Jr. and Weller, R. H., eds., 1981, pp. 227–67. [G: U.S.]

Clawson, Marion. Natural Resources of the Great Plains in Historical Perspective. In Lawson, M. P. and Baker, M. E., eds., 1981, pp. 3–10. [G: U.S.]

Collins, Keith J. and Glade, Edward H., Jr. Regional and Functional Disaggregation of the Cotton Industry in a National Input–Output Model. Southern J. Agr. Econ., July 1981, 13(1), pp. 111–18. [G: U.S.]

Courchene, Thomas J. A Market Perspective on Regional Disparities. Can. Public Policy, Autumn 1981, 7(4), pp. 506–18. [G: Canada]

Cromley, Robert G. and Leinbach, Thomas R. The Pattern and Impact of the Filter Down Process in Nonmetropolitan Kentucky. Econ. Geogr., July 1981, 57(3), pp. 208–24. [G: U.S.]

Cunningham, Edward. Regional Development and the Changing Economy. In Gaskin, M., ed., 1981, pp. 152–64. [G: U.K.; OECD]

Dabrowski, P. H. Regional Disparities in Agriculture. Europ. Rev. Agr. Econ., 1981, 8(2–3), pp. 199–209. [G: Europe]

Diejomaoh, V. P. and Anusionwu, E. C. The Structure of Income Inequality in Nigeria: a Macro Analysis. In Bienen, H. and Diejomaoh, V. P., eds., 1981, pp. 89–125. [G: Nigeria]

Dreifelds, Juris. Economic Development in Individual Regions in the USSR: Belorussia and Baltics. In Koropeckyj, I. S. and Schroeder, G. E., eds.,

1981, pp. 323–85. **[G: U.S.S.R.]**

Dunning, John H. Multinational Enterprises, Locational Strategies and Regional Development. In *Dunning, J. H.*, 1981, pp. 249–71. **[G: U.K.; Belgium]**

Eason, Warren W. Selected Problems of Regional Development in the USSR: Population and Labor Force. In *Koropeckyj, I. S. and Schroeder, G. E., eds.*, 1981, pp. 11–91. **[G: U.S.S.R.]**

Enderle, Georges. Wanderungen und sozio-ökonomische Entwicklung, Korreferat. (Migration and Socio-Economic Development—A Rejoinder. With English summary.) *Schweiz. Z. Volkswirtsch. Statist.*, September 1981, *117*(3), pp. 393–406. **[G: Switzerland]**

Engerman, Stanley L. Agriculture as Business: The Southern Context. In *Bateman, F., ed.*, 1981, pp. 17–26. **[G: U.S.]**

Eraydin, Ayda. Foreign Investment, International Labour Migration and the Turkish Economy. In *Hamilton, F. E. I. and Linge, G. J. R., eds.*, 1981, pp. 225–64. **[G: Turkey]**

Erickson, Rodney A. Corporations, Branch Plants, and Employment Stability in Nonmetropolitan Areas. In *Rees, J.; Hewings, G. J. D. and Stafford, H. A., eds.*, 1981, pp. 135–53. **[G: U.S.]**

Faye, Jacques. Zonal Approach to Migration in the Senegalese Peanut Basin. In *Colvin, L. G., et al.*, 1981, pp. 136–60. **[G: Senegal]**

Fisher, James S. and Mitchelson, Ronald L. Extended and Internal Commuting in the Transformation of the Intermetropolitan Periphery. *Econ. Geogr.*, July 1981, *57*(3), pp. 189–207. **[G: U.S.]**

Fox, William F. Fiscal Differentials and Industrial Location: Some Empirical Evidence. *Urban Stud.*, February 1981, *18*(1), pp. 105–11. **[G: U.S.]**

Freudenberger, Herman and Mensch, Gerhard. Regional Differences, Differential Development and Generative Regional Growth. In *Bairoch, P. and Lévy-Leboyer, M., eds.*, 1981, pp. 199–209. **[G: Czechoslovakia]**

Frost, M. and Spence, N. The Timing of Unemployment Response in British Regional Labour Markets, 1963–76. In *Martin, R. L., ed.*, 1981, pp. 208–31. **[G: U.K.]**

Garrison, Charles B. and Chang, Hui S. Subregional Income Differentials: A Study of the Tennessee Valley Region. *Rev. Reg. Stud.*, Winter 1981, *11*(3), pp. 22–37. **[G: U.S.]**

Gerking, Shelby D. and Barrington, Joseph L. Are Regional Share Effects Constant over Time? *J. Reg. Sci.*, May 1981, *21*(2), pp. 163–74. **[G: U.S.]**

Gessaman, Paul H. Rugged Individualism: Recurring Myth or Reemerging Giant? In *Lawson, M. P. and Baker, M. E., eds.*, 1981, pp. 267–75. **[G: U.S.]**

Ghali, Moheb A.; Akiyama, Masayuki and Fujiwara, Junichi. Models of Regional Growth: An Empirical Evaluation. *Reg. Sci. Urban Econ.*, May 1981, *11*(2), pp. 175–90. **[G: U.S.]**

Gibson, Lay James and Worden, Marshall A. Estimating the Economic Base Multiplier: A Test of Alternative Procedures. *Econ. Geogr.*, April 1981, *57*(2), pp. 146–59. **[G: U.S.]**

Gibson, N. J. and Spencer, J. E. Unemployment and Wages in Northern Ireland. In *Crick, B., ed.*, 1981, *1981*, pp. 100–14. **[G: U.K.]**

Gillula, James W. Selected Problems of Regional Development in the USSR: The Growth and Structure of Fixed Capital. In *Koropeckyj, I. S. and Schroeder, G. E., eds.*, 1981, pp. 157–93. **[G: U.S.S.R.]**

Goldfield, David R. The Urban South: A Regional Framework. *Amer. Hist. Rev.*, December 1981, *86*(5), pp. 1009–34. **[G: U.S.]**

Gömmel, R. The Development of a Growth Pole in the Nineteenth Century Illustrated by the Example of Nuremberg. In *Bairoch, P. and Lévy-Leboyer, M., eds.*, 1981, pp. 210–15. **[G: Germany]**

Goodman, D. E. Rural Structure, Surplus Mobilisation and Modes of Production in a Peripheral Region: The Brazilian Northeast. In *Mitchell, S., ed.*, 1981, pp. 10–40. **[G: Brazil]**

Goodstein, Marvin E. The Study of Southern Economic and Business History: Challenges and Opportunities. In *Bateman, F., ed.*, 1981, pp. 1–7. **[G: U.S.]**

Gordijew, Ihor. Economic Development in Individual Regions in the USSR: Moldavia. In *Koropeckyj, I. S. and Schroeder, G. E., eds.*, 1981, pp. 305–22. **[G: U.S.S.R.]**

Gordijew, Ihor and Koropeckyj, I. S. Economic Development in Individual Regions in the USSR: Ukraine. In *Koropeckyj, I. S. and Schroeder, G. E., eds.*, 1981, pp. 267–304. **[G: U.S.S.R.]**

Grady, Stephen T. Estimation and Evaluation of State Price Indexes for the Period 1967–1978: An Empirical Note. *Rev. Reg. Stud.*, Winter 1981, *11*(3), pp. 51–62. **[G: U.S.]**

Granberg, A. G. Siberia in the National Economic Complex. *Prob. Econ.*, January 1981, *23*(9), pp. 53–76. **[G: U.S.S.R.]**

Graziani, A. Regional Inequalities in Italy. In *Bairoch, P. and Lévy-Leboyer, M., eds.*, 1981, pp. 319–30. **[G: Italy]**

Greenhut, Melvin L. Spatial Pricing in the United States, West Germany and Japan. *Economica*, February 1981, *48*(189), pp. 79–86. **[G: U.S.; W. Germany; Japan]**

Griffin, Adrian H.; Martin, William E. and Wade, James C. Urban Residential Demand for Water in the United States: Comment. *Land Econ.*, May 1981, *57*(2), pp. 252–56. **[G: U.S.]**

Gustely, Richard D. and Ballard, Kenneth P. Regional Macro-economic Impact of Federal Grants: An Empirical Analysis. In *Burchell, R. W. and Listokin, D., eds.*, 1981, pp. 665–91. **[G: U.S.]**

Hainsworth, Paul. Northern Ireland: A European Role? *J. Common Market Stud.*, September 1981, *20*(1), pp. 1–5. **[G: EEC; U.K.]**

Hamilton, F. E. Ian. Economic Development in Individual Regions in the USSR: The European USSR. In *Koropeckyj, I. S. and Schroeder, G. E., eds.*, 1981, pp. 197–234. **[G: U.S.S.R.]**

Hanham, R. Q. and Chang, H. Wage Inflation in a Growth Region: The American Sun Belt. In *Martin, R. L., ed.*, 1981, pp. 75–95. **[G: U.S.]**

Harmston, Floyd K. A Study of the Economic Relationships of Retired People and a Small Community. *Reg. Sci. Persp.*, 1981, *11*(1), pp. 42–56.

Hekman, John S. and Strong, John S. The Evolution of New England Industry. *New Eng. Econ. Rev.*, March–April 1981, pp. 35–46. **[G: U.S.]**

Herget, J. Barlow. Industrial Growth: An Alternative for North Carolina's Tobacco Farmers. **In** *Finger, W. R., ed.*, 1981, pp. 103–08. **[G: U.S.]**

Hoch, Irving. Energy and Location. **In** *Hawley, A. H. and Mazie, S. M., eds.*, 1981, pp. 285–356. **[G: U.S.]**

Hodge, James H. A Study of Regional Investment Decisions. **In** *Henderson, J. V., ed.*, 1981, pp. 1–65. **[G: U.S.]**

Hodne, Fritz and Gjølberg, Ole. Market Integration during the Period of Industrialisation in Norway. **In** *Bairoch, P. and Lévy-Leboyer, M., eds.*, 1981, pp. 216–25. **[G: Norway]**

Honea, R. B. The Southeast's Energy Prospects: A Realistic Appraisal. *Rev. Reg. Stud.*, Fall 1981, *11*(2), pp. 74–87. **[G: U.S.]**

Horiba, Yutaka and Kirkpatrick, Rickey C. Factor Endowments, Factor Proportions, and the Allocative Efficiency of U.S. Interregional Trade. *Rev. Econ. Statist.*, May 1981, *63*(2), pp. 178–87. **[G: U.S.]**

Howes, Candace and Markusen, Ann R. Poverty: A Regional Political Economy Perspective. **In** *Hawley, A. H. and Mazie, S. M., eds.*, 1981, pp. 437–63. **[G: U.S.]**

Ingene, Charles A. and Yu, Eden S. H. Determinants of Retail Sales in SMSAs. *Reg. Sci. Urban Econ.*, November 1981, *11*(4), pp. 529–47. **[G: U.S.]**

Inoki, Takenori and Suruga, Terukazu. Migration, Age, and Education: A Cross-Sectional Analysis of Geographic Labor Mobility in Japan. *J. Reg. Sci.*, November 1981, *21*(4), pp. 507–17. **[G: Japan]**

Isard, W. and Reiner, Th. A. Megalopolitan Decline and Urban Redevelopment in the United States, an Analysis of Evolutionary Forces. **In** *Klaassen, L. H.; Molle, W. T. M. and Paelinck, J. H. P., eds.*, 1981, pp. 225–48. **[G: U.S.]**

Johnson, Marc A. Current and Developing Issues in Interregional Competition and Agricultural Transportation. *Southern J. Agr. Econ.*, July 1981, *13*(1), pp. 59–68. **[G: U.S.]**

Johnston, R. J. Regional Variations in British Voting Trends—1966–1979: Tests of an Ecological Model. *Reg. Stud.*, 1981, *15*(1), pp. 23–32. **[G: U.K.]**

Jörberg, Lennart and Bengtsson, Tommy. Regional Wages in Sweden during the Nineteenth Century. **In** *Bairoch, P. and Lévy-Leboyer, M., eds.*, 1981, pp. 226–43. **[G: Sweden]**

Kale, Steven. Industrial Development Trends in the Northern Plains States. **In** *Lawson, M. P. and Baker, M. E., eds.*, 1981, pp. 205–19. **[G: U.S]**

Kau, James B. and Sirmans, C. F. The Demand for Urban Residential Land. *J. Reg. Sci.*, November 1981, *21*(4), pp. 519–28. **[G: U.S.]**

Keeble, David. Manufacturing Dispersion and Government Policy in a Declining Industrial System: The United Kingdom Case, 1971–76. **In** *Rees, J.; Hewings, G. J. D. and Stafford, H. A., eds.*, 1981, pp. 197–215. **[G: U.K.]**

Kiesewetter, Hubert. Regional Disparities in Wages: The Cotton Industry in Nineteenth-century Germany—Some Methodological Considerations. **In** *Bairoch, P. and Lévy-Leboyer, M., eds.*, 1981, pp. 248–58. **[G: Germany]**

Kirk, Robert. Convergence and Differentials in State Investment Patterns. *Rev. Reg. Stud.*, Fall 1981, *11*(2), pp. 18–24. **[G: U.S.]**

Klep, Paul M. M. Regional Disparities in Brabantine Urbanisation before and after the Industrial Revolution (1374–1970): Some Aspects of Measurement and Explanation. **In** *Bairoch, P. and Lévy-Leboyer, M., eds.*, 1981, pp. 259–69. **[G: Belgium]**

Kofman, Eleonore. Functional Regionalism and Alternative Regional Development Programmes in Corsica. *Reg. Stud.*, 1981, *15*(3), pp. 173–81. **[G: France]**

Koropeckyj, I. S. Selected Problems of Regional Development in the USSR: Growth and Productivity. **In** *Koropeckyj, I. S. and Schroeder, G. E., eds.*, 1981, pp. 92–117. **[G: U.S.S.R.]**

Kort, John R. Regional Economic Instability and Industrial Diversification in the U.S. *Land Econ.*, November 1981, *57*(4), pp. 596–608. **[G: U.S.]**

Kozlowski, Paul J. Forecasting Cyclical Turning Points in Local Market Areas. *Bus. Econ.*, September 1981, *16*(4), pp. 43–49. **[G: U.S.]**

Krumme, Günter. Making it Abroad: The Evolution of Volkswagen's North American Production Plans. **In** *Hamilton, F. E. I. and Linge, G. J. R., eds.*, 1981, pp. 329–56. **[G: U.S.; W. Germany]**

Kumar, Dharma and Krishnamurty, J. Regional and International Economic Disparities since the Industrial Revolution: The Indian Evidence. **In** *Bairoch, P. and Lévy-Leboyer, M., eds.*, 1981, pp. 361–72. **[G: India]**

Lakshmanan, T. R. Regional Growth and Energy Determinants: Implications for the Future. *Energy J.*, April 1981, *2*(2), pp. 1–24. **[G: U.S.]**

Lawlor, Ann C. and Reid, Jack T. Hierarchical Patterns in the Location of Physician Specialists among Counties. *Inquiry*, Spring 1981, *18*(1), pp. 79–90. **[G: U.S.]**

Leistritz, F. Larry and Murdock, Steve H. Implications of Energy Development for Economic Growth and Social Change in the Great Plains. **In** *Lawson, M. P. and Baker, M. E., eds.*, 1981, pp. 247–64. **[G: U.S.]**

Lever, William F. The Inner City Employment Problem in Great Britain, 1952–76: A Shift–Share Approach. **In** *Rees, J.; Hewings, G. J. D. and Stafford, H. A., eds.*, 1981, pp. 171–96. **[G: U.K.]**

Linthorst, Joop M. and van Praag, Bernard M. S. Interaction-Patterns and Service-Areas of Local Public Services in the Netherlands. *Reg. Sci. Urban Econ.*, February 1981, *11*(1), pp. 39–56. **[G: Netherlands]**

Lithwick, N. H. and Cohen, Gad. The Israeli Experience: Some Economic Aspects of Population Distribution Policies. *Growth Change*, July 1981, *12*(3), pp. 23–31. **[G: Israel]**

Lombardini, Siro. Italy: Experiences, Problems and

Development Strategies. In *Mauri, A., ed.*, 1981, pp. 161–69. [G: Italy]

Lorch, Brian J. Mergers and Acquisitions and the Geographic Transfer of Corporate Control: Canada's Manufacturing Industry. In *Rees, J.; Hewings, G. J. D. and Stafford, H. A., eds.*, 1981, pp. 123–34. [G: Canada]

Macnaughton, Bruce D. and Winn, Conrad J. Economic Policy and Electoral Self Interest: The Allocations of the Department of Regional Economic Expansion. *Can. Public Policy*, Spring 1981, 7(2), pp. 318–27. [G: Canada]

Mair, Douglas. Urban Unemployment: A Comment [Urban Unemployment in England]. *Econ. J.*, March 1981, 91(361), pp. 224–30. [G: U.K.]

Majumdar, Badiul Alam. Effectiveness of Indirect "Operational Control" over the Private Sector: The Case of Pakistan. *Pakistan Econ. Soc. Rev.*, Summer 1981, 19(1), pp. 69–81. [G: Pakistan]

Malecki, Edward J. Recent Trends in the Location of Industrial Research and Development: Regional Development Implications for the United States. In *Rees, J.; Hewings, G. J. D. and Stafford, H. A., eds.*, 1981, pp. 217–37. [G: U.S.]

Mark, Shelley M. and Ono, Mitsuo. Accounting for Subnational Economic Growth: The Hawaiian Experience, 1900–1976. *Rev. Reg. Stud.*, Fall 1981, 11(2), pp. 41–53. [G: U.S.]

Markusen, Ann R.; Saxenian, Annalee and Weiss, Marc A. Who Benefits from Intergovernmental Transfers? In *Burchell, R. W. and Listokin, D., eds.*, 1981, pp. 617–64. [G: U.S.]

Martin, R. L. Wage-change Interdependence Amongst Regional Labour Markets: Conceptual Issues and Some Empirical Evidence for the United States. In *Martin, R. L., ed.*, 1981, pp. 96–135. [G: U.S.]

Martin, Randolph C. A Note on the Cost per Job Created by Federal Regional Development Programs. *Reg. Sci. Persp.*, 1981, 11(2), pp. 49–55. [G: U.S.]

Massey, Doreen. The UK Electrical Engineering and Electronics Industries: The Implications of the Crisis for the Restructuring of Capital and Locational Change. In *Dear, M. and Scott, A. J., eds.*, 1981, pp. 199–230. [G: U.K.]

Matley, Ian M. Economic Development in Individual Regions in the USSR: Central Asia and Kazakhstan. In *Koropeckyj, I. S. and Schroeder, G. E., eds.*, 1981, pp. 417–53. [G: U.S.S.R.]

Matlon, Peter. The Structure of Production and Rural Incomes in Northern Nigeria: Results of Three Village Case Studies. In *Bienen, H. and Diejomaoh, V. P., eds.*, 1981, pp. 323–72.
[G: Nigeria]

Mattsson, Lars-Göran and Weibull, Jörgen W. Competition and Accessibility on a Regional Labour Market. *Reg. Sci. Urban Econ.*, November 1981, 11(4), pp. 471–97. [G: Sweden]

Maxwell, Stephen. The Politics of Unemployment in Scotland. In *Crick, B., ed.*, 1981, *1981*, pp. 88–99. [G: U.K.]

Mayer, Jean. Regional Development in Portugal (1929–1977): An Assessment. In *Bairoch, P. and Lévy-Leboyer, M., eds.*, 1981, pp. 331–45.
[G: Portugal]

McDougall, Gerald and Bunce, Harold. Evaluating the Distributional Consequences of Local Service Delivery Systems—An Alternative Perspective. *Rev. Reg. Stud.*, Fall 1981, 11(2), pp. 25–40.
[G: U.S.]

McNicoll, I. H. Intertemporal Changes in a Rural Economy: A Case Study. *Econ. Develop. Cult. Change*, October 1981, 30(1), pp. 107–16.
[G: U.K.]

McRae, James J. An Empirical Measure of the Influence on Transportation Costs on Regional Income. *Can. J. Econ.*, February 1981, 14(1), pp. 155–63. [G: Canada]

Meir, Avinoam. Innovation Diffusion and Regional Economic Development: The Spatial Diffusion of Automobiles in Ohio. *Reg. Stud.*, 1981, 15(2), pp. 111–22. [G: U.S.]

Miller, E. Willard. Spatial Organization of Manufacturing in Nonmetropolitan Pennsylvania. In *Rees, J.; Hewings, G. J. D. and Stafford, H. A., eds.*, 1981, pp. 155–69. [G: U.S.]

Miller, Edward M. Differences in Productivity by Size of Firm and Region. In *Hogan, J. D. and Craig, A. M., eds., Vol. 2*, 1981, pp. 839–53.
[G: U.S.]

Mitchell, Simon. The Logic of Poverty: Introduction. In *Mitchell, S., ed.*, 1981, pp. 1–9.
[G: Brazil]

Moland, John, Jr. The Black Population. In *Hawley, A. H. and Mazie, S. M., eds.*, 1981, pp. 464–501. [G: U.S.]

Mollenkopf, John H. Paths toward the Post Industrial Service City: The Northeast and the Southwest. In *Burchell, R. W. and Listokin, D., eds.*, 1981, pp. 77–112. [G: U.S.]

Moomaw, Ronald L. Productive Efficiency and Region. *Southern Econ. J.*, October 1981, 48(2), pp. 344–57. [G: U.S.]

Moore, B. and Rhodes, J. The Convergence of Earnings in the Regions of the United Kingdom. In *Martin, R. L., ed.*, 1981, pp. 46–59. [G: U.K.]

Mountain, Dean C. The Spatial Distribution of Electricity Demand: Its Impact upon Input Usage. *Land Econ.*, February 1981, 57(1), pp. 48–62.
[G: Canada]

Murray, Steven W. and Tweeten, Luther. Some Trade-Offs: Culture, Education, and Economic Progress on Federal Indian Reservations. *Growth Change*, April 1981, 12(2), pp. 10–16. [G: U.S.]

Myers, George C. The Demographically Emergent South. In *Poston, D. L., Jr. and Weller, R. H., eds.*, 1981, pp. 268–82. [G: U.S.]

Nelson, Richard R. Regional Life-Cycles and U.S. Industrial Rejuvenation. In *Giersch, H., ed. (II)*, 1981, pp. 281. [G: U.S.]

Niemi, Albert W., Jr. Business in the New South: The Modern Success: Comment. In *Bateman, F., ed.*, 1981, pp. 154–56. [G: U.S.]

Norton, R. D. Regional Life-Cycles and U.S. Industrial Rejuvenation. In *Giersch, H., ed. (II)*, 1981, pp. 253–80. [G: U.S.]

Nove, Alec. Economics of Soviet Regions: Overview. In *Koropeckyj, I. S. and Schroeder, G. E., eds.*, 1981, pp. 1–8. [G: U.S.S.R.]

O'Connell, Martin. Regional Fertility Patterns in the United States: Convergence or Divergence? *Int.*

Reg. Sci. Rev., Fall 1981, 6(1), pp. 1–14.
[G: U.S.]

O'Farrell, P. N. and O'Loughlin, B. The Impact of New Industry Enterprises in Ireland: An Analysis of Service Linkages. *Reg. Stud.*, 1981, 15(6), pp. 439–58. [G: Ireland]

Okyay, Vildan. Bati Anadolu Bölgesinde Ulaşim Sistemindeki Değişikliğin Merkezler Kademelenmesi Üzerindeki Etkileri (1844–1914). (With English summary.) *METU*, 1981, 8(3&4), pp. 649–82. [G: Turkey]

Orlando, Giuseppe and Antonelli, Gervasio. Regional Policy in EC Countries and Community Regional Policy: A Note on Problems and Perspectives in Developing Depressed Rural Regions. *Europ. Rev. Agr. Econ.*, 1981, 8(2–3), pp. 213–46. [G: EEC]

Osmond, John. Wales: Will Unemployment Breed Unrest or Apathy? In *Crick, B., ed.*, 1981, *1981*, pp. 127–34. [G: U.K.]

Pagoulatos, Angelos and Anschel, Kurt R. An I-O Study of the Economic Structure of Appalachian Kentucky. *Growth Change*, October 1981, 12(4), pp. 2–8. [G: U.S.]

Parmar, H. S. Regional Inequalities in Himachal Pradesh. *Econ. Aff.*, January–March 1981, 26(1), pp. 51–58. [G: India]

Payne, Geoff; Ford, Graeme and Ulas, Marion. Occupational Change and Social Mobility in Scotland Since the First World War. In *Gaskin, M., ed.*, 1981, pp. 200–17. [G: U.K.]

Perrons, D. C. The Role of Ireland in the New International Division of Labour: A Proposed Framework for Regional Analysis. *Reg. Stud.*, 1981, 15(2), pp. 81–100. [G: Ireland]

Persson, Lars Olof and Bolin, Olof. Agricultural Planning for Regional Balance. *Europ. Rev. Agr. Econ.*, 1981, 8(4), pp. 499–518. [G: Sweden]

Pickvance, C. G. Policies as Chameleons: An Interpretation of Regional Policy and Office Policy in Britain. In *Dear, M. and Scott, A. J., eds.*, 1981, pp. 231–65. [G: U.K.]

Pimlott, Ben. The North East: Back to the 1930s? In *Crick, B., ed.*, 1981, *1981*, pp. 51–63.
[G: U.K.]

Polese, Mario. Regional Disparity, Migration and Economic Adjustment: A Reappraisal. *Can. Public Policy*, Autumn 1981, 7(4), pp. 519–25.
[G: Canada]

Porell, Frank W. and Hua, Chang-I. An Econometric Procedure for Estimation of a Generalized Systemic Gravity Model under Incomplete Information about the System. *Reg. Sci. Urban Econ.*, November 1981, 11(4), pp. 585–606.
[G: U.S.]

Poston, Dudley L., Jr. An Ecological Explanation of Southern Population Redistribution, 1970–1975. In *Poston, D. L., Jr. and Weller, R. H., eds.*, 1981, pp. 137–54. [G: U.S.]

Poston, Dudley L., Jr.; Serow, William J. and Weller, Robert H. Demographic Change in the South. In *Poston, D. L., Jr. and Weller, R. H., eds.*, 1981, pp. 3–22. [G: U.S.]

Pursell, Donald E. Natural Population Decrease: Its Origins and Implications on the Great Plains. In *Lawson, M. P. and Baker, M. E., eds.*, 1981,

pp. 53–66. [G: U.S.]

Rees, R. D. and Miall, R. H. C. The Effect of Regional Policy on Manufacturing Investment and Capital Stock within the U.K. between 1959 and 1978. *Reg. Stud.*, 1981, 15(6), pp. 413–24.
[G: U.K.]

Reiner, Thomas A. and Wolpert, Julian. The Non-Profit Sector in the Metropolitan Economy. *Econ. Geogr.*, January 1981, 57(1), pp. 23–33.
[G: U.S.]

Reis, Jaime. Hunger in the Northeast: Some Historical Aspects. In *Mitchell, S., ed.*, 1981, pp. 41–57. [G: Brazil]

Rindfuss, Ronald R. The Population of the South: Fertility. In *Poston, D. L., Jr. and Weller, R. H., eds.*, 1981, pp. 23–54. [G: U.S.]

Rosenberg, Harry M. and Burnham, Drusilla. The Population of the South: Mortality. In *Poston, D. L., Jr. and Weller, R. H., eds.*, 1981, pp. 55–108. [G: U.S.]

Rossi, José W. Income Distribution in Brazil: A Regional Approach. *J. Devel. Stud.*, January 1981, 17(2), pp. 226–34. [G: Brazil]

Rowthorn, Bob. Northern Ireland: An Economy in Crisis. *Cambridge J. Econ.*, March 1981, 5(1), pp. 1–31.

Rugg, Dean S. and Rundquist, Donald C. Urbanization in the Great Plains: Trends and Prospects. In *Lawson, M. P. and Baker, M. E., eds.*, 1981, pp. 221–46. [G: U.S.]

Schmidt, Elsa T. Key Issues of Land Use Planning in West Germany. *Growth Change*, April 1981, 12(2), pp. 44–52. [G: W. Germany]

Schroeder, Gertrude E. Selected Problems of Regional Development in the USSR: Regional Living Standards. In *Koropeckyj, I. S. and Schroeder, G. E., eds.*, 1981, pp. 118–56.
[G: U.S.S.R.]

Seley, John E. Targeting Economic Development: An Examination of the Needs of Small Businesses. *Econ. Geogr.*, January 1981, 57(1), pp. 34–51.
[G: U.S.]

Seninger, Stephen F. and Smeeding, Timothy M. Poverty: A Human Resource–Income Maintenance Perspective. In *Hawley, A. H. and Mazie, S. M., eds.*, 1981, pp. 382–436. [G: U.S.]

Serow, William J. An Economic Approach to Population Change in the South. In *Poston, D. L., Jr. and Weller, R. H., eds.*, 1981, pp. 198–226.
[G: U.S.]

Shakow, Don. The Municipal Farmer's Market as an Urban Service. *Econ. Geogr.*, January 1981, 57(1), pp. 68–77. [G: U.S.]

Short, Cameron; Turhollow, Anthony F., Jr. and Heady, Earl O. A Regional Problem in a National Context: The Ogallala Aquifer. *Reg. Sci. Persp.*, 1981, 11(2), pp. 70–82. [G: U.S.]

Short, John. Defence Spending in the U.K. Regions. *Reg. Stud.*, 1981, 15(2), pp. 101–10. [G: U.K.]

Singelmann, Joachim. The Population of the South: Southern Industrialization. In *Poston, D. L., Jr. and Weller, R. H., eds.*, 1981, pp. 175–97.
[G: U.S.]

Singh, J. P. Patterns of Urbanization in a Developing Region: A Demographic Perspective. In *Karna, M. N., ed.*, 1981, pp. 87–103. [G: India]

Singh, R. B.; Dey, B. K. and Roy, N. D. Demand–Supply Balance of Foodgrains in Bihar in 1982–83 and 1988–89—A Study. In *Karna, M. N., ed.*, 1981, pp. 29–44. [G: India]

Singleton, J. Clay; Schmidt, James R. and Matzke, Jane. Regional Bond Yields and Economic Activity: Theory and Application. *Reg. Sci. Persp.*, 1981, *11*(2), pp. 83–93. [G: U.S.]

Sinha, Amareshwar Prasad. Economic Backwardness of Bihar and Certain Relevant Aspects of Census Data. In *Karna, M. N., ed.*, 1981, pp. 15–27. [G: India]

Sly, David F. The Population of the South: Migration. In *Poston, D. L., Jr. and Weller, R. H., eds.*, 1981, pp. 109–36. [G: U.S.]

Smith, Tony E. A Representational Framework for the Joint Analysis of Regional Welfare Inequalities and National Expenditure Priorities. *J. Reg. Sci.*, May 1981, *21*(2), pp. 187–202.

Sokolow, Alvin D. Local Governments: Capacity and Will. In *Hawley, A. H. and Mazie, S. M., eds.*, 1981, pp. 704–35. [G: U.S.]

Sommers, Paul M. Analysis of Net Interstate Migration Revisited. *Soc. Sci. Quart.*, June 1981, *62*(2), pp. 294–302. [G: U.S.]

Soubeyroux, Nicole. The Spread of Agricultural Growth over the Departments of France from the Mid-nineteenth to the Mid-twentieth Century. In *Bairoch, P. and Lévy-Leboyer, M., eds.*, 1981, pp. 290–301. [G: France]

Soumah, Moussa. Regional Migrations in Southeastern Senegal, Internal and International. In *Colvin, L. G., et al.*, 1981, pp. 161–82.

[G: Senegal]

Stamas, George D. The Puzzling Lag in Southern Earnings. *Mon. Lab. Rev.*, June 1981, *104*(6), pp. 27–36. [G: U.S.]

Stephens, John D. and Holly, Brian P. City System Behaviour and Corporate Influence: The Headquarters Location of US Industrial Firms, 1955–75. *Urban Stud.*, October 1981, *18*(3), pp. 285–300. [G: U.S.]

Tarling, R. and Wilkinson, F. Regional Earnings Determination in the United Kingdom Engineering Industry, 1964–1979. In *Martin, R. L., ed.*, 1981, pp. 60–74. [G: U.K.]

Taylor, Stan. De-industrialisation and Unemployment in the West Midlands. In *Crick, B., ed.*, 1981, *1981*, pp. 64–73. [G: U.K.]

Tekeli, Ilhan. Dört Plan Döneminde Bölgesel Politikalar ve Ekonomik Büyümenin Mekânsal Farklilaşmasi. (Regional Policies in Four Plans and Spatial Differentiation of Economic Growth. With English summary.) *METU*, Special Issue, 1981, pp. 369–90. [G: Turkey]

Thomson, Lydia. Industrial Employment Performance and Regional Policy, 1952–71: A Cross-Sectional Approach. *Urban Stud.*, June 1981, *18*(2), pp. 231–38. [G: U.K.]

Thoroe, Carsten S. Changes in the Regional Growth Pattern in the European Community. In *Giersch, H., ed. (II)*, 1981, pp. 283–311.

[G: W. Germany; France; Italy; U.K.]

Till, Thomas E. Manufacturing Industry: Trends and Impacts. In *Hawley, A. H. and Mazie, S. M., eds.*, 1981, pp. 194–230. [G: U.S.]

Todd, D. Regional Variations in Naval Construction: The British Experience, 1895–1966. *Reg. Stud.*, 1981, *15*(2), pp. 123–42. [G: U.K.]

Tomic, Dušan. The Regional Economic Development and Political Aims, Methods and Measures in the Regional Development of Agriculture: The Yugoslav Example. *Europ. Rev. Agr. Econ.*, 1981, *8*(2–3), pp. 287–314. [G: Yugoslavia]

Toutain, Jean-Claude. The Uneven Growth of Regional Incomes in France from 1840–1970. In *Bairoch, P. and Lévy-Leboyer, M., eds.*, 1981, pp. 302–15. [G: France]

Ubaidullaeva, R. A. The Twenty-fifth Congress of the CPSU and Current Problems of Employment of Female Labor in the Republics of Central Asia. *Prob. Econ.*, Sept.–Oct.–Nov. 1981, *24*(5–6–7), pp. 147–55. [G: U.S.S.R.]

Upton, Graham J. G. Log-Linear Models, Screening and Regional Industrial Surveys. *Reg. Stud.*, 1981, *15*(1), pp. 33–45. [G: U.K.]

Van der Wees, Gerrit. Multinational Corporations, Transfer of Technology, and the Socialist Strategy of a Developing Nation: Perspectives from Tanzania. In *Hamilton, F. E. I. and Linge, G. J. R., eds.*, 1981, pp. 529–47. [G: Tanzania]

Vitali, Ornello. Lo sviluppo dell'urbanizzazione in Emilia-Romagna (1951–1977). (The Development of Urbanization in Emilia-Romagna (1951–1977). With English summary.) *Statistica*, April–June 1981, *41*(2), pp. 285–99. [G: Italy]

de Vries, Jan. Regional Economic Inequality in the Netherlands since 1600. In *Bairoch, P. and Lévy-Leboyer, M., eds.*, 1981, pp. 189–98.

[G: Netherlands]

Walker, Alan. South Yorkshire: The Economic and Social Impact of Unemployment. In *Crick, B., ed.*, 1981, *1981*, pp. 74–87. [G: U.K.]

Walker, David F. Regional Industrial Development Policy in Canada since 1973. In *Rees, J.; Hewings, G. J. D. and Stafford, H. A., eds.*, 1981, pp. 239–55. [G: Canada]

Walton, A. L. Variations in the Substitutability of Energy and Nonenergy Inputs: The Case of the Middle Atlantic Region. *J. Reg. Sci.*, August 1981, *21*(3), pp. 411–20. [G: U.S.]

Walzer, Norman and Stablein, Ralph. Small Towns and Regional Centers. *Growth Change*, July 1981, *12*(3), pp. 2–8. [G: U.S.]

Wasylenko, Michael. The Location of Firms: The Role of Taxes and Fiscal Incentives. In *Bahl, R., ed.*, 1981, pp. 155–90. [G: U.S.]

Weinstein, Bernard L. Business Development in the American South of Post-World War II. In *Bateman, F., ed.*, 1981, pp. 65–99. [G: U.S.]

Weiss, Thomas. Southern Business Never had it so Good!! A Look at Antebellum Industrialization. In *Bateman, F., ed.*, 1981, pp. 27–34. [G: U.S.]

West, Douglas S. Tests of Two Locational Implications of a Theory of Market Pre-Emption. *Can. J. Econ.*, May 1981, *14*(2), pp. 313–26.

[G: Canada]

Wheeler, James O. Effects of Geographical Scale on Location Decisions in Manufacturing: The Atlanta Example. *Econ. Geogr.*, April 1981, *57*(2), pp. 134–45. [G: U.S.]

Whitehouse, F. Douglas and Kamerling, David S.

Economic Development in Individual Regions in the USSR: The Asiatic RSFSR. In *Koropeckyj, I. S. and Schroeder, G. E., eds.*, 1981, pp. 235–66. [G: U.S.S.R.]

Williams, J. Allen, Jr.; White, Lynn K. and Johnson, David R. The Social and Demographic Character of the Quality of Life on the Great Plains by the Year 2000. In *Lawson, M. P. and Baker, M. E., eds.*, 1981, pp. 67–80. [G: U.S.]

Williamson, Jeffrey G. Inequality and Regional Development: The View from America. In *Bairoch, P. and Lévy-Leboyer, M., eds.*, 1981, pp. 373–91. [G: U.S.]

Winsberg, Morton D. Agriculture and the Interstate: A Note on Locational Impacts in the South. *Growth Change*, July 1981, *12*(3), pp. 41–46. [G: U.S.]

Woodman, Harold D. Agriculture and Business in the Postbellum South: The Transformation of a Slave Society. In *Bateman, F., ed.*, 1981, pp. 51–61. [G: U.S.]

Wright, Gavin. Black and White Labor in the Old New South. In *Bateman, F., ed.*, 1981, pp. 35–50. [G: U.S.]

Yadava, Gorelal. Industrialization of Bihar: Some Major Constraints and Possible Solutions. In *Karna, M. N., ed.*, 1981, pp. 45–56. [G: India]

Zidar, Milovan. Regional Development in the Economic Policy of Yugoslavia. *Europ. Rev. Agr. Econ.*, 1981, *8*(2–3), pp. 131–36. [G: Yugoslavia]

Ziemer, Rod F.; White, Fred C. and Clifton, Ivery D. An Analysis of Factors Affecting Differential Assessment Legislation. *Public Choice*, 1981, *36*(1), pp. 43–52. [G: U.S.]

Zinam, Oleg. Economic Development in Individual Regions in the USSR: Transcaucasus. In *Koropeckyj, I. S. and Schroeder, G. E., eds.*, 1981, pp. 386–416. [G: U.S.S.R.]

Zuiches, James J. Residential Preferences in the United States. In *Hawley, A. H. and Mazie, S. M., eds.*, 1981, pp. 72–115. [G: U.S.]

9413 Regional Economic Models and Forecasts

Barnard, J. R.; Dent, W. T. and Reznek, A. P. An Econometric Model of a State Government Sector. *Reg. Sci. Persp.*, 1981, *11*(1), pp. 3–21. [G: U.S.]

Baxter, Mike and Ewing, Gordon. Models of Recreational Trip Distribution. *Reg. Stud.*, 1981, *15*(5), pp. 327–44.

Black, Philip A. Injection Leakages, Trade Repercussions and the Regional Income Multiplier. *Scot. J. Polit. Econ.*, November 1981, *28*(3), pp. 227–35. [G: U.K.]

Brown, Ralph J. Simulating the Impact of an Irrigation Project on a Small Regional Economy. *Growth Change*, April 1981, *12*(2), pp. 23–30. [G: U.S.]

Burford, Roger L. and Katz, Joseph L. A Method for Estimation of Input-Output Type Output Multipliers When no I-O Model Exists. *J. Reg. Sci.*, May 1981, *21*(2), pp. 151–61. [G: U.S.]

Carlberg, Michael. A Neoclassical Model of Interregional Economic Growth. *Reg. Sci. Urban Econ.*,

May 1981, *11*(2), pp. 191–203.

Duobinis, Stanley F. An Econometric Model of the Chicago Standard Metropolitan Statistical Area. *J. Reg. Sci.*, August 1981, *21*(3), pp. 293–319. [G: U.S.]

Filippucci, Carlo. Gli impieghi intermedi dei settori agricoli: il caso dell'Emilia Romagna. (Agriculture's Inputs: A Case Study. With English summary.) *Statistica*, January–March 1981, *41*(1), pp. 95–113. [G: Italy]

Ghali, Moheb A.; Akiyama, Masayuki and Fujiwara, Junichi. Models of Regional Growth: An Empirical Evaluation. *Reg. Sci. Urban Econ.*, May 1981, *11*(2), pp. 175–90. [G: U.S.]

Goodman, D. E. Rural Structure, Surplus Mobilisation and Modes of Production in a Peripheral Region: The Brazilian Northeast. In *Mitchell, S., ed.*, 1981, pp. 10–40. [G: Brazil]

Gordon, Peter and Ledent, Jacques. Towards an Interregional Demoeconomic Model. *J. Reg. Sci.*, February 1981, *21*(1), pp. 79–87.

Granberg, A. Modelling the Processes of Coordinating National Economic and Regional Planning Decisions. In *Janssen, J. M. L.; Pau, L. F. and Straszak, A. J., eds.*, 1981, pp. 187–93.

Granberg, A. G. A Modified Version of the Optimal Multisectoral Interregional Model. *Matekon*, Summer 1981, *17*(4), pp. 72–93.

Hanseman, Dennis J. and Gustafson, Elizabeth F. Stochastic Input–Output Analysis: A Comment [Input–Output as a Simple Econometric Model]. *Rev. Econ. Statist.*, August 1981, *63*(3), pp. 468–70.

Hansen, Jørgen Drud. Om regionale uligheder i neoklassisk vækstteori. (The Regional Level of Income per Capita in a Neoclassical One-Sector Growth Model. With English summary.) *Nationaløkon. Tidsskr.*, 1981, *119*(3), pp. 392–408.

Harrigan, F.; McGilvray, J. W. and McNicoll, I. H. The Estimation of Interregional Trade Flows. *J. Reg. Sci.*, February 1981, *21*(1), pp. 65–78. [G: U.K.]

Hayton, K. A Linear Programming Land Selection Model for Structure Planning: A Case Study of Tyne and Wear. *Reg. Stud.*, 1981, *15*(6), pp. 425–37. [G: U.K.]

Henry, Mark S., et al. A Cost-effective Approach to Primary Input-Output Data Collection. *Rev. Public Data Use (See J. Econ. Soc. Meas. after 4/85)*, December 1981, *9*(4), pp. 331–36.

Hodge, James H. A Study of Regional Investment Decisions. In *Henderson, J. V., ed.*, 1981, pp. 1–65. [G: U.S.]

Hodgson, M. John. A Location-Allocation Model Maximizing Consumers' Welfare. *Reg. Stud.*, 1981, *15*(6), pp. 493–506. [G: Canada]

Ishitani, H., et al. Modelling of Geographical Distribution of Population in a Region and Its Application for Regional Planning. In *Janssen, J. M. L.; Pau, L. F. and Straszak, A. J., eds.*, 1981, pp. 213–20. [G: Japan]

Johnson, Manuel H. and Bennett, James T. Regional Environmental and Economic Impact Evaluation: An Input-Output Approach. *Reg. Sci. Urban Econ.*, May 1981, *11*(2), pp. 215–30.

Jones, Philip C. A Network Model of Economic Growth: A Regional Analysis. *Reg. Sci. Urban Econ.*, May 1981, *11*(2), pp. 231–37.

Koch, Donald L. and Mass, Nathaniel J. The Florida Economy—Elements of a System Dynamics Approach. *Bus. Econ.*, January 1981, *16*(1), pp. 21–25. [G: U.S.]

Kort, John R. and Cartwright, Joseph V. Modeling the Multiregional Economy: Integrating Econometric and Input–Output Models. *Rev. Reg. Stud.*, Fall 1981, *11*(2), pp. 1–17. [G: U.S.]

Kulikowski, R. Modelling of Rural–Urban Development. In *Janssen, J. M. L.; Pau, L. F. and Straszak, A. J.*, eds., 1981, pp. 195–99.

Ledent, Jacques and Gordon, Peter. A Framework for Modeling Interregional Population Distribution and Economic Growth. *Int. Reg. Sci. Rev.*, Fall 1981, *6*(1), pp. 85–90.

Maki, Wilbur R. Regional Economic Forecast System for Resource Development Planning. *Reg. Sci. Persp.*, 1981, *11*(1), pp. 22–31.

Mattei, Aurelio. Un modèle économétrique pour le Canton du Valais. (An Econometric Model of Valais. With English summary.) *Schweiz. Z. Volkswirtsch. Statist.*, December 1981, *117*(4), pp. 605–16. [G: Switzerland]

Mattsson, C. and Bubenko, J. A. Regional Energy Modelling. In *Janssen, J. M. L.; Pau, L. F. and Straszak, A. J.*, eds., 1981, pp. 201–06. [G: Sweden]

Miglierina, Claudio and Folloni, Giuseppe. Significato economico di proiezioni spaziali di tavole input-output nazionali: alcune verifiche. (The Economic Meaning of the Spatial Projections of I/O National Tables: Some Tests. With English summary.) *Giorn. Econ.*, March–April 1981, *40*(3–4), pp. 199–215. [G: Italy]

Milne, William J. Migration in an Interregional Macroeconometric Model of the United States: Will Net Outmigration from the Northeast Continue? *Int. Reg. Sci. Rev.*, Fall 1981, *6*(1), pp. 71–83. [G: U.S.]

Nader, George A. The Delineation of a Hierarchy of Nodal Regions by Means of Higher-order Factor Analysis. *Reg. Stud.*, 1981, *15*(6), pp. 475–92. [G: Canada]

Nakamura, Masahisa; Brill, E. Downey, Jr. and Liebman, Jon C. Multiperiod Design of Regional Wastewater Systems: Generating and Evaluating Alternative Plans. *Water Resources Res.*, October 1981, *17*(5), pp. 1339–48.

Nijkamp, Peter and Lojenga, Frans Kutsch. Natural Resources as Spatial Development Potentials in Developing Countries: A Case Study of Surinam. In *Chatterji, M.*, ed., 1981, pp. 245–54. [G: Surinam]

Nijkamp, Peter and Rietveld, Piet. Multi-Objective Multi-Level Policy Models: An Application to Regional and Environmental Planning. *Europ. Econ. Rev.*, January 1981, *15*(1), pp. 63–89. [G: Netherlands]

Ocanas, Gerardo and Mays, Larry W. A Model for Water Reuse Planning. *Water Resources Res.*, February 1981, *17*(1), pp. 25–32.

Olson, Dennis O. Neoclassical Growth Models and Regional Growth in the U.S.: A Comment. *J. Reg. Sci.*, August 1981, *21*(3), pp. 425–30. [G: U.S.]

Park, Se-Hark; Mohtadi, Malek and Kubursi, Atif A. Errors in Regional Nonsurvey Input–Output Models: Analytical and Simulation Results. *J. Reg. Sci.*, August 1981, *21*(3), pp. 321–39. [G: U.S.]

Parvin, Manoucher and Grammas, Gus W. Capacity, Energy, and Environment Planning in Developing Industries. In *Chatterji, M.*, ed., 1981, pp. 153–66. [G: LDCs]

Persson, Lars Olof and Bolin, Olof. Agricultural Planning for Regional Balance. *Europ. Rev. Agr. Econ.*, 1981, *8*(4), pp. 499–518. [G: Sweden]

Plaut, Thomas R. An Econometric Model for Forecasting Regional Population Growth. *Int. Reg. Sci. Rev.*, Fall 1981, *6*(1), pp. 53–70. [G: U.S.]

Puig, Jean-Pierre. La migration régionale de la population active. (Regional Migration of the Labor Force. With English summary.) *Ann. INSEE*, October–December 1981, (44), pp. 41–79. [G: France]

Richter, Josef and Zelle, Karl. Interregionale Lieferverflechtungen in Österreich 1976: Möglichkeiten der Schätzung einer multiregionalen Input-Output-Tabelle durch ein "information minimizing model." (With English summary.) *Empirica*, 1981, (1), pp. 73–110. [G: Austria]

Seiver, Daniel A. Projecting the Income Distribution in a Regional Economy. *Growth Change*, October 1981, *12*(4), pp. 9–15. [G: U.S.]

Shoji, K., et al. A Man-Machine Interactive Sensitivity Analysis Feature for the Kinki Regional Model. In *Janssen, J. M. L.; Pau, L. F. and Straszak, A. J.*, eds., 1981, pp. 207–12. [G: Japan]

Smith, Donald Mitchell. Neoclassical Growth Models and Regional Growth in the U.S.: A Reply. *J. Reg. Sci.*, August 1981, *21*(3), pp. 431–32. [G: U.S.]

Smith, Eldon D.; Hackbart, Merlin M. and Van Veen, Johannes. A Modified Regression Base Multiplier Model. *Growth Change*, July 1981, *12*(3), pp. 17–22.

Snickars, F. and Granholm, A. A Multiregional Planning and Forecasting Model with Special Regard to the Public Sector. *Reg. Sci. Urban Econ.*, August 1981, *11*(3), pp. 377–404. [G: Sweden]

Straszak, A. and Owsinski, J. W. Imbedding Perceptions of Regional Problems in the Integrated Modelling Framework. In *Janssen, J. M. L.; Pau, L. F. and Straszak, A. J.*, eds., 1981, pp. 231–45. [G: U.S.; U.S.S.R.; Japan; Bulgaria]

Tatarevic, Ljiljana. Teorijsko-metodološke osnove tabela međusektorskih odnosa privrednih delatnosti SR srbije van teritorije Socijalistickih Autonomnih Pokrajina u 1976 godini. (Theoretical-Methodological Bases of an Input-Output Table for the Socialist Republic of Serbia Proper in 1976. With English summary.) *Econ. Anal. Worker's Manage.*, 1981, *15*(2), pp. 219–30. [G: Yugoslavia]

Treyz, George I. Predicting the Economic Effects of State Policy Initiatives. *Growth Change*, April 1981, *12*(2), pp. 2–9. [G: U.S.]

Walsh, P. K., et al. Models for Forecasting Residential Populations—The Geometric Programming Approach. *Reg. Stud.*, 1981, *15*(6), pp. 521–31. [G: Australia]

Topical Guide
To Classification Schedule

TOPICAL GUIDE TO CLASSIFICATION SCHEDULE

This index refers to the subject index *group, category,* or *subcategory* in which the listed topic may be found. The subject index classifications include, in most cases, related topics as well. The term *category* generally indicates that the topic may be found in all of the *subcategories* of the 3-digit code; the term *group,* indicates that the topics may be found in all of the *subcategories* in the 2-digit code. The classification schedule (p. xxxiv) serves to refer the user to cross references.

ABSENTEEISM: 8240

ACCELERATOR: 0233

ACCOUNTING: firm, 5410; national income, 2210, 2212; social, 2250

ADMINISTERED PRICES: theory, 0226; empirical studies, 6110; industry, 6354

ADMINISTRATION: 513 category; business, 5131; and planning, programming, and budgeting: national, 5132, 3226, state and local, 3241; public, 5132

ADVERTISING: industry, 6354; and marketing, 5310

AFFLUENT SOCIETY: 0510, 0110

AGENT THEORY, 0228

AGING: economics of, 9180

AGGREGATION: 2118; in input-output analysis, 2220; from micro to macro, 0220, 0230

AGREEMENTS: collective, 832 category; commodity, 4220, 7130; international trade, 4220

AGRIBUSINESS: *see* CORPORATE AGRICULTURE

AGRICULTURAL: commodity exchanges, 3132, 7150; cooperatives, 7150; credit, 7140; research and innovation, 621 category; employment, 8131; marketing, 7150; outlook, 7120; productivity, 7110, 7160; situation, 7120; supply and demand analysis, 7110; surpluses, 7130

AGRICULTURE: 710 group; government programs and policy, 7130; and development, 7100, 1120

AIR TRANSPORTATION: 6150

AIRPORT: 6150, 9410

AIRCRAFT MANUFACTURING: 6314

ALLOCATION: welfare aspects, 0242; and general equilibrium, 0210

ALUMINUM INDUSTRY: 6312

ANCIENT ECONOMIC HISTORY: 043 category

ANCIENT ECONOMIC THOUGHT: 0311; individuals, 0322

ANTITRUST POLICY: 6120

APPLIANCE INDUSTRY: 6313

APPRENTICESHIP: 8110

ARBITRATION: labor, 832 category

ASSISTANCE: foreign, 4430

ATOMIC ENERGY: conservation and pollution, 7220; industries, 6352, 7230

AUCTION MARKETS: theory, 0227

AUSTRIAN SCHOOL: 0315; individuals, 0322

AUTOMATION: employment: empirical studies, 8243, theory, 8210

AUTOMOBILE MANUFACTURING: 6314

BALANCE OF PAYMENTS: 431 category; accounting, 4310; empirical studies, 4313; theory, 4312

BANK FOR INTERNATIONAL SETTLEMENTS: 4320

BANKS: central, 3116; commercial, 3120; investment, 3140; other, 3140; portfolios, 3120; savings and loan, 3140; savings, 3140; supervision and regulation of, 3120, 3140, 3116

BARGAINING: collective, 832 category; theory, 0262

BAYESIAN ANALYSIS: 2115

BENEFIT-COST ANALYSIS: theory 0242; applied, see individual fields

BEQUESTS: empirical, 9211; theoretical, 0243

BEVERAGE INDUSTRIES: 6318

BIBLIOGRAPHY: 0110; see also the GENERAL heading under each subject

BIOGRAPHY: businessmen, 040 group; history of thought, 0322

BOND MARKET: 3132

BOOK PUBLISHING: 6352

BOYCOTTS, LABOR: 833 category; 832 category

BRAIN DRAIN: 8230, 8410

BRAND PREFERENCE: 5310; and consumers, 9212

BREAK-EVEN ANALYSIS: 5120

BRETTON WOODS AGREEMENT: 4320

BUDGETS: consumers, 9211; governments: theory, 3212, national studies, 3226, state and local studies, 3241

BUILDING: construction industry, 6340; materials industry, 6317